CULINARY LANDMARKS
A Bibliography of Canadian Cookbooks, 1825–1949

ELIZABETH DRIVER

CULINARY LANDMARKS

A Bibliography of Canadian Cookbooks

1825–1949

UNIVERSITY OF TORONTO PRESS
Toronto Buffalo London

Published by University of Toronto Press Incorporated
Toronto Buffalo London
Printed in Canada

ISBN 978-0-8020-4790-8

Printed on acid-free paper

Library and Archives Canada Cataloguing in Publication

Driver, Elizabeth
Culinary landmarks : a bibliography of Canadian
cookbooks, 1825–1949 / Elizabeth Driver.

Includes bibliographical references and index.
ISBN 978-0-8020-4790-8

1. Cookery – Canada – Bibliography.   I. Title.

Z5776.G2D74 2008   016.64150971   C2006-902604-1

University of Toronto Press acknowledges the financial assistance to its publishing program of the
Canada Council for the Arts and the Ontario Arts Council.

University of Toronto Press acknowledges the financial support for its publishing activities of the
Government of Canada through the Book Publishing Industry Development Program (BPIDP).

Contents

Illustrations

Front cover: Image from the front cover of *Dainty and Delicious Dishes*, Toronto: Cowan Co. Ltd, nd [1915] (O336.1)

1. *'The Black Whale' Cook Book*, by Mrs Ethel Renouf, Montreal, 1948 (Q314.1). Credit: Nancy Rahija, Toronto
2a. *Five Roses Cook Book*, Lake of the Woods Milling Co., Montreal and Winnipeg, 1915 (Q79.3). Credit: Nancy Rahija, Toronto
2b. *La cuisinière Five Roses*, Lake of the Woods Milling Co., Montreal, 1915 (Q79.4). Credit: Nancy Rahija, Toronto
3a–b. *The Canadian Economist*, by the Ladies' Association of Bank Street Church, Ottawa, 1881; two facing colour lithographs, between pp vi and vii (O28.1). Credit: Nancy Rahija, Toronto
4. Watercolour illustration by the Toronto artist Augusta Helene Carter in *'Cowan's Cocoa Recipes,'* Cowan Co., Toronto, nd [1921], p 44 (O468.1). Credit: Nancy Rahija, Toronto
5. An up-to-date kitchen illustrated in *McClary's Household Manual*, McClary's, London, Ontario, 1922, p 9 (O488.1). Credit: The J.J. Talman Regional Collection, The D.B. Weldon Library, The University of Western Ontario
6a–d. Four cover designs for editions of *The Magic Cook Book and Housekeepers Guide*, E.W. Gillett Co. Ltd, Toronto, published in the period 1912–27 (O285.3, O285.10, O285.12, O285.18). Credit: Nancy Rahija, Toronto
7. *The Magic Cook Book*, E.W. Gillett Co. Ltd, Toronto, nd [about 1930–5] (O702.3). Credit: Nancy Rahija, Toronto
8. *The Art of Sandwich Making*, Canada Bread Co., Toronto, nd [about 1926] (O576.1). Credit: Nancy Rahija, Toronto
9. *Canadian Grown Apples*, Department of Agriculture, Ottawa, 1939 (O496.13). Credit: Nancy Rahija, Toronto
10. *The Maple Leaf Canadian Recipe Book*, by Mrs Kathleen Bowker, nd [about 1931] (GB2.1). Credit: Nancy Rahija, Toronto
11. *Margene Recipe Book*, by Brenda York, nd [1949] (O1230.1)
12. *D M S Cook Book*, by the Daughters of the Midnight Sun, Yellowknife, [1947] (NWT2.1)
13. Oil painting of the fictional Rita Martin, reproduced in *Robin Hood Prize Winning Recipes* (Q306.1)
14. *La cuisinière bourgeoise*, by Menon, Quebec City, 1825 (Q1.1). Credit: Library and Archives Canada, Ottawa
15. *La cuisinière canadienne*, Montreal, 1840 (Q3.1). Credit: Library and Archives Canada, Ottawa
16. *Directions diverses données par la révérende mère Caron*, Montreal, 1878 (Q15.1). Credit: Library and Archives Canada, Ottawa
17. *The Cook Not Mad*, Kingston, Upper Canada, 1831 (O1.1). Credit: Toronto Reference Library
18. *The Frugal Housewife's Manual*, by A.B. of Grimsby, Toronto, 1840 (O2.1). Credit: Toronto Reference Library
19. *The Female Emigrant's Guide*, by Mrs Catharine Parr Traill, Toronto, 1854 [1855] (O5.1). Credit: University of Toronto, Thomas Fisher Rare Book Library
20. *Dr Chase's Recipes*, by Dr Alvin Wood Chase, twenty-third edition, London, 1865 (O8.1). Credit: University of Toronto, Thomas Fisher Rare Book Library
21. *The Home Cook Book*, by ladies of Toronto and other cities and towns, Toronto, 1877 (O20.1). Credit: Kings County Historical Society Museum, Hampton
22. *Cuisine*, by the ladies of Saint John, New Brunswick, 1878 (NB2.1). Credit: Legislative Library of New Brunswick, Fredericton
23. Advertisement for *Mrs Clarke's Cookery Book*, by Mrs Anne Clarke, Toronto, 1883, in *Toronto World* 13 November 1883 (O35.1). Credit: Toronto Reference Library
24. *Church of England Institute Receipt Book*, by Mrs

Foreword

Even in my own lifetime, indeed in the latter half of it, the quality and status of bibliographies of cookery books have changed dramatically. Throughout most of the twentieth century such few of them as existed were patently intended as references for librarians and private collectors, most of whom were interested in the actual books, as artifacts which called for identification and accurate descriptions, rather than in their context and content. This is not to belittle in any way the work of earlier bibliographers. They did what they set out to do, with diligence and occasionally with hints of the broader perspectives in which the books they catalogued could be viewed; but only hints.

In reality, a good bibliography with accurately defined boundaries, whether of subject, language, geographical area, or period (or of course all four), can be used as a sort of prism through which to perceive, with a fresh illumination, many matters other than the publishing history of the books. As Elizabeth Driver says herself, the range of relevant interests, besides food history, is great: 'women's studies, social history, archaeology, museum studies, folklore, ethnology, even English literature.' To her list I would add the work of mainstream political historians (how often are great political events found to be partly explicable by food matters!), that of both general economists and students of economic botany, and that of dietitians and practitioners of medicine, including nursing. And I would further add agriculture, and those many forms of biology, including ichthyology, which are relevant to the use of animals as food. Finally, I warmly endorse the idea that studies of food in literature can be greatly helped by good bibliographies. I am, as it happens, just embarking on an investigation of food in novels, and find that the only relevant bibliography (by the late Professor Norman Kiell) is just about indispensable.

Of course the extent to which a bibliography fulfils the manifold purposes to which it can be put depends on how good a bibliography it is. On this, I am happy to say that they don't come any better than the present one. More than twenty years ago I was one of only a dozen or so people who had become aware of Elizabeth Driver's talents as a bibliographer. She was just starting work on what was to become her *Bibliography of Cookery Books Published in Britain 1875–1914*, and I could tell from the way that this was being planned (with the help of yet another Canadian, Dr Lynette Hunter) that it was going to be a model of its kind. In 1989 my wife and I had the privilege of being the book's publishers. We had never published a book so large, nor one on which we had had to contribute so little editorial work. It was a masterpiece.

The same could and will be said of the present volume, but in my opinion it deserves special and additional praise on two counts. First, its geographic and ethnic scope is so much wider, giving it a more international flavour. It is remarkable how a reading of the chapters on the provinces conveys what might be called their various personalities, reflecting the varied origins of the communities which settled in them. Second, like Elizabeth's earlier book but perhaps even more, the present one does so much to bring alive the books which it catalogues and their authors. I will never forget mère Caron, still less her nun who wept when cooking because the flame under the pan reminded her of the fires of Hell which she had so often deserved. Catharine Parr Traill is another outstanding figure, now firmly imprinted in my memory. These are but three characters from a cast of hundreds.

Here, then, is a book which is a precious gift to Canada and which will also be useful to and cherished by many people outside Canada. I wish it the success it deserves – although this wish may seem superfluous in the case of a book of such manifest excellence and with such a long life assuredly ahead of it.

Alan Davidson
Chelsea, London
October 2002

Acknowledgments

Culinary Landmarks is the offspring of my first publication in the field, *A Bibliography of Cookery Books Published in Britain 1875–1914*, which appeared in 1989 as one title in a series under the imprint of Prospect Books in London, England. To Alan Davidson, founder of the publishing house and the person who conceived of the idea of the British bibliographical series, and to Dr Lynette Hunter, the series editor, I am indebted for introducing me to the world of antiquarian cookbooks. Alan contributed the Foreword to this bibliography well in advance of its publication and about one year before his death on 2 December 2003. I regret that Alan could not see the work in its final form and dedicate *Culinary Landmarks* to his memory. I thank Lynette in particular for pursuing queries on my behalf at the British Library.

The research for *Culinary Landmarks* began in spring 1990, when I proposed the idea of a bibliography of Canadian cookbooks to Jo Marie Powers, then Associate Professor at the School of Hotel and Food Administration at the University of Guelph, and we launched the project together. Over more than a decade since then, many generous individuals, associations, institutions, and businesses have helped to bring the work to a successful conclusion.

My heartfelt thanks go to Jo Marie, who supported the project in countless ways, practical and intangible, over the entire course of the research. At the outset, she arranged for the bibliography to be located at the University of Guelph, whose long connection with agriculture, food, and home economics made it a perfect base. As I am an independent scholar, the association with the university was crucial for the fund-raising process and also for gaining the assistance of others for research purposes. It was an adventure to carry out the early stages of the research with Jo Marie, and I am especially grateful to her for enlarging the scale of the search through her many useful contacts and for shouldering the burdens of project administration and grant applications. Above all, her enthusiasm for culinary history and her commitment to preserving Canadian cookbooks were a constant inspiration and extended beyond the formal limits of the project when, with the co-operation of the Archival and Special Collections department of the University of Guelph Library, she helped to found the Canadian Cookbook Collection, which became the repository for donations of cookbooks from the public and an ongoing legacy of this bibliography. Since her retirement from the university, I have continued to benefit from her encouragement and advice.

From 1999 to 2002 the bibliography's home was Massey College in Toronto. I am grateful to John Fraser, the college's master, for welcoming the project, and to Peter Lewis, the bursar, for overseeing the account. Lunch breaks in the college's dining hall, in the company of Massey fellows, nourished the body and replenished the spirit.

The project's association with the University of Toronto Press dates almost from the conception of the project. Over the years, Bill Harnum's letters of support, his trust that the project would be completed, and his good humour were appreciated more than he could ever know. I am also beholden to the experienced and skilful team that transformed the manuscript into its final published form, especially editors Suzanne Rancourt, Barbara Porter, and Judy Williams, designer Val Cooke, and production manager Ani Deyirmenjian. Byron Moldofsky, Jane Davie, and Mariange Beaudry at the Cartography Office, Department of Geography, University of Toronto, converted raw data into informative maps in record time.

Many public institutions have participated in the project. Most of the Canadian libraries, archives, and museums listed under 'Libraries and Collections' on p xli sent information, and, when I was able to visit, the staff invariably made my research trips as efficient and profitable as possible. I made intensive use of certain collections and reference services. First among these is Library and Archives Canada, Ottawa, where I spent many fruitful hours in the stacks near the start of the project. Later, Michel Brisebois and Elaine Hoag helped track down volumes in the Rare Book Collection; Mary Bond introduced me to the AMICUS database before it was possible to search it from my home computer; Nicole Watier in the Reference and Information Services Division responded to all manner of queries; Anne Goddard, Patricia Kennedy, and Wilma MacDonald dealt expertly with archival matters; and the staff at the Canadian Institute for Historical Microreproductions, based at Library and Archives Canada, happily fielded questions. The Archival and Special Collections department of the University of Guelph Library has been a partner in the project from the beginning, first under the leadership of Tim Sauer, then Bernard Katz, and Lorne Bruce, and it was a challenge to keep up with the donations of cookbooks that flowed to the library as word of the project spread. I thank the staff of McGill University's Rare Books and Special Collections for their assistance as I worked my way through the many cookbooks there, especially Bruce Whiteman during my first visits and then Raynald Lepage, for answering questions of all sorts. I also thank the staff of the Bibliothèque nationale du Québec in Montreal, especially Renée Beaumier, Normand Cormier, Jean-René Lassonde, and Richard Thouin, for their aid in capturing all the French-language titles in the library's collection. In Toronto, I became a fixture in the Toronto Reference Library, where I relied on the help of Rita Ness and Norman McMullen in the Interlibrary Loan department and of the staff in the Special Collections, Genealogy and Maps Centre, under Christine Mosser. I also depended on the expert knowledge of the staff at the Thomas Fisher Rare Book Library, University of Toronto, especially Sandra Alston and Anne Dondertman; David Bain and John Jakobson at the Gladys Allison Canadiana Room in the North York Central Library; and staff at the York University Archives and Special Collections.

I am also indebted to a host of other librarians, archivists, curators, and museum board members across the country, some now working at other institutions or retired: In Newfoundland, Suzanne Sexty and Jackie Hillier, Memorial University of Newfoundland, St John's; Howard Brown, Provincial Archives of Newfoundland and Labrador, St John's; in Nova Scotia, Elizabeth Boyd and Karen Smith, Dalhousie University, Halifax; Garry D. Shutlak, Nova Scotia Archives and Records Management Library, Halifax; Susan White, Nova Scotia Museum, Halifax; Valerie Inness, Queens County Museum, Liverpool; Edith Haliburton and Patricia Townsend, Acadia University, Wolfville; Laura Bradley, Yarmouth County Museum; in New Brunswick, Sylvia Yeoman, Keillor House Museum, Dorchester; Peter Dickinson, Kings Landing Historical Settlement, Fredericton; Jean-Claude Arcand and Margaret Pacey, Legislative Library, Fredericton; Patricia Belier and Patricia Ruthven, University of New Brunswick, Fredericton; Kelly McKay, York-Sunbury Historical Society Museum, Fredericton; Brenda Orr, Moncton Museum; Cheryl Ennals, Mount Allison University, Sackville; Andrea Kirkpatrick, New Brunswick Museum, Saint John; Marcia Koven, Saint John Jewish Historical Museum; in Prince Edward Island, Mary Beth Harris, University of Prince Edward Island, Charlottetown; in Quebec, Miss Phelps and Arlene Royea, Brome County Historical Society, Knowlton; Lucille Potvin, Soeurs des Saints Noms de Jésus et de Marie, Service central des archives SNJM, Longueuil; Daniel Olivier, Bibliothèque de la ville de Montréal, Salle Gagnon; Ron Finegold and Eddie Paul, Jewish Pub-lic Library, Montreal; Florence Bertrand, Le service des Archives de la Congrégation de Notre-Dame, Montreal; Victoria Dickinson, McCord Museum, Montreal; Lan Tran, Musée de la civilisation, Quebec City; Jules Morin, Bibliothèque des Frères du Sacré-Coeur, Sainte-Foy; Hélène Liard and other staff, La société d'histoire de Sherbrooke; Sylvia Bertolini and Elizabeth Brock, Stanstead Historical Society; Germaine Blais, Archives des Ursulines, Trois-Rivières; Suzanne Girard, Archives du Séminaire de Trois-Rivières; in Ontario, Pat Zimmer, Aylmer and District Museum; Jim Quantrell, City of Cambridge Archives; Irene Arthur, Chatham-Kent Public Library; Karen Wagner, Wellington County Museum and Archives, Fergus, and Ian Easterbrook, Wellington County Historical Society; Bev Dietrich, Guelph Civic Museum; Brian Henley and Margaret Houghton, Hamilton Public Library; Stuart Renfrew and Vivien Taylor, Queen's University, Kingston; Marcia Shortreed, Elizabeth Hardin, and Tom Reitz, Doon Heritage Crossroads, Kitchener; Susan Burke, Joseph Schneider Haus, Kitchener; Susan Hoffman, Kitchener Public Library; Glen Curnoe and Arthur McClelland, London Public Library; Ann Morris and Theresa Resnier, University of Western Ontario, London; Jennifer Bunting, Lennox and Addington County Museum and Archives, Napanee; Dan Hoffman, Nepean Museum; Pam Handley, North Bay and Area Museum; Lisa Miettinen, Norwich and District Archives; Bill MacLennan, Canadian Agriculture Library, Ottawa; Joan Hyslop, Grey Roots Museum and Archives, Owen Sound; Noreen Gerrish, Queenston Community Library; Arden Phair, St Catharines Museum; Gail Banjafield and Elizabeth Finnie, St Catharines Public Library; Susan McNichol, Heritage House Museum, Smiths Falls; Frank vanKalmthout, Archives of Ontario, Toronto; Jennifer Rieger, the Grange at the Art Gallery of Ontario, Toronto; Diane Gilday, Archives of the Hospital for Sick Children, Toronto, who alerted me to the Minutes of the Ladies Committee referring to the Chicago source of O20.1, *The Home Cook Book*; Roma Dick, Imperial Order Daughters of the Empire national office, Toronto; staff of the United Church of Canada and Victoria University Archives, Toronto; Susan Saunders Bellingham, University of Waterloo; in Manitoba, Audrey Harburn, Carberry Plains Museum; Sandra Head, Daly House Museum, Brandon; M. McKenzie, Beautiful Plains Museum, Neepawa; Dr Philippe Mailhot, Le musée de Saint-Boniface; Eva Barclay, Hillcrest Museum, Souris; Mary Revel, Teulon and District Museum; Ann E. Wheatley, Manitoba Museum of Man and Nature, Winnipeg; Jody Baltessen and Elizabeth Blight, Provincial Archives of Manitoba, Winnipeg; Roy A. McLeod, Winnipeg District Archives, Sons of Scotland; Karen Hunt and Brett Lougheed, University of Manitoba, Winnipeg; in Saskatchewan, Roger Martin, Homestead Museum, Biggar; Timothy Beech, Biggar Museum and Gallery; Marj Redenbach, Melville Heritage Museum; Sandra Massey, Regina Plains Museum; Elizabeth Kalmakoff, Saskatchewan Archives Board, Regina; Maureen Fox, Saskatchewan Archives Board, Saskatoon; Ruth Bitner, Saskatchewan Western Development Museums, Saskatoon; Rose Marie Fedorak, Ukrainian Museum of Canada, Saskatoon; Margaret Baldock and Shirley Martin, University of Saskatchewan, Saskatoon; Lavine Stepp, Soo Line Historical Museum, Weyburn; in Alberta, M.L. Ludvigsson, Alix Wagon Wheel Museum Association; Bill Henderson, Bowden Pioneer Museum; Lindsay Moir, library of the Glenbow Museum, Calgary; Sylvia Harnden, Heritage Park Historical Village, Calgary; Apollonia Lang Steele, University of Calgary; Vera Kunda and Jeanine Green, University of Alberta, Edmonton; Barbara Wilberg, my first contact at the provincial government's Historic Sites and Archives Service, Edmonton, and Bill Gnatovich at the Provincial Museum of Alberta, and Joy Schellenberg and others at the Ukrainian Cultural Heritage Village; Dianne Vallée, Museum of the Highwood, High River; D. White, Medicine Hat Museum and Art Gallery; Valerie Miller, Red Deer and District Museum and Archives; in British Columbia, Susan Green, Burnaby Village Museum; Jim Bowman, Chilliwack Museum and Historical Society; Priscilla Davis, Cowichan Valley Museum; Leigh Hussey, Delta Museum and Archives; Elisabeth Duckworth, Kamloops Museum and Archives; Ursula Surtees, Kelowna Museum; Ursula Richardson,

Summerland Museum; Jennifer Jones, BC Sugar Museum, Vancouver; Norah McLaren, Vancouver Museum; Angela Haaf, Elizabeth Johnston, and Andrew Martin, Vancouver Public Library; George Brandak and Anne Yandle, University of British Columbia, Vancouver; Linda Wills, Greater Vernon Museum and Archives; David Mattison, British Columbia Archives, Victoria; Patricia Somerton, Legislative Library, Victoria; Virginia Careless, Royal British Columbia Museum, Victoria; and in the Northwest Territories, Peter Harding, Prince of Wales Northern Heritage Centre, Yellowknife. In the United States, I was aided by Jan Longone, curator of American culinary history, William L. Clements Library, University of Michigan; Barbara Wheaton, honorary curator of the culinary collection, Radcliffe Institute for Advanced Study, Schlesinger Library on the History of Women in America, Cambridge, Massachusetts; and David Schoonover, Curator of Rare Books, University of Iowa, Iowa City. To all these persons and many unnamed others who, in their official capacities, contributed information to the bibliography or otherwise helped in the quest, I extend my thanks.

I was fortunate to have the co-operation of several experts in their respective fields, among them: David Chun, of the William Cobbett Society, for providing material about the Cobbett family; Nathalie Cooke at McGill University, for her insights into the use of pseudonyms; Gwendolyn Davies at the University of New Brunswick, for help with Alice Jones's biographical note; Judy Donnelly, for sharing her knowledge of almanacs; Dr Serge Durflinger, Historian at the Canadian War Museum, whose answers to queries helped to date several wartime books; Janet Friskney, for introducing me to the papers of the Methodist Publishing House at the United Church Archives, Victoria University; Charlotte Gray, Elizabeth Hopkins, and Michael Peterman, for illuminating aspects of Catharine Parr Traill's life and writings; Amber Lloydlangston, for sharing information she had gathered about female employees of the federal Department of Agriculture; Stephen Otto, for searching the Gooderham and Worts archives for information about Betty Supplee; George L. Parker, for information about the Montreal printer Hew Ramsay and about cookbook author Sarah Lovell, the wife of another Montreal printer; Dr Miriam Ross at the Acadia Centre for Baptist and Anabaptist Studies, Acadia University, Wolfville, Nova Scotia, for guidance regarding the co-authors Annie Martell and Julia Hamm; Carl Spadoni at McMaster University, Hamilton, for additions to entries for McClelland and Stewart imprints and for assistance with an item related to Stephen

Leacock (Q95.1, *British, French, Italian, Russian, Belgian Cookery*); Basil Stuart-Stubbs, retired University Librarian and Director of the School of Librarianship at the University of British Columbia, for his research into the lives of Vancouver co-authors Florence Elizabeth Stewart and Gretchen Day Ross; and Joan Winearls for her good counsel about maps. I have learned a lot over the years about Ontario's food history from fellow members of the Culinary Historians of Ontario, especially Fiona Lucas (one of the founders of the group) and Elizabeth Nelson-Raffaele, and from Dorothy Duncan, retired Executive Director of the Ontario Historical Society.

The launch of the History of the Book in Canada project, under the general editorship of Patricia Fleming and Yvan Lamonde, was a boon for *Culinary Landmarks*. The founding conference for Volume 2 allowed me to develop ideas about the community-cookbook genre, and research carried out by others for the project, generously shared, strengthened the text.

My thanks go to the following Canadian home economists, who added to the life stories of past colleagues and revealed the identities of the women who worked behind corporate pseudonyms: Kathleen Hodgins, the original 'Brenda York'; Christine Robb Hindson, the second 'Martha Logan'; Mary Adams, for information about the fictional 'Ann Adam' and 'Anna Lee Scott'; Phyllis Dennett, for explaining the roles of the women who worked at the *Vancouver Sun*'s Edith Adams Cottage in the late 1940s; and Beatrice M. Millar, for the history of Jean Mutch at BC Electric. Ruth E. Berry expanded the biography of Margaret Speechly. Mary Leah DeZwart helped with the lives of Mary Hiltz and Alice Stevens. Helen Wattie and Elinor Donaldson Whyte shared their story of the 1953 revision of Nellie Pattinson's *Canadian Cook Book*. Jill Snider, at Robin Hood Multifoods Inc. in Markham, Ontario, facilitated access to the company's archives. Joanne Mackie and Marie Tyler disseminated my queries to the community of home economists and helped make connections. The Ontario Home Economists in Business Hall of Fame tribute to Elaine Collett was an essential source for her career. For sharing their personal papers and knowledge of Robin Hood's history, I am also grateful to Douglas Parker, Toronto, former Vice-President of Robin Hood Mills, and George Blanchard, Port Colborne, Ontario, former employee of the Port Colborne mill. Not long before Helen Gougeon died in May 2000, she told me the story of her first publishing venture, O1137.1, *Cooking with an Accent*.

Biographical material, such as family histories and photographs, came from author's or publisher's descendants or relatives: Bonnie Adie, Dora Fairfield's great-granddaughter; Marcel Anctil, a relation of Jeanne Anctil; Gordon Bourgard, son of Grace Bourgard, one of the several 'Anna Lee Scotts'; Heather Claggett, Jessie Read's daughter; Mrs Barbara Kincaide, daughter of Elizabeth Sieniewicz, behind the 1934 Evangeline Chapter IODE cookbook (NS43.1); Shirley Kirby, wife of Frederick Kirby, the illustrator of two New Brunswick cookbooks (NB39.1, NB41.1); W. Gordon Love, son of Robert W. Love, founder of Love – The Flavor Man, which published advertising cookbooks (Gordon Love also provided information about a Love flavours client, Gertrude Dutton, a cookbook author); Graeme Miltimore, a descendant of Grace Miltimore; and Fred Sherratt, Clarry Hunt's grandson.

Many new titles came to my attention through booksellers, and their contributions of information and their interest in the progress of the research were greatly appreciated. My special thanks go to Hugh Anson-Cartwright, Toronto; David Ewens, North Gower, Ontario; Ann Hall of the Bridgeburg Bookstore, Fort Erie, Ontario, when it was under the name of William Matthews and run by co-proprietors Matthews and Hall; Jill Reville Hill, when she was proprietor of Travellers' Tales Books in Ottawa; Janet Inksetter, Annex Books, Toronto; Denise Kenny, when she was in business in Bath, Ontario; Mary Lee MacDonald and John Townsend, Schooner Books Ltd, Halifax; David and Ann Skene-Melvin, Ann's Books, Toronto; Garry and Janice Shoquist, Northland Books, Saskatoon; Richard Spafford, Regina; Cameron Treleaven, Aquila Books, Calgary, and his wife, Marion; Bjarne Tokerud, Bjarne's Books, Edmonton; and Tom Williams, Calgary. In the later stages of the project, Jim Anderson of Anderbooks (now in Winnipeg), who specializes in cookbooks, made substantial additions to the bibliography, for which I am most grateful.

Since many Canadian culinary titles have not yet found their way into public institutions, the bibliography would have been much less comprehensive without the generous co-operation of many individual owners of old cookbooks, usually passed down in the family or sometimes rescued from a neighbour's house-clearing. I received thousands of letters from the public in response to appeals in the media and, on the research trips I took east and west of Ontario, and on shorter forays from my home base of Toronto, I fitted in as many visits as possible to private homes, where I not only had the pleasure of examining the owner's treasured volumes but would often be served a delicious meal. Early in the project, Carol Ferguson and Margaret Fraser let me see the cookbooks they had borrowed from friends and colleagues in preparation for co-writing *A Century of Canadian Home Cooking: 1900 through the '90s* (Toronto: Prentice Hall Canada, 1992). I am grateful to all these contributors for contacting me with information, for patiently answering my queries about their books, and for their hospitality in the case of those I visited.

I am also indebted to a number of private cookbook collectors whose passion for developing their libraries rivalled mine for pursuing the publishing history. The weeks spent in autumn 1990 exploring Una Abrahamson's magnificent private collection in her Don Mills, Ontario, home laid the foundation for the bibliography. Later, new titles would be added to the bibliography and new locations noted, but some of the titles first seen at Una's remain the only known copies. Before Una died on 28 February 1999, she donated her books to the University of Guelph, ensuring that the collection would remain intact and guaranteeing public access to what is now known as the Una Abrahamson Canadian Cookery Collection. The bibliography is richer for Una's early and prescient collecting of culinary Canadiana.

Over the course of the research, Mary F. Williamson, Fine Arts Bibliographer (retired), York University, Toronto, shared information about her personal collection and new acquisitions. Her friendship and encouragement were an invaluable support and I depended immensely on her bibliographical expertise. The manuscript was greatly improved by her suggestions of avenues of inquiry and by the searches she voluntarily undertook on a variety of fronts, from combing periodicals to pin down dates of publication to scouring cemetery records for biographical data. Many entries in the bibliography bear a silent acknowledgment to Mary for her help.

As Gary Draper's personal collection grew over the years, so did the bibliography, as Gary passed on news of his many finds, and his friendly and enthusiastic emails from the Department of English at St Jerome's University in Waterloo kept the project moving ahead at critical times. Assistance also came from Pat Rogal in Toronto, whose collection of culinary ephemera enriched the bibliography, and Elizabeth Baird, who let me examine her many volumes gathered during a long career championing Canadian food and cookery in print, radio, and television. The inclusion of an article about the project in *Canadian Living* (October 1991, p 15), where Elizabeth is the magazine's food editor, garnered a huge response from the public, adding many new titles to the record.

Away from my base in Toronto, Julian Armstrong, food editor of the *Montreal Gazette*, let me explore her home library and further helped by writing several articles about the project for her Montreal readers, who subsequently sent me details about their books. Julian's article in the 5 July 2000 issue of the newspaper resulted in the donation of a copy of the rare first edition of *La cuisinière canadienne* to the National Library of Canada, by André Sylvestre. I also had the privilege of viewing Ruth Spicer's collection in St Andrew's, New Brunswick, before she donated it to the Kings Landing Historical Settlement in Fredericton, and Eleanor Robertson Smith's collection in Shelburne, Nova Scotia. From Brooklyn, New York, Andrew F. Smith, the American author of books about tomatoes, ketchup, popcorn, peanuts, and soon turkey, and editor-in-chief of *The Oxford Encyclopedia of Food and Drink in America* (New York: Oxford University Press, 2004), sent me reports of new Canadian titles in his collection (including the only known copy of the Worcester, Massachusetts, edition of *La cuisinière canadienne*, which he subsequently donated to the University of Guelph) and shared his research about the American family trio, Cora, Bob, and Rose Brown. From Dunedin, New Zealand, collector Duncan Galletly sent information about two previously unknown editions of *The Home Cook Book* published in that country.

For the translation of texts in a language other than English or French, several persons freely gave their help: For Shirō Watanabe's *An English-Japanese Conversational Guide and Cook Book* (US3.1), Susan Michi Sirovyak at the Japanese Canadian National Museum in Burnaby, Lynne Kutsukake, Japanese Information Specialist at the University of Toronto Libraries, and Toshiko Yamashita at the Japanese Canadian Cultural Centre, Toronto; for 'Nordwesten'-Kochbuch (M127.1), Richard Mehringer, Malvern Collegiate Institute, Toronto; and for Ukrainian-language cookbooks, Roma Sanocka, Toronto Reference Library.

For technical advice and assistance I thank Nancy Crozier, who input the majority of the entries and guided me in the use of software; Nancy Rahija, for designing stationery and for photographing several of the cookbooks; Ulf Bein at Central Technical School in Toronto, for scanning Nellie Pattinson's portrait in an old school yearbook; and Dan Taylor of DanT's Inferno Foods Ltd, Mississauga, for scanning many of the images (for individual credits, see p vii). My husband, Edwin Rowse, his partner, Michael McClelland, and their staff at E.R.A. Architects Inc. in Toronto gave indispensable office support over the years.

On research trips I enjoyed the hospitality of friends and family: in Montreal, David Walker and the late Ann Duncan, and Julian Armstrong; in Ottawa, Maureen Cech and Carl Toole, Anne Newlands and Howard Duncan, and Christine and Jack Vanderloo; in Guelph, Jo Marie and Tom Powers; in Woodstock, Ontario, my aunt and uncle, Jean and Bill Sedgwick; in Winnipeg, Pat and Bruno Malis; in Saskatoon, my cousin Caroline Hlady and her husband, Gerald; in Calgary, Janet Wright and Jim Taylor; and in North Vancouver, my brother and sister-in-law, Michael and Susan Driver.

Midway through the project, there was an interlude where I had the pleasure of working with David P. Silcox on *David B. Milne: Catalogue Raisonné of the Paintings* (University of Toronto Press, 1998), which he co-authored with David Milne Jr. The experience gained improved the final form of *Culinary Landmarks*, and when I resumed the research for the cookbook bibliography, David Silcox supported my efforts in numerous ways. As someone who had just seen published a monumental reference work, his encouraging comments carried special weight.

The successful completion of the bibliography depended on financial support from several sources. I thank the University of Guelph for funds received over the course of the project, including seed money from the School of Hotel and Food Administration and additional grants from the Office of Research. Crucial aid came from the Social Sciences and Humanities Research Council and from E.R.A. Architects Inc. I am also indebted to the Canadian Home Economics Association for its contribution. The award of a Tremaine Fellowship from the Bibliographical Society of Canada funded research in British Columbia in 1992. The Albert and Temmy Latner Family Foundation, the George Cedric Metcalf Charitable Foundation, and the T.R. Meighen Foundation contributed generously to the project. On my behalf, Dr Linda McCargar at the University of Alberta, Edmonton, kindly sponsored a request for a grant from the Alberta Heritage Resources Foundation, and we thank the foundation for assisting with the printing costs of the Alberta section. Three consecutive annual grants from the Women's Culinary Network gave a helpful boost near the end of the project. I am grateful to Canada's food producers, notably Best Foods Canada Inc. and Nabisco Brands Ltd, who not only provided financial assistance but allowed me to use their company archives. Support has also come from Canada's bakers and restaurateurs, Ace Bakery (through the Haynes-Connell Foundation) and Pronto Restaurants Inc. (Barbara Prevedello). And my special thanks go to the following individual donors: Christine Bourchier, Alberta; Nathalie Cooke, Montreal; Honor de Pencier, Toronto; Lynda C. Hamilton, Toronto; Fiona Lucas, Toronto; Harrison McCain, Florenceville, New Brunswick; Mary Pratt, St John's, Newfoundland; Edwin Rowse; and anonymous.

I would not have reached the end goal without the unwaivering support of my husband, Edwin Rowse, and the patience over the years of our children, Michael and Alexandra. The publication of *Culinary Landmarks* is theirs to celebrate, too.

Introduction

This work, *Culinary Landmarks*, takes its title from two Ontario fund-raising cookbooks of the same name, produced by church women's groups in Sault Ste Marie and Port Colborne, at the turn of the last century (O84.1, O169a.1). Landmarks may be prominent features in a landscape, acting as signposts to guide the way, or events in history, signalling an important stage or turning point. Whether in physical space or time, landmarks help make sense of large-scale phenomena. Since the story of Canada's cookbooks unfolded over a vast expanse of land and within the continuum of time, *Culinary Landmarks* seemed a fitting title for this bibliography, which has two overarching purposes: to map the publishing history of the books and to identify the most significant works.

Culinary Landmarks describes 2,276 individual cookbooks published from 1825 to 1949, all in Canada except for seven texts about Canadian cooking published in Great Britain or the United States. The bibliography begins in the colonial era with the appearance of *La cuisinière bourgeoise* bearing the imprint of a Quebec City bookseller, but actually an edition of a text from France and printed in France (Q1.1), and ends at the mid-point of the twentieth century, when the war years were clearly over and new conditions were about to reshape Canadian society. Soon, in 1953, the National Library of Canada would be founded and a new copyright-deposit system put in place to preserve the country's printed heritage. The body of cookbooks documented here represents an aspect of Canadian publishing that until now has remained virtually unknown and unexplored, but which has a special fascination. No other category of book evokes such an emotional response across generations and genders and is freighted with so much cultural and historical meaning. Unlike the typical volumes on a library shelf, cookbooks are meant for daily reference in the kitchen, where they are subjected to the dangers of water, fire, and spills. The spots and annotations on the most-used pages are tangible and poignant links with the past user of the book, whether a mother or grandmother, or someone whose identity is now lost, but with whom one can still share the common bond of cooking and eating the same dish made from the same recipe. At the simplest level, cookbooks are collections of printed recipes – directions explaining how to cook – but cookbooks should not be mistaken for just instructional manuals. Food is at the very heart of living. It determines our health, defines our cultural and ethnic identity, and binds us together socially. Food is the main subject of the genre, but the cookbooks described in this bibliography also illuminate many other aspects of Canadian life across a broad sweep of time, especially the world of women (in the home, in philanthropic and political associations, and in the workplace), but also developments in agriculture, aquaculture, industry, education, medicine, publishing, and literature. Canadian writers who have turned their pens to the subject of food include Catharine Parr Traill in Canada West, George Stewart Jr at the time of his move from New Brunswick to Ontario, Mary Jane Lawson and Alice Jones in Nova Scotia, Grace Denison of Toronto's *Saturday Night* magazine, and Valance Patriarche in Winnipeg, but, with the exception of Traill, their contributions, and the contributions of many others (named and unnamed), to Canada's culinary literature have gone unremarked. This bibliography celebrates cookbooks and their authors as an incontrovertible part of Canada's literary history.

Canadian culinary manuals belong to a long tradition in the Western world of printed cookbooks. Not long after Johannes Gutenberg developed a system for printing with movable type and the beginning of the mass production of bibles and other religious material in the mid-fifteenth century, cookbooks began to issue from presses in Europe. If one were to draw a rudimentary family tree for Canadian cookbooks, one might trace lines back to the first printed cookbook in France, *Le viandier* by Taillevent, which appeared in about 1490, and the first in England, *A Noble Boke of Cokery*, published in 1500, keeping in mind, however, that there were other early European relations. Searching further into the past, one might also note the only known cookery text to survive from the days of the Roman Empire, attributed to 'Apicius' and first published in Milan in 1498.[1] Also in the family, but closer in time, is the earliest culinary manual published in what is now the United States, Eliza Smith's *The Compleat Housewife*, an edition of an English text, printed in Williamsburg, Virginia, in 1742. Other cookbooks would be published in the United States before *La cuisinière bourgeoise* was published in Quebec City in 1825, most notably Amelia Simmons's *American Cookery* of 1796, the first locally authored American text. Documenting the publishing history of Canadian cookbooks is crucial for understanding Canada's place in this family tree – its connections with, and differences from, these earlier, but continuously evolving, culinary and publishing traditions.

Scope and Arrangement of the Bibliography

The bibliography aims to identify every printed cookbook of 16 pages or more, published within the borders of present-day Canada, whether a locally authored text or a Canadian edition of a foreign work, from the beginning to 1949. The handful of texts discovered about cooking in Canada, but published outside the country, are also included, for example, *The Anglo-Canadian Cook Book* (GB3.1), probably for British war brides, and *An English-Japanese Conversational Guide and Cook Book* (US3.1), published in California for Japanese immigrants to the United States and Canada, especially British Columbia. In addition to cookbooks, the bibliography contains entries for what are sometimes called compendia – encyclopaedic household reference works, popular in the nineteenth century – if they incorporate a significant amount of culinary information; an example is Richard Moore's *The Universal Assistant* of 1879 (O23.1), which has a 'Baking and Cooking Department' and a section of 'Grocers and Confectioners' Receipts.' Recipes were sometimes printed in almanacs and advertising booklets for patent medicines, and these items are included in the bibliography if the culinary content is referred to in the title, for example, Northrop and Lyman's *Family Receipt Book* of about 1864 (O7.1) and *Le livre de ménage, recettes utiles par Mme Winslow, pour 1869* (Q8.1). It was not possible to make a thorough

search of all patent-medicine brochures and almanacs produced in the period covered by the bibliography; therefore, items with recipes in the text but no culinary content mentioned in the title are included only if they surfaced in the course of other research.[2]

Wherever possible, a copy of each edition of every work was examined and detailed information recorded: a transcription of the title-page, dimensions, pagination, whether illustrated, price, type of binding, and the contents. Also noted for each edition are citations in other bibliographies, as many locations as possible where copies may be consulted, and the existence of microfilm copies. Modern facsimile editions have full entries. Other later editions (1950 and after) and foreign editions are listed only. Biographical information about individual authors, including their other writings, or information about the history of publishers, corporations, institutions, and associations is often provided, especially where it helps to establish the date of publication or otherwise illuminates the context of the book's creation. See 'Explanation of Bibliography Entries' for the rules governing the presentation of the information.

The bibliography is arranged chronologically, by province and territory, to create a picture of cooking and dining customs in each part of the country over one-and-a-quarter centuries. Many of the cookbooks described here were local productions and well known in their own town, but not elsewhere; others had a regional profile; some were national bestsellers. The introductions to each provincial and territorial section highlight the most popular or interesting local or regional recipe collections, note the important developments and trends in cookbook publishing in the province or territory, and identify the nationally distributed titles. Most (but not all) of the nationally distributed cookbooks were published in Montreal and Toronto, Canada's largest cities in the two largest and most populous provinces; therefore, persons interested in cookbooks used in the Atlantic or Western provinces, and in the territories, should also read the introductions for Quebec and Ontario. Similarly, the story of Quebec cookbooks is not complete without reading the Ontario introduction, and vice versa. Note also that evidence of where a cookbook was distributed by its publisher (or carried by its owner) may sometimes be gleaned from the 'Copies' line in the individual entries: If the location is for a small museum or library – types of institution that invariably build their cookbook collections through donations from local residents – the cookbook likely originally belonged to a family in the same province as the museum or library.

A 'Chronology of Canadian Cookbook History' on p xxxiii helps to link the important events across the country, and maps on pp lxi–lxvi illustrate the pattern of publication. Four indexes serve as handy cross-references to the material: Subject Index; Place-of-Publication Index; Name Index (person, association, institution, or company); and Short-Title Index.

The Search for Canadian Cookbooks

The hunt for Canadian titles was more difficult than the search carried out for *A Bibliography of Cookery Books Published in Britain 1875–1914*. Most pre-1950 Canadian cookbooks were produced outside of the conventional publishing realm, by food companies, kitchen equipment manufacturers, and women's groups, not by regular publishers such as McClelland and Stewart. Many are physically unimpressive, almost ephemeral: small items of under 100 pages, with paper covers, stapled rather than sewn, and with a hole punched at the top left corner for hanging up in the kitchen, on a nail. Until the founding of the National Library of Canada, no institution in the country consistently collected and recorded cookbooks as did the national copyright-deposit libraries in Britain, France, and the United States, although for a brief period early in the twentieth century, a small number of Canadian cookbooks were deposited for copyright purposes at the British Library. These joined a part of the collection known as the Colonial Dump at the library's Woolwich Arsenal, but – in a cruel twist of fate – the cookbook section was hit by a German bomb during the Second World War and many were destroyed.

Bibliographies, the standard tools and usual first step in the pursuit of publishing history, and other printed sources, were generally of little help in my research. It was discouraging, for example, to find that Bruce Peel, in his 1973 *A Bibliography of the Prairie Provinces to 1953, with Biographical Index*, included just a handful of culinary titles; and the 2003 third edition, *Peel's Bibliography of the Canadian Prairies to 1953*, prepared by Ernie Ingles and Merrill Distad, increased the number of titles to just twenty-four. Likewise, cookbooks are just as scarce in Margaret Edwards's 1975 work, *A Bibliography of British Columbia: Years of Growth 1900–1950*. Agnes O'Dea's 1986 *Bibliography of Newfoundland* was the exception among regional bibliographies. Her good coverage of cookbooks may be a recognition of their usefulness in folklore studies, a long-time special interest at Memorial University of Newfoundland in St John's,

where she was a librarian; it is certainly a sign of the thoroughness of her research. *Publications of the Canada Department of Agriculture 1867–1974/Publications du Ministère de l'agriculture du Canada 1867–1974* was a useful guide to the many titles, in multiple editions, in French and English, from that federal department (especially as most items were not in the Canadian Agriculture Library electronic catalogue). I also benefited from Patrick O'Neill's *A Checklist of Canadian Copyright Deposits in the British Museum, 1895–1923*; although the volume including cookbooks is not yet published, the author kindly shared his valuable research with me. Three otherwise excellent histories of the Women's Institutes of Ontario, Manitoba, and Alberta were almost silent about or made no mention of cookbooks published by these groups, but their lists of branches, with dates of founding and disbanding, helped to limit dates of publication in the case of undated cookbooks.[3] *Legacy: A History of Saskatchewan Homemakers' Clubs and Women's Institutes, 1911–1988* offered information about two post-1950 cookbooks from the province's clubs, but only a passing mention to earlier 'cookbooks in the past.'[4] Nanci Langford, on the other hand, discusses the publishing success of *Recipes* (A59.1), by the United Farm Women of Alberta, in her 1997 history, *Politics, Pitchforks and Pickle Jars: 75 Years of Organized Farm Women in Alberta*. When *A Century of Canadian Home Cooking, 1900 through the '90s* appeared in 1992, it became the best printed source of references, with its 'Selected Cookbook Bibliography' and full-page colour photographs of 'Cookbook Samplers' for each decade. The co-authors, Carol Ferguson and Margaret Fraser, assembled their bibliography and photographs mainly from books borrowed from individuals across the country – a sort of amalgamated, but temporary, private collection, which they let me examine before it was dispersed. At the time I began my research, no Canadian bookseller specialized only in cookbooks or issued catalogues devoted to the subject. New items occasionally surfaced in booksellers' catalogues, but I learned about more titles directly from the bookdealers themselves or by visits to their shops. A few new titles were revealed through a search of the Canadian Institute for Historical Microreproductions database, and the microfilms themselves provided invaluable access to the texts; however, one great satisfaction of my work has been to pass on many previously unknown titles to the Institute for subsequent microfilming and dissemination. Easy access to, and searching of, on-line databases, such as individual library catalogues and Library and Archives Canada's AMICUS (which incorporates

Canada's Union Catalogue), only became possible near the end of the project. A full list of sources cited in this bibliography is under 'References' on p li.

I travelled across the country looking for Canadian cookbooks in libraries, museums, archives, and private collections. The three largest collections of pre-1950 Canadian cookbooks in the country are (in descending order) at Library and Archives Canada in Ottawa, the University of Guelph in Ontario, and McGill University in Montreal. The strength of the Library and Archives Canada collection is that the institution continues to collect material from across the country, but it is weak in English-language nineteenth-century cookbooks. The magnificent collection of Canadian, American, British, and French antiquarian cookbooks donated to the University of Guelph by the late Una Abrahamson is a rich resource for food historians; I was privileged to visit the collection in her home at the outset of the project. About 250 volumes in the University of Guelph's Canadian Cookbook Collection were donated by individuals, many of whom first shared their books with me in the course of my research for this bibliography, and donations continue to flow in. The culinary collection at McGill came from a variety of sources (including, long in the past, prescient purchases by a librarian, probably from the annual university fund-raising book sales). The records for many of the titles that were uncatalogued when I first examined them are now accessible on-line in the 'Cookery Book Collection,' part of the Digital Collections Program (http://digital.library.mcgill.ca/cookbooks/). Institutional collections in Canada tend to be regional in character: strict acquisitions policies sometimes limit collections to locally produced cookbooks; or collections have grown by donations from the region and, therefore, they reflect the cookbooks in use there. I often found small gold mines of material in local museums where the curators and supporting community have recognized, without question, how eloquently old cookbooks express their past. It was impossible, however, to contact and visit every museum in the country and no doubt further material remains to be discovered in out-of-the-way and unexpected places. Although many cookbooks have been preserved in museums, they have usually been treated as artifacts, not books, and often are not catalogued in even the most rudimentary way. And because books as artifacts in museums are not part of the same system as books in libraries, they have not yet, for the most part, been 'captured' in databases such as AMICUS. This bibliography is a first effort to bring to light a still largely inaccessible body of cookbooks in Canadian museums. In contrast, although university libraries are organized to share cataloguing information about their collections through electronic means, some universities are devoid of old cookbooks or nearly so, despite the potential they offer for scholarly inquiry. It was simple to identify significant collections at provincial archives, such as the British Columbia Archives or the Provincial Archives of Manitoba, but it was difficult to know whether cookbooks might be part of a unique fonds, without the archivist's assistance and without physically checking the contents of boxes, as, for instance, when cookbooks were found in the papers of Ethel McKnight at the Provincial Archives of Manitoba.[5] All public or private institutions where cookbooks were found are listed in 'Abbreviations and Symbols' on p xli. The best collections of pre-1950 Canadian cookbooks in each province are identified at the end of the introduction for each province.

Looking for cookbooks in private homes required a different strategy. In 1991 a press release about the project generated a lot of publicity and elicited thousands of letters from individuals, and people continued to come forward with information as they heard news of the bibliography. The frequency with which respondents reported the same title, and their addresses, helped me assess the popularity of a particular text and how widely it may have been distributed; and their letters often contained crucial evidence about dating or comments about the role the book played in their lives.[6] Of the 2,275 titles and their various editions that are described in the bibliography, over 1,000 were found only in private hands. Can there be a more dramatic example in the field of Canadian literature of ordinary citizens being the keepers of the country's printed heritage? Most cookbooks were written for use in the home; their authors were often homemakers; the books themselves illuminate that intimate and normally private world; and in the heart of the home, passed down in families, is also where many of the books survive. On my research trips, I not only visited institutions large and small, but also hundreds of individuals who asked me into the warmth of their homes to see their treasured volumes. I was also privileged to have access to the private libraries of several committed cookbook collectors, who are acknowledged on p xv. Near the end of the project, my belief in the importance of the media as an aid to research was reinforced when an article by Julian Armstrong in the *Montreal Gazette* brought to light a rare copy of the first edition of *La cuisinière canadienne* (Q3.1) in a private collection, which the owner subsequently donated to Library and Archives Canada and which is now available on microfilm to any researcher.

The Evolution of the Genre in Canada

Before 1825

The publication of *La cuisinière bourgeoise* in Quebec City in 1825 signalled the beginning of cookbook publishing in Canada, but culinary information was available to colonists from a variety of sources before (and after) this date. Some early immigrants brought manuscript recipes and printed cookbooks with them, and eventually they could buy cookbooks imported from overseas and from the United States, before and after the American Revolution. In Marius Barbeau's ground-breaking 1944 study, *Saintes artisanes* (Q287.1), the Quebec anthropologist recorded the French and English eighteenth- and early nineteenth-century cookbooks used by the religious orders in Quebec. As early as 17 August 1754, the auctioneer William Craft was advertising a book of 'Cookery' for sale in the *Halifax Gazette*. A notice for the English author Hannah Glasse's 'Cookery' [i.e., *The Art of Cookery Made Plain and Easy*] appeared in the *Nova Scotia Chronicle* of 31 July 1770, followed by ones for Martha Bradley's *The British Housewife* in the *Nova Scotia Gazette and Weekly Chronicle* of 22 October 1772 and 15 June 1773; and records show an increasing number of imported culinary titles, including American texts and American editions of British texts, available for purchase in the Canadian colonies in the nineteenth century. Recipes were also being circulated in locally printed and published almanacs, such as *The British Lady's Diary, and Pocket Almanack* for 1790, which was advertised in the *Quebec Herald* of 10 December 1789 as containing 'several useful recipes in cookery, pickling, preserving, &c.' (no copy located), in *Tiffany's Upper-Canada Almanac* for 1802 (CIHM A01075), and in *The Nova-Scotia Almanack* for 1820 (CIHM A01160). A recipe for that most Canadian of beverages, Spruce Beer, was reproduced on a broadsheet in 1783.[7] A section of 'Recette [*sic*] pour quelques poudings' concludes *Traité sur les maladies des enfans*, a French translation of a book by the English doctor Michael Underwood, published in Quebec City in 1801 (QTS). The *Farmers Journal* of 2 July 1828 (a St Catharines, Ontario, newspaper) reprinted 'Receipts for the Ladies ... copied from the manuscript receipt book of a first rate housekeeper.' Early sources are discussed in more depth in Williamson, *History of the Book*.[8]

The Beginnings, 1825 to 1876

The early history of cookbook publishing in Canada belongs almost exclusively to the provinces of Quebec and Ontario, and developments in those provinces are described in detail in their introductions (pp 73 and 273). From 1791 to 1841 the two jurisdictions were separately administered colonies called Lower Canada and Upper Canada; in 1841 they were joined in a legislative union as Canada East and Canada West in the Province of Canada; from Confederation on 1 July 1867, they became the provinces of Quebec and Ontario in a self-governing Dominion.

The first two cookbooks published in Lower and Upper Canada were editions of foreign works, and both were printed elsewhere. *La cuisinière bourgeoise* (Q1.1), by Menon, was a famous eighteenth-century cookbook from France, which, in the period from its first edition to the 1825 Quebec City edition, had been reprinted multiple times in France, Belgium, and England. *The Cook Not Mad* (O1.1), published in Kingston, Upper Canada, in 1831, was an edition of a recent American work, from just across the border in Watertown, New York, and likely not known outside its own state. These were followed, in 1840, by the first French-language cookbook and the first English-language cookbook to be compiled in Canada – *La cuisinière canadienne* (Q3.1) and *The Frugal Housewife's Manual* (O2.1) credited to 'A.B., of Grimsby.'[9] It is remarkable that these two landmark works appeared in the same year, but it was coincidental, and the character of their texts and the extent to which they penetrated their respective markets were very different. *La cuisinière canadienne* is unattributed but was probably compiled by someone in the circle of Louis Perrault, the publisher, and Mme Gamelin, one of the founders in 1843 of the Institute of Providence, a religious order. Here, for the first time, was a recipe collection addressed to 'the Canadian cook,' i.e., French-Canadian cook, and featuring familiar dishes made from local ingredients (for example, Purée aux poix, Beignets, Ragoût de pattes de cochon, Pouding à la farine de blé d'Inde), plus various English-style boiled puddings adopted from Montreal's English community. It was the only French-Canadian cookbook on the market up to 1878,[10] and continued to be reprinted as late as the mid-1920s, reaching several generations of Quebeckers through multiple editions over eight decades. In contrast, *The Frugal Housewife's Manual* was not reprinted and only two copies of the 1840 Toronto edition survive, despite the fact that it was undoubtedly a useful and carefully chosen collection: the one hundred numbered recipes are thoughtfully arranged in two parts, a 'Housewife's Manual' and a section of entries for vegetables, from Asparagus to Turnip, with instructions for growing and cooking.

Whereas the French-speaking market was well served in this early period by several editions of *La cuisinière canadienne*, A.B.'s manual was followed by a succession of titles from elsewhere: in 1845, *Modern Practical Cookery* (Q4.1), by the Edinburgh cookery teacher Mrs Nourse; in 1846, *Every Lady's Book* (O4.1), uncredited but by the American Mrs Crowen; in 1848, *The Skilful Housewife's Guide* (Q5.1), uncredited but extracted from a text by the American Mrs Abell; in 1865, the American *Dr Chase's Recipes* (O8.1); and in 1868, *The Dominion Home Cook-Book* (O11.1), actually an edition of *The American Home Cook Book*. In 1861, the Hamilton printer Henry Richards, seeing the need for a cookbook 'withal local in its aim,' selected appropriate recipes 'from the best English, French & American works' for publication in *The Canadian Housewife's Manual of Cookery* (O6.1).

There were only two notable exceptions to this run of 'foreign' texts: *The Female Emigrant's Guide* of 1854 (O5.1), by Catharine Parr Traill, who lived near Peterborough in Canada West; and *Household Recipes or Domestic Cookery* (Q7.1), by a Montreal lady [Constance Hart], of 1865. Until the person behind the initials 'A.B., of Grimsby' is discovered, Traill and Hart stand as the only positively identified women up to 1877 who were writing in English specifically for Canadian kitchens. Traill's aim was to characterize for immigrants the unique aspects of cooking in Canada, especially in the 'backwoods,' and she wrote in a way that was at once authoritative, detailed, reassuring, engaging, and particular to the country. She gave instructions for growing and cooking and described eating and dining customs, such as the preference for Buckwheat Pancakes at breakfast. When she contradicts a doctor's assertion that Dandelion Coffee is 'equal in ... flavour to the best Mocha coffee,' the modern reader is convinced that her judgment is reliable, and her comment that 'Canada is the land of cakes' (by which she meant a variety of sweet baked goods) still rings true. No further editions of *The Female Emigrant's Guide* were published after 1862, partly because the contents became increasingly out-of-date toward the end of the nineteenth century as the backwoods way of life in Ontario gave way to a more settled and technologically advanced society. Hart's father and husband were early advocates for Jewish civil liberties in Quebec, and her *Household Recipes* is the first Canadian cookbook by a Jewish author.

The Emergence of New Types, 1877 to 1900

The last quarter of the nineteenth century saw the emergence of three new types of culinary manual in Canada: community cookbooks, also called fund-raising or charitable cookbooks; advertising or promotional cookbooks; and texts for cookery classes. The appearance in 1877 of the first example of the community type, *The Home Cook Book* (O20.1), 'compiled from recipes contributed by ladies of Toronto and other cities and towns ... for the benefit of the Hospital for Sick Children,' marked the beginning in Canada of a grassroots publishing phenomenon that would help to shape Canadian cooking for the next one hundred years and more. Community cookbooks, which first emerged in the United States during the Civil War, are usually a co-operative effort on the part of an organization (often a church women's auxiliary, but also many other sorts of group). Recipes are solicited from the community and usually credited to the individual contributor; the text is edited by a committee; then the volumes are sold by members of the organization to raise money for a charitable purpose. In Canada, where conventional publishers routinely issued editions of foreign texts, community cookbooks were a means by which women could produce recipe collections uniquely suited to their own tastes and cooking practices, and they were especially valued as a source of favourite dishes, making them an important historical record of Canadian food. They also proved to be effective fund-raising tools for all kinds of philanthropic projects, through which women could contribute to the building of Canada's fast-growing civil society. As the best-selling Canadian culinary manual of the nineteenth century, *The Home Cook Book* popularized the concept of the community cookbook in Canada, although the story is complicated by the fact that the Hospital for Sick Children's name was removed from the volume after the hospital's Ladies' Committee severed its relationship with the publisher in 1879. Nevertheless, the title-page reference to the Toronto ladies was retained and the book continued to be reprinted, essentially unchanged, up to 1929, and was widely distributed in large numbers.[11] Since *The Home Cook Book* had an early connection with Saint John, New Brunswick,[12] it is not surprising that Canada's second community cookbook, *Cuisine* (NB2.1), emerged from that city in 1878. Soon, other fundraisers followed in Ontario (Ottawa, 1881, O28.1), Nova Scotia (Halifax, 1888, NS1.1), and Quebec (Montreal, 1888, Q21.1). Community cookbooks remained, for the entire period of this bibliography, primarily an English-language, Protestant publishing phenomenon. Relatively few were produced by English Catholic institutions, and none was found exclusively in the French language.[13] In the twentieth century, Jewish women's groups adopted the idea, both as a useful fund-raising tool and as a way to share their kosher and festival recipes, but the number of Jewish community cookbooks was relatively small, reflecting their proportion of the population.

From about mid-century, patent medicine companies had published promotional brochures that contained a few recipes, sometimes drawing attention to the culinary content in the title, such as *Family Receipt Book* by Northrop and Lyman (O7.1). Often, pages of recipes alternated with calendars and astronomical information, in what came to be called 'almanac cook books' or 'calendar cook books.' All these promotional vehicles for medicines were a sort of advertising cookbook, and *Wrigley's Practical Receipts in the Arts, Manufactures, Trades, and Agriculture* (O13.1), a compendium published in 1870 by the Toronto makers of an Antiseptic Solution and Preserving Powder, might also be considered in this category; however, in the 1880s, there was a new development: the advent of cookbooks openly promoting cooking ingredients or kitchen equipment. The earliest ones advertised baking powder, which at the time was usually concocted by druggists, the same people who distributed patent-medicine literature.[14] *Cook's Friend Cook Book* (O29.1), published in Toronto in 1881, featured recipes using Cook's Friend Baking Powder as an ingredient; and these recipes were later reprinted in *The Art of Cooking Made Easy* (O48.1), various editions of which, from 1890, advertised different proprietary baking powders made by druggists in Ontario, Nova Scotia, and Newfoundland. The earliest baking-powder cookbook to surface in Quebec, *The Princess Baker* for 'Princess' Baking Powder (Q17.1), dates from about the same time as *Cook's Friend Cook Book*. In about 1888, a Toronto publication, *The Breadmaker's Recipe Book* (O42.1), promoted the use of Breadmaker's Yeast and Baking Powder. The early 1890s saw recipe collections for a cooking fat called Cottolene – a mixture of cotton-seed oil and beef fat invented by an American company whose Canadian office was in Montreal (Q26.1) – and for Ontario canned goods (O61.1). The earliest cookbook in this bibliography from a stove maker also dates from the early 1890s: *Happy-Thought-Range Cookery Book* (O53.1) by Buck's Stove Works in Brantford, Ontario. The first cookbook for Church and Dwight's baking soda, a product still marketed today under the 'Cow Brand,' appeared simultaneously in Toronto and Montreal in 1897 (O82.1). By 1898, the first cookbook promoting Canadian flour was published in Peterborough by McAllister Milling Co.: *Good Flour and How to Use It* (O85.1). As the nineteenth century drew to a close, therefore, advertising cookbooks embraced the essential manufactured baking ingredients: raising agents, fat, and flour.

Education in Canada has been a provincial jurisdiction since Confederation in 1867; therefore, the development of cookery teaching in the school curriculum, within the subject of domestic economy, later called household science, then home economics (and later in the twentieth century, family studies), followed its own path in each province. The history of the teaching of the subject in the various provincial education systems is beyond the scope of this bibliography, but textbooks mark some of the changes. The earliest English-language textbook in Canada to touch upon food and cookery was likely *Health in the House* (O19.1), authorized by the Ontario minister of education and published in Toronto in 1877. It was an edition of a British text by Catherine Buckton, the first female member of the Leeds School Board and a pioneering advocate of cookery classes for girls. (Although several Toronto editions of *Health in the House* surfaced, no Canadian edition was located of her 1879 work, *Food and Home Cookery: A Course of Instruction in Practical Cookery and Cleaning, for Children in Elementary Schools, as Followed in the Schools of the Leeds School Board*.)[15] In England, universal public education was introduced in 1870, the first training school for cookery teachers opened its doors in 1874 (the privately run National Training School for Cookery in London), and cookery became a grant-supported subject in the Education Code of 1882. Similar developments in Canada's provinces for the training of cookery teachers and the support of cookery classes in the education system came decades later in some cases. Nevertheless, after *Health in the House*, locally authored textbooks incorporating cookery began to be produced, and three English-language titles were found from the period before the turn of the century. In 1889, Alice Clark, an instructor in the Provincial Normal School of New Brunswick (the institution for teacher training), saw published her *Domestic Economy and Plain Sewing and Knitting: A Manual for Teachers and Housekeepers* as an approved text in the New Brunswick School Series (NB7.1). The 'Preface' acknowledges her debt to another British textbook from the 1870s – *Domestic Economy: A Class Book for Girls* – and adds that the subjects covered within were now required elements on the syllabus for female candidates for school licence. In Ontario, Adelaide Hoodless, motivated by the tragic death of her baby son from drinking bad milk, arose as the most vigorous promoter of the teaching of domestic science to girls. In 1894, she started a school for the subject (outside of the provincial education system) in Hamilton's YWCA, and her 1898 book titled *Public School Domestic Science* (O86.1) contributed to the development of the curriculum in the province.[16] In 1900, in Hamilton, she opened the Ontario Normal School of Domestic Science and Art for training teachers, the first of its kind in the province, and a few years later she was responsible for securing the funding to establish the Macdonald Institute in Guelph in 1903, to which her Hamilton teacher-training program was transferred. Hoodless became famous nationally for these and other initiatives (not the least of which was helping to found the first Women's Institute in Stoney Creek in 1897). A lesser-known but influential figure in Nova Scotia was Helen Bell, whose *Elementary Text-book of Cookery* (NS4.1) was published in Halifax in 1898, the year she began teaching in the city what have been credited as the first domestic-science classes in a public school system.[17]

The signal event for French-language cookbooks in Quebec in the last quarter of the nineteenth century was the publication in Montreal in 1878 of *Directions diverses données par la rev. mère Caron ... pour aider ses soeurs à former de bonnes cuisinières* (Q15.1), which may be based on cooking classes Caron taught in 'une école ménagère' that she organized for the sisters and children at the Institute of Providence in the 1860s, in between her two terms as mother superior. Although probably conceived originally as a handy reference for the sisters and not as a formal textbook, *Directions diverses* was the first recipe manual by a member of a religious order for use in a Catholic institution. Caron begins by illuminating the moral dimensions of cookery and the scope for practising virtue in the kitchen. In Quebec, even after 1950, cookery instruction for francophones, like female education in general, was usually delivered by teaching nuns, overseen by the Catholic bureaucracy, and the discourse on Catholic values with which Caron began her text became a typical feature of textbooks produced by Quebec's écoles ménagères in the twentieth century. *Directions diverses* quickly found favour with the French-Canadian public, running through eight editions up to 1913.

Outside of the emerging new categories of cookbook (community, advertising, and educational), ones by named, local authors were rare in the last quarter of the nineteenth century, as they had been in the preceding half-century. In Ontario, accolades go to three women for compiling their own texts: Anne Clarke in Toronto for *Mrs Clarke's Cookery Book* of 1883 (O35.1); Dora Fairfield in Bath, for *Dora's Cook Book* of 1888 (O43.1); and Mrs James McDonald in

Orangeville, for *The Cook's True Friend* of 1889 (O47.1). Of these, only *Mrs Clarke's Cookery Book* made a real impact; it was the first Canadian culinary manual to be issued in an American edition, in Chicago, in 1889, and from 1898 it was a money maker for a variety of Toronto publishers and manufacturers, under various titles, such as *The Dominion Cook Book* and *The Hudson's Bay Cook Book* (after Canada's famous trading and retail company). In Nova Scotia and New Brunswick, two lone men produced books with recipes and other information: Edwin Lockett compiled *Cape Breton Hand-Book and Tourist's Guide* in about 1889 (NS2.1) and Ely Tree, a steward at Saint John's Union Club, wrote *The Little Helpmate or How to Keep Husbands at Home* in 1894 (NB13.1). In Quebec in 1895, two anglophone women compiled cookbooks, both likely for the purposes of earning a living: Sarah Allen's *The Common Sense Recipe Book* (Q27.1) and Amy G. Richards's *Cookery* (Q28.1). It was more common for Canadians to find for sale in bookstores reprints of cookbooks by rising American culinary stars, such as Marion Harland and Sarah Tyson Rorer, or occasionally a British author, such as Mary Jewry.

The Twentieth Century: Cookbooks of All Types, from East to West, and North

After 1900, culinary titles were published in increasing numbers and covered a wide range of subjects. The new types of cookbook that had begun to find their way into Canadian homes before the turn of the century became familiar and commonplace in the kitchen. Soon, community and advertising cookbooks and school textbooks were joined by recipe collections published by various departments of the federal and provincial governments. More and more cookbooks emanated from the Prairie provinces and British Columbia as new settlers poured into the West and the population boomed in the first few decades of the century. Many Canadians relocating to the West brought cookbooks from their old homes with them, and copies of these have sometimes found their way into the collections of Western libraries, archives, and museums. Whereas some recipe collections were intensely local in their expression and limited in their distribution, such as the 1917 fund-raiser *How We Cook in Strathroy* (O386.1) by a chapter of the Imperial Order Daughters of the Empire in a small town in Ontario or *The Powell River Cook Book* (B108.1) of 1941 from a British Columbia pulp-and-paper town, others were national in concept and widely disseminated in thousands of copies over several years, such as the 1921 federal government publication *How We*

Cook in Canada by Dr Helen MacMurchy (O469.1). Although there were many more Canadian-authored cookbooks produced in the first half of the twentieth century, many of which did enjoy national distribution, Toronto publishers especially continued to issue reprints of foreign works. And a growing outside influence were the Canadian editions of advertising cookbooks produced by mostly American, but also a few British, companies with branch plants in Canada.

The concept of the community cookbook was well established in the Maritimes, Quebec, and Ontario by the turn of the twentieth century, and by 1907, examples had appeared in every province (the colony of Newfoundland included). The genre blossomed over the next few decades, as all kinds of women's groups across the country turned to compiling and publishing cookbooks to raise money for building projects or their charitable work. Most of these cookbooks emanated from churches, the focus of community life. In the East, growing congregations needed new or enlarged buildings, while in the West, places of worship had to be constructed in new settlements. As hospitals sprang up in developing towns, the women's auxiliary attached to the institution often produced a fund-raising cookbook, just as the Toronto ladies had done for the children's hospital in that city in 1877. Many recipe manuals also came from branches of various philanthropic or patriotic associations that were founded about the turn of the century, such as the Women's Institutes (1897) and the Imperial Order Daughters of the Empire (1900), or, a little later, organizations of farm women in the Prairie provinces. Cookbooks were also published to boost tourism, to aid temperance causes and missionary work, to support the war effort during two World Wars, and even on occasion to benefit a political party – the Co-operative Commonwealth Federation (O1088.1) or the Alberta Social Credit Party (A108.1). Some community cookbooks were terrifically successful fund-raisers, such as the second edition of *The Blue Bird Cook Book*, whose profits paid for a furnished club house for the American Women's Club in Calgary in the 1920s (see notes for A28.1), or *The Victory Cook Book* (NB51.1) by the Women's Institutes of Carleton County, New Brunswick, whose 1942 first edition bought two ambulances for the Canadian military and whose second edition covered the construction of a manse and garage for the Anglican church in Florenceville. But beyond fund-raising, they also served other functions, sometimes as an educational tool for rural women, or as a vehicle to promote the values of the group, such as the ideals of the co-operative movement or the Zionism of Hadassah.

Some recorded aspects of local history in words and pictures, or marked a royal visit or a coronation. Others were valuable collections of recipes for a particular ethnic group; for example, the Icelandic specialties in a cookbook from Winnipeg's First Lutheran Church (M54.1) and the Ukrainian recipes collected together by St Josaphat's Ladies' Auxiliary in Edmonton (A95.1). Sometimes, a cookbook might be compiled for a simple social benefit, as a publication (O286.1) from North Broadview Presbyterian Church in Toronto explained in about 1912: 'This book is not only compiled for the raising of funds for our Sunday School but as an aid to introduce and enable us to become better acquainted with our surrounding members and friends.' Some charitable cookbooks were issued in multiple editions, over several decades, were influential locally for a long period, and remain well known, such as the *Victory Cook Book* in New Brunswick (NB51.1), the series of *Tested Recipes* (listed at NS29.1) issued by the Evangeline Chapter of the IODE in Halifax, the *Naomi Cook Book* (O627.1) in Toronto's Jewish community, or *Recipes* (A59.1) from the United Farm Women of Alberta.

In *American Cookbooks and Wine Books 1797–1950*, p 32, a catalogue for an exhibition held at the Clements Library, University of Michigan, in 1984, Janice Longone wrote: 'In many ways, [charitable] cookbooks are an American phenomenon. Although some books have appeared in Britain, Canada and other parts of the former British Empire, *there are only a small number of them, and they do not seem to have gained much prominence* [italics added]. Nowhere else do charitable cookbooks play the major role that they do in American cookbook publishing history.' Longone's comment is understandable given the lack of information about Canadian cookbooks at the time, but incorrect given the outcome of my research, which shows an astonishing number of community cookbooks created by Canadian women in the first half of the twentieth century. Fund-raisers made up a large part of the cookbook landscape in almost every province, as these percentages (which include the handful of nineteenth-century examples) demonstrate: about half or more of the total number of culinary titles published in Newfoundland (50%), Nova Scotia (74%), New Brunswick (51%), Prince Edward Island (80%), Manitoba (54%), Saskatchewan (83%), Alberta (61%), and British Columbia (44%). The three cookbooks to surface from the Yukon and the Northwest Territories were community cookbooks. In Ontario, 40% of all culinary titles were the community type, despite the many advertising items produced by the province's commercial sector and all the cookbooks

(Canadian and foreign) emanating from the offices of publishers in Toronto, the country's centre for English-language publishing. In fact, the number of Ontario community cookbooks discovered – 507 – exceeds the total number of cookbooks of all types published in Quebec (or any other province) for the entire period covered by this bibliography. Quebec is the only province where community cookbooks made up a small proportion (18%), because none appears to have been produced by the majority French-speaking and Catholic population and those that were published by the smaller English-speaking population (58) were outnumbered by other types. All the percentages quoted reflect the findings of my research, but the actual number of community cookbooks may be much higher because this type has tended to remain in private hands. The numbers are impressive, but it is also significant that these books arose out of the grassroots of Canadian society and, therefore, are a powerful and authentic expression of the culture. And they show Canadian women engaging, with enthusiasm, in all aspects of book production – as authors, editors, distributors, sometimes even as printers[18] – a sophisticated enterprise, which they often carried out with style and acumen. Although Longone and other scholars have commented on the role of community cookbooks in the United States, where the idea began, their importance within Canadian cookbook publishing, or, indeed, within the context of Canadian print culture generally, remains to be investigated.[19]

The twentieth century saw small, local or regional businesses evolve into national industries, and when these larger entities published cookbooks to promote food products and kitchen equipment, the publications were usually printed in large numbers for distribution across the country. Of all the twentieth-century advertising cookbooks, those produced by flour companies were the most commonly owned, the most influential, and the most typically Canadian. Canada is famed for its wheat, and it was the discovery of the hardy and early-maturing Marquis variety in 1903 by Charles E. Saunders and its commercial use on the Prairies a few years later that spurred on the opening of the West.[20] In the first half of the new century, bread-making was still a vital, daily chore in most families. Huge milling companies fought for market share, and cookbooks – often lavishly illustrated in colour – were an essential part of their arsenal. *Ogilvie's Book for a Cook* (Q55.1) of 1905, a recycled American text, was the first widely distributed flour-company cookbook, but the one that reached the most homes was probably the Canadian-

made *Five Roses Cook Book* (Q79.1) of 1913, by Lake of the Woods Milling Co. Reprintings surpassed 950,000 copies. As the publisher's blurb for the 1915 edition boasted, there was 'practically one copy [of the *Five Roses Cook Book*] for every second Canadian Home.' Starting in 1917, Western Canada Flour Mills, which made Purity Flour, published a series of cookbooks (listed at O394.1). The year 1932 saw a head-to-head marketing battle when both Lake of the Woods Milling and Western Canada Flour Mills issued new recipe collections – for Five Roses Flour, *A Guide to Good Cooking* (Q203.1), and for Purity, *The Purity Cook-Book* (O771.1). Robin Hood Mills Ltd, the maker of Robin Hood Flour, published its first cookbook in about 1915 (S16.1, commissioned by the company's American owners from Mrs Rorer, a famous American culinary authority), but Robin Hood Mills made its biggest impact in the 1940s, producing ones by the fictional Rita Martin (a name easy for English and French Canadians to pronounce, but also used in the unilingual American market). Editions of cookbooks for Purity Flour spanned the years 1917 to the mid-1970s. Customers could still order a Five Roses cookbook in 2008 – ninety-five years after the first edition! As each new edition was prepared, the favourite recipes of the past would be carried forward and other recipes added, reflecting changes in fashion or technology, so that in the 1967 edition of *The All New Purity Cook Book*, for example, the contents included instructions for baking bread and biscuits with the company's flour, a standard feature of every edition; Carrot Pudding, a version of a recipe from *The Home Cook Book* of 1877; Butter Tarts, a Canadian specialty from the turn of the twentieth century; Jellied Perfection Salad, popular in the 1920s; a section of 'Refrigerator Cookies,' called ice-box cookies in the 1930s, when the method was developed for the new cooling appliances; traditional preserving recipes (using bottles), but also a section about home freezing as a method of food preservation. The decades-long runs of editions of Purity Flour and Five Roses Flour cookbooks, designed to win the customer's loyalty by adhering closely to Canadian traditions and tastes, illustrate well the evolution of the country's home cooking through the twentieth century.

Also on offer to housewives were cookbooks advertising many other kinds of foodstuff, manufactured and harvested. A few major brands of baking powder replaced the variety of local brands sold in the 1880s and 1890s. In Winnipeg, the Blue Ribbon Manufacturing Co., which sold its own-name baking powder, spices, and other dry goods throughout the West, published *The Blue Ribbon Cook Book* in 1905

(M7.1). In Toronto, in the second decade of the century, E.W. Gillett Co. published *Magic Cook Book and Housekeepers Guide* to promote Magic Baking Powder (O285.1). These were not the only recipe collections for baking powder, but they were the most ubiquitous as many editions were issued up to mid-century (and beyond in the case of Blue Ribbon). Other Canadian manufactured products advertised through cookbooks include corn starch, sugar (from several different companies), corn syrup (promoted during the Second World War as a substitute for sugar), maple syrup, shortening, margarine (after its legalization in 1948), milk, cheese, cocoa, flavouring extracts, vinegar, mustard, canned foods, Tea-Bisk (the instant biscuit mix), even marshmallows. Since most manufacturers were located in Quebec or Ontario, the majority of advertising cookbooks were compiled and published in those provinces; however, important food industries in other parts of the country also issued recipe collections, for example, *48 Famous Sardine Meals* (NB33.1) by Connors Bros Ltd in Black's Harbour, New Brunswick, 1925, various titles (listed at A31.1) for cooking with Shamrock-brand meat from the famous Calgary meat-packer P. Burns and Co. Ltd, starting in about 1915, or several books for cooking with British Columbia fruit, such as *Yello Fello, the Apple Elf*, about 1920–5 (B46.1). Promotional cookbooks for kitchen equipment followed the introduction of new technologies, usually accompanying the purchase of a new appliance. At about the turn of the century, gas companies in Ottawa and Vancouver published cookbooks to promote the use of the new cooking fuel. The 1910s and 1920s were a period of transition for stoves, and the 1915 *Moffat Standard Canadian Cook Book* (O342.1) introduced women to the variety available, which included ones that ran on a single fuel (coal, gas, or electricity), combination gas-and-coal or gas-and-electricity, or a combination of all three fuels, but by the 1930s publications from stove manufacturers were for gas or electric cooking only. In the mid-1920s ice-boxes began to give way to electric refrigerators, although it would be some time before every home had this convenience (the hard times of the Depression slowed the technology's adoption). The earliest collection of recipes for preparing food using a refrigerator appeared in about 1929–32: *The Miracle of Cold* (O656.1), for those lucky enough to have a new Kelvinator electric refrigerator, an American make. Cookbooks also introduced food choppers, cream separators, aluminium saucepans, pressure cookers, and food mixers to the novice public. Firms often paid for special artwork to enhance their publications, and the reproductions in this bibli-

ography convey only a small degree of the invention and delight found in advertising cookbooks. When American and British companies promoted their brands of food or equipment in Canada, they generally reprinted texts from home, although there were occasional exceptions. Most of the branch plants for these foreign concerns were based in Montreal or Toronto and their books are discussed in the provincial introductions for Quebec and Ontario, on pp 73 and 273. Their brands, such as the American Jell-O and Crisco or the British Oxo and Fry-Cadbury, remain major players in the marketplace.

After 1900, cookery became increasingly organized as a subject of study for schoolgirls, in tandem with the development of home economics in the new university departments and colleges established for the subject. In the East, the Lillian Massey School of Household Science and Art at the University of Toronto was founded in 1902, the Macdonald Institute at the Ontario Agricultural College in Guelph opened in 1903, and the School of Household Science at Macdonald College at McGill University in Montreal accepted its first students in 1907; in the West, Manitoba Agricultural College in Winnipeg welcomed household science students in 1910. The staff of these institutions helped to develop curricula for schools and wrote cookery textbooks for use in their own courses and for school classes, and many graduates became teachers of cookery in schools (or found a career in the food industry). The pre-eminent school textbook in English was *Canadian Cook Book* (O506.1) by Nellie Pattinson, director of domestic science at Central Technical School in Toronto. It was republished multiple times from 1923 to 1949, then had a new life after its 1953 revision by Elinor Donaldson and Helen Wattie, the last edition appearing in 1991. A close second in popularity and longevity was *The Country Cook or the M.A.C. Cook Book* (soon abbreviated to just *The M.A.C. Cook Book*) (M37.1), first published in 1922 and compiled by Mary Hiltz and Mary Moxon, both on the staff of the Manitoba Agricultural College. Both *Canadian Cook Book* and *The M.A.C. Cook Book* were distributed nationally[21] and made the leap from being classroom texts to trusted kitchen bibles in the home; however, there were also other English-language textbooks for the provinces of Saskatchewan (S28.1) and British Columbia (B59.1), and the cities of Saint John, New Brunswick (NB54.1), Toronto (O528.1), and Winnipeg (M46.1, M98.1), that made a significant impact in their jurisdictions. In about 1900–10, the Quebec Department of Agriculture published *La bonne ménagère* (Q48.1), lessons for girls in rural schools, but the most influential school textbook in French was *Manuel de cuisine raisonnée* (Q102.1) (later simply *La cuisine raisonnée*), produced in 1919 for the students of the École normale classico-ménagère de Saint-Pascal, but subsequently used in classes and homes throughout the province of Quebec, and in print up to the 1980s (plus a 2003 edition).

The earliest provincial governments to publish recipe collections were Quebec and Ontario (*La bonne ménagère* and the Ontario Department of Agriculture's *Uses of Fruits, Vegetables and Honey* of 1905, O158.1). From the mid-1910s, the federal and other provincial governments also issued cookbooks. These publications often had two aims: to promote locally produced foods and to educate the public. Good examples of this double purpose are the *Use of Honey and of Maple Sugar in Cooking* (Q109.1) published by the Quebec Department of Agriculture in about 1920 and *Saskatchewan Fish Cookery* (S101.1) from that province's Department of Natural Resources and Industrial Development in about 1946. Sometimes, government publications were intended more to assist the food producer than the public at large, such as *Cheese-Making on the Farm*, *The Potato*, and *The Beef Ring*, in the Manitoba Farmers' Library, although the booklets were available free to any Manitoba citizen (cooking-related titles in the series are listed at M26.1). Canning, pickling, and other ways of preserving food, such as drying and salting, were still an important part of the seasonal cycle in Canadian kitchens before 1950, when fresh ingredients were in short supply over the winter. As a British cookbook of 1947 remarked, 'In Canada they say, "Use all you can, and can what you can't ..."'[22] The impetus to conserve the food supply during the First World War led to the publication by the food controller for Canada in 1917 of *Can, Dry and Store for Victory* (O376.1), and other titles with the same aim. Also in 1917, female employees at the Central Experimental Farm in Ottawa began to develop improved canning and pickling methods (especially from the point of view of safety) and the Department of Agriculture published the results of their work in cookbooks, beginning in 1919 with Margaret Macfarlane's *Preservation of Fruits and Vegetables for Home Use* (O424.1). Knowing how to preserve food was so essential to the economy, health, and safety of the family that publications on the topic were available from the federal Department of Agriculture through the period covered by this bibliography, and most provincial Departments of Agriculture also published them. The variety of federal and provincial government cookbooks is discussed further in the provincial introductions, the Ontario introduc-

tion including titles by the federal government in Ottawa.

Another notable development in Canadian culinary literature blossomed in the 1930s and 1940s: the individual author as a cooking authority, sometimes a celebrity, even media star. The advent of radio, the new photographically illustrated women's magazines, such as *Chatelaine*, cookery pages in newspapers, the popularity of cooking demonstrations, the advertising needs of food companies and other businesses, and a more developed and mature publishing industry – all these factors increased opportunities for Canadian women to build a reputation, locally or nationally. The ingredients common to their success were, in varying degrees, an entrepreneurial instinct, creative flair, energy, and sometimes, but not always, training in home economics. Earlier in the century, Grace Denison had used her connections as society reporter for *Saturday Night* magazine to collect recipes from Toronto ladies in the best circles, and published them as *The New Cook Book* by 'Lady Gay of Saturday Night' – her well-known pen name (O130.1). Of all the authors in this bibliography, the most masterful at creating a public profile were Ontario-born Kate Aitken and Montrealer Jehane Benoît (whose early cookbooks appear here under her maiden name, Patenaude). Aitken's nation-wide culinary fame came largely through radio; she was so successful in the medium that her work eventually embraced political and cultural affairs and later in life she was appointed to the Board of Governors of the Canadian Broadcasting Corporation. Benoît was a little younger than Aitken and, although she began publishing and doing radio shows in the war years, her star rose mostly after 1950 through television. Remarkably, this bilingual French Canadian became as popular in the rest of Canada as in her native Quebec. Other cookbook authors from the two decades leading up to mid-century who made their names first in radio or print journalism include Gertrude Dutton, Mary Moore, Jessie Read, Cynthia Brown (pseudonym of Rose Marie Armstrong Christie), Marie Holmes (pseudonym of Marie Wallace), and Helen Gougeon. The United States and Britain had long had their culinary experts, whose works were widely available in Canada. Although the country's home-grown authors had to compete for sales with foreign writers and they faced the constraints of a small market, they shared the advantage that they were attuned to the requirements of Canadian families. In a perceptive 1942 Toronto newspaper review of cookbooks for Christmas gift-giving, Jean Brodie recommended highly the works of Jessie Read, Marie Holmes, and

Nellie Pattinson (the Central Technical School teacher) for just this reason.[23] 'In Canada,' she stated, 'we have had far too few cookery books compiled by Canadians for Canadian households.' As she explained, Canadian cookbooks could not match the high production values of American ones, whose publishers had lower costs because of large print runs in a larger market. Instead, according to Brodie (who was musing about the plain, blue-cloth binding of Pattinson's *Canadian Cook Book*), they followed the British tradition of eliminating some of the attractive features to keep the price of the book within the reach of most families, but without sacrificing the quality of the contents. The benefit of cookbooks written for Canadian households was that the menus appealed to Canadian appetites, cuts of meat were those found in Canadian butcher shops, recipes for desserts called for less sugar than Americans liked to use, measurements followed the Canadian system (at the time, 20-ounce pints and 40-ounce quarts, not the American 16 and 32 ounces), and the flour specified was Canadian flour (not the American blended 'all purpose').[24]

Sharing the limelight with the real personalities were the fictional characters created by food companies, such as Anna Lee Scott for Maple Leaf Mills, Brenda York for Canada Packers, Martha Logan for Swift Canadian Co., and Rita Martin for Robin Hood Flour Mills, or Edith Adams, who was created by the *Vancouver Sun* newspaper. A real woman, usually a trained home economist, would be hired to represent the character on radio, in cookery demonstrations, or in print, with the assistance of others working out of the company's 'test kitchen.' From 1947, Edith Adams even had her own 'cottage' adjacent to the newspaper's building, where Vancouver residents would flock to see Marianne Linnell as 'Edith' demonstrate recipes. In one exceptional instance, Kay Caldwell Bayley of Toronto formed Ann Adam Homecrafters in about 1930, then contracted out services to Canada's major food companies, for whom she and her team of home economists would write cookbooks under the pseudonym Ann Adam or under the company's proprietary pseudonym; and for many decades Bayley prepared newspaper columns and ran a radio cooking school as Ann Adam.[25] Although make-believe, all these characters, through their real-life representatives, forged a bond with the Canadian public, who avidly listened to their radio shows, attended their demonstrations, sent letters to them about cooking problems, and consulted their cookbooks. And like the real personalities, the professional women standing in the fictional shoes understood the preferences of Canadian families and the nature of their kitchens.

Their relationship with the public, however, was more complex, and was unique for each character.[26] Although the real personalities sometimes authored advertising cookbooks (Aitken and Benoît), the sole purpose of the fictional characters was to promote the company's products. Moreover, whereas Ann Adam, Anna Lee Scott, Brenda York, and Edith Adams were Canadian creations, the women who wrote cookbooks as Rita Martin and Martha Logan were, in large part, interpreting material sent from their companies' twin test kitchens in the United States, making sure that it was adapted for Canadian households.

Conclusion

Culinary Landmarks is a record of the publishing history of Canadian cookbooks, and the entries that make up the whole are based on physical descriptions of individual volumes. The process of documenting the books was long and painstaking, yet the stories of the authors, publishers, and readers that emerged were a reminder that books, generally, and cookbooks, specifically, are not just objects to be catalogued, but expressions of the values and aspirations of the people who produced them. Sometimes, publishing events were momentous, such as when the anonymous compiler(s) of *La cuisinière canadienne* and its printer, Louis Perrault, produced the first French-Canadian recipe collection in 1840, putting into action the ideals of a political movement that aimed to preserve French culture in the British colony. Catharine Parr Traill's persistence in finding subscribers and a printer for *The Female Emigrant's Guide*, despite her poverty and isolation in the backwoods, was emblematic of the courage of the early pioneers of Canada West in their quest for a better life. In the first few years after Confederation, as citizens took on the task of building a nation, a group of Toronto ladies displayed an inspiring degree of pluck and social commitment when they founded the country's first children's hospital in 1875 and two years later compiled *The Home Cook Book*, the first of the fundraising type, setting in motion a major development in Canadian cookbook publishing. Even the humblest of the many community cookbooks that followed can be read as a small-scale manifestation of a larger subject – the importance for Canadian women of associational life as a means of contributing to their society. And writing cookbooks opened up a new path for self-motivated women in the working world, either as employees of a kitchen-related business, of government, or of an educational institution, or as independent food journalists. Aspects of Canada's early economic and industrial development were played out in the pages of cookbooks, especially the twentieth-century rivalry of the great flour-milling enterprises, and the many copies of flour-company cookbooks still found in Canadian homes and their owners' attachment to them are a testament to the quality of the culinary texts and to Canadians' baking skills. These are just some of the themes, major and minor, that can be traced through the chronological sequence of cookbooks described in this bibliography. Whether the texts contain a sophisticated discourse on gastronomy or offer a basic selection of recipes, whether they were published long in the past or more recently, whether they are regional or national productions – each one contributes in some way to our understanding of Canadian history.

NOTES

1 For information about this text, usually called *Apicius* after its supposed author, including a summary of published editions, see Alan Davidson's entry for Apicius, in his *The Oxford Companion to Food*, p 23. See also Sally Grainger and Christopher Grocock, eds, *Apicius: A Critical Edition with an Introduction and English Translation*, Totnes, Devon: Prospect Books, 2006.

2 For almanacs published in Canada, see the records of Anne Dondertman, Patricia Fleming, and Judy Donnelly for *A Bibliography of Canadian Almanacs, 1765–1900* [in progress].

3 For the history of the Women's Institutes in Ontario, see Ambrose; for Manitoba, see *The Great Human Heart: A History of the Manitoba Women's Institute, 1910–1980*, [Winnipeg:] Manitoba Women's Institute, 1980; for Alberta, see Cole/Larmour.

4 SWI, p 56.

5 There was no reason to expect cookbooks in Miss McKnight's papers (she was not a home economist, for example), but the archivist remembered seeing some, and suggested I search the boxes.

6 Correspondence received in the course of my research will be deposited at the University of Guelph, along with other documentation related to the project.

7 Patricia Lockhart Fleming and Sandra Alston, *Early Canadian Printing: A Supplement to Marie Tremaine's A Bibliography of Canadian Imprints, 1751–1800*, Toronto: University of Toronto Press, 1999, No. 400. Tremaine identified the broadsheet as having been

printed on 24 January 1783 by William Brown for Johnston and Purss, but neither Tremaine nor Fleming and Alston were able to locate a copy.

8 All the booksellers' advertisements, almanac titles, and the newspaper reference cited here were found by Williamson in the course of research for her entry in *The History of the Book in Canada*.

9 In 1834, Richard Hoit published *The Canadian Farrier*, with a section of 'Valuable Recipes' (Q2.1). Although it predates *The Frugal Housewife's Manual*, it is a compendium, rather than a cookbook proper.

10 Cookery was not the main topic of P. Hirbet's *La chimie* of 1859 (Q6.1).

11 See O20.1 for the number of variants printed and copies sold. In the course of my research, copies of *The Home Cook Book* have surfaced in all ten provinces, further evidence of its wide distribution.

12 See the New Brunswick introduction, pp 38–9, concerning *The Home Cook Book*'s connection with Saint John.

13 This phenomenon is discussed in the Quebec introduction, p 76. In a few rare instances, French-language recipes were incorporated in mainly English texts; for example, *Mother's Own Cook Book* (NB37.1) and *'The Black Whale' Cook Book* (Q314.1).

14 Baking powder, a combination of bicarbonate of soda and tartaric acid, was developed in the 1850s and available for sale in Upper Canada in that decade (Catharine Parr Traill refers to Durkee's brand in O5.1, *The Female Emigrant's Guide* of 1854). For more information about this raising agent and its earlier forms, see Davidson, pp 50–1.

15 No. 167.1 in Driver.

16 'Public school' in Canada means a school supported by taxes, not a private school as in Great Britain.

17 The claim is made in NS9.2.

18 Women's groups usually turned to local job printers, but sometimes they reproduced the text themselves by various multigraphing methods, such as hectograph in the 1940s. In a few cases, they made carbon copies of typed text; for example, M93.1.

19 A 1997 collection of essays by academics from various disciplines explored different ways of understanding community cookbooks: *Recipes for Reading: Community Cookbooks, Stories, Histories*, edited by Anne L. Bower, Amherst: University of Massachusetts Press. The writers discuss mainly American cookbooks, but 'Voices, Stories, and Recipes in Selected Canadian Community Cookbooks' by Elizabeth J. McDougall examines a few Canadian cookbooks from the second half of the twentieth century in the context of current literary

theory. The essay collection contains generalizations about the genre that may be true for community cookbooks from any country, but it does not illuminate the role of Canadian community cookbooks within the context of the history of Canadian cookbook publishing. For more comment on the genre in Canada, see Driver 2006.

20 Marquis wheat was sent to the Prairies for testing in 1907 and it was the established crop on farms by 1911.

21 Other textbooks were also used outside their province, as inscriptions by students in the copies often reveal; see, for example, the 1913 edition of Lillian Massey School recipes used at Mount Allison Ladies' College in Sackville, New Brunswick (O241.2), and the 1936, 1938, and 1949 editions of the British Columbia Department of Education *Foods, Nutrition and Home Management Manual* used in Alberta and Ontario schools (B59.5, B59.6, B59.14).

22 Mollie Stanley Wrench, *A Winter's Tale*, London: Porosan Publishing Ltd, April 1947, p 1.

23 Jean Brodie, 'These Cook Books Can Help You,' *Star Weekly* (Toronto) 5 December 1942, Magazine Section No. 2, p 2.

24 The characteristics of a Canadian kitchen mentioned by Brodie typify her time, in the 1940s.

25 For further information about Ann Adam Homecrafters, see O877.1.

26 Nathalie Cooke examines the power and function of what she calls these 'fictional folk' in 'Getting the Mix Just Right for the Canadian Home Baker,' *Essays on Canadian Writing* No. 78 (Winter 2003).

Chronology of Canadian Cookbook History

1754   Auctioneer William Craft advertises a book of 'Cookery' for sale in the *Halifax Gazette*, 17 August, the earliest reference to cookbooks for sale in the British colonies.

1825   *La cuisinière bourgeoise* by Menon, Quebec City, first French-language cookbook published in the area of present-day Canada, an edition of a work from France (Q1.1).

1831   *The Cook Not Mad*, Kingston, first English-language cookbook in the area of present-day Canada, an edition of a work from the United States (O1.1).

1840   *La cuisinière canadienne*, Montreal, first locally authored cookbook in French (Q3.1); *The Frugal Housewife's Manual* by 'A.B., of Grimsby,' Toronto, first locally authored cookbook in English (O2.1).

1860   *The Canadian Settler's Guide* by Catharine Parr Traill published in London, England (a retitled edition of *The Female Emigrant's Guide* of 1854), the first Canadian cookbook to appear in a British edition, but most of the culinary information is removed by the publisher (O5.1).

1865   *Household Recipes* by Constance Hart, Montreal, first by a Jewish author (Q7.1).

1877   *The Home Cook Book* by ladies of Toronto and other cities and towns, for the benefit of the Hospital for Sick Children, Canada's first community cookbook (O20.1); see also 1889 and 1906.

1878   *Cuisine* by ladies of Saint John, first locally authored cookbook in New Brunswick (NB2.1), although a compendium with recipes had appeared earlier, in 1871 (NB1.1, Richard Moore's *Secret Knowledge Disclosed*); *Directions diverses données par la révérende mère Caron*, first cookbook by a member of a religious order for use in Quebec's Catholic institutions (Q15.1).

1881   *Cook's Friend Cook Book*, promoting Cook's Friend Baking Powder and the first dated culinary manual advertising an ingredient (O29.1; Q17.1, *The Princess Baker*, may be one year or so earlier, but its date is uncertain).

1888   *Church of England Institute Receipt Book* by Mary Jane Lawson and Alice Jones, Halifax, first locally authored cookbook in Nova Scotia (NS1.1); *Clever Cooking for Careful Cooks* by a few ladies of the Church of St John the Evangelist, Montreal, the earliest dated community cookbook in Quebec (Q21.1); *Dr Chase's drittem, letzen und vollständigem Recept-Buch und Haus-Arzt*, Detroit, Michigan, and Windsor, Ontario, first cookbook published in Canada in a language other than English or French, a German-language edition of a work by an American doctor (O40.3).

1889   Retitled American editions of *Mrs Clarke's Cookery Book* of 1883, the first Canadian cookbook published in the United States (O35.1; American editions of Richard Moore's compendia, NB1.1 and O23.1, appeared earlier, but culinary recipes were a fraction of the text); Australian edition of *The Home Cook Book* of 1877, the first Canadian cookbook published in the southern hemisphere (New Zealand editions followed in 1891 and 1892); *Domestic Economy and Plain Sewing and Knitting* by M. Alice Clark, the first English-language textbook compiled in Canada for teachers of domestic economy, a subject that included cookery (NB7.1).

1896   *The Souvenir Cook Book* by Ladies' Aid Society of Grace Church, Winnipeg, first locally authored cookbook in Manitoba (M2.1).

1897   *Jubilee Cook Book* by Ladies' Aid Society of the First Methodist Church, Charlottetown, first locally authored cookbook in Prince Edward Island (P1.1).

1898   *Good Flour and How to Use It*, Peterborough:

McAllister Milling Co., the first flour-company cookbook (O85.1).

1901 *The Souris Branch Cook Book* by Ladies' Aid Society, Carnduff, first locally authored cookbook in the area of present-day Saskatchewan (S1.1).

1904 *The King's Daughters Cookery Book* by Mrs Margaret McMicking, first locally authored cookbook in British Columbia (B5.1).

1905 *The L.C.A.S. Cook Book* by Ladies' College Aid Society of the Methodist Church, St John's, first locally authored cookbook in Newfoundland (NF1.1); *Ogilvie's Book for a Cook*, Montreal: Ogilvie Flour Mills Co., the first widely distributed flour-company cookbook (Q55.1), but based on an American source.

1906 The first Canadian recipe collections published in Britain: *The Home Cook Book* of 1877, likely in 1906, and *The New Cook Book* by Grace Denison of 1903 (O130.1), certainly in 1906.

1907 *Clever Cooking* by Woman's Guild of Holy Trinity Church, Strathcona (A5.1), *Cook Book*, by Ladies' Branch 'E' Aid of Knox Church, Calgary (A6.1), and *High River Cook Book* by Ladies' Aid of Chalmer's Church (A7.1), first locally authored cookbooks in Alberta (A4.1, *A Book of Cookery* by Union Ladies' Aid, Lamont, may be earlier, but its year of publication is uncertain; A8.1, *Rising Sun Cook Book*, 1907, may or may not have been compiled locally).

1913 *Five Roses Cook Book*, Montreal: Lake of the Woods Milling Co. Ltd, first widely distributed flour-company cookbook written in Canada (Q79.1).

1914 *Fish and How to Cook It*, Department of the Naval Service, Ottawa, first cookbook published by the federal government (O319.1).

1915 *The Economical Cook Book* by Ottawa Ladies Hebrew Benevolent Society, first collection of Jewish recipes published in Canada (O337.1).

1917 *Ukrains'ko-angliiskyi kukharare* by Michael M. Belegai, Edmonton, earliest known edition of first cookbook in Ukrainian language published in Canada (A34.1).

1919 *Manuel de cuisine raisonnée*, École normale classico-ménagère, Congrégation de Notre-Dame, Quebec: Saint-Pascal, the most widely used French-language classroom textbook, then home-kitchen bible, last edition 2003 (Q102.1).

1923 *Canadian Cook Book* by Nellie Lyle Pattinson, Toronto, the most widely used English-language classroom textbook, then home-kitchen bible, last edition 1991 (O506.1); see also 1953.

1941–2 *D M S* by Daughters of the Midnight Sun, Yellowknife, first cookbook in the Northwest Territories (NWT1.1).

1942 *Choice Recipes* by Yukon Chapter No. 1, Order of the Eastern Star, Dawson, first cookbook in the Yukon (Y1.1).

1953 *Nellie Lyle Pattinson's Canadian Cook Book*, a revision by Helen Wattie and Elinor Donaldson, incorporating for the first time in a Canadian cookbook a special section of 'Regional Dishes' prefaced by comments on culinary history; National Library of Canada founded in Ottawa, Canadian cookbooks begin to be collected systematically by a public institution for the first time.

1979 Books for Cooks opens in September at 850 Yonge Street, Toronto, the first store in Canada to specialize in cookbooks; April 1983, renamed the Cookbook Store and continuing under new ownership, in the same location.

1998 Inauguration of annual Culinary Book Awards, the first Canadian cookbook prizes, conceived by Jo Marie Powers and sponsored by Cuisine Canada, a national association of food professionals; since 2003, co-sponsored with University of Guelph.

Explanation of Bibliography Entries

Arrangement of the Entries in the Bibliography

The entries are arranged by the province or territory in which the book was published. In most cases, a single place of publication is clearly indicated in the book; however, if more than one location is given in the imprint, the first-cited city or the city printed in the largest font, or other clues in the book, have guided the placement of the entry. Where no place of publication is recorded, but the location of the head office of the association or company that originated the book is known from outside sources, the entry is placed in the appropriate provincial section, and the reasons given in the 'Notes' part of the entry. In a few cases, no province of publication could be determined; these entries are in the section 'No Province of Publication.'

Occasionally, a book originally published in one province was subsequently published in another province, or editions of a book were published simultaneously by different publishers in different provinces; examples are the first edition of *The Home Cook Book* by a Toronto publisher in 1877, followed the next year by editions in Saint John, New Brunswick (O20.5, O20.6), and the multiple editions of *Good Bread* published in about the same year by druggists in Quebec, Ontario, and Nova Scotia (see O321.1). In such cases, entries for all the editions are kept together and located in the province of the first edition or, if the first edition is unknown, wherever most appropriate. Cross-references guide the reader from one provincial section to the specific entry in another provincial section where the run of editions is located. Multiple provinces of publication are also reflected in the Place-of-Publication Index.

In each provincial section, the entries are arranged chronologically by the date of publication of the first edition. For undated books where the designated approximate date of publication is a span of time, the first year in the period determines the placement. The following is an example of the ordering system for dates of publication: 1930; about 1930–3; about 1930–5; 1931; 1932; about 1932–3. Where more than one book was published in a year or particular span of years, the entries are arranged by their headings, following letter-by-letter alphabetical order. The heading '[Title unknown]' comes before the start of the alphabetical run. Entries for books with confirmed and approximate dates of publication, i.e., 1930 and about 1930, are considered the same for the purposes of ordering. Occasionally, two or more books with the same title were published in the same year. In these cases, the entries are arranged alphabetically by the compiling organization: *Selected Recipes*, 1934, by the Imperial Order Daughters of the Empire, Princess of Wales Chapter (O833.1), precedes *Selected Recipes*, 1934, by Livingston United Church (O834.1).

Since entries are arranged chronologically by date of publication, entries for two or more titles by the same person or organization will be in different places if they were published in different years. In such cases, all the titles are listed at the earliest entry and there are cross-references from the later entries to the earliest one. Also, all titles by an author or organization are listed in the Name Index.

Elements of a Typical Entry

The information in a typical entry takes the following form:

Heading
Author biography and/or corporate, institutional, or
    associational history
Entry number
Edition number and date
Title-page transcription
Description
Contents
Citations
Copies
Notes
Other editions
Foreign editions

Heading

The heading is the name of the person who wrote the book or who is designated as the editor or as the person who compiled or selected the recipes. The author's place and date of birth and death, if known, follow the name (if this information comes from a source other than Library and Archives Canada, the Library of Congress, or the British Library, then the source is usually recorded in the biographical part of the entry immediately below). If the author goes by a pseudonym, then the pseudonym is the heading: York, Brenda [pseudonym]. If the real name behind the pseudonym is known, it follows the pseudonym: Brown, Cynthia [pseudonym of] Mrs Rose Marie Claire Armstrong Christie (Ottawa, Ont., 18 February 1894–1939, Toronto, Ont.). In the case of two or more named authors, the heading lists the names in the order given on the title-page.

If there is no named person as the author and the book emanated from a government (federal, provincial, or municipal), then the government department or other unit is the heading: Ontario, Department of Agriculture. If there is no named person and the book is not a government publication, then the short-title is the heading. The names of corporations, institutions, and associations are not used as headings, but they are listed in the Name Index, along with all other names.

If the only extant copy of a book lacks its binding and title-page, and there are no other clues about author or title, the heading appears as [Title unknown].

Author Biography and/or Corporate, Institutional, or Associational History

In the course of my research, especially when attempting to establish the date of publication of an undated book, information often surfaced about the life of the author or about an organization's history. Relevant or interesting aspects of this information are recorded after the heading. If there are entries for more than one book by the author or organization at different places in the bibliography, then the biography or history is at the earliest entry and there are cross-references from the later entries to this information in the earliest one. For example: For information about Kate Aitken and her other cookbooks, see Q214.1.

Also included in this element of the entry are cross-references to all entries for later books by the same person or organization. Sometimes a person or organization produced other works not within the boundaries of this bibliography, perhaps because they were too short, published outside of Canada, or not deemed cookbooks. These works are listed here if they illuminate the trajectory of an author's culinary career or an organization's history.

Entry Number

Each entry has been given a unique identifier, made up of a letter or letters denoting the provincial (or other) section and a number in two parts, for example: Q3.1, Q3.2, Q3.3. The letters for the sections are: NF (Newfoundland and Labrador); NS (Nova Scotia); NB (New Brunswick); P (Prince Edward Island); Q (Quebec); O (Ontario); M (Manitoba); S (Saskatchewan); A (Alberta); B (British Columbia); Y (Yukon); NWT (Northwest Territories); NP (no province of publication); GB (Great Britain); and US (United States). No cookbooks are known to have been published in the area of what is now called Nunavut before 1950. The first part of the number refers to the work and these numbers run consecutively to the end of each section. The second number distinguishes each edition or variant of a work (it does not necessarily correspond to any edition number recorded in the book). In the case of a few late additions to the bibliography, the letter 'a' makes a new identifier; for example, O169a.1, which follows O169.1.

Since the publication in 1989 of *A Bibliography of Cookery Books Published in Britain 1875–1914*, scholars, booksellers, and others have referred to entries in that work as, for instance, Driver 300.1. References to entries in *Culinary Landmarks* will be distinguished by the initial letter(s) signifying the geographical section in which the entry is found.

Edition Number and Date

Information about edition number and date is extracted from the entry for quick reference and presented to the right of the entry number. If the information comes from a place other than the title-page, the particulars appear in square brackets. For undated books, an approximate date of publication is offered in square brackets, and, where possible, the suggested date is limited to a five-year span: nd [about 1905–10] or nd [about 1930–5]; however, for books judged to be from the period just before the First or Second World War, the suggested date is usually about 1910–14 or about 1935–9. Often, internal or external evidence limits the approximate date of publication to a particular span of years; for example, about

1930–2. The evidence for an approximate date (perhaps a dated testimonial or a company's address) is stated in the 'Notes.' If no evidence is offered, then the approximate date is based on aspects of the appearance of the book (such as typographic style) or on the contents (cooking fashions, technologies, or ingredients).

Title-Page Transcription

A transcription of the entire title-page (title, imprint, any quotations or other text) is given for every edition of every book that has been seen. If it was not possible to examine a book, every effort was made to obtain a photocopy of the title-page from which to transcribe the title. If the book has no title-page, the cover-title is transcribed, followed by 'cover-title' in square brackets.

The transcription reproduces the original spelling, including accents or the lack thereof, and punctuation, but does not preserve the publisher's differentiation between upper and lower case or the type style, such as italic or bold. Instead, the title-page transcription is in all lower case except for the initial letter of the first word, proper and place names, and the titles of books within the title, which have their main words capitalized. A single slash (/) indicates a line ending; a double slash (//) is inserted where the absence of punctuation may confuse the meaning.

The title-page transcription of a lone edition or the first edition in a run of editions is flush left on the page. A dash precedes all subsequent editions.

In the case of unseen books, information about edition number, title, imprint, dimensions, and number of pages is presented in square brackets, in place of the title-page transcription: [An edition of *The Canadian Cook Book: Cookery and Domestic Economy*, compiled by Lucy Bowerman, a graduate of the Toronto General Hospital, Toronto: Printed by National Press Ltd for Toronto Graduate Nurses Club, copyright 1908]. The source of the information is noted in 'Citations,' 'Copies,' or 'Notes.'

Description

The 'Description' encompasses the following aspects: dimensions of the leaves; pagination; illustrations; price; and binding.

The first measurement is the height of the leaves; the second is the width. Both measurements are rounded to the nearest half-centimetre.

The system for describing pagination generally follows the rules developed for the series *Cookery and*

Household Books Published in Britain 1800–1914, edited by Dr Lynette Hunter, of which my *A Bibliography of Cookery Books Published in Britain 1875–1914* was a part. The first page of a volume is considered to be the recto side of the first leaf with any print on either side. The last page of the volume is considered to be the last printed page. The pagination is recorded as it stands, including any irregularities. The listing of the pagination follows the printer's enumeration, with commas inserted between runs of arabic and roman numbers or whenever needed for clarity. Pages without numbers are noted in square brackets, following the pattern set by the publisher: [i–iii] iv–viii, 1–44 [45–8] for front matter and text, respectively. Unpaginated but printed pages, preceding a group of pages enumerated in small roman numerals at the start of the work, are collated in arabic numerals within square brackets: [1–2], i–viii, ... Unpaginated but printed pages, preceding a group of pages enumerated in arabic numerals, are collated in small roman numerals within square brackets: [i–ii], 1–48. Similarly, unpaginated concluding pages not part of the text, such as advertisements, are collated in small roman numerals if preceded by a group in arabic, and in arabic if preceded by a group in roman. If the entire text is unpaginated, the number of pages is noted in arabic numerals in square brackets: [1–48]; or the number of leaves may be noted.

Information about illustration occurs in the order: frontispiece; title-page illustration; plates; full-page illustrations; illustrations. If no indication is given of the colour, then the image is printed in black only. 'Col,' or a specific description of the colour, means the image is printed in colour, not hand-coloured.

A plate is defined as a full-page illustration, printed separately from the text, often on different paper. Where plates are unnumbered, they are described as: 6 pls; where they are numbered: 6 numbered pls. Numbered and unnumbered plates in one volume are described separately: 9 numbered pls, 6 pls. Where the frontispiece and plates are unnumbered, they are described together: 6 pls incl frontis [i.e., a frontispiece and 5 plates]; where both frontispiece and plates are numbered in the same sequence: 6 numbered pls incl frontis. The term 'double-sided plate' means that images are printed on both sides of a leaf and the leaf counts as one: 3 double-sided pls [i.e., images on both sides of three leaves].

An illustration is printed on the same paper as the text, often with text surrounding it or on the other side of the page. The presence of illustrations is noted as 'illus'; full-page illustrations are counted: 3 fp illus.

If the price is recorded as part of the title-page

transcription, it is not repeated in the description; however, if the price is known from the binding, an advertisement, or another source, the price and source are noted in square brackets: [$1.00, on binding].

The material of the binding is noted, typically paper, paper-covered boards, cloth (sometimes specified as oil cloth, a washable fabric), and limp cloth (sometimes limp oil cloth). In the rare case of leather, full leather denotes a volume covered with leather on all exterior surfaces – front, back, and spine; half leather, leather on the spine and corners only (cloth is usually the material on the remaining exterior surfaces); and quarter leather, leather on the spine only. If the original binding has been replaced with a new binding, the volume is described as 'Rebound.' Any images on the front face of the binding are noted after the material: Cloth, with image on front of a loaf of bread. Volumes bound in cloth are assumed to be sewn; other forms of fastening are recorded: Paper; stapled [or] Paper; bound by a ribbon through two punched holes. The fastening is at the left edge of the closed book, unless otherwise noted: Paper; stapled at top edge. Often, a book was designed to be hung from a nail or hook on the kitchen wall (see, for example, the printer's order for *Dwight's Cow-Brand Cook-Book*, quoted at O82.1), in which case the binding description may include the phrase: with hole punched at top left corner for hanging [or] with hole punched at top left corner, through which runs a string for hanging.

Contents

The contents of the volume are described from beginning to end, following the page numbering system set out in the 'Description.' The elements of the front matter (half-title, title-page, copyright information, any preface, etc.) and end matter (glossary, index, etc.) are specified, but judgment has been exercised in describing the contents of the body of the text: A run of chapters may be specified simply as 'text' or as 'recipes credited with the name of the contributor' (in the case of many fund-raisers), or the description of the contents may reflect an idiosyncratic arrangement of the material. The presence of advertisements is noted. Where part of the contents is unknown, for any reason, the unknown part is indicated by ellipses; for example: 1 tp; ...; 48 index.

Citations

Citations of the cookbook in printed sources are recorded here, using the abbreviations for 'References'

listed on p li. The abbreviated citations are arranged in alphabetical order.

Copies

Locations of copies in institutions are recorded by the abbreviation for the institution listed under 'Libraries and Collections,' pp xli–li. Other specified locations include booksellers' stock, company collections (when a copy is in the ownership of the company that published the book), and private collections, plus microfiches made by the Canadian Institute for Historical Microreproductions (CIHM). An asterisk before a location denotes the copy examined for the bibliographic information or the copy that was photocopied to obtain the title-page transcription or other information.

Locations are arranged by country. Canadian locations always appear first, followed by those in Great Britain and the United States. British and American locations are introduced by the headings 'Great Britain' and 'United States,' but no heading precedes Canadian locations. (The same system is used, when necessary, for listing locations in 'Notes,' 'Other editions,' or 'Foreign editions.') Abbreviations for institutional locations and CIHM microfiches are listed together alphabetically, followed by Bookseller's stock, Company collection, and Private collection. Wherever possible, the call number, acquisition number, or fonds information is given in parentheses after the institutional abbreviation. Some Library and Archives Canada call numbers end with 'p***' to indicate Preservation Collection.

Notes

This element of the entry presents additional information about the book not recorded elsewhere. The 'Notes' may, for example, contain the reasons for the ordering of a run of editions or the evidence for the suggested date of an undated book.

Other Editions

Editions that were published in 1950 or later are listed here, except for modern facsimile editions, which generally have full entries.

Foreign Editions

Many cookbooks described in this bibliography are Canadian editions of British, American, or French texts, or occasionally of texts from other countries.

Foreign editions are listed by country, after the country heading: British editions: *Foulsham's Universal Cookery Book*, London: W. Foulsham and Co., [about 1930] (Great Britain: LB). 'Driver,' the abbreviation for *A Bibliography of Cookery Books Published in Britain 1875–1914*, is sometimes cited as the source of information for British and American editions. In these cases, readers may find more information in the British bibliography.

Very occasionally, Canadian cookbooks were issued in foreign editions, in which case the foreign editions are listed in the usual way, and a statement in the 'Notes' points out the Canadian origin of the text.

Abbreviations and Symbols

/	used in a transcription or quotation to indicate a line break
//	used in a transcription or quotation where the absence of punctuation may confuse the meaning for the reader
*	used before a library or other location symbol to denote the copy examined for the bibliographic information
Acc.	Accession [number]
btwn	between
b/w	black and white
CIHM	Canadian Institute for Historical Microreproductions [followed by microfiche number]
col	colour
ECO	Early Canadiana Online (books available on-line at: www.canadiana.org)
ed., eds	edition(s), editor(s)
fp illus	full-page illustration
frontis	frontispiece
ht	half-title
illus	illustration(s) or illustrated
incl	including, included
IODE	Imperial Order Daughters of the Empire
IOOF	International Order of Odd Fellows
LOBA	Ladies' Orange Benevolent Association
micro	microfilm or microfiche
OES	Order of the Eastern Star
nd	no date
pl	black-and-white plate; 'double-sided pl' refers to a plate with an image printed on both sides
pl col	colour plate
publ	publisher
rev.	revised
tp	title-page
uncat	uncatalogued
WI	Women's Institute
YMCA	Young Men's Christian Association
YWCA	Young Women's Christian Association

Libraries and Collections

Canada

Abbreviations for libraries and collections in Canada are the standard library symbols assigned by Library and Archives Canada and published at its web site under Interlibrary Loans. In the case of institutions for which no symbol has been assigned (usually small museums and historical societies), abbreviations have been devised following the same principles; these new abbreviations are distinguished by a plus sign (+) at the end of the abbreviation.

Alberta:

AALIWWM+	Alix Wagon Wheel Museum
AALM+	Alliance and District Museum
ABA	Whyte Museum of the Canadian Rockies, Archives Library, Banff
ABARRCM+	Barrhead Centennial Museum
ABOM	Bowden Pioneer Museum
AC	Calgary Public Library
ACFCHP+	Fort Calgary Historic Park
ACG	Glenbow Museum, Library, Calgary
ACHP+	Heritage Park Historical Village, Calgary
ACIA	Parks Canada, Western Canada Service Centre, Library, Calgary
ACU	University of Calgary, MacKimmie Library
ACUM	University of Calgary, Health Sciences Library
ADEAHM+	Anthony Henday Museum, Delburne

ADTMP	Royal Tyrrell Museum of Palaeontology, Drumheller		BDEM	Delta Museum and Archives
AE	Edmonton Public Library		BDUCVM	Cowichan Valley Museum, Duncan
AEAG	Alberta Agriculture and Public Works, Neil Crawford Library, Edmonton		BFSJNPM+	North Peace Museum, Fort St John
			BKM	Kamloops Museum and Archives
			BKOM	Kelowna Centennial Museum and National Exhibition Centre
AEARN	Alberta Association of Registered Nurses Museum and Archives, Edmonton		BLCK	Kaatza Historical Museum, Lake Cowichan
AEE	Alberta Government Library, Devonian Building Site, Edmonton		BNEM	Nelson Museum
			BNW	New Westminster Public Library
AEEA	City of Edmonton, Archives		BPAM	Alberni Valley Museum, Port Alberni
AEPAA	Provincial Archives of Alberta, Edmonton		BPGRM	Fraser–Fort George Regional Museum, Prince George
AEPMA+	Provincial Museum of Alberta, Edmonton		BPM	Penticton Museum and Archives
AEPRAC+	Edmonton Parks and Recreation Department, Artifact Centre		BPORH	Powell River Historical Museum Association
AEU	University of Alberta, Edmonton		BPSIC+	SS *Sicamous*, historic ship moored in the harbour at Penticton, administered by SS *Sicamous* Restoration Society
AEUCHV+	Ukrainian Cultural Heritage Village, east of Edmonton			
AFFC	Fairview College, Fairview		BRMA	Richmond Cultural Centre, Richmond Museum
AHCESM+	End of Steel Heritage Museum and Park, Hines Creek		BSORM	Sooke Region Museum
AHRMH+	Museum of the Highwood, High River		BSUM	Summerland Museum
			BTCA	Trail City Archives
ALAGM+	Sir Alexander Galt Museum, Lethbridge		BVA	Vancouver Public Library
			BVAA	Vancouver City Archives
ALU	University of Lethbridge		BVABSM	BC Sugar Museum, Vancouver
AMHM	Medicine Hat Museum and Art Gallery		BVAMM	Vancouver Museum
			BVAU	University of British Columbia, Vancouver
AOYCM	Crossroads Museum, Oyen			
APRCM+	Peace River Centennial Museum and Archives		BVAUW	University of British Columbia, Woodward Biomedical Library, Vancouver
APROM	Fort Ostell Museum, Ponoka			
ARDA	Red Deer and District Museum and Archives		BVI	Greater Victoria Public Library
			BVICC+	Craigdarroch Castle, Victoria
ASPMHC+	Multicultural Heritage Centre, Stony Plain		BVIHH+	Helmcken House, Interpretation Collection, Victoria
AWWDM+	Wetaskiwin and District Museum		BVIP	British Columbia Legislative Library, Victoria
			BVIPA	British Columbia Archives, Victoria
British Columbia:			BVIPEH+	Point Ellice House Museum, Victoria
BBH	BC Hydro, Corporate Research and Information Services, Burnaby		BVIPM	Royal British Columbia Museum, Library, Victoria
BBJCNM+	Japanese Canadian National Museum, Burnaby		BVIV	University of Victoria
			BVMA	Greater Vernon Museum and Archives
BBVM	Burnaby Village Museum			
BCHM	Chilliwack Museum and Historical Society		BWV	West Vancouver Memorial Library
BCOM	Courtenay and District Museum and Archives		Manitoba:	
BCVM	Creston and District Historical and Museum Society		MAUAM+	Manitoba Agricultural Museum, Austin

MBDHM+	Daly House Museum, Brandon
MCDHM+	Dufferin Historical Museum, Carman
MCM+	Carberry Plains Museum
MG+	Ukrainian Museum and Village Society Inc., Gardenton
MNBPM+	Beautiful Plains Museum, Neepawa
MRIP	Prairie Crocus Regional Library, Rivers
MSM+	Le musée de Saint-Boniface
MSOHM+	Hillcrest Museum, Souris
MSPCL	Lower Fort Garry National Historic Park, Selkirk
MTM+	Teulon and District Museum
MTP	The Pas Public Library
MVPHM+	Pioneer Home Museum, Virden
MW	Winnipeg Public Library
MWASM+	Sipiweske Museum, Wawanesa
MWE	Manitoba Education, Citizenship and Youth, Instructional Resources Unit, Winnipeg
MWHWC+	Hadassah-Wizo Council of Winnipeg
MWIAP	Parks Canada, Western Canada Service Centre, Winnipeg
MWM	University of Manitoba, Neil John Maclean Health Sciences Library, Winnipeg
MWMM	Manitoba Museum of Man and Nature, Winnipeg
MWP	Manitoba Legislative Library, Winnipeg
MWPA	Provincial Archives of Manitoba, Winnipeg
MWU	University of Manitoba, Winnipeg

New Brunswick:

NBCOM+	Pioneer Historical Connors Museum, Connors, Madawaska
NBDKH	Keillor House Museum, Dorchester
NBFBA+	Brunswick Street United Baptist Church Archives, Fredericton
NBFKL	Kings Landing Historical Settlement, Fredericton
NBFL	Legislative Library of New Brunswick, Fredericton
NBFU	University of New Brunswick, Fredericton
NBFUA	University of New Brunswick, Fredericton, Archives and Special Collections
NBFY	York-Sunbury Historical Society and Museum, Fredericton

NBMOM	Moncton Museum
NBMOU	Université de Moncton
NBMOUA	Université de Moncton, Centre d'études acadiennes
NBS	Saint John Library Region
NBSAM	Mount Allison University, Sackville
NBSCU	Université de Moncton, Shippigan
NBSJHM+	Saint John Jewish Historical Museum
NBSM	New Brunswick Museum, Saint John
NBSU	University of New Brunswick, Ward Chipman Library, Saint John
NBSUH	Kings County Historical Society Museum, Hampton

Newfoundland and Labrador:

NFSA	Provincial Archives of Newfoundland and Labrador, St John's
NFSCF	Memorial University, Fisheries and Marine Institute, Dr C.R. Barrett Library
NFSG	Provincial Information and Library Resource Board, St John's
NFSM	Memorial University of Newfoundland, St John's

Northwest Territories:

NWY	Yellowknife Public Library
NWYWNH	Prince of Wales Northern Heritage Centre, Northwest Territorial Archives, Yellowknife

Nova Scotia:

NSAS	St Francis Xavier University, Antigonish
NSBCSH	Cape Sable Historical Society, Barrington
NSDB	Fisheries and Oceans Canada, Bedford Institute of Oceanography, Library, Dartmouth
NSH	Halifax Regional Library
NSHCN	Halifax Citadel National Historic Site
NSHD	Dalhousie University, Halifax
NSHMS	Nova Scotia Museum, Halifax
NSHP	Nova Scotia Archives and Records Management Library, Halifax
NSHPL	Nova Scotia Provincial Library, Halifax
NSHV	Mount Saint Vincent University, Halifax

NSKKR	Nova Scotia Community College, Kingstec Campus, Kentville
NSKR	Agriculture and Agri-Food Canada, Atlantic Food and Horticultural Research Centre, Library, Kentville
NSLFP	Fort Point Museum, LaHave
NSLQCM	Queens County Museum, Liverpool
NSME	Eastern Counties Regional Library, Mulgrave
NSNRM+	Ross Farm Museum, New Ross
NSPHM	Port Hastings Museum and Archives
NSPHOCM+	Chestico Museum and Historical Society, Port Hood
NSSXA	University College of Cape Breton, Beaton Institute, Research Library, Sydney
NSWA	Acadia University, Wolfville
NSYHM	Yarmouth County Museum and Historical Research Library, Yarmouth

Ontario:

OADUEL+	United Empire Loyalist Heritage Centre and Park, Adolphustown
OAUH	Aurora Museum
OAYM	Aylmer and District Museum
OBBM	Brant County Museum, Brantford
OBEHCM+	Hastings County Museum, Belleville
OBM	Brockville Museum
OBMBMM+	Bruce Mines Museum
OBRACWM+	Woodchester Villa and Museum, Bracebridge
OBRAPM+	Region of Peel Museum, Peel Heritage Complex, Brampton
OBUJBM+	Joseph Brant Museum, Burlington
OC	Cornwall Public Library
OCALNHM+	North Himsworth Museum, Callander
OCCA+	City of Cambridge Archives
OCHA	Chatham-Kent Public Library
OCHAK	Chatham-Kent Museum
OCLCLM+	Clarke Museum and Archives, Clarington
OCN	Parks Canada Agency, Cornwall
OCOLM+	Collingwood Museum
OCUM+	Cumberland Township Museum, Cumberland
OFERWM	Wellington County Museum and Archives, Fergus
OFFRH+	Ross Township Historical Society, Foresters Falls
OG	Guelph Public Library

OGAL	Cambridge Public Library
OGM+	Guelph Civic Museum
OGOWSM+	Whitchurch-Stouffville Museum, Gormley
OGU	University of Guelph (Una Abrahamson Canadian Cookery Collection signified by 'UA' before call number; Canadian Cookbook Collection, by 'CCC'; Edna Staebler Collection, by 'EA')
OH	Hamilton Public Library
OHALM+	Haliburton Highlands Museum, Haliburton
OHM	McMaster University, Hamilton, Mills Memorial Library
OHMA	McMaster University, Hamilton, William Ready Division of Archives and Research Collections
OHMB	McMaster University, Hamilton, Health Sciences Library
OHWHH+	Whitehern Historic House, Hamilton
OK	Kingston Frontenac Public Library, Central Branch
OKCKT	King Township Public Library, King City (Lady Eaton Estate Collection includes her cookbooks)
OKELWM+	Lake of the Woods Museum, Kenora
OKIT	Kitchener Public Library
OKITD	Doon Heritage Crossroads, Kitchener
OKITJS+	Joseph Schneider Haus, Kitchener
OKITWN+	Woodside National Historic Site, Kitchener
OKLPV+	Lang Pioneer Village, Keene
OKQ	Queen's University, Kingston
OKR	Royal Military College, Kingston
OL	London Public Library
OLA	Lakefield Public Library
OLDUCA+	Dundas Street Centre United Church, Archives, London
OLIAF+	Anderson Farm Museum, Lively
OLLLA+	London Life Insurance Co., corporate archives, London
OLU	University of Western Ontario, London
OMAHM	Markham District Historical Museum
OMARH+	Robin Hood Multifoods Inc., Markham
OMATTM+	Thelma Miles Museum, Matheson
OME	University of Toronto, Erindale College, Mississauga

OMIH	Huronia Historical Parks, Resource Centre, Midland
OMIHM	Halton Region Museum, Milton
OMIHURM+	Huronia Museum, Midland
OMINL+	Minden Library and Cultural Centre
OMMM	Moore Museum, Mooretown
OMSA	Simcoe County Archives, Minesing
OMSLSA+	St Lawrence Starch Co. Ltd, corporate archives, Port Credit
OMUC	Upper Canada Village, Morrisburg
ONBNBM+	North Bay and Area Museum
ONDA	Norwich and District Archives
ONENM+	Newmarket Museum
ONF	Niagara Falls Public Library
ONHI	Niagara Historical Society and Museum, Niagara-on-the-Lake
ONLAM	Lennox and Addington County Museum and Archives, Napanee
ONM+	Nepean Museum
OOA	National Archives of Canada, Ottawa; in 2004 amalgamated with National Library of Canada (OONL) and renamed Library and Archives Canada
OOAG	Agriculture and Agri-Food Canada, Canadian Agriculture Library, Ottawa
OOAKHS+	Oakville Historical Society
OOAKM	Oakville Museum at Erchless Estate
OOAOA	Anglican Church of Canada, Diocese of Ottawa, Archives
OOBEM+	Billings Estate Museum, Ottawa
OOC	Ottawa Public Library
OOCC	Carleton University, Ottawa
OOCIHM	Canadian Institute for Historical Microreproductions Library, Ottawa
OOG	Natural Resources Canada, Earth Sciences Sector, Earth Sciences Information Centre, Ottawa
OOHI	Bytown Historical Museum, Ottawa
OOJA+	Ottawa Jewish Archives
OONDH	National Defence, Directorate of History and Heritage, Archives, Ottawa
OONG	National Gallery of Canada, Ottawa
OONL	National Library of Canada, Ottawa; 'p***' after call number signifies Preservation Collection; in 2004 amalgamated with National Archives of Canada (OOA) and renamed Library and Archives Canada
OONMC	Canadian War Museum, Ottawa
OONMM	Canadian Museum of Civilization, Ottawa
OONMS	Canada Science and Technology Museum, Ottawa
OOP	Library of Parliament, Ottawa
OORADCM+	Dufferin County Museum, Orangeville
OORD	Indian and Northern Affairs Canada, Departmental Library, Gatineau, Quebec
OOSCA	Soeurs de la charité d'Ottawa, Archives
OOSH	Oshawa Public Library, McLaughlin Branch
OOSS	Canadian Heritage, Library and Research Centre, Knowledge Centre, Gatineau, Quebec
OOU	University of Ottawa
OOWM	Grey Roots Museum and Archives, Owen Sound
OPAL	Lakehead University, Chancellor Paterson Library, Thunder Bay
OPEMO	Champlain Trail Museum, Pembroke
OPET	Trent University Library, Peterborough
OPETA	Trent University Archives, Peterborough
OPETCM	Peterborough Centennial Museum and Archives
OPPSSHM+	Scugog Shores Historical Museum, Port Perry
OPREFM+	Forwarders' Museum, Prescott
OPS	Parry Sound Public Library
OSCELM+	Erland Lee Museum, Stoney Creek
OSGM+	Goulbourn Museum, Stittsville
OSHT	Sharon Temple
OSIDM	Eva Brook Donly Museum, Simcoe
OSMFHHM+	Heritage House Museum, Smiths Falls
OSPFAM+	Forge and Anvil Museum, Sparta
OSPTM	Timmins Museum
OSTC	St Catharines Public Library
OSTCB	Brock University, St Catharines
OSTCM	St Catharines Museum
OSTM	Sault Ste Marie Public Library
OSTMYM	St Marys District Museum
OSTPA	Stratford-Perth Archives, Stratford
OSTT	St Thomas Public Library
OSTTECPM+	Elgin County Pioneer Museum, St Thomas
OSUL	Laurentian University, J.N. Desmarais Library, Sudbury

OSUU   University of Sudbury
OTAF   Ontario Ministry of Agriculture and
            Food, Toronto
OTAG   Art Gallery of Ontario, Toronto
            (The Grange)
OTAR   Archives of Ontario, Toronto
OTB   Thunder Bay Public Library,
            Waverley Resource Library
OTBFA+   Best Foods Canada Inc., corporate
            archives, Toronto
OTBH   Thunder Bay Historical Society
            Museum
OTBNL   Canadian National Institute for the
            Blind, Library for the Blind, Toronto
OTBPM+   Paipoonge Museum, Thunder Bay
OTCC   United Church of Canada and
            Victoria University Archives,
            Toronto
OTCDA+   Church and Dwight Ltd, corporate
            archives, Toronto
OTCHAR   Anglican Church of Canada, General
            Synod, Archives, Toronto
OTCJCA+   Canadian Jewish Congress Ontario
            Region Archives, Toronto
OTCNE+   Canadian National Exhibition
            Archives, Toronto
OTDGA+   Davis Germantown (Canada) Inc.,
            corporate archives, Toronto
OTDM   Ontario Ministry of Northern Devel-
            opment and Mines, Mines Library,
            Sudbury
OTEUC+   Eglinton United Church Archives,
            Toronto (to be transferred to OTCC)
OTEYBE   East York Board of Education (now
            part of the Toronto District School
            Board), Education Centre Library
OTHFY+   Historic Fort York, Toronto
OTHSC   Hospital for Sick Children, Toronto
OTL   Ontario Legislative Library, Toronto
OTMCL   Toronto Reference Library
OTMLMA+   Maple Leaf Mills Consumer Prod-
            ucts Co., corporate archives, Toronto
            (collection seen in 1991, before major
            changes in the renamed company,
            Maple Leaf Foods, from 1995 on;
            current location of books unknown)
OTNBA+   Nabisco Brands Ltd, corporate
            archives, Toronto
OTNY   North York Central Library, Gladys
            Allison Canadiana Room, Toronto
            (now amalgamated with Toronto
            Public Library)
OTNYE   North York Board of Education (now

            part of the Toronto District School
            Board), Toronto
OTP   Toronto Public Library
OTR   Ryerson University Library, Toronto
OTRM   Royal Ontario Museum, Toronto
OTSBM+   Toronto District School Board,
            Sesquicentennial Museum, Toronto
OTSCC   University of Toronto at
            Scarborough
OTSCE+   St Clement Eglinton Anglican
            Church, Archives, Toronto
OTSHH+   Spadina Historic House and Gar-
            dens, Toronto
OTTHOCI   University Health Network, Toronto
            General Hospital, Fudger Health
            Sciences Library
OTU   University of Toronto
OTUAR   University of Toronto, Archives
OTUED   Ontario Institute for Studies in
            Education, R.W.B. Jackson Library,
            Toronto
OTUFP   University of Toronto, R.O. Hurst
            Pharmacy Library
OTUNE   University of Toronto, Noranda
            Earth Sciences Library
OTUTF   University of Toronto, Thomas
            Fisher Rare Book Library
OTV   Victoria University, E.J. Pratt
            Library, Toronto
OTWTJHS+   West Toronto Junction Historical
            Society archives, at Annette Street
            Public Library, Toronto
OTY   York University, Toronto
OTYA   York University Archives and Spe-
            cial Collections, Toronto
OUSH   Uxbridge-Scott Museum, Uxbridge
OVOH+   Osgoode Township Historical Soci-
            ety and Museum, Vernon
OW   Windsor Public Library
OWA   University of Windsor, Leddy
            Library
OWASRM+   Spruce Row Museum, Waterford
OWE   Welland Public Library
OWINLM+   Nor'westers and Loyalist Museum,
            Williamstown
OWOM   Woodstock Museum
OWOOXH+   Oxford Historical Society,
            Woodstock
OWSJ   St Jerome's University, Waterloo
OWT   Waterloo Public Library
OWTL   Wilfrid Laurier University, Waterloo
OWTU   University of Waterloo
OWWCM+   Windsor's Community Museum

OWYL   Lambton County Public Library, Wyoming

Prince Edward Island:
PCL   Confederation Centre Public Library, Charlottetown
PCM+   Prince Edward Island Museum, Charlottetown
PCU   University of Prince Edward Island, Charlottetown

Quebec:
QECCH   La société d'histoire musée du Comté de Compton, Cookshire
QGMG   Musée de la Gaspésie, Gaspé
QHQAR   Archives nationales du Québec, Gatineau
QKB   Brome County Historical Society, Knowlton
QLB   Bishop's University, Lennoxville
QLNLB   Institut Nazareth et Louis-Braille, Longueuil
QLOSNJMA+   Soeurs des Saints Noms de Jésus et de Marie, Service central des Archives SNJM, Longueuil
QMAC   McGill University, MacDonald College, Ste-Anne-de-Bellevue
QMACN   Le service des Archives de la Congrégation de Notre-Dame, Montreal
QMBM   Bibliothèque de la ville de Montréal, Salle Gagnon
QMBN   Bibliothèque nationale du Québec, Montreal
QMEP   École polytechnique de Montréal
QMJ   Jewish Public Library, Montreal
QMM   McGill University, Montreal
QMMARC+   McGill University Archives, Montreal
QMMDA+   Ville de Montréal, Service du greffe, Gestion de documents et archives
QMMMCM   McCord Museum, Montreal
QMOLF   Québec, Office de la langue française, Montreal
QMPRA   Archives Providence, Montreal
QMTH   Institut de tourisme et d'hôtellerie du Québec, Montreal
QMU   Université de Montréal
QNICS   Séminaire de Nicolet
QPC   Collège de Sainte-Anne-de-la-Pocatière, La Pocatière
QQACJ   Archives de la Compagnie de Jésus, Saint-Jérôme

QQFO   Québec, Ministère des Ressources naturelles, Bibliothèque des Ressources naturelles, Charlesbourg
QQL   Assemblée nationale du Québec, Bibliothèque
QQLA   Université Laval, Bibliothèque générale, Sainte-Foy
QQLAS   Université Laval, Bibliothèque scientifique, Sainte-Foy
QQS   Séminaire de Québec, Bibliothèque, Quebec City, 'fonds ancien' under administration of Musée de l'Amérique française, a branch of Musée de la civilisation
QQSCA   Archives des Soeurs de la charité de Québec, Beauport
QQU   Couvent des Ursulines de Québec, Archives, Quebec City
QQUQT   Université du Québec, Télé-université, Sainte-Foy
QRCB   Collège Bourget, Rigaud
QRMSF+   Manoir Seigneurial Fraser, Rivière-du-Loup
QRUQR   Université du Québec en Abitibi-Témiscamingue, Rouyn-Noranda
QSFBP   Maison généralice des Soeurs du Bon-Pasteur, Sainte-Foy
QSFFSC+   Bibliothèque des Frères du Sacré-Coeur, Sainte-Foy
QSH   Stanstead Historical Society
QSHERSH   La société d'histoire de Sherbrooke
QSHERU   Université de Sherbrooke
QSTHS   Séminaire de Saint-Hyacinthe
QTS   Archives du Séminaire de Trois-Rivières
QTU   Université du Québec à Trois-Rivières
QTURA   Archives des Ursulines, Trois-Rivières
QVE   Bibliothèque municipale de Verdun
QVMVS+   Musée régional de Vaudreuil-Soulanges, Vaudreuil
QWSMM   Westmount Public Library, Montreal

Saskatchewan:
SAMH+   Motherwell Homestead National Historic Park, Abernethy
SBIHM+   Homestead Museum, Biggar
SBIM+   Biggar Museum and Gallery
SBIN   Fort Battleford National Historic Park
SEEK+   Kaposvar Historic Site, Esterhazy
SELH+   Elrose Heritage Society

SFLM+	Foam Lake Museum
SMELM+	Melville Heritage Museum
SMJ	Moose Jaw Public Library
SMM+	McCord Museum
SR	Regina Public Library
SRA	University of Regina, Saskatchewan Archives Board
SRBJ+	Beth Jacob Synagogue, archives, Regina
SRED	Saskatchewan Education and Post-Secondary Education Skills Training Resource Centre, Regina
SRL	Saskatchewan Legislative Library, Regina
SRP	Saskatchewan Provincial Library, Regina
SRRPM+	Regina Plains Museum
SRU	University of Regina
SS	Saskatoon Public Library
SSA	Saskatchewan Archives Board, Saskatoon
SSU	University of Saskatchewan, Saskatoon
SSUMC	Ukrainian Museum of Canada, Saskatoon
SSWD	Saskatchewan Western Development Museums, Saskatoon
SWSLM+	Soo Line Historical Museum, Weyburn

Yukon:

YDAWM+	Dawson City Museum and Historical Society
YWA	Yukon Department of Education, Yukon Archives, Whitehorse

The United States

Abbreviations for American libraries and collections are the old *National Union Catalog* symbols, also used in Driver's *A Bibliography of Cookery Books Published in Britain 1875–1914*. A plus sign (+) at the end of an abbreviation indicates a symbol that has been assigned for the purposes of this bibliography.

AJacT	Jacksonville State University, Jacksonville, Alabama
AzTeS	Arizona State University, Tempe
CL	Los Angeles Public Library, Los Angeles, California
CLCM	Natural History Museum of Los Angeles County Foundation, Los Angeles, California
CLob	Long Beach Public Library, Long Beach, California
COMC	Mills College, Oakland, California
CTo	Thousand Oaks Public Library, Newbury Park, California
CU	University of California, Berkeley
CU-A	University of California, Shields Library, Davis
CU-S	University of California, San Diego
CU-SB	University of California, Santa Barbara
CoDJW+	Johnson and Wales University, Denver, Colorado
CoDU	University of Denver, Penrose Library, Denver, Colorado
CoGrU	University of Northern Colorado, Greeley
CtNh	New Haven Free Public Library, New Haven, Connecticut
DHEW	United States Department of Health, Education and Welfare, Washington, District of Columbia
DLC	United States Library of Congress, Washington, District of Columbia
DNLM	National Library of Medicine, Bethesda, Maryland
DSI-D	Smithsonian Institution, Dibner Library of the History of Science and Technology, Washington, District of Columbia
DeU	University of Delaware, Newark
FM	Miami-Dade Public Library System, Miami, Florida
FMU	University of Miami, Coral Gables, Florida
FTaSU	Florida State University, Tallahassee
ICJ	University of Chicago, John Crerar Library, Chicago, Illinois
ICRL	Center for Research Libraries, Chicago, Illinois
ICU	University of Chicago, Chicago, Illinois
IEuC	Eureka College, Eureka, Illinois
ILfB	Barat College, Lake Forest, Illinois
INap-N+	Naperville Public Library, Nichols Library, Naperville, Illinois
ISUM	Southern Illinois University, School of Medicine, Springfield, Illinois
IaAS	Iowa State University, Ames
IaU	University of Iowa Library, Iowa City; holds Louis Szathmary Collection of cookbooks

IdU	University of Idaho, Moscow, Idaho Library
InU	Indiana University, Lilly Library, Bloomington, Indiana
KMK	Kansas State University, Manhattan
LU	Louisiana State University, Baton Rouge
MB	Boston Public Library, Boston, Massachusetts
MBAt	Boston Athenaeum, Boston, Massachusetts
MBrNCM	Newbury College, Mewshaw Library, Brookline, Massachusetts
MCR	Radcliffe Institute for Advanced Study, Schlesinger Library on the History of Women in America, Cambridge, Massachusetts
MChB	Boston College, Chestnut Hill, Massachusetts
MFmT	Framingham State College, Framingham, Massachusetts
MH	Harvard University, Cambridge, Massachusetts
MSaE	Peabody Essex Museum (formerly Essex Institute), Salem, Massachusetts
MU	University of Massachusetts, Amherst
MWA	American Antiquarian Society, Worcester, Massachusetts
MdPM	University of Maryland, Eastern Shore, Princess Anne
MiD	Detroit Public Library, Detroit, Michigan
MiEM	Michigan State University, East Lansing, Michigan
MiU	University of Michigan, Ann Arbor, Michigan
MnHi	Minnesota Historical Society, St Paul, Minnesota
MnM	Minneapolis Public Library and Information Center, Minneapolis, Minnesota
MnSU	University of Minnesota, Magrath Library, St Paul
MoK	Kansas City Public Library, Kansas City, Missouri
MoU	University of Missouri, Columbia
MoU-St	University of Missouri, St Louis
MtBC	Montana State University, Bozeman, Montana
NBPu	Brooklyn Public Library, Brooklyn, New York
NBuBE	Buffalo and Erie County Public Library, Buffalo, New York
NCaS	Saint Lawrence University, Canton, New York
NHyCIA	Culinary Institute of America Library, Hyde Park, New York
NIC	Cornell University, Ithaca, New York
NN	New York Public Library, New York City
NNF	Fordham University, Bronx, New York
NNNAM	New York Academy of Medicine, New York City
NNStJ	Saint John's University Library, Jamaica, New York
NNU	New York University, New York City, Elmer Holmes Bobst Library
NPV	Vassar College, Poughkeepsie, New York
NRM	Rochester Museum and Science Center, Rochester, New York
NRMW	Strong Museum, Rochester, New York
NRRI	Rochester Institute of Technology Library, Rochester, New York
NcD	Duke University Library, Durham, North Carolina
NcGU	University of North Carolina, Greensboro
NcMoB+	Burke County Public Library, Morganton, North Carolina
NcSppA	Avery-Mitchell-Yancey Regional Library, Spruce Pine, North Carolina
NjN	Free Public Library of Newark, Newark, New Jersey
OAU	Ohio University, Athens, Ohio
OAkU	University of Akron, Akron, Ohio
OBgU	Bowling Green State University, Bowling Green, Ohio
OC	Public Library of Cincinnati/ Hamilton County, Cincinnati, Ohio
OCU	University of Cincinnati, Cincinnati, Ohio
OCl	Cleveland Public Library, Cleveland, Ohio
OClW	Case Western Reserve University, Cleveland, Ohio
OFH	Rutherford B. Hayes Presidential Center, Fremont, Ohio
OKentU	Kent State University, Kent, Ohio
OLak	Lakewood Public Library, Ohio
OO	Oberlin College, Oberlin, Ohio
OOxM	Miami University, Oxford, Ohio

OTU	University of Toledo, Toledo, Ohio (same as a Canadian abbreviation, but always preceded by 'United States:')	ViFGM	George Mason University, Fairfax, Virginia
OU	Ohio State University, Columbus, Ohio	ViNJW+	Johnson and Wales University, Norfolk, Virginia
Or	Oregon State Library, Salem	ViSwC	Sweet Briar College Library, Sweet Briar, Virginia
OrP	Public Library of Portland and Multnomah County, Portland, Oregon	ViU	University of Virginia, Charlottesville
PP	Free Library of Philadelphia, Philadelphia, Pennsylvania	WaE	Everett Public Library, Everett, Washington
PPC-C+	College of Physicians of Philadelphia, Children's Hospital of Philadelphia, Philadelphia, Pennsylvania	WaS	Seattle Public Library, Seattle, Washington
PPD	Drexel University, Philadelphia, Pennsylvania	WaU	University of Washington, Seattle, Washington
PPPL	Philadelphia Board of Education, Pedagogical Library, Philadelphia, Pennsylvania	WaWW	Whitman College, Walla Walla, Washington
PPSJ	St Joseph's University, Philadelphia, Pennsylvania	WLac	La Crosse Public Library, La Crosse, Wisconsin
RCJW	Johnson and Wales University, Culinary Library, Cranston, Rhode Island	WLacU	University of Wisconsin, La Crosse
RPB	Brown University, Providence, Rhode Island	WM	Milwaukee County Federated Library System, Milwaukee, Wisconsin
RPJW	Johnson and Wales University Library, Providence, Rhode Island	WU	University of Wisconsin, General Library System, Madison
RUn	University of Rhode Island, Kingston	WyU-AH	University of Wyoming, American Heritage Center, Laramie, Wyoming
ScCJW+	Johnson and Wales University, Charleston, South Carolina		
ScRhW	Winthrop College, Rock Hill, South Carolina		

Great Britain

Abbreviations for British and Australian libraries and collections follow the system devised for Driver's *A Bibliography of Cookery Books Published in Britain 1875–1914.*

SdB	South Dakota State University, Brookings	AnB	Central Library, Belfast, County Antrim
TxAbC	Abilene Christian University, Abilene, Texas	BeRU	University Library, Reading, Berkshire
TxCM	A and M University, College Station, Texas	DuSB	Beamish North of England Open Air Museum, Stanley, Durham
TxDN	University of North Texas, Denton	LB	British Library, London (regarding Canadian copyright material at the British Library, see the comments for O'Neill on p lvii)
TxDW	Texas Woman's University Library, Denton		
TxDaM	Southern Methodist University, Central Libraries, Dallas, Texas	LB(S)	Science Reference Library, British Library, London
TxLoL	Letourneau University, Margaret Estes Library, Longview, Texas	LCS	Swiss Cottage Library, Borough of Camden, London
TxSalA	Angelo State University, San Angelo, Texas	LCoF	Cookery and Food Association, London
TxSmS	Southwest Texas State University, San Marcos	LG	Guildhall Library, London
TxU	University of Texas, Austin	LWel	Wellcome Institute for the History of Medicine, London
UU	University of Utah, Salt Lake City	LaOP	Public Library, Oldham, Lancashire

LoEN — National Library of Scotland, Edinburgh, Lothian

NtCo — County Library, Nottingham, Nottinghamshire

NtU(S) — Science Library, University Library, Nottingham, Nottinghamshire

OB — Bodleian Library, Oxford, Oxfordshire

OPo(F) — Fuller Collection, Headington Library, Oxford Brookes University (formerly Polytechnic), Oxford, Oxfordshire

WyLUB — Brotherton Library, Leeds University, Leeds, West Yorkshire

Australia

ACN — National Library of Australia, Canberra, Australian Capital Territory

NSM — Mitchell Library, State Library of New South Wales, Sydney, New South Wales

SAS — State Library of South Australia, Adelaide, South Australia

VMRoT — Royal Melbourne Institute of Technology, Melbourne, Victoria

VMU — Monash University Library, Monash, Victoria

France

PBNF — Bibliothèque nationale de France, Paris

References

AbCat — Abigail Books, London, England, sales catalogue

Abrahamson — Abrahamson, Hilary. *Victorians at Table: Dining Traditions in Nineteenth-Century Ontario.* Toronto: Ministry of Culture and Recreation, Heritage Administration Branch, 1981

Ag 1867–1974 — Canada, Department of Agriculture. *Publications of the Canada Department of Agriculture 1867–1974/Publications du Ministère de l'agriculture du Canada 1867–1974.* 2nd rev. ed., prepared by Headquarters Library, Ottawa. Ottawa: Canada Department of Agriculture, 1975. This is a revised and updated edition of *Publications of the Canada Department of Agriculture 1867–1959,* compiled by Ella S.G. Minter. It does not include reprints.

Allen — Allen, Colonel Bob. *A Guide to Collecting Cookbooks and Advertising Cookbooks: A History of People, Companies and Cooking.* Paducah, Ky: Collector Books, Division of Schroeder Publishing Co. Inc., 1990

Ambrose — Ambrose, Linda McGuire. *For Home and Country: The Centennial History of the Women's Institutes in Ontario.* Erin, Ont.: Boston Mills Press, 1996

AMICUS — AMICUS database at Library and Archives Canada, Ottawa

AnderCat — Anderbooks, Regina (Jim Anderson, bookseller, now in Winnipeg), on-line sales catalogue

Anderson/ Mallinson — Anderson, Carol, and Katharine Mallinson. *Lunch with Lady Eaton: Inside the Dining Rooms of a Nation.* Toronto: ECW Press, 2004

Anson-Cart-wrightCat — Hugh Anson-Cartwright, Toronto, sales catalogue

Armstrong 2000 — Armstrong, Julian. 'History on a Platter.' *Gazette* (Montreal) 28 June 2000, pp F1–F2. Reprinted in *Citizen* (Ottawa) 12 July 2000, but with fewer illustrations

Armstrong 2004 — Armstrong, Julian. 'Ghost of Kitchens Past.' *Gazette* (Montreal) 2 June 2004, p D2

Arndt — Arndt, Alice, ed. *Culinary Biographies: A Dictionary of the World's Greatest Historic Chefs, Cookbook Authors and Collectors, Farmers, Gourmets, Home Economists, Nutritionists, Restaurateurs, Philosophers, Physicians, Scientists,Writers, and Others Who Influenced the Way We Eat Today.* Houston: Yes Press Inc., 2006

Attar — Attar, Dena. *A Bibliography of Household Books Published in Britain 1800–1914.* London, England: Prospect Books, 1987

Axford — Axford, Lavonne Brady. *English Language Cookbooks, 1600–1973.* Detroit: Gale Research Co., 1976

Baird — Baird, Elizabeth. *Classic Canadian Cooking.* Toronto: James Lorimer and Co., 1974

Barile — Barile, Mary. *Cookbooks Worth Collect-*

ing: *The History and Lore of Notable Cookbooks, with Complete Bibliographic Listings and Up-to-Date Values.* Radnor, Pa: Wallace-Homestead Book Co., 1994

Barss 1980 Barss, Beulah M. *The Pioneer Cook: A Historical View of Canadian Prairie Food.* Calgary: Detselig Enterprises Ltd, [1980]

Bates Bates, Christina. *Out of Old Ontario Kitchens: A Collection of Traditional Recipes of Ontario and the Stories of the People Who Cooked Them.* Toronto: Pagurian Press Ltd, 1978.

BCat Booktique, Halifax, Yorkshire, England, sales catalogue

Beaulieu Beaulieu, André, Jean-Charles Bonenfant, and Jean Hamelin. *Répertoire des publications gouvernementales du Québec de 1867 à 1964.* Québec: Roch Lefebvre, 1968

Beaulieu, Supp. 1965–1968 Beaulieu, André, Jean Hamelin, and Gaston Bernier. *Répertoire des publications gouvernementales du Québec, supplément 1965–1968.* Québec: Assemblée nationale, 1970

Bechtel Bechtel, George. *The 1914 Look: Landscapes and Gardens of Waterloo County.* Waterloo, Ont.: Doon Heritage Crossroads, Regional Municipality of Waterloo, 1991

Bédard Bédard, Francine. *Les livres de recettes publiés au Québec ainsi que quelques articles sur la cuisine québécoise.* Ottawa: Centre de recherches et de bibliographie, École de bibliothécaires, Université d'Ottawa, April 1967

Beeson Beeson, Patricia. *Macdonald Was Late for Dinner: A Slice of Culinary Life in Early Canada.* Peterborough, Ont.: Broadview Press, 1993

Benoît Benoît, Bernard. 'Jehane Benoît: An Intimate Biographical Essay.' In *Madame Jehane Benoît: 14 Years of Microwave Cooking,* pp 7–30. Commemorative edition. [Saint Lambert, Que.: Les Éditions Héritage Inc., copyright 1988]

Berton Berton, Pierre and Janet. *The Centennial Food Guide: A Century of Good Eating.* Canadian Centennial Library.

Toronto: Weekend Magazine/ McClelland and Stewart Ltd, 1966

Bibliothèque municipale de Montréal Bibliothèque municipale de Montréal, Salle Gagnon. *L'alimentation traditionnelle au Canada, une bibliographie.* Ville de Montréal, Service des loisirs et du developpement communautaire, August 1988

Biographical Cyclopaedia *The Biographical Cyclopaedia of American Women.* Compiled under the supervision of Mabel Ward Cameron. Vol. 1. New York: Halvord Publishing Co. Inc., 1924. Republished by Gale Research Co., Detroit, 1974

Bishop Bishop, Olga Bernice. *Publications of the Governments of Nova Scotia, Prince Edward Island, New Brunswick, 1758–1952.* Ottawa: National Library of Canada, 1957

Bitting Bitting, Katherine Golden. *Gastronomic Bibliography.* First published 1939. Reprint. London, England: Holland Press, 1981

Bloomfield Bloomfield, Elizabeth. *Waterloo County to 1972: An Annotated Bibliography of Regional History.* Waterloo Regional Heritage Foundation, 1993

Bloomfield/ Stelter Bloomfield, Elizabeth, and Gilbert A. Stelter. *Guelph and Wellington County: A Bibliography of Settlement and Development since 1800.* Guelph: University of Guelph, 1988

Bly Bly, David. 'Cookbooks Offer Food for Thought.' *Calgary Herald* 15 March 2002, p B4

BMCat British Museum on-line integrated catalogue

BN *Books and Notions.* Toronto. Vol. 1, No. 1 (August 1884)–Vol. 11 (1895). [Continued as *Canada Bookseller and Stationer;* see BS, below]

BouquinsCat Librairie O Vieux Bouquins, Drummondville, Que., sales catalogue

Bower Bower, Anne L., ed. *Recipes for Reading: Community Cookbooks, Stories, Histories.* Amherst: University of Massachusetts Press, 1997

BQ Bibliothèque nationale du Québec. *Bibliographie du Québec, 1821–1967.* Montréal: Bibliothèque nationale du Québec, 1980–

BQ Exposition 1974 — Bibliothèque nationale du Québec. *Exposition 'Du livre à la table' du 26 avril au 22 juin 1974.* Montréal: Bibliothèque nationale du Québec, 1974

Breckenridge — Breckenridge, Muriel. *The Old Ontario Cook Book.* Toronto: McGraw-Hill Ryerson Ltd, 1976

Brisebois — Brisebois, Michel. *Impressions: 250 Years of Printing in the Lives of Canadians.* Catalogue of an exhibition held at the National Library of Canada, Ottawa, April 1999–January 2000. Fitzhenry and Whiteside and the National Library of Canada in co-operation with the Department of Public Works and Government Services, 1999. French-language edition, *250 ans d'imprimerie dans la vie des Canadien(ne)s*

Brodie 5 Dec 1942 — Brodie, Jean. 'These Cook Books Can Help You.' *Star Weekly* (Toronto) 5 December 1942, Magazine Section No. 2, p 2

Brodie 12 Dec 1942 — Brodie, Jean. 'Give a Modern Cook Book for Christmas.' *Star Weekly* (Toronto) 12 December 1942, Magazine Section No. 2, p 11

Brown/ Brown — Brown, Eleanor, and Bob Brown. *Culinary Americana: Cookbooks Published in the Cities and Towns of the United States of America during the Years from 1860 through 1960.* New York: Roving Eye Press, 1961

BS — *Canada Bookseller and Stationer* [previously *Books and Notions*; see BN, above]. Toronto. Vol. 12, No. 1 (January 1896)–Vol. 13, No. 4 (April 1897); retitled *Bookseller and Stationer* from Vol. 13, No. 5 (May 1897); retitled *Bookseller and Stationer and Canadian Newsdealer* from Vol. 24, No. 1 (January 1908); retitled *Bookseller and Stationer and Office Equipment Journal* from Vol. 26, No. 4 (April 1910)

Cagle — Cagle, William R. *A Matter of Taste: A Bibliographical Catalogue of International Books on Food and Drink in the Lilly Library, Indiana University.* New Castle, Del.: Oak Knoll Press, 1999. 2nd ed., revised and expanded, of *A Matter of Taste: A Bib-liographical Catalogue of the Gernon Collection of Books on Food and Drink,* New York: Garland Publishing, 1990

Cagle/ Stafford — Cagle, William R., and Lisa Killion Stafford. *American Books on Food and Drink: A Bibliographical Catalog of the Cookbook Collection Housed in the Lilly Library at the Indiana University.* New Castle, Del.: Oak Knoll Press, 1998

Can 1867–1900 — Canada. National Library. *Canadiana, 1867–1900, Monographs: Canada's National Bibliography.* Microfiche ed. Ottawa: National Library of Canada, 1980

Canadian Women of Note — *Canadian Women of Note (C.W.O.N.),* compiled by Media Club of Canada. 2nd ed. [reprint]. 2 vols. [North York, Ont.: Institute for Social Research, York University, 1994]

Careless — Careless, Virginia. *Bibliography for the Study of British Columbia's Domestic Material History.* Ottawa: National Museums of Canada, 1976

Carrière — Carrière, Francine. *Bibliographie: l'alimentation traditionnelle au Canada.* Université de Montréal, Faculté des arts et des sciences, École de biblio-théconomie, December 1978 (copies at QMBM and QMBN)

CBCat — Cooks Books, Rottingdean, Sussex, England, sales catalogue

CBSCat — Corner Book Shop, New York City, sales catalogue

CCat — *The Canadian Catalogue of Books Published in Canada ..., with Imprint 1921–1949.* 2nd ed. Toronto: Toronto Public Libraries, 1967

CCB — 'Canadian Cook Books.' Typescript catalogue of display at National Library of Canada, summer 1968

CEWW — *Canada's Early Women Writers.* [Digital resource on Simon Fraser University library web site.] [Burnaby, BC: Carole Gerson, Simon Fraser University, Dept of English, 2001]

Chatelaine — *Chatelaine;* various issues of the Canadian women's magazine

Chatelaine 1935 — 'Build a Reference Library for Your Kitchen.' *Chatelaine* Vol. 8, No. 2 (February 1935), pp 64, 82. Lists free publications, including many cook-

	books, available from manufacturers of foods, household supplies, and equipment
CHO	Culinary Historians of Ontario. Newsletter (titled *Culinary Chronicles* from No. 40, Spring 2004)
CIHM	Canadian Institute for Historical Microreproductions. *Canada, the Printed Record: A Collection of Pre-1900 Printed Canadiana.* Microfiche. Ottawa: CIHM, 1980–
Claflin	Claflin, Kyri Watson. 'Cookbook Charity Aids Victims of War.' *Radcliffe Culinary Times* Vol. 1, No. 1 (Spring 1991), p 4
Cole/ Larmour	Cole, Catherine C., and Judy Larmour. *Many and Remarkable: The Story of the Alberta Women's Institutes.* [Edmonton:] Alberta Women's Institutes, [1997]
Cook	Cook, Margaret. *America's Charitable Cooks: A Bibliography of Fund-raising Cook Books Published in the United States, 1861–1915.* Kent, Ohio: 1971
Cooke 2002	Cooke, Nathalie. 'Cookbooks and Culture.' In *Encyclopedia of Literature in Canada.* William H. New, ed. Toronto: University of Toronto Press, 2002
Cooke 2003	Cooke, Nathalie. 'Getting the Mix Just Right for the Canadian Home Baker.' *Essays on Canadian Writing* No. 78 (Winter 2003)
Crawford	Crawford, Trish. 'Pages from the Past: Vintage Cookbook Collectors Know These Tomes Hold More Than Recipes.' *Star* (Toronto) 13 June 2001, pp D1–D2
Dagg	Dagg, Anne Innis. *The Feminine Gaze: A Canadian Compendium of Non-Fiction Women Authors and Their Books, 1836–1945.* Waterloo, Ont.: Wilfrid Laurier University Press, [2001]
Davidson	Davidson, Alan. *The Oxford Companion to Food.* Oxford: Oxford University Press, 1999
DCB	*Dictionary of Canadian Biography.* Toronto: University of Toronto Press, 1966–
Dewalt	Dewalt, Bryan. *Technology and Canadian Printing: A History from Lead Type to Lasers.* Ottawa: National Museum of Science and Technology, 1995
Dickinson	Dickinson, Linda J. *A Price Guide to Cookbooks and Recipe Leaflets.* Paducah, Ky: Collector Books, 1997
Dionne	Dionne, Narcisse-Eutrope. *Inventaire chronologique des livres, brochures, journaux et revues publiés en langue anglaise dans la province de Québec, depuis l'établissement de l'imprimerie en Canada jusqu'à nos jours 1764–1906.* Originally published by Société royale du Canada, 1905–9, and first supplement, 1912. Reprint. New York: Burt Franklin, 1969
Driver	Driver, Elizabeth. *A Bibliography of Cookery Books Published in Britain 1875–1914.* London: Prospect Books, 1989 [copies are available in Canada at BVAU, OONL, OTMCL, and OTU]
Driver 2001, All New Purity	Driver, Elizabeth. 'Historical Notes.' In *The All New Purity Cook Book,* inside front cover. Facsimile ed. of 1967. Classic Canadian Cookbook Series. North Vancouver: Whitecap Books, 2001, 6th and later printings
Driver 2001, 'Entrepreneurs'	Driver, Liz. 'Entrepreneurs of Kitchens Past.' *Women's Culinary Network News* (March 2001): p 4
Driver 2001, Wellington County	Driver, Elizabeth. 'Cookbooks of Wellington County.' Paper delivered at Annual General Meeting of Wellington County Historical Society, Fergus, Ont., 5 June 2000. *Wellington County History* Vol. 14 (2001), pp 85–98
Driver 2002, Five Roses	Driver, Elizabeth. 'Historical Notes.' In *Five Roses Cook Book,* p 4. Facsimile ed. of 1915. Classic Canadian Cookbook Series. North Vancouver: Whitecap Books, 2002, 7th and later printings
Driver 2002, Home Cook Book	Driver, Elizabeth. 'Introduction.' In *The Home Cook Book,* pp xi–xxiii. Facsimile ed. of 1878. Classic Canadian Cookbook Series. North Vancouver: Whitecap Books, 2002
Driver 2003, 'Canadian Cookbooks'	Driver, Elizabeth. 'Canadian Cookbooks (1825–1949): In the Heart of the Home.' Text of lecture for Savoir Faire seminar series, National Library of Canada, Ottawa, 22 January

	2002. *Petits Propos Culinaires* No. 72 (March 2003), pp 19–39
Driver 2003, Five Roses	Driver, Elizabeth. 'Historical Notes.' In *Five Roses: A Guide to Good Cooking,* p 1. Facsimile ed. of 1967. Classic Canadian Cookbook Series. North Vancouver: Whitecap Books, 2003
Driver 2003, Ogilvie's Book	Driver, Elizabeth. 'Historical Notes.' In *Ogilvie's Book for a Cook,* inside front cover. Facsimile ed. of 1905. Classic Canadian Cookbook Series. North Vancouver: Whitecap Books, 2003
Driver 2003, Robin Hood	Driver, Elizabeth. 'Historical Notes.' In *Robin Hood Flour Cook Book,* by Sarah Tyson Rorer, pp 84–8. Facsimile ed. Classic Canadian Cookbook Series. North Vancouver: Whitecap Books, 2003
Driver 2004	Driver, Elizabeth. 'Kate and Her Cookbook.' In *Kate Aitken's Canadian Cook Book,* pp iii–viii. Facsimile ed. of 1945. Classic Canadian Cookbook Series. North Vancouver: Whitecap Books, 2004
Driver 2005	Driver, Elizabeth. 'Cookbooks.' In *History of the Book in Canada.* Vol. 2, *1840–1918,* pp 408–12. Fiona A. Black, Patricia Lockhart Fleming, and Yvan Lamonde, eds. Toronto: University of Toronto Press, 2005. Also published in French as *Histoire du livre et de l'imprimé au Canada,* Les presses de l'Université de Montréal
Driver 2005, letter	Driver, Elizabeth. 'Simmering Controversy' [letter to editor]. *Beaver* Vol. 85, No. 6 (December 2005–January 2006), pp 6–7
Driver 2006	Driver, Elizabeth. 'Home Cooks, Book Makers and Community Builders in Canada.' In *Food, Culture and Community*, edited by Lynette Hunter. *Moving Worlds* Vol. 6, No. 2 (Autumn 2006), pp 41–60
DucharmeCat	Ducharme, G., bookseller, Montreal, sales catalogue
Duncan	Duncan, Dorothy. *Nothing More Comforting: Canada's Heritage Food.* Toronto: Dundurn Group, 2003
DuSablon	DuSablon, Mary Anna. *America's Collectible Cookbooks: The History, the Politics, the Recipes.* Athens: Ohio University Press, 1994
Eade	Eade, Ron. 'A Taste for History: Library and Archives Canada Savours Our Culinary Past through Cookbooks.' *Ottawa Citizen* 26 May 2004, pp E1–E2
Edwards	Edwards, Margaret H. *A Bibliography of British Columbia: Years of Growth 1900–1950.* Victoria: University of Victoria, 1975
EngCat	*The English Catalogue of Books.* New York: Kraus Reprint, 1963
FabreCat	Fabre, Edouard-Raymond, bookseller, Montreal, sales catalogue
Feeding America	*Feeding America: The Historic American Cookbook Project.* Digital collection. Michigan State University Library. http://digital.lib.msu.edu/projects/cookbooks/index.html
Ferguson/ Fraser	Ferguson, Carol, and Margaret Fraser. *A Century of Canadian Home Cooking: 1900 through the '90s.* Toronto: Prentice Hall Canada Inc., 1992
FirstSearch	FirstSearch on-line catalogue: http://firstsearch.oclc.org [subscription service, available at reference libraries]
FitzPatrickCat	FitzPatrick Books, Fredericton, NB, sales catalogue
Fleming	Fleming, Patricia. *Upper Canadian Imprints 1801–1841: A Bibliography.* Toronto: University of Toronto Press in co-operation with the National Library of Canada and the Canadian Government Publishing Centre, 1988
Fowler	Fowler, Marian. *The Embroidered Tent; Five Gentlewomen in Early Canada: Elizabeth Simcoe, Catharine Parr Traill, Susanna Moodie, Anna Jameson, Lady Dufferin.* Toronto: Anansi, 1982
Garrett	Garrett, Blanche Pownall. *Canadian Country Preserves and Wines.* Toronto: James Lewis and Samuel, 1974
Goldenberg	Goldenberg, Susan. 'Cooking with Nellie.' *Beaver* Vol. 85, No. 5 (October–November 2005): pp 41–3
Golick	Golick, Greta. '"One quart milk, five eggs I should say": Marginalia in Anglo-Canadian Cookbooks.' *Variants: Reading Notes* [journal of the European Society for Textual Scholarship] Vol. 2/3 (2004), pp 95–113

Golick 2005 Golick, Greta. 'Bookselling in Town and Country.' In *History of the Book in Canada*. Vol. 2, *1840–1918*, pp 214, 525 (note 68). Fiona A. Black, Patricia Lockhart Fleming, and Yvan Lamonde, eds. Toronto: University of Toronto Press, 2005. Also published in French as *Histoire du livre et de l'imprimé au Canada*, Les presses de l'Université de Montréal

Haight 1896 Haight, Willet Ricketson. *Canadian Catalogue of Books. Part One*. Toronto: Haight and Co., 1896

Haight 1904 Haight, Willet Ricketson. *1897 Annual Canadian Catalogue of Books. Second Supplement to the Canadian Catalogue of Books 1791–1895*. Toronto: Haight and Co., 1904

Hale Hale, Linda L. *Vancouver Centennial Bibliography: A Project of the Vancouver Historical Society*. [Vancouver:] Vancouver Historical Society, 1986

Howsam Howsam, Leslie. 'Food for Thought.' *Rare Book Review* (April 2004), pp 32–6

Hughes Hughes, Kathryn. *The Short Life and Long Times of Mrs Beeton*. London: Fourth Estate, 2005

Hulse Hulse, Elizabeth. *A Dictionary of Toronto Printers, Publishers, Booksellers and the Allied Trades, 1798–1900*. Toronto: Anson-Cartwright Editions, 1982

HuroniaCat Huronia Canadiana Books, Alliston, Ont., sales catalogue

Jarvits Janet Jarvits, bookseller, Pasadena, Calif., web site (www.cookbkjj.com)

JCCat Janet Clarke, bookseller, Bath, England, sales catalogue

JLCat John Lyle, bookseller, Sidmouth, Devon, England, sales catalogue

JPCat Joseph Patrick Books, Toronto, sales catalogue

Lafrance/ Lafrance, Marc, and Yvon Desloges.
Desloges *A Taste of History: The Origins of Québec's Gastronomy*. Les Éditions de la Chenelière and Environment Canada, Canadian Parks Service, 1989

LakeCat D. & E. Lake Ltd, Toronto, sales catalogue

Lambert, C. Lambert, Carole. 'Survivance d'usages culinaires anciens dans la cuisine québécoise.' In *Ethnologie* Vol. 12, No. 3, papers presented at 'Manger: de France à Nouvelle-France,' colloquium of the Société Québécoise des Ethnologues, at Université Laval, Quebec City, 27–9 May 1989

Lambert, T. Lambert, Thérèse. *Histoire de la Congrégation de Notre-Dame de Montréal*. Vol. 11, 1900–50, Tomes 1 and 2. Montreal: Congrégation de Notre-Dame de Montréal, 1974

Landsberg Landsberg, Michele. 'The Real Books of Love: How Recipes Reveal History.' *Toronto Star* 24 December 2000, p A2

Lang Lang, Marjory. *Women Who Made the News: Female Journalists in Canada, 1880–1945*. Montreal and Kingston: McGill-Queen's University Press, 1999

Langford Langford, Nanci. *Politics, Pitchforks and Pickle Jars: 75 Years of Organized Farm Women in Alberta*. Calgary: Detselig Enterprises Ltd, 1997

Leduc Leduc, Louise. 'Historienne de la bouffe: Elizabeth Driver a consacré les dix dernières années à retracer tous les livres de cuisine écrits entre 1825 et 1950.' *Le devoir* (Montreal) 24 December 2000, p A9

LongoneCat The Wine and Food Library: An Antiquarian Bookshop, Ann Arbor, Mich., Janice Longone, proprietor, sales catalogue

Longone/ *American Cookbooks and Wine Books*
Longone *1797–1950 Being an Exhibition from the Collections of, and with Historical Notes by, Janice Bluestein Longone and Daniel T. Longone ... at the William L. Clements Library of American History ... University of Michigan ... January and February, 1984*. Ann Arbor, Mich.: Janice B. Longone, copyright 1984

Lowenstein Lowenstein, Eleanor. *Bibliography of American Cookery Books 1742–1860*. Worcester, Mass.: American Antiquarian Society; New York: Corner Book Shop, 1972

Lowther Lowther, Barbara J. *A Bibliography of British Columbia: Laying the Foundations 1849–1899*. Victoria: University of Victoria, 1968

Lucas	Lucas, Fiona. *Hearth and Home: Women and the Art of Open-Hearth Cooking.* Toronto: James Lorimer and Co. Ltd, 2006
MacDonald	MacDonald, Cheryl. *Adelaide Hoodless: Domestic Crusader.* Toronto: Dundurn Press, 1986
MacFarlane	MacFarlane, William Godsoe. *New Brunswick Bibliography: The Books and Writers of the Province.* Saint John, NB: Press of the Sun Printing Co. Ltd, 1895
MacGillivray	MacGillivray, Royce. *Bibliography of Glengarry County.* Alexandria, Ont.: Glengarry Historical Society, 1996
Maclean	Maclean, Virginia. *A Short-Title Catalogue of Household and Cookery Books Published in the English Tongue, 1701–1800.* London, England: Prospect Books, 1981
Macmillan Dictionary	Wallace, W. Stewart, ed. *The Macmillan Dictionary of Canadian Biography.* 4th ed., edited by W.A. McKay. Toronto: Macmillan of Canada, 1978
MacTaggart	MacTaggart, Hazel I. *Publications of the Government of Ontario 1901–1955: A Checklist Compiled for the Ontario Library Association.* Toronto: University of Toronto Press for the Queen's Printer, 1964
MBPHCat 1876–7	*General Catalogue of Books, Published and on Sale at the Methodist Book and Publishing House, 80 King Street East, Toronto, and at the Branch Book Room, Montreal, P.Q.,* Toronto: Printed at the Guardian Book and Job Establishment, 1876–7
MCat	Marylebone Book Shop, London, England, sales catalogue
Montreal-BACat	Montreal Book Auctions Ltd/ L'Encan des livres de Montréal, auction catalogue
Morgan	Morgan, Henry James, ed. *The Canadian Men and Women of the Time: A Hand-Book of Canadian Biography of Living Characters.* 2nd ed. Toronto: William Briggs, 1912
Nakonechny/ Kishchuk	Nakonechny, Patricia, and Marie Kishchuk, with the assistance of Liudmilla Marivtsan-Soroka and Patricia Tymchatyn. *The Monograph Collections of the Ukrainian Museum of*
	Canada: An Integrated Catalogue. Saskatoon: The Museum, 1988
Neering	Neering, Rosemary. *The Canadian Housewife: An Affectionate History.* North Vancouver: Whitecap Books, 2005
Newman	Newman, Lenore. 'For More Than 60 Years Food Preserving Information in Demand.' *Ag-Rapport* [Agriculture Canada internal newsletter] (June 1983), p 4
Nightingale 1970	Nightingale, Marie. *Out of Old Nova Scotia Kitchens: A Collection of Traditional Recipes of Nova Scotia and the Story of the People Who Cooked Them.* [Halifax, NS: Printed by McCurdy Printing Co. Ltd], August 1970. Other editions, New York: Scribner, [1971], Toronto: Pagurian Press, 1971, and Toronto: Pagurian, 1976
Nightingale 1989	Nightingale, Marie. 'IODE's Recipes Bring Back Good Food, Fond Memories.' *Chronicle-Herald Mail-Star* (Halifax, NS), 8 March 1989
NUC	*National Union Catalog, Pre-1956 Imprints.* [London, England:] Mansell Information and the American Library Association, 1968–81
O'Dea	O'Dea, Agnes C. *Bibliography of Newfoundland.* Toronto: University of Toronto Press in association with Memorial University of Newfoundland, 1986. 2 vols
OHS	*Serve It Forth! Festive Desserts from the Nineteenth Century Adapted for Modern Times.* Toronto: Ontario Historical Society, 1984
Olafson-Jenkyns	Olafson-Jenkyns, Kristin. *The Culinary Saga of New Iceland: Recipes from the Shores of Lake Winnipeg.* Guelph, Ont.: Coastline Publishing, 2001
Oldfield/ Landon	Oldfield, Philip, and Richard Landon. *Ars Medica: Medical Illustration through the Ages: An Exhibition to Commemorate the Seventieth Anniversary of the Founding of Associated Medical Services.* Catalogue for exhibition at Thomas Fisher Rare Book Library, University of Toronto, January–April 2006. Toronto: University of Toronto Library, 2006
O'Neill	O'Neill, Patrick B. *A Checklist of Canadian Copyright Deposits in the*

British Museum, 1895–1923. Halifax, NS: School of Library and Information Studies, Dalhousie University, 1984–. [The volume incorporating cookbooks is not yet published; however, O'Neill has shared his research material with me and references to it are cited as O'Neill (unpublished). Many of the British Library's Canadian cookbooks were destroyed during the Second World War when a bomb fell on the Colonial Dump – uncatalogued, copyright material received from various parts of the British Empire and kept at the Woolwich Arsenal; they are recorded, with titles from other subject areas, in a British Museum typescript headed 'List of Missing Canadian Books.' These books are identified as 'LB (destroyed)' in the 'Copies:' section of the entry. Those cookbooks that survived are identified as 'LB (Woolwich).' The Colonial Dump is now stored at Boston Spa.]

Oxford — Oxford, Arnold Whitaker. *English Cookery Books to the Year 1850.* Reprint. London, England: Holland Press, 1977

PAC Library — Public Archives of Canada, Ottawa. *Catalogue of the Public Archives Library.* 12 vols. Boston: G.K. Hall and Co., 1979

PAC Pamphlets — Public Archives of Canada, Ottawa. *Catalogue of Pamphlets in the Public Archives of Canada.* Vol. 1, 1843–77; Vol. 2, 1878–1931. Prepared by Magdalen Casey. Ottawa: F.A. Acland, printer, 1931–2

Parker — Parker, George L. *The Beginnings of the Book Trade in Canada.* Toronto: University of Toronto Press, 1985

Peel — Peel, Bruce Braden. *A Bibliography of the Prairie Provinces to 1953, with Biographical Index.* 2nd ed. Toronto: University of Toronto Press, 1973. 'Micro' after Peel number indicates microfiche copy of book. See also Peel's Bibliography

Peel's Bibliography — Ingles, Ernie B., and N. Merrill Distad, eds and comps. *Peel's Bibliography of the Canadian Prairies to 1953.* 3rd ed., revised and enlarged, of *A Bibliography of the Prairie Provinces to 1953, with Biographical Index,* by Bruce Braden Peel. Toronto: University of Toronto Press, 2003

Peterat/ DeZwart — Peterat, Linda, and Mary Leah DeZwart, eds. *An Education for Women: The Founding of Home Economics Education in Canadian Public Schools.* Charlottetown: Home Economics Publishing Collective, University of Prince Edward Island, 1995

Phelps — Phelps, Edward Charles Howard. *A Bibliography of Lambton County and the City of Sarnia, Ontario.* Petrolia, Ont.: Printed by the Advertiser-Topic, 1970

Poulain– Le FurCat — Poulain–Le Fur, commissaires-priseurs associés, Paris, France. Auction catalogue. Issues cited include: La bibliothèque gourmande de M. Ulf Löchner, 4–5 February 2000; Deux bibliothèques gastronomiques: bibliothèque de M. Christian Guy, bibliothèque d'un cuisinier Quercynois, 13 January 2001

Powers/ Stewart — Powers, Jo Marie, and Anita Stewart, eds. *Northern Bounty: A Celebration of Canadian Cuisine.* Proceedings of symposium held at the Chefs School, Stratford, Ont., in September 1993. Toronto: Random House of Canada, 1995

Reitz — Reitz, Thomas A. 'Musings on Cookbooks and Christmas Dinner.' *Waterloo County Times* [publication of Heritage Resources Department, Regional Municipality of Waterloo, Ont.] Vol. 6, No. 3 (November 1991), p [4]

Rhodenizer — Rhodenizer, Vernon Blair. *Canadian Literature in English.* Montreal: Quality Press, 1965. For index, see Lois M. Thierman, *Index to Vernon Blair Rhodenizer's Canadian Literature in English,* Edmonton: La Survivance Printing, 1968

Rome et al. — Rome, David, Judith Nefsky, and Paule Obermeir. *Les juifs du Québec: bibliographie rétrospective annotée.* Institut Québécois de recherche sur la culture, 1981

Rowe	Rowe, Trent. 'Recipes Record Century of Cooking.' *Spectator* (Hamilton, Ont.) 22 February 1984, p D1
Rudolph	Rudolph, G.A. *Kansas State University Receipt Book and Household Manual*, Bibliography Series No. 4. Manhattan, Kans.: Kansas State University Library, 1968
RushCat	John Rush Books, bookseller, Hamilton, Ont., sales catalogue
Saberi/ Davidson	Saberi, Helen, and Alan Davidson. *Trifle*. Totnes, England: Prospect Books, 2001
Saturday Night	*Saturday Night;* various issues of the Canadian magazine
Simon	Simon, André Louis. *Bibliotheca Gastronomica: A Catalogue of Books and Documents on Gastronomy*. London, England: Wine and Food Society, 1953. Reprint. London, England: Holland Press, 1978
Simpson	Simpson, Lesley. 'Recipes for Reaching Out.' *Hamilton Spectator* 9 October 1999, pp W16–17
Spadoni 1989	'A Bibliography of Macmillan of Canada Imprints, 1906–1980: First Supplement with Corrigenda.' In *Papers of the Bibliographical Society of Canada* Vol. 28 (1989)
Spadoni 1998	Spadoni, Carl. *A Bibliography of Stephen Leacock*. Toronto: ECW Press, 1998
Spadoni/ Donnelly	Spadoni, Carl, and Judy Donnelly. *A Bibliography of McClelland and Stewart Imprints, 1909–1985: A Publisher's Legacy.* Toronto: ECW Press, 1994
Sullivan	Sullivan, Elinor. *A Bibliography of Simcoe County, Ontario, 1790–1990: Published Works and Post-Graduate Theses Relating to the British Colonial and Post-Confederation Periods.* Penetanguishene, Ont.: SBI, 1992
SWI	Saskatchewan Women's Institute. *Legacy: A History of Saskatchewan Homemakers' Clubs and Women's Institutes, 1911–1988.* Regina: Focus Publishing, 1988
Tapper	Tapper, Lawrence F. *A Biographical Dictionary of Canadian Jewry, 1909–1914: From the Canadian Jewish Times.* Teaneck, NJ: Avotaynu Inc., [1992]
Tennyson	Tennyson, Brian Douglas. *Cape Bretoniana: An Annotated Bibliography.* Toronto: University of Toronto Press, 2005
THEA 1988	Toronto Home Economics Association. *Toronto Home Economics Association, 1938–1988: Golden Memories.* Edited by Margaret Thibeault. Printed by Canada Yearbook Services (1988), Whitby, Ont.
Thomas/ Marchant	Thomas, Dave, and Bob Marchant. *When Milk Came in Bottles: A History of Toronto Dairies.* Port Hope, Ont.: Cowtown Publications, 1997
Tod/ Cordingley	Tod, Dorothea D., and Audrey Cordingley. *A Check List of Canadian Imprints 1900–1925.* Ottawa: Canadian Bibliographic Centre, Public Archives of Canada, 1950
TPL	*A Bibliography of Canadiana.* Toronto: Toronto Public Library, 1934; First Supplement, 1959; Second Supplement, 1985–9, 4 vols
TPL Scrapbooks	[Scrapbooks – biographies]. Microfilm. Toronto: Toronto Public Library. There is a card index to the biographical scrapbooks in Special Collections
Vicaire	Vicaire, Georges. *Bibliographie gastronomique.* Facsimile ed. London, England: Holland Press, 1978. 1st ed., Paris: P. Rouquette et fils, éditeurs, 1890
Vintage	The Vintage Cookbookery, bookseller, Albuquerque, NM, web site
Waddington Cat	Waddington's Auctioneers, Toronto, auction catalogue
WaiteCat	John Waite Rare Books, Ascutney, Vt, in conjunction with Kevin Rita Brick Walk Bookshop, West Hartford, Conn., sales catalogue
Walker	Walker, Kathleen. 'Homemakers Resourceful Combatants on Home Front.' *Calgary Herald* 8 June 1994, p B5
Wallace	Wallace, W. Stewart. *The Ryerson Imprint: A Check-list of the Books and Pamphlets Published by the Ryerson Press since the Foundation of the House in 1829.* Toronto: Ryerson Press, [1954]
Waterston	Waterston, Elizabeth, with Ian Easterbrook, Bernard Katz, and

	Kathleen Scott. *The Travellers – Canada to 1900: An Annotated Bibliography of Works Published in English from 1577.* Guelph: University of Guelph, 1989
Watier	Watier, Nicole. 'Canadian Cookbooks (1825–1949): In the Heart of the Home.' Report on Savoir Faire lecture by Elizabeth Driver. *Bulletin* [National Library of Canada] Vol. 34, No. 3 (May–June 2002), pp 7–8
Watters	Watters, Reginald Eyre. *A Checklist of Canadian Literature and Background Materials, 1628–1960.* 2nd ed. Toronto: University of Toronto Press, 1972
We Are Tomorrow's Past	*We Are Tomorrow's Past: History of the Canadian Home Economics Association.* Ottawa: Canadian Home Economics Association, 1989
Wheaton 1996	Wheaton, Barbara Ketcham. *Savoring the Past: The French Kitchen and Table from 1300 to 1789.* New York: Simon and Schuster, 1996. 1st ed., 1983
Wheaton/ Kelly	Wheaton, Barbara Ketcham, and Patricia Kelly. *Bibliography of Culinary History: Food Resources in Eastern Massachusetts.* Boston: G.K. Hall and Co., [1987?]
Whiteman et al.	Whiteman, Bruce, Charlotte Stewart, and Catherine Funnell. *A Bibliogra-*
	phy of Macmillan of Canada Imprints, 1906–1980. Toronto: Dundurn Press, 1985
Williamson	Williamson, Mary F. *'To fare sumptuously every day': Rambles among Upper Canadian Dishes and Repasts together with Authentic Menus and Culinary Receipts.* Occasional Paper 25. Peterborough, Ont.: Peterborough Historical Society, November 2004
Williamson, History of the Book	Williamson, Mary F. 'Recipe and Household Literature.' In *History of the Book in Canada.* Vol. 1, *Beginnings to 1840,* pp 275–7. Patricia Lockhart Fleming, Gilles Gallichan, and Yvan Lamonde, eds. Toronto: University of Toronto Press, 2004. Also published in French as *Histoire du livre et de l'imprimé au Canada,* Les presses de l'Université de Montréal
Wilson May 1991	Wilson, Susan. 'A Kitchen Full of Cookbooks.' *This Week in the Highlands* [insert in *Minden Times*] (Minden, Ont.) 24–30 May 1991, pp 7–8
Wilson July 1991	Wilson, Susan. 'Cooking for Summer Visitors a Full Day's Work.' *This Week in the Highlands* [insert in *Minden Times*] (Minden, Ont.) 19–25 July 1991, p 14

Maps

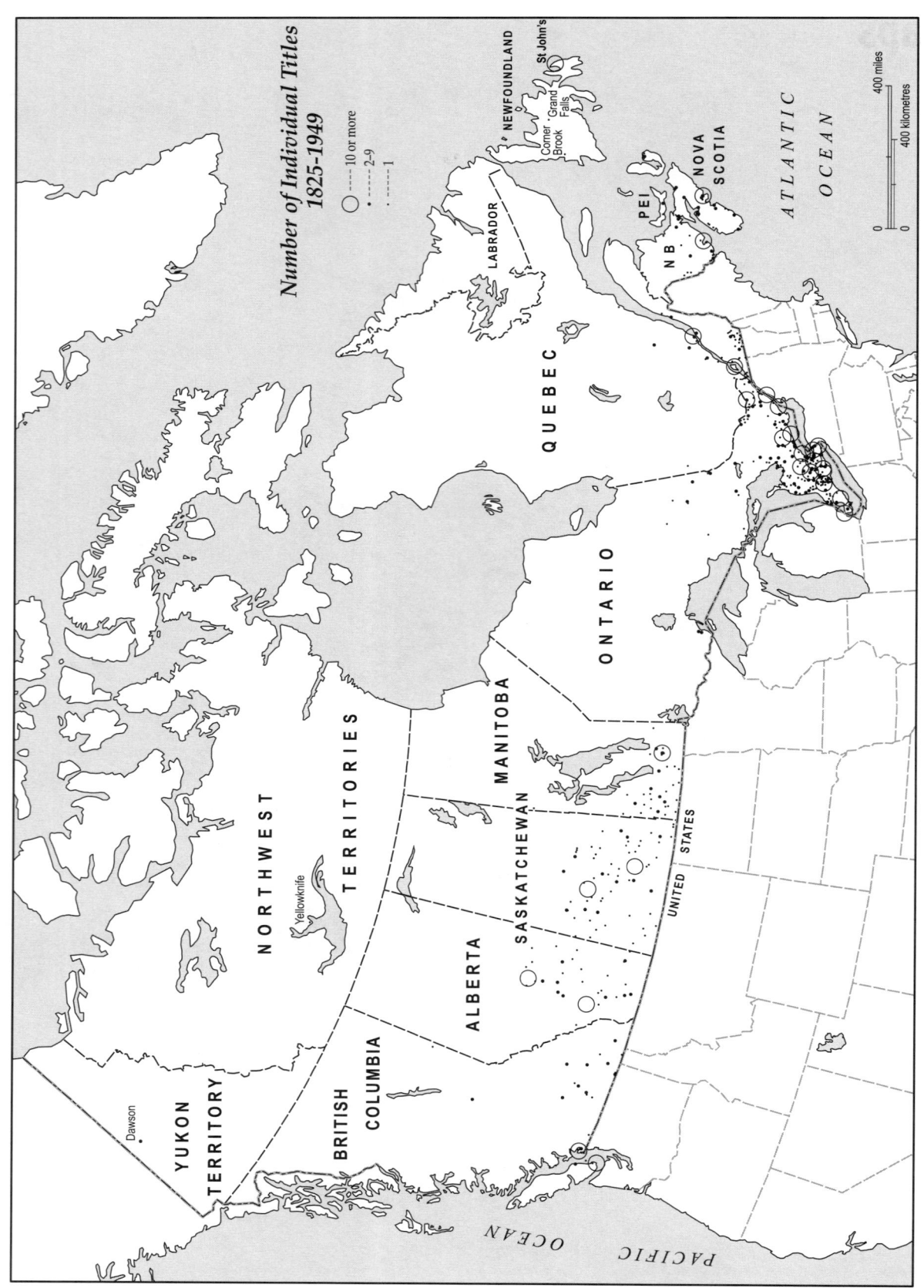

The Cartography Office, Department of Geography, University of Toronto.

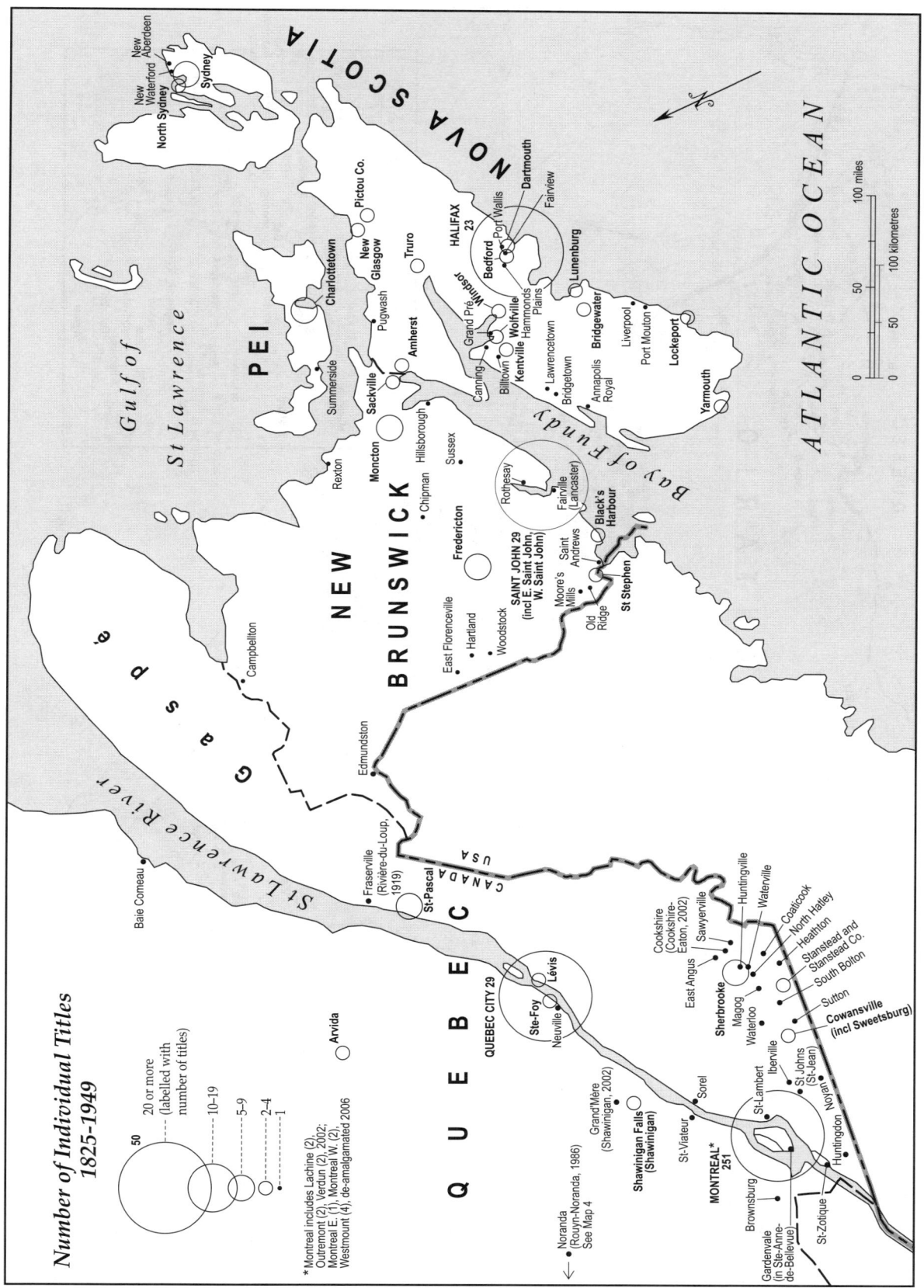

Number of Individual Titles 1825–1949

50 — 20 or more (labelled with number of titles)
10–19
5–9
2–4
1

* Montreal includes Lachine (2), Outremont (2), Verdun (2), 2002; Montreal E. (1), Montreal W. (2), Westmount (4), de-amalgamated 2006

NOVA SCOTIA

New Aberdeen
New Waterford
North Sydney
Sydney

Pictou Co.
New Glasgow
Truro
Charlottetown
Pugwash
HALIFAX 23
Port Wallis
Bedford
Dartmouth
Fairview
Windsor
Grand Pré
Hammonds Plains
Lunenburg
Wolfville
Kentville
Billtown
Canning
Lawrencetown
Bridgetown
Bridgewater
Liverpool
Port Mouton
Lockeport
Annapolis Royal
Yarmouth

PEI
Gulf of St Lawrence
Summerside
Sackville
Amherst

Rexton
Moncton
Hillsborough
Sussex
Chipman
Rothesay
Fairville (Lancaster)
Black's Harbour
Bay of Fundy

NEW BRUNSWICK
Fredericton
SAINT JOHN 29 (incl E. Saint John, W. Saint John)
Saint Andrews
Moore's Mills
St Stephen
Old Ridge
East Florenceville
Hartland
Woodstock

Campbellton
Gaspé
St Lawrence River
Baie Comeau
Edmundston
Fraserville (Rivière-du-Loup, 1919)
St-Pascal

ATLANTIC OCEAN

100 miles
100 kilometres
50
50

CANADA USA

QUEBEC

QUEBEC CITY 29
Ste-Foy
Neuville
Lévis

Arvida

Noranda Rouyn-Noranda, 1986) See Map 4

Grand'Mère (Shawinigan, 2002)
Shawinigan Falls (Shawinigan)
St-Viateur
Sorel

MONTREAL* 251
St-Lambert
Iberville
St Johns (St-Jean)
Noyan
Huntingdon
St-Zotique
Brownsburg
Gardenvale (in Ste-Anne-de-Bellevue)

Cookshire (Cookshire-Eaton, 2002)
Sawyerville
Huntingville
Waterville
Coaticook
North Hatley
Heathton
Stanstead and Stanstead Co.
South Bolton
East Angus
Sherbrooke
Magog
Waterloo
Sutton
Cowansville (incl Sweetsburg)

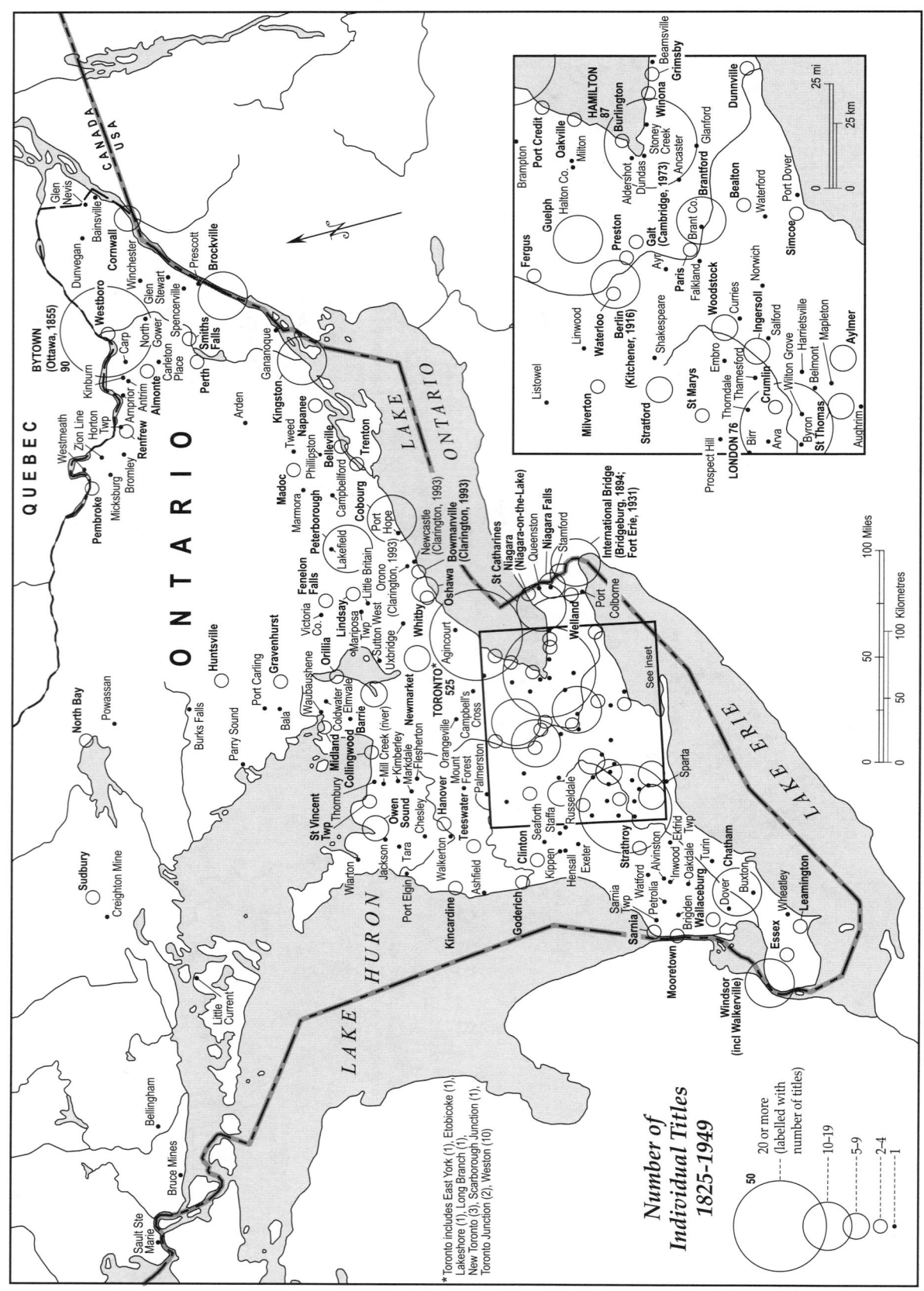

*Toronto includes East York (1), Etobicoke (1),
Lakeshore (1), Long Branch (1),
New Toronto (3), Scarborough Junction (1),
Toronto Junction (2), Weston (10)

**Number of
Individual Titles
1825–1949**

50
20 or more
(labelled with
number of titles)
10–19
5–9
2–4
1

The Cartography Office, Department of Geography, University of Toronto.

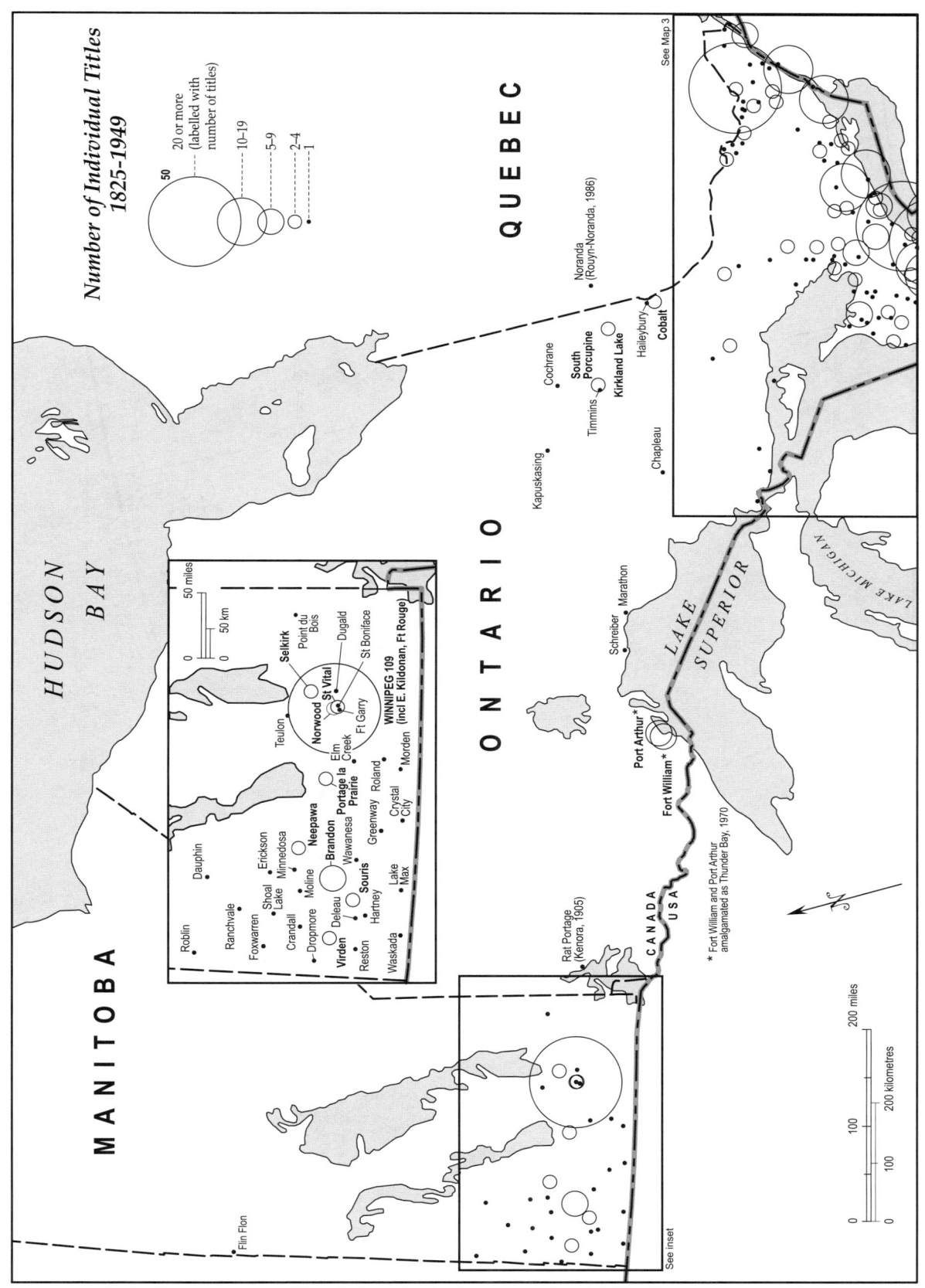

Number of Individual Titles
1825-1949

50
20 or more
(labelled with
number of titles)

10-19
5-9
2-4
1

HUDSON
BAY

QUEBEC

ONTARIO

MANITOBA

LAKE MICHIGAN

LAKE SUPERIOR

Noranda
(Rouyn-Noranda, 1986)

Cochrane

South
Porcupine

Kirkland Lake

Timmins

Chapleau

Kapuskasing

Schreiber

Marathon

Haileybury
Cobalt

Port Arthur *

Fort William *

CANADA
USA

* Fort William and Port Arthur
amalgamated as Thunder Bay, 1970

Rat Portage
(Kenora, 1905)

Flin Flon

See Map 3

See inset

Selkirk
Point du
Bois
Dugald

Norwood St Vital
St Boniface

Ft Garry
WINNIPEG 109
(incl E. Kildonan, Ft Rouge)

Teulon

Elm
Creek

Morden

Portage la
Prairie

Greenway Roland

Crystal
City

Neepawa

Brandon
Wawanesa

Souris

Lake
Max

Dauphin

Shoal
Lake Minnedosa

Erickson

Moline

Hartney

Roblin

Ranchvale

Foxwarren

Crandall

Dropmore
Deleau

Virden
Reston

Waskada

50 miles
50 km

0
0

200 miles
200 kilometres
100
100
0
0

The Cartography Office, Department of Geography, University of Toronto.

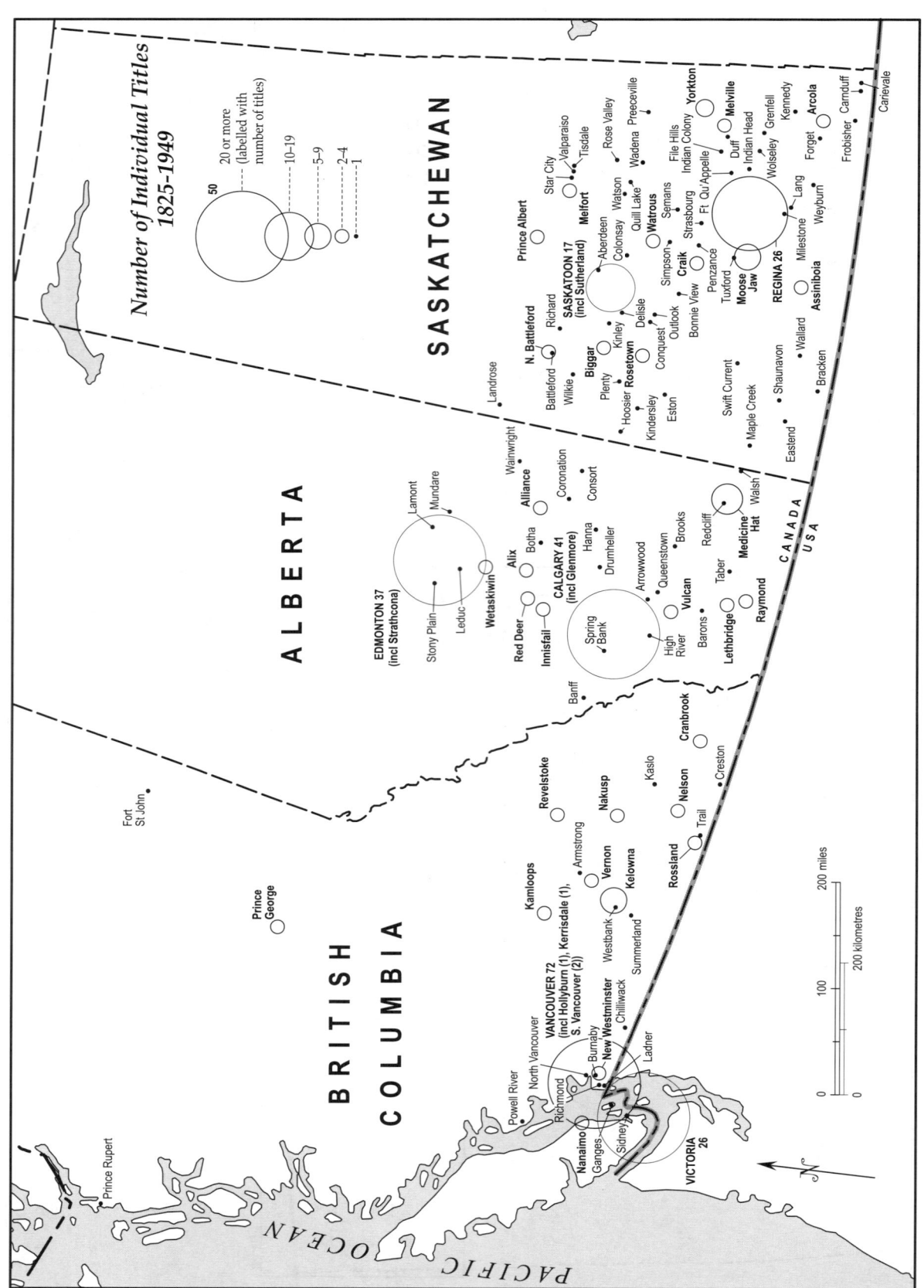

*Number of Individual Titles
1825-1949*

50 — 20 or more
(labelled with
number of titles)
10-19
5-9
2-4
1

BRITISH COLUMBIA

ALBERTA

SASKATCHEWAN

PACIFIC OCEAN

Prince Rupert

Fort St. John

Prince George

Powell River

Kamloops

Armstrong

Vernon

Kelowna

Westbank

Summerland

Kerrisdale (1),
S. Vancouver (2)

VANCOUVER 72
(incl Hollyburn (1),

North Vancouver

Burnaby

New Westminster

Chilliwack

Richmond

Ladner

Nanaimo

Ganges

Sidney

VICTORIA 26

Revelstoke

Nakusp

Kaslo

Nelson

Creston

Trail

Rossland

Cranbrook

Banff

EDMONTON 37
(incl Strathcona)

Lamont

Mundare

Stony Plain

Leduc

Wetaskiwin

Red Deer

Innisfail

Spring Bank

High River

CALGARY 41
(incl Glenmore)

Alix

Botha

Alliance

Coronation

Consort

Hanna

Drumheller

Arrowwood

Queenstown

Vulcan

Barons

Taber

Lethbridge

Raymond

Brooks

Redcliff

Medicine Hat

Walsh

CANADA
USA

Wainwright

Landrose

N. Battleford

Battleford

Wilkie

Plenty

Biggar

Hoosier

Rosetown

Kindersley

Eston

Conquest

Prince Albert

Star City

Valparaiso

Tisdale

Rose Valley

Wadena

Preeceville

Melfort

Watson

Colonsay

Quill Lake

SASKATOON 17
(incl Sutherland)

Aberdeen

Richard

Kinley

Delisle

Outlook

Bonnie View

Semans

Simpson

Craik

Penzance

Tuxford

Moose Jaw

Swift Current

Maple Creek

Shaunavon

Eastend

Bracken

Wallard

Milestone

Weyburn

Assiniboia

REGINA 26

File Hills

Indian Colony

Ft Qu'Appelle

Strasbourg

Lang

Indian Head

Wolseley

Grenfell

Milestone

Yorkton

Melville

Duff

Kennedy

Arcola

Forget

Frobisher

Carnduff

Carievale

Watrous

Carievale

200 miles

100

200 kilometres

0

The Cartography Office, Department of Geography, University of Toronto.

Culinary Landmarks

Newfoundland and Labrador

Blueberry Wine

1 gal. crushed blueberries
3 qts. water
3 qts. molasses
1 pkg. raisins

Place in container, cover or cork for two months, strain, bottle.

Mr. J.C. Goobie

Cod Tongues in Cream Sauce

Boil cod tongues in small amount of water for 20 minutes. Make a white sauce, using the liquid from the tongues. Add the tongues to the cooked sauce and stir gently. Serve with green peas or beans and creamed potatoes.

[Uncredited]

Both recipes, NF11.1, *Cook Book,* United Church Girls' Club, Corner Brook, [2nd ed., 1948], pp 7, 47

The section for Newfoundland and Labrador,[1] Canada's easternmost province, begins this bibliography, which is arranged from east to west to reflect the first contact by Europeans and the pattern of their gradual settlement of the land. It was in the tenth century, a millennium ago, that Viking explorers lived for a short while at L'Anse aux Meadows, on Newfoundland's north shore. The earliest known European visitors to North America, they arrived long before the 'discovery' of Terra Nova by John Cabot in 1497. The majority of Newfoundlanders are descended from later immigrants from southwest England and southern Ireland, although there are also some people of Scottish origin (whose forebears arrived via Cape Breton) and some of French descent (Acadians). The irony of Newfoundland's first-place position in the bibliography is that all the cookbooks in this section were published when Newfoundland was a British colony, before it became Canada's most recent province by joining in Confederation on 31 March 1949. Newfoundland food traditions, like other aspects of the province's culture, have evolved along a unique path, and there are several distinctive dishes, especially for codfish, the mainstay of the economy for centuries, until the collapse of the fishery in the 1990s.[2] Recipes for seafood, and also for some of the wild berries harvested by families in summer, feature in the cookbooks, along with the standard fare found on Canadian tables in the first half of the twentieth century. Despite the long history of settlement in Newfoundland, the population remained small, and in 1901, just after cookbooks began to be published, the number of citizens was only 220,984, growing to 361,416 by 1951.

The earliest cookbook to surface, *The Art of Cooking Made Easy* (O48.9), was published in 1900 by O'Mara's

Drug Store in St John's, to promote the use of Emerald Baking Powder. The same text, likely reprinted from an American source, was issued by Ontario druggists in the preceding decade (hence, the Newfoundland edition is located in the Ontario section). An advertisement in the O'Mara edition for the St John's bookseller S.E. Garland is especially interesting because it lists 'The Best Cookery Books' for sale in the city at that time: one Canadian title (an edition of O20.1, *The Home Cook Book,* Canada's first community cookbook), eight British titles (including three by Isabella Beeton), and two American recipe collections. The calendar or almanac cookbooks issued by McMurdo's drugstore in 1905 and 1909 (NF2.1, NF3.1), and likely other annual editions not yet located, also reprinted what are probably American texts, as did Bowring Brothers Ltd's *What to Cook and How to Cook It* of 1917 (NF4.1).

The first cookbooks compiled in Newfoundland were produced by three different denominations of church women's groups in St John's, beginning in 1905 with *The L.C.A.S. Cook Book* from the Ladies' College Aid Society of the Methodist Church (NF1.1), followed in 1924 by *Tested Recipes* from the Presbyterian Ladies' Aid (NF5.1), and in about 1926 by the *C.L.A. Cook Book* from the Columbus Ladies' Association, a Catholic group (NF6.1). All three works recommended their recipes in a similar fashion ('tried and proven' or 'tested,' 'endorsed' by the contributing lady or 'guaranteed' by the contributor's signature), and each was fondly called after the initials of the sponsoring group, including *Tested Recipes,* which was officially retitled *The P.L.A. Cook Book* in three subsequent editions from 1925 to 1939. My research revealed only two cookbooks published outside St John's, both the community type and from pulp-and-paper towns, one from Grand Falls in 1937 (NF7.1, by Girl Guides) and the other from Corner Brook in 1941 (NF11.1, by the United Church Girls' Club). The latter, *Corner Brook's Favourite Recipes,* highlighted local ingredients, such as dogberries and cod tongues, in many of the dishes, and enjoyed a huge success: 7,800 copies printed over the course of two decades. No less a personage than Joseph Smallwood, who would soon lead Newfoundland into Confederation, signed the foreword of the 1940s collection of *Fish Favourites* (NF12.1) by the Jubilee Guilds, a Newfoundland organization devoted to improving the difficult living conditions faced by many in the colony. The last cookbook in the section, the *NCOW Club Cook Book,* compiled in 1948 by the Non-Commissioned Officers' Wives Club and (like the earliest Newfoundland recipe collections) called after the sponsoring group's initials, brought 'dishes from many lands' to St John's tables (NF13.1).

Although agriculture has always been a small part of the province's economy because of poor soil and an unfavourable climate, there are pockets of fertile land and a need (perhaps felt more in the past) to produce food for local consumption. With this view in mind, the Department of Agriculture and Rural Reconstruction published three editions of *The Vegetable Garden* (NF9.1) during the Second World War, which offered, complete in one volume, gardening and cooking advice.

The largest collection of pre-1950 Canadian cookbooks in the province is at Memorial University of Newfoundland in St John's. Modest numbers are also held by the Provincial Archives of Newfoundland and Labrador, and by the Provincial Information and Library Resource Board.

NOTES

1 The name of the province changed legally on 6 December 2001, from Newfoundland to Newfoundland and Labrador, a reference to the mainland part of the province that lies to the northwest, which, although much larger in area (about three-quarters of the whole), is sparsely populated. No cookbooks were found from Labrador before 1950.

2 For an annotated bibliography encompassing the history of Newfoundland cooking and an introduction that draws attention to food-related issues specific to the province, see Maura Hanrahan and Marg Ewtushik, *A Veritable Scoff: Sources on Foodways and Nutrition in Newfoundland and Labrador,* St John's, Nfld: Flanker Press, 2001. The compilers describe monographs and articles, and items concerning food history are found mainly in the categories for 'Foodways' and 'Social History.' They do not include cookbooks ('due to the sheer number of such publications'), which nevertheless remain an essential source of information. Especially illuminating are the recipe selections and commentary in cookbooks that aim to characterize the province's distinctive food traditions, which began to appear in the second half of the twentieth century.

1900

The art of cooking made easy

The first editions of this title were published in Ontario, in 1890. For the edition published by O'Mara's Drug Store in St John's in 1900, and advertising Emerald Baking Powder, see O48.9.

1905

The L.C.A.S. cook book

NF1.1   1905
The / L.C.A.S. / cook book / arranged from / tried and proven recipes. / Published by the / Ladies' College Aid Society of the Methodist Church, / St. John's, Newfoundland. / St. John's, Nfld., / Robinson & Currie, printers and publishers. / 1905.
DESCRIPTION: 19.0 × 13.0 cm   Pp [i–ii], [1–3] 4–94, [i–ii], 95–6   Cloth; stapled
CONTENTS: i–ii ads; 1 tp; 2 untitled note signed the Committee and verse by Owen Meredith [pseudonym of Edward Robert Bulwer-Lytton] beginning, 'We may live without poetry, music or [*sic*; should be 'and'] art' [from *Lucile*, Part I, Canto ii]; 3–91 recipes credited with the name of the contributor and ads; 92–4 'Miscellaneous'; i ads; ii index; 95–6 blank for 'Memoranda'
CITATIONS: O'Dea 1331
COPIES: NBSAM   NFSA   *NFSG   NFSM (TX715 L22 1905)
NOTES: The note on p 2 comments, 'Each recipe is endorsed by the lady who has contributed it, ...'

NF1.2   1930
—The / L.C.A.S. / cook book / arranged from / tried and proven recipes. / Published by the / Ladies' College Aid Society / of the United Church, / St. John's, Newfoundland. / Dicks & Co. Limited / 1930
DESCRIPTION: 20.5 × 13.5 cm   Pp 1–176   Lacks paper(?) binding; stapled
CONTENTS: 1–15 ads; 16 blank except for '(Donated)'; 17 tp; 18 untitled note by the compilers and verse by Owen Meredith beginning, 'We may live without poetry, music or [*sic*] art'; 19–157 recipes and ads; 158 blank for 'Memoranda'; 159–60 ads; 161–3 'Miscellaneous'; 164 blank; 165 index; 166–76 ads
CITATIONS: O'Dea 1331
COPIES: *NFSG   NFSM (TX715 L22 1930, 3 copies)

McMurdo's 1905 calendar cook book

Thomas McMurdo opened Newfoundland Apothecaries' Hall on 1 March 1831, the first drugstore in Newfoundland. It burned down in 1846, and when it reopened, he named it Thomas McMurdo Co., chemists. See also NF3.1.

NF2.1   1905
McMurdo's / 1905 1905 / calendar / cook book / Published by / Thos. McMurdo & Co. / chemists and druggists / St. John's, Newfoundland.
DESCRIPTION: 17.5 × 13.0 cm   Pp [1–3] 4–31 [32]   Illus of astrological symbols   Paper, with image on front of a mortar and pestle; stapled
CONTENTS: 1 tp; 2–32 astronomical information, monthly calendars, jokes, recipes, and publ ads
COPIES: *OHMB (Serial)   OTUTF (uncat patent medicine)
NOTES: The cover-title is 'McMurdo and Coy's 1905 Almanac and Cook Book.' On the inside front face of the binding, under the heading 'To Our Friends and Customers,' the company refers to this book as 'our first venture in this way.'

There are four culinary sections: 'Cakes, etc.,' 'Meat, etc.,' 'Fish, etc.,' and 'Desserts, etc.' The recipes on p 4 are the same as on p 4 of A2.1, *Almanac and Cook Book 1905*, published in Edmonton: Soft Gingerbread, Spanish Bun, Dewey Icing, Raisin Layer Cake, Rice Griddle Cakes, Beautiful Layer Cake, and Oatmeal Macaroons.

1909

McMurdo's 1909 Newfoundland almanac and cook book

NF3.1   1909
McMurdo's / 1909 / Newfoundland / almanac and cook book / Seventh / year / Thos. McMurdo & Co. / chemists and druggists St. John's, N.F.
DESCRIPTION: 17.0 × 13.0 cm   Pp [1–3] 4–32   Illus of astrological symbols   Paper; stapled, and with hole punched at top left corner, through which runs a string for hanging
CONTENTS: Inside front face of binding untitled introductory note signed Thos McMurdo and Co.; 1 tp; 2 publ ad; 3–27 astronomical information, recipes, monthly calendars, 'Practical Breaks' [i.e., jokes], and publ ads; 28–mid 1st column 30 'Poisons and Antidotes'; mid 1st column 30–2nd column 30 medical information; 1st column 31–mid 2nd column 31 'Worth Knowing'; bottom 2nd column 31–32 'Things to Remember'

COPIES: *OTUTF (uncat patent medicine)
NOTES: The recipes are the same as listed for NB25.1, *Brown's New Brunswick Almanac and Cook Book 1909* (see that entry for the titles of other almanac or calendar cookbooks with the same recipes). 'Seventh year' in the title suggests that the first of McMurdo's annual cookbooks was published in 1902; however, in NF2.1 the company refers to the 1905 edition as 'our first venture in this way.'

1917

What to cook and how to cook it

NF4.1   [copyright 1917]
Price 25 cents / What to cook / and / how to cook it / Compliments of / Bowring Brothers, Limited / Saint John's, Newfoundland. / Copyright 1912 by Almanac Advertising Agency Westfield, N.J. [cover-title]
DESCRIPTION: 23.5 × 15.0 cm   Pp [3–4] 5–66   Paper, with image on front of a maid carrying a tray; stapled, and with hole punched at top left corner for hanging
CONTENTS: 3 'Introduction' and 'Entered according to Act of Congress, in the year 1917, by Almanac Advertising Agency, Woolworth Bldg., New York, in the office of the Librarian of Congress at Washington.'; 4 index; 5–mid 6 'General Suggestions'; mid–bottom 6 'Weights and Measures'; 7–66 recipes credited with the names of American contributors, most from New York State, Pennsylvania, New Jersey, Illinois, Michigan, and Virginia.
COPIES: *NFSA
NOTES: The cover-title records copyright 1912; p 3 records copyright 1917.

1924

Tested recipes

NF5.1   1924
Tested recipes / by / Presbyterian Ladies' Aid / St. John's, Newfoundland / 1924 [cover-title]
DESCRIPTION: 23.5 × 15.5 cm   Pp [1] 2–34 [35–6]   Paper, with image on front of St Andrew's Presbyterian Church; stapled, and with hole punched at top left corner for hanging
CONTENTS: 1–31 recipes; 32 ads; 33–4 'Household Hints'; 35 ads; 36 'Index' [i.e., table of contents]
COPIES: *NFSG

NF5.2   1925
—The / P.L.A. / cook book / Arranged from / tried and proven recipes / Published by the / Ladies' Aid Society of / St. Andrew's Presbyterian Church / Manning & Rabbitts, printers and publishers, / St. John's, Newfoundland, / 1925
DESCRIPTION: 19.5 × 13.5 cm   Pp [i–xxii], [1–3] 4–177 [178], [i–xxiv]   Cloth
CONTENTS: i–xxii ads; 1 tp; 2 blank; 3–167 recipes credited with the name of the contributor and blank pages for 'Notes:'; 168–72 'Household Hints'; 173 blank for 'Notes:'; 174–7 'Useful Tables'; 178 'Index' [i.e., table of contents]; i–xxiv ads
CITATIONS: O'Dea 1839
COPIES: NFSA   NFSM (TX715 P7 1925)   *OGU (CCC TX715.6 P52)   OONL (TX715.6 P53 1925)   OTUTF (B-12 7872)
NOTES: See pl 31. A comparison of recipes reveals that *The P.L.A. Cook Book* is a later, retitled edition of NF5.1, *Tested Recipes*.
    The OTUTF copy is inscribed on the front endpaper, in black ink, 'C.[I.?] Williamson 1926–.'

NF5.3   2nd ed., May 1928
—The / P.L.A. / cook book / (Second edition) / Arranged from tried / and proven recipes / Published by the / Ladies' Aid Society of / St. Andrew's Presbyterian Church / St. John's, Newfoundland, May, 1928. / Manning & Rabbitts, printers.
CITATIONS: O'Dea 1839
COPIES: *Private collection
NOTES: O'Dea records the 1928 edition as 19.0 cm and pp 181.

NF5.4   3rd ed., July 1939
—The / P.L.A. / cook book / (Third edition) / Arranged from tried / and proven recipes / Published by the / Ladies' Aid Society of / St. Andrew's Presbyterian Church / Printed by / the Evening Telegram, Ltd. / St. John's, Newfoundland, July, 1939
DESCRIPTION: 21.5 × 14.0 cm   Pp [i–xvi], [1–3] 4–183 [184], [i–xxii], [1–2]   Paper; stapled
CONTENTS: i–xvi ads; 1 tp; 2 'Index' [i.e., table of contents]; 3–183 recipes, 'Household Hints,' 'Useful Tables,' 'Planning Daily Meals,' and 'Miscellaneous'; 184 blank for 'Notes:'; i–xxii ads; 1–2 blank for 'Notes:'
COPIES: NFSA   *NFSG   NFSM (TX715 O52 1939)
NOTES: The NFSA copy lacks its binding and some leaves of advertisements.
    In 1992, the Kirk Association of St Andrew's Presbyterian Church, the successor of the Ladies' Aid,

compiled and published *150th Anniversary Cookbook: The New P.L.A.*, printed by L. Rasmussen Co. Ltd, Winnipeg, pp 150 (NFSM), to celebrate the 150-year history of the church. The first section of the book (10 pp) is called 'P.L.A. Favourites' and reprints recipes from the original work. The introductory paragraph to the section comments that 'many ... are still often used' and that, later in the book, the reader 'will also find recipes for a wedding cake and Christmas pudding, and no doubt some others, which were originally P.L.A. but updated.'

1926

C.L.A. cook book

NF6.1   nd [about 1926]
C.L.A. / cook book / compiled and contributed by / the members / of the Columbus Ladies' Association / Preface or Foreword / In compiling this book we have / endeavoured to use everyday, prac- / tical recipes contributed by the / members of the Columbus Ladies' / Association. The signature with / each recipe is sufficient guarantee, / K. Northcott, / A. Gallishaw.
COPIES: NFSM (TX715 C52 1926)
NOTES: NFSM records the book as published in St John's, [1926?]. There is an advertisement opposite the title-page for T. McMurdo and Co. Ltd, chemists and druggists, 'Inc. 1920.' The Columbus Ladies' Association acted as an auxiliary of the Knights of Columbus, a Roman Catholic men's organization.

1937

Favourite recipes

NF7.1   1937
Favourite recipes / collected by / the 2nd Grand Falls / Guide Co. / Grand Falls / 1937 [cover-title]
DESCRIPTION: 17.5 × 11.0 cm   Pp [i–iv], 1–88 [89] (versos not included in the pagination)   Paper; bound at top edge by a ribbon through two punched holes
CONTENTS: i 'Index' [i.e., table of contents]; ii blank; iii 'An Excellent Recipe' [i.e., mock recipe beginning 'Two equal quantities of generosity, ...']; iv blank; 1–88 recipes credited with the name of the contributor; 89 'Wit & Wisdom'
COPIES: *Private collection

1938

Prince, Charles A.

NF8.1   nd [about 1938]
An / up-to-date / recipe book / containing one hundred pages of / the most up-to-date recipes by / the celebrated chefs from abroad. / Compiled by / Chas. A. Prince / P.O. Box E5391 / Advertising Specialist / The book is presented to the general public / of St. John's entirely free of any charge. The / complete cost of the production is borne by / the advertisers. / Long Brothers / printers / 130 Water Street / St. John's, Newfoundland
DESCRIPTION: 24.0 × 17.5 cm   Pp [1] 2–140   Paper, with image on front of an aproned woman holding a pie(?); stapled
CONTENTS: 1 tp; 2 ad; 3–140 recipes and ads
CITATIONS: O'Dea 2329
COPIES: *NFSG   NFSM (TX715 U6)
NOTES: O'Dea dates the book [1938?].

1939

Newfoundland, Department of Agriculture and Rural Reconstruction

NF9.1   1939
Department of Agriculture and / rural reconstruction / Honorable J.H. Gorvin, C.B.E. / Commissioner / The / vegetable garden / Bulletin No. 10 / St. John's, Nfld., / 1939 / Long Bros., printers. [cover-title]
DESCRIPTION: 23.5 × 15.5 cm   Pp [1–3] 4–59   Illus   Paper, with image on front of a vegetable garden
CONTENTS: 1 index; 2 blank; 3–49 gardening text; 50–9 'Appendix A' [culinary information and recipes]
CITATIONS: O'Dea 2185
COPIES: NFSA   NFSG   *NFSM

NF9.2   rev. ed., 1941
—Department of Agriculture and / Rural Reconstruction / Honourable J.H. Gorvin, C.B.E. / Commissioner / The / vegetable garden / Bulletin No. 10 (Revised) / St. John's, Nfld. / 1941 / Long Brothers, printers. [cover-title]
DESCRIPTION: 23.0 × 15.0 cm   Pp [1–3] 4–40   Illus   Paper; stapled
CONTENTS: 1 index; 2 blank; 3–37 gardening text; 38–9 'Appendix A' ['Seed or Plant Requirements' on p 38 and 'Do Not Overcook Vegetables' on p 39]; 40 'Appendix B. Time-Table for Cooking Vegetables'

CITATIONS: O'Dea 2185
COPIES: *NFSM
NOTES: There are no recipes in this edition.

NF9.3 reprint, 1942
—Department of Agriculture and / Rural Reconstruction / Honourable P.D.H. Dunn, O.B.E. / Commissioner / The / vegetable garden / Bulletin No. 10 / St. John's, Nfld. / 1941 / (Reprinted 1942) / Robinson & Co., Ltd., printers [cover-title]
DESCRIPTION: Pp [1–3] 4–40   Illus
CONTENTS: 1 index; 2 blank; 3–37 gardening text; 38–9 'Appendix A' ['Seed or Plant Requirements' on p 38 and 'Do Not Overcook Vegetables' on p 39]; 40 'Appendix B. Time-Table for Cooking Vegetables'
CITATIONS: O'Dea 2185
COPIES: NFSA   *NFSM

1941

[Title unknown]

NF10.1   [about 1941]
[Cover-title lacking?]
DESCRIPTION: 21.0 × 13.5 cm   Pp [i–x], 1–216 [217–18], [i–iv]   Lacks binding; stapled
CONTENTS: i–x ads; 1–216 text and ads; 217 blank; 218 index; i–iv ads
CITATIONS: Ferguson/Fraser, p 234
COPIES: *Private collection
NOTES: Although no fund-raising purpose is specified, the book conforms to this type. The book's owner identifies it on the recto of the first leaf, in pencil, as 'Legion Ladies C/Book 1941.' Although an illustrated advertisement of a Nafco Range (coal-fuelled?) manufactured by the United Nail and Foundry Co. Ltd, St John's, gives the appearance of an earlier date of publication than 1941, a recipe for Rice Krispies Marshmallow Squares (p 139) indicates that the book could not have been published before 1941, the year the recipe was first tested and published by the Kellogg Test Kitchen in Battle Creek, Michigan. There are advertisements for businesses in Corner Brook and St John's.

Cook book

NF11.1   [2nd ed., 1948]
United Church / Girls' Club / Cook book / Corner Brook / Newfoundland

DESCRIPTION: 22.5 × 15.0 cm   Pp [i–x], [1] 2–338 [339], [i–iii]   Paper; sewn
CONTENTS: i tp; ii blank; iii dedication 'to Mrs. A.W. Bentley in appreciation of her untiring efforts to organize and build successfully the Girls' Club of the First United Church of Corner Brook. Corner Brook, May 12, 1948.'; iv blank; v introduction dated Corner Brook, 12 May 1948; vi blank; vii–x ads; 1–333 recipes credited with the name of the contributor and ads; 334–8 blank for 'Memoranda'; 339 'Index' [i.e., table of contents]; i blank; ii–iii ads
COPIES: *NFSM (TX715 F57 1948)
NOTES: The cover-title is 'Corner Brook's Favourite Recipes'; the running head is 'U.C. Girls' Club Cook Book.' The introduction refers to this as 'the second edition of "Corner Brook's Favourite Recipes."' There are recipes for Blueberry Syrup, Rose of Summer Cup (a strawberry and rose-extract drink), Plum Port, Dogberry Jelly, Wop Salad (a dish of tomatoes, hard-boiled eggs, and lettuce, whose title is an ethnic slur), and several fish recipes; for example, Cod Tongues in Cream Sauce, Fisherman's Brewis, and Pickled Herring.

According to Joan Ritcie, a librarian at NFSAM, this was a popular cookbook, widely used in Protestant homes from 1941, the year of the first edition, and still consulted today. See 'Other editions,' below, for the year and number of copies printed of all four editions. No copy of the first edition has been located.

OTHER EDITIONS: 4th ed., 1960, printed and bound by Western Star, Corner Brook; the following publishing history is on the verso of the title-page: '1st edition, 1941 – 800 copies // 2nd edition, 1948 – 1,000 copies // 3rd edition, 1954 – 2000 copies // 4th edition, 1960 – 4,000 copies' (NFSG).

1945–9

Fish favourites

The Jubilee Guilds were established in 1935 with the aim of providing relief to the local population. One focus was on home industry, such as the production of homemade jams and preserved fruit. An article about the Guilds in Atlantic Advocate *(July 1957; clipping in vertical file at NFSPR) refers to the 'circulation of fish recipes' and the 'publication of a number of "Partridgeberry Recipes."' The story of the Jubilee Guilds is told by Agnes M. Richard in* Threads of Gold: Newfoundland and

Labrador Jubilee Guilds Women's Institutes, *St John's, Nfld: Creative Publishers, 1989.*

NF12.1   nd [about 1945–9]
Fish / [same initial 'F' as for 'fish']avourites
DESCRIPTION: 19.0 × 12.5 cm   Pp [1–4] 5–31 [32]   Illus blue-and-green   Paper, with image on front of a sailboat at sea; stapled
CONTENTS: 1 foreword signed Joseph R. Smallwood; 2 'Compiled and distributed by the Jubilee Guilds of Newfoundland and Labrador // Cover illustration by I.W. Humber // Printed by the Evening Telegram Limited, St. John's, Nfld.'; 3–4 'Index' [i.e., table of contents]; 5–6 'Introduction'; 7–31 recipes under the following headings: 'Codfish,' 'Herring,' 'Salmon,' 'Other Fish Recipes,' 'Fish Dishes,' 'Soups and Chowders,' 'Fish Roe,' 'Sauces,' 'Dressings,' and 'Shellfish Recipes'; 32 blank for 'Notes'
CITATIONS: O'Dea 2406
COPIES: *NFSG

NOTES: Smallwood comments, 'You can help our fishermen, farmers and factory workers by buying and eating Newfoundland fish.' The text is printed aptly in blue. O'Dea dates the book [194?].

1948

NCOW Club cook book

NF13.1   1948
NCOW Club / cook book / compiled and edited / by / the Non-Commissioned Officers' Wives' Club / of / Fort Pepperrell / St. John's Newfoundland. / Tempting, tasty dishes, some old, / some new – from many lands. / 1948
DESCRIPTION: [28 leaves]   Top-hinged
COPIES: NFSM (TX715 N66 1948)
NOTES: The text is multigraphed.

Nova Scotia

Bloaters on Toast

Remove heads, tails and backbones from two or three National Bloaters ... Rub over with butter and fry until hot through. Then sprinkle with pepper and serve on fingers of hot buttered toast.

Mrs W.G. DeBay, Dartmouth, NS

Scalloped Clams

Chop up 12 clams and put in a well-buttered dish with alternate layers of sliced raw potatoes. Sprinkle each layer with a little onion, salt, pepper and butter. Put layers of crumbs on top, pour on liquor from clams, fill dish with milk and bake two hours.

Miss Nora E. Smith, 146 Shirley Street, Halifax

Both recipes, NS27.1, *National Sea Food Recipes*, Halifax: National Fish Co., 1923, p 3

Nova Scotia was one of the four founding provinces of Confederation on 1 July 1867, along with New Brunswick, Quebec, and Ontario. The first cookbook published in Nova Scotia – *Church of England Institute Receipt Book*, an Anglican fund-raiser from Halifax (NS1.1) – appeared only in 1888, a decade or so after the first cookbook published in New Brunswick, about six decades after the start of cookbook publishing in Quebec (then Lower Canada) and Ontario (Upper Canada), and long after Bartholomew Green set up the first press in Halifax in 1751. Yet, recipes were printed and circulated as early as 1820, as an 8-page section in Pythagoras's *Nova-Scotia Almanack* for that year, called 'Collection of Highly Approved and Valuable Receipts, for Domestic Economy.' Although it is always possible that an earlier cookbook for Nova Scotia may be discovered, one landmark event in North American culinary history belongs to the province: the founding in 1606 of what has been called the first gastronomical society on the continent, the Order of Good Cheer (L'ordre de bon temps), by Samuel de Champlain at the colony of Port-Royal in the land the new French settlers called Acadie. The colony, estab-

lished in 1605 near present-day Annapolis Royal, is also recognized as the first agricultural settlement by Europeans in Canada. L.M. Fortier recounted the meal-time rituals that Champlain devised for his men, as a way to ward off scurvy through the winter, in his 1928 book *Champlain's Order of Good Cheer and Some Brief Notes Relating to Its Founder*, described in the Ontario section of this bibliography (O622.1).[1] The early French settlers (Acadians), the British who arrived next (founding Halifax in 1749), and the influx of immigrants from New England (in the 1760s and Loyalists at the time of the American Revolution), all had a lasting influence on Nova Scotia's cuisine,[2] and elements of their food traditions can be traced through the cookbooks described here. The most important physical assets to have shaped the province's development are the proximity of the sea and its rich fishing grounds, Halifax's great natural harbour and favoured location on the eastern seaboard, the fertile Annapolis and Cornwallis river valleys, Cape Breton coal, and Nova Scotia's natural beauty. Many of the cookbooks recorded in this section feature recipes for seafood or for produce from the province's farms and orchards, and, not surprisingly, most of the advertising and government cookbooks promote fish, apples, molasses (an industry based in Halifax's port), and tourism. (The few exceptions are a vinegar cookbook, O1114.2, and reprints of American texts distributed by druggists or, in one case, by a hardware store: O48.10, O99.4, O118.1, O321.3.)

Of the eighty culinary titles found to have been published in Nova Scotia before 1950,[3] 74% were community cookbooks sold to raise money for a church or other organization, including the first-published title, *Church of England Institute Receipt Book* by Mary Jane Lawson and Alice Jones. The authors, both part of Halifax's lively social and literary scene, were well placed to see the potential of producing and selling a cookbook for the benefit of the Institute and to know how to realize the goal. In the period up to the First World War, community cookbooks came mostly from Protestant church groups, in Halifax (NS1.1, Church of England Institute; NS6.1, Charles Street Methodist Church; NS16.1, Fort Massey Church; NS17.1, All Saints Cathedral), Yarmouth (NS3.1, an unidentified missionary group), Bedford (NS10.1 and NS11.1, All Saints Church), Bridgewater (NS14.1, St John's Church), Truro (NS15.1, St John's Branch of the Woman's Auxiliary; the book contains an advertisement for Truro's famous maker of undergarments, Stanfield's Ltd, and Mrs John Stanfield's recipes), and Kentville (NS18.1, St Paul's Church); and church cookbooks predominated in the ensuing decades. In an unidentified title from St Philip's Church in Pictou County, during the First World War, the reader is transported to a typical meeting of the Young Ladies' Branch, by a 'casual observer's' description of their activities – hymn singing, sewing shirts for soldiers, studying the lives of missionaries, performing plays (NS19.1). In 1939, the Ladies' Aid of Lower Horton United Church in Grand Pré published the first of several editions of *Grand Pre Cook Book* (NS52.1), which was to become a major fund-raiser for the congregation: the thirteenth edition of 1987 marked 51,000 copies, many likely sold to tourists visiting the land of Evangeline, who would have appreciated the historical notes, photographs of the Evangeline statue and Memorial Chapel, and 'Recipes for Nova Scotia Apples.' In the late 1940s, the Ladies' Auxiliary of Kentville Baptist Church, also in the apple-growing region of the Annapolis Valley, compiled *Cook Book with Special Apple Recipes* (NS62.1).

A series of cookbooks published by chapters of the Imperial Order Daughters of the Empire in Halifax, Truro, and Sydney were influential in their respective cities. The Evangeline Chapter in Halifax issued six different recipe collections in 1924, 1926, 1929, 1934, 1947, and 1952 (entry numbers listed at NS29.1);[4] and the Nova Scotia Bureau of Information reprinted some of the Evangeline Chapter recipes in a 1935 pamphlet for the hotel trade (NS46.1). The Scotia Chapter in Truro published three editions of its *I.O.D.E. Recipes*, beginning in about 1930 (NS37.1). The Louisbourg Chapter in Sydney produced a recipe collection in 1936, 1942, and 1948 (NS48.1, NS59.1, NS71.1), and a 1985 collection is numbered thirteenth edition. These cookbooks were (and remain) celebrated locally, but are virtually unknown outside of Nova Scotia. IODE chapters in Windsor, Kentville, Bedford, Annapolis Royal, Dartmouth, and Wolfville also compiled recipe collections (NS30.1, NS38.1, NS44.1, NS54.1, NS57.1, NS60.1). Other groups that produced community cookbooks include the Amherst Hospital Aid Society in 1903 (NS7.1), Red Cross Society of Wolfville and vicinity in 1915 (NS20.1), Local Council of Women of West Pictou in 1920 (NS23.1), Rebekah Lodges of Nova Scotia (part of the International Order of Odd Fellows) in 1921 (NS25.1), Halifax Co-operative Society in 1942 (NS58.1), and in 1948, both the Halifax Senior Chapter of Hadassah (NS68.1, with a chapter of 'Special Festival Delicacies') and the Ladies' Auxiliary of the YMCA in Yarmouth (NS70.1). Women from Halifax's upper class contributed to a 1940s recipe collection, but the organization behind the publication remains unknown (NS61.1)

One phenomenon, apparently unique to the Maritimes, was the creation of fund-raising cookbooks by publishers in co-operation with a variety of charitable organizations. Two examples appeared in about 1920: *The Modern Cook Book for Nova Scotia and Prince Edward Island* (NS24.1) for a cross-section of groups, from the IODE to the Woman's Christian Temperance Association; and *The Modern Cook Book for New Brunswick* (NB31.1), to benefit hospitals. In the late 1930s, *Royal Cook Book* appeared, 'issued in aid of the various hospitals throughout the Maritimes' (NB45.1).

Nova Scotia was at the forefront when it came to introducing the teaching of cookery in public schools. In 1898, Helen Bell launched domestic science classes in rooms at St Patrick's Boys' School, on Brunswick Street in Halifax, and had published her *Elementary Text-Book of Cookery*, part of the 'Progressive School Series' (NS4.1). During the school year 1905–6, Bell had her pupils collect and arrange material for *Tried Recipes from Domestic Science School, Halifax* (NS9.1).

The expansion of the coal and steel industries in the 1890s brought increased settlement to Cape Breton. In about 1889, to meet the new interest in the area, Edwin Lockett published *Cape Breton Hand-Book and Tourist's Guide* (NS2.1). In addition to a section of 'Culinary & Gastronomic Receipes [*sic*],' which includes a good selection of fish dishes, there is also a Cape Breton poem ('The Bras-d'Or') and 'useful information' about Sydney and Cape Breton. By the 1930s the provincial government was promoting tourism and Nova Scotian apples. *Set a Good Table!* (NS50.1), published by the Bureau of Information and Publicity in about 1937 (and which followed another pamphlet on the same subject two years earlier, NS46.1), encouraged hotels and restaurants to serve 'distinctive Nova Scotian menus' and proposed six menus each for breakfast, lunch, and dinner; for example, for breakfast, Nova Scotia Strawberries, Creamed Finnan Haddie, and Sally Lunn; for lunch, Fish Chowder, Moulded Salmon with Cucumber Sauce, Tea Biscuit, and Crumb Cake; and for dinner, Tomato Juice Cocktail, Nova Scotia Spring Lamb Roasted, Green Peas, Mashed Potatoes, Mint Jelly, and Cranberry Meringue Pie. In the period 1933–40, the Department of Agriculture, in support of the Nova Scotia Fruit Growers Association, published three editions of *65 Apple Recipes* (NS41.1) by Helen J. MacDougall, who had served as superintendent of the province's Women's Institutes since 1917 (and was to retain the position until 1945). About 1939, for the Land Settlement Board, MacDougall adapted an Ontario government text to Nova Scotia conditions: *Economical Recipes and Household Hints* (NS53.1) was a guide for families who had accepted land instead of direct unemployment relief and who aimed to be self-sufficient. The book offered detailed information about domestic topics, from keeping a wood pile and banking a house (to prevent drafts) to uses for baking soda.

The molasses and fishing industries produced their own advertising cookbooks, some of which were distributed nation-wide. From Dominion Molasses Co., which had been founded in Halifax in 1900, came *The Molasses Cook Book* in 1911 (NS13.1) and *Come In, My Dear!* in about 1920 (NS22.1). Robin, Jones and Whitman Ltd, whose roots in the fish trade go back to 1766 on the Gaspé Peninsula, published *Ladies You Will Find Herein a Number of Useful Recipes for Cooking Codfish* in about 1910 (NS12.1) and *Fish Recipes for Preparing Boneless Salt Cod Fish* in about 1930–5 (NS39.1). The National Fish Co. Ltd in Halifax, mimicking the method of community cookbooks, solicited recipes from Maritime women, then had the manager of Halifax's Woodcock Inn and the superintendent eastern division of the CNR Dining Car Service make a selection from the more than 5,000 submissions for its 1923 *National Sea Food Recipes* (NS27.1). So successful was the compilation that 30,000 copies of the first edition were sold within a few

weeks. For a later edition, the company incorporated material from Mrs Evelene Spencer, an American 'Fish Evangelist.' In the 1930s, the company gave permission to the Quebec Department of Colonization, Game and Fisheries to reprint the book three times (French and English editions) to encourage Quebeckers to eat more fish, as both a health benefit and as an incentive for the fishing industry, in the process disseminating in Quebec the favourite recipes of Maritime women and Spencer's American contributions.

This bibliography contains a few examples of printed and bound volumes designed for handwritten recipes. One such 'manuscript cookbook,' nostalgically called *Mother and the Things She Used to Make* and sold as a gift for brides, was prepared by Rosamond M. de Wolfe Archibald, who was descended from the de Wolfe family after whom Wolfville is named, and illustrated by Annie Louise Ricker, a local art teacher (NS67.1).

The largest collections of pre-1950 Canadian cookbooks in Nova Scotia are at Acadia University in Wolfville and the Nova Scotia Museum in Halifax, followed by the Yarmouth County Museum and the Nova Scotia Archives and Records Management Library, Halifax. Smaller collections are at Dalhousie University, Halifax, and Queens County Museum, Liverpool. For a full list of Nova Scotia locations, see 'Abbreviations,' p xliii.

NOTES

1 For further information about Champlain's innovative strategy, see Jo Marie Powers, 'L'ordre de bon temps – Good Cheer as the Answer,' in *Feasting and Fasting*, Proceedings of Oxford Symposium on Food and Cookery, 1990, London, England: Prospect Books, 1990.

2 See Marie Nightingale, 'The Enduring Influences on Today's East Coast Cooking,' in *Northern Bounty: A Celebration of Canadian Cuisine*, edited by Jo Marie Powers and Anita Stewart, Toronto: Random House of Canada, 1995, pp 209–16.

3 There are seventy-four numbered entries in the Nova Scotia section, plus Nova Scotia editions of five advertising cookbooks described in the Ontario section (O48.10, O99.4, O118.1, O321.3, O1114.2) and a fund-raiser for hospitals in the Maritime provinces described in the New Brunswick section (NB45.1).

4 Marie Nightingale tells the story of the Evangeline Chapter cookbooks in 'IODE's Recipes Bring Back Good Food, Fond Memories,' *Chronicle-Herald Mail-Star* (Halifax, NS), 8 March 1989.

1888

Lawson, Mary Jane Katzmann [Mrs William Lawson] (1828–90), and Miss Alice C. Jones (Halifax, NS, 26 August 1853–27 February 1933, Menton, France)

Mary Jane Lawson and Alice Jones were prominent figures in the social and literary circles of Halifax. In the early 1850s, Mary Jane published the Provincial, *a periodical containing literary contributions, and she ran a bookstore before her marriage. She later wrote* History of the Townships of Dartmouth, Preston and Lawrencetown, Halifax County, Nova Scotia, *Halifax: Akins Historical Prize Essay, Nova Scotia: Morton, 1893, part of which was reprinted in NS65.1. For more information about Lawson, see Dagg, pp 165–6.*

Alice was one of two daughters and four sons in the family of Margaret Wiseman Stairs and Alfred Gilpin Jones. She travelled widely in the 1880s and 1890s, to Europe, Egypt, and the Caribbean, and during this time she wrote short stories and nonfiction pieces for publication in various Canadian periodicals. Her five novels, all published after the turn of the century, were popular at home and abroad. Church of England Institute Receipt Book, *co-edited with Lawson, is one of the earliest of her publications, since it appeared in the same year as her first known article (in Toronto's the* Week, *27 September 1888, pp 702–3). From 1900 to 1906, when her father was lieutenant-governor of Nova Scotia, she helped organize the banquets and entertainments at Govern-ment House. In 1907 she moved to Menton, in the south of France, near her sister, Frances Jones Bannerman. For more information about Alice Jones, see Gwendolyn Davies's entry for Jones in* Canadian Writers, 1890–1920, *edited by W.H. New, Dictionary of Literary Biography, Vol. 92, Detroit: Gale Research Inc., [1990], pp 165–8; Gwendolyn Davies's entry for Jones in* The Oxford Companion to Canadian Literature, *2nd ed., edited by Eugene Benson and William Toye, Toronto: Oxford University Press, 1997, pp 584–5; Gwendolyn Davies, 'Art, Fiction and Adventure: The Jones Sisters of Halifax,'* Journal of the Royal Nova Scotia Historical Society *Vol. 5 (2002), pp 1–22; and Eva-Marie Kröller,* Canadian Travellers in Europe, 1851–1900, *Vancouver: University of British Columbia Press, 1987, pp 82–8 and Plate 14, photograph of Jones. Gwendolyn Davies is editing Jones's diaries, which begin about 1899 and do not refer to the cookbook.*

NS1.1   1888
Church of England Institute / receipt book / Edited by / Mrs. William Lawson and Miss Alice Jones. / 1888 / Printed by Holloway Bros. / Halifax, N.S.
DESCRIPTION: Lacks binding
CITATIONS: Driver 2003, 'Canadian Cookbooks,' p 30
COPIES: *NSHMS (NSM 2001.13.25)
NOTES: See pl 24. The curator reports that the book has 126 pages, and that the title-page (the first page in the volume) is on p 3 and the 'Introduction,' on p 5. The 'Introduction' is a three-verse poem signed M.J.K.L., i.e., Mary Jane Katzmann Lawson. The poem makes a connection between a woman's duty to cook and the story of Adam and Eve: 'And woman since then fulfilling love's law, / Having lost man his Eden through edibles raw, / Has been doing her best by gastronomic lore / This lost Eden at least in his home to restore, / ...' At the end of the poem she refers to the cookbook's fund-raising purpose: 'Then buy it while Christmas with gladness illumes, / and help us to furnish our Institute rooms.' The archivist for the Diocese of Nova Scotia and Prince Edward Island could find no reference to the first edition in the Church of England Institute annual reports.

NSHP has an incomplete copy of the first edition, pp 15–98 only. The copy is inscribed 'Jean Hall [i.e., Mrs Harry Hall] // Sheet Har. N.S. Jan. 17/1962.'

NS1.2   2nd ed., 1898
—Church of England Institute / receipt book. / Edited by / Mrs. William Lawson and Miss Alice Jones. / Second edition. / 1898. / Morton & Co., publishers, / 143 Barrington St., Halifax, N.S.
DESCRIPTION: 19.0 × 14.0 cm   Pp [1–5] 6–123   Paper; stapled
CONTENTS: 1 tp; 2 blank; 3 'Introduction' [three-verse poem] signed M.J.K.L.; 4 two untitled notes, the first about the second edition, the second about the source of the recipes; 5–123 recipes and ads, and at bottom p 123, 'Press of J.R. Findlay, 211 Brunswick St., Halifax.'
CITATIONS: Nightingale 1970, pp 27, 68, 88
COPIES: CIHM (95369)   *NBSM (SPEC TX715 C58)
NOTES: The words 'receipt book' in the title are in an organic typeface, formed by wooden branches.

The 'Annual Report of the Woman's Auxiliary' in the *Church of England Institute, Twenty-fifth Annual Report for the Year Ending January 31st, 1899*, pp 11–12, tells the story of the second edition: 'Nothing was done during the year by the Auxiliary, with the exception of adding a few (sixteen) new members, ...; until October, when it having been thought a desirable way of adding a small sum to the, I might say gigantic undertaking of the Auxiliary, it was decided to reprint the Cook Book, which was first given to us by the late Mrs. Wm. Lawson, and Mrs. A. DeB.

Tremaine with the assistance of Mrs. R.T. LePine and Mrs. Milsom, (Dartmouth), undertook the onerous duty of securing the necessary advertisements, etc. in which they were most successful, as your Treasurer was handed not only sufficient to pay for the printing, but to add the sum of forty dollars and fifty cents to that made at the Sale of Work, held in November, which realized two hundred and six dollars twelve cents. The sum of two hundred dollars was handed to the Treasurer of the Parent Society, toward reducing the mortgage.'

Nightingale 1970 reprints the recipes for Black Bean Soup, Game Omelette, and Stuffed Cauliflower, with slight revisions.

1889

Lockett, Edwin

NS2.1 [1st ed.], nd [about 1889]
Cape Breton / hand-book / and / tourist's guide, / containing in addition / valuable – recipes, / and other / useful information. / Compiled by / E. Lockett, / North Sydney and Sydney.
DESCRIPTION: 20.5 × 13.0 cm   Pp 1–2 [3–4] 5–204   Paper; stapled
CONTENTS: 1–2 ads; 3 tp; 4 preface signed Edwin Lockett, publisher; 5–9 ads; 10 table of contents; 11–12 ads; 13 'The Bras-d'Or' [poem]; 14 ads; 15–116 text for hand-book and tourist's guide, and ads; 117–49 'Culinary & Gastronomic Receipes [sic]' and ads; 150 ads; 151–61 'Medical: Department' and ads; 162–204 text for hand-book and tourist's guide, and ads
CITATIONS: Tennyson No. 2186
COPIES: NBSAM   *NSHD
NOTES: On p 4 Lockett refers to this as the first edition. There are recipes for Salt Cod, commonly called 'Salt-Fish,' Lobster Salad, and Boiled Salmon on p 121; and Scalloped Oysters, Stewed Oysters, and Fried Trout on p 123. The culinary part of the book is poorly organized. The recipe numbering goes to seventeen, then ceases. The section headings do not accurately reflect the contents; for example, under 'Game' one also finds recipes for sweet puddings, vegetables, veal, and poultry.

The book was published about 1889. There is a reference on p 41 to a government building erected in Sydney in 1889; a reference on p 109 to a church dedicated in 1889; and a list on p 197 of barristers and attorneys of Cape Breton and the dates they were admitted, the latest on 19 September 1889.

1895–1900

Missionary recipe book

NS3.1 nd [about 1895–1900]
Missionary / recipe book. / We may live without poetry, music and art; / We may live without conscience, and live / without heart; / We may live without friends, / We may live without books, / But civilized man cannot live without cooks. / Herald Print. [cover-title]
DESCRIPTION: 21.0 × 14.0 cm   Pp 1–20   Paper; stapled
CONTENTS: 1 ad for Edward Allen's store, which sold baking powders, extracts, spices, and 'other goods required for successful cooking'; 2 ad for Crowells Shoe Store; 3–20 recipes, most credited with the name of the contributor, and ads
COPIES: *NSYHM
NOTES: The church or other institution responsible for *Missionary Recipe Book* is not named. The advertisements are for Yarmouth businesses. NSYHM catalogues the book under the name Edward Allen, from the advertisement on p 1. Herald Print was the print shop for the *Yarmouth Herald*, the local newspaper.

1898

Bell, Helen N. (25 March 1850–)

The 1901 Census records her birth date, her place of origin as Scotland, and 1864 as her year of immigration to Canada. See also NS9.1, for which Helen Bell wrote the 'Introduction.'

NS4.1 1898
Elementary text-book / of / cookery. / By / Helen N. Bell, / Principal School of Cookery, Halifax, N.S. / There are scientific principles lying at the foundation of the art / of cookery as of every other human art; and if you neglect to apply / them – if you neglect to educate your cooks in them – you must expect / to suffer. – Dr. Lankester. / Halifax, N.S. / T.C. Allen & Company. / 1898.
DESCRIPTION: 17.5 × 12.0 cm   Pp [1–6], [i–vii] viii–xi [xii], 1–108 [109–10], [i–iv]   Paper-covered thin card
CONTENTS: 1 endpaper publ ad; 2–6 blank; i ht; ii blank; iii tp; iv 'Entered according to Act of the Parliament of Canada, in the year 1898, by T.C. Allen & Co., in the Department of Agriculture (Copyright Branch).'; v preface signed Helen N. Bell, Halifax; vi blank; vii–xi table of contents; xii blank; 1–23 Sections I–V;

24–108 recipes; 109 'Rules for Cleaning'; 110 'Handy Measures, etc.'; i–ii publ ads; iii blank endpaper; iv endpaper publ ad

CITATIONS: Driver 2003, 'Canadian Cookbooks,' pp 31–2   O'Neill (unpublished)

COPIES: *NSHP (LT/C77); Great Britain: LB (07944.df.29 destroyed)

NOTES: 'Progressive School Series' is printed on the front face of the binding. Bell states on p v, 'The special purpose of this little book is to aid in the teaching of cookery in public schools.'

The new Windsor cook book

NS5.1   1898
The new / Windsor / cook book / Containing thoroughly tested recipes from the most re- / liable sources, beside many new and valuable / ones which are here given to the public / for the first time. / Adapted for use in our own homes. / Price 25 cents. / Windsor, N.S.: / Printed at the office of the "Windsor Tribune," / 1898.

DESCRIPTION: 16.5 × 12.0 cm   Pp [1–3] 4–72   Paper; stapled

CONTENTS: 1 tp; 2 ad; 3–72 recipes and ads

COPIES: CIHM (95407)   *OGU (UA s048 b42)

NOTES: The recipes are not credited. The text was likely produced by the *Tribune* newspaper, not by a community group.

The OGU copy is inscribed, beside the recipe for Delicious Cake on p 56, 'Very good // Same as in Bap. Cook Bk.' Which early Maritime Baptist cookbook has not been identified (it is not NB12.1).

1900

The art of cooking made easy

The earliest editions of this title were published in Ontario, in 1890. For the edition published by Hattie and Mylius Ltd, Halifax druggists, in 1900, see O48.10.

Hints on health and tested receipts for plain cooking

Editions of this title were published by three Ontario druggists. For the edition published by Taylor's Drug Store in Bridgewater, in about 1900, see O99.4.

1902

Gem Chopper cook book

This cookbook was distributed by various Ontario, Quebec, and Nova Scotia companies. For an edition distributed by Dunlap Bros and Co. Ltd in Amherst, see O118.1.

Sims, Miss Sarah (Sadie) Jane (Sherbrooke, NS, 23 August 1874–), and Miss Bessie E. Hills (about 1874–)

Sadie Sims and Bessie Hills both taught in the Sabbath School at Charles Street Methodist Church. In addition, they served on the executives of the Epworth League (Sadie) and the Woman's Missionary Society (Bessie). Sadie married William Sargent Theakston (same last name as the cookbook's printer) on 18 June 1907. Bessie married widower Frederick A. Evans on 9 September 1914, when she was forty years old. The new building for Charles Street Methodist Church opened in 1903 and was renamed J. Wesley Smith Church after its main benefactor. It closed in 1993. Information about the authors is from the 1901 Census, the Quarterly Herald *[newsletter of Halifax West Circuit] Vol. 1, Nos. 1–3 (29 October 1897–19 March 1898), and records at the Maritime Conference Archives of the United Church of Canada.*

NS6.1   [1902]
Tried and true / a handbook of / choice cooking recipes / Compiled by / the Misses S.J. Sims and B.E. Hills / in aid of / Building Fund / Charles St. Meth. Church / Halifax, Nova Scotia

DESCRIPTION: Pp [ii–viii], [1] 2–92, [i–iii]

CONTENTS: ii–iii ads; iv blank; v tp; vi ad; vii–viii 'Index' [i.e., table of contents]; 1–89 recipes and ads; 90–2 'Household Hints'; i–ii blank; iii ad

COPIES: *NSHP

NOTES: I examined the microfilm copy; the original is stored off-site. The NSHP catalogue records the volume as Halifax: Theakston's Printing, [1902], illus, 22 cm. There were Theakstons in the congregation.

1903

The Amherst cook book

NS7.1   1903
[An edition of *The Amherst Cook Book*, edited by the Amherst Hospital Aid Society, Amherst, Nova Scotia, 1903]

COPIES: Private collection

1905

Hill, Miss Katherine (Kate) Foss (Halifax, NS, 14 June 1846–5 September 1936, Windsor, NS), and Miss Florence Seeley (April 1867–)

Although the British Library catalogue gives only the initials and last names of the authors, they must be Miss Katherine Foss Hill and Miss Florence Seeley, two Nova Scotia artists, both cited in J. Russell Harper's Early Painters and Engravers in Canada, Toronto: University of Toronto Press, 1970 (Hill, p 157; Seeley, p 283).

Hill's obituary (Hants Journal, 9 September 1936) indicates that she trained in Paris and New York. She is listed in Halifax city directories from 1890–1 to 1914–15. She began teaching drawing in the city's public schools in November 1891 and retired because of ill health in 1913 (Report of the Board of School Commissioners, City of Halifax, for the years 1891–1913). She taught drawing at the Halifax Academy and also, in the period 1892–3, elementary drawing at the Victoria School of Art and Design. She exhibited her work at the Art Loan Exhibition, 6–11 August 1894; NSHP has a catalogue of this exhibition annotated by Harry Piers, which includes his remarks about Hill's work. In 1914 she moved to Windsor, Nova Scotia.

Seeley painted landscapes, genre, and flowers in oil, and she exhibited at the Royal Canadian Academy in 1886 and 1888. She is listed in Halifax city directories from 1907–8 to 1917, but not in the period when the cookbook was published. In 1907–8 she was living in Dartmouth, on Pleasant Street. The 1911 Census and most city directories (except 1914 and 1915) use the spelling Seeley.

NS8.1 [1905]
[An edition of *Souvenir Receipts, Nova Scotia*, by K.F. Hill and F. Seely [sic], Dartmouth, NS: [1905]]
CITATIONS: O'Neill (unpublished)
COPIES: Great Britain: LB (07943.f.76 destroyed)
NOTES: The book is known only from the British Library catalogue and copyright records, which do not give the number of pages. Why Hill and Seeley compiled the cookbook is a mystery, but perhaps its sales were to benefit a cause both artists supported.

1906

Tried recipes from Domestic Science School, Halifax

See also NS4.1 by Helen Bell.

NS9.1 1906
Tried recipes / from / Domestic Science School, / Halifax, N.S [sic, no period] / Halifax, N.S.: / McAlpine Publishing Company, Limite[d] / 1906.
DESCRIPTION: 18.5 × 12.0 cm   Pp [1–7] 8–48   Paper; stapled
CONTENTS: 1 tp; 2 blank; 3 'Introduction' signed Helen N. Bell, principal, Domestic Science School, Halifax, Nova Scotia, 29 June 1906; 4 blank; 5 'Index' [i.e., table of contents]; 6 blank; 7–48 'Tried Recipes'
COPIES: *NSHD
NOTES: The cover-title is 'One Hundred Recipes from Domestic Science School, Halifax.' Bell states on p 3: 'The recipes contained in this little book have all been worked out by the pupils of the Domestic Science School, during Session 1905–1906. They have also collected and arranged them in the order in which they here stand.' For each recipe, the price of the ingredients follows the ingredients list.

NS9.2 [1976, facsimile of 1906]
—Tried recipes / from / Domestic Science School, / Halifax, N.S / Halifax, N.S.: / McAlpine Publishing Company, Limite[d] / 1906.
DESCRIPTION: 18.0 × 11.5 cm   Pp [i–ii], [1–7] 8–48, [i–ii]   Paper; stapled
CONTENTS: i 'Publisher's Note'; ii 'Copyright 1976   ISBN 0-919380-20-4 Published by Petheric Press // Printed by McCurdy Printing Co. Ltd.'; 1 tp; 2 blank; 3 'Introduction' signed Helen N. Bell, principal, Domestic Science School, Halifax, Nova Scotia, 29 June 1906; 4 blank; 5 'Index' [i.e., table of contents]; 6 blank; 7–48 recipes; i blank; ii 'Titles by Petheric Press' and 'Printed & bound by McCurdy Printing Co. Ltd Halifax, Nova Scotia, Canada'
COPIES: *NSHP   NSME (641.5)   NSWA   OGU (CCC TX715.6 D63)   OONL (TX715 D65 1976)
NOTES: The 'Publisher's Note' states: 'This cookbook is a facsimile reproduction of the one produced in 1906 for the first domestic science school in Canada, under the public school system. The school began operation in 1898, in rooms fitted out for the purpose in St. Patrick's Boys' School, Brunswick Street, Halifax. In 1906 a separate building was constructed on Cunard St. to house the Cooking School ... the copy of it for our reproduction was provided by Mr. Barry Edwards.'

1908

The Bedford recipe book

NS10.1   1908
The Bedford / recipe book / "We may live without poetry, music and art; / We may live without conscience and live / without heart; / We may live without friends; we may live / without books; / But civilized man cannot live without cooks." / – Owen Meredith / Compiled by / the ladies of / All Saints Church Guild / Bedford, Nova Scotia. / 1908.
DESCRIPTION: About 16.0 × 11.0 cm [dimensions from photocopy]
COPIES: *Private collection
NOTES: See also NS11.1.

1910

The Bedford recipe book

NS11.1   1910
The Bedford / recipe book / "We may live without poetry, music and art; / We may live without conscience and live / without heart; / We may live without friends; we may live / without books; / But civilized man cannot live without cooks." / – Owen Meredith. / Compiled by / the ladies of / All Saints Church Guild / in aid of Building Fund / Bedford, Nova Scotia / 1910
COPIES: *NSHMS (84.92.11)
NOTES: This may be a reprint or revised edition of NS10.1, or a new collection of recipes. Here, the Building Fund is named on the title-page as the beneficiary of any profit from sales. The volume has 42 pp.

Ladies you will find herein ...

NS12.1   nd [about 1910]
Ladies / you will find / herein a num- / ber of useful / recipes for / cooking cod- / fish – Try them! [cover-title]
DESCRIPTION: 11.0 × 7.5 cm   Pp [1] 2–15   Paper; sewn
CONTENTS: 1 cover-title; 2 symbol of Atlantic Fish Companies Ltd and 'This booklet was prepared with the idea of giving a few particularly good recipes for cooking fish ... we should appreciate any new ideas or suggestions with regard to fish cooking which cooks or housekeepers may send. The Atlantic Fish Companies, Limited, Lunenburg, N.S.'; 3 untitled comments about the quality of AFC fish and the company's Halifax and Acadia brands; 4 'Shredded Codfish a la Mode' and 'Creamed Codfish Very Easy to Make'; 5 'German Method Cooking Codfish and Potatoes'; 6 'For a Dinner of Boiled Codfish' and 'Codfish on Toast'; 7 'Atlantic Cod Gems' and 'Freshening Process'; 8 'Codfish and Cheese' and 'A Chafing Dish Recipe'; 9 'To Make Croquettes' and 'Escalloped Codfish'; 10 'Escalloped Codfish // A Popular Recipe in Nova Scotia' and 'Fish Patties'; 11 'Fish Patties' [two versions on p 11]; 12 'Baked Codfish,' 'Croquettes,' and 'Minced Fish'; 13 'Old-fashioned Codfish Dinner'; 14 'Codfish Stew' and 'Codfish on Toast'; 15 'Fish Souffle'
COPIES: *NBSAM
NOTES: On pp 2–3 of the NBSAM copy, 'The Atlantic Fish Companies, Limited' is crossed out and 'Robin, Jones & Whitman, Limited' is stamped above, in purple ink. In 1910, C. Robin, Collis Co. Ltd amalgamated with A.G. Jones and Co. of Halifax and the Atlantic Fish Companies Ltd to form Robin, Jones and Whitman Ltd (see the history at NS39.1). The stamped name change in *Ladies You Will Find Herein ...* suggests that the book was published about the time of the amalgamation.

1911

The molasses cook book

The Dominion Molasses Co. was founded by Hugh Russell Silver (5 July 1865–14 August 1954) in Halifax in 1900. The company is listed in Halifax city directories up to 1959.

NS13.1   1911
The / molasses cook book / The daintiest food, without a perhaps, / Is certainly found in Gingerbread Snaps; / Delectable dainties, prepared for all classes, / Is made by the Gingerbread Brand of molasses. / – J.B. / Published by / the Dominion Molasses Co., Ltd. / Halifax, N.S. / 1911
DESCRIPTION: 17.0 × 12.5 cm   Pp [1] 2–32   Paper, with image on front of a can of Gingerbread Brand Molasses; stapled
CONTENTS: 1 tp; 2 publ ad; 3–24 recipes, publ ads, and ads; 25 note about Gingerbread Brand Molasses; 26 ad; 27 blank 'for writing your own favorite recipes'; 28 'A Big Industry and Still Enlarging' [about Moirs Ltd, the chocolate manufacturer]; 29 blank for manuscript recipes; 30 publ ad; 31–2 blank for manuscript recipes
COPIES: *OTYA (CPC 1911 0133)

NOTES: 'Compliments of the Dominion Molasses Co. Limited. Halifax, Canada // McAlpine Pub. Co. Ltd. Halifax, N.S.' is on the binding.

NS13.2 1912

—The / molasses cook book / The daintiest food, without a perhaps, / Is certainly found in Gingerbread Snaps; / Delectable dainties, prepared for all classes, / Is made by the Gingerbread Brand of molasses. / – J.B. / Published by / the Dominion Molasses Co., Ltd. / Halifax, N.S. / 1912

DESCRIPTION: 17.0 × 12.5 cm   Pp [1] 2–32   Illus centre spread of 'A Typical Scene in British West Indies'   Lacks binding

CONTENTS: 1 tp; 2 publ ad for Domolco and Gingerbread Molasses; 3–27 'Recipes' and publ ads; 28–9 blank 'for writing your own favorite recipes'; 30 publ ad; 31–2 blank for manuscript recipes

COPIES: *AEPMA   ASPMHC (641 DOM)   CIHM (74464)   OAYM   OKQ (F5012 1912 D671 Special Coll)

NOTES: On the binding of the ASPMHC copy there is an image of a can of Gingerbread Brand Molasses.

1912

The LaHave cook book

NS14.1 1912

The LaHave / cook book / A collection of tested recipes in cookery / and housekeeping, compiled by the / Managers' Auxiliary of / St. John's Church, / Bridgewater, N.S. / 1912. / C.J. Cragg & Co., / printers and publishers, / Bridgewater, N.S.

DESCRIPTION: 20.5 × 14.0 cm   Pp [1] 2–88   Tp illus of view of Bridgewater   Paper; stapled

CONTENTS: 1 tp; 2–4 ads; 5 'Foreword,' a poem by R.C. Stewart; 6–86 recipes; 87 'In Conclusion,' a poem signed 'LaHave' [i.e., Lahave, on the south shore, southeast of Bridgewater], and in manuscript, 'B. MacG. T'; 88 table of contents and table of weights and measures

COPIES: NSHMS   NSLFP   *OGU (UA s047 b30)

NOTES: '1912 Bridgewater Bulletin Print.' is on the front face of the binding. The title-page of the OGU copy is inscribed, 'With compliments of Cook Book committee.'

1913

The favorite cook book

NS15.1 1913

The / favorite cook book / a collection of up-to-date / and favorite recipes, pub- / lished under the auspices / of / St. John's Branch of the / Woman's Auxiliary / Truro, Nova Scotia / 1913

DESCRIPTION: 21.5 × 14.5 cm   Pp [1–3] 4–112   Paper; stapled

CONTENTS: Inside front face of binding 'Printed by the News Publishing Co. Ltd, Truro, N.S.'; 1 tp; 2 'A Word about Our Advertisers'; 3 'Index' [i.e., table of contents], abbreviations, and 'Table of Measures and Weights'; 4 ad; 5–112 text and ads

COPIES: *OGU (UA s063 b01)

NOTES: The Woman's Auxiliary was part of St John's Anglican Church. Some of the recipes were contributed by Mrs John Stanfield, whose husband and brother-in-law Frank owned Stanfield's Ltd, the famous underwear maker in Truro, an advertisement for which is on p 20. A yeast recipe, bread-making instructions, and bread recipes (pp 5–6) are from Miss Blanche Harris, domestic science teacher. Other recipes are attributed to Macdonald College School of Household Science.

The 'Golden Rule' cook book

NS16.1 1913

The / "Golden Rule" / cook book / "Cooking is become an art, / a noble science." / – Robert Burton. / Compiled by / members of the 'Golden Rule' Circle / of Fort Massey Church, / Halifax, N.S.

DESCRIPTION: 17.0 × 12.0 cm   Pp [1–7] 8–49, [i–vii]   Paper; stapled

CONTENTS: 1 tp; 2–4 ads; 5 preface signed Cook Book Committee, Golden Rule Circle, Halifax, Nova Scotia, March 1913; 6 ad; 7–49 recipes; i–vii ads

COPIES: *NSWA

Tested recipes

NS17.1 nd [1913]

Tested / recipes / Wash cover with damp cloth [cover-title]

DESCRIPTION: 18.0 × 12.0 cm   Pp [1–2] 3–116   Illus on p 1 of All Saints Cathedral, Halifax   Cloth

CONTENTS: 1 illus and introductory note; 2 blank;

3–10 ads; 11–103 recipes; 104–6 'Index' [i.e., table of contents]; 107–16 ads
COPIES: *OGU (2 copies: UA s047 b27, UA s047 b28)
NOTES: The introductory note states that money raised from the book's sale will be applied to 'the Building Fund of All Saints Cathedral, Halifax, through the Diocesan Women's Cathedral League.' An advertisement on p 116 for 'Wm. Stairs, Son & Morrow, Limited, Halifax 1810 1913' is evidence that *Tested Recipes* was published in 1913.

1914

Good bread

This title was published by druggists in Quebec, Ontario, and Nova Scotia. For the edition by L.C. Gardner and Co. of Yarmouth, in about 1914, see O321.3.

The helping hands cook book

NS18.1   1914
The helping hands / cook book / Tested recipes / Compiled by / the ladies of St. Paul's Church / Kentville, N.S. / Kentville, Nova Scotia / 1914 / Weeks Printing Company, Limited 83 Granville Street, Halifax, N.S.
DESCRIPTION: 22.0 × 14.0 cm   Pp [1–2] 3–4, [i–ii], 5–189   Cloth-covered boards; stapled
CONTENTS: 1 tp; 2 blank; 3–4 ads; i table of contents; ii blank; 5 quotation from Ruskin and from 'a widow in Treasure Trove and Short Cuts'; 6–8 'Measurements for Cooking'; 9–189 recipes credited with the name of the contributor and ads
CITATIONS: Nightingale 1970, p 60
COPIES: *Private collection
NOTES: A copy in another private collection has '1915' printed on the binding and no title-page; otherwise, it appears to be the same as described here. Yet another private collector reports her copy as dated 1915. Nightingale 1970 reprints the recipe for Sweetbreads.

1914–18

[Title unknown]

NS19.1   [about 1914–18]
[Title unknown of a book produced by the Young Ladies' Branch of St Philip's Presbyterian Church, Westville, Pictou County, NS]
DESCRIPTION: 21.0 × 14.5 cm [dimensions from photocopy]   Lacks paper(?) binding; stapled
COPIES: *Private collection
NOTES: Information about this book is gleaned from a photocopy supplied by the book's owner of an unnumbered page of introductory text – likely the first page in the volume – that is headed, 'St. Philip's Y.L.B.' The introductory text describes a monthly meeting of the Young Ladies' Branch of St Philip's Church, as witnessed by a 'casual observer.' The meetings took place on the second Tuesday evening of each month, at 8 o'clock. In this account, the president is named Bertha, the secretary, Lizzie, and the representative of the Sewing Committee, Tena. Activities of the group include putting on plays to raise money for missionary purposes and 'sewing shirts for soldiers.' The book appears to have been published about the time of the First World War, which would accord with the reference to soldiers' shirts. The book's owner reports that the advertisements in the book are for businesses in Pictou County.

1915

The Red Cross cook book

NS20.1   [1915]
The Red Cross / cook book / That cookery is a science / Who can doubt? / Domestic bliss were incomplete without! / A book of tested recipes / Compiled by / the ladies of the Red Cross Society / of Wolfville and vicinity / Wolfville, N.S.
DESCRIPTION: 20.0 × 14.0 cm   Pp [1–2] 3–204 [205–12]   Small tp illus of roast poultry on a platter   Paper, with image on front of a red cross; stapled
CONTENTS: 1 tp; 2 blank; 3 'Preface' signed Committee for the Red Cross Cook Book; 4–6 'The Foodstuffs' signed Julia A. McIntyre; 7–8 ads; 9–200 recipes credited with the name of the contributor and ads; 201 'Thanks' [to the advertisers and recipe contributors] signed Mrs Frances Burgess Elderkin for the committee, Wolfville, Nova Scotia, 16 August 1915; 202 'Table of Weights and Measures'; 203 note about baking powder, suggesting the use of Royal brand; 204 ad; 205–12 'Contents' [i.e., index]
COPIES: *BDEM
NOTES: The cover-title is 'Book on Cookery.' The year of publication, 1915, is on the front face of the binding. The 'Preface' states, 'The "Red Cross" work and the demands made upon that noble organization, especially during the present European war, have been the inspiration and the objective point of the committee for the Red Cross Cook Book.'

1918

The reliable cook book

See also NS49.1 from the same church.

NS21.1 191[8?]
The / reliable cook book / Issued by / the ladies of
First Presbyterian Church / in aid of / the Organ
Fund / New Glasgow, Nova Scotia / 191[8?]
DESCRIPTION: 20.5 × 14.5 cm [dimensions from photo-
copy]   Small tp illus of a woman, in profile, carrying
a tray   Lacks binding; stapled
CONTENTS: [First page] tp; ...; 22 ad for McLellan's
Ltd, New Glasgow, a home furnishings store; 23 reci-
pes credited with the name of the contributor; ...
COPIES: *Private collection
NOTES: The copy is inscribed on the title-page, 'Mrs
DW Cameron.'

1920

Come in, my dear!

NS22.1 nd [about 1920]
Come in, / my dear! [cover-title]
DESCRIPTION: 17.5 × 13.0 cm   Pp [i–ii], [1–2] 3–32,
[i]   Paper, with image on front of an aproned grandmother in a doorway
CONTENTS: i ad for the company's 'Domolco' brand
molasses, on a yellow leaf; ii blank; 1 '"Come in, my
dear" is Grandma's invitation to you, to learn how to
make *her* kind of gingerbread, ginger snaps and molasses cookies – *real* baked beans and brown bread –
old time mince meat and plum puddings – smacking
good taffy – and a lot of other things ...'; 2–29 text; 30–
2 blank for manuscript recipes; i book-order form to
be sent to the Dominion Molasses Co. Ltd, Halifax
COPIES: MWPA (MG14 C50 McKnight, Ethel)   *OGU
(UA s070 b76)   OONL (A-5301)
NOTES: The appearance of the book points to publication in about 1920. The symbol of 'Royal Print &
Litho Limited Halifax' is on the inside back face of
the binding. This printer is first listed in the Halifax
city directory for 1913–14.

Cook book

NS23.1 1920
Cook book / compiled by / the Ladies Bursary
Committee / of the / Local Council of Women /
of West Pictou [i.e., western part of Pictou County],

N.S. / 1920 / [illus of building] [cover-title]
DESCRIPTION: 22.0 × 15.0 cm [dimensions from photo-
copy]
CONTENTS: i [first page] ad for Cash Shoe Store
COPIES: *Private collection

The modern cook book for Nova Scotia and Prince Edward Island

NS24.1 nd [about 1920]
The / modern cook book / for / Nova Scotia / and
/ Prince Edward Island / Published in co-operation
with / the various women's organiza- / tions in
Nova Scotia and Prince / Edward Island.
DESCRIPTION: 21.5 × 14.0 cm   Pp 2–151   Cloth, with
image on front of a woman lifting the cover of a
chafing dish
CONTENTS: 2–4 endpaper ads; 5 tp; 6 'Women's
Organizations Interested'; 7 'Introduction'; 8 ad; 9
'A Word as to Our Advertisers'; 10 table of contents;
11 ad; 12 'Table of Weights and Measures'; 13 'Time
Tables for Cooking'; 14–151 recipes and ads
COPIES: CIHM (9-92248)   *NSHP   OONL (TX715.6
M63 1911)   Private collection
NOTES: The 'Women's Organizations Interested' on p
6 are listed alphabetically by town: Antigonish, Red
Cross; Amherst, Tantramar Chapter, IODE (Imperial
Order Daughters of the Empire); Annapolis, IODE;
Dartmouth, Shannon Chapter, IODE; Glace Bay,
Women's Institute; Halifax, Ladies' Auxiliary of the
GWVA (Great War Veterans Association) and Catho-
lic Women's League; Kentville, IODE; Lunenburg,
IODE; Liverpool, WCTU (Woman's Christian Tem-
perance Union); Middleton, Ladies' Auxiliary of the
GWVA; New Glasgow, Ladies' Aid of Aberdeen Hos-
pital; Sydney, Ladies' Aid of Ross Memorial Hospi-
tal; Truro, IODE and Ladies' Auxiliary of the GWVA;
Windsor, IODE; Yarmouth, Markland Chapter, IODE;
and, lastly, the only organization from Prince Edward Island, the Hospital Aid in Summerside.

An advertisement on p 27 for Rakwana Tea suggests a publication date of about 1911: '[Rakwana Tea
is] the first blend of India and Ceylon teas to be
marketed in Nova Scotia ... That was in 1891, for
twenty years Rakwana has led in its territory ...' However, the cookbook must have been published later
because three of the participating groups belonged to
the Great War Veterans Association, which was
formed in 1917 to assist Canadians returning from
the conflict overseas. It was likely published about
the same time as NB31.1, *The Modern Cook Book for
New Brunswick* of 1920, which follows the same model

(it, too, is 'published in co-operation with' various women's groups). *The Modern Cook Book for Nova Scotia and Prince Edward Island* was published no later than 1925, when a meeting of the GWVA and similar organizations resulted in the founding of the Canadian Legion of the British Empire Services League, which issued its first charter in 1926.

No printer or place of publication is recorded; however, the last advertisement in the book is for News Publishing Co. Ltd, Truro, Nova Scotia. OONL gives [Halifax].

The private collector reports that her mother purchased her copy on 26 August 1931.

1921–2

Kirkpatrick, Mrs Lilla A.

NS25.1   1921–2
Home recipes / over five hundred / tried formulas / By / Mrs Lilla Kirkpatrick / President of Rebekah Assembly, I.O.O.F., / of Maritime Provinces of Canada / 1921–22
DESCRIPTION: 20.5 × 14.0 cm   Pp [1–4] 5–72   Paper; stapled
CONTENTS: 1 tp; 2 'FLT 1921–22' and portrait of Mrs Lilla Kirkpatrick; 3 preface signed Lilla A. Kirkpatrick; 4 'Table of Proportions' and 'Household Hints'; 5–72 recipes
COPIES: *NSWA
NOTES: In the preface, which Kirkpatrick addresses 'To the officers and members of the Rebekah Lodges of Nova Scotia,' she says: 'My object in view in planning out this little culinary key to home recipes, is to raise money for the good of our Order. The proceeds, except printing, etc., to be given to aid our Home Fund, and such other fund deemed necessary to carry on the work of our Order.' Recipes for 'Cordials' are on pp 70–1 and for 'Invalid Cookery,' on p 72. IOOF stands for the International Order of Odd Fellows.

1923

Cook book

NS26.1   1923
Cook book / Mizpah Bible Class of Pugwash / Baptist Sunday School / Organized May 20th, 1923 / by / Mrs. W.J. Hamilton [cover-title]
DESCRIPTION: 20.5 × 13.0 cm [dimensions from photocopy]

COPIES: *Private collection
NOTES: The book's owner reports that the recipes are contributed by residents of Pugwash.

National sea food recipes

NS27.1   [copyright 1923]
National / sea food / recipes / by the women of / the Maritime provinces [cover-title]
DESCRIPTION: 19.5 × 13.0 cm   Pp 1–20   Paper, with images on front of a fishing boat at sea and a cooked fish on a plate; stapled
CONTENTS: 1–2 'Facts about Fish and This Book' and at bottom p 2, 'Copyrighted 1923 by National Fish Co. Ltd. Halifax, Canada'; 3–20 recipes credited with the name and town of the contributor
CITATIONS: Ferguson/Fraser, p 233, illus col on p 57 of closed volume   O'Neill (unpublished)
COPIES: *Private collection; Great Britain: LB (Woolwich 41190)
NOTES: On p 1, National Fish Co. explains how the book was compiled: '... we summoned the most skilful cooks in the Maritime provinces to share their recipes. More than five thousand recipes were thus secured, ...' Mr Leopold Braichet, manager, Woodcock Inn, Halifax, and Mr E.E. Cameron, superintendent eastern division CNR Dining Car Service, selected the recipes for inclusion. They are arranged alphabetically as follows: bloaters, clams, cod, devilled fish, fillets, flounder, haddock, halibut, herring, lobster, mackerel, oysters, salmon, and scallops.

NS27.2   [2nd ed., copyright 1924]
—National / sea food / recipes / The book of a / thousand cooks [cover-title]
DESCRIPTION: 18.5 × 12.5 cm   Pp 1–32   Paper, with images on front of a fishing boat at sea and a cooked fish on a plate; stapled
CONTENTS: 1–2 'Facts about Fish and This Book' and at bottom p 2, 'Copyrighted 1924 by National Fish Co. Limited Halifax, Canada'; 3–32 recipes credited with the name of the contributor
COPIES: *MWPA (MG14 C50 McKnight, Ethel)   OONL (TX747 N36 1924); United States: NRMW
NOTES: The text on p 1 begins, 'This is a second, and much enlarged edition, of a book that met with such favor that thirty thousand copies of the original issue were sold and distributed within a few weeks of publication.' It states that the National Fish Co. supplies one-sixteenth of the total amount of fish consumed in Canada. The text is printed in green. The MWPA copy is stamped on the inside front face of

the binding, 'W.R. Spooner // 119 Youville Square Montreal, Que. Selling agent National Fish Co. Ltd. products for Central and Western Canada.'

NS27.3   [3rd ed., copyright 1925]
—National / sea food / recipes / The book of a / thousand cooks [cover-title]
DESCRIPTION: 18.5 × 12.5 cm   Pp 1–32   Paper, with images on front of a fishing boat at sea and a cooked fish on a plate; stapled
CONTENTS: 1 'Facts about Fish and This Book' and 'Copyrighted, 1925, by National. Fish Co. Limited Halifax, Canada'; 2–32 recipes credited with the name of the contributor, under the following headings: 'The Spencer Hot Oven Method,' 'Bloater Recipes,' 'Cod,' 'Fillet Recipes,' 'Finnan Haddie,' 'Haddock Recipes,' 'Halibut Recipes,' 'Herring Recipes,' 'Lobster Recipes,' 'Mackerel Recipes,' 'Salmon Recipes,' 'Scallop Recipe,' 'Soles,' and 'Soup Recipes'
COPIES: *Private collection
NOTES: Page 1 begins, 'This, the third edition of the National Cook Book, has been contributed to by Mrs. Evelene Spencer, the "Fish Evangelist," ...' Spencer is identified as the co-author, with Professor Cobb, of *Fish Cookery*, i.e., Mrs Evelene Spencer, née Armstrong (1867–), and John N. Cobb, *Fish Cookery*, Boston: Little, Brown, and Co., 1921. She is described as having worked 'for the past eight years' for the United States Bureau of Fisheries in an educational capacity and as now working for the National Fish Co. Also on p 1, the company is said to supply more than one-sixteenth of all fish consumed in Canada. The text is printed in green.

NS27.4   unnumbered ed., nd [about 1930–5]
—Sea food / recipes / With the compliments of / Dept. Colonization, Game & Fisheries / Province of Quebec. [cover-title]
DESCRIPTION: 18.5 × 12.5 cm   Pp [1–3] 4–32   Paper, with small image on front of a fish in silhouette; stapled
CONTENTS: Inside front face of binding 'Printed by courtesy of National Fish Company Limited'; 1 'Eat More Fish' signed Department of Colonization, Game and Fisheries, Province of Quebec; 2 blank; 3–32 recipes credited with the name and city or town of the contributor, arranged under the following headings: 'Bloater Recipes,' 'Cod,' 'Cod Fillet,' 'Fillet Recipes,' 'Finan [sic] Haddie,' 'Haddock Recipes,' 'Halibut Recipes,' 'Herring Recipes,' 'Lobster Recipes,' 'Mackerel Recipes,' 'Salmon Recipes,' 'Scallop Recipe,' 'Soles,' and 'Soup Recipes'
COPIES: *Private collection
NOTES: This retitled, undated edition, distributed by

the Government of Quebec, was likely published during the Depression, since the introductory note on p 1 refers to 'these days of so much unemployment.' Readers were encouraged to eat more fish to benefit their health and to boost employment in the fishing industry.

NS27.5   unnumbered ed., nd
—Comment apprêter / le poisson / de notre province / Offert gratuitement par / le ministère de la colonisation / de la chasse et des pêcheries / Province de Quebec [cover-title]
DESCRIPTION: Inside front face of binding 'Publié avec la bienveillante permission de la National Fish Company Limited'; 1 'Mangeons plus de poisson' signed Le ministère de la colonisation, de la chasse et des pêcheries; 2 blank; 3–42 recipes credited with the name and city or town of the contributor
COPIES: *QSFFSC

NS27.6   unnumbered ed., nd
—Sea food / recipes / With the compliments of / Dept. Colonization, Game & Fisheries / Province of Quebec [cover-title]
DESCRIPTION: 19.0 × 13.5 cm   Pp [1–3] 4–40   Paper; stapled
CONTENTS: Inside front face of binding 'Printed by courtesy of National Fish Company Limited'; 1 'Eat More Fish' signed Department of Colonization, Game and Fisheries, Province of Quebec; 2 blank; 3–40 recipes credited with the name and city or town of the contributor, arranged under the following headings: 'Bloater Recipes,' 'Cod,' 'Cod Fillet,' 'Fillet Recipes,' 'Finnan Haddie,' 'Haddock Recipes,' 'Halibut Recipes,' 'Herring Recipes,' 'Lobster Recipes,' 'Mackerel Recipes,' 'Salmon Recipes,' 'Scallop Recipes,' 'Soles,' and 'Soup Recipes'
COPIES: *QMBN (191960 CON)
NOTES: This English-language edition has more pages than NS27.4. Here, there is no image of a fish on the binding and the section heading 'Finnan Haddie' is spelled correctly.

St Andrews Church cook book

NS28.1   1923
St. Andrews Church / cook book / Halifax, N.S. / 1923 / The Ross Print Ltd, / Halifax [cover-title]
DESCRIPTION: 22.0 × 14.5 cm   Pp [1–2] 3–29 [30–4] Paper, with small illus on front of a plate of six rolls or pastries(?); stapled
CONTENTS: 1 dedication 'To the members of St. Andrew's Presbyterian Church Halifax, Nova Scotia

in appreciation of their encouragement in promoting the publishing of this book on behalf of the choir'; 2 ads; 3–29 recipes credited with the name of the contributor; 30–3 ads; 34 index

COPIES: *Private collection

NOTES: The following names are listed on p 1: Mrs J.M. Murdoch, president; Marguerite Schulze, secretary-treasurer; and Committee: Mrs W.T. Francis, Jr, and Mrs H. Coleman. There is a mock recipe on p 26, Infallible Recipe to Preserve Children, submitted by Mrs J.M. Murdoch, and another mock recipe on p 29, How to Cook Husbands.

1924

Tested recipes

The Evangeline Chapter was formed in 1915 and disbanded in 1966.

NS29.1   1924
Tested recipes / compiled by members of / Evangeline Chapter / I.O.D.E. / Halifax, N.S. / Royal Print and Litho Ltd. / 1924
DESCRIPTION: 19.0 × 13.0 cm   Pp [i–ii], [1–27] 28–140 [141–78]   Tp illus of IODE symbol   Cloth, with IODE symbol on front
CONTENTS: i tp; ii blank; 1–26 ads; 27 part-title to recipes and an acrostic verse, where the initial letter of each line spells 'EVANGELINE'; 28–139 recipes credited with the name of the contributor; 140 blank for handwritten recipes; 141–74 ads; 175 'Contents' [i.e., index]; 176 'Useful Information'; 177–8 ads
CITATIONS: Nightingale 1989
COPIES: *Private collection
NOTES: This is the earliest of the several cookbooks compiled by the Evangeline Chapter. According to the chapter's annual statement for 1925–6 (quoted in Nightingale 1989), 'Between the first edition and the reprint, the chapter made a profit of $1,609.10 from the sale of the book and advertisements.' The reference to a reprint may be to a second printing of the 1924 edition or perhaps to the 1926 edition.

The other cookbooks (all new collections of recipes) are: NS32.1, *Tested Recipes*, 1926; NS35.1, *New Cook Book of Tested Recipes*, 1929; NS43.1, *New Cook Book of Tested Recipes*, 1934; NS66.1, *Tested Recipes*, 1947; and *Tested Recipes*, 1952 (outside the bounds of this bibliography; copy at OONL). In 1935, the Nova Scotia Bureau of Information reprinted recipes from the Evangeline Chapter's cookbooks in NS46.1.

Another Nova Scotia IODE chapter – the Haliburton Chapter in Windsor – also used an acrostic to spell out its name in a 1920s cookbook; see NS30.1.

1925

Recipes tried, tested and proved

NS30.1   nd [about 1925]
Recipes / tried, tested and proved / compiled by members of / Haliburton Chapter / I.O.D.E. / [IODE symbol] / "Loyal, true, ready to do." / Windsor, N.S.
DESCRIPTION: 19.0 × 14.0 cm   Pp [i–x], [1–3] 4–115, [i–xxi]   Paper
CONTENTS: i tp; ii blank; iii–ix ads; x blank; 1 introductory poem, an acrostic where the first letter of each line is printed in bold to spell out 'HALIBURTON CHAPTER IODE'; 2 'Table of Weights and Measures'; 3–115 recipes; i–v blank; vi–xxi ads
COPIES: NSWA   *OGU (UA s062 b06)
NOTES: The Haliburton Chapter was organized on 22 November 1923; it disbanded in 1964. The appearance of the book points to publication in the 1920s; it was likely one of the chapter's earliest fund-raising ventures.

Another Nova Scotia IODE chapter – the Evangeline Chapter in Halifax – also used an acrostic to spell out its name in a cookbook; see NS29.1.

1926

Port Mouton cook book

NS31.1   1926
Port Mouton / cook book / 1926 / Recipes gathered / by the / young girls / of the / "Fullerton" Mission Circle / of the / United Church / Port Mouton [cover-title]
COPIES: *Private collection

Tested recipes

For other cookbooks by the Evangeline Chapter, see NS29.1.

NS32.1   December 1926
Tested recipes / compiled by members of / Evangeline Chapter / I.O.D.E. / Halifax, N.S. / December, 1926 / [IODE symbol] / Wm. MacNab & Son, Halifax, N.S.
DESCRIPTION: 19.5 × 13.0 cm   Pp [1–6] 7–119   Cloth-covered boards; sewn
CONTENTS: 1 tp; 2 blank; 3 'Contents' [i.e., alphabetical list of sections]; 4 'Useful Information'; 5 part-title to recipes and an acrostic verse, spelling out

'EVANGELINE': 'Each day for something new you're looking / Variety is the spice of cooking – / And to supply a clamorous call / New books we've printed for you all. / Guaranteed recipes, old and new, / Each name means she makes it – likes it too! / Lots of good cooks have praised it well, / It's proved an easy thing to sell. / Now changes are many; – proud editors we / Evangeline Chapter, I.O.D.E.'; 6–119 recipes credited with the name of the contributor
COPIES: *Private collection
NOTES: The cover-title is 'New Tested Recipes.' Nightingale 1989, an article about the Evangeline Chapter cookbooks, does not list December 1926 in the run of editions.

Tried and true recipes

NS33.1 1926
Tried and true / recipes / by the Ladies Guild / of / Falmouth Street Church / Sydney, N.S. / 1926
DESCRIPTION: Cloth
COPIES: *Private collection
NOTES: The recipes, which begin on p 5, are credited with the name of the contributor. The volume has 120 pp. The cover-title is 'Recipes.'

1928

Peters, Mrs J.W.

The author is likely Amanda Peters, born 21 November 1865, wife of James W. Peters, both Baptist and living in Bridgetown at the time of the 1901 Census.

NS34.1 [March] 1928
Cook book / 1928 / Printed at the Monitor Office, Bridgetown, N.S [cover-title]
DESCRIPTION: 22.0 × 14.5 cm   Pp [1–47] Paper; stapled
CONTENTS: 1 blank; 2 ad; 3 'Introduction' signed Mrs J.W. Peters, 'Teacher of Class,' Bridgetown, Nova Scotia, March 1928; 4 ad; 5–39 recipes and ads; 40–3 blank for 'Memo'; 44 ads; 45 'Canning Chart' by Miss Jessie A. Hartt; 46 ad for the *Weekly Monitor*, Bridgetown; 47 'Members of Philathea Class of the Bridgetown Baptist Church'
COPIES: OGU (UA s070 b69)   *Private collection
NOTES: In the 'Introduction' Mrs Peters says, 'As compiler of the "Philathea Class Cook Book," I desire to acknowledge the large debt of gratitude which I owe to the many members of the class who have contributed so largely from their store-house of choice and

tested receipts.' Mrs Ray Miller, graduate nurse, contributed 'Invalid Cookery' on p 5. Miss Jessie A. Hartt, director of the Science Department, New Albert School, Saint John West, contributed 'Pastry' directions on pp 7–8. 'Children's School Sandwiches & Lunches' follow 'Pastry.' A notice on p 10 about the Philathea Class indicates that it 'meets every Sunday from 12 noon to 1 P.M.' An advertisement on p 32 for Evangeline Pale Dry Ginger Ale, made by M.W. Graves and Co. Ltd of Bridgetown and 'on the market for only nine months now,' is followed on p 33 by 'Graves' Recipes' using the Ginger Ale as an ingredient.

The OGU copy is in poor condition and lacks the binding and nine leaves.

1929

New cook book of tested recipes

For other cookbooks by the Evangeline Chapter, see NS29.1.

NS35.1 December 1929
New cook book of tested recipes / Evangeline Chapter I.O.D.E. / December, 1929 / Halifax, N.S. / [IODE symbol] / MacNab Print, 7–9–11 Bedford Row, / Halifax, N.S.
DESCRIPTION: 19.5 × 13.0 cm   Pp [1–6] 7–123   Cloth-covered boards, with IODE symbol on front
CONTENTS: 1 first tp; 2 blank; 3 'Useful Information'; 4 'Contents' [i.e., alphabetical list of sections]; 5 second tp; 6–121 recipes credited with the name of the contributor; 122–3 'Menus'
CITATIONS: Nightingale 1989
COPIES: NSHL   *Private collection

1930

Cook book

NS36.1 1930
Calvin United Church / New Waterford, N.S. / Cook book / Compiled by / the Grant Guild / 1930 / Printed by / Brodie Printing Service / Glace Bay, N.S.
DESCRIPTION: 22.5 × 15.0 cm   Pp [i–ii], [1] 2–78   Paper; stapled
CONTENTS: i tp; ii blank; 1 'Weights and Measures'; 2–73 recipes and ads; 74–7 blank for 'Additional Recipes'; 78 'Index' [i.e., table of contents]
COPIES: *Private collection

I.O.D.E. recipes

NS37.1   nd [about 1930]
I.O.D.E. recipes / [IODE symbol] / compiled by / Scotia Chapter / Truro, Nova Scotia / The Ross Print Limited / 95 Argyle Street, Halifax, N.S.
COPIES: *Private collection
NOTES: This edition was printed by Ross Print, Halifax, not Tribune Press, Sackville, as for NS37.2 and NS37.3. An 'Errata' list is pasted in at the back of the book, giving corrections for pp 9, 14, 19, 20, 27, 41, 45, and 46. For Luncheon Rolls on p 9, for example, read ¼ cup lukewarm water instead of 1¼ cups.

The 'Oven Temperatures' table has columns for 'Type of Oven' [i.e., slow, moderate, hot, and very hot] and corresponding Fahrenheit degrees [250°–350°, 350°–400°, 400°–450°, 450°–500°).

NS37.2   nd
—I.O.D.E. recipes / compiled by / Scotia Chapter / Truro, Nova Scotia / The Tribune Press / Sackville, New Brunswick
DESCRIPTION: 19.5 × 13.5 cm   Pp [1–6] 7–119   Cloth
CONTENTS: 1 tp; 2 blank; 3 quotation from Ruskin and from Shakespeare; 4 'Useful Information' [i.e., measurements]; 5 'Oven Temperature'; 6 table of contents; 7–119 recipes credited with the name of the contributor
COPIES: *OGU (UA s048 b10)
NOTES: This edition follows NS37.1 because the amount of lukewarm water called for in Luncheon Rolls on p 9 has been corrected to read ¼ cup. 'Christmas Recipes' are on pp 30–4.

NS37.3   nd
—I.O.D.E. recipes / compiled by / Scotia Chapter / Truro, Nova Scotia / The Tribune Press, Limited / Sackville, New Brunswick
DESCRIPTION: 19.5 × 13.0 cm   Pp [1–6] 7–119   IODE symbol on tp   Paper; stapled
CONTENTS: 1 tp; 2 blank; 3 quotations from Ruskin and from Shakespeare; 4 'Useful information'; 5 'Oven Temperature'; 6 table of contents; 7–119 recipes
COPIES: *Private collection
NOTES: The form of the printer's name (includes 'Limited') and the binding (paper) differ from NS37.2. The cover-title is 'Recipes' and it is in a more modern typeface than that on the title-page. The owner of the book reports that it was used in her family before 1950.

Olympic cook book

NS38.1   1930
Olympic / cook book / published by / Olympic Chapter, I.O.D.E. / Kentville, Nova Scotia / 1930
DESCRIPTION: 22.5 × 15.0 cm   Pp [1–3] 4–97 [98]   Paper, with image on front of a ship and seagulls; stapled
CONTENTS: 1 tp; 2 blank; 3–97 text and ads; 98 'Printed in Canada by the Kentville Publishing Company, Limited'
CITATIONS: Ferguson/Fraser, p 234
COPIES: *OGU (UA s048 b49)
NOTES: The poem on p 3, which is signed M.L.W., ends, 'So buy one [i.e., this book], please, it will dispense with your ills, / It will sharpen your wits and help pay their bills.'

1930–5

Fish recipes

For an earlier cookbook by the same company, see NS12.1.

NS39.1   nd [about 1930–5]
Fish / recipes / [company symbol: 'Robin Jones & Whitman Ltd Est. 1766 Trade mark registered'] / for preparing / boneless salt / cod fish [cover-title]
DESCRIPTION: 15.0 × 11.5 cm   Pp 1–23 [24]   Paper, with image on front of three fish; stapled
CONTENTS: 1 untitled introductory text signed Robin, Jones and Whitman Ltd, Lunenburg, Nova Scotia; 2 'The Value of Fish'; 3 'Robin, Jones & Whitman, Limited' [company history]; 4 'The Story of Lunenburg Fishing'; 5 'Freshening'; 6–23 'Salt Codfish Recipes'; 24 index
COPIES: *Private collection
NOTES: The company's boneless salt codfish was packed under the brand names Halifax and Acadia (p 1). The company history (p 3) states that Robin, Jones and Whitman Ltd is 'the third oldest company in Canada having been established in the year 1766 by Charles Robin on the Gaspe Peninsula.' In 1891, the company was amalgamated with John and Elias Collis to form Charles Robin, Collis and Co. Ltd. In 1904, it became known as C. Robin, Collis Co. Ltd. In 1910, it amalgamated with A.G. Jones and Co. of Halifax and the Atlantic Fish Companies Ltd of Lunenburg to form Robin, Jones and Whitman Ltd. The head office was in Halifax.

1930–9

Tested recipes

NS40.1   nd [about 1930–9]
Tested / recipes / by / the John Pringle Women's
Auxiliary / of St. Andrew's United Church /
Sydney, N.S. [cover-title]
DESCRIPTION: 16.5 × 12.5 cm [dimensions from
photocopy]   With small image on front of a manser-
vant, in profile, carrying aloft a covered dish   Prob-
ably stapled
COPIES: *Private collection

1933–9

MacDougall, Miss Helen J.

*Helen J. MacDougall was superintendent of Women's
Institutes in Nova Scotia from 1917 to 1945. Everyone
referred to her as 'Miss MacDougall' and she was said to
have had 'a commanding personality' (e-mail, July 2000,
from David Robinson, economist in the Nova Scotia
government). See also NS53.1, for which MacDougall
revised Ontario material to suit Nova Scotia conditions.*

*This author is not the Miss Helen MacDougall who
wrote M32.1.*

NS41.1   nd [about 1933–9]
65 / apple recipes [cover-title]
DESCRIPTION: 23.0 × 12.5 cm   Pp [1–24]   A few small
illus   Paper, with image on front of an aproned
woman coring a red apple
CONTENTS: 1 'This booklet is prepared for your per-
manent kitchen use; hang it up in some convenient
place for continual reference // John A. McDonald
Minister of Agriculture'; 2 'The Nova Scotia Fruit
Growers Association and the Department of Agricul-
ture approve of the 65 recipes in this book ...'; 3 'Just a
Word on Apples' and a map of Nova Scotia; 4 'Food
Value of Apples'; 5–23 '65 Ways to Prepare Apples';
24 'This booklet is published by authority of the
Honourable J.A. McDonald Minister of Agriculture
// Material for this booklet compiled by Helen J.
MacDougall, Director, Home Economics'
COPIES: OGU (2 copies: *UA not on shelf, CCC CA2NV
A 35S32)
NOTES: The text is printed in green and yellow. John
A. McDonald was minister of agriculture from 1933
to 1945; *65 Apple Recipes* dates from this period. From
appearances, NS41.1 and NS41.2 were both published
about 1933–9, but the order of publication of the two

editions is unknown. In NS41.1, the compiler's name
is on p 24; in NS41.2, it is on p 2.

NS41.2   nd [about 1933–9]
—65 / apple recipes [cover-title]
DESCRIPTION: 23.0 × 13.0 cm   Pp [1–23]   Illus green-
and-yellow on p 1 of a bushel basket of apples, on p 3
of a branch of apples and a map of Nova Scotia, and
on p 4 of apples on a plate   Paper, with image on
front of an aproned woman coring a red apple; stapled
CONTENTS: 1 'This booklet is prepared for your permanent kitchen use; hang it up in some convenient
place for continual reference // John A. McDonald
Minister of Agriculture' and 'The Nova Scotia Fruit
Growers Association and the Department of Agriculture approve all the 65 recipes in this book ...'; 2 'This
booklet is published by authority of the Honourable
J.A. McDonald Minister of Agriculture' and 'Material
for this booklet compiled by Helen J. MacDougall,
Director, Home Economics // Nova Scotia Department of Agriculture'; 3 'Just a Word on Apples' and a
map of Nova Scotia; 4 'Food Value of Apples'; 5–23
'65 Ways to Prepare Apples'
COPIES: *Private collection
NOTES: 'Nova Scotia Apple Calendar' is on the outside back face of the binding.

NS41.3   nd [about 1940]
—Apple recipes / with / Nova Scotia / apples
[cover-title]
DESCRIPTION: 22.0 × 13.0 cm   Pp [1–22]   Tp illus
green of a bushel basket of apples and a branch of
apples   Paper, with image on front of a woman pin-
ning an apple blossom to her hat, and below, a map of
Nova Scotia; stapled
CONTENTS: 1 'Use apples freely // This booklet is
prepared for your permanent kitchen use; hang it up
in some convenient place for continual reference //
John A. McDonald Minister of Agriculture // Mate-
rial for this booklet compiled by Helen J. MacDougall,
Director, Home Economics Nova Scotia Department
of Agriculture // Issued by authority of Honourable
John A. McDonald, Minister of Agriculture, Halifax';
2 'A Word about Apples'; 3–21 'Fifty Ways to Use
Apples and Apple Products'; 22 'Dehydrated and
Evaporated Apples'
COPIES: *Private collection
NOTES: The text is printed in green. 'Nova Scotia
Apple Calendar' is on the outside back face of the
binding. In this edition, MacDougall is credited as
the author on p 1. The book is undated, but it was
acquired by the owner's family before 1943; it was
likely published about 1940. I have not compared the

text of *Apple Recipes*, which contains only fifty recipes, with NS41.1 and NS41.2, *65 Apple Recipes*, but it is likely an edition of the same work.

1934

The community cook book

NS42.1 [November 1934]
The community / cook book / First Baptist Church / Hammonds Plains, N.S. [cover-title]
DESCRIPTION: Paper; stapled
COPIES: *Private collection
NOTES: The 'Foreword' (on the first page) is signed E. [i.e., Ethel] C. Jones, 'The Parsonage,' Hammonds Plains, November 1934. Jones, who describes herself as not a native of the village, writes: 'The "Community Cook Book" is being brought to the public by the ladies of the First Baptist Church ... Much credit is due Miss Dell Moren, who so faithfully collected these recipes and arranged them for publication ...' The 1901 Census records Della E. Moren born 2 October 1892 into a Baptist family in Hammonds Plains. Below the 'Foreword' there is a list of the branches of cooking covered in the text. The owner describes the recipes as 'traditional N.S.'

The front face of the binding is inscribed by the original owner of the book (the current owner's grandmother): 'Mrs Gertrude Bond Jones.' Ethel C. Jones, the writer of the 'Foreword,' was the wife of the Rev. H.B. Jones, the minister of the First Baptist Church in the 1930s (and the current owner's uncle).

New cook book of tested recipes

For a list of other cookbooks by the Evangeline Chapter, see NS29.1.

NS43.1 1934
New cook book / of / tested recipes / Evangeline Chapter I.O.D.E. / December 1934 / Halifax, N.S. / [IODE symbol] / The Ross Print Limited / 95 Argyle Street, Halifax, N.S.
DESCRIPTION: 19.0 × 13.0 cm   Pp [3–6] 7–132   Cloth-covered boards, with IODE symbol on front
CONTENTS: 3 tp; 4 blank; 5 'Useful Information'; 6 'Contents'; 7–132 recipes
CITATIONS: Driver 2001, Wellington County, pp 97–8 (note 12)   Nightingale 1989
COPIES: OGU (CCC TX715.6 N4756)   OTYA (TX715.6 N49 1934)   *Private collection

NOTES: This is the Evangeline Chapter's fourth new collection of recipes in ten years. Although not credited as such in the published volume, Mrs Elizabeth (Bess) Hazelett Sieniewicz, née Dobson (1893–1938), was the chair of the organizing committee, which met weekly, around the dining-room table at her home. She had graduated in 1912 from the Macdonald Institute, Guelph, Ontario, with a certificate as a domestic science teacher. Women who contributed recipes include Miss Edith Courser, secretary to Lieutenant-Governor Tory, Marjorie Dimock, a professional woman (unusual for the time), and Miss Bertha (Bertie) Donkin, also a 'working woman,' in the insurance business. Apparently, in the process of preparing the manuscript, it was necessary to fill out the text with more recipes, many of which Mrs Sieniewicz supplied. Most are credited to her under different forms of her name and initials (Mrs Sieniewicz, Mrs T.M. Sieniewicz, E.H. Sieniewicz, E.H.S.), but several of the unattributed recipes in the book are also hers; for example, Broiled Live Lobsters, p 16, Scalloped Oysters and Creamed Scallops, p 17, Almond Cookies, p 98, and Heavenly Jam, p 114, to name but a few. (Mrs Sieniewicz had also contributed recipes to NS32.1; see, for example, Lemon Pudding, p 42, and Orange Charlotte, p 51, in that book.) In her leadership role on *New Cook Book of Tested Recipes*, Mrs Sieniewicz had the example of her sister, Barbara Kein Dobson, who, in 1916, had helped to compile NB29.1, for the de Monts Chapter of the IODE in Saint John, New Brunswick. Mrs Sieniewicz's daughter, Mrs Barbara Kincaide of Toronto, is my source of information about NS43.1.

1935

Cook book of tested recipes

The Bedford Chapter was organized on 2 January 1923 and disbanded in 1969.

NS44.1 nd [about 1935]
Cook book / of / tested recipes / [IODE symbol] / Bedford Chapter / I.O.D.E. / Bedford, N.S.
DESCRIPTION: 22.0 × 15.0 cm   Pp [1–3] 4–72   Paper; stapled
CONTENTS: 1 tp; 2 'Contents' [i.e., alphabetical list of subject headings]; 3–72 text and ads
COPIES: *Private collection
NOTES: The book's owner commented that it was published before she was married in 1939. It appears to have been produced in the mid-1930s.

Mission Circle cook book

NS45.1 [1935]
Mission Circle / cook book [cover-title]
DESCRIPTION: About 19.5 × 12.5 cm [dimensions from photocopy]
COPIES: *Private collection
NOTES: The table of contents on the first page lists fourteen sections, but no corresponding page numbers: 'Soups'; 'Fish'; 'Meat'; 'Supper Dishes'; 'Salads and Salad Dressing'; 'Relishes'; 'Quick Breads'; 'Yeast Breads'; 'Desserts and Sauces'; 'Pies'; 'Small Cakes and Cookies'; 'Cakes'; 'Candy'; and 'Sandwich Suggestions.' The following is printed below the table of contents: 'This book contains recipes which have been tested, and are recommended by the members of the Mission Circle of First United Church, of Truro, N.S., 1935.'

Nova Scotia, Bureau of Information

NS46.1 [1935]
Be prepared for / our summer / guests / Compiled by / Bureau of Information / Government of Nova Scotia / Published by authority of / Hon. A.S. MacMillan / Minister of Highways / Nova Scotia
DESCRIPTION: 18.5 × 11.0 cm   Pp [1–2] 3–40   Paper; stapled
CONTENTS: Inside front face of binding 'Index'; 1 tp; 2 'Foreword' signed Bureau of Information; 3–39 text; 40 'Tourist Publications // Nova Scotia Government 1935'
COPIES: *OGU (CCC CA2NV IF 35B26)   OONL (COP.NS.2.2001-12)
NOTES: The 'Foreword' states that the pamphlet gives 'practical hints in the successful running of a hotel.' The introductory text on pp 3–14 includes sections on 'Manager and Staff,' 'Exterior of the Hotel,' 'Interior of the Hotel,' 'Sport and Recreation,' 'Dining Room and Menus,' 'Balanced Meals,' 'Steak and Coffee,' which advises that 'our neighbors across the border expect to find [steak and coffee] served to perfection,' and 'Importance of Fish on the Menu.' Recipes follow 'Suggestions for Menus' on pp 15–18. Recipes for cooking game conclude the recipe section. A footnote on p 21 states, 'Recipes marked with star are reproduced by courtesy of Evangeline Chapter I.O.D.E., Halifax, from their series of cookbooks entitled "New Tested Recipes."' The first cookbook by the Evangeline Chapter, NS29.1, appeared in 1924, and all the chapter's titles are listed at that entry.

See also a later booklet on the same subject by the Bureau of Information and Publicity, NS50.1, *Set a Good Table!*

1935–9

Tested recipes

In 1925, the congregations of St Matthew's Church and the Methodist Church joined to become St Matthew–Wesley United Church.

NS47.1 nd [about 1935–9]
Tested / recipes / St. Matthew–Wesley / Ladies Guild / North Sydney – Nova Scotia
DESCRIPTION: 20.5 × 13.5 cm   Pp [1–3] 4–70   Tp illus of St Matthew–Wesley Church   Paper, with tp illus on front; stapled
CONTENTS: 1 tp; 2 'Abbreviations' and 'Thank You!'; 3 'Contents'; 4–70 recipes credited with the name of the contributor and ads
COPIES: *OTMCL (641.86 T26)

1936

I.O.D.E. cook book

The Louisbourg Chapter was formed in 1910 and celebrated its Silver Jubilee in 1935.

NS48.1 1936
I.O.D.E. / cook book / Compiled by members of the / Louisbourg Chapter / Sydney, Nova Scotia / 1936
DESCRIPTION: 22.0 × 14.5 cm   Pp [1–4] 5–80   Paper, with IODE symbol on front; stapled
CONTENTS: 1 tp; 2 'Louisbourg Chapter – Sydney'; 3 'Aims and Objects of the Order'; 4 unattributed poem beginning, 'We may live without poetry, music and art' [from *Lucile*, Part I, Canto ii, by Owen Meredith, pseudonym of Edward Robert Bulwer-Lytton]; 5–79 recipes credited with the name of the contributor and ads; 80 'Table of Weights and Measures'
COPIES: NSSXA (MG14 122 D. 9)   *Private collection
NOTES: Page 2 records information about the history and activities of the Louisbourg Chapter and states that 'All monies from the sale of this book will be devoted to the work of the Order.' The cover-title is 'I.O.D.E. Recipe Book.'

The Louisbourg Chapter also published NS59.1, *Recipe Book*, 1942, and NS71.1, *Recipe Book*, 1948. I have not determined whether these later books are related to NS48.1 or not. NSHP has *A Collection of Recipes Compiled by the Members of the Louisbourg Chapter I.O.D.E.*, 7th ed., Sydney, NS: Printed by LeBlanc Printing Co. Ltd, nd [after 1950]; AnderCat (June 2002, No. 21425) lists the 13th ed. of the same title, 1985.

The ter-jubilee cook book

See also NS21.1 from the same church.

NS49.1 1936
The ter-jubilee / cook / book / [small symbol of a burning bush surrounded by the Latin phrase 'Nec tamen consumebatur,' i.e., Burning but not consumed] / 1786–1936 / Sponsored by the Ladies / Guild First Presbyterian /Church, New Glasgow, / Nova Scotia. [cover-title]
DESCRIPTION: 22.5 × 15.0 cm [dimensions from photocopy]   Probably stapled
CONTENTS: ...; 6 ads; 7 recipes for 'Small Cakes and Cookies,' credited with the name of the contributor
COPIES: *Private collection

1936–9

Royal cook book

See NB45.1 for a cookbook 'issued in aid of the various hospitals throughout the Maritimes.'

1937

Nova Scotia, Government Bureau of Information and Publicity

NS50.1   nd [about 1937]
Set a good / table! / Our summer visitors are quick to appreciate / good service, but are slow to forget bad / Compiled by / Government Bureau of Information and Publicity / Published by authority of / Hon. A.S. MacMillan / Minister of Highways / Nova Scotia [cover-title]
DESCRIPTION: 21.0 × 14.0 cm   Pp [i–ii], [1] 2–26   Paper; stapled
CONTENTS: Inside front face of binding letter dated 24 January 1937 to Mr A.J. Campbell, director, Bureau of Information, from Louis Brustein, Connecticut News Association, criticizing Nova Scotia cooking in hotels and inns; i index; ii blank; 1–4 introductory text; 5–top 25 recipes; mid 25–26 'Timely Tips for the Amateur Cook'
CITATIONS: Driver 2003, 'Canadian Cookbooks,' pp 37–8
COPIES: *Private collection
NOTES: *Set a Good Table!* was published for the Nova Scotia tourist trade. Businesses were encouraged to 'put distinctive Nova Scotian menus on ... hotel

tables ...' (on back face of binding). Suggested menus for breakfast, luncheon, and dinner are on pp 3–4.

The cookbook was likely published in 1937, the same year as the dated letter to Campbell, in which Brustein complains about inns and hotels outside Halifax, where he found 'a hodge podge of the traditional dreary British cooking combined with the worst aspects of the United States variety.' The book was likely published before the start of the Second World War, and certainly before Alexander Stirling MacMillan's last day as minister of highways and public works, on 24 February 1941. No place of publication is recorded, but the seat of the provincial government is in Halifax.

See also an earlier booklet on the same subject by the Bureau of Information, NS46.1.

1938

Favorite recipes

Woodside-Imperoyal United Church was at 11 Everette Street in Dartmouth. In 1998 the congregation amalgamated with Cole Harbour Church to become Cole Harbour Woodside United Church, after which the Woodside-Imperoyal property was sold.

NS51.1   [September 1938]
Favorite / recipes / of / the Ladies' Aid / of / the United Church / of / Woodside and Imperoyal [cover-title]
DESCRIPTION: Photograph on p [1] of Woodside-Imperoyal United Church   Stapled
CONTENTS: 1 photograph of the church and 'Foreword' signed the Committee, September 1938
COPIES: *Private collection
NOTES: The recipes are credited with the name of the contributor. The booklet has 72 pp.

1939

Grand Pre cook book

NS52.1   1939
Grand Pre / cook book / published by / Ladies' Aid of the Grand Pre / United Church / Grand Pré, Nova Scotia / 1939
DESCRIPTION: 21.5 × 14.0 cm   Pp [1–6] 7–40   Tp illus of Railway Depot, Grand Pré; illus on p 5 of 'Faed's Evangeline,' illus on p 6 of 'The Old Covenanter Church, Grand Pre'   Paper, with image on front of

the Memorial Chapel and Evangeline statue; stapled
CONTENTS: 1 tp; 2 'Printed by Kentville Publishing
Company, Limited Kentville, Nova Scotia'; 3–4 'History of Grand Pre, N.S.' by Annie M. Stuart; 5 illus
of 'Faed's Evangeline' and 'A Recipe for a Day'
[unattributed verse]; 6 illus and history of 'The Old
Covenanter Church, Grand Pre, Nova Scotia' and untitled verse by Mrs L.P. Dennison; 7–36 recipes and
ads; 37 ads; 38 'To Preserve a Husband'; 39–40 blank
for 'Memorandum'
COPIES: NSHMS *NSWA (2 copies) OONL (TX715
G74)
NOTES: In some editions, the 'History of Grand Pre' is
signed Annie M. Stuart; in others, Annie M. Stewart.
The OONL copy is rebound.

NS52.2 1940
—Grand Pre / cook book / published by / Ladies'
Aid of the Grand Pre / United Church / Grand Pre,
Nova Scotia / 1940
DESCRIPTION: Tp illus of Railway Depot, Grand
Pré With image on front of the Memorial Chapel
and Evangeline statue
CITATIONS: FitzPatrickCat 110 (February 1993) No.
142 FitzPatrickCat 111 (April 1993) No. 13
COPIES: *Private collection
NOTES: The owner reports that the 1940 edition, printed
by Kentville Publishing Co., has 24 pp.

NS52.3 1947
—Grand Pre / cook book / published by / the
Ladies' Aid / of the / Lower Horton United Church
/ Grand Pre, Nova Scotia / 1947
DESCRIPTION: Tp illus of Railway Depot, Grand
Pré With image on front of 'Memorial Park and
Evangeline Statue // Grand Pre, N.S.'
COPIES: *Private collection; United States: MCR
(641.6971 G75)
NOTES: The MCR catalogue describes the volume as
having 27 pp.

NS52.4 1949
—Grand Pre / cook book / published by / the
Ladies' Aid / of the / Lower Horton United Church
/ Grand Pre, Nova Scotia / 1949
DESCRIPTION: 22.5 × 15.0 cm Pp [1–5] 6–28 Tp illus
of Lower Horton United Church, illus on p 2 of the
Old Presbyterian Church Paper, with image on front
of 'Memorial Church and Evangeline Statue, Grand
Pré, N.S.'; stapled
CONTENTS: 1 tp; 2 'The Old Presbyterian Church' and
poem by Kate Osborne MacLatchey; 3 poem, 'The
Old Church,' by Kate Osborne MacLatchey; 4–5 'His-

tory of Grand Pre, N.S.' signed Annie M. Stewart; 6
'The Valley Song,' 'Home Makers' Prayer,' and 'My
Summer Travel Plan'; top–mid 7 'Wedding Anniversaries,' 'To Preserve a Husband,' and 'For Orderly
Management'; mid 7–mid 8 'Recipes for Nova Scotia
Apples'; mid 8–mid 10 'Breads'; mid 10–top 14 'Cakes';
mid 14–mid 19 'Cookies and Little Cakes'; mid 19–
mid 20 'Puddings'; mid 20–top 21 'Desserts'; mid 21–
top 22 'Pies'; mid–bottom 22 'Salads'; 23–mid 25
'Luncheon and Supper Dishes'; mid 25–mid 26 'Dressings and Sauces'; mid–bottom 26 'Jellies and Pickles';
27 'Candy'; 28 'Do Not Overlook These ...'
COPIES: OTYA (TX715 G52 1949) *Private collection

OTHER EDITIONS: The 1951 edition (OGU, OONL)
records the following publishing history on the title-
page: 'This booklet, which with each edition has become more popular with the homemaker, has grown
from 300 copies to a grand total of 10,000 copies. The
first copy came out in 1946 [sic] // the second was
published in 1947, third in 1949, and the 1951 booklet
of 3,000 copies is just off the press.' The first edition
was not published in 1946, as stated on the title-page
of the 1951 edition, but in 1939 (NS52.1). I have not
located a copy of the 1946 edition.
    The title-page of the 1959 edition (Private collec-
tion) refers to a total of 'Seven editions // 21,000
copies.' The title-page of the 1965 edition (Private
collection) refers to '2300 copies,' but an extra zero
has been handwritten to make the correct figure of
23,000. The title-page of the 1973 edition (OONL)
refers to 'Nine editions // 32,000 copies.' The title-
page of the 1987 edition (Private collection) refers to
'Thirteen editions // 51,000 copies.'

Nova Scotia, Land Settlement Board

NS53.1 nd [1939 or later]
The Nova Scotia / Land Settlement Board /
Economical recipes / and / household hints /
Issued from Office of the Nova Scotia / Land
Settlement Board / S.A. Logan, Chairman [cover-
title]
DESCRIPTION: 23.5 × 15.5 cm Pp [1] 2–33 Paper;
stapled
CONTENTS: Inside front face of binding 'We wish to
express to the Relief Land Settlement Committee,
of the Ontario Department of Land & Forests, our
appreciation of their courtesy in allowing us to use
material appearing in their publication, "Economical
Recipes and Household Hints"; also to Miss Helen
McDougall [sic], Superintendent of Women's Insti-

tutes of the Province of Nova Scotia, for her assistance in revising this material to suit Nova Scotia conditions.' and index; 1–33 text

COPIES: *Private collection

NOTES: Relief Land Settlement was an unemployment relief measure 'for helping worthy people to help themselves by affording them an opportunity of self-support on the land' (*First Report of the Relief Land Settlement Committee of Ontario for the Years 1932 and 1933*, Toronto: Herbert H. Ball, 1934, p 3). The idea was advanced in 1932 by Wesley A. Gordon, federal minister of labour, as an alternative to Direct Relief, i.e., straight financial support. The three levels of government shared the expenditures, the provinces administered the plan, and participating municipalities recommended families suited to a life of self-sufficiency on a farm. NS53.1 was based on a publication of the Ontario government; however, no copy has surfaced of the original source. NS53.1 was published no earlier than 1939, when the Provincial Farm Loan Board was renamed the Nova Scotia Land Settlement Board, and no later than 1945, the last year Helen MacDougall was superintendent of Women's Institutes. No place of publication is recorded, but the provincial government sits in Halifax.

The recipes are followed by household hints on such topics as 'Soft Soap,' 'To Soften Hard Water,' 'The Wood Pile,' 'Banking the House' [i.e., how to bank a house with sods, earth, or strawey manure to prevent drafts and to prevent frost on stored vegetables in the cellar], 'Mosquitoes,' 'Flies,' 'Frost Bites,' 'Sunburn,' 'Uses for Common Baking Soda,' 'A Use for Old Newspaper' [i.e., how to make a bed comforter from newspaper], and 'Knitting.'

For more information about Helen MacDougall, see NS41.1.

1939–45

War time recipes

NS54.1   nd [about 1939–45]
War time / recipes / Fort Anne Chapter / I.O.D.E. [cover-title]
DESCRIPTION: 21.0 × 14.0 cm   Pp 1–64   Paper, with IODE symbol on front; stapled
CONTENTS: 1 'A Recipe for a Day Requiring No Sugar' [poem] contributed by Hortense Spurr Gilliatt; 2 table of contents; 3–64 recipes
CITATIONS: Ferguson/Fraser, p 234, illus col on p 103 of closed volume
COPIES: *OGU (UA s063 b18)

NOTES: There is no indication of the place of publication in the book, but the Fort Anne Chapter, which was disbanded in 1969, was located in Annapolis Royal.

1940

Community cook book

NS55.1   1940
Community cook book / tried and tested recipes / "A blessing be upon the cook / Who, seeing, buys this little book, / And buying tries and tests its wares / And testing, throws away her cares; / And, carefree, tells her neighbor cook / To get another such a book." / Compiled by / the Ladies' Aid / of / St. Andrew's United Church / Lockeport, N.S. / 1940 [cover-title]
DESCRIPTION: 23.0 × 15.5 cm   Pp [1–4] 5–38   Paper; stapled
CONTENTS: 1–2 ads; 3 'Index' [i.e., table of contents]; 4 ad; 5–38 'Tried and Tested Recipes' credited with the name of the contributor
COPIES: *Private collection

Kitchen army nutrition and receipt book

NS56.1   nd [about 1940]
Kitchen army / nutrition / and / receipt book / Prepared under direction of / Sydney Nutrition Committee / Sydney, N.S. [cover-title]
DESCRIPTION: 22.5 × 15.0 cm   Pp [1] 2–40   Paper; stapled
CONTENTS: 1 table of contents; top–mid 2 'Nutrition Campaign,' 'Object and Importance of Campaign,' and 'Foods to Be Emphasized in This Course'; mid 2–mid 3 'What Are the Right Foods?'; mid 3–5 'Calories'; 6 'Suggestions in Planning Meals'; 7 'How to Divide the Food Dollar' and 'Marketing Hints'; 8 'Cooking Terms'; 9 'Abbreviations,' 'Measures,' 'Quantities,' and 'Substitutes'; 10 'Milk and Cheese'; 11–37 ninety-eight numbered recipes; 38 'Household Economies'; 39–40 'Index' [i.e., numerical list of recipes]
COPIES: *NSHP

NOTES: The object of the Nutrition Committee's campaign was 'To improve nutrition of Canadians and to emphasize its importance in the national war effort.' Health-promoting recipes include Cranberry Juice, Boston Baked Beans, Chocolate Yeast Drink, several salads, Apple Pie with Whole Wheat Pastry, Wheat

Germ Cheese Spread, and dishes featuring fish and offal as ingredients. The printer's name, 'Cameron – Sydney,' is on the outside back face of the binding.

1942

Cook book of favourite receipts

NS57.1   1942
Cook book / of / favourite receipts / [IODE symbol] / H.M. Shannon Chapter, / I.O.D.E. / March 1942 / Dartmouth, N.S.
DESCRIPTION: 21.0 × 14.0 cm   Pp [i–ii], [1–2] 3–94   Paper; stapled
CONTENTS: i 'Contents' [i.e., alphabetically arranged index of section headings]; ii blank; 1 tp; 2–90 recipes credited with the name of the contributor; 91 'Useful Information'; 92–4 'Household Hints'
COPIES: *OGU (CCC TX715.6 C658)
NOTES: Page 2 is inscribed, in ink, 'B. Mitchell.' 'H.M. Shannon' on the title-page is a typographical error; it should say, 'H.M.S. Shannon.'

Co-op cook book

NS58.1   [1942]
Page 1. / Co-op cookbook [*sic*, one word] / The Women's Guild / of the / Halifax Co-operative Society. / This little book has been / compiled by the Women's Guild, / with the forethought of ec- / onomy in war-time baking needs. / As far as possible the recipes / herein contained, are simple, / nutritious dishes that will / save you time, energy & money. / Co-op / cook book
DESCRIPTION: 21.5 × 14.0 cm   Pp 1–95 [96]   Paper, with still-life on front of ingredients and kitchen utensils, and image on back of two boats sailing along the coast; stapled
CONTENTS: 1 tp; 2 blank, except for folio; 3 'Contents'; 4 'Throw Nothing Away'; 5–mid 6 'Hints'; bottom 6 'Beware of Substitutes'; 7 'Minimum Adequate Diet for One Day' and 'Vitamin Sources'; 8 'Why Co-operatives?'; 9–87 recipes credited with the name of the contributor, interspersed with information about the co-operative movement (pp 12, 13, 18, 40, 42, 58, 59, 62, 66, 74, 83), a poem ('Good Cooks – Take Notice' by M. Ells) on p 46, and statistics about the distribution of 'Canada's Wealth' on p 57; 88 'The Co-operative Movement'; 89–95 'Index' and, at bottom p 95, 'Printed by the Women's Guild Gestetner Service, 27 Gottingen St.'; 96 'Printed by the Gestetner Service

of the Women's Guild of the Co-operative Society in Halifax.'
COPIES: *Bookseller's stock
NOTES: The year of publication, 1942, is printed on the front face of the binding. The leaves are green. The text is arranged in the following sections: 'Meat Cooking'; 'Meat Dishes'; 'Supper Dishes'; 'Fish'; 'Soups'; 'Salads'; 'Breads'; 'Cookies, Little Cakes'; 'Cakes'; and 'Puddings, Desserts.' Among the fish recipes is Hugger in Buff, subtitled 'A very old Nova Scotian recipe,' made of salt codfish, diced potatoes, salt fat pork, and onion. On p 77, one finds Canadian Carrot Pudding, a favourite dish in Canada since its first appearance in O20.1, *The Home Cook Book* of 1877, and English Carrot Pudding 1942, subtitled '"Portman Pudding" The Ministry of Food.' Both are essentially the same plum pudding–type recipe, calling for raw grated carrot and raw grated potato.

Recipe book

See also NS48.1 and NS71.1 by the same chapter.

NS59.1   1942
Louisbourg Chapter / I.O.D.E. / Sydney, N.S. / Recipe book / 1942 [cover-title]
DESCRIPTION: 23.0 × 15.0 cm   Pp [1–2] 3–100   Paper, with IODE symbol on front; stapled
CONTENTS: 1 unattributed poem beginning, 'We may live without poetry, music and art' [from *Lucile*, Part I, Canto ii, by Owen Meredith, pseudonym of Edward Robert Bulwer-Lytton]; 2 'Index' [i.e., table of contents], 'The income from the sale of this book will be devoted exclusively to the War Fund of the Chapter,' and 'Useful Information'; 3–98 recipes credited with the name of the contributor; 99–100 blank for 'Additional Recipes'
COPIES: NSSXA (MG14 122 D. 9)   OGU (CCC TX715.6 R42)   *Private collection
NOTES: The private collector's copy is inscribed on p 1, 'Mrs. Ken Petrie // 126 Main St., Glace Bay.'

1943

Victory cook book

NS60.1   nd [about 1943]
Victory / cook book / published by / Sir Robert Borden Chapter / I.O.D.E. / Wolfville, Nova Scotia [cover-title]
DESCRIPTION: 23.5 × 16.0 cm   Pp [1] 2–16   Paper, with image on front of DeWolf House; stapled

CONTENTS: 1 foreword signed Ronald S. Longley, Acadia University; 2 ads; 3–16 recipes and ads
COPIES: *NSWA (2 copies)
NOTES: In the foreword, Longley writes on behalf of the 'recently organized Wolfville Historical Society' and congratulates the members of the IODE on the publication of this cookbook. DeWolf House, which is illustrated on the binding, was the headquarters of the historical society, and Longley states that it was built 126 years ago. Since local-history sources record the construction of DeWolf House in 1817, the cookbook was published in about 1943 (1817 + 126 years). (The building has since been demolished.) The Wolfville Historical Society was founded in 1941.

1945–6

[Title unknown]

NS61.1 nd [about 1945–6]
[Title unknown]
DESCRIPTION: 24.0 × 18.5 cm Pp [1–46] Rebound in cloth; previously stapled?
CONTENTS: 1 'Recipes of Her Royal Highness Princess Alice // Government House Ottawa, Canada'; 2 'Suggestions by Hotel Nova Scotian // Halifax Canada'; 3 'Suggestions by Lord Nelson Hotel // Halifax Canada'; 4–46 recipes credited with the name of the contributor
COPIES: *Private collection
NOTES: The text is reproduced from typing and multigraphed. The cloth binding is newer than the interior leaves, but it is not clear whether there was an earlier binding or cover-title.
Princess Alice, whose recipes begin the text, was the wife of the Earl of Athlone, Canada's governor-general from 2 June 1940 (date of appointment) to 1946. After his term at Rideau Hall, the couple returned to England. Most cookbooks published during the Second World War reveal evidence of the era, sometimes specific references to wartime or recipes adapted to rationing. Since there is no indication that this cookbook was printed in the war years, it may have appeared in 1945–6.
Recipes on pp 4–46 are credited to Mrs Elkins, Mrs Sidney Oland, Mrs G.C. Jones, Mrs Vernon Gordon, Mrs W.A. Henry, Mrs G. McG. Mitchell, Mrs Courtney, Mrs S.L. Curry, Mrs Ralph P. Bell, Mrs Ralph Balders, Mrs Alan Curry, Mrs S.S. Bonham-Carter, Mrs R.L. Latcham, Mrs J. McG. Stewart, Mrs B. Armit, Mrs A.G.S. Griffin, Mrs Evat Mathers, Mrs Oxner, Mrs Norwood Duffus, Mrs M. Jean Sinclair, Mrs Norman

Stanbury, Mrs W.B. Almon, Mrs T.R. Robertson, Mrs F.F. Mathers, Mrs Turnbull, Mrs Victor Oland, Mrs MacC. Grant, Mrs R.M. Boyd, Mrs McMinn, Mrs Charles Allen, Mrs L.C. Goodeve, and Mrs Canavan. Mrs S.S. Bonham-Carter was likely the wife of British Rear-Admiral S.S. Bonham-Carter.

1945–9

Cook book with special apple recipes

NS62.1 nd [about 1945–9]
Cook/book / with special apple recipes / Compiled by / Ladies' Auxiliary / Kentville Baptist Church / Price $1.00 [cover-title]
DESCRIPTION: 23.0 × 15.5 cm Pp [1] 2–109, [i] Paper, with image on front of apple blossom; stapled
CONTENTS: 1 'Our First Edition' [i.e., preface]; 2–109 text and ads; i ads
COPIES: *OGU (UA s070 b08)
NOTES: 'Our First Edition' states, '... by the purchase of this book you are helping ... the treasury of the Ladies' Auxiliary of the Kentville United Baptist Church.' The first section is 'Apple Recipes.' An advertisement on the inside front face of the binding for the School of Home Economics, Acadia University, Wolfville, lists the staff, including Elizabeth MacMillan, dean. MacMillan was dean from 1943 to 1971. *Cook Book with Special Apple Recipes* was likely published after the Second World War, about 1945–9.

Kent Vinegars recipe book and household hints

Editions of this text were published in Ontario, Nova Scotia, and in the western provinces. For the edition published in Canning, Nova Scotia, see O1114.3.

1946

Favourite recipes

NS63.1 1946
Favourite / recipes / compiled by / Zion Guild / of / United Church of Canada / Liverpool, N.S. / 1946 [cover-title]
DESCRIPTION: 15.5 × 11.5 cm Pp [1–2] 3–70 [71–2] Paper; stapled
CONTENTS: 1 'Useful Information'; 2 'How to Preserve a Husband'; 3–62 recipes; 63–72 ads

COPIES: *Private collection

NOTES: Recipes for Baked Fish Fillets and Kippered Herring are included in an advertisement on the inside front face of the binding for Nickerson Bros Ltd, Liverpool, producers of Mersey Brand fillets and haddies and dealers in fresh, frozen, salt, and smoked fish.

1947

Our favorite recipes

NS64.1 [1947]
Our favorite / recipes / The Young Ladies' Auxiliary / Lawrencetown Baptist Church [cover-title]

DESCRIPTION: 22.0 × 14.5 cm [dimensions from photocopy] With image on front of the church

CONTENTS: 1 'List of Auxiliary Members 1947'; ...

COPIES: *Private collection

NOTES: This copy is inscribed on the front face of the binding, 'Mrs. I. Allen.' The cookbook was produced in Lawrencetown near Bridgetown, not Lawrencetown near Halifax.

Port Wallis cook book

NS65.1 1947
Port Wallis / cook book / Published by / Choir of St. Andrew's / Anglican Church / Port Wallis / 1947

DESCRIPTION: 21.5 × 14.5 cm Pp [1–4] 5–19 Paper; stapled

CONTENTS: 1 tp; 2 'History of Port Wallis // Halifax County, Nova Scotia ... (Extracts from History of Dartmouth by Mrs. William Lawson)'; 3 table of contents; 4 'Recipe for a Day' [mock recipe in one verse], 'Acknowledgements,' 'Table of Measures and Weights,' 'Oven Temperatures,' and 'Animal Crackers' [poem]; 5 'Useful Suggestions'; 6–19 recipes

COPIES: *Private collection

NOTES: Mrs Lawson, extracts of whose work are reprinted in *Port Wallis Cook Book*, co-edited NS1.1 with Alice Jones. According to the 'Acknowledgements,' the choir of St Andrew's Anglican Church sponsored a baking contest in June 1946. The entries, submitted by Port Wallis ladies, were 'judged by a competent dietitian and the winners' recipes are found within the pages of this book.' The 'Useful Suggestions' include advice relevant for East Coast families; for example, 'Removing Sand from Clams' and 'When Cooking Fish.'

Tested recipes

For a list of other cookbooks by the Evangeline Chapter, see NS29.1.

NS66.1 1947
Tested recipes / compiled by members of / Evangeline Chapter / I.O.D.E. / 1947 / Halifax, N.S. / Each day for something new you're looking, / Variety's the spice of cooking – / And here's a book we hope you'll read / Nor fail to praise if it fills your need. / Guaranteed recipes, old and new, / Each name means she makes it – likes it too, / Learn to cook the newest way, / In pressure cooker, it's almost play, / Now the editor's name is, you may see, / Evangeline Chapter, I.O.D.E.

CITATIONS: Nightingale 1989

COPIES: OGU (CCC TX715.6 T458) *Private collection

NOTES: The first letter in each line of the acrostic verse together spell out 'EVANGELINE.' Opposite the title-page, the Evangeline Chapter acknowledges 'the untiring efforts of the late Mrs. T.B. Cooke which made possible the publication of this book.' Nightingale 1989 reprints a few of the recipes.

1948

Archibald, Miss Rosamond Mansfield de Wolfe (Truro, NS, 17 November 1882– 19 May 1953, Wolfville, NS)

Rosamond de Wolfe Archibald of Wolfville, an only child, was descended from the de Wolfes, one of the original 1760s settler families from New England and the family after whom the town is renamed. She earned a BA (1904) and MA (1905) from Acadia University, and a BA (1907) and MA (1909) from Smith College. The Acadia Record outlines her career, which included several years as head of the Department of English Language and Literature at the Acadia Seminary (1914–26), teaching at the Nova Scotia Summer School in Halifax (1925–50), and lecturing on 'Better English' in Canada, the United States, and England. She was the first secretary of the Wolfville Historical Society when it was formed in 1941. The Acadia Record lists three of her publications, but not Mother and the Things She Used to Make.

Annie Louise Ricker, the cookbook's illustrator, was born in Glenwood, Yarmouth County, on 9 November 1894, and died in Truro on 9 September 1942 (so says The Acadian Record, although the cookbook is copyrighted 1948). She had a BA (1931) and an MA (1932)

from Acadia University, and she was on the staff of the university's Art Department from 1934 to 1942. Gwen Hales, who signed one drawing in the cookbook, taught art at Acadia University; she died in 1979.

For information about Archibald, see Mud Creek: The Story of the Town of Wolfville, Nova Scotia, *edited by James Doyle Davison, Wolfville, NS: Wolfville Historical Society, 1985. For information about Archibald and Ricker, see Acadia University, Associated Alumni,* The Acadia Record, 1838–1953, *[4th ed.], revised and enlarged by Watson Kirkconnell, Wolfville, NS: Acadia University, 1953.*

NS67.1   copyright 1948
Mother / and the things / she used to make / by / Rosamond M. de Wolfe Archibald. / Illustrated by / Annie Louise Ricker.
DESCRIPTION: 23.5 × 15.5 cm   Pp [1–114]   Tp illus of bowl and plate, illus   Paper; punched with two holes and bound with cord
CONTENTS: 1 tp; 2 blank; 3 dedication 'To all old fashioned mothers –'; 4 blank; 5 foreword; 6 blank; 7–17 'An Old Fashioned Kingdom'; 18 blank; 19–20 blank for 'His Wooing'; 21–2 blank for 'Their Marriage'; 23–6 blank for 'Her Guests'; 27–30 blank for 'Her Gifts'; 31–2 blank for 'Their New Home'; 33–6 blank for 'Their Frolics'; 37–8 blank for 'Mother'; 39–40 blank for 'Home'; 41–4 blank for 'Babyhood Days'; 45–8 blank for 'School Days'; 49–52 blank for 'College Days'; 53–6 blank for 'Her Breads'; 57–60 blank for 'Her Buns'; 61–4 blank for 'Her Cakes // Her Christmas Cake'; 65–6 blank for 'Her Birthday Cake'; 67 'Her Wedding Cake'; 68 blank; 69–72 blank for 'Her Candy'; 73–6 blank for 'Her Doughnuts and Cookies'; 77 'Grandmother's Cookies'; 78 blank; 79–80 blank for 'Her Frostings'; 81–4 blank for 'Her Fish'; 85–8 blank for 'Her Invalid Cookery'; 89 'Her Jams and Jellies // My Mother's Strawberry Preserve'; 90–2 blank; 93–6 blank for 'Her Meats'; 97–8 blank for 'Her Pancakes'; 99–102 blank for 'Her Pickles'; 103–6 blank for 'Her Pies'; 107–10 blank for 'Her Puddings'; 111 'Aunt Jeanie's Dropped Scones'; 112 blank; 113 blank for 'Her Vegetables'
CITATIONS: 'Seeking Unique Cookbook,' *Advertiser* (Kentville, NS), 16 April 2002, p 23
COPIES: *NSHP   NSWA (HQ759 A7)
NOTES: 'Copyrighted 1948' is inscribed on the title-page, in ink; on the verso of the title-page, also in ink, is: 'Out of 100 signed copies this book is – No. 40 // Rosamond Archibald // Wolfville, N.S. August, 1948.'

'Gift book' is printed below the cover-title. The book serves as a manuscript cookbook for brides. The author comments in the foreword, 'For all lovers of old fashioned homes this book is especially designed.' The text has been handwritten, then reproduced.

The NSWA copy is numbered three of one hundred numbered and signed copies. It was donated to the university by Helen Beals, a local artist.

Cook book

NS68.1   1948
Halifax Senior Chapter / of Hadassah / Cook book / 1948 [cover-title]
DESCRIPTION: 23.0 × 15.0 cm   Pp 1–104   Paper; stapled
CONTENTS: 1 'In Appreciation' signed Betty Arron, president, Halifax Senior Chapter of Hadassah, thanking 'the committee responsible for the compiling and arranging of this book'; 2 ad; 3 'Index' [i.e., table of contents]; 4 ad; 5 'Introduction,' 'Table of Equivalents,' and 'Substitutes'; 6 ad; 7 'Balanced Meals' and 'Oven Temperatures'; 8 ad; 9–104 recipes credited with the name of the contributor and ads
COPIES: * NBSJHM
NOTES: The chapter of 'Special Festival Delicacies' has recipes for Passover Beet Preserves, Passover Orange Pudding, Passover Cookies, Apple Pudding (Passover), Matzo Kneidlech, Pesach Mandlech, Passover Squares, Pesach Orange Torte, Poppy Seed Mixture for Haman Tashen, Pesach Doughnuts, and Fluffy Kneidlech.

Delicious dishes

NS69.1   14 July 1948
Delicious / dishes / from our / kitchen to yours / 1948 / St. John's / Evening Guild / Fairview, N.S. [cover-title]
CONTENTS: 1 poem beginning, 'We may live without poetry, music and art' [from *Lucile*, Part I, Canto ii, by Owen Meredith, pseudonym of Edward Robert Bulwer-Lytton] and 'Published by the Evening Guild, St. John's Church, Fairview, N.S. July 14, 1948'; ...
COPIES: *Private collection
NOTES: The text is reproduced from typing.

Famous Yarmouth recipes

NS70.1   1948
Famous Yarmouth / recipes / compiled by / Ladies' Auxiliary / Y.M.C.A. / 1948 [cover-title]

DESCRIPTION: About 23.5 × 15.5 cm [dimensions from photocopy] Pp [1–2] 3–108 With small image on front of an open Bible; stapled
CONTENTS: 1 unattributed poem beginning, 'We may live without poetry, music and art' [from *Lucile*, Part I, Canto ii, by Owen Meredith, pseudonym of Edward Robert Bulwer-Lytton]; 2 'Contents'; 3–108 recipes credited with the name of the contributor and ads
COPIES: *Private collection

OTHER EDITIONS: 3rd ed., retitled *Bluenose Cook Book: Famous Yarmouth Recipes*, [Yarmouth, NS: nd], OONL dates the book [1960?], but a private collector reports receiving the book as a wedding present in 1958 (OONL, OTMCL, Private collection); 4th ed., [Yarmouth, NS: 1964?] (NSAS, NSH); 4th ed., [Halifax, NS:] Nimbus, [1992] (NSHP, OONL, OOSH).

Recipe book

See also NS48.1 and NS59.1 by the same chapter.

NS71.1 1948
[IODE symbol] / Louisbourg Chapter / I.O.D.E. / Sydney, N.S. / Recipe book / 1948 [cover-title]
DESCRIPTION: 23.0 × 15.0 cm Pp [1–2] 3–107 Paper; stapled
CONTENTS: 1 untitled introductory note; 2 'Index' [i.e., table of contents], 'Abbreviations,' and 'Oven Temperatures'; 3–107 recipes credited with the name of the contributor and ads
COPIES: NSSXA (MG14 122 D. 9) *OGU (CCC TX715.6 R42 1948)
NOTES: The note on p 1 says, 'All monies from the sale of this book will be devoted to the work of the Order.'

1949

Favorite recipes

NS72.1 [May 1949]
Favorite / recipes / of / Young Ladies Guild / of / Warden United Church / New Aberdeen, N.S. [cover-title]
DESCRIPTION: About 21.0 × 13.5 cm Paper, with small image on front of a boar's head on a platter
COPIES: *Private collection
NOTES: The 'Forward [*sic*]' is signed the Committee, May 1949. A 'Table of Weights and Measures' on p 10 and a 'Quantity Table' on p 11 precede the 'Table of

Contents' on p 12. The recipes, which begin on p 13, are credited with the name of the contributor. The last item listed in the 'Table of Contents' is 'Miscellaneous' on p 82. The text pages are sandwiched between pages of advertisements for local businesses. Brodie Printing Service Ltd, Glace Bay, printed the book.

The text includes several recipes by Mrs Murdock Angus (Lena) MacDonald (1903–88), the mother of the book's owner, who was a life member of the Guild, later called the United Church Women. Although not stated in the volume, the cookbook was published to help defray the cost of a new sanctuary, whose foundation stone was laid on 1 November 1947.

The Jean Rushton Auxiliary cook book of the Billtown Baptist Church

NS73.1 1949
The Jean Rushton Auxiliary / cook book / of the / Billtown Baptist Church / 1949 / Tempting – true and tried / recipes / solicited from members of the Jean Rushton Auxiliary / "Eat plenty, wisely and waste nothing." / A Recipe for a Day / [twelve-line verse beginning, 'Take a dash of water cold, ...'] / The generosity of the advertisers made the publication of this book / possible. / We trust you will all try to show your appreciation by patronizing / them in every way possible.
COPIES: Bookseller's stock *Private collection
NOTES: The volume has 44 pp. The bookseller adds the description 'compliments of Palmeters Ltd, Kentville, Nova Scotia.'

Lockeport cooking beacon

NS74.1 1949
Lockeport / cooking beacon / Compiled by / ladies of Lockeport Baptist Congregation / 1949 [cover-title]
DESCRIPTION: 19.0 × 13.5 cm Pp [3–4] 5–86 Very thin card, with image on front of church; stapled
CONTENTS: 3 'Contents' [i.e., alphabetical list of section headings]; 4 blank; 5 quotations from Ruskin and Shakespeare; 6 'Roasting Temperatures for Meats and Poultrys'; 7–65 recipes credited with the name of the contributor; 66–76 ads; 77–86 blank except for folio
COPIES: *Private collection

New Brunswick

Fricot

Mettez de l'eau dans une marmite, ajoutez trois à quatre oignons tranchés, un poulet en quartier, sel et laissez mijoter jusqu'à ce quel le poulet soit presque cuit. Ajoutez des pommes de terre tranchées. Lorsque cuites, ajoutez une pincée de sarriette; aussitôt mettez des 'dumplings' avant de servir.

Acadian recipe from NB47.1, *The New Brunswick Cook Book* by Aida Boyer McAnn, [1938], p 48

Moose Meat Pie

First make a strong beef stock; pour a glass of port wine over some thin slices of the fat off a leg of mutton; let soak some hours, then cut up your moose meat into nice sized pieces (about 2½ inches square and 1 inch thick), put the moose meat and wine-soaked fat in layers in a brown stone crock with a cover; also with it, put pieces of onions stuck with cloves between each layer; season very sparingly with pepper and salt. Pour over this the beef stock till the crock is almost full; cover tightly, and tie over it a cloth to keep in the steam. Put the crock into a pot of boiling water, and boil 1½ hours; let cool in the gravy before uncovering crock. Rub the inside of a pie dish well with a piece of garlic; put a small cup (inverted) in centre of dish to collect gravy, lay in the moose meat with a piece of fat on each piece. Take enough of the gravy from crock to fill the dish; season well with port wine, red currant jelly, and a little cayenne; cover with a rich puff paste and bake.

Also good for venison pastie.

Mrs John Robinson

NB23.1, *Fredericton Cathedral Organ Fund Cookery Book*, 1907, p 11

New Brunswick became a separate colony in 1784, when Britain divided Nova Scotia at the Chignecto Isthmus, and it joined in Confederation with Nova Scotia, Quebec, and Ontario on 1 July 1867. New Brunswick cooking has been shaped by the same pattern of immigration as in Nova Scotia: first the Acadians of French origin; the British, who arrived from the mid-eighteenth century on, bringing their varied food customs (Scottish, Irish, Welsh, and some of the regional differences within England itself); and the settlers from New England (pre–American Revolution and the Loyalists fleeing the Revolution). Fish caught off the north and east shores and in the Bay of Fundy, the products of mixed farming in the Fundy lowlands, potatoes grown in the Upper Saint John River Valley, wild game and fish caught in the interior, wild berries, and maple syrup from the forests are the key ingredients of New Brunswick's cuisine. The province's food traditions are powerfully evoked in *The New Brunswick Cook Book* of 1938 (NB47.1), by Aida Boyer McAnn. She brings together history and recipes in sections devoted to Acadian, Yorkshire, Loyalist, Irish, and Scottish dishes, and to all the local ingredients, even dulse.

This section records a total of sixty-nine[1] cookbooks published in New Brunswick before 1950. The several nineteenth-century cookbooks are greater in numbers and in significance than those for the same period in Nova Scotia, despite the fact that Nova Scotia's population was (and still is) larger. The first work in this section, *Secret Knowledge Disclosed* of 1871 (NB1.1), is by Richard Moore, who had moved from Ontario to the Parish of Stanley in York County. It is a compendium, 'designed for the use of every business man' and containing culinary recipes for grocers and food manufacturers, but also including some family recipes contributed, in one confirmed instance, by Margaret Moore, the author's wife. Two of Moore's other works were published outside New Brunswick, but it is interesting to note that Montreal editions of his *Artizans' Guide and Everybody's Assistant* (Q12.1, Q12.2) directed readers to order copies by writing a business of machinists in Fredericton. Other nineteenth-century New Brunswick works are important for the history of Canadian cookbook publishing: early examples of community cookbooks; Alice Clark's *Domestic Economy and Plain Sewing and Knitting* of 1889 (NB7.1), the first manual for teachers compiled by a Canadian; and Ely Tree's *The Little Helpmate* of 1894 (NB13.1), the first cookbook by a male chef or other male professional in the food-service industry.[2] Herman H. Pitts of Fredericton printed an early New Brunswick cookbook in about 1880, *Canadian Family Cook Book* (NB3.1), but the most prolific publisher in the last two decades of the nineteenth century was R.A.H. Morrow of Saint John. He published three editions of *The Home Cook Book*, Canada's first community cookbook, in the years 1878–9 (O20.5, O20.6, O20.8), *Morrow's Practical Guide to Housekeeping in All Its Departments* in 1882 (NB5.1), two editions of *Breakfast, Dinner and Supper* (O81.4, O81.5) by the American Maud Cooke, the first in about 1897; and *The New Household Manual and Ladies' Companion* (NB17.1) in 1901 (purportedly by the same author as *Morrow's Practical Guide*). In addition to Maud Cooke's work, there were several other New Brunswick reprints of foreign culinary texts before 1900. Except for the Englishwoman Mary Jewry's *Warne's Cookery Book for the Million* (O21.2) issued by H.L. Spencer Medical Warehouse in Saint John, in the 1870s, they were all American: *The Successful Housekeeper* (NB4.1) and *The Queen of the Household* (NB9.1) attributed to one or both of the Ellsworth husband-and-wife team and issued in 1882 and 1890 by the Earle Publishing House in Saint John, and in the period 1882–99, the St Croix Soap Manufacturing Co. in St Stephen offered as advertising premiums American cookbooks by Mrs Jennie Taylor, Mrs Jane Warren, and Marion Harland (NB6.1, NB10.1, NB15.1). The same soap company also distributed an edition of a Toronto cookbook (O35.7).

Only a small number of advertising cookbooks surfaced for the first fifty years of the twentieth century, a reflection of the province's small industrial base (excepting the growth of pulp and paper in the 1930s; New Brunswick's food-processing industry, especially frozen food, developed mostly after 1950). In the first decade, the series of almanac cookbooks from the Saint John druggist E. Clinton Brown (NB22.1, NB24.1, NB25.1, NB27.1) are likely reprints of American text, although *20th Century Cook Book* (NB21.1, and an earlier version, NB16.1) from W.F. Hatheway Co. Ltd, the Saint John seller of Tiger Tea, Jewel Wheat Meal, and other goods, may contain recipes from local residents. The proprietor of Sackville's *Tribune* newspaper surely hoped that *The Tribune Cook Book* (NB28.1) of 1912 would boost the profile of his business. When the biscuit-maker J.A. Marven opened a new and larger factory in Moncton, he celebrated by publishing the 1917 *White Lily Brand Cook Book* (NB30.1). The processing plant for Atlantic Sugar Refineries Ltd, established in 1912, was in Saint John, but the directors were mainly Montreal businessmen and the company's two 1918 booklets – *The Lantic Sugar Recipe Book*, with a charming boy-sailor on the cover, and *Luscious Lantic Recipes* (Q97.1, Q98.1) – give Montreal before Saint John in the imprint; therefore, entries for the books are located in the Quebec section. Black's Harbour, on the Bay of Fundy, is famous for its sardine industry, run by Connors Bros Ltd since 1893. For the 1925 booklet *48 Famous Sardine Meals* (NB33.1), and the 1935 version (NB42.1), the company turned to well-known Canadian and American hotel chefs, among others, to select, test, and approve the recipes for Brunswick-brand sardines. Another leading national brand that originated in New Brunswick was Red Rose Tea, first launched on the market in 1899 by Theodore H. Estabrooks of Saint John. The company's mid-1920s *Tea-Time Tasties* (NB36.1) enticed the reader with recipes bearing oriental names, such as Simla Sandwiches.

Of the total number of culinary titles published in New Brunswick before 1950, 51% are community cookbooks. The first Canadian charitable cookbook was published in Toronto in spring 1877 by the Toronto firm Belford Brothers on behalf of the Ladies Committee of the Hospital for Sick Children, but residents of Saint John, New Brunswick, were a vital part of the book's early history in two respects. Firstly, R.A.H. Morrow published two variants of *The Home*

Cook Book in the city in 1878 (O20.5, O20.6) and another in 1879 (O20.8), and he is also known to have distributed the book in the 1880s (O20.17), so the cookbook was in use in Saint John homes almost from the beginning. But of particular interest to scholars of Canadian literature is the role of George Stewart Jr in the cookbook's initial promotion. Stewart ran a drugstore in Saint John to support his family, but he made his mark as the founder of *Stewart's Literary Quarterly* and as an early champion of Canadian writers. In the fall of 1877, not long after the devastating fire of June 1877 in which his home and business had been destroyed, Belford Brothers offered him a job in Toronto, which he accepted, moving to Toronto in spring 1878 to become editor of *Rose-Belford's Canadian Monthly and National Review*. Some time around this period, whether before or after the move to Toronto is unknown, he reviewed *The Home Cook Book*, and his erudite and entertaining comments are reprinted as a 'Letter to the Publishers' in editions from 1878 to about the mid-1880s, lending *The Home Cook Book* a certain distinction it would not otherwise have had. Today, New Brunswickers retain a special connection with *The Home Cook Book* because the only known extant copy of the first edition is in Kings County Historical Museum in Hampton.

If the ladies of Saint John were familiar with *The Home Cook Book* by 1878, it may not be a coincidence that they compiled Canada's second community cookbook in the same year: the humble, 28-page *Cuisine*, published in aid of the funds of their 'benevolent institutons [*sic*]' (NB2.1). Perhaps the proceeds went to alleviate the hardships felt after the 1877 fire. Other charitable cookbooks followed: in 1892, from the ladies of the Baptist Church in Fredericton (NB11.1); in about 1893, by Mrs C.H. Martell and Miss Julia Hamm of Fairville Baptist Church (NB12.1); and in 1895, in Hillsborough, also likely for a Baptist cause (NB14.1). In the first two decades of the new century, the ladies of Fredericton Cathedral had great success with their *Fredericton Cathedral Organ Fund Cookery Book* (NB23.1), which went through three editions, each raising money for a different cause: 1907, for the organ; November 1911, for the Reconstruction Fund to repair damage caused by the lightning strike and fire the previous summer; and 1920, for the Memorial Hall building fund. When it came time to make revisions for the 1920 edition, temperance advocates in the group must have held sway because, as the foreword explains, recipes using wine were weeded out, where the wine could not be replaced with fruit syrup or fruit juice. Women from Baptist, Anglican, and Methodist churches, and from 1925 the United Church of

Canada, all published cookbooks, as did the Catholic women of St Cecilia's Sodality at St Bernard's Church in Moncton in the 1930s (NB44.1). Several New Brunswick branches of the Catholic Women's League and a few other Catholic organizations contributed recipes to *Mother's Own Cook Book* (NB37.1) of about 1930, which were printed in their original language, English or French – a rare example of French-language content in a community cookbook. Only one recipe collection surfaced by a Jewish group, the Shaarei Zedek Sisterhood of the Saint John synagogue in 1947 (NB58.1). Other institutions that produced cookbooks include, during the Second World War, Fredericton High School (NB52.1), the Ladies' Auxiliary of the Canadian Legion in Campbellton (NB53.1), and the Fort Monckton and Barrington Memorial chapters of the Imperial Order Daughters of the Empire (NB49.1, in Moncton; NB56.1, in Edmundston). From the Passamaquoddy Division of the Canadian Girl Guides came a recipe collection with the punning title *The Cooking Guide of Charlotte County* (NB59.1).

The introduction to the Nova Scotia section refers to the advent, in 1920, of a type of fund-raising cookbook particular to the Maritimes, where a publisher issued a book that was distributed on behalf of a number of different groups. In the case of *The Modern Cook Book for New Brunswick* (NB31.1), which was 'published in co-operation with the various Women's Hospital Aids of the Province of New Brunswick and L'Assomption Society of Moncton,' S.K. Smith Advertising Agency in Saint John had the responsibility of arranging the advertising and selecting and classifying the recipes. Other examples of this type are the one published for women's groups in Nova Scotia and Prince Edward Island (NS24.1), and *Royal Cook Book* (NB45.1), sold to aid hospitals in the Maritimes.

The best-known of all the New Brunswick cookbooks described in this bibliography is undoubtedly one compiled in 1942 by the Women's Institutes of Carleton County to raise money for a war project (NB51.1): *Victory Cook Book*. Its wide distribution and ensuing popularity were due largely to the forceful determination of the project's organizer (unnamed in the book itself), Laura McCain, whose sons later founded McCain Foods. Many thousands of copies were printed – 10,000 of the 1946 second edition and 20,000 of the 1949 third edition. From 1954, it was published under the imprint of G.E. Barbour Co., the Sussex food producer, and the many later editions came to be known as *Barbour's Cook Book*.

From 1943 to at least the 1960s, Saint John schoolgirls learned to cook from *Food Manual for Use in Classes of Home Economics Department* (NB54.1), prepared by teachers in the city schools. Recipes and menus tested in the Home Economics Department of Saint John's Vocational School were reproduced in a 1949–50 booklet (NB63.1). At the end of the Second World War, the Department of Agriculture published *Cook Right – Eat Right – Live Right* (NB57.1) to help British war brides adapt to cooking in their new homes in the province.

The largest resource of pre-1950 Canadian cookbooks in New Brunswick is at the Kings Landing Historical Settlement, Fredericton, which has the Ruth Spicer Cookbook Collection. Modest numbers of cookbooks may be consulted at the following institutions: Keillor House Museum, Dorchester; Legislative Library of New Brunswick, York-Sunbury Historical Society and Museum, and University of New Brunswick, in Fredericton; Moncton Museum; Mount Allison University, Sackville; and New Brunswick Museum, Saint John. For a full list of New Brunswick locations, see 'Abbreviations,' p xliii.

NOTES

1 There are sixty-three numbered entries in the New Brunswick section plus six titles with New Brunswick editions described in the sections for Ontario (O20.5, O20.6, O20.8; O21.2; O35.7; O81.4, O81.5) and Quebec (Q97.1, Q98.1). See also Mrs Anne Cobbett's *Instructions for Using Meal and Flour of Indian Corn*, 1846 (GB1.1).

2 *La cuisinière canadienne* of 1840 (Q3.1) is advertised in Montreal newspapers as 'extraites du Journal d'un ancien confiseur de Montréal,' but the thus far unidentified confiseur is not mentioned in the book and he is unlikely to have had a personal connection with its creation, if indeed he actually existed.

1871

Moore, Richard (about 25 October 1830–28 March 1883, Brooklyn, NY)

Richard Moore also wrote Q12.1, The Artizans' Guide and Everybody's Assistant, *first published in Montreal in 1872, and O23.1,* The Universal Assistant, and Complete Mechanic, *Whitby, Ontario, [copyright 1879].*

Richard married Margaret Mercer in Galt, Ontario, on 31 October 1854. In the marriage announcement (Dumfries Reformer, 1 November 1854), both are described as 'of Galt.' Richard is not in the 1851 or later Galt Censuses, but Margaret is listed in the 1851 Galt Census as born in Scotland, a Presbyterian, and twenty years of age. He may have been in the nursery business in Galt (see references in 1855 and 1856 to agreements between Richard Moore and Robert Cairns concerning Cairns's nursery, and in 1857 to the sale of the nursery to Moore, in the Dickson papers, A988.213.83/84/85 MG8 Vol. II, at OCCA). There is also an earlier reference to 'Richard Moore, yeoman' buying land from W. Dickson Jr on 26 February 1845 (Dickson papers, A988.213.189 MG8 Vol. V). One of Richard and Margaret's children was born 'near Galt' on 28 August 1856 – David Richard Moore (he later became a doctor in Stanley, New Brunswick, and was elected to the House of Assembly for York County [1886–90]; he died in 1926; see Graves papers, New Brunswick Political Biography, MG H107, p 94, NBFUA).

Two editions of The Artizans' Guide and Everybody's Assistant *(Q12.1, 1872, and Q12.2, 1873) link Moore to a manufacturing business in St Mary's, New Brunswick, a village on the north side of the Saint John River, opposite Fredericton. In the 1872 edition readers are directed to order copies of the book from Richard Moore, care of Walter McFarlane of St Mary's. McFarlane was presumably part of McFarlane, Thompson, and Anderson, the machinists from whom lists of the contents of the book could be ordered. The 1873 edition also directs orders to McFarlane, Thompson, and Anderson.*

It is not known when Richard and Margaret moved to New Brunswick or how long they stayed there, but they likely left Galt before the 1861 Census and were in New Brunswick in the 1860s, since a source of information for their son David (Graves papers, MG H107, p 94) refers to the family moving from Ontario to Cross Creek (about 4 km north of Stanley) in York County, and to David being educated at the Stanley Public School (Stanley is north of Fredericton). Richard does not appear in the 1861 Census for any part of York County, but the following family members are listed in the 1871 Census for the

parish of Stanley in York County: Richard, aged forty, a farmer; his wife Margaret, aged thirty-seven; David R., aged fourteen; Mary E., aged twelve; Isabel, aged eight; Margaret J.[or I.], aged five; and Annie, aged three (all the children are listed as born in Scotland, likely an error). In the period 1872–4, Richard was granted land in Stanley (see Grantee Name Index: New Brunswick and Nova Scotia Land Company, 1833–1918, *compiled by Don Dixon, p 16, No. 678), but he appears to have left New Brunswick for Brooklyn, New York, by 1881. In the 1881 Census for Stanley, only his son David is listed; and Richard is not listed in the 1881 Census for Fredericton. Richard's death in Brooklyn, in 1883, was reported in a Fredericton paper: 'd[ied] of pneumonia, 28th March, at his residence 363 10th St. South Brooklyn, New York, Richard Moore, age 52 years 5 mos. 3 days [i.e., born about 25 October 1830]' (in Daniel F. Johnson,* Vital Statistics from New Brunswick Newspapers, *Vol. 60, 5 April 1883, No. 321). After Richard's death, Margaret returned to live in Fredericton. She is described as a widow of Richard, living on St John Street, in McAlpine's York and Carleton Counties Directory for 1884–5.*

NB1.1   nd [1871]

Secret knowledge disclosed; / or, / a plain way to wealth. / Comprising a collection of / rare and practical receipts / and valuable tables, / designed for the use of every business man. / Revised and corrected throughout, and many new receipts added. / By Richard Moore, / Bonnie Braes, N.B. / Stereotype edition: / Printed for the proprietor. / (Copyright secured.)

DESCRIPTION: 18.0 × 10.5 cm   Pp [1–3] 4–210 [plus 4 blank leaves]   Rebound

CONTENTS: 1 tp; 2 'Preface to the British American Edition' signed R.M.; 3–mid 27 'Farmer's Department'; mid 27–top 47 'Druggists' Department'; mid 47–top 87 'Grocers' and Manufacturers' Department'; mid 87–mid 165 'Rare and Valuable Receipts and Tables for Mechanical Purposes'; mid 165–188 various tables; 189–210 'Miscellaneous Receipts'

CITATIONS: LongoneCat 99, No. 215

COPIES: United States: DLC (master microform) *FTaSU (Sci TX153 M6 1924)

NOTES: In the 'Preface,' Moore says that the purpose of the book is to provide recipes so that businessmen can make the products themselves, thereby ensuring the purity of their products and saving money. He acknowledges his 'indebtedness to several [unnamed] works published on both sides of the Atlantic, for material ...'; he expresses his gratitude to 'the vast multitudes, both in the United States and British Provinces, who patronized the former editions of these Receipts'; and he thanks 'thousands of merchants, mechanics, &c., with whom he has had intercourse during the last ten years, for that readiness to impart information, ...'

There is no printed date in the FTaSU copy; however, both that library and DLC date this edition 1871. I could identify no town in New Brunswick called Bonnie Braes, but 'N.B.' on the title-page certainly stands for the province. The FTaSU catalogue spells Bonnie as 'Bonnir'; however, Bonnie is the spelling on the title-page.

There are some culinary recipes in the 'Farmer's Department,' on pp 13–19, including one from the author's wife, Mrs Margaret Moore's Ne Plus Ultra Buckwheat Cake. Most of the culinary recipes, however, are in the 'Grocers' and Manufacturers' Department,' where they make up most of the section, beginning with Vinegar for Family Use in Three Weeks on p 47 and ending with candy recipes on pp 80–7.

LongoneCat 99, No. 215, describes a copy with 'original black cloth,' which it dates [about 1869].

AMERICAN EDITIONS: FirstSearch lists four, attributed to various authors: Burns, J.H., *Secret Knowledge Disclosed, or, a Plain Way to Wealth: Comprising a Collection of Rare and Practical Receipts and Valuable Tables, Designed for the Use of Every Business Man*, Indianapolis: Geo. H. Adams, nd; Moore, Richard, *Professor Cameron's Secret Knowledge Disclosed; or Plain Way to Wealth ...*, no place: 1871; Van Cleve, B. Frank, *Secret Knowledge Disclosed: ... Comprising a Collection of about 1900 Rare and Practical Receipts ... Combination of Prof. Cameron's English and R. Moore's American Celebrated Copyright Recipes*, Boston: H.H. and T.W. Carter, 1870; Van Cleve, B. Frank, 'Van Cleve's Receipts:' *Being Secret Knowledge Disclosed; or, a Plain Way to Wealth. Comprising a Collection of about 1900 Rare and Practical English and American Receipts and Valuable Tables, Designed for the Use of Every Mechanic and Business Man*, Philadelphia: Inquirer Book and Job Printing Office, 1873 (United States: DLC).

1878

Cuisine

NB2.1   1878
Cuisine; / a compilation of / valuable recipes / known to be reliable. / Published by ladies of St. John, in aid of the funds / of our benevolent institutons [sic]. / "To be good, be useful; to be useful, / Always be making something good." / St. John, N.B.: / Printed at the Christian Visitor Office. / 1878.

DESCRIPTION: 21.5 × 14.0 cm   Pp [1–3] 4–28, [i–iv] Paper; sewn

CONTENTS: 1 tp; 2 untitled introductory text; 3–7 'Breakfast and Tea'; 8–13 'Pies and Puddings'; 14–20 'Cake'; 21–4 'Fancy Dishes'; 25–8 'Miscellaneous'; i–iv ads

CITATIONS: Driver 2002, Home Cook Book, p xix Driver 2003, 'Canadian Cookbooks,' p 30

COPIES: CIHM (95362)   *NBFL (pamphlet file)

NOTES: See pl 22. In June 1877 almost a third of the city of Saint John was destroyed by fire. This book must have helped to replace family recipe collections lost in the conflagration, in addition to raising funds for the city's benevolent institutions, which are not named specifically. This is Canada's second charitable cookbook. The first, O20.1, *The Home Cook Book*, had been published in Toronto the year before, in 1877; two variants of *The Home Cook Book* were published in Saint John, in the same year as *Cuisine*.

The introductory text is the same as noted for NB11.1, *Good Home Cookery*, published in Fredericton in 1892. There are two blank leaves, not included in the pagination, between pp 8–9, 16–17, and 24–5.

The home cook book

For editions of The Home Cook Book *published in Saint John in 1878 and 1879, see O20.5, O20.6, and O20.8. A Toronto edition, O20.17, was distributed in Saint John in the 1880s.*

1870s

Jewry, Mary

For an edition of Warne's Cookery Book for the Million *by the British author Mary Jewry, published in Saint John, see O21.2.*

1880

Canadian family cook book

NB3.1   nd [about 1880]
Canadian / family / cook book. / This book contains all the latest, best, and most reliable / receipts of the day. / Fredericton, N.B.: / Press of Herman H. Pitts, Queen Street.

DESCRIPTION: 17.5 × 12.0 cm   Pp [1–3] 4–56, [i–ii]
Limp oil cloth; sewn

CONTENTS: 1 tp; 2 blank; 3–15 'Cake'; 16–24
'Puddings'; 25–32 'Pies'; 33–9 'Soups'; 40–52 'Miscellaneous'; 53–6 'Food for Invalids'; i ad for McMurray
and Burkhardt, photographers, and ad for D. Mc-
Catherine, Phoenix Square, Fredericton, seller of sewing machines; ii ad for M.S. Hall, bookseller and
stationer

COPIES: *NBDKH

NOTES: The advertisement for McMurray and
Burkhardt, photographers, is a clue to the date of
publication. *McAlpine and Co's Fredericton and York
County Directory* for 1877–8 lists James F. McMurray
as a photographer and picture framer, but there is no
listing for Burkhardt or for the cookbook's printer,
H.H. Pitts. *McAlpine's Maritime Provinces Business Directory* for 1880–1 lists McMurray and Burkhardt photographers on Queen (Fredericton section, p 336) and
H.H. Pitts, printer and bookbinder, on Queen (p 337).
Since this is the only directory found where McMurray
and Burkhardt are listed as together in the photography business and it is the earliest identified listing for
H.H. Pitts, the cookbook was likely published about
1880 and certainly no earlier than 1878 or later than
1883. (*McAlpine's York and Carleton Counties Directory*
for 1884–5 lists James F. McMurray as of McMurray
and Co., books, stationery, pianos, and organs, but
there is no listing for Burkhardt. *Gatchell's Pocket Directory* of 1886 lists George A. Burkhardt as a photographer on his own, and J.F. McMurray still under the
business name of McMurray and Co. Later directories
continue to list Burkhardt as a photographer on his
own, and McMurray as a bookseller.) Herman Henry
Pitts was born in 1858, so he was a young man, not
long in business, when he printed the cookbook.

1882

Ellsworth, Milon W., and/or Mrs Mary Wolcott Janvrin Ellsworth (1830–70)

DLC records the author of the 1882 American edition of
The Successful Housekeeper *as Milon W. Ellsworth,
i.e., the publisher; Bitting, p 143, gives co-authors: Milon
W. Ellsworth and his wife Tinnie; the title-page of NB9.1,*
The Queen of the Household, *states that Mrs M.W.
Ellsworth is the author of* The Successful Housekeeper.
Also by husband and wife (according to Bitting) are: Our
Society Cook Book, *Harrisburg: Pennsylvania Publishing Co., 1888 (United States: DLC); the American
edition of NB9.1, 1889; and* The Home Economist,
Detroit: F.B. Dickerson Co., 1895 (United States: DLC).

NB4.1   [copyright 1882]
The / successful / housekeeper / [A?] / manual of
universal application, / especially adapted to the
every day wants of / American housewives; /
embracing / several thousand thoroughly tested
and approved recipes, care / and culture of children,
birds, and house plants; flower / and window
gardening, etc.; with many valuable / hints on home
decoration. / The Earle Publishing House. / St.
John, N.B.

DESCRIPTION: 20.5 × 15.0 cm   Pp [leaf lacking] [i–v]
vi, 13–608   3 pls col opp pp 248, 320, and 509;
illus   Cloth

CONTENTS: i tp; ii 'Copyright by M.W. Ellsworth and
F.B. Dickerson, 1882.'; iii dedication; iv 'Illustrations'
[lists only black-and-white illus]; v–vi 'Preface'; 13–
593 text in forty-nine chapters; 594 'Glossary of Terms
Used in Cooking'; 597–608 'Contents'

CITATIONS: Golick, pp 100, 104 (note 23)

COPIES: *OTUTF (B-12 7873)

NOTES: Chapters I–XXVI are devoted to cookery. Culinary information is also in the chapters for 'Kitchen,'
'The Sick Room,' 'The Dining-Room,' and 'The Picnic.' There is an illustration for Bride's Cake on p 45,
Christmas Cake on p 50, and Wedding Cake on p 72.

The OTUTF copy has no pp 7–12 (the beginning of
the 'Bread-making' chapter) and no pp 595–6 (likely
the rest of the 'Glossary'). There may also have been a
frontispiece, now lacking. The volume is inscribed,
on the front endpaper, 'Mrs Edward Lohnes // Middle
La H[ave?] // Lunenburg [illegible],' [i.e., in Nova
Scotia].

OWWCM (640 SUL) has a copy of *The Successful
Housekeeper* that lacks its title-page and which may be
the Canadian or American edition.

AMERICAN EDITIONS: [Ellsworth, Milon W.], *The Successful Housekeeper*, Detroit: M.W. Ellsworth and Co.,
1882 (United States: DLC).

Morrow's practical guide to housekeeping in all its departments

*Perhaps the publisher R.A.H. Morrow (Ireland, 28 April
1835–) enlisted the help of his wife, Jane A. (New
Brunswick, 6 May 1838–), and daughters Grace and
Mary in the production of this cookbook. See also
NB17.1,* The New Household Manual and Ladies'
Companion, *from the same publisher and described on
its title-page as 'By the author of "Practical Guide to
Housekeeping."'*

NB5.1 1882

Morrow's / practical / guide to housekeeping / in / all its departments, / comprising a repository of / valuable information / designed to promote / domestic happiness and comfort. / St. John, N.B.: / R.A.H. Morrow. / 1882.

DESCRIPTION: 22.0 × 14.0 cm   Pp [1–6] 7–136   Paper; sewn

CONTENTS: 1 tp; 2 'Entered according to Act of Parliament of Canada, in the year 1881, by R.A.H. Morrow, in the office of the Minister of Agriculture. Printed at the Daily Telegraph Steam Job Rooms, Canterbury Street, St. John, N.B.'; 3 preface dated Saint John, New Brunswick, December 1881; 4 blank; 5 table of contents; 6–8 'Alphabetical Index' and at bottom p 8, 'Eratta' [*sic*]; 9–136 text and ads

CITATIONS: MacFarlane, p 59   Rhodenizer, p 994

COPIES: CIHM (88757)   *NBFL

NOTES: The preface states, 'This volume is designed to be a permanent hand-book of practical information for everyday use in the family ... the latest and best works on the subject have been consulted, and in some cases freely used.' Some of the recipes were also furnished by the ladies of Saint John, according to the preface.

For culinary information, see: 'Art of Good Cooking,' pp 82–4; 'Directions for Cake Making,' pp 84–6; 'Science of Bread Making,' pp 86–8; 'Details of Practical Cookery,' pp 88–120; 'Table of Weights and Measures,' p 120; and 'Rules for Marketing,' p 122. Most of the text is devoted to housekeeping, from general matters, such as 'The House: Situation, Arrangement, etc.' and 'Systematic Routine of Labor,' to the specifics of dusting, paper-hanging, carpet sweeping, fires and lights, dish-washing, decoration, and house plants, and there are sections on medicine, etiquette, and children.

Taylor, Mrs Jennie

NB6.1 [about 1882 or later]

[An edition of *The Surprise Cook Book*, St Stephen, NB: St Croix Soap Co., [about 1882 or later]]

NOTES: There is a full-page advertisement for *The Surprise Cook Book* by Jennie Taylor in an undated promotional leaflet for the St Croix Soap Manufacturing Co. of St Stephen, New Brunswick (OONL). The advertisement describes the book, part of the company's 'Surprise Series,' as 'a veritable encyclopedia, containing 1000 practical recipes,' with 185 pages and a paper cover. It would be sent on receipt of twenty-five Surprise Soap wrappers. *The Surprise Cook Book* by Jennie Taylor is an American work. No copy of the New Brunswick edition has been located, but it was published in the same year or after the 1882 American editions.

The St Croix Soap Co. published many books in the 'Surprise Series,' including editions of other cookbooks (one American, one Canadian), also under the title *The Surprise Cook Book*: NB15.3 and O35.7. All were published no later than 1912, when the St Croix Soap Manufacturing Co. amalgamated with John Taylor and Co. of Toronto, to form a new corporation called Canadian Soaps Ltd (see 'Soap Merger,' *Monetary Times* Vol. 48, No. 19 (11 May 1912), p 1939).

AMERICAN EDITIONS: *The People's Cook Book; Being a Collection of Nearly One Thousand Valuable Cooking Recipes* compiled by Mrs Jennie Taylor, New York: J.S. Ogilvie and Co., [c1882] (United States: DLC); *The Popular Cook Book; Nearly 1000 Valuable Cooking Recipes* by Jennie Taylor, Brooklyn, NY: Abraham Strauss, 1882 (Axford, p 324); possibly another edition of the same book, *Universal Cookbook*, J. Taylor, 1888 (Dickinson, p 176).

1889

Clark, Miss Margaret Alice

NB7.1 1889

Domestic economy / and / plain sewing and knitting. / A manual for teachers and housekeepers. / Compiled by / M. Alice Clark, / Instructor in the Provincial Normal School of New Brunswick. / St. John, N.B. / J. & A. McMillan, 98 Prince William Street. / 1889.

DESCRIPTION: 17.0 × 11.5 cm   Pp [1–2] 3–150   Cloth

CONTENTS: 1 tp; 2 '(Approved by the Board of Education for New Brunswick.),' letter of recommendation signed William Crockett, chief superintendent of education, and dated Fredericton, 2 July 1889, and 'Entered according to the Act of Parliament of Canada, in the year 1889, by J. & A. McMillan, in the Office of the Minister of Agriculture, at Ottawa.'; 3 preface; 4 blank; 5 table of contents; 6 blank; 7–8 'Domestic Economy. Introduction.'; 9 half-title; 10 blank; 11–40 Part I, 'Food'; 41–76 Part II, 'Clothing and Cleanliness'; 77–120 Part III, 'Health and Sickness'; 121–50 Part IV, 'Plain Needlework'

CITATIONS: Driver 2005, p 410   Rhodenizer, p 994

COPIES: CIHM (95244)   *OONL (TX145 C53 1889)

NOTES: The series name, 'New Brunswick School Series,' is on the binding. The preface explains that the subjects of Domestic Economy, Plain Sewing, and Knitting have been added to the syllabus of examination for female candidates for school licence, by a recent regulation of the Board of Education. It adds that this manual 'is compiled largely from an excellent work included in the Royal School Series of T. Nelson & Sons, entitled Domestic Economy: A Class Book for Girls' (Attar 61.1 records the 1877 new edition of this British textbook). 'Advice and assistance in preparing the book' were received from Clark's colleague, Mr H.C. Creed (Herbert Clifford Creed, on staff at the Normal School since 1874; see Morgan, pp 223–4). The manuscript was 'examined and approved' by Lady Tilley (wife of Sir Leonard Tilley, New Brunswick's lieutenant-governor at the time).

The 'Introduction' sets down the purpose and importance of the study of domestic economy, and why 'this science ... belongs specially to the education of girls.' The following sections are in Part I, 'Food': 'What Food Has to Do'; 'The Sources of Food'; 'The Selection of Food'; 'The Preparation of Food'; and 'Hints and Helps.' Part III includes a section on 'Nourishment of the Sick.'

MacFarlane, p 20, does not record the 1889 edition, but cites St John: J. and A. McMillan, 1890. I have not located a copy dated 1890.

1890

[Title unknown]

NB8.1   [about 1890]
[Title-page lacking?; running head: 'Modern Recipes']
DESCRIPTION: 22.0 × 14.5 cm   Pp [leaf lacking] 3–92 [93–4, corner with folio torn off] [leaf lacking]   Lacks binding
CONTENTS: 3–80 ads on rectos, recipes on versos; 81–mid 92 ads on rectos, 'Household Hints' on versos; mid–bottom 92 'When and What to Eat'; 93 ad; top 94 index to recipes from 'Puddings' to 'Vegetables'; mid–bottom 94 'Index to Advertisers'
COPIES: *NBFKL (Ruth Spicer Cookbook Collection)
NOTES: The 'Index to Advertisers' cites an advertisement for Henri Jonas and Co. on p 1, which indicates that the NBFKL copy is lacking the initial leaf; a note on p 94 refers to 'Index to Recipes, page 96,' evidence that the copy also lacks a final leaf.

Advertisements are mainly for businesses in New Brunswick towns (Carleton, Saint John, Moncton, Fredericton, and Sussex), but there are also advertisements for businesses in Montreal and Halifax.

The advertisements date the book about 1890: e.g., an advertisement on p 47 for Progress, a Saint John periodical, 'Average circulation for the six months ending October 18th, 1890, 8,835'; another on p 73 for G.W. Schleyer, artist photographer with 'Diploma and Honorable Mention for First-Class Work, at Saint John Exhibition, 1890'; and one on p 89 for 'Davis' Patent Folding Umbrella Stand, patented August 25th, 1890.'

The running head on the recipe pages is 'Modern Recipes –' followed by the section heading.

Ellsworth, Mary Wolcott Janvrin (1830–70)

Concerning Mary Ellsworth and her husband Milon W. Ellsworth, see NB4.1.

NB9.1   1890
The / queen / of the / household / A guide / to the accomplishment of the home work in all its various / departments, and the supplying of the home / wants of the families of our land. / Thoroughly practical, rigidly economical, / and in every way reliable. / Compiled by / Mrs. M.W. Ellsworth, / author of / The Successful Housekeeper. / St. John, N.B. / The Earle Publishing House. / 1890.
DESCRIPTION: Frontis of 'A happy home' [scene of a mother and children], illus
CONTENTS: Tp verso 'Copyright, 1889, by Ellsworth & Brey.'; next recto page 'Publishers' Preface'; next verso page 'Preface' signed Mrs M.W. Ellsworth, Detroit, Michigan, 1 May 1889; next recto page 'List of Illustrations'; ...; 717–37 'Index'
COPIES: *Private collection
NOTES: The title suggests a work about the household generally, but the text is mainly recipes. The 'Publishers' Preface' refers to 'our first venture [i.e., in 1882] in this line of publication in The Successful Housekeeper ... Nearly one hundred thousand copies have been sold ...' The reference must be to sales of the American edition, since only one copy of the Canadian edition has surfaced. The owner of the copy described here reports that it was 'given to [her] grandmother as a bride.'

AMERICAN EDITIONS: Detroit: Ellsworth and Brey, 1889 (United States: DLC).

1891

Warren, Mrs Jane

Also by Warren is B1.1, The Handy Reliable Cook Book.

NB10.1 [copyright 1891]
The / ladies' own home cook book / A / practical and economical guide to cook- / ing, canning, curing and / preserving, / including also / a chapter on confectionery, showing how to / make all kinds of candies, ice cream, / etc., etc. / By / Mrs. Jane Warren. / The St. Croix Soap Manufacturing Co. / St. Stephen, N.B.
DESCRIPTION: Pp [i–ii], [1–5] 6–120, ...
CONTENTS: i tp; ii 'Copyright, 1891, by Hurst & Company.'; 1 'Preface'; 2 blank; 3 'Contents'; 4 blank; 5–114 recipes; 115–20 'Index' [for the first section]; 3–208 'The Household'
COPIES: *Private collection
NOTES: The 'Preface' says that the majority of the cake and pudding recipes are 'made by cup measure, to avoid the trouble of weighing.' The text is in two sections, each with a separate run of page numbers. The first section has a 'Contents' page listing fifteen parts, the last called 'Miscellaneous' and starting on p 106. The second section, called 'The Household,' has no table of contents or index; it is divided into 'Cooking Recipes,' 'The Home Physician,' 'The Toilet,' 'Laundry,' and 'Hints and Helps.'

AMERICAN EDITIONS: The first section of *The Ladies' Own Cook Book*, New York: Hurst and Co., copyright 1891 (OKITD; United States: DLC), may be the same as NB10.1; the pagination runs: [1–5] 6–120 (i.e., text in fifteen parts), [1–20] (i.e., 'How to Choose Meat, Fish, Poultry &c.'), [7] 8–96 (i.e., 'Canning, and Otherwise Curing and Preserving, Meats, Poultry, Game, &c., &c.'), [i–x] (blank for manuscript recipes and clippings).
   The first section of *The Economical Cook Book* (see B1.1, 'American editions') may also be the same as NB10.1.

1892

Good home cookery

NB11.1 1892
Good home cookery, / published by the / ladies' [*sic*] of the Baptist Church / in aid of their / church work. / "To be good, be useful." / Fredericton, N.B.: / "Reporter" Steam Publishing Office, York Street. / 1892.
DESCRIPTION: 21.0 × 14.0 cm   Pp [1–3] 4–58 [leaves lacking?]   Paper
CONTENTS: 1 tp; 2 untitled introductory text; 3–16 'Breakfast and Tea Dishes'; 17–29 'Soups, Meats, Fish, &c.'; 30 blank; 31–6 'Vegetebles' [*sic*]; 37–45 'Pies and Puddings'; 46 blank; 47–58 'Cake'
COPIES: NBFBA   *NBFKL (Ruth Spicer Cookbook Collection)
NOTES: The introductory text begins, 'These receipts have been contributed by housekeepers, who have used and proved them ...' (the text echoes the wording of NB2.1, *Cuisine*, published in Saint John in 1878); hints and advice follow about butter, cakes, sugar, and other matters.
   The book was published in 1892, but apparently copies remained unsold two years later. An entry for 6 February 1894 in 'Fredericton Baptist Church Record Book of the Sisters' Committee on Church Work' (at NBFBA) urges members to sell copies of the book: 'Mrs. Phillips then read a letter from the Pres. concerning the cook-books, and all the Sisters present consented to take a number & try to sell them, as the proceeds of the sales were to aid our Fund.'
   The NBFKL copy is in poor condition. The volume includes some blank leaves, not included in the pagination, but it is impossible to be sure where they fall within the run of pages because the binding is loose. The NBFBA copy was donated in the year 2000 by Mrs Lois Booker, a member the church, now called Brunswick Street United Baptist Church; she received the book as a gift from Mrs Winslow.

1893

Martell, Mrs Charles Holmes, née Annie C. MacDonnell (1853–20 July 1942, Wolfville, NS), and Miss Julia Travis Hamm (about 1863–)

Mrs Martell is a well-known figure from the early days of the Woman's Baptist Missionary Union of the Maritime Provinces (WBMU). She was elected to the Executive Committee at the first annual meeting on 24 August 1885. From 1890 to 1891 she was provincial secretary for New Brunswick; from 1892 to 1895 and 1900 to 1904, she was corresponding secretary, a position she also held from 1911 to 1915 for the UBWMU (the amalgamation of the WBMU with the Free Baptist Society). She was a frequent contributor to the Maritime Baptist *and*

Tidings, *and the author of* Historical Sketch of the United Baptist Woman's Missionary Union of the Maritime Provinces, *no place, nd [about 1920]. Her photograph is in* Tidings: The Official Organ of the U.B.W.M.U. *(Amherst, NS) Vol. 32, No. 4 (April 1925): 1 (NSWA Archives). On 13 September 1878, in Pugwash, Nova Scotia, she married Charles Holmes Martell. In the same year as their wedding, Charles graduated from Newton Theological Seminary. His pastorates were mostly in Nova Scotia (Onslow, 1878–88; Canard, 1894–1901; Great Village, 1904–5; Clements, 1906–8; Ohio, 1908–11; Little River, 1911–13;), but also in Fairville, New Brunswick, from 1888 to 1894, where Mrs Martell co-compiled the cookbook.*

After 1913 he lived in Wolfville, Nova Scotia, without a pastoral charge. The Martells had one daughter, identified in Mrs Martell's obituary as Mrs G.A. Foote of Sudbury, Ontario.

Church records show Julia Hamm – Mrs Martell's co-compiler – baptised at the Fairville Baptist Church on 19 November 1882 and dismissed from the church on 2 January 1899. She was the sixth of eleven children born to David Hamm Jr (1827–1904) and Mary Ann Hayter (died 1873), both of Grand Bay. In the 1861 Census for Westfield Parish she is listed as eight years old and born in New Brunswick (i.e., likely in 1863); in the 1881 Census for Westfield Parish, she is listed as eighteen years old; oddly, she is not listed in the 1891 Census for Westfield. Julia never married.

Information about Mrs Martell is from the following sources: Miss Mary Cramp, RETROSPECTS: A History of the Formation and Progress of the Women's Missionary Aid Societies of the Maritime Provinces, *Halifax, NS: Holloway Bros, 1892, p 33; Mrs F.H. Beals,* Mrs J.W. Manning: A Tribute, *Kentville, NS: Tidings, 1932, p 24; Mrs Martell's obituary in* The United Baptist Year Book of the Maritime Provinces of Canada 1942, *edited by L.H. Crandall, Saint John, NB: Barnes and Co. Ltd, 1942, p 177; A Catalogue of the Maritime Baptist Historical Collection in the Library of Acadia University, *Kentville, NS: Kentville Publishing Co. Ltd, 1955; Earl Chauncey Merrick,* These Impossible Women – 100 Years, *[Fredericton, NB], Brunswick Press, 1970, p 106. Her husband's obituary is in* The United Baptist Year Book of the Maritime Provinces of Canada 1927–1928; *see also his entry in Watson Kirkconnell,* The Acadia Record: 1838–1953, *4th ed., Kentville, NS: Kentville Publishing Co., 1953, p 19. Information about Julia Hamm is from Edith Rowena Nase,* Westfield: An Historical Sketch, *[Saint John, NB?], no publisher, [1925?], pp 49–51 for Hamm family; 'Membership Records of First United Baptist Church, Fairville, 6th Sept. 1881 to 6th Sept. 1946,'*

compiled by Rev. Edward M.B. Wheelock (NSWA Archives); and genealogical information provided by a Hamm family descendant.

NB12.1 nd [about 1893]
The / young housekeeper's / guide.
DESCRIPTION: Pp 5–50 Tp illus of ferns emerging from behind the rectangular frame containing the text of the title Probably lacks binding
CONTENTS: 5 tp; 6 ad for Manchester, Robertson and Allison, a Saint John dry goods store; 7–14 section I, 'Housekeeping' signed A.C. Martell [introductory text]; 15–16 ads; 17–50 sections II–VIII of recipes, and ads
CITATIONS: MacFarlane, p 95
COPIES: NBFUA (photocopy) *Private collection
NOTES: Mrs Martell begins her detailed discourse on housekeeping thus: 'In placing this book before the public we have a two-fold purpose. First, the profits from the sale are for the benefit of the Fairville Baptist Church to aid in paying a debt on the parsonage, and second, it is with a view of helping the young and inexperienced housekeeper, ... Mostly all cook books fail to meet the limited means of the so-called medium classes whose income may be from $1.50 to less than $1.00 per day – from these pages it is hoped this need may be met.' The date of publication and Julia Hamm's name do not appear in the private collector's copy, although perhaps the information was printed on the binding, which appears to be lacking; however, both are known from the entry for the book in W.G. MacFarlane's 1895 *New Brunswick Bibliography*, where he refers to 'a cook book [by Mrs C.H. Martell, formerly of Fairville, St John County] prepared in collaboration with Miss Julia Hamm and published a couple of years ago,' i.e., about 1893, two years before the publication of the bibliography. Mrs Martell's use of the first person plural ('we have a two-fold purpose') confirms the participation of another person.

The town once known as Fairville is about 15 km west of Saint John. Fairville Baptist Church, also called First United Baptist Church, was renamed Lancaster United Baptist Church after the community's incorporation as the city of Lancaster in 1953.

In 1895, about two years after *The Young Housekeeper's Guide* was published, Cooperstown Pudding, credited to Mrs C.H. Martell, was printed in NB14.1, *The Union Cook Book*, p 30. The recipe is not in *The Young Housekeeper's Guide*, so perhaps Mrs Martell submitted it directly to the compilers of *The Union Cook Book*. In 1895 Mr Martell's pastorate was in Canard, Nova Scotia, across the Bay of Fundy from Hillsborough, where *The Union Cook Book* was published.

1894

Tree, Ely M.

In the 1893–4 and 1894–5 Saint John directories, Ely M. Tree is listed as living at 226 Prince William. As steward of the Union Club, his job encompassed the following duties: '... custody of supply cellar, plate, cutlery, china, glass, linen, and all furniture and provisions of the club ... general control and superintendence of the Cook and men and women servants, ... charge of all wines and liquors ... account daily to the Secretary for all receipts of moneys, prepare bills of fare, ... good order of the house generally ... cater for the club, ... add up and receive from members the amount of their bills for meals' ('House Rules: Steward' in Constitution of the Union Club, St. John, N.B. with List of Officers for 1893–94 and List of Members, pp 23–4; copy in club archives). The Union Club was formed in 1890 by the joining of two Saint John's businessmen's clubs. Since that time the club has been located in the same building, at 123 Germain Street.

NB13.1 1894

The little helpmate / or / how to keep husbands at home. / A dictionary of useful inform- / ation not generally known ... / what dishes are good as well as / cheap ... the cost, and how it / is done by professional cooks / together with several valuable / household recipes, including the / wonderful / carpet shampoo / which is alone worth many times the price. / By / E.M. Tree / Late Steward St. James's Club, Montreal. Late Manager Montreal Cafe Company. / Steward Union Club, Saint John, N.B. Author of "Seasonable Recipes." / Saint John, N.B. / Ellis, Robertson and Company / "Globe" Press.

DESCRIPTION: 14.5 × 11.5 cm   Pp [1–8] 9–52, [i–iv] Paper, with image on front, in 3.5-cm-diameter circle, of a winged chef stirring the contents of a heart-shaped receptacle; stapled

CONTENTS: 1 tp; 2 blank; 3 'Entered according to Act of the Parliament of Canada in the year 1894, by E.M. Tree, in the office of the Minister of Agriculture, at Ottawa.'; 4 blank; 5 preface signed E.M.T.; 6–7 'Introductory'; 8 blank; 9–52 entries for recipes and advice arranged alphabetically from 'Anchovy' to 'Vermin, to Clear a House of'; i–iv testimonials

CITATIONS: MacFarlane, p 79

COPIES: CIHM (35507)   ECO   *NBSM

NOTES: In the preface Tree gives the objects of the book: 'to help make the home cooking equal to the club or high class restaurant, treating only on such things as our patrons tell us they "cannot get the same at home"' and to tell 'how to live well at small cost.' As the 'Introductory' states, '... the art of cooking, as it is now practiced [sic] in the best hotels, restaurants, and clubs, has reached such a stage of perfection that the majority of men ... prefer to dine at their club or restaurant rather than at home.'

'Seasonable Recipes,' cited on the title-page, was apparently a column (not a book), according to a testimonial on p [i].

The title-page touts 'the wonderful carpet shampoo.' Pages 28–34 are devoted to the shampoo, whose use avoided the usual carpet-cleaning method of lifting and beating. According to p 29, 'Carpet Shampoo was invented by the writer, and introduced to the St. John public in the spring of 1893, but is now for the first time made public property in the following pages.' The ingredients were 7 gallons water, 2 pounds good common soap, and 1 pound borax.

1895

The union cook book

NB14.1 1895

The / union cook book, / a / collection of valuable receipts. / We may live without poetry, music and art; / We may live without conscience and live without heart; / We may live without friends; we may live without books; / But civilized man cannot live without cooks. / – Bulwer. / Hillsborough, N.B., / Albert Star Publishing Co., / 1895.

DESCRIPTION: 22.0 × 15.0 cm   Pp [1–3] 4–48   Paper, with ads on front and back

CONTENTS: 1 tp; 2 blank; 3–4 table of contents; 5–6 'Preface'; 7–8 ads; 9–48 recipes and ads

COPIES: CIHM (95363)   NBFKL (Ruth Spicer Cookbook Collection)   *NBFL

NOTES: The 'Preface' defends the size of the book: '... we have given only tried receipts. The ordinary cook book of three or four hundred pages contains everybody's way of doing everything, and therefore can only be used with any degree of success by the initiated.'

No organizing group is identified; however, it was likely a community cookbook for a Baptist cause since several (although not the majority) of the recipes are credited and two of the contributors can be identified as Baptist. Perhaps the cookbook was a fund-raiser in connection with the United Baptist Woman's Missionary Union of the Maritime Provinces. The following names are attached to the recipes: Mrs C.J. Osman [wife of Chas J. Osman, sec[retary] A.M. Co.,

Hillsborough], Miss Blair, Mrs Howard Scott [possibly the wife of Howard D. Scott, street commissioner, Moncton], Mrs I.B. Colwell [wife of Rev. I.B. Colwell, Baptist, Riverside], Mrs E. Hickson, Mrs Kilbum [*sic*; possibly Mrs Ivory Kilburn, the only Kilburn listed for Albert County in *McAlpine's New Brunswick Directory for 1896*], Mrs C.H. Martell (wife of a Baptist minister; see NB12.1), Mrs James Scott [wife of an engineer in Hillsborough], and Mrs J.A.B. There is one advertisement in the book for Union Blend Tea, after which the cookbook could have been named, but this seems unlikely, since there are also advertisements for many other businesses.

Ruth Spicer's copy has pp 5–44 only.

1897

Cooke, Maud C.

Editions of this American author's Breakfast, Dinner and Supper *were published in Ontario. Two editions were also published in Saint John by R.A.H. Morrow: O81.4 and O81.5, the latter retitled* Twentieth Century Cook Book.

1899

Harland, Marion [pseudonym of] Mrs Mary Virginia Terhune, née Hawes (Amelia County, Va, 21 December 1830–3 June 1922, New York City)

For information about this American author and her other cookbooks, see O18.1.

NB15.1   1899 [copyright 1894]
The / premium cook book / to which is added / the preparations of foods for / infants / by / Marion Harland / New York / Prudential Book Company / 1899
DESCRIPTION: With image on front of a male and female cook working at a kitchen table
COPIES: *NBDKH
NOTES: The cover-title, parts of which are lacking in the NBDKH copy, reads, 'M[arion] Harl[and's] Cook Book // Made expressly for the St. Croix Soap M'f'g Co. St. Stephen, N.B.' NBDKH reports that this edition was copyrighted by the Home Book Co. in 1894.

The St Croix Soap Manufacturing Co. was established in St Stephen by Ganong Bros and Pickard; the factory was built in 1879 (see the introduction to NB15.4).

NB15.2   [copyright 1894]
—The / premium cook book / to which is added / the preparations of foods for / infants / by / Marion Harland / The St. Croix Soap Manufacturing Co. / St. Stephen, N.B.
DESCRIPTION: 15.5 × 11.0 cm   Pp [1–2] 3–224   Paper, with image on front of a male and female cook in a kitchen
CONTENTS: 1 tp; 2 'Copyrighted, 1894, by Home Book Company'; 3–224 recipes
COPIES: CIHM (95411)   *OGU (UA s043 b31)
NOTES: The cover-title is 'Marion Harland's Cook Book // Made expressly for the St. Croix Soap M'f'g Co., St. Stephen, N.B.' Unlike NB15.1, which has a New York imprint, here the title-page has been customized for the St Croix Soap Manufacturing Co.

NB15.3   [copyright 1894]
—The / Surprise cook book / to which is added / the preparation of foods for / infants / by / Marion Harland / The / St. Croix Soap Manufacturing Co. / manufacturers of "Surprise" Soap / St. Stephen, N.B.
DESCRIPTION: 14.0 × 9.5 cm   Pp [i–iii] iv–xxviii, 3–210 [leaves lacking]   Lacks paper binding
CONTENTS: i tp; ii 'Copyrighted, 1894, by Home Book Company'; iii–xxviii 'Index' [i.e., table of contents]; 3–210 recipes
COPIES: CIHM (95366)   *NBSAM
NOTES: The last page cited in the index is p 277; therefore, the NBSAM copy lacks pp 211–77 or more.

The St Croix Soap Co. published editions of other cookbooks (one American, one Canadian), also under the title *The Surprise Cook Book:* see NB6.1 and O35.7. All were published no later than 1912, when the St Croix Soap Manufacturing Co. amalgamated with John Taylor and Co. of Toronto, to form a new corporation called Canadian Soaps Ltd.

NB15.4   reprint, [copyright 1990]
—The premium cook book / by / Marion Harland / Originally published in 1894 by the / St. Croix Soap Manufacturing Company / ANE Heritage Reprint
DESCRIPTION: 15.0 × 11.0 cm   Pp [i–ii] iii–vi [vii–viii], [1–2] 3–224   Paper, with image on front of St Croix Soap Manufacturing Co., St Stephen
CONTENTS: i tp; ii 'Copyright © 1990 Atlantic–New England Heritage Committee ... ISBN 0-9694769-0-6'; iii–vii introduction signed Philip F. Christie; viii blank; 1 tp: 'The / premium cook book / to which is added / the preparations of foods for / infants / by / Marion Harland / The St. Croix Soap Manufacturing Co / St. Stephen, N.B.'; 2 'Copyrighted, 1894, by Home Book Company'; 3–224 recipes

COPIES: NBFL   *NBFU

NOTES: This facsimile was a fund-raiser for the Atlantic–New England Heritage Committee. The earliest St Croix edition was 1899, not 1894 as stated on the facsimile's title-page.

AMERICAN EDITIONS: *The Premium Cook Books*, New York: American Technical Book Co., 1894 (United States: DLC); *The Premium Cook Book ... In two volumes – Vol. I*, New York: Prudential Book Co., 1899 [copyright 1894 by Home Book Co.] (United States: InU); *The Premium Cook Book to Which Is Added the Preparation of Foods for Infants ... In two volumes – Vol. II*, on cover: 'No. 23 Wakefield series. Part 2 // Marion Harland's Cook Book,' New York: Prudential Book Co., nd (OKITD).

1899–1912

Clarke, Mrs Anne

See O35.7, The 'Surprise' Cook Book, *for a revised and retitled edition of* Mrs Clarke's Cookery Book *'made specially for' the St Croix Soap Manufacturing Co. in St Stephen.*

1900

[Title unknown]

NB16.1   [about 1900]
[Title unknown of a book published in Saint John, New Brunswick, and related to NB21.1, *20th Century Cook Book*]
DESCRIPTION: 22.0 × 14.5 cm [dimensions from photocopy] Pp [first page unnumbered]–74 Lacks paper binding; stapled
CONTENTS: [First page] ad for Pratt's Astral Oil sold by Eastern Oil Co., Saint John, New Brunswick, and ad for Higgins' British Liniment sold by Canadian Drug Co. Ltd, Saint John; ...; 28 ad for Sunlight Soap that has the maker's Royal Warrant as soap manufacturers to Her Majesty Queen Victoria; 29 recipes (section of 'Pies and Puddings' starts at bottom 2nd column) and running head, '"Mandarin" Air-Tight Packets Have Full Strength.'; 30 ad for Crown Brand Extracts made by Robert Greig and Co., Montreal; 31 recipes credited with initials of contributor, and running head, 'If Its [*sic*] Tea and Its [*sic*] Good, It's "Eagle."'; ...; 74 under the heading 'Index': 'Illustrations' and 'General,' and at bottom of page, ad for Visible Writing Machines, i.e., a make of typewriter sold by W.H. Underhill, Saint John

COPIES: *Private collection

NOTES: Information about this book is gleaned from photocopies of the first page, and pp 28–9, 30–1, and 74 (last page). The recipes appear to be from local contributors; for example, the recipe for Apple Pie from Mrs A.D. (p 29, continued on p 31) advises that the best apples are Gravenstein or New Brunswick apples.

A comparison of p 74 with the corresponding index page (p 3) in NB21.1, *20th Century Cook Book*, shows that the texts are related. Under 'Illustrations,' both books list four illustrations of cuts of meat, although on different pages (here, that for Beef is on p 11, Mutton is on p 19, Pork is on p 23, and Veal is on p 15). Under the 'General' index, the headings are mostly the same, although there are occasional minor revisions; for example, here the list reads, '... Lard, to Make 58 // Lime Water 58 // Liver 25,' whereas *20th Century Cook Book* reads, 'Lard, to Make 23 // Lime Water 21 // Liver, Meat Balls, etc. 55.' This book specifies Golden Eagle Flour in the recipes; on the binding of *20th Century Cook Book* there is an illustration that includes a barrel of Golden Eagle Hungarian Patent Flour. This book was likely published not long before Queen Victoria's death in 1901; *20th Century Cook Book* is dated 1905–6, just a few years later, and has more pages.

1901

The new household manual and ladies' companion

NB17.1   [1901]
The new / household manual / and / ladies' companion, / embracing / a repository of valuable recipes, / and other practical information covering the / whole field of domestic life; / also, including / the essential principles of hygienic and scientific cookery, / chemistry of the different animal and vegetable foods / in general use, chemical elements of the human body and / the nature and quantity of food required for its complete / nourishment; together with the causes of fermentation in the / process of light bread-making, &c., the whole forming a / complete directory in every department of household affairs. / By the author of "Practical Guide to Housekeeping," [i.e., NB5.1] / "The Home Circle, [*sic*, no closing quotation marks] &c. / Saint John, N.B.: / R.A.H. Morrow, / 59 Garden Street.
DESCRIPTION: 22.0 × 14.5 cm   Pp [i–ii], [1–5] 6–160 Double-sided frontis: on recto, 'A rural cottage ... on the western bank of the St. John River, at "Beulah

Camp" Grounds, 20 miles from St. John city.'; on verso, 'An ideal home ...' Thin, paper-covered boards, with image on front of a woman standing beside a table; stapled

CONTENTS: i blank; ii 'Publisher's Notice' signed R.A.H. Morrow; 1 tp; 2 errata, for pp 78 and 83, 'Entered according to Act of Parliament of Canada, in the year 1901, by R.A.H. Morrow, in the office of the Minister of Agriculture, at Ottawa. Printed by James Seaton, 85 Germain Street, St. John, N.B.'; 3 'Preface' dated Saint John, New Brunswick, October 1901; 4 table of contents; 5–8 index; 9–160 text

CITATIONS: Ferguson/Fraser, p 232, illus col on p 11 of closed volume   O'Neill (unpublished)

COPIES: NBS   *OGU (2 copies: UA s045 b35, UA s050 b02); Great Britain: LB (07945.h.52 destroyed)

NOTES: The 'Publisher's Notice' says of the distribution strategy for the book: 'In order that it may have general circulation we have decided to sell it through agents, who are expected to visit every home in their allotted districts, ... It will not be for sale in any book store, and when it cannot be had from an agent we will send a copy by mail to any address, postpaid, for 50 cents.'

In addition to cooking information and recipes, there are dissertations on a variety of other subjects related to home life; for example, aspects of housework (cleaning, lighting lamps, making fires), 'How to Promote Health and Prevent Disease,' 'Family Medicine Chest,' 'The Family Tool Chest,' 'Best Mode of Marketing,' 'Directions for Dry Goods Shopping,' 'Home Amusements,' 'Care and Management of Children,' 'Forbearance at Home,' 'Literature in the Family,' 'Punctuality in the Household,' 'Family Etiquette,' 'Sobriety in the Household,' 'The Family Altar,' 'Family Bereavements,' 'How to Beautify Home,' and 'Cultivation of House Plants.' In 'Review of the Home Institution,' pp 9–13, the author sets out the Christian context for domestic life: 'The household is the most important association on earth; it is the germ of Society, the nursery of Church and State, the foundation of all our relationships of life, and the grand centre of all moral and physical interests.'

1902

The Rothesay cook book

NB18.1   1902

The / Rothesay / cook book / tested recipes / compiled by the / ladies of the Sewing Society / of Saint Paul's Church / Rothesay, N.B. / Saint John,

N.B. / The Saint John Globe Publishing Company Limited / 1902

DESCRIPTION: 19.0 × 12.0 cm   Pp [i–iv], [1–2], [i–iv], 3–95, [i]   Tp illus of a Christmas pudding   Cloth; stapled

CONTENTS: i–iii ads; iv blank; 3 tp; 4 blank; i–iv blank; 3–92 recipes credited with the name of the contributor, and some blank leaves not incl in pagination; 93–5 index; i ads

COPIES: NBSUH   *Private collection

NOTES: The running head is 'Tested Recipes.' Saint Paul's Church is Anglican.

1904

The home cook book

NB19.1   1904

The / home cook book / breakfast dishes, soups, / meats, cakes, etc. / St. John, N,B, [*sic*]: / December, 1904.

DESCRIPTION: 21.0 × 14.5 cm   Pp [1] 2–32   Paper

CONTENTS: 1 tp; 2–32 recipes and ads

COPIES: CIHM (9-90868)   *OONL (TX715 H75 1904)

NOTES: 'Compliments of Woman's Exchange' is stamped on the binding. There is an advertisement on p 12 for Miss Hanson's Woman's Exchange, 193 Charlotte Street, which 'supplie[d] best home cooking, also girls, cooks and housemaids.'

1905

St John initial recipe book

NB20.1   nd [about 1905]

St. John initial / recipe book / "We may live without poetry, music and art; / We may live without conscience and live / without heart; / We may live without friends; we may live / without books; / But civilized man cannot live without cooks." / – Owen Meredith. / Compiled by the / Woman's Alliance

DESCRIPTION: 16.5 × 11.5 cm   Pp [1–2] 3–24   Paper; stapled

CONTENTS: 1 tp; 2 ads; 3–24 recipes credited with the initials of the contributor

COPIES: *NBFL (pamphlet file)

NOTES: 'E.J. Armstrong, printer' [i.e., Edward J. Armstrong] is on the outside back face of the binding. The title of the book must derive from the fact that the recipe contributors are identified only by initials.

1905–6

20th century cook book

NB21.1 1905–6

1905–6. / 20th century / cook book. / Preface. / A collection of the latest and most improved / cooking recipes – practicable and workable by persons / of ordinary means and intelligence – is the object of / this book. / Great pains have been taken to be certain that in / all cases they have been tried successfully by reliable operators. / If it be a fact that the race is improved by a variety / of healthful and appetizing foods, any help toward such an end / should be welcomed, and the object of this cook will be / attained. / A nos lecteurs français. / Ce livre est un receuil de recettes pour la cuisine. Voyez les gravures / aux pages 37–43. Nous espérons que toutes ces recettes peuvent aider / Madame, quand elle assiste dans la cuisine. Notez la page 38 en français. / Ça nous plaira de recevoir vos lettres françaises et nous espérons que vous / commanderez le Tigre Thé. / Nous vous saluons sincèrement, / W.F. Hatheway Co. Ltd., / St. John, N.B. / Press of Geo. E. Day.

DESCRIPTION: 22.5 × 15.0 cm   Pp [1] 2–80   Illus of cuts of meat on p 35 (mutton), p 37 (veal), p 39 (pork), p 41 (beef)   Paper, with image on front of a woman holding a sack of Gritz and, in the foreground, a barrel of Golden Eagle Hungarian Patent Flour; stapled

CONTENTS: 1 tp; 2 ad; 3 list of illustrations and index; 4 ad; 5–77 'Family Recipes to Make Cooking Easy' and ads; 78–top 79 'Sundry Recipes'; bottom 79 'Antidotes for Poisons'; 80 ad; inside back face of binding 'Recipes for Candies'

COPIES: NSHMS   OGU (UA s045 b41)   *Private collection

NOTES: The running head is '20th Century Tiger Tea Cook Book.' The advertisement on p 4 says that Tiger Teas are sold by W.F. Hatheway Co. Ltd, Saint John, New Brunswick. Many of the advertisements in the book are for products available at Hatheway's; for example, Gritz, Jewel Wheat Meal, and Tiger Tea. An advertisement on p 44 for St John Business College, which refers to the college as established in 1867 and now thirty-eight years old, confirms the publication date of 1905–6.

Of the five copies that I have seen (three in private collections, two in public collections), all are in poor condition and only two are complete (one of these is catalogued above). The NSHMS copy lacks the binding and pp 1–4 and 77–80. The OGU copy lacks the binding and pp 1–2 and 79–80.

20th Century Cook Book is related to a slightly earlier text, NB16.1. For a discussion of the links between the two books, see that entry.

1906

Brown's New Brunswick almanac and cook book 1906

For later issues of Brown's almanac cookbooks (1908, 1909, and 1911), each with a different selection of recipes, see NB24.1, NB25.1, and NB27.1.

NB22.1 1906

Brown's New Brunswick almanac / and / cook book / 1906 1906 / Published by / E. Clinton Brown, druggist, / cor. Union and Waterloo streets, St. John, N.B. / sole agent for the Regal Remedies. [cover-title]

DESCRIPTION: 17.5 × 13.5 cm   Pp [1–3] 4–27, [i–v] Illus of astrological symbols Paper, with image on front of E. Clinton Brown's corner store; stapled, and with hole punched at top left corner, through which runs a string for hanging

CONTENTS: Inside front face of binding 'To Our Customers' signed E. Clinton Brown; 1–2 publ ads; 3–27 astronomical information, recipes, monthly calendars, 'Practical Breaks' [i.e., jokes], and publ ads; i–v publ ads

CITATIONS: Oldfield/Landon, illus col p 15

COPIES: *OTUTF (uncat patent medicine)

NOTES: The recipes begin on p 4 with Ginger Bread, Neapolitan Cake, Nut and Raisin Cake, and Plain Cake, and continue on p 5 with Sally Lunns, Spanish Bun, Jelly or Layer Cake, Scones, and Corn Muffins. The p 5 recipes (but not the p 4 recipes) match those listed for the second page of recipes in A3.1, *Geary's 1906 Central Alberta Almanac and Housewife's and Bachelor's Favorite Cook Book.*

1907

Fredericton Cathedral Organ Fund cookery book

NB23.1 1907

Fredericton / Cathedral Organ Fund / cookery book / Saint John, N.B. / J. & A. McMillan, printers / 1907

DESCRIPTION: 17.5 × 12.0 cm   Pp [1–5] 6–162   Cloth, with image on front, in a 3.5-cm circle, of a winged chef stirring the contents of a heart-shaped receptacle

CONTENTS: 1 tp; 2 blank; 3 untitled introductory text; 4 blank; 5–128 recipes credited with the name of the contributor; 129–32 'Miscellaneous' [recipes and other information credited with the name of the contributor]; 133–43 'Useful Information'; 144 blank; 145–8 'Index'; 149–62 ads

COPIES: CIHM (86599) *NBFL OGU (UA s058 b34) OTCHAR

NOTES: The cover-title is 'The Fredericton Recipe Book for Cathedral Organ Fund.' Also printed on the binding is 'Wash cover with damp cloth if soiled.'

The NBFL copy is inscribed on the recto of the leaf before p 1, in pencil, 'Mrs A. Dunn, Harcourt, NB Feby 19. 1908.'

NB23.2   2nd ed., November 1911
—Fredericton / Cathedral Organ Fund / cookery book / Second edition / containing / many additional recipes. / November, 1911.
DESCRIPTION: Tp illus of the cathedral
COPIES: *Private collection
NOTES: Although the second edition is titled after the Organ Fund (following the example of the first edition), the profits from its sale also went to another cause, as stated in the untitled introductory text: 'The proceeds of the sales of the second edition of this cookery book are to be contributed to the Restoration Fund of Christ Church Cathedral, Fredericton, which was struck by lightning and partially destroyed by fire on the night of July 3rd, 1911.' The cover-title is 'Fredericton Recipe Book // Second edition // For Cathedral Organ Fund and Restoration Fund.'

NB23.3   3rd ed., 1920
—Fredericton / Cathedral Memorial Hall / cookery book / Third edition / containing / many additional recipes / 1920
DESCRIPTION: 18.5 × 12.0 cm   Pp [1–5] 6–167, [i], [i–ii], [1] 2–6   Tp illus of the cathedral   Cloth, with image on front, in a 3.5-cm circle, of a winged chef stirring the contents of a heart-shaped receptacle
CONTENTS: 1 tp; 2 blank; 3 foreword; 4 blank; 5–167 recipes credited with the name of the contributor and ads; i ad; i part-title for index; ii blank; 1–6 index
COPIES: *NBFKL (Ruth Spicer Cookbook Collection)
NOTES: The cover-title is 'Fredericton Recipe Book.' The foreword refers to the purpose of the third edition and to its contents, which reflect a temperance sensibility: 'It is proposed and intended by the editors of this third edition, to apply the proceeds to the building fund of the Memorial Hall, ... The recipes contained in the first and second editions of this book have been again carefully revised, and only the most useful of them are reproduced herein. Some of the old recipes containing wine as an ingredient have been retained, but care has been taken to select of such recipes only those that permit of the satisfactory substitution of fruit syrups or fruit juices for the wine. Many additional recipes appear in this edition, especially recipes for canning of fruit, vegetables, fish and meats.'

1908

Brown's New Brunswick almanac and cook book 1908

For a list of Brown's other almanac cookbooks, see NB22.1.

NB24.1   1908
Brown's / New Brunswick almanac / and / cook / book / 1908 / Published by / E. Clinton Brown, druggist / cor. Union and Waterloo streets, St. John, N.B. / sole agent for the Regal Remedies [cover-title]
DESCRIPTION: 17.5 × 13.5 cm   Pp [1–3] 4–27, [i–v]   Illus of astrological symbols   Paper, with image on front of E. Clinton Brown's corner store; stapled, and with hole punched at top left corner, through which runs a string for hanging
CONTENTS: Inside front face of binding 'To Our Customers' signed E. Clinton Brown; 1 'Where Two Years Meet // A Word of Appreciation' offering Brown's best wishes for a happy and prosperous New Year; 2 publ ads; 3–27 astronomical information, recipes, monthly calendars, 'Practical Breaks' [i.e., jokes], and publ ads; i–v publ ads
COPIES: *OTUTF (uncat patent medicine)
NOTES: The recipes begin with Almond Cakes, Cream Cake, Walnut Cake, and Ribbon Cake – the same recipes as noted for O189.1, *Bogardus and Co.'s Almanac and Cook Book of Tested Recipes 1908*, and O199.1, *Robson's Calendar Cook Book 1908*.

1909

Brown's New Brunswick almanac and cook book 1909

For a list of Brown's other almanac cookbooks, see NB22.1.

NB25.1   1909
Brown's / New Brunswick / almanac and / and [*sic*] / cook / book / 1909 / Published by / E. Clinton

Brown, druggist / corner Union and Waterloo streets St. John, N.B. / sole agent for the Regal Remedies [cover-title]

DESCRIPTION: 17.0 × 13.5 cm   Pp [1–3] 4–32   Illus of astrological symbols   Paper, with image on front of E. Clinton Brown's corner store; stapled, and with hole punched at top left corner, through which runs a string for hanging

CONTENTS: Inside front face of binding 'To Our Friends' signed E. Clinton Brown; 1 publ ad; 2 'Best Wishes for 1909'; 3–27 astronomical information, recipes, monthly calendars, 'Practical Breaks' [i.e., jokes], and publ ads; 28–31 'Scrap Book' and publ ads; 32 publ ad

COPIES: *OTUTF (uncat patent medicine)

NOTES: The recipes on p 4 are Rice Griddle Cakes, Spice Cake, Raisin Puff, Shortbread, and Plum Cake; on p 6, Jellied Apples, Maple Ice Cream, Fig Cake, and Banana Cake; and on p 8, Jelly Roll, Beautiful Layer Cake, Drop Cookies, Whole Wheat Gems, and Boston Brown Bread. The same recipes appear in the following publications: NF3.1, *McMurdo's 1909 Newfoundland Almanac and Cook Book*; O215.1, *Gunn's Household Calendar Cook Book 1909*; O220.1, *Robson's Household Calendar Cook Book 1909*; A12.1, *The Taber Calendar Cook Book 1909*; B10.1, *Calendar Cook Book 1909*; and B11.1, *Campbell's Calendar Cook Book 1909.*

Tried and proved recipes

NB26.1   1909

Tried and proved / recipes / compiled by ladies / of / Exmouth Street Methodist Church, / St. John, N.B. / October, 1909. / For additional copies phone Main 2170. / Barnes & Co., Ltd., printers, St. John, N.B.

DESCRIPTION: 21.5 × 15.0 cm   Pp [1–4] 5–57, [i–vi]   Cloth; stapled

CONTENTS: 1 tp; 2 blank; 3 untitled two-verse poem; 4 blank; 5–7 'Index' [i.e., table of contents]; 8 ad; 9–57 'Recipes'; i–vi ads

COPIES: NBFKL   *OGU (UA s047 b14)

1911

Brown's New Brunswick almanac and cook book 1911

For a list of Brown's other almanac cookbooks, see NB22.1.

NB27.1   1911

Brown's / New Brunswick / almanac and / cook / book / 1911 / Published by / E. Clinton Brown – druggist / cor. Union and Waterloo streets, St. John, N.B. / sole agent for the Regal Remedies [cover-title]

DESCRIPTION: 17.5 × 13.5 cm   Pp [1–3] 4–32   Illus of astrological symbols   Paper, with image on front of E. Clinton Brown's corner store; stapled, and with hole punched at top left corner, through which runs a string for hanging

CONTENTS: Inside front face of binding 'A Valuable Daily Companion' signed E. Clinton Brown; 1 publ ad; 2 'Read This – Important'; 3–29 astronomical information, recipes, monthly calendars, and publ ads; 30 menus; 31–2 'Superstitions'

COPIES: *OTUTF (uncat patent medicine)

1912

The Tribune cook book

NB28.1   1912

The / Tribune cook book / containing a collection of / the best known cooking / recipes, compiled and edit- / ed by culinary experts / Sackville, N.B. / The Tribune Printing Company, Limited / 1912

DESCRIPTION: 22.0 × 15.0 cm   Pp [1–4] 5–78   [$0.25, on binding]   Paper; stapled

CONTENTS: 1 tp; 2 ad; 3–78 recipes and ads

COPIES: *Private collection

NOTES: The 'culinary experts' are not identified.

1916

Tested recipes

NB29.1   1916

Tested recipes / compiled by members of / De Monts Chapter / [IODE symbol] / Saint John, N.B. / The Saint John Globe Publishing Company, Limited / 1916

DESCRIPTION: 18.5 × 12.0 cm   Pp [1–3] 4–66, [i–iii], [i] ii–iii   Cloth, with IODE symbol on front

CONTENTS: 1 tp; 2 'Useful Information'; 3–66 recipes; i–iii ads; i–iii index

COPIES: *OGU (UA s048 b29)

NOTES: Although not revealed in the book, Barbara Kein Dobson, a teacher and a member of the Senate of the University of New Brunswick for many years, was one of the principal organizers of *Tested Recipes*.

Her sister, Mrs Sieniewicz, was the chair of the organizing committee of NS43.1, published by the Evangeline Chapter of the IODE in Halifax in 1934. (For this information I am grateful to Mrs Sieniewicz's daughter, Mrs Barbara Kincaide of Toronto.) Throughout the recipe pages there are leaves of advertisements not included in the pagination.

1917

The J.A. Marven Limited cook book

J.A. Marven's biscuit factory was on Main Street in Moncton until 1916, after which the plant moved to larger premises on King Street. In 1926 Marven merged his business with four other companies to form the Canada Biscuit Co., later called McCormick's, after one of the larger partners. Although Marven died in 1931, and the ownership subsequently changed, baking continued at the plant until 1978.

NB30.1 [1917]
The / J.A. Marven Limited / cook book / J.A. Marven Limited / manufacturers White Lily Brand Biscuits / Moncton: N.B. / Branches: / Halifax, / N.S. / St. John, / N.B.
DESCRIPTION: 20.5 × 12.5 cm   Pp [1–2] 3–32   Illus on p 2 of 'Our New Home' of J.A. Marven Ltd   Lacks binding
CONTENTS: 1 tp; 2 illus of the new J.A. Marven plant on King Street; 3–4 'We Welcome You to Our New Home' signed J.A. Marven, Moncton, New Brunswick, January 1917; 5–32 130 numbered recipes
COPIES: *NBMOM (2 copies)   NBSM
NOTES: Marven's introduction on pp 3–4 relates the company's history: 'Dear Madam, It is just ten years since I came to Moncton and entered into the manufacturing of biscuits, selecting for my trademark the beautiful White Lily, the emblem of Purity.' Under the White Lily Brand, Marven made 'Sodas, Fig Bars, Social Teas, Graham Wafers, White Lily Cream Bar, Arrowroot, etc.' and the recipes specify some of these products as ingredients.
  NBMOM copy 2 is bound in paper, with the image of a white lily on the front. It is stapled and there is a hole punched at the top left corner to take a string for hanging. The cover-title is 'White Lily Brand Cook Book.'

1918

Lantic Sugar recipe book

See Q97.1, published simultaneously in Montreal and Saint John.

Luscious Lantic recipes

See Q98.1.

1920

The modern cook book for New Brunswick

NB31.1   1920
The / modern cook book / for New Brunswick / containing / carefully selected recipes / recommended / for practical use in / every household / Published in co-operation with / the various Women's Hospital / Aids of the Province of New / Brunswick and L'Assomption / Society of Moncton / St. John: / J. & A. McMillan / 1920
DESCRIPTION: 22.5 × 14.5 cm   Pp 3–206   Tp illus of a man seated at table, holding a carving knife and fork   Cloth, with image on front of a woman lifting the cover of a chafing dish
CONTENTS: 3 ad; 4 blank; 5 tp; 6 'Women's Organizations Interested'; 7 'Introduction'; 8 blank; 9 'A Word as to Our Advertisers'; 10 ad; 11 table of contents; 12 'Time Tables for Cooking'; 13 weights and measures; 14–206 recipe chapters
CITATIONS: CBCat 61, No. 90   Ferguson/Fraser, p 233   Wheaton/Kelly Nos. 1043 and 4489
COPIES: CIHM (75440)   NBFKL   NBFL   NBFU (TX715 M623)   NBMOM   NBSM   NBSU (TX715 M6)   *OGU (UA s043 b39)   OOAG (641.5 M689)   OONL (TX715.6 M62 1920, 2 copies)   OTMCL (641.5 M57)   OTUTF (B-12 7857, 2 copies)   OWTU (F0221)   QMM (RBD TX715.6 M64 1920)   SSWD; United States: MCR (641.6971 M68 and uncat, and microfilm SLC 76 #580)
NOTES: 'Women's Organizations Interested' on p 6 records the organizations that distributed the book in each city: Saint John, Women's Hospital Aid; St Stephen, Ladies' Auxiliary of the GWVA [Great War Veterans Association]; Fredericton, Women's Hospital Aid; Moncton, Ladies of L'Assomption Church; and local hospitals at Bathurst, Newcastle, Chatham, and Woodstock. The 'Introduction' says that not just women were interested in contributing to the vol-

ume, but also 'Mr. Peter Clinch, of St. John, whose camp cooking is said by those who know him best to be nothing short of a delight, submits four recipes ...' S.K. Smith Advertising Agency in Saint John 'had entire charge of the arrangement of the advertising and the selection and classification of the recipes' (p 9).

Wheaton/Kelly list the book twice, No. 1043 under Canada, St John, New Brunswick, and No. 4489, incorrectly, under Nova Scotia, St John.

At about the same time as *The Modern Cook Book for New Brunswick* was published, women's groups in the other two Maritime provinces produced a cookbook on the same model: NS24.1, *The Modern Cook Book for Nova Scotia and Prince Edward Island*. About ten years later, the Catholic Women's Leagues of New Brunswick, in another co-operative effort, produced NB37.1.

NB31.2   [copyright 1980]
—The / New Brunswick / cook book / for 1920 / containing / carefully selected recipes / recommended / for practical use in / every household / Published in co-operation with / the various Women's Hospital / Aids of the Province of New / Brunswick and L'Assomption / Society of Moncton / Coles
DESCRIPTION: 21.0 × 13.5 cm   Pp [3–14] 15–190 Tp illus of a man seated at table, holding a carving knife and fork   Paper
CONTENTS: 3 tp; 4 '© copyright 1980 and published by Coles Publishing Company Limited Toronto – Canada // Printed in Canada'; 5–10 ads; 11 'Contents'; 12 'Time Tables for Cooking'; 13 'Table of Weights and Measures'; 14–190 fifteen chapters and ads
COPIES: NBFL   OONL (TX715 N45 1980)   *Private collection
NOTES: Excluded from the facsimile are 'Women's Organizations Interested' and 'A Word as to Our Advertisers' found at the beginning of the original edition, and the last few leaves, pp 191–206.

1924

Cook book

NB32.1   1924
[An edition of *Cook Book* by the World Wide Guild, Charlotte Street Baptist Church, West Saint John, New Brunswick, 1924, pp 19]

CITATIONS: FitzPatrickCat 110 (February 1993) No. 143   FitzPatrickCat 111 (April 1993) No. 25
NOTES: McAlpine's city directory for 1923–4 lists a Baptist church at 162–8 Charlotte Street, Saint John.

1925

48 famous sardine meals

For a later Connors recipe book, see NB42.1.

NB33.1   [copyright 1925]
Price / 25¢ / 48 / famous / sardine / meals [cover-title]
DESCRIPTION: 14.0 × 9.5 cm   Pp [1–15]   Paper, with image on front of a sailboat; stapled
CONTENTS: 1 cover-title; 2 'Fish Essential in Healthy Diet'; 3 'Tested and Approved' [i.e., a list of chefs and 'leaders in household science' who selected and tested the recipes] and 'Copyright, 1925, by Connors Bros. Limited'; 4–15 recipes and publ ads; outside back face of binding 'Connors Bros. Limited // Black's Harbour, N.B. Canada [company symbol] Largest packers of sardines in the British Empire'
COPIES: *MWPA (MG14 C50 McKnight, Ethel)   NBFL (pamphlet file)
NOTES: Auguste Gois, chief chef at the Windsor Hotel, Marcel Thomas, chief chef at the Mount Royal Hotel, and B.M. Philip of Macdonald College's Household Science Department, all in Montreal, are three of the several named persons who selected and tested the recipes. The text is printed in blue and orange.

NB33.2   nd
—Price / 25¢ / 48 / famous / sardine / meals [cover-title]
DESCRIPTION: About 14.0 × 9.5 cm [dimensions from photocopy]   Pp [1–15]   Paper, with image on front of a sailboat; stapled
CONTENTS: 1 cover-title; 2 'Fish Essential in Healthy Diet'; 3 'Tested and Approved' [i.e., a list of chefs and 'leaders in household science' who selected and tested the recipes]; 4–? recipes and publ ads; outside back face of binding 'Connors Bros. Limited // Black's Harbour, N.B. Canada [company symbol] Largest packers of sardines in the British Empire'
COPIES: *Private collection
NOTES: Unlike NB33.1, there is no copyright date on p 3.

Progressive Club cook book

NB34.1 1925
Progressive Club / cook book / Old Ridge /
Charlotte County, N.B. / 1925 [cover-title]
COPIES: OGU (CCC)   OONL (TX715 P7585 1925 missing)
NOTES: 'Our Debut' on p 1 is an introduction in the form of a poem, by M.A. Maxwell, in which the writer quotes the cookbook's price of $0.50 and refers to the Progressive Club '... building a hall, / Which [it hopes] to have ready for suppers by Fall.' Recipes and other text are on pp 13–53; advertisements end on p 63. The running head is 'Old Ridge Progressive Club Cook Book.' Old Ridge is in Charlotte County, about 6 km north of St Stephen.

Recipes for desserts

NB35.1 nd [about 1925]
Recipes / for / desserts / Geo. M. Fairweather, – druggist / Sussex, N.B. [cover-title]
DESCRIPTION: 16.5 × 11.5 cm   Pp 1–24   Paper; stapled
CONTENTS: 1 publ ad for Vinol; 2–18 recipes and publ ads; 19–24 publ ad
COPIES: *NBFL
NOTES: 'Sunset Soap Dyes at G.M. Fairweather // Sussex, N.B.' is stamped on the front face of the binding. See NB35.5, regarding the date of publication of the various editions.

NB35.2 nd [about 1925]
—Recipes / for / desserts / Frederic T. Hill, – druggist / New Westminster, B.C. [cover-title]
COPIES: *BDEM

NB35.3 nd [about 1925]
—Recipes / for / desserts / J.W. Crooks & Co., – druggists / Port Arthur, Ont. [cover-title]
DESCRIPTION: 16.5 × 11.5 cm   Pp 1–24   Paper; stapled
CONTENTS: 1 publ ad for Vinol; 2–18 recipes and publ ads; 19–24 publ ad
COPIES: *Private collection
NOTES: J.W. Crooks and Co. also published a 24-page, undated booklet of about the same time, called *Aunt Rebecca Says*, which has one page of culinary information (Private collection). (OONL has an edition of *Aunt Rebecca Says* published by W.J. Hughes, Carleton Place, Ontario, catalogued by the library as a trade catalogue.)

NB35.4 nd [about 1925]
—Recipes / for / desserts / P.B. Willits & Co., – druggists / Kelowna, B.C. [cover-title]
COPIES: *BVAU
NOTES: BVAU records the place of publication and publisher as Windsor, Ontario: Chester Kent and Co. Chester Kent and Co. manufactured Vinol, for which this cookbook was a promotional vehicle.

NB35.5 nd [about 1925]
—Recipes / for / desserts / Wallace's Drug Store, Limited / Napanee, Ont. [cover-title]
DESCRIPTION: 16.5 × 11.5 cm   Pp 1–24   Paper; stapled
CONTENTS: 1 publ ad for Vinol; 2–18 recipes and publ ads; 19–24 publ ads
COPIES: *ONLAM
NOTES: In a testimonial on p 5, O. Walker, College Street, Toronto, refers to himself as 'a dispenser at a soda fountain.' Toronto city directories for 1924, 1925, and 1926 list Orton Walker as a soda dispenser for Binghams Ltd (directories for 1921 and before list him as a clerk). *Recipes for Desserts*, therefore, was likely published about 1925, a date consistent with the appearance of this and other editions of the booklet.

Tea-time tasties

Theodore H. Estabrooks started an import-export company in Saint John on 1 May 1894, and soon began to specialize in tea. He registered his Red Rose trademark on 16 October 1899. His business became a limited company on 4 May 1911. In 1929, he introduced tea bags to the New Brunswick market, a revolutionary idea at the time. In 1931, Brooke, Bond and Co. Ltd acquired the company, which it later sold to Unilever. (This history is from the Red Rose web site, www.time-for-tea.com, December 2001.)

NB36.1 nd [about 1925]
Tea-time tasties / This little book is dedicated / to the enjoyment and instruction of / all lovers of good tea / "The Muses' friend, tea, doth our fancy aid, / Repress the vapours which the head invade, / And keeps the palace of the soul serene." / So wrote the poet Waller centuries / ago, and now we add dainty, tasty / trifles and things gathered from far / distances and culled from carefully / guarded recipe books in private / homes, and bearing the musical / names of the Orient, for many of / them came from Eastern lands where / afternoon tea originated. /

Printed in Canada for the / T.H. Estabrooks Co., Limited / Proprietor: Red Rose Tea and Coffee
DESCRIPTION: 15.0 × 10.0 cm   Pp [1] 2–20   Illus green Paper, with cover-title printed on a stylized sign-board; stapled
CONTENTS: 1 tp; 2–20 recipes and information about tea, and at bottom p 20, 'T.H. Estabrooks Co., Limited Head office: Saint John, N.B. Branches: Montreal; Toronto; Winnipeg; Portland, Me. // St. John's, Nfld.'
COPIES: *QMM (RBD 1540)
NOTES: The recipes have exotic names, such as Ayah Tidbits, Ranee Ribbons, Nirvana Sandwiches, Delhi Dainties, Darjeeling Delights, Celestials, Kota Rajas, and Kashmir Lilies. The text is printed in green, on purple-printed leaves. Since there is no mention of tea bags, the book was likely published before 1929, when the company introduced the new product.

1930

Mother's own cook book

NB37.1   nd [about 1930]
Mother's own / cook book / "May Providence aid the tireless cook" / Who seeing buys a mother's book, / And tries and tests its many wares, / And testing throws away her cares; / Your efforts will not be in vain / Your family will not suffer pain / And kindly ask your neighbor cook / To buy another Mother's Book. [cover-title]
DESCRIPTION: 22.5 × 15.0 cm   Pp [1–3] 4–96   Illus on p 93 of Hôtel-Dieu de l'Assomption, Moncton   Paper, with image on front of a grandmother knitting; stapled
CONTENTS: 1 'Introduction'; 2 'Index' [i.e., table of contents]; 3 'Table of Weights and Measures'; 4–96 text and ads
COPIES: *Private collection
NOTES: The 'Introduction' states: 'Recipes contained in this book have been supplied by ladies in New Brunswick ... The Catholic Women's League in Canada consists of 30,000 members nationally organized June 17, 1920.' In a box below the 'Introduction,' the following organizations are thanked for their contribution to the book: 'Branches – Catholic Women's Leagues – Campbellton – Dalhousie – Bathurst – Fredericton – Devon – Minto – Woodstock – Newcastle – Chatham and Moncton Auspices Hôtel Dieu – Grand Falls – Assumption of the B.V.M. – Dominican Fathers, Sackville – St. John's R.C. Church, Springhill.' There are recipes in French and English, organized without regard to language. 'Directions for Reducing

Diet' are on p 78, and a 'Diebetic [sic] Diet' is on p 80. Information on p 92 about Hôtel-Dieu de l'Assomption, Moncton, refers to the hospital having opened on 15 June 1928. From appearances, the cookbook was published about 1930.

1931

The guild cook book

NB38.1   1931
"We may live without poetry, music and art; / We may live without conscience, we may live without heart: / We may live without friends, we may live without books, / But civilized man cannot live without cooks." / – Lord Lytton. / The / guild / cook book / Compiled by the / ladies of All Saints' Church / East St. John, N.B. / 1931 / "Cookery is become an art, a noble science." / – Burton. / Hopkins Press Limited printers / 95–97 Prince Edward Street, Saint John, N.B.
DESCRIPTION: 20.5 × 13.0 cm   Pp [1] 2–39   Paper, with image on front of two identical trees; stapled
CONTENTS: 1 tp; 2 'Useful Table of Weights, Measures & Signs'; 3–38 recipes and ads; 39 ads
COPIES: *Private collection

1934

B.Y.P.U. cook book

NB39.1   [1934]
B.Y.P.U. [i.e., Baptist Young People's Union] / cook book / After much meditation and experience, I have / divined that it takes as much sense and refinement / and talent to cook a dinner, to wash and wipe a dish, / make a bed and dust a room, as goes to the writing of / a novel or shining in high society. / – Rose Terry Cooke / Cover design graciously contributed by / Frederick P. Kirby / student artist at Toronto University of Arts.
DESCRIPTION: 22.5 × 15.0 cm   Pp [1–3] 4–64   Photograph on p 1 of First Moncton United Baptist Church, tp illus of a turkey and a fish, illus on pp 16, 26, and 37 of roast poultry, a pie, and a cake   Thin card, with image on front of a woman carrying a cake(?) on a plate; stapled
CONTENTS: Inside front face of binding '1934 B.Y.P.U. Executive'; 1 'This Cook Book' signed Henry R. Boyer, minister, and untitled note of appreciation signed

James Davison, president [of the BYPU]; 2 ad; 3 tp; 4–mid 64 text, mostly recipes credited with the name of the contributor, and ads; mid–bottom 64 'Table of Contents'

COPIES: *Private collection

NOTES: The running head is '1934 B.Y.P.U. Cook Book' on the recto pages and 'B.Y.P.U. Cook Book 1934' on the verso pages. Boyer says on p 1, '... in buying [the book] you are assisting the B.Y.P.U. of the First Church.' This copy is inscribed by Frederick Kirby, on the title-page, in ink: 'Will this do you any good? Fred' and, beside the printed phrase 'Toronto University of Arts,' the comment, 'Heh! [The?] Ontario College of Art affiliated with Toronto "U."' Frederick Palmer Kirby (1911–99) graduated with a BA from Mount Allison University in Sackville, then studied at the Ontario College of Art in Toronto. He went on to have a successful career in Toronto in advertising and promotion. Kirby also did the cover design for NB41.1.

1935

Neverfail cook book

NB40.1 nd [about 1935]
Neverfail / cook book / The recipes in this book / were collected by the members / and leaders of the Neverfail / Mission Band of the High- / field Baptist Church, Monc- / ton. The proceeds from sale / to be used for missions. / The compilers of this cook book wish to express their apprecia- / tion for the advertising given by the various firms and request / that the users of this book read these advertisements carefully.

DESCRIPTION: 22.5 × 14.5 cm   Pp [1] 2–22   Paper; stapled, and with hole punched at top left corner for hanging

CONTENTS: 1 tp; 2 ads; 3–22 recipes and ads

COPIES: *Private collection

The pantry shelf

NB41.1 [1935]
The / pantry shelf / Compiled by / the Young People's Society / of / Wesley Memorial United Church / Moncton, N.B. / Cover design contributed / by / Frederick P. Kirby

DESCRIPTION: 22.5 × 15.0 cm   Pp [1–2] 3–102   Tp photograph of the church   Paper, with stylized

image on front of a chef with a large hat, carrying a plate; stapled, and with hole punched at top left corner for hanging

CONTENTS: 1 tp; 2 'Appreciation' signed the Committee; 3 table of contents; top 4 'Proportions'; mid 4–5 'Equivalents'; 6 'Substitutions' and 'Shortening Table'; 7–101 recipes and ads; 102 'Helpful Hints'

COPIES: *NBFL

NOTES: The year of publication, 1935, appears at the top of pp 3–102. Frederick Kirby also did the cover design for NB39.1; see that entry for information about the artist.

Recipes and premium list for Connors famous sea foods

For an earlier Connors recipe book, see NB33.1.

NB42.1 [new ed., copyright 1935]
Recipes / and / premium list / for / Connors / famous / sea foods / Connors Bros. Limited / quality canners of sea foods / Black's Harbour, N.B. Canada [cover-title]

DESCRIPTION: 16.5 × 11.0 cm   Pp [1] 2–15   Illus col of Connors products; illus on pp 8–9 (centre spread) of premiums for Connors coupons, such as scissors, brushes, table silver, playing cards, irons, and toasters   Paper, with image on front of a sailing vessel at sea, the book's title printed in the yellow sun in the sky; stapled

CONTENTS: 1 cover-title; 2 'Proved and Approved' and 'This New Edition'; 3 'There Was an Oak in That Acorn!' and 'Copyright 1935 by Connors Bros. Limited // Lithographed in Canada'; 4–7 recipes; 8–9 'Valuable Premiums for Connors Coupons'; 10–15 recipes; back face of binding 'World's Largest Sardine Plant // Connors Bros. Plant at Black's Harbour, N.B.'

COPIES: NSLQCM   *Private collection

NOTES: Under 'Proved and Approved' on p 2 there is a list of those who selected, tested, and approved the recipes. The first three persons worked in Canada; the remainder, in the United States: Auguste Gois, chief chef, Windsor Hotel, Montreal; Marcel Thomas, chief chef, Mount Royal Hotel, Montreal; B.M. Philip, Macdonald College; Mable Jewett Crosby, *Ladies Home Journal*; Sarah Field Splint, editor of *Delineator*, New York; Katherine Clayberger, *Peoples Home Journal*, New York; F.W. Howe, School of Household Science, Brooklyn; Victor Hirtzler, chief chef, Hotel St Francis, San Francisco; Ruth Axtell Chalmers, *Modern Priscilla*, Boston; and Boston School of Cooking.

'This New Edition' on p 2 states, 'Over half a million copies of previous editions of the Connors Recipe Book have now been distributed, and this new edition points out many appetizing ways of serving Connors Famous Sea Foods.'

Chatelaine 1935, p 82, cites 'Connors Famous Sea Foods (fish recipes),' free upon request from Connors Bros Ltd.

Y.L.A. recipes

See also NB60.1, from the same group.

NB43.1   1935
Y.L.A. / recipes / St. John's United Church / Moncton, N.B. / 1935 [cover-title]
DESCRIPTION: Pp [1–3] 4–99 [100]
CONTENTS: 1 'Foreword'; 2 'How to Cook a Husband ... Copied from "Favorite Recipes, Ladies Aid Society, Rosemont First United Church, Montreal [i.e., Q182.1]"'; 3–4 'Table Setting and Service'; 5 ads; 6–93 recipes credited with the name of the contributor and ads; 94–8 blank for 'Additional Recipes' and ads; 99 'Table of Weights and Measures' and ad; 100 'Index' [i.e., table of contents] and ad
CITATIONS: FitzPatrickCat 111 (April 1993) No. 28
COPIES: NBFKL   *Private collection
NOTES: YLA stands for Young Ladies' Association or Auxiliary.

1935–9

Over 275 tested recipes

NB44.1   nd [about 1935–9]
St. Cecilia's Sodality / Over 275 / tested recipes / in aid of the Organ Fund / St. Bernard's Church, Moncton, N.B. [cover-title]
DESCRIPTION: 22.0 × 14.5 cm [dimensions from photocopy]
CONTENTS: 1 recipes, beginning with the section 'Bread, Rolls, etc.'; ...
COPIES: *Private collection
NOTES: The recipes, which specify a general oven heat plus Fahrenheit equivalent (for example, hot oven or 400–425°F), suggest a publication date in the 1930s, although the cover design looks a bit older. A sodality is a charitable association of the Roman Catholic laity.

1936–9

Royal cook book

NB45.1   nd [about 1936–9]
Royal cook book / tested recipes [cover-title]
DESCRIPTION: 22.0 × 14.5 cm   Pp [1–2] 3–120   Paper, with portraits on front of King George and Queen Elizabeth; stapled
CONTENTS: 1 'Introduction' and 'A Word as to Our Advertisers'; 2 table of contents and ads; 3 'Table of Weights and Measures'; 4–120 recipes and ads
COPIES: *NBFL
NOTES: George VI reigned from 1936 to 1952. From appearances, *Royal Cook Book* was published before the Second World War, in about 1936–9. It may have been produced in 1937, the year of George's coronation, or on the occasion of the King and Queen's visit to Canada in 1939. The running head is 'Royal Book of Domestic Science.'

According to 'A Word as to Our Advertisers,' the book was 'issued in aid of the various hospitals throughout the Maritimes.' No place of publication is recorded and there are about the same number of advertisements for New Brunswick and Nova Scotia businesses, with a few from PEI.

1937

Coronation cook book

NB46.1   1937
Coronation cook book / tried and tested recipes / "A blessing be upon the cook, / Who, seeing, buys this little book, / And buying, tries and tests its wares / And testing, throws away her cares; / And, carefree, tells her neighbor cook / To get another such a book." / Compiled by / the Ladies' Aid / of the / United Church of Canada / Hartland, N.B. / 1937 [cover-title]
DESCRIPTION: 22.5 × 15.0 cm [dimensions from photocopy]   Stapled
COPIES: *Private collection
NOTES: Information about this book is gleaned from photocopies of the binding and of two facing pages in the text. The left page is an advertisement for Hartland's *Observer* newspaper, which states, 'This cook book was printed by our commercial printing department.' The right page is the first page of recipes; it is headed 'Tried and Tested Recipes' and

begins with 'Cakes.' The recipes are credited with the name of the contributor. *Coronation Cook Book* was named for the coronation of King George VI on 12 May 1937.

1938

McAnn, Aida Maud Boyer (Victoria Corner, Carleton Co., NB, 7 March 1896–1994)

Given the name Ada at birth, the author later changed it to Aida, after Verdi's opera. Her mother died soon after she was born and her father died when she was eleven years old, after which she was raised in Moncton by her aunt and uncle, who was Moncton's mayor. After studies at Mount Allison University (BA in English), University of Toronto (Certificate in Education, 1917), and Columbia University in New York (MA in English, 1930), Aida McAnn worked as a freelance writer and journalist, including nine years for the New Brunswick Travel Bureau. At about the time The New Brunswick Cook Book *was published, she directed 'The Cooking School of the Air' on CHSJ radio each weekday morning in June, sponsored by G.E. Barbour Co. (FitzPatrickCat 157, July 2001, No. 7 lists a poster for the show: 'Out of the Sky! A New Service to Maritime Women, "The Cooking School of the Air."') She is remembered for her support of public libraries in New Brunswick and for founding the Kindness Club, a children's organization concerned with animal protection and environmental issues. On 20 August 1946, Aida married Hugh John Flemming, premier of New Brunswick from 1952 to 1960 and federal member of Parliament from 1962 to 1972. (A short first marriage to Major Douglas Vincent White, just after the First World War, had ended in divorce, as had a second brief marriage.)*

For more information, see Carolyn Atkinson's two articles: 'Aida Flemming ... the Early Years,' Officers' Quarterly [journal of York-Sunbury Historical Society] Vol. 10, No. 4 (Fall 1994), pp 12–14; 'Aida Flemming ... the Later Years,' Officers' Quarterly Vol. 11, No. 1 (Winter 1995), pp 10–13. In the first article, p 14, Atkinson refers to a draft of a recipe book that McAnn prepared for Prince Edward Island but 'it is not currently known if this was ever published.'

NB47.1 [copyright 1938]
The New Brunswick / cook book / treasured recipes / collected and edited by / Aida Boyer McAnn, M.A. / With illustrations by / Mrs. Edward Hart / The Tribune Printing Company, Limited / publishers / Sackville, New Brunswick

DESCRIPTION: 23.0 × 15.0 cm   Pp [1–3] 4–80   1 illus red-and-black on p 28 of a lobster, illus   Lacks paper(?) binding; stapled

CONTENTS: 1 tp; 2 illus of 'The Botsford House at Westcock, N.B.' and 'Copyright, 1938 by Aida Boyer McAnn All rights reserved'; 3 'New Brunswick Calling!'; 4 'The Romance of New Brunswick Agriculture'; 5–6 lacking in this copy; 7–9 potato recipes; 10–14 'New Brunswick Apples'; 15–17 'New Brunswick Blueberries'; 18–19 'New Brunswick Strawberries'; 20–2 'New Brunswick Rhubarb'; 23–5 'New Brunswick's Sweet Symphonies' [maple syrup recipes]; 26–41 'The Fisheries of New Brunswick'; 42–5 'New Brunswick Game and Game Birds'; 46 'New Brunswick Dulse'; 47–8 'A Few New Brunswick Pioneer Recipes'; 49 'Yorkshire Settlers' Recipes'; 50–mid 51 'Loyalist Recipes'; bottom 51 'An Irish Stew'; 52 'Scotch Pioneer Recipes'; 53–4 'Camping Out in New Brunswick'; 55–70 'Favorite New Brunswick Recipes'; 71 'Classification and Proportions of Batter and Dough Mixtures,' 'Chemistry in the Kitchen,' and 'Basic Recipe for All Scalloped Dishes'; 72 'Deep Fat Frying Tips,' 'Syrup Proportions for Canning Fruits,' and 'Time Table for Sterilizing Fruits and Vegetables'; 73 'Time Table for Cooking Cereals,' 'Table of Measures,' and 'Oven Temperatures'; 74 'Time Table for Boiling Vegetables'; 75 'Visitors Have Always Been Welcome to New Brunswick'; 76–80 index

COPIES: NBFU (TX715 N397)   *Private collection

NOTES: The book is a collection of traditional New Brunswick recipes using New Brunswick products. Each section begins with an informative introduction touching on the history and lore of the topic. On pp 47–8, three 'Typical French Acadian Recipes' are given, first in English, then in French: Poutines Râpées, Pâté Râpé, and Fricot. The text is printed in red and black.

Carolyn Atkinson, in her article about McAnn's early life, p 14, writes of the cookbook: 'In 1938 [Aida] had published a book of *Treasured Recipes* and in 1939 the Tribune Printing Company Ltd. in Sackville was running an ad suggesting that "people get more fun out of life" by buying, for only 50 cents, the attractive and useful New Brunswick Cook Book containing 225 new and different recipes edited by Aida Boyer McAnn.'

The New Brunswick Home Economics Association drew upon McAnn's work when it published *New Brunswick Recipes* in 1958. In the foreword, President Beatrice Mahoney thanks 'Mrs. Hugh John Flemming, from whose book of "Treasured Recipes", published in 1938, many valuable suggestions were taken.'

1940

Celestial cook book

NB48.1 1940
Celestial cook book / tried and tested recipes / [symbol of WA on a cross] / Compiled by / the Senior W.A. / of / Christ Church Parish Church / Fredericton, N.B. / 1940 [cover-title]
DESCRIPTION: 23.5 × 15.5 cm   Pp [1–4] 5–40   Photograph on p 1 of an interior view of Christ Church Parish Church   Paper; stapled
CONTENTS: 1 photograph; 2 '... a word of appreciation to the advertisers ...' signed A.S. Coster, rector; 3 'Index' [i.e., table of contents]; 4 ads; 5–40 recipes credited with the name of the contributor and ads
COPIES: *OONL (TX715.6 C45 1940 p***)
NOTES: The OONL copy is inscribed on the front face of the binding, 'Mary Young.'

1941

I.O.D.E. recipe book

The Fort Monckton Chapter was founded in Moncton on 1 April 1936 and disbanded on 31 December 1996.

NB49.1 1941
I.O.D.E. / recipe book / 1941 / Compiled by / the / Fort Monckton Chapter / Moncton, New Brunswick [cover-title]
DESCRIPTION: With image on front of a Union Jack
CITATIONS: FitzPatrickCat 111 (April 1993) No. 9
COPIES: *Private collection
NOTES: Another private collector has a copy that lacks its binding, but is likely the same as this edition: the running head is 'Fort Monckton Chapter Recipe Book' and the volume has 88 pp. FitzPatrickCat records 104 pp.

1942

Moore's Mills and St David Willing War Workers' cook book

NB50.1 1942
Moore's Mills / and / St. David / Willing War Workers' / cook book / Price fifty cents / Entire proceeds of this book for war purposes / 1942 [cover-title]
DESCRIPTION: 23.0 × 15.0 cm   Pp [1] 2–61 [62–3]   Very thin card, with image on front of the Union Jack in a shield-shape; stapled
CONTENTS: 1 'Congratulations to Willing War Workers of Moore's Mills and St. David ... Marven's Limited' and list of officers (president, Hazel Grearson; vice-president, Ruth Murray; secretary, Alice Gilman; treasurer, Florence Sinclair; buying committee, Elsie McBride; publicity chairman, Marion White); 2–3 ads; 4 'Table of Equivalents,' 'Temperature Chart,' and 'Time Table for Roasting'; 5–60 recipes and ads; 61 ads; 62 table of contents; 63 'Courier Press // St. Croix Printing & Pub. Co. St Stephen N.B.'
COPIES: OONL (TX715 M655 1942)   *Private collection
NOTES: The village of Moore's Mills is in the parish of St David.

Victory cook book

NB51.1 1942
Victory cook book / tried and tested recipes / "We may live without poetry, music and art, / We may live without conscience, / We may live without heart, / We may live without friends, / We may live without books, / But civilized man cannot live without cooks." / – Lord Lytton. / Compiled by / the Women's Institutes / of / Carleton County, New Brunswick / 1942 [cover-title]
DESCRIPTION: 23.0 × 15.5 cm   Pp [1–7] 8–109   Paper; stapled
CONTENTS: 1 'Preface' signed Clare A. Smith, East Florenceville, New Brunswick; 2 'Note to Advertisers'; 3 'Index' [i.e., table of contents]; 4 'Tables of Weights and Measures'; 5 'Time Tables for Cooking'; 6 'One View of Cooking' and 'Married Woman's Cake'; 7–109 recipes and ads
COPIES: *NBFU
NOTES: Clare Smith writes in the 'Preface': 'It would not be a misnomer to call this cook book "Recipes of Famous Women" as within its pages may be found recipes graciously donated by Her Royal Highness Princess Alice, Mrs. Franklin D. Roosevelt and many others ... It is proposed and intended that the net proceeds of the sale of this book be devoted entirely to one war project.'
It is widely known among the older generation of New Brunswick women that Mrs Andrew Davis McCain was the organizer behind *Victory Cook Book.* Although her name does not appear in the volume, her role was reported to me by several women and confirmed by her sons Harrison and Wallace McCain. Harrison (in a letter to Mary Pratt, May 2000) writes:

'[The proceeds from the first edition netted] about $40,000 ... and were used to purchase two ambulances for the Canadian Forces. The second Victory Cookbook was to build a new Manse for the Rector of the Anglican Church in Florenceville and it raised enough money to build a good house and a garage as a bonus. The third edition was for the Women's Institute Home in Woodstock, a flourishing Rest Home.' According to Mary Pratt, the successful sales were in part due to the way Mrs McCain kept her friends supplied with boxes of books to distribute.

Mrs McCain was born Laura Blanche Perley on 3 October 1891 in Maugerville, New Brunswick. After earning her education certificate in 1909 and teaching for a few years in Alberta, she took a one-year course for teaching household science at Mount Allison Ladies' College in Sackville in 1915. In 1916 she was hired to teach household science by A.D. McCain (then school board chairman). They married two years later. After her husband died in 1953, she took over the family business, McCain Produce Co. Ltd. Her sons went on to found the frozen food empire, McCain Foods. She died on 11 March 1982.

Paul Waldie, with Kate Jennison, in *A House Divided: The Untold Story of the McCain Family*, Toronto: Viking, 1996, p 46, refers to Laura McCain's community activities, which included '[publishing] a cookbook to raise money for local projects,' but the authors do not give the title and are vague about the period of publication. The reference is undoubtedly to *Victory Cook Book*. The authors also recount other aspects of her life.

NB51.2   2nd ed., 1946
—[Second edition of *Victory Cook Book*, 1946]
NOTES: This edition of 10,000 copies is cited in NB51.3. A private collector reported seeing the 1946 edition in a bookseller's stock; he described it as revised and having 84 pp.

NB51.3   [3rd ed.], 1949
—Revised / Victory cook book / tried and tested recipes / "We may live without poetry, music and art, / We may live without conscience, / We may live without heart, / We may live without friends, / We may live without books, / But civilized man cannot live without cooks." / – Lord Lytton / Reprint / Compiled by / the Women's Institutes / of / Carleton County, New Brunswick / 1949 / Price 50c [cover-title]
DESCRIPTION: 23.0 × 15.0 cm   Pp [1–5] 6–84   Paper; stapled

CONTENTS: 1 untitled introductory text; 2 ad; 3 'Index' [i.e., table of contents]; 4 'Time Tables for Cooking' and 'Tables of Weights and Measures'; 5–84 recipes and on p 84, 'Courier Press // St. Croix Printing & Pub. Co. // St. Stephen N.B.'
COPIES: *NBFY   OONL (TX715 V53 1949)
NOTES: The text on p 1 states: 'The Carleton County Cook Book was first printed to raise money for war work. It was revised and a second edition of 10,000 was printed in 1946. The book has been so popular that the N.B. Women's Institutes decided to have a third edition of 20,000 copies printed, the proceeds from sales to augment their fund to establish a home for aged W.I. members ... We ... bring our thanks to the G.E. Barbour Co., Ltd., Saint John, for continuing their advertisement ... in our third edition.'

OTHER EDITIONS: *Victory Cook Book ... Originally Compiled by the Women's Institutes of Carleton County, N.B.*, Saint John, NB: [Printed by University Press of New Brunswick for] G.E. Barbour Co. Ltd, 1954 (OGU); retitled *Barbour's Cook Book*, Saint John, NB: G.E. Barbour Co. Ltd, nd, pp 88, publisher's note on p 88: 'We would like to thank the members of the Women's Institute of Carleton County, New Brunswick, for making this third edition possible' (NBFKL); *Barbour's Cook Book*, 3rd ed., [Sussex, NB?: G.E. Barbour Co.?, about 1967], pp 97, caption opposite p 6 refers to a centennial project of the company (OONL); *Barbour Cook Book*, 'revised third edition,' nd [1990], 'Barbour Cook Books are assembled by the students of the Frank S. Kierstead Memorial School, Sussex Branch, C.A.M.R.' (OGU, OONL); *Barbour Cook Book: An Outstanding Collection of Favorite Home Recipes from the Atlantic Provinces*, 4th ed., [Saint John, NB: Barbour Foods, 1991?] (OONL).

War-time recipe book

NB52.1   1942
The Fredericton / High School / War-time / recipe book / 1942 [cover-title]
DESCRIPTION: 22.5 × 15.0 cm   Pp [1–3] 4–112   Paper; stapled

CONTENTS: 1 '... this book is prepared in loving acknowledgement of the sacrifice of Fredericton High School boys ...'; 2 blank; 3 'Household Hints'; 4–9 'Planning the Meal'; 10–13 'War-time Menus'; 14–97 recipes; 98–112 ads
CITATIONS: FitzPatrickCat 157, July 2001, No. 36
COPIES: *Private collection

1943

Cook book

NB53.1   1943
Ladies' Auxiliary / Campbellton Branch / Canadian Legion / British Empire Service League / Cook book / 1943 / Price $1.00 [cover-title]
DESCRIPTION: 23.0 × 15.0 cm   Pp [1] 2–80   Very thin card; stapled
CONTENTS: 1 poem entitled 'L-A-D-I-E-S A-U-X-I-L-I-A-R-Y B-E-S-L' and 'Appreciation' thanking the advertisers; 2 'Index' [i.e., table of contents]; 3–80 text and ads
COPIES: *Private collection
NOTES: 'Sugar Substitutes Chart' is on p 7; 'Meat Stretchers' are on pp 9–13.

Saint John, Board of School Trustees

NB54.1   1944
[An edition of *Food Manual for Use in Classes of Home Economics Department*, published by the Board of School Trustees of Saint John, New Brunswick, 1944]
COPIES: Private collection
NOTES: The title-page of the 1948 edition implies that the first edition was in 1943.

NB54.2   3rd ed., 1948
—Food manual / for use in / classes of Home Economics Department / Third edition / Compiled by the teachers of Home Economics Department of the Saint John / city schools in 1943. / Revised 1948. / Published by the Board of School Trustees / of Saint John, N.B. / 1948
DESCRIPTION: 22.5 × 15.0 cm   Pp [1–5] 6–62   A few illus   Cloth
CONTENTS: 1 tp; 2 'Published by the Board of School Trustees of Saint John, New Brunswick for use in the classes of the Home Economics Department. Approved by the Superintendent of Education of New Brunswick for use in the Home Economics Department // Saint John, N.B. Barnes-Hopkins, Limited 1948'; 3 table of contents; 4 blank; 5 'Cookery Methods and Terms'; top 6 'Abbreviations' and 'Table of Weights and Measures'; mid 6–top 7 'Measurements'; mid 7 'Rules for Dishwashing'; bottom 7–mid 8 'Rules for Table-Setting'; bottom 8 'Table Service'; 9 'Table Etiquette' and 'Suggestions for Meal Planning'; 10–62 recipes
COPIES: *Private collection

NOTES: The owner of the book used it when she was in Grades 7 and 8 in Saint John.
   There were at least ten editions of this textbook. The tenth edition was published in 1963 and the textbook was still in use in 1967, since it is cited (with no edition number or date) in *Teacher Work Material for New Brunswick Home Economics Curriculum*, Fredericton: New Brunswick Department of Education, Vocational Branch, 1967, Vol. 1 [of 3], p 83, in a Grade 9 Unit called 'An Environment for Growing – Food and Health Development – "Meat."'

OTHER EDITIONS: 1952 (Private collection); 10th ed., 1963 (Private collection). Ruby MacNeil, who worked as a home economist in New Brunswick, reported that she helped revise the tenth edition of the *Food Manual*.

Tested recipes

NB55.1   nd [about 1943]
Tested / recipes / [YPU symbol] St. Andrews Young Peoples Union / Rexton, New Brunswick
DESCRIPTION: 18.5 × 13.0 cm   Pp [1–4] 5–39   Frontis of St Andrews United Church, Rexton   Paper; stapled
CONTENTS: 1 tp; 2 'Giving you something good to remember us by' and 'The Tribune Press, Sackville, New Brunswick, Canada'; 3 table of contents; 4 blank; 5–39 recipes credited with the name of the contributor
COPIES: *Private collection
NOTES: Rev. David C. Jackson of Rexton Pastoral Charge (letter to me of 12 August 1992) comments regarding the date of *Tested Recipes*: '... 1943 is the date that the members of the Congregation who were involved in that project ascribe to that publication. Mind you, no one wants to say that it was "1943" exactly but by the determination of a number of factors, it would seem that 1943 is fairly accurate.'

1944

Cook booklet

Barrington Memorial Chapter was founded in Edmundston in 1929. It disbanded in 1991.

NB56.1   1944
[IODE symbol] / Cook / booklet / Compiled by / Barrington Memorial Chapter / Souvenir of the Street Fair, / Dominion Day 1944

DESCRIPTION: 20.0 × 12.5 cm   Pp [1–28]   [$0.25, on inside front face of binding]   Paper; stapled, and punched with three holes

CONTENTS: 1 tp; 2 untitled introductory text; 3–27 recipes and ads; 28 blank for 'Notes'

COPIES: *NBFY

NOTES: Text on the inside front face of the binding acknowledges the kindness of Edmundston and Fredericton businesses and states, 'All the proceeds from the sale of this booklet are for the war work of the order.' Text on p 2 states: 'If the booklet proves popular it is planned to compile another one for the next annual Street Fair. Provisions [*sic*] has been made so that booklets may be fastened together later with a ring [i.e., through the punched holes].' The printer, 'Madawaska Printing Office,' is on the outside back face of the binding. The text is printed in blue ink throughout.

1945

Weldon, Alma E., and Elsie E. Estabrooks

NB57.1   1945

Cook right – / eat right – / live right ... / Women's Institute Division / Alma E. Weldon / Director, Home Economics Service / Elsie E. Estabrooks, B.Sc. / Girls' Work Supervisor / Issued by the authority of / Hon. A.C. Taylor, / Minister of Agriculture / Fredericton, N.B. / 1945 [cover-title]

DESCRIPTION: 23.0 × 15.5 cm   Pp [1–4] 5–98 [99–112] A few illus   Paper, with images on front of the six categories of food (milk and cheese, meat, eggs, vegetables, fruit, bread and cereals); stapled

CONTENTS: 1 'Preface' signed Harriet D. Thompson; 2 blank; 3 table of contents; 4 blank; 5–98 twenty-five chapters, the last titled 'School Lunches'; 99–106 'Index' [i.e., table of contents]; 107–12 blank for 'Menus'

CITATIONS: Bishop, p 159

COPIES: NBCOM   *NBFKL (Ruth Spicer Cookbook Collection)   NBFL   OOAG (641.5 W445 1945)

NOTES: This cookbook was designed to help 'war brides,' i.e., women who were newly arrived in Canada after marrying Canadian servicemen they had met overseas during the Second World War. The 'Preface' is a poem, which begins, 'The N.B.W.I. present / This cook book as a compliment / To you who came from far away / As brides, in Canada to stay.'

1947

Cook book

NB58.1   1947

Shaarei Zedek Sisterhood / Cook book / Mav 1947 [cover-title]

DESCRIPTION: 28.0 × 21.5 cm   Pp [1–69]   Chapter head illus   Paper; punched with two holes and held with a metal fastener

CONTENTS: 1 untitled acknowledgment signed Shaarei Zedek Sisterhood; 2 blank; 3 ads; 4 blank; 5–65 recipes credited with the name of the contributor and ads, printed on rectos only; 66 blank; 67 'Useful Hints'; 68 blank; 69 ads

COPIES: *NBSJHM

NOTES: The Shaarei Zedek Sisterhood is the women's organization at Shaarei Zedek Synagogue in Saint John, New Brunswick. On p 1, the reader is 'cordially invited to consult the contributor whose name accompanies the recipe' if any difficulty is experienced.

1948

The cooking Guide of Charlotte County

NB59.1   1948

The cooking Guide / of / Charlotte County / compiled by the / Passamaquoddy Division / of the / Canadian Girl Guides / 1948 / Price 50c [cover-title]

DESCRIPTION: 24.0 × 15.5 cm   Pp [1–2] 3–80   Thin card, with Girl Guide shamrock symbol on front; stapled

CONTENTS: 1 'The Guide Promise,' 'The Guide Law,' and 'Motto'; 2 foreword signed E.M. Caughey, division commander, St Andrews, New Brunswick; 3–top 79 recipes credited with the name of the contributor and ads; mid 79–80 'Household Hints' and at bottom p 80, 'Courier Press St. Croix Printing & Pub. Co. St. Stephen N.B.'; inside back face of binding 'Substitutions,' 'Equivalents,' and 'Capacity of Canned Food Containers'

COPIES: *NBSM   OGU

OTHER EDITIONS: Rev. ed., [St Andrews, NB:] 1968 (OONL); golden anniversary ed., St Andrews, NB: Black Swan Publishing, c1998 (OONL).

Y.L.A. recipes

See also NB43.1, from the same group.

NB60.1   1948
Y.L.A. / recipes / St. John's United Church /
Moncton, N.B. / 1948 [cover-title]
DESCRIPTION: 22.0 × 14.5 cm   Pp [i–ii], [1–2] 3–108
Paper; stapled
CONTENTS: i 'Errata'; ii blank; 1 'Foreword'; 2 ad; 3–
103 recipes credited with the name of the contributor
and ads; 104 'Miscellaneous' and ads; 105 'Table of
Weights and Measures' and ads; 106 'Index' [i.e., table
of contents]; 107–8 blank for 'Menus'
COPIES: *NBFL

1949

Cook book

NB61.1   1949
Cook book / St. Paul's Service Club 1949 [cover-title]
DESCRIPTION: 17.5 × 10.5 cm   Pp [1–253]   Paper, with
image on front of a woman lifting the lid of a sauce-
pan; bound at top edge by string through two punched
holes
CONTENTS: 1–253 recipes on rectos only, versos blank
COPIES: *Private collection
NOTES: The Service Club was part of St Paul's United
Church in Fredericton, at the corner of York and
George streets.

The guild cook book of tasty and tested recipes

NB62.1   1949
The / guild cook book / of tasty and tested / recipes
/ Compiled / and / distributed by / the / Chipman
United Church / Guild / 1949 [cover-title]
CONTENTS: 1–62 recipes credited with the name of the
contributor and ads; 63 'Index' [i.e., table of contents]
COPIES: *Private collection

1949–50

Recipes and menus you may like

NB63.1   1949–50
Recipes and menus / you may like / Tested and
tried / in the / Home Economics Department /
Vocational School / Saint John, N.B. / 1949–50
DESCRIPTION: 21.5 × 13.5 cm   Pp [1] 2–49   Paper,
with image on front of a woman stirring the contents
of a bowl; stapled
CONTENTS: 1 tp; 2–49 text
COPIES: *NBFKL (Ruth Spicer Cookbook Collection)
NOTES: The cover-title is 'Menus for You // Home
Economics Teacher Education // Vocational School
Saint John.' The text is mimeographed.

Prince Edward Island

Walnut Cake

One cup sugar, half cup butter, two eggs, half cup sweet milk, one and one half cups flour, one and one half teaspoons baking powder, one large cup chopped walnuts.
Frosting – One and one half cups white sugar, half cup water, white of one egg.

Mrs D. Farquharson

P1.1, *Jubilee Cook Book* by Ladies' Aid Society, First Methodist Church, Charlottetown, [1897], p 17

Canada's smallest province joined Confederation in 1873. Although blessed with rich agricultural land and fishing grounds, it was without the resources to develop an industrial base, and by 1891 its population was in decline, dropping from 109,078 in 1891 to 88,038 in 1931, as people left to search for jobs in Central and Western Canada and the United States. Only in the fourth decade of the twentieth century did the population begin to grow again, to 98,429 by 1951. It is not surprising, therefore, that only a small number of cookbooks appear to have been produced in Prince Edward Island, and that the only advertising cookbook to surface was a 1909 almanac-type recipe collection promoting a Charlottetown drugstore (P3.1).

Prince Edward Island has been described as the most culturally homogeneous province in Canada,[1] the great majority of its citizens being descended from immigrants from the British Isles. The other significant group are descendants of a few hundred Acadians who escaped deportation in the eighteenth century (less than 10% of today's population); however, no cookbooks written by the French community before 1950 were found. Fittingly, the first cookbook published in Prince Edward Island celebrated the sixtieth or diamond anniversary of Queen Victoria's accession to the throne: *Jubilee Cook Book* (P1.1) by the Ladies' Aid Society of the First Methodist Church in Charlottetown in 1897. Although the interior text is

poorly organized, the printer, James D. Taylor, put considerable thought into the cover design, which features the Queen's head and shoulders, the title, and various decorative devices arranged within a diamond shape (pl 25). Other community cookbooks – a category that makes up 80% of all culinary titles recorded in this section – were produced to raise money for the province's hospitals and an orphanage. The earliest example is *Tested Recipes* (P2.1) by the Ladies' Aid of the Prince Edward Island Hospital in Charlottetown, of about 1905–10, and the same women may have compiled another recipe collection for the hospital in about 1920 (P4.1). The Summerside hospital benefited from the sale of *The Modern Cook Book for Nova Scotia and Prince Edward Island* in about 1920 (NS24.1), and in the 1930s, *Royal Cook Book* (NB45.1) was issued on behalf of hospitals throughout the Maritimes, likely including one or more in the province, since there are advertisements for island businesses. Recipes from *Mrs Flynn's Cookbook* (P5.1), published about 1930 to help St Vincent's Orphanage, were later prepared in the kitchen at Government House, when Katherine Flynn's daughter, Agnes, was resident there with her husband, Willibald Joseph MacDonald, the province's twenty-third lieutenant-governor.

Two cookbooks with an educational purpose emanated from the Women's Institute. In 1932, the Women's Institute Branch of the Department of Agriculture published *Cook Book for Use in Short Course Classes* (P6.1). During the Second World War, in response to the federal government's promulgation of 'Canada's Official Food Rules,' the Institute produced *Cook Book of Home Recipes* 'in the interest of nutrition work,' organizing the sections according to the new rules (P8.1). At the same time, the cookbook offered guidance to beginners in the hotel trade in a special 'Tourist Section.' In 1939, the Women's Institute Branch contributed recipes to *The Maritime Cook Book* (Q258.1), compiled by the Maritime Women's Club of Montreal to commemorate the visit to Canada of King George VI and Queen Elizabeth.

Aida McAnn, a New Brunswicker, is reported to have prepared a manuscript for a Prince Edward Island recipe book.[2] Her text would likely have followed the model of *The New Brunswick Cook Book* (NB47.1), and it is unfortunate that it was likely never published.

There are no significant collections of pre-1950 Canadian cookbooks in Prince Edward Island public institutions.

NOTES

1 *The Canadian Encyclopedia Online*, feature article for Prince Edward Island, section about 'People.'
2 Carolyn Atkinson, 'Aida Flemming ... the Early Years,' *Officers' Quarterly* [journal of the York-Sunbury Historical Society] Vol. 10, No. 4 (Fall 1994), p 14.

1897

Jubilee cook book

P1.1 [1897]
[Running head:] Jubilee cook book. / [Title:] Jubilee cook book / Valuable recipes / personally tested and vouched for / by the ladies whose names / appear under the recipes / Published by the / Ladies' Aid Society / of the / First Methodist Church / Charlottetown, P.E. Island / Printed by Jas. D. Taylor, Queen Street
DESCRIPTION: 18.5 × 12.5 cm   Pp [i–ii], [1] 2–42, 45–6, 43–4, 47–9, 54–5, 52, 56, 50–1, 56, [i–viii], 57–72   [$0.25, on binding]   Pink-paper-covered boards, with image on front of head-and-shoulders of Queen Victoria; stapled
CONTENTS: i–ii ads; 1 tp; 2–2nd 56 and i–viii ads on versos, recipes on rectos; 57–72 ads
COPIES: *PCM   Private collection
NOTES: See pl 25. The cookbook celebrates the sixtieth anniversary of Queen Victoria's reign; the years of her reign, '1837 1897,' are printed on the front face of the binding. The recipes are arranged in five chapters ('Cakes,' 'Salads,' 'Puddings,' 'Jellies,' and 'Biscuits'); however, the page numbers are printed out of order and some pages of recipes are not positioned in the appropriate chapter; for example, there is a page of preserves and pickles in the 'Biscuits' chapter.

1905–10

Haszard, Mrs F.L., Mrs A.A. Bartlett, Mrs Wesley Frost, et al.

Some of the women named on the title-page are recorded in the 1901 Census: Elizabeth (New Brunswick, 14 September 1853–), wife of Francis L. Haszard, a 'Stipendiary Magistrate'; Margrett D. (PEI, 24 April 1865–), wife of Arthur A. Bartlett, an 'Agent [General?]'; likely Matilda (PEI, 2 May 1865–), wife of John S. Bagnall, a 'Dr Dentist'; and Perle Taylor (PEI, 9 January 1878–), daughter of Mary A. and Francis Perle, a 'Medical Dr.' See also P4.1, possibly also compiled by the Ladies' Aid of the Prince Edward Island Hospital, Charlottetown.

P2.1   nd [about 1905–10]
Tested recipes by / the Ladies' Aid of / the Prince Edward / Island Hospital / Edited and arranged by / Mrs. F.L. Haszard, – Mrs. A.A. Bartlett, / Mrs. Wesley Frost, – Mrs. Geo. E. Full, / Mrs. J.S. Bagnall, Mrs. W.F. Tidmarsh, Miss Perle Taylor.
DESCRIPTION: 21.5 × 14.5 cm   Pp [1–5] 6–105 [106]   Tp illus (2.1 × 1.7 cm) of a man holding up a pheasant on a plate   Paper, with tp illus on front; stapled
CONTENTS: 1 tp; 2 blank; 3 part-title: 'Cook Book // Published by the Ladies' Aid of the Prince Edward Island Hospital'; 4 'Preface'; 5–105 recipes credited with the name of the contributor and ads; 106 'Index' [i.e., table of contents]
COPIES: *BDEM   Private collection
NOTES: The cover-title is 'Cook Book.' In the illustrated advertisement on p 52 for Carter and Co. Ltd, there is a small image of a calendar for the month of May 1904. The private collector's copy is inscribed on p 3, 'Margaret V. McKay // New Glasgow 1910.' The cookbook, therefore, was published about 1905–10. There is an errata slip glued to the inside front face of the binding of the BDEM copy.

1909

Hughes' 1909 household calendar cook book

P3.1   1909
Hughes' / 1909 / household / calendar cook book / Geo. E. Hughes, Apothecaries' Hall / Charlottetown P.E. Island
DESCRIPTION: 18.0 × 13.5 cm   Pp [1–3] 4–32   Small symbols of zodiac and phases of moon   Paper; stapled
CONTENTS: 1 tp; 2 publ ad; 3 eclipses, morning and evening stars, and chronological cycles for 1909; 4–27 recipes and ads on versos, calendar for a month and humorous dialogue on rectos; 28–top 30 'Poisons and Antidotes'; 30 'Relation of Pulse to Temperature,' 'Handy Household Drugs,' and first-aid measures for sunstroke, frozen limbs, foreign bodies in the throat, and hiccoughs; 31 'Worth Knowing' [mainly first aid] and 'Things to Remember'; 32 continuation of 'Things to Remember'
CITATIONS: Ferguson/Fraser, p 232, illus col on p 11 of closed volume
COPIES: PCU (TX715 H85 1909 photocopy)   *Private collection
NOTES: The private collector's copy may be a modern facsimile, although there is nothing to indicate who reproduced the book or when.

1920

[Title unknown]

P4.1 [about 1920]
[Title unknown]
DESCRIPTION: About 22.0 × 13.5 cm [dimensions from photocopy]   Pp [leaves lacking] 7–101 [102]   Lacks binding
COPIES: *Private collection
NOTES: This entry is based on photocopies of some of the pages of an incomplete copy. The 'Index' [i.e., table of contents], which is on p 102 (the last printed page), lists the following sections: 'Bread, Biscuits, &c.,' p 5; 'Cocktails,' p 12; 'Soups,' p 13; 'Fish,' p 16; 'Meats,' p 22; 'Vegetables,' p 32; 'Salads,' p 35; 'Puddings,' p 39; 'Pies and Pastry,' p 46; 'Invalid Dishes,' p 49; 'Ices,' p 52; 'Creams,' p 55; 'Cake,' p 59; 'Beverages,' p 77; 'Luncheon Dishes,' p 79; 'Preserves,' p 84; 'Pickles,' p 87; 'Confections,' p 93; and 'Things Worth Remembering,' p 97. The advertisements are for Charlottetown businesses.

I have compared pp 7, 28–9, 51, 60, and 76–7 with P2.1, *Tested Recipes*, by the Ladies' Aid of the Prince Edward Island Hospital. Some of the recipe contributors are the same (for example, Mrs Wesley Frost, Mrs F.L. Haszard, Mrs J.S. Bagnall, and Mrs H.J. Palmer), and there are a few duplicate recipes: White Bread from Mrs Norman McLeod (p 7 in this book, p 6 in P2.1); Jugged Hare from Mrs James Simpson (p 29 in both books); and Dandelion Wine from Mrs Charles McGregor (p 77 in this book, p 84 in P2.1). Yet, whereas Mrs W.S. Stewart contributed a recipe for Sponge Cake to both books, her recipe in this book (p 60) is different from that in P2.1 (p 77). The text of this book is divided into the same sections, in the same order, as P2.1; however, this book has five extra sections ('Cocktails,' 'Vegetables,' 'Invalid Dishes,' 'Creams,' and 'Things Worth Remembering' are not in P2.1). From appearances, this book was published later than P2.1, in about 1920. Since the differences far outweigh the similarities, this book must be considered a different text, possibly compiled by the same organization of ladies.

The modern cook book for Nova Scotia and Prince Edward Island

See NS24.1.

1930

Flynn, Mrs Katherine C. Lewis (Cardigan, PEI, 1874–)

According to the author's biography in the cookbook, she was born in 1874 in Cardigan and married William M. Flynn, a CNR station agent; however, the 1901 Census gives 25 January 1875 as the birth date of Katie Flynn, wife of W.M. Flynn, 'S. Agent & Operator,' Charlottetown.

P5.1   1981 reprint of [about 1930]
Mrs. / Flynn's / cookbook / selected and tested / recipes / compiled by / Mrs. Katherine C. Lewis Flynn / Published by / the ladies of St. Elizabeth's and [sic] Society / in aid of St. Vincent's Orphanage / Reprinted by / the Prince Edward Island Heritage Foundation / 1981
DESCRIPTION: 22.0 × 14.5 cm   Pp [i–iv], [1–4] 5–190   Tp illus of a striding woman with a basket and umbrella, fp illus on p iv of the author   Paper, with tp illus on front, slightly reduced in size
CONTENTS: i tp; ii 'Copyright: Prince Edward Island Heritage Foundation ... Printed by William's & Crue, Summerside // Published by: Prince Edward Island Heritage Foundation ...'; iii 'Prologue' signed C.G. Hennessey, May 1981 [i.e., Catherine Hennessey, former director of the Prince Edward Island Museum]; iv illus of author; 1 biography of author; 2 'This work is reprinted ... with the assistance of the Heritage Endowment Trust and the support of the following firms ...'; 3 'Preface' signed Mrs Katherine C. Lewis Flynn; 4–190 text; inside back face of binding 'Errata'
CITATIONS: Duncan, pp 133–4, 194–5   Ferguson/ Fraser, pp 12 and 234, illus col on p 80 of closed volume   Reddin (see 'Notes')
COPIES: OONL (TX715 F59 1981, 2 copies)   PCL   PCM   PCU (TX715 F59 1981)   *Private collection
NOTES: On the title-page the author's name is Mrs Katherine C. Lewis Flynn; on p 1 her maiden name is recorded as Catherine Clemintine [sic] Carruthers Lewis. According to the author's biography, Flynn came to the aid of the St Elizabeth's Aid Society of St Vincent's Orphanage when she lived in Charlottetown in 1930 (the orphanage needed a new boiler). The biography also refers to the 1931 annual report of the Society in Aid of St Vincent's Orphanage, which records a donation of $1,000 from the cookbook's sale. There is an advertisement on p 35 that asks, 'Have you seen the 1930 Nash car.' The cookbook,

therefore, was published about 1930. One thousand copies were printed by the Irwin Printing Co. for $370. The cookbook was later used at Government House in Charlottetown, by Mr and Mrs Flynn's only daughter, Agnes Smith Rosa, when her husband, Willibald Joseph MacDonald, was the province's lieutenant-governor, from 1963 to 1969. There are menus on p 4 for Christmas Dinner, Easter Dinner, and Thanksgiving Dinner.

No copy of the original cookbook was located. For two reviews of the facsimile by Estelle Reddin, see *Island Magazine* [Prince Edward Island Heritage Foundation] No. 10 (Fall–Winter 1981), pp 39–40, and 'Enthusiasm and a Spirit of Adventure,' *Atlantic Provinces Book Review* Vol. 9, No. 3 (November 1982), p 2. Ferguson/Fraser, p 12, refer to the cookbook's recipe for Crab Rabbit.

1932

Prince Edward Island, Department of Agriculture

P6.1 1932
Prince Edward Island / Department of Agriculture / Cook book / for use in / short course classes / under direction of / Women's Institute / Branch / Index on page 80 / Printed by / the Journal Publishing Co. Limited / Summerside, P.E.I. [*sic*] / 1932
DESCRIPTION: 21.5 × 15.0 cm   Pp [1–3] 4–80   Rebound in cloth, but retaining original paper
CONTENTS: 1 tp; 2 blank; 3 'General Information'; 4–79 text; 80 'Index' [i.e., table of contents]
COPIES: *PCU

1936–9

Royal cook book

See NB45.1 for a cookbook 'issued in aid of the various hospitals throughout the Maritimes.'

1939

Recipes tried and tested

The International Order of the King's Daughters and Sons, a philanthropic organization, was founded in New York in 1886.

P7.1 1939
Recipes / tried and tested / by the good housekeepers / of / the cabbage patch / of / the King's Daughters / Charlottetown, P.E.I. / 1939
DESCRIPTION: 22.5 × 15.0 cm   16 leaves numbered 1–16 on rectos only   Paper; stapled
COPIES: *Private collection

1943

Cook book of home recipes

P8.1 1943
Women's Institute / Cook book / of / home recipes / Published in the interest of / nutrition work / Printed by the Patriot Job Print / Charlottetown, Prince Edward Island / 1943
DESCRIPTION: 23.0 cm [height from photocopy]   [$0.25, on binding]   Stapled
COPIES: *Private collection
NOTES: The cover-title is 'Prince Edward Island "Home" Recipes [PEI–WI symbol] Compiled by Prince Edward Island Women's Institute members // Head office: Charlottetown Prince Edward Island Price 25¢.' Printed on the inside front face of the binding, opposite the title-page, is 'A Poem' beginning, 'Lord of all pots and pans and things, ...' The 'Index' [i.e., table of contents], which is on p [107] (the last printed page), lists the following items: 'Forward' [*sic*], p 3; 'Canada's Official Food Rules,' p 5; 'General Information,' p 5; 'Breads,' pp 6–16; 'Vegetables,' pp 18–20; 'Fish,' pp 21–3; 'Meat,' pp 23–5; 'Supper or Luncheon Dishes,' pp 26–33; 'Sauces for Meat, Fish and Vegetables,' p 28; 'Fish Dishes,' pp 30–1; 'Vegetable Dishes,' pp 32–3; 'Desserts and Sauces,' pp 34–44; 'Cakes and Cookies,' pp 45–64; 'Icings,' pp 65–6; 'Fillings,' p 67; 'Salads,' pp 68–72; 'Pickles and Relishes,' pp 73–9; 'Pastry and Pie Fillings,' pp 80–5; 'Jams, Jellies, Marmalades and Preserves,' pp 86–9; 'Canning,' pp 90–3; 'Wartime Section,' pp 94–6; 'Tourist Section,' pp 98–102; and 'Household Hints,' pp 103–6.

The owner of the 1943 edition reports that the text of the foreword matches that quoted for P8.2, except that there is an additional sentence following '... beginners in the Tourist Trade' that says, 'When planning this book the committee thought it advisable to include some recipes, which though impractical during the war years, will be useful in peace time.'

P8.2   nd [about 1945–9]

—Prince Edward Island / Women's Institute / Cook book / of / home recipes / Published in the interest of / nutrition work

DESCRIPTION: 22.5 × 15.0 cm   Pp [1–4] 5–112   [\$0.50, on binding]   Very thin card, with PEI–WI symbol on front; stapled

CONTENTS: 1 tp; 2 blank; 3 'Foreword'; 4 blank; 5–111 text; 112 'Index' [i.e., table of contents]

COPIES: *OONL (TX715.6 P766 1900z p***)

NOTES: There is a new section for 'School Lunches' on pp 109–11 and no 'Wartime Section.' The cover-title is the same as the 1943 edition, as is the poem printed on the inside front face of the binding. The 'Foreword' reads: 'This cook book has been compiled by the Women's Institutes of Prince Edward Island from home recipes contributed by individual members. Special attention is paid to Canada's Official Food Rules which are carried through as headings for each section. A novel part of the book is the Tourist Section, compiled from recipes contributed by leading Tourist Homes with hints for beginners in the Tourist Trade. Money from the sale of this cook book is to be used for Charitable Purpose [*sic*] connected with Institute Work.' The running head is 'P.E.I. Home Recipes.'

Quebec

Purée aux poix

Une pinte de pois dans un gallon d'eau froide. Faites bien bouillir le tout, que vous jetterez ensuite dans la passoire; écrâsant les pois avec une cuiller, pour les réduire en purée; remettez cette dernière dans la marmite, y ajoutant de l'ognon [sic] tranché fin et fris dans le beurre; des herbes salées hachées bien fines, et une pincée de sariette. Faites bouillir le tout encore une demie heure; on la mange avec des tranches de pain grillé, qu'on émiette ou casse.

Plum Pouding

Une douzaine d'oeufs bien battus, six cuillerées de fleur, trois demiards de lait froid, du raisin suivant le goût, de la muscade et cannelle, un peu d'écorse d'orange bien pilée, un peu de suif de mouton, ébouillantez votre sac, et faites bouillir trois heures, au bout d'une demie heure que votre pouding aura bouilli, tournez le, et brassez le sac afin que le raisin se mêle.

Both recipes from Q3.1, *La cuisinière canadienne*, 1840, pp 11, 47

Quebec is the only province where the vast majority of the population is French-speaking, their origins going back to 1608, when Samuel de Champlain established the first permanent French settlement (the Habitation of Quebec) where Quebec City now stands, and the ensuing one and a half centuries, when French settlers colonized the fertile St Lawrence River Valley. After the Conquest of New France by the British in 1759, the French population remained the large majority, despite the ongoing arrival of immigrants of British origin. The first significant influx of English-speakers were Loyalists fleeing the American Revolution, who settled the arable lands of what are now called the Eastern Townships, near the American border (and also areas of present-day Ontario, then part of the colony of Quebec), followed by a huge wave of immigration from the British Isles, mainly Ireland and Scotland, in the period 1815–60. In the first four decades or so of the twentieth century, Montreal saw the arrival of many Eastern European Jews, who generally chose English as their other tongue. Even the large out-migration of French-speaking Quebeckers to the United States from about 1840 to 1930, in search of jobs, did not much alter the balance between the French-speaking majority and the English-speaking minority. The dynamics within and between the two groups of language, culture, religion, and their relative positions of power within Quebec society, have affected the development of French- and English-language publishing in the province and made the story of cookbook publishing in Quebec more complex than elsewhere. Contemporary sensibilities compel us to look for differences between the two groups and to keep their stories on different tracks, but their paths were not entirely separate, with respect to either the business of cookbook publishing or the culinary content of the texts. Cookbooks written in one language were sometimes translated and published in the other, and both language groups shared a common culinary heritage evolved from the cooking practices of medieval Europe. In *All Manners of Food: Eating and Taste in England and France from the Middle Ages to the Present*, Stephen Mennell has explained how French cookery had an early and continuing influence on English cookery and that by the end of the nineteenth century it enjoyed an 'international culinary hegemony' that stretched as far as North America.[1] In Quebec, where Canadians of French and British origin lived together in a shared land, there were cross-currents in both directions, through the exchange of recipes, the use of common, local ingredients, and sometimes instruction by the same revered and bilingual cookery teachers – such as Sister St Mary Edith/soeur Sainte-Marie Edith of the Montreal Cooking School in the 1920s and 1930s or the later, national culinary celebrity, Jehane Benoît. The cookbooks described in this section are an important resource for studying the transmission of food customs within the province,[2] especially since they span a considerable period of time – 125 years from the first-published cookbook in 1825, when the citizens lived in a separately administered British colony called Lower Canada, to the end-date for this bibliography. The cookbooks may show an increasing influence of British and American cooking on French cooking (a reversal of the earlier trend elaborated by Mennell). In their pages are certainly found the everyday and festival dishes, recipes for the celebrated food products of the province (such as pork, dairy, maple syrup, fish, wild fowl, and game), and both the continuation of traditions and the introduction of new fashions.

More English than French culinary titles were published in nineteenth-century Quebec. Yet, the first French-language reprint of a foreign text and the first French-language cookbook written in Quebec for a Quebec readership came earlier than their English counterparts, and the long and overlapping runs of editions of two titles written for French-speaking Quebec families meant that cookbooks were always available for francophones who could afford to buy them. The two long-running titles – *La cuisinière canadienne* of 1840 (Q3.1) and *Directions diverses données par la révérende mère Caron* of 1878 (Q15.1) – served as agents of continuity within the culture.

The first cookbook published in Quebec (then Lower Canada), and the first in all of the area of present-day Canada, was *La cuisinière bourgeoise* (Q1.1), an 1825 edition of a 1746 book from France, by Menon (first name unknown), printed in France but bearing the title-page imprint of the Quebec City bookseller Augustin Germain. Menon was renowned for defining a new French cuisine, one built on the perceived strengths of middle-class cooking rather than the traditions of the royal court and the upper classes.[3] By the time of the 1825 Quebec City edition, *La cuisinière bourgeoise* was no longer a revolutionary tome, but a classic text, which continued to be regularly reprinted in France into the 1860s (and which had been translated for London, England, editions in the 1790s). In the early days of the book trade in Canada, before there was a homegrown literature, booksellers and publishers of necessity turned to foreign works to meet the public's growing demand for books. Augustin Germain's edition of *La cuisinière bourgeoise* is an interesting case of a bookseller acting as publisher.[4] Remarkably, it appeared twenty years before the first English-language cookbook to be published in Quebec,[5] which was also printed abroad: *Modern Practical Cookery* of 1845 (Q4.1), by the Scottish cookery teacher Mrs Nourse, printed in Edinburgh and published by the Scottish-born Montreal publishers Armour and Ramsay.

The first cookbook written in Canada in French was *La cuisinière canadienne*, published by Louis Perrault in Montreal in 1840, the same year that the first English-language cookbook compiled in Canada appeared (*The Frugal Housewife's Manual* printed in Toronto, O2.1), but twenty-five years before the first English-language cookbook written in Quebec (*Household Recipes or Domestic Cookery* by a Montreal lady [Mrs Hannah Constance Hart], 1865, Q7.1). Perrault, with his brother-in-law and business partner Édouard-Raymond Fabre, was part of a movement determined to break the economic hold of the colony's British elite and to preserve French-Canadian culture, and this nationalistic impulse may have been behind the publishing of the cookbook. If only one could have been a fly on the wall during the discussions leading to its eventual launch, both to hear the reasons for its publication and to learn who prepared the text. An advertisement in *Aurore des Canadas*, 10 April 1840, referred to the recipes as extracted from the 'Journal d'un ancien confiseur de Montréal,' but the confiseur has not been identified and other evidence suggests that the text was compiled by someone close to Perrault's family and the supporters of Mme Gamelin's charitable work (which eventually led to the founding in 1843 of the Institute of Providence). The recipes range from the standard dishes of French and English cuisine (Boeuf à la mode, Plum Pouding) to recipes featuring local ingredients (muskellunge, dried peas, pork, cornmeal). Perrault could never have foretold the success of his venture: his firm reissued the book several times up to 1865, then it appeared under the Beauchemin imprint until the 1920s, including a twentieth-century Worcester, Massachusetts, edition for francophones who had emigrated to the

United States, and a heavily revised version from the presses of the Montreal newspaper *La patrie* in about 1910.

Mère Caron's 1878 *Directions diverses* is a direct descendant of *La cuisinière canadienne*, from which it borrows many recipes. Originally compiled for use in the Institute of Providence and likely a summary of information mère Caron presented in cookery classes in the 1860s, *Directions diverses* begins by setting out the moral context for cooking. It soon found favour with the public, eventually appearing in eight numbered editions up to 1913. It was the first of several cookbooks prepared explicity for use by girls within Catholic institutions – a genre unique to Quebec, where the Catholic Church was omnipresent in the lives of the French-speaking population and controlled their education system. Another nineteenth-century example was *Manuel d'économie domestique* of 1896 (Q33.1), by B.A.T. de Montigny, Chevalier de l'Ordre militaire de Pie IX, in which the author set out the virtues and vices that would help or hinder the good practice of domestic economy.

One nineteenth-century French-language cookbook emanated from the community of Quebeckers who had settled in the United States: *Collection de recettes éprouvées, les plus en usage dans les meilleures cuisines du Canada et des États-Unis*, collected by Mme Charles Rouillard of St Johnsbury, Vermont, but printed on the presses of a Sherbrooke newspaper in 1884 (Q19.1). Most, if not all, nineteenth-century French-language advertising cookbooks (as in the next century) were translations from English texts; for example, the ones promoting the American Mrs Winslow's Soothing Syrup (Q8.1, 1869), the American cooking fat called Cottolene (Q29.1, about 1895–1900), and Montreal-made Diamond Dyes (Q38.2, about 1899).

English-language cookbook publishing in the province began with Nourse's Scottish text, *Modern Practical Cookery* of 1845 (Q4.1), and, three years later, a reprint of an American work, *The Skilful Housewife's Guide* (Q5.1), both published by the Montreal firm Armour and Ramsay for distribution in Canada East and Canada West, and there were other reprints of foreign texts later in the century.[6] The first of two landmark events for English Quebec cookbooks occurred in 1865 with the appearance of Mrs Hart's *Household Recipes or Domestic Cookery*. This work was not only the first English-language cookbook written in Quebec, it was the first cookbook by a Jewish author in all of Canada, and it followed the first Jewish cookbook published in England[7] by less than twenty years. The compiler's identity (name and religion) is veiled in the book: She is 'a Montreal lady' on the title-page; the copyright statement on the title-page verso gives only her first name (C. Hannah); and only one recipe, Ball Soup, can be considered Jewish. Nevertheless, she was likely recognized as the author within Montreal society since she came from a prominent family and, as she states in the preface, the excellence of the recipes had been commended by many ladies in the city's fashionable circles. Mrs Hart's family was likely supportive of her publishing venture: Her husband was an author and a lawyer, and both her husband and father were well known for their work in advancing Jewish civil liberties (Mrs Hart's son Gerald, who was in his mid-teens when his mother wrote the cookbook, went on to become a noted bibliophile). *Household Recipes* enjoyed some success, as a second edition was printed by John Lovell in 1867, but, despite Mrs Hart's ground-breaking publication and the increase in Montreal's Jewish population in the twentieth century, only a few other cookbooks surfaced from Quebec's Jewish community, in the 1920s and 1940s.[8] Two other nineteenth-century female authors deserve mention for making their way into print, both in 1895: Sarah Allen (*The Common Sense Recipe Book*, nine editions up to 1903, Q27.1) and Amy G. Richards (*Cookery*, Q28.1). Unlike Mrs Hart, Allen (a widow in business for herself) and Richards (a cookery teacher) turned to writing cookbooks to support themselves.

The second landmark event was the publication of Quebec's first community cookbook in 1888, *Clever Cooking for Careful Cooks* (Q21.1). Its recipes were collected and arranged by the ladies of the Church of St John the Evangelist in Montreal, and the ones for German Gulasch [*sic*] and Polish Salad show other influences on Montreal tables besides British and French cooking. Quebec's first fund-raiser came eleven years after Toronto's *The Home Cook Book* (Canada's first, 1877, O20.1) and followed three others (one in New Brunswick in 1878, and two in Ontario in the 1880s),[9] but the idea quickly caught on with English-speaking women's groups in the province, who produced a steady stream of fifty-eight community cookbooks in the years up to 1950 (18% of all cookbooks in this section). Early ones include *The Peerless Cook Book* (Q23.1), about 1890, from Montreal's St James Methodist Church; *The Huntingdon Cook Book* (Q32.1), three editions of which were published between 1896 and 1907 to benefit St Andrew's Church in Huntingdon, close to the US border; and *The Sutton Souvenir* (Q41.1), 1899, organized by the Methodist pastor of this Eastern Townships village, which was just rebuilding after a serious fire the year before. Most later fund-raisers were also from Montreal and environs[10] (one Montreal company, United Publications Ltd, specialized in printing community cookbooks in the 1930s), from places in the Eastern Townships, such as Heathton, Waterville, North Hatley, Sherbrooke, Waterloo, Magog, Sweetsburg, Lennoxville, Cookshire, East Angus, South Bolton, and Sawyerville, or from the area directly south of Montreal (now called Montérégie, but then southern counties or southwestern Quebec), such as Noyan and St Johns. The exceptions were a 1949 cookbook (Q316.1) from Brownsburg, near Lachute, northwest of Montreal, and a 1933 volume (Q208.1) from Noranda, much farther northwest; a 1900 collection of *My Pet Recipes* (Q44.1) by the ladies of St Andrew's Church in Quebec City; the 1936 *Shawinigan Falls Cook Book* (Q242.1) and 1949 *Grand'Mère Favourite Recipes* (Q315.1), from towns north of Trois Rivières; four cookbooks from Arvida, north of Quebec City (the earliest, Q257.1, *International Cook Book*, 1939, reflecting the multicultural character of the town that sprang up with the new aluminium smelter; Q290.1, *Saguenay Cook Book*, 1944; Q318.1, *Saguenay Cook Book IV*, 1949); one from Baie Comeau, northeast of Quebec City, on the St Lawrence River north shore (Q271.1, 1941); and one from Percé, on the Gaspé Peninsula, the farthest east of all (Q314.1, 1948). The latter, 'The Black Whale' Cook Book, in which Ethel Renouf presents 'fine old recipes from the Gaspé Coast going back to pioneer days,' is one of the most delightful of the community-cookbook type in this bibliography, bringing together, in a volume decorated with woodcuts by Canadian artists, traditional recipes and evocative descriptions of the life and lore of a part of the province noted for its extraordinary natural environment. Another exceptional fund-raiser was *British, French, Italian, Russian, Belgian Cookery* (Q95.1), arranged by the sisters Grace Clergue Harrison and Gertrude Clergue 'to aid the war sufferers in the devastated districts of France' in 1916. It included a preface from the satirical pen of Stephen Leacock and recipes contributed by famous chefs, was published in the United States (as *Allied Cookery*) and in France in translation, and won the French Legion of Honor for the Clergue sisters. Although most community cookbooks in Quebec came from church groups, a variety of other organizations also produced them, such as chapters of the Imperial Order Daughters of the Empire, the Westmount Soldiers' Wives' League (Q86.1 features the art of Quebec book illustrators and a Montreal cartoonist), Rebekah Assembly of the Independent Order of Odd Fellows, branches of the Women's Institute, the Montreal Amateur Athletic Association (the text of Q142.1 gives diets for ath-

letes), St John Ambulance Brigade, Karnak Temple Arab Patrol (part of the Shriners organization in Montreal), Maritime Women's Club of Montreal, and the Leah Echenberg Chapter of Hadassah in Sherbrooke.

It is extraordinary, in light of the many successful publishing projects carried out by English-speaking women's groups in Quebec, that no French-language community cookbooks appear to have been published in the province in the entire period covered by this bibliography ('The Black Whale' Cook Book reprinted a few recipes in the original French, but even this limited incorporation of the language was a rare occurrence). The phenomenon likely has to do with religious denomination and social class since a similar trend occurs in the rest of Canada where community cookbooks from Protestant churches greatly outnumber those from Roman Catholic institutions. Catholic women's groups usually placed more emphasis on spiritual concerns than fund-raising projects, and tended to be less able to donate to the latter.[11] The authority the Catholic Church exercised over the lives of women, especially québécoises, and over the publication of printed material emanating from the church,[12] may have been another factor that inhibited Catholic women's groups from making cookbooks. Whatever the reasons, even if a few French-language community cookbooks were to surface, they would not change the fundamental pattern.

Advertising cookbooks outnumbered all other types of culinary manual published in Quebec in the first half of the twentieth century, and most were originally written in English, to be distributed nationally. Many Canadian food and manufacturing companies had their head offices and plants in Montreal, the country's banking and transportation centre at the time,[13] and several British and American businesses also located their Canadian operations in the city. Large Canadian companies that published cookbooks include several flour millers (Ogilvie Flour Mills Co. Ltd, Lake of the Woods Milling Co. Ltd, St Lawrence Flour Mills Co., Brodie and Harvie Ltd, Dominion Flour Mills Ltd), the Canada Starch Co. (makers of cornstarch, corn syrup, corn oil), Dominion Glass Co. (preserving jars), C.H. Catelli Ltd (pasta), sugar refiners (Canada Sugar Refining Co., Atlantic Sugar Refineries Ltd), W. Clark Ltd (canned foods), Lion Vinegar Co., and General Steel Wares Ltd (makers of McClary stoves and refrigerators). Of all these companies, Lake of the Woods Milling Co. Ltd had the most success using cookbooks as a promotional tool: the 1913 and 1915 editions of its *Five Roses Cook Book* (Q79.1) reached into over 950,000 Canadian kitchens, and the 1932 successor, *A Guide to Good Cooking* (Q203.1), was continuously revised and reprinted through the twentieth century. From 1938, the Robin Hood Flour cookbooks by the fictional Rita Martin (listed at Q249.1) were stiff competition for Five Roses, and copies are still commonly found in Canadian homes. Although Robin Hood Flour Mills was privately owned by an American, Robin Hood Flour was a Canadian brand, first milled in Moose Jaw, Saskatchewan, in 1909; it came to dominate the American market only after the Second World War, through a brilliant marketing strategy devised and executed by a Canadian, Charles Ritz. American products advertised through cookbooks include Church and Dwight's Cow Brand Baking Soda, Walter Baker and Co. Ltd chocolate (recipes by the celebrated American author and lecturer Maria Parloa), Price Baking Powder, Knox Gelatine, Royal Baking Powder, Fleischmann's Yeast, Borden's canned milk, Kraft-MacLaren and later Kraft-Phenix cheeses (originally the Canadian firm of MacLaren), and the flavourings, baking powder, and spices of J.R. Watkins Co. and W.T. Rawleigh Co. Ltd. British brands promoted through cookbooks include Cox's Gelatine, Lea and Perrins' Sauce, Keen's Mustard (*Culinary Art* of 1947, Q303.1, has a striking mustard-yellow cover), Oxo beef extract, and Fry-Cadbury cocoa and chocolate. Although the latter was a British product, the company employed Canadian authors: Mary Moore, a native of Hamilton, Ontario, whose syndicated cookery columns ran in newspapers across the country, compiled *Favourite Cocoa and Chocolate Recipes* (Q189.1) in about 1930–3; and Jehane Patenaude, a Montrealer, wrote *Chocolate around the Clock* (Q273.1) in 1941 – the very first cookbook from the woman who would soon become nationally famous through print, radio, and television, under her married name of Benoît.

Although mandated bilingualism for packaging or in the workplace, whether through federal or provincial law, would not be in force until the last decades of the twentieth century,[14] most of the Canadian, American, and British makers of brand-name products produced French translations of their cookbooks for the Quebec market (and for the smaller French-speaking populations in other provinces), as did at least twenty-six Ontario-based companies.[15] It was unusual, however, for translations to incorporate revisions for the francophone community. One example was *La cuisinière Five Roses* (Q79.4, a 1915 edition of *Five Roses Cook Book*), where the flour miller added a recipe for Tire à la Saint-Catherine, a special festival-day molasses candy in Quebec, and commissioned a new and more sophisticated illustrated binding de-

sign. It was rarer still for a company to produce a new text for Quebec, such as *Farine Purity, recettes anciennes et modernes* from Western Canada Flour Mills in about 1934–5 (Q222.1), which is not a translation of *The Purity Cook-Book* of 1932 (O771.1), or *Recettes de choix qui amélioreront vos menus* from Canada Starch Co. Ltd in the late 1930s (Q252.1), which is uniform with a series of four booklets written in English by Kate Aitken, but which does not appear to match any of them. In the case of *Recettes pour tous les jours* (O466.1) published in 1921 by the Hamilton, Ontario, branch of the American firm Procter and Gamble, the author, Miss Katherine M. Caldwell, consulted French-Canadian cooking authorities. In the 1930s, Canadian General Electric Co. Ltd in Toronto used a different method to reach the francophone market when it published *Entremets et boissons glacés* (O885.1) by an expert in electric cookery from France, Gabriel Dumont-Lespine. In the same period, Maple Leaf Milling Co. Ltd in Toronto used the French name of Marthe Miral in place of Anna Lee Scott for the fictional author of French translations of the Easy Way Series, in what was more a marketing ploy than a meaningful accommodation to a distinctive culture. Only a few advertising cookbooks written and published by French Canadians surfaced, for example: *Recettes et conseils utiles pour tous* (Q105.1) to promote the flour of La cie des farines naturelles, about 1919–23; *L'érable, orgueil du Québec* (Q152.1; English edition, *The Maple, Pride of Quebec*) from the Société des producteurs de sucre d'érable de Québec, in the 1920s; *Les recettes de grand'maman* (Q165.1) for Magasins indépendants Victoria, LaPorte, Martin ltée, in 1928; and in the 1930s, *Les recettes des mamans modernes* (Q194.1) for Maison J. Corbeil, *Poisson Primo Seafood* (Q223.1) from Louis-T. Blais ltée, *Catalogue des produits Rena* (Q225.1) from J.A. Renaud, a purveyor of kitchen utensils, two items from Familex Products Co., founded by R. Parent (Q226.1, Q232.1), and two from the co-operative Les épiciers modernes ltée, which distributed its goods through Magasins E-M Stores (Q241.1, Q262.1). In 1928 the Shawinigan Water and Power Co. published *Recettes utiles pour la cuisine électrique* (Q169.1) for local residents; however, the source of the text has not been determined. Since English businesses dominated the commercial life of the province, it is not surprising that translations of English-language advertising cookbooks from Quebec- and Ontario-based companies overwhelmed ones from the French community, but it does raise the issue of the effect of these translations on French-Canadian culinary traditions. And there were other outside influences: the French translations of the

American Fannie Farmer's *The Boston Cooking-School Cook Book* from 1941 on (O144.11; in French, *Le livre de cuisine de l'École de cuisine de Boston*);[16] and the French editions of federal government publications, usually written by anglophones, with the exception of Estelle LeBlanc, who collaborated on the 1938 Department of Fisheries cookbook, *100 Tempting Fish Recipes* (O936.1; in French, *100 délicieuses recettes de poisson*).

In the first half of the twentieth century, the Catholic education system continued to be a powerful mode of cultural transmission, and the textbooks produced for cookery classes in the schools were, perhaps, an antidote to the advertising cookbooks from English businesses and other translations that found their way into Quebec homes. After the start of girls' schooling in Quebec City in 1639, under the Ursuline sisters (the first school in all of North America), the education of Catholic girls remained largely in the hands of nuns for more than three hundred years. In the nineteenth century an extensive network of religious teaching congregations was established throughout the province, and the Catholic bureaucracy assumed control of curriculum and ideology and of the publication and distribution of textbooks. The infrastructure of day and boarding schools run by nuns remained in place until after 1950, and from 1905 many nuns also taught in public schools. The most influential of the teaching orders was the Congrégation de Notre-Dame. In 1905, in Saint-Pascal-de-Kamouraska, these sisters, at the invitation of the local priest, Alphonse Beaudet, opened a specialized school for teaching household arts (École de Saint-Pascal, renamed École normale classico-ménagère in June 1913, then Institution chanoine-Beaudet in May 1935), and the success of their program influenced the evolution of home-economics teaching in the province, especially the educational reforms of 1923. Most of the textbooks described in this bibliography emanated from the Congrégation de Notre-Dame and, like Caron's *Directions diverses*, most set the subject of cookery and home-making in an explicitly Christian context: *Hygiène de l'alimentation et propriétés chimiques des aliments*, 1912, by Amélie DesRoches, a teacher in Neuville (Q74.1); *Art culinaire*, 1916 (Q94.1); *Manuel de cuisine raisonnée*, 1919 (Q102.1); *The Whys and Wherefores of Cooking: A Simple Text Book for Elementary Cooking Schools*, about 1919, published by the order's Montreal Cooking School (Q104.1); *Cours d'enseignement ménager: art culinaire*, 1922 (Q122.1); *La cuisine à l'école primaire*, 1922, by soeur Sainte-Marie-Vitaline (Q128.1); *L'économie domestique à l'école primaire ... IIIe année*, 1924, by soeur Sainte-Marie-Vitaline (Q134.1), plus all the titles listed at this entry for the

newly reformed courses; *Science and Arts of Home Life for Elementary Grades: Beginners Course* and *More Advanced Course*, both copyright 1925 (Q144.1, Q145.1); and *235 recettes pour dîners et soupers*, 1942, by soeur Sainte-Marie-Vitaline (Q279.1). In 1928, Sister St Mary Edith, principal of the Montreal Cooking School (Congregation of Notre Dame), had published English and French editions of *Secrets of Good Cooking* (Q171.1, Q171.2). Intended for the 'average housewife,' the book was a distillation of the material she and her colleagues taught at the school. Former students, all society ladies (francophone for the French editions, mainly anglophone for the other), happily endorsed her work by signing the Preface, and the book was eventually issued in three French and three English editions. Of all these publications, however, it was *Manuel de cuisine raisonnée*, 'adapté aux élèves des cours élémentaires de l'École normale classico-ménagère de Saint-Pascal,' later called simply *La cuisine raisonnée*, that was to become the pre-eminent reference in French Quebec kitchens. *La cuisinière canadienne* and mère Caron's *Directions diverses* had run their long courses, the last editions appearing in the mid-1920s and 1913, respectively. *La cuisine raisonnée* carried the torch of cultural continuity for the next six decades, from 1919 to 1985. Other religious orders published cookbooks (Soeurs grises de Montréal,[17] Soeurs des Saints Noms de Jésus et de Marie,[18] and Servantes du Coeur immaculé de Marie[19]), but none gained the same enduring popularity in the French community as *La cuisine raisonnée*. One recipe collection was produced in connection with Montreal's Écoles ménagères provinciales, a secular institution that opened in 1907 and which in 1937 became affiliated with the University of Montreal: *350 recettes de cuisine* (Q73.1), 1912, by Jeanne Anctil, the school's director. Only two items surfaced for pupils in the Protestant School Board for Greater Montreal, from the early 1940s: *Lesson Outlines in Cookery for Sixth Year* and for the seventh year (Q275.1, Q276.1).

The earliest Quebec Department of Agriculture publication to touch upon cookery was *La bonne ménagère: notions d'économie domestique et d'agriculture à l'usage des jeunes filles des écoles rurales de la province de Québec*, of about 1900–10 (Q48.1). The Department of Agriculture also published the 1916 edition of Amélie DesRoches's textbook (Q74.3) and another title of a general nature, *Manuel de la cuisinière économe et pratique*, 1922, by Mme Alphonse Désilets (Q123.1). The department's other cookbooks treated more specific subjects: the traditional method of making *Le fromage raffiné de l'Isle-d'Orléans* (Q68.1) by Jean-

Charles Chapais, 1911, editions in both languages of Joseph-Évariste Grisé's booklets on home canning (Q96.1, 1917; Q184.1, 1930), *How to Save Wheat and Meat* (Q99.1) in the face of food restrictions during the First World War, editions in both languages of *Use of Honey and of Maple Sugar in Cooking* (Q109.1) by Blanche Lajoie-Vaillancourt, 1920, *Eat More Cheese* (Q137.1), 1924, *Le pain de ménage* (Q220.1) by Eugénie Paré, 1934, *Mangeons plus de légumes* (Q251.1), about 1938–9, and *Les volailles et les oeufs* (Q259.1), 1939. Cookbooks also emanated from the Department of Roads (*La bonne cuisine canadienne*, 1927, to assist the hotel trade; Q162.1) and the Department of Colonization, Game and Fisheries (*Sea Food Recipes*, about 1930–5, to encourage the consumption of fish, but based on a Nova Scotia advertising booklet; NS27.4–27.6).

Three professional male chefs produced cookbooks. Henry Schneider, whose career embraced Montreal's St James' Club and the Ritz Carlton Hotel, wrote *Practical Cookery* in 1910 (Q67.1). The instructions include the killing and preparation of a turtle for Turtle Soup, not the mundane tasks of home cooking as the title might suggest. Médéric L'Huillier, chef pâtissier at the Arcade Grill in the Montreal department store of Henry Morgan and Co., compiled a 1928 treatise on modern pastry-making (Q166.1). Ovila Charbonneau, chef at the Hôtel Corona in Coaticook, celebrated local ingredients and dishes in *La cuisine nationale* (Q235.1), 1936, designed for both the hotel trade and home cooks. If sophisticated hotel and private-club kitchens were the domain of men before 1950, so were the kitchens in lumber camps, where living conditions were notoriously poor. In 1936, J.E. Caron of Price Brothers and Co. (the lumber firm founded by Sir William Price and headquartered in Quebec City) prepared *Feeding Men in Camps* (Q238.1), for the Woodlands Section of the Canadian Pulp and Paper Association. The subject of outdoor cooking was a key element in *Camp Craft and Woodlore* (Q132.1), a booklet published in the 1920s by Canadian National Railways, to promote train travel. The author is unnamed, but the intended readers were undoubtedly men, who after hunting and fishing for food in the wilderness needed instruction on preparing the game and cooking it over a campfire, such as the one illustrated on the binding. *Saintes artisanes* (Q287.1), 1944, by the renowned anthropologist Marius Barbeau is included in this bibliography for his account of the role of the religious orders in Quebec's food history, his identification of the cookbooks they used, and his early recognition of the interest and importance of the province's culinary past.

Notable cookbooks by women after 1900, which fall outside of the classifications discussed above, include *Meals of the Day* (Q54.1) by Mrs Sarah Lovell, 1904. Married to the printer of the 1867 edition of Mrs Hart's *Household Recipes*, Sarah was a founding member of the Montreal Women's Club and well known in the city's literary and musical circles. She wrote the cookbook in her mid-seventies, several years after her husband's death. *Helps for Young Housekeepers* (Q77.1) of about 1912–15 reprints the personal recipe collection of the late Miss Minnie Crawford, as gathered together by Miss E.S. Crawford. Their family had lived in Verdun House on Montreal's Lower Lachine Road for over half a century before the lot was sold for development and the building torn down in 1911. The neighbourhood names attached to some of the dishes (Mrs Ellegood, Old Margaret, Aunt Chloe) evoke the 'generous hospitality' of Verdun House's past, while the titles of nineteenth-century cookbooks given as sources for some of the recipes offer a glimpse of a typical bookshelf. In the 1930s, two entrepreneurial francophone women each self-published a book about menus and entertaining. Mme Hélène Durand-La Roche's *Menus de réceptions* (Q237.1) of 1936 covered every significant social occasion and festival day in the year of a French-Canadian family, from baptisms to réveillons (the traditional Christmas Eve or New Year's Eve party), in 214 pages; from 1957 to 1977 it was republished as *Madame reçoit ... menus de réceptions* or just *Madame reçoit*, by Éditions Beauchemin, then Éditions de l'homme. Marie-Blanche Clément's self-published *Le repas d'apparat* (Q253.1) of 1939 was a humbler affair of just 25 pages.

All of Kate Aitken's publications fall in the Quebec section because the advertising cookbooks she wrote were for companies with Montreal head offices (the 1934 Famous Royal Household Recipes series for Ogilvie Flour Mills, Q214.1–218.1, and the 1940 '52' series for Canada Starch, Q263.1–266.1) and because her 1945 *Kate Aitken's Canadian Cook Book* was published by the *Montreal Standard* when she was the newspaper's food editor (Q292.1). Yet, she is more associated with Ontario, where she was born, where her culinary career was launched, and where she lived all of her life, commuting from her Toronto base to Montreal as needed, often weekly. She became a national icon, through her broadcasts on CBC radio (on cooking and other topics) and through *Kate Aitken's Canadian Cook Book*. Published in several editions up to 1992, this title stands as one of the most popular English-language Canadian cookbooks of the mid-twentieth century. There were no French translations.

McGill University in Montreal has the largest collection in Quebec of pre-1950 Canadian cookbooks, one of the top three holdings in the country (the others are Library and Archives Canada and University of Guelph). The Bibliothèque nationale du Québec focuses on material published in the province. Other collections of a significant size are at the following institutions: Brome County Historical Society, Knowlton; Bibliothèque de la ville de Montréal; McCord Museum, Montreal; library of the Séminaire de Québec, Quebec City (administered by Musée de l'Amérique française); and Bibliothèque des Frères du Sacré-Coeur (many uncatalogued) and Université Laval, Sainte-Foy. At the Archives des Ursulines in Trois-Rivières is one of only two known surviving copies of the first edition of *La cuisinière canadienne*. The archives of the Soeurs des Saints Noms de Jésus et de Marie in Longueuil and the archives of the Congrégation de Notre-Dame in Montreal contain an important record of the cookbooks published by these orders. For a full list of Quebec locations, see 'Abbreviations,' p xlvii.

NOTES

1 Oxford and New York: Basil Blackwell, 1987; the quoted phrase is on p 134. (A second edition was published by University of Illinois Press, Urbana, in 1996.)

2 In *All Manners of Food*, Mennell used the evidence of cookbooks up to about the turn of the twentieth century, but for the period after, he based his study on a selection of women's magazines, giving these reasons, on pp 232–3: 'By the twentieth century there were many sources of influence besides the cookery book. In any case, cookery books were becoming *too numerous and diverse to be easily studied* [italics added] as a medium of influence. Merely drawing a representative sample poses insoluble problems. Their variety and specialisation are significant facts in themselves, but it is much easier to follow trends in fashion through the cookery columns which appeared in the popular mass-circulation women's magazines in France and England.' He cites the large circulation of magazines, but admits that 'of course books are retained much longer than a magazine.' Women's periodicals are, indeed, rich sources of information for Europe and Canada. Where Mennell faced the problem of choosing representative titles of English and French cookbooks from a huge body of publications, the Canadian corpus is smaller and this bibliography provides a remedy for anyone wishing to pursue similar questions in Canadian food history.

3 For the history of French eighteenth-century cooking, see Wheaton 1996.

4 For the role of booksellers as publishers, see Parker, p 18.

5 *The Canadian Farrier* of 1834 (Q2.1), which was published midway between *La cuisinière bourgeoise* and *Modern Practical Cookery*, is not a cookbook proper, but a compendium of of various types of information, including recipes. It was printed in the Eastern Townships.

6 In 1871, *The Manuscript Receipt Book and Household Treasury*, from the United States (Q9.1); in 1877, *Cookery for the Million*, from Great Britain (Q13.1); in 1898, *Home Helps* by the American Sarah Tyson Rorer (Q37.1); and in 1899, *Cooking Hints* by the American Marion Harland (Q40.1).

7 *The Jewish Manual*, edited by a lady [Lady Judith Cohen Montefiore], London: T. and W. Boone, 1846; facsimile ed., with introduction by Chaim Raphael, New York: Nightingale, 1983, also London: Sidgwick and Jackson, 1985.

8 In about 1922 the National Council of Jewish Women published *The Council Kosher Cook Book* compiled by Miss Libbie Jacobs (Q127.1). Mrs Tina Lohman's 1942 *Book of Jewish Recipes* (O1051.1) was published simultaneously in Toronto and Montreal; I have not determined whether she was a Quebecker. In the late 1940s, the Leah Echenberg Chapter of Hadassah in Sherbrooke compiled the *Eastern Townships' Third Annual Shoppers' Guide and Cook Book* (Q319.1), and, one assumes, two earlier annual issues. The much-loved and frequently reprinted *A Treasure for My Daughter: A Reference Book of Jewish Festivals with Menus and Recipes*, edited by Bessie W. Batist and published by the Ethel Epstein Ein Chapter of Hadassah in Montreal in 1950, falls just outside the bounds of this bibliography.

9 The other three are: *Cuisine*, Saint John, New Brunswick, 1878 (NB2.1); *The Canadian Economist*, Ottawa, Ontario, 1881 (O28.1); and *The Housekeeper's Help*, Hamilton (O44.1). Since the revised edition of *The Housekeeper's Help* was published in 1888, the first edition likely appeared before *Clever Cooking for Careful Cooks*.

10 Including, of course, Westmount, the separately incorporated anglophone city, just west of Montreal's downtown area. Westmount amalgamated with Montreal on 1 January 2002, but de-amalgamated in 2006.

11 See Lynne Marks, *Revivals and Roller Rinks: Religion,*

Leisure, and Identity in Late-Nineteenth-Century Small-Town Ontario, Toronto: University of Toronto Press, 1996, pp 70–1, discussing Brian Clarke, *Piety and Nationalism: Lay Voluntary Associations and the Creation of an Irish-Catholic Community in Toronto, 1850–1895*, McGill-Queen's University Press, 1993, p 83.

12 Pierre Hébert explains how the clergy 'by tacit agreement ... exercised control over printed materials in Quebec' from 1840 until the Quiet Revolution, in 'From Censoring Print to Advising Readers in Quebec,' in *History of the Book in Canada*, Vol. 3, *1918–1980*, pp 475–80, Carol Gerson and Jacques Michon, eds, Toronto: University of Toronto Press, 2007; also published in French as *Histoire du livre et de l'imprimé au Canada*, Les presses de l'Université de Montréal.

13 Montreal's port lost its privileged position for shipping in 1959 when the St Lawrence Seaway opened, allowing larger vessels passage between the Great Lakes and the Atlantic Ocean. After the separatist Parti québécois came to power in 1976, banks, insurance companies, and other large businesses shifted their headquarters to Toronto.

14 Federal measures were enacted in the Official Languages Act of 1969 and 1988. Quebec made French the sole official language of the province in 1974.

15 The following are some of the Ontario-based companies who published French translations of their cookbooks: Campbell Soup Co. Ltd; Canada Bread Co. Ltd; Canada Packers Ltd (meat); Canadian General Electric Co. Ltd (Hotpoint stoves); Canadian Shredded Wheat Co. Ltd; Canadian Westinghouse Co. Ltd (refrigerators); Carnation Co. Ltd (canned milk); Davis Gelatine (Canada) Ltd; Dodds Medicine Co. Ltd; Douglas-Pectin Ltd (Certo); E.W. Gillett Co. Ltd, later Standard Brands Ltd (maker of Magic Baking Powder, Royal Yeast); General Foods Ltd (Swans Down Cake Flour); Genesee Pure Food Company of Canada Ltd (Jell-O); H.J. Heinz Co. ('57 Varieties' of prepared foods); Imperial Oil Co. Ltd (distributor of New Perfection stoves); Kellogg Company of Canada Ltd (breakfast cereals); Kelvinator of Canada Ltd (refrigerators); Lydia E. Pinkham Medicine Co.; Maple Leaf Milling Co. Ltd; Metropolitan Life Insurance Co.; Moffats Ltd (stoves); National Pressure Cooker Co. (Canada) Ltd; Swift Canadian Co. Ltd (meat); Western Canada Flour Mills Co. Ltd (Purity Flour); W.T. Rawleigh Co. Ltd (flavourings); and Zam-Buk Co. (skin ointment). These companies' cookbooks are described in the Ontario section; to identify entry numbers, check the Name Index.

16 French-speaking Quebec families also consulted the English editions of Farmer's work; see the biographical note for Farmer at O144.1.

17 *Manuel de diététique à l'usage des écoles ménagères*, 1927 (Q161.1).

18 *La cuisine pratique à l'école primaire et dans la famille* by soeur Catherine-de-Cardone, 1930 (Q178.1).

19 *Aliments et nutrition*, 1946 (Q299.1), and *La cuisinière économe et avisée*, 1947 (Q305.1), both by soeur Marie de Sainte-Thérèse de Jésus.

1825

Menon (fl. 1739–95)

Cookbook writing flourished in mid-eighteenth-century France. Menon – a proponent of 'la cuisine moderne' over 'la cuisine ancienne' – was the most productive and influential of French culinary authors of the time. His cookbooks were published in multiple editions, in various languages, in Europe and England, yet no biographical information has surfaced about his life. In addition to La cuisinière bourgeoise, *other titles that bear his name are:* Nouveau traité de la cuisine, *Vols 1–2, Paris: Michel-Étienne David, 1739 (Vicaire 588), and Vol. 3, titled* La nouvelle cuisine, *Paris: David père, 1742 (Vicaire 589);* La science du maître d'hôtel cuisinier, *Paris: Paulus-du-Mesnil, 1749 (United States: InU; Vicaire 590); and* La science du maître d'hôtel, confiseur, *Paris: Paulus-du-Mesnil, 1750 (United States: InU; Vicaire 590; Simon No. 1040 says the first edition was Paris, 1749).*

Traditionally attributed to Menon are: Les soupers de la cour, *Vols 1–4, Paris: Guillyn, 1755 (United States: DLC, InU; Vicaire 591);* Cuisine et office de santé propre, *Paris: Le Clerc, Prault père, and Babuty père, 1758 (United States: InU; Simon No. 1037, Vicaire 591); and* Traité historique et pratique de la cuisine, *Vols 1– 2, Paris: Cl. J.B. Bauche, 1758 (United States: DLC, InU; Simon No. 1043, Vicaire 592). Barbara Ketcham Wheaton explains why she doubts these attributions, in Wheaton 1996, pp 207–8, and pp 298–9, note 45.*

Other titles attributed to Menon by Vicaire are: Le manuel des officiers de bouche, *Paris: Le Clerc, 1759 (United States: DLC; Simon No. 1042, Vicaire 592);* Almanach de cuisine, pour l'année M.DCC.LXI, *Paris: Leclerc, 1761 (Vicaire 593); and* Almanach d'office, pour l'année M.DCC.LXI, *Paris: Leclerc, 1761 (Vicaire 593).*

Q1.1   1825
La / cuisinière / bourgeoise, / précédée / d'un manuel / prescrivant les devoirs qu'ont a remplir les / personnes qui se destinent a entrer en / service dans les maisons bourgeoises. / Cet ouvrage contient, en outre: / 1°. Les recettes pour faire une bonne cuisine à peu de frais; / les moyens les plus utiles pour vider et trousser la volaille et / le gibier, ainsi que la dissection de toute sorte de viandes; / 2°. La pâtisserie et les confitures de différentes espèces; les / liqueurs, ratafias; la composition des vinaigres et des boissons / les plus économiques, etc., etc.; / 3°. Les soins à apporter pour élever la volaille, pour faire / le beurre, les fromages, et

conserver les liqueurs et les fruits; / 4°. Enfin, l'art de gouverner la cave et les vins; la manière / de servir les tables, et d'en faire les honneurs. / Troisième édition, / revue par une maitresse de maison. / Prix: 2 francs. / A Québec, / chez Augustin Germain, libraire. / M. DCCC. XXV.

DESCRIPTION: 17.0 × 9.5 cm   Pp [i–iii] iv, [5] 6–312 Frontis titled 'La propreté est l'ornement de nos tables et l'honneur d'une bonne cuisinière.'   Rebound

CONTENTS: i tp; ii blank; iii–iv 'Avis sur cette seconde édition.'; 5–303 text in nineteen chapters; 304–12 'Table des matières' and at bottom p 312, 'Imprimerie de J^H. Moronval, rue Galande, no°. 65.'

CITATIONS: Armstrong 2000, p F2   BQ 20-0993 Brisebois No. 99, p 25, illus   Carrière No. 104   Cooke 2002, p 234   Driver 2002, Home Cook Book, p xii Driver 2003, 'Canadian Cookbooks,' p 27   FabreCat June 1837, p 12   Watier, p 7   Williamson, History of the Book, p 276   Neering, p 23

COPIES: CIHM (95315)   OONL (TX707 M45 1825) *QMBM (641.5 C966cu)   QMBN (TX719 M45 1825 RES. and 160037 CON)

NOTES: See pl 14. This 1825 Quebec City edition of *La cuisinière bourgeoise* by Menon is the first cookbook published in what is now Canada. It was first published in Paris more than three-quarters of a century before. The author is not named, but his identity is known from earlier French editions. Michel Brisebois notes in his exhibition catalogue entry that the Quebec City edition, including the title-page, was printed in Paris. In June 1837 the Montreal bookseller Édouard-Raymond Fabre listed the title in his catalogue at the price of 3s 4d.

The QMBM copy is inscribed on the verso of the frontispiece, in ink, 'Marie Anne Esther Nelson Guy 1835.'

Philip and Mary Hyman, in their entry for 'French Cookbooks' in Davidson, p 319, comment that *La cuisinière bourgeoise* was the first French cookbook addressed to women, in this case to females working as cooks in middle-class homes (all earlier ones were written for men, by men – usually professional chefs in the employ of the aristocracy). Their research shows that *La cuisinière bourgeoise* went through more than 120 editions from 1746, some of which I have listed below.

FRENCH EDITIONS: There was apparently more than one edition dated 1746: *La nouvelle cuisinière bourgeoise*, Paris: Guillyn, 1746, pp 322 (United States: InU; Cagle No. 336 proposes that this edition, with its unique title and only 322 pp, is the first); and *La cuisinière bourgeoise*, Paris: Guillyn, 1746, pp 400

(France: PBNF; Bitting, p 320, Vicaire 235 and 589), Paris: Deckherr frères, 1746 (France: PBNF), and Paris: Deckher ... et Barbier, 1746 (France: PBNF). Marius Barbeau, in Q287.1, p 105, cites an edition dated 1745 at the General Hospital in Quebec City; 1745 may be a typographical error.

The many later editions, titled *La cuisinière bourgeoise* except where indicated otherwise, include: Paris: Guillyn, 1748 (France: PBNF; United States: InU; Vicaire 236); Paris: 1750 (United States: InU; Vicaire 236); Paris: Guillyn, 1752 (France: PBNF; United States: InU; Vicaire 236); Paris: Guillyn, 1756 (United States: InU); Paris: Guillyn ..., 1762 (United States: DLC); Paris: Guillyn, 1764 (www.abebooks.com, 19 July 2000); Paris: Guillyn, 1767 (Rudolph Nos. 137 and 137a); Paris: Guillyn, 1769 (France: PBNF; Rudolph No. 143, Vicaire 236); Paris: Monory, 1769 (Vicaire 236); 1774 (Bitting, p 320); Paris: Guillyn, 1775 (Rudolph No. 155); Paris: P. Guillaume Cavelier, 1777 (United States: DLC, InU); Paris: 1778 (Wheaton 1996, p 300, note 1); Paris: L. Cellot, 1779 (France: PBNF); Lyon: Amable Leroy, 1783 (Rudolph No. 172, Vicaire 236); Paris: P.-M. Nyon le jeune, 1788 (France: PBNF); Paris: Nyon, 1789 (Vicaire 236); Paris: Louis, 1794 (Simon No. 1039); Paris: André, An VI de la République [1797 or 8] (United States: DLC); Paris: Batillot fils, 1801 (Rudolph No. 210); Lyon: Leroy, 1802 (Poulain-Le FurCat 13 Jan 2001, No. 344); Paris: Les libraires associés, 1807 (Private collection); Paris: H. Nicolle, 1807 (www.abebooks.com, 19 July 2000); Paris: 1814 (cited by Barbeau in Q287.1, p 108, as at Hôtel-Dieu hospital in Quebec City); Avignon: Guichard, 1815 (France: PBNF); Avignon: imp. Guichard, 1816 (Vicaire 236); Paris: Lécrivain, 1817 (France: PBNF; Vicaire 236); Besançon: impr. d'A. Montarsolo, 1821 (France: PBNF; Vicaire 236); Paris: Guillaume, 1822 (France: PBNF; Vicaire 236); *La plus nouvelle cuisinière bourgeoise*, Paris: Vauquelin, 1822 (Bitting, p 320); Paris: Lecomte et Durey, 1823 (Vicaire 237); new ed., Paris: Moronval, 1823 (Vicaire 237); 2nd ed., Paris: Moronval, 1823 (Vicaire 237); Paris: Moronval, 1824 (Vicaire 237); Paris: Chassaignon, 1825 (France: PBNF; Vicaire 237); Montbéliard: impr. Deckherr, 1825 (Vicaire 237); Paris: Moronval, 1826 (Vicaire 237); Paris: Moronval, 1827 (Vicaire 237); Paris: Moronval, 1828 (Vicaire 237); Paris: Moronval, 1829 (Vicaire 237); Paris: Moronval, 1830 (Vicaire 237); Paris: Moronval, 1831 (Vicaire 237); Paris: Moronval, 1832 (Vicaire 237); Montbéliard: Deckherr, [1834] (France: PBNF); Montbéliard: Deckherr, 1835 (Vicaire 237); Paris: Moronval, 1836 (Vicaire 237); Paris: Moronval, 1838 (Vicaire 237); Paris: J. Moronval, 1841 (Bitting, p 321, Vicaire 237); Paris: Moronval, 1844 (Vicaire

237); Paris: Moronval, 1845 (Vicaire 237); Paris: Moronval, 1851 (Vicaire 237); Montbéliard: Barbier, 1852 (Vicaire 237); Paris: Moronval, 1855 (Vicaire 237); Paris: Moronval, 1857 (Vicaire 237); Paris: Moronval, 1866 (Vicaire 238); facsimile of Paris: Guillyn, 1746, Luzarches: D. Morcrette, 1977 (France: PBNF); facsimile of Bruxelles: François Foppens, 1774, [Paris:] Temps actuels, [1981] (France: PBNF; United States: NcD).

BELGIAN EDITIONS: Bruxelles: François Foppens, 1764 (Vicaire 236); Bruxelles: François Foppens, 1767 (Vicaire 236); Bruxelles: François Foppens, 1771 (Bitting, p 320); Bruxelles: François Foppens, 1774 (United States: DLC catalogue); Bruxelles: François Foppens, 1775 (France: PBNF; Simon No. 1038, Vicaire 236); Bruxelles: 1777 (Wheaton 1996, p 300, note 1); Bruxelles: F. Foppens, 1779 (United States: DLC); Liège: C. Plomteux, 1788 (Vicaire 236); Bruxelles: François Foppens, 1790 (Rudolph Nos. 189 and 189a).

BRITISH EDITIONS: *The French Family Cook: Being a Complete System of French Cookery ...*, London: Printed for J. Bell, 1793 (United States: InU; Bitting, p 554; Maclean, p 101, lists locations of copies; Oxford, pp 121–2); 4th ed., enlarged by S. Taylor, retitled *The Complete Family Cook; Being a System of Cookery*, London: Printed [for?] J. Annereau, 1796 (Maclean, p 101, lists one location); *The Accomplished Family Cook*, by A. Glasse (the name was pirated, to boost sales, according to Oxford), London: Printed for J. Bell, 1797 (Maclean, p 57; Oxford, pp 124–5).

1834

The Canadian farrier

Q2.1 1834
The / Canadian farrier, / or / farmer's manual / for the treatment of / horses, net cattle, sheep & swine. / By a practical farrier. / To which is added the / family physician; / or useful / family guide, / containing / plain and simple directions / for the treatment of the most / common diseases, / with a great variety of / medical and other recipes. / Published by Richard C. Hoit[.?] / Walton & Gaylord, / printers, Stanstead and Sherbrooke, L.C. / 1834.
DESCRIPTION: 16.0 × 10.0 cm   Pp [iii–vii] viii–xi [xii], [13] 14–132 [133–42 lacking]   Rebound
CONTENTS: iii tp; iv blank; v 'Preface' dated Stanstead, June 1834; vi blank; vii–xi 'Contents'; xii blank; 13–40

'Part I. Of Horses.'; 41–mid 51 'Part II. [Of Cattle.]'; mid 51–54 'Part III. Of Sheep.'; 55–7 'Part IV. [Of Swine.]'; 58–67 'Additions, from Various Authors'; 68 blank; 69–118 'The Family Physician'; 119–21 'Baiting'; 122–32 'Valuable Recipes, on Different Subjects'; 133–42 lacking, but table of contents gives heading 'Cookery'

COPIES: *QMBN (619.02 H688 SIC) QTU; United States: DLC (SF749 H72)

NOTES: The section of 'Valuable Recipes' includes some culinary ones: To Imitate Green Tea, p 124; Native Tea, pp 124–5; To Purify Water, p 125; Soda Powders (for making beverages), p 126; To Preserve Eggs, p 127; To Restore and Improve Flour, p 130; To Salt Beef, pp 131–2; and To Pickle Pork or Mutton Hams, p 132. The table of contents lists the following under 'Cookery': Beer; Cup Cake; Currant Jelly; Currant Wine; Dyspepsia Bread; Emptings, Hard; Gingerbread; Loaf Cake; Oatmeal Cake; Puddings; Pudding Sauce; Pies; Pie Crust; Preserves; Pickles; Raspberry Shrub; Sponge Cake; Tea Cake; and Wedding Cake.

AMICUS lists OLU as a location for *The Canadian Farrier*, but the book is not held by the library.

1840

La cuisinière canadienne

Q3.1 [1st ed., May 1840]
La / cuisinière / canadienne, / contenant tout ce qu'il est nécessaire de savoir dans / un ménage, pour préparer les diverses / soupes grasses et maigres, / cuire le boeuf, le veau, le mouton, le cochon, la volaille, / le gibier et le poisson: appreter les poudings / de toute espèce, ainsi que les patisseries en général, / comprenant la manière de / faire la pate feuilletée, / et une grande variété de / patés, tartes, biscuits, beignes et pains de savoie; / les confitures et les gelées de toutes sortes; / la préparation des oeufs et des crêmes, / enfin des recettes pour les / liqueurs et autres breuvages, / et des notes sur les marinades, les légumes et salades. / Montreal: / imprimée et publiée par Louis Perrault, / rue Ste. Thérèse, ancienne place du Vindicator. / Prix un ecu.

DESCRIPTION: 17.5 × 10.0 cm   Pp [3–7] 8–114   Rebound in full leather; original paper cover included in new binding

CONTENTS: 3 tp; 4 'District de Montréal. Bureau des protonotaires. No. 38. Vingt-septième jour de mai 1840. Qu'il soit notoire que le vingt-septième jour de mai, dans l'année mil-huit-cent-quarante, Louis Per-

rault, imprimeur-libraire de Montréal, a déposé dans ce Bureau le titre d'un livre dans les mots suivants, savoir: "La cuisinière canadienne &c." Au sujet du quel il réclame le droit propriété. Enrégistré [*sic*] conformément à l'Acte provincial, intitulé, "Acte pour protéger la propriété littéraire." L.S. Monk et Morrogh, P.B.R.' and below the copyright notice, a note about the increase in price since the first advertisement of the book: 'Les dépenses encourrues, pour rendre l'ouvrage plus complet; et la quantité d'articles ajoutés au plan que nous nous étions d'abord tracé, sont les raisons qui nous forcent d'augmenter le prix fixé par la première annonce:'; 5 'Préface'; 6 'Avis essentiels'; 7–108 text in fifteen chapters (I, 'Soupes grasses,' 'Soupes maigres'; II, 'Du boeuf'; III, 'Du veau'; IV, 'De l'agneau ou du mouton'; V, 'Du cochon'; VI, 'De la volaille'; VII, 'Du gibier'; VIII, 'Du poisson'; IX, 'Des poudings'; X, 'Pâtisseries en général,' 'Des biscuits,' 'Des beignes,' 'Pain de Savoie,' 'Macarons'; XI, 'Des confitures,' 'Des gelées'; XII, 'Des oeufs'; XIII, 'Des crêmes'; XIV, 'Recettes pour les liqueurs,' 'Autres breuvages'; XV, 'Des marinades,' 'Des légumes et salades'; 109–14 'Table des articles contenus dans la cuisinière canadienne'

CITATIONS: Armstrong 2000, p F2, illus F2   Armstrong 2004, p D2   Cooke 2002, p 234   Driver 2002, Home Cook Book, p xii   Driver 2003, 'Canadian Cookbooks,' pp 24, 27, 28   Driver 2005, pp 409, 552 (note 78)   DucharmeCat 27, January 1928, No. 4333, p 149   Eade, p E1   FabreCat June 1845, p 55   Ferguson/Fraser, p 232   Lafrance/Desloges, pp 103–4   Leduc, illus   Neering, pp 28, 32 (cites title incorrectly)   Powers/Stewart, pp 175–6 (Yvon Desloges, 'Quebec's Culinary Traditions: An Overview')   Watier, p 7   Williamson, History of the Book, pp 276–7

COPIES: CIHM (95419)   *OONL   QQS (missing)   QTURA (641.5 C966)

NOTES: See pl 15. The printer and publisher, Louis Perrault, announced the book for sale in an advertisement dated 10 April 1840, in *Aurore des Canadas*, which says that *La cuisinière canadienne* is 'sous presse et paraîtra incessamment ... Livret in 12, prix: un écu.' A description of the work follows: 'Ouvrage indispensable aux mères de famille, aux jeunes femmes, et généralement à toutes les personnes qui veulent apprendre à bien préparer et cuire les viandes, faire les pâtisseries et confitures, aussi recettes pour les liqueurs, boissons, &c. &c. N.P. Les directions sont toutes garanties infaillibles, étant extraites du Journal d'un ancien confiseur de Montréal, et ont été éprouvées par plusieurs familles.' Again in *Aurore des Canadas*, but two months later, in an advertisement dated 2 June 1840, Perrault announces the book 'en vente chez Louis Perrault ... aussi chez E.R. Fabre, rue St. Vincent.' An advertisement in *La canadienne* of 6 August 1840 states that 'Louis Perrault offre maintenant en vente La cuisinière canadienne contenant tout ce qu'il est nécessaire de savoir dans un ménage ... 4 juin.' The 1840 edition was apparently still available for sale five years later, since Édouard-Raymond Fabre (Perrault's brother-in-law) listed the title in the June 1845 catalogue for his bookstore (not *Nouvelle cuisinière canadienne*, as Q3.2); no price is given.

La cuisinière canadienne is the first French-language cookbook written in Canada. Q1.1, *La cuisinière bourgeoise* of 1825, is an edition of a text from France. *La cuisinière canadienne* is, therefore, an important record of French-Canadian cooking and it was published in the period when the cuisine 'finally found its identity' (Lafrance/Desloges, p 103). Lafrance and Desloges comment on the book's significance: '*La cuisinière canadienne* ... was for Quebec what La Varenne's *Le cuisinier français* was for France, or Simmons' *American Cookery* [was] for the United States.' Likely with reference to one of the later editions, which were retitled *La nouvelle cuisinière canadienne*, they compare the text with *La cuisinière bourgeoise*, citing borrowed recipes, and find the book's contents 'much less modern' than contemporary French cookbooks. They remark upon the English influences (especially the pudding recipes), and identify the distinctly Québécois recipes, ingredients, and 'rudimentary style of cooking' (there are twenty-two recipes called 'Canadian-style' plus others). The 'Préface' explains what guided the choice of recipes: 'Nous nous sommes borné à n'insérer dans ce livre, que ce que recommandait une sage économie domestique, et proportionnée aux moyens des familles canadiennes.'

The compiler of the text is unknown, but was undoubtedly someone close to Louis Perrault. I have not identified the 'ancien confiseur,' whose journal is credited in Perrault's advertisement as the source for the recipes. The confiseur may be fictitious, devised by Perrault to give authority to the collection or to hide the identity of a female compiler. If the journal existed (a good possibility, since it would have provided a convenient source of recipes for the cookbook), it may be significant that Perrault's father, Julien Isadore Perrault, was at one time a master baker (DCB, Vol. 9, p 633). Mary F. Williamson has checked an 1820 Montreal city directory for professionals in the baking and confectionery trade and found one name with a possible connection to Perrault's circle: Benjamin Berthelet, baker, shares the

same last name as Olivier Berthelet, who attended school with Perrault's brother-in-law Édouard-Raymond Fabre and who donated land to the Institute of Providence (regarding this institution, see below); further research is required to confirm a family connection.

The most important evidence linking the text to Perrault's immediate milieu are the recipes linked to individuals: three pastry recipes, 'à la manière de Fournier, cuisinier' on p 57, and 'Façon de P. Marcelais' and 'Façon de Mme Tulloch [*sic*]' on p 58; Pain de Savoie, 'manière de Fournier le cuisinier' on p 77; and Macarons 'à la façon de Mdlle. Thibeaudeau [*sic*]' on p 78. Only P. Marcelais remains unidentified. Both Mme Tullock and Mlle Thibodeau were part of the group of women supporting the charitable work of Mme Gamelin (born Marie Emmélie Eugene Tavernier, 19 February 1800 in Montreal, died 23 September 1851), which led, in 1843, to the founding of the Institute of Providence, with Mme Gamelin as the first mother superior; and 'Fournier le cuisinier' may be related to the three Fournier sisters, one of whom later joined the religious order, or another member of their family. The multi-volume history of the order records information about Mme Tullock, Mlle Thibodeau, and the Fournier family, and also reveals the close connection between Perrault's family and supporters of the Institute of Providence (*L'Institut de la Providence: histoire des Filles de la charité servantes des pauvres dites Soeurs de la Providence*, 6 vols, Montreal: Providence (Maison mère), 1925–40; subsequently published in English as *The Institute of Providence: History of the Daughters of Charity Servants of the Poor Known as the Sisters of Providence*, 6 vols, Montreal: Providence Mother House, 1927–58; page references below are to the French edition). Mme Tullock, née Marie Anne Josephte Hogue, was 'une des collaboratrices les plus dévouées de notre fondatrice' and five of her grandchildren would eventually join the order (Vol. 1, p 523); her husband, Augustin Tullock, was a major benefactor and in 1842 was chosen as a trustee of the proposed Providence Asile (Vol. 1, pp 238, 523). Mlle Marie Marguerite Thibodeau (1817–94), who had been a teacher in Montreal, was an 'inséparable collaboratrice' of Mme Gamelin (Vol. 1, p 245); she became a novice of the Institute of Providence in 1843 (Vol. 4, p 381), and took the religious name mère de l'Immaculée-Conception. The three Fournier sisters (born to Joseph Fournier and Apolline Racicot) – Hippolyte, Clotilde, and Luce – ran the École Saint-Jacques for girls from 1836 to 1846, when Clotilde joined the order of the Institute of Providence and, a year later, Hippolyte and Luce joined the order of Bon-Pasteur (Vol. 2, p 139; Vol. 4, pp 214–15). Mme Léon Fournier assisted Mme Gamelin at the time of the Institute's founding (Vol. 1, pp 287, 380), and Mmes Léon and E. Fournier were elected 'conseillères' of the Dames de l'Association de charité in 1845 (Vol. 2, p 35). Mme Gamelin herself had been brought up, after the death of her mother, in the family of Louis Perrault's aunt and uncle, Marie Anne Tavernier and Joseph Perrault (Marie Anne was Mme Gamelin's mother's sister; Joseph was Louis Perrault's father's brother). In 1829, both Mme Tullock and Louis Perrault's mother assisted Mme Gamelin in her charitable work (Vol. 1, pp 70–1). In 1831, Mme Gamelin formed 'une société de dames' to help in visiting the poor and in collecting money, which was composed of her relatives and friends and included, among others, Louis Perrault's sister Luce (Mme Édouard-Raymond Fabre), his Aunt Agathe (Mme Maurice Nowlan, his father's sister), and Mrs Tullock (Vol. 1, p 78). In 1841, Louis Perrault's mother, his sister Luce, and two aunts (Agathe and her sister Marie Claire) were among the first ladies elected to the Corporation of the Montreal Asile for Aged and Infirm Women, and his sister Delphine was elected in 1852 (Vol. 1, pp 545–8). It is interesting to note that Mme Gamelin's supporters had been holding fund-raising bazaars to aid her charitable work since 1833 and that one bazaar was held on 27 August 1840, not long after the publication of *La cuisinière canadienne* (Vol. 1, p 476). One wonders whether the cookbook was offered for sale at the bazaar or whether the ladies prepared food for the bazaar following its recipes. Regarding the possible involvement of Mme Gamelin in the book's preparation, it may be significant that she considered herself an excellent cook, especially of puff pastry (letter to Mme Maurice Nowlan, 19 February 1821, quoted in Vol. 1, p 33: 'Savez-vous qu'à Québec je passe pour une parfaite cuisinière? Il n'y en a pas de pareille à moi pour les pâtisseries surtout la pâte feuilletée.'); however, if she or the other ladies had been involved, one would expect a reference to *La cuisinière canadienne* in the multi-volume history. There can be no question that *La cuisinière canadienne* was used in the kitchens of the Institute of Providence after its founding in 1843, as mère Caron borrowed heavily from it when she compiled her 1878 recipe collection used by the sisters, Q15.1, *Directions diverses*.

The OONL copy of *La cuisinière canadienne* was part of the collection of Canadiana amassed by Georges-Alphonse Daviault of Berthierville, Quebec. It was bequeathed to his grandson, who donated it to the National Library in 2001.

The QTURA copy, which is rebound in cloth, measures 18.0 × 10.0 cm. The first and last leaves are in poor condition: the printing on the title-page is partially obscured along the right edge by a strip of fabric adhering to the surface of the paper; and the printing on p 114 is also partially obscured along the left edge by a strip of fabric.

The Musée de l'Amérique française in Quebec City, which is now in charge of the Séminaire de Québec's old and rare books ('fonds anciens'), has a record in its card catalogue for *La cuisinière canadienne* of 1840, but the volume has been missing for years. In the mid-1950s, the 'cover' (actually the title-page) of the now-missing volume was reproduced in *We Can Cook, Too! Recipes Hot off the Press*, compiled by the Montreal Branch of the Canadian Women's Press Club, nd [about 1956?], p 44. The date of publication, '1840,' is inscribed below the price, likely in a later hand; the library's stamp is at bottom right. The caption for the reproduction identifies it as from 'the oldest cook book in Laval University's archives in Quebec City.' (The reproduction from *We Can Cook, Too!* is illustrated in Armstrong 2000, p F2.)

Cookbook lovers will regret not being able to buy the copy of the first edition of *La cuisinière canadienne* offered for sale for $1.00 by the Montreal bookdealer G. Ducharme, in 1928.

Q3.2   nd [about 1850–5]
—Nouvelle / cuisiniere / canadienne, / contenant tout ce qu'il est nécessaire de savoir dans un / ménage, tel que l'achat de diverses sortes de denrées, – la / manière de préparer les soupes grasses et maigres, cuire et / assaisonner les potages et rôtis de toute espèce, ainsi que les / pâtisseries, confitures et gelées; la préparation des oeufs et / des crêmes; enfin des recettes pour les liqueurs et autres / breuvages, – sur les marinades, les légumes et les salades; / aussi, quelques recettes diverses. Le tout précédé par quel- / ques aphorismes sur la science du bien vivre. / Edition / revue, corrigee et considerablement augmentee. / Montreal: / imprimée et publiée par Louis Perrault, / rue Saint Vincent.
DESCRIPTION: 16.5 × 9.0 cm   Pp [1–4] 5–108   Leather
CONTENTS: 1 tp; 2 'Enregistrée conformément à l'Acte provincial, intitulé: "Acte pour protéger la propriété littéraire."'; 3 'Introduction'; 4–7 'Aphorismes sur la science du bien vivre'; 8–mid 9 'Du choix des viandes'; mid 9–mid 10 'Du choix des volailles'; bottom 10–12 'Du choix des poissons'; 13–104 text in fifteen numbered chapters, but no chapter numbered XIV; 105–8 'Table des matières'

CITATIONS: Brisebois No. 100, p 25   Possibly Cooke 2002, p 234   MontrealBACat, 15–16 Sept 1977, sale 103, No. 420 (sold for $210)

COPIES: *OONL (TX719 N695 1850z)   OTMCL (641.5 N595)   QMBN (138379 CON)   QMM (TX715.6 N65 1850z Lande)

NOTES: OONL dates this edition [185?]. It could not have been published before 1844, when the publisher Perrault was at Ste Thérèse Street. Montreal city directories for 1844–5 to 1853 list Perrault at 7 St Vincent Street; directories for 1854 to 1864–5 list him at 22 St Vincent; and the directory for 1865–6 lists him at 36 St Vincent. In the 1866–7 directory he is called Louis Perrault and Co. (cf Q3.4), at 36 St Vincent. Although unnumbered, this edition (Q3.2) is likely the second by Perrault. The title-page of this edition is distinguished by the use of large, decorative capital letters for 'CUISINIERE' in the title. From appearances, it was likely published about 1850–5.

The OONL copy is stamped, in red ink, on the front endpaper, 'Rejean Olivier Bibliothecaire ex libris.' The OTMCL copy is bound in half leather. The QMM copy has a cloth spine and paper-covered boards.

Wheaton/Kelly No. 4488 cites Montreal: Louis Perrault, nd (imperfect copy at MWA). I have not identified the edition.

Q3.3   3rd ed., nd [about 1859]

—Nouvelle / cuisinière / canadienne, / contenant: / tout ce qu'il est nécessaire de savoir dans un ménage, tel / que l'achat des diverses sortes de denrées; les recettes / les plus nouvelles et les plus simples de préparer les / potages, les rôtis de toute [sic] espèces, la pâtisserie, / les gelées, glaces, sirops, confitures, fruits, / sauces, puddings, crêmes, charlottes, / poissons, volailles, gibiers, oeufs, / légumes, salades, marinades, / différentes recettes pour / faire diverses sortes / de breuvages et / liqueurs, / etc. / 3e edition / revue, corrigée et considérablement augmentée. / Montréal: / imprimée et publiée par Louis Perrault, / rue Saint-Vincent.

DESCRIPTION: 14.0 × 9.0 cm   Pp [i–iii] iv [v] vi–x, [11] 12–288   Illus on p x of a beaver   Cloth

CONTENTS: i tp; ii 'Enregistrée conformément à l'Acte provincial, intitulé: "Acte pour protéger la propriété littéraire."'; iii–iv 'Introduction'; v–x 'Vocabulaire des termes de cuisine'; 11–13 'Aphorismes'; 14–top 15 'Du choix des viandes'; mid 15–mid 16 'Du choix des volailles'; mid 16–17 'Du choix des poissons'; 18–270 text in nineteen chapters; 271–88 table of contents and at bottom p 288, 'Des presses mécaniques et à vapeur de Louis Perrault.'

CITATIONS: TPL 6174, p 276

COPIES: *NSWA   OTMCL (641.5 N59.11)   QMM (RBD   TX715.6 N65 1860z Lande)   QQS (218.4.37) Private collection

NOTES: The NSWA copy is inscribed on the front endpaper, in ink, 'Mde de Martigny // Varenne [sic] 1859.'; Varennes is on the south shore of the St Lawrence River, not far from Montreal. The private collector's copy is inscribed on p v, in purple pencil, 'Locadie Bureau // Ste Anne de la Perade 1883.' The OTMCL copy is rebound.

Q3.4   4th ed., 1865

—Nouvelle / cuisinière / canadienne / contenant: / tout ce qui est nécessaire de savoir dans un ménage, tel que l'achat / des diverses sortes de denrées; les recettes les plus nouvelles / et les plus simples de préparer les potages, les rotis de / toutes espèces, la pâtisserie, les gelées, glaces, sirops, / confitures, fruits, sauces, puddings, crêmes, et / charlottes; poissons, volailles, gibiers, oeufs, / légumes, salades, marinades; différentes / recettes pour faire diverses sortes de / breuvages, liqueurs, etc., etc. / Quatrieme edition, / revue, corrigée et considérablement augmentée. / Montréal: / imprimée et publiée par Louis Perrault & cie., / rue Saint Vincent. / 1865.

DESCRIPTION: 14.0 × 9.0 cm   Pp [i–iii] iv [v] vi–viii, [9] 10–256   Marbled-paper-covered boards, cloth spine

CONTENTS: i tp; ii 'Enregistrée conformément à l'Acte provincial, intitulé: "Acte pour protéger la "propriété littéraire." [sic, no second closing quotation-marks] // Des presses de Louis Perrault et cie., Montréal.'; iii–iv 'Introduction'; v–viii 'Vocabulaire des termes de cuisine qui se trouvent dans cet ouvrage'; 9–top 11 'Aphorismes sur la science du bien vivre'; mid–bottom 11 'Du choix des viandes'; top–near bottom 12 'Du choix des volailles'; bottom 12–13 'Du choix des poissons'; 14–238 text in nineteen chapters; 239–56 'Table des matières'

COPIES: *QQS (218.4.30)

NOTES: There were two editions numbered fourth and dated 1865: this one with 'Louis Perrault & cie.' on the title-page and Q3.5 with 'C.O. Beauchemin & Valois.' Vicaire 238 may be Q3.4 or Q3.5.

Q3.5   4th ed., 1865

—Nouvelle / cuisinière / canadienne / contenant: / tout ce qui est nécessaire de savoir dans un ménage, tel que l'achat / des diverses sortes de denrées; les recettes les plus nouvelles / et les plus simples de préparer les potages, les rotis de / toutes espèces, la pâtisserie, les gelées, glaces, sirops, / confitures, fruits, sauces, puddings, crèmes et / charlottes; poissons, volailles, gibiers, oeufs, / légumes, salades, marinades; différentes / recettes pour faire diverses sortes de / breuvages, liqueurs, etc., etc. / Quatrieme edition, / revue, corrigée et considérablement augmentée. / Montréal: / C.O. Beauchemin & Valois, / libraires-éditeurs, / rue St. Paul, nos. 237 et 239. / 1865.

DESCRIPTION: 14.0 × 9.0 cm Pp [i–iii] iv [v] vi–viii, [9] 10–256 Cloth

CONTENTS: i tp; ii 'Enregistrée conformément à l'Acte provincial, intitulé: "Acte pour protéger la propriété littéraire." Des presses de Louis Perrault et cie., Montréal.'; iii–iv 'Introduction'; v–viii 'Vocabulaire'; 9–top 11 'Aphorismes sur la science du bien vivre'; near top–bottom 11 'Du choix des viandes'; top–near bottom 12 'Du choix des volailles'; bottom 12–13 'Du choix des poissons'; 14–238 text in nineteen chapters; 239–56 'Table des matières'

CITATIONS: Cagle No. 25 DucharmeCat 32, January 1929, No. 12997, p 406 Powers/Stewart, p 184 (James MacGuire, 'The Art and Science of Good Bread') TPL 6174, p 277 Wheaton/Kelly No. 4486

COPIES: BVAU *OTMCL (641.5 N59) QMBN (179189 CON) QTS; United States: InU MWA NN

NOTES: The BVAU copy retains its original cloth binding. The QTS copy has a bookseller's label on the front endpaper, opposite the title-page: 'M.L. Cremazie, libraire, no. 12, rue Buade, Québec.'

Q3.6 5th ed., 1879
—[Fifth edition, Montreal: J.B. Rolland, 1879, pp ix, 270, 15.0 cm]
COPIES: OONL (TX719 N695 1879b missing)

Q3.7 5th ed., 1879
—Nouvelle / cuisinière / canadienne / contenant / tout ce qu'ii [sic] est nécessaire de savoir dans un ménage, tel que l'achat / des diverses sortes de denrées; les recettes les plus nouvelles / et les plus simples pour préparer les potages, les rôtis de / toutes espèces, la pâtisserie, les gelées, glaces, sirops, / confitures, fruits, sauces, puddings, crèmes et / char- / lottes; poisson, volaille, gibier, oeufs, légumes, / salades, marinades; différentes recettes pour / faire diverses sortes de breuvages, / liqueurs, etc., etc. / Cinquième édition / revue, corrigée et considérablement augmentée. / Montréal / Beauchemin & Valois, libraires-imprimeurs / 256 et 258, rue Saint-Paul / 1879

DESCRIPTION: 14.0 × 9.5 cm Pp [i–iii] iv [v] vi–ix [x], [1] 2–270 Cloth; sewn

CONTENTS: i tp; ii 'Enregistré conformément à l'Acte du Parlement du Canada, en l'année mil huit cent soixante-dix-neuf, par Beauchemin & Valois, librai-res, au bureau du ministre de l'Agriculture.'; iii–iv 'Introduction'; v–ix 'Vocabulaire des termes de cui-sine'; x blank; 1–top 3 'Aphorismes sur la science du bien-vivre'; near top 3–5 'Du choix des viandes,' 'Du choix des volailles,' and 'Du choix des poissons'; 6–251 text in nineteen chapters; 252 blank; 253–70 'Table des matières'

COPIES: OGU (CCC TX715.6 N67 1879) *QMM (RBD TX715.6 N65 1879 Lande)

Q3.8 5th ed., nd [about 1886–1902]
—Nouvelle / cuisinière / canadienne / contenant / tout ce qu'il est nécessaire de savoir dans un ménage, tel que l'achat / des diverses sortes de denrées; les recettes les plus nouvelles / et les plus simples pour préparer les potages, les rôtis de / toutes espèces, la pâtisserie, les gelées, glaces, sirops, / confitures, fruits, sauces, puddings, crèmes et char- / lottes; poisson, volaille, gibier, oeufs, légumes, / salades, marinades; différentes recettes pour / faire diverses sortes de breuvages, / liqueurs, etc., etc. / Cinquième édition / revue, corrigée et considérablement augmentée. / Montreal / C.O. Beauchemin & fils, libraires-imprimeurs / 256 et 258, rue Saint-Paul

DESCRIPTION: 14.0 × 9.5 cm Pp [i–iii] iv [v] vi–ix [x], [1] 2–270 Rebound

CONTENTS: i tp; ii 'Enregistré conformément à l'Acte du Parlement du Canada, en l'année mil huit cent soixante-dix-neuf, par Beauchemin & Valois, libraires, au bureau du ministre de l'Agriculture.'; iii–iv 'Intro-duction'; v–ix 'Vocabulaire des termes de cuisine'; x blank; 1–5 'Aphorismes sur la science du bien-vivre'; 6–251 text in nineteen chapters; 252 blank; 253–70 'Table des matières'

CITATIONS: Carrière No. 163

COPIES: CIHM (13725) OONL (TX719 N695 1879, 2 copies) *QMBM (641.5 N934no) QMBN (253230 CON) QSFFSC (641.5 n)

NOTES: Montreal city directories list 'C.O. Beauchemin & fils' at 256 and 258 St Paul Street from 1886 to 1902. The page numbers for pp iii–iv of the QMBM copy are torn off; I have indicated the pagination for this leaf following the example of the OONL copies. The OONL copies are in their original cloth, each a differ-ent colour and with a different style of lettering on the spine.

DucharmeCat 32, January 1929, No. 12998, p 406, lists, after an entry for the fourth edition of *Nouvelle cuisinière canadienne* (Q3.5): 'Même, 1900, ix–270 p., toile, 40 [i.e., $0.40].' The reference may be to an edition dated 1900 that I have not located, or it may be to one of the undated 270-page editions, i.e., Q3.8, Q3.9, and Q3.11, perhaps with an inscribed date.

Q3.9   6th ed., nd [about 1886–1902]
—Nouvelle / cuisinière / canadienne / contenant / tout ce q'ii [*sic*] est nécessaire de savoir dans un ménage, tel que l'achat / des diverses sortes de denrées; les recettes les plus nouvelles / et les plus simples pour préparer les potages, les rôtis de / toutes espèces, la pâtisserie, les gelées, glaces, sirops, / confitures, fruits, sauces, puddings, crêmes et char- / lottes; poisson, volaille, gibier, oeufs, légumes, / salades, marinades; différentes recettes pour / faire diverses sortes de breuvages, / liqueurs, etc., etc. / Sixième édition / Revue, corrigée et considérablement augmentée. / Montreal / C.O. Beauchemin & fils, libraires-imprimeurs / 256 et 258, rue Saint-Paul
DESCRIPTION: 15.0 × 9.5 cm   Pp [i–iii] iv [v] vi–ix [x], [1] 2–270   Lacks paper binding; sewn
CONTENTS: i tp; ii 'Enregistré conformément à l'Acte du Parlement du Canada, en l'année mil huit cent soixante-dix-neuf, par Beauchemin & Valois, libraires, au bureau du ministre de l'Agriculture. // Les soussignés ont acquis de Beauchemin & Valois la propriété du présent ouvrage. [signed] C.O. Beauchemin & fils.'; iii–iv 'Introduction'; v–ix 'Vocabulaire des termes de cuisine'; x blank; 1–top 3 'Aphorismes sur la science du bien-vivre'; near top 3–bottom 3 'Du choix des viandes'; top 4 'Du choix des volailles'; bottom 4–5 'Du choix des poissons'; 6–251 text in nineteen chapters; 252 blank; 253–70 'Table des matières'
COPIES: *OONL (TX719 N695 1880z reserve)   QTURA (641.15 N934)
NOTES: Montreal city directories list 'C.O. Beauchemin & fils' at 256 and 258 St Paul Street from 1886 to 1902. The OONL copy is inscribed on the title-page, in ink, 'Madame Georges Daviault 1916'; and in another hand, in ballpoint pen, 'Mme Cécile Daviault décembre 1959.' The rebound QTURA copy includes the front and back faces of the original paper binding; on the front face, printed in red and black, there is an image of a woman in a kitchen.

Q3.10   nd [about 1910]
—La / cuisinière / canadienne / Publié par / La patrie / Montreal / Canada [cover-title]
DESCRIPTION: 21.0 × 15.0 cm   Pp [1–2], [v] vi, [1–2], vii–x, [1–2], xv–xviii, [3] 4–398, [1–2], [xix] xx, [1–2], xxi–xxvi   Illus of cuts of meat, poultry, and fish   Cloth, with image on front of an aproned woman holding roast poultry on a platter
CONTENTS: 1–2 ads; v–xviii 'Introduction // Choix

des viandes et des poissons' with illus of cuts of meat, poultry, and fish, and two unnumbered leaves of ads; 3–10 'Art de découper les viandes et les poissons'; 11–335 recipes in twelve numbered chapters; 336–94 'Recettes diverses'; 395–8 'Termes spéciaux de cuisine'; 1–2 ads; xix–xxvi 'Table des matières' [i.e., index] and one unnumbered leaf of ads
COPIES: *Private collection
NOTES: The newspaper *La patrie* produced this heavily revised edition of *La cuisinière canadienne*, and there are advertisements for the newspaper in the volume, including a photograph of 'Les bureaux d'administration de "La patrie"' opposite p xv and a photograph of 'L'une des énormes presses de "La patrie"' opposite p 83. No other edition has illustrations of cuts of meat, poultry, and fish. Although there are many new, modern recipes, some recipes are reprinted with almost the same wording as the original 1840 text; for example, the run of fish recipes on p 88 – Doré roti, Doré bouilli, Esturgeon en ragoût, Morue sèche – are almost word-for-word the same as the recipes on pp 40–1 and p 42 of the first edition published about seven decades before.

Two advertisements limit the date of publication of this editon to the period 1900–11. The appearance of the book is consistent with publication in about 1910. A search of issues of *La patrie* would likely pinpoint the year of publication. The advertisement opposite p xix is for Sultana Manufacturing, 313 St Paul Street, Montreal, a maker of stove polish. Since Sultana's address changes to 102 Amherst Street in the 1912–13 city directory, this editon was published in 1911 or earlier. The advertisement opposite p vii limits publication to no earlier than 1900: it is for Frank L. Benedict and Co., a Montreal agent for Chocolate 'Suchard,' which won a prize in Paris in 1900.

The copy described here may be lacking its title-page. The following is a transcription of the title-page of another private collector's copy: 'La / cuisinière / canadienne / de / La patrie / On peut se procurer des exemplaires de ce / livre sur demande et paiement de $1.00 / (en timbres, mandats de poste ou d'express.) / Publié par / La cie de publication de La patrie, ltee / Edifice La patrie / Montréal, Canada.'

Q3.11   nd [about 1924–7]
—Nouvelle / cuisinière / canadienne / contenant / tout ce qu'il est nécessaire de savoir dans un ménage, tel que l'achat / des diverses sortes de denrées; les recettes les plus nouvelles / et les plus simples pour préparer les potages, les rôtis de / toutes espèces, la pâtisserie, les gelées, glaces, sirops, / confitures, fruits, sauces, puddings, crèmes

et char- / lottes; poisson, volaille, gibier, oeufs, légumes, / salades, marinades; différentes recettes pour / faire diverses sortes de breuvages, / liqueurs. etc., etc. / Revue, corrigée et considérablement augmentée. / Montréal / Librairie Beauchemin limitée / 30, rue Saint-Gabriel, 30

CONTENTS: Tp verso 'Enregistré conformément à l'Acte du Parlement du Canada, en l'année mil huit cent soixante-dix neuf, par Beauchemin & Valois, libraires, au bureau du ministre de l'Agriculture. // La cie soussignée a acquis de Beauchemin & Valois la propriété du présent ouvrage. Librairie Beauchemin limitée. No 1441 Printed in Canada. – Imprimé au Canada.'; opposite tp verso 'Introduction'; ...

CITATIONS: Wheaton/Kelly No. 4487

COPIES: MCR (641.6971 N93 and micro SLC 82 #617)

NOTES: Librairie Beauchemin limitée was at 30 St Gabriel from 1924 to 1927. This edition has pp ix, 270.

Q3.12 [1984]

—La / cuisinière / canadienne

DESCRIPTION: 21.0 × 15.0 cm   Pp [i–xx], [3] 4–398, [1–2], [i–viii]   Illus of cuts of meat, poultry, and fish   Cloth, with image on front of an aproned woman holding roast poultry on a platter

CONTENTS: i tp; ii 'Edi-Courtage Inc. ISBN 2-89309-000-1 Dépôt légal, 3e trimestre 1984 Bibliothèque nationale du Québec // Bibliothèque nationale du Canada // © 1984 Edi-Courtage Inc.'; iii 'Avant-propos' signed Éditeur; iv blank; v–xviii 'Introduction // Choix des viandes et des poissons'; xix–xx blank; 3–10 'Art de découper les viandes et les poissons'; 11–335 recipes in twelve numbered chapters; 336–94 'Recettes diverses'; 395–8 'Termes spéciaux de cuisine'; 1–2 blank; i–viii 'Table des matières'

COPIES: *BVA (641.59 Ca2C9a)   QMBM QMPRA QQLA

NOTES: This is a reprint of Q3.10, with a few changes: On the title-page, references to La patrie and the price are not included; the front matter is not paginated with roman numerals; all the pages of advertisements are now blank; 'A nos lectrices' has been retitled 'Avant-propos,' the one reference to La patrie has been replaced with 'nous pensons,' and it is signed Éditeur instead of the newspaper's name; and the 'Table des matières' is printed on fewer pages. The lettering and image on the front face of the binding are the same, except that the phrase 'Publié par La patrie Montreal Canada' is omitted. The copy described here has a dust-jacket on which is printed 'Les entreprises Radio-Canada.'

AMERICAN EDITIONS: Nouvelle cuisinière canadienne, 6th ed., Worcester, Mass.: J.A. Jacques, libraire-importateur, [Enregistrée ... en l'année mil huit cent soixante-dix-neuf, par Beauchemin & Valois, libraires ...], and below the copyright date: 'Les soussignés ont acquis de Beauchemin & Valois la propriété du présent ouvrage. C.O. Beauchemin & fils. // Les soussignés ont acquis des parties ci-dessus mentionnées, la propriété du présent ouvrage. Librairie Beauchemin (à resp. limitée).' The last-cited form of the publisher's name, Librairie Beauchemin (à resp. limitée), is used in Montreal city directories from 1902 to 1909, and there is a bookseller's advertisement on the back face of the binding for Q64.1, La cuisinière des familles, which was published no earlier than 1909; therefore, the Worcester, Massachusetts, edition likely appeared in 1909. The front face of the binding bears the same image of a woman in a kitchen as on the binding of the Montreal sixth edition, Q3.9. The Worcester edition was donated by the American food historian Andrew F. Smith to OGU in 2006 (it is not held by MWA).

1845

Nourse, Mrs Elizabeth

A partial check of Edinburgh and Scottish directories has revealed Mrs Nourse's first name – Elizabeth – various addresses for her pastry school at different times, and that she also rented out furnished lodgings. In 1808–9 (when the first edition of her cookbook appeared), her pastry school is listed at 38 Princes Street, in the New Town. In 1810 the school is at 7 George Street, also in the New Town. In 1814–15, her 'pastry-school and furnished lodgings' are at 13 and 15 George Street. Directory of Midlothian (Edinburgh, Leith, and Dalkeith) for 1820 gives her first name and another address, under 'Confectioners': Elizabeth Nourse, 6 George Street. In 1822–3 her pastry school is at 11 Frederick Street. In 1832–3 it is at 3 Hanover Street. In 1833–4, Mrs Nourse, confectioner, is still at 3 Hanover Street. In 1837, Elizabeth Nourse, pastry cook, is at 79 Princes Street.

I found only one marriage with the spelling 'Nourse' in the Old Parish Records at the General Register Office for Scotland: on 18 November 1793, in Edinburgh, John Nourse, 'gentleman servant,' Old Gray Friars Parish, married Elisabeth Burn, of the same parish, daughter of the deceased Walter Burn, gardener at Hawick (southeast of Edinburgh, near the border with England). Elizabeth (spelled thus in her birth record) was born at Hawick, on 24 November 1763; her mother was Janet Ker. Elizabeth and John Nourse had three children: William, born 15 January 1794, christened 19 January 1794, in Dunfermline; a daughter Jassey Nurse [sic], christened on 15 March 1795, in Dunfermline (likely Jessie Nourse, who married on 24 August 1835); and Mary Nurse [sic], christened on 26 June 1796 (likely the baby Nurse born on 6 June in Dunfermline). William's christening record describes John as an innkeeper. In the children's christening and birth records, Mrs Nourse's name is given variously as Elisabeth or Eliza, and Burn or Burne. Dunfermline is not far from Edinburgh, across the Firth of Forth. The location of this family, John Nourse's occupation as innkeeper, and Elisabeth/Elizabeth/Eliza Nourse's age make her a good match for the author of Modern Practical Cookery; however, further research is needed to confirm the link. No death record was found for the author, but she likely died no later than 1855, after which Scottish death records are comprehensive.

The following directories were checked: Edinburgh post office directory for 1808–9, 1810, Whitsunday 1814–Whitsunday 1815, Whitsunday 1822–Whitsunday 1823, and 1832–3; Directory of Midlothian (Edinburgh, Leith, and Dalkeith) for 1820; Gray's Annual Directory, 1833–34, ... Edinburgh and Its Vicinity, pp 109, 249; and Pigot and Co.'s National Commercial Directory of the Whole of Scotland, 1837, p 62.

Q4.1 new ed., 1845
Modern / practical cookery, / pastry, confectionery, / pickling, and preserving; / with / a great variety of useful and economical receipts. / By Mrs. Nourse, / teacher of these arts, Edinburgh. / A new edition, corrected and improved. / Montreal – Armour & Ramsay. / Kingston – Ramsay, Armour & Co. / Hamilton – Ramsay & McKendrick. / 1845.
DESCRIPTION: 16.0 × 10.0 cm   Pp [i–ii] [2 leaves missing] vii [viii], [1] 2–413 [414]   Illus of trussing in Chapter XXIII   Marbled-paper-covered boards and quarter leather
CONTENTS: i tp; ii blank; iii–vi lacking; vii last page of author's 'Preface'; viii blank; 1–398 twenty-five chapters; 399–413 'Index'; 414 'Edinburgh: Printed by Andrew Shortreed, Thistle Lane.'
CITATIONS: Bates, pp 27, 34–5, 60–1 (note 12), 61–2, 63 (note 19), 70, 70–1 (note 23), 73–4 (note 3), 77 (note 11), 79 (notes 16, 17, 18), 80, 84 (note 30), 87 (note 39), 88, 96–7, 116–17 (notes 26, 27, 28), 123 (note 41), 134–5, 140 (note 26), 147, 148 (note 22), 149 (note 24), 150   Driver 2002, Home Cook Book, p xii   Driver 2003, 'Canadian Cookbooks,' p 28   Garrett, pp 31, 65, 103, 117, 131   Lafrance/Desloges, p 87   TPL 7799
COPIES: CIHM (89546)   *OTMCL (641.5 N594)
NOTES: This is the third English-language cookbook to be published in Canada, after O1.1, *The Cook Not*

Mad, 1831, and O2.1, *The Frugal Housewife's Manual*, 1840. It is an edition of a Scottish text. Several cookery and pastry schools flourished in eighteenth-century Edinburgh, run by their women owners, and some of these cookery teachers wrote cookbooks to serve as classroom texts. In *Modern Practical Cookery*, Mrs Nourse follows the example of such teachers as Elizabeth Cleland (*A New and Easy Method of Cookery*, 1755), Susanna MacIver (*Cookery and Pastry*, 1773), and MacIver's successor, Mrs Frazer (*The Practice of Cookery, Pastry, Pickling, Preserving*, 1791). Mrs Nourse writes in the first person and has an engagingly direct style of presenting her instructions. Chapter XXV is 'Dinner Bills' [i.e., menus].

The publishing company, Armour and Ramsay, was owned by Andrew Harvie and his brother-in-law, Hew Ramsay, both Scots. In the same year that Armour and Ramsay published *Modern Practical Cookery*, the company was printing and publishing a number of other Scottish titles, arranged through the original publishers, as a way to offset the flood into the Canadas of cheap American reprints of British works. I have been unable to confirm what seems a possible connection between George Ramsay and Co. of Edinburgh, who printed the 1809 and 1811 Edinburgh editions of *Modern Practical Cookery*, and Hew Ramsay's family. Hew Ramsay's obituary (*Montreal Gazette* 24 February 1857, p 83 verso) states that he was born in Edinburgh in 1811, and that before emigrating to Montreal in 1832, he worked in the office of a writer to the *Signet* and studied Scottish law.

The printer of the Canadian edition, Andrew Shortreed, is my great-great-great uncle, on my mother's side (I am descended from his brother Thomas, who emigrated to Guelph, Ontario, in 1831).

Modern Practical Cookery was advertised as selling for 6s 3d by the Montreal bookseller John McCoy, in the cookery section of an undated catalogue (OTMCL).

For information about cooking schools (day and boarding) in eighteenth-century Edinburgh, see Alexander Law, *Education in Edinburgh in the Eighteenth Century*, London: University of London Press Ltd, 1965, pp 183, 186–7.

BRITISH EDITIONS: Edinburgh: Printed by George Ramsay and Co. for the author, 1809 (LB; United States: DLC, KMK); 2nd ed., Edinburgh: Printed by George Ramsay and Co. for the author, 1811 (WyLUB); 3rd ed., Edinburgh: Printed for and sold by the author, 1813 (LB, LoEn; United States: KMK); 4th ed., 1820 [see note, below] (Bitting, p 347; Oxford, p 148); 4th ed., Edinburgh: Printed by Michael Anderson, sold by the author et al., 1821 (LB, WyLUB);

Edinburgh: Blackwood, 1831 (Simon No. 1104, p 107); 1838 (Bitting, p 347; Oxford, p 148).

There may be only one edition numbered fourth, that dated 1821, at LB and WyLUB. Oxford, p 148, says with reference to the fourth edition, which he dates 1820: 'The only copy I have seen has lost its title page ... the advertisement to the fourth edition gives the date ... 336 pp, seems a good book ...' He adds, 'Blackwoods published an edition in 1838 but can find no earlier edition published by them.' The Bitting citations are to the information in Oxford.

1848

The skilful housewife's guide

Q5.1   1848

The skilful / housewife's guide; / a book of domestic cookery, / compiled from the best authors. / Montreal: Armour & Ramsay. / Quebec: P. Sinclair. / Kingston: Ramsay, Armour and Co. / Toronto: Scobie and Balfour. / Hamilton: Ramsay and McKendrick. / Bytown [i.e., Ottawa]: A. Bryson. / London: T. Craig. / Niagara; [sic] J. Simpson. / 1848.

DESCRIPTION: 14.0 × 8.5 cm   Pp [i–iii] iv–xii, [1] 2–132   Paper-covered boards, quarter leather

CONTENTS: i tp; ii 'Montreal: Armour and Ramsay.'; iii–xii table of contents; 1–132 text and at bottom p 132, 'Montreal: Armour and Ramsay.'

CITATIONS: Bates, p 60 (note 10), 81, 126   Collard, Edgar Andrew, 'All Our Yesterdays,' *Montreal Gazette*, 23 May 1964, p 6   Driver 2002, Home Cook Book, p xii   Driver 2003, 'Canadian Cookbooks,' p 28   JPCat 130, No. 43   *Literary Garland* Vol. 6, No. 3 (March 1848), p 144   *Montreal Gazette* 18 February 1848

COPIES: CIHM (30587)   *OGU (UA s043 b11)   OTAG (The Grange, 641.5)   OTMCL (641.5 S44)   QMM (RBD S2078); Great Britain: LB (Mic.F.232); United States: DLC (TX715 S635)

NOTES: There are eight chapters covering the following subjects: I, 'Choice of Meats, etc.' and 'Regulations of Time in Cooking'; II, 'Cooking Fish, Soups, Meats, etc.' and 'Eggs'; III, 'Vegetables,' 'Salads,' 'Pickles,' and 'Ketchups'; IV, 'Pies, Puddings, Cakes, etc.'; V, 'Making Vinegar, Beer, etc.'; VI, 'Cookery for the Sick and for the Poor,' 'Sick Cookery,' 'Cookery for the Poor,' and 'General Remarks and Hints'; VII, 'Dairy'; and VIII, 'Directions to Servants.'

The book was positively reviewed in the *Montreal Gazette* of 18 February 1848: '... the system is both good and economical, and along with all standard English dishes there is a goodly array of recipes for Irish, Scotch, and American ones. Ample instructions are given relative to dishes peculiar to this continent, a point which has not been sufficiently attended to in previous works of this nature. The price is low – one shilling, and we are confident that every housewife in Canada will not hesitate to part with that same to encourage this, the first Canadian attempt, to initiate them on the mysteries of the cooking craft.' The *Literary Garland* summed up its approval thus: 'With this little work, (and a good supply of the necessary material,) it will be their [i.e., fair readers'] own fault if their husbands, or fathers, or brothers, ever get crusty at the "mahogany."'

Mary F. Williamson has compared *The Skilful Housewife's Guide* with the first edition of *The Skilful Housewife's Book, or Complete Guide to Domestic Cookery, Taste, Comfort, and Economy*, by Mrs L.G. Abell, New York: D. Newell, [entered 1846], pp 208 (United States: MWA). (All other American editions of Abell's book were published after the Canadian edition.) Williamson found that the Canadian book is made up of a selection of recipes from the American work; it does not include the American book's preface and omits much of the non-culinary material, such as the sections about flowers, birds, and plants.

Collard's article about *The Skilful Housewife's Guide* is based on the QMM copy.

1859

Hirbet, P.

Q6.1   1859

La / chimie, / applique'e [sic] aux / arts et metiers, / a l'usage de / toutes les familles, / par / P. Hirbet. / Extrait des meilleurs auteurs français / et autres. / Quebec: / Imprime par St. Michel et Darveau, / no. 11, rue La montagne, Basse-ville. / 1859.

DESCRIPTION: 14.0 × 9.0 cm   Pp [1–5] 6–152   Paper; sewn

CONTENTS: 1 tp; 2 blank; 3 'Avant-propos'; 4 blank; 5–146 text; 147–52 'Table des matières'

COPIES: CIHM (45054)   OONL (TX149 H57, 3 copies)   *OTMCL (640.09714 H39)   QMBN (233251 CON)   QTU

NOTES: The 'Avant-propos' states: 'C'est aux dames canadiennes, à qui cet ouvrage est particulièrement offert; elles y puiseront des connaissances qui leur seront d'un grand secours, en leur enseignant la manière de faire les crèmes, les syrops[,] les savons, les vinaigres; la manière de nettoyer la soie, le drap, la toile, etc. Le meilleur mode de faire le vernis, le ciment, l'encre et les boissons de toutes espèces.' The text includes a variety of culinary recipes; for example, Pot-au-feu, Crèmes de fraises, Crèmes en neige, Boisson canadienne par M. Jean Taylor, Fromage fondu, Marinades ou conserves, Salades, Sirops, Vins, and Vinaigres.

The OTMCL copy is stamped on the front face of the binding, 'Chls Frs Painchaud.'; and on the inside front face, 'Université de Montréal biblioth[è]ques // Volume en surplus.'

1865

Hart, Mrs Hannah Constance Hatton
(26 February 1826–13 December 1898)

OONL attributes Household Recipes or Domestic Cookery *to Constance Hatton Hart, one of eight surviving children of the sixteen born to Benjamin Hart and Harriot Judith Hart. Her mother came from a wealthy family. Her father was a prominent businessman in Trois-Rivières and Montreal, and an advocate of Jewish civil liberties. On 12 December 1844 Constance married her cousin Adolphus Mordecai Hart (Benjamin's brother Ezekiel's son). Adolphus, a lawyer and author, also worked for equal rights for Jews in Lower Canada, along with Constance's father and one of her brothers. Genealogical charts in Stern, 1991, show that Constance and Adolphus had three sons and two daughters, and one baby, Asher, who died in infancy (the DCB entry for Adolphus notes three daughters and two sons). Adolphus, presumably accompanied by his family, moved to the United States in 1850, returning to Canada in 1857. The Notman Photographic Archives (at QMMMCM) contain two photographs of the interior of Constance Hart's home at Prince Arthur and Durocher streets in Montreal. QMMMCM also has a painted photographic portrait, in a small silver oval frame, that may be of Constance (Acc. No. MP-0000.154.30).*

The above biographical information is taken from entries for various members of the Hart family in DCB, Vols 8 and 10, and from the genealogical charts for the Hart family in Malcolm Stern, First American Jewish Families, *Baltimore: Ottenheimer Publishers, 1991, pp 95 and 96.*

Q7.1 1865
Household recipes / or / domestic cookery, / by / a Montreal lady. / Montreal: / Printed by A.A. Stevenson, St. Francois Xavier St. / 1865.

DESCRIPTION: 16.5 × 11.0 cm   Pp [1–5] 6–81, [i] ii–ix Lacks binding
CONTENTS: 1 tp; 2 'Entered according to Act of the Provincial Legislature, in the year one thousand eight hundred and sixty-five, by C. Hannah, in the Office of the Registrar of the Province of Canada.'; 3 preface dated Montreal, December 1865; 4 blank; 5–81 274 numbered recipes; i–ix table of contents citing both recipe number and page
CITATIONS: Driver 2002, Home Cook Book, p xiii Driver 2003, 'Canadian Cookbooks,' pp 28, 29   Driver 2005, p 409   Leduc
COPIES: CIHM (91705)   *OONL (TX715 H394 1865)
NOTES: The author's preface begins, 'Many ladies in the fashionable circles of Montreal have urgently commended the excellence of the recipes contained in the following pages ... particular attention has been bestowed on the mode of preparing side-dishes or entremets, ...' (side dishes are on pp 25–31). The text is for a general, rather than Jewish, audience. The only recipe that can be considered Jewish is Ball Soup, p 7.

Q7.2 1867
—Household receipts / or / domestic cookery, / by / a Montreal lady. / Montreal: / Printed by John Lovell, St. Nicholas Street. / 1867.
CONTENTS: 1 tp; 2 'Entered according to Act of the Provincial Legislature, in the year one thousand eight hundred and sixty-five, by C. Hannah, in the Office of the Registrar of the Province of Canada.'; 3 preface dated Montreal, December 1865; 4 blank?; 5–81 274 numbered recipes; i–ix table of contents citing both recipe number and page
CITATIONS: DCB, Vol. 10, p 337   Haight 1896, p 52
COPIES: *OONL (TX715 H394 1867 reserve, photocopy)
NOTES: The original volume from which the OONL photocopy was made is inscribed by Gerald Ephraim Hart, Constance Hart's son and a noted book collector. The first of his two pencil inscriptions is on the title-page, below 'a Montreal lady': 'Constance H. Hart'; the second is on the endpaper(?): 'Personal property of Gerald E. Hart.'

About ten years after publication of the second edition, the cookbook was still in print and for sale at the Methodist Book and Publishing House (likely the Branch Book Room in Montreal): *Household Recipes* by a Montreal lady, price $0.15, is cited in MBPHCat 1876–7, p 47.

Dionne, Vol. 3, No. 1335 cites *Household Receipts, or, Domestic Cookery*; the spelling of 'receipts' in Dionne's citation corresponds with this edition.

1869

Winslow, Madame

Q8.1 1869

Le livre de ménage, / recettes utiles / par / Mme Winslow, / pour / 1869. / Ce livre sera publié annuellement et contiendra des recettes / entièrement nouvelles qui, ajoutées à celles de l'année pré- / cédente, formeront au bout de quelques années le recueil / le plus complet de recettes utiles pour les familles, qu'il y / ait dans le pays. / Entered, according to Act of Congress, in the year 1868, / by Jeremiah Curtis & Sons, and John I. Brown & Sons, / in the Clerk's office of the District Court of the United States, / for the Eastern District of New York. [cover-title]

DESCRIPTION: 16.0 × 9.5 cm   Pp [1–2] 3–32   Paper; sewn

CONTENTS: 1 calendar for 1869; 2–32 recipes and publ ads

COPIES: CIHM (61488)   *QQS (219.1.C.#5)

NOTES: An advertisement on the inside front face of the binding indicates that Mrs Winslow's Soothing Syrup can be obtained from 'dépots' in New York, London, and in Montreal, at 441 St Paul Street.

AMERICAN EDITIONS: *Mrs. Winslow's Domestic Receipt Book, for 1869*, [No place:] Entered 1868, by Jeremiah Curtis and Sons and John I. Brown and Sons (United States: InU).

Also at InU are the annual editions for 1862 (contains statement, 'it is now three years since Mrs. Winslow's Domestic Receipt Book was first offered to the public ...'), 1863, 1865, 1866, 1867, 1868, 1870, 1871, 1872, 1873, 1874, 1875, 1876, 1877, 1878, and 1879. Axford, p 283, records editions to 1886. Editions are also at DLC.

1871

The manuscript receipt book and household treasury

Q9.1 1871

The / manuscript receipt book / and / household treasury. / "The turnpike-road to people's hearts I find, / Lies through their mouths, or I mistake mankind." / Montreal: / Dawson Brothers / 1871.

DESCRIPTION: 20.0 × 16.0 cm   Pp [iii–iv] v [vi–viii] ix [x], [11] 12–192   Tp illus of fruit in a basket   Cloth, with images on front of a fork and covered serving dish; new cloth on spine

CONTENTS: iii tp; iv 'Printed by Plinguet & LaPlante 30 St. Gabriel Street, Montreal.'; v 'Preface'; vi blank; vii 'Contents'; viii blank; ix part-title: 'The Household Treasury,' and an eight-line verse; x blank; 11–192 text, i.e., blank pages for manuscript recipes, set off by chapter titles and running heads and with quotations and verses for interest

COPIES: *OWTU (F15203)

NOTES: The cover-title is 'The Household Treasury.' The 'Preface' points out the usefulness of a manuscript recipe book:

Receipts, without number, are constantly given to the public by newspapers, magazines, and larger works, under various headings; and yet, who is there that does not desire to retain a memorandum of familiar home-dishes, – some entirely out of date, and some unknown to compilers of cookbooks, – but still most savory, because once prepared in the old homestead, and, perhaps, by hands made more dear by remembrance.

Besides, many persons gather in, day by day, receipts used by familiar friends, and which are not to be found in print; and this Household Treasury, with its complete classification, – presented in an attractive form, – will be found admirably adapted for their reception.

The OWTU copy is inscribed on the front endpaper, in ink, 'Susie E. Benson St. Catharines'; her manuscript recipes partly fill the pages of the volume. Susan Elizabeth Benson (1855–1926), born into a prominent St Catharines family, was the youngest daughter of Senator James Rea Benson. (OWTU is incorrect in transcribing the name as 'Sadie E. Benton.')

Q9.2 1872

—The / manuscript receipt book / and / household treasury. / "The turnpike-road to people's hearts I find, / Lies through their mouths, or I mistake mankind." / Toronto: / The Canadian News and Publishing Company / 1872.

DESCRIPTION: 20.5 × 16.0 cm   Pp [iii–viii] ix [x], [11] 12–186   Tp illus of a cherub holding up a platter on which sits a joint of meat   Quarter leather, with images on cloth front of a fork and covered serving dish

CONTENTS: iii tp in decorative border; iv 'Printed by Plinguet & Laplante 30 St. Gabriel Street, Montreal.'; v 'Preface'; vi blank; vii table of contents; viii blank; ix part-title: 'The Household Treasury,' and an eight-line verse; x blank; 11–186 text, i.e., blank pages for manuscript recipes, set off by chapter titles and running heads and with quotations and verses for interest

COPIES: *OGU (UA XM1 MS A117058) OONMM
Private collection
NOTES: The 'Preface,' which is revised, now reads:
'Receipts, without number, are constantly being given
to the public by newspapers, magazines, and larger
works, which, for want of a convenient method of
reference, are forgotten or lost. Moreover, there are
many familiar home dishes not to be found in cookery books, ...; to keep such receipts on permanent
record is one of the chief objects of the present work.'

The OONMM copy is inscribed 'Marion Osler //
Christmas 1873 From E.W.W.' The book was a gift
from someone in the Wyld family to Marion Wyld
Osler (Brantford, Upper Canada, 1847–86), the first
owner of the book and writer of the manuscript recipes. Marion Osler gave it to her daughter, who passed
it down to her daughter, from whom it passed to her
daughter (the donor of the book to OONMM) – in
total, four generations of owners.

Q9.3 1905
—The / manuscript receipt book / and / household
treasury. / "The turnpike road to people's hearts I
find, / Lies through their mouths, or I mistake
mankind." / Montreal: / W.V. Dawson / 1905
DESCRIPTION: Tp still-life of pineapples, grapes, and
other fruit   With still-life on front of game birds, a
crab, and a lobster
COPIES: OHWHH (974.B.54.3.1278)

AMERICAN EDITIONS: 2nd ed., Philadelphia: Claxton,
Remsen and Haffelfinger, 1870 (United States: OOxM,
WyU-AH).

The Pain-Killer annual and household physician 1871

*See also Q11.1, Pain Killer Annual 1871 and 1872, and
Q20.1, Pain Killer Calendar and Cookery Book 1886
(the latter published by Davis and Lawrence Co. Ltd, a
later incarnation of the company). The following issues of
the company's almanac have no cookery recipes: 1873,
1890, 1891, 1896, 1897, 1908 (all at OTUTF).*

Q10.1 1871
1871. / The / Pain-Killer / annual / and /
household physician. / Perry Davis & Son /
Montreal / publishers. [cover-title]
DESCRIPTION: 14.0 × 9.0 cm   Pp [1–32]   Paper, with
image on front of a reclining man reaching up to a
bottle of Pain-Killer, which is being offered to him by
a hand emerging from a cloud; sewn

CONTENTS: Inside front face of binding 'Preface' signed
Perry Davis and Son, 1 January [no year]; 1 'A Dozen
Reasons Why the Pain-Killer Manufactured by Perry
Davis & Son Is the Best Family Medicine of This
Age'; 2, 4, 6, 8, 10, 12, 14, 16, 18, 20 'Sick Room
Cookery'; 22, 24, 26 'Miscellaneous Receipts'; 29, 31
'Right Food for Infants' [recipes]; all other pages medi-
cal information and testimonials and ads for the publ's
products
COPIES: *OTUTF (uncat patent medicine)
NOTES: The 'Preface' implies that the first issue of this
title was in 1870: 'The Pain-Killer Annual and House-
hold Physician has been received with unexpected
favor. We now present a new and much improved
edition for the ensuing year.' The 'Preface' continues,
'In [the annual's] preparation the best authorities upon
"Sick Room Cookery", have been consulted, ...' The
printer's name is on the outside back face of the
binding: 'Printed at l'Ordre office, Montreal, Canada.'

Anne Dondertman mentions the Pain Killer almanacs in 'Patent Medicine Collection,' *Halcyon* [news-
letter of Friends of the Thomas Fisher Rare Book
Library] 23 (June 1999), p 9.

AMERICAN EDITIONS: The following may be related to
the Montreal edition for the same year: *Pain Killer
Annual 1871*, Providence, RI: Perry Davis and Son,
1871 (WaiteCat 5, No. 360). The following serial at
DLC is also likely related: *The Pain-Killer Annual and
Home Physician*, Cincinnati: J.N. Harris and Co. (United
States: DLC).

Pain Killer annual 1871 and 1872

Q11.1 1871
Pain Killer / annual / 1871 & 1872. / Perry Davis &
Son / Montreal / publishers. [cover-title]
DESCRIPTION: 16.0 × 10.0 cm   Pp [1–36]   Paper; sewn
CONTENTS: Inside front face of binding 'Preface' signed
Perry Davis and Son; 1 'Calendar for 1871'; 2, 4, 6, 8,
10, 12, 14, 16, 18, 20, 22, 24, 26, 28–9, 31, 33, 35 'Sick
Room Cookery,' including sections for 'Broths and
Meat Teas,' 'Gruels,' 'Drinks for Invalids,' 'Miscella-
neous Dishes for Invalids,' and 'Food for Infants'; 3,
5, 7, 9, 11 'The Annual'; 13, 15, 17, 19, 21, 23, 25, 27, 30,
32, 34, 36 publ ads
COPIES: *OKQ (F5012 1871 P144)
NOTES: This issue does not include a calendar for
1872, despite the wording of the title. The 'Preface'
begins in the same way as Q10.1, by referring to the
annual's reception 'with unexpected favor' and by
asserting, 'We now present a new and much im-

proved edition for the ensuing year.' The company's Pain-Killer had been sold for thirty years, according to the 'Preface.' The printer's name is on the outside back face of the binding: 'Printed by Plinguet & La Plante, Montreal.' Perry Davis and Son's address was 377 St Paul Street, Montreal.

1872

Moore, Richard (about 25 October 1830– 28 March 1883, Brooklyn, NY)

Although The Artizans' Guide and Everybody's Assistant *was published in Montreal, Moore had married in Galt, Ontario, compiled the book while living in New Brunswick, and died in New York. For information about the author and his other two works, see NB1.1.*

Q12.1 1872
The / artizans' guide / and / everybody's assistant: / containing over / two thousand new and valuable / receipts and tables / in almost every branch of business connected with civilized / life, from the household to the manufactory. / By R. Moore. / Published for the proprietor. / Montreal: / Printed by John Lovell, St. Nicholas Street. / 1872.
DESCRIPTION: Pp [1–3] 4–258, 1–7 [8] 9–22
CONTENTS: 1 tp; 2 'Preface' signed R.M. and 'Entered according to Act of Parliament in the year one thousand eight hundred and seventy-two, by R. Moore, in the office of the Minister of Agriculture and Statistics of the Dominion of Canada.'; 3–258 text; 1–22 'Ready Reckoner' and various tables
COPIES: *CIHM (61496)   QQS
NOTES: The microfiche includes what appear to be the original paper wrappers, on the front of which is printed 'Price $2 ... Issued Jan. 24th 1872 ... This work can be procured post-free by remitting $2 to Richard Moore, care Walter McFarlane, St. Mary's, near Fredericton, N.B., Canada.'; printed on the back is 'Large outline list of contents sent free on application. Agents wanted ... direct all orders to R. Moore, care of McFarlane, Thompson, & Anderson, machinists, &c., Fredericton, N.B., Canada.' In the 'Preface' the author says, 'With a view to the future enlargement of the work it has been arranged in departments, omitting an index for the present, the "mechanical" receipts being placed near the end; and copies of the additions made to this part will be fowarded to purchasers who send their address.' Unlike Moore's *Secret Knowledge Disclosed*, NB1.1, the text begins with a section devoted to culinary recipes: 'Baking and Cook-

ing Department,' pp 3–mid 19; there are also recipes in 'Grocers and Confectioners' Receipts,' pp 64–96. Although many recipes from *Secret Knowledge Disclosed* are repeated here, the material is rearranged.

The QQS copy is inscribed on the title-page, in ink, 'JW Renaud,' and stamped three times with the stamp of the Séminaire de Québec.

OONL (AC901 P3 No. 1116 p***; filmed as CIHM 36271) has a variant of this edition, without pp 217–58 and with fewer tables at the end; the pagination runs: [1–3] 4–216, 1–18. It is inscribed on the title-page, in ink, 'Copy deposited No. 294.' The OONL copy lacks its binding.

Q12.2 1873
—The / artizans' guide / and / everybody's assistant: / containing over / two thousand new and valuable / receipts and tables / in almost every branch of business connected with civilized / life, from the household to the manufactory. / By R. Moore. / Published for the proprietor. / Montreal: / Printed by John Lovell, St. Nicholas Street. / 1873.
DESCRIPTION: 17.0 × 10.5 cm   Pp [i–ii], [1] 2–284, [1] 2–57, [i], 1–7 [8] 9–22   Cloth
CONTENTS: i tp; ii 'Preface' dated March 1873 and '(Entered according to Act of Parliament, in the year one thousand eight hundred and seventy-two, by R. Moore, in the office of the Minister of Agriculture and Statistics of the Dominion of Canada.)'; 1–2 'Index'; 3–284 text; 1–57 'Appendix to "The Artizan's [*sic*] Guide"' [religious tract]; i 'New Church Books and Pamphlets'; 1–22 'Ready Reckoner' and various tables
COPIES: AEU (T49 M66 1873)   CIHM (35298) *OONL (T49 M78 1873)
NOTES: There are two editions dated 1873. In Q12.2 the title-page refers to 'over two thousand ... receipts and tables'; in Q12.3, the title-page refers to 'over three thousand ...'

Glued to the inside front face of the OONL copy is a sheet that describes the book's contents and ends with the information: 'Free by mail, for $2.00. Agents wanted. Direct all orders to McFarlane, Thompson, & Anderson, Fredericton, N.B., Canada.'

Q12.3 1873
—The / artizans' guide / and / everybody's assistant: / containing over / three thousand new and valuable / receipts and tables / in almost every branch of business connected with civilized / life, from the household to the manufactory. / By R. Moore. / Price in cloth binding, $2. / Parties in the United States will please address orders to John Lovell & / Sons, Rouse's Point, N.Y. / Those in

Canada will address the publisher, John Lovell, St. Nicholas St., / Montreal / Montreal: / Printed by John Lovell, St. Nicholas Street. / 1873.
DESCRIPTION: 16.5 × 10.5 cm   Pp [i–ii], [1] 2–284, 1–2 [3] 4–6 [7–8] 9–22, [1] 2–57, [i]   A few illus   Cloth
CONTENTS: i tp; ii preface dated March 1873 and '(Entered according to Act of Parliament, in the year one thousand eight hundred and seventy-two, by R. Moore, in the office of the Minister of Agriculture and Statistics of the Dominion of Canada.)'; 1–2 'Index' [i.e., table of contents]; 3–284 text; 1–22 'Ready Reckoner' and various tables; 1–57 'Appendix to "The Artizan's Guide"' [religious tract]; i ad for 'church books'
COPIES: NFSM (AG105 M66 1873)   *OGU (UA s070 b72)   OKQ (HD2341 M66 1873t)   OWTU (F2078)

Q12.4   1874

—The / artizans' guide / and / everybody's assistant: / containing over / three thousand new and valuable / receipts and tables / in almost every branch of business connected with civilized / life, from the household to the manufactory. / By R. Moore. / Price in cloth binding, $2. / Parties in the United States will please address orders to John Lovell & / Sons, Rouse's Point, N.Y. / Those in Canada will address the publisher, John Lovell, St. Nicholas St., / Montreal / Montreal: / Printed by John Lovell, St. Nicholas Street. / 1874.
DESCRIPTION: 17.0 × 11.0 cm   Pp [i–ii], [1] 2–284, 1–2 [3] 4–6 [7–8] 9–22, [1] 2–71, [i]   A few illus   Cloth
CONTENTS: i tp; ii 'Preface' dated March 1873 and 'Entered according to Act of Parliament, in the year one thousand eight hundred and seventy-two, by R. Moore, in the office of the Minister of Agriculture and Statistics of the Dominion of Canada.'; 1–2 'Index' [i.e., table of contents]; 3–top 19 'Baking and Cooking Department'; mid 19–mid 31 'Farmers and Stock Owners' Department'; bottom 31–mid 40 'Dyers, Bleachers, and Clothiers' Department'; mid 40–mid 64 'Druggists' Department'; mid 64–top 96 'Grocers and Confectioners' Receipts'; mid 96–mid 106 'Tanners, Curriers, Boot, Shoe and Harness Makers, Marble Workers, &c.'; bottom 106–near bottom 140 'Receipts for Cabinetmakers, Painters, Gilders, Bronzers, Glass Stainers, &c.'; bottom 140–near bottom 167 'Watchmakers, Jewellers, Gilders, &c., Receipts'; bottom 167–mid 281 'Receipts for Machinists, Engineers, Millowners, Blacksmiths, Locomotive Builders, &c., &c., and Metal Workers of Every Kind'; mid 281–284 'Useful Items for Daily Remembrance'; 1–22 various tables; 1–71 'Appendix to "The Artizan's Guide"'; i ad for 'church books'

CITATIONS: BQ 05-0977
COPIES: CIHM (28164)   *OTUTF (sci)

Q12.5   [new ed.], 1875

—The / artizans' guide / and / everybody's assistant, / embracing nearly / four thousand new and valuable / receipts, tables, &c., / in almost every branch of business connected / with civilized life, from the household / to the manufactory. / By R. Moore. / Price in cloth binding, $2.00, in Morocco, $3.00. / This work will be supplied by mail to any address in the United States, on remit- / ting $2.00 to John Lovell and Sons, Rouses Point N.Y. In Canada, address orders / to the Lovell Printing and Publishing Co., Montreal. Parties will save express / charges by ordering single copies sent by mail, instead of by express C.O.D. Agents / wanted. Books sent to agents C.O.D. Send for circular. / Montreal: / Printed by the Lovell Printing and Publishing Co. / 1875.
DESCRIPTION: 16.0 × 10.5 cm   Pp [1–5] 6–479, [i]   Tp illus of an oil lamp on a book, a few illus   Cloth
CONTENTS: 1 tp; 2 'Preface to the New Edition' dated April 1875 and 'Entered according to Act of Parliament, in the year one thousand eight hundred and seventy-five, by R. Moore, ...'; 3–4 'General Index' [i.e., table of contents]; 5–479 text; i ad for 'New Church Books and Pamphlets'
COPIES: CIHM (33848 and 54941)   MW (608.3 M78)   OKQ (HD2341 M66 1875t)   OTMCL (602 M58)   *OTU (CAN T 9 M824 ROMC)
NOTES: The text has been repaginated so that there is one run of numbers, from beginning to end. 'Baking and Cooking Department' is on pp 5–20; 'Grocers and Confectioners' Receipts' are on pp mid 85–118.

The OTU copy is inscribed on the front endpaper, in pencil, 'Martin A Howell [Jr?] Chicago Ill.'

1877

Cookery for the million

Q13.1   1877

A book for the times. / How to live cheaply and well. / Cookery for the million / with / useful hints to housewives. / "Good cooking means economy, / bad cooking means waste." / – London Times. / Price, ten cents. / Montreal: / Wm. Drysdale & Co., publishers, 232 St. James Street. / 1877.
DESCRIPTION: 14.5 × 10.5 cm   Pp [1–3] 4–47   Paper
CONTENTS: 1 tp; 2 blank; 3–6 'Index'; 7–8 ads; 9–11 'Hints to Housewives'; 12–43 eighty-six numbered

recipes headed 'Cheap and Wholesome Cookery'; 44–7 ads

CITATIONS: BQ 12-0975   BQ Exposition 1974, p 14   Carrière No. 102

COPIES: *CIHM (04164)   QMBN (159999 CON)

NOTES: 'Hints to Housewives' explains that the book is meant for Canadian housewives with modest resources: 'No such schools [of cookery in Europe, for the middle and upper classes] exist in Canada, however, and even if they did, they would be practically closed to those for whom this little book is especially intended ... the object has been to show how persons of very limited means can have a large choice of dishes, which, while economical, shall be wholesome and savory' (p 9). The recipes (and tone), however, are unequivocally British; for example, Bubble and Squeak, Crowdie – a Scotch Broth, Cornish Pie, Oatmeal Porridge, Plum Pudding, Baked, Toad-in-the-Hole, and Treacle Pudding. In 1871 the British author Mary Jewry had published, in London, a similarly titled work, *A Cookery Book for the Million*, which was subsequently published in Canada about the same time, as *Warne's Cookery Book for the Million* (O21.1, O21.2). The latter and Q13.1 described here are both short volumes (64 and 47 pp, respectively). A comparison of the texts might reveal a connection. Another similarly titled British work is William Kitchiner's *The Shilling Kitchener; or Oracle of Cookery for the Million, with Dr Kitchiner's celebrated advice to cooks ... By the editors of 'The Dictionary of Daily Wants,'* London, 1861 (Great Britain: LB).

Tuttle, Charles Richard (Wallace, NS, 14 March 1848–)

According to Macmillan Dictionary, p 845, Tuttle spent most of his career as a journalist in the United States, first in Boston, Massachusetts, then (after a stint in Manitoba from 1879 to the mid-1880s) in Chicago, Illinois. He saw published many non-fiction works, the last in 1918.

Q14.1   1877

The Dominion / encyclopaedia / of / universal history / and / useful knowledge. / Compiled and edited under the direction and management of / Charles R. Tuttle, / author of "History of the Dominion of Canada," "History of the / Countries of America," "History of the Border Wars of / Two Centuries," etc., etc. / Illustrated. / Vol. II. / Sold only by canvassing agents. / Montreal: / H.B. Bigney & Brother, publishers. / 1877.

DESCRIPTION: 20.5 × 13.5 cm   Pp [1–3] 4–701, [i]   Illus   Cloth

CONTENTS: 1 tp; 2 'Entered according to Act of Parliament of Canada, in the year 1877, by Charles R. Tuttle, in the office of the Minister of Agriculture and Statistics, at Ottawa.'; 3–5 preface; 6 blank; 7–669 text; 670 blank; 671–701 index; i publ ad

COPIES: BVAU (AE5 D645)   CIHM (88988)   *OGU (UA s039 b08)   OTMCL (031.9 T79)   QMM (AE T98 Cutter)

NOTES: Volume 1 covers universal history; Volume 2, described here, is useful knowledge. There are recipes in the 'Household and Culinary' section, pp 63–155, and in the 'Appendix to Household,' pp 156–78. The latter begins by stating, 'The following pages of the "Household Department," are designed to assist the wives of working men especially, and also to be a medium whereby young girls can be instructed in *Simple Modes of Economical Cookery* – ...' The 'Confectioners' section, pp 281–92, is for professional candymakers, not the home cook.

1878

Caron, mère Emélie (Rivière-du-Loup-en-Haut, now Louiseville, Que., 8 May 1808–13 August 1888, Montreal, Que.)

The daughter of Ambroise Caron and Marie-Josephte Langlois, Emélie was one of the seven foundresses of the Institute of Providence, established in 1843, and the only one assigned responsibility for culinary matters. Her first job title was treasurer, and her duties were 'guardian of the outhouses, messenger, singer, apothecary, dyer, weaver, candle-maker, cook, stewardess, baker, gardener, shoemaker, soap-maker, and charged of the poultry yard' (The Institute of Providence, *Vol. 2, Montreal: Providence Mother House, 1930, p 24). In 1849 the Institute opened St Elizabeth Convent under Caron's supervision. 'Always on her guard against excessive comfort,' she furnished the convent with 'old cracked iron stoves; mended kitchen-ware, and even ... discarded razors converted into use for table knives!' (The Institute of Providence, Vol. 4, 1932, pp 250–1). In 1851, she was elected mother superior of the Institute, serving until 1858, and she was elected to a second term from 1872 to 1878. According to Auclair, Caron's biographer, in the time between her two terms as mother superior, she organized housekeeping classes, which would have included instruction in cookery. About her life in the 1860s, Auclair writes: 'Elle excellait en particulier dans l'art culinaire. Les Soeurs et les enfants formées sous sa direction se sont trouvées à assister, sans s'en douter peut-être, et avec un peu de bruit en moins, à ce qu'on croyait naguère si nouveau à Montréal: aux cours d'une école ménagère!' (p 86).* Caron is buried in the Institute of Providence cemetery at Longue-Pointe.

For Caron's biography, see Auclair, *Élie Joseph Arthur,* Vie de mère Caron, l'une des sept fondatrices et la deuxième supérieure des Soeurs de la charité de la Providence, 1808–1888, *Montreal: 1908. For a history of the Institute of Providence, see:* Notes historiques: livre dédié aux vénérables jubilaires de l'Institut des Filles de la charité servantes de pauvres dites Soeurs de la Providence, *Montreal: Providence (Maison mère), 1922; and* L'Institut de la Providence: histoire des Filles de la charité servantes des pauvres dites Soeurs de la Providence, *6 vols, Montreal: Providence (Maison mère), 1925–40, subsequently published in English as* The Institute of Providence: History of the Daughters of Charity Servants of the Poor Known as the Sisters of Providence, *6 vols, 1927–58 (a portrait of Caron in 1855 is in Vol. 3 of both editions, and is reproduced here as pl 33.*

Q15.1   1878

Directions diverses / données par / la rev. mere Caron sup. gen. / des / Soeurs de la Providence / pour aider ses soeurs / a former de bonnes cuisinieres. / Montréal, / 1878.

DESCRIPTION: 14.0 × 9.5 cm   Pp [1–5] 6–182   Paper-covered boards, cloth spine

CONTENTS: 1 ht; 2 blank; 3 tp; 4 blank; 5–170 text in eleven chapters; 171–82 'Table des matières'

CITATIONS: Armstrong 2000, p F2, illus p F2   Driver 2002, Home Cook Book, p xii   Driver 2003, 'Canadian Cookbooks,' pp 31, 38   Driver 2005, pp 409, 410, 552 (note 78)   Lafrance/Desloges, p 104   Leduc   PAC Library, Vol. 3, 1979, p 128   Powers/Stewart, p 176 (Yvon Desloges, 'Quebec's Culinary Traditions: An Overview')   Watier, p 8

COPIES: CIHM (02193)   ECO   *OONL (TX715 C37 1878)   QMBN (173874 CON)   QMPRA; Great Britain: LB (Mic.F.232)

NOTES: See pl 16. Copyright for *Directions diverses* was registered a few years after publication, on 28 October 1884, along with four other books by the Sisters of Providence (see *Notes historiques,* 1922, p 131). *Directions diverses* was the second French-language cookbook written in Canada, published nearly four decades after the first edition of Q3.1, *La cuisinière canadienne,* and like its predecessor it enjoyed wide distribution (Q6.1, P. Hirbet, *La chimie, appliquée aux arts et métiers,* 1859, is more a compendium of household information than a recipe book).

The text borrows heavily from *La cuisinière canadienne,* and, in many places, the same recipes are presented in the same order. Compare, for example, the recipes for beef or the run of recipes in Chapter 9, 'Des confitures, gelées et crèmes.' Given the close connection between Louis Perrault, the printer and publisher of *La cuisinière canadienne,* mère Gamelin, the first mother superior of the Institute of Providence, and other supporters of the religious order (see Q3.1), one can assume that *La cuisinière canadienne* had been a treasured culinary reference in the kitchen of the Institute of Providence since the order's founding in 1843 and that mère Caron, as the person responsible for food and cooking, consulted it regularly. If *Directions diverses* owed a debt to the earlier work, it also embodied Caron's thirty-five years of practical experience and may be a distillation of the material she used as a teacher of cookery classes in the 1860s (see Auclair, cited above). Regarding the differences between *La cuisinière canadienne* and *Directions diverses,* Lafrance and Desloges comment, 'Caron takes us further and further from the middle-class and professional French cuisine; the "Canadianization" process and English influence are present more than ever in her collection.' The text includes general directions and recipes for 'Des pâtés ou tourtières' and fourteen recipes for beignes (i.e., doughnuts), a traditional food in Quebec at Christmas and New Year. Of the English recipes in Caron's repertoire, some keep their English names, such as Sponge Cake, and she also includes the North American Johnny Cake.

Directions diverses is notable as the first cookbook written by a member of a religious order, for use in Quebec's Catholic institutions. Its first chapter sets out the moral dimensions of cooking, in ten numbered points, under the heading 'Du soin qu'il faut prendre pour former de bonnes cuisinières.' If cooking provides specific opportunities to exercise virtue, it also allows one to reflect on one's failings, as the tenth point illustrates: A cook, who carried out her culinary duties perfectly, was asked why she always cried; she explained, 'Le feu de la cuisine que j'ai toujours sous les yeux ... me fait penser aux flammes de l'enfer que j'ai si souvent méritées.'

The first edition of *Directions diverses* was printed at the Mother House for the use of the sisters, but it became popular outside of the order, eventually running through eight editions up to 1913. In 1908, Auclair recounted the publishing history of the book thus: 'La mère Caron se fit un petit recueil de ses recettes les plus usitées. En 1878, on l'imprima aux ateliers de la maison mère, et il fut distribué dans toutes les maisons de la Providence. Naturellement, il fut connu au dehors, et, pour tout dire, le recueil est aujourd'hui à sa 7me édition, on en distribue huit cents par année!' (p 86).

The OONL copy of *Directions diverses* is inscribed on the outside back and front faces of the binding, in pencil: 'Demoiselle Delima Aubertin.'

E. Donald Asselin reprints seventeen recipes from Q15.1 in *A French-Canadian Cookbook*, [Edmonton: Hurtig Publishers, 1975].

Q15.2 2nd ed., 1883
—Directions diverses / données en 1878, / par la révérende mère Caron / alors supérieure générale / des Soeurs de charité de la Providence / pour aider ses soeurs à former de / bonnes cuisinières. / Seconde edition / Montreal, / 1883.
DESCRIPTION: 14.0 × 9.5 cm   Pp [1–5] 6–196   Paper-covered boards, cloth spine
CONTENTS: 1 ht; 2 blank; 3 tp; 4 blank; 5–178 text in twelve chapters; 179–96 'Table des matières'
CITATIONS: BQ 09-0968
COPIES: CIHM (26821) *OGU (UA s043 b24) OONL (TX715 C37 1883) OOU QMBN (159993 CON); Great Britain: LB (Mic.F.232)

Q15.3 3rd ed., 1889
—[Third edition of *Directions diverses données en 1878 par la révérende mère Caron*, Montreal: 1889, pp 248]
CITATIONS: BQ 23-4867
COPIES: QMBN (TX714 C36 1889) SSU (TX715 C29)

Q15.4 4th ed., 1891
—Directions diverses / données en 1878 / par la reverende mere Caron / alors supérieure générale / des Soeurs de charité de la Providence / pour aider ses soeurs a former de / bonnes cusinieres. / Quatrieme edition / revisée et augmentée / Montreal / 1891.
DESCRIPTION: 14.0 × 9.0 cm   Pp [1–5] 6–269   Paper-covered boards, cloth spine
CONTENTS: 1 ht: 'Cuisinière de la réverénde mère Caron.'; 2 'Enrégistré [sic] conformément à l'Acte du Parlement du Canada, en l'année mil huit cent quatre vingt-quatre, par la communauté des Soeurs de cha-rité de la Providence, au bureau du ministre de l'Agriculture.'; 3 tp; 4 blank; 5–252 text in twelve chapters; 253–69 'Table des matières'
CITATIONS: BQ 09-0965 Carrière No. 95
COPIES: CIHM (91290) QMBN (159995 CON) QMPRA *Private collection
NOTES: There is no printed text on the spine or either face of the original binding. The private collector's copy is inscribed on the binding, in ink, 'Fernande

Renaud. Recettes'; and on the front endpaper, in ink, 'Melle Fernande Renaud. Recettes –.'

Printing of 4,000 copies of the fourth edition began on 17 December 1891 (see *Notes historiques*, 1922, p 153).

Q15.5 5th ed., 1898
—Directions diverses / données en 1878 / par la reverende mere Caron / alors supérieure générale / des Soeurs de charite de la Providence / pour aider ses soeurs a former dr [sic] / bonnes cuisinières. / Cinquieme edition / revue, corrigée et augmentée / Montreal / 1898.
DESCRIPTION: 15.5 × 10.0 cm   Pp [1–5] 6–302   Paper-covered boards, cloth spine
CONTENTS: 1 ht: 'Cuisinière de la révérende mère Caron.'; 2 'Enrégistré [sic] conformément à l'Acte du Parlement du Canada en l'année mil huit cent quatre-vingt-quatre, par la communauté des Soeurs de charité de la Providence, au bureau du ministre de l'Agriculture.'; 3 tp; 4 blank; 5–284 text; 285–302 'Table' [i.e., index]
CITATIONS: Armstrong 2000, p F2 BQ 09-0966
COPIES: *OGU (UA s043 b22) OONL (TX715 C37 1898) QMBN (TX715 C37 1898) QMPRA
NOTES: The QMBN copy is inscribed on the front endpaper, 'Mademoiselle Florianne Guyon // Verechères 1898.'

Q15.6 6th ed., 1903
—Directions diverses / données en 1878 / par la reverende mere Caron / alors supérieure générale / des Soeurs de charite de la Providence / pour aider ses soeurs a former de / bonnes cuisinières. / Sixieme edition / revue, corrigée et augmentée. / Montreal / 1903.
DESCRIPTION: 15.5 × 10.0 cm   Pp [1–5] 6–312   Paper-covered boards, cloth spine
CONTENTS: 1 ht: 'Cuisinière de la révérende mère Caron.'; 2 'Enrégistré [sic] conformément à l'Acte du Parlement du Canada en l'année mil huit cent quatre-vingt-quatre, par la communauté des Soeurs de charité de la Providence, au bureau du ministre de l'Agriculture.'; 3 tp; 4 blank; 5–293 text in thirteen chapters; 294–312 'Table'
CITATIONS: Carrière No. 95 Powers/Stewart, p 184 (James MacGuire, 'The Art and Science of Good Bread') Tod/Cordingley, p 59
COPIES: CIHM (73720) *OONL (TX715 C37 1903) QMBM (641.5 C293di)

Q15.7 7th ed., 1907
—Directions diverses / données en 1878 / par la / reverende mere Caron / alors supérieure générale /

des Soeurs de charité de la Providence / pour aider ses soeurs à former de / bonnes cuisinières. / Septieme edition / revue, corrigée et augmentée. / Montreal / 1907.

DESCRIPTION: 14.5 × 10.5 cm Pp [1–5] 6–296 Paper-covered boards, with image on front of beehive, cloth spine

CONTENTS: 1 ht; 2 'Enregistré conformément à l'Acte du Parlement du Canada en l'année mil huit cent quatre-vingt-quatre, par la communauté des Soeurs de charité de la Providence, au bureau du ministre de l'Agriculture.'; 3 tp; 4 blank; 5–277 text in thirteen chapters; 278–96 'Table'

CITATIONS: BQ 09-0967 BQ Exposition 1974, p 14 Carrière No. 95 Dionne, first supplement, 1912, No. 315, p 21 Tod/Cordingley, p 59

COPIES: CIHM (73732) *OONL (TX715 C37 1907 p***) QMBN (TX715 C37 1907) QMPRA Private collection

NOTES: See Q15.1 for Auclair's reference to the seventh edition, of which he says that 800 copies were distributed per year. The private collector, in St Paul, Alberta, who has a French surname, reported that her copy 'was given to my mother by her mother in 1911 to come out West.'

Q15.8 8th ed., 1913
—Directions diverses / données en 1878 / par la / reverende mere Caron / alors supérieure générale / des Soeurs de charité de la Providence / pour aider ses soeurs à former de / bonnes cuisinières. / Huitième édition / revue, corrigée et augmentée / Montréal / 1913.

DESCRIPTION: 15.5 × 10.5 cm Pp [1–5] 6–256 Paper-covered boards, with image on front of beehive, cloth spine

CONTENTS: 1 ht: 'Cuisinière de la révérende mère Caron.'; 2 'Enrégistré [sic] conformément à l'Acte du Parlement du Canada, en l'année mil huit cent quatre-vingt-quatre, par la communauté des Soeurs de charité de la Providence, au bureau du ministre de l'Agriculture.'; 3 tp; 4 blank; 5–240 text in thirteen chapters; 241–56 'Table'

COPIES: CIHM (81511) *OONL (TX715 C37 1913) OW (641.5 C22) QMM (RBD TX715 C37 1913 Joubert) QMPRA QQLA (TX715 C293 1913) QTU QVMVS

OTHER EDITIONS: 'Réédition de la troisième,' Montreal: [printed by Raymond Litho Offset Inc. on 1 November 1975 for Les Éditions de Montréal], 1975 (OONL, QMBM, QMBN, QMPRA).

Downs' Elixir recipe book

Q16.1 3rd ed., nd [about 1878]
The third edition / of the / Downs' Elixir / recipe book. / This book contains a choice collection of / cooking and coloring recipes, / and other interesting and instructive knowledge, / and is well worth preserving. / Few truths so obvious that the mind conceives / At once their force, and fixedly believes. / See all human wants in these combined / A healthful body, and a peaceful mind. / Published by / Wheeler & Johnson, / Montreal, P.Q. [cover-title]

DESCRIPTION: 17.5 × 10.5 cm Pp 1–24 Paper; sewn

CONTENTS: Inside front face of binding untitled introductory text for the third edition and 'To the Suffering' [recommendation of listed medicines: N.H. Downs' Balsamic Elixir, Henry and Johnson's Arnica and Oil Liniment, Baxter's Mandrake Bitters, Henry's Worm Lozenges, Johnson's Ginger, Henry's Electric Ointment, and Carpenter's Botanic Asthma Cure]; 1 'A Medical Mistake Corrected' and 'How to Get Along'; top 2 'Special Directions for Using N.H. Downs' Vegetable Balsamic Elixir'; mid 2–4 information about the treatment of particular illnesses, from Common Cold to Catarrh, including appropriate administration of the Elixir, and amusing conversation between John and Mrs Smith at bottom p 4; 5 testimonial for Downs' Elixir and untitled poem; 6 testimonial, recipes for Scotch Oatmeal Porridge, Liebig's Beef Tea, and Vinegar for Family Use in Three Weeks, and 'A Nice Thing of It' [humorous conversation]; 7 publ ad for Dr Rolls' Stomach and Liver Pills and Dr Rolls' Worm Killer; 8 culinary recipes for Preserving Eggs and Restorative Milk, plus recipes for general household use, and publ ad for Glenn's Sulphur Soap; 9 publ ad for Constitutional Catarrh Remedy; 10 testimonials; 11 'Family Matters' [includes culinary information and recipes] and publ ads; 12 publ ad for Baxter's Mandrake Bitters and recipes for general household use; 13 testimonials, non-culinary recipes, and publ ad; 14–15 fifteen numbered 'Recipes for Coloring'; 16 'Family Matters' [includes recipe for Home-made Cream Candy]; 17 publ ad; 18–19 general household recipes, including To Cure a Pig; 20–1 publ ads; 22 general household recipes, including instructions for chocolate icing; 23–4 publ ads, including reference to letter dated 30 March 1878

COPIES: *OTUTF (uncat patent medicine)

1880

The Princess baker

Q17.1   nd [about 1880]
The / Princess / baker / Containing practical recipes for making superior / bread, biscuit, cakes, &c., compiled carefully with / a view to be used by those who regard economy as / well as excellence. / Published by / Wm. Lunan & Son, / manufacturers of / The "Princess" Baking Powder, / Sorel, Que., Canada. / J. Theo. Robinson, printer, Montreal. [cover-title]
DESCRIPTION: 14.0 × 9.0 cm   Pp [1] 2–16   Paper, with image on front of a Princess Baking Powder container; sewn
CONTENTS: 1 'Are You Using Poisonous or Adulterated Baking Powder?'; 2 'The "Princess" Baking Powder'; top–mid 3 untitled introduction; mid 3–16 thirty-two numbered recipes
CITATIONS: Driver 2005, p 410
COPIES: CIHM (95270)   *QMM (RBD uncat)
NOTES: On p 3, Wm Lunan and Son refer to themselves as 'the proprietor (practical bakers and confectioners for over one-third of a century) of the "Princess" Baking Powder.' They comment that 'this book will be issued annually, and ... the next number will contain entirely new recipes.' No other editions have been located.

This edition was likely published about 1880: on p 1 there is a reference to a Canadian Government report of 1878 that analysed the composition of baking powder; on the outside back face of the binding there is a testimonial dated 22 October 1879. If it could be proven that *The Princess Baker* was published before O29.1, *Cook's Friend Cook Book* of 1881, then it would be the first cookbook in Canada advertising an ingredient.

1882

Recueil de recettes et le médecin à la maison

Q18.1   1882
Recueil / de / recettes / et le / medecin a la maison / Sommaire: – Un extrait de cuisine – Manière de faire différents / bouillons, soupe à la purée de divers légumes, le boudin, la / saucisse, le fromage, le cervelas, l'andouille, le petit salé – / Manière de faire toute espèce de pâtisseries, d'entremets sucrés, / confitures, sirops – Manière de faire cuire toute espèce de / poissons – La conservation du gibier,

des viandes, du poisson, / des oeufs, du beurre, du lait, des légumes – Salaison des / viandes, du jambon, du beurre – Blanchissage et repassage du / linge – Entretien des vêtements – Maladies et indispositions – / Pharmacie de ménage. / Québec / Imprimerie Leger Brousseau, / 9, rue Buade, 9 / 1882
DESCRIPTION: Pp [1–3] 4–82 [83]   Small illus on p 24 of how to fold 'Feuilletage' pastry
CONTENTS: 1 tp; 2 'Antoine Langlois, éditeur.'; 3–4 'Préface'; 5–82 text in three parts: 'Cuisine,' 'Linge, lessive, repassage et blanchissage,' and 'Maladies et indispositions'; 83 'Table des matières'
CITATIONS: BQ Exposition 1974, p 15   Carrière No. 178
COPIES: *CIHM (04903)   OONL (TX719 R428 1882)   QMBN (109493 CON)   QQS (219.1.28)
NOTES: The 'Préface' comments, 'Nous devons à l'esprit d'entreprise et à l'encouragement de MM. Bernard & Allaire, marchands de musique, de pouvoir offrir au public canadien un livre aussi utile sous tous les rapports.'

Q18.2   1882
—[An edition of *Receuil de recettes et le médecin à la maison*, Québec: Imprimerie Léger Brousseau, 1882, in four parts]
DESCRIPTION: Pp [1–3] 4–103 [104]   Lacks paper binding
CONTENTS: 1 tp; 2 'Antoine Langlois, éditeur.'; 3–4 'Préface'; 5–103 text in four parts: 'Cuisine,' 'Linge, lessive, repassage et blanchissage,' 'Maladies et indispositions,' and 'Certificates' [for harmoniums, pianos, and sewing machines]; 104 'Table des matières'
COPIES: *QMM (TX145 L3x)   QQS (219.1.29)
NOTES: Unlike Q18.1 and Q18.3, this edition has four parts. The QQS copy retains its paper binding; printed on the outside front face is the publication date 1883.

Q18.3   [2nd ed.], 1883
—Recueil / de / recettes / et le / medecin a la maison / Sommaire: – Un extrait de cuisine – Manière de faire différents / bouillons, soupe à la purée de divers légumes, le boudin, la / saucisse, le fromage, le cervelas, l'andouille, le petit salé – / Manière de faire toute espèce de pâtisseries, d'entremets sucrés, / confitures, sirops – Manière de faire cuire toute espèce de / poissons – La conservation du gibier, des viandes, du poisson, / des oeufs, du beurre, du lait, des légumes – Salaison des / viandes, du jambon, du beurre – Blanchissage et repassage du / linge – Entretien des vêtements –

Maladies et indispositions – / Pharmacie de ménage. / Québec / Imprimerie Léger Brousseau / 9, rue Buade, 9 / 1883

DESCRIPTION: 19.5 × 12.0 cm   Pp [1–3] 4–82 [83]   Small illus on p 24 of how to fold pastry   Paper; sewn

CONTENTS: 1 tp; 2 'Enregistré conformément à l'Acte du Parlement du Canada, en l'année 1882, par Antoine Langlois, au bureau de l'Agriculture, Ottawa. Antoine Langlois, éditeur.'; 3–4 'Préface'; 5–82 text in three parts; 83 'Table des matières'

COPIES: *OONL (TX719 R428)

NOTES: 'Deuxième édition' is on the front face of the binding. The OONL copy is inscribed on the title-page, in ink, '[?] de Beaufare [?] 1893'; the title-page bears the stamp of 'Bibliotheca FF Minorum Quebec.'

1884

Rouillard, Mme Charles

Q19.1   1884

Collection / de / recettes eprouvees, / les plus en usage dans les meilleures / cuisines du / Canada et des Etats-Unis / Recueillies par / Mme. Charles Rouillard, / St. Johnsbury, Vt. / Imprimé aux ateliers du Pionnier de Sherbrooke. / 1884.

DESCRIPTION: 15.0 × 9.5 cm   Pp [1–4] 5–109 [110]   Cloth

CONTENTS: 1 tp; 2 blank; 3 'Aux dames' signed Madame Chs Rouillard; 4–102 recipes; 103–9 'Index' [i.e., list of the recipes in their text order]; 110 ad for *Le pionnier de Sherbrooke*

COPIES: CIHM (91702)   *OONL (TX715 R675 1884)

NOTES: The OONL copy is inscribed on the front endpaper, in ink, 'Ce livre appartient à Madame Augustine Biotteau // Concord. N.H 1892'; and in another hand, 'Camille Ernest Biotteau // Leavitts Hill // Deerfield, N.H 1931.'

Q19.2   2nd ed., 1888

—La cuisiniere / du / "Pionnier." / Recettes les plus en usage / dans les / meilleures cuisines du Canada / par / Madame Charles Rouillard. / Deuxième édition, revue et augmentée. / En vente au bureau du "Pionnier" à Sherbrooke. / Prix: 15 centins. / 1888 [cover-title]

DESCRIPTION: About 14.5 × 9.0 cm [dimensions from photocopy]   With small image on front of a beaver

COPIES: * Private collection

1886

Pain Killer calendar and cookery book 1886

See Q10.1 for information about Pain Killer annuals.

Q20.1   1886

Pain Killer / calendar / and / cookery book / 1886. [cover-title]

DESCRIPTION: Pp [1–64]

CONTENTS: 1 'Bank Holidays in Ontario,' 'Holidays Observed in Public Offices in the Province of Quebec,' illus of astrological symbols, and 'Eclipses' for 1886; 2–25 publ ads on versos, monthly calendars from January to December on rectos; 26 publ ad; 27–63 'Selected Cooking Recipes' and publ ads; 64 publ ad

CITATIONS: Brisebois No. 233, p 57

COPIES: *CIHM (00679)   OONL   SSU (AY419 H7P35 1886)

NOTES: The publisher, Davis and Lawrence Co. Ltd of Montreal, is identified in many of the advertisements for the company's medical products, such as Pain Killer. The OONL copy bears the stamp of Dr G.W. Prentiss, Grenville, Quebec.

1888

Clever cooking for careful cooks

Q21.1   1888

Clever cooking / for / careful cooks. / Tried recipes, collected and arranged by a / few ladies of the Church of St. John / the Evangelist, Montreal. / Montreal: / Printed by John Lovell & Son. / 1888.

DESCRIPTION: 20.5 × 14.0 cm   Pp 3–8, [1–5] 6–102, [i–xiii], 103 [104–5]   Cloth, impressed with pattern simulating alligator(?) skin

CONTENTS: 3–8 ads; 1 tp; 2 unattributed poem beginning, '"We may live without poetry, music and art' [from *Lucile*, Part I, Canto ii, by Owen Meredith, pseudonym of Edward Robert Bulwer-Lytton] and remarks by DuPlaty, president of the French Assembly, about the relative importance of the discovery of a new pudding; 3 preface; 4 ad; 5–97 text; 98 blank; 99–102 index; i–xii blank, ruled leaves for manuscript recipes; xiii blank; 103–5 ads

CITATIONS: Driver 2003, 'Canadian Cookbooks,' p 30   Driver 2005, p 552 (note 82)

COPIES: OGU (2 copies: *UA s050 b16, UA s050 b17)   OTNY (uncat); United States: NNNAM (S.21.B)

NOTES: This is the first community cookbook published in Quebec. The preface states, 'Many of these recipes have never been published before, and some are more than a hundred years old.' There is a recipe for Gulasch [sic] (German Recipe) on p 31 and for Polish Salad on p 85.

Some of the blank, ruled leaves for manuscript recipes are lacking in one of the OGU copies (UA s050 b17). The end pagination in the OTNY copy runs ... 102, [i], 103, [ii–iii]; the unnumbered page between 102 and 103, and the unnumbered pages following p 103 are advertisements.

1890

Mother Seigel's 1890 almanac

Q22.1   1890
Mother / Seigel's / 1890 / almanac / Sabiston Lith. & Pub. Co Montreal [cover-title]
DESCRIPTION: 19.5 × 14.5 cm   Pp [1] 2–32   Paper, with image on front of a waterfall; sewn
CONTENTS: Inside front face of binding–32 'Shaker Cooking Receipts,' monthly calendars, medical information, and publ ads
COPIES: *OHMB (Serial)   OTUTF (uncat patent medicine)
NOTES: This almanac is a promotional vehicle for Mother Seigel brand medicines, which were American products, sold by A.J. White and Co., Montreal. An advertisement on p 26 points out 'What the People of Canada Say about Mother Seigel's Curative Syrup.'

On the outside back face of the OTUTF copy is 'For sale by [stamped in blank space:] A Herbold, general merchant, Chippewa, Ont.'

Whereas the 1890 almanac has many culinary recipes, there are no recipes in the following issues: 1885, 1888, 1889, 1891, 1892, 1893, 1898, 1900, 1901, 1903, 1907, 1909, 1911, and 1912 (all at OTUTF).

The peerless cook book

Q23.1   nd [about 1890]
The / peerless / cook book / a compilation of / tested recipes. / Published by the / ladies of St. James Methodist Church, / St. Catherine Street, / Montreal. / Babcock & Son, book and job printers, 4 Bleury Street
DESCRIPTION: 19.0 × 12.0 cm   Pp [3–13] 14–99, [i–vi]   Tp illus of the church   Cloth
CONTENTS: 3–8 ads; 9 tp; 10 ad; 11 preface; 12 ads;

13–91 text; 92–4 ads; 95–9 table of contents; i blank; ii–vi ads
COPIES: CIHM (88760)   *OGU (UA s043 b36)
NOTES: On p 10 there is a testimonial for Heintzman pianos dated October 1888.

1890–5

[Title unknown]

Q24.1   [about 1890–5]
[Title unknown]
DESCRIPTION: 18.5 × 12.0 cm   Pp [leaves lacking] 11–116 [five or more leaves lacking]
CONTENTS: 11–116 recipes credited with the name of the contributor and ads for products made by Amherst Manufacturing Co., 57 Amherst St., Montreal
COPIES: *Private collection
NOTES: Amherst Manufacturing Co. products advertised in the book include Lady Amherst Tablet (a soap), Hood's Triumph Laundry Powder, Silver Soap, 'Harry Lewis' Dog Soap, and Herpetic Tar Soap. The first surviving page, p 11, has a recipe for Lobster Croquettes from Miss Lang and the first part of Oyster Fritters from Miss Leslie. There are recipes for Haggis from Miss Gault and Pot Pie from Mrs David Liddell (both on p 14), Fricassee of Calves Tongues from Miss Lang (pp 14–15), Roast Sucking Pig (no source given, p 15), and the first part of Genuine Irish Stew from Mrs S. Cline (p 15). There are extensive instructions for To Bone a Turkey from Mrs W. Colquhoun, Toronto, starting on p 21.

1891–8

Rogers' tested recipes

Q25.1   nd [about 1891–8]
Rogers' / tested / recipes / A practical everyday / cook book / Published by / W.B. Rogers, / Medical Hall, 16 Fabrique St. / Quebec.
COPIES: *Private collection
NOTES: William B. Rogers, a chemist and druggist, sold baking powder and flavouring extracts, which he recommends in his note 'To Our lady Patrons and Friends': 'We have purposely advised the use of our Chemically Pure Baking Powder, and our full strength Flavoring Extracts in the recipes ...' The book has 32 pages, according to its owner. It originally belonged to the owner's grandmother, who lived in Quebec City.

Quebec City directories list Rogers at 16 Fabrique Street in the volumes for 1891–2 through to 1898–9, after which the address changes to 44 Fabrique; therefore, the cookbook was published about 1891–8, a date consistent with its appearance.

1892

Cottolene the new shortening

For other cookbooks promoting Cottolene, see Q29.1, 266 recettes choisies, Q30.1, 600 Selected Recipes, and Q37.1, Rorer, Mrs Sarah Tyson, Home Helps. See Arndt, pp 157–9 (Alice Ross, 'N.K. Fairbank'), for the story of Fairbank and his business.

Q26.1   nd [about 1892]
Cottolene / the new shortening. / For sale by all first-class grocers / everywhere. / If your grocer does not / sell Cottolene please / write to the manufacturers. / Cottolene ... / Made only by / N.K. Fairbank & Co. / Chicago. St. Louis. Montreal. / New York. Boston. Philadelphia. [cover-title]
DESCRIPTION: 11.5 × 10.0 cm   Pp [1–16]   Paper; stapled
CONTENTS: 1 'The New Shortening // What Is Cottolene?'; 2 'How to Use Cottolene' and 'Life and Health'; 3 'Read the Following from "Eleanor Kirk's Idea," May, 1892.'; 4 'Recipe for Making and Cooking Doughnuts'; 5 'Croquettes of Rice' and 'A Vegetable Lard as a Substitute for the Animal Material'; 6 'Marion A. McBride, in "The Cottage Hearth" for May, 1892, under "Domestic Science."'; 7–16 more recipes and information about Cottolene
CITATIONS: Driver 2003, 'Canadian Cookbooks,' p 33   Watier, p 8
COPIES: *QMM (RBD uncat)
NOTES: 'What Is Cottolene?' on p 1 states: '[It] is a pale yellow material, of the consistency, texture and substance of lard ... a simple preparation of cotton-seed oil and beef fat ... It meets the public demand for a pure, healthful, digestible substitute for swine fat ... the name Cottolene is duly registered in the Patent Office of the United States ...'

1895

Allen, Mrs Sarah, née Lawless

The 1901 Census records the widow and 'teacher' Sarah Allen, born 23 September 1848, living in Saint-Antoine Ward, with her single siblings, Rose, William, and Lucinda E. Lawless, and two younger nephews. During the 1881 Census she was a 'school teacher' living with her parents, John and Sarah, and several siblings, the eldest of whom, Thomas, was a printer – perhaps he suggested the idea of publishing a cookbook? Sarah's age given in the 1881 Census, thirty-one years, implies a different birth year than that in the 1901 Census.

Entries in Lovell's Montreal Directory *around the time of publication of* The Common Sense Recipe Book *indicate that Sarah Allen was a widow of Michael and in business for herself. The directory for 1894–5 records her business as 'underwear, etc.' Although the first edition of her cookbook is dated 1895, there is no business given in the directory for 1895–6; however, the directories for 1897–8 and 1898–9 list 'publisher'; and the directories for 1902–3 and 1903–4, 'agent and publisher.' The third edition of her cookbook, published in 1898, records her address as 181 St James Street, but her personal name is not listed under this address in any of the street indexes I consulted; instead, several businesses, some of them publishers, occupied 181 St James Street. There is a connection, however, between one business at this address and Sarah Allen: In the 1898–9 directory, under 181 St James Street, one of the businesses is William Keys, publisher. In the same directory, under Keys, and before the entry for William Keys, is Redmond Keys, agent, 181 St James Street, 'bds [i.e., boards at] 329 Laval Av.' This is the home address recorded for Sarah Allen in 1898–9. What publishing interests or activities Allen shared with her boarder Redmond and his relative(?), William Keys, is unknown, but the 181 St James Street address on the title-page of the third edition points to their involvement in its publication.*

Over the eight-year period when the various editions of her book were published, Allen moved residence several times: In 1894 she was at 295 St Antoine Street, then she lived at 327 Laval Avenue, 329 Laval, 107 Anderson, 142½ St Antoine, and 46 Victoria.

Q27.1   1st ed., 1895
The / common sense / recipe book / containing all the / latest recipes / on / cooking with economy / and also very valuable / medicinal recipes / First edition / Montreal: / Printed by John Lovell & Son / 1895 / Entered according to Act of Parliament, in the year 1895, by Mrs. Sarah / Allen, in the office of the Minister of Agriculture and Statistics at Ottawa.
DESCRIPTION: 21.0 × 13.0 cm   Pp 3–250   Cloth
CONTENTS: 3–4 ads; 5 tp; 6 ad; 7 preface; 8 ad; 9 'Index'; 10 ad; 11–248 text and ads; 249–50 ads
CITATIONS: Driver 2005, pp 409–10   O'Neill (unpublished)

COPIES: CIHM (01519) *OGU (UA s043 b29) OONL (TX715 C652 1895); Great Britain: LB (07944.g.18 destroyed)

NOTES: Several recipes have been reprinted from an unidentified edition of *The Home Cook Book* (O20.1); for example, those attributed to Mrs Ayer, Mrs J. Beaty, Mrs McMaster, and Helena Smith. Q27.1 has no 'Index to Advertisers.'

Q27.2 2nd ed., 1896
—[Second edition of *The Common Sense Recipe Book Containing All the Latest Recipes on Cooking with Economy and Also Very Valuable Medicinal Recipes*, Montreal: John Lovell and Son, 1896, pp 250, paper-covered boards, cloth spine]
COPIES: Bookseller's stock

Q27.3 3rd ed., 1898
—The / common sense / recipe book / containing all the / latest recipes / on / cooking with economy / and also very valuable / medicinal recipes / by Mrs. Sarah Allen, / 181 St. James Street Montreal / Third edition / Printed by John Lovell & Son / 1898. / Entered according to Act of Parliament, in the year 1898, by Mrs. Sarah Allen, in the office of the Minister of Agriculture and Statistics at Ottawa.
DESCRIPTION: 21.0 × 13.0 cm Pp 3–250 Cloth
CONTENTS: 3–4 ads; 5 tp; 6 ad; 7 preface; 8 ad; 9 'Index to Advertisers'; 10 ad; 11 table of contents; 12 ad; 13–249 text and ads; 250 ad
COPIES: *OGU (UA s043 b15)
NOTES: The preface refers to a revision of the first edition: 'It was with considerable diffidence that the Common Sense Recipe Book first made its appearance before the public in 1895, but ... now it comes before you with more courage and in a much improved form.' The sentiment and phrasing echo the text quoted for Q36.1, *The Diamond Dye Cook Book No. 2*, published about the same year.

Q27.4 9th ed., 1903
—[Ad:] Benson's Prepared Corn / used by best cooks for / over forty years / Pure corn. Filtered water. Great care. / [title:] The / common sense / recipe book / containing all the / latest recipes / on / cooking with economy / and also very valuable / medicinal recipes / by Mrs. Sarah Allen, / 142½ St. Antoine St., – Montreal / Ninth edition / Printed by John Lovell & Son / 1903 / Entered according to Act of Parliament, in the year 1903, by Mrs Sarah Allen / in the office of the Minister of Agriculture and Statistics at Ottawa. / [ad:] It's all in the service

/ and that of the Toilet Laundry is the best. / 290 Guy St. Phones, Up 2601 – 2602
DESCRIPTION: 21.0 × 13.0 cm Pp [3] 4–206 Cloth
CONTENTS: 3 tp; 4 ad; 5 'Preface' and ads; 6 ad; 7 'Index to Advertisers' and ads; 8 ad; 9 'Contents' [i.e., alphabetical list of topics] and ads; 10 ad; 11–203 text and ads; 204–6 ads
CITATIONS: Ferguson/Fraser, p 232
COPIES: *SSWD (641.5 A429c)
NOTES: The 'Preface' asserts that the recipes have been thoroughly tested and most 'are safe even for those whose digestions are impaired.' The SSWD copy is inscribed on the title-page, 'Donated by J.W. Brown 322 – 9th St Saskatoon.'

Richards, Amy Gertrude (Birmingham, England, 10 August 1862–)

Since Amy Richards dedicates the book to her 'Canadian pupils' and uses the British system for measuring ingredients in cake recipes (flour in ounces and milk in gills), she was likely a visiting cookery teacher from England. There is one clear match in the 1901 Census for England and Wales: Amy G. Richards, daughter of Sarah L. Richards (widow), living at Stonelea [sic], Bewdley, Worcestershire, born in Birmingham, Warwickshire, thirty-eight years old, single, occupation: cookery teacher, employment status: 'own account' (Public Record Office reference: RG13, Piece 2784, Folio 144, Page 34, Schedule No. 245). There is still a house called Stoneleigh in Bewdley, in an area called Bark Hill. No monumental inscriptions or burial registry entries were found in Bewdley for Amy or her mother. Amy's birth certificate identifies her father as Joseph, a Master Coach Axle Maker, and Smith as the maiden name of her mother, Sarah Lilley.

Q28.1 1895
Cookery. / By / Amy G. Richards. / "But for life the universe were nothing, and all that has life / requires nourishment." / "In compelling man to eat that he may live, nature gives / appetite to invite him, and pleasure to reward him." / – Brillat-Savarin. / Montreal: / E.M. Renouf, publisher. / 1895.
DESCRIPTION: 18.5 × 12.0 cm Pp [1–2], [i–viii], [1–3] 4–436, [i–x] Cloth
CONTENTS: 1–2 ads; i tp; ii 'Entered according to Act of Parliament of Canada, in the year one thousand eight hundred and ninety-five, by E.M. Renouf, in the office of the Minister of Agriculture. Printed from

Linotype Bars at "Witness" Office.'; iii author's dedication 'To my Canadian pupils, ...'; iv blank; v preface signed Amy G. Richards, Montreal, April 1895; vi blank; vii table of contents; viii blank; 1–6 introduction; 7–400 recipes; 401–14 'Glossary of Terms'; 415–24 'English and French Names of Articles of Food'; 425–36 index; i–x ads

CITATIONS: Dionne, Vol. 3, No. 2512 Driver 2005, pp 409–10 Eade, pp E1, E2 MCat Neering, p 69 O'Neill (unpublished)

COPIES: CIHM (12438) ECO *OGU (UA s043 b42) OONL (TX715 R477 1895) OTUTF (B-12 7850); Great Britain: LB (07944.f.20 destroyed)

NOTES: The OTUTF copy is inscribed on the recto of the first leaf of advertisements, in ink, 'Lavinia Thompson.' Dionne incorrectly cites the author's first name as Anny.

1895–1900

266 recettes choisies

For the titles of other works promoting the shortening Cottolene, see Q26.1.

Q29.1 nd [about 1895–1900]
266 recettes choisies / par / Melle [*sic*, in all three instances] Juliet Corson, / Mme F.L. Gillette, / Marion Harland, / Mme D.A. Lincoln, / Mme Frances F. [*sic*] Owens, / Melle Maria Parloa, / Mme Eliza R. Parker, / Mme S.T. Rorer, / Melle Margaret Wister. / Editées par / N.K. Fairbank Company, / Montreal / Chicago. St. Louis. New York. [cover-title]

DESCRIPTION: 17.0 × 12.5 cm Pp [i], [1–2] 3–70 Paper, with images on front of a cow in a circular frame and a pail of Golden Cottolene; stapled

CONTENTS: i 'Cottolene. Une graisse végétale.'; 1 'Préface' signed N.K. Fairbank Co.; 2 'Table des matières'; 3–7 'Certificats' [i.e., testimonials for Cottolene by the recipe contributors and others]; 8–66 266 numbered recipes; 67 'Table des poids et mesures de la cuisine'; 68–70 'Index'

COPIES: *QSH (555)

NOTES: In the cover-title, Mrs Owens's middle initial should be E. for Emugene. The 'Préface' refers to the recipes as from 'les meilleurs auteurs culinaires des États-Unis.' The undated *266 recettes choisies* was likely published about the same time as Q30.1, *600 Selected Recipes*. Unusually, the even page numbers are printed on the rectos; the odd page numbers, on the versos.

600 selected recipes

For the titles of other works promoting the shortening Cottolene, see Q26.1.

Q30.1 nd [about 1895–1900]
600 selected recipes / by / Miss. Juliet Corson, / Mrs. F.L. Gillette, / Marion Harland, / Mrs. D.A. Lincoln, / Mrs. Frances E. Owens, / Miss. Maria Parloa, / Mrs. Eliza R. Parker, / Mrs. S.T. Rorer, / Miss. Margaret Wister. / Published by / N.K. Fairbank & Co. / Chicago, / St. Louis, Montreal, New York. / Copyrighted by N.K. Fairbank [illegible]

DESCRIPTION: 18.0 × 12.5 cm Pp [i], [1–2] 3–131 [Free, on p 1] Paper, with image on front of a can of Golden Cottolene and the branch of a cotton plant; stapled

CONTENTS: Inside front face of binding 'The recipes in this book were contributed by the following well-known authorities on cooking, ...' [information about the cooks and titles of their published books]; i 'Cottolene, a Vegetable Fat' [facts about the product]; 1 'Preface' signed N.K. Fairbank and Co.; 2 table of contents; 3–6 testimonials for Cottolene; 7–124 600 numbered recipes, each attributed to one of the cooks named on the binding; 125–30 index; 131 publ ad

COPIES: *Private collection

NOTES: The text on p i states that 'Cottolene is a pure, sweet preparation of refined and clarified Cottonseed Oil and choice selected Beef Suet' and that it contains no other ingredients such as salt, water, or colouring matter. N.K. Fairbank and Co. is identified on p 131 as one of the departments of the American Cotton Oil Co. The recipes are from American authors: Miss Juliet Corson (1841–97); probably Mrs Fanny Lemira Camp Gillette (1828–1926); Marion Harland, pseudonym of Mrs Mary Virginia Terhune, née Hawes (1830–1922); Mary Johnson Lincoln, née Bailey (1844–1921), principal of the Boston Cooking School before Fannie Merritt Farmer, who assumed the role in 1891; Mrs Frances Emugene Owens, née Johnston (1843–); Miss Maria Parloa (1843–1909); Mrs Eliza R. Parker; Mrs Sarah Tyson Rorer, née Heston (1849–1937); and Miss Margaret Wister.

The book is undated; however, it was likely published about 1895–1900 since there are testimonials dated 5 January, 18 June, and 19 September 1892, and the latest book cited on the inside front face of the binding is *Mrs Lincoln's Boston Cook Book* of 1893. The printer, 'Donaldson Brothers Lith[illegible],' is on the outside back face of the binding. Unusually, the recto pages are even-numbered; the verso pages, odd-numbered.

The private collector's copy is inscribed on the inside front face of the binding, in ink, 'Miss Ethel [C.?] Parker.'

The DLC catalogue (TX715 S633) lists Chicago: N.K. Fairbank, [ca. 1893], pp 131, which may correspond to the edition described here.

AMERICAN EDITIONS: Chicago, 1892 (Longone/Longone B10; Brown/Brown 722).

1896

Garneau, Dr Joseph-A. (29 January 1845–)

The 1901 Census records Dr Joseph-A. Garneau, 'médicin,' living in Quebec City with his wife, Marie B., and four children.

Q31.1 [1896]
[Premi?]ere edition, 100,000. / Recettes / et / connaissances utiles / a l'usage / des familles / Quebec / Leger Brousseau / imprimeur.
DESCRIPTION: About 18.5 × 11.0 cm [dimensions from photocopy] Paper, with portrait on front of Dr Garneau
CITATIONS: Carrière No. 124 O'Neill (unpublished)
COPIES: Great Britain: LB (7404.ee.3)
NOTES: The title-page is printed on the inside front face of the paper binding. 'Enregistré conformément à l'Acte du Parlement du Canada, l'an 1896 par J.A. Garneau, au Ministère de l'Agriculture ' is inscribed on the title-page, in ink; below the copyright inscription, in another hand, is 'Garneau.' On the front face of the binding, below Dr Garneau's portrait, are his signature and the following information: 'J.-A. Garneau, M.D. // Diplôme & Licencié, 1868 // Bureau; 70, rue de l'Église St-Roch, Quebec // Je donne une attention spéciale au traitement des différentes formes de dyspepsies et des différentes espèces de dérangements abdominaux chez l'homme et la femme ...' The text is composed of monthly calendars for 1896, advertisements for Dr Garneau's Sel hygiénique and La Catarrhina, and recipes. Information in this entry is from photocopies of the British Library copy (binding and pp 12, 13, and 40).

The Huntingdon cook book

Q32.1 1896
Tried. Tested. Proved. / The / Huntingdon cook book / compiled from recipes contributed by ladies of / Huntingdon and published in behalf of the / St. Andrew's Church, / Huntingdon, Que. / "We may live without books – what is knowledge but grieving? / We may live without hope – what is hope but deceiving? / We may live without love – what is passion but pining? / But where is the man who can live without dining?" / 1896. / Huntingdon. / The News and Enterprise Print.
DESCRIPTION: 16.5 × 12.0 cm Pp [1–5] 6–162 Cloth
CONTENTS: 1 tp; 2 'Our Advertisers'; 3 'Index of General Subjects'; 4 'A Table of Weights and Measures for Housekeepers'; 5–146 text; [9 blank leaves, 'Errata' glued to recto of first leaf]; 147–62 ads
COPIES: CIHM (95404) *OGU (UA s049 b09)
NOTES: The recipes are credited with the name of the contributor.

Q32.2 2nd ed., 1902
—Tried. Tested. Proved. / The / Huntingdon cook book / compiled from / recipes contributed by ladies of Huntingdon / and vicinity and published in / behalf of the / St. Andrews Church, / Huntingdon, P.Q. / First edition 500 copies in 1896. / Second edition, revised and enlarged, 500 copies. / "We may live without books – what is knowledge but grieving? / We may live without hope – what is hope but deceiving? / We may live without love – what is passion but pining? / But where is the man who can live without dining? [*sic*, no closing quotation-marks] / 1902. / News and Enterprise Print. / Huntingdon.
COPIES: *Private collection

Q32.3 3rd ed., 1907
—Tried. Tested. Proved. / The / Huntingdon cook book / compiled from / recipes contributed by ladies of / Huntingdon and vicinity and / published in behalf of the / St. Andrews Church / Huntingdon, P.Q. / First edition, 500 copies in 1896. / Second edition revised and enlarged 500 copies 1902. / Third edition revised and enlarged, 1000 copies 1907. / "We may live without books – what is knowledge but grieving? / We may live without hope – what is hope but deceiving? / We may live without love – what is passion but pining? / But where is the man who can live without dining? [*sic*, no closing quotation-marks] / 1907. / News and Enterprise Print, / Huntingdon.
DESCRIPTION: 16.5 × 12.0 cm Pp [i–ii], [1–7] 8–210 [211–23], [i] ii–ix [x] xi–xxv Frontis of St Andrews Church, 'dedicated January 4th, 1906' Cloth, with leaf-pattern endpapers
CONTENTS: i tp; ii blank; 1 'Index of General Subjects';

2–3 'Our Advertisers'; 4 'A Table of Weights and Measures for Housekeepers'; 5 'Time Required for Cooking the Following Meats and Vegetables'; 6 'Time for Baking'; 7–11 'Table Service'; 12–205 recipes credited with the name of the contributor; 206–10 'Things Useful to Know'; 211 'Our Advertisements'; 212–23 blank; i–xxv ads
COPIES: OGU (CCC TX715.6 H8723 1906)   *Private collection
NOTES: The OGU copy lacks the title-page and last leaf of advertisements.

Montigny, Benjamin Antoine Testard de (1838–99)

Q33.1   1896
Manuel / d'économie domestique / par / Le Recorder Testard de Montigny, / Chevalier de l'Ordre militaire de Pie IX. / Montréal / Librairie Saint-Joseph / Cadieux & Derome / 1603 rue Notre-Dame / 1896
DESCRIPTION: 18.5 × 12.0 cm   Pp [i–vi], [1] 2–327 Paper-covered boards(?), new cloth spine
CONTENTS: i ht; ii blank; iii tp; iv 'Enregistré conformément à l'Acte du Parlement du Canada, en l'année mil huit cent quatre-vingt-seize par Cadieux & Derome, au bureau du ministre de l'Agriculture et de la statistique, à Ottawa. Eusèbe Senécal & fils, imprimeurs, 20 rue St-Vincent, Montréal.'; v–vi 'Mon but' signed B.A.T. de Montigny, Montreal, 6 October 1896; 1–311 text; 312–13 'Rapports approximatifs des poids et mesures françaises et anglaises'; 314–18 'Table d'intérêt'; 319–27 'Table des matières'
CITATIONS: BQ 23-4923   O'Neill (unpublished)
COPIES: CIHM (04693)   OOCC (TX145 M65)   OONL (TX167 M65 1896, 2 copies)   OONMS   OTMCL (640 M58)   *QMBN (106112 CON)   QMM (RBD TX145 M65 1896)   QQLA (TX167 M792 1896)   QQS (218.4.23); Great Britain: LB (07944.f.28 destroyed)
NOTES: The author defines domestic economy, on p 2, as 'l'art de régler sagement sa manière de vivre.' He sets the subject in a Christian context, identifying the vices that work against its good practice (le luxe, la luxure, la gourmandise, la colère, la paresse), on pp 5–11, and the virtues favourable to its good practice (le travail, de l'ordre), on pp 11–24. Practical information follows, including recipes, some of which are attributed to individuals; for example, Pâté de foie gras (Dicté par Mde Adolphe Germain), p 265, and Beignes de Mde Laurent (Les meilleures), p 266. There is also information about bee-keeping, gardening, maple syrup–making, keeping pigeons, rabbits, and other animals, cheese-making, wine, cider, and vinegar.

The QMBN copy is inscribed on p i, in ink, 'Mlle. Marie-Anne Garneau // Cap-Santé.' The QQS copy is stamped on p i, 'J.O. Filteau, libraire, 27 rue Buade. 27 Quebec.'

1897

The Diamond cook book No. 1

For other cookbooks in the series, see Q36.1 (No. 2), Q38.1 (No. 3), and Q50.1 (No. 5?). There is an unidentified edition (the copy lacks its binding) at ONLAM (Walters-Wagar Collection, Box 20).

Q34.1   nd [about 1897]
The / Diamond / cook / book / No. 1 / Published by / Wells, Richardson & Co. Montreal / Geo. Bishop Eng. & Ptg. Co. Montre[al] [cover-title]
DESCRIPTION: 18.0 × 13.0 cm   Pp 1–32   Paper, with image on front of women working in the kitchen of a 'School of Cookery'; stapled
CONTENTS: Inside front face of binding 'The Diamond Cook Book; or the Young Housekeeper's Friend' signed Wells, Richardson and Co., Montreal; 1–32 text
COPIES: CIHM (88759)   NSBCSH NSHD NSHMS (88.40.32)   QQU   *Private collection
NOTES: If one of the editions of No. 3 in the series was entered for copyright in 1899, Nos. 1 and 2 were published earlier, perhaps in 1897 and 1898. See the quotation in Q36.1, which refers to 700,000 copies printed of No. 1 and which indicates that No. 2 was published one year after No. 1.

Diamond was the trade name of Wells, Richardson and Co. of Burlington, Vermont, and Montreal. Recipes are interspersed with articles offering advice, such as 'A Mother's Experience,' p 1, about feeding baby, which recommends the company's Lactated Food. Household information is on pp 24–32; for example, about dyeing, using Diamond Dyes. Testimonials for the company's products on p 7 are dated 1888.

Dwight's Cow-Brand cook-book

The earliest editions of this cookbook bear two places of publication, Toronto and Montreal; some later editions were published only in Toronto or only in Montreal. For all editions, see O82.1.

Nursing the sick

Q35.1 [6th ed.], 1900
Nursing the sick / Practical ... / information / by a / trained nurse / directions for amateur nursing / at home. / Entered according to Act of the Parliament of Canada, in the year 1897 by / Davis & Lawrence Co., Ltd., at the Department of Agriculture. / Published by / Davis & Lawrence Co., Ltd. / Montreal. / 1900.
DESCRIPTION: 18.0 × 12.5 cm   Pp [1–3] 4–27 [28–32] Paper, with image on front of a woman carrying a tray; stapled
CONTENTS: 1 tp; 2 'Preface' signed Davis and Lawrence Co. Ltd, Montreal, August 1900; 3–27 text in ten chapters: 'Nursing at Home,' 'Ventilation,' 'Bathing,' 'The Bed,' 'Poultices,' 'Stimulating Applications,' 'Liquid Food,' 'Solid Food,' 'Nursing in Special Diseases,' and 'Accidents & Emergencies'; 28–32 publ ads
COPIES: *QMM (N9747 1897 Osler Robertson)
NOTES: The recipes are in the chapters for 'Liquid Food' and 'Solid Food.' The 'Preface' refers to 'our 5th edition, making in all about two million books, ...' 'Sixth edition' is on the binding. The first edition likely appeared in 1897.

1898

The Diamond Dye cook book No. 2

See Q34.1 for a list of other numbers in the same series.

Q36.1   nd [about 1898]
The / Diamond / Dye / cook / book / No. 2 / Published by / Wells, Richardson & Co. Montre[torn off] / Geo. Bishop [rest of printer information torn off] [cover-title]
DESCRIPTION: 18.0 × 13.0 cm   Pp [1] 2–32 Paper, with image on front of women working in the kitchen of a 'School of Cookery'; stapled
CONTENTS: Inside front face of binding 'Index'; top 1 'To the Housekeepers'; mid 1–32 recipes and publ ads
COPIES: *Private collection
NOTES: 'To the Housekeepers' on p 1 indicates that the Diamond Dye cookbooks were annual publications (at least the first two in the series): 'It was with considerable diffidence that we came before you last year in this form; but as you patronized us to the extent of 700,000 copies, we make our appearance with more courage this year, ...' If one of the editions of No. 3 in the series (Q38.3) was entered for copy-

right in 1899, No. 2 was published earlier, perhaps in 1898. The latest testimonial, on p 9, is dated 7 January 1889. The image on the front face of the binding is the same as on No. 1, and many of the recipes are the same. Printed on the outside back face of the binding is 'With compliments of Geo. Fierheller & Co chemists and druggists, Sunderland, Ont.'

Rorer, Mrs Sarah Tyson, née Heston (Richboro, Bucks County, Pa., 1849–1937, Colebrook, Lebanon County, Pa.)

For information about this American author and her other books, see O56.1. For the titles of other works promoting the shortening Cottolene, see Q26.1.

Q37.1   1898
Home helps / With illustrations. / A practical and useful book of / recipes with much / valuable information on cook- / ing and serving / breakfasts, / luncheons, / dinners / and teas. / Edited by / Mrs. Sarah Tyson Rorer, / Principal Philadelphia Cooking School. / Published by the N.K. Fairbank Company, / Chicago, St. Louis, New York, Montreal. / 1898. / Copyright, 1898, The N.K. Fairbank Company, Chicago.
CITATIONS: Arndt, p 316 (Sandra L. Oliver, 'Sarah Tyson Rorer')
COPIES: United States: CU-S   MCR (641.5 R78h) MiEM

Q37.2   1900
—Home helps / With illustrations. / A practical and useful book of / recipes with much / valuable information on cooking / and serving / breakfasts, / luncheons, / dinners / and teas. / Edited by / Mrs. Sarah Tyson Rorer, / Principal Philadelphia Cooking School. / Published by the N.K. Fairbank Company, / Chicago, St. Louis, New York, Montreal, / 1900. / Copyright, 1900, The N.K. Fairbank Company, Chicago.
DESCRIPTION: 18.0 × 13.0 cm   Pp [i–ii] iii–iv, [1–2], v–vi, 1–74 [75–77]   Fp portrait on p ii of Rorer; illus on p viii of table glassware   Thin card, with floral design on front; stapled
CONTENTS: i tp; ii portrait of Rorer; iii 'Mrs. Rorer Recommends Cottolene' signed Sarah Tyson Rorer, principal, Philadelphia Cooking School; iv 'Greeting' from N.K. Fairbank Co.; 1 illus of pail of Cottolene; 2–v 'How to Use Cottolene for Shortening'; vi testimonials for Cottolene from Emma P. Ewing, director, Model Home School of Household Economics, and

Rorer; 1–48 on each page, left column of recipes, printed in black, and right column of 'Helps,' printed in red, and publ ads; 49–74 recipes; 75 publ ad; 76–7 'Contents'

CITATIONS: Arndt, p 158 (Alice Ross, 'N.K. Fairbank') Dickinson, p 98

COPIES: *Private collection; United States: CoDU FTaSU MFmT NN

NOTES: The title-page is printed in red and black. The 1900 edition has the same recipes as the 1898 edition. They are credited to famous American cooks of the day, such as Rorer, Miss Parloa, Mrs Lincoln, and Juliet Corson. There are occasional roman-numbered pages through the text (mostly advertisements for N.K. Fairbank products), with the result that the last verso page in the volume is an odd, not even, number. Fairbank products advertised are Cottolene, Gold Dust Washing Powder, and Fairy Soap.

Copies of a 1906 edition are at CL and TxDN in the United States; the 1906 edition may or may not have Montreal on the title-page.

Despite the same short-title, *Home Helps: A Pure Food Cook Book*, Chicago, New York, St Louis, New Orleans and Montreal: N.K. Fairbank Co., 1910 (Private collection), is a new text except for a handful of duplicate recipes from previous editions. The book is not described as edited by Rorer, but rather as a 'collection of up-to-date, practical recipes by five of the leading culinary experts in the United States: Mrs. Mary Lincoln // Lida Ames Willis // Mrs. Sarah Tyson Rorer // Mrs. Helen Armstrong // Marion Harland.'

1899

Diamond Dye cook book No. 3

See Q34.1 for a list of other numbers in the same series.

Q38.1 nd [about 1899]
Diamond / Dye / cook / book / No. 3 / Published by / the Wells Richardson Co Limited / Montreal / Que [cover-title]
DESCRIPTION: 18.5 × 13.5 cm   Pp [1] 2–32 Paper, with image on front, in 6-cm-high oval frame, of a woman rolling dough; stapled
CONTENTS: Inside front face of binding index; 1–28 recipes and publ ads; 29 'How to Make Art Colors from Diamond Dyes'; 30–1 'To Color Photographs'; 32 'Ivory-type or Cameo Painting' and 'Water Color Painting with Diamond Art Colors'; inside back face index
COPIES: CIHM (51194) *NSYHM OKQ (F5012 nd D537) OPETCM Private collection

NOTES: In this edition of No. 3, there is a woman depicted on the front face of the binding; the company name, in the cover-title, is 'Wells Richardson' without an ampersand; and there is no copyright date on the inside front face of the binding. Q38.3 is described as entered for copyright at the Department of Agriculture in 1899; Q38.1 and Q38.2 were likely published about the same time.

The NSYHM copy has 'With compliments of ... L.C. Gardner & Co. druggists Yarmouth, N.S.' on the outside back face of the binding. The private collector's copy is stamped on the outside back face: 'With compliments of J.A [sic, no period] Joudrey, general merchant, Mahone Bay, N.S.'

QKB has an incomplete copy of *Diamond Dye Cook Book*, which lacks pp 1–2 and the binding, but which may be Q38.1 or Q38.3.

Q38.2 nd [about 1899]
—Livre / de / cuisine / de / Teintures / diamant / no. 3 [remainder of cover-title torn off]
DESCRIPTION: 18.5 × 14.0 cm   Pp [1] 2–31 Paper, with image on back of a woman dying cloth in a tub; stapled
CONTENTS: 1–27 recipes and publ ads; 28–31 publ ads
COPIES: *MSM
NOTES: The MSM copy is in poor condition: the paper binding has been reattached, apparently with the front and back switched. The advertisements give the company name as Wells, Richardson Co. Ltd, Montreal.

Q38.3
nd [entered 1899]
—Diamond / Dye / cook / book / No. 3 / Published by / Wells & Richardson Co. / Montreal. [cover-title]
DESCRIPTION: 19.0 × 13.5 cm   Pp [1] 2–32 Paper; stapled
CONTENTS: Inside front face of binding 'Index' and 'Entered according to Act of the Parliament of Canada, in the year 1899 by Wells & Richardson Co., at the Department of Agriculture.'; 1–28 recipes and publ ads; 29 'How to Make Art Colors from Diamond Dyes'; 30–1 'To Color Photographs'; 32 'Ivory-type or Cameo Painting' and 'Water Color Painting with Diamond Art Colors'; inside back face of binding 'Index' continued
CITATIONS: O'Neill (unpublished)
COPIES: *ARDA; Great Britain: LB (not located)
NOTES: Wells and Richardson Co. is the form of the company name that is found on dated editions of the company's publications from 1899 (see AMICUS). O'Neill's entry for *Diamond Dye Cook Book No. 3*, which is based on the copyright material at the British

Library, corresponds to this edition rather than Q38.1, since he records the company name as 'Wells and Richardson'; the British Library records 1899 as the year of publication.

No human figures are depicted on the front of the binding. Instead, the organic design features two long stems running vertically up each side, topped by stylized budding flowers or berries.

Quatrième recueil de médecines et recettes

See also Q43.1, Cinquième recueil de médecines et recettes. Another cookbook from the same company, but published after Morin's death, is Q91.1. See that entry for information about Dr Morin.

Q39.1   1899
Quatrieme recueil / de / medecines et recettes / a l'usage des familles / Publié par / Dr Ed Morin & cie., Quebec / [in two columns: introductory text and a recipe for Ananas confits]
DESCRIPTION: 16.0 × 12.5 cm   Pp 1–32   Paper, with image on front of a package of Dr Morin's Cardinal Pills, at which points a hand; stapled
CONTENTS: 1 tp, including introductory text and a recipe; 2–32 publ ads and recipes
COPIES: CIHM (64482) *OKQ (F5012 1899 M858)   OONL (RM671 A1 P38 No. 07)
NOTES: The cover-title is 'Pilules cardinales du Dr Morin.' On the package of Dr Morin's Cardinal Pills depicted on the binding, the pills are described as 'for pale and weak people; and all female diseases.' The following publishing information is offered on p 1: 'C'est avec un véritable plaisir que nous présentons notre recueil de 1899. Ce petit travail ... est distribué tous les ans, par milliers, tant aux États-Unis qu'au Canada.' The Morin company address was 48, rue St-Pierre, in Quebec City.

Harland, Marion [pseudonym of] Mrs Mary Virginia Terhune, née Hawes (Amelia County, Va., 21 December 1830–3 June 1922, New York City, NY)

For information about this American author and her other cookbooks, see O18.1.

Q40.1   [entered 1899]
Bits of / Common Sense Series / Cooking hints / by / Marion Harland / author of "Common Sense in the Household" / Montreal / John Lovell & Son / 23 St. Nicholas Street

DESCRIPTION: 14.0 × 9.5 cm   Pp [1–4] 5–119   Paper; stapled
CONTENTS: 1 tp; 2 'Entered according to Act of Parliament, in the year 1899, by John Lovell & Son, in the office of the Minister of Agriculture and Statistics at Ottawa.'; 3 table of contents; 4 blank; 5–119 text in nine chapters (I, 'How to Be Hospitable though Rural'; II, 'Eggs; – Their Uses and Abuses'; III, 'Diet and Homes'; IV, 'The Modern Luncheon "for Ladies Only"'; V, 'The Invariable Potato'; VI, 'Between Seasons'; VII, 'Hot Weather Dishes'; VIII, 'Under Protest?'; IX, 'Oil Stoves and John')
COPIES: *Private collection
NOTES: Most of the culinary advice is offered in a narrative style, although there are some recipes. 'Vol. 1 // "Bits of Common Sense" Series // No 4' is on the front face of the binding; on the back face there is a list of the four titles in the series: I, 'Health Topics'; II, 'Home Topics'; III, 'Household Management'; IV, 'Cooking Hints.'

AMERICAN EDITIONS: [No series number], *Cooking Hints*, New York: Home Topics Publishing Co., [copyright 1899] (OGU). Copies of No. 2, *Home Topics*, and No. 3, *Household Management*, both New York: Home Topics Publishing Co., [copyright 1899], are at OWTU.

Tucker, William Bowman (London, England, 27 February 1859–1934)

In September 1886, Tucker married Emily, the third daughter of Peter Miller of Napanee, Ontario. A Methodist minister, he held various pastorates in Quebec and Eastern Ontario, including at the Methodist Church in Sutton, Quebec. Information about Tucker is in Who's Who, *1912, p 1112.*

Q41.1   [1899]
The / Sutton souvenir [cover-title]
DESCRIPTION: 19.0 × 11.0 cm   Pp [1] 2–32   Illus on p 3 of 'Methodist Church and Parsonage, Sutton, Que. With the compliments of the Ladies' Aid Society.'   Cloth
CONTENTS: 1 preface in poem-form signed 'local poet' and dated Sutton, Quebec, September 1899; 2 ad; 3 illus and ad; 4–31 text; 32 index of recipes and 'C.H. Remick, Typ., Barnston.'
COPIES: CIHM (25040)   *OONL (TX715 T934 1899)
NOTES: The OONL copy is inscribed on the endpaper opposite p 1, in ink: 'Entered according to Act of Parliament, in the year 1899, by William Bowman Tucker, in the office of the Minister of Agriculture, Ottawa.' The recipes are few in number: Lightning

Yeast, Breadmaking, Excelsior Pudding, Chocolate Pudding, Cholera Medicine, Marble Cake, Mrs Ball's Fruit Cake, Delicate Cake, Can Tomatoes, Meat Loaf, Salad Dressing, Soft Ginger Bread, Mother Wisdom's Scripture Cake, Lemon Pie, Chow-chow, Ginger Snaps, Economy Cake, Lemon Foam, Johnny Cake, Dandy Cake, Pumpkin Pie, Mustard Pickles, and Ginger Snaps. They are signed variously E.M.T. [possibly Tucker's wife, Emily], W.B.T. [the author], Mrs H.S.B., Miss B.A.E., anonymous, E.L.C., Rev. T.C.C., C.D.G., Mrs I.C., I.A., and Mrs J.J.L.

The text also includes a section about Sutton by W.B.T., on pp 23–7, that refers to the town being 'lost in ashes' on 15 April 1898 (a fire had started in a sawmill and tannery and spread to the centre of the town). This section names W. Bowman Tucker, MA, PhD, as pastor of the Methodist Church, and tells about Sutton's businesses, the churches, the landscape, the waterworks, the societies, and the mayor. On p 17 there is an advertisement for a book of Sunday School outlines by Rev. Dr Tucker, i.e., *Sunday School Outlines: Being Normal Studies for Teachers' Meetings, Normal Classes, Normal Institutes, Young People's Societies and Individual Students*, Toronto: W. Briggs, 1898.

1900

Almanach pour tous pour l'année 1900

See Q49.1 for the 1901 issue.

Q42.1 1900
Almanach / pour tous / pour l'année / 1900 / Contenant / recettes utiles, notes historiques, etc. / Publié par Jos. Beauchamp / Enregistré conformément à l'Acte du Parlement du Canada, / en l'année 1896, par Jos. Beauchamp, au bureau du / ministre d'Agriculture à Ottawa. / Québec / Imprimerie Darveau, / 80, rue de la montagne.
COPIES: QQS
NOTES: Cooking recipes are on pp 44–7, under the heading 'Recettes utiles pour tous.'

Cinquième recueil de médecines et recettes

See also Q39.1 and Q91.1

Q43.1 1900
[An edition of *Cinquième recueil de médecines et recettes à l'usage des familles*, 'publié par Dr. Ed. Morin & cie., Québec,' 1900, pp 32]

COPIES: OONL (RM671 A1 P38 No. 08)
NOTES: The cover-title is 'Pilules cardinales du Dr Morin.'

My pet recipes

Q44.1 1900
My / pet recipes / tried and true / contributed by the ladies and friends / of St. Andrew's Church / Quebec / "We may live without poetry, music and art; / We may live without conscience, and live without heart; / We may live without friends; we may live without books; / But civilized man cannot live without cooks." / – Owen Meredith. / Quebec / "Daily Telegraph" Printing House / 1900
DESCRIPTION: 21.5 × 14.0 cm   Pp i–vi, [1–2] 3–156 [157–8], vii–xii   Cloth
CONTENTS: i–vi ads; 1 tp; 2 'Rhymes to Remember'; 3–156 recipes credited with the name of the contributor; 157 'Index' [i.e., table of contents]; 158 blank; vii–xii ads
CITATIONS: BQ 23-4927
COPIES: CIHM (38328)   ECO   OGU (CCC TX715.6 M97)   *OKQ (TX715 M88 1900t)   QMBN (158973 CON)   QQLA (TX715 M995 1900)   QQS (218.4.25)
NOTES: The recipe selection includes Manitoba Pudding, five different recipes for Plum Pudding, Scripture Cake (the ingredients and their amounts associated with verses in the Bible), and Canadian Tomato Chutney (the title is followed by the qualifier 'Splendid'). The last recipe, Scotch Haggis, is accorded the honour of a separate section in the 'Index.'

The QQS copy is inscribed on p i, in pencil, 'Angéline Hamel Carrièr // 6, rue Laporte Cap –.'

Tried recipes

Q45.1 1900
Tried recipes / published by / the Ladies' Aid Society / of / Heathton, Que. / 1900 [cover-title]
DESCRIPTION: 14.0 × 9.0 cm   Pp [1–13]   Paper; stapled
CONTENTS: 1–13 recipes credited with the name of the contributor
COPIES: *QSH (0440)
NOTES: No church is named in the book. There are eight leaves, but three of the pages have no printing.

1900–5

Souvenir cook book

Q46.1   nd [about 1900–5]
Souvenir cook book / tried and tested recipies [*sic*] / arranged by the ladies of the / Waterville Congregational Church [cover-title]
DESCRIPTION: 20.5 × 14.5 cm   Pp 3–44   Illus on p 7 of Waterville Congregational Church   Thin card, with image on front of the church; sewn
CONTENTS: 3–6 ads; 7 'Introduction'; 8 untitled three-verse poem; 9 'Index' [i.e., table of contents]; 8 ads; 9–44 recipes credited with the name of the contributor and ads
COPIES: *QLB (Township TX703 S6)
NOTES: There are two leaves numbered 8–9.

1900–6

Recipe book

In 1858 William T. Benson opened the first Canadian cornstarch manufacturing plant in Edwardsburg, Canada West (now Cardinal, Ontario), which he named the Canada Starch Works. Before this date, American-made cornstarch was available in Canadian stores; see O5.1, Traill, Mrs Catharine Parr, The Female Emigrant's Guide, *pp 121, 127. In 1865 the company was reorganized and renamed the Edwardsburg Starch Co. In 1906 Edwardsburg amalgamated with two other starch companies to form Canada Starch Co. In 1919 Corn Products Refining Co. in the United States purchased a controlling interest in Canada Starch, and its Mazola Oil was introduced to the Canadian market. The company papers are at OOA (MG28 III 94). See also George Frederick Benson,* Historical Record of the Edwardsburg and Canada Starch Companies, *[Montreal: Canada Starch Co., 1959]; according to this source, p 261, the company began to advertise its products only in 1899. For other cookbooks by the Canada Starch Co. see: Q83.1,* Edwardsburg Recipe Book; *Q110.1,* Mazola Recipes; *Q177.1,* Canada's Prize Recipes; *Q252.1,* Recettes de choix qui amélioreront vos menus; *and Q263.1–266.1, Aitken, Mrs Katherine,* 52 Baking Secrets, 52 Cakes, 52 Desserts, *and* 52 Pies.

Q47.1   nd [about 1900–6]
Recipe book / How to make / candy / delicacies / and / tasty / appetizing / puddings / The Edwardsburg Starch Comp'y / Limited / Offices, Montreal, P. Que. Toronto, Ont. [cover-title]

DESCRIPTION: 15.0 × 9.0 cm   Pp 1–48   Paper, with image on front of a tin of Edwardsburg Corn Syrup and a package of Benson's Prepared Corn [i.e., cornstarch]; stapled
CONTENTS: 1–20 'Candy Recipes'; 21–7 'Cake Recipes'; 28–31 'Pie Recipes'; 32–48 'Pudding Recipes'
COPIES: *Company collection (Best Foods Canada, Toronto, Ont.)
NOTES: This cookbook was published before the company changed its name to Canada Starch, some time in 1906. The order of publication of the two editions is unknown. From appearances, both were published about 1900–6.

This edition is distinguished from Q47.2 by the spelling of the company name in the cover-title: here 'Comp'y' is abbreviated; in Q47.2, 'Company' and a comma is the form used. Another difference is that here 'How to make' is in roman all-capital letters; in Q47.2, the phrase is in italic all-capitals.

Q47.2   nd [about 1900–6]
—Recipe book / How to make / candy / delicacies / and / tasty / appetizing / puddings / The Edwardsburg Starch Company, / Limited / Offices: Montreal, P. Que. Toronto, Ont. [cover-title]
DESCRIPTION: 15.0 × 9.0 cm   Pp 1–48   Paper, with image on front of a tin of Edwardsburg Corn Syrup and a package of Benson's Prepared Corn; stapled
CONTENTS: 1–20 'Candy Recipes'; 21–7 'Cake Recipes'; 28–31 'Pie Recipes'; 32–48 'Pudding Recipes'
COPIES: *Private collection

1900–10

Quebec, Department of Agriculture

For other cookbooks from Quebec's Department of Agriculture, see (under Quebec, Department of Agriculture, where no author is cited): Q68.1, Chapais, Jean-Charles, Le fromage raffiné de l'Isle-d'Orléans; *Q74.3, DesRoches, Amélie,* Hygiène de l'alimentation et propriétés chimiques des aliments; *Q96.1, Grisé, Joseph-Évariste,* De la fabrication des conserves alimentaires à la maison; *Q99.1,* How to Save Wheat and Meat; *Q109.1, Lajoie-Vaillancourt, Mrs Blanche,* Use of Honey and of Maple Sugar in Cooking; *Q123.1, Désilets, Mme Rolande Savard,* Manuel de la cuisinière économe et pratique; *Q137.1,* Eat More Cheese; *Q184.1, Grisé, Joseph-Évariste,* Les conserves; *Q220.1, Paré, Eugénie,* Le pain de ménage; *Q251.1,* Mangeons plus de légumes; *and Q259.1,* Les volailles et les oeufs.

Q48.1 nd [about 1900–10]
La / bonne ménagère / Notions d'economie domestique et d'agriculture / à l'usage des jeunes filles des écoles rurales / de la province de Québec. / Publié par le / département de l'Agriculture / de la province de Québec.
DESCRIPTION: 16.5 × 11.0 cm   Pp [1–5] 6–96   Tp illus of a basket of flowers, illus   Lacks binding
CONTENTS: 1 ht; 2 blank; 3 tp; 4 blank; 5–7 'Préface'; 8 blank; 9–90 thirty-six numbered lessons in three parts; 91–3 'Conclusion'; 94 blank; 95–6 'Table des matières'
CITATIONS: Beaulieu, p 142   Bibliothèque municipale de Montréal, p 7   Carrière No. 273   Driver 2003, 'Canadian Cookbooks,' p 38
COPIES: BVAU   CIHM (48243)   OONL (COP.QU.2. 1993-1125, 2 copies)   QMBM (640.2 Q3bo)   *QMBN (161764 CON)   QQL (B.C. 1800 003)   QQS (2 copies: 218.4.35, 359.2.10.3)
NOTES: QMBN dates the book about 1900; Beaulieu dates it about 1910. The QQS copy is stapled and retains its paper binding, with the title-page illustration on the front face.
There are two editions, this one with 96 pp and Q48.2 with 104 pp. The order of publication is unknown.

Q48.2 nd [about 1900–10]
—La / bonne ménagère / Notions d'economie domestique et d'agricul- / ture a l'usage des jeunes filles des écoles / rurales de la province de Québec / Publié par le / departement de l'Agriculture / de la province de Québec.
DESCRIPTION: 17.0 × 12.0 cm   Pp [1–5] 6–104   Tp illus of a basket of flowers, illus   Paper, with tp illus on front; stapled
CONTENTS: 1 ht; 2 blank; 3 tp; 4 blank; 5–7 'Préface'; 8 blank; 9–97 thirty-six numbered lessons; 98–100 'Conclusion'; 101–2 blank; 103–4 'Table des matières'
COPIES: *QTURA

1901

Almanach pour tous pour l'année 1901

See also Q42.1.

Q49.1 1901
Almanach / pour tous / pour l'année / 1901 / Contenant / recettes utiles, notes historiques, etc. / Publié par Jos. Beauchamp / Enregistré conformément à l'Acte du Parlement du Canada, / en l'année 1896, par Jos. Beauchamp, au bureau du /

ministre d'Agriculture à Ottawa. / Québec / Imprimerie Darveau, / 80, côte de la montagne.
COPIES: QQS
NOTES: Cooking recipes are on pp 41–53, under the heading 'Recettes utiles pour tous.'

Diamond Dye cook book [No. 5?]

See Q34.1 for a list of other numbers in the same series.

Q50.1 nd [about 1901]
[Cover-title of NSWA copy covered in cloth]
DESCRIPTION: 19.0 × 13.5 cm   Pp [1] [2 obscured by clipping?] 3–32   Paper, later covered in limp cloth; stapled
CONTENTS: Inside front face of binding index; 1–28 recipes; 29 'How to Make Art Colors from Diamond Dyes'; 30–2 'To Color Photographs'; inside back face index continued
COPIES: *NSWA
NOTES: The NSWA copy is inscribed on the front face of the applied cloth, 'No. 5 D.D. Cook Book.' If one of the editions of No. 3 in the series was entered for copyright in 1899, No. 5 was published later, perhaps in 1901.
OWTU (F14537) has an unidentified edition that lacks its binding. The first recipe page matches the NSWA copy described here.

Oliphant, Mrs Nelson B.

Q51.1 [copyright 1901]
A / dainty cook book / by / Mrs. Nelson Oliphant / The / Abbey Press / publishers / 114 / Fifth Avenue / New York / London Montreal
DESCRIPTION: 21.0 × 13.5 cm   Pp [1–4] 5–178   A few small illus   Cloth, with image on front of a steaming kettle and a ladle
CONTENTS: 1 tp; 2 'Copyright, 1901, by the Abbey Press'; 3 quotation from Henrion de Pensey; 4 blank; 5–6 table of contents; 7–178 text
CITATIONS: Axford, p 108   Bitting, p 350   Driver 784.1
COPIES: *OGU (UA s053 b36); United States: DLC
NOTES: The book is designed for the owner to add manuscript recipes: Text and illustrations are interspersed with blank spaces and blank pages. There are six parts: I, 'Ancient and Curious Recipes'; II, 'Local Recipes'; III, 'Calendar'; IV, 'Special Occasions'; V, 'Breakfast, Lunch, Dinner'; and VI, 'Miscellaneous.' Although most of the culinary history and lore is

British, one of the recipes – Fig Pudding, p 146 – is described as a 'Recipe from Montreal.' There is information about gingerbread eaten on Guy Fawkes' Day, on p 65, and about food associated with the city of Shrewsbury, on p 32. The title-page is printed in red and black.

DLC dates the book [1902], based on the date it received the two deposit copies, 2 April 1902. The copyright entry was made on 9 December 1901.

1902

Gem Chopper cook book

This cookbook was distributed by various Ontario, Quebec, and Nova Scotia companies. For editions distributed by Lewis Bros Ltd in Montreal, see O118.1 and O118.3; by Caverhill Learmont and Co., Montreal, see O118.2.

Parloa, Miss Maria (Mass., 1843–1909, Bethel, Conn.)

Maria Parloa opened her own cooking school in Boston in 1877, taught at the Boston Cooking School for a short time from its founding in 1879, and started another cooking school in New York City in 1883. Her articles appeared frequently in the Ladies' Home Journal, *which she part-owned. See her biography in Arndt, pp 282–4 (Nancy Harmon Jenkins, 'Maria Parloa').*

Her recipes were included in various American promotional cookbooks, some of which were issued in Canadian editions: Q52.1, Choice Recipes; Q153.1, Chocolate and Cocoa Recipes ... Home Made Candy Recipes, also by Walter Baker and Co. Ltd; and two booklets for the shortening Cottolene, Q29.1 and Q30.1. Other books published by Walter Baker are Q173.1, Chocolate and Cocoa Recipes, and O747.1, Baker's Best Chocolate Recipes.

Also by Parloa, but not published in Canada, are: The Appledore Cook Book, *Boston: Graves and Ellis, 1872 (United States: DLC, InU);* Camp Cookery, *Boston: Graves, Locke and Co., [c1878] (United States: DLC, InU);* First Principles of Household Management and Cookery, *Boston: Houghton, Osgood and Co., 1879 (United States: DLC, InU);* Lectures on Cooking ... as Reported in the Morning Mail, *Lowell, Mass.: Stone, Bacheller and Livingstone, 1880 (WaiteCat 5, No. 121);* Miss Parloa's New Cook Book, *Boston: Estes and Lauriat, 1880 (United States: InU);* Practical Cookery, with Demonstrations, *New York: Tribune, 1884 (United States: DLC);* Miss Parloa's Kitchen Com-

panion, *Boston: Estes and Lauriat, 1887 (United States: DLC, InU);* Miss Parloa's Young Housekeeper, *Boston: D. Estes and Co., [c1893] (United States: DLC);* Home Economics, *New York: Century Co., 1898 (United States: DLC, InU);* Canned Fruit, Preserves and Jellies, *Washington, DC: United States Agriculture Department, 1904, Farmer's Bulletin 203 (referred to in Cagle/Stafford No. 590); and* Government Cook Book: Economical Use of Meat in the Home, *Brooklyn: [Brooklyn Daily Eagle], 1910 (United States: DLC). She contributed to* Handbook of Ideas in China, Crockery, Silver and Art Pottery ... *and* Miss Parloa's Advice on Setting the Dinner Table, *[2nd ed.], Boston: Morey, Churchill and Morey, c1888 (United States: DLC), and to* New England Cook Book, *by Mrs D.A. Lincoln, Maria Parloa, and others, [compiled by Gertrude Strohm], Boston: C.E. Brown, c1894 (United States: DLC).*

Miss Parloa's Kitchen Companion *and* Miss Parloa's New Cook Book *were sold by the Methodist Book and Publishing House in Toronto; see the following entries in 'Stock Book 1909' (OTCC, Acc. 83.061C, UCC Board of Publication, Series III, Box 39, p 49): '5 [copies] Parloa's New Cook Bk ... 3 [copies] Parloa's Kitchen Compan.' There is also an entry for '2 [copies] Miss Parloa's Kitchen' in 'Stock Book 1913' (Box 41, p 10).*

Q52.1 copyright 1902
Gold Medal, Paris, 1900 / Choice / recipes / by / Miss Maria Parloa / and other noted / teachers, lecturers and / writers. / Walter Baker & Co. Ltd. / Dorchester, / Mass., U.S.A. / Copyrighted 1902 by / Walter Baker & Company, Ltd.
DESCRIPTION: 15.0 × 8.5 cm   Pp [1] 2–78 [79–80]   Illus on p 4 of the company mill, Dorchester, Massachusetts; illus on p 6 of a group of demonstrators, on p 75 of parts of a cocoa plant, on p 79 of cocoa pods, and on p 80 of company machine   Paper, with image on front of cocoa pods; stapled
CONTENTS: 1 tp; 2–3 'The House of ... Walter Baker & Co. Limited'; 4 illus of mill; 5–27 'Choice Recipes by Miss Maria Parloa'; 28–34 'Recipes Specially Prepared by Miss Elizabeth Kevill Burr'; 35–43 'Recipes from Other Noted Teachers'; 44–55 'State Recipes'; 56–7 'Miscellaneous Recipes'; 58–70 'Some Notes on the Food Value of Cocoa and Chocolate'; 71–5 'Walter Baker & Co.'s Cocoa and Chocolate Preparations'; 76–8 'Index to Recipes'; 79–80 illus
COPIES: *AALIWWM   OTYA (CPC 1902 0051)   Private collection
NOTES: The cover-title of the AALIWWM and OTYA copies is 'Canadian edition / Choice / recipes / by / Miss Parloa and other / noted teachers. / Compliments of / Walter Baker & Co., Limited, / manufac-

turers of / cocoa and chocolate preparations / Branch house / 12 and 14 St. John St. / Montreal, P.Q.' Printed on the outside back face of the binding is 'Duncan Litho. Co. Hamilton.'

The private collector's copy appears to be identical except for the text on the binding, which reads, on the front: 'Canadian edition. / Choice / recipes / by / Miss Parloa / and other / noted teachers. / Walter Baker & Co. Ltd. / Manufacturers of / cocoa and chocolate preparations. / Branch house / 86 St. Peter St. Montreal, P.Q.'; on the back, the printing company is not named. Since the company address on the binding (St Peter Street) matches that on the title-page of the 1906 edition (Q52.2), the private collector's copy follows those bearing the St John Street address.

The following notice for *Choice Recipes* appeared in *Canadian Grocer* Vol. 16, No. 17 (25 April 1902), under the heading 'A New Recipe Book': 'Walter Baker & Co. Limited, Dorchester, Mass., ... are about to issue a new and greatly enlarged edition of their booklet of choice recipes, prepared by Miss Parloa, and other noted teachers of cooking. It is a very attractive publication of 80 pages, illustrated with half-tones and colored lithographs, and contains the most complete collection ever made of recipes in which cocoa or chocolate is used for eating and drinking. Vassar College and Smith College contribute their famous recipes for making fudge.' The book could be ordered, free by mail to any applicant in the US or Canada, by writing the company in Dorchester.

Q52.2   copyright 1906
—Canadian edition / Choice / recipes / by / Miss Maria Parloa / and other noted / teachers / Walter Baker & Co. / Limited / Dorchester, Mass. / Branch house / 86 St. Peter St., Montreal. / Copyright, 1906, by / Walter Baker & Co., Ltd.
DESCRIPTION: 16.5 × 10.0 cm   Pp [1] 2–64   4 double-sided pls col between pp 16–17, 32–3 (2 pls), and 48–9; 1 fp illus on p 2 of company mills at Dorchester and Milton, Massachusetts; 1 fp illus on p 8 of demonstrators   Paper, with decorative border on front of cocoa pods, leaves, and flowers; stapled
CONTENTS: 1 tp; 2 illus of mills; 3–4 'The House of Walter Baker & Co., Ltd.'; 5–7 'Index to Recipes'; 8 illus of demonstrators; 9–25 'Choice Recipes by Miss Maria Parloa'; 26–32 'Recipes Specially Prepared by Miss Elizabeth Kevill Burr'; 33–41 'Recipes from Other Noted Teachers'; 42–50 'State Recipes'; 51–2 'New Recipes by Miss Burr'; 53–8 'Some Notes on the Food Value of Cocoa and Chocolate'; 59–63 'Walter Baker & Co.'s Cocoa and Chocolate Preparations'; 64 publ ad

COPIES: CIHM (76501)   ONHI (987.1)   OONL (TX715 C3465 No. 13 reserve)   *Private collection

AMERICAN EDITIONS: *Choice Receipts ... Specially Prepared for Walter Baker and Company,* by Maria Parloa, Dorchester, Mass.: Walter Baker and Co., 1893, c1892 (United States: DLC); *Choice Recipes,* 1895 (Dickinson, p 52); *Choice Recipes,* by Maria Parloa and Elizabeth K. Burr, Dorchester, Mass.: Walter Baker and Co. Ltd, c1899 (cited in DLC catalogue); *Choice Recipes,* Dorchester, Mass.: W. Baker and Co. Ltd, 1904 (United States: DLC); Dorchester, Mass.: Walter Baker and Co. Ltd, copyright 1906 (United States: InU; Cagle/ Stafford No. 904 states that this is the 2nd printing of the 1st ed. of 1904; illus of No. 904 incorrectly identified as No. 905 and vice versa); 1909 (Longone/ Longone Q6).

1903

Cook book

Q53.1   1903
[First edition of *Cook Book,* by the Ladies' Aid Society of the First Universalist Church, North Hatley, Quebec, 1903]
NOTES: See Q53.3 for the facsimile of 1903. The cookbook is cited in *The Unitarian-Universalist Church of North Hatley, Québec: A Memoir,* [Women's Alliance, 1986], p 13: 'The women of the congregation were very inventive and creative in their money-raising activities, as their "Souvenir Cook Book" (1903) illustrates.'; the title-page is reproduced on p 15. The First Universalist Church in Hatley had been founded in 1895. Some of the funds raised from publication of the cookbook in 1903 went toward the cost of a new parsonage, built in 1904 (conversation with Phyllis Skeats, local historian, April 2001; no minutes of the Ladies' Aid Society survive).

Q53.2   2nd ed., 1910
—Second edition souvenir / Cook book / containing choice receipts from / practical housekeepers / Compiled by the / Ladies' Aid Society / of the / First Universalist Church / North Hatley, Que. / 1910
DESCRIPTION: 20.5 × 14.5 cm   Pp [1–7] 8–72 [73]   Paper; sewn
CONTENTS: 1–2 ads; 3 tp; 4 ads; 5 'Index' [i.e., table of contents] and acknowledgment of contributors' generosity; 6 'The Church of Our Father' [i.e., information about the First Universalist Church]; 7 untitled

six-line verse; 8–mid 10 'A Sketch of North Hatley and Lake Massawippi' signed A.R.M.; mid 10–11 ads; 12–72 'Recipes'; 73 'Household Help and Hints'
COPIES: *QSH
NOTES: The cover-title is 'Cook Book and Business Directory.'

Q53.3   nd [facsimile of 1903, 1980]
—[Running head:] Title page [folio:] 3 / Souvenir / Cook book / containing choice receipts from / practical housekeepers / compiled by the / Ladies' Aid Society / of the / First Universalist Church / North Hatley, Que. / 1903. / "Thou shalt not die for lack of dinner." – / Shakespeare. / Geo. Gale & Sons Print, Waterville, Que.
DESCRIPTION: 21.0 × 13.5 cm   Pp 3–23, 25–70 [71] Paper, with image on front of the church; stapled
CONTENTS: 3 tp; 4 ad; 5 'Index' [i.e., table of contents]; 6 notice about the church (its pastor, beliefs, services, and meetings); 7 untitled poem signed C.A.C.; 8–11 'A Sketch of North Hatley and Lake Massawippi' signed A.R.M., and ads; 12 ads; 13–70 'Recipes' credited with the name of the contributor and ads; 71 ad
COPIES: QSH   *Private collection
NOTES: Page 24 is omitted from the pagination so that, from p 25 onward, odd-numbered pages are versos and even-numbered pages are rectos. No publication date is recorded in the facsimile, but it was published in 1980 (conversation with Phyllis Skeats, April 2001).

1904

Lovell, Mrs Sarah, née Kurczyn (Montreal, Que., 22 August 1829–24 June 1917, Montreal)

The author's great-great-granddaughter, who owns a copy of the cookbook passed down to her in 1973 by her grandmother (not the one catalogued here), informed me (letter, June 1991) that Sarah Lovell was the wife of the printer and publisher John Lovell (1810–93) (i.e., not Sarah and John Lovell's daughter Sarah). She was the child of Sarah Wurtele and N.P.M. Kurczyn, a wealthy merchant. In 1849, she married John Lovell. They lived in a large house on St Catherine Street and had six sons and six daughters, two of whom died as babies. In 1877 Sarah opened a school for young ladies. She was a charter member of the Montreal Women's Club, founded in 1892. A close friend described her as 'a woman of commanding presence and great intellectual power as an educationalist' (DCB, Vol. 12, p 573). In 1908, four years after the

publication of her cookbook, she had published Reminiscences of Seventy Years *(Montreal: John Lovell and Son Ltd) dedicated to her children and grandchildren (photocopy at OKQ). Oddly, these memoirs make no mention of* Meals of the Day.

It is interesting to note that 'once or twice' Sarah entertained at her home Susanna Moodie, the sister of Catharine Parr Traill, author of O5.1, The Female Emigrant's Guide *(see Charlotte Gray,* Sisters in the Wilderness: The Lives of Susanna Moodie and Catharine Parr Traill, *Toronto: Viking, 1999, p 160, regarding Susanna's visits with the Lovells).*

See George L. Parker's entry for John Lovell in DCB, Vol. 12, and Sarah Lovell's obituary in the Montreal Gazette *25 June 1917, p 4. The 1901 Census records her birth date. Dionne incorrectly cites the author as 'Miss' Sarah Lovell.*

Q54.1   1904
Meals of the day / a guide / to the young housekeeper / by / Sarah Lovell / Montreal / John Lovell & Son, Limited / 1904
DESCRIPTION: 21.5 × 14.0 cm   Pp [3–10] 11–186   Cloth
CONTENTS: 3 ht; 4 blank; 5 tp; 6 'Entered according to Act of Parliament of Canada, in the year of our Lord one thousand nine hundred and four, by Sarah Lovell in the office of the Minister of Agriculture and Statistics at Ottawa.'; 7 preface; 8 blank; 9–169 text; 170 blank; four blank leaves not incl in pagination; 171–86 index
CITATIONS: Dionne, Vol. 3, No. 2872   Ferguson/Fraser, p 232   O'Neill (unpublished)
COPIES: QMU (641.5 L911m)   *Private collection; Great Britain: LB (07945.i.39 destroyed); United States: IaU
NOTES: Another private collector reports that her mother 'received this book on marriage at Aylmer Que. June 29, 1904 – 21 years old.'

1905

Denison, Mrs Grace Elizabeth

For the 1905 Montreal edition of Grace Denison's The New Cook Book, *see O130.3.*

Ogilvie's book for a cook

The Ogilvie family began milling flour in Canada in 1801, soon after their emigration from Scotland. In 1902, William Watson Ogilvie's executors sold the business to a

Canadian-owned syndicate, at which point it was re-named Ogilvie Flour Mills Co. Ltd. The company's papers are at MWU.

Earlier cookbooks had been published by other milling companies to promote the use of their flour; for example, the pre-1900 editions of O85.1, Good Flour and How to Use It, *by the McAllister Milling Co. in Peterborough, and O95.1,* The Beaver Mills Cook Book, *by the T.H. Taylor Co. in Chatham, of about 1900; however, these were local publications.* Ogilvie's Book for a Cook *by the newly organized Ogilvie Flour Mills Co. was the first of the genre to be distributed nationally in multiple editions, in English and French – editions have been identified for almost every year, from 1905 to 1922, the last published in 1931.*

There are unidentified, incomplete copies of Ogilvie's Book for a Cook *at the following places: ACG, lacks most of title-page, but inscribed on p 4, 'Miss Jeanie Thomson. Pincher Creek Alberta. Sep 12th 1911.'; AHRMH, pp 5–122 only; ONLAM (Walters-Wagar Collection, Box 20), pp 5–124 only; and OOWM (1979.7.1), lacking pp 1–4.*

The following are not later editions of Ogilvie's Book for a Cook, *but editions of another text:* Le livre de recettes Ogilvie, *1st ed., August 1950 (QMM);* The Ogilvie Cook Book, *10th ed., revised, Toronto: 1957 (OONL, QMBM, QMM); and* Le livre de cuisine Ogilvie, *10th ed., revised, September 1957 (QMM).*

For other cookbooks published by Ogilvie Flour Mills see: Famous Royal Household Recipes *series, Q214.1– 218.1, under Aitken, Mrs Katherine, and Q219.1, under McKenzie, Mildred Mae; and Q261.1,* Royal Household Flour Basic Sponge Recipes.

Q55.1 1905

Ogilvie's / book for a cook / A selection of recipes and other / things adapted to the needs of / the average housekeeper, / some entirely new, and / all have been / thoroughly / tested / Ogilvie / Montreal, Canada / 1905 / Entered according to Act of Parliament of Canada, in the year one thousand nine hundred / [obscured by collector's bookplate: 'and five, by the Ogilvie Flour Mills'] Company, Limited, of Montreal, / [obscured by bookplate: 'at the Department of'] Agriculture, Ottawa.

DESCRIPTION: 20.0 × 13.5 cm   Pp [1–5] 6–124 [125–8] Tp illus of a windmill; illus (many of the company's mills)   Paper, with image on front of a seated woman reading 'Ye Cooke's Booke'

CONTENTS: 1 tp; 2 'Introduction' by Ogilvie Flour Mills Co.; 3 fp illus of a small testing mill and electric oven; 4 blank; 5 'Correspondence'; 6–124 text; 125–7 table of contents; 128 'Note'

CITATIONS: Armstrong 2000, p F2   Driver 2003, 'Canadian Cookbooks,' p 36   Driver 2003, Robin Hood, p 85   Ferguson/Fraser, p 232, illus col on p 11 of closed volume may be this edition

COPIES: BDEM BDUCVM BKOM BVMA CIHM (80162) MTM NBFKL *OGU (3 copies: UA s045 b24, UA s045 b25, and CCC TX715.6 O35) MWU (Archives and Special Collections, Ogilvie Collection, MSS 120, Box 82, Folder 1) NBSUH OONL (TX715.6 O45 1905) OTAG (The Grange, 641.5971) QMM (RBD TX715 O37x 1905) QMBM QKB (87-74) SBIHM

NOTES: *Ogilvie's Book for a Cook* is the earliest known collection of recipes published by Ogilvie Flour Mills Co. Introductory text in *The Ogilvie Cook Book* of September 1957 (not related to Q55.1) suggests that there was an earlier cookbook: 'The earliest Ogilvie Cook Book available on our files dates back to the early 1900's, but it is generally acknowledged that an Ogilvie Cook Book existed long before even this.' I have found no evidence to support this claim.

The text and design are clearly derived from *A Book for a Cook* published in the same year, 1905, by Pillsbury Flour Mills of Minneapolis, Minnesota. The 'Introduction' of the American work states that Mrs Nellie Duling Gans compiled the recipes for Pillsbury at the 1904 World's Fair in St. Louis. How or whether Ogilvie secured permission to use the American text is unknown.

Q55.2 1906

—[An edition of *Ogilvie's Book for a Cook*, Montreal, Que.: Ogilvie Flour Mills Co., 1906, pp 124]
CITATIONS: O'Neill (unpublished)
COPIES: Great Britain: LB (7942.h.44 destroyed)

Q55.3 1907

—Ogilvie's / book for a cook / A selection of recipes and other / things adapted to the needs of / the average housekeeper, / some entirely new, / all have been / thoroughly / tested / Ogilvie / Montreal, Canada / 1907 / Entered according to Act of Parliament of Canada, in the year one thousand / nine hundred and seven, by the Ogilvie Flour Mills Company, Limited, of / Montreal, at the Departement [*sic*] of Agriculture, Ottawa.
DESCRIPTION: 20.5 × 14.0 cm   Pp [1] 2–124 [125–8]   Tp illus of a windmill, illus   Paper, with image on front of a seated woman reading a book
CONTENTS: 1 tp; 2 'Introduction' by Ogilvie Flour Mills Co.; 3 fp illus of a small testing mill and electric oven; 4 blank; 5 'Correspondence'; 6–124 text; 125–7 'Contents' [i.e., index]; 128 'Note'

COPIES: AHRMH (998-043-001) ARDA NSYHM (2 copies) OONL (TX715.6 O45 1907) *Private collection

Q55.4 1907
—Le livre de cuisine / d'Ogilvie / Choix de recettes et autres / connaissances utiles et indispen- / sables au besoin de la généralité / des maitresses de maison, chacune / de ces recettes a été essayée / et plusieurs d'entre elles sont / entièrement nouvelles. / Ogilvie / Montreal, Canada / 1907 / Enregistré d'après l'Acte du Parlement en l'année 1907 par The Ogilvie / Flour Mills Company Limited, de Montréal, au département / de l'Agriculture, Ottawa.
DESCRIPTION: Tp illus of a windmill With image on front of a seated woman reading a book
CITATIONS: Powers/Stewart, p 184 (James MacGuire, 'The Art and Science of Good Bread')
COPIES: *Private collection
NOTES: The cover-title is 'Recettes Ogilvie pour la cuisinière moderne.'

In Powers/Stewart, p 184, MacGuire refers to what is likely this edition in the 'Ogilvie-Five Roses archives in Montreal'; however, I did not find the volume when I visited in September 2000 (the company is now called ADM Milling Co.).

Q55.5 1908
—Recettes Ogilvie / pour la cuisiniere moderne / Choix de recettes et autres / connaissances utiles et indispen- / sables au besoin de la généralité / des maitresses de maison, chacune / de ces recettes a été essayée / et plusieurs d'entres elles sont / entièrement nouvelles. / Ogilvie / Montreal, Canada / 1908 / Enregistré d'après l'Acte du Parlement en l'année 1908 par The Ogilvie / Flour Mills Company Limited, de Montréal, au département / de l'Agriculture, Ottawa.
DESCRIPTION: Pp [1–2] 3–124 [125–8] Tp illus of a windmill, illus
CONTENTS: 1 tp; 2 'Introduction'; 3 fp illus of 'Moulin expérimental et four électrique en usage au laboratoire et au département de la boulangerie'; 4 blank; 5 'Correspondence'; 6 publ ad; 7–119 text and ads; 120–2 'Conseils pratiques'; 123 'Poids et mesures'; 124 'Temps pour cuire'; 125–7 'Index'; 128 'Notice'
CITATIONS: BQ 24-4837
COPIES: OTYA (TX715 R43 1908) QMBN (114290 CON and *MIC B5801 GEN)

Q55.6 1909
—Ogilvie's / book for a cook / A selection of recipes and other / things adapted to the needs of /

the average housekeeper, / some entirely new, / all have been / thoroughly / tested / Ogilvie / Montreal, Canada / 1909 / Entered according to Act of Parliament of Canada, in the year one thousand / nine hundred and nine, by the Ogilvie Flour Mills Company, Limited, / of Montreal, at the Department of Agriculture, Ottawa.
DESCRIPTION: 20.5 × 14.0 cm Pp [1] 2–128 Tp illus of a windmill, illus Paper, with image on front of a seated woman reading a book
CONTENTS: 1 tp; 2 'Introduction' by Ogilvie Flour Mills Co.; 3 fp illus of a small testing mill and electric oven; 4 blank; 5 'Correspondence'; 6–124 text; 125–7 'Contents' [i.e., index]; 128 'Note'
COPIES: NSHMS (84.92.10) Company collection (ADM Milling Co., Montreal) *Private collection

Q55.7 1909
—Recettes Ogilvie / pour la cuisinière moderne / Choix de recettes et autres / connaissances utiles et indispen- / sables au besoin de la généralité / des maitresses de maison, chacune / de ces recettes a été essayée / et plusieurs d'entres elles sont / entièrement nouvelles. / Ogilvie / Montreal, Canada / 1909 / Enregistré d'après l'Acte du Parlement en l'année 1909 par The Ogilvie / Flour Mills Company Limited, de Montréal, au département / de l'Agriculture, Ottawa.
DESCRIPTION: 20.5 × 14.0 cm Pp [1] 2–128 Tp illus of a windmill, illus Paper, with image on front of a seated woman reading a book; stapled
CONTENTS: 1 tp; 2 'Introduction'; 3 fp illus of 'Moulin expérimental et four électrique'; 4 blank; 5 'Correspondence'; 6–123 text and publ ads; 124–7 index; 128 'Notice'
COPIES: *MSM QMM (RBD uncat Soeur Berthe 488)

Q55.8 1910
—Ogilvie's / book for a cook / A selection of recipes and other / things adapted to the needs of / the average housekeeper, / some entirely new, / all have been / thoroughly / tested / Ogilvie / Montreal, Canada / 1910 / Entered according to Act of Parliament of Canada, in the year one thousand / nine hundred and nine [sic], by the Ogilvie Flour Mills Company, Limited, / of Canada, at the Department of Agriculture, Ottawa.
DESCRIPTION: 20.5 × 14.0 cm Pp [1] 2–128 Tp illus of a windmill, illus Paper, with image on front of a seated woman reading a book
CONTENTS: 1 tp; 2 'Introduction' by Ogilvie Flour Mills Co.; 3 fp illus of 'Small Testing Mill & Electric Oven Used in Laboratory and Baking Dept.'; 4 blank; 5 'Correspondence'; 6–7 'Yeast'; 8 publ ad; 9–119 reci-

pes and publ ads; 120–2 'Useful Hints'; 123 'Weights and Measures'; 124 'Time for Baking'; 125–7 'Contents' [i.e., index]; 128 'Note'
COPIES: OKITD (986.040.003) OMUC OSMFHHM OTBPM QKB (4 copies: 72-5, 76-94, 79-23, 80-7) QQUQT SBIM *SRRPM
NOTES: That four copies of this edition have found their way into the collection of the Brome County Historical Society in Knowlton indicates that this book enjoyed widespread use in the town.

Q55.9 1911
—Ogilvie's / book for a cook / A selection of recipes and other things / adapted to the needs of the average / housekeeper, some entirely / new, all have been / thoroughly tested / Ogilvie / Montreal, Canada / 1911 / Entered according to Act of Parliament of Canada, in the year one thousand nine hundred and / nine, by the Ogilvie Flour Mills Company, Limited of Montreal, at the Department of / Agriculture, Ottawa.
DESCRIPTION: 20.5 × 14.0 cm Pp [1] 2–127 [128] Tp illus of a windmill, illus Paper, with image on front of a seated woman reading a book; stapled
CONTENTS: 1 tp; 2 'Introduction' by Ogilvie Flour Mills Co.; 3 fp illus of 'Small Testing Mill & Electric Oven Used in Laboratory and Baking Dept.'; 4 blank; 5 'Correspondence'; 6–124 text and publ ads; 125–7 'Contents' [i.e., index]; 128 'Note'
COPIES: *ACG BVIPM OBEHCM QMM (RBD ckbk 1878)

Q55.10 1912
—Ogilvie's / book for a cook / A selection of recipes and other things / adapted to the needs of the average / housekeeper, some entirely / new, all have been / thoroughly tested / Ogilvie / Montreal, Canada / 1912 / Entered according to Act of Parliament of Canada, in the year one thousand nine hundred and / nine, by the Ogilvie Flour Mills Company, Limited of Montreal, at the Department of / Agriculture, Ottawa.
DESCRIPTION: 20.5 × 14.0 cm Pp [1] 2–127 [128] Tp illus of a windmill, illus Paper, with image on front of a seated woman reading a book; stapled
CONTENTS: 1 tp; 2 'Introduction' by Ogilvie Flour Mills Co.; 3 fp illus of a small testing mill and electric oven; 4 blank; 5 'Correspondence'; 6–124 text; 125–7 table of contents; 128 'Note'
COPIES: NSYHM OKELWM QKB QMM (RBD ckbk 1879) *Private collection
NOTES: A loose leaf (16.5 × 25.5 cm, folded twice) is inserted in the private collector's copy: 'Supplement to Ogilvie's Book for a Cook containing some new and economical recipes.'

Q55.11 1913
—[An edition of *Recettes Ogilvie pour la cuisinière moderne*, Montreal: Ogilvie, 1913, pp 123]
CITATIONS: Brisebois No. 102, p 25
COPIES: *Private collection

Q55.12 1914
—Ogilvie's book / for a cook / A selection of recipes and other / things adapted to the needs of / the average housekeeper, some / entirely new, all have been / thoroughly tested / Ogilvie / Montreal, Canada / 1914
DESCRIPTION: 20.0 × 14.0 cm Pp [1] 2–127 [128] Tp illus of a windmill, illus Paper, with image on front of a baker holding a tray of baked goods and standing beside a sack of Ogilvie flour; stapled
CONTENTS: 1 tp; 2 'Introduction' by Ogilvie Flour Mills Co.; 3 fp illus of 'Small Testing Mill & Electric Oven Used in Laboratory and Baking Dept.'; 4 blank; 5 'Correspondence'; 6–124 text; 125–7 'Contents'; 128 'Note'
COPIES: AALM ACHP (HP 5109.46) BSUM MAUAM OKITD (985.032.002) QMM (RBD ckbk 1880) Company collection (ADM Milling Co., Montreal, photocopy) *Private collection
NOTES: This edition has a new image on the binding: a male baker instead of a seated woman. The BSUM copy is stamped on the title-page, 'Penticton Dep't Stores, Penticton, – B.C. Local agency of Brantford Bicycles, bicycle supplies, general merchan[ts?].'

Q55.13 1916
—Ogilvie's book / for a cook / A selection of recipes and other / things adapted to the needs of / the average housekeeper, some / entirely new, all have been / thoroughly tested / Ogilvie / Montreal, Canada / 1916
DESCRIPTION: 20.5 × 14.0 cm Pp [1] 2–127 [128] Tp illus of a windmill, illus Paper, with image on front of a baker holding a tray of baked goods and standing beside a sack of Ogilvie flour; stapled
CONTENTS: 1 tp; 2 'Introduction'; 3 fp illus of 'Small Testing Mill & Electric Oven Used in Laboratory and Baking Dept.'; 4 blank; 5 'Correspondence'; 6–124 text; 125–7 'Contents' [i.e., index]
CITATIONS: Bly Ferguson/Fraser, p 232, illus col on p 35 of closed volume
COPIES: MWPA OAYM *OGU (CCC TX715.6 O35 1916) SSWD

Q55.14 1916
—Recettes Ogilvie / pour la cuisinière moderne / Choix de recettes et autres connaissances / utiles et indispensables au besoin de la / generalite des maitresses de maison. / Chacune de ces recettes a ete / essayee et plusieurs d'entres / elles sont entierement / nouvelles. / Ogilvie / Montreal, Canada / 1916 / Enregistré d'après l'Acte du Parlement en l'année 1909 par The Ogilvie Flour / Mills Company, Limited, de Montréal, au département / de l'Agriculture, Ottawa.
DESCRIPTION: 20.0 × 14.0 cm Pp [1] 2–123 [124–8] Tp illus of a windmill, illus Paper, with image on front of a baker holding a tray of baked goods and standing beside a sack of Ogilvie flour; stapled
CONTENTS: 1 tp; 2 'Introduction'; 3 fp illus of 'Moulin expérimental et four électrique en usage au laboratoire et au département de la boulangerie.'; 4 blank; 5 'Correspondence'; 6–123 text; 124–7 index; 128 'Avis'
COPIES: *OGU (UA s041 b30)   OONL (TX715.6 R3966 1916)

Q55.15 1921
—Ogilvie's book / for a cook / A selection of recipes and other / things adapted to the needs of / the average housekeeper, some / entirely new, all have been / thoroughly tested / Ogilvie / Montreal, Canada / 1921
DESCRIPTION: Tp illus of a windmill, illus With image on front of a baker holding a tray of baked goods and standing beside a sack of Ogilvie flour
COPIES: BVAMM *Private collection

Q55.16 copyright 1922
—Ogilvie's / book / for / a / cook / By appointment to His Majesty the King / A new, thoroughly revised and en- / larged edition. This book contains / a selection of well tested recipes, / together with a large number of / cooking pointers of value and service / to all housekeepers / Copyrighted, Canada, 1922, by / the Ogilvie Flour Mills Co. / Limited / Head office, Montreal, Que., Canada / Mills at / Montreal, Que. Fort William, Ont. Winnipeg, Man. / Medicine Hat, Alta. / Branch offices at / St. John, N.B. Quebec, Que. Ottawa, Toronto, Hamilton / London, Fort William, Ont. Winnipeg, Man. Regina / Moose Jaw, Sask. Medicine Hat, Calgary, Edmonton, Alta. / Vancouver, B.C. / Also 170 grain receiving and flour distributing stations throughout / Manitoba, Saskatchewan and Alberta
DESCRIPTION: 23.0 × 15.0 cm Pp [1–3] 4–160 Frontis on p 2 of 'The Ogilvie Mills,' illus blue headpieces for

chapters Paper, with image on front, at bottom, of a baker holding a tray of baked goods, and at top, of two men and a woman, walking to the right, each carrying a tray of food; sewn
CONTENTS: 1 note about the book-order coupons located at the back of the book; 2 frontis; 3 tp; 4–5 'Introduction'; 6 'Correspondence'; 7–150 text; 151–5 blank for 'Other Favourite Personal Recipes'; 156–60 'Alphabetical Index to Recipes'
CITATIONS: O'Neill (unpublished)
COPIES: AHRMH MVPHM QKB *SSWD; Great Britain: LB (Woolwich 41296)
NOTES: This edition has a new image on the binding. The title-page is printed in blue and black. Between pp 88 and 89, but not included in the pagination, is a centre spread advertising Ogilvie products, printed in colour. A leaf of book-order coupons was originally glued to the gutter of the endpaper opposite p 160, but it is lacking in the SSWD copy.

Q55.17 1922
—Recettes / Ogilvie / pour la / cuisinière moderne / By appointment to His Majesty the King / Une nouvelle édition revue et aug- / mentée. Ce livre renferme un choix / de recettes éprouvées ainsi qu'un / grand nombre de conseils utiles aux / ménagères. / Enrégistré [sic] d'après l'Acte du Parlement du Canada en 1922 / The Ogilvie Flour Mills Co. / Limited / au département de l'Agriculture à Ottawa / Bureau chef: Montreal, Que., Canada / Moulins à / Montreal, Que. Fort William, Ont. Winnipeg, Man. / Medicine Hat, Alta. / Succursales à / St. John, N.B. Quebec, Que. Ottawa, Toronto, Hamilton / London, Fort William, Ont. Winnipeg, Man. Regina / Moose Jaw, Sask. Medicine Hat, Calgary, Edmonton, Alta. / Vancouver, C.A. / Aussi 170 entrepôts pour grains et farines dans le Manitoba, / la Saskatchewan et l'Alberta
DESCRIPTION: With image on front, at bottom, of a baker holding a tray of baked goods, and at top, of two men and a woman, walking to the right, each carrying a tray of food
CITATIONS: O'Neill (unpublished)
COPIES: OONL (TX715.6 R3966 1908 missing) *Private collection; Great Britain: LB (Woolwich 41297)
NOTES: This edition has 176 pp.

Q55.18 copyright 1931
—Ogilvie's / book for a cook / A new, thoroughly revised and / enlarged edition, containing a / selection of well tested recipes, / together with a number of cooking / pointers of value and service

to all / housekeepers / Copyright, Canada, 1931, by / the Ogilvie Flour Mills Co. / Limited / Executive offices: / Montreal, Que., Canada / Mills at / Montreal, Que. Fort William, Ont. Winnipeg, Man. / Medicine Hat, Alta. Edmonton, Alta. / Branch offices at / Saint John, N.B. Quebec, Que. Ottawa Toronto Hamilton / London Fort William, Ont. Winnipeg, Man. Regina / Moose Jaw, Sask. Medicine Hat Calgary / Edmonton, Alta. Vancouver, B.C. / Also 157 grain receiving and flour distributing stations throughout / Manitoba, Saskatchewan and Alberta

DESCRIPTION: 22.5 × 15.0 cm   Pp [i–ii], [1–3] 4–159 [160–2]   Frontis of executive offices of Ogilvie Flour Mills, place d'Youville, Montreal; illus purple   Paper   CONTENTS: i untitled note about where in the text to find instructions for ordering additional copies of the book; ii frontis; 1 tp; 2–3 'Introduction'; 4 'Correspon-dence'; 5–159 text; 160 index; 161 three book-order coupons; 162 'Complete List of Ogilvie Products'   COPIES: NSWA   OCOLM   OTYA (TX715 O34 1931) *Private collection

NOTES: The title-page and text are printed in black and purple.

Q55.19   [facsimile ed., copyright 1975] —Old / Canadian / recipes / compiled by / the Ogilvie Flour Mills Co. Ltd. / in 1905 / Note: Brand name products may be substituted with equivalents. / Coles

DESCRIPTION: 21.5 × 14.0 cm   Pp [5–6] 7–124 [125–30]   Illus   Soft cover, with still-life on front of apples and a serving of apple pudding   CONTENTS: 5 tp; 6 '© Copyright 1975 and published by Coles Publishing Company Limited Toronto – Canada'; 7–124 text; 125–7 table of contents; 128 'Note'; 129 blank; 130 'Printed in the United States'   CITATIONS: AbCat spring 1981   Carrière No. 168   COPIES: OONL (TX715 O38 1975)   *Private collection

Q55.20   [facsimile ed., copyright 1979] —Old / Canadian / recipes / compiled by / the Ogilvie Flour Mills Co. Ltd. / in 1905 / Note: Brand name products may be substituted with equivalents. / Coles

DESCRIPTION: 21.0 × 13.5 cm   Pp [5–6] 7–124 [125–8]   Illus   Paper, with still-life on front of apples and a serving of apple pudding   CONTENTS: 5 tp; 6 '© Copyright 1979 and published by Coles Publishing Company Limited Toronto – Canada // Printed in Canada'; 7–8 'Yeast'; 9–119 reci-pes; 120–2 'Useful Hints'; 123 'Weights and Measures'; 124 'Time for Baking'; 125–7 'Contents'; 128 'Note'

COPIES: *Private collection

Q55.21   [facsimile ed. of 1905, copyright 2003] — Ogilvie's / book for a cook / A selection of recipes and other / things adapted to the needs of / the average housekeeper, / some entirely new, and / all have been / thoroughly / tested / Ogilvie / Montreal, Canada / 1905 / Entered according to Act of Parliament of Canada, in the year one thousand nine hundred / and five, by the Ogilvie Flour Mills Company, Limited, of Montreal, / at the Department of Agriculture, Ottawa.

DESCRIPTION: 20.5 × 13.5 cm   Pp [1–5] 6–124 [125–8]   Tp illus of a windmill; illus (many of the company's mills)   Thin card, with image on front of a seated woman reading 'Ye Cooke's Booke'   CONTENTS: Inside front face of binding 'Historical Notes' by Elizabeth Driver; 1 tp; 2 'Copyright © 2003 Whitecap Books'; 3 'Introduction' by Ogilvie Flour Mills Co.; 4 fp illus of a small testing mill and electric oven; 5 'Correspondence'; 6–124 text; 125–7 'Contents'; 128 'Note'   COPIES: OONL   *Private collection

NOTES: The 'Historical Notes' were written before the original American edition had been identified.

AMERICAN EDITIONS: *A Book for a Cook*, Minneapolis: Pillsbury, copyright 1905 (United States: DLC); fac-simile ed. of 1905, Bedford, Mass.: Applewood Books, 1994 (Private collection; United States: DLC).

West, L.C.

Q56.1   August 1905 The / royal / recipe book / [to left of a vine-shaped, vertical decorative device:] Valuable / recipes / on / cookery, / menus, / drinks / for the / sickroom, / etc., etc. / [to right of the decorative device:] Contributed by / ladies connected with the in- / stitution in aid of which this / book was published, supplement- / ed by tested recipes from Ameri- / can schools of cookery / [below decorative device:] Edited by L.C. West / Montreal / August, 1905 / Entered according to Act of the Parliament of Canada in the year one thousand nine / hundred and five, by L.C. West, at the Department of Agriculture.

CITATIONS: O'Neill (unpublished)   COPIES: Great Britain: LB (07945.i.49 destroyed); United States: NNNAM (S.21.B)

NOTES: The 'Preface' refers to this as 'the first edition of the Royal Recipe Book' and mentions 'announce-ments from various Montreal firms' throughout the text. The NNNAM catalogue records the volume as having 142 pages. The book's title and the sickroom recipes suggest that the book was a fund-raiser for Montreal's Royal Victoria Hospital (opened in 1893), although there is no reference to the hospital in the book. The identity of L.C. West remains a mystery: no link could be made between Wests in Montreal city directories and the hospital, and there was no West on staff at McGill University at the time.

The Wingate almanac 1905

Q57.1   1905
The / Wingate / almanac / 1905 1905 / McGales Sprucine / trade mark / Published by / the Wingate Chemical Co. Limited / Montreal, Canada. [cover-title]
DESCRIPTION: 18.5 × 13.0 cm   Pp [1–32]   Illus portrait of Dr J. Emery Coderre   Paper; stapled
CONTENTS: 1–2 'A Short Sketch of the Life of the Late Dr. J. Emery Coderre'; 3–4 '... Standard Remedies and Proprietary Preparations' of the Wingate Chemical Co. Ltd, Montreal; 5 'Eclipses for 1905,' 'Morning and Evening Stars for 1905,' 'Church Festivals, Holidays, etc.,' and 'Legal and Bank Holidays'; 6 publ ad; 7 statistics for January and below, jokes and publ ads; 8 'Veterinary' and publ ad; 9 February, jokes, and publ ads; 10 'Recipes for Cooking' and publ ads; 11 March, jokes, and publ ads; 12 'Recipes for Cooking' and publ ads; 13 April, jokes, and publ ads; 14 'Recipes for Cooking' and publ ads; 15 May, jokes, and publ ads; 16 'Recipes for Cooking' and publ ads; 17 June, jokes, and publ ads; 18 'Recipes for Cooking' and publ ads; 19 July, jokes, and publ ads; 20 'Recipes for Cooking' and publ ads; 21 August, jokes, and publ ads; 22 'Recipes for Cooking' and publ ads; 23 September, jokes, and publ ads; 24 'Recipes for Cooking' and publ ads; 25 October, jokes, and publ ads; 26 'Recipes for Cooking' and publ ads; 27 November, jokes, and publ ads; 28 'Notes on the Care of Horses' and publ ads; 29 December, jokes, and publ ads; 30–2 publ ads
COPIES: *Private collection
NOTES: Many of the Wingate products advertised in the book bear Dr Coderre's name; for example, Dr Coderre's Infants' Syrup. The biographical sketch of Dr Coderre (St Denis, County of Richelieu, 14 November 1814–9 September 1888) refers to his appointment in 1847 as professor of the School of Medicine and Surgery, Montreal.

1905–10

Get flourwise

The following cookbooks also advertised Five Roses Flour: Q79.1, Five Roses Cook Book; Q203.1, A Guide to Good Cooking; Q246.1, Baker, Aunt Hattie, Helpful Household Hints and Recipes; and M102.1, A Diary of Celebrated Christmas Recipes.
Lake of the Woods Milling Co. was formed in 1887; its Keewatin mill was built the same year (Monetary Times Vol. 20, No. 49 (3 June 1887), p 1432).

Q58.1   nd [about 1905–10]
Get / flourwise / says the grocer / [symbol of Lake of the Woods Milling Company, Keewatin] / Issued by / Lake of the Woods Milling / Company Limited / Montreal
DESCRIPTION: 15.5 × 8.5 cm   Pp [1] 2–16   Illus brown Paper, with scene, extending over front and back, of a grocer placing a sack of Five Roses Flour on a counter, before which sits a woman customer on a stool; stapled
CONTENTS: 1 tp; 2–9 'Get Flourwise' [the dialogue of Mr Jones, the grocer, as he sells the virtues of Five Roses Flour to his customer, Mrs Brown]; 10–14 'Recipes'; top–mid 15 'Hints Regarding Measures'; bottom 15–16 'Useful Hints'
COPIES: *OONL (TX769 G47 1890z p***)
NOTES: This booklet was likely published before the first edition of Q79.1, *Five Roses Cook Book,* in 1913. The text is printed in brown and red.

1906

A., Mme M.H.

Q59.1   [1906]
[An edition of *La cuisine sanitaire, économique, pratique, adaptée à l'usage des personnes de moyens ordinaires. Par Mme. M... H... A...,* [etc.], Lévis, Que.: Mercier et cie, [1906], pp 160]
CITATIONS: O'Neill (unpublished)
COPIES: Great Britain: LB (07943.i.36 destroyed)

Table and kitchen

Q60.1   nd [about 1906]
Table and kitchen / a compilation of / approved cooking / receipts / carefully selected for the use of families / and / arranged for ready reference / Supplemented by brief hints for / the table and

kitchen / Published by / Price Baking Powder Co. / Chicago / [stamped:] Factories at, Chicago & Montreal.
DESCRIPTION: 18.5 × 12.0 cm Pp [i–iii], [1] 2–57, [i–iii] Paper, with decorative border on front featuring a stylized grape-vine and bunches of grapes; stapled, and with hole punched at top left corner for hanging
CONTENTS: i tp; ii–iii publ ads; 1–52 recipes; 53 'Hints for the Table and Kitchen'; top 54 'Weights and Measures'; mid 54–57 index; i–iii publ ads
COPIES: *AEEA (88.37.126)
NOTES: *Table and Kitchen* is a Canadian edition of an American text. On the outside back face of the binding there is an advertisement for Dr Price's Cream Baking Powder, 'fifty years the standard.' The Price Baking Powder Co. was established in Chicago, in 1853 (see Allen, p 144), which suggests a date of publication of about 1903 (1853 + 50 years); however, this edition could not have been published then since there is a testimonial on p i (after p 57) that is dated 1905. Moreover, the edition of the book that is copyrighted 1916 (Q60.3) refers to the baking powder as 'sixty years the standard.' If, at the time of the 1916 edition, the baking powder had been the standard for ten more years, then Q60.1 was published about 1906 (1916 – 10 years). At the time of publication of the 1916 edition, the baking powder had actually been manufactured for sixty-three years, despite the reference to 'sixty years the standard.'

This is the only edition where the spelling 'receipts' is used on the title-page (the editions described below use 'recipes'). Unusually, the arabic numbering starts on the verso of a leaf so that recto pages are even-numbered and versos, odd-numbered.

'Compliments of James Ramsey Ltd. Edmonton, Alberta' is on the outside back face of the AEEA copy.

Q60.2 nd [about 1916]
—Table / and kitchen / a practical cook book / Dr Price's Cream Baking Powder / Manufactured by / Royal Baking Powder Co. / New York Chicago Montreal [cover-title]
DESCRIPTION: 18.0 × 12.0 cm Pp [i–ii], [1] 2–57, [i] Paper; stapled
CONTENTS: i–ii publ ads; 1–52 recipes; 53 'Hints for the Table and Kitchen'; top 54 'Weights and Measures' and 'Utensils for Miners or Ranchmen'; mid 54–57 'Index' [i.e., table of contents]; i publ ad
COPIES: AMHM   *Private collection
NOTES: An advertisement on the inside front face of the binding refers to the baking powder as 'a sixty-year standby'; therefore, this edition was published about the same time as Q60.3, which is described in

the same way and copyrighted 1916. The Price Baking Powder Co. was owned by Royal Baking Powder Co. by 1915 (see Allen, p 144, and the 1915 American edition of *Table and Kitchen* by Royal Baking Powder, under 'American editions,' below).

The text on p 54 suggests the following 'Utensils for Miners or Ranchmen': 1 iron pot, 2 saucepans, 1 gridiron, 1 frying-pan, and a poor man's jack for toasting.

The AMHM copy is stamped on the front face of the binding, 'Cassidy's Limited.'

Q60.3 copyright 1916
—Table and kitchen / a compilation of / approved cooking / recipes / carefully selected for the use of families / and arranged for ready reference / Supplemented by brief hints for / the table and kitchen / Published by Royal Baking Powder Co. / New York – Chicago – Montreal / manufacturers of / Dr. Price's Cream Baking Powder / Copyright, 1916, by Royal Baking Powder Co.
DESCRIPTION: 18.0 × 12.0 cm Pp [i–iv], [1] 2–57, [i–iii] Paper; stapled
CONTENTS: i tp; ii–iv publ ads; 1–52 recipes; 53 'Hints for the Table and Kitchen'; top–mid 54 'Weights and Measures' and 'Utensils for Miners or Ranchmen'; mid 54–57 'Index'; i–iii publ ads
COPIES: BDUCVM BNEM BSUM *BVMA
NOTES: 'Compliments of the Okanagan Grocery // Vernon, B.C.' is stamped on the front face of the BVMA copy.

Q60.4 copyright 1924
—Table and kitchen / a compilation of / approved cooking / recipes / carefully selected for the use of families / and arranged for ready reference / Supplemented by brief hints for / the table and kitchen / Published by Royal Baking Powder Co. / New York – Chicago – Montreal / manufacturers of / Dr. Price's Cream Baking Powder / Copyright, 1924, by Royal Baking Powder Co.
DESCRIPTION: 18.5 × 12.0 cm Pp [i–iv], [1] 2–57, [i–iii] Paper; stapled
CONTENTS: i tp; ii–iv publ ads; 1–52 recipes; 53 'Hints for the Table and Kitchen'; top–mid 54 'Weights and Measures' and 'Utensils for Miners or Ranchmen'; mid 54–57 'Index'; i–iii publ ads
COPIES: *Private collection
NOTES: The advertisement on the inside front face of the binding begins, 'A sixty-year standby // For over sixty years Dr. Price's Cream Baking Powder has been the standby ...'

Stamped on the front face of another private

collector's copy is 'Stinson's Self Serving Grocery Phone N1745 – 1818 Centre Street N.'

AMERICAN EDITIONS: Chicago: Price Baking Powder Co., nd [about 1892–3], '40 years the standard' on binding and a notice on the title-page verso regarding the amount of Dr Price's Cream Baking Powder ordered by the US Government in the first five months of 1892 (OKITJS, OWTU); World's Columbian Exposition issue, 1893 (Allen, p 144); Chicago: Price Baking Powder Co., nd [about 1895], '40 years the standard' on binding and a testimonial on the inside back face of binding dated 25 November 1895 (Private collection); 1896 (Allen, p 144); Chicago: Price Baking Powder Co., nd, advertisement opposite p 57 with date of 1905 and reference to 'fifty years the standard' (OGU); 1908 (Allen, p 144); 1913 (Allen, p 144); Royal Baking Powder Co., 1915 (Allen, p 144); 1916 (Allen, p 144).

1906–10

Selected recipes for Cox's Gelatine

From 1903 to 1939, the Edinburgh-based J. and G. Cox Ltd published several British editions of A Manual of Gelatine Cookery *by Bertha Roberts (Driver 899.1–899.9); this title is advertised in Q61.1. In the United States, Miss Marion Harris Neil revised the text, which was published in 1909 and 1914 under the title* Cox's Manual of Gelatine Cookery *(Driver, p 522). Later, the Cox Gelatine Co. published* Cox's Gelatine Recipes, *revised by Neil, New York: copyright 1920 (Driver, p 522). I have not determined whether these British and American texts are related to Q61.1.*

Q61.1 nd [about 1906–10]
Selected recipes / for / Cox's Gelatine / Issued by / J. and G. Cox, Limited / Gorgie Mills, Edinburgh, Scotland
DESCRIPTION: 18.0 × 12.0 cm Pp [1–2] 3–37 Tp illus of a container of Cox's Instant Powdered Gelatine; tp in checkerboard border Paper, with tp illus and border on front; stapled
CONTENTS: 1 tp; 2 'Important Notice. These recipes are carefully calculated for use with Cox's ... only ...' and 'Cox's Manual of Gelatine Cookery containing over 200 selected recipes will be sent free on application to our Canadian representatives ...'; 3–6 'Introduction'; 7 index; 8–37 100 numbered recipes
COPIES: *BBVM Private collection
NOTES: 'Canadian edition' is printed on the outside

back face of the binding. Arthur P. Tippet and Co., Montreal, Tees and Persse Ltd, Winnipeg, and Martin and Robertson Ltd, Vancouver, are cited on p 2 as the Canadian representatives for Cox's Gelatine.

The 'Introduction' states: 'Cox's Gelatine was the first gelatine introduced to the Canadian public ... It has been on the markets of the world for over sixty years, ...' The Scottish company established a New York office in 1845 (Allen, p 194) and the 'Introduction' of Q61.3 refers to the product in its checkerboard box being used by housewives since 1845. The year of publication of this edition, therefore, is later than 1905 (1845 + over 60 years).

In the private collector's copy, the following is printed on the inside front face of the binding: 'With compliments from H. Ward 108 St. Viateur // We stock and recommend "Cox's Gelatine."'

There is an advertisement in the February 1921 issue of *Western Home Monthly* for 'Cox's Book of Selected Recipes,' but the edition is not identified.

Q61.2 nd [about 1925]
—Selected recipes / for use with / Cox's / Instant Powdered / Gelatine / The Cox Tartan / registered / [caption:] "The checkerboard package" / The Cox Gelatine Co. Limited / Montreal / Canada [English cover-title on one face of binding] Recettes choisies / Cox's / Instant Powdered / Gelatine / The Cox Tartan / registered / [caption:] "The checkerboard package" / The Cox Gelatine Co. Limited / Montreal / Canada [French cover-title on other face]
DESCRIPTION: 17.5 × 11.0 cm Pp 1–16 [on English rectos only]; 1–16 [on French rectos only] Paper, with image on English and French faces of a container of Cox's Instant Powdered Gelatine and a checkerboard border; stapled at top edge
CONTENTS: [English and French texts:] 1–2 'Introduction'; 3–15 recipes; 16 index
COPIES: *NBMOM OTMCL (641.5971 H39 No. 51) QMM (RBD uncat; 2 copies)
NOTES: The 'Introduction' states, 'Cox's Gelatine has been the standard both in this country and abroad for over seventy-five years.' The year of publication of this bilingual edition, therefore, is later than 1920 (1845 + over 75 years). Since the first listing for Cox Gelatine Co. Ltd in Montreal city directories is in the volume for 1925–6, the cookbook was likely published about 1925.

Q61.3 nd [about 1931–2]
—Selected recipes / for use with / Cox's / Instant Powdered / Gelatine / The Cox Tartan / registered / [caption:] "The checkerboard package" / The Cox

Gelatine Co. Limited / Montreal / Canada [cover-title]

DESCRIPTION: 17.5 × 11.0 cm   Pp 1–24   Paper, with image on front of a container of Cox's Instant Powdered Gelatine and a checkerboard border; stapled

CONTENTS: 1 'Introduction' and 'Important Notice'; 2–3 index; 4–24 recipes

COPIES: OKELWM   OONL (TX814.5 G4 S45 1920z, 2 copies)   OTMCL (2 copies: 641.5971 H39 No. 45 and No. 120)   QMM (RBD ckbk 1465)   *Private collection

NOTES: The 'Introduction' states, 'Cox's Gelatine in the familiar red, white and blue checkerboard box has been used by good housewives since 1845 ... [it] has been the standard in this country and abroad for over eighty-five years.' This suggests publication after 1930 (1845 + over 85 years). Another private collector has a copy inscribed, 'Thelma Briggs Mar 12. 1932.' The date of publication, therefore, is about 1931–2.

Page 24 states that 'copies of this Cookery Book may be had in English or French [i.e., probably Q61.4] ...' A free booklet, 'Selected Recipes for Use with Cox [sic] Gelatine (French and English),' is listed in Chatelaine 1935, p 82; the reference may be to this edition and Q61.4. One of the OTMCL copies (No. 45) lacks its binding.

Q61.4   nd [about 1931–2]
—Recettes choisies / Cox's / Instant Powdered / Gelatine / The Cox Tartan / registered / [caption:] "The checkerboard package" / The Cox Gelatine Co. Limited / Montreal / Canada [cover-title]

DESCRIPTION: 17.5 × 11.0 cm   Pp 1–24   Paper, with image on front of a container of Cox's Instant Powdered Gelatine and a checkerboard border

CONTENTS: 1 'Introduction' and 'Avis important'; 2–3 'Index'; 4–24 recipes

COPIES: *QMBN (TX814.5 G4R42 1930 and 115094 CON)

NOTES: See Q61.3 regarding the date of publication.

1907

The Canadian cook book

Q62.1   nd [about 1907]
The / Canadian cook / book / A collection of original / recipes furnished by the / housekeepers of Canada. / Each recipe bears the / author's name and address. / Published by / Davis & Lawrence Company / Montreal / Manufacturers of Royal Flavoring Extracts

DESCRIPTION: 20.5 × 12.0 cm   Pp [1–2] 3–48   Paper; stapled, and with hole punched at top left corner to take string for hanging

CONTENTS: 1 tp; 2–10 publ ads; 11–46 recipes credited with the name of the contributor and publ ads; 47–8 publ ads

COPIES: BDEM   NBSAM   *OGU (UA s047 b32)

NOTES: There is a testimonial on p 21 for Royal Flavoring Extracts dated 1 February 1906; however, an advertisement for *The Canadian Cook Book* in Davis and Lawrence's *Painkiller Almanac 1908* (OTUTF) points to 1907 as the year of publication: '"The Canadian Cook Book." – This last publication has only recently been issued, and is composed solely of original recipes sent in by ladies all over Canada in response to our request in last year's Painkiller Almanac. Each recipe bears the name and address of its author, and this book is in all ways the most unique and interesting collection of choice cooking recipes which has ever been gotten out. A neatly bound copy of the Canadian Cook Book can be had by sending 10c. to the undersigned [i.e., Davis and Lawrence Co., Montreal].' In this edition of *The Canadian Cook Book*, advertisements give the company's address as 356 St Antoine Street, Montreal.

The BDEM copy is stamped on the front face of the binding, 'Fisher's Drug & [?] Ladner' [Ladner is south of Vancouver, in the Fraser Delta]; the NBSAM copy is not stamped on the front.

Q62.2   nd [about 1935]
—The / Canadian cook / book / A collection of original / recipes furnished by the / housekeepers of Canada. / Each recipe bears the / author's name and address. / Published by / Davis & Lawrence Company / Montreal / Manufacturers of Royal Flavoring Extracts

DESCRIPTION: 21.0 × 12.5 cm   Pp [1] 2–48   [$0.25, on binding]   Paper; stapled, and with hole punched at top left corner to take string for hanging

CONTENTS: 1 tp; 2–4 publ ads; 5–47 recipes credited with the name of the contributor and publ ads; 48 publ ad

COPIES: *BVAMM

NOTES: Unlike Q62.1, there is no dated testimonial on p 21. In this edition, advertisements give the company's address as 1910 St Antoine Street, Montreal. This address is first cited in the Montreal city directory for 1928–9 (previously, the address was 356 St Antoine Street). An advertisement on the outside back face of the binding for Perry Davis's Painkiller refers to the product's existence 'for more than 95 years.' This suggests a publication date for this edition of about 1935, since the formulation was invented in 1839 and placed on the market soon after. The appearance of the book confirms publication in the 1930s. (See at OTUTF: *Painkiller Almanac 1908*, p 13: 'In the year 1839 Perry Davis, ... finally originated the combination of drugs and gums ... In course of time Painkiller was put up for sale, ...'; *Perry Davis' Pain Killer Almanac 1890*, opposite July calendar: '50 years experience proves that the Pain-Killer is the best family remedy ...'; *Pain-Killer Annual 1873*, p [2]: 'The Pain-Killer has been before the public over thirty years, ...')

1909

Cooling drink and frozen desserts

See also Q65.1, [Title unknown], by the same company.

Q63.1   1909
[An edition of *Cooling Drink and Frozen Desserts Made with Montserrat Lime Fruit Juices*, Montreal: National Drug and Chemical Company of Canada, 1909]
CITATIONS: O'Neill (unpublished)
COPIES: Great Britain: LB (not located)
NOTES: National Drug and Chemical Company of Canada Ltd was formed on 1 February 1906, when eighteen independent Canadian drug wholesalers amalgamated (*Centennial/Anniversary Souvenir: A Commemorative Volume Celebrating Canada's Centenary and National Drug's 60 Years of Service*, [Montreal:] National Drug and Chemical Company of Canada Ltd, 1967, p 110); therefore, the company was only about three years old at the time this recipe collection was deposited for copyright purposes at the British Library.

La cuisinière des familles

Q64.1   nd [about 1909]
La / cuisinière / des familles / contenant / les recettes les plus pratiques / et les plus simples pour préparer les / potages, viandes et poisson; oeufs et salades, / légumes, marinades; pâtisseries, gelées, fruits, / sauces, crèmes, poudings, plats sucrés, con- / serves, breuvages divers, etc., etc., / ainsi que plusieurs conseils très / utiles dans un ménage. / En vente chez tous les libraires
DESCRIPTION: 15.0 × 10.0 cm   Pp [1–3] 4–115   Paper, with image on front of a woman tasting the contents of a saucepan; stapled
CONTENTS: 1 tp; 2 obscured by QMBM bookplate; 3–104 text in eighteen chapters; 105–15 'Table des

matières' and at middle p 115, 'No. 1379'
CITATIONS: Bibliothèque municipale de Montréal, p 3
COPIES: *QMBM (641.5 C9665cu)
NOTES: 'Montréal // Librairie Beauchemin limitée 79, rue Saint-Jacques, 79' is printed on the front face of the binding. Montreal directories list Librairie Beauchemin limitée at this address from 1909 to 1923. From appearances, the book was published closer to 1909 than 1923, and it was advertised for sale for $0.20 on the binding of the Worcester, Massachusetts, edition of Q3.1, *La cuisinière canadienne* (see 'American editions' for that title). See comment at Q82.1.

1910

[Title unknown]

Q65.1   [about 1910]
[Cover-title lacking?; heading on p 1: 'Some Plain Talk to Housewives']
DESCRIPTION: 16.5 × 10.5 cm   Pp 1–48   Illus   Lacks [paper?] binding; stapled
CONTENTS: 1–4 'Some Plain Talk to Housewives'; 5, 7, 9, 11, 13, 15, 17, 19, 21, 23, 25, 27, 29 'Marie – French Maid' [a narrative in eleven roman-numbered sections]; 6, 8, 10, 12, 14, 16, 18, 20, 22, 24, 26, 28, 30–44 recipes; 45–8 Christmas dinner menu and recipes
COPIES: *NSHP
NOTES: The text begins on p 1 with two sections headed 'The Wiles of the Adulterator' and 'There's Only One Protection.' The latter indicates that the cookbook was published to promote the use of St George's Baking-Powder, Sovereign Spices, Sovereign Flavouring Extracts, and Montserrat Sauce, all made by the National Drug and Chemical Company of Canada Ltd. From appearances, the book was published about 1910. No place of publication is cited in this copy, but the company's head office was in Montreal and O'Neill records Montreal as the place of publication for Q63.1 by the same company.

The handy home book

See also Q125.1, The Family Herald Cook-Book.

Q66.1   nd [about 1910]
The handy home book / An encyclopedia of useful / information compiled from / the columns of the Family / Herald and Weekly Star, / Montreal, Canada.
DESCRIPTION: 20.0 × 12.5 cm   Pp [1–3] 4–192   Paper, with image on front of leaves; stapled

CONTENTS: 1 tp; 2 blank; 3–186 text; 187–92 index

CITATIONS: Ferguson/Fraser, p 232

COPIES: BDUCVM   *OGU (3 copies: *UA s048 b30, UA s048 b31, and CCC TX715.6 H336)   OTNY (031.02 H)   OTU (AG105 H36 ROMU)   OTUTF (B-12 7860, 2 copies)   QKB

NOTES: This is a compendium of household information, including 'Dainty Dishes' on pp 109–24. 'Published by the Family Herald and Weekly Star // Montreal, Canada' is on the outside front face of the binding; on the inside front, 'All the information printed in this useful home book has been gathered from the columns of the "Family Herald and Weekly Star of Montreal" during the past two years.' Although undated, evidence points to publication in about 1910: p 11 refers to the foundation of a fund by Andrew Carnegie in April 1904; and the entry for 'Canadian V.C.'s' mentions soldiers from the Boer War, but not from World War I.

One of the OTUTF copies is bound in cloth, with leaves on the front; the other has a paper binding, as described for the OGU copy. The OTNY and OTU copies are bound in paper.

Schneider, C. Henry

Schneider contributed recipes to Q95.1, Harrison, Mrs Grace Eugenie Clergue, and Miss Alice Gertrude Clergue, British, French, Italian, Russian, Belgian Cookery. He also endorsed the recipes in Q83.5, Edwardsburg Recipe Book. A letter from Schneider to the Soeurs grises is reprinted in Q161.1, Manuel de diététique à l'usage des écoles ménagères.

Q67.1   1910

Practical cookery / by / Henry Schneider / Chef de cuisine / Montreal, 1910

DESCRIPTION: 21.5 × 12.5 cm   Pp [1–8] 9–69, [i–x]   Tp illus portrait of author   Cloth

CONTENTS: 1–4 ads; 5 author's dedication to members of the St James' Club and 'Copyright, Canada, 1910, by Henry Schneider.'; 6 'Au riche,' a poem by Joseph de Berchoux from *La gastronomie*; 7 tp; 8–68 recipes; 69 table of contents; i–x ads

CITATIONS: Ferguson/Fraser, p 233

COPIES: QMM (TX725 A1 S3 1910)   *Private collection; Great Britain: Private collection

NOTES: On p 5, Schneider says his collection of recipes is 'all classical.' Turtle Soup, p 10, includes full instructions for killing and eviscerating a turtle.

1911

Chapais, Jean-Charles (1850–1926)

Chapais wrote books on subjects related to agriculture, including the pork, lamb, milk, and forestry industries, and agriculture schools. For the titles of other cookbooks published by the Quebec Department of Agriculture, see Q48.1.

Q68.1   1911

J.-C. Chapais / Monographie / Le fromage raffiné / de / l'Isle-d'Orléans / Bulletin / Publié par le ministère de l'Agriculture / de la province de Québec. / 1911

DESCRIPTION: 26.0 × 17.5 cm   Pp [1–5] 6–30   Illus   Paper; stapled

CONTENTS: 1 ht; 2 blank; 3 tp; 4 blank; 5–26 text; 27–30 'Index alphabétique'

CITATIONS: Beaulieu, p 96

COPIES: QMBM   QMBN (A38A1 P83 03a OFF)   *QTS

NOTES: The text tells about the origin of the cheese and how to make it. There are photographs of equipment, the finished cheese, and Madame Joseph-P. Roberge ('l'une des meilleures fabricantes de fromage raffiné de la paroisse de Saint Pierre'). The printer's name is on the outside back face of the binding: 'Imprimerie Dussault & Proulx // 30, rue Garneau // Québec.'

Dainty desserts for dainty people

See also Q185.1, Knox Gelatine Desserts, Salads, Candies, and Frozen Dishes, for the same product.

Q69.1   nd [about 1911]

Dainty / desserts / for / dainty / people / Knox / Gelatine / Trade mark reg U.S Pat. Off. [cover-title]

DESCRIPTION: 17.0 × 12.0 cm   Pp [1] 2–41   Illus col, illus   Paper, with image on front of a cow's head in a wreath, to the right of which stands a black-skinned child-cook, and to the left, a white-skinned child-cook, each holding a moulded jelly; stapled

CONTENTS: 1 'Knox Dainty Desserts for Dainty People' [i.e., introductory text]; 2 description of the contents of No. 1 and No. 3 boxes of Knox Gelatine; 3 'Quantity of Liquid Jellied by a Package of Knox Sparkling Gelatine' and 'To Mold and Unmold Gelatine Mixtures Quickly'; 4–5 'Hints on Serving'; 6 index; 7–41 'Recipes'

COPIES: ACG   *NSWA

NOTES: In the NSWA copy, a pasted-on recipe clipping obscures the imprint, which is on the inside front face of the binding; however, the publisher – Charles B. Knox Co., Johnstown, New York, and Montreal – is clearly visible on the gelatine packages illustrated in the book. Pp 38–9 contain instructions 'For the Invalid and Convalescent's Tray.'

A Knox Gelatine advertisement in *Canadian Courier* Vol. 11, No. 10 (3 February 1911) advises the reader to 'Send for recipe book ... "Dainty Desserts for Dainty People."' An advertisement in *Everywoman's World* (May 1916) refers to 'Knox New Recipe Book.' Another advertisement in *Everywoman's World* (June 1917) says, 'Dainty Desserts for Dainty People send on receipt of your grocer's name.' The first listing for C.B. Knox Gelatine Co. in Montreal city directories is in the volume for 1910–11, where Wm H. Dunn is recorded as the agent and the factory's address is 589 St Paul. The ACG and NSWA copies were likely published about 1911, the year of the *Canadian Courier* advertisement and close to the time of the first city directory listing; however, the date of publication is uncertain because the advertisements in Canadian periodicals may refer to American editions of the book. The ACG copy lacks its binding.

AMERICAN EDITIONS: Allen, pp 195–6, lists the following, presumably all American: 1896; 1898; 1900; 1909, compiled by Rose Markward Knox; rev. ed., 1909; 1915 (United States: DLC); and 1924 (also cited in Barile, p 187, and Dickinson, p 65 and illus p 66). ONLAM has an edition dated 1896, numbered third edition, compiled by Rose Markward (Walters-Wagar Collection, Box 20). DLC has *Dainty Desserts for Dainty People: Salads, Savories, and Dainty Dishes Made with Knox Gelatine*, compiled by Janet McKenzie Hill, Johnstown, NY: Charles B. Knox Co., c1909, pp 37. The 1915 edition has 41 pp, the same as Q69.1.

The family cook book

Q70.1 1911
The / family / cook book, / compiled by / the ladies of Noyan, / Province of Quebec, / Canada. / 1911 / Printed by / A.T. Gould, printer and stationer, / Bedford, Que.
DESCRIPTION: 21.5 × 15.0 cm   Pp [1–6] 7–130 [131–2] Cloth
CONTENTS: 1 tp; 2 blank; 3 two verses beginning, 'We may live without poetry, music, and art' [from *Lucile*, Part I, Canto ii, by Owen Meredith, pseudonym of Edward Robert Bulwer-Lytton]; 4 'Food'; 5 table of contents; 6 blank; 7–116 text; 117–18 blank for manuscript recipes; 119–30 ads; 131 blank; 132 'Printed by A.T. Gould, printer and stationer, Bedford, Que.'
CITATIONS: BQ 22-4888
COPIES: *OGU (UA s061 b42)   OWTU (F3937) QMBN (160003 CON); United States: IaU (SPEC SZAT TX715.6 F27 1911)
NOTES: The recipes are credited with the name of the contributor. The 'ladies of Noyan' are not identified as belonging to a particular institution in the town.

Royal baker and pastry cook

Royal Baking Powder Co. was an American firm. In 1929 it merged with other companies to form Standard Brands Inc. See also NP7.1, New Royal Cook Book, and Q207.1, Royal Cook Book.

Q71.1   1911
Royal / baker / and / pastry cook / [line of text obscured by label glued on binding, probably 'A manual,' as American 1911 edition] / of practical / receipts for / home baking / and cooking / Royal / Baking Powder / Company / New York, U.S.A. / [over-printed?:] Canadian factory – Montreal [cover-title]
DESCRIPTION: 20.0 × 12.5 cm   Pp [i–ii], [1] 2–44, [i–ii]   Paper, with image on front of a woman holding up a pan of baked goods, a young child reaching up for them; stapled
CONTENTS: Inside front face of binding 'Copyright, 1911, by Royal Baking Powder Co.'; i 'Index to Receipts'; ii publ ad; 1–43 text; 44 'Glossary of Terms Used in Cookery'; i–ii publ ads
COPIES: OKQ (F5012 1911 R888B)   QMM (RBD ckbk 1976)   *SSWD
NOTES: On the inside back face of the binding there is a statement from the Public Analyst, Ontario, Dominion of Canada, concerning the strength of the product. The SSWD copy is inscribed on the front face of the binding, in ink, 'Eva Dec. 21st, 1920.'

AMERICAN EDITIONS: *The Royal Baker and Pastry Cook*, compiled by G[iuseppi] Rudmani, New York: Royal Baking Powder Co., copyright 1877 [1878] (United States: DLC); New York: Royal Baking Powder Co., [copyright 1882] (United States: DLC); New York: Royal Baking Powder Co., [1884?] (United States: DLC); New York: Royal Baking Powder Co., copyright 1888 (United States: DLC); New York: Royal Baking Powder Co., copyright 1892 (OKITD); German-language ed., New York: Royal Baking Powder

Co., copyright 1895 (United States: DLC); New York: Royal Baking Powder Co., copyright 1896 (United States: DLC, InU); New York: 1897 (CBCat 25); 1898 (Allen, p 145); New York: Royal Baking Powder Co., 1902 [from this year, without Rudmani's name] (OGU; United States: DLC); 1903 (Cagle/Stafford, p 708); New York: Royal Baking Powder Co., copyright 1906 (OGU, OWTU); New York: Royal Baking Powder Co., 1907 (United States: DLC); New York: Royal Baking Powder Co., copyright 1911 (OWTU; United States: DLC, InU); New York: Royal Baking Powder Co., copyright 1913 (United States: InU).

BRITISH EDITIONS: *The Royal Baker and Pastry Cook ... with Original Receipts by Ch. Herman Senn, Hon. Director, Universal Cookery and Food Association, London, Eng.*, New York: Royal Baking Powder Co., 1902 (Great Britain: LCoF, LoEN; United States: DLC, ICJ); New York: Royal Baking Powder Co., 1906 (Great Britain: LCoF); New York: Royal Baking Powder Co., 1912 (Great Britain: LCoF); *Royal Baker and Pastry Cook ... with Original Receipts by Ch. Herman Senn, G.C.A., Hon. Director, Universal Cookery and Food Association, London*, New York: Royal Baking Powder Co., [copyright 1913] (Great Britain: Private collection). Driver 914.1 discusses revisions for the British reader.

FINNISH EDITIONS: 1903 (United States: DLC).

1911–15

Tried recipes

Westmount Methodist Church, founded in 1889, became Westmount Park United Church in 1925.

Q72.1   nd [about 1911–15]
Our cook book / Tried recipes / Selected and approved by the / Ladies' Aid Society of / Westmount Methodist Church [cover-title]
DESCRIPTION: 21.5 × 14.5 cm   Pp 1–96   Paper, with image on front of the Union Jack and the flag of France; stapled
CONTENTS: Inside front face of binding 'Westmount Methodist Church Directory'; 1–2 ads; 3–94 recipes credited with the name of the contributor and ads; 95 blank for 'Additional Recipes'; 96 'Index' [i.e., table of contents]
COPIES: *Private collection
NOTES: The Church Directory opposite p 1 records W.E. Baker as the pastor of Westmount Methodist Church, at the intersection of Lansdowne and West-

ern avenues. Montreal city directories for the years 1911–12 to 1915–16 list Baker as pastor (different pastors are listed before and after); therefore, the cookbook was published about 1911–15. There is a full-page advertisement on p 88 for Babcock and Son, printers, 157 Craig Street West, possibly the printer of the cookbook.

1912

Anctil, Mlle Jeanne (Ste-Anne-de-la-Pocatière, Que., 27 December 1875–December 1926)

Jeanne Anctil (pl 37) was the second youngest of twelve children in the family of Barthélémie Anctil and Zélie Pelletier. Early in her career, she worked as a private tutor to the Beaudry family in Montreal. In November 1904 she began studies in Paris, France, then Fribourg, Switzerland, in preparation for teaching at the Écoles ménagères provinciales, which officially opened in Montreal in January 1907 (the secular institution's legal name was plural, but referred to a single school). She was the school's director from its opening until her death in 1926. During the First World War, at the request of Quebec's Department of Agriculture, she lectured in rural centres throughout the province. When she died, the following appeared in a Montreal newspaper: 'Avec Mademoiselle Anctil disparaît la fondatrice des maisons d'enseignement ménager dans la province de Québec. Mademoiselle Anctil a su ... montrer la véritable noblesse ... de la vie domestique ... et indiquer à nombre de jeunes filles des directions sensées. Toute sa vie fut consacrée au service des siens.' She was buried on 7 December 1926 in Montreal's Côte-des-Neiges Cemetery, Lot 00200C.

Marcel Anctil has self-published a history of his family, *Les familles Anctil en Amérique.* In 1937, the Écoles ménagères provinciales became affiliated with the University of Montreal; in 1953, it was renamed École des sciences ménagères. The records for the school are at the university archives (fonds E81, École ménagère provinciale, 1906–59). See also Chapter 4, 'Une école laïque et urbaine: "les Écoles ménagères provinciales,"' in Nicole Thivierge, Histoire de l'enseignement ménager-familial au Québec 1882–1970, *Institut québécois de recherche sur la culture*, 1982. The quotation from the Montreal newspaper is in the biographical entry for Anctil by Monique Papineau, in Cent soixante femmes du Québec, 1834–1994, *[2nd ed.]*, Montreal: Section Jacques-Viger de la Société Saint-Jean-Baptiste de Montréal, [1996], p 33 (the quotation is reprinted from *the autobiography of Mme F.-L. Béique, the founder of* Écoles ménagères provinciales, *Quatre-vingt ans de souvenirs, Montreal: B. Valiquette, 1939).*

Q73.1   1912
350 recettes / de cuisine / par / Mademoiselle Jeanne Anctil / directrice / Les écoles ménagères / provinciales. / 1912. / Imprimerie "La Patrie", Montréal.
DESCRIPTION: 16.0 × 11.5 cm   Pp [i–ii], [1–3] 4–265
Paper-covered boards, cloth spine
CONTENTS: i–ii 'Préface' signed 'Un ami de l'école'; 1 tp; 2 blank; 3–12 'Qu'est-ce que la cuisine?'; 13–17 'Principaux termes employés dans le langage culinaire'; 18–211 300 numbered recipes; 212–49 '12 menus de cuisine fine' [menus plus recipes numbered 2–53]; 250–2 continuation from 17 of 'Principaux termes employés dans le langage culinaire'; 253–65 'Table des matières'
CITATIONS: O'Neill (unpublished)
COPIES: CIHM (75991) *OONL (TX715 A488 1912) QMBN (158976 CON); Great Britain: LB (07943.ee.51 destroyed)
NOTES: The 'Préface,' which begins by quoting Paul the Apostle to the Philippians ('Quorum deus venter est' – Whose god is their belly), sets cooking and eating in a Christian context. 'Le christianisme,' it asserts, 'n'a pas complètement balayé l'épicurianisme ... Si c'est un devoir pour tous de se tenir en bonne santé pour être toujours d'humeur agréable et en état de faire son travail, il faut en prendre les moyens. Le premier et principal moyen est une bonne nourriture.'

Q73.2   1915
—350 recettes / de cuisine / par / Mademoiselle Jeanne Anctil / directrice / Les écoles ménagères / provinciales. / 1915. / Imprimerie H.F. Lauzon, Montréal.
DESCRIPTION: Cloth
CITATIONS: Bibliothèque municipale de Montréal, p 1   BQ 07-0985   O'Neill (unpublished)   Poulain-Le FurCat 4–5 Feb 2000, No. 13
COPIES: QQLA (TX715 A542 1915) *Private collection; Great Britain: LB (07943.e.26 destroyed)
NOTES: This edition has 265 pp.

Q73.3   1924
—350 recettes / de cuisine / par / Mademoiselle Jeanne Anctil / directrice / Les écoles ménagères / provinciales / 1924 / Montréal / Librairie Beauchemin limitée / 430, rue Saint-Gabriel, 430
DESCRIPTION: 17.0 × 11.5 cm   Pp [i–iv], [1–3] 4–265
2 pls, 7 double-sided pls   Cloth
CONTENTS: i 'Impr. Alliés Syndicats Cathol. –

Nationaux Montréal, Can. // 20'; ii blank; iii tp; iv 'Enregistré conformément à l'Acte du Parlement du Canada, en l'année dix-neuf cent quinze, par Mademoiselle Jeanne Anctil, Montréal, au bureau du ministère de l'Agriculture, à Ottawa.'; 1–2 'Préface // Quorum deus venter est.'; 3–249 text; 250 blank; [251–2 not included in numbering]; 253–65 'Table des matières'
CITATIONS: BQ 02-0939   BQ Exposition 1974, p 14   Carrière No. 55
COPIES: *OGU (UA s043 b13)   OONL (TX715 A488 1924)   QMBN (73138 CON)
NOTES: Some of the plates show scenes at the school and equipment used in the classes.

DesRoches, Amélie

Q74.1   1912
Amelie DesRoches / Professeur, Congrégation N.-D., Neuville, P.Q. / Hygiene de l'alimentation / et / propriétés chimiques des / aliments / suivi d'un cours théorique sur / l'art culinaire / Le sage ne recherche pas l'abondance / des mets; il ne se préoccupe que de / leur saveur et de leur délicatesse. / Epicure. / Première édition / Enregistré conformément à l'Acte du Parlement du Canada au / bureau du ministre de l'Agriculture. / Tous droits reserves / Neuville, Co. de Portneuf, P.Q. / 1912
DESCRIPTION: 17.0 × 12.0 cm   Pp [i–v] vi–viii [ix] x–xix [xx], [1] 2–490 [491]   Tp illus of cherub, illus
Cloth, with tp illus on front
CONTENTS: i tp; ii blank; iii 'Sommaire'; iv blank; v–viii 'Avant-propos' signed Amélie DesRoches; ix–xix 'Table des matières'; xx blank; 1–490 text in four parts: 'Hygiène de l'alimentation et propriétés chimiques des aliments,' two parts both titled 'Art culinaire,' and 'Pain, pâtisseries, entremets sucrés, dessert'; 491 'Errata'
CITATIONS: BQ 09-0971   O'Neill (unpublished)
COPIES: CIHM (72603)   OONL (TX165 D48 1912, 3 copies)   QMBN (TX651 D48 1912)   *QMM (RBD Soeur Berthe, ckbk 387)   QQLA (TX551 D474 1912) QQS (218.1.11); Great Britain: LB (07943.k.69 destroyed)
NOTES: The title-page text differentiates the two editions dated 1912. Here, for example, the author is described as 'Professeur, ...' and no price is recorded; Q74.2 does not give the author's profession, but records the price.

In the United States, DLC (TX551 D4) and DNLM have copies of a 1912 edition, but I have not identified which version.

Q74.2 [copyright] 1912
—Amelie DesRoches / Hygiene de l'alimentation / et / propriétés chimiques des / aliments / suivi d'un cours théorique sur / l'art culinaire / Le sage ne recherche pas l'abondance / des mets; il ne se préoccupe que de / leur saveur et de leur délicatesse. / Epicure. / Première édition / Ouvrage approuvé par le Comité de l'instruction publique / comme livre du maître. / Prix: Relié, $1.50; Broché, $1.25 / Neuville, Co, [sic] de Portneuf, P.Q. / 1912
DESCRIPTION: 17.5 × 12.0 cm Pp [i–v] vi–viii [ix] x–xix [xx], [1] 2–490 [491] Tp illus of cherub, illus Cloth, with tp illus on front
CONTENTS: i tp; ii 'Enregistré conformément à l'Acte du Parlement du Canada au bureau du ministre de l'Agriculture ... Copyright 1912, by Amélie DesRoches, in the United States of America ...'; iii 'Sommaire'; iv blank; v–viii 'Avant-propos' signed Amélie DesRoches; ix–xix 'Table des matières'; xx blank; 1–490 text in four parts; 491 'Errata'
CITATIONS: BQ 09-0970
COPIES: QMBN (158968 CON) *QTURA (641.3 D474h)

Q74.3 1916
—Bulletin no 20 / Hygiène de l'alimentation / et / propriétés chimiques des / aliments / suivi d'un cours theorique sur / l'art culinaire / Premiere edition / Ouvrage approuvé par le Comité de l'instruction publique / comme livre du maître. / Publié par le ministère de l'Agriculture de Québec / 1916
DESCRIPTION: 17.0 × 11.5 cm Pp [i–v] vi–viii [ix] x–xix [xx], [1] 2–490 [491] Illus Paper; sewn
CONTENTS: i tp; ii 'Enregistré conformément à l'Acte du Parlement du Canada au bureau du ministre de l'Agriculture ... Copyright 1912, by Amélie DesRoches, in the United States of America ...'; iii 'Sommaire'; iv blank; v–viii 'Avant-propos'; ix–xix 'Table des matières'; xx blank; 1–490 text in four parts; 491 'Errata'
COPIES: QQL (A38A1 P84 020) QQLA (S159 Q3b 20) *QSFFSC (641.3 D474h)
NOTES: The QSFFSC copy is inscribed on the inside front face of the binding, in ink, 'Madame Lin Grandmont // Champlain // Que'; it is stamped on the outside back face, 'Compliments of A. Désilets, B.S.A. Agronome officiel' (Alphonse Désilets was the husband of Rolande Savard Désilets, who wrote Q123.1). For the titles of other cookbooks published by the Quebec Department of Agriculture, see Q48.1.

Perfect preserving with Perfect jars

Dominion Glass Co. was formed in 1912 by the amalgamation of Diamond Flint Glass Co. and Sydenham Glass Co. For other books published by Dominion Glass, see Q154.1, Home Canning, Q212.1, Preserving and Canning, and Q310.1, Dominion Home Canning Guide.

Q75.1 nd [about 1912 or later]
Perfect preserving / with / Perfect jars / Helpful hints on the / home canning and / preserving of / fruits, / vegetables, / etc. / Issued with / the compliments of / Dominion Glass Co., Limited / Montreal, Toronto, Hamilton, Wallaceburg, / Redcliff, Alta.
DESCRIPTION: 15.5 × 9.0 cm Pp [1–2] 3–46 Illus Paper, with image on front of a Perfect Seal jar; stapled
CONTENTS: 1 tp; 2 fp illus of Perfect Seal jar; 3–46 text
COPIES: OOWM (980.141.182) *SSWD
NOTES: I have not compared the text of this undated edition of *Perfect Preserving with Perfect Jars* with Q75.2–75.5, which have the same cover-title, but Q75.1 is likely an earlier edition of the same work.

Q75.2 1919
—Helpful hints / on the / preserving and canning / of / fruits, vegetables, meats, / soups, etc. / 1919 / edition / Presented with the compliments of / Dominion Glass Company Limited / Head office: Montreal / Factories at / Montreal, Toronto, Hamilton, Wallaceburg, / Redcliff, Alta.
DESCRIPTION: 17.0 × 12.5 cm Pp [1] 2–31 Illus of 'The "Perfect Seal" Jar,' 'The "Improved Gem" Jar,' and 'The "Crown" Jar,' and 2 illus of 'The Adjustable Feature of the Perfect Seal Jar' Paper, with image on front of a woman preparing fruit, with a preserving kettle and jars on the table; stapled
CONTENTS: 1 tp; 2–6 illus; 7–11 'Home Canning'; 12–31 recipes and at bottom p 31, 'Stationery Supply Co., printers, Unity Building, Montreal.'
COPIES: *Private collection
NOTES: The cover-title is 'Perfect Preserving with Perfect Jars.'

Q75.3 1922
—Useful hints / on the / preserving and canning / of / fruits, vegetables, meats, / soups, etc. / 1922 / edition / Presented with the compliments of / Dominion Glass Company Limited / Head office: Montreal / Factories at / Montreal, Toronto, Hamilton, Wallaceburg, / Redcliff, Alta.

DESCRIPTION: 17.0 × 12.5 cm   Pp [1] 2–31   Illus of jars   Paper, with image on front of a woman cutting or peeling fruit; stapled
CONTENTS: 1 tp; 2 Fig. 1, 'The "Perfect Seal" Jar'; 3 Fig. 2, 'The "Improved Gem" Jar'; 4 Fig. 3, 'The "Crown" Jar'; 5–6 Figs 1–2 showing 'The Adjustable Feature of the Perfect Seal Jar'; 7–11 general information about 'Home Canning'; 12–31 'Canning Recipes' and at bottom p 31, 'Birch-Hinds Printing Co., Limited, Montreal.'
COPIES: *Private collection
NOTES: The cover-title is 'Perfect Preserving with Perfect Jars.'

Q75.4   1924

—Useful hints / on the preserving and canning / of fruits, vegetables / meats, soups, etc. / Presented with the / compliments of / Dominion Glass Company, Limited / Head office / Montreal / Factories at Montreal, Toronto, / Hamilton, Wallaceburg, Redcliff, Alta. / 1924 edition
DESCRIPTION: 17.0 × 13.0 cm   Pp [1] 2–32   Tp illus of a still-life of a basket, jar, and fruit; illus   Paper, with image on front of a woman cutting or peeling fruit; stapled
CONTENTS: 1 tp; 2–8 general information about home canning; 9 illus of 'The "Perfect Seal" Jar'; 10 'The Adjustable Feature of the Perfect Seal Jar'; 11 illus of 'The "Improved Gem" Jar'; 12 illus of 'The "Crown" Jar'; 13–32 'Canning Recipes'
COPIES: APROM   *NSWA   SRRPM
NOTES: Copies at OBEHCM (980.029/002) and OKITJS (991.23.11) have no title-page illustration.

Q75.5   1925

—Suggestions utiles / sur la / mise en conserves / et en bocaux / des / fruits, legumes, viandes, soupes, etc. / Présenté avec les compliments de la / Dominion Glass Company, limitée / Bureau principal / Montreal / Manufactures à Montreal, Toronto, / Hamilton, Wallaceburg, Redcliff, Alta. / Edition 1925
DESCRIPTION: 17.5 × 13.0 cm   Pp [1] 2–32   Illus of jars   Paper, with image on front of a woman cutting or peeling fruit; stapled
CONTENTS: 1 tp; 2–8 'Comment préparer les conserves chez soi'; 9–12 illus of Perfect Seal, Improved Gem, and Crown jars; 13–32 'Recettes à conserves'
COPIES: *QMBN (194342 CON)
NOTES: The cover-title is 'Conserver parfaitement dans des bocaux Parfaits.' No printer is named.

Really reliable recipes

Q76.1   1912

Really reliable / recipes / contributed by the ladies of St. Matthias' / Church, Westmount, P.Q. / "We may live without poetry, music and art: / We may live without conscience, and live without heart; / We may live without friends; we may live without books; / But civilized man cannot live without cooks." / – Owen Meredith / Montreal / Printed by John Lovell & Son, Limited / 1912
DESCRIPTION: 22.0 × 14.5 cm   Pp [1–16] 17–132   Cloth
CONTENTS: 1–10 ads; 11 tp; 12 blank; 13 table of contents; 14 blank; 15 'Rhymes to Remember'; 16 'Table of Measures'; 17–129 recipes credited with the name of the contributor; 130–2 'Household Hints'
COPIES: OONL (TX715.6 R36 1912)   QWSMM (Westmount 641.5 R288)   *Private collection
NOTES: The cover-title is 'Cookery Book.' The private collector reports that her copy, handed down in the family, was originally a gift from Mrs H.E. Suckling of Montreal, who contributed a curry recipe to the book. The recipe is annotated by her mother as 'Grandmother's Curry Learned in India,' i.e., when Grandfather Suckling was stationed there.

1912–15

Crawford, Miss Mary A.E. (called Minnie) (Que., 26 October 1849–)

Verdun House was on what at the turn of the last century was called Lower Lachine Road, in Verdun (later called La Salle Road). QVE (Reference Department) has material relating to the site: four photographs of Verdun House and four photographs of John Crawford. Text accompanying the photographs states: '"Verdun House" Erected and so named by John Crawford, owner of Crawford Park, the original "fief" granted by the French Government to Major Zacharie Dupuis in 1671. The building was demolished in 1911 when the land was sold by John Crawford [for subdivision].'

The 1901 Census gives Mary Crawford's birth date and records her living with her parents, John and Marguerite, and two sisters, Lilian and Aliza (i.e., Eliza S. in the 1911 Census and the writer of the letter discussed on p. 135).

A search of Montreal city directories reveals some information about the Crawford family. Only John Crawford, Councillor, is listed at Verdun House in the

1900–1 directory, but in the 1906–7 directory (alphabetical index) and the 1908–9 directory (street index) there are three Crawfords on Lower Lachine Road: Miss E.S. Crawford (i.e., Eliza), Miss Mary A.E. Crawford, and A.E.H. Crawford (Arthur E.H. in the 1911 Census). The last certain reference to Miss Mary A.E. Crawford is in the 1910–11 directory, when she is still living on Lower Lachine Road.

After 1911, the year Verdun House was demolished, members of the Crawford family are listed at other addresses. The 1914–15 directory shows Miss E.S. Crawford at 450 Clark Avenue in Westmount. In the intervening years (i.e., the directories for 1911–12 and 1912–13), Miss Mary A.E. and Miss E.S. are not positively identified, although there is a listing in both directories for Misses Crawford at 468 Clarke Avenue, Westmount, which may refer to the two women.

Q77.1 nd [about 1912–15]
Helps for / young housekeepers / by the late / M.A.E. Crawford / Verdun House

DESCRIPTION: 20.0 × 15.0 cm   Pp [i–iv] v–viii, 1–52
Cloth

CONTENTS: i tp; ii blank; iii 'The recipes in this book have been tested and considered worth keeping in a house whose name, for more than fifty years, stood for Generous Hospitality. E.M.G. [possibly Mrs Greenshields; see notes]'; iv blank; v–viii 'Index'; 1–top 6 'General Directions'; mid 6–52 recipes credited with the source, either an individual or a book or magazine

COPIES: *Private collection

NOTES: Slipped into the private collector's copy is a letter to 'Mary' from E.S. Crawford, dated Friday, which indicates that the late M.A.E. Crawford was unmarried and called Minnie. The note reads: 'I am sending you a small cook book with some of Miss Minnie's receipts which I have had printed. Perhaps you will get some old "Verdun" receipts out of it.'

The cookbook was published after Mary A.E. Crawford's last positive listing in the city directory for 1910–11 and likely no later than 1915, since E.S. Crawford (Eliza), who had the cookbook printed, is not identified in the 1915–16 directory. The appearance of the book is consistent with this period.

The recipes are in random order, sweet and savoury together. Some are credited to the following individuals (listed in the order they appear in the text): Mrs Ellegood [possibly the wife of Reverend Canon Ellegood, canon of Christ Church Cathedral and rector of St James the Apostle, listed in the 1906–7 city

directory], A. Hall, Lizzie, Mrs S. Greenshields [probably in the same family as Mrs Em [*sic*] Greenshields and Miss Mary Greenshields, both on Lower Lachine Road in the 1906–7 directory], Mrs Gibb, C. Gent Sr (also C. Gn., the same person?), Miss Harrington, Old Margaret, M. Duffy, Mrs Sutherland, Mrs Kingston, Mrs Paley, Mrs Courtney, T.B.G., E. Crawford, Mrs Adams, Miss Miller, Miss Simpson, Mrs Baker, Miss Burrage, Aunt Chloe, Emily, Mrs Parker, Polly, Kate O'Rourke, Felinda [*sic*] Duell, Miss McDonnell, Mrs Duvernet, N. Livingstone, Mrs Morkill, Lily, Mrs Duff, and 'Molly.'

Several printed sources are also given, some of which can be identified. Where recipes have been clearly borrowed from a source, it is interesting to note how Mary Crawford has revised the instructions in the light of her own cooking experience. 'Can. Home Ck. Bk,' from which Molasses Candy, Chocolate Caramels, Cup Pudding, Tomato Ketchup, and Sally Lunn were taken, is one of the many editions of O20.1, *The Home Cook Book,* compiled from recipes contributed by ladies of Toronto and other cities and towns, 1877. 'Diamond Ck. Bk,' the source for Mountain Cake, is Q34.1, *The Diamond Cook Book No. 1,* Montreal: Wells, Richardson and Co., [about 1897]. 'Revised edition, Home Made Ck. Bk.,' from which Queen of Puddings (Bread) and Souffle de Russe were taken, is likely O50.1, *The Home Made Cook Book,* rev. ed., Toronto: William Bryce, [entered 1890]. I have not identified 'St. John's Ck. Bk.,' the source for Fig Pudding and Fig Mould. Some recipes are attributed to the American author Miss Parloa, who wrote several cookbooks. Although the specific cookbook is not named, Ladies' Fingers, Jelly Roll, Swiss Pudding, Nut Cake, and Delicate Indian Pudding are all found in *Miss Parloa's New Cook Book,* Minneapolis: Washburn, Crosby Co., 1880. Four recipes are from the American magazine *Ladies' Home Journal.* One recipe is from 'Royal Baker,' probably *Royal Baker and Pastry Cook:* The first of many American editions appeared in 1877; one Canadian edition was published in Montreal in 1911. Nine recipes credited to 'C.P.R.' may have been used on the Canadian Pacific Railway, or the initials may stand for a person's name. I have not identified 'Am. Home Ck. Bk.,' the source for Ginger Snaps. The following are probably British sources: 'Dedham Ck. Bk.' (for Leap Year Cake), 'Nottingham School Ck. Bk.' (Stuffed Haddock and Soda Scones), and the credit for Meg Dodds (Shrewsbury Cakes), which may refer to *The Cook and Housewife's Manual* by Margaret Dods, 1826.

1913

Almanach Rolland ... 1913

See also Q100.1, Almanach Rolland ... 1919.

Q78.1   1913
Almanach / Rolland / agricole, / commercial et des familles / de / la compagnie J.-B. Rolland & fils / 1913 / Quarante-septième année / Enregistré conformément à l'Acte du Parlement du Canada, en l'année mil neuf / cent douze par la compagnie J.-B. Rolland & fils, au bureau du ministre / de l'Agriculture à Ottawa. / Canada / En vente chez tous les libraires / et les principaux marchands / N.B. – Cet almanach contient beaucoup de matières d'un intérêt général et / mérite d'être conservé à titre de renseignements utiles.
DESCRIPTION: Tp still-life of globe, ruler, books, agricultural tools, and wheat sheaf
COPIES: QQS
NOTES: 'Cuisine des malades et des convalescents' is on pp 154–62; the thirty-four numbered recipes give proportions for one person. J.-B. Rolland et fils was a Montreal business.

Five Roses cook book

Five Roses Cook Book (La cuisinière Five Roses *in the French-language editions) is an early example of a flour-company cookbook and the most successful of them all. In its first incarnation, published in 1913, and again in 1915, it reached into over 950,000 Canadian homes. This is a phenomenal number of copies as the population of Canada in 1915 was only 7,981,000 (by 1920, 8,556,000); as the publisher's blurb boasted, there was 'practically one copy [of* Five Roses Cook Book*] for every second Canadian home.' In 1932 the company published a new collection of recipes, Q203.1,* A Guide to Good Cooking, *which continued to be popularly known as the 'Five Roses Cook Book.' Numerous editions were issued through the century and Canadian cooks can still order a copy of the latest edition through the company.*

Five Roses Cook Book *served as the source for the 'Anglo' recipes in a Ukrainian-language cookbook published in Edmonton in 1917: A34.1,* Ukrains'ko-angliiskyi kukhar, *by Michael Belegai.*

OPREFM has a copy of Five Roses Cook Book, *but I have not determined its date. There are incomplete copies of* Five Roses Cook Book *at MSM and SBIM.*

For the titles of other cookbooks advertising Five Roses Flour, see Q58.1.

Q79.1   [copyright 1913]
Five Roses / cook book / being a manual of good recipes / carefully chosen from the contributions of over two / thousand successful users of Five Roses / Flour throughout Canada / also / useful notes on the various classes of good things / to eat, all of which have been carefully / checked and re-checked by / competent authority / [symbol of Lake of the Woods Milling Co., Keewatin] / Issued by / Lake of the Woods Milling / Company Limited / Montreal
DESCRIPTION: 25.5 × 18.0 cm   Pp [1–4] 5–144   Many small illus orange of girl and boy cooks   Paper, with image on front of a girl cook stirring the contents of a bowl, which sits on a stool
CONTENTS: 1–2 three coupons for ordering the cookbook; 3 tp; 4 'Copyright, Canada, 1913 by Lake of the Woods Milling Company Limited // Compiled and designed by Advertising Department Lake of the Woods Milling Company Limited // Engraved and printed by the Herald Press at Montreal'; 5–7 'List of Recipes'; 8 'A Page of Weights and Measures'; 9–11 'The Making of Bread (Editor's Note)'; 12–140 recipes, some credited with the name of the contributor; 141–4 blank 'For Additional Recipes'
CITATIONS: Armstrong 2000, p F2   Cooke 2002, p 235   Crawford, p D2   Driver 2001, Wellington County, p 96   Driver 2003, 'Canadian Cookbooks,' p 36   Driver 2003, Five Roses, p 1   Driver 2003, Ogilvie's Book, inside front cover   Driver 2003, Robin Hood, pp 85, 87   *Everywoman's World* (September 1914), p 4   O'Neill (unpublished)   Watier, p 9
COPIES: ABOM   AEUCHV (UV 85.312.13)   BCHM   BSUM   NBFKL   OAUH   OFERWM (A1978.4.16)   OGU (CCC TX715.6 F54, 2 copies)   OKELWM   OMARH   OMIHURM   ONLAM (Walters-Wagar Collection 975.9.7, Box 20)   OPETCM   OSMFHHM   OWTU (G14358)   QKB (2 copies: 80-7, 92-33)   QMM (RBD uncat)   SSWD   *Private collection; Great Britain: LB (not located)
NOTES: The coupons indicate that the book was sent free to the customer, upon receipt of the coupon and money to cover postage. The title-page is printed in orange and black. Decorative initial capital letters begin each section. The book's attractive design contributed to its success. There are advertisements throughout the text, illustrating the company's mills and showing how Five Roses Flour was sold in bags of various weights (7, 14, 24, 49, and 98 pounds) and in half barrels (98 pounds) and whole barrels (196 pounds). There are no colour plates illustrating pre-

pared recipes in the 1913 edition, as there are in the 1915 edition.

In some sections, the introductions are described as 'specially written [or prepared] for the Five Roses Cook Book.' The recipes, however, are from various sources. Some are credited to individuals in particular towns, such as Mrs Dan Lynch, Esterhazy, Saskatchewan (Nut Bread, p 19); Plain Biscuits, p 37, is described as a 'Women's Institute recipe'; others are described as 'Selected,' but no source is given (for example, Dumplings with Stews, p 65); Marshmallows, p 89, is from the *Canadian Farm Cook Book* (O257.1); How to Preserve Ginger, p 127, is from *The New Home*; Bursting a Loaf Right, p 16, is from *Bakers' Magazine;* Honey Bread, p 19, is a 'Boston Cooking School Recipe'; and How to Make Patty Cases, p 74, is from *Gold Medal Cook Book,* probably *Gold Medal Flour Cook Book,* published by the American firm Washburn Crosby Co. in 1900 and later. Rye Bread, p 20, is not credited, but it is the same recipe, with a few minor revisions, as Rye Bread in the 1896 first American edition of Fannie Farmer's *The Boston Cooking-School Cook Book,* p 60, and in the 1924 Canadian edition, p 52 (O144.3); the recipe may have been submitted by an individual, as her trusted recipe, as opposed to being added, without credit, by the compilers of the Five Roses cookbook.

There is a full-page advertisement for *Five Roses Cook Book* in the Toronto periodical *Everywoman's World* of September 1914, which states that the cookbook 'has already satisfied every baking ambition of over 100,000 housewives,' i.e., by September 1914, over 100,000 copies had been distributed.

The coupons on p 2 of the QMM copy are stamped 'Jun 20 1914'; the coupons on p 2 of the QKB copies are stamped: 'Sep 22 1914' (92-33) and 'May 13[?] 1915' (80-7). Both the OFERWM and OSMFHHM copies have the lower part of the title-page, including the imprint, torn or cut off.

Q79.2 [copyright 1915]

—Five Roses / cook book / being a manual of good recipes / carefully chosen from the contributions of over two / thousand successful users of Five Roses / Flour throughout Canada / also / useful notes on the various classes of good things / to eat, all of which have been carefully / checked and re-checked by / competent authority / [symbol of Lake of the Woods Milling Co., Keewatin] / Issued by / Lake of the Woods Milling / Company Limited / Montreal

DESCRIPTION: 24.0 × 17.5 cm   Pp [1–4] [part of third leaf missing where folios 5–6 are printed in other copies] 7–140 [two leaves missing]   4 double-sided

pls col, many small illus orange of girl and boy cooks   Thin card, with image on front of a girl cook stirring the contents of a bowl, which sits on a stool

CONTENTS: 1–2 three coupons for ordering the cookbook; 3 tp; 4 'Copyright, Canada, 1915 by Lake of the Woods Milling Company Limited // Compiled and designed by Advertising Department Lake of the Woods Milling Company Limited // Printed by Gazette Printing Company Limited Montreal'; 5–7 'List of Recipes'; 8 'A Page of Weights and Measures'; 9–11 'The Making of Bread (Editor's Note)'; 12–140 recipes, some credited with the name of the contributor

CITATIONS: Bitting, p 552   Driver 2001, Wellington County, pp 86, 94   Reitz, p [4]   Wheaton/Kelly No. 3427

COPIES: AALIWWM   AC (Pam file 641.5 Fiv) ACG   ACHP (HP 6209.1)   AEPMA   AEPRAC AOYCM   APROM   BBVM   BKM   BKOM   BPGRM (987.56.46)   BSUM   BVMA   CIHM (78539) MBDHM (2 copies)   MSOHM   MTM   OAUH OBEHCM (1976.28.3)   OBUJBM   OFERWM (A1997.133 MU235)   OGU (CCC TX715.6 F54, 2 copies)   OKIT   OKITD (968.137.017)   OKITJS (991.40.1)   OONL (TX715 F575 1915 fol. copy 2; copy 1 missing)   OOWM   (2 copies: 989.6.11, 976.40.9) OSMFHHM   OVOH   OWTU (G10398 and a second copy)   QMM (RBD ckbk 1746)   SSWD   *Private collection; United States: MCR (641.81 F56 and micro SLC 42 #310)

NOTES: There was more than one English-language edition with the copyright date 1915. The one described here has only one place of publication on the title-page – Montreal – and the printer is Gazette Printing Co. Ltd. Like the 1913 edition, the title-page is printed in orange and black and decorative initial capital letters begin each section. A note on the coupon page indicates that the book was available in French as *La cuisinière canadienne.*

Some copies of the 1915 edition have a publisher's blurb printed on the inside front face of the binding that celebrates the Canadian production and specifies how many copies of the cookbook had been printed to date. The blurb in the private collector's copy states: '"The Five Roses Cook Book" is an all-Canadian publication. The recipes were supplied by Canadian housewives ... The book was printed in a Canadian shop, and the paper, both inside and cover stock, was produced in a Canadian mill. No cook book published anywhere has received such popular appreciation. Already, nearly 650,000 copies are in daily use in Canadian kitchens – practically one copy for every second Canadian home.' The blurbs in the BVMA, OKIT, and OKITJS copies, and in one of the copies at MBDHM and the second copy at OWTU, also have '650,000 copies.' The OOWM copy (989.6.11) has '600,000 copies.' The BKOM, OONL, and SSWD copies, and one of the OGU copies, have '700,000 copies.' The AALIWWM, AC, and BBVM copies have '850,000 copies.' There is no blurb in the copies at ACG, AEPMA, BSUM, MSOHM, MTM, OAUH, OFERWM, and OKITD, or in the other copies at MBDHM, OGU, and OOWM (976.40.9). A copy at AMHM lacks its title-page, but the blurb refers to '650,000 copies'; the coupons are stamped 'Aug 6 1923.' A clipping covers the BKM copy's blurb.

The BPGRM copy is inscribed on the title-page, in ink, 'From K. Sharp With all good wishes 1925 To Mrs. Harold Lee's.' The publisher's blurb refers to '[?]00,000 copies.'

The OWTU copy (G10398) is complete. Its pagination runs [1–4] 5–144; pp 141–4 are blank for 'Additional Recipes.' The inside front face of its binding is inscribed 'Mrs R.[G. or C.] MacBride.'

The QMM copy appears to match the edition described here. Newspaper clippings obscure the publication date on the verso of the title-page and also the text on the inside front face of the binding; the coupons are stamped 'Mar 9 1923.'

The OSMFHHM copy lacks pp 1–2, pp 139 onward, and the binding.

The Wheaton/Kelly citation for the copy at the Schlesinger Library likely refers to the edition described here. Duncan, pp 94–5, may refer to Q79.2 or Q79.3.

OOWM has a third copy (973.57.23) of a 1915 edition, but it was temporarily unavailable for examination to determine whether it matches Q79.2 or Q79.3.

Copies at NSHMS (76.67.37) and OTMCL (641.6311 F395), and at IaU in the United States (SPEC SZAT TX763 F38 1915), were printed by the Gazette Printing Co. Ltd, but have two places of publication – Montreal and Winnipeg. The publisher's blurb in the OTMCL and IaU copies refers to '900,000 copies.'

Q79.3 [copyright 1915]
—Five Roses / cook book / being a manual of good recipes / carefully chosen from the contributions of over two / thousand successful users of Five Roses / Flour throughout Canada / also / useful notes on the various classes of good things / to eat, all of which have been carefully / checked and re-checked by / competent authority / [symbol of Lake of the Woods Milling Co., Keewatin] / Issued by / Lake of the Woods Milling / Company Limited / Montreal Winnipeg
DESCRIPTION: 24.0 × 17.5 cm   Pp [1–4] 5–144   4

double-sided pls col, many small illus orange of girl and boy cooks   Thin card, with image on front of a girl cook stirring the contents of a bowl, which sits on a stool
CONTENTS: 1–2 three coupons for ordering the cookbook; 3 tp; 4 'Copyright, Canada, 1915 by Lake of the Woods Milling Company Limited // Compiled and designed by Advertising Department Lake of the Woods Milling Company Limited // Printed by Southam Press Montreal Limited'; 5–7 'List of Recipes'; 8 'A Page of Weights and Measures'; 9–11 'The Making of Bread (Editor's Note)'; 12–140 recipes, some credited with the name of the contributor; 141–4 blank for 'Additional Recipes'
CITATIONS: Armstrong 2000, p F2, illus p F1 Ferguson/Fraser, pp 46, 65, and 232, illus col on p 35 of closed volume
COPIES: AEUCHV   MWASM   MWU (Archives and Special Collections, Ogilvie Collection, MSS 120, Box 164) *OGU (CCC TX715.6 F54 1915)   OHALM (988.43.3)   OPETCM   SBIM   Private collection
NOTES: See pl 2a. This edition has two places of publication on the title-page – Montreal and Winnipeg – and the printer is Southam Press. The publisher's blurb on the inside front face of the binding refers to 'over 950,000 copies' (the same number is quoted in the copies at AEUCHV, MWASM, OGU, and OPETCM). The copy at SBIM has '900,000 copies.' All these copies were likely distributed in about 1928 or later because there is an advertisement in an Essex, Ontario, fund-raiser of about 1928 (O616.1, *Cook Book*) for the 'famous Five Roses Cook Book ... used in over 850,000 Canadian homes.'

A copy at OKELWM has only one place of publication – Montreal – but was printed by Southam, as Q79.3. The publisher's blurb refers to over 950,000 copies.

Q79.4 [copyright 1915]
—La cuisiniere / Five Roses / comprenant 1001 recettes eprouvées / et autorisées par l'emploi qu'en ont fait au delà de 2,000 / ménagères canadiennes. Cet ouvrage contient en / plus un très grand nombre d'observations utiles / destinées à l'emploi de la farine Five Roses / dans les différents genres de mets. / Le tout vérifié et approuvé / [symbol of Lake of the Woods Milling Co.] / Editeurs / Lake of the Woods Milling / Company Limited / Montréal
DESCRIPTION: 24.5 × 17.0 cm   Pp [1–4] 5–151 [152]   Many small illus orange of girl and boy cooks   Paper, with image on front of an aproned woman consulting this book; stapled, and with hole punched at top left corner for hanging

CONTENTS: 1–2 three coupons for ordering the cookbook; 3 tp; 4 'Tous droits réservés, Canada, 1915 par Lake of the Woods Milling Company Limited // Compilé et vérifié par le Bureau de publicité de la Lake of the Woods Milling Company Limited Montréal // Imprimé par The Gazette Printing Company Limited Montréal'; 5–7 'Table alphabétique des recettes'; 8 'Des poids et mesures'; 9–11 'Cuisson du pain de ménage'; 12–151 recipes; 152 publ ad
CITATIONS: Bédard, p 2   Carrière No. 114   Leduc   Watier, p 8   Wheaton/Kelly No. 3426
COPIES: MSM   OONL (TX715 L252 1915)   QMBN (TX714 C85f 1915 and 158971 CON)   QMM (2 copies: RBD ckbk 789; RBD Vanna Garnier, ckbk 793)   QSFFSC (641.5 L192c)   QTS   SSWD Company collection (ADM Milling Co., Montreal)   *Private collection; United States: MCR (641.81 F56f)
NOTES: See pl 2b. The French-language edition is not a straight translation of the English edition. The most obvious change is a new title – *La cuisinière Five Roses*, meaning 'The Five Roses Cook' – and a new design for the binding in an art-nouveau style. Instead of an image of a child stirring the contents of a bowl, there is an image of an elegant woman ('la cuisinière') reading this cookbook; the image is signed by the artist M.C. Perley. The design of the English edition could be characterized as cute; the design of the French edition, as sophisticated.

Within the text, some chapters are placed in a different order. Occasionally, the order of recipes is changed. In some cases, the change may have been made for design reasons (translations into French inevitably create more text). In the English edition, for example, the last recipe in the chapter 'Recipes for Fancy Bread' is Bread from Five Roses Breakfast Food (p 21); the French translation of this recipe is Bon pain de gruau, but it would not fit on the last page of the same chapter and instead appears in the chapter 'Un bon gruau de blé ou semoule pour le déjeuner' (called 'A Pure Wheat Breakfast Food' in the English edition). In other instances, the change may have been made to improve the logic of the text. In the English edition, for example, the two recipes for Christmas Pudding and the three variations of Plum Pudding are separated by nineteen other recipes, which are not necessarily associated with the holiday season. In the French edition, the Pouding à la Christmas recipes are followed immediately by the Pouding de Noël recipes. Sometimes, but not always, the recipe contributor's name is omitted from the French edition, perhaps for reasons of space: for example, Pain de riz à la Louisiane (p 22) – Southern Rice Bread (p 20) in the English edition – is not credited to Mrs

A.W. Fraser, Iron Springs, Alberta. The most interesting changes, however, are the additions to the French edition of new introductory text for chapters and new recipes. On p 9, for example, there is additional text explaining how to judge the quality of flour. New to the Bonbons chapter (i.e., Candies) is Tire à la Saint-Catherine, a Quebec molasses candy made especially on the saint's day. A full examination of the extensive revisions made for the French edition is not possible here, but would illuminate the differences between the two cultures.

Like the English editions, the title-page is printed in orange and black. Unlike the 1915 English editions, the copy catalogued here has no double-sided colour plates; however, BQ 22-4874 records a copy with colour plates.

The QSFFSC copy is stamped on the outside front face of the binding, 'Rec'd Oct 1934'; 'Déjà, au delà de 850,000 exemplaires ...' is printed on the inside front face. The SSWD copy has 'Déjà, au delà de 600,000 exemplaires ...'

Q79.5 [copyright 1939]
—La cuisiniere / Five Roses / comprenant 1001 recettes eprouvées / et autorisées par l'emploi qu'en ont fait au delà de 2,000 / ménagères canadiennes. Cet ouvrage contient en / plus un très grand nombre d'observations utiles / destinées à l'emploi de la farine Five Roses / dans les différents genres de mets. / Le tout vérifié et approuvé / [symbol of Lake of the Woods Milling Co.] / Editeurs / Lake of the Woods Milling / Company Limited / Montréal
DESCRIPTION: 23.5 × 15.0 cm   Pp [1–4] 5–152   4 double-sided pls col, illus   Card; wire-bound
CONTENTS: 1–2 coupons for ordering the cookbook on remittance of $0.40; 3 tp; 4 'Tous droits réservés, Canada, 1939 par Lake of the Woods Milling Company Limited ...'; 5–7 'Table alphabétique des recettes'; 8 'Des poids et mesures'; 9–151 text; 152 'Table de températures et durée de cuisson'
COPIES: *OONL (TX715 L252 1939)
NOTES: The title-page is printed in black only.

Q79.6 [facsimile ed., 1999]
—Five Roses / cook book / being a manual of good recipes / carefully chosen from the contributions of over two / thousand successful users of Five Roses / Flour throughout Canada / also / useful notes on the various classes of good things / to eat, all of which have been carefully / checked and re-checked by / competent authority / [symbol of Lake of the Woods Milling Co., Keewatin] / Issued by / Lake of the Woods Milling / Company Limited / Montreal

DESCRIPTION: 24.5 × 18.0 cm   Pp [1–4] 5–144   Many small illus orange of girl and boy cooks, illus portrait on p 2 of Caroline Ada Richardson   Thin card, with image on front of a girl cook stirring the contents of a bowl, which sits on a stool

CONTENTS: 1 tp; 2 dedication to 'my mother, Caroline Ada Richardson. The *Five Roses Cook Book* was given to my mother as a young bride ... she passed her treasured copy of the book on to me.' signed Carol Ann Shipman [owner of the volume from which the facsimile was made], 'Copyright © 1999 by Carol Ann Shipman // Whitecap Books Vancouver/Toronto/ New York // First published in 1915 ...'; 3 'Foreword' by Elizabeth Baird; 4 blank; 5–7 'List of Recipes'; 8 'A Page of Weights and Measures'; 9–11 'The Making of Bread (Editor's Note)'; 12–140 recipes, some credited with the name of the contributor; 141–4 blank 'For Additional Recipes'

CITATIONS: Neering, p 127

COPIES: *Private collection

NOTES: This is a facsimile of Q79.2; however, it does not include all four double-sided colour plates from the 1915 edition, only two colour plates, and these are not in their original position, but on the inside front face and inside back face of the binding. This is the first title in what was to become Whitecap's Classic Canadian Cookbook Series. Although the early printings of the facsimile are not identified as such, the seventh printing in 2002 bears the series name and has 'Historical Notes' by Elizabeth Driver on p 4.

Hiller, Mrs Elizabeth O.

This American author also wrote: O408.1, The Corn Cook Book; O436.1, The Calendar of Cakes, Fillings and Frostings; O437.1, The Calendar of Luncheons, Teas and Suppers; O438.1, The Calendar of Sandwiches and Beverages; O439.1, New Calendar of Salads; *and* O440.1, New Dinners for All Occasions.

Also by Hiller, but not published in Canada, are: Leftover Foods and How to Use Them, *Kendallville, Ind.: McCray Refrigerator Co., copyright 1910* (OKITD; *United States:* DLC); The Practical Cook Book, *New York: Doherty Operating Co., [c1910]* (United States: DLC, MCR); The Calendar of Dinners, *Chicago, New York: P.F. Volland, [1915?]* (United States: MCR); Delicious Dishes, *[Denver:] Morey Mercantile Co., c1915* (United States: DLC); The Calendar of Desserts, *New York: P.F. Volland and Co., [1916]* (United States: MH); The Calendar of Salads, *Chicago and New York: P.F. Volland and Co., nd [1916]* (QMM; United States:

MCR); Your Daily Kitchen Companion, *Chicago, New York [etc.]: P.F. Volland Co., [c1918]* (United States: DLC); New Calendar of Desserts, *New York: P.F. Volland, [192-?]* (United States: MCR).

Q80.1   copyright 1913
[An edition of *Fifty-two Sunday Dinners*, Chicago, New York, St Louis, New Orleans, and Montreal: N.K. Fairbank Co., copyright 1913]
COPIES: OGU; United States: DLC (TX737 H7)   MCR

Johnston's year book 1913

Q81.1   1913
Hang me up in a handy place. I'm worth while. / Johnston's / year book / 1913 / A convenient household guide / containing / reliable cooking recipes / health helps / a birthday horoscope and / monthly calendar / George W. Johnston / druggist / Cowansville. Que. [cover-title]
DESCRIPTION: 17.5 × 13.5 cm   Pp [1] 2–32   Illus of zodiac signs and a decorative headpiece for each month in the year   Paper; stapled, and with hole punched at top left corner for hanging
CONTENTS: 1 'Calendar for 1913'; 2 'Keep This Book'; 3 'Table of Measures and Weights,' 'Table of Proportions,' and 'Pigs in Blankets'; 4–32 for each month of the year: moon phases, historical events, rising and setting of the sun and moon, weather predictions, recipes, and other information
COPIES: *QLB (Townships TX159 J5 1913)

Manuel de la ménagère

Q82.1   [1st ed., 1913]
Manuel / de la menagere / contenant environ 500 recettes les plus / pratiques et les plus simples pour pre- / parer les potages, viandes, poissons / oeufs, salades, legumes, marina- / des, patisseries, gelées, fruits, / sauces, poudings, plats sucrés, / conserves, breuvages di- / vers, etc. etc., etc, ainsi / que plusieurs bons / conseils tres uti- / les dans un / ménage. / Tirage: / cent mille / exemplaires / Publié par / Montreal Advertising Agency / Montreal, Canada
DESCRIPTION: 22.5 × 15.5 cm   Pp [1–3] 4–192   Paper, with image on front of a woman pouring extract(?) into a spoon; stapled
CONTENTS: 1 'Madame: –'; 2 coupon for ordering this free book; 3 tp; 4 ad; 5 'Préface' signed 'les éditeurs,'

1 December 1913; 6 ad; 7–178 text and ads; 179–mid 187 'Index des recettes de cuisine' and ads; mid 187–91 'Index des annonceurs' and ads; 192 ad
COPIES: *OTYA (CPC 1913 0118)
NOTES: The 'Préface' refers to this as the first edition. Printed on the front face of the binding, in a blank space below the image, is 'Avec les compliments de Arthur Thibodeau, bonbons, etc., 2333 Clarke, Montréal.' The OTYA copy is inscribed on the front face of the binding and on pp 41 and 135, 'Dr L. Laberge.'

The sub-title closely matches Q64.1. I have not compared the texts.

Q82.2 [1917]
—Manuel / de la menagere / contenant environ 500 recettes les plus / pratiques et les plus simples pour pre- / parer les potages, viandes, poissons / oeufs, salades, legumes, marina- /des, patisseries, gelees, fruits, / sauces, poudings, plats sucres, / conserves, breuvages di- / vers, etc. etc., etc, ainsi / que plusieurs bons / conseils tres uti- / les dans un / menage. / Publié par / La compagnie de publicité nationale / 97 St-Jacques, / Montreal.
DESCRIPTION: 22.0 × 15.0 cm   Pp [2–3] 4–144   Illus of astrological signs   [$0.25, on binding]   Paper, with image on front of a woman trimming the crust of a pie, two children at the kitchen window; stapled
CONTENTS: 2 'Tous droits réservés.'; 3 tp; 4 ad; 5–6 'Préface' signed 'éditeur'; 7 'Introduction'; 8 ad; 9–129 text; 130 blank; 131–42 monthly calendar, including astrological signs and 'Pronostics de la température pour le mois de [name of month] 1917'; 143–4 ads
COPIES: *QMBN (153599 CON)
NOTES: The British Library catalogue (07945.m.52 destroyed) cites *Manuel de la ménagère contenant environ 500 recettes ...*, Montreal: [1916], pp 84, under the name of Oscar Gladu. It seems likely that the Gladu reference is to the same book, although the number of pages in the British Library copy does not match Q82.1 or Q82.2. The Montreal city directory for 1913–14 lists Oscar Gladu as a notary in the firm of Boisseau and Gladu, Room 12, 92 Notre Dame East, living at 755 Durocher, Outremont; the 1915–16 directory also lists him as with the firm of Boisseau and Gladu, but there is no listing under the firm's name; the directory for 1916–17 lists neither Oscar Gladu nor the firm and his name is not listed thereafter. It may be that Gladu did not produce the book, but only submitted it to the British Library for copyright purposes.

1914

Good bread

This title was published by druggists in Quebec, Ontario, and Nova Scotia. For the edition by Geo. W. Johnston of Cowansville, see O321.2.

1914–18

Edwardsburg recipe book

For information about the Canada Starch Co. and its cookbooks, see Q47.1

Q83.1   nd [about 1914–18]
Edwardsburg / recipe / book / The Canada Starch Co. Limited. [cover-title]
DESCRIPTION: 15.5 × 11.5 cm   Pp [1] 2–31 [32]   Illus   Paper, with image on front of a pyramid of cans of Edwardsburg Corn Syrup, behind which stands a child-chef holding up a jar of Edwardsburg Corn Syrup on a plate; previously stapled, now sewn by library
CONTENTS: 1 illus of a can of Edwardsburg Corn Syrup, a girl pouring syrup on pancakes, and a can of Lily White Corn Syrup, 'Specially Selected Recipes' [introductory text], and at bottom, 'Prepared and guaranteed by the Canada Starch Company Limited // Head office: Montreal // Works: Brantford, Cardinal and Fort William, Ont.'; 2–30 recipes for 'Candy Making,' 'Cake Recipes,' 'Frostings,' 'Delicious Desserts,' 'Sweet Sauces,' 'Pie Recipes,' 'Ice Creams and Desserts,' 'Soups,' 'Gravies and Sauces,' 'Vegetables,' 'Souffles,' 'Entrees,' 'Omelets,' 'Fritters,' 'Griddle Cakes and Waffles,' 'Recipes with Potato Flour,' and 'Preserving'; 31 'Suggestions'; 32 'C.R. Corneil Limited Montreal'
COPIES: CIHM (76500)   *OONL (TX715 C3465 No. 15 reserve)
NOTES: The order of the early editions is uncertain; however, all editions without a reference to Mazola Oil were published in 1919 or before (see notes for Q83.4). A Canada Starch advertisement in the March 1914 issue of *Everywoman's World* refers to 'our free recipe book,' but does not cite the publication's title; the reference is likely to *Edwardsburg Recipe Book*.

This edition has no index. The introductory text says, 'This is a new and larger edition of our famous "Edwardsburg Cook Book." Many novel recipes have been added ...' The recipes are for cooking with the company's corn syrup and cornstarch. There is a recipe for War Cake on p 7.

An advertisement for Lily White Corn Syrup in the November 1919 issue of *Western Home Monthly* refers to 'our new illustrated cook book.' The advertisement may or may not refer to this edition.

Q83.2 nd [about 1914–18]
—Edwardsburg / recipe book [cover-title]
DESCRIPTION: 15.0 × 11.5 cm   Pp [1] 2–32   Several small illus   Paper, with image on front of a woman holding a cake on a plate and looking down at a young girl; stapled
CONTENTS: 1 publ ad for Crown Brand and Lily White corn syrups and Benson's Prepared Corn; 2–29 recipes for 'Candy,' 'Cake Recipes,' 'Cake Fillings and Frostings,' 'Puddings, Desserts, &c.,' 'Sweet Sauces,' 'Pie Recipes,' 'Ice Cream and Ices,' 'Soups,' 'Gravies and Sauces,' 'Vegetables,' 'Souffles,' 'Entrees,' 'Omelets,' 'Fritters,' 'Griddle Cakes,' and 'Potato Flour Recipes'; 30 'Suggestions'; 31–2 index and, at bottom p 32, 'C.R. Corneil Limited Montreal'
COPIES: *Private collection
NOTES: There is no reference on p 1 to any edition of the *Edwardsburg Recipe Book.* There is no mention of Mazola.

Q83.3 nd [about 1914–18]
—Edwardsburg / recipe book / The Canada Starch Co. Limited / Montreal Cardinal Brantford / Fort William
DESCRIPTION: 15.0 × 11.5 cm   Pp [i–ii], [1] 2–32, [i–ii]   Centre spread pl col between pp 16 and 17 of 'Crown' Toffee, 'Crown' Fudge, 'Crown' Divinity, Corn Gems, Griddle Cakes, Waffles, Cream Cake, and Sponge Cake; several small illus   Paper, with image on front of a woman holding a cake on a plate and looking down at a young girl; stapled
CONTENTS: i tp printed in col; ii blank; 1 publ ad; 2–29 recipes for 'Candy,' 'Cake Recipes,' 'Cake Fillings and Frostings,' 'Puddings, Desserts, &c.,' 'Sweet Sauces,' 'Pie Recipes,' 'Ice Cream and Ices,' 'Soups,' 'Gravies and Sauces,' 'Vegetables,' 'Souffles,' 'Entrees,' 'Omelets,' 'Fritters,' 'Griddle Cakes,' and 'Potato Flour Recipes'; 30 'Suggestions'; 31–2 index, and at bottom p 32, 'C.R. Corneil Limited Montreal'; i blank; ii publ ad
COPIES: BBVM (2 copies)   *OGU (CCC TX715.6 E38)
NOTES: The title-page is printed with a blue background. There is no mention of Mazola.

Q83.4 nd [about 1919]
—Edwardsburg / recipe / book / The Canada Starch Co. Limited. / Montreal [cover-title]
DESCRIPTION: 16.0 × 12.5 cm   Pp 3–66   Many illus col of prepared dishes   Paper, with image on front of prepared dishes above title, company products (including a can of Mazola Oil) below title; stapled
CONTENTS: 3 'Start with the Right Products'; 4 information about company products; 5–64 recipes; 65–6 index
COPIES: *Private collection
NOTES: The text on p 3, under 'Start with the Right Products,' indicates a publication date during or shortly after the First World War: 'The importance of good wholesome food economically prepared cannot be over-estimated – especially in these times ... variety in the daily menus is more difficult of achievement than ever under the necessary food restrictions.' The probable date of publication is about 1919, since Mazola Oil is the first-mentioned company product on p 4 and it was introduced to the Canadian market in 1919 (the year that Corn Products Refining Co. (USA) bought a controlling interest in Canada Starch Co.).

The text on p 3 refers to 'this edition of the Canada Starch Cook Book.' In this edition there is no endorsement by C.H. Schneider (Q83.5) or by Canadian housewives (Q83.6, Q83.7, Q83.8). The printer, 'C.R. Corneil, Limited Montreal,' is on the outside back face of the binding.

Q83.5 nd [about 1919]
—Recipes / endorsed by C.H. Schneider / of the Ritz Carlton Hotel / Montreal / Published by / the Canada Starch Co., Limited / Montreal Toronto / Fort William Cardinal / Form A-1
DESCRIPTION: 16.0 × 13.0 cm   Pp [1–2] 3–67   Illus col   Paper, with image on front of prepared dishes above title, company products (including a can of Mazola Oil) below title; stapled
CONTENTS: 1 tp; 2 'Endorsement' by C.H. Schneider, chef de cuisine, Ritz Carlton Hotel; 3 'Start with the Right Products'; 4 information about company products; 5–64 recipes; 65–6 index; 67 table of 'Energy Values of Foods – Calories per LB.'
COPIES: *Private collection
NOTES: Like Q83.4, p 3 discusses the difficulty of achieving menu variety 'under the necessary food restrictions' and refers to 'this edition of the Canada Starch Cook Book.' The cover-title is 'Edwardsburg Recipe Book.' The printer's name, 'C.R. Corneil, Limited Montreal,' is on the outside back face of the

binding. This is the only edition where the recipes are endorsed by Henry Schneider. Schneider was an author in his own right; see Q67.1.

Q83.6 nd [about 1920–2]
—Popular and economical / recipes / Published by / the Canada Starch Co. Limited / Montreal Toronto / Cardinal Fort William / Form A-1
DESCRIPTION: 16.0 × 12.5 cm   Pp [1] 2–63   Illus col   Paper, with image on front of prepared dishes above title, company products below title; stapled
CONTENTS: 1 tp; 2 'The recipes contained in this book have the hearty endorsement of thousands of housewives throughout Canada. Send one of these books to your friends, see page 63.' and reference to 'this edition of the Edwardsburg Recipe Book'; 3 information about company products; 4–59 recipes; 60–1 index; 62 table of 'Energy Values of Foods – Calories per LB.'; 63 book-order form
COPIES: OMAHM (993.16.13)   OONL (TX715 C3465 No. 14 copy 2)   OTMCL (641.5971 P58)   OWTU (F0861)   *Private collection
NOTES: The cover-title is 'Edwardsburg Recipe Book.' The printer, 'C.R. Corneil Limited Montreal,' is on the outside back face of the binding. Both Q83.6 and Q83.7 are called *Popular and Economical Recipes*; see the notes for Q83.7 regarding the distinguishing features.

Q83.7 nd [about 1920–2]
—Popular and economical / recipes / Published by / the Canada Starch Co. Limited / Montreal Toronto / Cardinal Fort William / Quebec Vancouver / Form A-2
DESCRIPTION: 16.0 × 13.0 cm   Pp [1] 2–62 [63–4]   Many illus col of prepared dishes   Paper, with image on front of prepared dishes above title, company products below title; stapled
CONTENTS: 1 tp; 2 'The recipes contained in this book have the hearty endorsement of thousands of housewives throughout Canada // Send one of these books to your friends ...' and reference to this book as 'The Edwardsburg Recipe Book'; 3 information about company products; 4 'Measurements,' 'Oven Heat,' and 'Time Required for Average Gas Oven to Get These Heats before Putting in Cake'; 5–62 recipes; 63 book-order form; 64 'C.R. Corneil, Limited Montreal'
COPIES: AWWDM   *Company collection (Best Foods Canada, Toronto, Ont.)
NOTES: The cover-title is 'Edwardsburg Recipe Book.' Whereas in Q83.6 the recipes begin on p 4, in this edition information about measurements and oven

heat are on p 4, and the recipes begin on p 5. Also, here the printer's name is on p 64, not on the binding. There is no reference to 'food restrictions'; therefore, Q83.6 and Q83.7 were published after Q83.4 and Q83.5, likely in the early 1920s.

MCM has a copy that lacks pp 1–2, but which may be this edition.

Q83.8 nd [about 1920–2]
—Recettes / faciles et economiques / Edité par / The Canada Starch Co., Limited / Montréal Toronto / Cardinal Fort William / Québec Vancouver / Form A-2
DESCRIPTION: 16.0 × 12.5 cm   Pp [1] 2–62 [63–4]   Many illus col of prepared dishes   Paper, with image on front of prepared dishes above title, company products below title; stapled
CONTENTS: 1 tp; 2 'Les recettes continues dans ce livret sont hautement recommandées par des milliers de ménagères, par tout le Canada // Expédiez l'un de ces livrets à vos amis ...' and reference to this book as 'la "Cuisinière Edwardsburg"'; 3 information about company products; 4 'Mesures,' 'Température du four,' and 'Temps requis pour produire ces chaleurs dans un four à gaz ordinaire, avant d'enfourner'; 5–62 recipes; 63 book-order form; 64 'C.R. Corneil, Limited Montreal'
COPIES: OONL (TX715 R43533 1930z p***)   *Company collection (Best Foods Canada, Toronto, Ont.)
NOTES: The cover-title is 'Edwardsburg livret de recettes.' This French-language edition of 'Popular and Economical Recipes' corresponds to Q83.7.

Q83.9 [Serial No. 1], nd [about 1923]
—The secrets / of / menu variety / Prepared by / the Canada Starch Co., Limited / Montreal / Quebec Toronto Cardinal / Fort William Vancouver / Edwardsburg / products
DESCRIPTION: 17.0 × 12.5 cm   Pp [1] 2–63 [64–70] 71 [72]   Tp illus col of a maid with a tea tray, centre spread illus col of Edwardsburg products, illus col   Lacks binding; stapled
CONTENTS: 1 tp; 2–3 'Let Your First Thought Be the Ingredients'; 4 measurements and information about oven heat; 5–63 recipes; 64 index; 65–70 blank pages, first of which is headed 'Write Your Own Recipes on These Pages'; 71 book-order form; 72 'Serial No. 1'
COPIES: BBVM   OGU (CCC TX715.6 N48)   OTMCL (641.5971 S24)   *Private collection
NOTES: Another collector's copy and the OTMCL copy retain their paper binding: on the front face, in a rectangular frame, there is a still-life of a cake,

pie, and two salads; the cover-title is 'The New Edwardsburg Recipe Book.'

The introductory text states, 'For over 65 years some of these famous Edwardsburg products have been a household necessity ...' Since William Benson founded the Canada Starch Works in 1858, Serial No. 1 was published about 1923 (1858 + 65 years). The introductory text carries an endorsement from 'M. Thomas ... Chef of the Mount Royal, Canada's famous Hotel at Montreal, ...' Marcel Thomas, with others, selected and tested the recipes in NB33.1, *48 Famous Sardine Meals*.

Another collector's copy has a label on the back face of the binding indicating that her book was given away, compliments of the Groceteria, T. Eaton Co., Montreal. The OGU copy lacks pp 1–2 and the front face of the binding.

Q83.10   [Serial No. 1], nd [about 1923]
—Les secrets / de la / variété dans les menus / Préparé par / The Canada Starch Co., Limited / Montréal / Québec Toronto Cardinal / Fort-William Vancouver / Produits / Edwardsburg

DESCRIPTION: 17.0 × 12.5 cm   Pp [1] 2–63 [64–70] 71 [72]   Tp illus black-and-orange of a maid with a tea tray, centre spread illus col of Edwardsburg products, illus col   Paper, with image on front, above title, of prepared dishes; stapled

CONTENTS: 1 tp; 2–3 'Que votre première pensée soit pour les ingrédients'; 4 measurements and information about oven heat; 5–63 recipes; 64 'Tables des matières'; 65–70 blank pages, the first of which is headed 'Écrivez vos propres recettes sur ces pages'; 71 book-order form; 72 'Serial No. 1'

COPIES: *QMBN (176584 CON)

NOTES: The cover-title is 'Le nouveau livret de recettes Edwardsburg.' As in Q83.9, the introductory text on p 3 states, 'Depuis plus de 65 ans, ces fameux produits Edwardsburg sont des choses absolue nécessité dans la maison'; therefore, the French-language edition of Serial No. 1 was also published about 1923.

Q83.11   [Serial No. 5], nd [about 1926]
—The secrets / of / menu variety / prepared by / the Canada Starch Co., Limited / Montreal / Quebec Toronto Cardinal / Fort William Vancouver / Edwardsburg / products

DESCRIPTION: 17.0 × 12.5 cm   Pp [1] 2–66 [67–70] 71 [72]   Tp illus col of a maid with a tea tray, centre spread illus col of Edwardsburg products, illus col   Paper, with image on front of a woman pushing a tea trolley

CONTENTS: 1 tp; 2–3 'Let Your First Thought Be the Ingredients'; 4 measurements and information about oven heat; 5–65 recipes; 66 index; 67–70 blank pages, first of which is headed 'Write Your Own Recipes on These Pages'; 71 book-order form; 72 'Serial No. 5'

COPIES: ACG   APROM   MBDHM   SBIHM   *Company collection (Best Foods Canada, Toronto, Ontario)

NOTES: The cover-title is 'The New Edwardsburg Recipe Book.' The introductory text on p 3 states, 'For over 68 years Benson's Prepared Corn has been a household necessity ...' Serial No. 5, therefore, was published about 1926 (1858 + 68 years).

In Ferguson/Fraser, the reference on p 233 and the colour illustration on p 57 of the closed volume are likely of this edition, the one consulted by the authors for their *A Century of Canadian Home Cooking*.

OGU (CCC TX715.6 N48 1933 copy 2) has the book-order form with the serial number torn out; however, it may be this edition since the text refers to '68 years.' QGMG has a copy of an English-language edition, which may match Q83.11 or a later entry.

Q83.12   [Serial No. 5], nd
—Les secrets / de la / variété dans les menus / préparé par / The Canada Starch Co., Limited / Montréal / Québec Toronto Cardinal / Fort-William Vancouver / Produits / Edwardsburg

DESCRIPTION: 17.5 × 12.5 cm   Pp [1] 2, 9–63 [64], 71 [72]   Tp illus col of a maid with a tea tray, centre spread illus col of Edwardsburg products, illus col   Paper, with image on front of prepared dishes in a rectangular frame; stapled

CONTENTS: 1 tp; 2 'Que votre première pensée soit pour les ingrédients'; 9–63 recipes; 64 'Tables des matières'; 71 book-order form; 72 'Serial No. 5'

COPIES: *OONL (TX715.6 S377 1940 p***)

NOTES: The cover-title is 'Le nouveau livret de recettes Edwardsburg.' Although the index lists recipes on pp 4, 5, 6, and 7, this copy has no pp 3–8 bound in and no blank pages between the index and the book-order form.

Q83.13   [Serial No. 10], nd [about 1927]
—The secrets / of / menu variety / prepared by / the Canada Starch Co., Limited / Montreal / Quebec Toronto Cardinal / Fort William Vancouver / Edwardsburg / products

DESCRIPTION: 17.0 × 12.5 cm   Pp [1] 2–66 [67–72]   Tp illus black-and-orange of a maid with a tea tray, centre spread illus col of Edwardsburg products, illus col   Paper, with image on front of a woman pushing a tea trolley

CONTENTS: 1 tp; 2–3 'Let Your First Thought Be the Ingredients'; 4 measurements and information about oven heat; 5–65 recipes; 66 index; 67–71 blank pages, first of which is headed 'Write Your Own Recipes on These Pages'; 72 'Serial No. 10'
COPIES: BDUCVM NSLQCM OKQ (F5012 nd C212Ne) QKB (87-74) QMM (RBD uncat) *Private collection
NOTES: The cover-title is 'The New Edwardsburg Recipe Book.' The introductory text on p 3 states, 'For over 69 years Benson's Prepared Corn has been a household necessity ...' Serial No. 10, therefore, was published about 1927 (1858 + 69 years).

Q83.14 [Serial No. 14], nd [about 1927]
—Les secrets / de la / variété dans les menus / Préparé par / The Canada Starch Co., Limited / Montréal / Québec Toronto Cardinal / Fort-William Vancouver / Produits / Edwardsburg
DESCRIPTION: 17.0 × 12.5 cm Pp [1] 2–66 [67–72] Tp illus black-and-orange of a maid with a tea tray, centre spread illus col of Edwardsburg products, illus col Paper, with image on front of a woman pushing a tea trolley; stapled
CONTENTS: 1 tp; 2–3 'Que votre première pensée soit pour les ingrédients'; 4 measurements and information about oven heat; 5–65 recipes; 66 'Tables des matières'; 67–71 blank pages, first of which is headed 'Écrivez vos propres recettes sur ces pages'; 72 'Serial No. 14'
COPIES: *QMBN (153603 CON)
NOTES: The cover-title is 'Le nouveau livret de recettes Edwardsburg.' The introductory text on p 3 states, 'Depuis plus de 69 ans, le Maïs Préparé Benson est un article de première nécessité ...' Serial No. 14, therefore, was published about 1927 (1858 + 69 years). In 1930, the Canada Starch Co. published a new cookbook, Q177.1, *Canada's Prize Recipes*.

Recipes ancient and modern

The Duke of Wellington Chapter of the IODE was formed in March 1911. In 1974 it amalgamated with two other chapters in the city (Sir Dudley Pound Chapter, Fifty-Third Regiment Chapter) to form the Sherbrooke Chapter.

Q84.1 nd [about 1914–18]
Recipes / ancient and modern / Compiled by / Duke of Wellington Chapter / of the / Imperial

Order of Daughters / of the Empire.
DESCRIPTION: 22.5 × 15.0 cm Pp [1–2] 3–30, [i–vi] Paper; stapled
CONTENTS: 1 tp; 2 'Index' [i.e., table of contents]; 3–30 recipes; i–vi ads
CITATIONS: Ferguson/Fraser, pp 44 and 233, illus col on p 35 of closed volume
COPIES: QSHERSH (641.5 W452w) *Private collection
NOTES: The cover-title is 'War Time Cook Book for the Benefit of Our Soldiers and Sailors by Daughters of the Empire.' The advertisements are for businesses in Sherbrooke, Quebec, where the Duke of Wellington Chapter was based. One of the modern recipes is Ginger Ale Salad on p 10, described as 'the latest novelty in salads.'

1915

Cook book

Q85.1 April 1915
Cook book / Economical recipes for the women / of Canada during the war / Compiled by / the Longfellow Chapter of the Imperial / Order of the Daughters of the Empire / Waterloo, Quebec / April, 1915 / Proceeds of sale to be devoted to / work for the soldiers
DESCRIPTION: 22.0 × 15.5 cm Pp [1–2] 3–32 Paper; stapled
CONTENTS: 1 tp; 2 'Index' [i.e., table of contents]; 3–32 recipes credited with the name of the contributor
COPIES: CIHM (9-92259) *QKB (80-7) QSH

The cook book

Q86.1 1915
The / cook book / edited by the / Westmount Soldiers' / Wives' League / Westmount, Canada.
DESCRIPTION: 22.5 × 15.0 cm Pp [1–5] 6–106 [107–21] Small tp illus of soldier (2 cm high) Thin card, with image on front, drawn in art-nouveau style, of a woman carrying a plate; stapled
CONTENTS: 1 tp; 2 blank; 3 'Objects of Publication'; 4 'Grateful acknowledgement to A.G. Racey, for cover design and to A.S. Brodeur // A. Bourgeois // F. de Quoy // G. La Tour // P. Leclerq // M. Boisvert // Nap. Savard for heading sketches'; 5 'The Crown of

Empire' by Frederick George Scott, 1st Canadian Division, France, December 1915; 6 'Good Rules of Housekeeping' and 'How to Preserve a Husband'; 7–101 recipes; 102 'Table of Measures'; 103–4 'Odds & Ends'; 105–6 'Quotations'; 107–16 ads; 117–21 table of contents

COPIES: *NBMOM

NOTES: The aim of publication, according to p 3, was 'to augment [the league's] Treasury and provide further comforts, etc., for "Our Soldier Boys at the Front."' Arthur G. Racey (1870–1941), who did the cover design, was a cartoonist at the *Montreal Star* at the time *The Cook Book* was published. Albert Samuel Brodeur, Albéric Bourgeois, Georges La Tour (worked for *La patrie* from 1898; died 1946), and Napoléon Savard were book illustrators.

Excellent recipes for baking raised breads

For the titles of other books about cooking with Fleischmann's Yeast, see O131.1.

Q87.1 copyright 1915
Form 481 D Rev. Can. / Excellent recipes / for / baking raised breads / also directions for making / refreshing summer drinks / (Index page 46) / Send one of these books / to your friends – See page 47 / Copyright, 1915, by / the Fleischmann Company
DESCRIPTION: 17.0 × 12.0 cm   Pp [1] 2–47 [48]   Small tp illus of a wheat sheaf; 1 double-sided pl col btwn pp 12–13, 2 double-sided pls col btwn pp 24–5 (i.e., the centre spread is a double-sided colour plate), 1 double-sided pl col btwn pp 36–7   [Free, on p 47]   Paper, with image on front of a woman in a red-striped dress removing a loaf of bread from an oven; stapled, and with hole punched at top left corner for hanging
CONTENTS: 1 tp; 2–6 'Valuable Suggestions on the Use of Fleischmann's Yeast'; 7–45 recipes; 46 index, notice about a new Fleischmann's cookbook ('"Good Things to Eat Made with Bread" by Marion H. Neil,' possibly an edition of Q103.1, *Sixty-five Delicious Dishes Made with Bread*), and 'The Fleischmann Company // Montreal Toronto St. John Winnipeg Calgary Vancouver'; 47 order form for the company's cookbooks; 48 'The Fleischmann Co. Agencies throughout the Dominion of Canada and St. John's, Newfoundland.'
CITATIONS: Garrett, p 131
COPIES: BSUM   QKB   *Private collection
NOTES: The cover-title is 'Fleischmann's Recipes.' The

refreshing summer drinks are Lemon Pop, Root Beer, Kumyss, and Dandelion Wine (pp 43–5).

'Our book, "Excellent Recipes for Baking"' is advertised by the Fleischmann Co. on p 221 of O347.1, *Red Cross Cook Book*, published in Newmarket, Ontario, in 1915. Before this Canadian edition of *Excellent Recipes for Baking Raised Breads* was published in 1915, Canadian cooks could order an American edition, as p 2 of the 1910 Cincinnati edition explains: 'One of these recipe books will be mailed free of charge to any address in the United States, or Canada, upon request ... The Fleischmann Co., No. 427 Plum Street, Cincinnati, Ohio.' The fact that copies of American editions are found in Canadian public collections confirms that Canadians did place orders.

Q87.2 copyright 1917
—Form 481D Rev. Can. / Excellent recipes / for / baking raised / breads / also directions for making / refreshing / summer drinks / Index page forty-six / Send one of these books to your friends / See page forty-seven / The Fleischmann Company / Copyright 1917
DESCRIPTION: 17.0 × 11.5 cm   Pp [1] 2–47 [48]   1 double-sided pl col btwn pp 12–13, 2 double-sided pls col btwn pp 24–5 (i.e., the centre spread is a double-sided colour plate), 1 double-sided pl col btwn pp 36–7   [Free, on p 47]   Paper, with image on front of a woman in a red-striped dress removing a loaf of bread from an oven; stapled
CONTENTS: 1 tp; 2–6 'Valuable Suggestions on the Use of Fleischmann's Yeast'; 7–45 recipes; 46 index; 47 order form for Fleischmann's cookbooks; 48 'The Fleischmann Co. Agencies throughout the Dominion of Canada and Newfoundland.'
COPIES: AWWDM BSUM MWPA NSHMS (84.92.12) NSWA OGU (CCC TX715.6 E92) QMBM (Env. 7865) SRRPM *Private collection
NOTES: The plates in the 1917 edition differ from those in the 1915 edition. The OGU copy has a different image on the binding: a woman in a yellow dress and a blue-and-white checked apron, cutting a loaf of bread, and a child beside her. The BSUM copy lacks its binding.

AMERICAN EDITIONS: New York and Cincinnati: Fleischmann Co., [copyright 1910] (ACHP, BDEM, BKOM, OSMFHHM; Wheaton/Kelly No. 2168); New York and Cincinnati: Fleischmann Co., copyright 1912 (APROM); Cincinnati: 1914 (Wheaton/Kelly No. 2169); 1915 (Longone/Longone, illus in Photo R; Wheaton/Kelly No. 2170); New York: Fleischmann

Co., copyright 1916, 'Form 481 D Rev.' (United States: InU; Cagle/Stafford No. 943, illus; Wheaton/Kelly No. 2171); [New York:] Fleischmann Co., copyright 1917 (BDUCVM; United States: InU); New York, Chicago: copyright 1920 (Wheaton/Kelly No. 2172).

1915–18

New book of practical cooking recipes and household hints

Q88.1   nd [about 1915–18]
New book / of / practical cooking / recipes / and / household hints / specially prepared for the / Canadian housewife / Presented by / the St. Lawrence Flour Mills Co., Limited / Montreal
DESCRIPTION: 22.0 × 15.0 cm   Pp [1–4] 5–128   Illus   Paper; stapled
CONTENTS: 1 tp; 2 blank; 3–4 introductory text signed St Lawrence Flour Mills Co. Ltd, Montreal; 5–128 text
COPIES: NBDKH   *Private collection
NOTES: The cover-title (transcribed from a photocopy of the NBDKH copy) is 'Regal / The / flour / which makes / possible the / delicious cakes / and pastry that / satisfy the ex- / perienced house- / wife / Pastries that are / crisp, delicious, / and gratifying.' There is an image on the front face of the binding of a woman holding a cake on a plate in her right hand and resting her left hand on a 24-pound sack of Regal Flour produced by the St Lawrence Flour Mills Co. Ltd, Montreal, Quebec.

This is probably the first of several cookbooks published by St Lawrence Flour Mills since there is no reference in the introductory text to other company cookbooks. The text on p 3 indicates that the cookbook was published during the First World War, when it refers to 'the enormous purchases of [St Lawrence] flours, to feed the armies at the front.' Mr Thomas Williamson and General A.E. Labelle are named as the 'heads of this great enterprise,' i.e., of the company.

According to the Personnel Records Unit at OOA, Alfred E. Damase Labelle had joined the Canadian Expeditionary Force (CEF) in the rank of colonel on 22 September 1914, and was appointed to the rank of brigadier (the first rank of general) on 21 October 1915, under General Order 129 of 1915. He left the CEF to return to the Permanent Force on 30 May 1920 (keeping his rank of brigadier). The cookbook was published no earlier than October 1915, when Labelle was made a brigadier. The entry for Labelle in Morgan, p 623, states that in 1910 Labelle retired from his

job as sales manager at Ogilvie Flour Mills to become managing director of St Lawrence Flour Mills Co.

I have not compared the text of this cookbook with others by St Lawrence Flour Mills to see whether they are related, i.e., Q143.1, *The 'Regal' Cook Book*; Q160.1, *The Jubilee Recipe Book*; and Q191.1, *The Regal Recipe Book*.

Q88.2   nd [about 1915–18]
—Nouveau livre / de / recettes pratiques / de / cuisine et d'économie / domestique / a l'usage des / familles canadiennes / Offert par / The St. Lawrence Flour Mills Co., Limited / Montreal
DESCRIPTION: 22.0 × 15.0 cm   Pp [1–5] 6–128   Illus   Thin card, with image on front of a woman carrying a cake on a plate; stapled
CONTENTS: 1 tp; 2 blank; 3–4 introductory text signed St Lawrence Flour Mills Co. Ltd, Montreal; 5–128 text
CITATIONS: BQ 23-4929
COPIES: *QMBN (158974 CON)
NOTES: The French-language edition also refers to 'des quantités énormes de ces farines pour l'alimentation des armées sur le front'; however, only General A.E. Labelle (and not Thomas Williamson) is named as 'l'âme dirigeante de ce grand établissement.' QMBN incorrectly dates this edition [194–?].

1915–19

Guide de la bonne cuisinière

Q89.1   nd [about 1915–19]
Guide / de la / bonne cuisiniere / Offert par / l'imprimerie "Le St-Laurent", limitée / Atelier de typographie moderne / Impressions en tous genres / à des prix modérés. / Demandez nos prix. / Fraserville, P.Q. [cover-title]
DESCRIPTION: 22.0 × 14.0 cm [dimensions from photocopy]   Paper; stapled
COPIES: *QRMSF
NOTES: Although the 'Introduction,' which is on p 7 (probably the first page), is written in the first person singular, the author is not identified by name. The 'Introduction' has the following sub-headings: 'Propreté et entretien de la cuisine'; 'Du service de la table'; 'Des proportions'; and 'Généralités.' The volume has 52 pp.   QRMSF's curator reports that, according to Mme Marthe Paré, 'fille du propriétaire,' the cookbook was published about 1915, a date that is consistent with the appearance of the volume. It could not have been published after 1919, when Fraserville became Rivière-du-Loup.

1915–20

For your kitchen

The Catelli brand had its start in 1867, when Carlo Onorato (Charles Honoré) Catelli, formerly of Vedano, Italy, established Montreal's first pasta plant, on St Paul Street, where macaroni and vermicelli were made by hand (Catelli web site, May 2004). Montreal city directories list the Catelli family in the 1860s, in the statuary business, but the first reference to pasta-making is in the directory for 1870–1, where Pietro Catelli is described as a manufacturer of macaroni, vermicelli, and Italian paste, at 59 Perthius, and living at 318 Craig. It was a family business: the 1872–3 directory lists three Catellis – Pietro, Charles, and Charles Jr, 'of Cattelli [sic] & frère, cooks and vermicelli manufacturers' – all living at 318 Craig. The corporate name, C.H. Catelli Co. Ltd, first appears in the city directory for 1910–11.

Q90.1   nd [about 1915–20]
For your kitchen / 6 / exquisite / varieties / L'Étoile / macaroni, / spaghetti, / vermicelli, etc. / The C.H. Catelli Co. Limited. / Montreal, Canada. [cover-title]
DESCRIPTION: 15.0 × 8.5 cm   Pp 1–22   Illus of packages of L'Étoile-brand pasta and of dishes of steaming pasta   Paper, with image on front, in an oval frame, of a woman holding up a box of L'Étoile pasta, five other varieties on the table beside her; stapled
CONTENTS: 1–mid 3 untitled note about 'macaroni, spaghetti, vermicelli, noodles and the smaller kinds of pastes'; mid–bottom 3 'Preliminary Hints on Cooking L'Étoile Pastes'; 4–22 recipes for pasta dishes
COPIES: *Private collection
NOTES: There is an illustration, on the outside back face of the binding, of 'View of the C.H. Catelli Co., Limited, factory, Montréal, 5 stories. 120 ft. × 150 ft. total area: 90.000 ft.' This is the building at 201 Comte East, later called Bellechasse, where the company relocated in about 1911; therefore, *For Your Kitchen* was published no earlier than 1911. (In May 2001, the factory building was still standing, and the Catelli name, painted on the brick wall, was worn but still visible.) On p 1, pasta is promoted as an aid to economy since '[t]he high cost of living is getting more and more acute; ...' Another Canadian cookbook of about 1916 addressed the same problem (O361.1, *Helps to Overcome the High Cost of Living*), an indication that *For Your Kitchen* was published as prices rose during the First World War. If, however, mechanization in 1920 allowed the company to make spaghetti and other special shapes (Catelli web site, May 2004), then *For Your Kitchen* was published later,

in about 1920. Whatever the date, it likely preceded the company's other cookbook, Q114.1, *The Girl at Catelli's*.

Le compagnon de la ménagère

Other publications from the same company are Q39.1 and Q43.1.

Q91.1   nd [about 1915–20]
Le compagnon / de la / ménagère / Dr. Ed. Morin & cie, limitée. / Quebec, Canada. / Avec conseils vétérinaires. [cover-title]
DESCRIPTION: 17.0 × 13.0 cm   Pp 1–32   Illus portrait on p 1 of Dr Édouard Morin   Paper, with image on front of a woman at a kitchen table, measuring flour(?) from a sack; stapled
CONTENTS: Inside front face of binding 'Poids et mesures'; 1 'Feu le Dr Édouard Morin'; 2 publ ad; 3–8 'Conseils à la ménagère' and publ ads; 9 publ ad; 10–15 'Recettes de cuisine' and publ ads; 16–17 publ ads; 18–26 'Conseils vétérinaires' and publ ads; 27 publ ads; 28–mid 30 'L'âge des chevaux' and publ ads; mid–bottom 30 'Le soin des jeunes enfants'; 31 publ ads; 32 'Pour prédire le temps'
COPIES: *QMM (RBD uncat)
NOTES: The biography of Dr Morin on p 1 says that he was born on 1 April 1854, in Quebec City, became a doctor in 1878, then practised medicine in Quebec City for seven years, after which he established a drug business. He died in June 1909, and two years later, 'le tuteur qui administrait les affaires de la succession forma une compagnie ... Les succès de la compagnie du Dr Édouard Morin ltée, ont toujours grandi d'année en année, ...' The 1901 Census gives a slightly later birth date, 20 April 1854; in 1901 he was living with his wife, Georgiana, and five sons and three daughters. The advertisements are for the company's pharmaceutical products, such as Pilles Cardinales, Crême des dames parisiennes, and Élixir d'huile de foie de morue. The QMM copy is stamped, 'Vendu par H, [*sic*]E. Menard 2542 N.D.O.'

1915–25

Bliss cook book

Q92.1   nd [about 1915–25]
Bliss cook book / Livre de / cuisine / de Bliss / Published by / the Alonzo O. / Bliss Medical / Company / Montreal, Can. / Presented by: Presente par: / [blank space] [cover-title]

DESCRIPTION: 23.0 × 14.5 cm   Pp [1] 2–35   Portraits of testimonial writers   Paper, with image on front of stout chef; stapled

CONTENTS: 1 cover-title; 2–5 information about Bliss Native Herbs; 6–31 recipes, and testimonials for Bliss Native Herbs; 32–5 [inside back face of binding] information about Bliss Native Herbs

COPIES: *Private collection

NOTES: Each page has a vertical rule that divides the text into two columns, one English and one French. The first section of recipes is for 'Invalid Cookery.' On the outside back face of the binding, there is an illustration of the Bliss Building and the comment: 'It is the house-wife's duty to look after the health of the family, as well as the kitchen economy. This useful book will help you do both.' Bliss Native Herbs were sold for medical, not culinary purposes.

The address of the company on p 35 – 124 St Paul Street East, Montreal – helps to date the book. The company is first listed at this address in the Montreal city directory for 1915–16 and it remained there at least into the mid-1920s. The introductory text states, 'Over twenty-seven years ago, Alonzo O. Bliss, the maker of Bliss Native Herbs, began compounding this well known remedy ...' Knowing the year that Bliss Native Herbs were introduced to the market would date the book more precisely. The first listing for the business in Montreal city directories is in the volume for 1897–8, and twenty-seven years after 1897 was 1924; however, if Alonzo Bliss began his compounding in Washington, DC (the American location cited in the cover-title of Q93.1, *Bliss Native Herbs Cookbook*) or elsewhere than Montreal, then the calculation of the year of publication might be different. Nevertheless, the appearance of this book and Q93.1, which bears the same address, is consistent with publication in the period 1915–25.

In another collector's copy, 'Andrew Mittleholtz, Zurich, Ont.' is stamped on the front face of the binding, in the blank space under 'Presented by:'; another collector's copy has 'Mde. H. Cimon, 88a King Street, Sherbrooke' in the blank space.

Bliss Native Herbs cookbook

Q93.1   nd [about 1915–25]

Bliss / Native / Herbs / cookbook / Published by / Alonzo O. Bliss Medical Co., / 124 St. Paul St., East, Montreal, Canada. / Bliss Building, Washington, D.C. [cover-title]

DESCRIPTION: 22.5 × 15.0 cm   Pp [1] 2–35   Paper, with image on front of a woman standing before a

kitchen cupboard and consulting a cookbook; stapled, and with hole punched at top left corner for hanging

CONTENTS: 1 cover-title; 2, 4, 6, 8, 10, 12, 14, 16, 18, 20, 22, 24, 26, 28, 30, 32, 34 'Beauty,' 'La beauté'; 3 'Soups, Broths,' 'Soupes'; 5 'Fish,' 'Poisson'; 7, 9 'Meats,' 'Viandes'; 11 'Game,' 'Volailles, Gibiers'; 13 'Eggs,' 'Oeufs'; 15 'Vegetables,' 'Légumes'; 17 'Salads,' 'Salades'; 19 'Bread, Biscuits,' 'Pain, Biscuits'; 21 'Puddings,' 'Poudings'; 23 'Pies,' 'Tartes'; 25, 27 'Cakes,' 'Gâteaux'; 29 'Pastry,' 'Pâtisseries'; 31 'Ices, Drinks,' 'Breuvages'; 33, 35 'Jellies, Preserves,' 'Confitures et marmelades'

COPIES: CIHM (9-92244)   ONLAM (Walters-Wagar Collection, Box 20)   *Private collection

NOTES: Each page has two columns of text: one in English, one in French. The testimonials are all from Canadian towns across the country. The book records branches of the company in Kansas City, Missouri, London, England, San Francisco, California, and Kadina, South Australia. Regarding the date of publication, see Q92.1.

The private collector's copy is stamped on the front face of the binding, 'E.A. St. Dizier // Massawippi Que.' The ONLAM copy is stamped on the front face, 'Wallace's Drug Store Ltd // Prescription druggist // Napanee Ont.'

1916

Art culinaire

For references to other books produced by the same school in St Pascal, see Q134.1, L'économie domestique à l'école primaire ... IIIe année. St Pascal is on the south shore of the St Lawrence River, northeast of Quebec City.

Q94.1   1916

Art culinaire / Différentes manières d'utiliser les restes / et / quelques recettes culinaires / à l'usage des malades. / [symbol of École normale classico-ménagère, Congrégation de Notre-Dame, and below symbol:] / Saint-Pascal / Co Kamouraska. / P.Q. / 1916 / Publié pour la partie d'ens. ménager / des "Cours abrégés d'Agriculture".

DESCRIPTION: 17.5 × 10.5 cm   Pp [i–ii], [1] 2–64   Paper; stapled

CONTENTS: i tp; ii blank; 1–60 text; 61–4 'Tables des matières'

COPIES: CIHM (79169)   *OONL (TX715.6 A777 1916 p***)   QQL (B.C. 1916 005)   QQLA (TX651 A784 1916)

NOTES: The following is printed on the outside back

face of the binding: 'Des ateliers d'imprimerie, de papeterie et de reliure de A.E. Mignault, St-Pascal, Que. Tel. Kam. no62 [*sic*, no space before '62'].'

Harrison, Mrs Grace Eugenie Clergue (1869–1944), and Miss Alice Gertrude Clergue (Bangor, Maine, 1871–20 August 1951, Montreal, Que.)

Gertrude and Grace were the youngest sisters in a family of five girls and three boys born to a French father (Joseph Hector Clergue) and an American mother (Frances Clarissa Lombard). Their childhood home was in Bangor, Maine. One brother, Francis Hector Clergue, is remembered for his pioneering industrial development in Sault Sainte Marie, Ontario, where his business concerns encompassed water power, pulp and paper, steel, and a railway. An article about Gertrude in the column 'Canadian Women in the Public Eye,' Saturday Night *(18 August 1923), lists her pursuits (sports, art, literature, journalism, love of animals, patriotism, and social service), names the many clubs and organizations to which she belonged, and reproduces her portrait. At the time of the article, in 1923, Gertrude was living with her brother Francis on Sherbrooke Street in Montreal, and the two had recently acquired a farm at St Bruno; Grace was living in London, England.*

See also the entry for Gertrude in Biographical Cyclopaedia, Vol. 1, pp 376–7. OSTM has biographical information about the Clergue family on file, including a typescript of a newspaper article about the wedding of Grace and William Lynde Harrison on 12 November 1900 ('A Brilliant Society Event,' Bangor Daily News, *13 November 1900, p 2), and a photograph of Gertrude's gravestone. Gertrude's obituary is in the* Gazette *(Montreal), 21 August 1951. Grace is buried in the Castine Town Cemetery, Maine, Section I, Lot 363.*

See also Q236.1, Delectable Dishes, *compiled by Gertrude for the Women's Guild of St George's Church, to which she belonged. She also contributed recipes to O84.1,* Culinary Landmarks, *published by the Woman's Auxiliary of St Luke's Cathedral in Sault Ste Marie.*

Q95.1 [1916]
British / French Italian Russian / Belgian / cookery / Arranged by / Grace Clergue Harrison / and / Gertrude Clergue / to aid the war sufferers in the devastated districts of France / Introduction by / Hon. Raoul Dandurand / Commandeur de la Légion d'honneur / Preface by / Prof. Stephen Leacock / McGill University, Montreal. [cover-title]

DESCRIPTION: 21.5 × 14.5 cm   Pp [1–6] 7–38   [$0.50, on p 1]   Paper, with image on front of five flags; stapled

CONTENTS: 1 'The Purpose' signed Mrs Wm Lynde Harrison, Milestone House, Branford, Connecticut, and Miss Gertrude Clergue, 597 Sherbrooke Street West, Montreal; 2 'Copyright, Canada 1916, by Gertrude Clergue.'; 3–4 'Allied Food (A special preface written for this volume and inserted only after strong protest from the editors)' by Stephen Leacock; 5–6 letter in French to Mrs Harrison and Miss Clergue from Raoul Dandurand, Comité France-Amérique (Section canadienne), chambre-31, Édifice 'Duluth,' Montréal; 7 recipe for Charlotte de pommes from Elise Jusserand, Ambassade de France aux États-Unis, 2 March 1916; 8–38 recipes, many identified by nationality

CITATIONS: Biographical Cyclopaedia, Vol. 1, p 376   JPCat 130, No. 84   O'Neill (unpublished)   Saturday Night (18 August 1923)   Spadoni 1998 B4a

COPIES: CIHM (87619)   OONL (TX725 A1 A45 1916 reserve)   OTNY (uncat)   *OTUTF (cap); Great Britain: LB (07945.k.51 destroyed)

NOTES: The OONL and OTNY copies have a tipped-in errata slip opposite p 1, where the compilers regret the errors caused in the haste to produce the book 'in time to help in the planting season [i.e., spring] of 1916.' On p 1, they state: 'The purpose of this little book is to procure funds in aid of the farmers in that part of France which was devastated by the invasion of the German armies, but which was subsequently regained by the French ... Its proceeds will be destributed [*sic*] by Le secours national, of France, ... The recipes have been arranged with the kind aid of many house keeping friends; we believe the collection comprises some that will be novel to many households, ...'

The OTUTF copy has no errata slip and there is no sign that one was tipped in. None of the errata has been corrected in the OTUTF copy, except the first-listed erratum, which indicates that 'so distinctive' should be substituted for 'no distinctive' on p 3; in the OTUTF copy, the 'n' is erased and 's' added by hand, with pen and ink. There are no handwritten corrections in the OTNY copy.

Many of the recipes are identified as from the five allied countries of the title and/or as contributed by particular persons, mostly chefs; a few are specified as Canadian (Leg of Mutton Pie, Canadian, from A.A.B., chef; Rillettes de Tours, Cretons canadiens; Oat Cakes, Canadian; Gingerbread, Gaspé Fashion); there is one Japanese recipe, Salmon Teriyaki. The contributing chefs were from Montreal institutions:

A.A.B. of the Mount Royal Club; H.S. of the Ritz-Carlton Hotel; A.L. of the Windsor Hotel; and J.T. of the Engineers Club. H.S. is Henry Schneider, author of Q67.1, *Practical Cookery*.

Stephen Leacock may have been asked to contribute the 'special preface' because of his own fundraising efforts for the Belgium Relief Fund. As Spadoni 1998 B4a states, Leacock had been giving public readings of his work for the cause in February 1916, about the time the cookbook was being produced.

The printer, 'Consolidated Lithographing & Manufacturing Co., Limited, Montreal,' is on the inside back face of the binding. Spadoni 1998 B4a states that the OONL copy has '4200' stamped on the inside front face of the binding, suggesting a print run of that number.

The *Saturday Night* profile of Gertrude Clergue says of *Allied Cookery*: 'During some years of travel [in?] many countries, previous to the war, the sisters collected recipes of various appetising dishes, so the book much later resulted, is of unique [tone?] for its international character ... The "Figaro" thought the book of sufficient importance to devote a leading article of one and a half columns to it. The work was very successful, and in recognition of [Gertrude Clergue's] services the French Government bestowed upon her the decoration of the Médaille de la Reconnaissance francaise.'

A typescript at OSTM describes the cookbook's launch in the summer of 1917 (i.e., after production of both the Canadian and American editions), in the garden of Gertrude's home on Sherbrooke Street in Montreal:

It's [sic] cause ... attracted personnages of influence and importance. Jusserand the French ambassador to Washington, George Haven Putnam, the publisher, and President Taft gave rousing speeches. The Clergues enjoyed doing things in style. Allied flags decorated the tables and trees. Bands played the National anthems. The white cockatoo raised his yellow crest and swore in Portuguese and the little black scottie ran to hide in the house.

AMERICAN EDITIONS: The one American edition followed the smaller, 38-page Canadian edition. The American edition, which has a title-page, was retitled: 'Allied / cookery / British / French / Italian / Belgian / Russian / arranged by / Grace Clergue Harrison / and / Gertrude Clergue / to aid the war sufferers in the devastated districts / of France /

Introduction by / Hon. Raoul Dandurand / Commandeur de la Légion d'honneur / Prefaced by / Stephen Leacock and Ella Wheeler Wilcox / G.P. Putnam's Sons / New York and London / The Knickerbocker Press / 1916' (OONL, OTUTF, QMM; United States: DLC, InU; cited in Barile, pp 77, 177, illus p 77, Cagle/Stafford No. 337, Claflin, p 4, Longone/Longone Q4 with illus, and Spadoni 1998 B4b). The OTUTF copy of the American edition is inscribed on the front endpaper, 'To Mrs LeMoyne from J.[O.?] Vaughan Xmas 1916,' which indicates that the American edition was on sale by December 1916. It includes a table of contents and Ella Wheeler Wilcox's 'Foreword,' neither of which is found in the Canadian edition. It has more pages (108) and more recipes, which are now arranged in sections: 'Soups'; 'Fish'; 'Meats and Entrées'; 'Curries'; 'Pastes, Cheese, etc'; 'Sauces'; 'Salads'; 'Vegetables'; and 'Puddings, Cakes, etc.' In the case of the recipes common to both editions, some recipe titles vary; for example, Salmon Tidnish contributed by H.L. in the Canadian edition is Salmon Tidnish (Canadian) with no named contributor in the American edition. There are minor revisions to the text throughout, including 'The Purpose' by the compilers, Leacock's essay (Spadoni B4a specifies the differences between the essays), Dandurand's letter (titled 'Introduction' in the American edition), and occasional slight rewordings of the recipes; in the American edition, Dandurand's letter precedes, rather than follows, Leacock's essay.

The American edition appears to have been the source for several recipes in Q119.1, *The Tried and True Cook Book of St George's,* which is not surprising since Gertrude Clergue was a member of St George's Church.

FRENCH EDITIONS: The one French edition is titled *La cuisine des alliés: recettes américaines, anglaises, belges, françaises, italiennes, japonaises, russes, serbes, etc.,* Paris: L'Édition française illustrée, 1918, pp 128, price 3 francs (OONL). It retains the Wilcox preface, excludes Leacock's, and has a new preface by Monsieur Gabriel Hanotaux, président du Comité France-Amérique. Hanotaux describes the French edition as 'revue, et augmentée de savoureuses nouveautés'; he adds, 'Déja Mmes Clergue ont souscrit 2000 exemplaires pour l'Amérique et pour le Canada.' Claflin, p 4, states, 'This volume ..., translated into French in a 1918 Paris edition, was so successful that its authors, Grace Clergue Harrison and Gertrude Clergue, were awarded the French Legion of Honor.'

1917

Grisé, Joseph-Évariste (1892–)

Grisé also wrote Q184.1, Bulletin 102, Les conserves, for the Department of Agriculture. For the titles of other cookbooks published by the department, see Q48.1.

Q96.1   September 1917
Ministere de l'Agriculture de la province de Quebec / Service de l'horticulture septembre, 1917 / Bulletin no 49 / De la fabrication des / conserves alimentaires / a la maison / par / J.E. Grisé, B.S.A. / [Quebec provincial symbol] / Publié par ordre de l'hon. Jos.-Ed. Caron, ministre de l'Agriculture de la province de Québec.
DESCRIPTION: 24.0 × 16.0 cm   Pp [1–5] 6–69 [70–1] 8 pls, illus   Cloth
CONTENTS: 1 tp; 2 'Tous droits réservés'; 3 'Introduction' signed J.-É. Grisé, Québec, le 10 septembre 1917; 4 'Explications utiles aux lecteurs'; 5–65 text in four parts; 66 blank; 67–9 'Table des matières'; 70 blank; 71 'Errata'
CITATIONS: Beaulieu, p 99   Bibliothèque municipale de Montréal, p 4   Carrière No. 266
COPIES: *OONL (TX603 G75 1917 p***) QMBN (A38A1 P83 49 OFF); Great Britain: LB (C.S.E. 322/5)
NOTES: The author's first names are not printed in the book; they are noted at QMBN and in the British Library copyright records. The OONL copy is stamped on the inside front face of the binding, 'Copy deposited No. [inscribed: '33799']'; the following is printed in the gutter of the front endpaper: 'Jeremie Richard relieur, regleur, et imprimeur Quebec.' The 'Introduction' of the French-language edition is dated one day earlier than Q96.2.

Q96.2   September 1917
—Department of Agriculture of the Province of Quebec / Horticultural Service September, 1917 / Bulletin No 49 / Home canning of / food products / by / J.E. Grisé, B.S.A. / [Quebec provincial symbol] / Published by order of the Hon. Jos.-Ed. Caron, Minister of Agriculture of the Province of Quebec.
DESCRIPTION: 23.5 × 16.0 cm   Pp [1–5] 6–69 [70–1] 8 pls, illus   Cloth
CONTENTS: 1 tp; 2 'All rights reserved'; 3 'Introduction' signed J.É. Grisé, Quebec, 11 September 1917; 4 'Useful Explanations to Readers' [glossary of terms]; 5–65 text in four parts; 66 blank; 67–9 'Index' [i.e., table of contents]; 70 blank; 71 'Errata'
CITATIONS: Beaulieu, p 99   O'Neill (unpublished)

COPIES: *OONL (TX603 G752 1917 p***); Great Britain: LB (C.S.E. 322/5)
NOTES: The OONL copy is stamped on the inside front face of the binding, 'Copy deposited No. [inscribed: '33800']'; the following is printed in the gutter of the front endpaper: 'Jeremie Richard relieur, regleur, et imprimeur Quebec.'

In the 'Introduction' Grisé refers to 'the continual increase in the price of canned goods and the considerable annual losses of the sub-products of the vegetable-garden.' He indicates that the book is to assist the 'District Representatives, the Household Science Schools and the Women's Institutes in their home economics propaganda and ... [to give] a new impetus to this branch of agriculture [i.e., the branch concerned with the preservation of animal and vegetable food products].'

Q96.3   1918
—[Another edition of *De la fabrication des conserves alimentaires à la maison. Bulletin 49*, Quebec: 1918]
CITATIONS: O'Neill (unpublished)
COPIES: Great Britain: LB (not located)

Q96.4   1919
—[Another edition, titled *Préparation de conserves de légumes, de fruits et de viandes* [cover-title], 'Résumé du Bulletin no 49,' [Quebec City:] ministère de l'Agriculture, Service de l'horticulture, 1919, pp 16, illus]
COPIES: QMBN (161611 CON)
NOTES: A shorter version of the résumé appeared a year earlier: Beaulieu, p 99, states, 'On a publié un résumé [of the 1917 edition of *De la fabrication des conserves alimentaires à la maison*]: *Préparation de conserves de légumes, de fruits et de viandes.* (1918), 7p.'

Q96.5   [new ed.], 1921
—[New edition of *Préparation de conserves de légumes, de fruits et de viandes* [cover-title], Bulletin 49, [Quebec City:] ministère de l'Agriculture, Service de l'horticulture, 1921, pp 24, illus]
CITATIONS: Beaulieu, p 99
COPIES: QMBN (161610 CON)
NOTES: Beaulieu lists Bulletin 49 as in série 4.

Rexall cook book

The first two editions of Rexall Cook Book *were published in Ontario, in 1890, under the title* The Art of Cooking Made Easy. *For the edition distributed in Cowansville, Quebec, in about 1917, see the notes for O48.18.*

1918

Lantic Sugar recipe book

Atlantic Sugar Refineries was organized in 1912 (see Monetary Times Vol. 49, No. 23 (7 December 1912), p 859). The directors were mostly Montreal men (Monetary Times Vol. 60, No. 26 (28 June 1918), p 16).

Q97.1   nd [about 1918]
Lantic Sugar / recipe book / Atlantic Sugar Refineries Limited / Montreal – St. John / [folio:] 1
DESCRIPTION: 18.0 × 14.0 cm   Pp 1–20   Tp illus col of a running boy-sailor holding a container of Lantic Sugar under his left arm and holding up his cap with his right hand; centre spread illus col on pp 10–11 of prepared dishes; illus   Paper, with image on front of several boy-sailors, each carrying a container of Lantic Sugar, running beside, and in front of, an over-size container of sugar; stapled
CONTENTS: 1 tp; 2 'List of Recipes'; 3 'Foreword'; 4–20 recipes; inside back face of binding illus of 'The refinery where Lantic Sugars are made – St. John, N.B.'
COPIES: OKQ (F5012 nd A881)   *Private collection
NOTES: The printer's name, 'Howell Lithographic Co.,' is on the outside back face of the binding. According to p 3, one must use cane sugar, not beet sugar, for success in cooking. *Lantic Sugar Recipe Book* and Q98.1, *Luscious Lantic Recipes*, were likely published about 1918: An advertisement in the March 1918 issue of *Everywoman's World* tells the reader to 'write for our little library of three cook books, "Lantic Sweets."'

Luscious Lantic recipes

Q98.1   nd [about 1918]
Lantic / Sugar / Luscious Lantic / recipes / for use with / Lantic Brown Sugar [cover-title]
DESCRIPTION: 14.5 × 9.0 cm   Pp 1–24   Paper, with image on front of a grandmother stirring the contents of a bowl; stapled
CONTENTS: 1–2 'Breads'; 3–7 'Cakes'; 8–9 'Cookies'; 10–14 'Puddings'; 15–17 'Desserts'; 18–20 'Candies'; 21–3 'Preserves'; 24 'Miscellaneous'
COPIES: OKQ (F5012 nd L296)   QGMG   *Private collection
NOTES: The text is printed on blue leaves. The company name is printed on the bag of sugar illustrated on the outside back face of the binding: Atlantic Sugar Refineries Ltd, Montreal and Saint John. 'The Sterling Printing Service Limited' is printed below the illustration of the bag of sugar. On the inside front face of the binding there is an explanation of 'The Difference

between Lantic Granulated and Lantic Old-fashioned Brown.' Concerning the date of publication, see Q97.1.

There is a recipe for War Cake on p 4, using rye flour and cornmeal instead of wheat flour. An unusual hint is on p 16: 'Campers and fishermen make a good mock lemonade by boiling together a pint of Old-fashioned Brown with a cup of vinegar and one of water, adding a few sticks of dry ginger. If water is ill-flavored or brackish this greatly improves it.' A Nursery Pudding on p 10 is made by cooking together 1 cup graham flour, 1 cup boiling water, and 1 cup hot milk, to be served with milk and sugar as a children's supper.

Another private collector has a copy that matches the description above, except that the cover-title is 'Grandmother's / Recipes / for Use with Lantic / Old-fashioned Brown Sugar.' This title is cited in an advertisement in the April 1919 issue of *Everywoman's World*. It is likely one of the 'library of three cook books' mentioned in the March 1918 issue.

Quebec, Department of Agriculture

For the titles of other cookbooks published by the Quebec Department of Agriculture, see Q48.1.

Q99.1   nd [about 1918]
Department of Agriculture of the Province of Quebec / Bulletin No. 58 / How to save wheat and meat / Forty tested recipes / Prepared by the instructors of the School of Household Science, / Macdonald College. / [caption:] War bread / 1. Rye Bread, 2. Oatmeal Bread, 3. Rye and Corn- / meal Bread, 4. Steamed Brown Bread, / 5. Whole Wheat Grain Bread. / Published by order of the Hon. J.-Ed. Caron, Minister of Agriculture, / Province of Quebec.
DESCRIPTION: Pp [1–2] 3–14   Illus
CONTENTS: 1 tp or cover-title?; 2 'Measurements,' 'Oven Temperatures,' and 'Flour Mixtures'; 3–4 'Muffins'; 5–mid 6 'Baking Powder Biscuits'; mid 6–7 'Miscellaneous'; 8–mid 10 'Meat Substitutes'; mid 10–mid 11 'Fish and Rice Loaf'; mid 11–13 'Bread'; 14 'Suggestions'
CITATIONS: Beaulieu, p 100
COPIES: *CIHM (83678)   OOAG
NOTES: The OOAG copy is stamped on p 1, 'Jun 24 1918 I[illegible] Agr. Inst.' Although this booklet has only 14 pp, it contains mainly recipes. Beaulieu lists Bulletin 58 as série 4.

At about the same time, the Ontario Department of Agriculture published a booklet on war breads, O380.1.

1919

Almanach Rolland ... 1919

See also Q78.1.

Q100.1   1919
Almanach / Rolland / agricole, / commercial / et des / familles / de / la compagnie J.-B. Rolland & fils / 1919 / Cinquante-troisième année / Enregistré conformément à l'Acte du Parlement du Canada, en l'année mil / neuf cent dix-huit, par la compagnie J.-B. Rolland & fils, au / bureau du ministre de l'Agriculture à Ottawa. / Canada / En vente chez tous les libraires / et les principaux marchands. / N.-B. – Cet almanach contient beaucoup de matières d'un intérêt / général et mérite d'être conservé à titre de renseignements utiles. / [folio:] 11
DESCRIPTION: Tp still-life of globe, ruler, books, agricultural tools, and wheat sheaf
COPIES: QQS
NOTES: Cooking recipes are on pp 193–201.

Les recettes pour bières, porters, vins, cidres, liqueurs, etc.

Q101.1   3rd ed., copyright 1932
Les recettes / pour / bières, porters, vins, / cidres, liqueurs, / etc. / Troisieme edition / Procédés faciles de fabrication / a la maison / En vente chez tous les libraires, 25c.
DESCRIPTION: 15.0 × 10.5 cm   Pp [1–3] 4–28   Tp illus of fruits in a comport   Thin card, with tp illus on front; stapled
CONTENTS: 1 tp; 2 'Droits réservés, Canada 1919, 1925, 1932. Propriété de J.-E. Bélanger, Québec.'; 3–6 'À votre santé ...' [introduction]; 7–mid 26 recipes; mid 26–mid 27 'Bouche-bouteilles'; mid 27–28 'Remarques'
COPIES: *OTYA
NOTES: The copyright notice on p 2 indicates that the first edition was likely published in 1919. In 'À votre santé,' the author comments on the healthful properties of various drinks, especially when made at home, without the 'contrefaçons, falsifications, colorations ou additions' found in factory-made drinks. He also recommends the making of drinks at home as 'une petite industrie domestique très intéressante pour les dames et les jeunes filles' and goes on to moralize about the proper place of men and women and to express his opposition to the Suffragette movement and to women serving in the Legislature. The recipes are mainly for alcoholic drinks, but there are also non-alcoholic ones; for example, Bière blanche au gingembre and Bière d'épinette (p 8), Limonade, Orangeade, and Eau de vinaigre (p 25), and Eau de fruits et miel and Thé de camomille (p 26). The following is printed on the outside back face of the binding: 'Pourquoi payer $2.00 ou $3.00 pour un gallon de vin? Lorsque nous pouvons faire nos vins et liqueurs pour quelques sous seulement. 50 recettes.' A list of the recipes follows.

Manuel de cuisine raisonnée

Q102.1   1919
Manuel / de / cuisine raisonnée / adapté aux élèves des cours élémentaires / de l'École normale classico-ménagère / de Saint-Pascal / par / l'École normale / de Saint-Pascal / 1919 / Imprimerie l'Action sociale ltée, / Québec.
DESCRIPTION: 19.0 × 12.0 cm   Pp [1–5] 6–410   A few illus   Rebound?
CONTENTS: 1 ht; 2 blank; 3 tp; 4 'Tous droits réservés'; 5–6 'Préface' signed 'L'abbé A. Beaudet, principal de l'École normale classico-ménagère. Saint-Pascal, en la fête de SS. Anges gardiens, 1919.'; 7–10 'Introduction'; 11–387 text in two parts; 388 blank; 389–92 'Table des matières'; 393–410 'Index alphabétique'
CITATIONS: Armstrong 2004, p D2   BQ Exposition 1974, p 15   Carrière No. 156   Driver 2003, 'Canadian Cookbooks,' p 38   Ferguson/Fraser, p 232   Lambert, T., p 94°   O'Neill (unpublished)
COPIES: *OGU (UA s020 b30)   OONL (TX715 M339 1919)   QMACN (570.620 (1))   QMBM (641.59714 M294ma)   QMBN (181683 CON)   QNICS (641.5 E275m)   QQLA (TX715 C966 1919)   QTURA (641.15 E19m); Great Britain: LB (07942.ccc.22 destroyed); United States: NNNAM (S.21.B)
NOTES: *Manuel de cuisine raisonnée,* later retitled *La cuisine raisonnée,* was to francophone Quebeckers what Nellie Lyle Pattinson's *Canadian Cook Book* (O506.1, first edition in 1923) was to English Canadians: the preeminent school textbook, also widely used in homes for decades. As the 'Préface' states, '[Le livre] n'enseigne rien d'irréalisable, mais uniquement ce qui a déjà été essayé et pratique à l'école ... notre livre aura son utilité non seulement pour nos élèves et la classe féminine étudiante en général, mais pour toutes les maîtraisses de maison.' The book held its superior place for years, despite competition from textbooks from other religious orders, such as Q178.1, *La cuisine pratique,* by soeur Catherine-de-Cardone. For a 1935 abridged edition of the text, see Q228.1, *La cuisine à l'école complémentaire.*

The OGU copy is inscribed on the half-title, 'A ma chère bonne et dévouée soeur Olie[?] // Ma reconnaisance vous [?] fidèle toujours – sr Ste-Marie-de-la Repara[?] C. [?].' The QMBM copy has a label for 'Librairie Granger frères' obscuring the imprint on the title-page. The QTURA copy is rebound, but the front face of the original binding has been preserved under clear plastic.

Katherine Caldwell, in O466.1, *Recettes pour tous les jours*, acknowledges *Manuel de cuisine raisonnée* as 'une aide précieuse.' Marius Barbeau, in Q287.1, *Saintes artisanes*, p 91, refers to the medicinal recipes in *Manuel de cuisine raisonnée*. Ferguson/Fraser, p 232, cite the 1919 edition but incorrectly give the later title.

Q102.2   2nd ed., 1926
—Manuel / de cuisine / raisonnée / [symbol of École normale classico-ménagère, Congrégation de Notre-Dame] / Deuxième édition / revue, corrigée et augmentée / Québec / l'Action sociale, limitée / 1926
DESCRIPTION: 19.5 × 14.0 cm   Pp [i–iii] iv [v] vi [vii] viii [ix] x, [1] 2–524   Illus   Paper, with image on front of stalks of wheat(?); sewn
CONTENTS: i tp; ii 'Nihil obstat. Chs Gagné, ptre, chan. Archevêché de Québec, 20 avril 1926. Permis d'imprimer. J.-Alfred Langlois, Év. de Titop., Vic.-Cap. Archevêché de Québec, 20 avril 1926. Enregistré conformément à l'Acte du Parlement du Canada, en l'année mil neuf cent vingt-six, au bureau du ministère de l'Agriculture, à l'Ottawa. Tous droits réservés'; iii–iv 'Préface' signed Alphonse Beaudet, chanoine, principal, École normale classico-ménagère, Saint-Pascal, en la fête de l'Annonciation, 1926; v–vi 'Répartition 7ème année'; vii–viii 'Répartition 8ème année'; ix–x 'Répartition 9ème année'; 1–304 first part of text, 'Théorie et exercises appliqués,' in three parts for the seventh, eighth, and ninth years; 305–11 'Lexique'; 312–510 second part of text, 'Pratique'; 511–16 'Table des matières'; 517–24 'Index alphabétique'
CITATIONS: BQ 08-0961
COPIES: OONL (TX715 M339 1926) *QMACN (570.620 (2))   QMBN (138435 CON and MIC/B5528 GEN)   QQLA (TX715 C966 1926)   QQS (missing) QTS   QTURA

Q102.3   4th ed., 1936
—La cuisine raisonnée / à / l'École supérieure / et à / l'École normale / Quatrième édition / entièrement refondue / Québec / 1936
DESCRIPTION: 23.0 × 15.5 cm   Pp [i–iii] iv [v] vi, [1] 2–744   Pl col of 'Valeur nutritive des aliments' between

pp 48 and 49 and between pp 100 and 101, illus   Cloth
CONTENTS: i tp; ii list of 'Auteurs consultés' and 'Avec permission de l'Ordinaire // Tous droits réservés par la Congrégation de Notre-Dame de Montréal'; iii–iv 'Table des matières'; v–vi 'Avant-propos'; 1–732 twenty-nine chapters in two parts; 733–44 'Index des recettes'
CITATIONS: Bédard, p 1   BQ 08-0956   Lambert, T., p 94°
COPIES: AEU (TX715 C74 1936)   QMACN (570.620 (3)) QMBM (641.5 C749cu)   QMBN (TX715.6 C87 1937 and 126589 CON)   QQS (missing)   *Private collection
NOTES: The 'Avant-propos' sets out the moral context for cooking and home-making. The date 1937 is printed on the binding of the QMBN copy.

Q102.4   4th ed., 1943
—La cuisine / raisonnée / Aux élèves finissantes, futures maitresses de maison, / et aux ménagères chargées de l'alimentation familiale, / ce manuel est humblement dédié. / [symbol of École normale classico-ménagère, Congrégation de Notre-Dame] / Approuvé par le Comité catholique / du Conseil de l'instruction publique / Quatrième édition, / revue, augmentée. / Québec MCMXLIII
DESCRIPTION: 23.0 × 15.5 cm   Pp [iii–vii] viii, [1] 2–725 [726], [1] 2–15   Frontis of 'Élèves finissantes (1943) de l'École supérieure de sciences domestiques,' illus   Cloth, with image on front of a steaming dish, the cover-title printed within the shape of the rising steam
CONTENTS: iii ht; iv blank; v tp; vi 'Auteurs consultés: [list of ten sources] Nihil obstat: Edgar Chouinard, ptre, censor librorum. 31a maii 1943. Imprimatur: Ulric Perron, V.G., Quebici, die 31a maii 1943. Enregistré conformément à l'Acte du Parlement du Canada, en l'année mil neuf cent vingt-six, au bureau du ministère de l'Agriculture, à Ottawa. Tous droix réservés par la Congrégation de Notre-Dame de Montréal.'; vii–viii 'Avant-propos'; 1–707 text; 708 fp illus of 'Moulin à farine (antique)'; 709–mid 712 'Table des matières'; mid–bottom 712 'Table des planches spéciales'; 713–25 'Index alphabétique des recettes'; 726 fp illus of an outdoor bake oven; 1–15 'Supplément (suite du chapitre troisième, page 48)'
CITATIONS: BQ Exposition 1974, p 14   Lambert, T., p 94°
COPIES: *OONL (TX715 C655 1943)   QMACN (570.620(4))   QMBN (189148 CON)

Q102.5   5th ed., 1946
—La cuisine / raisonnée / aux élèves finissantes, futures maîtresses de maison, / et aux ménagères

chargées de l'alimentation fami- / liale, ce manuel est humblement dédié. / [symbol of École normale classico-ménagère, Congrégation de Notre-Dame] / Approuvé par le Comité catholique / du Conseil de l'instruction publique / Cinquième édition / revue, augmentée / Québec MCMXLVI

DESCRIPTION: 22.5 × 15.5 cm   Pp [i–vii] viii, [1] 2–721 [722], [1] 2–53   Frontis of 'Élèves finissantes (1943) ...,' tables in col, illus   [$2.25, on binding]   Cloth, with image on front of a steaming dish, the cover-title printed within the shape of the rising steam

CONTENTS: i ht; ii blank; iii–iv frontis; v tp; vi 'Auteurs consultés: [list of ten sources] Nihil obstat: Edgar Chouinard, ptre, censor librorum. 8. sept. 1945. Imprimatur: Ulric Perron, V.G., Quebeci, die 8a septembris 1945. Droits réservés – copyright – Ottawa, 1926. Institution chanoine-Beaudet, Saint-Pascal (Kamouraska), P.Q.'; vii–viii 'Avant-propos'; 1–6 'Préliminaire'; 7–704 text in two parts; 705–mid 708 'Table des matières'; mid–bottom 708 'Table des planches spéciales'; 709–21 'Index alphabétique des recettes'; 722 'Index alphabétique du supplément'; 1–53 'Supplément'

COPIES: *QMACN (570.620 (8))   QTS

NOTES: Lambert, T., p 94°, records an edition of 1945, but not one for 1946. Ferguson/Fraser, p 35, illustrate in colour a closed volume of *La cuisine raisonnée* that may be Q102.5 or Q102.6 or a later edition (the reference on p 232 incorrectly gives Institution chanoine-Beaudet – the publisher of Q102.5 and Q102.6 – as the publisher of the 1919 edition).

Q102.6   6th ed., 1949

—La cuisine / raisonnée / aux élèves finissantes, futures maîtresses de maison, / et aux ménagères chargées de l'alimentation fami- / liale, ce manuel est humblement dédié. / [symbol of École normale classico-ménagère, Congrégation de Notre-Dame] / Approuvé par le Comité catholique / du Conseil de l'instruction publique / Sixième édition / revue, augmentée / Québec MCMXLIX

DESCRIPTION: 22.5 × 15.0 cm   Pp [i–vii] viii, [1] 2–721 [722], [1] 2–53   Frontis of 'Élèves finissantes (1943) ...,' tables in col, illus   Cloth, with image on front of a steaming dish, the cover-title printed within the shape of the rising steam

CONTENTS: i ht; ii blank; iii–iv frontis; v tp; vi 'Auteurs consultés: [list of ten sources] Nihil obstat: Edgar Chouinard, ptre, censor librorum. 28 oct. 1948. Imprimatur: Geo.-E. Grandbois, V.G. Quebeci, die 28a oct. 1948. Droits réservés – copyright – Ottawa, 1926. Institution chanoine-Beaudet, Saint-Pascal (Kamouraska), P.Q.'; vii–viii 'Avant-propos'; 1–3 'Lexique';

4 blank; 5–10 'Préliminaire'; 11–704 text in two parts; 705–mid 708 'Table des matières'; mid–bottom 708 'Table des planches spéciales'; 709–21 'Index alphabétique des recettes'; 722 'Index alphabétique du supplément'; 1–53 'Supplément'

CITATIONS: Lambert, T., p 94°

COPIES: *QMACN (570.620 (5))   QMBM

OTHER EDITIONS: The following are at QMACN, unless otherwise indicated: 7th ed., 1954 (also at QTS); 8th ed., 1957 (also at OONL); 8th ed., 1959; 9th ed., 1961; 9th ed., 1963 (only at QMBN); 10th ed., 1966 (only at QMBM); another ed., Montreal and Paris: Fides, 1967 (also at OMIH, QSFFSC); another ed., 1976; 10th ed., Montreal: Éditions Fides, 1979 (only at OONL); Braille ed., [Longueuil, Que.: Institut Nazareth et Louis-Braille, 197-?] (QLNLB); 11th ed., 1984 (Private collection); metric ed., Montreal: Fides, 1985 (OOC, QMBM, QMBN, QMOLF); nouvelle éd. abrégée, Saint-Laurent, Québec: Les soeurs de la Congrégation de Notre-Dame et les Éditions Fides, 2003 (OONL).

Neil, Marion Harris

For information about this author and the titles of her other cookbooks, see O307.1. For the titles of other books about cooking with Fleischmann's Yeast, see O131.1.

Q103.1   copyright 1919

Sixty-five delicious dishes / made with bread / containing tested recipes compiled for / the Fleischmann Co. / by / Marion Harris Neil / author of / "Economical Cookery," Salads, Sand- / wiches and Chafing Dish Recipes, and / "How to Cook in Casserole Dishes" / This booklet is intended to show the various uses of / bread combined with other things which make whole- / some, economical and tempting dishes. / Bread is your best food – eat more of it. / Copyright, 1919, by / the Fleischmann Co. / Form 1044. Canadian.

DESCRIPTION: 17.5 × 12.5 cm   Pp [1] 2–30 [31–2]   Illus   Paper, with image on front, in a circular frame, of a woman (shown from waist up) carrying a prepared dish; stapled

CONTENTS: 1 tp; 2–3 'General Uses for Bread'; 4–8 'Fish and Meat Dishes'; 9–10 'Stuffings'; 11–20 'Toast, Vegetables and Savories'; 21–30 'Puddings, Tarts and Muffins'; 31 book-order form; 32 addresses of Canadian offices of the Fleischmann Co. in Montreal, Quebec, Saint John, New Brunswick, Calgary, Alberta, Toronto, Ontario, Winnipeg, Manitoba, and Vancouver, British Columbia

COPIES: BDUCVM NBFKL OONL (TX769 N44 1919 p***) OTBPM *Private collection

NOTES: 'Niagara Litho Co. Buffalo–New York 9999' is printed on the outside back face of the binding. On the front face of the binding of the OONL copy, 'The Fleischmann Co.' is blocked out and a new name is over-printed above: 'Sanitary Bakery Ltd., Regina.'

This may be an edition of the new Fleischmann book that is referred to as 'Good Things to Eat Made with Bread' by Neil, on p 46 of Q87.1, *Excellent Recipes for Baking Raised Breads*.

AMERICAN EDITIONS: Philadelphia: Printed by Donovan-Armstrong, 1919 (QKB).

The whys and wherefores of cooking

Q104.1 nd [about 1919]
The whys and wherefores / of cooking / a simple text book for / elementary cooking schools / The Montreal Cooking School / 1010 Sherbrooke St. / Montreal

DESCRIPTION: 19.0 × 14.0 cm Pp [1–3] 4–68 Paper; stapled

CONTENTS: 1 tp; 2 blank; 3–68 text in a question-and-answer format

CITATIONS: Lambert, T., p 94°

COPIES: *QMACN (570.625 (1)) QMBN (TX663 W49 1910 and 83775 CON)

NOTES: The QMBN copy is inscribed on the blank leaf before the title-page, in ink, 'Gladys Darling. Cooking class. 1919.'; stamped above this inscription is 'Cuisine ménagère.' This textbook received its 'approbation officielle' from the Conseil de l'instruction publique in 1924 (*Rapport du surintendant de l'instruction publique* for the year 1924–5, p 378); that its approval came several years after it was first published was not unusual. The address 1010 Sherbrooke Street [West] was the location of the Mother House of the Congregation of Notre Dame.

1919–23

Recettes et conseils utiles pour tous

Q105.1 nd [about 1919–23]
Recettes et conseils / utiles pour tous / Hygiene alimentaire / La vraie farine naturelle / pour / la fabrication / du pain du bon vieux temps / qui a fait la race forte et vigoureuse! / La farine naturelle / moulue sur des meules de pierre et blutee a 85% /

afin de conserver tous les principes nutritifs et digestifs / du ble / Marque de commerce / enregistree / Louis Hebert / Manufacturee par / La cie des farines naturelles / enrg. / Cette vraie farine naturelle est le complement / necessaire et pratique au celebre volume du Dr. / Aurele Nadeau: La grande erreur du pain blanc. / Publie et distribue par le ministere de l'Agriculture / de la province de Quebec / Essayez la de suite! / 100 lbs quand mis en sac / Pour etre gardee dans un endroit froid et sec / C.A. Paradis, / agent et / distributeur. / Quebec / Imp. l'Action sociale, ltée. / 103, rue Sainte-Anne, Québec. [cover-title]

DESCRIPTION: 13.5 × 10.0 cm Pp [1–3] 4–30 Paper, with image on front of the company's trademark: Louis Hebert holding up stalks of wheat in his left hand; stapled

CONTENTS: 1 'Revenons au pain, fait de farine naturelle ...'; 2 blank; 3–5 untitled introduction signed 'La compagnie des farines naturelles enrg. // C.-A. Paradis, agent distributeur, 83 rue Dalhousie, Québec, tél. 1324.'; 6 blank; 7–24 recipes using Farine naturelle as an ingredient; 25–8 quotations from various professors and doctors on health issues; 29 'Les sept commandements de Fleischmann' [i.e., the yeast manufacturer]; 30 quotation from Hon. J.-É. [i.e., Joseph-Édouard] Caron beginning, 'Depuis cette terrible guerre, ...' [i.e., the First World War]

CITATIONS: BouquinsCat 212, No. 389

COPIES: *Private collection

NOTES: Aurèle Nadeau's *La grande erreur du pain blanc* (English edition, *The Great Fallacy of White Bread*), which is cited in the cover-title and quoted on p 4, was published by the Quebec Department of Agriculture in 1916. The introductory text argues for a return to cooking with less-processed flour ('farine naturelle'): '... depuis cinq ans, les autorités médicales les plus hautes et les pouvoirs civils ont signalé les dangers d'une alimentation qui pêche par sa base, et, nous avons aujourd'hui en mains le grand remède ...: c'est le retour à une alimentation plus frugale et plus substantielle par les végétaux et le pain naturel.' There are recipes for bread (two), Crêpes canadiennes, Pâtés aux fruits, Biscuits à la mélasse, Grands-pères aux fruits, Bouillie pour les convalescents et les enfants, Gruau de farine naturelle, Buns, Beignets, Gâteau économique, Petits gâteaux, Pudding éponge, Sauce, Pâte brisée, Viandes rôties, and Poissons rôtis.

C.A. Paradis is identified as a distributor of Farine naturelle in Quebec City directories from 1919–20 to 1922–3 (no product name is given before or after). The appearance of the booklet is consistent with publication in about 1919–23. The reference to 'depuis cinq ans' in the introductory text might be to the year of publication of Nadeau's book, in which case *Recettes et conseils utiles pour tous* was published in about 1921 (1916 + 5 years).

1920

Borden's Eagle Brand book of recipes

The American Gail Borden Jr (1801–74) took out his first patent for a system for condensing milk in vacuum pans in 1856 and soon founded the New York Condensed Milk Co., later called Borden's Condensed Milk Co., then Borden Co. The company's first Canadian office was in Montreal: The first listing in the Montreal city directory was in the volume for 1909–10, under Borden's Condensed Milk Co.; in the directory for 1912–13, the name changes to Borden Milk Co. Ltd; from 1920–1, it is Borden Co. Ltd. In 1928 the company established a presence in Toronto when it bought Canadian Milk Products, and in 1929 and 1930 it purchased two other top Toronto firms, Caulfield's Dairy and City Dairy; the scale of its Toronto operations grew so quickly that on 31 January 1931, Borden's moved its headquarters from Montreal to George Street in Toronto (Thomas/Marchant, pp 40, 45–6, 67, 134). In 1944, the New York office withdrew American staff from their positions in Canada and placed the operating direction of the Canadian company in the hands of Canadian officers ('Borden Company Set Up All-Canadian Organization,' Industrial Canada Vol. 45, No. 7 (November 1944), p 147).

For other books from the Borden Co., see: Q149.1, Borden's St Charles Milk; Q196.1, New Magic in the Kitchen; O707.1, The Particular Cook's Cook Book; O761.1, The Good Provider's Cook Book; O784.1, Magic!; O534.3, Easy Camp Cooking Recipes; O825.1, Magic Recipes; O913.1, Easy Recipes for Camp and Kitchen; O1038.1, Eagle Brand Recipes; O1126.1, Borden's Eagle Brand Magic Recipes; and O1171.1, Skillet Skills for Camp and Cottage.

Q106.1   nd [about 1920]
Borden's / Eagle Brand / book of recipes / The Borden Company, Limited / "Leader of Quality" / Established 1857 Montreal
DESCRIPTION: 11.5 × 16.0 cm   Pp [1] 2–32   Tp illus col of meal tray, illus col   Paper, with image on front, in a circular frame, of a woman in a checkered apron, consulting this book at a kitchen table; stapled
CONTENTS: 1 tp; 2–3 'Borden's Eagle Brand Improves All Cooking Where Recipes Call for Both Milk and Sugar'; 4–6 'Breads and Muffins'; 7–9 'Cakes and Cookies'; 10–14 'Pies and Pastries'; 15–21 'Puddings and Sauces'; 22 'Salads'; 23–mid 24 'Entrees'; bottom 24–26 'Ice Cream'; 27–30 'Candies'; 31 'Beverages'; 32 index
COPIES: APROM   OKELWM   OTMCL (641.5971 H39 No. 56A)   *Private collection
NOTES: The recipes are for cooking with Borden's Eagle Brand Condensed Milk. The introductory text on p 2 states, 'When following your regular recipes, and where you use Borden's Eagle Brand Milk in place of ordinary fluid milk, no additional sugar will be required in many instances.'

Since the company's first listing in Montreal city directories as Borden Co. Ltd is in the volume for 1920–1, the cookbook was published in 1920 or later. It may be the free 'recipe booklet' offered in the advertisement for Borden's Eagle Brand Condensed Milk in the August 1920 issue of *Western Home Monthly*. The appearance of the book is consistent with 1920.

Q106.2   nd [about 1920]
—Borden's / Marque Eagle / livre de recettes / The Borden Company, Limited / "Au tout premier rang" / Fondé en 1857 Montreal
DESCRIPTION: 11.5 × 16.0 cm   Pp [1] 2–32   Tp illus col of meal tray, illus col   Paper, with image on front, in a circular frame, of a woman in a checkered apron, consulting this book at a kitchen table; stapled
CONTENTS: 1 tp; 2–3 'Comment économiser le lait et le sucre par l'usage du Lait Eagle Borden'; 4–6 'Pains et gâteaux'; 7–9 'Entremets et croquets'; 10–14 'Tartes et pâtisseries'; 15–21 'Poudings et sauces'; 22 'Salades'; 23–mid 24 'Entrées'; bottom 24–26 'Glaces'; 27–30 'Bonbons'; 31 'Boissons'; 32 'Table des matières'
COPIES: *Private collection

A few selected recipes for fruit season

See also Q108.1, Jellies That Jell, from the same company. In 1854, John Redpath built Canada's first sugar refinery in Montreal, beside the Lachine Canal. From 1880 to 1930 the business was called the Canada Sugar Refining Co. After a merger in 1930 with the Dominion Sugar Co. Ltd, it became the Canada and Dominion Sugar Co. Ltd. In 1959 a new Toronto plant started production; refining at the Montreal plant ceased in 1980. In 2004, the business (then part of Tate and Lyle North American Sugars Ltd) celebrated 150 years of sugar refining in Canada, and could boast that the Redpath brand, registered as a trademark in 1883, was 'the oldest unmodified and continually used trademark for a Canadian food product' (corporate web site, May 2004). For information about Redpath Sugar and the Canadian sugar industry, visit the Redpath Sugar Museum in Toronto and see three titles by Richard Feltoe: Redpath: The History of a Sugar House, *Toronto: Natural Heritage/Natural History, 1991;* Let Redpath Sweeten It, *Toronto: Natural Heritage/Natural History, 1993; and* A Gentleman of Substance: The Life and Legacy of John Redpath, 1796–1869, *Toronto: Natural Heritage/ Natural History, 2004.*

Q107.1   nd [about 1920]
A few / selected / recipes / for / fruit / season [cover-title]
DESCRIPTION: 15.0 × 9.0 cm   Pp [1] 2–16   Paper, with image on front of six small jars of preserved fruit; stapled
CONTENTS: 1–top 3 'Who Does Not Love Fruit?'; near top 3–15 recipes; 16 'Use Only the Very Best Sugar'
COPIES: ONLAM (Walters-Wagar Collection, Box 20) OTNY (uncatalogued pamphlet file, cookery) *Bookseller's stock   Private collection
NOTES: This booklet was published by the Canada Sugar Refining Co. Ltd, Montreal, to promote the sale of Redpath Sugar. An illustration of a 5-pound box of Redpath Extra Granulated Sugar is on the outside back face of the binding, evidence that the booklet was published after 1912, when the company began to sell granulated sugar ready-packaged in small amounts (previously sugar was sold only in bulk). After the First World War, until the mid-1920s, the company produced a lot of advertising to promote its new packaged goods. From appearances, *A Few Selected Recipes for Fruit Season* was published in this period. The text begins with recipes for preserves, but there are also recipes for 'Frozen Desserts,' 'Frostings,' and 'Candies.'

The OTNY copy lacks its binding; the library files the pamphlet by the heading on p 1, 'Who Does Not Love Fruit?' The private collector's copy has 'Geo. A. Robertson // Glen Fruit Farm // St. Catharines, Ontario' printed on the front face of the binding, at the bottom.

Jellies that jell

See also Q107.1.

Q108.1   nd [about 1920]
Jellies / that jell / Some new light / on an old / problem

DESCRIPTION: 14.0 × 9.0 cm   Pp [1] 2–16   Paper, with images on front of a bunch of grapes and a jar of jelly; stapled
CONTENTS: 1 tp; 2–16 text
CITATIONS: Leduc
COPIES: QMM (RBD uncat)   *Private collection
NOTES: The cover-title is 'Fruit Jellies That "Jell."' The booklet was published by the Canada Sugar Refining Co. Ltd, Montreal, to promote the sale of Redpath Sugar. On the outside back face of the binding there is an illustration of a 5-pound package of Redpath Extra Granulated Sugar. *Jellies That Jell* was published about the same time as Q107.1, for the same reasons.

The text, p 4, explains 'The Pectin Test': A tablespoon or two of alcohol is added to an equal quantity of fruit juice, and left to cool; the amount of jelly-like substance that separates from the liquid and which can be gathered up with a spoon indicates the level of pectin in the juice. The instructions for making jellies are presented as general procedures and principles; there are no formal recipes where specific amounts of juice and sugar are called for.

Lajoie-Vaillancourt, Mrs Blanche

See also Q121.1, Vaillancourt, Cyrille, and Mme Blanche Lajoie-Vaillancourt, Produits de choix du Québec: sirop d'érable, sucre d'érable et miel. *Blanche's name is on the following illustrated leaflet of recipes using maple syrup and maple sugar:* These Recipes Are Contributed by the Women's Institutes of the Province of Quebec and Mrs. Blanche Lajoie-Vaillancourt, *distributed by the Province of Quebec Maple Sugar Producers, Plessisville, Quebec, nd [about 1925], one sheet folded three times (Private collection). For the titles of other cookbooks published by the Quebec Department of Agriculture, see Q48.1.*

Q109.1   [1st English-language ed.], 1920
Department of Agriculture of the Province of Quebec / Division of Apiculture / and Sugar Making / September 1920 / Bulletin No. 68 / Use of honey and of maple sugar / in cooking / by / Mrs. Blanche Lajoie-Vaillancourt / [caption:] Nothing better / Published by order of the Hon. J.E. Caron, Minister of Agriculture.
DESCRIPTION: Pp [1–3] 4–16   Tp illus of honey being poured into a bowl
CONTENTS: 1 tp; 2 blank; 3–top 4 'Composition and Nutritive Value of Honey'; mid 4 'Honey Supplies' and 'Different Kinds of Honey'; bottom 4–top 5 'How to Keep Honey'; mid 5 'How to Liquefy Honey,' 'Sale

of Honey on the Market,' 'Use of Honey in Cooking,'
and 'Honey Is a Delicious Food'; bottom 5–top 6
'Honey in the Preparation of Food'; mid 6–mid 14
'Various Recipes'; bottom 14 'Use of Maple Sugar';
15–16 recipes using maple sugar
CITATIONS: Driver 2003, 'Canadian Cookbooks,' p 37
COPIES: *CIHM (85556)   OOAG

Q109.2   [1st French-language ed.], 1920
—Ministere de l'Agriculture de la province de
Quebec / Service de l'apiculture / et de l'industrie
sucrière septembre 1920 / Bulletin no 68 / Emploi
du miel / et du / sucre d'erable / a la cuisine / par
/ Madame Blanche Lajoie-Vaillancourt / [caption:]
Rien de meilleur / Publié par ordre de l'hon. J.-Ed.
Caron, ministre de l'Agriculture. [cover-title]
DESCRIPTION: Pp [1–3] 4–16   Tp illus of honey being
poured into a bowl, fp illus on p 2 of three children
reaching up for a piece of bread, presumably spread
with honey, in the hand of their mother
CONTENTS: 1 tp; 2 fp illus; 3 'Composition et valeur
nutritive du miel' and 'Le miel est indispensable'; 4
'Le miel est utile,' 'Valeur nutritive du miel,' and 'Le
miel fournit'; top–near bottom 5 'Différentes sortes de
miel,' 'Conservation du miel,' 'De quelle manière
liquéfier le miel,' 'La vente du miel sur le marché,'
and 'Emploi du miel à la cuisine'; bottom 5–top 6 'Le
miel est un mets exquis'; mid 6 'Le miel dans la
préparation des aliments'; bottom 6–mid 14 'Recettes
diverses'; mid 14–16 'Emploi du sucre d'érable'
('L'industrie sucrière' on p 14, recipes on pp 15–16)
CITATIONS: Beaulieu, p 102   Bibliothèque municipale
de Montréal, p 5   Carrière No. 269
COPIES: *CIHM (85555)   OOAG
NOTES: Beaulieu lists Bulletin 68 as in série 4.

Q109.3   1924
—VIIth International Congress of Bee-keepers,
September 1924 / Use of honey / and of / maple
sugar / in cooking / by / Mrs Blanche Lajoie-
Vaillancourt / [symbol of La fédération apicole,
Québec] / Distributed with the compliments of the
Hon. J.-E. Caron, Minister of Agriculture / Province
of Quebec [cover-title]
DESCRIPTION: 22.5 × 15.0 cm   Pp [1] 2–16   Paper;
probably originally stapled, but now sewn into new
library binding
CONTENTS: Inside front face of binding illus of 'Pack-
ing Used by Members of La fédération apicole of
Quebec'; 1–mid 3 'Composition and Nutritive Value
of Honey'; bottom 3–mid 5 'Different Kinds of Honey,'
'How to Keep Honey,' 'How to Liquefy Honey,' 'Use
of Honey in Cooking,' 'Honey Is a Delicious Food,'

and 'Honey in the Preparation of Food'; mid 5–13
'Culinary Preparations with Honey' [i.e., recipes]; top–
mid 14 untitled introductory text about maple sugar;
mid 14–16 recipes using maple sugar; inside back
face of binding illus of 'Four Products of Equal Value'
[i.e., 7 ounces honey, 1 quart milk, 15 ounces codfish,
10 eggs]
COPIES: *QMBN (163814 CON)

Q109.4   1924
—VIIieme Congres international d'apiculture,
septembre 1924 / Emploi du miel / et du / sucre
d'erable / a la cuisine / par / Madame Blanche
Lajoie-Vaillancourt / [symbol of La fédération
apicole, Québec] / Distribué avec les compliments
de l'hon. J.-Ed. Caron, ministre de l'Agriculture /
Province de Québec [cover-title]
DESCRIPTION: About 21.5 × 14.0 cm   Pp [1] 2–16   Probably paper; stapled
CONTENTS: Inside front face of binding illus of
'Emballage utilisé par les membres de La fédération
apicole de Québec'; 1–mid 3 'Composition et valeur
nutritive du miel'; mid–bottom 3 'Différentes sortes
de miel,' 'Conservation du miel,' and 'De quelle
manière liquéfier le miel'; top 4 'Emploi du miel à la
cuisine' and 'Le miel est un mets exquis'; mid 4–top 5
'Le miel dans la préparation des aliments'; mid 5–
mid 13 'Préparations culinaires au miel' [i.e., recipes];
bottom 13–top 14 'Emploi du sucre d'érable'; mid 14–
16 recipes using maple sugar; inside back face illus of
'Quatre produits d'égale valeur // 7 onces de miel
// 1 pinte de lait // 15 onces de morue // 10 oeufs'
COPIES: *QMBN (TX767 M5L34f 1924 and 163813
CON)

Mazola recipes

For information about the Canada Starch Co., see Q47.1.

Q110.1   nd [about 1920]
Mazola / recipes / introducing the pure oil / from
corn for salads, deep / frying and shortening. / The
Canada Starch Co. Limited / Montreal / Serial A-6
DESCRIPTION: 16.0 × 11.0 cm   Pp [1–2] 3–28   Paper;
stapled
CONTENTS: 1 tp; 2 blank; 3–4 'Mazola Cook Book' [i.e.,
introductory text]; 5 'Contents' [i.e., index]; 6–28 recipes using Mazola Oil as an ingredient, some recipes
credited to Mrs Lincoln, Mrs Scott, and Mrs Wood
COPIES: *Private collection
NOTES: Mazola Oil was introduced to the Canadian
market in 1919, the year that the Canada Starch Co.

was acquired by Corn Products Refining Co. (USA). The product was first launched in the American market in June 1911. From appearances, *Mazola Recipes* was published about 1920. The introduction on p 3 defines the product: 'Mazola is a pure, refined vegetable oil – for salad dressings and cooking. The name "Mazola" is formed from "maize" (the Indian name for corn).' The text is printed in brown.

Q110.2   nd [about 1920]
—Recettes / Mazola / pour introduire cette huile / pure, extraite du blé d'inde. / S'emploie pour les salades, la / friture et les pâtisseries. / The Canada Starch Co. Limited / Montréal
DESCRIPTION: 16.0 × 11.5 cm   Pp [1–2] 3–28   Paper; stapled
CONTENTS: 1 tp; 2 blank; 3–4 'Livre de cuisine Mazola' [i.e., introductory text]; 5 'Table des matières'; 6–28 recipes, some credited to Mrs Lincoln, Mrs Scott, and Mrs Wood
COPIES: *QSFFSC

Seasoning suggestions

See also the company's 1946 cookbook, O1142.1, The Secret of Seasoning.

Q111.1   nd [about 1920]
Seasoning / suggestions / Revealing the chef's seasoning / secrets for improving over one / hundred and fifty dishes with / Lea & Perrins' Sauce / Lea & Perrins / Montreal, Canada
DESCRIPTION: 20.5 × 13.0 cm   Pp [1] 2–32   Paper, with the same image on front and back of a bottle of Lea and Perrins' Worcestershire Sauce and with a decorative border incorporating images of prepared dishes; previously stapled, now sewn by library, and with hole punched at top left corner for hanging
CONTENTS: Inside front face of binding information about Lea and Perrins' Sauce and 'For additional copies of this book, write Lea & Perrins // Montreal, Canada'; 1 tp; 2 'Alphabetical Index to Recipes'; 3 'Contents'; 4–32 nine chapters; inside back face blank space for 'Telephone Directory,' address for ordering additional copies of the cookbook, and 'Montclair, N.J. – The Globe Press, Inc. – New York, N.Y.'
COPIES: *OONL (TX715 C3465 No. 23 reserve)
NOTES: The recipes are for a bottled sauce made by Lea and Perrins Ltd, a firm based in Worcester, England. The sauce was concocted by the chemists John Lea and William Perrins and first marketed in Britain in 1837. The cookbook is undated, but the only listing

in Montreal city directories for Lea and Perrins is in the 1920–1 volume, where Harold Seddon, 137 McGill Street, is described as 'sole Canadian agent.' (In 1923, the company appears in Toronto city directories.)

AMERICAN EDITIONS: Lea and Perrins, 1920 (Dickinson, p 160); New York: copyright 1922, by John Duncan's Sons (United States: InU; Cagle/Stafford No. 982, illus).

Standard of portions, prices and table service

Q112.1   1 July 1920
Canadian Pacific Railway / Dining car service / Standard of portions, prices / and / table service / Montreal, July 1st, 1920 / Copyright, Canada, 1920 / by Canadian Pacific Railway Company.
COPIES: *OONMS (TF668 C36 1920)
NOTES: Copies of a facsimile edition of the original 1920 book are at OK, OORD, and OOSS (TF 668 C36). I have examined the OK copy, which measures 13.0 × 10.0 cm, has pp i–xxv [xxvi], 1–159 [leaves lacking?], and the following contents: i–xxv 'Index and Price List'; xxvi blank; 1–14 'General Instructions'; 15–147 'Orders and Preparation and Service'; 148–59 'Terminal Kitchen Recipes.' Printed on the outside back face of the paper binding is 'CP Bygones // Reprint facsimile.' Pages 15–147 are arranged in three columns headed 'Orders,' 'Single Portion,' and 'Preparation and Service'; the latter column includes cooking information. The OK copy is in poor condition; pp xix–xxvi are incorrectly rebound in the volume after p ii.

1920–5

Cuts of meat and how to use them

Q113.1   nd [about 1920–5]
Cuts of meat / and how / to use them / How the whole side of / beef and lamb is cut – / with useful cookery / hints for every joint. / Presented with the / compliments of / Stanford's Limited [cover-title]
DESCRIPTION: 15.5 × 10.0 cm   Pp [1–2] 3–30   Illus red-and-black   Paper, with images on front of a man bowing and a cut of meat; stapled
CONTENTS: 1 cover-title; 2 blank; 3 'Beef Tenderloin Steak'; 4 'Sirloin Roast'; 5 'Rib Roast of Beef'; 6 'The Fifth Rib'; 7 'The Club Steak'; 8 'The Round of Beef'; 9 'The Chuck Roast'; 10 'The Brisket'; 11 'The Plate'; 12 'Flank of Beef'; 13 'The Rump'; 14 'The Foreshank';

15 'Do You Like Fresh Fish'; 16 'The Side of Beef'; 17 'The Side of Lamb'; 18 'The Hindquarter of Lamb'; 19 'The Forequarter'; 20 'Leg of Lamb'; 21 'Loin of Lamb'; 22 'The Crown Roast'; 23 'Rolled Shoulder Roast'; 24 'Shoulder of Lamb'; 25 'Breast and Shank'; 26 'Lamb Chops'; 27–9 'A Word about the Stanford Store'; 30 'Delivery Time Table'; inside back face of binding 'Dodd-Simpson Press Limited, Montreal'; outside back face illus of Stanford's Ltd store, 128 Mansfield Street, Montreal

COPIES: *QMM (RBD ckbk 2036)

NOTES: Stanford's Ltd was a butcher. From appearances, the book was published about 1920–5. This approximate date is consistent with the company's listing in Montreal city directories, which record the address 128 Mansfield Street in the period 1916–26 (other addresses are listed before and after).

The girl at Catelli's

See Q90.1 for the company's history.

Q114.1 nd [about 1920–5]
The / girl at / Catelli's [cover-title]
DESCRIPTION: 15.0 × 11.0 cm   Pp 1–36   Illus blue and illus blue-and-orange   [Free, on p 36]   Paper, with image on front, in oval frame, of a woman carrying a steaming pasta dish; stapled, and with hole punched at top left corner for hanging
CONTENTS: Inside front face of binding recipe for Tomatoes Stuffed with Macaroni or Spaghetti; 1–34 sixty-eight numbered recipes using Catelli's pasta products; 35 illus of Catelli products; 36 order form for free copy of this cookbook from C.H. Catelli Co. Ltd, 201 Bellechasse Street, Montreal; inside back face illus of various pasta shapes (macaroni, spaghetti, noodles, vermicelli, stars, alphabets, ready cut [macaroni], animals, and oats)
COPIES: OTYA (CPC 19-? 0071)   QMM (RBD ckbk 1428)   *Private collection
NOTES: The corporate name – C.H. Catelli Co. of Montreal – is first listed in the Montreal city directory for 1910–11, at 25 William. In the 1911–12 directory, the company is at 201 Comte East. In the 1913–14 directory and onward, the company is at 201 Bellechasse (the new street name for Comte East). All editions bearing the 201 Bellechasse address, therefore, were published in 1913 or later. If the company began producing special pasta shapes in 1920 (Catelli web site, May 2004), then editions illustrating the special shapes were published in 1920 or later. The appearance of the various editions is consistent with publication in the 1920s.

The order of the editions of *The Girl at Catelli's* is uncertain. The setting of the text on p 1 is a distinguishing feature. In this edition, the first line of text on p 1 ends, 'perfect'; the last line of text reads, 'washed. Let it boil until it yields easily to pressure' (sentence continues on next page). There is a reference on p 10 to 'former editions of this book, ...' On p 28, there is a reference to the Catelli plant doubling in size and capacity 'in the past two years.' There is no bookseller's name on the inside back face of the binding as there is in Q114.3. The text of this edition is printed in blue.

Ferguson/Fraser, p 233, and the colour illustration on p 57 of the closed volume, may be Q114.1, Q114.2, Q114.3, or Q114.4. Armstrong 2000, p F2, refers to this book, but not by title.

Q114.2 nd [about 1920–5]
—The / girl at / Catelli's [cover-title]
DESCRIPTION: 15.0 × 11.0 cm   Pp 1–36   Illus blue and illus blue-and-orange   [Free, on p 36]   Paper, with image on front, in oval frame, of a woman carrying a steaming pasta dish; stapled, and with hole punched at top left corner for hanging
CONTENTS: Inside front face of binding recipe for Tomatoes Stuffed with Macaroni or Spaghetti; 1–34 sixty-eight numbered recipes; 35 illus of Catelli products; 36 order form for free copy of this cookbook from C.H. Catelli Co. Ltd, 201 Bellechasse Street, Montreal; inside back face illus of various pasta shapes (macaroni, spaghetti, noodles, vermicelli, stars, alphabets, ready cut [macaroni], animals, and oats)
COPIES: *Private collection
NOTES: This edition has a different setting of type. The first line of text on p 1 ends, 'perfect'; the last line reads, 'cloth, but not washed. Let it boil until it yields' (sentence continues on p 2). There is no bookseller's name on the inside back face of the binding as there is in Q114.3. The text is printed in blue.

Q114.3 nd [about 1920–5]
—The / girl at / Catelli's [cover-title]
DESCRIPTION: 15.0 × 10.5 cm   Pp 1–36   Illus blue and illus blue-and-red   [Free, on p 36]   Paper, with image on front, in oval frame, of a woman carrying a steaming pasta dish; stapled
CONTENTS: Inside front face of binding recipe for Tomatoes Stuffed with Macaroni or Spaghetti; 1–34 sixty-eight numbered recipes; 35 illus of Catelli products; 36 order form for free copy of this cookbook from C.H. Catelli Co. Ltd, 201 Bellechasse Street; inside back face illus of various pasta shapes (macaroni, spaghetti, noodles, vermicelli, stars, alphabets, ready

cut [macaroni], animals, and oats) and at bottom, 'Librairie Beauchemin limitée'

COPIES: *SSWD

NOTES: This edition has a different setting of type. The first line of text on p 1 ends, 'perfect re-'; the last line reads, 'boiling fast, throw into it the macaroni, wiped with' (sentence continues on next page). The company 'Librairie Beauchemin limitée' began using this form of its name in 1909 (the firm began as bookbinders in the 1840s).

Q114.4 nd [about 1925]
—The / girl at / Catelli's [cover-title]

DESCRIPTION: 15.5 × 10.5 cm   Pp 1–37   Illus col   Paper, with image on front, in oval frame, of a woman carrying a steaming pasta dish; hole punched at top left corner for hanging

CONTENTS: Inside front face of binding 'Macaroni and Cheese [illus col] See page 2. Recipe No. 3.' and 'On Buying Macaroni'; 1–34 114 numbered recipes; 35 illus of pasta shapes entitled 'Catelli's Products' and showing 'exact thickness of each' (macaroni, spaghetti, noodles, vermicelli, stars, alphabets, ready cut or elbow macaroni, and animals); 36 reprint of illus and text from inside front face of binding, but illus is black-and-white; 37 [inside back face] Recipe No. 115, Tomatoes Stuffed with Macaroni or Spaghetti

COPIES: OKQ (F5012 193- C358)   *Private collection

NOTES: The text is printed in black. There is a reference on p 11 to 'former editions of this book,' and on p 26 to the Catelli plant doubling in size and capacity 'in the past two years.'

Q114.5 nd [about 1925]
—The / girl / at / Catelli's [cover-title]

DESCRIPTION: 15.5 × 10.5 cm   Pp 1–36   Illus [Free, on p 36]   Paper, with image on front of a woman (not in oval frame) carrying a steaming pasta dish; stapled

CONTENTS: Inside front face of binding table of contents; 1–4 Recipe Nos. 1–13; 5–6 'Macaroni and Cheese'; 7–14 Recipe Nos. 14–43; 15 'Why It Pays to Eat Macaroni'; 16–17 Recipe Nos. 44–53; 18–19 illus of Recipe Nos. 19, 87, 16, 70, 58, and 93; 20 continuation of Recipe No. 53 and Recipe Nos. 54–6; 21 'Who Put the Hole in Macaroni?'; 22–4 Recipe Nos. 57–69; 25 'The Home of the Girl at Catelli's'; 26–8 Recipe Nos. 70–83; 29 'How to Cook Catelli's Milk Macaroni'; 30–2 Recipe Nos. 84–97; 33 'A Fair Exchange'; 34–5 Recipe Nos. 98–110; 36 'So Handy to Use // Catelli's Ready Cut Milk Macaroni'; inside back face illus of various pasta shapes (macaroni, spaghetti, noodles, vermicelli, stars, alphabets, ready cut or

elbow macaroni, and animals), showing the 'exact thicknesses of each'

COPIES: *Private collection

NOTES: The text and illustrations are printed in black. Unlike the editions described above, the woman depicted on the front face of the binding is not within an oval frame. From appearances, this edition and Q114.6, its French-language counterpart, are the latest editions.

Q114.6 nd [about 1925]
—La / fille / chez / Catelli [cover-title]

DESCRIPTION: Paper, with image on front of a woman (not in oval frame) carrying a steaming pasta dish; stapled

COPIES: QSTHS

NOTES: The last page says, 'Si commodes à employer Coquilles au lait de Catelli (the same text, in translation, as Q114.5). On the inside back face of the binding, various pasta shapes are illustrated (the same as Q114.5), showing 'les épaisseurs précises de chacun ces produits.' Below the illustrations of the pasta shapes is the following text: 'Préparée par A. McKim limitée, Montréal // Imprimer [sic] par la Federated Press limitée.'

1921

Cheese: The ideal food

See also Q120.1, The Perfectly Digestible Cheese, by the same company.

Q115.1 nd [about 1921]
Cheese / the ideal food / healthful / nutritious / economical / many delicious ways / to serve it / Kraft-MacLaren Cheese Co. / Montreal Canada

DESCRIPTION: 18.0 × 12.5 cm   Pp [1–3] 4–32   Illus col, illus   [$0.10, on binding]   Paper, with image on front of a rectangular block of Kraft Cheese from which two slices have been cut; stapled

CONTENTS: 1 tp; 2 five interior scenes of a factory and one exterior 'View of Chicago Plant'; 3 'Foreword' signed Kraft-MacLaren Cheese Co.; 4–7 information about cheese generally and Kraft Cheese specifically; 8–31 recipes; 32 index

COPIES: *OONL (TX759.5 C48 C44 1930z copy 2)

NOTES: The cover-title is 'Cheese and Ways to Serve It.' The 'Foreword' dedicates the book 'to the housewives of America.' The American printer's name is on the outside back face of the binding: 'Printed in U.S.A. Walton & Spencer Co. Chicago, Ill.'

The form of the company name is a guide to the date of publication of the various editions of *Cheese: The Ideal Food:* In 1920 J.L. Kraft and Bros Co. purchased MacLaren's Imperial Cheese Co. Ltd and the Canadian business became known as Kraft-MacLaren Cheese Co.; in 1928 the business was renamed Kraft-Phenix Cheese Co. Ltd; in 1940 the name changed to Kraft Cheese Ltd, then in 1945 to Kraft Foods Ltd. This edition and Q115.2, Q115.3, and Q115.4, therefore, were published in the period 1920–8. Q115.1 is the earliest because there are no references to Canadian cheese in the 'Foreword' (as added to the other editions) and there is no 'Limited' in the company's name on the title-page (as found in the other editions). Q115.1 was likely published in about 1921, the same year as the American edition cited in Allen, p 112 (both have the same image on the binding).

OONL copy 1 is missing.

Q115.2 nd [about 1921–8]
—Cheese / the ideal food / healthful / nutritious / economical / many delicious ways / to serve it / Published by Home Economics Dept. / Kraft-MacLaren Cheese Co. – Limited / Montreal Canada
DESCRIPTION: 18.0 × 12.5 cm   Pp [1–3] 4–32   Illus col, illus   [$0.10, on binding]   Paper, with image on front of two men seated at a table, on which sits a plate of cheese; stapled
CONTENTS: 1 tp; 2 four interior scenes of a factory and one exterior view of a factory; 3 'Foreword' signed Kraft-MacLaren Cheese Co. Ltd; 4–7 information about Kraft Cheese specifically and cheese generally; 8–31 recipes; 32 'Index'
COPIES: ACG   *BKOM   QMMMCM (ARM2000.62. 10)
NOTES: The cover-title is 'Cheese – and Ways to Serve It.' 'Printed in U.S.A. R. Gair Co. N.Y.' is on the outside back face of the binding. Like Q115.1, the 'Foreword' begins, 'To the housewives of America ...'; however, where the last paragraph in Q115.1 has no heading and makes no mention of Canada, here it is headed 'Varieties of Kraft Cheese' and refers to 'the most popular being Canadian, ... and Old English (Sharp Canadian).'

Q115.3 nd [about 1921–8]
—Cheese / the ideal food / healthful / nutritious / economical / many delicious ways / to serve it / Published by Home Economics Dept. / Kraft MacLaren Cheese Co. / Limited / Montréal Canada
DESCRIPTION: 17.5 × 12.5 cm   Pp [1–3] 4–32   Illus col, illus   [$0.10, on binding]   Paper, with image on front of two men seated at a table, on which sits a plate of cheese; stapled
CONTENTS: 1 tp; 2 five numbered interior scenes of a factory and one unnumbered exterior view of a factory; 3 'Foreword'; 4–7 information about Kraft Cheese specifically and cheese generally; 8–31 recipes; 32 'Index'
COPIES: *NBFKL (Ruth Spicer Cookbook Collection) OTNY (uncat)
NOTES: The cover-title is 'Cheese – and Ways to Serve It.' The Canadian printer is on the outside back face of the binding: 'Printed in Canada // Standard Litho.'

Q115.4 nd [about 1921–8]
—Le fromage / l'aliment idéal / hygiénique / nourrissant / economique / mille manières délicieuses / de le servir / Kraft-MacLaren Cheese Co. / Limited / Montréal Canada
DESCRIPTION: 17.0 × 12.5 cm   Pp [1–3] 4–32   Illus col, illus   [$0.10, on binding]   Paper, with image on front of a rectangular block of Kraft Cheese from which two slices have been cut; originally stapled, but now sewn by library
CONTENTS: 1 tp; 2 five interior scenes of a factory and one exterior view of Kraft Cheese factory; 3 'Avant-propos' signed Kraft-MacLaren Cheese Co. Ltd; 4–7 information about Kraft Cheese specifically and cheese generally; 8–31 recipes; 32 'Index'
CITATIONS: BQ 22-4892
COPIES: *QMBN (135216 CON)
NOTES: 'Printed in Canada // The Mortimer Co. Limited' is on the outside back face of the binding. The 'Avant-propos' dedicates the book 'aux ménagères de l'Empire britannique ...' The cover-title is 'Le fromage et mille manières de le servir.' QMBN incorrectly dates this edition [195-?].

Q115.5 [copyright 1928]
—Cheese / the ideal food / healthful / nutritious / economical / many delicious ways / to serve it / Home Economics Department / Kraft-Phenix Cheese Company Limited / Montreal, Canada
DESCRIPTION: 17.0 × 12.0 cm   Pp [1–2] 3–32   Tp illus col of a maid serving two women at table, illus col, illus   Paper, with image on front of cheese dishes; stapled
CONTENTS: Inside front face of binding 'Copyrighted Kraft-Phenix Cheese Company Limited 1928 Printed in Canada'; 1 tp; 2 illus of Kraft office, dinette, and kitchen; 3–5 'What Shall I Serve?'; 6–31 recipes; 32 'Proper Grating of Cheese' and 'Proper Cooking of Cheese'; inside back face 'Index' and at bottom,

'Sampson-Matthews Limited, Toronto and Montreal'
CITATIONS: Ferguson/Fraser, p 233, illus col on p 57 of closed volume
COPIES: OKQ (F5012 nd K89C)   *Private collection; United States: Company collection (Kraft Foods Inc., Archives Department, Morton Grove, Ill.)
NOTES: The cover-title is 'Cheese – and Ways to Serve It.' The text on p 5 states, 'In the following pages we have included a group of choice recipes for Kraft and Velveeta Cheese, Nukraft, MacLaren Cream Cheese and Kay.' The centre spread (pp 16–17) illustrates in colour various Kraft cheese products.

The reference in Chatelaine 1935, p 82, to 'Cheese and Ways to Serve It,' free upon request from Kraft-Phenix Co., may refer to this edition or Q115.6.

Q115.6   nd [about 1937]
—Cheese / and ways to / serve it [cover-title]
DESCRIPTION: 7.5 × 14.5 cm   Pp [1–2] 3–47   Several illus col of prepared dishes, photograph on p 3 of Marye Dahnke, illus on pp 4–5 of Kraft products and on p 47 of Kraft Dinner, several small illus of women in various poses   Paper, with all-over pattern of women in various poses against a black background; stapled
CONTENTS: 1 cover-title; 2 'Cheese // The Ideal Food // Many Delicious Ways to Serve It // Healthful Nutritious Economical // Home Economics Department Kraft-Phenix Cheese Company Limited Outremont, P.Q., Canada'; 3 'So Many Good Things to Make with Cheese' signed Marye Dahnke, director of Home Economics Department; 4–5 'There's a Cheese for Every Taste in the Kraft Line'; 6 'For the Lover of Cheese // A "Cave Cured" Flavor'; 7 'Velveeta – the Delicious New Cheese Food'; 8–42 recipes using cheese; 43–5 menus; 46 'A Meal for Four in Nine Minutes' [i.e., information about Kraft Dinner]; 47 [inside back face of binding] illus of package of Kraft Dinner
COPIES: *Private collection
NOTES: This edition was likely published not long after Kraft Dinner was introduced to the Canadian and American markets in 1937. Page 46 refers to three years of research to produce Kraft Dinner and explains how to cook it. This edition of *Cheese and Ways to Serve It* is in the same format as Q244.1, *Kitchen Fresh Ideas*.

The following information about Marye Dahnke is from the 'Acknowledgments' of *The Ogilvie Cook Book*, tenth edition, September 1957: 'Marye Dahnke is director of Kraft Foods Consumer Service ... Miss Dahnke was born in Union City, Tennessee, and holds a B.S. degree from Columbia University. Prior to join-ing Kraft 33 years ago [i.e., about 1924], she was a hospital dietician and also managed a resort in Maine for two summers. She is a member of the American Home Economics Association, the American Deitetic [*sic*] Association and the Institute of Food Technologists.'

AMERICAN EDITIONS: *Cheese and Ways to Serve It* [cover-title], 1921, image of rectangular block of Kraft Cheese on binding (Allen, p 112 and illus col on p 16); *Cheese: The Ideal Food*, Chicago: Kraft-Phenix Cheese Co., 1928 (Axford, p 59); Chicago: Kraft Cheese Co., nd [about 1928], image of 'tavern interior' on binding (United States: InU); *Cheese and Ways to Serve It*, Chicago: Kraft-Phenix Cheese Corp., copyright 1933, signed on p 3 by Marye Dahnke (OGU).

Good eats

In the early 1930s, the same church produced another cookbook; see the notes for Q200.1.

Q116.1   nd [1921]
Good / eats / and how to prepare them / Recommended by / Ladies' Guild / St. Philips Church, Montreal West / Thos. V. Bell, Limited / Montreal
DESCRIPTION: 22.0 × 15.0 cm   Pp [1–2] 3–32   Tp illus of St Philips Church   Paper, with tp illus on front; stapled
CONTENTS: 1 tp; 2 'Special Note' and 'A Card'; 3–32 recipes credited with the name of the contributor and ads
COPIES: *QMM (RBD ckbk 1983)
NOTES: The book is undated; however, there is an advertisement on p 24 that says, 'Beginning Sunday, October 2nd, 1921 ... Jones' Pharmacy will open on Sundays ...'

The Memphremagog cook book

Q117.1   1921
The Memphremagog / cook book / of / receipts tried and tested / Published under the auspices / of the / Women's Guild / of / St. Luke's Anglican Church / Magog, Que., / 1921.
DESCRIPTION: 17.5 × 13.5 cm   Pp [1–3] 4–72 [73–4] [$0.60, on binding]   Paper, with image on front of church; stapled
CONTENTS: 1 '"Let me cook the meals of my country, / And I care not who makes her laws."'; 2 blank; 3 tp;

4 'Magog // Population 5000' [brief description of the town]; 5–9 ads; 10 'Index' [i.e., table of contents]; 11–70 recipes credited with the name of the contributor; 71–2 ads; 73 blank; 74 'Printed by the Enterprise Print, Magog, Que.'
COPIES: *QKB

Miltimore, Mrs Grace Rebecca, née Chadsey (East Farnham, Que., 17 November 1874– 15 August 1946, Dunham Township, Que.)

Grace was the daughter of the Rev. and Mrs E.G. Chadsey. On 12 June 1895 she married William George Miltimore. She is buried in the Winchester Cemetery in Sweetsburg, now part of Cowansville.

Q118.1 1921
"Our / President's cook book" / of over / "500 home recipes" / By / Mrs. Grace R. Miltimore, / President of Rebekah Assembly I.O.O.F. of Qnebec [sic], / Sweetsburg, Que. / R.M.D. No. 2. / [text torn off; another private collector's copy has: 'Published by / E.R. Smith Co. Limited, / 1921']
DESCRIPTION: 19.0 × 14.0 cm Pp [1–4] 5–98 Photograph on p 1 of Grace Miltimore Lacks binding; stapled
CONTENTS: 1 '1921–1922' above photograph of the author, who is described in the caption below as 'also Vice-President of the Cowansville Branch of the Women's Institute'; 2 blank; 3 tp; 4 'Copyright reserved by the author. 1921.'; 5 'Preface' addressed to the officers and members of Rebekah Lodges, IOOF, of Quebec and signed Mrs Grace R. Miltimore; 6 'Service'; 7–74 recipes; 75–8 'Things Well to Know and Do'; 79 'Weights and Measures' and 'Birth Days'; 80 'Birth Stones' and 'Wedding Anniversaries'; 81 'Language of Gems'; 82–mid 83 'Language of Flowers'; bottom 83 'The Eight Wonders'; 84 'The Footpath to Peace' and 'My Friends'; 85–98 'Index'
COPIES: *Private collection
NOTES: In the 'Preface' the author refers to her 'twenty-six years of experience' in culinary work in her own home, i.e., the twenty-six years since she was married in 1895. The object of the book, she says, is 'to raise money to start a fund for an Odd Fellows' and Rebekahs' Home in the Province of Quebec.' All the proceeds, except the cost of printing, were to be given 'to aid in the establishment and maintenance of a home for the aged and indigent Odd Fellows, and a home for the care, education and support of orphans of deceased Odd Fellows and of deceased sisters of the Rebekah Degree in the Province of Quebec.'
The many recipes that are described as 'Original' must be Grace Miltimore's own creations. She annotates the recipe for New York Corn Hash, 'My visit there, 1911.' Other recipes are credited to family and probably friends, for example, Grandma, Aunt Eliza, Aunt Ella, Aggie, Mrs Quackenboss, and Mrs Jim Carlin. The owner of the copy described here reports that her copy originally belonged to Grace Miltimore and that it was a gift from one of her descendants.

The tried and true cook book of St George's

Q119.1 nd [about 1921]
The / tried and true / cook book / of / St. George's / Price / one dollar
DESCRIPTION: 20.0 × 12.5 cm Pp [1–8] 9–91 Cloth
CONTENTS: 1 tp; 2 blank; 3–8 ads; 9–80 recipes credited with the name of the contributor; 81–8 ads; 89–91 'Contents' and at bottom p 91, 'The Mortimer Co. Limited Ottawa Montreal & Toronto'
COPIES: OTMCL (641.5 M58) *OTUTF (B-12 7868)
NOTES: The running head is 'Tried and True Recipes.' The recipes are credited with the names of well-known women in Montreal society and the names of a few chefs; for example, Réné Anjard of the Waldorf-Astoria. Since Miss Gertrude Clergue was a member of St George's Church in Montreal, it is not surprising that several recipes are reprinted from Q95.1, a cookbook that she co-wrote in 1916 with her sister Grace, or from the enlarged American edition published later the same year. That two of the reprinted recipes in *The Tried and True Cook Book* (Lettuce Soup and Pot-au-feu) are only in the enlarged American edition, not in the Canadian edition, points to the American edition as the source. Further evidence supporting the American edition as the source is the wording of the Borcht recipe, which follows the American edition, but varies slightly from the Canadian one. In the case of Salmon Tidnish, the attribution is different in all three books: in the Canadian edition of the 1916 book, the recipe is identified as contributed by H.L.; in the American edition, it is unattributed; in *The Tried and True Cook Book*, it is attributed to Miss G. Clergue.
There is an advertisement on p 82 for Cowan's Cocoa that refers to 'Our new 64 page Recipe Book illustrated with 16 pages in full color,' probably O468.1, '*Cowan's Cocoa Recipes,*' [1921]; therefore, *The Tried and True Cook Book* was published about 1921.
The book plate in the OTUTF copy reads, 'Robert Jewett Mercur // Ex libris Catherine Aishton.' The OTMCL copy was presented to the library by Mr and Mrs S. Temple Blackwood of Toronto.
In 1936 Gertrude Clergue compiled Q236.1, *Delectable Dishes,* as a fund-raiser for the same church.

1921–4

The perfectly digestible cheese

See also Q115.1, by the same company.

Q120.1   nd [about 1921–4]
The perfectly / digestible cheese / new and most
delicious ways / to serve it / Compliments of the
Kraft-MacLaren Cheese Co. / Ltd. / Montreal,
Quebec. [cover-title]
DESCRIPTION: 16.0 × 10.5 cm   Pp 3–39   Illus orange-
and-black   Paper, with images on front of a tin of
Kraft Pimento Cheese at top and of a hand unwrap-
ping an opened tin of Swiss Cheese at bottom; stapled
CONTENTS: 3–7 'Kraft Cheese (Elkhorn) in Tins';
8–36 'Cheese Recipes'; 37 'Many Varieties in Tins';
38 'Kraft's New Cheese Loaf'; 39 [inside back face of
binding] 'Index'
COPIES: *AEPMA
NOTES: The recipes are arranged in four groups:
'Cheese Dishes Which Serve as Meat Substitutes';
'Cheese Soups and Vegetables Cooked with Cheese';
'Cheese Salads and Sandwiches and Similar Dishes';
and 'Cheese Pastry, Cheese Sweets and Similar Dishes.'
The text, originally prepared for the United States
market, has not been revised for the Canadian reader;
it begins on p 3, 'In the United States we do not
appreciate to the full ...'

In 1920 MacLaren's Imperial Cheese Co. Ltd became known as Kraft-MacLaren Cheese Co., after its
purchase by J.L. Kraft and Bros Co. In 1928 the business was renamed Kraft-Phenix Cheese Co. Ltd. *The
Perfectly Digestible Cheese*, therefore, was published in
the period 1920–8, likely about the same time as the
American edition, in about 1921–4.

AMERICAN EDITIONS: nd, but dated [about 1921–4] by
the company (Kraft Foods Inc., Archives Department,
Morton Grove, Ill.).

1921–5

Vaillancourt, Cyrille (1892–1969), and Mme Blanche Lajoie-Vaillancourt

Vaillancourt is credited as the sole author of Usage du
miel à la cuisine, *3ième série, ministère de l'Agriculture, Québec, 1918 (CIHM, QMBN); this 10-page
pamphlet includes 'Recettes' on pp 5–8. Beaulieu, p 112,
lists Vaillancourt as sole author of* De l'usage du miel à
la cuisine dans la province de Québec, *1919, Circu-*

*laire 39, pp 10, also published in English. The same
circular was published a year later:* De l'usage du miel
à la cuisine, *Circulaire 39, 4ième série, ministère de
l'Agriculture de la province de Québec, 1920 (CIHM,
QMBN); 'Conserves au miel' [recipes] are on pp 5–6, and
'Recettes,' on pp 7–10. See also Q109.1, by Blanche
Lajoie-Vaillancourt.*

Q121.1   nd [about 1921–5]
Produits / de choix / du Québec / [caption below
illus of maple leaf:] La vraie feuille d'érable / a sucre
/ Sirop d'érable / sucre d'érable / et miel [cover-
title]
DESCRIPTION: About 17.5 × 12.0 cm   Pp [1–2] 3–24
Illus   With image on front of a maple leaf
CONTENTS: 1 cover-title; 2 blank; 3–8 'L'industrie du
sucre d'érable dans la province de Québec par C.
Vaillancourt, chef du Service de l'apiculture et de
l'industrie du sucre d'érable avec la collaboration de
Madame Blanche Lajoie-Vaillancourt'; 9–14 recipes
using maple syrup; 15–mid 16 'Composition et valeur
nutritive du miel de Québec'; bottom 16–top 17
'Différentes sortes de miel de Québec'; mid 17 'Con-
servation du miel de Québec' and 'Emploi du miel de
Québec à la cuisine'; bottom 17–mid 18 'Le miel de
Québec dans la préparation des aliments'; bottom 18–
24 'Préparations culinaires au miel' [recipes]
COPIES: *QMBN (A38A1 A14 V31 1920 OFF and 161748
CON)
NOTES: The can of maple syrup, illustrated on p 8, has
'Emballé par les producteurs de sucre d'érable de
Québec' printed on it. A note on p 9, before the maple
syrup recipes, says, 'Ces recettes ont été fournies par
diverses institutions ménagères du Québec ...'

The booklet is undated, but p 3 discusses the production of maple-syrup products and states, 'En 1920,
d'après le rapport du bureau des statistiques de la
province de Québec, la récolte dépassa les 31,000,000
de livres.' *Produits de choix du Québec* was published
after the report for 1920, but in the same period as
Q109.1, Lajoie-Vaillancourt's 16-page booklet on the
same subject. The order of publication of Q121.1 and
Q121.2 is unknown.

Q121.2   nd [about 1921–5]
—Quebec / standard / products / [caption below
illus of maple leaf:] The true representation of a /
real maple leaf / Maple syrup / and / maple sugar
[cover-title]
DESCRIPTION: Pp [1–2] 3–16   Illus   With image on
front of a maple leaf; stapled
CONTENTS: 'Greetings from the Province of Quebec';
2 blank; 3–10 'Maple Sugar Industry in Quebec';

11–16 recipes using maple syrup and maple sugar
COPIES: *Private collection
NOTES: In this edition, there is no information about honey and there are no attributions to C. Vaillancourt or Blanche Lajoie-Vaillancourt. Like Q121.1, the maple sugar industry's yield for 1920 is recorded. A note at the top of the first page of recipes states, 'These recipes are contributed by the Women's Institutes of the Province of Quebec, and aim to show the use of maple products in the home.' There are illustrations of cans used by Les producteurs de sucre d'érable de Québec/ Quebec Maple Sugar Producers Association.

1922

Cours d'enseignement ménager: art culinaire

Q122.1 1922
[An edition of Cours d'enseignement ménager: art culinaire, Montreal, Que.: Soeurs de la Congrégation de Notre-Dame, 1922]
CITATIONS: O'Neill (unpublished)
COPIES: Great Britain: LB (Woolwich)
NOTES: O'Neill's citation for 1922 likely corresponds to the volume seen by Dr Lynette Hunter in 1999 (Woolwich 418-F), which she describes as Cours d'enseignement ménager: art culinaire, lessons from 3rd to 8th year, 20.8 × 16.3 cm, 57 unnumbered pages, plain card, stapled.

Désilets, Rolande Savard (Mme Alphonse Désilets)

Madame Désilets's husband, Alphonse (1888–1956), helped organize the first Cercles de fermières in the province (like the Women's Institutes started in 1897 in Ontario, but for francophone women) and in 1923 he became the first chief of the Department of Agriculture's new Domestic Economy Service. He contributed the introduction to Q237.1, Durand-La Roche, Mme Hélène, Menus de réceptions. For the titles of other cookbooks published by the Quebec Department of Agriculture, see Q48.1.

Q123.1 1922
Ministere de l'Agriculture de la province de Quebec / Bulletin no 77 / Manuel / de la / cuisinière / économe et pratique / par / Madame Alphonse Desilets / Diplômée de l'Ecole ménagère de Roberval. / Publie par ordre de l'honorable Jos.-Ed. Caron, ministre de l'Agriculture / 1922 [cover-title]

DESCRIPTION: 24.5 × 17.0 cm Pp [1–4] 5–32 Paper; probably originally stapled, but now sewn by library
CONTENTS: 1 cover-title; 2 'Sommaire'; 3 'À toutes les bonnes ménagères' signed R.S.D.; 4–32 recipes
CITATIONS: Beaulieu, p 101 Carrière No. 265
COPIES: *QMBN (163819 CON) QQLAS (S159 Q3b Sér.4 77)
NOTES: Beaulieu lists Bulletin 77 as in série 4, and indicates that there was an English-language edition.

Excellent recipes for baking with Fleischmann's Yeast

For the titles of other books about cooking with Fleischmann's Yeast, see O131.1.

Q124.1 copyright 1922
Excellent recipes / for baking with / Fleischmann's Yeast / Send one of these / books to your / friends / See page forty-seven / The Fleischmann Company / Copyright 1922 / Form R.B.1
DESCRIPTION: 16.0 × 9.5 cm Pp [1] 2–48 Many illus of young children Paper; stapled, and with hole punched at top left corner, through which runs a string for hanging
CONTENTS: 1 tp; 2 'Index'; 3 'Introduction'; 4 'Yeast Wisdom'; 5 'The Mixing' and 'The Kneading'; 6 'The Rising,' 'The Moulding,' and 'The Baking'; 7 'Accurate Measurements' and 'Little Helpful Hints'; 8–45 recipes; 46 'The New Importance of Yeast in Diet'; 47 order form for the book to be sent to Fleischmann's nearest offices in Montreal, Quebec, Toronto, Ontario, Saint John, New Brunswick, Winnipeg, Manitoba, Calgary, Alberta, and Vancouver, British Columbia; 48 'The Fleischmann Company // Agencies throughout the Dominion of Canada and Newfoundland'
COPIES: *Private collection
NOTES: The cover-title is 'Fleischmann's Recipes.' The book is printed in brown ink.

Q124.2 copyright 1924
—Excellent recipes / for baking with / Fleischmann's Yeast / Send one of these / books to your / friends / See page forty-seven / The Fleischmann Company / Copyright 1924 / Form R.B.1. Can. Printed in Canada
DESCRIPTION: 16.0 × 10.0 cm Pp [1] 2–48 Amusing illus of children eating or cooking [Free, on p 47] Paper; stapled
CONTENTS: 1 tp; 2 index; 3 'Introduction'; 4 'Yeast Wisdom'; 5 'The Mixing' and 'The Kneading'; 6 'The Rising,' 'The Moulding,' and 'The Baking'; 7 'Accu-

rate Measurements' and 'Little Helpful Hints'; 8–45 recipes; 46 'Yeast and the Family's Health'; 47–8 order form for free copies of this book

CITATIONS: Ferguson/Fraser, p 233, illus col on p 57 of closed volume

COPIES: AMHM BDUCVM BSUM OGOWSM OONL (AC901 A7 1924 No. 0100) OTMCL (641.5971 H39 No. 15) *Private collection

NOTES: The cover-title is 'Fleischmann's Recipes.' The book is printed in brown ink.

AMERICAN EDITIONS: New York: Fleischmann Co., 1910 (Allen, p 180); New York: Fleischmann Co., 1912 (United States: Bookseller's stock); [New York:] Fleischmann Co., copyright 1922 (BDUCVM; Allen, p 180).

The Family Herald cook book

See also Q66.1, by the same newspaper.

Q125.1 nd [1922]
The Family Herald / cook book / Published by / the Family Herald and Weekly Star / Montreal
DESCRIPTION: Pp [1–4] 5–215 [216] With image on front of a daughter watching her mother, who is seated at a kitchen table
CONTENTS: 1 tp; 2 blank; 3 'Contents' [i.e., alphabetical list of sections]; 4 'Introduction' signed Family Herald and Weekly Star, Montreal; 5–215 text; 216 publ ad
COPIES: OMATTM OPETCM *Private collection
NOTES: There is no date or statement of edition number on the verso of the title-page. This is likely the first edition, published in November 1922 according to Q125.2. The 'Introduction' sets out the contents and contributors of the text: 'Much of the material used is the valued contribution of our women readers, ... Added to these practical recipes are chapters setting forth the fundamental principles of various branches of cookery, ... This part of the book is the work of a skilled domestic science graduate, ... And, ... there have been kindly supplied to us "Favorite Recipes" by a number of Canada's women of note.'

Q125.2 [2nd ed., May 1923]
—The Family Herald / cook book / Published by / the Family Herald and Weekly Star / Montreal
DESCRIPTION: 21.5 × 14.0 cm Pp [1–3] 4–213, [i] ii–vii 10 pls Rebound, but including the front face of the binding, with image of a daughter watching her mother, who is seated at a kitchen table

CONTENTS: 1 tp; 2 'First edition November, 1922 // Second edition May, 1923'; 3 'Introduction'; 4–213 text; i–vii 'Index'
COPIES: OBBM *QMM (TX715 F223 1923)
NOTES: 'Favorite Recipes (Contributed to the Family Herald Cook Book by Canadian Women of Note)' is on pp 209–13.

Q125.3 [3rd ed., March 1924]
—The Family Herald / cook book / Published by / the Family Herald and Weekly Star / Montreal
DESCRIPTION: 22.5 × 15.0 cm Pp [1–3] 4–217, [i] ii–vii 10 pls Paper, with image on front of a daughter watching her mother, who is seated at a kitchen table; stapled
CONTENTS: 1 tp; 2 'First edition November, 1922 // Second edition May, 1923 // Third edition March, 1924'; 3 'Introduction'; 4–217 text; i–vii index
COPIES: OONL (TX715.6 F35 1924) OWASRM QMM (RBD ckbk 1547) *Private collection

The fine art of carving

In 1927, five years after the publication of The Fine Art of Carving, *Sheet Metal Products Co. of Canada Ltd merged with four other firms to become General Steel Wares; for more information about the merger, see O162.1.*

Q126.1 [copyright 1922]
The / fine art / of / carving [cover-title]
DESCRIPTION: 15.0 × 8.0 cm Pp [1–32] Illus red-and-black Paper, with image on front of a man sharpening a knife as he stands behind roast poultry on a platter; stapled
CONTENTS: 1 cover-title; 2 same illus as on the binding, but printed in black, and a poem titled 'The Fine Art of Carving'; 3 'Carving Should Be Listed among the Fine Arts'; 4 'Have You Ever Witnessed Anything Like This!'; 5 'Take Lessons from Your Butcher'; 6–7 'Buy Yourself One of the New Covered Enameled Roasters' [i.e., the SMP Covered Enameled Ware Roaster]; 8 'Reduces Your Meat Bill $24.00 a Year'; 9 'They Roast without Shrinking the Meat'; 10 'Cooking Odors Can't Spread All through the House'; 11 'You Don't Have to Baste!'; 12–16 'Valuable Hints on Roasting'; 17–22 'Valuable Hints on Carving'; 23 'There's One in Every Family'; 24 'Dont [sic] Forget to Care for Your Carvers'; 25 'Note the Smooth China-like Interior Surface; Easy to Clean'; 26–7 'And Now Let Us Show You Some Pictures of These Wonderful SMP Roasters'; 28 'The SMP Vegetable Steam Cooker';

29 'SMP Savoy Tea Kettle'; 30 'SMP Enameled Ware Is the Finest Kitchen Ware You Can Buy in Any Store To-day'; 31 [inside back face of binding] 'Mr. SMP Copyright, Canada, 1922, by the Sheet Metal Products Co. of Canada, Limited Montreal // Toronto // Winnipeg // Edmonton // Vancouver // Calgary'; 32 [outside back face] SMP symbol and roast poultry in a roasting pan
COPIES: *QMM (RBD ckbk 2001)

Jacobs, Miss Libbie (29 May 1886–)

The 1901 Census gives the birth date of Libby [sic] Jacobs and records her living in Montreal with her parents, Wm and Anna Jacobs, and seven siblings, one of whom was Samuel W. Jacobs, a lawyer. His wife was the first president of the Montreal Section of the National Council of Jewish Women, the organization that sponsored the cookbook. Lawrence F. Tapper, in A Biographical Dictionary of Canadian Jewry, 1909–1914: From the Canadian Jewish Times, *[1992], indexes Libbie's social activities in the years 1909–12.*

Mrs A.M. Bilsky was married to Alex M. Bilsky, the son of Mrs Moses Bilsky of Ottawa, 'an active charitable worker' before there were organized Jewish societies in that city and subsequently honorary president of the Ottawa Ladies' Hebrew Benevolent Society, which, in 1915, published O337.1, The Economical Cook Book, *Canada's first Jewish community cookbook (for Mrs Moses Bilsky, see Arthur Daniel Hart,* The Jew in Canada, a Complete Record of Canadian Jewry from the Days of the French Régime to the Present Time, *Toronto and Montreal: Jewish Publications, 1926, p 548). According to entries in Tapper, Mr and Mrs Alex M. Bilsky were living in Cobalt, Ontario, in 1909 (pp 67, 84), but moved to Toronto in 1912 (p 67); on 6 July 1910, they had a daughter, named Annie (pp 8, 67). The Bilskys visited Montreal regularly and were living there at the time of the cookbook's publication. Montreal city directories of 1922–3, 1923–4, and 1924–5 list Alex M. Bilsky as a mine manager; in 1920–1 he is recorded as a commercial traveller; in 1921–2, no position is recorded.*

The last listing for Mr A.H. Jackson, president of Northern Fur Mfg Co., is in the Montreal city directory for 1921–2. He may be the husband of Mrs A.H. Jackson named on the cookbook's title-page; however, there is some uncertainty since a reference in Tapper indicates that Mr and Mrs A.H. Jackson had a son who was also called A.H. Jackson (see Tapper, p 32, for a reference to the 1909 wedding of Mr and Mrs A.H. Jackson's daughter Sadie, which was attended by Sadie's brother A.H. Jackson).

Q127.1   nd [about 1922]
The / Council kosher / cook book / Compiled by / Miss Libbie Jacobs / Assisted by / Mrs. A.M. Bilsky and / Mrs. A.H. Jackson/ All recipes according to the / Jewish dietary laws, with / the rules for kashering. / Price $2.25
COPIES: *QMJ (uncat, Jewish Canadiana section, 'Institutions,' in box labelled 'National Council of Jewish Women – Publications')   Private collection
NOTES: The volume has 197 pp. QMJ dates the book about 1922. Although the name of the sponsoring organization is nowhere in the volume, QMJ records that it was published by the Montreal Section of the National Council of Jewish Women. The Montreal Section was founded in 1918, as part of the National Council of Jewish Women in the United States. In January 1924 it formally changed its name to the Council of Jewish Women of Montreal and ceased sending fees to the American headquarters.

La cuisine à l'école primaire

Q128.1   1922
La cuisine / a l'école primaire / théorie et pratique / [symbol of École normale classico-ménagère, Congrégation de Notre-Dame] / Saint-Pascal / 1922 / Des presses de l'Action sociale, limitée, / Québec.
DESCRIPTION: 19.5 × 13.5 cm   Pp [i–v] vi–vii [viii–ix] x, [1] 2–317   Frontis of 'Mater Admirabilis' and 4 pls numbered 2–5, illus   Paper; sewn
CONTENTS: i ht; ii blank; iii tp; iv 'Tous droits réservés'; iv–vii 'Préface' signed Congrégation de Notre-Dame, Maison mère, 22 July 1922; viii blank; ix–x 'Avant-propos'; 1–293 text incl 227 numbered recipes; 294–305 'Lexique'; 306–12 'Table des matières // Leçons théoriques'; 313–17 'Table des matières // Exercices pratiques' and at bottom p 317, 'Enregistré conformément à la loi du Parlement du Canada, l'an 1922, par l'École normale classico-ménagère de Saint-Pascal, au ministère de l'Agriculture, à Ottawa.'
CITATIONS: BQ 23-4937   Lambert, T., p 93°   O'Neill (unpublished)
COPIES: OTYA (TX663 C8)   *QMACN (570.600 (1)) QMBN (160000 CON)   QMM (RBD TX663 C85 1922)   QQLA (TX715 C9663 1922); Great Britain: LB (7942.ppp.41 destroyed)
NOTES: No author is named, but she was soeur Sainte-Marie-Vitaline (Anna Fournier, 1873–1954) (Lambert, T., p 93°). This sister had taught at the École normale classico-ménagère since its opening in 1905 and became 'directrice de l'enseignement ménager' at the

end of its first year (see Lambert, T., p 305, and Appendix I, 'Personnel de l'école ménagère de Saint-Pascal,' in *L'oeuvre d'un grand éducateur: le chanoine Alphonse Beaudet ...*, Montréal: Soeurs de la Congrégation Notre-Dame, 1947).

The 'Préface' begins, 'Le Comité catholique du Conseil de l'instruction publique, en donnant une place de choix, dans son nouveau programme, à l'enseignement ménager a rendu à notre province un service dont il convient de la remercier.' It goes on to give the advantages of studying household science: 'esprit de dévouement ... de souplesse ... de décision ... de simplicité ...' The text is arranged in four parts, for the third, fourth, fifth, and sixth years of study, and each part has individually numbered lessons. Plate 5 shows 'Une installation modèle pour leçons de démonstrations à une classe entière. Académie St-Joseph, Verdun, Montréal.' On the outside back face of the binding there is an illustration of 'École normale classico-ménagère, Saint-Pascal, comté de Kamouraska, P.Q., Canada.'

Later, texts were published for individual years of study in domestic science, following the new levels established in 1923 for the provincial education system; see Q134.1, *L'économie domestique à l'école primaire ... IIIe année,* and other books cited in that entry.

Other books attributed to soeur Sainte-Marie-Vitaline are: Q134.1; Q140.1, *L'économie domestique à l'école primaire ... IVe année;* Q141.1, *L'économie domestique à l'école primaire ... Ve et VIe années;* Q228.1, *La cuisine à l'école complémentaire;* Q267.1, *L'économie domestique à l'école primaire ... 4e, 5e, 6e et 7e années;* and Q279.1, *235 recettes pour dîners et soupers.*

The masterpiece

Q129.1 nd [about 1922]
The / masterpiece / R & L [cover-title]
DESCRIPTION: About 15.0 × 8.5 cm [dimensions from photocopy] Pp [1] 2–24 19 numbered illus on pp 4–8 of cakes and other baked goods; fp illus on p 22 of floral buds produced by 'a prominent baker in Victoria, B.C.'; illus on p 24 of a cake top decorated by Mr E.G. Barber, Claresholm, Alberta, January 1922 Stapled
CONTENTS: 1 'This book derives its title from the distinctive character of Mer-Ang Whites and its functions. Symbolized by nineteen illustrations and their respective formulas, everyone a masterpiece'; 2 'Chart of Cake Illustrations'; 3 'Foreword' signed Rose and Laflamme Ltd, Montreal; 4–8 nineteen numbered illus; 9 'In the twenty-six years that we have been in busi-

ness our one big aim has been to make something for which there was a common need ... 19 valuable formulas follow'; 10–? recipes; 22 fp illus of floral buds; 23 'Just a Word' [about Mer-Ang Whites]; 24 illus of cake top
COPIES: *Private collection
NOTES: This recipe collection was published to promote the sale of Mer-Ang Whites, a meringue product, to Canadian bakers. E.G. Barber, whose 1922 cake top is illustrated on p 24, once submitted a manuscript of his own recipes to Maclean Publishing Co., in about 1911 (see A21.1).

Whereas *The Masterpiece* was produced and published by Rose and Laflamme, the company also distributed a British cookbook to its Canadian customers: *Marzipan Recipes,* England: Crimony Co. Ltd, nd, 16 unnumbered leaves, 'Rose & Laflamme, Limited // sole Canadian distributors // Montreal Toronto' stamped on binding (Private collection). Two pages have been tipped in by Rose and Laflamme, one explaining the English terms used for various ingredients, the other referring to Rose and Laflamme as 'flavor specialists for 42 years.' Since the company is first listed in the Montreal city directory for 1893–4, *Marzipan Recipes* was distributed about 1935 (1893 + 42 years).

1924

Bradley, Alice (1875–1946)

For information about this American author's other works, see O375.1. For editions of an earlier book of recipes for Cow Brand Baking Soda, see O82.1, Dwight's Cow-Brand Cook-Book. *In the 1930s, the company issued editions of another booklet of the same title as Q130.1, but with the recipes 'tested and approved in the Cow Brand Baking Soda Kitchen by Martha Lee Anderson':* Q210.1, Good Things to Eat Made with Cow Brand Baking Soda. Q312.1, New Fashioned, Old Fashioned Recipes *followed in 1948.*

Q130.1 copyright 1924 [about 1927–30]
De bonnes / choses à manger / faites avec le / bicarbonate de soude / (soda a pate) / Cow Brand / Compilé par / Alice Bradley, directrice / Ecole de cuisine de Miss Farmer / Boston, Mass. / Church & Dwight, ltée. / 91, rue Reading / Montreal / Copyright 1924, Church & Dwight, ltée.
DESCRIPTION: Tp illus of box of Dwight's Baking Soda   Paper, with image on front of a woman mixing the contents of a bowl; stapled

COPIES: *Private collection

NOTES: Four editions have the copyright date of 1924; however, the company address on the title-page is a guide to the actual date of publication. According to Montreal city directories, Church and Dwight was at 37 Nazareth from 1924 to 1926, after which it was concurrently at two addresses – 37 Nazareth and 91 Reading (these two addresses last listed in the 1929–30 directory). The 1930–1 and 1931–2 directories list the company at both 2715 Reading and 25 Brennan; the 1932–3 and 1933–4 directories list three addresses: 2715 Reading, 25 Brennan (factory), and 37 Nazareth (warehouse). Q130.1, where the address is 91 Reading, was, therefore, published about 1927–30. Editions with the address 25 Brennan Street (Q130.2 and Q130.3) or 2715 Reading Street (Q130.4) were likely published no earlier than 1930. The 1924 copyright date may refer to the year the American edition was registered for copyright.

Q130.2   copyright 1924 [about 1930 or later]
—Good things to eat / made with / Cow Brand / Baking Soda / (bicarbonate of soda) / Compiled by / Alice Bradley, Principal / Miss Farmer's School of Cookery / Boston, Mass. / Church & Dwight, Ltd. / 25 Brennan Street / Montreal / Copyright 1924 by Church & Dwight, Ltd.

DESCRIPTION: 14.0 × 9.0 cm   Pp [1] 2–32   Tp illus of box of Dwight's Baking Soda, illus on p 13 of box of Dwight's Baking Soda   Paper, with image col on front of a woman mixing the contents of a bowl; stapled

CONTENTS: 1 tp; 2–30 text; 31–2 index; inside back face of binding 'Try This for Cooking Green Peas' and 'Also for Cooking String Beans'

COPIES: MBDHM   ONLAM (Walters-Wagar Collection, Box 20)   *Private collection

NOTES: See Q130.1 regarding the year of publication. On the title-page of this edition the product is called 'Cow Brand Baking Soda (bicarbonate of soda)' and the company address is 25 Brennan Street. Where Q130.3 has an illustration of a bottle of Dwight's Baking Soda on p 29, this edition has two additional recipes, Doughnuts and Peanut Brittle.

'Making Mixtures Light' on p 2 describes three ways of producing a light and porous texture: '... by fermentation, as with yeast in the making of bread and rolls, by using eggs and beating the mixture to enclose air in it as in popovers, sponge cake, cream cakes, and some pound cake, and by chemical action as with bicarbonate of soda combined with other agents.' The book recommends baking soda as the simplest method (no time waiting for yeast to grow

and no effort beating eggs) and as cheaper than using eggs.

A comparison of this work with O82.10, *Cook Book and Facts Worth Knowing*, copyright 1922, shows that, although many of the recipe names are the same, this is essentially a new text.

A copy of Bradley's book at ARDA could not be found when I visited in 1993. It may match Q130.2, Q130.3, or Q130.4.

Q130.3   copyright 1924 [about 1930 or later]
—Good things to eat / made with / Cow Brand / Bicarbonate of Soda / (baking soda) / Compiled by / Alice Bradley, Principal / Miss Farmer's School of Cookery / Boston, Mass. / Church & Dwight, Ltd. / 25 Brennan Street / Montreal / Copyright 1924 by Church & Dwight, Ltd.

DESCRIPTION: 14.0 × 8.5 cm   Pp [1] 2–32   Tp illus of box of Dwight's Baking Soda, illus on p 13 of box of Dwight's Baking Soda, illus on p 29 of bottle of Dwight's Baking Soda   Paper, with image col on front of a woman mixing the contents of a bowl; stapled

CONTENTS: 1 tp; 2–30 text; 31–2 index; inside back face of binding 'Try This for Cooking Green Peas' and 'Also for Cooking String Beans'

COPIES: OGU (CCC TX715.6 B695)   OONL (A-12124) QMM (RBD ckbk 1447)   *Private collection

NOTES: See Q130.1 regarding the year of publication. On the title-page of this edition the product is called 'Cow Brand Bicarbonate of Soda (baking soda)' and the company address is 25 Brennan Street.

Q130.4   copyright 1924 [about 1930 or later]
—Good things to eat / made with / Cow Brand / Baking Soda / Compiled by / Alice Bradley, Principal / Miss Farmer's School of Cookery / Church & Dwight Limited / 2715 Reading Street / Montreal, Canada / Copyright 1924 Printed in Canada

DESCRIPTION: 14.0 × 9.0 cm   Pp [1] 2–32   Illus on p 13 of package of Dwight's Baking Soda   Paper, with black-and-white image on front of a woman stirring the contents of a bowl; stapled

CONTENTS: 1 tp; 2–mid 4 'Making Mixtures Light'; mid–bottom 4 'How to Add Cow Brand Soda'; top 5 'Baking Powder Not Needed'; mid 5–top 6 'To Measure with Spoons'; mid 6 'Butter and Shortening'; bottom 6–top 7 'Liquids'; mid 7 'To Measure with Cups'; bottom 7 'Dry Ingredients'; 8 'Butter or Other Fat' and 'Soda and Acids'; top–mid 9 'Proportions'; bottom 9–mid 10 'Time and Temperature'; mid 10–top 11 'Use of Honey in Cooking'; near top 11–13

'Rules for Baking'; 14 'Time Table for the Cook'; 15 'Kitchen Weights and Measurements'; 16–30 recipes; 31–2 'Index'; inside back face of binding 'Try This for Cooking Green Peas' and 'Also for Cooking String Beans'

COPIES: *AEUCHV (UV 85.17.159) QSH (0534)

NOTES: See Q130.1 regarding the year of publication. On the title-page of this edition the product is called 'Cow Brand Baking Soda' (with no further description) and the company address is 2715 Reading Street. There is no title-page illustration and the image on the binding is black and white, not colour.

AMERICAN EDITIONS: *Good Things to Eat Made with Arm and Hammer Baking Soda*, 1924 (Dickinson, p 87, illus p 89 of 78th ed., but year not cited); 93rd ed. [on binding], New York: Church and Dwight Co. Inc., copyright 1925 (Private collection).

Cake secrets

Carnol was a tonic for the relief of coughs, colds, and run-down conditions generally. Carnol Ltd also published Q135.1, Original Cooking Recipes.

Q131.1 nd [about 1924]

Cake / secrets / Carnol Limited / 40 St. Urbain St. Montreal, P.Q. [cover-title]

DESCRIPTION: 16.5 × 12.5 cm Pp 1–32 Paper; stapled

CONTENTS: 1 'Cake Secrets // A Complete Description of What They Are'; 2–30 recipes and testimonials; 31 testimonials; 32 verse about Carnol submitted by Charlotte Carr, 52 St James Street, Saint John, New Brunswick, and dated 1 March 1924

COPIES: BDEM OGU (UA s050 b36) OONL (TX765 C34 1924, 2 copies) QMM (RBD ckbk 1426) *Private collection

NOTES: The following note is on the inside front face of the binding: 'All the cake recipes in this booklet call for the use of "Swans Down Flour". All recipes tested and approved by Mrs. Helen R. Farquhar, Cake Specialist and Director of Domestic Science Department, Igleheart Bros., Evansville, Ind. We are indebted to this firm for giving us permission to use these recipes in full.' Carnol's *Cake Secrets* was likely published about 1924 since all the dated testimonials are from that year.

Igleheart Bros published several American editions of a cookbook, also called *Cake Secrets*, from 1915 to 1928 (see, for example, Allen, p 157). OFERWM (A1977.122.15) and OGU (CCC TX715.6 C33 1925) have *Cake Secrets*, Evansville, Indiana: Igleheart Bros,

copyright 1925, but, instead of Helen R. Farquhar as the source of the recipes, it has 'All recipes tested and approved by Mary Jean Hart, Director of Domestic Science Department'; an advertisement on p 36 for a Cake Set that cites the price for readers ordering from Canada indicates that copies were distributed in Canada. Another American edition at OGU, copyright 1926 (CCC TX715.6 C33), also gives the price for Canadians on p 36.

Copies of Carnol's *Cake Secrets* at OKITJS (991.23.3) and at OTBPM match the description above except for the cover-title, where there is clearly a comma in 'Urbain St,' (instead of 'St.'). FitzPatrickCat 111 (April 1993) No. 7 describes a copy of *Cake Secrets*, but records the date as 1921.

Q131.2 nd [about 1924]

—Good / cake / recipes / Carnol Limited / 40 St. Urbain St. Montreal, P.Q. [cover-title]

DESCRIPTION: 17.0 × 12.5 cm Pp 1–32 Paper; stapled

CONTENTS: 1 'Cake Secrets // A Complete Description of What They Are'; 2–30 recipes and testimonials; 31 testimonials; 32 verse about Carnol submitted by Charlotte Carr, 52 St James Street, Saint John, New Brunswick, and dated 1 March 1924

CITATIONS: JPCat 130, No. 140

COPIES: OONL (TX765 G66 1924 p***) OTUTF (uncat patent medicine) *Private collection

NOTES: This is a retitled edition of Q131.1. The order of publication of the two editions is unknown. The text is printed from another setting of the type.

Camp craft and woodlore

Q132.1 nd [about 1924]

Camp craft / and / woodlore / Issued by / Canadian National Railways

DESCRIPTION: 14.5 × 8.5 cm Pp [1–3] 4–48 Paper, with image on front of two cooking pots suspended over a campfire, and on back, image of a canoe on a shore; stapled

CONTENTS: 1 tp; 2 blank; 3 'Foreword'; 4 'Table of Contents'; 5–44 text; 45 'Publications'; 46–7 information about Canadian National Railways; 48 blank for 'Notes'

COPIES: *OONL (COP.CA.2.1999-764) OONMS

NOTES: The cover-title is in an organic typeface simulating sticks of wood. The OONL copy is blind-stamped on the title-page, 'Dept of the Interior // Canada // Forestry Branch'; stamped in ink, in the middle of this blind-stamp, is the date 'Jul 13 '24.' This edition is likely the earliest because it has the fewest pages and only '29 Well-Tested Hints' in the text (other editions have forty-nine hints), and there are no illustrations. It could not have been issued earlier than 1918, when Canadian National Railways was formed. 'Printed in Canada' is on the inside front face of the binding.

Concerning the order of editions, those with the image of two cooking pots on the binding and the cover-title in an organic typeface precede those with the image of one pot and the cover-title in block capital letters; those with 'Issued by Canadian National Railways' on the title-page precede those with 'Compliments of Canadian National–Grand Trunk Railways'; and those without the list of girls' and boys' camps precede those with the list.

Q132.2 nd
—Camp craft / and / woodlore / Issued by / Canadian National Railways
DESCRIPTION: With image on front of two cooking pots suspended over a campfire, and on back, image of a canoe on a shore
COPIES: *ABA OKQ (F5012 nd C186)
NOTES: The cover-title is in an organic typeface simulating sticks of wood. 'Printed in Canada' is on the inside front face of the binding. ABA reports that this undated edition has 96 pp.

Q132.3 1926
—Camp craft / and / woodlore / Issued by / Canadian National Railways / 1926
DESCRIPTION: 14.5 × 8.5 cm Pp [1] 2–96 Illus of Schafer's Method of resuscitation and illus of pressure points in case of arterial haemorrhage Paper, with image on front of two cooking pots over a campfire, and on back, image of a canoe on a shore; stapled
CONTENTS: 1 tp; 2 'Sturdy's Table of Weight for Length of Salmon and Trout'; 3 'Foreword'; 4 'Table of Contents'; 5–92 text; 93–6 information about Canadian National Railways
COPIES: *OONL (GV191.7 C28 1926 copy 1 p***)
NOTES: 'Printed in Canada' is on the inside front face of the binding. Cooking information is on pp mid 12–mid 27: 'What to Eat'; 'Hudson's Bay Company's Scale of Provisions'; 'Field Cooking' [i.e., recipes]; 'Cooking Meats' [i.e., recipes for game]; 'Cooking Fish'; 'Cooking Vegetables'; 'Cooking Utensils'; and 'The Cook Fire.'

Q132.4 1927
—Camp craft / and / woodlore / Compliments of / Canadian National–Grand / Trunk Railways / 1927

DESCRIPTION: Pp [1] 2–96 Illus of Schafer's Method of resuscitation and illus of pressure points in case of arterial haemorrhage With image on front of two cooking pots suspended over a campfire, and on back, image of a canoe on a shore; stapled
CONTENTS: 1 tp; 2 'Sturdy's Table of Weight for Length of Salmon and Trout'; 3 'Foreword'; 4 'Table of Contents'; 5–92 text; 93–6 information about Canadian National Railways
COPIES: *QMBM (Env. 4502)
NOTES: The cover-title is in an organic typeface simulating sticks of wood. Food-related sections are 'What to Eat' beginning on p 12, 'Field Cooking, with Recipes,' p 14, and 'The Cook Fire,' p 27. There is also detailed information about fishing and hunting and what to do with fish and wild game to prepare it for eating or to preserve it for later use. 'Printed in Canada' is on the inside front face of the binding.

Q132.5 1928
—Camp craft / and / woodlore / Compliments of / Canadian National–Grand / Trunk Railways / 1928 / Printed in Canada
DESCRIPTION: 14.5 × 8.5 cm Pp [1] 2–96 Illus of Schafer's Method of resuscitation and illus of pressure points in the case of arterial haemorrhage Very thin card, with image on front of a tent-and-campfire scene (only one cooking pot suspended over fire) and, on back, continuation of same landscape, with two men paddling a canoe; stapled
CONTENTS: 1 tp; 2 'Sturdy's Table of Weight for Length of Salmon and Trout'; 3 'Foreword'; 4 'Table of Contents'; 5–92 text; 93–6 information about Canadian National Railways
COPIES: OONL (2 copies: C.O.P. C.O.P.CA.T27, *GV191.7 C28 1928 p***) OONMM (SK601 C36 1928)
NOTES: The cover-title is rendered in block capital letters. 'Printed in Canada' is on the inside front face of the binding. 'Beans in the Hole,' a method of cooking beans by burying them in a pot in the ground, follows 'Field Cooking.' The month and year of printing, '1/28,' i.e., January 1928, are on p 96.

The OONL copy catalogued here is inscribed on the title-page, in ink, 'Betty Lester // Edith Phillips.'

Q132.6 1929
—Camp craft / and / woodlore / Compliments of / Canadian National / Grand Trunk Railways / 1929 / Printed in Canada
DESCRIPTION: 14.5 × 8.5 cm Pp [1] 2–96 Illus of Schafer's Method of resuscitation and illus of pres-

sure points in case of arterial haemorrhage   Cloth; sewn

CONTENTS: 1 tp; 2 'Table of Contents'; 3 'Foreword'; 4 'Sturdy's Table of Weight for Length of Salmon and Trout'; 5–87 text; 88–91 'Camps for Boys and Girls'; 92–6 information about Canadian National Railways
COPIES: *OONL (C.O.P. C.O.P.CA.TN.27)
NOTES: There is no image on the binding. The month and year of printing, '2/29,' i.e., February 1929, are on p 96.

Q132.7   nd [about 1930]
—Camp craft / and / woodlore / Compliments of / Canadian National Railways / Printed in Canada
DESCRIPTION: 14.5 × 8.0 cm   Pp [1] 2–80   Illus of Schafer's Method of resuscitation and illus of pressure points in case of arterial haemorrhage   Very thin card, with image on front of a tent-and-campfire scene (only one cooking pot suspended over fire); stapled
CONTENTS: 1 tp; 2 'Table of Contents'; 3–4 'Foreword'; 5–75 text; 76–80 information about Canadian National Railways
COPIES: *OONL (GV191.7 C28 1926 copy 2)
NOTES: The cover-title is in block capital letters. The 'Foreword' is an abridged version of Q132.6. On the inside back face of the binding, there is a list of three publications available from C.K. Howard, manager, Convention Bureau, Canadian National Railways, Montreal; of these, *Canoe Trips and Nature Photography* was published in 1930 and 1931. The reference to *Canoe Trips and Nature Photography* and the binding design suggest a publication date for this edition of *Camp Craft and Woodlore* of about 1930.

500 tested recipes

Q133.1   1924
500 / tested recipes / issued by the / members / of the / Women's Institutes / of / Stanstead County / Quebec / 1924
DESCRIPTION: 20.0 × 12.5 cm   Pp [i–ii], 1–116 [117] [$0.75, on binding]   Paper; stapled
CONTENTS: Inside front face of binding 'Weights and Measures'; i tp; ii 'Balfour & Beck printers, Lennoxville Que.'; 1–2 'Sketch of Stanstead County'; 3–116 recipes credited with the name of the contributor and ads; 117 'Contents'
COPIES: *QMM (RBD ckbk 1561)
NOTES: The QMM copy is inscribed on the front face of the binding, in ink, 'Myrtle M. Wheeler.'

L'économie domestique à l'école primaire ... IIIe année

Q134.1   1924
L'économie domestique / à / l'école primaire / [symbol of École normale classico-ménagère, Congrégation de Notre-Dame] / IIIe année / Québec / Des presses de l'Action sociale ltée / 1924
CITATIONS: BQ 08-0977   Lambert, T., p 92º
COPIES: *QSTHS
NOTES: The text is in four parts: 'Tenue de la maison'; 'Blanchissage et repassage'; 'Couture – Raccommodage – Tricot – Coupe'; and 'Art culinaire.' The 'Table des matières' shows the first lesson of 'Art culinaire' starting on p 79 and the eighth (last) lesson starting on p 106. No author is named, but she was soeur Sainte-Marie-Vitaline (Anna Fournier, 1873–1954) (Lambert, T., p 92º); for information about her and her other books, see Q128.1.

The publication in 1924 of this domestic economy textbook for the third year was prompted by reforms in the organization of the Quebec education system. The year before, in 1923, a seven-year elementary program and a complementary course were created to replace the previous progression of three levels: primary (five or six years); model (two years); and academy (two years) (Micheline Dumont, *Girls' Schooling in Quebec, 1639–1960*, Historical Booklet No. 49, Ottawa: Canadian Historical Association, 1990, p 17).

See Q140.1 and Q140.2 for a text covering the fourth year of study (published in 1925 and 1927, respectively), and Q140.3, Q140.4, and Q140.5, which incorporate both the third and fourth years (published in 1931, 1934, and 1938). Q141.1, Q141.2, Q141.3, and Q141.4 have lessons for the fifth and sixth years (published in 1925, 1928, 1932, and 1936). In 1940 Q267.1 was published incorporating lessons for the fourth, fifth, sixth, and seventh years.

See also Q94.1, *Art culinaire*, of 1916, and Q128.1, *La cuisine à l'école primaire*, of 1922, both of which treat cooking as their main subject. The latter presents lessons and recipes for the third, fourth, fifth, and sixth years of study, under the old system. Q228.1, *La cuisine à l'école complémentaire*, of 1935, presents lessons in cooking for the seventh and eighth years of study; the 1939 edition of the same title, Q228.2, presents lessons for the seventh, eighth, and ninth years. École normale classico-ménagère also produced *L'économie domestique à l'école complémentaire et aux cours de lettres-sciences*, editions in 1950 (QTURA) and 6 July 1954 (QMM).

Marius Barbeau, in Q287.1, *Saintes artisanes*, reprints a recipe for Citrouille à la mélasse au four, which he identifies as from *Manuels de cuisine et d'économie domestique.* I have not pinpointed the specific volume from which the recipe was taken.

Q134.2 1926
—[Another edition, 1926]
CITATIONS: Lambert, T., p 92°

Original cooking recipes

Carnol Ltd also published Q131.1.

Q135.1 nd [about 1924]
Original / cooking / recipes / Carnol Limited / 40 St. Urbain St. / Montreal. [cover-title]
DESCRIPTION: 18.5 × 12.5 cm Pp [1] 2–32 Paper; stapled
CONTENTS: 1–2 'Principles of Food Selection'; bottom 2 'Comparative Measurements'; top 3 'How to Measure'; mid 3–10 'Quick Breads' and testimonials; 11–12 'Griddle Cakes, Waffles and Crullers'; 13 'Baking by Temperature'; 14–23 'Cakes for All Occasions' and testimonials; 24 'Icings'; 25 testimonials; 26–8 'Pastry and Pies' and recipes for Foamy Sauce, Creamed Sweetbreads, and Scraped Beef; 29–30 testimonials; 31 'Invalid Cookery'; 32 notice of contest run by Carnol Ltd that 'closes May 1st. 1924'
CITATIONS: FitzPatrickCat 111 (April 1993) No. 8
COPIES: AMHM OAYM OONL (TX765 O75 1924 p***) OTMCL (641.5 C1264) OTUTF (flem pam 0064) OWTU (F15911) *Private collection
NOTES: Carnol was 'an appetizer, a restorative, a nutrient and a nerve tonic,' according to p 17.

An uncatalogued and incomplete copy of this book (pp 3–32 only) is found with the OONL copy of O20.5, *The Home Cook Book.*

Plymouth Church cook book

Q136.1 December 1924
[An edition of *Plymouth Church Cook Book,* compiled by the Women's Association of Plymouth Church, Sherbrooke, Quebec, December 1924, printed by Page Printing and Binding Co., Sherbrooke, pp 80]
COPIES: Private collection
NOTES: The recipes are credited with the name of the contributor.

Quebec, Department of Agriculture

For the titles of other cookbooks published by the Quebec Department of Agriculture, see Q48.1.

Q137.1 1924
Eat more / cheese / Recipes / A well balanced meal having cheese / for a basis is economical as well as / appetizing and nourishing. / Domestic Economy Service / Department of Agriculture / Province of Quebec / 1924
DESCRIPTION: 17.5 × 12.5 cm Pp [1–12] Tp illus blue-and-yellow of a wheel of cheese, illus blue-and-yellow Paper, with image on front of a slice of cheese and a steaming casserole dish; stapled
CONTENTS: 1 tp; 2–3 'A Wholesome Food – Economical and Nourishing' signed A. Désilets, B.S.A., chief of Domestic Economy Service; 4–12 'Delicious Ways to Cook and Serve Canadian Cheese' [recipes]; inside back face of binding 'Designed and printed by Canadian Advertising Agency, Limited Montreal'
COPIES: *QMM (RBD ckbk 1933)
NOTES: The cover-title is 'Cheese Recipes for Every Day.'

1925

Brodie's recipe book

For later cookbooks by Brodie and Harvie, see Q289.1, Recipe Calendar for Brodie's Self-Raising Flour [1944], Q293.1, Recettes et calendrier pour La farine préparée Brodie [1945], and Q294.1, Recipes for Brodie's Self-Raising Flour.

Q138.1 nd [about 1925]
Brodie's / recipe book / Contains a collection of tested and tried recipes dependable / and practical for the quick and economical pre- / paration of pastries and desserts / Brodie & Harvie, Limited / Montreal, P.Q.
DESCRIPTION: 17.5 × 12.5 cm Pp [1] 2–39 [40] Tp illus of a white-haired woman holding up a three-layer cake, and on the surface in front of her, a plate of biscuits and a package of Brodie and Harvie Flour; illus Paper, with tp illus on front; stapled
CONTENTS: 1 tp; 2 'Index to Recipes'; 3 'Accuracy Means Success in Every Phase of Home Cooking' signed Brodie and Harvie Ltd, Montreal; 4–39 recipes; 40 'Save the Coupons'
COPIES: *Private collection
NOTES: The cover-title is 'Brodie's Labor-Saving Reci-

pes.' Text on the inside front face of the binding states: 'In 1863. Just sixty two years ago, Brodie's XXX Self-Raising Flour made according to a formula discovered by Prof. Horsford, of Philadelphia, Pa., was introduced to Canadian housewives.' The cookbook's year of publication, therefore, is about 1925 [1863 + 62 years]. The same text says that each package of Brodie's Flour contained a coupon 'towards the free gift of valuable premiums,' such as china cups and saucers. Other Brodie's products mentioned in the publisher's advertisements and illustrated on the outside back face of the binding are custard powder, jelly powder, pearl hominy, Brose meal, farina, buckwheat flour, self-raising pancake flour, and rolled oats.

Q138.2   nd [about 1925]
—Recettes pratiques / de / Brodie / Une collection de recettes pratiques et éprouvées pour la / préparation rapide et économique de / pâtisseries et desserts. / Brodie & Harvie, limitée / Montréal, P.Q.
DESCRIPTION: 17.5 × 12.5 cm   Pp [1] 2–40   Tp illus of a white-haired woman holding up a three-layer cake, and on the surface in front of her, a plate of biscuits and a package of Brodie and Harvie Flour; illus col, illus   Paper, with tp illus on front; stapled
CONTENTS: 1 tp; 2 'Table des matières'; 3 'Pour la cuisinière, la précision est un gage de succès' signed Brodie et Harvie ltée, Montreal; 4–39 recipes; 40 'Conservez les coupons'
COPIES: *OONL (TX773 R4)
NOTES: The cover-title is 'Recettes économiques de Brodie.'

Delicious mustard recipes

For later books published by Colman-Keen (Canada) Ltd., see Q167.1, Martin, Virginia, Salad Secrets; *Q193.1,* Keen's Cook Book; *Q248.1,* Hostess Delights; *and Q303.1,* Culinary Art, *the latter under the new name, Reckitt and Colman (Canada) Ltd.*

Q139.1   nd [about 1925]
Delicious / mustard / recipes [cover-title]
DESCRIPTION: 16.0 × 8.5 cm   Pp 1–24   Paper, with image on front of a mother adding mustard to a bowl, boy watching; stapled, and with hole punched at top left corner for hanging
CONTENTS: Inside front face of binding 'Delicious Mustard Recipes compiled by the Advertising Department Colman-Keen (Canada) Limited' and 'Index' [i.e., table of contents]; 1–2 'About Mustard'; 3–7 'Mayonnaise Dressings'; 8–mid 9 'Mayonnaise Sauces';

mid 9–11 'Salads'; 12–mid 15 'Pickles'; mid 15–mid 17 'Sandwiches'; mid 17–top 22 'Various Dishes'; mid 22–24 'The Medicinal Use of Colman's D.S.F. Mustard'
COPIES: OTMCL (641.5971 H39 No. 38)   *Private collection
NOTES: 'Printed in Canada // The Federated Press Limited, Montreal' is on the outside back face of the binding. The Montreal printer indicates that it was published after 1922, the year Colman-Keen (Canada) Ltd moved its Canadian head office to Montreal from Toronto (where it was first established immediately after the First World War by its English parent company). From the appearance of the mother and boy on the binding, the book was likely published in the mid-1920s. An advertisement for Keen's Mustard in the Toronto *Globe* newspaper of 10 July 1925 offers a 'Recipe Book free'; the reference is probably to *Delicious Mustard Recipes*.
'Wallbridge's Belleville' is stamped on the front face of the binding of the OTMCL copy.

Q139.2   nd [about 1925]
—Recettes de / mets délicieux / à la moutarde [cover-title]
DESCRIPTION: 16.0 × 8.5 cm   Pp 1–24   Paper, with image on front of a woman adding Keen's Mustard to a bowl, boy watching; stapled, and with hole punched at top left corner for hanging
CONTENTS: Inside front face of binding 'Compilées par le Service de publicité de la Compagnie Colman-Keen (Canada) Limited' and 'Index' [i.e., table of contents]; 1–2 'À propos de moutarde'; 3–22 culinary recipes; 23–4 'Usages médicinaux de la Moutarde "Colman" ou "Keen"'
COPIES: *MSM
NOTES: 'Printed in Canada // The Federated Press Limited, Montreal.' is on the outside back face of the binding.

L'économie domestique à l'école primaire ... IVe année

Q140.1   1925
L'économie domestique / à / l'école primaire / théorie et pratique / IVe année / [symbol of École normale classico-ménagère, Congrégation de Notre-Dame] / Québec / Des presses de l'Action sociale ltée / 1925
DESCRIPTION: 18.5 × 12.5 cm   Pp [i–iii] iv–v [vi–ix] x–xii [xiii] xiv–xv [xvi], [1] 2–177 Illus [$0.40, on binding]   Paper, with images on front of a woman at a spinning wheel and bulrushes; sewn

CONTENTS: i blank; ii illus of subjects covered in the text; iii tp; iv illus of soeur Bourgeoys in November 1686; v 'Préface' in the form of a letter from Marguerite Bourgeoys to her 'Chères enfants' as if written 225 years after her death; vi 'Nihil obstat. Chs-E. Gagné, ptre, censeur. 26 janvier 1925. Imprimatur. L.-N. card. Bégin, arch. de Québec. Archevêché de Québec, 26 janvier 1925.'; vii–viii letter from Cardinal Bégin to la révérende mère provinciale, Congrégation de Notre-Dame, Québec, dated 27 December 1924; ix–xii 'Introduction'; xiii–xv 'Répartition du programme // 4e année' from September to June; xvi blank; 1–174 text in five parts: 'Tenue de la maison,' 'Blanchissage et repassage du linge,' 'Travaux à l'aiguille,' 'Art culinaire,' and 'Horticulture'; 175 ...
CITATIONS: BQ 08-0979   Lambert, T., p 92°
COPIES: *QTURA   QSTHS
NOTES: The fourth part, 'Art culinaire,' is on pp 105–60. No author is named, but she was soeur Sainte-Marie-Vitaline (Anna Fournier, 1873–1954) (Lambert, T., p 92°); for information about her and her other books, see Q128.1. For references to other texts presenting lessons for different years, see Q134.1.

Q140.2   1927
—L'économie domestique / à / l'école primaire / théorie et pratique / IVe annee / [symbol of École normale classico-ménagère, Congrégation de Notre-Dame] / Québec / Des presses de l'Action sociale ltée / 1927
DESCRIPTION: 18.0 × 12.5 cm   Pp [i–iii] iv–v [vi–ix] x–xii [xiii] xiv–xv [xvi], [1] 2–177   Illus   [$0.40, on binding]   Paper, with images on front of a girl in a kitchen and bulrushes; sewn
CONTENTS: i blank; ii illus of subjects covered in the text; iii tp; iv illus of soeur Bourgeoys in November 1686; v 'Préface' in the form of a letter from Marguerite Bourgeoys to her 'Chères enfants' as if written 225 years after her death; vi 'Nihil obstat. 19 juillet 1927. Chs-E. Gagné, ptre, censeur. Imprimatur. Archevêché de Québec, 19 juillet 1927. Mgr I.-O.-P. Cloutier, V.G.'; vii–viii letter from Cardinal Bégin to la révérende mère provinciale, Congrégation de Notre-Dame, Québec, dated 27 December 1924; ix–xii 'Introduction'; xiii–xv 'Répartition du programme // 4e année' from September to June; xvi blank; 1–174 text in five parts: 'Tenue de la maison,' 'Blanchissage et repassage du linge,' 'Travaux à l'aiguille,' 'Art culinaire,' and 'Horticulture'; 175 ...
CITATIONS: BQ 08-0980   Lambert, T., p 92°
COPIES: *QTURA

Q140.3   [3rd ed.], 1931
—L'économie domestique / à / l'école primaire / IIIe et IVe années / [symbol of École normale classico-ménagère, Congrégation de Notre-Dame] / Approuvé, par le Comité catholique du / Conseil de l'instruction publique, le / 23 septembre 1925 / Québec / Des presses de l'Action sociale, ltée / 1931
DESCRIPTION: 19.5 × 13.0 cm   Pp [i–v] vi, [1] 2–221   Illus   [$0.40, on binding]   Paper, with image on front of bulrushes; sewn
CONTENTS: i tp; ii illus of subjects covered in the text; iii 'Préface' in the form of a letter from Marguerite Bourgeoys to her 'Chères enfants' as if written 225 years after her death; iv illus of soeur Bourgeoys in November 1686; v–mid vi letter from Cardinal Bégin to la révérende mère provinciale, Congrégation de Notre-Dame, Québec, dated 27 December 1924; bottom vi 'Nihil obstat. 19 juillet 1927. Chs-E. Gagné, ptre, censeur. Imprimatur. Archevêché de Québec, 19 juillet 1927. Mgr I.-O.-P. Cloutier, V.G.'; 1–218 text in four parts: 'Tenue de la maison,' 'Le vêtement,' 'Alimentation,' and 'Horticulture'; 219–21 'Table des matières'
CITATIONS: Lambert, T., p 92°
COPIES: *QTURA
NOTES: 'Troisième édition revue, corrigée et augmentée' is on the front face of the binding. The third part, 'Alimentation,' is on pp 143–98.

Q140.4   [4th ed.], 1934
—L'économie domestique / à / l'école primaire / IIIe et IVe années / [symbol of École normale classico-ménagère, Congrégation de Notre-Dame] / Approuvé, par le Comité catholique du / Conseil de l'instruction publique, le / 23 septembre 1925 / Québec / Des presses de l'Action sociale, ltée / 1934
DESCRIPTION: 19.5 × 13.0 cm   Pp [i–v] vi, [1] 2–216   Illus   [$0.35, on binding]   Rebound in cloth; original paper applied to new cloth; with image on front of bulrushes
CONTENTS: i tp; ii illus of subjects covered in the text; iii 'Préface' in the form of a letter from Marguerite Bourgeoys to her 'Chères enfants' as if written 234 years after her death; iv illus of soeur Bourgeoys in November 1686; v–mid vi letter from Cardinal Bégin to la révérende mère provinciale, Congrégation de Notre-Dame, Québec, dated 27 December 1924; bottom vi 'Nihil obstat. Edgar Chouinard, ptre, censor // Imprimatur. B. Ph. Garneau, V.G. 6 août 1934.'; 1–213 text in four parts: 'Tenue de la maison,' 'Le vêtement,' 'Alimentation,' and 'Horticulture'; 214–16 'Table des matières'
CITATIONS: Lambert, T., p 92°

COPIES: *QTURA

NOTES: 'Quatrième édition revue, corrigée et augmentée' is on the front face of the binding. The third part, 'Alimentation,' is on pp 139–93.

Q140.5 [5th ed.], 1938

—L'économie domestique / à / l'école primaire / IIIe et IVe années / [symbol of École normale classico-ménagère, Congrégation de Notre-Dame] / Approuvé, par le Comité catholique du / Conseil de l'instruction publique, le / 23 septembre 1925 / Québec / Des presses de l'Action sociale ltée / 1938

DESCRIPTION: 21.5 × 14.5 cm   Pp [i–iii] iv, [1] 2–217 [218], [i–ii], 1–16   Illus   [$0.35, on binding]   Paper, with image on front of bulrushes; sewn

CONTENTS: i tp; ii illus of soeur Bourgeoys in November 1686; iii–mid iv letter from Cardinal Bégin to la révérende mère provinciale, Congrégation de Notre-Dame, Québec, dated 27 December 1924; bottom iv 'Nihil obstat. Chan. Edgar Chouinard, ptre. Librorum censor ex officio. Imprimatur. B.-Ph. Garneau, V.G. Quebeci, die 11a julii 1938.'; 1–214 text in four parts: 'Tenue de la maison,' 'Le vêtement,' 'Alimentation,' and 'Horticulture'; 215–17 'Table des matières'; 218 illus signed Gérard Morisset; i part-title: 'Supplément à l'économie domestique IIIe et IVe années // Causerie sur les bienséances.'; ii blank; 1–16 text

CITATIONS: Lambert, T., p 92°

COPIES: *QTURA

NOTES: 'Cinquième édition revue, corrigée et augmentée' is on the front face of the binding. The third part, 'Alimentation,' is on pp 139–92.

L'économie domestique à l'école primaire … Ve et VIe années

Q141.1 1925

L'économie domestique / à / l'école primaire / théorie et pratique / Ve et VIe années / [symbol of École normale classico-ménagère, Congrégation de Notre-Dame] / Québec / L'Action sociale ltée / 1925

CITATIONS: BQ 08-0981   Lambert, T., p 92°

COPIES: QSTHS

NOTES: No author is named, but she was soeur Sainte-Marie-Vitaline (Anna Fournier, 1873–1954) (Lambert, T., p 92°); for information about her and her other books, see Q128.1. For references to texts presenting lessons for different years, see Q134.1.

Q141.2 1928

—L'économie domestique / à / l'école primaire / théorie et pratique / Ve et VIe années / [symbol of École normale classico-ménagère, Congrégation de Notre-Dame] / Québec / L'Action sociale ltée / 1928

DESCRIPTION: 18.0 × 12.5 cm   Pp [i–vii] viii [ix] x–xii [xiii] xiv–xvii, [1] 2–253   Illus   Rebound; sewn

CONTENTS: i illus of subjects covered in the text; ii tp; iii illus of soeur Bourgeoys in November 1686; iv blank; v 'Préface' in the form of a letter from Marguerite Bourgeoys to her 'Chères enfants' as if written 125 [sic] years after her death; vi 'Nihil obstat. Arthur Robert, pter, censor deputatus. Imprimatur. f.R.M. card. Rouleau, o.p. Archiepus Quebecensis // Quebeci, 10 maii 1928. Enregistré, conformément à la loi du Parlement du Canada, l'an 1925, … par l'École normale classico-ménagère de Saint-Pascal.'; vii–viii letter from Cardinal Bégin to la révérende mère provinciale, Congrégation de Notre-Dame, Québec, dated 27 December 1924; ix–xii 'Introduction'; xiii–xvii 'Répartition du programme' from September to June (Ve année) and September to June (VIe année); 1–250 text in five parts: 'Tenue de la maison,' 'Blanchissage et repassage,' 'Couture – Broderie – Raccommodage – Tricot – Coupe,' 'Art culinaire,' and 'Horticulture'; 251–3 'Table des matières' and at bottom p 253, 'Ouvrage approuvé … le 23 septembre 1925'

CITATIONS: Lambert, T., p 92°

COPIES: *QTURA

NOTES: The roman numbering begins on the verso of the first printed leaf. 'Art culinaire' is on pp 149–237.

Q141.3 1932

—L'économie domestique / à / l'école primaire / théorie et pratique / Ve et VIe années / [symbol of École normale classico-ménagère, Congrégation de Notre-Dame] / Québec / Des presses de l'Action sociale, ltée / 1932

DESCRIPTION: 20.0 × 13.5 cm   Pp [i–iv] v [vi], [1] 2–231   Illus   [$0.50, on binding]   Paper, with image on front of a fireplace; sewn

CONTENTS: i tp; ii illus of soeur Bourgeoys in November 1686; iii 'Préface' in the form of a letter from Marguerite Bourgeoys to her 'Chères enfants' as if written 125 [sic] years after her death; iv–mid v letter from Cardinal Bégin to la révérende mère provinciale, Congrégation de Notre-Dame, Québec, dated 27 December 1924; bottom v 'Nihil obstat. Arthur Robert, pter, censor deputatus. Imprimatur. Mgr J.-O.-P. Cloutier. Québec, 19 juillet 1927. Enregistré, conformément à la loi du Parlement du Canada, l'an 1925, … par l'École normale classico-ménagère de Saint-Pascal.'; vi blank; 1–228 text in five parts: 'Tenue de la maison,' 'Blanchissage et repassage,' 'Couture – Broderie – Raccommodage – Tricot – Coupe,' 'Art

culinaire,' and 'Horticulture'; 229–31 'Table des matières' and at bottom p 231, 'Ouvrage approuvé ... le 23 septembre 1925'
CITATIONS: BQ 08-0982   Lambert, T., p 92°
COPIES: *QTURA
NOTES: 'Art culinaire' is on pp 134–214.

Q141.4 1936
—L'économie domestique / à / l'école primaire / théorie et pratique / Ve et VIe années / [symbol of École normale classico-ménagère, Congrégation de Notre-Dame] / Québec / Des presses de l'Action sociale, ltée / 1936
DESCRIPTION: 20.0 × 13.5 cm   Pp [i–iv], [1] 2–252   Illus   [$0.50, on binding]   Paper, with image on front of a fireplace; sewn
CONTENTS: i tp; ii illus of soeur Bourgeoys in November 1686; iii 'Préface' in the form of a letter from Marguerite Bourgeoys to her 'Chères enfants' as if written 235 years after her death; iv 'Nihil obstat. Edgar Chouinard, ptre // Imprimi potest. B.-Ph. Garneau, V.G Quebeci 14 febr. 1936.'; 1–224 text in five parts: 'Tenue de la maison,' 'Blanchissage et repassage,' 'Couture – Broderie – Raccommodage – Tricot,' 'Art culinaire,' and 'Sciences naturelles et horticulture'; 225–7 'Table des matières'; 228 illus signed Gérard Morisset; 229 part-title: 'Supplément à l'Économie domestique Ve et VIe années // Causeries sur les bienséances'; 230 'Pour faire suite aux études qui précèdent, ... nous exposons dans ce nouveau chapitre (Supplément) les règles essentielles du savoir-vivre.'; 231–52 text
CITATIONS: Lambert, T., p 92°
COPIES: *QTURA
NOTES: 'Art culinaire' is on pp 122–98.

Morrison, Gladys Earle

The 1911 Census and Montreal city directories indicate that the author was likely born in December 1885 and married to W.J. Morrison, sporting editor at the Gazette.

Q142.1 [1925]
Our best recipes / M.A.A.A. [cover-title]
DESCRIPTION: 22.0 × 14.0 cm   Pp [3–5] 6–184, [i–xxiv]   Cloth; sewn
CONTENTS: 3 'Our Best Recipes' signed Gladys Earle Morrison, convenor, and dated '"Cookery Corner" M.A.A. Carnival, April 15–16–17–18 1925'; 4–5 table of contents; 6–7 'Diets // Reducing Diet'; 8 'Diet for

Athletes' signed A.A. MacKay, M.D.; 9–10 'Tables & Measures'; 11–184 recipes; i–xxiv ads and at bottom p xxiv, 'Southam Press Limited Montreal & Toronto'
CITATIONS: Armstrong 2000, p F2
COPIES: OGU (CCC TX715.6 M6677)   OONL (TX715 M5787 1925)   QMM (2 copies: RBD ckbk 1844; RBD Vanna Garnier, ckbk 579)   QMMMCM (RB-1046)   *Private collection
NOTES: The recipes were submitted by members and friends of the Montreal Amateur Athletic Association. The QMMMCM copy is inscribed by the author, on the front endpaper, in ink, 'Presented to the McCord Museum by Gladys Earle Morrison Montreal May 7th/1925.'

The 'Regal' cook book

Q143.1 nd [about 1925]
The "Regal" / cook book [cover-title]
DESCRIPTION: 22.5 × 15.0 cm   Pp [i–iv], 1–122   2 pls col ('Mills' opp p 8 and ad for Regal Flour opp p 26), many small illus orange   Thin card, with pl col mounted on front face of binding of a woman measuring Regal Flour
CONTENTS: i 'The Regal Cook Book contains 1000 recipes tested by leading housewives of Canada ... The St. Lawrence Flour Mills Company, Limited ... Montreal'; ii blank; iii 'A Word to Canadian Housewives on "Regal Flour" and the St. Lawrence Flour Mills'; iv blank; 1–117 text; 118–22 'Table of Contents' [i.e., alphabetical index]
COPIES: *Private collection
NOTES: Page iii begins, 'In presenting this third issue of our cook book, ...' I have been unable to compare the text of this book with other cookbooks by St Lawrence Flour Mills to determine whether they are related, i.e., Q88.1, Q160.1, and Q191.1.

Q143.2 nd [about 1925]
—Les recettes / "Regal" [cover-title]
DESCRIPTION: Pl (probably col) mounted on front face of binding of a woman measuring Regal Flour
COPIES: *Private collection
NOTES: The book's owner reports that this volume of 146 pp was printed in Montreal by L'agence cndne de publicité ltée. The first page begins, 'Le livre de recettes Regal comprend 1000 recettes éprouvées par nos meilleures ménagères canadiennes et recueillies spécialement pour cet ouvrage ...,' and is signed La cie St. Lawrence Flour Mills, limitée.

Science and arts of home life for elementary grades: Beginners course

Q144.1   1929 [copyright 1925]
Science and arts / of / home life / for elementary grades / Beginners course / [symbol of Congrégation de Notre-Dame, Montreal] / Montreal / 1929
DESCRIPTION: 18.5 × 12.5 cm   Pp [i–vii] viii–x, [1–2] 3–166 Illus [$0.50, on binding]   Paper, with three small images on front: a girl standing at a kitchen table, symbol of Congrégation de Notre-Dame, and a woman gardening; sewn
CONTENTS: i blank; ii 'Nihil obstat. 19 juillet 1927. Chs.-E Gagné, ptre. censeur. Imprimatur. Archevêché de Québec, 19 juillet 1927, mgr I.-O-P. Cloutier, VG. Nil obstat. 18-VII-29 M.-Léo Derome, SAC, censor delegatus. Imprimatur: George Coadjutor Archbishop of Montreal. Copyright. Ottawa, 1925.'; iii blank; iv seven illus headed 'Science and Arts of Home Life Teaches:'; v tp; vi fp illus of 'Our Pioneer School of Domestic Arts November, 1686'; vii–x 'Introduction'; 1–41 'Part One // Housekeeping'; 42–56 'Part Two // Washing and Ironing'; 57–93 'Part Three // Needlework, Knitting, Cutting'; 94–148 'Part Four // Cooking'; 149–62 'Part Five // Gardening'; 163–6 'Contents'
COPIES: OONL (TX167 S36 1929)   *QMACN (570.565 (1))   QMBN (TX167 S36 1929)   QQLA (TX167 S416 1929)
NOTES: 'Volume I' is on the spine. 'La "Croix" Printing, 309 Notre-Dame East, Montreal.' is on the outside back face of the binding. Lambert, T., p 93º, cites the 1925 edition, but not 1929.

Science and arts of home life for elementary grades: More advanced course

Q145.1   1929 [copyright 1925]
Science and arts / of / home life / for elementary grades / more advanced course / [symbol of Congrégation de Notre-Dame, Montreal] / Montreal / 1929
DESCRIPTION: 18.5 × 13.0 cm   Pp [iii–ix] x [xi] xii–xiv, [1–2] 3–179 Illus [$0.50, on binding]   Paper, with image on front of a house; sewn
CONTENTS: iii blank; iv 'Nihil obstat. 19 juillet 1927. Chs.-E. Gagné, ptre. censeur. Imprimatur. Archevêché de Québec, 19 juillet 1927, mgr I.-O.-P. Cloutier, V.G. Nihil obstat: 18-VII-29 M.-Léo Derome, SAC., censor delegatus. Imprimatur: George Coadjutor Archbishop of Montreal. Copyright, Ottawa, 1925.'; v blank; vi seven illus headed 'Science and Arts of Home Life Teaches:'; vii tp; viii fp illus of 'Our Pioneer School of Domestic Arts 1686'; ix–x letter from L.N. [i.e., Louis-Nazaire] cardinal Bégin, Arch. de Québec, to Reverend Mother Provincial, Congrégation de Notre Dame, Quebec, 27 December 1924; xi–xiv 'Introduction'; 1–36 'Part One // Housekeeping'; 37–56 'Part Two // Washing and Ironing'; 57–97 'Part Three // Needlework'; 98–161 'Part Four // Cooking'; 162–75 'Part Five // Gardening'; 176 blank; 177–9 'Contents'
CITATIONS: BQ 08-0984   Lambert, T., p 93º
COPIES: *QMACN (570.565 (2))   QMBN (TX167 S365 1929)
NOTES: Lambert, T., p 93º, cites the 1929 edition, but not 1925.

Victory recipes

The Dominion Flour Mill [sic] Ltd is first listed in the Montreal city directory for 1914–15. In the directories for 1918–19 on, it is listed as Dominion Flour Mills Ltd. According to the 1918–19 directory, William B. Wood was general manager.

Q146.1   nd [about 1925]
Victory recipes / [Caption:] Montreal plant. / One of the six mills in which / Victory Flour is made. Daily / capacity, 3,000 barrels. / Dominion Flour Mills, Limited / Montreal, Canada [cover-title]
DESCRIPTION: 17.0 × 12.5 cm   Pp [1–2] 3–31   A few illus   Paper, with image on front of the company's Montreal plant; stapled, and with hole punched at top left corner for hanging
CONTENTS: 1 cover-title; 2 'Put your hand in the strong, pure hand of Victory and smile at baking day'; 3–4 'Introduction'; 5 'Kitchen Wisdom'; 6–9 'Victory Recipes'; 10–12 'Biscuits and Muffins'; 13–19 'Cakes and Cookies'; 20–1 'Cake Filling and Frosting'; 22–5 'Pastry and Pudding'; 26–7 'Pudding Sauces'; 28 'Victory Truths'; 29–31 'Index to Recipes'
COPIES: *NBMOM
NOTES: 'Victory' in the book title does not refer to wartime, but to the name of the flour. 'Designed and printed in Montreal by Dodd-Simpson Press' is on the outside back face of the binding. The 'Introduction' states: 'The Dominion Flour Mills, Limited, is incorporated under a federal charter with an authorized capital of $1,500,000. Its directorate embraces a number of the ablest financiers of the City of Montreal, and an equal number of the best and most successful flour millers of Western Canada. Its general manager began business in a little grist mill in the County of Brant over thirty years ago, ...'

Watkins cook book

For information about the J.R. Watkins Co. and the titles of its other cookbooks, see M36.1.

Q147.1 copyright 1925
Watkins / cook book / [caption:] A composite grouping of all the manufacturing and / administrative properties of the J.R. Watkins Company. / These many buildings house the model facilities so / essential to creation of superior products for the home. / Copyright, 1925, by / the J.R. Watkins Company / The J.R. Watkins Company / From ocean to ocean / New York Chicago Boston Newark Columbus Kansas City / Winona Memphis Oakland / Montreal Hamilton Winnipeg Vancouver
DESCRIPTION: 15.5 × 11.5 cm   Pp [1–2] 3–64   Tp illus of Watkins Co. properties, illus col   Paper, with image on front of four prepared dishes; stapled
CONTENTS: 1 tp; 2 table of contents; 3–6 'The Secret of Artistic, Appealing Meals'; 7–60 recipes; 61 'Kitchen Weights and Measures'; 62–3 'Index to Recipes'; 64 'Watkins Products' and at bottom, 'Printed in U.S.A.'
COPIES: BNEM   OWASRM   *Private collection
NOTES: The centre spread on pp 32–3 is a colour illustration of the company's products.

Q147.2 copyright 1926
—Watkins / cook book / [caption:] A composite grouping of all the manufacturing and / administrative properties of the J.R. Watkins Company. / These many buildings house the model facilities so / essential to creation of superior products for the home. / Copyright, 1926, by / the J.R. Watkins Company / The J.R. Watkins Company / From ocean to ocean / New York Chicago Newark Columbus Kansas City / Winona Memphis Oakland / Montreal Hamilton Winnipeg Vancouver
DESCRIPTION: 15.0 × 11.5 cm   Pp [1–2] 3–64   Tp illus of Watkins Co. properties, illus col   Paper, with image on front of four prepared dishes; stapled
CONTENTS: 1 tp; 2 table of contents; 3–6 'The Secret of Artistic, Appealing Meals'; 7–60 recipes; 61 'Kitchen Weights and Measures'; 62–3 index; 64 list of Watkins products and at bottom, 'Printed in U.S.A.'
COPIES: SBIHM   SBIM   *Private collection
NOTES: The centre spread on pp 32–3 is a colour illustration of the company's products. Page 3 states that 'sixty years ago Watkins set out to build a business ...'

Q147.3 copyright 1935
—Watkins / cook / book / Copyright, Canada, 1935 / Printed in Canada / The J.R. Watkins Co. / Montreal, Winnipeg, Vancouver
DESCRIPTION: 19.0 × 12.5 cm   Pp [1] 2–48   Illus on pp 24–5 of company buildings   Paper, with image on front of a woman carrying a steaming dish; stapled
CONTENTS: 1 tp; 2–45 text; 46–7 index; 48 'A Handy Checking List of Watkins Products'
CITATIONS: Ferguson/Fraser, p 234, illus col on p 80 of closed volume
COPIES: ADEAHM   AEPMA (2 copies)   ARDA   BVIPM   MBDHM   MTM   OGU (UA s070 b04)   OONL (TX715 W333 1935)   OTMCL (641.5971 H39 No. 50)   OTUTF (uncat patent medicine)   *Private collection
NOTES: The colour illustration in Ferguson/Fraser is of the copy catalogued here. The BVIPM copy is stamped on the title-page, 'H.R. Fowler Phone 1046L 474 Milton St. Nanaimo, B.C.' The OTMCL copy is inscribed on p 48, in the blank space for 'Your Watkins Dealer,' in ink, 'C. Wilson // Byron Ont.' Another private collector's copy (not the one catalogued here) is inscribed on p 48, in the blank space, in pencil, 'Benjamin J. Amiro, Lower East Pubnico' [i.e., in Nova Scotia].

Q147.4 copyright 1935
—[An edition of *Livre de recettes culinaires Watkins*, Montreal: J.R. Watkins Co., copyright 1935, pp 48, illus, 20 cm]
COPIES: OONL (TX715.6 L58 1935, not on shelf)

Q147.5 copyright 1938
—Watkins / cook book / Price $1.50 / Copyright, 1938, by the J.R. Watkins Company / The J.R. Watkins Company / Newark Memphis Winona Oakland / Montreal Winnipeg Vancouver / AS902 Printed in U.S.A.
DESCRIPTION: 21.0 × 15.0 cm   Pp [1–4] 5–288   Double-sided pls col between pp 48–9, 120–1, 192–3, and 240–1 of Watkins's products; illus on p 288 of salad-dressing bottle with measurements
CONTENTS: 1 tp; 2 blank; 3 'To all Watkins customers:' signed Elaine Allen; 4 table of contents; 5–285 recipes; 286 'Well-Balanced Meals'; 287 'Kitchen Weights, Measures and Temperatures'; 288 'Watkins Special Salad Dressing'
COPIES: *Private collection
NOTES: Printed on p 288 is 'AS902-400M-638-1951'; on the inside back face of the binding, 'Wire-O Bind-

ing Patents pending.' The letter on p 3 informs the reader: 'The Watkins New Cook Book of 200 pages issued in June 1936, proved an instantaneous success; the first printing of 175,000 copies was exhausted within three months. A second printing of 500,000 copies was distributed within eighteen months ... another printing was necessary and it was decided to print an enlarged book ...'

Elaine Allen wrote Q298.1, *Watkins Salad Book*.

Q147.6   7th ed., copyright 1948
—[Watkins] / cook book / by Elaine Allen / author of / Watkins Salad Book / Watkins Household Hints Book / Watkins Economy Recipe Book / Price $2.00 / Copyright, 1948, by the J.R. Watkins Company / The J.R. Watkins Company / Newark Memphis Winona Oakland / Montreal Winnipeg Vancouver / Seventh edition / Printed in U.S.A.
DESCRIPTION: 21.0 × 15.0 cm   Pp [1–2] 3–288   2 double-sided pls col btwn pp 96–7 and 192–3, 1 double-sided pl btwn pp 144–5   Cloth; wire
CONTENTS: 1 tp; 2 table of contents; 3–288 text
COPIES: OONL (TX715 W333 1948)   SEEK   *Private collection

Q147.7   8th ed., copyright 1948
—Watkins / cook book / by Elaine Allen / author of / Watkins Salad Book / Watkins Household Hints Book / Watkins Economy Recipe Book / Price $2.00 / Copyright, 1948, by the J.R. Watkins Company / The J.R. Watkins Company / Newark Memphis Winona Oakland / Montreal Winnipeg Vancouver / Eighth edition / Printed in U.S.A.
DESCRIPTION: 20.5 × 15.0 cm   Pp [1–2] 3–288   2 double-sided pls col incl frontis, 1 double-sided pl, illus on p 288 of bottle with measurements for 'Watkins Special Salad Dressing'   Cloth; wire
CONTENTS: 1 tp; 2 'Table of Contents'; 3–288 text
COPIES: *QMM (RBD ckbk 1251)

AMERICAN EDITIONS: 1926 (Allen, p 175); Winona, Minn.: J.R. Watkins Co., copyright 1930 (United States: InU); Winona, Minn.: J.R. Watkins Co., copyright 1936 (BSUM, OONL; United States: DLC, InU); Winona, Minn: J.R. Watkins Co., copyright 1938 (BKOM, OGU; United States: InU); 4th ed., Racine, Wis.: J.R. Watkins Co., copyright 1943 (Private collection); 5th ed., Newark: J.R. Watkins Co., copyright 1945 (Private collection; United States: DLC); 6th ed., Newark, Memphis, Winona, Oakland: J.R. Watkins Co., copyright 1945 (OFERWM, OVOH).

1925–7

The 'Oxo' cook book

Oxo is a British beef extract. For other Oxo recipe collections, see Q172.1, How to Make Many Tasty Dishes, *and Q229.1,* New Recipes of Flavor.

Q148.1   nd [about 1925–7]
[An edition of *The 'Oxo' Cook Book* [cover-title], [Montreal: Oxo Ltd, nd], pp 16, illus, 18 cm]
COPIES: OONL (TX715.6 O86 1930z missing)
NOTES: See Q148.2 regarding the date of publication.

Q148.2   nd [about 1925–7]
—Livre de cuisine / "Oxo" / L'ami de la / bonne ménagère / "Le puissant atome" [cover-title]
DESCRIPTION: 18.0 × 12.0 cm   Pp 1–16   Illus brown Paper, with image on front of a woman adding an Oxo cube to a saucepan; stapled
CONTENTS: Inside front face of binding 'Avez-vous une bonne recette? Les recettes contenues dans ce livre sont en grande partie choisies parmi une foule de ces recettes que nous envoient les femmes qui, dans la préparation de leurs aliments, emploient le cordial "Oxo" avec une grande satisfaction ...,' illus of 6-ounce and 16-ounce bottles, and 'Oxo Limited, 356, rue St. Antoine, Montréal, P.Q.'; 1 'Faire meilleur avec le cordial "Oxo"'; 2–16 recipes
COPIES: *QMM (Env. 7849)
NOTES: The company address indicates a publication date of about 1925–7: Oxo Ltd is first listed in the Montreal city directory for 1924–5, at 232 Lemoine; in the directories for 1925–6 and 1927–8, the company is at 356 St Antoine; in the directory for 1928–9, the address changes to 1910 St Antoine. The text is printed in brown, an appropriate colour for recipes using beef extract.

1925–8

Borden's St Charles Milk

For information about the company and its other books, see Q106.1.

Q149.1   nd [about 1925–8]
Borden's / St. Charles Milk / The Borden Company, Limited / Established 1857 / 180 St. Paul St West Montreal P.Q.
DESCRIPTION: 16.5 × 12.5 cm   Pp [1–3] 4–32   Tp illus col of table set with desserts, coffee, and a vase of

flowers; illus col; illus on p 2 of Gail Borden   Paper, with two images on front: at top, a building on a hill; at bottom, a kitchen table; stapled
CONTENTS: 1 tp; 2–3 'Gail Borden' and at bottom p 3, 'All Measures Are Level'; 4–31 recipes; 32 index and 'Southam Press Ltd. Montreal'
COPIES: ACG   BSUM   QMM (RBD ckbk 1338)   *Private collection
NOTES: According to p 3, 'Many of the recipes in this book were prize recipes received from every part of the country, others are by leading food experts.'

From appearances, Q149.1 and Q149.2 were published in the mid-1920s. Listings for the company in Montreal city directories show that the two editions must have been published within the period 1920–8. The directory for 1919–20 (and before) gives the name Borden Milk Co. Ltd; directories from 1920–1 and onward give the name Borden Co. Ltd, as used in the cookbooks. From the 1915–16 directory to the 1927–8 directory, the company's address is 180 St Paul West, as in the cookbooks; in the 1928–9 directory (and to the early 1930s), the address changes to 140 St Paul West. The order of publication of the two undated editions is unknown.

Q149.1 and Q149.2 are differentiated in three ways: by the lettering on the front face of the binding (in Q149.1, the letters in the word EVAPORATED are all the same height and square on the page, as printed here; in Q149.2, although the bottom of the word follows a straight line, the top of the word is curved, with the outside letters tallest and the middle letters shortest); by the printer recorded on p 32; and by the punctuation in Borden's address on the title-page.

A copy at OONL (TX715.6 B67 1920z p***) has the same title-page and same printer on p 32 as Q149.1, but the front face of the binding matches the description for Q149.2. An unidentified edition is at SBIHM.

Q149.2   nd [about 1925–8]
— Borden's / St. Charles Milk / The Borden Company, Limited / Established 1857 / 180 St. Paul St. West Montreal, P.Q.
DESCRIPTION: 16.5 × 12.5 cm   Pp [1–3] 4–32   Tp illus col of table set with desserts, coffee, and a vase of flowers; illus col; illus on p 2 of Gail Borden   Paper, with two images on front: at top, a building on a hill; at bottom, a kitchen table; stapled
CONTENTS: 1 tp; 2–3 'Gail Borden' and at bottom p 3, 'All Measures Are Level'; 4–31 recipes; 32 index and 'Standard Litho Co. Limited Montreal'
COPIES: BDEM   *Private collection
NOTES: See the notes for Q149.1.

AMERICAN EDITIONS: *Borden's Evaporated Milk Book of Recipes*, nd [about 1919], pp 32 (Allen, p 202, illus on p 44 shows front face of binding with same design as the Canadian editions).

37 *delightful breads and some cakes*

For the titles of other books about cooking with Fleischmann's Yeast, see O131.1.

Q150.1   nd [about 1925–8]
37 / delightful / breads / and / some cakes / The Fleischmann Company / Offices in all principal cities / [folio:] 3
DESCRIPTION: 16.0 × 10.0 cm   Pp [1–2] 3–48   Illus brown   Paper, with image on front of a man and woman, in formal dress, standing in a pantry, eating and drinking; stapled
CONTENTS: 1 'Variety in Bread Delicious and So Easy'; 2 blank; 3 tp; 4 untitled introduction; 5–8 index; 9 'Are You Serving a Variety of Breads?'; 10–14 'Little Arts in Bread Baking'; 15–22 '12 Breads the Clever Hostess Serves'; 23–6 'Bread Easily Becomes Rolls and Biscuits'; 27–30 'The Magic Touch That Makes Bread Buns'; 31–6 'Muffins Griddle Cakes Waffles & Doughnuts Are Bread, Too –'; 37–40 'Breads That Masquerade as Cakes'; 41–4 'Breads That Are Really Desserts'; 45–7 'Yeast – and the Family Health'; 48 book-order form and at bottom, 'Printed in Canada'
COPIES: ACG   *Private collection
NOTES: The cover-title is 'Delicious Recipes.' The clothes worn by the man and woman on the binding point to publication in the mid-1920s, and they are an earlier style than those depicted in Q150.2, published in 1928. The recipes were to be made with Fleischmann's Yeast. The book-order form cites company offices in Montreal, Toronto, Vancouver, Winnipeg, Saint John, New Brunswick, Halifax, and Calgary.

Q150.2   1928
—Delightful / breads / and buns / and / coffee cakes / 1928 edition / The Fleischmann Company / Offices in all principal cities
DESCRIPTION: 16.5 × 10.0 cm   Pp [3–4] 5–50   Illus   Paper, with image on front of a woman and man seated at a table set for tea; stapled
CONTENTS: 3 tp; 4 fp illus captioned 'For elaborate meals and for simple meals the most satisfactory appetizer is variety'; 5–8 table of contents; 9–10 'Variety in Breads Stimulates Their Appetite'; 11–14 'Little Arts in Bread Baking'; 15–20 'Breads the Clever Hostess Serves'; 21–4 'Bread Easily Becomes Rolls and

Biscuits'; 25–30 'The Magic Touch That Makes Bread Buns'; 31–6 'Muffins Griddle Cakes Waffles and Doughnuts Are Breads Too'; 37–40 'The Famous Sally Lunn and Other Fancy Breads'; 41–5 'Breads That Masquerade as Cakes'; 46–8 'Yeast – and the Family Health'; 49–50 book-order form and at bottom p 50, 'Printed in Canada'
COPIES: *BSUM   OGU (CCC TX715.6 D4555)   OONL (TX769 D45 1928, 2 copies)   SSWD
NOTES: The cover-title is 'Recipes for Delicious Varieties of Breads.'

Q150.3   1931
—Delightful / breads / and buns / and / coffee cakes / 1931 edition / Standard Brands Limited / Offices in all principal cities
DESCRIPTION: 16.5 × 10.0 cm   Pp [3–4] 5–50   Illus   Lacks binding; stapled
CONTENTS: 3 tp; 4 fp illus of persons at a formally set table; 5–8 index; 9–10 'Variety in Breads Stimulates Their Appetite'; 11–14 'Little Arts in Bread Baking'; 15–20 'Breads the Clever Hostess Serves'; 21–4 'Bread Easily Becomes Rolls and Biscuits'; 25–30 'The Magic Touch That Makes Bread Buns'; 31–6 'Muffins Griddle Cakes Waffles and Doughnuts Are Breads Too'; 37–40 'The Famous Sally Lunn and Other Fancy Breads'; 41–5 'Breads That Masquerade as Cakes'; 46–8 'Yeast – and the Family Health'; 49–50 book-order form and at bottom p 50, 'Printed in Canada'
COPIES: OONL (TX769 D44 1931, 2 copies)   QMM (RBD ckbk 2035)   *Private collection
NOTES: In 1929 Fleischmann Co. joined a merger to become Standard Brands; hence, the new publisher of this edition. The OONL catalogue incorrectly records the title as 'Delightful bread ...'

Q150.4   1934
—Delightful / breads / and buns / and / coffee cakes / 1934 edition / Standard Brands Limited / Offices in all principal cities
DESCRIPTION: 16.5 × 10.0 cm   Pp [3–4] 5–46   Illus   Paper, with image on front of a man and woman seated by a tea tray; stapled
CONTENTS: 3 tp; 4 fp illus captioned 'For elaborate meals and for simple meals the most satisfactory appetizer is variety'; 5–6 index; 7–8 'Variety in Breads Stimulates Their Appetite'; 9–12 'Little Arts in Bread Baking' and on p mid 12, 'Things That Are Helpful to Know'; 13–18 'Breads the Clever Hostess Serves'; 19–23 'Bread Easily Becomes Rolls and Biscuits'; 24–8 'The Magic Touch That Makes Bread Buns'; 29–33 'Muffins Griddle Cakes Waffles and Doughnuts Are Breads Too'; 34–7 'The Famous Sally Lunn and Other Fancy Breads'; 38–42 'Breads That Masquerade as

Cakes'; 43–4 [lacking in BVIPM copy]; 45–6 information about the health-giving properties of yeast
COPIES: *BVIPM
NOTES: The cover-title is 'Recipes for Delicious Varieties of Breads.' On the outside back face of the binding is 'Printed in Canada.'

Chatelaine 1935, p 82, lists 'Recipes for Delicious Varieties of Breads,' free upon request from Standard Brands, but does not specify the edition.

Q150.5   [1986, reprint of 1934]
—Delightful / breads / and buns / and / coffee cakes / 1934 edition / Standard Brands Limited / Offices in all principal cities
DESCRIPTION: 16.5 × 10.0 cm   Pp [3–4] 5–46   Illus   Paper, with image on front of a man and woman by a tea tray
CONTENTS: Inside front face of binding note about Cumberland Township Museum and 'This cookbook is a 1986 reprint of an original from the museum's collection. It is reprinted with the permission of Nabisco Brands Ltd., formerly Standard Brands Ltd., ... © 1934 Nabisco Brands Ltd ...'; 3 tp; 4 fp illus of persons at a formally set table; 5–6 index; 7–8 'Variety in Breads Stimulates Their Appetite'; 9–12 'Little Arts in Bread Baking'; 13–18 'Breads the Clever Hostess Serves'; 19–23 'Bread Easily Becomes Rolls and Biscuits'; 24–8 'The Magic Touch That Makes Bread Buns'; 29–33 'Muffins Griddle Cakes Waffles and Doughnuts Are Breads Too'; 34–7 'The Famous Sally Lunn and Other Fancy Breads'; 38–42 'Breads That Masquerade as Cakes'; 43 'How to Obtain Additional Copies of This Cookbook,' from Cumberland Township Museum for $3.75 by mail or $2.50 from the Museum Shop; 44–6 'Yeast – and the Family Health'
COPIES: ONBNBM   *OTHFY

1925–30

Favorite recipes

The Cookshire Women's Institute, which was organized in 1911, was one of the earliest Women's Institutes in Quebec (the first was established at Dunham on 27 January 1911; see John Ferguson Snell, Macdonald College of McGill University: A History from 1904–1955, *Montreal: McGill University Press, 1963, p 185).*

Q151.1   nd [about 1925–30]
Favorite recipes / by / Cookshire members / of the / Women's Institute [cover-title]
DESCRIPTION: Bound at top edge by a cord through two holes

COPIES: *Private collection

NOTES: The 'Preface' (on the first page) says that the aim of the book is 'to provide further funds towards [the Women's Institute's] campaign for the Cookshire Cemetery.' The text includes two pages of text describing 'Cookshire as It Is To-day.' The recipes are credited with the name of the contributor. The cover text is professionally printed; the interior text is reproduced from typed copy.

L'érable, orgueil du Québec

Q152.1   nd [about 1925–30]

Marque / Citadelle / 100% pur / L'érable / orgueil / du / Québec [cover-title]

DESCRIPTION: 23.0 × 15.0 cm   Pp 1–16   Illus col opp p 1 of prepared dishes, illus   Paper, with image on front of a man emptying a pail of sap, sled drawn by two horses in the background; stapled

CONTENTS: 1–2, 4, 6, 8, 10, 12–14, 16 'L'industrie du sucre d'érable dans la province de Québec' by C. Vaillancourt; 3, 5, 7, 9, 11, 15 recipes using maple syrup; inside back face of binding note about Société des producteurs de sucre d'érable de Québec, Lévis; outside back face illus col of Citadelle products

COPIES: *QMBN (SB239 E7V35 1920 and 192480 CON)   QSFFSC

NOTES: The person(s) who contributed the recipes is not identified. QMBN dates this 16-page edition [192-?].

Q152.2   nd

—Citadelle / Brand / 100% pure / The maple / pride / of / Quebec [cover-title]

DESCRIPTION: 22.0 × 14.5 cm   Pp 1–22   Illus col opp p 1 of prepared dishes, illus   Paper, with image on front of a man emptying a pail of sap, sled drawn by two horses in the background; previously stapled, now sewn by library

CONTENTS: 1–8 'The Maple Syrup Industry in the Province of Quebec' by Cyrille Vaillancourt; 9 'Foreword' to Second Part by Cyrille Vaillancourt; 10–11 'Culinary Suggestions' by Mme Hélène Durand LaRoche and Mlle Véronique Durand; 12–22 'Culinary Recipes'

COPIES: *OONL (TX767 M3 V32)

NOTES: Hélène Durand-LaRoche is the author of Q237.1, *Menus de réceptions.*

Q152.3   nd

—Citadelle / and / Camp / brands / 100% pure / The maple / pride / of / Quebec [cover-title]

DESCRIPTION: 22.5 × 15.0 cm   Pp 1–24   Illus col opp p 1 of prepared dishes, illus   Paper, with image on front of a man emptying a pail of sap, sled drawn by two horses in the background

CONTENTS: 1–8 'The Maple Syrup Industry in the Province of Quebec' by Cyrille Vaillancourt; 9 'Foreword' to Second Part by Cyrille Vaillancourt; 10–11 'Culinary Suggestions' by Mme Hélène Durand LaRoche and Mlle Véronique Durand; 12–24 'Culinary Recipes'

COPIES: *QMBN (TX767 E8M36 1930 and 109266 CON)

NOTES: Unlike Q152.1 and Q152.2, which refer only to the Citadelle brand in the cover-title, this edition and Q152.4 refer to Citadelle and Camp brands. The 'Foreword' states that Hélène and Véronique are sisters and that they are graduates of, and former teachers at, Les écoles ménagères provinciales, Montreal, and lecturers on domestic economy for the province's Department of Agriculture. 'The Maple Sugar Producers of Quebec // Head office, 5 Bégin Street, Levis' and illustrations of maple products are on the outside back face of the binding.

Q152.4   nd [about July 1932]

—Marques / Citadelle / et / Camp / 100% pur / L'érable / orgueil / du / Québec [cover-title]

DESCRIPTION: 23.0 × 15.5 cm   Pp 1–24   Illus col opp p 1 of prepared dishes, illus   Paper, with image on front of a man emptying a pail of sap, sled drawn by two horses in the background; stapled

CONTENTS: 1–8 'L'industrie du sucre d'érable dans la province de Québec' by C. Vaillancourt; 9 'Introduction' to Deuxième partie by Cyrille Vaillancourt; 10–11 'Suggestions culinaires' by Mme Hélène Durand-LaRoche and Mlle Véronique Durand, dated July 1932; 12–24 'Recettes culinaires'

CITATIONS: Probably Carrière No. 196

COPIES: *QMBN (192479 CON)

Q152.5   nd [about July 1932]

—Nos / produits / de / l'érable [cover-title]

DESCRIPTION: 23.5 × 15.5 cm   Pp 1–24   Illus   Paper, with image on front of over-size maple products (can and bottle of syrup, two bricks of maple sugar, and a bowl of 'Tire d'érable') set in the foreground of a maple forest, a sugar shack in the background; stapled

CONTENTS: 1–8 'L'industrie du sucre d'érable dans la province de Québec' by C. Vaillancourt; 9 'Introduction' to Deuxième partie by Cyrille Vaillancourt; 10–11 'Suggestions culinaires' by Mme Hélène Durand-LaRoche and Mlle Véronique Durand, dated July 1932; 12–24 'Recettes culinaires'

COPIES: *QMBN (192478 CON)

NOTES: This retitled edition is from a different setting of type than Q152.4, and it has no colour illustration of prepared dishes opposite p 1. Instead, the inside front face of the binding is blank; the QMBN copy has the bookplate of the Bibliothèque Saint-Sulpice applied in the blank space.

Q152.6 nd
—L'erable / orgueil du Quebec [cover-title]
DESCRIPTION: 23.0 × 15.0 cm   Pp 1–16   Illus col opp p 1 of prepared dishes, illus   Paper, with image on front of a boy offering a girl maple syrup candy on a stick; stapled
CONTENTS: 1–2, 4–6, 8–10, 12–14, 16 'L'industrie du sucre d'érable dans la province de Québec'; 3, 7, 11, 15 recipes using maple syrup
COPIES: *QSFFSC
NOTES: In this edition, the text about the maple syrup industry and the recipes are not attributed. On p 1, after the figures for production in 1911, the text states, 'Depuis ce temps cependant, il y a eu mouvement ascendant si bien qu'en 1930 la production dépassa 25,000,000 lbs.'

1926

Chocolate and cocoa recipes ... home made candy recipes

For the titles of other cookbooks by the same company, see Q52.1.

Q153.1   copyright 1926
Chocolate / and / cocoa / recipes / by celebrated cooks / Home made / candy / recipes / by Mrs. Janet McKenzie Hill / Compliments of / Walter Baker & Co., Ltd / Established 1780 / Dorchester, Mass [*sic*, no period] / Canadian mills at Montreal / Copyright, 1926 / by Walter Baker & Co., Ltd.
DESCRIPTION: 16.5 × 10.0 cm   Pp [1–2] 3–64   6 double-sided pls col, 1 fp illus on p 2 of 'Canadian mills at Montreal'   Paper, with image on front of the 'Chocolate Girl–La belle chocolatière' carrying a tray of drinks, within a decorative border featuring cocoa pods and flowers
CONTENTS: 1 tp with decorative border; 2 fp illus; 3–6 'Cocoa and Chocolate'; 7 'How to Use Recipes'; 8–11 'Beverages'; 12–17 'Cakes'; 18–20 'Icings and Fillings'; 21–2 'Sauces'; 23–4 'Hot Desserts'; 25–30 'Cold Desserts'; 31 'Frozen Desserts'; 32–6 'Miscellaneous Recipes'; 37–9 'Children and Invalids'; 40–55 'Home Made Candy Recipes Specially Prepared by Mrs. Janet McKenzie Hill'; 56–7 'Walter Baker & Co., Limited'; 58–61 'Walter Baker & Co.'s Cocoa and Chocolate Preparations'; 62–4 'Index to Recipes' and on p 64, 'Printed in U.S.A.'

COPIES: *OGU (UA s076 b22)   OMIHURM   ONLAM (Walters-Wagar Collection, Box 20)   QKB   QMMMCM (AR-M2000.92.39)
NOTES: The cover-title is 'Choice Recipes'; 'Canadian edition' is printed on the front face of the binding. The introductory section, 'Cocoa and Chocolate,' tells the story of La belle chocolatière, the company's trademark image taken from a 1760 painting of a Viennese beauty, by Jean-Étienne Liotard. Individual recipes are credited variously to Maria Parloa, Mrs A. Louise Andrea, Fannie Merritt Farmer, *Good Housekeeping*, M.E. Robinson, *Mrs Rorer's Cook Book*, and others.

Q153.1 differs from the 1924 American edition published two years before. In the American edition, the recipes are arranged according to the contributor (Miss Parloa, Mrs Andrea, Miss Farmer, Miss Robinson, Mrs Peck, and Mrs Hill). In Q153.1, the recipes have been rearranged by type of recipe (beverages, cakes, etc.); although the candy section remains attributed to Hill, the recipe order has been changed.

AMERICAN EDITIONS: *Chocolate and Cocoa Recipes by Miss Parloa and Home Made Candy Recipes by Mrs Janet McKenzie Hill*, Dorchester, Mass.: Walter Baker and Co. Ltd, copyright 1909 (NBFKL; United States: DLC); copyright 1913 (SBIHM); *Chocolate and Cocoa Recipes by Miss Parloa // Home Made Candy Recipes by Mrs Janet McKenzie Hill*, Dorchester, Mass.: Walter Baker and Co. Ltd, copyright 1914 (United States: InU; Cagle/Stafford No. 905, illus of No. 905 incorrectly identified as No. 904 and vice versa; Cagle/Stafford incorrectly describes as 1st ed.); Dorchester, Mass.: Walter Baker & Co. Ltd, copyright 1916 (OGU; United States: DLC); 1922 (OBUJBM; cited in Longone/Longone Q6); *Chocolate and Cocoa Recipes by Miss Parloa and Other Celebrated Cooks // Home Made Candy Recipes by Mrs Janet McKenzie Hill*, copyright 1924 (OGU).

Home canning

For information about Dominion Glass Co. Ltd and its other cookbooks, see Q75.1.

Q154.1   1926
Home canning / a compilation of recipes / and useful hints on the / preserving and canning / of fruits, vegetables, / meat and soups / 1926 / Dominion Glass Company Limited / Head office Montreal
DESCRIPTION: 22.5 × 15.0 cm   Pp [1–3] 4–32   Illus   Lacks binding; stapled

CONTENTS: 1 tp; 2 'Canning Time-Table'; 3 'Home Canning'; 4–8 general information about canning; 9 'The Adjustable Feature of the Perfect Seal Jar'; 10 'The "Perfect Seal" Jar'; 11 'The "Improved Gem" Jar'; 12 'The "Crown" Jar'; 13 'The "Best" Jar'; 14–32 text
COPIES: *BDEM   Private collection
NOTES: I have not compared the text of *Home Canning* with editions of Q75.1, *Perfect Preserving with Perfect Jars*, but it may be related. The private collector's copy retains its binding, printed with a small image of a house and a fruit pattern.

Q154.2   reprint, 1927
—Home canning / a compilation of recipes / and useful hints on the /   preserving and canning / of fruits, vegetables, / meat and soups / Reprinted 1927 / Dominion Glass Company Limited / Head office Montreal
COPIES: *OSTPA   Private collection

Q154.3   reprint, 1929
—Home canning / a compilation of recipes / and useful hints on the /   preserving and canning / of fruits, vegetables, / meat and soups / Reprinted 1929 / Dominion Glass Company Limited / Head office Montreal
DESCRIPTION: 23.0 × 15.0 cm   Pp [1–3] 4–32   Illus   Paper, with image on front of two preserving jars; stapled, and with hole punched at top left corner for hanging
CONTENTS: 1 tp; 2 'Canning Time-Table' and 'Designed, engraved and printed in Canada by the Ronalds Company Limited, Montreal, Que.'; 3 'Home Canning'; 4–8 general information about canning; 9 'The Adjustable Feature of the Perfect Seal Jar'; 10 'The "Perfect Seal" Jar'; 11 'The "Improved Gem" Jar'; 12 'The "Crown" Jar'; 13 'The "Best" Jar'; 14–32 recipes
COPIES: AMHM   APROM   *BVIPM   OONL (TX603 D6 1929)   SSWD

Rawleigh's good health guide cook book almanac 1926

For information about Rawleigh's annual almanac cookbooks and other publications, see M22.1.

Q155.1   1926
Rawleigh's / Trade mark reg. U.S. Pat. Off. / good health guide / cook book almanac / 1889 1926 / [five paragraphs of introductory comments] / Published by / the W.T. Rawleigh Co., Ltd. / Montreal – Winnipeg / Freeport, Memphis, Chester,

Oakland, / Minneapolis, Richmond, Denver / Hayden Press Ltd., London, Ont. / Printed in Canada
DESCRIPTION: Tp illus portrait of W.T. Rawleigh Image on front face of binding of a woman holding a bouquet of flowers; hole punched at top left corner for hanging
COPIES: *BBVM   OONL (RC81 R38)

Systematic cookery

Q156.1   1926
Systematic cookery / recipes // food values / tabulated cooking forms / cooking and household / suggestions / Compiled for the benefit / of the Building Fund / under the auspices of the Women's Association of / Trinity Memorial Church / Montreal / 1926
DESCRIPTION: 22.0 × 15.0 cm   Pp [1–7] 8–199 [200], [1–2] 3–8 [9] 10–42   Cloth
CONTENTS: 1 tp; 2 'Copyright Canada 1926'; 3–4 'Foreword' signed the Committee; 5 table of contents; 6 blank; 7–192 text; 193–9 'Index to Recipes'; 200 'Please patronize the advertisers ...'; 1 'Index to Advertisers'; 2–42 ads
CITATIONS: BQ 22-4946
COPIES: QMBN (160036 CON)   *Private collection
NOTES: In the 'Foreword' the Committee explains its ambitious effort to make a 'systematic Cook Book,' by asking the recipe contributors to use level measurements and to state the yield of each recipe and the number of servings. The Committee also refers to 'the variety of the suggestions obtained from British, French and American practice in this city, and which is here offered as representative of Montreal cookery.' Under 'Standards of Weights and Measures' on p 7, there is a discussion of the confusion in Canada because of the difference between British and American measuring systems: 'The Imperial gallon is legal in Canada; and so far as we have been able to ascertain, it is this Imperial standard which is indicated when most Montreal women speak of the pint, quart or gallon. On the other hand, when a "cup" is mentioned, it seems that it is the Wine Measure half-pint cup [i.e., the American or Wine Measure containing 8 ounces] which is indicated. In accordance with that usage which appears to be most common in Montreal we have used the Imperial gallon, quart and pint, but the Wine Measure cup and spoons.'

Q156.2   2nd ed., 1927
—Systematic cookery / recipes // food values / tabulated cooking forms / cooking and household /

suggestions / Second edition / Compiled for the benefit / of the Building Fund / under the auspices of the Women's Association of / Trinity Memorial Church / Montreal / 1927
DESCRIPTION: 22.0 × 15.0 cm   Pp [1–7] 8–212, 1–2 [3] 4–43   Cloth
CONTENTS: 1 tp; 2 'Copyright Canada 1926'; 3–4 'Foreword' signed the Committee; 5 table of contents; 6 blank; 7–205 text; 206–12 'Index to Recipes'; 1–43 ads and blank pages for 'Recipes'
COPIES: *OONL (TX715.6 S97 1927 p***)

1926–30

Rawleigh recipe book

For information about Rawleigh's annual almanac cookbooks and other publications, see M22.1.

Q157.1   nd [about 1926–30]
Rawleigh / Trade mark / recipe book / jellies – jams – preserves / made with / Rawleigh's Ideal / Fruit Pectin / Published by / the W.T. Rawleigh Co., Ltd. / Montreal Winnipeg [cover-title]
DESCRIPTION: 12.0 × 8.0 cm   Pp [1–2] 3–23   Many illus   Paper, with still-life on front of fruit and packages of Rawleigh's Fruit Pectin, Extract of Orange, and Extract of Lemon; stapled
CONTENTS: 1 cover-title; 2 'Table of Contents' [i.e., alphabetical list of recipes]; 3 'Rawleigh's Ideal Fruit Pectin' [information about the product]; 4–5 'Suggestions'; 6–23 recipes
COPIES: *Private collection
NOTES: From appearances, the book was published in the 1920s, but likely no earlier than 1926, when the company's almanac cookbooks begin to bear the imprint 'Montreal Winnipeg.'

1927

Choice recipes

Q158.1   1927
Choice recipes / by / members / of / Ladies' Guild / Christ Church / East Angus, Que. / Nineteen twenty-seven [cover-title]
COPIES: *Private collection
NOTES: The cookbook begins with a page of information about Christ Church (the minister's name, Rev. T. Lloyd; times of services; and meeting days of the Ladies' Guild and the Women's Auxiliary) and two pages of information about East Angus (situated about 20 miles, i.e., 32 kilometres, from Sherbrooke on the St Francis River) and its major industry, the Brompton Pulp and Paper Co. Ltd. The text points out that '[t]he cover on this booklet is Brompton Regular Kraft Embossed.'

Clark's food delicacies

W. Clark Ltd was founded in 1877; see 'Clark Quarter-of-a-Century Club,' Canadian Food Packer Vol. 17, No. 6 (June 1946), p 43. For a later cookbook by the company and a list of its products, see Q180.1, Clark's Recipe Book.

Q159.1   nd [about 1927]
Clark's / food / delicacies
DESCRIPTION: 18.0 × 14.0 cm   Pp [1–32]   Tp illus col of mother, father, and daughter at dining table; centre spread illus col of 'Correct Table Arrangement'; many illus col of Clark products and prepared dishes; fp illus on p 32 of 'The Clark Laboratory'   Paper; stapled
CONTENTS: 1 tp; 2–3 'What the Name Clark Means to You'; 4–15, 18–31 information about Clark products, including advice on preparing and serving them; 16–17 centre spread illus col; 32 fp illus
CITATIONS: Ferguson/Fraser, p 233, tp illus on p 51
COPIES: *Private collection
NOTES: The company name, W. Clark Ltd, Montreal, is on the food labels of the illustrated products. The cover-title is 'Clark's Prepared Foods.' The introductory text explains the two-fold purpose of the book: 'It is first a Suggestion Book planned to encourage good housekeeping, to lighten kitchen work, to promote higher standards – greater variety and daintiness – in the meals prepared at home. It also demonstrates ... how you may best attain these wholly desirable ends with Clark's Prepared Foods, ...' (p 2). The introductory text also refers to the Clark kitchens, 'situated at Montreal and St. Remi, Quebec, and at Harrow, Ontario' (p 2) and to 'half a century of constant, unwavering effort to better methods and improve quality' (p 3). Since the company was founded in 1877, *Clark's Food Delicacies* was published about 1927 (1877 + 50 years). Earlier advertisements in the *Western Home Monthly* may or may not refer to the cookbook: In the March 1923 issue, the company advertised a booklet for 'Clark's Prepared Foods'; in the July 1922 issue, the company advertised a 'booklet in colors.'

The jubilee recipe book

Q160.1 [1927]

The jubilee / recipe book / A collection of practical and / tested recipes to guide the / housewife in the baking of / bread, cake and pastry. / The St. Lawrence Flour Mills Company, / Limited / Montreal, Canada.

DESCRIPTION: 17.5 × 12.5 cm   Pp [3] 4–31   Illus col Paper, with Canada's coat of arms on front and two images in circular frames: a traditional mill powered by a waterwheel and the modern Regal Flour mill with silos

CONTENTS: Inside front face of binding 'Equivalents of Capacity' and 'Approximate Weights of Some Common Dry Commodities'; 3 tp; 4–31 [inside back face of binding] recipes

COPIES: *OGU (UA s070 b92)

NOTES: The cover-title is '1867 [Canada's coat of arms] 1927 / / Regal jubilee cook book / / The St. Lawrence Flour Mills Company Limited.' The jubilee likely refers to the sixtieth anniversary of Confederation. I have not compared the text of this cookbook with others by St Lawrence Flour Mills to determine whether they are related, i.e., Q88.1, Q143.1, and Q191.1.

Q160.2 nd

—Le livre de / recettes / Régal / Une collection de recettes / pratiques et éprouvées / pour guider la ménagère / dans la préparation de ses / gâteaux et pâtisseries / La compagnie / St. Lawrence Flour Mills, limitée

DESCRIPTION: Paper, with Canada's coat of arms on front and two images in circular frames: a traditional mill powered by a waterwheel and the modern Regal Flour mill with silos

COPIES: *Private collection

NOTES: The cover-title is 'Les recettes Régal.' There are no dates on the front face of the binding and no reference to Canada's jubilee, indicating that the French-language edition was likely published later than the English edition. The private collector reports that her copy has 31 pp. It is inscribed on the title-page, above the printed company name, in ink, 'En souvenir de ton grand'père, Brig. gen. A.E. Labelle qui fut le fondateur et président de' [printed: 'La compagnie St. Lawrence Flour Mills, limitée']. For information about Labelle, see Q88.1.

Manuel de diététique à l'usage des écoles ménagères

Q161.1 1927

Manuel / de / diététique / a l'usage des ecoles menageres / des Soeurs grises de Montreal / Filialement dédié à notre vénérable mère d'Youville / à l'occasion de sa fête patronale, / ce 20 juillet, 1927. / Imprimerie des Sourds-Muets, 7400, boul. St-Laurent, Montréal / [printer's symbol]

DESCRIPTION: 22.5 × 15.0 cm   Pp [3–5] 6–422   Paper, with floral border on front; sewn

CONTENTS: 3 tp; 4 'Nihil obstat, Marianopoli, die 11° septembris 1927. Canonicus Aemilius Chartier, censor librorum. † Em.-Alph. Deschamps, V.G., Év. de Thennesis, Adm. 12 septembre 1927. Droits réservés, Ottawa, 1927.' and stamped 'Approuvé par le Comité catholique du Conseil de l'instruction publique en février 1928'; 5–11 five letters to révérendes Soeurs grises: from J.A. Beaudoin, directeur, École d'hygiène sociale appliquée, Université de Montréal, 24 janvier 1927, from C.H. Schneider, chef du Ritz Carlton, 11 mai 1927, from Abbé Henri Jasmin, 16 juin 1927, from H. Bois, ptre, inspecteur des écoles ménagères, 18 juin 1927, from A. Désilets, chef du Service de l'économie domestique au ministère provincial de l'Agriculture, 21 septembre 1927; 12 'Préface' signed Hôpital général des Soeurs grises, Montréal, 24 juin 1927; 13 'Manuel de diététique destiné aux élèves de 4ème année du cours de l'enseignement ménager'; 14–382 text in sixty-two lessons, followed by 'Application des menus diététiques aux enfants et à certaines maladies'; 383–422 'Table des matières'

CITATIONS: BouquinsCat 229, No. 361   BQ 23-4914   CCat No. 6, p H20

COPIES: QMBN (TX354 M358 1927 and 104000 CON) *QMM (RBD Soeur Berthe, ckbk 445; 2 copies)   QQLA (WB405 M294 1927)

Quebec, Department of Roads

Q162.1   March 1927

La bonne cuisine / canadienne / Traité d'art culinaire à l'usage / des hôtels de la province / de Québec / Avec dix planches originales / en couleur / Préparé et publié sous la direction du / ministère de la Voirie / Quebec / mars, 1927 / Prix: $1.00 / Hon. J.-L. Perron / ministre / Jos.-L. Boulanger / sous-ministre

DESCRIPTION: 21.0 × 14.0 cm   Pp [1–3] 4–173   10 pls col, illus of cuts of meat   Thin card, with image on front of a maid serving a man seated at table; sewn

CONTENTS: 1 ht and 'Imprimé au Canada // Tous droits réservés, 1927'; 2 blank; 3 tp; 4 'Table des matières'; 5–6 'Avant-propos'; top-mid 7 'Qualités requises d'une bonne directrice d'hôtel'; mid 7–9 'Nécessité de savoir faire la cuisine'; 10 'Les mesures en cuisine'; 11 'Temps de cuisson approximatif de certains aliments'; 12–14 'Principaux termes culinaires'; 15–18 'Liste alphabétique des recettes'; 19–173 recipes

CITATIONS: Beaulieu, Supp. 1965–1968, p 337   CBSCat C22   Ferguson/Fraser, p 233, illus col on p 57 of closed volume

COPIES: QMBN (165400 CON)   *QMM (RBD Soeur Berthe, ckbk 260)   QQSCA   QSFFSC (641.5 Q3b)   QTU (TX715 Q84)

NOTES: Beaulieu, Supp. 1965–1968, p 337, records the author as Mme Émile Gauthier. The title-page of the QMM copy is stamped 'École supérieure des arts et métiers // Congrégation de Notre-Dame ... Montreal.'

Q162.2   April 1929
—La bonne cuisine / canadienne / traité d'art culinaire à l'usage / des hôtels de la province / de Québec / Avec dix planches originales / en couleur / Préparé et publié sous la direction du / ministère de la Voirie / Quebec / avril, 1929 / Prix: $1.00 / Hon. J.-L. Perron / ministre / Jos.-L. Boulanger / sous-ministre

DESCRIPTION: 22.5 × 14.5 cm   Pp [1–3] 4–173   10 pls col, illus   Thin card, with image on front of a maid serving a man at table and below, 'Publié ... 1927'; sewn

CONTENTS: 1 ht and 'Imprimé au Canada // Tous droits réservés, 1929'; 2 blank; 3 tp; 4 'Table des matières'; 5–6 'Avant-propos'; top-mid 7 'Qualités requises d'une bonne directrice d'hôtel'; mid 7–9 'Nécessité de savoir faire la cuisine'; 10 'Les mesures au cuisine'; 11 'Temps de cuisson approximatif de certains aliments'; 12–14 'Principaux termes culinaires'; 15–18 'Liste alphabétique des recettes'; 19–173 recipes

CITATIONS: Armstrong 2000, p F1, illus col   Bédard, p 4   Bibliothèque municipale de Montréal, p 7   Carrière No. 277

COPIES: *QMM (RBD TX715 Q44 Joubert)

OTHER EDITIONS: Retitled *Fine cuisine du Québec d'autrefois*, Montreal: F.L. de Martigny, [1981], pp 131, described on p 4 as 'extrait de "La bonne cuisine canadienne" publié par le ministère de la Voirie du Québec en 1927' (QMBM, QMBN).

Rawleigh's good health guide cook book almanac [1927]

For information about Rawleigh's annual almanac cookbooks and other publications, see M22.1.

Q163.1   [1927]
Rawleigh's / good health guide / cook book / almanac / Table of contents / [above page numbers:] Page / Astronomical calculations 4 / Almanac and weather forecasts 6, 10, 12, 14, 16, 18 / Health & dietetical information 24, 27, 38, 41, 43, 44, 46, 48, 52 / Cooking recipes 29, 30, 36, 40, 42, 45, 46, 47, 51, 56, 59, 61 / Beauty and toilet hints 35, 50 / Housekeeping helps 31, 57 / The Rawleigh retailer 2, 3 / Back of the Rawleigh retailer 3, 5, 7, 17, etc. / Factories and branches 8, 9, 11, 13, 15, 32, 33 / Rawleigh products 20, 22, 26, 28, 31, 34, 37, 50, 57, 58, 60, 62, 64 / Live stock and poultry 35, 58, 60, 62 / Foreign activities 20, 22, 54 / Published by / the W.T. Rawleigh Co., Ltd. / Montreal – Winnipeg / Freeport, Memphis, Chester / Oakland, Minneapolis / Richmond, Denver / Printed in Canada

DESCRIPTION: 24.0 × 16.5 cm   Pp [1] 2–64   Tp illus border of a man and woman in a rural landscape, illus   Paper, with portrait on front of W.T. Rawleigh; stapled, and with hole punched at top left corner for hanging

CONTENTS: 1 tp; 2 'When the Rawleigh Retailer Comes'; 3 'Back of the Rawleigh Retailer'; 4 'Astronomical Calculations'; 5 'The Desire to Serve'; 6 January, February; 7 'Years of Service and Progress'; 8–9 'The Rawleigh Factories'; 10 March, April; 11 'Rawleigh's Makes Everything It Sells'; 12 May, June; 13 'Making Bottles at Rawleigh's'; 14 July, August; 15 'Building for Future and Larger Service'; 16 September, October; 17 'Products That Are Right'; 18 November, December; 19 'Direct and Complete Service'; 20–1 'Taking the Mystery Out of Spices'; 22–3 'The World's Most Popular Flavor' [i.e., vanilla]; 24–5 'Food and Its Function'; 26 'When Nature Cries for Help'; 27 'Vitamin Foods'; 28 'Protection against Infection'; 29 'Forage Foods for Humans'; 30 'Summer Beverages'; 31 'Helps for Better Housekeeping'; 32–3 'A Composite Picture Showing the Rawleigh Factories, Distributing Branches, Farms and Three of the Nine Foreign Branches'; 34 'If You Want Attractiveness and Health'; 35 'Rawleigh's Ideal Farms'; 36 'Winter Garden Dishes'; 37 'Avoid the Common Cold'; 38–9 'Will You Be Young at 50?'; 40 'Sea Foods'; 41 'Mineral Foods'; 42 'Fruits and Nuts in the Diet'; 43 'The

Fountain of Youth Is Right Living'; 44 'The Business of Keeping Well'; 45 'Regulative and Laxative Foods'; 46 'Balanced Menus'; 47 'Foods for Vegetarians'; 48–9 'Sleep a Main Need'; 50 'Beneficial to Health and Beauty'; 51 'Frozen Desserts'; 52–3 'Corrective Eating'; 54–5 'The Lighter Things of Japan'; 56 'Foods from Cans'; 57 'Good Health Food Products'; 58 'The Poultry Industry'; 59 'Preserves in the Diet'; 60 'The Purpose of a Pig'; 61 'Pickles and Relishes Correctly Used'; 62–3 'The Dairy Cow'; 64 'Couldn't Keep House without Them'

COPIES: AMHM BBVM NSWA SWSLM *Private collection

NOTES: The year of publication, 1927, is on the front face of the binding.

Q163.2   [1927]

—Guide de bonne santé / Rawleigh / Trade mark / Livre de cuisine / almanach / Table des matières / Calculs astronomiques 1 / Almanach et pronostics de la température 4, 8, 10, 21, 23, 25 / Informations diététiques et de santé 13, 22, 28 / Recettes de cuisine 12, 13, 24, 26, 27, 29 / Aides de beauté et pour la toilette 22 / Le détaillant Rawleigh 2, 3 / Appuyant le détaillant Rawleigh 3, 5, 9 / Les manufactures et les succursales 6, 7, 16, 17 / Les produits Rawleigh 11, 14, 15, 18, 19, 20, 22, 30, 31, 32, 33 / Le bétail et les volailles 30, 31, 32 / Les activités à l'etranger 9, 14, 15, 18, 19 / Publie par / The W.T. Rawleigh Co., Ltd / Montreal Winnipeg / Freeport, Memphis, Chester / Oakland, Minneapolis, / Richmond, Denver / Imprime au Canada / Imprime au Canada par The W.T. Rawleigh Co., Ltd, [*sic*]

DESCRIPTION: 24.0 × 16.5 cm   Pp 1–32   Illus   Paper, with illus portrait on front of W.T. Rawleigh; stapled, and with hole punched at top left corner for hanging

COPIES: *QMM (RBD ckbk 1623)

NOTES: The year of publication, 1927, is on the front face of the binding.

AMERICAN EDITIONS: *Rawleigh* [*sic*] *Health Almanac Cookbook*, 1927 (Dickinson, p 149).

1928

The bride's book

The earliest edition of this book was published in Vancouver, as The Real Home-Keeper. *For the editions published in Montreal as* The Bride's Book *in 1928 and 1932, see B21.6 and B21.8; for the French-language editions of 1930 and 1934, see B21.7 and B21.9.*

Fry's book of recipes

Q164.1   nd [about 1928]

200 years of excellence / By appointment / Fry's / book of / recipes / economical / and simple / Made with Fry's Cocoa & Chocolate [cover-title]

DESCRIPTION: 14.0 × 11.0 cm   Pp 3–21 [22]   Illus col, illus   Paper, with image on front of chocolate desserts; stapled

CONTENTS: Inside front face of binding 'Aeroplane view of the new Fry factory in a garden at Somerdale // Bristol, England'; 3–mid 5 'J.S. Fry & Sons Limited Bristol and Montreal Established 1728 ... The House That Fry Built // Two hundred years of achievement' [company history]; mid 5–6 'The History of Cocoa and Chocolate'; 7–20 'A Selection of Choice Tested Recipes'; 21 'The Food Value of Cocoa and Chocolate'; 22 'Index' [i.e., table of contents]; inside back face 'Canadian factory of the historic house of Fry at Montreal'

COPIES: AEUCHV (UV 85.264.26)   MWPA (MG14 C50 McKnight, Ethel)   OONL (TX767 C5 F788 1928 p***)   *Private collection

NOTES: The cookbook was published about 1928, since the company, established in 1728, was celebrating its two-hundredth anniversary. The private collector's copy is inscribed on p 3, in pencil, 'Thelma Briggs Mar 12. 1932.'

Q164.2   nd [about 1928]

—200 years of excellence / By appointment / Fry's / book of / recipes / economical / and simple / The T. Eaton Co Limited / Made with Fry's Cocoa & Chocolate [cover-title]

DESCRIPTION: 14.5 × 11.0 cm   Pp 3–21 [22]   Illus col, illus   Paper, with image on front of chocolate desserts; stapled

CONTENTS: 3–mid 5 'J.S. Fry & Sons Limited Bristol and Montreal Established 1728 ... The House That Fry Built // Two hundred years of achievement' [com-

pany history]; mid 5–6 'The History of Cocoa and Chocolate'; 7–20 'A Selection of Choice Tested Recipes'; 21 'The Food Value of Cocoa and Chocolate'; 22 'Index' [i.e., table of contents]
COPIES: *Private collection
NOTES: This edition was distributed through Eaton's department stores.

Les recettes de grand'maman

Q165.1   nd [1928]
Les recettes de / grand'maman / Magasins indépendants Victoria [cover-title]
DESCRIPTION: 31.0 × 23.0 cm   Pp 1–112   Paper, with image on front of a seated grandmother holding a bowl in her left hand and a spoon in her right hand
CONTENTS: 1 ad for 'Magasins indépendants Victoria // Coopération de LaPorte, Martin, limitée Montréal'; 2 list of the many 'Magasins Victoria,' their addresses and telephone numbers; 3 'Introduction'; 4 ad; 5 'Index'; 6–105 recipes, household hints, and ads; 106–11 blank for 'Recettes personnelles'; 112 ad for La gomme Wrigley
CITATIONS: BQ 22-4934
COPIES: *QMBN (TX715 R3805 1920 FOL. and 160029 CON)
NOTES: The book is undated, but there is an advertisement on p 23 for Sel Windsor, i.e., Windsor Salt, with the heading '1896 1928 Lorsque grand'maman avait trente ans de moins.'

L'Huillier, Médéric

Q166.1   1928
L'aide-mémoire / du / patissier moderne / par / Mederic L'Huillier / chef pâtissier à l'Arcade Grill / de la / Maison Henry Morgan & Co. / Droits de reproduction et de traduction réservés. / [symbol of Librairie Beauchemin] / Montreal / Librairie Beauchemin limitée / 430, rue Saint-Gabriel, 430 / 1928
DESCRIPTION: 22.0 × 15.0 cm   Pp [1–5] 6–251, [i–v]   Frontis opp p 5 of four-tier wedding cake   Cloth
CONTENTS: 1 ht; 2 blank; 3 tp; 4 blank; 5–6 'Avant-propos' signed 'l'auteur'; 7–9 'Aux ménagères'; 10–11 'Aux commençants'; 12 'À mes confrères'; 13–216 recipes; 217–19 'Le vocabulaire du pâtissier'; 220–34 'Table des matières'; 235–49 'Table alphabétique'; 250 blank; 251 'Table alphabétique des matières'; i blank; ii–v ads

CITATIONS: BQ 22-4921   BQ Exposition 1974, p 20
COPIES: OONL (TX773 L5)   *QMBN (TX773 L48 1928)
NOTES: As well as recipes for baked goods, such as cakes and cookies, there are recipes for jams and puddings. Henry Morgan and Co. was a large Montreal department store. Established in 1845, the family business was sold to the Hudson's Bay Co. in 1960 (company records at QMMARC (MG 1002)).

Q166.2   1928
—L'aide-mémoire / du / patissier moderne / par / Mederic L'Huillier / chef pâtissier à l'Arcade Grill / de la / Maison Henry Morgan & Co. / Droits de reproduction et de traduction réservés. / [symbol of Librairie Beauchemin] / Montreal / Librairie Beauchemin limitée / 430, rue Saint-Gabriel, 430 / 1928
DESCRIPTION: 24.0 × 16.0 cm   Pp [1–5] 6–190   Paper; sewn
CONTENTS: 1 ht; 2 blank; 3 tp; 4 blank; 5–6 'Avant-propos'; 7–9 'Aux ménagères'; 10–11 'Aux commençants'; 12 'À mes confrères'; 13–190 recipes
COPIES: *QSFFSC (641.5 L692a)
NOTES: This edition has larger dimensions and fewer pages than Q166.1 (no leaves are missing). There is no 'Le vocabulaire du pâtissier' and no indexes. The order of the two editions is unknown.

Martin, Virginia [pseudonym]

For the titles of other cookbooks by the same company, see Q139.1.

Q167.1   1928
Salad / secrets / by / Virginia Martin / Colman-Keen (Canada) Limited / Montreal / 1928
DESCRIPTION: 20.5 × 14.0 cm   Pp [i–ii], 1–22   Tp illus of a bowl of salad, illus of elegant dining scenes and some kitchen scenes   Paper, with image on front of a woman preparing salad dressing
CONTENTS: i tp; ii 'Copyright 1928 by Colman-Keen (Canada) Limited' and 'Printed in Canada'; 1–mid 2 'Some Facts about Salads'; mid 2–4 'Dressings and Sauces'; 5–9 'Salads'; 10–11 'Recipes from Chefs in Canadian Hotels'; 12–14 'Savouries'; 15–17 'Pickles'; 18–20 'Sandwich Recipes'; 21 'Mustard as a Condiment'; 22 'The Remedial Value of Keen's D.S.F. Mustard'
CITATIONS: Ferguson/Fraser, p 233, illus col on p 57 of closed volume
COPIES: ACG   AEPMA   BBVM   BDEM   MAUAM

MWPA NSHMS (88.74.10) OGU (CCC TX715.6 M377) OONL (TX740 M328 1928) OSMFHHM QGMG QMM (RBD ckbk 1800) *Private collection
NOTES: 'The Remedial Value of Keen's D.S.F. Mustard' describes how to prepare a mustard plaster or mustard bath and when to use each.

Q167.2 1928
—Le secret de / bonnes salades / par / Virginia Martin / Colman-Keen (Canada) Limited / Montreal / 1928
DESCRIPTION: Tp illus of a bowl of salad   Image on front face of binding of a woman preparing salad dressing
COPIES: QQU *Private collection
NOTES: This edition has 22 pp.

Rawleigh's good health guide and cook book [1928]

For information about Rawleigh's annual almanac cookbooks and other publications, see M22.1.

Q168.1 [1928]
Rawleigh's / good health guide / and cook book / Table of contents / [flush right, above page numbers:] Page / Cooking recipes 11, 13, 15, 19, 21, 23, 24, 29, 30 / Dietetical information 6, 10, 12, 25, 26, 28 / Things women should know 2, 4, 5, 7, 14 / The Rawleigh factories 3, 8, 9 / Foreign activities 16, 17 / Good health products 7, 14, 16, 17, 18, 20, 22, 32 / Ideal farms 31 / The W.T. Rawleigh Co., Ltd. / Montreal – Winnipeg / Freeport Memphis Chester Oakland / Minneapolis Richmond Denver / Printed in Canada by the W.T. Rawleigh Co., Ltd.
DESCRIPTION: Tp illus of W.T. Rawleigh and a landscape with a mother and two children in the foreground   With image on front of a mother pouring hot Rawleigh's cocoa for two children seated at table; hole punched at top left corner for hanging
COPIES: ACG (2 copies, each lacking binding) *BBVM
NOTES: The date of publication is not part of the cover-title or on the title-page, but can be deduced from various statements in the text; for example, on p 2 there is a reference to '39 years still actuated by the desire to serve' and on p 3 to the company's '39 years of study and successful experience.' Since Rawleigh started his business in 1889, this issue was published in 1928 [1889 + 39 years].

Recettes utiles pour la cuisine électrique

Q169.1 February 1928
Recettes utiles / pour la / cuisine électrique / Compliments / The / Shawinigan Water & Power / Company / Fevrier 1, 1928 [cover-title]
COPIES: *Private collection

St Barnabas Guild cook book

Q170.1 nd [about 1928]
[Caption:] Photo by Ward & Davidson / St. Barnabas Church, St. Lambert / Rector, Rev. F. Gwynne Lightbourn, B.D. / St. Barnabas Guild / cook book / Officers of the Guild / Hon. President Mrs. A.W. Thompson / President Mrs. Eldred Archibald / Vice-President Mrs. Kenneth Chalmers / Secretary Mrs. E. Swayne / Treasurer Mrs. C. Flint
DESCRIPTION: 23.0 × 15.0 cm   Pp [1–6] 7–71, [i–xiii] Tp illus of St Barnabas Church   Cloth
CONTENTS: 1 tp; 2 ads; 3 'Appreciation' [alphabetical list of twenty-one women's names, followed by name of Mrs John H. Horsfall, convenor]; 4 ads; 5 'Index' [i.e., table of contents]; 6 ad; 7–8 'Weights and Measures'; 9–69 'Recipes'; 70–1 blank for 'Additional Recipes'; i–xiii ads
COPIES: *QKB (79-21)   Private collection
NOTES: There is an advertisement on p v for Molson's Ale that refers to the establishment of the business in 1786 and the ale as 'brewed in Montreal for 142 years'; therefore, the cookbook was published about 1928 (1786 + 142 years). Mrs Eldred Archibald, president of St Barnabas Guild, is Irene Archibald, who wrote O520.1, under the pseudonym of Margaret Currie.

The private collector's copy is inscribed with her grandmother's name, 'Minnie K. [i.e., Kate] Brown. Bridge Prize Dec. 5th 1930. St Barnabas Card Party. 57 Mercille Ave. St Lambert.'

Sainte-Marie Edith, soeur (1876–1949)

Soeur Sainte-Marie Edith (pl 39) was born Mary Theodora Turner. The 'head dietitian and associates' of the Montreal Cooking School were credited with judging, testing, and approving the recipes in Q177.1, Canada's Prize Recipes.

Q171.1 [copyright 1928]
Les secrets / de la bonne / cuisine / contenant la substance des cours de cuisine / donnés à l'Ecole ménagère (Congrégation de / Notre-Dame) de

Montréal, avec plus de / 1500 recettes, toutes mises à l'épreuve / dans la cuisine de l'ecole / par / soeur Sainte-Marie Edith, / directrice de l'Ecole ménagère / de Montréal. / Publié par / La compagnie de l'imprimerie et de lithographie / canadienne limitée, Montréal.

DESCRIPTION: 25.0 × 17.5 cm   Pp [i–ii] iii [iv–vi] vii [viii] ix–xiii [xiv] xv–xvi, 1–319   6 pls col, 2 double-sided pls, 7 pls, illus on p 46 of carving   Cloth, with grid pattern of blue lines

CONTENTS: i ht; ii 'Tous droits réservés, Canada. (1928) Imprimé au Canada.'; iii dedication to Madame P.R. du Tremblay; iv blank; v tp; vi blank; vii 'Préface' signed by four former francophone students of the school (Caroline Leman, Paule de Martigny, Angeline R. Leclerc, Minette R. Dupré); viii blank; ix–x 'L'importance de la bonne cuisine' signed *La presse;* xi–xiii 'Introduction de l'auteur'; xiv blank; xv 'Table alphabétique des matières'; xvi 'Table des illustrations'; 1–304 text; 305–19 'Index alphabétique détaillé'

CITATIONS: BQ 24-4866   BQ Exposition 1974, p 16   Carrière, p 186   Driver 2003, 'Canadian Cookbooks,' p 38   Probably Ferguson/Fraser, p 233, illus col on p 57 of closed volume   Lambert, T., p 94°

COPIES: OONL (TX715 S1274 fol.)   *QMACN (570.610 (2))   QMBN (TX715.6 S35 1928 and 114971 CON)

NOTES: Armstrong 2000, pp F1–F2, discusses the book, but does not identify the edition.

Q171.2 [1st English-language ed., copyright 1928] —The secrets / of good / cooking / containing the substance of the courses, given / at the Montreal Cooking School, (Congregation / of Notre-Dame), and a choice of more than / 1500 recipes, all tested in the laboratory- / kitchen of the school / by / Sister St. Mary Edith, / Principal of the Montreal / Cooking School / Published by / the Canadian Printing and Lithographing / Company, Limited, Montreal

DESCRIPTION: 25.0 × 17.0 cm   Pp [i–ii] iii [iv–vi] vii [viii] ix–xiii [xiv] xv–xvi, 1–292, [i–ii], 293–309   6 pls col, 2 double-sided pls, 7 pls, 1 fp illus on p 50   Cloth, with grid pattern of blue lines

CONTENTS: i ht; ii 'Copyright, 1928, by the Canadian Printing & Lithographing Company, Ltd. Printed in Canada'; iii dedication to Madame P.R. du Tremblay; iv blank; v tp; vi blank; vii preface signed by former students of the school, all well-known members of Montreal society (Lady Shaughnessy, Lady Gouin, Lady Forget, Mrs Walter Molson, Mrs Allan Magee, Mrs Winthrop Brainerd, and Mrs W.P. O'Brien); viii blank; ix–x 'The Importance of Good Cooking' signed

La presse; xi–xiii 'The Author's Introduction'; xiv blank; xv table of contents; xvi index of illustrations; 1–292 text; i 'Sandwich Recipes'; ii blank; 293–309 index

CITATIONS: Bitting, p 414   Cooke 2002, p 235   Dickinson, p 160   Driver 2003, 'Canadian Cookbooks,' p 38   Lambert, T., p 94°

COPIES: BVAU (Woodward Biomedical Library)   NBMOU   OGU (2 copies: *UA s048 b06, TX715 M3)   OKQ (Special Collections uncat)   OONL (TX715 S12742 fol. copy 1)   OTAG   OTNY (uncat)   OTUTF (D-11 0984)   QMACN (570.610 (3))   QMM (3 copies: TX715 S23; RBD ckbk 2010; RBD Soeur Berthe, ckbk 523)   QMMMCM (RB-1480); United States: DLC (TX715.6 S8 1928)

NOTES: The English-language editions are not numbered, but Q171.2 must be the first because the BVAU copy is inscribed by the author and dated 1928. It is inscribed in blue ink, on the front endpaper: 'To my ever dear Suzanne, in the hope that our "Secrets" may prove helpful when upheavals threaten your household – [?] devotedly, Sister St. Marie Edith, [?] September the ninth, 1928.' Although this edition has fewer leaves than Q171.5, it is printed on thicker paper so that the volume is 3.0 cm thick.

Una Abrahamson's copy at OGU is marked with changes, likely by a student. See, for example, the pencil revisions on p 284 for 'The Utensils Necessary for a Kitchen' where a tea kettle, double boiler, one steamer, and a toaster have been added to the first column, and custard cups, a nutmeg grater, quart measure, and doughnut cutter have been deleted from the first column. There is a pencil inscription on p 225, next to Sponge Cakes, which refers to an earlier publication of the Montreal Cooking School, Q104.1, *The Whys and Wherefores of Cooking:* 'See under Cake folder – & use "Hows & Whys" receipt.' There are also references in pencil to Fannie Farmer's *The Boston Cooking-School Cook Book;* for example, on p 264: 'See Boston page 98 for best method.'

One of the QMM copies (Soeur Berthe, ckbk 523) has an addendum, headed 'After Thoughts and Suggestions' and measuring 12.5 × 12.5 cm, glued to the gutter of the double-sided plate opposite p 293; there is also a loose leaf (i.e., not bound in) opposite p 292 that is headed 'Sandwich Recipes.' There are recipes for Doughnuts and Crullers on p 291, and Boston Baked Beans, Mexican Beans, and New York Beans on p 292. QMM (ckbk 2010) and the OTAG copy are the same, except there is no addendum of 'After Thoughts and Suggestions' and the leaf of 'Sandwich Recipes' is glued to the gutter of the double-sided plate opposite p 292. The OTNY copy has the addendum opposite p 293, and the leaf of 'Sandwich Recipes' is glued to the gutter of p 292. The OONL copy has no unpaginated leaf of 'Sandwich Recipes'; it has the addendum glued to the gutter opposite p 293. The OTUTF copy matches the OGU Abrahamson copy, i.e., it has the unpaginated leaf of 'Sandwich Recipes,' but no glued-in addendum. The other OGU copy (TX715 M3), which is rebound, is the same as the Abrahamson copy, except that it has the addendum of 'After Thoughts and Suggestions' tipped in, opposite p 293.

Glued to the front endpaper of the OTUTF copy is the card of Alfred O. Beardmore, 75 St George Street, Toronto. The NBMOU copy lacks p 309. The NFSM catalogue records a 309-page, unnumbered edition that probably matches the OGU volume catalogued here; the copy (TX715 S3) is missing.

CCat No. 7, p I4, cites *The Secrets of Good Cooking*, published in 1928, but does not record the number of pages. The reference is likely to Q171.2.

Q171.3   [2nd ed., copyright 1928]
—Les secrets / de la bonne / cuisine / contenant la substance des cours de cuisine / donnés à l'Ecole ménagère (Congrégation de / Notre-Dame) de Montréal, avec plus de / 1500 recettes, toutes mises à l'épreuve / dans la cuisine de l'ecole / par / soeur Sainte-Marie Edith, / directrice de l'Ecole ménagère / de Montréal. / Publié par / La compagnie d'imprimerie et de lithographie / canadienne limitée, Montréal.
DESCRIPTION: 25.0 × 17.0 cm   Pp [i–ii] iii [iv–vi] vii [viii] ix–xvi, 1–320   6 pls col, 2 double-sided pls, 6 pls, illus on p 46 of carving   Cloth, with grid pattern of blue lines
CONTENTS: i ht; ii 'Tous droits réservés, Canada. (1928) Imprimé au Canada.'; iii dedication to Madame P.R. du Tremblay; iv 'Deuxième édition revue et augmentée'; v tp; vi blank; vii 'Préface' signed by four former francophone students at the school; viii blank; ix–x 'L'importance de la bonne cuisine' signed *La presse*; xi–xiii 'Introduction de l'auteur'; xiv 'Remarques'; xv 'Table alphabétique des matières'; xvi 'Table des illustrations'; 1–304 text; 305–20 'Index alphabétique détaillé'
CITATIONS: BQ 24-4867
COPIES: *MWIAP   OONL (TX715 S1274 1928 fol.) QMBN (TX715.6 S35 1928a and 114984 CON)
NOTES: The text is partly in a question-and-answer format, described in the 'Introduction de l'auteur' as 'la forme catéchistique.'

The MWIAP copy is in its original dust-jacket, which features a colour illustration of 'Truite saumonée rôtie.' The QMBN copy, which is rebound, has seven black-and-white plates.

Carrière No. 186, which does not identify an edition number but records 320 pp, may refer to this edition.

Q171.4   [3rd ed., copyright 1928]
—Les secrets / de la bonne / cuisine / contenant la substance des cours de cuisine / donnés à l'Ecole ménagère (Congrégation de / Notre-Dame) de Montréal, avec plus de / 1500 recettes, toutes mises à l'épreuve / dans la cuisine de l'ecole / par / soeur Sainte-Marie Edith, / directrice de l'Ecole ménagère / de Montréal. / Publié par / La compagnie d'imprimerie et de lithographie / canadienne limitée, Montréal.
DESCRIPTION: 23.5 × 15.5 cm   Pp [i–ii] iii [iv–vi] vii–xvi, 1–336   18 fp illus of, for example, serving uniforms, made dishes, table settings, china and cutlery, and serviettes and table cloths   Paper-covered boards, cloth spine
CONTENTS: i ht; ii 'Tous droits réservés, Canada. (1928) Imprimé au Canada.'; iii dedication to Madame P.-R. du Tremblay; iv 'Troisième édition revue, augmentée et corrigée.'; v tp; vi blank; vii préface; viii fp illus of serving uniforms; ix–x 'L'importance de la bonne cuisine' signed *La presse*; xi–xiii 'Introduction de l'auteur'; xiv 'Remarques'; xv 'Table alphabétique des matières'; xvi 'Table des illustrations'; 1–320 text; 321–36 'Index alphabétique détaillé'
CITATIONS: Bédard, p 4
COPIES: *OGU (UA s048 b50)   OONL (TX715 S1274 1928b fol.)   QMACN (570.610 (1))

Q171.5   [copyright 1928]
—The secrets / of good / cooking / containing the substance of the courses, given / at the Montreal Cooking School, (Congregation / of Notre-Dame), and a choice of more than / 1500 recipes, all tested in the laboratory- / kitchen of the school / by / Sister St. Mary Edith, / Principal of the Montreal / Cooking School / Published by / the Canadian Printing and Lithographing / Company, Limited, Montreal
DESCRIPTION: 23.5 × 16.0 cm   Pp [i–ii] iii [iv–vi] vii–xiii [xiv] xv–xvi, 1–327   18 fp illus   Paper-covered boards, cloth spine
CONTENTS: i ht; ii 'Copyright, 1928, by the Canadian Printing & Lithographing Company, Ltd. Printed in Canada'; iii dedication to Madame P.R. du Tremblay; iv blank; v tp; vi blank; vii preface; viii fp illus of two maids in uniform; ix–x 'The Importance of Good Cooking' signed *La presse*; xi–xiii 'The Author's Introduction'; xiv blank; xv table of contents; xvi index of illustrations; 1–309 text; 310 blank; 311–27 index
COPIES: OONL (TX715 S12742 fol. copy 2)   QMACN

QMM (RBD Soeur Berthe, ckbk 524) *Private collection

NOTES: This edition is not numbered, but it probably corresponds to the French-language third edition, Q171.4 (note the matching binding, the same number of full-page illustrations, and the increased number of pages from earlier editions). Although this edition has more leaves than Q171.2, it is printed on thinner paper so that the volume is only 1.0 cm thick. The text finishes with 'Sandwich Recipes' on pp 308–mid 309, followed by Boston Baked Beans, Mexican Beans, and New York Beans under the general heading 'Pork and Beans.'

The QMACN copy could not be found when I visited; however, a comparison of photocopies of the title-pages shows that the QMACN copy matches Q171.5 (the title-page text does not vary; however, the three-line border here is absolutely plain, whereas the outer line in Q171.2 is punctuated by a small, decorative pattern).

An owner of a later English edition (probably this one) reported that the book 'was put out in a cheaper edition [than the first] in both English and French, and was available in bookstores in Montreal into the 1940s.'

1928–31

How to make many tasty dishes

For the titles of other Oxo books, see Q148.1.

Q172.1 nd [about 1928–31]
How to make many / tasty dishes / With the compliments of / Oxo Limited, / 1910, St. Antoine Street, / Montreal. [cover-title]
COPIES: *Private collection
NOTES: The book's owner reports that there is no date and no table of contents or index; there are the following sections: 'The Oxo Story' (7 pp); 'Invalid Recipes'; 'Tasty Dishes Easily Prepared'; 'The Oxo Habit – a World-Wide Benefit'; 'Household Economy'; 'What to Do in Cases of Emergency'; and 'Kitchen Hints.' The company name and address indicate a publication date of about 1928–31: Oxo Ltd is listed at 1910 St Antoine in the Montreal city directories for 1928–9 to 1931–2. (In the directories for 1932–3 to 1934–5 Oxo Ltd is at 428 St Peter, and in the directory for 1935–6 the company name changes to Oxo Canada Ltd.) The appearance of the book is consistent with publication in about 1928–31.

BRITISH EDITIONS: *How to Make Many Tasty Dishes*, [London: Oxo Ltd, 193?] (Great Britain: LB).

1929

Chocolate and cocoa recipes

For the titles of other cookbooks by the same company, see Q52.1.

Q173.1 [copyright 1929]
Presented with the compliments of / Walter Baker & Co., / of Canada, / Limited / Established 1780 / Montreal, Canada / The world's most popular chocolate and cocoa recipes [cover-title]
DESCRIPTION: 17.5 × 12.5 cm Pp 1–24 Paper, with image on front of a two-layer white cake with chocolate icing and a dessert in a tall-stemmed glass; stapled
CONTENTS: 1–4 general information about chocolate and cooking with chocolate, and at top p 1, 'World-Famous Chocolate and Cocoa Recipes'; 5–6 'Beverages'; 7–top 11 'Cakes and Cookies'; mid 11–13 'Frostings, Fillings, and Sauces'; 14 'Pastry'; 15–17 'Puddings'; 18–19 'Frozen and Chilled Desserts'; 20–2 'Candies'; 23–4 'Index to Recipes' and at bottom p 24, 'Copyrighted 1929 Canadian Postum Company, Ltd. (5799) Printed in Canada'
CITATIONS: Armstrong 2000, illus p F2 (not identified in caption)
COPIES: AEUCHV SSWD *Private collection
NOTES: There are two possible short-titles: 'The World's Most Popular Chocolate and Cocoa Recipes' or 'Chocolate and Cocoa Recipes.'

Q173.2 [copyright 1929]
—Présenté avec les compliments de / Walter Baker & Co., / of Canada / Limited / Maison fondée en 1780 / Montreal, Canada / Les plus fameuses recettes pour préparer le chocolat et le cacao [cover-title]
DESCRIPTION: 17.0 × 12.0 cm Pp 1–27, [i–iv] Paper, with image on front of a two-layer white cake with chocolate icing and a dessert in a tall-stemmed glass; stapled
CONTENTS: 1–4 general information about chocolate and cooking with chocolate, and at top p 1, 'Les fameuses recettes'; 5–top 7 'Breuvages'; mid 7–12 'Gâteaux et biscuits'; 13–14 'Entremets glacés et rafraîchis'; 15–mid 18 'Bonbons'; mid 18–mid 21 'Sauces, garnitures, glaçage'; mid 21–24 'Poudingues'; 25–mid 26 'Pâtisseries'; mid 26–27 untitled table of contents and at bottom p 27, 'Copyrighted, 1929, Canadian Postum Company, Ltd. (5780) Imprimé au Canada'; i–iv publ ads
COPIES: *QMBN (198106 CON)

Home made banana recipes

Q174.1 [copyright 1929]
Yes! / Home / made / banana / recipes / Canada–
West Indies Fruit Co. Ltd. / 1171 St. James Street
West / Montreal, Canada / Toronto Halifax /
Printed in U.S.A. [cover-title]
DESCRIPTION: 18.0 × 12.5 cm   Pp 3–22   Illus col Paper, with image on front of Banana and Nut Salad;
stapled, and with hole punched at top left corner,
through which runs a string for hanging
CONTENTS: Inside front face of binding 'Introductory'
and 'Copyright 1929 Bauerlein, Inc., New Orleans';
3 'Index'; 4–22 recipes
COPIES: *QSFFSC

Rawleigh's good health guide and cook book 1929

*For information about Rawleigh's annual almanac
cookbooks and other publications, see M22.1.*

Q175.1   1929
1889 1929 / Rawleigh's / Trade mark reg. U.S. Pat.
Off. / good health guide / and / cook book / Table
of contents / Cooking recipes 4-7-9-10-11-12-13-19-
21-24-25-30-31 / Health and diet information 6-7-8-
12-13-18-30 / Good health products 14-23-26-27-29-
31-32 / Palatable foods 16-17 / Secrets for women
19-20-22-23-28-29 / Rawleigh service 2-3-5-15-16-32
/ An opportunity for you 30 / Published by / the
W.T. Rawleigh Co., Ltd. / Montreal – Winnipeg /
Melbourne, Australia / Freeport Memphis Chester /
Oakland Minneapolis Richmond / Denver and
Albany, U.S.A. / 40th anniversary number
DESCRIPTION: 23.5 × 16.0 cm   Pp [1] 2–32   Tp illus
black-and-brown of W.T. Rawleigh and a man and a
horse-drawn cart; illus black-and-brown   Lacks paper binding; stapled, and with hole punched at top
left corner for hanging
CONTENTS: 1 tp; 2–3 '40 Years Ago and Today'; 4
'When We Were Five and Six' [recipes]; 5 '40 Years of
Service'; 6 'Sunshine Essential for Health'; 7 'Child
Body-Building Foods' [recipes]; 8–9 'Breakfast – the
Best Meal of All' [recipes]; 10 'Food from the Sea'
[recipes]; 11 'Attractive and Corrective Salads'; 12
'Vegetables for Vitamins and Vitality' [recipes]; 13
'Fruits for Health'; 14 'Two Most Common Body Ills';
15 'From the Ends of the Earth'; 16 'For Distinctive
Flavor in Foods'; 17 'Good Health Foods'; 18–19
'Foods That Reduce Weight'; 20 'A Charming Personality'; 21 'Simple Puddings'; 22–3 'Helpful Kitchen

Ways'; 24 'Foods You May Can' [recipes]; 25 'Campfire Cooking'; 26–7 'When Emergencies Come'; 28–9
'Cleaning Hints'; 30–1 'Nourishing Soups'; 32 'The
Choice of Four Generations'
COPIES: AEUCHV (UV 85.188.8)   AHRMH (994-001-
035) ARDA BBVM OMAHM (993.16.11a)
OTUTF (uncat patent medicine) SSWD *Private
collection
NOTES: On the front face of the binding of the BBVM
copy, there is an image of a mother and daughter
preparing food at a kitchen table.

AMERICAN EDITIONS: The following descriptions are
probably of the same American edition: *Rawleigh's
Good Health Guide and Cook Book*, '40th anniversary
number,' Freeport, Ill.: W.T. Rawleigh Co., 1928 [the
year recorded in the OBgU record for the book]
(United States: OBgU); *Rawleigh's 40th Anniversary*,
1929 (Dickinson, p 149).

77 winning recipes

*For the history of Robin Hood Mills Ltd and the titles of
the company's other cookbooks, see S16.1, Rorer, Mrs
Sarah Tyson, Robin Hood Flour Cook Book.*

Q176.1 [copyright 1929]
77 winning / recipes / home tested methods / for
making cakes, pastries and bread / Every recipe /
prepared and tested / in a home kitchen / under the
supervision of / Robin Hood Mills Limited [cover-
title]
DESCRIPTION: 19.0 × 13.0 cm   Pp 1–36   Illus col Paper, with image on front of Robin Hood Angel Food
cake; stapled
CONTENTS: 1 'Your Complete Guide to Baking Success'; 2 'Insure Successful Baking'; 3–11 'Cakes'; 12–
13 'Cookies'; 14–17 'Pies'; 18–top 20 'Desserts'; mid
20–22 'Tea Dainties'; 23–6 'Bread'; 27–8 'Quick Breads';
29 'Muffins'; 30 'Popovers'; 31–mid 32 'Waffles and
Griddle Cakes'; mid 32–33 'Doughnuts'; 34–5 'Rolled
Oats Sweets'; 36 'How to Win Prizes on Baked Products'
COPIES: ACG ARDA MCM OONL (TX765 S48
1929) OTMCL (641.5971 H39 No. 42) *Company
Collection (Robin Hood Multifoods Inc., Markham,
Ont.)
NOTES: 'Copyright, Canada, 1929' is on the inside
front face of the binding. The location of the company's
offices – Montreal, Moose Jaw, Calgary, and Vancouver
– are also recorded there. No single place of publication is given, but headquarters were in Montreal.

The text on p 1 vouches for the quality of the illustrated recipes: 'The illustrations shown in this booklet were not touched by an artist's brush. The baked products were brought right from the home kitchen to the photographer, ...'

Q176.2 [copyright 1931]
—77 winning / recipes / home tested methods / for making cakes, pastries and bread / Every recipe / prepared and tested / in a home kitchen / under the supervision of / Robin Hood Mills Limited [cover-title]
DESCRIPTION: 19.0 × 13.0 cm   Pp 1–40   Illus col   Paper, with image on front of Robin Hood Angel Food cake; stapled, and with hole punched at top left corner for hanging
CONTENTS: 1–2 'Your Complete Guide to Baking Success'; 3–13 'Cakes'; 14–15 'Cookies'; 16–19 'Pies'; 20 'Puddings'; 21–2 'Desserts'; 23–5 'Tea Dainties'; 26–9 'Bread'; 30 'Sandwiches'; 31–2 'Quick Breads'; 33 'Muffins'; 34 'Popovers'; 35 'Waffles'; 36–7 'Doughnuts'; 38–9 'Oats Sweets'; 40 'Easy to Win Prizes on Home Baking with Robin Hood Flour'
COPIES: AHRMH (987-035-003)   OGU (CCC TX715.6 S48)   *Private collection
NOTES: 'Copyright, Canada, 1931' is on the inside front face of the binding. Page 40 begins, 'The year 1930 again recorded sweeping victories for Robin Hood Flour at Canadian Home Baking Contests.'

Copies of *77 Winning Recipes* were ordered by people attending the 1931 Saskatchewan Provincial Exhibition in Regina, according to the article 'Friends Old and New at Western Exhibitions' in Robin Hood Mills Ltd's in-house magazine *Grist* (October 1931), p 10: '... the complete baking book, "77 Winning Recipes," was prominently displayed [at the company's booth] and some thousands of names and addresses of those desiring the book secured.' The article also reports that 'quantities of bread baking recipe leaflets in various languages' were distributed at the booth. Although the accounts of the fairs at Brandon, Manitoba, and at Yorkton, Saskatoon, Prince Albert, North Battleford, Weyburn, and Estevan, Saskatchewan, do not mention the cookbook, it was probably also offered to the public at these fairs, in conjunction with cookery demonstrations and displays.

The January 1932 issue of *Grist*, p 18, features 'More Cook Book Requests.' Letters received by the company's Vancouver and Montreal offices requesting *77 Winning Recipes* are reprinted. The Montreal letter is from a young girl, whose teacher had instructed all the pupils to write away for a copy of the cookbook.

The October 1932 issue of *Grist*, p 27, tells of a cookbook request addressed 'Montreal, Moose Jaw, Calgary, Vancouver,' with no company name. The Post Office correctly guessed the intended destination, writing on the envelope, 'Try Robin Hood Mills, Montreal.'

Q176.3 [about 1931]
—77 recettes / merveilleuses / méthodes eprouvées à la maison / pour faire le pain, les gâteaux et les pâtisseries / Chaque recette / préparée et eprouvée / dans une cuisine / sous la surveillance de / Robin Hood Mills Limited [cover-title]
DESCRIPTION: Paper, with image on front of Robin Hood Angel Food cake; stapled
COPIES: *Private collection
NOTES: Page 40 refers to the number of prizes won by Robin Hood Flour in exhibitions in 1930.

Q176.4 [copyright 1931; about 1933]
—77 / winning / recipes / Robin Hood Flour [cover-title]
DESCRIPTION: 19.0 × 13.0 cm   Pp 1–44   Illus col   Paper, with image on front of Robin Hood Angel Food cake; stapled, and with hole punched at top left corner for hanging
CONTENTS: 1 'Your Complete Guide to Baking Success'; 2 'Insure Successful Baking'; 3–13 'Cakes'; 14–17 'Pies'; 18–21 'Special Occasions'; 22–5 'Bread'; 26 'Sandwiches'; 27–8 'Quick Breads'; 29 'Muffins'; 30 'Popovers'; 31 'Waffles and Griddle Cakes'; 32–3 'Doughnuts'; 34 'Puddings'; 35–6 'Desserts'; 37–9 'Tea Dainties'; 40–1 'Oats Sweets'; 42–4 'Cookies'
COPIES: *Private collection
NOTES: 'Copyright, Canada, 1931' is on the inside front face of the binding; however, on the inside back face there is a reference to 'the 1933 Canadian National Exhibition at Toronto.' *Chatelaine* 1935, p 82, cites *77 Winning Recipes*, but does not specify the edition.

1930

Canada's prize recipes

For information about the Canada Starch Co., see Q47.1.

Q177.1 [copyright 1930]
Canada's / prize / recipes / This book contains the prize / winning recipes selected / from over 75,000 received / from all parts of Canada – / contributed by the users of / the famous Edwardsburg / products – and which were / judged, tested and

approved / by the Montreal Cooking / School. / Compiled by / the Canada Starch Co., Limited / Montreal / Quebec Toronto Cardinal / Fort William Vancouver

DESCRIPTION: 22.5 × 15.0 cm   Pp [1–3] 4–128   Frontis of place setting, 1 fp illus on p 13 of 'The Maid and Her Uniform,' centre spread illus on pp 64–5 of Canada Starch Co.'s products, many illus of prepared dishes   [$0.10, on binding]   Paper

CONTENTS: 1 'Copyright, Canada 1930 by the Canada Starch Co., Limited // Head office: Montreal // Works: Cardinal and Fort William // Sales offices: Montreal Quebec Toronto Fort William Winnipeg Vancouver'; 2 frontis; 3 tp; 4 'How This Book Became Possible'; 5 'The Important Part Corn Plays in Your Daily Menu'; 6 'Edwardsburg Products' (Crown Brand Corn Syrup, Benson's Golden Syrup, Lily White Corn Syrup, Benson's Prepared Corn, Canada Corn Starch, Challenge Corn Starch, Casco Potato Flour, Mazola Oil); 7–10 'The Necessity of a Modern Kitchen'; 11–12 'The Value of Good Utensils'; 13–14 'The Maid and Her Uniform'; 15–16 'Table Service'; top 17 'Correct Table Etiquette'; bottom 17–19 'How to Carve'; 20–2 'Foods and Their Relative Values'; 23–top 25 'The Feeding of Children'; bottom 25 'Table of Measurements'; 26–top 27 'Reduction or Gaining of Weight'; bottom 27 'A Few Reminders'; 28 'Average Length of Time for Cooking Meat'; 29–31 'A Few Suggestions That May Add Variety to Your Menu' [menus for three meals a day, Sunday to Saturday]; 32 list of Canada Starch Co.'s products; 33–123 'Canada's Prize Recipes'; 124–6 index of recipes; 127 ad for Linit Starch; 128 book-order form

CITATIONS: Armstrong 2000, p F2   Chatelaine 1935, p 82   Duncan, p 180   Ferguson/Fraser, pp 90 and 233, illus col on p 80 of closed volume   Golick, p 101

COPIES: ACHP (HP 6209.2)   BVIPM   NBDKH OBUJBM   OFERWM (A1977.122.16 not on shelf, December 1999)   OGU (CCC TX715.6 C355) OKELWM   OMATTM   OONL (TX715 C34 1930 p***)   OTBH   OTMCL (641.5971 C1178 missing) OTYA (CPC 1930 0047)   OWTU (G10684)   QMBM (641.5971 C212ca)   QMM (RBD ckbk 1397)   *Private collection

NOTES: Canada's Prize Recipes superseded 'a little recipe book' that had been issued in various editions 'from year to year' (p 4), i.e., Q83.1, Edwardsburg Recipe Book. It is not surprising that the Canada Starch Co., whose head office was in Montreal, should ask the Montreal Cooking School to judge the many thousands of recipes that were submitted in response to the company's public appeal. The school was famous in the city, and only two years before, in 1928, its principal, Sister St Mary Edith, had seen published

Q171.1, Les secrets de la bonne cuisine, a substantial text that went through three editions in French and three in English.

Canada Starch advertisements in Nor'-West Farmer and Farm and Home Vol. 50, No. 5 (5 March 1931), and Vol. 50, No. 6 (20 March 1931), include a book-order form for Canada's Prize Recipes.

Q177.2 [copyright 1930]

—Les / meilleures / recettes / du Canada / Ce livre contient les recettes / primées choisies parmi plus / de 75,000 que nous ont en- / voyées, de toutes les parties / du Canada, des consomma- / teurs des célèbres produits / Edwardsburg, et qui ont été / jugées, mises à l'essai et ap- / prouvées par la Montreal / Cooking School (Ecole de / cuisine de Montréal). / Compilées par / The Canada Starch Co., Limited / Montreal / Quebec Toronto Cardinal / Fort-William Vancouver

DESCRIPTION: 22.5 × 15.0 cm   Pp [1–3] 4–128   Frontis of place setting, 1 fp illus on p 15 of 'La servante et son uniforme,' centre spread illus on pp 64–5 of Canada Starch Co.'s products, many illus of prepared dishes   [$0.10, on binding]   Paper; stapled

CONTENTS: 1 'Droits de publication réservés au Canada 1930 par The Canada Starch Co., Limited // Siège social: Montreal // Ateliers: Cardinal et Fort-William // Succursales de vente: Montreal Quebec Toronto Fort-William Winnipeg Vancouver'; 2 frontis; 3 tp; 4 'Ce qui a donné lieu à la publication de ce livre'; 5 'L'importance du rôle du maïs dans votre menu quotidien'; 6 'Produits Edwardsburg'; 7–mid 10 'Nécessité de la cuisine moderne'; bottom 10–mid 12 'La valeur de bons ustensiles'; bottom 12–16 'Service de la table'; top 17 'La parfaite étiquette à table'; bottom 17–19 'Comment faire le dépeçage; 20–2 'Les aliments et leur valeur relative'; 23–mid 25 'L'alimentation des enfants'; mid–bottom 25 tables of measurement; 26–mid 27 'Diminution ou augmentation de poids'; bottom 27 'Quelques conseils à retenir'; 28 'Durée moyenne de la cuisson de la viande'; 29–31 'Quelques suggestions qui vois aideront à varier votre menu'; 32 list of company products; 33–123 'Les meilleures recettes du Canada'; 124–6 'Table des matières'; 127 ad for Linit Starch; 128 book-order form

CITATIONS: Armstrong 2000, p F2   BQ 23-4920

COPIES: OONL (TX715 C34 1930b)   QMBN (TX715.6 M475 1930 and 105058 CON)   QQUQT   *Company collection (Best Foods Canada, Toronto, Ont., 2 copies)   Private collection

NOTES: The QQUQT copy is inscribed on the front face of the binding, in ink, 'PA Picard mars 1932.' The private collector's copy belonged originally to her mother, who lived in Quebec City.

Q177.3 [facsimile, 1975]
—Prize / Canadian / recipes / Compiled by / the
Canada Starch Co. Ltd. / in 1930 / Note: Brand
name products may be substituted with equivalents.
/ Coles
CONTENTS: 3 tp; 4 '© copyright 1975 and published by
Coles Publishing Company Limited Toronto –
Canada'; ...
COPIES: OONL (TX715 C34 1975, 2 copies)

Catherine-de-Cardone, soeur (Bernardine Archambault) (1877–1959)

*The religious order of Soeurs des Saints Noms de Jésus et
Marie was founded by Sister Marie-Rose (Marie-Rose
Durocher) in Longueuil, Quebec, in 1843.*

Q178.1 1930
J.M. / La cuisine pratique / à l'école primaire / et /
dans la famille / Révérendes Soeurs des Saints
Noms / de Jésus et de Marie / Montréal, 1930
DESCRIPTION: 22.5 × 15.0 cm   Pp [1–5] 6–122 [123]
Paper; stapled
CONTENTS: 1 tp; 2 'Droits réservés'; 3–122 text; 123
'Table des matières'
COPIES: *QLOSNJMA (641.1 C363c)
NOTES: The printer's name is on the outside back face
of the binding: 'Imprimerie des Sourd[s-Muets] 7400,
Saint-Laure[nt] Montréal.' The author is not recorded
in the book, but she was soeur Catherine-de-Cardone,
according to biographical information on a single,
typed sheet that describes a painting of the sister (at
QLOSNJMA). Founder of the École classico-ménagère
de Sainte-Martine, she had an interest in 'tout le
secteur des sciences familiales aux cours primaire,
secondaire et supérieur dans les écoles et les
pensionnats dirigés par les SNJM.' Regarding the cookbook, the sheet states: 'Le nom de soeur Catherine est
buriné pour toujours dans le "classique" de notre
héritage culinaire québécois, *La cuisine pratique*,
retouchée, améliorée dans chacune des cinq [*sic*]
éditions successives, de son vivant, aux Ateliers des
Sourds-Muets. À la demande de milliers d'anciennes
élèves, Libre Expression l'a rééditée en 1981, 1984 et,
en l'année centenaire du Couvent de Ste-Martine, au
4e trimestre 1996.'

Q178.2 [copyright 1936]
—J.M. / La cuisine / pratique / a l'ecole et dans /
la famille / Choisir une nourriture saine et /
économique, c'est s'orienter vers / le bonheur et la
prospérité.

DESCRIPTION: 22.0 × 15.0 cm   Pp [1–5] 6–156 [157]
Symbol on tp of Soeurs des Saints Noms de Jésus et
de Marie   Paper, with SNJM symbol on front; sewn
CONTENTS: 1 tp; 2 'Table des matières'; 3–141 text;
142–52 'Recettes supplémentaires'; 153–6 'Index des
recettes'; 157 'Index des recettes supplémentaires'
CITATIONS: BQ 24-4765
COPIES: *QMBN (94631 CON)
NOTES: This and later editions are retitled *La cuisine
pratique à l'école et dans la famille,* without the adjective
'primaire.' The following is on the outside back face
of the binding: 'Prix: 45 sous // En vente chez tous
les libraires et à la Procure des Soeurs des Saints
Noms de Jésus et de Marie 1430, boulevard Mont-
Royal, Outremont. Droits réservés, Canada 1936.
Imprimé aux Ateliers des Sourds-Muets 7400, boul.
St-Laurent Montréal.'

Q178.3 [22nd thousand, January 1944, copyright
1941]
—J.M. / La cuisine / pratique / a l'ecole et dans /
la famille / Choisir une nourriture saine et /
économique, c'est aller vers le / bonheur et la
prospérité.
DESCRIPTION: 22.5 × 15.0 cm   Pp [1–3] 4–166 [$0.50,
on binding]   Paper; sewn
CONTENTS: 1 tp; 2 'Table des matières'; 3–161 text; 162
blank; 163–6 'Index des recettes'
COPIES: *QMM (RBD ckbk 2023)
NOTES: The following is printed on the outside back
face of the binding: 'Prix: 50 sous // En vente chez
tous les libraires et à la Procure des Soeurs des Saints
Noms de Jésus et de Marie 1430, boulevard Mont-
Royal, Outremont. 22e mille janvier 1944 Droits
réservés Canada 1941. Imprimé aux Ateliers des
Sourds-Muets 7400, boul. St-Laurent Montréal.'
QLOSNJMA (641.1 C363c) has a rebound copy of
what may be the same edition as that described here.

Q178.4 [40th thousand, March 1948, copyright 1941]
—J.M. / La cuisine pratique / a l'ecole et dans la
famille / Les Soeurs des Saints Noms / de Jésus et
de Marie / Outremont / Montréal
DESCRIPTION: 22.5 × 15.0 cm   Pp [1–3] 4–176   Sym-
bol on tp of Soeurs des Saints Noms de Jésus et de
Marie, illus   Paper; sewn
CONTENTS: 1 tp; 2 'Table des matières'; 3–171 text; 172
blank; 173–6 'Index des recettes'
CITATIONS: BQ 24-4766
COPIES: *QMBN (TX714 C84 1948 and 94632
CON)   QQLA (TX715 C9662 1948)
NOTES: The following is on the outside back face of
the binding: 'Prix: 75 sous // En vente chez tous les

libraires et à la Procure des Soeurs des Saints Noms de Jésus et de Marie 1430, boulevard Mont-Royal, Outremont. 40ᵉ mille mars 1948 Droits réservés Canada 1941. Imprimé aux Ateliers des Sourds-Muets 65 ouest, rue De Castelnau Montréal.'

OTHER EDITIONS: [55th thousand, November 1953, copyright 1941] (QLOSNJMA, QMBN, QMM, QTURA); [65th thousand, September 1954, copyright 1941] (QSFFSC); new ed., retitled *La cuisine pratique des Soeurs des Saints Noms de Jésus et de Marie*, Montreal: Éditions Libre expression, 1981, 'Annexe' reprints most of the preliminary text from an earlier edition, probably that of 1953 (OONL, QLOSNJMA, QMBN); Montreal: Libre expression, 1984 (OONL, QQLA); and Montreal: Libre expression, 1996 (OONL, QMBN).

Church of the Ascension recipe book

Q179.1 [1930]
Church of the / Ascension / recipe book / Published under the auspices / of the Women's Guild of the / Church of the Ascension / Park Ave., Montreal [cover-title]
DESCRIPTION: 23.0 × 15.0 cm   Pp 1–112   Paper, with image on front of a slice of a three-layer cake; stapled
CONTENTS: 1–2 ads; 3 'Index' [i.e., table of contents]; 4 'Foreword'; 5 ad; 6 'Church of the Ascension Women's Guild // Officers for 1930'; 7–111 text and ads; 112 ads
COPIES: *QMM (RBD Vanna Garnier, ckbk 757)
NOTES: According to the 'Foreword,' the book had 'the double object of helping along our own good cause and also providing for our readers a cook book full of useful, practical information.' The QMM copy is inscribed on the front face of the binding, in ink, 'Marjorie [I.?] Adams.'

Clark's recipe book

For an earlier publication by W. Clark Ltd, see Q159.1.

Q180.1 nd [about 1930]
Clark's / recipe / book / Let the / Clark kitchen / help you for / quicker and / better meals [cover-title]
DESCRIPTION: 16.5 × 13.0 cm   Pp [1–24]   Illus col of Clark products and prepared dishes, illus   Paper, with image on front of a steaming casserole of baked beans(?) on a dining table; previously stapled, now sewn by library
CONTENTS: 1 'Appetising Recipes // Kitchen Efficiency'; 2–3 'Clark's Prepared Foods' [information about the company]; 4–24 recipes using Clark's products
COPIES: *OONL (TX715 C3465 No. 19 reserve)
NOTES: The company name, W. Clark Ltd, Montreal, is on the food labels of the illustrated products, which include canned beans (this brand of beans remains popular today), canned soups, spaghetti with tomato sauce and cheese, pâté de viande, smoked Vienna-style sausage, Cambridge-style sausages, ox tongue, Canadian boiled dinner, sliced smoked beef, cooked corned beef, corned beef hash, bottled tomato ketchup, chili sauce, and many other prepared foods. The text on p 1 gives the book's two purposes: '... to show you handy, labour-saving ways in which Clark's Prepared Foods can cut down the time you spend in the kitchen ... [and to] introduce some practical recipes that provide pleasant and tasty changes in the family menu.' The text on pp 2–3 notes that the Clark kitchens are in Montreal and St Rémi, Quebec, and in Harrow, Ontario; it refers to the founding of the business by William Clark 'over fifty years ago.' Since William Clark Ltd was established in 1877, *Clark's Recipe Book* was published after 1927 (1877 + 50 years), likely about 1930. The binding has a striking yellow-and-black design. 'The Montreal Lithographing Co. Limited' is on the outside back face.

Cook book

Q181.1 nd [about 1930]
South Bolton / Women's Institute / Cook book [cover-title]
DESCRIPTION: 34.0 × 21.5 cm   Pp [1–23]   Paper; bound at top edge
CONTENTS: 1–23 recipes credited with the name of the contributor
COPIES: *QKB
NOTES: The text is reproduced from typed copy, and printed on the rectos only; the versos are blank.

Favorite recipes

Q182.1 nd [about 1930]
Favorite / recipes / Ladies' Aid / Society / Rosemont First / United Church / Montreal [cover-title]
DESCRIPTION: 17.0 × 13.0 cm   Pp 1–127   Thin card; stapled
CONTENTS: 1 'Foreward' [*sic*]; 2 blank; 3–4 'How to Cook a Husband' [i.e., mock recipe] copied from 'Ladies Aid Cook Book, Beverly, Mass.' [not cited in Cook]; 5–126 recipes credited with the name of the

contributor and ads; 127 'Index' [i.e., table of contents]
COPIES: *QMM (RBD ckbk 1968)
NOTES: 'How to Cook a Husband' was copied from Q182.1 for NB43.1.

Good cooks of the Quebec Women's Institute

Q183.1   nd [about 1930]
[An edition of *Good Cooks of the Quebec Women's Institute*, nd]
COPIES: Private collection
NOTES: The book's owner reports that there is no date or publisher recorded and that the volume was likely published about 1930.

Grisé, Joseph-Évariste (1892–)

Grisé also wrote Q96.1, Bulletin 49, De la fabrication des conserves alimentaires à la maison, for the Quebec Department of Agriculture. For the titles of other cookbooks published by the department, see Q48.1.

Q184.1   1930
Ministère de l'Agriculture de la province de Québec / Les conserves / par J.E. Grisé, L.S.A. / [on image of can:] Légumes / fruits / viandes / variées / [below can:] en tout temps de l'année / Bulletin no 102 / Publié par ordre de l'honorable ministre de l'Agriculture / 1930 [cover-title]
DESCRIPTION: 23.0 × 15.5 cm   Pp 1–31 [32] Illus   Paper, with image on front of a mother and daughter making preserves at a kitchen table, and a still-life of raw and preserved foods; stapled
CONTENTS: 1 'Les conserves' [introductory text]; 2 'Qu'est-ce que la mise en conserve?'; 3 'Bactérie, levure, moisissure'; 4–8 'Stérilisation'; 9–15 'Matériel nécessaire pour la mise en conserve'; 16–17 'Comment faire la mise en conserve à la maison' [twelve numbered and illustrated steps]; 18–23 'Les légumes'; 24–6 'Les fruits'; 27–8 'Les viandes'; 29–mid 30 'Le poisson'; mid 30–31 'Notes importantes'; 32 'Temps alloué pour le blanchiment et la stérilisation'
CITATIONS: Beaulieu, p 102
COPIES: QMBN (161614 CON)   *QSFFSC
NOTES: The 1937, 1943, and 1948 editions all have the same image on the front face of the binding.

Q184.2   1932
—Ministère de l'Agriculture de la province de Québec / En tout temps de l'année / Les conserves / par J.E.

Grisé L.S.A / Bulletin no 102 / Publié par ordre de l'honorable ministre de l'Agriculture / 1932 [cover-title]
DESCRIPTION: 22.5 × 15.0 cm   Pp [1] 2–56 Illus   Paper, with image on front of cans and bottles of preserved foods at top and a still-life of raw foodstuffs at bottom; stapled
CITATIONS: Beaulieu, p 102
COPIES: *QSFFSC
NOTES: This is the only edition without the kitchen scene of mother and daughter on the binding.

Q184.3   1937
—Ministère de l'Agriculture de la province de Québec / Les conserves / par J.E. Grisé, L.S.A. / [on image of can:] Légumes / fruits / viandes / variées / [below can:] en tout temps de l'année / Bulletin no 102 / Publié par ordre de l'honorable ministre de l'Agriculture / 1937 [cover-title]
DESCRIPTION: 23.0 × 15.5 cm   Pp [1] 2–63 [64] Illus   Paper, with image on front of a mother and daughter making preserves at a kitchen table, and a still-life of raw and preserved foods; stapled
CITATIONS: Beaulieu, p 102
COPIES: QMBN (A38A1 P83 102 1937 and microform SEM 105P2950)   *QSFFSC   QTS   QVMVS (641.42)

Q184.4   1943
—Ministère de l'Agriculture de la province de Québec / Les conserves / par J.E. Grisé, L.S.A. / [on image of can:] Légumes / fruits / viandes / variées / [below can:] en tout temps de l'année / Bulletin no 102 / Publié par ordre de l'honorable ministre de l'Agriculture / 1943 [cover-title]
DESCRIPTION: 22.5 × 15.0 cm   Pp [1] 2–63 [64] Illus   Paper, with image on front of a mother and daughter making preserves at a kitchen table, and a still-life of raw and preserved foods; stapled
COPIES: QMBN (A38A1 P83 102 1943)   *QSFFSC

Q184.5   [new ed.], 1945
—[New edition of *Les conserves*, Bulletin 102, [Quebec City:] Ministère de l'Agriculture de la province de Québec, 1945, pp 55, illus]
COPIES: QMBN (161616 CON)

Q184.6   1948
—[Ministè]re de l'Agriculture de la province de Québec / Les conserves / par J.E. Grisé, L.S.A. / [on image of can:] Légumes / fruits / viandes / variées / [below can:] en tout temps de l'année / Bulletin no 102 / Publié par ordre de l'honorable ministre de l'Agriculture / 1948 [cover-title]

DESCRIPTION: 23.0 × 15.0 cm   Pp [1] 2–56   Illus   Paper, with image on front of a mother and daughter making preserves at a kitchen table, and a still-life of raw and preserved foods; stapled
CITATIONS: Beaulieu, p 102
COPIES: *QSFFSC (641.4 G869c)

Knox Gelatine desserts, salads, candies and frozen dishes

An earlier cookbook for Knox Gelatine is Q69.1.

Q185.1   nd [about 1930]
Knox / Gelatine / desserts / salads / candies and / frozen dishes [cover-title]
DESCRIPTION: 17.0 × 11.0 cm   Pp [1–2] 3–23   Centre spread illus col of twelve prepared dishes, each keyed to a page in the book; illus on p 3 of Knox Gelatine packages   Paper, with image on front of three women in nineteenth-century dress at a small table
CONTENTS: 1 cover-title; 2 note beginning, 'This book is dedicated to the improved package of Knox Sparkling Gelatine with its 4 convenient, ready-measured envelopes ...,' index, and 'Charles B. Knox Gelatine Company, Inc. Johnstown, New York, U.S.A. and Montreal, Canada'; 3 note about 'Yellow (No. 1 package)' and 'Blue (No. 3 package)'; 4 directions for using the gelatine; 5–23 recipes and at bottom p 23, 'Printed in Canada'
CITATIONS: Chatelaine 1935, p 82
COPIES: ACG   OONL (TX814.5 G4 G4313 1950z p***)   *Private collection
NOTES: OONL's suggested date of publication in the 1950s is incorrect.

Q185.2   nd [about 1930]
—Knox / Gelatine / desserts / salades / bonbons et / mets congelés [cover-title]
DESCRIPTION: 17.0 × 11.0 cm   Pp [1–2] 3–23   Centre spread illus col of twelve prepared dishes, each keyed to a page in the book; illus on p 3 of Knox Gelatine packages   Paper, with image on front of three women in nineteenth-century dress at a small table; stapled
CONTENTS: 1 cover-title; 2 note beginning, 'Ce livre de recettes est destiné au carton amélioré de la Gélatine brillante Knox, ...,' 'Table des matières,' and 'Charles B. Knox Gelatine Company, Inc. Johnstown, New York, É.U.A. et Montréal, Canada'; 3 note about 'le carton jaune no. 1 et le carton bleu no. 3'; 4 directions for using the gelatine; 5–23 [inside back face of binding]

recipes and at bottom p 23, 'Imprimé au Canada'
CITATIONS: BQ 24-4786
COPIES: OONL (TX814.5 G4 G43 1950z p***)   QMBN (124887 CON)   *QMM (RBD uncat)
NOTES: The QMM copy is inscribed on the front face of the binding, in ink, 'H. Lortie // Hawkesbury, Ont.' OONL's suggested date of publication is incorrect.

AMERICAN EDITIONS: *Knox Gelatine Desserts, Salads, Candies and Frozen Dishes*, copyright 1933 (Private collection); [Johnstown, NY: Charles B. Knox Gelatine Co. Inc., copyright 1941] (OGU). A similarly titled, earlier publication by the company – *Knox Gelatine Dainty Desserts, Candies, Salads* – is related; editions of this title include: Johnstown, NY: Charles B. Knox Gelatine Co., nd [about 1925] (WaiteCat 5, No. 347); Johnstown, NY: C.B. Knox Gelatine Co., copyright 1927 (OGU); [Johnstown, NY:] Charles B. Knox Gelatine Co. Inc., copyright 1929 (OGU, SSWD); [Johnstown, NY:] Charles B. Knox Gelatine Co. Inc., copyright 1930 (AHRMH); Charles B. Knox Gelatine Co. Inc., 1931 (BSUM; Dickinson, p 112, illus p 113). Allen, p 196, lists other variations of this title: *Knox Gelatine Dainty Desserts, Salads, Candies*, 1927; *Dainty Desserts, Salads, Candies*, 1936.

1001 emplois du vinaigre

See also Q297.1, New and Delicious Recipes, *by the same company.*

Q186.1   nd [about 1930]
1001 emplois du / vinaigre / Compliments / de / Lion Vinegar Co. / Limited / Montreal et Quebec [cover-title]
DESCRIPTION: About 15.5 × 7.5 cm [dimensions from photocopy]   Pp [1] 2–24   Illus on p 1 of a bottle of Lion Malt Vinegar and a bottle of Lion Spirit Vinegar   With same illus on front
CONTENTS: 1 'Employez toujours la marque Lion'; 2–mid 3 'Fruits marines'; mid 3–mid 6 'Produits de tomates'; mid 6–mid 7 'Produits d'oignons'; mid 7–mid 9 'Sauces'; mid 9–12 'Assaisonnements'; 13–mid 17 'Pickles (Marinades)'; mid 17–mid 18 'Ketchups'; mid 18–mid 19 'Breuvages'; mid 19–22 'Emplois divers'; 23 'Liste commode de poids et mesures de ménage' and 'Temps pour la cuisson des légumes'; 24 continuation of 'Emplois divers'
COPIES: *QMBN (TX819 V5M55 1900 and 153608 CON)

Panomalt recipes

For the titles of other books about cooking with Fleischmann's Yeast, see O131.1.

Q187.1 [3rd ed.], nd [about 1930]
Panomalt / recipes / To bring larger cookie / sales to the retail baker [cover-title]
DESCRIPTION: 25.5 × 17.5 cm Pp [1–2] 3–35 Illus Paper; stapled, and with hole punched at top left corner for hanging and with two holes punched in gutter for holding the book in a ring binder
CONTENTS: 1 illus of a plate of baked goods and a coffee pot, with the caption 'As good to eat as they are to look at. – As easy to sell as they are to make.'; 2 'Third edition // Printed in Canada.'; 3–5 'To Help You Sell Many More Cookies Than You Do Now' [i.e., introductory text]; 6–7 'Index'; 8–33 recipes for cookies; 34 untitled concluding text and 'Table of Weights and Measures'; 35 'The New Faucet for Fleischmann's Panomalt'
COPIES: *Private collection
NOTES: 'Fleischmann Company of Canada Limited // Fleischmann's Yeast // Service // Panomalt' is printed on the inside back face of the binding. The recipes are for various kinds of malt cookies. The text on p 5 explains that 'Panomalt may be used to advantage in replacing molasses in cookie and cake recipes.' No place of publication is recorded, but the company had offices in Montreal; a branch office was in Toronto.

Rawleigh's good health guide and cook book 1930

For information about Rawleigh's annual almanac cookbooks and other publications, see M22.1.

Q188.1 1930
Rawleigh's / Trade mark reg. U.S. Pat. Off. / 1889 1930 / good health / guide / and / cook book / W.T. Rawleigh / President and founder of the Rawleigh Industries / The W.T. Rawleigh Co., Ltd. / Winnipeg Montreal Melbourne / Freeport Memphis Chester Oakland / Minneapolis Richmond Denver Albany / "Good health is better than great riches" / Copyright 1929, The W.T. Rawleigh Co. All rights reserved. Printed in Canada
DESCRIPTION: 24.0 × 16.5 cm Pp [1] 2–32 Tp illus of W.T. Rawleigh; fp illus col on inside front face of binding of Rawleigh's factories; many illus, some

printed in black and orange Paper, with image on front of three children and a dog under a tree, one child slipping flowers under the dog's collar; hole punched at top left corner for hanging
CONTENTS: 1 tp; 2–3 'Review of the Growth of the Rawleigh Industries'; 4–5 'Rawleigh Policies, Principles and Methods'; 6 'The Growth of the Rawleigh Industries'; 7 'Buying and Manufacturing'; 8 'Printing and Bottle Making'; 9 'Satisfaction or No Sale'; 10 'Dates – Figs and Raisins' [recipes]; 11 'Guarding Family Health'; 12–13 'Sunshine and Growth'; 14 'Honey' [recipes]; 15 'The Apple' [recipes]; 16 'The Flavor You Like'; 17 'Food Specialties'; 18 'Bran for Health' [recipes]; 19 'Macaroni – a Valuable Food' [recipes]; 20 'The Health of the Child'; 21 'Household Suggestions' [culinary hints]; 22 'Gardening for Health'; 23 'Citrus Fruits' [recipes]; 24–5 'Care of the Skin'; 26 'Nutritive Value of Corn' [recipes]; 27 'Cocoa and Chocolate' [recipes]; 28 'Hygiene in Clothing'; 29 'Milk, the Protective Food' [recipes]; 30 'Household Sanitation'; 31 'Know Your Calories'; 32 'Necessities for Every Home'
COPIES: AEUCHV *OGU (UA s070 b63)
NOTES: In the imprint, 'Montreal' is in a larger typeface than 'Winnipeg.'

1930–3

Moore, Mary Allen (Mrs Harry Forrester Moore, divorced), née Clark (Hamilton, Ont., 21 February 1903–22 May 1978, Hamilton, Ont.)

For fifty years, 1928–78, Mary Moore wrote a daily cookery column, which, at the peak of her career, appeared in twenty-two newspapers across Canada, from St John's, Newfoundland, to Victoria, British Columbia, and reached an estimated million readers. In the London Free Press, *her columns appeared under the name Mary Allen because other papers in the region carried the same column under Mary Moore. She wrote four cookbooks: Q189.1,* Favourite Cocoa and Chocolate Recipes, *and O1104.1,* Fruit-Kepe Recipes, *both of which bear her name; O1054.1,* The Bee Hive Cook Book, *where she is not credited as the author; and at the end of her life,* The Mary Moore Cookbook, *edited by her son Peter Moore, Toronto: Mary Moore Cookbook, Marianne Moore Pitts and Peter Moore, [1978] (OONL). The latter, which was published just days before the author died and sold about 50,000 copies in its first year in print, has her photograph on the binding. In the 'Foreword,' where she reflects on her career, she mentions taking courses in dietetics in Toronto and studies at Missouri State Teachers' College and at McMaster University in Hamilton, Ontario. In 1938, together with her two sisters, Pearl and Doris, and with financial backing from her brother, Wilfrid, she started a canning company in Hamilton, called Mary Miles Foods (after the silent film star Mary Miles Minter, because her first two names fitted well on can labels); however, rationing of tin during the Second World War forced the family to sell the business to Fearman's in 1942. According to her daughter, Marianne, Mary Moore developed the first chocolate cake mix for Monarch Flour, in the 1940s. After her mother's death, Marianne continued to publish her recipes in a weekly column called 'Best of Mary Moore,' in eleven newspapers; the last of these columns was published in 1998, in the* Beacon Herald *in Stratford, Ontario.*

For further information about this author, including references to articles about her, see Canadian Women of Note *No. 633. 'Meet Mary Moore: The Food Columnist Who Always Has the Answers' by Carroll Allen,* Homemaker's Digest *Vol. 7, No. 4 (July/August 1972), includes biographical information and photographs. Lang, pp 184–5, discusses Pearl's career and incorrectly attributes the syndicated Mary Moore cookery columns to her sister Pearl, implying that Mary Moore was a pseudonym. The confusion may stem from differing accounts of the genesis of the columns. According to Doris, Pearl, who worked in an advertising agency, thought of the career idea for Mary, encouraged her to write the columns, and helped her with the first few (conversation with Doris Ludwig, née Clark, August 2002). Peter Moore related that Pearl was asked by the* Edmonton Journal *in 1928 to write a food column, but she was too busy, so Mary took on the job; the* Edmonton Journal, *therefore, was the launching pad for Mary's syndicated columns (conversation with Peter Moore, February 2002). For Mary's photograph, see pl 44.*

Doris Clark helped produce Q204.1, How We Do It.

Q189.1   nd [about 1930–3]
Chocolate ... / the world's favourite flavour / Favourite / cocoa and chocolate / recipes / Prepared by Mary Moore / Published by Fry-Cadbury Ltd. / Montreal [cover-title]
DESCRIPTION: 21.5 × 13.5 cm   Pp [1–2] 3–23   Illus
Paper, with image on front of two women drinking cocoa; stapled
CONTENTS: 1 cover-title; 2 letter to cooks signed Mary Moore; 3 table of contents; 4–5 'Beverages'; 6–10 'Chocolate Cakes'; 11–15 'Cookies and Small Cakes'; 16–17 'Chocolate Desserts'; 18–top 19 'Chocolate Pies'; mid 19–mid 21 'Chocolate Frostings and Fillings'; mid 21–23 'Homemade Chocolate Candies'

COPIES: *NSWA   OGU (CCC TX715.6 M67)
NOTES: There is a reference to the company on pp 12–13 that indicates a publication date after 1928: 'Since 1728 ... for over 200 years ... the name Fry's ...' Unlike Q189.2, there is no mark on the outside back face of the binding that points to a specific year of publication, but it was likely some time after Moore began her cookery column in 1928 and not long before Q189.3, of which there were variants in 1934 and 1935.

The short-title, 'FAVOURITE COCOA AND CHOCOLATE RECIPES,' is in block capital letters. The text and illustrations are printed in brown, appropriate for a chocolate cookbook.

Q189.2   nd [1934]
—[Le] chocolat / [la] saveur préférée de tous / Recettes / choisies au chocolat / et cacao / Préparées par Mary Moore / Publiées par Fry-Cadbury Ltd. / Montreal [cover-title]
DESCRIPTION: 21.0 × 13.5 cm   Pp [1–3] 4–23   Illus
Paper, with image on front of chocolate desserts; stapled
CONTENTS: 1 cover-title; 2 letter to a cook signed Mary Moore; 3 'Table des matières'; 4–5 'Breuvages'; 6–8 'Gâteaux au chocolat'; 9–11 'Cookies [sic] et petits gâteaux'; 12–13 illus of Fry-Cadbury products; 14–15 'Desserts au chocolat'; 16–17 'Tartes au chocolat'; 18–19 'Glaçages, garnitures et sirops'; 20–1 'Faites vos bonbons vous-même'; 22 'Une industrie ravitaillant tout un empire'; 23 [inside back face of binding] notice about the use of Fry-Cadbury coupons
COPIES: *QMBN (84667 CON)
NOTES: This edition was likely published in 1934 because '8-34 Imprimé au Canada' is on the outside back face of the binding. Like Q189.3, the short-title is in the form of upper- and lower-case hand-writing. The text and illustrations are printed in brown. The QMBN copy has a label on pp 13 and 23 announcing that coupons are no longer issued. Part of the cover-title is torn off the QMBN copy.

Q189.3   nd [1935]
—Chocolate – / the world's favourite flavour / Favoured / chocolate and cocoa / recipes / Prepared by Mary Moore / Published by Fry-Cadbury Ltd. / Montreal [cover-title]
DESCRIPTION: 21.5 × 13.5 cm   Pp [1–3] 4–23   Illus
Paper, with image on front of chocolate desserts; stapled
CONTENTS: 1 cover-title; 2 letter to a cook signed Mary Moore; 3 table of contents; 4–5 'Beverages'; 6–8 'Chocolate Cakes'; 9–11 'Cookies and Small Cakes'; 12–13 illus of Fry-Cadbury products; 14–15 'Choco-

late Desserts'; 16–17 'Chocolate Pies'; 18–19 'Frost-ings, Fillings and Syrup'; 20–1 'Make Your Own Candy'; 22 'An Industry That Serves an Empire'; 23 notice about the use of Fry-Cadbury coupons
CITATIONS: Canadian Women of Note No. 633   Chatelaine 1935, p 82   Vancouver Sun, 5 March 1937
COPIES: AEUCHV (UV 85.264.27)   BBVM   OONL (TX767 C5 M66 1935)   OTMCL (641.5971 H39 No. 62)   *Private collection
NOTES: The new short-title, 'Favoured Chocolate and Cocoa Recipes' [i.e., not 'Favourite Cocoa and Chocolate …'], is in the form of upper- and lower-case hand-writing, not block capital letters. Like Q189.1, the text and illustrations are printed in brown and there is a reference to the company on pp 12–13 that indicates a publication date after 1928: 'Since 1728 … for over 200 years … the name Fry's …' This edition was likely published in 1935 since '3–35 Produced in Canada' is on the outside back face of the binding. On pp 13 and 23 there is a yellow sticker pasted over the notice about coupons, saying that the coupons are no longer being issued, but that those now in the hands of customers will be redeemed.

BSUM has a copy that appears to be identical to the private collector's copy described here, except that '8–34 Produced in Canada' is on the binding, indicating a publication date of 1934, and there are no yellow stickers. A copy at OTNY (uncat) also has the mark '8–34.' Another private collector has a copy with no indication of the year of printing before 'Produced in Canada' and no yellow stickers. Canadian Women of Note No. 633 records 1934 as the year of publication of *Favoured Chocolate and Cocoa Recipes*.

Chatelaine 1935 cites 'Favored Chocolate and Cocoa Recipes (French and English),' free upon request. Fry-Cadbury advertised Q189.3 in the *Vancouver Sun*, 5 March 1937: 'Write today for illustrated booklet "Favoured Recipes for Cocoa and Chocolate" … Sent free.'

1930–5

Palmer, Miss Lilian L. (18 October 1898–January 1976)

Lilian Palmer, of German and English ancestry, was the third generation of her family settled in the Eastern Townships. She lived in Bury, between Cookshire and Scotstown, and worked as a secretary in the lumber business, at one time for Arthur Hunt, and at another time for Clifford Anderson. She is buried in the cemetery at Bury. A photograph of Palmer is in the files amassed for this bibliography, to be deposited at OGU.

The Hunting family began milling on the Salmon River, in what became known as Huntingville, in about 1815 (see Elizabeth Hearn Milner, Huntingville, 1815–1980: A Story of a Village in the Eastern Townships, [Lennoxville, Que.]: E.H. Milner, 1981). In addition to a flour mill, W.H. Hunting and Sons had a grist mill and a sawmill. The Hunting flour mill burned down in about 1960.

Q190.1   nd [about 1930–5]
The / Hunting / cook / book [cover-title]
DESCRIPTION: 18.0 × 13.5 cm   Pp [1–16]   Paper, with image on front of a sack of Hunting's flour; stapled
CONTENTS: Inside front face of binding 'The Hunting Cook Book is sent to you with the compliments of W.H. Hunting & Sons, Reg'd // Huntingville, Que. millers of: whole wheat flour // all-wheat cereal // granulated wheat cereal // graham // table bran // old fashioned corn meal'; 1 untitled introductory note signed Lilian L. Palmer; 2–16 general instructions followed by sixty-eight numbered recipes, mostly for baked goods and porridge
COPIES: CIHM (81254)   *OONL (TX763 H85 1900z)
NOTES: In her introductory note, Palmer comments, 'East meets West in Hunting's Whole Wheat Flour! The high gluten content of Western Canada hard wheat, combined with that rich, nutty flavor of our Eastern Townships hard wheat, makes a Whole Wheat Flour that cannot be rivalled … [Hunting products] are a product of our Eastern Townships, made by Eastern Townships people, in that beautiful little town of Huntingville.' Palmer's recipes and instructions are detailed and comprehensive. The printer's name is on the outside back face of the binding: 'Beck Press, Reg'd., Lennoxville, Que.'

Harold Hunting told me (September 2001) that in the mid-1920s his father, William Herbert Hunting, sold the family business to another son, Kenneth. It was Kenneth who arranged for Palmer to write the cookbook, in the 1930s. Kenneth may have known her through the lumber side of the Hunting business. CIHM has filmed the book, judging it to be published before 1920 (the physical appearance of the book is deceiving), but Palmer's text stresses accurate measurements, gives Fahrenheit degrees for older temperature classifications (moderate, moderate hot, and hot oven), and specifies shortening (or butter as a substitute for shortening) – all features consistent with the publication date reported by the Hunting family.

OTHER EDITIONS: Reprint, retitled *Recipes from My Father's Mill*, published by Mrs Jean Brooks, née Hunting (Kenneth's daughter), about 1975, and distributed mainly in the Eastern Townships, through her rag-doll, mail-order business called Kermeen Ltd. The reprint does not include Palmer's introductory text; Jean Brooks has replaced it with her own introductory note and a 'Metric Conversion Chart.'

Quebec, Department of Colonization, Game and Fisheries

For Sea Food Recipes *and* Comment apprêter le poisson de notre province *published by this department, see entries NS27.4–27.6.*

The Regal recipe book

Q191.1   nd [about 1930–5]
The Regal / recipe book / A collection of practical and / tested recipes to guide the / housewife in the baking of / bread, cake and pastry. / The St. Lawrence Flour Mills Company, / Limited / Montreal, Canada.
DESCRIPTION: 17.5 × 12.5 cm   Pp [3] 4–31   Illus col Paper, with two images on front, in circular frames: a traditional mill powered by a waterwheel and the modern Regal Flour mill with silos
CONTENTS: Inside front face of binding 'Equivalents of Capacity' and 'Approximate Weights of Some Common Dry Commodities'; 3 tp; 4–31 [inside back face] recipes
COPIES: *Private collection
NOTES: The cover-title is 'Regal Flour Cook Book.' From appearances, *The Regal Recipe Book* was published about 1930. It has the same mill images on the binding as for Q160.1, *The Jubilee Recipe Book* of 1927. I have not compared the text of this book with other cookbooks by St Lawrence Flour Mills to determine whether they are related, i.e., Q88.1, Q143.1, and Q160.1.

Q191.2   nd [about 1930–5]
—Le livre de / recettes / Régal / Une collection de recettes / pratiques et éprouvées / pour guider la ménagère / dans la préparation de ses / gâteaux et pâtisseries / La compagnie / St. Lawrence Flour Mills, limitée
DESCRIPTION: 16.5 × 12.5 cm   Pp [3] 4–31   Illus col   Paper, with two images on front, in circular frames: a traditional mill powered by a waterwheel and the modern Regal Flour mill with silos; stapled
CONTENTS: Inside front face of binding 'L'équivalent des mesures' and 'Poids approximatifs de quelques articles secs ordinaires'; 3 tp; 4–31 [inside back face] recipes

CITATIONS: BQ 22-4922
COPIES: *QMBN (160010 CON)
NOTES: The cover-title is 'Les recettes Régal.'

Q191.3   nd
—[Another edition of *The Regal Recipe Book*]
COPIES: *Private collection
NOTES: This edition has 30 numbered pp and there is no text and no folio on the inside back face of the binding. The cover-title is 'Regal Cook Book.'

OTHER EDITIONS: Probably in the 1950s, St Lawrence Flour Mills Ltd published another undated booklet of the same length, *Livre de cuisine Régal* (OONL), which may or may not be related to the earlier cookbooks.

Tested recipes

Q192.1   nd [about 1930–5]
Tested recipes. / Summerlea United / Mrs. Walker's Group [cover-title]
COPIES: *Private collection
NOTES: Summerlea United Church is in Lachine. The year of publication is uncertain, but it was after the formation of the United Church of Canada in 1925. The owner reported that Summerlea was his wife's mother's church and that some of the recipe contributors 'have been dead many years.'

1931

Keen's cook book

For the titles of other cookbooks by the same company, see Q139.1.

Q193.1   1931
Keen's / cook book / "Mustard maketh Methuselahs" / Colman-Keen (Canada) Limited / Montreal / Vancouver Toronto / 1931 / Lithographed in Canada
DESCRIPTION: 21.0 × 14.5 cm   Pp [i–ii], 1–30   Tp illus red-and-black of an animated mustard pot, illus red-and-black   Paper, with image on front of a woman seen through a kitchen window, carrying a bowl; stapled
CONTENTS: i tp; ii 'Table of Contents' [i.e., alphabetical list of section headings] and illus red-and-black of five adults at a dinner table; 1 foreword; 2 'Table Service'; 3–28 culinary text; 29–30 'Mustard's Medicinal Value'

COPIES: AEUCHV (UV 85.213.5) ARDA OFERWM (A1991.100) SSWD *Private collection
NOTES: There are sections about 'The Bridge,' 'Chafing Dishes,' and 'Stag Suppers.' The latter comments on the type of foods and the presentation appropriate for these men-only meals.

Q193.2 1931
—Livre de recettes / Keen / "Vieux et fort vous deviendrez / si moutarde vous consommez" / Colman-Keen (Canada) Limited / Montréal / Vancouver Toronto / 1931 / Lithographié au Canada
DESCRIPTION: 21.0 × 14.5 cm Pp [i–ii], 1–30 Tp illus red-and-black of an animated mustard pot, illus red-and-black Paper, with image on front of a woman seen through a kitchen window; stapled
CONTENTS: i tp; ii 'Table des matières' [i.e., alphabetical list of section headings]; 1 'Avant-propos'; 2 'Service de table'; 3–28 culinary text; 29–30 'Propriété médicinale de la moutarde'
COPIES: *OONL (TX819 M87 L58 1931 p***)

Les recettes des mamans modernes

Q194.1 [copyright April 1931]
Les recettes / des / mamans modernes / [Com]pliments de la Maison J. Corbeil / [corner of binding lacking] rue St-Hubert, angle Beaubien, Montréal / [?] Crescent 4137 4138 [cover-title]
DESCRIPTION: With image on front of the Corbeil store; stapled
CONTENTS: Inside front face of binding 'Tous droits réservés, Ottawa // Avril 1931'
COPIES: *Private collection

Menu variations

Q195.1 [May 1931]
[IODE symbol] / Menu / variations / By / Nolan-Cornell Chapter / I.O.D.E. [cover-title]
DESCRIPTION: 23.0 × 15.5 cm Pp [1] 2–40 Paper, with IODE symbol on front; stapled
CONTENTS: 1 'Foreword' dated Montreal, May 1931; 2 ad; 3 'Table of Measures and Weights,' 'Oven Temperatures,' and a note about level measurements used in this book; 4 ads; 5 'Invalid Cookery'; 6 ad; 7–36 menus for 'Luncheon and Supper Dishes,' 'Afternoon Tea Suggestions,' 'Suggested Dinner Combinations,' and 'Extra Dinner Suggestions' (pp 7, 21, 26, 27), 'Recipes,' and ads; 37–40 blank for manuscript 'Recipes'

COPIES: *Private collection
NOTES: The 'Foreword' states that the 'contents of this book have been compiled from the personal recipes of the chapter members' and that 'proceeds from [the book's] sale will be used to assist in carrying on the patriotic, educational and child welfare work of the chapter.' The printer was probably Westmount News Co. Ltd, whose advertisement on p 2 boasts, 'It has been the happy privilege – particularly during the last few years – to execute the printing requirements of many of the prominent women's organizations of this city.'

New magic in the kitchen

For information about the company and its other books, see Q106.1.

Q196.1 nd [about 1931]
New magic / in the kitchen / 180 delicious dishes made / with Eagle Brand Condensed Milk [cover-title]
DESCRIPTION: 19.0 × 12.0 cm Pp [1–2] 3–62 Many illus col; 1 illus on p 59 of a coffee cup Paper, with image on front of a woman turning out a moulded dish, beams of light focusing on the upside-down mould, image signed 'Merritt Cutler'; stapled
CONTENTS: 1 cover-title; 2 blank; 3 'Dear Reader' and at bottom, 'Lithographed in Canada'; 4–mid 6 table of contents; mid 6–8 'Read about This Interesting Experiment'; 9 'How to Measure in Cooking' and 'Weight and Measurement Equivalents'; 10–56 recipes using Eagle Brand Milk and St Charles Evaporated Milk; 57–8 'Advantages of Eagle Brand Condensed Milk in Cooking'; 59–top 60 'Cream and Sugar Your Coffee with Eagle Brand Milk'; mid 60 'The Borden Brands of Sweetened Condensed Milk'; bottom 60–61 'Eagle Brand Sweetened Condensed Milk as a Food for Children'; 62 'Other Borden Milks and Their Uses' and 'Send for the "St. Charles Evaporated Milk Recipe Book"' [likely Q149.1 or O707.1]; inside back face of binding 'Serial No. 42'
COPIES: OGU (2 copies: CCC TX715.6 E555, TX715.6 M572 No. 526) OKQ (F5012 nd B728) OTMCL (641.67142 N266) *Private collection
NOTES: There is an illustration on p 61 of a can of Eagle Brand condensed milk; on the can label is 'The Borden Co. Limited Montreal, Canada.' The company's address, 140 St Paul Street West, Montreal, is on p 62. This is the address listed in Montreal city directories for 1928–9 to 1931–2 (the 1932–3 and 1933–4 directories give 361 Place Royale). Another private

collector's copy is inscribed on p 3, in pencil, 'Thelma Briggs Feb 13. 1932.' The address and the dated inscription point to publication in about 1931, the same year as the American edition cited in Allen and the year that the company moved its Canadian headquarters to Toronto.

Q196.2 nd
—La magie / culinaire / 180 recettes succulentes / a base de Lait condensé Eagle [cover-title]
DESCRIPTION: With image on front of a woman turning out a moulded dish, beams of light focusing on the upside-down mould, image signed 'Merritt Cutler'
COPIES: *Private collection
NOTES: There is an illustration on p 61 of a can of Eagle Brand condensed milk; on the can label is 'The Borden Co. Limited Montreal, Canada.'

AMERICAN EDITIONS: *New Magic in the Kitchen*, 1931 (Allen, p 202); the same or another ed., Ellison, Jane, *New Magic in the Kitchen: 208 Delicious Dishes Made with Sweetened Condensed Milk*, New York City: Borden Company, nd (United States: DLC); *New Magic in the Kitchen*, '175 dishes,' Borden, [about 1942] (Dickinson, p 130).

Rawleigh's good health guide cook book almanac 1931

For information about Rawleigh's annual almanac cookbooks and other publications, see M22.1.

Q197.1 1931
1889 Year book 1931 / Rawleigh's / Trade mark reg. U.S. Pat Off / good health guide / cook book almanac / [caption:] W.T. Rawleigh / President & founder – Rawleigh Industries / Preface / [three paragraphs of 'Preface'] / The W.T. Rawleigh Co., Ltd. / Montreal – Winnipeg / Freeport Memphis Richmond Chester Albany / Minneapolis Denver Oakland / Melbourne Wellington / The largest industries of their kind in the world
DESCRIPTION: 23.5 × 16.5 cm   Pp [1] 2–32   Tp illus portrait of W.T. Rawleigh, many illus orange-and-black, illus   Paper, with two images on front: Rawleigh's car approaching a farmstead and Rawleigh's factory complex; stapled, and with hole punched at top left corner for hanging
CONTENTS: 1 tp; 2 'The Year 1930'; 3 'World Wide Service'; 4 'Rawleigh Research'; 5 'Manufacture';

6 calendars for January, February; 7 'The Rawleigh Good Health Service'; 8 'The Island of Sicily // Its Lemons and Oranges'; 9 'Madagascar and Mexican Vanilla'; 10 March, April; 11 'Spices from Many Countries'; 12 May, June; 13 'Coughs and Colds'; 14 July, August; 15 'Food Delicacies'; 16–17 'The Rawleigh Factories // United States, Canada and Australia'; 18 September, October; 19 'Frozen Desserts'; 20 November, December; 21 'Health and Beauty'; 22 'New Ways to Serve Onions'; 23 'Cabbage and Sauerkraut'; 24 'The Tomato'; 25 'Cakes'; 26 'Salad Greens'; 27 'Balanced Menus'; 28 'Acidity and Constipation'; 29 'Some Good Soups'; 30 'Diet in Old Age'; 31 'Vegetable Greens'; 32 'Your Stocks on Hand'
COPIES: OGU (UA s050 b25)   OONL (RC81 R38) OTUTF (uncat patent medicine)   *Private collection
NOTES: The cover-title is 'Rawleigh's Good Health Guide Year Book 1931.' On p 17 there are illustrations of the Montreal factory that supplied Eastern Canada and the Winnipeg factory that supplied the Western provinces, the Peace River country, and the Hudson Bay territory.

The private collector's copy is stamped on the outside back face of the binding, in the space for the Rawleigh dealer's name, 'E.G. Stickle, Newcastle Ont.'

Q197.2 1931
—1889 Livre annuel 1931 / Rawleigh / Trade mark / Guide de bonne santé / Livre de / cuisine / et / almanach / [caption:] W.T. Rawleigh / président & fondateur – Industries Rawleigh / Preface / [three paragraphs of 'Preface'] / The W.T. Rawleigh Co., Ltd. / Montreal – Winnipeg / Freeport Memphis Richmond Chester Albany / Minneapolis Denver Oakland / Melbourne Wellington / Les plus grandes industries de leur genre dans l'univers
DESCRIPTION: 24.0 × 16.5 cm   Pp [1] 2–32   Tp illus portrait of W.T. Rawleigh, illus orange-and-black, illus   Paper, with two images on front: Rawleigh's car approaching a farmstead and Rawleigh's factory complex; stapled, and with hole punched at top left corner for hanging
COPIES: *QMM (RBD ckbk 1624)

Recipe book

Q198.1 1931
[An edition of *Recipe Book*, published under the auspices of the St John Ambulance Brigade, Montreal, January 1931, pp 100]
COPIES: Private collection

Recipe book

Q199.1 [1931]
St. Luke's / United / Church / Recipe book /
Under the auspices / of the Women's As- / sociation
of the / St. Luke's United / Church, Montreal. /
Published by Benefit Publications Reg'd / 961
Inspector Street, Montreal [cover-title]
DESCRIPTION: 23.5 × 15.5 cm Pp 1–112 Paper, with
image on front of a plate of muffins; sewn
CONTENTS: 1 ad for Woman's Institute Canada Ltd,
Montreal; 2 ad; 3 'Index' [i.e., alphabetical list of sec-
tions]; 4 'St. Luke's United Church' [i.e., history of the
church, including the announcement that the new
church building will be 'in full operation' in 'this
coming spring of 1931']; 5 ad; 6 'Officers and Committees of St. Luke's Women's Association for 1931'; 7
ad; 8–111 recipes, other text, and ads; 112 ad
COPIES: *Private collection
NOTES: The running head is 'St Luke's United Church
Recipe Book.' The recipes are not credited with the
name of the contributor.

1932

Cookery recipe book

Q200.1 [1932]
St. Andrew's United Church / Cookery / recipe
book / Published under the auspices of / the Young
Women's Club of St. Andrews [sic, no apostrophe]
United Church [cover-title]
DESCRIPTION: Pp [1–8] 9–136
CONTENTS: 1–5 ads; 6–9 'Index' and ads; 10 'Our Sup-
porters "Message" ... Go to church every Sunday'; 11–
12 ads; 13–136 recipes and ads
COPIES: *Private collection
NOTES: The running head is '1932 Church Recipe Book.'
The following text is on the outside back face of the
binding:

> The series of church Cookery Recipe Books is is-
> sued under the auspices of the ladies' organisations
> attached to the following churches: – St. Cyprian's,
> Maisonneuve [i.e., St Cyprian's Anglican Church,
> Morgan Boulevard, corner of Adam], St. Luke's,
> Rosemount [i.e., St Luke's Anglican Church, cor-
> ner of Holt and Eighth avenues], St. Mary's
> Hochelaga [i.e., St Mary's Anglican Church, corner
> of Prefontaine and Adam; according to Canadian
> Churchman (October 1934), the church used to min-
> ister to the troops at Hochelaga], Taylor East End
> United Church [which produced Q201.1], Mount

> Royal United [i.e., Mount Royal Avenue United
> Church, 206 Boulevard St Joseph East, Montreal],
> Mac Vicar Presbyterian [i.e., MacVicar Memorial
> Presbyterian Church, 5570 Hutchison, Outremont],
> St. Matthews, Snowdon [i.e., St Matthews Angli-
> can Church, Hampstead; in the Snowdon neigh-
> bourhood], All Saints, St. Denis Street [i.e., All Saints
> Anglican Church, corner of St Denis and Marie
> Anne East], Church of the Redeemer, Côte St. Paul
> [i.e., Church of the Redeemer (Anglican), corner of
> Galt Avenue and Angers], St. Columba's, N.D.G.
> [i.e., St Columba Anglican Church on Hingston
> Avenue], Wesley United, N.D.G. [i.e., Wesley United
> Church, 5964 Notre Dame de Grace Avenue,
> Montreal], Verdun United [which produced
> Q202.1], St. Phillips, Montreal West [i.e., St Phillip's
> Anglican Church, between 7 and 37 Brock Avenue
> North, Montreal West; Q116.1, Good Eats, is from
> the same church], St. Andrew's Lachine [i.e., St
> Andrew's United Church, 326 St Joseph, Lachine,
> which produced Q200.1] ... Published by United
> Publications Limited // 1502 St. Catherine Street
> West // Montreal.

Church names and addresses in square brackets are
from the Montreal city directory for 1932–3; many
Montreal street names and numbers have changed
since then.

Cookery recipe book

Q201.1 nd [about 1932]
Taylor East End United Church / Cookery / recipe
book / Published under the auspices of / the
Ladies' Aid, Taylor East End United Church [cover-
title]
COPIES: *Private collection
NOTES: The Montreal city directory for 1932–3 lists
Taylor East End United Church on Papineau Avenue,
at the corner of Logan East. The owner of the book
reports that it has 136 pp. A photocopy of one face of
the binding (not the cover-title) has the same text as
quoted in Q200.1, indicating that several Montreal
and area churches turned to the same Montreal publisher, United Publications Ltd. See also Q202.1.

Cookery recipe book

Q202.1 1932
Verdun United Church / Cookery / recipe book /
Published under the auspices of / the Ladies' Aid
Society of Verdun United Church [cover-title]

COPIES: *Private collection

NOTES: The book's owner reports that it was published in 1932 and has 136 pp. Her copy is inscribed on the front face of the binding, 'Mrs. Marsdon // Pinehurst // Eastgreenfield // Mrs. Marsdon // Mrs. Marsdon.' The volume has the same title, the same binding design, and the same number of pages as Q200.1 and Q201.1, and Verdun United Church is listed in those books as one of the churches participating in the 'series of church Cookery Recipe Books' published by United Publications Ltd, Montreal.

Each taste a treat: 87 delicious recipes

See O752.1, distributed by various Ontario dairies and also by Borden's Farm Products Co. Ltd of Montreal.

A guide to good cooking

First published in 1932, A Guide to Good Cooking *followed the earlier success of Q79.1,* Five Roses Cook Book, *first published in 1913.* A Guide to Good Cooking *may have been a new collection of recipes, but, in the words of Ferguson/Fraser, p 93, it was 'known forever as the* Five Roses Cookbook.' *There was no French-language edition of* A Guide to Good Cooking *in the period covered by this bibliography. Instead, in 1939, the company issued another edition of its 1915 text,* La cuisinière Five Roses *(Q79.5). In the same year that* A Guide to Good Cooking *first appeared, Western Canada Flour Mills published a competing recipe collection, O771.1,* The Purity Cook-Book. *For the titles of other cookbooks advertising Five Roses Flour, see Q58.1.*

Q203.1 [copyright 1932]
A guide to good cooking / being a collection of good recipes / carefully tested and approved by expert / authority, under the supervision of / Jean Brodie / to which have been added recipes chosen / from the contributions of over / fifteen thousand users of / Five Roses Flour / throughout Canada / together with / many economical and time-saving cookery / suggestions of value to the modern / housekeeper. / Published by / Lake of the Woods Milling Company, / Limited / Montreal Winnipeg
DESCRIPTION: 22.5 × 15.0 cm   Pp [i–ii], [1–4] 5–161 [162]   4 double-sided pls col, illus at head of each chapter   Paper
CONTENTS: i–ii endpaper printed with coupons for ordering the book on remittance of $0.40; 1 tp; 2 'Copyright, Canada, 1932, by Lake of the Woods Milling Company, Limited // Compiled under the supervision of Jean Brodie and designed by the Advertising Department of Lake of the Woods Milling Company, Limited.'; 3 dedication to 'the housewives of Canada'; 4 'Introduction'; 5–154 text; 155–61 index; 162 'Substitutions'
CITATIONS: Armstrong 2000, p F2   Chatelaine 1935, p 82   Cooke 2002, p 235   Driver 2003, 'Canadian Cookbooks,' p 36   Driver 2003, Five Roses, p 1   Ferguson/Fraser, pp 93 and 233   Wilson July 1991
COPIES: ACG   AEPRAC   AHRMH   BDEM   NSPHOCM   OGU (CCC TX715.6 G844 1932)   OMMM   OONL (TX715 L25 1932)   OTMCL (641.5 L12 1932)   QKB (76-94)   Company collection (ADM Milling Co., Montreal)   *Private collection
NOTES: The 'Introduction' states:

> Twenty years ago [i.e., 1912], Lake of the Woods Milling Company, Limited decided that the most useful cook book for Canadian housewives should be written by the housewives themselves. Recipes were collected from all over Canada, tested, and compiled in the Five Roses Cook Book. The wisdom of this policy has been definitely proven. The Five Roses Cook Book is now a household name. Over a million copies are in use – one for almost every second home in Canada.
>
> Great changes have taken place during the past two decades, and with this in mind, we decided to publish a more complete and up-to-date cook book. Another appeal was therefore made to Canadian women – and thousands of recipes and suggestions were received. We now offer the result of this work – "A Guide to Good Cooking" – the new Five Roses Cook Book, ...
>
> ... We have not given the names of contributors, as in many cases several suggestions have been combined in one recipe.

The company collected the recipes by running a series of contests through the pages of Canadian magazines; for example, an advertisement in *Nor'-West Farmer and Farm and Home* Vol. 50, No. 4 (20 February 1931), p 23, asked for 'your favourite dessert recipe' for the contest closing 31 March 1931, and the advertisement in Vol. 50, No. 6 (20 March 1931), p 31, announced the cookie-category winners and called for submissions in four other categories. The issue for November 1932, Vol. 51, No. 19, p 15, advertised the publication of the cookbook, which 'embod[ied] the suggestions of 15,000 Canadian women who entered their ideas, recipes and menus in the Big Prize Contest held in 1930–1.'

The BDEM copy is bound in dark-blue-paper-covered boards; the OTMCL copy, in black-paper-covered boards.

A private collector has a single-sheet pamphlet (three folds) called 'Proven Recipes // A few sample recipes from "A Guide to Good Cooking,"' which includes an order form for the book. The pamphlet refers to Jean Brodie as an 'eminent Canadian cooking expert' of Toronto. Brodie is the author of O562.1, *100 Tested Recipes*, published for Farmers' Dairy in Toronto.

Q203.2   [copyright 1938]
—A guide to good cooking / being a collection of good recipes / carefully tested and approved by expert / authority, under the supervision of / Jean Brodie / to which have been added recipes chosen / from the contributions of over / fifteen thousand users of / Five Roses Flour / throughout Canada / together with / many economical and time-saving cookery / suggestions of value to the modern / housekeeper. / Published by / Lake of the Woods Milling Company, / Limited / Montreal – Winnipeg
DESCRIPTION: 22.0 × 14.5 cm   Pp [1–4] 5–166   4 double-sided pls col, illus at head of each chapter   Thin card; wire-bound
CONTENTS: 1 tp; 2 'How to Get a Copy' [of *A Guide to Good Cooking*], 'A Guide to Good Cooking Is an All-Canadian Book,' and 'Copyright, Canada, 1938, by Lake of the Woods Milling Company, Limited // Compiled under the supervision of Jean Brodie and designed by the Advertising Department of Lake of the Woods Milling, Company, Limited.'; 3 dedication to 'the housewives of Canada'; 4 'Introduction'; 5–154 text; 155–61 index; 162 'Substitutions'; 163 'Food Equivalents'; 164 'Time and Temperature Chart'; 165–6 recipes beginning with 'Bride's Cake' and ending with 'Filling for German Buns'
CITATIONS: Driver 2001, Wellington County, p 94   Driver 2003, Five Roses, p 1
COPIES: OKELWM   SSWD   *Private collection
NOTES: The SSWD copy ends at p 164.

Q203.3   rev. and enlarged ed., [copyright 1938]
—A guide to good cooking / being a collection of good recipes / carefully tested and approved by expert / authority, under the supervision of / Jean Brodie / to which have been added recipes chosen / from the contributions of over / fifteen thousand users of / Five Roses Flour / throughout Canada / together with / many economical and time-saving cookery / suggestions of value to the modern / housekeeper. / Revised & enlarged edition / [symbol of Lake of the Woods Milling Co.] /

Published by / Lake of the Woods Milling Company, / Limited / Montreal – Winnipeg
DESCRIPTION: 22.5 × 14.5 cm   Pp [i–ii], [1–4] 5–191   4 double-sided pls col, illus at head of each chapter, illus on pp 102–4 of cuts of meat   Card; 'Wire-O-Binding'
CONTENTS: i–ii coupons for ordering the book on remittance of $0.40; 1 tp; 2 'How to Get a Copy' [of *A Guide to Good Cooking*], '[this book] Is an All-Canadian Book,' 'Copyright, Canada, 1938, by Lake of the Woods Milling Company, Limited // Compiled under the supervision of Jean Brodie and designed by the Advertising Department of Lake of the Woods Milling, Company, Limited.'; 3 dedication to 'the housewives of Canada'; 4 'Introduction'; 5–181 text; 182 blank; 183–91 index
CITATIONS: Driver 2001, Wellington County, p 96   Driver 2003, Five Roses, p 1   Neering, pp 153, 157
COPIES: ACG   AEPMA   BKOM   BVAMM   MWMM   OFERWM (A1978.189.51)   OGU (CCC)   OONL (TX715 L25 1938, 2 copies)   QMM (RBD uncat)   Company collection (ADM Milling Co., Montreal)   *Private collection
NOTES: The OFERWM copy lacks pp 1–8 and 177 onward. The AEPMA copy lacks pp 183 onward.

OTHER ENGLISH-LANGUAGE EDITIONS: *A Guide to Good Cooking*, 'under the supervision of Jean Brodie // Pauline Harvey,' completely rev., Montreal and Winnipeg: Lake of the Woods Milling Co. Ltd, 1954 (BKOM, QMM); 15th ed., 1956 (Private collection); 16th ed., Montreal and Winnipeg: Lake of the Woods Milling Co. Ltd, 1957 (OGU); 17th ed., 1958 (Private collection); 18th ed., 1959 (BKOM, OFERWM, OVOH); 19th ed., Montreal and Winnipeg: Lake of the Woods Milling Co. Ltd, 1960 (OGU; United States: IaU); 20th ed., 1962 (OGU, OPETCM, QMM, Company collection, ADM Milling Co., Montreal); 21st ed., nd (Company collection, ADM Milling Co., Montreal, photocopy; private collector reports this to be the Centennial ed. of 1967); 22nd ed., nd [1969] (QMBN); 23rd ed., nd (Private collection); 24th ed., [1975] (OGU, OONL, QMM); 25th ed., [1980?] (OONL, Company collection, ADM Milling Co., Montreal); 25th ed., 1983 (OONL); *The Five Roses Complete Guide to Good Cooking*, 26th ed., Montreal: Ogilvie Mills Ltd, 1989 (OONL, Company collection, ADM Milling Co., Montreal); *Five Roses: A Guide to Good Cooking*, facsimile of 21st ed., with 'Historical Notes' by Elizabeth Driver, North Vancouver: Whitecap Books, copyright 2003 (OONL).

OTHER FRENCH-LANGUAGE EDITIONS: *La cuisinière Five Roses*, unnumbered ed., nd, pp 183 (Private collection); *La cuisinière Five Roses*, 17th ed., Montreal: Lake of the Woods Milling Co. Ltd, 1960 (BQ 22-4873); *La cuisinière*, 21st ed., nd [1967?] (OONL, QMBN); 22nd ed., nd (Company collection, ADM Milling Co., Montreal); *La cuisinière*, 24th ed., Lake of the Woods Milling Co., [1976?] (OONL); *La cuisinière*, 25th ed., [1980?] (OONL); *La cuisinière Five Roses*, 26th ed., Montreal: Ogilvie Mills Ltd, 1989 (OONL).

How we do it

Q204.1 nd [1932]
How / we / do / it. / Price 25 cents [cover-title]
CONTENTS: [First page] 'Foreword' signed Emergency Unemployment Relief Committee of Montreal, 1027 St George Street; ...
COPIES: *Private collection
NOTES: The 'Foreword' explains that the book was compiled at the request of 'families in receipt of unemployment relief' and that the information in the book 'was obtained through a contest conducted amongst those who are actually living on relief rations.' The handbook shows 'how families manage their three meals a day on food purchased with the orders supplied through this committee.' Trained dietitians checked that the menus submitted by contestants could be made from the orders. Lastly, the 'Foreword' notes that the first page (the one on which the 'Foreword' is printed) 'has been perforated and may be torn out, thus removing all reference to unemployment relief' in the hope that the booklet 'will be of value long after unemployment relief is finished.'

The date of publication is from Doris Ludwig, née Clark, who helped produce *How We Do It* when she was working in a welfare office in Montreal, dispensing vouchers to needy members of the English Protestant community in the 1930s. She tells the story of those times and comments on the 1932 book in an article by Suzanne Bourret, 'Stretching Your Food Dollar,' in the *Spectator* (Hamilton, Ontario) 8 June 1994, p D1. In the article readers are advised of where to write for a copy of the facsimile (Q204.2). A further reference to the 1994 facsimile is in Bourret's 'Foodstuff' column on 6 July 1994. Doris and Mary Moore, née Clark, another author in this bibliography, are sisters; see Q189.1 for more information about the family. The copy of Q204.1 described here is stamped on the front face of the binding with Mary's name and address, 'M.A. Moore [8?]2 Churchill Ave. Hamilton, Ontario L9A 1J5.'

Q204.2 [facsimile ed., June 1994]
—How / we / do / it / Smart food management / Budget-designed recipes from the 1930's / A report of thrifty and imaginative / food planning and preparation by / Montreal's homemakers in the / troubled times of the thirties [cover-title]
DESCRIPTION: 21.5 × 13.5 cm Pp [i–ii], 1–22 Very thin card; stapled
CONTENTS: i 'Foreword' signed Emergency Unemployment Relief Committee of Montreal, 1027 St George Street, and 'First issued in 1932'; ii names of the nine firms that 'have defrayed the entire cost' of publication; 1–3 'A Week's Supply of Food' for families of two, three or four, and five or six persons; 4–14 'Weekly Menus from Orders Listed' [i.e., from the food orders listed on pp 1–3]; 15–21 'Economical Recipes' credited with the initials of the contributor; 22 'Pass It Along' [i.e., hints extracted from letters] and 'List of Contents'
COPIES: *Private collection
NOTES: The facsimile was made from a copy of the original book in the possession of Doris Clark Ludwig. The cover text of the facsimile is new. The publishers' names and address, and the date, are on the outside back face of the binding: 'Publishers: Doris and Robert Ludwig ... Hamilton, Ont. ... June 1994.' On p i, 'First issued in 1932' is an addition to the original text.

In the United States, the DLC catalogue records the title as undated (MLCM 98/03018 (H) FT MEADE). The record may refer to the original edition.

The icing room

For other cookbooks published by Nulomoline Ltd, see Q209.1, Freshness from Oven to Consumer, and Q268.1, 'Practo-fax' Cookies.

Q205.1 [copyright 1932]
The / icing / room [cover-title]
DESCRIPTION: 21.5 × 13.5 cm Pp [1–2] 3–47 [48] Tp illus of an iced cake, illus Paper; stapled
CONTENTS: 1 tp; 2 'Copyright 1932 Nulomoline Limited Montreal, Quebec'; 3 'The Icing Room' [introductory text]; 4–45 text; 46 'Table of Contents'; 47 'Formula Index'; 48 'Printed in U.S.A'
COPIES: *OONL (TX771 I35 1932 p***)
NOTES: The book is for professional bakers and many of the recipes specify Nulomoline, 'a non crystallizable sugar that attracts and retains moisture,' manufactured by the company 'for nearly a quarter of a

century,' i.e., since about 1907 (1932 – 25 years). The standard package for Nulomoline was a barrel of 650 pounds or trial pails of 50 pounds (p 3). Although the ingredient amounts are out-of-scale for home use, the text is informative and the illustrations of commercial baking scenes are interesting.

The OONL copy is stamped opposite the title-page, 'The property of the Library of Parliament,' and on the title-page with the Copyright Act 1931 stamp, which is inscribed with the deposit number 231.

Rawleigh's good health guide cook book– year book 1932

For information about Rawleigh's annual almanac cookbooks and other publications, see M22.1.

Q206.1   1932
1889 1932 / Rawleigh's / Trade mark reg. U.S. Pat. Off. / good health guide / cook book–year book / In presenting Rawleigh's Good Health Guide, Cook Book and Year / Book for 1932 we desire to express our appreciation to all the mil- / lions of consumers throughout Canada, the United States, Australia and / other countries for your continuous and steadfast patronage which has / been the most important factor in the unparalleled growth and expan- / sion of our business since it was founded 43 years ago. / [four additional introductory paragraphs] / Published by / the W.T. Rawleigh Company, Ltd. / Montreal – Winnipeg / and its subsidiary corporations with the following / other factories and branches / Freeport Memphis Richmond Chester Albany / Minneapolis Denver Oakland Melbourne Wellington / Copyright 1931. The W.T. Rawleigh Co., Ltd. All rights reserved.
COPIES: ARDA   SWSLM   *Private collection

Q206.2   1932
—1889 1932 / Guide / de bonne santé / Rawleigh / Trade mark / Livre de cuisine – livre annuel / En presentant le Guide annuel Rawleigh de bonne santé et / livre de cuisine pour 1932 [...] / Publié par / The W.T. Rawleigh Company, Ltd. / Montréal – Winnipeg / et ses compagnies subsidiaires avec les autres manufactures / et succursales suivantes / Freeport Memphis Richmond Chester Albany / Minneapolis Denver Oakland Melbourne Wellington / Copyright 1931. The W.T. Rawleigh Co. Ltd. Tous droits réservés.
DESCRIPTION: 23.5 × 16.5 cm   Pp [1] 2–32   Illus orange-and-black, illus   Paper, with image on front of

'Copie d'une belle mosaïque faite à Florence, ...'; stapled, and with hole punched at top left corner for hanging
COPIES: *QMM (RBD ckbk 1625)

Royal cook book

For the titles of other Royal Baking Powder cookbooks, see Q71.1.

Q207.1   [copyright 1932]
Royal / cook book / Standard Brands / Limited / Montreal, Canada [cover-title]
DESCRIPTION: Pp [1–4], i–? Small illus on p i of teaspoon measurements   Images on front face of binding of cupcakes, doughnuts, cake, waffles, and tea biscuits
CONTENTS: Inside front face of binding 'Since 1878 the Royal Cook Book has been the popular handbook ...' [i.e., introductory text] and 'Copyright, 1932, by Standard Brands Incorporated R.C.B. 2-32'; 1 'Royal Cakes Keep Fresh Longer'; 2 'Cream of Tartar'; 3–4 'Royal Cook Book Index to Recipes'; i 'How to Measure'; ...
COPIES: Bookseller's stock
NOTES: The bookseller reports that the volume has 45 pp. A comparison of a photocopy of the index with Q207.2 reveals that this edition has more pages and more recipes.

Royal Cook Book is a Canadian edition of an American book promoting Royal Baking Powder. Standard Brands Ltd was incorporated in Canada on 27 August 1929, the same year that Standard Brands Inc. was formed in the United States by the merging of Royal Baking Powder Co., Chase and Sanborn Coffee Co., and the Fleischmann Yeast Co. The 1932 Montreal edition, therefore, was published only a few years after the formation of Standard Brands Ltd.

The order of publication of the editions of *Royal Cook Book* is uncertain. Q207.1 may be the first (the cover design matches the 1930 American edition, and the title and number of pages match the 1932 American edition), followed by 17-page abridged editions for the Canadian market, first under the title *Royal Cook Book* (Q207.2), then under a new title, *Magic Cook Book* or *Le pâtissier Magic* (Q207.3 and Q207.4, which promote Magic Baking Powder). Another possibility is that the 17-page editions, abridged from earlier American editions, were published in Canada shortly after the incorporation of Standard Brands Ltd in 1929, followed by the longer 1932 edition (Q207.1).

Also unknown is whether any or all of the editions of *Royal Cook Book* were published before or during the run of 'black-background' editions of the company's *The Magic Cook Book* (O702.1–702.4). Both books were offered free, upon request, in *Chatelaine* 1935, p 82: 'Royal Cook Book (English and French)' and 'Magic Baking Powder Cook Book (English and French).'

The reference in the introductory text to editions of *Royal Cook Book* dating from 1878 is to the American *Royal Baker and Pastry Cook,* the first Canadian edition of which was published in 1911 (Q71.1).

Q207.2 nd
—Royal / cook book [cover-title]
DESCRIPTION: 24.0 × 17.0 cm Pp [1] 2–17 Small illus on p 2 of teaspoon measurements Paper, printed all over with a fabric texture, and with image on front of a stylized chef in a 4.0-cm circle; stapled
CONTENTS: 1 'Royal Cook Book published by Standard Brands Limited ...' and 'Index'; top–mid 2 'How to Measure,' 'Tables of Measures and Equivalents,' and 'Correct Temperatures'; bottom 2–3 'Ingredients in General'; 4–17 [inside back face of binding] recipes
COPIES: OONL (TX765 R68 1930z missing) *Private collection
NOTES: The 'Index' and binding design of this edition, which promotes Royal Baking Powder, match Q207.3 for Magic Baking Powder. Both have the same illustration of a factory on the inside front face of the binding, but Q207.2 has the caption 'This is where Royal Baking Powder is made,' whereas Q207.3 has 'This is where Magic Baking Powder is made'; in both cases, the company's Toronto street address and 'Printed in Canada' are at the bottom of the inside front face.

Q207.3 nd
—Magic / cook book [cover-title]
DESCRIPTION: 24.0 × 17.0 cm Pp [1] 2–17 Small illus on p 2 of teaspoon measurements Paper, printed all over with a fabric texture, and with image on front of a stylized chef in a 4.0-cm circle
CONTENTS: 1 'Magic Cook Book published by Standard Brands Limited ...' and 'Index'; 2–17 text
COPIES: AEPMA MWPA (MG14 C50 McKnight, Ethel) OGU (2 copies: *UA s070 b33, CCC TX715.6 M34) SBIM SSWD
NOTES: See 'Notes' for Q207.2. The SBIM copy lacks the front face of the binding.

For the titles of other cookbooks promoting Magic Baking Powder, see O285.1.

Q207.4 nd
—Le pâtissier / Magic [cover-title]
DESCRIPTION: 24.0 × 17.0 cm Pp [1] 2–17 Small illus on p 2 of teaspoon measurements Paper, printed all over with a fabric texture, and with image on front of a stylized chef in a 4.0-cm circle
CONTENTS: 1 'Livre culinaire "Magic" publié par Standard Brands Limited ...' and 'Index'; 2–17 [inside back face of binding] text
COPIES: *QSFFSC
NOTES: The following is opposite p 1: 'Standard Brands Limited // Produits Gillett // Fraser Avenue et Liberty Street // Toronto // Montreal Winnipeg Vancouver // Imprimé au Canada.' This is the French-language version of Q207.3.

AMERICAN EDITIONS: The following, all titled *Royal Cook Book,* may be editions of the same work (I have examined only the 1929 edition): 1920s (Allen, p 145); New York: Royal Baking Powder Co., c1925 (United States: DLC); 1927 (Allen, p 145); New York: Royal Baking Powder Co., copyright 1929 (OKITJS); New York: Standard Brands Inc., [copyright 1930], same cover design as Q207.1 (AEUCHV); Standard Brands Inc., 1932 (Allen, p 145); 1937 (Allen, p 145).

Scott, Anna Lee [pseudonym]

See O773.7 and O773.10, O776.6 and O776.9, and O777.3 and O777.7, for editions of Scott's The Easy Way Cake Book, Marketing and Meal Planning, *and* Planning the Party, *published in Montreal by the Family Herald and Weekly Star and the Montreal Daily Star. French-language editions, copyrighted 1934, were issued under the pseudonym Marthe Miral: O773.15,* L'art de réussir des gâteaux, *and O777.9,* L'art de recevoir.

1933

The cookery nook

Q208.1 1933
The / cookery / nook / 1933 / Noranda-Rouyn / United Church / Noranda / Quebec / Printed by / Rouyn-Noranda Press [cover-title]
CONTENTS: 3 'Foreword' signed ladies of the Noranda United Church Guild and 'Index' [i.e., table of contents]
COPIES: *Private collection
NOTES: The owner reports that the volume has 96 pp.

Freshness from oven to consumer

For the titles of other cookbooks by Nulomoline Ltd, see Q205.1.

Q209.1 [copyright 1933]
Freshness / from / oven to consumer [cover-title]
DESCRIPTION: 21.5 × 14.0 cm   Pp [1–2] 3–37 [38–40]
Illus   Paper
CONTENTS: 1 publisher's note and name: 'Nulomoline Limited 1410 Stanley Street Montreal'; 2 'Copyright 1933 Nulomoline Limited Montreal'; 3–37 text; 38–9 index; 40 publ ad
CITATIONS: CCB
COPIES: *OONL (TX765 F74 1933)
NOTES: Nulomoline is the brand name for a standardized invert sugar (p 6): 'When spread as thin as paper and allowed to stand ..., Nulomoline always remains soft and wet.' The product, which is for commercial use, helps to keep baked products fresh. The amount of Nulomoline to be substituted for a portion of sugar in recipes is given on p 9: for example, for pound cake using 10 pounds sugar, substitute 5 ounces of Nulomoline. The recipes are illustrated. According to p 37, the New York–based company published a monthly periodical called *Baking Sketches*.

CCB incorrectly cites the publisher as 'Numoline Ltd.'

Good things to eat made with Cow Brand Baking Soda

For the titles of other publications advertising the baking soda, see O82.1.

Q210.1 copyright 1933
Good things to eat / made with / Cow Brand / Baking Soda / (pure bicarbonate of soda) / All recipes have been tested and / approved in the Cow Brand / Baking Soda Kitchen / by / Martha Lee Anderson / Church & Dwight Limited / 2715 Reading Street / Montreal, Canada / Copyright 1933 Printed in Canada
DESCRIPTION: 14.5 × 9.0 cm   Pp [1] 2–32   Paper, with image on front of a woman in a checked apron, stirring the contents of a bowl; stapled
CONTENTS: Inside front face of binding 'Additional copies of this booklet sent free on request'; 1 tp; 2 'Good Things to Eat and How to Make Them' signed Martha Lee Anderson; 3 'Sour Milk, Buttermilk and Baking Soda'; 4 'Directions Point the Way to Success'; 5–29 recipes; 30–1 index; 32 'Table of Weights and Measures' and 'Temperature and Time Table'; inside back face 'Vegetable Cookery' and 'Time Table for Vegetables'
COPIES: AMHM   MWMM   *NSWA

Q210.2 copyright 1933
—[An edition of *Bonnes choses à manger faites avec le Soda à pâte (bicarbonate de soude pur) 'Cow Brand'; toutes les recettes ont été éprouvées dans la cuisine du Soda à pâte 'Cow Brand' par Martha Lee Anderson*, Montreal: Church and Dwight, copyright 1933]
CITATIONS: BQ 12-0964
COPIES: QMBN (TX765 A53 1933)

Q210.3 1st ed., copyright 1937
—Good things / to eat / made with / Cow Brand Baking Soda / (pure bicarbonate of soda) / All recipes have been / tested and approved in / the Cow Brand Baking / Soda Kitchen / by / Martha Lee Anderson / Church & Dwight Limited / 2715 Reading Street / Montreal, Canada / Edition No. 1 / (Copyright, 1937, by Church & Dwight Limited, Montreal, Canada) / Litho'd in Canada
DESCRIPTION: 14.0 × 8.5 cm   Pp [1] 2–32 Illus Paper; stapled
CONTENTS: 1 tp; 2 'Good Things to Eat ... and How to Make Them'; 3 'Sour Milk, Buttermilk and Baking Soda'; 4 'Substitutes for Sour Milk and Buttermilk'; 5–24 recipes; 25 'How to Bake'; 26–7 'Facts Regarding Plain White Flour'; 28–9 'Kitchen Tested Methods'; 30–1 index; 32 'Table of Weights and Measures' and at bottom, 'S–100M–8-37'
COPIES: *Private collection

Q210.4 2nd ed., copyright 1937 [April 1938]
—Good things / to eat / made with / Cow Brand Baking Soda / (pure bicarbonate of soda) / All recipes have been / tested and approved in / the Cow Brand Baking / Soda Kitchen / by / Martha Lee Anderson / Church & Dwight Limited / 2715 Reading Street / Montreal, Canada / Edition No. 2 / (Copyright, 1937, by Church & Dwight Limited, Montreal, Canada) / Litho'd in Canada
DESCRIPTION: 14.0 × 8.5 cm   Pp [1] 2–32 Illus Paper, with blue abstract design; stapled
COPIES: *Private collection
NOTES: 'S–100M–4-38' is printed on p 32, indicating that the booklet was printed in April 1938.

Q210.5 6th ed., copyright 1937
—Bonnes choses / à manger / faites avec le / Soda à pâte / (bicarbonate de soude pur) / "Cow Brand" / Toutes les recettes / ont été éprouvées / et

approuvées dans / la cuisine du Soda / à pâte "Cow Brand" / par / Martha Lee Anderson / Church & Dwight Limited / Edifice Sun Life / Montréal, Canada / Edition no 6 / (Copyright, 1937, par Church & Dwight Limited, Montreal, Canada / Lithographié au Canada)

DESCRIPTION: 14.5 × 8.5 cm Pp [1] 2–32 Illus Paper, with blue abstract design; stapled

CONTENTS: 1 tp; 2 'Bonnes choses à manger ... et comment les préparer' signed Martha Lee Anderson; 3 'Lait sur, lait de beurre et soda à pâte'; 4 'Pour faire du lait sur vite et simplement'; 5–11 'Pains chauds'; 12–16 'Gâteaux'; 17–20 '"Cookies"'; 21–2 'Poudings et beignes'; 23–4 'Glaces et sauces'; 25 'Préparation et cuisson de la pâte'; 26–7 'Employez le soda à pâte dans la cuisine'; 28–30 'Autres usages du soda à pâte'; 31 'Table des matières'; 32 'Table des poids et mesures' and 'Température et durée de cuisson'; inside back face of binding 'Cuisine aux légumes'

COPIES: *OONL (TX715 A493 1937 p***)

NOTES: Q210.7, a French-language edition, copyright 1939 and printed in 1941, is numbered third edition. It is odd, therefore, that this edition is numbered sixth.

Q210.6   3rd ed., copyright 1937 and 1939
—Good things / to eat / made with / Cow Brand Baking Soda / (pure bicarbonate of soda) / All recipes have been / tested and approved in / the Cow Brand Baking / Soda Kitchen / by / Martha Lee Anderson / Church & Dwight Limited / 2715 Reading Street / Montreal, Canada / Edition No. 3 / (Copyright, 1937 and 1939, / by Church & Dwight Limited, Montreal, Canada)

DESCRIPTION: 14.5 × 8.5 cm   Pp [1] 2–32 Illus Paper, with blue abstract design; stapled

CONTENTS: 1 tp; 2 'Good Things to Eat ... and How to Make Them' signed Martha Lee Anderson; 3 'Sour Milk, Buttermilk and Baking Soda'; 4 'To Make Sour Milk Quickly and Simply'; 5–11 'Hot Breads'; 12–16 'Cakes'; 17–20 'Cookies'; 21–2 'Puddings and Doughnuts'; 23–4 'Frostings and Sauces'; 25 'How to Bake'; 26–7 'Use Baking Soda in Cooking'; 28–30 'Other Baking Soda Uses'; 31 'Index'; 32 'Table of Weights and Measures,' 'Temperature and Time Table,' and at bottom, 'S–100M–5-39'; inside back face of binding 'Vegetable Cookery'

COPIES: AEUCHV (UV 85.17.157)   *Private collection

Q210.7   3rd ed., copyright 1937 and 1939 [May 1941]
—Bonnes choses / à manger / faites avec le / soda à pâte / (bicarbonate de soude pur) / "Cow Brand" / Toutes les recettes / ont été éprouvées / et

approuvées dans / la cuisine du Soda / à pâte "Cow Brand" / par / Martha Lee Anderson / Church & Dwight Limited / 2715, rue Reading, / Montréal, Canada. / Troisième édition / (Copyright 1937 & 1939, / par Church & Dwight Limited, Montréal, Canada)

DESCRIPTION: 14.5 × 8.5 cm   Pp [1] 2–32 Illus Paper, with blue abstract design; stapled

CONTENTS: 1 tp; 2 'Bonnes choses à manger ... et comment les préparer' signed Martha Lee Anderson; 3 'Lait sur, lait de beurre et soda à pâte'; 4 'Pour faire du lait sur vite et simplement'; 5–11 'Pains chauds'; 12–16 'Gâteaux'; 17–20 '"Cookies"'; 21–2 'Poudings et beignes'; 23–4 'Glaces et sauces'; 25 'Préparation et cuisson de la pâte'; 26–7 'Employez le soda à pâte dans la cuisine'; 28–30 'Autres usages du soda à pâte'; 31 'Table des matières'; 32 'Table des poids et mesures' and at bottom, 'S–50M–5-41'; inside back face of binding 'Cuisine aux légumes'

COPIES: *OONL (TX715 A493 1939)

NOTES: The printer's mark on p 32 indicates the book was printed in 1941.

Q210.8   4th ed., copyright 1937 and 1939
—[Fourth edition of *Good Things to Eat Made with Cow Brand Baking Soda*, copyright 1937 and 1939]

COPIES: Private collection

Q210.9   5th ed., copyright 1937 and 1939 [May 1941]
—Good things / to eat / made with / Cow Brand Baking Soda / (pure bicarbonate of soda) / All recipes have been / tested and approved in / the Cow Brand Baking / Soda Kitchen / by / Martha Lee Anderson / Church & Dwight Limited / 2715 Reading Street / Montreal, Canada / Edition No. 5 / (Copyright, 1937 and 1939, / by Church & Dwight Limited, Montreal, Canada)

DESCRIPTION: 14.5 × 8.5 cm   Pp [1] 2–32 Illus Paper; stapled

CONTENTS: 1 tp; 2 'Good Things to Eat ... and How to Make Them' signed Martha Lee Anderson; 3 'Sour Milk, Buttermilk and Baking Soda'; 4 'To Make Sour Milk Quickly and Simply'; 5–11 'Hot Breads; 12–16 'Cakes'; 17–20 'Cookies'; 21–2 'Puddings and Doughnuts'; 23–4 'Frostings and Sauces'; 25 'How to Bake'; 26–7 'Use Baking Soda in Cooking'; 28–30 'Other Baking Soda Uses'; 31 'Index'; 32 'Table of Weights and Measures,' 'Temperature and Time Table,' and at bottom, 'S–100M–5-41'

COPIES: *Private collection

NOTES: The printer's mark on p 32 indicates the book was printed in 1941.

Q210.10 6th ed., copyright 1937 and 1939 [December 1947]

—Good things / to eat / made with / Cow Brand Baking Soda / (pure bicarbonate of soda) / All recipes have been / tested and approved in / the Cow Brand Baking / Soda Kitchen / by / Martha Lee Anderson / Church & Dwight Limited / Sun Life Building / Montreal, Canada / Edition No. 6 / (Copyright, 1937 and 1939, / by Church & Dwight Limited, Montreal, Canada)

DESCRIPTION: 14.5 × 8.5 cm   Pp [1] 2–32   Illus   Paper, with blue abstract design; stapled

CONTENTS: 1 tp; 2 'Good Things to Eat ... and How to Make Them' signed Martha Lee Anderson; 3 'Sour Milk, Buttermilk and Baking Soda'; 4 'To Make Sour Milk Quickly and Simply'; 5–11 'Hot Breads'; 12–16 'Cakes'; 17–20 'Cookies'; 21–2 'Puddings and Doughnuts'; 23–4 'Frostings and Sauces'; 25 'How to Bake'; 26–7 'Use Baking Soda in Cooking'; 28–30 'Other Baking Soda Uses'; 31 'Index'; 32 'Table of Weights and Measures,' 'Temperature and Time Table,' and at bottom, 'S–80M–12-47'; inside back face of binding 'Vegetable Cookery'

COPIES: *Private collection

NOTES: The printer's mark on p 32 indicates the book was printed in 1947.

AMERICAN EDITIONS: *Good Things to Eat,* promoting Arm and Hammer Baking Soda, 1930 (Dickinson, p 26); *Good Things to Eat,* promoting Arm and Hammer or Cow Brand Baking Soda, recipes tested by Martha Lee Anderson, 114th ed., New York: 1936 (WaiteCat 5, p 61); *Good Things to Eat,* signed Martha Lee Anderson, 125th ed., New York: Church and Dwight Co. Inc., copyright 1939, 'Form No. F2000–12-39, Litho in U.S.A.' on p 15 (Private collection); *Some of My Favorite Good Things to Eat,* by Martha Lee Anderson, 129th ed., New York: Church and Dwight Co. Inc., copyright 1940, 'Form No. F2000–8-41. Litho in U.S.A.' on p 15 (Private collection). The Canadian and American editions share the same (or similar) title, the basic Soda Biscuits recipe, and the association with Martha Lee Anderson, but little else.

The mixing bowl

Q211.1 1933
The / mixing / bowl / 1933 / Trinity United Church / Sherbrooke, Quebec [cover-title]
DESCRIPTION: Photograph on p 1 of the church Stapled

CONTENTS: 1 photograph of the church, 'Preface,' and 'Compiled by the Ladies' Circle // Trinity United Church // Sherbrooke, Quebec.'; ...; 40 ads and 'Index' [i.e., table of contents]
COPIES: *Private collection
NOTES: The book has 40 pp. See O729.1 regarding the wording of the 'Preface.'

Preserving and canning

For information about Dominion Glass Co. Ltd and its other cookbooks, see Q75.1.

Q212.1 1933
Preserving and / canning / The housekeeper's guide / to success in preserving and canning of / fruits, vegetables, meat, fowl and soups, / to which have been added / other chosen recipes. / A compilation of good recipes / and useful hints, carefully tested and / approved by expert authority. / A Canadian publication / for Canadian housewives, by / Dominion Glass Company Limited / Head office: Montreal / 1933
CITATIONS: Armstrong 2000, p F2
COPIES: Bookseller's stock   *Private collection
NOTES: The bookseller describes the volume as having 40 pp.

Q212.2 1938
—Preserving and / canning / The housekeeper's guide / to success in preserving and canning of / fruits, vegetables, meat, fowl and soups, / to which have been added / other chosen recipes. / A compilation of good recipes / and useful hints, carefully tested and / approved by expert authority. / A Canadian publication / for Canadian housewives, by / Dominion Glass Company Limited / Head office: Montreal / 1938
DESCRIPTION: 22.5 × 15.5 cm   Pp [1] 2–39 [40]   Illus   Paper, with image on front of two full preserving jars (a Crown jar and a Perfect Seal jar); stapled, and with hole punched at top left corner for hanging
CONTENTS: 1 tp; 2 'Processing Time-Table'; 3–4 table of contents; 5–mid 6 'Preserving and Canning' [introductory text]; mid 6–top 7 'Why Foods Spoil'; near top 7–top 8 'Equipment for Canning'; mid 8 'Methods of Canning'; bottom 8–top 13 'Steps in Canning' and 'New Style "Perfect Seal" Jar' on p 9, 'The Adjustable Feature of the Old Style Perfect Seal Jar with Neck Wire' on p 11, and 'The Adjustable Feature of the New Style Perfect Seal Jar with No Neck Wire' on

p 12; near top 13–mid 14 'Detailed Directions'; mid 14–15 'Canned Fruit'; top 16 'Examine Canned Food before Using' and 'Advantages of Canned Foods'; bottom 16–mid 21 'Canned Foods for the Family Menu' and '"Crown" Jar' on p 18; mid 21–mid 25 'Jelly' and '"Improved Gem" Jar' on p 24; mid 25 'Conserves'; bottom 25–mid 26 'Marmalade'; bottom 26–top 28 'Jellies and Jams for the Family Menu'; near top 28–top 29 'Fruit Juices'; near top 29 'Wild Fruits'; mid 29–top 33 'Pickles' and '"Dominion Special" Jar' on p 30; near top 33–mid 34 'Meats'; mid 34–mid 35 'Poultry'; bottom 35 'Fish'; 36 '"Best" Jar'; 37 'Soup'; 38 untitled concluding text; 39–40 blank for 'Memorandum' and at bottom p 40, 'Designed, engraved and printed in Canada by the Ronalds Company Limited Montreal'
COPIES: *Private collection

Q212.3   1942
—Preserving and / canning / The housekeeper's guide / to success in preserving and canning of / fruits, vegetables, meat, fowl and soups, / to which have been added / other chosen recipes. / A compilation of good recipes / and useful hints, carefully tested and / approved by expert authority. / A Canadian publication / for Canadian housewives, by / Dominion Glass Company Limited / Head office: Montreal / 1942
DESCRIPTION: 23.0 × 15.5 cm   Pp [1] 2–39 [40] Illus   Paper, with image on front of two full preserving jars; stapled, and with hole punched at top left corner for hanging
CONTENTS: 1 tp; 2 'Processing Time-Table'; 3–4 'Contents'; 5–37 text; 38–40 blank for 'Memorandum' and at bottom p 40, 'Designed, engraved and printed in Canada by the Ronalds Company Limited Montreal'
COPIES: OONL (AC901 A7 1942 No. 0065 p***)   *Private collection

Rawleigh's good health guide cook book year book 1933

For information about Rawleigh's annual almanac cookbooks and other publications, see M22.1.

Q213.1   1933
1889 1933 / Rawleigh's / Trade mark reg. U.S. Pat. Off. / good health guide / cook book year book / [caption:] The Raleigh Expedition 1584 / Adapted by permission from the beautiful painting by Turner on the lobby wall / of the Raleigh Hotel, Washington, D.C. It pictures the departure of Sir

Walter / Raleigh's first expedition to colonize America. For further details see page 4. / Published by / the W.T. Rawleigh Co., Ltd. / Montreal – Winnipeg / Freeport Memphis Richmond Chester Albany Minneapolis / Denver Oakland Melbourne Wellington [cover-title]
DESCRIPTION: With image on front face of binding of the Turner painting
COPIES: ARDA

1934

Aitken, Mrs Katherine (Kate) May, née Scott (Mrs Henry Mundell Aitken) (Beeton, Ont., 6 April 1891– 11 December 1971, Mississauga, Ont.)

Kate Aitken (pl 45) – fondly known across Canada as 'Mrs A' – had no formal home economics training, but she was a practical woman with boundless energy and an entrepreneurial spirit. She was the first of seven children of Anne (née Kennedy) and Robert Scott, who ran the Beeton general store. After first working as a teacher, Kate married Henry Aitken in 1914. They moved for a brief period to Virginia, Minnesota, but then returned to Beeton (northwest of Toronto), where Henry ran a mill and Kate established a poultry farm and a canning business, using her own fruit and poultry. The couple had two daughters: Mary (Mrs Robert Hortop) and Anne (Mrs Clinton Thompson). One of Kate's early ventures, using products from the farm, was to make up food baskets to sell to families in Toronto. Kate was the first president of the Beeton Women's Institute, and until 1928 she lectured to rural women, on behalf of the Ontario Department of Agriculture.

Her nearly thirty-year association with the Canadian National Exhibition (CNE) in Toronto began in 1923 when she set up a 'Country Kitchen' in the Women's Building to promote her preserves and baked goods. She was soon asked to organize an annual cooking school (according to her autobiography, Making Your Living Is Fun, her first experience at organizing cooking schools was in Montreal cinemas, at the request of an unnamed sponsor) and, in 1938, she became director of women's activities at the CNE. By all accounts a dynamo, in a typical day at the CNE she gave cooking demonstrations, ran competitions, did two daily, live, one-hour radio broadcasts, and supervised three restaurants. She retired from the CNE after the 1952 exhibition.

Her radio shows, sponsored by Canada Starch, Ogilvie Flour Mills, or Tamblyn Drug Stores, were carried first on CFRB in Toronto, starting in 1934, later on CJAD in Montreal, then on the CBC national network, from 1948.

During the Second World War, she served as supervisor of conservation, Consumers Branch, Wartime Prices and Trade Board, and in August 1945 she completed a six-week tour of the British Isles and the Continent, at the invitation of the British Ministry of Food, to see how Canadian women could help alleviate food shortages there. From 1941 to 1951 her usual schedule included a weekly commute from Toronto to Montreal, where she was women's editor of the Standard newspaper.

Her most successful publication, and one still used in Canadian homes after half a century, is Q292.1, Kate Aitken's Canadian Cook Book, first published in 1945 by the Montreal Standard and in several later editions and reprints. The Famous Royal Household Recipes series of cookbooks published by Ogilvie Flour Mills are described below. For a series published by Canada Starch, see: Q263.1, 52 Baking Secrets; Q264.1, 52 Cakes; Q265.1, 52 Desserts; and Q266.1, 52 Pies. See also Q277.1, Feeding Your Family in Wartime, and Q278.1, How to Save Sugar in Cooking, compiled in her first years at the Standard; S78.1, The Doughnut Book of Recipes, which includes her recipes; and O1091.1, Household Helps for 1944, which has an article by her on clothing. She also wrote Kate Aitken's Guernsey Gold Recipes for Christmas, no place: Christie's Dairy Ltd, nd [after 1950] (Private collection). For her broadcasts she prepared recipe leaflets – for example, Cooking Gossip bulletins for Canada Starch and the monthly Good News for Tamblyn Drug Stores – and various small pamphlets were printed in connection with her cooking demonstrations, such as My Book of Happy Days by Mrs. Canada, leaflet numbered Chapter I for 25 August 1939 (OTCNE), and Mrs. Aitken's Cooking School, 10 pp of recipes (OFERWM).

Her broadcasting and public speaking extended beyond the culinary to cultural and political affairs. She travelled widely, and after her trips to such places as post-war Japan and South Africa, she would speak frankly about her findings, sometimes eliciting official responses from criticized parties (see, for example, 'The Significant Case of Mrs. Aitken' by Alexander Steward in South Africa: The Complex Country, distributed by the South African Information Officer, Ottawa, September 1953, copy in TPL Scrapbooks, Vol. 67, pp 37–40).

In the winter of 1953–4 she opened the Kate Aitken Spa in Streetsville, Ontario. She retired from radio work on 28 June 1957. From 1959 to 1962 she served as director of the Board of Governors of the CBC. She is buried in Beeton United Church Cemetery.

For more information about Aitken, see: Kate Aitken papers at OOA (MG30 D206), which include indexes to her various broadcasts; the autobiography of her childhood, Never a Day So Bright, Toronto: Longmans, Green and Co., 1956, and of her adult life, Making Your Living Is Fun, Toronto: Longmans, Green and Co., 1959; Jean Bannerman, Leading Ladies, Canada, 1639–1967, Dundas, Ont.: 1967, pp 277–9; Canadian Women of Note No. 9; Nancy Kee, 'The Incredible Mrs. A,' in Once upon a Century: 100 Year History of the 'Ex,' Toronto: J.H. Robinson Publishing Ltd, 1978; articles about Aitken in TPL Scrapbooks; articles by Neil Brochu, Margo Oliver, Fiona Lucas, and Ed Lyons in CHO No. 40 (Spring 2004); Susan Sampson, 'A Finger in Every Pie,' Star (Toronto) 2 June 2004, p D4; and Elizabeth Driver's entry for Aitken in Arndt, pp 9–10.

For information about Ogilvie Flour Mills Co. Ltd, see Q55.1.

Q214.1 No. 1, [1st ed., copyright 1934]
Famous / Royal / Household / recipes / [Seri]es No. 1 / [Hot] breads / [(tea bis]cuits, etc.) / Compiled by Mrs. H.M. Aitken / for / the Ogilvie Flour Mills Co., Limited [cover-title]
DESCRIPTION: 1st leaf, 20.5 × 12.5 cm; 2nd–15th leaves graduate in size from 10.0 × 12.5 cm to 20.5 × 12.5 cm, in about 0.8-cm increments   Card; metal spiral–bound at top edge
CONTENTS: Inside back face of binding 'Copyright, Canada, 1934 by the Ogilvie Flour Mills Co., Limited Montreal, Que. Spirax Binding.'
COPIES: *OONL (TX763 F35 1934 Vol. 1 p***)   OTMCL (641.5971 H39 No. 35)
NOTES: This first edition is credited to Mrs H.M. Aitken, whereas later editions are attributed to Mildred Mae McKenzie; the same recipes are in the later editions. Text on the inside front face of the binding indicates that this book may be obtained from Ogilvie's by sending $0.15 plus six Royal Household recipe coupons or $0.25 without coupons. Each bag of Royal Household Flour contained one recipe coupon on which was printed 'a complete list of the wire-bound and visible-indexed Famous Royal Household Recipe Books.'

Many Canadian home cooks, past and present, would concur with the initial statement of the 'Fore-word': 'In the whole field of cookery there is no recipe more adaptable than what we call the plain tea biscuit recipe. Using the same foundation we can make hot breads, tea biscuits, puddings, fruit loaves and even a very good emergency bread.'

Q214.2 No. 1, 2nd ed., [copyright 1934]
—Famous / Royal / Household / recipes / Series No. 1 / Second edition / Hot breads / (tea biscuits, etc.) / Compiled for / the Ogilvie Flour Mills Co., Limited / by / Mildred Mae McKenzie [cover-title]

DESCRIPTION: 1st leaf, 20.0 × 12.5 cm; 2nd–15th leaves graduate in size from 10.0 × 12.5 to 20.0 × 12.5 cm Pp [1–29]   Thin card; metal spiral–bound at top edge
CONTENTS: Inside front face of binding 'Copyright, Canada, 1934 by the Ogilvie Flour Mills Co., Limited Montreal, Que.'; 1 'Foreword'; 2 blank; 3–29 recipes on rectos, blank versos
COPIES: *AMHM (M76.39.5f)

Q214.3   No. 1, 4th ed., [copyright 1934]
—Famous / Royal / Household / recipes / Series No. 1 / Fourth edition / Hot breads / (tea biscuits, etc.) / Compiled for / the Ogilvie Flour Mills Co., Limited / by / Mildred Mae McKenzie [cover-title]
COPIES: *Private collection

Q214.4   No. 1, 5th ed., [copyright 1934]
—Famous / Royal / Household / recipes / Series No. 1 / Fifth edition / Hot breads / (tea biscuits, etc.) / Compiled for / the Ogilvie Flour Mills Co., Limited / by / Mildred Mae McKenzie [cover-title]
DESCRIPTION: 1st leaf, 20.0 × 12.5 cm; 2nd–15th leaves graduate in size from 10.0 × 12.5 cm to 20.0 × 12.5 cm Pp [1–29]   Card; metal spiral–bound at top edge
CONTENTS: Inside front face of binding notice about coupons for ordering this series of cookbooks, found in each bag of Royal Household Flour, and 'Copyright, Canada, 1934 by the Ogilvie Flour Mills Co., Limited Montreal, Que. ...'; 1 'Foreword'; 2 blank; 3–29 recipes on rectos, blank versos
COPIES: *Private collection

Q215.1   No. 2, [1st ed., copyright 1934]
Famous / Royal / Household / recipes / [Serie]s No. 2 / [Ca]kes / [fillings a]nd icings / Compiled by Mrs. H.M. Aitken / for / the Ogilvie Flour Mills Co., Limited [cover-title]
DESCRIPTION: 1st leaf, 20.5 × 12.5 cm; 2nd–15th leaves graduate in size from 10.0 × 12.5 cm to 20.5 × 12.5 cm, in about 0.8-cm increments   Pp [1–29]   Card; metal spiral–bound at top edge
CONTENTS: 1 'Foreword'; 2 blank; 3–29 recipes on rectos, blank versos; inside back face of binding 'Copyright, Canada, 1934 by the Ogilvie Flour Mills Co., Limited Montreal, Que. Spirax binding.'
COPIES: *OONL (TX763 F35 1934 Vol. 2 p***)
NOTES: The first edition is attributed to Mrs H.M. Aitken; later editions are credited to Mildred Mae McKenzie.

Q215.2   No. 2, 2nd ed., [copyright 1934]
—Famous / Royal / Household / recipes / Series No. 2 / Second edition / Cakes / fillings and icings / Compiled for / the Ogilvie Flour Mills Co.,

Limited / by / Mildred Mae McKenzie [cover-title]
CONTENTS: Inside front face of binding notice about coupons found in each bag of Royal Household Flour, on which is printed 'a complete list of the wire-bound and visible-indexed Famous Royal Household Recipe Books ...,' and 'Copyright, Canada, 1934 by the Ogilvie Flour Mills Co., Limited Montreal, Que. Spirax Binding.'
COPIES: *Private collection

Q215.3   No. 2, 4th ed., [copyright 1934]
—Famous / Royal / Household / recipes / Series No. 2 / Fourth edition / Cakes / fillings and icings / Compiled for / the Ogilvie Flour Mills Co., Limited / by / Mildred Mae McKenzie [cover-title]
DESCRIPTION: 1st leaf, 20.0 × 12.5 cm; 2nd–15th leaves graduate in size from 10.0 × 12.5 cm to 20.0 × 12.5 cm, in about 0.8-cm increments   Pp [1–29]   Card; metal spiral–bound at top edge
CONTENTS: Inside front face of binding notice about coupons found in each bag of Royal Household Flour, on which is printed 'a complete list of the wire-bound and visible-indexed Famous Royal Household Recipe Books ...,' and 'Copyright, Canada, 1934 by the Ogilvie Flour Mills Co., Limited Montreal Que. Spirax Binding. Patented Canada 1932. No. 326518'; 1 'Famous Royal Household Recipes Compiled and Tested Exclusively for the Ogilvie Flour Mills Co., Limited by Mildred Mae McKenzie // Series No. 2 // Fourth edition // Cakes, Fillings and Icings'; 2 blank; 3–29 recipes on rectos, blank versos
COPIES: AMHM   *Private collection

Q215.4   No. 2, 5th ed., [copyright 1934]
—Famous / Royal / Household / recipes / Series No. 2 / Fifth edition / Cakes / fillings and icings / Compiled for / the Ogilvie Flour Mills Co., Limited / by / Mildred Mae McKenzie [cover-title]
DESCRIPTION: 1st leaf, 20.0 × 12.5 cm; 2nd–15th leaves graduate in size from 10.0 × 12.5 cm to 20.0 × 12.5 cm, in about 0.8-cm increments   Pp [1–29]   Card; metal spiral–bound at top edge
CONTENTS: Inside front face of binding notice about coupons found in each bag of Royal Household Flour, on which is printed 'a complete list of the wire-bound and visible-indexed Famous Royal Household Recipe Books ...,' and 'Copyright, Canada, 1934 by the Ogilvie Flour Mills Co., Limited Montreal, Que. ...'; 1 'Famous Royal Household Recipes Compiled and Tested Exclusively for the Ogilvie Flour Mills Co., Limited by Mildred Mae McKenzie // Series No. 2 // Fifth edition // Cakes, Fillings and Icings // Foreword' [general information about baking cakes]; 2 blank; 3–29 recipes on rectos, blank versos
COPIES: *Private collection

Q216.1 No. 3, [1st ed., copyright 1934]
Famous / Royal / Household / recipes / [Serie]s
No. 3 / [Pud]dings / [and pudd]ing sauces /
Compiled by Mrs. H.M. Aitken / for / the Ogilvie
Flour Mills Co., Limited [cover-title]
DESCRIPTION: 1st leaf, 20.5 × 12.5 cm; 2nd–15th leaves
graduate in size from 10.0 × 12.5 cm to 20.5 × 12.5 cm,
in about 0.8-cm increments Pp [1–29] Thin card;
metal spiral–bound at top edge
CONTENTS: 1 'Foreword'; 2 blank; 3–29 recipes on
rectos, blank versos; inside back face of binding 'Copy-
right, Canada, 1934 by the Ogilvie Flour Mills Co.,
Limited Montreal, Que. Spirax binding ...'
COPIES: *OONL (TX763 F35 1934 Vol. 3 p***)
NOTES: The first edition is attributed to Mrs H.M.
Aitken; later editions are credited to Mildred Mae
McKenzie.

Q216.2 No. 3, 2nd ed., [copyright 1934]
—Famous / Royal / Household / recipes / Series
No. 3 / Second edition / Puddings / and pudding
sauces / Compiled for / the Ogilvie Flour Mills Co.,
Limited / by / Mildred Mae McKenzie [cover-title]
DESCRIPTION: 1st leaf: 20.0 × 12.5 cm; 2nd–15th leaves
graduate in size from 10.0 × 12.5 cm to 20.0 × 12.5 cm
Pp [1–29] Thin card; metal spiral–bound at top edge
CONTENTS: Inside front face of binding 'Copyright,
Canada, 1934 by the Ogilvie Flour Mills Co., Limited
Montreal Que.'; 1 'Foreword'; 2 blank; 3–29 recipes
on rectos, blank versos
COPIES: *AMHM (M76.39.5d)

Q216.3 No. 3, 4th ed., [1934]
—Famous / Royal / Household / recipes / Series
No. 3 / Fourth edition / Puddings / and pudding
sauces / Compiled for / the Ogilvie Flour Mills Co.,
Limited / by / Mildred Mae McKenzie [cover-title]
COPIES: *Private collection

Q216.4 No. 3, 5th ed., [copyright 1934]
—Famous / Royal / Household / recipes / Series
No. 3 / Fifth edition / Puddings / and pudding
sauces / Compiled for / the Ogilvie Flour Mills Co.,
Limited / by / Mildred Mae McKenzie [cover-title]
DESCRIPTION: 1st leaf, 20.0 × 12.5 cm; 2nd–15th leaves
graduate in size from 10.0 × 12.5 cm to 20.0 × 12.5 cm,
in about 0.8-cm increments Pp [1–29] Card; metal
spiral–bound at top edge
CONTENTS: Inside front face of binding notice about
coupons for ordering this series of cookbooks, found
in each bag of Royal Household Flour, and 'Copyright, Canada, 1934 by the Ogilvie Flour Mills Co.,

Limited Montreal, Que. ...'; 1 'Foreword'; 2 blank;
3–29 recipes on rectos, blank versos
COPIES: *Private collection
NOTES: 'All recipes serve six portions, except Christmas puddings,' according to the 'Foreword.' The recipes in the fifth edition are the same as in the first
edition.

Q217.1 No. 4, [1st ed., copyright 1934]
Famous / Royal / Household / recipes / [Serie]s
No. 4 / [Co]okies / Compiled by Mrs. H.M. Aitken
/ for / the Ogilvie Flour Mills Co., Limited [cover-
title]
DESCRIPTION: 1st leaf, 20.5 × 12.5 cm; 2nd–15th leaves
graduate in size from 10.0 × 12.5 cm to 20.5 × 12.5 cm,
in about 0.8-cm increments Pp [1–29] Card; metal
spiral–bound at top edge
CONTENTS: 1 'Foreword'; 2 blank; 3–29 recipes on
rectos, blank versos; inside back face of binding 'Copy-
right, Canada, 1934 by the Ogilvie Flour Mills Co.,
Limited Montreal, Que. Spirax binding.'
COPIES: *OONL (TX763 F35 1934 Vol. 4 p***)
NOTES: The first edition is attributed to Mrs H.M.
Aitken; later editions are credited to Mildred Mae
McKenzie.

Q217.2 No. 4, 2nd ed., [copyright 1934]
—Famous / Royal / Household / recipes / Series
No. 4 / Second edition / Cookies / Compiled for /
the Ogilvie Flour Mills Co., Limited / by / Mildred
Mae McKenzie [cover-title]
CONTENTS: Inside front face of binding notice about
coupons found in each bag of Royal Household Flour,
on which is printed 'a complete list of the wire-bound
and visible-indexed Famous Royal Household Recipe
Books ...,' and 'Copyright, Canada, 1934 by the Ogilvie
Flour Mills Co., Limited Montreal, Que. Spirax Bind-
ing.'
COPIES: *Private collection

Q217.3 No. 4, 4th ed., [copyright 1934]
—Famous / Royal / Household / recipes / Series
No. 4 / Fourth edition / Cookies / Compiled for /
the Ogilvie Flour Mills Co., Limited / by / Mildred
Mae McKenzie [cover-title]
DESCRIPTION: 1st leaf, 20.0 × 12.5 cm; 2nd–15th leaves
graduate in size from 10.0 × 12.5 cm to 20.0 × 12.5 cm
Pp [1–29] Thin card; metal spiral–bound at top edge
CONTENTS: Inside front face of binding 'Copyright,
Canada, 1934 by the Ogilvie Flour Mills Co., Limited
Montreal, Que.'; 1 'Foreword'; 2 blank; 3–29 recipes
on rectos, blank versos
COPIES: *AMHM (M76.39.5c)

Q217.4   No. 4, 5th ed., [copyright 1934]
—Famous / Royal / Household / recipes / Series
No. 4 / Fifth edition / Cookies / Compiled for / the
Ogilvie Flour Mills Co., Limited / by / Mildred Mae
McKenzie [cover-title]
DESCRIPTION: 1st leaf, 20.0 × 12.5 cm; 2nd–15th leaves
graduate in size from 10.0 × 12.5 cm to 20.0 × 12.5 cm
Pp [1–29]   Thin card; metal spiral–bound at top edge
CONTENTS: Inside front face of binding 'Copyright,
Canada, 1934 by the Ogilvie Flour Mills Co., Limited
Montreal, Que.'
COPIES: *Private collection

Q218.1   No. 5, [1st ed., copyright 1936 [sic]]
Famous / Royal / Household / recipes / Series No.
5 / Plain and fancy breads / white and brown /
Compiled by Mrs. H.M. Aitken / for / the Ogilvie
Flour Mills Co., Limited [cover-title]
DESCRIPTION: 1st leaf: 20.0 × 12.5 cm; 2nd–15th leaves
graduate in size from 10.0 × 12.5 cm to 20.0 × 12.5 cm
Pp [1–29]   Thin card; metal spiral–bound at top edge
CONTENTS: Inside front face of binding notice that
book will be sent free upon receipt of six Royal House-
hold Flour coupons or receipt of $0.25 without cou-
pons; 1 'Foreword'; 2 blank; 3–29 recipes on rectos,
blank versos; inside back face 'Copyright, Canada,
1936 [sic] by the Ogilvie Flour Mills Co., Limited
Montreal, Que. ...'
COPIES: *AMHM (M76.39.5a)   OONL (TX763 F35 1934
Vol. 5 p***)
NOTES: The first edition is credited to Mrs H.M. Aitken;
the second, fourth, and fifth editions, to Mildred Mae
McKenzie. The first edition bears the copyright date
1936, but this is probably a typographical error since
all subsequent editions of *Plain and Fancy Breads* and
all other titles in the series are copyright 1934.

Q218.2   No. 5, 2nd ed., [copyright 1934]
—Famous / Royal / Household / recipes / Series
No. 5 / Second edition / Plain and fancy breads /
white and brown / Compiled for / the Ogilvie Flour
Mills Co., Limited / by / Mildred Mae McKenzie
[cover-title]
COPIES:* Private collection

Q218.3   No. 5, 4th ed., [copyright 1934]
—Famous / Royal / Household / recipes / Series
No. 5 / Fourth edition / Plain and fancy breads /
white and brown / Compiled for / the Ogilvie Flour
Mills Co., Limited / by / Mildred Mae McKenzie
[cover-title]
DESCRIPTION: Metal spiral–bound at top edge

CONTENTS: Inside front face of binding 'Copyright,
Canada, 1934 by the Ogilvie Flour Mills Co., Limited
Montreal, Que. Spirax binding. Patented Canada
1932.'
COPIES: *Private collection

Q218.4   No. 5, 5th ed., [copyright 1934]
—Famous / Royal / Household / recipes / Series
No. 5 / Fifth edition / Plain and fancy breads /
white and brown / Compiled for / the Ogilvie Flour
Mills Co., Limited / by / Mildred Mae McKenzie
[cover-title]
DESCRIPTION: 1st leaf, 20.0 × 12.5 cm; 2nd–15th leaves
graduate in size from 10.0 × 12.5 cm to 20.0 × 12.5 cm,
in about 0.8-cm increments   Pp [1–29]   Card; metal
spiral–bound at top edge
CONTENTS: Inside front face of binding notice about
coupons for ordering this series of cookbooks, found
in each bag of Royal Household Flour, and 'Copyright, Canada, 1934 by the Ogilvie Flour Mills Co.,
Limited Montreal, Que. ...'; 1 'Foreword'; 2 blank;
3–29 recipes on rectos, blank versos
COPIES: OGU (CCC TX715.6 P53)   *Private collection

McKenzie, Mildred Mae

In the Famous Royal Household Recipes *series, the
first editions of Nos 1–5 are attributed to Mrs H.M.
Aitken (i.e., Kate Aitken), and subsequent editions to
Mildred Mae McKenzie. The only exception in the series
is Q219.1, No. 6,* Pies and Pastry, *where all editions are
credited to McKenzie. No. 6 is described here, under
McKenzie's name; all the other numbers are under
Aitken, Q214.1–218.1. What prompted the change in
author's credit is a mystery.*

*Mildred Mae McKenzie may be Mrs M.M. Mackenzie
[sic], widow of H.B. Mackenzie, listed as living at
11 Severn Avenue, Westmount, in the 1931–2 and 1932–3
Montreal city directories. Before 1931, the directory
listing is under her husband's name: H.B. Mackenzie,
general manager of Royal Trust Co. and assistant general
manager of Bank of Montreal, home address at 4302
Montrose Avenue, Westmount. Inexplicably, Mrs M.M.
Mackenzie is not listed in the 1933–4 or 1934–5 directories, which cover the period when the* Famous Royal
Household Recipes *series was probably being compiled.
Perhaps she was in the process of moving to another
address or to another city, or perhaps she remarried.*

Q219.1   No. 6, [1st ed., copyright 1934]
Famous / Royal / Household / recipes / Series No.
6 / Pies and pastry / Compiled for / the Ogilvie

Flour Mills Co., Limited / by / Mildred Mae McKenzie [cover-title]

DESCRIPTION: 1st leaf, 20.0 × 12.5 cm; 2nd–15th leaves graduate in size from 10.0 × 12.5 cm to 20.0 × 12.5 cm Pp [1–29] Thin card; metal spiral–bound at top edge

CONTENTS: Inside front face of binding 'Copyright, Canada, 1934 by the Ogilvie Flour Mills Co., Limited Montreal Que.'; 1 'Foreword' [general information about making pies and pastry]; 2 blank; 3–29 recipes on rectos, blank versos

COPIES: *AMHM OONL (TX763 F35 1934 Vol. 6 p***)

NOTES: The first recipes are for Plain Pastry, Hot Water Pastry, Apple Pie, Dutch Apple Pie, and Custard Pie.

Q219.2 No. 6, 3rd ed., [copyright 1934]
—Famous / Royal / Household / recipes / Series No. 6 / Third edition / Pies and pastry / Compiled for / the Ogilvie Flour Mills Co., Limited / by / Mildred Mae McKenzie [cover-title]

CONTENTS: Inside front face of binding 'Copyright, Canada, 1934'; 1 'Foreword'; ...

COPIES:* Private collection

Q219.3 No. 6, 4th ed., [copyright 1934]
—Famous / Royal / Household / recipes / Series No. 6 / Fourth edition / Pies and pastry / Compiled for / the Ogilvie Flour Mills Co., Limited / by / Mildred Mae McKenzie [cover-title]

DESCRIPTION: 1st leaf, 20.0 × 12.5 cm; 2nd–15th leaves graduate in size from 10.0 × 12.5 cm to 20.0 × 12.5 cm, in about 0.8-cm increments Pp [1–29] Card; metal spiral–bound at top edge

CONTENTS: Inside front face of binding notice about coupons for ordering this series of cookbooks, found in each bag of Royal Household Flour, and 'Copyright, Canada, 1934 by the Ogilvie Flour Mills Co., Limited Montreal, Que. ...'; 1 'Foreword'; 2 blank; 3–29 recipes on rectos, blank versos

COPIES: *Private collection

Miral, Marthe [pseudonym]

See O773.15, L'art de réussir des gâteaux, and O777.9, L'art de recevoir, for French-language editions of The Easy Way Cake Book and Planning the Party, published in Montreal and attributed to Marthe Miral instead of Anna Lee Scott, the pseudonym used by Maple Leaf Milling Co. Ltd for the English-language editions.

Paré, Eugénie

For the titles of other cookbooks published by the Quebec Department of Agriculture, see Q48.1.

Q220.1 1934
[First edition of *Le pain de ménage*, Bulletin 131, série 4, Quebec: ministère de l'Agriculture, 1934, pp 32, illus]

CITATIONS: Beaulieu, p 104

COPIES: QMBN (A38A1 P83 131 OFF)

Q220.2 1940
—[New edition of *Le pain de ménage*, Bulletin 131, Quebec: ministère de l'Agriculture, 1940, pp 29, illus]

CITATIONS: Beaulieu, p 104

COPIES: QMBN (A38A1 P83 131 1940 OFF)

Recipes for every-day use in the home

Q221.1 [1934]
[Title at top p 1:] Recipes / for every-day use / in the home

DESCRIPTION: 15.0 × 14.0 cm Pp 1–24 Paper, with 'sketch' on front by Lorne K. Smith, Toronto, of the schooner Bluenose; stapled, and with hole punched at top left corner, through which runs a string for hanging

CONTENTS: 1–16 'Recipes for Every-Day Use in the Home' and ads for Dr Hamilton's Pills; 17 'Homely Hints for the Housewife' and ad for Dr Hamilton's Pills; 18–24 'Hints of Value to Housekeepers' and ads for the Catarrh-o-zone Inhaler; inside back face of binding ad for Dr Hamilton's Pills, plus 'Measurements for These Recipes,' 'Table of Equivalents,' 'Cooking Times and Temperatures,' and 'Water and Syrup Temperatures'; outside back face calendars for 1934 and 1935, and 'Published by the Catarrhozone Co., Montreal, Canada'

COPIES: *OTUTF (uncat patent medicine)

NOTES: There is no cover-title or title-page.

1934–5

Farine Purity, recettes anciennes et modernes

For information about Western Canada Flour Mills and other cookbooks for Purity Flour, see O394.1.

Q222.1 nd [about 1934–5]
Farine / Purity / recettes / anciennes / et / modernes / [Western Canada Flour Mills Co.

symbol] / Prix – 15 sous l'exemplaire / Publié par / Western Canada Flour Mills Co. Limited / Montreal, Canada / Meuniers de la Farine Purity, Farine d'avoine Purity et Farine Hovis / Moulins à / Goderich Winnipeg Brandon Calgary Victoria / Bureaux à / Saint-John Montreal Ottawa Toronto Winnipeg Calgary / Vancouver New-Westminster Victoria

DESCRIPTION: 24.0 × 16.5 cm   Pp 1–48   Illus col, illus Paper, with image on front of a windmill ('érigé il y a 300 ans Isle aux Coudres, Québec'); stapled

CONTENTS: 1 tp; 2 fp illus of the monument to Louis Hébert in Quebec City ('... il moissona le premier champ de blé semé au Canada.'); 3 introductory note signed by the company's Département de sciences domestiques, Montreal, and 'L'équivalent des mesures'; 4 publ ad; 5–46 recipes; 47 book-order coupons; 48 *Canadian Home Journal* 'certificat d'approbation' dated 4 April 1934, but over-printed 1934–5; inside back face of binding 'Created and produced by Harris Lithographing Co. Limited, Toronto'

COPIES: QMBN   *Private collection

NOTES: The introductory note states, 'Les recettes modernes ont été choisies par notre autorité canadienne-française, les recettes de l'ancien temps sont des souvenirs de vieilles familles historiques de vieux Québec.' On pp 42–6 there are 'Des recettes populaires du bon vieux temps,' which were collected from the following sources: 'les archives à Ottawa, des filières de vieux couvents, des cuisines de manoirs historiques, et des chaumières modestes des campagnes et villages.'

The book-order coupons indicate that the work was available in French and English. In 1932, the company had published O771.1, *The Purity Cook-Book*. Perhaps *Farine Purity, recettes anciennes et modernes* was the corresponding new cookbook in French, but prepared especially for the Quebec market.

1934–9

Poisson Primo seafood

Q223.1   nd [about 1934–9]
Poisson / Primo / seafood [cover-title]
DESCRIPTION: 9.5 × 9.5 cm   Pp [1–28]   Paper binding and leaves cut in oyster-shape; stapled

CONTENTS: Inside front face of binding 'Tous nos produits marque Primo portent le sceau d'inspection du ministère provincial des pêcheries. Louis-T. Blais, limitée // distributeurs des produits Primo // 52,

rue Saint-Pierre, Québec, P.Q.'; 1 'Présentation'; 2–28 and inside back face recipes using Primo products, such as lobster, salmon, trout, etc.

COPIES: *QMM (RBD ckbk 1325)

NOTES: The 'Présentation' states, '... tous nos poissons sont pris par des pêcheurs de la province de Québec, ...' From appearances, *Poisson Primo Seafood* was published in the 1930s. The first listing in Quebec City directories for Louis-T. Blais at 52 St-Pierre is in the directory for 1934–5.

1935

Better meat curing

Q224.1   nd [about 1935]
Better / meat curing / Complete directions for / choosing, butchering and / curing meat so as to assure the best results / for hams and bacon, also beef, lamb, fish, / wild game, etc. / Habacure / ha(m)-ba(con) cure / Habacure Canada Limited, Montreal [cover-title]

DESCRIPTION: 22.0 × 14.5 cm   Pp [1–3] 4–21 [22]   Illus red-and-black, illus   Paper, with two images on front: at top, a pig's head in a circular frame, and at centre, three pigs watching another pig, in a gown and mortar board, who is pointing at bacon slices and a ham on a plate; stapled

CONTENTS: 1 cover-title; 2 'Your Habacure dealer offers you this complete modern way to "better meat curing" // This booklet aims to be practical and helpful to all farmers who butcher and cure meats at home, ...'; 3 'Habacure – It Smokes // Cures // Flavors' and map of Canada; 4–5 'Better Meat Curing' [introductory text]; 6–9 'Bleed Well // Chill Well // Trim Well'; 10–12 'Proper Chilling Very Important'; 13–18 'How to Habacure Hams and Bacon' including 'The Dry Cure' and 'The Sweet Pickle Cure'; 19 'Beef'; 20 'Lamb and Mutton'; 21 'Large & Small Game, Poultry & Fish'; 22 'Directions for Using Habacure Meat Pump'; inside back face of binding publ ad for 'The Habacure Meat Pump'; outside back face 'Printed and copyright in Canada'

COPIES: *Private collection

NOTES: Full instructions are given for slaughtering and butchering hogs, and for curing with Habacure. Directions for Corned Beef, Corned Lamb, and for corning tongue are on p 20. The private collector's copy is stamped on the front face of the binding, 'Scott, Bathgate Company, Ltd. Winnipeg, Man.'

Q224.2 [copyright 1944]
—Better / meat curing / with / Habacure /
Complete directions for / choosing, butchering /
and home-curing. / Habacure Canada Limited /
Montreal, Canada / Scott-Bathgate Co. Ltd. Western
distributors / Winnipeg Calgary Edmonton Fort
William Vancouver [cover-title]
DESCRIPTION: 21.5 × 13.5 cm   Pp 3–30   Illus   Paper,
with image on front of a 'teacher' pig pointing out
slices of bacon and a ham to three other pigs; stapled
CONTENTS: 3 'Habacure Means Easy, Safe, Thrifty
Home Curing'; 4 'Planning for Butchering'; ...; 7–19
'Bleed Well, Chill Well, Trim Well'; 20 'Now You Are
Ready to Use Habacure' and 'How to Habacure Hams
and Bacon'; 21–mid 25 'The Dry Sugar Cure'; mid 25–
26 'The Sweet Pickle Cure'; 27 'The Habacure Meat
Pump'; 28 'Directions for Using Meat Pump'; 29 'Beef';
30 'Lamb and Mutton'; inside back face of binding
'Fish' and 'Large and Small Game and Poultry'
COPIES: *Private collection
NOTES: 'Copyright in Canada 1944' is on the outside
back face of the binding. This copy is stamped by a
Manitoba co-operative, on the front face, 'This booklet is sent through the courtesy of Deleau Cons. Co-
op. Deleau, who stock Habacure.'

Catalogue des produits Rena

Q225.1   nd [about 1935]
L'ami du peuple / The people's friend / Catalogue
/ des / Produits / Rena / Products / catalogue /
J.A. Renaud / 752, Rachel E., Montreal Tel. Fa. 1125*
/ No. 5 [cover-title]
DESCRIPTION: 22.5 × 10.0 cm   Pp [1] 2–48   Illus   Paper, with image on front of J.A. Renaud building
CONTENTS: Inside front face of binding recipes; 1 letter from J.A. Renaud to his customers, in French and
in English; ...
COPIES: *Private collection
NOTES: This catalogue of kitchen utensils and other
items has a few pages of recipes. On p 1 Renaud
comments that he has 'been obliged to make the
acquisition of a four Storey's [sic] Building, to be able
to fill all the orders,' and the building is illustrated on
the binding. The first listing for Renaud at 752 Rachel
East is in the Montreal city directory for 1934–5, where
he is described as a seller of patent medicines; the
first listing at 752 Rachel East using the business
name Rena Products is in the directory for 1935–6.
Renaud boasts that he is 'Un canadien au service
des canadiens avec des produits canadiens'; and in
English, 'A Canadian to serve the Canadians with
Canadian products.'

Familex

*Familex is first listed in the Montreal city directory for
1932–3, at 570 St Clement. In 1944 the company's
address changed to 1600 Delorimier Avenue. This address
change helps to date the company's publications. A
librarian at QMBN remembers vividly the sight, as one
crossed the Jacques Cartier Bridge toward downtown
Montreal, of the Familex factory on one side and
Molson's (the beer company) on the other. He also remembers the 'Familex man' selling toiletries and food products
door to door in his Montreal neighbourhood. See also
Q232.1, Culinary Secrets.*

Q226.1   nd [about 1935]
Familex [cover-title]
DESCRIPTION: 23.0 × 15.0 cm   Pp 1–32   Photograph
on inside front face of binding of Mr R. [i.e., Roméo]
Parent, to whom the company 'owes its origin'; illus
of Familex products   Paper, with image on front of a
Familex representative chatting with a housewife on
her doorstep
CONTENTS: 1 'A Real "Home" Service // Familex';
2–29 catalogue of company products; 30–2 price list
COPIES: *Private collection
NOTES: This publication is a catalogue of Familex products; recipes using the products are on pp 25 and 27
only. The company address on the outside back face
of the binding is 570 St Clement Street, the address
recorded in Montreal city directories from 1932–3 to
1943 (in 1944 the address changed). The dress of the
woman depicted on the binding points to publication
in about 1935.

Jubilee cook book

*Westmount Baptist Church, at 411 Roslyn Avenue, was
founded in 1902. The congregation has always had strong
links to Britain and it was David Lloyd George (British
prime minister, 1916–22) who turned the sod for the new
church building in 1923.*

Q227.1   1935
Jubilee / cook book / 1935 / Westmount Baptist
Church / Westmount, Que. [cover-title]
DESCRIPTION: 23.0 × 15.5 cm   Pp [1–4] 5–28, [i–iv]
Silver paper; stapled
CONTENTS: 1–4 ads; top 5 preface and 'Published by
the Women's Mission Circle of the Westmount Bap-
tist Church'; mid 5–28 recipes credited with the name
of the contributor; i–iv ads
COPIES: *Private collection
NOTES: The cookbook, which is bound in silver paper,

likely celebrates the twenty-fifth (or silver) jubilee of the reign of George V, who ascended the throne in 1910.

La cuisine à l'école complémentaire

Q228.1   1935
La cuisine / à / l'école complémentaire / [symbol of École normale classico-ménagère, Congrégation de Notre-Dame] / Édition abrégée de / "La cuisine raisonnée" / Des ateliers de / l'Action catholique, Québec. / 1935
DESCRIPTION: 23.0 × 16.0 cm   Pp [1–3] 4–240   Illus [$0.50, on binding]   Paper, with tp symbol on front; sewn
CONTENTS: 1 tp; 2 'Nihil obstat chan. Edgar Chouinard, censeur. Imprimateur Quebeci, die dec. 1934. B. Ph. Garneau, V.G. [*sic*] Tous droits réservés'; 3–4 'Préface' signed Alphonse Beaudet, chanoine, principal, École normale classico-ménagère, Saint-Pascal, 'En la fête de l'Annonciation,' 1926; 5–236 text arranged in two parts, for the seventh and eighth years; 237–40 'Table de matières'
CITATIONS: BQ 08-0974   Lambert, T., p 94°
COPIES: *QMACN (570.600 (2))   QMBN (160001 CON)   QQLA (TX715 C966 1935)
NOTES: No author or editor is named, but she was soeur Sainte-Marie-Vitaline (Anna Fournier, 1873–1954) (Lambert, T., p 94°); for information about her and her other books, see Q128.1. *La cuisine raisonnée* was first published in 1919 as *Manuel de cuisine raisonnée* (Q102.1). This abridged edition is arranged for the seventh and eighth years of school. The 1939 edition, Q228.2, also covers the ninth year.

On 8 May 1935, École normale classico-ménagère de Saint-Pascal became Institution chanoine-Beaudet. For references to other books produced by the same school, see Q134.1.

Q228.2   2nd ed., 1939
—La cuisine / à / l'école complémentaire / [symbol of École normale classico-ménagère, Congrégation de Notre-Dame] / 2e édition abrégée de / "La cuisine raisonnée" / revue et corrigée / Endroits de vente / Procure des missions / rue Atwater, 1520 Montréal, – rue Saint-Joseph, 228, Québec. / Institution chanoine Beaudet / Saint-Pascal de Kamouraska, Qué. / 1939
DESCRIPTION: 23.5 × 15.5 cm   Pp [1–3] 4–240 Illus   Quarter leather and cloth, probably rebound
CONTENTS: 1 tp; 2 'Nihil obstat chan. Edgar Chouinard, censeur. Imprimateur Quebeci, die 5 juin 1939. B. Ph. Garneau, V.G. Tous droits réservés'; 3–4 'Préface'

signed Alphonse Beaudet, chanoine, principal, École normale classico-ménagère, Saint-Pascal, 'En la fête de l'Annonciation,' 1926; 5–234 text arranged in two parts, for the seventh, eighth, and ninth years; 235–mid 238 'Table de matières'; mid 238–240 'Table alphabétique'
CITATIONS: Lambert, T., p 94°
COPIES: *QMACN (570.600 (3))   QQLA (TX715 C966 1939)   QRCB (E V-175)
NOTES: The QRCB copy has the price of $0.50 printed on the binding.

New recipes of flavor

For the titles of other Oxo books, see Q148.1.

Q229.1   nd [about 1935]
New / recipes / of / flavor [cover-title]
DESCRIPTION: 19.0 × 13.0 cm   Pp [1] 2–36   Illus   Paper, with image on front of a chef carrying a giant Oxo cube on a stick and leading a crowd of women, each of whom is holding a copy of this cookbook; stapled
CONTENTS: 1 'Oxo // The Basis of Flavor and Good Cooking,' acknowledgment by Oxo (Canada) Ltd to five 'dietitians of national reputation' for their co-operation in compiling the book (Katherine M. Caldwell, Helen G. Campbell, Helen Gagen, M. Frances Hucks, and Marjorie Mills, all but Mills based in Canada), 'Index' [i.e., table of contents], and 'Price: Ten cents'; 2–5 untitled introductory text; 6–26 recipes using Oxo; 27 'Table of Equivalent Weights and Measures'; 28–9 'Time Table'; 30–1 'Carving'; 32–3 'Table Setting'; 34–5 'Menu Page'; 36 publ ad
COPIES: *OGU (CCC TX715.6 O996)
NOTES: Illustrations on pp 2 and 3 indicate the book was published before 1936: The illustration on p 2 shows the Prince of Wales, i.e., Edward before he ascended the throne and abdicated in 1936; p 3 shows the Duke of York, i.e., George before he ascended the throne in 1936 after Edward's abdication. Since the first listings of the name Oxo (Canada) Ltd are in the Montreal city directory for 1935–6 and the Toronto city directory for 1935, the cookbook was published about 1935 (directories before 1935 give Oxo Ltd). The appearance of the book is consistent with this year.

There is no place of publication recorded in the volume and, at the time, Oxo (Canada) Ltd had offices in both Montreal and Toronto; however, a book-order coupon for *New Recipes of Flavor* that is slipped into the OGU copy asks readers to send their orders to the Montreal address, 428 Peter Street.

Rawleigh's good health guide 1935

For information about Rawleigh's annual almanac cookbooks and other culinary publications, see M22.1.

Q230.1 1935
[*Rawleigh's Good Health Guide 1935*, W.T. Rawleigh Co.]
COPIES: OONL (RC81 R38 p***, not on shelf)

Recettes et méthodes éprouvées par Fleischmann

For the titles of other books about cooking with Fleischmann's Yeast, see O131.1.

Q231.1 nd [about 1935]
Recettes et methodes / éprouvées par / Fleischmann / pain, petit [*sic*] pains, / brioches, biscuits [cover-title]
DESCRIPTION: With image on front face of a package of La levure Fleischmann
COPIES: QHQAR (Fonds Boulangerie Larose P41)
NOTES: The book has 37 pp. Montreal, Fleischmann's location, is printed on the yeast package depicted on the binding. The QHQAR copy is inscribed on the front face of the binding, 'Mr. Perras Gaston Thurso.'

1935–9

Culinary secrets

For information about Familex and for a catalogue that includes recipes, see Q226.1, Familex. The OONL copy of Culinary Secrets *(TX715.6 C855 1950z) was not on the shelf, so I could not compare it with the two English editions described below; the catalogue records* Culinary Secrets / Familex, *Montreal: Familex Products Co., [195-?], pp 119, illus, 24 cm.*

Q232.1 nd [about 1935–9]
Culinary / secrets / Familex / 50¢ [cover-title]
DESCRIPTION: 23.0 × 15.0 cm Pp 1–119 [120–8] Illus col Thin card, with image on front of a woman carrying a steaming tureen; wire-bound
CONTENTS: 1 'Culinary Secrets' [i.e., introductory text]; 2 illus col of Familex products; 3–113 text; 114–19 index; 120–8 blank for 'Memorandum'
COPIES: *Private collection
NOTES: This edition was likely published a few years after the company's establishment, but before the

Second World War. The text on p 1 comments that 'the Familex Products Company is an out-and-out Canadian organization, owned and controlled by a Canadian pharmacist.' The private collector's copy has a label, glued on p 1, for a Winnipeg business: 'Vernon Luff Familex dealer // 338 Albany St. Winnipeg, Man. Tel: 61052.' The copy at NBDKH is likely the same edition as Q232.1.

Q232.2 nd [about 1935–9]
—Secrets / culinaires / Familex / 50¢ [cover-title]
DESCRIPTION: 22.5 × 15.0 cm Pp [1–2] 3–123 [124–9] Illus col, illus portrait on p 1 of Roméo Parent, propriétaire-gérant Very thin card, with image on front of a woman carrying a steaming tureen; wire-bound
CONTENTS: 1 introductory text signed Roméo Parent; 2 publ ad; 3–117 text and publ ads; 118–23 'Index'; 124–9 blank, lined pages for 'Memorandum'
CITATIONS: BQ 24-4881
COPIES: *QMBN (119555 CON)
NOTES: The company address, '570 rue St-Clement,' is on the outside back face of the binding. Editions with the St Clement address were published before 1944.

QQS lists a 123-page edition of *Secrets culinaires 'Familex'* in its card catalogue, but the copy is missing. It may match Q232.2 or Q232.5.

Q232.3 nd [about 1944–5]
—Culinary secrets / Familex / Practical suggestions // Model menus / 50¢ [cover-title]
DESCRIPTION: 23.0 × 15.0 cm Pp [i–ii], 1–119 [120–6] Illus on p 1 of Familex building at 1600 Delorimier Street, illus col of Familex products and prepared dishes Paper; Wire-O Binding
CONTENTS: i blank; ii 'Culinary Secrets'; 1 illus of Familex building and information about the company; 2 illus col; 3–113 text; 114–19 index; 120–6 blank for 'Memorandum'
COPIES: *Private collection
NOTES: There is no image on the front face of the binding, which is printed in blue and a dark, mustard yellow; the name 'Familex' is in all capitals, formed as if by paint strokes. The text on p 1 says that 'about 250 preparations' of medicines, toilet articles, food products, and farm necessities are sold door-to-door through a thousand dealers. The text adds, 'During the war, they have been used to satisfy the needs of our Armed Forces, whether it be from the Army, Navy or Air Force Supply Depots.' Editions with the Delorimier address date from 1944.

Q232.4   nd [about 1944–5]
—Culinary secrets / Familex / Practical suggestions / Model menus / 50¢ [cover-title]
DESCRIPTION: Illus on p 1 of Familex building at 1600 Delorimier   With image on front of a chef indicating a secret by bringing his finger to his lips
COPIES: *Private collection
NOTES: The text on p 1 is as described for Q232.3, but the binding is as Q232.5.

Q232.5   nd [about 1944–9]
—Secrets culinaires / Familex / Conseils pratiques / Menus modèles / 50¢ [cover-title]
DESCRIPTION: 22.5 × 14.5 cm   Pp [i–ii], [1] 2–123 [124–6]   Illus col on pp 2, 13, 31, 52, 71, 84, 87, and 96 of Familex products; illus col of prepared dishes; illus on p ii of the company factory at 1600 rue Delorimier; illus portrait on p 1 of the company owner Roméo Parent   Thin card, with image on front of a chef indicating a secret by bringing his finger to his lips; Wire-O binding
CONTENTS: i blank; ii illus of the Familex factory and information about the company; 1 illus portrait; 2 publ ad; 3–117 text; 118–23 'Index'; 124–6 blank for 'Memorandum' and at bottom p 126, 'Wire-O Binding patented 1936, Semi-Exposed patented 1939 // Printed by Sampson-Matthews Limited, Toronto'
CITATIONS: Bédard, pp 4–5   BQ 24-4882   BQ Exposition 1974, p 3   Carrière No. 193
COPIES: QMBN (2 copies: *TX714 S437 1943, 119556 CON)   QSFFSC (641.5 F198s)
NOTES: QMBN dates this edition 1943, but the company is first listed on Delorimier in the 1944 Montreal directory. Other evidence of a later date is that there is no reference in the text to the Second World War, as there is in Q232.3.

100 tested recipes

Q233.1   nd [about 1935–9]
100 / tested recipes / supper dishes / & / desserts / Compiled by / members of the / Sawyerville Women's Institute [cover-title]
COPIES: QECCH (missing)

Recipes

Q234.1   nd [about 1935–9]
Montreal-West Presbyterian Church / corner Nelson St. and Ballantyne Ave. / Minister: Rev. H.R. Pickup, B.A. / Recipes / compiled by / the Ladies' Aid Society
DESCRIPTION: Tp illus of the church   Stapled

COPIES: *Private collection
NOTES: H.R. Pickup was pastor of the church from 1935 to 1946. From the appearance of the title-page, the book dates from before the Second World War. The book's owner reports that it has 92 pp and advertisements throughout.

1936

Charbonneau, Ovila (St-Agathe-des-Monts, Que., about 1901–)

Q235.1   1936
Bien faire ce que l'on fait / La cuisine nationale / secrets d'une bonne cuisine / avec illustrations / par le chef / Charbonneau / Ste-Agathe des Monts / Province de Québec. / 1936 / Prix $2.00
DESCRIPTION: 19.5 × 12.5 cm   Pp [3–9] 10–309   12 pls incl frontis portrait of Le chef Ovila Charbonneau   Rebound
CONTENTS: 3 ht; 4 'Tous droits réservés 1936 Imprimé au Canada.'; 5 tp; 6 'Lettres de recommandation' from Willie A. St-Pierre, maire de Coaticook, dated 18 March 1935, and from la directrice de l'enseignement ménager, Congrégation de Notre-Dame, Richmond; 7 'Préface'; 8 blank; 9–13 'Conseils généraux'; 14–mid 26 'Menus'; mid 26–27 'Utilisation d'un quartier de boeuf'; 28 blank; 29–299 recipes; 300 blank; 301–9 'Table des matières' and at bottom p 309, 'L'imprimerie d'Arthabaska, Inc.'
CITATIONS: Bibliothèque municipale de Montréal, p 3   BQ 13-0973   Carrière No. 97
COPIES: *OONL (TX715 C4734 1936 p***)   QMBM (641.572 C469li)   QMBN (159998 CON)   QTURA (641.5 C469c)
NOTES: St-Pierre's letter says that Charbonneau, age thirty-four years, is the chef at the Hôtel Corona in Coaticook and that he was born in St-Agathe. Since St-Pierre's letter is dated 1935, Charbonneau was born about 1901.

The cover-title is 'Livre de la cuisine nationale.' The 'Préface' explains that the book is for Quebec's hotel cooks and for concerned homemakers ('maîtresses de maison soucieuses') and that the dishes are diverse, 'obtenu avec le minimum de produits, surtout dans un pays comme le nôtre où les légumes saisonniers sont peu variés et viennent tard.' The recipe titles reflect the Quebec origin of many of the dishes; for example, Truite des Laurentides, Soupe aux pois à la canadienne, Tartes aux groseilles fraîches, Gâteau 'Baie des Chaleurs' aux dattes, and Glace au sirop d'érable.

The QTURA copy is sewn in its original paper binding.

Clergue, Miss Alice Gertrude (Bangor, Maine, 1871–20 August 1951, Montreal, Que.)

Q236.1   1936
Delectable / dishes / Published / by / the Women's Guild / of / St. George's Church / Montreal / Canada / 1936
DESCRIPTION: 20.5 × 13.0 cm   Pp [i–iv] v [vi] vii–ix [x–xii], 1–137, [i–x]   Cloth
CONTENTS: i ht; ii blank; iii tp; iv 'The Garden City Press Gardenvale, Que. Printed in Canada'; v 'To the Women's Guild of St. George's Church' signed Gertrude Clergue, Montreal, May 1936; vi blank; vii–viii preface signed Gordon J. Laing; ix table of contents; x blank; xi ht; xii blank; 1–130 recipes credited with the name of the contributor; 131 'Envoi'; 132 blank; 133–7 'Index'; i–x ads
CITATIONS: Ferguson/Fraser, p 233, illus col on p 80 of closed volume
COPIES: *OGU (UA s048 b25)   QMM (RBD ckbk 1494)
NOTES: In her note to the Women's Guild, Gertrude Clergue refers to herself as the compiler and says that the purpose of the book is 'to augment our funds.' The text includes recipes credited to Clergue and to her sister, Mrs William Lynde Harrison, called Grace. The OGU copy is inscribed on the front endpaper, in ink, 'Marion T. Osler.'

There is an unidentified newspaper clipping about the recent publication of *Delectable Dishes* in the files of OSTM. The notice states that Gertrude Clergue 'has already two cook-books to her credit.' One of these is Q95.1, *British, French, Italian, Russian, Belgian Cookery*, co-authored with Grace in 1916. The other may be Q119.1, *The Tried and True Cook Book of St George's*, about 1921, also from St George's Church and which reprints recipes from the earlier work. Biographical information about the sisters is at Q95.1.

Durand-La Roche, Mme Hélène (24 January 1894–)

Hélène and her sister Véronique Durand contributed recipes to some editions of Q152.1, L'érable, orgueil du Québec. Also by Hélène are: Plaisirs de la table, *Montreal: Beauchemin, 1961 (QMBM, QMBN);* La cuisine des 4 saisons, *Montreal: Les Éditions de l'homme, 1973 (OONL); and [Cartes-recettes Provigo], [Montreal: Les Éditions de l'homme, 1973], a box of 320 cooking cards (OONL). The author's file at OONL contains a newspaper or magazine clipping about the 1966 edition of* Madame reçoit, *which features a photograph of Hélène and her daughter Marie-Louise.*

Q237.1   [1936]
Hélène Durand-La Roche / diplômée ès sciences domestiques de / l'Ecole ménagère provinciale / Menus / de / réceptions / fêtes de famille – goûters / – grands dîners – parties de plaisir / – réunions sociales – / repas de cérémonie – réveillons / – soirées de gala – / thés / Toutes les recettes de ce volume / ont été expérimentées / par l'auteur [cover-title]
DESCRIPTION: 20.5 × 14.5 cm   Pp [1–6] 7–214, [i–vii] [$1.00, 'En vente chez l'auteur à 3445, ave Laval, Montréal,' on outside back face of binding]   Paper
CONTENTS: 1 blank; 2 'Droits réservés Édition 1936 – 10,000'; 3 'Introduction' signed Alphonse Désilets, directeur général de l'Enseignement ménager, Quebec, December 1935; 4 'Choix des menus' [i.e., table of contents]; 5–208 text; 209–14 'Table alphabétique des recettes'; i–vii ads
CITATIONS: BouquinsCat 229, No. 335   BQ 22-4881
COPIES: *OONL (TX715 L3 1936, 2 copies)   QMBN QMM (RBD Soeur Berthe, ckbk 451)
NOTES: Menus are offered for a variety of ages and occasions, from baptisms and birthday parties to New Year, Hallowe'en, and Christmas.

OTHER EDITIONS: Retitled *Madame reçoit ... menus de réceptions*, Montreal: Éditions Beauchemin, 1957 (OONL, QMBN); 2nd ed., Montreal: Éditions Beauchemin, 1957 (OONL) [1966 ed. refers to 2nd ed. as published in 1961]; Montreal: Les Éditions de l'homme, [copyright 1966] (OONL, QMBN); retitled simply *Madame reçoit*, Montreal: Les Éditions de l'homme, [copyright 1966], tirage de [1977] (OONL).

Feeding men in camps

For a later book prepared at the request of the Canadian Pulp and Paper Association, see O1206.1, Canada, Department of National Health and Welfare, Recettes – 100 portions pour les hommes qui travaillent dur.

Q238.1   1936
Woodlands Section, Canadian Pulp & Paper Association / Feeding / men in camps / A manual / of commissary practice / prepared by the Commissariat / Department of Price Brothers & Co., Limited / at the instance of and in cooperation / with the Woodlands Section of the / Canadian Pulp & Paper / Association / Layout and equipment of camp kitchens / and dining rooms; food values; menus / for various situations; recipes; waste / elimination and economy hints; miscel- /laneous information. / First edition / National Business

Publications, Limited / Gardenvale, Que., Canada / 1936

DESCRIPTION: 23.0 × 15.0 cm   Pp [iii–iv] v [vi] vii [viii], 1–214   Frontis of 'A Fine Depot Kitchen and Dining Room,' illus   Cloth

CONTENTS: iii tp; iv 'Copyright, 1936, by National Business Publications, Ltd.' and 'Printed by the Garden City Press, Gardenvale, Que.'; v preface signed Woodlands Section, Canadian Pulp and Paper Association; vi blank; vii table of contents; viii blank; 1–5 'Foreword // To the Cook:'; 6–208 text; 209–14 index

CITATIONS: CCat No. 15, p Q20

COPIES: ACG   *NBFU

NOTES: The preface states, 'This book is prepared by J.E. Caron, manager of Price Bros. Commissariat Department, who has had more than thirty years supervisory experience in feeding woodsmen ... The bulk of practical information contained in the manual was taken from the cook book of Price Brothers' Commissariat Department.' The recipes were compiled 'on the basis of a crew of 25 men' (p 1). CCat records the volume's price: $2.00.

The NBFU copy is inscribed on the title-page, in ink, 'Woodlands Section Index No. 76 (B-2).'

Q238.2   1937

—[First French-language edition of *L'alimentation des hommes dans les camps: manuel pratique preparé par le Commissariat de Price Brothers and Co. Limited à la demande et avec la collaboration du Département forestier de la Canadien Pulp and Paper Association,* Montreal: Printed by Garden City Press, Gardenvale, Quebec, for Woodlands Section, Canadian Pulp and Paper Association, 1937, pp 175]

COPIES: QMM (RBD TX820 F444 1937)

Rawleigh's good health guide almanac catalog 1936

For information about Rawleigh's annual almanac cookbooks and other publications, see M22.1.

Q239.1   1936

1889 1936 / Rawleigh's / Trade mark reg. U.S. Pat. Off. / good health guide / almanac catalog / [caption:] The Morning Bath / An interesting family scene from a famous Italian painting / Published by / the W.T. Rawleigh Co., Ltd. / Montreal – Winnipeg / Freeport Memphis Richmond Chester Albany Minneapolis / Denver Oakland Melbourne Wellington [cover-title]

DESCRIPTION: 24.0 × 16.0 cm   Pp 1–32   Illus black-and-orange   Paper, with image on front of a mother

bathing a baby, observed by a child, grandmother, and grandfather; stapled, and with hole punched at top left corner for hanging

CONTENTS: 1 '1912 1936 // 24 Years of Unusual Service Makes Millions of Canadians Friends' [i.e., the company opened its first Canadian factory in Winnipeg in 1912]; 2 'Facts about the 1936 Calendar Year'; 3 'Welcome Your Rawleigh Dealer'; 4, 6, 8, 10, 14, 18 January–December calendar for 1936; 5, 7, 9, 11, 13, 16, 19, 20, 24–32 publ ads, including ads for Rawleigh food products entitled 'Delightful Extracts & Flavors,' 'Food Specialties,' and 'The World's Best Spices'; 12 'Light Creamy Desserts'; 15 'The Family Nurse-Doctor'; 17 'What to Do with Cocoa'; 21 'Spicy Ways to Make Foods Tasty'; 22 'Tempting Cakes and Bread'; 23 'Jellies, Jams, Salad Dressings'

COPIES: OKQ (F5012.1936 R258)   *Private collection

NOTES: Stamped on the front face of the binding of the collector's copy is 'Fred Thompson // The Rawleigh dealer // Victoria Road, Ont.'

Recipe book

Karnak Temple, a charitable men's association in Montreal, received its charter from the Imperial Council of the Ancient Arabic Order of the Nobles in 1900. At the time of the cookbook's publication, Karnak Temple headquarters were in the Masonic Memorial Temple on Sherbrooke Street West at the corner of St Mark Street.

Q240.1   nd [about 1936]

Recipe / book / Issued by / Karnak Temple Arab Patrol / Montreal

DESCRIPTION: 20.5 × 13.0 cm   Pp [i–vi], 1–91, [i–xiii]   Paper, with image on front of a Karnak hat; stapled

CONTENTS: i tp; ii–vi ads; 1–91 recipes and ads; i–xiii ads

COPIES: OONL (TX715 R436)   *QMM (RBD ckbk 1260)

NOTES: 'Practical Recipes' is the cover-title. 'Barwick Limited, printers, Montreal' is on the outside back face of the binding. The QMM copy is inscribed on the title-page, in pencil, 'Flo. [i.e., Florence?] Feb. 1936.' The book appears to have been published about that date. The recipes are not credited with the name of the contributor.

Régals gastronomiques

For another publication from Les épiciers modernes ltée, see Q262.1, [Title unknown].

Q241.1   [1936]

Recettes, conseils, / informations pour / la ménagère / Régals / gastronomiques / [in a circle:] Magasins / E.M. / Stores

DESCRIPTION: Illus on p 4 of the office and warehouse of Les épiciers modernes ltée   Stapled

CONTENTS: 1 tp; ...; 4 'Les épiciers modernes ltée en coopération avec Magasins E-M Stores,' illus of 'Bureaux et entrepôts,' the date 1936, and the address '50 est, St-Viateur Montréal'; 5 'Les épiciers modernes ltée // Quelques notes brèves' dated Montreal, December 1936; ...

COPIES: QMM (ckbk 2227)

NOTES: According to the history on p 5, Les épiciers modernes ltée was an all-Canadian co-operative founded in May 1927 by Mr P.-E. Guilbeault. The co-operative operated as a wholesaler, importer, and manufacturer, and its members were in business under the name Magasins E.M. Stores.

The cookbook was distributed by individual stores throughout the province: The QMM copy has 'Avec les compliments de Magasin E-M Store // P.-E. Éthier, prop. // Épicier – boucher 1251 St-Zotique ...' on the front face of the binding; a bookseller reports a copy with 'Avec les compliments de Magasin E-M Store, Iberville.'

Shawinigan Falls cook book

Q242.1   [1936]

Shawinigan Falls / cook book / in aid of the / Rectory Building Fund / Compiled under the auspices of / the Ladies' Guild of the Church of St. John the Evangelist / Shawinigan Falls, Que.

DESCRIPTION: 22.0 × 14.5 cm   Pp [3–6] 7–216   Cloth

CONTENTS: 3 tp; 4 blank; 5 'Foreword' signed the Committee, December 1936; 6 photograph and history of St John the Evangelist (the first service in the church building was held in February 1901); 7 'Graces before Meals'; 8–179 recipes; 180–214 ads; 215 table of contents; 216 ad

CITATIONS: Ferguson/Fraser, p 234

COPIES: *OGU (UA s059 b22)   OONL (TX715.6 S43 1936)

NOTES: The 'Foreword' identifies the source of the recipes: 'a large circle of friends' and the '"Better Homes and Gardens" Cook Book' [an American text]. There are 'Camping and Picnic Menus' and 'Christmas Party Menus and Games for Young Children.' An errata slip is bound in before the blank leaf preceding the title-page.

What do you really know about bread?

Q243.1   copyright 1936

[An edition of *What Do You Really Know about Bread? Prepared by the Department of Applied Research, Standard Brands Limited* [cover-title], Montreal, Que.: Standard Brands Ltd, copyright 1936, 26.0 cm, pp 24, illus]

COPIES: OONL (TX769 W42 1936 fol.)

1937

Kitchen fresh ideas

Q244.1   nd [about 1937]

Kitchen fresh / ideas [cover-title]

DESCRIPTION: 7.5 × 14.5 cm   Pp [1] 2–47   Illus red-and-black on p 2 of Miracle Whip Salad Dressing, several illus col of prepared dishes, several small illus of women in various poses, illus on p 4 of Kraft Dinner and on pp 44–5 of Kraft products   Paper, with all-over pattern of prepared dishes against a grid of blue lines; stapled

CONTENTS: 1 cover-title; 2 'Fresh Every Few Days!' [information about Miracle Whip Salad Dressing]; 3 'Salads and Sandwiches You'll Love to Make ...' signed Marye Dahnke, director Home Economics Kitchen; 4 illus of package of Kraft Dinner; 5 'A Meal for Four in Nine Minutes' [i.e., Kraft Dinner]; 6–43 recipes using Miracle Whip Salad Dressing and menus; 44–5 illus of Kraft products; 46 'We Suggest Miracle Whip Salad Dressing'; 47 [inside back face of binding] 'Millions Prefer ... Miracle Whip!'

COPIES: *Private collection

NOTES: The manufacturer named on the label of the Miracle Whip bottle illustrated on p 2 is Kraft-Phenix Cheese Co. Ltd, Outremont, Montreal. The company was known in Canada by the name Kraft-Phenix Cheese Co. Ltd from 1928 to 1940, when it became Kraft Cheese Ltd. Miracle Whip was introduced to the market in 1933, and Kraft Dinner, in 1937 (information from Kraft Foods Inc., Archives Department, Morton Grove, Ill.); therefore, this undated Canadian edition was published about 1937. *Kitchen Fresh Ideas* is in the same format as Q115.6, *Cheese and Ways to Serve It*. For information about Marye Dahnke, see Q115.6.

Chatelaine 1935, p 82, cites 'Kitchen Fresh Ideas (English and French),' free upon request from Kraft-Phenix Co. The Chatelaine reference indicates that there were English- and French-language Canadian editions before 1937, possibly published about the time of the American editions of 1931 and 1933.

Q244.2 nd [about 1937]
—Produits / kitchen fresh / quelques / suggestions [cover-title]
COPIES: United States: Company collection (Kraft Foods Inc., Archives Department, Morton Grove, Ill.)
NOTES: There are photographs of Kraft Dinner on pp 3 and 44, and the product is described on p 4.

AMERICAN EDITIONS: *Kitchen Fresh Ideas,* 1931 (Kraft Foods Inc., Archives Department, Morton Grove, Ill.); [Chicago: Kraft-Phenix Cheese Corp., copyright 1933], with pages perforated so that they may be detached for filing in an index-card box (Private collection; United States: DLC, Kraft Foods Inc., Archives Department, Morton Grove, Ill.).

Rawleigh's good health guide almanac cook book 1937

For information about Rawleigh's annual almanac cookbooks and other publications, see M22.1.

Q245.1 1937
1889 1937 / Rawleigh's / Trade mark reg. U.S. Pat. Off. / good health guide / almanac cook book / [caption:] First Steps / This interesting family scene shows three generations, depicting life in a home of / southern Europe, by a leading artist of international reputation / Published by / the W.T. Rawleigh Co., Ltd. / Montreal Winnipeg Melbourne Wellington Freeport Memphis / Richmond Chester Albany Minneapolis Denver Oakland [cover-title]
COPIES: ACG AWWDM *BDEM OTYA (TX1 R38 1937)

1938

Baker, Aunt Hattie

For the titles of other cookbooks advertising Five Roses Flour, see Q58.1.

Q246.1 nd [about 1938]
Helpful / household hints / and recipes [cover-title]
DESCRIPTION: 17.5 × 13.5 cm Pp [1–28] Illus brown Paper, with image on front of Aunt Hattie Baker in foreground and, behind her, several small scenes of women performing household tasks; stapled

CONTENTS: 1 illus of Aunt Hattie Baker and 'Dedicated fondly to all of my "nieces," the housewives of Canada. Aunt Hattie Baker'; 2 ad for Five Roses Flour; 3 'Foreword' signed Aunt Hattie Baker; 4–18 'Helpful Hints,' each credited with the name and town of the contributor; 19 'A Guide to Good Cooking!' [information about, and illus of, *A Guide to Good Cooking;* the edition illustrated is one of the two copyrighted in 1938, probably Q203.2]; 20–4 'A Few Choice Recipes' selected 'from the famous 166-page Five Roses Cook Book,' i.e., Q203.2; 25 'Cooking Time and Temperature Chart,' 'Roasting Temperatures,' and 'Other Baking Temperatures'; 26–inside back face of binding 'Scrap-Book Notes'; outside back face book-order coupon for 'Five Roses Cook Book' and 'Printed in Canada'
CITATIONS: BouquinsCat 212, No. 394
COPIES: *Private collection
NOTES: In the 'Foreword,' Baker states: 'In this little booklet I have gathered together and am publishing some of the best household hints and recipes that you yourselves have contributed to my column in "The Family Herald and Weekly Star [a Montreal newspaper]." ... I am offering the work with the compliments of the Lake of the Woods Milling Company, the millers of the famous Five Roses Flour.'

Baking made easy

For information about Robin Hood Flour Mills and its other cookbooks, see S16.1.

Q247.1 [copyright 1938]
Baking / made / easy [cover-title]
DESCRIPTION: 22.5 × 15.0 cm Pp [1] 2–62 [63–4] Illus Paper, with image on front of a loaf of bread being sliced; stapled
CONTENTS: 1 'Dear Madam' signed Robin Hood Flour Mills Ltd; 2 table of contents; 3 'General Instructions'; 4–61 recipes; 62–3 '"In Prairie Sunshine"' [history of Robin Hood Flour]; 64 'Recipes prepared and tested by Ruth Davison Reid, B.A. // Approved by the Chatelaine Institute // Method photographs by Arnott & Rogers // Artwork designed by Carl Mangold // Printed in Canada by Canadian Printing & Lithographing Company Limited // Baking Made Easy // Copyright by Robin Hood Flour Mills Limited 1938'
CITATIONS: Bly
COPIES: ACG BKOM *NSWA OFERWM (A1977 .122.13)

NOTES: The introductory text for 'Bread' on p 5 is signed Evangeline. Ruth Reid, who is credited on p 64 with preparing and testing the recipes for *Baking Made Easy,* also tested the recipes in Q285.1, *Ration Recipes.* The Canadian Printing and Lithographing Co. and the headquarters of Robin Hood Flour Mills Ltd were in Montreal. The artist, Carl Mangold, was born in 1901.

'Moose Jaw News' in Robin Hood's in-house magazine *Grist* (February 1939), p 23, refers to the international reach of *Baking Made Easy:* 'Of the several thousand copies of our cook book, "Baking Made Easy," that we have distributed in the recent months, the two that have gone the greatest distance are those to Umtata, Transkei, South Africa, and also the Gold Coast Colony, South Africa ... the Gold Coast Colony letter was from a General and Produce Merchant interested in distributing our flour in that territory.' In the same issue of *Grist,* p 30, 'Moncton News' tells of a lady whose house had burned down and who is reported to have written immediately to request a replacement copy of *Baking Made Easy.* In an article about *Ration Recipes* in the June 1943 issue of *Grist, Baking Made Easy* is referred to as 'our famous cook book.'

In 'New Exhibitor at Ontario Fairs Succeeds by Using Exact Methods' by Evangeline (clipping from unidentified magazine or newspaper, about 1940), Mrs W.E. (Lillian) Williamson extols the 'clearly defined instructions' for the baking of bread in *Baking Made Easy.* She was soon winning prizes for her bread at fairs. (Mrs W.E. Williamson is the aunt of Mary F. Williamson, credited in this bibliography's Acknowledgments for her assistance.)

The BKOM copy lacks its binding. The citation for the 1938 edition in Powers/Stewart, p 292 (Bibliography), may refer to Q247.1 or Q247.2.

Q247.2 [copyright 1938]
—Baking / made / easy [cover-title]
DESCRIPTION: 23.0 × 15.0 cm Pp [1] 2–62 [63–4] Illus Paper, with image on front of a loaf of bread being sliced; stapled
CONTENTS: Inside front face of binding label with text that begins, 'Baking Made Easy is not an ordinary advertising Cook Book ...' signed Robin Hood Flour Mills Ltd, Moose Jaw, Saskatoon, Calgary, Vancouver, Winnipeg, Toronto, Quebec, Moncton, and Montreal (the last-cited city is in the largest typeface); 1 'Dear Madam' signed Robin Hood Flour Mills Ltd; 2 'Table of Contents'; 3 'General Instructions'; 4–61 recipes; 62–3 '"In Prairie Sunshine"' [history of Robin Hood Flour]; 64 'Recipes prepared and tested by Ruth Davison Reid, B.A. // Approved by the Chatelaine

Institute // Method photographs by Arnott & Rogers // Artwork designed by Carl Mangold // Baking Made Easy // Copyright by Robin Hood Flour Mills Limited 1938 // Printed in Canada'
COPIES: OONL (TX765 R45 1938) *Private collection
NOTES: Page 64 differs from p 64 in Q247.1: here there is no 'Printed in Canada by Canadian Printing & Lithographing Company Limited' after Mangold's name; instead, 'Printed in Canada' appears after the copyright date.

'"In Prairie Sunshine"' offers the following history of Robin Hood Flour: 'In 1909 a little mill on the banks of Thunder Creek in Moose Jaw, Saskatchewan, began to turn out a flour named after the great English hero – Robin Hood. Its daily output was about 150 barrels. Today Robin Hood mills can supply more than a third of the flour used by all the people in the Dominion of Canada.'

Q247.3 [copyright 1938]
—Cuissons / faciles [cover-title]
DESCRIPTION: 23.0 × 15.0 cm Pp [1] 2–62 [63–4] Illus Paper, with image on front of loaf of bread being sliced; stapled
CONTENTS: Inside front face of binding label with text that begins, 'Notre livre de recettes intitulé "Cuissons faciles" n'est pas un simple livre de publicité' signed Robin Hood Flour Mills Ltd, Moose Jaw, Saskatoon, Calgary, Vancouver, Winnipeg, Toronto, Quebec, Moncton, and Montreal (the last-cited city is in the largest typeface); 1 letter to 'Madame' signed Robin Hood Flour Mills Ltd; 2 'Table des matières'; 3 'Avant propos'; 4–61 recipes; 62–3 'Dans les prairies de l'ouest'; 64 'Notre garantie' and at bottom, 'Cuissons faciles enregistré par Robin Hood Flour Mills, Limited 1938 Imprimé au Canada'
COPIES: *NBMOM QSFFSC
NOTES: The introductory text for 'Le pain' on p 5 is signed Evangeline.

Q247.4 [reprint, 1941]
—Baking / made / easy [cover-title]
DESCRIPTION: 22.5 × 15.0 cm Pp [1] 2–62 [63–4] Illus Paper, with image on front of a loaf of bread being sliced; metal spiral
CONTENTS: 1 'Dear Madam' signed Robin Hood Flour Mills Ltd; 2 table of contents; 3 'General Instructions'; 4–61 recipes; 62–3 '"In Prairie Sunshine"'; 64 'Dear Robin Hood User:' signed Evangeline, and at bottom, 'Copyright by Robin Hood Flour Mills Limited, 1938 Reprinted 1941'
CITATIONS: Ferguson/Fraser, p 233, reproduction on p 76 of illus from the book, illus col on p 80 of closed volume

COPIES: SSWD   *Private collection
NOTES: The Ferguson/Fraser reference does not specify the 1941 reprint, but the illustration shows the metal spiral binding of the reprint, rather than the staples of 1938 (Q247.1).

Q247.5 [reprint, 1941]
—Cuissons / faciles [cover-title]
DESCRIPTION: With image on front of a loaf of bread being sliced; metal spiral
CONTENTS: First page letter to 'Madame' signed Robin Hood Flour Mills Ltd, Montreal and Quebec, Quebec; ...; last page letter to 'Madame' signed Evangéline, Service de l'art culinaire, and 'Tous droits réservés par Robin Hood Flour Mills Limited, 1938 // Réimprimé 1941'
CITATIONS: BouquinsCat 229, No. 354
COPIES:* Private collection
NOTES: The private collector's copy belonged originally to her mother, who lived in Quebec City.

Hostess delights

For the titles of other cookbooks by the same company, see Q139.1.

Q248.1   nd [about 1938]
Hostess / delights / by / Colman-Keen (Canada) Limited / Montreal
DESCRIPTION: 21.0 × 14.5 cm   Pp [i–ii], [1] 2–32, [i–ii]   Tp illus col of a stylized food trolley, illus   Paper, with image on front of a woman standing behind a food trolley; stapled
CONTENTS: i–ii gummed leaf with perforations marking fourteen labels for 'Mustard Pickles'; 1 tp; 2 'Table of Contents'; 3 'Foreword'; 4–5 'Table Service'; 6–7 'Hors d'Oeuvres'; 8 'Soups'; 9 'Fish'; 10–11 'Meats'; 12–17 'Salads and Dressings'; 18–22 'Sandwiches'; 23–4 'Left Overs'; 25–9 'Pickles'; 30 'Kitchen Secrets'; 31–2 'Medicinal'; i–ii gummed leaf with perforations marking fourteen labels for 'Pickles'
COPIES: MBDHM   MCM   OGU (CCC TX715.6 H67) OONL (TX819 M87 H67 1920z, 2 copies)   OTMCL (641.5971 H39 No. 121)   *Private collection
NOTES: In the 'Foreword' the publisher refers to 'the many favourable comments we have received regarding former editions of our cook book' (probably Q167.1, *Salad Secrets*, or Q193.1, *Keen's Cook Book*), and says that the recipes in *Hostess Delights* 'have been sent to [the company] by women all over Canada.'
A Keen's Mustard advertisement in the April 1938

issue of *National Home Monthly* offers *Hostess Delights* for 'free.' The appearance of the cookbook is consistent with publication in about 1938. *Hostess Delights* continued to be presented to the public in the June 1942 issue of *Chatelaine*, p 54.

Q248.2 nd
—[An edition of *Les délices de l'hôtesse*, Montreal: Colman-Keen (Canada) Ltd, nd, pp 32, illus]
CITATIONS: BouquinsCat 228, No. 277

Martin, Rita [pseudonym]

For the history of Robin Hood Flour Mills Ltd and its other cookbooks, see S16.1. From about 1938, Rita Martin (easy to say in English and French) was the fictional character used to promote Robin Hood Flour, and the person considered to be the Canadian Rita was the home service director at the Montreal headquarters, who presided over the Canadian Rita Martin Test Kitchen there (the American Rita Martin Test Kitchen was in Minneapolis). In 1938, Robin Hood Flour Mills Ltd also used the name Evangeline; see Q247.1, Baking Made Easy. In addition to Q249.1, Simplified Method for Making Refrigerator Sweet Dough, Rita Martin is credited as the author of the following books: Q295.1, Favourite Rita Martin Robin Hood Recipes; Q296.1, Bread Baking Made Easy; Q302.1, 12 New Recipes for the Modern Homemaker; and Q306.1, Robin Hood Prize Winning Recipes. Her name is also associated with Q308.1, Velvet Cake and Pastry Recipes.

Other books bearing the Rita Martin name, but not included in this bibliography because they have too few pages or were published outside the bibliography's time period, are: Cooking School Featuring Rita Martin Recipes, nd, pp 14 (OONL); Cooking School Featuring Recipes by Rita Martin, nd [about 1953], pp 20 (OGU, 2 copies, both inscribed 1953 on the binding); The Velvet Touch, nd [1950s] (see notes at Q308.1); Robin Hood Mix Magic: Exciting New Ways to Use Robin Hood Mixes, nd [1960s?] (OONL).

In the mid-1940s, Rex Woods, a Toronto artist, was commissioned to paint a portrait of the fictitious Rita Martin, to be used in promotional material. A photograph of the painting, held up by a company employee, illustrates the article '"Rita Martin" Painting Hung in Minneapolis: Home Service Bureau Personality Portrayed on Canvas by Artist Rex Wood [sic] for Robin Hood' in the company's in-house magazine Grist (February 1947), p 4. The article refers to the painting as a 'composite portrait' or 'picturization of ... Rita Martin,' which had been brought from Canada to hang on the wall outside the office of the company's president, Charles Ritz (for information about Ritz, a Canadian citizen, see S16.1). According to the article, the painting was 'originally prepared for the Canadian Sales Department' and 'may soon find its way into the promotional programs of the United States Sales Divisions.' Rex Woods's image of Rita Martin (pl 13) is reproduced in several cookbooks; for example, Q302.1 and Q306.1. The artist's papers are at OTRM, and it is possible that further information about the portrait may be found there.

The identity of the person(s) behind the pseudonym Rita Martin in Canada is uncertain for the early days; however, issues of Grist *record some developments. On 15 September 1947 Miss Dorothy Shantz became Rita when she was appointed director of the Home Service Department in Montreal (appointment announced in Autumn 1947 issue, p 25; her photograph in Holiday issue, 1947, p 21). Before her appointment, she had graduated from the University of Toronto with a BA in household economics in 1933, done post-graduate studies at Columbia University in New York City, worked at New York's Montefiore Hospital, and then was a nutrition consultant for the Toronto Department of Health (file for Dorothy Margaret or Marguerite Shantz at OTUAR, A73-0026, Box 407, file 74; the OTUAR file also contains family information). About the time of Shantz's appointment with Robin Hood, a new Rita Martin Test Kitchen was built in Montreal. Two photographs of the new kitchen and a description of its special features (including built-in shelves for Robin Hood cookbooks and framed colour spreads 'from our cook book' on the wall) are in* Grist *(Autumn 1948), p 8. In 1948 Miss Jeannette Albert, home economist for the Quebec Division, resigned her position and was replaced by Miss Henriette Rouleau, a graduate of Laval University (Holiday issue 1948, p 27); Frances Marceau became a 'new member of the Home Service Department (same issue, p 19). Miss Albert later returned to work for the company in 1950 (the Fall 1950 issue, p 13, describes Shantz as assisted by the newly appointed Miss Jeanette [sic] Albert and by Miss Irene Lahoud). At a Robin Hood cooking school in Moncton, New Brunswick, Shantz presided while Muriel Bellefleur demonstrated (Spring 1950, p 31). Shantz left her job as Rita Martin before 14 January 1952, when Frances Little took over (personal communication with Frances Little, who said that Shantz then worked for Versafood Services).*

In Ontario, in the 1940s, Mrs Lereine Ballantyne was the company's most visible cookery demonstrator, but she was not considered to be Rita Martin. In 1948 she was director of the Home Service Department for the Ontario Sales Division, assisted by Betty Kirby, 'a recent addition' (Holiday issue 1948, p 33). Ballantyne received her

five-year pin at a banquet on 5 October 1948 (Holiday issue 1948, p 33), which indicates she began her employment with Robin Hood in 1943; however, a caption to a photograph in the 1951 Fall issue, p 8, indicates that her connection with the company stretches back further: 'Mrs. Lereine Ballantyne is known to Canadian women as Rita Martin's first assistant in the Dominion, as a demonstrator and home economics lecturer, as a writer (she's authored two books), and, in Robin Hood's Ontario Division, she's often called "chief salesman." Mrs. Ballantyne got her college degree in Toronto where she now lives. From 1938 to 1943 she toured Canada writing features on Robin Hood Flour.' Ballantyne also appears in other photographs in Grist, *taken of various Robin Hood Cooking School classes; one, of an Ottawa class, shows her on stage with Mrs Violet Scriver, 'a newcomer to the Home Service Department' (Holiday issue, 1950, p 13). Ballantyne is credited in an issue of* Grist *with developing the recipes in a 1943 Robin Hood booklet, Q285.1,* Ration Recipes *(for further information, see that entry). According to the on-line database of 'Canada's Early Women Writers' at Simon Fraser University, Lereine Katherine Hoffman (Chesley, Ont., 6 October 1890–16 November 1962, Hamilton, Ont.) married Robert Ballantyne on 14 June 1915, had three children (Bruce, Thomas, and Harley), and, after being widowed in 1920, turned to editing and writing to support herself and her children. She lived in Weston, 1920–41; in Toronto, 1941–56; and in Hamilton, 1956 until her death. Her father was Joseph Hoffman; her mother, Catherine Hoffman, née Smith.*

After the period covered by this bibliography, Rita Martin's shoes were filled by Frances Little, 14 January 1952–31 May 1961. Little was followed by Vivian Merrill, at least until April 1968 (she is home service director in that issue of Grist); *born Vivian Narsted, she graduated from McGill University with a degree in home economics in 1949. Other women associated with the Montreal Rita Martin Test Kitchen include the home economists Jacqueline April (Christmas 1962 issue of* Grist) *and Cecile Hamel (March 1966 and Pre-holiday issue, 1968).*

I surveyed issues of Grist *in the archives of Robin Hood Multifoods Inc., Markham, Ontario, and in the collection of a former employee.*

Q249.1 [copyright 1938]
Simplified method for making / Refrigerator Sweet Dough / (will keep fresh and sweet in the refrigerator for 7 full days) / with 4 varied and delicious recipes / by / Rita Martin / Director, Home Service Department / Robin Hood Flour Mills Limited / [caption:] Use this easy new

kitchen-tested way for making and / baking tasty, economical sweet dough. The "batch" will / keep fresh in any good refrigerator one whole week ... / will serve 4–6 persons four times!

DESCRIPTION: 23.0 × 15.0 cm   Pp [1] 2–24   Tp illus of a father and daughter watching mother mix ingredients in a bowl at a kitchen table, illus   Paper, with image on front of four baked variations of the basic recipe; stapled

CONTENTS: Inside front face of binding 'Baking Success Depends Primarily on Flour' signed Robin Hood Flour Mills Ltd, Vancouver, Calgary, Moose Jaw, Saskatoon, Winnipeg, Humberstone, Toronto, Montreal, Quebec, and Moncton, and 'Special note – The entire contents of this book, both text and photos, is original material of which copyright is registered in Canada.'; 1 tp; 2–3 'All the Family Will Be "Sweet" on These Sweet-Dough Hot Breads' signed Rita Martin; 4 'Step-by-Step Directions for Making Basic Recipe for Refrigerator Sweet Dough' [i.e., introductory text]; 5–12 'Simplified Method for Making Refrigerator Sweet Dough' [i.e., twenty-two numbered and illustrated steps]; 13–24 'Variations' (Pan Buns, 13–15; Fan Tans, 16–18; Jelly Braid, 19–21; Hungarian Coffee Cake, 22–4); inside back face 'Copyright by Robin Hood Flour Mills Limited, 1938 // Printed in Canada'

COPIES: *Private collection

NOTES: The cover-title is 'Refrigerator Sweet Dough Recipe.' The title-page and text are printed in brown and black. Only this edition has an illustration on the title-page.

Q249.2   nd

—Simplified method for making / Refrigerator / Sweet Dough / (will keep fresh and sweet in the refrigerator for 7 full days) / with 4 varied and delicious recipes / by Rita Martin / Director, Home Service Department / Robin Hood Flour Mills Limited / Use this easy new kitchen-tested way for making and baking tasty, / economical sweet dough. The "batch" will keep fresh in any good / refrigerator one whole week ... will serve 4–6 persons four times!

DESCRIPTION: 23.0 × 15.0 cm   Pp [1] 2–23 [24] Illus   Paper, with image on front of four baked variations of the basic recipe; stapled

CONTENTS: 1 tp; 2–3 'All the Family Will Be "Sweet" on These Sweet-Dough Hot Breads' [unsigned]; 4 'Step-by-Step Directions for Making Basic Recipe for Refrigerator Sweet Dough' [i.e., introductory text]; 5–11 'Simplified Method for Making Refrigerator Sweet Dough' [i.e., nineteen numbered and illustrated steps];

12–23 'Variations' (Pan Buns, 12–14; Fan Tans, 15–17; Jelly Braid, 18–20; Hungarian Coffee Cake, 21–3); 24 'Baking Success Depends Primarily on Flour' and at bottom, 'Special note – The entire contents of this book, both text and photos, is original material of which copyright is registered in Canada.'

COPIES: MWMM   OONL (TX765 M37, 2 copies) *Company collection (Robin Hood Multifoods Inc., Markham, Ont.)

NOTES: No copyright date is given. This edition has only nineteen numbered steps for making the dough (Q249.1 has twenty-two steps). The title-page and text are printed in red and black.

A private collector has a copy that appears to be identical to the copy in the company collection except for the style of Rita Martin's signature on the title-page: in the company collection the signature slants to the right; in the private collector's copy, the signature stands straight, slanting neither right nor left (i.e., the newer signature style found in Q249.4 and after).

Q249.3   nd

—Méthode simplifiée de pâte / sucrée / à la glacière / avec 4 recettes délicieuses / par Rita Martin / directrice, Département d'art culinaire / Robin Hood Flour Mills Limited / Utilisez cette nouvelle manière de préparer et de cuire la pâte / sucrée. Cette pâte se conservera une semaine entière dans la glacière / ... et servira 4 à 6 personnes à 4 repas différents.

DESCRIPTION: 23.0 × 15.0 cm   Pp [1] 2–23 [24]   Illus Very thin card, with image on front of four baked variations of the basic recipe; stapled

CONTENTS: 1 tp; 2–3 'La famille sera enchantée de ces pains délicieux!'; 4 'Préliminaires pour préparer' [introductory text]; 5–11 'Méthode simplifiée de la pâte sucrée à la glacière' [nineteen numbered and illustrated steps]; 12–23 'Variétés'; 24 'Base du succès' and at bottom, 'Robin Hood Flour Mills Limited Montréal et Québec // Remarque – Le contenu, texte et images, de ce livre est un document original pour lequel des droits d'auteur ont été enregistrés au Canada.'; inside back face of binding 'Imprimé au Canada'

COPIES: *OONL (TX765 M37 1940z p***)

Q249.4   nd

—Simplified method for making / Robin Hood / Sweet Dough / (will keep fresh and sweet in the refrigerator for 7 full days) / with twelve variations / by Rita Martin / Director, Home Service Department / Robin Hood Flour Mills Limited /

Use this easy new kitchen-tested way for making and baking tasty, / economical sweet dough. The "batch" will keep fresh in any good / refrigerator one whole week ... will serve 4–6 persons four times! [folio:] 1

DESCRIPTION: 23.0 × 15.0 cm Pp 1–32 Illus Paper, with images on front and back of five baked variations of the basic recipe; stapled

CONTENTS: 1 tp; 2–3 'All the Family Will Be "Sweet" on These Sweet-Dough Hot Breads' [unsigned]; 4 'Picture Index'; 5–11 'Step-by-Step Directions for Making Basic Recipe for Robin Hood Sweet Dough' [nineteen numbered steps]; 12–32 'Variations'

COPIES: *ACG   AEPMA   OONL (TX765 M38 1900z p***)

NOTES: The new title is *Simplified Method for Making Robin Hood Sweet Dough* (i.e., not 'Refrigerator Sweet Dough'). The cover-title is 'Robin Hood Sweet Dough Recipes.' The title-page now boasts twelve variations. On the title-page, 'Robin Hood Sweet Dough' is in plain, block letters; the Rita Martin signature stands straight, slanting neither right nor left. This and the following editions may have been published in the 1950s.

Q249.5 nd
—Simplified method for making / Robin Hood / Sweet Dough / (will keep fresh and sweet in the refrigerator for 7 full days) / with twelve variations / by Rita Martin / Director, Home Service Department / Robin Hood / Flour Mills Limited / Use this easy new kitchen-tested way for making and baking tasty, / economical sweet dough. The "batch" will keep fresh in any good / refrigerator one whole week ... will serve 4–6 persons four times! [folio:] 1

DESCRIPTION: 23.0 × 15.0 cm Pp 1–32 Illus Paper, with images on front and back of five baked variations of the basic recipe; stapled

CONTENTS: 1 tp; 2–3 'All the Family Will Be "Sweet" on These Sweet-Dough Hot Breads' [unsigned]; 4 'Picture Index'; 5–11 'Step-by-Step Directions for Making Basic Recipe for Robin Hood Sweet Dough' [nineteen numbered steps]; 12–32 'Variations' (Pan Buns, 12–14; Fan Tans, 15–17; Jelly Braid, 18–20; Hungarian Coffee Cake, 21–3; Swedish Tea Ring, 24–6; Butterscotch Pecan Treats, 27–9; Twirls, Butterflies, 30; Parker House Rolls, Cloverleaf Rolls, 31; Bowknots, Crescents, 32); inside back face of binding 'Special note – The entire contents of this book, both text and photos, is original material of which copyright is registered in Canada.'

COPIES: OGU (CCC TX715.6 M3757) SBIHM *Company collection (Robin Hood Multifoods Inc., Markham, Ont.)

NOTES: Unlike Q249.4, on the title-page of this edition, the letters in the words 'Robin Hood' are in a calligraphic style, as if formed by a stick pen with a broad, flat nib.

Q249.6 nd
—Méthode simplifiée de / pâte sucrée / Robin Hood / et douze recettes délicieuses / par Rita Martin / directrice, Service d'art culinaire / Robin Hood / Flour Mills Limited / Utilisez cette nouvelle manière de préparer et de cuire la pâte sucrée. / Cette pâte se conservera une semaine entière dans le réfrigérateur ... / et servira 4 à 6 personnes à 4 repas différents. [folio:] 1

DESCRIPTION: 23.0 × 15.0 cm Pp 1–32 Illus Paper, with image on front and back of five baked variations of the basic recipe; stapled

CONTENTS: 1 tp; 2–3 'Toute la famille raffolera de ces pains délicieux!'; 4 'Table alphabétique des 12 variétés'; 5–12 'Méthode simplifiée de la pâte sucrée Robin Hood' [nineteen numbered steps]; 13–32 'Variétés'

COPIES: *QMM (RBD Soeur Berthe, ckbk 464)

NOTES: Like Q249.5, on the title-page of this edition, the letters in the words 'Robin Hood' are in a calligraphic style, as if formed by a stick pen with a broad, flat nib.

Rawleigh's good health guide almanac cook book 1938

For information about Rawleigh's annual almanac cookbooks and other publications, see M22.1.

Q250.1 1938
1889 1938 / Rawleigh's / Trade mark reg[.] U[.] S[.] Pat[.] Off[.] / good health guide / almanac cook book / [caption:] The First Sewing Lesson / The third scene showing three generations in a south European home / Published by / the W.T. Rawleigh Co., Ltd. / Montreal – Winnipeg / Freeport Memphis Richmond Chester Albany Minneapolis / Denver Oakland Melbourne Wellington [cover-title]

COPIES: *BDEM   OONL (RC81 R38)   OTYA (TX1 R38 1938)

NOTES: In the trade-mark line, the intended periods were obscured in the printing process.

1938–9

Quebec, Department of Agriculture

For the titles of other cookbooks published by the Quebec Department of Agriculture, see Q48.1.

Q251.1 nd [about 1938–9]
Mangeons / plus de / légumes / Bulletin no 136 / Cent façons d'apprêter / les / légumes / Ministère de l'Agriculture / Québec [cover-title]
DESCRIPTION: Probably paper, with image extending over front and back, of a woman checking a steaming saucepan on the stove, and behind her, a table laden with vegetables; stapled
COPIES: *QQL (A38A1 P84 136)
NOTES: This booklet of 32 pages, Bulletin 136, was likely published in the same year, or a year earlier, than Q259.1, Bulletin 140, *Les volailles et les oeufs*, which is dated 1939. It could not have been published before 1937, and probably not in 1937, because there is a reference in the introductory text (headed '"Mangeons plus de légumes" // Notre santé sera meilleure') that says, 'Dans un rapport publié en 1937, la commission technique du Bureau de santé de la Société des nations ...'
Beaulieu, p 104, cites Estelle Leblanc as the author of Bulletin 136, [copyright 1937]. The QQS catalogue records *Quelques recettes pratiques; mangeons plus de légumes*, by Estelle Leblanc, Quebec Department of Agriculture, [about 1938], pp 31. The copy is missing so a comparison of the texts could not be made. It may or may not match the edition described here. Leblanc's name is also associated with a 1938 federal Department of Fisheries book, O936.1, *100 Tempting Fish Recipes*.

OTHER EDITIONS: *Mangeons plus de légumes: cent façons de les apprêter*, no. 136, ministère de l'Agriculture et de la colonisation, 1970.

1938–40

Recettes de choix qui amélioreront vos menus

For information about the Canada Starch Co., see Q47.1.

Q252.1 nd [about 1938–40]
Recettes / de choix / qui amélioreront / vos menus / Créées et réalisées par / Le service de / l'économie domestique / The / Canada Starch Company / Limited [cover-title]

DESCRIPTION: 23.0 × 15.0 cm Pp 1–16 Paper, with image on front of many prepared dishes; stapled
CONTENTS: 1–16 recipes under the headings 'Gâteaux,' 'Glaçage,' 'Desserts,' 'Tartes,' 'Pâtisseries,' 'Pains et biscuits,' 'Poisson,' and 'Divers'; inside back face of binding 'Secrets pour réussir les crêpes' and 'Fritures à la Mazola'
COPIES: *Company collection (Best Foods Canada, Toronto, Ont.)
NOTES: This book is uniform with the series of cookbooks written by Kate Aitken for Canada Starch and copyrighted 1940 (Q263.1–266.1); however, Aitken is not cited as author here. On the outside back face of the binding, there is a reference to Canadians using Canada Starch products 'au delà de 80 ans.' Since Canada Starch was founded in 1858, the cookbook was published in 1938 or later [1858 + 80 years], likely about the same time as the Aitken series.

1939

Clément, Marie-Blanche

Q253.1 1939
Le / repas d'apparat / par / Marie-Blanche Clément / maîtresse d'enseignement / ménager / Montréal / 1939
DESCRIPTION: 22.5 × 15.0 cm Pp [1–25] Paper; stapled
CONTENTS: 1 tp; 2 blank; 3–15 text under the following headings: 'Notre table,' 'Les invitations,' 'L'apéritif,' 'Le menu,' 'La mise du couvert,' 'Détails sur la mise du couvert,' 'Choses à éviter'; 16–23 'Indicateur des mets pouvant servir à chacune des parties d'un repas'; 24–5 'Tableau du service des vins'
CITATIONS: BQ 12-0974
COPIES: QMBN (2 copies: *160042 CON, TX731 C44 1939)
NOTES: The book is about entertaining and menu-planning.

The community cook book

Q254.1 [1939]
Montreal-East Community Church / The United Church of Canada / St. Cyr Avenue, Montreal-East / Minister: Rev. W.C. Mercer, B.A., B.D. / The community cook book / in aid of / Church Mortgage Fund / All recipes tested and signed
DESCRIPTION: 22.0 × 15.5 cm Pp [1] 2–88 [89–96] Paper; stapled

CONTENTS: 1 tp; 2 ad; 3 poem titled 'A Recipe for a Day'; 4 ad; 5–85 'Tested Recipes'; 86–8 'Kitchen Wisdom' [i.e., tables and measures]; 89 table of contents; 90–6 blank for 'Additional Recipes'
COPIES: QMM (RBD ckbk 1841)   *Private collection
NOTES: The cover-title is '... The Community Cook Book // Published under auspices of the Ladies' Aid Society 1939.' In 1939 no eyebrows would have been raised by the recipe name Copper Indians (p 61), a racial description for a brownie-like sweet.

Favorite recipes

Q255.1   1939
Favorite / recipes / 1939 / The Unity Group / of the / St. Johns United Church, / St. Johns, Que. [cover-title]
DESCRIPTION: 23.0 × 15.0 cm   Pp [1] 2–66   Very thin card; stapled
CONTENTS: 1 'Foreword'; 2 ad; 3–64 'Our Best Recipes' credited with the name of the contributor and ads; 65 'Miscellaneous'; 66 ad and 'Index' [i.e., table of contents]
COPIES: *OONL (TX715.6 F387 1939 p***)
NOTES: The 'Foreword' informs the reader, '*Our special economy recipes we have marked by a star.' St Johns is now known as St Jean.

The OONL volume has two copies of the last leaf, pp 65–6, bound in. The front face of the binding is inscribed in ink, 'Joan Shepherd. from Dorothy Pratt. Christmas 1939.'

How to use your McClary Range

For other books about cooking with McClary appliances and for information about the company, see O162.1.

Q256.1   [1939]
How to use / your McClary / Range / McClary / since 1847 [English cover-title on one face of binding] Comment vous / servir de / votre poêle / McClary / McClary / since 1847 [French cover-title on other face]
DESCRIPTION: 20.5 × 12.5 cm   Pp [English:] [1] 2–24, [French:] [1] 2–24   Illus   Paper; stapled at top edge
CONTENTS: [English:] 1 introductory text and 'General Steel Wares Limited // Branches across Canada // 8-39'; 2 'The Cooking Elements'; 3 'The Cooking Top'; 4 'The Oven'; 5 'The Oven Heat Control'; 6 'Special Advantages of Heat Control'; 7 'The Broiler'; 8 'High Shelf,' 'Warming Cabinet,' 'Utility Drawer,'

'Care of the Range,' and 'Care of the Smokeless Broiling Grid'; 9–10 'Baking Suggestions'; 11–12 'Temperature and Time Chart for Baking'; 13 'Roasting'; 14 'Temperature and Time Chart for Roasting'; 15 'Deep Fat Frying'; 16 'Whole Meal Cooking'; 17 'Meat Dishes'; 18 'Standard Soup Stocks'; 19–22 'Cakes, Cookies and Pies'; 23–4 'Bread, Muffins, Rolls and Pastry'; [French:] 1 introductory text and 'General Steel Wares Limited // Succursales à travers le Canada // 8-39'; 2 'Les éléments de cuisson'; 3 'La surface de cuisson'; 4 'Le four'; 5 'Le régulateur de chaleur du four'; 6 'Avantages spéciaux du régulateur de chaleur'; 7 'Le grilleur'; 8 'Tablette supérieure,' 'Réchaud,' 'Tiroir-utilité,' 'Soins à donner au poêle,' and 'Soin à prendre du nouveau gril'; 9–10 'Pâtisserie'; 11–12 'Tableau de température et de temps pour cuire au four'; 13 'Rôtissage'; 14 'Tableau de température et de temps pour le rôtissage'; 15 'Friture dans la graisse'; 16 'Cuisson d'un repas entier'; 17 'Plats de viande'; 18 'Bouillons ordinaires'; 19–22 'Gâteaux, gâteaux secs et tartes'; 23–4 'Pain ordinaire, brioches, petits pains et pâtisserie'
COPIES: *Private collection
NOTES: This edition is for cooking with the McClary Electric Range. The information on p 2, for example, concerns the electric cooking elements. The printer's mark on p 1, '8-39,' indicates that the book was published in 1939. No place of publication is cited, but the head office of General Steel Wares was in Montreal at this time.

Q256.2   [1940]
—How to use / your McClary / Range / McClary / since 1847 [English cover-title on one face of binding] Comment vous / servir de / votre poêle / McClary / McClary / since 1847 [French cover-title on other face]
DESCRIPTION: 20.0 × 12.5 cm   Pp [English:] [1] 2–24, [French:] [1] 2–24   Illus   Paper; stapled at top edge
CONTENTS: [English:] 1 introductory note and 'General Steel Wares Limited // Branches across Canada // 3-40'; 2 'The Burners'; 3 'The Cooking Top'; 4 'The Oven'; 5 'The Oven Heat Control'; 6 'Special Advantages of Heat Control'; 7 'The Broiler'; 8 'Utility Drawer,' 'Care of the Range' and 'Care of the Smokeless Broiling Grill'; 9–12 'Baking'; 13–14 'Roasting'; 15 'Deep Fat Frying'; 16 'Whole Meal Cooking'; 17 'Meat Dishes'; 18 'Standard Soup Stocks'; 19–22 'Cakes, Cookies and Pies'; 23–4 'Bread, Muffins, Rolls and Pastry'; [French:] 1 introductory note and 'General Steel Wares Limited // Succursales à travers le Canada // 3-40'; 2 'Les brûleurs'; 3 'La surface de cuisson'; 4 'Le four'; 5 'Le régulateur de chaleur

du four'; 6 'Avantages spéciaux du régulateur de chaleur'; 7 'Le grilleur'; 8 'Tiroir – utilité,' 'Soins à donner au poêle,' and 'Soin à prendre du nouveau gril'; 9–12 'Pâtisserie'; 13–14 'Rôtissage'; 15 'Friture dans la graisse'; 16 'Cuisson d'un repas entier'; 17 'Plats de viande'; 18 'Bouillons ordinaires'; 19–22 'Gâteaux, gâteaux secs et tartes'; 23–4 'Pain ordinaire, brioches, petits pains et pâtisserie'
COPIES: *Private collection
NOTES: This edition is for cooking with the McClary Gas Range. The information on p 2, for example, concerns the gas burners. The printer's mark on p 1, '3-40,' indicates that the book was published in 1940. No place of publication is cited.

Q256.3   [6th ed., 1943]
—How to use / your McClary / Range / McClary / since 1847 [English cover-title on one face of binding] Comment vous / servir de / votre poêle / McClary / McClary / since 1847 [French cover-title on other face]
COPIES: *OONL (Reserve Z7916 A7 H62 No. 05)
NOTES: OONL describes the volume as having 23 pp of English text and 23 pp of French text. '6th edition 3-43' and '6ème édition 3-43' are at the bottom of the page with the introductory note in each case.

Q256.4   nd [1940s]
—How to use / your / McClary / Range [English cover-title on one face of binding] Comment vous / servir de votre / poêle / McClary [French cover-title on other face]
DESCRIPTION: 20.5 × 13.5 cm   Pp [English:] [1] 2–14, [French:] [1] 2–14   Illus   Paper, with same image on front and back of roast beef on a platter; stapled
CONTENTS: [English:] 1 'How to Use Your Range' [i.e., introductory text] and 'General Steel Wares Limited Montreal Toronto London Winnipeg Calgary Edmonton Vancouver // 6188-B'; 2 'How to Use the Cooking Top'; 3 'General Instructions'; 4–top 5 'How to Use the Oven'; mid 5 'How to Use the Storage Drawer'; mid 5–top 6 'To Bake or Roast'; mid 6–8 'Automatic Controls'; 9 'How to Use the Broiler'; 10 'How to Use the Range'; 11–12 'How to Care for Your Range'; 13 'Temperature and Time Chart for Roasting'; 14 'Deep Fat Frying' and 'Table of Measures and Weights'; [French:] 1 'Apprenez à bien connaître votre poêle' [introductory text] and 'General Steel Wares Limited Montréal Toronto London Winnipeg Calgary Edmonton Vancouver'; 2 'Utilisation des éléments de surface'; 3 'Instructions générales'; 4–top 5 'Utilisation du four'; mid 5 'Utilisation du tiroir à ustensiles'; mid 5–top 6 'Pâtisserie et rôtis'; mid 6–8 'Commandes

automatiques'; 9 'Utilisation du grilloir'; 10 'Comment obtenir le maximum de rendement'; 11–12 'Entretien de votre poêle'; 13 'Température et durée de cuisson des rôtis'; 14 [first heading illegible, but about deep fat frying] and 'Correspondance des mesures et des poids'
COPIES: OGU (CCC TX715.6 H688)   *Private collection
NOTES: This edition includes general advice about cooking, but no recipes. The guarantee on the inside front face of the binding of the OGU copy has the space for 'Date of delivery' filled in as 'Jan 11/57.'

Q256.5   nd [about 1948 or later]
—How to use your / McClary / Range .... / [4-paragraph introductory note] / General Steel Wares / Limited / Montreal Toronto London / Winnipeg Calgary Vancouver
DESCRIPTION: 20.5 × 14.0 cm   Pp [1] 2–23 [24]   Illus   Paper, with image on front of roast beef and potatoes on a platter, and image on back of strawberry-topped cake and cherry pie or tart; stapled
CONTENTS: 1 tp and introductory note; 2–3 'How to Use the Cooking Top'; 4–5 'How to Use the Oven'; 6–top 7 'How to Use the Broiler'; bottom 7 'How to Use the Warming Oven'; 8 'How to Use the Storage Drawer'; 9 'How to Use the Range'; 10–11 'How to Care for Your Range'; 12 'Temperature and Time Chart for Roasting'; 13 'Deep Fat Frying' and 'Table of Measures and Weights'; 14–15 'Meats'; 16–17 'Casserole Dishes'; 18–19 'Quick Breads'; 20–1 'Pies, Puddings'; 22–3 'Cakes, Cookies'; 24 'Over 100 Years of Progress'
COPIES: *Private collection
NOTES: This edition is for cooking with a gas range. Since McClary's was founded in 1847, this edition was published about 1948 or slightly later (1847 + 'Over 100 Years of Progress').

Q256.6   nd [late 1940s]
—How to use your / McClary / Range .... / [4-paragraph introductory note] / General Steel Wares / Limited / Montreal Toronto London / Winnipeg Calgary Vancouver
DESCRIPTION: 20.5 × 14.0 cm   Pp [1] 2–27 [28]   Illus   Paper, with image on front of roast beef and potatoes on a platter, and image on back of strawberry-topped cake and cherry pie or tart; stapled
CONTENTS: 1 tp; 2–3 'How to Use the Cooking Top'; 4–5 'How to Use the Oven'; 6–7 'How to Use the Automatic Timer and Selector Switch on De Luxe Models'; 8–mid 9 'How to Use the Broiler'; bottom 9 'How to Use the Warming Oven'; 10 'How to Use the Storage Drawer'; 11 'How to Use the Range'; 12–13

'How to Care for Your Range'; 14 'Temperature and Time Chart for Roasting'; 15 'Deep Fat Frying' and 'Table of Measures and Weights'; 16–19 'Meats'; 20–1 'Quick Breads'; 22–3 'Pies, Puddings'; 24–5 'Cakes, Cookies'; 26–7 publ ads; 28 'General Steel Wares Limited Warranty' [not dated]

COPIES: *Private collection

NOTES: This edition is for cooking with an electric range.

International cook book

For later cookbooks from the same church, see Q290.1, Saguenay Cook Book, and Q318.1, Saguenay Cook Book IV.

Q257.1 1939

International cook book / Compiled by / the Womens Association / of the / Arvida First United Church / Arvida, P.Q. / November, 1939

DESCRIPTION: 21.5 × 17.5 cm   Pp [i–vi], 1–57 [58, corner of page on which folio possibly printed is torn off]   A few small illus   Limp oil cloth; stapled

CONTENTS: i tp; ii blank; iii 'To Be a Good Cook'; iv blank; v 'Index' [i.e., table of contents]; vi blank; 1–58 text

COPIES: *OGU (CCC TX715.6 I57)

NOTES: The leaves are printed and numbered on the rectos only; the versos are blank and not included in the pagination. The recipes are credited with the name of the contributor and her nationality. Most contributors describe themselves as Canadian, but some are Finnish, Russian, German, Slovakian, Ukrainian, Swiss, English (many), Danish, American, and Scotch. There are also some Japanese and Chinese recipes bearing decidedly Western names, such as Carter. The town of Arvida (now part of the city of Jonquière) came into existence when the Aluminum Company of Canada (now called Alcan) established an aluminium smelter there in 1926. The international flavour of the cookbook reflects the cultural make-up of the people who came to work at the plant.

The Maritime cook book

Q258.1 [1939]

The / Maritime / cook book / Maritime Women's Club / of Montreal, Inc.

DESCRIPTION: 22.0 × 15.0 cm   Pp [1] 2–127 [128]   Tp illus of the symbols of the three Maritime provinces   Cloth, with the tp symbols on front

CONTENTS: 1 tp; 2 untitled verse by Amy Bissett England; 3 'Foreword' signed Florence Russell Lapraik, president, Mary Duncan Mitchell, chairman Special Committee, and six other names, dated December 1939; 4 'Our Appreciation' [list of advertisers]; 5 table of contents; 6 weights and measures; 7 cooking time; 8–110 recipes credited with the name of the contributor; 111–15 ads; 116 'Maritime Apple Calendar'; 117–27 ads; 128 printer's name, 'Church, Baines & Company Montreal'

CITATIONS: BQ 24-4802

COPIES: NBMOU (TX715 M37)   *OONL (TX715.6 M37 1939 p***)   OONMM (TX715 M37 1939)   QMBN (120106 CON)   QWSMM

NOTES: The 'Foreword' states the purpose of the book: 'To commemorate the visit of Their Majesties King George VI and Queen Elizabeth, the Maritime Women's Club of Montreal is publishing this book. It has been the aim of the editors, to use as many recipes as possible identified with old days, and new, in the Maritime Provinces. They have also been so fortunate as to receive recipes in use at Government House, Ottawa, and furnished by Her Excellency, the Lady Tweedsmuir. Mrs. Franklin D. Roosevelt, wife of the President of the United States has also been kind enough to contribute.' The 'Foreword' also expresses the hope that the book will be useful during wartime conditions when 'the first line of defense lies in the kitchen.' There is a recipe for War Cake on p 67, and, on p 74, recipes for Scones and Pineapple Squares served at Government House when George and Elizabeth visited on 15 June 1939. The book also includes recipes sent in by the Women's Institute Branch of the Department of Agriculture of Prince Edward Island.

The QWSMM copy is stamped 'Feb 1940' on the title-page.

Quebec, Department of Agriculture

For the titles of other cookbooks published by the Quebec Department of Agriculture, see Q48.1.

Q259.1 1939

Les volailles / et les oeufs / recettes culinaires / préparées par / le Service de / l'économie / domestique / Bulletin no 140 / Distribué par le / Service de la publicité / Ministère de / l'Agriculture, / Québec / 1939 [cover-title]

DESCRIPTION: 23.0 × 15.0 cm   Pp 1–32   Illus on outside back face of binding of 'Manière de brider une poule, un poulet ou un chapon'   Paper, with image on front of a bowl of eggs, a steaming saucepan, and various fowl; stapled

CONTENTS: 1–6 'Les volailles'; 7–32 'Recettes culinaires'
CITATIONS: Beaulieu, p 104
COPIES: *QMBN (189630 CON)
NOTES: The text includes information about 'Dindes – Dindons – Dindonneaux,' 'Canes, canards, canetons,' 'Oies,' and 'Pigeons – Pigeonneaux.' Beaulieu lists Bulletin 140 as in série 4.

Q259.2 1946
—Les volailles / et les oeufs / recettes culinaires / Bulletin / n° 140 / Ministère / de / l'Agriculture / Québec / 1946 [cover-title]
DESCRIPTION: 22.5 × 15.0 cm   Pp 1–32   Illus on outside back face of binding of 'Manière de brider une poule, un poulet ou un chapon'   Paper, with image on front of a bowl of eggs, a steaming saucepan, and – all in a row – a turkey, goose, chicken, duck, and pigeon; stapled
CONTENTS: 1–6 'Les volailles'; 7–22 'Recettes culinaires'; 23–mid 26 information about 'Les oeufs'; mid 26–32 egg recipes
CITATIONS: Beaulieu, p 104   Bédard, pp 3–4
COPIES: *OONL (C.O.P. COP.QU.8128, 2 copies)
NOTES: Bédard says, 'Cette petite brochure décrit entre autre la valeur nutritive de la volaille, sa cuisson, quelques recettes appropriées aux différentes sortes de volaille, ainsi que la manière de brider une poule, un poulet ou un chapon.'

Rawleigh's 50th anniversary good health guide almanac cook book

For information about Rawleigh's annual almanac cookbooks and other publications, see M22.1.

Q260.1 1939
Hang me up for future reference / 1889 1939 / Rawleigh's / Trade mark reg. U.S. Pat. Off. / 50th anniversary / good health guide / almanac cook book / [caption:] The boyhood farm home where W.T. Rawleigh, the founder of our business, was / raised, from where he attended school, made and sold inks and sold books – / "Deeds of Daring by Blue and Gray" – Historical Incidents of the Civil War. / Published by / the W.T. Rawleigh Co., Ltd. / Montreal Winnipeg / Freeport Memphis Richmond Chester Albany Minneapolis / Denver Oakland Melbourne Wellington / The largest industries of their kind in the world [cover-title]
DESCRIPTION: 24.0 × 16.5 cm   Pp [1–2] 3–32   Illus orange-and-black, illus   Paper, with image on front of the boyhood home and portrait of W.T. Rawleigh; stapled, and with hole punched at top left corner for hanging
CONTENTS: 1 '50 Golden Years Service & Progress'; 2–3 '50 Years Service Pioneering and Progress'; 4 'Rawleigh's Zodiacal Planting Chart'; 5 'The 1939 Calendar Year'; 6 'Time Savers for Busy Cooks'; 7 'Attractive and Corrective Salads'; 8 'How Raw Materials Are Bought'; 9 'Interesting Rare Packages'; 10 January, February; 11 'Health Should Be in Tune // How Vitamins and Tonics Aid Nature'; 12 March, April; 13 'Look Your Best and Be Happy!'; 14 May, June; 15 'About Diet and Laxatives'; 16 July, August; 17 '50 Years Service That Satisfies'; 18 September, October; 19 'Pies for Variety'; 20 November, December; 21 'Accidents'; 22 'Choose Your Stuffing'; 23 'Roots, Herbs, Buds, etc. for Coughs and Colds'; 24–5 'Crisp Spicy Pickles'; 26 'Some Facts about Flavors and Spices'; 27 'Chicken Fit for a King'; 28 'Cakes – New and Different'; 29 'Pork & Vegetables'; 30 'Helps in the Fight against Insects and Dirt' and 'For Better Cleansing'; 31 'Success with Livestock and Poultry'; 32 'Tortes ... Growing in Popularity'
COPIES: NBMOM OKQ (F5012 1939 R258 Special Coll)   *Private collection
NOTES: The history on pp 2–3 says that Rawleigh made his first sale of Liniment and Salve on 6 April 1889, at the age of eighteen years, and that he incorporated his business in 1895. Regarding the firm's Canadian business, it says that a factory opened in Winnipeg in 1912, and in Montreal, in 1926. By 1932, there were branches in the United States, Canada, Australia, and New Zealand. The collector's copy is stamped on the outside back face of the binding, in the space for 'Your Rawleigh Dealer': 'Ira D Rusnell / / Stouffville' [i.e., in Ontario].

Q260.2 1939
—Suspendez-moi pour référence future / 1889 1939 / Guide de bonne sante / du 50ieme anniversaire / Rawleigh / Trade mark reg. U.S. Pat. Off. / almanach livre de cuisine / [caption:] Maison paternelle de cultivateur ou W.T. Rawleigh fut eleve, d'ou il allait a l'ecole, ou il / faisait et vendait des encres et vendait des livres – "Deeds of Daring by Blue and Gray" – / Evenements historiques de la guerre civile. / Publie par / The W.T. Rawleigh Co., Ltd. / Montreal Winnipeg / Freeport Memphis Richmond Chester Albany Minneapolis / Denver Oakland Melbourne Wellington / Les plus grandes industries de leur genre au monde [cover-title]
COPIES: OONL (RC81 G83 1939)   QPC

1939–40

Royal Household Flour basic sponge recipes

See Q55.1 for information about Ogilvie Flour Mills Co. Ltd and its other cookbooks.

Q261.1 nd [about 1939–40]
Royal / Household / Flour / basic sponge recipes / A modern / time-saving / money-saving / home baking idea [cover-title]
DESCRIPTION: 21.5 × 14.0 cm   Pp [1–16]   Illus   Paper, with image on front of baked goods; stapled
CONTENTS: 1 cover-title; 2 [inside front face of binding] untitled introductory text signed Ogilvie Flour Mills Co. Ltd, Montreal, Fort William, Winnipeg, Medicine Hat, Edmonton, and (in a smaller typeface) the names of other Canadian cities; 3 'A Modern Home Baking Idea!' and Royal Household 'Basic Sponge' Recipe; 4–14 recipes; 15 'Causes of Common Baking Failures'; 16 [outside back face] 'Published by the Ogilvie Flour Mills Co. Limited ...'
COPIES: OONL (B-18999)   *Private collection
NOTES: The text on p 2 refers to Royal Household Flour being 'chosen for use on the Royal Train which conveyed Their Majesties, King George VI and Queen Elizabeth, on their historic tour across our fair Dominion.' The cookbook was likely published not long after the royal visit, which took place in 1939.

1940

[Title unknown]

For another book from Les épiciers modernes ltée and for information about the co-operative, see Q241.1.

Q262.1 [about 1940]
[Title unknown]
DESCRIPTION: 24.5 × 17.0 cm   Pp [leaves lacking] 7–124 [leaves lacking?]   Illus portraits of P.-E. Guilbeault, directeur et gérant-général of Les épiciers modernes ltée, members of the company's Bureau de direction, and other men associated with the company   Lacks paper(?) binding; stapled
CONTENTS: 7 'Les épiciers modernes ltée en coopération avec Magasins E-M Stores' and illus portrait of Guilbeault; 8–10 illus portraits of men associated with Les épiciers modernes ltée and lists of other persons associated with the company; 11 'Magasins E-M Stores' and 'Les produits "Moderne"'; 12 ad; 13–15 'Informations pour la cuisinière' and ad on p 14;

16–17 'Le petit dictionnaire de "Cordon bleu"' [glossary from A to Z]; 18 ads; 19–86 recipes and ads; 87–8 ad; 89–124 miscellaneous household information and ads
COPIES: *QMM (RBD Soeur Berthe, ckbk 344)
NOTES: QMM dates the book [1940], later than Q241.1, *Régals gastronomiques*, which bears the printed date 1936. The librarian reports that the photographs of people associated with the co-operative look older in Q262.1 than in Q241.1 (for example, A. Laniel, P.E. Éthier, and A. Rouleau).

The incomplete volume at QMM may be the same as the following book described in the QMBN catalogue: *Cordon bleu: recettes, conseils, informations pour la ménagère*, rédigé par Monsieur P.E. Guilbeault, assisté de son secrétaire Monsieur Paul E. Leboeuf, Magasins E-M Stores, [1940], pp 128, cover-title: *Cordon bleu: livre de recettes*, one copy 'Avec la [sic] compliments de La boulangerie provinciale' (246482 CON), another copy 'Avec la [sic] compliments de R. Desmarchais, Magasins E.-M. Stores, épicier licencié, boucher' (281254 CON).

Aitken, Mrs Katherine (Kate) May, née Scott (Mrs Henry Mundell Aitken) (Beeton, Ont., 6 April 1891–11 December 1971, Mississauga, Ont.)

For information about Kate Aitken and her other cookbooks, see Q214.1. For information about the Canada Starch Co., see Q47.1.

Q263.1 [copyright 1940]
52 / baking / secrets / A different and / delicious recipe / for every week / in the year / Created and tested by / Mrs. H.M. Aitken / Canada Starch / Home Service Department [cover-title]
DESCRIPTION: 23.0 × 15.0 cm   Pp 1–16   Paper, with image on front of many plates of baked goods; stapled
CONTENTS: Inside front face of binding introductory note signed 'Kate Aitken' and 'Index' [i.e., table of contents]; 1–16 recipes; inside back face 'Cooking Gossip' and '"52 Baking Secrets" – Copyright 1940, The Canada Starch Company, Limited.'
COPIES: NSWA   OGU (CCC TX715.6 A562)   *Company collection (Best Foods Canada, Toronto, Ont.)
NOTES: The text headings are 'Bread Secrets,' 'Cookie Secrets,' 'Doughnut Secrets,' 'Fish Secrets,' 'Meat Secrets,' 'Pancake Secrets,' 'Salad Secrets,' 'Vegetable Secrets,' and 'Deep Frying in Mazola.' Canada Starch's offices were in Montreal and Toronto.

This is one of four titles by Aitken in the '52' series.

Aitken prepared the series in the Toronto offices of Canada Starch's advertising agents, Vickers and Benson, where she set up her own cooking equipment (see George Frederick Benson, *Historical Record of the Edwardsburg and Canada Starch Companies*, [Montreal: Canada Starch Co., 1959], p 188). See also the unattributed Q252.1, *Recettes de choix qui amélioreront vos menus*, which is uniform with the '52' series.

Q264.1   nd [about 1940]
52 / cakes / A different and delicious / recipe for every week / in the year / Created and tested by / Mrs. H.M. Aitken / Director / Canada Starch / Home Service Department [cover-title]
DESCRIPTION: 22.5 × 15.0 cm   Pp 1–16   Paper, with many cakes on front; stapled
CONTENTS: Inside front face of binding introductory note signed 'Kate Aitken'; 1 two cake recipes and 'Index'; 2–16 recipes; inside back face 'Cooking Gossip'
COPIES: OGU (CCC TX715.6 A563)   OONL (B-19329)   *Company collection (Best Foods Canada, Toronto, Ont.)
NOTES: On the outside back face of the binding there is a reference to 'over 80 years' of the company's policy of quality. The booklet must have been published after 1938 since the company was established in 1858 (1858 + 80 years). It was likely published in 1940, at the same time as other titles in the '52' series.

Q265.1   nd [about 1940]
52 / desserts / A different and / delicious recipe / for every week / in the year / Created and tested for / Canada Starch / Home Service Department / by / Mrs. H.M. Aitken [cover-title]
DESCRIPTION: 23.0 × 15.0 cm   Pp 1–16   Paper, with image on front of many desserts; stapled
CONTENTS: Inside front face of binding introductory text signed 'Kate Aitken' and 'Index' [i.e., table of contents]; 1–16 recipes for 'Cake Desserts,' 'Corn Starch Desserts,' 'Chilled Desserts,' 'Frozen Desserts,' 'Fruit Desserts,' 'Rice and Tapioca Desserts,' 'Steamed Desserts,' 'Upside-down Desserts,' and 'Sauces'; inside back face 'Cooking Gossip'
CITATIONS: Chatelaine Oct 1940
COPIES: OGU (CCC TX715.6 A564)   OONL (B-20190)   *Company collection (Best Foods Canada, Toronto, Ont.)
NOTES: This title in the '52' series has no date; however, there is an order form at bottom p 16 for other Canada Starch titles, including Q263.1, *52 Baking Secrets*, and Q266.1, *52 Pies*, both copyright 1940. Also,

52 Desserts was advertised in *Chatelaine* in 1940. The year of publication of *52 Desserts*, therefore, is likely 1940.

Q266.1   [copyright 1940]
52 / pies / A different and / delicious recipe / for every week / in the year / Created and tested for / Canada Starch / Home Service Department / by / Mrs. H.M. Aitken [cover-title]
DESCRIPTION: 22.5 × 15.0 cm   Pp 1–16   Paper, with image on front of many pies; stapled
CONTENTS: Inside front face of binding introductory note signed 'Kate Aitken' and 'Index' [i.e., table of contents]; 1–16 recipes; inside back face 'Cooking Gossip' and '"52 Pies" – Copyright 1940, The Canada Starch Company, Limited'
CITATIONS: Chatelaine Nov 1940, p 77
COPIES: OGU (CCC TX715.6 A565)   *Company collection (Best Foods Canada, Toronto, Ont.)
NOTES: *52 Pies* is advertised in *Chatelaine* as free with one label from a Canada Starch product.

L'économie domestique à l'école primaire 4e, 5e, 6e et 7e années

Q267.1   1940
L'économie / domestique / à l'école primaire / 4e, 5e, 6e & 7e années / [symbol of Congrégation de Notre-Dame, Montreal] Édition refondue / Québec MCMXL
DESCRIPTION: 22.0 × 14.5 cm   Pp [i–ii], [1] 2–262, [1] 2–20, [i–iii]   Illus   [$0.60, on binding]   Cloth
CONTENTS: i tp; ii 'Nihil obstat: Edgar Chouinard, pter, censor librorum. Imprimatur: Ulric Perron, V.G., Quebeci, die 28a maii 1940 … En vente: Procure des missions // rue Atwater, 1520, Montréal, – rue Saint-Joseph, 228, Québec. Institution chanoine-Beaudet // Saint-Pascal de Kamouraska, Qué. 1940'; 1–262 text; 1–20 'Supplément // Bienséance (Causeries)'; i–iii 'Table des matières' and at bottom p iii, letter from Marguerite Bourgeoys to her 'Chères enfants' as if written 240 years after her death
CITATIONS: BQ 08-0978   Lambert, T., p 92°
COPIES: *QTURA
NOTES: The text is in the following sections: 'Tenue de la maison'; 'Soin du linge'; 'Alimentation'; 'Hygiène, anatomie et physiologie'; 'Horticulture'; and 'Leçons modèles.' No author is named, but she was soeur Sainte-Marie-Vitaline (Anna Fournier, 1873–1954) (Lambert, T., p 92°); for information about her and her other books, see Q128.1. For references to earlier texts presenting lessons for different years, see Q134.1.

Q267.2 —[Another edition, 1942]
CITATIONS: Lambert, T., p 92°

Q267.3 —[Another edition, 1945]
CITATIONS: Lambert, T., p 92°

'Practo-fax' cookies

*For the titles of other cookbooks by Nulomoline Ltd, see
Q205.1.*

Q268.1 [copyright 1940]
"Practo-fax" / cookies / including crackers, biscuits,
/ flour-confections and small cakes / Practical
application / of scientific facts / Nulomoline
Limited – 1410 Stanley Street – Montreal
DESCRIPTION: 21.5 × 14.0 cm   Pp [1–2] 3–96   Tp illus
col of a cookie, illus col, illus   Very thin card, with
several photographs on front of commercial baking
scenes; stapled, and with three punched holes for
storing the book in a ring-binder
CONTENTS: 1 tp; 2 'Copyright, 1940 Nulomoline Ltd.
Montreal'; 3–90 text; 91 'Acknowledgment' that the
fly-leaves in the volume are 'Alligator Embossed
Chocolate Glassine' made by the McDowell Division
of the Glassine Paper Co., manufacturers of glassine
papers for the baking industry, and the remark that
both the fly-leaves and the text pages of the book
contain Nulomoline as a plasticizer; 92–mid 93 'Table
of Contents'; mid 93–96 'Index of Formulas' and at
bottom p 96, 'Printed in U.S.A. by John E. Weiss &
Son N.A. 72 Ltd. – 1-40–1M'
COPIES: *OONL (TX765 P73 1940 p***)
NOTES: The OONL copy is stamped on the inside
front face of the binding, 'The property of the Library
of Parliament,' and on the title-page with the Copyright Act 1931 stamp inscribed with the deposit number 1269.

Rawleigh's good health guide almanac cook book 1940

*For information about Rawleigh's annual almanac
cookbooks and other publications, see M22.1.*

Q269.1 1940
Hang me up for future reference / 1889 1940 /
Rawleigh's / Trade mark reg. U.S. Pat. Off. / good
health guide / almanac cook book / [caption:] The
Prodigal Son / From a famous oil painting /
Published by / the W.T. Rawleigh Co., Ltd. /

Montreal – Winnipeg / Freeport Memphis
Richmond Chester Albany Minneapolis / Denver
Oakland Melbourne Wellington / The largest
industries of their kind in the world [cover-title]
COPIES: ACG   *BDEM   OGU (CCC TX715.6 R38)
SWSLM

1940s

Bourassa, Jean

Q270.1 nd [about 1940s]
[An edition of *Au camp –: cuisine pratique pour la
patrouille au camp*, Saint-Viateur, Que., nd [194–?],
18.0 cm, pp 32, cover-title: 'Cuisine pratique pour la
patrouille au camp']
COPIES: OONL (TX823 B68 1940z missing)

1941

Cook book

Q271.1 1 December 1941
Ladies' Guild / Church of St. Andrew & St. George /
Baie Comeau, Que. / Cook book / Issued Dec. 1, 1941
[cover-title]
DESCRIPTION: Bound by string through two punched
holes
CONTENTS: 1st page 'Index' [i.e., table of contents]
and 'Abbreviations'; ...
COPIES: *Private collection
NOTES: The text is multigraphed. The 'Index' lists the
following contents: 'Luncheon, Casserole, Oven
Dishes, etc.,' p 1; 'Cakes,' p 33; 'Frostings,' p 50;
'Breads, Rolls,' p 52; 'Cookies, Shortbreads, Small
Cakes,' p 56; 'Puddings, etc.,' p 67; 'Salads,' p 75;
'Pickles, Relishes,' p 78; 'Soups,' p 85; 'Miscellaneous,'
p 91; and 'Last Minute Additions,' p 95.

Food and the family income

Q272.1 2nd ed., [copyright 1941]
Food and the / family income / low cost recipes /
Second edition revised / Prepared by / the
Nutrition Committee / of the / Health Service of
the Federated Agencies / of Montreal /
Philadelphia London Montreal / J.B. Lippincott
Company
DESCRIPTION: 23.0 × 15.0 cm   Pp [1–2] 3–72   Illus on
p 18 of 'Fireless Cooker'   Paper; stapled

CONTENTS: 1 tp; 2 list of members of the Nutrition Committee and '2nd edition revised // Copyright 1941 by J.B. Lippincott Company // Printed in Canada'; 3 table of contents; 4 'Unless otherwise stated recipes in this book make from 4 to 6 servings'; 5–6 'Food and Health'; 7–11 'Budgeting Our Income'; 12 'Requirements' and 'Meal Planning and Marketing'; 13 'Menus'; 14 'Summer Menu Suggestions'; 15 'Lunch and Supper Suggestions,' 'Meals Which May Be Prepared on a Single Burner Stove,' and 'Cleansers'; 16 'Abbreviations,' 'Weights and Measures,' and 'Oven Temperatures'; 17 'Cooking Hints'; 18–19 'Fireless Cooker'; 20–68 recipes; 69–70 index; 71–2 blank for 'Notes'
CITATIONS: BQ 24-4778
COPIES: QMBN (121713 CON)   *Private collection

Q272.2   2nd ed., 1945 printing
—Food and the / family income / low cost recipes / Second edition / New 1945 printing / with additions and corrections / Prepared by / the Nutrition Committee / of / Welfare Federation / Montreal / Philadelphia London Montreal / J.B. Lippincott Company
DESCRIPTION: 23.0 × 15.0 cm   Pp [1–2] 3–72   Illus on p 20 of 'Fireless Cooker'   Paper; stapled
CONTENTS: 1 tp; 2 list of members of the Nutrition Committee and 'Copyright 1941, by J.B. Lippincott Company // Second edition // New 1945 printing with additions and corrections // Printed in Canada'; 3 table of contents; 4 'Canada's Food Rules Approved by the Canadian Council on Nutrition – 1944'; 5–6 'Food and Health'; 7–11 'Budgeting Our Income'; 12 'Requirements' and 'Meal Planning and Marketing'; 13 'How Well Do You Eat?'; 14 'Plan for Daily Meals'; 15 'Menus' [i.e., general information]; 16 'Summer Menu Suggestions'; 17 'Lunch and Supper Suggestions,' 'Meals Which May Be Prepared on a Single Burner Stove,' and 'Cleansers'; 18 'Abbreviations' and 'Weights and Measures'; 19 'Oven Temperatures' and 'Cooking Hints'; 20–1 'Fireless Cooker'; 22–70 recipes for 'Beverages,' 'Cereals,' 'Left Overs,' 'Sauces,' 'Soups,' 'Vegetables,' 'Salads,' 'Eggs,' 'Cheese,' 'Meat,' 'Poultry,' 'Fish,' 'Desserts,' 'Flour Mixtures,' 'Marmalades and Relishes,' 'Canning,' 'Sandwich Fillings,' and 'Sweets' and suggestions for 'The Lunch Box,' including a recipe for 'Doubling Butter'; 71–2 index
CITATIONS: Ferguson/Fraser, p 234
COPIES: *Private collection
NOTES: *Food and the Family Income* is recommended in O1095.1, *Canadian Cook Book for British Brides*.

L'art nouveau dans l'achat, la conservation et la préparation des aliments

See O810.11, the French-language edition of The New Art of Buying, Preserving and Preparing Foods *published in Montreal by Canadian General Electric Co. Ltd.*

Patenaude, Jehane-Cécile (Montreal, Que., 22 March 1904–24 November 1987, Cowansville, Que.)

Jehane Patenaude (better known by her married name, Madame Benoît, usually spelled without the circumflex in her English-language publications) was the eldest daughter of Alfred Patenaude and Marie-Louise Cardinal. She began her cooking career in Paris at the Sorbonne, where she took a four-year food science course, under Édouard de Pomiane, the new chair of Culinary Physics and Chemistry (after completing a Bachelor of Arts at the Dames du Sacré-Coeur in Paris). In 1940, when she met her future (second) husband Bernard-Camille-Joseph Benoît, she was running her own business out of the ground floor of her home on Sherbrooke Street: a restaurant during the day, called the Salad Bar; and a cooking school at night, called Au fumet de la vieille France. A fire on the premises in January 1942 forced her to leave this location, bringing an end to the restaurant and school. She began her radio work in the war years and became well known across Canada through her appearances on television, beginning in 1952. The publication for Fry-Cadbury, Q273.1, Chocolate around the Clock, *is her earliest cookbook, followed by Q309.1,* 70 New Chocolate and Cocoa Recipes. *She apparently also wrote a cookbook during the war years, intended for publication by Paul Péladeau, but which never appeared because of paper rationing; the manuscript is lost (see the 1988 biography by her husband, p 15; full reference, below).*

Within the period covered by this bibliography, she compiled Mes fiches culinaires, chaque fiche une leçon de cuisine, 1947–1948, *Montreal, 1948 (QMBN). This hybrid form of publication could be used either as a booklet or as tear-out cards filed in a box. The introductory text for No. 13 (Private collection) explains the system: 'Ce numéro 13 de* Mes fiches culinaires *marque le commencement d'une deuxième année de publication. Le format présent a été adopté pour satisfaire à toutes les exigences: ainsi on pourra continuer de classer les fiches dans un fichier ou conserver* Mes fiches culinaires *en cette forme de livret. Le service d'informations établi par* Mes fiches culinaires *opère pour les abonnées seulement. Jehane Benoît répondra à toutes leurs questions à l'adresse suivante: Mes Fiches Culinaires // B.P. 189, Station L (Westmount) Montréal, Qué. Fitzroy 2357 Tous droits réservés – Canada 1947.'*

Her many other works fall outside the chronological bounds of this bibliography, but the most famous is Encyclopedia of Canadian Cuisine, *produced by the editors of* Canadian Homes Magazine, *[Montreal: Messageries du Saint-Laurent, c1963] (NSH), the French edition titled* L'encyclopédie de la cuisine canadienne, *and later editions called* The New and Complete Encyclopedia of Cooking, *Montréal: Messageries du St-Laurent, copyright 1970 (QMBN),* La nouvelle encyclopédie de la cuisine, *Montréal: Messageries du Saint-Laurent, [copyright 1970] (QMBN), and* Madame Benoît's Library of Canadian Cooking, *[Montréal:] Messageries du Saint-Laurent, 1972, 12 vols (QMM). Over her lifetime, which spanned most of the twentieth century, she cooked on wood, gas, and electric stoves, and finally, in microwave and convection ovens. She was an early proponent of microwave cooking in* Madame Benoît's Microwave Cookbook, *Toronto: McGraw-Hill Ryerson, [1975] (OONL), the French edition titled* La cuisine micro-ondes, *Montréal: Éditions de l'homme, c1976 (OONL), and she wrote other cookbooks on the subject, plus* Madame Benoît's Convection Oven Cookbook, *Toronto: McGraw-Hill Ryerson, 1981 (OONL), French edition,* Cuisiner avec le four à convection, *Montréal: Éditions de l'homme, copyright 1982 (QMBN). She also produced recipe collections for such products as Bovril, Dainty Rice, Sealtest Cottage Cheese, Outspan citrus fruit, and Dow beer.*

She had a daughter, Monique, from her first marriage (when she went by the name Patenaude-Zimmerman). She married her second husband, Bernard Benoît, on 28 August 1945. For the last two decades of her life, she lived on a sheep farm called Noirmouton, in Sutton, Quebec (purchased in 1956). She is buried in Sutton. Bernard Benoît wrote an 'Intimate Biographical Essay' for Madame Jehane Benoît: 14 Years of Microwave Cooking, *[Saint Lambert, Que.: Les Éditions héritage inc., copyright 1988], published to commemorate her fourteen-year association with Panasonic, which manufactured microwave ovens. See also Fiona Lucas's entry for Jehane Benoît in Arndt, pp 62–3.*

Q273.1 [1941]
Chocolate / around the clock / chocolate and cocoa / tested culinary treats / prepared by Jehane Patenaude / Published by / Fry-Cadbury Ltd. / Montreal [cover-title]
DESCRIPTION: 22.0 × 16.0 cm   Pp 1–31 [32]   Illus

brown   Paper, with stylized image on front of the head-and-shoulders of a Mexican man wearing a sombrero, and a clock behind him; stapled
CONTENTS: Inside front face of binding 'Dedicated to You' signed Jehane Patenaude; 1 'Contents Including [red star] Recipes'; 2 'Table of Measurements'; 3–4 'Breakfast'; 5–6 'Mid-Morning Bite'; 7–12 'Lunch'; 13–15 'After School Delight'; 16–17 'Around the World with Chocolate Lovers'; 18–22 'Bridge Game'; 23–5 'Five O'Clock de Madame'; 26–8 'Dinner Time'; 29–32 'Midnight Snack'; inside back face '100M-8-41'
CITATIONS: Armstrong 2000, p F2   Driver 2003, 'Canadian Cookbooks,' p 37
COPIES: OGU (CCC TX715.6 P26)   OONL (TX767 C5 P37 1941)   QMMMCM (AR-M2000.62.19)   *Private collection
NOTES: There are references to wartime on p 16: 'England: In war time as well as in peace time, the British are always cocoa lovers.'; 'Europe: When peace returns to Europe, once again men and women will sit in sidewalk cafés, ...' Appropriately for a chocolate cookbook, the text and illustrations are printed in brown. A Fry's Cocoa advertisement in the *Star Weekly* (13 December 1941), p 10, describes *Chocolate around the Clock* as 'the new, illustrated book of latest recipes.' In Bernard Benoît's 1988 biography of Jehane, p 24, he refers to *Chocolate around the Clock* as 'her first one,' i.e., her first advertising cookbook, and he dates it 1940; he adds, 'We did it together.'

Rawleigh's good health guide almanac cook book 1941

For information about Rawleigh's annual almanac cookbooks and other publications, see M22.1.

Q274.1 1941
Hang me up for future reference / 1889 1941 / Rawleigh's / Trade mark reg. U.S. Pat. Off. / good health guide / almanac cook book / [caption:] Bountiful Autumn / From a famous oil painting / Published by / the W.T. Rawleigh Co., Ltd. / Montreal – Winnipeg / Freeport Richmond Chester Albany Minneapolis / Denver Oakland Melbourne Wellington / The largest industries of their kind in the world [cover-title]
DESCRIPTION: 24.0 × 16.5 cm   Pp 1–32   Illus black-and-orange, illus   Paper, with image on front of an oil painting of a still-life; stapled, and with hole punched at top left corner for hanging
COPIES: *Private collection

1941–2

Household science: Lesson outlines ... sixth year

See also Q276.1.

Q275.1   nd [about 1941–2]
Household / science / Lesson / outlines / in / cookery / for / sixth year [cover-title]
DESCRIPTION: 20.0 × 12.5 cm   Pp 1–24   Illus on p 17 of 'Table Service'   Paper; stapled
CONTENTS: 1 'Introductory Lesson'; 2–18 fifteen numbered lessons; 19–24 blank for 'Notes'
COPIES: *Private collection
NOTES: The heading on p 1 is 'Lesson Outlines in Cookery for Household Science Classes // Sixth Year.' The textbook was published by the Protestant School Board for Greater Montreal. The copy described here is stamped throughout the volume, 'Property of Iona Avenue School // 5000 Iona Avenue, Montreal.' The book's owner reports that it was her class text in 1947. Another owner reports that she used her copy of the same book and the one for the seventh year, also at Iona Avenue School, in the years 1941–2.

Household science: Lesson outlines ... seventh year

See also Q275.1.

Q276.1   nd [about 1941–2]
Household / science / Lesson / outlines / in / cookery / for / seventh year [cover-title]
DESCRIPTION: 20.5 × 12.5 cm   Pp 1–40   2 fp illus numbered 1–2 of cuts of meat   Paper; stapled
CONTENTS: 1–35 fifteen numbered lessons; 36–40 blank for 'Notes'
COPIES: *Private collection
NOTES: The textbook was published by the Protestant School Board for Greater Montreal. The book's owner reports that it was her class text in 1948. Another owner reports that she used her copy of the same book and the one for the sixth year, at Iona Avenue School, in the years 1941–2.

1941–5

Aitken, Mrs Katherine (Kate) May, née Scott (Mrs Henry Mundell Aitken) (Beeton, Ont., 6 April 1891–11 December 1971, Mississauga, Ont.)

For information about Aitken and her other cookbooks, see Q214.1.

Q277.1   nd [about 1941–5]
Feeding your family / in wartime / Meals for five on $12.50 a week / Kate Aitken – The Standard [cover-title]
DESCRIPTION: With image on front of a mother serving three children and their father at table; stapled
COPIES: *Private collection
CITATIONS: Neering, p 184
NOTES: Aitken worked at the *Standard* newspaper from 1941, commuting weekly from Toronto.

1942

Aitken, Mrs Katherine (Kate) May, née Scott (Mrs Henry Mundell Aitken) (Beeton, Ont., 6 April 1891–11 December 1971, Mississauga, Ont.)

For information about Aitken and her other cookbooks, see Q214.1.

Q278.1   nd [1942]
How to / save sugar / in cooking 10¢ [cover-title]
DESCRIPTION: 23.0 × 15.0 cm   Pp 1–16   Illus   Paper, with image on front of a milk bottle, bee and honeycomb, sugar ration coupons, and a hand dropping sugar crystals (?) into a measuring cup; stapled
CONTENTS: Inside front face of binding seven numbered suggestions for saving sugar; 1 'Sugar Substitutes'; 2–4 'Quick Breads'; 5–6 'Yeast Breads'; 7–8 'Cookies'; 9–11 'Cakes'; 12–13 'Pies'; 14–15 'Desserts'; 16 'Beverages'
COPIES: *Private collection
NOTES: This cookbook was published shortly after the introduction of sugar rationing, in April 1942. The private collector's copy is inscribed on the front face of the binding, in ink, 'E.[L.?] Green 1942'; this person lived in Cowansville, Quebec (her address was on another book owned by the same collector). 'The Standard,' i.e., the name of the Montreal newspaper, is printed at the bottom of pp 2–16. On the outside back face of the binding, there are comments

about the efforts of those in the Standard Kitchen 'to create new and different recipes that will help you with your sugar ration'; the comments are signed Kate Aitken, of the Standard.

235 recettes pour dîners et soupers

Q279.1 1942
Exercices pratiques / d'art culinaire / 235 recettes / pour dîners et soupers / CND / $0.10 Québec 1942 [cover-title]
DESCRIPTION: 22.5 × 15.0 cm   Pp [1] 2–80   Paper; stapled
CONTENTS: 1–19 '8e année'; 20–37 '9e année'; 38–56 '10e année'; 57–75 '11e année'; 76 'Table pour les conserves de légumes'; 77–80 'Les conserves alimentaires' and at bottom p 80, 'Des ateliers de l'Action catholique, Québec.'
CITATIONS: Lambert, T., p 94°
COPIES: *QMACN (570.630 (1))   QSFFSC
NOTES: No author is named, but she was soeur Sainte-Marie-Vitaline (Anna Fournier, 1873–1954) of the Congregation of Notre Dame (Lambert, T., p 94°); for information about her and her other books, see Q128.1.

Q279.2 rev. ed., 1948
—Exercices pratiques / d'art culinaire / 8e, 9e, 10 et 11 années / 235 recettes / pour dîners et soupers / CND / Edition revue, corrigée et augmentée / $0.25 Montréal 1948 [cover-title]
DESCRIPTION: 22.5 × 15.0 cm   Pp [i] ii–iv, [1] 2–84   Paper; stapled
CONTENTS: i 'Règles alimentaires officielles au Canada'; ii–iv 'Quelques conseils à propos des menus, de la cuisson, etc.'; 1–19 '8e année'; 20–37 '9e année'; 38–56 '10e année'; 57–top 76 '11e année'; mid–bottom 76 'Table pour les conserves de légumes'; 77–80 'Les conserves alimentaires'; 81–4 index
CITATIONS: BouquinsCat 229, No. 355   BQ 08-0973 Lambert, T., p 94°
COPIES: OONL (TX715.6 E96 1948)   *QMACN (570.630 (2))   QMBN (160034 CON)   QQLA (TX715 E96 1948)   QSFFSC (641.5 S681e)

Lohman, Mrs Tina

See O1051.1 for Lohman's Book of Jewish Recipes, published simultaneously in Toronto and Montreal.

Rawleigh's consumers catalog with cooking recipes

For information about Rawleigh's annual almanac cookbooks and other publications, see M22.1.

Q280.1 nd [about 1942]
Rawleigh's / Trade mark / good health products / consumers catalog / with cooking recipes / Your / shopping / center / is your home / For over half a century / Independent competitive progressive [cover-title]
DESCRIPTION: 20.5 × 11.5 cm   Pp [1] 2–23   Illus col   Paper, with image on front of a Rawleigh's agent and housewife on doorstep; stapled, and with hole punched at top left corner for hanging
CONTENTS: 1 cover-title; 2 'President's Greeting'; 3–23 catalogue of Rawleigh's products and recipes
COPIES: *ACG
NOTES: No publication date is cited, but the 'President's Greeting' refers to 'over 50 years' of quality products. Since the company was founded in 1889, the catalogue was published in 1939 or later. The likely year was 1942 if one takes 'Printed in Canada 42-1' (printed on the outside back face of the binding) to mean 1942. No place of publication is recorded, but all the company's almanac cookbooks in this period were published in Montreal and Winnipeg (Montreal being the first-cited city). The ACG copy is stamped on the outside back face of the binding, in the space for 'Your Rawleigh Dealer,' with the name of C. Butler and his Calgary address.

Rawleigh's good health guide almanac cook book 1942

For information about Rawleigh's annual almanac cookbooks and other publications, see M22.1.

Q281.1 1942
Be sure to keep. Hang up for future reference / 1889 1942 / Rawleigh's / Trade mark reg. / good health guide / almanac cook book / [caption:] Man's most faithful friend / confidence well placed / Published by / the W.T. Rawleigh Company, Ltd. / Montreal Winnipeg / Freeport Memphis Richmond Chester Albany Minneapolis / Denver Oakland Melbourne Wellington / Independent competitive progressive since 1889 [cover-title]
DESCRIPTION: With image on front of a boy bandaging his dog's leg
COPIES: *AEUCHV (UV 85.17.158)

1942–5

An open secret of exciting dishes

Q282.1 nd [about 1942–5]
An open secret / of / exciting / dishes / made with
Cox's / Instant Powdered / Gelatine [cover-title]
DESCRIPTION: 18.5 × 13.0 cm   Pp [1] 2–31 [32]   Illus
Paper, with image on front of Orange Chiffon Pie;
stapled
CONTENTS: 1 'The Whys and Wherefores of Cox's
Gelatine' and at bottom, 'The Cox Gelatine Company
439 West Street, New York, N.Y. // The Cox Gelatine
Company, Ltd. 370 Lemoyne Street, Montreal,
Canada'; 2 'Quick Tips That Bring Perfect Results'
and 'Recipes compiled and tested by Mrs. Sylvia B.
Young // Home Economics authority'; 3–30 recipes;
31 'Cooking Hints'; 32 index and at bottom, 'Printed
in U.S.A.'
COPIES: *NSLQCM
NOTES: The text on p 1 refers to Cox's Gelatine being
made in Scotland 'for about a hundred years' and
'sold in the United States and Canada since 1845.'
Since the company began manufacturing powdered
gelatine in checkerboard boxes in Scotland in 1842
(see Allen, p 194), the publication date is about 1942
(1842 + 100 years) and certainly no later than 1945.

Q282.2 nd [about 1942–5]
—An open secret / of / exciting / dishes / made
with Cox's / Instant Powdered / Gelatine [cover-
title]
DESCRIPTION: 18.5 × 13.0 cm   Pp [1] 2–31 [32]   Illus
Paper, with image on front of Orange Chiffon Pie;
stapled
CONTENTS: 1 'The Whys and Wherefores of Cox's
Gelatine' and at bottom, 'The Cox Gelatine Company, Ltd. 370 Lemoyne Street, Montreal, Quebec,
Canada.'; 2 'Quick Tips That Bring Perfect Results'
and 'Recipes compiled and tested by Mrs. Sylvia B.
Young // Home Economics authority'; 3–30 recipes;
31 'Cooking Hints'; 32 'Index' and at bottom, 'Printed
in Canada'
COPIES: *Private collection
NOTES: The text on p 1 refers to Cox's Gelatine being
made in Scotland 'for about a hundred years' and
'sold in Canada since 1845.' This edition was printed
in Canada and has only the Montreal address on p 1
(Q282.1 was printed in the United States and has the
Montreal and New York addresses on p 1).

Q282.3 nd [about 1942–5]
—Un secret dévoilé / sur des / plats / succulents /
faits avec la / Gelatine / non / aromatisée Cox
[cover-title]
DESCRIPTION: 18.0 × 12.5 cm   Pp [1] 2–31 [32]
Illus   Paper, with image on front of Tarte chiffon à
l'orange; stapled
CONTENTS: 1 'Les comments et les pourquois de la
Gélatine Cox' and at bottom, 'The Cox Gelatine Company, Ltd. Casier postal 73, Montréal, Québec,
Canada.'; 2 'Suggestions rapides qui donnent des
résultats merveilleux' and at bottom, 'Recettes
compilées et experimentées par Madame Sylvia B.
Young // autorité au économie domestique'; 3–30
recipes; 31 'Avis pour la cuisson'; 32 'Index' [no place
of printing]
COPIES: *OONL (TX814.5 G4 S42 1950 p***)
NOTES: There is a reference on p 1 to Cox's Gelatine
'faite en Écosse il y a peu près cent ans' and in Canada,
'depuis 1845.'

1943

Cooper, Lenna Frances (1884–), Edith Michael Barber (1892–), and Helen Swift Mitchell (1895–)

For meatless recipes by Lenna Cooper, see M33.1,
Rawleigh's Almanac Cook Book and Guide to
Health 1919. *Cooper also wrote* The New Cookery,
Battle Creek, Mich.: Good Health Publishing Co.,
[c1913], and How to Cut Food Costs, *Battle Creek,*
Mich.: Good Health Publishing Co., [c1917] (both United
States: DLC).

Edith Barber is the author of the following: What
Shall I Eat?, *New York: Macmillan Co., 1933;* Edith
Barber's Cook Book, *New York: G.P. Putnam's Sons,*
[c1940]; Speaking of Servants, *New York, London:*
Whittlesey House, McGraw-Hill Book Co. Inc., [c1940];
The Short-Cut Cook Book, *New York: Sterling Pub.*
Co., [1952]; Short Cut to Etiquette, *New York: Sterling*
Pub. Co., [c1953]; 101 Best Party Recipes and Menus,
New York: Sterling, [c1960] (all United States: DLC).

Q283.1 9th ed., [7th impression, copyright 1943]
Nutrition / in health / and disease / by / Lenna F.
Cooper, B.S., M.A., M.H.E. / Chief, Department of
Nutrition, Montefiore Hospital, New York City;
formerly / Food Director, University of Michigan;
Dean of School of Home Economics, / Battle Creek
College; Supervising Dietitian, U.S. Army, 1918–
1919; / President, American Dietetic Association,

1937–1938 / Edith M. Barber, B.S., M.S. / writer and consultant, food and nutrition; editor food column New York "Sun" / and food column, Bell Syndicate; lecturer on history of cookery, / Teachers College, Columbia University / Helen S. Mitchell, B.A., Ph.D. / Chief Nutritionist, Office of Foreign Relief and Rehabilitation Operations, State / Department; formerly Principal Nutritionist, Office of Defense Health / and Welfare Services; Research Professor in Nutrition, / Massachusetts State College / Ninth edition, revised / 99 illustrations and 7 colored plates / Philadelphia Montreal London / J.B. Lippincott Company

DESCRIPTION: 20.0 × 13.5 cm   Pp [i–iv] v–viii [ix–x] xi–xiv, [1–2] 3–716   7 pls col incl frontis, illus   Cloth

CONTENTS: i ht; ii blank; iii tp; iv 'Copyright, 1943, by J.B. Lippincott Company // Copyright, 1928, 1929, 1930, 1931, 1933, 1935, 1938, 1941 by J.B. Lippincott Company Ninth edition Seventh impression ... Under government regulations for saving paper during the war, the thickness of this book has been reduced below the customary peacetime standards. The text is complete and unabridged. Printed in the United States of America'; v–vi 'Preface to the Ninth Edition' signed the authors; vii–viii 'Preface to the First Edition'; ix 'Acknowledgments'; x blank; xi–xiv 'Contents'; 1–685 text; 686–7 'Reference Books and Scientific Journals'; 688 blank; 689–93 'Glossary'; 694 blank; 695–716 'Index'

COPIES: *QMBN (RM216 C66 1943 and 88139 CON)

NOTES: Of culinary interest are Part 5, 'Food Selection and Cookery,' pp 425–512, and Part 6, 'Cooking for the Sick and the Convalescent,' pp 513–606. Part 4, Chapter 35, 'Racial Differences in Dietary Habits,' discusses how a public health nurse should approach modifying the food habits of immigrants from other cultures, who may be suffering health problems because their customary foods are unavailable in North America or because they are poor. The text argues that the nurse should be sensitive to immigrants' religious ideas and customs.

AMERICAN EDITIONS: *Nutrition in Health and Disease*, [1st ed.–2nd ed.], 2 vols, Philadelphia: Lippincott, copyright 1928–9, serial (United States: DLC); *Nutrition in Health and Disease for Nurses*, 3rd ed.–6th ed., 4 vols, Philadelphia: Lippincott, copyright 1930–5, serial (United States: DLC); *Nutrition in Health and Disease*, 7th ed., Philadelphia: Lippincott, copyright 1938–, serial (United States: DLC).

Economy recipes for Canada's 'housoldiers'

Q284.1   [March 1943]

Economy recipes / for / Canada's "housoldiers" / Home Service Department / The Canada Starch Company Limited – Montreal – Toronto [cover-title]

DESCRIPTION: 23.0 × 15.0 cm   Pp 1–21   Paper, with image on front of a woman saluting, and with her other hand, holding a wooden spoon like a rifle resting on her shoulder

CONTENTS: 1 note signed 'Jane Ashley // Canada Starch Home Service Department March 1943,' Canada's food rules, and table of contents; 2–21 text

CITATIONS: Ferguson/Fraser, p 99, illus on p 96 of front face of binding   Landsberg   Walker

COPIES: ACG   AEPMA   ARDA   BKOM   MTM   OGU (*UA s070 b62 and CCC TX715.6 E36, 3 copies)   OKQ (F5012 1943 C213 Special Coll)   OOA (MG28 III 94 Vol. 40, file 8)   OOAG (641.55)   OONL (TX715.6 E38 1943)   OPETCM   Company collection (Best Foods Canada, Toronto, Ont.)

NOTES: Text on the inside front face of the binding refers to the housewives of Canada as 'the "housoldiers", serving the nation.' Jane Ashley states on p 1 that the booklet has 'the purpose of guiding Canadian housewives in the preparation of nourishing and economical meals, within the possibilities of a restricted budget.' Listed below the table of contents are 'Timely Recipes which will help replace foods not being canned in wartime' and 'Meat Substitutes.' Cookies are recommended on p 5 for inclusion in overseas parcels. Jane Ashley and Marie Gelinas in Q284.2 may be pseudonyms.

Q284.2   [March 1943]

—Recettes économiques / pour vous du / "front domestique" / Service de l'économie domestique / The Canada Starch Company Limited – Montréal [cover-title]

DESCRIPTION: 23.0 × 15.0 cm   Pp 1–21   Paper, with image on front of a woman saluting, and with her other hand, holding a wooden spoon like a rifle resting on her shoulder

CONTENTS: 1 note signed 'Marie Gelinas // Service de l'économie domestique // The Canada Starch Company, Limited mars, 1943,' 'Règlements alimentaires du Canada,' and table of contents; 2–21 text

COPIES: OONL (TX715.6 E382 1943)   *Company collection (Best Foods Canada, Toronto, Ont.)

NOTES: In the French-language edition, a different name is appended to the p 1 note.

Ration recipes

*For information about Robin Hood Mills and its other
cookbooks, see S16.1.*

Q285.1   nd [1943]
Ration recipes / Robin Hood Flour Mills Limited
[cover-title]
DESCRIPTION: 8.0 × 16.0 cm   Pp 3–22   Illus   Paper,
with image on front of the figure of Robin Hood
against a maple leaf; stapled
CONTENTS: 3–4 untitled introductory text signed
Evangeline, director, Robin Hood Kitchen, and at bottom p 4, 'Tested and approved by Ruth Davidson [*sic*]
Reid // recipe and nutrition consultant'; 5–21 recipes; 22 'High in Food Value – Low in Cost' and 'Note'
about ordering copies of this book
CITATIONS: 'Evangeline Develops Some Meat-Savers,'
Grist [Robin Hood's in-house magazine] (June 1943),
illus
COPIES: *Private collection
NOTES: Text on the inside front face of the binding
explains that '[t]his folder tells how to prepare nutritious, economical meals in spite of rationing and shortages.' Recipes for Beef Loaf, Stuffed Veal Birds,
Wartime Meat Cakes, and others are recommended
as a way to extend the meat ration. Additional copies
of the book could be ordered from Robin Hood Flour
Mills offices in Vancouver, Calgary, Moose Jaw, Saskatoon, Winnipeg, Toronto, Montreal, and Moncton, according to p 22. No single place of publication is
given, but company headquarters were in Montreal.
The landscape format of *Ration Recipes* mimics the
shape of the ration booklets distributed by the government during the Second World War, which contained perforated stamps to be torn out at the time of
use (examples of ration books are at OONMC).

Lereine Ballantyne developed the recipes, then Ruth
Reid tested them, according to an account of the genesis of the booklet in the June 1943 issue of *Grist*:

Sensing opportunity to spread the gospel of Robin
Hood Oats, (milled in Canada only) Mrs. L.
Ballantyne of the Sales Promotion Department
started experiments to employ oats as a meat extender in anticipation of meat rationing which
started in Canada May 21. Mrs. Ballantyne ... [who]
has raised a family of three sons, who are all in the
Armed Forces of the Empire, started experimenting with a meat loaf. Within a few weeks, she had
developed an oat soup, (almost) sugarless muffin,
sausage griddle cakes, and simple fruit pudding –
not to mention several other new dishes – all made

with Robin Hood Oats ... [At] meetings of the
famed Women's Institute throughout Central
Ontario ... she handed out mimeographed copies
of the new recipes ... enthusiastic reports came
back ... With this evidence before us we arranged
with Mrs. Reid who developed most of the recipes
in our famous cook book, 'Baking Made Easy'
[Q247.1] – to test the new recipes and improve
them if possible ... The Sales Promotion Department decided to produce [with these recipes] a
new recipe folder to be called, 'Ration Recipes.' ...
As a service to our Robin Hood employees in
Canada, we are distributing the new folder,
'Ration Recipes' [free] to every member of the organization.

For further information about Lereine Ballantyne, see
the biographical note about Rita Martin at Q249.1.

Rawleigh's good health guide almanac cook book 1943

*For information about Rawleigh's annual almanac
cookbooks and other publications, see M22.1.*

Q286.1   1943
Hang me up for future reference / 1889 1943 /
Rawleigh's / Trade mark reg. / good health guide /
almanac cook book / Printed in Canada by / the
W.T. Rawleigh Co., Ltd. / Montreal Winnipeg
Freeport Memphis Richmond Chester Albany /
Denver Oakland Minneapolis Melbourne
Wellington / Independent – competitive –
progressive [cover-title]
DESCRIPTION: 24.0 × 16.0 cm   Pp [1] 2–32   Illus red-
and-black, illus   Paper, with image on front of a
young girl tasting from a big spoon; stapled, and
with hole punched at top left corner for hanging
CONTENTS: 1 'President's Message ...'; 2 'Some Impor-
tant Facts about How You Can Save ...'; 3 'Rawleigh's
Zodiacal Planting Chart'; 4 'Year 1943'; 5 '$3 1/3 Billion
a Year for Accidents and Injuries ...'; 6 January, February, and 'Health Affected by Weather'; 7 'For Good
Health and Energy ...'; 8 March, April, and 'Safety
and Short Cuts ...'; 9 'Nature Often Needs Help of
Regulative Laxative Medicines'; 10 May, June, and
'To Do Things Easier and Better'; 11 'Fighting De-
structive Insects'; 12 July, August, and 'Movable
Church Feasts'; 13 'The Danger from Coughs and
Colds'; 14 September, October; 15–18 'Sources of Raw
Materials Become Scenes of War!'; 19 'For Defense
and Victory'; 20 November, December, and 'Interest-

ing Facts about Almanacs'; 21 'Fancy Breads and Rolls'; 22 'Muffins'; 23 'Tasty Nourishing Foods Your Family Will Enjoy'; 24–5 'Stretching the Meat Dollar!'; 26–7 'New Faces for Familiar Vegetables'; 28–9 'You'll Like These New Cake Recipes'; 30 '9 New Delicious Leftover Dishes'; 31 'Vitamins for Health'; 32 'Your Loveliness and Enjoyment'
COPIES: ONLAM (Walters-Wagar Collection, Box 20) SWSLM *Private collection
NOTES: The 'President's Message' discusses difficulties faced in wartime.

1944

Barbeau, Marius (Ste-Marie de Beauce, Que., 5 March 1883–1969)

Barbeau won a Rhodes Scholarship to Oxford University, where he studied anthropology. From 1911 to 1948, he was on staff at what became the National Museum of Man in Ottawa (now the Canadian Museum of Civilization). He is renowned for his pioneering research in native studies and French-Canadian folk culture.

Q287.1   nd [1944]
Saintes artisanes / II – Mille petites adresses / Marius Barbeau / Editions Fides / Montréal
DESCRIPTION: 21.5 × 16.5 cm   Pp [1–8] 9–157 [158–9]   Tp illus by Grace Melvin of two angels kneeling at the foot of a stylized tree, 8 double-sided pls after p 159   Cloth
CONTENTS: 1 'Saintes artisanes – 1'; 2 blank; 3 'Saintes artisanes II – Mille petites adresses'; 4 'Fides à l'étranger // C.P. 258b, Sao Paulo, Brésil // 5, rue de Mézières, Paris VIe, France // 110 East La Salle Ave, South Bend, Ind., U.S.A.'; 5 tp; 6 blank; 7 '"Berceaux et feuillage" et chambres d'oeuvres'; 8 blank; 9–24 'Tissage, dentelle, roberie'; 25–50 'Sculpture, dorerie et carnation'; 51–82 'Peinture, reliure et autres ouvrages'; 83–148 'Boulangerie, pâtisseries et friandises'; 149–53 'Bibliographie et références'; 154 blank; 155–7 'Table des matières'; 158 blank; 159 parttitle: 'Illustrations'
CITATIONS: Bibliothèque municipale de Montréal, p 1
COPIES: OONL (NK841 B3, 4 copies)   OTMCL (746 B13 v. 2)   QMBM   *QMBN (NK842 Q8B37 1944 v. 2) QTU (NK841 B37)
NOTES: In Volume 2, pp 83–148, Barbeau discusses the history of various dishes eaten in the earliest days of New France, and the influence of the religious orders on Quebec's food history, with reference to manuscript and printed sources. He gives recipes used by the religious orders and cites specific titles and editions of eighteenth- and early-nineteenth-century French and English cookbooks used by them. Volume 2 is undated, but the author's acknowledgments in Volume 1 are dated 20 August 1943. QMBN dates the book 1944.

The OTMCL copy is bound in paper and has no pp 1–2.

Rawleigh's good health guide almanac cook book 1944

For information about Rawleigh's annual almanac cookbooks and other publications, see M22.1.

Q288.1   1944
1889 Our 55th year 1944 / Rawleigh's / Trade mark reg. [U.S. Pat. Off.] / good health guide / almanac cook book / Printed in Canada by / the W.T. Rawleigh Co., Ltd. / Montreal Winnipeg / Freeport Memphis Richmond Chester Albany Minneapolis / Denver Oakland Melbourne Wellington / Independent – competitive – progressive since 1889 / The largest industry of its kind in the world [cover-title]
DESCRIPTION: With image on front face of a farm woman reading a letter
COPIES: *ACG   SWSLM

Recipe calendar for Brodie's Self-Raising Flour [1944]

For other titles by Brodie's, see Q138.1.

Q289.1   [1944]
Recipe / calendar / for / Brodie's / Self-Raising / Flour / Nothing new to learn ... simply less to do / With the compliments of / Brodie & Harvie, Limited / 6600 Hutchison St. / Montreal, Canada [covertitle]
DESCRIPTION: 21.0 × 13.5 cm   Pp [1–24]   Fp illus green on inside front face of binding of a woman in a kitchen, stirring the contents of a bowl, illus   Paper, with image on front of a package of Brodie's Self-Raising Flour; stapled, and with hole punched for hanging on the wall as a calendar
CONTENTS: Rectos monthly calendar for four years on each recto page, beginning with May 1944–7 and ending with April 1945–8; versos recipes and mixing methods
COPIES: *OGU (CCC TX715.6 R432)

Saguenay cook book

For other cookbooks from the same church, see Q257.1 and Q318.1.

Q290.1 [June 1944]
Saguenay / cook book [cover-title]
DESCRIPTION: 22.5 × 15.0 cm   Pp [1] 2–95   Illus on p 1 of Arvida First United Church   Paper, with woodcut on front of a woman putting a tray into an outdoor bake oven, woodcut signed 'L.B.'; stapled
CONTENTS: 1 'Arvida First United Church Jct. Moissan and Rodin Rd. // The Community Church Rev. M.W. Booth, B.A., B.D., Minister ...'; 2 'The Saguenay Churches Cook Book // Preface' dated June 1944; 3 'Table of Contents'; 4–95 culinary information and recipes credited with the name of the contributor
COPIES: *QMM (RBD Vanna Garnier, ckbk 613)
NOTES: The 'Preface' says that the cookbook was 'made possible by the ladies of the Saguenay District' and refers to 'this fifth year of war.'

Woody, Elizabeth

Q291.1 [6th printing, September 1944]
The pocket / cook book / Elizabeth Woody / Director of Foods, McCall's Magazine / and / members of McCall's / food staff / Pocket Books of Canada, Ltd.
DESCRIPTION: Small tp illus of a kangaroo
CONTENTS: Tp verso 'The Printing History // The Pocket Cook Book // Published October, 1942 // 1st printing August, 1942 // 2nd printing October, 1942 // 3rd printing December, 1942 // 4th printing March, 1943 // 5th printing September, 1943 // 6th printing September, 1944 // Printed in Canada ... Copyright, 1942, by Pocket Books, Inc.'
COPIES: *Private collection
NOTES: No place of publication is recorded, but Q291.5 gives Montreal. Despite the number of printings of *The Pocket Cook Book,* I did not find many copies, likely because the book was not sturdily constructed and easily falls apart with use.

Q291.2 [10th printing, March 1945]
—The pocket / cook book / Elizabeth Woody / formerly Director of Foods, McCall's Magazine / and / members of McCall's / food staff / Pocket Books of Canada, Ltd.
DESCRIPTION: 16.0 × 10.5 cm   Pp [i–viii], 1–494, [i–vi]   Paper, with image on front of a stylized open book behind a lobster and a casserole of baked beans

CONTENTS: i 'Buy War Savings Stamps and Certificates'; ii 'Important – This is a new publication written especially for Pocket Books.'; iii tp; iv 'The Printing History of The Pocket Cook Book // Published October, 1942 // 1st printing August, 1942 // 2nd printing October, 1942 // 3rd printing December, 1942 // 4th printing March, 1943 // 5th printing September, 1943 // 6th printing September, 1944 // 5th printing September, 1943 // 6th printing September, 1944 // 10th printing March, 1945 // Printed in Canada ...' [*sic*; information about 5th and 6th printings repeated; 7th, 8th, and 9th printings not mentioned]; v–vi table of contents; vii–viii 'About This Book and Why I Think You'll Like It' signed Elizabeth Woody; 1–459 text; 460 blank; 461–90 index; 491–2 'About the Authors'; 493–4 'A Suggestion for the Reader'; i–vi 'A List of Pocket Books' dated March 1945
COPIES: OGU (CCC)   *Private collection
NOTES: 'About the Authors' says of Elizabeth Woody that she was born in Kentucky and graduated from Wellesley College in Massachusetts; she lived for four years in England and France, and worked in New York City; in 1935 she was appointed director of foods at *McCall's.* Gertrude Lynn is described as 'past six years senior Associate Food Editor at McCall's.' Margaret Murray's title was associate food editor.

Q291.3 [13th printing, May 1945]
—The pocket / cook book / Elizabeth Woody / formerly Director of Foods, McCall's Magazine / and / members of McCall's / food staff / Pocket Books of Canada, Ltd.
DESCRIPTION: 16.0 × 10.5 cm   Pp [i–viii], 1–494, [i–viii]   Thin card
CONTENTS: i 'Buy War Savings Stamps and Certificates'; ii 'Important – This is a new publication written especially for Pocket Books.'; iii tp; iv 'The Printing History of The Pocket Cook Book // Published October, 1942 ... 13th printing May, 1945 ...'; v–vi 'Contents'; vii–viii 'About This Book ...'; ...
COPIES: *Private collection

Q291.4 [16th printing, October 1945]
—The pocket / cook book / Elizabeth Woody / formerly Director of Foods, McCall's Magazine / and / members of McCall's / food staff / Pocket Books of Canada, Ltd.
DESCRIPTION: 16.0 × 10.5 cm   Pp [i–viii], 1–494, [i–viii]   Lacks original binding; rebound by home cook in card
CONTENTS: i 'Buy War Savings Stamps and Certificates'; ii 'Important – This is a new publication written especially for Pocket Books.'; iii tp; iv 'The Printing

History // The Pocket Cook Book // Published October, 1942 // 1st printing August, 1942 // 2nd printing October, 1942 // 3rd printing December, 1942 // 4th printing March, 1943 // 5th printing July, 1943 // 6th printing September, 1943 // 7th printing April, 1944 // 8th printing June, 1944 // 9th printing September, 1944 // 10th printing February, 1945 // 11th printing March, 1945 // 12th printing April, 1945 // 13th printing June, 1945 // 14th printing June, 1945 // 15th printing September, 1945 // 16th printing October, 1945 Printed in Canada ... Copyright, 1942, by Pocket Books, Inc.'; v–vi 'Contents'; vii–viii 'About This Book and Why I Think You'll Like It' signed Elizabeth Woody; 1–459 text; 460 blank; 461–90 'Index'; 491–2 'About the Authors'; 493–4 'A Suggestion for the Reader'; i–viii 'A List of Pocket Books' dated October 1945
COPIES: *OFERWM (A1978.189.65)
NOTES: In 'The Printing History,' the year recorded for the sixth printing and the months recorded for the tenth and thirteenth printings do not match the dates given in those printings, i.e., Q291.1, Q291.2, and Q291.3.

Q291.5 [18th printing, April 1946]
—The pocket / cook book / Elizabeth Woody / formerly Director of Foods, McCall's Magazine / and / members of McCall's / food staff / Pocket Books, of Canada, Ltd. / Montreal, Canada
DESCRIPTION: 16.0 × 10.5 cm Pp [i–ii] iii–iv [v–vi], 1–416, [i–ii] Paper, with image on front of a stylized open book behind a lobster and a casserole of baked beans
CONTENTS: i tp; ii '... Published by Pocket Books, Inc., October, 1942 // 1st printing August, 1942 // 2nd printing October, 1942 // 3rd printing December, 1942 // 4th printing March, 1943 // 5th printing July, 1943 // 6th printing September, 1943 // 7th printing April, 1944 // 8th printing June, 1944 // 9th printing September, 1944 // 10th printing December, 1944 // 11th printing January, 1945 // 12th printing March, 1945 // 13th printing April, 1945 // 14th printing July, 1945 // 15th printing September, 1945 // 16th printing October, 1945 // 17th printing November, 1945 // 18th printing April, 1946 // Printed in the U.S.A.'; iii–iv table of contents; v 'About This Book and Why I Think You'll Like It' signed Elizabeth Woody; vi blank; 1–382 text; 383–412 index; 413–14 'About the Authors'; 415–16 'A Suggestion for the Reader'; i–ii publ ads
COPIES: ARDA QMM (RBD uncat) *Private collection
NOTES: On p ii, the year recorded for the sixth print-ing and the months recorded for the tenth and thirteenth printings do not match the dates given in those printings, i.e., Q291.1, Q291.2, and Q291.3.

Q291.6 newly rev., [1948]
—['Newly revised' edition of *The Pocket Cook Book*, Pocket Book No. 181, [Pocket Books of Canada Ltd, 1948], pp 467]
COPIES: QMM (Soeur Berthe, ckbk 168)

Q291.7 [25th printing, January 1949]
—[Twenty-fifth printing of *The Pocket Cook Book*, Pocket Books Inc. and Pocket Books of Canada, [January 1949]]
COPIES: Private collection

OTHER EDITIONS: Cardinal ed., Montreal: Pocket Books of Canada, 1955, c1947 (OONL); Montreal: Pocket Books of Canada, 1961, c1947 (OONL).

AMERICAN EDITIONS: New York: Pocket Books Inc., [1942] (United States: DLC); New York: Pocket Books, [1947, c1942] (United States: DLC); 50th printing, 1964 (Private collection).

1945

Aitken, Mrs Katherine (Kate) May, née Scott (Mrs Henry Mundell Aitken) (Beeton, Ont., 6 April 1891–11 December 1971, Mississauga, Ont.)

For information about Aitken and her other cookbooks, see Q214.1.

Q292.1 copyright 1945
Kate Aitken's / Canadian cook book / by / Kate Aitken / Food Editor / The Standard / First edition / Copyright 1945 / The Standard / Montreal / All rights reserved – no part of this book / may be reproduced in any form without / permission in writing from the publisher. / Printed in Canada
DESCRIPTION: 19.5 × 12.5 cm Pp [1–7] 8–283 [284–8] Fp illus portrait of author on p 2, illus of cuts of meat Paper-covered boards
CONTENTS: 1 tp; 2 fp illus portrait of author; 3 'Foreword'; 4 'Chapter Index' [i.e., table of contents]; 5–268 text; 269 'Kate Aitken' [a brief biography]; 270–83 'Recipe Index'; 284–8 blank for 'Recipe Clippings'
CITATIONS: Arndt, pp 9, 10 (Elizabeth Driver, 'Kate Aitken') Bédard, p 9 BQ 02-0936 BQ Exposition 1974, p 13 Canadian Women of Note No. 9 CCat

No. 24, p Z19   Cooke 2002, p 235   Driver 2001, 'Entrepreneurs,' p 4   Driver 2003, 'Canadian Cookbooks,' p 39   Ferguson/Fraser, p 234
COPIES: OGU (CCC TX715.6 A57)   OOA (MG30 D206 Vol. 33)   OONL (TX715 A3 1945)   OTMCL (641.5 A39)   OW (641.5 AIT)   QMBN (158975 CON)   QMM (RBD ckbk 1246)   *Private collection
NOTES: The OOA copy, which is in the Kate Aitken papers, is inscribed by the author on the front endpaper, in red pencil, 'Kate Aitken office copy'; and above the author's inscription, in pencil, probably referring to her daughter, 'Anne's.' The private collector's copy is inscribed in ink, on the front endpaper, 'Marie Ironside September '47.'

The 'Foreword' asserts, 'In the hands of Canadian women lies the health of the people of Canada. Food is our business.' The first chapter, 'Daily Menu Building,' begins with a discussion about the vitamins and minerals necessary for health, then presents a list of what the average adult and average child (10–12 years) should eat daily. CCat records the price of the book: $1.50.

Q292.2   [facsimile ed. of 1945, copyright 2004]
— Kate Aitken's / Canadian cook book / by / Kate Aitken / Food Editor / The Standard / First edition / Introduction by Elizabeth Driver / Essays by the Aitken family / Whitecap
DESCRIPTION: 19.5 × 12.5 cm   Pp [i–iii] iv–xiii, [2–7] 8–283 [284]   Fp illus portrait of author on p 2, illus of author with family essays on pp ix–xiii, illus of cuts of meat
CONTENTS: i tp; ii 'Copyright © 2004 Estate of Kate Aitken'; iii–viii 'Kate and Her Cookbook' by Elizabeth Driver; ix–xiii essays 'From Her Family'; 2 fp illus portrait of author; 3 'Foreword'; 4 'Chapter Index' [i.e., table of contents]; 5–268 text; 269 'Kate Aitken' [i.e., a brief biography]; 270–83 'Recipe Index'; 284 blank for 'Recipe Clippings'
COPIES: OONL   *Private collection
NOTES: The facsimile is part of the 'Classic Canadian Cookbook Series.'

OTHER EDITIONS: Later editions appeared under various titles: *Kate Aitken's Canadian Cook Book*, White Circle Pocket ed., Toronto: [Wm Collins Sons and Co. Ltd, copyright 1950] (MSOHM, OGU, OOA, OONL, OOWM); *Kate Aitken's Canadian Cook Book*, Tamblyn ed., Toronto: [Wm Collins Sons and Co. Ltd, copyright 1950] (OFERWM); *Kate Aitken's Ogilvie Cook Book*, Montreal: Ogilvie Flour Mills, [copyright 1950] (NBCOM, OGU, OOA; the OOA copy, in the Kate Aitken papers, is marked up with the author's revi-

sions); *The New Kate Aitken Cook Book*, Tamblyn ed., [copyright 1953] (OOA, OONL; the OOA copy, in the Kate Aitken papers, lacks its title-page, is inscribed 'Anne T.' for Mrs Anne Thompson, Kate's daughter, and 'K.A.,' and the text is marked up with revisions); *The New Kate Aitken Cook Book*, Good Luck Margarine ed., [Toronto: Wm Collins Sons and Co. Ltd, copyright 1953] (Private collection); *Kate Aitken's Cook Book*, White Circle Book ed., Toronto: Collins, 1964 (OGU, OOA, OONL, OTMCL; inserted in OOA copy, in the Kate Aitken papers, are file cards headed 'Cook Book Corrections'; 'Star Home Library' is printed on the binding of the OONL copy); *Kate Aitken's Canadian Cook Book*, reprint of White Circle Book ed., prepared by R.M. Darragh and Associates Ltd, Toronto, Special Projects Division for Wm Collins Son and Co. Canada Ltd, 1965 (OONL); Toronto: Collins, 1967 (OGU); *Kate Aitken's Cook Book*, reprint, Toronto: Totem Books, [1982], publishing history on title-page verso: 'First published 1950 by Collins White Circle Books, Toronto // Second edition 1953 // Third edition 1964 // Reprinted 1965, 1966, 1967, 1968, 1969, 1970, 1971, 1973, 1975 // First reprinting 1982 Totem Books a division of Collins Publishers' (OONL); *Kate Aitken's Cook Book*, 1st HarperPerennial ed., HarperCollins Publishers Ltd, [1992], title-page verso refers to 1987 reprint of 3rd ed. by Totem Books and a 1990 reprint by HarperCollins Publishers (OONL).

Recettes et calendrier pour La farine préparée Brodie [1945]

For other titles by Brodie's, see Q138.1.

Q293.1   [1945]
Recettes / et / calendrier / pour / La farine / préparée / Brodie / Rien de difficile / à apprendre ... / Simplement moins / à faire / Avec les hommages de / Brodie & Harvie, Limited / 6600 rue Hutchison / Montréal, Canada [cover-title]
DESCRIPTION: 21.0 × 13.5 cm   Pp [1–24]   Illus   Paper, with image on front of a package of La farine préparée Brodie; stapled, and with hole punched for hanging on the wall as a calendar
CONTENTS: Rectos monthly calendar for four years on each recto page, beginning with January for 1945, 1946, 1947, and 1948; versos illus and recipes; inside back face of binding 'Conseils utiles sur l'emploi de La farine préparée Brodie,' 'Pesées et mesures,' and 'Température du four'
COPIES: *OONL (TX773 R412 1945)

Recipes for Brodie's Self-Raising Flour

For other titles by Brodie's, see Q138.1.

Q294.1   nd [about 1945]
Recipes / for / Brodie's / Self-Raising / Flour / Nothing new to learn ... Simply less to do / With the compliments of / Brodie & Harvie, Limited / 6600 Hutchison St. / Montreal, Canada [cover-title]
DESCRIPTION: 21.0 × 13.5 cm   Pp [1] 2–19 [20]   Fp illus green opp p 1 of a woman in a kitchen, stirring the contents of a bowl; illus   Very thin card, with image on front of a package of Brodie's Self-Raising Flour; stapled
CONTENTS: 1 'More Leisure ... More Pleasure'; 2–19 recipes and, on pp 10–11, 'Proper Mixing Method'; 20 'Index'
COPIES: OGU (CCC TX715.6 R458)   *Private collection
NOTES: The illustration opposite p 1 of a woman in a kitchen is the same as an illustration in Q293.1, which contains a calendar for 1945. This edition of *Recipes for Brodie's Self-Raising Flour* and its French-language counterpart, Q294.2, were likely published about the same time. According to p 6, the company was founded in 1863 by James Parkin, who shortly after took into partnership R. and J. Brodie; the firm later became Brodie and Harvie.

In the OGU copy, the illustration opposite p 1 is printed in brown on yellow paper.

Q294.2   nd [about 1945]
—Recettes / pour / La farine / préparée / Brodie / Rien de difficile / à apprendre ... / Simplement moins / à faire / Avec les hommages de / Brodie & Harvie, Limited / 6600 rue Hutchison / Montréal, Canada [cover-title]
DESCRIPTION: 21.0 × 13.5 cm   Pp [1] 2–19 [20]   Fp illus opp p 1 of a woman in a kitchen, stirring the contents of a bowl; illus   Paper, with image on front of a package of La farine préparée Brodie; stapled
CONTENTS: 1 'Plus de loisirs ... plus de plaisir'; 2–19 recipes; 20 'Index'
COPIES: *QMBM (Env. 7837)

Q294.3   nd [about 1945–9]
—Recipes / for / Brodie's / Self-Raising / Flour / Nothing new to learn ... Simply less to do / With the compliments of / Brodie & Harvie, Limited / 6600 Hutchison St. / Montreal, Canada [English cover-title on one face of binding] Recettes / pour / La farine / préparée / Brodie / Rien de difficile / à

apprendre / Simplement moins / à faire / Avec les hommages de / Brodie & Harvie, Limited / 6600 rue Hutchison / Montréal, Canada [French cover-title on other face]
DESCRIPTION: 20.5 × 13.5 cm   Pp [English:] [1–10], [French:] [1–10]   Illus   Paper, with small image on each face of a package of Brodie's Self-Raising Flour; stapled
CONTENTS: [English:] 1 'Eat Right – Feel Right // The Reason Why Brodie's Self-Raising Flour Has Extra Nourishment Value'; 2–10 'Tested Recipes ...'; [French:] 1 'Qui mange bien, se porte bien // Pourquoi La farine préparée Brodie posséde une plus grande valeur nutritive'; 2–10 'Recettes éprouvées ...'
COPIES: OAUH   *Private collection
NOTES: On p 5 there is a reference to Brodie and Harvie as 'an old established Canadian company ... founded in 1863 by James Parkin, who shortly afterwards took into partnership R. and J. Brodie, the title of the firm later becoming Brodie and Harvie.'

1945–7

Martin, Rita [pseudonym]

For the history of Robin Hood Flour Mills Ltd and its other cookbooks, see S16.1. Regarding Rita Martin, see Q249.1.

Q295.1   nd [about 1945–7]
Favourite / Rita Martin / Robin Hood / recipes [cover-title]
DESCRIPTION: 15.5 × 8.5 cm   Pp [1] 2–16   A few small illus   Paper, with image on front of a woman holding up a hot pie; stapled
CONTENTS: Inside front face of binding statistics about the winning entries at 1,196 agricultural fairs over a three-year period by baking made with Robin Hood Flour; 1 introductory text entitled 'Favourite Robin Hood Recipes' and signed Rita Martin, director, Home Service Department; 2–14 recipes; 15–16 'Household Hints'
COPIES: *Private collection
NOTES: The introductory text comments: 'These are simple economical recipes, planned for helping out during a period of rationing, shortages and restrictions.' Rationing of various foodstuffs was instituted in Canada from 1942 to 1947. There are no references to wartime in the book, which suggests that it was published about 1945–7. The volume is in the same format as another Rita Martin booklet, Q302.1,

12 New Recipes for the Modern Homemaker, [about 1946–7], and both make reference to winning entries at 1,196 agricultural fairs.

On p 14, the reader is advised to write Rita Martin, Robin Hood Flour Mills Ltd, Moncton, Montreal, Toronto, Winnipeg, Moose Jaw, Calgary, and Vancouver, 'for extra copies and other recipes.' No single place of publication is given, but company headquarters and the Rita Martin Test Kitchen were in Montreal. The text is printed in red and green.

There may have been a French-language edition. The company's in-house magazine *Grist* (Holiday issue, 1948), p 27, refers to '2,000 booklets "Recettes Préférées"' being distributed at the Provincial Fair in Quebec. A later, 1950s edition of what is probably the same booklet is at OONL (TX765 M3666 1950z): *Rita Martin présente ses recettes préférées*, nd, pp 16.

1945–8

Martin, Rita [pseudonym]

For the history of Robin Hood Flour Mills Ltd and its other cookbooks, see S16.1. Regarding Rita Martin, see Q249.1.

Q296.1 nd [about 1945–8]
Bread baking / made easy / By Rita Martin / This simple, new easy bread-baking / method makes 4 large, delicious loaves / in 6 hours. No fuss with overnight rising
DESCRIPTION: 23.0 × 15.0 cm   Pp [1] 2–24 Tp illus red-and-black of a boy watching his mother mix dough in a bowl with her hands, illus red-and-black, illus   Thin card, with two images on front, one of a woman mixing dough at 9 AM, the other of the same woman glancing at four baked loaves as she pulls on her gloves to go out at 3 PM; stapled
CONTENTS: Inside front face of binding 'Baking Success Depends Primarily on the Flour You Use' signed Rita Martin, director, Home Service Department, Robin Hood Flour Mills Ltd; 1 tp; 2–3 'Knocking the "Knack" out of Bread-Making'; 4–5 'The Ten Important High Spots in "Bread-Baking Made Easy"'; 6–23 fifty numbered and illustrated steps for making bread; 24 'Short Method for Experienced Bakers'
CITATIONS: Cooke 2003, p 201   Probably Ferguson/Fraser, p 234, illus col on p 124 of front face of binding
COPIES: ACG   MWMM   OONL (TX769 M377 1940z copy 1)   *Company collection (Robin Hood Multifoods Inc., Markham, Ont.)
NOTES: This edition has fifty numbered steps. An

enamel double-boiler is depicted in the illustrated steps. The following note is on the inside front face of the binding: 'The entire contents, text and pictures of this book is original material of which copyright is registered in Canada.' The locations of the company's several Canadian offices are recorded on the inside back face of the binding. No single place of publication is given, but company headquarters and the Rita Martin Test Kitchen were in Montreal.

The various editions of *Bread Baking Made Easy* are undated, but Q296.1 and Q296.2 are the earliest. They predate those that use the 'rolled dough method' introduced to the public in 1949.

Q296.2 nd [about 1945–8]
—Une croute / dorée / dans six heures / par Rita Martin / Cette formule simple et nouvelle de pani- / fication donne quatre pains savoureux. / [folio:] 1
DESCRIPTION: 23.0 × 15.0 cm   Pp 1–24 Tp illus red-and-black of a boy watching his mother mix dough in a bowl with her hands, illus red-and-black, illus   Thin card, with two images on front, one of a woman mixing dough at 9 AM, the other of the same woman glancing at four baked loaves as she pulls on her gloves to go out at 3 PM; stapled
CONTENTS: Inside front face of binding 'Aux ménagères du Québec' signed Rita Martin; 1 tp; 2–3 'Habilité superflue' and at bottom p 3, 'Publié pour faciliter la panification à la maison par Robin Hood Flour Mills Limited … Montréal et Québec …'; 4–5 'Dix points importants dans la "panification"'; 6–23 fifty numbered and illustrated steps for making bread; 24 'Méthode rapide'; inside back face 'Base du succès' signed Rita Martin and at bottom, 'Remarque – Le contenu, texte et images de ce livre est un document original pour lequel des droits d'auteur ont été enregistrés au Canada.'
COPIES: *OONL (TX769 M378 1950z p***)
NOTES: Like Q296.1, this French-language edition has fifty numbered steps.

Q296.3 nd [about 1949]
—Bread baking / made easy / by Rita Martin / This simple, new rolled dough / method makes 4 large, delicious loaves / in 6 hours. No fuss with overnight rising.
DESCRIPTION: 23.0 × 15.0 cm   Pp [1] 2–20 Tp illus red-and-black of a boy watching his mother mix dough in a bowl with her hands, illus red-and-black, illus   Thin card, with two images on front, one of a woman mixing dough at 9 AM, the other of the same woman glancing at four baked loaves as she pulls on gloves to go out at 3 PM; stapled

CONTENTS: 1 tp; 2–3 'Knocking the "Knack" out of Bread-Making'; 4–5 'The Ten Important High Spots in "Bread-Baking Made Easy"'; 6–19 thirty-five numbered and illustrated steps for making bread; 20 'Short Method for Experienced Bakers'
COPIES: *ACG   QMM (RBD Soeur Berthe, ckbk 1796)
NOTES: This edition has only thirty-five numbered steps. Note the change in the title-page text from 'This simple, new easy bread-baking / method ...' of Q296.1 to 'This simple, new rolled dough / method ...' The binding image is the same as Q296.1 and Q296.2. Unlike the 1950s editions, there is no recipe for Oat Bread or Pain au gruau at the end of the text.

The 'rolled dough method' was introduced to the public in 1949. The article 'Robin Hood Rolled Dough Method Wins Acclaim in Canada and the United States' in the company's in-house magazine *Grist* (Spring 1949), pp 16–17, states that the 'new' method is 'currently being widely publicized throughout Western Canada and the United States.' This edition was likely published about the same time.

In spring 1949, in Winnipeg, Manitoba, there was a strike at the four big bakeries that supplied 90% of the city's daily bread. A report by W.H. Shingleton in *Grist* (Spring 1949), p 10, describes how requests poured into Robin Hood's Winnipeg office for copies of *Bread Baking Made Easy,* as housewives turned to baking their own bread. Shingleton states that, at the time of writing his report, 'over 2500 requests' for the cookbook had been received. In the next issue of *Grist* (Summer 1949), p 10, Shingleton refers again to the bread strike and *Bread Baking Made Easy,* adding that a local radio station was inspired to run a bread-baking contest, in which the first and second prize winners used Robin Hood Flour. Winnipeg's strike was Robin Hood's gain!

OTHER EDITIONS: An undated 24-page, English-language edition, *Bread Baking Made Easy* (ACG, OONL, TX769 M377 copy 2, and Company collection, Robin Hood Multifoods Inc., Markham, Ont.), and an undated 24-page, French-language edition, *Une croûte dorée en six heures* (QMM, RBD Soeur Berthe, ckbk 289), were published in about 1953. Two distinguishing features of these editions are the glass double-boiler (not enamel) depicted in the thirty-five steps for making bread and the eight numbered and illustrated steps on pp 22–4 for making Oat Bread or Pain au gruau. The clue to the approximate date of publication is the text on the inside front face of the binding, which describes how Robin Hood Flour is enriched with Riboflavin, Thiamine, Niacin, and Iron. These vitamins and minerals were 'recently' added to the flour, according to the article 'Canadian Advertising Announces Robin Hood's Vita-Mineral Enrichment' in *Grist* (Summer 1953), inside back face of binding.

1945–9

New and delicious recipes

See also Q186.1.

Q297.1   nd [about 1945–9]
New and / delicious / recipes / Use / Lion Vinegar [English cover-title on one face of binding]
Nouvelles et / délicieuses / recettes / Employez le / Vinaigre Lion [French cover-title on other face]
DESCRIPTION: With same image on both faces of a woman holding a bottle of Lion Vinegar in her left hand and stirring the contents of a bowl with her right hand; stapled
CONTENTS: Inside front face of binding 'This booklet of old and new recipes is presented to you with the compliments of the Lion Vinegar Company Limited, who have manufactured Deluxe Pickling, White, Malt and Cider Vinegars under government supervision for over fifty years ... If more of these booklets are required for yourself or your friends, write to: The Lion Vinegar Company Limited 4537 Drolet Street, Montreal // 74 Renaud Street, Quebec City ...'; 1 'Catsups' and 'Dressings'; ...
COPIES: *Private collection
NOTES: The recipes use vinegar as an ingredient. This edition presents the recipes in English and French. The order of the two undated editions is unknown.

Q297.2   nd [about 1945–9]
—New and / delicious / recipes / Use / Lion Vinegar [cover-title on one face of binding]
Household / uses for / vinegar / Use / Lion Vinegar [cover-title on other face]
DESCRIPTION: 15.0 × 8.0 cm   Pp [*New and Delicious Recipes:*] [1] 2–26; [*Household Uses for Vinegar:*] [1] 2–6 Illus Paper, with image on *Recipes* face of a woman holding a bottle of Lion Vinegar in her left hand and stirring the contents of a bowl with her right hand; four small images on *Household Uses* face of a woman employing vinegar for various household uses; stapled
CONTENTS: [*New and Delicious Recipes:*] Inside front face of binding 'Index'; 1 'Foreword' signed Lion Vinegar Co. Ltd, Montreal and Quebec City; 2–23 recipes for 'Beverages,' 'Candies,' 'Catsups,' 'Dress-

ings,' 'Onion Products,' 'Pickles,' 'Pickled Fruits,' 'Sauces,' and 'Tomato Products'; 24–mid 25 'Helpful Cooking Hints'; bottom 25–mid 26 'Handy List of Household Weights and Measures'; mid–bottom 26 'Time for Cooking Vegetables'; [*Household Uses for Vinegar:*] Inside front face of binding 'Index'; 1 'Foreword' signed Lion Vinegar Co. Ltd, Montreal and Quebec City; 2–6 uses for vinegar under the headings 'For the Toilet Table,' 'Medicinal Uses,' 'Laundry Uses,' 'For Cleaning Purposes,' and 'Miscellaneous Uses'

COPIES: *QMM (RBD ckbk 1772)

NOTES: This English-only edition presents culinary and household uses for vinegar.

1946

Allen, Elaine

For information about the J.R. Watkins Co. and the titles of its other cookbooks, see M36.1. The seventh and eighth editions of Watkins Cook Book, *Q147.6 and Q147.7, are attributed to Elaine Allen.*

Q298.1 copyright 1946

Watkins / salad book / by Elaine Allen / author of Watkins Cook Book, Watkins Household / Hints Book and Watkins Economy Recipe Book / Price $1.50 / Copyright, 1946, by the J.R. Watkins Company / The J.R. Watkins Company / Newark Memphis Winona Oakland / Montreal Winnipeg Vancouver

DESCRIPTION: 20.5 × 15.0 cm   Pp [1–4] 5–251 [252–64]   Cloth; metal spiral–bound

CONTENTS: 1 tp; 2 blank; 3 table of contents; 4 blank; 5–251 text; 252–63 index; 264 'Watkins Products' and at bottom, 'Printed in U.S.A.'

CITATIONS: Axford p 414   Cagle/Stafford No. 1035

COPIES: BVAU (Beatrice M. Millar papers)   *Private collection; United States: Probably DLC (TX807 A5)   InU

Q298.2 2nd ed., copyright 1946

—Watkins / salad book / by Elaine Allen / author of Watkins Cook Book, Watkins Household / Hints Book and Watkins Economy Recipe Book / Price $2.00 / Copyright, 1946, by the J.R. Watkins Company / The J.R. Watkins Company / Newark Memphis Winona Oakland / Montreal Winnipeg Vancouver /Melbourne, Australia / Second edition

COPIES: *Private collection

Marie de Sainte-Thérèse de Jésus, soeur (Lawrence, Mass., 17 May 1882– 7 February 1957)

See also Q305.1, La cuisinière économe et avisée, *by the same author. Sister Marie de Sainte-Thérèse de Jésus was born Alma-Angéline-Eugénie Bolduc. Her parents were Wilfrid-Archélas Bolduc and Césarine Goddaire dit Lacaillade. In 1884, the family moved from Lawrence to Haverhill, Massachusetts, where she grew up. A 10-page biography, published by the Maison-Mère du Bon-Pasteur on 25 March 1957, describes her education and her career teaching household science and cooking, with special attention to nutrition (copy at QSFBP).*

Q299.1 1946

Aliments et nutrition / par / une soeur Servante du Coeur immaculé de Marie / du / Bon-Pasteur de Québec / 1946

CITATIONS: BQ 15-0970

COPIES: QMBN (158994 CON)   QQLA (TX354 M334 1946)   QSFBP

NOTES: Sister Marie de Sainte-Thérèse de Jésus began writing this textbook in 1940 (see p 7 of the 10-page biography referred to above). The 191-page volume is in two parts ('Importance des aliments et de la bonne alimentation' and 'Nos trois repas') and there is an 'Appendice.' The 'Table des matières' indicates that the information about menus and cooking is in the second part: Chapter XIV, 'Les menus'; Chapter XIX, 'Cuisson des viandes'; and Chapter XXII, 'Cuisson des légumes.'

The official name of the religious order, founded in the mid-nineteenth century, is Servantes du Coeur immaculé de Marie (often abbreviated to SCIM); however, the members are also known as Soeurs du Bon Pasteur ('sisters of the good shepherd') because of charitable work they did with women prisoners. The order is based in Sainte-Foy.

Q299.2 new ed., 1948

—Aliments et nutrition / par / soeur M. de Sainte-Thérèse de Jésus / Servante du Coeur immaculé de Marie / du / Bon-Pasteur de Québec / Nouvelle edition, revisée / 1948

DESCRIPTION: With three images on front of individual place-settings with food served

CITATIONS: BQ 15-0969

COPIES: OONL (TX353 S34 1948, 2 copies)   QMBN (158995)   *QQLA (TX354 M334 1948)   QSFBP (4 copies)

NOTES: This edition has 232 pp. There is no place of publication recorded. OONL and QQLA record the date as 1948, c1947. Information about menus is in Chapters XIV–XVI. Chapter XIX is 'Cuisson des viandes' and Chapter XXII, 'Cuisson des légumes.' A section called 'Cuisson de la fève de soya' is in Chapter XXIII.

Minute magic with the Ecko Pressure Cooker

Q300.1 [copyright 1946]
Minute magic / with the / Ecko / Pressure / Cooker [cover-title]
DESCRIPTION: 23.0 × 15.0 cm Pp [1] 2–34 Illus Paper, with image on front of a pressure cooker filled with meat and vegetables and a platter of mixed vegetables; stapled
CONTENTS: 1 cover-title; 2–3 'A Miracle Comes to Your Kitchen!' and at bottom p 1, 'Copyright 1946 by Ecko Products Company'; 4 'Ecko Cooking Is Economy Cooking 6 Ways!'; 5 'Only Ecko Gives You All These Extra Features!'; 6–7 'Always Open and Close Your Ecko Pressure Cooker This Easy Way ...'; 8–9 'So Easy to Cook With ...'; 10 'To Keep Your Ecko Looking (and Cooking!) Like New!'; 11 'Before You Start to Cook May We Say a Word on Ecko Cooking Time'; 12–30 timetables and recipes; 31 'A Star in the Kitchen ... Shines at the Table!'; 32 'How to Order Replacement Parts for Your Ecko Pressure Cooker Model Nos. 6002, 6022, 6004, 6024'; 33 order form with address of company, 3580 St Antoine Street, Montreal; 34 illus of cooking cover; inside back face of binding 'Printed in Canada'
COPIES: OONL (TX840 P7 E53 1946) *Private collection

Notes on spices

See O1141.1 for copies of Notes on Spices *distributed by companies with Montreal offices and O1141.2 for the French-language edition.*

Rawleigh's good health guide almanac cook book 1946

For information about Rawleigh's annual almanac cookbooks and other publications, see M22.1.

Q301.1 1946
Hang me up for future reference / 1889 1946 / Rawleigh's / Trade mark reg. / good health guide / almanac cook book / [caption:] From a noted Italian painting / Printed in Canada by / the W.T. Rawleigh Co., Ltd. / Montreal – Winnipeg / Freeport Memphis Richmond Chester Albany Minneapolis / Denver Oakland Melbourne Wellington / Independent – competitive – progressive for 57 years [cover-title]
DESCRIPTION: With image on front of a painting by E. Zempighi showing a man standing beside a seated woman
COPIES: ACG *SWSLM
NOTES: The ACG copy lacks its binding.

Q301.2 1946
—Veuillez conserver pour consulter plus tard / 1889 1946 / Rawleigh's / Trade mark reg. / guide de bonne sante / almanach livre de cuisine / [caption:] Reproduction d'une peinture italienne / Imprime au Canada par / The W.T. Rawleigh Co., Ltd. / Montreal Winnipeg / Freeport Memphis Richmond Chester Albany Minneapolis / Denver Oakland Melbourne Wellington / Independante – competitrice – progressive depuis 57 ans [cover-title]
COPIES: QPC

1946–7

Martin, Rita [pseudonym]

For the history of Robin Hood Flour Mills Ltd and its other cookbooks, see S16.1. Regarding Rita Martin, see Q249.1.

Q302.1 nd [about 1946–7]
Rita Martin / presents / 12 new recipes / for the / modern homemaker / Robin Hood Flour Mills Limited [cover-title]
DESCRIPTION: 15.5 × 8.0 cm Pp [1] 2–19, [i] Illus Paper, with portrait on front of Rita Martin (regarding portrait, see pp 236–7); stapled
CONTENTS: Inside front face of binding statistics about the winning entries at 1,196 agricultural fairs over a three-year period by baking made with Robin Hood Flour; 1 introductory note signed Rita Martin, director, Home Service Department, Robin Hood Flour Mills Ltd; 2–16 recipes; 17–19 'Baking Hints'; i ad for Robin Hood oats
COPIES: MWPA *Private collection
NOTES: The introductory note begins, 'The recipes in this booklet are old favourites in modern dress, ...' Another private collector's copy (not the one catalogued here) is dated on the outside back face of the

binding, in ink, 'Mrs Kellar Jan. 28 1947.' From appearances, the book was published about that time. There is still an element of wartime thrift and rationing in the selection of recipes; for example, Sugarless Cake, Economy White Bread, which uses less yeast, and the instruction 'To economize on sugar when making jam, ...' The volume is in the same format as another Rita Martin booklet, Q295.1, *Favourite Rita Martin Robin Hood Recipes,* [about 1945–7], and both make reference to winning entries at 1,196 agricultural fairs. No place of publication is recorded, but company headquarters and the Rita Martin Test Kitchen were in Montreal.

Q302.2   nd [late 1940s]
—12 / new / Robin / Hood / recipes / by / Rita Martin / Kitchen proved [cover-title]
DESCRIPTION: 10.0 × 15.0 cm   Pp [1–16]   Illus brown-and-orange   Paper, with image on front of a sliced loaf of bread; stapled
CONTENTS: Inside front face of binding illus of the Home Service Department kitchen; 1 '12 New Recipes for the Modern Homemaker' signed Rita Martin; 2–13 recipes; 14–15 'Kitchen Hints'; 16 'Robin Hood Rolled Oats'
COPIES: *BSUM   Private collection
NOTES: This may be a later edition of Q302.1, but produced in a landscape format; however, I have not compared the recipes. The heading on p 1 is the same as the cover-title of Q302.1 and the introductory note on p 1 also makes reference to old favourites: 'Old favourites are best favourites – ...'

The private collector's copy is stamped on the binding, 'The T. Eaton Co Limi[ted] // Western.'

1947

Culinary art

Reckitt and Colman made Keen's Mustard. Reckitt's merged with Colman's in the United Kingdom in 1938, after which their overseas interests were also joined together. For four cookbooks published under the earlier company name, Colman-Keen (Canada) Ltd, see Q139.1.

Q303.1   nd [1947]
Culinary / art / Reckitt & Colman (Canada) Limited Montreal.
DESCRIPTION: 23.0 × 15.0 cm   Pp [i–ii], [1] 2–28, [i–ii]   Tp illus col of a woman standing beside an over-sized artist's palette, on which are arranged prepared dishes, fp illus col, illus col   Paper, with image on front of a woman reading this cookbook; stapled
CONTENTS: i–ii sheet of gummed and perforated 'Mustard Pickles' labels; 1 tp; 2 table of contents; 3 foreword; 4 'Table Service'; 5 fp illus col; 6–25 recipes, illus col, and fp illus col; 26 'Kitchen Secrets'; 27–8 'Medicinal'; i–ii sheet of gummed and perforated 'Pickles' labels
CITATIONS: Chatelaine (May 1947), p 96
COPIES: *NSLQCM   OGU (CCC TX715.6 M572 No. 202)   OONL (TX819 M87 A7913 1950z p***)   OTMCL (641.5971 H39 No. 10)
NOTES: *Culinary Art* is advertised and illustrated in *Chatelaine* Vol. 20, No. 5 (May 1947), p 96: 'Free // We have prepared a new and beautifully illustrated recipe book "Culinary Art" which is just off the press.' Yellow – the colour of mustard – is a prominent feature of the book's design.

The OTMCL copy lacks its binding and the leaves of gummed labels.

Q303.2   nd [about 1947]
—Art / culinaire / Reckitt & Colman (Canada) Limited Montreal.
DESCRIPTION: 23.0 × 15.0 cm   Pp [i–ii], [1] 2–28, [i–ii]   Tp illus col of a woman standing beside an over-sized artist's palette, on which are arranged prepared dishes, fp illus col, illus col   Paper, with image on front of a woman reading this cookbook; stapled, and punched with two holes for storing in a ring-binder
CONTENTS: i–ii sheet of gummed and perforated 'Marinades à la moutarde' labels; 1 tp; 2 table of contents; 3 'Avant-propos' signed Reckitt and Colman (Canada) Ltd, Station T, Montreal; 4 'Comment dresser la table'; 5 fp illus col; 6–25 recipes, illus col, and fp illus col; 26 'Secrets culinaires'; 27–8 'Usages médicinaux'; i–ii sheet of gummed and perforated 'Marinades' labels; inside back face of binding 'Lithographié au Canada'
COPIES: *OONL (TX819 M87 A79 1950z p***)

Q303.3   [2nd ed.], nd
—How to win friends and influence appetites / with Culinary Art / Reckitt & Colman (Canada) Limited, Montreal
DESCRIPTION: 23.0 × 15.0 cm   Pp [i–ii], [1–3] 4–32, [i–ii]   Tp illus col of a cupid-chef, illus col   [$0.25, on binding]   Paper, with image on front of a roast ham on a platter held up by a miniature male figure; stapled
CONTENTS: i–ii sheet of gummed and perforated 'Mustard Pickles' labels; 1 tp; 2 table of contents and 'Acknowledgment'; 3 'To the Culinary Artist:' signed Reckitt and Colman (Canada) Ltd, Montreal; 4 'Helpful Facts'; 5 fp illus col; 6–32 recipes and illus col, and at bottom p 32, 'Printed in Canada'; i–ii sheet of gummed and perforated 'Pickles' labels

COPIES: QMM (RBD Soeur Berthe, ckbk 297)   *Private collection

NOTES: 'To the Culinary Artist:' refers to this publication as 'the second edition of "Culinary Art."' The 'Acknowledgment' is to the following 'leading Canadian food editors and home economists': Miss M.T. Chandler, Consumers' Gas Co., Toronto; Miss Elaine Collett, Moffats Ltd [see O1220.1, *Moffat Cook Book*]; Mrs E. Dighton, Hydro Electric Power Commission of Ontario; Mrs Marjorie Elwood, Toronto *Star Weekly*; Miss Marie Holmes, *Chatelaine* magazine [see her O854.1 and O1005.1]; Miss Jay M. Laws, Aluminum Co. of Canada; and Miss Louise Moore, Toronto *Evening Telegram*.

Hallaure, Jean

Q304.1   1947

Jean Hallaure / A ma femme / Montréal, 1947 / Madame / est / servie / Les Éditions B.D. Simpson / 1459 ouest, rue Dorchester, Montréal 25, P.Q. [*sic*], Canada

DESCRIPTION: 23.5 × 15.0 cm   Pp [3–5] 6–231 [232], i–vi   Small tp illus of a man in silhouette, illus   Rebound

CONTENTS: 3 ht; 4 'Du même auteur // Lettres gourmandes // Suite à Monselet à paraître en 1947 aux Éditions B.D. Simpson'; 5 tp; 6 'Menu' and 'Plats du jour'; 7 'Sonnet en guise de préface // à Jean Hallaure' by 'André Maurois [1885–1967], de l'Académie française'; 8 blank; 9–231 text in the following chapters: 'Hors d'oeuvre,' 'Soupes et potages,' 'Les oeufs,' 'Crustacés – mollusques, poissons,' 'Viandes,' 'Oiseaux de chasse et de basse-cour,' 'Plats du jour,' 'Divers,' 'Salades – légumes,' 'Entremets – Pâtisserie,' 'Fruits,' 'Auxiliaires indispensables,' and 'Matériel'; 232 blank; i–vi 'Table alphabétique des recettes' and at bottom p vi, 'Les illustrations de ce volume ont été faites par Claire Fauteux [born 1890]'

CITATIONS: BQ 04-0984

COPIES: *NBMOU   OONL (TX719 H38 1947, 2 copies)   QMBM (641.5 H182ma)   QMBN (TX715 H27 and 29499 CON)   QRCB (641.5 H182m)

NOTES: The recipes are interspersed with poems and amusing illustrations about particular foodstuffs, such as sugar, wine, tongue, and turkey, giving the book a literary feel. In a letter to 'Chère madame' on p 230, the author and publisher note that they left the recipes in metric measurements because 'nous avons voulu les [recettes] reproduire intégralement, ne nous reconnaissant pas le droit de modifier un texte rédigé par un roi de France ou un grand littérateur.' 'Équiv-alences' for converting from metric to imperial are on p 231. The QMBN catalogue notes, 'Certains exemplaires n'ont pas de mention d'illustrateur à la p. vi.'

Marie de Sainte-Thérèse de Jésus, soeur (Lawrence, Mass., 17 May 1882– 7 February 1957)

For information about the author, see Q299.1.

Q305.1   1947

La cuisinière / économe et avisée / Menus et recettes pratiques / conformes aux nécessités des temps / par / soeur M. de Ste-Thérèse de Jésus, S.C.I.M. / religieuse du Bon Pasteur de Québec / 1947

DESCRIPTION: 25.5 × 17.0 cm   Pp [i–ii], [1–15] 16–370 [371–2]   Illus   Paper, with image on front of a basket of fruits and vegetables; sewn

CONTENTS: i 'La cuisinière économe et avisée // Menus et recettes pratiques conformes aux nécessités des temps.' and binding illus; ii blank; 1 ht; 2 blank; 3 tp; 4 'Droit d'auteur 1947 Imprimé au Canada.'; 5 'À la Vierge de Nazareth, je dédie mon humble travail.'; 6 blank; 7 'Préface' signed 'l'auteur'; 8 'Remerciements' signed 'l'auteur'; 9–11 'Les aliments protecteurs'; 12 blank; 13–335 text in twenty-nine chapters; 336–41 'Appendice'; 342–5 'Bibliographie'; 346 blank; 347 'Table des tableaux'; 348 blank; 349–66 'Index des recettes'; 367–70 'Table des matières'; 371 blank; 372 'Des ateliers de l'Institut St-Jean-Bosco'

CITATIONS: BouquinsCat 229, No. 344   BQ 15-0971   BQ Exposition 1974, p 15   Carrière No. 159

COPIES: OONL (TX715 S12745 1947 fol.)   QMBM (641.5 M334cu)   QMBN (TX715 M15 1947 and 119994 CON)   *QMM (RBD TX715.6 M37 1947)   QQLA (TX715 M334 1947)   QSFBP   QSFFSC (641.5 M334c)

NOTES: The 10-page biography of Sister Marie de Sainte-Thérèse de Jésus, published by the Maison-Mère du Bon-Pasteur on 25 March 1957, says of *La cuisinière économe et avisée*, on p 7: 'Imprimé dans un but d'utilité communautaire, ce travail suscita des appréciations dans le monde, et connut le succès surtout aux États-Unis ... On la recommande [i.e., la diététique] même dans certains Sanatorium de tuberculeux. Rien d'étonnant qu'à l'approbation du département de l'Instruction publique et de la Santé dans la province de Québec, se soit ajoutée celle du semblable département dans le Maine [i.e., the state of Maine].' The place of publication is not recorded, but the religious order is based in Ste-Foy.

Martin, Rita [pseudonym]

For the history of Robin Hood Flour Mills Ltd and its other cookbooks, see S16.1. Regarding Rita Martin, see Q249.1.

Q306.1 [copyright 1947]
Robin Hood / prize winning / recipes / selected by / Rita Martin / Robin Hood Flour Mills Limited / Moose Jaw Saskatoon Calgary Vancouver / Winnipeg Toronto Humberstone Quebec Moncton / Montreal
DESCRIPTION: 21.5 × 15.5 cm   Pp [i–ii], [1–4] 5–136 Small tp illus red of the figure of Robin Hood, 6 double-page illus col on pp 24–5, 38–9, 50–1, 68–9, 82–3, and 120–1; 8 fp illus col, incl half-length portrait of Rita Martin on p 4, illus   Paper, with all-over photographic image on front of loosely woven fabric; Cerlox-type binding
CONTENTS: i–ii perforated tear-out coupons; 1 tp; 2 'Printed in Canada // Copyright by Robin Hood Flour Mills Limited, 1947 ...'; 3 table of contents; 4 fp illus col of Rita Martin; 5 'Foreword' signed Rita Martin; 6–130 text; 131–6 'Index'
CITATIONS: Ferguson/Fraser, p 234
COPIES: ACG   AEPMA   BVAU (Beatrice M. Millar Papers)   OONL (TX763 R63 1947, 2 copies)   OOWM (989.6.14)   OPETCM   OTMCL (641.5 M133)   SEEK   SSWD   *Private collection
NOTES: No single place of publication is given, but company headquarters and the Rita Martin Test Kitchen were in Montreal. The portrait on p 4 of the imaginary Rita Martin (pl 13 in this volume) is signed by Rex Woods, a well-known Canadian graphic artist (for information about the portrait, see pp 236–7). The title-page and text are printed in red and black.

The OTMCL copy is inscribed on the title-page, in ink, 'Helen B. Sulman.'

The Toronto report in the company's in-house magazine *Grist* (Holiday issue 1947), p 21, tells of Mrs Ballantyne, of the Ontario Home Service Department, giving a Robin Hood cooking school in Windsor, where all 1,500 cookbooks shipped down for the event were sold and orders were taken for 150 more; the reference is likely to *Robin Hood Prize Winning Recipes*. The Quebec report in the 1948 Holiday issue of *Grist*, p 27, refers to 'eight thousand cook books' distributed at the Provincial Fair, many of which were likely copies of Q306.1 or Q306.2. The previous issue of *Grist* (Autumn 1948), p 16, tells the story of a lady in Holland writing the Toronto office for a copy of *Robin Hood Prize Winning Recipes*.

Q306.2 [1947]
—Recettes choisies / Robin Hood / par / Rita Martin / Robin Hood Flour Mills Limited / Moose Jaw Saskatoon Calgary Vancouver / Winnipeg Toronto Humberstone Quebec Moncton / Montreal
DESCRIPTION: 21.5 × 15.5 cm   Pp [i–ii], [1–4] 5–136 Small tp illus red of the figure of Robin Hood, 6 double-page illus col on pp 24–5, 38–9, 50–1, 68–9, 82–3, and 120–1; 8 fp illus col, incl half-length portrait of Rita Martin on p 4, illus   Thin card, with all-over photographic image on front of loosely woven fabric; Cirlox-type binding
CONTENTS: i–ii perforated tear-out coupons; 1 tp; 2 'Imprimé au Canada // Publié par Robin Hood Flour Mills Limited. (1947) ...'; 3 table of contents; 4 fp illus col of Rita Martin; 5 'Avant-propos' signed Rita Martin; 6–129 text; 130–6 'Index'
COPIES: *OONL (TX715 M57135 1947)
NOTES: The title-page and text are printed in red and black.

OTHER EDITIONS: [Rev. ed., 1950] (AC, ACHP, OGU, OONL, QMM); [rev. ed., 1953] (BKOM, OONL). In the article 'Yukon Mother Lauds Robin Hood, Rita Martin Canadian Cook Book,' in *Grist* [company's in-house magazine] (Fall 1953), p 11, a reprinted letter from a Yukon mother to Robin Hood Flour Mills tells how her daughter learned to bake bread using 'the Rita Martin Prize Winning recipe book' – likely one of the 1950s editions.

Pour des plats savoureux

Q307.1   nd [about 1947]
[An edition of *Pour des plats savoureux d'après des recettes continentales traditionnelles, de préparation facile*, Montreal: La compagnie Pastene ltée, nd [about 1947], pp 16]
CITATIONS: BouquinsCat 212, No. 393
COPIES: Bookseller's stock
NOTES: The Pastene Co., an importer of Italian packaged goods, began in Boston, Massachusetts, in the mid-nineteenth century. Its Montreal branch, now called Pastene Inc., was established in the early twentieth century. The suggested date of publication is the bookseller's.

1947–8

Velvet cake and pastry recipes

For the history of Robin Hood Flour Mills Ltd and its other cookbooks, see S16.1. Regarding Rita Martin, see Q249.1.

Q308.1   nd [about 1947–8]
Velvet / cake and pastry / recipes [cover-title]
DESCRIPTION: 9.5 × 15.5 cm   Pp 1–20   Portrait opp p 1 of Rita Martin (by Rex Woods, as in Q306.1), illus opp p 20 of 1940s kitchen   Paper, with image on front of draped red velvet behind the words 'Velvet Cake and Pastry'; stapled
CONTENTS: Inside front face of binding 'To the Canadian Homemaker' signed Rita Martin, Robin Hood Flour Mills Ltd, Montreal; 1–20 recipes for sweet baked goods (cakes, pies, cookies); inside back face illus of kitchen
COPIES: *Private collection
NOTES: This cookbook promotes the use of Velvet Cake Flour and Velvet Cake and Pastry Flour made by Robin Hood Flour Mills Ltd. In 'To the Canadian Homemaker,' the pseudonymous Rita Martin refers to 'new [my italics] superfine Velvet Cake and Pastry Flour.' The Velvet brand was launched in the Canadian market, first in southern Ontario, on 5 June 1947, having already been a popular seller in the United States by Henkel and the International Milling Co. (see the in-house magazine Grist (June–July 1947), p 15; the February 1947 issue, p 2, announces the winner of a slogan contest for the new flour; the Autumn 1947 issue, p 34, describes the marketing campaign). The cookbook was likely published about 1947–8, close to the time when the product was introduced to the marketplace.

Likely in the 1950s, the company published another 20-page booklet advertising Velvet Cake and Pastry Flour, The Velvet Touch, by Rita Martin. A copy at QMM (RBD ckbk 1962) has an image of a cherry pie on the binding; a copy at OONL (TX715 M5715) has an image of a strawberry shortcake.

1947–9

Patenaude-Benoît, Mrs Jehane-Cécile (Montreal, Que., 22 March 1904–24 November 1987, Cowansville, Que.)

For information about this author and her other books, see Q273.1.

Q309.1   nd [about 1947–9]
70 / new / chocolate and cocoa / recipes / prepared by Mme. Jehane Patenaude-Benoit, / dietitian and graduate of la Sorbonne, / Paris, France. / Independently panel-tested – and found to be 100% prac- / tical under all everyday, normal conditions – / by a group of average Canadian housewives. / Presented in simplified ultra-modern form – for / quick and easy reading and reference. / Featuring extra blank pages at the back for mounting / your own collection of favorite recipes. / Produced – for your meal and / refreshment-time enjoyment – / with the compliments of / Fry-Cadbury Ltd., Montreal, Quebec
DESCRIPTION: 23.0 × 15.0 cm   Pp [i] ii–iv, 1–37 [38–44]   Illus brown   Paper, with image on front of a Fry's Cocoa container, bowl, and spoons; stapled
CONTENTS: i tp; ii–iv 'Index' [i.e., table of contents]; 1–38 text; 39–44 blank for 'Notes'
COPIES: OGU (CCC TX715.6 S458)   OONL (TX767 C5 B45 1940z, 2 copies)   QMM (RBD ckbk 1581) SWSLM   *Private collection
NOTES: The cover-title is '70 Tested Cocoa and Chocolate Recipes.' The author is identified as Mme Jehane Patenaude-Benoit [sic], evidence that the book was published after her marriage to Bernard Benoît in August 1945, and after her return from Europe in January 1946 (she had travelled to England to marry Bernard at the end of the war). It took a while for the couple to re-establish their lives. In Bernard Benoît's 1988 commemorative biography of his wife, pp 19–20 (full reference at Q273.1), he describes the period after their return: 'Jehane had burnt all her bridges before leaving Canada ... Jehane went back to radio work gradually. She gave lectures, she contracted for a few advertising appearances, and she wrote two or three recipe booklets for food manufacturers.' The cookbook was likely published about 1947–9.

Q309.2   nd [about 1947–9]
—70 / plats nouveaux / au / chocolat et au cacao / préparés par Jehane Patenaude-Benoit; / diplômée en diététique de la Sorbonne, / Paris, France. / Vérifiés indépendamment par un groupe de

ménagères / canadiennes et trouvés 100% pratiques pour la cuisine / de tous les jours dans des conditions normales. / Présentés sous une forme ultra-moderne – et très simple / – qui permet une lecture rapide et facile de chaque recette. / Des pages blanches supplémentaires au dos du livre / pour y coller votre collection de recettes favorites. / Publiés – pour ajouter au plaisir / gourmet de vos repas et goûters – / avec les hommages de / Fry-Cadbury Ltd., Montréal, Québec

DESCRIPTION: 23.0 × 15.0 cm   Pp [i] ii–iv, 1–39 [40–4]   Illus brown   Paper, with image on front of a Fry's Cocoa container, bowl, and spoons; stapled

CONTENTS: i tp; ii–iv 'Index' [i.e., table of contents]; 1–39 text; 40–4 blank for 'Notes'

COPIES: *OONL (TX767 C5 B45 1940y copy 1 p***)

NOTES: There are three variants of the French-language edition: OONL (copy 1) catalogued here, where the last-numbered page is 39 and the 'Notes' begin on p 40; OONL (copy 2), where the last-numbered page is 36 and the 'Notes' begin on p 39; and QMBN (160057 CON), where the last-numbered page is 37 and the 'Notes' begin on p 39 (BQ 12-0967).

1948

Dominion home canning guide

For information about Dominion Glass Co. Ltd and its other cookbooks, see Q75.1.

Q310.1   1948

Dominion home canning / guide / "The key to successful canning" / Western edition / The Dominion Glass Company, Limited / General offices: Montreal, Que. / Western Division / Factory: Redcliff, Alta. / Sales offices: / Winnipeg, Man. Redcliff, Alta. Vancouver, B.C. / Eastern Division / Factories: / Montreal, Que. Hamilton, Ont. Wallaceburg, Ont. / Sales offices: / Montreal, Que. Toronto, Ont. Hamilton, Ont. / Nineteen hundred and forty-eight

DESCRIPTION: 20.5 × 13.0 cm   Pp [1–3] 4–72 [73–6]   Tp illus of a seated woman reading 'How to Can' book, illus   Paper, with image on front of fruits and vegetables; stapled

CONTENTS: 1 tp; 2 blank; 3 'Introduction' signed Dominion Glass Co. Ltd; 4–72 text and at bottom p 72, 'Litho'd in Canada // Mann Lithograph Co. Ltd. Van., B.C.'; 73–5 'Index'; 76 blank for 'My Favorite Recipes'

COPIES: *Private collection

NOTES: The title-page is printed in blue and black. The 'Introduction' begins, 'We are pleased to once again present for Canadian housewives everywhere, a completely new and up-to-the-minute Canning Book.' The Vancouver Daily Province Kitchen and the Home Economics departments of the University of Alberta and of Saskatchewan are thanked for their assistance.

OONL (TX603 D62 1948 p***) matches the above description except that on p 72 there is no 'Litho'd in Canada // Mann ...'

Q310.2   nd

—Dominion home canning / guide / "The key to successful canning" / Western edition / The Dominion Glass Co., Limited / General offices: Montreal, Que. / Western Division / Factory: Redcliff, Alta. / Sales offices: Winnipeg, Man. Redcliff, Alta. Vancouver, B.C. / Eastern Division / Factories: Montreal, Que. Hamilton, Ont. Wallaceburg, Ont. / Sales offices: Montreal, Que. Quebec, Que. Toronto, Ont. / Hamilton, Ont.

DESCRIPTION: 21.0 × 13.5 cm   Pp [1–3] 4–72 [73–6]   Tp illus of fruits and vegetables, illus black-and-yellow, illus   Lacks binding

CONTENTS: 1 tp; 2 blank; 3 'Introduction' signed Dominion Glass Co. Ltd; 4–72 text in thirteen numbered sections; 73–5 'Index'; 76 blank for 'My Favourite Recipes'

COPIES: *Private collection   OONL (TX603 D62 1900z p***)

NOTES: The OONL copy is bound in paper and stapled; there is an image on the front of empty jars and various fresh fruits and vegetables. The 'Introduction' refers to this as 'a completely new and up-to-the-minute Canning Book.' This edition may have been published in the early 1950s: I have seen an 'Eastern edition' (Private collection) that matches this one, where the owner has written the year '1953' next to some recipes (i.e., the year she prepared the recipe); OGU (CCC TX715.6 D64) is the same 'Eastern edition' and the binding looks 1950s.

How to use your McClary Refrigerator

For information about the company and other books about cooking with McClary appliances, see O162.1.

Q311.1   nd [about 1948]

How to use your / McClary / Refrigerator ... / [four-paragraph introductory note] / General Steel Wares / Limited / Montreal Toronto London / Winnipeg Calgary Vancouver

DESCRIPTION: 20.5 × 14.0 cm   Pp [1–24]   Illus   Paper, with image on front and back of various foodstuffs (e.g., bottle of milk, bottle of ginger ale, meat, eggs, carrots, tomatoes, peas, celery, radishes, beans, lemon, two tall-stemmed dessert glasses); stapled
CONTENTS: 1 tp; 2 'Selection of Location'; 3 'Starting and Stopping'; 4 'Temperature Control'; 5 'Freezer Compartment'; 6 'Food Arrangement'; 7 'Defrosting'; 8 'How to Care for Your McClary Refrigerator'; 9 'Meats and Garnishes'; 10–11 'Vegetable Salads'; 12–13 'Fruit Salads'; 14–mid 15 'Ice Cream // Sherbets'; mid–bottom 15 'Ice Cream Specialties'; 16–17 'Refrigerator Desserts'; 18–19 'Refrigerator Cookies, Pies'; 20 'Refrigerator Rolls'; 21 'Refrigerator Sandwiches'; 22–3 'Cold Beverages'; 24 'Over 100 Years of Progress'
COPIES: OFERWM (A1977.119.4)   *Private collection
NOTES: The OFERWM copy is inscribed, on the title-page, 'Refrigerator bought 1948,' which indicates that the book was published about that year. The statement on p 24 referring to 'Over 100 Years of Progress' confirms publication in about 1948 since McClary's was founded in 1847. The head office of General Steel Wares was in Montreal.

Q311.2   nd [about 1948–50]
—How to use your / Admiral / Refrigerator ... / [four-paragraph introductory note] / Canadian Admiral Corporation, Ltd. / London, Ontario
DESCRIPTION: 20.5 × 14.0 cm   Pp [1–24]   Illus   Paper, with image on front and back of various foodstuffs (e.g., bottle of milk, bottle of ginger ale, meat, eggs, carrots, tomatoes, peas, celery, radishes, beans, lemon, two tall-stemmed dessert glasses); stapled
CONTENTS: 1 tp; 2 'Selection of Location'; 3 'Starting and Stopping'; 4 'Temperature Control'; 5 'Freezer Compartment'; 6–top 7 'Food Arrangement'; mid–bottom 7 'Defrosting'; 8 'How to Care for Your Admiral Refrigerator'; 9 'Meats and Garnishes'; 10–11 'Vegetable Salads'; 12–13 'Fruit Salads'; 14–mid 15 'Ice Cream // Sherbets'; mid–bottom 15 'Ice Cream Specialties'; 16–17 'Refrigerator Desserts'; 18–19 'Refrigerator Cookies, Pies'; 20 'Refrigerator Rolls'; 21 'Refrigerator Sandwiches'; 22–3 'Cold Beverages'; 24 'A Pledge of Quality'
COPIES: *Private collection
NOTES: The binding design and recipe pages are the same as Q311.1. In the introductory text on p 1, the only change is the substitution of 'Admiral Refrigerator' for 'McClary Refrigerator.' The text for 'Food Arrangement' has been revised; it now continues from p 6 to p 7 and refers to the 'Butter Conditioner' that can be seen on the inside of the refrigerator door in the new illustration on p 6. The text for 'Defrosting'

has also been revised; it now describes two methods of defrosting, 'Regular Method ...' and 'Fast Method ...' The text on p 24 is new.
    Canadian Admiral Corp. was incorporated on 4 June 1946; it became bankrupt in 1981.

New fashioned, old fashioned recipes

For the titles of other publications advertising the baking soda, see O82.1.

Q312.1   [copyright 1948]
New fashioned / old fashioned / recipes [cover-title]
DESCRIPTION: 11.5 × 15.0 cm   Pp [1–16]   Illus brown   Paper, with image on front of a three-layer cake within a picture frame, and image on back of a box of Dwight's Baking Soda within a picture frame
CONTENTS: Inside front face of binding introductory note signed Martha Lee Anderson, Home Economics Department, Church and Dwight Ltd, Sun Life Building, Montreal, and 'Copyright 1948'; 1–11 recipes; 12–inside back face 'Household Hints,' 'Medicinal Uses,' and 'In the Nursery'
COPIES: *OGU (UA s070 b65)
NOTES: The text and illustrations are printed in brown.

Q312.2   [2nd ed., copyright 1948]
—New fashioned / old fashioned / recipes [cover-title]
DESCRIPTION: 11.5 × 15.0 cm   Pp [1–16]   Illus brown   Paper, with image on front of a three-layer cake within a picture frame, and image on back of a box of Dwight's Baking Soda within a picture frame; stapled
CONTENTS: Inside front face of binding introductory note signed Martha Lee Anderson, Home Economics Department, Church and Dwight Ltd, Sun Life Building, Montreal, and 'Copyright 1948 2nd. edition'; 1–11 recipes; 12–14 'Household Hints'; 15–16 'Medicinal Uses'; inside back face 'In the Nursery'
COPIES: *Private collection

Q312.3   [2nd ed., copyright 1948]
—Recettes / d'antan / modernisées [cover-title]
DESCRIPTION: 11.5 × 15.0 cm   Pp [1–16]   Illus brown   Paper, with image on front of a three-layer cake within a picture frame, and image on back of a box of Dwight's Baking Soda within a picture frame
CONTENTS: Inside front face of binding introductory note signed Martha Lee Anderson, Home Economics Department, Church and Dwight Ltd, Sun Life Building, Montreal, and 'Droits réservés 1948 Deuxième

édition'; 1–11 recipes; 12–14 'Conseils domestiques'; 15–16 'Usages médicinaux'; inside back face 'Dans la pouponnière'
COPIES: *Private collection
NOTES: The text and illustrations are printed in brown.

OTHER EDITIONS: *New Fashioned, Old Fashioned Recipes,* numbered '1st edition,' but actually a rev. ed. of 1948, Montreal: Church and Dwight Ltd, copyright 1953 (OONL); [Montreal, Que.: Church and Dwight Ltd, copyright 1969] (OTMCL).

AMERICAN EDITIONS: *New Fashioned, Old Fashioned Recipes,* New York: Church and Dwight Co. Inc., copyright 1948 (Private collection); '7th edition,' New York: Church and Dwight Co. Inc., 1953 (Private collection).

Rawleigh's good health guide almanac cook book 1948

For information about Rawleigh's annual almanac cookbooks and other publications, see M22.1.

Q313.1 1948
Hang me up for future reference / Our 59th year / 1889 1948 / Rawleigh's / Trade mark reg. U.S. Pat. Off. / good health guide / almanac cook book / [caption:] European Street Scene, from a noted oil painting / Printed in Canada by / the W.T. Rawleigh Co., Ltd. / Montreal – Winnipeg / Freeport Memphis Richmond Chester Albany Minneapolis / Denver Oakland Melbourne Wellington / Independent competitive progressive [cover-title]
DESCRIPTION: 24.0 × 16.5 cm   Pp 1–31 [32]   Illus orange-and-black   Paper, with reproduction on front of an oil painting signed F. Freuer; stapled, and with hole punched at top left corner for hanging
CONTENTS: 1 'President's Message 1948 ...' signed W.T. Rawleigh; 2 'Year 1948'; 3 'Your Family Welcomes an Old Friend and Valued Service'; 4 'Rawleigh's 1948 Zodiacal Planting Chart'; 5 'For Health and Vigor You Need Vitamins'; 6, 8, 10, 12, 14, 18 monthly calendars; 7 'Bad Luck of Colds'; 9 'Housekeeping Helps'; 11 'Delightful Drinks and Rich Flavoring Extracts'; 13 'Lessen the Suffering from Injuries, Strains, Congestions, Pains'; 15 'Stock and Poultry Supplies'; 16 'The Best of Care for Skin, Teeth, Hair'; 17 'Top of the Morning to You or Any Time o' Day' [egg recipes]; 19 'More Bodily Fitness – Less Pain'; 20 'Foods You'll Enjoy'; 21 'Easy Economical Desserts'; 22–3 'Macaroni and Spaghetti'; 24–5 'Different Ways to Cook

Vegetables'; 26 'Try These New Ways to Serve Apples'; 27 'Happy Enjoyment of Living'; 28 'Soup's On'; 29 'Some New Salad Dressings'; 30 'Rawleigh's Insect Control Chart'; 31 'New and Better Weapons to Defeat Flies and Insects'; 32 'Ways of Enjoyment'
COPIES: *OTUTF (uncat patent medicine)   QMBN (Z-9432)

Renouf, Mrs Ethel Scott, née Lindsay (21 September 1881–23 September 1958)

Mrs Renouf is described on p 3 of the cookbook as the daughter of Mrs Lindsay, 'one of the most gracious hostesses in Gaspé of the last generation.' Her husband was Herbert Philip Renouf, manager of the Robin, Jones, and Whitman store located next door to the Black Whale craft shop (see the fish company's history at NS39.1). Mr Renouf contributed 'A Trip to Robin Jones and Whitmans – a Hundred Years Ago' to the cookbook, p 50. The Renoufs lived across from the craft shop. They had one son, Lindsay. Ethel and her husband are buried in St Paul's Anglican Church cemetery in Percé. St Paul's Anglican Church celebrated its centennial in 1962, the same year as the reprint edition of 'The Black Whale' Cook Book.

Q314.1 1948
"The Black Whale" / cook book / Famous old recipes handed down from mother to daughter. / Compiled by Mrs. Ethel Renouf / Wood cuts by: / V.C. Wynn-Edwards, / André Bieler, / Irene Tuzo / Gnaedinger Printing Co. / Montreal / 1948
DESCRIPTION: 23.0 × 15.0 cm   Pp [1–4] 5–64   Tp woodcut of a house, with horse and sleigh coming into view, 2 double-sided pls, illus woodcuts   Paper, with woodcut on front of a whale
CONTENTS: 1 tp; 2 'We will be glad to receive any Gaspé recipes that have been omitted from this book, for possible publication in a second edition. They should be addressed to – "The Black Whale" Percé, Gaspé County, P.Q.'; 3 'Preface' signed Alice M.S. Lighthall, president, Quebec Provincial Branch, Canadian Handicrafts Guild; 4–5 'Expeditions'; 6–9 'Autumn in the Woods'; 10–16 'Deep Sea Fishing'; 17–19 'The Salmon Pool'; 20–1 'Fishing for Your Breakfast'; 22–7 'The Butcher's Dog'; 28–9 'Sunday on the Coast'; 30–1 'The Iron Pot'; 32–4 'The Kitchen Garden'; 35–8 'The Out Door Oven – and Home Made Bread'; 39–49 'Desserts for the Men Folk'; 50 'A Change in the Weather'; 51–2 'Famous Old French Canadian Recipes'; 53–7 'Celebrations'; 58–61 'Swapping Recipes'; 62–4 'Grandma's Spare Time'
CITATIONS: Armstrong 2000, p F2, illus p F2   BQ Ex-

position 1974, p 23   Carrière No. 179   Driver 2001, Wellington County, p 88   Driver 2003, 'Canadian Cookbooks,' p 35   Ferguson/Fraser, p 234, illus col on p 103 of closed volume   Landsberg

COPIES: OONL (TX715.6 B53 1948, 2 copies)   QMBN (185987)   QMMARC (MG 1001, Black Whale, 1934–1975, file 18)   QMMMCM (Old information file – cookery)   *Private collection; United States: KMK

NOTES: See pl 1. The cover-title is 'The Black Whale Cook Book: Fine Old Recipes from the Gaspé Coast Going Back to Pioneer Days.' The Black Whale was a community shop run by the Percé Handicraft Committee for the craftspeople of the district. In the 'Preface,' Lighthall describes the Black Whale as more than a shop: '... it is the centre of a very active revival of local arts, in and around Percé.' Documents relating to the Black Whale craft shop, including three photographs of Ethel Renouf and the store interior, were donated to QMMARC (MG 1001, Black Whale, 1934–1975). QMMARC describes the history behind the shop thus:

In 1934 the Percé Handicrafts Guild was formed by a group of women, many of them wealthy 'summer people' from Montréal, to encourage Gaspé handicrafts both for their intrinsic value and as a means of alleviating the financial hardships of the Depression. The Guild organized lectures, competitions and exhibits and in 1936 opened a shop in Percé called 'The Black Whale'. Guild members manned the shop on a volunteer basis, and profits were used for community projects, such as the Dental Clinic, staffed in the summer by McGill professors Roland Lamb and Arthur Walsh. The shop was a centre for the study of Gaspé history and natural science, and sponsored a number of publications.

File 18 of MG 1001 contains material related to the cookbook: a copy of the book (1948 edition); a handwritten outline; a typewritten draft of pp 4–5; draft material from page 50; and handwritten versions of five recipes given to Mrs Renouf and signed by B.E. Tardif, Mrs Thos Gorman, and Mrs Isaac E. Kennedy. A summary entry for 1948 in the Percé Handicraft Guild Minute Book records information about the book's production: 'At a meeting held on April [blank space for day] at Mrs Renoufs. There being present Mrs H.P. Renouf Mrs Valpy and Miss B. Tardif ... A Black Whale cookbook compiled by Mrs Ethel Renouf our President – was completed and was to be put on sale that year. Mrs Phyllis Birks undertook to see about editing & printing & also did the proof reading.'

The book is remarkable for the detail it provides on local lore, customs associated with specific celebrations such as weddings or New Year, and the region's traditional foodways. The volume is also unusual because it is illustrated by Canadian artists. Irene Tuzo, one of the three artists who contributed woodcuts, also submitted a recipe for Scallop Croquettes, p 21. Recipes signed Captain's Cottage came from Mrs Phyllis Birks, née Ross, who vacationed in the cottage of that name in Percé; Phyllis was married to Gerald Birks of the Montreal jewellery-store family. Recipes signed Cod Cottage came from the Ross family, of the well-known Montreal accounting firm P.S. Ross and Sons. Cod Cottage was Phyllis Birks's childhood summer home. Recipes signed Miss Jean Lindsay are from Ethel Renouf's sister.

The 1948 edition was still available for sale in Percé in 1957, reports a private collector who bought her copy at that time.

Information about the Renoufs and about Captain's Cottage and Cod Cottage is from Joyce Quinn of Quebec City (a relative of Mrs Laura Valpy and Miss Betty Tardif, whose recipes are in the cookbook), and from Mrs Margaret Lamb of Montreal (also a relative of Valpy and Tardif). Margaret was the first assistant clerk in the shop, beginning, she says, in the summer of 1935; she later married Roland Lamb, who, in the summer of 1939, served as the community's first volunteer dentist. The Renoufs' birth and death dates are from the headstones in the cemetery.

OTHER EDITIONS: Montreal: Typo-Press, 1962 (OGU, OKQ, OONL, OTMCL, QGMG).

1949

Grand'Mère favourite recipes

Q315.1   1949

Bethel United Church, / Grand'Mère, Quebec. / The Women's Association / of / Bethel United Church / presents / Grand'Mere favourite recipes

DESCRIPTION: 22.0 × 14.5 cm   Pp [1] 2–124   Tp illus of Bethel United Church signed Don Inman   Paper, with image on front of steps going up a hill; stapled

CONTENTS: 1 tp; 2 ads; 3 'Foreword' signed Women's Association, Bethel United Church, Grand'Mère, Quebec, August 1949; 4 ads; 5–122 text and ads; 123 'Index' [i.e., table of contents]; 124 ads

COPIES: *NBFY

NOTES: The recipes are credited with the name of the contributor.

Our favourite recipes

Q316.1   1949
Our favourite / recipes / Compiled by / the /
Junior Women's Association / Brownsburg United
Church / Brownsburg, Que. / 1949 [cover-title]
COPIES: *Private collection

Rawleigh's 60th anniversary good health guide almanac cook book 1949

*For information about Rawleigh's annual almanac
cookbooks and other publications, see M22.1.*

Q317.1   1949
1889 Rawleigh's 60th anniversary 1949 / good
health guide / almanac cook book / Printed in
Canada by / the W.T. Rawleigh Co., Ltd. / Montreal
– Winnipeg / Freeport Memphis Richmond Chester
Albany Minneapolis / Denver Oakland Melbourne
Wellington [cover-title]
DESCRIPTION: 24.0 × 16.5 cm   Pp 1–31 [32]   Illus
black-and-orange   Paper, with portrait on front of
W.T. Rawleigh; stapled, and with hole punched at top
left corner for hanging
CONTENTS: 1 'An Appreciation and Some Recollections for 60 Years' signed W.T. Rawleigh, president
and founder; 2 'The Year 1949'; 3 'Late News about
Products'; 4 'Rawleigh's 1949 Zodiacal Planting Chart';
5 'Your Family Medicine Chest'; 6–31 monthly calendars, health information, advice about housework,
culinary recipes, and information about insect pests
and livestock; 32 '1949 Fishing Calendar'
COPIES: OHMB (Serial)   OSPTM   OTUTF (uncat
patent medicine)   *SWSLM

Saguenay cook book IV

Q318.1   [1949]
Saguenay / cook book / IV [cover-title]
DESCRIPTION: With stylized image on front of a
Saguenay scene (cliff and water)
COPIES: *Private collection
NOTES: The introductory note on p 2 states: 'This
fourth church cook book of the Saguenay region is
offered by the Woman's Association of Arvida First

United Church ... the year of its publication marks the
completion of plans for our new church building.'
The note is signed July 1949, Cook Book Committee,
followed by the names of the four women on the
committee (Gladys Thomson, Ida Woodwark, Dorothy James, and Haroldine Crerar). The executive of
the Woman's Association is listed below. Another private collector reports that his copy has 105 pp.
Two of the earlier cookbooks are Q257.1, *International Cook Book*, and Q290.1, *Saguenay Cook Book*. The
other has not been identified.

Before 1950

Eastern Townships' third annual shoppers' guide and cook book

Q319.1   nd [before 1950]
Eastern Townships' / third annual / shoppers'
guide / and / cook book [cover-title]
CONTENTS: 1 thank-you to advertisers signed Leah
Echenberg Chapter of Hadassah, Sherbrooke, Quebec, Mrs Abe Schachter, president
COPIES: *QLB (TX715.6 E27)
NOTES: The volume has 72 pp. It was likely published
before 1950 because the advertisers' street addresses
use the old names of Drummond, Wolfe, Lansdowne,
and St Sacrement, which became Galt, Belvedere,
Grand Fourches, and 1st Avenue, respectively, in 1950.
The only evidence that would indicate a later date is
an advertisement for a business celebrating its sixtieth anniversary: if the business was established in
1892, as the QLB Special Collections Archivist informs me it was, the book would have been published in 1952 (1892 + 60 years). How the business
counted its anniversary is a less reliable indicator
than the change in street names; therefore, the pre-
1950 date of publication is the more likely. In any
case, the first annual edition of this cookbook (no
copy found) must have been published within the
period covered by this bibliography.
The title of the cookbook suggests that the Leah
Echenberg Chapter was following the successful series of annual cookbooks published by the Winnipeg
Hadassah Council, starting in about 1928; for this
series, see M73.1.

Ontario

Pumpkins

This vegetable, or rather fruit, is extensively grown in Canada; being always planted with Indian corn. It is given in the fall of the year to the cattle and swine, which feed upon it eagerly; it is fattening and nourishing, and imparts no bad flavour to the milk, as turnips are apt to do.

Among the old-fashioned settlers, the pumpkin is much esteemed for pies, and a sort of molasses, which they prepare from the fruit by long boiling. When properly made, there is not a better dish eaten than a good pumpkin-pie. Now I must tell you, that an English pumpkin-pie, and a Canadian one, are very differently made, and I must give the preference, most decidedly, to the American dish; which is something between a custard and a cheese-cake, in taste and appearance. I will now give you a recipe or two for

Pumpkin-Pie*

Select a good, sweet pumpkin, fully ripe: to ascertain if it be a sweet one, for there is a great difference in this respect, cut a piece of the rind and taste it, or cut several, and then you can judge which is best. The sweetest pumpkins require less sugar, and are much richer.

Pare and cut the fruit into slices, removing the seeds and also the fibrous, spongy part, next to the seeds. Cut it into small pieces, and put it on the fire with about a pint of water, covering the pot close: you are not to bruise or stir it. Should the water boil away so as to endanger the pumpkin burning to the bottom of the pot, a small quantity more of water may be added. It will take three or four hours to boil quite soft, and of a fine brownish yellow. Some improve the color and richness by setting the pot on a few embers, near the fire, and keeping the pot turned as the pulp browns at the sides: but this requires to be carefully attended to.

When the pumpkin is as soft as mashed turnips, pass it through a hair-sieve or a colander; then add new milk and two or three eggs well beaten, with grated ginger; as much sugar as will make it sweet enough to be pleasant. Pounded and sifted cinnamon is frequently used as spice or nutmeg; but ginger and cinnamon are preferable to any other spice for pumpkin-pies. The milk must not be sufficient to thin the pumpkin too much: it should be about the consistence, when ready for the oven, of finely mashed turnips: if too thin you will need more eggs to set it; but it absorbes a great deal of milk, and is better to stand some little time after the milk is added, before being baked.

Make a nice light paste; line your dishes or plates, and then put in your mixture. These pies are always open; not with a cover of paste over them.

A very rich pumpkin-pie may be made by adding cream, lemon-peel, the juice of a lemon, and more eggs.

A finer dish, than a good pumpkin-pie, can hardly be eaten: and it is within the power of any poor man's family to enjoy this luxury. If you do not grow this fruit, any neighbour will give you one for the asking.

*I had this recipe from a Canadian lady who is celebrated for the excellence of her pumpkin-pies. I can vouch for their goodness from my own experience.

O5.1, *The Female Emigrant's Guide*, by Catharine Parr Traill, 1854 [1855], pp 127–8

Before 1950, 1,240 culinary titles were published in Ontario[1] – almost four times as many as in Quebec, and more than the total number of culinary titles published in all of the rest of Canada, Quebec included. In 1825, the year *La cuisinière bourgeoise* (Q1.1) was published in Quebec City, the population of what is now Ontario was lower than that of its eastern neighbour, but by the first Census of 1851, the tables were turned.[2] Moreover, since Quebec has always had a francophone majority, Ontario's mostly English-speaking population has long outstripped the number of anglophones in Quebec, as it has the populations in other provinces. The earliest European settlement in the area of present-day Ontario was the French Jesuit mission called Ste Marie among the Hurons, near Midland, close to Georgian Bay, but it was abandoned in 1649. Today's Franco-Ontarians, a relatively small group, are descended from Quebeckers who arrived in the late 1800s and after, or are new arrivals. Large-scale immigration began only after the American Revolution, with the arrival of Loyalists of British and German extraction (the latter, Pennsylvania Mennonites, settled mostly in Waterloo County, where they have maintained many of their food traditions). After this first influx, people from the United States and Britain continued to settle the southern part of the province, carving out farms in what turned out to be the largest amount of the best agricultural land in all of Canada and which included the favoured Niagara Peninsula at the west end of Lake Ontario, where conditions were ideal for growing peaches, grapes, and other soft fruit. In the period covered by this bibliography, therefore, Ontarians were overwhelmingly of British ancestry. By 1867, the year of Confederation with the other three founding provinces (Quebec, Nova Scotia, and New Brunswick), Ontario was the leader in manufacturing, owing in part to its abundance of natural resources (water, timber, minerals), good transportation routes (first by waterways, then by rail), and its proximity to American markets, and the shift of population to the cities had begun. By 1900, Toronto had secured its place as the centre of English-language publishing for Canada, and many of the developments in early Canadian publishing described by Parker are evident in the body of nineteenth-century Ontario cookbooks, such as the reprinting of American and British works, the advent of 'cheap' series of books in 1879, the establishment of the textbook industry in Toronto, the vogue for subscription book publishing in the 1880s and 1890s, the proliferation of new publishing houses in the 1890s, and the significant role of the Methodist Book and Publishing House.[3] Over time,

many of the successful makers of kitchen appliances and food products expanded their markets and opened additional offices and plants in other parts of the country so that many of the advertising cookbooks in this section were distributed nationally, as were all the culinary publications produced by the federal government, which are described in this section because the nation's capital, Ottawa, is in Ontario. A legacy of Ontario's nineteenth-century development is the large stock of historic houses and sites, many of which have been turned into museums with working kitchens, where staff or volunteers prepare foods from the past to offer to the visiting public. Ontario is also the first province where an association was formed of those interested in foodways research: the Culinary Historians of Ontario, founded in 1994 to research, interpret, preserve, and celebrate Ontario's (and since 2006, Canada's) culinary heritage.

The first cookbook published in Ontario (then Upper Canada), and the earliest English-language cookbook for all of Canada, was *The Cook Not Mad; or Rational Cookery* of 1831 (O1.1), an edition of an American work of regional significance.[4] The Kingston edition was likely printed in Watertown, New York, by Knowlton and Rice, the original American publisher. The text was not revised in any way for Upper Canadian homes (the Preface, for example, retains the reference to 'good Republican dishes'), but since it was directed at an audience not far across the border, Kingstonians probably found *The Cook Not Mad* to be a useful reference.

Nine years passed before the next cookbook was published in Upper Canada: *The Frugal Housewife's Manual* by the as-yet-unidentified 'A.B.,' who is described as from Grimsby, although the volume was printed in Toronto, in 1840 (O2.1). This slim volume of 100 numbered items, arranged in two complementary sections, the second combining growing and cooking instructions for vegetables, is the first English-language cookbook compiled in Canada. Although the title brings to mind two well-known British and American works, both called *The Frugal Housewife*, by Susannah Carter and Lydia Child respectively, the text appears to be original, with the exception of some growing instructions extracted from an American seed catalogue and a few recipes from *Mackenzie's Five Thousand Receipts in All the Useful and Domestic Arts*, a British compilation (also published in American editions). *The Frugal Housewife's Manual* appeared in the same year as the first French-language cookbook compiled in Canada – *La cuisinière canadienne* (Q3.1) – but it did not have the long-lasting impact of its popular French counterpart (issued in multiple editions into the twentieth century), despite its ground-breaking role as the first locally compiled cookbook in English. The single edition was printed at the office of the *Christian Guardian*, the influential Methodist newspaper. Through the period covered by this bibliography, several other cookbooks were to roll off its press or to be distributed through the bookselling side of the business (the Wesleyan Book Room, later the Methodist Book Room), including imported works.[5]

Of all Canada's nineteenth-century culinary writers in English, the most authentic voice belonged to Catharine Parr Traill, who had published in 1854–5 *The Female Emigrant's Guide, and Hints on Canadian Housekeeping* (O5.1), after much difficulty in arranging a printer and with little remuneration for her efforts in the end. As she states in the book, she did not set out to make 'a regular cookery-book,' but rather to explain for new immigrants the aspects which were different from British practice. Bringing food to the table entailed more than preparing a recipe, and Traill covered the whole process from growing, harvesting, and preserving, to cooking and tasting. Her comments range from the traditional food customs of the native people and typical farmhouse dishes to the merits of the new cookstoves and baking powders. As a novelist and story-writer from a literary family, she presented the information with an eye for the telling detail and from the perspective of someone with nearly a quarter-century of experience in the backwoods, who was sensitive to the mid-century changes in settler society and to all the influences (physical and cultural) that shaped cooking in the colonial kitchen. As the century progressed, however, her text became increasingly out of date, and, although she began to prepare a revised version in the 1880s, it was never published.

Cookbooks by named, local authors, such as 'A.B.' and Traill, were the exception rather than the rule in nineteenth-century Ontario. When the Hamilton printer Henry Richards saw the need for 'a decided Canadian vade-mecum of cookery' he selected recipes 'from the best English, French & American works' and reprinted them in *The Canadian Housewife's Manual of Cookery* of 1861 (O6.1). One is left to wonder whether his wife, Elizabeth, helped make the choice. Little is known of Mrs Anne Clarke, author of *Mrs Clarke's Cookery Book* of 1883 (O35.1), except that she lived at the same Toronto address as George Clarke, an English tea merchant. Her comprehensive collection features local recipes and versions of recipes (uncredited) from a well-known 1877 English textbook, *The Official Handbook for the National Training School for Cook-*

ery Containing the Lessons on Cookery Which Constitute the Course of Instruction in the School. The lady superintendent of the NTSC was Mrs Edith Clarke, which suggests a possible family connection with Anne and George. Clarke's cookbook came to be a standard reference for Ontario housewives in the first two decades of the twentieth century, long after its first publication, when it was reissued several times as *The Dominion Home Cook Book* or *The Dominion Cook Book* by various publishers (J.L. Nichols and Co., J.S. Brown and Sons, McLeod and Allen, and George J. McLeod), as *The Ideal Cook Book* by other publishers (Westminster Co. Ltd and Dominion Phelps Ltd), and as an advertising vehicle, under different titles, for three soap makers (John Taylor and Co., St Croix Soap Manufacturing Co., and Pugsley, Dingman and Co. Ltd), a flour miller (Campbell Flour Mills Co. Ltd), and three national retailers (Hudson's Bay Co., T. Eaton Co., and Robert Simpson Co. Ltd). *Mrs Clarke's Cookery Book* is also notable as the first Canadian cookbook to be issued in an American edition, in 1889, in Chicago (and in later American editions). Two other Ontario women, Dora Fairfield of Bath, near Kingston, and Mrs James McDonald of Orangeville, northwest of Toronto, produced cookbooks in the 1880s, but neither of their works sold in large numbers. Fairfield compiled *Dora's Cook Book* (O43.1), 1888, from recipes 'furnished by leading ladies of Canada and the United States.' The Fairfields were a well-known Loyalist family and *Dora's Cook Book*, which records the source of some recipes, is a significant record of her Loyalist culinary heritage. McDonald's text for *The Cook's True Friend* (O47.1), 1889, is authoritative, offering, for example, explicit instructions for making pastry and roasting coffee. At the very end of the century, Adelaide Hoodless's *Public School Domestic Science* (O86.1) of 1898 made an important contribution to the early development of the subject within the provincial school system.

Of the ninety-six culinary titles published before 1900 in Ontario,[6] thirty-seven are known to be reprints of foreign texts, mostly American, and there are more cookbooks in this section that likely originated outside Canada, but which have not yet been positively identified. For the fledgling publishing industry in the colony, and from 1867 new province, issuing local editions of successful foreign titles (pirated or with permission) was the most practical way to meet the increasing appetite for literature, especially for books of 'useful knowledge,' a category to which cookbooks belonged. It was easiest for publishers to reprint American, rather than British, works for various reasons,[7] but American cookbooks had another advantage: some recipes called for North American ingredients, such as corn, peaches, cranberries, and maple syrup – items not normally found in British recipe collections; and one can imagine that descendants of Loyalists might find the contents of American texts familiar and especially suited to their family tables. Yet readers might not always be aware of the source of a text because, while some reprints clearly stated their authorship and printing history, others disguised their identities to varying degrees. *The Cook Not Mad*, for example, did not refer to the first Watertown edition, but neither did it delete the reference to Republican dishes. The owners of the Montreal firm of Armour and Ramsay, which had branch plants in Kingston and Hamilton, were applauded in the 1840s for their efforts to bring authorized editions of British works to the Canadian public.[8] The title-page of their 1845 edition of *Modern Practical Cookery* (Q4.1), a Scottish text, correctly records the author, Mrs Nourse, as an Edinburgh cookery teacher, but the American Mrs Abell goes uncredited in the company's 1848 edition of *The Skilful Housewife's Guide* (Q5.1), which is based entirely on material extracted from Abell's *The Skilful Housewife's Book*. Likewise, Alexander Davidson did not credit the American Mrs Crowen in his 1846 Niagara edition of *Every Lady's Book* (O4.1). From 1865, multiple editions of the American *Dr Chase's Recipes* flooded the Canadian market, to be followed by *Dr Chase's Third, Last and Complete Receipt Book and Household Physician* and *Dr Chase's New Receipt Book* (O8.1, O40.1, O45.1). The success of these books in Canada derived from the huge reputation south of the border of the Ann Arbor, Michigan, doctor. In 1868 the Toronto publisher Adam Miller retitled his edition of *The American Home Cook Book*, a New York recipe collection of the mid-1850s, as *The Dominion Home Cook-Book* (O11.1), likely fooling many buyers (and future researchers!), and in 1874, the Hamilton or Toronto publisher of the *Housekeeper's Companion* did not reveal that many of the recipes came from *Mackenzie's Five Thousand Receipts*, first published in England half a century before (O17.1). There would be a few later cases of hidden origins (for example, O27.1, *The Seaside Cook Book* of 1880, likely a version of *The Lakeside Cook Book* from Chicago, and O31.1, *Mother Hubbard's Cupboard* of 1881, misleadingly subtitled 'Canadian Cook Book' but from Rochester, New York); however, in the last quarter of the century, the trend was for Ontario publishers to capitalize on the fame of the new American culinary celebrities, such as Marion Harland (O18.1, O22.1, O46.1), Eliza Parker (O39.1), and Sarah Tyson Rorer, founder of the Philadelphia School of Cookery (O56.1,

O57.1), and sometimes also well-known English cooks or educators, such as Mary Jewry (O14.1, O21.1), Catherine Buckton (O19.1), and Matilda Lees Dods, who, in 1879–80, enjoyed a successful lecture tour in the United States, and in Toronto and London, Ontario (O26.1). At the same time, Ontario branches of American subscription publishing houses marketed American culinary titles to Canadians: The Brantford branch of the Philadelphia subscription firm Bradley, Garretson and Co. sold books by three American authors, Julia McNair Wright (O24.1), Laura Holloway (O37.1), and Maud Cooke (O75.1, O81.1), and in 1895 the Toronto branch of a Naperville, Illinois, firm began selling *The Household Guide or Domestic Cyclopedia*, which included a cookery section by the publisher's wife, Elizabeth Nichols (O70.1). And the Guelph-based subscription business World Publishing Co. sold orders for the 1883 American work, *The Housewife's Library* (O38.1). At the very end of the century, Copp Clark Co. Ltd published a Toronto edition of *The White House Cook Book* (O93.1), an immensely popular American work of 1887 by Hugo Ziemann (steward of the White House) and Mrs F.L. Gillette. Two Toronto editions followed where the reference to the US president's home was replaced by new titles – *The Premier Cook Book* (O93.2) and *The Union Life Cook Book* (O93.3) – but the retitling was more to distinguish these editions as advertising premiums than an aversion to the original title. American editions of *The White House Cook Book* and the condensed version called *The Presidential Cook Book* were widely distributed in Canada and the large numbers of copies still found in Canadian private collections attest to the welcome this large, well-illustrated volume received. How all these nineteenth-century American and British recipe collections influenced cooking practices in Ontario (and in other parts of the country when distributed nationally) is an important question that has yet to be explored, but every recipe disseminated through a printed cookbook had the potential of being adopted into a family's repertoire and from there to enter the traditions of the wider community.

One of the most significant events in the history of English-language Canadian cookbooks was the publication in Toronto in 1877 of *The Home Cook Book* (O20.1), to raise money for the Hospital for Sick Children, which had been founded just two years before by a group of women led by the indomitable Mrs McMaster. *The Home Cook Book* was Canada's first community cookbook; it was the best-selling Canadian cookbook of the nineteenth century; and it is the only Canadian cookbook in this bibliography to be published in an Australian edition (Sydney, about 1889) and in New Zealand editions (1891, 1892), and one of only two in the bibliography to be published in a British edition (London, England, likely 1906).[9] By 1885, over 100,000 copies were purported to have been sold. By 1929 (the date of the last edition), it had been republished almost fifty times, by various firms in Ontario, New Brunswick, and Manitoba. When *The Home Cook Book* first appeared, the novelty of the text would have been apparent – most of the recipes were credited with the name of the contributor, many of whom were familiar figures in Toronto society. *The Home Cook Book* was an example for other women of how they could create their own cookbooks and sell them to support a cause in their own communities. It launched a new type of recipe collection in Canada, one that would be suited to local kitchens and more personal than the ubiquitous foreign reprints and imports. Ironically, *The Home Cook Book* itself was based on *The Home Cook Book of Chicago*, an 1874 fund-raiser for the Home for the Friendless in that city, although the Toronto ladies did add their own new recipes. In 1879, when the Chicago publisher levelled a charge of piracy, the hospital ladies turned to one of their trustees to craft a letter, which seems to have solved the problem; however, the affair likely prompted the hospital to disassociate itself from the cookbook in the same year. Although the volume was no longer described as a benefit for the hospital after 1879, it remained essentially unchanged in other respects for the next fifty years.[10] Its widespread distribution ensured that not only did it continue to serve as a model for other Canadian fund-raisers, several of which borrowed its title-page guarantee of 'Tried, tested, proved' (Q32.1, M2.1, M20.1, S5.1, A18.1), but the recipe collection itself must have helped to shape Canadian cooking. Mrs McMaster's Carrot Pudding (p 197), for example, is the first instance in a Canadian cookbook of this lighter type of plum pudding; versions of the recipe were subsequently reprinted in most English-Canadian cookbooks up to 1950 and beyond, and the recipe became a classic Christmas dessert in English-Canadian homes.

The Home Cook Book's appearance in 1877 signalled the start of a Canadian publishing phenomenon that had its greatest expression in Ontario: an astonishing 507 community cookbooks surfaced for the years up to 1950 – more than the total number of culinary titles published in Quebec in the same period – and there are likely many more to be discovered. The 12 community cookbooks found from before 1900 came from a variety of sources, but 7 were produced by church

women's groups (O28.1, O44.1, O58.1, O66.1, O84.1, O89.1, O91.1). An undated 1890s cookbook supported the work of the Epworth League in Leamington (O51.1); one 1895 cookbook raised funds for Toronto's Grace Hospital (O69.1), as *The Home Cook Book* had done for the city's children's hospital; another 1895 cookbook was described simply as 'by the ladies of Wallaceburg' (O67.1); and an 1897 Windsor recipe collection celebrated the diamond jubilee of Queen Victoria's ascent to the throne (O83.1). In every decade after 1877, there were significant or unusual examples, including three of these early charitable cookbooks. The 594-page *The Canadian Economist* (O28.1) by the Ladies' Association of Bank Street Church was the third community cookbook published in Canada (after *The Home Cook Book* and NB2.1, *Cuisine*, Saint John, New Brunswick, 1878) and the most lavish of all. Eight colour lithographs were produced by the publisher Alexander Mortimer especially for the volume: a frontispiece of the church, two illustrations (a beaver and an eagle) for a poem that mysteriously refers to family ties with the United States, and interior and exterior views of an ideal 'home cottage.' *The Galt Cook Book* of 1892 (O58.1), another lengthy volume of 534 pages, but not illustrated, is notable for its global distribution and long local popularity. Copies of the first edition were sent through the network of Presbyterian ladies to destinations across Canada and to the United States, England, Scotland, China, Egypt, India, South Africa, Australia, and 'other remote countries'; and it was republished another four times up to about 1916–20, the last edition sold through T. Eaton Co., the national department store. The 1898 edition was the only Canadian cookbook to be listed in the Toronto Public Library's subject catalogue for the circulating library, in the period 1889–99. All compilers of community cookbooks faced submissions of duplicate recipes and most exercised some degree of editorial control, but the food historian should be thankful to the ladies of the Parry Sound Baptist Church who included every variation, however similar, in *The B.Y.P.U. Cook Book* (O89.1), because the frequency with which certain recipes were offered is evidence of the favourite foods of the time – for example, seventeen numbered recipes for Doughnuts and ten for Lemon Pie.

From 1900 onward there was an explosion in the number of community cookbooks produced in Ontario: this bibliography records 96 titles in the first thirteen years; 26 for 1914–18 (the First World War period); 93 for 1919–29; 134 for 1930–8; 84 for 1939–45 (Second World War); and 62 to the end of the 1940s. The books emanated from large- and medium-sized cities and from small towns, all around the province, including many places in Northern Ontario, some recently established.[11] To nineteenth-century examples from Sault Ste Marie, Parry Sound, and North Bay (O84.1, O89.1, O91.1), one can add other early ones from Huntsville and Gravenhurst in 1900 (O97.1, O98.1), Orillia in 1902 (O123.1), Burks Falls in 1903 (O138.1), Wiarton in 1904 (O139a.1), Powassan in 1905 (O160a.1), Port Arthur in about 1905–10 (O165.1), Cobalt in 1908 (O204.1), North Bay and Fort William in 1910 or so (O226.1, O246.1), Bala in 1913 (O296.1), Schreiber in 1914 (O327.1), and Bruce Mines in 1916 (O359.1). In the 1920s there were others from Haileybury (O522.1), Manitoulin Island (O561.1), Chapleau (O567.1), and South Porcupine (O581.1), and later ones from Sudbury (O836.1, O1135.1), Kirkland Lake (O912.1, O1138.1), Creighton Mine (O937.1), Kapuskasing (O964.1), New Liskeard (O1167.1), Cochrane (O1176.1), Marathon (O1215.1), and again South Porcupine (O1232.1). Sometimes, the early northern cookbooks are more attractive than one might perhaps expect. The paper cover of the Burks Falls volume (O138.1) is decorated with a printed ribbon border and the volume itself is bound by a real ribbon through punched holes. *Cobalt Souvenir and Cook Book* (O204.1) celebrated a town that had sprung up only five years before, when silver was discovered there, with photographs of streetscapes and bush scenes; in 1924 the Silver Chapter of the Imperial Order Daughters of the Empire in Cobalt published a cookbook where the binding featured silver lettering on dark blue card (O519.1).

Many fund-raisers were produced for churches and hospitals, but there were also other causes, occasionally ambitious or odd, or relying on unusual marketing methods. The Women's Temperance Auxiliary in Sparta, for example, published five editions of *The Spartan Cook Book* (O124.1) between 1902 and about 1915 to help purchase the local hotel-cum-bar and transform it into a dry community centre where citizens could read 'good periodic literature.' In 1906 users of *Bright Ideas: A Book of Home Secrets* (O168.1) learned of another money-making scheme for the County of Carleton General Protestant Hospital; the advertisement for the Toronto publisher Musson explained that if they bought one of the listed novels, Musson would send 10% of the price of the book to the hospital. *The Essex Cook Book* (O176.1) of 1907 by the ladies of the Methodist Church was promoted as a souvenir of the disastrous explosion at the Essex Station that year. *C.L.C. Tombola Cook Book* (O208.1) was a 1909 fund-raiser for the Cornwall Lacrosse Club; on the front cover, a lacrosse player is depicted

against a maple leaf – a national symbol to signify the national sport. The first Women's Institute in the world was founded in 1897 in Stoney Creek, near Hamilton, and among the earliest of the many fund-raisers by the various branches was the *Laura Secord Memorial Cook Book* (O249.1) of about 1910–12, which the Queenston branch hoped would help pay for a 'Greek style hall' in honour of Canada's heroine of the War of 1812.[12] In the case of *The Wimodausis Club Cook Book* (O294.1) of 1912 or 1913, a small but influential group of Toronto women likely exceeded their initial fund-raising goals for the club's social service work when the continued demand for copies led to a second edition of 224 pages in 1922 and a further enlarged third edition of 528 pages in 1934. Mrs Hart, a Montrealer and Canada's first Jewish culinary author, had included a recipe for Ball Soup in her 1865 *Household Recipes* (Q7.1), but *The Economical Cook Book* (O337.1) of 1915, produced by the Ottawa Ladies Hebrew Benevolent Society 'to alleviate the sufferings of their poor,' is the country's first Jewish recipe collection. The best-known Jewish cookbook, however, was *Naomi Cook Book* (O627.1), by the Toronto Hadassah chapter of the same name, where the profits of the first edition were directed specifically to the work of Hadassah in Palestine; it went through four editions in 1928, 1934, 1948, and 1960, and treasured family copies are still consulted today. The headquarters of the Imperial Order Daughters of the Empire has been in Toronto since 1901, a year after the organization's founding. Toronto's St George Chapter published the earliest Ontario IODE cookbook (O358.1), a 1916 fund-raiser for St Dunstan's Hostel for Blinded Soldiers in London, England, where injured Canadian soldiers were treated. Many Ontario women's groups published cookbooks during the two World Wars to support the national war effort, the Red Cross Society being the usual beneficiary in 1914–18. However, in the unique case of Mrs Powell's *The Toronto Cook Book* (O345.1) of 1915, money raised by selling 25,000 copies was to be disbursed by a committee of Toronto businessmen to the city's wartime unemployed, but it appears that the organizers overestimated the potential for sales and leftover copies were distributed later with the wartime preface carefully torn out. During the Second World War, to raise money for war and welfare work, the Scandinavian Canadian Club of Toronto compiled a collection of recipes from Denmark, Finland, Norway, and Sweden – the only such collection in this bibliography (O983.1). In 1944 or 1945, near the end of the Second World War and anticipating peace soon, the women of the Co-operative Commonwealth Federation (the

Canadian socialist political party, precursor to today's New Democratic Party) published a cookbook under the auspices of the CCF National Council in Ottawa (O1088.1). As Lucy Woodsworth, wife of the party's founder, explained in the 'Foreword,' the women members focused 'their first united effort' on food since one of the immediate aims of the party was to develop a high standard of health in Canada. Far from being a prescriptive tome on nutrition, the text is a typical collection of 'recipes submitted by housewives across the country' – *Canadian Favourites*, as the title so aptly states, including British, Scandinavian, Eastern European, and Mediterranean dishes. The American Women's Club in Toronto was founded in 1917, but it was not until 1948 that they compiled their *Favorite Recipes from American Kitchens* (O1183.1), publishing no fewer than three editions in two years. These two titles, and the twenty-five Ontario community cookbooks in the 1930s called *Favorite Recipes* or the variation *Favorite Recipes Cook Book*, reinforce the fact that this genre of cookbook, more than any other, best reflects local food preferences.

The earliest advertising cookbooks in Ontario were the annual series of *Family Receipt* (or *Recipe*) *Book*s by the patent medicine company Northrop and Lyman, beginning in about 1864 (O7.1), the same period as similar publications appeared in Quebec. Soon, other Ontario businesses turned to cookbooks as promotional vehicles for their products, typically cooking ingredients or kitchen appliances, and it was in Ontario that this development began. The first dated culinary manual advertising a raising agent was *Cook's Friend Cook Book* of 1881 (O29.1), named after Cook's Friend Baking Powder, a trademark owned by a Montrealer, although the book was published in Toronto and the recipes are likely from an American source. *The Breadmaker's Book of Cooking Lessons* (O41.1) and *The Breadmaker's Recipe Book* (O42.1) followed in about 1888, both probably published to advertise Breadmaker's Yeast and Baking Powder made by Churchill and Co. in Toronto. The first for baking soda appeared in 1897, *Dwight's Cow-Brand Cook-Book* (O82.1) printed in Toronto for Church and Dwight Co., the Canadian branch of an American firm. The earliest recipe collections from Canadian stove manufacturers, canning companies, and flour millers were all published in Ontario in the 1890s: *Happy-Thought-Range Cookery Book* (O53.1) for cookstoves made in Brantford; *The Story of Canned Goods and How to Use Them* (O61.1), which employs a literary device to present the benefits of Ontario canned goods; and *Good Flour and How to Use It* (O85.1) from Peterborough's McAllister Milling Co. There were also

two Toronto titles intended for the trade: Dane and McIndoe's 1891 treatise on tea-blending, with recipes (O54.1), and Fletcher Manufacturing Co.'s 1896 guide for candy-making (O74.1).

In the twentieth century there would be cookbooks from a myriad of different Ontario businesses, usually intended for national distribution and often translated into French (mainly for the Quebec market), but stoves, flour, and raising agents remained the most advertised products. Stove manufacturing was an important and growing industry in nineteenth-century Ontario and several of the firms represented in this section were already a half-century old when they published their first cookbooks, among them Burrow, Stewart and Milne Co. in Hamilton (founded in 1864), McClary's in London (1847; amalgamated in 1927 with other Canadian companies, including Brantford's Happy Thought Foundry Co. Ltd, to form General Steel Wares, which carried on the McClary's brand), Gurney Foundry Ltd in Hamilton (1843), Moffat Stove Co. Ltd in Weston (1882), and Findlays Ltd in Carleton Place (1860).[13] A company cookbook often accompanied the purchase of a new stove, not just as a welcome gift of recipes, but sometimes to offer hints on kitchen design and to explain the operation and features of the appliance. Manuals such as *The Moffat Standard Canadian Cook Book* of 1915 (O342.1) helped Canadian women navigate technological changes in the first three decades of the twentieth century as they moved from wood- or coal-heated stoves to those run on gas or electricity. Cookbooks from this era also reveal how varied kitchens could be. In 1929, for example, General Steel Wares offered three separate editions of *The Modern Housekeepers' Guide*, each with special reference to either 'coal and wood cookery,' electric cookery, or gas cookery (O645.1–645.3), but by 1939, the company offered manuals only for electricity or gas (Q256.1, issued when the head office was in Montreal). Also published in Ontario were cookbooks for stoves and refrigerators made by Canadian General Electric in Toronto and Canadian Westinghouse in Hamilton – both originally American brand names, although the Westinghouse texts attributed to Anna May Cornell seem to have originated in Canada.

Following amalgamations in the first decade of the twentieth century, Western Canada Flour Mills Co., the maker of Purity Flour, and Maple Leaf Milling Co., the maker of Monarch Flour and Tea-Bisk (the instant biscuit mix introduced in 1931), emerged as the two largest Toronto-based milling companies. (Other major players in the industry were headquartered in Montreal.) Beginning with *Purity Flour Cook*

Book by Miss E. Warner (O394.1), Western Canada Flour Mills published a series of 'Purity Flour' cookbooks in 1917 (O394.1), 1923 (O504.1), 1932 (O771.1; this version revised and reissued in 1937, in 1945 with new illustrations by the Canadian artist A.J. Casson, and three times in the 1950s), and another in 1967, always carrying forward the best recipes from the previous publication, sometimes amended to suit the times (making this run of editions a good case study of the constants and changes in twentieth-century Canadian home cooking). The first Maple Leaf Milling cookbook, which bore the sentimental title *Old Homestead Recipes* (O444.1), appeared in about 1920, but from the mid-1920s to the 1960s, the company's many publications, plus newspaper and radio publicity, came out under the pseudonym Anna Lee Scott (except for French editions of two titles in the 1930s, under the pseudonym Marthe Miral, O773.15, O777.9). Cookbooks from these two flour giants reached into homes across the country and remain ubiquitous today. Canadian women – grandmothers, mothers, daughters – still feel a special attachment to the centennial edition of *The All New Purity Cook Book* in particular, as sales of the 2001 Whitecap Books facsimile edition have shown.

In the 1880s and 1890s, factory brands of baking powder, such as Cook's Friend, and baking powders mixed by individual druggists,[14] competed for customers; however, by the second decade of the new century Magic Baking Powder made by E.W. Gillett Co. Ltd in Toronto began to dominate the market. (The familiar maroon packaging still graces grocery store shelves in the twenty-first century.) From about 1912, the company produced multiple editions, in French and English, of the smaller-format *Magic Cook Book and Housekeepers Guide* (O285.1), and in the 1930s, multiple editions of the larger-format *Magic Cook Book* (O702.1), published after Gillett was taken over by Standard Brands in 1929. That so many copies survive today must be as much because of the colourful and amusing front covers as the huge numbers printed. The small format features variations of mustachioed or stout chefs, or bug-like creatures; the large format depicts a woman revealing a plate of biscuits for the magician-like 'Presto!' version or the faces of a mother, grandmother, and daughter to convey 'A family tradition.'

Other major Ontario food manufacturers also published advertising cookbooks. Canadian Milk Products Ltd, for example, was a Toronto firm that made powdered milk. Klim (milk spelled backward) was the name of their product for the general market. Their several titles were aimed at different clients: the

bakery trade (O374.1, O559.1); the housewife (O397.1, O453.1, O674.1); and the outdoorsman, who would take Klim on his hunting and fishing expeditions in the Canadian bush (O534.1). When Borden Co. Ltd (the next owner of the Klim brand) issued *Skillet Skills for Camp and Cottage* (O1171.1), a 1947 retitled version of *Camp Cooking* (O534.1), it incorporated humorous text by Jack Hambleton and cartoons by Jim Frise (both well-known figures in the pages of Toronto newspapers at the time); this version belongs in the small category of humorous camping cookbooks by men. Publications from Cowan Co. Ltd, the Toronto cocoa and chocolate maker, were attractively illustrated, typically with figures of children, but the 1921 'Cowan's Cocoa Recipes' stands out for the specially commissioned colour reproductions of watercolours by local artist Helene Carter (O468.1). Several brands of shortening – a new ingredient in the second decade – were promoted in cookbooks by the Toronto companies Gunns Ltd (O353.1, O426.1, O560.1), William Davies Co. Ltd (O455.1), and Harris Abattoir Co. Ltd (O456.1, O587.1), and by Canadian branches of the American firms Procter and Gamble, which invented Crisco shortening (O332.1, O343.1, O362.1, O363.1, O387.1, O390.1, O465.1, O582.1, O588.1, O735.1), and Swift, the maker of Jewel, Swift'ning, and Vreamay (O564.1, O575.1, O695.1, O863.1, O871.1, O894.1, O898.1, O1018.1, O1120.1). Canada Packers Ltd, the powerful entity created in 1927 by the amalgamation of Gunns, Davies, Harris Abattoir, and one other concern, produced recipe collections for meat in 1933 (O804.1), for large-scale baking in 1941 (O1023.1), and for Margene (its brand of recently legalized margarine) in 1949 (O1230.1), the latter employing the design talents of A.J. Casson (also illustrator of the 1945 *Purity Cook Book*, O771.3). Other striking examples of graphic art were *The Art of Sandwich Making* (O576.1) published by the Canada Bread Co. in about 1926 and the early 1930s style of *100 Dainty Dishes for Your Table* (O737.1), a collection of recipes for cooking with left-overs stored in waxed paper made by Appleford Paper Products in Hamilton. Even *The Bee Hive Cook Book* (O1054.1), promoting St Lawrence Starch Co. Ltd's corn syrup as a substitute for sugar during the Second World War, featured a tempting full-colour image of a slice of lemon meringue pie on the front cover. Many other advertising cookbooks came from Ontario businesses, to which could be added recipe collections published by the following Ontario newspapers and magazines since they served as promotional vehicles for the periodicals as much as money-earning publications: Toronto's *Vogue* in 1908 (O202.1), *Canadian Farm* magazine in 1911 (O257.1), the *London Free Press* in 1914 (O316.1), *MacLean's* [*sic*] in 1927 (O610.1), and newspapers in Flesherton, Cornwall, and Sarnia (O569.1, O749.1, O902.1). Most of these followed the community-cookbook model by soliciting recipes from readers.

Advertising cookbooks for American brands usually reprinted texts from the United States. Crisco and Canadian General Electric have already been mentioned, but there were many others, such as New Perfection cookstoves (O164.1), Shredded Wheat cereal (the Canadian and American plants were located across the border from each other at Niagara Falls; O222.1, O242.1, O521.1, O1116.1), Certo pectin (made in Cobourg; O480.1, O491.1, O600.1, O608.1, O714.1, O753.1, O835.1, O905.1), Minute Tapioca (O717.1, O848.1), Campbell's Soup (O744.1, O746.1, O1214.1), and Jell-O – 'America's most famous dessert' (O212.1, O487.1, O502.1, O503.1, O524.1, O557.1, O730.1, O759.1). Some of the collectible pamphlets for Jell-O were reprinted by the Genesee Pure Food Company of Canada in Bridgeburg, with the claim that Jell-O was 'Canada's most famous dessert' (the 1923 edition has a cover illustration by American artist Norman Rockwell).

Continuing a trend from the last quarter of the nineteenth century, Toronto publishers reprinted cookbooks by high-profile American and British authors, for distribution across Canada. One effect of the 1900 amendment to the Copyright Act of 1875 was to encourage the reprinting or importing of foreign books through agency arrangements with foreign firms. In Parker's words, 'foreign book agencies proliferated like rabbits in the first decade of the twentieth century.'[15] In the first two decades, three publishers – Musson, Copp Clark, and McClelland and Goodchild (later McClelland, Goodchild and Stewart, then McClelland and Stewart) – between them published one or more American authors almost every year. The '365' series (O100.1, O111.1, O125.1, O139.1),[16] Emily Holt (O132.1), Sarah Tyson Rorer (O137.1), Fannie Farmer (O144.1, O262.1), Jennie B. Williams (O224.1),[17] Marion Harris Neil (O306.1, O325.1),[18] and Alexander Filippini (O320.1)[19] were all under the Musson imprint. Mary Ronald (O115.1, O141.1), Paul Pierce (O182.1, O183.1, O184.1), Laura Davenport (O193.1), Emma Paddock Telford (O290.1), and Helen Cramp (O301.1) were under Copp Clark. McClelland and Goodchild (or its later incarnations) represented Janet McKenzie Hill (O264.1), Ellye Howell Glover (O302.1), Linda Hull Larned (O304.1), Mildred Maddocks (O324.1), Eugene Christian (O357.1), Vance Thompson (O370.1), Alice Bradley (O375.1), Anna

Merritt East (O382.1), Alfred McCann (O389.1), Mary Elizabeth Evans (O406.1), and also Marion Harris Neil (O391.1, O425.1). Bell and Cockburn, another Toronto firm, represented Marion Harland's daughter, Christine Terhune Herrick (O282.1). In 1939 McLean Publishers Syndicate in Toronto published *The Canadian Woman's Cook Book* by Ruth Berolzheimer (O961.1). This massive, highly illustrated tome was, in fact, an edition of *The American Woman's Cook Book*, evolved from a series of 1890s pamphlets, but the full-colour endpapers depicting petits fours on a silver tray helped to make the book irresistible to buyers on either side of the border. In the 1940s McClelland and Stewart published the first two Canadian editions of Irma Rombauer's American classic, *The Joy of Cooking* (O1057.1); however, in the course of my research, only one copy surfaced (the 1945 edition), an indication that the book did not become popular in Canada until after 1950. Another American standard reference, *The Good Housekeeping Cook Book* (O1046.1), was first published in Canada in 1942 by its New York publisher, Farrar and Rinehart. Probably few Americans (or Canadians) realized that the Good Housekeeping Institute in New York was under the leadership of a Canadian from 1924 to 1953: Katharine Fisher, who signed the 'Preface' of *The Good Housekeeping Cook Book*, was born and educated in Ontario and began her career as head of the School of Household Science at Macdonald College in Montreal.

Fewer British cookbooks were published in Toronto than American ones in the first half of the twentieth century, but popular titles and authors featured in every decade. The years 1908 and 1909 saw *Pot-Luck* by H.E.C. (O192.1), *French Dishes for English Tables* by Claire de Pratz (O194.1), and two titles by Arthur Payne (O198.1, O219.1). In the second decade, there were editions of Isabella Beeton's cookbooks (O231.1, O256.1, O272.1, O273.1, O315.1), the unattributed *Cooking by Gas* (O234.1) and *A Thousand and One Cookery Recipes and Kitchen Hints* (O291.1), *The Everyday Pudding Book* by F.K. (O238.1), *The One Maid Book of Cookery* by Mistress A.E. Congreve (O299.1), three titles by May Byron (O317.1, O333.1, O355.1), *More Up-to-Date and Economical Cookery* by Dora Groome and May Little (O313.1), and Little's *The Complete Cake Book* (O341.1). Louisa Thorpe's 1921 *Bonbons and Simple Sugar Sweets* (O473.1) was the solitary English title of its decade. In the 1930s, there were cookbooks by Florence White, founder of the English Folk Cookery Association (O782.1, O839.1), X.M. Boulestin, the French chef who made his career in London (O845.1, O906.1), and Mabel Osborne, who wrote about meatless and raw-food diets (O952.1). In 1934 the English firm William Heinemann Ltd published in Toronto *Recipes for Successful Dining* (O815.1), by Elsie de Wolfe, an American interior decorator who was renowned on both sides of the Atlantic for her style and taste. Cookbooks by the English novelist Sheila Kaye-Smith (O1099.1) and the Irish broadcaster and writer Maura Laverty (O1139.1), plus the uncredited *The Universal Cookery Book* (O1059.1), followed in the 1940s.

As the centre for English-language publishing in Canada, Toronto was the place from which these editions of American and British cookbooks were distributed, but it was also the milieu from which home-grown culinary authors began to emerge, especially through the city's vibrant newspaper and magazine print culture and through the growing medium of radio. The first journalist to make a mark was Grace Denison, society editor and staff reporter of *Saturday Night* magazine since the early 1890s, who compiled *The New Cook Book* (O130.1) in 1903 mostly from recipes submitted to her by ladies well known in Toronto society, whom she listed at the front. By 1906 the cookbook had been published in Montreal, Winnipeg, and Victoria, and in Toronto by E.W. Gillett, the maker of Magic Baking Powder; in 1914 (the year Denison died) it was reissued as *The Canadian Family Cook Book*, and in 1932 as *The Canadian Home Cook Book*. Its initial success was due in part to Denison's public profile as a writer for *Saturday Night*; however, it was likely also the result of a conscious strategy to model the collection after the best-selling *Home Cook Book* of 1877, but to market it as the 'new' cookbook for the new century. It was published in London, England, in 1906 (likely the same year as the London edition of *The Home Cook Book*, the only other Canadian title in this bibliography to be published in a British edition), 1907, and 1912. It was also distributed in the United States, under the guise of *The American Home Cook Book* (and various other titles) in 1913 and 1932 (a rare reversal of the usual pattern).

Jessie Read, author of *Three Meals a Day* (O954.1) published by Musson in six numbered editions from 1938 to 1949, first came to public attention in the late 1920s through her broadcasting and demonstrating work for the Home Service Department of Toronto's Consumers' Gas Co. In 1934, to great fanfare, the Toronto *Evening Telegram* announced the start of her daily cookery column in the newspaper, and two years later she starred in *Kitchen Talks*, billed as the first cooking-school movie made in Canada and reported to have been shown in over three hundred Ontario towns. In 1942, two years after her death at the tragically young age of thirty-five, she was re-membered as 'one of the most popular demonstrators of cookery methods that Toronto has ever known.'[20] Three other Toronto cookbook authors who first became known through print journalism were Mona Purser, editor of the *Globe and Mail*'s Home-maker Page for almost thirty years (O927.1); Marie Wallace, for many years food editor of the Toronto *Star* under the pseudonym Marie Holmes and, from 1947, director of *Chatelaine* magazine (O854.1, O1005.1); and Mrs Rose Marie Armstrong Christie, like Denison a writer for *Saturday Night*, whose 'Concerning Food' columns appeared under the pseudonym Cynthia Brown (O935.1). To this list of journalists (although an Ottawa resident), one might also add Helen Gougeon, who gathered recipes from various national embassies as a young reporter for the city's *Journal* newspaper in 1946, and self-published them in *Cooking with an Accent* (O1137.1). In the period covered by this bibliography, Kate Aitken, from Beeton, Ontario, was Canada's greatest culinary star. Her cooking career began in the 1920s at the annual Canadian National Exhibition in Toronto, but she won national fame through her radio broadcasts on CBC. She expended her prodigious capacity for work between Toronto and Montreal, supported by a large team of assistants, but because her cookbooks were published by firms based in Montreal (Ogilvie Flour Mills, Canada Starch, and the Montreal *Standard* newspaper), entries for her books are in the Quebec section and further information about her is in the Introduction for that province and at Q214.1.

School textbooks for cooking classes chart the evolution of the teaching of Home Economics (earlier called Domestic Science, then Household Science) in Ontario in the first half of the twentieth century. The first two institutions established to train teachers are both represented: the Lillian Massey School of Household Science and Art at the University of Toronto, which opened in 1902, and the Macdonald Institute at the Ontario Agricultural College in Guelph, founded in 1903 thanks to the lobbying of Adelaide Hoodless. Soon after the Lillian Massey School's founding, it published *Individual Recipes for Class Work* (O128.1), and in about 1910, *Recipes in Individual and Large Amounts for Home and School* (O241.1, plus other re-titled editions up to 1933). 'Individual recipes' meant recipes for students to make single servings in class; 'large amounts' in the 1910 title referred to family-size recipes. Both books were addressed to student-teachers and teachers of Household Science across Canada, and by 1910 the text was also deemed to be suitable for use in the home. Hoodless's *Public School Domestic Science* had been published in 1898 and was directed partly at teachers, for whom no officially sanctioned courses in the subject yet existed, but in 1905 a new edition, retitled *Public School Household Science* (O86.2), was issued with the elements for teachers removed and revised to conform with the provincial curriculum; the revisions were likely made by the Macdonald Institute's principal, Mary Urie Watson, who is credited as the co-author, not by Hoodless. In 1916 and 1918 the Ministry of Education authorized two titles in the series of Ontario Teachers' Manuals, *Household Management* (O364.1) and *Household Science in Rural Schools* (O410.1), the latter offering statistics about the proportion of rural (5,697) and urban (903) schools in the province and promoting the 'hot noon-day lunch' as a means of teaching cookery and of increasing the 'efficiency' of pupils. In 1923 Ryerson Press published *Canadian Cook Book* (O506.1) by Nellie Pattinson, director of Domestic Science at Central Technical School in Toronto, which, like the Lillian Massey School textbooks, specified individual and family amounts of ingredients. Who instigated the book is unknown – author or publisher, or Dr Peter Sandiford, a professor in the Faculty of Education at the University of Toronto, who is not named in the volume, but who received a 1% royalty. It was 'compiled, primarily, to satisfy a demand for a book of recipes conveniently arranged for use of teachers and students in technical schools [i.e., at the secondary level],' and many students used it over the years at 'Central Tech' and in classrooms across the country. It also found a wider audience among the Canadian public. There were twenty printings up to 1949, then, after Helen Wattie and Elinor Donaldson updated the text, it was republished as *Nellie Lyle Pattinson's Canadian Cook Book* in 1953 (the year that Pattinson died) and in further new editions to 1991 – a run of nearly seventy years! Despite the plain, blue-cloth binding of all the editions up to 1949, *Canadian Cook Book* is one of the best remembered twentieth-century English-language Canadian cookbooks, partly because of the many school students who used it and the new life it was given by Wattie and Donaldson, whose perceptive revisions featured a special section of 'Regional Dishes.' One year after the first edition of *Canadian Cook Book*, in 1924, the Toronto Board of Education published *Handbook of Practical Cookery for the Use of Household Science Classes in the Public Schools of Toronto* (O528.1), compiled by Margaret Davidson, then director of Household Arts for city schools and Pattinson's predecessor at Central Technical School. Editions of the textbook were used in Toronto public schools up to at least 1950, and its influence extended beyond Toronto when

it was reprinted by the Stratford Board of Education for its pupils and probably also by the Hamilton Board (O528.5, O1090.1). Ryerson Press, Pattinson's publisher, introduced another textbook in 1932: *Junior Home Economics* (O751.1) by Ruth Dean and Elspeth Middleton, for beginners at the secondary level. Dean had taught under Pattinson at Central Technical School in the late 1920s, and Middleton was teaching under her at the time of the book's publication. Although *Junior Home Economics* was reprinted several times up to 1946, their textbook did not have the long life of Pattinson's.

Numerous recipe collections were published by various departments of the federal government, for national distribution in English and French, usually with the aim of encouraging the consumption of particular farm or fishery products as a boost for the industry.[21] Another ongoing, important purpose of federal government cookbooks was to set safe standards for home preserving at a time when most families routinely bottled fruits and vegetables, or used other methods to preserve food for storage over the winter (often in the 'root cellar,' a term no longer in general use). During both World Wars, the emphasis was on promoting the economical use of certain ingredients, such as meat, butter, wheat, or sugar, and the increased use of substitute foods, such as honey, offal, and lobster (*Economical Lobster Recipes*, O996.1, is one of the more surprising titles for twenty-first-century readers). Cooking manuals were also produced for all three branches of the military (O356.1, O997.1, O1094.1, O1152.1, O1175.1), for new immigrants to Canada in 1921 (O469.1), for British war brides in 1945 (O1095.1 illuminates distinctive Canadian tastes, such as the liking for the combination of bacon and marmalade), and even for catering at the many new summer recreational camps that opened in the post–Second World War period (O1127.1). One federal publication, *The Maple Leaf Canadian Recipe Book* by Kathleen Bowker (GB2.1), was issued in London, England, in 1931, by the director of Canadian Trade Publicity, to encourage British consumers to buy Canadian products; requests from home eventually led to the printing of a Canadian edition. Also included in this bibliography is Frederick Waugh's illustrated study of *Iroquis* [sic] *Foods and Food Preparation* (O371.1) in the Anthropological Series of the Geological Survey of Canada, 1916. Early federal government cookbooks, such as *Fish and How to Cook It* (O319.1), issued by the Department of the Naval Service in 1914, and *Two Hundred and Nine Recipes* (O323.1) from the Department of Trade and Commerce in about the same year, relied on material from

British and American sources; however, by 1919, the Department of Agriculture was publishing recipe collections credited to named women working for its various branches, beginning with *Preservation of Fruits and Vegetables for Home Use* by Margaret Macfarlane, a recipe tester at the Central Experimental Farm in Ottawa (O424.1). In the 1920s, Helen Campbell and Ethel Hamilton became familiar names through the Department of Agriculture's free distribution of their booklets, especially Campbell's *Why and How to Use Cheese* (O477.1) and *Why and How to Use Milk* (O478.1). Campbell's reputation soared when she left the civil service to be director of the Chatelaine Institute from 1930 to 1946. In the 1930s and 1940s, Edith Elliot and Laura Pepper were the prominent names, and Elliot's *Jams, Jellies, and Pickles* (O721.1) is just one of her booklets still commonly found today.

Ontario government cookbooks treated preserving, bread making, wartime foods, recipes for Ontario's fruits and vegetables, and in the 1940s, information about freezing food, salads, and how to get *Your Money's Worth in Food* in the face of increased prices (O1224.1).[22] Often the booklets emanated from the Women's Institutes Branch of the Department of Agriculture, including three by Ethel Chapman, who was known throughout the province for her work with rural women (O379.1, O380.1, O516.1). One unusual booklet was published by the provincial secretary in response to public requests for the recipes used by inmates at the Ontario Reformatory in Guelph, where a farm and canning plant had been established as a form of occupational therapy (O573.1).

Belonging to the small category of men's camping cookbooks, along with *Skillet Skills for Camp and Cottage*, are James Edmund Jones's *Camping and Canoeing* of 1903, which has a section called 'Camp Cook-Book' (O133.1), and *Famous Pointe Mouillée Club Recipes* (O422.1), produced in 1919 by the 'chef' of a duck-hunting club located by Lake St Francis, near Bainsville. Although the former was a conventional book, for sale to the general public, and the latter was intended originally to be a gift for a few intimate friends, both were written in a humorous vein, by men for men (see the entries for samples of the wit).

The two largest collections of pre-1950 Canadian cookbooks in the country are in Ontario, at Library and Archives Canada in Ottawa and at the University of Guelph. Library and Archives Canada has the most volumes, but nineteenth-century English-language cookbooks are poorly represented. The University of Guelph has the Una Abrahamson Canadian Cookery Collection, the Rural Heritage Collection (books previously held by the Ontario Agricultural Museum),

plus a large and growing number in the Canadian Cookbook Collection, and the library is attracting the papers and cookbook collections of Canadian home economists and cookbook authors. The Una Abrahamson collection encompasses not just the pre-1950 Canadian titles recorded in this bibliography and other later Canadian titles, but also American, British, and French antiquarian cookbooks and studies on complementary subjects, such as gastronomy and etiquette, making the University of Guelph the best centre in Canada for food-history research. The Toronto Reference Library has a substantial number of pre-1950 Canadian cookbooks, including early and rare examples, the legacy of a long history of making acquisitions. Significant collections are also at the North York Public Library, the Thomas Fisher Rare Book Library at the University of Toronto, York University Archives and Special Collections in Toronto, the Hamilton Public Library, Queen's University in Kingston, and the University of Waterloo. For a full list of Ontario locations, see 'Abbreviations,' p xliv.

NOTES

1 In the Ontario section there are 1,233 numbered entries plus eight late additions, O109a.1, O139a.1, O160a.1, O169a.1, O194a.1, O319a.1, O1055a.1, and O1210a.1. Please note that, late in the bibliography's production, it was discovered that O300.1, *Cook Book*, although printed in Smiths Falls, Ontario, was compiled by a church in Grenfell, Saskatchewan (not Grenfell, Ontario). See also A111.1.

2 In 1851, there were 952,004 persons in what was then Canada West versus 890,261 in Canada East; in 1871, just after Confederation, 1,620,851 versus 1,191,516 (by 1881, the difference was more than a half-million); in 1951, after the end-point of this bibliography, 4,597,542 versus 4,055,681.

3 George L. Parker, *The Beginnings of the Book Trade in Canada*, Toronto: University of Toronto Press, 1985.

4 *The Cook Not Mad* was not as well known and widely distributed as Amelia Simmons's *American Cookery* (first edition, 1796) or Lydia Child's *The Frugal Housewife*, later retitled *The American Frugal Housewife* (first edition, 1829).

5 The first edition of Catharine Parr Traill's *The Female Emigrant's Guide*, 1854 [1855], was printed at the Guardian office (O5.1). Titles bearing the imprint of William Briggs, the Methodist book steward, were also printed there: the American Marion Harland's *House and Home*, 1889 (O46.1); the American Mrs Porter's *New World's Fair Cook*

Book, 1891 (O55.1); the 1898 and 1902 editions of *The Galt Cook Book* (O58.2, O58.3); editions of *Dwight's Cow-Brand Cook-Book*, an 1897 advertising book for baking soda (O82.1, O82.2); James Edmund Jones's *Camping and Canoeing*, 1903 (O133.1); the American *Mrs Allen's Cook Book*, 1917 (O372.1); and a 1918 Ontario textbook, *Household Science in Rural Schools* (O410.1). In 1919 the business was renamed Ryerson Press, which published the following titles: *Canadian Cook Book* by Nellie Pattinson, 1923 (O506.1); *Junior Home Economics* by Ruth Dean and Elspeth Middleton, 1932 (O751.1); the American *June Platt's Plain and Fancy Cook Book*, 1941 or 1942 (O1037.1); *Let's Cook* by the American Nancy Hawkins, 1942 (O1048.1); and *The Cook's Recipe Manual* by Elspeth Middleton, Muriel Ransom, and Albert Vierin, 1943 (O1078.1). Various 'Stock Books' of the Methodist Book and Publishing House at OTCC (Acc. 83.061C, UCC Board of Publication) record several foreign culinary titles in stock, probably imported editions.

6 There are ninety-four numbered entries in the Ontario section before 1900, plus two titles in the Quebec section that include Ontario places of publication in the imprint (Q4.1, Q5.1).

7 Ontario's proximity to the United States made transportation and communication faster and cheaper. Another reason was the ambiguity of various aspects of copyright law in the nineteenth century, which encouraged Canadian publishers to consider American publications over British ones.

8 Parker, p 113.

9 The other was *The New Cook Book* by Grace Denison, of 1903, also published in London, England, in 1906 (O130.1). *The Female Emigrant's Guide* had been pub-lished in London in 1860 as *The Canadian Settler's Guide*, but the English publisher removed most of the culinary part of Traill's text.

10 The only significant changes occurred sometime in the 1880s, when George Stewart Jr's letter to the publishers was dropped, and a page of two recipes for Breakfast Dal and Bengal Soup, both credited to Mrs Keer, were added (p 235).

11 Places such as Parry Sound, Huntsville, Gravenhurst, Orillia, and Bala are now designated the 'Near North' for tourism purposes, but were considered part of Northern Ontario in the period covered by this bibliography.

12 The earliest Women's Institute cookbook to surface was O194a.1, *Good Things and How to Prepare Them*, by the Welland branch in 1908.

13 See under the company name in the Name Index for cookbooks published by each stove manufacturer.

14 See, for example, the cookbook advertising Strong's Baking Powder by the London druggist of the same name (*The Art of Cooking Made Easy*, 1892, O48.4), or editions of *Gems of Fancy Cookery* by three different Ontario druggists (O68.1, about 1895).

15 Parker, p 259.

16 The volumes in the '365' series were compilations of recipes from famous American cooks.

17 Jennie B. Williams, author of *Us Two Cook Book* (O224.1), published by Musson in 1909, may be American, although her nationality is uncertain. Her text is an amalgam of British and American elements, and includes a recipe for Governor's Sauce, a Canadian favourite. Perhaps she had a Canadian family connection. She is credited with '[arranging] for the Canadian table' Fannie Farmer's *Catering for Special Occasions* (O262.1).

18 Neil trained in Glasgow, Scotland, but worked for most of her career in the United States.

19 Filippini, a native of Switzerland and author of *The International Cook Book* (O320.1), had made his name as chef at Delmonico's Restaurant in New York City.

20 Brodie 5 December 1942.

21 All federal government cookbooks are listed in the Subject Index under 'Government publications, Canada' and in the Name Index under 'Canada, [department name].'

22 Ontario government cookbooks are listed in the Subject Index under 'Government publications, Ontario' and in the Name Index under 'Ontario, [department name].'

1831

The cook not mad

O1.1 1831

The / cook not mad; / or / rational cookery: / being / a collection of original and selected / receipts, / embracing not only the art of curing various / kinds of meats and vegetables for future / use, but of cooking, in its general / acceptation, to the taste, habits, / and degrees of luxury, pre- / valent with the / Canadian public, / to which are added, / directions for preparing comforts for the sick / room – together with sundry miscellaneous / kinds of information of importance to house- / keepers in general, nearly all tested by / experience. / Kingston, U.C. / Published by James Macfarlane. / 1831.

DESCRIPTION: 13.5 × 7.5 cm   Pp [i–iii] iv–v [vi], [7] 8–120   Paper-covered boards

CONTENTS: i tp; ii blank, with pasted-on 'Errata' slip; iii–v 'Preface'; vi blank; 7–116 310 numbered recipes and other items; 117–20 'Contents' [i.e., index]

CITATIONS: Bates, pp 27, 31, 80, 85, 89, 90–1, 105 (note 22), 106–7, 110 (notes 5, 6, 10), 112, 114 (notes 20, 21), 115 (note 24), 120 (note 37), 126, 128 (note 10), 132 (note 15), 140, 142 (notes 3, 4), 145, 154, 156   CHO No. 29 (Summer 2001)   Cooke 2002, p 234   Crawford, p D2   Dewalt, p 37   Driver 2001, Wellington County, p 86   Driver 2002, Home Cook Book, p xii   Driver 2003, 'Canadian Cookbooks,' p 27   Duncan, pp 171–2, 216, 219–20   Eade, p E1   Ferguson/Fraser, p 232   Fleming 523   Garrett, pp 11, 89, 100, 131   Golick, p 98   Lafrance/Desloges, p 87   Longone/Longone E4   Neering, pp 44, 46–7, 51, 52, 55   Parker, p 75   Reitz, p [4]   Rhodenizer, p 992   TPL 1634 (illus)   Williamson, History of the Book, p 276

COPIES: CIHM (89823)   *OTMCL (641.5 C58)   Private collection

NOTES: See pl 17. *The Cook Not Mad* is often incorrectly referred to as Canada's first printed cookbook (this description appears, for example, on the dust-jacket of the twentieth-century reprints). It is more accurate to describe it as the first English-language cookbook bearing a Canadian imprint. (The first French-language cookbook with a Canadian imprint had been published six years before: Q1.1, *La cuisinière bourgeoise*, Quebec City: 1825.) *The Cook Not Mad* is an American text, first published in Watertown, New York, in 1830. The Kingston edition may be a stereotype edition of the American book. Parker and Dewalt both discuss the publisher James Macfarlane's earlier printing from imported stereotype plates, with reference to *The Cook Not Mad*. Alternatively, the Kingston edition may have been printed entirely in Watertown, then shipped across the border. Supporting this possibility is the fact that the paper and the title-page design are dissimilar to known Macfarlane stereotyped books. Moreover, Mary F. Williamson, who has examined both the Kingston and Watertown editions, reports that both editions are the identical size, and have the same text paper and blue-paper-covered boards. It is unlikely to have been printed in Watertown, then had a local title-page added by Macfarlane in Kingston, because the title-page is integral to the volume, not pasted in.

Only three copies of the Kingston edition are known to exist: one at OTMCL, the one used by Roy Abrahamson for the twentieth-century reprints, and one in another Canadian private collection. Oddly, Macfarlane didn't advertise the book in his Kingston newspaper, the *Chronicle* (so states Roy Abrahamson, p 4 of the 1972 reprint; confirmed by a search of the paper by Mary F. Williamson). Nevertheless, he must have realized sales because in June 1834 he ordered additional copies – of the American edition – from Knowlton and Rice (see Macfarlane's account and letterbook for 1832–4 at OKQ, Fairfield Family Collection 2193b). Joseph Wilson, publisher of the *Hallowell Free Press* and a bookseller in Picton in Hallowell Township, advertised 'Rational Cookery' in a list of books 'just received' for sale, in the issue of 28 December 1830 (the first issue of the paper) and for the six months following. Wilson may have been selling the Kingston or Watertown editions. An advertisement for 'Rational Cookery' also appeared in the *Picton Gazette* of 4 January 1831.

The 'Preface' of *The Cook Not Mad* argues that the contents of a cookbook should match the circumstances and habits of its readers: 'A work of cookery should be adapted to the meridian in which it is intended to circulate. It is needless to burden a country cookery book with receipts for dishes depending entirely upon seaboard markets, ... Still further would the impropriety be carried were we to introduce into a work intended for the American Publick such English, French and Italian methods of rendering things indigestible, ...' Although American, this cookbook originated not far across the border from Kingston, so it was 'adapted to the meridian' of its Canadian readers.

The OTMCL copy is inscribed on the (loose) front endpaper, in ink, 'C. Robertson Kingston.'

CHO (Summer 2001) contains the following articles about *The Cook Not Mad:* Mary F. Williamson, 'A

Beginning: A Publication History'; Dorothy Duncan, 'Yes I Have Met the Real Cook!'; Fiona Lucas, 'Fiona's Musings'; and 'Jumbles, No. 115.'

OTHER EDITIONS: There were four editions of a modern reprint of *The Cook Not Mad*, all copyright Roy A. Abrahamson and all described on the title-page as 'A reprint of Canada's first cookbook published in 1831 to which have been added recipes for present-day use and explanatory notes': Toronto: Roy A. Abrahamson and Associates, [1972], 'prepared for Diana Sweets Limited, Toronto's longest-established restaurateurs, to commemorate their 60th anniversary in 1972' (OGU, OKITWN, OKQ, OONL, OTMCL, OTU; United States: MWA); [2nd ed.], Toronto: Cherry Tree Press, [1973], one private collector's copy with original dust-jacket, on which is printed 'This edition distributed in Canada exclusively by Kiwanis Clubs in support of their philanthropic activities,' and another collector's copy with no reference to the Kiwanis Clubs on the dust-jacket (BVAU, BVIV, MW, MWMM, NSHMS, OGU in Rural Heritage Collection uncat, OH, OMIH, OONL, OWYL; United States: DLC); 3rd ed., revised, 1982 (OSIDM); [Ontario Bicentennial ed.], Toronto: Cherry Tree Press, [1984], note on p i signed Dennis R. Timbrell, Minister, Ontario Ministry of Agriculture and Food, revised 'Introductory Notes' credit Joan Graham for the 'present-day' recipes, 'Agricultural Firsts in Ontario' on last page (MWIAP, OGU, OKQ, ONBNBM, OSMFHHM, OTSBM, OTAR, OTR, OWTL).

In all the reprints, the text is reset, and the volume has larger dimensions than the original Canadian edition. Roy Abrahamson was Una Abrahamson's husband, and he produced his reprint from a copy of the book that was originally part of Una's collection of Canadian and other cookbooks. Regarding Una's efforts to have her copy reprinted, as a fund-raiser for Black Creek Pioneer Village, see Duncan in CHO (Summer 2001). Roy Abrahamson characterizes *The Cook Not Mad* as 'a reading cookbook rather than a "how to" cookbook' (p 3 of 1972 reprint). In his view, 'it is inadvisable and hardly possible to use the receipts in the 1831 edition' because 'our ingredients are different, our flour and sugar are much more refined, our eggs are larger, and our tastes are more sophisticated.' Anyone who has cooked or tasted the delicious dishes made from early cookbooks would attest to how wrong-headed this view is. In fact, recipes from *The Cook Not Mad* are regularly used, with success, in the kitchens of various historic sites in Ontario. Readers should also be wary of the reprint's twenty-two 'recipes for present-day use,'

which are poor modern equivalents, some specifying canned soup or monosodium glutamate – hardly indicative of more sophisticated modern tastes! Sometimes, the 'present-day' recipes are completely unrelated to the original recipe; see, for example, No. 88, Carrot Pudding, which is a baked dish using cooked carrots, five eggs, and rose-water flavouring, and the present-day Steamed Carrot Pudding (p 69, 1972 reprint), which is the well-known steamed suet pudding (here with shortening, not the traditional suet) using raw carrot and potato, candied fruit, and cinnamon, cloves, and nutmeg. For further comments on Roy Abrahamson's introductory text and on the modern-day recipes, see Lucas in CHO (Summer 2001).

AMERICAN EDITIONS: Watertown, NY: Knowlton and Rice, 1830 (United States: DLC, MWA); Watertown, NY: Knowlton and Rice, 1831 [deposited 11 October 1830] (OGU; United States: InU, MCR, MWA, NN); Watertown, NY: Knowlton and Rice, 1841 (MWA); reprint [title-page reproduction based on copy at MWA], Toronto and Buffalo: Roy A. Abrahamson and Associates, [1975] (OONL); Sunnyvale, Calif.: Colonial Publications, c1982 (United States: DLC).

1840

B., A.

O2.1 1840
The / frugal housewife's manual: / containing / a number of useful receipts, / carefully selected, and well adapted to the use / of families in general. / To which are added / plain and practical directions / for the / cultivation and management of some of the most useful / culinary vegetables. / By A.B., of Grimsby. / Toronto: / Guardian office, No. 9, Wellington Buildings. / J.H. Lawrence, printer. / 1840.

DESCRIPTION: 14.0 × 9.0 cm   Pp [i–iv], [1] 2–66 [67] Paper-covered boards, cloth spine

CONTENTS: i tp; ii blank; iii 'Advertisement' signed A.B.; iv blank; 1–31 'Housewife's Manual' [recipes numbered 1–72]; 32 blank; 33–66 'Practical Directions for the Cultivation of Vegetables' [entries for individual vegetables, with instructions for cultivation and cooking, numbered 73–100 and arranged alphabetically from Asparagus to Turnip]; 67 'Index' [i.e., numbered list of recipes and entries for vegetables, in the order in which they appear in the text]

CITATIONS: Armstrong 2000, p F2 Bly Cooke 2002, p 234 Crawford, p D2 Driver 2001, Wellington

County, pp 86, 96–7 (note 5)   Driver 2002, Home Cook Book, p xii   Driver 2003, 'Canadian Cookbooks,' pp 27–8   Driver 2005, p 409   Ferguson/ Fraser, p 232   Fleming 1389   Golick, p 98   Lafrance/ Desloges, p 87   Reitz, p [4]   TPL 7561   Wallace, p 12   Watier, p 7   Williamson, p 20 (note 71), note 76   Williamson, History of the Book, p 277
COPIES: CIHM (90013)   *OHMA (TX157 A3)   OTMCL (641.5 B11)
NOTES: See pl 18. *The Frugal Housewife's Manual* was the first English-language cookbook compiled in Canada, and it appeared in 1840, the same year as the first French-language cookbook compiled in Canada – Q3.1, *La cuisinière canadienne*. It was printed at the Guardian office and advertised in the *Christian Guardian* newspaper of 8 April 1840 as 'Just published, and for sale at the Wesleyan Book Room, Wellington Buildings, Toronto, ... By a Canadian lady.' The slim volume of modest dimensions is distinguished by the charm and simplicity of the arrangement of the text, which presents just 100 numbered items in two complementary sections. The idea of marrying instructions for the cultivation and cooking of vegetables has a long tradition in English-language cookery writing, going back as far as *A Book of Fruit and Flowers*, 1653.

Mary F. Williamson has determined that some of the recipes match ones in *Mackenzie's Five Thousand Receipts in All the Useful and Domestic Arts* by Colin Mackenzie (first British edition, 1823; first American edition, 1825) and that most of the directions for cultivation are derived from an 1835 booklet by Charles Crossman of the Shakers of Mount Lebanon, New York, *The Gardener's Manual*, which was distributed widely in conjunction with seed sales, including in Upper Canada (copy at MWA in the United States). Despite extensive research, she has not been able to identify with certainty the person behind the initials A.B.

A.B.'s text is not related to either of two earlier cookbooks with a similar title: *The Frugal Housewife* by the British author Susannah Carter, London: F. Newbery, [about 1765], and other British and American editions; or *The Frugal Housewife ... by the author of Hobomok* [Lydia Maria Child], Boston: Marsh and Capen, and Carter and Hendee, 1829, second and subsequent editions retitled *The American Frugal Housewife*.

The OHMA copy has the library's bookplate, with the donor's name, 'Mr. Gordon Allison'; the copy is inscribed, likely by the donor, on the front endpaper, in ballpoint pen, 'G.H. Allison'; on the other face of the front endpaper, opposite the title-page, there is

more information about the provenance of the book, probably inscribed by library staff, in pencil, 'Cookbook of Mrs Wm. M. Allison nee Elizabeth Lister.'

The OTMCL copy has an errata slip before the 'Advertisement' page. The free front endpaper is inscribed, in ink, 'Mrs. J. Wm. Collins // presented by her affectionate sister Mary Gibbs Augst. 15th. 44.' Mrs J. Wm. Collins may be the wife of John Collins of the Nag's Head Inn on Yonge Street, who is listed in the Toronto city directory for 1843–4. Opposite the Collins/Gibbs inscription, on the front endpaper applied to the binding, in a later hand and in purple pencil, is 'Mrs Skinner // 35 St. Patrick St // Go with Dr Adams about 11 A.M. Find his voting pla[ce?].' A handwritten recipe for Baking Powder is glued on the inside back face of the binding.

The OHMA and OTMCL copies are printed from the same setting of type, but likely at different times. Both copies have paper-covered boards and a cloth spine, but whereas the original paper colour of the OHMA copy is difficult to discern (possibly off-white or light brown) and its spine features a raised floral pattern, the OTMCL copy has blue-green paper and cloth with diagonal ribbing. Since the OHMA copy has no evidence of an errata slip, it probably represents the first printing of the book in 1840. The OTMCL copy may have been printed about the date of the 1844 inscription. The OTMCL copy shows more signs of real use in the kitchen: There are spots of grease on pp 1–15, containing recipes Nos. 1–41, for such dishes as cakes, fritters, and puddings; the marks are less frequent from 'Jellies' onward; and the gardening section of the book is clean.

Goodrich, Charles Augustus (1790–1862)

This prolific American author wrote books on a variety of subjects, from Christian martyrs and prayer to tourism and a history of the United States.

O3.1   1840
A new / family encyclopedia / or / compendium / of / universal knowledge: / comprehending / a plain and practical view of those subjects most inter- / esting to persons in the ordinary professions of life. / Illustrated by numerous engravings. / Seventh edition – revised and improved. / Edited / by Charles A. Goodrich. / Published by Thomas Belknap, / for G. Collins Tremaine. / Kingston, U.C. / 1840.
DESCRIPTION: 18.5 × 11.0 cm   Pp [1–3] 4–8, [13] 14–483   5 fp illus, many illus   Full leather

CONTENTS: 1 tp; 2 blank; 3–8 table of contents; 13–483 text

COPIES: CIHM (95403)   *OGU (UA s041 b02)

NOTES: Part II, 'Aliments,' pertains to food; Sections 1–7 in Part II discuss artificial aliments, fruits, drinks, condiments, animals, fish, and fowl. This title is not recorded in Fleming.

AMERICAN EDITIONS: *A New Family Encyclopedia*, New York: 1831 (United States: DLC); *The Family Encyclopedia*, new ed., New York: J.W. Smith and Co., 1860 (United States: DLC); new ed., revised, improved, and enlarged by J.R. Bigelow, New York: J. Whorter Smith and Son, 1868 (OGU).

1845

Nourse, Mrs Elizabeth

See Q4.1 for the 1845 edition of Nourse's Modern Practical Cookery, *published in Montreal, Kingston, and Hamilton.*

1846

Crowen, Mrs Thomas J.

Mrs Crowen's The Management of the Sick Room, with Rules of Diet, *New York: J. Mowatt, 1844 (United States: DLC), appeared in the same year as the first American edition of her* Every Lady's Book. *She later wrote* The American System of Cookery, *1847, some later editions of which were titled* The American Lady's System of [or for] Cookery *or* Mrs Crowen's American Lady's Cookery Book.

O4.1   1846

Every lady's book: / An / instructor / in the art of making every variety / of / plain & fancy cakes, / pastry, confectionery, / blanc mange, jellies, ice creams, / and / other useful information for ordinary / and holiday occasions. / By a lady. / Niagara: / Printed and published by A. Davidson, / at the Niagara Mail office. / 1846 / Price – 1s. 3d.

CITATIONS: DCB, Vol. 8, pp 203, 204 Driver 2002, Home Cook Book, p xii Driver 2003, 'Canadian Cookbooks,' p 28

COPIES: ONHI (x987.5.4.134)

NOTES: The author is not named, but Mary F. Williamson has compared the Canadian publication with the first edition of *Every Lady's Book ... By a lady*

of New York. (Mrs. Thomas J. Crowen.), New York: published by T.J. Crowen, 1844 [copyright 1843], and found that the Canadian text is identical except for the omission of the last recipe, Albany Cake, for which there was not space on the page. Williamson has also determined that the publisher, Alexander Davidson (1794–1856), printed the book from his own resetting of the type. Davidson, who 'disliked the extensive use of American textbooks in Upper Canadian schools' (DCB, Vol. 8, p 202), wrote and had published in 1840, *The Canada Spelling Book*. It is odd that he had no compunction about publishing an American cookbook.

No advertisements have been found in Niagara newspapers for the title *Every Lady's Book*; however, the runs of extant copies of the various Niagara newspapers are incomplete, and an advertisement for *Every Lady's Book* may be in one of the missing copies. Nevertheless, Davidson did place several advertisements in the years 1844–7 for a cookbook he called 'Domestic Receipt Book': On 10 July 1844, in the *Niagara Chronicle*, 'Just published by Alex. Davidson the "Domestic Receipt Book"'; on 20 November 1844, in the *Niagara Argus*, the same title for 7½ d; on 5 February 1845, 7 January 1846, and February 1846, all in the *Niagara Argus*; and on 13 January 1847, in the *Niagara Mail*, 'By A. Davidson // The "Domestic Receipt Book," a useful compendium for families, to be had at the book store ...' These advertisements for 'Domestic Receipt Book' may not refer to *Every Lady's Book* for several reasons: The earliest advertisement for 'Domestic Receipt Book' appeared at least eighteen months before the date (1846) on the title-page of *Every Lady's Book*; the advertised title ('Domestic Receipt Book') bears no relation to the title of the Crowen text and the description of the contents ('useful compendium for families') does not accurately depict *Every Lady's Book*, which is mainly confectionery; it is unlikely that the Canadian edition of *Every Lady's Book* would have appeared in the same year (1844) as the first American edition; and the price of 7½ d quoted in one of the *Argus* advertisements is half the cost printed on the title-page of *Every Lady's Book*. The 'Domestic Receipt Book' is also unlikely to be an edition of *Miss Beecher's Domestic Receipt Book* by Catherine Esther Beecher, New York: Harper and Brothers, 1846 (Bitting, p 32), which, like *Every Lady's Book*, was first published at least eighteen months after Davidson's first advertisement. It is likely, therefore, that the advertisements for 'Domestic Receipt Book' refer to a book for which no copy has yet been found. The possibility remains, however, that Davidson used the phrase 'Domestic Receipt Book' as a general description for a collection of recipes for the home and that there was a delay between his first advertisement and the actual publication of *Every Lady's Book*. The DCB entry for Davidson (Vol. 8, pp 203 and 204) states, without qualification, that in 1847 he published *The Domestic Receipt Book*, an assertion probably based on the 1847 advertisement.

The cookbook is incorrectly attributed to Alexander Davidson's daughter in *Catalogue of Articles in Memorial Hall, the Historical Building of the Niagara Historical Society*, Toronto: 1911, p 21, No. 917: 'Cookery Book, by a Niagara lady (Miss Davidson, afterwards Mrs. Sanderson), 1846.' The misattribution is repeated in Janet Carnochan, *History of Niagara (in Part)*, Toronto: William Briggs, 1914, p 286.

The ONHI copy was donated by Miss Crouch of Virgil.

AMERICAN EDITIONS: *Every Lady's Book: An Instructor in the Art of Making Every Variety of Plain and Fancy Cakes, Pastry, Confectionery, Blanc Mange, Jellies, Ice Creams, and Other Useful Information for Ordinary and Holiday Occasions. By a lady of New York. (Mrs. Thomas J. Crowen.)*, New York: T.J. Crowen, 1844 (Bitting, p 109); 2nd ed., New York: J.K. Wellman, 1845 (United States: DLC, InU); 3rd ed., 1845 (referred to in Cagle/Stafford No. 204); 3rd ed., 2nd printing, New York: J.K. Wellman, 1846 (United States: InU); retitled *Every Lady's Cook Book*, 4th ed., 1st printing, New York: Kiggins and Kellogg, [copyright 1854] (United States: InU, MB, MWA, NN, MSaE); Toledo, Ohio: Sawyer, Brother and Co., 1854 (United States: DLC); New York: Kiggins and Kellogg, [copyright 1854, cover dated 1856] (United States: MCR, MWA); New York: Kiggins and Kellogg, [copyright 1854, front wrapper dated 1857] (United States: InU, MWA).

1848

The skilful housewife's guide

See Q5.1 for The Skilful Housewife's Guide, *extracted from a cookbook by the American Mrs Abell and published simultaneously in Montreal, Quebec City, Kingston, Toronto, Hamilton, Bytown, London, and Niagara, in 1848.*

1855

Traill, Mrs Catharine Parr, née Strickland (Rotherhithe, Kent, England, 9 January 1802– 29 August 1899, Lakefield, Ont.)

Catharine Parr Strickland was one of six daughters and two sons in the family of Elizabeth and Thomas Strickland. Six of these eight children became published authors and, of these, Catharine's younger sister, Susanna Moodie, is noted in Canada for her Roughing It in the Bush, or, Life in Canada, *London: Richard Bentley, 1852, and Samuel Strickland for his* Twenty-seven Years in Canada West; or, the Experience of an Early Settler, *London: Richard Bentley, 1853. As a young, unmarried woman living with her family in England, Catharine herself had already had published several books and contributed to various annuals and periodicals.*

Catharine married Thomas Traill on 13 May 1832, and that summer Catharine and Thomas, and Susanna and her husband, emigrated to Canada. Catharine and Thomas first settled in Douro Township, north of Peterborough, on a lot next to her brother Samuel, who had emigrated in 1825. Over the years, Catharine lived in various locations: Peterborough East (Ashburnham), the area of Rice Lake (where she wrote O5.1, The Female Emigrant's Guide), and Lakefield. She had nine children.

Catharine recounted the experience of her first three years in Canada in The Backwoods of Canada: Being Letters from the Wife of an Emigrant Officer, Illustrative of the Domestic Economy of British America, *London: Charles Knight, 1836 (OTMCL). Her aim was 'to afford every possible information to the wives and daughters of emigrants of the higher class who contemplate seeking a home amid our Canadian wilds.' In the body of the text there are occasional comments about food and also information about maple-sugar making on pp 155–8. Shortly before publication, Charles Knight requested more material for the book and, in response, Catharine sent recipes and domestic instructions, which Knight added as Appendix A (pp 315–25), organized in the following sections: 'Maple-Sugar'; 'Vinegar'; 'Hop-Rising'; 'Salt-Rising'; 'Soft Soap'; 'Candles'; and 'Pickling.' A note at the head of the appendix explained the inclusion of the extra matter thus: 'The following communications have been received from the writer of this work during its progress through the press.' Although the culinary information in the appendix is detailed and useful, it is not integral to the text and is a small part of the whole; therefore,* The Backwoods of Canada *is not included in this bibliography. The first Canadian edition of* The Backwoods of Canada *was published in 1929 by McClelland and Stewart. The full publishing history of this title is presented in the scholarly edition edited by Michael A. Peterman, Ottawa: Carleton University Press, 1997, Centre for Editing Early Canadian Texts series. Peterman explains the story of the appendix material on p xli; in his edition, he repositions the recipes as end notes following the relevant text section.*

For further information about Traill, see: Traill Family Collection (OOA); Carl Ballstadt, Catharine Parr Traill and Her Works, *Downsview, Ont.: ECW Press, [1984?]; Carl Ballstadt, Elizabeth Hopkins, and Michael A. Peterman, editors,* I Bless You in My Heart: Selected Correspondence of Catharine Parr Traill, *Toronto: University of Toronto Press, 1996; Michael Peterman's entries for Traill in DCB, Vol. 12, pp 995–9, and in Eugene Benson and William Toye, editors,* The Oxford Companion to Canadian Literature, *second edition, Toronto: Oxford University Press, 1997, both of which include the essential references to literature about Traill; Charlotte Gray,* Sisters in the Wilderness: The Lives of Susanna Moodie and Catharine Parr Traill, *Toronto: Viking, 1999, especially pp 237–9 regarding* The Female Emigrant's Guide *(but note that for* The Backwoods of Canada, *on p 115, Gray incorrectly implies that the appendix material was not included in the first edition); Dagg, pp 297–9; and Fiona Lucas's entry for Traill in Arndt, pp 357–8. Material about Traill is also at the Library and Archives Canada web site, under 'Memorable Canadians.'*

O5.1 1st thousand, 1854 [1855]
The / female emigrant's / guide, / and / hints on Canadian housekeeping. / By Mrs. C.P. Traill, / authoress of the "Backwoods of Canada," "Forest / Gleanings," "The Canadian Crusoes," &c., &c. / (First thousand.) / Toronto, C.W: / Sold by Maclear and Company, / and all the principal booksellers throughout Canada, the / British American provinces, and the United States. / 1854. / Price twenty-five cents, or one shilling and three-pence, each part, / postpaid to any part of Canada, the British American provinces, / and the United States.
DESCRIPTION: 17.5 × 10.5 cm Pp [iii–v] vi [vii–ix] x–xii, [13] 14–218 [219–31], [i], [1] 2–40 6 pls before tp, a few illus Rebound
CONTENTS: iii tp; iv dedication of the first part of the volume to the Earl of Elgin and Kincardine, governor-general of British North America; v–vi 'Table of Contents' [i.e., index]; vii 'Contents of Appendix'; viii blank; ix–xii 'Preface' signed Canadian emigrant; 13–58 'Introductory Remarks'; 59–226 text; 227–30 'Conclusion'; 231 'The Scottish Emigrant's Song'; i blank; 1–40 'Appendix' and at bottom p 40, 'Book Post. (From The Old Countryman March 12, 1855.)' [giving the most recent regulations about book postage]

CITATIONS: Arndt (Traill entry by Fiona Lucas) CHO No. 46 (Autumn 2005), p 11, illus Dagg, p 298 DCB, Vol. 12, p 998 Driver 2002, Home Cook Book, pp xii–xiii Driver 2003, 'Canadian Cookbooks,' pp 28–9, 36 Driver 2005, p 409 Fowler, pp 62, 78, 80, 82, 84 Lucas, p 22 Traill, *The Backwoods of Canada*, Michael A. Peterman, ed., Ottawa: Carleton University Press, 1997, p xlviii Wallace, p 14 Watier, p 7
COPIES: *OTUTF (B-10 5356)
NOTES: See pl 19. Traill explains in the 'Preface' that she intends *The Female Emigrant's Guide* to remedy the deficiencies of her earlier work, *The Backwoods of Canada*. That book had been addressed to women of her own class and was based on 'but a short time resident in the country.' The new book has 'been written for all classes, and more particularly for the wives and daughters of the small farmers, and a part of it is also addressed to the wives of the labourer and mechanics ...' In selecting and presenting the 'points of knowledge' she considered 'essential for the instruction of the emigrant's wife,' Traill could now draw on twenty years' experience of living in Canada. On p xi, she describes her work as 'a manual of Canadian housewifery,' and later, on p 50, as instruction in 'the simple elements of Canadian housekeeping.' Whereas the culinary information in *The Backwoods of Canada* was added in an appendix as an afterthought, here it is at the core of the book's usefulness.

Traill's correspondence illuminates the development of the text (page numbers cited for correspondence refer to the Traill Family Collection at OOA). In a letter of 6 January 1854 to her sister Susanna Moodie, she put out a call for recipes from friends and neighbours:

Eliza [an older sister, living in England] ... highly approves of the Female Emigrants Manual and bids me hasten it. Now this requires more arrangement than invention. I must get all my friends to help me with good recipes about Canadian management and all such things in cooking and making and baking as are needful – any good useful practical receipts that you can glean up for me among farmers wives will be thankfully received but I do not want you to trouble about writing them because you have too much to do but if you can get any written for me I shall be equally obliged. I want to supply a book that will give instruction in every branch that may be needed by the family of a new settler, a book such as I should have been glad to have had myself when I came out.

The native Canadians and Yankees are after all the most practical people and from them I shall glean many hints. (p 2339)

Traill also sought recipes for the book within her local community. We know, for example, that one recipe, unidentified, came from Traill's friend Eliza Brown (see letter to Ellen Dunlop, 17 September [1854], incorrectly dated [1855] by OOA, p 1953, quoted below). She also used material that she had contributed as articles to the *Old Countryman* edited by Henry Payne Hope (1803–68) and to the *Canadian Agriculturist* (see, for example, her 'Prize Essay on Butter Making' in Vol. 6, May 1854, pp 140–2, which she dates Oakland, Rice Lake, 1853).

In a letter of 3 April 1854, her sister Agnes Strickland gave advice on the content of the book: 'Your Female Emigrants Hand Book might have some illustrative anecdotes of warning and encouragement ... be sure you warn ladies not to make the worst of everything for no one can avoid trials even in the most luxurious homes' (p 550). On 4 April, probably also in 1854, Catharine's sister Jane wrote offering 'a large stock of recipes almost big enough for a whole book written out by Thay [i.e., her sister Sarah] in her widowhood'; she also suggests, 'In the first and second vol of Home Circle most recipes were furnished by me which you could add' (p 567). Jane also offered to tell 'how indexes are made, always done after the book is printed, a plague to do, but easy when learned.'

Other evidence for the sources of the recipes is found in the book itself. Of the Pumpkin-Pie recipe on p 128, for example, Traill writes: 'I had this recipe from a Canadian lady who is celebrated for the excellence of her pumpkin-pies.' Silver Cake on p 104 is noted as 'from the "Maple-Leaf,"' a Montreal monthly (the December 1854 issue carried a notice about *The Female Emigrant's Guide*, which it described as 'written in that easy, truthful style that characterizes [Traill's] productions'). One recipe, Excellent Bread without Yeast on p 99, is identified as 'From Mrs. Child's Frugal Housewife,' the well-known American cookbook first published in 1829, and Traill occasionally refers to American gardening instructions; for example, on p 87. In the 'Preface' she acknowledges her indebtedness to Mr W. McKyes, Mrs McKyes, and Miss McKyes (the family of Willis McKyes lived near Amherst in Hamilton Township); Mrs Stewart (i.e., Mrs Frances Stewart) of Auburn, Douro, and her kind family; Misses A. and M. Ferguson; and 'many others, by whose instruction [she has] been largely benefitted.' An in-depth study of Traill's recipe sources remains to be done, especially for the purpose of identifying British, American, or Canadian origins.

Traill's correspondence also contains many references to the difficulties she faced having her manuscript published. On 20 June 1854 Traill wrote to Ellen Dunlop about her efforts to find a publisher and subscribers for the book:

I had a very friendly visit from Mr Hope of Toronto [editor of the *Old Countryman*] who is very zealous to serve me about my new work – He wants me to bring it out on my own risk and get subscription lists opened at the principal towns for the work – A great many of the great folks are advising the same plan and Mr Sherwood thinks the Government will help me – or order 200 copies as a starting point – I am waiting to hear Mr Armours estimate of the expences of printing and then I shall decide – also to hear from Agnes in answer to my proposal to a London House.

I want much to go up to Toronto this next month but I have not the means either for supplying myself with decent outer clothes – such as I could present myself in at the houses of the gentry who are desirous of seeing me – or to pay for a weeks board and lodging at some decent house.

... I should think that I might get some names on my list in Peterboro, it will not be a dear book – About 75 cents I think may be the price, and it will be useful to all housekeepers old and young – (pp 1935–6)

In a letter dated 17 September [1854], Traill tells Ellen Dunlop about Hope's efforts to publicize the book and her further trials finding subscribers:

I send you one of the circulars that my zealous friend Mr. Hope has sent me – I do not quite like the method he employs to make the work known. These sort of things are out of my quiet way and I am a little nervous about being brought so publickly forward ... I have not yet heard if there are any signatures for the work at Nicholls's [Nicholls and Hall general store] – nor do I know how many Dr Bird has got for me, but my good old Doctor Bird has sent me 42 subscribers all good men and true he says ... and I am sure of a great number at Coburg ... Many wait to see the book out – ... I'm sure Mr. Sedgewick would take a copy for Tom [his son] is a great book buyer and this book is the sort of thing for young men to buy to give to their wives or sweethearts – Mr. Hope wishes me to have one or two short stories illustrative of Canadian life. I have sent home for the ms. of 'The Old Log House' – also for the 'Curse of the Colony' which is a Temperance tale and would make the book sell with the Sons of Temperance. If these do not come in time I must substitute others. I am sure Templeton Brown will take a copy for Eliza and she will see one of her own receipts among my list. I fear owing to a want of funds there will be some delay on the printing. The printer wants now to have his pay for the paper beforehand, and this we cannot do – James must go up to arrange it – but if we get a good list of names that should be assurance of the money sufficient I think to satisfy them. (pp 1951–3)

The Female Emigrant's Guide was originally issued in four monthly parts. According to Thomas Maclear and Co.'s advertisement for the four parts in the *Christian Guardian* of 15 November 1854, the first part was to appear on 1 December and 'the three following [to] be published at intervals of about three weeks each, ...' The first part did appear at the end of 1854, but publication of the other parts was delayed until 1855 because of lack of money to pay the printer for paper, as Traill explained to Ellen Dunlop in a letter of 19 February 1855:

We have been stopped in issuing the last part of my book for want of paper for the printing, few of the subscribers having paid in advance on the second part. This has been a drawback for we relied on some of the proceeds to get out the last part – I am not liable myself to any risk but of course I am anxious on account of the friends who have already paid for the whole – Mr Hope says it will be all out in March – I have not yet heard one word from home about the English edition, but an English mail may bring me news tomorrow night. I have waited with some anxiety for the issue of any negociation at home. (p 1941) [For Agnes's unsuccessful efforts to secure an English or Scottish publisher, see Agnes's letters to Catharine, 3 April [1854], p 550; [Summer 1854], pp 553–4; 17 September 1854, pp 556–7; 21 January 1855, p 560; 2 June 1855, p 568.]

In the same letter Traill refers to reviews of the first part, in which the critics 'speak well of it,' although she claims to put more store in the 'unbiased judgment' of Ellen Dunlop 'on whose truth and candor [she] can rely' (p 1941).

The first part, first thousand, bears the imprint 'Toronto, C.W.: Sold by Maclear and Company ... 1854,' and has an advertisement on the inside back face of the binding dated 24 November 1854 (OONL (Casey 854 (2)), OTMCL (917.1 T67.2 1854), OTUTF (B-12 4633), cited TPL 8388). The second part, first thousand, has the same imprint as the first, but there is a 'Notice' on the inside front face of the binding that begins, 'A few days delay in the publication of the present part, has been caused by the impossibility of getting paper. The same reason will probably necessitate the publication of the two remaining parts of the work at one time – about the middle of February.' An advertisement on the inside back face of the binding for Henry Bovell Hope, conveyancer (and son of Henry Payne Hope), dated 1 January 1855, confirms publication of the second part in 1855. The actual day of publication of the second part was likely 18 January since an advertisement of that date in the *Christian Guardian* of 24 January states, 'This day first thousand of the second part.' (OONL (Casey 1854 (2)) has two copies of the first two parts, first thousand; copy 2 of the second part is a variant: cf, for example, the position of p 73 in each copy.) I have not located any copies of the third or fourth part, but they were advertised as if ready for sale in February: An advertisement dated 15 February 1855 in the *Christian Guardian* of 28 February announces, 'In a few days the fourth, and concluding, part, ...'; an advertisement dated 5 March 1855 in the *Christian Guardian* of 7 March announces, 'Now ready second thousand of the first, second and third parts.' It is possible, but unlikely, that the last two parts were superseded by the publication of the complete volume and never issued.

The first edition of the book is dated 1854 on the title-page; however, it was not actually published until 1855, after publication of the parts. The table of contents in the first part was revised and reset for the first edition of the book. An advertisement dated 5 March 1855 in the *Christian Guardian* of 7 March heralds the publication of the complete volume: 'Mrs. Traill's New Work. The Female Emigrant's Guide. Or Hints to Canadian Housekeepers, of All Classes, will be ready for delivery on Monday next [i.e., 12 March]. The volume complete, price – one dollar. Each part may be had separately at one shilling and three pence ...' In the book, Traill's text for the month of January, p 203, seems to imply publication in 1856: 'This year 1855, there was snow about the middle of November which lay till the 22nd, then the weather was mild again. We had intense cold the week before Christmas, but a thaw commenced on the 23rd and the snow disappeared, the ground being bare till the 13th of January.' If, as Elizabeth Hopkins explained to me, Traill occasionally labelled a winter by its January rather than December date, then this quotation confirms publication of the book in 1855, not 1856.

There is no printer's name in the rebound volume

at OTUTF; however, 'T.H. Bentley, pr.' is on the outside back face of the paper wrapper of the first part at OTMCL. Wallace, in reference to a copy of the book at the University of Toronto (presumably the one now at OTUTF, which came into the collection in 1890), cites the imprint as Toronto: T.H. Bentley, 1854. Perhaps the printer information was lost in the rebinding. According to Hulse, p 21, Thomas Hugh Bentley was the printer at the Christian Guardian Newspaper Office and his name appeared on publications of the Wesleyan Methodist Book Room in the period 1850–5 (Hulse located no imprints with his name after May 1855). There is an entry in a ledger for the Wesleyan Methodist Book Room that may refer to *The Female Emigrant's Guide* (OTCC (Acc. 83.061C, UCC Board of Publication, Series III, Box 50, 'Oversize ledger Meth. Bk & Pub. House 1854–1859,' p 155)). The entry, under 'H.P. Hope' [i.e., Traill's agent], states, '23 July 1855 // To Mrs Traill // 131 [i.e., copies?] // 39 10 6 [probably the price in pounds, shilling, pence].'

It is not clear where the 'Introductory Remarks' end in the 1854 edition of *The Female Emigrant's Guide* or in the other early editions, O5.2–5.4. Although the table of contents printed in the first part shows 'Natural Productions of the Woods' as the last item in 'Introductory Remarks,' in the 1861 edition 'Introductory Remarks' clearly ends before 'Natural Productions of the Woods.' For the 1854 and other editions where the text division is not clear, I have followed the example of the 1861 edition and, in the 'Contents' section of the entries, indicated that the 'Introductory Remarks' ends before the page headed 'Natural Productions of the Woods.'

The book sold well, going through several Canadian editions and one British edition. The numbering of the known editions is inconsistent: first thousand, 1854 [1855]; second thousand, 1854 [1855]; fifth edition, 1855; seventh edition, 1857; tenth edition, 1860, in London, England; fifth thousand, 1861; and 1862 unnumbered. A possible 'third edition' was advertised in May 1855 (see O5.2), and a possible Canadian 'tenth edition' reviewed in 1865 (see O5.6). In a 'Supplement to the Old Countryman' of 1 October 1859, Hope refers to 'nine editions ... exhausted' and says he will be producing a 'tenth.' The gaps in the numbering of the known editions may indicate editions published but not yet located, or they may simply point to irregularities in Hope's numbering. One sign of the book's popularity was an appearance in another author's emigration tale – *Cedar Creek* by Elizabeth Walshe, London: Religious Tract Society, nd [1863?], p 21 – where the character Arthur is dis-

covered 'lying in his berth, reading Mrs. Traill's "Emigrant's Guide."' Also, recipes and descriptive material from the book were reproduced later in periodicals. Apple-Pie and Dried Apples, for example, were reprinted, uncredited, in the *Farmers' Journal*, a Montreal publication, on 4 December 1858, p 92; and Susanna reported in a letter to Catharine, 18 November 1870, that she had 'read a harmony extract in the Ontario paper, on the Indian Summer from Settlers in Canada' (Carl Ballstadt, Elizabeth Hopkins, and Michael Peterman, eds, *Susanna Moodie: Letters of a Lifetime*, University of Toronto Press, 1985, Letter 102, p 283).

Despite the book's success, Traill received little financial benefit because of the self-serving dealings of her agent. Hope, it seems, was less concerned in representing the interests of his author than in using her work to bolster his own business of promoting immigration to Canada. In March 1860, for example, in his evidence to a Select Committee of the Legislative Assembly, he took considerable credit for the text when he referred to 'my edition of Mrs. Traill's "Canadian Settler's Guide," to which I made considerable additions' (*Journals of the Legislative Assembly of the Province of Canada, from February 28 to May 19, 1860, ...*, Vol. 18, Appendix 4, p 24). He also arranged for bulk sales of the book to the Canadian government without, apparently, passing on any of the proceeds to Traill (at OOA, see material in Submission to Council for 14 December 1855, RG 1 E7, Ex Agriculture File 826, and in Department of Agriculture, RG 17, Sub Group A1, Section 1861–1865). In a letter of 21 July 1861 (p 653), Agnes warned Catharine about her 'foxlike friend' Hope's activities in England. It must have been Hope who, in the English edition, removed her name from the title-page (although acknowledging her in the 'Preface') and who excised most of the culinary information. In notes made later in life (Vol. 6, p 8967), Traill remembered what she considered the mismanagement of the publication of *The Female Emigrant's Guide*: '1854 The Emigrants Guide printed in Toronto by subscription, badly got up – a vexatious failure – sold the copyright to Revd Mr Hope for which he paid me with a bad note of hand & 50 unbound copies. Afterwards he treated with an Eng^l[ish] printer and got a situation for his son in Liverpool – I was told after his death that he had obtained a money grant from the Can^n Gov^n as in my behalf but I never received or was told of the gift.' An article printed in the *Ottawa Citizen* about a year before Traill died recounted similar details ('Mrs. Catharine Parr Traill: Her Life and Work,' 27 June 1898): '"A Guide for Female Emigrants" was published in Toronto in 1855, and a seventh edition in 1857. For this Mrs. Traill received personally no remuneration; but a clergy man named Hope, who had undertaken to publish it, procured £300 from the Canadian Government to recuperate him the losses he alleged that he had incurred in publication.'

If Hope's treatment of Traill was unfair, as the evidence indicates, it was especially unwarranted in view of the quality of her work. In *The Female Emigrant's Guide* one finds the freshest and most authentic voice in Canadian English-language cookbooks to the mid-nineteenth century and, one could argue, well beyond. Most English-language cookbooks published in Canada before 1855 were editions of British or American texts, and no Canadian cookbook before 1855 had presented its recipes in a Canadian context with Traill's convincing narrative force. As Traill explains in the 'Preface,' p x, it was the difference between British and Canadian practices that determined the scope of her subject: 'As even materials differ, and the method of preparing food varies greatly between the colony and the Mother-country, I have given in this little book the most approved recipes for cooking certain dishes, the usual mode of manufacturing maple-sugar, soap, candles, bread and other articles of household expenditure; in short, whatever subject is in any way connected with the management of a Canadian settler's house ...' It was not 'intended for a regular cookery-book' (p 106 and see also p 153), where comprehensive collections of recipes are arranged in a conventional form. Rather, her recipes were selected and her comments crafted to explain specifically Canadian cooking customs.

The range of food-related information is extensive, as the following items listed in the table of contents indicate: apples, pears, cherries; beer; bread-making; buckwheat; cakes; cheese; coffee and tea, substitutes for; corn, Indian; curing of fish; curing of meat; dairy [includes the making at home of butter and cheese]; fish; fruits; game; gardening; oatmeal; peaches; potatoes; pumpkins; rice, Indian; sugar, making of maple; vegetables; venison; and wild fruits. Since pioneer families had to provide many of their own raw materials (hops for raising bread, apples from their own orchards, wild fruits from the forest), Traill's instructions for growing or gathering food are integral to the food's preparation. Her text is a model of precision and thoroughness, from when and how to plant a fruit or vegetable, its appearance when ready for harvesting, the taste raw and cooked, different methods of preserving or storing it, and its health benefits. In addition, she indicates the essential things to know. In her opinion, for example, 'the making and baking

of REALLY GOOD HOUSEHOLD BREAD [her capital letters] is a thing of the greatest consequence to the health and comfort of a family' (p 16), so she gives first place in the text to detailed instructions for the making of barm and bread. Her advice extends to the merits and methods of various cooking technologies, including the open hearth, cook-stove, and outdoor clay oven.

Traill notes Canadian eating and dining customs, especially for country families living on modest incomes. She says, for example, that 'Canada is the land of cakes [where a] tea-table is generally furnished with several varieties of cakes and preserves,' and the cake recipes she provides are for those 'in common use in the farm-houses' (p 106). One also learns that in Canada 'preserves are always placed on table at the evening meal, and often in the form of tarts' (p 90); that '[in] Canadian farm-houses meat is generally cooked twice and sometimes thrice a day' (p 124); and that 'Buckwheat pancakes are a favourite breakfast-dish with the old Canadian settlers' (p 110). Traill also includes recipes for the humblest dishes, such as Brown Supporne (porridge made with inferior flour), and Farmers' [mock] Rice (p 100), and refers to the kinds of tea that lumbermen drank – 'the New-Jersey tea, when out at their work, and also the Labrador-tea' (p 134). She mentions that few Canadians brew their own beer and gives the reasons why (pp 136–7). She also remarks that maple-sugar making had become less important for Canadian settlers as West India sugars were more available (p 141). Her comments about coffee substitutes (p 135) instil confidence in the reliability of her judgment: 'Dr. Harrison, of Edinburgh, reports that Dandelion Coffee may be safely used as a substitute for the Arabian berry, (he adds,) "being equal in substance and flavour to the best Mocha coffee." This is going too far: it is the best substitute that has been found, but certainly not equal in flavour to really fine coffee.' Traill suggests adding a small quantity of good coffee to Dandelion Coffee as an economical measure to improve the flavour. Many more examples could be offered to illustrate how well Traill describes eating and cooking in Upper Canada. In *Sisters in the Wilderness*, p 126, Charlotte Gray remarks that '[Susanna] was a better cook than her sister [Catharine],' without offering supporting evidence. We cannot know for sure which of the sisters was the more skilled in the kitchen because we can never eat at their tables, but *The Female Emigrant's Guide* is a testament to Catharine's practical knowledge, the trustworthiness of her taste, and her close familiarity with local foodways.

Scholarly assessments of *The Female Emigrant's Guide* have generally been equivocal in their praise or incomplete in their analysis in so far as they have not considered the work in relation to other culinary writing of the period. Clara Thomas, in her 'Introduction' to the 1969 McClelland and Stewart reprint, offers the most comprehensive explanation of the strengths of the work. *The Female Emigrant's Guide* barely registers in Gray's 1999 biography of the two sisters. Michael Peterman, otherwise a great champion of Traill, in his entry in *The Oxford Companion to Canadian Literature*, 1997, misses what lies at the core of her achievement when he refers to *The Female Emigrant's Guide* as 'providing supportive counsel and practical information,' but 'repetitive, anecdotal, and uneven.' Peterman has commented that Traill's botanical writing has not been fully explored or appreciated and offers a variety of reasons, among them the literature student's lack of scientific expertise and resistance to science *per se*, the difficulty of getting beyond generalizations in describing scientific contributions, and the danger of seeing Traill too exclusively within the context of a contemporary thesis ('"Splendid Anachronism": The Record of Catharine Parr Traill's Struggles as an Amateur Botanist in Nineteenth-Century Canada,' in *Re(dis)covering Our Foremothers: Nineteenth-Century Canadian Women Writers*, edited by Lorraine McMullen, Reappraisals: Canadian Writers 15, Ottawa: University of Ottawa Press, 1990, pp 173–85). Her culinary writing has been equally disregarded and for similar reasons, especially the limiting boundaries of scholarly inquiry to date, a lack of knowledge about the history of Canadian cookery writing (which this bibliography aims to remedy), and a general tendency to dismiss cookbooks as 'how to' manuals, without considering how they might be evaluated. It is hoped that this bibliography will prompt a reappraisal of *The Female Emigrant's Guide* within the context of nineteenth-century Canadian culinary writing.

Watters, p 988, records the 1854 edition, with pp xi, ... (as O5.2), but for the copy at OTUTF (O5.1). The following references to the 1854 edition do not distinguish between the first and second thousand: Breckenridge, p 132; Cooke 2002, p 234 (title cited incorrectly); Dagg, pp 298, 299.

O5.2 2nd thousand, 1854 [1855]
—The / female emigrant's / guide, / and / hints on Canadian housekeeping. / By Mrs. C.P. Traill, / authoress of the "Backwoods of Canada," "Forest / Gleanings," "The Canadian Crusoes," &c., &c. / Second thousand. / Toronto, C.W: / Sold by Maclear and Company, / and all the principal

booksellers throughout Canada, the / British American Provinces, and the United States. / 1854. / Price twenty-five cents, or one shilling and three-pence, each part, / postpaid to any part of Canada, the British American Provinces, / and the United States.

DESCRIPTION: 18.0 × 11.0 cm   Pp [iii–v] vi [vii–ix] x–xi [xii], [13] 14–218 [219–34], [1] 2–28 [29] 30–40, [i–xvi]   9 pls, illus   Rebound

CONTENTS: iii tp; iv dedication to the Earl of Elgin and Kincardine; v–vi 'Table of Contents' [i.e., index]; vii 'Contents of Appendix'; viii blank; ix–xii 'Preface' signed Canadian emigrant; 13–58 'Introductory Remarks'; 59–230 text; 231–4 'Conclusion'; 1–40 'Appendix'; i–xvi ads

CITATIONS: Haight 1896, p 100   PAC Library, 1979, Vol. 9, p 689   TPL 3486   Williamson, pp 5, 7, 9, 10, 11, 12, 13, 15 (note 52), 15–16, 21, 22, 23, illus on pp 10, 11, 19

COPIES: CIHM (41417)   ECO   *OONL (F5016.1 T7 1854b)   OTMCL (917.1 T67.2); Great Britain: LB destroyed (7955.c.27)

NOTES: Like the first thousand, the second thousand was apparently also issued in four parts, and the printing of the second thousand followed soon after the first thousand. The advertisement dated 18 January 1855 in the *Christian Guardian* of 24 January that announces 'This day first thousand of the second part' also announces the second thousand of the first part. By mid-February the second thousand of the second part was available (see the advertisement dated 15 February 1855 in the *Christian Guardian* of 28 February that announces 'Now ready second thousand of the first and second part,' after the reference to what must be the first thousand of the fourth part, quoted in O5.1). The second thousand of the third part is described as 'Now ready' in an advertisement dated 5 March 1855 in the *Christian Guardian* of 7 March. The complete volume, second thousand, probably followed not long after.

At the back of the complete volume there are several advertisements dated 1855 and, on p 36 of the 'Appendix,' a notice from the Government Emigration Department, Toronto, dated 5 March 1855.

The OTMCL copy is rebound; it is stamped on the title-page 'Joseph Lesslie' (in the Toronto city directory for 1856, Joseph Lesslie is listed as a postmaster).

An advertisement dated [19?] April 1855 in the *Christian Guardian* of 9 May announces: 'Third edition Mrs. Traill's new work, The Canadian Housekeeper and Female Emigrant's Guide, 300 pages. Price $1. Post free. For sale at the Wesleyan Book Room.'

This advertisement may refer to an as yet unlocated new edition, or, more likely, simply a reprinting of the book. It is also possible that there was no 'third edition' and that the advertisement was a ploy on Hope's part to boost sales.

O5.3 5th ed., 1855

—The / Canadian settler's guide: / By / Mrs. C.P. Traill, / authoress of / The "Backwoods of Canada," &c., &c., &c. / Fifth edition. / [caption:] Christmas day in the backwoods. / Toronto, C.W.: / Printed at the Old Countryman office. / 1855.

DESCRIPTION: 18.0 × 11.0 cm   Pp [i–v] vi [vii–ix] x–xi [xii], [13] 14–218 [219–34], [1] 2–40   Tp illus of children travelling through snow in a cutter, fp illus, illus   Rebound

CONTENTS: i tp; ii 'Entered according to the Act of the Provincial Legislature, in the year one thousand eight hundred and fifty-five, in the office of the Registrar of the Province of Canada.'; iii blank; iv fp illus of 'The emigrant's home in the back woods of Canada'; v–vi 'Table of Contents' [i.e., index]; vii 'Contents of Appendix'; viii blank; ix–xii 'Preface' signed Canadian emigrant; 13–58 'Introductory Remarks'; 59–229 text; 230 blank; 231–4 'Conclusion'; 1–40 'Appendix' and at bottom p 40, 'Book Post. (From the Old Countryman March 12, 1855.)'

CITATIONS: Dagg, pp 298, 299   Garrett, pp 25, 132   Haight 1896, p 100   PAC Library, 1979, Vol. 9, p 689   TPL 3487   Watters, p 987

COPIES: BVAU (F5016.1 T7 1855)   CIHM (37099) ECO   OKQ (F5016.1 T73 1855)   OLU (F1013 T76, 3 copies)   *OONL (F5016.1 T7 1855 reserve) OOP   OTMCL (917.1 T67.21 and 917.1 T67.22) OTUTF (2 copies: B-10 5355, flem 0212)   OTV (F1032 T8 1855)   QLB (FC480 I6 T8); United States: DLC (F1013 T76)

NOTES: The title-page illustration of children riding in a cutter through a winter landscape presents a merry picture of backwoods life. The full-page illustrations are included in the pagination.

OONL has a small broadside (FC41 T732 1862 xxfol.) advertising this edition for $0.50.

The DLC copy of *The Canadian Settler's Guide*, fifth edition, is described as having an added title-page: 'The female emigrant's guide, and hints on Canadian housekeeping. / By Mrs. C. P. Traill. – (First thousand) – Toronto, C.W.: Sold by Maclear and company ..., 1854'; and pagination: [2], [xii], [3]–132, 5–8, [16], 133–218, [18], 9–40; and [6] leaves of plates.

A review of *The Canadian Settler's Guide* published at the Old Countryman office in 1855 (no edition number cited) appeared in the *Canadian Agriculturist*

Vol. 7 (December 1855), p 374. The anonymous reviewer praises Traill for 'compiling an amount of practical information, suited to the every day wants of the immigrant settler, that is not to be found in any other single work with which [he or she is] acquainted'; surprisingly, the reviewer's list of the book's contents does not mention the recipes.

The fifth edition of 1855 was reprinted in 1969 by McClelland and Stewart as No. 64 in the New Canadian Library (see 'Other editions,' below). Christina Bates's many references to Traill in *Out of Old Ontario Kitchens* are to the 1969 reprint: see Bates, pp 28, 39, 41, 51, 53–4, 65 (notes 1 and 3), 66, 69, 73 (note 1), 74, 89 (note 43), 90 (notes 45, 46, 49), 91, 99 (notes 2 and 3), 101, 102 (notes 13 and 14), 105, 109, 113 (note 17), 114 (notes 19 and 22), 117, 119, 120, 128, 141 (notes 1 and 2), 144, 146, 151, 156. References to Traill in Barss 1980 are also to the 1969 reprint: pp 73, 80, 109; Barss comments that 'it is not known if [Traill's book] was used in the Western Interior.'

'Settler's Guide (Canadian)' by Mrs C.P. Traill is listed in A. Boisseau, *Catalogue des livres de la bibliothèque de l'Institut-canadien*, Montreal: 1870, p 44, but the edition number is not specified.

O5.4 7th ed., 1857

—The / Canadian settler's guide: / By / Mrs. C.P. Traill, / authoress of / The "Backwoods of Canada," etc., etc. / Seventh edition – considerably enlarged. / Toronto, C.W.: / Printed at the office of the "Toronto Times." / 1857.

DESCRIPTION: 18.5 × 11.5 cm   Pp [i–v] vi [vii–ix] x–xi [xii], [13] 14–218 [219–34], [1] 2–40, [1] 2–14, [i–ii], [1–44]   Fp illus, illus   Rebound; original cloth applied to new binding

CONTENTS: i tp; ii 'Entered according to the Act of the Provincial Legislature, in the year one thousand eight hundred and fifty-five, in the office of the Registrar of the Province of Canada, and at Stationers Hall, London.'; iii–iv 'Preface to the Seventh Edition' dated Toronto, Canada West, 1 January 1857; v–vi 'Table of Contents' [i.e., index]; vii 'Contents of Appendix'; viii blank; ix–xii 'Preface' signed Canadian emigrant; 13–58 'Introductory Remarks'; 59–228 text; 229–33 'Conclusion'; 234 blank; 1–40 'Appendix'; 1–14 'Appendix' containing 'The Future of Western Canada from Maclear's Almanac for 1856'; i–ii blank; 1–44 'Appendix'

CITATIONS: Abrahamson, pp 39, 62   Eade, p E2   TPL 3489   WaddingtonCat 20 Jan 2000, lot 81

COPIES: BVIPA (NW971 T766c)   NBFL   OGU (s0097 b25)   OKQ (F5016.1 T73 1857)   OLU (F1013 T77) *OONL (F5016.1 T7 1857 copy 1 reserve)   OPET

(F5505 T72 C 1857 bstc) OTMCL (917.1 T67.25) OTRM (FC41 T73 1857 RB CAN) OTUTF (B-10 5812) OTYA (FC41 T73 1857) SRL; Great Britain: LB (10470.aaa.16)

NOTES: The 'Preface to the Seventh Edition' says that the 'Appendix' has been added by the publisher; i.e., the enlargement of this edition is not to Traill's text, but to the end matter. The full-page illustrations are included in the pagination.

OONL has three copies of this edition. Copy 1, catalogued here, has a book plate, 'Ex libris Fred G. Ketcheson'; the title-page is inscribed, in brown ink, '[G?]P.R. James.'

OONL copy 2 is in its original cloth binding, which is a different colour and different impressed pattern from copy 1. Copy 2 is inscribed on the title-page, in brown ink, 'Ecole normale Laval.' Copy 2 does not have the 14-page 'Appendix' containing 'The Future of Western Canada ...' The end pagination runs ... 218, [i–ii], [219–34], [1] 2–40, [1–44]; there is a blank leaf between pp 218 and 219.

OONL copy 3 is in its original cloth binding, which is a different colour from copies 1 and 2, but has the same impressed pattern as copy 2. The pagination is the same as copy 1.

The end pagination of the OTYA copy runs ... 218 [219–30], [1] 2–40, [i–iv], [1–44]; the contents are: ... 59–229 text; 230 blank; 1–40 'Appendix'; i–iv 'Conclusion'; 1–44 'Appendix.' Unlike the OONL copies, the 'Conclusion' is sandwiched between the two appendices, rather than following immediately after the main text. There is no 14-page 'Appendix' containing 'The Future of Western Canada ...' The volume is bound in quarter leather and marbled-paper-covered boards.

The seventh edition of 1857 was also issued in two parts, but under the title *The Emigrant Housekeepers Guide to the Backwoods of Canada*. OTAR (microfilmed as CIHM 55497; ECO) has 'Part the second,' which begins at p 59, with 'Natural Productions of the Woods'; the last numbered page is 218; the last part of the 'Appendix' is on the last page and carries 'Toronto Market Report. December, 11, 1856.'

O5.5 5th thousand, 1861
—The / Canadian / emigrant housekeeper's / guide. / By Mrs. C.P. Traill. / Published by authority. / [coat of arms] / Fifth thousand. / Price two shillings, post paid. / Published by James Lovell, / Montreal, Quebec and Toronto. / 1861.
DESCRIPTION: 17.5 × 12.0 cm Pp [i–iv], [1–3] 4–150 Frontis of 'Emigrant's first home in the back woods,' illus Rebound in cloth, with original paper applied to front and back face of new cloth

CONTENTS: i tp; ii blank; iii–iv, 1 'Contents' [i.e., index]; 2 blank; 3–10 'Introductory Remarks'; 11–133 text headed 'The Canadian Housekeeper's Guide'; 134 blank; 135–50 various tables, notices, and other information that in earlier editions was headed 'Appendix'
CITATIONS: Cagle No. 26, illus PAC Library, 1979, Vol. 9, p 689
COPIES: CIHM (41581) ECO *OONL (FC88 T7 1861 rare); United States: InU
NOTES: In this edition there is no 'Contents of Appendix,' and the end matter is not incorporated in 'Contents' (pp iii–iv, 1) as it is in O5.6. On the back face of the original paper binding there is an advertisement for Traill's *The Settler's Guide to Canada*, 10th thousand. The OONL copy is blind-stamped twice on the title-page: 'Dominion Archives' and 'Soldiers Institute Toronto.'

The copy at InU does not have as many pages of end matter as the OONL copy; Cagle records the pagination of the InU copy as 70 leaves, pp [2] [1–3] 4–133 [134–8].

O5.6 1862
—The / Canadian / emigrant housekeeper's / guide. / By Mrs. C.P. Traill. / Published by authority. / [Canada's coat of arms] / Price two shillings, sterling (50 cents.) / Toronto: / Published by Lovell & Gibson, Yonge Street. / 1862.
DESCRIPTION: 18.5 × 12.0 cm Pp [i–ii], [1] 2–150 Illus Cloth spine, paper-covered boards, with coat of arms on front; sewn
CONTENTS: i tp; ii blank; 1–2 'Contents' [i.e., index]; 3–10 'Introductory Remarks'; 11–133 text; 134–50 various tables, notices, and other information
CITATIONS: PAC Library, 1979, Vol. 9, p 689 TPL 3490 Watters, p 987
COPIES: AEU (FC41 T755 1862) CIHM (49781) OKQ (F1013 T7C) OONL (FC41 T73 reserve, 3 copies) OTMCL (640 T67) OTUTF (B-12 4341) *QMBM (G641.5971 O59 cat) QMBN (285519 CON) QQL (BC 1862 053) QQS (216.1.8)
NOTES: OONL copy 1 is rebound; the original paper is applied to the front and spine of the new cloth. The title-page is inscribed, in ink, with an illegible name. OONL copies 2 and 3 are also rebound. The OKQ copy is inscribed on the title-page, 'A.E. Morgan, 1865.' Cagle records a copy of this edition at BVAU, but it is the CIHM microfilm of the OONL copy.

The 1862 edition may not be the last in Traill's lifetime since there is a review for a 'tenth edition' of 150 pages, published by Lovell and Gibson, in the *Irish Canadian* Vol. 3, No. 13 (5 April 1865), p 5. The review begins, 'A demand for another edition of this very useful publication ... affords the best evidence of the value attached to it.' Michael Peterman suggested to me that the review may be for a reprinting of an earlier edition or it may have been prompted by a remarketing of left-over copies from an earlier print run.

Some time in the 1880s, Traill worked on an updated version of the book that was never published. Her marked-up copy, new manuscript additions, and other related material are at OOA (Traill Family Collection, Vol. 4, Folders 1, 2, 3, and 4, pp 5782–6252; Folder 1 has marked-up copy of parts of *The Female Emigrant's Guide*, 1854 [1855] (O5.1 or O5.2) or *The Canadian Settler's Guide*, fifth edition, 1855 (O5.3); Folder 2 has marked-up copy of parts of the 1862 edition). One proposed title for the updated version was 'The Female Emigrants Friend and Household Guide' (p 5829). In a letter (pp 6214–17) to an unnamed person, presumably a publisher, she offered another choice of titles, none of which, she said, quite pleased her: 'The Emigrants Household Guide: A Book for the Emigrants Wife'; 'The Emigrants Wife: A Household Book for the Dominion of Canada'; or 'The Canadian Settlers Guide: A Household Book for the Wives of Emigrants' (p 6214). If he could give the book a more suitable heading, Traill asked him to do so, suggesting that 'the simpler [the title] the better for the class for whose benefit the vol. was written.' She briefly recounted the book's history: 'The book in pamphlet form was published many years ago – in 1854 – long ago out of print but approved and valued by many Canadian householders and by men of mark in the then Government of the country.'

In previous published editions of her guide, Traill had reflected on the changes in settlers' lives since the time of her arrival in Canada in 1832. Traill's 1880s revisions reflect further improvements in living conditions. In her new 'Introduction' she mentions the new villages, stores, roads, mills, and churches, all making life easier for settlers (p 5787). Elsewhere she cites new industries and telegraph offices as sources of employment, the proliferation in Ontario of cheese factories, and the system of universal education. She notes that, although her book is more particularly suited to emigrants to Ontario, many are now travelling farther west, to the Northwest Territory of Manitoba (p 5807).

The deletions or amendments to parts of the text that offer advice or instructions on specific topics are especially telling. For example, Traill has struck out the section on 'Furnishing Log House' (p 5810). With regard to drying apples, she adds: 'I have lately learned that the stringing of apples is discontinued as useless labor ... Dried apples are now sold at a much

lower price as orchards have increased everywhere' (p 5856). Whereas in earlier editions she had recommended Durkee's Baking Powder, she now inserts the sentence: 'There are many kinds [of baking powders] now in use "Cooks Friend" "Snow flake" Dunns Best C.F. – directions on the packets for using –' (p 5881); or, in another suggested revision of the same text: 'The most approved of these articles for raising dough for small bread buns cakes etc is that sold by the name of "The Cooks Friend". Another "The Snow flake" and there are others well approved of – ' (p 6104). Where she had previously cited lard as a substitute for oil in parlour lamps, 'Kerosene or Coal Oil is now used in all houses – but in far off places in the woods lard lamps are still used for light' (p 5933), and, a few pages on, she adds 'coal oil or petroleum has taken the place of candles all over the country' (p 5950). She also notes other changes in household technology, such as the use of 'the modern washing machine and wringer,' the latter saving 'much hand labor' (p 5947). She remarks on the many new varieties of apple and small fruit (p 6083) and the disappearance of the Passenger Pigeon (p 6162).

Traill also suggests to the (unnamed) editor that the section for making bread should be moved to before the fruit recipes (see p 5878, between pp 6099 and 6100, and p 6215). Some recipes are deleted and others added. The new recipes represent a little-known and thus far unexamined trove of culinary information. Traill explained what guided the recipe changes in a note at the end of the 'Cakes' section (p 6116): 'I have crossed out such recipes as I thought unnecessary – retaining those only of a more homely character –'

OTHER EDITIONS: *The Canadian Settler's Guide*, [reprint of O5.3], New Canadian Library 64, general editor, Malcolm Ross, introduction by Clara Thomas, Toronto: McClelland and Steward Ltd, [1969] (BVAU, MWMM, OH, OKQ, OLA, OLU, OMIH, OOCC, OONL, OOSH, OPET, OTU, OWSJ, OWTL, OWTU, QLB, QMM; United States: DLC; Duncan, pp 16, 164, 207–8). For the story behind the New Canadian Library edition, including quotations from readers' reports that reveal attitudes toward Traill and her book, see Janet B. Friskney, 'On a Mission for Culture: The New Canadian Library and Its Milieu, 1953–1978,' Ph.D. dissertation, Ottawa: Carleton University, Department of History, 1999, pp 361–3.

The Canadian Settler's Guide, introduction by Carl Ballstadt, Vancouver: Alcuin Society, 1971–5; limited ed. of 450 numbered copies of 2 fascicles in slip case; fascicle 1 is an abridged version of the first 60 pages of *The Canadian Settler's Guide*; fascicle 2 takes Traill's references to the seasons from O5.3 and rearranges them in calendar form (BVAU, BVIPA (partial), OGU, OH, OKQ, OLU, OONL, OPET, OTMCL, OTU, OWTU, QLB, QMM; Great Britain: LB; United States: DLC).

BRITISH EDITIONS: *The Canadian Settler's Guide*, 10th ed., considerably enlarged, London: Edward Stanford, 1860 (BVAU, CIHM, ECO, OLU, OOCC, OONL, OTP, OWTU, QMM; Great Britain: LB; United States: DLC).

The Stanford edition differs significantly from the Canadian editions. The first of three parts, pp 1–85, is written by Traill, but although it begins with 'Introductory Remarks' and has the information about ovens and cooking stoves, 'Maple Sugar,' and 'Indian Rice,' it does not have the recipes and other culinary information found in the Canadian editions. The second part, pp 86–155, comprises official documents added by the publisher. The third part, pp 156–92, is Traill's 'Letters from Canada.' The text ends with an 'Appendix' of what the publisher calls 'official information.'

In a letter dated 29 October 1861 to her sister Agnes Strickland (OTUTF), Catharine commented on the Stanford edition: '[*The Female Emigrant's Guide*] is now reprinted by Stanford, London and the proprietor has divided the book into two portions and changed the title – which I am not sure he could do without my full approbation. It now appears as "The Canadian Emigrants Housekeepers Guide" by Mrs. C.P. Traill but the second and more valuable part of the book has not my name on the title page. The preface it is true acknowledges the author but I consider it is scarcely just to with hold it from the title page. The work is enlarged and rendered more generally valuable no doubt by the additions but I think it is these that should have been acknowledged while the original work should have retained the authors name. The dismembering of the book involves a future difficulty.' In the next paragraph, she voices concerns about her financial security. Traill was correct about her name not appearing on the title-page of the Stanford edition, but wrong about the title, which was *The Canadian Settler's Guide*.

1861

The Canadian housewife's manual of cookery

According to the 1861 Census, carried out in the same year that the cookbook appeared, Henry Ilett Richards

(the publisher) and his wife Elizabeth were living in St Patrick's Ward in Hamilton. Both were 45 years old in 1861. Henry was from the Isle of Guernsey; Elizabeth, from Hampshire, England. Henry retired from the Spectator *newspaper in the summer of 1866, at which point he had been in the printing business for forty years, the last eleven years and six months in the* Spectator's *jobbing office (see letters in the* Hamilton Evening Times, *4 August 1866). It appears that he had no surviving children in 1866.*

O6.1 1861
The / Canadian housewife's / manual of cookery / carefully compiled / from the best / English, French & American works, / especially adapted to this country. / Hamilton, C.W. / Printed by William Gillespy, "Spectator" office, / Prince's Square. / MDCCCLXI.

DESCRIPTION: 8.0 × 12.5 cm   Pp [1–8], [i] ii–x, [v] vi–x, [11] 12–360, 1–12   Illus of carving   Cloth

CONTENTS: 1 blank; 2 'The Canadian Housewife's Multiplication and Market Table'; 3 tp; 4 'Published by Henry I. Richards, printer, Spectator office, Hamilton, C.W., and may be had of all the principal booksellers in the province.'; 5–6 preface signed H.I.R.; 7 table of contents; 8 blank; i–x 'Directions for Carving'; v–x 'Introductory Observations for the Use of the Mistress of a Family ... The following practical hints are abridged from a very valuable English work entitled "Domestic Cookery."'; 11–360 text (the recipes are numbered within each chapter); 1–12 ads

CITATIONS: Bates, pp 27–8, 48, 49–50, 50 (note 13), 51 (note 16), 52, 55 (note 3), 56, 57 (note 6), 62 (note 17), 63, 66 (notes 9 and 11), 67 (note 14), 68, 69 (note 17), 69, 70, 73 (note 2), 76 (note 8), 81, 82 (note 26), 83 (note 29), 84 (note 31), 85 (notes 34, 36), 88, 91 (note 51), 95 (note 1), 97 (note 6), 100 (notes 6, 7), 100–1, 103, 104, 112 (note 13), 115 (note 23), 116, 119 (note 35), 125 (notes 1, 2), 127 (note 6), 131 (note 13), 137, 145 (note 11), 147, 149, 154 (note 10), illus of tp on p 29   Berton, pp 18, 24, 31, 33, 35, 54   Driver 2002, Home Cook Book, p xii   Driver 2003, 'Canadian Cookbooks,' p 28   Garrett, pp 90, 106, 120, 131   Golick, p 98   Lafrance/Desloges, p 87   Wheaton/Kelly No. 1046

COPIES: CIHM (64026)   *OGU (UA s049 b01)   OH (R641.5 C167 CESH)   OTMCL (641.5 R37); United States: MWA

NOTES: Mary F. Williamson reports that the MWA copy is bound with the front face of its original blue-paper binding, which has the title 'The Canadian cook book / Hamilton / George Barnes & Co. / King Street' and the price of 12½ cents.

Richards states in the preface that he has 'carefully

culled and collated' from various sources 'all that was valuable and applicable to this country' because he has 'seen the want of a decided Canadian vade-mecum of cookery ...' Since all other publications 'invariably [had] a cosmopolitan character, a work more restricted and withal local in its aim, was much required.' He names two of his English, French, and American sources: 'a very valuable English work entitled "Domestic Cookery,"' i.e., *A New System of Domestic Cookery* by a lady [Mrs Maria Eliza Ketelby Rundell (1745–1828)], and 'a late work of M. Soyer's.' There were many English and American editions of Rundell's work, first published in London in 1806 (see *Petits Propos Culinaires* No. 16, p 8), some of which were undoubtedly in use in Canada. Soyer, although properly described by Richards as 'the celebrated French cook,' built his reputation in England as chef of London's Reform Club, as advisor to British army kitchens during the Crimean War, as the promoter of his own patented kitchen equipment, and as a cookbook writer. I have not determined which title Richards consulted of Soyer's cookbooks, some of which appeared in several English and American editions: *A Shilling Cookery for the People*, London: 1845; *The Gastronomic Regenerator*, London: 1846; *The Modern Housewife or Ménagère*, London: 1849; *The Pantropheon*, London: 1853 (Soyer's name is on the book, but it was actually written by Adolphe Duhart-Fauvet; see Michael McKirdy, 'Who Wrote Soyer's Pantropheon?' *Petits Propos Culinaires* No. 29, pp 18–21); and *Soyer's Culinary Campaign*, London: 1857.

One source that Richards does not identify is *The Housekeeper's Almanac, or the Young Wife's Oracle, for 1842*, by 'a lady of this city, who has kept an extensive boarding-house, for twenty-two years in Pearl St.,' New York: Elton, 1842 (OTAR). Baked Apple Pudding, p 213, Hasty Pudding, p 215, and Bread and Butter Pudding, p 211, for example, are all found in this American periodical. (I am grateful to Fiona Lucas, Toronto, for bringing this source to my attention.)

Lafrance/Desloges incorrectly cite 1867 as the date of the book.

1864

Family receipt book

In about 1864, when Family Receipt Book *was published, Henry Northrop and John Lyman were manufacturers and wholesale dealers of patent medicines, supplying individual retail druggists. The business had* begun in Newcastle, in 1854, as a retail drugstore called Tuttle, Moses and Northrop, which was a branch of the Auburn, New York, firm of Tuttle and Moses. Lyman bought out the American part of the business between 1859 and 1862, at which point it was renamed Northrop and Lyman. The business moved to Toronto in 1874, where its first location, a warehouse, was at 40 Scott Street. About 1879, the company established itself in larger quarters at 21 Front Street West. In April 1904, the Front Street building was destroyed by fire. In March 1905 the company moved from a temporary location to 86–8 Richmond Street West; about 1917 it moved again, to 462, 464, 466 Wellington Street West. Unfortunately, none of the editions of* Family Receipt Book *that I examined included the company's street address, which would have helped establish the year of publication. In the mid-1960s, the company name changed to Northrop-McGillivray.*

I have checked the following issues of the company's Family Almanac Guide to Health and Recipe Book, *later retitled* Almanac and Guide to Health, *and they contain no cookery: 1885, 1887, 1888, 1890, 1892, 1898, 1901, 1906, 1907, 1910, 1912, 1924 (Nalco almanac and calendar) (all at OTUTF).*

Information about the company is from Catherine Sullivan, 'The Bottles of Northrop and Lyman, a Canadian Drug Firm,' Material History Bulletin, *No. 18 (Fall 1983), pp 13–30.*

O7.1   nd [about 1864]
Family / receipt book. / This book will be found to contain a large / number of colouring, cooking and / other receipts, very useful / to every family. / Newcastle, C.W.: / Published by Northrop & Lyman. / Printed at the Globe Steam Job Press, Toronto, C.W. [cover-title]
DESCRIPTION: 17.0 × 11.0 cm   Pp [1] 2–26 [folios torn off 27–32]   Paper; sewn
CONTENTS: Inside front face of binding 'To the Public' [i.e., a note about Dr Ransom's Hive Syrup and Tolu] signed Northrop and Lyman; 1–2 publ ad for Canadian Pain Destroyer; 3, part of 10 and 13, 25, 30 'Domestic Receipts'; 4–6, 8–9, part of 10, 11–12, bottom 14–15, 18–mid 19, 21–mid 23, 26–9, 31–2 publ ads; 7 'Recipes for Coloring'; bottom 13–mid 14 'Coloring and Other Useful Receipts'; 16, bottom 19–top 20, mid 23–24 'Wit and Humor'; 17 'Miscellaneous'; mid–bottom 20 'Pickles'
COPIES: *OTMCL (640.4 F12)
NOTES: This edition was published before Confederation on 1 July 1867, likely in about 1864. There is a testimonial dated 5 February 1864 on p 8 and several testimonials for 1864 on p 9. This is the only edition

that I have seen where the spelling 'receipt' is used in the title; all later editions are called *Family Recipe Book* (in French, *Livre de recettes des familles*), *Northrop and Lyman's Family Recipe Book*, or *Northrop and Lyman Co's Family Recipe Book* (the last two sometimes extended by 'and guide to health').

O7.2   nd [about 1869–73]

—Family / recipe book. / This book will be found to contain a large / number of colouring, cooking and / other receipts, very useful / to every family. / Newcastle, Ont., / Published by Northrop & Lyman. / Globe Printing Company, King St. East, Toronto. [cover-title]

DESCRIPTION: 17.5 × 10.5 cm   Pp 1–32   Paper; sewn
CONTENTS: 1 'Directions for Using the Canadian Pain Destroyer'; 2–3 'Caution' and testimonials for Pain Destroyer, one dated 1 August 1869; 4–6 testimonials for Trask's Magnetic Ointment; 7 'Domestic Receipts, &c.'; 8–9 testimonials for Ransom's Hive Syrup and Tolu and at bottom p 9, 'Sundry Useful Receipts'; 10 'Wit and Humor'; 11 publ ad for Bryan's Pulmonic Wafers; 12 publ ad for Job Moses' Periodical Pills; 13 'Domestic Receipts'; 14 ad for Dr Fowler's Extract of Wild Strawberry; 15 publ ad for Warner's blacking and 'Miscellaneous'; 16 publ ad for Hall's Vegetable Sicilian Hair Renewer; 17 'Wit and Humour'; 18–19 publ ad for Darley's Arabian Oil; 20 publ ad for Canadian Arnica Strengthening Plasters and 'Pickles' [2 recipes]; 21–3 ads for Ayer's products; 24 'Wit and Humor'; 25 'Domestic Receipts'; 26 publ ads for Darley's products and Dr Kellogg's Catarrh Snuff; 27 publ ads for Ayer's Hair Vigor and Bryan's Pulmonic Wafers; 28 publ ads for Holloway's Worm Lozenges and Canadian Pain Destroyer; 29 'Miscellaneous'; 30–1 'Recipes for Coloring'; 32 'Domestic Recipes' and 'Curious Epitaphs'
COPIES: *OONL (TX715 F35)
NOTES: OONL dates the book [1869?], probably following the dated testimonial. According to Hulse, p 107, the Globe Printing Co. was incorporated in 1866, and the business was at 26–8 King Street East from 1864 to 1890. This issue of *Family Recipe Book* precedes O7.5 of about 1874, where Northrop and Lyman is located in Toronto, but described as 'late of Newcastle.'

OTMCL (640.4 F12 1869) is a variant. The only difference is p 16, where the advertisement is for W.H. Hall's Chemical Hair Invigorator, not Hall's Vegetable Sicilian Hair Renewer. In the cover-title, there is no period and comma after 'Ont'; however, the punctuation may simply have not registered during printing.

O7.3   nd [about 1872–3]

—Family / recipe book. / This book will be found to contain a / large number of colouring, cooking / and other receipts, very useful / to every family. / Newcastle, Ont., / published by Northrop & Lyman. / Printed by J.A. Plinguet, 30 St. Gabriel Street, Montreal. [cover-title]

DESCRIPTION: 16.5 × 10.5 cm   Pp 1–32   Paper; sewn
CONTENTS: 1–6 publ ads; 7–10 lacking; 11 'Extracts from letters'; 12–13, 22, 26, 29 'Domestic Receipts'; 14–21, 23–5, 27–8, 30 publ ads and at bottom p 28, 'Fine Pickled Cabbage' and 'Pickled Peaches'; 31–2 'Recipes for Coloring'
COPIES: OTUTF (uncat patent medicine)   QKB (89-8) *QSH
NOTES: The OTUTF copy has pp 7–10, which are publisher's advertisements. The advertisements include testimonials dated 1872, and on p 9 there is a note regarding Job Moses' Periodical Pills dated 1 March 1872. This edition predates Northrop and Lyman's move to Toronto in 1874.

O7.4   nd [about 1874]

—Livre de recettes / des / familles. / Ce livre contient un grand nombre / de recettes pour la teinture, / l'art culinaire et autres / très utiles a toutes / les familles. / Toronto, Ont., / publié par Northrop & Lyman. / Imprimé par J.A. Plinguet, 30 rue St. Gabriel, Montréal. [cover-title]

DESCRIPTION: 16.5 × 10.5 cm   Pp 1–32   Paper; sewn
CONTENTS: 1–11, 14–21, 23–5, 27–8, 30 publ ads; 12–13, 22, 26, 29 'Recettes domestiques'; 31–2 'Recettes pour teinture'
COPIES: CIHM (61489)   *QMM (RBD uncat 0110) QQS
NOTES: On p 3 there is a testimonial dated 20 June 1872; however, the book must have been published no earlier than 1874, the year that Northrop and Lyman moved the business from Newcastle to Toronto.

The arrangement of text and advertisements matches that for O7.3, an English-language edition published about 1872–3; the recipes, for example, are on the same pages.

O7.5   nd [about 1874]

—Family / recipe book. / This book will be found to contain a / large number of coloring, cooking, / and other receipts, very useful / to every family. / Published by / Northrop & Lyman, / Toronto, (late of Newcastle), Ont. / Presbyterian Printing Company, 102 Bay Street, Toronto. [cover-title]

DESCRIPTION: 16.5 × 10.5 cm   Pp 1–32   Paper; sewn

CONTENTS: 1–2 publ ad for Thomas' Excelsior Eclectric Oil; 3 testimonials for the oil; 4–top 7 publ ad for Canadian Pain Destroyer and testimonials; mid–bottom 7 humorous text and the population of principal cities; 8 publ ad for Ayer's Sarsaparilla; 9 'Cooking Receipts'; 10 publ ad for Dr Ransom's Hive or Croup Syrup; 11 testimonials for the syrup; 12 publ ad for Darley's Condition Powders; 13 'Domestic Receipts'; 14–20 publ ads for various products; 21 humorous text and information about the length of days; 22–mid 25 publ ads for various products; mid–bottom 25 humorous text; top 26 publ ad for indelible ink; mid–bottom 26 humorous text; 27–8 'Domestic Receipts' and publ ad for Holloway's Worm Lozenges; 29–30 publ ads for various products; 31–2 'Recipes for Coloring'

COPIES: *QQS (219.1.Cart.4)

NOTES: This edition was likely published shortly after Northrop and Lyman moved their business from Newcastle to Toronto in 1874. The latest testimonial is dated 1 June 1874 (p 23). The Presbyterian Printing Co. was at 102 Bay Street from November 1872 to 1877 (Hulse, p 208).

O7.6 1876
—Northrop & Lyman's / family / recipe book. / 1876. / This book contains a careful collection of the latest / colouring, cooking and other receipts, and / many facts worth knowing. / New every year, and is well worth preserving. / Published by / Northrop & Lyman, / Toronto, Ont. [cover-title]
DESCRIPTION: 16.5 × 11.5 cm   Pp 1–32   Paper, with still-life on front of an open volume about 'Family Medicine,' stacked books, and a mortar and pestle; sewn, and with string running through top left corner for hanging
CONTENTS: 1–5, 7–12, 14–20, 22–8, 30 publ ads and 'Humorous Clippings'; 6, 13, 21, 29 'Domestic Receipts'; mid 27, 31–2 'Recipes for Coloring'
COPIES: *OTUTF (uncat patent medicine)
NOTES: The recipes begin on p 6 with Sweet Apple Pickles, Cream Nectar, Tomato Catsup, and To Take Out Mildew.

OTUTF has a second copy, where the year in the cover-title is overprinted with Canada's coat of arms. This overprinted copy was probably distributed later, possibly in 1877. On the outside back face of the overprinted copy is 'Presented by A.R. Stephen, Collingwood, dealer in drugs, medicines & chemicals.'

O7.7 1878
—Northrop & Lyman's / family / recipe book. / 1878. / This book contains a careful collection of the latest / colouring, cooking and other receipts, and / many facts worth knowing. / New every year, and is well worth preserving. / Published by / Northrop & Lyman, / Toronto, Ontario. [cover-title]
DESCRIPTION: 17.5 × 11.5 cm   Pp 1–32   Paper, with still-life on front of an open book, mortar and pestle, etc.
CONTENTS: 1–32 text and publ ads
COPIES: *OGU (UA s076 b22)
NOTES: 'Domestic Receipts' are on pp 4, 10, and 21. 'Presented by L.A. Gamsby, Orono, dealer in drugs, medicines and chemicals, ...' is printed on the back face.

O7.8 nd [about 1881]
—Northrop & Lyman's / family / recipe book / and / guide / to / health. / Globe Printing Co., printers and engravers, / Toronto, Ontario. [cover-title]
DESCRIPTION: 18.0 × 11.5 cm   Pp 1–32   Paper, with small images on front of a bird and open fan; sewn, and with string running through top left corner for hanging
CONTENTS: 1–4, 6–top 2nd column 11, 12, 1st column 14, 15, 1st column 16, 17, 19–20, 1st column 22, 23–top 2nd column 30, 1st column 31, 32 publ ads, jokes, and miscellaneous information; 5, near top–bottom 2nd column 11, 2nd column 14, 2nd column 16, 18, 2nd column 22, near top 2nd column 30 'Domestic Recipes'; 13, 21, 2nd column 31 'Dyeing'
CITATIONS: Oldfield/Landon, illus col p 15
COPIES: *OTUTF (uncat patent medicine)
NOTES: The first four recipes on p 5 are Yeast Cake, Corn Meal Bread, Buckwheat Cakes, and Potato Rolls. There are two testimonials referring to the year 1881: on p 6, 'Mr. T.C. Berchard ... writes: "During the year 1881, I was much troubled ..."'; and on p 22, 'After I commenced my spring work in 1881, ...' signed Henry Colton. (Mr Colton sent another letter to the company, dated March 1885, published in O7.12.)

O7.9 nd [1883 or later, possibly 1888]
—Northrop & / Lyman Co's / family / recipe book / and / guide to health / Published by / Northrop & Lyman Co (Limited) / Toronto Canada / Toronto Lith Co [cover-title]
DESCRIPTION: 19.0 × 13.0 cm   Pp 1–31 [32]   Paper, with image on front of a seated woman reading 'Recipe Book' in a kitchen; stapled
CONTENTS: 1–32 recipes and publ ads
COPIES: *NSYHM

NOTES: The first column of recipes is on p 4, beginning with Beef Soup, Veal Soup, and Scotch Broth. The last column of recipes is on p 31, ending with To Make an Ornamental Pyramid for a Table.

Northrop and Lyman was incorporated in 1883 (see Sullivan's article, p 15, and also the text on the binding of the company's *Almanac and Guide to Health*, 1907, at OHMB); therefore, this edition of *Family Recipe Book*, which carries the name 'Northrop & Lyman Co,' was published in 1883 or later. It may have appeared in 1888, when Northrop and Lyman Co. used the same printer (Toronto Lithographing Co.) for its almanac (OHMB). The Toronto Lithographing Co. was active from 1878; it changed its name to Stone Ltd in 1909 (Hulse, p 261).

O7.10   nd [about 1884–96]
—Northrop & Lyman Co's / family / recipe / book / and / guide to / health / Published / by / Northrop & Lyman Co Limited / Toronto, Canada / J.L. Jones, / Toronto. / Printed by R.G. McLean, Toronto. [cover-title]
DESCRIPTION: 20.0 × 13.0 cm   Pp 1–32   Paper; stapled
CONTENTS: 1–32 recipes and publ ads
COPIES: *NSYHM
NOTES: The letter R in 'Recipe' in the cover-title is organic, decoratively transforming into a trailing vine that encircles the phrase 'Family Recipe Book.' The first column of recipes is on p 3, beginning with To Fry Salmon Steaks, Broiled Fresh Mackerel, and Chili Sauce. The last column of recipes is on p 30, ending with Broiled Venison Steaks and To Restore Frozen Plants.

'Presented by [stamped in blank space:] J.A. Craig, Yarmouth' is on the outside back face of the NSYHM copy.

This edition was published between 1884, when J.L. Jones is recorded as in business for himself, and 1896, when he became proprietor of the Jones Engraving Co. (see Hulse, p 139). The printer, R.G. McLean, was active 1879–1905 (Hulse, p 163).

O7.11   nd [about 1884–96]
—Northrop & Lyman Co's / family / recipe / book / and / guide to / health / Published by / Northrop & Lyman Co / Toronto Canada / J.L. Jones, Toronto. [cover-title]
COPIES: *OPEMO
NOTES: At the top of the cover-title, 'Northrop & Lyman Co's' is in an oval shape and surrounded by radiating lines. Swirls of acanthus-like leaves run from the letter R in 'Recipe' at mid-left to the bottom right corner.

For the same reasons as O7.10, this edition of *Family Recipe Book* was published about 1884–96. The OPEMO copy was distributed by 'A & L Cameron Beachburg Ont.,' whose stamp appears at the back of the book, under 'Presented by.'

O7.12   nd [about 1885]
—Northrop & / Lyman Co's / family / recipe / book / and / guide to / healt[h] / Published by / Northrop & L[yman, Co. (Limited)] / Toront[o, Canada.] / J.L. Jones – Engraver, Toronto [cover-title]
DESCRIPTION: 18.0 × 11.5 cm   Pp 1–32   Paper, with image on front of a vase of wheat stalks (?) and flowers; stapled
CONTENTS: 1–32 recipes and publ ads
COPIES: *NSYHM   OTUTF (2 copies: uncat patent medicine)   QSH
NOTES: The first column of recipes is on p 5, beginning with Brown Bread, Boston Corn Bread, and Plain Corn Bread. The last column of recipes is on p 31, ending with Tapioca Cream.

'March, 1885. – Mr. Colton informs us ...' is on p 21, suggesting a publication date of about that year. The book was certainly published no later than 1896, when J.L. Jones became proprietor of J.L. Jones Engraving Co. (Hulse, p 139).

'Presented by [stamped in blank space:] CC Richards // Yarmouth' is on the outside back face of the NSYHM copy. 'Presented by [stamped in blank space:] J.S. Mills, Brantford, Ont.' is on the outside back face of one of the OTUTF copies; a printed label is in the same position on the other OTUTF copy: 'Presented by L.A. Gamsby, Orono, Ont. ...' The Mills stamp confirms a publication date of about 1885: The 1885 Brantford city directory lists Jesse S. Mills, druggist, but directories from 1887 onward list him in connection with Snow Drift Co., a spice and baking powder manufacturer. Mills was more likely to be distributing Northrop and Lyman booklets as a druggist than as a Snow Drift salesman.

O7.13   nd [about 1887–96]
—Northrop & Lyman / Co's / family / [in very small type:] J.L. Jones, Toronto. [in large type:] recipe / book / and guide to health / Published by / Northrop & Lyman Co: / Toronto, Canada [cover-title]
DESCRIPTION: 20.0 × 12.5 cm   Pp 1–32   Paper [see description below]; sewn
CONTENTS: 1–2 'Northrop & Lyman's Vegetable Discovery'; 1st column 3 'Dr. J.D. Kellogg's Eye Water'; 2nd column 3 and 5 and 7 and 11 and 12, 15, 2nd

column 19 and 21 and 22 and 27 and 29, 31 'Cooking Recipes'; 4–1st column 5 and 1st column 6 'Dr. Thomas' Eclectric Oil'; 2nd column 6 'Sparkles'; 1st column 7 'Darley's Condition Powders'; 8 'Dr. J.D. Kellogg's Healing Ointment' and 'Brieflets'; 9 'Handy Package Dyes' and 'Merryisms'; 10 'Carboline'; 1st column 11 'Dr. Kellogg's Catarrh Snuff'; 1st column 12 'Northrop & Lyman's Beef, Iron & Wine'; 13 'Parmelee's New Vegetable Pills' and 'Humor'; 14 'Northrop & Lyman's Vegetable Discovery'; 16 'Holloway's Corn Cure' and 'Fun'; 17 'Dr J.D. Kellogg's Dysentery Cordial' and 'House – Cleaning Times'; 18 'Parmelee's New Pills'; 1st column 19 'Persian Beautifier'; 20 'Mother Graves' Worm Exterminator' and 'Scraps'; 1st column 21 'Sparkles'; 1st column 22 and 1st column 23 'Dr Thomas' Eclectric Oil'; 2nd column 23 'Funnigrams'; 1st column 24 'Coplands Castor Oil'; 2nd column 24–25 'Coloring Recipes'; 26 'Bickles' Anti-Consumptive Syrup'; 1st column 27 'Canadian Liquid Hair Dye'; 28–1st column 29 'Laughlets' and 'Northrop & Lyman's Vegetable Discovery'; 30 'Northop & Lymans Quinine Wine'; 32 'Dr. Thomas' Eclectric Oil'

COPIES: *OKQ (F5012 1879? N877)

NOTES: There is a testimonial on p 10 dated 10 March 1879, which accounts for OKQ's suggested date of publication of [1879?]; however, a later testimonial on p 12 refers to spring 1887. The book was certainly published no later than 1896, when J.L. Jones became proprietor of the J.L. Jones Engraving Co. (Hulse, p 139).

The binding design is much simpler than other editions; the only decorative features are a series of lines radiating from the centre of the capital R in 'Recipe' (the largest word in the cover-title), and four solid circles clustered at the centre of the R, two aligned with the vertical line and two with the horizontal line. The lettering style has characteristics in common with that on the binding of 1890 and 1893 editions of *The Art of Cooking Made Easy* (O48.1–48.3 and O48.5–48.6), all printed by the London Printing and Lithographing Co. This edition of *Family Recipe Book* was not printed by the London company, but the stylistic similarities point to a publication date about the same time, in the early 1890s.

The following is on the outside back face of the OKQ copy: 'Presented by [stamped in blank space:] James Williams // Brockville Ont.'

O7.14 nd [about 1897]
—Northrop & Lyman / Co's / family / recipe / book / This book contains a careful / collection of the latest / coloring, cooking / and other recipes /

Published by / Northrop & Lyman Co. Limited / Toronto, Canada. / J.L. Jones Eng. Co. Toronto. / Murray Printing Co., Toronto. [cover-title]

DESCRIPTION: 20.0 × 13.0 cm   Pp 1–32   Paper, with a stylized leaf design on front; stapled

CONTENTS: 1–2 'Parmelee's New Vegetable Pills'; 3, 6, 10, 13, 16, 20, 26, 30 'Cooking Recipes'; 4 information about Dr Thomas' Eclectric Oil; 5 'Persian Beautifier' and 'Witticisms'; 7 'Dr. Kellogg's Asthma Remedy'; 8 'Mother Graves' Worm Exterminator'; 9 'Beef, Iron & Wine' and 'Album Verses'; 11 'Vegetable Discovery' [a blood medicine]; 12 'Dr. Thomas' Eclectric Oil'; 14 'Jokelets' and 'Dr. J.D. Kellogg's Eye Water'; 15 'Holloway's Corn Cure'; 17 'Parmelee's New Vegetable Pills'; 18 'Dr. J.D. Kellogg's Carbolic Healing Ointment'; 19 'Dr. Kellogg's Catarrh Snuff' and 'Laughlets'; 21 'Bickles Anti-Consumptive Syrup'; 22 'Brieflets' and 'Darley's Condition Powders'; 23 'Dr. J.D. Kellogg's Dysentery Cordial'; 24–1st column 25 'Coloring Recipes'; 2nd column 25 'Brieflets'; 27 'Dr. Thomas' Eclectric Oil'; 28 testimonials for Kellogg's Asthma Remedy and 'Jokelets'; 29 'Parmelee's New Vegetable Pills'; 31 'Quinine Wine'; 32 'Dr. Thomas' Eclectric Oil'

COPIES: OFERWM (A1999.83 MU278)   OHMB (Ephemera QV772 N877n 1896)   OTUTF (uncat patent medicine)   *Bookseller's stock

NOTES: The first recipes are Egg Balls for Soup, Mutton Soup, and Tomato Soup.

A testimonial on p 28 is dated 11 December 1896. In the same year, 1896, the J.L. Jones Engraving Co. was established (Hulse, p 139). The Murray Printing Co. had been active since 4 February 1893 (Hulse, p 186).

O7.15 nd [about 1897]
—Northrop and Lyman Co's / family / recipe / book / This book contains a careful / collection of the latest / coloring, cooking / and other recipes / Published by / Northrop & Lyman Co Limited / Toronto, Canada. / Murray Printing Co., Toronto. [cover-title]

DESCRIPTION: 20.0 × 13.0 cm   Pp 1–32   Paper, with stylized leaf-and-flower design on front; sewn, and with string running through top left corner for hanging

CONTENTS: 1–32 publ ads, 'Cooking Recipes,' 'Jokelets,' 'Laughlets,' 'Wit,' and 'Coloring Recipes'

COPIES: OONL (TX715 F35 1896 p***)   *OTUTF (uncat patent medicine)

NOTES: The 'Cooking Recipes' are on pp 3, 6, 10, 13, 16, 20, 26, and 30, beginning with Coloring for Soups and Gravies, Chicken Broth, Plain White Soup, and

Veal Broth. The latest testimonial is dated 11 December 1896 (p 19).

O7.16   nd [1905]
—Northrop & Lyman Co's / family / recipe / book / This book / contains a careful collection of the / latest cooking, coloring / and other recipes / Published by / Northrop & Lyman Co., Limited. / Toronto, Canada. / O5 J.L. Jones. Eng Co Toronto. [cover-title]
DESCRIPTION: 19.5 × 13.0 cm   Pp 1–32   Paper; stapled, and with hole punched at top left corner for hanging
CONTENTS: 1–2, 4–5, 7–9, 11–12, 14–15, 17–19, 21–1st column 24, 27–8, 30, 32 publ ads and 'Humor of the Hour'; 3, 6, 10, 13, 16, 20, 2nd column 24–top 2nd column 26 'Cooking Recipes'; near top–bottom 2nd column 26, 29 'Coloring Recipes'; 31 'The Time to Spray'
COPIES: *OTNY (641.5971 N)   OTUTF (uncat patent medicine)   OTYA (CPC 1873 0037)   *Private collection
NOTES: The first recipes are Stock, Economical Soup, Tomato Soup, and Chicken Soup. The recipes end on p 6 with Cheese Omelet.

1865

Chase, Dr Alvin Wood (Cayuga County, NY, 20 March 1817–25 May 1885, Ohio)

The American Dr Chase earned his 'M.D.' from the Cincinnati Eclectic Medical Institution, after a short course. Dr Chase's Recipes; or, Information for Everybody, *which he compiled, printed, and marketed himself, met with great success and was published in many editions from 1856 onward. In 1869, Chase sold the copyright for* Dr Chase's Recipes *and many of his other assets to Rice Aner Beal, an action he later regretted. In 1872, in an effort to regain lost income and return to the publishing field, he produced* Dr Chase's Family Physician, Farrier, Bee-keeper, and Second Receipt Book, *a move that embroiled him in a legal battle with Beal. Just before he died, Chase finished writing* Dr Chase's Third, Last and Complete Receipt Book and Household Physician, *which was subsequently published with an 'In Memoriam' recounting the details of his life, by L. Davis, secretary of the Washtenaw County Pioneer Society. Chase is buried in Forest Hill Cemetery, Ann Arbor, with his wife, Martha.*

Dr Chase's Recipes *and* Dr Chase's Third, Last and Complete Receipt Book and Household Physi-

cian *were both published in several Canadian editions (O8.1 and O40.1); however, no Canadian edition of* Dr Chase's Family Physician, Farrier, Bee-keeper, and Second Receipt Book *has been found (although it appears to have been for sale in Nova Scotia and New Brunswick; see the $2.50 price quoted on p ii of the 1875 Toledo, Ohio, edition, CIHM 01767).* O45.1, Dr Chase's New Receipt Book, *first published in Toronto by Rose Publishing Co. in 1889, does not correspond to any of the three texts written by Chase in his lifetime; for a discussion of* Dr Chase's New Receipt Book, *see that entry.*

Long after Chase's death, the following cookbooks were issued under the imprint of the Dr A.W. Chase Medicine Co.: *O129.1,* Dainty Dishes for the Invalid; *O142.1,* 100 Special Receipts Selected from Dr. A.W. Chase's Receipt Book; *O206.1,* Dr Chase's Candy Book; *and various annual almanacs with culinary recipes, from 1925 to 1928 and in 1935 (O535.1, O578.1, O594.1, O613.1, and O847.1).*

For information about Dr Chase, see [Marsha E. Ackermann], A Man, a Book, a Building: The Story of Dr Chase's Steam Printing House, *Ann Arbor, Mich.: Dobson-McOmber Agency, 1994.*

O8.1   23rd ed., [87th thousand], 1865
Dr. Chase's recipes; / or, / information for everybody: / An invaluable collection of / about eight hundred / practical recipes / for / merchants, grocers, saloon-keepers, physicians, druggists, / tanners, shoe makers, harness makers, painters, / jewelers, blacksmiths, tinners, gunsmiths, farriers, / barbers, bakers, dyers, renovators, farmers and / families generally. / To which have been added / a rational treatment of pleurisy, inflammation of the lungs, / and other inflammatory diseases, and also for general / female debility and irregularities. / All arranged in their appropriate departments. / By A.W. Chase, M.D., / practical therapeutist. / Twenty-third edition. / Stereotyped. / Carefully revised, illustrated, and much enlarged, / with remarks and full explanations. / We learn to live, by living to learn. / London, C.W., / published by J. Moffat, bookseller & stationer. / 1865.
DESCRIPTION: 17.0 × 11.0 cm   Pp [i–v] vi–xi [xii] xiii–xxv [xxvi] xxvii–xxxii, [33] 34–384   Cloth
CONTENTS: i ht: 'Dr. Chase's Recipes; or, Information for Everybody. Eighty-seventh thousand.'; ii publ ads; iii tp; iv testimonial for the book dated Fort Gratiot, Michigan, 13 July 1864, and '"Advertiser" Print, London, C.W.'; v–xi 'Preface to the Tenth Edition' signed the author; xii–xxv 'Index'; xxvi–xxxii 'References'; 33–384 text

CITATIONS: Driver 2002, Home Cook Book, p xii
Driver 2003, 'Canadian Cookbooks,' p 28
COPIES: CIHM (01773)   OLU (TX153 C48 1865)
*OTUTF (jah)   QMM
NOTES: See pl 20. This is the earliest Canadian edition
of a hugely popular American cookbook. The numbering of this Canadian edition (twenty-third edition,
eighty-seventh thousand) corresponds to the numbering of the American editions in the same year: It
fits between the twenty-second edition, seventy-sev-
enth thousand, and the twenty-fourth edition, both
published in Ann Arbor, Michigan, by the author in
1865. This is the only Canadian edition to follow the
American numbering; subsequent Canadian editions
are numbered as 'Second Canadian edition,' 'Fourth
Canadian edition,' etc. London, the home of J. Moffat's
business, is not far from Ann Arbor. 'Bakers' and
Cooking Department' is on pp 280–302. Culinary information is also in other departments.

O8.2   2nd Canadian ed., 1866
—Dr. Chase's recipes; / or, / information for
everybody: / An invaluable collection of / about
eight hundred / practical recipes / for / merchants,
grocers, saloon-keepers, physicians, druggists, /
tanners, shoemakers, harness makers, painters, /
jewellers, blacksmiths, tinners, gunsmiths, far- /
riers, barbers, bakers, dyers, renovators, / farmers,
and families generally. / To which have been added
/ a rational treatment of pleurisy, inflammation of
the lungs, / and other inflammatory diseases, and
also for general / female debility and irregularities.
/ All arranged in their appropriate departments. /
By A.W. Chase, M.D., / practical therapeutist. /
Second Canadian edition. / Stereotyped. / Carefully
revised, and much enlarged, with remarks and / full
explanations. / We learn to live, by living to learn. /
London. C.W., / published by Moffat & Gillean,
booksellers and stationers. / 1866.
DESCRIPTION: 17.0 × 11.0 cm   Pp [i–v] vi–xi [xii] xiii–xxv
[xxvi] xxvii–xxxii, [33] 34–385   Cloth
CONTENTS: i ad for Middlesex Seminary at Komoka,
Canada West, of which A.M. Moffat was principal; ii
publ ad; iii tp; iv testimonial for the book dated Fort
Gratiot, Michigan, 13 July 1864, and 'Stereotyped at
the "Globe" Stereotype Foundry, Toronto, C.W. Printed
at the "Globe" Steam Press, Toronto, C.W.'; v–xi 'Pref-
ace to the Tenth Edition' signed the author; xii–xxv
'Index'; xxvi–xxxii 'References'; 33–385 text
COPIES: *OL (P49)
NOTES: There is culinary material in 'Merchants' and
Grocers' Department' on pp 33–51, in 'Saloon Depart-
ment' on pp 51–75, in 'Bakers' and Cooking Depart-

ment' on pp 280–302, and in parts of 'Miscellaneous
Department' on pp 302–42.

O8.3   2nd Canadian ed., 1867
—Dr. Chase's recipes; / or, / information for
everybody: / An invaluable collection of / about
eight hundred / practical recipes / for / merchants,
grocers, saloon-keepers, physicians, druggists, /
tanners, shoemakers, harness makers, painters, /
jewellers, blacksmiths, tinners, gunsmiths, far- /
riers, barbers, bakers, dyers, renovators, / farmers,
and families generally. / To which have been added
/ a rational treatment of pleurisy, inflammation of
the lungs, / and other inflammatory diseases, and
also for general / female debility and irregularities.
/ All arranged in their appropriate departments. /
By A.W. Chase, M.D., / practical therapeutist. /
Second Canadian edition. / Stereotyped. / Carefully
revised, and much enlarged, with remarks and / full
explanations. / We learn to live, by living to learn. /
London. C.W., / published by John Moffat & Co.,
booksellers and stationers. / 1867.
DESCRIPTION: 17.0 × 11.0 cm   Pp [i–v] vi–xi [xii] xiii–xxv
[xxvi] xxvii–xxxii, [33] 34–385   Cloth
CONTENTS: i ad for Middlesex Seminary, Komoka,
Canada West, of which A.M. Moffat was principal; ii
publ ad; iii tp; iv testimonial for the book dated Fort
Gratiot, Michigan, 13 July 1864, and 'Stereotyped at
the "Globe" Stereotype Foundry, Toronto, C.W. Printed
at the "Globe" Steam Press, Toronto, C.W.'; v–xi 'Pref-
ace to the Tenth Edition' signed the author; xii–xxv
'Index'; xxvi–xxxii 'References'; 33–385 text
CITATIONS: Wheaton/Kelly No. 1151
COPIES: *OKITD (956.019.037)   OTMCL (615.88 C34);
United States: MWA (G320 C487 D876L)
NOTES: There were two London editions dated 1867:
this one published by John Moffat and Co. and O8.4,
published by E.A. Taylor.
      The OKITD copy is incribed on the inside front face
of the binding, in pencil, 'Mr Wm Abra // Blair
Ontario'; and on the verso of p 385, in pencil, 'Jacob F.
Abra // Dumfries // Blair Ont.' The OTMCL copy is
inscribed on the front endpaper, in ink, 'James Blair
March 1868.'

O8.4   2nd Canadian ed., 1867
—Dr. Chase's recipes; / or, / information for
everybody: / An invaluable collection of / about
eight hundred / practical recipes / for / merchants,
grocers, saloon-keepers, physicians, druggists, /
tanners, shoemakers, harness makers, painters, /
jewellers, blacksmiths, tinners, gunsmiths, far- /
riers, barbers, bakers, dyers, renovators, / farmers,

and families generally. / To which have been added / a rational treatment of pleurisy, inflammation of the lungs, / and other inflammatory diseases, and also for general / female debility and irregularities. / All arranged in their appropriate departments. / By A.W. Chase, M.D., / practical therapeutist. / Second Canadian edition. / Stereotyped. / Carefully revised, and much enlarged, with remarks and / full explanations. / We learn to live, by living to learn. / London, Ont., / published by E.A. Taylor, bookseller and stationer. / 1867.

DESCRIPTION: 17.0 × 11.0 cm   Pp [iii–v] vi–xi [xii] xiii–xxv [xxvi] xxvii–xxxii, [33] 34–385   Cloth

CONTENTS: iii tp; iv testimonial for the book dated Fort Gratiot, Michigan, 13 July 1864, and 'Stereotyped at the "Globe" Stereotype Foundry, Toronto, C.W. Printed at the "Globe" Steam Press, Toronto, C.W.'; v–xi 'Preface to the Tenth Edition'; xii–xxv 'Index'; xxvi–xxxii 'References'; 33–385 text

CITATIONS: Bates, pp 20 (note 7), 95–6 (note 2), 101–2, 137, 138, 142, 146, 151 (note 3)

COPIES: OHMB (TX C487d 1867)   OTAR (640.3 CHA) *Private collection

NOTES: E.A. Taylor had started his business in 1858, about a decade before publishing Chase's book (*Commercial Industries of Canada*, 1890, p 55).

The OHMB copy is inscribed on the front end paper, in ink, 'March 13/[68?] G.K. Foster, Jr.'

O8.5   2nd Canadian ed., 1868
—Dr. Chase's recipes; / or, / information for everybody: / An invaluable collection of / about eight hundred / practical recipes / for / merchants, grocers, saloon-keepers, physicians, druggists, / tanners, shoemakers, harness makers, painters, / jewellers, blacksmiths, tinners, gunsmiths, far- / riers, barbers, bakers, dyers, renovators, / farmers, and families generally. / To which have been added / a rational treatment of pleurisy, inflammation of the lungs, / and other inflammatory diseases, and also for general / female debility and irregularities. / All arranged in their appropriate departments. / By A.W. Chase, M.D., / practical therapeutist. / Second Canadian edition. / Stereotyped. / Carefully revised, and much enlarged, with remarks and / full explanations. / We learn to live, by living to learn. / London, Ont., / published by E.A. Taylor, bookseller and stationer. / 1868

DESCRIPTION: 16.5 × 10.0 cm   Pp [i–v] vi–xi [xii] xiii–xxv [xxvi] xxvii–xxxii, [33] 34–385, [i–iii]   Rebound

CONTENTS: i publ ad; ii blank; iii tp; iv testimonial for the book dated Fort Gratiot, Michigan, 13 July 1864, but no indication of the printer; v–xi 'Preface to the

Tenth Edition'; xii–xxv 'Index'; xxvi–xxxii 'References'; 33–385 text; i blank; ii–iii publ ads

COPIES: CIHM (11865)   OFFRH   OGU (2 copies: UA s052 b06, UA s045 b23)   OKQ (TX153 C49 1868t)   OL (P69)   *OONL (TX153 C49 1868 copy 1)   OTU (TX153 C49 1869 Gerstein)   OTUTF (jah)

NOTES: On the title-page, the third digit in the year, '6,' barely registers. OONL (TX153 C49 1868 copy 2) matches O8.8, not this one. OONL (TX153 C49 1868 copy 3) is missing.

One copy at OGU (UA s045 b23), which is in its original cloth binding, lacks the first leaf of advertisements; the advertisement on the last page is for job printing at the London Free Press Office. Otherwise the copy matches the description here for the OONL copy. The other copy at OGU (UA s052 b06), also in its original cloth binding, has 'Printed at the London Free Press Steam Printing Office.' on p iv; it is inscribed on the front endpaper, in ink, 'John Bee's book // Cavan // Durham // March 1873.' The OKQ copy also has 'Printed at the London Free Press Steam Printing Office.' on p iv.

The OTU copy, which is in its original cloth binding, differs from the OONL copy catalogued here in the following ways. It has no leaf of publisher's advertisements before the title-page, but the leaf may simply be lacking because the binding is loose. The verso of p 385 bears the place and year of printing, 'London, Ontario. Printed at the Free Press Office, Richmond St. 1869 [*sic*].' The OTU copy has advertisements for various London businesses on the last two pages, not publisher's advertisements. The OL copy, also in its original binding, matches the OTU copy; the only difference is that it has a leaf of advertisements before the title-page (the recto bears a publisher's advertisement; the verso, advertisements for other London businesses).

The OTUTF copy is rebound, lacks p 385, and has no publisher's advertisements. The library dates it 1868, i.e., 1869.

O8.6   nd [about 1870–2]
—Chase's receipts; / or, / information for everybody: / Consisting of / a large number of medical recipes: / Also, / practical recipes / for / merchants, grocers, shopkeepers, physicians, / druggists, tanners, shoemakers, harness- / makers, painters, jewellers, black- / smiths, tinners, gunsmiths, &c., &c. / By A.W. Chase, M.D. / Toronto: / W. Warwick, / 36, Wellington Street.

COPIES: *NBFKL

NOTES: The NBFKL copy is inscribed on the title-page, '1858.' This handwritten date must be wrong because Hulse, p 273, says that William Warwick moved to Toronto in 1868 and that his business was located at 36 Wellington Street East from 1870–2, after which it moved to 8–10 Wellington Street East.

William Warwick may have published another edition of *Dr Chase's Recipes* in about 1876, a copy of which has not been located. In his 'Cottage Library Catalogue' bound in Henry Kingsley, *Recollections of Geoffry Hamlyn*, Toronto: W. Warwick, 1876, p 11, under 'Miscellaneous' (OTMCL), there is a listing for 'Chase's Receipes [*sic*] or Information for Everybody, with Upwards of 1000 Practical Recipes,' $0.75. Since the title-page of O8.6 does not record the number of recipes, it is uncertain whether the catalogue listing is for O8.6 or not (earlier editions had 800 recipes; later ones, 1,000). The catalogue, which illustrates the company's building at 8–10 Wellington Street, was printed after the move from 36 Wellington. As William Warwick and Sons, the company published a later edition of *Dr Chase's Recipes*, O8.17, in about 1885–93.

William Warwick published one other cookbook in this bibliography, an edition of a British work: O14.1, *Warwick's Every-day Cookery*, by Mary Jewry, nd.

O8.7   1871
—[Another edition of *Dr Chase's Recipes*]
COPIES: Bookseller's stock
NOTES: On the title-page there is no indication of the edition number; the imprint is London, Ont.: E.A. Taylor and Co., booksellers and stationers, 1871.

O8.8   2nd Canadian ed., nd [about 1873]
—Dr. Chase's recipes; / or, / information for everybody: / An invaluable collection of / about eight hundred / practical recipes / for / merchants, grocers, saloon-keepers, physicians, druggists, / tanners, shoemakers, harness makers, painters, / jewellers, blacksmiths, tinners, gunsmiths, far- / riers, barbers, bakers, dyers, renovators, / farmers, and families generally. / To which have been added / a rational treatment of pleurisy, inflammation of the lungs, / and other inflammatory diseases, and also for general / female debility and irregularities. / All arranged in their appropriate departments. / By A.W. Chase, M.D., / practical therapeutist. / Second Canadian edition. / Stereotyped. / Carefully revised, and much enlarged, with remarks and / full explanations. / We learn to live, by living to learn. / London, Ont., / published by E.A. Taylor, bookseller and stationer.
DESCRIPTION: 16.5 × 10.5 cm   Pp [i–v] vi–xi [xii] xiii–

xxv [xxvi] xxvii–xxxii, [33] 34–385   Quarter black leather, green cloth
CONTENTS: i–ii publ ads dated London, Ontario, 1873; iii tp; iv testimonial for the book dated Fort Gratiot, Michigan, 13 July, 1864; v–xi 'Preface to the Tenth Edition'; xii–xxv 'Index'; xxvi–xxxii 'References'; 33–385 text
COPIES: AMHM CIHM (21202) NBFKL NBSM NSHD NSHMS (72.351.7) *OGU (UA s039 b02) OKQ (TX153 C4) OL (P64) OONL (TX153 C49 1868 copy 2) OPET (TX153 C49 1873) OTUTF (3 copies: flem 0571; jah copy 1; jah 'Another state') QKB (71-24)
NOTES: Of the three copies at OTUTF, flem 0571 is bound in quarter black leather and black cloth, and the publisher's advertisement on p i is dated 1873; jah copy 1 is bound in quarter red leather and brown cloth, and the publisher's advertisement on p i is indistinctly dated, probably 1873; and jah, 'Another state,' is bound in quarter black leather and green cloth, like the OGU copy, and, although the publisher's advertisement on p i is clearly dated 1873 (like flem 0571), the advertisements are printed from a different setting of type.

The OL copy is bound in quarter blue leather and brown cloth; the publisher's advertisement on p i is clearly dated 1873. The publisher's advertisement on p i of the OONL copy is also clearly dated 1873, but a comparison of photocopies of pp i–ii with the OL copy reveals that the advertisements are printed from a different setting of type. The OONL copy is bound in quarter black leather and brown cloth.

The publisher's advertisement on p i of the QKB copy is dated 1872.

The OKQ copy is stamped on p v, 'Mr. Henry. Robertson. his book // Vernon // Osgoode –. Ont.'

The publisher's advertisement on p i of the AMHM copy is dated 1878, and p ii is blank.

The NBSM copy has advertisements for Saint John businesses opposite the title-page, not publisher's advertisements.

O8.9   unnumbered ed., nd
—Dr. Chase's recipes; / or, / information for everybody: / An invaluable collection of / upwards of a thousand / practical recipes / for / merchants, grocers, shop-keepers, physicians, / druggists, tanners, shoemakers, harness ma- / kers, painters, jewellers, blacksmiths, / tinners, gunsmiths, barbers, bakers, / dyers, renovators, farmers, and / families generally. / To which have been added / recipes for the diseases of horses, cattle, / sheep and

dogs; together with the com- / plete art of brewing and innkeeping, / &c., &c. / All arranged under their appropriate departments. / London, Ontario. / Published by E.A. Taylor & Co., booksellers & stationers.

DESCRIPTION: 16.5 × 10.5 cm   Pp [i] ii–viii, 9–384 Cloth

CONTENTS: i tp; ii–viii 'Contents'; 9–373 text in various departments; 374–84 'Explanation of Technical Terms Used in Medical Works' and at bottom p 384, 'Milner & Company, publishers, Halifax'

COPIES: *OKITD (x962.098.001)

NOTES: The title-pages of this and subsequent editions refer to a 'thousand practical recipes,' whereas the title-pages of previously cited editions record 'about eight hundred practical recipes,' with the exception of O8.6, where the number is not specified. This unnumbered and undated edition looks newer than other editions published by E.A. Taylor and Co., but the year of publication is unknown.

The OKITD copy is signed on the inside front face of the binding, in pencil, 'Arthur D. Walford // Galt Ont'; and on the front endpaper, in ink, 'A.D. Walford // AM Walford.'

O8.10   1878 [1879]

—One thousand / practical recipes / for / merchants, grocers, saloon-keepers, physicians, druggists, / tanners, shoemakers, harness makers, painters, / jewellers, blacksmiths, tinners, gunsmiths, / farriers, barbers, bakers, dyers, reno- / vators, farmers, and families / generally. / Being / Dr. Chase's celebrated recipe book, / improved and enlarged. / London, Ont.: / Published by John Cameron & Co., / Advertiser Office. / 1878.

DESCRIPTION: 16.5 × 10.5 cm   Pp [1–2], [i–xii] xiii–xxv [xxvi] xxvii [xxviii], [33] 34–416, [i–vi]   [Free, on binding]   Paper-covered boards, cloth spine; sewn

CONTENTS: 1–2 ads; i–viii ads; ix tp; x ads; xi 'Preface' dated London, 1 January 1879; xii–xxv 'Index'; xxvi–xxvii 'Index to Appendix'; xxviii blank; 33–385 text; 386–416 'Appendix'; i–vi ads

CITATIONS: Reitz, p [4]

COPIES: OKITD (x962.269.001)   OLU (TX153 C48 1878)   OSTMYM   OTU (TX153 C49 1879 RB ROMU)   *OTUTF (jah, 2 copies)

NOTES: The following is printed on the binding: 'Published by John Cameron & Co., for gratuitous distribution to subscribers to the "Western Advertiser and Weekly Liberal," for 1879. // 1878.' The 'Preface' refers to a new chapter on emergencies.

The other OTUTF copy is bound in paper, not paper-covered boards; it is in poor condition, possibly lacking leaves of advertisements at the front. The OTU copy is bound in paper-covered boards.

O8.11   4th Canadian ed., 1879

—Dr. Chase's recipes / or / information for everybody / An invaluable collection of about / one thousand practical recipes / for / merchants, grocers, saloon keepers, physicians, druggists / tanners, shoemakers, harnessmakers, painters, / jewellers, blacksmiths, tanners [sic], gunsmiths, / farriers, barbers, bakers, dyers, ren- / ovaters, farmers, and families / generally; / to which has been added / additional treat- / ment of pleurisy, inflamma- / tion of the lungs, and other inflam- / matory diseases; and also, for general / female debility and irregularities, all arranged / in their appropriate departments, together with an / appendix of 30 pages, / never before published in book form. / By A.W. Chas [sic], M.D. / Fourth Canadian edition. Revised. / London, Ontario, Canada: / Published by Wm. Bryce, 168 and 215 Dundas Street. / 1879.

DESCRIPTION: 16.5 × 10.5 cm   Pp [3] 4 [5] 6–12, [ix–xii] xiii–xxv [xxvi] xxvii [xxviii], [33] 34–416, [i–ii]   Paper-covered boards, cloth spine

CONTENTS: 3–12 publ ads; ix tp; x 'Publisher's Notice' citing the price of $0.30 to have the book mailed to an address; xi preface dated London, 1 January 1879; xii–xxv 'Index'; xxvi–xxvii 'Index to Appendix'; xxviii blank; 33–385 text; 386–416 'Appendix'; i–ii publ ads

COPIES: *OGU (UA s039 b01)

NOTES: On the title-page, 'tanners, gunsmiths' is a typographical error for 'tinners, gunsmiths.'

O8.12   5th Canadian ed., 1880

—Dr. Chase's recipes / or / information for everybody / An invaluable collection of about / one thousand practical recipes / for / merchants, grocers, saloon keepers, physicians, druggists, / tanners, shoemakers, harnessmakers, painters, / jewellers, blacksmiths, tanners [sic], gunsmiths, / farriers, barbers, bakers, dyers, ren- / ovaters, farmers, and families / generally; / to which has been added / additional treat- / ment of pleurisy, inflamma- / tion of the lungs, and other inflam- / matory diseases; and also, for general / female debility and irregularities, all arranged / in their appropriate departments, together with an / appendix of 30 pages, / never before published in book form. / By A.W. Chase, M.D. / Fifth Canadian edition. Revised. / London, Ontario, Canada: / Published by Wm. Bryce, 168 and 215 Dundas Street. / 1880.

DESCRIPTION: Pp [ix–xii] xiii–xxi [xxii] xxiii–xxv [xxvi–xxvii] xxviii, [33] 34–416

CONTENTS: ix tp; x 'Preface' dated London, 1 April 1880; xi 'Publisher's Notice'; xii–xxv 'Index'; xxvi publ ad; xxvii–xxviii 'Index to Appendix'; 33–385 text; 386–416 'Appendix'

COPIES: *CIHM (26928)   OONL (TX153 C49 1880)

O8.13   6th Canadian ed., 1881
—Dr. Chase's recipes / or / information for everybody. / An invaluable collection of about / one thousand practical recipes / for / merchants, grocers, saloon keepers, physicians, druggists, / tanners, shoemakers, harnessmakers, painters, / jewellers, blacksmiths, tinners, gunsmiths, / farriers, barbers, bakers, dyers, ren- / oavters [*sic*], farmers, and families / generally; / to which has been added / additional treat- / ment of pleurisy, inflamma- / tion of the lungs, and other inflam- / matory diseases; and also, for general / female debility and irregularities, all arranged / in their appropriate departments, together with an / appendix of 30 pages, / never before published in book form. / By A.W. Chase, M.D. / Sixth Canadian edition. Revised. / London, Ontario, Canada: / Published by Wm. Bryce, 123 and 168 Dundas Street. / 1881.

DESCRIPTION: Pp [ix–xii] xiii–xiv [xv] xvi–xxi [xxii] xxiii–xxv [xxvi–xxvii] xxviii, [33] 34–416

CONTENTS: ix tp; x blank; xi 'Preface' dated London, 1 August 1881; xii–xxv 'Index'; xxvi blank; xxvii–xxviii 'Index to Appendix'; 33–385 text; 386–416 'Appendix'

COPIES: *CIHM (01771)   OVOH (986.232.1)   QMM

O8.14   7th Canadian ed., London, 1882
—Dr. Chase's recipes / or / information for everybody. / An invaluable collection of about / one thousand practical recipes / for / merchants, grocers, saloon keepers, physicians, druggists, / tanners, shoemakers, harnessmakers, painters, / jewellers, blacksmiths, tinners, gunsmiths, / farriers, barbers, bakers, dyers, ren- / ovaters farmers and families / generally; / to which has been added / additional treat- / ment of pleurisy, inflamma- / tion of the lungs, and other inflam- / matory diseases; and also for general / female debility and irregularities all arranged / in their appropriate departments, together with an / appendix of 30 pages, / never before published in book form. / By A.W. Chase, M.D. / Seventh Canadian edition. Revised. / London, Ontario, Canada: / Published by Wm. Bryce, 123 and 168 Dundas Street. / 1882.

DESCRIPTION: Pp [ix–xii] xiii–xiv [xv] xvi–xxi [xxii] xxiii–xxv [xxvi–xxvii] xxviii, [33] 34–416

CONTENTS: ix tp; x blank; xi 'Preface' dated London, 1 August 1882; xii–xxv 'Index'; xxvi blank; xxvii–xxviii 'Index to Appendix'; 33–385 text; 386–416 'Appendix'

COPIES: *CIHM (41643)   OONL (TX153 C49 1882 p***)

O8.15   7th Canadian ed., Toronto, 1882
—Dr. Chase's recipes / or / information for everybody. / An invaluable collection of about / one thousand practical recipes / for / merchants, grocers, saloon keepers, physicians, druggists, / tanners, shoemakers, harnessmakers, painters, / jewellers, blacksmiths, tinners, gunsmiths, / farriers, barbers, bakers, dyers, ren- / ovaters farmers and families / generally; / to which has been added / additional treat- / ment of pleurisy, inflamma- / tion of the lungs, and other inflam- / matory diseases; and also for general / female debility and irregularities all arranged / in their appropriate departments, together with an / appendix of 30 pages, / never before published in book form. / By A.W. Chase, M.D. / Seventh Canadian edition. Revised. / Toronto, Ont: / The Toronto News Company, 42 Yonge St., and Niagara Falls. / 1882.

DESCRIPTION: Pp [ix–xii] xiii [xiv–xv] xvi–xxi [xxii] xxiii–xxv [xxvi–xxvii] xxviii, [33] 34–416

CONTENTS: ix tp; x blank; xi 'Preface' dated Toronto, 1 August 1882; xii–xxv 'Index'; xxvi blank; xxvii–xxviii 'Index to Appendix'; 33–385 text; 386–416 'Appendix'

COPIES: *CIHM (91094)   OLU

O8.16   8th Canadian ed., 1883
—Dr. Chase's recipes / or / information for everybody. / An invaluable collection of about / one thousand practical recipes / for / merchants, grocers, saloon keepers, physicians, druggists, / tanners, shoemakers, harnessmakers, painters, / jewellers, blacksmiths, tinners, gunsmiths, / farriers, barbers, bakers, dyers, ren- / ovators, farmers, and families / generally; / to which has been added / additional treat- / ment of pleurisy, inflamma- / tion of the lungs, and other inflam- / matory diseases; and also for general / female debility and irregularities, all arranged / in their appropriate departments, together with an / appendix of 30 pages, / never before published in book form. / By A.W. Chase, M.D. / Eighth Canadian edition. Revised. / London, Ontario, Canada: / Published by Wm. Bryce, 123 and 168 Dundas Street. / 1883.

DESCRIPTION: 17.0 × 10.5 cm   Pp [ix–xvi] xvii–xx [xxi–xxii] xxiii–xxiv [xxv–xxvii] xxviii incorrectly numbered as xxvii, [33] 34–416   [$0.35, on binding]   Paper-covered boards

CONTENTS: ix tp; x blank; xi preface dated London, 1 August 1883; xii–xxv 'Index'; xxvi blank; xxvii–xxviii 'Index to Appendix'; 33–385 text; 386–416 'Appendix'

COPIES: OL (P4)   OTUTF (jah)   *Private collection

O8.17   nd [about 1885–93]
—Dr. Chase's recipes; / or, / information for everybody: / An invaluable collection of / upwards of a thousand / practical recipes / for / merchants, grocers, shop-keepers, physicians, / druggists, tanners, shoemakers, harness ma- / kers, painters, jewellers, blacksmiths, / tinners, gunsmiths, barbers, bakers, / dyers, renovators, farmers, and / families generally. / To which have been added / recipes for the diseases of horses, cattle, / sheep and dogs; together with the com- / plete art of brewing and innkeeping, / &c., &c. / All arranged under their appropriate departments. / Toronto, Ontario: / Published by William Warwick and Sons, / booksellers.

COPIES: *OKQ (TX153 C49 1858)

NOTES: Hulse, p 273, states that Warwick and Sons was active from 1 October 1885 to 30 September 1893 (previously, the company had been known as Warwick and Son). Unfortunately, there is no publisher's address in the volume, which would help to determine a more specific date of publication. An earlier edition of *Dr Chase's Recipes*, O8.6, was published by the company in about 1870–2.

O8.18   8th Canadian ed., 1887
—Dr. Chase's receipes [*sic*] / or / information for everybody / An invaluable collection of about / one thousand practical recipes / for / merchants, grocers, saloon keepers, physicians, druggists, / tanners, shoemakers, harnessmakers, painters, / jewellers, blacksmiths, tinners, gunsmiths, / farriers, barbers, bakers, dyers, ren- / ovators [*sic*, no comma] farmers and families / generally; / to which has been added / additional treat- / ment of pleurisy, inflamma- / tion of the lungs, and other inflam- / matory diseases: and also for general / female debility and irregularities, all arranged / in their appropriate departments together with an / appendix of 30 pages, / never before published in book form. / By A.W. Chase, M.D. / Eighth Canadian edition. Revised. / Toronto, Ontario, Canada: / Published by William Bryce. / 1887.

DESCRIPTION: 17.5 × 11.5 cm   Pp [1–2], [ix–xiv] xv [xvi] xvii–xx [xxi–xxii] xxiii–xxiv [xxv–xxvii] xxviii, [33] 34–416, [i–ii]   [$0.50, on binding]   Paper-covered boards

CONTENTS: 1–2 publ ads; ix tp; x blank; xi preface dated Toronto, 1 August 1887; xii–xxv 'Index'; xxvi blank; xxvii–xxviii 'Index to Appendix'; 33–385 text; 386–416 'Appendix'; i–ii publ ads

COPIES: *OGU (UA s043 b35)

NOTES: William Bryce, the publisher, had moved to Toronto from London, Ontario, in 1886. There is an advertisement on the binding for O27.1, *The Seaside Cook Book* (see that entry for the text of the advertisement).

O8.19   10th Canadian ed., nd
—Dr. Chase's recipes; / or, / information for everybody: / An invaluable collection of / about eight hundred / practical recipes / for / merchants, grocers, saloon-keepers, physicians, druggists, / tanners, shoemakers, harness makers, painters, / jewellers, blacksmiths, tinners, gunsmiths, far- / riers, barbers, bakers, dyers, renovators, / farmers, and families generally. / To which have been added / a rational treatment of pleurisy, inflammation of the lungs / and other inflammatory diseases, and also for general / female debility and irregularities. / All arranged in their appropriate departments. / By A.W. Chase, M.D., / practical therapeutist. / Tenth Canadian edition. / Stereotyped. / Carefully revised, and much enlarged, with remarks and / full explanations. / Toronto, Ontario, Canada: / Published by William Bryce.

COPIES: *Private collection

NOTES: Another private collector reports that her copy of 385 pp is bound in green cloth and has margin notes dated 1916.

AMERICAN EDITIONS: In the 'Preface to the Tenth Edition' of *Dr Chase's Recipes*, the author related the early publishing history of his book: 'The author ... began in "Fifty-six," [i.e., 1856] ... to publish [his recipes] in a pamphlet of only a few pages, since which time he has been traveling between New York and Iowa, selling the work and prescribing, so that up to this time, "Sixty-three," [i.e., 1863] over twenty-three thousand copies have been sold ... [The need to revise], with a desire to add to the various departments, at every edition, has kept us from having it stereotyped until the present, tenth edition' (quoted from O8.1).

The following is not an exhaustive list of all the American editions, but it shows the regularity with which they were issued and the large numbers printed: *Dr Chase's Recipes, or, Information for Everybody: An Invaluable Collection of about Six Hundred Practical Recipes*, 8th ed., Ann Arbor, Mich.: the author, 1860 (United States: DLC); *Dr Chase's Recipes; ... an Invaluable Collection of about Eight Hundred Practical Recipes*, 9th ed., Ann Arbor, Mich.: the author, 1862 (OTUTF); 12th ed., 30th thousand, Ann Arbor, Mich.: the author, 1863 (OGU); Ann Arbor, Mich.: the author, 1864 (Private collection); 22nd ed., 77th thousand, Ann Arbor, Mich.: the author, 1865 (OTUTF); 24th ed., Ann Arbor, Mich.: the author, 1865 (United States: DLC); 25th ed., Ann Arbor, Mich.: the author, 1865 (OTUTF; United States: MH); 34th ed., Ann Arbor, Mich.: A.W. Chase, 1866 (United States: MCR); 39th ed., Ann Arbor, Mich.: the author, 1866 (NSHMS); 46th ed., 322nd thousand '– English and German,' Ann Arbor, Mich.: the author, 1867 (United States: InU), and another copy dated 1867 (United States: MCR); 50th ed., 375th thousand '– English and German,' Ann Arbor, Mich.: the author, 1869 (United States: DLC); 6th ed., Ann Arbor, Mich.: R.A. Beal, 1870 (Barile, p 187), and two copies published by Beal and dated 1870 (United States: MH); Ann Arbor, Mich.: R.A. Beal, 1871 (United States: MH); [62nd ed.], 520th thousand, Ann Arbor, Mich.: R.A. Beal, 1872 (United States: DLC); Ann Arbor, Mich.: R.A. Beal, 1874 (United States: DLC, MH); [7th new and enlarged ed., 70th thousand, 730th thousand small ed.], Ann Arbor, Mich.: R.A. Beal, 1875 (ONLAM); 73rd ed., 730 thousand, Ann Arbor, Mich.: R.A. Beal, 1876 (United States: InU); [14th new and enlarged ed., 140th thousand, 730th thousand small ed.], Ann Arbor, Mich.: R.A. Beal, 1878 (ONLAM); 74th ed., 740th thousand, Ann Arbor, Mich., 1880 (cited in John Foster Kirk, *A Supplement to Allibone's Critical Dictionary of English Literature and British and American Authors*, Philadelphia: J.B. Lippincott Co., 1891, p 317); Ann Arbor, Mich.: R.A. Beal, 1881 (NSYHM); Ann Arbor, Mich.: R.A. Beal, 1896 (United States: MH); Chicago: Thompson and Thomas, [copyright 1902] (OGU); Chicago: Stanton and Van Vliet Co., publishers [copyright 1902 by Thompson and Thomas] (OSTC); modern facsimile of 9th ed., Ann Arbor, Mich.: the author, 1862, [Pointe-Claire: A.W. Chase, 1972], with label on inside face of binding that reads, 'A.W. Chase // A division of Laurentian Laboratories Limited // 70 Hymus Blvd., Pointe-Claire 730, Canada' (OONL, QMBN); modern facsimile of 38th ed., Ann Arbor, Mich.: the author, 1866 (OTSHH).

American editions in German: *Recepte von Dr. Chase*, Ann Arbor, Mich.: Verlag des Verfassers, 1865 (United States: DLC, InU); Ann Arbor, Mich.: Verlag des Verfasser[paper torn, year missing?], [copyright 1866] (OKITD).

1867

The Canadian receipt book

O9.1 1867

The / Canadian receipt book; / containing over / 500 valuable receipts / for the farmer / and / the housewife. / Ottawa: / Printed for the compiler at "The Ottawa Citizen" / 1867. [cover-title]

DESCRIPTION: 15.0 × 10.0 cm   Pp [3–4] 5–190   Paper-covered boards, cloth spine

CONTENTS: 3 note entitled 'The Canadian Receipt Book'; 4–top 46 'Domestic Cookery'; mid 46–48 'Home Brewery, Wines, &c.'; bottom 48–56 'Receipts for Dyeing'; 57 ad; 58–mid 62 'Toilet Receipts'; bottom 62–mid 72 'Hints to Housekeepers'; mid 72–mid 84 'Diseases of Cattle and Their Remedies'; bottom 84–92 'Diseases of Sheep and Their Remedies'; bottom 92–mid 108 'The Diseases of the Horse and Their Remedies'; mid 108–top 116 'Diseases of Pigs and Their Remedies'; mid 116–top 138 'Poultry and Their Diseases'; mid 138–mid 172 'Miscellaneous Department,' which includes instructions for preserving fruit and meat; bottom 172–189 'Payne's Bee-Keeping for the Many'; 190 ad

COPIES: CIHM (95405)   *OGU (UA s041 b06)

NOTES: A title-page (pp 1–2) may be missing in this copy. Page 3 states, 'In selecting the recipes for this work, care has been taken to make use of those ... which are likely to prove of practical use in the Canadian country house.'

Cumming, William Henry

O10.1 1867

Food for babes; / or, / artificial human milk, / and / the manner of preparing it and administering / it to young children. / By Wm. Henry Cumming, M.D. / Toronto: / Printed for the author, by the Globe Printing Company. / 1867.

DESCRIPTION: 14.0 × 9.5 cm   Pp [iii–v] vi–viii, [9] 10–100   Frontis of a bottle   Cloth

CONTENTS: i tp; ii blank; iii–viii 'Introduction' dated Toronto, Canada, December 1867; 9–100 text

COPIES: CIHM (01144)   *OTUTF (jah small books)

NOTES: The 'Introduction' states: 'We send forth this little work with the hope of extending the use of artificial human milk, ...' Without discouraging breast-feeding, Cumming wanted to promote a form of artificial milk prepared from cow's milk that he considered better for mothers who were not healthy enough to breast-feed. He was, however, critical of the 'evils of female education and training during the period of early womanhood, and ... their disastrous influence on infants, both before and after birth' (p viii).

The OTUTF copy is inscribed on the front endpaper, in ink, 'Dr. Thorburn with the respects of the author.' There is also a bookplate: 'Presented to the Library of the University of Toronto by [handwritten:] Executors of the late James Thorburn [M.D.?] A.D. 1905.'

1868

The dominion home cook-book

O11.1 1868
The dominion / home cook-book, / with / several hundred excellent receipes [*sic; and comma may be obscured by library stamp*] / selected and tried with great care, and with a view to be / used by those who regard economy, and containing / important information on the arrangement and / well-ordering of the kitchen. / The whole based on many years of experience. / By a thorough housewife. / Illustrated with engravings. / Toronto: / Published by Adam Miller, / and for sale by all booksellers. / 1868.
DESCRIPTION: 17.5 × 11.5 cm   Pp [1–3] 4–133   Many illus of utensils and carving instructions   Paper, with image on front of two women in a kitchen; sewn
CONTENTS: 1 tp; 2 blank; 3–4 'Preface'; 5–21 'Introductory Remarks'; 22–mid 23 'Marketing'; bottom 23–25 'Important Hints to Cooks'; 26–37 'Directions for Carving'; 38–122 recipes for 'Soups and Broths,' 'Fish,' 'Meats,' 'Poultry,' 'Gravies,' 'Sauces,' 'Vegetables,' 'Eggs, Omelettes, &c.,' 'Pickles,' 'Ketchup,' 'Pies and Puddings,' 'Pancakes and Fritters,' 'Custards,' 'Creams and Ices,' 'Jellies – Preserving, Bread, &c.,' 'Fruit Cakes, &c.,' 'Coffee, Tea, Chocolate, and Cocoa'; 123–33 'Index'
CITATIONS: Driver 2002, Home Cook Book, p xii   Driver 2003, 'Canadian Cookbooks,' p 28   Wheaton/ Kelly No. 1742   Williamson, p 20 (note 70), illus p 17 of woodcuts of utensils
COPIES: CIHM (27128)   ECO   *QQS (218.1.15); United States: MCR (641.6971 D67 and micro SLC 31 #239)
NOTES: This Toronto edition was published about ten years after the Dick and Fitzgerald edition of its American source, *The American Home Cook Book*. The image on the binding of the Toronto edition is the same as the one on the binding of the Dick and Fitzgerald

edition (DLC copy). In the lively 'Preface,' the 'authoress' says that this book was written 'with a view to practical utility' and 'designed expressly for the use of housekeepers who study simplicity and economy in the preparation of food, and who require explicit directions for their guidance.' The method of preparing each recipe is, indeed, fully and clearly presented, although the number of utensils described at the beginning of the book could be considered to have gone beyond the bounds of economy. All the utensils, nevertheless, serve a particular purpose. At the close of the 'Preface,' the author announces that she has in preparation a 'Home Receipt Book' designed to be a 'complete manual for all that relates to house cleaning – dying [*sic*] – repairing – home made beverages – accidents – emergencies – the sick room – remedies – and all the thousand and one things that the head of a family requires to know.' This publication (if it was completed) has not been located.

Nine years after publishing *The Dominion Home Cook-Book*, an American book, Adam Miller published a British culinary text, O19.1, Buckton, Catherine M., *Health in the House*.

AMERICAN EDITIONS: *The American Home Cook Book, with Several Hundred Excellent Recipes, Selected and Tried with Great Care, and with a View to Be Used by Those Who Regard Economy, and Containing Important Information on the Arrangement and Well Ordering of the Kitchen ... By an American lady*, New York: Garrett and Co., [entered 1854], pp 123 (United States: MSaE, NPV; Lowenstein No. 604). Lowenstein Nos. 605–7 refer to three variants of an edition with the imprint New York: Dick and Fitzgerald, [entered 1854]; each has 133 numbered pages, followed by a different number of unnumbered pages. Bitting, pp 515–16, is the copy at DLC, also New York: Dick and Fitzgerald, [entered 1854 by Garrett and Co.]; DLC dates the copy [1858], probably based on evidence in Dick and Fitzgerald's book list following p 133.

1870

Ometa recipe book

William Henry Comstock was an American whose family patent-medicine business was based in New York City, but marketed a large proportion of its products in the backwoods of Canada West. In about 1860 W.H. Comstock established himself in Brockville, and in 1867 the company built another manufacturing plant directly across the St Lawrence River, in Morristown, New York. In 1902, W.H. Comstock Co. Ltd, the Canadian corporation, took over the Morristown part of the business, previously run as a sole proprietorship. Dr Morse's Indian Root Pills, originally developed by Andrew B. Moore in the 1850s, were the company's most famous medicine ('Dr Morse' was a fictitious character used in company advertising). W.H. Comstock was an important figure in Brockville, elected mayor of the city three times, and a member of Parliament once. When he died in 1919, his son, William Henry Comstock II, took over the business. It is interesting to note that Brockville was home to another patent medicine, manufactured by a local doctor: Dr Williams' Pink Pills.

The Comstock company promoted its products through travelling salesmen and by printing massive numbers of almanacs and flyers (see, for example, Morse's Indian Root Pills Almanac *of 1889 at DLC). For an 1894 recipe book by the company, see O63.1,* Cook Book. *For a history of the company, see Robert B. Shaw,* History of the Comstock Patent Medicine Business and Dr. Morse's Indian Root Pills, *Washington, DC: Smithsonian Institution Press, 1972 (DLC).*

O12.1 [1870]
Ometa / recipe book / "Truth stranger than fiction." / [to left of image, in vertical lines:] Canadian / branch of / [image of head-and-torso of a man, with caption:] Ometa / [to right of image, in vertical lines:] W.H. Comstock. / Brockville, Ont. / [below image:] Presented by / Oliver & Co., / Barrie, Ont. / agent for / Judson's Mountain Herb Pills / McKenzie's Dead Shot Worm Candy, / Carlton's Condition Powders / Dr. Morse's Indian Root Pills. / The Judson's and Morse's pills are put up both sugar coated / and plain, and can be procured through the agent. [cover-title]
DESCRIPTION: 16.5 × 10.0 cm   Pp 1–22, [i–ii]   Paper, with image on front, in an oval frame, of Ometa; sewn
CONTENTS: Inside front face of binding calendar for 1870 and six months of 1871; 1 'To the Public'; 2–16 'Medical Recipes,' which includes recipes for invalid cookery and recipes for general use, plus testimonials for Judson's Mountain Herb Pills; 17–21 'Miscellaneous Recipes,' which includes a Recipe to Make a Ham Better Than a Westphalia; 22 'Dyeing Recipes' and 'Artificial Manures'; i–ii publ ads
COPIES: *OTUTF (uncat patent medicine)

Wrigley, William

O13.1   1870
Wrigley's / practical receipts / in the / arts, manufactures, trades, & agriculture, / including / medicine, pharmacy and domestic economy; / with copious remarks on the valuable properties of / creosote, glycerine and pyroligneous, carbolic / and cresylic acids, / and their efficacy in curing and preserving / meats, fish, fruits, / and all animal and vegetable substances, / and a large amount of valuable information of every-day use and of / general utility to / merchants, manufacturers, tradesmen, storekeepers, farmers, / mechanics and families generally. / With a copious alphabetical index. / Carefully compiled from the most recent and authentic sources by / William Wrigley. / Edited by / Louis E. Vergette, / practical chemist. / Toronto: / Wrigley & Vergette, publishers. / Printed at the Leader office, King Street East / 1870.
DESCRIPTION: 20.0 × 12.0 cm   Pp [i–iii] iv [v] vi–xi [xii], [1] 2–192, 1–22 [23–4]   Rebound
CONTENTS: i tp; ii '(Entered according to Act of the Parliament of Canada, in the year of our Lord one thousand eight hundred and seventy, in the office of the Minister of Agriculture.)'; iii–iv preface signed William Wrigley, compiler, and Louis E. Vergette, editor; v–xi index; xii blank; 1–192 text; 1–24 ads
COPIES: CIHM (95406)   *OGU (UA s050 b18) OONMS (TX153 W74 1870)   OTU (T W PASC Gerstein)   OTUTF (jah)
NOTES: Wrigley and Vergette state on p 3, 'It is now nearly two years ago since we first introduced our Antiseptic Solution to public notice.' They name the chemicals that form the basis of their Antiseptic Solution and the active agents in their Preserving Powder. The text covers the preservation of various kinds of food, and also gives recipes and advice for beers and sodas, baking, butter making, cider, coffee, eggs, fruits, honey, ice cream, ketchups, lard, meats, fish, milk, pickles, syrups, tea, vinegar, and domestic wines.

The OTU and OTUTF copies are in their original cloth bindings.

1871–80

Jewry, Mary

See O21.1, Jewry, Mary, Warne's Cookery Book for the Million, *for a Canadian edition of another cookbook by this British author.*

Jewry also compiled Warne's Model Cookery and Housekeeping Book, *London: Frederick Warne and Co., 1868 (Great Britain: LB); a later edition was retitled* Warne's New Model Cookery, *edited by Mabel Wijey, London: F. Warne, 1926 (OGU). No Canadian editions have been identified, but in 1876* Warne's Model Cookery and Housekeeping *(publisher and year of publication not given) was advertised for sale at the price of $2.25 by the Methodist Book and Publishing House, which had Book Rooms in Toronto and Montreal; see MBPHCat 1876–7, p 25. What must be a smaller edition,* Warne's Model Cookery Book, *$0.30, was advertised for sale in the same catalogue: MBPHCat 1876–7, p 48. One of the 728-page editions (likely London and New York: F. Warne & Co., [1879], as at LB) was used in Ontario, because a copy in a bookseller's stock (unfortunately, lacking the title-page) is inscribed on the front endpaper, 'Mrs. C.A. Weller // Peterboro' Feb 4th 1879.' OSTCM has a copy of the condensed edition, which is inscribed 'Mrs Burridge April 1875.'*

O14.1   nd [about 1871–80]
Warwick's / every-day cookery. / Containing / one thousand eight hundred and fifty-eight / distinct receipts. / Compiled and edited by / Mary Jewry, / author of "Warne's Model Cookery," and "Warne's Cookery Book / for the Million." / With original illustrations printed in colours. / Toronto: / W. Warwick.
DESCRIPTION: 18.0 × 12.0 cm   Pp [i–vi], 1–364   3 pls col, illus   Cloth
CONTENTS: i tp; ii blank; iii preface; iv blank; v table of contents; vi blank; 1–356 text; 357–64 index
CITATIONS: Berton, pp 33, 44, 45
COPIES: *OTMCL (641.5 J266)
NOTES: The preface reveals that the book was intended for persons of moderate income. The text contains 1,858 numbered recipes, not '1900 receipts' as described on the binding. The book was printed in England by Billing in Guildford, Surrey. The Toronto edition was published no earlier than 1871, the year of the first London/New York edition of *Warne's Everyday Cookery* and the year of the first edition of *Warne's Cookery Book for the Million;* and no later than 1880, when the publisher's name changed from William Warwick to Warwick and Son (Hulse, p 273).

W. Warwick published one other cookbook in this bibliography, an edition of an American work: O8.6, *Chase's Receipts,* and a later edition, O8.17, as William Warwick and Sons.

What may be the English edition is cited in MBPHCat 1876–7, p 25: *Warne's Every Day Cookery,* 'Containing 1858 different receipts,' edited by Mary Jewry, illustrated, $0.75.

OTHER EDITIONS: EngCat cites *Warne's Everyday Cookery,* London, 1872. NUC records *Warne's Every-day Cookery,* London: F. Warne and Co., and New York: Scribner, Welford and Co., [1871] (United States: MIU, OU); and London: Frederick Warne and Co., [1872] (United States: MB, MH). DLC has London: F. Warne, and New York: Scribner, Welford and Co., [1872]. BMCat records editions published in London by Frederick Warne and Co., dated [1881?] and 1887. NN holds London: F. Warne and Co., 1899. A new edition, edited by Mrs Mabel Wijey, was published in 1929 (Great Britain: LB).

1872

The manuscript receipt book and household treasury

For the edition published in Toronto, see Q9.2.

1873

Philp, Robert Kemp (Falmouth, England, 1819–82)

Philp produced cheap publications, mostly on domestic subjects, for the English mass market. His two best-known titles were the periodical The Family Friend, *first issued in 1849, and the compendium* Enquire Within upon Everything, *London: Houlston and Stoneman, 1856 (Attar 230.1).*

O15.1   1873
The / domestic world / A / practical guide / in all the / daily difficulties of the higher branches / of domestic and social economy / By the / author of "Enquire Within' [*sic,* single closing quotation-mark] / Toronto: / Adams, Stevenson, & Co. / 1873.
DESCRIPTION: 18.5 × 12.0 cm   Pp [i–ii], [1–5] 6–396, 397–400, [i–ii]   Cloth
CONTENTS: i endpaper ads; ii blank; 1 tp; 2 blank; 3 'Preface'; 4 blank; 5–381 alphabetically arranged entries, from A to Zodiac; 382 blank; 383–96 'Index'; 397–400 ads; i blank; ii endpaper ad
COPIES: *OONL (A-21433)
NOTES: The author is unnamed in the volume, but identified on the title-page by the reference to his *Enquire Within.* The date of publication, 1873, is printed clearly on the title-page, although the earliest English edition cited by Attar is 1878 (copy at LB). The advertisements are all for London, England, businesses.

In the 'Preface' Philp describes *The Domestic World*

as a 'supplement' to his other domestic books. The text, he says, 'will concern more the occupations for the parlour than the kitchen.' Nevertheless, there are many food-related entries; for example, the following at the start of the alphabetical arrangement: Adulterations; Anchovies; Apple Wine; Arrowroot; Aspic; Barley Sugar, To Make; Bath Buns; Biscuits, Anise; Biscuits and Bread; and more for the letter B. On p 222, under Pie Juice, he discusses the question of how to catch juice that would otherwise boil over. He explains why the method of placing an inverted cup in the pie plate does not work (the method supported by Catharine Parr Traill for Apple Pie, in O5.1, *The Female Emigrant's Guide*), and suggests, instead, making a small hole in the cup.

The copy described here is inscribed on the title-page, in pencil, 'M. Whitson.'

BRITISH EDITIONS: London: Hodder and Stoughton, 1878 (Attar 235.1); London: Haughton and Co., nd (Attar 235.2); 1887 (Attar 235.3); 838th thousand, with advertisement for 63rd ed. (Attar 235.4).

1874

The Canadian household guide

O16.1 1874
The / Canadian / household guide. / In four parts. / Part I. – Medical Department. / Part II. – Miscellaneous and Receipt Department. / Part III. – Cookery Department. / Part IV. – Farmer's Department. / Complete in one volume. / Toronto: / James Spencer, / 1874.
DESCRIPTION: 18.5 × 12.0 cm   Pp [iii–vii] viii–x [xi] xii, [13–14] 15–100, [5–8] 9–100, [1–3] 4–96, [5–9] 10–100   I: illus; III: fp illus on pp 13 and 14, illus; IV: fp illus on pp 6, 35, 37, and 38, illus   Cloth
CONTENTS: iii tp; iv blank; v part-title for *The Family Doctor* by S. Remington, Toronto: James Spencer, 1874; vi blank; vii–x introduction; xi–xii index; 13–100 text; 5 part-title for *The Canadian Family Receipt Book*, Toronto: James Spencer, 1874; 6 blank; 7 preface; 8–12 'Contents' [i.e., index]; 13–100 text; 1 part-title for *The Frugal Housekeeper's Kitchen Companion* by Mrs Eliza Ann Wheeler, Toronto: James Spencer, 1874; 2 note 'To the Purchaser'; 3–6 table of contents; 7–8 carving instructions; 9–14 'Introduction. Meats.'; 15–87 'Practical Cookery,' i.e., 330 numbered recipes; 88–96 'An Appendix ... written by a physician, ...'; 5 blank; 6 fp illus of horse; 7 part-title for *Farmer's Guide in the Management of Domestic Animals, and the Treatment of Their Diseases* by Thomas B. Williams, Toronto: James

Spencer, 1874; 8 blank; 9–10 preface; 11–12 table of contents; 13–100 text
COPIES: CIHM (95400)   OAUH   *OGU (UA s041 b04) OONMS
NOTES: The OGU copy is inscribed on the front endpaper, in ink, 'Angus Martin's book // Galt July 15 1874.'

When I examined the book at Una Abrahamson's home (before it was donated to OGU), I saw the publisher's promotional leaflet, which reprints the part-titles for the four parts and the indexes and tables of contents; the leaflet, which was shelved separately from the book, did not apparently follow the book to OGU. The back page of the leaflet gives the following 'Prices and Conditions': 'The Canadian Household Guide is printed from beautiful, clear type, on strong, heavy paper, made expressly for this work, in one volume of over 400 pages, 12mo., and appropriately illustrated, and will be furnished to subscribers, in neat and substantial muslin binding, with gold back and side stamp, at $1.75 per copy.' The publisher's printed address of 65 Colborne Street, Toronto, is corrected with the stamp 'Removed to 61 King St. East.' The printed branch office address is '7 Bleury Street, Montreal.' The publisher also issued an undated single sheet headed 'Confidential Terms to Agents for the Canadian Household Guide,' filmed by CIHM (45948) and incorrectly dated 1870 in the CIHM record.

The parts were also issued separately. The undated 'Catalogue of Maps, Charts and Books Furnished by James Spencer' (OTMCL, incorrectly dated [1840?]), which was a 'confidential circular for agents only,' lists each part at the price of 12½ cents wholesale and 25 cents retail. Mary F. Williamson reports that MWA has one of the parts bound separately, but not in its original binding, with the title: 'The Canadian / family receipt book / A new collection of nearly / 500 / rare and valuable recipes / for the production and use of / things essential / to the / health, wealth, comfort & convenience / of / every household.'; the imprint is Toronto: James Spencer, 1874; the running head, 'Universal Receipt-Book' (Wheaton/Kelly No. 1045). MWA also has, bound separately, Eliza Ann Wheeler's *The Frugal Housekeeper's Kitchen Companion*, Toronto: James Spencer, 1874 (Wheaton/Kelly No. 6458).

See also O17.1, which has similarities with Part II, *The Canadian Family Receipt Book*.

AMERICAN EDITIONS: The following of Wheeler, Eliza Ann, *The Frugal Housekeeper's Kitchen Companion*: New York: H. Phelps, 1847; New York: Ensign, Bridgman and Fanning, 1847; New York: H. Phelps, 1848; New

York: Ensign and Thayer, 1849; New York: Phelps, Fanning, 1852; New York: Ensign, Bridgman and Fanning, 1854 (all at MWA).

Housekeeper's companion

O17.1   1874
Housekeeper's / companion; / being / a guide to economical household / management, / containing / advice and domestic recipes of inestimable value to every housewife, / carefully compiled from the latest, the most approved, / and reliable sources. / Also, / a diary for the entire year, / and / account sheets for all expenditures connected with / the household, arranged to exhibit the outlay / for each day, week, month, and total / for the year. / Designed for the use of housekeepers for the yar [*sic*] 1874. / Published by / Sharratt & Davidson. / 1874.
DESCRIPTION: 17.5 × 11.5 cm   Pp iii–xii [xiii] xiv [xv] xvi, [7–8] 9–100, [97] 98–350, [i–ii]   Cloth
CONTENTS: iii–xii ads for Hamilton businesses; xiii tp; xiv Hamilton ad; xv 'Preface' signed the publishers; xvi Hamilton ad; 7 unsigned 'Preface'; 8–12 'Contents' [i.e., index]; 13–100 'The Universal Receipt-Book'; 97 'Housekeeper's Companion,' 'Introduction,' and 'Entered according to the Act of the Parliament of Canada, in the year one thousand eight hundred and seventy-three, by Sharrat [*sic*] & Davidson, in the office of the Minister of Agriculture.'; 98 ad for Toronto business; 99–346 diary for every day in the year, and weekly and monthly account sheets; [i–ii, not included in pagination] fold-out account sheet for the year and ad; 347–50 Hamilton ads; i ad for Hamilton and Dundas business; ii 'Postal Regulations'
COPIES: *Bookseller's stock
NOTES: The first part of the text, called 'The Universal Receipt-Book,' is a compendium of household formulas, items of advice, and some culinary recipes; the second part, called 'Housekeeper's Companion,' is for diary entries and account-keeping. The publishers' 'Preface' on p xv is directed to Canadians and dedicates the book to 'the careful and successful housekeepers of the Dominion.' The unsigned 'Preface,' reprinted from an earlier source, describes the text (i.e., the first part) as a 'Hand-Book of Economy and a Self-Instructor in a spacious department of useful knowledge.' Several recipes are from the British author Colin Mackenzie's *Five Thousand Receipts in all the Useful and Domestic Arts* (first British edition, 1823; first American edition, 1825); for example, To Make Acorn Coffee on p 51, To Bottle Damsons on p 80, To Pickle Salmon on p 80, To Preserve Barberries on p 80, To Clarify Honey on p 81, To Preserve Fruits in Brandy or Other Spirits on p 81, and To Preserve Cucumbers and Melons on p 81; and the running head 'Universal Receipt-Book' is the same phrase used for the Philadelphia 1856 edition. Whereas Mackenzie's recipes are well organized in sections according to subject, this is not the case for the *Housekeeper's Companion*, which may include recipes from other sources than Mackenzie; however, a thorough comparison was not possible.

The bookseller's copy has a plate mounted on the outside back face of the binding. Although most of the gilt lettering has been rubbed off, the company name 'Canada Life Assurance' is just visible. Perhaps the book was offered as a premium to the company's customers.

It was not possible to compare O17.1 side-by-side with O16.1, but the first part of O17.1 appears to correspond with Part II of *The Canadian Household Guide*. The title of the first part of O17.1 matches the running head for Part II of O16.1; wording in each preface matches; in both cases, the pagination runs 13–100; and the Colin Mackenzie recipes mentioned above are also found in O16.1 and on the same pages (except To Make Acorn Coffee, which is on p 33 in O16.1).

1876

Harland, Marion [pseudonym of] Mrs Mary Virginia Terhune, née Hawes (Amelia County, Va, 21 December 1830–3 June 1922, New York City, NY)

See this novelist's biography in Arndt, pp 202–5 (Nancy Carter Crump, 'Marion Harland') and in Feeding America. In Marion Harland's Autobiography: The Story of a Long Life, *New York and London: Harper and Brothers, 1910, she reflects on the unexpected success of her first cookbook,* Common Sense in the Household, *which, according to her account, went through 'ten editions ... in as many months' and reached the million mark in sales. When her husband found her gloating over a copy, the week after it was published, and suggested that she took more pride in that book than in all her novels, she replied, 'It will do more good than all of them put together' (pp 344–5). In addition to* Common Sense in the Household, *several of her other works were also published in Canadian editions: O22.1,* The Dinner Year Book; *O46.1,* House and Home; *Q40.1,* Cooking Hints; *and NB15.1,* The Premium Cook

Book. *Her recipes are included in the following: Q29.1, 266 recettes choisies; Q30.1, 600 Selected Recipes; and O82.2, Dwight's Cow-Brand Cook-Book.*

Other cookbooks by this author, but not published in Canada, are: Breakfast, Luncheon and Tea*, New York: Scribner, Armstrong and Co., 1875 (United States: InU);* The Cottage Kitchen*, New York: C. Scribner's Sons, 1883 (United States: DLC);* Cookery for Beginners*, Boston: D. Lothrop and Co., [copyright 1884] (United States: InU);* The Art of Cooking by Gas*, New York: American Technical Book Co., 1896 (Bitting, p 215);* The National Cook Book *by Marion Harland and her daughter Christine Terhune Herrick, New York: C. Scribner's Sons, 1896 (Bitting, p 215);* Breakfast, Dinner and Supper*, New York: G.J. McLeod and Co., [about 1897] (Bitting, p 215);* The Comfort of Cooking and Heating by Gas*, New York: William M. Crane and Co., [copyright 1898 by American Technical Book Co.] (United States: InU); and* The Helping Hand Cook Book*, by Marion Harland and Christine Terhune Herrick, New York: Moffat, Yard and Co., 1912 (United States: InU).* Marion Harland's Complete Cook Book*, Indianapolis: Bobbs-Merrill Co., [copyright June 1903] (OTU; United States: DLC), includes a frontispiece portrait of the author. O24.1,* Peerless Cook Book*, by Mrs Julia McNair Wright, contains bills of fare by Harland. Harland also contributed to* The New England Cook Book*, Boston: Chas E. Brown Publishing Co., 1905 (Bitting, p 215).*

For a Canadian edition of her daughter Christine's cookbook, Like My Mother Used to Make, *see O282.1.*

O18.1   1876

Common sense / in the household: / A manual of / practical housewifery. / By / Marion Harland. / "We go upon the practical mode of teaching, Nickleby. When a boy knows / this out of a book, he goes and does it. This is our system. What do you think / of it?" – Nicholas Nickleby. / Toronto: / Belford Bros., publishers, / 11 Colborne Street, / 1876.

DESCRIPTION: 17.0 × 11.0 cm   Pp [iii–v] vi–xv [xvi], [17] 18–320   Rebound

CONTENTS: iii tp; iv 'Toronto: Printed at the Monetary Times Office, 64 and 66 Church Street.'; v–xv table of contents; xvi blank; 17–25 'Familiar Talk with My Fellow-Housekeeper and Reader' signed Marion Harland; 26 blank; 27–320 recipes

COPIES: *OGU (UA s004 b24)

NOTES: See also O41.1, *The Breadmaker's Book of Cooking Lessons*, whose unnamed author acknowledges consulting *Common Sense in the Household*.

O18.2   nd [about 1886]

—Common sense in the / household: / A manual of / practical housewifery. / By / Marion Harland. / "We go upon the practical mode of teaching, Nickleby. When a boy / knows this out of a book, he he [*sic*] goes and does it. This is our system. What / do you think of it?" – Nicholas Nickleby. / Toronto: / Rose Publishing Company.

DESCRIPTION: 18.0 × 12.0 cm   Pp [1–6] 7–319   Cloth simulating brown leather

CONTENTS: 1 tp; 2 'Hunter Rose & Co // printers & binders // Toronto' in publ's symbol; 3 author's dedication 'To my fellow housekeepers, ...'; 4 'Note' indicating that recipes marked ‡ are 'certainly safe, and for the most part simple.'; 5–308 recipes; 309–19 'Index' [i.e., table of contents]

COPIES: CIHM (91674)   *OGU (UA s070 b71)   OONL (TX715 H373 1879, 2 copies)   OTUTF (jah, copies 1 and 2)   QMM (RBD TX715 H2644 1879)   Private collection

NOTES: Rose Publishing Co. was active from 1 May 1883 to 1894 (Hulse, p 223). An inscription in the QMM copy establishes a publication date of about 1886; other inscribed dates are later. The QMM copy is signed in ink, on the back endpaper, 'Miss Kate. J. Ashton London Jan 23d 1886'; also in ink, on the front endpaper, 'Kate. Jewell Ashton the year 1888'; and signed in three other places by the same person and with the date 1888. OTUTF copy 2 is inscribed on the front endpaper, in blue ink, 'M.M. Macklem // Chippawa Ont Feb 1st 1888'; the same name and place are inscribed on the back endpapers, in pencil. The OGU copy is inscribed on the front endpaper, 'M.E. Walker Toronto Mar. 27/91.' OTUTF copy 1 is inscribed in ink, on the front endpaper, 'A.C. Cawthra 1893.' The private collector's copy is signed on the front endpaper, in pencil, 'Jessie from Mrs Quaid Christmas 1906.'

The two OTUTF copies are identical except for the binding, the setting of the dedication page, and the thickness of the paper. Copy 1 is bound in cloth simulating leather, like the OGU copy catalogued here, whereas copy 2 is bound in cloth simulating wood grain. Both OTUTF copies are from the same setting of type, with the exception of the dedication page: one difference is that copy 2 has a hyphen in 'To my fellow-housekeepers,' but copy 1 does not. Copy 1 is printed on thinner paper: the volume measures about 1.8 cm in thickness, excluding the binding. Copy 2 has thicker paper and measures about 2.3 cm. Copy 1 is incomplete, lacking pp 309–16 of the index. The CIHM microfilm is of OONL copy 2, which has no hyphen in 'fellow housekeepers.' (I have not examined the other OONL copy.)

MWMM has only the title-page leaf and the blank endpaper(?); the rest of the volume is missing. These two leaves are incorrectly filed in a copy of *The Home Cook Book* that lacks its own title-page.

O18.3   nd [about 1896–8]
—Common sense in the / household: / A manual of / practical housewifery. / By / Marion Harland. / "We go upon the practical mode of teaching, Nickleby. When / a boy knows this out of a book, he he [*sic*] goes and does it. This is our / system. What do you think of it?" – Nicholas Nickleby. / Toronto: / G.M. Rose & Sons.
DESCRIPTION: 18.0 × 12.0 cm   Pp [i–iv], [1–6] 7–308, [i–xviii], [309] 310–19   Cloth
CONTENTS: i endpaper ad; ii blank; iii–iv ads; 1 tp; 2 blank; 3 dedication 'To my fellow housekeepers, ...'; 4 'Note' indicating that recipes marked ‡ are 'certainly safe, and for the most part simple.'; 5–308 recipes and leaves of ads not included in pagination; i–ii ads; iii–ix 'Dinner Etiquette'; x–xv 'Bills of Fare' and ads; xvi blank; xvii–xviii ads; 309–19 'Index' [i.e., table of contents]
CITATIONS: Abrahamson, pp 29 (note 6), 31, 60
COPIES: *OGU (UA s070 b70)   OTMCL (641.5 T26 1879)
NOTES: Printed on the binding of the OGU copy is the name of a London, Ontario, grocer (his store address on Dundas Street is given in an advertisement opposite p 144): 'Compliments of Scandrett Bros. London.' An advertisement opposite p 129 for the St Lawrence Sugar Refining Co. features a chemist's Certification of Purity dated 8 April 1895. The publisher, G.M. Rose and Sons, took this name on 1 November 1895, incorporated in 1898, and dissolved in 1901 (Hulse, p 222).

The OTMCL copy has no advertisements and is bound in cloth simulating wood grain. OTMCL dates the book 1879, but there is no evidence to support this date.

AMERICAN EDITIONS: New York: [Printed by New York Printing Co. for] Charles Scribner and Co., 1871 (OGU; United States: InU); New York: C. Scribner and Co., 1872 (Bitting, p 214); New York: Scribner, Armstrong and Co., 1872 (Barile, p 184); New York: Scribner, Armstrong and Co., 1876 (OGU); New York: [Printed by Trow's Printing and Bookbinding Co. for] Charles Scribner's Sons, [entered 1871], with a publisher's advertisement dated 1878 following p 556 (OGU, OTU); rev. ed., New York: C. Scribner's Sons, 1881

(United States: DLC); New York: C. Scribner, 1882 (OWTU microfilm); Majority ed., [No place: 1892] (United States: DLC). More than fifty years after the first edition, and after Harland's death, the book was republished as *The New Common Sense in the Household, Being 'Common Sense in the Household,' by Marion Harland, Revised for Gas and Electricity by Her Daughter, Christine Terhune Herrick*, New York: Frederick A. Stokes Co., 1926 (United States: DLC).

1877

Buckton, Catherine M.

In 1873, the year this British author was elected as the first woman on the Leeds School Board, she saw published Two Winters' Experience in Giving Lectures to My Fellow Townswomen of the Working Classes, on Physiology and Hygiene, *third edition, Leeds: William Wood, 1873 (Great Britain: LB). She also wrote:* Food and Home Cookery: A Course of Instruction in Practical Cookery and Cleaning, for Children in Elementary Schools, as Followed in the Schools of the Leeds School Board, *London: Longmans and Co., 1879 (Driver 167.1);* Town and Window Gardening ... A Course of Sixteen Lectures Given ... to Pupil-Teachers and Children Attending the Leeds Board Schools, *London: Longmans and Co., 1879 (Great Britain: LB);* Our Dwellings Healthy and Unhealthy Addressed to Girls Attending the Leeds Board Schools, *London: Longmans, Green and Co., 1885 (Attar 37.1); and* Comfort and Cleanliness: The Servant and Mistress Question, *London: Longmans, Green and Co., 1898 (Attar 362.1).*

O19.1   8th ed., [entered 1877]
Authorized by the Minister of Education. / Health in the house. / Twenty-five lectures on elementary physiology in its / application to the daily wants of man and animals, / delivered to the wives and children of / working-men in Leeds and Saltaire / by / Catherine M. Buckton, / member of the Leeds School Board. / Revised throughout. / Eighth edition. / Toronto: / Adam Miller & Co.
DESCRIPTION: 18.0 × 11.0 cm   Pp [v–ix] x–xiii [xiv–xv] xvi–xviii [xix] xx, [1] 2–207   Illus   Cloth
CONTENTS: v tp; vi 'Entered according to Act of the Parliament of Canada, in the year one thousand eight hundred and seventy-seven, by Adam Miller & Co., in the office of the Minister of Agriculture. Globe Printing Company, Toronto.'; vii 'Preface to the Sixth Edition' signed Catherine M. Buckton, 4 Moorland

Terrace, 4 February 1876; viii blank; ix–xiii 'Preface to the First Edition'; xiv blank; xv–xviii 'Contents'; xix–xx 'List of Illustrations'; 1–186 twenty-five lectures; 187–200 'Appendices'; 201–7 'Index'
COPIES: CIHM (26714)   OLU (QP38 B9 1877)   OONL (QP38 B83 1877)   OTU (613 1877 B926H OISE/UT OHEC)   *QMM (Osler Robertson B9267h 1877)
NOTES: 'French Cooking' is discussed in Lecture XVI. Lectures XVIII–XXI cover 'Foods' and 'Cooking.'

O19.2   10th ed., 1879
—Miller & Co's Educational Series. / Health in the house. / Twenty-five lectures on elementary physiology / in its application to the daily wants of / man and animals, delivered to the / wives and children of work- / ing-men in Leeds and / Saltaire. / By / Catherine M. Buckton, / member of the Leeds School Board. / Authorized by the Minister of Education. / Tenth edition. / Toronto: / Adam Miller & Co. / 1879.
CONTENTS: Tp verso 'Entered according to Act of the Parliament of Canada, in the year one thousand eight hundred and seventy-seven, by Adam Miller & Co., in the office of the Minister of Agriculture.'
COPIES: *OLU (LT1001.612 B83 1879)

O19.3   10th ed., 1880
—Miller & Co's Educational Series. / Health in the house. / Twenty-five lectures on elementary physiology / in its application to the daily wants of / man and animals, delivered to the / wives and children of work- / ing-men in Leeds and / Saltaire. / By / Catherine M. Buckton, / member of the Leeds School Board. / Authorized by the Minister of Education. / Tenth edition. / Toronto: / W.J. Gage & Co. / 1880.
DESCRIPTION: 17.5 × 11.5 cm   Pp [iii–ix] x–xiii [xiv–xv] xvi–xviii [xix] xx, [1] 2–207, [i–iii]   Illus   Cloth
CONTENTS: iii endpaper publ ad; iv blank; v tp; vi 'Entered according to Act of the Parliament of Canada, in the year one thousand eight hundred and seventy-seven, by Adam Miller & Co., in the office of the Minister of Agriculture.'; vii 'Preface to the Sixth Edition' signed Catherine M. Buckton, 4 Moorland Terrace, 4 February 1876; viii blank; ix–xiii 'Preface to the First Edition'; xiv blank; xv–xviii 'Contents'; xix–xx 'List of Illustrations'; 1–186 twenty-five lectures; 187–200 'Appendices'; 201–7 'Index'; i–ii blank; iii endpaper publ ad
COPIES: OLU (LT1001.612 B83 1880)   *OTU (613 1877 M647 B926H OISE/UT OHEC)
NOTES: There were two editions numbered tenth and dated 1880: this one with the series name 'Miller &

Co's Educational Series' on the title-page and O19.4 with the series name 'W.J. Gage & Co.'s Educational Series' on the title-page. Although the series name 'Miller & Co's ... ' is on the title-page of this edition, 'Gage & Co.'s Educational Series' is printed on the binding.

O19.4   10th ed., 1880
—W.J. Gage & Co.'s Educational Series. / Health in the house. / Twenty-five lectures on elementary physiology / in its application to the daily wants of / man and animals, delivered to the / wives and children of work- / ing-men in Leeds and / Saltaire. / By / Catherine M. Buckton, / member of the Leeds School Board. / Authorized by the Minister of Education. / Tenth edition. / Toronto: / W.J. Gage & Co. / 1880.
DESCRIPTION: 17.5 × 11.0 cm   Pp [iii–ix] x–xiii [xiv–xv] xvi–xviii [xix] xx, [1] 2–207, [i–iii]   Illus   Cloth
CONTENTS: iii endpaper publ ad; iv blank; v tp; vi 'Entered according to Act of the Parliament of Canada, in the year one thousand eight hundred and seventy-seven, by Adam Miller & Co., in the office of the Minister of Agriculture.'; vii 'Preface to the Sixth Edition' signed Catherine M. Buckton, 4 Moorland Terrace, 4 February 1876; viii blank; ix–xiii 'Preface to the First Edition'; xiv blank; xv–xviii table of contents; xix–xx 'List of Illustrations'; 1–186 text; 187–200 'Appendices'; 201–7 index; i–ii blank; iii endpaper publ ad
COPIES: *AEU (QP 37 B92 1880)

O19.5   11th ed.
—[Eleventh edition of *Health in the House*]
COPIES: OTU (613 1877 G134 B926H OISE/UT OHEC, not on shelf)
NOTES: Although OTU records the imprint as Toronto: W.J. Gage, 1877, the title-page is probably undated, as the twelfth edition. The London eleventh edition is dated 1880.

O19.6   12th ed., nd
—W.J. Gage & Co's Educational Series. / Health in the house. / Twenty-five lectures on elementary physiology / in its application to the daily wants of / man and animals, delivered to the / wives and children of work- / ing-men in Leeds and / Saltaire. / By / Catherine M. Buckton, / member of the Leeds School Board. / Authorized by the Minister of Education. / Twelfth edition. / Toronto and Winnipeg: / W.J. Gage & Co.
DESCRIPTION: 18.5 × 11.5 cm   Pp [v–ix] x–xiii [xiv–xv] xvi–xviii [xix] xx, [1] 2–207   Illus   Cloth

CONTENTS: v tp; vi 'Entered according to Act of the Parliament of Canada, in the year one thousand eight hundred and seventy-seven, by Adam Miller & Co., in the office of the Minister of Agriculture.'; vii 'Preface to the Sixth Edition' signed Catherine M. Buckton, 4 Moorland Terrace, 4 February 1876; viii blank; ix–xiii 'Preface to the First Edition'; xiv blank; xv–xviii 'Contents'; xix–xx 'List of Illustrations'; 1–186 text in twenty-five numbered lectures; 187–200 'Appendices'; 201–7 'Index'
COPIES: CIHM (35827)   OONL (QP38 B83 1870z) *OTU (613 1877 G134 B926H2 OISE/UT OHEC)

BRITISH EDITIONS: London: Longmans and Co., 1875 (Great Britain: LB); 3rd ed., London: Longmans and Co., 1875 (Great Britain: LB); 6th ed., London: Longmans and Co., 1876 (Great Britain: LB); 7th ed., London: Longmans, Green and Co., 1876 (OWTU); 11th ed., London: Longmans, Green and Co., 1880 (United States: DLC); 19th impression, London, New York, and Bombay: Longmans, Green and Co., 1905 (United States: DLC).

The home cook book

O20.1 1877
Tried, tested, proved. / The / home cook book. / Compiled from recipes contributed by ladies of Toronto and / other cities and towns: Published for the benefit / of the Hospital for Sick Children. / Toronto, Canada: / Belford Brothers, publishers. / MDCCCLXXVII.
DESCRIPTION: Pp [i–iv] [v–vi lacking] [vii–viii], [9] 10–384, [i–vi]
CONTENTS: i ht; ii blank; iii tp; iv 'Entered according to Act of the Parliament of Canada, in the year one thousand eight hundred and seventy-seven, by Belford Brothers, in the office of the Minister of Agriculture. Trout & Todd, printers and stereotypers. Hunter, Rose & Co., binders, Toronto.'; v–vi [leaf lacking, but 'Index' lists 'Preface' on p v]; vii 'Index' [i.e., table of contents]; viii blank; 9–384 text; i–vi ads
CITATIONS: Armstrong 2000, p F2 Bly *Canadian Monthly and National Review* Vol. 11 (April 1877), p 452   Cooke 2002, p 234   Crawford, p D2   Driver 2001, All New Purity, inside front cover   Driver 2001, Wellington County, pp 95, 97 (note 7)   Driver 2003, 'Canadian Cookbooks,' pp 29–30, 35   Driver 2005, pp 410, 552 (note 80)   Driver 2005, letter, p 7   Landsberg   Simpson, p W17   Watier, p 7
COPIES: *CIHM (95365)   NBSUH
NOTES: *The Home Cook Book* (pl 21) was the first ex-

ample in Canada of what are variously called fund-raising, charitable, or community cookbooks. The title-page of *The Home Cook Book* plainly states that it was 'published for the benefit of the Hospital for Sick Children,' and the 'Preface,' written by the hospital's treasurer, Mrs Samuel Fenton McMaster (pl 34; born Elizabeth Jennet Wyllie, Toronto, 27 December 1847, died 3 March 1903, Chicago, Illinois), appeals for the reader's support of the institution's important work. Mrs McMaster had been the motivating force behind the founding of the hospital – Canada's first for children – in March 1875, and retained control of the hospital, through the Ladies' Committee, until 1891. (The 'Preface,' which is listed in the 'Index' of the 1877 edition, is missing in the NBSUH copy.)

In addition to its fund-raising purpose, another novelty of *The Home Cook Book* was that the recipes were credited to individuals. Toronto citizens would have been familiar with many of the recipe contributors. Connected with the hospital were Mrs McMaster and her mother, Mrs G.B. Wyllie, and a relative, Miss Wyllie; the hospital's matron, Mrs Spence; Mrs Christopher Patterson, the wife of a hospital trustee; and other women associated with the Ladies' Committee (Mrs Snider, Miss Knapp, Mrs F. Knapp, Mrs John Morse, Mrs Thomas A. Hill, and Mrs D. McCraney). On the publisher's side, the wives of Charles and Robert Belford contributed recipes, as did Mrs James Beaty (probably the wife of the Belford brothers' great-uncle James) and two of her relatives (Mrs Robert Beaty and Miss Kate Beaty). The appeal for recipes extended beyond the hospital and publisher to many other women in the middle to upper echelons of Toronto society. These included, for example, the wives of two diplomats, a former mayor of Toronto, a homoeopathist, a French professor, another publisher, an artist, a lumber merchant, and a jeweller. There were also recipe contributors from lower in the social order, such as Mrs Joseph Saulter, wife of a mail clerk. More information about the recipe contributors is in the 'Introduction' to the 2002 Whitecap Books facsimile, O20.52. Although *The Home Cook Book* lost its connection with the hospital after 1879, all subsequent reprints still credited the ladies of Toronto on the title-page and assigned the recipes to individuals.

As the first recipe manual of this type in Canada, *The Home Cook Book* served as a model for other women's groups to follow. Ironically, however, it was itself based on a Chicago text: *The Home Cook Book of Chicago*, 'compiled from recipes contributed by ladies of Chicago and other cities and towns: Published for the benefit of the Home for the Friendless.' There were editions in 1874, 1875, 1876, 1877, and later, published by J. Fred Waggoner (descriptions and locations are in Margaret Cook, *America's Charitable Cooks: A Bibliography of Fund-raising Cook Books Published in the United States, 1861–1915*, Kent, Ohio: 1971, pp 57–8). I was able to examine a complete copy of the 1874 edition and photocopies of selected parts of the 1876 edition. Several points of correspondence with the 1876 edition suggest that it is the likely source of the Toronto text. The Toronto title-page guarantee of 'Tried, tested, proved' matches the 1876 edition (1874 has 'Tried and true recipes'). The Toronto book has the same headings for a one-page 'Index' as the 1876 edition, with one minor difference ('Sickroom and medicinal receipts' instead of 'Sick-room'), whereas 1874 has a different style of 'Index' (multipage) at the back. The 'Vegetables' chapter has fifteen recipes found in the 1876 edition, but not in 1874, plus a quotation from Thompson new to 1876.

Two entries in the minutes of the Ladies' Committee make oblique reference to the Chicago book, the first for the meeting on 14 May 1879:

Some unpleasant correspondence was then referred to by Mrs McMaster, from a Chicago publisher, in reference to the 'Home Cook Book' averring that it had been copied from a book previously issued from their press in the interests of a charity in their city. Although the charge was not strictly founded on fact, and the responsibility of the book does not happily rest with the Lady Managers, it was decided as the most prudent course, to apply to Mr Justice Patterson to dictate the reply, which should if necessary be given.

An entry for the next meeting on 2 June reads, 'The correspondence in reference to "Home Cook Book" again read, as some of the ladies had not heard it. All united in condemning the publication and any connection with it.' The charge of piracy and any real or imagined difficulties relating to the charge may have led to the Ladies' Committee being disassociated from the book some time in 1879. The hospital's name last appears in an 1879 edition, and a cryptic entry in the minutes for 2 April 1879 may point to a possible final reckoning with Belford Brothers. It states, '$75 had been recovered from Belford.'

At the time, outside of the small circle of the Ladies' Committee and Belford Brothers, it is unlikely that many people knew that *The Home Cook Book* was modelled after the Chicago work. More than a century later, it may not be possible to learn who acquired a copy of the Chicago book, who conceived of using it as part of a fund-raising project for the hospi-

tal, and who had responsibility for compiling the amalgamated Chicago/Toronto text, although it is likely that Belford Brothers played a significant role in all these aspects of the book's production. An 1879 Rose-Belford *Catalogue of Books* refers to *The Home Cook Book* as 'the joint effort of the publishers and a number of Toronto ladies' (copy at OTUTF, p 8). In the mid-1870s, Belford Brothers had been exploiting what they saw as an ambiguity between the Canadian Copyright Act of 1875 and the Imperial copyright law, by reprinting editions of certain American and British books, sometimes without permission. The Chicago cookbook may have come to their attention in the course of this aspect of their business. It is also possible that Mrs McMaster or someone in her circle knew the Chicago book. There are two instances of an unusual last name – Knapp and Odell – that can be matched with a Toronto person, but which also appears in the Chicago book; perhaps the Chicago Mrs Knapp or Mrs Odell sent a copy to her relation in Toronto.

In the 'Introduction' to the 2002 facsimile, O20.52, pp xvi–xviii and Note 16, I compared the Toronto text with the 1874 Chicago edition to show the extent of the Canadian content and to illuminate the editorial process followed by the Toronto ladies. Those findings must be revised and a new assessment of Canadian content done, based on a comparison with a complete copy of the 1876 edition. Generally, recipes credited to women in known Toronto families are Canadian additions, although sometimes Toronto names were added to Chicago recipes. Definitely new to the Toronto book is a recipe for Carrot Pudding, contributed by Mrs McMaster, which is the earliest example I have found of what became a classic Christmas dish in English Canada.

Partly pirated or not, *The Home Cook Book* was embraced by the public and sold in huge numbers. It was the most successful Canadian cookbook of the nineteenth century. It was continuously reprinted through the 1880s and 1890s, and into the twentieth century. An advertisement for *The Home Cook Book* in O29.1, *Cook's Friend Cook Book*, 1881, cites 'Over 25,000 sold in Canada.' By 1885, over 100,000 copies had been sold (Elizabeth Hulse, 'The Hunter Rose Company: A Brief History,' *Devil's Artisan* Vol. 18 (1986), p 6), at a time when Canada's population was only about four and a half million. The publisher numbered the last edition, in 1929, the one hundredth, but the edition numbering is inconsistent and misleading, and my research has uncovered fifty-two variant title-pages (Canadian and other). (I have not attempted to track resettings of type, a difficult task because the variants are scattered across the country in public and private collections.) The book was published in five Ontario cities – Toronto, London, Paris, Barrie, and Whitby – in Saint John, New Brunswick, and in Winnipeg; and there were editions in Sydney, Australia, in Wellington, New Zealand, and in London, England.

The order of publication of the various editions is not always certain because only some title-pages are dated. In the case of undated editions, library cataloguers and others have sometimes incorrectly taken the 1877 copyright date (on the verso of the title-page of most nineteenth-century editions) to be the year of publication. The form of the publisher's name is a guide to ordering the editions. The two earliest editions bear the name Belford Brothers. In 1878 George Maclean Rose established Rose-Belford Publishing Co., which operated under this name until 1883, when it became Rose Publishing Co. The Rose Publishing Co. failed in 1894, but the family's Hunter Rose and Co. survived. (Hulse records the Rose Publishing Co. active only until 1894, but its imprint is on cookbooks dated 1903 and 1906; see O130.1 and O130.4, for Grace Elizabeth Denison's *The New Cook Book*.) From 1894, Hunter Rose and Co., the printer and binder of most of the preceding editions, became the publisher of some editions. Editions published by G.M. Rose and Sons date from the period 1895 to 1901, when the business (incorporated in 1898) was dissolved. The Musson Book Co. was established in 1898, but its editions of *The Home Cook Book* probably all date from after the turn of the century (Charles Joseph Musson, manager then president of the company, had worked for Hunter Rose and Co. in 1893–4). The Musson Book Co. published the last edition of *The Home Cook Book* in 1929.

The first edition was favourably received in the *Canadian Monthly and National Review* Vol. 11 (April 1877), p 452, although the unnamed reviewer 'look[ed] in vain for a recipe for "strawberry short-cake," ... such a favorite institution.' There are, in fact, instructions for this seasonal dish on p 280. Another review, by George Stewart Jr, is reprinted as the 'Letter to the Publishers' in editions from 1878 to about the mid-1880s. Stewart, who lived in Saint John, New Brunswick, was the founder of *Stewart's Literary Quarterly* and an early champion of Canadian literature. In the fall of 1877, Belford Brothers had offered him a job in Toronto, which he accepted, moving to Toronto in spring 1878. Whether the publisher requested the review before or after the move to Toronto is unknown. Stewart's review is an amusing, but erudite, rumination on the topic of gastronomy and the im-portance of a national cuisine, and it ends with a hearty recommendation of the cookbook (a clipping from an unidentified newspaper or magazine, containing the complete text of the review, is at NBSAM, George Stewart Scrap Books 29 (1878): 61, call number FC2472.99 S84 Bell). It is curious that the only known copy of the first edition is in New Brunswick. The museum has no record of the provenance of its copy, but it probably belonged originally to a New Brunswick family. It is not impossible to imagine that the museum's copy is George Stewart Jr's review copy, left behind when he moved to Toronto.

Ferguson/Fraser, pp 232 and 233, refer incorrectly to the first edition as *The Canadian Home Cook Book*. None of the fifty-two variants of *The Home Cook Book* that appeared between 1877 and 1929 was called *The Canadian Home Cook Book*, the title that appears on the fake title-page in the facsimile editions of 1970, 1971, and 1980 (O20.49–20.51). Abrahamson, p 60, refers incorrectly to an edition published by Rose-Belford dated 1877.

There is an unidentified edition of *The Home Cook Book* at OTU (TX715 H6 1884 Gerstein). It is rebound and lacks its title-page. It is inscribed on p iii (the first page of the 'Contents'), in ink, 'J.E. McLa[n?]dress // Little Current // 1884.' Golick, p 111, discusses this copy. OTU catalogues this edition as published by Rose Publishing Co.

Another unidentified edition of *The Home Cook Book* is at OGM (979.7.8). The pagination runs as follows: [leaves lacking] [iii] iv–xi [xii], [9] 10–384.

Another unidentified edition of *The Home Cook Book*, retaining only pp 17–366, is at OKITD (982.011.001).

Various nineteenth-century Canadian cookbooks refer to *The Home Cook Book*. O29.1, *Cook's Friend Cook Book*, reprints the 'Housekeeping' and 'Table Talk' sections, and includes an advertisement for the book. The unnamed author of O41.1, *The Breadmaker's Book of Cooking Lessons*, acknowledges consulting *The Home Cook Book*. A Hamilton bookseller advertises *The Home Cook Book* in O44.1, *The Housekeeper's Help*, 1888, as the only Canadian title among British and American works (see that entry for the text of the advertisement). Montrealer Sarah Allen reprinted several recipes and a bill of fare from *The Home Cook Book* in her 1895 work, Q27.1, *The Common Sense Recipe Book*. And fund-raising cookbooks from across the country mimicked *The Home Cook Book*'s title-page guarantee of 'Tried, Tested, Proved.': M2.1, *The Souvenir Cook Book*, 1896; Q32.1, *The Huntingdon Cook Book*, 1896; S5.1, *The Guild Cook Book*, 1910; A18.1, Pinkham, Miss Mary, *The W.A. Cook Book*, [about 1910]; and M20.1, *The Minnedosa Cook Book*, 1914.

Pierre and Janet Berton reprinted several recipes from *The Home Cook Book* in their *Centennial Food Guide* of 1966. They identify the edition consulted as 'published in 1877,' but give no other information about the specific imprint; see Berton, pp 19, 30, 44. Duncan, pp 22 and 165, also refers to *The Home Cook Book*, but does not identify the edition.

In 1983 the Women's Auxiliary of the Hospital for Sick Children published *Hospitality: Our Cook Book* (OTY) to raise money for the hospital. The 'Introduction,' p 5, refers to *The Home Cook Book*: 'The Ladies Committee continued to have financial problems. They compiled The Home Cook Book to publicize the hospital and to raise funds. The quotations in this book [i.e., quotations from Stewart's 'Letter to the Publishers'] have been plucked from that publication.' A reproduction of the only known photograph of Mrs McMaster is opposite p 6.

The Toronto *Home Cook Book* is not related to *The American Home Cook Book by Ladies of Detroit and Other Cities*, Detroit and Chicago: Rose-Belford Publishing Co., 1878 (United States: ICU, NBuBE). According to Hulse (*Devil's Artisan*, p 5, cited above), soon after George Maclean Rose formed the Rose-Belford Publishing Co. in 1878 with Robert J. Belford and other investors, Robert and his brother Alexander left for Chicago and New York. *The American Home Cook Book* must have been one of their first ventures in Chicago. The only shared text (with slight revisions) is the table of 'Weights and Measures.'

The minutes of the Ladies Committee are in the Archives of the Hospital for Sick Children. For information about Mrs McMaster, see Gina Feldberg's entry for her in DCB, Vol. 13, pp 1118–19; and Judith Young, 'A Divine Mission: Elizabeth McMaster and the Hospital for Sick Children, Toronto, 1875–92,' *Canadian Bulletin of Medical History* Vol. 11 (1994), pp 71–90. For the early history of the hospital, see Diane L. Gilday, 'The Founding and the First Quarter Century of Management of the Hospital for Sick Children,' 2000 Paper for degree of MA in History, University of Toronto, 25 January 1991. There is no mention of the cookbook in Max Braithwaite, *Sick Kids: The Story of the Hospital for Sick Children in Toronto*, Toronto: McClelland and Steward Ltd, 1974. For information about George Stewart Jr, see Carol Fullerton, 'George Stewart, Jr., a Nineteenth-Century Canadian Man of Letters,' *Papers of the Bibliographical Society of Canada* Vol. 25, pp 82–108; Fullerton's entry for Stewart in DCB, Vol. 13, pp 988–90; and George L. Parker's entry for Stewart in *The Oxford Companion to Canadian Literature*, second edition, edited by Eugene Benson and William Toye, Toronto, Oxford, New York:

Oxford University Press, 1997, pp 1096–7. Hulse is the source for the dates of operation for the various publishers of *The Home Cook Book*.

O20.2   1878
—Tried, tested, proved. / The / home cook book. / Compiled from recipes contributed by ladies of Toronto and / other cities and towns: Published for the benefit / of the Hospital for Sick Children. / Toronto: / Belford Brothers, publishers. / MDCCCLXXVIII.
DESCRIPTION: 18.0 × 12.0 cm   Pp [i–v] vi [vii–viii], [9] 10–384   Cloth
CONTENTS: i ht; ii blank; iii tp; iv 'Entered according to Act of the Parliament of Canada, in the year one thousand eight hundred and seventy-seven, by Belford Brothers, in the office of the Minister of Agriculture. Printed and bound by Hunter, Rose & Co., Toronto.'; v–vi 'A Letter to the Publishers' signed Geo. Stewart Jr; vii 'Index' [i.e., table of contents]; viii blank; 9–384 text
COPIES: *OGU (UA s048 b32)   OKQ (Special Collections uncat)

O20.3   1878
—Tried, tested, proved. / The / home cook book. / Compiled from recipes contributed by ladies of Toronto and / other cities and towns: Published for the benefit / of the Hospital for Sick Children. / Toronto: / Rose-Belford Publishing Company. / MDCCCLXXVIII.
DESCRIPTION: 18.0 × 12.0 cm   Pp [i–v] vi [vii–viii], [9] 10–384   Cloth
CONTENTS: i ht; ii blank; iii tp; iv 'Entered according to Act of the Parliament of Canada, in the year one thousand eight hundred and seventy-seven, by Belford Brothers, in the office of the Minister of Agriculture. Printed and bound by Hunter, Rose & Co., Toronto.'; v–vi 'A Letter to the Publishers' signed Geo. Stewart Jr; vii 'Index' [i.e., table of contents]; viii blank; 9–384 text
COPIES: OTHSC   *Private collection
NOTES: The OTHSC copy lacks its half-title; the volume was donated to OTHSC in 1977 by Miss Grace McBride, Glencairn Avenue, Toronto. The 2002 facsimile, O20.52, was made from the private collector's copy described here. A copy at OW (641.5 H75) has the same title-page as O20.3, but has Mrs McMaster's 'Preface' on p [iii], as O20.4.

O20.4   1878
—Tried, tested, proved. / The / home cook book. / Compiled by / ladies of Toronto and other cities and

towns / in Canada. / Toronto: / Rose-Belford
Publishing Company. / MDCCCLXXVIII.
DESCRIPTION: 18.0 × 12.0 cm   Pp [i–v] vi [vii–viii], [9]
10–384   Cloth
CONTENTS: i tp; ii 'Entered according to Act of the Parliament of Canada, in the year one thousand eight hundred and seventy-seven, by Belford Brothers, in the
office of the Minister of Agriculture. Printed and
bound by Hunter, Rose & Co., Toronto.'; iii 'Preface'
signed Mrs S.F. McMaster, Treasurer, Hospital for Sick
Children; iv blank; v–vi 'A Letter to the Publishers'
signed Geo. Stewart Jr; vii 'Index' [i.e., table of con-
tents]; viii blank; 9–384 text
COPIES: *NFSM   ONLAM   QMM (RBD Vanna
Garnier, ckbk 865)
NOTES: There is no reference to the Hospital for Sick
Children on the title-page. The ONLAM copy is inscribed on the front endpaper, in pencil, 'Mrs. R.G.
Wright // Napanee Ontario.'

O20.5   1878
—Tried, tested, proved. / The / home cook book. /
Compiled from recipes contributed by ladies of
Toronto and / other cities and towns: Published for
the benefit / of the Hospital for Sick Children.
/ St. John, N.B. / R.A.H. Morrow, publisher. /
MDCCCLXXVIII.
DESCRIPTION: 18.0 × 12.0 cm   Pp [iii–v] vi [vii–viii], [9]
10–384   Cloth
CONTENTS: iii tp; iv 'Entered according to Act of the
Parliament of Canada, in the year one thousand eight
hundred and seventy-seven, by Belford Brothers, in
the office of the Minister of Agriculture. Printed and
bound by Hunter, Rose & Co., Toronto.'; v–vi 'A Letter to the Publishers' signed Geo. Stewart Jr; vii
'Index' [i.e., table of contents]; viii blank; 9–384 text
COPIES: BKOM   CIHM (29260)   *OONL (TX715 H76
1878***)

O20.6   1878
—Tried, tested, proved. / The / home cook book. /
Compiled from recipes contributed by ladies
of Toronto and / other cities and towns. /
St. John, N.B. / R.A.H. Morrow. / MDCCCLXXVIII.
DESCRIPTION: 18.0 × 12.0 cm   Pp [i–v] vi [vii–viii],
[9] 10–384   Cloth
CONTENTS: i tp; ii blank; iii 'Preface' signed Mrs S.F.
McMaster, Treasurer, Hospital for Sick Children; iv
blank; v–vi 'A Letter to the Publishers' signed Geo.
Stewart Jr; vii 'Index' [i.e., table of contents]; viii blank;
9–384 text
COPIES: NBFU   *NSHP

NOTES: In this edition the verso of the title-page is
blank.

O20.7   1879
—Tried, tested, proved. / The / home cook book. /
Compiled by / ladies of Toronto and other cities and
towns / in Canada. / Toronto: / Rose-Belford
Publishing Company. / MDCCCLXXIX.
DESCRIPTION: 18.0 × 11.5 cm   Pp [1–2], [i–iii] iv [lacks
v–vi], [9] 10–384   Cloth
CONTENTS: 1 ht; 2 blank; i tp; ii 'Entered according to
Act of the Parliament of Canada, in the year one
thousand eight hundred and seventy-seven, by
Belford Brothers, in the office of the Minister of Agri-
culture. Printed and bound by Hunter, Rose & Co.,
Toronto.'; iii–iv 'A Letter to the Publishers'; v–vi lack-
ing; 9–384 text
COPIES: *Private collection
NOTES: The private collector's copy is stamped on the
title-page 'R.A.H. Morrow, 28, Charlotte Street, Saint
John, N.B.'

O20.8   1879
—Tried, tested, proved. / The / home cook book. /
Compiled by / ladies of Toronto and other cities and
/ towns in Canada. / Sold only by subscription. /
St. John, N.B.: / R.A.H. Morrow. / MDCCCLXXIX.
CONTENTS: Tp verso: 'Entered according to Act of the
Parliament of Canada, in the year one thousand eight
hundred and seventy-seven, by Belford Brothers, in
the office of the Minister of Agriculture. Printed and
bound by Hunter, Rose & Co., Toronto.'
COPIES: NSHMS (76.104.1)   *NSSXA   Private collec-
tion
NOTES: The NSSXA copy has the 'Preface' signed Mrs
S.F. McMaster, treasurer, Hospital for Sick Children.

Of the two copies found in private collections, one
is inscribed on the title-page, '"Liz" Xmas, 1879';
the book's owner reported that Liz was her late
husband's grandmother, Mrs Norman Cunningham
of Dartmouth, Nova Scotia, the former Elizabeth
McQueen from Sutherlands River, near New Glasgow.
A copy in another private collection is inscribed on
the endpaper, by the owner's great-grandmother, 'Mrs
Chas Vanwart // Woodstock May 27th 1883.'

O20.9   1879, entered 1880
—Tried, tested, proved. / The / home cook book. /
Compiled by / ladies of Toronto and other cities and
towns / in Canada. / Entered according to Act of
the Parliament of Canada, in the year one thousand
eight hundred / and eighty, by the Rose-Belford

Publishing Company, in the office of the Minister / of Agriculture. / Toronto: / Rose-Belford Publishing Company. / MDCCCLXXIX.

DESCRIPTION: 18.0 × 12.0 cm   Pp [1–2], [i–iii] iv–v [vi], [9] 10–384, [i]   Cloth

CONTENTS: 1 ht; 2 ad for W.J. Smith, 'manufacturer and dealer in coffees, spice, ginger // pepper, &c. self-raising flour and buckwheat,' 247 King Street West, Toronto; i tp; ii ad for Cook's Own Baking Powder manufactured by Hossack, Woods and Co., Quebec, which includes testimonials from Montreal and Quebec dated February and March 1880; iii–v 'A Letter to the Publishers' signed Geo. Stewart Jr; vi 'Index' [i.e., table of contents]; 9–384 text; i ad for G. Coleman, 111 King Street West, Toronto, and publ ad for Rose-Belford Publishing Co., Toronto, that lists books for sale (but not this cookbook)

COPIES: *Private collection

NOTES: On the title-page, the date entered for copyright (1880) is a year later than the date of publication in roman numerals (1879).

The private collector's copy is inscribed on the front endpaper, in ink, 'Miss Zorada Phelps // Knowlton // Quebec // Feb. 10th 1882.'

O20.10

—Tried, tested, proved. / The / home cook book. / Compiled by / ladies of Toronto and other cities and towns / in Canada. / Toronto: / Rose-Belford Publishing Company. / Paris: John S. Brown.

DESCRIPTION: 18.0 × 12.0 cm   Pp [i–iii] iv–v [vi–viii], [9] 10–384   Cloth imitating wood

CONTENTS: i tp; ii symbol of 'Hunter Rose & Co printers & binders. Toronto' and 'Entered according to Act of the Parlament [sic] of Canada, in the year one thousand eight hundred and seventy-seven, by Belford Brothers, in the office of the Minister of Agriculture.'; iii–v 'A Letter to the Publishers' signed Geo. Stewart Jr; vi blank; vii 'Index' [i.e., table of contents]; viii blank; 9–384 text

COPIES: *QKB

O20.11

—Tried, tested, proved. / The / home cook book. / Compiled by / ladies of Toronto and other cities and towns / in Canada. / Toronto: / Rose-Belford Publishing Company. / Paris: / John S. Brown.

CONTENTS: Tp verso symbol of 'Hunter Rose & Co printers & binders. Toronto' and 'Entered according to Act of the Parlament [sic] of Canada, in the year one thousand eight hundred and seventy-seven, by Belford Brothers, in the office of the Minister of Agriculture.'

COPIES: *OSTMYM

NOTES: Unlike the title-page of O20.10, 'Paris:' and 'John S. Brown' are on two lines, not one.

O20.12   1881

—Tried, tested, proved. / The / home cook book. / Compiled by / ladies of Toronto and other cities and towns / in Canada. / Toronto: / Rose-Belford Publishing Company. / 1881.

DESCRIPTION: 18.0 × 12.0 cm   Pp [i–iii] iv–v [vi], [9] 10–384   Cloth simulating leather

CONTENTS: i tp; ii 'Entered according to Act of the Parliament of Canada, in the year one thousand eight hundred and seventy-seven, by Belford Brothers, in the office of the Minister of Agriculture. Printed and bound by Hunter, Rose & Co. Toronto.'; iii–v 'A Letter to the Publishers' by Geo. Stewart Jr; vi 'Index' [i.e., table of contents]; 9–384

CITATIONS: Golick, pp 103, 105–7, 108–9, 109, illus p 106

COPIES: ACHP   BVAMM   OKITD (x962.275.001) OKQ (Special Collections uncat)   OTNY (641.5971 H)   *OTUTF (B-12 7843)   QSHERSH (641.5971 H765)

NOTES: The OKITD copy has a half-title, pp [1–2], but the page is loose in the volume. The OTNY copy lacks pp v–vi. Golick illustrates an ink drawing of a bird with ribbons in its beak, made on the front fly-leaf of the OTNY copy, and records the multiple inscriptions of versions of the name Mrs John Scott, Killean (in Puslinch Township, Wellington County, Ontario), one of which is dated 31 May 1881.

In 1881, the same year that this edition was published, Rose-Belford advertised *The Home Cook Book* in O29.1, *Cook's Friend Cook Book*, citing the price of $1.00 and boasting, 'Over 25,000 sold in Canada.'

O20.13   50th ed., [about 1881]

—Tried, tested, proved. / The / home cook book. / Compiled by / ladies of Toronto and other cities and towns / in Canada. / Fiftieth edition/ Toronto: / Rose-Belford Publishing Company.

DESCRIPTION: 18.0 × 12.0 cm   Pp [1–2], [i–iii] iv–v [vi], [9] 10–384   Cloth

CONTENTS: 1 ht; 2 blank; i tp; ii symbol of 'Hunter Rose & Co. Toronto printers & binders' and 'Entered according to Act of the Parlament [sic] of Canada, in the year one thousand eight hundred and seventy-seven, by Belford Brothers, in the office of the Minister of Agriculture.'; iii–v 'A Letter to the Publishers' signed Geo. Stewart Jr; vi 'Index' [i.e., table of contents]'; 9–384 text

COPIES: OKITD (x962.273.001)   *OL (R641.5 H752)

NOTES: On the title-page, the phrase 'other cities and towns' distinguishes this edition from O20.14, which has 'chief cities and towns.' The front endpaper advertisement (glued to the inside face of the binding) is for Cook's Friend Baking Powder.

The OL copy is inscribed on the front endpaper, in pencil, 'Mrs Harry Rundle. Exeter. Ontario.' The OKITD copy is inscribed on the front endpaper, in ink, 'Miss Sarah Snyder May 7th 1881'; it lacks pp v–vi.

O20.14   50th ed., [about 1882]
—Tried, tested, proved. / The / home cook book. / Compiled by / ladies of Toronto and chief cities and towns / in Canada. / Fiftieth edition. / Toronto: / Rose-Belford Publishing Company.
DESCRIPTION: 18.0 × 12.0 cm   Pp [1–2], [i–iii] iv–v [vi], [9] 10–384   Cloth imitating brown leather
CONTENTS: 1 ht; 2 blank; i tp; ii symbol of 'Hunter Rose & Co Toronto printers & binders' and 'Entered according to Act of the Parlament [sic] of Canada, in the year one thousand eight hundred and seventy-seven, by Belford Brothers, in the office of the Minister of Agriculture.'; iii–v 'A Letter to the Publishers' signed Geo. Stewart Jr; vi 'Index' [i.e., table of contents]; 9–384 text
COPIES: BVIPM   *OGU (UA s048 b35)   OTMCL (641.5971 H58 copy 2)
NOTES: The BVIPM copy is inscribed on the front endpaper, 'Mrs. John Macpherson // Fredericton November 1882.' The OTMCL copy lacks pp v–vi and 384.

O20.15   1882
—Tried, tested, proved. / The / home cook book. / Compiled by / ladies of Toronto and other cities and / towns in Canada. / Whitby, Ont. / J.S. Robertson & Bros., / 1882.
COPIES: *Private collection

O20.16   50th ed., [about 1883 or later]
—Tried, tested, proved. / The / home cook book. / Compiled by / ladies of Toronto and chief cities and towns / in Canada. / Fiftieth edition. / Toronto: / Rose Publishing Company.
COPIES: *OOWM (980.72.1)   OWTU (F0126)   Private collection
NOTES: On p ii there is no reference to the Canada Paper Co., as there is in O20.17. Rose Publishing Co. was active from 1 May 1883 to 1894, according to Hulse. Note, however, that in 1903 and 1906 Rose Publishing Co. published editions of *The New Cook Book* by Grace Denison (O130.1 and O130.4).

The OOWM copy is inscribed on the title-page, '(Margaret Cunningham Kilsythe) Mrs. David Douglas // Chesley Ont'; and opposite the title-page, 'An 1877 Cook Book. Donated to the Grey County Museum by her daughter Miss Myrtle Douglas // Chesley, Ontario.'

O20.17   50th ed., [about 1883–4]
—Tried, tested, proved. / The / home cook book. / Compiled by / ladies of Toronto and chief cities and towns / in Canada. / Fiftieth edition. / Toronto: / Rose Publishing Company.
DESCRIPTION: 18.0 × 12.0 cm   Pp [1–2], [i–iii] iv–v [vi], [9] 10–384   Cloth imitating brown leather
CONTENTS: 1 ht; 2 blank; i tp; ii 'Paper manufactured by Canada Paper Co Montreal & Toronto' [at top of page], 'Entered according to Act of the Parlament [sic] of Canada in the year one thousand eight hundred and seventy-seven, by Belford Brothers, in the office of the Minister of Agriculture.,' and symbol of 'Hunter Rose & Co printers & binders'; iii–v 'A Letter to the Publishers' signed Geo. Stewart Jr; vi 'Index' [i.e., table of contents]; 9–384 text
CITATIONS: Golick, p 111, illus   Wheaton/Kelly No. 6057 (cites incorrectly as 15th ed.)
COPIES: ACIA (No. LL.70.3.3)   ACU   BFSJNPM (968.74.01)   BKM   MBDHM   NBMOM   OAYM   OFFRH   OGOWSM   OGU (CCC TX715.6 H64 50th ed)   OKITJS (997.24.1)   OOAG (OB 641.5 H765)   OONL (TX715 H76 1877 p***)   OOSS (TX715 H66)   OOWM (x980.71.1)   OTMCL (641.5971 H58 copy 1)   OTNY (641.5971 H)   OWTU (F14431)   *Private collection; United States: MCR (641.6971 H76)
NOTES: The information on p ii about the Canada Paper Co. distinguishes this edition from O20.16. The MBDHM copy is inscribed with a ballpoint pen (i.e., in a modern hand), 'Given as a wedding gift to Mrs. Wm Snider in 1880.' If the publisher only began to use the name 'Rose Publishing Company' from 1883, then the year of the gift must be inaccurate. The ACIA copy, held at Fort Langley National Historic Park, is inscribed 'To Katie Taylor from Amie Dunn May 24th 1884 // KA[?] Willis // Dublin Castle.' The BFSJNPM copy is inscribed, opposite the title-page, '[first name illegible] Lowery // West Gravenhurst' and dated on the back endpaper, '[illegible] 1884.' The private collector's copy is inscribed on the front endpaper, 'Mrs Hosley // Shelburne [Onto?] 1889.' Another private collector's copy is inscribed with the date 2 January 1884. The OGU copy is inscribed on the front endpaper, in ink, 'Ella M Henry // Mono Mills Ontario.' The OWTU copy is stamped on the title-page, 'R.A.H. Morrow, 28 Char-

lotte Street, Saint John, N.B.' The OOAG copy lacks its binding.

O20.18   50th ed.
—Tried, tested, proved. / The / home cook book. / Compiled by / ladies of Toronto and chief cities and towns / in Canada. / Fiftieth edition. / Toronto and Whitby: / J.S. Robertson & Brothers.
CONTENTS: Tp verso symbol of Canada Paper Co., 'Entered according to Act of the Parlament [*sic*] of Canada in the year one thousand eight hundred and seventy-seven, by Belford Brothers, in the office of the Minister of Agriculture.,' and symbol of 'Hunter Rose & Co printers & binders.'
COPIES: *APROM
NOTES: This edition has 'A Letter to the Publishers' by George Stewart Jr. The front endpaper advertisement is for Cook's Friend Baking Powder and cites medals won in 1882. The APROM copy is inscribed on the front endpaper, 'Mrs D. Watt.'

O20.19   50th ed.
—Tried, tested, proved. / The / home cook book / Compiled by / ladies of Toronto and chief cities and towns / in Canada. / Fiftieth edition. / Whitby: / J.S. Robertson & Brothers.
DESCRIPTION: 18.0 × 12.0 cm   Pp [i–iii] iv–xi [xii], [9] 10–384   Cloth
CONTENTS: i tp; ii 'Paper manufactured by Canada Paper Co Montreal & Toronto // Entered according to Act of the Parlament [*sic*] of Canada in the year one thousand eight hundred and seventy-seven, by Belford Brothers, in the office of the Minister of Agriculture,' and symbol of Hunter Rose and Co., printers and binders; iii–xi 'Contents' [i.e., index]; xii blank; 9–384 text
COPIES: *OTUTF (B-12 7844)
NOTES: O20.18 has 'Toronto and Whitby' on the title-page; this edition has only 'Whitby.' Here there is an index on pp iii–xi called 'Contents'; all previously cited editions that I examined have a one-page table of contents called 'Index.'

The title-page is printed on a leaf of smaller dimensions (about 17.0 × 11.5 cm) than the rest of the volume and it is glued to p iii at the left edge. The endpaper advertisement opposite the title-page is for Cook's Friend Baking Powder and cites medals won in 1882.

O20.20   50th ed.
—Tried, tested, proved. / The / home cook book / Compiled by / ladies of Toronto and chief cities and towns / in Canada. / Fiftieth edition. / Whitby: / Robertson Brothers.
COPIES: *Private collection
NOTES: Like O20.19, this edition has only 'Whitby' on the title-page; however, the publisher's name is 'Robertson Brothers' (no initials, no conjunction), not 'J.S. Robertson & Brothers.' Like O20.19, the title-page appears to be glued to p iii at the left edge (evident in the photocopy of the title-page supplied by the book's owner); and there is an endpaper advertisement opposite the title-page for Cook's Friend Baking Powder that cites medals won in 1882.

O20.21   1883
—Tried, tested, proved. / The / home cook book. / Compiled by / ladies of Toronto and other cities and towns / in Canada. / Sold by subscription. / Toronto and Whitby: / J.S. Robertson & Bros., / 1883.
DESCRIPTION: 18.0 × 11.5 cm   Pp [1–2], [i–iii] iv–v [vi], [9] 10–384   Cloth
CONTENTS: 1 ht; 2 blank; i tp; ii blank; iii–v 'A Letter to the Publishers' signed Geo. Stewart Jr; vi 'Index' [i.e., table of contents]; 9–384 text
COPIES: *Private collection

O20.22   60th ed.
—Tried, tested, proved. / The / home cook book. / Compiled by / ladies of Toronto and chief cities and towns / in Canada. / Sixtieth edition. / Toronto: / J.S. Robertson & Brothers.
DESCRIPTION: Pp [i–iii] iv–xi [xii], [9] 10–...   Cloth
CONTENTS: i tp; ii 'Entered according to Act of the Parliament of Canada, in the year one thousand eight hundred and seventy-seven, by Belford Brothers, in the office of the Minister of Agriculture.' and symbol of 'Hunter Rose & Co. printers & binders'; iii–xi 'Contents' [i.e., index]; xii blank; 9– text
COPIES: OONMM (TX715 H6)   *Private collection

O20.23   60th ed.
—Tried, tested, proved. / The / home cook book. / Compiled by / ladies of Toronto, and chief cities and towns / in Canada. / Sixtieth edition. / Toronto: / Rose Publishing Company.
DESCRIPTION: 18.0 × 12.0 cm   Pp [1–2], [i–iii] iv–v [vi], [9] 10–384   Cloth imitating wood grain
CONTENTS: 1 ht; 2 blank; i tp; ii 'Paper manufactured by Canada Paper Co Montreal & Toronto' [at top of page], 'Entered according to Act of the Parlament [*sic*] of Canada in the year one thousand eight hundred and seventy-seven, by Belford Brothers, in the office of the Minister of Agriculture.,' and symbol of 'Hunter Rose & Co. printers & binders'; iii–v 'A Letter to the Publishers' signed Geo. Stewart Jr; vi table of contents; 9–384 text

COPIES: NBFKL   OKITD (x962.277.001)   OW   *Private collection

NOTES: On the title-page, note the comma after 'ladies of Toronto,' – not in O20.24. The design also varies; for example, here there is a wavy rule above the short-title, which has tall initial capitals (H, C, B) – O20.24 has a straight rule and same-size capitals. A front endpaper advertisement for Cook's Friend Baking Powder cites medals awarded in 1882.

O20.24   60th ed., [about 1887]
—Tried, tested, proved. / The / home cook book. / Compiled by / ladies of Toronto and chief cities and towns / in Canada. / Sixtieth edition. / Toronto: / Rose Publishing Company.

DESCRIPTION: 18.0 × 12.0 cm   Pp [i–iii] iv–xi [xii], [9] 10–384   Cloth

CONTENTS: i tp; ii 'Entered according to Act of the Parliament of Canada, in the year one thousand eight hundred and seventy-seven, by Belford Brothers, in the office of the Minister of Agriculture.' and symbol of 'Hunter Rose & Co. printers & binders'; iii–xi 'Contents' [i.e., index]; xii blank; 9–384 text

CITATIONS: Driver 2001, Wellington County, p 95

COPIES: *OFERWM (A1990.7)   OGU (CCC TX715.6 H64)   OKITD (956.019.019)   OSTC (640.2 Hom)

NOTES: Unlike O20.23, there is no reference to the Canada Paper Co. or 'A Letter to the Publishers.'

The OFERWM copy of O20.24 is inscribed on the front endpaper, in ink, 'Miss Margret [*sic*] Gregson's book // Erin Apr 29/1887 A.D. Ont' (Erin is in Ontario, east of Fergus and south of Orangeville). This edition was likely published in the same year as the inscription.

The OKITD copy has an advertisement on the inside front face of the binding for Cook's Friend Baking Powder that cites medals won in 1883. The OKITD copy is stamped on the front endpaper, 'Polly B Gropp.'

O20.25   60th ed., 1887
—Tried, tested, proved. / The / home cook book. / Compiled by / ladies of Toronto and chief cities and towns / in Canada. / Sixtieth edition. / London: / McDermid & Logan, / 1887.

COPIES: *Bookseller's stock

O20.26   70th ed., 1887
—Tried, tested, proved. / The / home cook book. / Compiled by / ladies of Toronto and chief cities and towns / in Canada. / Seventieth edition. / Toronto: / Rose Publishing Company. / Barrie: – W.B. Baikie. / 1887.

DESCRIPTION: 18.0 × 12.0 cm   Pp [i–iii] iv–xi [xii], [9] 10–382 [leaf lacking]   Cloth, with floral pattern

CONTENTS: i tp; ii 'Entered according to Act of the Parliament of Canada, in the year one thousand eight hundred and seventy-seven, by Belford Brothers, in the office of the Minister of Agriculture.' and symbol of Hunter, Rose and Co., printers and binders, Toronto; iii–xi 'Contents' [i.e., index]; xii blank; 9–382 text

CITATIONS: Golick, p 33

COPIES: *AMHM   OBM   OTNY (641.5971 H)   OTUTF (B-12 7845)

NOTES: The OTUTF copy is complete and includes the last leaf, pp 383–4. It is bound in cloth coloured brown with tinges of red and green, and marked with a pattern of veins. The volume is inscribed on the front endpaper, in pencil, 'Mother Barclay's cook book.'

The OTNY copy is bound in cloth simulating leather(?); the cloth has no floral pattern.

O20.27   70th ed., 1887
—Tried! Tested! Proven! / The / home cook book. / Compiled by / ladies of Toronto and chief cities and towns / in Canada. / Seventieth edition. / Toronto: / J.S. Robertson & Brothers. / 1887.

COPIES: *Private collection

NOTES: On the title-page of this and subsequent editions, the recipes are described as 'Tried! Tested! Proven!' where previously they were 'Tried, Tested, Proved.'

O20.28   70th ed., 1887
—Tried! Tested! Proven! / The / home cook book. / Compiled by / ladies of Toronto and chief cities and towns / in Canada. / Seventieth edition. / Toronto: / Rose Publishing Company. / 1887.

DESCRIPTION: 18.0 × 12.0 cm   Pp [i–iii] iv–xi [xii], [9] 10–384   Cloth, with floral pattern

CONTENTS: i tp; ii 'Entered according to Act of the Parliament of Canada, in the year one thousand eight hundred and seventy-seven, by Belford Brothers, in the office of the Minister of Agriculture.' and symbol of 'Hunter Rose & Co printers & binders. Toronto'; iii–xi 'Contents' [i.e., index]; xii blank; 9–384 text

COPIES: *NBDKH   OKITD (978.081.013)   OKITJS (991.41.1)   OMIHURM   OPETCM   QMM (RBD TX715.6 H65 1887)

NOTES: The cloth binding of the OKITD and QMM copies has a pattern simulating wood grain, not a floral pattern. The OKITD copy is inscribed on the front endpaper, in ink, 'Lydia Witmer, Berlin, Ont. My first Cook Book purchased in Guelph, Ontario, Nov. or Dec. 1887.' The OKITJS copy is stamped on the front endpaper, 'Amos Shantz, Berlin, Ont.'

O20.29 70th ed., 1888

—Tried! Tested! Proven! / The / home cook book. / Compiled by / ladies of Toronto and chief cities and towns / in Canada. / Seventieth edition. / Toronto: / Rose Publishing Company. / 1888

DESCRIPTION: 18.0 × 12.0 cm   Pp [i–ii] [lacks iii–iv] v–xi [xii], [9] 10–350 [lacks 351 onward]   Lacks binding

CONTENTS: i tp; ii 'Entered according to Act of the Parliament of Canada, in the year one thousand eight hundred and seventy-seven, by Belford Brothers, in the office of the Minister of Agriculture.' and symbol of 'Hunter, Rose & Co., printers & binders. Toronto'; iii–iv lacking; v–xi index; xii blank; 9–350 text

CITATIONS: Driver 2001, Wellington County, p 95

COPIES: CIHM (06848)   OCN (FJ.XX.252)   OFERWM (A1991.92)   OGU (2 copies: *CCC TX715.6 H66 1888, UA s068 b30)   OONL (TX715 H76 1888)   OTU (TX715 H6 1888 Gerstein)   Private collection

NOTES: The Abrahamson copy at OGU is inscribed on the front endpaper, in pencil, 'Minnie H[i?]nson July 20th 1889 Toronto Canada // [In another hand, in ink:] Mrs Thos. Dowswell // Goodwood Ont.' The OONL and OTU copies are rebound; neither has advertisements. The OTU copy is from the estate of Effie M.K. Glass.

A private collector has a copy in its original cloth binding. The front endpapers have advertisements for Cook's Friend Baking Powder, for the pianos and organs of W. Bell and Co., Guelph, Ontario, and for Kerry, Watson and Co. The pagination at the end of the text runs: –384, [i–viii]; pp i–viii are advertisements.

The OFERWM copy matches the private collector's copy, except that it lacks pp 378 onward. It is inscribed on the recto of the blank leaf before the title-page, in blue pencil: 'Mary / Jean [crossed through] / Smith' ('Jean' may have been crossed through later and 'Mary' added then). The copy is also inscribed on the back endpaper, in red pencil, 'Jean Smith / wife Donald Smith' and 'Jean [Ramsay?].'

On the title-page of some copies of this edition, a printed period registered after '1888,' but in other copies no period is visible.

O20.30 70th ed., 1889

—Tried! Tested! Proven! / The / home cook book. / Compiled by / ladies of Toronto and chief cities and towns / in Canada. / Seventieth edition. / Toronto: / Rose Publishing Company. / 1889.

DESCRIPTION: 18.0 × 12.0 cm   Pp [i–iii] iv–xi [xii], [9] 10–384   Cloth

CONTENTS: i tp; ii 'Entered according to Act of the Parliament of Canada, in the year one thousand eight hundred and seventy-seven, by Belford Brothers, in the office of the Minister of Agriculture.' and symbol of 'Hunter, Rose & Co. printers & binders Toronto'; iii–xi 'Contents' [i.e., index]; xii blank; 9–384 text

COPIES: ACG   ACHP (HP 3223/8)   OGU (TX715.6 H66 1889)   OKITWN   OPPSSHM   OSHT   OTUTF (B-12 7846)   *Private collection; Great Britain: LCoF

NOTES: On the title-page of the private collector's, ACG, and OTUTF copies, 'Seventieth edition.' is set in italic. On the title-page of the ACHP, OKITWN, and OPPSSHM copies, the edition number is set in roman. I did not note this variation for the OGU and OSHT copies.

The private collector's copy is inscribed by the owner's great-grandmother, on the blank leaf before the title-page, in pencil, 'Mrs Maurice Downing // Kingsville // St John N.B.' [Mrs Downing's maiden name was Sarah Olive Pond].

O20.31 70th ed., 1889

—Tried! Tested! Proven! / The / home cook book. / Compiled by / ladies of Toronto and chief cities and towns / in Canada. / Seventieth edition. / London: / McDermid & Logan, / 1889.

DESCRIPTION: 18.0 × 12.0 cm   Pp [i–iii] iv–xi [xii], [9] 10–384   Cloth

CONTENTS: i tp; ii 'Entered according to Act of the Parliament of Canada, in the year one thousand eight hundred and seventy-seven, by Belford Brothers, in the office of the Minister of Agriculture.' and symbol of 'Hunter Rose & Co. printers & binders. Toronto'; iii–xi 'Contents'; xii blank; 9–384 text

COPIES: *QKB (72-20)

O20.32 70th ed.

—Tried! Tested! Proven! / The / home cook book. / Compiled by / ladies of Toronto and chief cities and towns / in Canada / Seventieth edition / Toronto: / Rose Publishing Company.

DESCRIPTION: 17.5 × 11.5 cm   Pp [i–iii] iv–xi [xii], [9] 10–384   Rebound

CONTENTS: i tp; ii 'Entered according to Act of the Parliament of Canada, in the year one thousand eight hundred and seventy-seven, by Belford Brothers, in the office of the Minister of Agriculture.' and symbol of 'Hunter, Rose & Co. printers & binders Toronto'; iii–xi 'Contents' [i.e., index]; xii blank; 9–384 text

COPIES: BKM   BRMA   BVA   MWPA   NSYHM   *OONL (TX715 H76 1888 copy 2)   OTAG   OUSH   OWOOXH   OWTU (TX715 H58 1877 Conrad Grebel College); United States: IaU (SPEC SZAT TX715 H76 1877)

NOTES: In the printing of the title-page of this edition, sometimes the period after 'Canada' did not register (for example, the copy at OONL). The BKM copy is inscribed on the front endpaper, in pencil: 'Miss Beattie // Kamloops B.C. July 7th 1900 // Minnie Beattie // Kamloops. B.C. July 7th 1900.' A private collector has a copy of the seventieth edition by Rose Publishing Co., likely O20.32, which she describes as 'purchased in Toronto February 23rd, 1894.'

O20.33   70th ed., 1894
—Tried! Tested! Proven! / The / home cook book. / Compiled by / ladies of Toronto and chief cities and towns / in Canada / Seventieth edition. / Toronto: / Hunter, Rose and Company. / 1894.
DESCRIPTION: 18.0 × 12.0 cm   Pp [i–iii] iv–xi [xii], [9] 10–384   Cloth imitating leather
CONTENTS: i tp; ii 'Entered according to Act of the Parliament of Canada, in the year one thousand eight hundred and seventy-seven, by Belford Brothers, in the office of the Minister of Agriculture.' and symbol of 'Hunter, Rose & Co. printers & binders Toronto'; iii–xi 'Contents' [i.e., index]; xii blank; 9–384 text
COPIES: OMINL   OONL (TX715 H76 1894 p***)   *Private collection
NOTES: This edition was published in the same year that the Rose Publishing Co. failed. The OONL copy is inscribed on the front endpaper, in ink, 'Edith Brown. 1896'; and it is stamped on the title-page, 'Golden Lion Book Dep't Books & Stat'y at reduced prices. R. Walker & Sons, Toronto.'

O20.34   70th ed., [about 1897]
—Tried! Tested! Proven! / The / home cook book. / Compiled by / ladies of Toronto and chief cities and towns / in Canada. / Seventieth edition. / Toronto: / Hunter, Rose and Company.
DESCRIPTION: 18.0 × 12.0 cm   Pp [i–iii] iv–xi [xii], [i–iv], [9] 10–384, [i–iv]   Cloth
CONTENTS: i tp; ii 'Entered according to Act of the Parliament of Canada, in the year one thousand eight hundred and seventy-seven, by Belford Brothers, in the office of the Minister of Agriculture.' and symbol of 'Hunter Rose & Co printers & binders Toronto'; iii–xi table of contents; xii blank; i–iv Michie and Co. ads; 9–384 text and several leaves of ads not included in the pagination; i–ii blank; iii–iv endpaper ads for Michie and Co.
COPIES: *OTYA (TX715 H6 1888)
NOTES: 'The Home Cook Book. Compliments [of?] Michie & [Co.?], Tor[onto]' is stamped in gold on the front face of the binding. Michie and Co., founded in

1835, had stores at 51–2 and 7 King Street West, 6 and 8 Melinda Street, and 466 and 468 Spadina Avenue, and the unpaginated leaves of advertisements throughout the book are for products they offered for sale, such as Edwardsburg Starches, Kingsford's Oswego Corn Starch, Queen City Mills Flour, and Charles Wilson's ginger ale.

This edition was likely published about 1897, the year of a pencil annotation next to Sweet Manchester Pudding on p 185, 'Have made this. Aug. 1897.' A publication date of about 1897 is confirmed by the advertisement opposite p 156 for Smith's Toronto Dye Works, 75 King Street West, 'Established 50 years': the earliest identified listing in Toronto city directories for David Smith, dyer, 62 King Street West (he later moved to 75 King), is in the 1846–7 directory (there is no listing for David Smith for 1843–4). The book is unlikely to have been published earlier than the 1897 annotation since an advertisement after p xii (blank) for Edwardsburg Starches refers to 'nearly half a century' that the product has had the highest reputation, and the Canada Starch Works was founded in 1858. At the possible time of the book's publication (1897), therefore, Edwardsburg Starches had been manufactured for thirty-nine years. The book could not have been published before the founding of the Queen City Flour Mills in 1893. The advertisement for Kingsford's Oswego Corn Starch, opposite p 28, cites an award of 1893, further evidence that this edition could not have been published before 1893.

The OTYA copy is inscribed on the front endpaper, in pencil, 'Mrs John Ransford // [S. or G.?]H. Clinton // Ontario Canada March 22th [sic] 1901.'

O20.35   70th ed., [about 1895–8]
—Tried! Tested! Proven! / The / home cook book. / Compiled by / ladies of Toronto and chief cities and towns / in Canada. / Seventieth edition. / Toronto: / G.M. Rose & Sons.
DESCRIPTION: 18.0 × 12.0 cm   Pp [i–iii] iv–xi [xii], [9] 10–384   Cloth imitating leather(?)
CONTENTS: i tp; ii 'Entered according to Act of the Parliament of Canada, in the year one thousand eight hundred and seventy-seven, by Belford Brothers, in the office of the Minister of Agriculture.' and symbol of 'Hunter, Rose & Co. printers & binders Toronto'; iii–xi 'Contents' [i.e., index]; xii blank; 9–384 text
COPIES: OONMM (TX715 H6 1877)   *Private collection
NOTES: G.M. Rose and Sons was active from 1 November 1895, incorporated in 1898, and dissolved in 1901.

O20.36 79th ed., [about 1895–8]
—Tried! Tested! Proven! / The / home cook book. / Compiled by / ladies of Toronto and chief cities and / towns in Canada. / Seventy-ninth edition. / Toronto: / G.M. Rose & Sons.
DESCRIPTION: 18.0 × 12.0 cm   Pp [i–iii] iv–xi [xii], [9] 10–384   Cloth
CONTENTS: i tp; ii 'Entered according to Act of the Parliament of Canada, in the year one thousand eight hundred and seventy-seven, by Belford Brothers, in the office of the Minister of Agriculture.' and symbol of 'Hunter, Rose & Co. printers & binders Toronto'; iii–xi 'Contents' [i.e., index]; xii blank; 9–384 text
CITATIONS: Armstrong 2000, p F2
COPIES: OTSHH   OVOH (976.59.1)   *Private collection

O20.37 79th ed., [about 1898–1901]
—Tried! Tested! Proven! / The / home cook book. / Compiled by / ladies of Toronto and chief cities and / towns in Canada. / Seventy-ninth edition. / Toronto: / G.M. Rose & Sons Co. Limited.
DESCRIPTION: 18.0 × 12.0 cm   Pp [i–iii] iv–xi [xii], [9] 10–380 [381–4]   Cloth
CONTENTS: i tp; ii 'Entered according to Act of the Parliament of Canada, in the year one thousand eight hundred and seventy-seven, by Belford Brothers, in the office of the Minister of Agriculture.' and symbol of 'Hunter, Rose & Co. printers & binders Toronto'; iii–xi 'Contents' [i.e., index]; xii blank; 9–384 text
COPIES: MAUAM   *OGU (CCC TX715.6 H64 79th ed)   SSWD
NOTES: Here the publisher's name is given as 'G.M. Rose & Sons Co. Limited,' indicating that the book was published no earlier than 1898, when the business was incorporated. The OGU copy is stamped on the title-page, 'Baysville [i.e., in Ontario] Public Library.'

O20.38 [about 1901]
—Tried! Tested! Proven! / The / home cook book / Compiled by / ladies of Toronto and chief cities and towns / in Ontario / Winnipeg / Russell Lang & Company
DESCRIPTION: 19.0 × 12.5 cm   Pp [i–iii] iv–xi [xii], [9] 10–380 [381–4]   Cloth
CONTENTS: i tp; ii 'Entered according to Act of the Parliament of Canada, in the year one thousand eight hundred and seventy-seven, by Belford Brothers in the office of the Minister of Agriculture.'; iii–xi 'Contents' [i.e., index]; xii blank; 9–384 text
COPIES: *Private collection
NOTES: The first listing for Russell Lang and Co. (W.D. Russell and Lisgar L. Lang), booksellers and statio-

ners, in Henderson's Winnipeg city directory is in the volume for 1901 (before 1901, the business was called Russell and Co.). The appearance of this edition of *The Home Cook Book* is consistent with publication in 1901. The owner's grandmother (probably the book's original owner) moved out West just after the turn of the century.

O20.39 [about 1908]
—Tried! Tested! Proven! / The / home cook book / Compiled by / ladies of Toronto and chief cities and towns / in Canada / The Musson Book Co., Limited / Toronto
DESCRIPTION: Pp [i–iii] iv–xi [xii], [9] 10–380 [381–4]
CONTENTS: i tp; ii 'Entered according to Act of the Parliament of Canada, in the year one thousand eight hundred and seventy-seven, by Belford Brothers in the office of the Minister of Agriculture.'; iii–xi 'Contents' [i.e., index]; xii blank; 9–384 text
COPIES: *MCDHM   OTUTF (B-12 7847)
NOTES: The Musson Book Co. was active from 1898. The order of publication of the various undated and unnumbered Musson editions (O20.39–20.42) is unknown. The MCDHM copy is inscribed on the front endpaper, in ink, 'Mrs John R Waddell Dec 25 1908. Sperling Man.' The OTUTF copy has the lower right corner of the title-page torn off so that 'Co., Limited' is missing.

O20.40
—Tried! Tested! Proven! / The / home cook book / Compiled by / ladies of Toronto and chief cities and towns / in Ontario / Toronto: / The Musson Book Company, Limited
DESCRIPTION: 19.0 × 12.5 cm   Pp [i–iii] iv–xi [xii], [9] 10–380 [381–4]   Cloth
CONTENTS: i tp; ii 'Entered according to Act of the Parliament of Canada, in the year one thousand eight hundred and seventy-seven, by Belford Brothers in the office of the Minister of Agriculture.'; iii–xi 'Contents' [i.e., index]; xii blank; 9–384 text
COPIES: *OKITD (970.094.002)
NOTES: The OKITD copy is stamped on the back endpaper, 'E.P. Stewart druggist & stationer Rouleau, Sask.' Here the title-page refers to 'cities and towns in Ontario'; O20.39 says, 'in Canada.' For the differences between O20.40 and O20.41, see O20.41.

O20.41
—Tried! Tested! Proven! / The / home cook book / Compiled by / ladies of Toronto and chief cities and towns / in Ontario / Toronto / The Musson Book Company, Limited

CONTENTS: i tp; ii 'Entered according to Act of the Parliament of Canada, in the year one thousand eight hundred and seventy-seven, by Belford Brothers in the office of the Minister of Agriculture.'; iii– 'Contents' [i.e., index]; ...

COPIES: *OOWM (974.17.1)

NOTES: There are two differences between the title-pages of O20.40 and this edition. Here there is no full colon after 'Toronto' in the imprint. Also, each imprint is in a different setting of type: in O20.40, 'Toronto:' is clearly in a smaller type size than the publisher's name; here, city and publisher are set in the same size type.

The OOWM copy is inscribed on p ii, 'Mrs. I.A. Lamson // Owen Sound Ontario 787 10th str. East.'

O20.42   nd

—Tried! Tested! Proven! / The / home cook book / Compiled by / ladies of Toronto and chief cities and towns / in Canada / The Musson Book Co., Limited / Toronto

DESCRIPTION: 19.0 × 12.5 cm   Pp [i–iii] iv–xi [xii], [9] 10–380 [381–4]   Cloth, with floral pattern

CONTENTS: i tp; ii blank; iii–xi index; xii blank; 9–384 text

COPIES: *MWPA

NOTES: There is no copyright notice on the title-page verso of this edition or O20.45–20.48.

O20.43   nd [before 1917]

—Tried! Tested! Proven! / The / home cook book / Compiled by / ladies of Toronto and chief cities and towns / in Canada / Consolidated Stationery Co., Limited / Winnipeg

COPIES: *OKELWM

NOTES: The small decorative device on the title-page (a spherical shape with vertical stripes) is identical to the one found on the title-pages of O20.39–20.42, all published by Musson, and the one on the title-page of O20.47 published by Hunter Rose. From 1917, Winnipeg city directories list the publisher as Consolidated Stationery and Fancy Goods Co. Ltd, marking a change from the simpler name, Consolidated Stationery Co. Ltd. This edition, therefore, was published before 1917, but likely after the turn of the century.

Consolidated Stationery Co. Ltd published the first community cookbook in Manitoba, M2.1, *The Souvenir Cook Book* of 1896, which uses the phrase 'Tried! Tested! Proved!' from earlier editions of *The Home Cook Book*.

O20.44   100th ed., 1918

—Tried! Tested! Proven! / The / home cook book / Compiled by / ladies of Toronto and chief cities and towns / in Canada / One hundredth edition / Toronto: / The Musson Book Co., Limited. / 1918

COPIES: OUSH   *OW

NOTES: There were two 1918 editions, numbered one hundredth: this one with Musson Book Co. on the title-page and O20.45 with Hunter-Rose Co. The title-page transcription is from a photocopy of the title-page received from OW in 1991. What is probably the same volume now lacks its title-page.

O20.45   100th ed., 1918

—Tried! Tested! Proven! / The / home cook book / Compiled by / ladies of Toronto and chief cities and towns / in Canada / One hundredth edition / Toronto: / The Hunter-Rose Co., Limited / 1918

DESCRIPTION: 19.0 × 12.5 cm   Pp [i–iii] iv–xi [xii], [9] 10–379 [380–4]   Cloth, with 'Musson' on the spine

CONTENTS: i tp; ii blank; iii–xi 'Contents' [i.e., index]; xii blank; 9–384 text

COPIES: *QMM (RBD ckbk 1667)

O20.46   100th ed., 1923

—Tried! Tested! Proven! / The / home cook book / Compiled by / ladies of Toronto and chief cities and towns / in Canada / One hundredth edition / Toronto: / The Hunter-Rose Co., Limited / 1923

DESCRIPTION: 18.5 × 12.0 cm   Pp [i–iii] iv–xi [xii], [9] 10–379 [380–4]   Cloth, with 'Household Library // Musson' on the spine

CONTENTS: i tp; ii blank; iii–xi 'Contents' [i.e., index]; xii blank; 9–384 text

CITATIONS: Ferguson/Fraser, p 233, illus col on p 57 of closed volume   Golick, p 108

COPIES: OH (R641.5 H752 CESC)   OTUTF (B-12 7849)   *Private collection

O20.47   nd

—Tried! Tested ! Proven! / The / home cook book / Compiled by / ladies of Toronto and chief cities and towns / in Canada / Toronto: / The Hunter-Rose Company, Limited

DESCRIPTION: 18.5 × 12.5 cm   Pp [i–iii] iv–xi [xii], [9] 10–379 [380–4]   Cloth with blue veins

CONTENTS: i tp; ii blank; iii–xi 'Contents' [i.e., index]; xii blank; 9–384 text

COPIES: *OTUTF (B-12 7848)

NOTES: There is no date or edition number, but from appearances, this edition was published in the twentieth century.

O20.48 100th ed., 1929
—Tried! Tested! Proven! / The / home cook book /
Compiled by / ladies of Toronto and chief cities and
towns / in Canada / One hundredth edition /
Toronto / The Musson Book Company / 1929
DESCRIPTION: 18.5 × 12.0 cm   Pp [i–iii] iv–xi [xii], [9]
10–379 [380–4]   Cloth
CONTENTS: i tp; ii blank; iii–xi 'Contents' [i.e., index];
xii blank; 9–384 text
CITATIONS: Ferguson/Fraser, p 233
COPIES: *OGU (UA s048 b39)   OONL (TX715 H76
1929)   OTNY (641.5971 H)

O20.49 [facsimile, 1970]
—Tried! Tested! Proven! / The Canadian / home
cook book / Compiled by / ladies of Toronto and
chief cities and towns / in Canada / Toronto /
Hunter, Rose and Company. / 1877
DESCRIPTION: 21.0 × 13.5 cm   Pp [i–iv] v–xi [xii], [9]
10–380 [381–4]   Paper
CONTENTS: i tp; ii 'A reprint of the original edition //
1970 Ontario Reprint Press Toronto'; iii–xi 'Contents'
[i.e., index]; xii blank; 9–384 text
CITATIONS: Ferguson/Fraser, p 232
COPIES: OMIH   OONL (TX715 C35 1970)   OTNYE
(641.5971 CAN)   OTU (TX715 H65 1970)   OTYA
(TX715 C23 1970)   *Private collection
NOTES: The title-page is a fake: No contemporary edi-
tions include 'Canadian' in the title; the only known
copy of the 1877 edition gives the date in roman
numerals, not arabic; and the earliest edition where
Hunter, Rose and Co. appears on the title-page is
O20.33, dated 1894 (Hunter, Rose bound the first
edition, and printed and bound editions from 1878).
The 1970, 1971, and 1980 facsimiles were made from
a later, unidentified edition (an edition without
Stewart's 'Letter to the Publishers'). Although these
facsimiles served to bring this important book to a
wide audience, they have obscured the real history of
the cookbook and perpetrated an incorrect title.

O20.50 [facsimile, 1971]
—Tried! Tested! Proven! / The Canadian / home
cook book / Compiled by / ladies of Toronto and
chief cities and towns / in Canada / Toronto /
Hunter, Rose and Company. / 1877
DESCRIPTION: 21.0 × 13.5 cm   Pp [i–iv] v–xi [xii], [9] 10–
380 [381–4]   Paper, identical to 1970 facsimile
except for 'Coles Canadiana Collection' on spine
CONTENTS: i tp; ii 'Coles Canadiana Collection //
Originally published in 1877 in Toronto, Canada by
Hunter Rose and Co. Facsimile edition reprinted by

Coles Publishing Company, Toronto © Copyright
1971.'; iii–xi 'Contents'; xii blank; 9–384 text
CITATIONS: Carrière No. 90   Ferguson/Fraser, p 232
COPIES: AC   ACU   AEU (TX715 C19 1971)   BVAU
MRIP   NBSU (TX715.C3 1877a)   NSHMS   NSWA
OCN   OKQ (TX715 C3 1971t)   OL (R641.5
C16)   OLU (TX715 C18 1971)   OOC (641.5
C2121)   OOCC (TX715.6 C35)   OONMM (TX415 C36
1971)   OOSH (641.5971   CAN)   OPETCM
OTEYBE (641.5 CAN)   OTMCL (641.5971 H58
1971)   OTNY (uncat)   OTY (TX415 C22)   OTYA
(TX415 C22)   OWT   OWYL   QMAC (TX715 C3)
QMBM (641.5 C212ca)   QMM (TX715 C3x 1971; 2
copies)   *Private collection; United States: MCR
(641.6971 C212c)

O20.51 [facsimile, 1980]
—Tried! Tested! Proven! / The Canadian / home
cook book / Compiled by / ladies of Toronto and
chief cities and towns / in Canada / Toronto /
Hunter, Rose and Company. / 1877
CONTENTS: Tp verso 'Coles Canadiana Collection //
Originally published in 1877 in Toronto, Canada by
Hunter Rose and Co. // Facsimile edition reprinted
by Coles Publishing Company, Toronto © Copyright
1980.'
COPIES: *MW   OGOWSM   OGU (Rural Heritage
Collection uncat and UA s066 b11)   OKQ (TX715 C35
1980t)

O20.52 [facsimile, 2002]
—Tried, tested, proved. / The / home cook book. /
Compiled from recipes contributed by ladies of
Toronto and / other cities and towns: Published for
the benefit / of the Hospital for Sick Children. /
Whitecap
DESCRIPTION: 19.0 × 12.5 cm   Pp [i–vi] vii–ix [x–xi] xii–
xxiii [xxiv], [9] 10–384   Paper-covered boards, with
photograph on front of Mrs McMaster
CONTENTS: i ht; ii blank; iii tp; iv information about the
facsimile, 'Copyright © Elizabeth Driver 2002 //
Whitecap Books,' publisher's disclaimer concern-
ing the nineteenth-century recipes, and 'Printed in
Canada'; v 'Contents'; vi–vii 'Guidelines for Modern
Cooks'; viii–ix 'A Letter to the Publishers' signed
George Stewart Jr; x 'Preface' signed Mrs S.F.
McMaster; xi–xxiii 'Introduction' by Elizabeth Driver;
xxiv blank; 9–384 text
CITATIONS: Hobsbawn-Smith, Dee, 'Old-fashioned
Baking a Virtue,' *Calgary Herald* 20 June 2002, p E7
Neering, pp 61, 63, 67–8, 69, 78, 81
COPIES: *Private collection

NOTES: This edition celebrates the 125th aniversary of the book's first publication. The facsimile is of O20.3, one of the two 1878 variants by Rose-Belford. Added to the facsimile are a resetting of Mrs McMaster's 'Preface' from O20.4, 'Guidelines for Modern Cooks' explaining how to interpret the recipes, and an 'Introduction' relating the story behind the book.

AUSTRALIAN EDITIONS: The following describes an edition published in Sydney in what was then the British colony of New South Wales:

Tried! Tested! Proven! / The / home cook book. / Compiled by / ladies of Toronto and chief cities and / towns in Canada. / Seventy-fifth edition. / Sydney, N.S.W.: / Fraser & Fraser. / Toronto, Canada: Rose Publishing Co.
DESCRIPTION: 17.5 × 11.5 cm   Pp [i–iii] iv–xi [xii], [9] 10–380 [leaves lacking?]   Lacks binding
CONTENTS: i tp; ii 'Entered according to Act of the Parliament of Canada, in the year one thousand eight hundred and seventy-seven, by Belford Brothers, in the office of the Minister of Agriculture.' and symbol of 'Hunter, Rose & Co. printers & binders Toronto'; iii–xi 'Contents' [i.e., index]; xii blank; 9–380 text
COPIES: OGU *Private collection; Australia: ACN (641.5 H 765–75)   NSM (2 copies: 641.5 408, 641.5 408A)   SAS (not on shelf)   VMU (641.5 H 765/75)
NOTES: That Rose Publishing Co. entered into an agreement with Fraser and Fraser to publish an antipodean edition of The Home Cook Book is a testament to the popularity of the book. The Sydney edition was probably printed and bound in Canada, then shipped to the colony. The copy catalogued here, belonging to a woman in Northern Ontario, was passed down through her Canadian family, which has no known connection with Australia; this copy must have escaped shipment 'Down Under' and remained in Canada. One of the NSM copies (641.5 408A) has advertisements for Canadian companies and products on the endpapers: Cook's Friend Baking Powder; W. Bell and Co. of Guelph, maker of pianos and organs; and Gray's Syrup of Red Spruce Gum. The other NSM copy, which has no advertisements, was given by one woman in Victoria (then a colony south of New South Wales, now a state) to another, also in Victoria. It is inscribed on the front endpaper, in ink, 'Presented to Mary M. McKenzie by Mrs Dunlop of Fasse Fern Cottage // Wangaratta 28/6/91'; and on p v, in the gutter, in pencil: 'Mary Morrison McKenzie // Stanley Road. Stanley via Beachworth // Victoria' (the address indicates that mail was to go via Beachworth to the small town of Stanley). Another Canadian private collector's copy, purchased from an Australian bookseller, has the same advertisements as one of the NSM copies and is inscribed in ink, 'Martha Crozia / Jannury [sic] 20th 1st. 1889 / Hunter [sic] Hill / Sydney / New S. Wales.' In the inscription, '1st' probably refers to January, a repetition of the month and a small error, like the spelling mistakes. Hunters Hill is now a metropolitan suburb of Sydney. The dated inscription is proof that Fraser and Fraser's 'seventy-fifth edition' (the only one so numbered) was published no later than 1889, although one would expect the 'seventy-fifth' to have followed all editions numbered 'seventieth,' including O20.33, dated 1894, and O20.35, published 1895 or later. The Sydney edition, therefore, predated the first community cookbook compiled in Australia (W.M.U. Cookery Book of Tried Recipes, in Aid of the Queensland Presbyterian Missions, [Brisbane: Printed by Muir and Morcom, 1894]. Both NSM copies and the Crozia copy have a brown cloth binding of the same type as many of the Canadian editions.

The Fraser and Fraser edition of The Home Cook Book is not cited in: Bette R. Austin, A Bibliography of Australian Cookery Books Published Prior to 1941, Melbourne: RMIT Libraries, 1987; John Alexander Ferguson, Bibliography of Australia, Vol. 6, Canberra: National Library of Australia, [1977]; or Susan Radvansky, Irene MacDonald, and Eric Archer, The Monash University Library Supplement to John Alexander Ferguson's Bibliography of Australia, Clayton, Victoria: Monash University Library, 1980. Of Fraser and Fraser, I know only that its imprint also appeared on an American book: Conversations on the Bible, by Enoch Pond, president of Bangor Theological Seminary, Bangor, Maine, published in Sydney, NSW, by Fraser and Fraser, 1887 (No. 14244 in Ferguson, Vol. 6).

NEW ZEALAND EDITIONS: Two Wellington, New Zealand, editions followed soon after the Australian edition: seventy-eighth edition in 1891 and eightieth edition in 1892 (both private collection). No Canadian copies with these edition numbers have surfaced. As for Australia, the Wellington editions predated the first fund-raiser compiled in New Zealand (St Andrew's Cookery Book, Dunedin, 1905). The tipped-in title-pages of both editions bear the name of Clara Pinny Yerex, who had recently, in 1890, married Ontario-born George Manley Yerex. George left Canada for Australia in 1883 'to represent a Canadian company in Australia' and for five years travelled through New South Wales and Queensland before relocating his business to New Zealand, where he imported American office equipment and also (according to *Yerex of TACA;* citation below) sold copies of *The Family Doctor.* The New Zealand editions of *The Home Cook Book,* although bearing Clara's name, likely came about through George's connections, possibly with Rose Publishing in Toronto or with Fraser and Fraser in Australia, although no evidence has yet arisen to link him directly with either company (one can also imagine George as agent bringing the Toronto book to the Sydney firm). Clara's brother Frederick James, an importer of musical instruments, also had North American business connections. The title-page of the first New Zealand edition reads: 'Tried! Tested! Proven! / The / home cook book. / Compiled by / ladies of Toronto and chief cities and towns / in Canada. / Seventy-eighth edition. / Wellington, New Zealand: / Clara Pinny Yerex. / Toronto, Canada: Rose Publishing Company. / 1891.' Unique to both New Zealand editions, on the title-page verso, is the 'Explanation of Some Words and Expressions Used in This Volume' for such North American terms as squash ('a variety of pumpkin') and spider ('a frying pan'). Also on the title-page verso is the 'post paid' price of 7 shillings and the usual Rose Publishing Co. 1877 copyright date. Clara died in Tegucigalpa, Honduras, during the Second World War. For information about Clara and George and family photographs, see David Yerex, *Yerex of TACA,* Carterton, NZ: Ampersand Publishing Associates, 1985; biographical entries for George Yerex and for Frederick James Pinny are in *Cyclopaedia of New Zealand.*

BRITISH EDITIONS: A description follows of an edition from the De La More Press, which had been founded by Alexander Moring in 1895. Moring's purpose was 'the production of ordinary commercial work in a manner worthy of the craft and at a price which was not prohibitive' (G.S. Tomkinson, *A Select Bibliography of the Principal Modern Presses Public and Private in Great Britain and Ireland,* London: First Edition Club, 1928, facsimile ed., San Francisco: A. Wofsy Fine Arts, 1975, p 210). The press's specialty was reprints of classics and liturgical books, but they also published books of poetry and general literature. There is no indication that the De La More Press edition of *The Home Cook Book* was a success in the British market. The title does not appear in Tomkinson's list, or in William Ridler's *British Modern Press Books: A Descriptive Check List of Unrecorded Items,* London: Covent Garden Press, 1971. No copy was deposited for copyright at the British Library.

Tried! Tested! Proven! / The / home cook book / Compiled by / ladies of Toronto and chief cities and

towns / in Ontario / London, W. / Alexander Moring, Limited / The De La More Press, 32 George Street, Hanover Square

DESCRIPTION: 19.0 × 12.5 cm   Pp [i–iii] iv–xi [xii], [9] 10–380 [381–4]   Cloth

CONTENTS: i tp; ii 'Entered according to Act of the Parliament of Canada, in the year one thousand eight hundred and seventy-seven, by Belford Brothers in the office of the Minister of Agriculture.'; iii–xi 'Contents' [i.e., index]; xii blank; 9–384 text

COPIES: OONL (TX715 H76 1877b p***)   *Private collection; United States: DLC (TX715 H65x 1900z)

NOTES: The copy catalogued here is inscribed by the owner's aunt (born 1884), on the front endpaper, in ink, 'M.F. Kervin 1913.' Since Alexander Moring Ltd was active from 1902, the inscription is evidence that this unnumbered edition was published about 1902–13. Another private collector's copy is inscribed on the front endpaper, in pencil, 'Mrs Edwin Farmer – Got in Brockville – Aug. 2/19' (Emma Farmer, née Johnston, likely acquired the book on a visit to Brockville because, at the time, her home was in Arnprior, north of Brockville and west of Ottawa). The only citation in EngCat for *The Home Cook Book* is for an edition by Port Pub. Co., August 1906, price 4s. There is no listing in EngCat for an edition by Alexander Moring. Port Pub. Co. is not listed in the 'Directory of Publishers' at the back of EngCat 1906–10 or EngCat 1911–15, but EngCat 1901–5 lists Port Publ. Co. at Mansion House Chambers, Queen Victoria Street, London E.C. Since five copies have been found with the Alexander Moring imprint (at OONL, DLC, and in three private collections) and no copies found with the Port imprint, the 1906 EngCat listing may in fact refer to the Alexander Moring edition, although why EngCat recorded Port as the publisher remains a mystery.

Bitting, p 610, cites the Alexander Moring edition, but she likely copied the title incorrectly: instead of 'cities and towns in Ontario,' she records 'cities of Ontario.'

1878

Jewry, Mary

See O14.1 for information about this British author.

O21.1   [1878]

[An edition of *Warne's Cookery Book for the Million. Compiled and edited by Mary Jewry ... with Upwards of Two Hundred Useful Economical Receipts,* London:

F. Warne and Co., and New York: Scribner, Welford and Co., [1878], pp 64, illus; the cover imprint is Brockville, Ont.: McMullen and Co., 1878.]
COPIES: United States: TxU

O21.2 nd [1870s]
—[An edition of *Warne's Cookery Book for the Million* [cover-title], Saint John, N.B.: H.L. Spencer Medical Warehouse, nd [187-?], 14.0 cm, pp [8], 64, [8], illus; publisher on added title-page: London, Frederick Warne]
COPIES: OONL (TX652.7 J48 1870z)
NOTES: The order of publication of O21.1 and O21.2 is unknown. Although H.L. Spencer Medical Warehouse is not in Saint John city directories, H.L. Spencer himself is listed from 1871, when he is recorded as a purveyor of patent medicines, to 1879–80, when he is a patent medicine manufacturer. In the volumes for 1877–8 and 1878–9 he is part of Spencer and Wortman, manufacturers of patent medicines, which suggests that O21.2 appeared before or after the collaboration with Wortman.

BRITISH EDITIONS: *A Cookery Book for the Million. Compiled and edited by M.J.*, London, [1871] (United States: possibly DLC; Great Britain: LB).

1879

Harland, Marion [pseudonym of] Mrs Mary Virginia Terhune, née Hawes (Amelia County, Va, 21 December 1830–3 June 1922, New York City, NY)

For information about this American author and her other cookbooks, see O18.1.

O22.1 1879
Robertsons cheap series. / The / dinner year book. / By / Marion Harland, / author of "Common Sense in the Household," "Breakfast Dinner / and Tea," etc. / Toronto: / J. Ross Robertson, 67 Yonge Street / 1879.
DESCRIPTION: 20.5 × 14.0 cm Pp [1–3] 4–264 Cloth
CONTENTS: 1 tp; 2 blank; 3–4 'Familiar Talk with the Reader'; 5–6 'Touching Saucepans'; 7–255 a menu and accompanying recipes for every day in the year, January–December; 256 blank; 257 'Company Dinners,' a company menu for every month in the year; 258 blank; 259–64 index
COPIES: CIHM (93646) *OGU (UA s041 b29) OONL (TX737 H37 1879)

NOTES: The OONL copy is inscribed on the front endpaper, in ink, 'Mrs. Robert R[or?]therford July 1882.' John Ross Robertson advertised *The Dinner Year Book* in the *Telegram* (Toronto) 28 January 1880, and for several weeks afterward, at the price of $1.00, or paper edition, $0.50.

AMERICAN EDITIONS: New York: Charles Scribner's Sons, [copyright 1878] (OGU; United States: InU); New York: Charles Scribner's Sons, 1887 (United States: InU); New York: Charles Scribner's Sons, 1891 (Private collection).

Moore, Richard (about 25 October 1830– 28 March 1883, Brooklyn, NY)

For information about the author and his other works, see NB1.1.

O23.1 [copyright 1879]
The / universal assistant, / and / complete mechanic, / containing over / one million industrial facts, / calculations, receipts, processes, trade secrets, rules, / business forms, legal items, etc., in every / occupation, from the / household to the manufactory, / by R. Moore. / Illustrated with 500 engravings. / "Let us have facts, real, certain, unmistakable facts, there can be / no science without them." – Robert Dick. / Price in cloth binding, $3.00; in leather binding, $4.00. Free by mail to any / address in Canada, or Great Britain, by remitting the price to J.S. Robertson / & Bros., subscription book publishers, Deverell's Block, Whitby, Ont. Parties / will save express charges by ordering single copies sent by mail, instead of by / express, C.O.D. Agents wanted. / Whitby, Ont. / J.S. Robertson & Bros., subscription book publisher, / Deverell's Block.
DESCRIPTION: 18.0 × 11.5 cm Pp [3–4] 5–1016 Frontis of New York and Brooklyn Suspension Bridge; tp still-life of books, pen, paper, and an oil lamp; illus Rebound
CONTENTS: 3 tp; 4 'Table Showing the Time in Various Parts of the World When It Is Noon at Washington, D.C.,' 'Copyright R. Moore, 1879, ...,' and notice that agents are wanted to sell the book; 5–6 'Preface'; 7–8 'General Index'; 9–1016 text
COPIES: CIHM (11146) *OONL (T49 M8, 2 copies)
NOTES: The 'Preface' says: 'This work is issued with the design of supplying very important omissions in the author's antecedent writings and compilations ... to make the information more comprehensive and

complete, he has quoted largely from his previously published works, wherever he judged it necessary to do so.' Culinary recipes are in the 'Baking and Cooking Department,' pp 9–30, and in 'Grocers and Confectioners' Receipts,' pp 201–39.

In Moore's 'Table Showing the Time in Various Parts of the World ...' he includes the following Canadian places: Halifax, Nova Scotia; Hamilton, Ontario; Moncton, New Brunswick; Montreal, Quebec; Ottawa, Ontario; Port Hope, Ontario; Quebec City; Saint John, New Brunswick; St John's, Newfoundland (then a British colony); St Stephen, New Brunswick; Sault St Marie, Ontario; and Toronto, Ontario.

AMERICAN EDITIONS: New York: R. Moore, 1880 (OTU (T49 M85 1880 ROMC RB)).

Wright, Mrs Julia McNair (1840–1903)

This American author wrote several books on the subject of temperance. She is also featured as the main author of a 532-page volume, Ladies' Home Cook Book: A Complete Cook Book and Manual of Household Duties *... Compiled by Julia Mac Nair [sic] Wright, et al. ... Together with Bills of Fare for All Seasons, by Marion Harland [i.e., Mrs Mary Virginia Terhune], Philadelphia: Manufacturers' Book Co., [c1896] (United States: DLC). This book may have been distributed in Canada under a different title. A Kingston, Ontario, private collector has an edition with no place of publication or printing. The title on the spine is* Peerless Cook Book *and the title-page reads, 'Food / for the hungry / a complete manual / of household duties / [...] / Compiled by / Julia MacNair [sic] Wright, et al / author of "The Complete Home" / Together with / bills of fare for all seasons / by / Marion Harland'; 'Copyrighted 1896 by L.M. Palmer' is on the title-page verso. Another copy is at BKM; it also has 'Peerless Cook Book' on the spine, but the title-page is missing.*

O24.1 1879
The complete home: / An / encyclopaedia of domestic life and affairs. / The household, / in its / foundation, order, economy, beauty, healthfulness, emergencies, / methods, children, literature, amusements, religion, / friendships, manners, hospitality, servants, / industry, money, and history. / A volume of practical experiences popularly illustrated. / By / Mrs. Julia McNair Wright. / "O fortunate, O happy day, / When a new household takes its birth, / And rolls on its harmonious way / Among the myriad homes of earth." / – Longfellow. / Bradley, Garretson & Co., / Philadelphia, 66 North Fourth Street. / Brantford, Ont. / William Garretson & Co., / Columbus, O.; Chicago, Ill.; Nashville, Tenn.; / St. Louis, Mo.; San Francisco, Cal. / 1879.
DESCRIPTION: 22.0 × 14.0 cm   Pp [1–2] 3–4, v–xiii [xiv], 11–584   5 pls col incl frontis   Cloth
CONTENTS: 1 tp; 2 'Copyright, by Julia McNair Wright, 1879.'; 3–4 preface; v–xiii table of contents; xiv blank; 11–573 text; 574–80 'Index'; 581–4 'Supplemental Index to Chapter on "Valuable Home Knowledge"'
COPIES: *OGU (UA s018 b27 copy 1)
NOTES: This edition is dated 1879 on the title-page. It has no black-and-white plates and no black-and-white presentation plate. The OGU copy is inscribed on the front endpaper, in ink, 'Mrs. James Ker 1880.'

McNair uses a literary device to construct her text: She claims that the book is a selection of writings from Aunt Sophronia's journals. Aunt Sophronia is described on p 11 as 'the relative of many of the townspeople – the Oracle of all.'

Only pp 533–61 of Chapter 22, 'Valuable Home Knowledge,' deal with cooking in any depth and contain recipes; however, there are occasional culinary references in other parts of the text, as the following entries from the general index show: 'Cooking for the sick'; 'Cooking utensils of the Romans'; 'Food and sleep'; 'Food for invalids'; 'Food for young children'; 'Food in patriarchal times'; 'Kitchen, made beautiful'; 'Kitchen furniture of'; 'Kitchen economizing in'; 'Salad, how to make'; 'Salad dressing for'; and 'Salad for fish.'

O24.2 1883
—The complete home: / An / encyclopaedia of domestic life and affairs. / The household, / in its / foundation, order, economy, beauty, healthfulness, emergencies, / methods, children, literature, amusements, religion, / friendships, manners, hospitality, servants, / industry, money, and history. / A volume of practical experiences popularly illustrated. / By / Mrs. Julia McNair Wright. / "O fortunate, O happy day, / When a new household takes its birth, / And rolls on its harmonious way / Among the myriad homes of earth." / – Longfellow / Bradley, Garretson & Co., / Philadelphia, 66 North Fourth Street; / Brantford, Ont. / William Garretson & Co., / Columbus, O.; Chicago, Ills.; Nashville, Tenn.; / St. Louis, Mo.; San Francisco, Cal. / 1883.
COPIES: *NSYHM

NOTES: There are 584 pages. The only difference between the title-page of this edition and that of O24.3 is in the address for Bradley, Garretson. Here it is given with the city first and a semicolon at the end of the line: 'Philadelphia, 66 North Fourth Street;' In O24.3, the city is last and followed by a period: '66 North Fourth Street, Philadelphia.'

O24.3 1883
—The complete home: / An / encyclopaedia of domestic life and affairs. / The household, / in its / foundation, order, economy, beauty, healthfulness, emergencies, / methods, children, literature, amusements, religion, / friendships, manners, hospitality, servants, / industry, money, and history. / A volume of practical experiences popularly illustrated. / By / Mrs. Julia McNair Wright. / "O fortunate, O happy day, / When a new household takes its birth, / And rolls on its harmonious way / Among the myriad homes of earth." / – Longfellow / Bradley, Garretson & Co., / 66 North Fourth Street, Philadelphia. / Brantford, Ont. / William Garretson & Co., / Columbus, O.; Chicago, Ills.; Nashville, Tenn.; / St. Louis, Mo.; San Francisco, Cal. / 1883.
DESCRIPTION: 22.0 × 14.0 cm   Pp [1–2] 3–4, v–xiii [xiv], 11–584   4 pls col, frontis of 'Journey of Life,' presentation pl   Cloth
CONTENTS: 1 tp; 2 'Copyright, by Julia McNair Wright, 1879.'; 3–4 'Preface'; v–xiii 'Contents'; xiv blank; 11–573 text; 574–80 'Index'; 581–4 'Supplemental Index to Chapter on "Valuable Home Knowledge"'
COPIES: OBUJBM   *OFERWM (A1988.9)
NOTES: See comments for O24.2.

O24.4 nd
—The complete home: / An / encyclopaedia of domestic life and affairs. / The household, / in its / foundation, order, economy, beauty, healthfulness, emergencies, / methods, children, literature, amusements, religion, / friendships, manners, hospitality, servants, / industry, money, and history. / A volume of practical experiences popularly illustrated. / By / Mrs. Julia McNair Wright. / "O fortunate, O happy day, / When a new household takes its birth, / And rolls on its harmonious way / Among the myriad homes of earth." / – Longfellow. / Bradley, Garretson & Co., / 66 North Fourth Street, Philadelphia. / Brantford, Ont. / William Garretson & Co., / Columbus, O.; Chicago, Ill.; Nashville, Tenn.; / St. Louis, Mo.; San Francisco, Cal.
DESCRIPTION: 22.0 × 14.0 cm   Pp [1–2] 3–4, v–xiii [xiv], 11–584   4 pls col, presentation pl, frontis of 'Journey of Life'   Cloth
CONTENTS: 1 tp; 2 'Copyright, by Julia McNair Wright, 1879.'; 3–4 preface; v–xiii table of contents; xiv blank; 11–573 text; 574–80 'Index'; 581–4 'Supplemental Index to Chapter on "Valuable Home Knowledge"'
COPIES: *NBSAM   OCN
NOTES: O24.4 and O24.5 have no date on the title-page; here the state for Chicago is given as 'Ill.'; in O24.5, the state is given as 'Ills.' O24.4 has 584 pp; O24.5 has 588 pp.

OONL (HQ734 W94 1879; CIHM 92074) is a variant: Like O24.4 it has 584 pp, but on the title-page there is a semicolon after Philadelphia and the state abbreviation is 'Ills.' I have not examined the second OONL copy with the same call number.

O24.5 nd
—The complete home: / An / encyclopaedia of domestic life and affairs. / The household, / in its / foundation, order, economy, beauty, healthfulness, emergencies, / methods, children, literature, amusements, religion, / friendships, manners, hospitality, servants, / industry, money, and history. / A volume of practical experiences popularly illustrated. / By / Mrs. Julia McNair Wright. / "O fortunate, O happy day, / When a new household takes its birth, / And rolls on its harmonious way / Among the myriad homes of earth." / – Longfellow / Bradley, Garretson & Co., / 66 North Fourth Street, Philadelphia. / Brantford, Ont. / William Garretson & Co., / Columbus, O.; Chicago, Ills.; Nashville, Tenn.; / St. Louis, Mo.; San Francisco, Cal.
DESCRIPTION: 22.0 × 14.0 cm   Pp [1–2] 3–4, v–xiii [xiv], 11–588   3 pls col incl frontis; 9 pls incl presentation pl; 1 pl missing opp p 48 (probably col since the tissue-paper protective leaf is still in place) and 1 pl (col?) missing opp p 460   Cloth
CONTENTS: 1 tp; 2 'Copyright, by Julia McNair Wright, 1879.'; 3–4 preface; v–xiii table of contents; xiv blank; 11–577 text; 578–84 'Index'; 585–8 'Supplemental Index to Chapter on "Valuable Home Knowledge"'
COPIES: *OGU (UA s018 b28 copy 2)
NOTES: At first glance the copyright date looks like 1870, but it is probably 1879. This is the only Canadian edition that I have examined with 588 pp. The OGU copy's presentation plate is inscribed with a twentieth-century date: 'Rev. F.A. Kidson [to] William J. Kidson March 21s- 193_.'

AMICUS cites a 588-page 'People's edition,' [No place: No publisher], 1889, but no location is recorded; it may have been published in Canada or the United States.

AMERICAN EDITIONS: Philadelphia, Cincinnati, Chicago, and St Louis: J.C. McCurdy and Co., nd [title-page verso: copyright by Julia McNair Wright, 1879] (OGU, QMM, NSHV microfilm, OWTU; United States: DLC); Philadelphia: Bradley, Garretson and Co., [1879] (OWTU; United States: DLC microform); Philadelphia: J.C. McCurdy, 1882 (Axford, p 74); printings of 1883 and 1884 (referred to in Cagle/Stafford No. 837); Philadelphia: 1903 (United States: InU).

1880

The art of baking

O25.1 1880
The / art of baking / giving / receipts and full instructions / how to make bread / and all kinds of / cakes and pastry / plain, fancy and ornamental. / By / a practical baker and confectioner. / Entered according to Act of the Parliament of Canada, in the year one / thousand eight hundred and eighty, by James D. Dunlop, / in the office of the Minister of Agriculture. / Woodstock: / Woodstock "Times" Steam Book and Job Print / 1880.
COPIES: *ONF (LHC 641.5 D922)

Dods, Miss Matilda Lees

Dods, an early graduate of the South Kensington School of Cookery in London, England, began lecturing on cookery in London in 1876. Probably in December 1878, she travelled to the United States, where she lectured in New York and Philadelphia, extending further the influence of the South Kensington School. The Culinary Art, Philadelphia: Enterprise Publishing Co., 1879, was a 64-page souvenir of her Philadelphia lectures (United States: DLC).

She also visited Canada, about the time that O26.1, the Toronto edition of The Art of Cooking, *was published. Her first set of lectures was at Shaftesbury Hall in Toronto, commencing 17 November 1879 (see* Globe *(Toronto) 15 November 1879). The twenty-four 'demonstrative lectures' were divided into two courses, 'Superior Cookery' in the afternoon and 'Plain Cookery' in the evening. They were held under the patronage of HRH Princess Louise and by invitation of the Misses Macdonald, Government House, and many other well-known ladies and gentlemen. A report about the ongoing lectures in the* Globe, *22 November 1879, p 8, describes them as 'daily becoming more interesting and profitable.' She also gave twenty lectures at Bishop Cronyn Hall in London, Ontario, commencing 6 February 1880 (see*

Free Press (London) 3 February 1880). The London lectures were divided into the same two courses, afternoon and evening, and they were also under the patronage of HRH Princess Louise and the invitation of several ladies, whose names are cited in the Free Press *article. The 6 February 1880 diary entry of Lucy Ronalds Harris (Mrs George Becher Harris) refers to her attending the first lecture: '... in the afternoon went to Miss Dod's [sic] class for cooking' (The Eldon House Diaries, Toronto: Champlain Society, 1994, p 464).*

For Dods's other culinary publications, American and British, see Driver, pp 224–6.

O26.1 1880
The art of cooking / A series of / practical lessons / by / Matilda Lees Dods / of the South Kensington School of Cookery / Edited by / Henrietta de Condé Sherman / Toronto / Hart & Rawlinson / 5 King Street, West / 1880
DESCRIPTION: 17.0 × 12.0 cm   Pp [i–iii] iv–v [vi–viii], [1] 2–226, [i–iii]   Cloth, with four small images on front of prepared dishes
CONTENTS: i tp; ii blank; iii–v preface; vi blank; vii table of contents; viii blank; 1–222 recipes; 223–6 index; i–iii ads
CITATIONS: MCat item 116
COPIES: CIHM (95401)   *OGU (UA s041 b03)
NOTES: 'Putnam' is the publisher printed on the spine. The Canadian edition is a reprint of the American edition of the same year. In the preface Dods refers to her British training and subsequent teaching in Britain and the United States: 'I was so fortunate as to obtain one of the earliest first-class diplomas issued by the South Kensington School of Cookery [in London], ... It is pleasant to be able to state, as well for the credit of the school whose teachings I have carried out, as for my own satisfaction, that such instruction as I have attempted to give in Great Britain and this country [i.e., the United States], through lessons and practical examples with demonstration before classes, has been most cordially and favorably received in all quarters, ...' The recipes are followed by useful notes about technique or alternative ingredients.

Hart and Rawlinson, Toronto booksellers, advertised *The Art of Cooking* for $1.25 in the *Daily Globe* on 24 January 1880 and 7 February 1880, the latter referring to the book as 'Just published – Canadian edition.'

'Dods. Art of Cooking D 441' is listed in the Toronto Public Library's *Catalogue of the Books in the Circulating Library ... 1889*, Toronto: 'Week' Office, 1889, p 228, but whether the entry refers to the 1880 Toronto edition or another edition is unknown.

AMERICAN EDITIONS: *The Art of Cooking: A Series of Practical Lessons*, edited by Henrietta de Condé Sherman, New York: G.P. Putnam's Sons, 1880 (Great Britain: LWel; United States: DLC, MCR, NNNAM); retitled *My Mother's Cook Book: A Series of Practical Lessons in the Art of Cooking*, edited by Henrietta de Condé Sherman, Chicago: Charles C. Thompson Co., [copyright 1902] (OGU; United States: DLC, NNNAM).

BRITISH EDITIONS: *A Handbook of Cookery: A Series of Practical Lessons*, London, Edinburgh, and New York: T. Nelson and Sons, 1881 (Great Britain: LG, OB, OPo(F); United States: MB); retitled *Handbook of Practical Cookery*, London, Edinburgh, and New York: T. Nelson and Sons, 1886 (Great Britain: LB, LoEN missing, OB); London, Edinburgh, and New York: T. Nelson and Sons, 1892 (Great Britain: OPo(F)); London, Edinburgh, and New York: Thomas Nelson and Sons, 1900 (Great Britain: LB, LG, LWel); miniature ed., London, Edinburgh, and New York: Eyre and Spottiswoode (Bible Warehouse) Ltd, 1906 (OGU; Great Britain: LB, LoEN missing, OB missing; United States: OCl).

The seaside cook book

O27.1   1880
The seaside / cook book / A complete manu[obscured by pasted-on newspaper clipping] / palata[obscured by clipping] / coo[obscured by clipping] / Price, 25 cents. / Entered according to the Act of Parliament of Canada, in the year one / thousand eight hundred and eighty, by Wm. Bryce, in the / office of the Minister of Agriculture. / London, Ont.: / Wm. Bryce, 168 & 215 Dundas Street. / 1880.
DESCRIPTION: 17.0 × 11.0 cm   Pp [i–ii] iii–x, [9] 10–192   Paper, with image on front of a woman rolling dough; sewn
CONTENTS: i tp; ii–x 'Index' [i.e., table of contents]; 9–192 text
COPIES: CIHM (95343)   *NBMOM
NOTES: This book is advertised on the binding of O8.18, *Dr Chase's Receipes* [sic], published by William Bryce in 1887: 'The Sea Side Cook Book // A complete manual of practical, economical, palatable, and healthful cookery // No household can afford to be without this book. Paper cover, 25 cents. Over 1000 best recipes ever published. William Bryce, publisher, Toronto, Ont.'
No reason is given for 'seaside' in the title; however, following the first chapter of soups are chapters for 'Fish' and 'Shellfish.' The latter includes recipes for Maryland Stewed Oysters and Soft Shell Crabs, suggesting that *The Seaside Cook Book* is an edition of an originally American text, possibly from the Eastern Seaboard, perhaps Baltimore. On the other hand, 'seaside' is more likely to be William Bryce's revision of 'lakeside' since the title and sub-title of the cookbook echo those for an American work by Naomi A. Donnelley: *The Lakeside Cook Book: A Complete Manual of Practical, Economical, Palatable and Healthful Cookery*, Chicago: Donnelley, Loyd and Co., 1878, pp 47 (United States: DLC); Bitting, p 127, designates this as No. 1. According to Parker, p 195, Donnelley, Loyd had started a series called the Lakeside Library in 1875; perhaps 'Lakeside' referred to Lake Michigan, beside which Chicago is situated. The companion work is *The Lakeside Cook Book No. 2: A Manual of Recipes for Cooking, Pickling, and Preserving ... By N.A.D.*, Chicago: Donnelley, Gassette and Loyd, [1878], pp 48 (United States: DLC). Bitting, p 127, describes the two numbers as bound together. A comparison of *The Seaside Cook Book* with Nos. 1 and 2 of *The Lakeside Cook Book* would reveal the relationship of the Canadian edition with the probable American source.

Also attributed to Naomi Donnelley is *The Homemade Cook Book: A Complete Manual of Practical, Economical, Palatable, Healthful and Useful Cookery*, New York: M.J. Ivers and Co., [1885], pp 47 (United States: DLC). DLC records this as an edition of *The Lakeside Cook Book*. William Bryce, the London, Ontario, publisher of *The Seaside Cook Book*, published O33.1, *The New Home-made Cook Book*, also an edition of an American book, but by a male author, and O50.1, *The Home Made Cook Book*, which may be related to the lakeside/seaside text.

1881

The Canadian economist

At the time The Canadian Economist *was published, Bank Street Presbyterian Church, founded in 1865, was located on Bank Street, at Slater, in Ottawa. In 1913, the congregation built a new church at 355 Cooper Street and took the name Chalmers Presbyterian, which became Chalmers United in 1925. See O801.1,* The Pantry Shelf, *for a cookbook by the Women's Association of Chalmers United Church. The records of the Ladies' Association of Bank Street Church survive in the archives of Dominion-Chalmers United Church, the new name from 1962.*

O28.1 1881

The / Canadian economist, / a book of / tried and tested receipts. / Compiled by / members of the Ladies' Association of Bank Street Church, Ottawa. / The profits to be devoted to the church. / Price $2.00 / Ottawa: / Published by Alexr. Mortimer. / Toronto: – Hunter, Rose & Co. / 1881.

DESCRIPTION: 18.0 × 12.0 cm   Pp [i–vii] viii–ix [x–xi] xii–xiii [xiv] xv–xvi [xvii] xviii–xx [xxi] xxii [xxiii] xxiv, [1] 2–594   8 pls col lith incl frontis of Bank Street Presbyterian Church; all lithos by A. Mortimer, Ottawa   Rebound

CONTENTS: i tp; ii 'Entered according to Act of Parliament of Canada, in the year one thousand eight hundred and eighty-one, by Alexr. Mortimer, in the office of the Minister of Agriculture. Printed by Hunter, Rose & Co., Toronto.'; iii untitled and unattributed three-verse poem; iv blank; v introduction; vi blank; vii–ix preface; x blank; xi–xiii 'The Kitchen'; xiv–xvi 'The Dining-Room'; xvii–xx 'The Parlour'; xxi–xxii 'The Bedrooms'; xxiii–xxiv table of contents; 1–574 text; blank leaf not included in pagination; 575–94 index

CITATIONS: Axford, p 52   Berton, pp 22, 34, 110   Bitting, p 527   Driver 2002, Home Cook Book, p xix   Driver 2003, 'Canadian Cookbooks,' p 30

COPIES: BVIPM   CIHM (07261)   OGU (UA s043 b07)   OOC (641.5 C2125)   *OTMCL (641.5 O76)   OTNY (641.5 C)   OTRM   OTUTF (sci 5640)   QMBM (641.5 L155ca)   Private collection; United States: DLC (TX715 O87)

NOTES: This early Canadian fund-raising cookbook – the second in Ontario, after O20.1, *The Home Cook Book* – is notable for its confident expression of Canadian national identity through striking colour lithographs and verse. The opening poem was written expressly for the book, the first letter of each line spelling out 'THE CANADIAN ECONOMIST.' The poem's topic is gastronomy in Canada: 'Canada is the land in which this art flourishes, / And whose soil is fertile in rich materials, ...'

The introduction refers to the book's dual purpose, to raise money for the church and to benefit the general public, both in Canada and the United States. A note at the end of the preface says that a recent 'wicked act of incendiarism,' which defaced the interior of the church, has created a greater need to raise funds through sales of the cookbook.

The two facing plates between pages vi and vii point to the congregation's American connections. See pl 3a-b. The left plate shows a beaver gnawing a branch beside a stream, flowering plants adorning the riverbank opposite. The verse below reads, 'In

this book you will find various contributions / From brave chivalric sons and fairest daughters, / Who, worshipping Canadian soil and institutions / Love, the emblems of the lands of their fathers, / And desire to unite them, with their own dear nations / Beautiful, Maple-leaves, and very popular, Beavers.' The right plate depicts an eagle standing on a crest of stars and stripes. The verse continues from the plate opposite, 'And also to live, in close fraternal conjunction / With their beloved brethren, over the borders. / Farewell: Be not dismayed at the construction / Of verses, and rhythm, by such stupid rhymers, / But look on the "Cookery Book" with compassion / Friends, patrons, high, low, and good neighbours, all.'

The anonymous writer of the preface recognizes the importance of recipes proven by experience, especially when living away from civilization as she has, 'far up the Ottawa River.' She says that the book takes 'as a model of a pleasant home, a cottage consisting of a kitchen, dining room, parlour, bed-rooms, etc, presided over by a mistress who is ably assisted by one general servant ...' Facing page ix of the preface is a colour lithograph entitled 'The Home Cottage.' Accompanying each of the separate accounts for the kitchen, dining room, parlour, and bedrooms is a colour lithograph of the particular room.

The source of most of the recipes is given, either an individual's name and her city or town, or the title of a book or periodical. The 'Conclusion,' p 574, apologizes 'for culling so freely from books and magazines,' and offers the excuse that 'the time given in which to get up this one was so short that originality [was] out of the question.' Many printed sources are cited, including: *Warne's Every-day Cookery* (for the Canadian edition, see O14.1); *Young Ladies' Journal* (an English magazine, published 1864–1920); *Godey's Book* (an American women's magazine); *Home Messenger* of Detroit (possibly Mary B. Duffield's *The Home Messenger Book of Tested Receipts*, 1873 and later editions); *Miss Parloa's Working Women's Lectures*; *How to Cook Potatoes in a Hundred Different Ways* (likely *Upwards of a Hundred Ways of Dressing and Serving Potatoes*, 1866, by the British author, Georgiana Hill, whose other titles have an equivalent phrasing, for example, *How to Cook Vegetables in One Hundred Different Ways*); *Cookery for Invalids* (possibly Mary Hooper's book of that title, first published in London, England, in 1876, Driver 509.1); *The Presbyterian; French Domestic Cookery* (possibly Louis-Eustache Audot's work, of which there was a New York edition in 1855, and earlier editions in English published in London); *Little Dinners* (probably Mary Hooper's book of that title, first published in England in 1874); *Home Cook Book* (an edition of O20.1); *What I Know* (possibly Elizabeth Nicholson's *What I Know; or, Hints on the Daily Duties of a Housekeeper*, Philadelphia: 1856, or Sarah Annie (Frost) Shields's *What I Know about Cooking*, Philadelphia: [copyright 1872]); *Cassell's Household Guide* (a multi-volume English work, [1869–71] and later editions, Attar 44); and *Family Friend* (possibly the popular British periodical edited by Robert Kemp Philp, first issued in 1849 and published into the twentieth century). The original works would have to be checked against the recipes in *The Canadian Economist* to confirm each source. Two of the cited sources were sold by the Methodist Book and Publishing House, which had Book Rooms in Toronto and Montreal; see MBPHCat 1876–7 for *Warne's Every Day Cookery*, p 25, and *How to Cook Potatoes in 100 Different Ways*, p 47.

A few recipes are credited to American women; for example, Mrs Humphreys of Providence, Rhode Island, and Mrs White of Bradford, Pennsylvania. Most of the individual contributors, however, are local, such as Mrs Thomas McKay of New Edinburgh (the 'Conclusion' relates a story of her late husband's servant), or from elsewhere in Ontario. Mrs James Young of Galt, who contributed the Carrot Pudding recipe, was the sister of Miss Frances McNaught, named as the co-compiler of later editions of O58.1, *The Galt Cook Book*.

The private collector's copy is inscribed on the front endpaper, in ink, 'Annie B. Viets from C.H. Thorburn May 6th 1923 Ottawa // To be kept till called for.'

Cook's friend cook book

O29.1 1881
Cook's friend / cook book. / A book of / tried and tested recipes. / Price 25 cents. / Toronto: / Published by Hopkins & Virtue. / 1881.
DESCRIPTION: 18.0 × 12.0 cm Pp iii–iv [v] vi [vii–viii], [1] 2–86 Cloth simulating brown leather(?)
CONTENTS: iii–iv ads; v tp; vi ads; vii 'Introduction,' 'Index to Recipes,' and 'Index to Advertisements'; viii fp illus of the premises of 'Norman's Electric Belt Institution'; 1–62 text; 63–4 ads; 65–86 blank pages for 'Memorandum' and fp ads
CITATIONS: Driver 2002, Home Cook Book, p xx (note 1) Driver 2005, p 410
COPIES: CIHM (95414) *OGU (UA s043 b02)
NOTES: *Cook's Friend Cook Book* is the first dated culinary manual published in Canada to advertise an

ingredient. The recipes specify Cook's Friend Baking Powder, and the book is titled after the product. The advertisement on p ii states that the name Cook's Friend Baking Powder and the trademark are the property of W.D. McLaren, 55 and 57 College Street, Montreal.

Pages ii and 87 are endpapers glued to the inside face of the binding. The recipes are headed 'Family Recipes' and begin on p 13 with Potato Yeast credited to Mrs De Freest, Another credited to Mrs Morgan, and Bread, to Mrs H. Galusha. These same recipes also begin the various editions of O48.1, *The Art of Cooking Made Easy* (earliest edition, 1890), all of which promote the sale of proprietary baking powders sold by particular druggists. The sections on 'House-Keeping' and 'Table Talk' are from O20.1, *The Home Cook Book*, the first edition of which was published in 1877 by Belford Brothers, Toronto, and there is an advertisement for *The Home Cook Book* on p vi. Note also several jam recipes from *The Home Cook Book*.

The OGU copy is annotated on p 75, in brown ink, probably by the first owner of the book, 'Mrs [F.?] Oct. 5th 1881 Age 26 yrs'; there are various other pencil annotations in the same hand – for example, on p 65, 'Toronto June 26th 1881 I saw the comet at halfpast nine.' The volume probably passed to a new owner who inscribed the title-page and p iii, in pencil, 'Martha M. Stokes // Kingston'; she also stencilled her name, set in a simple leaf pattern, in black ink, on p vii.

A variant copy of *Cook's Friend Cook Book* is at OKITJS (992.11.5), in which pp iii–vi (which include the title-page) are not bound into the volume. Rather, the volume starts with p vii, the 'Introduction,' etc.

Freedley, Edwin Troxell (1827–1904)

O30.1 1881
The / secret of success in life; / or, / common sense in business and the home. / A compendium of practical information: / showing / how to acquire correct business habits and education; manage / a farm successfully; become a skilful mechanic; accumu- / late wealth by manufacturing and in mercantile pur- / suits; form and dissolve partnerships; contract / a prudent marriage; effect leases and insu- / rance; avoid lawsuits and failure in / business; and make a valid will. / Also, / the best methods of saving money in the household; making / home comfortable and happy; of purchasing and prepar- / ing food economically; preserving health and beauty; / curing children's

diseases, and prolonging life. / By / Edwin T. Freedley, / author of "Practical Treatise on Business," "Legal Adviser," "Opportunities for Industry," / "Philadelphia and Its Manufactures." / Handsomely illustrated. / Whitby, Ontario. / J.S. Robertson & Bros. / 1881.

DESCRIPTION: 20.5 × 14.0 cm   Pp [1–2], i–xxxi [xxxii], 33–721   2 pls col of prepared dishes, 22 pls incl frontis   Cloth

CONTENTS: 1 tp; 2 'Copyright, 1881, by Edwin T. Freedley. All rights reserved. Ferguson Bros. & Co., printers and electrotypers, Philadelphia.'; i–ii 'Publisher's Preface'; iii–xviii 'Contents. Part I.'; xix–xxxi 'Contents. Part II.'; xxxii blank; 33–368 'Part I. Common Sense in Business.'; 369–698 'Part II. Home Comforts.'; 699–708 'Index. Part I.'; 709–21 'Index. Part II.'

COPIES: *BVAMM

NOTES: The following chapters in Part II contain culinary information: I, 'Elements of Comfort' (comments on cooking and the 'value of cook-books to housekeepers'); IV, 'Household Conveniences Not in General Use' (discusses cooking utensils); V, 'The Art of Marketing – Housekeeping Hints' (on selecting food); VI, 'On Fuels and Fires, Saving Gas, etc.'; VII, 'About Eating and Articles of Food'; VIII, 'Cheap Living and Economical Food'; IX, 'Valuable Secrets Known to Good Cooks'; X, 'Dainty Dishes for Dainty Palates: 1. Domestic Cookery'; and XI, 'Dainty Dishes for Dainty Palates: 2. High-class Cookery.' Some of the recipes are credited to specific sources, such as Marion Harland (p 523), Alexis Soyer (p 527), Eliza Leslie (p 526), and Mrs Freedley (p 533).

AMERICAN EDITIONS: Philadelphia: Thayer, Merriam and Co., 1881 (United States: DLC microfilm).

'Mother Hubbard's cupboard'

O31.1   1881

"Mother Hubbard's cupboard." / Or, / Canadian cook book / "Double, double, toil and trouble; / Fire burn, and cauldron bubble." / Published by / G.C. Briggs & Sons, / Hamilton, Ontario. / Hamilton: / Spectator Printing Company. / 1881.

DESCRIPTION: 17.5 × 11.0 cm   Pp [2 leaves lacking] [7–9] 10–112 [113–24]   Trademark for 'Baby Cordial' on p 72 and for 'Star Cement' on p 75   Cloth; stapled

CONTENTS: 3–6 ads, according to 'Contents'; 7 tp; 8 'Contents' [alphabetical list of topics]; 9–112 text; 113–24 ads

CITATIONS: Simpson, p W17 (includes photograph)

COPIES: CIHM (91815)   OGU (s0249 b22)   OH (R641.5971 MOT CESH)   OHMA (TX715 M66)   *OTUTF (jah copy 2)   OWTU (F12253)

NOTES: Unlike O31.2, this edition does not have the title-page phrase 'Over five hundred practical receipts.' The unnamed author of O41.1, *The Breadmaker's Book of Cooking Lessons*, acknowledges consulting 'Mother Hubbard.' Neering, pp 79 and 80, may refer to O31.1 or O31.2.

O31.2   1881

—"Mother Hubbard's cupboard." / Or, / Canadian cook book / "Double, double, toil and trouble; / Fire burn, and cauldron bubble." / Over five hundred practical receipts. / Published by / G.C. Briggs & Sons, / Hamilton, Ontario. / Hamilton: / Spectator Printing Company / 1881.

DESCRIPTION: 17.5 × 11.0 cm   Pp [3–9] 10–112 [113–26]   Trademark for 'Baby Cordial' on p 72 and for 'Star Cement' on p 75   Cloth simulating brown leather

CONTENTS: 3–6 ads; 7 tp; 8 'Contents' [alphabetical list of topics]; 9–112 text; 113–26 ads

CITATIONS: Brisebois No. 101, p 25   Eade, p E2

COPIES: *OGU (UA s043 b01)   OONL (TX715.6 M743 1881 and a second copy)   OPET (TX157 C3 B7)   OTMCL (641.5971 M59)   OTUTF (jah, copies 1 and 3)

NOTES: This edition has the title-page phrase 'Over five hundred practical receipts.' OTUTF copy 3 is inscribed on the title-page, in ink, 'W.H. Montray.'

AMERICAN EDITIONS: *Mother Hubbard's Cupboard*, published by the Young Ladies' Society, First Baptist Church, Rochester, NY, printed by Daily Democrat and Chronicle Book and Job Print, 1880 (Private collection); [Rochester, NY:] E.R. Andrews, 1880 (United States: DLC); 4th ed., 20th thousand, Rochester: Scrantom, Wetmore and Co., 1887 (United States: DLC); possibly another ed. of the same work, *Mother Hubbard's Modern Cupboard*, Battle Creek, Mich.: Little-Preston Co. Ltd, [1903] (Bitting, p 580).

1882

Fowler, Charles Henry (Burford, Ont., 11 August 1837–1908) and William Harrison De Puy (1821–1901)

Fowler moved from Canada to Illinois with his family at a young age. He was elected president of Northwestern University in 1872. In 1876 he became editor of the New

York Christian Advocate, *and in 1884, he was made a bishop of the Methodist Episcopal Church. He is also remembered for his vindictive treatment of Frances Willard, his former fiancée, who was president of Northwestern Female College when Fowler was elected president of Northwestern University. Willard resigned her position at Northwestern and went on to help found the Woman's Christian Temperance Union and serve as its president, and to become a famed orator and suffragist. Willard wrote the introduction to O49.1,* Woman; Her Character, Culture and Calling, *by B.F. Austin, and two 1930s Ontario cookbooks celebrated the centenary of her birth, O938.1 and O970.1.*

O32.1 1882
Home and health / and / compendium of useful knowledge: / A cyclopedia of facts and hints for all / departments of home life, health, / and domestic economy, / and / hand book of general / information. / London, Ont.: / The Advertiser Printing and Publishing Co. / 1882.
DESCRIPTION: 17.0 × 11.0 cm   Pp [3–7] 8–346   A few illus   Paper
CONTENTS: 3 tp; 4 dedication to 'our mothers ... wives ... daughters ... [and] our readers ...' signed 'the authors'; 5 preface; 6 quotations; 7–8 'General Topics' [i.e., table of contents]; 9–330 text in four parts (I, 'Home'; II, 'Health'; III, 'Home Economics'; IV, 'Useful Knowledge'); 331–46 'Index'
COPIES: CIHM (91598)   *OGU (UA s049 b07)   OLU
NOTES: No authors are named in the Canadian editions. There is a small amount of information about food and cooking: In Part I, 'Table Manners,' pp 40–3; in Part II, 'Food and Health,' pp 71–7, 'Hints about Healthful Eating,' pp 77–81, 'Food for the Sick,' pp 82–6, and 'Summer Beverages,' pp 92–5; and in Part III, 'Waste in the Kitchen,' pp 290–1, and 'Rules for Carving.'

O32.2 1883
—Home and health / and / compendium of useful knowledge: / A cyclopedia of facts and hints for all / departments of home life, health, / and domestic economy, / and / hand book of general / information. / London, Ont.: / The Advertiser Printing and Publishing Co. / 1883.
DESCRIPTION: 17.0 × 11.0 cm   Pp [3–7] 8–346   A few illus   Paper-covered boards
CONTENTS: 3 tp; 4 dedication to 'our mothers ... wives ... daughters ... [and] our readers ...' signed 'the authors'; 5 preface; 6 quotations; 7–8 'General Topics' [i.e., table of contents]; 9–330 text; 331–46 'Index'

CITATIONS: Abrahamson, pp 23 (note 27), 59   Neering, p 73
COPIES: *OGU (UA s041 b31)   OTUTF (jah, 2 copies)
NOTES: A private collector has a copy identical to that at OGU except that there is no period after 1883 on the title-page. Like the OGU copy, it is bound in paper-covered boards, but a second sheet of paper has been applied over the first (only the border of the underneath sheet is visible and it is different from the top sheet). The top sheet reads, 'The Canadian Post premium. [book title] Lindsay, Ont.: Chas. D. Barr, Prop'r of the Canadian Post.' One of the OTUTF copies matches the OGU copy; the other matches the private collector's.

O32.3 1884
—Home and health / and / compendium of useful knowledge: / A cyclopedia of facts and hints for all / departments of home life, health, / and domestic economy, / and / hand book of general / information. / Winnipeg, Man.: / The Nor' West Farmer Publishing House. / 1884
DESCRIPTION: 17.5 × 11.5 cm   Pp [3–7] 8–346   A few illus   Paper; sewn
CONTENTS: 3 tp; 4 'Dedication' signed 'the authors'; 5 'Preface'; 6 quotations; 7–8 'General Topics' [i.e., table of contents]; 9–57 'Home'; 58–289 'Health'; 290–317 'Home Economics'; 318–30 'Useful Information'; 331–46 'Index'
COPIES: *OTUTF (jah)
NOTES: The cover-title is 'Nor'West Farmer Premium / / Home and Health and Compendium of Useful Knowledge.' *The Nor' West Farmer* was a monthly publication established in 1882.

AMERICAN EDITIONS: Fowler, C.H., and W.H. De Puy, *Home and Health and Home Economics: A Cyclopedia of Facts and Hints for All Departments of Home Life, Health, and Domestic Economy*, New York: Phillips and Hunt, 1880 [c1879] (United States: KMK); *The New Home and Health and Home Economics*, illustrated ed., with revisions and additions, New York: Printed for the author, Hunt and Eaton Press, 1896 (United States: DLC).

The new home-made cook book

O33.1 1882
The new / home-made cook book / A practical guide / to / healthful, tasteful, cheap, / as well as / refined cooking of soups, fish, meats, game, / poultry, vegetables, pastry, cakes / and bread. / To

which are added / numerous household recipes / for / pickling, preserving, &c. / all tried and tested / in families of taste, but of moderate expenditure. / London, Ont. / Wm. Bryce, publisher, 168 & 123 Dundas St., London, Ont. / 1882

DESCRIPTION: 20.5 × 15.0 cm   Pp [1–3] 4–48   Paper, with image on front of a young woman carrying a steaming cup on a tray; sewn

CONTENTS: 1 tp; 2 'Entered according to Act of Parliament of Canada, in the year one thousand eight hundred and eighty-two, by Wm. Bryce, in the office of the Minister of Agriculture.'; 3–48 recipes

COPIES: *OTNY (641.59713 N)

NOTES: '[H?] Beech,' the signature of the engraver of the image of the young woman on the binding, is visible to the left of her legs. See the notes for O27.1, *The Seaside Cook Book*, concerning other publications by Bryce.

AMERICAN EDITIONS: [Williams, Jr, Henry Llewellyn], *The New Home-Made Cook-Book*, New York: M.J. Ivers and Co., [c1882] (United States: DLC).

1883

The Canadian home, farm and business cyclopaedia

O34.1   [1883]

The Canadian / home, farm and business / cyclopaedia. / A treasury of useful and entertaining knowledge / on the art of making home happy, and an aid in self-education; the laws of / etiquette and good society; home amusements; out-door sports, / and other interesting matters of social / and educational value. / The / science and practice of farming: / with special reference to Canada; / giving the most complete and practical information on the culture of the / soil; the management of farm animals; the erection of farm / buildings; the garden, etc., etc. / Also, / Goodwin's practical book-keeping / complete. / A treatise on arithmetic, penmanship, forms of business correspondence; a / digest of mercantile law, and various forms of legal documents. / The farm department, specially written for this work, by / Prof. William Brown, / of the Ontario Experimental Farm, Guelph. / The business department under the supervision of / George Maclean Rose, / ex-President of the Board of Trade, Toronto. / The entire work carefully edited by / a syndicate of Canadian specialists. /

Handsomely illustrated. / Price, $4.00. / Paris, Ont.: / J.S. Brown & Sons.

DESCRIPTION: 23.0 × 16.0 cm   Pp [i–v] [vi incorrectly numbered iv] [vii] viii–xv [xvi], [17] 18–816   Many pls   Cloth, with floral design on front and spine

CONTENTS: i ht; ii blank; iii tp; iv 'Entered according to Act of the Parliament of Canada, in the year one thousand eight hundred and eighty-three, by Hunter, Rose & Co., in the office of the Minister of Agriculture. Printed and bound by Hunter, Rose & Co., Toronto.'; v–vi preface dated Toronto, 1 December 1883; vii–xv table of contents; xvi blank; 17–816 text

CITATIONS: Driver 2001, Wellington County, p 94

COPIES: OKQ (Special Collections uncat)   SSU (FC23 C37 1883)   *Private collection

NOTES: The first main text division is 'Home,' which includes the following subdivisions related to food and cooking: 'The Amenities of Home,' pp 33–99; 'Hints to Housekeepers' with sections on 'Choices of Articles of Food,' 'Seasonable Food,' 'Names and Situations of Joints,' and 'Instructions for Cooking,' pp 139–70; 'Etiquette for Ladies' with sections on 'Morning and Evening Parties,' 'The Dinner Party,' and 'Staying at a Friend's House – Breakfast,' pp 238–56; 'Etiquette for Gentlemen' with sections on 'Morning and Evening Parties' and 'The Dinner Table,' pp 257–73; and 'Etiquette of Courtship and Marriage' with a section on 'The Wedding Breakfast,' pp 294–314. George Maclean Rose, who supervised the business department, was a co-owner of Hunter, Rose and Co., who printed the book.

The private collector's copy is inscribed opposite p i, in brown ink, 'Elam H. Smith // St Thomas Ont Jan 9th/92 // JB Smith Esq St Thomas Ont // [JB?] Smith'; and on p i, in brown ink, 'Mr Chas [A.?] Smith // St Thomas Ont Feb 4th 96.' Another copy of the same edition, also in a private collection, has a frontispiece.

O34.2   1884

—The Canadian / home, farm and business / cyclopaedia. / A treasury of useful and entertaining knowledge / on the art of making home happy, and an aid in self-education; the laws of / etiquette and good society; home amusements; out-door sports, / and other interesting matters of social / and educational value. / The / science and practice of farming: / with special reference to Canada; / giving the most complete and practical information on the culture of the soil; / the management of farm animals, the erection of farm / buildings, the garden, etc., etc. / Also, / Goodwin's practical book-keeping / complete. / A treatise on arithmetic, penmanship, forms of business correspondence; a digest / of mercantile law, and various forms of legal documents. / The farm department, specially written for this work, by / Prof. William Brown, / of the Ontario Experimental Farm, Guelph. / The business department under the supervision of / George Maclean Rose, / ex-President of the Board of Trade, Toronto. / The entire work carefully edited by / a syndicate of Canadian specialists. / Handsomely illustrated. / Toronto and Whitby: / J.S. Robertson and Brothers. / 1884.

DESCRIPTION: 23.5 × 16.0 cm   Pp [i–v] [vi incorrectly numbered iv] [vii] viii–xv [xvi], [17] 18–816   Many pls incl frontis of 'Returning Home,' presentation pl col   Cloth, with floral design on front

CONTENTS: i ht; ii blank; iii tp; iv 'Entered according to Act of the Parliament of Canada, in the year one thousand eight hundred and eighty-three, by Hunter, Rose & Co., in the office of the Minister of Agriculture. Printed and bound by Hunter, Rose & Company, 25 Wellington St. West.'; v–vi 'Preface' signed the Editors, Toronto, 1 December 1883; vii–xv 'Contents'; xvi blank; 17–806 text; 807–16 'Miscellaneous Tables'

CITATIONS: Driver 2001, Wellington County, p 94

COPIES: CIHM (03837)   OGU (s0518 b10)   OKQ (AG105 C2)   OONL (AG6 C35, 3 copies)   OONMS   OOU (FC2 C295 1883)   *OTMCL   OTY (FC23 C42 1884)   QQS (211.7.16)

NOTES: The presentation plate in the OTMCL copy is inscribed to 'John E. Gordon' by 'Duncan' and dated 25 December 1893.

Clarke, Mrs Anne

O35.1   [1883]
Mrs. Clarke's / cookery book / comprising a collection of / about fourteen hundred / practical, useful, and unique / receipts. / Including "sick room cookery," and a number of / excellent receipts entitled "The Doctor." / Also / what to name the baby. / A complete dictionary of Christian names; their origin / and signification. / Toronto: / The Grip Printing and Publishing Co. / 55 & 57 Adelaide Street East. / (Copyright.)

DESCRIPTION: 18.5 × 11.5 cm   Pp [iii–xii], [17] 18–402   Rebound

CONTENTS: iii tp; iv 'Entered according to Act of Parliament of the Dominion of Canada in the year 1883, by George Clarke, in the office of the Minister of Agriculture.'; v 'Preface' signed Anne Clarke, 38 Pem-

broke Street, Toronto, 1 November 1883; vi blank; vii–viii table of contents; ix–xii 'Introductory Observations'; 17–341 cookery text of 1,276 numbered recipes; 342–74 'The Doctor'; 375–85 'What to Name the Baby'; 386 blank; 387–402 index

CITATIONS: Berton, pp 15, 32, 36, 37, 45, 58   Breckenridge, p 2   Cooke 2002, p 234   Driver 2003, 'Canadian Cookbooks,' pp 32–3   Driver 2005, p 409   Duncan, pp 43, 141–2   Ferguson/Fraser, p 232   Golick, p 103 (note 22)   Valerie Legge, 'Foremothers, a New Nation, and Women's History,' in *Facsimile* [CIHM newsletter], No. 17 (May 1997), p 10

COPIES: CIHM (01114)   OGU (CCC TX715.6 C54)   OHMA (TX715 C6 1883)   OLU   OONL (TX715 C5773 1883)   *OTMCL (641.5 C473)   OTNY (641.5 C)   OTUTF (sci)

NOTES: Numbers 13–16 are omitted in the pagination. No text appears to be missing. The text contains 1,349 numbered recipes and other instructions. *Mrs Clarke's Cookery Book* was the first Canadian cookbook to be published in an American edition, in Chicago, in 1889. It is not an American text as stated in Cooke 2002, p 234.

Anne Clarke is not in Toronto city directories for the 1880s; however, George Clarke (her husband?), who registered the book's copyright, is first listed in the 1882 directory as general manager of Li-Quor Tea Co. of England, living at 473 Sherbourne Street. George Clarke had come to Toronto from England in 1881 (see the entry for Li-Quor Tea Co. in *History of Toronto and County of York Ontario*, Vol. 1, Toronto: C. Blackett Robinson, 1885, p 466). In the 1883 city directory, George Clarke is again listed as general manager of Li-Quor Tea Co., but living at 38 Pembroke Street, the address appended to Anne Clarke's 'Preface.' He continues to be listed as living at 38 Pembroke Street up to and including 1887, the last year that he appears in the directory, but the description of his business changes. In 1884, his business is 'books' at 100 Yonge Street, and he is in the 'Businesses' section of the directory under 'Booksellers and Stationers.' In 1885, his business is 'teas' at 295 Yonge Street. In 1886, his business is 'real estate' at 47 Toronto Arcade and proprietor of the Li-Quor Tea Co. at 295 Yonge. In 1887, a fuller form of his name is given, George K.M. Clarke, but his only business is real estate. It appears that George Clarke was involved in bookselling for only one year, about the time of the cookbook's publication in November 1883. (Hulse found no other information about George Clarke, apart from that in the 1884 Toronto directory.) The fact that the earliest identified American edition of the cookbook was published in 1889 in Chicago, two years after George

Clarke disappeared from the Toronto directory, suggests that he may have moved to the United States, or that his business interests turned to that country; however, I could find no clear match in Chicago city directories for 1888–90. Another possibility is that Clarke moved to Halifax or Winnipeg, where the Li-Quor Tea Co. is supposed to have had branch houses (*History of Toronto and County of York Ontario*, Vol. 1, p 466); however, I found no listing for Clarke or the Li-Quor Tea Co. in Halifax directories for the period 1888 to 1890 or in the Winnipeg directory for 1890.

Identical advertisements for *Mrs Clarke's Cookery Book* appear in the newspaper *Toronto World* on 13 November 1883, p [3] (see pl 23), and on 15 November 1883, p [2], both indicating that the cookbook 'is now ready at all booksellers. Wholesale at Wm. Warwick & Sons.' A feature of the advertisement is a six-verse poem called 'She Does Not Know Chicken from Turkey,' which ends: 'Now, here comes the moral of this little tale, / Which showed that Helene did not know the word "fail," / For she went where cookery books were for sale, / And made known her desire to the clerk. He, / From several volumes, immediately took / A copy of "Mrs. Clarke's Cookery Book," / And said, "You'll soon know, if through this you will look, / What to do with a chicken or turkey."' If George Clarke is known to have emigrated from England, a reference in the third verse to Helene knowing 'every stitch of the Kensington school' reveals another English connection. South Kensington, in London, was the location of the South Kensington School of Art (which gave its name to Helene's stitch) and also of the National Training School for Cookery (NTSC), founded in 1874. The latter was the pre-eminent English cookery school at the time *Mrs Clarke's Cookery Book* was published in 1883. Some recipes in *Mrs Clarke's Cookery Book* are, in fact, from *The Official Handbook for the National Training School for Cookery Containing the Lessons on Cookery Which Constitute the Course of Instruction in the School*, compiled by R.O.C. [Miss Rose Owen Cole], London: Chapman and Hall, 1877 (I consulted an 1878 edition, Driver 219.2); however, they have been rewritten so that instead of Cole's lengthy numbered steps in the first person plural, designed for classroom use, the instructions are contracted and in the imperative. If, for example, one compares the English recipe for Tapioca Cream, Lesson No. 2 of 'Soups,' with No. 4, Tapioca Soup in *Mrs Clarke's Cookery Book*, one finds that the ingredients lists specify the same amounts of the same ingredients in the same order, and the method is the same; however, where *Mrs Clarke's Cookery Book* says simply, 'Put stock on to boil, then

stir in gradually the tapioca, ...,' the Engish recipe gives the following lengthy instruction: 'Now we will show you how to make Tapioca Cream. 1. We take one pint of white stock (see "Lesson on Stock,") and pour it in a stewpan. 2. We put the stewpan on the fire to boil. 3. We take one ounce of prepared crushed tapioca. 4. When the white stock boils, we stir in gradually the tapioca.' Other soup recipes that derive from *The Official Handbook for the National Training School for Cookery* are No. 1, Crowdie or Scotch Soup (the Training School's Crowdie, Lesson No. 10), No. 3, Milk Soup (Milk Soup, Lesson No. 11), and No. 2, Macaroni Soup (Macaroni Soup, Lesson No. 15). No. 630, Seed Cake corresponds to Seed Cake, Lesson No. 4; and No. 689, Oatmeal Biscuits to Oatmeal Biscuits, p 373, no lesson number. (It is possible, although less likely, that Anne Clarke used the one American edition of *The Official Handbook*, retitled *Lessons in Cookery: Hand-book of the National Training School for Cookery*, New York: D. Appleton and Co., 1878.) The lady superintendent of the NTSC was Mrs Edith Clarke from 1875 to 1919, and further research may reveal a family connection between Mrs Edith Clarke (husband, Charles Clarke) and George Clarke. It should be noted that Ontario residents had already been exposed to the culinary ideas of the NTSC through the cookbook and lectures of Matilda Lees Dods (see O26.1).

In her 'Preface,' Anne Clarke refers to 'the valuable assistance [from] friends in the British Isles, France, Germany and the United States.' Much of the text, for example, the meat, fish, and puddings sections, clearly comes from other sources than *The Official Handbook*. Some recipes, such as No. 616, Johnny Cake, and others using Indian meal, are North American by virtue of their ingredients. No. 308, Governor's Sauce, and No. 577, Corn Bread Steamed, are described specifically as 'Canadian recipe,' and the name of No. 627, New York Plum Cake, identifies its origin. George Clarke may have supplied the history of tea in the introductory text for the 'Beverages' chapter since he was in the tea business (he might have written it himself or culled it from reference books about tea in his possession). More research is required to identify other possible sources for the recipes and for the 'Observations' that introduce each section in *Mrs Clarke's Cookery Book*.

Mrs Clarke's Cookery Book was an early publication of the Grip Printing and Publishing Co., which started business in March 1882 (Hulse, p 113). Grip's office at 55–7 Adelaide Street East (1883) and 26–8 Front Street West (from 1884) was close to the 1883 location of George Clarke's book business at 100 Yonge Street.

The OTUTF copy has its original cloth binding; however, it lacks pp iii–iv (i.e., the title-page) and pp 401–2 (the last leaf).

See also O41.1, *The Breadmaker's Book of Cooking Lessons*, of 1888, whose unnamed author acknowledges consulting *Mrs Clarke's Cookery Book*.

O35.2 1889
—The latest and the best. / The people's cook book. / Economy, wealth and comfort / in the home. / 1,349 / new, useful and unique recipes / in / cookery and all departments of housekeeping. / Rules for the preservation of health, and valuable / medical prescriptions by eminent physicians / for family use. / By Mrs. Anne Clarke, / assisted by some of the most successful housekeepers and home- / makers in the United States, Canada, France, / Germany and Great Britain. / Wm. Briggs, publisher, / 30–36 Temperance Street, / Toronto, Ontario. / 1889.
COPIES: *Private collection
NOTES: The half-title is 'Mrs. Clarke's Cookery Book.' There is a frontispiece depicting a woman grating a piece of fruit(?) at a kitchen table, with the caption 'The queen at home.' The following is on the title-page verso: 'Copyright, 1889, by F.J. Schulte.' This Briggs edition came out in the same year as the first two American editions, one of which has the same title and the other of which has F.J. Schulte as publisher.

O35.3 3rd ed., [entered 1898]
—The dominion / home / cook book / and / cyclopedia of recipes. / By Anne Clarke. / Third edition, / which has been carefully revised and enlarged; all recipes / containing "spirituous liquors" having been / eliminated and substituted by others. / Published by / J.L. Nichols & Co., / 33 Richmond St. W., Toronto, Can. / Agents wanted.
DESCRIPTION: 18.0 × 12.0 cm   Pp [1–6] 7–319   Illus part-title on p 269 for 'A Complete Cyclopedia of Family Receipts'; fp illus on pp 265–8, and 271; a few illus in 'Poultry and Game' and 'Meats' sections and in 'A Complete Cyclopedia of Family Receipts'   Cloth, with all-over flower pattern
CONTENTS: 1 tp; 2 'Not for sale in bookstores. This volume will be sent postpaid on receipt of $1.00 to any address. Agents wanted. Entered according to Act of Parliament of Canada in the year one thousand eight hundred and ninety-eight by J.L. Nichols & Co. at the Department of Agriculture.'; 3 'Preface' signed Anne Clarke; 4 blank; 5 'Preface to the Second Edition' signed Anne Clarke; 6 blank; 7–10 'Introduc-

tory Observations'; 11–264 cookery text of 954 numbered recipes; 265–8 fp illus; 269–310 'A Complete Cyclopedia of Family Receipts'; 311–17 'Index of Dominion Cook Book'; 318–19 'Index of Cyclopedia Department'
CITATIONS: O'Neill (unpublished)
COPIES: *OGU (UA s070 b39); Great Britain: LB (7942.g.36 destroyed)
NOTES: In the 'Preface to the Second Edition' Anne Clarke writes, '... I have issued a second edition, the Canadian edition being exhausted, though in the United States many thousands of copies have been sold, and the remainder is still having a very large sale. The present edition has been thoroughly revised and corrected.'

'A Complete Cyclopedia of Family Receipts,' on pp 269–310, appears only in O35.3 and not in later editions that I have examined. It may also be in O35.4, another J.L. Nichols and Co. edition, which I have not examined. This text is taken from another book published by J.L. Nichols: See the section on 'Family Receipts' in Book III of *The Household Guide or Domestic Cyclopedia*, by Prof. Benjamin Grant Jefferis, James Lawrence Nichols, and Mrs J.L. Nichols, the editions entered for copyright in 1897 (I compared O70.9, twenty-third edition, entered in 1897, but likely published about 1899–1903). The illustrated part-title on p 269 of O35.3 also appears in O70.2, sixteenth edition, 1896.

O35.4 3rd ed., [entered 1898]
—The dominion / home / cook book / and / cyclopedia of recipes. / By Anne Clarke. / Third edition, / which has been carefully revised and enlarged; all recipes / containing "spirituous liquors" having been / eliminated and substituted by others. / J.S. Brown & Sons, / Paris, / Ontario.
CONTENTS: Tp verso 'Not for sale in bookstores. This volume will be sent postpaid on receipt of $1.00 to any address. Agents wanted. Entered according to Act of Parliament of Canada in the year one thousand eight hundred and ninety-eight by J.L. Nichols & Co. at the Department of Agriculture.'
COPIES: *Private collection

O35.5 1899
—The / ideal cook book / containing / valuable recipes in all the departments, / including sickroom cookery. / By / Anne Clarke / Toronto: The Westminster Company / Limited, Confederation Life Building / 1899
DESCRIPTION: 18.5 × 12.0 cm   Pp [3–6] 7–309 [310]   A few illus   Cloth

CONTENTS: 3 tp; 4 'Entered according to Act of Parliament of Canada in the year one thousand eight hundred and ninety-nine by Geo. J. McLeod at the Department of Agriculture.'; 5 preface signed Anne Clarke; 6 blank; 7–10 'Introductory Observations'; 11–265 cookery text of 955 numbered recipes; 266–301 'The Doctor' with items numbered 956–1034; 302 blank; 303–9 'Index of Dominion Cook Book'; 310 'Index of Medical Department'

COPIES: NSHCN *OGU (CCC TX715.6 C52) OSTPA

NOTES: American editions, in 1889 and 1891, were titled *The Ideal Cookery Book*. One other Canadian edition, O35.9, was titled *The Ideal Cook Book*. The Westminster Co. was a publishing house, active from 15 April 1896 to 1921 (Hulse, pp 277–8).

The OGU copy was originally a Christmas present. It is inscribed on the blank leaf before the title-page, in ink, 'To Mabel. From. [A.?] Tod. Dec. 25th 1899.'; and on the front endpaper, 'Mrs John M Tod // RR no 5 Embro Ontario Canada'; and on the back endpaper, in pencil, 'Mrs John Mable [*sic*] Tod // RR no 5 Embro Ontario Canada.'

O35.6 [entered 1899; about 1899–1912]

—The / Eclipse cook book / containing / valuable recipes in all the departments, / including sickroom cookery. / By / Anne Clarke / Published for / John Taylor & Company / Toronto / Sole manufacturers of Eclipse Soap.

DESCRIPTION: 18.5 × 12.0 cm Pp [3–6] 7–309 [310] A few illus Cloth

CONTENTS: 3 tp; 4 'Entered according to Act of Parliament of Canada in the year one thousand eight hundred and ninety-nine by Geo. J. McLeod at the Department of Agriculture.'; 5 preface signed Anne Clarke; 6 blank; 7–10 'Introductory Observations'; 11–265 cookery text of 955 numbered recipes; 266–301 'The Doctor' with items numbered 956–1034; 302 blank; 303–9 'Index of Dominion Cook Book'; 310 'Index of Medical Department'

COPIES: *ACG; United States: NIC (TX715.6 C51 1899)

NOTES: *The Eclipse Cook Book* was published no later than 1912, when John Taylor and Co. amalgamated with St Croix Soap Manufacturing Co. of St Stephen, New Brunswick, to form a new entity called Canadian Soaps Ltd (see 'Soap Merger,' *Monetary Times* Vol. 48, No. 19 (11 May 1912), p 1939). St Croix also published an edition of Anne Clarke's cookbook; see O35.7.

The title-page of the ACG copy is inscribed 'Martha Murray.'

O35.7 [entered 1899; about 1899–1912]

—The / "Surprise" cook book / containing / valuable recipes in all the departments, / including sickroom cookery / By / Anne Clarke / Made specially for / St. Croix Soap Manufacturing Co. / St. Stephen, N.B.

DESCRIPTION: 18.5 × 12.0 cm Pp [3–6] 7–309 [310] A few illus Cloth

CONTENTS: 3 tp; 4 'Entered according to Act of Parliament of Canada in the year one thousand eight hundred and ninety-nine by Geo. J. McLeod at the Department of Agriculture. The Dominion Cook Book'; 5 preface signed Anne Clarke; 6 blank; 7–10 'Introductory Observations'; 11–265 cookery text of 955 numbered recipes; 266–301 'The Doctor' with items numbered 956–1034; 302 blank; 303–9 'Index of Dominion Cook Book'; 310 'Index of Medical Department'

COPIES: CIHM (95360) NBFL *NSSCM

NOTES: The NBFL copy has eighteen unnumbered pages for manuscript recipes after p 310, of which pp 311–20 are blank and pp 321–8 are blank, but headed 'Recipes // My Friends' & My Own.'

The 'Surprise' Cook Book was published no later than 1912, when the St Croix Soap Manufacturing Co. amalgamated with John Taylor and Co. of Toronto, to form a new corporation called Canadian Soaps Ltd (see 'Soap Merger,' *Monetary Times* Vol. 48, No. 19 (11 May 1912), p 1939). John Taylor and Co. also published an edition of Anne Clarke's cookbook; see O35.6.

The St Croix Soap Co. published editions of two American cookbooks, also under the title *The Surprise Cook Book*: see NB6.1 and NB15.3.

O35.8 [entered 1899; about 1901–15]

—Revised edition / The / dominion cook book / containing / valuable recipes in all the departments, / including sickroom cookery. / By / Anne Clarke / Toronto: / McLeod & Allen / publishers

DESCRIPTION: 18.5 × 12.5 cm Pp [3–6] 7–309 [310–18] A few illus Cloth

CONTENTS: 3 tp; 4 'Entered according to Act of Parliament of Canada in the year one thousand eight hundred and ninety-nine by Geo. J. McLeod at the Department of Agriculture. The Dominion Cook Book'; 5 'Preface' signed Anne Clarke; 6 blank; 7–10 'Introductory Observations'; 11–265 cookery text of 955 numbered recipes; 266–301 'The Doctor' with items numbered 956–1034; 302 blank; 303–9 'Index of Dominion Cook Book'; 310 'Index of Medical Department'; 311–18 blank, ruled leaves for 'Recipes // My Friends' & My Own'

CITATIONS: O'Neill (unpublished) Powers/Stewart, p 105 (Dorothy Duncan, 'Ontario Cooking')

COPIES: ACHP (HP 4334.15) AHRMH (997-017-040) BCOM BKOM BVAU BVMA OCALNHM *OGU (UA s039 b07) OH (R641.5 C55 CESC) OKLPV OMINL ONF OTNY (uncat) OTUTF (sci) OWTU (F3878) QMM (RBD ckbk 1449); Great Britain: LB (not located)

NOTES: George J. McLeod and Thomas Allen formed a partnership in 1901 under the business name McLeod and Allen (Parker, p 251). The partnership dissolved early in 1916, after which the business operated under the name of George J. McLeod (see BS, Vol. 32, No. 2 (February 1916), p 29).

The BKOM copy lacks its binding. A copy seen at a bookseller's had its original dust-jacket, which was printed in green and featured, on the front face, in an oval frame, the image of an aproned woman adding an ingredient to a saucepan; the dust-jacket was titled 'The Dominion Cook Book // A Household Necessity // 1000 Practical Recipes Which Always Come Out Right.'

The references in Duncan, pp 133, 159, and 246–7, are to O35.8, O35.13, O35.14, or O35.17.

O35.9 [entered 1899; about 1903–6]

—The / ideal cook book / containing / valuable recipes in all the departments, / including sickroom cookery. / By / Anne Clarke / Price, $1.00 / Toronto: / Dominion Phelps, Limited, / Morang Building.

DESCRIPTION: 18.5 × 12.0 cm Pp [3–6] 7–309 [310] A few illus Cloth

CONTENTS: 3 tp; 4 'Entered according to Act of Parliament of Canada in the year one thousand eight hundred and ninety-nine by Geo. J. McLeod at the Department of Agriculture. The Dominion Cook Book'; 5 preface signed Anne Clarke; 6 blank; 7–10 'Introductory Observations'; 11–265 cookery text of 955 numbered recipes; 266–301 'The Doctor' with items numbered 956–1034; 302 blank; 303–9 'Index of Dominion Cook Book'; 310 'Index of Medical Department'

COPIES: OKITJS (992.15.1) *Private collection

NOTES: Dominion Phelps Ltd was a publishing house. It is listed in Toronto city directories for the years 1903–6 only, at 90 Wellington Street West, George N. Morang, vice-president.

American editions, in 1889 and 1891, were titled *The Ideal Cookery Book.* One other Canadian edition, O35.5, was titled *The Ideal Cook Book.*

O35.10 [entered 1899; about 1909–19]

—Revised edition / The / comfort cook book / It's all right! / Containing / valuable recipes in all the departments, / including sick room cookery. / By / Anne Clarke / Toronto: / Pugsley, Dingman & Co., Limited / publishers.

DESCRIPTION: 19.0 × 13.0 cm Pp [3–6] 7–309 [310], 24–5, 6–8, 11, 14, 17–18 [19] A few illus Lacks paper binding except part of spine, which reads, 'Comfort Cook Book'; sewn

CONTENTS: 3 tp; 4 'Entered according to Act of Parliament of Canada in the year one thousand eight hundred and ninety-nine by Geo. J. McLeod at the Department of Agriculture. The Dominion Cook Book'; 5 'Preface' signed Anne Clarke; 6 ad for Comfort Soap; 7–10 'Introductory Observations'; 11–265 cookery text of 955 numbered recipes; 266–301 'The Doctor' with items numbered 956–1034; 302 blank; 303–9 'Index of Dominion Cook Book'; 310 'Index of Medical Department'; 24–5, 6–8, 11, 14, 17–19 ads

COPIES: *QKB (75-10)

NOTES: Toronto city directories list Pugsley, Dingman and Co. as manufacturers of soaps and blues. *The Comfort Cook Book* was likely given as a premium to encourage sales of the company's laundry products. Pugsley, Dingman was at various addresses from 1899 (when this edition was registered for copyright); however, only in the period 1909–19 do the entries for the company list a Premium Department (located at 287 Queen Street West).

O35.11 copyright 1899 [about 1911–19]

—Revised edition / Ye old miller's / household book / (formerly Dominion Cook Book) / valuable recipes in all the departments, including / sickroom cookery; also medical department / Toronto: / The Campbell Flour Mills Company, Limited / publishers / Copyright, Canada, 1899 by George J. McLeod. The Dominion Cook Book.

DESCRIPTION: 18.0 × 12.5 cm Pp [3–6] 7–309 [310–18] Tp illus of a miller leaning on a sack of flour, a few illus Cloth

CONTENTS: 3 tp; 4 publ ad; 5 preface signed the publishers; 6 publ ad; 7–10 'Introductory Observations'; 11–265 cookery text of 955 numbered recipes; 266–301 'The Doctor' with items numbered 956–1034; 302 blank; 303–9 'Index of Dominion Cook Book'; 310 'Index of Medical Department'; 311–18 blank, ruled leaves for 'Recipes // My Friends' & My Own'

COPIES: *OGU (CCC TX715.6 Y34)

NOTES: Campbell Milling Co. Ltd was formed in 1904 (from Queen City Mills), and in 1911 became Campbell Flour Mills Co. Ltd; in 1919 it was bought by Maple

Leaf Milling Co. This and the following edition of *Ye Old Miller's Household Book*, therefore, were published in the period 1911–19. Anne Clarke is not credited as the author in the Campbell Flour Mills editions. For another cookbook published by the same milling company, see O153.1.

O35.12 [about 1911–18]
—Revised edition / Ye old miller's / household book / (formerly Dominion Cook Book) / valuable recipes in all the departments, including / sickroom cookery; also medical department / Toronto: / The Campbell Flour Mills Company, Limited / publishers
DESCRIPTION: 18.0 × 12.0 cm   Pp [3–6] 7–309 [310–18], [i–ii]   Tp illus of a miller leaning on a sack of flour, a few illus   Cloth
CONTENTS: 3 tp; 4 publ ad; 5 preface; 6 publ ad; 7–10 'Introductory Observations'; 11–265 cookery text of 955 numbered recipes; 266–301 'The Doctor' with items numbered 956–1034; 302 blank; 303–9 'Index of Dominion Cook Book'; 310 'Index of Medical Department'; 311–18 blank, ruled leaves for 'Recipes // My Friends' & My Own'; i–ii publ ads
CITATIONS: Golick, p 104   JPCat Recent Acquisitions, June 1994, No. 33
COPIES: *OGU (UA s045 b38)   OL (641.5 Y3)   OTUTF (sci)   Private collection
NOTES: Unlike O35.11, there is no copyright date on the title-page. The private collector's copy is inscribed on the title-page, in ink, July 2[7?]th/18 Mary E Codlin.'; therefore, this edition was published no later than 1918. See O35.11 regarding the date of the Campbell Flour Mills editions.

O35.13 [entered 1899; 1916 or later]
—Revised edition / The / dominion cook book / containing / valuable recipes in all the departments, / including sickroom cookery. / By / Anne Clarke / Toronto: / George J. McLeod / publisher.
DESCRIPTION: 18.5 × 12.0 cm   Pp [3–6] 7–309 [310]   A few illus   Cloth
CONTENTS: 3 tp; 4 'Entered according to Act of Parliament of Canada in the year one thousand eight hundred and ninety-nine by Geo. J. McLeod at the Department of Agriculture. The Dominion Cook Book'; 5 preface signed Anne Clarke; 6 blank; 7–10 'Introductory Observations'; 11–265 cookery text of 955 numbered recipes; 266–301 'The Doctor' with items numbered 956–1034; 302 blank; 303–9 'Index of Dominion Cook Book'; 310 'Index of Medical Department'

COPIES: OKQ (TX715 C55 1899t)   OONL (TX715 C577 1899b p***)   *Private collection
NOTES: The title-page differs from O35.14 in that there is no 'Limited' following 'McLeod' and 'publisher' is singular. 'Presented with the Montreal Herald' is printed on the front face of the binding.

In early 1916, Mr Allen left the publishing company of McLeod and Allen, and his partner took over, operating the firm under his own name, George J. McLeod (see BS, Vol. 32, No. 2 (February 1916), p 29). This edition and O35.14, therefore, were published in 1916 or later.

O35.14 [entered 1899; 1916 or later]
—Revised edition / The / dominion cook book / containing / valuable recipes in all the departments, / including sickroom cookery. / By / Anne Clarke / Toronto: / George J. McLeod, Limited / publishers
DESCRIPTION: 18.5 × 12.0 cm   Pp [3–6] 7–309 [310–18]   A few illus   Cloth
CONTENTS: 3 tp; 4 'Entered according to Act of Parliament of Canada in the year one thousand eight hundred and ninety-nine by Geo. J. McLeod at the Department of Agriculture.'; 5 preface signed Anne Clarke; 6 blank; 7–10 'Introductory Observations'; 11–265 cookery text of 955 numbered recipes; 266–301 'The Doctor' with items numbered 956–1034; 302 blank; 303–9 'Index of Dominion Cook Book'; 310 'Index of Medical Department'; 311–18 blank for 'Recipes // My Friends' & My Own'
COPIES: OHMB (TX C597d 1899)   OKELWM (988.18.1)   OTUTF (sci)   *Private collection; United States: OC
NOTES: Unlike O35.13, ', Limited' follows 'McLeod' and 'publishers' is plural.

Ferguson/Fraser, p 232, cite *The Dominion Cook Book*, revised edition, Toronto: George J. McLeod Ltd, 1901. The date 1901 is incorrect; the reference is likely to O35.13 or O35.14. The closed volume is illustrated in colour on p 11.

O35.15 [entered 1899; 1916 or later]
—[First tp:] The / new Canadian / cook book / Price one dollar / Stone & Cox Limited / 7 Jordan Street – Toronto
[Second tp:] Revised edition / The / dominion cook book / containing / valuable recipes in all the departments, / including sickroom cookery. / By / Anne Clarke / Toronto: / George J. McLeod, Limited / publishers
DESCRIPTION: 17.5 × 12.5 cm   Pp [i–ii], [1–6] 7–309 [310–18]   A few illus   Paper

CONTENTS: i first tp; ii 'Entered according to Act of Parliament of Canada in the year one thousand eight hundred and ninety-nine by Geo. J. McLeod at the Department of Agriculture'; 1–2 blank; 3 second tp; 4 'Entered according to Act of Parliament of Canada in the year one thousand eight hundred and ninety-nine by Geo. J. McLeod at the Department of Agriculture'; 5 preface signed Anne Clarke; 6 blank; 7–10 'Introductory Observations'; 11–265 cookery text with 955 numbered recipes; 266–301 'The Doctor' with items numbered 956–1034; 302 blank; 303–9 'Index of Dominion Cook Book'; 310 'Index of Medical Department'; 311–18 blank for 'Recipes // My Friends' & My Own'
COPIES: *Private collection
NOTES: The cover-title is 'The New Canadian Cook Book // A Household Necessity // 1,000 Tried and Tested Recipes and Household Helps.'

O35.16   [entered 1899]
—Revised edition / The Hudson's Bay / cook book / containing / valuable recipes in all the departments, / including sickroom cookery. / By / Anne Clarke / The Hudson's Bay Company / publishers
DESCRIPTION: 18.5 × 12.5 cm   Pp [3–6] 7–309 [310–18]   A few illus   Cloth
CONTENTS: 3 tp; 4 'Entered according to Act of Parliament of Canada in the year one thousand eight hundred and ninety-nine by Geo. J. McLeod at the Department of Agriculture. The Dominion Cook Book'; 5 preface signed Anne Clarke; 6 blank; 7–10 'Introductory Observations'; 11–265 cookery text of 955 numbered recipes; 266–301 'The Doctor' with items numbered 956–1034; 302 blank; 303–9 'Index of Dominion Cook Book'; 310 'Index of Medical Department'; 311–18 blank, ruled leaves for 'Recipes // My Friends' & My Own'
COPIES: MWMM   OGU (2 copies: CCC TX715.6 C52 1899, *UA s039 b19)
NOTES: The Hudson's Bay Co. is Canada's oldest corporation, created in 1670 to exploit the fur trade. By the 1880s its focus had shifted to retail.

O35.17   [entered 1899]
—Revised edition / The / dominion cook book / containing / valuable recipes in all the departments, / including sickroom cookery. / By / Anne Clarke / The T. Eaton Co Limited / Toronto and Winnipeg
DESCRIPTION: 18.0 × 12.0 cm   Pp [3–6] 7–309 [310–18]   A few illus   Rebound
CONTENTS: 3 tp; 4 'Entered according to Act of Parlia-

ment of Canada in the year one thousand eight hundred and ninety-nine by Geo. J. McLeod at the Department of Agriculture.'; 5 'Preface' signed Anne Clarke; 6 blank; 7–10 'Introductory Observations'; 11–265 cookery text of 955 numbered recipes; 266–301 'The Doctor' with items numbered 956–1034; 302 blank; 303–9 'Index of Dominion Cook Book'; 310 'Index of Medical Department'; 311–18 blank for 'Recipes // My Friends' & My Own'
COPIES: CIHM (26962)   *OONL (TX715 C577 1899)
NOTES: Another Toronto department store, Robert Simpson Co., also published an edition of Anne Clarke's book; see O35.18.

O35.18   [entered 1899]
—Revised edition / The / white / cook / book / containing /cooking and household recipes, to which / is added a compendium of   health / suggestions and useful / medical knowledge. / By / Anne Clarke. / The / Robert Simpson / Co. / Limited / Toronto, Canada
CONTENTS: Tp verso 'Entered according to Act of Parliament of Canada in the year one thousand eight hundred and ninety-nine by Geo. J. McLeod at the Department of Agriculture. The Dominion Cook Book'
COPIES: United States: *IaU (SPEC SZAT TX715.6 C5 1899)
NOTES: The cookbook's title may refer to the colour of the cloth binding, probably originally white, although now reported to be a 'dirty gray' by the curator of Rare Books at IaU. The publisher, Robert Simpson Co., was a Toronto department store and competitor of the T. Eaton Co., which published O35.17. The volume has 309 pp.

AMERICAN EDITIONS: *The People's Cook Book. Economy, Wealth and Comfort in the Household. 1,349 New, Useful and Unique Recipes in Cookery and All Departments of Housekeeping,* half-title: *Mrs Clarke's Cookery Book,* Chicago: The People's Publishing Co., 1889 (BVICC); *The Ideal Cookery Book ...,* Chicago: F.J. Schulte and Co., [1889] (United States: DLC); *... The Ideal Cookery Book ... 1,349 New, Useful and Unique Recipes in Cookery and All Departments of Housekeeping,* Chicago: F.J. Schulte and Co., 1889, 1891 (Axford, p 224); *The Ideal Cookery Book ... 1,178 New, Useful and Unique Recipes in Cookery and All Departments of Housekeeping,* [Philadelphia:] Edgewood Publishing Co., 1891 (United States: ICJ microform); possibly *Mrs Clarke's Cook Book: Containing Over One Thousand of the Best Up-to-Date Recipes ...,* Washington, DC: National Tribune, 1906, [c1899] (United States: CoDU, OBgU).

Health in the household

O36.1 1883
Health / in the / household / a valuable collection of information / and / practical recipes / for the / preservation / of / health / and / cure of disease. / Published by T. Milburn & Co. / Toronto, Ont. / 1883. [cover-title]
DESCRIPTION: 18.5 × 12.0 cm Pp [1–3] 4–31, [i] Paper, with image on front of two Chinese figures (woman and child) and a crane(?), plus three other birds and a head in silhouette; sewn, and with string through top left corner for hanging
CONTENTS: 1 'Contents' and 'Classification of Diseases'; 2 'Introduction' signed the publishers; 3–top 7 Part I, 'Health Hints, or Hygiene at Home'; near top 7–mid 29 Part II, 'Diseases and Their Treatment'; bottom 29–31 Part III, 'Cookery for the Sick'; i ad for Burdock Blood Bitters
COPIES: *OTUTF (uncat patent medicine)
NOTES: The 'Introduction' explains the book's purpose: 'To teach a better understanding of the human system in health and disease, and a more compatible living with nature's requirements, in plain, simple truths, imparting such knowledge and giving such hints as shall be of practical benefit in every home and to every individual, is the earnest endeavor of this little book.' There are sections on 'Diet' and 'Drink' on pp 5–top 7. Printed on the outside back face of the binding is 'This book is presented by,' and stamped in the following blank space, 'J.D Fitch Grimsby Ont.'

O36.2 nd [about 1885–90]
—Health in the / household / and / practical / recipes / for the sick / [printer's name in very small letters:] Grip Co. / Published by / T. Milburn & Co. / Toronto [cover-title]
DESCRIPTION: 18.0 × 12.0 cm Pp [1–3] 4–31, [i] Paper; stapled, and with hole punched at top left corner, through which runs a string for hanging
CONTENTS: 1 'Contents' and 'Classification of Diseases'; 2 'Introduction' signed the publishers; 3–top 7 Part I, 'Health Hints, or Hygiene at Home'; near top 7–mid 29 Part II, 'Diseases and Their Treatment'; bottom 29–31 Part III, 'Cookery for the Sick'; i ad for Burdock Blood Bitters
COPIES: *OTUTF (uncat patent medicine, 2 copies)
NOTES: From appearances, this edition is later than that of 1883. On p 1, in the table of contents, Part IV, 'Practical Recipes and Useful Information' is listed, but there is no Part IV at the end of the book. The printing of 'Part IV' in the table of contents may be a typographical error. In the 1883 edition, no 'Part IV' is

listed and the phrase 'Practical Recipes and Useful Information' appears as an extension of the Part III title, i.e., 'Cookery for the Sick, Including Practical Recipes ...'
The only apparent difference between the two OTUTF copies of O36.2 is that the advertisements on the inside faces of the binding are reversed, i.e., one copy has an advertisement for Petrolina at the front and an advertisement for Burdock Blood Bitters at the back, the other has Petrolina at the back and Burdock Blood Bitters at the front. Printed on the outside back face of the binding is 'Presented with compliments of [blank space].'

O36.3 nd [about 1939]
—Health / in the / household / and hints / for the / preservation / of health / Published by / the T. Milburn Co. Limited / Toronto, Ont. [cover-title]
DESCRIPTION: 17.0 × 11.5 cm Pp 1–32 Paper, with image on front of a miniature woman and man, the woman cutting the bloom of the plant that the man is watering; stapled
CONTENTS: Inside front face of binding 'Just a Few Hints for the Sick' [i.e., introductory text] signed T. Milburn Co. Ltd, Toronto; 1–32 medical information and testimonials, including 'Cookery for the Sick' on p 24
COPIES: *OTUTF (uncat patent medicine)
NOTES: There is only one page of recipes in this edition, which looks much later than O36.1 and O36.2. 'Just a Few Hints for the Sick' refers to the organization of T. Milburn and Co. Ltd in 1874 and lists its preparations that have been used 'during the last 65 years,' suggesting a publication date of about 1939. Preparations made by T. Milburn Co. included Burdock Blood Bitters, Dr Fowler's Extract of Wild Strawberry, Milburn's Heart and Nerve Pills, Hagyard Remedies, and Dr Low's Remedies.
Printed on the outside back face of the binding is 'Presented with the compliments of your dealer.,' and stamped in the blank space that follows, 'E.R. Wigle, druggist // successor to Jas. Wilson, Goderich, Ont.'

Holloway, Laura Carter (1848–)

Another food-related work by this American author is The Buddhist Diet-Book, *New York: Funk and Wagnalls, 1886 (United States: DLC). She also wrote about social and domestic life in the White House, and about the mothers and wives of great men. Some of her titles appeared under the last name of Holloway Langford.*

O37.1   1883 [copyright 1883]

The / hearthstone; / or, / life at home. / A household manual. / Containing / hints and helps for home making; home furnishing; decorations / amusements; health directions; the sick-room; the nursery / the library; the laundry; etc. / together with / a complete cookery book, / by / Laura C. Holloway, / author of "Ladies of the White House," etc. / Bradley, Garretson & Co., / Philadelphia, 66 North Fourth Street, / Brantford, Ont. / William Garretson & Co., / Columbus, O.; Chicago, Ills.; Nashville, Tenn. St. Louis, Mo. / 1883.

DESCRIPTION: 21.5 × 15.5 cm   Pp [i–ii] iii–v [vi] vii [viii] ix–xix [xx], 25–582   11 pls incl frontis of 'The Hearth Stone' (6 pls incl in pagination, pp 376–88), 4 fp illus, illus   Cloth, with image on front of a house and children playing

CONTENTS: i tp; ii 'Copyright by Laura C. Holloway, 1883.'; iii–v preface; vi blank; vii list of illustrations; viii blank; ix–xix table of contents; xx blank; 25–582 text

COPIES: CIHM (95409)   *OGU (UA s050 b13)

NOTES: The frontispiece is copyrighted: 'Copyright by J.W. Bradley, 1882.' There are recipes for invalid cookery in the chapter 'In the Sick-Room.' 'The Kitchen in the Home,' pp 395–402, is followed by 'Cookery Recipes,' pp 403–549.

O37.2   [copyright 1883]

—The / hearthstone; / or, / life at home. / A household manual. / Containing / hints and helps for home making; home furnishing; decorations / amusements; health directions; the sick-room; the nursery / the library; the laundry; etc. / together with / a complete cookery book, / by / Laura C. Holloway, / author of "Ladies of the White House," etc. / Bradley, Garretson & Co., / 66 North Fourth Street, Philadelphia. / Brantford, Ont. / William Garretson & Co., / Columbus, O.; Chicago, Ill.; Nashville, Tenn.; / St. Louis, Mo.; San Francisco, Cal.

DESCRIPTION: 21.5 × 16.0 cm   Pp [i–ii] iii–v [vi] vii [viii] ix–xix [xx], 25–582   11 pls incl frontis of 'The Hearth Stone,' fp illus, illus   Rebound

CONTENTS: i tp; ii 'Copyright by Laura C. Holloway, 1883.'; iii–v 'Preface'; vi blank; vii 'Illustrations'; viii blank; ix–xix 'Contents'; xx blank; 25–582 text

COPIES: *OTU (TDS H Gerstein)

NOTES: The imprint differentiates this edition from O37.1: San Francisco is a place of publication and there is no date on the title-page.

O37.3   [copyright 1883; about 1885–7]

—The / hearthstone; / or, / life at home / A household manual. / Containing / hints and helps for home making; home furnishing; decoration [*sic*] / amusements; health directions; the sick-room; the nursery / the library; the laundry; etc. / together with / a complete cookery book / by / Laura C. Holloway, / author of "Ladies of the White House," etc. / International Book and Bible House, / 46 and 48 Front Street, East, / Toronto, Ontario.

COPIES: *OMUC

NOTES: International Book and Bible House was in business from 1 January 1885 to 1887 (Hulse, p 132).

The housewife's library

O38.1   [copyright 1883]

The / housewife's library: / (Many volumes in one.) / Furnishing / the very best help in all the necessities, intricacies, emergencies, / and vexations that puzzle a housekeeper in every department / of her duties in the home. / Household management, / domestic cookery, home furnishing, / home decoration, polite deportment, / trying emergencies, care of children, / games, amusements, etc., / general hints. / Very carefully prepared after laborious research by a skilled / corps of experts in the different departments. / Appropriately illustrated. / World Publishing Co., / Guelph, Ont.

DESCRIPTION: 19.5 × 13.0 cm   Pp [i–ii] iii–xi [xii], [13–14] 15–644   6 pls col; frontis of 'Mother. The Queen of Home'; 2 pls, incl in pagination; many illus of stoves, ranges, kitchen utensils, furniture   Cloth

CONTENTS: i tp; ii 'Copyright by George A. Peltz, 1883.'; iii–iv preface signed the publishers; v–viii table of contents; ix–xi list of illustrations; xii quotation from James A. Garfield; 13–632 text; 633–44 index

CITATIONS: Abrahamson, p 59   Driver 2001, Wellington County, p 94

COPIES: CIHM (95402)   OCN (FX91.36.1)   *OGU (UA s062 b11)   SR (uncat)

NOTES: Of culinary interest are Part I, 'Domestic Cookery,' pp 13–296; Part II, 'Household Management,' pp 297–388; and Part IX, 'General Hints,' pp 627–32, which includes hints for the kitchen.

World Publishing Co. had been established in Guelph by Mr J.W. Lyon, to publish books for distribution in Canada and through agencies in South America, South Africa, Hindostan, Ceylon, Australia (which he visited in 1876), and New Zealand. It is unknown whether this Canadian-published, but American-authored cookbook (or a later American-authored cookbook by the company, O119.6, Gregory, Annie R., *Woman's Favorite Cook Book*) reached these distant places. (See 'Canadian Books Abroad,' *Monetary Times* Vol. 20, No. 43 (22 April 1887), p 1257, and the advertisement for World Publishing reproduced in Parker, p xviii.)

AMERICAN EDITIONS: *The Housewife's Library*, [edited by George A. Peltz], Philadelphia, New York: Hubbard Bros, [c1883] (United States: DLC); *The Housewife's Library with Suggestions on Self-Supporting Employment for Southern Ladies ...*, [edited by George A. Peltz], Richmond, Va: B.F. Johnson and Co., [c1885] (United States: DLC).

1886

Parker, Mrs Eliza R.

This American author's recipes were included in promotional books for the shortening Cottolene: Q29.1, 266 recettes choisies; and Q30.1, 600 Selected Recipes. She contributed recipe columns to such periodicals as Home Magazine *of Washington, DC (for example, Vol. 8, No. 6 (July 1896)) and* Cooking Club *of Goshen, Ind. (for example, 8th year, No. 3 (March 1902)).*

O39.1   1886 [copyright 1885]
Economical / housekeeping. / A complete system of household management / for those who wish to live well at a moderate cost. All / branches of cookery are carefully treated, and in- / formation given on canning fruits, curing meats, / making butter, washing, ironing, dyeing, renovat- / ing, the toilet, care of the sick, rearing of chil- / dren, cultivating flowers, bee culture, silk / culture, the poultry yard, and much else / that is valuable to every housekeeper. / By Mrs. Eliza R. Parker. / Illustrated. / Toronto: / J.S. Robertson & Bros., publishers, / 1886.
DESCRIPTION: 20.5 × 15.0 cm   Pp [i–v] vi–viii, [1] 2–598   4 pls col incl frontis, 11 fp illus, many illus   Cloth
CONTENTS: i tp; ii 'Copyrighted by M.T. Richardson, 1885.'; iii preface; iv blank; v–viii table of contents; 1–585 text, mainly recipes; 586 blank; 587–98 index; [eight blank, ruled leaves for manuscript recipes]
COPIES: CIHM (08841)   *OGU (UA s050 b14)   OWTU (F8799)
NOTES: In the preface, the author thanks the Lalance and Grosjean Manufacturing Co., New York, for 'the use of the cuts representing their Patent Agate Iron Ware.' Chapter 49, 'Cooking School,' relates the teaching methods and useful information disseminated at the New York Cooking School.

AMERICAN EDITIONS: *Mrs Parker's Complete Housekeeper, a System of Household Management for All Who Wish to Live Well at a Moderate Cost*, New York: M.T. Richardson, 1888 (United States: DLC, LU, MoU, OAkU, TxSalA, ViFGM); *Mrs Parker's Complete Housekeeper*, rev. ed., New York: M.T. Richardson Co., 1894 (United States: DLC).

1887

Chase, Dr Alvin Wood (Cayuga County, NY, 20 March 1817–25 May 1885, Ohio)

For information about Dr Chase and his publications, see O8.1.

O40.1   1887
"Memorial edition" / Dr. Chase's / third, last and complete / receipt book / and / household physician, / or / practical knowledge for the people, / from / the life-long observations of the author, embracing the choicest, most valuable / and entirely new receipts in every department of medicine, mechanics, / and household economy; including a treatise on / the diseases of women and children, / in fact, / the book for the million, / with remarks and explanations which adapt it to the every-day wants / of the people, arranged in departments and most / copiously indexed. / By A.W. Chase, M.D. / author of "Dr. Chase's Receipts; or Information for Everybody;" also "Dr. Chase's / Family Physician, Farrier, Bee Keeper and Second Receipt Book." / "Why conceal that which relieves distress." / Published by / F.B. Dickerson & Co. / Detroit, Mich. and Windsor, Ont. / To whom all correspondence should be addressed. / 1887.
DESCRIPTION: 21.0 × 15.7 cm   Pp 808   Frontis portrait of the author, three woodcut illus   Cloth
CONTENTS: Tp verso 'Copyright, 1884, by A.W. Chase. Copyright, 1887, by F.B. Dickerson. All rights reserved.'
CITATIONS: Cagle/Stafford No. 142
COPIES: United States: InU
NOTES: This is Dr Chase's third collection of recipes, which he compiled shortly before his death. Information about this edition is from the Cagle/Stafford entry.

O40.2 1888

—"Memorial edition" / Dr. Chase's / third, last
and complete / receipt book / and / household
physician, / or / practical knowledge for the people,
/ from / the life-long observations of the author,
embracing the choicest, most valuable /
and entirely new receipts in every department of
medicine, mechanics, / and household economy;
including a treatise on / the diseases of women and
children, / in fact, / the book for the million, / with
remarks and explanations which adapt it to the
every-day wants / of the people, arranged in
departments and most / copiously indexed. / By
A.W. Chase, M.D. / author of "Dr. Chase's Receipts;
or Information for Everybody;" also "Dr. Chase's /
Family Physician, Farrier, Bee Keeper and Second
Receipt Book." / "Why conceal that which relieves
distress." / Published by / F.B. Dickerson & Co. /
Detroit, Mich. and Windsor, Ont. / To whom all
correspondence should be addressed. / 1888.

DESCRIPTION: 20.5 × 15.0 cm   Pp [i–vii] viii–ix [x–xi]
xii–xiv [xv–xvi], 1–865   Frontis portrait of the author, fp illus on pp iv, vi, x, xvi   Cloth, with images
on front of flowers and, in a circular frame, a small
landscape

CONTENTS: i tp; ii 'Copyright, 188[last digit illegible], by
A.W. Chase. Copyright, 1887, by F.B. Dickerson. All
rights reserved.'; iii 'Dedication' signed A.W. Chase;
iv fp illus; v 'Publishers' Preface'; vi fp illus; vii–ix
'Author's Preface'; x fp illus; xi–xiv 'In Memoriam'
signed Rev. L. Davis, secretary of the Washtenaw
County Pioneer Society, Ann Arbor, 28 November
1886; xv table of contents; xvi fp illus; 1–816 text; 817–
31 'Glossary'; 832 'Publishers' Notice'; 833–43 'Medical Index'; 844–65 'General Index'

COPIES: *OTUTF (jah 19652, 2 copies)

NOTES: At the end of the 'Author's Preface,' on p ix, the
publishers have added, 'Just two months after completing this work, and writing the foregoing preface,
the "Old Doctor" passed away [i.e., in 1885] ...'

   OTUTF copy 2 is signed in purple pencil, 'Wm
Buckland // Amabel Ont.'

O40.3 1888

—[Another edition, *Deutsche Ausgabe von Dr. Chase's
drittem, letzten und vollständigem Recept-Buch und
Haus-Arzt, oder praktische Lehren für das Volk*, Detroit,
Mich., and Windsor, Ont.: F.B. Dickerson and Co.,
1888 [copyright 1886, 1888]]

COPIES: United States: MH (TX153 C38 G3 1888)

NOTES: This edition has 873 pages and is bound in
cloth.

O40.4 1889

—"Memorial edition" / Dr. Chase's / third, last
and complete / receipt book / and / household
physician, / or / practical knowledge for the people,
/ from / the life-long observations of the author,
embracing the choicest, most valuable /
and entirely new receipts in every department of
medicine, mechanics, / and household economy;
including a treatise on / the diseases of women and
children, / in fact, / the book for the million, / with
remarks and explanations which adapt it to the
every-day wants / of the people, arranged in
departments and most / copiously indexed. / By
A.W. Chase, M.D. / author of "Dr. Chase's Receipts;
or Information for Everybody;" also "Dr. Chase's /
Family Physician, Farrier, Bee Keeper and Second
Receipt Book." / "Why conceal that which relieves
distress." / Published by / F.B. Dickerson & Co. /
Detroit, Mich. and Windsor, Ont. / To whom all
correspondence should be addressed. / 1889.

DESCRIPTION: 20.5 × 15.0 cm   Pp [i–vii] viii–ix [x–xi]
xii–xiv [xv–xvi], 1–865   Frontis portrait of the author, fp illus on pp iv, vi, x, xvi   Cloth

CONTENTS: i tp; ii 'Copyright, 188[last digit illegible] by
A.W. Chase. Copyright, 1887, by F.B. Dickerson. All
rights reserved.'; iii 'Dedication' signed A.W. Chase;
iv fp illus; v 'Publishers' Preface'; vi fp illus; vii–ix
'Author's Preface'; x fp illus; xi–xiv 'In Memoriam';
xv 'Contents'; xvi fp illus; 1–816 text; 817–31 'Glossary'; 832 'Publishers' Notice'; 833–43 'Medical Index'; 844–65 'General Index'

COPIES: CIHM (01772)   OKITD (x962.081.001) *QMM
(Osler Robertson C487r 1889)

NOTES: On p ii of the OKITD copy, the last digit of
Chase's copyright date is also badly printed, but it
may be 1884.

O40.5 1889

—"Zum Angedenken." / Deutsche Ausgabe von
Dr. Chase's / drittem, letzten und vollständigem /
Recept-Buch / und Haus-Arzt, / oder praktische
Lehren für das Volk. / Das Resultat langjähriger /
Beobachtungen des Verfassers, enthaltend die
werthvollsten und neuesten / Recepte in allen
Zweigen der Medizin, und Gemeinnütziges für den
Haushalt, / einschliesslich einer Abhandlung über /
Frauen- und Kinder-Krankheiten, / –:thatsächlich:–
/ Das Buch für Millionen, / Mit Bemerkungen und
Erklärungen für den täglichen Gebrauch der Menge,
in interessanten / Abschnitten geordnet, und mit
leicht übersichtlichem Inhaltsverzeichniss /
versehen. / Von A.W. Chase, M.D., / Verfasser von
"Dr. Chase's Recept-Buch, oder Rathschläge für

Jedermann," sowie "Dr. Chase's Haus- / arzt,"
"Thierarzt," "Bienenzüchter," und "Zweites
Recept-Buch." / "Warum verschweigen, was das
Leid vermindert?" / Herausgegeben von / F.B.
Dickerson & Co., / Detroit, Mich., u. Windsor, Ont.
/ 1889.
DESCRIPTION: 21.0 × 15.0 cm   Pp [i–vi] vii–ix [x] xi–xv
[xvi], 1–873   Frontis portrait of the author, a few fp
illus   Cloth
CONTENTS: i tp; ii 'Copyright, 1886. By A.W. Chase.
Copyright, 1888. By F.B. Dickerson. All rights re-
served.'; iii 'Widmung' signed the author; iv fp illus;
v 'Vorwort der Herausgeber'; vi fp illus; vii–ix
'Vorwort des Verfassers'; x fp illus; xi–xiv 'In Memoriam'; xv 'Inhalt'; xvi fp illus; 1–850 text; 851–8
'Inhaltsverzeichniss des medicinischen Theils'; 859–
73 'Allgemeines Inhaltsverzeichniss'
COPIES: *OGU (CCC TX715.6 C4515)
NOTES: The OGU copy originally belonged to Old Order Mennonites in Waterloo County, Ontario, according to the donor of the book.

O40.6   1891
—Memorial edition / Dr. Chase's / third / last /
and complete / receipt book / and / household /
physician / or practical knowledge for the people, /
from the life-long observations of the author,
embracing the choicest, most valuable / and entirely
new receipts in every department of medicine,
mechanics, and household / economy; including a
treatise on / the diseases of women and children, /
in fact, / the book for the million, / with remarks
and explanations which adapt it to the every-day
wants of the people, / arranged in departments and
most copiously indexed. / By A.W. Chase, M.D., /
author of "Dr. Chase's Receipts; or Information for
Everybody." Also Dr. Chase's / Family Physician,
Farrier, Bee Keeper and Second Receipt Book." /
"Why conceal that which relieves distress." /
Published by / F.B. Dickerson Co / Detroit, Mich.,
and Windsor, Ont. / to whom all correspondence
should be / addressed. / 1891
DESCRIPTION: Frontis portrait of the author
CONTENTS: Tp verso 'Copyright, 188[last digit illegible]
by A.W. Chase. Copyright, 1887, by F.B. Dickerson.
All rights reserved.'
COPIES: OKQ (2 copies: *TX153 C49 1891t, WBA C487t
1891)

O40.7   1892
—Memorial edition / Dr. Chase's / third / last /
and complete / receipt book / and / household /
physician / or practical knowledge for the people, /

from the life-long observations of the author,
embracing the choicest, most valuable / and entirely
new receipts in every department of medicine,
mechanics, and household / economy; including a
treatise on / the diseases of women and children, /
in fact, / the book for the million, / with remarks
and explanations which adapt it to the every-day
wants of the people, / arranged in departments and
most copiously indexed. / By A.W. Chase, M.D., /
author of "Dr. Chase's Receipts; or Information for
Everybody." Also [sic, no opening quotation-marks]
Dr. Chase's / Family Physician, Farrier, Bee Keeper
and Second Receipt Book." / "Why conceal that
which relieves distress." / Published by / F.B.
Dickerson Co. / Detroit, Mich., and Windsor, Ont. /
to whom all correspondence should be / addressed.
/ 1892
DESCRIPTION: 20.5 × 15.0 cm   Pp [iii–vii] viii–ix [xi] xii–
xiii [xiv–xv], 1–865   Frontis portrait of the author, 16
pls   Cloth
CONTENTS: iii tp; iv 'Publishers' Notice' seeking agents
and 'Copyright, 1884, by A.W. Chase. Copyright, 1887,
by F.B. Dickerson. All rights reserved.'; v dedication:
'This, my third and last receipt book, is ... dedicated
to the twelve hundred thousand families, throughout
the United States and Dominion of Canada, who have
purchased one or both of my former books, ...'; vi
'Publishers' Preface'; vii–ix 'Author's Preface'; xi–xiv
'In Memoriam'; xv table of contents; 1–816 text; 817–
31 glossary; 832 'Publishers' Notice' seeking agents;
833–43 'Medical Index'; 844–65 'General Index'
COPIES: BCHM   OTAR (640.3 Cha 1892)   *Private
collection
NOTES: Page x is omitted in the pagination of the front
matter: The table of contents indicates that 'In Memoriam' starts on p xi, which is actually the verso of p ix,
i.e., which should be numbered as p x.

O40.8   1900
—Memorial edition. / Dr. Chase's / third, last and
complete / receipt book / and household physician,
/ or practical knowledge for the people, / from the
life-long observations of the author, embracing the
choicest, most valuable and / entirely new receipts
in every department of medicine, mechanics,
and / household economy; including a treatise on /
the diseases of women and children; / in fact, /
the book for the million. / With remarks and
explanations which adapt it to the every-day wants
of the people, / arranged in departments and most
copiously indexed. / By A.W. Chase, M.D., / author
of "Dr. Chase's Receipts, or Information for
Everybody." Also "Dr. Chase's / Family Physician,

Farrier, Bee-Keeper and Second Receipt Book." / "Why conceal that which relieves distress?" / Published by / F.B. Dickerson Company, / Detroit, Mich., and Windsor, Ont. / to whom all correspondence should be addressed. / 1900.

DESCRIPTION: 21.0 × 15.5 cm   Pp [iii–vii] viii–ix [xi] xii–xiii [xiv–xv], 1–865, [i–iii]   Frontis portrait of the author, pls   Full leather

CONTENTS: iii tp; iv 'Publishers' Notice' and 'Copyright, 188[4?], by A.W. Chase. Copyright, 1887, by F.B. Dickerson. All rights reserved.'; v 'Dedication'; vi 'Publishers' Preface'; vii–ix 'Author's Preface'; xi–xiv 'In Memoriam' by L. Davis, secretary of the Washtenaw County Pioneer Society, Ann Arbor, Michigan; xv 'Contents'; 1–816 text; 817–31 'Glossary'; 832 'Publisher's Notices'; 833–43 'Medical Index'; 844–65 'General Index'; i–iii publ ads

COPIES: ACHP (HP 5109.36)   *Private collection

NOTES: The title-page is printed in red and black. Page x is omitted from the pagination.

O40.9   1901

—[Another edition, Toronto: Edmanson, Bates and Co., 1901]

COPIES: Private collection

O40.10   1903

—Authorized Canadian edition. / Memorial edition. / Dr. Chase's / third, last and complete / receipt book / and household physician, / or practical knowledge for the people, / from the life-long observations of the author, embracing the choicest, most valuable and / entirely new receipts in every department of medicine, mechanics, and / household economy; including a treatise on / the diseases of women and children; / in fact, / the book for the million. / With remarks and explanations which adapt it to the every-day wants of the people, / arranged in departments and most copiously indexed. / By A.W. Chase, M.D., / author of "Dr. Chase's Receipts, or Information for Everybody." Also "Dr. Chase's / Family Physician, Farrier, Bee-keeper and Second Receipt Book." / "Why conceal that which relieves distress?" / Published by / Edmanson, Bates & Co., / Toronto, Ontario. / 1903.

COPIES: OSTC (640.2 Cha M)   *Private collection

AMERICAN EDITIONS: *Dr Chase's Third, Last and Complete Receipt Book and Household Physician*, Detroit: F.B. Dickerson and Co., 1891 [copyright 1884] (United States: MCR, MH); Detroit: F.B. Dickerson, 1897, copy-right 1887 (United States: DLC); Detroit and Minneapolis: F.B. Dickerson Co., 1907 (Private collection); Detroit and Minneapolis: F.B. Dickerson Co., 1908 (OGU; United States: InU).

1888

The breadmaker's book of cooking lessons

O41.1   entered 1888

The breadmaker's / book of / cooking lessons / compiled from / original and selected formulae. / Entered according to Act of Parliament of Canada, in the year one thousand / eight hundred and eighty-eight, by T.H. Churchill, in the office of / the Minister of Agriculture. / Churchill & Co., / Toronto, Ont.

DESCRIPTION: 17.5 × 12.0 cm   Pp [iii–v] vi [vii–viii], [9] 10–188, [i] ii–iv   Illus on p 24 of breadmaker's kneading pan   Limp cloth; stapled

CONTENTS: iii tp; iv dedication 'To the bread-winners and bread-makers of America ...'; v–vi 'Preface' signed the author; vii 'Contents'; viii 'Comparative Values of Foods'; mid 9 'Our Plan'; bottom 9–top 10 'Weights and Measures'; mid 10–25 'Lessons in Breadmaking'; 26–top 54 'Lessons in Cakemaking'; mid 54–71 'Pies, Puddings, Tarts, etc.'; 72–mid 98 'Animal Food' [i.e., recipes for meat and poultry]; bottom 98–mid 107 'Sauces, Gravies, Salads and Relishes'; bottom 107–mid 115 'Soups'; mid 115–mid 129 'Vegetables'; bottom 129–136 'Pickles'; 137–mid 138 'Catsups'; bottom 138–139 'Eggs'; 140–mid 146 'Drinks'; mid 146–mid 157 'Fruit'; bottom 157–163 'Food for the Sick'; 164–mid 174 'Family Prescriptions, etc.'; bottom 174–mid 177 'Disinfectants'; mid 177–179 'Materia Medica'; 180–8 'Miscellaneous'; i–top iv 'Index' [culinary]; mid iv index for 'Medical and General Department'

CITATIONS: Golick, pp 99, 101, 105

COPIES: CIHM (88781)   *OTNY (uncat)

NOTES: The cover-title is 'The Breadmakers [*sic*] Cooking Lessons.' In the 'Preface' the unnamed author identifies the source of some of the recipes: '... we are indebted to an enthusiastic housewife who placed at our disposal a bulky scrap book, ... In some instances we have consulted other publications, notably Marion Harland's ... "Common Sense in the Household," "Mrs. Clark's Cookery Book," "The Home Cook Book," "Mother Hubbard," and "Soyer's English Cook Book," ...' All but the last are catalogued in this bibliography. 'Our Plan' explains the organization of the text: 'We shall depart from the usual routine of [cookbooks] and instead, we shall commence with bread as the most important food of mankind, ...' The section on breadmaking includes prize bread recipes from women living in various small Ontario towns, such as Courtland, Staffa, and Wellandport.

See also O42.1, *The Breadmaker's Recipe Book*. Both books were published by Churchill and Co. and there are some parallels in the two texts; however, *The Breadmaker's Book of Cooking Lessons*, the longer of the two, has no apparent promotional purpose, whereas *The Breadmaker's Recipe Book* promotes Breadmakers' baking products.

The breadmaker's recipe book

O42.1 nd [about 1888]
The breadmaker's / recipe book / compiled from / original and selected formulae. / To the / bread-winners and bread-makers / of America / the two most important personages in every family, around whom / cluster its minor members, by sheer force of affection and / gratitude – in trial and prosperity, in sickness and in / health; and by whose superior wisdom, self- / denial and love that place called home / is made the safest, happiest, and / dearest place on earth: / To these / this book is most respectfully dedicated.
DESCRIPTION: 18.5 × 12.5 cm   Pp [1–5] 6–31 [32] [Free, on p 32]   Paper, with two scenes on front of Toronto; stapled
CONTENTS: 1 cover-title: 'The Breadmakers Recipe Book dedicated to the breadmakers and bread winners of America'; 2 'Comparative Values of Foods' signed the author (unnamed); 3 tp; 4 'Table of Contents' and 'Weights and Measures'; 5–21 recipes under the headings 'Art of Cakemaking,' 'Biscuit,' 'Pancakes,' 'Bread,' 'Bread Directions,' 'First Prize Bread,' 'Pies,' 'Puddings,' and 'Home-made Candy,' plus many Canadian testimonials for Burdock Blood Bitters and other medical products; 22–30 'Miscellaneous Department' and testimonials; 31 'Proof for the Public' regarding Burdock Blood Bitters, signed T. Milburn and Co., Toronto, 'Medical Index,' and a testimonial; 32 'Published by Churchill & Co Toronto. Manufacturers of the Breadmakers' goods // For free distribution to consumers. With compliments of [blank space where the following is stamped, in purple ink:] Chas. A. Nairn // importer & [illegible] groceries fruit china & glassware // Goderich, Ont.'
COPIES: *OTUTF (uncat patent medicine)
NOTES: The latest testimonial is dated 15 March 1888

(p 23). Both Toronto scenes on the binding are dated, but only the date on the lower scene, 1888, is legible. The book was sold to promote Breadmakers' goods. According to p 12, 'One hundred and thirty-two prizes were taken with bread made with Breadmaker's Yeast at agricultural fairs in Canada in 1887.' Breadmakers Dry Hop Yeast and Baking Powder are referred to on the front face of the binding.

See also O41.1, *The Breadmaker's Book of Cooking Lessons*, a related text, which is advertised on p 4 of *The Breadmaker's Recipe Book* as 'sold everywhere' for $0.25.

Fairfield, Dora Estelle (Stratford, Ont., 17 May 1862–11 June 1941, San Diego, Calif.)

Dora Fairfield (pl 35) was descended from a prominent Loyalist family that settled near Kingston, Ontario, and built Fairfield House (completed in 1793; now numbered 4575 Bath Road and a historic site). Her parents, Charles D. Fairfield and Sarah Minerva Davy of Bath, married in 1861 and had two daughters, both born in Stratford: Dora, called Dolly, but baptized Mary Ham Fairfield; and her younger sister, Birdie Perry Fairfield, baptized Hannah. By 1871 the family had moved to Bath. In the year after the publication of Dora's Cook Book, *on 19 October 1889, at Fargo, North Dakota (where her brother-in-law was a jeweller), Dora married William Henry Stevenson. The couple had one child, Dorita Davy Stevenson, born 1890 in Kingston. The 1901 Census records the family still living in Kingston (the Census gives 1863 as Dora's birth year). Dora is buried in the Greenwood Mausoleum in San Diego, California, as are her sister and brother-in-law. This information is found in the Davy family file, p 92, H.C. Burleigh Collection 2324, at OKQ; information about the author in the Fairfield family file, p 14, same collection, is not as extensive and may be inaccurate.*

O43.1 1888
Dora's / cook book; / containing / over one thousand tested and / tried recipes, / furnished by / leading ladies of Canada and the United / States. / Compiled by / Dora E. Fairfield, / Bath, Ont. / Toronto: / Hunter, Rose & Co. / 1888.
DESCRIPTION: 18.0 × 12.0 cm   Pp [i–v] vi–vii [viii], [9] 10–311   Cloth
CONTENTS: i ht; ii blank; iii tp; iv blank; v–vii 'Preface' signed Dora E. Fairfield; viii blank; 9–299 text; 300 blank; 301–11 'Index'
CITATIONS: Beeson, pp 79, 191   CHO, No. 26 (Au-

tumn 2000), p 1   Driver 2003, 'Canadian Cookbooks,' p 25   Driver 2005, p 409

COPIES: OADUEL   ONLAM (uncat)   *Private collection; United States: CL   IaU (SPEC SZAT TX714 F218 1888)

NOTES: At the time her cookbook was published, in 1888, Dora was twenty-six years old and unmarried. Her mother had died in the same year (31 August 1888), whether before or after Dora began writing or had published the cookbook is unknown. Despite Dora's young age, she professed a long interest in cookery. She writes in the 'Preface': 'This is essentially a cook book. I have thought it best to omit the subjects, "Social Observances," "The Internal Arrangement of Your Home," "Etiquette," etc., and leave these for specialists in such departments. I have devoted many years of my life to the collection and trial of the best recipes obtainable.' Dora's comment about 'Social Observances' and other omitted subjects is a reference to the type of material that introduced O20.1, *The Home Cook Book*, the best-selling Canadian cookbook of her day. In that book, 'Housekeeping,' 'Table Talk,' 'Dinner Etiquette,' 'Social Observances,' 'The Little Housekeepers,' 'Our Susan's Opinions of a Kitchen,' and 'Utensils' precede the recipes. Interestingly, most editions of *The Home Cook Book* were printed by Hunter, Rose, the publisher of *Dora's Cook Book*. Both *The Home Cook Book* and *Dora's Cook Book* conclude with a section of menus.

On the title-page Dora proudly identifies her recipes as from both American and Canadian sources and the recipe names often identify the origin: for example, Mrs Gen. Sherman's Recipe for 'Claret Punch,' p 263, or Bay [of] Quinte Cake, p 185, and Ontario Cake, p 188. The inclusion of American recipes is not surprising, given the family's Loyalist roots on her father's side. Also, Dora's mother spent some part of her formative years in the United States, when, at a young age, she and her sister (Dora's Aunt Mary) had been sent to live in a convent (probably Episcopal or other Protestant denomination) in Monroe, Michigan, after Dora's maternal grandmother died.

The ONLAM copy is inscribed on the front endpaper, in pencil, 'J.E. Ham 23/8/88,' evidence that the book was published by August 1888. J.E. Ham must be a member of the author's family, on her paternal side (Dora's father's mother was baptized Elizabeth Ham).

There is a note in the H.C. Burleigh Collection (Fairfield family file, p 14) that Mrs Gutzeit, who owned an autographed copy of *Dora's Cook Book*, gave it to Mrs Marjorie Fairfield McCaw in 1968.

Beeson reprints two recipes from the book.

The housekeeper's help

See also O901.1, The Mixing Bowl, from the same church.

O44.1   rev. ed., 1888
The / housekeeper's help / Revised edition. / [quotation in two columns of two lines each; first column:] "She looketh well / to the / [small illus positioned between the two columns] / [second column:] ways of her / household." / Compiled by the / Ladies' Aid Society / of the / Central Presbyterian Church, / Hamilton, Ontario. / 1888. / Hamilton, Ont.: / Robt. Raw & Co., printers and wood-engravers, 28 & 30 John St. North.
DESCRIPTION: 21.0 × 14.5 cm   Pp [1–2] 3–43 [44]   Small tp illus of peacock feathers(?) in a hanging vase   Thin card; sewn
CONTENTS: 1 tp; 2–43 recipes credited with the initials of the contributor and ads; 44 'Index' [i.e., alphabetical list of sections]
COPIES: CIHM (94611)   *OH (641.5 C333h CESH)
NOTES: Page 10 is a 'List of Cookery Books' for sale at J. Eastwood and Co., booksellers, stationers, bookbinders, 16 King Street East, Hamilton; all the titles on the list are British or American, with the exception of this cookbook, *The Housekeeper's Help*, which is described as 'an excellent book, with many valuable recipes, at a low price,' and an unidentified edition of O20.1, *The Home Cook Book*, by the ladies of Toronto, promoted as 'The Canadian Cook Book [which] merits a place in every home. Price $1.00.'

I found no copy of the first edition of *The Housekeeper's Help*, and any information about its date of publication in the records of the Ladies' Aid Society did not survive the church fire in 1906.

1889

Chase, Dr Alvin Wood (Cayuga County, NY, 20 March 1817–25 May 1885, Ohio)

For information about Dr Chase and his publications, see O8.1.

O45.1   1889
Dr. Chase's / new / receipt book, / or / information for everybody. / The life-long observations of the author, embracing / the choicest, most valuable and / entirely new receipts / in every department of / medicine, mechanics and household economy. / In fact a book for everybody, with remarks and

explanations / which adapt it to the every-day wants of the people, / arrarged [sic] in departments, and copiously indexed. / Toronto: / Rose Publishing Company. / 1889.

DESCRIPTION: 18.0 × 12.0 cm   Pp [13–17] 18–397   Frontis portrait of author   Cloth

CONTENTS: 13 tp; 14 'Hunter Rose & Co printers & binders Toronto'; 15 table of contents; 16 blank; 17–366 text; 367–82 individual indexes for medical, cookery, dairy, mechanical, miscellaneous, drinks, canaries, toilet, horses, cattle, and hogs; 383–97 'Index – General'

CITATIONS: Driver 2001, Wellington County, p 95

COPIES: NSYHM   OFERWM (A1975.64.21a)   OONL (TX153 C49 1889 p***)   *Private collection

NOTES: The source of this text, issued under Dr Chase's name two years after his death, is a mystery. There appears to be no correlation between the contents of *Dr Chase's New Receipt Book* and any of the three texts known to have been compiled by him: *Dr Chase's Recipes*, the earliest Canadian edition of which was published in 1865 (O8.1); *Dr Chase's Family Physician, Farrier, Bee-keeper, and Second Receipt Book*, first published in the United States in 1872, but never in Canada; and *Dr Chase's Third, Last and Complete Receipt Book and Household Physician*, first published in Canada in 1887 (O40.1). Moreover, a search for American editions titled *Dr Chase's New Receipt Book* turned up nothing except for one late 1920s edition: *Dr Chase's New Receipt Book and Medical Advisor or Information for Everybody; an Invaluable Collection of Practical Receipts*, Chicago and New York: M.A. Donohue and Co., [copyright 1927]. If the text of *Dr Chase's New Receipt Book* did not derive from a previous American edition, where did Rose Publishing Co. obtain it?

The 'Index – General' brings together items from the preceding individual indexes and arranges them alphabetically. There is a variant of the 1889 edition that matches the description above, except that the 'Index – General' is shorter (pp 383–93 only) and does not incorporate items from the medical index (copies at BCHM, NBFKL, OFERWM (A1955.49.2), OH (R640.3 CHA CESC), and QMM, the latter filmed by CIHM (01769)). In all other editions of *Dr Chase's New Receipt Book* that I have examined the 'Index – General' ends on p 397, except for this variant of the 1889 edition. The variant, therefore, may represent an error in the compiling of the 'Index – General'; the publisher noticed the omission of the medical references, added them, then reissued the 1889 edition with the corrected 'Index – General.' The variant is evidence that the 1889 edition preceded O45.2, the undated edition by Rose Publishing Co. that has the corrected index.

The OFERWM copy (A1975.64.21a) is inscribed on the front endpaper, in pencil, 'Mrs Wm. Luxton Keldon Aug 16th 1893.'

O45.2   nd [about 1890–4]

—Dr. Chase's / new / receipt book, / or / information for everybody. / The life-long observations of the author, embracing / the choicest, most valuable and / entirely new receipts / in every department of / medicine, mechanics and household economy. / In fact a book for everybody, with remarks and explanations / which adapt it to the every-day wants of the people, / arrarged [sic] in departments, and copiously indexed. / Toronto: / Rose Publishing Company.

DESCRIPTION: 18.0 × 12.0 cm   Pp [13–17] 18–397   Frontis portrait of author   Cloth

CONTENTS: 13 tp; 14 'Hunter Rose & Co printers & binders Toronto' symbol; 15 table of contents; 16 blank; 17–160 'Medical Department'; 161–98 'Cookery Department'; 199–207 'Recipes for the Dairy'; 208–24 'Mechanical'; 225–74 'Miscellaneous Recipes'; 275–9 'Drinks'; 280–5 'Care of Canaries'; 286–91 'The Toilet'; 292–7 'Interest'; 298–325 'Horses'; 326–34 'Cattle'; 335–43 'Sheep'; 344–8 'Hogs'; 349–66 'Dictionary of Medical Terms'; 367–97 indexes

COPIES: *ACG   OBRAPM   OTUTF (jah)

NOTES: Rose Publishing Co. was active in the period 1 May 1883–1894 (Hulse, p 223); however, this undated edition probably follows the 1889 edition, O45.1, because the 'Index – General' ends on p 397. It could not have been published before summer 1882 because there is a reference on p 44 to 'the present summer (in the month of August, 1882).'

O45.3   1895

—Dr. Chase's / new / receipt book, / or / information for everybody. / The life-long observations of the author, embracing / the choicest, most valuable and / entirely new receipts / in every department of / medicine, mechanics and household economy. / In fact a book for everybody, with remarks and explanations / which adapt it to the every-day wants of the people, / arrarged [sic] in departments, and copiously indexed. / Toronto: / Hunter, Rose & Company. / 1895.

DESCRIPTION: 18.0 × 12.0 cm   Pp [13–17] 18–397   Cloth

CONTENTS: 13 tp; 14 'Hunter Rose & Co printers & binders Toronto' symbol; 15 table of contents; 16 blank; 17–348 text; 349–66 'Dictionary of Medical Terms Used in This Work'; 367–82 index by departments; 383–97 'Index – General'

COPIES: *NSHMS

O45.4   nd [1895 or later]
—Dr. Chase's / new / receipt book / or / information for everybody. / The life-long observations of the author, embracing / the choicest, most valuable and / entirely new receipts / in every department of / medicine, mechanics and household economy. / In fact a book for everybody, with remarks and explanations / which adapt it to the every-day wants of the people, / arrarged [sic] in departments, and copiously indexed. / Toronto: / The Hunter, Rose Co., Limited.
DESCRIPTION: 18.0 × 12.0 cm   Pp [13–17] 18–397 Cloth imitating wood
CONTENTS: 13 tp; 14 blank; 15 table of contents; 16 blank; 17–366 text; 367–82 index by departments; 383–97 'Index – General'
COPIES: *OGU (UA s048 b40)   ONENM   ONLAM
NOTES: The publisher was known as Hunter, Rose Co. Ltd from 1895 (Hulse, p 128).

O45.5   Paris, nd [about 1895]
—Dr. Chase's / new / receipt book, / or / information for everybody. / The life-long observations of the author, embracing / the choicest, most valuable and / entirely new receipts / in every department of / medicine, mechanics and household economy. / In fact a book for everybody, with remarks and explanations / which adapt it to the every-day wants of the people, / arrarged [sic] in departments, and copiously indexed. / Paris: / John S. Brown & Sons.
DESCRIPTION: 18.0 × 12.0 cm   Pp [13–17] 18–397 Cloth
CONTENTS: 13 tp; 14 'Hunter Rose & Co printers & binders Toronto' symbol; 15 'Table of Contents'; 16 blank; 17–348 text; 349–66 'Dictionary of Medical Terms Used in This Work'; 367–82 index by departments; 383–97 'Index – General'
COPIES: *Bookseller's stock

O45.6   nd [about 1895–8]
—Dr. Chase's / new / receipt book, / or / information for everybody. / The life-long observations of the author, embracing / the choicest, most valuable and / entirely new receipts / in every department of / medicine, mechanics and household economy. / In fact a book for everybody, with remarks and explanations / which adapt it to the every-day wants of the people, / arrarged [sic] in departments, and copiously indexed. / Toronto. / George Maclean Rose & Sons.
COPIES: *Private collection
NOTES: The publisher used the name George Maclean

Rose and Sons from 1895 to 1898; in 1898 the business was incorporated (Hulse, p 222).

O45.7   nd [about 1898–1901]
—Dr. Chase's / new / receipt book / or / information for everybody. / The life-long observations of the author, embracing / the choicest, most valuable and / entirely new receipts / in every department of / medicine, mechanics and household economy. / In fact a book for everybody, with remarks and explanations / which adapt it to the every-day wants of the people, / arrarged [sic] in departments, and copiously indexed. / Toronto: / G.M. Rose & Sons Co. Limited.
COPIES: *Private collection
NOTES: G.M. Rose and Sons incorporated in 1898 and dissolved in 1901 (Hulse, p 222).

O45.8   nd [about 1900–5]
—Dr. Chase's / new / receipt book / or / information for everybody. / The life-long observations of the author, embracing / the choicest, most valuable and / entirely new receipts / in every department of / medicine, mechanics and household economy. / In fact a book for everybody, with remarks and explanations / which adapt it to the every-day wants of the people, / arrarged [sic] in departments, and copiously indexed. / Toronto: / The Musson Book Company, Limited
DESCRIPTION: Pp [13–17] 18–397
CONTENTS: 13 tp; 14 blank; 15 'Table of Contents'; 16 blank; 17–160 'Medical Department'; 161–98 'Cookery Department'; 199–207 'Recipes for the Dairy'; 208–24 'Mechanical'; 225–74 'Miscellaneous Recipes'; 275–9 'Drinks'; 280–5 'Care of Canaries'; 286–91 'The Toilet'; 292–7 'Interest'; 298–325 'Horses'; 326–34 'Cattle'; 335–43 'Sheep'; 344–8 'Hogs'; 349–66 'Dictionary of Medical Terms'; 367–97 indexes
COPIES: *CIHM (01768)   QMM
NOTES: The Musson Book Co. was established in 1898 (Hulse, p 187). From appearances, this edition was published about the turn of the century.

O45.9   nd [about 1920]
—Dr. Chase's new / receipt book / and / medical advisor / or / information for everybody / an invaluable collection of / practical receipts / for / merchants, grocers, manufacturers, physicians, druggists, / tanners, shoemakers, harness makers, painters, jewelers, / blacksmiths, miners, gunsmiths, furriers, barbers, bakers, / dyers, renovators, farmers and families generally / All arranged in their appropriate departments by /

A.W. Chase, M.D. / based on the life-long observations of the author / Toronto / The Musson Book Company / Limited

DESCRIPTION: 18.5 × 12.5 cm   Pp [i–vi], 367 [368–98], [17] 18–366   Frontis portrait of author   Cloth

CONTENTS: i tp; ii 'All rights reserved // Printed in Canada // Press of the Hunter-Rose Co., Limited'; iii 'The Interesting Life Story of Dr. A.W. Chase'; iv blank; v table of contents; vi blank; 367–82 'Index' [of departments]; 383–97 'Index – General'; 398 blank; 17–348 text; 349–66 'Dictionary of Medical Terms Used in This Work'

COPIES: OGU (CCC TX715.6 C45 19--)   OTUFP (RS127 C43)   *OTUTF (jah)

NOTES: From appearances, this Musson edition was published considerably later than O45.8, another Musson edition. The indexes are bound in at the front of the volume, yet the first page of the indexes is numbered 367 and the table of contents lists the two indexes as on pp 367 and 383.

The OTUFP copy is inscribed on the front endpaper, in ink, 'HW Shoemaker Druggist Kitchener.'

AMERICAN EDITIONS: *Dr Chase's New Receipt Book and Medical Advisor or Information for Everybody; an Invaluable Collection of Practical Receipts*, Chicago and New York: M.A. Donohue and Co., [copyright 1927] (United States: CU-A, CU-SB, MiU, MnM, OAU, WaU).

Harland, Marion [pseudonym of] Mrs Mary Virginia Terhune, née Hawes (Amelia County, Va, 21 December 1830–3 June 1922, New York City, NY)

For information about this American author and her other cookbooks, see O18.1.

O46.1 [copyright 1889]

House and home: / A / complete / housewife's guide / by / Marion Harland. / "God help us on the common days, / The level stretches, white with dust!" / Margaret E. Sangster. / With original engravings. / By / L.A. Shafer, Walter Satterlee, Rue & Hoelffler, B.G. Goodline[comma?] / Will Phillip Hooper and F.L.V. Hoppin. / William Briggs, publisher, / Toronto, Canada.

DESCRIPTION: 23.0 × 17.0 cm   Pp [1–2], i–vii [viii] ix [x], 11–532   Frontis portrait of author, 4 pls col, 27 pls incl in pagination   Cloth, with image on front of a fireplace

CONTENTS: 1 tp; 2 'Copyrighted by Mary Virginia Terhune, 1889.'; i–vii table of contents; viii blank; ix

list of illustrations; x blank; 11–526 text; 527–32 index of recipes

COPIES: CIHM (95416)   *OGU (UA s043 b40)

NOTES: The title-page is printed in red and black. The following chapters concern food: 'The Dining-Room, Meals and Serving'; 'Vagaries of the American Kitchen'; 'Breakfast as It Should Be'; 'The Tea Table'; 'What Our Children Eat'; 'Introduction to Menus'; 'Spring Bills of Fare'; 'Summer Bills of Fare'; 'The Dinner Pail'; 'Autumn Bills of Fare'; 'Thanksgiving Dinner'; 'Winter Bills of Fare'; 'Christmas Dinner'; 'Pickles'; 'Fruit Jellies'; 'Preserves, Jams and Marmalades'; and 'A Few Dishes for the Invalid.'

AMERICAN EDITIONS: Philadelphia and St Louis: P.W. Ziegler and Co., 1889 (OGU; United States: DLC); New York: C. Scribner's Sons, 1895 (Bitting, pp 214–15); 1897 (Bitting, p 215).

McDonald, Mrs James, née Martha Jane Falconer (Chinguacousy Township, Ontario, 14 December 1861–18 February 1928)

Martha Jane Falconer was the daughter of Alexander Falconer and Elizabeth Irving. In 1885 she married James McDonald, a Scottish builder and contractor, and they had two sons and four daughters. She was an active member of the Women's Missionary Society at the Orangeville Methodist Church. Minutes of the society for 1894–1903 (OTCC) record some of her activities; for example, on 3 January 1903, it was decided that she would 'give the [society's] first social,' where 'bread and butter and cake and tea or coffee' would be offered for refreshments. In 1907, the family moved to Toronto, where they joined High Park Avenue Methodist Church. Martha McDonald's obituaries are in the Orangeville Banner *23 February 1928 and in the* Orangeville Sun *of the same date.*

Mrs James McDonald (first name, Esther), who lived in Camilla, in the countryside outside of Orangeville, but never in Orangeville itself, is unlikely to be the cookbook's author.

O47.1 1889

The / cook's true friend. / Compiled by / Mrs. James McDonald, / Orangeville, Ont. / Toronto: / Printed by Hunter, Rose & Company. / 1889.

DESCRIPTION: 18.0 × 12.0 cm   Pp [1–3] 4–152 [153–5]   Cloth printed with a pattern incorporating a scene of geese or ducks

CONTENTS: 1 tp; 2 Hunter, Rose and Co. symbol and 'Entered according to the Act of Parliament of Canada, in the year one thousand eight hundred and eighty-nine, by Mrs. James McDonald, at the Department of Agriculture.'; 3–153 text; 154 blank; 155 'Index' [i.e., table of contents]

CITATIONS: Driver 2005, p 409

COPIES: CIHM (95243) *OGU (UA s001 b14) OORADCM OONL (TX715.6 M33 1889) OTNY (641.5971 M)

NOTES: The author's instructions are detailed and authoritative; for example, her five variations for making doughnuts are followed by Hints on Making Doughnuts. She advises readers to avoid ground coffee, which she says is generally adulterated, and explains how to roast and store coffee beans.

1890

The art of cooking made easy

O48.1   Toronto, 1890
Strong's Baking Powder should always be used to / insure satisfactory results, as all baking powders are / not of uniform strength, and some are not pure. / The / art of cooking / made easy. / Presented by / A.E. Fawcett, / chemist and druggist, / 67 King Street, West, Toronto, Ont. / Only authorized agent in Toronto for Strong's Baking Powder. / London, Ont. / London Printing and Lithographing Company. / 1890.

DESCRIPTION: 18.0 × 10.0 cm   Pp [3–5] 6–118   Paper; sewn

CONTENTS: 3 tp; 4 blank; 5–10 'Index'; 11 publ ad; 12 blank; 13–118 recipes and publ ads

CITATIONS: Driver 2003, 'Canadian Cookbooks,' p 33

COPIES: CIHM (88756)   *Private collection

NOTES: On p 77 and on the outside back face of the binding, there are advertisements for W.T. Strong, druggist, 184 Dundas Street, London, Ontario, the maker of Strong's Baking Powder. The graphic design of the cover-title is the same for this edition, O48.2, O48.3, O48.5, and O48.6.

The recipes begin on p 13, under the heading 'Family Recipes,' with Potato Yeast, credited to Mrs De Freest, Another, by Mrs Morgan, Bread, by Mrs H. Galusha, and Salt Rising Bread, not credited. The same recipes begin O29.1, *Cook's Friend Cook Book*, 1881, which promotes the use of Cook's Friend Baking Powder. The 1881 book may be the source for the recipes in *The Art of Cooking Made Easy*.

The private collector's copy is inscribed on the front endpaper, in brown ink, 'J.G. Clogg St Catherines [*sic*] Canada'; and in what appears to be a more re-

cent hand, on the back endpaper, in blue pencil, 'Mrs Jas Clogg.'

O48.2   Stratford, 1890
—Strong's Baking Powder should always be used to / insure satisfactory results, as all baking powders are / not of uniform strength, and some are not pure. / The / art of cooking / made easy. / Presented by / C.E. Nasmyth & Co., / City Drug Store, / Market Square, / Stratford, Ontario. / Manufacturer of Strong's Baking Powder. / London, Ont.: / London Printing and Lithographing Company. / 1890.

COPIES: *CIHM (90105)   OSTPA

NOTES: The graphic design of the cover-title is the same as O48.1, O48.3, O48.5, and O48.6. The following is printed at the bottom of the front face of the binding: 'Entered according to Act of the Parliament of Canada, in the year 1890, at the Department of Agriculture, Ottawa.'

O48.3   St Catharines, 1890
—Strong's Baking Powder should always be used to / insure satisfactory results, as all baking powders are / not of uniform strength, and some are not pure. / The / art of cooking / made easy. / Presented by / Seymour's Central Drug Store, / St. Paul Street, corner of Queen, / St. Catharines, Ontario. / Branch, Grimsby Park. / London, Ont.: / London Printing and Lithographing Company. / 1890.

DESCRIPTION: Pp [i–ii], [1–3] 4–126

CONTENTS: i–ii publ ads; 1 tp; 2 publ ad; 3–8 'Index'; 9–10 publ ads; 11– recipes; ...

COPIES: *OSTC (641.5971 Art M)   Private collection

NOTES: Central Drug Store was the 'only authorized agent in St. Catharines for Strong's Baking Powder,' according to text on the binding. Copyright information is on the binding: 'Entered according to Act of the Parliament of Canada, in the year 1890, at the Department of Agriculture, Ottawa.' The graphic design of the cover-title is the same as O48.1, O48.2, O48.5, and O48.6.

O48.4   1892
—Strong's Baking Powder should always be used to / [insur]e satisfactory results, as all baking powders are / [not o]f uniform strength, and some are not pure. / The / art of cooking / made easy. / Published and presented by / W.T. Strong, / druggist, / [Lo]ndon, Ontario. / London, Ont.: / [L]ondon Printing and Lithographing Company. / 1892.

DESCRIPTION: 18.5 × 11.0 cm   Pp [1–3] 4–120   Lacks binding

CONTENTS: 1 tp; 2 publ ad; 3–8 'Index'; 9 ad for London Free Press; 10 publ ad; 11–mid 105 'Family Recipes'; mid 105–mid 110 'Household Recipes'; bottom 110–113 'Recipes for Coloring'; 114–20 'Poisons' and publ ads

COPIES: *OLU (TX715 S76 1892)

NOTES: The recipes begin on p 11 and are the same as listed for O48.1. The OLU copy is inscribed on the title-page, in ink, 'Miss [Ca]ssie Corbett // Ingersoll Ontario Canada.' Tape applied to the left-hand side of the title-page obscures some of the printed text.

O48.5   ['First edition'], 1893

—Stewart's Baking Powder should always be used to / insure satisfactory results, as all baking powders are / not of uniform strength, and some are not pure. / The / art of cooking / made easy. / Presented by / Alex. Stewart, / druggist, / Guelph, Ontario. / London, Ont.: / London Printing and Lithographing Company. / 1893.

DESCRIPTION: 18.5 × 10.5 cm   Pp [1] 2–152   Thin card; stapled

CONTENTS: 1 tp; 2 ad; 3–9 'Index'; 10 ad; 11–mid 139 'Family Recipes,' publ ads, and ads; mid 139–mid 144 'Household Recipes'; bottom 144–147 'Recipes for Coloring'; 148–52 'Poisons' and publ ad

COPIES: OBBM   *OGM (977.83.1)

NOTES: 'First edition' is printed on the front of the binding. The recipes begin on p 11 and are the same as listed for O48.1. The graphic design of the cover-title is the same as O48.1–48.3 and O48.6.

OGU (CCC TX715.6 A77 19-) has an incomplete copy that may match the one described here or O48.6. Golick, p 102, refers to an 1893 edition by Alex Stewart.

O48.6   ['First edition'], 1893

—Stewart's Baking Powder should always be used to / [ins]ure satisfactory results, as all baking powders are / [no]t of uniform strength, and some are not pure. / The / art of cooking / made easy. / Published by / Alex. Stewart, / druggist, / Guelph, Ontario. / London, Ont.: / London Printing and Lithographing Comp[any.?] / 1893[.?]

COPIES: *Private collection

NOTES: The title-page of this edition is identical to O48.5 except for 'Published' in place of 'Presented'; the binding design is the same and bears the description 'First edition.' The volume has 152 pp. The title-page of this copy is torn in places so that some text is lacking.

O48.7   nd [about 1895]

—[Top left of tp lacking]der should always be used to insure / [lacking] baking powders are not of uniform / [lacking]re. / The art of / cooking / made easy / Analysis of Strong's Baking Powder by Franklin T. Harrison, Professor of / Analytical Chemistry. / London, August 25th, 1895. / W.T. Strong, Esq / Dear Sir, – [letter follows] / Published by / W.T. Strong / druggist / London, Ontario. / Advertiser Job Dept. [cover-title]

DESCRIPTION: 22.0 × 14.5 cm   Pp 3–142 [leaves lacking]   Paper; stapled, and with hole punched at top left corner, through which runs a string for hanging

CONTENTS: 3–mid 2nd column 125 'Family Recipes' and ads; mid 2nd column 125–mid 130 information about homoeopathic remedies, antidotes for poisons, and accidents, and ad; mid 130–mid 135 'The Horse'; bottom 135–137 'When to Spray'; 138–42 'Index'

COPIES: *OGU (CCC TX715.6 A77); United States: NNNAM (S.21.B Strong)

NOTES: This edition is distinguished by Dr Harrison's dated letter in the cover-title. The NNNAM copy has 144 pp and the suggested date '1903?' inscribed in pencil on the title-page.

O48.8

—[Another edition of *The Art of Cooking Made Easy* with advertisements for Alex. Stewart, family and dispensing chemist, Guelph, Ontario]

DESCRIPTION: 19.0 × 11.0 cm   Pp [probably lacks tp, lacks some index pages, fragments of other index pages remaining] 7–211   Rebound(?) in cloth

CONTENTS: [fragments of index pages, folios torn off]; 5–10 index; 11–12 ads; 13–207 recipes, many credited with the name of the contributor, and ads, some for Alex. Stewart, family and dispensing chemist, Guelph; 208–top 209 'Recipes for Coloring'; mid 209–11 'A Full Stock of Homoeopathic Medicines for Sale at Alex. Stewart's Drug Store, Guelph // Diseases. What Homoeopathic Remedies to Take.' [alphabetical list of diseases from Abscess to Worms]

COPIES: OFERWM (A1996.129 MU312)   *OGM (972.1.1)

NOTES: The running head is 'The Art of Cooking Made Easy.' The pagination of this edition differs from earlier editions advertising Alex. Stewart.

Page 211 of the OGM copy is stuck to the inside back face of the binding. The OFERWM copy has only pp 37–180 and no binding.

O48.9   1900

—Emerald Baking Powder should always be used to insure / satisfactory results, as all baking powders are not of uniform / strength, and some are not pure. / The / art of cooking / made easy. / Published / and presented by / O'Mara's Drug Store, / Military / Road, / St. John's, N.F. / Evening Herald Job Print. / St. John's, N.F. 1900.

DESCRIPTION: 20.0 × 12.0 cm   Pp 1–128   Paper, with image on front of young girl carrying tray on which sits a steaming cup-and-saucer; stapled

CONTENTS: 1–2 ads; 3 tp; 4 ads; 5–10 index; 11–12 ads; 13–mid 107 'Family Recipes' and ads; mid 107–116 'Household Recipes' and ads; 117–mid 122 'Receipt for Coloring' and ads; mid 122–126 'Poisons' and ads; 127–8 ads

COPIES: *MWU

NOTES: Like O48.1, the recipes begin on p 13, under the heading 'Family Recipes,' with Potato Yeast, credited to Mrs De Freest, Another, by Mrs Morgan, Bread, by Mrs H. Galusha, and Salt Rising Bread, not credited.

An advertisement on p 2 for S.E. Garland, bookseller, lists 'The Best Cookery Books': 'Mrs Beeton's Household Management and Cookery // Beeton's Every Day Cookery // Beeton's All about Cookery // Miss Parloe's [sic] Cook Book // The Home Cook Book // Enquire Within upon Everything // Cassel's [sic] Dictionary of Cookery // Dainty Meals for Small Households [by Marguerite Ninet] // The Skilful Cook by Mary Harrison // The Household Oracle by A.H. Miles // Chase's New Receipt Book.' Only one of these titles – an unidentified edition of O20.1, *The Home Cook Book* – is Canadian. Most are British; only Miss Parloa and Dr Chase are American authors. For a discussion of *Dr Chase's New Receipt Book*, see O45.1.

O48.9 is not recorded in O'Dea.

O48.10   nd [about 1900]
—Diadem Baking Powder should always be used to / insure satisfactory results, as all baking powders are not / of uniform strength, and some are not pure. / The / art of cooking / made easy. / Published and presented by / Hattie & Mylius, / Limited, / wholesale druggists, / Halifax, – Nova Scotia / Imperial Publishing Co., Limited, printers, Halifax, N.S.

DESCRIPTION: 16.0 × 11.0 cm   Pp [1–5] 6–128   Paper, with image on front of woman pointing to over-sized container of Diadem Baking Powder; stapled

CONTENTS: 1–2 ad and publ ad; 3 tp; 4 publ ad; 5–10 index; 11 publ ad; 12 ad; 13–mid 107 'Family Recipes' and ads; bottom 107–125 'Household Recipes' and ads; 126–8 'Poisons' and publ ad

COPIES: NSHMS   NSLQCM   *NSYHM

NOTES: Like O48.1, 'Family Recipes' are credited to De Freest, Galusha, et al. There is a homily at the bottom margin of most pages; for example, 'Of two evils, choose the least' on p 73. An advertisement on p 117 for Johnson's Anodyne Liniment, manufactured by I.S. Johnson and Co., Boston, Massachusetts, refers to the liniment as 'originated in 1810,' then adds that 'the century mark is reached.' The century mark could mean 1900, i.e., the turn of the century, or the hundred-year mark of the liniment's manufacture, 1910. From appearances, however, the book was published about 1900.

The incomplete NSHMS copy has pp 9–120 only. The NSLQCM copy lacks the last leaf.

O48.11   nd [about 1904]
—Zimmerman's Baking Powder should / always be used to insure satisfactory results, as / all baking powders are not of uniform strength, / and some [sic, no 'are'] not pure. / The / art of cooking / made easy / Zimmerman's Baking Powder is always / put up in original air tight cans, thus insuring / cleanliness and dryness. / Published by / J.A. Zimmerman, chemist and druggist, / Hamilton, Ontario.

DESCRIPTION: 18.0 × 10.0 cm   Pp [1] 2–208   Paper, with image on front of interior view of what is probably J.A. Zimmerman's store; stapled

CONTENTS: 1 tp; 2 ad and publ ad; 3 'Index to Advertisements'; 4 ad; 5–11 'Index to Recipes'; 12 ad; 13–top 201 'Family Recipes' and ads; mid 201–204 'Homoepathic [sic] Medicines ... for sale at Zimmerman's Drug Store' and publ ad; 205–6 'Remedies'; 207–top 208 'Antidotes for Poisons'; mid–bottom 208 'Help, in Case of Accidents'

COPIES: *OH (R641.5 ART CESH)

NOTES: Another chemist's name is stamped on the outside back face of the binding, in purple ink: 'John P. Hennessey chemist Hamilton.' This edition is undated; however, there is a testimonial on p 25 dated 15 November 1903, which suggests publication no earlier than 1904.

O48.12   Woodstock
—[Another edition of *The Art of Cooking Made Easy*]

DESCRIPTION: 18.5 × 10.5 cm   Pp [leaves lacking] 21–134 [leaves lacking]   Lacks binding; stapled

COPIES: *ONDA

NOTES: The running head is 'The Art of Cooking Made Easy.' The recipes are credited with the name of the contributor. The advertisements are for Woodstock, Ontario, businesses, including W.A. Karn's drugstore. Karn's published a later edition, O48.13, in a larger format.

O48.13   [6th ed.], nd [about 1910]
—Karn's Baking Powder should always / be used to insure satisfactory results, as all / baking powders are not of uniform strength, / and some are not pure. / The art / of / cooking / made easy / Best domestic science re- / ports are that we have a pure pow- / der, and upon test has proven to be free / from adulteration of alums or phosphates. / They say it is equal to the powders which sell at 75c a / pound, and is highly recommended by all who have used / it. / W.A. Karn. / Published / by / W.A. Karn / druggist / Woodstock / Ontario
DESCRIPTION: 22.0 × 15.0 cm   Pp [1–3] 4–184   Illus on p 3 of the construction of a fireless cooker   [Free, on binding]   Paper; stapled
CONTENTS: 1 tp; 2 ad; 3–171 text and publ ads; 172–84 'Index' and publ ads
COPIES: ARDA   OGU (UA s066 b07)   *OTUTF (jah 19669)
NOTES: I have compared the first section of this edition with the first section of O48.1. The original recipes are reprinted here, including Potato Yeast, Another [yeast], Bread, and Salt-Rising Bread; however, they are not credited with the names of the contributors and there are more recipes added to the text.

An advertisement on p 114 cites 'Nineteen years unbroken record of success // Dodd's Kidney Pills.' The pills were introduced to the market in about 1891 (see *Dodd's Almanac and Calendar 1899*, p 48, at OTUTF: '... eight years ago, Dodd's Kidney Pills were given to the world by a medical man who had undertaken the treatment of Bright's Disease and Diabetes ...'). This edition, therefore, must have been published in about 1910 (1891 + 19 years), and three years before O48.15, where the advertisement for Dodd's cites 'twenty-two years' unbroken record of success.' Dodds Medicine Co. Ltd first appears in the Toronto city directory in 1894.

Printed on the front face of the binding is 'Sixth edition' and Karn's address, 423 Dundas Street in Woodstock. The edition number may refer to the sixth edition by Karn (i.e., not the sixth from all the various drugstores). The printer's name is on the outside back face of the binding: 'Advertiser, London, Ont.' 'Family Recipes' begin on p 6, starting with General Directions, Wheat Bread (continued on p 7), Compressed Yeast Bread, Home-made Yeast, and Unrivaled Yeast. This and other later editions are in a larger format than earlier editions.

New information about the fireless cooker begins the text. Fireless cookers were a means of saving fuel and in vogue at the time this and other later editions were published. In 1909, a cookbook devoted solely to this cooking technique was published in the United States: *The Fireless Cook Book: A Manual of the Construction and Use of Appliances for Cooking by Retained Heat, with 250 Recipes*, by Margaret Johnes Mitchell, New York: Doubleday, Page and Co., 1909. Other American and British editions followed.

The ARDA copy lacks its binding and may or may not be numbered as the sixth edition.

See also O48.12, which contains advertisements for the same Woodstock druggist.

O48.14   20th ed., nd
—[Twentieth edition of *The Art of Cooking Made Easy*, London, Ont.: W.T. Strong, druggist, nd, pp 184]
COPIES: Bookseller's stock

O48.15   21st ed., nd [about 1913]
—Strong's Baking Powder should always be used to / insure satisfactory results, as all baking powders are not / of uniform strength, and some are not pure. / The art of / cooking / made easy / Published by / W.T. Strong, druggist / London, Ontario
DESCRIPTION: 22.0 × 14.5 cm   Pp [1] 2–184   Small tp illus of two girls sitting on a bench, illus on p 3 of the construction of a fireless cooker   Paper, with hole punched at top left corner, through which runs a string for hanging
CONTENTS: Inside front face of binding testimonial dated September 1908; 1 tp; 2 publ ad; 3–175 text and ads; 176–84 'Index'
COPIES: *OTUTF (jah 19307)
NOTES: 'Twenty-first edition' is printed on the binding. 'Family Recipes' begin on p 6. The text pages are the same as O48.13, the sixth edition published by W.A. Karn in Woodstock, except that Strong's Baking Powder is specified instead of Karn's and the full-page advertisements are in different positions, thereby changing the page references for the recipes. The index, therefore, has been reset.

An advertisement on p 111 cites 'twenty-two years' unbroken record of success' for Dodd's Kidney Pills. Since the pills were introduced to the market in about 1891 (see O48.13), this edition was published in about 1913 (1891 + 22 years). The edition number on the binding may refer to the twenty-first edition by W.T. Strong or to the twenty-first of all the various drugstores over the years. The earliest identified editions of *The Art of Cooking Made Easy* were promotions for Strong's Baking Powder: O48.1–48.3, all dated 1890. It is likely that an edition of the cookbook was published, on average, once a year, in the period 1890–1913.

O48.16 22nd ed., nd
—Strong's Baking Powder should always be used to / insure satisfactory results, as all baking powders are not / of uniform strength, and some are not pure. / The art of / cooking / made easy / For analysis of Strong's Baking Powder / see page 154 / Strong's Drug Store / The Rexall store / London 184 Dundas St. Ontario
DESCRIPTION: 22.0 × 15.0 cm   Pp [1] 2–184   Small tp illus of two girls sitting on a bench, illus on p 3 of fireless cooker   [Free, on binding]   Paper; stapled
CONTENTS: 1 tp; 2 publ ad; 3–mid 5 'A Home-made Fireless Cooker'; mid–bottom 5 'Good Health in One Simple Exercise'; 6–175 text headed 'Family Recipes,' publ ads, and ads; 176–84 'Index'
COPIES: *OL (London Room Box 66)
NOTES: 'Twenty-second edition // The art of cooking made easy ... Published by Strong's Drug Store // London Canada // The Rexall store' is on the binding. 'Family Recipes' begin with General Directions, Wheat Bread, Compressed Yeast Bread, Home-made Yeast, and Unrivaled Yeast. There is a testimonial for Strong's Baking Powder dated September 1908 on p 154 .

O48.17
—[Another edition of *The Art of Cooking Made Easy*(?), published by Strong's Drug Store, London, Ontario]
DESCRIPTION: 22.0 × 15.0 cm   Pp [leaves lacking] 7–168, [leaf from index, but page numbers unknown], [leaves lacking?]
COPIES: *OL (London Room Box 66)
NOTES: The running heads advertise products from Strong's Drug Store in London. The volume is incomplete and in poor condition; however, a comparison of p 7 with the same page in O48.15 and O48.16, the twenty-first and twenty-second editions, also by Strong's, shows that this is a different edition. Here, p 7 has the following recipes: an unidentified recipe (the top left corner of the page is torn off, so this first recipe is either a continuation of one from p 6 or a new recipe, title unknown), Salt-Rising Bread, Good Bread, Brown Bread, Corn Bread, etc. In the twenty-first and twenty-second editions, p 7 has Wheat Bread (a continuation from p 6), Compressed Yeast Bread, Home-made Yeast, and Unrivaled Yeast. Where this edition fits in the run of editions is unknown.

O48.18 nd [about 1917]
—Rexall / cook book / The art of cooking / made easy / Published by / the United Drug Company, Limited / Toronto – Ontario – Canada / Every scholar should commit this to / memory. / 1. Three little words you often see, / Are articles *a, an* and *the*. / 2. A noun is the name of anything / As *school* or *garden, hoop* or *swing*. / 3. Adjectives, the kind of noun, / As *great, small, pretty, white* or *brown*. / 4. Instead of nouns the pronouns stand – / *her* hair, *his* face, *your* arm, *my* hand. / 5. Verbs tell something to be done – / To *read, count, laugh, sing, jump* or *run*. / 6. How things are done the adverbs tell, / As *slowly, quickly, ill* or *well*. / 7. Conjunctions join the words together / As men *and* women, wind *or* weather. / 8. The preposition stands before / the noun as *in*, or *through* the door. / 9. The interjection shows surprise, / As *oh!* how pretty, *ah!* how wise. / The whole are called nine parts of speech / Which reading, writing, speaking teach, / Rexall Remedies. / The Advertiser Job Printing Co,. [*sic*] Limited, London, Ont. Canada.
DESCRIPTION: 22.0 × 15.0 cm   Pp [1] 2–176   Illus on p 3 of the construction of a fireless cooker   Paper; stapled
CONTENTS: 1 tp; 2 ad; 3–167 text and publ ads; 168–76 index
COPIES: OTUTF (uncat patent medicine)   *Private collection
NOTES: *Rexall Cook Book* is a retitled, later edition of *The Art of Cooking Made Easy*. This edition and O48.19, O48.20, and O48.21 were sold by Rexall druggists and published by the United Drug Co. Ltd, Toronto. I have compared the first section of this edition with the first section of O48.15, the twenty-first edition of about 1913. This edition does not include the home-made yeast recipes and the bread recipes based on homemade yeast (i.e., Salt-Rising Bread, Bread by Mrs Galusha, Potato Yeast, and Another [yeast] are omitted). Instead, Royal Yeast is specified. This text reflects a move away from older bread-making methods, and follows previously described editions.

Printed on the front face of the binding of the private collector's copy is 'This book can only be procured through Rexall Druggists // Sent by mail to any Canadian address on receipt of 25 cents' and below, 'Geo. W. Johnston // Rexall Drug Store // Cowansville, Quebec.' This copy is inscribed on the front face of the binding, in pencil, '... G.M. 1917'; and inscribed on p 78, beside a recipe, 'Fine Mar. 9 – 1919.' The OTUTF copy has 'A. Dulmage, Limited // Rexall Drug Store // Saskatoon, Sask.' instead of the Cowansville drugstore.

OSTC (641.5 Uni M) has an incomplete copy that probably matches the edition described here. The last remaining page is p 174, on which are printed index entries for 'Cakes.' The name of 'Macartney's Drug Store // Rexall trade mark drug store // Thorold Ontario' is on the binding.

NBFKL reports in its collection a copy of a Rexall Drug Co. cookbook that lacks the binding and several initial leaves. A private collector has a copy that may match O48.18, O48.19, or O48.20; it has the name of John Thomson, Rexall Drug Store, Bracebridge, Ontario, on the binding.

O48.19 [copyright 1910, about 1917]
—Rexall / cook book / The / art of cooking / made easy / Published by / the United Drug Company, Limited / Toronto – Ontario – Canada / Every scholar should commit this to / memory. / 1. Three little words you often see, / Are articles *a*, *an* and *the*. / 2. A noun is the name of anything / As *school* or *garden, hoop* or *swing*. / 3. Adjectives, the kind of noun, / As *great, small, pretty, white* or *brown*. / 4. Instead of nouns the pronouns stand – / *her* hair, *his* face, *your* arm, *my* hand. / 5. Verbs tell something to be done – / To *read, count, laugh, sing, jump* or *run*. / 6. How things are done the adverbs tell, / As *slowly, quickly, ill* or *well*. / 7. Conjunctions join the words together / As men *and* women, wind *or* weather. / 8. The preposition stands before / the noun as *in*, or *through* the door. / 9. The interjection shows surprise, / As *oh!* how pretty, *ah!* how wise. / The whole are called nine parts of speech / Which reading, writing, speaking teach, / Rexall Remedies.
DESCRIPTION: 22.0 × 14.5 cm   Pp [1] 2–184   Illus on p 3 of fireless cooker   Paper; stapled, and with hole punched at top left corner for hanging
CONTENTS: 1 tp; 2 publ ad; 3–175 text and ads; 176–84 index
COPIES: *BVIPEH
NOTES: Unlike O48.18, there is no printer on the title-pages of O48.19–48.21.
Printed on the front face of the binding is 'Rexall Cook Book // The art of cooking made easy containing over one thousand tested recipes // Sent by mail to any Canadian address on receipt of 25 cents. We are prompt ...' and below, 'Campbell's Prescription Store cor. Fort and Douglas sts. Victoria, B.C. P.O. Box 260 Phones 135 and 2859 O.' On the inside back face of the binding, D.E. Campbell says that this book is 'the product of 35 years in the retail drug business, ...' Since Campbell established his drugstore in 1882 (see Vertical Newspaper Clipping files, reel 22, at BVIPA), this edition was published about 1917 (1882 + 35 years). Printed on the outside back face is 'United Drug Co. Boston, Mass. Chicago, Ill. Toronto, Canada. Copyright, 1910, United Drug Company.' D.E. Campbell published a series of *Campbell's Calendar Cook Books*, from 1900; see B3.1.

O48.20 [copyright 1910]
—Rexall / trade mark / cook book / The / art of cooking / made easy / Published by / the United Drug Company, Limited / Toronto Ontario Canada / Every scholar should commit this to / memory. / 1. Three little words you often see, / Are articles *a*, *an* and *the*. / 2. A noun is the name of anything / As *school* or *garden, hoop* or *swing*. / 3. Adjectives, the kind of noun, / As *great, small, pretty, white* or *brown*. / 4. Instead of nouns the pronouns stand – / *her* hair, *his* face, *your* arm, *my* hand. / 5. Verbs tell something to be done – / To *read, count, laugh, sing, jump* or *run*. / 6. How things are done the adverbs tell, / As *slowly, quickly, ill* or *well*. / 7. Conjunctions join the words together / As men *and* women, wind *or* weather. / 8. The preposition stands before / the noun as *in*, or *through* the door. / 9. The interjection shows surprise, / As *oh!* how pretty, *ah!* how wise. / The whole are called nine parts of speech / Which reading, writing, speaking teach, / Rexall Remedies.
DESCRIPTION: 22.0 × 15.0 cm   Pp [1] 2–184   Tp illus of boar's head on a platter, illus on p 3 of the construction of a fireless cooker   Paper, with hole punched at top left corner for hanging
CONTENTS: 1 tp; 2 ad; 3–175 text; 176–84 'Index'
COPIES: *OGU (UA s066 b08)
NOTES: Printed on the front face of the binding is 'This book can only be procured through Rexall Druggists // Sent by mail to any Canadian address on receipt of 25 cents' and advertisement for Gould's Drug Store, Cobourg, Ontario. Printed on the outside back face is 'Copyright, 1910, United Drug Company.'

O48.21 [copyright 1910]
—Rexall / trade mark / cook book / The / art of cooking / made easy / Published by / the United Drug Company, Limited / Toronto Ontario Canada / Every scholar should commit this to / memory. / 1. Three little words you often see, / Are articles *a*, *an* and *the*. / 2. A noun is the name of anything / As *school* or *garden, hoop* or *swing*. / 3. Adjectives, the kind of noun, / As *great, small, pretty, white* or *brown*. / 4. Instead of nouns the pronouns stand – / *her* hair, *his* face, *your* arm, *my* hand. / 5. Verbs tell something to be done – / To *read, count, laugh, sing, jump* or *run*. / 6. How things are done the adverbs tell, / As *slowly, quickly, ill* or *well*. / 7. Conjunctions join the words together / As men *and* women, wind *or* weather. / 8. The preposition stands before / the noun as *in*, or *through* the door. / 9. The interjection shows surprise, / As *oh!* how pretty, *ah!* how wise. / The whole are called nine parts of speech / Which

reading, writing, speaking teach, / Rexall Remedies.
DESCRIPTION: 22.0 × 15.0 cm   Pp [1] 2–184   Tp illus
of boar's head on a platter, illus on p 3 of the con-
struction of a fireless cooker   Paper; stapled, and
with hole punched at top left corner, through which
runs a string for hanging
CONTENTS: 1 tp; 2 ad; 3–175 text and ads; 176–84
'Index'
COPIES: *OTNY (uncat)
NOTES: 'F.R. Smith druggist // The Rexall store //
Brussels – Ontario – Canada' is on the outside front
face of the binding; 'Copyright, 1910, United Drug
Company' is on the outside back.

Austin, Benjamin Fish (Brighton, Ont., 21 September 1850–1932)

O49.1   1890
Woman; / her / character, culture and calling. / A
full discussion of / woman's work in the home, /
the school, the church and the social / circle; with
an account of her successful / labors in moral and
social reform, her heroic work / for God and
humanity in the mission field, her success as a /
wage-earner and in fighting life's battle alone; with
/ chapters on all departments of woman's training /
and culture, her claims to the higher / education,
and the best methods / to be pursued therein. / By
/ a galaxy of distinguished authors / in the United
States and Canada. / With / introduction/ by /
Miss Frances E. Willard / President of the /
Women's Christian Temperance Union. / Edited by
the Rev. Principal Austin, A.M., B.D. / of Alma
Ladies' College, St. Thomas, Ont. / The Book &
Bible House / Brantford, Ont. / 1890.
COPIES: CIHM (06583)   ECO   OONL
NOTES: Chapter XVIII, beginning on p 247, is entitled
'Importance of a Knowledge of Cookery to Women'
and covers such ideas as 'Food holds an important
place in the human economy ... Things we eat and
drink materially affect our opinions, beliefs and preju-
dices ... The Drink question and the Food question
neighbors ... The relation of bad food to perfect man-
hood ... Home is the primary school ...' Chapter XIX,
beginning on p 249, includes recipes.
   Austin also discusses 'Woman in Literature' and
the work of Canada's female writers, including
Catharine Parr Traill. Although he comments on p
105 that Traill 'gives an insight into the primitive
domestic life and the privations and toils of the early
settler,' he does not cite O5.1, *The Female Emigrant's
Guide.*

The home made cook book

O50.1   rev. ed., [entered 1890]
The home made / cook book / A complete manual
of practical, economical, / palatable and healthful /
cookery. / Revised edition. / Toronto, Ont.: /
William Bryce, [*sic*]
DESCRIPTION: 18.0 × 12.5 cm   Pp [i–iii] iv–xii, [17] 18–
233, [i–xi]   Cloth, with flower-and-horse pattern
CONTENTS: i tp; ii 'Entered according to the Act of
Parliament of Canada, in the year one thousand eight
hundred and ninety, by Wm. Bryce, in the office of
the Minister of Agriculture.'; iii–xii 'Index' [i.e., table
of contents]; 17–233 text; i–ix publ ads; x ad; xi publ
ad
COPIES: NSHP   OMUC   *Private collection
NOTES: See the notes for O27.1, *The Seaside Cook Book,*
concerning other publications by Bryce.

1890–5

Epworth League cook book

*The Epworth League was a Methodist youth group,
formally organized in Cleveland, Ohio, in 1889, whose
membership grew rapidly across North America.*

O51.1   nd [about 1890–5]
Epworth League / cook book / This book was
printed by the Post Printing Co., Leamington. /
If you want to know / how to cook horse meat /
you will have to consult a French cook book. But
anyone can tell you / that the proper place to buy /
books, school supplies, stationery / wall paper and
window shades / is / Geo. W. Jackson's,
Leamington. / Corner store. Sign of the Big Book.
[cover-title]
DESCRIPTION: 14.5 × 13.5 cm   Pp [i–ii], [1] 2–12, [i–ii],
13–24, [i–ii]   Paper, with small image on front of
flowers; stapled
CONTENTS: i–ii ads; 1–12 recipes credited with the name
of the contributor; i–ii ads; 13–24 recipes
credited with the name of the contributor; i–ii ads
COPIES: CIHM (93744)   *OONL (TX715.6 C657 1890z
p***)

Greenwood's tested recipes

O52.1   nd [about 1890–5]
Greenwood's / tested / recipes / A / practical /
everyday / cook book / Published for / A.J.

Greenwood's / Dispensary, / cor. St. Paul & St. James sts., / 187 St. Paul Street East, St. Catharines. / (Copyrighted) [cover-title]

COPIES: *Private collection

NOTES: The owner reports that the book has 32 pp. St Catharines city directories list A.J. Greenwood, druggist, at 187 St Paul Street East from the 1870s to 1903 (the 1904 directory lists A.J. Greenwood and Co. at 149 St Paul). From appearances, the book was published in the first half of the 1890s.

Happy-Thought-Range cookery book

In 1927, what was then called the Happy Thought Foundry Co. Ltd in Brantford merged with four other firms to become General Steel Wares; for more information about the merger, see O162.1, McClary's Gas Range and Cook Book.

O53.1   nd [about 1890–5]
Happy-Thought-Range / cookery book. / Manufactured by / William Buck, Buck's Stove Works, Brantford / 35,000 "Happy Thought Ranges" now in use in Canada. / For sale at / R. Bigley's, 96 & 98 Queen St. East, Toronto [cover-title]

DESCRIPTION: 18.5 × 12.0 cm   Pp [1] 2–56 [57–64]   Illus of company ranges   Paper, with image on front of Happy Thought Range; stapled

CONTENTS: 1 'Directions for Operating "The Happy Thought Range"'; 2–56 illus of ranges and heaters, recipes, and a list of names and addresses of the many people in Toronto who have Happy Thought Ranges; 57–64 blank for 'Memoranda'

CITATIONS: Driver 2003, 'Canadian Cookbooks,' p 33

COPIES: *OTMCL (683.88029 W38.3)

NOTES: Happy Thought Ranges were adapted to burning wood, coal, or gas, according to information on the inside front face of the binding. In Toronto city directories, the first listing for the stove-seller Richard Bigley at 96 and 98 Queen Street East is in 1890 (before this date his business was at 92–4 Queen Street East).

'Toronto Lith. Co.' is on the outside back face of the binding. The Toronto Lithographing Co. was active from 1878; it changed its name to Stone Ltd in 1909 (Hulse, p 261).

1891

Dane, Frederick (1861–), and Robert S. McIndoe (14 April 1856–)

Toronto city directories list Dane as a tea broker (1890) or in 'teas' (1891), in business at 23 Scott Street. They list Robert S. McIndoe as a broker (1890) or manufacturer's agent (1891), at 24 Front Street East. The 1901 Census records McIndoe living in Toronto with his wife, Agness, and twelve-year-old daughter.

O54.1   1891
A sketch / of the / growth and history of tea / and / the science of blending / particularly adapted / to the / Canadian trade / Entered according to Act of the / Parliament of Canada in the year 1891 / By / Frederick Dane and R.S. McIndoe / at the Department of Agriculture / Toronto: / Mail Job Printing Co., Ltd.

DESCRIPTION: 18.0 × 11.5 cm   Pp 3–4 [5] 6–116 [117–18]   Cloth

CONTENTS: 3–4 ads; 5 tp; 6 ad; 7 'Contents'; 8 blank; 9–16 lacking in OTMCL copy; 17–103 text and ads; 104 ad; 105–16 'Index'; 117–18 blank for 'Memorandum'

COPIES: CIHM (02262, 95415)   OGU (UA s048 b41)   OONL (TP650 D36 1891)   *OTMCL (663.9 D12)   OWTU (F8878)   QMM (GT2905 D3 1891)

NOTES: The cover-title is 'Tea and the Science of Blending.' The OGU copy lacks the title-page, but retains p 7 onward. The 'Introduction,' which is on p 9, is dated Toronto, 1891, and states, 'This book is written with the intention of giving to those engaged in the retail tea trade in Canada, and who desire to take an interest in blending, an idea of the classes of tea most suitable to their trade, with hints on blending, which will enable any intelligent person to gain a proficiency in the art, ...'; the author is described as having 'practical experience in this work both in Canada and the Old Country, ...' A poem titled 'The Tea Leaf' by William H. Seyler, dated 29 May 1890, is on pp 13–14. The text contains historical information and statistics about tea consumption, including figures for tea imports into Canada. There are twenty-six numbered recipes for 'Specimen Blends' on pp 81–101. The directions for 'How to Make Tea' on p 102 advise the retailer 'to print on every wrapper or bag the following instructions ...'

Porter, Mrs M.E.

O55.1 [1891]
The new / World's Fair cook book / and / housekeepers' companion: / Containing / carefully prepared and practically tested recipes for all kinds of / plain and fancy dishes; making of wholesome and pal- / atable confections; valuable hints on setting / of the table; rules for the proper / care of food; together / with / things every housekeeper should know, / such as / how to preserve health; how to make plants grow, and how to / make them fresh; hints for the toilet; how to receive / and entertain; timely antidotes for poisons; / what to name the baby; and many / valuable tables useful / for every-day / reference. / By Mrs. M.E. Porter, / Prince George Court House, Virginia. / Elegantly illustrated. / Toronto: / William Briggs.
COPIES: *OGOWSM

O55.2 1974
—Mrs. / Porter's / cook.book [*sic*] / and / housekeepers' / companion / ... containing carefully prepared and / practically tested recipes for all kinds / of plain and fancy dishes; making of / wholesome and palatable confections; / valuable hints on setting of the table; / rules for the proper care of food; together / with things every housekeeper / should know such as how to preserve / health; how to make plants grow, and / how to make them fresh; hints for the / toilet; how to receive and entertain; what / to name the baby; notes for the modern / cook; and many valuable tables useful for / every-day reference. / By / Mrs. M.E. Porter / McGraw-Hill Ryerson Limited / Toronto Montreal New York
DESCRIPTION: 21.5 × 13.5 cm   Pp [i–iv] v–xxxvii [xxxviii], 1–391   Cloth
CONTENTS: i ht; ii blank; iii tp; iv 'Mrs. Porter's New Cook Book and Housekeepers' Companion // Originally published in 1891 by William Briggs, Toronto, with the title The New World's Fair Cook Book and Housekeeper's Companion // Reprinted in 1974 by McGraw-Hill Ryerson Limited, 330 Progress Avenue, Scarborough [now part of the amalgamated city of Toronto], Ontario ...'; v–x introduction to reprint signed Elma E. [i.e., Elizabeth] Perrin; xi–xxxiii table of contents; xxxiv blank except for folio; xxxv–xxxvi original publisher's preface; xxxvii 'Weights and Measures'; xxxviii blank; 1–top 388 text; mid 388 'A Note to the Modern Cook' giving oven temperatures; bottom 388–391 'Editor's Notes' [i.e., glossary of terms with modern explanation]

COPIES: OKITWN   *OONL (TX715 P6 1974)
NOTES: Elma Perrin's introduction to the reprint says that Porter published her first cookbook of American recipes in 1870 [*sic*], and that this text, *The New World's Fair Cook Book and Housekeepers' Companion*, is her second book. In fact, the latter is an enlarged edition of her *New Southern Cookery Book* of 1871.

Although Longone/Longone H16 refers to 'several American and Canadian editions,' I have identified only two American editions and one nineteenth-century Canadian edition. The original volume from which the 1974 reprint was made could not be found in the book collection at McGraw-Hill Ryerson in Whitby. I found no reference to the book in *Books and Notions* for 1891, or in Wallace.

AMERICAN EDITIONS: *Mrs Porter's New Southern Cookery Book*, Philadelphia, New York: J.E. Potter and Co., [c1871] (United States: DLC, IaU); enlarged ed., re-titled *The New World's Fair Cook Book and Housekeepers' Companion: Containing Carefully Prepared and Practically Tested Recipes for All Kinds of Plain and Fancy Dishes*, Philadelphia: J.E. Potter, [copyright 1891] (OBUJBM; United States: DLC); *Mrs Porter's New Southern Cookery Book*, introduction and suggested recipes by Louis Szathmáry, New York: Arno Press, 1973 [c1871] (United States: DLC, IaU)

Rorer, Mrs Sarah Tyson, née Heston (Richboro, Bucks County, Pa, 18 October 1849–27 December 1937, Colebrook, Lebanon County, Pa)

Sarah Heston married William Albert Rorer in 1871 and bore two sons, Billy and James. In spring 1880, following a short course in cookery at the New Century Club in Philadelphia, Pennsylvania, she agreed to direct the New Century Club cooking school. In 1883 she founded her own Philadelphia School of Cookery, which she ran until 1903. She lectured widely, attracting huge numbers to her talks, including close to a quarter of a million people during the Chicago World's Fair in 1893; and she was a prolific writer of over fifty cookbooks and advertising pamphlets and of regular columns in Table Talk *and* Ladies' Home Journal. *The personal qualities behind her success – her charisma, wit, the forcefulness with which she delivered her opinions – are described by Emma Seifrit Weigley in 'The Philadelphia Chef: Mastering the Art of Philadelphia Cookery,'* Philadelphia Magazine of History and Biography *Vol. 96, No. 2 (April 1972), pp 229–40, and in Weigley's* Sarah Tyson Rorer: The Nation's Instructress in Dietetics and

Cookery, *Philadelphia: American Philosophical Society, 1977. Canadians experienced her magnetism first-hand when, in 1898, she travelled to London, Ontario, to give six lectures on various subjects at the YMCA, on 7–12 March; the series of six lectures cost $2.50 or $0.50 for one class only (see* Free Press *(London) for 4, 5, 7, 8, 9, 10, 11, 12 March 1898). Her London visit was also reported in the* Farmer's Advocate *of 15 April 1898, pp 160, 189, under the heading 'Travelling Schools of Cookery.'*

A few of her titles were published in Canada: O56.1, Home Candy Making; *O57.1,* Hot Weather Dishes; *Q37.1,* Home Helps; *O137.1,* Mrs Rorer's New Cook Book; *and S16.1,* Robin Hood Flour Cook Book. *The latter was prepared specifically for the Canadian market by the American owners of Robin Hood Mills, which was based in Moose Jaw, Saskatchewan. Rorer's recipes were included in two Canadian-published promotional books for the shortening Cottolene: Q29.1,* 266 recettes choisies; *and Q30.1,* 600 Selected Recipes.

One of her books, My Best 250 Recipes, *Philadelphia: Arnold and Co., [1907], was probably sold by the Methodist Book and Publishing House in Toronto; see the following entry in 'Stock Book 1909' (OTCC (Acc. 83.061C, UCC Board of Publication, Series III, Box 39, p 49)): '11 [copies] Mrs Orers [sic] Best Riceps [sic].' Another entry in 'Stock Book 1909,' under 'Public Schools,' p 170, may also be for one of her titles: '3 [copies] Canning and Preserving.'*

The following titles by Rorer were published only in the United States, except for one British edition where noted: How to Use Olive Butter, *Philadelphia: Washington Butcher's Sons, 1883 (United States: DLC, InU);* Mrs Rorer's Philadelphia Cook Book, *Philadelphia: Arnold and Co., [1886] (OGU; Great Britain: LB; United States: DLC), and Philadelphia: G.H. Buchanan and Co., 1886 (United States: DLC);* Canning and Preserving, *Philadelphia: Arnold and Co., 1887 (OONMS; United States: DLC);* Questions and Class Book of the Philadelphia Cooking School ..., *Philadelphia: Press of G.H. Buchanan and Co., [1887] (United States: DLC);* Bread and Bread-Making, *Philadelphia: Arnold and Co., [c1889] (United States: DLC);* Good Ways in Cooking, *New York: Syndicate Trading Co., [1889] (United States: DLC);* Dainty Dishes for All the Year Round, *Part I, Philadelphia: American Machine Co., 1890 (United States: DLC);* How to Cook Vegetables, *Philadelphia: W.A. Burpee and Co., 1891 (United States: DLC);* Cream of Maize Recipes, *Dayton: Dayton Cereal Co., 1893 (Weigley 1977, p 188);* Recipes Used in Illinois Corn Exhibit Model Kitchen, Woman's Building, Columbian Exposition, Chicago, 1893, [Philadelphia: Printed by G.H. Buchanan and Co., 1893] (United*

States: DLC); Colonial Recipes, *Philadelphia: Arnold and Co., [1894] (United States: DLC);* Dainties, *Philadelphia: Arnold and Co., [1894] (United States: DLC);* Fifteen New Ways for Oysters, *Philadelphia: Arnold and Co., [c1894] (United States: DLC);* How to Use a Chafing Dish, *Philadelphia: Arnold and Co., [c1894] (United States: DLC);* Quick Soups, *Philadelphia: Arnold and Co., [1894] (United States: DLC);* Sandwiches, *Philadelphia: Arnold and Co., 1894 (Weigley 1977, p 189);* Twenty Quick Soups, *Philadelphia: Arnold and Co., [c1894] (United States: DLC);* Dainty Dishes for All the Year Round, *Part II, Philadelphia: North Brothers Mfg Co., 1896 (United States: DLC);* For Serving Shredded Wheat, *[New York: Cereal Machine Co., 1896] (United States: DLC);* New Salads for Dinners, Luncheons, Suppers and Receptions, *Philadelphia: Arnold and Co., [copyright 1897] (United States: InU);* Good Cooking, *Philadelphia: Curtis Publishing Co., and New York: Doubleday and McClure Co., [1898] (OKITD; United States: DLC);* Left Overs, *Philadelphia: Arnold and Co., [1898] (United States: DLC);* Cereal Foods and How to Cook Them, *Chicago: American Cereal Co., 1899 (Weigley 1977, p 188);* How to Set the Table, *Wallingford, Conn., and New York [etc.], London: R. Wallace and Sons Mfg Co., [1901] (United States: DLC);* Made Over Dishes, *Philadelphia: Arnold and Co., [1901] (United States: DLC);* New Ways for Oysters, *Philadelphia: Arnold and Co., [1903] (United States: DLC);* World's Fair Souvenir Cook Book ... Louisiana Purchase Exposition, St. Louis, 1904, *Philadelphia: Arnold and Co., [1904] (United States: DLC);* Mrs Rorer's Cakes, Icings and Fillings, *Philadelphia: Arnold and Co., [copyright 1905] (United States: DLC, InU);* Mrs Rorer's Every Day Menu Book, *Philadelphia: Arnold and Co., [c1905] (United States: DLC);* Many Ways for Cooking Eggs, *Philadelphia: Arnold and Co., copyright 1907 (United States: DLC);* My Best 250 Recipes, *Philadelphia: Arnold and Co., [1907] (United States: DLC);* Mrs Rorer's Vegetable Cookery and Meat Substitutes, *Philadelphia: Arnold and Co., [copyright 1909] (United States: DLC, InU), and a British edition, London, Leipsic: T. Fisher Unwin, printed in United States, [1911] (Great Britain: LB);* Recipe Book for the Mudge Patent Processor, *Philadelphia: John L. Glaumer Co., 1912 (Weigley 1977, p 189);* Ice Creams, Water Ices, Frozen Puddings, *Philadelphia: Arnold and Co., 1913 (United States: DLC);* McIlhenny's Tabasco Sauce Recipes, *Philadelphia: McIlhenny Co., 1913 (Weigley 1977, p 189);* Snowdrift Secrets, *Savannah, New Orleans, Chicago: Southern Cotton Oil Co., 1913 (United States: DLC);* Mrs Rorer's Diet for the Sick, *Philadelphia: Arnold and Co., [1914] (AEU; United States: DLC);* Mrs

Rorer's Brand New Salads, *Philadelphia: Arnold and Co., [c1915] (United States: DLC); Recipes, Savannah, New Orleans [etc.]: Southern Cotton Oil Co., c1915 (United States: DLC);* Domestic Science Teaching in Rural District, *Massachusetts State Board of Agriculture Circular No. 62, January 1916 (Weigley 1977, p 188); and Mrs Rorer's Key to Simple Cookery, Philadelphia: Arnold and Co., [1917] (United States: DLC). See Weigley 1977, p 189, for books to which Rorer contributed recipes.*

See also Sandra L. Oliver's biography of Rorer in Arndt, pp 315–17, especially regarding Rorer's collaboration with the food industry.

O56.1 1891
[An edition of *Home Candy Making*, Toronto: Hart and Co., 1891, cloth, $0.75, 'uniform with Hot Weather Dishes [O57.1]']
CITATIONS: BN, Vol. 7, No. 10, p 8
NOTES: BN incorrectly gives 'R.T.' as the author's initials. The Toronto edition probably had 74 pp, as did the American edition.

AMERICAN EDITIONS: Philadelphia: Arnold and Co., [1889] (United States: DLC, NN); Philadelphia: Arnold and Co., [c1911] (United States: DLC).

O57.1 1891
[An edition of *Hot Weather Dishes*, Toronto: Hart and Co., 1891]
CITATIONS: BN, Vol. 7, No. 8, p 10
NOTES: BN states, 'Mrs. Rarer's [*sic*] Hot Weather Dishes ... Hart & Company issue the book in this city [i.e., Toronto].' It probably had 104 pp, as did the American edition. See also O56.1, Mrs Rorer's *Home Candy Making*, which is described as uniform with this book.

AMERICAN EDITIONS: Philadelphia: Arnold, [c1888] (SRU; United States: DLC).

1892

The Galt cook book

In 1937 the ladies of the same church produced O930.1, The West End Circle Recipe Book.

O58.1 [Christmas 1892]
The / Galt cook book / comprising / a large number of tested recipes / for the kitchen, dining /

room and sick room. / Compiled and edited by / a committee of the Ladies' Aid Society / of the Central Presbyterian / Church, Galt. / Printed by / Robt. G. McLean, Lombard Street, / Toronto.
DESCRIPTION: 17.5 × 12.0 cm   Pp 3–12 [13–15] 16 [17–18] 19–528 [3 leaves lacking]
CONTENTS: 3–12 ads; 13 tp; 14 blank; 15–16 preface signed the Committee, Galt, Christmas 1892; 17 'What Does Cookery Mean?' [quotation from Ruskin]; 18–517 recipes credited with the name of the contributor and chapters on 'Simple Cures,' 'Useful Hints,' 'Window Gardening,' 'A Few Words about Manners,' 'Breakfast,' 'Lunch,' 'Tea,' and 'Dinner'; 518 blank; 519–25 'Contents' [i.e., index]; 526 blank; 527–8 ads
CITATIONS: Bechtel, p 169   Bloomfield 3207   Driver 2001, Wellington County, p 95   Landsberg   Reitz, p [4]   RushCat List 1, 2002, No. 83
COPIES: OCCA   OKITD (2 copies: x967.372.001, 984.027.007)   OKITJS (981.3.3)   OWTU (2 copies: F8207, F19037)   *Private collection
NOTES: The Committee's preface reads: 'Our chief aim in preparing [this cookbook] has been to make it a thoroughly practical guide for housekeepers. To this end we have carefully supervised its contents, selecting only such recipes as are suitable to our community, and such as either our contributors or ourselves can vouch for as valuable from actual experience ... We gratefully acknowledge and thank the ladies of Galt, Hamilton, Berlin, Ayr, St. George and Waterloo, and other places, who have given us their generous assistance ...' Pages 514–17 describe in detail the preparations and menu for a Christmas dinner.

The endpaper on the inside back face of the binding is printed with an advertisement and numbered as p 535. The private collector's copy, therefore, lacks pp 529–34. The OKITJS copy retains pp 529–34 (all advertisements), although they are loose from the binding, as are some leaves at the front of the volume. The OKITJS copy is inscribed on p 14, in pencil, 'Mrs. George Kalbfleisch Berlin Ont.' One of the OKITD copies (x967.372.001) is inscribed on p 3, in ink, 'Kate Bauman // Doon, Ont.'

Although the first edition is attributed to a committee of the Ladies' Aid Society, all later editions are described as compiled by Margaret Taylor and Frances McNaught, and an obituary for Margaret Taylor's daughter (also called Margaret; middle initial, A.) clearly connects her mother with the first edition of the book (obituary dated 28 October 1972, on file at OCCA, p T3). The obituary states: '... her mother is credited with editing the first cookbook ever published by a local group in the city. Proceeds from the sale of it were used to help pay for repairs to the manse [of Central Presbyterian Church]. Today, [fundraising cookbooks are common], but away back in 1892 when Mrs. Taylor asked the women of Central Church to turn in their favorite recipes for what came to be known as the Galt Cookbook, it was unheard of. Members brought their recipes to Mrs. Taylor's home and they worked for three days, pasting them on to brown paper sheets prior to being sent to the publisher. The women "made a day of it" and everyone stayed for dinner. Local firms paid for the printing of the book.' Margaret Taylor (11 September 1849–15 February 1929), the daughter of Mr and Mrs Alex Fisher, married Alfred Taylor. She was the second president of the Ladies' Aid Society, which had been formed in 1880, two years before the construction of Central Presbyterian Church in 1882. She is buried in Mount View Cemetery. She is still remembered for her contribution to the church community: The Margaret Taylor Circle of the Ladies' Aid Society is named after her, and in 1954 her daughter Margaret donated a stained glass window to the church in her parents' honour.

Her co-compiler, Miss Frances McNaught, died on 6 March 1919, but her obituary (dated 7 March, on file at OCCA) makes no reference to the cookbook, although it does refer to her character and offer family information. Born in Fergus, she had been a resident of Galt for 'upwards of 50 years' and was a member of Central Presbyterian Church. At her death she was survived by one sister, Mrs James Young, and two brothers, Thomas of Toronto and David in the West. She is described as 'well informed on political topics,' 'an omniverous [sic] reader and an exceedingly interesting reviewer of events, local and general,' and 'keenly interested in many topics allied to social reform and social progress' to which she 'gave a practical turn in her activities.' This last-mentioned aspect of her character is certainly consistent with her taking on the project of *The Galt Cook Book*. Miss McNaught was the fifth president of the Ladies' Aid Society, serving from 1890 to 1911. The 1911 Census clearly records her as being born in 1848 and sixty-two years old (the handwriting of the 1901 Census can be read as 1848 and fifty-two years). She is buried in Mount View Cemetery.

Various publications about the history of Central Presbyterian Church (all in the archives of the church) refer to the cookbook. As early as 1904, the first minister of the church, James A.R. Dickson, in his account *'Ebenezer': A History of the Central Presbyterian Church, Galt, Ontario* (Toronto: William Briggs, 1904, p 190),

wrote: 'One thing deserves special mention, and that was the "publication of the Galt Cook Book," which was prepared by a committee of the Ladies' Aid Society in 1893 [sic], and an edition of 1000 copies printed, which by 1897 was entirely disposed of, and netted in profits for the Society the handsome sum of $470.37.' In *The Story of Our Ladies' Aid Society, Central Presbyterian Church*, 1965, p 4, Agnes G. Burgess offered more information: '... on September 22, 1892, a special meeting was called to discuss "Ways and Means" [of raising money to improve the Manse]. Six ladies were present, – Miss McNaught, President – Mrs. Risk, Secretary – Mrs. A. Taylor, Mrs. Dietrich, Miss Addison and Mrs. Capron. After much discussion, the suggestion of publishing a cook book was decided on, and committees set up, – one to solicit advertising to help defray the cost, – and one to secure and compile recipes. This undertaking entailed a great deal of work and it was Mrs. Alfred Taylor's home, I believe, that became the headquarters for weeks and months of preparation. Eventually 1000 copies were published in the first edition, and some of these actually found their way to the four corners of the earth. A total of $470.37 was cleared on this project, although it was about five years before the full accounting was made.' *A Century at Central, 1882–1982*, p 20, refers to the 1893 [sic] edition and to the 1974 Coles Canadiana Collection facsimile of the 1898 edition, and reprints two recipes.

The amount of money raised by the book was substantial, and the monthly receipts from the cookbook are recorded in the 'Treasurer's Book' for the Ladies' Aid, in the volume covering 1890–1912 (at the church archives). Revenues are recorded from 1 June 1893: in the period June–December 1893, receipts totalled $82.51; 1894, $157.40; 1895, $65.91; 1896, $100.15; and 1897, $58.40. By December 1897, therefore, the first edition had reaped $464.37 (the difference between this figure and Dickson's figure of $470.37 may have to do with a few small amounts identified as 'Talent CB' entered in 1899, 1900, and 1901). The only other entry in the 1890–1912 'Treasurer's Book' that almost certainly has to do with the cookbook is the one for 1 May 1902, when Miss McNaught and Mrs Taylor submitted for deposit $200.00, an amount that, although it is not identified further, is probably a payment from Briggs for sales of the 1898 edition (it is unlikely to be for the 1902 edition because the compilers had signed the contract for the 1902 edition only one month before, on 2 April).

O58.2 [2nd ed.], 1898
—The / Galt cook book / (revised edition) /
comprising / a large number of tested recipes /
for the kitchen, dining / room and sick room /
Compiled and edited by / Margaret Taylor and
Frances McNaught / Toronto: / William Briggs /
29–33 Richmond St. West / 1898

DESCRIPTION: 18.0 × 12.0 cm   Pp [i–iii] iv–v [vi], [7]
8–454   Cloth

CONTENTS: i tp; ii 'Entered according to Act of the
Parliament of Canada, in the year one thousand eight
hundred and ninety-eight, by Margaret Taylor and
Frances McNaught, at the Department of Agriculture, Ottawa.'; iii–v 'Preface' signed Frances Mc-
Naught and Margaret Taylor, Galt, 25 November 1898;
vi 'What Does Cookery Mean?' [quotation from
Ruskin]; 7–422 recipes credited with the name of the
contributor; 423–9 'Simple Cures'; 430–40 'Useful
Hints'; 441 'Dinner' [menu for Christmas dinner and
menu for a family dinner]; 442 blank; 443–54 'Contents'

CITATIONS: Cooke 2002, p 234   JCCat 6   O'Neill
(unpublished)   Toronto Public Library, *Subject Catalogue of Books in the Central Circulating Library*, Vol. 3,
Part II, Toronto: Murray Printing Co., 1899, p 56

COPIES: *MCDHM   OKITD (974.107.001)   Private collection; Great Britain: LB (7945.e.40 destroyed)

NOTES: In the 'Preface' McNaught and Taylor explain
the revisions that have been made for this 'second
edition': 'Some duplicate recipes have been omitted,
others have been corrected and improved, and a valuable addition of new plain, practical, common-sense
recipes have been added.' They comment that the
first edition of one thousand copies had been 'completely exhausted' for 'over a year,' despite the fact
that the book was not advertised in the press, and
they refer to the book's wide distribution: '[Copies of
the first edition] were all speedily absorbed in Galt
and neighborhood, Waterloo, Woodstock, and other
surrounding places. The book ... not only found its
way all over Canada, but quite a number have gone
to the United States, England and Scotland. Copies of
the work have also been sent to China, Egypt, India,
South Africa, Australia and other remote countries,
either sent as presents by Canadian friends, or written for by persons in those lands who had chanced in
some way to see or hear of the book.' By way of
example, letters are quoted, such as one from Mrs
Ogilvie, who, in August 1895 in Cairo, Egypt, saw a
copy at the house of an American missionary. The
popularity of *The Galt Cook Book* is confirmed by the
fact that the revised edition is listed in the 1899 volume of the Toronto Public Library's *Subject Catalogue*
of Books in the Central Circulating Library – the only
Canadian cookbook to be listed in the ten-year period, 1889–99 (of the many other cookbooks listed,
about half are British, half American).

The OKITD copy is inscribed on the title-page, in
ink, 'Kate W. Morden.' The private collector's copy is
inscribed on the title-page, in ink, 'Elizabeth Bally //
Prince Albert Sask. Sept – 10th 190[last digit unclear].'

O58.3 [3rd ed.], 1902
—The / Galt cook book / (revised edition) /
comprising / a large number of tested recipes /
for the kitchen, dining / room and sick room /
Compiled and edited by / Margaret Taylor and
Frances McNaught / Toronto: / William Briggs /
29–33 Richmond St. West / 1902

DESCRIPTION: 18.0 × 12.5 cm   Pp [i–iii] iv–v [vi], [7]
8–454   Cloth

CONTENTS: i tp; ii 'Entered according to Act of the
Parliament of Canada, in the year one thousand eight
hundred and ninety-eight, by Margaret Taylor and
Frances McNaught, at the Department of Agriculture, Ottawa.'; iii–v 'Preface' signed Frances Mc-
Naught and Margaret Taylor, Galt, 25 November 1898;
vi 'What Does Cookery Mean?' [quotation from
Ruskin]; 7–422 recipes credited with the name of the
contributor; 423–9 'Simple Cures'; 430–40 'Useful
Hints'; 441 'Dinner' [menu for Christmas dinner and
menu for a family dinner]; 442 blank; 443–54 'Contents'

CITATIONS: Bloomfield 3227

COPIES: BVAMM   *OKITD (998.186.001)

NOTES: Various records relating to the publication of
the 1902 edition are at OTCC (Acc. 83.061C, UCC
Board of Publication), including the 'Memorandum
of Agreement' for publishing the 'third edition,' dated
2 April 1902 and signed by William Briggs, book
steward of the Methodist Book and Publishing House,
Frances McNaught, and Margaret Taylor (Series I,
Box 8, William Briggs Agreements 135–98, Contract
155). For the sum of $208, the publisher agreed 'to
make plates from the existing matrices ... and print
one thousand copies, being the Third Edition of the
Author's book "The Galt Cook Book," and to bind
five hundred of such copies in cloth, the printing and
binding ... to be equal in style and quality to the book
heretofore printed and bound for the Author by the
Publisher [i.e., O58.2].' The publisher also agreed to
bind the other copies, if ordered in lots of at least one
hundred each, at the rate of $8 per hundred. The
retail price was to be $1 per copy. An entry in 'Bound
Index Books of Printing Jobs ... 1901–1906' (Series I,
Box 4) states, '4686 [i.e., ticket no.] June 13/02 1000

[copies] 213.79 [price] McNaught, Miss F. Galt Cook Bk (2nd [*sic*] Edition) cast plates from matrices Bind 482.'

The publisher's record of copies bound for sale (Series III, Box 43, 'Books for Sale 1899–1916,' p 265) indicates that of the thousand copies printed, all were bound by 24 June 1903. Under the heading 'Galt Cook Book // Miss F. McNaught' there are entries for 1902 and 1903. The left column for 1902 records 200 copies 'From Bindery' on 16 May, 64 copies on 19 May, and 218 copies on 21 May [making a total of 482 in 1902]; the right column for 1902 notes, 'May Edition 1000 // Bind 500.' The left column for 1903 records 482 copies 'To T Eaton Coy [the department store] in June [no day specified], 500 copies 'From Bindery' on 24 June, plus another 18 from the bindery [making a total of 518 in 1903]; the right column for 1903 notes, 'June 10 Bind 500 // L-10 ...'

The Methodist Book and Publishing House held copies of the book in stock for several years: In 'Stock Book 1909' (Series III, Box 39), on p 86, under the heading 'Subscription Books,' 52 copies of 'New Galt Cook Book' are listed; in 'Stock Book 1910' (Series III, Box 40), on p 88, again under 'Subscription Books,' 45 copies of 'Galt Cook Book' are listed; and in 'Stock Book 1913' (Series III, Box 41), on p 74, under 'Subscription Stock,' 34 copies of 'New Galt Cook Book' are listed. These entries probably refer to the later editions retitled *The New Galt Cook Book*.

Bloomfield 3227 records the 1902 edition at OCCA; however, the archives holds the 1892 edition, not 1902.

O58.4 [entered 1898; about 1904–9]

—The new / Galt cook book / (revised edition) / a comprehensive treatment of the subject of / cookery with abundant instructions in / every branch of the art – soups, fish, / poultry, meats, vegetables, salads, / bread, cakes, jellies, fruits, / pickles, sauces, beverages, / candies, sick room diet, / canning, &c., &c. / including / valuable tested recipes in all departments, / prepared for the housewife – not / for the chef. / Compiled and edited by / Margaret Taylor and Frances McNaught / Toronto / McLeod & Allen / publishers

DESCRIPTION: 18.0 × 12.5 cm   Pp [1–2], [i–iii] iv–v [vi], [7] 8–454 [455–62]   Cloth

CONTENTS: 1 blank; 2 'Time for Cooking'; i tp; ii 'Entered according to Act of the Parliament of Canada, in the year one thousand eight hundred and ninety-eight, by Margaret Taylor and Frances McNaught, at the Department of Agriculture, Ottawa.'; iii–v preface signed Frances McNaught and Margaret Taylor,

Galt, 25 November 1898; vi quotation from Ruskin; 7–442 text; 443–54 'Contents'; 455–62 blank for 'Recipes // My Friends' & My Own'

CITATIONS: Abrahamson, pp 41, 61   Bloomfield 3227

COPIES: BNEM   BVIPM   CIHM (38741)   OGU (UA S043 b08)   OH (R641.5971 TAY CESC)   OKQ (TX715 T243 1898t)   OTUTF (B-12 7870)   OWTU (F3871)   SSWD   *Private collection; Great Britain: OPo(F)

NOTES: The first listing in Toronto city directories for the publisher McLeod and Allen is in 1902; Thomas Allen left the business early in 1916, after which the firm operated under the name of George J. McLeod (see BS, Vol. 32, No. 2 (February 1916), p 29). This edition, therefore, was published no earlier than 1902. It was likely published in 1904 or later because Briggs was still binding copies of the 1902 edition (O58.3) in June 1903; it was published by 1909 because Briggs's 'Stock Book 1909' lists the new title, 'New Galt Cook Book.'

OGM has a copy (979.41.1) that lacks the title-page; however, it is probably the same edition as that described here since it has 454 numbered pages plus blank pages for 'Recipes // My Friends' & My Own.' Bloomfield 3227 incorrectly records two copies at OWTL; there are no copies of *The New Galt Cook Book* at OWTL.

Berton, pp 52, 72, and 73, reprints recipes from 'The New Galt Cookbook, 1898,' probably O58.4 or O58.5. Duncan, pp 48, 144, and 240, refers to O58.4 or O58.5.

O58.5 [entered 1898; about 1916–20]

—The new / Galt cook book / (revised edition entirely re-set) / a book of tried and tested recipes / Compiled by / Margaret Taylor / and / Frances McNaught / Toronto / George J. McLeod, Limited / publishers

DESCRIPTION: 18.5 × 12.5 cm   Pp [3–6] 7–282 [283–8]   Paper, with image on front, in an oval frame, of a woman stirring the contents of a bowl

CONTENTS: 3 tp; 4 'Entered according to Act of the Parliament of Canada, in the year one thousand eight hundred and ninety-eight, by Margaret Taylor and Frances McNaught, at the Department of Agriculture, Ottawa.'; 5 table of contents; 6 blank; 7–274 text; 275–82 index; 283–8 blank for 'Recipes // My Friends' & My Own'

CITATIONS: Bloomfield 3227 (note)   Driver 2001, Wellington County, p 95   Powers/Stewart, p 105 (Dorothy Duncan, 'Ontario Cooking')

COPIES: OCCA   OFERWM (A1984.51)   OGU (*UA S062 b02)   OTMCL (641.5971 T138)   OTNY

(uncat) OTUTF (B-12 7871) QMM (RBD TX715.6 T39 1898); United States: DLC (TX715 T243 1898)
NOTES: This edition was published after Thomas Allen left the company McLeod and Allen, early in 1916; it was published no later than the earliest dated inscription, 1920 (in the OTMCL copy, transcribed below). This edition has no preface and no quotation from Ruskin. 'The T. Eaton Co Limited Toronto Canada' (the Canadian department store) is on the front face of the paper binding of the OGU copy catalogued here; it is inscribed, opposite the title-page, 'Mrs G.A. Holland 329 Buller Street Woodstock.' The OFERWM copy has the same paper binding as the OGU copy, and it is inscribed on the second blank leaf at the front of the book, in ink, 'Presented by Grandma to Hazel W. Reichard.'

The OTNY, OTUTF, and QMM copies are bound in cloth, with an image on the front face of a maid carrying a Christmas pudding. The OTNY copy is inscribed on the front endpaper, in ink, 'To Tootsie from Vernie // Toronto Sept 13th 1921.' The OTMCL copy, which is rebound, is inscribed on the front endpaper, in pencil, '1920,' and in ink, 'Mrs Ewart-Walker 5 Clarendon Crescent // Earthmore.' (The Toronto city directory shows B. Ewart Walker at 5 Clarendon Crescent in 1920.)

O58.6 [facsimile ed., copyright 1974]
—The / early Canadian / Galt cook book / (revised edition) / comprising / a large number of tested recipes / for the kitchen, dining / room and sick room / Compiled and edited by / Margaret Taylor and Frances McNaught / Toronto: / William Briggs / 29–33 Richmond St. West / 1898
DESCRIPTION: 21.0 × 13.5 cm   Pp [i–iii] iv–v [vi], [7] 8–454   Thin card
CONTENTS: i tp; ii 'Coles Canadiana Collection // Originally published in 1898 by William Briggs Toronto. Facsimile edition published by Coles Publishing Company, Toronto © Copyright 1974.'; iii–v preface signed Frances McNaught and Margaret Taylor, Galt, 25 November 1898; vi quotation from Ruskin; 7–442 text; 443–54 'Contents'
CITATIONS: AbCat March 1977   Bloomfield 3226   Carrière No. 145   Ferguson/Fraser, pp 65 and 232
COPIES: ACU   BVIV   NBSU (TX715 E37)   NFSM (TX715 T243 1974)   OGAL (641.5971 Tay, 2 copies)   OGU (Rural Heritage Collection uncat)   OKIT   OKQ (TX715 T242 1974)   OLU (TX715 E27 1974)   OONL (TX715 E3, 2 copies)   OONMM (TX715 E37 1974)   OPET (missing)   OSUL (TX715 E27 1974)   OTMCL (641.59713 E13)   OTNY (641.5971 E)   OTP (641.5971

EAR)   OTU   OWA (TX715 G3 1974)   OTY (TX715 E27 1974)   *Private collection
NOTES: Another private collector has a hard-cover edition with a dust-jacket. Coles Publishing Co. added 'early Canadian' to the original title.

O58.7 [facsimile ed., copyright 1980]
—The / early Canadian / Galt cook book / (revised edition) / comprising / a large number of tested recipes / for the kitchen, dining / room and sick room / Compiled and edited by / Margaret Taylor and Frances McNaught / Toronto: / William Briggs / 29–33 Richmond St. West / 1898
DESCRIPTION: 21.0 × 13.5 cm   Pp [i–iii] iv–v [vi], [7] 8–454   Soft cover
CONTENTS: i tp; ii 'Coles Canadiana Collection // Originally published in 1898 by William Briggs Toronto. Facsimile edition published by Coles Publishing Company, Toronto © Copyright 1980.'; iii–v preface signed Frances McNaught and Margaret Taylor, Galt, 25 November 1898; vi quotation from Ruskin; 7–442 text; 443–54 'Contents'
CITATIONS: Neering, pp 68, 96, 98, 107
COPIES: *OGU (UA s066 o10)

Hollingsworth, Mrs H.E. (Adelaide)

O59.1 [copyright 1892]
The / Columbia / cook book / Toilet, household, medical, and cooking recipes, / flowers and their culture, health suggestions, / carving, table etiquette, dinner giving, menus, / care of the sick, facts worth knowing, etc., [etc.?] / Embracing all the points necessary for ,/ successful housekeeping. / A complete home instructo[r?] / By / Mrs. H.E. Hollingsworth. / Illustrated. / C.R. Parish & Co., / Philadelphia, Pa., and Toronto, Canada.
DESCRIPTION: 24.0 × 18.5 cm   Pp [leaf or leaves lacking?] [5–9] 10–792 [leaves lacking]   Pls, illus   Cloth, with images on front of a man's head and a ship
CONTENTS: 5 tp; 6 'Copyright, 1892, by Mrs. H.E. Hollingsworth.'; 7 'Preface' signed the author; 8 blank; 9–10 'Index' [i.e., alphabetical list of sections]; 11–774 text, beginning with 'A Talk with the Housekeeper' on pp 11–13; [leaves lacking?]; 779–80 blank; 781–92 'Index'
COPIES: *OMAHM (983.48.65)   Private collection
NOTES: The 'Preface' refers to the 'American housewife' and describes the book as 'essentially a simply expressed and economical treatise on the subject of cooking.' The plate opposite p 32 portrays Thomas

W. Palmer, president of the National World's Fair Commission; other plates depict buildings at the fair. The book takes its title from the World's Columbian Exposition, also called the Chicago World's Fair, held in 1893.

The OMAHM copy is detached from its binding; some of the leaves are loose and others are lacking. Pages 5–18 have been trimmed to the body of the text; in the case of the title-page, a few letters at the end of two lines have been cut off. The OMAHM copy is inscribed on the title-page, in pencil, 'Mrs I Fleming // Markham.'

The private collector's copy came from his father's homestead in Chezzetcook, Nova Scotia, but he does not know how it was originally acquired. The only copy located in the United States is at DSI-D (TX715 C72). It lacks the title-page and other front matter.

AMERICAN EDITIONS: Probably Adelaide Hollingsworth, *The Home Cook Book: A Choice Collection of Thoroughly Tested and Reliable Recipes, Including Practical and Economical Suggestions for Every Department of the Home, a Guide to Successful House-keeping*, Philadelphia: Premier Pub. Co., 1895, pp 792 (United States: PPC-C).

1892–6

Good pickles and preserves

Parke and Parke advertised their business extensively. In addition to editions of this cookbook, the company also issued annual almanacs. 'Progressive Hamilton Drug Store ...,' The Times (Hamilton), 2 May 1914, refers to the twentieth consecutive issue of Parke and Parke's almanac that year.

O60.1 nd [about 1892–6]
Good / pickles / and / preserves / Compiled by / an experienced housekeeper. / Price 25 cents / Published by / Parke & Parke, / wholesale and manufacturing druggists, / McNab [*sic*] Street, cor. York, Hamilton. / V.B. Whipple, printer, Hamilton. [cover-title]
DESCRIPTION: 17.0 × 12.5 cm   Pp 3–30 Rebound; original paper cover-title mounted on new card
CONTENTS: 3–8 'Pickling and Preserving' and publ ads; 9 publ ad; 10 'Catsup'; 11 publ ad; 12–14 'Sweet Pickles' and publ ad; 15 publ ad; 16 'Canning and Preserving'; 17 publ ad; 18–22 'Canned Fruit' and publ ads; 23 publ ad; 24–30 'Jelly Making' and publ ads

COPIES: *OH (R641.4 P22 CESH)
NOTES: There are blank spaces throughout the text for the reader to 'Write Your Own Recipes Here.'

The order and date of the various editions can be partly determined by the course of the expansion of Parke and Parke's business, as related in various articles about the company in Hamilton newspapers (indexed at OH) and as summarized in the entries for George and Walder Parke, brothers and the firm's founders, in *Dictionary of Hamilton Biography* (Vol. III, Hamilton, Ont.: 1992, p 164). According to the latter source, Parke and Parke was founded in 1892, when George bought out an established drugstore at the corner of York and MacNab streets, and the store made its first move, in 1896, to 16 Market Square. Since O60.1, *Good Pickles and Preserves*, bears the company's first address, it was published before the move to 16 Market Square, i.e., about 1892–6. Unlike later editions, *Good Pickles and Preserves* has no illustration of the firm's premises on the binding.

The biographical entries refer to the company moving to the corner of Market and MacNab streets in 1904. The move was, in fact, a two-stage process. The article 'Parke and Parke: ... Has New Magnificent Quarters' (*Evening Times*, 12 January 1905, p 4) tells the story of their purchase of the property to the west of their old premises at 16 Market Square 'a few months ago' (i.e., late 1904) and their renovation of the four-storey building that stood at the corner of MacNab Street and Market Square; in the renovated building, the store occupied 17, 18, and 19 Market Square, with an entrance on MacNab Street North. A year and a half later, in the article 'Still Extending: Parke and Parke ... Take in a Corner' (*Spectator*, 19 July 1906, p 1), one learns that the druggists had originally leased the corner of the building to the Molsons bank, which was now moving out, allowing Parke and Parke to extend their retail space once again, to take in the entire corner. All the editions described below were published after this final 1906 expansion since all feature, on the binding, an illustration of the Parke and Parke store, which clearly occupies the whole building, replete with flags and extensive signage.

O60.2 nd [about 1909–15]
—[Illus of Parke and Parke building] / The most complete drug store in Canada / Tested recipes for pickles / jellies and preserves / Compiled by an experienced housekeeper for / Parke & Parke / druggists / 17, 18, 19, 20 Market Square, and 22, 24 McNab [*sic*] St. / Hamilton, Canada / Price 25 cents [cover-title]

DESCRIPTION: 17.0 × 13.0 cm Pp [1–16] Paper, with image on front of Parke and Parke building; stapled
CONTENTS: 1 cover-title; 2 publ ad; 3–6 'Jelly Making'; 7–10 'Pickling and Preserving'; 11–12 'Sweet Pickles'; 13 'Canned Fruit'; 14 blank for 'Write Own Recipes Here' and publ ad; 15–16 [back face of binding] publ ads
COPIES: *OH (R641.852 REC CESH)
NOTES: In the cover-title of this edition, all the text is below the image of the building. The booklet is printed on pinkish orange (or faded orange) paper. There are spaces throughout the text for the reader to 'Write Own Recipes Here.' There is a testimonial on p 15 dated 20 July 1909.

O60.3 nd [about 1917 or later]
—Parke & Parke / Limited / Recipe book / containing / tested recipes / for / pickles, jellies and preserves / Compiled by an experienced housekeeper / [illus of Parke and Parke building] / Wholesale & retail / chemists & druggists / corner McNab [sic] St. & Market Sq. Hamilton, Ont. [cover-title]
DESCRIPTION: 17.0 × 13.0 cm Pp [1–16] Paper, with image on front of Parke and Parke building; stapled
CONTENTS: 1 cover-title; 2 publ ad; 3–5 'Pickling and Preserving' and publ ad; 6 publ ad; 7 'Sweet Pickles'; 8 publ ad; 9–11 'Jelly Making' and publ ad; 12 publ ad; 13 'Canned Fruit'; 14 recipes for Lemon Pie, Special Mayonnaise Dressing for Salad, Dandelion Wine, and Special – Grapefuit Marmalade, and publ ad; 15–16 [back face of binding] publ ads
COPIES: *OH (R641.852 REC CESH)
NOTES: In 1917 the company was incorporated as Parke and Parke Ltd (*Dictionary of Hamilton Biography, 1925–1939*, Vol. III, 1992, p 164, entries for George and Walder Parke); therefore, all editions bearing the name Parke and Parke Ltd were published in 1917 or later. The OH copy is printed on orange paper.
OHMB (Serial) has a copy that matches the above description for the OH copy, except for a slight variation in typeface on the cover-title: in the OH copy, below the company name and above the illustration of the building, 'for' is in roman capital letters and 'compiled by' is roman; in the OHMB copy, 'for' is in italic upper- and lower-case letters and 'compiled by' is italic. Otherwise, the company name at top and address at bottom, the illustration of the building, and the ornamental frame that encloses text and illustration are identical.
A private collector has a copy that also matches the above description for the OH copy, but which has another variation in the typeface in the cover-title:

below the company name and above the illustration of the building, the private collector's copy matches the OH copy's use of upper- and lower-case letters; however, whereas the OH copy uses only serif type, the private collector's copy uses sans serif for the words 'containing,' 'for,' and 'compiled by an experienced housekeeper.' A comparison of p 3 reveals that where the OH copy has no punctuation after the heading 'Pickling and Preserving' or after the recipe titles, the private collector's copy has a period.

O60.4 nd [about 1917 or later]
—Parke & Parke / Limited / Recipe book / containing / tested recipes / for / pickles, jellies and preserves / Compiled by an experienced housekeeper / [illus of Parke and Parke building] / Wholesale & retail / chemists & druggists / corner McNab [sic] St. & Market Sq. Hamilton, Ont. [cover-title]
DESCRIPTION: 17.0 × 12.5 cm Pp [1–16] Paper, with image on front of Parke and Parke building; stapled
CONTENTS: 1 cover-title; 2 publ ad; 3 'Sweet Pickles'; 4 publ ad; 5 recipes from Pickles, Cauliflower to Mushroom Catsup [i.e., part of the 'Pickling and Preserving' section, which starts on the next recto page]; 6 publ ad; 7 'Pickling and Preserving'; 8 publ ad; 9 'Jelly Making'; 10 recipes for Lemon Pie, Special Mayonnaise Dressing for Salad, Dandelion Wine, and Special – Grapefruit Marmalade, and publ ad; 11–12 publ ads; 13 'Canned Fruit'; 14 publ ad; 15 recipes from Crab-Apple Jelly to Strawberry Jam [i.e., part of the 'Jelly Making' section, which starts on p 9]; 16 [outside back face of binding] publ ad
COPIES: *OTUTF (uncat patent medicine)
NOTES: In this edition, some text pages are printed out of order. The cover-title is identical to O60.3, the copy at OH, except that the part of the title below 'Recipe book' has been reset; most noticeably, in the OTUTF edition, the word 'for' is in all lower case, not all upper case, as in the OH copy. A copy at OSTPA also has the word 'for' in all lower case.

O60.5 nd [about 1917 or later]
—Tested recipes for pickles, jellies and preserves / Compiled by an experienced housekeeper for / Parke & Parke / Limited / druggists / corner MacNab Street and Market Square, Hamilton, Ont. / [illus of Parke and Parke building] / Parke's Preservine / used in your canned tomatoes and fruit will keep them from spoiling. / It does not alter the taste or color. / Price, 25c per package, or will be sent postpaid anywhere on receipt of 30 cents. / By

/ Parke & Parke Limited, druggists, Hamilton, Ont. [cover-title]

DESCRIPTION: 17.5 × 13.0 cm   Pp [1–16]   Paper, with image on front of Parke and Parke building; stapled

CONTENTS: 1 cover-title; 2 publ ad; 3–6 'Pickling and Preserving' and publ ads; 7–8 'Sweet Pickles' and publ ad; 9–12 'Jelly Making' and publ ads; 13–14 'Canned Fruit' and publ ad; 15–16 back face of binding

COPIES: OPETCM   *OTUTF (uncat patent medicine)

NOTES: There are blank spaces throughout where one may 'Write Own Recipes Here.'

O60.6   nd [about 1920]

—Tested recipes for pickles, jellies and preserves / Compiled by an experienced housekeeper for / Parke & Parke / Limited / druggists / corner MacNab Street and Market Square, Hamilton, Ontario / [illus of Parke and Parke building, still-life of druggists' equipment in foreground] / Parke's Rennet Wine / makes the most delicious junket / A very nutritive and easily digested food for infants and in- / valids. Price 25c per bottle, or will be sent postpaid anywhere on / receipt of 30 cents, by / Parke & Parke Limited, druggists / Hamilton, Ontario. [cover-title]

DESCRIPTION: 17.0 × 13.0 cm   Pp [1–16]   Paper, with image on front of Parke and Parke building and still-life of druggists' equipment in foreground; stapled

CONTENTS: 1 cover-title; 2 publ ad; 3–6 'Pickling and Preserving' and publ ads; 7–8 'Sweet Pickles' and publ ads; 9–12 'Jelly Making' and publ ads; 13 'Canned Fruit'; 14 recipes for Lemon Pie, Special Mayonnaise Dressing for Salad, Dandelion Wine, and Special – Grapefruit Marmalade, and publ ads; 15–16 [outside back face of binding] publ ads

COPIES: OHMB (Serial)   *Private collection

NOTES: This edition, which features a still-life of druggists' equipment on the binding, looks newer than O60.5 and older than O60.7. The binding is illustrated in *Downtown Hamilton: The Heart of It All*, Hamilton: Fountain Foundation, [1995], p 110.

O60.7   nd [about 1925–30]

—Parke and Parke / Limited / Recipe book / containing tested recipes / for / pickles, jellies and preserves / Compiled by an experienced housekeeper / High / quality / P. & P. / household / drugs / Flavoring / extracts / spices / oils / and / essences / Wholesale and retail / Chemists and druggists / corner McNab [*sic*] St. and Market Sq. Hamilton, Ontario [cover-title]

DESCRIPTION: 17.0 × 12.5 cm   Pp [1] 2–16   Paper, with photograph on front of Parke and Parke storefront; stapled

CONTENTS: 1 cover-title; 2 Recipe for Ice Cream and publ ads; 3 'Pickling and Preserving'; 4 publ ads; 5–7 'Sweet Pickles,' recipes for Parke's Condensed Orangeade, Special – Raspberry Vinegar, Dandelion Wine, and Imperial Drink, and publ ads; 8 recipes for Apple Dumplings, Pickled Onions, and Ice Box Rolls, and publ ads; 9–11 'Jelly Making,' recipes for Celery Sauce and Suet Pudding, and publ ads; 12 publ ads; 13–14 miscellaneous recipes and publ ads; 15 'Canned Fruit'; 16 [outside back face of binding] publ ads

COPIES: *Private collection

NOTES: I have compared the copy catalogued here with photocopies of pp 2–3 of another private collector's copy, which appears to be another printing of the same edition (identical cover-title and matching recipe sections), but with differences in the publisher's advertisements. On p 2 of both copies, the advertisements for the various Parke and Parke products are headed '"Aids to Efficiency" in Canning'; however, the advertisements are arranged differently on the page, the prices cited in the copy catalogued here are lower (for example, Catsup Flavor is $0.35, but $0.59 in the other copy), and whereas here the accompanying recipe is for Ice Cream, in the other copy the recipe is for Chili Con Carne. On p 3 of this copy there is a line of advertising inserted between the recipes for Pickling and Cucumber Pickles that says, 'Parke's Catsup Flavor may be used in place of ground spices in any of these recipes.'; in the other copy the line begins, 'Parke's Catsup Flavor and Preservative may be used ...'

1893

The story of canned goods and how to use them

O61.1   nd [about 1893]

The / story of / canned goods / and / how to use them [cover-title]

DESCRIPTION: 10.0 × 15.0 cm [dimensions from photocopy]   Pp [1–2] 3–16   Fp illus on p 1 of several persons seated at a dinner table, with the caption 'Table delicacies from the gardens and orchards of Ontario'   Paper, with image on front of a woman holding up her apron filled with fruit and vegetables; stapled

CONTENTS: Inside front face of binding 'Officers of the Canadian Packers' Association' (W. Boulter, president;

W.A. Ferguson, vice-president; W.C. Breckenridge, secretary-treasurer; and the names of those on the Executive Committee and Auditing Committee) and a list of 'reliable firms'; 1 fp illus; 2 'Preface' signed Simcoe Canning Co., Strathroy Canning Co., Ontario Canning Co., A.C. Miller and Co., Lakeport Canning Co., Erie Preserving Co., Delhi Canning Co., Bay of Quinte Canning Co., and Aylmer Canning Co.; 3–mid 9 'Her Secret'; mid 9–mid 13 'Receipts'; mid–bottom 13 'Notes' about using various canned products; 14–16 'Testimony for Canned Goods'; inside back face untitled text signed by the nine canning companies who signed the 'Preface'
COPIES: *OONMS

NOTES: The latest testimonial, on p 14, is dated 5 April 1893. The 'Preface' gives the purpose of the book: 'to increase the consumption of canned goods, and disabuse the minds of the good people of Canada of any prejudice existing against the use of canned fruits and vegetables.' The trademarks of the nine Ontario canning firms that sign the 'Preface' are illustrated at the tops of the following pages. 'Her Secret' is the story of how Sylvia Blissington makes a happy home on limited means, using canned goods. The 'Receipts' are Sylvia's as copied by another character in the story, Miss Alice Mason, who wanted them in preparation for her marriage six weeks hence. Sylvia's last name expresses happiness; Alice's brings to mind the Mason jars used for home preserving. Tomato Soup No. 1 is the version my mother made in my Toronto childhood and which I still use, although I heat the canned tomatoes briefly, not for 30 minutes.

1893–5

Slocum's cook book

For a later cookbook by the same company, see O94.1, Coltsfoote Cook Book and Fortune Teller.

O62.1   nd [about 1893–5]
Slocum's / cook book / Published by / T.A. Slocum & Co., 186 Adelaide Street West, / Canada, Toronto. / Price 25 cents / John M. Poole & Co., printers, / Toronto. [cover-title]
DESCRIPTION: Paper, with image on front of a large codfish being carried by five elves, with the following text printed on the fish: 'Doctor Slocum's Oxygenized Emulsion of Pure Cod Liver Oil'
COPIES: *OAUH

NOTES: On p 32 (the last page), there are testimonials dated 4 March 1893, 14 March 189[digit torn off], and

10 December 18[digits torn off]. The company was called T.A. Slocum and Co. up to and including 1895 (from 1896 to 1903 it is listed in Toronto city directories as T.A. Slocum Chemical Company of Canada; and from 1904, as Dr T.A. Slocum Ltd). *Slocum's Cook Book*, therefore, was published about 1893–5.

1894

Cook book

For information about the W.H. Comstock Co., see O12.1.

O63.1   [1894]
Cook book / Dr. / Morse's / Indian / Root Pills / Toronto Lithographing Co [cover-title]
DESCRIPTION: 15.0 × 16.5 cm   Pp [1–32]   Paper, with image on front of an Indian, mounted on horseback and spearing a bear; stapled, and with hole punched at top left corner, through which runs a string for hanging
CONTENTS: Inside front face of binding 'Dr Morse's Indian Root Pills Cook Book' [i.e., introductory text] and at bottom, 'The W.H. Comstock Co., Limited ... Brockville, Ont., and Morristown, St. Lawrence Co., N.Y.'; odd-numbered pages, 1–23 recipes; even-numbered pages, 2–24, and all following pages, 25–32 medical information and testimonials for Dr Morse's Indian Root Pills and other Comstock products
COPIES: *OTUTF (uncat patent medicine)

NOTES: The introductory text begins: 'We present to you again Dr. Morse's Indian Root Pills Cook Book. We think it is a better cook book than we have ever issued before ... It is printed on a new perfecting press, especially designed for this purpose, more than a hundred thousand cook books each day. Our issue for 1894 runs far up into the millions ...' The testimonials are from addresses mainly in the United States, but also from Canada and the West Indies.

O63.2   nd [about 1895]
—Cook book / Dr. / Morse's / Indian / Root Pills [cover-title]
DESCRIPTION: 15.0 × 16.5 cm   Pp [1–32]   Paper, with image on front of an Indian, mounted on horseback and spearing a bear; stapled, and with hole punched at top left corner, through which runs a string for hanging
CONTENTS: Inside front face of binding 'Our Cook Book. Full of Valuable Recipes' [i.e., introductory text] and at bottom, 'The W.H. Comstock Co., Limited ... Brockville, Ont., and Morristown, St. Lawrence Co.,

N.Y.'; odd-numbered pages, 1–25 recipes; even-numbered pages, 2–26, and all following pages, 27–32 medical information and testimonials for Dr Morse's Indian Root Pills and other Comstock products

COPIES: *OKQ (F5012 nd C739D)

NOTES: There is no printer on the binding of this edition. The introductory text implies that there were several previous editions of this work: 'The appearance of this book is looked for as regularly as Christmas, …' This edition is undated, but there are two testimonials dated 1895, the latest being 10 July 1895 (p 24). Text on the outside back face of the binding states, 'For more than forty years these pills [Indian Root] have been before the public, …'

Home Comfort cook book

O64.1   1894

[Cover-title lacking of *Home Comfort Cook Book*, Toronto, Ont., and St Louis, Mo.: Wrought Iron Range Co., 1894]

DESCRIPTION: 26.0 × 18.0 cm   Pp [1] 2–122   Illus col, illus   [Free, on p 3]   Lacks paper binding; stapled

CONTENTS: 1 ad for Wrought Iron Range Co., 70–6 Pearl Street, Toronto, Ontario, and St Louis, Missouri, and '[month(?) torn off] edition, 1894.'; 2 'The Wrought Iron Range Company. Business History.' and 'Notice – Special' [about conditions of sale of the range]; 3 'Home Comfort Steel Range No. 66' [information about the range] and at bottom, 'Our Home Comfort Range Cook Book is not for sale, but is printed solely for gratuitous distribution among our customers.'; 4 'Directions for Operating Home Comfort Ranges'; 5 illus of Range No. 66; 6 illus of 'Solid Steel Cooking Utensils'; 7 illus of 1893 exhibit; 8 illus col of ribbon won by the Wrought Iron Range Co. at the World's Columbian Exposition, Chicago, 1893; 9 reprint of newspaper articles about the company; 10 illus of medals; 11 'Our Method of Doing Business'; 12–16 'Breakfast'; 17 'Morning Beverages' and 'The Largest Kitchen in the World'; 18–21 'Bread'; 22–55 'Dinner'; 56–62 'Supper'; 63–1st column 71 'Home Remedies'; 2nd column 71 'Rates of Postage'; 72 'Hints for the Household'; 73–5 'A Few of the Hotels, Restaurants, etc., Using Home Comfort Ranges'; 76–111 'What Hotel Men and Others Think' [includes 'Canada References' on p 91]; 112–14 'Three Uncertain Young Men'; 115–17 'Laboratory Tests'; 118 'Our Material'; 119–21 'Sectional Parts of Range No. 66'; 122 illus of Range Series No. 810-3-D

COPIES: CIHM (88754)   *OTMCL (683.88029 W68)

O64.2   August 1901

—Home Comfort / cook book / Wrought Iron / Range Co. (Limited.) / Toronto, Ontario. / August, 1901. [cover-title]

DESCRIPTION: 26.5 × 18.5 cm   Pp [1] 2–110   Illus col, illus   [Free, on p 4]   Paper, with image on front of a woman carrying roast poultry on a platter, and behind her, in a circular frame, a Home Comfort Range; stapled

CONTENTS: 1 publ ad and 'August edition, 1901.'; 2 'The Wrought Iron Range Co. (Limited.) Business History' and 'Notice – Special' [about conditions of sale of the range]; 3 'Our Method of Doing Business'; 4 'Home Comfort Steel Range'; 5 illus of Range No. 99; 6 'Solid Steel Cooking Utensils'; 7 'Directions for Operating Home Comfort Ranges'; 8–16 'Home Comfort Victories' [i.e., prizes won]; 17–25 illus of, and testimonials from, public buildings and ships that have Home Comfort cooking equipment, including these Canadian places: three New Glasgow, Nova Scotia, hotels, Victoria Industrial School in Mimico, Ontario, Walker House in Toronto, the Steamer Majestic in Collingwood, Ontario, Hotel Quinte in Belleville, Ontario, Pictou County Insane Asylum, Stellarton, Nova Scotia, and New Union Station in Toronto; 26–30 'Breakfast'; 31 'Morning Beverages' and 'Welsh "Welsh Rabbit"'; 32–5 'Bread'; 36–69 'Dinner'; 70–6 'Supper'; 77–mid 1st column 85 'Home Remedies'; mid 1st column 85–86 'Rates of Postage'; 87 'Hints for the Household'; 88–92 'Canada Testimonials'; 93–7 'A Few of the Hotels, Restaurants, etc., Using Home Comfort Ranges'; 98–101 'What Hotel Men and Others Think'; 102–4 'Laboratory Tests'; 105 'Our Material'; 106–7 'Sectional Parts of Range'; 108 'Home Comfort Center Range Series No. 810-3-D'; 109 'Home Comfort Black Enamel'; 110 'Home Comfort Steel Hot-Air Furnaces'

COPIES: *OTSHH

NOTES: Page 4 states, 'This Home Comfort Cook Book is not for sale, but is printed solely for gratuitous distribution among our customers.' The company was founded in 1864 and had factories at 70–6 Pearl Street, Toronto, and in St Louis, Missouri (p 1). There is a colour illustration of the Pearl Street factory on the outside back face of the binding. The company employed nearly 400 salesmen in Canada, the USA, and other countries to sell its products (p 3).

AMERICAN EDITIONS: Rev. ed., St Louis: Wrought Iron Range Co., [1914?] (United States: MCR); 54th anniversary ed., St Louis: Wrought Iron Range Co., 1918 (Allen, p 109); St Louis: Wrought Iron Range Co.,

1924 (Allen, p 109; Barile, pp 55, 195, illus p 56; Barile discusses the company's cookbooks in general on p 133); Wrought Iron Range Co., 1925 (Allen, p 109 and illus col on p 16; Dickinson, p 98); St Louis: Wrought Iron Range Co., nd [1930s], pp 211 (Vintage, May 2000).

Wilson's calendar cook book for 1895

O65.1 [entered 1894]
Wilson's / calendar / cook book / for 1895. / Published by / J. Wilson, / prescription drug store, / Goderich, Ontario.
DESCRIPTION: 18.0 × 13.0 cm   Pp [1–3] 4–32   Illus of astrological symbols   Paper; stapled, and with hole punched at top left corner for hanging
CONTENTS: Inside front face of binding calendars for 1895 and 1896; 1 tp; 2 'To Our Customers' signed J. Wilson; 3 'Eclipses' for 1895; 4–30 recipes, publ ads, monthly calendars, and jokes; 31 'Hints on Dyeing'; 32 'Curious and Interesting Facts'
COPIES: *Private collection
NOTES: The following is printed on the front face of the binding: 'Entered according to Act of the Parliament of Canada, in the year 1894, in the Department of Agriculture.' The note 'To Our Customers' on p 2 suggests that this edition may be the first published by J. Wilson; it reads, 'We present you in this, our Calendar Cook Book, with a new idea in almanac literature, ...'

1895

[Title unknown]

See also O109a.1, Recipes, from the same church.

O66.1 [1895]
[Title unknown of a 'cook book containing recipes collected by the young ladies of St. Paul's Presbyterian Church, Ingersoll, in 1895 ... for the benefit of the church']
CITATIONS: E.G. Sumner, 'Cook Book Was Business Directory of Its Day,' *London Free Press* 20 November 1943, p 33; microfiche (OL) and newspaper clipping in *Oxford County Scrapbook*, Vol. 2, p 47 (OL)
NOTES: Sumner identifies many of the advertisers in the book and, through them, relates some of the early history of Ingersoll.

The gem cook book

O67.1 1895
The / gem cook book. / Compiled by the ladies of Wallaceburg. / Wallaceburg: / Herald Printing House. / 1895.
COPIES: *Private collection
NOTES: The owner reports that the book has 92 pages and that the last three recipes are Oatmeal Gruel, To Candy Orange and Lemon Peel, and A Cure for Love. The book belonged to her husband's grandmother.

Gems of fancy cookery

O68.1 nd [about 1895]
Gems / of / fancy cookery / A collection of / reliable and useful / household recipes / Published by / F. Jordan, / dispensing chemist, / Medical Hall, Goderich, Ontario.
DESCRIPTION: 16.5 × 11.0 cm   Pp [1–5] 6–48   Lacks paper binding; stapled
CONTENTS: 1 tp; 2 blank; 3 'Preface' signed F. Jordan; 4 'Housekeepers' Weights and Measures'; 5–48 recipes, publ ads, and ad on p 25 for Glasgow House, a store selling general and fancy drygoods and managed by Mrs R.B. Smith
COPIES: CIHM (01604)   *OTUTF (uncat patent medicine)
NOTES: The 'Preface' states: 'This little work, Gems of Fancy Cookery, was first published some time ago, and ran rapidly through three editions, being sold at 15 cents per copy. It was compiled chiefly from the columns of a household magazine ... Since the work has been out of print it has been repeatedly asked for, and in presenting it now in a revised form, adding some of the newest acquisitions of the culinary art, to our customers, we trust that its value will be duly appreciated.' O68.2 and O68.3 have the same 'Preface.' See O68.2 and O68.4 regarding the date of publication.

The recipes are organized under the following headings (I have regularized the punctuation): 'Bread, etc.'; 'Cakes'; 'Cookies, etc.'; 'Jellies'; 'Meats, etc.'; 'Pies, etc.'; 'Puddings, etc.'; 'Pickles'; 'Preserves'; 'Relishes'; 'Soups, etc.'; 'Summer Drinks, etc.'; 'Sweetmeats, etc.'; and 'Miscellaneous.' The first few recipes are Bread, Boston Brown Bread, Baker's Rolls, Breakfast Rolls, No. 1, and Breakfast Rolls, No. 2. The recipes specify Jordan's Baking Powder and Essence Vanilla.

O68.2   nd [about 1895]
—Gems / of / fancy cookery / A collection of useful / and reliable / household recipes. / Published by / H.N. Packert, Phm. B. / Gold Medallist of the Ontario College Pharmacy; / Honor Graduate of Toronto University; and / Honor Graduate of the State Board of Michigan. / Muir's Block, Port Elgin.
DESCRIPTION: 16.0 × 10.5 cm   Pp [1–5] 6–48   Lacks paper binding; stapled
CONTENTS: 1 tp; 2 blank; 3 'Preface' signed H.N. Packert; 4 'Housekeepers' Weights and Measures'; 5–48 'Family Recipes' and publ ads
COPIES: *Private collection
NOTES: The recipes, which specify Packert's Baking Powder, are organized under the same headings as O68.1. The first few recipes are also the same.

Herman N. Packert graduated from the University of Toronto with a Bachelor's degree in Pharmacy (Phm. B.) in 1893. This edition, and also O68.1 and O68.3, were likely published in the mid-1890s. The student register of graduates at OTUAR indicates that Packert was originally from Stratford. The student register, which was published in 1910, gives the spelling Packert, as found in the cookbook. The convocation roll for 1893 uses the spelling Paeckert where it cites his Phm. B., and the spelling Paechert where it cites his name in connection with the Ontario College of Pharmacy.

O68.3   nd [about 1895]
—Gems / of / fancy cookery / A collection of / reliable and useful / household recipes / Published by / R.A. Scarlett / chemist, / Oshawa, Ontario.
DESCRIPTION: 16.5 × 11.0 cm   Pp [1–5] 6–46   Lacks paper binding; stapled
CONTENTS: 1 tp; 2 blank; 3 'Preface' signed R.A. Scarlett; 4 'Housekeepers' Weights and Measures'; 5–45 recipes and publ ads; 46 publ ad
COPIES: *Private collection
NOTES: See O68.2 and O68.4 regarding the date of publication. Scarlett's address, cited in the advertisements, was Simcoe Street South, Oshawa. The recipes specify such Scarlett products as baking powder and various flavouring essences.

The private collector's copy is inscribed on p 2, with a recipe for 'Mrs Watson's Hermits.'

O68.4   [about 1895]
—[Title unknown]
DESCRIPTION: 16.5 × 10.5 cm   Pp [5] 6–43 [44–5]   Lacks binding; sewn
CONTENTS: 5–44 recipes and ads; 45 ad(?)
COPIES: *MSM

NOTES: The book is in very poor condition and is held in a folder on which is inscribed 'Mother's cook book of 1882.' The inscribed date, however, is too early. Although the title is unknown, the text on p 5 is exactly the same as for O68.1, *Gems of Fancy Cookery*, of which there are three Ontario editions, all published about 1895. As O68.1, the recipes on p 5 are Bread, Boston Brown Bread, and Baker's Rolls.

The advertisements for J.H. Rose, chemist, 302 Main Street, Winnipeg (pp 9, 11, 19, 25, 34, 37, 42, and 45?) are evidence of the date of publication. In Winnipeg city directories, J.H. Rose is first called a druggist in the volume for 1886, and he lives on 4 Dagmar (in 1884 and 1885 his occupation is 'assistant'). In the volumes for 1890 and 1895 he is a druggist and his business address is 302 Main Street, as in the cookbook. From 1896 onward, his business is called Rose Drug Co., at the same Main Street address. The cookbook, therefore, was published no later than 1895.

The Grace cookery book

In 1895 the hospital was at the corner of Huron and College streets, in an old hotel building. In 2005, a century later, it was at 650 Church Street.

O69.1   1895
Now, good digestion wait on appetite, / And health on both. / Published by / the Young Ladies' Auxiliary / of / Grace Hospital / Toronto, Ont. / 1895 / A copy of this book can be obtained at any time from the Young Ladies' / Auxiliary, Grace Hospital, for 25 cents.
DESCRIPTION: 19.0 × 13.5 cm   Pp [1–5] 6–90, [i–ii]   Cloth; stapled
CONTENTS: 1 publisher, date, and price, as transcribed above (the title is on the binding); 2 ads; 3 ad and 'Index' [i.e., table of contents]; 4 ad; 5–90 recipes and ads; i–ii ads
COPIES: CIHM (95413)   *OGU (UA s004 b29)   OTAG (641.5971 Gra)   QMMMCM (RB-0970)
NOTES: The cover-title is 'The Grace Cookery Book.' Funds raised by the sale of the cookbook likely went to support the hospital, which at the time was 'on the verge of bankruptcy' (Jesse Edgar Middleton, *The Municipality of Toronto: A History*, Toronto and New York: Dominion Publishing Co., 1923, Vol. II, p 639).

Jefferis, Prof. Benjamin Grant (1851–1929), James Lawrence Nichols (Coburg, Germany, about 1851–18 August 1895, Naperville, Ill.), and Mrs Elizabeth Nichols, née Barnard (Mrs J.L. Nichols) (–1946)

James Nichols and Elizabeth Barnard married on 18 August 1886 and had three children: Grace, James II, and Laura. Some years after James's death, Elizabeth married William C. Simpson. For biographical information about James and Elizabeth, see: dedication speech of Nichols Library, 9 June 1898, reported in Naperville Clarion, *15 June 1898;* Autobiography of James L. Nichols as Told to His Wife, Elizabeth Barnard Nichols *and* History of Nichols Library *by Miriam B. Fry, Librarian, [No place, nd], typescript pamphlet; and Genevieve Towsley,* A View of Historic Naperville from the Sky-Lines, Naperville Sun, *[1990], 1975 (all in Local History Collection of INap-N).*

O70.1 15th ed., 1895
The / household guide / or / domestic cyclopedia. / Home remedies for man and beast; / a complete receipt book. / Home nursing and home treatment; / insect extermination; / Prof. Henkel's illustrations of / the effects of alcohol & cigarettes; / care of children; / how to cook for the sick, etc. / by / Prof. B.G. Jefferis, M.D., Ph.D., Chicago, Ill., / and / J.L. Nichols, A.M. / Also, / a complete cook book, / by / Mrs. J.L. Nichols. / Fifteenth edition. / Published by / J.L. Nichols & Co., / 33 Richmond Street West, Toronto, Ont., / to whom all communications must be addressed. / Sold only by subscription. / 1895.
DESCRIPTION: 18.0 × 12.0 cm   Pp [1–4] 5–512   Frontis of 'Mother Away from Home,' illus   Cloth
CONTENTS: 1 tp; 2 'This volume will be promptly sent, in cloth postpaid, on receipt of $1.00, ...' and 'Entered, according to the Act of the Parliament of Canada, in the year one thousand eight hundred and ninety-four, by John A. Hertel, ...'; 3 'The Good Samaritan' [a poem]; 4 'Publisher's Preface' signed J.L. Nichols, Naperville, Illinois; 5 fp illus of 'Guardian Angel'; 6–14 'A Complete Medical Dictionary'; 15–505 text; 506–top 511 'Alphabetical Index'; mid 511–mid 512 'Index of Cooking Department'; bottom 512 publ ad
COPIES: OONL (RC81 J47 1895)   OTUTF (flem 0688)   *Private collection
NOTES: Editions published by J.L. Nichols and Co., 33 Richmond Street West, Toronto, date from 1895 to 1903 (the last year for the publisher at this address). John Adam Hertel was manager of the company from 1894 to 1896; David E. Hughes was manager from 1897. J.L. Nichols and Co. reprinted material from

The Household Guide in O35.3. *The Dominion Home Cook Book;* see that entry. Neering, pp 70, 72, 84, and 87, cites an unidentified Toronto edition of *The Household Guide.*

O70.2 16th ed., 1896
—The / household guide / or / domestic cyclopedia. / Home remedies for man and beast; / a complete receipt book. / Home nursing and home treatment; / insect extermination; / Prof. Henkel's illustrations of / the effects of alcohol & cigarettes; / care of children; / how to cook for the sick, etc. / By / Prof. B.G. Jefferis, M.D., Ph.D., Chicago, Ill., / and / J.L. Nichols, A.M. / Also, / a complete cook book, / by / Mrs. J.L. Nichols. / Sixteenth edition. / Published by / J.L. Nichols & Co., / U.S. address: / Naperville, Ill. / 33 Richmond St. West, / Toronto, Can. / Sold only by subscription. / 1896.
DESCRIPTION: 18.0 × 12.0 cm   Pp [1–4] 5–521, [i]   Frontis of 'Mother Away from Home,' illus   Cloth
CONTENTS: 1 tp; 2 'The Good Samaritan' [a poem], 'Entered according to Act of the Parliament of Canada, in the year one thousand eight hundred and ninety-four, by John A. Hertel, at the Department of Agriculture.,' and 'This volume will be sent to any address on receipt of $1.00. Agents wanted.'; 3 'Publisher's Preface' signed J.L. Nichols, Naperville, Illinois; 4 fp illus of 'Guardian Angel'; 5–505 text; 506–14 'A Complete Medical Dictionary'; 515–mid 520 'Alphabetical Index'; mid 520–521 'Index of Cooking Department'; i publ ad
COPIES: *OTAG (640 Jef)

O70.3 17th ed., 1896
—The / household guide / or / domestic cyclopedia. / Home remedies for man and beast; / a complete receipt book. / Home nursing and home treatment; / insect extermination; / Prof. Henkel's illustrations of / the effects of alcohol & cigarettes; / care of children; / how to cook for the sick, etc. / By / Prof. B.G. Jefferis, M.D., Ph.D., Chicago, Ill., / and / J.L. Nichols, A.M. / Also, / a complete cook book, / by / Mrs. J.L. Nichols. / Seventeenth edition. / Published by / J.L. Nichols & Co., / U.S. address: / Naperville, Ill. / 33 Richmond St. West, / Toronto, Can. / Sold only by subscription. / 1896.
DESCRIPTION: Frontis of 'Mother Away from Home'
COPIES: *Private collection

O70.4 18th ed., 1897
—[Eighteenth edition of *The Household Guide or Domestic Cyclopedia,* Naperville, Ill., and Toronto, Ont.: J.L. Nichols and Co., 1897, pp 521]
COPIES: United States: ISUM

O70.5 19th ed., 1897
—[Nineteenth edition of *The Household Guide or Domestic Cyclopedia*, Atlanta, Ga, and Toronto, Ont.: J.L. Nichols and Co., 1897]
COPIES: United States: DLC (microfilm 16544 RC)

O70.6 20th ed., 1897
—[Twentieth edition of *The Household Guide or Domestic Cyclopedia ... by Prof. B.G. Jefferis ... and J.L. Nichols. Also a Complete Cook Book ...*, Toronto: J.L. Nichols and Co., 1897, pp 539]
CITATIONS: Haight 1904, pp 21–2 O'Neill (unpublished)
COPIES: Great Britain: LB (07944.f.38 destroyed)
NOTES: Haight describes this edition as sold only by subscription, in cloth for $1.00, leather for $1.50.

O70.7 20th ed., 1899
—The / household guide / or / domestic cyclopedia. / A practical family physician. Home remedies / and home treatment on / all diseases. / An instructor on nursing, housekeeping and / home adornments. / By / Prof. B.G. Jefferis, M.D., Ph.D., / and / J.L. Nichols, A.M. / Also / a complete cook book / by / Mrs. J.L. Nichols. / Twentieth edition. / Published by / J.L. Nichols & Co. / Atlanta, Ga. Toronto, Ont. / Naperville, Ill. / Sold only by subscription. / 1899
DESCRIPTION: 18.0 × 12.0 cm   Pp [7] 8–9, [x] xi–xx, 21–539, [i–ii]   Frontis of 'A Sweet Face,' illus   Cloth
CONTENTS: 7 tp; 8 'The Good Samaritan' [a poem] and 'This volume will be sent to any address bound in leather on receipt of $1.50; in cloth $1.00. Agents wanted. Entered according to Act of the Parliament of Canada, in the year one thousand eight hundred and ninety-four, by John A. Hertel, at the Department of Agriculture. Entered according to Act of the Parliament of Canada, in the year one thousand eight hundred and ninety-seven, by J.L. Nichols & Co., at the Department of Agriculture.'; 9 'Publisher's Preface' signed J.L. Nichols; x illus of 'Mother Away from Home'; xi–xx table of contents; 21–244 Book I; 245–326 Book II; 327–98 Book III; 399–490 Book IV, 'Woman's Friend. A Complete Cook Book.'; 491–521 Book V; 522–30 'A Complete Medical Dictionary'; 531–9 index; i–ii publ ads
COPIES: *NSHD   OFERWM (A1980.116)
NOTES: A copy in a private collection appears to match this edition, but it has a label, mounted over the original imprint, that says, 'The People's Supply House, Winnipeg, Manitoba.'
O'Neill (unpublished), which is a record of copyright information at the British Library, cites *The House-*

hold Guide by John A. Scanlon, Winnipeg, Manitoba: 1907. O'Neill describes the item as a 'book' but does not give the number of pages, and the volume was not located at the British Library. It is unlikely that Scanlon was the author: the 1907 Winnipeg city directory describes him as a clerk, living at 623 Spence; the 1909 directory as an advertising agent, living at 670 Victor; and the 1910 directory, as a traveller, living at 684 Victor. It is possible that the copyright record is for O70.7, the copy with the Winnipeg People's Supply House label.

O70.8 20th ed., 1899
—The / household guide / or / domestic cyclopedia. / A practical family physician. Home remedies / and home treatment on / all diseases. / An instructor on nursing, housekeeping and / home adornments. / By / Prof. B.G. Jefferis, M.D., Ph.D., / and / J.L. Nichols, A.M. / Also / a complete cook book / by / Mrs. J.L. Nichols. / Twentieth edition. / J.L. Nichols & Co. / Atlanta, Ga. Toronto, Ont. / Naperville, Ill. / Sold only by subscription. / 1899
DESCRIPTION: 17.5 × 12.0 cm   Pp [7] 8–9, [x] xi–xx, 21–539   Frontis of 'A Sweet Face,' illus   Cloth
CONTENTS: 7 tp; 8 'The Good Samaritan' [a poem] and 'This volume will be sent to any address bound in leather on receipt of $1.50; in cloth $1.00. Agents wanted. Entered according to Act of the Parliament of Canada, in the year one thousand eight hundred and ninety-four, by John A. Hertel, at the Department of Agriculture. Entered according to Act of the Parliament of Canada, in the year one thousand eight hundred and ninety-seven, by J.L. Nichols & Co. at the Department of Agriculture.'; 9 'Publisher's Preface' signed J.L. Nichols; x illus of 'Mother Away from Home'; xi–xx table of contents; 21–244 Book I; 245–326 Book II; 327–98 Book III; 399–490 Book IV, 'Woman's Friend. A Complete Cook Book.'; 491–521 Book V; 522–30 'A Complete Medical Dictionary'; 531–9 index
COPIES: BFSJNPM   *Private collection
NOTES: Unlike O70.7, there is no 'Published by' on the title-page. The cover-title is 'Family Recipes.'

O70.9 23rd ed., [entered 1897; about 1899–1903]
—The / household guide / or / domestic cyclopedia. / A practical family physician. Home remedies / and home treatment on / all diseases. / An instructor on nursing, housekeeping and / home adornments. / By / Prof. B.G. Jefferis, M.D., Ph.D., / and / J.L. Nichols, A.M. / Also / a complete cook book / by / Mrs. J.L. Nichols. / Twenty-third edition. / Published by / J.L. Nichols & Co., /

33 Richmond St. W., Toronto, Can. / Agents wanted.
DESCRIPTION: 18.0 × 12.0 cm Pp [7] 8–9, [x] xi–xx, 21–539 Frontis, 17 fp illus, many illus Cloth
CONTENTS: 7 tp; 8 'The Good Samaritan' [a poem] and 'This volume will be sent to any address bound in leather on receipt of $1.50; in cloth $1.00. Agents wanted. Entered according to Act of the Parliament of Canada, in the year one thousand eight hundred and ninety-four, by John A. Hertel, at the Department of Agriculture. Entered according to Act of the Parliament of Canada, in the year one thousand eight hundred and ninety-seven, by J.L. Nichols & Co., at the Department of Agriculture'; 9 'Publisher's Preface' signed J.L. Nichols; x fp illus of 'Mother Away from Home'; xi–xx table of contents; 21–521 Books I–V; 522–30 'A Complete Medical Dictionary'; 531–9 'Alphabetical Index'
COPIES: AHRMH *OGU (UA s043 b34) OTNY (uncat) OTUTF (B-12 7869)
NOTES: The twenty-third edition is unlikely to have been published earlier than 1899, the date of two editions numbered twentieth (O70.7 and O70.8). O70.9 was published no later than 1903, the last year that J.L. Nichols and Co. was at 33 Richmond Street West. O70.9 and O70.10 have different publishers.

O70.10 23rd ed., [entered 1897; 1899 or later]
—The / household guide / or / domestic cyclopedia. / A practical family physician. Home remedies / and home treatment on / all diseases. / An instructor on nursing, housekeeping and / home adornments. / By / Prof. B.G. Jefferis, M.D., Ph.D., / and / J.L. Nichols, A.M. / Also / a complete cook book / by / Mrs. J.L. Nichols. / Twenty-third edition. / The Guide Publishing Co. / Toronto, Canada.
DESCRIPTION: 18.0 × 12.0 cm Pp [7] 8–9, [x] xi–xx, 21–539 Frontis, fp illus, illus Half leather, marbled-paper-covered boards
CONTENTS: 7 tp; 8 'The Good Samaritan' [a poem] and 'This volume will be sent to any address bound in leather on receipt of $1.50; in cloth $1.00. Agents wanted. Entered according to Act of the Parliament of Canada, in the year one thousand eight hundred and ninety-four, by John A. Hertel, at the Department of Agriculture. Entered according to Act of the Parliament of Canada, in the year one thousand eight hundred and ninety-seven, by J.L. Nichols & Co., at the Department of Agriculture.'; 9 'Publisher's Preface' signed J.L. Nichols; x fp illus of 'Mother Away from Home'; xi–xx table of contents; 21–521 Books I–V; 522–30 'A Complete Medical Dictionary'; 531–9 'Alphabetical Index'
COPIES: *Private collection

O70.11 unnumbered ed., [entered 1897; about 1904–10]
—The / household guide / or / domestic cyclopedia. / A practical family physician. Home remedies / and home treatment on / all diseases. / An instructor on nursing, housekeeping and / home adornments. / By / Prof. B.G. Jefferis, M.D., Ph.D., / and / J.L. Nichols, A.M. / Also / a complete cook book / by / Mrs. J.L. Nichols / Manufactured and published by / the J.L. Nichols Company, Limited / 292 Wellington West / Toronto, Canada / Agents wanted
DESCRIPTION: 18.0 × 12.0 cm Pp [7–8] 9, [x] xi–xx, 21–539 Frontis of head-and-shoulders of a young girl, fp illus, illus Cloth
CONTENTS: 7 tp; 8 'The Good Samaritan' [a poem] and 'This volume will be sent to any address bound in leather on receipt of $1.50 Agents wanted. Entered according to Act of the Parliament of Canada, in the year one thousand eight hundred and ninety-four, by John A. Hertel, at the Department of Agriculture. Entered according to Act of the Parliament of Canada, in the year one thousand eight hundred and ninety-seven, by J.L. Nichols & Co. at the Department of Agriculture.'; 9 'Publisher's Preface' signed J.L. Nichols; x fp illus of 'Mother Away from Home'; xi–xx 'Table of Contents'; 21–244 Book I; 245–326 Book II; 327–98 Book III; 399–490 Book IV, 'Woman's Friend. A Complete Cook Book.'; 491–521 Book V; 522–30 'A Complete Medical Dictionary'; 531–9 'Alphabetical Index'
COPIES: CIHM (91779) OKITD (956.019.021) OONL (RC81 J47 1894) *QMM (Osler Robertson J453h 1897Z)
NOTES: From 1904 to 1910 Toronto city directories list J.L. Nichols Co. Ltd at 292 Wellington Street West; D.E. Hughes remained the manager.

O70.12 unnumbered ed., [entered 1897; about 1904–10]
—The / household guide / or / domestic cyclopedia. / A practical family physician. Home remedies / and home treatment on / all diseases. / An instructor on nursing, housekeeping and / home adornments. / By / Prof. B.G. Jefferis, M.D., Ph.D., / and / J.L. Nichols, A.M. / Also / a complete cook book / by / Mrs. J.L. Nichols. / Manufactured and published by / the J.L. Nichols Company Limited / 292 Wellington West / Toronto Canada
DESCRIPTION: 18.0 × 12.0 cm Pp [7–8] 9, [x] xi–xx, 21–539 Frontis of head-and-shoulders of a young girl, fp illus, illus Lacks binding, except for fragment of leather spine

CONTENTS: 7 tp; 8 'The Good Samaritan' [a poem], a section of printing erased (probably regarding the price), and 'Entered according to Act of the Parliament of Canada, in the year one thousand eight hundred and ninety-four, by John A. Hertel, at the Department of Agriculture. Entered according to Act of the Parliament of Canada, in the year one thousand eight hundred and ninety-seven, by J.L. Nichols & Co., at the Department of Agriculture.'; 9 'Publisher's Preface' signed J.L. Nichols; x fp illus of 'Mother Away from Home'; xi–xx 'Table of Contents'; 21–521 Books I–V; 522–30 'A Complete Medical Dictionary'; 531–9 'Alphabetical Index'

COPIES: *OTMCL (616.024 J24.2)

NOTES: Unlike O70.11, there is no 'Agents wanted' on the title-page. The title-page and p 8 are printed in blue ink, not black. On p 8 a section of printing has been erased between the poem and the copyright information.

O70.13 unnumbered ed., [entered 1897; 1911 or later]
—The / household guide / or / domestic cyclopedia. / A practical family physician. Home remedies / and home treatment on / all diseases. / An instructor on nursing, housekeeping and / home adornments. / By / Prof. B.G. Jefferis, M.D., Ph.D., / and / J.L. Nichols, A.M. / Also / a complete cook book / by / Mrs. J.L. Nichols. / Manufactured and published by / the J.L. Nichols Co. Limited / 182 Spadina Avenue / Toronto, Canada / Agents wanted

DESCRIPTION: 18.0 × 12.0 cm Pp [7–8] 9, [x] xi–xx, 21–539 Frontis of head-and-shoulders of a young girl, illus Cloth

CONTENTS: 7 tp; 8 'The Good Samaritan' [a poem] and 'Agents wanted. Entered according to Act of the Parliament of Canada, in the year one thousand eight hundred and ninety-four, by John A. Hertel, at the Department of Agriculture. Entered according to Act of the Parliament of Canada, in the year one thousand eight hundred and ninety-seven, by J.L. Nichols & Co. at the Department of Agriculture.'; 9 'Publisher's Preface' signed J.L. Nichols; x fp illus of 'Mother Away from Home'; xi–xx table of contents; 21–244 Book I; 245–326 Book II; 327–98 Book III; 399–490 Book IV, 'Woman's Friend. A Complete Cook Book.'; 491–521 Book V; 522–30 'A Complete Medical Dictionary'; 531–9 'Alphabetical Index'

COPIES: *NFSM

NOTES: From 1911, Toronto city directories list J.L. Nichols Co. Ltd at 182 Spadina Avenue; D.E. Hughes was still the manager. The cover-title is 'Family Recipes.'

O70.14 facsimile ed., [copyright 1972]
—The / household guide / or / domestic cyclopedia. / A practical family physician. Home remedies / and home treatment on / all diseases. / An instructor on nursing, housekeeping and / home adornments. / By / Prof. B.G. Jefferis, M.D., Ph.D., / and / J.L. Nichols, A.M. / Also / a complete cook book / by / Mrs. J.L. Nichols. / Manufactured and published by / the J.L. Nichols Company Limited / 292 Wellington West / Toronto – Canada

CONTENTS: Tp verso: 'Coles Canadiana Collection // Originally published in 1894 by the J.L. Nichols Company Limited, 292 Wellington West, Toronto, Canada. Facsimile edition published by Coles Publishing Company, Toronto // Printed in Canada © Copyright 1972.'

COPIES: AEU (RC81 J45 1972) BVAU (WB 120 J44 1894a; not on shelf, not in storage) MWIAP MWMM NSFM (RC81 J4 1972) OKITWN OLU (RC81 J47) OONL (RC81 J47 1972, 2 copies) OOU (RC81 J47 1972) OSTPA *OTMCL (616.024 J24) OTNY (616 J) OTSHH OTU (TX145 J44 1894a) OWTU (RC81 J47 1972) QLB (RC81 J47 1972) QRUQR (RC81 J4H6 1972 UQ) SS (640 JEF) SSU (RC81.A2J45 1972 Shortt Spec; not on shelf)

NOTES: Unlike the abridged O70.15, this is a complete facsimile of the original work.

O70.15 facsimile ed., [copyright 1978]
—The great / nineteenth century / household / guide / Grandma Nichols / Coles / Looking / Back / Series

DESCRIPTION: 21.0 × 13.5 cm Pp [i–viii], 1–245 Illus Paper, with image on front of two women at a kitchen table, filling preserving jars

CONTENTS: i tp; ii 'Coles Looking Back Series // Originally published in 1894 by the J.L. Nichols Company Limited, 292, Wellington West, Toronto, Canada. © Copyright 1978 and published by Coles Publishing Company Limited Toronto – Canada // Printed in Canada'; iii–vii table of contents; viii 'Publisher's Preface' signed J.L. Nichols; 1–232 text; 233–41 'A Complete Medical Dictionary'; 242–5 'Alphabetical Index'

CITATIONS: Duncan, p 143

COPIES: OKITWN OONL (TX145 N53, 3 copies) *Private collection; United States: DLC (RC81 N58 1978)

NOTES: This edition does not have a facsimile title-page; the new title and attribution to 'Grandma' Nichols are the inventions of Coles. The text has been abridged and rearranged; the 'Alphabetical Index' is new to this edition and is referenced to the renumbered pages.

AMERICAN EDITIONS: The title of the earlier American editions differs from that of the Canadian editions: *The Household Guide; or Practical Helps for Every Home ... by Prof. B.G. Jefferis ... Also a Complete Cook Book by Mrs. J.L. Nichols and Anna Holverson*, 6th ed., Naperville, Ill.: J.L. Nichols, 1893 [entered ... 1892] (OGU); Holverson is cited as co-author, but her name does not appear in the Canadian editions. Other American editions have this title, but include J.L. Nichols as co-author with Jefferis: 10th ed. [see next paragraph]; and 12th ed., Naperville, Ill.: J.L. Nichols, 1894 (OTUTF, QLB). A comparison of the American 6th ed. of 1893 with O70.9 reveals that the cookery material is essentially the same, although the order of some parts is rearranged.

The tenth American edition was sold in Canada: *The Household Guide; or Practical Helps for Every Home ... Also a Complete Cook Book by Mrs. J.L. Nichols and Anna Holverson*, 10th ed., Naperville, Ill.: J.L. Nichols, 1893 [entered according to the Act of the Congress, in the year 1892], sold only by subscription; a copy of this edition in a private collection in Toronto is stamped twice on the title-page, in purple ink: 'From Wm. F. Currie, Gen'l Agent, Box 112, Fredericton, N.B. Office York St:'

The thirteenth American edition has the title of the Canadian editions: *The Household Guide or Domestic Cyclopedia ... by Prof. B.G. Jefferis ... and J.L. Nichols ... Also, a Complete Cook Book, by Mrs. J.L. Nichols*, 13th ed., Naperville, Ill.: J.L. Nichols, 1894 [entered in 1892] (United States: KMK).

Silico standard cook book

O71.1 nd [about 1895]
Silico / standard cook book / Price 10 cents. / [left of illus:] Cats / scratch / but / [right of illus:] Silico / does not, / it cleans. / [below illus:] The household's friend / The Hoffman Co. / International Bridge. / Ontario. [cover-title]
DESCRIPTION: 19.5 × 12.0 cm   Pp [1] 2–48   Paper, with image on front of two cats standing on a window sill, their backs arched, ready for a fight; stapled
CONTENTS: Inside front face of binding 'Index'; 1 introductory text extolling the qualities of Silico scouring soap produced by Hoffman Co.; 2–48 testimonials and ads for Silico on even-numbered pages, recipes on odd-numbered pages
COPIES: CIHM (88761)   *Private collection
NOTES: Most of the even-numbered pages present lists of women by Canadian city (mostly from Ontario), often with each woman's street address and

her comments about Silico, such as 'Like it very much' or 'Good for scouring.' The introductory text on page 1 refers to the sample of soap sent to the reader of the cookbook; presumably, the cookbook accompanied the soap sample. Page 1 also comments that the recipes 'have been selected with great labor from the very best authorities.' The testimonial on p 34, dated 3 October 1894, from Thomas McBean, caretaker at Massey Music Hall, Toronto, suggests 1895 as the year of publication, but certainly no later because International Bridge was renamed Bridgeburg in 1894. Hoffman's American location, New Rochelle, New York, is recorded on p 46..

1895–1900

Hamilton Jewel cook book

In 1864 William Burrow and Charles Stewart founded the Hamilton Malleable Iron Works; in 1872 the company was renamed Burrow, Stewart and Milne.

O72.1 nd [about 1895–1900]
Hamilton Jewel / cook book / [caption for illus of factory:] Where Hamilton Jewel Gas Ranges are made / Issued by / the Burrow, Stewart & Milne Co. / Limited / Hamilton, Canada / largest makers of gas goods in Canada
DESCRIPTION: 16.5 × 10.0 cm   Pp [1] 2–24   Tp illus of factory, illus of gas appliances   Lacks paper binding; stapled
CONTENTS: 1 tp; 2 'About Hamilton Jewel Gas Stoves'; 3 'About Cooking // Read These General Directions'; 4–24 'Choice Cooking Recipes'
COPIES: CIHM (78635)   *OH (R641.5 HAM CESH)
NOTES: The title-page and the text are printed in red and black. The recipes are interspersed with illustrations of gas appliances and information about them. The appliances illustrated include: No. 200 Hamilton Jewel Gas Range, p 4; No. 220 Hamilton Jewel Gas Range, p 5; Jewel Hood, p 6; Nos. 73, 83, and 93, p 7; No. 230, p 8; and many more.

Three editions of a text by Burrow, Stewart and Milne, called *Jewel Cook Book* or *Choice Cooking Recipes* (O179.1, O179.2, O179.3), all start with the same recipes: Rye and Corn Meal Bread; Steamed Corn and Graham Bread; Plain White Family Bread; and Graham Bread. *Hamilton Jewel Cook Book* shares with two of these editions the heading 'Choice Cooking Recipes,' but it begins with a different selection of recipes: Bread and Brown Bread, p 4; Steamed Boston Brown Bread and Corn Bread, p 5; and English Muffins and

Graham Muffins, p 7. *Hamilton Jewel Cook Book* has fewer pages than the other books, and, from appearances, it likely predates them and another work from the company, O169.1, *Choicest Cooking Recipes*.

Hayden, P.T.

O73.1 nd [about 1895–1900]
King / of / receipt books / 100 receipts, tried, tested and guaranteed / to give satisfaction, each of which has / cost me from $1.00 to $5.00, and are to / be sold for the small price of $1.00. / Satisfaction guaranteed or money / refunded. / Lawson & Jones, printers, London, [*sic*] [cover-title]
DESCRIPTION: 14.5 × 10.5 cm   Pp [1–3] 4–39   Card; stapled
CONTENTS: 1 'Introductory'; 2 blank; 3–39 recipes
COPIES: CIHM (88758)   *Private collection
NOTES: The following text is printed on the inside back face of the binding: 'This book has been put up in the most compact form possible, and nothing but the most useful recipes have been put in, ... This work contains 100 recipes. Price $1.00 post paid. Address: P.T. Hayden, Box 82, Coldwater, Ont.' Most of the recipes are for cosmetics or medicines (for example, rouge, freckle remover, lip salve, dandruff cure) or for household needs (cleaning wallpaper, making soap, gold plating solution, how to iron shirts), but there are some culinary recipes: Baking Powder, How to Make Ice Cream, Lemonade Powders, Lemon Cream, Maple Syrup and Sugar, and Artificial Honey. The final section is about 'Female Complaints.'

1896

The candy maker's guide

See also O237.1, Ice Cream and Candy Makers' Factory Guide, *in which is glued a Fletcher Manufacturing Co. label.*

O74.1 [1896]
The / candy maker's guide / A collection of / choice recipes for sugar boiling / compiled and published by / the Fletcher Mnf'g Co. / manufacturers of / confectioners' and candy makers' tools and machines / tea and coffee urns / bakers' confectioners and hotel supplies / importers and dealers in / pure fruit juices, / flavoring extracts, / fruit oils, / essential oils, / malt extract, / XXXX glucose, etc. / [caption:] Prize medal and diploma awarded at Toronto Industrial Exhibition / 1894, for general excellence in style and finish of our goods. / 440–442 Yonge St., – Toronto, Can.
DESCRIPTION: 20.5 × 13.5 cm   Pp [i–ii], [1–3] 4–111 [112]   Many illus of candy-making equipment [$1.00, on binding]   Cloth
CONTENTS: i blank; ii 'Toronto // J Johnston printer & stationer 105 Church St // 1896'; 1 tp; 2 list of items manufactured or sold by the company; 3 'Introduction'; 4–112 text, including recipes and illus of equipment, and ads
COPIES: *OTMCL (664.15 C12)
NOTES: The recipes are for Canadian professional candy makers and call for commercial amounts of ingredients. The 'Introduction' draws attention to the importance of the branch of candy-making called sugar boiling: 'Of the entire make of confectionery in Canada, at least two-thirds of it may be written down under the name of boiled sugar.'

Cooke, Maud C.

See also O81.1, Breakfast, Dinner and Supper, *by the same American author.*

O75.1 [entered 1896]
Social etiquette / or / manners and customs of / polite society / containing / rules of etiquette for all occasions, including calls; / invitations; parties; weddings; receptions; dinners / and teas; etiquette of the street; / public places, etc., etc. / Forming a / complete guide to self-culture / the art of dressing well; conversation; courtship; / etiquette for children; letter-writing; / artistic home and interior / decorations, etc. / By / Maud C. Cooke / the well-known and popular author. / Embellished with superb phototype engravings / J.L. Nichols & Co. / Atlanta, Ga., Naperville Ill., Toronto, Ont.
DESCRIPTION: 20.0 × 14.5 cm   Pp [i–ii] iii–vi, 17–508   9 pls col incl presentation pl and frontis; 8 double-sided pls; 16 fp illus; many illus   Cloth, with image on front of a woman playing a piano
CONTENTS: i tp; ii 'Entered according to Act of Congress, in the year 1896, by J.R. Jones, in the office of the Librarian of Congress, at Washington, D.C. All rights reserved.'; iii–iv preface; v–vi table of contents; 17–508 text
CITATIONS: Abrahamson, pp 10 (note 12), 11 (note 16), 17 (notes 1, 2, 4, 5), 21 (notes 16, 17), 22 (note 24), 25 (note 42), 29 (note 2), 30 (notes 7, 9), 31–2 (notes 13, 14), 35 (note 6), 36 (note 9), 37 (note 13), 40 (notes 7, 8), 60

COPIES: *OGU (UA s050 b08)
NOTES: The title-page is printed in red and black. Information about meals is in the chapters for 'Dinner Giving' on pp 189–210, 'Table Etiquette' on pp 211–26, and 'Breakfasts, Luncheons and Teas' on pp 274–95.

AMERICAN EDITIONS: *Social Etiquette*, Philadelphia: National Publishing Co., [1896] (United States: DLC); possibly *Our Deportment*, by Maude [*sic*] C. Cooke, Philadelphia: National Publishing Co., [1902] (United States: DLC); possibly *Modern Etiquette*, by Maude [*sic*] C. Cooke, Philadelphia: National Publishing Co., [c1907] (United States: DLC).

The Goderich almanac and cook book for 1897

O76.1   1897 [1896]
The Goderich / almanac / and / cook book / for 1897. / This book is / worth / preserving. / It contains / much valuable / information. / Published by / W.C. Goode, / chemist, / Goderich, Ontario. / (Copyrighted) [cover-title]
DESCRIPTION: Pp [1–3] 4–32
CONTENTS: Inside front face of binding calendar for 1897; 1 'To the Public' signed W.C. Goode; 2–3 publ ads; 4– 1st column 28 recipes, publ ads, monthly calendars, and 'Crisp Conversations'; 2nd column 28 'Diet and Digestion'; 29 'Domestic Hints'; 1st column 30 'Hints on Dyeing'; 2nd column 30–mid 1st column 32 'Coloring Recipes'; mid 1st column 32–2nd column 32 'Bridal Superstition' and 'Weather Wisdom'
COPIES: *CIHM (A02130)   OLU
NOTES: In 'To the Public,' W.C. Goode writes, 'At the approach of another year [i.e., the end of 1896] we desire to present you with an improved edition of our Almanac and Cook Book.' The recipes begin on p 4 with Baked Soup, Stewed Brisket of Beef, and Soup without Meat.

Hyde, Frank (1871 or 1872?–1953)

No copy of Hyde's cookbook has been located, but later in life, he published his memoirs as a pharmacist in Woodstock, from the start of his apprenticeship in a Woodstock drugstore on 5 November 1888 and purchasing the store in 1896, to 1946: Romance of 100 Years of Pharmacy in Woodstock, [Woodstock, Ont.: Frank Hyde, 1946] (OTU, photocopy at OWOM). The cover-title describes the author as 'Frank Hyde who has been in business in Woodstock fifty-eight years 1888–1946 and has lived here for seventy-five years 1871–1946.' The book is inscribed by Hyde and includes photographs of the author, his wife, Carrie, and son, Francis T., called Frank Jr, and his Rexall Drug Store on Dundas Street in 1946. Page 23 records his printed works, but not the cookbook. Hyde is buried in Old St Paul's Cemetery, Woodstock. The 1901 Census records the birth date 25 September 1872. The file for Hyde at OWOM contains local newspaper articles about him.

O77.1   [1896]
[An edition of *Hydes's* [*sic*] *Tested Recipes; a Practical Everyday Cook Book*, Woodstock, Ont.: Lawson and Jones, [1896], pp 32]
CITATIONS: O'Neill (unpublished)
COPIES: Great Britain: LB (07944.df.8 destroyed)
NOTES: *Hydes's Tested Recipes* was published in the year that Hyde bought the drugstore where he had apprenticed. The cookbook is not cited in his memoirs.

The ladies' book of useful information

O78.1   1896
The ladies' book / of / useful information – / Compiled from many sources. / London, Ont.: / London Printing & Lithographing Co. (Ltd.) / 1896.
DESCRIPTION: Pp [1–3] 4–208, [i] ii–vi
CONTENTS: 1 tp; 2 stamp: 'Entered according to Act of the Parliament of Canada, in the year 1897, on behalf of the unnamed author, by P.J. Edmunds, at the Department of Agriculture. All rights reserved.'; 3–12 'Preface'; 13–19 'Contents'; 20 blank; 21–208 text in eighteen chapters; i–vi index
CITATIONS: O'Neill (unpublished)
COPIES: *CIHM (08380)   OONL (missing); Great Britain: LB (07944.g.33 destroyed)
NOTES: The only culinary information is in Chapter XI, 'Things for the Sick Room,' pp 157–65, a collection of recipes for invalids. Otherwise, the text is about health and beauty. The 'Preface' dedicates the book 'to the ladies of America.'

1897

Carter's almanac and cook book for 1897

O79.1   1897
Carter's / almanac / and / cook book / for 1897. / Published by / H.R. Carter, / White Drug Store, /

20 King St. West, Berlin, Ont. / Telephone 20. [cover-title]
DESCRIPTION: Paper
CITATIONS: Bloomfield No. 3200
COPIES: *OKITD

A collection of reliable recipes

O80.1 1897
[An edition of *A Collection of Reliable Recipes: Cake Baking*, London, Ont.: Lawson and Jones, 1897]
CITATIONS: O'Neill (unpublished)
COPIES: Great Britain: LB (not located)
NOTES: No further information could be found about this publication, which is noted in copyright records at the British Library. O'Neill describes the item as a 'book.'

Cooke, Maud C.

See also O75.1, Social Etiquette, *by the same American author.*

O81.1 Brantford and Toronto, [entered 1897]
Breakfast, dinner and supper / or / what to eat and how to prepare it / containing / all the latest approved recipes in every department / of cooking; instructions for selecting meats / and carving; descriptions of the best / kitchen utensils, etc. / including / hygienic and scientific cooking / rules for dinner giving; use of the chafing dish; menu / cards for all special occasions; cooking for / invalids; valuable hints for economical / housekeeping, etc. / the whole forming / a standard authority on the / culinary art / by / Maud C. Cooke / author of "Social Etiquette," etc., etc. / Superbly embellished with engravings in colors / and phototype illustrations / The Bradley, Garretson Co., Limited. / Brantford, Ont. & Toronto, Ont.
CONTENTS: Tp verso 'Entered according to Act of Congress, in the year 1897, by G.W. Bertron, in the office of the Librarian of Congress, at Washington, D.C. All rights reserved.'
COPIES: OGOWSM   *Private collection

O81.2 Brantford and Toronto, [entered 189–]
—Breakfast, dinner and supper / or / what to eat and how to prepare it / containing / all the latest approved recipes in every department / of cooking;

instructions for selecting meats / and carving; descriptions of the best / kitchen utensils, etc. / including / hygienic and scientific cooking / rules for dinner giving; use of the chafing dish; menu / cards for all special occasions; cooking for / invalids; valuable hints for economical / housekeeping, etc. / the whole forming / a standard authority on the / culinary art / by / Maud C. Cooke / author of "Social Etiquette," etc., etc. / Superbly embellished with engravings in colors / and phototype illustrations / The Bradley, Garretson Co., Limited / Brantford, Ont. & Toronto, Ont.
DESCRIPTION: 20.0 × 15.0 cm   Pp [3–4] 5–8, 17–608   4 pls col incl presentation pl and frontis, 8 double-sided pls, illus incl many of kitchen utensils   Cloth, with image on front of a family at table and a maid serving
CONTENTS: 3 tp; 4 'Entered according to Act of Congress, in the year 189[blank] by G.W. Bertron, in the office of the Librarian of Congress, at Washington, D.C. All rights reserved.'; 5–6 introduction; 7–8 'Contents' [alphabetically arranged]; 17–587 text; 588–608 'Alphabetical Index'; [six blank, ruled leaves for manuscript recipes]
COPIES: CIHM (95408)   OFERWM (A1997.44)   *OGU (UA s050 b12)
NOTES: The title-page is printed in red and black. The presentation plate in the OGU copy is inscribed, 'Xmas 1904. [Presented to] Sister Alma [by] Maude, Rae & Frank.'

A private collector has a copy of *Breakfast, Dinner and Supper* with no imprint below 'phototype illustrations' on the title-page; like O81.2, the copyright date on the title-page verso is '189[blank].'

O81.3 London, [entered 189[7?]]
—Breakfast, dinner and supper / or / what to eat and how to prepare it / containing / all the latest approved recipes in every department / of cooking; instructions for selecting meats / and carving; descriptions of the best / kitchen utensils, etc. / including / hygienic and scientific cooking / rules for dinner giving; use of the chafing dish; menu / cards for all special occasions; cooking for / invalids; valuable hints for economical / housekeeping, etc. / the whole forming / a standard authority on the / culinary art / by / Maud C. Cooke / author of "Social Etiquette," etc., etc. / Superbly embellished with engravings in colors / and phototype illustrations / McDermid & Logan / London, Ontario
DESCRIPTION: 20.0 × 14.5 cm   Pp [3–4] 5–8, 17–608

[leaves lacking?] 3 pls col incl presentation pl 8 double-sided pls grouped together, illus Cloth, with image on front of a family at table and a maid serving
CONTENTS: 3 tp; 4 'Entered according to Act of Congress, in the year 189[7,?] by G.W. Bertron, in the office of the Librarian of Congress, at Washington, D.C. All rights reserved.'; 5–6 introduction; 7–8 'Contents' [alphabetically arranged]; 17–587 text; 588–608 'Alphabetical Index'
COPIES: *Private collection
NOTES: The title-page is printed in red and black.

O81.4   Saint John, [entered 1897]
—Breakfast, dinner and supper / or / what to eat and how to prepare it / containing / all the latest approved recipes in every department / of cooking; instructions for selecting meats / and carving; descriptions of the best / kitchen utensils, etc. / including / hygienic and scientific cooking / rules for dinner giving; use of the chafing dish; menu / cards for all special occasions; cooking for / invalids; valuable hints for economical / housekeeping, etc. / the whole forming / a standard authority on the / culinary art / by / Maud C. Cooke / author of "Social Etiquette," etc., etc. / Superbly embellished with engravings in colors / and phototype illustrations / R.A.H. Morrow, / St. John, New Brunswick.
DESCRIPTION: 20.0 × 15.0 cm   Pp [3–4] 5–8, 17–608 [609–24]   4 pls col incl presentation pl and frontis, 8 double-sided pls, illus incl many of kitchen utensils Cloth, with image on front of a family at table and a maid serving
CONTENTS: 3 tp; 4 'Entered according to Act of Congress, in the year 1897, by G.W. Bertron, in the office of the Librarian of Congress, at Washington, D.C. All rights reserved.'; 5–6 introduction; 7–8 'Contents' [alphabetically arranged]; 17–587 text; 588–608 'Alphabetical Index'; 609–24 blank, ruled leaves for 'Miscellaneous Recipes'
COPIES: NBFKL   *OGU (UA s050 b11)   OTUTF (B-12 7876)
NOTES: The title-page is printed in red and black.

O81.5   Saint John, [entered 1897]
—Twentieth century / cook book / containing / all the latest approved recipes in every department / of cooking; instructions for selecting meats / and carving; descriptions of the best / kitchen utensils, etc. / including / hygienic and scientific cooking / rules for dinner giving; use of the chafing dish; menu / cards for all special occasions; cooking

for / invalids; valuable hints for economical / housekeeping, etc. / the whole forming / a standard authority on the / culinary art / by / Maud C. Cooke / author of "Social Etiquette," etc., etc. / Superbly embellished with engravings in colors / and phototype illustrations / R.A.H. Morrow, / St. John, New Brunswick.
COPIES: *Private collection
NOTES: The following information is on the title-page verso: 'Entered according to Act of Congress, in the year 1897, by Horace C. Fry, in the office of the Librarian of Congress, at Washington, D.C.'

O81.6   [entered 1897]
—[Another edition of *Twentieth Century Cook Book*]
COPIES: OGU (UA S059 b27)   OWOM
NOTES: The text on the title-page matches O81.5 except that there is no imprint following '… phototype illustrations'; printed on the title-page verso is 'Entered according to Act of Congress, in the year 1897, by Horace C. Fry, in the office of the Librarian of Congress, at Washington, D.C.' A copy at QKB matches those at OGU and OWOM except for the date on the title-page verso, '189'; the fourth digit is blank and may not have registered.

AMERICAN EDITIONS: These appeared under different titles: *Breakfast, Dinner and Supper*, Philadelphia: National Publishing Co., [1897] (United States: DLC); *Montgomery Ward and Co.'s Common Sense Cookery*, Philadelphia: National Publishing Co., [1897] (United States: DLC); *Twentieth Century Cook Book*, Chicago: W.S. Reeve Publishing Co., [1897] (SRRPM); *The Colorado Cook Book*, Philadelphia: National Publishing Co., [1901] (United States: DLC).

The following publication may be related to *Breakfast, Dinner and Supper: Three Meals a Day: A Collection of Valuable and Reliable Recipes in All Classes of Cookery*, by Miss M.C. Cooke, Chicago: Acme Publishing House, [c1887] (United States: DLC); *Three Meals a Day*, by Maude [sic] C. Cooke, Chicago: Educational Co., [189-?] (Bitting, p 98).

Dwight's Cow-Brand cook-book

John Dwight and Co., established by Dr Austin Church and John Dwight in New York City in 1847, was the first commercial manufacturer in the United States of baking soda. The company adopted its famous Cow Brand trademark in 1876. In 1867, as the market for baking soda grew, two sons of one of the original founders started Church and Co., and six years later, in 1873, they introduced the Arm and Hammer trademark. The two firms were friendly competitors for nearly thirty years, until their merger in 1896 and the renaming of the new entity, Church and Dwight Co. Whereas both brand names were used in the United States, in Canada the company sold only Cow Brand. Its Canadian head office was in Montreal until 1972, when it moved to Don Mills, Ontario, now part of Toronto. (The preceding information is derived from a 3-page document titled 'History of the Company,' given to me by Church and Dwight in 1992.)

Cow Brand Soda was introduced to Canada in 1897, when free samples and copies of Dwight's Cow-Brand Cook-Book *were distributed: An article headed 'Cow Brand Soda' in the Toronto* Globe *(29 January 1898) states, 'Nearly a year ago this pure soda was placed on the market in Canada, and by January 1 [1898] over 142,000 sample packages and cook books had been given away.'*

The earliest editions of Dwight's Cow-Brand Cook-Book *bear two places of publication: Toronto and Montreal. Since Toronto is cited first and since O82.2 and probably also O82.1 were printed by William Briggs in Toronto, the entries for all editions are positioned here, in the Ontario section. Some later editions were published only in Montreal, and others, only in Toronto.*

Except for O82.1, all editions of Dwight's Cow-Brand Cook-Book *up to and including that of 1903 bear the corporate name John Dwight and Co., which is at odds with the company history recounted above. I cannot explain the discrepancy.*

See also Q130.1, Bradley, Alice, De bonnes choses à manger faites avec le bicarbonate de soude (soda à pâte) Cow Brand; *Q210.1,* Good Things to Eat Made with Cow Brand Baking Soda; *and Q312.1,* New Fashioned, Old Fashioned Recipes.

O82.1 [1897]
Dwight's / Cow-Brand cook-book / Established half a century. / Church & Dwight Co. / Toronto. – Montreal. – New York. [cover-title]
DESCRIPTION: Paper, with image on front of a cow in a rectangular frame; with hole punched at top left corner, through which runs a string for hanging
CONTENTS: Inside front face of binding portrait of Queen Victoria, 'Sixty years a queen.'; 1 'First, best, cheapest. Cheapest because best[.?]'
COPIES: *Private collection
NOTES: This edition was published in 1897, sixty years after Queen Victoria ascended the throne in 1837 and 'half a century' after the establishment of the baking soda company in 1847. Unlike O82.2, there is no printer's name on p 1 (or elsewhere in the volume,

according to the book's owner). Note that in the cover-title, the company name is Church and Dwight Co., and New York is a third place of publication.

A letter relating to the printing of what may be this or the following edition is in the papers of the Methodist Book and Publishing House at OTCC (Acc. 83.061C, UCC Board of Publication, Box 6, Agreements 1–68): On 25 June 1897, William Briggs, book steward, wrote to Church and Dwight Co., 65 Wall Street, New York, accepting its order to print 500,000 copies of 'Cow Brand Cook Book' to be delivered to the company's Toronto office in packages of 1,000 copies. The book was 'to be bound, wire stitched and cover drawn on with paste, with hole and string hanger on top of left hand corner: [and] to be printed in brown ink, [the publisher] to be furnished with printed covers and one set of Electro plates, ...'

O82.2 nd [about 1897]
—Dwight's / Cow-Brand cook-book / Established half a century. / John Dwight and Company, / Toronto. – Montreal. [cover-title]
DESCRIPTION: 13.0 × 8.5 cm   Pp [1–5] 6–32 Paper, with image on front of a cow in a rectangular frame; stapled, and with hole punched at top left corner for hanging
CONTENTS: Inside front face of binding crest-shape featuring the provincial symbols for Ontario, Quebec, New Brunswick, Nova Scotia, Manitoba, British Columbia, and Prince Edward Island; 1 'First, best, cheapest. Cheapest because best. William Briggs, Toronto.'; 2–3 'To Make Home Happy'; 4–20 'Valuable Receipts'; 21 'Things Well to Know' and 'Weights and Measures for Cooks, etc.'; 22 'What Housekeepers Should Remember' and 'For the Bath'; 23 'Useful Household Remedies'; 24 information about Dwight's Cow Brand Soda; 25 'Useful Information for Farmers' and 'Estimating Measures'; 26–7 'Tables of Weights and Measures'; 28 'Valuable Facts'; 29 'Rates of Postage'; 30 'Amount of Barbed Wire Required for Fences' and 'A Table of Daily Savings'; 31–2 'Simple Remedies'
COPIES: *NBFKL (Ruth Spicer Cookbook Collection) OKQ (F5012 nd D992) QMM (RBD ckbk 1522) SSWD
NOTES: Page 5 carries the credit: 'Seventeen of the following receipts marked [diamond symbol] are taken from "Common Sense," and "Book of Forty Puddings," compiled by Marion Harland, and are published by permission.'; these recipes are noted as copyrighted by Chas. Scribner's Sons, 1882.

This edition is undated; however, the words 'Established half a century' on the binding indicate a publication date of about 1897 since the company was founded in 1847. This edition was likely published not long after O82.1.

The SSWD copy lacks its binding.

O82.3 1899
—[An edition of *Cow Brand Soda. Recipe Book.*, Montreal and Toronto: John Dwight and Co., 1899]
CITATIONS: O'Neill (unpublished)
NOTES: O'Neill's entry, based on Canadian copyright material at the British Library, says that the book was 'possibly not received' by the library. No other editions have the phrase 'recipe book' in the title; however, if the book was not received, then the library's information was not taken from the book itself and may be inaccurate. Perhaps the British Library record refers to O82.4.

O82.4 copyright 1899
—Cow Brand Soda / Cow Soda book / of / facts worth knowing. / Established half a century / Copyrighted, 1899, by John Dwight & Co. Montreal & Toronto. [cover-title]
DESCRIPTION: 14.5 × 9.0 cm   Pp 1–32   Illus on pp 1 and 5 of rectangular Dwight's Soda symbol   Paper, with image on front of a cow's head bursting through paper; stapled, and with hole punched at top left corner for hanging
CONTENTS: 1 'First! Best! Cheapest! Cheapest, because best!' and list of company offices; 2–3 'To Make Home Happy'; 4 'Valuable Receipts'; 5 'Marion Harland's Receipts' and 'To Make a Delicious Biscuit'; 6–20 recipes; 21 publ ad; 22 'Things Well to Know' and 'Weights and Measurements for Cooks, etc.'; 23 'What Housekeepers Should Remember,' 'For the Bath,' and notice about publ's bird picture cards; 24 'Useful Household Remedies'; 25 'Carbonic Acid Gas in the Soda'; 26 'Useful Information for Farmers'; 27–8 'Tables of Weights and Measures'; 29 'Valuable Facts'; 30–1 'Rates of Postage'; 32 'Amount of Barbed Wire Required for Fences' and 'A Table of Daily Savings'
COPIES: *ARDA

O82.5 copyright 1903
—Cow Brand / Baking Soda / Book of / valuable recipes / Established over half a century. / Copyrighted, 1903, by John Dwight & Co. Toronto. [cover-title]
DESCRIPTION: 15.0 × 9.0 cm   Pp [1–3] 4–31 [32]   Circular Cow Brand symbol on p 4; rectangular Cow Brand symbol on p 6; illus on p 7 of an aproned woman carrying a steaming tureen, with caption 'All in the soup'; other amusing illus on pp 9, 10, 11, 14,

15, 16, 17, 19, 20, 22, 24, 28   Paper, with image on front of a rectangular package of Dwight's Baking Soda; stapled, and with a string at top left corner for hanging
CONTENTS: 1 'Index' [i.e., table of contents]; 2 'Introduction'; 3 'Do Not Buy Baking Powder'; 4–5 'The Great "Cow Brand" Best in the World'; 6 'The Use of Dwight's Cow Brand Soda is recommended in all receipts where soda is to be used. Marion Harland's Receipts. (Copyright, 1882, by Chas. Scribner's Sons.) Seventeen of the following receipts marked [bullet:] • are taken from "Common Sense," and "Book of Forty Puddings," compiled by Marion Harland, ...' and note about 'complete set of beautiful picture cards' available from John Dwight and Co., Toronto; 7–29 'Valuable Receipts Prepared and Tested by Expert Cooks'; 30 'Useful Information for Farmers'; 31 'Dwight's Cow Brand Soda in Packages' and 'Raising Young Calves and Pigs'; 32 'Cow Brand Soda in the Sick Room and for Toilet Purposes'
COPIES: BVMA   ONLAM (Walters-Wagar Collection, Box 20)   QMM (RBD uncat)   *Private collection
NOTES: The cover-titles of O82.5 and O82.6 are identical; however, the interior text differs; for example, in O82.5, 'Valuable Receipts' starts on p 7, whereas in O82.6, it starts on p 8.

O82.6 copyright 1903
—Cow Brand / Baking Soda / Book of / valuable recipes / Established over half a century. / Copyrighted, 1903, by John Dwight & Co. Toronto. [cover-title]
DESCRIPTION: 15.0 × 9.5 cm   Pp [1] 2–32   Circular Cow Brand symbol on p 4; rectangular Cow Brand symbol on p 6; illus on p 8 of an aproned woman carrying a steaming tureen, with caption 'All in the soup'; other illus on pp 10, 11, 12, 14, 15, 16, 17, 19, 20, 21, 23, 26   Paper, with image on front of a rectangular package of Dwight's Baking Soda; stapled, and with hole punched at top left corner, through which runs a string for hanging
CONTENTS: 1 'Index' [i.e., table of contents]; 2 'Introduction'; 3 'Do Not Buy Baking Powder'; 4–5 'The Great "Cow Brand." Best in the World'; 6 'The use of Dwight's Cow Brand Soda is recommended in all receipts where soda is to be used. Marion Harland's Receipts. (Copyright, 1882, by Chas. Scribner's Sons.) Seventeen of the following receipts marked [bullet:] • are taken from "Common Sense," and "Book of Forty Puddings," compiled by Marion Harland, ...' and note about 'complete set of beautiful picture cards' available from John Dwight and Co., Toronto; 7 'Hints on Baking'; 8–27 'Valuable Receipts Prepared and Tested

by Expert Cooks'; 28 'Raising Young Calves and Pigs' and 'Dwight's Cow Brand Soda, in packages ...'; top–mid 29 'Useful Information for Farmers'; bottom 29–mid 30 'Things Well to Know'; mid 30 'Dwight's Cow Brand Soda in Packages'; bottom 30–31 twenty numbered 'Facts for Housekeepers'; 32 'Cow Brand Soda in the Sick Room and for Toilet Purposes'
COPIES: *Private collection

O82.7 copyright 1913
—Cow Brand Soda / Cook book / and / facts worth knowing. / Copyrighted 1913 by Church & Dwight, Limited, Montreal. [cover-title]
DESCRIPTION: 14.5 × 9.0 cm   Pp 1–32   Circular Cow Brand symbol on p 4, rectangular Cow Brand symbol on p 6; illus on p 7 of an aproned woman carrying a steaming tureen, with caption 'All in the soup'   Paper, with circular Cow Brand symbol on front; stapled, and with hole punched at top left corner, through which runs a string for hanging
CONTENTS: 1–2 'Rates of Postage'; 3 'Introduction'; 4–5 'The Great "Cow Brand"'; 6 'Important Reasons'; 7–22 'Valuable Receipts Prepared and Tested by Expert Cooks'; 23–mid 24 'What to Do with Left-overs'; bottom 24–25 'Economical Menus'; 26 'The Cooking of Meats'; 27 'The Cooking of Vegetables'; 28 'Time Tables for the Cook'; 29 'The Meal-Maker'; 30 'Birthday Stones'; 31 'Cow Brand Soda (Bi-carbonate) in the Sick Room'; 32 'Cow Brand Soda in the Bath'
COPIES: NBFKL   OONL (TX715.6 C697 1913)   OTNY (uncat)   OTUTF (flem pam 0131)   OWTU (E1052)   QMM (RBD ckbk 1446)   *Private collection

O82.8 1918
—Cow Brand Soda / Cook book / and / facts worth knowing. / Copyrighted 1918 by Church & Dwight, Limited, Montreal. [cover-title]
DESCRIPTION: 14.5 × 9.0 cm   Pp 1–30 [31–2]   [Free, on p 1]   Circular Cow Brand symbol opp p 1, rectangular Cow Brand symbol on p 3   Paper, with circular Cow Brand symbol on front; stapled, and with hole punched at top left corner, through which runs a string for hanging
CONTENTS: 1 'Much Inferior Soda Is Put Up in Kegs'; 2 'Dedication' and 'A Woman's Business'; 3 'How to Be Popular'; 4 'Do Not Buy Baking Powder'; 5 'Raising Agents'; 6 'Various Uses of the Cow Brand Soda in Cooking'; 7–21 'Valuable Receipts Prepared and Tested by Expert Cooks'; 22–mid 23 'What to Do with Left-overs'; mid–bottom 23 'Economical Menus'; 24 'Health for the Baby'; 25 'Kitchen Weights and Measures'; 26 'Time Tables for the Cook'; 27 'Preserving Eggs for Long Periods'; 28 'Cow Brand Soda (Bicar-

bonate) in the Sick Room'; 29 'Useful Information for the Farmer'; 30 'Birthday Stones' and 'Formula for Telling a Girl's Age'; 31–inside back face of binding 'Parcel Post Regulations' and postage rates
CITATIONS: O'Neill (unpublished)
COPIES: OGOWSM   *Private collection; Great Britain: LB (Woolwich)
NOTES: The private collector's copy is inscribed on the front face of the binding, in pencil, 'John A Morgan.'

O82.9 1918
—"Soda" à pâte / Cow Brand / Livre de la cuisinière / et / faits qu'il importe de connaître / Copyrighted 1918 by Church & Dwight, Limited, Montreal. [cover-title]
DESCRIPTION: 14.5 × 9.0 cm   Pp 1–30 [31–2]   Circular Cow Brand symbol opp p 1, rectangular Cow Brand symbol on p 3   Paper, with circular Cow Brand symbol on front; stapled, and with hole punched at top left corner, through which runs a string for hanging
CONTENTS: 1 'Une grande quantité de "Soda" de qualité inférieure est mis en baril' and 'Ménagères'; 2 'Dédicace' and 'Le travail de la ménagère'; 3 'Comment devenir populaire'; 4 'N'achetez pas de poudre à pâte'; 5 'Moyens à employer pour faire lever la pâte'; 6 'Divers usages du "Cow Brand" à la cuisine'; 7–21 'Recettes précieuses préparées et contrôlées par des cuisiniers experts'; 22–near bottom 23 'Que faire avec les restes'; bottom 23–mid 24 'Menus économiques'; bottom 24 'La santé pour le bébé'; 25 'Poids et mesures à l'usage de la cuisinière'; 26 'Horaire de la cuisinière'; 27 'Conservation des oeufs'; 28 'Soda Cow Brand (Bicarbonate) dans la chambre du malade'; 29 'Renseignements utiles aux cultivateurs'; 30 'Pierres de naissance'; 31–inside back face of binding 'Règlements des colis postaux'
CITATIONS: O'Neill (unpublished)
COPIES: *QSFFSC; Great Britain: LB (Woolwich)

O82.10 copyright 1922
—Cow Brand / Baking Soda / Cook book / and / facts worth knowing / Established over 70 years. / Copyrighted 1922 by Church & Dwight Ltd. Montreal [cover-title]
DESCRIPTION: 14.5 × 9.0 cm   Pp [1–2] 3–31 [32]   Paper, with image on front of box of Cow Brand Baking Soda; stapled, and with hole punched at top left corner, through which runs a string for hanging
CONTENTS: Inside front face of binding 'Perpetual Calendar' specifying years 1914–25; 1 'Contents'; 2 'Raising Agents'; 3 'Do Not Buy Baking Powder'; 4–6

'Various Uses of Cow Brand Baking Soda'; 7 'General Directions'; 8 'Sour Milk and Buttermilk' and 'Substitute for Sour Milk'; 9–28 recipes; 29 'Time Tables for the Cook'; 30 'Kitchen Weights and Measures'; 31 'Origin of Common Vegetables and Fruits' and 'World's Crops'; 32 'Useful Birds of America' [series of colour pictures distributed in packages of soda]
CITATIONS: O'Neill (unpublished)
COPIES: ARDA BSUM OMIHURM OTMCL (641.5971 H39 No. 3) *Private collection; Great Britain: LB (not located)

AMERICAN EDITIONS: *Dwight's Cow-Brand Cook-Book,* 1894 (Longone/Longone Q1); *Arm and Hammer Soda Book of Valuable Recipes,* 34th ed. 'of one million each,' New York: Church and Dwight Co., copyright 1900 (Dickinson, p 26, illus p 25); *Arm and Hammer Valuable Recipes,* 1921 (Dickinson, p 26).

The jubilee cook book

O83.1   1897
The / jubilee cook book / A selection of tested receipts. / "Cooking is a fine art to which you must bring / common sense and judgment." / 1897. / The Record Printing Company, Ltd. / of Windsor.
DESCRIPTION: 21.0 × 14.5 cm   Pp [1–3] 4–106   Limp cloth
CONTENTS: 1 tp; 2 blank; 3–106 text and ads
COPIES: *Private collection
NOTES: The recipes are credited with the name of the contributor, but no women's group is identified as the compiler of the book, which was likely published to mark the sixtieth jubilee of Queen Victoria's reign, 1837–97.

1898

Culinary landmarks

St Luke's Anglican Cathedral was established in 1870.

O84.1   3rd ed., 1909
Culinary landmarks / or / half-hours with Sault Ste. Marie / housewives / Third edition / Revised and enlarged / 1909
DESCRIPTION: 19.5 × 13.0 cm   Pp [1–9] 10–208   Cloth
CONTENTS: 1–4 ads; 5 tp; 6 ad; 7 preface signed Annie M. Reid, president, Sault Ste Marie, March 1909; 8 ad; 9–200 text and ads; 201–4 index; 205–8 ads
CITATIONS: Ferguson/Fraser, p 232, illus col on p 11

of closed volume   Golick, p 101 (note 14)   Golick 2005, pp 214, 525 (note 68)
COPIES: CIHM (87507)   OTNY (uncat)   *Private collection
NOTES: The preface relates the cookbook's publishing history: 'It is just five years [i.e., in about 1904] since "Culinary Landmarks" was placed by St. Luke's Woman's Auxiliary [i.e., the Auxiliary of St Luke's Anglican Cathedral] before the public as a successor to the "Handy Cook Book." ... The first edition was compiled by Mrs. Rennison and Mrs. Arthur Bennetts in 1898, and was called the "Handy Cook Book," their efforts realizing the sum of one hundred dollars. The second edition "Culinary Landmarks," was compiled, and added to, by Mrs. Kennedy and Mrs. Capp, and was nearly double the size. The demand has been so great that a third edition has been found necessary.' No copies of the first and second editions were found.

The text includes recipes from Gertrude Clergue and Mrs Bertrand J. Clergue. For information about the Clergue family, prominent in Sault Ste Marie, see Q95.1.

This bibliography, *Culinary Landmarks,* takes its title from O84.1 and from a 1906 fund-raising cookbook of the same name, O169a.1.

Good flour and how to use it

The earliest listings found for Charles B. McAllister and the McAllister Milling Co. are in the Peterborough and Ashburnham directory for 1895. The company had a short life since the last listings for McAllister and company are in the 1905–6 city directory; see also an article in the Peterborough Daily Examiner, *29 November 1906, which refers to propositions for the mill's future. An early photograph of the mill appears in the* Peterborough Weekly Examiner, *14 July 1950. According to the caption, the mill was torn down in 1930 by the Quaker Oats Co.*

O85.1   nd [about 1898]
Good flour / and / how to use it / Compliments of / the McAllister Milling Co. / Peterborough
DESCRIPTION: 13.0 × 8.0 cm   Pp [1–2] 3–24   Cloth; stapled
CONTENTS: 1 tp; 2 'Our Brands'; 3–5 'The Manufacturing of Wheat Flour' signed C.B. McAllister; 6–7 'A Talk on Bread'; 8–10 'Breakfast Cakes'; 11–12 'Pastry'; 13–15 'Puddings'; 16–23 'Cakes' and 'Icing and Filling'; bottom 23–24 'Hints'
CITATIONS: CHO No. 46 (Autumn 2005), p 12, illus   Driver 2003, 'Canadian Cookbooks,' p 33

COPIES: CIHM (95412)   *OGU (UA s041 b05)

NOTES: *Good Flour and How to Use It* is the earliest known Canadian cookbook from a flour company. This undated edition is likely the first because it has the fewest pages. It was published no earlier than 1895, the date of McAllister's first listing in Peterborough directories. Since O85.2 and O85.3 appeared in two consecutive years, 1899 and 1900, perhaps O85.1 was published in 1898.

In 'A Talk on Bread,' on p 6, readers are advised to make their own yeast rather than use cakes of commercial pressed yeast: 'In the first place we must make our yeast, as the old fashioned yeast makes the sweetest bread. Take 6 raw potatoes, grate them; 1 large hand-ful of hops, cover with water and simmer (not boil) 15 or 20 minutes, pour in the grated potatoes, add ½ cup of salt and 2 teaspoonsful of ginger, seal up tight.'

O85.2   1899

—Good flour / and / how to use it / Compliments of / the McAllister Milling Co. / Peterborough. / 1899

DESCRIPTION: 13.0 × 7.5 cm   Pp [1–2] 3–36   Cloth; stapled

CONTENTS: 1 tp; 2 'Our Brands'; 3–5 'The Manufacturing of Wheat Flour' signed the McAllister Milling Co.; 6–36 recipes

COPIES: *ARDA

O85.3   [1900]

—Good / flour and / how to / use it / Compliments of the / McAllister Milling / Co'y, Peterborough.

COPIES: *OPETCM (2 copies: L.59.37, L.67.151)

NOTES: The year of publication, 1900, is clearly printed on the front face of the binding of one OPETCM copy, L.67.151; this copy is inscribed on the title-page, 'Mrs. Jas. Pakenham.' The other copy (L.59.37) is inscribed opposite the title-page, 'Mrs Telford.'

Hoodless, Adelaide Sophia, née Hunter (Mrs John Hoodless) (farm near St George, Ont., 27 February 1858–26 February 1910, Toronto, Ont.)

Galvanized by the death of her baby son in 1889 from drinking impure milk, Hoodless took up the cause of promoting domestic science education for girls, believing that such tragedies could be avoided if girls were properly prepared for their role as mothers. Hoodless worked to establish the National Council of Women of Canada in 1893 and organized the founding meeting of the national body of the Young Women's Christian Association in the same year. In 1894 she opened a school for domestic science at the Hamilton YWCA. Three years later, on 19 February 1897, she addressed a meeting of women in nearby Stoney Creek, which led to the founding of the first Women's Institute. The organization quickly expanded to include national and international federations. Although Hoodless is venerated as the organization's founder, her involvement was limited mainly to public events (see Cheryl MacDonald, cited below). When the Victorian Order of Nurses was established by Lady Aberdeen in 1897, Hoodless supported the cause in Hamilton.

Hoodless determined to replace the domestic science classes at the Hamilton YWCA with a school for training domestic science teachers and, in 1900, with herself as president, the Ontario Normal School of Domestic Science and Art opened; however, the institution soon faced financial and other difficulties. Hoodless secured funding from William Macdonald, the tobacco magnate, to establish the Macdonald Institute at the Ontario Agricultural College in Guelph, and the Hamilton program moved there in September 1903. The Macdonald Institute was to become one of the pre-eminent institutions for the teaching of home economics in Ontario. Terry Crowley, in his DCB entry for Hoodless, comments, 'During the last five years of her life Adelaide Hoodless lessened her commitments as she was increasingly pushed to the periphery of the home economics movement by better-qualified individuals.' Nevertheless, she was, Crowley says, 'the last of the non-professionals to have a significant impact on the provincial school system in Ontario.'

Hoodless is buried in Hamilton Cemetery on York Street. According to Crowley, the birth year recorded on her gravestone (1857) is incorrect. For more information about Hoodless, see Cheryl MacDonald, Adelaide Hoodless: Domestic Crusader, Toronto and Reading: Dundurn Press, 1986; Crowley's entry for her in DCB, Vol. 13, pp 488–93; Ambrose, pp 17–22; and Dagg.

Miss Mary Urie Watson (Ayr, Ont., 1866–1950), who is credited as co-author in the 1905 retitled edition of Public School Domestic Science, was first hired by Hoodless to teach domestic science at the Hamilton YWCA. To further her education, she attended the Philadelphia Cooking School, graduating in 1895; and, from 1898 to 1900, she studied for the two-year Domestic Art Diploma at Columbia University's Teachers College. In 1900, she returned to Hamilton to work under Hoodless at the Ontario Normal School of Domestic Science and Art. Shortly after the Macdonald Institute opened in 1903, she was made principal, a post she held until her retirement in 1920. She was an active member of the Canadian Home Economics Association from its establishment in 1939, and in 1950 the association awarded her honorary life membership (We Are Tomorrow's Past, p 54). In 1909 she served as vice-president of the American Home Economics Association. See O236.2, Harcourt, Robert, and Miss M.A. Purdy, Flour and Breadmaking, *for which she prepared and 'criticized' the recipes. Watson's 'The Educational Value of Sewing,' 1901, is reprinted in Peterat/DeZwart. For more information about Watson, see Mary Leah DeZwart, 'Mary Urie Watson,'* Canadian Home Economics Journal *Vol. 48, No. 2 (Spring 1998), pp 63, 65; Dagg, pp 305–6; and her biography at the Waterloo County Hall of Fame.*

O86.1 1898
Public school / domestic science / By / Mrs. J. Hoodless, / President School of Domestic Science, Hamilton. / This book may be used as a text-book in any high or public school, if so ordered by / a resolution of the trustees. / Toronto: / The Copp, Clark Company, Limited, / 1898.
DESCRIPTION: 18.0 × 12.0 cm   Pp [i–ii] iii [iv] v–xiii [xiv] xv–xvi, 1–196   Frontis of 'A Young Housekeeper,' 4 numbered illus of cuts of meat   [$0.50, on binding]   Cloth
CONTENTS: i tp; ii 'Entered according to Act of the Parliament of Canada, in the year one thousand eight hundred and ninety-eight, by the Copp, Clark Company, Limited, Toronto, Ontario, in the office of the Minister of Agriculture.'; iii quotations from Sir Henry Thompson, Herbert Spencer, and Ruskin; iv blank; v–viii 'Preface' signed Adelaide Hoodless, 'Eastcourt,' Hamilton, June 1898; ix–xi 'Suggestions to Teacher'; xii table of 'Composition of Food Materials'; xiii table of 'Pecuniary Economy of Food'; xiv blank; xv–xvi 'Contents'; 1–191 text in nine chapters; 192 blank; 193–6 'Appendix'
CITATIONS: Dagg, pp 138–9   DCB, Vol. 13, pp 490, 492   Driver 2003, 'Canadian Cookbooks,' p 31   MacDonald, pp 82–5, 168, 178–9   O'Neill (unpublished)
COPIES: CIHM (08944)   OH   *OONL (TX663 H6)   OTUED (640 1898 H777P OHEC Coll); Great Britain: LB (7942.g.35 destroyed)
NOTES: The first eight chapters cover 'The Relation of Food to the Body,' 'Food Classification,' 'Nutrition,' 'Food and Economy,' 'Foods Containing Protein or Nitrogenous Matter,' 'Fats and Oils,' 'Carbohydrate Foods,' and 'Fruits.' The ninth chapter comprises 'Preparing Food,' recipes beginning on p 60, 'General Hints,' 'Suggestions for Young Housekeepers,' 'Car-

ing for Invalids,' 'General Hints for School Children,' 'Suggestions for School Children's Diet,' 'Infants' Diet,' 'Planning and Serving Meals,' 'Consideration of Menus,' 'Suggestive Questions,' and 'Schedule of Lessons for Public School Classes.'

Canadian Women of Note No. 398 refers to Hoodless's recipe book, but does not specify the edition.

O86.2 1905
—Public school / household science / By / Mrs. J. Hoodless / (Hamilton) / and / Miss M.U. Watson / Home Economics Department, Ontario Agricultural College, Guelph / Toronto / The Copp, Clark Company, Limited / 1905
DESCRIPTION: 18.0 × 12.0 cm   Pp [i–ii] iii–xi [xii], 1–164   4 numbered illus on pp 154–5 of cuts of beef, veal, pork, and mutton   [$0.50, on binding]   Cloth
CONTENTS: i tp; ii 'Entered according to Act of the Parliament of Canada, in the year one thousand nine hundred and five, by the Copp, Clark Company, Limited, Toronto, Ontario, in the office of the Minister of Agriculture.'; iii–iv 'Preface'; v–xi table of contents; xii blank; 1–157 text; 158 blank; 159–64 index
CITATIONS: Dagg, pp 138–9, 306   Driver 2001, Wellington County, p 94   Ferguson/Fraser, p 232, illus col on p 11 of closed volume   MacDonald, p 83   O'Neill (unpublished)
COPIES: OTU (TDS Hoo Gerstein)   *Private collection; Great Britain: LB (07943.k.20 destroyed)
NOTES: The 'Preface' states, 'Now that special provision has been made for the training of teachers of household science, those parts of the first edition which were intended chiefly for the teacher have been omitted, and the remainder revised in conformity with the course in household science prescribed by the Department of Education for the public schools of Ontario.' The 'Introductory Chapter' comments: 'Nearly every woman is called upon, at some time, to direct the affairs of a household. Therefore, a systematic study of household operations will enable girls to obtain knowledge which will greatly conduce to the physical, mental and moral well-being of a people.' There are 126 numbered recipes in Chapters IV–XII, and 20 numbered recipes in Chapter XIV, 'Caring for Invalids.' The OTU copy is rebound.

O86.3 [entered 1905]
—Public school / household science / By / Mrs. J. Hoodless / and / Miss M.U. Watson / Home Economics Department, Ontario Agricultural College, Guelph / Toronto / The Copp, Clark Company, Limited

DESCRIPTION: 18.0 × 12.0 cm   Pp [i–ii] iii–xi [xii], 1–164   4 numbered illus on pp 154–5 of cuts of beef, veal, pork, and mutton   [\$0.50, on binding]   Cloth
CONTENTS: i tp; ii 'Entered according to Act of the Parliament of Canada, in the year one thousand nine hundred and five, by the Copp, Clark Company, Limited, Toronto, Ontario, in the office of the Minister of Agriculture.'; iii–iv 'Preface'; v–xi table of contents; xii blank; 1–157 text; 158 blank; 159–64 index
CITATIONS: Driver 2001, Wellington County, p 94
COPIES: OGU (CCC TX715.6 H666)   *OONL (TX663 H6 1905 p***)
NOTES: This edition has no date on the title-page. The year of publication is unknown.

Scott's calendar cook book 1898

See also O92.1, Scott's Calendar Cook Book 1899, and O122.1, Scott's Calendar Cook Book 1902.

O87.1   1898
1898 / 1898 / Scott's / calendar / cook / book / Published by / Stuart Scott, M.D. / chemist and druggist, / next post office, Main Street, / Newmarket. [cover-title]
COPIES: *OSHT

Southcott's almanac and cook book for 1898

O88.1   1898
Southcott's / almanac   and / cook book / for / 1898. / Published by / Harry Southcott, / 97 St. Paul Street, / St. Catharines. / [to left of 'St. Catharines.' and in a smaller typeface:] Branch store: / Niagara on the Lake. / [below both addresses:] Bring your prescriptions to us, our charges are moderate. / (Copyrighted.)
DESCRIPTION: 18.0 × 13.5 cm   Pp [1–3] 4–32   Illus of astrological symbols   Paper; stapled, and with string through top left corner for hanging
CONTENTS: Inside front face of binding 'To Our Customers' signed Harry Southcott; 1 tp; 2 publ ad; 3–27 astronomical information, recipes, monthly calendars, jokes, and publ ads; 28–top 2nd column 32 'The Common Uses of Drugs'; near top–bottom 2nd column 32 'Antidotes of Common Poisons'
COPIES: OSTC (317.1351 Sou)   *OWTU (F15102)
NOTES: The cover-title is 'Southcott's Almanac for 1898 and Cook Book No. 2.' In 'To Our Customers,' the publisher writes, 'Our almanac for this, our second season, will be found full and complete ...', while the recipes are all selected from the latest, up-to-date cook books published during the past year.' The recipes begin on p 4, under the heading 'Miscellaneous,' with Lunch Cake, Apple Custard Pie, Cookies, Roly Poly Pudding, Kisses, and Omelet.

1899

The B.Y.P.U. cook book

O89.1   1899
"Good cooking can not be made / out of bad marketing." / The / B.Y.P.U. cook book / A / selection / of / tested recipes / prepared / by the ladies / of the / Parry Sound Baptist Church / 1899 / Ireland & Bundy, printers, / Parry Sound.
DESCRIPTION: 22.5 × 15.0 cm   Pp [1–9] 10–208   Illus on p 2 of Parry Sound Baptist Church   Cloth
CONTENTS: 1 ad; 2 illus of church and 'Note'; 3 tp; 4 ad; 5 'Preface' signed the Committee; 6 ad; 7 'Index' [i.e., table of contents]; 8 ads; 9–196 recipes credited with the name of the contributor and ads; 197–9 'Miscellaneous' [information and advice about housekeeping matters, such as cleaning types of fabric or making furniture polish]; 200–3 'Medical Department'; 204 'Essences'; 205–8 'Invalid Cooking'
CITATIONS: Crawford, p D2   Simpson, p W17
COPIES: *Private collection
NOTES: The 'Note' on p 2 explains that an indebtedness of \$2,500 remains from the cost of \$6,200 to erect the church in 1889 and that 'The B.Y.P.U. of the church have undertaken to pay off this debt and the publication of this cook book is one of the enterprises adopted to raise the amount.' The 'Note' adds that 'Our Young People have also pledged themselves to raise \$240.00 yearly by subscription.' BYPU stands for Baptist Young People's Union and the 'Preface' refers to the book as 'a Baptist Young People's Union Cook Book.'

Invariably, the compilers of fund-raising cookbooks receive from their many contributors more than one recipe for a specific dish and the usual course of action is to choose one recipe and apologize in the published book for not printing all submissions. This text follows an inclusive policy: There are, for example, ten numbered recipes for Lemon Pie, eighteen numbered recipes for Fruit Cake, eight for Jelly Cake, and five for Ginger Cookies; these variations are from different contributors and specify different ingredients or amounts and various cooking methods. The recipes in this book, therefore, could serve as the basis for a study of how a dish may vary within a single community at a particular time. (Another cookbook that has multiple recipes for the same dish is O280.1, *Halton Women's Institute Cook Book.)*

The private collector's copy belonged to her grandmother, Mrs D. Johnston (Annie). Although Mrs Johnston was a Methodist, she supported the Baptists' cause – as other neighbours in the community did – by contributing recipes (for example, Lemon Pie, No. 6, p 150) and by purchasing a copy of the book. Mrs Johnston came to Parry Sound as a bride in 1895, from the Collingwood/Thornbury area.

Merrill's cook book

O90.1 nd [about 1899]
Merrill's / cloth bound / cook book / and miscellaneous hints / Price 50 cents / A practical and invaluable aid to the careful / housewife. / 1000 selected recipes all tried, tested and / pronounced perfect and economical. / Prepared by / Merrill / the reliable / druggist / Brantford, Ont. / The Corner Drug Store, opp. Big 22 [cover-title]
DESCRIPTION: 14.5 × 11.0 cm Pp 1–48 Limp cloth; stapled
CONTENTS: 1 'Do You Know Merrill'; 2 'Contents of Merrill's Cook Book'; 3–48 text and publ ads
COPIES: OWASRM *Private collection
NOTES: The Corner Drug Store was located at the corner of Market and Colborne streets (p 1). The name of Frank W. Merrill is printed on the outside back face of the binding, the same person cited in O187.1, *Merrill's Handy Cook Book*, published by the Merrill Medical Co., Toronto. The advertisements are for such products as Merrill's Baking Powder, Merrill's Wizard Lightning (it cured women's 'periodical pains,' among other ailments), and 4 T's Cough and Cold Cure.

An advertisement on p 23 refers to Merrill's Corner Drug Store as established in 1843 and 'for 56 years the popular drug store,' which indicates that the cookbook was published about 1899 [1843 + 56 years]. The advertisement for 4 T's Cough and Cold Cure, on the inside back face of the binding, says that the medicine was compounded in October 1892 and boasts, 'Nearly half a million bottles sold in five years.' Although the Cough and Cold Cure advertisement suggests publication in about 1897 [1892 + 5 years], the advertisement on p 23 is probably a better guide to the date of publication.

Our own cook book

O91.1 1899
Our own cook book. / A publication by the / ladies of / St. John's Church, / North Bay, Ont. / 1899. / "What's this?" / "Things for the cook, sir; / But I know not what." / – Romeo and Juliet / North Bay, Ont. / The North Bay Despatch Print. / 1899.
COPIES: *Private collection
NOTES: '160 recipes for 25 cents' is printed on the binding. The private collector's copy is inscribed on the title-page, 'Original owner the late Mrs George Cockerline.' For an article about this copy and a reproduction of a recipe page and an advertisement page, see Inez Murray, 'Cook Book of 1899 Vintage Tells N. Bay Story,' *North Bay Nugget*, 29 March 1973, p 10. The recipes are not credited to individuals.

In 1905, the women of the East Victoria Women's Institute appear to have copied the title-page text from O91.1 for O159.1, *Our Own Cook Book*.

Scott's calendar cook book 1899

For Scott's other annual cookbooks, see O87.1.

O92.1 1899
Scott's / 1899 / calendar / cook book / Published by / Stuart Scott, M.D. / chemist and / druggist, / next post office, Main Street, / Newmarket. [cover-title]
COPIES: *OSHT

Ziemann, Hugo, and Mrs Fanny Lemira Camp Gillette (Ann Arbor, Mich., 1828–1926, Beverly Hills, Calif.)

Gillette's recipes are included in promotional books for the shortening Cottolene: Q29.1, 266 recettes choisies, and Q30.1, 600 Selected Recipes. Also by her is Mrs Gillette's Cook Book, New York, Akron, Ohio, Chicago: Werner Co., [1899] (Bitting, p 184). See her biography in Feeding America.

O93.1 [copyright 1899]
The White House / cook book / A comprehensive cyclopedia of information / for the home / containing / cooking, toilet and household recipes, menus, dinner-giving, table / etiquette, care of the sick, health suggestions, / facts worth knowing, etc.

/ Hugo Zieman [*sic*] / Steward of the White House / and Mrs. F.L. Gillette / Toronto / The Copp Clark Co., Limited

DESCRIPTION: 24.0 × 18.0 cm   Pp [1–2], [i–ii] iii–vi, 7–588 [last leaf, 589–90, mostly lacking in OGU copy]   17 pls incl frontis; illus of cuts of meat, carving meat and fish, and arrangement of glasses on table   Cloth, with image on front, in a circular frame, of the White House

CONTENTS: 1 tp; 2 'Copyright, 1887, by F.L. Gillette. Copyright, 1894, by the Werner Company. Copyright, 1899, by the Werner Company. Made by the Werner Company Akron, Ohio'; i author's dedication 'To the wives of our presidents, ...'; ii stag's(?) head; iii–iv 'Publisher's Preface'; v–vi table of contents; 7–575 text; 576–90 index

CITATIONS: Abrahamson, p 62

COPIES: AMHM   *OGU (UA s050 b20)   ONBNBM

NOTES: The 'Publisher's Preface' gives a brief biography of the co-author, whose name is incorrectly spelled Zieman on the title-page. There is a portrait of Ziemann included in the plate opposite p 38.

The ONBNBM copy has a faintly printed folio '(i)' on the dedication page that may not have registered on the OGU copy. All editions of *The White House Cook Book* are printed on poor-quality paper, which has become brittle with age.

The White House Cook Book was the source for the American recipes in A34.1, *Ukrains'ko-angliiskyi kukhar*, by Michael M. Belegai. Part of the text of M128.1, *Ukrainian-English Cook Book*, is also translated from *The White House Cook Book.*

O93.2   nd [about 1900–5]

—The / premier / cook book / Toronto / The Copp Clark Co., Limited

DESCRIPTION: 21.0 × 15.0 cm   Pp [i–iv], [1] 2–440   Illus of cuts of meat and carving   Cloth, with image on front of a male cook sitting on a flour barrel and holding a frying pan in one hand, spoon in the other

CONTENTS: i tp; ii blank; iii table of contents; iv blank; 1–428 text; 429–40 index

COPIES: CIHM (78893)   OONL (TX715.6 P74 1910z)   *Private collection

NOTES: This is a retitled edition of *The White House Cook Book*. Its American origins are disguised by the maple leaves on the binding (three leaves on the flour barrel on the front face, and one on the spine). A copy of *The Premier Cook Book* in a bookseller's stock was reported to have a 'presentation book plate from Toronto Daily World [i.e., the newspaper].'

O93.3   nd [about 1900–5]

—The / Union Life / cook book / Printed and published for / the Union Life Assurance Co. / Toronto / Copies of this book may be obtained upon application and the payment of $1.00 / (in stamps, express or money order). / Postage 14c extra.

DESCRIPTION: 21.0 × 15.0 cm   Pp [i–iv], [1] 2–440   Illus of cuts of meat and carving   Cloth, with image on front of a male cook sitting on a flour barrel and holding a frying pan in one hand, spoon in the other

CONTENTS: i tp; ii blank; iii table of contents; iv blank; 1–428 text; 429–40 index

COPIES: QMM (RBD ckbk 2076)   *Private collection

NOTES: This is a retitled edition of *The White House Cook Book*. Like the binding of O93.2, there are three maple leaves on the flour barrel.

AMERICAN EDITIONS: Although no Canadian places of publication appear in the many editions cited here, they were widely sold in Canada and sometimes given away for free (see, for example, the 1908 edition of *The Presidential Cook Book*, below). All the following editions titled *The White House Cook Book* were found in Canadian collections: Chicago, Philadelphia, and Stockton, Calif.: L.P. Miller and Co., [copyright 1887 by F.L. Gillette and copyright 1890 by R.S. Peale] (Private collection); Chicago, Akron, Ohio, and New York: Saalfield Publishing Co., [copyright 1900] (BVAU, OTBPM; United States: DLC); New York, Akron, Ohio, and Chicago: Saalfield Publishing Co., [1902] (Private collection); New York, Akron, Ohio, and Chicago: Saalfield Publishing Co., 1904 (MVPHM photocopy); New York, Akron, Ohio, and Chicago: Saalfield Publishing Co., 1905 (BKM; United States: DLC); New York, Akron, Ohio, and Chicago: Saalfield Publishing Co., 1906 (BDEM); New York, Akron, Ohio, and Chicago: Saalfield Publishing Co., 1907 (Private collection); New York, Akron, Ohio, and Chicago: Saalfield Publishing Co., 1910 (BKOM, OGU); New York, Akron, Ohio, and Chicago: Saalfield Publishing Co., 1911 (Private collection); Akron, Ohio, and Chicago: Saalfield Publishing Co., 1912 (Private collection; Great Britain: LB); New York, Akron, Ohio, and Chicago: Saalfield Publishing Co., 1913 (Private collection); New York, Akron, Ohio, and Chicago: Saalfield Publishing Co., 1916 (Private collection); New York, Akron, Ohio, and Chicago: Saalfield Publishing Co., 1922 (Private collection); revised by Mrs Mary E. Dague, Akron, Ohio: Saalfield Publishing Co., 1928 (OFERWM).

The following editions of *The White House Cook*

Book are cited in American sources or located in American institutions: New York: Gillette Publishing Co., 1887 (United States: DLC); Chicago: R.S. Peale and Co., 1887 (United States: DLC); Chicago: L.P. Miller and Co., 1889 (Bitting, p 184; WaiteCat 5, No. 79); Chicago: Werner Co., [copyright 1890] (United States: InU); Chicago: Werner Co., [copyright 1894] (United States: InU); 'special edition with colored plates sold by subscription only,' Chicago and Philadelphia: Monarch Book Co., [copyright 1894] (United States: InU); Chicago: Werner Co., 1897 (Barile, p 214); New York, Akron, Ohio, and Chicago: Saalfield Publishing Co., 1903 (United States: InU); New York, Akron, Ohio, [etc.]: Saalfield Publishing Co., 1915 (United States: DLC); revised by Mrs Mary E. Dague, Akron, Ohio: Saalfield Publishing Co., 1925 [c1924] (United States: DLC). The first German-language edition was *Das 'Weisse Haus' Kochbuch*, Chicago: R.S. Peale Co., 1891 (United States: InU); another German-language ed., 1899 (Dickinson, p 183).

More recent editions are: *The White House Cookbook: A Re-creation of a Famous American Cookbook ... edited and new material supplied by Frances R. Grossman*, New York: D. McKay Co., [1976] (United States: DLC); *The Original White House Cookbook*, Old Greenwich, Conn.: Devin Adair, c1983 (United States: DLC, FTaSU); *White House Cookbook ... with Healthy Updates by Patti Bazel Geil and Tami Ross*, rev. and updated centennial ed., Minneapolis: Chronimed Pub., c1996 (United States: DLC).

The White House Cook Book was condensed and sold at a lower price, under the title *The Presidential Cook Book Adapted from The White House Cook Book*. All the following editions were found in Canadian collections: Akron, Ohio, and Chicago: Saalfield Publishing Co., 1906 (ASPMHC); Akron, Ohio, New York, and Chicago: Saalfield Publishing Co., 1908 (OFERWM, OGM, OGU, and Private collection); Saalfield, 1909 (Private collection). The OFERWM copy of the 1908 edition is inscribed by an Ontario resident, 'Mrs. R.N. Jennings // Palmerston.' The OGM copy also belonged to Ontario residents; it is inscribed, on the back endpaper, 'Mrs. Charles Deruchie // Lancaster Ont. // [Leolu?] Deruchie // Lancaster Ont Dec.,' and in a later hand, 'Miss Lizzie D[?] // Monckland Ont.' The private collector's copy of the 1908 edition has a notice pasted to the front endpaper that reads, 'This cook book is presented with the compliments of the Toronto Daily World // Canada's leading and Toronto's favorite morning newspaper ...' The private collector's copy of the 1909 edition belonged originally to her grandmother, who moved west with her husband in about 1911 and made her home in various Alberta towns – Empress, Carbon, and Edson.

The following edition of *The Presidential Cook Book* is in an American location: Chicago, New York: Werner Co., [c1895] (United States: DLC). Also related is *The Capitol Cook Book, Adapted from the White House Cook Book*, Chicago, New York: Werner Co., [c1896] (United States: DLC).

1899–1903

Coltsfoote cook book and fortune teller

For another cookbook by the same company, see O62.1, Slocum's Cook Book.

O94.1   nd [about 1899–1903]
Coltsfoote / cook book / and fortune teller / Amusement and instruction for all // See that you get coupon on / page 21, worth / 10 cents / to you or anyone else // This valuable booklet is a free gift to all / Canadian homes by / the T.A. Slocum Chemical Co. / of Toronto / publishers // W.S. Johnston & Co., printers, 34 Adelaide Street West, Toronto [cover-title]
COPIES: *OONL (TX652.7 C64 1900z p***)
NOTES: The booklet has 22 pp. The address in the book for the T.A. Slocum Chemical Co. is 179 King Street West. Toronto city directories list the T.A. Slocum Chemical Company of Toronto from 1896 to 1903 (before 1896, the company name is T.A. Slocum and Co.; from 1904, it is Dr T.A. Slocum Ltd). In this period, the company was at 186 Adelaide Street West up to 1898; from 1899 it was at 179 King Street West. The *Coltsfoote Cook Book and Fortune Teller* was, therefore, published about 1899–1903. W.S. Johnston and Co. was active from 1892, and at 34 Adelaide Street West from 1896 to 1907 (Hulse, p 137).

1900

The Beaver Mills cook book

For a history of the T.H. Taylor Co., see Victor Lauriston, A Century of Milling 1848–1948: The Story of the T.H. Taylor Company Limited, Chatham, Ontario, no place, nd (copies at OCHA and OONL). This history does not cite the cookbook. See also articles about the company in issues of the Chatham Daily Planet:

30 October 1901; 29 November 1902; 14 May 1903; and 15 May 1903. The original Beaver Mill was erected in Chatham, in 1872, and enlarged in 1883 to mill 150 barrels in 24 hours; the smaller Daisy Mill was leased until its purchase in 1908. The founder of the business, Thomas Hulme Taylor, died on 3 November 1891, leaving his interest in the business to his sons Walter Hulme Taylor (called Jim) and William James Taylor (called Bill). In spring 1892 the business was incorporated. The decision to build a new, modern mill was made in 1900. The new mill building was completed by November 1902; the machinery was installed over the winter, and the mill formally opened on 14 May 1903.

O95.1 nd [about 1900]

The / Beaver Mills / cook book / Published by / the T.H. Taylor Co'y, Ltd. / Props. / of the Beaver and Daisy mills / capacity, 500 bbls per day / Chatham, Ont. [cover-title]

DESCRIPTION: 16.0 × 15.0 cm   Pp [1–3] 4–24   Paper; stapled

CONTENTS: 1 cover-title; 2 blank; 3–top 4 'Muffins, Biscuits, etc.'; mid 4–mid 7 'Puddings and Pastry'; mid 7–mid 9 'Custards and Jellies'; mid 9–16 'Cakes and Cookies'; 17–mid 18 'Meats and Fish'; bottom 18–19 'Made Dishes'; top–mid 20 'Soups'; mid 20–mid 21 'Salads'; mid 21–23 'Pickles and Sauces'; 24 'Wines'

COPIES: *Bookseller's stock

NOTES: This edition was published no earlier than spring 1892, when the business was incorporated, and before construction of the new mill, opened in 1903 (note that the total capacity of the Beaver and Daisy mills, quoted in the cover-title, is only 500 barrels; the *Chatham Daily Planet* of 30 October 1901 and 29 November 1902 cite a capacity of 400 barrels for the Beaver Mill). From appearances, this edition was likely published about 1900.

The recipes are credited with the name of the contributor and include some from the Taylor family: Mrs T.H. Taylor (i.e., Maria Lent Taylor, née Bogart, wife of the company's founder); Mrs W.J. Taylor (wife of William James Taylor); Mrs Fred Stone, the founder's daughter; Mrs McMullen, Evanston, Ill., possibly the founder's daughter, Mrs David S. McMullen, or a relation; and Mrs Stephenson, possibly the founder's daughter, Mrs E.F. Stephenson, or a relation. (T.H. Taylor's children are listed in the entry for Walter Hulme Taylor in *National Encyclopedia of Canadian Biography*, Toronto: Dominion Publishing Co., 1937, p 242.)

O95.2 nd [1902]

—The / Beaver Mills / cook book / Published by / the T.H. Taylor Co., Limited. / Chatham, Ont. [cover-title]

DESCRIPTION: 14.5 × 14.5 cm   Pp [1] 2–24   Paper, with a bird's-eye view on front of Beaver Mills (two buildings), Chatham Woolen Mills, and Daisy Mills; stapled

CONTENTS: 1 publ ad listing 'Our Specialties in Mixed or Whole Car Lots'; 2 'To Our Customers // Erecting a Modern Mill' quoted from *Canadian Grocer*; 3–mid 4 'Muffins, Biscuits and Bread'; mid–bottom 4 'Soups'; 5–mid 6 'Meats and Fish'; mid 6–top 8 'Salads'; mid 8–top 12 'Puddings and Pastry'; mid 12–19 'Cakes and Cookies'; top–near bottom 20 'Candies'; bottom 20–top 22 'Sherbets, Fruit Salads and Marmalades'; mid 22–top 24 'Pickles and Sauces'; mid 24 'Miscellaneous'; bottom 24 'Wines and Cordials'

COPIES: *Private collection

NOTES: The *Canadian Grocer* article, reprinted on p 2, is not dated, but it is in the 30 May 1902 issue (Vol. 16, No. 22, Export Number, p 36). It reports the company's development as follows: 'From a 75-barrel mill in 1885 to a 1,000-barrel, most modern milling plant in 1902, is the satisfactory record of the T.H. Taylor Co., Limited, of Chatham, Ont.'; the text goes on to note that the company is in the process of building a new mill that will have a capacity of 1,000 barrels per day. This edition, therefore, appeared after the *Canadian Grocer* article in May and before the end of 1902, when the new mill building was completed.

The first recipes on p 3 are Tea Biscuits from Mrs Geo. A. Gray (i.e., wife of a member of the office staff, who in 1911 was named a company director), Biscuits from A.M., Lemon Biscuits from Miss Smith, and Rolls. Most recipes are credited with the name of the contributor. 'London Ptg. & Litho. Co.' is printed on the outside back face of the binding. An advertisement opposite p 1 gives the company's telephone number: Telephone 1 (the first number for Chatham going to the town's major industry).

O95.3 nd [about 1903]

—The / Beaver Mills / cook book / Published by / the T.H. Taylor Co., Limited, / Chatham, Ont. [cover-title]

DESCRIPTION: 14.5 × 14.5 cm   Pp 1–48   Illus of views of mill interior and of equipment   Paper, with image on front of the company's flour mill; stapled

CONTENTS: 1–9 'Where "Beaver" Flour Is Made // The Mammoth New Mill of the T.H. Taylor Company, Chatham ...'; 10 publ ad; 11–46 recipes, most credited with the name of the contributor; 47–8 'Hints to Housewives' and at bottom p 48, 'London Printing & Litho. Co.'

COPIES: *Private collection

NOTES: The heading on p 1 citing 'the mammoth new mill' and the reference on p 3 to 'the new mill, which was built within the year, ...' suggest that this edition was published not long after O95.2 (likely about 1903, the year the mill opened). On p 9 the company's history is described thus: 'The firm is one of the oldest in the milling business in Canada, the founder, Mr. T.H. Taylor, having established the business in 1845. The present company was incorporated in 1892, ...' The first recipes on p 11 are Tea Biscuits from Mrs Geo. A. Gray, Biscuits from A.M., Lemon Biscuits from Miss Smith, and Rolls.

O95.4 nd [about 1909]
—Beaver Mills cook book / The T.H. Taylor Co., Limited, / Chatham, Ont. / "Busy as a beaver, with Beaver Flour." [cover-title]

DESCRIPTION: 14.5 × 14.5 cm Pp 1–48 Illus of views of mill interior and of equipment Paper, with image on front of a woman in a pink dress and white apron, standing behind a table and holding up a loaf of bread in her left hand, a barrel of Beaver Flour standing on the floor, beside the table, on her right side; stapled

CONTENTS: 1–9 'Where "Beaver" Flour Is Made // The Mammoth New Mill of the T.H. Taylor Company, Chatham ...'; 10 publ ad; 11–mid 46 recipes, most credited with the name of the contributor; mid 46–48 'Hints to Housewives'

COPIES: *Private collection

NOTES: Like O95.3, there is a reference on p 3 to 'the new mill ... built within the year'; unlike that edition, the definite article is dropped from the book's title and 'Hints to Housewives' begins on p 46. No printer is named anywhere in the volume; however, company records (in a private collection) reveal that the binding came from the presses of the *Chatham Daily Planet* newspaper in February 1909. The binding image is reproduced several times on a sheet in the private collection. The sheet is accompanied by a docket from the *Planet,* identifying T.H. Taylor Co. Ltd as the customer and dated 16 September 1908; the number supplied is noted as '50,000 covers' but changed to '51,000'; regarding colours, the docket states: 'Six or five if it will do. Submit sketch. No buildings to be shown.'; after 'Job completed' is the date 'Feby 2'; after 'Shipped,' 'Feby 2' [i.e., 1909].

The same private collector also has unsigned art-

work, probably for a cover that was never used. It shows a woman in a wheat field, holding a scythe and a sheaf of wheat. O95.5 and O95.6 feature a wheat-field scene, but not this image.

O95.5 nd [1925 or before]
—Beaver Mills / cook book / The T.H. Taylor Co., Limited / Chatham, Ont. [cover-title]

DESCRIPTION: 15.0 × 14.5 cm Pp 1–48 Paper, with a harvesting scene printed across front and back (on front, two men loading wheat onto a wagon pulled by two horses, and on back, the wheat is shown being cut); the image of a red ribbon runs horizontally in a band across the harvesting scene; stapled

CONTENTS: 1–4 'Where "Beaver" Flour Is Made // The Mammoth New Mill of the T.H. Taylor Company, Chatham – ...'; 5 publ ad; 6–43 recipes credited with the name of the contributor; 44–8 'Hints to Housewives'

COPIES: *Private collection

NOTES: There are no illustrations in this edition. The private collector's copy is inscribed by her aunt, Phyllis Dauphinee, on the outside back face of the binding, 'Earle gave me this book Nov 1925'; therefore, this edition was published in 1925 or before. No printer's name was found in this copy.

O95.6 nd
—Beaver Mills / cook book / The T.H. Taylor Co., Limited / Chatham, Ont. [cover-title]

DESCRIPTION: Pp 1–48 Illus of views of mill interior and of equipment Paper, with a harvesting scene printed across front and back (on front, two men loading wheat onto a wagon pulled by two horses, and on back, the wheat is shown being cut); the image of a ribbon runs horizontally in a band across the harvesting scene; stapled

CONTENTS: 1–9 'Where "Beaver" Flour Is Made // The Mammoth New Mill of the T.H. Taylor Company, Chatham – ...'; 10 publ ad; 11–mid 44 recipes; mid 44–8 'Miscellaneous'

COPIES: OCHA OCHAK OGU (CCC TX715.6 T49) *Private collection

NOTES: This edition has the same binding design as O95.5, but unlike that edition, there are illustrations and the recipes start on p 11 (not p 6). The recipes on p 11, which are not credited, are for Scones, Brown Bread, Gems, Hot Tea Biscuit, Cream Waffles, Buttermilk Waffles, Popovers, and Whole Wheat Bread (i.e., not the same recipes as O95.2 and O95.3). Whereas the introductory text in O95.3 describes the new mill as 'built within the year' (p 3), here it is described as 'very recently built' (p 1). The printer's name on the outside back face of the binding is difficult to decipher, but it is probably 'Duncan Litho Co Hamilton.' (A private collector, who owns some of the T.H. Taylor Co. records, has a form with the name of the Duncan Lithography Co. and the date 13 October 1908; the form is not identified with any edition of the cookbook, but it may be connected to O95.6.)

Dr King's guide to health, household instructor and family prize cook book 1900

See O117.1, O143.1, O170.1, and O213.1, for the 1902, 1904, 1906, and 1909 issues. Allen, p 104, cites the title Dr King's Guide to Health Cook Book for 1901, 1908, and 1910; Allen records no place of publication, but these years were probably also published in both Chicago and Windsor.

O96.1 [1900]
Dr. King's / Price 10 cents / guide to health / household / instructor / and / family / prize / cook book / H.E. Bucklen & Co. / Chicago, Ill. / 275 276 277 Michigan Ave. / Windsor, Can. / 53 54 Sandwich St West. [cover-title]
DESCRIPTION: 23.0 × 17.0 cm Pp [1] 2–32 Paper, with image on front of a building; stapled
CONTENTS: 1 calendars for 1900 and 1901; 1st column 2 'Introduction'; 2nd column 2–32 information about a variety of topics, including household matters, recipes on pp 24–31, publ ads, and testimonials
COPIES: *OTUTF (uncat patent medicine)
NOTES: The recipes begin on p 24, with Good Bread, Biscuit, Buns, and Waffles. The publisher's advertisements are for Electric Bitters, Bucklen's Arnica Salve, Dr King's New Discovery for Consumption, Coughs and Colds, and Dr King's Life Pills, all made by H.E. Bucklen and Co. This book appears in a colour photograph of a selection of almanacs from the Hannah Institute's History of Medicine Collection at OTUTF (*Preserving the Past, Preparing for the Future: The University of Toronto Libraries*, [1999], p 15).

Epworth League cook book

O97.1 1900
Epworth / League / cook book / A book of / tested family recipes / Compiled by / the ladies of Huntsville and vicinity. / Huntsville: / Printed at the office of the Forester, Main Street. / 1900.
DESCRIPTION: 22.0 × 15.0 cm Pp [1–5] 6–31 Paper; stapled

CONTENTS: 1 tp; 2 blank; 3 'Contents'; 4 blank; 5–31 recipes credited with the name of the contributor (from towns such as Novar and Gravenhurst, as well as Huntsville) and ads
COPIES: *Private collection
NOTES: The heading on p 5 is 'Epworth League Recipe Book // Tested Family Recipes.' A notice about the book in *Canadian Epworth Era* (April 1900), p 119, states: 'The Huntsville Forester [i.e., the local newspaper] tells of "something new under the sun" as follows: "We have published and issued from our office this week the first edition of the 'Epworth League Cook Book,' containing a choice collection of family recipes compiled by the ladies of Huntsville and vicinity. It is printed on choice coated paper, contains some full page advertisements and is sold at the nominal sum of 25c. Parties desirous of obtaining a copy, may do so either at this office or from the Epworth League executive."' It is interesting to note that O97.1 and O98.1, published in the same year and in towns only about 50 km apart, both use the subtitle 'A book of tested family recipes.'

Gravenhurst ladies' cook book

Methodist Church is now called Trinity United Church. For a later cookbook by the same congregation, see O925.1, The Old Home Cook Book.

O98.1 nd [about 1900]
Gravenhurst / ladies' / cook / book / A book of / tested family recipes / Compiled by / the ladies of Methodist Church, assisted by / ladies of the town.
DESCRIPTION: 22.0 × 15.0 cm Pp [5–7] 8–83 Illus of Gravenhurst subjects: on p 39, Gravenhurst Public School, below which is the Toronto printer's name, 'JL Jones Eng Co'; on p 52, a photograph of a boat; on p 56, 'Muskoka Christmas'; on p 67, Gravenhurst Sanitorium [*sic*] for Consumptives Card, with architectural drawing on front of Gravenhurst High School; stapled
CONTENTS: 5 tp; 6 blank; 7 'Introduction' signed R. Kimber Johns; 8 ad; 9–81 recipes credited with the name of the contributor and ads; 82 ad; 83 'Index' [i.e., table of contents]
COPIES: *OGU (CCC TX715.6 G7347)
NOTES: The 'Introduction,' by R. Kimber Johns, Gravenhurst's first clerk when the town incorporated in 1878, tells the history of Gravenhurst. The cookbook was published in about 1900: There is an advertisement on p 56 for the Muskoka Navigation Co., which is dated Gravenhurst, 1900; and an advertise-

ment on p 58, for John's Agency, Gravenhurst, 'Established 1873' and with 'experience of over a quarter of a century.'

The drawing of Gravenhurst High School on the binding is signed, lower right, 'C. [i.e., Charles] J. Gibson Architect [1895?].' Land for the school was purchased in 1895 and the school opened in 1896. Gibson (1862–1935) was a well-known Toronto architect, who worked in the Romanesque style (he also designed St John's Church Norway illustrated on the binding of O649.1, *The St John's Church Norway Cook Book*). It is odd to find a drawing of a high school on a cookbook compiled by a church group, but the building was the first purpose-built high school to be constructed in Muskoka, and the residents were proud of it. The printer of the cookbook, 'Gravenhurst "Banner" Print,' is on the binding, below the drawing. The front and back leaves of the OGU copy are loose, but the copy is probably complete.

Hints on health and tested receipts for plain cooking

See also O321.1, another cookbook advertising Vinol.

O99.1   nd [about 1900]
Hints on health / and / tested receipts for / plain cooking / Presented with the compliments of / J.S. Armitage, druggist / Paris, Ont. [cover-title]
DESCRIPTION: 18.5 × 12.5 cm   Pp 1–23 [24]   Paper, with image on front, in circular frame, of the head-and-shoulders of an old woman; stapled
CONTENTS: Inside front face of binding 'Introduction' and 'Three Reasons Why Vinol Is by Far the Best Strengthening Tonic'; 1, 3, 5 'Bread Making'; 7, 9 'Pies'; 11, 13 'Puddings'; 15, 17 'Hints on Cake Making'; 19, 21 'Feeding the Sick'; all even-numbered pages and 23 publ ads for Vinol and Vinlax
COPIES: *Private collection
NOTES: The text is the same as O99.3, published by Jury and Lovell, druggists, Bowmanville, Ontario. The testimonials bear American addresses. The publisher's advertisement on p 23 for Vinol is in French; the one on p 24, also for Vinol, is in German. The various editions were likely published about the same time.

O99.2   nd [about 1900]
—Hints on health / and / tested receipts for / plain cooking / Presented with the compliments of / H.C. Dunlop, druggist / Goderich, Ontario [cover-title]

DESCRIPTION: 18.0 × 13.0 cm   Pp 1–23 [24]   Paper, with image on front, in circular frame, of the head-and-shoulders of an old woman; stapled
CONTENTS: Inside front face of binding 'Introduction' and 'Three Reasons Why Vinol Is by Far the Best Strengthening Tonic'; 1, 3, 5 'Bread Making'; 7, 9 'Pie Making'; 11, 13 'Puddings'; 15, 17 'Hints on Cake Making'; 19, 21 'Feeding the Sick'; all even-numbered pages and 23 publ ads for Vinol and Vinlax
COPIES: *OTUTF (uncat patent medicine)
NOTES: The text is the same as O99.3. The testimonials bear American addresses. The publisher's advertisement on p 23 for Vinol is in French; the one on p 24, also for Vinol, is in German.

O99.3   nd [about 1900]
—Hints on health / and / tested receipts for / plain cooking / Presented with the compliments of / Jury & Lovell, druggists / Bowmanville, Ont. [cover-title]
DESCRIPTION: 18.5 × 12.5 cm   Pp 1–24   Paper, with image on front, in circular frame, of the head-and-shoulders of an old woman; stapled
CONTENTS: Inside front face of binding 'Introduction' and 'Three Reasons Why Vinol Is by Far the Best Strengthening Tonic'; 1, 3, 5 'Bread Making'; 7, 9 'Pies'; 11, 13 'Puddings'; 15, 17 'Hints on Cake Making'; 19, 21 'Feeding the Sick'; all even-numbered pages and 23 publ ads for Vinol and Vinlax
COPIES: CIHM (01605)   *OTUTF (uncat patent medicine)
NOTES: The testimonials bear American addresses and the 'Introduction' is directed at American readers: 'One of the objects of this little book is to place in every American home tested recipes for plain cooking which will materially contribute to the health of the family ... The recipes contained herein are the tested recipes of practical New England housekeepers ...' The publisher's advertisement on p 23 for Vinol is in French; the one on p 24, also for Vinol, is in German. The following is stamped on the front face of the binding, in purple ink: 'When you get your eyes tested at Jury & Lovell's it is done properly.'

O99.4   nd [about 1900]
—Hints on health / and / tested receipts for / plain cooking / Presented with the compliments of / Taylor's Drug Store / Bridgewater N.S. [cover-title]
COPIES: *Private collection

Nelson, Harriet Schuyler

For other books in this American series, see O111.1, 365 Breakfast Dishes; O125.1, 365 Luncheon Dishes; and O139.1, 365 Dinner Dishes. There were more titles in the series published in the United States, but only four have been identified as published by Musson Book Co. in Toronto. In Britain, Dean and Son Ltd picked up more of the American titles, and expanded the series by adding new, British works (see Driver, pp 614–15).

O100.1 [copyright 1900]
365 / desserts / a dessert for every day in the year / selected from / Marion Harland, Mrs. Lincoln / Good Housekeeping, Table Talk / and others / Toronto / Musson Book Co. / Limited
DESCRIPTION: Tp still-life of an open book, utensils, and ingredients
COPIES: *OKELWM
NOTES: The author is not identified in the book. The attribution is DLC's.

AMERICAN EDITIONS: Philadelphia: George W. Jacobs and Co., [1900] (United States: DLC).

BRITISH EDITIONS: London: Dent and Son Ltd, nd [1906] (Great Britain: LoEN, OB); London: Dean and Son Ltd, nd (Great Britain: LB, OPo(F)).

Recipes

See also O287.1, Recipes, a 1912 cookbook from the same church. The imposing Broadway Tabernacle (Methodist) church, completed in 1889 to the design of architect E.J. Lennox and now demolished, stood at the corner of College Street and Spadina Avenue. It could hold 2,000 worshippers and was 'one of the chief architectural ornaments in the north-west portion of Toronto' (Robertson's Landmarks of Toronto, Fourth Series, Toronto: J. Ross Robertson, 1904, pp 384–7).

O101.1 1900
Recipes / compiled and arranged / by the / Ladies' Aid Society / of / Broadway Tabernacle / Toronto / "Mens sana in corpore sano" / Toronto: / The Endeavor Herald Company / 1900
DESCRIPTION: 19.5 × 13.5 cm   Pp [1–5] 6–88   Paper; bound by a cord through three punched holes
CONTENTS: 1 quotation: '"Let me cook the meals of my country, and I care not who makes her laws."'; 2 dedication to 'the "Lords of Creation," dear to us as

fathers, brothers, husbands, or sons, keen critics always of the culinary art ...'; 3 tp; 4 quotation: '"She looketh well to the ways of her household."'; 5–80 recipes credited with the name of the contributor; 81–mid 82 'Table Hints'; mid 82–84 'Suggested Menus,' recipes for the luncheon menu, and 'Note – The luncheon menu and recipes were kindly furnished by Mrs. George McBeth [sic], of the Y.W.C.G. School of Domestic Science.'; 85 ad; 86 'Miscellaneous Rules'; 87–8 ads
COPIES: *Private collection
NOTES: Mrs George Macbeth, who contributed the luncheon menu and recipes, was the compiler of O180.1, Invalid Cookery. At the time of that book's publication, in 1907, she was chief dietitian at Toronto's Hospital for Sick Children.

Royal Victoria cook book

See also O260.1, The Coronation Cook Book, another text by the hospital's women's group.

O102.1 1900
Royal Victoria / cook book. / Compiled by / the Woman's Auxiliary / to / Royal Victoria / Hospital. / "We may live without friends, we may live without books, / But civilized man cannot live without cooks; / He may live without books – what is knowledge but grieving? / He may live without hope – what is hope but deceiving? / He may live without love – what is passion but pining? / But where is the man that live without dining?" / Barrie, / 1900. / S. Wesley, printer.
DESCRIPTION: 16.0 × 12.0 cm   Pp [3–9] 10–198 [199–204], [i–ii]   Fp illus on p 4 of 'Proposed New Hospital'   Cloth
CONTENTS: 3 tp; 4 fp illus; 5 preface; 6 ad; 7 table of contents; 8 ads; 9–204 text, mainly recipes credited with the name of the contributor; i–ii ads
CITATIONS: Berton, pp 56, 58, 66, 68, 114
COPIES: *OGU (UA s043 b12)   OMIHURM (2 copies) OMSA   OONL (TX715 R73)   OTMCL (641.59713 R598)
NOTES: The preface refers to the concept of the fundraising cookbook: '... the Woman's Auxiliary of the R.V. Hospital appeal to the generosity of a heretofore liberal people ... The scheme of a cook book is not a new one. Many other towns have adopted this way, and have been successful; ...'

The two copies at OMIHURM are in poor condition; one lacks its title-page. Ferguson/Fraser, p 232, cite *Royal Victoria Hospital W.A. Cook Book*, Barrie, Ont.: 1901. The year cited may be a typographical error for 1900.

Two hundred and fifty recipes

O103.1   1900
Two hundred and fifty / recipes. / Specially selected and recommended by / the Ladies / of / Grace Church / Sewing Circle. / Brantford: / Donovan & Henwood. / 1900.
DESCRIPTION: 18.0 × 12.0 cm   Pp [1–3] 4–86, [i–viii] Cloth
CONTENTS: 1 tp; 2 'The Modelling of a Kitchen Mechanic'; 3–82 recipes; 83–6 index; i–viii ads and at bottom p viii, 'Donovan & Henwood, publishers. The Courier Press, Brantford. 1900.'
COPIES: *OGU (UA s043 b23)   OTUTF (B-12 7864)
NOTES: '"Our best" An indispensible [*sic*] cook book ... Easter 1900.' is printed on the binding.

1900–1

Tried and true recipes

O104.1   nd [about 1900–1]
Tried and true / recipes / Arranged by the Young Women's / Guild of St. Andrew's Church, / Kingston. / "We may live without poetry, music or art; / We may live without conscience and live without / heart; / We may live without friends, we may live without / books, / But the civilized man cannot live without cooks." / Owen Meredith.
DESCRIPTION: 18.5 × 13.0 cm   Pp [1–8] 9–83 [84], [i–viii]   Paper-covered boards, with small floral decoration on front; stapled
CONTENTS: 1–5 ads; 6 blank; 7 tp; 8–84 recipes credited with the name or initials of the contributor; i–viii ads
CITATIONS: Likely Duncan, p 130
COPIES: *Private collection
NOTES: 'Invalid Cookery' is on pp 80–3; 'Sundries,' on p 84. An advertisement on p 4 for R. Uglow and Co., booksellers and stationers, which describes the company as 'removed to No. 141 Princess Street,' is evidence that the cookbook was published about 1900–1: Foster's Kingston directory for the period July 1900–July 1901 lists R. Uglow and Co. at 86 Princess Street; the directory for the period July 1901–July 1902 lists it at the new address of 141 Princess.

O104.2   2nd ed., nd
—Tried and true / recipes / Second edition / Arranged by the Young / Women's Guild of St. / Andrew's Church, / Kingston. / "We may live without poetry, music or art; / We may live without conscience and live without heart; / We may live without friends, we may live without books, / But the civilized man cannot live without cooks." / Owen Meredith.
DESCRIPTION: 21.0 × 14.5 cm   Pp [1–5] 6–128 [129–40]   Paper-covered boards and cloth spine, with image on front of St Andrew's Church; stapled
CONTENTS: 1–4 ads; 5 tp; 6–115 recipes credited with the name of the contributor and ads; 116 blank; 117–28 'Appendix' with sections for 'Potting' [of fish, meat, and poultry], 'Eggs,' and 'Bills of Fare'; 129–34 ads; 135–9 blank; 140 'Index' [i.e., table of contents]
CITATIONS: Crawford, p D1, illus col
COPIES: *Private collection
NOTES: At the head of each chapter is the name of the woman who arranged that chapter. The printer is named in an advertisement on p 130: 'This book is a product of our press // The British Whig // Kingston, Canada.'; and also on the outside back face of the binding: 'Press of British Whig // Kingston, Ont.'

1900–5

Coate's tested recipes

O105.1   nd [about 1900–5]
Coate's / tested / recipes / A / practical / everyday / cook book / Published at / Medical Hall, / W.D. Coate, / Rat Portage, Ontario. / (Copyrighted). [cover-title]
COPIES: *OKELWM
NOTES: Rat Portage was renamed Kenora in 1905. See also B4.1 and B4.2, both called *Hall's Tested Recipes* and with the same subtitle as *Coate's Tested Recipes*.

Cook book

O106.1   nd [about 1900–5]
Cook book / Containing recipes for a / number of excellent dishes / which can be made best with / this food chopper.
DESCRIPTION: 14.0 × 11.0 cm   Pp [1–21]   Illus on p 2 of numbered food-chopper parts, and on p 21 of sausage stuffer   Paper, with image on front of a food chopper and five individual cutters suspended in space; stapled

CONTENTS: 1 tp; 2 information about, and illustrations of, food chopper; 3–19 seventy-one numbered recipes; 20 'Unbreakable Steel Cutters'; 21 'Directions' and 'Sausage Stuffer'
COPIES: CIHM (95398) *Private collection
NOTES: The cover-title is 'Food Chopper Cook Book.' No food-chopper manufacturer is named and no publisher or place of publication is cited; however, there is space on the title-page possibly meant for a retailer's name-stamp. The caption under the illustration on p 2 is general: 'A modern household utensil that is needed in every kitchen. Carefully made, nicely tinned, self-cleaning, self-sharpening. It has steel cutters and is made in four sizes as described below: ...'

O106.2 nd
—Cook book / Containing recipes for a / number of excellent dishes / which can be made best with / this food chopper.
DESCRIPTION: 15.0 × 11.5 cm   Pp [1–21]   Illus on p 2 of numbered food-chopper parts, and on p 21 of sausage stuffer   Paper, with image on front of a food-chopper, clamped to the edge of a table; stapled
CONTENTS: 1 tp; 2 information about, and illustrations of, food chopper; 3–19 seventy-one numbered recipes; 20 'Description // Cutter Plates ... Use of Plates'; 21 'Directions' and 'Sausage Stuffer'
COPIES: *Private collection
NOTES: Like O106.1, no food-chopper brand is identified. Unlike O106.1, the binding illustrates a food chopper clamped to a table edge; on p 2, the heading 'A Modern Household Utensil' is printed above the illustration of the chopper parts, and the caption below reads, 'Carefully made, nicely tinned, self-cleaning, self-sharpening, needed in every kitchen.' Also, note that the heading on p 20 differs.

O106.3 nd
—Cook book / Containing recipes for a / number of excellent dishes / which can be made best with / Acme Food / Choppers / The / T. Eaton Co Limited / Toronto Canada [cover-title]
DESCRIPTION: 14.5 × 11.0 cm   Pp [1–20]   Illus on p 2 of food-chopper parts   Paper; stapled
CONTENTS: 1 cover-title; 2 information about, and illustrations of, food chopper; 3–19 seventy-one numbered recipes; 20 'Tempered Steel Knives and Cutter Plates for Acme Choppers'
COPIES: *Private collection
NOTES: On p 2, the heading 'Acme Food Choppers' is printed above the illustration of the chopper parts, and the text below begins, 'Cutter plates are of forged and tempered steel.'

O106.4 nd [about 1900–5]
—Cook book / Containing recipes for a / number of excellent dishes / which can be made best with / Jewel-Model and / Purity Food / Choppers / David Maxwell & Sons / manufacturers / St. Mary's, Ontario
DESCRIPTION: 15.0 × 11.0 cm   Pp [1–29]   Illus of food-chopper parts   [$0.10, on binding]   Paper, with image on front of three food choppers (Purity, Model, and Jewel types); stapled
CONTENTS: 1 tp; 2–4 information about Jewel Food Choppers; 5–6 information about Model Food Choppers; 7–8 information about Purity Food Choppers; 9–29 [inside back face of binding] eighty-six numbered recipes
COPIES: *OKITJS (991.23.2)
NOTES: An illustration of the St Mary's factory of David Maxwell and Sons is on the outside back face of the binding. The image shows trains and many horse-drawn buggies, but no cars.

I compared the recipes with those in O118.1, *Gem Chopper Cook Book* (copy at OKITJS). The David Maxwell *Cook Book* recipes are the same, but they are fewer and bear different numbers. Like the *Gem Chopper Cook Book*, the ingredients list for some recipes is in a box. Whereas the *Gem Chopper Cook Book* credits the recipes to Janet Hill and other writers, here there is no reference to the source of the recipes. Also, where the Gem Chopper text says 'Gem-Chop the apple,' the directions in the Maxwell edition instruct the reader simply to 'chop the apple.'

The secret of delicious desserts easily made

O107.1 nd [about 1900–5]
The / secret / of / delicious desserts / easily made / The / Pure Gold Mfg. Co. / Limited / Toronto, Canada [cover-title]
DESCRIPTION: 18.5 × 13.0 cm   Pp 1–19   Illus col of prepared dishes, illus col and illus of Pure Gold products   Paper, with image on front, in oval frame, of a woman holding a package of Pure Gold Quick Custard Pudding in one hand and holding a finger of her other hand to her lips as a sign to keep it secret; stapled, and tied with a cord through centre of gathering
CONTENTS: 1 'Pure Gold'; 2 'Some Pure Gold Products'; 3 'Purity First – Speed Next'; 4 'Pure Gold Baking Powder'; 5–8 'Baking Powder Recipes'; 9 'Pure Gold Quick Puddings'; 10 'Tapioca Recipes'; 11 'Gelatine Recipes'; 12 'Custard Recipes'; 13 'Pure Gold Jelly Powder'; 14 'Jelly Powder Recipes'; 15 'Pure

Gold Salad Dressing Powder'; 16 'Salads'; 17 'Salad Dressing'; 18 'Pure Gold Extracts'; 19 heading torn from a page promoting the qualities of Pure Gold goods

COPIES: *Private collection

NOTES: This book has an interesting and attractive design. The text is printed in grey; some of the pages are laid out in three columns, with the recipes placed in the outside columns and small colour illustrations of the dishes arranged, one above the other, in the centre column. The text follows the pattern of a page of information about a particular product, followed by pages of recipes for that product. From appearances, the book was published about 1900–5.

Pure Gold Manufacturing Co. is listed in Toronto city directories for the years 1893–1946.

1900–10

The making of Star

John Goldie started his first mill in Ayr in 1849. He began operating his second mill in Highgate, in 1893, and his third mill in Galt, in 1899. The Canadian Cereal and Milling Co. purchased all three mills from Goldie Milling Co. Ltd in 1910.

O108.1   nd [about 1900–10]

The making of Star. [cover-title]

DESCRIPTION: 12.5 × 17.0 cm   Pp [1–2] 3–32   Illus on p 1 of 'Our Three Mills' at Galt, Ayr, and Highgate, and illus on pp 3–10 of scenes relating to the milling of Star Flour   Paper, with cut-out on front revealing the three mills depicted on p 1; stapled

CONTENTS: 1 'Our Three Mills' and note about 'our splendid railway connections' signed Goldie Milling Co. Ltd; 2 'Introduction to the One Who Makes the Dough' signed Goldie Milling Co. Ltd; 3–10 illus and text describing the process of milling Star Flour; 11–14 [lacking in this copy]; 15–32 'Some Selected Recipes // Bread Biscuits etc.'

COPIES: *Private collection

NOTES: There is no indication of the place of publication, but the head office of Goldie Milling Co. was in Ayr. The cookbook appeared after Goldie Milling Co. acquired the Galt mill in 1899 and before the company sold all three mills in 1910. According to the 'Introduction,' the purpose of the pamphlet was '[t]o give the reader some idea of the process of manufacture of "Star" Flour ... To show ... the care used in the different departments of the mill, ... To convince [the reader] that "Star" ... [is] without exception, the best

flour in the world for all-round family use ... [and] to place in [the reader's] hands some selected recipes, ...'

This copy is inscribed on ɔ 15, in pencil, 'Digby N.S. // Digby N.S.' Star Flour was sold in the Maritimes, and this copy was purchased from a Nova Scotia antiquarian bookseller.

1901

Directions for preserving fruit, vegetables and liquids

O109.1   1901

[An edition of *Directions for Preserving Fruit, Vegetables and Liquids with Canadian Fruit Preserver,* Glen Stewart, Ont.: W.J. Hamilton, 1901]

CITATIONS: O'Neill (unpublished)

COPIES: Great Britain: LB (not located)

NOTES: There are two entries in O'Neill for the same title with the same date; nothing in the entries distinguishes the two.

Floreen Ellen Carter, in *Place Names of Ontario,* [London, Ont.: Phelps Publishing Co., 1984], identifies Glen Stewart as a small community, 40 miles (64 km) west of Cornwall and 9 miles (14 km) northwest of Iroquois Station, on the Grand Trunk Railway (population 100, in 1886; 75, in 1926). There was another equally small Ontario community of the same name, but spelled Glen Stuart, in Haldimand-Norfolk Township.

Recipes

See also O66.1, from the same church.

O109a.1   1901

The 20th century / cook book / Recipes / collected by / the young ladies / of / St. Paul's Church, Ingersoll / 1901. / "A good digestion to you all, and once more / I shower a welcome on you, welcome all." / Tribune Print.

DESCRIPTION: With photograph on back of the church; stapled

CONTENTS: 1 tp; 2 'An Old-fashioned Recipe for Home Comfort' signed 'a friend'; 3 'Index' [i.e., table of contents]; ...

COPIES: *OGU

NOTES: The volume has 87 pp. 'Tribune Job Print' is on the front face of the binding. On the title-page and on the binding, 'Recipes' is in a larger typeface than 'The 20th Century Cook Book.' The OGU copy is inscribed on the binding, 'Sara M. Cuthbert.'

Smiley's cook book and universal household guide

O110.1 copyright 1901
Smiley's / cook book / and / universal / household guide / A comprehensive collection / of recipes and / useful information / pertaining to every department / of housekeeping. / Profusely / illustrated / Chicago: / Smiley Publishing Company, / publishers. / Copyright 1894, by J.B. Smiley. Copyright 1895 and 1896, by Smiley Publishing Company. All rights reserved. / Copyright 1901, by Smiley Pub. Co. All right[s?] reserved[.?]
DESCRIPTION: 23.0 × 15.0 cm   Pp [i–ii], 1–991 [992]   5 pls col incl tp, fp illus on pp 650, 652, 654, and 656, many small illus   Cloth
CONTENTS: i tp; ii blank; 1 dedication 'To all those who are engaged in the noble work of housekeeping, ...'; 2 'This book is sold by subscription only. Those desiring a copy, and not knowing any agent, should write to the publishers.'; 3–4 preface signed the editor; 5–6 'Order of Departments' [i.e., table of contents] and at bottom p 6, 'Colored Plates'; 7–990 text, glossary, and index; 991–2 publ ads
COPIES: OGU (2 copies: *UA s068 b36, CCC TX715.6 S64 1901); Great Britain: OPo(F)
NOTES: 'The Toronto Daily Star edition // Smiley's new and complete guide for housekeepers. Illustrated' is on the binding. This is probably the American edition of 1901, marked on the binding for distribution through the Toronto newspaper.
  The Smiley Publishing Co.'s address is on p 991: 917 West Washington Street, Chicago, Illinois. There are four blank leaves between pp 416 and 417, and four blank leaves between pp 768 and 801.

O110.2 [copyright 1902]
—[An edition of *Smiley's Cook Book and New and Complete Guide for Housekeepers; a Complete and Comprehensive Collection of New, Choice and Thoroughly Tested Recipes, Including Every Department of Housekeeping*, Montreal: Montreal News Co., [copyright 1902], pp 990]
COPIES: United States: DLC (TX715 S649)

AMERICAN EDITIONS: *Smiley's Cook Book and Universal Household Guide*, edited by James Bethuel Smiley, Chicago: Smiley Publishing Co., c1895 (United States: DLC); Chicago: Smiley Publishing Co., c1896 (United States: DLC); Chicago: Smiley Publishing Co., c1901 (United States: DLC).
  Possibly also the same book is *Twentieth Century*

Cook Book and Practical Housekeeping ..., by James Bethuel Smiley, Chicago: Alhambra Book Co., [c1900] (United States: DLC); Barile, p 212, cites the same title and year, but gives Smiley Publishing Co. as the publisher.

365 breakfast dishes

For other Canadian editions in this American series, see O100.1.

O111.1 [copyright 1901]
365 / breakfast dishes / a breakfast dish for every day / in the year / selected from / Mrs. Lincoln, Mrs. Lemcke, Table / Talk, Boston Cooking School / Magazine and others / Toronto / Musson Book Co. / Limited
DESCRIPTION: 17.5 × 12.5 cm   Pp [i–ii], 1–169   Tp still-life orange of an open book, bowls, and other containers; many small illus orange of kitchen utensils   Paper-covered boards, with pl mounted on front of a chef twirling his moustache
CONTENTS: i tp; ii 'Copyright, 1901 by George W. Jacobs & Co.'; 1–161 recipes; 162 blank; 163–9 index
COPIES: *OGU (UA s045 b37)

AMERICAN EDITIONS: Philadelphia: George W. Jacobs and Co., [1901] (United States: DLC).

BRITISH EDITIONS: London: Dean and Son Ltd, nd [1906] (Great Britain: LoEN, OB); 1910 (Driver 1069.2).

Wright, Charles (Dudley, Worcestershire, England, 1839–)

O112.1 new ed., nd [about 1901]
For all ages. / Wright's / golden recipes / New edition. / Revised, corrected and improved by / Chas. Wright / Toronto Junction, Ont. / Price 50 cents. / Printed and published for the proprietor by / the Tribune Publishing Co'y / 22 Dundas St., Toronto Junction. [cover-title]
DESCRIPTION: 20.5 × 14.0 cm   Pp [1–2] 3–53   Paper; stapled
CONTENTS: 1 'Preface' signed Chas Wright, Toronto Junction; 2–3 'References'; 4–47 entries arranged alphabetically from A to Y containing medical, health, and food information; 48–51 'These Will Be Found a Mother's Friend' [alphabetically arranged entries]; 52–3 'Good Words' [alphabetically arranged entries]
CITATIONS: *Leader and Recorder* [West Toronto Junc-

tion Historical Society newsletter] (Spring 1993), p 5, illus

COPIES: OTWTJHS *Bookseller's stock

NOTES: According to text on the back face of the binding, there are 'upwards of four hundred valuable recipes and other facts worth knowing.' Many items concern the healthful properties of various foods, such as their digestibility or pleasing combinations. For example, Wright comments on p 14, 'Dates used in rice puddings cannot be too highly recommended'; and on p 17, 'A new-laid egg beaten with vinegar and pepper is superior to an oyster.'

Biographical information about Charles Wright on pp 2–3 relates that he came to Canada in 1871, became a member of the College of Pharmacy in Toronto on 15 May 1871, and practised medicine in Collingwood, Ontario. After twenty years, he moved to Toronto Junction, 'where he now resides.' This is evidence that the book was published no earlier than 1891 (1871 + 20 years). At the time of publication, however, his son, J.G. Wright, was carrying on 'the drug business he built up.' Toronto city directories up to and including the volume for 1900 list the business as C. Wright and Co. and Charles Wright as manager, and name Mrs Louisa M. Wright as his wife (perhaps Louisa contributed recipes or culinary advice). In the 1901 directory, the business is listed under the son's name, J.G. Wright, although Charles continued to live on the premises. The book, therefore, was likely published about 1901.

1902

[Title unknown]

See also O151.1, Polson and Co.'s Almanac 1904–5, by the same firm.

O113.1   [about 1902]
[Title unknown]
DESCRIPTION: 22.0 × 14.5 cm   Pp 1–32   Lacks binding
CONTENTS: 1–48 recipes and publ ads
COPIES: *NBFKL (Ruth Spicer Cookbook Collection)
NOTES: The running heads are 'N.C. Polson & Co., Kingston, Ont.' On p 10 there is a reference to a testimonial given on 4 November 1901; on p 26 there is a reference to the year 1900.

Almanac, cook book and index to health 1902

See also O140.1, Almanac of Dr Mack's Pills 1904, published by Walker and Abbs.

O114.1   1902
This valuable / 1902 / Almanac, / cook book / and / index to health / is published at our / new store, by / Walker & Abbs / the leading St. Catharines druggists, / and is presented to our cus- / tomers with our compliments. / Main store – Queen St., near the post office. Estab- / lished 1894. Telephone No. 102. / Branch store – 187 St. Paul St. Established 1898. Telephone No. 28. [cover-title]
DESCRIPTION: 18.0 × 13.3 cm   Pp [1–3] 4–32   Illus of astrological signs and symbols   Paper; stapled, and with hole punched at top left corner for hanging
CONTENTS: Inside front face of binding 'To Our Friends' signed Walker and Abbs; 1–3 publ ads; 4–30 recipes, publ ads, monthly calendars for 1902, and 'Practical Breaks' [i.e., jokes]; 1st–mid 2nd column 31 'Home Hints'; mid 2nd column 31–1st column 32 'For the Curious'; 2nd column 32 'Canada Postal Rates'
COPIES: *OTSC (317.1351 Alm M)
NOTES: The recipes begin on p 4 under the heading 'Cakes, etc.,' with Angel Cake, Fruit Cake without Eggs, White Cake (Cherry Filling), and Molasses Cake.

Arnold, Mrs Augusta, née Foote (1844–1903)

This American author's books were published under the pseudonym Mary Ronald, the last name being a rearrangement of the letters of her real surname, Arnold. On the title-pages of Luncheons *and editions of O141.1,* The Century Cook Book, *her name appears as a facsimile of a signature, which could be misread as Arnold, but which is actually Ronald.*

O115.1   1902
Luncheons / a cook's picture book / a supplement to the / Century Cook Book / By / Mary Ronald / author of The Century Cook Book / Illustrated with over / two hundred photographs / The Copp, Clark Company, Limited / Toronto / 1902
DESCRIPTION: 20.5 × 14.0 cm   Pp [i–vii] viii, [1–3] 4–223   208 numbered photographs on 25 pls and

29 double-sided pls   Cloth, with china-and-cutlery pattern on front and spine

CONTENTS: i ht; ii blank; iii tp; iv 'Copyright, 1902, by the Century Co. Published October, 1902 Printed in the United States by the De Vinne Press.'; v 'The Book'; vi blank; vii–viii table of contents; 1–211 text; 212 blank; 213–23 index

COPIES: *OGU (CCC TX715.6 R63644)

NOTES: The introductory text on p v explains: 'This book is intended as a supplement to the "Century Cook Book," hence no general rules for cooking are given. It is a book of illustrated receipts, a cook's picture-book, intended to be very useful in the way of suggestion.' Chapter 1 offers general information about luncheons, including garnishing and dishing, preparing butter, the pastry-bag, measures and terms, and order of courses. Each of Chapters 2–12 is devoted to a single course, numbered 'First Course' to 'Eleventh Course.' Chapters 13 and 14 are about cakes and icings, and breads, respectively.

The private collector's copy is inscribed on the front endpaper, in ink, 'Edith L. Bell // 1443 King St. W. Toronto.' The Toronto city directory for 1902 shows Wm C. Bell, 'trav Copp, Clark Co,' living at the same address. Edith likely received this book from William, directly from Copp, Clark stock.

AMERICAN EDITIONS: New York: The Century Co., 1902 (United States: DLC); New York: The Century Co., 1906 (Bitting, p 405).

Collection of choice recipes

McLaren's products, and later the company McLaren's Ltd, were named after John I. McLaren. Born in Goderich Township, Huron County, in 1865, McLaren had moved with his family to Hamilton at the age of thirteen years. After working with a Hamilton firm of wholesale grocers for eight years, he joined Hamilton Coffee and Spice Co. as a partner and remained with the firm for eighteen years. He left the business to serve as alderman, then mayor of Hamilton in 1909–10. (Information about McLaren is from the article 'Retires from Active Career,' Spectator (Hamilton), 4 January 1947.)

O116.1   nd [about 1902]
Collection / of / choice / recipes / Celebrated cooks. / The Hamilton Coffee and Spice Co. Limited, / manufacturers of / McLaren's Invincible Extracts, / Jelly Powder, Baking Powder, Coffee, &c. / Hamilton, Ontario. [cover-title]

DESCRIPTION: 15.0 × 11.5 cm   Pp [1–2] 3–32   8 pls col, mainly of dishes made with McLaren products; 6 fp illus of Hamilton sites: City Hall, Public Library, Gore Park, Geo. E. Tuckett's residence, Central School, and Bank of Hamilton   Paper

CONTENTS: 1 list of McLaren's products and the company name; 2 fp illus of Hamilton City Hall; 3 'Introduction'; 4–mid 6 'Jelly Powder'; mid 6–top 7 extracts; mid–bottom 7 'McLaren's Invincible Pure Cream of Tartar Baking Powder'; 8 fp illus of Hamilton Public Library; 9 'Tables of Weights and Measures'; 10–27 recipes; 28–31 'Coffee'; 32 'Index' [i.e., table of contents]

COPIES: CIHM (78598)   *OGU (CCC TX715.6 C64) OONL (TX715 C63)

NOTES: The 'Introduction' says that the Hamilton Coffee and Spice Co Ltd was established in 1885, and that the decision to build a modern factory at 25 and 27 MacNab Street South was made in 1898. The company's extract flavours included vanilla, orange, lemon, strawberry, almond, rose, pineapple, and pistachio.

On p 4 one learns that Miss Goff was the company's 'principal demonstrator' (i.e., the person who demonstrated how to use McLaren's products) and that she had made 'extensive tours ... [visiting] every large city in Canada.' The 1902 Hamilton city directory lists Miss Annie Goff as working at the Hamilton Coffee and Spice Co. and living at 269 John Street North (she is not listed under Goff in directories for 1903 onward). The book was likely published shortly after the end of the Boer War on 31 May 1902 (the date of the signing of the Treaty of Vereeniging) since there is a reference on p 29 to that conflict in the past tense: 'In the British army while engaged in South Africa, nothing was found to be appreciated so much by the soldiers as the rations of coffee, while their courageous enemies of the Transvaal and the Orange River, were equally fond of this nourishing drink.' The book was likely published before Hamilton Coffee and Spice Co. became known as McLaren's Ltd: The last separate listing in the city directory for Hamilton Coffee and Spice Co. is for 1905. The 1906 directory lists McLaren's Ltd, operating Hamilton Coffee and Spice Co.

The binding of the OGU copy is loose; the colour plates are loose and may not be complete or in their original position.

The OONL copy has 9 colour plates opposite pp 4, 6, 8, 12, 16, 18, 20, 24, and 26.

Dr King's guide to health, household instructor and family prize cook book 1902

See O96.1 for a list of other annual issues.

O117.1 [1902]

Price 10 cents. / Dr. King's / guide to health / household / instructor / and / family / prize / cook book / H.E. Bucklen & Co. / Chicago, Ill. / 275–276–277 Michigan Ave. / Windsor, Can. / 53–54 Sandwich St. West. [cover-title]

DESCRIPTION: Pp [1] 2–32   Paper, with three images on front: at centre, in a circular frame, a building; to the left of the building, a man in a laboratory; to the right, a man in a kitchen; stapled

CONTENTS: 1 calendars for 1902 and 1903; 1st column 2 'Introduction'; 2nd column 2–32 information about a variety of topics, including household matters, recipes on pp 24–32, and publ ads

CITATIONS: Allen, p 104

COPIES: United States: *Private collection

NOTES: Like O96.1, the recipes begin on p 24, with Good Bread, Biscuit, Buns, and Waffles.

Gem Chopper cook book

O118.1   copyright 1902

Gem / Chopper / cook / book / Valuable / recipes for / substantial / dishes and / dainty / desserts / Sargent & / Company / 149–151–153 / Leonard Street / New York / Copyright, 1902, by / Sargent & Co.

DESCRIPTION: 17.5 × 11.5 cm   Pp [1–93]   Illus of food chopper and parts, and other illus accompanied by captions extolling the chopper   Limp cloth; stapled

CONTENTS: 1 tp; 2 blank; 3–7 'Sargent's Gem Food Chopper'; 8–9 'Suggestions by Janet McKenzie Hill'; 10 'Janet McKenzie Hill's Recipes,' 'Other Proven Recipes,' and 'My Own Recipes'; 11–92 207 numbered recipes and blank pages for 'My Own Recipes'; 93 index and 'Cooking Measures'

COPIES: *Private collection

NOTES: This edition has more pages (93) and more recipes (207) than O118.2. Hill's 'Suggestions' promote using the food chopper to transform leftovers. The text on p 10 notes that, whereas many of the recipes have been prepared by Hill for the book, others are selected from '*Kohinoor* and *Ladies' Aid cook book*' (I have not identified these sources). The ingredients for each recipe are enclosed in a box – an unusual design feature.

On the front face of the binding, below the title, is the name 'Kemp Manufacturing Co., Toronto, Canada.' Other copies examined have different companies (or variations of the same company's name) printed below the title: 'Rice Lewis & Son, Limited, Toronto, Canada' (Private collection; and cited in JPCat 130, No. 39); 'Walter Woods & Co., Hamilton, Ontario' (SRRPM); 'The Hobbs Hardware Co., Ltd., London, Canada' (OKITJS (999.24.1)); 'The Hobbs Hardware Co., London, Canada' (Private collection); 'Lewis Bros. Limited. Montreal' (ADEAHM); 'L.H. Hebert, 297 & 299 rue St. Paul, et 21 rue St. Jean B[aptiste?], Montreal, Canada' (Private collection); 'Dunlap Bros. & Company, Limited. Amherst, N.S.' (NBDKH). OKITJS has a second copy of *Gem Chopper Cook Book* (991.24.1), where the company name is only partly legible: '[two initials and a last name, illegible] Sons & Co. Ltd.'

See also O106.4, *Cook Book*, for another manual promoting food choppers that has some of the same recipes as in the *Gem Chopper Cook Book*.

O118.2   copyright 1902

—Gem / Chopper / cook / book / Valuable / recipes for / substantial / dishes and / dainty / desserts / Sargent & / Company / 149–151–153 / Leonard Street / New York / Copyright, 1902, by / Sargent & Co.

DESCRIPTION: 17.5 × 11.5 cm   Pp [1–64]   Illus   Paper; stapled

CONTENTS: 1 tp; 2 blank; 3–7 'Sargent's Gem Food Chopper'; 8–9 'Suggestions by Janet McKenzie Hill'; 10–64 177 numbered recipes

COPIES: *OKIT   OMAHM (993.16.14)   Private collection

NOTES: This edition has fewer pages (64) and fewer recipes (177) than O118.1. 'Wood Vallance & Co., Hamilton, Ontario' is printed on the front face of the binding of the OKIT copy. 'Caverhill Learmont & Co., Montreal.' is on the private collector's copy. The OMAHM copy has no business name.

O118.3   copyright 1902

—Sargent / Gem / Chopper / cook / book / Valuable / recipes for / substantial / dishes and / dainty / desserts / Sargent & / Company / 149–151–153 / Leonard Street / New York / Copyright, 1902, by / Sargent & Co.

DESCRIPTION: 17.5 × 11.5 cm   Pp [1–64]   Illus of food chopper and parts, and other illus   Paper; stapled

CONTENTS: 1 tp; 2 'Sargent'; 3–7 'Sargent's Gem Food Chopper'; 8–9 'Suggestions by Janet McKenzie Hill'; 10–64 177 numbered recipes

COPIES: Bookseller's stock   *Private collection

NOTES: Unlike O118.2, the title-page of this edition

has 'Sargent' at the head of the page, and there is text on p 2 (p 2 of O118.2 is blank). This edition looks later than those described above.

'Lewis Bros., Ltd. Montreal, Canada' is printed on the front face of the binding. Another private collector's copy has 'Starke-Seybold Ltd. Montreal Canada.' The bookseller's copy has 'The Sheet Metal Products Co of Canada, Ltd. Toronto.'

AMERICAN EDITIONS: New York: Sargent and Co., copyright 1902, 50 leaves, unpaginated (United States: InU, MSaE); New York: Sargent, 1902, with the following stamped on the front face of the binding: 'Lemuel Du Bois & Co., Ellenville, N.Y.' (Barile, p 150, illus).

Gregory, Annie R.

O119.1   [copyright 1902]
Canada's favorite / cook book / by Annie R. Gregory / assisted by one thousand homekeepers / approved and endorsed by A. Chabrison, / for ten years chef of the Union League Club, Chicago, / now of Grand Pacific Hotel / There is no higher art than that which tends towards the / improvement of human food. H.W. Beecher. / The Bradley-Garretson Co., Limited, / Brantford, Canada.
DESCRIPTION: 23.5 × 17.5 cm   Pp [5–6] 7–10, 13–14, [i–ii], 15–578, [i]   Tp illus of four miniature children sitting on the handle of a ladle, 8 pls col incl frontis, 11 double-sided pls, many small illus and decorative headpieces   Cloth, with image on front of an aproned woman carrying a steaming chafing dish
CONTENTS: 5 tp; 6 'Copyright, 1902, by Annie R. Gregory' and a quotation from Ruskin; 7–8 publishers' preface; 9–10 author's introduction; 13–14 table of contents; i–ii list of illustrations; 15–406 [Book I]; 407–86 Book II; 487–551 Book III; 552–78 index; i ad
COPIES: OBM *OGU (UA s047 b19)   ONENM
NOTES: Canadian editions of this American book are called either *Canada's Favorite Cook Book* or *Woman's Favorite Cook Book*. The order of publication of the various editions is unknown, except for O119.7 and O119.8, copyright 1907, which follow all those copyrighted 1902. In this edition of *Canada's Favorite Cook Book*, Bradley-Garretson Co. Ltd is the only publisher cited on the title-page and its location is Brantford.

The publisher's preface refers to the author, Annie Gregory, as 'a skilled home caterer, successful housewife, and ideal mother.' Cooking, it says, should have a health-promoting purpose: 'Pure foods, pure water, and pure air, will give new power, and when the perverted appetite has approached its normal condition, many of the diseases that now assail the human frame will disappear, thus making our bodies fit temples for the dwelling of the human soul.' It describes the contents of the book thus: 'Book I. is intended for the inexperienced housekeeper ... as well as for the epicure ... whose pocket-book demands economy. Book II. is devoted to various health foods ... It is an up-to-date guide in brain-building, health-building and happiness. Book III. is devoted to household economics, nursing the sick, the toilet, the care of the kitchen, laundry, etc., etc.' There are a few Canadian references – for example, menus for Dominion Day and the King's Birthday, and a recipe for a Canadian Coffee Cake – but these are likely renamed recipes from the original American edition, as in the case of O262.1, Fannie Farmer's *Catering for Special Occasions*.

Bradley-Garretson was an American subscription publishing house, based in Philadelphia. Its Brantford branch was in operation from about 1876, and managed by Thomas S. Linscott by 1879 (Parker, p 200). The name of Linscott's own firm, Linscott Publishing Co., appears on two printings of the cookbook (O119.3, O119.4). Regarding Linscott's co-operation with James Walter Lyon of World Publishing Co. in Guelph, publisher of O119.6, see Parker, p 200.

O119.2   [copyright 1902]
—Canada's favorite / cook book / by Annie R. Gregory / assisted by one thousand homekeepers / approved and endorsed by A. Chabrison, / for ten years chef of the Union League Club, Chicago, / now of Grand Pacific Hotel / There is no higher art than that which tends towards the / improvement of human food. H.W. Beecher. / The Bradley-Garretson Co., Limited. / Brantford and Toronto.
CONTENTS: Tp verso 'Copyright, 1902, by Annie R. Gregory' and a quotation from Ruskin
COPIES: *OBEHCM
NOTES: Like O119.1, Bradley-Garretson Co. Ltd is the only publisher cited on the title-page, but here there are two locations, Brantford and Toronto.

O119.3   [copyright 1902]
—Canada's favorite / cook book / by Annie R. Gregory / assisted by one thousand homekeepers / approved and endorsed by A. Chabrison, / for ten years chef of the Union League Club, Chicago, / now of Grand Pacific Hotel / There is no higher art than that which tends towards the / improvement of human food. H.W. Beecher. / The Bradley-Garretson Co., Ltd. / Brantford, Canada. / The

Linscott Publishing Co. / Brantford, Canada.
DESCRIPTION: 23.5 × 17.5 cm   Pp [5–6] 7–578, [i]   Tp illus of four miniature children sitting on the handle of a ladle, 8 pls col incl frontis, 11 double-sided pls, many small illus and decorative headpieces   Cloth, with image on front of an aproned woman carrying a steaming chafing dish
CONTENTS: 5 tp; 6 'Copyright, 1902, by Annie R. Gregory' and quotation from Ruskin; 7–8 publishers' preface; 9–10 author's introduction; 11–12 'Contents'; 13–14 list of illustrations; 15–406 [Book I]; 407–86 Book II; 487–551 Book III; 552–78 index; i ad
CITATIONS: Ferguson/Fraser, pp 25 and 232, illus col on p 11 of closed volume
COPIES: *Private collection
NOTES: In this edition, there are two Brantford publishers cited on the title-page: Bradley-Garretson Co. Ltd and Linscott Publishing Co.

OCHAK, OHWHH, and another private collector have copies that are identical to the one described here, except that on the title-page, there is no period after 'Canada' (for either publisher), and on p 6, the last digit in the copyright date did not fully register (the tail of the '2' shows faintly). The OCHAK copy is inscribed by the original owner, 'M.E. Smith … 1904.'

O119.4   [copyright 1902]
—Canada's favorite / cook book / by Annie R. Gregory / assisted by one thousand homekeepers / approved and endorsed by A. Chabrison, / for ten years chef of the Union League Club, Chicago, / now of Grand Pacific Hotel / There is no higher art than that which tends towards the / improvement of human food. H.W. Beecher. / The Linscott Publishing Co. / Brantford, Canada.
DESCRIPTION: 23.5 × 17.5 cm   Pp [5–6] 7–578   Tp illus of four miniature children sitting on the handle of a ladle, 8 pls col incl frontis, 11 double-sided pls, illus   Cloth, with image on front of an aproned woman carrying a steaming chafing dish
CONTENTS: 5 tp; 6 'Copyright, 1902, by Annie R. Gregory' and quotation from Ruskin; 7–8 publishers' 'Preface'; 9–10 author's 'Introduction'; 11–12 'Contents'; 13–14 list of illustrations; 15–406 [Book I]; 407–86 'Book II'; 487–551 'Book III'; 552–78 'Index'
COPIES: *OFERWM (A1977.120.1); United States: DLC (TX715 G823)
NOTES: In this edition, Linscott Publishing Co. is the only publisher cited on the title-page.

O119.5   [copyright 1902]
—Woman's favorite / cook book / by Annie R. Gregory / assisted by one thousand homekeepers / approved and endorsed by A. Chabrison, / for ten

years chef of the Union League Club, Chicago, / now of Grand Pacific Hotel[.?] / There is no higher art than that which tends towards the / improvement of human food. H.W. Beecher. / J.M. MacGregor Publishing Co. / Vancouver, B.C.
DESCRIPTION: 23.5 × 17.5 cm   Pp [5–6] 7–578, [i]
CONTENTS: 5 tp; 6 'Copyright, 1902, by Annie R. Gregory'; …
COPIES: *Bookseller's stock
NOTES: There were three editions called *Woman's Favorite Cook Book*: this one, published by J.M. MacGregor Publishing Co.; O119.6, by World Publishing Co.; and O119.8, with no named publisher.

O119.6   [copyright 1902]
—Woman's favorite / cook book / by Annie R. Gregory / assisted by one thousand homekeepers / There is no higher art than that which tends towards the / improvement of human food. H.W. Beecher. / World Publishing Company, / Guelph, Ont.
DESCRIPTION: 23.5 × 18.0 cm   Pp [7–8] 9–610   Tp illus of four miniature children sitting on the handle of a ladle, 8 pls col incl frontis (plates incl in pagination), 8 double-sided pls (incl in pagination); illus   Cloth, with image on front of an aproned woman carrying a steaming chafing dish
CONTENTS: 7 tp; 8 'Copyright, 1902, by Annie R. Gregory' and quotation from Ruskin; 9–10 preface; 11–12 author's 'Introduction'; 13–14 'Contents'; 15–16 'Illustrations'; 17 blank; 18 pl col; 19–434 Book I; 435–518 Book II; 519–83 Book III; 584–610 index
CITATIONS: Driver 2001, Wellington County, p 94
COPIES: *BCHM (1956.008.001)   MSOHM
NOTES: See O38.1, *The Housewife's Library*, for information about World Publishing Co. and foreign distribution of the company's titles.

O119.7   [copyright 1907]
—Canada's favorite / cook book / by Annie R. Gregory / assisted by one thousand homekeepers / approved and endorsed by A. Chabrison, / for ten years chef of the Union League Club, Chicago, / now of Grand Pacific Hotel. / Embellished with many colored and photo engravings illustrating the art of / carving, table decoration, preparation of fancy dishes, etc. / There is no higher art than that which tends towards the / improvement of human food. H.W. Beecher.
DESCRIPTION: 23.5 × 17.5 cm   Pp [5–6] 7–578   Tp illus of four miniature children sitting on the handle of a ladle, 8 pls col incl frontis, 11 double-sided pls, many small illus and decorative headpieces   Cloth, with image on front of an aproned woman carrying a steaming chafing dish

CONTENTS: 5 tp; 6 'Copyright, 1907, by Annie R. Gregory' and quotation from Ruskin; 7–8 preface; 9–10 author's introduction; 11–12 'Contents'; 13–14 list of illustrations; 15–406 [Book I]; 407–86 Book II; 487–551 Book III; 552–78 index

CITATIONS: Berton, pp 43, 69, 71

COPIES: NSNRM OGM (986.21.1) OGOWSM OTMCL (641.5 G668) OTUTF (D-11 0986) *Private collection

NOTES: No publisher is cited on the title-page or elsewhere. The catalogue for QQLA (TX715 G822 1907) records this title, 1907, with the imprint Brantford: Bradley-Garretson Co. Ltd.

O119.8 [copyright 1907]
—[An edition of *Woman's Favorite Cook Book*, no publisher recorded on the title-page, [copyright 1907]]

COPIES: SRRPM

NOTES: The museum catalogue card comments, 'Found in a farm home in Edgely [Saskatchewan] ...' The copy lacks pp 577–8.

SSWD has a copy of *Woman's Favorite Cook Book*, where no publisher is recorded on the title-page and which is likely a bookseller's dummy. All the plates are grouped together, before the title-page, and the pagination is not continuous, e.g., [5–6] 7–12, 15–16, 27–32, [5–6] 7–12, etc. The last leaf presents information about ordering the book by subscription, at the price of $2.00.

AMERICAN EDITIONS: These were published under several different titles: *Woman's Favorite Cook Book*, Chicago: George S. Cline, [copyright 1902] (Private collection); *Woman's Favorite Cook Book*, [Chicago: Monarch Book Co., 1902] (United States: DLC); *The Ideal Cook Book*, Chicago: American Wholesale Co., 1902 (Axford, p 224; Bitting, p 200); *The American Family Receipt Book*, Chicago: A.B. Kuhlman Co., [1902] (United States: DLC); *The Blue Ribbon Cook Book*, Chicago: Monarch Book Co., [copyright 1902] (QKB); *The Blue Ribbon Cook Book*, Chicago: Monarch Book Co., 1906 (United States: DLC); *The Blue Ribbon Cook Book*, Chicago: L.W. Walter Co., successor [to] Monarch Book Co., [copyright 1907] (United States: InU); *The National Course in Home Economics; ... by Ruth Allen Beezley ... It contains also more than one thousand tested and approved economical recipes, ... by Annie R. Gregory*, [Chicago?:] National School of Home Economics, [c1917] (United States: DLC).

Harrison, Professor Francis Charles (Spain, 19 February 1871–)

The 1901 Census records the author as a 'bacteriologist,' living in Guelph with his wife, Maggie, and two children.

O120.1 January 1902
Bulletin 118. January, 1902 / Ontario Agricultural College and Experimental Farm. / Yeast and its household use. / By Prof. F.C. Harrison. [Title from top p 1]

DESCRIPTION: Pp 1–16 6 numbered illus

CONTENTS: 1 'Introduction'; 2–16 text, including recipes

COPIES: *CIHM (83965) OOAG

NOTES: Harrison identifies his readership on p 1: 'This bulletin is written more especially for those who make bread in their own homes; it may also be found helpful to professional bakers ...'

The reliable cook book

O121.1 1902
The / reliable / cook book. / 1902 / Compiled by the ladies of / Alvinston and vicinity.

DESCRIPTION: 17.5 × 13.0 cm Pp [1–5] 6–68 Paper; stapled

CONTENTS: 1 tp; 2 'Printed at the Alvinston Free Press Book and Job Rooms.'; 3 table of contents and table of weights and measures; 4 unattributed poem beginning, 'We may live without poetry, music and art' [from *Lucile*, Part I, Canto ii, by Owen Meredith, pseudonym of Edward Robert Bulwer-Lytton] and 'Time for Boiling Vegetables'; 5–68 text and ads

COPIES: *OGU (UA s048 b28)

NOTES: There is an advertisement on p 64 for the Alvinston Free Press, 'one of the best equipped in Western Ontario.'

Scott's calendar cook book 1902

For Scott's other annual cookbooks, see O87.1.

O122.1 1902
Scott's / calendar / 1902 cook book 1902 / Published by / Stuart Scott, M.D. / chemist and druggist. / Main Street, / next post office, Newmarket. [cover-title]

COPIES: *OSHT

Souvenir cook book

O123.1 1902
Souvenir / cook book. / Orillia, Ont. / 1902. [cover-title]
DESCRIPTION: 20.0 × 14.0 cm Pp [1–32] Paper; bound by a ribbon through two punched holes
CONTENTS: 1–2 ads; 3–32 recipes credited with the name of the contributor and ads
CITATIONS: HuroniaCat List 196, No. 332
COPIES: *Private collection
NOTES: The compiler of the book is not identified. The binding is especially attractive – purple paper with gold lettering, and tied with a ribbon. There is an advertisement on p 13 for the Times Printing Co. in Orillia, which probably printed the cookbook. The company did 'Wedding announcements // At-home cards // Ball programmes // Visiting cards // Cake boxes, etc.'

The Spartan cook book

O124.1 [1st ed.], 1902
Now good digestion wait on appetite and health on both. – Shakespeare. / The / Spartan / cook book / A / selection / of / tested recipes / compiled by / the ladies of / the Sparta W T. A [sic; lacking two periods] / 1902. / St. Thomas, Ont. / The Journal Book and Job Dept. / 1902
DESCRIPTION: About 21.0 × 15.0 cm [dimensions from photocopy] Pp [1–5] 6–152 Photograph on p 2 of Hotel Spartan Limp cloth
CONTENTS: 1 tp; 2 photograph of Hotel Spartan; 3 'Our Greeting' signed 'Committee. Mrs. H.B. Smith, Mrs G.H. Haight, Mrs. J. Gorvett, Mrs. J.W. Kirkpatrick, Miss Whiting, sec.'; 4 'To Whom It May Concern:' signed W.H. Graham, secretary, and G.A. Shannon, president; 5–152 recipes credited with the name of the contributor and ads
COPIES: OSPFAM *Private collection
NOTES: Temperance sentiment was strong in Sparta at the turn of the twentieth century. Only two of the town's original four bars remained open. After one closed voluntarily, the community rallied to stop the serving of liquor in the Sparta hotel. Their plans were ambitious, as related in the note 'To All Whom It May Concern': '... many of the petitioners [against granting a liquor licence to the Sparta hotel] expressed their willingness to stand by any organization, financially which would undertake to furnish entertainment to the public without the accessories of

intoxicants. The plan, speedily formed, included not only the idea expressed above, but also the purpose of furnishing in the house of entertainment, a drawing-room equipped with daily papers and good periodic literature, and of making the general surrounding of the place such, that it would be not only a hospitable home for the traveller, but also a centre of social and educational interest to the community at large. For carrying into effect these plans, a company was formed and stock subscribed by the people of the community ... while the ladies' organization [i.e., the Women's Temperance Auxiliary], under whose auspices the cook-book is being issued, assumed five hundred dollars of the cost.' This note is reprinted, with minor revisions, in the fourth and fifth editions.

According to the publishing history in the 1998 reprint of the 1970 facsimile, Mrs Hiram B. Smith introduced the idea of producing a fund-raising cookbook, and the proposal was moved by Miss Maria Haight, and seconded by Miss Reynolds. Mrs Hiram B. Smith is the first-listed of the Committee members who signed 'Our Greeting' on p 1. In 'Our Greeting' the Committee draws the reader's 'special attention to those [recipes] so kindly contributed by Miss Gray, of the School of Domestic Science, Toronto'; Miss Gray is probably Miss Annie M. Gray, who taught in the Domestic Science Department at Toronto's Central Technical School and who assisted Miss Nellie Lyle Pattinson with O506.1, *Canadian Cook Book*. In 'Our Greeting' the Committee also thanks the contributors, 'especially those philanthropic gentlemen whose generosity has [made the] undertaking an assured financial success.' The publishing history in the 1998 reprint states that 1,000 copies of the first edition were printed. Information about pagination and contents are from the 1998 reprint.

O124.2 2nd ed., 1903
—[Second edition, 1903]
NOTES: No copy has been found, but the date of the second edition is cited in the third edition, O124.3.

O124.3 [3rd ed.], 1904
—Now good digestion wait on appetite and health on both. – Shakespeare. / The / Spartan / cook book / A / selection / of / tested recipes / compiled by / the ladies of / the Sparta W.T.A. / 1904. / St. Thomas, Ont. / The Journal Book and Job Dept. / 1904.
DESCRIPTION: 21.5 × 15.0 cm Pp [1–4] 5–160 Photograph on p 2 of Hotel Spartan Limp cloth; stapled
CONTENTS: 1 tp; 2 photograph of Hotel Spartan;

3 'Preface' signed Committee No. 2, Mrs E. Yarwood, convener, and Mrs A.O. Clark, cor. secretary, September 1904, and 'Our Greeting' signed Committee No. 1, Mrs H.B. Smith, con., Mrs G. Haight, Mrs J. Gorvett, Mrs J.W. Kirkpatrick, and Miss Whiting, sec., September 1902; 4 'To All Whom It May Concern:' signed W.H. Graham, secretary, and G.A. Shannon, president; 5–6 ads; 7–159 recipes credited with the name of the contributor and ads; 160 ads

COPIES: OLU (Lloyd Walden Collection)   *Private collection

NOTES: The 'Preface' refers to the earlier editions: 'In 1902 the Women's Temperance Auxiliary, of Sparta, published the first edition of The Spartan Cook Book. In 1903 a second followed. This, the third edition, is published at the demand of the unsupplied public, previous editions having met with unlimited favor. New recipes have been added in the form of an appendix.' The 'Appendix' of new recipes is on pp 150–9. 'The Journal, St. Thomas' is on the outside back face of the binding.

O124.4   4th ed., 1908

—Now good digestion wait on appetite and health on both. – Shakespeare. / The / Spartan cook book / A selection of / tested recipes / compiled by / the ladies of / the Sparta W.T.A. / Fourth edition / London Ont. / A. Talbot & Co., printers. / 1908.

DESCRIPTION: 21.5 × 14.0 cm   Pp [1–4] 5–168   Photograph on p 2 of Hotel Spartan   Limp cloth; stapled

CONTENTS: 1 tp; 2 photograph of Hotel Spartan; 3 'Preface' signed Miss M.E. Haight, convenor of Committee, and Mrs A.O. Clark, cor. secretary; 4 'To All Whom It May Concern:' signed W.H. Graham, secretary, and G.A. Shannon, president; 5–6 ads; 7–top 163 recipes credited with the name of the contributor and ads; mid 163–167 'Miscellaneous'; 168 'Index' [i.e., table of contents]

COPIES: *OAYM   OSTT (R641.5 SPA, photocopy lacking tp)

NOTES: In the 'Preface' the Women's Temperance Auxiliary extends its thanks and refers to the purpose and contents of this new edition: 'Because many housewives are yet unprovided [with a copy of this book], and because the cost of our Public House is not yet defrayed, we offer another edition, the fourth, of this collection of recipes. This edition consists of three thousand copies, each of which will contain the recipes we published previously, together with one hundred and twenty new ones, and a new division made up of recipes for dishes suitable for the sick room.' The running head is 'The Spartan W.T.A. Cook Book.'

The publishing history in the 1970 facsimile edition and its 1998 reprint incorrectly refers to the fourth edition as 'printed in 1904'; it cites $345.30 as the price of reprinting.

Beeson, p 31, reprints a recipe from a 1908 edition, which she saw in the early 1990s at OSTTECPM; the edition, presumably the fourth, could not be located when I inquired in 1999.

O124.5   5th ed., nd [about 1915]

—Now good digestion wait on appetite and health on both. – Shakespeare. / The / Spartan cook book / A selection of / tested recipes / compiled by / the ladies of / the Sparta W.T.A. / Sparta, Ontario, Canada / Price 25c / Fifth edition / London, Ont. / A. Talbot & Co., printers.

DESCRIPTION: 21.0 × 14.0 cm   Pp [1–4] 5–189 incorrectly numbered 168   Illus on p 2 of Hotel Spartan Paper; stapled

CONTENTS: 1 tp; 2 illus of Hotel Spartan; 3 preface to fifth edition; 4 'To All Whom It May Concern:'; 5 'Yarmouth' [information about Yarmouth Township in Elgin County]; 6–188 recipes; 189 index

COPIES: *OGU (UA s047 b31)   OSPFAM (2 copies) Private collection; United States: MiU

NOTES: The book is undated; however, the private collector's copy is signed and dated on the front face of the binding, in ink, by the owner's husband's aunt, '1915 Meta McCrimmon.'

FACSIMILE EDITIONS: In 1970 the Sparta Community Society published a facsimile of the first edition, printed by Impressions, St Thomas, to promote the Sparta Old Boys Reunion in July of that year. The facsimile includes a page relating the book's publishing history.

In 1998 OSPFAM reprinted the 1970 facsimile and the page of publishing history; there is no indication of the date of the reprinting in the volume.

365 luncheon dishes

For other Canadian editions in this American series, see O100.1.

O125.1   [September 1902]

365 / luncheon dishes / a luncheon dish for every day / in the year / selected from / Marion Harland, Christine Terhune / Herrick, Boston Cooking School / Magazine, Table Talk, Good House- / keeping, and others. / Toronto / Musson Book Co. / Limited

DESCRIPTION: 17.0 × 12.0 cm   Pp [i–ii], 1–151   Tp

still-life orange of an open book, cooking utensils, and ingredients; many small illus orange of kitchen utensils   Rebound
CONTENTS: i tp; ii 'Copyright, 1902, by George W. Jacobs & Company // Published September, 1902'; 1–144 one recipe for each day in the year; 145–51 'Index'
COPIES: CIHM (79156)   *OHM (TX735 T48)
NOTES: This book was sold by the Methodist Book and Publishing House in Toronto since there is an entry in 'Stock Book 1914' at OTCC (Acc. 83.061C, UCC Board of Publication, Series III, Box 42, p 14) for '6 [copies] 365 Luncheon Dishes.'

AMERICAN EDITIONS: Philadelphia: G.W. Jacobs and Co., [1902] (United States: CL, CU, CoDU, ICJ, MCR, MoU, NIC, NN, OCl, WU).

BRITISH EDITIONS: London: Dean and Son Ltd, nd [1906] (Great Britain: LoEN, OB).

Williams, Mrs Mary Emma (1853–1916), and Katharine Rolston Fisher

O126.1   April 1902
Elements / of the / theory and practice of / cookery / A text-book of household science for / use in schools / by / Mary E. Williams / Supervisor of Cookery in the public schools of the / boroughs of Manhattan and the Bronx / New York City / and / Katharine Rolston Fisher / formerly teacher of cookery in these schools / Toronto / George N. Morang & Company, Limited / 1902
DESCRIPTION: 18.0 × 12.0 cm   Pp [i–iv] v–vii [viii] ix–xv [xvi] xvii–xix [xx] xxi [xxii], 1–347, [i–iii]   12 numbered pls incl frontis; 18 numbered illus incl 2 fp illus; 4 unnumbered fp illus   Cloth, with image on front of wheat stalks
CONTENTS: i ht; ii Macmillan Co. symbol; iii tp; iv 'Copyright, 1901, by the Macmillan Company. Set up and electrotyped February, 1901. Reprinted April, 1902. // Norwood Press // J.S. Cushing & Co. – Berwick & Smith // Norwood Mass. U.S.A.'; v–vii preface; viii blank; ix–xii 'Notes to Teachers'; xiii–xv bibliography; xvi blank; xvii–xix table of contents; xx blank; xxi quotation from Ruskin headed 'The Motto of the New York City Public School Kitchens'; xxii blank; 1–4 introduction; 5–318 twelve chapters; 319–27 appendices A and B; 328 blank; 329–47 index; i blank; ii–iii publ ads
COPIES: *OGU (UA s039 b12)

NOTES: There are 502 numbered recipes and other items in this American textbook.

AMERICAN EDITIONS: New York: Macmillan, 1901 (United States: DLC, ICJ, KMK, MB, MtBC, OClW, PPD, PPPL, WaS, WaWW); New York: Macmillan, and London: Macmillan, 1902 (United States: NIC); New York: Macmillan Co., and London: Macmillan and Co. Ltd, 1903 (OTAG; United States: OCU, PPD); New York: Macmillan Co., and London: Macmillan and Co. Ltd, 1907 (United States: OU); New York: Macmillan Co., and London: Macmillan and Co. Ltd, 1908, publishing history on the title-page verso: 'Copyright, 1901, ... Set up and electrotyped February, 1901. Reprinted April, July, September, 1902; June, 1903; April, 1905; January, September, 1906; March, October, 1907; January, August, 1908' (OTU; United States: MH, OCl, OOxM); New York: Macmillan Co., and London: Macmillan and Co. Ltd, 1909 (Great Britain: OB); New York and London: Macmillan Co., 1912 (United States: DHEW); New York: Macmillan Co., and London: Macmillan and Co. Ltd, 1913 (United States: ICRL, MH, NIC, PP, ViU); New York: Macmillan Co., and London: Macmillan and Co. Ltd, 1915, see Driver 1156.9 for the publishing history on the title-page verso (Great Britain: LB destroyed; United States: KMK, PP); New York: Macmillan Co., 1916 (United States: DLC, ICJ, NIC, OrP); New York, etc.: Macmillan Co., 1917 (United States: MH); New York: Macmillan, 1923 (OOxM).

Words of wisdom

Soon after founding the patent medicine business G.T. Fulford and Co. in Brockville, Ontario, in 1887, George Fulford (1852–1905) acquired the rights to Dr Williams' Pink Pills for Pale People and created the Dr Williams Medicine Co. to market the product. International success came quickly. Fulford was active in Brockville politics and appointed to the Canadian Senate in 1900. See also O201.1, Things Worth Knowing, *by the same company.*

O127.1   [1902]
Hang up this booklet where it can / be referred to when required. / Words of wisdom [cover-title]
DESCRIPTION: 23.0 × 15.5 cm   Pp 1–32   Paper, printed to look like half leather; stapled
CONTENTS: Inside front face of binding 'Contents' [i.e., alphabetical index of topics] and ad for Dr Williams'

Pink Pills for Pale People; 1 'Words of Wisdom // A Hand-Book of Useful Information' [introductory text] and 'Hints for the Kitchen' [i.e., recipes]; 2–32 information about various ailments at top of pages, continuation of 'Hints for the Kitchen' at bottom of verso pages to p 20, then 'How to Remove Stains' at bottom of verso pages to p 24, 'Household Hints' at bottom p 24, 'To Serve with Meats' at bottom p 26, 'How to Make Poultices' at bottom p 30, monthly calendars for 1902 and testimonials at bottom of most recto pages, 'Hints for the Kitchen' at bottom p 31
COPIES: CIHM (73886) *OONL (AY419 P3 W67 1901 p***)
NOTES: The text includes references to, and advertisements for, various products of the Dr Williams Medicine Co., Brockville, Ontario.

1902–7

Individual recipes for class work

See also another textbook for the Lillian Massey School, O241.1, Recipes in Individual and Large Amounts for Home and School.

O128.1   nd [about 1902–7]
Lillian Massey School / of / Household Science and Art / Individual recipes / for / class work.
DESCRIPTION: 16.5 × 12.0 cm   Pp [1–3] 4–47   Limp cloth; stapled
CONTENTS: 1 tp; 2 'These recipes are in individual amounts, and are especially designed for the use of Normal students and teachers of Household Science in Canada.' and information about measurements; 3–43 'Recipes'; 44–7 'Index'
COPIES: *QMM (RBD ckbk 1769)   Private collection
NOTES: The description 'individual recipes' refers to the fact that each recipe makes only one serving, i.e., the ingredients are proportioned for an individual. *Individual Recipes for Class Work* was published after the founding of the school in 1902 and before the dated inscription in the private collector's copy: 'Marion F. Coats. 7 Queen's Park. Oct. 1907.' The QMM copy is inscribed by the original owner, on the inside front face of the binding, in pencil, 'Nora [F.?] Wishart 235 Jarvis St Toronto.' Wishart has numbered the first page of recipes for 'Beverages' on p 3, 'Lesson 2.'

1903

Chase, Dr Alvin Wood (Cayuga County, NY, 20 March 1817–25 May 1885, Ohio)

For information about Dr Chase and his publications, see O8.1.

O129.1   nd [about 1903–6]
Dainty / dishes / for the invalid [cover-title]
DESCRIPTION: 19.0 × 13.5 cm   Pp [1] 2–32   Portrait of Dr Chase opp p 1   Paper, with image on front of a mother reading to a child on her lap, another child listening beside her; stapled
CONTENTS: 1 'Dr. Chase's Symptom Book' and 'Dainty Dishes for the Invalid' [introductory text pertaining to these two aspects of the book]; 2–31 information about various illnesses, recipes for invalid cookery, and publ ads; 32 'Table of Contents' [i.e., index]
COPIES: *OTUTF (uncat patent medicine)
NOTES: The address given for obtaining Dr Chase's products is Edmanson, Bates and Co., Toronto. On p 31 there is a certificate signed Thomas Heys, analytical chemist, 114 Bay Street. Toronto directories show Heys's business, which was established in 1873, at 114 Bay Street from 1903–6; therefore, *Dainty Dishes for the Invalid* was published about 1903–6.

Denison, Mrs Grace Elizabeth, née Sandys (Chatham, Ont., 10 September 1853– 1 February 1914, likely Toronto, Ont.)

According to her obituary in Saturday Night, *Grace Denison (pl 36) was born into 'a distinguished Irish family of strong literary inclinations.' The first of six children in the family of Elizabeth Sandys, née Moeren, and Archdeacon Francis Edward Sandys, of Christ Church (Anglican), Chatham, she attended Hellmuth College in London, Ontario. At the time of her death, she was sixty years old and had worked as society reporter and staff writer for* Saturday Night *for twenty-two years, less two months. Hector Charlesworth, in* Candid Chronicles, *states that her pen-name of Lady Gay was after Lady Gay Spanker, the heroine of Dion Boucicault's comedy* London Assurance, *but not long before Grace died, in conversation with Jean Graham, she contradicted this explanation and said that it was a childhood nickname. After separating from her husband, Albert Ernest Denison, she sought work as a journalist because of financial need. She had no children.*

For information about Grace Denison see: 1901 Census (under 'Dennison'), which gives her birth date; Morgan; Hector Charlesworth, 'The Late Grace E. Denison,' Saturday Night *(7 February 1914), p 26 [obituary, includes her photograph]; Jean Graham, 'Lady Gay's Pen-Name,'* Saturday Night *(7 February 1914), p 26; J.G. [Jean Graham?], 'A Brilliant Journalist,'* Canadian Courier *Vol. 15, No. 12 (21 February 1914), p 20; Hector Charlesworth,* Candid Chronicles: Leaves from the Note Book of a Canadian Journalist, *Toronto: Macmillan Company of Canada Ltd, 1925; Macmillan Dictionary; Marjory Lang, 'Separate Entrances: The First Generation of Canadian Women Journalists,' in* Re(dis)covering Our Foremothers, *edited by Lorraine McMullen, Ottawa, Ont.: University of Ottawa Press, 1988, p 86; Lang; Dagg; and newspaper clippings on microfilm at OTMCL. Eva-Marie Kröller explores Denison's travel writing in* Canadian Travellers in Europe, 1851–1900, *Vancouver: University of British Columbia Press, 1987.*

O130.1   1903
The / new cook book / a volume of / tried, tested and proven recipes / by / the ladies of Toronto and other cities and towns / Edited by / Grace E. Denison / (Lady Gay of Saturday Night) / Toronto: / Rose Publishing Company / 1903
DESCRIPTION: 19.5 × 13.0 cm   Pp [i–iii] iv [v–vi] vii incorrectly numbered vi, viii, [17] 18–405 [406]   14 numbered illus of carving   Brown cloth simulating leather
CONTENTS: i tp; ii 'Entered according to Act of the Parliament of Canada in the year one thousand, nine hundred and three, by Rose Publishing Company, at the Department of Agriculture.'; iii–iv 'Contents'; v 'Preface' signed Grace E. Denison (Lady Gay); vi–viii 'Contributors'; 17–396 text; 397–405 'Index'; 406 blank for 'Remarks'
CITATIONS: Driver 2005, letter, p 7   Ferguson/Fraser, p 232   Rhodenizer, p 992
COPIES: ACG   CIHM (86593)   *OTMCL (641.5 D25.2)   Private collection
NOTES: In the 'Preface' Denison thanks those who responded to her request for recipes. The 'Contributors' listed on pp vi–viii are from the upper crust of Toronto society; for example, Lady Thompson, Lady Mulock, Mrs Timothy Eaton (of the department store), Mrs Vogt, Mrs Nordheimer, Mrs R.S.F. McMaster, Mrs Fred W. Rose (the publisher's wife), Mrs Musson (another publisher's wife), Mrs Melfort Boulton and Mrs Athol Boulton, the Misses Gooderham (of the whisky distillery), and Mrs Goldwin Smith. A few

other sources are also recorded, such as London's Carleton Club and New York's Waldorf Astoria. Denison presents full instructions for 'dinner giving' on pages 385–96. The private collector's copy has an extra leaf, pp [407–8], blank for 'Remarks.'

Although Denison does not say so, this work follows the model of the best-selling Canadian cookbook of the previous quarter-century, O20.1, *The Home Cook Book,* whose title-page is headed 'Tried, tested, proved' and whose text was 'Compiled from recipes contributed by ladies of Toronto and other cities and towns.' Denison's recipes were also 'tried, tested and proven' and contributed 'by the ladies of Toronto and other cities and towns.' The early editions of *The New Cook Book* came from the same publishers as *The Home Cook Book* – Rose Publishing Co. and Musson Book Co. Rose Publishing Co. must have hoped that by naming Denison's work *The New Cook Book,* they would encourage potential buyers to see it as the successor of *The Home Cook Book,* which had dominated the market. Perhaps unwittingly, Grosset and Dunlap gave O130.11 the title *The Canadian Home Cook Book.* Very few Canadian cookbooks have been published in Britain: *The Home Cook Book* and Denison's *The New Cook Book* were the first and both appeared in London, England, in 1906.

For another cookbook written by a female columnist for *Saturday Night,* see O935.1, Brown, Cynthia, *Cooking – with a Grain of Salt,* 1938.

O130.2   [entered 1905]
—The / new cook book / a volume of / tried, tested and proven recipes / by / the ladies of Toronto / and other cities and towns / Revised edition. / Edited by / Grace E. Denison / (Lady Gay of Saturday Night) / Toronto / The Musson Book Co., Limited.
DESCRIPTION: 19.5 × 13.0 cm   Pp [i–iv] v [vi] vii–viii, [17] 18–407 [408]   14 numbered illus on pp 17–23 of carving   Cloth, with leaf-and-line pattern
CONTENTS: i tp; ii 'Entered according to Act of the Parliament of Canada, in the year one thousand nine hundred and five, by Dan A. Rose, at the Department of Agriculture.'; iii 'Preface' signed Grace E. Denison (Lady Gay); iv–v 'Contents'; vi–viii 'Contributors'; 17–398 text; 399–407 index; 408 blank for 'Remarks'
CITATIONS: Ferguson/Fraser, p 232, illus col on p 11 of volume opened at title-page   Landsberg
COPIES: OMMM   *Private collection
NOTES: The private collector's copy is inscribed on the front endpaper, in pencil, 'Beatrice MacKinnon // 2 Dundas Terrace // Water St.'

O130.3 Montreal, [entered 1905]
—The / new cook book / a volume of / tried, tested and proven recipes / by / the ladies of Toronto / and other cities and towns / Revised edition / Edited by / Grace E. Denison / (Lady Gay of Saturday Night) / Montreal / The Montreal News Company, Limited

DESCRIPTION: 20.0 × 13.0 cm   Pp [i–iv] v [vi] vii–viii, [17] 18–406 [leaf lacking]   Illus on pp 17–23 of carving   Cloth

CONTENTS: i tp; ii 'Entered according to Act of the Parliament of Canada, in the year one thousand nine hundred and five, by Dan A. Rose, at the Department of Agriculture.'; iii 'Preface' signed Grace E. Denison (Lady Gay); iv–v 'Contents'; vi–viii 'Contributors'; 17–398 text; 399–406 index

COPIES: *Private collection

O130.4 [entered 1906]
—The / new cook book / a volume of / tried, tested and proven recipes / by / the ladies of Toronto / and other cities and towns / Revised edition. / Edited by / Grace E. Denison / (Lady Gay of Saturday Night) / Toronto, Ont.: / Rose Publishing Co.

DESCRIPTION: 19.5 × 12.5 cm   Pp [i–iv] v [vi] vii–viii, [17] 18–407 [408]   14 numbered illus on pp 17–23 of carving   Rebound

CONTENTS: i tp; ii 'Entered according to Act of the Parliament of Canada, in the year one thousand nine hundred and six, by Rose Publishing Co., at the Department of Agriculture.'; iii 'Preface'; iv–v table of contents; vi–viii 'Contributors'; 17–398 text; 399–407 index; 408 blank for 'Remarks'

COPIES: BVA (641.5 D39N)   CIHM (86919)   OGU (3 copies: UA s027 b17, CCC TX715.6 N4755, CCC)   OKITJS (991.23.1)   *OTU (TX715 D4 1906)   Private collection

NOTES: The OTU copy is from the estate of Effie M.K. Glass. One OGU copy (UA s027 b17) is bound in cloth with a lily-of-the-valley pattern. Another OGU copy (CCC TX715.6 N4755) is inscribed by the publisher to the editor of the *Globe*: 'Stewart Lyon Esq // Compliments the publisher Fred W. Rose Oct 3rd 1907.' Another OGU copy (CCC) is inscribed on the front endpaper, in ink, 'To Effie from mother July/07.' The OKITJS copy, which is bound in cloth with a repeating pattern of roses in a vase, is inscribed 'Miss Alma Schill.'

Saberi/Davidson, pp 70–1, discuss the trifle recipes in a 1906 edition of *The New Cook Book* and reprint one of the two fig versions. They do not identify which of the 1906 editions they consulted. Likewise,

Berton, p 64, quotes from a 1906 edition of *The New Cook Book,* but does not record the publisher.

O130.5 [copyright 1906]
—The / new cook book / a volume of / tried, tested and proven recipes / by / the ladies of Toronto / and other cities and towns / Revised edition. / Edited by / Grace E. Denison / (Lady Gay of Saturday Night) / Published by / E.W. Gillett Co., Ltd. / Toronto, Ont.

DESCRIPTION: 19.5 × 13.0 cm   Pp [1–2], [i–iv] v [vi] vii–viii, [17] 18–406 [leaf missing?]   Illus   Cloth

CONTENTS: 1–2 endpaper publ ads; i tp; ii 'Copyright: Canada, 1906 – No. 63'; iii 'Preface' signed Grace E. Denison; iv–v 'Contents'; vi–viii 'Contributors'; 17–398 text; 399–406 index

CITATIONS: Reitz, p [4]

COPIES: OKITD (x962.278.001)   OTUTF (B-12 7861)   QKB (87-16)   *Private collection

NOTES: The private collector's copy has an errata slip headed 'Index Corrections' mounted on p 399. The following text is printed on the front face of the binding: 'From E.W. Gillett Company Limited Toronto, Ont. // The New Cook Book // Magic Baking Powder does not contain alum.' For information about E.W. Gillett and other cookbooks published by the company, see O285.1.

O130.6 [entered 1906]
—The / new cook book / a volume of / tried, tested and proven recipes / by / the ladies of Toronto / and other cities and towns / Revised edition. / Edited by / Grace E. Denison / (Lady Gay of Saturday Night) / Toronto, Ont.: / E.W. Gillett Co., Ltd.

DESCRIPTION: 19.5 × 13.0 cm   Pp [i–iv] v [vi] vii–viii, [17] 18–407 [408]   Illus   Cloth

CONTENTS: i tp; ii 'Entered according to Act of the Parliament of Canada, in the year one thousand nine hundred and six, by Rose Publishing Co., at the Department of Agriculture.'; iii 'Preface' signed Grace E. Denison; iv–v 'Contents'; vi–viii 'Contributors'; 17–398 text; 399–407 'Index'; 408 blank for 'Remarks'

COPIES: *OTSHH   Private collection

NOTES: The form of the imprint on the title-page and the text on the title-page verso differentiate this Gillett edition from O130.5. The OTSHH copy is inscribed in ink, on the front endpaper, 'Mrs H.[I.?] Taylor.'

O130.7 Victoria, [entered 1906]
—The / new cook book / a volume of / tried, tested and proven recipes / by / the ladies of Toronto / and other cities and towns / Revised edition. /

Edited by / Grace E. Denison / (Lady Gay of Saturday Night) / Victoria, B.C.: / T.N. Hibben & Co.

DESCRIPTION: 19.5 × 13.0 cm   Pp [i–iv] v [vi] vii–viii, [17] 18–407 [408]   Illus   Cloth

CONTENTS: i tp; ii 'Entered according to Act of the Parliament of Canada, in the year one thousand nine hundred and six, by Rose Publishing Co., at the Department of Agriculture.'; iii 'Preface' signed Grace E. Denison; iv–v 'Contents'; vi–viii 'Contributors'; 17–398 text; 399–407 index; 408 blank for 'Remarks'

COPIES: BVIPA   *Private collection

O130.8   Winnipeg, [1906]

—[*The New Cook Book ... Revised ed.*, Winnipeg, Man.: Robinson and Co., [1906], pp 407]

CITATIONS: O'Neill (unpublished)

COPIES: Great Britain: LB (07944.g.61 destroyed)

O130.9   1914

—The / Canadian family / cook book / a volume of / tried, tested / and proven recipes / by / prominent Canadian ladies / Edited by / Grace E. Denison / (Lady Gay of "Saturday Night") / Revised and enlarged edition / Toronto / McLeod & Allen / 1914

DESCRIPTION: 20.0 × 14.0 cm   Pp [i–viii], 1–538 [539–40]   14 pls incl frontis of 'Table set for luncheon'   Rebound, original cloth applied to front and back face of new binding; on front, image of aproned woman carrying a dish of steaming food

CONTENTS: i tp; ii blank; iii 'Weights and Measures'; iv blank; v table of contents; vi blank; vii–viii 'Contributors'; 1–528 text; 529–38 'Index'; 539 blank; 540 'Housekeeper's Time Table'

CITATIONS: Abrahamson, p 59   Anson-CartwrightCat 75 (May 1991), No. 108   Berton, p 69   Dagg, p 83   Golick, p 104 (note 23)   Rhodenizer, p 992

COPIES: CIHM (80496)   OGU (UA s051 b18, UA s059 b10)   OH (R641.5971 C16 CESC 1914)   OKQ (TX715 D45 1914)   OONL (TX715 D45 1914)   *OTMCL (641.5 D25)   OTSHH   OTUTF (B-12 7862)   OTYA (TX715.6 C36 1914)   OWTU (F17883)

NOTES: This retitled edition was published the year that Grace Denison died.

The initial four leaves of the OTMCL copy, catalogued here, have been rebound out of order. The OH, OTUTF, and OTYA copies are in their original bindings and the front matter runs as follows: i 'Weights and Measures'; ii blank; iii tp; iv blank; v 'Contents'; vi blank; vii–viii 'Contributors.'

The OONL copy, which is rebound, lacks pp 539–40. Mounted on the blank verso of 'Weights and Mea-

sures' is the bookplate 'Ex libris Household Science Department Univ. of Toronto.' The OWTU copy is rebound.

O130.10   nd [1916 or later]

—The / Canadian family / cook book / a volume of tried, tested / and proven recipes / by / prominent Canadian ladies / Edited by / Grace E. Denison / (Lady Gay of "Saturday Night") / Toronto / George J. McLeod, Limited / publishers

DESCRIPTION: 18.5 × 12.5 cm   Pp [i–viii], 1–538 [539–40]   16 pls incl frontis of 'Table set for luncheon'   Cloth, with image on front of an aproned woman carrying a dish of steaming food

CONTENTS: i 'Weights and Measures'; ii–iv blank; v tp; vi 'Printed in the United States of America'; vii 'Contents'; viii blank; 1–528 text; 529–38 'Index'; 539 blank; 540 'Housekeeper's Time Table'

COPIES: *OH (R641.5971 C16 CESC)   OTNY (uncat)   OTUTF (B-12 7863)

NOTES: George J. McLeod and Thomas Allen were partners in the Toronto firm of McLeod and Allen (publishers of O130.9). After Allen left the business early in 1916, the company operated under the name of George J. McLeod (see BS, Vol. 32, No. 2 (February 1916), p 29).

The OH copy is inscribed on the blank face of the frontispiece, in red ballpoint pen, 'To Ella. From Mother Fellingham June 13/64.'

O130.11   1932

—The Canadian / home cook book / a volume of / tested recipes / Edited by / Grace E. Denison / Grosset & Dunlap / publishers New York

DESCRIPTION: 19.5 × 12.5 cm   Pp [i–iv] v–vi, 1–537   4 pls col incl frontis, 2 pls, 5 double-sided pls   Rebound

CONTENTS: i tp; ii 'Copyright, 1932, by Grosset & Dunlap, Inc. Printed in the United States of America'; iii 'Contents'; iv blank; v–vi 'What Price a Good Meal?' signed the publishers, and at bottom p vi, acknowledgment to General Electric Co. for the recipes in the 'Icebox Recipes' chapter, which are reprinted from the company's *Silent Hostess Treasure Book* [O740.1]; 1–526 text; 527–37 index

COPIES: *OTMCL (641.5 D245)   OTNY (uncat); United States: NBuBE

NOTES: In 1932 Grosset and Dunlap published an edition called *The American Home Cook Book*. The edition described here, which was published in the same year under a different title, was distributed in Canada, despite the American imprint. During the course of research for this bibliography, several individuals reported to me that they owned a copy of this edition, often apologizing for submitting what they thought was an American cookbook! The OTNY copy is bound in its original cloth, with an image on front of an aproned woman holding a pie(?).

AMERICAN EDITIONS: There were many, with various titles: *The American Home Cook Book*, New York: Barse and Hopkins, [copyright 1913] (Great Britain: LB destroyed; United States: CoDU, DLC, ICU, IaAS, LU, NN, OFH, OLak, RPJW); *The American Home Cook Book*, New York: Grosset and Dunlap, [copyright 1932] (Great Britain: LB; United States: DLC, KMK, LU, MdPM, MnM, NBuBE, NHyCIA, NN, NcD, OBgU, RPJW, RUn, TxDW, WaE, WU); *Auerbach's Cook Book*, Salt Lake City, Utah: Auerbach, 1932 (United States: AJacT, DeU); *Brown Thomson's Cook Book*, Hartford, Conn.: Brown Thomson, 1932 (United States: IaU, MBrNCM); *Burdine's Cook Book*, Miami, Fla: Burdine's, and Grosset and Dunlap, [1932] (United States: FM, FTaSU); *Doerflinger's Cook Book*, La Crosse, Wisc.: Grosset and Dunlap, distributed exclusively by Doerflinger's, 1932 (United States: WLac); *The Pomeroy Cook Book*, Harrisburg, Pa: Pomeroy's, 1932 (United States: UU); and *Modern Home Cook Book*, New York and Kingsport, Tenn.: Southern Publishers Inc., [1938] (United States: CL, CU-SB, CoDU, DLC, FMU, IaU, MnM, RPJW, TxDW, UU).

BRITISH EDITIONS: There were three, all entitled *The New Cook Book*: Sampson Low, Marston and Co. Ltd, August 1906 (EngCat 1906–10); London: Sampson Low, Marston and Co. Ltd, nd [1907] (Great Britain: LB destroyed, LoEN, OB; United States: NN); and London: S. Low, Marston and Co., [1912] (BVIP; United States: ICJ).

Directions for using Fleischmann and Company's compressed yeast

Fleischmann and Co. is the earlier form of the firm's name, which subsequently changed to Fleischmann Co. For later books about cooking with Fleischmann's Yeast, see NP3.1, Fleischmann's Booklet; Q87.1, Excellent Recipes for Baking Raised Breads; Q103.1, Neil, Miss Marion Harris, Sixty-five Delicious Dishes Made with Bread; Q124.1, Excellent Recipes for Baking with Fleischmann's Yeast; Q150.1, 37 Delightful Breads and Some Cakes; O514.1, The Basic Sweet Dough Formula; Q187.1, Panomalt Recipes; and Q231.1, Recettes et méthodes éprouvées par Fleischmann.

O131.1 1903
[An edition of *Directions for Using Fleischmann and Company's Compressed Yeast*, Toronto, Ont.: 1903]
CITATIONS: O'Neill (unpublished)
COPIES: Great Britain: LB (not located)
NOTES: O'Neill describes this item as a 'book,' but does not record the number of pages.

O131.2 1906
—[Another edition, 1906]
CITATIONS: O'Neill (unpublished)
COPIES: Great Britain: LB (not located)

Holt, Emily

Also by this American author are Encyclopaedia of Etiquette, *New York: McClure, Phillips and Co., 1901 (United States: DLC), and* The Secret of Popularity, *New York: McClure, Phillips and Co., 1904 (United States: DLC).*

O132.1 1903
The complete / housekeeper / by / Emily Holt / author of Encyclopaedia of Etiquette / [publisher's logo of intertwined initials, 'MBCo'] / Illustrated / The Musson Book Company / Toronto London
CONTENTS: Tp verso 'Copyright, 1903, by McClure, Phillips & Co. // Published, October, 1903 N'
COPIES: *Private collection

AMERICAN EDITIONS: *Encyclopaedia of Household Economy*, New York: McClure, Phillips and Co., 1903 (United States: DLC); retitled ed., *The Complete Housekeeper*, [2nd impression], New York: McClure, Phillips and Co., 1904 (United States: DLC).

Jones, James Edmund (1866–1939)

O133.1 [1903]
Camping and canoeing / What to take / how to travel / how to cook / where to go / By / James Edmund Jones, B.A. / With forty-two illustrations. / Toronto / William Briggs
DESCRIPTION: Pp [i–v] vi, 7–154, [i–iii] Illus of camp scenes Binding has pattern of short horizontal lines suggesting birch bark and image on front of a man carrying a canoe
CONTENTS: i tp; ii 'Entered according to Act of the Parliament of Canada, in the year one thousand nine hundred and three, by James Edmund Jones, at the Department of Agriculture.'; iii dedication 'To my

comrades of Aura Lee Camp'; iv 'Preface'; v–vi 'Table of Contents'; 7–151 text; 152 blank; 153–4 'Index'; i–iii ads
CITATIONS: Benedickson, pp 100, 148, 173, 190, 197–8 (full reference, below) O'Neill (unpublished)
COPIES: *CIHM (73113) OONL (GV790 J65 1903, 2 copies); Great Britain: LB (7912.i.38 destroyed); United States: NCaS (GV191.76 J66 1903)
NOTES: In *Idleness, Water, and a Canoe: Reflections on Paddling and Pleasure,* Toronto: University of Toronto Press, 1997, Jamie Benedickson identifies Jones as a Toronto lawyer, later police magistrate, who paddled with the Aura Lee Club, and refers to Jones's book as an example of how experienced canoeists in the early part of the twentieth century passed on their canoeing and wilderness knowledge to the less skilled. He quotes Jones's instructions for making campfire coffee and his words against the drinking of alcohol when camping.

This is one of a small group of humorous, but informative, Canadian camping cookbooks written by men. The text covers everything one needs to know about canoeing, with the recipes and other culinary information gathered together in a section called 'Camp Cook-Book' on pp 75–93, which begins: 'Smile not, kind lady reader, at the depth of ignorance that the following notes presume on the part of the reader. You are perhaps not aware that the male ignoramus will be surprised if his directions are so incomplete as not to contain an injunction against allowing the water to burn.' The captions to illustrations are also amusing; for example, a photograph of 'A Dutch Oven and Buns' has the following footnoted comment: 'Camera shutter was not swift enough. Notice that the buns are blurred. They were rising so rapidly.' Amounts are given of provisions needed for six men for two weeks. Other parts of the text that treat food and cooking are: 'Dunnage and Provisions, How to Pack,' pp 33–4; 'Canned Goods, How to Carry,' p 39; 'Pots, Pans, Cups, etc.,' pp 41–5; and 'Lunch Basket,' p 58.

There is an entry for *Camping and Canoeing* in the papers of the Methodist Book and Publishing House (for which William Briggs was book steward) at OTCC (Acc. 83.061C, UCC Board of Publication Series III, Box 43, 'Books for Sale 1899–1916,' p 308): 'Camping & Canoeing June / Mr. Jones / [In left column:] 1903 / June 12 – / July 28 1004 bound / [In right column:] June Edition 1000.' Another entry for 'Camping & Canoeing by Jones' is in a record book, p 209 (UCC Board of Publication Series I, Box 5); the column head-

ing is 'Received from Bindery' and the dates run from 12 June to 28 [July?, year not specified].

The CIHM microfilm is made from the copy at OONL that was originally held by the Library of Parliament, whose stamp is on the binding.

The kitchen wall cook book

See also O259.1, The Coronation Cook Book, published to support the same hospital.

O134.1 1903
The kitchen wall / cook / book / Published by / the ladies of the Egyptian Booth of the Carnival of Nations, / held by the Ladies' Management Committee of the / General and Marine Hospital. / [at left of title:] 1903 [cover-title]
COPIES: *OCOLM
NOTES: The General and Marine Hospital was in Collingwood. The printer was the Bulletin Presses, Collingwood. The cookbook is bound at the top edge so the volume could be consulted while hanging on the kitchen wall, as suggested by the title.

Lemon's calendar cook book 1903

O135.1 1903 [1902]
Lemon's / calendar / 1903 cook book 1903 / Published by / F.A. Lemon & Co. / dispensing chemists / 587 Talbot St., St. Thomas. [cover-title]
DESCRIPTION: 17.5 × 13.0 cm Pp [1–3] 4–32 Illus of astrological symbols Paper; stapled, and with hole punched at top left corner, through which runs a string for hanging
CONTENTS: Inside front face of binding 'To Our Customers' signed F.A. Lemon and Co., St Thomas, Ontario; 1–2 publ ad; 3–29 astronomical information, recipes, monthly calendars, 'Practical Breaks, Conundrums and Jokelets,' and publ ads; 30–2 'The True Interpretation of Dreams'
COPIES: *OTYA (CPC 1903 0052)
NOTES: On the inside back face of the binding there is an advertisement for F.A. Lemon and Co. that indicates the book was published before 1903; it says, 'Let us tell you about what we are going to have for Christmas, 1902 ...' The recipes begin on p 4 with Vegetable Soup, Made without Stock, Stock, and Cream of Tomato Soup.

L.H. Yeomans and Co.'s almanac and cook book

O136.1 1903
1903 / L.H. Yeomans & Co.'s / almanac / ... and ... / cook book / Published by / L.H. Yeomans & Co. / chemists, druggists and grocers / Main Street, Mount Forest. / The best way to keep this book and save money is / to hang it in a handy place. [cover-title]
DESCRIPTION: 17.5 × 13.0 cm Pp [1–3] 4–32 Paper
CONTENTS: 1 'The Prescription Counter' signed L.H. Yeomans and Co.; 2 'To Our Customers' signed L.H. Yeomans and Co.; 3 'Our Grocery Department' signed L.H. Yeomans and Co.; 4–27 recipes and ads on verso pages and, on recto pages, one monthly calendar from January to December 1903, below which are 'Practical Breaks, Conundrums and Jokelets' by Chestnut Burr; 28–9 recipes; 30–2 'The True Interpretation of Dreams'
CITATIONS: Driver 2001, Wellington County, p 94
COPIES: *Bookseller's stock

Rorer, Mrs Sarah Tyson, née Heston (Richboro, Bucks County, Pa, 1849–1937, Colebrook, Lebanon County, Pa)

For information about this American author and her other books, see O56.1.

O137.1 [February 1903]
Mrs Rorer's / new / cook book / A manual / of / housekeeping / by / Sarah Tyson Rorer / author of Mrs Rorer's Philadelphia Cook Book, / Canning and Preserving, Bread and Bread Making, / and other valuable works on cookery; Principal of / Philadelphia Cooking School / Toronto / The Musson Book Company / Limited
DESCRIPTION: 20.0 × 13.5 cm Pp [1–3] 4–5 [6] 7–8, [i–iv], [9] 10–731, [i–ix] 3 frontispieces, several pls and double-sided pls Cloth
CONTENTS: 1 tp; 2 'Copyright 1902 by Sarah Tyson Rorer ... Published February 1903 // Printed by George H Buchanan and Company at the Sign of the Ivy Leaf in Sansom Street // Philadelphia'; 3–5 'Preface' signed Sarah Tyson Rorer; 6–8 table of contents; i–iv 'List of Illustrations'; 9–701 text; 702 blank; 703–31 'Index'; i–viii 'A List of Mrs. Rorer's Cookery Books Published by Arnold and Company // 420 Sansom Street, Philadelphia'; ix publ ad
CITATIONS: Driver 2003, Robin Hood, p 86

COPIES: CIHM (77075) *OONL (TX715 R665 1903 p***)
NOTES: The title-page is tipped in on p 3.

AMERICAN EDITIONS: Philadelphia: Arnold and Co., [copyright 1902] (United States: DLC, InU, MB, MCR); reprint, New York: Ladies' Home Journal Cook Book Club, 1970 (described as from an edition of 1898, but I have found no such original edition).

BRITISH EDITIONS: London, Leipsic: T. Fisher Unwin, printed in United States, 1911 (Great Britain: LB destroyed).

Tested cook book

O138.1 1903
Tested / cook / book / Burks Falls / Ontario / 1903 / Price / twenty-five / cents / Arrow Presses [cover-title]
DESCRIPTION: 21.0 × 14.0 cm Pp [1–3] 4–15 Paper, with ribbon-design border; sewn, and also bound by ribbon through three punched holes
CONTENTS: 1 'Recipes by the ladies of St. Andrew's Church'; 2 blank; 3–15 recipes credited with the name of the contributor
COPIES: CIHM (87515) *OTNY (uncat)
NOTES: The recipes are in seven numbered sections: 'Soups'; 'Meats and Fish'; 'Puddings and Pies'; 'Salads, Pickles and Sauces'; 'Cakes'; 'Bread and Biscuits'; and 'Miscellaneous.' The printed ribbon border and the actual tied ribbon make a sweet design.

365 dinner dishes

For other Canadian editions in this American series, see O100.1.

O139.1 [June 1903]
365 / dinner dishes / a dinner dish for every day in / the year / selected from / Table Talk, Good Housekeeping, / The Boston Cooking School / Cook Book, and others / Toronto / Musson Book Co. / Limited
DESCRIPTION: 17.0 × 12.0 cm Pp [i–ii], 1–177 Tp still-life orange of an open book, cooking utensils, and ingredients; many small illus orange of kitchen utensils Rebound
CONTENTS: i tp; ii 'Copyright, 1903, by George W. Jacobs & Company // Published June, 1903'; 1–169

one recipe for each day in the year; 170 blank; 171–7 'Index'
COPIES: CIHM (79155) *OHM (TX737 T48)

AMERICAN EDITIONS: Philadelphia: George W. Jacobs and Co., [June 1903] (United States: DLC, InU).

BRITISH EDITIONS: London: Dean and Son Ltd, nd [1906] (Great Britain: LoEN, OB, WyLUB).

1903–6

See O129.1.

1904

[Title unknown]

O139a.1
[First edition of a cookbook published by the *Echo* newspaper, Wiarton, Ont., about 1904]
NOTES: Regarding the first edition, see O139a.2.

O139a.2 [1907]
—Recipes / A booklet of / useful inform- / ation pertain- / ing to the art / of cooking [cover-title]
DESCRIPTION: 19.5 × 12.5 cm Pp [1–3] 4–38, [i] Paper; stapled
CONTENTS: 1 'To our subscribers' signed the *Echo*, Wiarton, 1 January 1907; 2 'Spoon and Cup Measure' and 'Table of Proportions'; 3–38 recipes credited with the initials or name of the contributor; i ad for Wm Armstrong, grocer, Wiarton
COPIES: *Private collection
NOTES: The letter 'To our subscribers' presents 'this enlarged edition of our Cook Book' and comments: 'The success that attended our venture three years ago was beyond our expectation, and we have received so many inquiries for this book, long after the issue had been exhausted, that we have determined to publish another.' The first issue, therefore, appeared in about 1904. The place of residence sometimes follows the recipe contributor's name: Gould Street (in Wiarton), Stokes Bay, Lions Head, L'Original, Lake Charles, Spry, McVicar (recipe from Mrs Wm McVicar), Shallow Lake, Hawkesbury, Oxenden, Fournier, and Chelsea, Quebec. 'From the presses // The Wiarton Echo' is on the back of the binding.

Almanac of Dr Mack's Pills 1904

See also O114.1, published by Walker and Abbs.

O140.1 1904
Almanac of / Dr. Mack's / Pills. / 1904 / Weak people made strong / by the use of / Dr. Mack's Pills / "The great tonic." / Walker & Abbs, / manufacturing druggists, / St. Catharines, Canada. [cover-title]
DESCRIPTION: 17.0 × 13.0 cm Pp [1–3] 4–32 Illus of astrological signs and symbols Paper, with image on front of two pointing hands; stapled, and with hole punched at top left corner for hanging
CONTENTS: 1 ad for the Dr Mack Medicine Co., St Catharines; 2 'How Dr. Mack's Pills Cure Disease'; 3 'Eclipses, 1904' and 'Morning and Evening Stars'; 4–27 recipes, publ ads, monthly calendars for 1904, and 'Comical Conversations'; 28 'Our Housekeepers' Note Book'; 29 'Miscellaneous' [i.e., culinary recipes]; 30 'As to Diet'; 31 'Weights and Measures,' 'Terms Used in French Menus Explained for the Benefit of the Canadian Hostess,' and 'Language of the Eyes'; 32 'Children and the Moon' and 'How to Sleep'
COPIES: *OSTC (317.1351 Alm M)
NOTES: The recipes begin on p 4 under the heading 'Cakes, etc.': Velvet Cake, Birthday Cake, and Walnut Cakes – the same recipe names as in A1.1, *Pingle's 1904 Calendar Cook Book*, published in Medicine Hat, in what is now Alberta, and O149.1, *Tuthill's Almanac and Cook Book 1904*, published in Toronto. M6.1, *Taylor's 1904 Calendar Cook Book* may also be related.

Arnold, Mrs Augusta, née Foote (1844–1903)

See O115.1, Luncheons, under Arnold, concerning the author's pseudonym Mary Ronald.

O141.1 1904
The / century cook book / by / Mary Ronald / This book contains directions for cooking in its various branches, / from the simplest forms to high-class dishes and ornamental pieces; / a group of New England dishes furnished by Susan Coolidge; / and a few receipts of distinctively Southern dishes. It gives also / the etiquette of dinner entertainments – how to serve dinners – / table decorations, and many items relative to household affairs / "Now good digestion wait on appetite / and health on both" / – Macbeth / The Copp, Clark Company, Limited / Toronto / 1904

DESCRIPTION: 20.0 × 14.0 cm   Pp [iii–viii] ix–xi [xii] xiii–xiv [xv–xvi], 1–588, [i–xii]   Frontis, pls, illus on p 387   Rebound, with original cloth applied to front and back faces and spine

CONTENTS: iii ht; iv blank; v tp; vi 'Copyright, 1895, by the Century Co. Printed in the United States by the De Vinne Press.'; vii quotation from Ruskin; viii 'Aphorisms – Brillat-Savarin'; ix–xi 'Preface'; xii blank; xiii–xiv table of contents; xv 'The Century Cook Book'; xvi blank; 1–562 text in twenty-seven chapters; 563–88 'Alphabetical Index' and 'General Index'; i–iv blank; v–xii 'Memoranda for the Cook' [pages of perforated slips, each with a blank space for recipe name and page number]

COPIES: CIHM (78337)   *OONL (TX715 R66)

NOTES: The 'Preface' states on p ix, 'The author believes that the women of to-day, because of their higher education, have a better understanding of domestic duties; that hygiene, economy, system, and methods are better understood and more generally practised.' The OONL copy is inscribed on the original front endpaper, in ink, 'L.M. [i.e., Lillian Massey] School'; it is also stamped on the original front endpaper and on the title-page, 'Department of Household Science.'

A private collector has a copy of the 1904 Copp, Clark edition with a title-page identical to that transcribed above, except that there is a blank space instead of 'by / Mary Ronald'; the name should appear as a facsimile of a signature.

O141.2   1909
—The / century cook book / by / Mary Ronald / This book contains directions for cooking in its various branches, / from the simplest forms to high-class dishes and ornamental pieces; / a group of New England dishes furnished by Susan Coolidge; / and a few receipts of distinctively Southern dishes. It gives also / the etiquette of dinner entertainments – how to serve dinners – / table decorations, and many items relative to household affairs / "Now good digestion wait on appetite / and health on both" / – Macbeth / The Copp, Clark Company, Limited / Toronto / 1909

DESCRIPTION: 20.0 × 14.0 cm   Pp [leaf missing?] [v–viii] ix–xi [xii] xiii–xiv [xv–xvi], 1–588, [i–x]   59 pls, illus on p 387   Cloth

CONTENTS: v tp; vi 'Copyright, 1895, by the Century Co. Printed in the United States by the De Vinne Press'; vii quotation from Ruskin; viii 'Aphorisms – Brillat–Savarin'; ix–xi preface; xii blank; xiii–xiv table of contents; xv 'The Century Cook Book'; xvi blank; 1–562 text; 563–88 'Alphabetical Index' and 'General

Index'; i–iv blank; v–x 'Memoranda for the Cook' [pages of perforated slips, each with blank space for recipe name and page number]

CITATIONS: Abrahamson, pp 25, 26 (note 44), 28 (note 47), 61

COPIES: *OGU (UA s043 b26)

NOTES: The binding of the OGU copy is loose and some plates may be missing.

AMERICAN EDITIONS: The following were published by the Century Co. in New York: 1895, 1896, 1900, 1901, 1902, 1903, 1905, 1909, 1913, 1917, 1920, and 1922 (all are cited in NUC or in Bitting, p 405, except for the 1905 edition, which is at NNNAM). The last American edition appeared nearly four decades after the first: New York and London: D. Appleton-Century Co. Inc., 1937 (Great Britain: LB, OPo(F); United States: DLC, NN, KMK, MoK, Or).

BRITISH EDITIONS: London: [printed in New York for] T.F. Unwin, 1895 (LB destroyed).

Chase, Dr Alvin Wood (Cayuga County, NY, 20 March 1817–25 May 1885, Ohio)

For information about Dr Chase and his publications, see O8.1.

O142.1   nd [1904 or later]
100 / special receipts / selected from / Dr. A.W. Chase's / Receipt Book. [cover-title]

DESCRIPTION: 19.0 × 13.0 cm   Pp [3] 4–34   Paper, with image on front of one volume of *Dr Chase's Last Receipt Book and Household Physician*; stapled

CONTENTS: 3–34 culinary and medicinal recipes, testimonials, and publ ads

COPIES: *Private collection

NOTES: The heading on p 3 is 'Dr. Chase's Receipts.' There is more medical than culinary information. 'Food for the Sick,' i.e., recipes for invalids, is at bottom p 14; 'Cooking Receipts' are at bottom pp 25, 26, 27, 28, 30, and 32.

The latest dated testimonial indicates that the booklet was likely published about 1904; it reads, 'In July, 1903 ... By September ... In December we began using Dr. Chase's Ointment, which has made a complete cure.'

Advertisements on p 34 and elsewhere advise readers that Dr Chase's family medicines can be bought from Edmanson, Bates and Co., 32 Colborne Street, Toronto, Ontario.

The private collector's copy is inscribed on the front face of the binding, possibly in a child's hand, in pencil, 'Mrs AF Dobsone'; and on the outside back face, in pencil, 'Wm Young Sunderland.'

O142.2   nd [about 1922]
—100 / special recipes / selected from / Dr. Chase's Receipt Book / [below Dr Chase's photograph:] Respectfully / A.W. Chase, M.D. / Published by / Dr. A.W. Chase Medicine Co. / Toronto, Can. [cover-title]
DESCRIPTION: 19.0 × 13.0 cm   Pp [3] 4–34   Paper, with photograph on front of Dr Chase; stapled
CONTENTS: 3–34 culinary and medicinal recipes, testimonials, and publ ads
COPIES: *OHMB (Ephemera QV772 A964o 1920) OTUTF (uncat patent medicine)
NOTES: The heading on p 3 is 'Dr. Chase's Recipes.' There is more medical than culinary information. The latest dated testimonial is 15 July 1922.

Dr King's guide to health, household instructor and family prize cook book 1904

See O96.1 for a list of other annual issues.

O143.1   [1904]
Price 10 cents / Dr. King's / guide to health / household / instructor / & family / prize / cook book / H.E. Bucklen & Co. / Chicago, Ill. / 275–276–277 Michigan Ave. / Windsor, Can. / 52–54 Sandwich St West. [cover-title]
DESCRIPTION: Three images on front face of binding: at centre, a building; to the left of the building, a man in a laboratory; to the right, a woman stirring steaming food and holding a cookbook; stapled, and with hole punched at top left corner, through which runs a string for hanging
COPIES: United States: *Private collection
NOTES: Calendars for 1904 and 1905 are on the first page.

Farmer, Miss Fannie Merritt (Boston, Mass., 23 March 1857–15 January 1915, Boston, Mass.)

Fannie Farmer was a graduate of the Boston Cooking School and its principal from 1891 to 1902, after which she opened her own School of Cookery, which she ran until her death. See her biography in Arndt, pp 159–61 (Alice Ross, 'Fannie Merritt Farmer') and in Feeding America.

Farmer's The Boston Cooking-School Cook Book *was the most popular cookbook in the United States from its first publication in 1896 to 1931, when it was overtaken by Irma Rombauer's* Joy of Cooking *(Longone/ Longone, p 9). The Boston Cooking-School Cook Book was also hugely successful in Canada, where the first Canadian edition was likely issued in 1904. Its influence was strong past 1950, in both English- and French-language homes. A francophone Quebecker, Hélène Dionne of the Musée de la civilisation in Quebec City, told me that it was the only English-language cookbook in her mother's kitchen and that it was widely distributed in Quebec. Another woman explained that her unilingual French-speaking mother sometimes had to ask her husband for help in translating the recipes in* The Boston Cooking-School Cook Book, *the only culinary manual in their Quebec home. It was my aunt's kitchen bible through the 1950s, and at Christmas, at the end of the twentieth century, we still enjoyed Popcorn Balls made from a recipe in the book. American editions of* The Boston Cooking-School Cook Book *were also used in Canada: One correspondent reported to me that her mother-in-law's copy of the 1918 Boston edition was the text for a course she took at the Macdonald Institute in Guelph in 1919.*

Farmer's Catering for Special Occasions *was published in a Canadian edition; see O262.1. Also by Farmer are:* Jaynes and Co.'s Economical Cook Book, *Boston: March 1895 (United States: InU);* Chafing Dish Possibilities, *Boston: Little, Brown and Co., 1898 (United States: DLC);* A Book of Good Dinners for My Friend, *1900 (Bitting, p 153);* Food and Cookery for the Sick and Convalescent, *Boston: Little, Brown and Co., 1904 (United States: DLC);* What to Have for Dinner, *New York: Dodge Publishing Co., [copyright 1905] (United States: DLC);* Cresca Dainties, *New York: Reiss and Brady, [1908] (United States: DLC);* A New Book of Cookery, *Boston: Little, Brown and Co., 1912 (United States: InU);* The Dinner Calendar, *New York: Sully and Kleinteich, c1915 (United States: DLC); and* The Rumford Cook Book, *Providence, RI: Rumford Chemical Works, nd (United States: InU). Janice Longone, in her introduction to the 1997 Dover reprint of the 1896 edition of* The Boston Cooking-School Cook Book, *p ix, says that Farmer also wrote advertising pamphlets and endorsed such products as Knox's Gelatine, Cleveland's Baking Powder, Read's 'Odorless' Refrigerator, and Quaker Crimped Crust Bread. She also wrote a cookery page in* Woman's Home Companion, *with her sister Cora.*

Farmer's What to Have for Dinner *was probably sold by the Methodist Book and Publishing House in Toronto; see the following entry in 'Stock Book 1909' (OTCC Acc. 83.061C, UCC Board of Publication, Series*

*III, Box 39, p 49): '8 [copies] What to have for Dinner.'
'Stock Book 1910' (Box 40, p 33) lists '15 [copies] What to
have for Dinner etc.' 'Stock Book 1913' (Box 41, p 10)
lists '9 [copies] What to Have for Dinner.'*

O144.1 [copyright 1904]
[An edition of *The Boston Cooking-School Cook Book*,
Toronto: Musson Book Co. Ltd, [copyright 1904],
cloth]
COPIES: Private collection
NOTES: The private collector describes the book as
'Revised // With an appendix of three hundred reci-
pes and an adden[dum?] of one hundred recipes,'
and printed by the University Press, John Wilson and
Son, USA.

O144.2 [copyright 1906]
—The / Boston Cooking-School / cook book / by /
Fannie Merritt Farmer / of Miss Farmer's School of
Cookery / author of "Chafing-Dish Possibilities,"
and "Food and Cookery / for the Sick and
Convalescent" / Revised / With one hundred and
twenty-five new recipes, the / recipes from the
appendix and the addenda / introduced in logical
order throughout / the book, and one hundred /
half-tone illustrations / Toronto / The Musson Book
Company / Limited
DESCRIPTION: 19.0 × 12.0 cm   Pp [i–ix] x [xi] xii–xv [xvi],
[1] 2–648   69 pls [this copy lacks the frontis, which
would make a total of 70 pls]   Cloth
CONTENTS: i tp; ii 'Copyright, 1896, 1900, 1901, 1902,
1903, 1904, 1905, 1906 by Fannie Merritt Farmer //
The University Press, Cambridge, U.S.A.'; iii dedication to Mrs William B. Sewall, president of the Boston
Cooking-School; iv blank; v quotation from Ruskin;
vi blank; vii 'Preface' signed F.M.F.; viii blank; ix–x
table of contents; xi–xv 'List of Illustrations'; xvi blank;
1–603 text in thirty-eight chapters; 604 blank; 605–6
'Glossary'; 607–16 'Miss Farmer's School of Cookery'
[information about courses]; 617–48 index
COPIES: *BKOM   OGU (TX715 F234 1906)   QMU
(641.5 F233b)
NOTES: In the 'Preface' Farmer predicts, 'I certainly feel
that the time is not far distant when a knowledge of
the principles of diet will be an essential part of one's
education.'

O144.3 [copyright 1924]
—The / Boston Cooking-School / cook book / by /
Fannie Merritt Farmer / New edition, revised and
enlarged / With 122 half-tone illustrations / Toronto
/ McClelland and Stewart
DESCRIPTION: 20.5 × 13.5 cm   Pp [i–xi] xii [xiii] xiv–xvi

[xvii–xviii], [1] 2–806   Frontis, 31 double-sided pls
Cloth
CONTENTS: i ht; ii blank; iii tp; iv 'Copyright, 1924, by
Cora D.[exter] Perkins'; v dedication to Mrs William
B. Sewall; vi quotation from Ruskin; vii 'Preface to
the New Edition' signed C.D.P., Boston, July 1923; viii
blank; ix 'Preface to the First Edition' signed F.M.F.;
x blank; xi–xii table of contents; xiii–xvi list of illus-
trations; xvii part-title: 'The Boston Cooking-School
Cook Book'; xviii blank; 1–756 text; 757–806 index
CITATIONS: Driver 2001, Wellington County, pp 95–6
Ferguson/Fraser, p 52   Spadoni/Donnelly No. 759
COPIES: ARDA   OFERWM   OHMA (TX715 F234
1924)   OWTU (F14639)   *Private collection
NOTES: Cora Dexter Perkins, née Farmer, was one of
Fannie Farmer's three sisters. In her 'Preface to the
New Edition,' she recounts the book's publishing
history: 'It is now twenty-seven years since "The Boston Cooking-School Cook Book" was first published.
Since that time it has been frequently revised and a
large number of new recipes have been added, first in
the form of an appendix and addenda, later incorporated in logical order throughout the volume. Meantime, in 1912, Miss Farmer published an entirely new
work, "A New Book of Cookery", ... [included in the
present revision are] most of the recipes heretofore
found in "A New Book of Cookery", as well as a
number of new recipes. "The Boston Cooking-School
Cook Book" ... [now contains] more than six hundred
recipes not found in previous editions.'
    Spadoni/Donnelly state, 'From the sheets of the
Little, Brown and Co., Ltd. edition of 1924.'

O144.4 1930
—The Boston / Cooking-School / cook book / by /
Fannie Merritt Farmer / New edition completely
revised / With illustrations / Toronto / McClelland
and Stewart / 1930
DESCRIPTION: 20.5 × 13.5 cm   Pp [i–xi] xii, [1–3] 4–
831 [832], [i–xxxii]   Frontis of 'Testing Recipes at Miss
Farmer's School of Cookery,' many illus   Cloth
CONTENTS: i ht; ii blank; iii tp; iv 'Copyright, 1896,
1900, 1901, 1902, 1903, 1904, 1905, 1906, 1912, 1914, /
by Fannie Merritt Farmer / Copyright, 1915, 1918,
1923, 1924, 1927, 1928, / by Cora D. Perkins / Copyright, 1930, / by Dexter Perkins / Original edition
published 1896 / 1st printing 3,000 copies / Reprinted
(twice) 1897 5,000 copies / Reprinted 1899 5,000 copies / Reprinted 1900 5,000 copies / Reprinted 1901
8,000 copies / Reprinted 1902 10,000 copies / Reprinted 1903 10,000 copies / Reprinted 1904 10,000
copies / Reprinted 1905 10,000 copies / Revised edition published 1906 / 1st printing 20,000 copies /

Reprinted 1907 20,000 copies / Reprinted 1908 20,000 copies / Reprinted 1909 20,000 copies / Reprinted 1910 45,000 copies / Reprinted 1911 30,000 copies / Reprinted 1912 50,000 copies / Reprinted 1913 50,000 copies / Reprinted 1914 50,000 copies / Reprinted 1915 50,000 copies / Reprinted 1916 50,000 copies / Reprinted 1917 50,000 copies / Revised edition published 1918 / 1st printing 50,000 copies / Reprinted 1919 25,000 copies / Reprinted (twice) 1920 100,000 copies / Reprinted (three times) 1921 60,000 copies / Reprinted (three times) 1922 100,000 copies / Revised edition published 1923 / 1st printing 50,000 copies / Reprinted 1923 50,000 copies / Reprinted (three times) 1924 105,000 copies / Reprinted 1925 50,000 copies / Reprinted (twice) 1926 100,000 copies / Reprinted 1927 50,000 copies / Reprinted 1928 50,000 copies / Reprinted (twice) 1929 75,000 copies / New edition completely revised published 1930 / 1st printing 50,000 copies / Making total printings 1,436,000 copies / Printed in the United States of America'; v dedication to Mrs William B. Sewall; vi quotation from Ruskin; vii 'Preface to the New Edition' [i.e., this edition of 1930] signed W.L.P. [i.e., Wilma Lord Perkins]; viii blank; ix 'Preface to the First Edition' signed F.M.F.; x blank; xi–xii 'Contents'; 1–771 text; 772 blank; 773–831 'Index'; 832 blank; i Little Brown and Co. symbol; ii blank; iii–xxxii ads

CITATIONS: Spadoni/Donnelly No. 972
COPIES: *QMM (TX715 F234 1930)

NOTES: In the 'Preface to the New Edition,' Wilma Lord Perkins comments: 'Of recent years new vegetables, new fruits, and new salad greens have come into use, as well as new ways of preparing the ones formerly known. New equipment, such as mechanical refrigeration, pressure cookers, and the like, have suggested changes in method. New material has, therefore, been included in this 1930 edition ...' Wilma was the wife of Herbert Perkins, the son of Fannie's sister Cora. Wilma later wrote O1056.1, *The Fannie Farmer Junior Cook Book*.

Spadoni/Donnelly state, 'From the sheets of the Little, Brown and Co., Ltd. edition.'

O144.5 1932
—The Boston / Cooking-School / cook book / by / Fannie Merritt Farmer / New edition completely revised / With illustrations / Toronto / McClelland and Stewart / 1932
DESCRIPTION: 20.0 × 13.5 cm   Pp [i–xi] xii, [1–3] 4–831   Frontis of 'Testing Recipes at Miss Farmer's School of Cookery,' many illus   Rebound
CONTENTS: i ht; ii probably blank (in the OTMCL copy the original endpapers, printed with various

tables, are glued to p ii and the verso of the frontis); iii tp; iv copyright information and publishing history as cited for O144.4, except for the following revision: '... New edition completely revised published 1930 / 1st printing 50,000 copies / Reprinted 1930 50,000 copies / Reprinted 1931 50,000 copies / Making total printings 1,541,250 copies / Printed / in Canada / on Canadian / paper / T.H [*sic*, no period] Best Printing Co., Limited / Toronto, Ont.'; v dedication to Mrs William B. Sewall; vi quotation from Ruskin; vii 'Preface to the New Edition' signed W.L.P. [i.e., Wilma Lord Perkins]; viii blank; ix 'Preface to the First Edition' signed F.M.F.; x blank; xi–xii 'Contents'; 1–771 text; 772 blank; 773–831 'Index'
COPIES: *OTMCL (641.5 F13 1932)

O144.6 [copyright 1934]
—The Boston / Cooking-School / cook book / by / Fannie Merritt Farmer / New edition completely revised / With illustrations / Toronto / McClelland and Stewart
DESCRIPTION: 20.5 × 13.5 cm   Pp [1–2], [i–xi] xii [xiii–xxviii], [1–3] 4–831   Frontis of 'Ham and Broccoli for Color Contrast,' many illus   Cloth
CONTENTS: 1 [endpaper recto] 'Ways to Use Sour Milk and Cream' and a list of recipes using 'Sour Milk, More Than 1 Cup'; 2 [endpaper verso] blank; i ht; ii blank; iii tp; iv copyright information and publishing history as cited for O144.4, except for copyright years for Dexter Perkins now '1930, 1931, 1932, 1933, 1934' and for the following revision: '... New edition completely revised published 1930 / 1st printing 50,000 copies / Reprinted 1930 50,000 copies / Reprinted 1931 50,000 copies / Reprinted 1933 50,000 copies / Reprinted 1934 50,000 copies / Making total printings 1,636,000 copies / Printed in Canada / T.H. Best Printing Co., Limited / Toronto, Ont.'; v dedication to Mrs William B. Sewall; vi quotation from Ruskin; vii 'Preface to the New Edition' signed W.L.P. [i.e., Wilma Lord Perkins]; viii blank; ix 'Preface to the First Edition' signed F.M.F.; x blank; xi–xii table of contents; xiii part-title: 'The Boston Cooking-School Cook Book'; xiv blank; xv–xxviii, 1–2 'Modern Menus for Many Occasions'; 3–771 Chapters 1–50; 772 blank; 773–831 index
COPIES: *Private collection

O144.7 [1936]
—The Boston / Cooking-School / cook book / by / Fannie Merritt Farmer / New edition, completely revised / With illustrations / McClelland & Stewart Limited / publishers Toronto
DESCRIPTION: 19.5 × 12.0 cm   Pp [iii–xi] xii–xiii [xiv],

[1–3] 4–838 Frontis of 'Making a Tray of Small Pastries,' many illus Rebound

CONTENTS: iii tp; iv copyright information and publishing history as cited for O144.6, except for copyright years for Dexter Perkins now '... 1934, 1936' and for the following revision: '... Reprinted 1934 50,000 copies / Reprinted 1935 50,000 copies / New edition completely revised published 1936 / 1st printing 50,000 copies / Making total printings 1,736,000 copies / Printed in Canada / T.H. Best Printing Co., Limited / Toronto, Ont.'; v dedication to Mrs William B. Sewall; vi quotation from Ruskin; vii 'Preface to the New Edition' signed Wilma Lord Perkins, Harvard, Massachusetts, 18 July 1936; viii blank; ix 'Preface to the First Edition' signed F.M.F.; x blank; xi–xiii table of contents; xiv blank; 1 part-title: 'The Boston Cooking-School Cook Book'; 2 blank; 3–772 text; 773–838 index

CITATIONS: Spadoni/Donnelly No. 1175

COPIES: *BVA OHMA (TX715 F234 1936) OTMCL (641.5 F13 1936) QMM (TX715 F234 1936)

NOTES: In the 'Preface to the New Edition' of 1936, Wilma Perkins comments that the recipes have been grouped so 'that their similarity was made obvious ... variations have been placed with the basic recipes to which they belong ... Other changes have been made to conform with modern fashions in food.' The chapter on canapés and hors d'oeuvres is longer; foreign and regional specialties have been added; and wine is more widely used as an ingredient.

The BVA copy lacks pp 67–74 and 173–4.

O144.8 1938

—The Boston / Cooking-School / cook book / by / Fannie Merritt Farmer / New edition completely revised / With illustrations / Toronto / McClelland and Stewart / 1938

DESCRIPTION: 20.5 × 13.5 cm Pp [1–2], [i–xi] xii–xiii [xiv], [1–3] 4–838, [i–ii] Frontis of 'Making a Tray of Small Pastries,' illus Cloth

CONTENTS: 1 [endpaper recto] 'Roasting Chart for Poultry and Game' and 'Deep-Fat Frying Chart'; 2 [endpaper verso] blank; i ht; ii blank; iii tp; iv copyright information and publishing history as cited for O144.7, except for the following revision: '... New edition completely revised published 1936 / 1st printing 50,000 copies / Reprinted 1937 100,000 copies / Reprinted 1938 50,000 copies / Making total printings 1,886,000 copies / Printed and bound in Canada by T.H. Best Printing Co. Limited, Toronto'; v dedication to Mrs William B. Sewall; vi quotation from Ruskin; vii 'Preface to the New Edition' signed Wilma Lord Perkins, Harvard, Massachussetts, 18 July 1936; viii

blank; ix 'Preface to the First Edition' signed F.M.F.; x blank; xi–xiii table of contents; xiv blank; 1 part-title: 'The Boston Cooking-School Cook Book'; 2 blank; 3–772 Chapters 1–54; 773–838 index; i [endpaper recto] blank; ii [endpaper verso] 'Substitutions,' 'Equivalents,' and 'Capacity of Canned-Food Containers'

COPIES: *Private collection

O144.9 1940

—The Boston / Cooking-School / cook book / by / Fannie Merritt Farmer / New edition completely revised / With illustrations / Toronto / McClelland and Stewart / 1940

DESCRIPTION: 20.5 × 13.5 cm Pp [1–2], [i–xi] xii–xiii [xiv], [1–3] 4–838, [i–iv] Frontis of 'Making a Tray of Small Pastries,' many illus Cloth

CONTENTS: 1 [endpaper recto] roasting and deep-frying charts; 2 [endpaper verso] blank; i ht; ii blank; iii tp; iv copyright information and publishing history as cited for O144.8, except for copyright years for Cora Perkins now '... 1924, 1928, 1929' (not '1924, 1927, 1928') and for the following revision: '... Reprinted 1938 50,000 copies / Reprinted 1939 50,000 copies / Reprinted 1940 20,000 copies / Making total printings 1,956,000 copies / Printed and bound in Canada by T.H. Best Printing Co. Limited, Toronto'; v dedication to Mrs William B. Sewall; vi quotation from Ruskin; vii 'Preface to the New Edition' signed Wilma Lord Perkins, Harvard, Massachussetts, 18 July 1936; viii blank; ix 'Preface to the First Edition' signed F.M.F.; x blank; xi–xiii table of contents; xiv blank; 1 part-title: 'The Boston Cooking-School Cook Book'; 2 blank; 3–772 Chapters 1–54; 773–838 index; i–iii blank; iv [endpaper] 'Substitutions,' 'Equivalents,' and 'Capacity of Canned-Food Containers'

COPIES: *Private collection

O144.10 [copyright 1941]

—The Boston / Cooking-School / cook book / by / Fannie Merritt Farmer / New edition completely revised / With illustrations / McClelland & Stewart Limited / publishers Toronto

DESCRIPTION: 20.0 × 13.0 cm Pp [i–xiii] xiv [xv–xvi], [1–3] 4–830 Illus Rebound

CONTENTS: i ht; ii blank; iii tp; iv copyright information and publishing history as cited for O144.9, except for copyright years for Dexter Perkins now '... 1936, 1941' and for the following revision: '... Reprinted 1940 20,000 copies / Reprinted 1941 5,000 copies / New edition completely revised published 1941 / 1st printing 75,000 copies / Making total printings 2,036,000 copies / Copyright, Canada, 1941 / by / McClelland & Stewart Limited / Printed in Canada

/ T.H. Best Printing Co., Limited / Toronto, Ont.'; v
dedication to Mrs William B. Sewall; vi blank; vii
quotation from Ruskin; viii blank; ix 'Preface to the
Seventh Edition' signed Wilma Lord Perkins; x blank;
xi 'Preface to the First Edition' signed F.M.F.; xii blank;
xiii–xiv table of contents; xv 'Fifty Basic Recipes (For
Students and Beginners)'; xvi blank; 1–756 text; 757–
830 index
CITATIONS: Spadoni/Donnelly No. 1260
COPIES: BVAU (TX715 F234 1941; not on shelf,
not in storage) *OTMCL (641.5 F13 1941) OTNY
(641.5 F) QMBN
NOTES: The rebound OTMCL copy has no frontispiece.

O144.11 [copyright 1941]
—[An edition of *Livre de cuisine de Boston*, Toronto:
McClelland and Stewart Ltd, [copyright 1941]]
CITATIONS: BQ Exposition 1974, p 14
COPIES: QMBN (TX715 F3 F)
NOTES: BQ Exposition 1974, p 14, refers to an edition,
[copyright 1941], with the call number TX715 F3 F,
exhibited in 1974. This same copy was exhibited in
1948 at Bibliothèque Saint-Sulpice, Vitrine 1, according to a typescript record of the exhibition, dated
23 December 1948 (at QMBN). When I visited QMBN
in September 2000, however, the only copy of *Livre de
cuisine de Boston* that I found recorded in the catalogue, and examined, was an eighth edition published in Montreal by Beauchemin, [copyright 1949],
but dated [1965] by the library; it has the new conservation number of 160004 CON, and the label TX715
F3 F 1965.

O144.12 [copyright 1944]
—Fannie Merritt Farmer / Le livre de / cuisine / de
/ l'Ecole de cuisine / de Boston / Nouvelle edition
revue et corrigée / Avec illustrations / Traduit de
l'anglais / par Madeleine Bodier / McClelland &
Stewart Limited / Editeurs Toronto
DESCRIPTION: 20.5 × 13.0 cm   Pp [i–xiii] xiv [xv–xvi],
[1–3] 4–842 Illus Cloth
CONTENTS: i ht; ii blank; iii tp; iv 'Copyright, Canada,
1944 par McClelland & Stewart Limited Imprimé au
Canada T.H. Best Printing Co., Limited Toronto, Ont.';
v dedication to Mrs William B. Sewall; vi blank; vii
quotation from Ruskin; viii blank; ix 'Préface à la
septième édition' signed Wilma Lord Perkins; x blank;
xi 'Préface à la premirèe [*sic*] édition' signed F.M.F.;
xii blank; xiii–xiv 'Table des matières'; xv 'Cinquante
recettes fondamentales'; xvi blank; 1–762 text; 763–
842 index
CITATIONS: Spadoni/Donnelly No. 1274

COPIES: *QMM (RBD Soeur Berthe, ckbk 434); United
States: DLC (TX715 F2343 1944)

O144.13 [copyright 1945]
—Fannie Merritt Farmer / Le livre de / cuisine / de
/ l'Ecole de cuisine / de Boston / Nouvelle edition
revue et corrigée / Avec illustrations / Traduit de
l'anglais / par Madeleine Bodier / McClelland &
Stewart Limited / Editeurs Toronto
DESCRIPTION: 20.0 × 13.5 cm   Pp [i–xiii] xiv [xv–xvi],
[1–3] 4–842 Illus Cloth
CONTENTS: i ht; ii blank; iii tp; iv 'Copyright, 1945 par
McClelland & Stewart Limited Imprimé au Canada
T.H. Best Printing Co., Limited, Toronto'; v dedication to Mrs William B. Sewall; vi blank; vii quotation
from Ruskin; viii blank; ix 'Préface à la septième
édition' signed Wilma Lord Perkins; x blank; xi
'Préface à la premirée [*sic*] édition' signed F.M.F.; xii
blank; xiii–xiv 'Table des matières'; xv 'Cinquante
recettes fondamentales pour étudiants et commençants'; xvi blank; 1–762 text; 763–842 'Index'
COPIES: QQSCA   *QSFFSC (641.5 F223L)
NOTES: Tables of temperature, times, measurement, and
substitutes are on the endpapers.

O144.14 8th ed., [copyright 1946]
—[Tp on two facing pages:] The Boston Cooking-
School / cook book / by / Fannie Merritt Farmer /
Eighth edition, / completely revised by / Wilma
Lord Perkins / Drawings by Martha Powell Setchell
// McClelland & Stewart, Limited / publishers
Toronto
DESCRIPTION: 20.0 × 13.5 cm   Pp [i–ix] x [xi–xiii] xiv
[xv–xvi], [1–3] 4–879 Illus Cloth
CONTENTS: i ht; ii–iii tp; iv copyright information and
publishing history as cited for O144.10, except for
copyright years for Dexter Perkins now '... 1941, 1942,
1946' and for the following revision: '... New edition
completely revised published 1941 / 1st printing
75,000 copies / Reprinted 1942 50,000 copies / Reprinted (twice) 1943 75,000 copies / Reprinted (twice)
1944 70,000 copies / Reprinted 1945 (four times)
190,000 copies / Reprinted 1946 25,000 copies / New
edition completely revised published 1946 / 85,000
copies / Making total printings 2,531,000 copies /
New revised Canadian edition / Copyright, Canada,
1946 / by / McClelland & Stewart Limited / Printed
and bound in Canada, by / the Hunter-Rose Co.
Limited, Toronto'; v dedication to Mrs William B.
Sewall; vi blank; vii quotation from Ruskin; viii blank;
ix–x 'Preface to the Eighth Edition' signed Wilma
Lord Perkins, Harvard, Massachusetts, 15 August
1946; xi 'Preface to the First Edition' signed F.M.F.; xii

blank; xiii–xiv table of contents; xv 'Fifty Basic Recipes'; xvi blank; 1–805 text; 806 blank; 807–79 index
CITATIONS: CCat No. 26, p ZB12
COPIES: *OWTU (F14635)   Private collection
NOTES: The endpapers are printed with 'Cooking Temperatures,' page references for various charts, 'Substitutions,' and 'Equivalents.' CCat records the price: $3.00.

A private collector has an edition that appears to be identical except that a different printer/binder is recorded on the title-page verso: instead of 'Printed and bound in Canada, by / the Hunter-Rose Co. Limited, Toronto,' her copy has '... by / T.H. Best Printing Co., Limited, Toronto.' Spadoni/Donnelly No. 1296 describe a rebound copy at OSU printed by T.H. Best Printing Co. Ltd.

O144.15   8th ed., [copyright 1949]
—Livre de cuisine / de Boston / (École de cuisine de Boston) / de / Fannie Merritt Farmer / Huitième édition / complètement revue et corrigée / par Wilma Lord Perkins / Traduction / de / Madeleine Bodier / McClelland & Stewart, Limited / éditeurs Toronto
DESCRIPTION: 20.0 × 13.5 cm   Pp [1–2], [i–vii] viii [ix–xi] xii [xiii–xiv], [1–3] 4–972 [973–5]   Illus   Cloth
CONTENTS: 1 ht; 2 illus of utensils and 'Illustrations par Martha Powell Setchell'; i tp; ii 'Copyright 1896, 1900, 1901, 1902, 1903, 1904, 1905, 1906, 1912, 1914, / par Fannie Merritt Farmer / Copyright 1915, 1918, 1923, 1924, 1928, 1929, par Cora D. Perkins / Copyright 1930, 1931, 1932, 1933, 1934, 1936, 1941, 1942, 1946, / par Dexter Perkins / Édition originale publiée en 1896 / 1ère impression 3,000 exemplaires / Réimprimé (deux fois) 1897 5,000 exemplaires / Réimprimé 1899 5,000 exemplaires / Réimprimé 1900 5,000 exemplaires / Réimprimé 1901 8,000 exemplaires / Réimprimé 1902 10,000 exemplaires / Réimprimé 1903 10,000 exemplaires / Réimprimé 1904 10,000 exemplaires / Réimprimé 1905 10,000 exemplaires / Édition revisée publiée en 1906 / 1ère impression 20,000 exemplaires / Réimprimé 1907 20,000 exemplaires / Réimprimé 1908 20,000 exemplaires / Réimprimé 1909 20,000 exemplaires / Réimprimé 1910 45,000 exemplaires / Réimprimé 1911 30,000 exemplaires / Réimprimé 1912 50,000 exemplaires / Réimprimé 1913 50,000 exemplaires / Réimprimé 1914 50,000 exemplaires / Réimprimé 1915 50,000 exemplaires / Réimprimé 1916 50,000 exemplaires / Réimprimé 1917 50,000 exemplaires / Édition revisée publiée en 1918 / 1ère impression 50,000 exemplaires / Réimprimé 1919 25,000 exemplaires / Réimprimé (deux fois) 1920 100,000 exemplaires / Réimprimé (trois fois) 1921 60,000 exemplaires / Réimprimé (trois fois) 1922 100,000 exemplaires / Édition revisée publiée en 1923 / 1ère impression 50,000 exemplaires / Réimprimé 1923 50,000 exemplaires / Réimprimé (trois fois) 1924 105,000 exemplaires / Réimprimé 1925 50,000 exemplaires / Réimprimé (deux fois) 1926 100,000 exemplaires / Réimprimé 1927 50,000 exemplaires / Réimprimé 1928 50,000 exemplaires / Réimprimé (deux fois) 1929 75,000 exemplaires / Nouvelle édition complètement revisée publiée en 1930 / 1ère impression 50,000 exemplaires / Réimprimé 1930 50,000 exemplaires / Réimprimé 1931 50,000 exemplaires / Réimprimé 1933 50,000 exemplaires / Réimprimé 1934 50,000 exemplaires / Réimprimé 1935 50,000 exemplaires / Nouvelle édition complètement revisée publiée en 1936 / 1ère impression 50,000 exemplaires / Réimprimé 1937 100,000 exemplaires / Réimprimé 1938 50,000 exemplaires / Réimprimé 1939 50,000 exemplaires / Réimprimé 1940 20,000 exemplaires / Réimprimé 1941 5,000 exemplaires / Nouvelle édition complètement revisée publiée en 1941 / 1ère impression 75,000 exemplaires / Réimprimé 1942 50,000 exemplaires / Réimprimé (deux fois) 1943 75,000 exemplaires / Réimprimé (deux fois) 1944 70,000 exemplaires / Réimprimé (quatre fois) 1945 190,000 exemplaires / Réimprimé 1946 25,000 exemplaires / Nouvelle édition complètement revisée publiée en 1946 / 85,000 exemplaires / Formant un tirage total de 2,531,000 exemplaires / Nouvelle édition canadienne revisée / Copyright, Canada, 1949 / par / McClelland & Stewart Limited / Imprimé et relié au / Canada par / Le Soleil – Québec'; iii dedication to Mrs William B. Sewall; iv blank; v uncredited quotation beginning, 'L'art culinaire exige tout à la fois la science de Médée, de Cercé, de ...'; vi blank; vii–viii 'Préface à la huitième édition'; ix 'Préface à la première édition'; x blank; xi–xii 'Table des matières'; xiii 'Cinquante recettes fondamentales'; xiv blank; 1–909 text; 910 blank; 911–72 index; 973–5 blank for 'Memo'
CITATIONS: Spadoni/Donnelly No. 1358
COPIES: QMM (2 copies: *RBD TX715 F2343 1949 Joubert, RBD Vanna Garnier 903)

OTHER EDITIONS: *Livre de cuisine de Boston*, 8th ed., Montreal: Librairie Beauchemin, [copyright 1949], dated [1965] in library catalogue (QMBN), and 8th ed., Montreal: Beauchemin, [1973] (NBSCU); *The Boston Cooking School Cook Book*, reprint, Toronto: Coles Publishing Co. Ltd, [copyright 1980] (OONL).

AMERICAN EDITIONS: *The Boston Cooking-School Cook*

Book, 1st ed., Boston: Little, Brown and Co., 1896 (United States: InU); 2nd ed., 1896 (Bitting, p 153); Boston: Little, Brown and Co., 1900 (United States: DLC); Boston: Little, Brown and Co., 1902 (United States: DLC); Boston: Little, Brown and Co., 1904 (United States: DLC); Boston: Little, Brown and Co., 1905 (United States: DLC); Boston: Little, Brown and Co., 1906 (United States: DLC); Boston: Little, Brown and Co., 1907 (United States: DLC); Boston: Little, Brown and Co., 1909 (United States: DLC); Boston: Little, Brown and Co., 1912 (OTMCL); Boston: Little, Brown and Co., 1913 (United States: DLC); Boston: Little, Brown and Co., 1914 (United States: DLC); 1915 (Dickinson, p 37); Boston: Little, Brown and Co., 1916 (WaiteCat 5, No. 67); Boston: Little, Brown and Co., [c1918] (United States: DLC); Boston: Little, Brown and Co., 1920 (NBFKL); Boston: Little, Brown and Co., 1922 (QMM); Boston: Little, Brown and Co., 1923 (OFERWM; United States: DLC); Boston: Little, Brown and Co., 1924 (United States: DLC); Boston: Little, Brown and Co., 1925 (QMM); Boston: Little, Brown and Co., 1926 (United States: DLC); Boston: Little, Brown and Co., 1927 (QMM); Boston: Little, Brown and Co., 1929 (Private collection); Boston: Little, Brown and Co., 1930 (QMM; United States: DLC); Boston: Little, Brown and Co., 1931 (WaiteCat 5, No. 69); Boston: Little, Brown and Co., 1933 (United States: DLC); Boston: Little, Brown and Co., 1934 (United States: DLC); new ed., Boston: Little, Brown and Co., 1936 (United States: DLC); 1938 (Dickinson, p 37); 7th ed., Boston: Little, Brown and Co., 1941 (United States: DLC); 1942 (Dickinson, p 37); Boston: Little, Brown and Co., 1943 (Private collection); New York: Garden City Publishing Co., 1945 (Private collection); 8th ed., Boston: Little, Brown and Co., [c1946] (United States: DLC); *Fannie Farmer's Handy Cook Book; Recipes from Her Famous Boston Cooking-School Cook Book,* abridged by Wilma Lord Perkins, [New York:] New American Library, [1950] (United States: DLC); *The Boston Cooking-School Cook Book,* 9th ed., Boston: Little, Brown, 1951 (QMM; United States: DLC); *The All New Fannie Farmer Boston Cooking-School Cookbook,* 10th ed., Boston: Little, Brown, [1959] (QMM; United States: DLC); *The All New Fannie Farmer Boston Cooking-School Cookbook,* 10th ed., New York: Bantam Books, [1959] (QMM); *The Fannie Farmer Cookbook,* 11th ed., Boston: Little, Brown, [1965] (NSH, NSWA, OTMCL, QMJ; United States: DLC); *The Boston Cooking-School Cook Book,* New York: Gordon Press, 1973 (United States: DLC); *The Original Boston Cooking-School Cook Book, 1896* [1st ed.], New York: H.L. Levin Associates, distributed by Crown Publishers, [1973?] (United States:

DLC); *The Fannie Farmer Cookbook,* 12th ed., rev. by Marion Cunningham with Jeri Laber, New York: Knopf, distributed by Random House, 1979 (United States: DLC); *The Fannie Farmer Large Print Cookbook,* edited by Marion Cunningham and Jeri Laber, large print ed. edited by Amy and Peter Pastan, Boston: G.K. Hall, 1985 (United States: DLC); *The Original Boston Cooking-School Cook Book, 1896,* New York: New American Library, 1988 (United States: DLC); *The Original Fannie Farmer 1896 Cook Book, The Boston Cooking School,* commemorative ed., Baltimore, Md: Ottrenheimer Publishers, 1996 (Private collection); *Original 1896 Boston Cooking-School Cook Book,* introduction by Janice Bluestein Longone, Mineola, NY: Dover Publications, c1997 (United States: DLC).

The housekeeper's perfect account book 1905

Later editions of the account book were published to promote different businesses, in 1912, 1917, 1930, 1931, 1932, and 1933 (O267.1, O385.1, O643.1, O731.1, O762.1, O794.1). For information about Cowan's Co., see O336.1, Dainty and Delicious Dishes.

O145.1   1905, entered 1904
Cowan's / cocoa and / chocolate / are the standard of purity and excellence / Every home needs them Ask your grocer for them / The / housekeeper's / perfect / account book / 1905 / Entered according to Act of the Parliament of Canada in the year nineteen hundred and four, by Geo. Shepard, at the Department of Agriculture at Ottawa. / Toronto: / George Shepard, 27 Widmer Street. / Price 25 cents. [cover-title]
DESCRIPTION: With image on front of a housekeeper holding a book
COPIES: *OBM
NOTES: The account book has printed recipes.

The Ladies' Aid cook book

O146.1   1904
The / Ladies' Aid / cook book / Edited by the Ladies' Aid of St. / Andrew's Presbyterian Church, / Campbellford, Ontario. / Campbellford: / Printed at the Despatch office / 1904.
COPIES: *Private collection
NOTES: The book is inscribed, opposite the title-page, by the current owner's grandmother, 'Mrs. D.S. Archer.'

Palmer, Mrs Ida M.

O147.1 [entered 1904]
Culinary / wrinkles / practical recipes / for using /
Armour's / Extract / of Beef / by / Mrs Ida M.
Palmer / Armour Limited / Toronto
DESCRIPTION: 19.5 × 13.5 cm Pp [3–7] 8–47 Illus
red-and-black Paper; one staple and sewn
CONTENTS: 3 small images in a circular frame of steaming dishes on a table; 4 symbol of Armour Press; 5 tp;
6 'Entered according to Act of the Parliament of
Canada in the year 1904, by Armour Limited, Toronto,
in the Department of Agriculture.'; 7 'Imprimus'
signed Armour Ltd, Toronto; 8–45 text; 46–7 'Index'
COPIES: *Private collection
NOTES: The title-page, printed in red and black, has a
decorative border in an ancient Celtic style; the Celtic
motif is used throughout the volume. The 'Imprimus'
says that the recipes were compiled by Mrs Ida M.
Palmer and have the commendation of 'ladies in all
parts of the United States and Canada.' The recipes
use the following products as ingredients: Armour's
Extract of Beef, Asparox ('selected asparagus juice
concentrated, and Armour's Extract of Beef ... designed to be used as a hot drink and for seasoning
purposes'), Armour's Tomato Bouillon, and Armour's
Soluble Beef. Armour Ltd is described on the outside
back face of the binding as 'Sole packers and shippers of Armour's Extract of Beef and Beef Extract
Products for Dominion of Canada, Armour Limited,
Toronto.'

O147.2 [entered 1904]
—Culinary / wrinkles / practical recipes / for using
/ Armour's / Extract / of Beef / by / Mrs Ida M.
Palmer / Armour Limited / Toronto
DESCRIPTION: 19.5 × 13.0 cm Pp [3–7] 8–44 [45–7] Illus
red-and-black Paper; stapled
CONTENTS: 3 small images in a circular frame of steam-
ing dishes on a table; 4 blank; 5 tp; 6 'Entered accord-
ing to Act of the Parliament of Canada in the year
1904, by Armour Limited, Toronto, in the Depart-
ment of Agriculture'; 7 'Imprimus' signed Armour
Ltd, Toronto; 8–45 text; 46–7 'Index'
COPIES: *OTMCL (641.5971 H39 No. 6)
NOTES: The title-page, printed in red and black, has a
decorative border in an ancient Celtic style. Unlike
O147.1, this edition is not sewn, there is no symbol of
Armour Press on p 4, no folios printed on pp 45–7 (or
the folios did not register), and no description of
Armour Ltd on the outside back face of the binding,
which is blank. In addition, some of the text varies;
for example, on p 27 Asparox is described as a 'se-

lected and concentrated Asparagus juice, retaining
all the flavor of fresh asparagus, and Armour's Extract of Beef ... intended to be used for basting fowl
and game of all kinds, and for seasoning, as well as
making a delicious hot drink' (cf the description for
Asparox quoted in O147.1). The order of publication
of the two editions is unknown.

The citation for this title in O'Neill (unpublished)
and the following copies may match O147.1 or O147.2:
OMIHURM, OONL (TX819 S8 P34 1904 missing);
and Great Britain: LB (not located).

AMERICAN EDITIONS: Chicago: Armour and Co., 1903 (Vintage, May 2000); Chicago: Armour and Co., 1905
(United States: CoDU, OBgU, UU); another ed.?, Chicago: Armour and Co., [1905] (United States: DLC).

Another Armour and Co. book has the cover-title
'Culinary Wrinkles,' but it is not related to Palmer's
work: *Recipes and Directions for the Use of Armour's
Extract of Beef*, by Helen Louise Johnson, Chicago:
[Printed by Armour Printing Works, Chicago, for]
Armour and Co., [copyright 1 January 1901] (OKITJS).

Sangster, Margaret Elizabeth Munson (New Rochelle, NY, 22 February 1838– 4 June 1912, Maplewood, NJ)

*This deeply religious American author wrote books,
essays, stories, and poems, for children and adults, from a
Christian perspective. She also worked as editor on the
magazines* Hearth and Home, Christian Intelligencer,
and Harper's Bazar. *See her autobiography,* From My
Youth Up: Personal Reminiscences, *New York and
Toronto: Fleming H. Revell, [copyright 1909], in which
she refers to a Canadian connection: her father emigrated
from Ireland to Canada at the age of eighteen years, then
moved to New York.*

O148.1 [copyright 1904]
The / little kingdom / of home / by / Margaret E.
Sangster / Toronto / McLeod & Allen / publishers
DESCRIPTION: 21.0 × 15.0 cm Pp [i–vi] vii–xii,
[13–14] 15–483 Cloth
CONTENTS: i ht; ii blank; iii tp; iv 'Copyright, 1904, by
J.F. Taylor and Company, New York'; v dedication;
vi blank; vii–viii foreword; ix–xii table of contents;
13–483 text
COPIES: *OGU (UA s024 b15) OWTL
NOTES: Chapter XV, pp 237–48, is titled 'Queen of
One's Own Kitchen' and is described in the table of
contents as follows: 'Just homely housework. The
independence of knowing how to do it. The comfort

of doing it by one's self.' The author conjures up an image of the ideal kitchen and the ideal home cook.

AMERICAN EDITIONS: New York: J.F. Taylor and Co., [1904] (United States: DLC); New York: Fox, Duffield and Co., 1905 (United States: DLC).

Tuthill's almanac and cook book 1904

O149.1 1904
Tuthill's / almanac / and / cook book / 1904 1904 / Published by / Robert Tuthill, / wholesale agent for the Dr. Massey's Remedies. / Market Drug Store, / 155 King Street East, Toronto. / All medicines advertised in this book are guaranteed by us or money refunded. [cover-title]
DESCRIPTION: 17.5 × 13.5 cm   Pp [1–3] 4–32   Illus of astrological symbols   Paper, with photograph on front of the head-and-shoulders of Robert Tuthill; stapled, and with hole punched at top left corner, through which runs a string for hanging
CONTENTS: 1–2 publ ads; 3–27 astronomical information, recipes, monthly calendars, 'Comical Conversations,' and publ ads; 28 'Our Housekeepers' Note Book'; 29 'Miscellaneous' [recipes]; 30 'As to Diet'; 31 'Weights and Measures,' 'Terms Used in French Menus Explained for Benefit of the Canadian Hostess,' and 'Language of the Eyes'; 32 'Children and the Moon' and 'How to Sleep'
COPIES: *OTUTF (uncat patent medicine)
NOTES: The recipes are the same as those listed for A1.1, *Pingle's 1904 Calendar Cook Book,* and for O140.1, *Almanac of Dr Mack's Pills 1904.* M6.1, *Taylor's 1904 Calendar Cook Book,* may also be related.

Weir, James Lachlin (18 May 1843– 6 January 1915, Chatham, Ont.)

The son of Malcolm Weir, a past treasurer of Chatham, he was 'born down the river' and lived most of his life in Chatham, working in the insurance business. He had also been connected with the dry-goods business in Detroit and Indianapolis, and with the Chatham dry-goods firm Thomas Stone and Son. The preceding information is from a report of the author's death, 'James Weir Found Dead on the Street,' in the Chatham Daily Planet, *7 January 1915, and from a notice regarding his death and funeral in the 8 January issue. Listings for Weir in Chatham city directories, however, make no mention of the insurance or dry-goods business. They reveal only*

that in 1876–7 he was a clerk; in 1882, a salesman; in 1885–6, a manufacturer of washing machines; in 1892, a mechanic; and in 1900–2 (just before the publication of Weir's Recipes for Mixed Foods) he was retired. His birth date is from the 1901 Census.

O150.1 1904
[An edition of *Weir's Recipes for Mixed Foods,* Chatham, Ont.: 1904]
CITATIONS: O'Neill (unpublished)
COPIES: Great Britain: LB (not located)

1904–5

Polson and Co.'s almanac 1904–5

See also O113.1, by the same company.

O151.1 1904–5
Twenty sixth annual Canadian edition. / Polson & Co.'s / almanac / 1904–5 / cook / and / receipt book / Copyrighted & published by / N.C. Polson & Company / Hartford, Conn. U.S. Kingston, Ont. / Canada. [cover-title]
DESCRIPTION: 22.0 × 14.0 cm   Pp 1–48   Illus   Paper
CONTENTS: Inside front face of binding 'Invalid Cookery'; 1–48 recipes and publ ads
COPIES: NSYHM   *OGU (UA s076 b25)   OTUTF (uncat patent medicine)
NOTES: The recipes are arranged under the following headings: 'Invalid Cookery'; 'Tasty Deserts [*sic*]'; 'Cakes'; 'Fruits'; 'Delicious Candies'; 'Salads'; 'Pickles & Sauces'; 'Icings & Fillings'; 'Bread & Biscuits'; 'Pies'; 'Handy Hints'; and 'Soups.'

1904–7

[Title unknown]

O152.1 [about 1904–7]
[Title unknown]
DESCRIPTION: 22.0 × 14.0 cm   Pp [leaves lacking?] 5–66 [leaves lacking?]   Lacks paper binding
CONTENTS: 5–66 recipes and ads
COPIES: *Private collection
NOTES: The book originally belonged to the present owner's grandmother, Mrs MacNamara, who contributed the recipe for Oyster Patties on p 6 and others. Although the binding and probably the first two leaves are lost so that the book's title and author

are not evident from the existing volume, the owner reports that it was published by the Women's Auxiliary of St John's Anglican Church in Winona, Ontario. She believes that it was published about 1904–10. The advertisements are for Winona, Hamilton, and Grimsby businesses. There is a full-page advertisement on p 65 for E.D. Smith, nurseryman, fruit grower, and manufacturer of pure jams, jellies, and preserves, of Winona, who is described as 'established over a quarter of century.' Since Ernest D'Israeli Smith started his fruit-transportation business in 1882, as an extension of his fruit-growing interest begun a few years earlier, the advertisement suggests that the cookbook was published about 1907 or so. It could not have been published before the preserving season of 1903, when Ernest started manufacturing jam, and likely not until 1905, when he built his first factory for large-scale jam production. The book includes recipes credited to Mrs E.D. Smith; for example, Nut Marmalade on p 43 and Chipped Pear on p 44. Mrs E.D. Smith was the first president of the first branch of the Women's Institute, established at Stoney Creek, near Hamilton, in 1897.

The dimensions and probable date of the cookbook are close to O177.1, *The Excelsior Cook-Book,* 1907, also published in Winona. I have not been able to compare the texts of these two volumes to determine whether they are the same or different works.

1904–11

Cook book

A few years later, the same milling company published O35.11 and O35.12, editions of a cookbook by Anne Clarke, retitled Ye Old Miller's Household Book.

O153.1 [about 1904–11]
The / Campbell Milling / Company, Limited / Toronto Junction / Canada / Operating the Queen City Mills / Daily capacity, 1,200 / bbls. of flour / Cook book
COPIES: *Private collection
NOTES: 'London Printing & Litho. Co., London, Ont.' is on p 32, the last page in the volume, which is stapled. 'General Hints' are printed on the inside back face of the binding, opposite p 32.

A photocopy of the front face of the binding shows an image of the company's mill; below the mill, in a circle, is 'The Campbell Milling Co. Toronto Junction Canada'; and, although the bottom left corner of the binding is lacking, one can read the following: 'as been compiled with care / [lacking]en City" Flour. It con- / [lacking] recipes and hints, which if / [lacking]e very satisfactory results.' The printer's name, 'London Print. & Litho. Co.,' is below the image of the mill, to the right of the circle.

The Campbell Milling Co. made the following brands of flour, listed in an advertisement on p 32: Cream of the West (60% Manitoba wheat); Toronto's Pride (80% Manitoba); Queen City (described as 'all purposes' and a blend of half Manitoba and half Ontario wheat); Monarch (75% winter wheat, for pastry); Crescent (90% winter wheat, for pastry); Tower ('feed flour'); and Gem ('low grade'). The company was formed in 1904 (from Queen City Mills), and in 1911 became Campbell Flour Mills Co. Ltd; therefore, the apparently undated cookbook was published in the period 1904–11.

1905

The capital cook book

O154.1 1st ed., 1905
The capital cook book / Published by the Ladies' Home Missionary / Society of St. Andrew's Church, / Ottawa, Canada / Entered according to Act of the Parliament of Canada in the year of our Lord / one thousand nine hundred and five, by the Ladies' Home Missionary Society / of St. Andrew's Church, Ottawa, Canada, in the office of the Department of / Agriculture at Ottawa. / First edition / Ottawa, Ontario / The Rolla L. Crain Company, Limited, printers / 1905
DESCRIPTION: 17.5 × 12.5 cm   Pp [i–viii], [1–3] 4–204, [i–viii]   3 pls of 6 numbered illus   Cloth
CONTENTS: i–vi ads; vii tp; viii ad; 1 'Preface'; 2 blank; 3–188 recipes; 189–204 'Index'; i–viii ads
CITATIONS: O'Neill (unpublished)
COPIES: CIHM (66642) *OOC (641.5 C244); Great Britain: LB (07943.h.56 destroyed)
NOTES: The 'Preface' comments on the book's production: 'The wealth of material received necessitated our enlarging this volume considerably, and therefore, we present a much larger work than was originally contemplated.' There is an advertisement for the printer, Rolla L. Crain Co. Ltd (p v at back).

The OOC copy is inscribed on the front endpaper, in ink, 'Christmas Greetings to my dear friend [illegible name] from Broughie 1905.'

The Catarrhozone receipt book

The Catarrhozone Co. manufactured Nerviline, Dr Hamilton's Pills, Dr Hamilton's Ointment, Ferrozone, Catarrhozone, and Putnam's Painless Corn Extractor, all of which are illustrated on the outside back face of the binding of O155.1. For other publications by the same company, see O251.1, Catarrhozone Health Message, and O378.1, Catarrhozone Almanac.

O155.1 nd [about 1905]
The / Catarrhozone receipt book / Published by the Catarrhozone Co. – Buffalo, NY. Kingston, Ont. [cover-title]
DESCRIPTION: 11.0 × 15.0 cm Pp 1–16 Paper, with image on front of an unhealthy-looking woman in apron and frilled cap, standing beside a range on which sit a steaming kettle and cauldron; she is probably preparing 'the healing fumes of Catarrhozone' (p 14); stapled
CONTENTS: Inside front face of binding 'The Cause and Cure of Biliousness'; 1 'How to Cure the Liver'; 2 'Is Your Color Bad?'; 3 'The Cause and Cure of Headaches'; 4 'The Evils of Constipation Explained'; 5 'The Worst Suffering of All – Indigestion'; 6 'When Appetite Fails – Invalidism Follows'; 7 'A Stab-like Pin [*sic*] in the Back'; 8 'Weights and Measures' and 'How to Tell the Age of Any Person'; 9–1st column 14 recipes for 'Meats,' 'Bread,' 'Eggs,' 'Vegetables,' 'Fowl,' 'Salads,' 'Cakes and Icings,' 'Puddings and Desserts,' 'Icings and Fillings,' 'Pies,' 'Soups,' 'Fish,' and on p 14, untitled section of recipes for various baked goods; 2nd column 14 'Cured My Cough in One Night'; 15–16 and continued on inside back face 'Directions for Use of Nerviline'
COPIES: *Private collection
NOTES: This copy is inscribed on the front face of the binding, in black ink, 'Annie M. Rolleston. Marlington, Que.' (a place in Stanstead County).

Choice recipes from Fenelon Falls ladies and friends

O156.1 reprint, 2003
Choice recipes / from / Fenelon Falls / ladies and friends / in aid of / Ladies' Aid / of the / Methodist Church / Fenelon Falls / 1905 / Mrs. Jas. Knox / President / Mrs. F.A. McDiarmid / Secretary [cover-title]
DESCRIPTION: 21.5 × 14.0 cm Pp [1] 2–36 Very thin card; stapled
CONTENTS: 1 'This booklet is sold by the Fenelon Falls

United Church Women to help with the expenses involved to bring the church up to the requirements of the Fire Marshal of Ontario // Some of the recipes have been re-typed due to the age of the paper. Spring 2003'; 2–36 recipes credited with the name of the contributor and ads
COPIES: *Private collection
NOTES: The 2003 reprint is a photocopy of the 1905 book, with new text on p 1 and the occasional recipe retyped and inserted in its original position. The running head on the recto pages is 'Tested Family Recipes'; the running head on the verso pages, 'Ladies' Aid Cook Book.' The 1905 volume appears to have smaller dimensions than the 2003 photocopy since one can clearly see the edges of the original leaves in the photocopied version.

Mackie Brothers' practical guide to candy making and soda dispensing

O157.1 nd [about 1905]
Mackie Brothers' / practical guide / to / candy making / and / soda / dispensing / containing over 300 recipes for / candy, soda syrups, ices, ice / cream, extracts, crushed fruits, / etc., etc.
DESCRIPTION: 14.0 × 11.0 cm Pp [1–3] 4–105 Limp cloth, with image on front of a stylized flaming torch; sewn
CONTENTS: 1 tp; 2 blank; 3–5 'The Art of Selling'; 6–97 text; 98–105 index
COPIES: *OKQ (F5012 [1905] M158)
NOTES: The recipes are for candy, ice cream, sweet syrups, and salads, in large amounts for retail. On the outside back face of the binding there is a photograph of 'Sectional View of Experimental Room' (for recipe development) and the printer's name, 'Chatham Banner-News Print.' There is an extra leaf, not included in the pagination, between pp 64 and 65; the recto of this leaf is printed in red, with recipes, and the verso is blank.

Ontario, Department of Agriculture

For other cookbooks published by the Ontario Department of Agriculture, see the following, under Ontario, Department of Agriculture, unless an author's name is given: O236.1, Harcourt, Robert, and Miss M.A. Purdy, Flour and Breadmaking; O379.1, Chapman, Miss Ethel Matilda, The Preservation of Food; O380.1, Chapman, Miss Ethel Matilda, War Breads; O413.1, Information and Recipes on War-Time Foods and

Cooking; *O414.1*, Drying of Fruits and Vegetables and Preservation of Vegetables by Fermentation and Salting; *O446.1*, Information and Recipes on Vegetables, Fruits, and Salads; *O516.1*, *Chapman, Miss Ethel Matilda*, Food for the Family; *O692.1*, Recipes for Ontario Fruits and Vegetables; *O1010.1*, Conserve by Canning; *O1019.1*, *Truscott, J.H.L.*, Quick Frozen Fruits and Vegetables in Locker Storages; *O1222.1*, Canning Ontario's Fruits and Vegetables; *O1223.1*, Salads – All the Year 'Round; *O1224.1*, Your Money's Worth in Food; *and O1229.1*, *Truscott, J.H.L.*, *E.C. Stillwell*, *and E.S. Snyder*, Frozen Foods.

O158.1 November 1905
[An edition of *Uses of Fruits, Vegetables and Honey*, Bulletin 146, November 1905, pp 20]
CITATIONS: MacTaggart, p 20
COPIES: OGU (CA2 ON AF6 B146, not on shelf)

O158.2 rev. ed., November 1910
—Bulletin 184. November, 1910 / A revised edition of No. 146, / Ontario Department of Agriculture / Women's Institutes. / Uses of vegetables, fruits and honey / [text follows]
DESCRIPTION: Pp [1] 2–32
CONTENTS: top 1 title; mid 1–8 'Vegetables'; 9–26 'Fruits'; 27–32 'Honey'
CITATIONS: MacTaggart, p 22
COPIES: OGU (Rural Heritage Collection) *OSUL (CA2 ON AF6 B184)

O158.3 rev. ed., May 1915
—Ontario Department of Agriculture / Women's Institutes / Bulletin 184 / (Revised, May, 1915) / Uses of vegetables, fruits / and honey / Toronto, Ontario, May, 1915 [cover-title]
DESCRIPTION: 24.5 × 16.5 cm Pp [1] 2–24 Paper; stapled
CONTENTS: top 1 'Bulletin 184 // November, 1910 // Ontario Department of Agriculture Women's Institutes (Revised, May, 1915) Uses of Vegetables, Fruits and Honey'; mid 1–top 2 'Large Vegetables'; mid 2–mid 3 'The Cooking of Vegetables'; mid 3–7 'Selected Recipes' [for vegetables]; 8–top 9 'Vegetable Salads'; mid–bottom 9 'Fruits'; top–mid 10 'Selection and Preparation of Fruit' and 'General Rules for Cooking'; mid 10–mid 14 'Canning Fruits and Vegetables'; mid 14–mid 17 'Jelly-Making'; mid 17–19 'Selected Fruit Recipes'; top 20 'Fruit Salad Combinations'; mid 20–24 'Honey' [includes 'Honey Cooking Recipes']
COPIES: OGU (Rural Heritage Collection) *Private collection
NOTES: On p 10, 'Canning Fruits and Vegetables' is identified as 'Extracts from a paper read by Mr. A.J.

Morton before the Wingham Women's Institute at one of their regular monthly meetings.' Some of the honey recipes are credited to Maria Fraser, Mrs E. Smith, Miss M. Chandler, C.C. Miller, and Mrs R.C. Aikin.

Our own cook book

O159.1 1905
Our own cook book / A publication by the / East Victoria Women's Institute / 1905. / "What's this?" / "Things for the cook, sir; / But I know not what." / – Romeo and Juliet / Victoria County, Ontario, Canada. / Fenelon Falls Star Print. / 1905
DESCRIPTION: With image on front of two flowers on stalks
COPIES: *OPETA (Bury's Green Women's Institute collection 01-011)
NOTES: OPETA reports that its copy has 16 pp, the back face of the binding is lacking, and there may also be leaves lacking. The title-page text of *Our Own Cook Book* matches O91.1, an 1899 church cookbook from North Bay, Ontario. The recipes, however, are different.

In the list of institutes in Ambrose, there is no individual branch for 'East Victoria' in Victoria County. In the section for Victoria East, however, there are three branches founded by 1905 – Bobcaygeon (1900), Omemee (1904), Fenelon Falls (1905), plus Haliburton (date of founding uncertain). All locations are east of Lake Simcoe and north of Lake Scugog.

Paul, Mrs Sara T.

O160.1 [copyright 1905]
The economical / cook book / a practical guide for house- / keepers in the preparation / of / every day meals / containing / more than one thousand domestic recipes, / mostly tested by personal experience / with / suggestions for meals, lists of meats / and vegetables in season, etc. / By / Mrs. Sara T. Paul / "The turnpike road to people's hearts I find / Is through their mouths, or I mistake mankind." / Peter Pindar / John C. Winston Company / Chicago Philadelphia Toronto
DESCRIPTION: Frontispiece of two views of 'A Model Kitchen'
CONTENTS: i tp; ii 'Copyright, 1905 The John C. Winston Co. Printed in the U.S.A.'; iii–? 'Contents'; …
COPIES: *Private collection
NOTES: The text is by an American author. NSPHOCM has a copy that may match this edition.

AMERICAN EDITIONS: *Cookery from Experience: A Practical Guide for Housekeepers in the Preparation of Every Day Meals,* Philadelphia: Porter and Coates, [c1875] (United States: DLC); retitled *The Economical Cook Book,* Philadelphia: 'International' Press, [c1905] (United States: DLC); *The Economical Cook Book,* No place: No publisher, c1905 (United States: DLC).

The P.M.L.A. cook book

O160a.1   1905

"If you eat to live, live on the best, / If you live to eat, eat the best." / The / P.M.L.A. cook book / a selection of / tested recipes, / prepared / by the Ladies' Auxiliary, / of the / Powassan / Methodist Church / 1905 / The Forester Printery, / Huntsville.
DESCRIPTION: Pp [5–14] 15–148 [149]   3 illus on p 6 of Rev. G.R. Kitching, pastor of Powassan Methodist Church, Mrs Kitching, and Powassan Methodist Parsonage, 'Erected in 1903'   Sewn
CONTENTS: 5 'Powassan // One of the most prosperous villages in the Eastern District of Parry Sound' [history]; 6 illus and 'The Ladies' Aid Society of the church have undertaken to pay off the indebtedness of the parsonage by publishing this cook book.'; 7 tp; 8 ad; 9 'Preface' signed Committee; 10 ad; 11–13 'Brief History of Cooking' [likely reprinted from another source] and ad; 14–140 recipes credited with the name of the contributor and ads; 141–8 'Useful Household Receipts' and ads; 149 'Index' [i.e., table of contents]
COPIES: *Private collection
NOTES: In the 'Preface' the Committee of Management claims that the book will be 'of excellent use ... based upon the ability and experience of the housekeepers of Powassan and vicinity.' The copy is inscribed on an initial blank leaf, 'Ina M. Magee.'

Practical cookery

O161.1   1905

Practical / cookery / over 300 recipes / ("Tried and true.") / from ladies of Lindsay and friends. / Compiled by the Women's Auxiliary of the Y.M.C.A. / of Lindsay, Ontario. / 1905
DESCRIPTION: 22.5 × 14.0 cm   Pp [1–3] 4–79, [i]   Lacks paper binding; stapled
CONTENTS: 1 tp; 2 'The Post Presses'; 3–76 text and ads; 77–9 'Index,' which lists the names of the recipe contributors for each chapter; i ads
COPIES: *OGU (UA s048 b45)

1905–7

McClary's gas range and cook book

McClary's was founded in London, Ontario, in 1847. Eighty years later, in 1927, McClary's amalgamated with four other firms to form General Steel Wares (the other four were Thos Davidson Manufacturing Co. Ltd of Montreal, Happy Thought Foundry Co. Ltd of Brantford, Ontario, and Sheet Metal Products Co. of Canada and Macdonald Manufacturing Co. Ltd, both of Toronto); for information about the merger, see: 'Merger Represents Over Half Industry,' Monetary Times *Vol. 79, No. 17 (21 October 1927), pp 5, 20–1, and 29; Business Index Cards at OTMCL; and the 1941 issue of* Hardware and Metal, *the Canadian trade magazine, p 216, also at OTMCL. For other cookbooks by McClary's, see: O200.1,* Tested Recipes; *O283.1,* The Kootenay Range in Your Kitchen *(?); O322.1, 'McClary's' Recipe Book; O334.1,* Cooking with Gas; *O409.1,* The Household Helper; *and O488.1, McClary's Household Manual. General Steel Wares published cookbooks for use with McClary brand appliances: O645.1,* The Modern Housekeepers' Guide; *O671.1,* The McClary Electric Range Cook Book; *Q256.1,* How to Use Your McClary Range; *and Q311.1,* How to Use Your McClary Refrigerator.

O162.1   nd [about 1905–7]

McClary's / gas range / and / cook book / Pocket edition catalogue. / Contains valuable instruction on the / management of gas ranges and / a special selection of thoroughly / tried cooking recipes / Quality is the foundation of McClary goods [cover-title]
DESCRIPTION: 15.0 × 11.0 cm   Pp 7–26   Illus of gas ranges   Paper; previously stapled, now sewn by library
CONTENTS: 7, 9, 11, 13, 15, 19, 23 'Recipes'; 8, 10, 12, 14, 16–18, 20–2, 24 illus of ranges
COPIES: *OLU (TX714 M34 1900z)
NOTES: No pages are lacking; the book starts on p 7. The printer's name, 'A Talbot & Co., London,' is on the outside back face of the binding. The following styles of McClary gas range are illustrated: Style E.S. No. 256; H, No. 258; G, No. 258; L, No. 220; M, No. 2058; B, No. 258; E, No. 258; C, Nos. 256–8; C, No. 258; D, Nos. 256–8; No. 2180; No. 218; and No. 212. *McClary's Gas Range and Cook Book* probably precedes the company's *Tested Recipes* of 1908 (O200.1), where the styles are numbered in the 30s and 300s.

O162.2 1912

—McClary's / gas range / and / cook book / Pocket edition 1912 catalogue / Contains valuable instruction on the / management of gas ranges and / a special selection of thoroughly / tried cooking recipes / Quality is the foundation of McClary goods [cover-title]

COPIES: *Private collection

1905–10

Cookery recipes

O163.1 nd [about 1905–10]

Cookery recipes / compiled and published by / the Mission Circle / of the / Dundas Methodist Churc[h?] / Dundas Ont.

DESCRIPTION: 14.5 × 10.0 cm   Pp [1–2] 3–72   Lacks binding?

CONTENTS: 1 tp; 2 blank; top 3 'A Recipe for a Day' [poem]; mid 3–4 'Time Table'; 5–12 ads; 13–72 recipes credited with the name of the contributor and ads

COPIES: *ABOM

NOTES: Dundas Banner Ltd is likely the printer of the cookbook; the company's advertisement is on p 65: 'Our first aim is to do good printing. The Dundas Banner Ltd. Ontario.'

New Perfection cook book

O164.1 nd [about 1905–10]

See page 1 for directions / New Perfection / cook book / For best results use "Royalite" Oil [cover-title]

DESCRIPTION: 18.5 × 12.5 cm   Pp [1] 2–72   Illus of New Perfection Stoves   Paper, with image on front of a woman removing baked bread from a stove; stapled, and with hole punched at top left corner for hanging

CONTENTS: 1–16 'Directions and Suggestions for Using Nos. 1, 2, 3, 4, 20, 25 and "Junior" New Perfection Wick Blue Flame Oil Cooking Stoves'; 17–70 'Recipes'; 71–2 index

COPIES: OFERWM (A1985.43)   *SBIHM

NOTES: On p 17 one learns that 'the recipes ... have been compiled by several prominent and successful users of the New Perfection Cook Stove ...'

No place of publication is recorded; however, the book was probably published in Ontario. In O164.3, Imperial Oil Co. Ltd is named as 'wholesale distributors,' and Imperial Oil Co. Ltd was based in Ontario

(it started in 1880 in London, Ontario; head office moved to Petrolia in 1883, Sarnia in 1899, Toronto in 1916, and Calgary in 2005). O164.4 was printed in London.

The OFERWM copy lacks pp 71–2 and the outside back face of the binding.

O164.2 nd

—[An edition of *New Perfection livre de recettes culinaires*, No place, nd, pp 70]

COPIES: Private collection

NOTES: The book's owner reports that the image on the front face of the binding is of a woman removing baked bread from a New Perfection stove.

O164.3 nd [about 1916]

—New Perfection / cook-book / and directions [for] / operating / New Perfection Oil Sto[ves] [cover-title]

DESCRIPTION: 18.5 × 13.0 cm   Pp [1] 2–96   Illus   [Free with purchase of stove, on p 22]   Paper, with image on front of a seated woman holding a plate on which sits a slice of cake; stapled

CONTENTS: 1–25 'Directions for Using New Perfection Oil Cooking Stoves'; 26–90 'Recipes'; 91–4 'Menus'; 95 'Perfection Smokeless Oil Heaters'; 96 index

CITATIONS: Reitz, p [4]

COPIES: *ACG   OKITD (972.111.003.004)

NOTES: Pages 1–25 contain extensive instructions accompanied by many illustrations for using the stoves. There is a reference on p 11 to 'the advent of the New Perfection Stoves Nos. 5, 6, 7 and 8, all with Fireless Cooking Oven, [which] marks an epoch in the evolution of both oil stove and fireless cookery.' On p 26 one learns that 'the following recipes have been prepared and carefully tested by Miss Nellie L. McCann, the well-known Domestic Science Expert.' In O164.4, McCann is described as from Gorham, Maine. Printed on the outside back face of the binding is 'Wholesale distributors // The Imperial Oil Company, Ltd. Toronto Montreal St. John Halifax Winnipeg Regina Saskatoon Calgary Edmonton Vancouver.' New Perfection Oil Stoves were made in Canada (see p 1 and other references in the text).

OBM has an incomplete copy, beginning on p 11, that probably matches O164.3.

O164.4 nd

—New Perfection / cook / book / and / directions / for operating / New Perfection Oil Stoves [cover-title]

DESCRIPTION: 18.5 × 12.5 cm   Pp [1] 2–96   Illus black-and-blue, illus   Paper, with image on front, in an

oval frame, of the upper half of a woman who holds, in both hands, a whole cake on a plate; stapled
CONTENTS: 1–23 'Directions for Operating New Perfection Oil Cook Stoves on Pages from 2 to 11 // Made in Canada ...' and directions for, and information about, other New Perfection appliances, including especially No. 37 New Perfection Oil Cook Stove with heat retaining oven on pp 12–13; 24–88 'Recipes'; 89–92 'Menus'; 93 'Perfection Smokeless Oil Heaters'; 94 'Index'; 95–6 'Special Cross-Index of Recipes' and at bottom p 96, 'London Printing & Litho. Co., London, Ont.'
COPIES: OKITJS (999.24.2)   *Private collection
NOTES: Page 24 states, 'The following recipes have been prepared and carefully tested by Miss Nellie L. McCann, Gorham, Maine, a New England Domestic Science Expert.' Since this edition refers to No. 37 in the line of New Perfection Oil Cook Stoves, it was likely published a little later than O164.3.

An advertisement in the May 1920 issue of *Western Home Monthly* suggests that the reader 'write for New Perfection booklet.' The reference may be to the cookbook, but which edition is unknown.

AMERICAN EDITIONS: *Directions for Using New Perfection Oil Cooking Stoves,* cover-title: *New Perfection Cook-Book and Directions for Operating New Perfection Oil Stoves,* Cleveland: nd [stamp on p 21: 'See Supplement enclosed showing illustrations of 1916 models'], number of pages and image on binding match O164.3 (United States: InU; Cagle/Stafford No. 1001, illus); *Directions for Using New Perfection Oil Cook Stoves and Ranges with Blue Chimney Burners and Cook Book,* Cleveland: Cleveland Metal Products Co., copyright 1922 (United States: InU).

Reliable recipes

In 1927 the same Ladies' Aid published O595.1, Choice Recipes.

O165.1   nd [about 1905–10]
Reliable recipes / issued by / the Ladies' Aid of the Railway, Marine and General / Hospital, Port Arthur. / [caption:] The new General Hospital / Editor Miss Alice Read / Contributors / [first column:] Mrs. T.N. Andrew / Mrs. Beaver / Mrs. D.F. Burk / Mrs. Horace Bray / Mrs. W.A. Brown / Mrs. D.R. Bruce / [second column:] Mrs. J.C. Dobie / Miss L. Dobie / Mrs. S. Downing / Miss Gibbs / Mrs. Haynes / Mrs. Hewish / [third column:]

Mrs. F.D. Jackson / Mrs. Langworthy / Mrs. I.L. Matthews / Mrs. Powley / Mrs. Pratt / [centred below columns of names:] Chronicle Job Presses, Port Arthur [cover-title]
DESCRIPTION: About 22.5 × 30.0 cm [dimensions from same-size photocopy]   12 leaves printed on rectos only   Architect's drawing of new General Hospital on front face of binding; top-hinged by a ribbon through one punched hole
COPIES: *Private collection
NOTES: *Reliable Recipes* was probably published to raise funds to pay for the new hospital. Since construction began in 1906 and the building was opened to the public in 1909, the cookbook likely dates from about 1905–10.

The Shirreff cook book

The Shirreff Manufacturing Co. was founded in Brockville in 1905 by Charles J. Shirreff (1844–1923). The business closed in 1918. In addition to food choppers, the company specialized in carpet sweepers and clothes wringers.

O166.1   nd [about 1905–10]
The Shirreff / cook book / a manual for busy housekeepers. / Showing dishes which can be prepared by / the use of the / Shirreff Food Cutter. / Published by / the Shirreff Mfg. Co. Limited, / Brockville, Ont. / William H. Albery, general job printer, / King Street, Brockville.
DESCRIPTION: 15.0 × 10.0 cm   Pp [1–2] 3–32   Tp illus of a steaming spherical pudding(?) on a plate, and a knife and fork embedded in the pudding; 2 fp illus; illus   Paper, with image on front of a Shirreff Food Chopper No. 20
CONTENTS: 1 tp; 2 still-life of fruits and vegetables; 3–7 'The Shirreff Food Cutter'; 8 'Getting the Most Out of Meat'; 9–29 'Useful Recipes'; 30 fp illus of '"General" Bread Maker'; 31 The "General"'; 32 'Cooking Measures'
COPIES: CIHM (95418)   *OGU (UA s043 b32)

1906

The Berlin cook book

O167.1   1906
The Berlin / cook book / Compiled by the ladies / of Berlin, Waterloo / and friends elsewhere. /

1906 / Berlin, Ont., Canada. / The News Record Print Shop

DESCRIPTION: 21.0 × 14.0 cm   Pp [1–5] 6–304   Cloth
CONTENTS: 1 tp; 2 'Foreword' signed the compilers; 3 'Contents' [i.e., alphabetical list of headings]; 4 'Table of Weights'; 5–304 text, mainly recipes credited with the name of the contributor, and blank leaves (included in the pagination) for manuscript recipes, and 'Menus' on pp 301–4
CITATIONS: Bloomfield 3198   Ferguson/Fraser, p 232   Reitz, p [4]
COPIES: CIHM (9-92334) OGU (UA s043 b04) OKIT OKITD (989.022.001) OKITJS (991.21.1) *OWTU (F14913)
NOTES: The 'Foreword' states, 'The contributors ... look for no other reward than lies in the pleasure of diffusing it [i.e., the information in the book] and in assisting a worthy cause.' The worthy cause is not identified. The first section is devoted to the important subject of 'Breads'; the first recipe is for making yeast. The front and back faces of the original cloth binding of the OWTU copy are obscured by a layer of paper applied later.

The OGU copy is inscribed on the title-page, in pencil, 'Mary Schwalm.' The OKITJS copy is inscribed on the front endpaper, in ink, 'Ida Hachbait Aug. 28th. 1907.' OKITJS has another copy (989.15.1), which lacks pp 1–2 and 302–4. It is inscribed twice on the front endpaper, in pencil, 'Mrs. D Fries.'

The OKITD copy lacks pp 1–4. Only the cloth spine remains of the binding so it is possible to see that the leaves are stapled together, not sewn. This is the copy cited in Reitz.

The OKIT copy lacks pp 1–2 and 301–4. It is inscribed on the front endpaper, in ink, 'Mrs. Richard Frickey Berlin Ont.' Without the benefit of the title-page, which bears the year of publication, the library dates its copy [about 1909]. Bloomfield 3198 refers to the OKIT copy. In her entry for the book, Bloomfield comments that 'the recipes seem to be typical of Canadian household cooking at the time rather than particular to Waterloo County.' On the contrary, the recipes should be taken as particular to the County in that they were gathered together from the collections of local women and the publication of the book served to reinforce their use in County homes. Community cookbooks, by definition, represent community customs (irrespective of whether other communities share similar customs).

During the First World War, on 3 July 1916, Berlin was renamed Kitchener (now the city of Kitchener-Waterloo).

Bright ideas

County of Carleton General Protestant Hospital was at 589 Rideau Street in Ottawa.

O168.1   nd [1906]

Bright ideas / a book of home secrets / Gathered by the / Woman's Auxiliary of the County of Carleton / General Protestant Hospital.
DESCRIPTION: 20.0 × 13.0 cm   Pp [i–ii], [1] 2–81   Small tp illus of a young girl   Paper-covered boards and cloth spine, with image on front of a standing woman in a floor-length gown, reading a book; stapled
CONTENTS: 1 tp; 2 'Introduction'; 3–80 text in eight chapters and ads; 81 ad
COPIES: *Private collection
NOTES: The binding has an attractive design: the paper is light purple; the woman's hair and long, flowing gown are printed in dark purple; and her shape and detail are defined in gold. 'Esdale-Martin Print, Ottawa' is on the outside back face of the binding.

The 'Introduction' explains that the book was published to raise funds to replenish 'the Treasury of our Hospital ... to meet the extra demands upon it.' It grew out of the idea of one of the members of the Auxiliary that 'every household held some secret for the furtherance of work or pleasure, known to itself alone.' The ideas for cleaning, thrift, decorating, cooking, and other subjects are personal and detailed, and illuminate how families lived in Ottawa in the first decade of the twentieth century. The eight chapters are 'Cleaning in General,' 'Around the House,' 'Odd Bits of Information,' 'Hints for Travellers,' 'Hints to Hostesses,' 'A Chapter of Choice Recipes,' 'A Chapter on German Cooking' by Mrs Otto Klotz, and 'Pot Pourri.' There is an errata slip glued to the title-page, headed 'Corrections for Bright Ideas.'

An advertisement on p 76 for the Musson Book Co. Ltd, Toronto, indicates that the book was published in 1906. The preamble to the list of advertised novels states: 'Reader will you assist our hospital fund? ... The publishers of the following list of novels which comprises all the most popular fiction of 1905 and 1906, offer to contribute 10 per cent. of the price of any book in the list on the following conditions ...' On 30 December 1906 the bookseller was to send a list to Musson of all the volumes purchased when customers showed this advertisement, and Musson would forward a cheque to the hospital for 10%. The book was completed close to Christmas 1906, for there is a note at the head of the last chapter that says, '['Pot Pourri'] was gathered during the holiday season, after the preceeding [sic] chapters had gone to press consequently it was impossible to classify the contents, ...' Another collector's copy is inscribed 'For [?]. Wishing you a very Merry Xmas [...] From Annie.' The copy described here is inscribed 'A.W.H. March – 1907.'

Choicest cooking recipes

O169.1 1906
This book contains cuts and descriptions / of many styles of / cooking ranges / and / heating stoves / for manufactured / and for natural / gas / also / gas hot plates, gas water heaters, / natural gas burners, / for use in ordinary cooking and heating stoves, and other / gas appliances / The book also contains a goodly number of the / [in all capital letters:] Choicest cooking recipes / for the use of those who do their cooking on the / Jewel Gas Ranges. / These goods are all / made in Canada / by / the Burrow, Stewart & Milne Co. / Limited / Hamilton
DESCRIPTION: With image on front of a woman opening the top compartment of a gas stove; stapled
COPIES: *Private collection
NOTES: The cover-title is '1906 1906 / Jewel / gas stoves / and gas appliances for cooking and heating / Made / in / Canada / by the / Burrow, Stewart & Milne Co. / Limited / Hamilton, Canada.' The bottom left corner of the back face of the binding is torn off, revealing the text for the last advertised item on the last page: No. 197 Garnet Burner. The information in this entry is from photocopies. I have not examined the book, whose text may or may not be related to O72.1, *Hamilton Jewel Cook Book*, or O179.1, *Jewel Cook Book*. Of all the Burrow, Stewart and Milne cookbooks, O169.1 is the only dated edition.

Culinary landmarks

O169a.1 [2001, facsimile of] 1906
Culinary landmarks / Recipes / collected by the ladies of St. James Church / Port Colborne 1906 / "Better wait on the cook than on the doctor"
DESCRIPTION: 15.5 × 13.0 cm Pp [i–ii], [6–7] 8–101 Cloth
CONTENTS: Inside front face of binding 'Reproduced by the Port Colborne Historical and Marine Museum in 2001'; i [endpaper] 'Recipes // Recipes collected by the ladies of St. James Church, Port Colborne, Ont. "I will tell you the beginning and if it please your

ladyship you will see the end." – As You Like It // Culinary Landmarks'; ii blank; 6 tp; 7 'Introduction' signed Mrs S.J. Sidey, president; 8–101 recipes credited with the name of the contributor and ads
COPIES: *Private collection
NOTES: In the 'Introduction,' the 'members of St. James Woman's Auxiliary ... acknowledge their appreciation of the business men and women of Port Colborne, Humberstone and other places who patronized the pages of their recipe book.'
This bibliography, *Culinary Landmarks*, takes its title from O169a.1 and from another fund-raising cookbook of the same name, O84.1.

Dr King's new guide to health prize cook book 1906

See O96.1 for a list of other annual issues.

O170.1 [1906]
[An edition of *Dr King's New Guide to Health Prize Cook Book*, Chicago, Ill., and Windsor, Canada [i.e., Ontario]: H.E. Bucklen and Co., 1906 and 1907 calendars on the last page]
COPIES: United States: eBay on-line auction, May 2001, No. 1431762600

The Leamington cook book and business guide

O171.1 1906
The / Leamington cook book / and business guide / A book of helpful hints / on / practical housekeeping / We may live without poetry, music and art; / We may live without conscience, and live without heart. / We may live without friends; we may live without books; / But civilized man cannot live without cooks. / – Owen Meredith. / Compiled by the Ladies' Aid Society of / the Leamington Baptist Church / 1906 / Post Printing Company, Leamington.
DESCRIPTION: About 23.5 × 15.0 cm [dimensions from photocopy] Paper, with faint line drawing underlying the title on front, of the church; stapled
CONTENTS: 1 tp; 2 ad; 3–53 recipes credited with the name of the contributor and ads
COPIES: *Private collection
NOTES: The private collector's copy is inscribed on the title-page, 'Mrs. William Nash.'

The right range and why

Edwin and Charles Gurney started an iron foundry in Hamilton, Ontario, in 1843. By the 1880s the business, called E. and C. Gurney Co. from 1863, had extended its operations to nearby Dundas and to Toronto, Winnipeg, and Montreal. After Charles's death in 1893, heirs created the Gurney Foundry Co. from some of the remaining assets. Another cookbook by the company is O601.1, Instructions for Operating Gurney Electric Ranges. *In 1930 McClelland and Stewart Ltd published an edition of Mildred Maddocks's American cookbook, retitled* Gurney Cook Book, *as an advertising vehicle for the company (O324.4).*

For more information about the company, see: The Queen's Jubilee and Toronto 'Called Back,' *Toronto: Wm Briggs, 1887, pp 256–7; the death notice for Edward in* Monetary Times *Vol 18, No. 22 (28 November 1884), p 606; the death notice for Charles in* Monetary Times *Vol. 26, No. 36 (10 March 1893), p 1066; and the digital collection* Industrial Hamilton: A Trail to the Future *(OH).*

O172.1   [entered 1906]
The right range / and why / being a little book / meant to tell about / the / Imperial Oxford / Range / together with some / hints about ways to / do better baking / Presented to the housewives of / Canada with compliments of / The Gurney Foundry Co., / Limited, Toronto, Hamilton, / Winnipeg, Vancouver; The / Gurney-Massey Co., Limited, / Montreal; The Gurney Standard / Metal Co., Limited, Calgary.
DESCRIPTION: 22.5 × 9.0 cm   Pp [1–4] 5–16   Illus brown   Very thin card, with two images on front: in the foreground, a loaf of bread in a tin, and in the background, a woman removing baked goods from the oven of a range, watched by a cat; stapled, and with hole punched at top left corner for hanging
CONTENTS: 1 tp; 2 'Entered according to Act of the Parliament of Canada, in the year one thousand nine hundred and six, at the Department of Agriculture.'; 3 untitled introductory text signed the Gurney Foundry Co. Ltd; 4 blank; 5–9, 11, 13, 15–16 'Imperial Oxford // It Does Bake Perfectly'; 10 the heading 'Good Recipes' followed by recipes for Imperial Oxford Bread, Bread Sticks, Gurney Pop-Overs; 12 Graham Bread, Gurney Gems, Toronto Loaf; 14 Ontario Rolls, Gourmet's Bread, Edinboro Waffles [made from oatmeal porridge]
COPIES: *Private collection
NOTES: The cover-title, which is depicted as stamped into the crust of the baked loaf, is 'The Master Baker';

below the loaf is the phrase, 'Which is the Imperial Oxford Range made by the Gurney Foundry Co., Limited.' The inside text is printed in dark brown; the illustrations are in a lighter brown. 'Press of J.J. Gibbons Toronto Montreal 3192' is on the outside back face of the binding.

Tested recipes for cakes, puddings and desserts

O173.1   June 1906
Tested / recipes / for cakes / puddings and / desserts / Made-in-Canada / Exhibition / June, 1906 / This collection of the best recipes of / St. Catharines housekeepers have [*sic*] been / carefully compiled, and can be recommended [cover-title]
DESCRIPTION: With image on front of a steaming chafing dish
COPIES: *OSTCM (1983.265.1)
NOTES: The book has 48 pp. The title-page states: 'Made and Produced in Canada Exhibition under the auspices of the Ladies of St. Catharines and vicinity // One week, June eighteenth to twenty-third, nineteen hundred and six // In the New Armouries // Proceeds in aid of the General and Marine Hospital, St. Catharines, Ont.' The recipes are credited with the name of the contributor.

The OSTCM curator of collections reports that the exhibition was opened by Lieutenant-Governor Mortimer Clark and featured a concert, wax exhibits, a maypole dance and drill, grand marches, high tea, palmistry, a Turkish Lounge, a fish pond, and extensive displays of edibles, fancy work, gardens, paper work, flowers, art, handicrafts, etc.

Tried and proven practical household recipes

O174.1   1906
1906 / Tried and proven / practical / household recipes / Carefully collated by the ladies of / Watford and vicinity.
DESCRIPTION: [$0.25, on binding]
CONTENTS: Tp verso 'Printed at the Watford Guide-Advocate Book and Job Office.'
COPIES: *OGU (CCC)
NOTES: The running head is 'Watford Methodist Church Ladies' Cook Book.' The recipes are credited with the name of the contributor. Watford is east of Sarnia.

1907

The Beaver Valley collection of the latest and best recipes

O175.1   [1st ed.], nd [about 1907]
The / Beaver / Valley / collection / of the / latest / and best / recipes / compiled by the / ladies of St. Paul's Presbyterian / Church, Thornbury and Clarksburg. / Herald Print, Thornbury [cover-title]
DESCRIPTION: Paper, with image on front of a beaver on a maple leaf; stapled
COPIES: *Private collection
NOTES: The owner reports that the book has 90 pp. The recipes are credited with the name of the contributor. One of the contributors (for example, of Bread and Apple Pudding, p 78) was the wife of Reverend Barton, who came to St Paul's in 1905.

There is an advertisement on p 7, paid for by a dealer in Clarksburg, for Ramsay's Paint, manufactured in Montreal. The advertisement states that 'Ramsay's Paints have been made in Canada for 65 years,' and the paint company was 'Established 1842,' according to the label on the illustrated paint can; therefore, the first edition of the cookbook was published about 1907 (1842 + 65 years).

O175.2   2nd ed., nd
—The / Beaver / Valley / collection / of the / latest / and best / recipes / compiled by the / ladies of St. Paul's Presbyterian / Church, Thornbury and Clarksburg. / Second edition. / Herald-Reflector Print. [cover-title]
DESCRIPTION: Paper, with image on front of a beaver on a maple leaf
CITATIONS: Beeson, p 47
COPIES: *Private collection
NOTES: The owner reports that the second edition has 92 pp. The recipes are credited with the name of the contributor. There is a recipe for Butter Tarts from Mrs S. Hooey on p 49 – an early printed example (I have found no references to Butter Tarts in nineteenth-century cookbooks).

O175.3   [3rd ed.], nd [about 1912]
—The Beaver Valley collection / of the / latest and / best recipes / compiled by the / ladies of St. Paul's Presbyterian Church / Thornbury and Clarksburg.
DESCRIPTION: Stapled
COPIES: *OOWM (969.18.1)
NOTES: The museum describes this as the third edition of 68 pp. The title-page is inscribed, 'Miss E.D.

McVittie Merry Xmas 1912'; and below this inscription, in a later hand, 'Muriel (Snider) Johnson's Aunt Della McVittie.'

The Essex cook book

For a later cookbook by the same church (renamed the United Church), see O616.1, Cook Book.

O176.1   1907
"Now good digestion wait on appetite and health on both." – Shakespeare. / The / Essex cook book / a selection / of / tested recipes / compiled by the / ladies of / the Essex Methodist Church / 1907 / The Journal Press / St. Thomas, Ont.
DESCRIPTION: 22.5 × 15.0 cm   Pp [1–3] 4–186 [lacks pp 187–8]   Photograph on p 2 of 'Essex Station after the explosion, August 10, 1907'   Limp cloth; stapled
CONTENTS: 1 tp; 2 photograph; 3 'Our Greeting' signed ladies of Essex Methodist Church, Mrs Wm Church, president; 4–5 ads; 6–186 recipes credited with the name of the contributor and ads
COPIES: *OAYM   OMMM
NOTES: 'Our Greeting' expresses the 'hope that this book will find a welcome to any home in the town or county of Essex, not only because of its intrinsic value, but because it will prove a valuable souvenir of the never-to-be-forgotten disaster of Saturday, August 10th, 1907.' On that morning a boxcar of nitroglycerine exploded, killing two men, injuring dozens of others, and causing extensive property damage. The OMMM copy retains pp 187–8.

The Excelsior cook-book

O177.1   1907
The / Excelsior / cook-book / Winona, 1907 [cover-title]
DESCRIPTION: About 21.5 × 14.0 cm [dimensions from photocopy]   Paper, with image on front of a bunch of cherries
COPIES: *Private collection
NOTES: The above information is from a photocopy of the front face of the binding, the only part of the book that survives. On the other side, there is an advertisement for the Robert Simpson Co. Ltd, Toronto, a department store that is no longer in business. See the notes for O152.1, [Title unknown], which may be the same or a different book.

Gunn's 1907 calendar cook book

See also O215.1, Gunn's Household Calendar Cook Book 1909.

O178.1   1907
Gunn's 1907 / calendar / cook book / Published by / C.H. Gunn & Co. / Central Drug Store / Chatham Ont.
COPIES: *OLU (J.J. Talman Regional Collection, pamphlet file: Chatham)

Jewel cook book

See also O72.1, Hamilton Jewel Cook Book, *and* O169.1, Choicest Cooking Recipes, *by the same company.*

O179.1   nd [about 1907 or later]
Jewel cook book / containing / choice cooking / recipes / and other valuable information / for the housewife [cover-title]
DESCRIPTION: 21.5 × 14.0 cm   Pp [1] 2–32   Several illus of Jewel stoves, ranges, and scales   Paper, with image on front of a young girl at table, with her hands together in prayer and her head bowed; stapled
CONTENTS: 1–27 'Cooking Receipts' and publ ads; 28–32 housekeeping information: 'The Housekeeper's Helpful Standard' [measurements and proportions of ingredients for standard recipes], 'Household "Ifs,"' 'Dainty Table Linen,' 'Just the Difference,' 'What Can You Use a Lemon For?,' 'In Canning Time,' 'How to Pop Corn,' 'Household Economies,' 'Flavoring Canned Pears,' and 'To Remove Stains from Table-cloths'
COPIES: OH   *Private collection
NOTES: Printed on the outside back face of the binding is 'Jewel stoves and ranges are for sale by A.E. Buttler [*sic*], Perth, Ont.' The OH copy appears to be identical except that a different retailer is printed on the outside back face of the binding: '... for sale by Kilpatrick Bros., hardware and stoves, sole agents in London for "Jewel" stoves & ranges Phone 2525. 602 Dundas St.' Robert G. Kilpatrick and William J. Kilpatrick opened their hardware store at this address in 1907; therefore, this edition was published about 1907, but likely no earlier ('Personal Touch Being Lost Says Hardware Store Veteran,' *London Free Press* 15 October 1969).
O179.1, O179.2, and O179.3 all begin with the same recipes: Rye and Corn Meal Bread, Steamed Corn and Graham Bread, Plain White Family Bread, and

Graham Bread. There are minor differences between the two editions of 32 pages (O179.1 and O179.2). In O179.1, the running head on the recto pages is 'Jewel Stoves and Ranges'; the running head on the verso pages is 'Burrow, Stewart & Milne Co., Ltd.'; and the advertisements are for the following: on p 5, the Royal Jewel Steel Range, no style specified and the advertisement is unillustrated; on p 6, Royal Jewel Steel Range, R, Style E; on p 8, Arctic Jewel Steel Range, Style E; on p 12, Dominion Jewel Cast Range, Style F; on p 16, Sterling Jewel Range; on p 18, Grand Jewel (four different models); on p 20, Ideal Jewel Heater; on p 23, Jewel Heating Stoves; on p 24, a scale; and on the inside back face of the binding, Hamilton Jewel Gas Ranges.

O179.2   nd
—[Cover-title lacking]
DESCRIPTION: 21.5 × 14.0 cm   Pp [1] 2–32   Illus of Jewel stoves and ranges   Lacks paper binding; stapled
CONTENTS: 1–27 'Cooking Recipes' and publ ads; 28–32 information about housekeeping, including directions for canning, popping corn, and flavouring canned pears
COPIES: *SBIHM
NOTES: Since the cover-title is lacking, the title of this edition is unknown. The running head on the recto pages is the same as O179.1: 'Jewel Stoves and Ranges'; however, here the running head on the verso pages uses the definite article: 'The Burrow, Stewart & Milne Co., Ltd.' The letter designation for Style on pp 6 and 8 of the advertisements also differentiates O179.1 and O179.2. In O179.2, the advertisements are for the following: on p 5, Royal Steel Range; on p 6, Royal Jewel, R, Style B; on p 8, Arctic Jewel Steel Range, Style F; on p 12, Dominion Jewel Cast Range; on p 16, Sterling Steel Range; on p 18, four different models; on p 20, Ideal Jewel Heater; on p 23, Jewel Heating Stoves; on p 24, scales; and on the inside back face of the binding, Hamilton Jewel Gas Ranges.

O179.3   nd
—Choice / cooking / recipes / compiled by / the makers of the celebrated / line of / Jewel / stoves / ranges, furnaces / and / gas ranges / For sale by [blank space for retailer's name; see notes, below] [cover-title]
DESCRIPTION: 21.5 × 14.5 cm   Pp [1] 2–40   Illus on p 2 of Jewel factory, several illus of Jewel stoves and ranges   Paper, with image on front of two female cooks, seated on stools and facing each other; stapled
CONTENTS: 1 'To the Public // The Burrow, Stewart &

Milne Company, Limited, Hamilton, Canada' [a recommendation to use Jewel stoves]; 2 company trademark and illus of factory; 3–34 'Cooking Recipes' and publ ads; 35–9 housekeeping information, including directions for canning, popping corn, and flavouring canned pears; 40 publ ad
COPIES: OH (R641.5 CHO CESH) OKITJS (984.4.1) *SSWD
NOTES: 'Reid Press Hamilton' is on the outside back face of the binding. The cover-title includes a blank space for the retailer's name and a different name is stamped on each of the copies located: on the SSWD copy, 'A,[E or B?], Jones, Milestone' (Milestone is in Saskatchewan); on the OH copy, 'W.F. Dibblee & Son // Woodstock N.B.'; and on the OKITJS copy, 'W. Strand // Queen and Bridge St. Ottawa.' An advertisement on p 12 refers to the Dominion Jewel Range as a '20th century range.'

Macbeth, Mrs George, née Emma Amelia Worthington (1861–1925)

Mrs Macbeth was the daughter of Philip Worthington, a Fenian Raid veteran. Her husband, George, was auditor of the Toronto General Trusts Corporation and, at the time of his death in 1918, they lived in the Alexandra Apartments. George and Emma had three children (Meta, Kenneth, and Dalton), plus a son who died in infancy (George Morrison). Emma and George are buried in Woodland Cemetery in London, Ontario. (This information is gleaned from cemetery records and George's obituary, TPL Scrapbooks, Vol. 7, p 512.)

See also O101.1, Recipes, for a luncheon menu and recipes contributed by Mrs Macbeth, who is described in this 1900 cookbook as 'of the Y.W.C.G. School of Domestic Science.'

O180.1 1907
Invalid cookery / for the use of the / trained nurse / and all others who have / to cook and serve food / for invalids. / Individual recipes / also a chapter / on / the feeding of infants / with full instructions / for every mother. / Issued by the alumnae / of / the Hospital for Sick Children / College Street, Toronto / Price fifty cents / Toronto / 1907
DESCRIPTION: 18.0 × 9.5 cm   Pp [1–4] 5–8, [i–ii], 9–16, [i–ii], 17–24, [i–ii], 25–32, [i–ii], 33–40, [i–ii], 41–8, [i–ii], 49–56, [i–ii], 57–64, [i–ii], 65–9, [i–vii]   Fp illus on p 61 of 'A Milk Bottle,' fp illus on p 64 of 'A Cream Dipper'   Cloth
CONTENTS: 1 tp; 2 'Entered according to Act of Parliament of Canada, in the year one thousand nine hun-

dred and seven, by the Hospital for Sick Children, Toronto, at the Department of Agriculture, Ottawa.'; 3 dedication by the alumnae to Mrs J. Ross Robertson in recognition of her 'deep interest shown in the welfare of the nurses' of the hospital; 4 blank; 5–6 preface; 7 'Points for the Reader'; 8–68 text; 69 table of contents; all roman-numbered leaves blank for 'Memorandum,' except pp i–iii following p 69 that are all blank
CITATIONS: O'Neill (unpublished)
COPIES: CIHM (98228)   OONL (RM219 I58 1907) *OTHSC   OTMCL (641.563 T59.2); Great Britain: LB (07943.k.31 destroyed)
NOTES: The preface identifies the compiler of *Invalid Cookery* as Mrs George Macbeth, 'the chief dietitian of the Hospital for Sick Children, Toronto'; it identifies the author of the chapter on infant feeding (pp 55–68) as Dr Alan Canfield, 'on the staff of the hospital.' The book was 'compiled for not only the use of the trained nurse, but for those of the public who desire to use its recipes.'

O180.2 2nd ed., 1912
—Second edition / Invalid cookery / for the use of the / trained nurse / and all others who have / to cook and serve food / for invalids / Individual recipes / also a chapter / on / the feeding of infants / with full instructions / for every mother / Issued by the alumnae / of / the Hospital for Sick Children / College Street, Toronto / Price fifty cents / Toronto / 1912
DESCRIPTION: 18.0 × 9.5 cm   Pp [1–4] 5–16, [i–ii], 17–20, [i–ii], 21–8, [i–ii], 29–32, [i–ii], 33–6, [i–ii], 37–44, [i–ii], 45–8, [i–ii], 49–52, [i–ii], 53–60, [i–ii], 61–4, [i–ii], 65–7   Fp illus on p 59 of 'A Milk Bottle,' fp illus on p 63 of 'A Cream Dipper'   Cloth
CONTENTS: 1 tp; 2 'Entered according to Act of Parliament of Canada, in the year one thousand nine hundred and seven, by the Hospital for Sick Children, Toronto, at the Department of Agriculture, Ottawa.'; 3 dedication by the alumnae to Mrs J. Ross Robertson; 4 blank; 5–6 preface; 7 'Points for the Reader'; 8–66 text; 67 table of contents; all roman-numbered leaves blank for 'Memorandum'
COPIES: OONL (RM219 I58 1907)   *OTHSC

Our own cook book

O181.1 [about 1907]
[An edition of *Our Own Cook Book*]
DESCRIPTION: Lacks binding; stapled
COPIES: *OOWM (962.23.1)

NOTES: The volume is incomplete and begins on p 7; the last extant page is p 68. The running head is 'Our Own Cook Book.' The recipes are credited with the name of the contributor, mostly Grey County ladies, from such places as Lake Charles, Annan, Owen Sound, and Chatsworth, plus a recipe from McClarty Bros, an Owen Sound grocery business. There are no advertisements. The museum's accession form indicates that the book's original owner was Mrs John Baird, a charter member of the Chatsworth Women's Institute in Grey County, and that the person who donated the book in 1962 suggested the publication date of 1907.

Pierce, Paul Ashville (1866–)

Pierce was an American. DLC holds forty volumes of the National Food Magazine, *Minneapolis [etc.]: Pierce and Pierce, 1896–1900; Chicago [etc.]: Pierce Publishing Co., 1900–16.*

O182.1   [copyright 1907]
Breakfasts and teas / novel suggestions for social / occasions / Compiled by / Paul Pierce / Editor and publisher of What to Eat, the National Food Magazine, / Superintendent of Food Exhibits at the St. Louis Worlds's [sic] Fair. / Honorary Commissioner of Foods at the Jamestown Exposition. / Toronto / The Copp, Clark Co., Limited.
DESCRIPTION: 15.0 × 11.0 cm   Pp [1–7] 8–96   Paper-covered boards, with image on front of a woman and a coffeepot(?)
CONTENTS: 1 tp; 2 'Copyrighted 1907 by Paul Pierce'; 3 'To Women Editors'; 4 'Publisher's Announcement'; 5–6 table of contents; 7–96 text in ten chapters
COPIES: *OKQ (TX733 P6)
NOTES: In 'To Women Editors,' the author indicates that *Breakfasts and Teas* may be used by women editors looking for new entertaining ideas for their cookery columns, provided proper credit to the book is given. In the text Pierce offers menus, recipes, and advice on serving and other aspects of entertaining, such as decorating.
The 'Publisher's Announcement' identifies the book as a companion volume to the following titles, all by Pierce: O183.1, *Dinners and Luncheons; Parties and Entertainments* (no entry in this bibliography; American edition, Chicago: Brewer, Barse and Co., [c1907], at DLC); O184.1, *Suppers;* and *Weddings and Wedding Celebrations* (no entry in this bibliography). In 1916, the texts of all four volumes appear to have been brought together in the 382-page *Novel Suggestions for Social Occasions,* New York: Barse and Hopkins, [1916] (United States: DLC).
The series was sold by the Methodist Book and Publishing House in Toronto; see, for example, the entry in 'Stock Book 1909' (OTCC, Acc. 83.061C, UCC Board of Publication, Series III, Box 39, p 50): '6 [copies] Dinner [sic] & Lucheons [sic] ... 4 [copies] Suppers ... 3 [copies] Breakfast & Teas ... 5 [copies] Parties & Entertainment.' Some of the titles are also listed in 'Stock Book 1910,' 'Stock Book 1913,' and 'Stock Book 1914' (Boxes 40, 41, 42).

AMERICAN EDITIONS: Chicago: Brewer, Barse and Co., [c1907] (United States: DLC).

O183.1   [copyright 1907]
Dinners / and luncheons / novel suggestions for social / occasions. / Compiled by / Paul Pierce / Editor and publisher of What to Eat, the National Food Magazine. / Superintendent of Food Exhibits at the St. Louis World's Fair. / Honorary Commissioner of Foods at the Jamestown Exposition. / Toronto / The Copp, Clark Co., Limited.
DESCRIPTION: 15.0 × 11.0 cm   Pp [1–6] 7–96   Paper-covered boards, with images on front of a dining table and dinner bells
CONTENTS: 1 tp; 2 'Copyrighted 1907 by Paul Pierce'; 3 dedication 'to the overworked, perturbed American hostess'; 4 untitled introductory note signed the publishers; 5 table of contents; 6 blank; 7–96 text in five chapters
COPIES: *OONL (TX737 P54 1907 p***)
NOTES: The OONL copy retains its original dust-jacket. The introductory note on p 4 refers to this title as 'the first of a series containing suggestions for entertaining, ...' For the titles of other volumes in the series, see O182.1, *Breakfasts and Teas.*

AMERICAN EDITIONS: Chicago: Brewer, Barse and Co., [c1907] (United States: DLC).

O184.1   [copyright 1907]
Suppers / novel suggestions for social / occasions / Compiled by / Paul Pierce / Editor and publisher of What to Eat, the National Food Magazine, / Superintendent of Food Exhibits at the St. Louis World's [sic] Fair. / Honorary Commissioner of Foods at the Jamestown Exposition. / Toronto / The Copp, Clark Co., Limited.
DESCRIPTION: 15.0 × 11.0 cm   Pp [1–7] 8–96   Paper-covered boards, with image on front of a steaming chafing dish

CONTENTS: 1 tp; 2 'Copyrighted 1907 by Paul Pierce'; 3 dedication 'To the Aristocracy of America'; 4 'Publisher's Announcement'; 5–6 table of contents; 7–17 Chapter I, 'Chafing Dish Suppers'; 18–26 Chapter II, 'German, Dutch and Bohemian Suppers'; 27–36 Chapter III, 'Entertaining in the Modern Apartment'; 37–52 Chapter IV, 'Suppers for Special Occasions'; 53–87 Chapter V, 'Miscellaneous Suppers'; 88–96 Chapter VI, 'Toasts and Stories for Suppers'
COPIES: *Private collection
NOTES: The dedication is to 'that much abused, but very eminent class, the society women of America.' Pierce comments that this aristocracy is one 'of real merit entree to which is attained by achievement, not by mere inheritance.'

His suggestions for suppers are wide-ranging and include 'Bohemian Suppers for Men' (men, he says, prefer substantial dishes with generous helpings, not 'a great number of fancy "messes"'), special occasions such as Hallowe'en, Thanksgiving, and birthdays, and a variety of miscellaneous suppers; for example, camping parties and clam bakes, a railroad party, and a literary supper.

For the titles of other volumes in the series, see O182.1, *Breakfasts and Teas*.

AMERICAN EDITIONS: New York: Barse and Hopkins, [c1907] (United States: DLC).

Practical cookery

O185.1 1907
Practical / cookery / Recipes / tried and true / by ladies of Trenton / Compiled by the / Epworth League of King / Street Church / Trenton, Ont. / 1907
COPIES: *Private collection

Recipes

O186.1 1907
A cook book / Recipes / tested and tried. / Collected by the ladies of Trinity Church, / Norwich. / Norwich: / Gazette Printing House, / 1907.
DESCRIPTION: 21.5 × 15.0 cm Pp [5–7] 8–46, [i–xviii] Lacks binding
CONTENTS: 5 tp; 6 blank; 7–46 recipes credited with the name of the contributor; i–xviii ads
COPIES: *ONDA
NOTES: At top p 7, under the heading for the 'Soups'

section, is the attribution 'From Washburn-Crosby's Co's New Cook Book.' The American firm Washburn-Crosby Co., which produced Gold Medal Flour, was based in Minneapolis. One of the various cookbooks it published was *Washburn, Crosby Co.'s New Cook Book* in 1894 (United States: DLC), and another edition, 1897 (Allen, p 156).

The ONDA copy is in poor condition: It lacks its binding, and the leaves are loose. Also at ONDA is a photocopy of another copy of the book (not in the museum's collection) that is in better condition. Its cover-title is 'The Norwich Cook Book [image of roast poultry on a platter] Recipes: "Tested and Tried."'

1907–14

Merrill's handy cook book

See also O90.1, Merrill's Cook Book.

O187.1 nd [about 1907–14]
Merrill's / handy cook book / 500 / prize recipes / for making / bread, biscuits, cakes / and the / pies mother used to bake / Price 25 cents / Published by / the Merrill Medical Co. / Toronto Ontario [cover-title]
DESCRIPTION: 14.0 × 8.5 cm Pp 1–64 Paper, printed on the front face to give the optical illusion of a thick, cloth-bound book; stapled
CONTENTS: 1 'How to Cook Successfully'; 2 'Time Table for Cooking'; 3 'Read and Learn the Truth'; 4 'What Does the Miller Take Out of the Flour?'; 5 'The Chemical Structure of a Grain of Wheat Magnified 1,000 Times'; 6 'Why Does He Do It?'; 7 'The Harmful Effects of Yeast'; 8 'Merrill's Nutrient Baking Powder'; 9 'The Poisonous Nature of Alum'; 10 'More Expert Opinion'; 11 'One Word about Flavors'; 12 'Ideal Bread' and 'Measures'; 13–63 recipes and publ ads; 64 'Index' [i.e., table of contents]
COPIES: *Private collection
NOTES: The Merrill Medical Co. made a variety of products, such as baking powder, fruit flavours, Preservine, Seven Spices, and Smokine. Page 7 refers to 'F. [i.e., Frank] W. Merrill, one of Canada's most proficient chemists,' who produced Merrill's Pure Nutrient Baking Powder. According to text on the inside front face of the binding, this baking powder was 'the only baking powder in the world that [made] fine white flour as wholesome and nourishing as whole wheat flour' by replacing 'wheat phosphates' and 'diastase,' which were bolted out by the miller. On the inside back face of the binding, there is a

photograph of the Merrill Medical Building, Toronto, and a reference to 'twenty years' experience in the drug business.' The first listing in Toronto city directories for the Merrill Medical Co. (at 93½ Church Street) and for Frank W. Merrill (described as manager of the company, living at 278 Jarvis Street) is in 1907. From 1915, the company is listed under the name Merrill Co. Ltd. The cookbook, therefore, was likely published in the period 1907–14. The appearance of the book is consistent with publication in this period.

1908

Barnett, Mrs Henrietta Octavia Weston, née Rowland (England, 1851–10 June 1936, Hampstead, London, England)

Henrietta and her husband, Samuel, whom she married in 1873, were fervent social reformers. One of Henrietta's most famous ideas was Hampstead Garden Suburb, an early-twentieth-century community designed to integrate rich and poor.

O188.1 1908
The making of / the home. A book of / domestic economy for home and / school use / By / Mrs. Samuel A. Barnett / Ninety-fifth thousand / Cassell & Company, Limited / London, Paris, New York, Toronto & Melbourne / MCMVIII / All rights reserved
COPIES: *Private collection
NOTES: There are five chapters about cooking and one about baking, plus other chapters about food.

BRITISH EDITIONS: *The Making of the Home: A Reading-Book of Domestic Economy for School and Home Use*, London: Cassell and Co. Ltd, [1885] (Great Britain: LB, OB); 65th thousand, London: Cassell and Co. Ltd (Great Britain: OPo(F)).

Bogardus and Co.'s almanac and cook book of tested recipes 1908

O189.1 1908
Bogardus & Co.'s / almanac and / cook book of tested recipes / 1908 / Published at / Opera House Pharmacy / Bogardus & Co. / chemists and druggists / Guelph Ontario [cover-title]
DESCRIPTION: 17.5 × 13.5 cm   Pp [1–3] 4–32   Small illus of astrological signs and symbols   Paper, with

photograph on front of drugstore interior; stapled, and with hole punched at top left corner, through which runs a string for hanging
CONTENTS: 1 'Our Specialty' signed Bogardus and Co. at the Opera House Pharmacy, Guelph; 2 'To Our Friends' dated 1 January 1908 and signed Bogardus and Co.; 3 'Eclipses, 1908,' 'Morning and Evening Stars, 1908,' and 'Chronological Cycles, 1908'; 4–top 1st column 29 recipes, monthly calendars, 'Practical Breaks,' and publ ads; bottom 1st column 29 'Frost on Windows'; 2nd column 29 'Magic Age Table'; 30 'Foods for Dyspeptics' and 'Antidotes of Common Poisons'; 1st column 31 'Human Models' and 'Cold Feet and Sleepy Hands'; 2nd column 31–1st column 32 'Hints for the Home'; 2nd column 32 'The Family Medicine Chest' and 'Number of Trees on an Acre'
COPIES: *OGM (976.40.42)
NOTES: On p 4, under the heading 'Cakes, etc.,' the recipes begin with Almond Cakes, Cream Cake, Walnut Cake, and Ribbon Cake – the same recipes as noted for O199.1, *Robson's Calendar Cook Book 1908*, and NB24.1, *Brown's New Brunswick Almanac and Cook Book 1908*.

Bowerman, Miss Lucy (6 October 1870–)

The 1901 Census records Miss Lucy Bowerman, nurse, born 6 October 1870, living in Toronto with her parents Lydia and James. She is not listed in the 1908 city directory, but in the 1907 directory she is identified as a nurse, living at 505 Sherbourne, a Nurses' Home, whose proprietor was Miss Sarah Gray.

O190.1 1908
[An edition of *The Canadian Cook Book: Cookery and Domestic Economy*, compiled by Lucy Bowerman, a graduate of the Toronto General Hospital, Toronto: Printed by National Press Ltd for Toronto Graduate Nurses Club, copyright 1908]
CITATIONS: O'Neill (unpublished)
COPIES: Private collection; Great Britain: LB (07942.k.7 destroyed)
NOTES: The book has 354 pp according to LB.

The Bruce County cook-book

O191.1 1908
The Bruce County cook-book. / Compiled by / the Ladies of the Walkerton Hospital Aid / Society from receipes [sic] supplied by / ladies of the county. / Published in aid of / the Bruce County Hospital. /

"We may live without poetry, music and art; / We may live without conscience and live without heart: / We may live without love, we may live without books, / But civilized man cannot live without cooks." / Walkerton, 1908. / Printed at / the Bruce Herald Office, / Walkerton.

DESCRIPTION: 21.5 × 14.5 cm   Pp [i–iv], [1–5] 6–107 [108], [i–vi] [$0.25, on binding and p 3] Paper; stapled

CONTENTS: i–iv ads; 1 tp; 2 blank; 3 preface; 4 table of contents; 5–107 text; 108 'Kitchen Time-Table'; i–vi ads

COPIES: *Private collection

NOTES: The front face of the binding states: 'Copies of this book may be obtained from Mrs. Norman Robertson, Walkerton, Ont. Price 25 cents. Postage 4 cents.' The preface explains: 'All the profit derived from its sale will be handed over to the Treasurer of the Hospital. The price has been fixed at only twenty-five cents so that a large edition may be sold.' Money was being raised because the hospital 'has many free patients who are unable to pay for the care and attention rendered, ...' The recipes are credited with the name and town of the contributor. There is a chapter of 'Drinks for Invalids.' An advertisement on p iii (back of the book) shows a cooking demonstration at the Macdonald Institute in Guelph. An advertisement on p iv (back) illustrates the Pfeffer Bros flour mill in Milverton; Pfeffer Bros published O430.1, *Cooking Recipes*.

C., H.E.

O192.1   nd [about 1908]
The / pot-luck / cookery book / compiled by / H.E.C. / The Musson Book Company / Toronto

DESCRIPTION: 18.5 × 12.0 cm   Pp [leaf lacking?] [iii–v] vi–x, [11] 12–160   4 pls col   Cloth, with image on front of animals and animated foodstuffs (e.g., eggs) dancing around a steaming cauldron

CONTENTS: iii tp; iv 'Edinburgh: Printed by McFarlane and Erskine'; v–x index; 11–160 recipes

COPIES: *Private collection

NOTES: This is a British text.

BRITISH EDITIONS: London: Maclaren and Co., nd [1908] (Driver 178.1); Edinburgh: W.P. Nimmo, Hay and Mitchell, nd [1921] (Driver 178.2).

Davenport, Mrs Laura

Also by this American author are: The Small Family Cook Book, *Chicago: Reilly and Britton, c1910 (United States: DLC); and* The Ideal Home Cook Book, *Chicago: Reilly and Britton Co., [c1913] (United States: DLC).*

O193.1   [copyright 1908]
The / bride's cook book / a superior collection of thoroughly tested / practical recipes / specially adapted to the needs of the young housekeeper / Selected and arranged / by / Laura Davenport / Toronto / The Copp, Clark Co., Limited / publishers

DESCRIPTION: 22.5 × 16.0 cm   Pp [1–14] 15–265 [266–74]   Frontis col of a bride in an oval frame, illus col part-titles   Cloth, with pl col mounted on front of a bride

CONTENTS: 1 ht; 2 blank; 3 tp; 4 'Copyright, 1908, by the Reilly & Britton Co.'; 5–6 'Introductory'; 7–9 table of contents; 10 'Note'; 11–265 text, beginning with a chapter of menus; 266–74 blank for 'Contributed Recipes'

COPIES: *Bookseller's stock   Private collection

NOTES: There is no index, but the text is thumb-indexed and the recipes in each chapter are arranged alphabetically. In the 'Introductory' the author says, 'The Bride's Cook Book is born of my own twenty years experience in housekeeping ...' The recipes serve two to three persons.

AMERICAN EDITIONS: Chicago: Reilly and Britton Co., [c1908] (United States: DLC).

De Pratz, Madame Claire (died 1934)

Day Monroe, the editor of the 1925 edition of De Pratz's cookbook, refers to her as Madame De Pratz. Also by De Pratz is France from Within, *London, New York: Hodder and Stoughton, [1912] (United States: DLC).*

O194.1   nd [about 1908]
French dishes for / English tables / by / C. de P. / Toronto / The Musson Book Co. / Limited

DESCRIPTION: 19.0 × 12.5 cm   Pp [i–viii], [1] 2–189, [i]   Cloth, with image on front of a male servant carrying a covered platter

CONTENTS: i ht; ii blank; iii tp; iv blank; v 'Contents'; vi blank; vii 'Preface' signed C. de P.; viii ad; 1–178 recipes; 179–83 'English Index'; 184–9 'French Index'; i ad

COPIES: CIHM (81214) *OONL (TX719 P73 1908 p***)
NOTES: The author's name, 'C. de Pratz,' is on the spine. The author explains her choice of recipes thus: 'This book is not a manual of cookery; it is a collection of cooking recipes used in most French households. I have therefore purposefully omitted joints and plainly boiled fish and vegetables, or the puddings and pies which form the staple cuisine of an English household.' The Canadian edition was likely published about the time of the original British edition, in 1908.

BRITISH EDITIONS: London and Edinburgh: Sands and Co., nd [1908] (Driver 298.1).

AMERICAN EDITIONS: Philadelphia: D. McKay, [1908] (NUC); retitled *French Home Cooking*, edited by Day Monroe, New York: E.P. Dutton and Co., [c1925] (United States: DLC); 2nd printing, December 1925 (1st printing was in May 1925) and 3rd printing, December 1926 (QMAC); rev. ed., edited by Georgia Lingafelt, with a chapter on wines by Jeanne Owen, New York: Dutton, 1956 (United States: DLC).

Good things to eat and how to prepare them

The Welland branch of the Women's Institute was founded in 1901 and disbanded in 1914; after reorganization in 1923, it was active for sixty years, disbanding again in 1983.

O194a.1 nd [1908]
Good things to eat / and / how to prepare them / "All mankind's concern is charity." – Pope. / This book has been prepared by the ladies of / the Welland branch of the Women's Insti- / tute, in aid of Welland County Hospital / Printed at the office of the Tribune, Welland, Ont.
DESCRIPTION: Pp ... 136 [137–8] 139 [140–1] 142
CONTENTS: ...; 132–6 'Miscellaneous' recipes; 137–9 'Time Table' and ad; 140 'Weights and Measures'; 141 'Committee' listing 'Mrs. Cowper, Pres. of Wom. Ins. Mrs. John Gaiser, Sec.-Treas. Wom. Ins. Mrs. F.C. Hobson, Convener of Com. Mrs. Wells. Mrs. Valencourt. Mrs. Cohoe. Mrs. Baldwin. Mrs. McNiece. Miss M. Smith. Miss F. Hobson.'; 142 'Index' [i.e., table of contents]
COPIES: *OWE
NOTES: The 'Greeting,' p 5, states, 'The Women's Institute of Welland, being desirous of helping to build the hospital, so sorely needed, have prepared this little book of tried recipes, ...' The 'Proportions,' under 'Weights and Measures' on p 140, are described as 'copied from Century Cook Book,' likely O141.1.

No date of publication appears in the book, but newspaper reports about the Welland branch's activities in the *Welland Tribune* and in the *People's Press*, another local paper, record 1908 as the year of the first edition. The project was launched in autumn 1907:

> It was decided to compile and publish a book of recipes to be sold and the proceeds to be given to the Welland hospital fund as a donation from the institute. The recipes are to be those that have been tested by members of the institute and found 'O.K.' A meeting is to be held in the court house at the usual hour tomorrow (Saturday) afternoon for the purpose of further arranging for getting up the recipe book. All members are requested to attend this meeting, and take with them the copy of recipes they have tried and found good, with their names attached to the same. (*Welland Tribune*, 6 September 1907, p 1)

On 11 and 15 October, the *Welland Tribune*, p 2, carried this message: 'Those who have not already handed in recipes for the Cook Book are invited to come and bring them [to the 16 October meeting].' The *Welland Tribune*, 18 October, p 1, recorded the motion passed at the 16 October meeting 'that every member should bring with her a recipe to give in answer to the roll call at the next meeting.' The *People's Press*, 5 November, p 2, stated that 'those interested in the Cook Book' are 'invited to be present' at the 6 November meeting. The cookbooks were printed by the following summer, as the *People's Press* reported on 28 July 1908, p 2, 'The cook books will be there [at the 5 August meeting] for those who wish them.' The *People's Press*, 11 August, p 2, reported about the 5 August meeting:

> Those present were glad to receive the new cook books. A number of the ladies have undertaken to sell the books in their different sections, as follows: Mrs. Misener, Mrs. Gainer, Mrs. Goodwillie, Mrs. Asher, Mrs. Gaiser, Mrs. Baldwin. They may also be obtained from Mrs. Cowper or Mrs. Cohoe. Every housekeeper should have one, as they are well worth the price, 35¢.

Welland County General Hospital opened on 1–2 March 1909. The Women's Institute met the next day to consider the gift of an ambulance, and the report of this meeting in the *People's Press,* 9 March, p 1, refers to money raised by the cookbook and remaining copies: 'Through the sale of cook books the Institute has about $250 on hand, but returns are not all in, and there are still books unsold.'

O194a.2 [2nd ed.], nd
—Good things to eat / and / how to prepare them / "All mankind's concern is charity." Pope. / This book has been prepared by the ladies of / the Welland branch of the Women's Insti- / tute, in aid of Welland County Hospital / Printed at the office of the Tribune, Welland.
DESCRIPTION: Pp [1–10] 11–135 [136]   Card; sewn
CONTENTS: 1 poem beginning, 'We may live without poetry, music and art' [from *Lucile,* Part I, Canto ii, by Owen Meredith, pseudonym of Edward Robert Bulwer-Lytton]; 2 blank; 3 tp; 4 'Committee' listing 'Mrs. Cowper, Pres. of Wom. Ins. Mrs. John Gaiser, Sec.-Treas Wom. Ins. Mrs. F.C. Hobson, Convener of Com. Mrs. Wells. Mrs. Valencourt. Mrs. Cohoe. Mrs. Baldwin. Mrs. McNiece. Miss M. Smith. Miss F. Hobson.'; 5 quotations from Francis Bacon and Montaigne, and 'Greeting:'; 6 ad; 7 'Good Things to Eat and How to Prepare Them' [introductory text]; 8 ad; 9–132 recipes credited with the name of the contributor and ads; 133–top 135 'Time Table' and ad; mid–bottom 135 'Weights and Measures'; 136 ad
COPIES: *Private collection
NOTES: Printed on the front face of the binding are the title, a quotation from Burns, and 'Second edition // This book is prepared by the Welland County Women's Institute, the proceeds to go towards the Welland County Hospital Price, 35 cents.' This edition is printed from a new setting of type. On the title-page, for example, there is no dash before 'Pope,' and no 'Ont.' at the end of the printer's line. The text of the 'Greeting' is identical, but it is reset and there is no initial ornamental letter. The 'Committee' list, previously on p 141, is now at the front of the book, on p 4; 'Proportions' have moved from p 140 to p 135.

Harrison's calendar cook book 1908

O195.1   1908
Harrison's / calendar / cook book / 1908 / Published by / R.A. Harrison / druggist and optician / Dunnville Ontario [cover-title]
DESCRIPTION: 17.5 × 13.0 cm   Pp [1–3] 4–31 [32]   Paper, with image on front of a mortar and pestle; stapled, and with hole punched at top left corner, through which runs a string for hanging

CONTENTS: 1 'Our Announcement' signed R.A. Harrison, druggist, Dunnville; 2 publ ad; 3–32 astrological information, monthly calendars, jokes, recipes, publ ads, and miscellaneous items
COPIES: *OHMB (Ephemera QV737 H321h 1908)
NOTES: On p 1 Harrison refers to his thirty years in business. The recipes are in three sections: 'Cakes, etc.,' 'Puddings, etc.,' and 'Miscellaneous Recipes.' There is also a section that specifies the 'Proper Sauces for Meats.'

The King's Daughter's cook book and domestic helps

O196.1   1908
The / King's Daughter's [*sic*] / cook book and / domestic helps / Compiled by / the Guelph Circle of / the King's Daughters / Guelph, Ont., 1908 / Mercury Print
DESCRIPTION: 16.5 × 12.5 cm   Pp [3–9] 10–246, [i]   Cloth; stapled
CONTENTS: 3 tp; 4 blank; 5 preface; 6 ad; 7 table of contents; 8 ad; 9–246 recipes credited with the name of the contributor and ads; i ad
CITATIONS: Driver 2001, Wellington County, p 89
COPIES: OGM (2 copies: 972.10.1, 998.30.1)   *OGU (UA s047 b15)   OWTU (F17882)
NOTES: The preface refers to the work of the Guelph Circle of the King's Daughters, i.e., the International Order of the King's Daughters and Sons, founded in 1886 in New York: 'Charity, Missions, General Hospital, Elliott Home, and wherever the call is made, in our own city or elsewhere.'

One of the copies at OGM (998.30.1) is inscribed on the title-page, in black ink, 'Agnes Taylor Gow from Janet McCrae // "Janefield" Christmas 1908.'; also inscribed on the title-page, but in ballpoint pen and, therefore, in a later hand, is 'Julie Pope.' Janet McCrae was the mother of John McCrae, famous for his First World War poem, 'In Flanders Fields.' Janefield was the name of the McCrae family home at 108 Water Street in Guelph, which is now a city museum called McCrae House.

Nearly two hundred tested recipes

O197.1   [1908]
[An edition of *Nearly Two Hundred Tested Recipes,* Napanee, Ont.: Ladies' Aid of Napanee Trinity Methodist Church, [1908]]
CITATIONS: O'Neill (unpublished)

COPIES: Great Britain: LB (7945.l.10 missing)
NOTES: O'Neill and the LB catalogue describe this item as 'cards.'

Payne, Arthur Gay

Payne also wrote O219.1, Choice Dishes at Small Cost. *Also by this author, but not published in Canada, are:* Common-sense Papers on Cookery, *London, Paris and New York: Cassell, Petter and Galpin, nd [1877] (Great Britain: LB, LCS, LoEN, OB);* The Housekeeper's Guide to the Use of Preserved Meats, Fruits, Vegetables, &c., *London and New York: Frederick Warne and Co., nd [1886] (Great Britain: LoEN, OB); and* Cassell's Vegetarian Cookery, *London, Paris and Melbourne: Cassell and Co. Ltd, 1891 (Great Britain: LoEN, OB). In about 1875, Payne contributed 'The Principles of Cookery' to* Cassell's Dictionary of Cookery *(see Driver 186.1 and 186.2).*

For a discussion of DLC's identification of A.G. Payne as a pseudonym of Mrs Sarah Sharp Hamer, née Heaton (1839–1927), see Driver, p 307.

O198.1   1908
[An edition of *Cassell's Shilling Cookery,* London, Paris, New York, Toronto and Melbourne: Cassell and Co. Ltd, 1908]
CITATIONS: Driver 805.13
COPIES: Great Britain: Private collection
NOTES: Cassell and Co. Ltd's Canadian agency was set up in Toronto in 1907 under Henry Button (see Spadoni/Donnelly, p 27, and the first listing for Cassell in the Toronto city directory for 1908). This book was an early publication of the new agency.

O198.2   nd [1910 or later]
—[An edition of *Cassell's Popular Cookery,* London, New York, Toronto and Melbourne: Cassell and Co. Ltd, nd]
CITATIONS: Driver 805.17
COPIES: Great Britain: OPo(F)
NOTES: An advertisement on p [iv] refers to King George V, who reigned 1910–35.

O198.3   1912
—Cassell's / cookery / edited by / A.G. Payne / author of "Choice Dishes," etc. / With coloured frontispiece / Cassell and Company, Ltd / London, New York, Toronto and Melbourne / 1912 / All rights reserved
DESCRIPTION: 18.0 × 12.0 cm   Pp [i–v] vi [vii–viii], [1] 2–360   Frontis brown, a few small illus   Cloth, with

image on front of an aproned woman standing beside a range and holding a frying pan in her left hand
CONTENTS: i ht; ii blank; iii tp; iv blank; v–vi 'Preface' and at bottom p v, 'A * Can. edn.'; vii table of contents; viii blank; 1–352 text; 353–60 index and at bottom p 360, 'Printed by Cassell & Company, Limited, La Belle Sauvage, London, E.C. // 30.1012'
COPIES: *Private collection

O198.4   nd [about 1917]
—Cassell's cookery / edited by / A.G. Payne / author of "Choice Dishes," etc. / With coloured frontispiece / Cassell and Company, Ltd / London, New York, Toronto and Melbourne
DESCRIPTION: 18.0 × 11.5 cm   Pp [i–v] vi [vii–viii], [1] 2–360   Frontis brown, a few small illus   Cloth
CONTENTS: i ht; ii blank; iii tp; iv 'All rights reserved'; v–vi preface and at bottom p v, 'A * Can. edn.'; vii table of contents; viii blank; 1–352 text; 353–60 index and at bottom p 360, 'Printed by Cassell & Company, Limited, La Belle Sauvage, London, E.C. 4 // 10.517'
COPIES: *OGU (UA s012 b08)
NOTES: If the printer's mark on p 360 follows the same pattern as for O198.3 (dated 1912 on the title-page; printer's mark 30.1012'), then this edition was published in 1917.

BRITISH EDITIONS: *Cassell's Shilling Cookery,* London, Paris, New York and Melbourne: Cassell and Co. Ltd, 1888 (Great Britain: LB destroyed, OB); retitled *Cassell's Popular Cookery,* London, Paris, New York and Melbourne: Cassell and Co. Ltd, 1889 (Great Britain: LB destroyed, OB); *Cassell's Shilling Cookery,* 40th thousand, London, Paris, New York and Melbourne: Cassell and Co. Ltd, 1889 (Great Britain: Private collection); 60th thousand, London, Paris, New York and Melbourne: Cassell and Co. Ltd, 1889 (Great Britain: Bookseller's stock); 1890 (CBCat 7/77); 95th thousand (Great Britain: DuSB); 1896 (Great Britain: NtCo); London, Paris, New York and Melbourne: Cassell and Co. Ltd, 1900 (Great Britain: OPo(F)); London, Paris, New York and Melbourne: Cassell and Co. Ltd, 1902 (Great Britain: Private collection); London, Paris, New York and Melbourne: Cassell and Co. Ltd, 1903 (Great Britain: LCS); 1905 (Great Britain: Private collection); London, Paris, New York and Melbourne: Cassell and Co. Ltd, 1907 (United States: DLC); 1908 (O198.1, above); 1910 (JLCat 118); *Cassell's Popular Cookery,* nd [1910 or later] (O198.2, above); retitled *Cassell's Cookery,* 1912 (O198.3, above); *Cassell's Shilling Cookery,* 1913 (BCat Parkinson, March 1975); nd, pp 369 (CBCat 9/76 and 7/77); *Cassell's Cookery,* nd [about 1917] (O198.4, above).

See also 'General comments' in Driver, p 477, regarding the 80th thousand, 110th thousand, and 135th thousand of *Cassell's Shilling Cookery.*

AMERICAN EDITIONS: *Cassell's Half-Dollar Cook Book,* New York: Cassell, nd (United States: NIC).

Robson's calendar cook book 1908

See also O220.1, Robson's Household Calendar Cook Book 1909.

O199.1 1908
Robson's / calendar cook book / 1908 / Published by / W.H. Robson, Phm.B. / druggist and optician / Fenelon Falls Ontario [cover-title]
DESCRIPTION: 18.0 × 13.5 cm   Pp [1–3] 4–30   Illus of astrological symbols   Paper; stapled, and with hole punched at top left corner, through which runs a string for hanging
CONTENTS: Inside front face of binding untitled introductory text signed W.H. Robson; 1–2 publ ads; 3–28 astronomical information, recipes, monthly calendars, 'Practical Breaks' [i.e., jokes], and publ ads; 29 'Proper Sauces for Meats,' 'Frost on Windows,' 'Magic Age Table,' and a tip about making mashed potatoes; 30 'Foods for Dyspeptics' and 'Antidotes of Common Poisons'
COPIES: *OTUTF (uncat patent medicine)
NOTES: The introductory text opposite p 1 indicates that the first of these publications appeared in 1902: 'We again take the pleasure of greeting you through this seventh edition of our Almanac and Cook Book.' The recipes begin on p 4 with Almond Cakes, Cream Cake, Walnut Cake, and Ribbon Cake – the same recipes as noted for O189.1, *Bogardus and Co.'s Almanac and Cook Book of Tested Recipes 1908,* and NB24.1, *Brown's New Brunswick Almanac and Cook Book 1908.*

Tested recipes

For information about McClary's and its cookbooks, see O162.1.

O200.1 [1908]
Tested recipes / These pages contain a number of most / useful and inexpensive recipes. / They have been thoroughly / tested and proven, and / can be relied / upon. / McClary's / London / largest makers in Canada of / stoves, ranges, heaters / for gas, coal or wood

DESCRIPTION: 19.0 × 11.0 cm   Pp [1–3] 4–48   Illus of gas ranges and burners   Paper, with image on front of a maid carrying meat in a pan, a gas range to her right; stapled
CONTENTS: 1 tp; 2 fp illus of a woman standing beside a gas range and 'Edited and published by McClary Manufacturing Co. London, Toronto, Montreal, Winnipeg, Vancouver, St. John, N.B., Hamilton, Calgary.'; 3 'Preface 1908'; 4–5 'Glossary of Terms Used in Cookery'; 6–48 recipes and information about McClary products
COPIES: *Private collection
NOTES: The cover-title is 'McClary's Cook Book // For sale by F.C. Kulow // Port Colborne, Ont.' The printer's name is on the outside back face of the binding, 'A. & A. Bot & Co., London, Ont.' Illustrated models include: E.S. Side Oven 'Caloric' Gas Range, Nos. 380-E.S. and 38-E.S. on p 22; 'Caloric' Gas Range, Nos. 36-B, 38-B, 360-B, and 380-B, all on p 25, and Nos. 38-E and 380-E on p 28, and Nos. 36-C, 38-C, 360-C, and 380-C, all on p 33, and Nos. 36-D, 38-D, 360-D, and 380-D, all on p 37; 'Pony Jubilee' Range, Nos. 22 and 33 on p 40; 'Jubilee' Hot Plate, Nos. 2 and 3 on p 44; and Gas Ovens, Cut No. 655 on p 47. The title-page and text are printed in red and black. The 'Preface' presents the advantages of gas:

> The use of the McClary 'Caloric' Gas Stoves is rapidly increasing owing to their convenience, cleanliness and economy.
> With the Gas Range there is no trouble of gathering kindling, carrying coal, carrying away and sifting ashes ...
> After a long series of experiments, it has been proven that meats roasted by gas lose less in weight than when cooked with other fuels, thus saving the nutritious juices which usually evaporate when cooked with other fuels.

The private collector's copy is inscribed on the front face of the binding, in pencil, 'Mrs Louis Augustine, Port Colborne, Ont.'

O200.2 2nd ed., 1909
—[Second edition of *Tested Recipes,* McClary's, 1909]
COPIES: Private collection

Things worth knowing

See also O127.1, by the same company.

O201.1 [1908]
Things worth / knowing / Reliable recipes, valuable formulas / and methods of home treatment / for common diseases [cover-title]
DESCRIPTION: 22.0 × 14.5 cm   Pp 1–32   Paper, with image on front of a family of five by the hearth; stapled, and with string through top left corner for hanging
CONTENTS: Inside front face of binding 'Things Worth Knowing' [introductory text] signed Dr Williams Medicine Co., Brockville, Ontario; 1–32 medical information, 'Household Recipes,' monthly calendars for 1908, and publ ads
COPIES: *OTUTF (uncat patent medicine)
NOTES: 'Household Recipes' begin on p 4 with Bread, Boston Brown Bread, and Grafton Milk Biscuit. The volume was published to promote the sale of Dr Williams' Pink Pills for Pale People.

O201.2 [1908]
—Choses dignes d'etre / connues. / Recettes utiles, formules et méthodes / indispensables pour bien se traiter chez / [illegible on microfilm] pour les maladies ordinaires [cover-title]
DESCRIPTION: Pp 1–32   Stapled
CONTENTS: Inside front face of binding 'Choses dignes d'être connues' [introductory text] signed Dr Williams Medicine Co., Brockville, Ontario; 1–32 information about various illnesses, testimonials for 'Les pilules roses du Dr Williams' [i.e., Dr Williams' Pink Pills for Pale People], monthly calendars for 1908 on recto pages, and 'Recettes domestiques' in the 1st column of pp 4–14
COPIES: *CIHM (74480)   OKQ (F5012 1908 D75C)

Vogue cook book

O202.1   nd [1908]
Vogue / cook / book / being a collection of / well proven recipes / contributed by readers / of the Vogue Page of / the News
DESCRIPTION: 21.0 × 15.0 cm   Pp [1–2] [3–4, folios likely printed, but torn off in this copy] [5] 6–170 [171, folio possibly torn off], [i, folio possibly torn off] Tp illus of two stylized men in profile, each carrying a tray   Cloth
CONTENTS: 1–10 ads; 11 tp; 12 ad; 13 'A Word from the Editor'; 14–162 text; 163 'Index' [i.e., table of contents]; 164 ad; 165–70 'Classified Index'; 171 blank, ruled leaf for 'Memoranda'; i ad
COPIES: OGU (2 copies: *UA s048 b18, TX715 V63)   OTUTF (B-12 7865)
NOTES: 'The News Publishing Co. Toronto' is on the front face of the binding. Recipes were contributed by readers of the Vogue Page of Toronto's *Daily News* newspaper.

An advertisement for 'Vogue Cook Book for Christmas Giving' in the *Daily News*, 19 December 1908, p 31, states that the cookbook 'will be issued on Wednesday, December 23rd.' The advertisement includes a coupon for the book, giving the price of $0.75, or $0.50 for recipe contributors.

The first leaf of the OTUTF copy is numbered 3–4; the volume may or may not be lacking a leaf before p 3. It does lack the last leaf, pp 171, i.

The Y.W.C.A. cook book

O203.1   1908
"Before the housewife now our book is laid – / 'Twill aid her, if its teachings be obeyed." / The Y.W.C.A. / cook book / A selection of tested recipes compiled / by the ladies of St. Thomas / 1908 / The Journal Press / St. Thomas, Ontario.
DESCRIPTION: 22.0 × 14.5 cm   Pp [1–3] 4–167 [168] Limp cloth, with image on front of the YWCA building; stapled
CONTENTS: 1 tp; 2 'Greeting' signed the Young Women's Christian Association, St Thomas, Ont.; 3 'Index to Advertisers'; 4 ads; 5 'Tables'; 6–mid 165 recipes credited with the name of the contributor and ads; mid 165–167 'Remedies'; 168 'Index to Recipes' [i.e., table of contents]
CITATIONS: Beeson, p 31
COPIES: CIHM (87075)   *OSTT (R641.5 YOU) OSTTECPM   OTNY (641.5971 Y)
NOTES: The 'Greeting' says that the proceeds of the sale of the cookbook were to go toward decreasing the debt on the association's new building. It goes on to explain that the YWCA has 'been in existence [in St Thomas] for some five years [i.e., since about 1903] ... It has a Boarding House Department which [does] good work among the young women who come as strangers and who are employed in various ways.' Once finances are stronger, the YWCA 'hopes to have a better equipped Gymnasium, classes in Domestic Science, etc., which are essential parts of Y.W.C.A. work ...' The running head is 'St. Thomas Y.W.C.A. Cook Book.'

Beeson reprints two recipes from the book. The OSTTECPM copy lacks pp 1–4 and 163–8.

1908–9

Cobalt souvenir and cook book

O204.1 1908–9

Cobalt souvenir / and cook book / a collection of / choice tested recipes / contributed and compiled by the ladies / of the Presbyterian Church / Cobalt, Ontario / For books apply to / "Ladies' Aid," Presbyterian Church / Cobalt, Ontario / 1908–09 / Cobalt Nugget Print

DESCRIPTION: 22.0 × 14.0 cm   Pp [1–4] 5–95 [96–102]   Many illus   Paper, with image on front of a camp site (two men by a cauldron over a fire, and one man in a canoe; in the background, man at tent entrance); stapled

CONTENTS: 1 tp; 2–3 fp illus; 4 ad; 5–101 text; 102 'Index (recipe section),' index for 'illustrated section,' and 'We are indebted to Messrs. Bogart and Seligman, and other friends, for photographs taken and assistance given in compilation of this book.'

CITATIONS: Driver 2003, 'Canadian Cookbooks,' illus p 20   Driver 2005, illus p 411

COPIES: CIHM (78190)   *OGU (UA s045 b40)   OONL (TX715 C5796 1908)   OTAR (Pamph 1909 #63) OTNY (641.59713144 C)

NOTES: See pl 28. The illustrations are of Cobalt streets, public buildings, churches, mines, and bush scenes, such as 'Breakfast in the Bush,' 'Biscuits for Tea (Not Like Mother Used to Make),' and 'Annual Gathering of Indians at Abitibi.' In 1903, only a few years before the cookbook's publication, the discovery of silver had sparked a mining boom and the town of Cobalt grew up almost overnight.

The OGU copy lacks pp 33–64.

1908–12

Recipes

The women of the same church, called Parkdale United Church from 1925, produced O732.1, The Mixing Bowl.

O205.1   nd [about 1908–12]

Recipes / compiled and arranged in the / interests of / the Bascom Mission Band / of / Parkdale Methodist Church, / Toronto.

DESCRIPTION: 20.0 × 13.5 cm   Pp [1–5] 6–87 [88–98] Illus on p 1 of Parkdale Methodist Church   Lacks binding?; stapled, and bound by a cord through three punched holes

CONTENTS: 1 illus of church; 2 dedication 'To the members of the Woman's Missionary Auxiliary // Parkdale Methodist Church'; 3 tp; 4 quotation; 5–87 recipes credited with the name of the contributor; 88–9 'Invalid Cookery'; 90 ad; 91–2 'Table Hints'; 93–7 ads; 98 'Glossary' and ad

COPIES: *Private collection

NOTES: The copy catalogued here is inscribed on p 1, in pencil, 'Mary E. Stauffer'; and on p 3, in pencil, 'Violet Stauffer.'

Another private collector has the copy that belonged originally to Mrs (Dr) Joseph Bascom. The copy was passed down from her mother, who had been adopted at the age of eight years by Mrs Bascom, whom she called 'aunt.' Mrs Bascom moved to Parkdale in 1892, from Uxbridge, to escape conditions that exacerbated her asthma. She was dominion secretary of the Women's Christian Temperance Union, and active in the Woman's Missionary Society (WMS); from 1897 to 1906 she was president of the WMS at the church (*Parkdale United Church, 60 Years of Service: 1878–1938*, [Toronto: 1938], p 23, copy at OTCC). 'Bands' were the children's organizations within the WMS, and the Bascom Mission Band, in whose interests the cookbook was published, was likely named in her honour. The cookbook predates Mrs Bascom's death in 1919.

Two advertisements point to publication in about 1908–12, and the appearance of the volume is consistent with publication in this period. The advertisement on p 95 for Hollands Florists, 1510 Queen Street West, sets the earliest date: Toronto city directories from 1908 onward list Harry Holland as a florist. The advertisement on p 98 for J.F. Holloway, grocer, at the corner of King Street and Spadina Avenue, determines the latest date: the last listing for John F. Holloway as a grocer is in the 1912 directory.

1909

Chase, Dr Alvin Wood (Cayuga County, NY, 20 March 1817–25 May 1885, Ohio)

For information about Dr Chase and his publications, see O8.1.

O206.1   nd [about 1909]

Dr Chase's / candy / book [cover-title]

DESCRIPTION: 19.0 × 13.5 cm   Pp [1] 2–32   Paper, with image on front of a boy and girl pulling taffy; stapled

CONTENTS: Inside front face of binding 'Life of Dr.

A.W. Chase' and his portrait; 1 'Home-made Candies for Boys and Girls' and 'Do You Know Dr. Chase?'; 2–32 publ ads and a few boxed recipes; inside back face '(C.B. '09)' on the corner of a coupon for a free trial

COPIES: QKB (80-7)   *Private collection

NOTES: The book was published after 1903 since a testimonial on p 23 says, 'In 1903 I broke out with small red blotches ...' It was published in 1909 if the number on the coupon (on the inside back face of the binding) is a date, which it probably is. On p 32 there is an advertisement for Edmanson, Bates and Co., Toronto, which sold Dr Chase's medicines and which is likely the publisher of the book. The testimonials have Canadian addresses.

'Home-made Candies for Boys and Girls' reveals the attitude to candy in the first decade of the twentieth century: 'Pure, wholesome candy is good for the system and seems to be particularly necessary for growing boys and girls. But do not eat candy every day. It is a very good plan to look forward to candy-making as a treat ...' By the end of the century, parents were more likely to see candy (and sugar in any form) as bad for health.

The QKB copy lacks its binding.

Choice recipes

See also O1075.1, The Golden Anniversary Cook Book Library, *from the same church.*

O207.1 1909
Choice recipes / from / the Ladies' Aid and friends / for the / Talent Workers' Fund / of / St. Giles' Presbyterian Church / Cor. Main Street East and Holton Avenue / Hamilton / 1909 / F.G. Smith, printer [union label] 107 West King Street

DESCRIPTION: 21.0 × 13.0 cm   Pp [i–iv], 1–36, [i]   Very thin card, with image on front of the church; stapled

CONTENTS: i tp; ii ad; iii 'Index' [i.e., table of contents]; iv ads; 1–36 recipes credited with the name of the contributor; i ad

COPIES: CIHM (84009)   OH (R641.5 G394 CESH) *SWSLM

NOTES: The cover-title is 'Three Hundred Choice Recipes.'

C.L.C. tombola cook book

O208.1 [1909]
C.L.C. tombola cook book / A book of recipes / tried and tested by the ladies of Cornwall and / friends of the Cornwall Lacrosse Club. [cover-title]

DESCRIPTION: 17.0 × 13.0 cm   Pp [1–2] 3–98 [99], [i–xvii]   Paper, with image on front of a lacrosse player stepping out of an oval shape, behind which is a large maple leaf; stapled

CONTENTS: 1 tp; 2 dedication to the '"Lords of Creation," dear to us as fathers, brothers, husbands or sons, keen critics always of the culinary art, ...' and 'Recipe for a Day' [i.e., mock recipe]; 3–88 recipes credited with the name of the contributor; 89 'Weights and Measures'; 90–2 'Household Hints'; 93–9 'Index' and at bottom p 99, ad and 'Printed at the office of the Cornwall Standard.'; i–xvii ads

CITATIONS: O'Neill (unpublished)

COPIES: *Private collection; Great Britain: LB (07943.de.9 destroyed)

NOTES: Copyright was registered in 1909 at the British Library by Mary Elizabeth MacPhee and Bertha Grace Kirkpatrick. Tombola is a kind of lottery sometimes played at fund-raising events.

The private collector's copy is covered in oil cloth in such a way as to obscure the title-page. The title-page of another collector's copy reads: 'C.L.C. / tombola / cook book / A book of recipes / tried and tested by ladies of Cornwall and / friends of the Cornwall Lacrosse Club. / "Let me cook the meals of my country, and I / care not who makes her laws."'

The Cobourg Congregational cook book

O209.1 1909
The Cobourg / Congregational / cook book. / A selection of tested recipes compiled by the / Ladies' Aid of the Cobourg Congregational / Church, Cobourg, Ont., 1909, and / contributed by the ladies of the / congregation and friends. / The Ladies' Aid desire to thank all kind con- / tributors whose generosity has been the means of / making their undertaking a success.

DESCRIPTION: 18.0 × 11.0 cm   Pp [1–2] 3–59 [60] Frontispiece photograph of the Congregational Church   Paper; stapled

CONTENTS: 1 tp; 2 ads; 3–59 text, mainly recipes credited with the name of the contributor, and ads; 60 'Index' [i.e., table of contents] and ad for the *Cobourg World* newspaper

COPIES: CIHM (84260)   OPET   *OTNY (641.59713 C)   OTYA (CPC 1909 0069)

NOTES: 'Cobourg World Print.' is on the front face of the binding. 'Useful Hints' is on p 56; 'Things Worth Knowing,' on pp 57–8; and 'Bread and Rolls – (Supplementary),' on pp bottom 58–59.

Cook book recipes tested and tried

O210.1 1909
Cook book / recipes / tested and tried. / Collected
by the Ladies Auxiliary of the / Y.M.C.A. /
Woodstock, Ont., 1909. / R.H. Constable, printer, /
over 484 Dundas St., Woodstock.
DESCRIPTION: 21.5 × 13.5 cm   Pp [i–ii], [1–2] 3–56   Paper; stapled
CONTENTS: i ad; ii blank; 1 tp; 2 blank; 3–56 recipes
credited with the name of the contributor and ads
COPIES: *OTUTF (cap 08543)
NOTES: The following note is printed on p 56: 'Owing
to lack of time the committee regret omitting many
good recipes.'

Cooking recipes

O211.1   16 December 1909
Cooking / recipes / Compiled by / North Perth
Women's / Institute / Price 25 cents / Milverton,
Ont., December 16th, 1909 [cover-title]
COPIES: *OSCELM (1978.031.001)

Desserts of the world

*For other books about cooking with the American gelatine
product, Jell-O, see: O487.1, Jell-O; O502.1, Jell-O;
O503.1, Jell-O Rhymes; O524.1, Jell-O Book; O557.1,
New Jell-O Recipes; O730.1, 48 New Jell-O Entrées,
Relishes, Salads, Desserts; and O759.1, 48 New Jell-O
Recipes.*

O212.1   copyright 1909
Desserts / of / the / world / Presented by / the
Genesee Pure Food Co. / Le Roy, N.Y., U.S.A. /
Copyright 1909 by the Genesee Pure Food Co.
[cover-title]
DESCRIPTION: 18.5 × 13.5 cm   Pp [1–20]   Illus col
Paper, with image on front of a girl's head in a circu-
lar frame (symbolizing the terrestial globe), framed
by fruit trees; stapled, and with hole punched at top
left corner for hanging
CONTENTS: Inside front face of binding 'Jell-O the
American Dessert' signed Genesee Pure Food Co., Le
Roy, New York, and Bridgeburg, Ontario; 1 untitled
introduction; 2–20 recipes and information about the
cuisines of other countries
CITATIONS: Allen, p 198
COPIES: *BKOM

NOTES: The introductory text presents a brief culinary
history of the world, and ends with the comment:
'Good cooks are found everywhere now, but France
and America lead in all that is best in cookery. A few
recipes for the American dessert that can be made
without cooks are given in this book.' The recipes are
for desserts made with Jell-O.

Dr King's new guide to health, household instructor and family prize cook book 1909

See O96.1 for a list of other annual issues.

O213.1   [1909]
Price 10 cents / Dr. King's / new / guide to health /
household instructor / and / family / prize / cook
book / H.E. Bucklen & Co / Chicago, Ill. / 275–277
Michigan Ave. / Windsor, Can. / Sandwich Street,
West [cover-title]
CITATIONS: Allen, p 104 and illus col on p 15
NOTES: Allen, p 104, incorrectly records Windsor as in
Connecticut.

Fifty recipes

O214.1   1909
Fifty recipes / specially selected and /
recommended by / the Ladies Guild / of / St. James
Church / Ingersoll / 1909 [cover-title]
DESCRIPTION: 18.5–19.5 × 13.5–14.0 cm [i.e., irregular
leaves]   Pp [1–10]   Paper; stapled
CONTENTS: 1 'The Modelling of a Kitchen Mechanic'
[mock recipe]; 2 blank; 3–10 recipes credited with the
name of the contributor
COPIES: *QMM (TX715.6 F54 1909)
NOTES: This copy was sent through the mail, stamped
and addressed on the outside back face of the bind-
ing to: 'Mrs. R. Boultbee, c/o Col. Tisdale // Simcoe
Ont.'

Gunn's household calendar cook book 1909

See also O178.1.

O215.1   1909
Gunn's / household / calendar cook book / 1909 /
Published by / C.H. Gunn & Co. / Central Drug
Store / Chatham Ontario
DESCRIPTION: 17.0 × 13.0 cm   Pp [1–3] 4–32   Illus of

astrological symbols   Paper; stapled, and with hole punched at top left corner, through which runs a string for hanging

CONTENTS: 1 tp; 2 'To Our Customers' signed C.H. Gunn and Co.; 3–27 astronomical information, recipes, monthly calendars, 'Practical Breaks' [i.e., jokes], and publ ads; 28–mid 1st column 30 'Poisons and Antidotes'; mid 1st column 30–bottom 2nd column 30 medical information; 1st column 31–mid 2nd column 31 'Worth Knowing'; bottom 2nd column 31–32 'Things to Remember'

COPIES: *OTUTF (uncat patent medicine)

NOTES: The address of Gunn's Central Drug Store, at the corner of King and Fifth streets, is printed on the outside back face of the binding. The recipes are the same as listed for NB25.1, *Brown's New Brunswick Almanac and Cook Book 1909,* and for other almanac or calendar cookbooks cited in that entry.

Johnson, Alice A., Mrs Janet McKenzie Hill (1852–1933), Dr Henry Hartshorne (1823–97), and other specialists

For cookbooks by Janet McKenzie Hill and information about her, see O264.1.

O216.1 [copyright 1909]
A practical reference work for housekeepers / The / household / companion / comprising / a complete cook book – practical household / recipes, aids and hints for household decorations; / the care of domestic plants and animals and a / treatise on domestic medicine / including a chapter on tuberculosis the great white plague / a curable and preventable disease / by / Dr. Lawrence F. Flick / Medical Director of the Henry Phipps Institute for the Study, / Treatment and Prevention of Tuberculosis / General editors of the work / Alice A. Johnson / graduate in Domestic Science of Drexel Institute, Philadelphia / Mrs. Janet McKenzie Hill / Editor of the Boston Cooking School Journal / Dr. Henry Hartshorne, M.D., LL.D. / author of "Essential of Practical Medicine" / and other specialists / Profusely illustrated / with color plates, half-tone / engravings and text pictures / The John C. Winston Co., Limited / Toronto, Canada

DESCRIPTION: 23.0 × 17.0 cm   Pp [vii–x] xi–xv [xvi], [17–18] 19–370   4 pls col incl frontis of 'A man's work is from sun to sun // But a woman's work is never done'; 16 pls; illus   Cloth, with image on front of a ring of house keys

CONTENTS: vii tp; viii 'Copyright, 1909 by M.L. Dewsnap.'; ix–x 'Introduction' signed the publishers; xi–xv 'Table of Contents'; xvi blank; 17–370 text in five books (I, 'The Model Cook Book'; II, 'Home Decorations'; III, 'Practical Mechanics'; IV, 'The Home Book of Etiquette'; V, Part I, 'Tuberculosis,' and Part II, 'The Family Doctor')

COPIES: *OONL (B-229)

NOTES: The title-page is tipped in and printed in red and black. The 'Introduction' dedicates the volume to 'the busy American housewife.' Each of the five books is also separately paginated at the top of the pages.

BBVM has two copies of an edition where the title-page is identical to that transcribed above, except that there is no imprint following the phrase 'engravings and text pictures'; 'Copyright 1909 by M.L. Dewsnap' is on the title-page verso.

O216.2 [copyright 1913]
—A practical reference work for housekeepers / The / household / companion / comprising / a complete cook book – practical household / recipes, aids and hints for household decorations; / the care of domestic plants and animals and a / treatise on domestic medicine / including a chapter on tuberculosis the great white plague / a curable and preventable disease / by / Dr. Lawrence F. Flick / Medical Director of the Henry Phipps Institute for the Study, / Treatment and Prevention of Tuberculosis / General editors of the work / Alice A. Johnson / graduate in Domestic Science of Drexel Institute, Philadelphia / Mrs. Janet McKenzie Hill / Editor of the Boston Cooking School Journal / Dr. Henry Hartshorne, M.D., LL.D. / author of "Essential of Practical Medicine" / and other specialists / Profusely illustrated / with color plates, half-tone / engravings and text pictures / The John C. Winston Company, Limited / Toronto, Canada

DESCRIPTION: 23.0 × 17.0 cm   Pp [vii–x] xi–xv [xvi], [17–18] 19–370   4 pls col incl frontis, 16 pls, illus   Cloth, with image on front of a ring of house keys

CONTENTS: vii tp; viii 'Copyright 1913 by L.T. Myers'; ix–x 'Introduction' signed the publishers; xi–xv table of contents; xvi blank; 17–96 Book I, 'The Model Cook Book'; 97–114 Book II, 'Attractive Home Decorations'; 115–52 Book III, 'The Practical Mechanic'; 153–228 Book IV, 'Book of Etiquette'; 229–44 Book V, Part I, 'Tuberculosis'; 245–370 Book V, Part II, 'The Family Doctor'

COPIES: OSTMYM OSTPA *Private collection; United States: DLC (TX158 J66 1913)

NOTES: The title-page is printed in red and black. The 'Introduction' dedicates the book to 'the busy American housewife.' Like O216.1, Books I–V are also paginated separately.

AMERICAN EDITIONS: *The Standard Book of Recipes and Housewife's Guide*, [Entered ... in the year 1901, by W.E. Scull, in the office of the Librarian of Congress, at Washington] (Private collection; United States: DLC, which suggests Philadelphia? as the place of publication); *The Household Companion*, Philadelphia: Uplift Publishing Co., [c1909] (United States: DLC).

Laurel cook book

O217.1   1909
Laurel cook book / compiled by / the Laurel Mission Circle / of / St. John Presbyterian Church / Hamilton, 1909.
DESCRIPTION: 22.0 × 15.0 cm   Pp [i–iv], [1–6] 7–69 Small tp illus of a stylized laurel wreath   Paper, with image on front of a small, stylized laurel wreath; stapled
CONTENTS: i tp; ii blank; iii–iv ads; 1–2 ads; 3 'Index' [i.e., table of contents]; 4–6 ads; 7–69 text and ads
CITATIONS: Ferguson/Fraser, p 232, illus col on p 11 of closed volume
COPIES: *Private collection
NOTES: 'The Davis Printing Co.' is on the inside back face of the binding. The private collector's copy is inscribed on the title-page, 'Edith Dickson.'

'Magnet' cook book

O218.1   nd [about 1909]
"Magnet" / cook / book / Please try these receipts / in your house, and if you / find them good, show your / appreciation by sending us / one or more receipts that / you have found extra good / [caption:] The "Magnet" / Price 25 cents / The Petrie M'f'g. Co., Limited / Head office and factory / Hamilton – Ontario – Canada / Branches: – Winnipeg, Man.; St. John, N.B.; Regina, / Sask.; Hamilton, Ont.; Vancouver, B.C.; / Calgary, Alta.; Montreal, Que. [cover-title]
DESCRIPTION: 20.5 × 13.5 cm   Pp [1–32]   Paper, with image on front of a Magnet Cream Separator; stapled
CONTENTS: 1–32 recipes and testimonials
COPIES: ASPMHC (641 MAG)   *BDUCVM
NOTES: The latest testimonial, on the inside back face

of the binding, from Geo. E. Gurney of Melford, Saskatchewan, is dated 3 August 1909 (the earliest testimonial is 1906, on p 27; most are for 1907). This is likely the first edition.

O218.2   [2nd ed., nd, 1910]
—Magnet / users / cook book / Price 25 cents. / The Petrie M'f'g Co., Limited / Head office and factory / Hamilton – Ontario – Canada / Branches: – Winnipeg, Regina, Vancouver, Calgary, Montreal, / St. John, N.B. [cover-title]
DESCRIPTION: 19.0 × 13.0 cm   Pp [1–48]   Paper, with image on front of a Magnet Cream Separator within a red heart; stapled
CONTENTS: 1 'Magnet Cream Separator Cook Book // Original recipes contributed by Magnet users and compiled by the Petrie M'f'g. Co., Limited Hamilton, Canada. Second edition' and introductory text; 2–48 recipes and publ ads
COPIES: CIHM (78529)   OONL (TX715.6 M34 1910) *Bookseller's stock
NOTES: The introductory text states: 'The large demand for the Magnet Users Cook Book has made it necessary to publish in 1910 a second edition. The number of this edition will be 75,000 [copies] ... We request from Magnet users still further contributions to this cook book ... the present edition of 75,000 will be followed, we hope with one of 100,000.' There is an illustration opposite p 1 of the Petrie factory on Lottridge Avenue in Hamilton.

O218.3   [4th ed., nd, about 1911]
—Magnet users / cook book. / Price 25 cents / An investment of over $1,000,000.00 / guarantees every "Magnet." [cover-title]
DESCRIPTION: 20.0 × 13.0 cm   Pp [1–48]   Paper, with image on front of a Magnet Cream Separator within a red heart
CONTENTS: 1 'Magnet Cream Separator Cook Book // Original recipes contributed by Magnet users and complied [*sic*] by the Petrie M'f'g. Co., Limited Hamilton, Canada, fourth edition' and introductory text; 2–48 recipes and publ ads
COPIES: OFERWM (A1985.43)   *OKQ (F5012 [1910?] P495)
NOTES: The introductory text states, 'The number of this [fourth] edition will be 75,000.' There is a reference on p 46 to the Dominion Exhibition, Regina, in 1911, which indicates a publication date for the fourth edition of about that year. The OFERWM copy lacks its binding.

O218.4 [5th ed., nd, about 1912]
—"Magnet" users / cook book. / Price 50 cents, / an investment of over $1,000,000.00 / guarantees every "Magnet." [cover-title]
DESCRIPTION: 19.5 × 13.0 cm   Pp [1–88]   Illus of a money bag   Paper, with image on front of a Magnet Cream Separator within a red heart; stapled
CONTENTS: 1 '"Magnet" Cook Book (Fifth edition) Original recipes contributed by "Magnet" users and compiled by the Petrie M'f'g. Co., Limited Hamilton, Canada' and introductory text; 2–85 recipes, testimonials, and publ ads; 86–8 testimonials and publ ads
COPIES: *BBVM   BVIPM   Private collection
NOTES: The introductory text states, 'The number of this [fifth] edition will be 75,000.' Further recipe contributions are requested of readers. The latest testimonial is dated 19 November 1912 (from J.W. McNicol, on p 40). The private collector's copy is inscribed on the front face of the binding, 'Muriel Topp 1933.'

O218.5   6th ed., nd
—The / "Magnet" / users' / cook book / Price 50 cents. / (Sixth edition) / Winnipeg Regina Calgary Edmonton / The Petrie Mfg. Co., Limited / Head office & factory, Hamilton, Can. / Vancouver Lethbridge Montreal St. John. [cover-title]
DESCRIPTION: 19.5 × 13.0 cm   Pp 1–80   Illus on p 1 of farm buildings in a landscape   Paper; stapled, and with hole punched at top left corner for hanging
CONTENTS: Inside front face of binding red-and-black illus of a Magnet Cream Separator; 1 '"Magnet" Cook Book (Sixth edition) Original recipes contributed by "Magnet" users and compiled by the Petrie Mfg. Co., Hamilton, ...' signed A.B. Petrie, president and general manager; 2 ad for Magnet gasoline engines; 3–73 recipes, testimonials for the Magnet Cream Separator, blank pages for 'Memo,' and publ ads; 74 publ ad; 75 blank for 'Memo'; 76–7 publ ads; 78–9 'Cost of Farming Operations'; 80 'Index' [i.e., alphabetical list of sections]
CITATIONS: JPCat 130, No. 41
COPIES: *Private collection
NOTES: The following text is on p 1: 'The number of this [sixth] edition will be 100,000, in the publishing of which over 12½ tons of paper will be used ... The big undertaking we have set ourselves in publishing the seventh edition ... requires over 31 tons of paper. The "Magnet" Printing Department is complete and takes care of all our printing, including calendars, posters, cook books, envelopes, letter paper, etc., etc.' The latest testimonial for the cream separator, on p 4,

is dated September 1910. This copy is stamped 'Sold by W.C. Brueckner, Baden Ont' on the front face of the binding. It is inscribed on the binding, with a ball-point pen, 'Mrs. Erma Grosz.'

O218.6   8th ed., nd [about 1917 or later]
—Magnet users / cook book / Eighth edition / Price 50 cents / Winnipeg. Regina. Calgary. Edmonton / The Petrie Mfg. Co., Limited / Head office & factory, Hamilton, Can. / Vancouver. Lethbridge. Montreal. St. John [cover-title]
DESCRIPTION: 20.0 × 13.0 cm   Pp 1–96   Illus on p 9 of Magnet trademark, on p 60 of Magnet gears, on p 95 of money bag   Thin card; stapled
CONTENTS: 1–2 'Magnet Cream Separator Users Cooking Receipts. Compiled by the Petrie Mfg. Co., Limited. Seventh edition.' and below this heading, a letter signed Petrie, president; 3–near bottom 88 recipes and testimonials; bottom 88–95 'Household Hints' and testimonials; 96 'Index' [i.e., table of contents]
COPIES: OMIHURM   *Private collection
NOTES: Petrie's letter on p 1 flatters Magnet users by pointing out the superior culinary skills of the Canadian home cook: '... the surprise came when we had showered upon us from all parts of Canada, tens of thousands of choice receipts ... We have compared many of these receipts furnished by Magnet users with those from the so called up-to-date Domestic Science Schools, and though not opposed to education along that line, the writer ... would much rather trust his life to the cooking of a Magnet user who cooks good substantial every day food ...'

This edition is identified as the seventh on p 1, and the eighth on the binding. The seventh edition was likely published in 1917 because on p 2 Petrie writes, 'Nineteen sixteen was a fine year, but so far this year our sales are nearly double those of last year ...'

O218.7   [9th ed.], copyright 1920
—Magnet users / cook book / Tested recipes with helps / and hints of value / to every house- / keeper / We may live without poetry, music and art; / We may live without conscience and live without heart; / We may live without friends and live without books; / But civilized men cannot live without cooks. / We may live without books – what is knowledge but grieving? / We may live without hope – what is hope but deceiving? / We may live without love – what is passion but pining? / But where is the man that can live without dining? / Copyright Canada, 1920 by / Petrie Mfg. Co.,

Limited. / Winnipeg; Regina; Lethbridge; Vancouver; St. John, N.B.; Charlottetown, / P.E.I.; Truro, N.S.; Prince Albert; London; Calgary; Edmonton.

DESCRIPTION: 21.0 × 13.5 cm   Pp [1–2] 3–94, [i–ii] Paper; stapled

CONTENTS: 1 tp; 2 'Introduction' signed A.B. Petrie, president; 3–4 'Terms and Processes Used in Cookery'; 5–mid 6 'Satisfactory Combinations'; mid 6–7 'Table of Weights and Measures'; 8–86 recipes credited with the name of the contributor and publ ads; 87 publ ad; 88–94 '101 Uses for Salt as Aunt Samanthy Saw It'; i–ii 'Index'

CITATIONS: O'Neill (unpublished)

COPIES: *OGU (CCC TX715.6 M362 1920); Great Britain: LB (7942.bbb.62 destroyed)

NOTES: The following is on the front face of the binding: 'Compiled by Petrie Manufacturing Co., Limited. Hamilton, Ontario, Canada. Ninth edition // Price 5[paper torn].' The 'Introduction' draws attention to the 'many new recipes' in 'this the ninth edition,' and refers to the company's 'twenty-one years' experience' making farm machinery.

Payne, Arthur Gay

For information about Payne and the titles of his other cookbooks, see O198.1.

O219.1   1909

Choice dishes / at small cost / By / A.G. Payne / With four full-page plates / Cassell and Company, Ltd. / London, New York, Toronto and Melbourne / 1909

CITATIONS: Driver 807.4

COPIES: *OGU (TX652 P39); Great Britain: LB LoEN   OB   OPo(F)

NOTES: The OGU copy has 379 pp. Editions before 1909 do not include Toronto as a place of publication.

BRITISH EDITIONS: London, Paris and New York: Cassell, Petter, Galpin and Co., 1882 (Great Britain: LB destroyed, LoEN, OB); 2nd ed., London, Paris and New York: Cassell, Petter, Galpin and Co., 1883 (Great Britain: OPo(F); United States: MU, RCJW); cheap ed., London, Paris, New York and Melbourne: Cassell and Co. Ltd, 1886 (Great Britain: Private collection).

Robson's household calendar cook book 1909

See also O199.1, Robson's Calendar Cook Book 1908.

O220.1   1909

Robson's / household / calendar / cook book / 1909 / Published by / W.H. Robson, Phm.B. / druggist and optician / Fenelon Falls Ontario [cover-title]

DESCRIPTION: 17.5 × 13.5 cm   Pp [1–3] 4–30 [31–2 lacking]   Illus of astrological symbols   Paper; stapled, and with hole punched at top left corner, through which runs a string for hanging

CONTENTS: Inside front face of binding untitled introductory text signed W.H. Robson; 1–2 publ ads; 3–27 astronomical information, recipes, monthly calendars, 'Practical Breaks' [i.e., jokes], and publ ads; 28–mid 1st column 30 'Poisons and Antidotes'; bottom 1st column 30–2nd column 30 'Relation of a Pulse to Temperature,' medical information, and 'Handy Household Drugs'

COPIES: *OTUTF (uncat patent medicine)

NOTES: The recipes are the same as listed for NB25.1, *Brown's New Brunswick Almanac and Cook Book 1909*, and for other almanac or calendar cookbooks cited in that entry.

Selected recipes

O221.1   1909

Selected / recipes / tested and furnished / by / the ladies / of / the Yonge Street / Methodist Church / Published under the auspices of / the Ladies' Aid / 1909

DESCRIPTION: 21.5 × 14.5 cm   Pp [1–3] 4–95, [i]   Rebound

CONTENTS: 1 tp; 2 ads; 3–95 text, mainly recipes credited with the name of the contributor, and ads; i ads

COPIES: CIHM (86748)   *OTMCL (641.5 Y58)

NOTES: On p 84 there is an advertisement for the Methodist Book and Publishing House, 29–33 Richmond Street West, which states, 'This book was printed and bound by us.' The OTMCL copy is inscribed on the title-page, in pencil, 'Mrs Coles 1912'; and in another hand, in pencil, '$3.00.'

The 'vital question'

The process for forming shredded wheat biscuits was invented by the American Henry Perky, who, by 1892, was making them in his bakery in Denver, Colorado; the

product won awards as early as 1895 at the Louisiana Purchase Exposition and the market for the biscuits grew rapidly thereafter (Allen, p 211). A factory in Niagara Falls, New York, began production in 1901. Across the border, in Niagara Falls, Ontario, in 1904, Edward Wallace established the Canadian Shredded Wheat Co., in an old factory building. Construction of a new plant began in 1913. In 1928 the National Biscuit Co. (renamed Nabisco Foods Ltd in 1954) bought the American and Canadian businesses, and in the same year built a new plant on Lewis Avenue, in Niagara Falls, Ontario. Shredded Wheat (the only product made at the Ontario plant until 1937) is still on the market, as are other early products, Triscuits (savoury biscuits), and the cereal Shreddies, which was introduced in 1939.

For other cookbooks promoting the breakfast cereal, see O242.1, Shredded Wheat Dishes; O521.1, Fifty Ways of Serving Shredded Wheat; and O1116.1, Delicious, Nourishing Dishes. For information about the Canadian Shredded Wheat Co., see: Monetary Times Vol. 50, No. 8 (22 February 1913), p 424; and the file for the company at ONF.

O222.1   copyright 1909

The / "vital question" / The food problem and its relation to / health and happiness with a de- / scription of the finest, clean- / est, most hygienic food / factory in the / world. / Also practical and economical recipes for / making simple, palatable and / nutritious / Shredded Wheat / dishes / Copyright 1909 / The Shredded Wheat Company / Niagara Falls, N.Y. / The Canadian Shredded Wheat Company, Ltd. / Niagara Falls, Ont.

DESCRIPTION: With two images on front: 'From the Wheat Field' [i.e., landscape featuring a field of wheat] and 'To the Table' [still-life of a bowl of Shredded Wheat, milk, sugar, and box of Shredded Wheat]

COPIES: United States: *Private collection

NOTES: The cover-title is 'The Vital Question Cook-Book.' O242.1, *Shredded Wheat Dishes*, may be a related text.

Advertisements in the *Canadian Home Journal* indicate that earlier editions were distributed in Canada; however, the earlier editions may not have had a Canadian imprint. In the December 1900 issue of *Canadian Home Journal*, an advertisement for the Shredded Wheat Co., Toronto, states: '... we will be glad to send you, free of any cost, our valuable booklet, "The Vital Question," with 262 recipes.' One month later, in the January 1901 issue, the company advertised 'our book of Food Facts and Food Values, containing 262 recipes for preparing and serving Shredded Wheat.' In the May 1901 issue, an advertisement for

'Our Cook Book' comments: '"The Vital Question" should be in every household in Canada // Besides 262 recipes for preparing healthful dishes, it contains much helpful information for the housekeeper. Mailed free ...' The only American edition that I have examined is the seventh edition, copyright 1899, which has 262 numbered recipes; it has one Canadian testimonial, on pp 13–14, from J.A. McConnell, a dyspeptic, of 'Sturgeon Falls, Can.,' and it was purchased by the current owner at a Toronto book fair.

AMERICAN EDITIONS: *The Vital Question*, 6th ed., Worcester, Mass.: 1899 (QMM); *The Vital Question* [cover-title], '7th edition of 100,000 each,' Worcester, Mass.: Cereal Machine Co., copyright 1899, printed by Providence Albertype Co., Phillipsdale, RI (Private collection); *The Vital Question, Devoted to Natural Food ...,* [Niagara Falls: Natural Food Co., c1901] (United States: DLC); *The 'Vital Question', Being a Discussion of the Food Problem and Its Relation to Health and Happiness: Including a Comprehensive Treatise on the Principles of Cookery, with Practical and Economical Recipes for Making Simple, Palatable, and Nutritious Shredded Wheat Dishes*, Niagara Falls, NY: Natural Food Co., c1908 (United States: DLC).

Waterford cook book

O223.1   1909

[An edition of *Waterford Cook Book*, by ladies of Trinity Church, Waterford, Ontario, 1909]

COPIES: Private collection

Williams, Jennie B.

The author's middle initial appears variously as B. or C. on the title-pages of her books. She 'arranged for the Canadian table' the text of O262.1, Farmer, Fannie Merritt, Catering for Special Occasions. She also wrote Just for Ourselves Cookery Book, *London, New York, and Toronto: Hodder and Stoughton, nd [1912] (Driver 1154.1), in* The Woman's Economical Series.

O224.1   [copyright 1909]

Us two / cook book / containing tested recipes for / two persons / by / Jennie B. Williams / Toronto / The Musson Book Company / Limited

DESCRIPTION: 18.5 × 12.5 cm   Pp [1–6] 7–319   Fp illus part-titles   Cloth

CONTENTS: 1 tp; 2 'Copyright, Canada, 1909, by the Musson Book Company, Limited'; 3 table of contents;

4 blank; 5 'Preface' signed Jennie B. Williams, Toronto, 1 July 1909; 6 blank; 7–319 text
COPIES: *BKOM
NOTES: There is no 'MBCo.' symbol on the title-page. The 'Preface' explains that the ingredients for each recipe have been 'reduced so as to supply the requirements of two.' Each chapter begins with an illustrated part-title, signed by the artist A.M. Wickson, that incorporates an aphorism or verse.

The BKOM copy is inscribed on the front endpaper, in ink: 'Dear bride-to-be // It seemed to me someone might overlook the fact that you, a "cook-to-be" would need this little book. From F.K. Sept. 1919.'

AEPMA has a copy with the 'Preface' dated 1 July 1909, but the title-page is missing, as are pp 317 onward; it may be O224.1 or O224.2. BMCat (07943.g.33 destroyed) and O'Neill (unpublished) record an edition, Toronto: Musson Book Co., [1909], which may be the edition described here or O224.2.

The book was sold by the Methodist Book and Publishing House in Toronto; see the entry in 'Stock Book 1909,' p 51, at OTCC (Acc. 83.061C, UCC Board of Publication, Series III, Box 39): '3 [copies] Just for two [the title used for British and American editions].'

O224.2 [copyright 1909]
—Us two / cook book / containing tested recipes / for / two persons / by / Jennie C. [sic] Williams / ['MBCo.' symbol] / Toronto / The Musson Book Company / Limited
DESCRIPTION: 18.5 × 12.5 cm   Pp [1–6] 7–319   Fp illus part-titles   Cloth
CONTENTS: 1 tp; 2 'Copyright, Canada, 1909, by the Musson Book Company, Limited.'; 3 table of contents; 4 blank; 5 'Preface' signed Jennie B. Williams, Toronto, 1 July 1909; 6 blank; 7–319 text
COPIES: ACHP (HP 3181.7c)   *AEPMA   BVIHH

O224.3 [copyright 1916]
—Us two / cook book / containing tested recipes / for / two persons / [probably 'by' poorly printed] / Jennie B. Williams / (Revised and enlarged edition) / ['MBCo.' symbol] / Toronto / The Musson Book Company / Limited
DESCRIPTION: 19.0 × 12.5 cm   Pp [1–6] 7–320   Fp illus part-titles   Cloth, with still-life on front of a steaming preserving pan, fruit, and bottled fruit
CONTENTS: 1 tp; 2 'Copyright Canada, 1916.'; 3 table of contents; 4 blank; 5 'Preface' signed Jennie B. Williams, Toronto, 1 July 1909; 6 blank; 7–320 text
CITATIONS: O'Neill (unpublished)

COPIES: BBVM   BKM   MCDHM   *OGU (UA s043 b05)   OONL (TX715.6 W547 1916)   OTUTF (B-12 7867); Great Britain: LB (07943.b.48 destroyed)
NOTES: The OTUTF copy has its original dust-jacket: On the front face there is an image of a woman in a floor-length white dress, holding a copper ladle in her hand and standing beside a counter on which sits a large copper kettle; on the back face, the publisher records 'over 25,000 copies sold' and the price of $1.00.

O224.4 [9th ed., 27th thousand, copyright 1924]
—Us two / cook book / containing tested recipes / for / two persons / by / Jennie B. Williams / (Revised and enlarged edition) / Toronto / The Musson Book Company / Limited
DESCRIPTION: 19.0 × 12.0 cm   Pp [1–6] 7–322   Illus part-titles   Cloth, with still-life on front of a steaming preserving pan, fruit, and bottled fruit
CONTENTS: 1 tp; 2 '... Copyright, Canada, 1924 by the Musson Book Company, Ltd. publishers Toronto // Ninth edition 27th thousand // Printed in Canada // Press of the Hunter-Rose Co., Limited'; 3 table of contents; 4 blank; 5 'Preface' signed Jennie B. Williams, Toronto, 1 July 1924; 6 blank; 7–322 text
CITATIONS: CCat No. 4, p F5   Golick, p 107
COPIES: OH (R641.5 W673 CESC)   OONL (TX715.6 W547 1924)   OTNY (uncat)   QMM (RBD ckbk 2111) *Private collection
NOTES: The recipes end on p 319; pp 320–2 are 'Time-Tables for Cooking.' CCat records the price: $1.35. Another private collector's copy has a different binding: instead of the still-life, there is a 2.5 × 6.5 cm pattern of fruit and vegetables impressed in the cloth, below the title. The OTNY copy is inscribed on the front endpaper, in pencil: 'Hoping that this may prove useful to you both. And an ever present help in time of trouble. Mabel [S.?] Williams.'

BRITISH EDITIONS: There were four published under the title *Just for Two Cookery Book:* London: Hodder and Stoughton, nd [1910] (Great Britain: LB, LoEN, OB); 2nd ed., London: Hodder and Stoughton, 1910 (Great Britain: Private collection); 3rd ed., London: Hodder and Stoughton, nd (QMM); 4th ed., London, New York, and Toronto: Hodder and Stoughton, nd (Great Britain: OPo(F)). *Just for Two Cookery Book,* like the author's *Just for Ourselves Cookery Book,* is in *The Woman's Economical Series.*

AMERICAN EDITIONS: *Us Two Cook Book,* New York: Barse and Hopkins, [copyright 1909] (United States:

DLC); *Us Two Cook Book,* New York: Harper and Brothers Publishers, 1920 (Vintage, May 2000).

Young, Miss Bertha M. (May 1881–)

The recipe compiler is recorded in the 1901 Census for Wellington Ward in Ottawa as Bertha Young, a 'saleswoman' employed at 'Gas Co.' and an Anglican of Scotch origin. She and Charles Young (her brother?, born 1874) lodged with Alfred Scott and his wife.

In the book, Miss Young is described as having earned her diploma from the City and Guilds of London Institute in England. Further research may reveal a family connection with an English author, Mrs Hannah M. Young (24 June 1858–2 June 1949), whose father sold gas cookers, who demonstrated gas cooking, and who wrote, among other titles, Domestic Cookery: With Special Reference to Cooking by Gas, *[1886], and* The Housewife's Manual of Domestic Cookery with Special Reference to Cooking by Gas, *nd. Or, the same last name of the Ottawa and Warrington, Lancashire, gas demonstrators may be a coincidence. (For more information about H.M. Young, see Driver 1189–94.)*

O225.1 nd [about 1909]
Domestic / science / recipes / Price, $1.00 / Ottawa Gas Co. / Ottawa, Canada
DESCRIPTION: 17.5 × 12.0 cm   Pp [1–5] 6–176   9 pls of gas stoves and other gas appliances   Cloth
CONTENTS: 1 tp; 2 'Monotyped and printed by Capital Press Limited Ottawa, Can.'; 3 'Contents' [i.e., alphabetical list of subjects]; 4 'These recipes have been compiled by Miss B.M. Young, First-Class Diploma, City and Guilds of London Institute, England, now Demonstrator for the Ottawa Gas Company, and used at all the company's demonstrations.'; 5 ad for the gas company, at 35 Sparks Street; 6–167 text; 168 blank; 169–76 index
COPIES: *OGU (UA s048 b23)   OKQ (TX765 D6 19--t)   OOC (641.5 Y74)   OONL (TX715 088)   OTMCL (641.5 Y594)   OWTU (F9435)
NOTES: In Ottawa city directories up to 1908, Ottawa Gas Co. is at 23 Sparks Street; from the 1909 directory on, the company is at 35 Sparks Street, the address given in the advertisement on p 5 of the cookbook. The appearance of the cookbook is consistent with publication about 1909. Ferguson/Fraser, p 233, give 1910 as the date, probably following Una Abrahamson's suggested year of publication.
The OOC copy has no plates.

1910

[Title unknown]

O226.1 [about 1910]
[Title unknown]
DESCRIPTION: 20.0 × 13.5 cm   Pp 9–56
CONTENTS: 9–56 recipes credited with the name of the contributor and ads
COPIES: *Private collection
NOTES: The advertisements are mainly for North Bay, Ontario, businesses, and include advertisements for the following professional men (all p 18): James H. McCurry, barrister, Ferguson Block; Dr D.A. Campbell, Campbell Block, telephone 377; Dr B.F. Nott, Pardiac Block, telephone 15; T.E. McKee, barrister. There is an illustrated advertisement for the Eureka Vacuum Cleaner. Since the Eureka brand was launched in the United States in 1909, the cookbook may have been published later than 1910.

[Title unknown]

O227.1 [about 1910]
[Title unknown]
DESCRIPTION: 21.5 × 15.0 cm   Pp [3–4] 5–122   Lacks binding; stapled
CONTENTS: 3 ad; 4–122 recipes and ads
COPIES: *OGU (CCC TX715.6 W65)
NOTES: The first leaf, which probably included the title-page, is likely missing; the 'Marmalades and Preserves' section ends on p 122, which indicates that probably no leaves are lacking at the back.

The OGU copy was donated to the library by the daughter-in-law of the original owner (born about 1882), whose family homestead was at Palermo, Ontario. Advertisements in the book are for businesses in Oakville, Milton, Acton, Burlington, Bronte, Hamilton, Ingersoll, and Palermo, all in Ontario. The donor remembers the volume being a Women's Institute publication and having a binding in the Institute colours – navy blue and gold. The book is undated but, from appearances, was published about 1910.

[Title unknown]

O228.1 1910
[An edition of a cookbook from Princess Street Methodist Church, Kingston, Ontario, 1910]
COPIES: Private collection

Adult Bible Class cook book

O229.1 nd [about 1910]
Adult Bible Class / cook / book / [photograph of church] / College Street Methodist Church, Toronto / Compiled by the ladies of / the class [cover-title]
DESCRIPTION: 21.5 × 14.5 cm   Pp 1–122   Illus on p 13 of cuts of beef, illus on p 118 of 'Our Adult Bible Class 1910'   Paper
CONTENTS: 1–2 ads; 3 'Greetings' signed 'Committee'; 4 ad; 5–118 text and ads; 119–20 ads; 121 'Index' [i.e., table of contents]; 122 ads
COPIES: *OGU (UA s043 b03)

Armstrong, George S.

London, Ontario, city directories for 1909–10 and 1910–11 list George Armstrong, grocer, 495 Richmond, possibly the same person recorded by LB.

O230.1 [1910]
[An edition of *Domestic Science Cook Book, Containing Only Reliable Recipes*, by George S. Armstrong, London, Ont.: Lawson and Jones, [1910], pp 32]
CITATIONS: O'Neill (unpublished)
COPIES: Great Britain: LB (07943.ee.48 destroyed)
NOTES: The following are likely related publications issued in the same year: A14.1, *Calgary's Domestic Science Cook Book Containing Only Reliable Recipes*; A15.1, *Cowles' Domestic Science Cook Book Containing Only Reliable Recipes*; and B16.1, *Gillanders' Domestic Science Cook Book Containing Only Reliable Recipes*.

Beeton, Mrs Isabella Mary, née Mayson (St Marylebone, Middlesex, England, 14 March 1836–6 February 1865, Greenhithe, Kent, England)

From its first publication in book form in 1861, Mrs Beeton's The Book of Household Management *ruled English kitchens for well over half a century. Her monumental text was recognized as a culinary authority throughout the Empire as emigrants carried the complete book, or the various shorter derivations of the original work, with them to their new homes. As the 'Preface' of O256.2, Mrs Beeton's Cookery Book, of 1912, states, '[Mrs Beeton's] Cookery Books have appeared amongst the wedding presents of every bride as surely as the proverbial salt cellars, and thousands of grateful letters from all English-speaking countries testify that they have often proved the most useful gifts of all.' And O273.1,*

Mrs Beeton's Every-day Cookery, of 1912, treated 'foreign cookeries,' including Canadian, 'so that Britons living under other skies may learn how to combine the dishes of their adopted country with those of the Mother-land.'

English editions of The Book of Household Management *and its derivations were sold in Canada. For example, the following three titles are cited in MBPH 1876–7, as for sale at the Methodist Book and Publishing House, which had Book Rooms in Toronto and Montreal: Book of Household Management, $2.25, and Dictionary of Practical Receipts and Every-day Information, $1.00, both on p 12 (the latter also on p 25); and Beeton's Dictionary of Every Day Cookery, $1.00, p 25.*

Some editions of the Beeton books include Toronto as a place of publication, after London (England) and Melbourne (Australia); however, it is difficult to identify such editions in institutional catalogue descriptions that list only the first city in the imprint. I have included 'Toronto' editions in this bibliography when I found copies of them in Canadian public or private collections. Since I have not examined the title-pages of all Beeton books listed in Canadian catalogues, my record of 'Toronto' editions may be incomplete. Yet, there is a pattern to the copies found in Canadian collections: the original book, plus all its derivations, were published with a 'Toronto' imprint, all in the period of about 1910 to 1915: O231.1 and O231.2, Mrs Beeton's All about Cookery, [about 1910] and 1913; O256.1 and O256.2, Mrs Beeton's Cookery Book, 1911 and 1912; O272.1 and O272.2, Mrs Beeton's Book of Household Management, 1912 and 1915; O273.1, Mrs Beeton's Every-day Cookery, 1912; O315.1, Mrs Beeton's Family Cookery, 1914. (The 'penny cookery books,' which bear the Beeton name, were apparently published only in England.) All the 'Toronto' imprints, therefore, postdate the 1906 revision of The Book of Household Management, *which is notable for the expanded recipe section by Charles Herman Senn (concerning the revision, see Howsam, p 36, and Hughes, pp 391–5).*

For a discussion of the derivations of The Book of Household Management, *see Hughes, pp 383–6, and Driver, pp 101–2. The most insightful biography is Kathryn Hughes's* The Short Life and Long Times of Mrs Beeton, *London, Eng.: Fourth Estate Ltd, 2005.*

O231.1 nd [about 1910]
Mrs. Beeton's / all about cookery / New edition. / With coloured plates and other illustrations. / Ward, Lock & Co., Limited, / London, Melbourne and Toronto.
DESCRIPTION: 20.0 × 12.5 cm   Pp [i–ii], [1–4] 5–584,

1–8 [9] 10–12 [13] 14–16 [17–18]   12 pls col incl frontis, 24 double-sided pls   Cloth

CONTENTS: i–ii endpaper ads; 1 ht; 2 blank; 3 tp; 4 blank; 5–8 'Preface to Mrs. Beeton's Cookery Books'; 9 'General Contents'; 10 blank; 11 'Coloured Plates'; 12–14 'List of Illustrations'; 15–563 text; 564 blank; 565 'General Index'; 566 blank; 567 'Index of Introductory Chapters'; 568 blank; 569–84 'Analytical Index of Recipes'; 1–18 ads

COPIES: *BBVM

NOTES: The recipes on pp 65 onward are arranged alphabetically from Alma Pudding to Zeltlinger Cup. An advertisement on p 4 at the back of the book cites medals awarded in 1906. The BBVM copy is inscribed on the half-title, in pencil, 'Jan 1. 1919.'

An earlier English edition – London, New York, and Melbourne: Ward, Lock and Co., 1905 – was distributed by a Toronto newspaper: A Toronto bookseller's copy has a presentation plate mounted on the front endpaper, which states, 'This cook book is presented with the compliments of the Toronto Daily World // Canada's leading and Toronto's favorite morning newspaper ... The World, 40 Richmond St. W., Toronto.'

O231.2 1913
—Mrs. Beeton's / all about cookery / New edition. / With coloured plates and other illustrations. / Ward, Lock & Co., Limited, / London, Melbourne and Toronto. / 1913.

DESCRIPTION: 20.0 × 13.0 cm   Pp [leaf lacking?] [3–4] 5–584, 1–2 [3] 4–8 [9–10]   Lacks frontis col; 11 pls col (excluding frontis), 24 double-sided pls   Cloth

CONTENTS: 3 tp; 4 blank; 5–8 'Preface to Mrs. Beeton's Cookery Books'; 9 'General Contents'; 10 blank; 11 'Coloured Plates'; 12–14 'List of Illustrations'; 15–563 text; 564 blank; 565 'General Index'; 566 blank; 567 'Index of Introductory Chapters'; 568 blank; 569–84 'Analytical Index of Recipes'; 1–10 ads

COPIES: *BKOM   Private collection

NOTES: The private collector's copy is inscribed by her Canadian-born grandmother (the original owner of the book) with the date 4 March 1915.

BRITISH EDITIONS: English editions of *All about Cookery* were published as early as 1871 (35th thousand). The 1905 edition was distributed in Canada by a Toronto newspaper (see notes for O231.1). *All about Cookery* was the new title for *Mrs Beeton's Dictionary of Every-day Cookery* (1865), an abridged version of the recipes from her *Book of Household Management*. For more information, see Driver, p 101. *Beeton's*

Dictionary of Every Day Cookery was advertised for sale by the Methodist Book and Publishing House (Book Rooms in Toronto and Montreal) in MBPH 1876–7, p 25.

The Brockville cook book

O232.1 1910
The Brockville / cook book / compiled by / the ladies of Brockville / and friends elsewhere / To be sold for the benefit of the General / Hospital. / [unattributed poem beginning, 'We may live without poetry, music and art' (from *Lucile*, Part I, Canto ii, by Owen Meredith, pseudonym of Edward Robert Bulwer-Lytton)] / The Recorder Printing Co., Limited. / 1910.

DESCRIPTION: Illus of Brockville General Hospital

COPIES: OBM   *Private collection

NOTES: The owner reports that the book has 168 pp.

O232.2   rev. ed., 1923
—The Brockville / cook book / compiled by / the women of Brockville / and friends elsewhere / To be sold for the benefit of the General Hospital. / Revised edition / "We may live without poetry, music and art; / We may live without conscience, and live without heart; / We may live without friends, we may live without books; / But civilized man cannot live without cooks. / He may live without books; – what is knowledge but grieving? / He may live without hope, – what is hope but deceiving? / He may live without love, – what is passion but pining? / But where is the man that can live without dining?" / The Recorder Printing Co., Ltd. / 1923.

DESCRIPTION: 22.0 × 15.5 cm   Pp [1] 2–98   Fp illus on p 1 of Brockville General Hospital   Cloth

CONTENTS: 1 fp illus; 2 ad; 3 tp; 4 table of contents; 5 'Foreword' signed the Committee; 6 ads; 7 'Time-table for Cooking'; 8 ad; 9 'Spoon and Cup Measure' and 'Table of Weights and Measures'; 10 ads; 11–94 recipes credited with the name of the contributor and ads; 95 'Household Suggestions'; 96 ad; 97–8 'Miscellaneous'

COPIES: OBM   *OGU (CCC TX715.6 B76 1923)

NOTES: The 'Foreword' states, 'The continued demand for a former cook book, published some years ago and now out of print, was incentive to the Woman's Auxiliary of the Brockville General Hospital to compile the present volume, containing the recipes used before, and many new ones.'

Some of the recipes also appeared in a 1918 Brockville collection, O420.1, *The Women's Patriotic League Cookery Book*; for example, Bean Soup contributed by Mrs D.M. Spaidal (p 14 in both books), Mincemeat without Meat (unattributed on p 132 in the 1918 book, attributed to M.M. Hutcheson on p 42 here), and Mustard Pickles contributed by Mrs Moody (p 145 in the 1918 book, p 80 here).

The OGU copy is inscribed on the front endpaper, in ink, by a friend of the donor: 'Elizabeth Y. Cole // Brockville. October: 1926.'

Cook book of well proven recipes

O233.1   1910
[An edition of *Cook Book of Well Proven Recipes*, collected by the Ladies' Aid of Caven Presbyterian Church, Exeter, 1910, cover-title: 'Select Recipes,' pp 55]
COPIES: Private collection

Cooking by gas

O234.1   1910
Cooking by gas / with four full-page plates / Cassell and Company, Ltd. / London, New York, Toronto and Melbourne / 1910
DESCRIPTION: 19.0 × 12.5 cm   Pp [1–2], [i–viii], [1] 2–270, [i–iv] Tp illus of two women working in a kitchen, 4 pls incl frontis, 8 numbered illus Cloth, with image on front of a woman standing beside a range and holding roast poultry on a platter
CONTENTS: 1–2 endpaper ads; i ht; ii blank; iii tp; iv 'All rights reserved'; v table of contents; vi blank; vii 'List of Plates'; viii blank; 1–261 text; 262 blank; 263–70 index and at bottom p 270, 'Printed by Cassell and Co., Ltd., La Belle Sauvage, London, E.C.'; i–ii blank; iii–iv publ ads
CITATIONS: Driver 245.1
COPIES: *Private collection; Great Britain: LB LoEN OB; United States: ICJ
NOTES: The 'Introduction' gives information about cooking by gas. Two chapters called 'The Model Kitchen' and 'Kitchen Methods' follow. The main body of the text comprises menus, with recipes, for the four seasons, April, July, October, Christmas, home dinners, luncheons, and breakfasts. The text ends with a chapter about 'Bread and Cakes.'

Cooking recipes

O235.1   1910
Cooking recipes / compiled and arranged by the Ladies' Aid / Society of St. Andrew's Church, Renfrew / Published for the Society by Smallfield & Son, printers, Renfrew, / December: 1910.
DESCRIPTION: 17.0 × 12.5 cm   Pp [1–7] 8–124 [125–6] Lacks paper(?) binding; stapled
CONTENTS: 1–4 ads; 5 tp; 6 'Preface' and quotations from Ruskin and Confucius; 7–124 recipes credited with the name of the contributor and ads; 125 ad; 126 'Finale' [poem beginning, 'We may live without poetry, music and art' (from *Lucile*, Part I, Canto ii, by Owen Meredith, pseudonym of Edward Robert Bulwer-Lytton)]
COPIES: *BBVM

Harcourt, Robert (1866–1943), and Miss M.A. Purdy

Harcourt also wrote Food Value of Milk and Its Products, *Bulletin 221, Toronto: Ontario Department of Agriculture, April 1914 (OGU). For the titles of other cookbooks published by the Ontario Department of Agriculture, see O158.1.*

O236.1   April 1910
Ontario Department of Agriculture / Ontario Agricultural College / Bulletin 180 / Flour and breadmaking / by / R. Harcourt, B.S.A., Professor of Chemistry, / and / Miss M.A. Purdy, Demonstrator. / Printed by L.K. Cameron, printer to the King's Most Excellent Majesty. / Toronto, Ont., April, 1910. [cover-title]
CITATIONS: MacTaggart, p 22
COPIES: CIHM (83737) *OGU (Rural Heritage Collection) OOAG (641.3/31 20)
NOTES: The 1910 edition has 40 pp.

O236.2   rev. ed., January 1922
—Bulletin 285. January, 1922 / Ontario Department of Agriculture / Ontario Agricultural College / A revised edition of No. 180. / Flour and breadmaking / by R. Harcourt and Miss M.A. Purdy. / Introduction. / [...]
CONTENTS: top 1 title; mid 1– 'Introduction'; ...
CITATIONS: MacTaggart, p 26
COPIES: OGU (Rural Heritage Collection) OSUL (CA2 ON A56 B285) *Private collection
NOTES: There are 48 pp containing information about flour and recipes for baking. The 'Acknowledgments'

on p 48 thank Professor Edwards for the part on yeasts and Miss Watson, i.e., Miss Mary Urie Watson, 'for her assistance in preparing and criticizing the recipes for bread, biscuits, and pastry.' Miss Watson was the former dean of the Macdonald Institute in Guelph and the co-editor, with Adelaide Hoodless, of O86.2, *Public School Household Science*, 1905.

Ice cream and candy makers' factory guide

See also O74.1, The Candy Maker's Guide, published by Fletcher Manufacturing Co.

O237.1   3rd ed., 1910
Ice cream and / candy makers' / factory / guide / Third edition / revised, with numerous additions / 1910
DESCRIPTION: 22.5 × 15.0 cm   Pp [i–ii], [1–2] 3–124   Paper
CONTENTS: i tp; ii blank; 1 part-title: 'Ice Creams'; 2 blank; 3 'Preface to Third Edition' signed the publishers, March 1910; 4–43 recipes for, and information about, making ice cream; 44 blank; 45 part-title: 'The Candy Kitchen'; 46–120 recipes for, and information about, candy; 121–4 'Index'
COPIES: *OTMCL (664.153 I17)
NOTES: Glued on the inside front face of the binding is the label of 'Fletcher Manufacturing Company Limited // 440–442 Yonge Street Toronto, Ont., Can.' Although the text is addressed to an American audience (note, for example, the reference on p 5 to the American 'National Pure Food Law'), the book was intended for international distribution, as the 'Preface to Third Edition' states, 'Its sale has extended more than half way round the world, even into Australia and India, and is achieving a steady sale on the Continent of Europe, while at home it has outrun all competitors, and is popular from coast to coast, and from Panama to British Columbia.' The recipes may specify large amounts of ingredients for commercial use, but the instructions are simple enough for an amateur to follow.

K., F.

F.K. may be Flora Klickmann (1867–November 1958); see Driver, p 356.

O238.1   nd [about 1910]
The / everyday pudding book / a tasty recipe for / every day in the year / by / F.K. / The Copp Clark Company, Ltd. / Toronto

DESCRIPTION: 18.0 × 12.0 cm   Pp [iii–vii] viii–ix [x] xi–xiii [xiv], [1] 2–130, [i–ii]   [$0.25, on binding]   Paper-covered boards, with image on front of a maid carrying a steaming bowl
CONTENTS: iii–iv ads; v tp; vi ad; vii–ix preface signed F.K.; x–xiii index; xiv ad for currants; 1–130 366 numbered recipes for puddings, 12 numbered recipes for sauces, 8 numbered recipes for pastry; i–ii ads
COPIES: *OGU (UA s048 b15)
NOTES: F.K. states in the preface, 'The pudding question comes back, with persistent regularity, every day of the year, and although husbands and children are willing to eat beef and mutton, in regular succession, they are not willing to eat apple-tart or rice pudding 365 days in the year.' This is a Canadian edition of a British work that was one of *The Everyday Series* edited by Gertrude Paul. No Canadian editions of the other titles in the series have been identified.

BRITISH EDITIONS: London: Stanley Paul and Co., nd [1910] (Great Britain: LB destroyed, LoEN, OB; United States: NN); 2nd ed., nd (Driver 563.2); 3rd ed., London: S. Paul and Co., nd (United States: ICJ); 4th ed., London: S. Paul and Co., [1917] (United States: NN); 5th ed. (Driver 563.5).

Preston cook book

O239.1   nd [about 1910]
Preston / cook book / by the / Women's Guild and Home Mission / of / St. John's Church. / President, Mrs. A.D. Pringle. / Vice-President, Mrs. W. Cunningham. / Treasurer, Mrs. Goodall. / Secretary, Mrs. E. Reuter.
DESCRIPTION: 21.5 × 14.0 cm   Pp [1–5] 6–49   Paper
CONTENTS: 1 tp; 2 blank; 3 preface; 4 untitled note; 5–49 text
COPIES: *Private collection
NOTES: 'Progress Print, Preston, Ont.' is on the back face of the binding.

Recipes

O240.1   1910
Recipes / collected by / the Girls' Friendly Society, / the proceeds of which are to be devoted / to the / Missionary Fund / of / St. George's Church, / corner Tom and Sophia streets. / Hamilton. / 1910 / The Criel Printing Co. [Typographical Union symbol] 89 James Street N.
DESCRIPTION: 19.5 × 13.5 cm   Pp [1–2] [3–4 lacking]

5–43 [44]   Paper, with image on front of St George's Church; stapled
CONTENTS: 1 tp; 2 ads; 3–43 recipes and ads; 44 'Index' [i.e., table of contents]
CITATIONS: Simpson, p W16 (photograph)
COPIES: *OH (R641.5 REC CESH)
NOTES: The cover-title is 'Cook Book.' The binding of the OH copy is loose; a previous owner has secured pp 41–3 with tape in an incorrect position, after the title-page leaf. The volume lacks pp 3–4, but the 'Index' indicates that 'Soups' are on p 3 and 'Fish,' on p 4.

Recipes in individual and large amounts for home and school

Miss Annie Lewisa Laird (Fergus, Ont., 1 August 1871– 31 May 1939, Toronto, Ont.) was associated with the Lillian Massey School of Household Science from its beginning, in 1902, first as a senior instructor, then in 1903 as principal, a post she held for thirty-four years, until her retirement in 1936. She was likely involved with the early, uncredited editions of the school's cookbook, although her name does not appear until the 1917 edition, as the copyright owner and also as co-editor with Miss Nellie Lyle Pattinson (for information about Pattinson, see O506.1, Canadian Cook Book, under her name). She may also have contributed in some way to O541.1, Economical Recipe Book, published by the Visiting Housekeepers Association, which she helped to organize in Toronto in 1925. Laird was the daughter of Rebecca LaPierre and John Guinness Laird, a Methodist minister. Her early education was in schools in Collingwood, Orangeville, and London, Ontario. She graduated from the Drexel Institute in Philadelphia, and was a founding member of the American Home Economics Association, the American Dietitians Association, and the Canadian Dietitians Association. A half-length portrait of Laird, painted in oil by Kenneth Forbes and dated April 1935, is in the University of Toronto Art Collection. The file for Laird at OTUAR (A73-0026/214 (02)) contains newspaper articles (with photographs) relating to her career; her obituary and a tribute in the Globe and Mail (Toronto), 1 June 1939 and 12 June 1939; a copy of the funeral address delivered on 2 June 1939 at Sherbourne United Church in Toronto; and 'A Resolution Respecting the Late Professor A.L. Laird,' 13 October 1939, by the university's Faculty of Household Science. An untitled article about the Lillian Massey School in the Toronto Daily News (25 January 1913, p 22) includes Laird's photograph. The file for her father at OTCC contains family information. See also an earlier book from the school, O128.1, Individual Recipes for Class Work.

O241.1   1910
Lillian Massey School / of / Household Science and Art / Recipes / in / individual and large amounts / for / home and school / Toronto, 1910
DESCRIPTION: 21.0 × 14.0 cm   Pp [1–2] 3–128   Limp cloth
CONTENTS: 1 tp; 2 'Abbreviations' and 'Table of Weights and Measures'; 3–86 'Recipes'; 87–91 'Index'; 92 introductory note: 'These recipes are in individual amounts, and are especially designed for the use of students and teachers of Household Science in Canada ...'; 93–125 'Individual Recipes'; 126–8 'Index'
COPIES: *Private collection
NOTES: The private collector's copy is inscribed on the inside front face of the binding, in ink, 'Mena Hanson // Victoria Hospital // London, 1910–1913.'

O241.2   1913
—Lillian Massey School / recipes / Individual and large amounts / for / home and school / Toronto, 1913
DESCRIPTION: 22.0 × 14.0 cm   Pp [1–2] 3–118   Limp cloth; stapled
CONTENTS: 1 tp; 2 'Abbreviations' and 'Tables of Weights and Measures'; 3–79 'Recipes'; 80–4 'Index'; 85 introductory note: 'The following recipes are in individual amounts, and are especially designed for the use of students and teachers of Household Science in Canada ...'; 86–115 'Individual Recipes'; 116–18 'Index'
COPIES: *Private collection
NOTES: The private collector's copy is inscribed on the title-page, in ink, 'Norma W. Spencer '16.' Norma Winnifred Spencer was a graduate of Victoria College, University of Toronto. Another private collector's copy is inscribed on the binding, in ink, 'A.E. Johnston // Mount Allison. Sackville.'

O241.3   1917
—L.M.S. / book of recipes / Individual and large amounts / for / home and school / Edited by / A.L. Laird and N.L. Pattinson / Toronto, 1917
DESCRIPTION: 22.0 × 14.5 cm   Pp [1–2] 3–129   Limp cloth; stapled
CONTENTS: 1 tp; 2 'Abbreviations,' 'Table of Weights and Measures,' and 'Copyright, Canada, 1917, by A.L. Laird'; 3–114 'Recipes'; 115–19 'Appendix I. Table of Food Values'; 120–1 'Appendix II. Table of Approximate Food Values'; 122–4 'Appendix III. Table of Approximate Values of Foods Prepared According to Foregoing Recipes (Large Amounts)'; 125–9 index
CITATIONS: Duncan, p 166   Ferguson/Fraser, p 232, illus col on p 35 of closed volume   O'Neill (unpublished)

COPIES: OPEMO *Private collection; Great Britain: LB (07942.d.11 destroyed)

O241.4 1923

—The / household science / book of recipes / (formerly the L.M.S. Book of Recipes) / Individual and large amounts / for / home and school / Edited by / Annie L. Laird and Edna W. Park / Toronto, 1923

DESCRIPTION: 22.0 × 14.0 cm   Pp [1–2] 3–135   Limp cloth; stapled

CONTENTS: 1 tp; 2 'Abbreviations,' 'Table of Weights and Measures,' and 'Copyright, Canada, 1917 and 1923. By A.L. Laird.'; 3–114 'Recipes'; 115–22 'Appendix I Table of Food Values'; 123–5 'Appendix II. Table of 100 Calorie Portions'; 126–9 'Appendix III Table of Approximate Food Values'; 130 blank; 131–5 index

COPIES: OONL (TX715.6 H685 1923)   *Private collection

NOTES: At the time Laird was preparing this revision, Pattinson would have been writing her *Canadian Cook Book*, also published in 1923, which perhaps explains the new co-editor, Edna Park.

O241.5 1933

—The / household science / book of recipes / Individual and large amounts / for / home and school / Edited by / Annie L. Laird and Edna W. Park / Toronto / The University of Toronto Press / 1933

DESCRIPTION: 22.0 × 14.0 cm   Pp [1–2] 3–124 [125–8] Limp cloth; stapled

CONTENTS: 1 tp; 2 'Abbreviations,' 'Table of Weights and Measures,' and 'Copyright, Canada, 1917 and 1923 by A.L. Laird'; 3–91 'Recipes'; 92–8 'Appendix I'; 99–103 'Appendix II'; 104–9 'Appendix III'; 110–15 'Appendix IV'; 116–19 'Appendix V'; 120–4 index; 125–8 blank for 'Notes'

COPIES: OONL (TX715.6 H685 1933 p***)   *Private collection

NOTES: The OONL copy is inscribed opposite the title-page, 'E. Malloch. Pembina Hall.,' which has been crossed through and a revised address added below: '8507–112 St. Edmonton.'; below this, in the same hand, is 'H. Ec. '38.' Inscribed on the title-page, in the same hand, is 'Esme Malloch // Home Ec. '38.'

O241.6 reprint, 1974

—The / household science / book of recipes / Individual and large amounts / for / home and school / Annie L. Laird and Edna W. Park / Reprinted on the occasion of the / first Edna Park

Lecture / for the Household Science alumnae / University of Toronto / 1974 / Toronto / The University of Toronto Press / 1933

DESCRIPTION: 21.5 × 14.0 cm   Pp [1–2] 3–124 [125–7] Paper; stapled

CONTENTS: 1 tp; 2 'Abbreviations,' 'Table of Weights and Measures,' and 'Copyright, Canada, 1917 and 1923 by A.L. Laird'; 3–91 'Recipes'; 92–8 'Appendix I'; 99–103 'Appendix II'; 104–9 'Appendix III'; 110–15 'Appendix IV'; 116–19 'Appendix V'; 120–4 index; 125–7 blank for 'Notes'

COPIES: *Private collection

Shredded Wheat dishes

See O222.1, for information about the company and other cookbooks promoting Shredded Wheat.

O242.1 copyright 1910

Shredded Wheat / dishes / some practical and economical recipes / for making Shredded Wheat dishes / in combination with fresh or / preserved fruits, creamed / meats or vegetables / together with a treatise on / the food problem / and its relation to health and / happiness, with a description / of the finest, cleanest, / most hygienic food / factory in the / world / Copyright 1910 / The Shredded Wheat Company / Niagara Falls, N.Y. / The Canadian Shredded Wheat Co., Ltd. / Niagara Falls, Ont.

DESCRIPTION: 17.5 × 13.0 cm   Pp [1–2] 3–82 [83–4]   2 double-sided pls col, illus   Paper, with two images on front: 'From the Wheat Field' [i.e., a landscape featuring a field of wheat] and 'To the Table' [a still-life of a bowl of Shredded Wheat, milk, sugar, and a box of Shredded Wheat]; stapled

CONTENTS: 1 tp; 2 fp illus of 'The Home of Shredded Wheat'; 3 'Some Interesting Facts about the World's Finest Food Factory'; 4 'Ten Reasons Why Shredded Wheat Should Be in Every Home'; 5–24 'Shredded Wheat Dishes' [discussion of the cereal's role in health and information about the cereal and its manufacture]; 25–42 'Unsolicited Letters of Gratitude and Appreciation'; 43–7 'General Principles of Cookery'; 48–59 'Shredded Wheat Biscuit Recipes' [i.e., the cereal]; 60–7 'Triscuit Recipes' [i.e., the cracker]; 68–71 blank for 'Housekeeper's Memoranda'; 72–4 'Index to Recipes'; 75–7 German-language text, including recipes; 78–80 French-language text, including recipes; 81 'Shredded Sermons'; 82 '"Come and See" // The Process of Making Shredded Wheat Biscuit and Triscuit Is Open to the World'; 83 fp illus of 'Views in

and about "The Home of Shredded Wheat"'; 84 fp illus of 'Interior Views of "The Home of Shredded Wheat"'
COPIES: *Private collection
NOTES: Slipped into the private collector's copy are a promotional leaflet for Shredded Wheat, copyright 1910, and a letter from the Canadian Shredded Wheat Co. Ltd to Miss L. Morlock, Morriston, Ontario, 16 February 1911. The letter indicates that the company sent the book to Miss Morlock at her request. The stationery features colour illustrations of Niagara Falls, the factory, and various Shredded Wheat dishes.
O222.1, The 'Vital Question,' may be a related text.

Sweetheart Brand cook book

IXL Spice and Coffee Mills Ltd was founded in 1909 by H. Daniel Gwalchmai, and incorporated in 1911. Gwalchmai was born in Wales and moved to London, Ontario, when he was seven years old; he died 25 May 1943. In 1928 IXL was acquired by Gorman Eckert and Co., another London, Ontario, firm and the publisher of O445.1, Olive Facts, O1026.1, Gaige, Crosby, Season to Taste, and O1073.1, Delicious Mustard and Spice Recipes. (Information about IXL and its founder is from H.W. Gardner, London, Ontario, Canada, 1914; a Presentation of Her Resources, Achievements and Possibilities, London, Ont.: London Free Press, 1914, pp 69, 92, and from 'H.W. Gwalchmai Taken by Death,' London Free Press, 26 May 1943.)

O243.1 nd [about 1910]
Trade mark of / quality / Sweetheart / Brand / cook book / Select recipes of the world's best authorities on / cooking and a list of valuable premiums / given away free to the users of / "Sweetheart Brand goods" / Ask your / grocer / for / Sweetheart / Brand / spices / coffees / mustards / jelly powders / baking powder / flavoring extracts / etc. etc. etc. / All up-to-date / grocers / handle / Sweetheart / Brand / Compliments of / IXL Spice & Coffee Mills / Limited / London Ontario / Advertiser Job., London, Ontario [cover-title]
DESCRIPTION: 25.5 × 16.5 cm Pp [1] 2–32 Illus col of Sweetheart Brand products Paper, with small image on front of the head of the smiling woman that appears on Sweetheart Brand products; stapled, and with hole punched at top left corner for hanging
CONTENTS: 1 ad for IXL Spice and Coffee Mills Ltd

and 'Advertiser Job, London, Ont.'; 2–mid 3 ad for Sweetheart Brand products; mid 3–32 'Select Recipes,' ads for IXL products, ads for items available through payment by coupons, and 'List of Premiums'
COPIES: OAYM OTBH *QMM (RBD TX714 S94 1900) Private collection
NOTES: The text is printed in blue. On the outside back face of the binding, along the edge of an illustration of the company's factory, is the note: 'Only 100,000 [of these cookbooks] given away.' From appearances, *Sweetheart Brand Cook Book* was published about 1910.
The private collector's copy is stamped on the front face of the binding, 'W.S. Sutherland // Wyoming'; the town of Wyoming is east of Sarnia, Ontario.

Tested recipes for making bread, rolls, cake and pastry

The Copeland Flour Mills was established in 1849, in Coldwater. In 1854, it began production in Penetanguishene, and by the 1880s it had acquired a mill in Midland. In about 1919, James Playfair and his associates purchased the business. They built a large, new mill in Midland in about 1921–2. (James Playfair's wife, Charlotte, contributed text to O265.2, Midland Cook Book.)

O244.1 nd [about 1910]
[Five Crowns Flour symbol] / Tested recipes / for / making bread, rolls / cake and pastry / Copeland Flour Mills, Limited / Midland, Ontario / Maritime representatives / The Smith Brokerage Co., Limited / Saint John, N.B.
DESCRIPTION: 18.0 × 11.0 cm Pp [1] 2–24 Paper; stapled
CONTENTS: 1 tp; 2 untitled introductory text; 3–5 information about making bread; 6–24 'Tested Five Crowns Recipes'
COPIES: *Private collection
NOTES: The cover-title is 'Cooking Secrets.' The earliest identified listing for Smith Brokerage in McAlpine's Saint John city directories is in the volume for 1905 (in the 1904 volume the listing is for Smith, Edward A., at a different address); therefore, the cookbook was published no earlier than about 1905. From appearances, it was published about 1910.

Tried and true recipes

O245.1 nd [about 1910]
Tried and true / recipes / compiled and arranged by the / Goforth Mission Band / of the / Glebe Presbyterian / Church, Ottawa. / No mean woman can cook well, it calls for a / generous spirit, a light hand and a large heart.
DESCRIPTION: 20.5 × 14.0 cm Pp [3–8] 9–112 [113–4] Paper-covered boards, cloth spine; stapled
CONTENTS: 3 'Index' [i.e., table of contents] and untitled acknowledgment of the ladies who contributed recipes and of the businessmen for advertisements; 4 ads; 5 tp; 6 ad; 7–112 recipes credited with the name of the contributor and ads; 113 'Table of Weights and Measures'; 114 'Time for Baking'
COPIES: *Private collection
NOTES: There is an advertisement on p 48 for the McKechnie Musical Co. that refers to 'A Perfect Day' by Carrie Jacobs-Bond as 'one of the prettiest songs of the year.' Jacobs-Bond was an American song writer and music publisher. 'A Perfect Day,' one of her most popular songs, was published in 1910. The appearance of the cookbook is consistent with publication in the same year, 1910.

Another collector's copy is bound in paper, not paper-covered boards.

Wesley cook book

O246.1 [1910]
Wesley / cook / book / Price 50 cents / Times-Journal Press [cover-title]
COPIES: *Private collection
NOTES: The owner describes the book as 'Tested Recipes by the Epworth League of Wesley Methodist Church, Fort William, Ont. 1910, and contributed by the ladies of the congregation.'

Y.M.C.A. cook book

O247.1 nd [about 1910]
Y.M.C.A. / cook book / Published by / Y.M.C.A. Ladies' Auxiliary / Owen Sound, Ont. [cover-title]
CONTENTS: 1 ads; 2 ad for text cards for Social Bible Readings, published and sold by Winnifred E. Doyle, Seldon House [a temperance hotel], Owen Sound; 3 'Foreword' signed ladies of the YMCA Auxiliary; ...
COPIES: *OOWM (961.4.10)
NOTES: 'Richardson, Bond and Wright Limited, print-ers' is on p 216, the last page. The OOWM copy is inscribed on p 3, 'This cook book blonged [sic] to late Mrs. Geo. Menzies Owen Sound. Donated by Mrs. R. Menzies.'

The Zam-Buk book of cookery recipes

O248.1 nd [about 1910]
[The] Zam-Buk book of / cookery / recipes / for / fish, soups, / meats, dressings / salads, sauces, / vegetables, / desserts, / pastry, cakes, / puddings, / beverages, / invalid cookery, / also / a collection of / reliable household / hints. [cover-title]
DESCRIPTION: 20.0 × 13.0 cm Pp 1–32 Illus on p 1 of a woman holding a book of 'Cookery Recipes' Paper, with image on front of a woman rolling dough; stapled
CONTENTS: Inside front face of binding 'Something Good for You' signed the Zam-Buk Co.; 1 untitled introductory text and 'Handy Weights and Measures'; 2 publ ad; 3–32 recipes and publ ads
COPIES: BDUCVM BVAU NSPHM OGU (CCC TX715.6 Z35) OTUTF (uncat patent medicine) *Private collection
NOTES: Under 'Something Good for You,' the Zam-Buk Co. states, 'This fall, instead of presenting our friends with a book of prophecies of weather and events, as we have done now for several years, we decided to get together a number of useful recipes, household hints, etc. ...' This cookbook, therefore, is the first of the four cookbooks published to promote the use of Zam-Buk, a skin ointment. The other cookbooks are: O270.1, *Cookery Recipes*; O361.1, *Helps to Overcome the High Cost of Living*; and O396.1, *Good Things and How to Cook Them. The Zam-Buk Book of Household Hints* (BDUCVM) has no cookery.

According to 'Something Good for You,' this collection of recipes was 'prepared by a lady of exceptional ability and experience.' A testimonial on p 11, dated 28 February 1910, suggests that *Zam-Buk Book of Cookery Recipes* was published about 1910. The testimonials are from Canadians and the book was published by the Toronto branch of the Zam-Buk Co., whose chief laboratory and head office were in London, England. The product was sold around the world. In 2007 the brand name was owned by Bayer Consumer Care.

In the private collector's copy catalogued here, 'The' in the cover-title is torn off.

1910–12

Laura Secord Memorial cook book

O249.1   nd [about 1910–12]
Laura Secord / Memorial / cook book / Published by / the Women's Institute / of Queenston, Ontario / Officers / President, Mrs. H.C. Bradley / Vice-Pres., Mrs. F.A. Sheppard / Sec'y-Treas., Miss E.L. Lowrey
CONTENTS: First page tp; second page 'Some History' signed Mrs H.C. Bradley and Miss Edna L. Lowrey; third page recipes; ...; 79 'An Easy Way to Clean Silver' and ad; two unnumbered leaves and another leaf(ves) possibly missing
COPIES: *Private collection
NOTES: 'Review Printery // Niagara Falls, Canada' is on the front face of the binding. 'Some History' tells the story of Laura Secord, a Queenston resident who had 'saved her country' in June 1813, by warning the British of an imminent American attack during the War of 1812. 'Some History' also explains that the Women's Institute of Queenston is 'working to erect a Memorial Hall at Queenston to honor the Canadian heroine.' The building 'is to be a substantial one containing an assembly room, library and museum, where records of this district may be preserved.' Contributions could be sent to the secretary. Although it is not explicitly stated, this cookbook was published as part of the fund-raising drive for the Memorial Hall, and the initiative to honour Laura Secord marked about a century since the start of the War of 1812.

The Queenston St Davids branch of the Women's Institute was founded in 1908 (Ambrose, p 236). In the same year, 1908, the membership of thirty women determined to ensure that Laura Secord was appropriately recognized and started their campaign to build a 'fine Greek style hall containing a Library.' They petitioned city councils in St Catharines and Niagara Falls, the Niagara Parks Commission, and the provincial and federal governments, and they solicited donations through pledge forms sent to Ontario villages and all Women's Institute branches, as well as schools. Records show the following amounts received: $99.40 from other Women's Institute branches, $85.70 from schools, $59.50 from personal donations, $30.00 from a concert, $50.00 from advertising in a cookbook (presumably *Laura Secord Memorial Cook Book*), and $480.50 in subscriptions from Queenston area residents. The plan was to start building in 1911 and complete the project by the centenary of her walk, June 1913 (the estimated completion date is from p 7 of the undated brochure cited below).

No record could be found of when Mrs H.C. Bradley was president (her officer's title on the title-page of the cookbook); however, she followed the first president Isabel Armstrong, who served from 29 May 1908 for two years. The cookbook, therefore, could not have been published before 1910, and was likely published about 1910–12, given the planned construction schedule.

The Memorial Hall was never built (the women failed to win the necessary support from the Niagara Parks Commission). Instead, the women lent their memorial money to help pay for a new, two-classroom Laura Secord Memorial School containing a Community Hall, which opened in 1914. In the 1920s, when the school repaid the Institute's loan, the women bought the then-unused Baptist Church for their meetings. This building, which the Institute sold in the mid-1950s, now houses the Queenston Community Library. It could be said that, in a small way, the publication of the *Laura Secord Memorial Cook Book* in about 1910–12 contributed to the community life of Queenston today.

Information about the activities of the Queenston St Davids branch of the Women's Institute is from the Jean M. Huggins Collection at ONF. An undated promotional brochure published by the Queenston branch to solicit donations for the memorial project contains the rationale and plan for the project, and a reproduction of the architect's drawing for the elevation (title of the brochure: *A National Memorial to Laura Secord;* copy at ONHI (x995.032)). See Colin M. Coates and Cecilia Morgan, *Heroines and History: Representations of Madeleine de Verchères and Laura Secord,* Toronto: University of Toronto Press, 2002, pp 200–2, concerning the branch's struggle to persuade the Niagara Parks Commission to support the Memorial Hall.

Recipes

O250.1   nd [about 1910–12]
Recipes / Compiled and arranged / by the / Ladies' Aid Society / of / St. Andrew's Church / Tweed / "She looketh well to the ways / of her household." / Tweed: / The Tweed News Press
DESCRIPTION: 17.5 × 12.5 cm   Pp [leaf lacking] [3–5] 6–118 [leaf lacking]   Stapled and with cord through two holes
CONTENTS: 3 tp; 4 'How to Cook a Husband' [mock recipe]; 5–117 recipes credited with the name of the contributor and ads; 118 ad
COPIES: *Private collection
NOTES: Advertisements point to publication in the

period 1910–12. One for Mathewson's Sons, wholesale grocers in Montreal, cites a report of 26 November 1910 by Dr J.T. Donald, dominion government analyst. Another advertisement is for Robin Hood Flour from Saskatchewan Flour Mills Co. Ltd in Moose Jaw. This company began production on 27 January 1909; on 12 April 1912, it changed its name to Robin Hood Mills Ltd. The cookbook, therefore, could not have been published before 1910 or after 1912.

Another privately owned copy retains pp 1–2, p 119, and the binding. Printed on p 2 is 'To the "Lords of Creation," dear to us as fathers, brothers, husbands or sons, keen critics always of the culinary art, this book is devotedly dedicated'; the following inscription is on the front face of the binding: 'Best Xmas wishes From the Manse [i.e., the minister's home].'

1910–15

Catarrhozone health message

For the titles of other publications by the same company, see O155.1.

O251.1 nd [about 1910–15]
Catarrhozone / health / message [cover-title]
DESCRIPTION: 11.5 × 15.0 cm Pp [1–4] 5–29 [30–2] Paper, with image on front of a man on horseback carrying an over-size package of Catarrhozone Ozonated Air Remedy; stapled, and with hole punched at top left corner, through which runs a string for hanging
CONTENTS: 1–4, 6, 8, 10, 12, 14, 16, 18, 20–8, 30–2 publ ads; 5 'Hints to Housekeepers'; 7, 9, 11 'Weights and Measures'; 13 'Time Table for the Cook'; 15, 17, 19 recipes for candy; 29 'Hair Washes'
COPIES: *ONLAM (Walters-Wagar Collection, Box 20)
NOTES: The company name and city – Catarrhozone Co., Kingston, Ontario, and Buffalo, New York – are recorded in the advertisements and in the illustrations of the company's products on the outside back face of the binding.

Dainty dishes

O252.1 nd [about 1910–15]
Dainty dishes / from the / Hamilton Woman's / Exchange
DESCRIPTION: 23.0 × 9.0 cm Pp [1] 2–24 Card; stapled

CONTENTS: 1 tp; 2–3 'Contents'; 4–24 recipes
CITATIONS: Simpson, p W16 (photograph)
COPIES: *OH (R641.5 DAI CESH) OKQ (F5012 nd H228) Private collection
NOTES: The leaves are printed on the rectos only; the versos are not included in the pagination. OH dates the book [192-]. It may be earlier since a copy was found in a box of other cookbooks, all dating about 1910–12.

The favorite cook book

O253.1 nd [about 1910–15]
Our motto: / "For home and country" / The / favorite / cook book / Compiled by / Millcreek [*sic*, one word] Women's Institute / President – Mrs. H.J. Lougheed / Vice-President, Mrs. Geo. Irwin / Sec.-Treas. – Mrs J.E. Clark / [in box, to right of officers' names:] Our Aims and / Objects / To do all the good we / can, / To all the people we / can, / In every way we can, / Just as long as ever / we can. / [below officers' names and boxed text:] We thank one and all for their assistance in the production / of this useful recipe book. We trust it will benefit every / one making use of its contents. [cover-title]
CONTENTS: 1st page 'Index to Recipes under Appropriate Headings' [i.e., table of contents]
COPIES: *Private collection
NOTES: The book's owner reports that the volume has 76 pp. The recipes are credited with the name of the contributor. There was more than one Women's Institute branch called Mill Creek, but an advertisement on p 12 for banks in Clarksburg and Thornbury confirms that the cookbook was published by the WI branch in Grey County East, founded in 1902 and disbanded in 1988 (Ambrose). The river called Mill Creek runs through Euphrasia, Osprey, and Collingwood townships. The copy is inscribed by the owner's father's sister – the original owner of the book – on the inside front face of the binding, in ink, 'Anne Burritt.'

Over one hundred tried receipes

O254.1 [about 1910–15]
Over / one hundred / tried receipes [*sic*]. / Table of contents. / [section headings and page numbers for 'Table of Contents']
DESCRIPTION: 21.5 × 14.0 cm Pp [1], [i], 2–15 [leaf lacking] Lacks paper binding; stapled
CONTENTS: 1 tp and 'Table of Contents'; i blank; 2–15 recipes

CITATIONS: Driver 2001, Wellington County, p 97 (note 7)

COPIES: *Private collection

NOTES: The recipes are not credited. The 'Table of Contents' lists 'Sherbet,' 'Drinks,' 'Candy,' and 'Washing Fluids' on p 16; 'Liniments and Lotions' on pp 16–17; and 'Table of Weights and Measures' on p 17. The place of publication is unknown, but it was probably Ontario since the copy catalogued here belongs to an elderly person in Guelph.

1910–16

'Dominion maid' recipes

O255.1   nd [about 1910–16]

"Dominion / maid" / recipes / being 103 selections from the / private cook books of some / of Canada's foremost homes. / Selected, tested and approved by / Dominion Sugar Company / Limited / Berlin Wallaceburg Chatham

DESCRIPTION: 26.0 × 11.5 cm   Pp [1] 2–32   Small tp illus of steaming dishes on a tray, illus   Paper, with image on front of a woman holding an iced cake on a plate; stapled, and with hole punched at top left corner for hanging

CONTENTS: 1 tp; 2–5 '"What Shall We Have for Breakfast?"'; 6–9 '"What Shall We Have for Luncheon?"'; 10–12 '"What Shall We Have for Dinner?"'; 13–20 blank for 'My Own Pet Recipes' and illus at top pp 16–17 of 'The Three Great Modern Plants of the Dominion Sugar Company, Limited'; 21–2 continuation of dinner recipes; 23–mid 27 'Cakes'; mid 27–30 'Candies'; 31 'In Your Preserving This Year Try – Dominion Crystal Sugar'; 32 index; inside back face of binding 'Rous and Mann Limited, Toronto & Montreal'

COPIES: *Private collection

NOTES: On the inside front face of the binding there are illustrations of the types and packaging of Dominion Crystal Sugar: Dominion Crystal Cut Loaf (i.e., cubed sugar, 'popular for five o'clock tea and for general table use'); Dominion Crystal Icing Sugar, in 25-pound pails and boxes; Dominion Crystal Granulated Sugar, in 300-pound barrels and 20- and 10-pound bags. Also illustrated are a 2-pound carton of Cut Loaf Sugar and a 5-pound carton of Granulated Sugar, but with the note that they are not currently sold because the Canadian public prefers to buy sugar in bulk; however, the company says it intends to make the smaller packages shortly. The cookbook

was published no earlier than 1910, when the printer, Rous and Mann Ltd, is first listed in Toronto city directories. It was most likely published a few years later, perhaps about 1912 when Redpath Sugar, a competing brand, began to be sold in ready-packaged sizes (see Q107.1). It certainly appeared no later than 1916, when Berlin was renamed Kitchener (now the city of Kitchener-Waterloo). In *Everywoman's World* (August 1916) the company advertises copies of *Dominion Maid Recipes: 100 Selected Recipes,* likely the same publication as that described here.

Probably in the 1950s, the company published another cookbook, also called *Dominion Maid Recipes,* [Chatham, Ont.: Canada and Dominion Sugar Co. Ltd, nd] (OGU).

1911

Beeton, Mrs Isabella Mary, née Mayson (St Marylebone, Middlesex, England, 14 March 1836–6 February 1865, Greenhithe, Kent, England)

For information about Mrs Beeton and her other cookbooks, see O231.1.

O256.1   1911

Mrs. Beeton's / cookery book / all about / cookery, household work, / marketing, trussing, / carving, etc / Fully illustrated with coloured / and photographic plates / New edition / Ward, Lock & Co., Limited / London, Melbourne and Toronto / 1911

COPIES: *Private collection

O256.2   1912

—Mrs. Beeton's / cookery book / all about / cookery, household work, / marketing, trussing, / carving, etc / Fully illustrated with coloured / and photographic plates / New edition / Ward, Lock & Co., Limited / London, Melbourne and Toronto / 1912

DESCRIPTION: 18.5 × 12.0 cm   Pp [i–ii], [1–4] 5–380, [i–vi]   6 pls col incl frontis, 16 double-sided pls, 3 fp illus on pp 350, 351, and 352 of serviette-folding [1 shilling, in publ ad on p iv at back]   Cloth, with four images impressed on front: game birds, two pedestal dishes on which food is arranged, and fish

CONTENTS: i–ii endpaper ads; 1 ht; 2 ads; 3 tp; 4 ad; 5–7 'Preface to Mrs. Beeton's Cookery Books [plural]'; 8 ad; 9 'General Contents'; 10 ad; 11 continuation of

'General Contents'; 12 ads; 13 'List of Coloured Illustrations'; 14 ads; 15–16 'List of Illustrations'; 17–368 text; 369–70 ads; 371–80 'Index to Recipes' and bottom p 380, 'Butler and Tanner The Selwood Printing Works Frome and London'; i–vi ads and publ ads
COPIES: *OGU (CCC TX715.6 B43 1912)

BRITISH EDITIONS: *Mrs Beeton's Cookery Book* is the shortened title for *Mrs Beeton's Cookery Book and Household Guide* (editions from 1890 onward), itself a new title for *The Englishwoman's Cookery Book ... Being a Collection of Economical Receipts Taken from Her 'Book of Household Management,'* sometimes called *Mrs Beeton's Shilling Cookery Book* (editions from 1862 to the 1880s). For more information, see Driver, p 101.

Canadian Farm cook book

O257.1   [copyright 1911]
Canadian Farm / cook book / Compiled by / the Woman's Department / Canadian Farm / Publishers / Canadian Farm / Toronto
DESCRIPTION: 18.5 × 13.0 cm   Pp [i–viii], [1] 2–408 Cloth marked with black veins, crudely simulating leather
CONTENTS: i ht; ii ad; iii tp; iv 'Copyright, Canada, 1911, by Canadian Farm Toronto' and the printer's symbol 'Press of the Hunter-Rose Company Limited'; v table of contents; vi ad; vii introduction signed 'Canadian Farm // Toronto Canada'; viii blank; 1–408 recipes credited with the name of the contributor
CITATIONS: Driver 2002, Five Roses, p 4   Ferguson/ Fraser, p 232   O'Neill (unpublished)
COPIES: CIHM (9-91639)   OBEHCM (974.9.54)   *OGU (UA s023 b28)   OH (R641.5 CAN CESC)   OPETCM OSIDM   OTUTF (B-12 7874)   Private collection; Great Britain: LB (07943.g.94 destroyed)
NOTES: The cookbook was originally intended to be ready for distribution by Christmas 1910, according to a notice headed 'Canadian Farm Cook Book a Winner' in the *Canadian Farm* magazine of 23 December 1910, p 13. The notice, from the editor of the 'Home and Fireside' section, states:

When the cook book idea was announced a couple of months ago, there were some misgivings as to whether enough recipes could be secured in so short a time to make the publication of a book worth while. But our kind friends, the women folk of the farm, have responded nobly. Recipes have simply poured in. The thousand limit was soon

reached ... It will be impossible to have it ready as a Christmas present ... We expect, however, to have it ready for distribution early in the new year ... The large number of recipes has made it necessary to do some selecting ... Everyone, however, who sent in recipes in the prescribed time will receive a copy of the book.

An advertisement for the cookbook in the 12 May 1911 issue, p 9, reveals that the first call for recipes was made in the issue of 28 October 1910, and a total of '2,150 acceptable recipes' were received. The advertisement explains that 2,000 copies of the book were printed, of which 1,450 copies were to be distributed to recipe contributors, leaving 550 copies to be sent to readers for free if they sent in three paid yearly subscriptions (subscriptions from three friends; the reader's own annual renewal, plus two friends' subscriptions; or the reader's renewal for two years and a friend's annual subscription).

The cookbook's introduction explains that 'Canadian Farm Cook Book is compiled from a large number of recipes submitted by our women readers from every province of Canada.' The private collector's copy includes a loose-leaf insert on which is printed a letter from Geo. M. Bertram, vice-president, The Farm Press Ltd, Toronto, 24 April 1911, who says that the delay in publishing the cookbook was caused by the receipt of 'so many more recipes ... [from the women readers] than expected ...'

The private collector's copy is inscribed on the front endpaper, in pencil, 'Mrs. P.D. McArthur.'

Cook book

O258.1   1911
Cook book / published by / the Ladies' Aid / of the / Christian Church / Newmarket / Newmarket: / Printed at "The Express-Herald Book" and Job Office / 1911
DESCRIPTION: 22.0 × 15.0 cm   Pp [1–4] 5–131 [132] Paper-covered limp cloth, with image on front of the church; sewn
CONTENTS: 1 tp; 2 ad; 3 'Table of Weights and Measures'; 4 'Preface'; 5–131 recipes credited with the name of the contributor and ads; 132 table of contents
CITATIONS: Garrett, pp 59, 131
COPIES: ONENM   *Private collection
NOTES: Garrett reprints the recipe for Cucumber Catsup.

The coronation cook book

See also O134.1, in support of the same hospital.

O259.1 August 1911
The coronation / cook book / compiled for / the Board of Lady Managers / of the / General and Marine / Hospital / Collingwood, Ont. / "We may live without friends, we may live without books, / But civilized man cannot live without cooks; / He may live without books – what is knowledge but grieving? / He may live without hope – what is hope but deceiving? / He may live without love – what is passion but pining; / But where is the man can live without dining? [*sic*, no closing quotation-marks] / Price 25 cents / Collingwood, August 1911 [cover-title]
COPIES: *OCOLM
NOTES: *The Coronation Cook Book* was named for the coronation of King George V on 22 June 1911. The museum's copy is inscribed on the binding, 'Mabel Darling.'

The coronation cook book

See also O102.1, an earlier text by the hospital's women's group.

O260.1 1911
The / coronation cook book / Compiled for / the Women's Auxiliary / of the / Royal Victoria Hospital / Barrie, Ont., June, 1911 / "To be a good cook means the knowledge of all / fruits, herbs, balms and spices, and of all / that is healing and sweet in field and groves, and / savory in meats; means carefulness, inventiveness, / watchfulness, willingness and readiness of appli- / ance. It means the economy of your great grand- / mothers, and the science of modern chemists. It / means much tasting and no wasting. It means / English thoroughness, French art and Arabian / hospitality. It means in fine, that you are to be / perfectly and always ladies (loaf-givers) and are to / see that everyone has something nice to eat" – Ruskin / To the business men who have given advertisements, thereby / assisting us materially in our work, and to all who may / purchase copies, we tender our grateful thanks. The / advertisements form a valuable feature of the / work, as they present to the reader only / reliable business houses.

DESCRIPTION: 22.5 × 15.0 cm Pp [1] 2 [3] 4, [i–iv], 5–72 Illus on p 5 of Royal Victoria Hospital Paper (front face lacking); stapled
CONTENTS: 1 tp; 2 ad; 3–4 'Beautiful Barrie' and 'Council of the Town of Barrie for 1911'; i illus of hospital 'Officers 1911' and 'Woman's [*sic*] Auxiliary'; ii ad; iii 'Royal Victoria Cook Book /,' Index' [i.e., table of contents]; iv ad; 5–71 text and ads; 72 ad
CITATIONS: Sullivan 78
COPIES: OMSA *Private collection
NOTES: There is an advertisement on p [iv] for the newspaper *Barrie Saturday Morning*, by Walls Bros, which says 'Society printing a specialty.' Walls Bros may be the printer of the cookbook. The book's title refers to the coronation of King George V on 22 June 1911.

The Electric Bean Chemical Co's calendar and household receipe book for 1911

See also O277.1, The Electric Bean Chemical Co's Calendar and Household Receipt Book for 1912.

O261.1 1911
Keep this book It is valuable / The Electric Bean Chemical Co's / calendar and household / receipe [*sic*] book for 1911 / also funnygrams, etc. / See that you get / the coupon on / page 30, it / is worth / 10 cents. / Electric Beans / are a / doctor's prescription / for tired people. / The experience of / the ages combined / with the marvellous / advancement made / in modern medical / science has alone / made possible such / a remedy as Electric / Beans – a remedy / that has proven it- / self to be as powerful / to cure as the chain- / ed electric current / is to obey the will of / man. [cover-title]
DESCRIPTION: 23.0 × 15.5 cm Pp 1–32 Illus Paper, with image on front of a man holding a package of Electric Beans, a pyramid behind him; cover-title and image within a border of Electric Beans; stapled
CONTENTS: 1–32 text incorporating monthly calendars, ads for publ's products, and recipes on pp 2–4, 6–10, 12–13, 15–18, 24–5, and 27–30
COPIES: OTUTF (uncat patent medicine) *Private collection
NOTES: The company address, 226–8 Albert Street, Ottawa, is on p 1.

Farmer, Fannie Merritt (Boston, Mass., 23 March 1857–15 January 1915, Boston, Mass.)

For information about Farmer and her famous The Boston Cooking-School Cook Book, *see O144.1.* Jennie B. Williams's Us Two Cook Book *was published in a Canadian edition; see O224.1.*

O262.1   nd [about 1911]
Catering / for / special occasions / with / menus and recipes / by / Fannie Merritt Farmer / author of / "The Boston Cooking-School Cook Book" / Arranged for the Canadian table / by / Jennie B. Williams / author of / "Us Two Cook Book" / Decorations by / Albert D. Blashfield / Toronto / The Musson Book Company / Limited
DESCRIPTION: 19.5 × 13.5 cm   Pp [i–vi] vii–x, [1–2] 3–240   6 pls incl frontis, of tables set for various occasions; tp illus of child angels in human formal dress, about to enter a vehicle, on their way to a 'special occasion'; many illus of child angels   Cloth, with pl col mounted on front of a baby angel sharpening a knife, a large turkey in the background
CONTENTS: i ht; ii blank; iii tp; iv 'Entered at Stationers' Hall, London, England // All rights reserved'; v quotation from Shelley; vi blank; vii–viii 'A Foreword' signed Fannie Merritt Farmer; ix table of contents; x list of illustrations; 1–229 text; 230 blank; 231–40 index
COPIES: *BVA   CIHM (65705)   OGU (UA s048 b16) OONL (TX739 F37 1919, 2 copies)   QMBM
NOTES: Although the title-page asserts that the text has been 'arranged for the Canadian table,' the revisions are minor and involve the renaming of overtly American holidays, recipes, and references. The 'Foreword' is identical to the American one, except for the substitution of 'Canadians' in the first sentence: 'Canadians of to-day are accused, somewhat unjustly, it seems to me, of being inhospitable.' (One hopes that Canadians were never accused of being inhospitable!) There are chapters for the following occasions: 'New Year's Afternoon Teas'; 'St. Valentine's Spreads'; 'St. Patrick's Day Luncheons'; 'Easter Dinners'; 'Victoria Day Spreads'; 'Dominion Day Spreads'; 'Hallowe'en Spreads'; 'Thanksgiving Dinners'; 'Christmas Dinners'; 'Wedding Receptions'; 'Birthday Feasting'; and 'Children's Parties.' The chapter for Victoria Day is actually 'Washington's Birthday Spreads' in the American text, and the chapter for Dominion Day is the 'Fourth of July Spreads.' George Washington Hatchets (a cookie recipe) is renamed Victoria Maple Leaves, with a corresponding change in the instruc-

tion to cut the cookies into leaf-shapes, not hatchet-shapes. The well-known recipe for Lady Baltimore Cake is renamed Lady Ottawa Cake, and Fourth of July Punch becomes Dominion Punch. In the Thanksgiving chapter, however, Puritan Pudding and New England Thanksgiving Pudding keep their American references. OONL dates the Canadian edition of *Catering for Special Occasions* [1911?].

AMERICAN EDITIONS: Philadelphia: David McKay, [copyright 1911] (United States: DLC, InU, NBuBE); Birmingham, Ala.: Oxmoor House, c1985 (United States: DLC).

Helpful hints for housekeepers [1911]

The Dodds Medicine Co. is first listed in the Toronto city directory for 1894, where the manager is John A. McKee, 'pro med,' office at 536 Bloor Street West. The first annual issue of Helpful Hints for Housekeepers *was published in 1911. For later issues, some published in English and French editions, see O281.1, O303.1, O360.1, O383.1, O407.1, O423.1, O435.1, O499.1, O523.1, O544.1, O584.1, O623.1, O820.1, O853.1, O941.1, and O1076.1. The company also published almanacs, copies of which are at OTUTF (uncat patent medicine).*

O263.1   nd [1911]
Hang me in the kitchen / Helpful / hints / for housekeepers / Compliments of / the Dodds Medicine Co. / Limited / Toronto, Can. [cover-title]
DESCRIPTION: 16.5 × 10.5 cm   Pp 1–[32 obscured by clipping]   Paper; stapled, and with hole punched at top left corner for hanging
CONTENTS: Inside front face of binding 'Table of Contents'; 1–32 text
COPIES: *NSWA
NOTES: See O281.1, regarding the date of publication.

Hill, Mrs Janet McKenzie (Westfield, Mass., 1852–1933)

Janet McKenzie first worked as a high school teacher; only long after her marriage in 1873 to Benjamin Hill did she train in cookery at the Boston Cooking School, graduating in 1892. She became the long-time editor of the school's magazine, which she founded in 1896. See her biography in Feeding America.
For other Canadian editions of her books, see O362.1, Balanced Daily Diet, *and O363.1,* The Whys of

Cooking. *Her recipes are included in: O118.1,* Gem Chopper Cook Book; *O216.1, Johnson, Alice A., Mrs Janet McKenzie Hill, Dr Henry Hartshorne, and other specialists,* The Household Companion; *and Q153.1,* Chocolate and Cocoa Recipes ... Home Made Candy Recipes, *where the 'home made candy recipes' are by Hill.*

Her other books (all at DLC unless otherwise indicated) include: Salads, Sandwiches and Chafing-Dish Dainties, Boston: Little, Brown and Co., 1899; Table Helps for Housewife and Hostess, [3rd ed.], Chicago: Tildesley and Co., 1904; The Up-to-Date Waitress, Boston: Little, Brown and Co., 1906; Cooking for Two, [Boston:] Little, Brown and Co., 1909; Dainty Desserts for Dainty People: Salads, Savories, and Dainty Dishes Made with Knox Gelatine, Johnstown, NY: Charles B. Knox Co., c1909; The Book of Entrées, Boston: Little, Brown and Co., 1911; Cooking and Serving en Casserole and Things We Relish, Meriden, Conn.: Meriden Silver Plate Co., [c1910]; The American Cook Book, Boston: Boston Cooking-School Magazine, 1914; Canning, Preserving and Jelly Making, Boston: Little, Brown and Co., 1915; Nyal Cook Book, Detroit: Nyal Co., [1916]; Cakes, Pastry and Dessert Dishes, Boston: Little, Brown and Co., 1917; Economical War-Time Cook Book, 1918 (Bitting, p 228, but not at DLC); War Time Recipes, Cincinnati: Procter and Gamble Co., [1918]; Recipes for Everyday, Cincinnati: Procter and Gamble Co., copyright 1919 (United States: DLC, InU); The Rumford Way of Cookery and Household Economy, Providence, RI: Rumford Co., nd (United States: InU).

O264.1   1911
Practical cooking / and serving / a complete manual of how to / select, prepare, and serve food / by / Janet McKenzie Hill / editor of "The Boston Cooking School Magazine" / author of "Salads, Sandwiches, and / Chafing-Dish Dainties" / With many illustrations / Toronto / McClelland & Goodchild / 1911
DESCRIPTION: 19.5 × 12.5 cm   Pp [v–vii] viii–xviii [xix–xx], 1–731   2 pls col incl frontis, 70 pls, illus   Rebound
CONTENTS: v tp; vi 'Printed in New York, U.S.A.'; vii–x 'Preface'; xi–xii table of contents; xiii–xviii 'List of Illustrations'; xix ht; xx blank; 1–712 text; 713–31 index
COPIES: CIHM (73018)   OONL (TX715 H55 1911) *SSU
NOTES: A comparison of the OONL copy, which is in its original cloth binding, with the SSU copy cata-

logued above indicates that the initial pages of the SSU copy have been rebound out of order. The pagination of the OONL copy runs [i–vii] viii ...; the contents are: i ht; ii blank; iii tp; iv 'Printed in New York, U.S.A. ...'; v quotation from *Elizabeth and Her German Garden* and from Hourion de Penesey (a learned French judge); vi blank; vii–x preface; ...

According to Spadoni/Donnelly No. 3690, *Practical Cooking and Serving* is cited in *Bookseller and Stationer* Vol. 26, No. 8 (August 1910). Spadoni/Donnelly found no copy of this title and I have found copies dated 1911 only.

BRITISH EDITIONS: London: Wm Heinemann, 1903 (Great Britain: LB destroyed, LCoF; United States: DLC); London, New York and Toronto: Hodder and Stoughton, nd [1913] (Great Britain: LB micro OB, LoEN, OB).

AMERICAN EDITIONS: New York: Doubleday, Page and Co., 1902 (United States: DLC); New York: Doubleday, Page and Co., 1906 (Great Britain: LCoF); New York: Doubleday, Page and Co., 1909 [Tp verso: 'Copyright, 1902, by Doubleday, Page & Company // Published October, 1902'] (OGM); Garden City, NY: Doubleday, Page and Co., 1911 (United States: NNNAM); Garden City, NY: Doubleday, Page and Co., 1912 (Bitting, p 228); Garden City, NY: Doubleday, Page and Co., 1916 (United States: DLC).

Midland cook book

O265.1   1911
Midland / cook / book / 1911 [cover-title]
DESCRIPTION: 19.5 × 13.0 cm   Pp [1–3] 4–168   Cloth
CONTENTS: 1 preface and 'W.G. Cave, printer, Midland.'; 2 blank; 3–166 text headed 'Midland Cook Book. 700 Receipts.' and ads; 167 ad; 168 'Index' [i.e., table of contents]
COPIES: *OGU (UA s048 b21)   OMIHURM
NOTES: The preface states, 'To prepare and complete a cook book ... was deemed a wise and popular means whereby a sum of money could be raised to aid the building of the new Catholic church; and the Women's Auxiliary of St. Margaret's Church have undertaken this task.'

The OMIHURM copy is inscribed on the front endpaper, in ink, 'Marie Morrow. Sylvandale // Midland. On.' This inscription has been crossed through and a later inscription added above, in ballpoint pen, 'Mrs. J.R. Morrow.'

O265.2   1922

—Midland / cook book / 1922 [cover-title]

DESCRIPTION: 20.0 × 13.5 cm   Pp [3–5] 6–246 [247]   Cloth

CONTENTS: 3 'Preface'; 4 blank; 5–246 text, mostly recipes credited with the name of the contributor, and ads; 247 'Index' [i.e., table of contents] and at bottom, 'Midland Free Press Print'

CITATIONS: Golick, p 108 (note 35 cites year incorrectly as 1911)

COPIES: OMIHURM (2 copies)   OONL (TX715 M5784)   OTNY (uncat)   *Private collection

NOTES: The 'Preface' states: 'The "Midland Cook Book" which the Auxiliary of St. Andrews Hospital now offers to the public for sale, is practically a revised version of the one published in 1911 by the Women's Auxiliary of St. Margaret's Church, with the addition of many new recipes. The idea came to us as the 1911 books are now out of print and are constantly in demand. Therefore we decided on this means of raising money for our Hospital, ...'

The first section of the text, titled 'General Suggestions' and 'Small Leakages of a Household' (suggestions for economy in cooking and cleaning), is signed Mrs Playfair, i.e., Charlotte Playfair, the wife of James Playfair, a leading member in the industrial and municipal affairs of Midland. Both Mrs Playfair and her husband were involved with the development of St Andrews Hospital at the time of the book's publication. James had purchased the new building for the town's hospital and renamed the institution after his birthplace in Scotland. In 1922, Charlotte herself purchased the house next door for a nurses' residence and paid for its interior furnishings. Charlotte was the daughter of Senator Alexander Walker Ogilvie of Montreal. A.W. Ogilvie and his two brothers had built the flour milling business, which, later, as Ogilvie Flour Mills Co., published the many editions of Q55.1, *Ogilvie's Book for a Cook*.

Recipes tried and proved

O266.1   1911

Recipes / tried and proved. / From / the Ladies' Aid / and friends / for the / First Congregational Church, / Hamilton. / 1911. / H.A. Martin, printer. 23 John St. North

DESCRIPTION: 21.0 × 13.5 cm   Pp [1] 2–96   [$0.25, on binding]   Paper, with image on front of 'Old Congregational Church, built 1858'; stapled

CONTENTS: [blank leaf]; 1 tp; 2 ad; 3 'Index' [i.e., table of contents]; 4 ad; 5–93 recipes credited with the name

of the contributor and ads; 94 ad; 95 'Cooking Measures' and ad for the printer, H.A. Martin, which includes his photograph; 96 ads

COPIES: *OONL (TX715.6 R4455 1911 p***)

NOTES: The cover-title is 'Over Three Hundred Recipes'; below the image of the church is 'Compiled by Building Fund Guild.' In the OONL copy, the blank leaf is stuck to the title-page so that the text can only be read by holding the page up to the light.

Shepard's practical housekeepers account book and kitchen companion 1912

See O145.1 for a list of other editions.

O267.1   1912, copyright 1911

Shepard's / practical housekeepers / account book / and / kitchen companion / 1912 / Shredded Wheat Biscuit / The delicious "breakfast food" / Good for any meal. / Triscuit the shredded wheat toast, for / luncheon, with cheese, butter or marmalade. / Entered according to Act of the Parliament of Canada in the year nineteen hundred and eleven, by Geo. Shepard, at / the Department of Agriculture at Ottawa [cover-title]

DESCRIPTION: 31.0 × 23.5 cm   Pp 1–64   Paper, with image on front of a boy unpacking a box of groceries at a kitchen table as a woman watches; stapled

CONTENTS: 1 'Published annually in December of each year at Toronto,' publ's address of 33 Scott Street, Toronto, and 'Preface to New Edition'; 2 ad; 3–63 blank weekly accounting tables for household expenses, a calendar for each month, recipes, and ads; 64 ad and 'Household List'

COPIES: *QMM (RBD uncat)

NOTES: 'Printed by Geo. Shepard Printing Co 33 Scott Street Toronto' is on the outside back face of the binding. The 'Preface to New Edition' says that the book is 'distributed free to housekeepers.'

The Smiths Falls cook book

O268.1   1911

The Smiths Falls / cook book / arranged by / the Ladies' Auxiliary of / the Methodist Church / Smiths Falls, Ontario. / To be sold for the benefit of the / new public hospital / "But for life the universe were nothing; / and all that has life requires nourishment." / 1911 / Rideau Record Press

DESCRIPTION: 22.5 × 15.0 cm   Pp [1–4] 5–135   Cloth

CONTENTS: 1 ad; 2 blank; 3 tp; 4 ad; 5–133 text and

ads; 134 blank; 135 ad; [twenty-nine blank leaves for manuscript recipes]
COPIES: *OGU (UA s043 b37)   OSMFHHM

Tried and true recipes

The Almonte branch of the Women's Institute was established in 1909 (Ambrose, p 229).

O269.1 [1911]
Tried and / true / recipes / This book has been arranged by the Women's / Institute of Almonte. / The money is to be used to furnish a bed in / the Women's Ward to be known as the / Women's Institute Cot. / The housewife will have ever before her a / reminder that jam, bread, buns, puddings, / and an occasional pie is always acceptable. / Also old linen or cotton, dish wipers and / dish cloths. / Proceeds in aid of the / Rosamond Memorial / Hospital.
DESCRIPTION: Paper-covered boards, with image on front of the hospital, and cloth spine
CITATIONS: Garrett, pp 109, 132
COPIES: *Private collection
NOTES: The private collector reports that the book has 94 pp, was published in 1911, and was printed on the press of the Almonte Gazette.

Garrett reprints the recipe for Rhubarb Marmalade. On p 109 she states that the book was published by the Hospital Auxiliary; on p 132, she gives Women's Institute.

1911–14

Cookery recipes

O270.1 nd [about 1911–14]
Cookery / recipes / "If only I / could read / it!" / Price / 10 / cents [cover-title]
DESCRIPTION: 20.0 × 12.5 cm   Pp 1–24   Paper, with image on front of a girl, in a kitchen, consulting a cookbook; stapled
CONTENTS: Inside front face of binding 'To Our Readers' signed the Zam-Buk Co.; 1 publ ad; 2–20 recipes and publ ads; 21–4 publ ads; inside back face 'Printed and published for C.E. Fulford, Limited'
COPIES: *AEPMA (2 copies: H79.114.194, H86.43.703) AEUCHV   OKQ (F5012 nd z24)   OTMCL (641.5971 H39 No. 7)
NOTES: 'To Our Readers' states: '... the demands for duplicate copies [of 'the last book of cookery recipes

which we sent out'] were so numerous that we decided this year to prepare another such booklet.' This text draws attention to the section of 'Invalid Cookery' and recommends Zam-Buk herbal balm and Zam-Buk Soap. Page 2 also refers to an earlier work: 'Once again we present our readers with a handy book of recipes, ...' *Cookery Recipes* may be the second of four cookbooks promoting Zam-Buk products. The earliest was O248.1, *Zam-Buk Book of Cookery Recipes* of [about 1910]. The others are O361.1, *Helps to Overcome the High Cost of Living*, and O396.1, *Good Things and How to Cook Them.*

O270.2 nd [about 1911–14]
—Cookery / recipes / "If only I / could read / it!" / Lecteurs / francais / lisez / en sens / inverse [English cover-title on one face of binding]
Recettes / de cuisine / "Si je / pouvais / seulement / le lire!" / English / readers / reverse / this / book [French cover-title on other face]
DESCRIPTION: 20.0 × 12.5 cm   Pp [English:] 1–10; [French:] 1–14   Paper, with same image on both faces of a girl, in a kitchen, consulting a cookbook; stapled
CONTENTS: [English:] 1–10 recipes for 'Soups,' 'Fish,' 'Meats,' 'Vegetables,' 'Pastry and Pies,' 'Puddings and Pudding Sauces,' and 'Cakes,' and publ ads; [French:] 1–14 recipes for 'Soupes,' 'Poissons,' 'Les viandes,' 'Sauces – mayonnaises et farces (remplissages),' 'Légumes,' 'Pâtisseries & tartes,' 'Pouding et sauces pour poudings,' and 'Gâteaux,' and publ ads
COPIES: *Private collection
NOTES: The introductory note on p 1 begins, 'Once again we present our readers with a handy book of recipes, ...' The section for 'Sauces – mayonnaises et farces' is not included in the English text.

Stockham, Mrs Alice Bunker (1833–1912)

O271.1 rev. ed., [about 1911–14]
Tokology / a book for every woman / by / Alice B. Stockham, M.D. / Illustrated / Maternal love! Thou word that sums up all bliss; / Gives and receives all bliss, fullest when most / Thou givest! – Pollock / Revised edition / Toronto / McClelland & Goodchild / Limited
DESCRIPTION: 20.5 × 13.5 cm   Pp [v–viii] ix–xiv, 17–373   Frontis portrait of author   Cloth
CONTENTS: v tp; vi 'Entered according to Act of Congress, in the year 1893, by Alice B. Stockham, M.D. in the office of Librarian of Congress, Washington, D.C. Entered according to Act of Congress, in the year 1886, by Alice B. Stockham, ... Entered according to

Act of Congress, in the year 1883, by Alice B. Stockham, M.D. ...'; vii dedication to 'my daughter' and 'all women'; viii blank; ix–xiv table of contents; 17–320 text in twenty-three chapters; 321–50 'A Familiar Letter to the Reader from the Author'; 351 'Author's Special Request'; 352–8 'Glossary'; 359–mid 366 'Index'; bottom 366–373 'Index of Dietetics'
CITATIONS: Neering, pp 111–12, 113
COPIES: CIHM (93583) *OONL (RG121 S86 1893 p***)
NOTES: Although the latest American copyright date on p vi is 1893, this Canadian edition was published no earlier than 8 March 1911 when McClelland and Goodchild became a limited company and no later than 29 May 1914 when the company's name changed to McClelland, Goodchild and Stewart Ltd. If the 1916 edition, O271.2, was from the sheets of the R.F. Fenno and Co. edition of 1911, this edition was likely also from the 1911 sheets; therefore, this edition was published about 1911–14.

The last chapter, 'Dietetics,' has 'nearly two hundred recipes' (p xiv) for 'Drinks for the Sick,' 'Cereals,' 'Bread,' 'Eggs as Food,' and various other recipes considered healthful. There is a separate index for the 'Dietetics' recipes. The rest of the text discusses issues to do with female health and sexuality. Tokology is a variant spelling for tocology, which is the practice of obstetrics or midwifery.

O271.2 rev. ed., [1916]
—Tokology / a book for every woman / by / Alice B. Stockham, M.D. / Illustrated / Maternal love! Thou word that sums all bliss, / Gives and receives all bliss, fullest when most / Thou givest! – Pollock / Revised edition / Toronto / McClelland, Goodchild & Stewart / Limited
DESCRIPTION: 19.5 × 13.5 cm Pp [v–viii] ix–xiv, 17–373 Cloth
CONTENTS: v tp; vi 'Copyright, Canada, 1916, by McClelland, Goodchild & Stewart, Limited.'; vii dedication to 'my daughter' and 'all women'; viii blank; ix–xiv table of contents; 17–320 text in twenty-three chapters; 321–50 'A Familiar Letter to the Reader from the Author'; 351 'Author's Special Request'; 352–8 'Glossary'; 359–mid 366 'Index'; bottom 366–373 'Index of Dietetics'
CITATIONS: Spadoni/Donnelly No. 261
COPIES: OHM (RG121 S78 1916) *OONL (RG121 S86 1916 copy 2 of 2)
NOTES: There are no illustrations, despite the description on the title-page; however, Spadoni/Donnelly refer to a 16-page pamphlet that is 'inside the pocket of the lower board' of the OHM copy and titled 'Color Plates Illustrating Maternity.' Spadoni/Donnelly state

that this edition is 'From the sheets of the R.F. Fenno & Co. edition of 1911.'

AMERICAN EDITIONS: Rev. ed., [No place:] 1886 (United States: DLC); New York: R.F. Fenno and Co., [c1911] (United States: DLC).

1912

Beeton, Mrs Isabella Mary, née Mayson (St Marylebone, Middlesex, England, 14 March 1836–6 February 1865, Greenhithe, Kent, England)

For information about Mrs Beeton and her cookbooks, including comments about The Book of Household Management, *see O231.1.*

O272.1 1912
Mrs. Beeton's / book of / household / management / a guide to / cookery in all branches / daily duties / mistress & servant / hostess & guest / marketing / trussing and carving / menu making / home doctor / sick nursing / the nursery / home lawyer / New edition / revised, enlarged, brought up to date / and fully illustrated / Ward, Lock & Co., Limited / London, Melbourne and Toronto / 1912
DESCRIPTION: 20.5 × 13.0 cm Pp [1–2], [i–iv] v–viii, 1–2040, [1] 2–16 [17–18] Many pls col incl frontis of 'Fish,' pls
CONTENTS: 1–2 ads; i ht; ii blank; iii tp; iv blank; v–viii 'Preface to New Edition'; 1–2 'Abridged Preface to the First Edition' signed Isabella Beeton, 1861; 3–4 'General Contents'; 5 'List of Coloured Plates'; 6–8 'List of Illustrations'; 9–1990 text; 1991–2040 'Analytical Index' and at bottom p 2040, 'Butler & Tanner // The Selwood Printing Works // Frome and London'; 1–18 ads
COPIES: ACHP *NSYHM
NOTES: Hughes, pp 197–220, describes how Mrs Beeton 'blend[ed] material' from many sources to create the original text of *The Book of Household Management*: cookbooks by the court chefs Antonin Carême, Louis Eustache Ude, and Charles Elmé Francatelli, Alexis Benoît Soyer of the Reform Club, the Marquis of Buckingham's chef Simpson, and the female British authors Hannah Glasse, Elizabeth Raffald, Maria Rundell, and Eliza Acton; William Kitchiner's *The Cook's Oracle*; Jean Anthelme Brillat-Savarin's *La physiologie du goût*; Thomas Webster's *Encyclopaedia of Domestic Economy*; and recipes from her circle of friends. This 'new edition' has 3,945

numbered recipes, more than half of which were added in 1906 by the London chef Charles Herman Senn (about the 1906 revision, see Howsam, p 36, and Hughes, pp 391–5).

O272.2   1915
—Mrs. Beeton's / book of / household / management / a guide to / cookery in all branches / daily duties / mistress & servant / hostess & guest / marketing / trussing & carving / menu making / home doctor / sick nursing / the nursery / home lawyer / New edition / revised, enlarged, brought up to date / and fully illustrated / Ward, Lock & Co., Limited / London, Melbourne and Toronto / 1915
DESCRIPTION: 21.0 × 13.0 cm   Pp [1–2], [i–iv] v–viii, 1–1997 [1998], [1] 2–4 [5] 6–11 [12] 13–16 [17–18] Many pls col incl frontis of 'Fish,' pls   Quarter leather
CONTENTS: 1–2 endpaper ads; i ht; ii blank; iii tp; iv blank; v–viii 'Preface to New Edition'; 1–2 'Abridged Preface to the First Edition' signed Isabella Beeton, 1861; 3–4 'General Contents'; 5 'List of Coloured Plates'; 6–8 'List of Illustrations'; 9–1948 text; 1949–97 'Analytical Index' and at bottom p 1997, 'Butler & Tanner // Frome & London'; 1998 blank; 1–18 ads
COPIES: *QMM (RBD TX717 B4 1915)

BRITISH EDITIONS: First issued as *The Book of Household Management* in twenty-four monthly parts by S.O. Beeton, London, November 1859–October 1861 (United States: InU), then in book form, London: S.O. Beeton, 1861 (United States: InU), and in many subsequent editions into the twenty-first century. Howsam, pp 33–6, and Hughes, pp 386–95, track the main changes to Beeton's master text through the nineteenth and early twentieth century.

In 1876 the Methodist Book and Publishing House, which had Book Rooms in Toronto and Montreal, advertised what was likely a British edition for $2.25; see MBPH 1876–7, p 12.

O273.1   1912
Mrs. Beeton's / every-day cookery / New edition. / With coloured plates and other illustrations. / Ward, Lock & Co., Limited / London, Melbourne and Toronto / 1912
DESCRIPTION: 20.0 × 12.5 cm   Pp [i–ii], [1–4] 5–752, 1–8, [i–ii]   Frontis col of 'Bacon & Ham,' 2 facing pls col of 'Dinner Table à la Russe' btwn pp 56–7, 17 pls col; 32 double-sided pls; illus   Cloth, with two images on front of hung gamebird and hung hare
CONTENTS: i–ii endpaper ads; 1 ht; 2 blank; 3 tp; 4 blank; 5–8 'Preface to Mrs. Beeton's Cookery Books';

9 'General Contents'; 10 blank; 11–12 'List of Coloured Plates'; 13–16 'List of Illustrations'; 17–30 'Introduction to Cookery'; 31–3 'Work in the Kitchen'; 34–44 'Marketing'; 45–106 'Food and Cookery'; 107–9 'Invalid Cookery'; 110–12 'Foreign, Colonial, and American Cookery'; 113–22 'Carving at Table'; 123–6 'Trussing, Poultry and Game'; 127–30 'Serviettes'; 131–8 'Menu-Making'; 139 'How to Wait at Table'; 140 'Note'; 141–730 'Recipes' arranged alphabetically from Alma Pudding to Zeltlinger Cup; 731 'General Index'; 732 blank; 733–4 'Index of Introduction to Cookery'; 735–52 'Analytical Index of Recipes' and at bottom p 752, 'Ward, Lock & Co., Ltd., London'; 1–8 ads; i–ii endpaper ads
COPIES: *ACFCHP
NOTES: The 'Preface' states on p 7, 'Australian, American, Canadian, South African, German, Italian, and all foreign cookeries, have been treated of, and included amongst the recipes are all the most popular and typical dishes of the Continental nations and the colonists, so that Britons living under other skies may learn how to combine the dishes of their adopted country with those of the Motherland.' The 'Analytical Index,' however, lists 'American and Canadian Dishes' under one heading, and of the over fifty dishes, most bear distinctly American names; for example, Washington Pie and Apples, Lexington Style.

The ACFCHP copy is inscribed on the title-page, in ink, 'To dearest Edie, from the Chocolate Soldier with all his best love & good wishes // Maisteg. 18.1.14.'

BRITISH EDITIONS: *Mrs Beeton's Every-day Cookery* is the twentieth-century, shortened title of *Beeton's Every-day Cookery and Housekeeping Book* (editions from 1872 onward), which, like *All about Cookery*, was a reissue of *Mrs Beeton's Dictionary of Every-day Cookery*, but with additional matter. For more information, see Driver, p 101.

Book of recipes

O274.1   February 1912
[An edition of *Book of Recipes: A Collection of Over 200 Thoroughly Tested Recipes*, compiled by the ladies of Westboro Methodist Church, Westboro, Ontario, February 1912, printed by Ottawa Printing Co. Ltd, pp 96, photograph of the church in winter by Latimer]
COPIES: Private collection
NOTES: The recipes are credited with the name of the contributor and there are advertisements from Ottawa firms; for example, Ottawa Gas and Murphy Gamble.

A cook book of nearly 300 well proven recipes

O275.1   1912
A cook book / of / nearly 300 / well proven recipes / Compiled by / the ladies of the / Autumn Booth / Peterborough Summer Fair / 1912 / [folio:] 1
DESCRIPTION: 21.5 × 14.0 cm   Pp 1 [2], [1–3] 4–92 Lacks limp cloth; stapled
CONTENTS: 1 tp; 2 blank; 1 'Index' [i.e., table of contents] and 'The Peterborough Examiner, Limited, printers'; 2 blank; 3–92 recipes
CITATIONS: Ferguson/Fraser, p 233
COPIES: *OGU (UA s048 b13)   OPETCM

O275.2   enlarged and rev. ed., 1915
—A cook book / of / over 300 / well proven recipes / Compiled by the ladies of the / Autumn Booth of the Peter- / borough Summer Fair, 1912. / Enlarged and revised by the F.H.S. Class / of George Street Methodist Church / Sunday School, December, 1915.
DESCRIPTION: 22.0 × 14.0 cm   Pp [1–5] 6–95 [96] Limp cloth, with illustrated ad on front for Belleghem's, depicting a woman seated at 'the famous Hoosier'; stapled
CONTENTS: 1 tp; 2 ad; 3 'Index' [i.e., table of contents] and 'The Peterborough Examiner, Limited, printers'; 4 ad; 5–96 recipes credited with the name of the contributor, blank pages for manuscript recipes, and ads
CITATIONS: CHO No. 46 (Autumn 2005), p 12, illus
COPIES: *Private collection
NOTES: The 'Index' incorrectly notes 'Soups' as starting on p 3; it starts on p 5.

Eclectic recipes

O276.1   1912
Eclectic recipes / tested and furnished / by / the ladies of the / Barton St. Methodist Church / Hamilton, Ontario / Published under the auspices of the / Mission Circle / 1912 / F.G. Smith, printer 107 West King St.
DESCRIPTION: 20.5 × 12.5 cm   Pp [i–ii], 1–34 [35–9] Thin card, with image on front of Barton Street Methodist Church, at the corner of Sanford Avenue and Barton Street; stapled
CONTENTS: i tp; ii ad; 1–34 recipes and ads; 35 ad; 36–8 blank for 'My Recipes'; 39 and inside back face of binding 'Wit and Humor'
COPIES: OBUJBM   OH (R641.5 ECL)   *Private collection

NOTES: The cover-title is 'Three Hundred Eclectic Recipes.'

The Electric Bean Chemical Company's calendar and household receipt book for 1912

See O261.1 for the company's 1911 issue.

O277.1   1912
Keep this book It is valuable / The Electric Bean / Chemical Company's / calendar and / household / receipt book for 1912 / also funnygrams, etc. / See $1,000 prize contest, page 16 / See that you get the coupon on page 14 / It is worth 10 cents / Electro Balm / for all / wounds / of the / flesh [cover-title]
DESCRIPTION: 20.0 × 14.5 cm   Pp 1–28 [leaves lacking]   Illus   Paper, with decorative border on front incorporating irises and two draped faces; stapled, and with hole punched at top left corner for hanging
CONTENTS: 1–28 text incorporating monthly calendars, ads for publ's products, and recipes
COPIES: *Private collection
NOTES: The company address, 226–8 Albert Street, Ottawa, is on p 2. The culinary text includes 'The Cook's Measures,' p 2, 'Kitchen Maxims,' p 3, and recipes on pp 3–4, 6–9, 12–14, and 19. A calendar for November is on p 28.

Garner's year book 1912

O278.1   1912
Hang me up in a handy place. I'm worth while. / Garner's / year book / 1912 / A valuable book / containing / tested recipes for tasty / dishes / Canadian facts, information / for your health. Also, a / monthly calendar and / birthday horoscope / A.W. Garner & Co. – St. Catharines, Ont. / 64 St. Paul St., opposite Queen St. / Phone 101 [cover-title]
DESCRIPTION: 18.0 × 13.5 cm   Pp [1] 2–32   Illus of astrological signs and symbols, illus headpieces for each monthly calendar   Paper
CONTENTS: 1 'Calendar for 1912. Eclipses – Standard Time,' 'The Twelve Signs of the Zodiac,' 'The Seasons,' and 'Morning and Evening Stars'; 2 'This Little Book'; 3–29 recipes, monthly calendars, monthly birthday horoscopes, and publ ads; 30 'Table of Weights and Measures' and 'Facts about Canada'; 31–2 'Household Hints'
COPIES: *OSTC (317.1351 Gar M)
NOTES: The recipes begin on p 3 under the heading 'Meats': Pork and Beans, How to Cook Young Chicken, Mock Duck, etc.

The Glengarry cook book

O279.1   26 December 1912
The / Glengarry / cook book. / Compiled by a few
of / the ladies of Glengarry / Glen Nevis, Ont., /
December 26th, 1912.
DESCRIPTION: About 20.0 × 14.5 cm [dimensions from
photocopy]   Pp [1–2] 3–43 [44]
CONTENTS: 1 tp; 2 'Contents'; 3–44 'Recipes' and at
bottom p 44, 'Printed at the News Job Press, Alexandria, Ont.'
COPIES: *OWINLM (979.1.3)
NOTES: The ladies of Glengarry County who compiled the cookbook are not identified by name. The
recipes are not credited. The text on the front of the
binding is in a floral border.

Halton Women's Institute cook book

O280.1   nd [about 1912]
Halton Women's Institute / cook book / Compiled
by the ladies of Halton County / District officers /
Mrs. Deverean, Pres. Mrs. R. Gorman, Vice-Pres. /
Mrs. Geo. Havil, Sec.-Treas. / Cook Book
Committee / [left column:] Mrs. W.C. Inglehart /
Mrs. W.J. McClenahan / Mrs. Robt. Gorman, /
Convener / [right column:] Mrs. E. Blanshard /
Miss M.G. Alton / Miss E. Hager, / Treasurer
DESCRIPTION: 22.0 × 15.5 cm   Stapled
COPIES: OGU (Rural Heritage Collection)   *Private
collection
NOTES: There are 128 numbered pages. The recipes
are credited with the name of the contributor. One of
the contributors is Mrs Edgar Williamson (Nut Bread
No. 6, p 68), who is a relative of the private collector
and who is known to have died on 29 January 1912.
The OGU copy is inscribed, on the title-page, '1912.'

Like O89.1, *The B.Y.P.U. Cook Book*, the Cook Book
Committee appears to have accepted all submissions
so that there are several variations of the same recipe,
numbered sequentially; for example, on pp 68–9, one
finds Nut Bread Nos. 3–10 and Walnut Bread No. 1
and No. 2.

This entry is based on information supplied by the
private collector. Although no printer is recorded in
her copy of the book, the owner believes that it was
printed by the *Burlingon Gazette*. Another private collector described her copy as 'Printed at Burlington
(Ontario) Gazette Office 1912.'

Helpful hints for housekeepers 1912

*See O263.1 for information about the company and other
issues of* Helpful Hints for Housekeepers.

O281.1   1912
1912 Volume II. 1912 / Hang me in the kitchen /
Helpful / hints / for housekeepers / Compliments
of / the Dodds Medicine Co. / Limited / Toronto,
Can. [cover-title]
DESCRIPTION: 17.0 × 11.5 cm   Pp 1–32   Paper;
stapled, and with hole punched at top left corner,
through which runs a string for hanging
CONTENTS: Inside front face of binding 'Volume II'
[introductory text]; 1 'Every Day Uses of Salt'; 2 'Uses
of Borax' and 'Uses of Ammonia'; 3 'Understand the
Subject'; 4, 6 'Uses of Soda' and 'Points for the
Kitchen'; 5 'Unconscious Health'; 7 'The Cost of Failing Health'; 8 'Removal of Stains'; 9 'Nature Cures';
10, 12 'Things Worth Remembering'; 11 'The Aching
Spot'; 13 'What to Shun'; 14 'Points in Laundering';
15 'A Seeming Paradox'; 16 'Ironing'; 17 'About Rheumatism'; 18 'Care of Flowers'; 19 'Insidious Disease';
20 'The Sewing Room'; 21 'Mysterious But True'; 22
'The Bedroom'; 23 'The Sentinel Off Guard'; 24 'The
Sickroom'; 25 'The Records of History'; 26 'Nursery';
27 'The Most Practical System'; 28 'Care of Furniture'; 29 'Diamond Dinner Pills'; 30 'Weights and
Measures' [for the kitchen]; 31 'Dodd's Dyspepsia
Tablets'; 32 'Comparative Value of Foods'; inside back
face 'Self Examination Page'
COPIES: *OTUTF (uncat patent medicine)
NOTES: The introductory text refers to the date of the
first issue: 'The first number of Household Hints issued in 1911 was such an immediate success ... that
the Dodds Medicine Co., Limited decided to make it
an annual publication.'

Herrick, Christine Terhune (1859–1944)

*For information about this American author's famous
mother, who wrote under the pseudonym Marion
Harland, see O18.1.*

O282.1   [copyright 1912]
[An edition of *Like My Mother Used to Make*, Toronto:
Bell and Cockburn, [copyright 1912 in the United
States of America by Dana Estes and Co.]]
COPIES: Private collection

AMERICAN EDITIONS: Boston: D. Estes and Co., [copy-
right 1912] (United States: DLC).

The Kootenay Range in your kitchen (?)

For information about McClary's and its cookbooks, see O162.1.

O283.1 nd [about 1912]
[Lacks tp and/or binding]
DESCRIPTION: 16.5 × 11.5 cm Pp 3–22 Illus orange-and-black Lacks paper(?) binding; stapled
CONTENTS: 3 'The Kootenay Range in Your Kitchen'; 4 'Burnished Top'; 5 'Great Capacity'; 6 'Convenient Reservoir'; 7 'Washable Oven'; 8 'Perfect Cooking'; 9 'Semi-Steel Linings'; 10 'Cooking by Thermometer'; 11 'A Kootenay Range Makes Fuel Bills Smaller!'; 12 'And Now!' and 'More Features'; 13–19 'Selected Recipes "à la Kootenay"'; 20–2 'Cookery Hints'
COPIES: *BVIPM
NOTES: 'The Kootenay Range in Your Kitchen' states: 'This booklet comes into your hands because you were interested enough to send for it. If it results in your getting a Kootenay Range, you will be well repaid. Twenty years ago or thereabouts, the first Kootenay Range was put on the market, ... it soon became one of the most successful ranges in Canada, ... If you will let the nearest McClary dealer demonstrate the Kootenay Range ...' The illustrated ranges bear the name 'McClary's' and the illustration on p 10 of a thermometer has 'McClary's stoves // leaders for 65 years ... London, Canada.' Since McClary's was founded in London, Ontario, in 1847, the cookbook was published about 1912 (1847 + 65 years).

London cook book

O284.1 1912
London cook book / Collected and compiled by / the Ladies' Aid of / Dundas Centre Methodist Church / London, Ont. / February, 1912 / The Ladies' Aid wish to thank most cordially all who have / assisted them in any way in getting out this book, which they / hope will prove of practical assistance to all who are interested / in the "good food" problem. / London, Ont. / A. Talbot & Co., printers and publishers / 1912
DESCRIPTION: 16.5 × 12.0 cm Pp [1–3] 4–73, [i–xxi] Cloth
CONTENTS: 1 tp; 2 'Weights and Measures' and 'Index' [i.e., table of contents]; 3–73 recipes credited with the name of the contributor; i–xxi ads
COPIES: OLDUCA OLU *Private collection
NOTES: The Pumpkin Pie recipe on p 31 is in verse.

Magic cook book and housekeepers guide

E.W. Gillett Co. was incorporated in 1902 (see Canadian Grocer *Vol. 16, No. 11 (14 March 1902), p 38), and its Toronto factory at the corner of Fraser Avenue and Liberty Street was built in 1912. Since all the earliest undated and unnumbered editions of* Magic Cook Book and Housekeepers Guide *include an illustration of the 1912 factory on the inside back face of the binding, they were published about 1912 or slightly later. It is possible that the first edition appeared after April 1916 because a full-page advertisement for Gillett products in the April 1916 issue of* Canadian Home Journal *does not mention the cookbook. All subsequent editions, except O285.20, were published before 27 August 1929, when Standard Brands Ltd was incorporated and took over Gillett products. There is an advertisement for* Magic Cook Book and Housekeepers Guide *on the outside back face of the* Farmer's Advocate *of 10 December 1925. An advertisement for* Magic Baking Powder *in* Canadian Home Journal *Vol. 25, No. 8 (December 1928), p 38, has a coupon for ordering a free copy of* Magic Cook Book and Housekeepers Guide. *Although it is not possible to know which editions are being advertised, one or more of the editions described below must have been published about 1925 or 1928.*

The editions can be roughly arranged by the image on the binding, in the following order: one male chef with beard and moustache, holding up a container of Magic Baking Powder in his left hand; five stout male chefs, marching one behind the other and each holding up a container of Magic Baking Powder; five bug-like creatures marching one behind the other, the last four carrying prepared dishes, the first carrying a container of Magic Baking Powder; and one stout male chef with an over-size head, holding up Magic Baking Powder in his right hand, spoon in his left (pls 6a–d).

For other publications promoting Magic Baking Powder, see: O470.1, The Magic Way; *O702.1,* The Magic Cook Book; *and Q207.3 and Q207.4,* Magic Cook Book *and* Le pâtissier Magic. *For other cookbooks from E.W. Gillett Co., see: O130.5 and O130.6, editions of* The New Cook Book *edited by Mrs Grace Elizabeth Denison; O369.1,* Royal Yeast Bake Book; *and O418.1,* War Time Cookery. *E.W. Gillett Co. also published an undated 16-page booklet called* A Little History of Baking, *which covers the subject from prehistory, through biblical times, to the present, and ends with a discussion of the superiority of Magic Baking Powder (Private collection).*

O285.1 unnumbered ed., nd [about 1912 or later]
The Magic / cook book. / A collection of / selected

recipes / suitable for home / cooking, also / various useful / hints to house- / keepers. / [printer's union label] / Published by / E.W. Gillett / Company Limited / Toronto, Ont. / Chicago[,?] Ill London, Eng[.?]

DESCRIPTION: 14.5 × 8.5 cm   Pp [i–ii], 1–59 [60–2]   Paper, with image on front of a male chef with beard and moustache, holding up a container of Magic Baking Powder; stapled

CONTENTS: i tp; ii 'Introduction' dedicating the book to the 'housewives of Canada'; 1–13 'Cake'; 14–16 'Bread and Rolls'; 17–mid 24 'Puddings'; bottom 24–mid 31 'Other Desserts and Sauces'; mid 31–33 'Preserves and Jellies'; 34–top 35 'Candies'; mid–bottom 35 'Mince Meat'; 36–top 38 'Pickles and Catsups'; mid 38 'Salads'; bottom 38–top 40 'Potatoes'; mid 40–mid 41 'Entrees, etc.'; mid 41–mid 46 'Soup'; mid 46–mid 50 'Fish'; mid 50–52 'How to Warm Over Cold Fragments'; 53–mid 55 'For the Sick'; mid 55–57 'Toilet Recipes'; 58 'Things to Remember' and 'Household Hints'; 59 'Weights and Measures'; 60–2 index

COPIES: *AEPMA (H86.43.696)   OKITJS (991.23.8)

NOTES: O285.1 and O285.2 are the only editions with a proper title-page. The cover-title is 'Magic Cook Book / and / Housekeepers Guide. / Published by / E.W. Gillett / Company Limited / Toronto, Ont.' On the inside back face of the binding of the AEPMA copy there is an illustration of the Gillett factory and the following text: 'Where Gillett's goods are made. Established 1852. The largest, cleanest, and best equipped factory of the kind in British America.' The year the factory was erected is not recorded.

The OKITJS copy lacks its binding. OFERWM has a copy (A1977.26.44a) that lacks the binding and pp i–ii and 61–2; since 'Bread and Rolls' starts on p 14, it is probably the edition described here or O285.2.

OOWM has a copy (980.141.14) which shares features of O285.1 and O285.2. Page i is the same as O285.1 except that it has a paragraph added after 'hints to house- / keepers.': 'If you already have a / Magic Cook Book, / kindly hand this copy to / a friend.' Although the added paragraph is the same as O285.2, the places of publication – Toronto, Chicago, and London, England – are as O285.1. Page ii has the same 'Introduction' as O285.1.

O285.2   unnumbered ed., nd [about 1912 or later]
—The Magic / cook book. / A collection of / selected recipes / suitable for home / cooking, also / various useful / hints to house- / keepers. / If you already have a / Magic Cook Book, / kindly

hand this copy to / a friend. / [printer's union label] / Published by / E.W. Gillett / Company Limited / Toronto, Ont. / Winnipeg. Montreal.

DESCRIPTION: 14.5 × 8.5 cm   Pp [i–ii], 1–59 [60–2]   Paper, with image on front of a male chef with beard and moustache, holding up a container of Magic Baking Powder; stapled

CONTENTS: i tp; ii publ ad; 1–13 'Cake'; 14–16 'Bread and Rolls'; 17–mid 24 'Puddings'; bottom 24–mid 31 'Other Desserts and Sauces'; mid 31–33 'Preserves and Jellies'; 34–top 35 'Candies'; mid–bottom 35 'Mince Meat'; 36–top 38 'Pickles and Catsups'; mid 38 'Salads'; bottom 38–top 40 'Potatoes'; mid 40–mid 41 'Entrees, etc.'; mid 41–mid 46 'Soup'; mid 46–mid 50 'Fish'; mid 50–52 'How to Warm Over Cold Fragments'; 53–mid 55 'For the Sick'; mid 55–57 'Toilet Recipes'; 58 'Things to Remember' and 'Household Hints'; 59 'Weights and Measures'; 60–2 index and at bottom p 62, dedication to the 'housewives of Canada'

COPIES: *BDEM

NOTES: Page i is the same as O285.1, except for the paragraph added after 'hints to house- / keepers.' and the places of publication – Toronto, Winnipeg, and Montreal. The cover-title is 'Magic Cook Book / and / Housekeepers Guide. / Published by / E.W. Gillett / Company Limited / Toronto, Ont.' Unlike O285.1, which has an 'Introduction' on p ii, here there is an advertisement for Magic Baking Powder emphasizing that it contains no alum. The dedication to the housewives of Canada is now on p 62. On the inside back face of the binding there is an illustration of the Gillett factory, but the year the factory was erected is not recorded.

O285.3   unnumbered ed., nd [about 1912 or later]
—Magic cook book / and / housekeepers guide. / Published by / E.W. Gillett / Company Limited / Toronto, Ont. [cover-title]

DESCRIPTION: 15.0 × 8.5 cm   Pp [i–ii], 1–59 [60–2]   Paper, with image on front of a male chef with beard and moustache, holding up a container of Magic Baking Powder; stapled

CONTENTS: i 'The Magic Cook Book,' dedication to 'the housewives of Canada,' and 'Published by E.W. Gillett Company Limited Toronto, Ont. Winnipeg Montreal'; ii ad for Magic Baking Powder; 1–top 15 'Cake'; mid 15–mid 18 'Bread and Rolls'; bottom 18–mid 25 'Puddings'; bottom 25–top 32 'Other Desserts and Sauces'; mid 32–mid 34 'Preserves and Jellies'; mid 34–mid 35 'Candies'; bottom 35–mid 36 'Mince Meat'; mid 36–38 'Pickles and Catsups'; top 39–mid

39 'Salads'; mid 39–mid 40 'Potatoes'; mid 40–mid 42 'Entrees, etc.'; bottom 42–mid 47 'Soup'; bottom 47–near bottom 51 'Fish'; bottom 51–53 'How to Warm Over Cold Fragments'; 54–top 56 'For the Sick'; mid 56–57 'Toilet Recipes'; 58 'Things to Remember' and 'Household Hints'; 59 'Weights and Measures'; 60–2 index

COPIES: AEPRAC QMM (RBD ckbk 1601) Company collection (Nabisco Brands Ltd, Toronto, Ont.) *Private collection

NOTES: In O285.1 and O285.2 'Bread and Rolls' begins on p 14; here 'Bread and Rolls' starts middle p 15.

See pl 6a. On the inside back face of the binding of the private collector's copy there is an illustration of the Gillett factory, oriented on the page in the same direction as the text, which reads, 'Where Gillett's goods are made. [illustration of factory] Established 1852 The largest, cleanest, and best equipped factory of the kind in British America.' No year is recorded for the erection of the factory. On the outside back face there is an illustration of a container of baking powder on which 'New Style Label' is printed. The Nabisco Brands Ltd copy matches this variation.

The same collector has another copy, which is identical except for the binding, where, on the inside back face, the illustration of the factory is larger and has been turned 90° so that it faces the gutter, and the text reads, 'Plant of E.W. Gillett Co. Ltd., Toronto, Ont. Erected 1912'; on the outside face, the baking powder container label reads, 'Contains no alum,' not 'New Style Label.' The AEPRAC copy matches this variation.

MAUAM and OGU (CCC TX715.6 M35 cover a) have copies where, in place of the dedication to 'the housewives of Canada' on p i, there is a note about 'Full weight 1 lb. cans Magic Baking Powder sell for 25c. ...'; the dedication to housewives is at the end of the index, on p 62.

O285.4 unnumbered ed., nd [after 24 January 1914] —['Magic' obscured by museum label] cook book / and / housekeepers guide. / Published by / E.W. Gillett / Company Limited / Toronto, On[paper torn] [cover-title]

DESCRIPTION: Pp [i–ii], 1–59 [60–2] Paper, with image on front of a male chef with beard and moustache, holding up a container of Magic Baking Powder; stapled

CONTENTS: i 'The Magic Cook Book // A collection of selected recipes suitable for home cooking, ... This little cook book is respectfully dedicated to the housewives of Canada ...' signed E.W. Gillett Co. Ltd, double

rule at about the middle of the page, followed by 'Magic Baking Powder Contains No Alum ...'; ii 'Beware of Fake Baking Powder Tests' with quotations dated September 1913 and 24 January 1914; 1–'Cake'; ...; bottom 51–53 'How to Warm Over Cold Fragments'; ...; 60–2 index

COPIES: *QSH (0439)

NOTES: On the inside back face of the binding, the illustration of the factory faces the gutter, and the text reads, 'Plant of E.W. Gillett Co. Ltd., Toronto, Ont. Erected 1912.'

O285.5 unnumbered ed., nd [after 24 January 1914] —Magic / cook book / and / housekeepers guide / Published by / E.W. Gillett Co. Ltd. / Toronto, Ont. / Winnipeg, Montreal. [cover-title]

DESCRIPTION: 15.0 × 8.5 cm Pp [i–ii], 1–59 [60–2] Paper, with image on front of five stout male chefs, marching one behind the other and each holding up a container of Magic Baking Powder; stapled

CONTENTS: i 'The Magic Cook Book // A collection of selected recipes suitable for home cooking, ...' signed E.W. Gillett Co. Ltd and 'Magic Baking Powder contains no alum ...'; ii 'Beware of Fake Baking Powder Tests' with quotations dated September 1913 and 24 January 1914; 1–top 15 'Cake'; mid 15–mid 18 'Bread and Rolls'; mid 18–mid 25 'Puddings'; mid 25–mid 32 'Other Desserts and Sauces'; mid 32–mid 34 'Preserves and Jellies'; mid 34–mid 35 'Candies'; bottom 35–mid 36 'Mince Meat'; mid 36–38 'Pickles and Catsups'; top–mid 39 'Salads'; bottom 39–mid 40 'Potatoes'; mid 40–mid 42 'Entrees, etc.'; bottom 42–mid 47 'Soup'; bottom 47–near bottom 51 'Fish'; bottom 51–53 'How to Warm Over Cold Fragments'; 54–top 56 'For the Sick'; mid 56–57 'Toilet Recipes'; 58 'Things to Remember' and 'Household Hints'; 59 'Weights and Measures'; 60–2 index

COPIES: APROM OONL (TX715 C3465 No. 2) OWTU (E0925) *Private collection

NOTES: Here, there are five stout male chefs and three cities in the cover-title: Toronto, Winnipeg, and Montreal. In this edition, unlike O285.6, the company name precedes the statement about alum on p i, and there are dated quotations on p ii.

There are copies at NBFKL and SSWD that match the above description except for the cover-title, where there is a period, not a comma, after Winnipeg. A copy at OHALM (984.25.51) may match the one catalogued here.

O285.6 unnumbered ed., nd [1917 or later]
—Magic / cook book / and / housekeepers guide / Published by / E.W. Gillett Co. Ltd. / Toronto, Ont. / Winnipeg. Montreal. [cover-title]
DESCRIPTION: 14.5 × 8.5 cm   Pp [i–ii], 1–59 [60–2] Paper, with image on front of five stout male chefs, marching one behind the other and each holding up a container of Magic Baking Powder; stapled
CONTENTS: i 'The Magic Cook Book // A collection of selected recipes suitable for home cooking, ...,' 'Magic Baking Powder contains no alum,' and at bottom, 'E.W. Gillett Company Limited.'; ii 'Beware of Fake Baking Powder Tests'; 1–top 15 'Cake'; mid 15–mid 18 'Bread and Rolls'; mid 18–mid 25 'Puddings'; mid 25–mid 32 'Other Desserts and Sauces'; mid 32–mid 34 'Preserves and Jellies'; mid 34–mid 35 'Candies'; bottom 35–mid 36 'Mince Meat'; mid 36–38 'Pickles and Catsups'; top–mid 39 'Salads'; bottom 39–mid 40 'Potatoes'; mid 40–mid 42 'Entrees, etc.'; bottom 42–mid 47 'Soup'; bottom 47–near bottom 51 'Fish'; bottom 51–53 'How to Warm Over Cold Fragments'; 54–top 56 'For the Sick'; mid 56–57 'Toilet Recipes'; 58 'Things to Remember' and 'Household Hints'; 59 'Weights and Measures'; 60–2 index
COPIES: OTYA (CPC 19-? 0042)   OWTU (E0894)   *Private collection
NOTES: Unlike O285.5, the company name follows the statement about alum on p i, and although there are no dated quotations, p ii quotes Bulletin No. 360, Inland Revenue Department, Ottawa, by A. McGill – an item (CIHM 97587) dated 17 January 1917.

O285.7 unnumbered ed., nd [1917 or later]
—Livre de cuisine / Magic / et / guide des ménagère's. / Publié par / E.W. Gillett Co. Ltd. / Toronto, Ont. / Winnipeg. Montreal. [cover-title]
DESCRIPTION: 14.5 × 9.0 cm   Pp [i–ii], 1–74 [75–8] Paper, with image on front of five stout male chefs, marching one behind the other and each holding up a container of Magic Baking Powder; stapled
CONTENTS: Inside front face of binding 'Les produits de Gillett sont les meilleurs'; i 'Le livre de cuisine Magic // Une collection de recettes choisies pour la cuisine domestique, ... Ce petit livre de cuisine est respectueusement dédié aux ménagères du Canada ...,' 'La poudre à pâte Magic ne contient pas d'alun ...,' and at bottom, 'E.W. Gillett Co. Ltd.'; ii–mid 1 'Méfiez-vous des démonstrations de fausses poudre à pâte'; mid 1–mid 20 untitled section of recipes described in 'Table' as 'gâteaux' and 'pain et petits pains'; mid 20–mid 30 'Puddings'; mid 30–top 39 'Autres desserts et sauces'; near top 39–top 42 'Confitures et gelées'; near top 42–mid 43 'Confise-

ries'; mid 43–mid 44 'Mince Meat'; mid 44–mid 47 'Marinades et catsups'; mid–bottom 47 'Salades'; 48–9 'Patates'; 50–mid 51 'Entrées, etc.'; mid 51–mid 57 'Soupe'; mid 57–mid 62 'Poissons'; mid 62–mid 66 'Comment on accommode les restes'; mid 66–mid 69 'Pour les malades'; mid 69–72 'Recettes de toilette'; 73 'Choses à se rappeler' and 'Conseils à la ménagère' 74 'Poids et mesures' 75–7 'Table'; 78 publ ad
COPIES: *QMM (RBD ckbk 1818)   QMBN (181019 CON)
NOTES: Like O285.6, the quotations on p ii are not dated, but Bulletin No. 360 is quoted.

O285.8 [6th ed., nd, about 1920]
—Livre de cuisine / Magic / et / guide des ménagère's. / Publié par / E.W. Gillett Co. Ltd. / Toronto, Canada / Winnipeg. Montreal. [cover-title]
DESCRIPTION: Paper, with image on front of five stout male chefs, marching one behind the other and each holding up a container of Magic Baking Powder; stapled
CONTENTS: [First page] 'Form 405. 6th edition – 256620. Le livre de cuisine Magic // Une collection de recettes choisies pour la cuisine domestique, ... Ce petit livre de cuisine est respectueusement dédié aux ménagères du Canada ...,' 'La poudre à pâte Magic ne contient pas d'alun ...,' and at bottom, 'E.W. Gillett Co. Ltd.'
COPIES: *Private collection

O285.9 [8th ed., nd, about 1921]
—Magic / cook book / and / housekeepers guide / Published by / E.W. Gillett Co. Ltd. / Toronto, Canada / Winnipeg. Montreal. [cover-title]
DESCRIPTION: 14.5 × 8.5 cm   Pp [1] 2–61 [62–4] Paper, with image on front of five stout male chefs, marching one behind the other and each holding up a container of Magic Baking Powder; stapled
CONTENTS: 1 '8th edition – 504721 The Magic Cook Book // A collection of selected recipes suitable for home cooking, ... This little cook book is respectfully dedicated to the housewives of Canada ...,' 'Magic Baking Powder contains no alum ...,' and at bottom, 'E.W. Gillett Company Limited.'; 2–3 'Beware of Fake Baking Powder Tests'; 4–16 'Cake'; 17–20 'Bread and Rolls'; 21–6 'Puddings'; 27–33 'Other Desserts and Sauces'; 34–mid 36 'Preserves and Jellies'; bottom 36 'Mince Meat'; 37 'Candies'; 38–mid 40 'Pickles and Catsups'; mid 40–41 'Salads'; 42 'Potatoes'; 43–5 'Entrees, etc.'; 46–9 'Soup'; 50–top 53 'Fish'; mid 53–54 'How to Warm Over Cold Fragments'; 55–top 61 'Recipes for Invalids'; mid–bottom 61 'Toilet Recipes'; 62–4 index

COPIES: BNEM OGM (975.16.32) OGU (CCC TX715.6 M35 cover b) Company collection (Nabisco Brands Ltd, Toronto, Ont.) *Private collection
NOTES: Unlike the ninth edition and some other later numbered editions, there is no number at the top left corner of p 62.

The Nabisco Brands Ltd copy has '8th edition – 5610120' on p 1. OGM, OGU, and two other private collectors have copies with '8th edition – 50121520.' The BNEM copy has '8th edition – 509120.' Another private collector's copy has '8th edition – 504721.'

SWSLM has a copy that lacks the first leaf, but which appears to match the description here.

O285.10 [9th ed., about 1923]
—Magic / cook book / and / housekeepers guide / Published by / E.W. Gillett Co. Ltd. / Toronto, Canada / Winnipeg. Montreal. [cover-title]
DESCRIPTION: 14.5 × 8.5 cm Pp [1] 2–61 [62–4] Paper, with image on front of five stout male chefs, marching one behind the other and each holding up a container of Magic Baking Powder; stapled
CONTENTS: 1 '9th edition – 10011120 The Magic Cook Book,' dedication 'to the housewives of Canada,' information about Magic Baking Powder, and at bottom, 'E.W. Gillett Company Limited'; 2–3 'Beware of Fake Baking Powder Tests'; 4–16 'Cake'; 17–20 'Bread and Rolls'; 21–6 'Puddings'; 27–33 'Other Desserts and Sauces'; 34–mid 36 'Preserves and Jellies'; bottom 36 'Mince Meat'; 37 'Candies'; 38–mid 40 'Pickles and Catsups'; mid 40–41 'Salads'; 42 'Potatoes'; 43–5 'Entrees, etc.'; 46–9 'Soup'; 50–top 53 'Fish'; mid 53–54 'How to Warm Over Cold Fragments'; 55–top 61 'Recipes for Invalids'; mid–bottom 61 'Toilet Recipes'; 62–4 index and at top left of p 62, '61923'
COPIES: BNEM ONM *Private collection
NOTES: This ninth edition has five stout chefs on the binding (see pl 6b); another edition numbered ninth (O285.11) has five bug-like creatures.

The ONM copy is exactly as the private collector's copy catalogued here, i.e., '9th edition – 10011120' on p 1 and '61923' on p 62. The same private collector has a second copy with '9th edition – 7511120' on p 1 and '28823' on p 62. The BNEM copy has '9th edition – 7511120' on p 1 (p 62 not checked). SBIM has a copy with '9th edition – 508122' on p 1 and '722' on p 62. Another private collector has a copy with '9th edition – 5051920' on p 1 and no number on p 62.

O285.11 [9th ed., about 1925]
—Magic / cook book / and / housekeepers guide / Published by / E.W. Gillett Co. Ltd. / Toronto, Canada / Winnipeg. Montreal. [cover-title]

DESCRIPTION: 14.5 × 8.5 cm Pp [1] 2–61 [62–4] Paper, with image on front of five bug-like creatures marching one behind the other, the last four carrying prepared dishes, the first carrying a container of Magic Baking Powder; stapled
CONTENTS: 1 '9th edition – 5011120' and information about Magic Baking Powder; 2–3 'Beware of Fake Baking Powder Tests'; 4 'Valuable Suggestions'; 5–61 recipes; 62–4 index and at top right of p 64, '75425'
COPIES: AMHM *NBFKL (Ruth Spicer Cookbook Collection) OGU (CCC TX715.6 M35 cover c) OKIT OWTU (E1010) SBIM SSWD
NOTES: All the copies listed above have '9th edition – 5011120' on p 1. Only the number at the back of the book differs: The AMHM and SBIM copies have '75524' on p 62; SSWD has '75824' on p 62; OGU, OKIT, and OWTU have '75824,' but on p 64.

APROM has a copy that lacks its binding; however, like the NBFKL copy catalogued here, it has '9th edition – 5011120' on p 1 and '75425' on p 64. ONBNBM has a copy that lacks its binding; like the SSWD copy, it has '9th edition – 5011120' on p 1 and '75824' on p 62. A copy at ACG is incomplete, having only pp 3–62; however, like the AMHM and SBIM copies, it has '75524' on p 62.

O285.12 [10th ed., about 1925]
—Magic / cook book / and / housekeepers guide / Published by / E.W. Gillett Co. Ltd. / Toronto, Canada / Winnipeg. Montreal. [cover-title]
DESCRIPTION: 14.5 × 9.0 cm Pp [1] 2–62 [63–4] Paper, with image on front of five bug-like creatures marching one behind the other (see plate 6c), the last four carrying prepared dishes, the first carrying a container of Magic Baking Powder; stapled
CONTENTS: '10th edition – 5011120 Magic Baking Powder contains no alum' followed by information about Magic Baking Powder, and at bottom, 'E.W. Gillett Company Limited'; 2–3 'Beware of Fake Baking Powder Tests'; 4 'Valuable Suggestions'; 5–62 recipes; 63–4 index and at top right of p 64, '501225'
COPIES: BBVM BVAMM ONM QSH (0441) *Private collection
NOTES: All the copies listed above have '10th edition – 5011120' on p 1, but the number on p 64 differs: the BBVM and BVAMM copies have '50326'; the ONM copy has '50226'; another private collector's copy has '50126'; I did not note the number for QSH.

QKB (87-74) has a copy of the tenth edition ('10th edition – 5011120' on p 1 and '37526' on p 64); however, its binding features the image of the stout chef found in O285.14 onward. NBFKL and OONL (TX715 C3465 No. 1 reserve copy 1) also have a copy of the tenth edition ('10th edition – 5011120' on p 1) where the binding features the stout chef; the OONL copy has '2851726' on p 64.

O285.13   nd [about 1925]
—Livre culinaire / Magic / et / guide des ménagères. / Publié par / E.W. Gill[e]tt Co. Ltd. / Toron[to, Cana]da. / Winnipeg. [Montr]eal. [cover-title]
DESCRIPTION: 14.5 × 8.5 cm   Pp [1] 2–62 [63–4]   Paper, with image on front of five bug-like creatures marching one behind the other, the last four carrying prepared dishes, the first carrying a container of Magic Baking Powder; stapled
CONTENTS: 1 'Form 405-25112625 La poudre à pâte Magique ne contient pas d'alun' followed by information about Magic Baking Powder, and at bottom, 'E.W. Gillett Company Limited'; 2–3 'Méfiez-vous des épreuves frauduleuses de poudre à pâte'; 4–17 'Gâteaux'; 18–top 22 'Pain et rouleaux'; near top 22–mid 28 'Pudding'; mid 28–mid 35 'Autres desserts et sauces'; mid 35–top 38 'Confitures et gelées'; mid 38 'Mince Meat'; bottom 38–mid 39 'Bonbons'; bottom 39–mid 42 'Conserves au vinaigre'; mid 42–top 44 'Salades'; mid 44–top 45 'Pommes de terre'; mid 45–46 'Entrées, etc.'; 47–top 48 'Hors d'oeuvres'; near top 48–mid 51 'Potages'; bottom 51–top 55 'Poisson'; mid 55–56 'Comment utiliser des restes froids'; 57–62 'Recettes pour des invalides'; 63–mid 64 'Table' and at bottom p 64, information about La poudre à pâte Magique
COPIES: *Company collection (Nabisco Brands Ltd, Toronto, Ont.)

O285.14   nd [about 1926]
—Livre culinaire / Magic / [...] / La cie. E.W. Gillett ltee. / [...] [cover-title]
DESCRIPTION: Paper, with image on front of a stout male chef with over-size head holding up a container of baking powder in his right hand, spoon in his left; stapled
CONTENTS: [First page] 'Form 405-509326 La poudre à pâte Magique ne contient pas d'alun' followed by information about Magic Baking Powder, and at bottom, 'E.W. Gillett Company Limited'
COPIES: *Private collection
NOTES: The first page of text is identical to O285.13, except for the form number. Whereas O285.13 has the five bug-like creatures on the binding, this copy has the one stout chef.

O285.15   nd [about 1926]
—Magic / cook book / and / housekeepers guide / Published by / E.W. Gillett Company Limited / Toronto, Canada / Vancouver – Winnipeg – Ottawa – Montreal – Quebec [cover-title]
DESCRIPTION: 14.5 × 8.5 cm   Pp [1] 2–62 [63–4]   2 illus on p 1 of scraping excess powder off a spoon and of a measuring cup   Paper, with image on front of a stout male chef with over-size head holding up a container of baking powder in his right hand, spoon in his left; stapled
CONTENTS: 1 'All Measurements Level,' 'Weights and Measures,' 'Baking Time and Temperatures,' and 'E.W. Gillett Company Limited Toronto 2, Canada.'; 2–3 'Beware of Fake Baking Powder Tests'; 4 'Valuable Suggestions'; 5–21 'Cakes'; 22–mid 24 'Bread and Rolls'; bottom 24–30 'Puddings'; 31–mid 37 'Other Desserts and Sauces'; bottom 37–mid 40 'Preserves and Jellies'; bottom 40–top 41 'Mince Meat'; mid–bottom 41 'Candies'; 42–mid 44 'Pickles and Catsups'; bottom 44–45 'Salads'; 46 'Potatoes'; 47–9 'Entrees, etc.'; 50–top 54 'Soup'; mid 54–56 'Fish'; 57–8 'How to Warm Over Cold Fragments'; 59–top 62 'Recipes for Invalids'; mid–bottom 62 'Household Recipes'; 63–4 index and at top p 64, '2851726'
COPIES: *BSUM   OWTU (E0923)
NOTES: This edition and O285.16, its French-language counterpart, are distinguished by the illustrations on p 1. Unlike earlier, numbered English-language editions, such as O285.9 and O285.10, 'Bread and Rolls' begins on p 22, not p 17.
   The BSUM copy lacks the back face of the binding. The OWTU copy has 'Form No. 404-7512326' at top p 64.

O285.16   nd [about 1926]
—Livre culinaire / Magic / et / guide des ménagères. / Publié par / La cie. E.W. Gillett ltee. / Toronto, Canada / Vancouver – Winnipeg – Ottawa – Montreal – Quebec [cover-title]
DESCRIPTION: 14.5 × 8.5 cm   Pp [1] 2–62 [63–4]   2 illus on p 1 of scraping excess powder off a spoon and of a measuring cup   Paper, with image on front of a stout male chef with over-size head holding up a container of Magic Baking Powder in his right hand, spoon in his left; stapled
CONTENTS: 1 'Toutes les mesures sont à niveau,' 'Poids et mesures,' 'Temps et températures,' and 'La cie. E.W. Gillett ltée. Toronto 2, Canada.'; 2–3 'Méfiez-vous des épreuves frauduleuses de poudre à pâte'; 4–17 'Gâteaux'; 18–top 22 'Pain et rouleaux'; mid 22–mid 28 'Pudding'; mid 28–mid 35 'Autres desserts et

sauces'; mid 35–top 38 'Confitures et gelées'; mid 38 'Mince Meat (de tante Marie)'; bottom 38–mid 39 'Bonbons'; bottom 39–mid 42 'Conserves au vinaigre'; mid 42–top 44 'Salades'; mid 44–top 45 'Pommes de terre'; mid 45–46 'Entrées, etc.'; 47–top 48 'Hors d'oeuvres'; near top 48–mid 51 'Potages'; bottom 51–top 55 'Poisson'; mid 55–56 'Comment utiliser des restes froids'; 57–top 60 'Recettes pour des invalides'; near top 60–62 'Bouillons et soupes'; 63–4 'Table' and publ ad, and at top p 64, 'Form 405-508326'
COPIES: *OKQ (F5012 1912 G479) OONL (TX715 C3465 No. 3 reserve) QSFFSC
NOTES: The OONL copy has 'Form 405-2091926' on p 64. The QSFFSC copy has 'Form 405-5012326.'

O285.17 nd [about 1927–9]
—Magic / cook book / and / housekeepers guide / Published by / E.W. Gillett Company Limited / Toronto, Canada / Vancouver – Winnipeg – Ottawa – Montreal – Quebec [cover-title]
DESCRIPTION: 14.5 × 8.5 cm Pp [1] 2–62 [63–4] Paper, with image on front of a stout male chef with over-size head holding up a container of Magic Baking Powder in his right hand, spoon in his left; stapled
CONTENTS: 1 'General Information' and at bottom, 'E.W. Gillett Company Limited Toronto 2, Canada.'; 2–3 'Beware of Fake Baking Powder Tests'; 4 'Valuable Suggestions'; 5–21 'Cakes'; 22–mid 24 'Bread and Rolls'; bottom 24–30 'Puddings'; 31–mid 37 'Other Desserts and Sauces'; bottom 37–mid 40 'Preserves and Jellies'; bottom 40 'Mince Meat'; top 41 'Mint Sauce'; mid–bottom 41 'Candies'; 42–mid 44 'Pickles and Catsups'; bottom 44–45 'Salads'; 46 'Potatoes'; 47–9 'Entrees, etc.'; 50–top 54 'Soup'; mid 54–56 'Fish'; 57–8 'How to Warm Over Cold Fragments'; 59–top 62 'Recipes for Invalids'; mid–bottom 62 'Household Recipes'; 63–4 index
COPIES: ACG AEUCHV (UV 85.258.1) APROM BTCA (77.71) MAUAM MSOHM MWPA (MG14 C50 McKnight, Ethel) OAYM OGU (2 copies: CCC TX715.6 M35 cover d, cover d1) OONL (TX715 C3465 No. 1 reserve copy 2) OPEMO OPETCM OWTU (2 copies: E0922, E0924) QKB (2 copies: 92-12, 87-74) SBIM *Private collection
NOTES: Unlike earlier English-language editions, O285.17 and O285.20 have 'General Information' on p 1 and Mint Sauce on p 41, before 'Candies.'

Different numbers appear at top p 64 in the various copies: 404-10032127 (ACG); Form No. 404-10071829 (AEUCHV, OGU cover d1); Form 404-10041327 (APROM); Form No. 404-1005629 (BTCA); Form No. 404-5841229 (MSOHM); Form 404-

10072827 (MWPA, OPEMO); Form No. 404-100728 (OAYM, OONL); Form 404-752927 (OGU cover d); Form 404-10032127 (OWTU E0922); Form No. 404-100928 (OWTU E0924 and QKB 92-12); Form No. 404-5841229 (QKB 87-74); Form No. 404-12531329 (SBIM); Form No. 404-100528 (MAUAM); Form No. 404-10021129 (another private collector's copy); Form No. 404-10022527 (bookseller's stock).

The text on the inside front face of the binding also varies. In the private collector's copy catalogued here, and in that at MWPA and OPETCM, the text, which is in one double-ruled box, begins, 'A better cake usually results if, ...' In the copies at AEUCHV, BTCA, MAUAM, MSOHM, OGU (cover d1), OWTU (E0924), QKB (92-12), and SBIM, the text is in two separate boxes, the first titled, 'A Better Cake,' and the second, 'How to Open Any Can of Magic Baking Powder.' In the ACG, OGU (cover d), and OWTU (E0922) copies, the text begins, 'For best results hold batter 20 minutes before baking ...' In a copy in a bookseller's stock, the text begins, 'The Magic Cook Book // A collection of selected recipes ...'

O285.18 nd [about 1927]
—Livre culinaire / Magic / et / guide des ménagères. / Publié par / La cie. E.W. Gillett ltée. / Toronto, Canada / Vancouver – Winnipeg – Ottawa – Montreal – Quebec [cover-title]
DESCRIPTION: 14.5 × 8.5 cm Pp [1] 2–62 [63–4] Paper, with image on front of a stout male chef with over-size head holding up a container of Magic Baking Powder in his right hand, spoon in left; stapled
CONTENTS: 'Renseignements généraux' and at bottom, 'La cie. E.W. Gillett ltée. Toronto 2, Canada'; 2–3 'Méfiez-vous des épreuves frauduleuses de poudre à pâte'; 4–17 'Gâteaux'; 18–top 22 'Pain et rouleaux'; mid 22–mid 28 'Pudding'; mid 28–mid 35 'Autres desserts et sauces'; mid 35–top 38 'Confitures et gelées'; mid 38 'Mince Meat (de tante Marie)'; bottom 38–mid 39 'Bonbons'; bottom 39–mid 42 'Conserves au vinaigre'; mid 42–mid 44 'Salades'; mid 44–mid 45 'Pommes de terre'; mid 45–46 'Entrées, etc.'; 47–top 48 'Hors d'oeuvres'; mid 48–mid 51 'Potages'; mid 51–mid 55 'Poisson'; mid 55–56 'Comment utiliser des restes froids'; 57–62 'Recettes pour des invalides'; 63–4 'Table' and publ ad, and at top p 64, 'Form No. 405-100527'
COPIES: *QMBN (172442 CON) Private collection
NOTES: See pl 6d. In this French-language edition, p 1 is headed 'Renseignements généraux,' not 'Information générale' as in O285.19. The private collector's copy has 'Form No. 405-50326' on p 64.

O285.19   nd [about 1929]
—Livre culinaire / Magic / et / guide des ménagères. / Publié par / La cie. E.W. Gillett ltee. / Toronto, Canada / Vancouver – Winnipeg – Ottawa – Montreal – Quebec [cover-title]
DESCRIPTION: 14.5 × 8.5 cm   Pp [1] 2–62 [63–4]   Paper, with image on front of a stout male chef with over-size head holding up a container of Magic Baking Powder in his right hand, spoon in his left; stapled
CONTENTS: 'Information générale' and at bottom, 'La cie. E.W. Gillett ltée. Toronto 2, Canada'; 2–3 'Méfiez-vous des démonstrations de poudres à pâte'; 4 'Excellents conseils'; 5–mid 25 'Gâteaux'; bottom 25–28 'Pains et petits pains'; 29–mid 35 'Poudings'; bottom 35–42 'Autres desserts et sauces'; 43–6 'Conserves et gelées'; 47 'Salades'; 48 'Pommes de terre'; 49–mid 52 'Entrées, etc.'; mid 52–mid 55 'Soupes'; mid–bottom 55 'Hachis (Mince Meat)'; 56 'Sucreries'; 57–mid 60 'Marinades et catsups'; mid 60–62 'Recettes pour malades'; 63–4 'Table alphabétique des recettes' and at top p 64, 'Form No. 405-50129'
COPIES: *OTNY (uncat)
NOTES: In this French-language edition, p 1 is headed 'Information générale.'

O285.20   nd [about 1929]
—Magic / cook book / and / housekeepers guide / Published by / E.W. Gillett Company Limited / Toronto, Canada / Vancouver – Winnipeg – Ottawa – Montreal – Quebec [cover-title]
DESCRIPTION: 14.5 × 8.5 cm   Pp [1] 2–62 [63–4]   Paper, with image on front of a stout male chef with over-size head holding up a container of Magic Baking Powder in his right hand, spoon in his left; stapled
CONTENTS: 1 'General Information' and at bottom, 'Standard Brands Limited successors to E.W. Gillett Company Limited // Toronto 2, Canada.'; 2–3 'Beware of Fake Baking Powder Tests'; 4 'Valuable Suggestions'; 5–21 'Cakes'; 22–mid 24 'Bread and Rolls'; bottom 24–30 'Puddings'; 31–mid 37 'Other Desserts and Sauces'; bottom 37–mid 40 'Preserves and Jellies'; bottom 40 'Mince Meat'; top 41 'Mint Sauce'; mid–bottom 41 'Candies'; 42–mid 44 'Pickles and Catsups'; bottom 44–45 'Salads'; 46 'Potatoes'; 47–9 'Entrees, etc.'; 50–top 54 'Soup'; mid 54–56 'Fish'; 57–8 'How to Warm Over Cold Fragments'; 59–top 62 'Recipes for Invalids'; mid–bottom 62 'Household Recipes'; 63–4 index and at top p 64, 'Form No. 404-13891329'
COPIES: *Company collection (Nabisco Brands Ltd, Toronto, Ont.)
NOTES: This is the latest identified edition since it was published by the company that succeeded Gillett, Standard Brands Ltd, which incorporated on 27 Au-

gust 1929. On the inside front face of the binding, the text is in two separate boxes: the first is titled 'A Better Cake,' and the second, 'How to Open Any Can of Magic Baking Powder.'

North Broadview Presbyterian Church cook book

In 1925, the congregation of North Broadview Presbyterian Church, located at 289 Broadview Avenue in Toronto, became part of the United Church of Canada. In 1966, the congregation amalgamated with Eastminster United Church on Danforth Avenue.

O286.1   nd [about 1912]
North Broadview / Presbyterian Church / cook book / Recipes and helps / selected by the Junior Bible Class / of North Broadview Presbyterian Church / for their usefulness, simplicity / and economy, in / practical homes. / Price 25 cents [cover-title]
DESCRIPTION: 22.0 × 15.0 cm   Pp 1–128   Limp cloth; stapled
CONTENTS: Inside front face of binding information about the church; 1–2 ads; 3 'Index' [i.e., alphabetical list of sections]; 4 ads; 5 'Introductory'; 6 ads; 7–124 recipes credited with the name of the contributor; 125–6 'Useful Helps and Hints'; 127 'Table of Weights and Measures'; 128 ad
COPIES: *OTYA (CPC 1910 0108)
NOTES: The 'Introductory' gives the cookbook's purpose: 'This book is not only compiled for the raising of funds for our Sunday School but as an aid to introduce and enable us to become better acquainted with our surrounding members and friends.' Page 18 is devoted to oyster recipes. On pp 49–50, there are 'Some Recipes from a Minister's Cook Book,' being twelve numbered items contributed by Peter F. Sinclair, the church's pastor. Some items are culinary, while others offer advice; their tone is light-hearted and humorous. Item 8, for example, is 'A Toronto Boy's Ideal Dinner Menu,' which lists sweet dishes for all the several courses plus turkey for two courses. The running head is 'North Broadview Cook Book.'

Several clues point to a publication date of about 1912. Firstly, Sinclair served as pastor from 1909 to 1914. Secondly, an advertisement on p 39 for Central Business College, whose president was W.H. Shaw, boasts '20 years successful work to its credit.' Shaw College, as it was known in 1999 when it went bankrupt, was established in 1892, which fixes the year of publication at 1912 (1892 + 20 years). Thirdly, the *Five Roses Cook Book* (first edition, 1913, Q79.1) is not mentioned in the advertisement for Five Roses Flour on p 41, confirming that the volume was published before 1913.

Recipes

See also O101.1, another cookbook by the ladies of Broadway Tabernacle.

O287.1   1912
Recipes / compiled and arranged / by the / Ladies' Aid Society / of / Broadway Tabernacle / Toronto / "Mens sana in corpore sano" / Toronto: / P.R. Wilson Ptg., Co. / 1912
DESCRIPTION: 20.0 × 12.0 cm   Pp [3–5] 6–95   Lacks paper binding; stapled, and with brown cord tied through two punched holes
CONTENTS: 3 tp; 4 'The Cook at Our House' by Jean Blewett [poem; 'cook book' in first verse is identified in footnote as *The Broadway Ladies Aid Cook Book*]; 5–8 'Soups' compiled by Mrs E. Harley; 9–12 'Fish' compiled by Mrs G.A. Saunders; 13–15 'Hot Dishes for Supper' compiled by Mrs A.W. Lee; 16–18 'Meats' compiled by Mrs Wm Vokes; top 19 'Meat Sauces'; bottom 19–21 'Poultry and Game'; 22–6 'Vegetables' compiled by Mrs Miles Vokes; 27–31 'Salads' compiled by Mrs L. Duncan; 32–8 'Pickles' compiled by Mrs Frank Stanley; 39–41 'Eggs' compiled by Mrs Wm M. Ronald; 42–5 'Bread, Biscuits, etc.' compiled by Mrs Morden and Miss Cheesbrough; 46–56 'Puddings and Pies' compiled by Miss Worth; 57–8 'Pudding Sauces'; 59–65 'Light Desserts' compiled by Miss D. Campbell; 66–9 'Cookies' compiled by Mrs Elsley; 70–9 'Cakes' compiled by Mrs Ketcheson and Mrs Shepherd; 80–3 'Fruit' compiled by Mrs Ira H.F. Patterson; 84–7 'Candies' compiled by Mrs G.T. Rooke; 88–91 'Table Hints' compiled by Mrs J.C. Baker, Mrs S. Milligan, and Mrs H.B. Somers; 92–5 'Helpful Hints for the Home' by the Cook Book Committee
COPIES: *Private collection
NOTES: This church cookbook is unusual in that the chapters are identified as compiled by a particular person(s). More conventionally, the individual recipes are credited with the name of the contributor.

Reliable recipes and helpful hints

The directors of the Egg-o Baking Powder Co., Philip Gershel and J. Dorsey, moved the company's plant from Regina, Saskatchewan, to Hamilton, Ontario, at the end of December 1910, when they took over a vacated factory on Mary Street. They wanted to move closer to the source of supply of cans and other raw materials, to save on freight charges. The company's aim was 'to thoroughly exploit the Ontario and Quebec trade as well as keep up its business relations in Manitoba, Saskatchewan, Alberta and British Columbia.' (See '$4,000,000 Capital in New Industries,' in Times Scrapbooks: Industry *at OH.)*

Other cookbooks by Egg-o Baking Powder Co. are O354.1, The Truth about Baking Powder, *and O367.1,* Modern Mixes for Bakers.

The company advertised its cookbooks in Canadian magazines, although it is not always possible to tell which title or which edition is being offered. An advertisement for Egg-o Baking Powder in the May 1917 issue of Everywoman's World, *for example, advises, 'Use the coupon in the can for recipe book.' An advertisement in the April 1918 issue of* Western Home Monthly *refers to 'the book of Reliable Recipes.'*

There are incomplete copies of Reliable Recipes and Helpful Hints *at ACG and MBDHM.*

O288.1   nd [about 1912]
Reliable recipes / and helpful hints / A concise compend of tested / recipes which make delicious / dishes, together with a compilation / of helps and hints of value to / every housekeeper. / Published by / Egg-o Baking Powder Co. / Limited / Hamilton
DESCRIPTION: 16.5 × 13.0 cm   Pp [1] 2–64   Illus   Paper, with image on front of a container of Egg-o Baking Powder sitting in a broken eggshell framed by heads of wheat; stapled
CONTENTS: 1 tp; 2 'Index'; 3 'Just a Word'; 4 'Baking Powder Facts of Value to You'; 5 'General Hints and Directions'; 6–53 recipes; 54–9 'Hints and Helps'; 60 quotations about Rochelle Salts; 61 'Court Testimony'; 62–3 'Time Tables for Cooking'; 64 'Table of Measures and Weights'
COPIES: ARDA   *BDEM (DE 969-121-10)   SBIHM
NOTES: There are testimonials on pp 40–1, the latest of which is dated 16 April 1912. From appearances, the book was published about that year. The ARDA copy appears to be identical to the BDEM copy except for differences on the front face of the binding: In the BDEM copy, the letters of the cover-title are outlined and only Hamilton is cited as the location of Egg-o Baking Powder Co.; in the ARDA copy, the letters of the cover-title are not outlined and Hamilton, Regina, and Vancouver are cited as company locations. The SBIHM copy lacks its binding.

O288.2   nd [about 1914–18]
—Reliable / recipes / and / helpful / hints. / A concise compend of tested / recipes which make

most de- / licious dishes, together with / a compilation of helps and / hints of value to every / housekeeper. Every baking / recipe given herein has been / repeatedly tested by and is / regularly used in the Egg-o / baking schools. / This is an Egg-o cook book and / the recipes contained in it are / proportioned for the use of / Egg-o Baking Powder. For the / best results use Egg-o exact- / ly according to directions. / Published by / Egg-o Baking Powder Co. / Hamilton Canada.

DESCRIPTION: 17.0 × 12.0 cm   Pp [1] 2–72   4 pls col, illus on p 4 of teaspoon measurements, illus on p 64 of a bottle of Rochelle Salts   Paper, with image on front of a woman adding a spoonful of Egg-o Baking Powder to a bowl, as she follows a recipe in a copy of *Reliable Recipes*

CONTENTS: 1 tp; 2 index; 3 'Baking Powder Facts'; 4 'General Hints and Directions'; 5–8 'Breads, Biscuits and Shortcakes'; 9–11 'Muffins, Waffles, Ginger-breads'; 12–13 'Griddle Cakes'; 14–15 'Fritters, Dough-nuts and Crullers'; 16 comparison of Egg-o Baking Powder and Trust Cream of Tartar Baking Powders by composition, residue left in food, efficiency, and price; 17 'Testimonials'; 18–31 'Cakes and Cookies'; 32 'Baking Powder Is Not a Food' and 'Alum Baking Powders Are Declared Not to Be Harmful'; 33–4 'Cake Fillings and Frostings'; 35 'Valuable Information' [i.e., a refutation of attacks in the media by the Royal Baking Powder Trust against Egg-o]; 36–8 'Pies'; 39–43 'Puddings'; 44 'Pudding Sauces'; 45–6 'Ice Cream and Ices'; 47–9 'Soups, Meats and Eggs'; 50 'Use Standard Goods'; 51 'What the U.S. Government Department of Agriculture Says about Rochelle Salts in Baking Powder' and quotations from two doctors; 52–3 'Salads'; 54–5 'Candies'; 56–8 'Fireless Cookers' and recipes for use with fireless cookers; 59–63 'Hints and Helps'; 64 quotations from two doctors about the harmful effects of Rochelle Salts and illus of a bottle of Rochelle Salts, 'the residue left in bread baked with one pound of "Royal Baking Powder"'; 65 'Court Testimony' proving 'the wholesomeness of alum bak-ing powders'; 66 'Time Tables for Cooking'; 67 'Time Table for Fireless Cooker' and 'Table of Measures and Weights'; 68–70 'Spring and Summer Menus'; 71–2 'Fall and Winter Menus'

COPIES: MCM   OH (R641.865 REL CESH)   ONLAM (Walters-Wagar Collection, Box 20)   *Private collection

NOTES: The private collector's copy includes a 9.5 × 14.5 cm loose-leaf insert published by Egg-o, which contains six recipes; the first is 'Canada's War Cake,' whose ingredients include no milk, eggs, or butter. Also suggesting a publication date during the First World War is an announcement on p 32 from the Department of Agriculture, Washington, DC, dated 1 May 1914.

'The Reid Press, Limited Hamilton, Ont.' is printed on the outside back face of the binding of the OH copy.

O288.3   nd
—Reliable / recipes / and / helpful / hints. / A concise compend of tested / recipes which make most de- / licious dishes, together with / a compilation of helps and / hints of value to every / housekeeper. Every baking / recipe given herein has been / repeatedly tested by and is / regularly used in the Egg-o / baking schools. / This is an Egg-o cook book and / the recipes contained in it are / proportioned for the use of / Egg-o Baking Powder. For the / best results use Egg-o exact- / ly according to directions. / Published by / Egg-o Baking Powder Co. / Hamilton Canada.

DESCRIPTION: 16.5 × 12.0 cm   Pp [1] 2–72   4 double-sided pls col, illus on p 67 of teaspoon measure-ments, illus on p 64 of Rochelle Salts   Lacks front face of paper binding; stapled

CONTENTS: 1 tp; 2 'Index'; 3–58 recipes, beginning with 'Breads, Biscuits and Shortcakes'; 59–63 'Hints and Helps'; 64 quotations about Rochelle Salts; 65 'Court Testimony'; 66 'Baking Powder Facts of Value to You'; 67 'General Hints and Directions'; 68–72 menus for spring and summer, fall and winter

COPIES: *Private collection

NOTES: The title-page is identical to O288.2, but the text has been rearranged. In this edition the recipes begin on p 3; the 'Baking Powder Facts' are at the back of the book, not on p 3.

O288.4   1 May 1919
—Reliable / recipes / and / helpful / hints. / A concise compend of tested / recipes which make most de- / licious dishes, together with / a compilation of helps and / hints of value to every / housekeeper. Every baking / recipe given herein has been / repeatedly tested by and is / regularly used in the Egg-o / baking schools. / This is an Egg-o cook book and / the recipes contained in it are / proportioned for the use of / Egg-o Baking Powder. For the / best results use Egg-o exact- / ly according to directions. / Published by / Egg-o Baking Powder Co. / Hamilton Canada. / May 1st, 1919.

DESCRIPTION: 16.5 × 12.0 cm   Pp [1] 2–72   4 double-sided pls col, illus on p 67 of teaspoon measure-ments   Paper, with image on front of a woman adding a spoonful of Egg-o Baking Powder to a bowl, as she follows a recipe in a copy of *Reliable Recipes*

CONTENTS: 1 tp; 2 index; 3 'What You Should Know about Egg-o Baking Powder'; 4–7 'Bread, Biscuit and Shortcakes'; 8–9 'War Breads and Substitutes'; 10–12 'Muffins, Waffles, Gingerbreads'; 13–14 'Griddle Cakes'; 15–16 'Fritters, Doughnuts and Crullers'; 17 publ ad; 18–31 'Cakes and Cookies' and publ ad on p 26; 32 publ ad; 33–4 'Cake Fillings and Frostings'; 35 publ ad; 36–8 'Pies'; 39–43 'Puddings'; 44 'Pudding Sauces'; 45–6 'Ice Cream and Ices'; 47–9 'Soups, Meat and Eggs' [soup recipes on p 47, meat on p 48, egg on p 49]; 50–1 publ ads; 52–3 'Salads'; 54–5 'Candies'; 56–8 'Fireless Cookers'; 59 publ ad; 60–4 'Hints and Helps'; 65 publ ad; 66 'Baking Powder Facts'; 67 'General Hints and Directions'; 68–70 'Spring and Summer Menus'; 71–2 'Fall and Winter Menus'

COPIES: *QMM (RBD ckbk 1531)

NOTES: The section of 'War Breads and Substitutes' on pp 8–9 reflects a government initiative to save wheat flour for the military. Ferguson/Fraser, p 233, and the colour illustration on p 35, may be O288.4 or O288.5.

O288.5 1 November 1919

—Reliable / recipes / and / helpful / hints. / A concise compend of tested / recipes which make most de- / licious dishes, together with / a compilation of helps and / hints of value to every / housekeeper. Every baking / recipe given herein has been / repeatedly tested by and is / regularly used in the Egg-o / baking schools. / This is an Egg-o cook book and / the recipes contained in it are / proportioned for the use of / Egg-o Baking Powder. For the / best results use Egg-o exact- / ly according to directions. / Published by / Egg-o Baking Powder Co. / Hamilton, Canada. / Nov. 1st, 1919.

DESCRIPTION: 16.5 × 12.0 cm Pp [1] 2–72 4 double-sided pls col, illus on p 67 of teaspoon measurements Paper, with image on front of a woman adding a spoonful of Egg-o Baking Powder to a bowl, as she follows a recipe in a copy of *Reliable Recipes*; stapled

CONTENTS: 1 tp; 2 index; 3 'What You Should Know about Egg-o Baking Powder'; 4–7 'Bread, Biscuit and Shortbread'; 8–9 'War Breads and Substitutes'; 10–12 'Muffins, Waffles, Gingerbreads'; 13–14 'Griddle Cakes'; 15–16 'Fritters, Doughnuts and Crullers'; 17 publ ad; 18–31 'Cakes and Cookies' and publ ad on p 26; 32 publ ad; 33–4 'Cake Fillings and Frostings'; 35 publ ad; 36–8 'Pies'; 39–43 'Puddings'; 44 'Pudding Sauces'; 45–6 'Ice Cream and Ices'; 47–9 'Soups, Meat and Eggs' [soup recipes on p 47, meat on p 48, egg on

p 49]; 50–1 publ ads; 52–3 'Salads'; 54–5 'Candies'; 56–8 'Fireless Cooker'; 59 publ ad; 60–4 'Hints and Helps'; 65 publ ad; 66 'Baking Powder Facts'; 67 'General Hints and Directions'; 68–70 'Spring and Summer Menus'; 71–2 'Fall and Winter Menus'

COPIES: CIHM (74198) OKIT OONL (TX765 E55 1919, 2 copies) *Private collection

O288.6 May 1926

—Reliable recipes / and / helpful hints / A concise compend of tested / recipes which make most deli- / cious dishes, together with a compila- / tion of helps and hints of value to / every housekeeper. Every baking / recipe given herein has been repeated- / ly tested by and is regularly used in / the Egg-o baking schools. / This is an Egg-o cook book and the / recipes contained in it are proportion- / ed for the use of Egg-o Baking Pow- / der. For the best results use Egg-o / exactly according to directions. / Published by / Egg-o Baking Powder Co. / Hamilton, Canada / May, 1926

DESCRIPTION: 15.5 × 11.0 cm Pp [1] 2–72 4 double-sided pls col Paper, with image on front of a girl eating a doughnut; stapled

CONTENTS: 1 tp; 2–top 3 'Index'; mid–bottom 3 'Measurements' and untitled note about the chemical action of baking powder; 4–5 'Some Principals [*sic*] of Baking'; 6–8 'Baking Powder Bread'; 9–mid 11 'Biscuit'; mid 11–13 'Special Bread Recipes (Sweet Dough)'; 14 'Here Is a Great Convenience That Is Distinctly an Egg-o Feature' [making a flour-and-shortening mixture to keep and use later]; 15–18 'The Soft Batter Baked Goods' [includes griddle cakes, muffins, waffles, fritters]; 19–21 'Cake Making'; 22–mid 24 'Plain White Cakes'; mid 24–28 'Plain Cakes (Yellow)'; 29–32 'Spice Cakes'; 33–4 'Eggless Cakes' [includes Canada's War Cake]; 35 'Chocolate Cakes'; 36 'Sponge Cakes'; 37 'Two Cake Oddities' [Ice Box Cake and Graham Cracker Cake] and 'Baking Powder' [information about the company's product]; 38–41 'Cookies'; 42–5 'Icings – Fillings – Frostings'; 46 'Eggs'; 47–50 'Puddings'; 51 'Pudding Sauces'; 52 'Ice Cream and Ices'; 53–5 'Pies'; 56–7 'Salads'; 58–9 'Candies'; 60–1 'Soups'; 62–3 'Meats'; 64–5 'Chicken Pie Supper for 25 to 30 People'; 66–7 'Left Overs'; 68–72 'Hints and Helps'

COPIES: *Private collection

AMERICAN EDITIONS: Possibly *Reliable Recipes* by the Calumet Baking Powder Co. of Chicago, Illinois; several editions (all cited in Allen, p 149): 1906; 1909; 10th ed., 1914; 1916; 1918 (also United States: DLC, which gives title *Reliable Recipes and Helpful Hints*); 1920; 16th ed., 1922. See also O367.1, *Modern Mixes for Bakers,* another Egg-o book with a title that matches a Calumet Baking Powder Co. publication.

Stamford Women's Institute cook book

O289.1   April 1912
[An edition of *Stamford Women's Institute Cook Book,* printed by the Tribune, Welland, Ontario, April 1912, pp 127]
COPIES: Private collection

Telford, Emma Paddock (1851–)

Also by this American author is The Evening Telegram Cook Book, *New York: Cupples and Leon Co., [c1908] (United States: DLC).*

O290.1   [copyright 1912]
Standard / paper-bag / cookery / by / Emma Paddock Telford / Household Editor of / the Delineator, New Ideas, and The Designer / Toronto / The Copp Clark Co., Limited
DESCRIPTION: 18.5 × 12.0 cm   Pp [1–8] 9–156, [i–iv] Cloth
CONTENTS: 1 ht: 'Standard Paper-Bag Cookery by Emma Paddock Telford adapted to the needs of American housewives' and quotation from Shakespeare; 2 'The paperbags required for paper-bag cookery can be obtained from your local stationer'; 3 tp; 4 'Copyright, 1912, by Cupples & Leon Company'; 5–6 table of contents; 7 foreword; 8 blank; 9–146 text; 147–56 index; i–iv ads
CITATIONS: Ferguson/Fraser, p 233
COPIES: *OGU (UA s045 b36)
NOTES: The advertisements are for American businesses; for example, on p i, the Continental Paper Bag Co., New York.

AMERICAN EDITIONS: New York: Cupples and Leon Co., [c1912] (United States: DLC).

A thousand and one cookery recipes and kitchen hints

O291.1   1912
A thousand and one / cookery recipes / and kitchen hints / alphabetically arranged / With 26 black-and-white illustrations / [for imprint, see Notes]

DESCRIPTION: 22.5 × 10.0 cm   Pp [i–ii], [1–7] 8–152, [i–ii]   6 pls incl frontis, 2 fp illus on pp 41 and 112, a few illus   [6d, on binding]   Paper-covered boards, with images on front of a woman weighing ingredients and a woman trimming a piecrust
CITATIONS: Driver 1067.1
COPIES: Great Britain: LB (missing) *OB; United States: ICJ   NN
NOTES: This is the first edition of March 1912 (see O291.2). The imprint is London, New York, Toronto, and Melbourne: Cassell and Co. Ltd, 1912. There are 1,001 numbered recipes and hints. Pages 139–52 are blank for memoranda.

O291.2   [reprint], 15th thousand, 1913
— A thousand and one / cookery recipes / and kitchen hints / alphabetically arranged / With 26 black-and-white illustrations / Fifteenth thousand / Cassell and Company, Ltd / London New York / Toronto Melbourne / 1913
DESCRIPTION: 23.0 × 10.0 cm   Pp [i–ii], [1–7] 8–152, [i–ii]   6 pls incl frontis, 2 fp illus on pp 41 and 112, a few illus   [6d, on binding]   Paper-covered boards, with images on front of a woman weighing ingredients and a woman trimming a piecrust
CONTENTS: i ad; ii blank; 1 ht; 2 publ ad; 3 tp; 4 'First edition March 1912. Reprinted March 1913. All rights reserved'; 5 'Introduction'; 6 ad; 7–138 1,001 numbered recipes and hints, and ads; 139–52 blank for 'Private Recipes and Memoranda'; i blank; ii publ ad
COPIES: *Private collection
NOTES: The advertisements are for British businesses; however, the private collector's copy was purchased from a Toronto bookdealer, which suggests that the book was originally distributed in Canada.

O291.3   nd
—[Another edition of *A Thousand and One Cookery Recipes and Kitchen Hints,* London, Toronto, New York, and Melbourne: Cassell and Co. Ltd, nd]
CITATIONS: Axford, p 391   Bitting, p 606   Driver 1067.2

Tried and tested recipes

O292.1   1912
"To be a good cook means the economy of your great-grand- / mother and the science of modern chemists. It means much tasting / and no wasting. It means English thoroughness, French art, and / Arabian hospitality. It means, in fine, that you are to see that / every one has something nice to eat." –

Ruskin. / Tried and tested / recipes / collected and compiled by / the Ladies' Aid Society of the / Talbot St. Baptist Church / and their friends / December, 1912 / London, Ontario / A. Talbot & Co., printers. / 1912.

DESCRIPTION: 21.0 × 13.5 cm Pp [3–5] 6–115 Cloth

CONTENTS: 3 tp; 4 'Measures and Weights' and table of contents; 5–92 recipes credited with the name of the contributor and ads; 93–115 ads

COPIES: CIHM (78014) OLU (TX715 T769 1912) *Private collection

Wilton Grove Women's Institute cook book

The Wilton Grove branch of the Women's Institute was established in 1909 (Ambrose, p 237).

O293.1 [1912]

Wilton Grove / Women's Institute / cook book / Price, twenty-five cents / Henry & Colerick the printers, London [cover-title]

DESCRIPTION: Pp [1] 2–108 Image on front of a maple leaf; stapled

CONTENTS: 1 ad for Bank of British North America dated 1912; 2 ad; 3 'Greeting'; 4 ad; 5 'The Women's Institutes of Ontario' signed Geo. A. Putnam, superintendent; 6 ads; 7 'Handy Weights and Measures'; 8 ads; 9–103 recipes credited with the name of the contributor and ads; 104–5 'Remedial Foods'; 106 ad; 107 'Index' [i.e., table of contents]; 108 ad

COPIES: *CIHM (79084) OLU (J.J. Talman Regional Collection, pamphlet)

NOTES: The 'Greeting' says: 'Our cook book has been compiled, not only with the convenience and advantage of the individual in view, but also with the object of forming the nucleus of a fund for the promotion of schemes in the interest of agriculture and social welfare in our rural community.' The first recipe sections are classified as 'Miscellaneous' and 'Remedies.'

1912–13

The Wimodausis Club cook book

O294.1 [1st ed.], nd [1912 or 1913]

The Wimodausis Club / cook book / These are all tried and tested / recipes, used by the ladies under / whose names they appear.

DESCRIPTION: 21.0 × 14.0 cm Pp [1–11] 12–124, [i–viii] Paper-covered boards, cloth spine; stapled

CONTENTS: 1 tp; 2–8 ads; 9 'Time Allowance for Baking'; 10 blank; 11–116 recipes credited with the name of the contributor and blank pages, with section headings, for manuscript recipes; 117–24 'Index' [i.e., table of contents]; i–ii blank; iii–viii ads

COPIES: *Private collection

NOTES: The Wimodausis Club, a volunteer social-service group in Toronto, took its name in 1906 (according to the history in O294.3) from the first syllables of the words wives, mothers, daughters, sisters. Several of the women who contributed recipes to the book are from well-known Toronto families; for example, Miss Muriel Larkin (Peter C. Larkin founded the Salada Tea Co.), Miss Clara Flavelle and Mrs Barrett, née Mina Flavelle (daughters of Sir Joseph Flavelle, a rich Toronto industrialist whose mansion stands at 78 Queen's Park Crescent), Mrs A.E. Ames (her husband owned a stock-brokerage business), Miss G.A. Gooderham (her family established Toronto's famous whisky distillery), Miss Martha Fudger (for three decades Harris Henry Fudger was president of the Robert Simpson Co. department store, which he purchased with Joseph Flavelle and A.E. Ames in 1897), and Mrs Tovell (i.e., Florence Tovell, née Bradshaw, not her sister-in-law Ruth Tovell, née Massey, who at the time of the book's publication was in Germany). There are also recipes from Miss Mona Cleaver, who, as Mrs Mona Cleaver Purser, edited the 'Homemaker Page' in the *Globe and Mail* newspaper from 1925 until her death in 1954, and who compiled O927.1, *The Homemaker's Guide Book.*

An advertisement on p 8 indicates that the first edition was published before Robins Ltd, a real estate company, moved to its new building. In the advertisement, Robins Ltd advises that it 'will shortly occupy their new building at the corner of Victoria and Richmond.' The company gives its 'present address' as 'Adelaide and Victoria // Telephone Main 7171.' The Toronto city directory for 1912 records the company at 22 Adelaide Street East, and the 1913 city directory records the new address, Victoria, northeast corner Richmond; therefore, the company moved to the new building in the period 1912–13.

O294.2 [2nd ed.], 1922

—The / Wimodausis Club / cook book / compiled by / members of the Wimodausis Club / Toronto / 1922

DESCRIPTION: 23.0 × 15.0 cm Pp [1–6] 7–224, 225–56 Cloth

CONTENTS: 1 tp; 2 'Copyright, Canada, 1922 by the Wimodausis Club Toronto // Printed and bound by the Hunter-Rose Co., Limited'; 3 table of contents; 4 blank; 5 foreword signed 'Editor'; 6 blank; 7–218 text; 219–24 index; 225–56 ads

CITATIONS: Ferguson/Fraser, p 233   Golick, p 101 (note 14)

COPIES: NFSM (TX715.6 W56 1922)   OGU (UA s047 b17)   *OTMCL (641.5 W386)   OTUTF (B-12 7856) OWTU (G12593)

NOTES: The anonymous editor writes in the foreword, 'The continued demand for a former cook book, published some years ago and now out of print, was incentive to the Wimodausis Club to compile the present volume, containing the recipes used before, and many new ones.' In the expanded 'Soups' chapter, for example, most of the original recipes have been retained; only Tomato Soup contributed by Mrs R.D. Hume and the unattributed Substitute for Cream have been omitted. Some of the original recipes bear the new names of their contributors who had married in the decade between the two editions: recipes submitted by Miss Alma Laing, for example, now appear as from Mrs C.S.F. Mitchell, and those submitted by Miss Clara Flavelle, as from Mrs Frank McEachren. There is a new, first chapter devoted to 'Hors d'Oeuvres, Canapés and Savouries,' and the following information has been added after the recipes, on pp 211–18: 'The Menu Maker'; 'Helpful Hints for the Home'; 'Time Allowance for Cooking' (i.e., an expanded table, which in the first edition was called 'Time Allowance for Baking'); 'Comparative Measurements'; 'Temperatures'; and 'Ordinary Tests.' The latter explains how to judge a warm, moderate, hot, and very hot oven by how long one can hold a hand in the centre back of the oven (if one can count from twelve to fifteen before having to withdraw the hand, the oven is warm; if only from five to eight, the oven is very hot).

O294.3   [3rd ed.], copyright 1934
—The / Wimodausis Club / cook book / compiled by / members of the Wimodausis Club / Toronto / Copyright 1934, Canada / Produced by / Grand & Toy Limited / Toronto
DESCRIPTION: 23.5 × 15.0 cm   Pp [1–6] 7–528, 529–44 Illus head each chapter   Cloth
CONTENTS: 1 tp; 2 'The Wimodausis Club' [a brief history of the club and its cookbook]; 3 table of contents; 4 blank; 5 'Advertisers'; 6 blank; 7–506 text; 507–28 index; 529–44 ads
CITATIONS: AbCat winter 1979   Garrett, pp 73, 132
COPIES: NFSM (TX715 W56 1934)   OGU (UA s064 b26)   OONL (TX715 W455 1934)   *OTMCL (641.5 W386 1934)

NOTES: 'Third edition' is printed on the front face of the binding. The history on page 2 says that by the year this third edition was published, the club had grown from the original five members to thirty-five.

The book is printed throughout on sections of variously coloured leaves and in various colours of ink. Many new recipes have been added to the text. The 'Ordinary Tests' for oven temperatures are omitted; the 'Household Hints' are rewritten, enlarged, and brought up to date. There are new chapters of recipes for 'Children's Hour,' 'Electric Refrigerator Recipes,' 'Invalid Cookery,' 'Sandwiches,' 'Sour Milk, Egg Whites and Egg Yolks,' and 'Left-overs.' The new menu chapters for 'Special Occasion Menus,' 'Inexpensive Family Meals,' and 'Hot Weather Menus' also include recipes.

1912–17

500 hints and helps for housekeepers

Cooke's Presbyterian Church was at Queen and Mutual streets. It was demolished in 1984, two years after the congregation dissolved.

O295.1   [1st ed.], nd [about 1912–17]
500 / hints and helps / for / housekeepers / Selected by the Women's Association of Cooke's Church, for / their tested value and usefulness in the homes of to-day. / Toronto: / The Armac Press, Limited
DESCRIPTION: 22.0 × 14.5 cm   Pp 1–144   Limp cloth, with image on front of the church
CONTENTS: 1–2 ads; 3 tp; 4 ads; 5 index and ad; 6–7 'Index to Advertisers'; 8 ads; 9 foreword signed the Committee; 10 ads; 11–141 text and ads; 142 blank for 'Additional Recipes'; 143–4 ads
COPIES: *OGU (2 copies: UA s043 b27, UA s043 b28)
NOTES: There is an advertisement for the Armac Press that gives the address 56–8 Agnes Street. Toronto city directories list the company at this address from 1912 to 1917.

O295.2   3rd ed., 1924
—500 / hints and helps / for / housekeepers / Selected by the Women's Association of Cooke's Church, for / their tested value and usefulness in the homes of to-day. / Third edition / Toronto / The Armac Press Limited / 1924
DESCRIPTION: 21.5 × 14.5 cm   Pp 1–144   Paper, with image on front of the church; stapled
CONTENTS: 1–2 ads; 3 tp; 4 ads; 5 'Index' [i.e., alpha-

betical list of sections] and ads; 6 'Index to Advertisers'; 7–8 ads; 9 'Foreword' signed the Committee; 10 ads; 11–142 recipes credited with the name of the contributor, blank pages for 'Additional Recipes,' 'Household Hints,' 'Toilet Recipes,' and ads; 143–4 blank pages for 'Additional Recipes'
COPIES: *Private collection

1913

The Bala ladies' cook book

O296.1 [1913]
The Bala ladies' / cook book. / [caption for illus of Bala Church:] Showing the Bala Church / for the support of which the ladies prepared this / recipe book. Visitors of all denomina- / tions are cordially invited to / attend all services.
DESCRIPTION: 21.0 × 15.0 cm   Pp [1–2] 3–40   Tp illus of Bala Church   Thin card; stapled
CONTENTS: 1 tp; 2 poem titled 'The Bala Ladies' Cook Book'; 3–top 38 recipes credited with the name of the contributor and ads; mid–bottom 38 'Miscellaneous'; 39 'Index' [i.e., table of contents]; 40 'Published for the ladies of Bala by the Bracebridge Gazette Printing and Publishing Company, Limited // Bracebridge, Ontario, June 30th, 1913.'
COPIES: *OGU (CCC TX715.6 G7347)
NOTES: On p 8 there is an advertisement for Bala Church (Presbyterian). Bala is in Muskoka.

The B.B.B. cook book

O297.1 1913
"Now good digestion wait on / appetite, and health on both" / Shakespeare. / The / B.B.B. cook book / a selection of / tested recipes / compiled by the young ladies / of / Wheatley Methodist Church / 1913.
DESCRIPTION: [16 unnumbered leaves]   Sewn
COPIES: *Private collection
NOTES: This volume, and presumably other multiple copies, were made entirely by the young ladies of the church, from the handwritten title-page and recipes to the cloth cover with three embroidered letter Bs. The recipes are credited with the name of the contributor. In 2002, no church members of what is now Wheatley United Church could identify the meaning behind the initials B.B.B. Wheatley is in the southwest corner of Ontario, east of Leamington.

The blue cook book

O298.1 nd [about 1913]
The blue / cook / book / 75 cents [cover-title]
DESCRIPTION: 18.0 × 13.0 cm   Pp [1–3] 4–90   Illus on p 3 of St Paul's Church, Fort William, Ontario   Paper; stapled
CONTENTS: 1 'The recipes in this book have all been tried and found successful'; 2 blank; 3 illus and 'This book is published for he [sic] purpose of applying the proceeds of its sale to the Talent Fund of St. Paul's Church, Fort William.'; 4 ad; 5–89 text and ads; 90 ads
COPIES: *OGU (CCC TX715.6 B56)   OTBH
NOTES: On p 87 there are five recipes for invalids supplied by Miss Muriel E. Farmer, dietitian at McKellar General Hospital. The OGU copy is inscribed on p 1, in ink, 'Marion Miller with Phyl's love March 1932,' but the book is older than the inscription. An advertisement on p 36 for the Union Bank of Canada cites profits for 30 November 1912. An advertisement on p 60 for Baker's Chocolate boasts 'For more than 133 years ...' and refers to the establishment of the company in 1780, indicating a date of publication of 1913 (1780 + 133 years).

Congreve, Mistress A.E.

O299.1 1913
The one maid / book of cookery / by Mistress / A.E. Congreve / First-class Diplomée / Toronto / Bell & Cockburn / MCMXIII
DESCRIPTION: 18.5 × 12.5 cm   Pp [1–8] 9–217, [i–vii]   Cloth, with image on front of a maid's silhouette
CONTENTS: 1 ht; 2 blank; 3 tp; 4 'The Mercat Press, Edinburgh'; 5 'Foreword' signed A.E. Congreve, Hove [in England], 1913; 6 blank; 7–8 'Contents'; 9–209 text; 210 blank; 211–17 'Index'; i blank; ii–iii ads; iv–v 'The One Maid House' by Mrs M.A.[Maud Adeline] Cloudesley Brereton; vi recipes using the ingredient Cakeoma; vii ad
COPIES: CIHM (9-90031)   *OONL (TX717 C66 1913 p***)
NOTES: The book was written to meet fast-changing living conditions where 'the number of gentle people living in small houses and flats run with One Maid, or with no maid at all is rapidly increasing' (p 5). The text begins with chapters on the following general topics: 'The Art of Cookery'; 'The Art of Catering'; 'The Art of Shopping'; 'The Kitchen and Utensils'; 'The Scullery and Washing Up'; 'The Store Cupboard'; 'The Larder'; and 'Cookery Methods and Their Prin-

ciples.' Recipes follow. The OONL copy is inscribed on the front endpaper, 'I Willcox, Toronto, Ont.'

BRITISH EDITIONS: London: Herbert Jenkins Ltd, 1913 (Driver 228.1); popular ed., 18th thousand, London: Herbert Jenkins Ltd, nd (Driver 228.2).

AMERICAN EDITIONS: New York: E.P. Dutton and Co., nd [foreword dated 1913] (NUC).

Cook book

O300.1 1913
Cook book / compiled by / the Woman's Auxiliary / of / St. Michael and All Angels' Church / Grenfell / 1913 / Rideau Record Press / Smiths Falls, Ont.
DESCRIPTION: 22.5 × 15.0 cm   Pp [1–4] 5–90   Cloth
CONTENTS: 1 tp; 2 blank; 3 table of contents; 4 blank; 5–90 text
COPIES: OTBH   *Private collection
NOTES: The cover-title and running head are 'Grenfell Cook Book.' See cross-reference between S13.1 and S14.1 for comment.

Cramp, Helen (1886–)

O301.1 [copyright 1913]
The Winston / cook book / planned for a family of four / economical recipes / designed to meet the / needs of the modern / housekeeper / including chapters on / entertaining fireless cooking / paper-bag cookery chafing-dish cookery / casserole cookery meat substitutes / By Helen Cramp / Ph.B., University of Chicago / Illustrated / Canadian agents / The Copp Clark Co., Limited / Toronto
DESCRIPTION: 20.0 × 14.0 cm   Pp [1–2], i–iv, [1–2] 3–507   8 pls col incl frontis; 24 pls; a few illus   Cloth
CONTENTS: 1 tp; 2 'Copyright 1913 by Helen Cramp'; i–ii preface; iii–iv table of contents; 1–484 text; 485–98 'General Index'; 499–507 'Alphabetical Index'
COPIES: OW (at library in 1991, not on shelf in 2001) *Private collection
NOTES: In 1926 the John C. Winston Co. published a cookbook of the same title, but under the name of Jane Eayre Fryer; see O583.1.

AMERICAN EDITIONS: These were published under various titles: *The Institute Cook Book*, Philadelphia: International Institute, [1913] (United States: DLC), and an abridged ed., *The Institute Cook Book*, Oakland, Calif.: Smithsonian Co., 1913 (United States: DLC);

The Universal Cook Book, Philadelphia: International Press, [copyright 1913] (OKITD; United States: DLC); *White Ribbon Cook Book*, Philadelphia: P.W. Ziegler Co., [1913] (United States: DLC); *The Winston Cook Book*, Chicago: Jordan [*sic*] C. Winston Co., [1913] (United States: DLC); *The Institute Cook Book*, Philadelphia: International Institute, [copyright 1921] (OGU); and *The Winston Cook Book*, Philadelphia and Chicago: John C. Winston Co., [copyright 1922] (BVAU Beatrice M. Millar Papers).

Glover, Ellye Howell (1868–1913)

O302.1 [October] 1913
"Dame Curtsey's" book of / candy making / by / Ellye Howell Glover / author of "Dame Curtsey's" Book of Party Pastimes, etc. / Toronto / McClelland & Goodchild / Chicago / A.C. McClurg & Co. / 1913
DESCRIPTION: 16.5 × 11.5 cm   Pp [1–4] [leaf torn out] [7–10] 11–110   Frontis of a woman with a chafing dish, entitled 'Nearly Ready'   Paper-covered boards, cloth spine
CONTENTS: 1 ht; 2 list of 'The "Dame Curtsey" Books' published by A.C. McClurg and Co., Chicago; 3 tp; 4 'Copyright A.C. McClurg & Co. 1913 // Published October, 1913 // W.F. Hall Printing Company, Chicago'; 5–6 lacking; 7 foreword; 8 blank; 9 table of contents; 10 blank; 11–106 text; 107–10 index
CITATIONS: Spadoni/Donnelly No. 67
COPIES: *OONL (TX791 G56 1913)   OTMCL (641.85 G48)
NOTES: The OONL copy is stamped on the front endpaper, 'The property of Scarboro Public Library.'

Spadoni/Donnelly state, 'From the sheets of the A.C. McClurg & Co. edition.' This title or another in the series was sold by the Methodist Book and Publishing House in Toronto; see the entry in 'Stock Book 1913' at OTCC (Acc. 83.061C, UCC Board of Publication, Series III, Box 41, p 10): '6 [copies] Dame Curtsey Book.'

The following titles in the series are listed on p 2: 'Dame Curtsey's' Book of Novel Entertainments for Every Day in the Year, 'Dame Curtsey's' Book of Guessing Contests, More Guessing Contests, 'Dame Curtsey's' Book of Etiquette, 'Dame Curtsey's' Book of Recipes, and 'Dame Curtsey's' Book of Party Pastimes for the Up-to-Date Hostess. Other titles in the series were published after 1913 (see the DLC catalogue).

AMERICAN EDITIONS: Chicago: A.C. McClurg and Co., 1913 (United States: DLC).

Plate 1. *'The Black Whale' Cook Book,* by Mrs Ethel Renouf, Montreal, 1948 (Q314.1). The front cover and interior pages are decorated with Canadian artists' woodcuts.

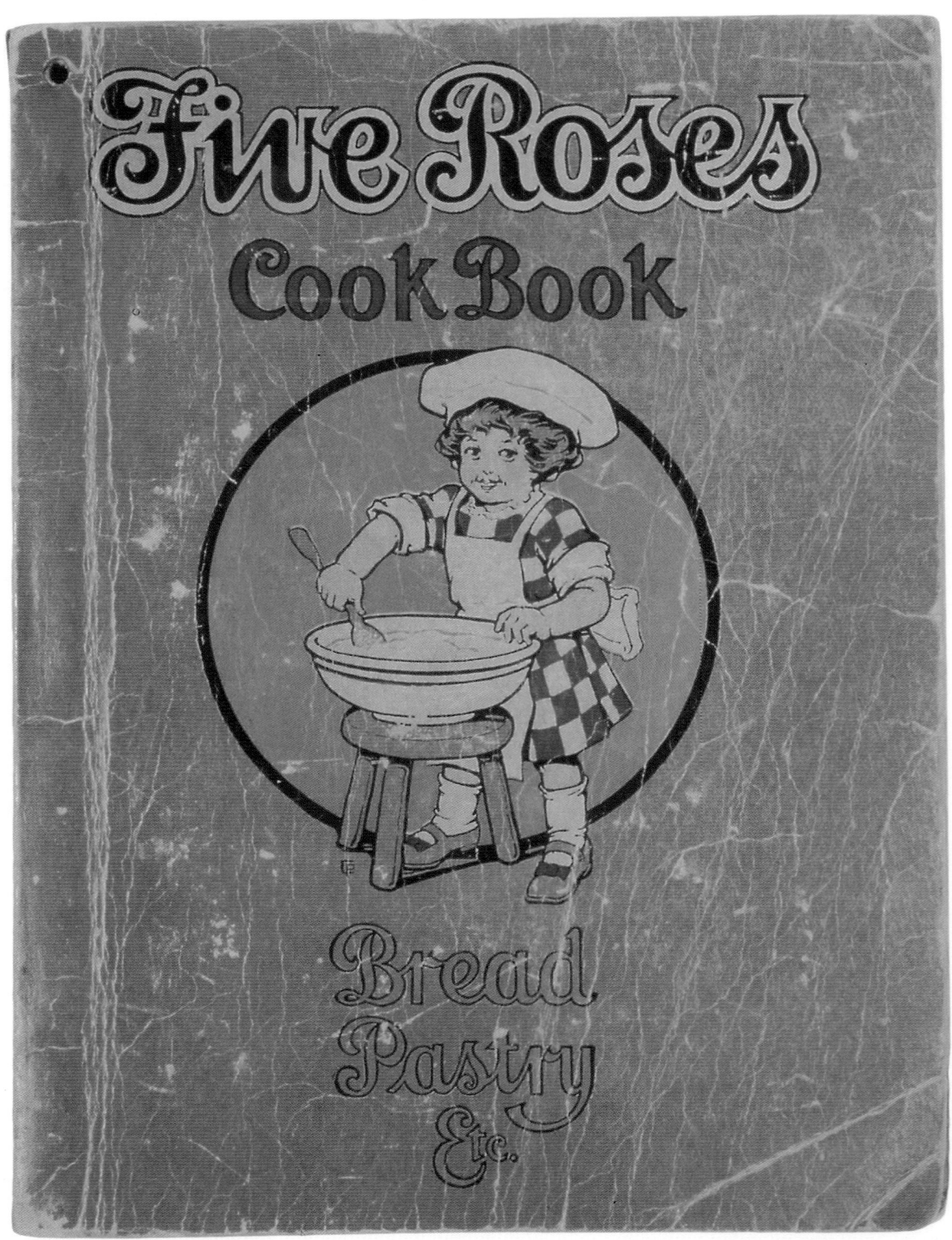

Plate 2a. *Five Roses Cook Book,* Lake of the Woods Milling Co., Montreal and Winnipeg, 1915 (Q79.3). For the French market, the company redesigned the cover and replaced the cute child-cook with an elegant woman (opposite).

Plate 2b. *La cuisinière Five Roses,* Lake of the Woods Milling Co., Montreal, 1915 (Q79.4)

In this Book you will find various contributions
From brave chivalric sons and fairest daughters,
Who, worshipping Canadian soil and Institutions
Love, the emblems of the lands of their fathers,
And desire to unite them, with their own dear nations
Beautiful, Maple-Leaves, and very popular, Beavers.

Plate 3a

Plates 3a–b. *The Canadian Economist,* by the Ladies' Association of Bank Street Church, Ottawa, 1881 (O28.1). Two facing colour lithographs, between pp vi and vii, illustrate a poem linking Canadians with their 'brethren' across the border in the United States.

And also to live, in close fraternal conjunction
With their beloved brethren, over the borders.
Farewell: Be not dismayed at the construction
Of verses, and rythm, by such stupid rhymers,
But look on the " Cookery Book " with compassion
Friends, patrons, high, low, and good neighbours, All.

Plate 3b

Plate 4. Watercolour illustration by the Toronto artist Augusta Helene Carter in *'Cowan's Cocoa Recipes,'* Cowan Co., Toronto, nd [1921], p 44 (O468.1). Other subjects painted by Carter for the book, such as a picnic scene, a young couple on a mansion's grand verandah, and children peaking through a window at a pie, also incorporate cocoa-flavoured desserts or cocoa-drinking.

FRESH PAINT AND A CAREFUL RE-ARRANGEMENT OF UTILITIES WILL
TRANSFORM THE MOST DRAB AND AWKWARD KITCHEN

Plate 5. An up-to-date kitchen illustrated in *McClary's Household Manual*, McClary's, London, Ontario, 1922, p 9 (O488.1). With the exception of the hide-away ironing board, this 1920s kitchen – as in earlier times – is essentially a room filled with freestanding pieces of furniture, from the table and cabinets to the coal-fired stove and the sink on legs (the ice-box is out of sight). Nevertheless, the furniture has been arranged for maximum efficiency, taps replace a hand pump for water supply, and on the floor there is boldly patterned linoleum, about which the text proclaims that 'modern invention ... has produced nothing to surpass a really good linoleum for the kitchen floor.' Not until the 1940s would Canadian kitchens begin to feature streamlined runs of built-in cupboards, counters and appliances.

Plate 6a. [About 1912 or later] (O285.3)

Plate 6b. [Ninth edition, about 1923] (O285.10)

Plates 6a–d. Four cover designs for editions of *The Magic Cook Book and Housekeepers Guide,* E.W. Gillett Co. Ltd, Toronto, published in the period 1912–27

Plate 6c. [Tenth edition, about 1925] (O285.12). The bug-like figures are reminiscent of the popular Brownies created by Quebec-born writer and illustrator Palmer Cox (1840–1924).

Plate 6d. [About 1927] (O285.18)

Plate 7. *The Magic Cook Book,* E.W. Gillett Co. Ltd, Toronto, nd [about 1930–5] (O702.3). Like a magician executing a trick, the woman lifts a napkin to reveal her baking-powder biscuits – Presto!

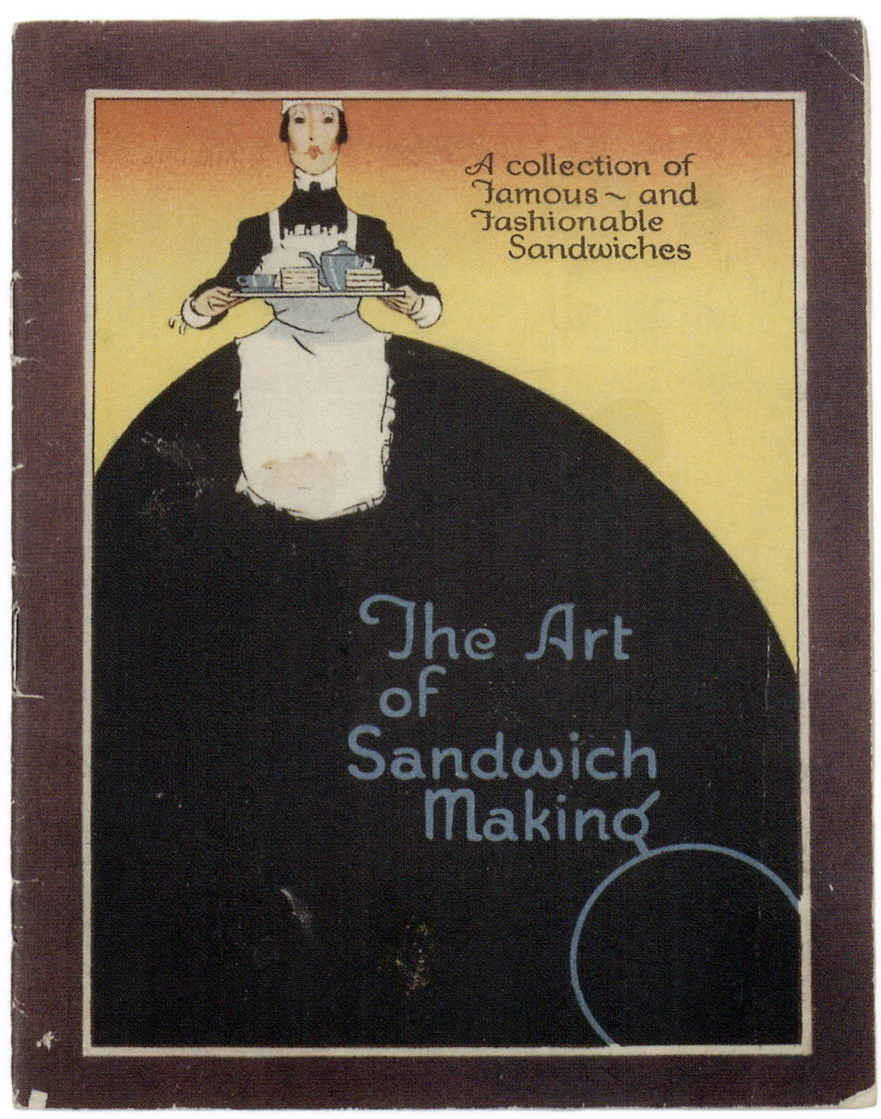

Plate 8. *The Art of Sandwich Making,* Canada Bread Co., Toronto, nd [about 1926] (O576.1). A stylish cover-design promotes the making of fashionable sandwiches with the company's factory-made bread, at a time when many women still made their own homemade loaves.

Plate 9. *Canadian Grown Apples,* Department of Agriculture, Ottawa, 1939 (O496.13). The luscious red fruit and patriotic cover-title are an irresistible invitation to try the apple recipes inside this long-running federal government booklet, first published in French in 1923.

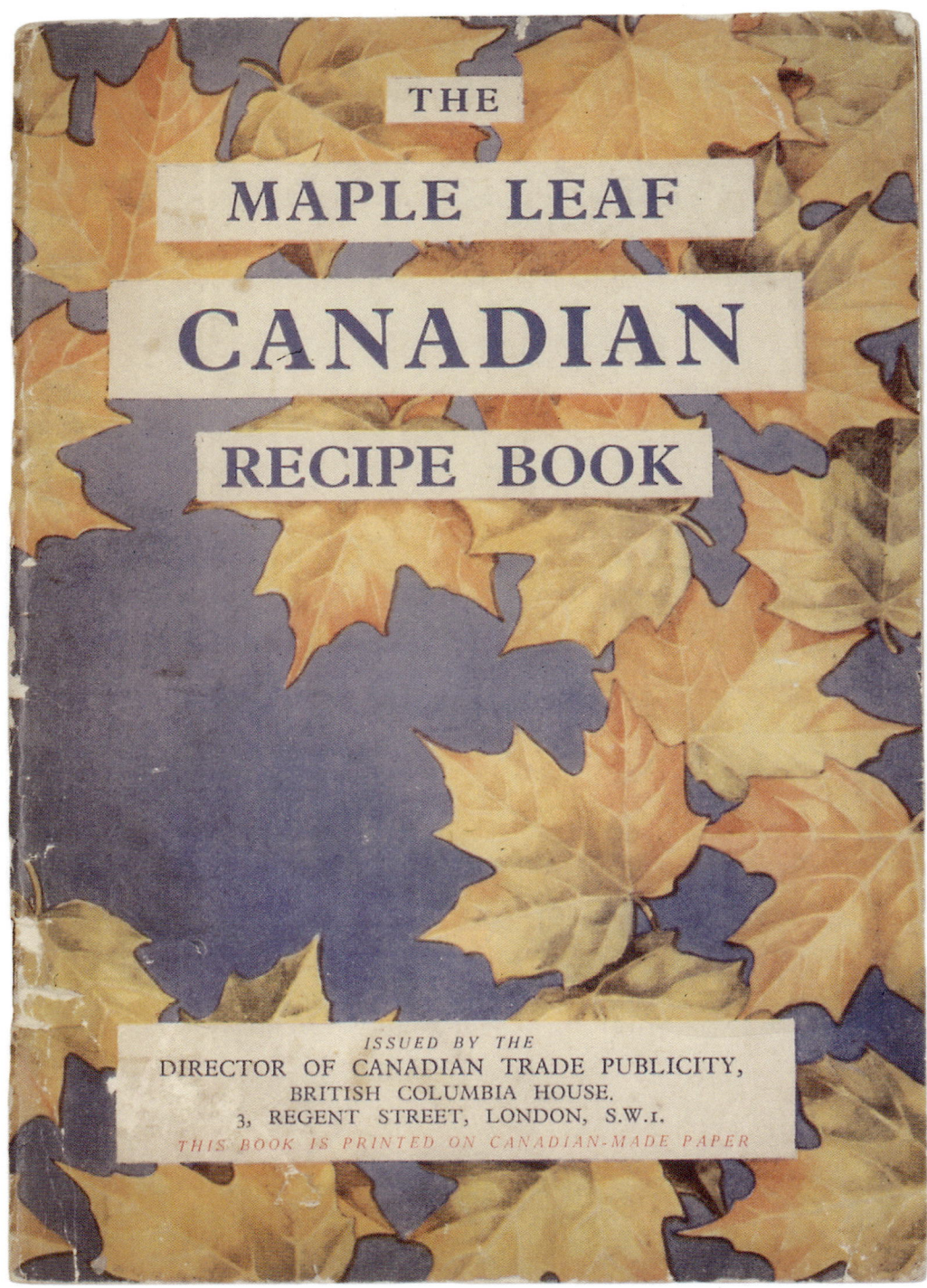

THE
MAPLE LEAF
CANADIAN
RECIPE BOOK

ISSUED BY THE
DIRECTOR OF CANADIAN TRADE PUBLICITY,
BRITISH COLUMBIA HOUSE.
3, REGENT STREET, LONDON, S.W.1.
THIS BOOK IS PRINTED ON CANADIAN-MADE PAPER

Plate 10. *The Maple Leaf Canadian Recipe Book,* by Mrs Kathleen Bowker, nd [about 1931] (GB2.1). The iconic fall-coloured maple leaves cascading across the cover helped sell Canadian products – dried pasta, cereals, canned foods, honey, milk powder, cheese, and fresh apples – to British housewives.

Plate 11. *Margene Recipe Book,* by Brenda York, nd [1949] (O1230.1), designed by Group-of-Seven artist A.J. Casson. Foil endpapers, imitating the margarine wrapping, peak through cut-outs in the cover of the first Canadian advertising cookbook for the newly legalized butter-substitute.

Plate 12. *D M S Cook Book,* by the Daughters of the Midnight Sun, Yellowknife, [1947] (NWT2.1). Designed by a club member, the front cover shows two polar bears greeting each other with an 'Eskimo kiss' and news of a new recipe. The purple-and-gold palette evokes the colours of the North's perpetually light summer sky, from which the DMS took its name.

RITA MARTIN

Plate 13. Oil painting of the fictional Rita Martin, commissioned by Robin Hood Flour Mills from the Toronto artist Rex Woods in the 1940s, reproduced in *Robin Hood Prize Winning Recipes* (Q306.1). Rita's steady, kind gaze encourages readers to believe her message printed on the cookbook's opposite page: 'If you ever have a baking problem or cooking difficulty that this book doesn't solve, won't you write me? For I shall be right here, still working on new recipes and methods for you, and I should love to hear from you.'

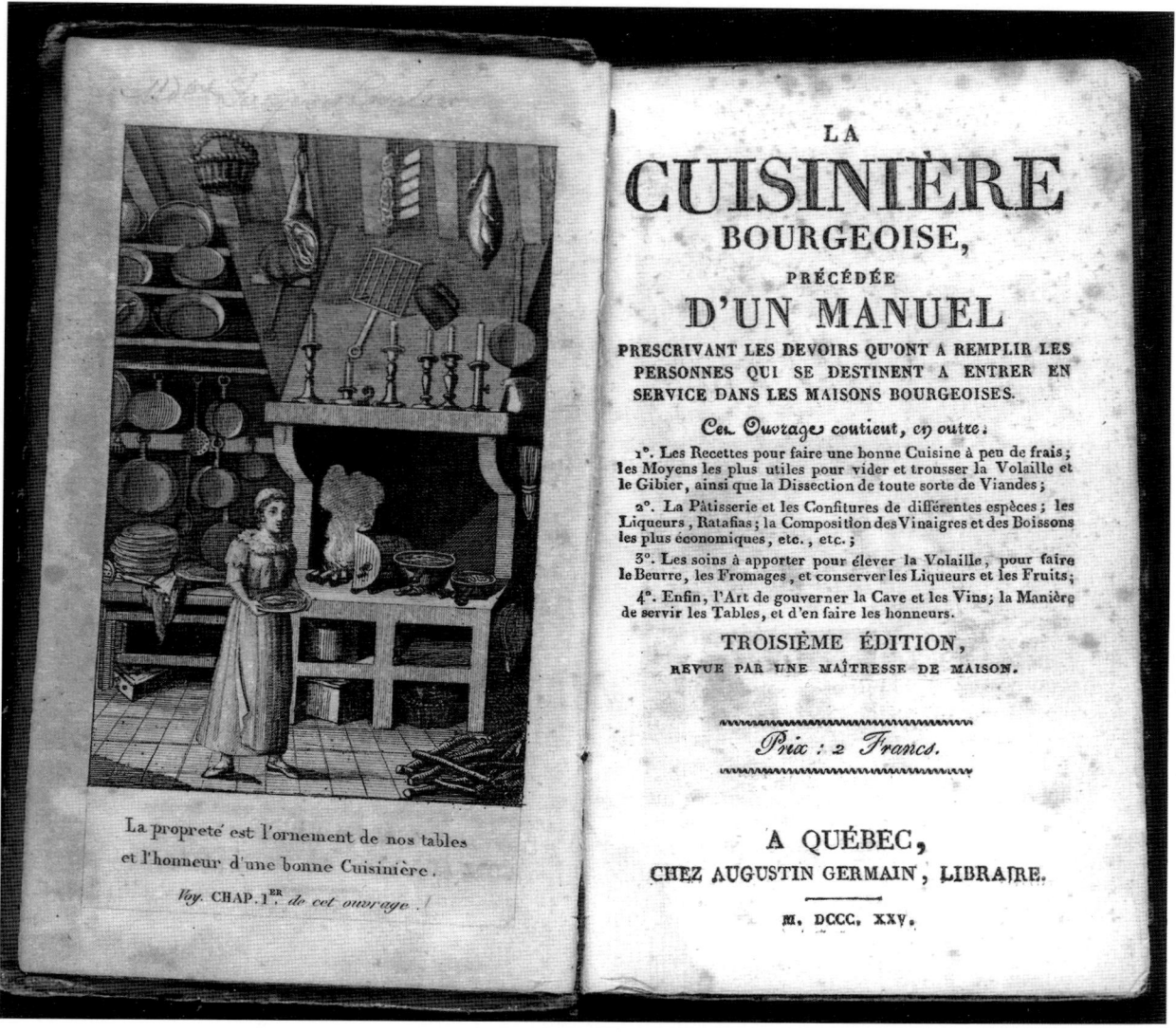

LA
CUISINIÈRE
BOURGEOISE,
PRÉCÉDÉE
D'UN MANUEL
PRESCRIVANT LES DEVOIRS QU'ONT A REMPLIR LES
PERSONNES QUI SE DESTINENT A ENTRER EN
SERVICE DANS LES MAISONS BOURGEOISES.

Cet Ouvrage contient, en outre :

1°. Les Recettes pour faire une bonne Cuisine à peu de frais ;
les Moyens les plus utiles pour vider et trousser la Volaille et
le Gibier, ainsi que la Dissection de toute sorte de Viandes ;

2°. La Pâtisserie et les Confitures de différentes espèces ; les
Liqueurs, Ratafias ; la Composition des Vinaigres et des Boissons
les plus économiques, etc., etc. ;

3°. Les soins à apporter pour élever la Volaille, pour faire
le Beurre, les Fromages, et conserver les Liqueurs et les Fruits ;

4°. Enfin, l'Art de gouverner la Cave et les Vins ; la Manière
de servir les Tables, et d'en faire les honneurs.

TROISIÈME ÉDITION,
REVUE PAR UNE MAÎTRESSE DE MAISON.

Prix : 2 Francs.

A QUÉBEC,
CHEZ AUGUSTIN GERMAIN, LIBRAIRE.

M. DCCC. XXV.

Caption under illustration:

La propreté est l'ornement de nos tables
et l'honneur d'une bonne Cuisinière.

Voy. CHAP. 1ᵉʳ. *de cet ouvrage.*

Plate 14. *La cuisinière bourgeoise,* by Menon, Quebec City, 1825 (Q1.1). This first cookbook published in Canada was entirely printed in France.

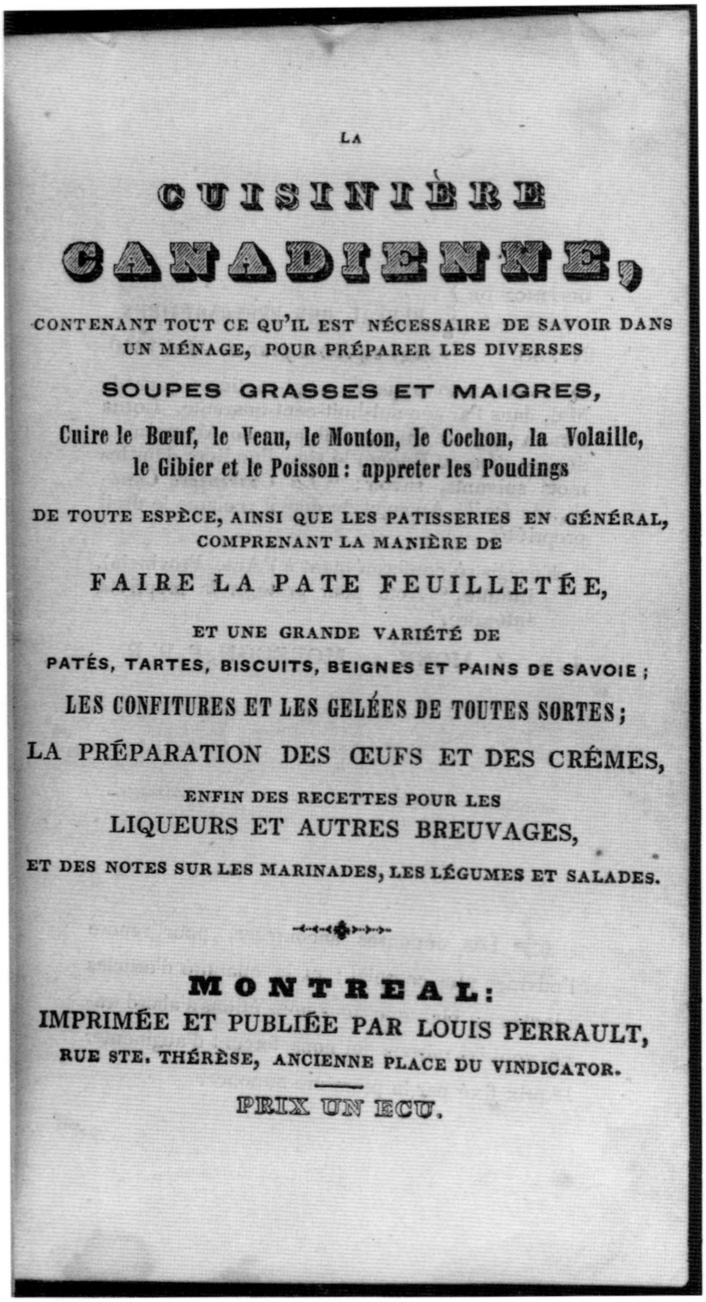

LA

CUISINIÈRE

CANADIENNE,

CONTENANT TOUT CE QU'IL EST NÉCESSAIRE DE SAVOIR DANS UN MÉNAGE, POUR PRÉPARER LES DIVERSES

SOUPES GRASSES ET MAIGRES,

Cuire le Bœuf, le Veau, le Mouton, le Cochon, la Volaille, le Gibier et le Poisson: appreter les Poudings

DE TOUTE ESPÈCE, AINSI QUE LES PATISSERIES EN GÉNÉRAL, COMPRENANT LA MANIÈRE DE

FAIRE LA PATE FEUILLETÉE,

ET UNE GRANDE VARIÉTÉ DE

PATÉS, TARTES, BISCUITS, BEIGNES ET PAINS DE SAVOIE;

LES CONFITURES ET LES GELÉES DE TOUTES SORTES;

LA PRÉPARATION DES ŒUFS ET DES CRÊMES,

ENFIN DES RECETTES POUR LES

LIQUEURS ET AUTRES BREUVAGES,

ET DES NOTES SUR LES MARINADES, LES LÉGUMES ET SALADES.

MONTREAL:

IMPRIMÉE ET PUBLIÉE PAR LOUIS PERRAULT,

RUE STE. THÉRÈSE, ANCIENNE PLACE DU VINDICATOR.

PRIX UN ECU.

Plate 15. *La cuisinière canadienne,* Montreal, 1840 (Q3.1). The first cookbook compiled in Canada in French captured in print traditional Quebec recipes, such as Tourtière au porc frais, Purée au pois, and Beignes, plus boiled Plum Pouding and other English-origin dishes.

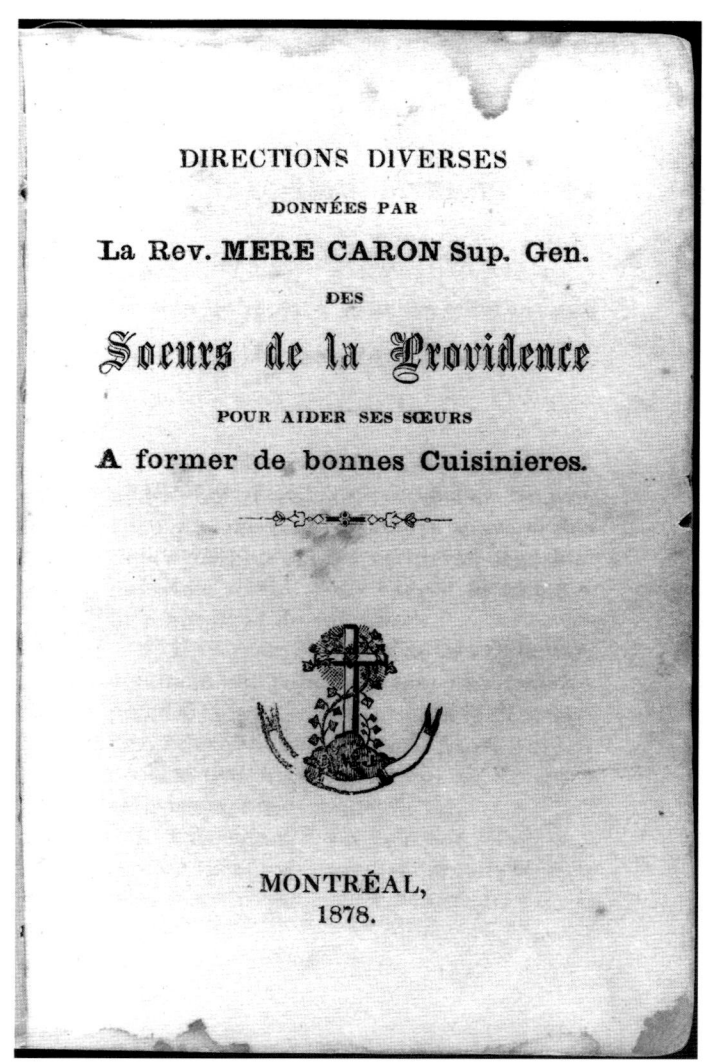

DIRECTIONS DIVERSES

DONNÉES PAR

La Rev. MERE CARON Sup. Gen.

DES

Sœurs de la Providence

POUR AIDER SES SŒURS

A former de bonnes Cuisinieres.

MONTRÉAL,
1878.

Plate 16. *Directions diverses données par la révérende mère Caron,* Montreal, 1878 (Q15.1). Caron, who was mother superior of the Institute of Providence, advises her readers to practise Christian virtues in the kitchen. The moral aspects of cooking and housekeeping would be a common aspect of French-language culinary textbooks to the mid twentieth century.

THE

COOK NOT MAD;

OR

RATIONAL COOKERY:

BEING

A COLLECTION OF ORIGINAL AND SELECTED

RECEIPTS,

Embracing not only the art of curing various kinds of Meats and Vegetables for future use, but of Cooking, in its general acceptation, to the taste, habits, and degrees of luxury, prevalent with the

CANADIAN PUBLIC,

TO WHICH ARE ADDED,

Directions for preparing comforts for the SICK ROOM—together with sundry miscellaneous kinds of information, of importance to housekeepers in general, nearly all tested by experience.

KINGSTON, U. C.
Published by James Macfarlane.
1831.

THE

FRUGAL HOUSEWIFE'S MANUAL:

CONTAINING

A NUMBER OF USEFUL RECEIPTS,

CAREFULLY SELECTED, AND WELL ADAPTED TO THE USE OF FAMILIES IN GENERAL.

To which are added

PLAIN AND PRACTICAL DIRECTIONS

FOR THE

CULTIVATION AND MANAGEMENT OF SOME OF THE MOST USEFUL

CULINARY VEGETABLES.

BY A. B., OF GRIMSBY.

Toronto:
Guardian Office, No. 9, Wellington Buildings.
J. H. LAWRENCE, PRINTER.
1840.

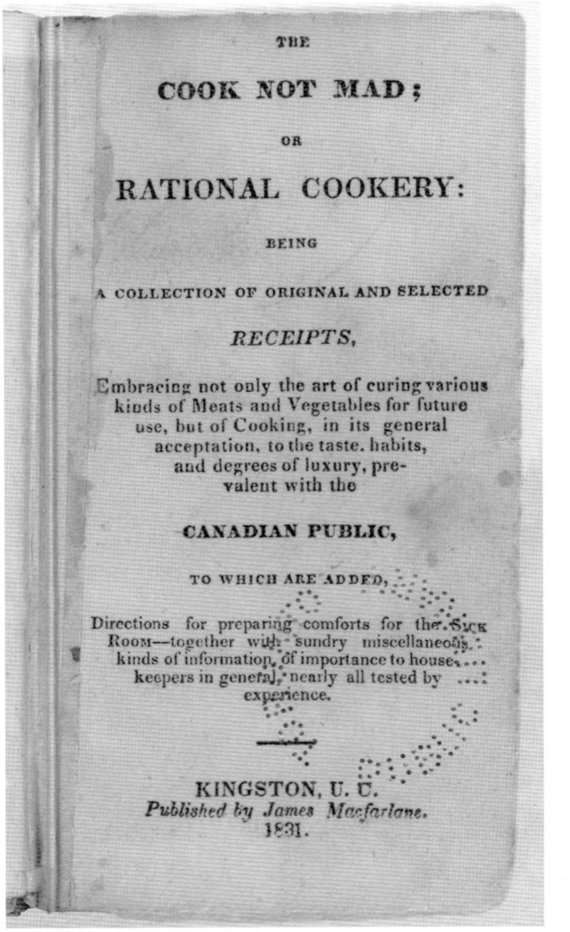

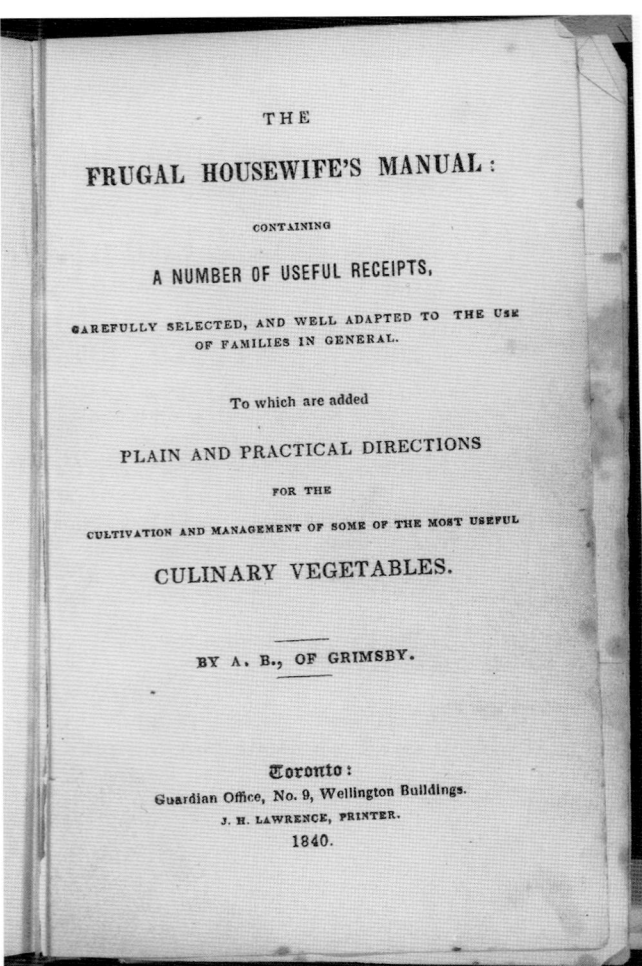

Plate 17. *The Cook Not Mad,* Kingston, Upper Canada, 1831 (O1.1). The first cookbook published in Canada in English was an edition of a work from Watertown, New York, but the recipes reflected Anglo-American tastes and practices shared on both sides of the border.

Plate 18. *The Frugal Housewife's Manual,* by A.B. of Grimsby, Toronto, 1840 (O2.1). The so-far unidentified author of the first cookbook compiled in Canada in English lived in a rich agricultural area, part of the Niagara Peninsula, and the text includes a section for growing and cooking 'the most useful culinary vegetables.'

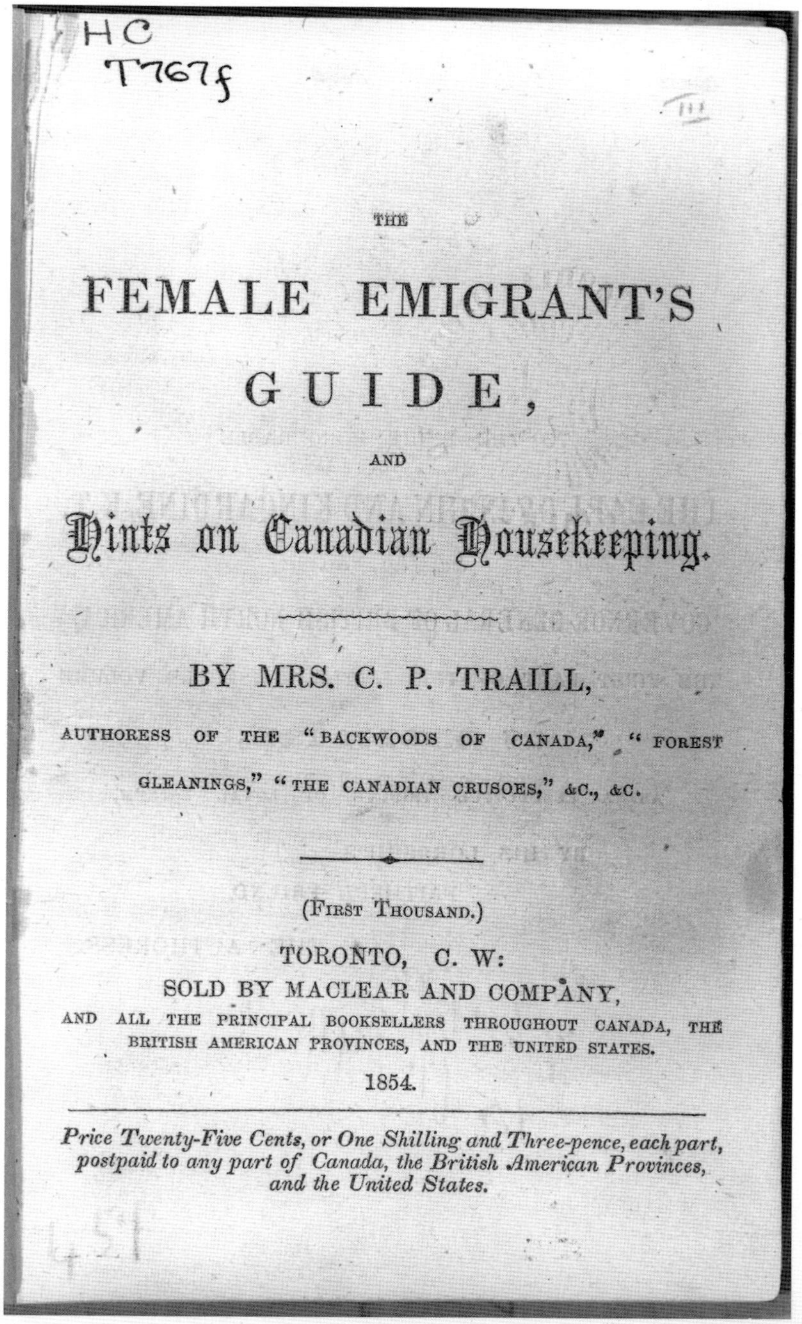

THE

FEMALE EMIGRANT'S GUIDE,

AND

Hints on Canadian Housekeeping.

BY MRS. C. P. TRAILL,

AUTHORESS OF THE "BACKWOODS OF CANADA," "FOREST GLEANINGS," "THE CANADIAN CRUSOES," &C., &C.

(FIRST THOUSAND.)

TORONTO, C. W:
SOLD BY MACLEAR AND COMPANY,
AND ALL THE PRINCIPAL BOOKSELLERS THROUGHOUT CANADA, THE
BRITISH AMERICAN PROVINCES, AND THE UNITED STATES.

1854.

Price Twenty-Five Cents, or One Shilling and Three-pence, each part, postpaid to any part of Canada, the British American Provinces, and the United States.

Plate 19. *The Female Emigrant's Guide,* by Mrs Catharine Parr Traill, Toronto, 1854 [1855] (O5.1). Not counting the elusive A.B. (plate 18), Traill is the first identifiable woman to write a cookbook in Canada. Drawing on over twenty years' experience living in the backwoods, near Peterborough, Ontario, she aimed to describe for English immigrants what was different about preparing food in the colony.

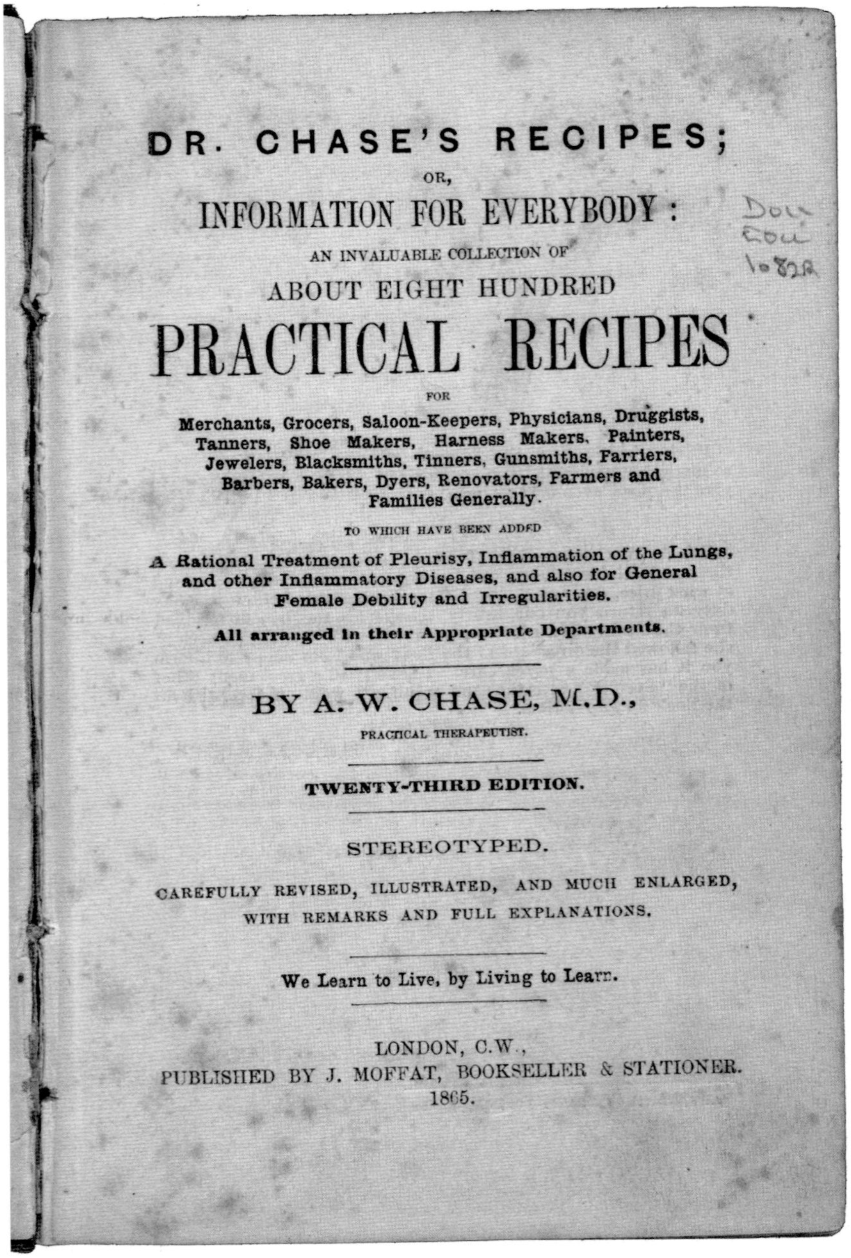

DR. CHASE'S RECIPES;

OR,

INFORMATION FOR EVERYBODY:

AN INVALUABLE COLLECTION OF

ABOUT EIGHT HUNDRED

PRACTICAL RECIPES

FOR

Merchants, Grocers, Saloon-Keepers, Physicians, Druggists,
Tanners, Shoe Makers, Harness Makers, Painters,
Jewelers, Blacksmiths, Tinners, Gunsmiths, Farriers,
Barbers, Bakers, Dyers, Renovators, Farmers and
Families Generally.

TO WHICH HAVE BEEN ADDED

A Rational Treatment of Pleurisy, Inflammation of the Lungs,
and other Inflammatory Diseases, and also for General
Female Debility and Irregularities.

All arranged in their Appropriate Departments.

BY A. W. CHASE, M.D.,

PRACTICAL THERAPEUTIST.

TWENTY-THIRD EDITION.

STEREOTYPED.

CAREFULLY REVISED, ILLUSTRATED, AND MUCH ENLARGED,
WITH REMARKS AND FULL EXPLANATIONS.

We Learn to Live, by Living to Learn.

LONDON, C.W.,
PUBLISHED BY J. MOFFAT, BOOKSELLER & STATIONER.
1865.

Plate 20. *Dr Chase's Recipes,* by Dr Alvin Wood Chase, twenty-third edition, London, 1865 (O8.1). Despite the numbering, this is the first of at least nineteen Canadian editions of the Ann Arbor, Michigan, doctor's compendium, a valuable reference work in a largely self-sufficient society before the era of professional medicine.

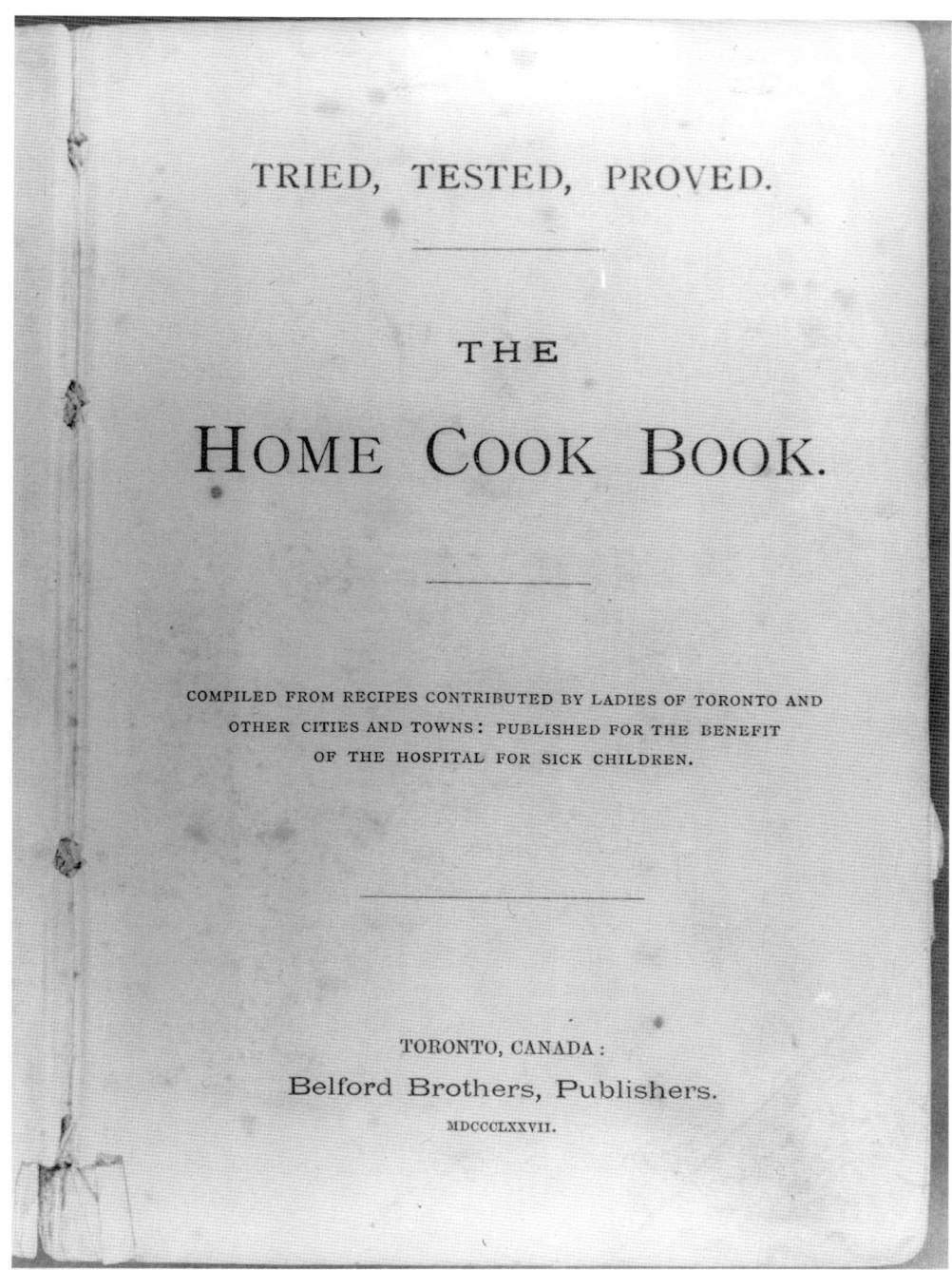

TRIED, TESTED, PROVED.

THE

HOME COOK BOOK.

COMPILED FROM RECIPES CONTRIBUTED BY LADIES OF TORONTO AND
OTHER CITIES AND TOWNS: PUBLISHED FOR THE BENEFIT
OF THE HOSPITAL FOR SICK CHILDREN.

TORONTO, CANADA:
Belford Brothers, Publishers.
MDCCCLXXVII.

Plate 21. *The Home Cook Book,* by ladies of Toronto and other cities and towns, Toronto, 1877, the only known copy of the first edition (O20.1). Canada's first community cookbook became the country's bestselling culinary manual of the nineteenth century.

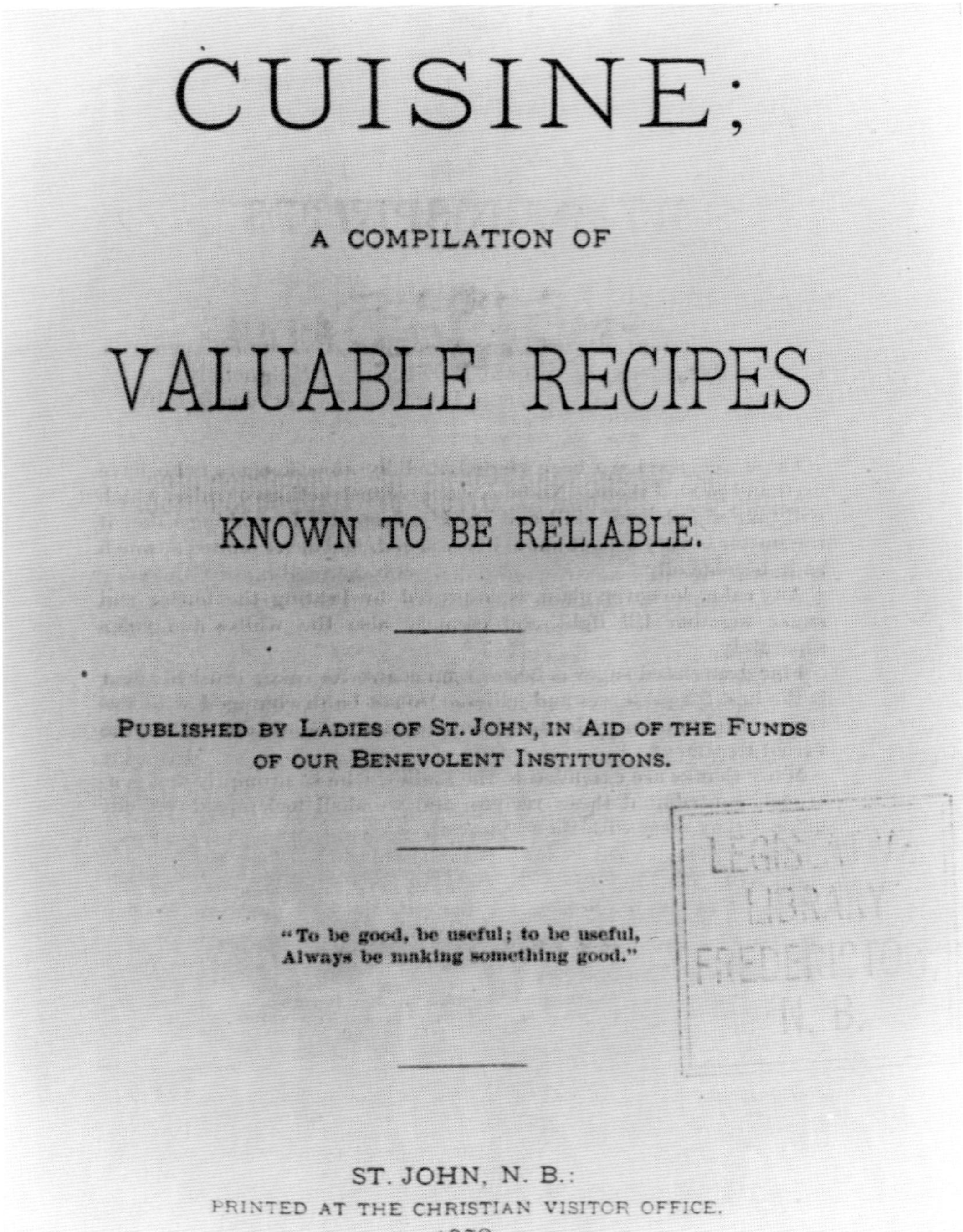

CUISINE;

A COMPILATION OF

VALUABLE RECIPES

KNOWN TO BE RELIABLE.

PUBLISHED BY LADIES OF ST. JOHN, IN AID OF THE FUNDS
OF OUR BENEVOLENT INSTITUTONS.

"To be good, be useful; to be useful,
Always be making something good."

ST. JOHN, N. B.:
PRINTED AT THE CHRISTIAN VISITOR OFFICE.
1878.

Plate 22. *Cuisine,* by the ladies of Saint John, New Brunswick, 1878 (NB2.1), the only known copy of Canada's second community cookbook

"She Does Not Know Chicken from Turkey."

Helene is the handsomest girl of her race,
She's an elegant form and an exquisite face,
And she dresses with perfectly consummate grace,
But she doesn't know chicken from turkey;
She knows many languages, living and dead;
In science and fiction is very well read,
But she cannot cook meat, and she cannot make bread,
And she doesn't know chicken from turkey.

She can play a "Fantasia" or "Nocturne" with skill;
Can sing up to "B"—has a wonderful trill;
Can write a good story or sonnet, but still
She doesn't know chicken from turkey.
She's been up the Tiber, the Rhine and the Nile,
She's a painter in every popular style—
Can decorate china, a plaque or a tile,
But she doesn't know chicken from turkey.

She's always self-satisfied, graceful and cool;
A critic, both just and correct as a rule;
And knows every stitch of the Kensington school,
But she doesn't know chicken from turkey.
She can work a design by Lansing or Burt;
But she cannot cut out for her children a skirt,
Or make for her husband a well-fitting shirt—
She doesn't know chicken from turkey.

I'm willing a girl should read Latin and Greek;
Should German and French and Italian speak;
And be "up" in the latest esthetical freak,
If she only knows chicken from turkey.
I'd like her in music and song to take part;
Read poetry, science and cultivate art,
If husband and children were first to her heart,
And if she knew chicken from turkey.

Knew barley from rice, knew a tart from a pie;
A boil from a stew, a broil from a fry;
And if she went into the market to buy,
Knew very well chicken from turkey.
For, to make a home happy, all knowledge must blend
Art, science and service their benefits lend;
Then, ladies so clever and wise, condescend
To know about chicken or turkey.

Now, here comes the moral of this little tale,
Which showed that Helene did not know the word "fail,"
For she went to where cookery books were for sale,
And made known her desire to the clerk. He,
From several volumes, immediately took
A copy of "Mrs. Clarke's Cookery Book,"
And said, "You'll soon know, if through this you will look,
What to do with a chicken or turkey."

MRS. CLARKE'S
COOKERY BOOK
IS
NOW READY AT ALL BOOKSELLERS.

WHOLESALE AT
WM. WARWICK & SONS'.

Plate 23. Advertisement for *Mrs Clarke's Cookery Book*, by Mrs Anne Clarke, Toronto, 1883, in *Toronto World* 13 November 1883 (O35.1)

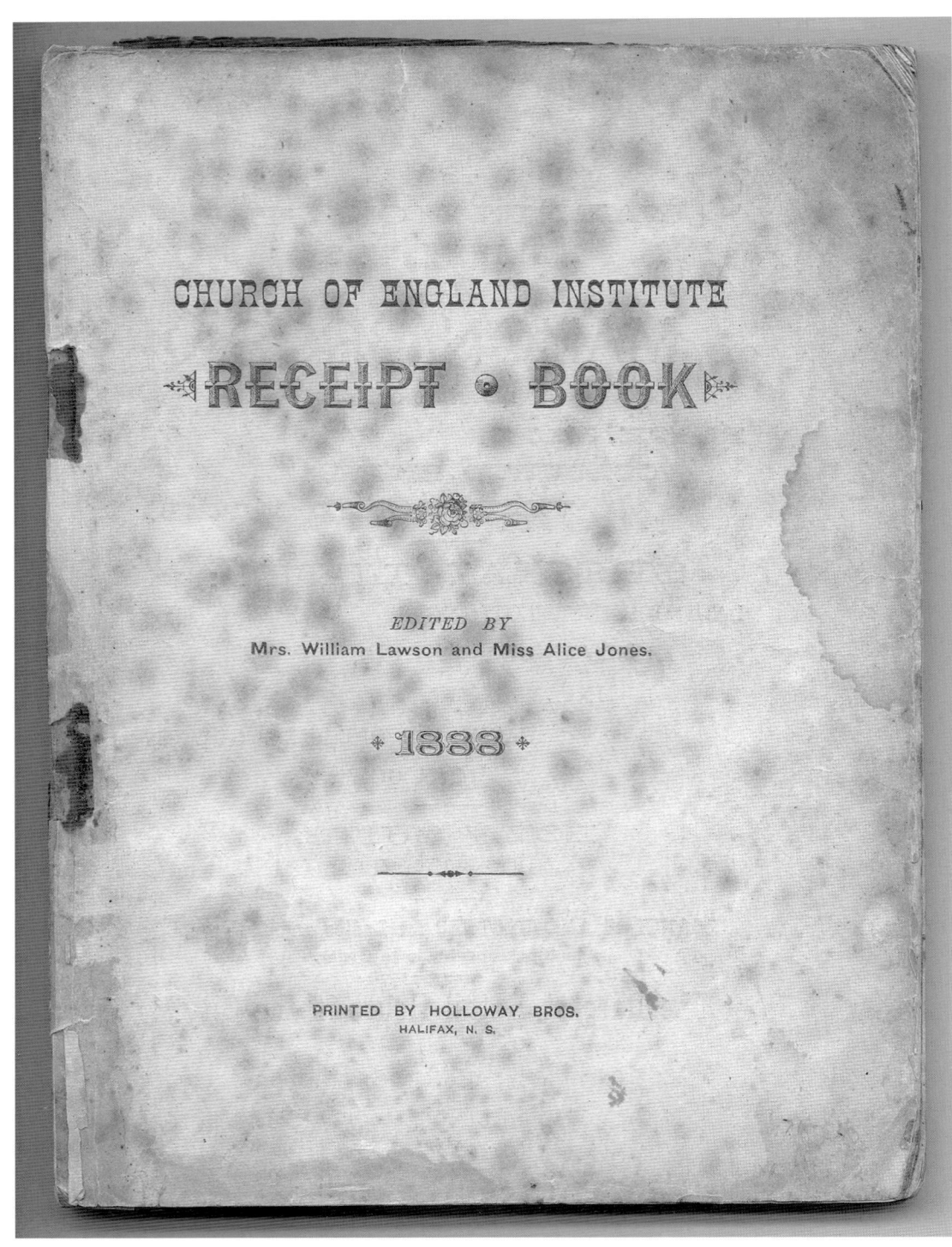

CHURCH OF ENGLAND INSTITUTE

RECEIPT · BOOK

EDITED BY
Mrs. William Lawson and Miss Alice Jones.

1888

PRINTED BY HOLLOWAY BROS.
HALIFAX, N. S.

Plate 24. *Church of England Institute Receipt Book,* by Mrs Mary Jane Lawson and Miss Alice C. Jones, Halifax, Nova Scotia, 1888 (NS1.1). Both editors of the first cookbook published in Nova Scotia contributed to Canada's early literary history as writers, and in Lawson's case, also as a bookseller and publisher.

Plate 25. *Jubilee Cook Book,* by the Ladies' Aid Society of the First Methodist Church, Charlottetown, Prince Edward Island, 1897 (P1.1). Age hides the pretty pink colour of the paper-covered boards of this book celebrating Queen Victoria's sixty-year reign.

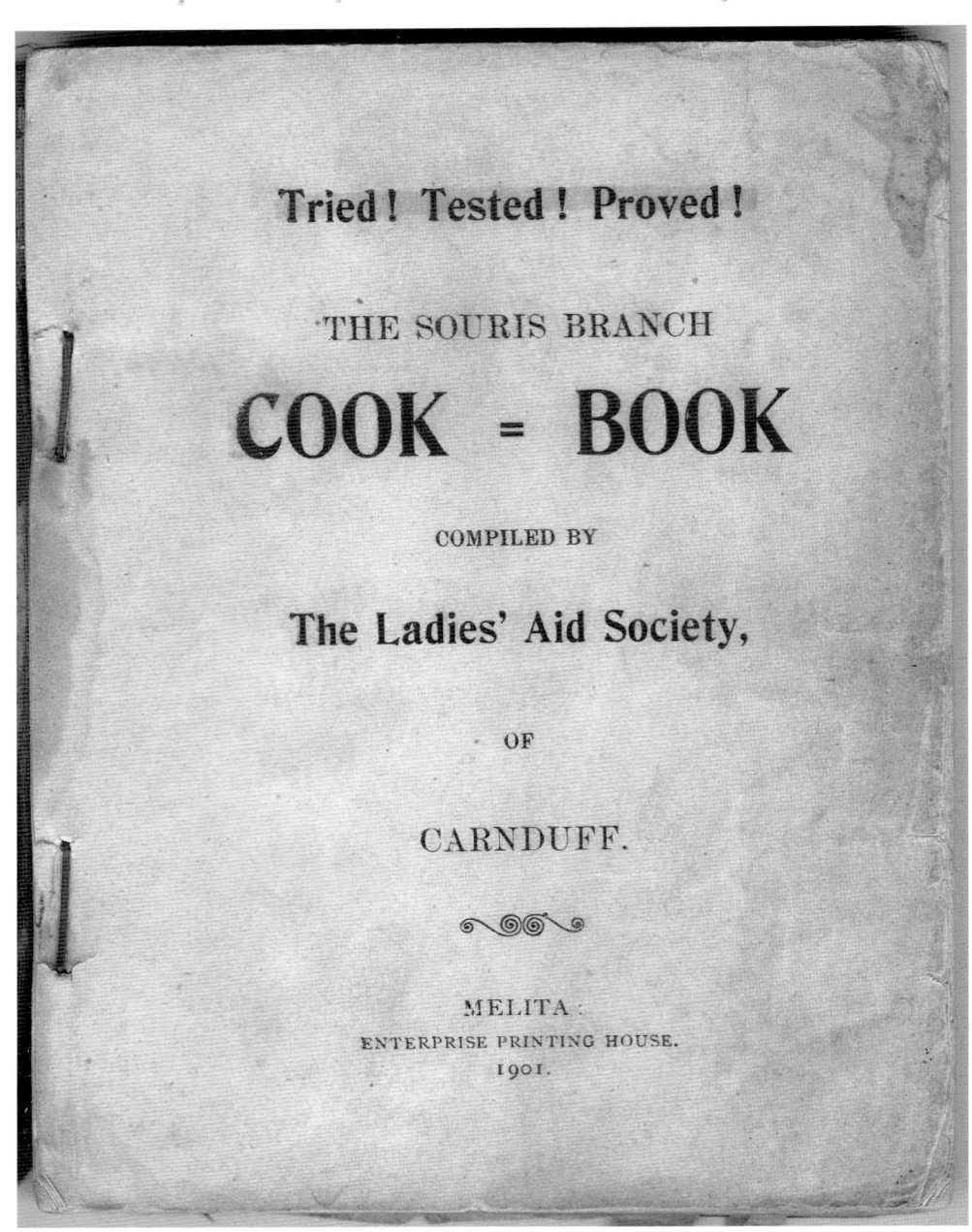

Plate 26. *The Souris Branch Cook Book,* by the Ladies' Aid Society of Carnduff, Melita, 1901 (S1.1), the only known copy of the first culinary manual published in what is now Saskatchewan. Typical of Canadian cookbooks, two staples secure the leaves.

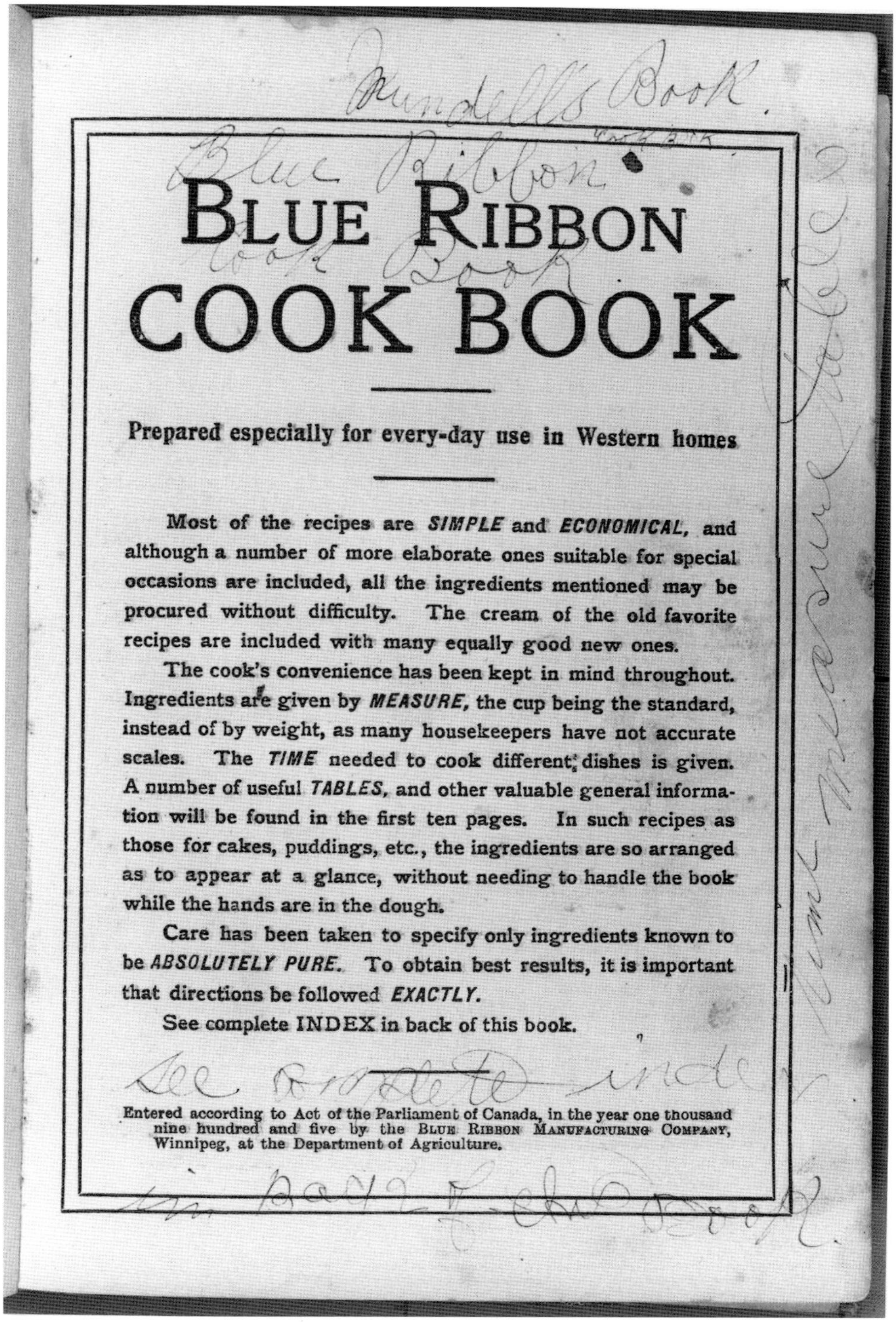

BLUE RIBBON
COOK BOOK

Prepared especially for every-day use in Western homes

Most of the recipes are *SIMPLE* and *ECONOMICAL*, and although a number of more elaborate ones suitable for special occasions are included, all the ingredients mentioned may be procured without difficulty. The cream of the old favorite recipes are included with many equally good new ones.

The cook's convenience has been kept in mind throughout. Ingredients are given by *MEASURE*, the cup being the standard, instead of by weight, as many housekeepers have not accurate scales. The *TIME* needed to cook different dishes is given. A number of useful *TABLES*, and other valuable general information will be found in the first ten pages. In such recipes as those for cakes, puddings, etc., the ingredients are so arranged as to appear at a glance, without needing to handle the book while the hands are in the dough.

Care has been taken to specify only ingredients known to be *ABSOLUTELY PURE*. To obtain best results, it is important that directions be followed *EXACTLY*.

See complete INDEX in back of this book.

Entered according to Act of the Parliament of Canada, in the year one thousand nine hundred and five by the BLUE RIBBON MANUFACTURING COMPANY, Winnipeg, at the Department of Agriculture.

Plate 27. *Blue Ribbon Cook Book,* Blue Ribbon Manufacturing Co., Winnipeg, 1905 (M7.1), an advertising vehicle for the company's coffee, tea, and flavouring products for over half a century. Many Prairie families, and later Easterners, owned editions of this book.

Plate 28. *Cobalt Souvenir and Cook Book,* by the ladies of the Presbyterian Church, Cobalt, Ontario, 1908–9 (O204.1). The ladies – community boosters for the new northern mining town – illustrated their fund-raiser with photographs of local scenes.

Plate 29. One of several cartoons in *The 'Shamrock' Girl,* P. Burns and Co. Ltd, Calgary, nd [about 1918] (A31.4), featuring two joke-cracking Irish meat inspectors, Shamrock (right) and Weaney (middle)

"*Friendship is the most pleasant of all things,
and nothing more glads the heart of man.*"

FAMOUS
POINTE MOUILLÉE
CLUB RECIPES

A.J.D., D. R. Pepin, C.M., Peter McK., " Blake."
THE " SHANTY," 1891

Plate 30. *Famous Pointe Mouillée Club Recipes,* [Bainsville, October 1919] (O422.1). The recipes are those served to the hunting club (mostly wealthy Montrealers). Their 'shanty' was located on Lake Francis, part of the St Lawrence River, where there was an abundance of migrating waterfowl to shoot – and eat.

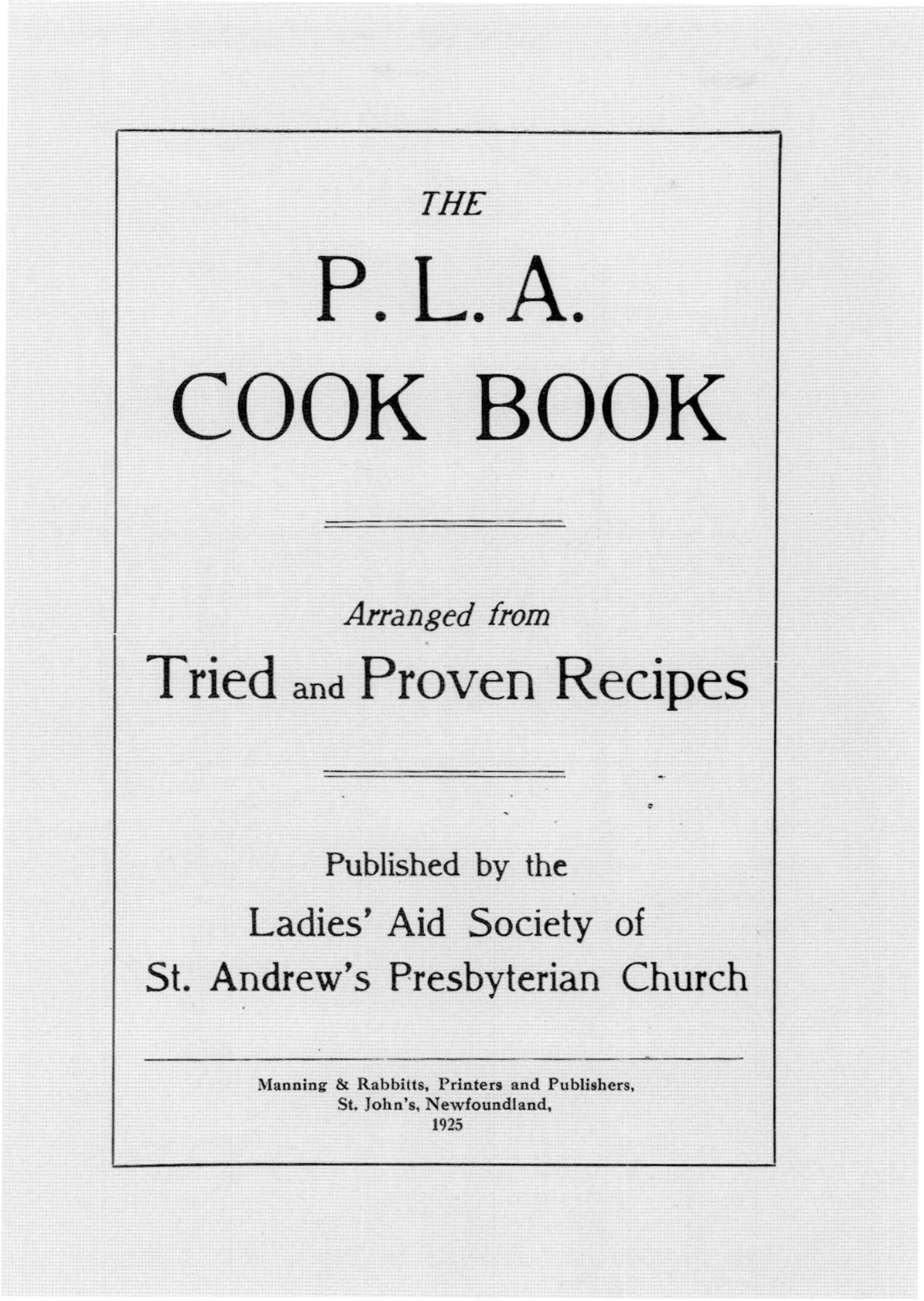

THE
P. L. A.
COOK BOOK

Arranged from

Tried and Proven Recipes

Published by the

Ladies' Aid Society of
St. Andrew's Presbyterian Church

Manning & Rabbitts, Printers and Publishers,
St. John's, Newfoundland,
1925

Plate 31. *The P.L.A. Cook Book,* by the Ladies' Aid Society of St Andrew's Presbyterian Church, St John's, Newfoundland, 1925 (NF5.2). The text encompasses frugal recipes (Bottled Fish and Salmon made from locally caught fish) and what were at the time sophisticated dishes for entertaining (Waldorf Salad, a New York chef's recipe).

Plate 32. *9th Annual Edith Adam's Wartime Cook Book,* published by *Vancouver Sun* newspaper, nd [1943] (B114.1). The artist Fraser Wilson devised a cheerful, animated building (the newspaper's headquarters) to introduce this issue of wartime recipes. His design perfectly reflects Edith's 'Preface,' in which she says to British Columbians, 'We are thankful our food situation is as happy as it is.'

Plate 33. Image of Mother Caron in 1855, twenty-three years before the publication of *Directions diverses* (Q15.1)

Plate 34. Elizabeth McMaster, the motivating force behind the founding of Toronto's Hospital for Sick Children in 1875, the treasurer of the hospital's Ladies' Committee, and the contributor of the 'Preface' to *The Home Cook Book*, 1877 (O20.1). Mrs McMaster is wearing a nurse's uniform, which suggests that the photograph was taken no earlier than 1889, when she began her two-year nurse training in Chicago, returning in 1891 to become lady superintendent.

Plate 35. Dora Stevenson, née Fairfield, a descendant of United Empire Loyalists and author of *Dora's Cook Book,* 1888 (O43.1), photograph taken in 1939, at the age of 77 years

Plate 36. Mrs Grace Denison, society reporter for *Saturday Night* magazine and author of *The New Cook Book,* 1903 (O130.1)

Plate 37. Mlle Jeanne Anctil, director of Les écoles ménagères provinciales in Montreal and author of *350 recettes de cuisine*, 1912 (Q73.1)

Plate 38. Miss Nellie Lyle Pattinson, author of *Canadian Cook Book*, 1923 (O506.1), and director of domestic science at Central Technical School from about 1920 to 1942, as pictured in the school's 1943 yearbook, p 28

Plate 39. Soeur Sainte-Marie Edith / Sister St Mary Edith, director of the Montreal Cooking School and author of *Les secrets de la bonne cuisine*, copyright 1928 (Q171.1)

Plate 40. Miss Gertrude Dutton depicted in *Specially Selected Recipes*, [about 1931] (M70.1), published by *Western Home Monthly*, where she ran the periodical's Better Cookery Department

Plate 41. Photograph of Jessie Read, demonstrator for Consumers' Gas Co. in Toronto, then columnist at the *Toronto Evening Telegram* and star of *Kitchen Talks* (Canada's first cooking-school movie), reproduced in her first book, *Three Meals a Day Recipe Review,* [1934], p 1 (O830.1)

Plate 42. Miss Edith Elliot, on staff at the federal Department of Agriculture from 1930, for two decades, and the compiler of several recipe collections, the first being *Canadian Vegetables for Every Day* (O665.1)

Plate 43. Miss Laura Pepper, federal Department of Agriculture employee from about 1930 to 1964, a colleague of Elliot, and author of several culinary titles, beginning with *Milk Desserts* (O676.1)

Plate 44. Mrs Mary Moore, for fifty years the writer of a daily cooking column published in newspapers across the country, photographed in about 1943, in the decade she wrote *The Bee Hive Cook Book* (O1054.1) and *Fruit-Kepe Recipes* (O1104.1)

Plate 45. Mrs Kate Aitken, in her kitchen at Sunny-bank Acres, near Streetsville, Ontario, 1955, ten years after the first edition of *Kate Aitken's Canadian Cook Book* (Q292.1)

Plate 46. Mrs Marianne Linnell (right), the person behind the fictional Edith Adams at the *Vancouver Sun* from 1 February 1947 to about 1960, with her colleague Zazu Pitts (left); Marianne is holding *Edith Adams' Thirteenth Prize Cook Book*, 1950.

Helpful hints for housekeepers 1913

See O263.1 for information about the company and other issues of Helpful Hints for Housekeepers.

O303.1   1913
1913 Volume III. 1913 / Hang me in the kitchen / Helpful / hints / for housekeepers / Compliments of / the Dodds Medicine Co. / Limited / Toronto, Can. [cover-title]
DESCRIPTION: 17.0 × 11.5 cm   Pp 1–32   Paper; stapled, and with hole punched at top left corner for hanging
CONTENTS: Inside front face of binding 'Volume III' [introductory text]; 1 'Every Day Uses of Salt'; 2 'Uses of Borax' and 'Uses of Ammonia'; 3 'Understand the Subject'; 4, 6 'Points for the Kitchen'; 5 'Nature Cures'; 7–8 lacking; 9 'Unconscious Health'; 10, 12 'Things Worth Remembering'; 11 'Insidious Disease'; 13 'The Sentinel Off Guard'; 14 'Here's a Handy List for Brides Who Intend to Begin Housekeeping'; 15 'The Records of History'; 16 'To Get Rid of Pests'; 17 'The Cost of Failing Health'; 18 'The Sewing Room'; 19 'The Aching Spot'; 20 'The Sick Room'; 21 'The Most Practical System'; 22 'Health and Beauty'; 23 'What to Shun'; 24 'Housecleaning Time'; 25 'A Seeming Paradox'; 26 'Linens'; 27 'Mysterious but True'; 28 'Care of Furniture'; 29 'Diamond Dinner Pills'; 30 'Weights and Measures'; 31 'Dodd's Dyspepsia Tablets'; 32 'Comparative Value of Foods'; inside back face 'Self Examination Page'
COPIES: *AALIWWM   OTUTF (uncat patent medicine)
NOTES: The introductory text refers to 'Volume Number One, published in 1911, ...' and 'Volume Number Two' published 'last year,' i.e., O263.1 and O281.1.

Larned, Mrs Linda Hull (1853–1939)

Also by this American author are: The Little Epicure, *New York: Baker and Taylor Co., [c1894] (United States: DLC);* One Hundred Cold Desserts, *New York: C. Scribner's Sons, 1914 (United States: DLC);* One Hundred Salads, *New York: Charles Scribner's Sons, 1914 (United States: DLC);* One Hundred Luncheon Dishes, *New York: Charles Scribner's Sons, 1915 (OTMCL); and* One Hundred Picnic Suggestions, *New York: Charles Scribner's Sons, 1915 (United States: DLC).*

O304.1   1913
The / new hostess / of to-day / by / Linda Hull Larned / With illustrations by / Mary Cowles Clark / Toronto / McClelland & Goodchild / publishers
DESCRIPTION: 20.0 × 13.5 cm   Pp [i–iv] v–vii [viii] ix–xiii [xiv] xv–xxiii [xxiv], 1–428   Tp illus of animated foodstuffs, many small illus   Cloth, with image on front of a nude imp toasting bread by a fire in an open hearth
CONTENTS: i ht; ii blank; iii tp; iv 'Copyright, 1913, by Charles Scribner's Sons // Published February, 1913 // The Scribner Press'; v–vii preface; viii blank; ix–xiii 'Hints to the Novice'; xiv blank; xv–xvi 'Please Read Carefully before Using This Book'; xvii–xxiii table of contents; xxiv blank; 1–399 text; 400 blank; 401–28 index
CITATIONS: Spadoni/Donnelly No. 3811 ('Imprints Not Located')
COPIES: *OGU (UA s047 b08)
NOTES: Larned states her purpose in the preface, '... to assist the housekeeper and hostess in selecting and serving a menu suitable for an elaborate repast or a simple meal; to show her how to prepare and serve each course and to provide a quantity sufficient for six persons.' There are 1,975 numbered recipes. According to Spadoni/Donnelly, this book is cited in *Bookseller and Stationer* Vol. 29, No. 3 (March 1913).

AMERICAN EDITIONS: New York: C. Scribner's Sons, 1899 (United States: DLC); February 1913 (cited in 1924 ed.); New York: Charles Scribner's Sons, 1916 (OGU); New York: Scribner's, 1920 (United States: DLC); New York: Charles Scribner's Sons, 1924 (OTMCL).

Merri or Meri, Mme

Probably also by this author is Art of Entertaining for All Occasions, *Toronto: McClelland and Goodchild Ltd, 1913, which BS, Vol. 29, No. 12 (December 1913), p 26, records as by 'Mms. [sic] Meri [sic].' Spadoni/Donnelly No. 3827, under 'Imprints Not Located,' incorrectly transcribe the title as 'Art of entertainment ...'*

O305.1   1913
[An edition of *Salads, Sandwiches and Beverages,* Toronto: McClelland and Goodchild Ltd, 1913, $1.00]
CITATIONS: BS, Vol. 29, No. 11 (November 1913), p 28   Spadoni/Donnelly No. 3828 ('Imprints Not Located')

Neil, Marion Harris

Miss Neil studied at the West End Training School of Cookery in Glasgow, Scotland, but she made her career in the United States, where most of her books were published. The following titles were published in Canada: O306.1, Candies and Bonbons and How to Make Them; O325.1, Canning, Preserving and Pickling; O343.1, The Story of Crisco; O390.1, A 'Calendar of Dinners' with 615 Recipes ... Including The Story of Crisco; possibly O391.1, The Economy Cook Book; Q103.1, Sixty-five Delicious Dishes Made with Bread; and O425.1, Economical Cookery.

By Neil, but not published in Canada, are: Alcono Cook Book, Newark, NY: J.M. Pitkin and Co., c1909 (United States: DLC); How to Cook in Casserole Dishes, Philadelphia: David McKay, [copyright 1912] (OGU; United States: DLC); Delicious Recipes Made with Mueller's Products, Jersey City, NJ: C.F. Mueller Co., c1914 (United States: DLC); The Something Different Dish, Philadelphia: David McKay, [c. 1915] (Bitting, p 340); Ryzon Baking Book, New York: General Chemical Co., copyright 1916 (OTNY uncat; United States: DLC, InU); Salads, Sandwiches and Chafing Dish Recipes, Philadelphia: D. McKay, [c1916] (United States: DLC); Good Things to Eat, San Francisco: California Packing Corp., c1917 (United States: DLC); The Thrift Cook Book, Philadelphia: David McKay, [c1919] (United States: DLC); and 43 Delicious Ways of Serving McMenamin's Crab Meat, Hampton, Va: McMenamin and Co., [192-?] (United States: DLC). She edited Favorite Recipes Cook Book, New York: F.M. Lupton, 1917 (United States: DLC).

O306.1 [copyright 1913]
Candies and bonbons / and / how to make them / by / Marion Harris Neil, M.C.A. / Cookery Editor, The Ladies' Home Journal, Philadelphia, and Principal, / the Philadelphia Practical School of Cookery; author of / "How to Cook in Casserole Dishes" / Toronto / The Musson Book Company / Limited
DESCRIPTION: 18.5 × 12.0 cm Pp [i–ii] iii [iv] v [vi] vii [viii], [9–10] 11–287, [i] 16 pls incl frontis Cloth, with image on front of a beribboned basket
CONTENTS: i tp; ii 'Copyright, 1913, by David McKay'; iii table of contents; iv blank; v 'Illustrations'; vi blank; vii 'Preface' signed Marion Harris Neil; viii blank; 9–275 text; 276 blank; 277–87 index; i publ ad for the author's *How to Cook in Casserole Dishes*
COPIES: *SBIM

NOTES: The SBIM copy is inscribed on the front end-paper, in ink, 'Mrs. A.J. Saich'; and stamped below the inscription, 'Dr. A.J. Saich // dentist // Biggar Sask.' The title-page is inscribed, in ink, 'To Alma [i.e., the dentist's wife] from Alex [i.e., Dr Alex Saich]. 1921.' (From the perspective of current medical practice, it is odd to find a candy cookbook in a dentist's family.) There is a later inscription, by a subsequent owner of the book, on the front endpaper, in ball-point pen, 'Mrs Alma Covey' (not apparently related to the Saich family).

AMERICAN EDITIONS: Philadelphia: D. McKay, [c1913] (United States: DLC).

BRITISH EDITIONS: London and Edinburgh: W. and R. Chambers Ltd, 1913 (Australia: VMRoT; Great Britain: LWel, LoEN, OB, OPo(F)); 1914 (Driver 752.3); London and Edinburgh: W. and R. Chambers Ltd, nd [1923] (Great Britain: LCoF, OPo(F)).

Our candi(e)d opinions

O307.1 nd [about 1913]
[An edition of *Our Candi(e)d Opinions: Recipes for Making Candies*, Kingston, Ont.: Alert Club, Cooke's Presbyterian Church, nd [about 1913], pp 16]
CITATIONS: AnderCat No. 7318
COPIES: OONL (A-12927)
NOTES: The title-page is inscribed with the original owner's name and the date 1913.

Recipes proved and approved

O308.1 1913
Recipes / proved and approved / compiled by / the ladies of St. George's Guild / Owen Sound / 1913 / The R-B-W Press, Owen Sound
DESCRIPTION: 16.5 × 12.5 cm Pp [1–2] 3–144 Fp illus on p 2 of St George's Church, Owen Sound Paper, with small image on front of a boar's head on a platter; stapled
CONTENTS: 1 tp; 2 illus; 3 ads; 4 'Preface' [i.e., poem about the usefulness of this cookbook]; 5–144 text
COPIES: *OGU (CCC TX715.6 R45)

Selected recipes and useful household information

O309.1 nd [about 1913]
Selected recipes / and / useful household information / [caption:] James St. Baptist Church, Hamilton, Ont. / Compiled and published by / Young Women's Mission Auxiliary / of the / James St. Baptist Church / for the benefit of home and foreign missions / Printed by F.G. Smith, 107 King St. West
DESCRIPTION: 22.5 × 15.0 cm   Pp [i–iv], 25 leaves of which the rectos are numbered 1–25 and contain recipes and the versos are unnumbered and contain ads, 26–54 incl one unnumbered page of ads btwn 30–1, [i–iv]   Tp illus of James Street Baptist Church   Paper; stapled
CONTENTS: i tp; ii blank; iii 'Foreword'; iv 'Index'; 1–54 recipes credited with the name of the contributor and ads; i ads; ii–iv blank for 'My Recipes'
COPIES: OH (R641.5 SEL CESH)   *Private collection
NOTES: The book is undated; however, there is an advertisement on p 22 that points to publication in 1913: Adam Clark's business was established in 1877 and he enjoys 'thirty-six years of unequalled reputation.'

Snow-Mellow 'goodies'

See also O546.1, Hip-o-lite Professional Recipes, *a later book of recipes for a marshmallow-like product called* Hip-o-lite. *In O310.1 the name is spelled without hyphens:* Hipolite.

O310.1 [copyright 1913]
Snow-Mellow / "goodies" / Connell-Ott Company / Canadian distributors / Toronto Canada [cover-title]
DESCRIPTION: 16.0 × 8.5 cm   Pp [1] 2–15   Paper, with image on front of a woman holding a slice of cake, and a cake in the foreground; stapled
CONTENTS: 1 cover-title; top–mid 2 'Read These Directions Carefully // Follow Them Exactly // Success Is Sure'; bottom 2–mid 15 recipes using Hipolite's Snow-Mellow as an ingredient; mid–bottom 15 'Notes' and 'Recipes on pages from 6 to 15, inclusive, prepared by Mrs. Jennie Dyer Wyse, teacher of Domestic Science, John Marshall High School, Chicago, Ill. // Copyright 1913 Connell-Ott Company, Toronto Canada.'
COPIES: *Private collection

NOTES: Snow-Mellow could be used as a filling for cakes, a meringue for pies, or a topping for fruit.

Some home made good things

O311.1 nd [about 1913 or later]
Some / home made / good things / as used in / the Mission / Tea Rooms / Toronto
DESCRIPTION: 16.5 × 12.0 cm   Pp [1] 2–16   Tp illus of five maids in profile, each carrying a prepared dish; illus on pp 4, 7, 10, 13, and 16 of individual women   Paper, with small image on front of two women facing each other; stapled
CONTENTS: 1 tp; 2–16 recipes
COPIES: *OGU (UA s048 b14)
NOTES: There is no printing on the versos of the sixteen leaves that make up the book, and the versos are not included in the pagination. The Mission Tea Rooms, at 87 King Street West, are listed in Toronto city directories from 1913 to 1927. The appearance of the book points to publication early in this period, when Lillian F. Billings, widow of Charles R. Billings, and Mrs May were in charge.

Souvenir cook book

O312.1 1913
[An edition of *Souvenir Cook Book,* compiled by a committee, North Toronto, 1913]
COPIES: Private collection

1913–14

Groome, Dora, and Miss May Little

The British author May Little also wrote O341.1, The Complete Cake Book, in about 1915, plus the following: Cookery Up-to-Date, London: T. Werner Laurie, nd [1908] (Driver 628.1); A Year's Dinners, London: T. Werner Laurie, nd [1910] (Driver 630.1); Simple Electric Cookery, London: Jarrold and Sons, nd [1913 or 1914] (Driver 629.1); Everywoman's Cook Book, London: Jarrold and Sons, nd [after 1914] (Driver, p 393); and How to Make and Bake Bread at Home, London: Jarrold and Sons, [1916] (Driver p 393).

O313.1 nd [about 1913–14]
More / up-to-date / and / economical / cookery / by / Dora Groome / and / May Little / Toronto / Bell & Cockburn

COPIES: *Private collection
NOTES: This is the sequel to Groome's *Up-to-Date and Economical Cookery,* first edition dated 1898, which May Little revised in 1912 (see Driver 452.1–452.3). The Canadian edition of the sequel may have been published in 1913–14, about the same time as the original British edition, or a little later.

BRITISH EDITIONS: London: Jarrold and Sons, nd, but LoEN and OB record [1913], and LB, [about 1914] (Great Britain: LB, LoEN, OB).

The maple leaf cook book

The Kimberley branch of the Women's Institute was established in 1897, the same year as the charter branch at Stoney Creek (Ambrose, p 235).

O314.1 nd [about 1913–14]
The maple leaf / cook book / compiled by / Kimberley Women's Institute / Our Aims and Objects / To do all the good we can, in every way that / we can, to all the people that we can, and / above all to study household good and any / line of work which makes for the betterment / of our homes, the advancement of our people / and the good of our country. / We thank one and all for their kind assis- / tance in the production of this useful recipe / book, and specially commend to the users the / wares of the merchants and manufacturers / whose advertisements appear herein. / President – Mrs. B.A. Carruthers. / Vice-Pres. – Mrs. Andrew Wallace. / Sec'y-Treas. – Mrs. E.H. Boyle. / [folio:] 1
DESCRIPTION: 22.0 × 14.5 cm   Pp 1–85   Tp illus of a maple leaf   Paper, with image on front of a green maple leaf; stapled
CONTENTS: 1 tp; 2 ad; 3 'Index' of 'Recipes' [i.e., table of contents] and 'Advertisements'; 4 'How to Cook a Husband' [mock recipe]; 5–83 recipes credited with the name of the contributor and ads; 84 ad; 85 'Table of Weights and Measures'
COPIES: *Private collection
NOTES: 'Markdale Standard Print' is on the front face of the binding. The book's owner suggests that the cookbook was published about 1913–14: she checked several advertisements against the *Dominion of Canada and Newfoundland Gazetteer and Classified Business Directory* and all the companies were listed in the volumes for 1913 and 1914, but not in 1912 or 1915. There is no reference to the First World War in the text or advertisements.

1914

Beeton, Mrs Isabella Mary, née Mayson (St Marylebone, Middlesex, England, 14 March 1836–6 February 1865, Greenhithe, Kent, England)

For information about Mrs Beeton and her other cookbooks, see O231.1.

O315.1 1914
Mrs. Beeton's / family cookery / New edition / With coloured plates and other illustrations / Ward, Lock & Co., Limited / London, Melbourne and Toronto / 1914
DESCRIPTION: 20.0 × 13.0 cm   Pp [leaf(ves) lacking] [3–4] 5–864, [i–x]   Lacks frontis col of 'Dinner Table à la Russe,' 17 pls col ('List of Coloured Plates' records 18 pls col, but one lacking in this copy), many double-sided pls, fp illus of serviette-folding on pp 207–13   Quarter leather
CONTENTS: 3 tp; 4 blank; 5–8 'Preface to Mrs. Beeton's Cookery Books'; 9 'Contents'; 10 blank; 11–12 'List of Coloured Plates'; 13–16 'List of Illustrations'; 17–844 text; 845 'General Index'; 846–8 'Index of Introduction to Cookery'; 849–64 'Analytical Index of Recipes'; i–x ads
COPIES: *Private collection
NOTES: Recipes on pp 237–826 are arranged alphabetically from Alma Pudding to Zeltinger Cup.

BRITISH EDITIONS: *Mrs Beeton's Family Cookery* is the later, shortened title of *Mrs Beeton's Family Cookery and Housekeeping Book* (editions 1893 onward), which was a slightly altered version of *Beeton's Every-day Cookery and Housekeeping Book* (see 'British editions' for O273.1, *Mrs Beeton's Every-day Cookery*). For more information, see Driver, p 101.

Blackburn, Walter J.

The 1913 and 1914 London city directories list W.J. Blackburn as manager director of the London Free Press Ptg Co. Ltd.

O316.1 1914
[An edition of *Free Press Prize Menu Contest. Which is being preliminarily published in separate articles in a newspaper or periodical.,* London, Ont.: 1914]
CITATIONS: O'Neill (unpublished)
NOTES: O'Neill's entry, based on Canadian copyright material at the British Library, records that the book

was 'not received' by the library. A search of 1914 issues of the *Free Press* newspaper for references to a 'Prize Menu Contest' may reveal whether the material was published as a book or not.

Byron, May Clarissa, née Gillington (died 1936)

Also by this British author are O333.1, May Byron's How-to-Save Cookery, *and O355.1,* May Byron's Jam Book. *She also wrote:* May Byron's Cake Book, *London: Hodder and Stoughton, 1915 (Great Britain: OB);* May Byron's Vegetable Book, *London: Hodder and Stoughton, 1916 (Great Britain: LB);* May Byron's Pudding Book, *London and New York: Hodder and Stoughton, 1917 (United States: DLC); and May* Byron's Rations Book, *London and New York: Hodder and Stoughton, [1918] (United States: DLC), plus many books outside the culinary sphere, including several about famous figures in English literature.*

O317.1 [1st ed., 1914]
[First edition of *Pot-luck or the British Home Cookery Book: Over a Thousand Recipes from Old Family Ms. Books,* collected and edited by May Byron, London, New York and Toronto: Hodder and Stoughton, [1914]]
DESCRIPTION: 19.0 × 13.0 cm   Pp [i–iv] v–xxxix [xl] xli–xlv [xlvi], 1–427   Rebound
CITATIONS: Driver 177.1
COPIES: Great Britain: *LB   LoEN   OB; United States: NN
NOTES: The publication date is on the title-page verso. There are 1,097 numbered recipes. Where possible, the author has indicated the origin of each recipe, or 'at least the county from which its possessor came.'

O317.2 [2nd ed., March 1915]
—[Second edition of *Pot-luck or the British Home Cookery Book,* London, New York and Toronto: Hodder and Stoughton, [March 1915]]
DESCRIPTION: 20.0 × 13.5 cm   Pp [i–iv] v–xxxix [xl] xli–xlv [xlvi], 1–427 [428]   Cloth, with pl col mounted on front of a woman peeling a potato(?)
CITATIONS: Axford, p 325   Bitting, p 70   Driver 177.2
COPIES: Great Britain: *OPo(F)   LB; United States: DLC (TX717 B9 1915)   NIC   NNNAM
NOTES: 'First edition in 1914 // Second edition March 1915' is on the title-page verso. New to this edition is a short section on made gravies and sauces, and fish sauces.

O317.3 [3rd ed., May 1916]
—Pot-luck / or the British home / cookery book / over a thousand recipes / from old family ms. books / collected & edited / by May Byron / "Old-fashioned ... but choicely good." Izaak Walton / "To be chronicled, and chronicled, and cut and / chronicled, and all to be praised" Fuller. / Hodder and Stoughton / London. New York. Toronto
DESCRIPTION: 20.0 × 13.5 cm   Pp [i–iv] v–xxxix [xl] xli–xlv [xlvi], 1–427 [428]
CONTENTS: i ht; ii list of May Byron's other books; iii tp; iv 'First edition in 1914 // Second edition March 1915 // Third edition May 1916'; v–viii preface signed M.B.; ix–xxxix table of contents; xl blank; xli–xliv 'Some Preliminary Remarks'; xlv 'Postscript'; xlvi blank; 1–427 1,097 numbered recipes; 428 'Printed in Great Britain by Hazell, Watson and Viney, Ld., London and Aylesbury.'
CITATIONS: Driver 177.3
COPIES: *OGU (UA s016 b14); United States: ICJ

O317.4 [4th ed., October 1917]
— [Fourth edition of *Pot-luck or the British Home Cookery Book,* [October 1917]]
CITATIONS: Driver 177.4   JCCat 4
NOTES: If the fourth edition follows the pattern of the other editions, then Toronto is part of the imprint.

O317.5 [5th ed., January 1922]
—[Fifth edition of *Pot-luck or the British Home Cookery Book,* [January 1922]]
DESCRIPTION: 19.0 × 12.5 cm   Pp [i–iv] v–xxxix [xl] xli–xlv [xlvi], 1–427 [428]   Cloth
CITATIONS: Driver 177.5
COPIES: Great Britain: *OPo(F)
NOTES: The publication date is on the title-page verso.

O317.6 [6th ed., January] 1923
—[Sixth edition of *Pot-luck or the British Home Cookery Book,* [January] 1923]
DESCRIPTION: 18.0 × 12.0 cm   Pp [i–iv] v–xxxix [xl] xli–xlv [xlvi], [1] 2–427   Rebound
CITATIONS: Driver 177.6
COPIES: *LCS

BRITISH EDITIONS: 7th ed., rev. and enlarged, London: Hodder and Stoughton Ltd, [August 1926] (Driver 177.7); 8th ed., rev. and enlarged, London: Hodder and Stoughton Ltd, [February 1932] (Driver 177.8); [abridged ed.], London: English Universities Press, [November 1940] (Driver 177.9); reprint of November 1940, [July 1941] (Driver 177.10); reprint of November 1940, [April 1942] (Driver 177.11).

Campbell, Matilda Gertrude (1870–)

O318.1 1914

A textbook of / domestic science / for high schools / by / Matilda G. Campbell / instructor in home economics, Jesup W. Scott High School, Toledo / Ohio, lecturer on home economics, University of / California, Summer School, 1911 / New York / The Macmillan Company / 1914 / All rights reserved

DESCRIPTION: 19.0 × 12.5 cm Pp [i–iv] v [vi] vii [viii], 1–219, [i–vii] Illus Cloth

CONTENTS: i ht; ii 'The Macmillan Company New York Boston Chicago Dallas Atlanta San Francisco // Macmillan & Co., Limited London Bombay Calcutta Melbourne // The Macmillan Co. of Canada, Ltd. Toronto'; iii tp; iv 'Copyright, 1913, by the Macmillan Company. Set up and electrotyped. Published November, 1913. Reprinted February, June, 1914. Norwood Press J.S. Cushing Co. – Berwick & Smith Co. Norwood, Mass., U.S.A.'; v preface; vi blank; vii table of contents; viii blank; 1–207 text; 208 'Reference Books'; 209–19 index; i blank; ii 'The following pages contain advertisements of a few of the Macmillan books on kindred subjects'; iii blank; iv–vii publ ads

CITATIONS: Bitting, p 73

COPIES: *OGU (CCC TX715.6 C35)

NOTES: The preface states that the book is meant to be 'a laboratory manual in the school, and ... a practical cookbook in the home.' It adds that the text is mainly about 'food and nutrition and the application of heat to foods'; sanitation, the chemistry of cleaning, shelter, and many other domestic science subjects are omitted.

AMERICAN EDITIONS: New York: Macmillan Co., 1913 (United States: DLC, 2 copies).

Canada, Department of the Naval Service

Department of the Naval Service was the name in use from 1914 to 1920, followed by Department of Marine and Fisheries from 1920 to 1930, and Department of Fisheries from 1930 to 1969. For later collections of fish recipes published by the federal government, see: O377.1, Canada, Food Controller for Canada, Eat More Fish; O401.1, Canada, Canada Food Board, Fish Recipes; O467.1, Canada, Department of Marine and Fisheries, Eat More Fish; O896.1, Canada, Department of Fisheries, Any Day a Fish Day; and O936.1, Canada, Department of Fisheries, 100 Tempting Fish Recipes.

O319.1 1914

Fish / and how to cook it / Issued by / the Department of the Naval Service, / Ottawa, / 1914 / Copies may be obtained by applying / to the department.

DESCRIPTION: 20.0 × 10.0 cm Pp [1–2] 3–72 Fp illus on pp 30, 34, 40, 42, 44, 46, and 59 of different types of fish Thin card, with images on front of a sailing ship and a still-life of fish and a fishing basket

CONTENTS: 1 tp; 2 blank; top 3 table of contents; mid 3–4 'Index of Recipes'; 5–7 preface dated Department of the Naval Service, Ottawa, 1 July 1914; 8 blank; top 9 'Special Notice to Housewives'; mid 9–mid 10 'Fish as Food'; mid 10–mid 11 'Comparative Value of Fish as Food'; mid 11 'Composition of Fish'; 12–14 tables for 'Composition of Fish'; 15 'Cost of Protein and Energy in Fish and Other Food Materials'; 16–17 tables for 'Cost of ...'; 18–mid 20 untitled text; mid 20–top 22 'Canned Fish'; mid 22 'The Value of Canada's Fisheries' and 'Classes of Fish'; bottom 22–mid 23 'Hints on Frying Fish'; mid 23–top 24 'Hints on Boiling Fish'; mid 24–mid 25 'Further Hints'; mid 25–28 'Terms Used in Cookery'; 29–72 'Recipes for Cooking Fish and Information Regarding Different Kinds of Fish'

CITATIONS: Ferguson/Fraser, p 232, illus col on p 35 of closed volume

COPIES: ACG CIHM (9-00596) OGU (CCC CA1 ND80 14F33) OONL (COP.CA.D.66, 2 copies) OW (641.5 C16, at library in 1991, not on shelf in 2001) *Private collection; United States: NNNAM

NOTES: In the preface, the department thanks 'the New England Fish Exchange, of Boston, for allowing it to use information and recipes contained in the valuable little work published by it, entitled "Recipes for Sea Foods"; ... the National Sea Fisheries' Protection Association of Great Britain, for permission to use recipes in the booklet ..."Tasty Ways of Cooking Fish; ..." The famous London chef Charles Herman Senn provided the recipes in the latter book (Driver 1048.1), which was published about 1909.

Another private collector has a copy stamped 'The Canadian Fish & Cold Storage Co. Ltd.' BQ Exposition 1974, p 6, cites this title, but no date is recorded.

O319.2 1915

—Fish / and how to cook it / Issued by / The Department of the Naval Service, / Ottawa, / 1915 / Copies may be obtained by applying / to the department.

DESCRIPTION: 20.0 × 10.0 cm Pp [1–2] 3–72 Fp illus on pp 30, 34, 40, 42, 44, 46, and 59 of different types of fish Thin card, with images on front of a sailing ship and a still-life of fish and a fishing basket

CONTENTS: 1 tp; 2 blank; 3–4 table of contents and 'Index of Recipes'; 5–7 preface dated Department of the Naval Service, Ottawa, 1 July 1914; 8 blank; 9–top 10 'Fish as Food'; bottom 10–top 22 'Comparative Value of Fish as Food'; mid 22 'The Value of Canada's Fisheries' and 'Classes of Fish'; bottom 22–mid 23 'Hints on Frying Fish'; mid 23–top 24 'Hints on Boiling Fish'; mid 24–mid 25 'Further Hints'; mid 25–28 'Terms Used in Cookery'; 29–72 'Recipes for Cooking Fish and Information Regarding Different Kinds of Fish'
COPIES: NFSM   OKQ (F5012 1915 C212F)   OTU (Gov. Doc. Can N) *Private collection; United States: NNNAM (uncat pamphlet)

O319.3   1915

—[An edition of *Le poisson et comment le cuire*, Ottawa: Département du service naval, 1915]
COPIES: Private collection

O319.4   2nd ed., 1932

—Department of Fisheries / Ottawa, Canada / Minister: / Hon. E.N. Rhodes, M.P. / Fish / and how to cook it / (Second and revised edition) / Prepared under the direction of / Mrs. Evelene Spencer / Specialist in fish cookery / (Cover design by the National Development Bureau of the Department / of the Interior, Ottawa) / Ottawa / F.A. Acland / printer to the King's Most Excellent Majesty / 1932 / Price: 10 cents
DESCRIPTION: 19.0 × 11.5 cm   Pp [1–3] 4–52   Paper, with image on front of two seabirds flying above a wavy sea; stapled
CONTENTS: 1 tp; 2 blank; 3 'The Value of Fish in the Diet' by Dr J.A. Amyot; 4–8 'Fish Foods and Health' [includes list of Canada's fish and the forms in which they are marketed]; 9 'The Purpose of "Fish and How to Cook It"'; 10–11 'Marketing Notes'; 12–17 'General Talk on Fish Cookery'; 18–50 recipes; 51–2 index
CITATIONS: CCat No. 11, p M23
COPIES: *BVIPEH   OONL (COP.CA.FS.325, 2 copies)
NOTES: See also O896.1, Canada, Department of Fisheries, *Any Day a Fish Day*, described on its title-page as a later edition of *Fish and How to Cook It*.

O319.5   3rd ed., 1935

—[Third edition of *Fish and How to Cook It*, Ottawa: Department of Fisheries, 1935]
COPIES: OONL (COP.CA.2.2000-1498)

Cook book

O319a.1   1914

[Running head:] The Westmeath Women's Institute cook book / Cook book / Published by the / Womens' [*sic*] Institute / of Westmeath / 1914 / The Westmeath Womens' [*sic*] Institute desire to thank / the merchants of Westmeath and Pembroke for the / interest and help given by taking advertising space, / thereby making possible the publishing of this book. / Page 9.
DESCRIPTION: 22.5 × 15.0 cm   Pp 1–119   Tp illus of three maple leaves   Limp cloth; stapled
CONTENTS: 1–8 ads; 9 tp; 10 'Index' [i.e., table of contents]; 11–108 recipes credited with the name of the contributor; 109 'Boil' [i.e., timetable for boiling various ingredients]; 110–11 'Miscellaneous'; 112–19 ads
COPIES: *Private collection
NOTES: An advertisement on p 8 for the German Post Printing and Publishing Co., Pembroke, proclaims in large type, 'We printed this book.' The front face of the binding is inscribed, in ballpoint pen, 'Mrs J.H. Bromley,' possibly the recipe contributor Mrs James H. Bromley and a relation of other contributors with the same last name (Mrs Alex Bromley, Mrs David Bromley, Mrs Harry G. Bromley, Mrs John G. Bromley, Miss Myrtle Bromley).

Filippini, Alexander

Alexander or Alessandro Filippini was a native of Switzerland, according to the 'Introduction' of The International Cook Book. *For many years, and before turning to writing, he was chef de cuisine at Delmonico's Restaurant in New York City, and his first cookbook is dedicated to Charles C. Delmonico:* The Table: How to Buy Food, How to Cook It, and How to Serve It, *New York: C.L. Webster and Co., 1889 (United States: DLC), some editions of which were retitled* The Delmonico Cook Book. *In 1892 and 1893 he saw published, in New York and London, three titles in a series:* One Hundred Desserts, One Hundred Ways of Cooking Eggs, *and* One Hundred Ways of Cooking Fish *(Driver 388.1, 389.1, 390.1). His only title published in a Canadian edition is* The International Cook Book.

O320.1   nd [about 1914]

The / international cook book / Over 3,300 recipes gathered from all over the / world, including many never before / published in English. With com- / plete ménus of the three meals / for every day in the year / By / Alexander Filippini / formerly of

Delmonico's, and Travelling Inspector of the International / Mercantile Marine Company. Author of "The Table" / [publisher's 'MBCo' symbol] / Toronto / The Musson Book Company / Limited

DESCRIPTION: Pp [i–iv] v ... 1059   Cloth

CONTENTS: i ht; ii blank; iii tp; iv 'Printed in New York, U.S.A. All rights reserved, including that of translation into foreign languages including the Scandinavian'; v– 'Introduction'; ...; –1059 'Index'

COPIES: *Bookseller's stock

NOTES: There is no date of publication in the Musson edition, but the bookseller's copy is inscribed on the front endpaper, in ink, 'M.F. 23/1/15.' If this volume was acquired in January 1915, the date of publication may have been 1914 (the same year as one of the American editions).

On p v Filippini recounts the creation of the book: 'This new work ... is the result of years of preparation ... A leave of absence for several months was obtained from my superiors of the International Navigation Company, a tour of the world was made, and personal visits paid to hotels, restaurants and homes of all countries. Indeed, I have been continually gathering new material and travelling for the past decade, and the work is truly international in its scope.'

AMICUS No. 11067814 records a copy with the imprint Toronto: Musson, [1906], at BVI, but the copy is no longer in the library's collection. It may or may not be the same as O320.1.

AMERICAN EDITIONS: New York: Doubleday, Page and Co., 1906 (United States: DLC), 1907 (BVA, OTMCL), 1911, 1913 (OTMCL), 1914, and 1917 (all NUC).

BRITISH EDITIONS: London: Doubleday, Page and Co., 1906 (Great Britain: LoEN, OB); London: Hodder and Stoughton, 1911 (Great Britain: LB destroyed, LCS, LoEN missing, OB, WyLUB).

Good bread

Vinol is also advertised in O99.1, Hints on Health and Tested Receipts for Plain Cooking. *Although there are some parallels in the culinary text between the two books, most of the recipes are different.*

O321.1   St Catharines, nd [about 1914]
Good bread / This book tells how / to make good bread / Presented with the compliments of / Abbs & McNamara, druggists / St. Catharines, Ont. [cover-title]

COPIES: *OSTC (641.815 Goo M)

NOTES: Abbs and McNamara, druggists, are listed in St Catharines city directories from 1914 to 1930 (before 1914, the business was called Walker and Abbs; from 1931, just Abbs). This edition and the editions distributed by other druggists all appear to have been published about the same time, likely about 1914 or slightly later.

O321.2   Cowansville, nd
—Good bread / This book tells how / to make good bread / Presented with the compliments of / Geo. W. Johnston druggist / Cowansville Quebec [cover-title]

DESCRIPTION: About 16.5 × 11.5 cm   Pp 1–24   With image on front, in a circular frame, of an old woman removing a loaf of bread from an oven

CONTENTS: 1–20 ads for Vinol, 'a cod liver and iron tonic without oil,' on rectos, and bread recipes on versos; 21–4 ads for Vinol

CITATIONS: BQ 22-4894

COPIES: *QMBN (TX769 G66 1900 and 160060 CON)

NOTES: See O321.1 regarding the date of publication.

O321.3   Yarmouth, nd
—Good bread / This book tells how / to make good bread / Presented with the compliments of / L.C. Gardner & Co., druggists / Yarmouth, N.S. [cover-title]

DESCRIPTION: With image on front, in a circular frame, of an old woman removing a loaf of bread from an oven

COPIES: *Private collection

NOTES: See O321.1 regarding the date of publication.

O321.4   Toronto, nd
—Good bread / This book tells how / to make good bread / Presented with the compliments of / Ernest A. Legge, druggist / Cor. College and Ossington Ave., Toronto, Ont. [cover-title]

DESCRIPTION: 16.5 × 11.5 cm   Pp 1–24   Paper, with image on front, in a circular frame, of an old woman removing a loaf of bread from an oven; stapled

CONTENTS: 1–20 ads for Vinol, a 'cod liver and iron tonic,' on rectos, bread recipes on versos; 21–4 ads for Vinol

COPIES: *OTUTF (uncat patent medicine)

NOTES: The testimonials are from Canadian and American sources. The advertisement on p 24 is in French.

In Toronto city directories, Ernest A. Legge is first listed in the business of drugs, at 814 College Street, in the 1903 directory. The address of his business changes in the 1905 directory to 831 College Street, which is at the corner of Ossington, the address recorded in the cover-title. This edition of *Good Bread*, therefore, was published in 1905 or later, but likely about the same time as O321.1, i.e., about 1914.

O321.5   Niagara Falls, nd
—Good bread / This book tells how / to make good bread / Presented with the compliments of / A.C. Thorburn, – druggist / Niagara Falls, Ont. [cover-title]
DESCRIPTION: 16.5 × 11.5 cm   Pp 1–24   Paper, with image on front, in a circular frame, of an old woman removing a loaf of bread from an oven; stapled
CONTENTS: 1–20 ads for Vinol on rectos, 'Recipes for Bread' on versos; 21–4 ads for Vinol and Vinlax
COPIES: *OTYA (CPC 1912 0128)
NOTES: The testimonials are from Canadian and American sources. The advertisement for Vinol on p 24 is in French. See O321.1 regarding the date of publication.

'McClary's' recipe book

For information about McClary's and its cookbooks, see O162.1.

O322.1   nd [about 1914]
[Running head:] "McClary's" Recipe Book [folio:] 1 / Introduction / to gas cook book / [four paragraphs, beginning, 'The convenience and cleanliness to be derived from cooking with gas ...'] / Wishing you the best success, / McClary's / "McClary" on goods is a "quality" name
DESCRIPTION: 20.0 × 11.5 cm   Pp 1–48   Several illus brown on pp 28–48 of McClary stoves and other equipment   Paper, with image on front of woman placing pan on McClary range; stapled
CONTENTS: 1 running head and 'Introduction to Gas Cook Book'; 2 'Index'; 3 'Hints on Serving'; 4–5 'Cookery Hints'; 6 'Advice for the Care of Kitchen Utensils'; 7 'Table of Comparative Measurements,' 'Measuring Hints,' and 'Mixing Hints'; 8–23 'Recipes'; 24 'Introduction to McClary Gas Ranges'; 25 'Leading Features'; 26–7 'The Champion'; 28–48 illus of McClary products
COPIES: *OKIT
NOTES: The running head is the source of the title; there is no title on the binding. Various references in the text point to publication in 1914: 'Our 1914 series of gas ranges' (p 24); 'The McClary Water Heater can be attached to any of our 1914 gas ranges' (p 39); 'An

entirely new 1914 feature, ...' (p 43). The book was published before the city of Berlin was renamed Kitchener in September 1916 (there is a stamp on the front face of the binding of the OKIT copy for 'H. Wolfhard & Co. Berlin, Ontario.' Printed on the front of the binding is the name 'McClary's' and the cities of London, Toronto, Montreal, Winnipeg, Vancouver, Hamilton, Saint John, Calgary, Saskatoon, and Edmonton. The cookbook promoted the use of the company's gas ranges, and also the Champion Interchangeable Range, which could burn either coal or gas (p 26).

MacKay, Miss Lucy Gertrude (1877–)

Apples were also the subject of this American author in her Housekeeper's Apple Book, *Baltimore: Advertising Committee, International Apple Shippers' Association, 1915 (Axford, p 212), and in* The Housekeeper's Apple Book; Over Two Hundred Ways of Preparing the Apple, *Boston: Little, Brown and Co., 1917 (United States: DLC). W.T. Macoun, who contributed the text about storing apples, was dominion horticulturalist from 1910 to 1933.*

O323.1   nd [about 1914]
Two hundred / and nine recipes / Dedicated to the / patriotic housewives / of Canada / Published by / Dept. of Trade and Commerce / Ottawa / Additional free copies of recipes on request
DESCRIPTION: 18.0 × 11.5 cm   Pp [1] 2–68   Illus of apple varieties   Paper, with image on front of a single red apple; stapled
CONTENTS: 1 tp; 2 'The Apple as an Article of Food'; 3–14 recipes; 15–29 'Famous Canadian Varieties'; 30 'How to Store Apples for the Winter' by W.T. Macoun; 31–68 recipes and at bottom p 68, 'Romance in an Apple Orchard' [a story incorporating the names of apple varieties as puns]
CITATIONS: Reitz, p [4]
COPIES: OGU (CCC CA1 TC 45T83)   OKITD (x962.260.001)   *Private collection
NOTES: The cover-title is 'The Book of Apple Delights // Two Hundred and Nine Recipes by Miss L. Gertrude MacKay.' The card catalogue at OOAG records a copy of *The Book of Apple Delights*, by L. Gertrude MacKay, Ottawa: Department of Trade and Commerce, 1914, pp 68; however, the volume is not on the shelf. The OOAG record may refer to the undated edition described here.
Two Hundred and Nine Recipes may be an edition of MacKay's *Two Hundred and Nine Ways of Preparing the*

Apple ..., Spokane: Shaw and Borden Co., printers, [c1913], pp 52 (United States: DLC). See also O404.1, Canada, Department of Agriculture, *160 Apple Recipes*, which reprints recipes from O323.1.

Maddocks, Mildred

Also by Maddocks (later Mildred Maddocks Bentley) is Good Housekeeping Family Cook Book, *New York, Springfield, Mass., and Chicago: Phelps Publishing Co., 1906 (Bitting, pp 36, 303). She became director of the Delineator Institute.*

O324.1 [copyright 1914]
The pure food cook book / The Good Housekeeping recipes / just how to buy – just how to cook / Edited by Mildred Maddocks / Associate Editor of Good Housekeeping Magazine / Editor of the "Family Cook Book"; "Every Day Dishes"; "Brosia / Meal Cook Book" / With an introduction and notes on food and food values by / Harvey W. Wiley, M.D. / Toronto / McClelland, Goodchild & Stewart / Limited
DESCRIPTION: 18.5 × 12.5 cm   Pp [i–iv] v–viii [ix–x], [1–2] 3–8, [i–ii], 9–417   32 pls incl frontis   Cloth, with small image on front of a covered casserole dish
CONTENTS: i ht; ii blank; iii tp; iv 'Copyright, 1914, by Hearst's International Library Co., Inc. ... Printed in the United States of America'; v–vi table of contents; vii–viii 'List of Illustrations'; ix 'Preface' signed Mildred Maddocks; x 'Important New Features'; 1–7 'Good Cooking' by H.W. Wiley; 8 blank; i part-title: 'The Pure Food Cook Book'; ii blank; 9–408 text in thirty-nine chapters; 409–17 'Complete Index to Recipes'
COPIES: OWOOXH   *Private collection
NOTES: Spadoni/Donnelly refer to this edition in their comments for O324.6 (Spadoni/Donnelly No. 1015) as published in November 1914 and cited in BS Vol. 30, No. 11.

O324.2 [copyright 1930]
—The Eaton / pure food cook book / just how to buy – just how to cook / Edited by Mildred Maddocks / Editor of the "Family Cook Book"; "Every Day Dishes"; / "Brosia Meal Cook Book". / With an introduction and notes on food values by / Harvey W. Wylie [*sic*], M.D. / Illustrated / The T. Eaton Co Limited / Canada
COPIES: *OGU (CCC TX715.6 E325)
NOTES: 'Copyright, Canada, 1930 All rights reserved Printed in Canada' is on the title-page verso.

O324.3 [copyright 1930]
—Good Housekeeping / cook book / Good Housekeeping recipes / just how to buy – just how to cook / Edited by Mildred Maddocks / former Associate Editor of Good Housekeeping Magazine / Editor of the "Family Cook Book"; "Every Day Dishes"; "Brosia / Meal Cook Book" / With an introduction and notes on food and food values by / Harvey W. Wiley, M.D. / A new impression of The Pure Food / Cook Book / Illustrated / Published in Canada by / McClelland & Stewart, Limited / publishers Toronto
DESCRIPTION: 20.5 × 13.5 cm   Pp [i–iv] v–vi [vii–viii], [1–2] 3–7 [8], [i–ii], 9–417   8 pls incl frontis   Cloth
CONTENTS: i ht: 'The Pure Food Cook Book'; ii blank; iii tp; iv 'Copyright, Canada, 1930 by McClelland & Stewart, Limited Toronto Printed in Canada'; v–vi table of contents; vii 'Important New Features'; viii blank; 1–7 'Good Cooking' by Harvey W. Wiley; 8 blank; i part-title: 'The Pure Food Cook Book'; ii blank; 9–408 text; 409–17 'Complete Index to Recipes' and at bottom p 417, 'Printed and bound in Canada // Press of the Hunter-Rose Co., Limited, Toronto'
COPIES: OGU (CCC TX715.6 G6555)   QMM (RBD Vanna Garnier, ckbk 843)   *Private collection

O324.4 [copyright 1930]
—Gurney / cook book / Good Housekeeping / recipes / Edited by Mildred Maddocks / Introduction by Harvey W. Wiley, M.D. / This Gurney Cook Book, together / with the special Instruction Book / enclosed with your Gurney Elec- / tric Range, will enable you to / achieve the results you have a / right to expect from a modern / cooking appliance. / McClelland & Stewart, Limited / publishers Toronto
DESCRIPTION: 20.5 × 13.5 cm   Pp [i–iv] v–vi [vii–viii], [1–2] 3–7 [8], [i–ii], 9–417   Cloth
CONTENTS: i ht: 'The Pure Food Cook Book'; ii blank; iii tp; iv 'Copyright, Canada, 1930 by McClelland & Stewart, Limited Toronto Printed in Canada'; v–vi table of contents; vii 'Important New Features'; viii blank; 1–7 'Good Cooking' by Harvey W. Wiley; 8 blank; i part-title: 'The Pure Food Cook Book'; ii blank; 9–407 text; 408 blank for 'More Ways of Making Coffee'; 409–17 index and at bottom p 417, 'Printed and bound in Canada // Press of the Hunter-Rose Co., Limited, Toronto'
COPIES: *Private collection
NOTES: For information about the company that made Gurney ranges and its cookbooks, see O172.1, *The Right Range and Why.*

O324.5 [copyright 1931]
—The Eaton / pure food cook book / just how to buy – just how to cook / Edited by Mildred Maddocks / Editor of the "Family Cook Book"; "Every Day Dishes"; / "Brosia Meal Cook Book". / With an introduction and notes on food values by / Harvey W. Wylie [*sic*], M.D. / Illustrated / The T. Eaton Co Limited / Canada
DESCRIPTION: 20.5 × 13.5 cm   Pp [i–iv] v–vi [vii–viii], [1–2] 3–417   8 pls incl frontis   Cloth
CONTENTS: i ht: 'The Pure Food Cook Book'; ii blank; iii tp; iv 'Copyright, Canada, 1931 All rights reserved Printed in Canada'; v–vi table of contents; vii 'Important New Features'; viii blank; 1–7 'Good Cooking' by Harvey W. Wiley; 8 blank; 9–408 text; 409–17 index
CITATIONS: Golick, p 103
COPIES: AHRMH (000-034-001)   *OGU (UA s042 b55)   OTUTF (B-12 7855)

O324.6 [copyright 1931]
—Good Housekeeping / cook book / Good Housekeeping recipes / just how to buy – just how to cook / Edited by Mildred Maddocks / former Associate Editor of Good Housekeeping Magazine / Editor of the "Family Cook Book"; "Every Day Dishes"; "Brosia / Meal Cook Book" / With an introduction and notes on food and food values by / Harvey W. Wiley, M.D. / A new impression of The Pure Food / Cook Book / Illustrated / Published in Canada by / McClelland & Stewart, Limited / publishers Toronto
DESCRIPTION: 20.5 × 13.5 cm   Pp [i–iv] v–vi [vii–viii], [1–2] 3–7 [8], [i–ii], 9–417   8 pls incl frontis   Cloth
CONTENTS: i ht: 'The Pure Food Cook Book'; ii blank; iii tp; iv 'Copyright, Canada, 1931 All rights reserved Printed in Canada'; v–vi table of contents; vii 'Important New Features'; viii blank; 1–7 'Good Cooking' by Harvey W. Wiley; 8 blank; i part-title: 'The Pure Food Cook Book'; ii blank; 9–417 text and index
CITATIONS: Spadoni/Donnelly No. 1015
COPIES: *OGU (UA s062 b10)   OHMA (TX715 M23 1931)
NOTES: Spadoni/Donnelly state, 'Photographically reprinted from the sheets of *The Pure Food Cook Book*, published in 1914 by Hearst's International Library Co.'

AMERICAN EDITIONS: *The Pure Food Cook Book, the Good Housekeeping Recipes*, edited by Mildred Maddocks, New York: Hearst's International Library Co., 1914 (Bitting, pp 36, 303).

Neil, Marion Harris

For information about this author and her other cookbooks, see O306.1.

O325.1 [copyright 1914]
Canning, preserving / and pickling / by / Marion Harris Neil, M.C.A. / Cookery Editor, The Ladies' Home Journal, Philadelphia, author of / "How to Cook in Casserole Dishes" and "Candies and Bonbons / and How to Make Them" / Toronto / The Musson Book Co. / Limited
DESCRIPTION: 18.0 × 11.5 cm   Pp [i–ii] iii [iv] v [vi] vii [viii], [9–10] 11–284   12 pls incl frontis, mainly of equipment   Rebound
CONTENTS: i tp; ii 'Copyright, 1914, by David McKay'; iii table of contents; iv blank; v list of illustrations; vi blank; vii author's preface; viii blank; 9–274 text; 275–84 index
COPIES: *OONL (TX601 N5)

AMERICAN EDITIONS: Philadelphia: David McKay, [c1914] (United States: DLC).

BRITISH EDITIONS: London and Edinburgh: W. and R. Chambers Ltd, 1914 (Great Britain: LB destroyed, LWel, LoEN, OB); London and Edinburgh: W. and R. Chambers Ltd, nd [1923] (Great Britain: LCS; United States: NN).

The real home-keeper

The earliest edition of this title was published in Vancouver. For the editions published in Hamilton and in Toronto in 1914, see B21.3 and B21.4.

Red Cross cook book

O326.1 [1914]
Red Cross / cook book / Compiled by the ladies of the / Women's Institute, Grimsby, Ont.
DESCRIPTION: Pp [1] 2–73   Tp illus of a cross   With image on front of a cross
CONTENTS: 1 tp; 2 ads; 3–72 recipes credited with the name of the contributor and ads, and at p mid 72, 'Index' [i.e., table of contents]; 73 'Weights and Measures'
COPIES: *Private collection
NOTES: The year of publication, 1914, is printed on the front face of the binding. 'Printed in Grimsby by the Independent Publishing House' is on the back face.

St Andrew's cook book

Schreiber is on the north shore of Lake Superior, between Nipigon and Marathon. St Andrew's Church was built in 1885 as a place of worship for travelling missions. In 1925, it became St Andrew's United Church. The congregation still meets in the original building.

O327.1 1914
St. Andrew's / cook book / 1914 [cover-title]
DESCRIPTION: 16.5 × 13.0 cm   Pp [1–2] 3–31   Paper; stapled
CONTENTS: 1 'St. Andrew's Cook Book // The recipes were contributed by the following ladies in connection with St. Andrew's Presbyterian Church, Schreiber. [column 1:] Mesdames Moodie Robson Smart Hogg Wilson Struthers McGladdery Davis Harrison Williamson Duncan Goldie Gerow [column 2:] Mesdames McLean Hepburn McCauig [*sic*] Reid Walker Coons Hastings McCuaig Moore West Scott Roser Currie [column 3:] Mesdames Nicholson Polliski Drake Hesson Hawke Hoskins McIntosh Sparks Spence Irvine Thurlow Lindsay Bosler'; 2 blank; 3–26 recipes; 27–30 'Miscellaneous'; 31 'Table of Proportions'
COPIES: *Private collection
NOTES: The original owner of the book has identified two recipes as Mrs Bosler's (the last-named recipe contributor on p 1), by writing her name in pencil next to them: Christmas Cake, p 15; and Doughnuts, p 18. Most of the recipes in this copy are ticked in pencil, to signify that they have been tried.

St James' cookery book

O328.1 1914
St. James' / cookery / book / Published by / the Women's Auxiliary / (St. James' Branch) / Price 25 cents
DESCRIPTION: 17.0 × 11.0 cm   Pp [1–4] 5–112   Tp illus of a manservant carrying a flaming pudding   Cloth-covered boards, with tp illus on front; stapled
CONTENTS: 1 tp; 2 blank; 3 preface signed Women's Auxiliary, St James' Church Branch, March 1914; 4 blank; 5–96 text and ads; 97–102 blank for 'Other Recipes'; 103 'Weights and Measures'; 104–11 blank for 'Other Recipes'; 112 'Index' [i.e., table of contents]
COPIES: *Private collection
NOTES: No address is given for the church; however, since many of the advertisements are for businesses near St James Anglican Church in Hamilton, Ontario,

it is most likely that church rather than St James in nearby Dundas. The preface says that revenue from the book's sale will go 'towards the building of a Sunday School and a Church for Divine worship.' (St James in Hamilton was established in 1909, but it took some time to build the church.) The printer's name, 'Times Print,' is on the front face of the binding.

Selected recipes

O329.1 1914
[*Selected Recipes* by the Gleaners' Mission Band of First Methodist Church, Hamilton, Ontario, 1914]
NOTES: This is the first of four cookbooks produced in the period up to 1948 by the women of First Methodist Church (called First United Church from 1925). The others are: O447.1, *Selected Recipes*; O799.1, *More Selected Recipes*; and O1178.1, *Cook Book*. No copies of the 1914 work were located, but it is referred to in O799.1 and in O1178.1; for more information, see those entries.

Tried and true recipes

The Sunday School building illustrated on the cookbook's title-page was dedicated on 19 March 1912. It was originally called the Westminster Sunday School Building, but from 1 May 1913, the congregation ceased holding services in the old church on Cross Street and began to worship in the Sunday School Building on Main Street, which then became known as Westminster Presbyterian Church. This information is from History of the Presbyterian Church in Canada: Serving in Weston 1847–1947, *[Northland Press], 1947, p 9.*

O330.1   nd [about 1914]
Tried and true recipes / compiled and arranged by the / Ladies Aid Society / of the / Westminster Presbyterian Church / Weston, Ontario / [caption for photograph:] Presbyterian Sunday School, Weston / No mean woman can cook well; it calls for a / generous spirit, a light hand and a large heart.
DESCRIPTION: 23.5 × 15.5 cm [dimensions from photocopy]   Tp illus of three-storey Presbyterian Sunday School building   [$0.35, on binding]   Stapled
COPIES: *Private collection
NOTES: The cover-title is 'Selected Recipes'; the printer, The Walker Press, Paris, Ontario, is recorded on the inside front face of the binding. An advertisement on

p 56 for H. Cousins and Son, Weston, guarantees 'lower prices on Ford cars effective from August 1, 1914, to August 1, 1915.' The cookbook was likely published in early 1914, when the congregation was settling into its new premises in the Sunday School Building, shortly after the move from the old church. The 'Index' shows the first section, 'Soups,' on pp 5–10, and the last two items, 'Proportions' and 'Times for Baking,' on p 94. A note on the 'Index' page states that 'Copies of this cook-book may be obtained from Mrs. J.C. Irvin, Dennison Ave., Weston, or any other member of the Ladies Aid.'

There is a full-page advertisement for the coal-fired Canada 'B' Steel Range manufactured by the Moffat Stove Co. Ltd, Weston, opposite a page of soup recipes. Members of the Moffat family belonged to the church (see, for example, p 9 of the church history).

1914–18

Tried and tested recipes

O331.1 nd [about 1914–18]
Tried and tested recipes / compiled and arranged / by the / Ladies' Patriotic Society / Brigden, Ontario / "We may live without poetry, music, and art, / We may live without conscience, and live without heart, / We may live without friends, we may live without books, / But civilized man cannot live without cooks." / – Lord Lytton. / Issued in connection with the / Red Cross Aid Fund. For sale / by the members of the society. / The officers and members of the Ladies' Pat- / riotic Society desire to thank the ladies who have / so kindly assisted them by contributing the / recipes. They also desire to thank the business men / of Brigden and vicinity for the generous way in / which they have assisted them by contributing / advertisements. / Page 1
DESCRIPTION: About 19.5 × 12.5 cm [dimensions from photocopy]   Paper
COPIES: *OMMM
NOTES: The volume has 78 pp. Brigden is southeast of Sarnia. In 1926, about a decade after this cookbook was published, the Women's Institute in Inwood, a few kilometres to the east of Brigden, published a similarly titled cookbook, O586.1, *Tried and Tested Receipts*, which they had printed in Brigden.

1915

Brown-Lewers, Mrs Mary

See also O582.1, a 1926 Crisco cookbook with the same title, but unattributed.

O332.1 nd [about 1915]
A few / cooking / suggestions / by / Mrs. Mary Brown-Lewers [cover-title]
DESCRIPTION: 18.5 × 11.5 cm   Pp [1–2] 3–17 [18–19]   Illus on p 17 of three-layer cake   Paper, with image on front of a woman rolling dough; stapled
CONTENTS: 1 cover-title; 2 'Why I Like Crisco' signed Mary Brown-Lewers; 3–mid 16 forty-three numbered recipes; mid 16–mid 17 blank for 'Notes'; bottom 17 a tear-out 'Cook Book Coupon' and illus of a cake; top 18 'Book of 250 Recipes Free' [information about Marion Harris Neil's *250 Tested Crisco Recipes*, i.e., O343.1, copyright 1915]; bottom 18 other face of the tear-out 'Cook Book Coupon' to be sent to Procter and Gamble Distributing Co. of Canada Ltd, Hamilton, Ontario; 19 [inside back face of binding] 'Important Points' [about Crisco]
COPIES: *OTYA (CPC 1915 0137)
NOTES: The recipes are for cooking with Crisco, the shortening. The text is printed in brown; '30-C-9-24-15' is on the outside back face of the binding. A private collector has a copy with '20M C-7 30-15' on the outside back face.

Byron, May Clarissa, née Gillington (died 1936)

For other cookbooks by this British author, see O317.1.

O333.1 1915
May Byron's / how-to-save cookery / a war-time cookery book / by / the author of "Pot-luck" / Hodder and Stoughton / London New York Toronto / MCMXV
DESCRIPTION: 20.0 × 13.0 cm   Pp [i–iv] v–xxii, 1–234   Cloth, with small image on front of a steaming double boiler
CONTENTS: i ht; ii blank; iii tp; iv 'Printed in Great Britain by Hazell, Watson & Viney, Ld., London and Aylesbury.'; v–xxii 'Contents'; 1–234 text including 620 numbered recipes
COPIES: *QMM (RBD ckbk 1604); Great Britain: LB (MICA.7222.(6))

Cooking with gas

For information about McClary's and its cookbooks, see O162.1.

O334.1   nd [about 1915]
McClary's [i.e., running head] / "In her very style of looking / There was cognizance of cooking! / From her very dress were peeping / Indications of housekeeping!" / Cooking with gas / [four paragraphs about gas cooking and McClary gas ranges, beginning, 'The convenience and cleanliness of a gas range ...'] / McClary's / London, Toronto, Montreal, Winnipeg, Vancouver, / St. John, N.B., Hamilton, Calgary, / Saskatoon, Edmonton.
DESCRIPTION: 23.0 × 15.5 cm   Pp [1] 2–47   Illus on p 4 of a table setting, illus of models of McClary gas range   Paper, with image impressed on front of a gas range; stapled
CONTENTS: 1 tp; 2 'Index'; 3–47 text, including recipes and information about the following models of McClary's gas range: Style E.S., No. 656; T, No. 656; B.R., No. 18–20; B, No. 458; E, No. 4585; C, Nos. 456 and 458; D, Nos. 456 and 458; E.S., No. 6518; No. 4390; No. 438; No. 425; No. 422; No. 183
COPIES: *OTMCL (683.88029 M11)
NOTES: On p 12, under the heading 'Sanitary Gas Ranges,' is the statement 'McClary's Gas Ranges have behind them the result of 68 years' consistent success ...' Since McClary's was founded in 1847, *Cooking with Gas* was published about 1915 (1847 + 68 years); the appearance of the book confirms this approximate date of publication.

Craig, Miss Sarah E. Woodworth

O335.1   [copyright 1911; about 1915]
Scientific cooking / with / scientific methods / AB / A.J. Freiman / Ottawa / Price $2.00 / Sarah E. Woodworth Craig [cover-title]
DESCRIPTION: 18.5 × 12.5 cm   Pp [1–6], [i–iv] v [vi] vii [viii] ix [x–xii], [1] 2–404, [i–viii]   Cloth
CONTENTS: 1 A-B Stove Co. ad; 2 blank; 3 A-B Stove Co. ad; 4 illus of 'Birdseye View of A-B Stove Company // Battle Creek, Michigan'; 5–6 and i–ii A-B Stove Co. ads; iii 'Copyright, 1911, by Sarah E. Woodworth Craig. Ellis Publishing Company // printers, electrotypers, binders // Battle Creek, Michigan'; iv 'Introduction'; v 'Oh, hours of all hours, the most blessed upon earth, // Blessed hour of dinner.' and poem beginning, 'We may live without poetry, music and art' [from *Lucile*, Part I, Canto ii, by Owen

Meredith, pseudonym of Edward Robert Bulwer-Lytton]; vi blank; vii 'Editor's Page'; viii blank; ix preface; x blank; xi table of contents; xii blank; 1–392 text; 393–404 index; i blank; ii–viii A-B Stove Co. ads
COPIES: *OGU (CCC TX715.6 C72)
NOTES: The copyright date is 1911, but the A-B Stove Co. advertisement on the recto of the first leaf cites awards won by the company at the Panama-California Exposition in San Diego, in 1915. The 'Introduction' refers to the author as 'Miss' Sarah E. Craig and says that she 'devoted a lifetime to the study of Scientific Cooking with Scientific Methods.' The 'Editor's Page' states that Miss Craig's mother was a direct descendant of Samuel Woodworth, who at one time edited the New York *Mirror*.

Archibald J. Freiman, whose name is on the binding, ran the Canadian House Furnishing Co. on Rideau Street, in Ottawa, from 1900. In 1918, he renamed the business the Archibald J. Freiman Department Store. Freiman's, as it was known, closed its doors in the early 1970s.

The leaves of the OGU copy are loose at front and back. Pages 399–400 of the index are lacking, and there may have been a title-page, now lacking.

AMERICAN EDITIONS: Cincinnati: Standard Pub. Co., 1911 (United States: DLC).

Dainty and delicious dishes

For other books by Cowan Co., see: O458.1, Cowan's Book of Jingles; O459.1, Cowan's Cocoa Insures a Wealth of Health; O460.1, Cowan's Cocoa Makes Good Things to Eat; O461.1, Cowan's Cocoa Recipes; and O468.1, 'Cowan's Cocoa Recipes.' All the Cowan cookbooks feature amusing illustrations and a high standard of design. In the case of O468.1, the company hired a Toronto artist, Helene Carter, to create the images for the colour plates. Before producing its own books, the company advertised its business by distributing O145.1, The Housekeeper's Perfect Account Book 1905, a publication of George Shepard.

The first listing for this cocoa and chocolate business in the Toronto city directory is in 1885: Cowan, Musgrave and Co. (John W. Cowan, Frederick J. Musgrave, and Alexander R. McFarlane), cocoa and chocolate manufacturers, at 7 and 9 Temperance Street. In the same year (and before), Cowan and McFarlane had a tea and coffee business at 52–4 Front Street East. In 1886, the city directory shows the two businesses amalgamated under a new name: J.W. Cowan and Co. The company's growth

*eventually led it to acquire a large site on Stirling Road.
'An Interesting Industry' in* Monetary Times *Vol. 34,
No. 33 (15 February 1901), pp 1061–2, describes a trip to
the Toronto factory of Cowan Co., which, it says, has
'done much to place [the cocoa and chocolate] industry, a
comparatively novel one for Canada, on an established
basis.' Upon John W. Cowan's death, his son, H.N.
Cowan, became general manager (see 'Historical,' p 3,
in O468.1).*

O336.1   [1st ed.], nd [1915]
Little Miss – / Maiden Canada / registered / Dainty
& delicious dishes / prepared from / Cowan's
Cocoa and Chocolate / The Cowan Company,
Limited / Stirling Road – Toronto
DESCRIPTION: 21.5 × 15.0 cm   Pp [1–2] 3–72   Tp illus
of Cowan's brand-name girl (Little Miss); pls col on
pp 17–18, 35–8, 55–6; many illus   Paper, with image
on front of a woman stirring the contents of a bowl;
stapled
CONTENTS: 1 tp; 2 fp illus of 'General offices, ware-
house and works' on Stirling Road; 3 history of the
Cowan Co.; 4 fp illus of cocoa pods; 5 'Description of
Manufacture' [of cocoa and chocolate]; 6 'Primary
Points'; 7–56 recipes; 57–69 'Chocolate Confections
Prepared by the Cowan Company, Limited'; 70 index; 71 order form for samples of Perfection Cocoa
and Supreme Chocolate; 72 'Other Lines'
CITATIONS: Watier, illus p 7
COPIES: *BKOM (PB-991-3-50)
NOTES: On p 71, 'Recipe Book No. 1' appears at top
right of the page, above a space for the date, but there
is no indication of the book's edition or the date of
publication. This is probably the first edition published in 1915 (the copyright date cited in the second
edition, O336.2). The cover-title is 'Cowan's Dainty
Recipes.' The image above the cover-title is reproduced on the dust-jacket of *Culinary Landmarks.*

   The history on p 3 says that the business's 'phenomenal career began in 1886, when the late J.W. Cowan
organized a company under the name of J.W. Cowan
& Company'; this statement accords with the evidence in Toronto city directories. The illustrations of
various products on pp 57–69 include the company's
famous Maple Buds. On the title-page, 'Little Miss –
/ Maiden Canada' refers first to the company's icon,
Little Miss; 'Maiden Canada' may be a pun for 'Made
in Canada.'

   The BKOM copy has a label mounted on the inside
front face of the binding: 'With the compliments of
McKenzie Co. Ltd., Kelowna, B.C. All ingredients in
these recipes may be obtained here.'

O336.2   [2nd ed., 1916]
—Little Miss – / Maiden Canada / registered /
Dainty & delicious dishes / prepared from /
Cowan's Cocoa and Chocolate / The Cowan
Company, Limited / Stirling Road – Toronto
DESCRIPTION: 21.5 × 15.0 cm   Pp [1–2] 3–72   Tp illus
of Cowan's brand-name girl (Little Miss); pls col on
pp 17–18, 35–8, 55–6; many illus   Paper, with image
on front of a woman stirring the contents of a bowl;
stapled
CONTENTS: 1 tp; 2 fp illus of Cowan's 'General offices,
warehouse and works' on Stirling Road; 3 history of
the Cowan Co.; 4 fp illus of cocoa pods; 5 'Description of manufacture' [of cocoa and chocolate]; 6 'Primary Points'; 7–56 recipes; 57–69 'Chocolate
Confections Prepared by the Cowan Company, Limited'; 70 index; 71 order form for samples of Perfection Cocoa and Supreme Chocolate; 72 'Other Lines'
COPIES: *BSUM   OKQ (F5012 1916 C874)
NOTES: On p 71, above a blank space for the date, is
'2nd edition, 1916'; and on the outside back face of
the binding, 'Copyrighted 1915, The Cowan Co. Limited.' The cover-title is 'Cowan's Dainty Recipes.'

   The BSUM copy has a label glued to the inside
front face of the binding: 'With the compliments of
the Penticton Department Stores // The ingredients
of the recipes may be obtained at our store.'

O336.3   [3rd ed., 1918]
—Little Miss – / Maiden Canada / registered /
Dainty & delicious dishes / prepared from /
Cowan's Cocoa and Chocolate / The Cowan
Company, Limited / Stirling Road – Toronto
DESCRIPTION: 21.5 × 15.0 cm   Pp [1–2] 3–72   Tp illus
of Cowan's brand-name girl (Little Miss); pls col on
pp 17–18, 35–8, 55–6; many illus   Paper, with image
on front of a young child
CONTENTS: 1 tp; 2 fp illus of Cowan's 'General offices
and works at Stirling Road, Toronto'; 3 history of the
Cowan Co.; 4 fp illus of cocoa pods; 5 'Description of
Manufacture' [of cocoa and chocolate]; 6 'Primary
Points'; 7–56 recipes; 57–69 'Chocolate Confections
Prepared by the Cowan Company, Limited'; 70 in-
dex; 71 order form for product samples; 72 'Other
Lines'
CITATIONS: Ferguson/Fraser, p 232, illus col on p 35
of closed volume
COPIES: CIHM (76493)   OGU (CCC TX715.6 D24)
OONL (TX715 C3465 No. 27)   QMM (RBD ckbk
1464)   *Private collection
NOTES: On p 71, at the top of the order form for
the product samples, is '3rd edition, 1918.' The cover-
title is 'Cowan's "Dainty Recipes."'

The economical cook book

The Ottawa Ladies' Hebrew Benevolent Society was founded in 1898.

O337.1 1915
The economical / cook book / Under the auspices of / the Ottawa Ladies Hebrew / Benevolent Society / Ottawa, Canada / 1915 / Crain Printers, Limited, Bank St., Ottawa, Ont.
DESCRIPTION: 17.0 × 13.0 cm   Pp [1–25] 26–114 [115] Illus on p 50 of cuts of meat   Cloth
CONTENTS: 1 'To the Ottawa Ladies Hebrew Benevolent Society who will use the proceeds from the sale of volume to alleviate the sufferings of their poor this book is sincerely dedicated by A.L.R.'; 2–6 'Index' [i.e., table of contents]; 7–22 ads; 23 tp; 24 blank; 25–114 text; 115 blank 'For Extra Recipes'; [6 blank leaves]
CITATIONS: DCB Vol. 15, entry for Lehman, Bertha (Rosenthal)   Neering, p 97
COPIES: CIHM (79899)   *OGU (UA s048 b46)   OOJA (2 copies)   OONL (TX715.6 E36 1915)
NOTES: The title-page is in an unconventional position, after the dedication, table of contents, and pages of advertisements. *The Economical Cook Book* is the first collection of Jewish recipes published in Canada. There are directions for Matzo Pancake, Potato Pancake, Pickled Herring, Noodles, Matzo Balls No. I, Matzo Balls No. II, Matzo Pudding, Matzo Crimsel, Matzo Pie Crust, and various pickle recipes. The cookbook also includes such non-kosher recipes as Lobster Salad. Instructions for making a Fireless Cooker are on pp 28–30.

The author of the cookbook and composer of the dedication, signed A.L.R., is Augusta Leonora Rosenthal, née Poznanski (Chippewa Falls, Wis., 29 April 1881–21 March 1946, buried in Beechwood Cemetery, Ottawa, Ont.). Evidence for the attribution is in a letter from Augusta's daughter, Audrey Dribben, to Shirley Berman (archivist at OOJA, where the letter is held), [1992], in which Audrey says:

I have a cook book, which my mother compiled during the First World War and it was called 'The Economical Cook Book', which was sold to raise money for those in need. On the first page it states,

To
THE OTTAWA LADIES HEBREW
BENEVOLENT SOCIETY
who will use the proceeds from the sale of
volume (sic) to alleviate the sufferings
of their poor
this book is sincerely dedicated
by A.L.R.

Augusta was the daughter of Leah and Edward Poznanski, whose origins on her birth certificate are given as 'Polish, Russia.' Her father had a dry-goods business and served as mayor of Chippewa Falls three times (1878, 1880, 1897). She married Samuel Rosenthal, the son of Bertha and Aaron Rosenthal, on 21 June 1909, and in 1915 the couple were living in Ottawa, where her in-laws were closely connected with the men's Hebrew Benevolent Society and its women's counterpart. Aaron had been instrumental in establishing the men's society; at the time of the cookbook's publication and until her death in 1922, Bertha was president of the ladies' society. Perhaps Augusta compiled the cookbook under Bertha's direction.

Government House cook book

O338.1 1915
1915 / Government House cook book / delectable recipes / and hints to the / hostess / Containing: / seating the guests / a luncheon for the bride-to-be / wedding breakfast // reception menus / new and pretty ways of serving / what to throw after the bride / floral decorations / entertaining / tango tea, afternoon tea / tea tray lore, tales of English tea / the Lenten luncheon hour / spring guest / packing picnic hampers and / appropriate menus / South American summer drinks / sunset teas / hors d'oeuvres, salads / entrees, cakes and desserts
DESCRIPTION: 23.0 × 12.5 cm   Pp [i–iv], 1–116   Illus on p iii of Parliament Buildings, Centre Block   Black binding textured to simulate snake(?) skin
CONTENTS: i tp; ii 'Copyright, Canada, 1914 by L.E. Plummer'; iii illus and 'Mail orders promptly sent prepaid upon receipt of seventy-five cents. Address // Government House Cook Book Dept. 2 – Post Office Box No. 234 Ottawa Canada'; iv preface; 1–109 text; 110–11 ads; 112–16 'Index to Contents' and at bottom p 116, 'Lowe-Martin Co., Limited printers'
CITATIONS: O'Neill (unpublished)
COPIES: *OGU (UA s041 b27); Great Britain: LB (07942.d.2 destroyed)
NOTES: '1915 edition' is printed on the binding. The British Library records Lowe-Martin Co., Ottawa, as the publisher. In the 1912, 1913, and 1914 Ottawa city directories, Lewis E. Plummer is listed as manager of the Neal Institute of Ottawa, where one could take the 'Three Day Drink Cure'; 373 Cooper, the address of the Neal Institute, was also Plummer's residence. In the 1915 city directory, Plummer is no longer associated with the Neal Institute (a different person is

named as manager) and his residence has changed to 289 Metcalfe. He is not listed in city directories from 1916 on. Perhaps this cookbook's publication marked a change in his career.

Jopson, Alfred (November 1874–)

The 1911 Census lists Jopson as emigrated from England in 1908, now working in Toronto as a steward.

O339.1 1915
[An edition of *The Standard System of Housekeeping and Key to Successful Economy*, Toronto, Ont.: 1915]
CITATIONS: O'Neill (unpublished)
NOTES: O'Neill records this book as 'not received' by the British Library. It may or may not have included cookery, if in fact it was ever published.

Laurin, J.-Philias

The 1915 Ottawa city directory lists J. Philias Laurin, marble and granite works and memorials, at 95–9 George.

O340.1 1915
L'ami du foyer / ou le / trésor de la cuisinière / receuil de 5000 recettes / compilées et classifiées / par / J.-P. Laurin, 95 rue George, / Ottawa. Ont. / 1915 / Imprime aux ateliers de l'Imprimerie / canadienne, 1023 rue Wellington, Ottawa, Ont.
DESCRIPTION: 21.0 × 14.0 cm   Pp [i–vi], [1] 2–465 [$2.00, on spine]   Cloth, with image on front of a woman rolling dough
CONTENTS: i tp; ii 'Tous droits de reproduction ou traduction réservés, Ottawa, août 1915.'; iii–iv 'Introduction' signed 'L'éditeur. Ottawa, août 1915'; v–vi 'Important avant-propos'; 1–446 text; 447–65 'Table des matières' [i.e., index]
CITATIONS: O'Neill (unpublished)
COPIES: CIHM (80976) *OONL (TX715 L393 1915); Great Britain: LB (07942.d.1 destroyed)
NOTES: The 'Introduction' asserts that 'il n'existe pas de livres de la cuisine canadienne, publié en français,' although there are many in English; however, the English cookbooks use technical words incomprehensible to French-speaking housewives and give recipes for dishes 'pas en usage dans notre pays' and featuring unusual or expensive ingredients. The author of *L'ami du foyer* has eliminated terms that are not current and chosen economical 'recettes canadiennes.'

Little, Miss May

For information about this British author, see O313.1.

O341.1 nd [about 1915]
The complete cake / book / by / May Little / author of "A Year's Dinners," "Cookery Up-to-Date," / "The Dinner Calendar." / Toronto / Bell and Cockburn
DESCRIPTION: 18.5 × 12.0 cm   Pp [vii–xii], xiii–xv [xvi], [1–2] 3–161 [162], [i–xiv]   [$1.00, on dust-jacket]
CONTENTS: vii ht; viii publ ad; ix tp; x blank; xi preface signed May Little, Cromer [Norfolk, England]; xii blank; xiii–xv table of contents; xvi blank; 1–158 text including 200 numbered recipes and 20 numbered 'Extra Recipes'; 159–61 index; 162 'Printed by the Northumberland Press // Thornton Street, Newcastle-upon-Tyne'; i–xiv publ ads
COPIES: *Bookseller's stock

BRITISH EDITIONS: London: T. Werner Laurie, nd [1912] (Great Britain: LB, LoEN, OB; United States: NN, ICJ); London: T. Werner Laurie, nd [1915 or 1916] (Great Britain: LoEN, OB); London: T. Werner Laurie, [reprinted 1929] (Great Britain: LoEN, OPo(F); United States: NN).

The Moffat standard Canadian cook book

Later, as Moffats Ltd, the company published: O500.1, How to Cook with Moffats 'Electric' Range; O585.1, McGill, Mrs D., Moffats Cook Book; O704.1, Moffats Blue Star Cook Book; O705.1, Moffats Cook Book; O1000.1, The Culinary Art Perfected to Pleasing Certainty; O1053.1, Moffat Cook Book; O1149.1, Adam, Ann, De la magie dans les menus avec le nouveau 'handi-chef'; and O1221.1, Moffat Cook Book.

O342.1 [copyright 1915]
The Moffat standard / Canadian cook book / favorite recipes of Canadian women carefully / selected from the contributions of over / 12,000 successful cooks throughout / Canada; thoroughly tried, / tested and checked by / competent auth- / orities. / Published by / the Moffat Stove Company Limited / Head office and factory: Weston, Ont. / Branches: Montreal Winnipeg Calgary Vancouver
DESCRIPTION: 22.0 × 15.0 cm   Pp [1–3] 4–128 8 fp illus (one of Moffat factory, others of Moffat ranges); illus on pp 4, 7–11, 32   Thin card, with silhouette on front of a woman stirring the contents of a bowl

CONTENTS: 1 tp; 2 'Copyright Canada, 1915 by the Moffat Stove Company Limited // Compiled by the Advertising Department of the Moffat Stove Company, Weston, Ont. Printed by the Acton Publishing Co., Toronto'; 3–4 table of contents, and illus at bottom p 4; 5 'Introduction'; 6 'Table of Weights and Measures'; 7–11 'Carving'; 12 fp illus of Moffat factory; 13–120 recipes; 121–2 'Hints for the Housewife'; 123–5 'Practical Menus'; 126–7 'Kitchen Talks'; 128 'Every Woman in Canada Should Have a Copy of This Standard Canadian Cook Book' and three book-order forms

CITATIONS: Driver 2003, 'Caanadian Cookbooks,' p 37 Ferguson/Fraser, pp 25, 33, and 232, illus col on p 35 of closed volume Golick, p 102 O'Neill (unpublished)

COPIES: OKQ (Jordan Special Collections uncat) OTNY (uncat) OTY (TX715.6 M63 1915) *Private collection; Great Britain: LB (07942.d.3 destroyed)

NOTES: The cover-title is 'Moffat Cook Book.' The book was 'published with the object of standardizing Canadian cookery' (p 5). The section of 'Kitchen Talks' discusses the arrangement of the kitchen. It also refers to the variety of heat sources available for cooking, in what was a transitional period for stove technology: 'Just think of it, a woman can obtain every conceivable style, size and finish of range she needs. The variety includes Coal Ranges, Gas Ranges, Electric, Combination Gas and Coal, Gas and Electricity, or all three, Coal, Gas and Electricity.'

In the October 1914 issue of *Everywoman's World*, p 22, the Moffat Stove Co. ran an advertisement soliciting recipes from the public for a cookbook, which was to be compiled by a teacher in the Domestic Science Department of the Toronto Technical School (later called Central Technical School), with the assistance of two other ladies. The cookbook in question must be *The Moffat Standard Canadian Cook Book*, published one year later. The school's Commencement program for 27 November 1915 (copy at the school's library) lists the names of the cookery teachers for the preceding academic year, 1914–15; one or more of these women is probably the unnamed compiler of *The Moffat Standard Canadian Cook Book*: Miss Lucie E. Bailey; Miss Lyle Burgess; Miss K. Campbell, B.A.; Miss Margaret Davidson, Director of the Domestic Science Department; Miss P. Forfar; Miss Annie M. Gray; Miss Isabel Pease; Miss Muriel Powell; Miss Agnes Robertson; and Miss Isabel Sutherland. Two of the women are associated with 1920s cookbooks: Annie Gray assisted with O506.1, Pattinson, Miss Nellie Lyle, *Canadian Cook Book*; Margaret Davidson's name is connected with O528.1, Toronto, Board of

Education, *Handbook of Practical Cookery for the Use of Household Science Classes in the Public Schools of Toronto.* Davidson, the department's director, is the most likely candidate for compiler of *The Moffat Standard Canadian Cook Book;* for information about her, see O528.1.

Neil, Marion Harris

For information about this author and her other cookbooks, see O306.1.

O343.1 [copyright 1915]
The story / of Crisco / 250 tested recipes / by Marion Harris Neil [cover-title]
DESCRIPTION: 19.0 × 12.5 cm Pp [1–3] 4–128 Illus Paper, with image on front of four persons looking at a giant-size cookbook
CONTENTS: 1 illustrated part-title with 'Form 82 25M 9-24-15 The Story of Crisco' and at bottom right, the artist's name, 'Fred Pegram 1912'; 2 table of contents; 3 quotations and 'Copyright 1915 The Procter & Gamble Distributing Co. of Canada, Ltd. Hamilton, Canada'; 4 'Introduction'; 5–17 'The Story of Crisco'; 18 'Things to Remember in Connection with These Recipes'; 19 'Remember That –'; 20 'Hints to Young Cooks'; 21–2 'Time Table for Cooking'; 23 'Weights and Measures'; 24–6 'The Art of Carving'; 27–128 'Two Hundred and Fifty Tested Recipes by Marion Harris Neil'
CITATIONS: Reitz, p [4]
COPIES: OKITD (969.098.014) *Private collection
NOTES: Crisco shortening was introduced to the American market in 1911. Procter and Gamble officially opened its first Canadian plant, in Hamilton, in 1915, the same year it published the Canadian edition of *The Story of Crisco*.

A note about the enlarged edition of this book is on the inside back face of the binding: 'De Luxe Edition of This Book // You may obtain the enlarged edition of this book for 5 two-cent stamps. It is bound in handsome blue and gold cloth ... it contains, in addition to everything printed in this book, 365 more recipes by Marion Harris Neil, and a "Calendar of Dinners" by the same author.' The first Canadian enlarged edition that I have located is dated copyright 1917 (O390.1, A *'Calendar of Dinners' with 615 Recipes*), but there were earlier American editions.

O343.2 copyright 1923
—Form C-82 / Mrs. Neil's / cooking secrets / by Marion Harris Neil / formerly Cookery Editor of / "The Ladies' Home Journal" / and / The story of

Crisco / Copyright 1923, Procter & Gamble, Hamilton, Canada

DESCRIPTION: 18.5 × 13.0 cm   Pp [i–ii], [1–2] 3–128 Illus   Paper, with image on front of a boy and a three-layer cake, and below, a pie and two eggs in a frying pan; stapled

CONTENTS: i letter from Procter and Gamble to the reader; ii blank; 1 tp; 2 'Introduction'; 3–13 'The Story of Crisco'; 14 'Things to Remember in Connection with These Recipes' and 'Remember That –'; 15–20 'How to Choose Foods'; 21–mid 28 'Methods of Cooking'; bottom 28 'Hints to Young Cooks'; 29–30 'Time Table for Cooking'; 31 'Weights and Measures'; 32–4 'The Art of Carving'; 35–128 recipes; inside back face of binding 'Table of Contents' and 'De Luxe Edition of This Book' [note about 'the enlarged edition of this book for 25 cents,' i.e., A 'Calendar of Dinners' with 615 Recipes]

COPIES: *QSFFSC (641.5 N398m)

NOTES: This is a retitled edition of O343.1.

AMERICAN EDITIONS: The Story of Crisco, Cincinnati: Procter and Gamble, 1911 (DuSablon, p 93).

Patriotic cook book

O344.1   1915

Patriotic / cook book / collected and compiled by / the ladies of Talbot St. School / Mothers' Club / for / Red Cross / and / War Contingent Funds / November 1915 / London, Ont. / The Advertiser Job Printing Co.

DESCRIPTION: 22.0 × 12.5 cm   Pp [1–4] 5–100 [101–4] 1 fp illus on p 20 of cuts of beef   Limp cloth, with image on front of a Union Jack and Red Ensign; stapled

CONTENTS: 1 tp; 2 'The following ladies have contributed valuable recipes:' [followed by two columns of names]; 3 three quotations (one unattributed, two from Hood); 4 'Preface'; 5–6 ads; 7–8 'Balanced Menus'; 9–97 recipes and ads; 98–101 'Helpful Hints'; 102–3 blank for 'Memorandum'; 104 'Index' [i.e., table of contents]

COPIES: *BPM   Private collection

NOTES: The private collector's copy belonged originally to her mother, Mrs Clark, who is listed as one of the recipe contributors.

Powell, Georgia Delia Sexton (Franklin, Mass., about 1865–January 1948, Cobourg, Ont.)

Mrs Powell, wife of Edwin James Powell and affectionately known as 'Georgie,' died aged eighty-three years; therefore, she was born about 1865. She is buried in Mount Pleasant Cemetery in Toronto. Her obituary is in the Toronto Telegram, *28 January 1948.*

O345.1   [copyright 1915]

The Toronto / cook book / by / Mrs. E.J. Powell / Toronto, Canada / No. 53 Glen Grove Ave

DESCRIPTION: 19.0 × 12.5 cm   Pp [1–2, 5] 6–352   16 pls, incl in pagination   [$1.00, on spine]   Cloth, with image on front of Toronto City Hall in a circular frame and two maple leaves

CONTENTS: 1 tp; 2 'Dedicated to the ladies of the Dominion of Canada by Mrs. Edwin James Powell compiler // Copyright, Canada, 1915 by Mrs. E.J. Powell // Printed by the Mortimer Company, Ottawa, Toronto, Montreal'; 3–4 [removed from this copy]; 5–8 'Introductory' and 'A Visit with the Housewife by Mrs. H.C. Tomlin'; 9–10 table of contents; 11–352 text

CITATIONS: Bitting, p 380   O'Neill (unpublished)

COPIES: ACG   CIHM (98740)   *OGU (UA s006 b03)   OTMCL (641.59713 P596)   Private collection; Great Britain: LB (07942.e.58 destroyed); United States: DLC (TX715 P88)

NOTES: The cover-title is 'The Toronto Queen City of Canada Cook Book.'

Two private collectors' copies have a 'Preface' on pp 3–4, written by Mrs Powell, that reveals the motivation for publishing the cookbook and the details of its production. The ACG, OGU, and OTMCL copies, and the CIHM fiche (made from the OTMCL copy), have no 'Preface,' and where it might have been, the leaf has been carefully torn out. It is likely that, some time after 1915, perhaps after the end of the First World War, copies of the book were distributed with the 'Preface' removed.

In the 'Preface' Mrs Powell begins by referring to her 'work in the aid of those who unfortunately have been financially embarrassed by the present war' and the need for more money to continue the work. She comments that this recipe book will meet the call of Toronto housewives for a 'cookbook of moderate cost' and will raise funds for her cause. She tells of a meeting, chaired by Rev. A.A. Wall [i.e., Alfred Adam Wall, pastor of Davisville Methodist Church], where a resolution was passed authorizing her to compile the cookbook under the direction of an executive committee. She identifies the committee members as: chairman: Rev. A.A. Wall; treasurers: Mr H. Waddington, president of Standard Reliance, and Mr E.J. Powell [her husband, manager of Greenshields Ltd, a wholesale dry goods business, and people's warden, Church of St Clement, Eglinton, 1919–23 and 1932–4]; secretary: Mrs P.F. Sexton [probably her relation by marriage]; compiler of book: Mrs Edwin James Powell; hon. chairmen: H.C. Hocken, Hon. Thomas Crawford, and Rev. A.J. Fidler Jr [Arthur J. Fidler, rector of Church of St Clement, Eglinton, 1910–41]; Committee of Ladies: Mrs H. Waddington [whose husband Herbert was rector's warden of Church of St Clement, Eglinton, for 1901–2, and people's warden, 1903–7], Mrs A.J. Fidler Jr [rector's wife, Church of St Clement, Eglinton], Mrs C.B. Cleveland, Mrs Aubrey O. Hurst, and Mrs A.K. Griffin. Below the list of names is a declaration headed 'Toronto Queen City Cook Book' and dated 27 October 1914: 'We, the undersigned, approve of the composition and distribution of this book, which is intended to be sold for $1.00. The proceeds of the first 25,000 copies, after paying expenses of preparation and distribution, will be placed in the hands of the Trustee Board to be distributed in the best way possible to give employment to the unemployed in our city. The intention of Mrs. E.J. Powell … is to have 25,000 copies of this book printed and distributed or sold to the citizens of Toronto.' The declaration is signed H.C. Hocken, mayor, 1914; Hon. Thos Crawford; Noel Marshall, president, Red Cross Society; Edwin J. Powell; and H.C. Cox. Following the declaration, Mrs Powell thanks her friends for their recipe contributions and for their help (Mrs H.C. Tomlin, Mrs Jenkins, Mrs J.R. Skinner, Mrs John Morrish, Mrs Whitehead, Mrs Willard R. Beatty of Pembroke, Ontario, Mrs R.E. Powell of Ottawa, Mrs William R. Hudson of Boston, Massachusetts, Mrs P.F. Sexton of Toronto, and Mrs T.W. Miller). She expresses the hope that 'every Christian church … will act as a sale centre' and comments that the Central Financial Committee of Business Men have volunteered to disburse the receipts from the sale of the book.

Recipes

See also O598.1, Daisy Recipe Book No. 2.

O346.1   1915
Recipes / Compiled and arranged by the / Daisy Bible Class / of the / Hyatt Avenue / Methodist Church / London Ontario / "L'appétit, vient en mangeant." / 1915

DESCRIPTION: About 22.5 × 15.0 cm   Pp 3–92   No photocopy of binding
CONTENTS: 3 quotations from Shakespeare, Ruskin, and an unidentified source; 4 'Our Greeting' and 'Officers'; 5 tp; 6 ads; 7–85 recipes, most credited with the name of the contributor, and ads; 86 'Table Hints'; 87 'Helpful Hints for the Home'; 88–mid 89 'Time Table'; mid–bottom 89 'Kitchen Rules'; 90–2 'The Art of Table Setting'
COPIES: *OL (R641.5 REC, photocopy)
NOTES: 'Our Greeting' thanks the contributors and especially the advertisers who have 'assured [our] financial success.' The printing plant of the *London Free Press* newspaper may have printed the cookbook since on every page, in the position for running heads, there are advertisements for the *Free Press*.

Red Cross cook book

O347.1   February 1915
Red Cross / cook book / Compiled by the ladies / of the / Red Cross Society, Newmarket. / February, 1915.

DESCRIPTION: 17.0 × 13.0 cm   Pp [tp lacking] [3–9] 10–240   1 fp illus on p 3 of 'Motor ambulance provided by the Newmarket Red Cross Society for Canadian Volunteers in France'   Cloth, with image on front of a red cross
CONTENTS: 3 fp illus; 4 ad; 5 'Preface'; 6 'How to Cook a Husband' [mock recipe]; 7–8 ads; 9–233 text; 234 'Index to Contents'; 235–8 [lacking]; 239–40 blank for 'Additional Recipes.'
COPIES: *OGU (UA s048 b22)   Private collection
NOTES: The title-page transcription is from a photocopy of the title-page supplied by the private collector (the title-page in the OGU copy is lacking). The Red Cross Society's cross symbol is printed on the title-page; an advertisement for the Bank of Toronto is on p [2].

The 'Preface' states, 'The Red Cross Society of Newmarket is endeavoring to raise sufficient funds to purchase an ambulance to send to the front with our second contingent, and this book is designed to help make up the desired sum.' It adds that a number of the recipes 'have been chosen with a view to economy, thereby fitting them for use during the stress of hard times.'

Ritter, T.J., Mrs Alice Gitchell Kirk, and W.C. Fair

Alice Kirk's The People's Home Recipe Book *was also published separately; see O441.1.*

O348.1 1915
The people's / home library / A / library / of / three / practical / books / The / people's / home / medical / book / by / T.J. Ritter M.D. / The / people's / home / recipe / book / by / Mrs. Alice G. Kirk. / The / people's / home / stock / book / by / W.C. Fair V.S. / Published by / the R.C. Barnum Co. / Cleveland, Ohio – Minneapolis, Minn. / Imperial Publishing Co. / Toronto, Canada / 1915
DESCRIPTION: 24.0 × 17.5 cm   Pp [1–6], i–iv, [1] 2–478 [479–80], [1–2], i–iv, 1–238 [239–42], [1–2], i–v [vi], [1] 2–315   Frontis portrait of R.C. Barnum; Book I: 9 pls col, 5 pls incl frontis portrait of T.J. Ritter; Book II: 9 pls incl frontis portrait of Alice Kirk; Book III: 2 pls col, 47 pls incl frontis portrait of W.C. Fair   Cloth
CONTENTS: 1 tp; 2 'Copyrighted 1910, by R.C. Barnum. All rights reserved. Copyrighted 1913, by the R.C. Barnum Company. Note. This is strictly a subscription book ...'; 3 'Compiler's Preface' signed R.C. Barnum; 4 dedication; 5 Book I tp; 6 'Copyrighted 1910, by R.C. Barnum. All rights reserved.'; i–ii 'Author's Preface'; iii 'Contents'; iv 'List of Illustrations'; 1–440 text; 441–3 blank for 'Supplement. (Additional Recipes.)'; 444–78 'Medical Index'; 479–80 blank; 1 Book II tp; 2 'Copyrighted 1910, by R.C. Barnum. All rights reserved.' and copyright notice for recipes credited to 'Mrs. Kirk's Card Index Cooking Recipes'; i–ii 'Author's Preface'; iii 'Contents'; iv 'List of Illustrations'; 1–219 text; 220–2 blank for 'Supplement. (Additional Recipes.)'; 223–38 'Culinary Index'; 239–42 blank; 1 Book III tp; 2 'Copyrighted 1910, by R.C. Barnum. All rights reserved.'; i–ii 'Author's Preface'; iii 'Contents'; iv–v 'List of Illustrations'; vi blank; 1–269 text; 270–91 'Glossary'; 292–4 blank for 'Supplement. (Additional Recipes.)'; 295–315 'Veterinary Index'
COPIES: *QMM (Osler Robertson P41993 1915)
NOTES: This is the earliest known edition with the name of Toronto's Imperial Publishing Co. printed on the title-page; however, I have seen a copy of the 1913 American edition with 'Imperial Publishing Co. Toronto, Canada' stamped in purple ink on the title-page (Private collection, Toronto).

O348.2 1916
—The people's / home library / A / library / of / three / practical / books / The / people's / home / medical / book / by / T.J. Ritter M.D. / The / people's / home / recipe / book / by / Mrs. Alice G. Kirk. / The / people's / home / stock / book / by / W.C. Fair V.S. / Published by / the R.C. Barnum Co. / Cleveland, Ohio – Minneapolis, Minn. / Imperial Publishing Co. / Toronto, Canada / 1916
DESCRIPTION: 24.5 × 17.5 cm   Pp [1–6], i–iv, [1] 2–478 [479–80], [1–2], i–iv, 1–238 [239–42], [1–2], i–v [vi], [1] 2–315   Frontis; Book I: 9 pls col, 5 pls incl frontis; Book II: 9 pls incl frontis portrait of Alice Kirk; Book III: 2 pls col, 46 pls incl frontis   Cloth
CONTENTS: 1 tp; 2 'Copyrighted 1910, by R.C. Barnum ... Copyrighted 1913, by the R.C. Barnum Company. Note. This is strictly a subscription book and will not be sold in stores ...'; 3 'Compiler's Preface' signed R.C. Barnum; 4 dedication; 5 Book I tp; 6 'Copyrighted 1910, by R.C. Barnum'; i–ii 'Author's Preface'; iii table of contents; iv list of illustrations; 1–440 text; 441–3 blank for 'Supplement. (Additional Recipes.)'; 444–78 'Medical Index'; 479–80 blank; 1 Book II tp; 2 'Copyrighted 1910, by R.C. Barnum' and copyright notice for recipes credited to 'Mrs Kirk's Card Index Cooking Recipes,' earliest copyright date cited being 1906; i–ii 'Author's Preface'; iii table of contents; iv list of illustrations; 1–219 text; 220–2 blank for 'Supplement. (Additional Recipes.)'; 223–38 'Culinary Index'; 239–42 blank; 1 Book III tp; 2 'Copyrighted 1910, by R.C. Barnum'; i–ii 'Author's Preface'; iii table of contents; iv–v list of illustrations; vi blank; 1–269 text; 270–91 glossary; 292–4 blank for 'Supplement. (Additional Recipes.)'; 295–315 'Veterinary Index'
COPIES: ACHP   SMM   *Private collection
NOTES: In her 'Author's Preface,' Alice Kirk describes her cooking career.

O348.3 city ed., 1916
—The people's / home library / A / library / of / very / practical / books / The / people's / home / medical / book / by / T.J. Ritter M.D. / City / edition / Nursing / Medicine / Domestic / science / The / people's / home / recipe / book / by / Mrs. Alice G. Kirk / Published by / the R.C. Barnum Co. / Cleveland, Ohio – Minneapolis, Minn. / Imperial Publishing Co. / Toronto, Canada / 1916
DESCRIPTION: 24.5 × 17.5 cm   Pp [1–6], i–iv, [1] 2–478 [479–80], [1–2], i–iv, 1–238   Frontis portrait of R.C. Barnum; Book I: frontis portrait of T.J. Ritter, 9 pls col,

4 pls; Book II: frontis portrait of Alice Kirk, 8 numbered pls opp p iv

CONTENTS: 1 tp; 2 'Copyrighted 1910, by R.C. Barnum. All rights reserved. Copyrighted 1913, by the R.C. Barnum Company. Note. This is strictly a subscription book and is not and will not be sold in stores ...'; 3 'Compiler's Preface' signed R.C. Barnum; 4 dedication; 5 Book I tp; 6 'Copyrighted 1910, by R.C. Barnum.'; i–ii 'Author's Preface'; iii table of contents; iv 'List of Illustrations'; 1–440 text; 441–3 blank for 'Supplement. (Additional Recipes.)'; 444–78 'Medical Index'; 479–80 blank; 1 Book II tp; 2 'Copyrighted 1910, by R.C. Barnum.' and copyright notice for 'Mrs. Kirk's Card Index Cooking Recipes,' earliest copyright date cited being 1906; i–ii 'Author's Preface'; iii table of contents; iv 'List of Illustrations'; 1–219 text; 220–2 blank for 'Supplement. (Additional Recipes.)'; 223–38 'Culinary Index'

COPIES: *AMHM

NOTES: The city edition omits Book III, *The People's Home Stock Book*.

O348.4 1917

—The people's / home library / A / library / of / three / practical / books / The / people's / home / medical / book / by / T.J. Ritter M.D. / The / people's / home / recipe / book / by / Mrs. Alice G. Kirk. / The / people's / home / stock / book / by / W.C. Fair V.S. / Published by / the R.C. Barnum Co. / Cleveland, Ohio – Minneapolis, Minn. / Boston, Mass. / Imperial Publishing Co. / Toronto, Canada / 1917

COPIES: SBIM *SSWD

O348.5 1919

—The people's / home library / A / library / of / three / practical / books / The / people's / home / medical / book / by / T.J. Ritter M.D. / The / people's / home / recipe / book / by / Mrs. Alice G. Kirk. / The / people's / home / stock / book / by / W.C. Fair V.S. / Published by / the R.C. Barnum Co. / Cleveland, Ohio – Minneapolis, Minn. / Boston, Mass. – Lincoln Nebr. / Seattle, Wash. / Imperial Publishing Co. / Toronto, Canada / 1919

COPIES: *SSWD

O348.6 [1926]

—[Another edition of *The People's Home Library*, Cleveland: R.C. Barnum Co., and Toronto: Imperial Publishing Co., [1926], three parts in one volume]

COPIES: United States: DLC (RC81 P4 1926)

NOTES: There is a second entry in the DLC catalogue for a volume that matches the description above except that the date is recorded as [c1926] (RC81 P4) instead of [1926] (RC81 P4 1926).

AMERICAN EDITIONS: Cleveland: R.C. Barnum Co., 1910 (United States: DLC); Cleveland: R.C. Barnum Co., 1911 (Private collection); Cleveland: R.C. Barnum Co., 1913 (United States: DLC); Cleveland: R.C. Barnum Co., 1914 (Private collection).

The Sarnian cook book

London Road West Methodist Church is now called London Road West United Church.

O349.1 [1915]

[An edition of *The Sarnian Cook Book*, published by the Ladies' Aid of London Road West Methodist Church, Sarnia Township, Ontario, [1915]]

COPIES: OWYL

NOTES: The OWYL copy is incomplete and lacks the binding; however, the library records the title, *The Sarnian Cook Book*. The 'Foreword' is signed B.H. Robinson, pastor, Point Edward, 17 December 1915. Robinson explains in the 'Foreword' that the Ladies' Aid had been organized in April 1915, and he names the members of the executive. The purpose of the Ladies' Aid was 'to encourage in every way possible those social tendencies, which make for a strong and happy community life' and 'to inaugurate a movement which shall at not too distant a date secure a church building better suited to the needs of this splendid section of Sarnia Township.' The publication of the cookbook, he writes, is 'perhaps [the Ladies' Aid's] largest venture, and indicates the aggressive and earnest spirit of the executive members.'

The story of Carnation Milk

The company that developed the product called Carnation Condensed Milk was founded in Kent, Oregon, in 1899, as Pacific Coast Condensed Milk Co. The brand name Carnation was created soon after and, in about 1915, the company was renamed Carnation Milk Products Co. Also in the First World War period, the company expanded into Canada, buying a creamery in Aylmer, Ontario, and calling the Canadian business Carnation Co. Ltd. In 1934, the company added Vitamin D to the milk by a process of irradiation. From 1945, the Vitamin D was added as a concentrate and the amount increased. In

1949, the fiftieth anniversary of the company's founding, its offices were reorganized and a new headquarters opened in Los Angeles, California. The Carnation Co. was bought by Nestlé in 1985.

For a 1922 book about cooking with Carnation milk, see O489.1, One Hundred Tested Recipes. From about 1923, Carnation cookbooks were generally attributed to the pseudonymous Mary Blake; for these titles, see O494.1. Ruth Crowley's name is associated with O1047.1, Growing Up with Milk.

Information about the company's history is from the biography Elbridge A. Stuart: Founder of Carnation Company, by James Marshall, Los Angeles: Carnation Co., [1949]. Allen, p 204, incorrectly states that Carnation Condensed Milk was introduced in 1923.

O350.1 [copyright 1915]
The story of / Carnation Milk / [caption below illus of cows:] From / contented cows / Carnation Milk / Products Co. Limited / Aylmer, Ontario. / In U.S.A. – General offices, Seattle, Wash. / Copyright, by Carnation Milk Products Co.
DESCRIPTION: 17.5 × 12.5 cm   Pp [1] 2–32   Tp illus of cows, centre spread col on pp 16–17 of prepared dishes, fp illus on p 2 of Carnation Stock Farm near Seattle, illus col, illus   Paper, with image on front of a mother and daughter looking at cows in a meadow; stapled
CONTENTS: Inside front face of binding 'Made in Canada // Aylmer Ontario'; 1 tp; 2 fp illus; 3–31 information about the product and recipes using it, with running head 'The Story of Carnation Milk and Carnation Milk Recipes'; 32 table of contents
COPIES: *Private collection
NOTES: The title-page is printed in red and black. 'Copyright, 1915, by Carnation Milk Products Co.' is on the outside back face of the binding.

The title-page text differentiates this edition from O350.2 (note, for example, 'In U.S.A. – General offices, Seattle, Wash.' in this edition; 'General offices / Seattle, U.S.A.' in O350.2). The order of publication of the two editions is unknown. The company's advertisements for *The Story of Carnation Milk* in the August 1918 issue of *Everywoman's World*, p 21, and in the May 1919 issue of *Western Home Monthly* may refer to either edition, as may the citation in Chatelaine 1935, p 82.

O350.2 [copyright 1915]
—The story of / Carnation Milk / [caption below illus of cows:] From / contented cows / Carnation Milk Products Co. / Limited / Aylmer, Ontario. / Carnation Milk / Products Co. / General offices /

Seattle, U.S.A. / Copyright, by Carnation Milk Products Co.
DESCRIPTION: About 18.0 × 12.5 cm (dimensions from photocopy)   Pp [1] 2–32   Tp illus of cows, fp illus on p 2 of Carnation Stock Farm near Seattle, illus col, illus   Paper, with image on front of a mother and daughter looking at cows in a meadow; stapled
CONTENTS: Inside front face of binding 'Made in Canada // Aylmer Ontario'; 1 tp; 2 fp illus; 3–31 information about the product and recipes using it, with running head 'The Story of Carnation Milk and Carnation Milk Recipes'; 32 table of contents
COPIES: *Private collection
NOTES: 'Copyright, 1915, by Carnation Milk Products Co.' is on the outside back face of the binding.

Tested recipe book

St Margaret's College was a boarding and day school for girls. It is listed in Toronto city directories for the period 1898–1921. Its initial location was 403 Bloor Street West, at the corner of Spadina. In 1915, when the cookbook was published, it was at 144–50 Bloor Street East; Mrs George Dickson was president, and Miss J.E. Macdonald, lady principal. The college specialized in preparing young women for university.

One pupil attending the college in fall 1917 was Amelia Earhart's sister Muriel (1899–1998). After visiting Muriel in Toronto in Christmas 1917, Amelia took a course in Red Cross First Aid, then cared for soldiers at Spadina Military Hospital in Toronto. Perhaps the Red Cross was a special cause of St Margaret's throughout the First World War, not just at the time of the cookbook's publication.

O351.1   June 1915
St. Margaret's College / Toronto / Household Science / Department / Tested recipe book / Published for / the benefit of the Red Cross Fund / June 1915
DESCRIPTION: 18.5 × 12.5 cm   Pp [1–4] 5–51   Paper; stapled
CONTENTS: 1 tp; 2 blank; 3 'St. Margaret's College' signed the Editor; 4 'Index'; 5–6 'Time Tables of Cooking'; 7–51 recipes
COPIES: *Private collection
NOTES: The text on p 3 says that the recipes 'have been tested by the Mistress and pupils of the Household Science Department of the college' and that the funds raised are for the Red Cross Fund. The printer's name is on the outside back face of the binding: 'Commercial Art Press, Toronto Limited.'

Tested recipes

See also O723.1, Favorite Recipes, from the same church (called Eglinton United Church from 1925).

O352.1 nd [1915]
Tested / recipes / Compiled and arranged / by the / Mission Circle / Eglinton Methodist Church [cover-title]
DESCRIPTION: 21.0 × 14.0 cm Pp [1] 2–59 Card; bound at top edge by two metal rings through punched holes
CONTENTS: 1 'Index' [i.e., table of contents]; 2 'Weights and Measures' and ad; 3–56 recipes credited with the name of the contributor and ads; 57 'Household Hints'; 58 ad; 59 'How to Cook a Husband' [mock recipe]
COPIES: *Private collection
NOTES: Minutes of the Mission Circle in the archives of Eglinton United Church (to be transferred to OTCC) record in detail the compiling and publishing of *Tested Recipes* in 1915, including the amount of money made from its sale. Blank, lined leaves for manuscript recipes follow p 59. A photocopy of the private collector's copy has been donated to the church's archives.

To make him say 'Delicious!'

For other cookbooks by Gunns Ltd, see: O426.1, Recipes: Wholesome, Nutritious, Economical; and O560.1, Recipes: Attractive, Nutritious, Economical. The foreword of O426.1 refers to the founding of the business in 1873. Toronto city directories in the 1910s describe Gunns Ltd as 'pork and beef packers and cotton oil refiners,' with head office in West Toronto.

O353.1 nd [about 1915]
To make / him say / "Delicious!" / Containing / forty selected recipes / and explaining the secret / of kitchen economy and / better food / Gunns Limited / Toronto and Montreal
DESCRIPTION: 18.0 × 12.5 cm Pp [1–2] 3–24 Tp illus of a man and woman seated at table, a few small illus [Free, on p 24] Very thin card, with image on front of a man seated at table; stapled
CONTENTS: 1 tp; 2–3 information about Gunns 'Easifirst' Shortening; 4–7 'Cakes'; 8–9 'Pies and Pastry'; 10–12 'Puddings'; 13–14 'For Afternoon Tea'; 15–16 'Salads'; 17–20 'Fish and Meat Dishes'; 21–2 'Vegetables'; 23 'Things You Should Know When Using Gunns "Easifirst"'; 24 'Table of Weights and Measures'

COPIES: *OGU (CCC TX715.6 T6)
NOTES: This is the book advertised by Gunns on p 22 of O347.1, *Red Cross Cook Book*, published by the Red Cross Society of Newmarket in February 1915; the advertisement commands the reader, 'Write us for booklet containing 40 recipes.' The book could not have been published after 1927, the year that Gunns Ltd merged with the William Davies Co., the Canadian Packing Co. Ltd, and the Harris Abattoir Co. to form Canada Packers Ltd.
   On pp 2–3, 'Easifirst' Shortening is described as 'a pure, creamy, snow-white substance that means double economy'; it is a Canadian product that is 'more than a substitute for lard and butter [and] destined to supersede them in every class of cookery.'

The truth about baking powder

See O288.1 for information about Egg-o Baking Powder Co. and its other cookbooks.

O354.1 nd [about 1915]
The truth about / baking powder / Trade mark registered / With special bread, / cake and biscuit / recipes / Egg-o Baking Powder / Company, Limited / Hamilton, Ontario [cover-title]
DESCRIPTION: 15.0 × 9.0 cm Pp 1–32 Paper, with image on front of an Egg-o Baking Powder container in an eggshell surrounded by a wheat wreath, i.e., the image that is printed on Egg-o Baking Powder containers; stapled
CONTENTS: 1 'The Reason Why'; 2 'Facts Worth Knowing'; 3–9 'Cakes'; 10 'Cookies'; 11 guarantee of the purity of Egg-o Baking Powder; 12–13 'Cake Fillings and Frostings'; 14 about the convenience of Egg-o Baking Powder; 15 'Biscuits'; 16–17 'Don't Take the Risk'; 18 'Griddle Cakes'; 19–21 'Bread'; 22–3 'Fritters, Doughnuts'; 24 'Muffins, Waffles'; 25 'Pudding Sauces'; 26–7 'Our Test // You Can Test –'; 28–9 'Puddings'; 30–1 'Pies'; 32 index and an invitation to order 'our larger cook-book, "Reliable Recipes"' of 72 pp [likely O288.2]
COPIES: *Private collection
NOTES: The binding is white and the cover-title is printed in blue. The inside text is black. Another private collector has what appears to be an identical copy except that the inside text is blue.

O354.2 nd
—[An edition of *La vérité sur la poudre à pâte: recettes pour pain spécial, gâteaux et biscuits*, Hamilton: Egg-o Baking Powder Co. Ltd, nd, pp 32]
CITATIONS: BouquinsCat 228, No. 286

O354.3 nd

—The truth about / baking powder / With special / recipes / for / Egg-o / Baking Powder [cover-title]

DESCRIPTION: 15.5 × 9.0 cm   Pp 1–26   Paper, with image on front of a container of Egg-o Baking Powder; stapled

CONTENTS: 1 '4 – Good Reasons – 4'; 2 'Facts Worth Knowing'; 3–7 'Cakes' and publ ad on p 6; 8 'Griddle Cakes'; 9 'Cookies'; 10 'Cake Fillings and Frostings'; 11 guarantee of the purity of Egg-o Baking Powder; 12 'Biscuits'; 13–14 'Don't Take the Risk'; 15 'Fritters, Doughnuts'; 16 'Muffins, Waffles' and 'Pudding Sauces'; 17–18 'Bread'; 19–20 'Our Test // You Can Test'; 21 about the convenience of Egg-o Baking Powder; 22–3 'Puddings'; 24–5 'Pies'; 26 index and an invitation to order 'our larger cook-book, "Reliable Recipes"' of 72 pp

COPIES: AMHM   OONL (TX409 T78 1945)   OWTU (E0918, 2 copies)   QMM (RBD ckbk 1530)   *Private collection

NOTES: The binding is printed with a blue background; the cover-title is reversed out in white. The inside text is all blue. Unusually, the odd page numbers are on the versos, and the even numbers, on the rectos.

1916

Byron, May Clarissa, née Gillington (died 1936)

For other cookbooks by this British author, see O317.1.

O355.1   1916

May Byron's / jam book / a handy guide to the preserving / of fruit with and without sugar / jams, jellies, marmalades / cheeses, pastes, butters / bottled, dried, spiced / syruped, brandied / and candied fruit / Containing over five hundred recipes / "It is ... my purpose to make my book ... a gentle- / woman's preserving pan." – John Gerarde ("Great Herball.") / Hodder and Stoughton / London New York Toronto / MCMXVI

DESCRIPTION: Cloth, with still-life on front of fruit and jars of preserves

COPIES: *Private collection

O355.2   1923

—May Byron's / jam book / a handy guide to the preserving / of fruit with and without sugar / jams, jellies, marmalades / cheeses, pastes, butters / bottled, dried, spiced / syruped, brandied / and candied fruit / Containing over five hundred

recipes / "It is ... my purpose to make my book ... a gentle- / woman's preserving pan." – John Gerarde "Great Herball." / Hodder and Stoughton Ltd. / Toronto London New York / MCMXXIII

DESCRIPTION: 19.0 × 12.0 cm   Pp [i–iv] v–ix [x] xi–xxi [xxii], [1] 2–276   Cloth, with still-life on front of fruit and jars of preserves

CONTENTS: i ht; ii list of 'May Byron's Cookery Books'; iii tp; iv 'Made and printed in Great Britain by Hazell, Watson & Viney, Ld., London and Aylesbury.'; v–xxi table of contents; xxii blank; 1–276 text incl 543 numbered recipes

COPIES: *QMM (RBD Vanna Garnier, ckbk 921)

BRITISH EDITIONS: London and New York: Hodder and Stoughton, 1916 (Great Britain: LB; United States: DLC).

AMERICAN EDITIONS: *Jams and Jellies: 543 Recipes*, New York: Dover Publications, 1975 (United States: DLC).

SPANISH EDITIONS: *Libro de confituras*, Barcelona: L. Gili, 1928 (United States: DLC).

Canada

O356.1   1916

Manual / of / military cooking / 1916 / Ottawa / Government Printing Bureau / 1916 / 4 M. 5-16. / H.Q. 70-55-94.

DESCRIPTION: 19.5 × 12.5 cm   Pp [1–3] 4–68   Illus   Paper-covered boards; sewn

CONTENTS: 1 tp; 2 blank; 3–68 text in eight numbered sections

COPIES: *OH (R641.573 C16 CANA)   OONMC (UC725 C2 M3 1916)

NOTES: Section 1 discusses the duties of various personnel, from company commander to quartermasters, cooks, butchers, and storemen. Section 2 covers messing arrangements in camp and on the march, cooking in the field, and the building and working of field apparatus. Section 3 includes 'The Diet Sheet' and information about the care of meat, fuels, cleaning, and utensils. Section 4 includes 'Inspection of Rations' and information about the quality of beef and mutton, frozen meat, the inspection of canned goods, bread, and vegetables. Section 5 has recipes for soups, roasting, stews, vegetables, and beverages, and information about condiments and seasonings, followed by other recipes. Section 6 has recipes for cooking for 100 men with canned meat. Section 7 is 'Miscellaneous Recipes.' Section 8 covers such topics as 'Economy,' 'Disposal of Refuse,' and 'Fireless Cookers,' and ends with detailed illustrations of various arrangements for cooking.

Christian, Eugene (1860–1930)

One of Christian's pupils was Miss Dickson Riley, author of M72.1, Eclipse Tempting Recipes, *published a year after he died. Christian wrote the following on the subject of food and health, some co-authored with his wife (all at DLC in the United States):* Uncooked Foods and How to Use Them, *by Mr and Mrs Eugene Christian, New York: Health-Culture Co., 1904;* Suncooked Food; a Treatise on How to Get the Highest Form of Human Energy from Food, *6th ed., New York: Christian's School of Applied Food Chemistry, 1909;* 250 Meatless Menus and Recipes to Meet the Requirements of People under the Varying Conditions of Age, Climate and Work, *New York: E. Christian and M.G. Christian, 1910;* Encyclopedia of Diet; a Treatise on the Food Question ..., *New York: Christian Dietetic Society, 1914;* How to Live 100 Years; What to Eat According to Your Age, Your Occupation, and the Time of the Year, *New York: Christian Dietetic Society, 1914;* Little Lessons in Scientific Eating, *New York: Corrective Eating Society Inc., [1916];* Fifty Corrective Eating Recipes, *New York City: Corrective Eating Society Inc., [c1917];* Meatless and Wheatless Menus, *New York: A.A. Knopf, 1917;* Encyclopedia of Cookery; 1001 Recipes, Menus and Rules for Modern, Scientific and Economic Cookery, *by Eugene Christian and Mollie Griswold Christian, New York: Corrective Eating Society, [c1920];* Why Die, *New York: E. Christian, [c1928];* Pounds Off; a System of Weight Control for Health, Beauty and Efficiency, *New York: MacFadden Book Co., [c1930].*

O357.1   [copyright 1916]
Eat and be well / eat and get well / Eugene Christian, F.S.D. / Toronto / McClelland, Goodchild & Stewart / publishers
DESCRIPTION: 18.0 × 12.5 cm   Pp [i–xiv], 1–133   Cloth
CONTENTS: i ht; ii 'If you will select, combine and proportion your food according to your age, your work and the time of year, you will get well and you will keep well; if you are overweight you will reduce and if you are underweight you will gain to normal. The author.'; iii tp; iv 'Copyright, 1916, by Eugene Christian // Printed in the United States of America'; v 'The Purpose of This Book' signed Alfred A. Knopf, publisher, The Borzoi, 25 April 1916; vi blank; vii 'Preface' signed Eugene Christian; viii blank; ix–xiv

'Contents'; 1–133 text
CITATIONS: BS, Vol. 32, Nos. 4 and 6 (April and June 1916)   Spadoni/Donnelly No. 4089 ('Imprints Not Located')
COPIES: *OKITD (969.043.003)
NOTES: Christian presents menus for persons with different conditions, for the different seasons. The publisher comments on p v: 'Dr. Christian is not a faddist and people who have followed his advice have almost invariably improved. The menus in this book are not experimental; ...'
The OKITD copy was transferred from the New Hamburg Public Library in 1969.

AMERICAN EDITIONS: New York: A.A. Knopf, 1916 (United States: DLC).

Cook book

O358.1   1916
Imperial Order / of the / Daughters of the Empire / St. George Chapter / Cook book / [IODE symbol]
DESCRIPTION: 22.5 × 15.0 cm   Pp [1–7] 8–118 [119]   Paper
CONTENTS: 1 tp; 2 'The Bryant Press Toronto'; 3 table of contents; 4 list of advertisers; 5 foreword dated Toronto, July 1916; 6 blank; 7–91 text; 92–119 ads
CITATIONS: Wheaton/Kelly No. 1044
COPIES: *OGU (UA s043 b43); United States: MBAt
NOTES: There is an errata slip glued to the gutter of p 3. The foreword states: 'The proceeds resulting from the sale of the book will be donated to St. Dunstan's Hostel for Blinded Soldiers, London, England, ... It has been decided by the Dominion Government that blinded Canadian soldiers shall be trained at St. Dunstan's, ...' Donations were to be sent to the treasurer of the St George Chapter, Upper Canada College, Toronto (p 91).
In 1925, almost ten years later, another Toronto-based organization, the Women's Auxiliary of the Canadian National Institute for the Blind, published O536.1, *Cook Book,* also in support of the blind. Although there is no reference in the 1925 text to the 1916 one, it is an enlarged version of the former: Most of the 1916 recipes are reprinted in the same order and organized in the same chapters; the new recipes are inserted throughout the original 1916 chapters. O536.1 also follows the style of the 1916 work, by listing the recipe names at the beginning of each chapter.

The cook's favorite

O359.1 [1916]
The cook's / favorite / Published by the W.A. of St.
George's Church / Bruce Mines, Ont. / Spectator
Printery, Bruce Mines [cover-title]
DESCRIPTION: 21.0 × 13.0 cm   Pp 3–78   Paper, with
image on front of a woman slicing a loaf of bread;
stapled
CONTENTS: 3 'Preface' signed Mrs Fraser Ingram, Mrs
O.T. Ballantyne, and Miss Gertrude Prout, Committee St George's Church, Bruce Mines, Ontario,
15 December 1916; 4 ad; 5–71 text, including recipes
credited with the name of the contributor, and ads;
72 ad; 73–8 blank for 'Some of My Useful Favorites'
COPIES: *OONL (TX715.6 C6694 1916 p***)
NOTES: The 'Preface' charts the beginning of cookbook publishing in Bruce Mines: 'It is just five years
since a cook-book was compiled in this town. It was
so successful, we have felt impelled to place before
the public a new book, ...' I have not located a copy of
the first Bruce Mines cookbook.

Helpful hints for housekeepers 1916

*See O263.1 for information about the company and other
issues of* Helpful Hints for Housekeepers.

O360.1   1916
1916 Volume VI. 1916 / Hang me in the kitchen /
Helpful / hints / for housekeepers / Compliments
of / the Dodds Medicine Co. / Limited / Toronto,
Can. [cover-title]
DESCRIPTION: 17.0 × 11.0 cm   Pp 1–32   Paper;
stapled, and with hole punched at top left corner for
hanging
CONTENTS: Inside front face of binding 'Volume VI'
[introductory text]; 1 'Don'ts for Mothers'; 2 'Understand the Subject'; 3, 5 'Points for the Kitchen'; 4
'Unconscious Health'; 6 'The Cost of Failing Health';
7 'Laundry Helps'; 8 'Nature Cures'; 9 'Use More
Lemons'; 10 'The Aching Spot'; 11 'The Care of Flowers' and 'Some Kitchen Helps'; 12 'What to Shun'; 13,
15 'Things Worth Remembering'; 14 'A Seeming Paradox'; 16 'About Rheumatism'; 17 'Removing Stains';
18 'Insidious Disease'; 19 'The Sick Room'; 20 'Mysterious but True'; 21 'The Care of Furniture'; 22 'The
Sentinel Off Guard'; 23 'The Uses of Salt and Soda';
24 'The Records of History'; 25 'Housekeeping Notes';
26 'The Most Practical System'; 27 'The Care of Children'; 28 'Dodd's Dyspepsia Tablets'; 29 'The Care of
Clothes'; 30 'Diamond Dinner Pills'; 31 'Sewing

Room'; 32 'Weights and Measures'
COPIES: *Private collection
NOTES: The introductory text refers to the First World
War and draws from the conflict a lesson for the
domestic sphere: 'At a time when nearly the whole
civilized world is in the turmoil of strife, ... it seems
fitting that in our homes affairs should be conducted
economically and orderly.'

O360.2   1916
—1916 Volume VI. 1916 / Suspendez-moi dans la /
cuisine / Indices / utiles / pour les menagères [*sic*]
/ Avec les compliments de / The Dodds Medicine
Co. / Limited / Toronto, Can. [cover-title]
DESCRIPTION: 17.0 × 11.5 cm   Pp 1–32   Paper;
stapled, and with hole punched at top left corner,
through which runs a string for hanging
CONTENTS: Inside front face of binding 'Volume VI'
[introductory text]; 1 'À lire par les mères'; 2
'Comprenez le sujet'; 3, 5 'Propos culinaires'; 4 'Santé
inconsciente'; 6 'Le coût de la santé défaillante'; 7 'À
propos de blanchissage'; 8 'La nature guérit'; 9 'Servez-
vous davantage des citrons'; 10 'L'endroit malade'; 11
'Le soin des fleurs' and 'Quelques conseils culinaires';
12 'Ce que l'on doit éviter'; 13, 15 'Choses à se
rappeler'; 14 'Un semblant de paradoxe'; 16 'À propos
de rhumatisme'; 17 'L'enlèvement des taches'; 18
'Malade insidieuse'; 19 'La chambre d'un malade';
20 'Mysterieux, mais vrai'; 21 'Le soin des meubles';
22 'Sentinelle ne montant pas la garde'; 23 'L'utilité
du sel et de la soude'; 24 'Les annales de l'histoire';
25 'Conseils aux ménagères'; 26 'Le système le plus
pratique'; 27 'Le soin des enfants'; 28 'Les tablettes de
Dodd contre la dyspepsie'; 29 'Le soin des vêtements';
30 'Pilules Diamond Dinner'; 31 'La salle de couture';
32 'Poids et mesures'; inside back face 'Page pour
faire son examen'
COPIES: *OTUTF (uncat patent medicine)

Helps to overcome the high cost of living

*Three other cookbooks were published to advertise Zam-
Buk: O248.1, O270.1, and O396.1.*

O361.1   nd [about 1916]
Helps / to / overcome / the / high cost / of / living
[cover-title]
DESCRIPTION: 20.0 × 12.5 cm   Pp 1–32   Illus on p 1
of a steaming pie(?)   Paper, with image on front of a
woman squatting to remove a pie(?) from an iron
stove; stapled
CONTENTS: Inside front face of binding 'To Our Read-

ers' signed C.E. Fulford Ltd, Toronto; top 1 'New Dishes from Old' [one paragraph about using leftovers]; mid 1–top 30 recipes and publ ads; mid–bottom 30 'A Few Hints on Economy' and 'Handy Weights and Measures'; 31–2 publ ads
COPIES: CIHM (76930) OKITJS (991.23.9) OONL (TX715 Z36 1910z) *QMM (RBD ckbk 1582)
NOTES: 'To Our Readers' advises that 'making up new dishes from "leftovers" is one way in which the housekeeper can solve [the] problem [of the present high cost of living]' that makes it difficult to provide varied and tasty meals. The same text also suggests that the housekeeper practise economy by buying Zam-Buk, a herbal balm for the skin. The advertisements in the text are for Zam-Buk.

An order form on p 32 for a picture of Sir Douglas Haig ('commander of the troops in France with which your own relations and friends are fighting') indicates that the cookbook was published during the First World War, after Haig took command in France in December 1915.

Hill, Mrs Janet McKenzie (Westfield, Mass., 1852–1933)

For this American author's other works, see O264.1.

O362.1 nd [about 1916]
Balanced / daily / diet / Janet McKenzie Hill / Hamilton, Canada / The Procter & Gamble Distributing Co. of Canada, Limited
DESCRIPTION: 18.0 × 12.5 cm Pp [1–2] 3–96 Tp still-life red of container of Crisco, fish, apple, head of grain, and spinach(?) leaf; illus col Thin card, with tp still-life on front; sewn
CONTENTS: 1 tp printed in red and black; 2 'Introduction' and at bottom, 'The price of this book is 10c.'; 3–6 'Balanced Daily Diet'; 7–14 'About Crisco'; 15–22 'Key How to Use the Well-Balanced Menus'; 23–32 'List of Foods'; 33–92 'Recipes'; 93–4 'Index'; 95 'Suggestions for Cooking at High Altitudes'; 96 'Other Helpful Books Which Every Housekeeper Should Have'
COPIES: OH (R613.2 HIL CESG) *OKIT
NOTES: The Canadian edition of *Balanced Daily Diet* was likely published in 1916, the same year as the American edition. Listed under 'Other Helpful Books ...' on p 96 is Janet Hill's *The Whys of Cooking*, the earliest American edition of which is dated 1916 (O363.1). Bitting, p 228, describes *Balanced Daily Diet* as 'uniform with' *The Whys of Cooking*.

Crisco shortening was introduced to the market in

1911. The 'Introduction' stresses the importance of fat in the diet: 'Fat is life's fuel – the greatest producer of human heat and human energy.' It tells how and where Crisco is made, explains how it is kosher, and remarks on its purity.

AMERICAN EDITIONS: Cincinnati: Procter and Gamble Co., 1916 (United States: DLC).

O363.1 nd [about 1916]
The / whys / of / cooking / by / Janet McKenzie Hill / Hamilton, Canada / The Procter & Gamble Distributing Co. of Canada, Limited.
DESCRIPTION: 17.5 × 12.0 cm Pp [1–2] 3–106, [i–ii] Tp illus red-and-black of two men and three women at table, illus col Paper, with small still-life on front of two jugs and a bowl; sewn
CONTENTS: 1 tp printed in red and black; 2 'Introduction' and 'The price of this book is 10c.'; 3–4 'The Whys of Cooking'; 5–11 'The Story of Crisco'; 12–19 'Modern Kitchens'; 20–8 'Serving'; 29–43 'Frying'; 44–59 'Cakes'; 60–72 'Pastry'; 73–83 'Breads'; 84–92 'Meats'; 93–100 'Vegetables'; 101 'Salad Dressings'; 102 'Suggestions for Cooking at High Altitudes'; 103–4 'Weights and Measures'; 105–6 'Index' [i.e., table of contents at top p 105, followed by index of recipes]; i publ ad for *A Calendar of Dinners* by Marion Harris Neil (O390.1) and *Balanced Daily Diet* by Janet McKenzie Hill (O362.1); ii publ ad listing four sizes of Crisco can
COPIES: *Private collection
NOTES: If the 1916 Cincinnati edition has 107 pp and the 1925 Cincinnati edition has 83 pp, then the Canadian editions of 106 pp and 84 pp were likely published in the same order.

O363.2 [copyright 1916]
—Form No. 449 / The / whys / of / cooking / by / Janet McKenzie Hill / The Procter & Gamble Distributing Co. of Canada, Ltd. / Hamilton, Canada
DESCRIPTION: 17.5 × 12.5 cm Pp [1–2] 3–84 Tp illus of two men and three women at table, illus Paper, with small still-life on front of two jugs and a bowl; stapled
CONTENTS: 1 tp; 2 'Introduction' and 'Copyright 1916 The Procter & Gamble Distributing Co. of Canada, Ltd. Hamilton, Canada'; 3–4 'The Whys of Cooking'; 5–11 'The Story of Crisco'; 12–19 'Modern Kitchens'; 20–8 'Serving'; 29–39 'Frying'; 40–51 'Cakes'; 52–60 'Pastry'; 61–71 'Breads'; 72–80 'Meats'; 81–2 'Weights and Measures'; 83–4 index
CITATIONS: Ferguson/Fraser, p 232

COPIES: AWWDM CIHM (75576) OONL (TX715 H554 1916 p***) *OONMS (TX715 H54 1916)

AMERICAN EDITIONS: 1st ed., Cincinnati: Procter and Gamble Co., 1916 (United States: DLC); 2nd ed., 1919 (United States: DLC); 2nd ed., 2nd printing, Cincinnati: Procter and Gamble Co., [copyright 1921] (United States: InU); 3rd ed., Cincinnati: Procter and Gamble Co., [copyright 1925], Form No. 449 (United States: InU).

Household management

See also O410.1, Household Science in Rural Schools, in the same series.

O364.1 [copyright 1916]
Ontario / Teachers' Manuals / Household management / Authorized by the Minister of Education / Toronto / The Copp, Clark Company, Limited
DESCRIPTION: 19.0 × 12.0 cm   Pp [iii–iv] v–xi [xii], 1–225   Frontis of 'A Household Management pupil in uniform,' illus   [$0.19, on binding]   Cloth
CONTENTS: iii tp; iv 'Copyright, Canada, 1916, by the Minister of Education for Ontario'; v–xi 'Contents'; xii blank; 1–4 'Public and Separate School Course of Study: Details'; 5–222 text in fourteen chapters; 223–5 'Bibliography'
COPIES: CIHM (76936)   OONL (TX167 H6)   OTUED (375.00971 O59DE)   *QKB (70-41)
NOTES: The QKB copy is inscribed on the front endpaper, in ink, 'C.L. Shufelt. I.N.S. no 206 '17–18.'

O364.2 [reprint, 1921]
—Ontario / Teachers' Manuals / Household management / Authorized by the Minister of Education / Toronto / The Copp Clark Company, Limited
DESCRIPTION: 19.0 × 12.0 cm   Pp [iii–iv] v–xi [xii], 1–225   Frontis of 'A Household Management pupil in uniform,' illus   [$0.19, on binding]   Cloth
CONTENTS: iii tp; iv 'Copyright, Canada, 1916, by the Minister of Education for Ontario // Reprinted, 1921'; v–xi 'Contents'; xii blank; 1–4 'Public and Separate School Course of Study // Details'; 5–222 text in fourteen chapters; 223–5 'Bibliography'
COPIES: OLU (TX354 O55 1921)   *OWTU (F15329)
NOTES: The OWTU copy has pencil notes for 'Mar. 5/ 23. Lesson 11' on the blank page after p 225.

O364.3 [reprint, 1926]
—[Reprint of *Household Management,* 1926]
COPIES: OONL (TX167 H6 copy 4)

O364.4 [reprint, 1929]
—Ontario / Teachers' Manuals / Household Management / Authorized by the Minister of Education / Toronto / The Copp Clark Company, Limited
DESCRIPTION: 19.0 × 12.0 cm   Pp [iii–iv] v–xi [xii], 1–225   Frontis of 'A Household Management pupil in uniform,' illus   [$0.33, on binding]   Cloth
CONTENTS: iii tp; iv 'Copyright, Canada, 1916, by the Minister of Education for Ontario // First edition, 1916 // Reprinted, 1923, 1924, 1926, 1929.'; v–xi 'Contents'; xii blank; 1–225 text
COPIES: *OGU (CCC CA2ON DE 16H55)
NOTES: The illustrations show typical equipment and classroom arrangements for Household Management, including on p 10, 'A Household Management class at work,' and on p 18, 'A class cupboard.'

Hutchison, Robert (1871–1960)

O365.1   4th ed., 1916
Food / and the / principles of dietetics / by / Robert Hutchison, M.D. Edin., F.R.C.P. / physician to the London Hospital; physician with charge of out-patients to the / Hospital for Sick Children, Great Ormond Street / author of 'Lectures on Diseases of Children,' 'Patent Foods and Patent Medicines,' / 'Applied Physiology,' joint-author of 'Clinical Methods' / With plates and diagrams / Fourth edition / London / Edward Arnold / Toronto / The Macmillan Company of Canada / 1916 / (All rights reserved)
DESCRIPTION: 22.0 × 13.5 cm   Pp [i–vi] vii [viii–ix] x–xx, 1–617   3 pls col (all of graphs), illus   Cloth
CONTENTS: i ht; ii blank; iii tp; iv blank; v dedication 'To the students of the London Hospital to whom its [the book's] contents were first addressed, ...'; vi blank; vii 'Preface to the Fourth Edition' signed R.H., London, May 1916; viii blank; ix–x 'Preface to the First Edition' dated London, October 1900; xi–xvii table of contents; xviii 'Table of Equivalents'; xix–xx 'List of Illustrations'; 1–580 text; 581–617 index and at bottom p 617, 'Billing and Sons, Ltd., printers, Guildford, England.'
COPIES: *OGU (CCC TX715.6 H88)
NOTES: 'Preface to the Fourth Edition' states: 'In this edition the whole book has been thoroughly revised, and many minor alterations and additions affected. A

section has been included on the subject of vitamines.' The text offers an insight into contemporary attitudes to various foods, food products, and food fads: gelatin and isinglass; soups, beef extracts, beef juices, beef tea, and beef powders; the pros and cons of vegetarianism; baking powders; wholemeal versus white bread; the 'grape cure'; advantages of slow cooking and a discussion of apparatus for slow cooking (bain marie, Norwegian cooker, Ede's apparatus, Aladdin Oven); substitutes for mother's milk in infant feeding; feeding of children; principles of feeding in disease; and dietetic 'cures' and 'systems.' The OGU copy originally belonged to Annie May Watson (1898–1970).

BRITISH EDITIONS: London: E. Arnold, 1900; London: Edward Arnold, 1906 [1905]; 3rd ed., London: Edward Arnold, 1911; 4th ed., London: Edward Arnold, 1916; 4th ed., 3rd impression, London: Arnold, 1919 (ACUM, QMM); 5th ed., London: E. Arnold and Co., 1922 [1921] (QMM); 6th ed., London: E. Arnold and Co., 1927 [1926]; 6th ed., 3rd impression, London: E. Arnold and Co., 1931; 7th ed., Hutchison and V.H. Mottram, London: E. Arnold and Co., 1933 (QMM); 8th ed., Hutchison and V.H. Mottram, London: Arnold, [1936] (OTU); and later editions, revised by V.H. Mottram and George Graham (all except 1919, Great Britain: LB).

AMERICAN EDITIONS: New York: Wood, 1901 (MWM); [2nd ed.], New York: Wood, 1906 (QMM); 3rd ed., New York: W. Wood and Co., 1911 (United States: DLC); 4th ed., New York: W. Wood, 1917 (QQLAS, SSU).

Maple leaf cookery book

O366.1 copyright 1916
Dedicated to / Her Royal Highness the Duchess of Connaught / by Her gracious permission / Maple leaf / cookery book / tested / home-nursing invalid-diet / recipes / Entire profits donated to the / Canadian Red Cross Society / Issued by their permission / Copyrighted 1916 [cover-title]
DESCRIPTION: 21.5 × 14.0 cm   Pp [i–iv], [1–2] 3–134 Card, with image on front of a maple leaf; punched with two holes at top edge and held by two metal rings
CONTENTS: Inside front face of binding 'All recipes were contributed by Red Cross workers throughout Canada. Compiled by the Maple Leaf Cookery Book

Committee. Mrs. W.F. Govinlock, Chairman // Mrs. H.P. Plumptre // Mrs. John Caven // Mrs. Frank Smith, Secretary // Offices: 217 Confederation Life Building Toronto, Ont. W.F. Govinlock, Business Manager // Extra copies will be mailed on receipt of price of book 75c. with 10c. added'; i 'Index' [i.e., alphabetical list of headings]; ii blank; iii 'Abbreviations' and 'Time for Cooking'; iv 'Terms Used in Cookery'; 1–mid 134 recipes credited with the name and city of the contributor; mid–bottom 134 'Household Hints'
COPIES: *BVIPM

Modern mixes for bakers

See O288.1 for information about Egg-o Baking Powder Co. and its other cookbooks.

O367.1   1916
[An edition of *Modern Mixes for Bakers*, Hamilton, Ont.: Egg-o Baking Powder Co., 1916, pp 64]
CITATIONS: O'Neill (unpublished)
COPIES: Great Britain: LB (Woolwich)

O367.2   4th ed., March 1925
—Modern / mixes / for bakers / Price $2.00 / Egg-o Baking Powder Co., Ltd. / Hamilton, Canada / Fourth edition March, 1925
DESCRIPTION: 22.0 × 12.0 cm   Pp [1] 2–67   Cloth
CONTENTS: 1 tp; 2 'Egg-o Bakers' Special Is Guaranteed in Every Particular' signed E.G. Willard, president; 3 'Introduction'; 4–6 index; 7 'Bakers' Special Baking Powder'; top 8 'Modern Cake Making'; mid 8–mid 9 'Mixing of Cakes'; mid–bottom 9 'Baking'; 10 'Baker of Today'; 11–mid 14 'Preparing Cakes for the Store'; mid 14–15 'Stock Icings for the Bake Shop'; 16 'Cake Baking Cost'; 17–67 123 numbered recipes and text on the topics 'Cake Philosophy,' 'Uses for Bread and Cake Crumbs,' 'Store Hints,' 'The Key to Bakeshop Success,' 'Suggestions,' 'How to Keep Your Trade at Home,' 'Oven Hints,' and 'Flour'
COPIES: *AALIWWM
NOTES: The 'Introduction' states, 'These recipes have been carefully selected from thousands submitted ...'

AMERICAN EDITIONS: Possibly *Modern Mixes for Bakers*, Chicago: Calumet Baking Powder Co., 1914 (United States: CLCM, DLC, LU, MiD, OBgU, WU). See also O288.1, *Reliable Recipes and Helpful Hints*, another Egg-o book with a title that matches a Calumet Baking Powder Co. publication.

Recipes

O368.1 [2nd ed., 1925]
Recipes / compiled and arranged / in the interests
of / the Ladies' Aid / of / Charlton United Church
/ of Canada / Hamilton, Canada
DESCRIPTION: 20.0 × 14.0 Pp [1–4] 5–130 [131–2] Paper
CONTENTS: 1 tp; 2 'Preface' signed Ladies' Aid Society, Charlton United Church of Canada, Hamilton, Ontario, 25 June 1925; 3 ads; 4–132 text, including recipes credited with the name of the contributor, and ads
CITATIONS: Golick, p 101 (note 14), 109
COPIES: OBUJBM *OTNY (uncat)
NOTES: The 'Preface' reveals that this is the second edition of 1925; it records the following publishing history: 'Some nine years ago [i.e., in about 1916] the first edition of this book was issued under the auspicies [sic] of "The Ladies' Aid Society of the Charlton Avenue Methodist Church" in aid of it's [sic] finances ... the edition [was] soon exhausted. Each year since it's [sic] issue, repeated requests have been made for further copies. For this reason, and also in aid of it's [sic] finances, the Ladies' Aid Society of the Charlton United Church of Canada, have issued this, the second edition ... There have been some depletions [sic] and many valuable additions made in this new edition.'

The second edition was published shortly after church union, which took place on 10 June 1925; hence, the name change from Charlton Avenue Methodist Church in the first edition to Charlton United Church of Canada in the second.

Royal Yeast bake book

For information about E.W. Gillett Co. and its other cookbooks, see O285.1.

O369.1 unnumbered, nd [about 1916]
Royal Yeast / bake / book [cover-title]
DESCRIPTION: Paper, with image on front of a stout woman removing one of two loaves of bread from oven; stapled
CONTENTS: 1 cover-title; 2 'Published by E.W. Gillett Company Limited Toronto, Ont. Winnipeg Montreal'; 3 'Concerning Bread as an Article of Food'; ...
COPIES: *QKB Private collection
NOTES: The yeast container depicted on the outside back face of the binding is cylindrical; it is printed on an otherwise blank page. The private collector's copy

has the dimensions 15.0 × 9.0 cm and pp [1–2] 3–31.

An advertisement for Gillett in the September 1916 issue of *Canadian Home Journal* offers free copies of *Royal Yeast Bake Book*. From appearances, this unnumbered and undated edition was published about 1916. The May 1917 issue of *Everywoman's World* also advertises the book, describing it as 'our new Royal Yeast Bake Book free.'

The stout woman depicted on the binding appears to be the same person as on the binding of E.W. Gillett Co.'s O470.1, *The Magic Way*, although in a different pose.

O369.2 unnumbered, nd [about 1916]
—Levure "Royal" / instructions / et / recettes [cover-title]
DESCRIPTION: 15.0 × 9.0 cm Pp [1–2] 3–31 Illus col on pp 9, 15, 21, 25; 12 step-by-step illus on pp 16–17 of making bread Paper, with image on front of a stout woman removing one of two loaves of bread from oven; previously stapled, but now sewn
CONTENTS: 1 cover-title; 2 'Publié par E.W. Gillett Company Limited Toronto, Ont. Winnipeg Montreal'; 3 'Le pain comme article de l'alimentation'; top–mid 4 'L'expérience n'est pas indispensable'; bottom 4 'Économie'; 5–top 6 'À propos de farine'; mid 6 'Pour faire le pain'; bottom 6–top 7 'Comment faire la levure liquide avec les pains de levure "Royal"'; mid 7–mid 8 'Pour faire deux pains'; mid–bottom 8 'Pour la cuisson au four'; 9 illus col; 10–11 'La recette suivante est imprimée sur chaque paquet de pains de levure "Royal"'; 12–31 recipes
COPIES: CIHM (76494) *OONL (TX715 C3465 No. 4 copy 2 p ***)
NOTES: Like O369.1, this edition is unnumbered and undated, and the yeast container depicted on the back face of the binding is cylindrical and is printed on an otherwise blank page. It was likely published in the same year as O369.1.

O369.3 unnumbered, nd [about 1921]
—Royal Yeast / bake / book [cover-title]
DESCRIPTION: 15.0 × 9.0 cm Pp [1–2] 3–31 Illus col on pp 9, 15, 21, 25; 12 step-by-step illus on pp 16–17 of making bread Paper, with image on front of a stout woman removing one of two loaves of bread from oven; stapled
CONTENTS: 1 cover-title; 2 'Published by E.W. Gillett Company Limited Toronto, Ont. Winnipeg Montreal'; 3 'Concerning Bread as an Article of Food'; top–mid 4 'No Experience Necessary'; bottom 4–top 5 'Economy'; mid 5–top 6 'A Word about Flour'; mid 6 'The Making of Bread'; bottom 6–mid 7 'To Make

Liquid Yeast with Royal Yeast Cakes'; mid 7–mid 8 'To Make Two Loaves of Bread'; mid–bottom 8 'To Bake'; 9 illus col of white loaf; 10 'The Following Recipe Is Printed on Each Package of Royal Yeast Cakes'; 11–31 [inside back face of binding] recipes

COPIES: ACG   ARDA (2 copies)   QMM (RBD ckbk 2201)   SSWD   *Company collection (Nabisco Brands Ltd, Toronto, Ontario)

NOTES: The yeast container depicted on the outside back face of the binding is a tall, rectangular container. The product name on the container is 'ROYAL / YEAST / CAKES': the word ROYAL is curved, with the Y at the top of the curve; YEAST follows a circumflex-shape (upside-down vee), with the A at the apex; and the lettering for CAKES follows a straight, horizontal line. The yeast container is framed in a plain circle, the same size as the circle on the front cover that frames the stout woman; below the circle is the phrase 'Royal Yeast Cakes make perfect bread' and the company name. This unnumbered and undated edition was likely published about the same time as the 14-page *Royal Yeast Cakes for Better Health* (not a cookbook), fourth edition, Toronto, Ont.: E.W. Gillett Co. Ltd, [copyright 1921], which has the same-style container illustrated on the outside back face of the binding (Private collection).

The first recipe on p 11 is for Bread, from Lady Eaton, Toronto. Lady Eaton (1881–1970) was the wife of Sir John Craig Eaton, knighted in 1915 and the third son of department-store-founder Timothy Eaton. Page 12 presents a short process for bread-making by Jean Archibald, 'Lecturer and Demonstrator in House [sic] Economics.' The last recipe is for Royal Yeast Breakfast Waffles.

O369.4   unnumbered, nd [about 1921]
—Levure "Royal" / instructions / et / recettes [cover-title]

DESCRIPTION: 15.5 × 9.0 cm   Pp [1–2] 3–31   Illus col on pp 9, 15, 21, 25; 12 step-by-step illus on pp 16–17 of making bread   Paper, with image on front of a stout woman removing one of two loaves of bread from oven; stapled

CONTENTS: 1 cover-title; 2 'Publié par E.W. Gillett Company Limited Toronto, Ont. Winnipeg Montreal'; 3 'Le pain comme article de l'alimentation'; top–mid 4 'L'expérience n'est pas indispensable'; bottom 4 'Économie'; 5–top 6 'À propos de farine'; mid 6 'Pour faire le pain'; bottom 6–top 7 'Comment faire la levure liquide avec les pains de levure "Royal"'; mid 7–mid 8 'Pour faire deux pains'; mid–bottom 8 'Pour la cuisson au four'; 9 illus col; 10–11 'La recette suivante

est imprimée sur chaque paquet de pains de levure "Royal"'; 12–31 recipes

COPIES: CIHM (76494)   *OONL (TX715 C3465 No. 4 reserve)

NOTES: The yeast container depicted on the outside back face of the binding is exactly as described for O369.3.

O369.5   unnumbered, nd
—Royal / Yeast / bake / book [cover-title]

DESCRIPTION: 15.5 × 9.0 cm   Pp [1–2] 3–31   Illus col on pp 9, 15, 21, 25; 12 step-by-step illus on pp 16–17 of making bread   Paper, with chequerboard pattern; stapled

CONTENTS: 1 cover-title; 2 'Published by E.W. Gillett Company Limited Toronto, Ont. Winnipeg Montreal'; 3 'Concerning Bread as an Article of Food'; top–mid 4 'No Experience Necessary'; bottom 4–top 5 'Economy'; mid 5–top 6 'A Word about Flour'; mid 6 'The Making of Bread'; bottom 6–mid 7 'To Make Liquid Yeast with Royal Yeast Cakes'; mid 7–mid 8 'To Make Two Loaves of Bread'; mid–bottom 8 'To Bake'; 9 illus col of white loaf; 10 'The Following Recipe Is Printed on Each Package of Royal Yeast Cakes'; 11–31 recipes

COPIES: *BPM   OONL (TX769 R6 copy 2 p***)

NOTES: This edition is unnumbered and undated. The outside front and back faces of the binding are decorated with a chequerboard pattern; the yeast container on the back is identical to that on O369.3, except that it appears within a rectangular frame with rounded corners. There is no recipe for Milk Loaf on p 13 (cf O369.9).

O369.6   [7th ed., nd, about 1924]
—Royal / Yeast / bake / book [cover-title]

DESCRIPTION: 15.5 × 9.0 cm   Pp [1–2] 3–31   Illus col on pp 9, 15, 21, 25; 12 step-by-step illus on pp 16–17 of making bread   Paper, with chequerboard pattern on front; stapled

CONTENTS: 1 cover-title; 2 'Published by E.W. Gillett Company Limited Toronto, Ont. Winnipeg Montreal 7th edition 100 912 24'; 3 'Concerning Bread as an Article of Food'; top–mid 4 'No Experience Necessary'; bottom 4–top 5 'Economy'; mid 5–top 6 'A Word about Flour'; mid 6 'The Making of Bread'; bottom 6–mid 7 'To Make Liquid Yeast with Royal Yeast Cakes'; mid 7–mid 8 'To Make Two Loaves of Bread'; mid–bottom 8 'To Bake'; 9 illus col of white loaf; 10 'The Following Recipe Is Printed on Each Package of Royal Yeast Cakes'; 11–31 recipes

COPIES: *NBFKL (Ruth Spicer Cookbook Collection)

O369.7 [8th ed., nd, about 1925]
—Royal / Yeast / bake / book [cover-title]
DESCRIPTION: 15.5 × 8.5 cm   Pp [1–2] 3–31   Illus col
on pp 9, 15, 21, 25; 12 step-by-step illus on pp 16–17
of making bread   Paper, with chequerboard pattern
on front; stapled
CONTENTS: 1 cover-title; 2 'Published by E.W. Gillett
Company Limited Toronto, Ont. Winnipeg Montreal
8th edition 2004125'; 3 'Concerning Bread as an Article of Food'; top–mid 4 'No Experience Necessary';
bottom 4–top 5 'Economy'; mid 5–top 6 'A Word
about Flour'; mid 6 'The Making of Bread'; bottom 6–
mid 7 'To Make Liquid Yeast with Royal Yeast Cakes';
mid 7–mid 8 'To Make Two Loaves of Bread'; mid–
bottom 8 'To Bake'; 9 illus col of white loaf; 10 'The
Following Recipe Is Printed on Each Package of Royal
Yeast Cakes'; 11–31 recipes
COPIES: ACHP (HP 3446.33A)   AMHM   *Private
collection
NOTES: The binding matches the description given for
O369.5. I was able to compare, side by side, copies of
the eighth edition with O369.9, the tenth edition: the
bindings and texts are the same except that there is no
recipe for Milk Loaf below Graham or Entire Wheat
Bread on p 13 of the eighth edition.

O369.8 [9th ed., nd, about 1926]
—Royal / Yeast / bake / book [cover-title]
DESCRIPTION: 16.0 × 8.5 cm   Pp [1–2] 3–31   Illus col
on pp 9, 15, 21, 25; 12 step-by-step illus on pp 16–17
of making bread   Paper, with chequerboard pattern
on front; stapled
CONTENTS: 1 cover-title; 2 'Published by E.W. Gillett
Company Limited Toronto, Ont. Winnipeg Montreal
9th edition 1005626'; 3 'Concerning Bread as an Article of Food'; top–mid 4 'No Experience Necessary';
bottom 4–top 5 'Economy'; mid 5–top 6 'A Word
about Flour'; mid 6 'The Making of Bread'; bottom 6–
mid 7 'To Make Liquid Yeast with Royal Yeast Cakes';
mid 7–mid 8 'To Make Two Loaves of Bread'; mid–
bottom 8 'To Bake'; 9 illus col of white loaf; 10 'The
Following Recipe Is Printed on Each Package of Royal
Yeast Cakes'; 11–31 recipes
COPIES: *ACG

O369.9 [10th ed., nd, about 1927]
—Royal / Yeast / bake / book [cover-title]
DESCRIPTION: 15.5 × 9.0 cm   Pp [1–2] 3–31   Illus col
on pp 9, 15, 21, 25; 12 step-by-step illus on pp 16–17
of making bread   Paper, with chequerboard pattern
on front; stapled
CONTENTS: 1 cover-title; 2 'Published by E.W. Gillett

Company Limited Toronto, Ont. Winnipeg Montreal
10th edition 1006427'; 3 'Concerning Bread as an Article of Food'; top–mid 4 'No Experience Necessary';
bottom 4–top 5 'Economy'; mid 5–top 6 'A Word
about Flour'; mid 6 'The Making of Bread'; bottom 6–
mid 7 'To Make Liquid Yeast with Royal Yeast Cakes';
mid 7–mid 8 'To Make Two Loaves of Bread'; mid–
bottom 8 'To Bake'; 9 illus col of white loaf; 10 'The
Following Recipe Is Printed on Each Package of Royal
Yeast Cakes'; 11–31 recipes
COPIES: OOWM (984.91.8)   OTMCL (641.5971 H39
No. 20)   OTNY (uncat)   *Private collection
NOTES: The binding matches the description given for
O369.5. I was able to compare, side by side, copies of
O369.7, the eighth edition, with the tenth edition: the
bindings and texts appear to be the same except that a
recipe for Milk Loaf has been added below Graham
or Entire Wheat Bread on p 13 of the tenth edition.
   The OOWM copy has '10th edition, 10081926' on
p 2.

O369.10 [11th ed., nd, about 1927]
—[Eleventh edition of *Royal Yeast Bake Book*, [Toronto,
Winnipeg, and Montreal: E.W. Gillett Co. Ltd], nd]
COPIES: MAUAM
NOTES: '11th edition 200927' is printed opposite p 3.

O369.11 nd
—Livre / culinaire / de Levain / Royal [cover-title]
DESCRIPTION: Paper, with chequerboard pattern on
front; stapled
COPIES: *Private collection

O369.12 unnumbered, nd [1931 or later]
—Royal / Yeast / bake book / Standard Brands
Limited / Gillett Products / Fraser Ave & Liberty St.
/ Toronto [cover-title]
DESCRIPTION: 16.0 × 9.0 cm   Pp [1] 2–15   Paper, with
plaid pattern on front and text printed in black; stapled
CONTENTS: 1 cover-title; 2–5 'The Art of Bread Mak-
ing'; 6–15 recipes
COPIES: ACG   MWPA (MG14 C50 McKnight,
Ethel)   *Private collection
NOTES: Editions bearing the name Standard Brands
were published after 27 August 1929, when Standard
Brands was incorporated. An advertisement for Stan-
dard Brands Ltd in *Nor'-West Farmer and Farm and
Home* Vol. 50, No. 7 (6 April 1931), p 15 includes an
order form for *Royal Yeast Bake Book* and illustrates
one of the editions with the chequerboard-pattern
bindings; therefore, the editions with the plaid pattern likely appeared after April 1931.

Like some earlier editions, O369.12 has a tall, rect-angular container of yeast depicted on the outside back face of the binding; however, here the lettering in the product name 'ROYAL / YEAST / CAKES' is arranged differently: whereas the word YEAST still forms a circumflex-shape (upside-down vee), with the A at the apex, ROYAL and CAKES follow a straight, horizontal line. Apart from a few places where the text of O369.12 corresponds with O369.7, the eighth edition (for example, the recipes for Salad Rolls and French Tea Ring are nearly the same), the text has been largely rewritten.

A comparison of O369.12 with O369.14, also from Standard Brands and with a plaid-pattern binding, reveals the following differences. Here the text on the binding and inside is printed in black (O369.14 is in blue). Here the headings on p 3 are 'A Word about Flour,' 'Temperature for Sponge,' and 'Liquid' (in O369.14 they are 'A Word about Flour,' 'Whole Wheat (Brown) Flour,' and 'Temperature for Sponge or Dough'). Most of the recipes are the same, but the order is sometimes different: for example, here Dainty Lemon Buns on p 15 follows Butterscotch Buns on p 14 (in O369.14 Dainty Lemon Buns on p 12 precedes Butterscotch Buns on p 13). The container of yeast on the back face of the binding of O369.14 has a simpler design; each word in the product name 'ROYAL / YEAST / CAKES' is horizontal.

Chatelaine 1935, p 82, lists 'Royal Yeast Bake Book (English and French),' free upon request from Stan-dard Brands Ltd, but does not specify which of the Standard Brands editions.

O369.13   unnumbered, nd [1931 or later]
—Royal / Yeast / bake book / Standard Brands Limited / Gillett Products / Fraser Ave & Liberty St. / Toronto [cover-title]
DESCRIPTION: 16.0 × 9.0 cm   Pp [1] 2–15   Paper, with plaid pattern on front; stapled
CONTENTS: 1 cover-title; 2–5 'The Art of Bread Mak-ing'; 6–15 recipes
COPIES: *APROM
NOTES: The design of the binding, including the im-age of the yeast container, matches O369.12; how-ever, the text, which is printed in black, is identical to O369.14 (printed in blue).

O369.14   unnumbered, nd [1931 or later]
—Royal / Yeast / bake book / Standard Brands Limited / Gillett Products / Fraser Ave & Liberty St. / Toronto [cover-title]
DESCRIPTION: 16.0 × 8.5 cm   Pp [1] 2–15   Paper, with plaid pattern on front and text printed in blue; stapled

CONTENTS: 1 cover-title; 2–5 'The Art of Bread Mak-ing'; 6–15 recipes
COPIES: AEUCHV (2 copies: UV 85.17.125, UV 85.17.126) QKB SWSLM *Private collection
NOTES: The text on the binding and inside is printed in blue. See O369.12 for a comparison of the two editions.

SWSLM has a second, identical copy except that the plaid pattern on the binding is printed in orange.

O369.15   unnumbered, nd [1931 or later]
—Livre de recettes du / Levain / Royal / Standard Brands Limited / Produits Gillett / Fraser Ave & Liberty St. / Toronto [cover-title]
DESCRIPTION: Paper, with plaid pattern
COPIES: *Private collection

Thompson, Vance (1863–1925)

Thompson, an American, also wrote Drink and Be Sober, *New York: Moffat, Yard and Co., 1915 (OONL; United States: DLC).*

O370.1   1916
[An edition of *Eat and Grow Thin: The Mahdah Menus,* Toronto: McClelland, Goodchild and Stewart, 1916]
CITATIONS: BS, Vol. 32, No. 2 (February 1916), p 30   Spadoni/Donnelly No. 4249 ('Imprints Not Located')
NOTES: Bitting, p 460, comments of the New York 1914 edition: 'Menus followed by recipes, and list of forbidden foods.'

AMERICAN EDITIONS: New York: E.P. Dutton and Co., [1914] (QLB); New York: E.P. Dutton and Co., [1916]; New York: E.P. Dutton and Co., [1920] (QMM); new ed., New York: E.P. Dutton and Co., [1924]; new ed., New York: E.P. Dutton and Co. Inc., [1931] (all United States: DLC).

Waugh, Frederick Wilkerson (1872–1924)

O371.1   1916
Canada / Department of Mines / Hon. P.E. Blondin, Minister; R.G. McConnell, Deputy Minister. / Geological Survey / Memoir 86 / No. 12, Anthropological Series / Iroquis [*sic*] foods and food / preparation / by / F.W. Waugh / [Department of Mines Geological Survey symbol] / Ottawa / Government Printing Bureau / 1916 / No. 1612
DESCRIPTION: 25.0 × 16.5 cm   Pp [1–2], [i] ii–v [vi],

[1] 2–235 [236], [i] ii–vii 39 numbered pls (1 col, 38 b/w), 2 illus Paper
CONTENTS: 1 tp; 2 blank; i–v table of contents and list of illustrations; vi blank; 1–154 text arranged under the headings 'Introduction,' 'Phonetic Key,' 'Agricultural Methods and Customs,' 'Cookery and Eating Customs,' 'Utensils Used in the Gathering, Preparation, and Eating of Food,' and 'Food Materials and Recipes'; 155–8 bibliography; 159–236 pls (incl in pagination); i–vii 'Publications of the Geological Survey'
CITATIONS: Armstrong 2004, p D2 Bitting, p 487 CBSCat C22 Poulain-Le FurCat 4–5 Feb 2000, No. 698
COPIES: ACU (CA1 MS 30 16M086) AEU (E99 I7 W35 1916) BVA (970.3 W35 REF) CIHM (82410) MWU (QE185 A2 No. 86) NFSG NSHMS NSHPL *OGU (UA s044 b06) OHM OKQ OMIH OOG (Govt TN26 E3 G3 M5 No. 86 1916) OONL (COP.CA.M.6208, 2 copies) OOU (E99 I7 W35 1916 MRT) OSUL (CA1 MS30 16M86) OSUU (E99 I7 W35) OTDM OTRM (E99 I7 W38 1916) OTSCC (E99 I7 W38) OTUNE (E99 I7 W38) OTV (E99 I7 W35) OWTU (CA1 GS M86) QMEP (CA1 MS30 16M086) QMU (E99 I7 W38) QQFO (QE 185 C212.65 86) QQLAS (QE185 A2 86) SRU (CA1 MS30 16M86); United States: DLC (E99 I7 W35) MB MH (2 copies)
NOTES: Waugh describes his idea: '... to deal with present-day customs, or with those which have been practised within the memory of the older people now living on the reservations, ... The subject matter as a whole is the result of personal investigations conducted by the writer during the years 1912–1915 among the Iroquois of Ontario, Quebec, and New York State, ...' The typographical error 'Iroquis' appears only on the title-page.

OTHER EDITIONS: Facsimile ed., Ottawa: National Museums of Canada, 1973 (ACU, AEU, OME, OOC, OONG, OPET, OSUU, OTRM, OWTU, QMM, QMU, SSU); Ohsweken, Ont.: Iroqrafts, 1991 (ACG, ACU, OKQ, OONL, OONMM, OPAL, OSTCB, QQLA, SSU; United States: MH)

1917

Allen, Mrs Ida Cogswell Bailey (Danielson, Conn., 1885–1973)

For Allen's biography and photograph, see Arndt, pp 17–19. See also O513.1, Mrs Allen on Cooking, Menus, Service, and O1040.1, Successful Entertaining. This

prolific American author also wrote (all at DLC, unless otherwise noted): The Golden Rule Cook Book, [Columbus, Ohio: Pfeifer Show Print Co.], c1916; Delicious Ham and Bacon Recipes, Ottumwa, Iowa: J. Morrell and Co., c1917; Mrs Allen's Book of Meat Substitutes, Boston: Small, Maynard and Co., [c1918]; Mrs Allen's Book of Sugar Substitutes, Boston: Small, Maynard and Co., [c1918]; (Mrs. Allen's) Book of Wheat Substitutes, Boston: Small, Maynard and Co., [c1918]; Temtor Tempting Recipes, St Louis: Temtor Corn and Fruit Products Co., c1920; For the Bride, Chicago: Reuben H. Donnelley Corp., c1922; Home Partners, [New York:] Priv. print., 1924; The Modern Method of Preparing Delightful Foods, New York: Corn Products Refining Co., copyright 1926 (Private collection); One Hundred Four Prize Radio Recipes with Twenty-four Radio Home-maker's Talks, New York: J.H. Sears and Co., [c1926]; Your Foods and You, Garden City, NY: Doubleday, Page and Co., 1926; Vital Vegetables, with Analyses, Menus, and Recipes, Garden City, NY: Doubleday, Page and Co., 1927; When You Entertain; What to Do, and How, [Boston: Forbes Litho. Mfg Co., c1932]; The Service Cook Book, Colorado Springs: Pub. exclusively for F.W. Woolworth Co. by Service Inc., copyright 1933 (also at OGU); (Ida Bailey Allen's) Wines and Spirits Cook Book, New York: Simon and Schuster, 1934; The Round-the-World Cook Book, [New York:] Best Foods Inc., [c1934]; The Budget Cook Book, [New York:] Best Foods Inc., [c1935]; Cooking within Your Income, Chicago: Pub. exclusively for F.W. Woolworth Co. by W.F. Hall Printing Co., [c1936]; Ida Bailey Allen's Everyday Cook Book; Tested Recipes, Balanced Menus, Money-Saving Hints, Setting the Table and Serving, Racine, Wis.: Whitman Pub. Co., c1938; Ida Bailey Allen's Kitchenette for Two Cook Book, Racine, Wis.: Whitman Publishing Co., [c1938]; The Common Sense Cook Book, Racine, Wis.: Whitman Publishing Co., [c1939]; Ida Bailey Allen's New Modern Cook Book; 2819 Delicious Recipes, Including the Famous Radio Recipes and a Chapter on Wines and Their Use, New York: Garden City Publishing Co., [c1939]; Ida Bailey Allen's Time-Saving Cook Book: With 465 Timed Recipes and Time-Table Meals the Year Round, Chicago: Rand McNally, c1940; Ida Bailey Allen's Money-Saving Cook Book, New York: Garden City Publishing Co., [c1940]; Successful Entertaining, Garden City, NY: Doubleday, Doran and Co., 1942; Double-Quick Cooking for Part-Time Homemakers, New York: M. Barrows and Co., 1943; Food for Two, [1st ed.], Garden City, NY: Garden City Pub. Co., [1947]; Pressure Cooking, Garden City, NY: Garden City Publishing Co., [1947]; ... Solving the High Cost of Eating: A Cookbook to Live By, *New York: Farrar, [c1952]*; Step-by-Step Picture Cook Book, *New York: Grosset and Dunlap, [1952]*; Sandwich Book, *Greenwich, Conn.: Fawcett Publications, c1955*; 159 Exciting Easy-Do-Meals with Sausage, *[No place:] Union Carbide Corp., c1957*; Gastronomique: A Cookbook for Gourmets, *Garden City, NY: Doubleday, [c1958]*; Best Loved Recipes of the American People, *[1st ed.], Garden City, NY: Doubleday, 1973*.

O372.1 1917

[An edition of *Mrs Allen's Cook Book*, Toronto: William Briggs, 1917, $2.00]

NOTES: This work is cited in an advertisement for Briggs in BS, Vol. 33, No. 11 (November 1917), p 24, which offers the following description: 'This book is really the official recipe collection grown out of the [Westfield Pure Food Movement].' The William Briggs edition was published in the same year as the American edition, but no copy of the Briggs edition has been found.

Mrs Allen's reach was international: in her 'Preface' to the 756-page American edition, she refers to 'thousands of letters from housewives all over the country [i.e., the United States], as well as from Canada and Mexico, and many from the old world.' An interesting feature of the American edition is the frontispiece showing 'Mrs. Allen in Her Own Kitchen.' According to the title-page, Mrs Allen lectured at the Westfield Domestic Science schools, and Professor Allyn, who wrote the 'Introduction,' was the former chemist of the Westfield Board of Health.

AMERICAN EDITIONS: *Mrs Allen's Cook Book*, introduction by Professor Lewis B. Allyn, illustrations from photographs by T.L. Allen and A.E. Sproul, Boston: [printed by S.J. Parkhill and Co., Boston, for] Small, Maynard and Co., [copyright 1917] (United States: DLC, IaAS).

Armstrong, Donald Budd (1886–)

Metropolitan Life Insurance Co., later renamed MetLife, is an American company, chartered in 1868 and based in New York City. In 1924 it established a Canadian head office in Ottawa (see 'Metropolitan Expands Canadian Business: Canadian Headquarters Established at Ottawa One Year Ago,' Monetary Times Vol. 74, No. 20 (15 May 1925), p 17). In addition to Food Facts, *the company published the following food-related books in Canada: O411.1,* The Metropolitan Life Cook Book; *O590.1,* All about Milk; *O619.1,* Family Food Supply; *and O631.1,* Three Meals a Day.

O373.1 [copyright] 1917

Food facts / by / Donald B. Armstrong / M.D., M.A., M.S. / Printed and distributed by the / Metropolitan Life Insurance Company / for the use of its policy-holders / 1917

DESCRIPTION: 19.0 × 13.0 cm   Pp [1–2] 3–32   Tp illus of the company's New York City headquarters, illus chapter headpieces   Paper, with image on front of a woman facing food-laden grocery-store shelves and beside her, a grocery-store clerk; stapled

CONTENTS: 1 tp; 2 author's acknowledgments and 'Copyright, 1917, by the Metropolitan Life Insurance Company'; 3 'Contents'; 4–32 text

COPIES: *Bookseller's stock

NOTES: 'N1316 Printed in Canada' is on the outside back face of the binding, but no city of publication is recorded. Statistics cited in the text are for New York City only. There are six chapters: 'Where to Buy'; 'How to Buy Cheaply'; 'Clean Food and Disease Prevention'; 'Wise Food and Health'; 'Cooking Foods' on pp 19–23; and 'Good Food Habits.' The entry for *Food Facts* is in the Ontario section because the Canadian head office was located there from 1924.

AMERICAN EDITIONS: [New York:] Printed by the Metropolitan Life Insurance Co., 1917 (United States: DLC).

The bakery book

Benjamin Gould founded Canadian Milk Products in 1903, and incorporated the business in 1908. The plant for making powdered milk was in Brownsville; head office was in Toronto. From 1909 the company used a spray process acquired from Merrell-Soule Co. in Syracuse, New York. New plants were built in Belmont in 1912, Burford in 1916, and Hickson in 1917. The company was sold to Borden Co. Ltd in 1928, but continued to operate under its original name into the 1930s. Canadian Milk Products Ltd also published: O397.1, Klim Cook Book; *O453.1,* The Wonderful Story of Klim; *O534.1,* Camp Cooking; *O559.1, Bradbury, Adam H.,* C.M.P. Bakery Formulas; *and O674.1,* Nationally Known Recipes.

For information about the company see: Edward S. Moore, When Cheese Was King: A History of the Cheese Factories in Oxford County, *[Norwich, Ont.: Norwich and District Historical Society, 1987], pp 21–2; and Thomas/Marchant, pp 67–8.*

O374.1 nd [about 1917]

The / bakery / [same capital 'b' as for 'bakery']ook / bakery methods & recipes / Canadian Milk Products Limited / Toronto [cover-title]

DESCRIPTION: 17.5 × 13.0 cm   Pp [1–2] 3–40   Frontis of Burford plant, 2 double-sided pls between pp 14–15 and 26–7 of 'A Good Baking Test' and baked goods, 1 pl opp p 40 of 'A Bacteriological Laboratory'   Very thin card, with small image on front, in circular frame, of a baker; stapled, and with hole punched at top left corner, through which runs a string for hanging
CONTENTS: 1 'Foreword'; 2–8 introductory text under the following headings: 'Service,' 'General Baking and Cooking Uses,' 'Advantages of C.M.P. Powdered Milk for Baking,' 'Directions for Restoring Powdered Milk for Bakery Use,' 'Powdered versus Liquid Milk – Quality, Cost, Yield,' 'In Yeast Raised Baked Goods,' and 'Milk Bread'; 9–mid 15 'Bread Formulas'; mid 15–mid 17 'Sweet Yeast Dough Goods'; mid 17–top 18 'Use of C.M.P. Powdered Milk in Cake Baking'; mid 18–mid 22 'Cake Recipes'; mid 22–27 'Sweet Doughs, Coffee Cakes, Hot Cross Buns, etc.'; 28–mid 30 'Cookies, Jumbles, Snaps, Drop Cakes and Fancy Cakes'; mid 30–39 'For Pie Baking'; 40 'Index' [i.e., table of contents] and at bottom, 'We are indebted to Merrell-Soule Company, Syracuse, N.Y. for much of the material in this book.'
COPIES: *Private collection
NOTES: The 'Foreword' states the book's purpose: '... to describe the general bakery uses of C.M.P. Powdered Milk; to give necessary technical information regarding the employment of these products as ingredients in the manufacture of baked goods, and to show the advantages gained by their use.' The frontispiece illustrates the Burford plant and lists other Ontario plants at Brownsville, Belmont, Hickson, and Glanworth; the head office and laboratories were in Toronto, and branch offices in Montreal, Saint John, and Winnipeg. *The Bakery Book* was published no earlier than 1917, the year the Hickson plant was built.

Bradley, Alice (1875–1946)

Also by Alice Bradley is Q130.1, De bonnes choses à manger faites avec le bicarbonate de soude (soda à pâte) Cow Brand, *and English editions titled* Good Things to Eat Made with Cow Brand Baking Soda. *Bradley wrote the 'Introduction' for O502.1,* Jell-O.

Also by this author, but published in the United States (and all at DLC unless otherwise indicated), are: Lessons in Food Values and Economical Menus, *[Boston: Printed by B.B. Nichols], 1917;* Thirty-Cents-a Day, *New York: Woman's Home Companion, [c1917];* Wheatless and Meatless Menus and Recipes, *[Boston: B.B. Nichols, printer], 1918;* Cooking for Profit, *Chicago: American School of Home Economics, 1922;* Fifty Family Budgets, *New York: Woman's Home Companion, c1923;* Low Cost Menus, *New York: Woman's Home Companion, copyright 1926 (United States: InU);* For Luncheon and Supper Guests, *Boston: M. Barrows and Co., 1927;* Desserts, *Boston: M. Barrows and Co., 1930 (United States: InU);* Meals Thrifty and Thrilling ... for the Woman's Home Companion, *New York: Crowell Publishing Co., copyright 1932 (United States: InU);* 100 Foundation Recipes, *New York: Woman's Home Companion, copyright 1932 (United States: InU);* Nutrition Simplified, *Boston: B. Humphries Inc., [1944].*

O375.1   1917
[An edition of *The Candy Cook Book*, Toronto: McClelland, Goodchild and Stewart, 1917, $1.00]
CITATIONS: BS, Vol. 33, No. 7 (July 1917), p 44, and Vol. 33, No. 10 (October 1917), p 67   Spadoni/Donnelly No. 4286 ('Imprints Not Located')

AMERICAN EDITIONS: Boston: Little, Brown and Co., 1917 (United States: DLC); new, rev. ed., Boston: Little, Brown and Co., 1924 (United States: DLC).

Canada, Food Controller for Canada

The Office of the Food Controller was created on 16 June 1917 and existed for less than eight months; its powers were assumed by the Canada Food Board on 11 February 1918. In Report of the Food Controller, *1918, p 19, W.J. Hanna explained one area of its activities: 'Realizing ... that the wholesale co-operation of the people with the aims of Food Control was an essential, and that they must know and understand what those aims are, an educational organization was established, which by means of the press, pamphlets, bulletins, cards, posters, sample bills of fare, cookery books, teachers, preachers, voluntary speakers, motion pictures, cartoons, women's societies, etc., etc., secured continued and very extensive publicity.' In addition to the works described below, the food controller published the 12-page* War Meals: Practical Suggestions to Save Beef, Bacon, Wheat and Flour to Meet the War-Needs Overseas, *Ottawa: J. de Labroquerie Taché, printer to the King's Most Excellent Majesty, two editions dated 1917, one with the letter from the food controller on p 2, the other with the letter on p 1; both editions are at OOAG (641.1 C212); one of the two is at OTU (Gov. Doc. Can. F Gerstein).*

O376.1   nd [about 1917]
Can, dry and store / for victory / conserve fruits and vegetables for home / consumption, and release wheat, / beef and bacon for export / The

armies must be fed / [caption:] Steps in the canning process. / 1. The jar ready for filling. / 2. A jar packed with cauliflower and filled with water and salt. / 3. A jar with the cover on and clamp left loose. Ready for boiling. / 4. Jar inverted after boiling to test for leaks. / Published by / the Food Controller for Canada / F. C. Pamphlet 2. [cover-title]

DESCRIPTION: 25.0 × 16.5 cm   Pp [1] 2–16   Illus   Paper, with image on front of four 'Steps in the Canning Process'; stapled

CONTENTS: 1 cover-title; 2 'Read These "Donts" [sic] before You Fail' and 'Note to Housewives'; 3 'Canadian Crops for Victory in France // Canning in the Home'; top–mid 4 'Steps in the Canning Process'; mid 4–near bottom 5 'Canning Recipes in Detail'; bottom 5–6 'Some Favourite Recipes'; 7–mid 9 'Drying Fruits and Vegetables'; bottom 9 'Recipes in Detail'; 10–11 'Winter Storage of Vegetables and Fruits'; 12–13 'Vegetables in Detail'; 14 'Fruit and Vegetable Canning Chart'; 15 'To Win the War'; 16 [outside back face of binding] 'Help the Fighters to Win' signed W.J. Hanna, food controller

COPIES: *ACG   OOAG (641.4)   OTMCL (338.1 C122)   OTU (Gov. Doc. Can. F Gerstein); United States: DLC (TX601 C3)

NOTES: This title was likely published about the same time as O377.1, *Eat More Fish.* OGU (CCC CA1 DA 42C15) has a copy with only 14 pp. DLC dates the book [1918].

See O402.1 for later editions, retitled *Fruit and Vegetables: Canning, Drying, Storing,* published by the Canada Food Board, then the Department of Agriculture.

O377.1   1917

Eat more fish / how to prepare cook and serve Canadian / fish, and so conserve Canadian beef / and bacon for the soldiers / at the front. / [caption for image of a fish:] Mackerel / [caption for national symbol:] Canada / Canadians consume 29 pounds of fish per head / of population in a year. The normal consumption / in Great Britain is 56 pounds per year. Canadian / consumption of meat is out of all proportion to the / food value of fish. / In time of war it is Canada's duty to do her / utmost in view of the demands of the armies upon / her supplies of beef and bacon, to make fullest / possible use of the abundant supplies of food fish / obtainable from Canadian waters. This is one / way of serving the country in the time of need. / W.J. Hanna. / Published by order of / the Food Controller for Canada / from the office of the King's Printer, / Ottawa, September 20, 1917. [cover-title]

DESCRIPTION: 24.5 × 16.5 cm   Pp [1] 2–14 [15–16] Illus of fish   Paper, with image on front of a mackerel; stapled

CONTENTS: 1 'Food Values of Fish'; top 2 'Preparation of Fish'; mid 2–mid 3 'Methods of Cooking'; mid–bottom 3 'Best Methods of Cooking Different Fish'; 4–9 'Canada's Chief Sea Fish'; top 10 'Canadian Shell Fish'; near top 10–12 'Canadian Fresh Water Fish'; 13 'Delicious Sauces for Fish'; 14 'Food Control in Canada' and 'Organization of Advisory Bodies'; 15 'Help the Fighters to Win' signed W.J. Hanna, food controller, 25 October 1917; 16 'Your Part in the War' [exhortation to buy Victory Bonds]

COPIES: CIHM (9-01823)   OONL (COP.CA.2.1999-1472)   *Private collection; United States: DLC (TX747 C3)

NOTES: The sections on each type of fish are accompanied by recipes. Another private collector's copy is stamped on the binding, 'The Canadian Fish & Cold Storage Co., Ltd. Prince Rupert, B.C.' See also O401.1, Canada, Canada Food Board, *Fish Recipes,* a retitled edition of 1918, and O467.1, Canada, Department of Marine and Fisheries, *Eat More Fish,* 1921.

O377.2   1917

—Mangeons du poissons / et laissons le boeuf et le bacon pour / les soldats au front. / Préparation, cuisson et service. / [caption for image of a fish:] Maquereau / [caption for national symbol:] Canada / Le poisson, qui est un mets très nourrissant, / est trop peu employé au Canada. Nous n'en / consommons que 29 livres par tête et par an, tandis / que la Grande-Bretagne en consomme le double, / 56 livres. Nous mangeons beaucoup trop de viande / et trop peu de poisson. / Les pêcheries canadiennes peuvent nous four- / nir des approvisionnements abondants. Sachons / les utiliser, afin de ménager le boeuf et le bacon / nécessaires aux armées. C'est un service à rendre / au pays en cette heure de crise. C'est donc pour / tous un devoir impérieux. / W.J. Hanna. / Publié par ordre / du Contrôleur des vivres du Canada / Bureau de l'Imprimeur du roi, / Ottawa, 20 septembre 1917. [cover-title]

DESCRIPTION: 24.0 × 15.5 cm   Pp [1] 2–14 [15–16] Illus of fish   Paper, with image of a mackerel

CONTENTS: 1 'Valeur alimentaire du poisson'; top 2 'Préparation du poisson'; mid 2–mid 3 'Cuisson'; mid–bottom 3 'Meilleurs modes de cuisson pour différentes sortes de poissons'; 4–mid 10 'Les principaux poissons de mer du Canada'; bottom 10 'Mollusques canadiens'; 11–13 'Poissons canadiens d'eau douce'; 14 'Sauces délicieuses pour servir avec le poisson';

15 'Le contrôle des vivres au Canada'; 16 'Aidons nos soldats à vaincre' signed W.J. Hanna, food controller, 25 October 1917

COPIES: *AEU (PN3215 C2 C4 1917 title 14)

Catarrhozone almanac

For the titles of other publications by the same company, see O155.1.

O378.1 [1917]

Catarrhozone almanac [cover-title]

DESCRIPTION: 21.5 × 15.0 cm   Pp 1–48   Paper, with image on front of polo players; stapled, and with hole punched at top left corner, through which runs a string for hanging

CONTENTS: Inside front face of binding calendar for July 1917–December 1918; 1–48 miscellaneous information, including 'Simple Puddings' on pp 12–14, 'Some Home Made Candies' on pp 14–15, 'Tested Cooking Receipts' on pp 15–20, 'Preserves and Jellies' on pp 20–1, 'How to Have Food [sic] Bread' on pp 21–2, various household hints on pp 27–38, 41–2, and 'Preserving Receipts' on p 48

COPIES: *OHMB (Serial)   OTUTF (uncat patent medicine)

NOTES: The company's address is on p 1: The Catarrhozone Co., Kingston, Ontario, and Buffalo, New York.

Chapman, Miss Ethel Matilda (Campbellville, Ont., 25 February 1888– 28 August 1976, Toronto, Ont.)

Also by this author is O516.1, Food for the Family, published by the Ontario Department of Agriculture in 1924. Chapman contributed 'Learn to Save Yourself' to O1091.1, Household Helps for 1944.

Ethel Chapman was the twelfth of thirteen children of Ephraim and Sarah Chapman of Campbellville. She grew up on the family farm. Following high school in Milton, she attended the Milton Model School in 1905 and the Hamilton Normal School in 1909–10. She earned a Domestic Science Teacher Certificate in one year of study at the Macdonald Institute in Guelph, graduating in 1912, after which she worked for the Women's Institute Branch of the Ontario Department of Agriculture. From 1927 to 1952 she was editor of the 'Home' section of Farmer's Magazine (title varied). In 1952 she joined the Federated Women's Institutes of Ontario office and began editing its Home and Country. In all these jobs her goal was to improve the lives of rural Ontario women. She

also wrote novels, short stories, and essays. In 1966 she received an honorary doctorate from the University of Guelph; and in 1974, the Ontario Agricultural College Centennial Medal. In 1980 she was inducted into the Ontario Agricultural Hall of Fame.

For more information about Ethel Chapman, see her file at the Ontario Agricultural Hall of Fame and archival material at OGU, including her Entrance Record, Registration No. 1438, for the Macdonald Institute. See also her obituary in the Toronto Star, 30 August 1976, p A6; and Acton Free Press, 1 September 1976, p 7, column 2. Information about the Chapman family, including a photograph of Ethel, is in Nassagaweya: A History of Campbellville and Surrounding Area; Its Land and People, Campbellville, Ont.: Campbellville Historical Society, copyright 1981, pp 167–8. Another photograph of Ethel is in Ambrose, p 183.

The birth year for Chapman in Entry 143 of Canadian Women of Note (1891) is incorrect.

For the titles of other cookbooks published by the Ontario Department of Agriculture, see O158.1.

O379.1   July 1917

Ontario Department of Agriculture / Women's Institutes / Bulletin 252 / The preservation of food / home canning / compiled by / Miss Ethel M. Chapman / [caption:] Canned vegetables in good types of jars. / [caption:] Canning surplus chickens in the fall. / Toronto, Ontario, July, 1917 [cover-title]

DESCRIPTION: 24.5 × 16.5 cm   Pp [1–2] 3–31   1 fp illus, illus   Paper, with 2 illus on front (see captions in cover-title transcription)

CONTENTS: 1 cover-title; 2 fp illus of canned fruit and vegetables and of canning equipment; 3–31 [inside back face of binding] text

CITATIONS: MacTaggart, p 25

COPIES: OFERWM (A1996.52 MU306)   OGU (2 copies: *UA s048 b47, CA2ON AF6 B252)   OOWM (984.91.11)

NOTES: The introductory text refers to wartime conditions: 'Food is going to be scarce this winter. The woman who can find time to preserve food which would otherwise be wasted, and who will sell or give away the surplus above what is required for her own family, will be doing a real patriotic work. Canned fruits, jams and jellies are needed for soldiers in the hospitals and in the trenches. Through the income derived from selling canned products at home markets many women would find a practical way of raising Red Cross funds.' In addition to recipes for canning, there are instructions for preserving eggs, drying fruit, curing pork and beef on the farm, and storing vegetables for winter use.

O379.2 rev. ed., May 1922
—Ontario Department of Agriculture / Women's Institutes / Bulletin 252 / Revised May, 1922 / The preservation of food / home canning / [caption:] Canned vegetables in good types of jars. / [caption:] Canning surplus chickens in the fall. / Toronto, Ontario [cover-title]
DESCRIPTION: 24.0 × 16.0 cm   Pp [1] 2–32   Illus on p 2 of bottled fruit and vegetables and wash boiler, illus on p 15 of 'Small steam pressure outfit for home canning,' illus on p 16 of 'Practical steam-pressure outfit with firebox'   Paper, with 2 illus on front (see captions in cover-title transcription); stapled
CONTENTS: 1 cover-title; 2 illus; top 3 'Importance of Preserving Food in the Home'; mid 3–top 5 'Why Foods Spoil'; near top 5–mid 6 'Methods of Canning'; mid 6 'Scalding, Blanching, Cold-Dipping'; bottom 6–7 'General Rules and Recipes for Canning Fruits'; 8–mid 10 'Fruit Jams and Relishes'; mid 10–top 12 'Preserving'; near top 12–mid 14 'Jelly Making'; mid 14–mid 17 'The Canning of Vegetables'; mid 17–mid 20 'Rules and Recipes for Canning Vegetables'; bottom 20–mid 21 'Preserving Vegetables in Brine'; mid 21–mid 22 'Pickles'; mid 22–top 25 'Canned Meats, Fish and Soups'; mid 25–top 26 'Preservation of Eggs'; near top 26–mid 27 'Drying Fruits'; mid 27–30 'Curing Pork and Beef on the Farm'; 31–2 'Storing Vegetables for Winter Use'
COPIES: *Private collection
NOTES: Chapman's name is not mentioned in this revised edition. References to wartime conditions have been deleted.

O379.3 rev. ed., July 1932
—Bulletin 252 July, 1932 / Ontario Department of Agriculture / Women's Institutes Branch / [provincial coat of arms] / The / preservation of food / home canning / Revised by Gertrude A. Gray / Published by direction of Colonel the Honourable Thos. L. Kennedy, Minister of Agriculture / Toronto, 1932 [cover-title]
DESCRIPTION: 24.0 × 16.5 cm   Pp [1] 2–40   Illus Paper, with image on front of a basket of vegetables and jars of preserves sitting on a counter; stapled
CONTENTS: 1–mid 16 general information about canning; bottom 16–20 'Jelly Making'; 21–mid 24 'Fruit Butters, Jams, Conserves, and Marmalades'; mid 24–25 'Canned Meat'; top 26 'Canned Fish'; mid 26 'Preserving Vegetables in Brine' and 'Dried Sweet Corn'; bottom 26–mid 32 'Pickles'; mid 32–top 34 'Drying Fruits'; near top 34–mid 37 'Curing Pork and Beef on the Farm'; bottom 37–near bottom 38 'Preservation of Eggs'; bottom 38–40 'Storing Vegetables for Winter Use'

COPIES: *Private collection
NOTES: Chapman's name is not mentioned in this revised edition.

O380.1 August 1917
Ontario Department of Agriculture / Women's Institutes / Bulletin 254 / War breads / How the housekeeper may help to save the country's / wheat supply / By Ethel M. Chapman / Toronto, Ontario, August, 1917.
DESCRIPTION: Pp [1–3] 4–16   Illus on p 1 of bread loaves
CONTENTS: 1 tp; 2 blank; top 3 introductory text; mid 3–11 recipes; 12–16 'Appendix // Announcement of Demonstration-Lecture Courses, 1917–18' [to be provided by the Women's Institutes] signed Geo. A. Putnam, superintendent, Toronto, 25 August 1917
CITATIONS: MacTaggart, p 25
COPIES: *CIHM (82551)   OGU (CA2ON AF6 B254) OMMM   OOAG
NOTES: The introductory text explains what measures must be taken in war time to save the nation's wheat supply: 'One of the lessons that Canadians have to learn from Europe is that white bread is not the bread for war-time; that when the supply of wheat is low, bread must be made of other grains than wheat; also that in the milling of the wheat the manufacturer must put a greater proportion of the grain into flour and less into cattle-feed ... The constant use of these coarser breads might not agree with some people, but as a rule they will be found more healthful than the finer white bread.'

At about the same time, the Quebec Department of Agriculture published a book of recipes for war breads, Q99.1, *How to Save Wheat and Meat.*

Cook book

O381.1 [1917]
Cook book / published by / the Ambulance Corps / of / the Women's Recruiting League / Hamilton, Canada / Price 25 cents [cover-title]
DESCRIPTION: 22.0 × 15.0 cm   Pp [1] 2–80   Paper, with image on front of a red cross
CONTENTS: 1 dedication; 2 ad; 3 names of officers in the Ambulance Corps; 4 ads; 5–78 text and ads; 79 'Index' [i.e., table of contents]; 80 blank for 'My Own Recipes' and at bottom, 'The Press of Robert Duncan & Co.'
CITATIONS: Ferguson/Fraser, p 233
COPIES: *Private collection

NOTES: Printed on p 1 is 'Red Cross Cook Book // To the soldier boy's [sic] of Hamilton, Ontario ... December 1917.' The running head is 'Red Cross Cook Book.'

East, Anna Merritt

This author is described as 'formerly New Housekeeping Editor, The Ladies' Home Journal' on the title-page of the 1917 Boston edition of Kitchenette Cookery.

O382.1 1917
[An edition of *Kitchenette Cookery,* Toronto: McClelland, Goodchild and Stewart, 1917, $1.00]
CITATIONS: BS, Vol. 33, No. 7 (July 1917), p 44, and Vol. 33, No. 10 (October 1917), p 67 Spadoni/Donnelly No. 4297 ('Imprints Not Located')

AMERICAN EDITIONS: Boston: Little, Brown and Co., 1917 (United States: DLC).

Helpful hints for housekeepers 1917

See O263.1 for information about the company and other issues of Helpful Hints for Housekeepers.

O383.1 1917
1917 Volume VII. 1917 / Hang me in the kitchen / Helpful / hints / for housekeepers / Compliments of / the Dodds Medicine Co. / Limited / Toronto, Can. [cover-title]
DESCRIPTION: 17.0 × 11.5 cm Pp 1–28 [29–32 lacking] Paper; stapled, and with hole punched at top left corner, through which runs a string for hanging
CONTENTS: 1 'For Young Housekeepers'; 2 'Just Kerosene'; 3, 5, 7, 9, 11, 13, 15, 17, 19, 21, 23, 25, 27 'Best Horoscope Is Health'; 4 'A Kitchen Timetable'; 6 'Some Uses for Old Paper'; 8, 10 'What Salt Will Do'; 12 'Potatoes for Cleaning'; 14, 16 'Points for the Kitchen'; 18, 20 'Things Worth Remembering'; 22 'Laundry Helps'; 24 'Linens'; 26 'Moths, etc.'; 28 'Removing Stains'
COPIES: *OHMB (Serial) OTUTF (uncat patent medicine)

Home making

O384.1 1917
Home making / The art of good / housekeeping / Toronto Household Exhibition / Arena, Toronto – April 9 to 14, 1917 / [ad for Toronto Grafonola Co.] [cover-title]
DESCRIPTION: 22.5 × 15.0 cm Pp 1–24 Paper; stapled
CONTENTS: 1–2 ads; 3–top 9 'The Ideal Home' and ad; near top 9–17 'Household Hints' and ads; 18 ads; 19–21 'Exhibitors Toronto Household Exhibition 1917,' 'Tea Room,' 'Patronesses,' and ads; 22 'A Good Cleaning Fluid' and ads; 23–4 ads
COPIES: *OTMCL (640.971 H58)
NOTES: There is a section about 'Table Service' under 'The Ideal Home.' Culinary information is under 'Household Hints'; for example, how to choose the right relish, cooking times, fish as a food, uses for dripping, how to reduce the meat bill, and how to cook meat.

The housekeepers' perfect account book 1917

See O145.1 for a list of other editions.

O385.1 1917
The / housekeepers' perfect / account book / 1917 / Even a dollar earns interest / [ad for Standard Reliance Mortgage Corp., head office, Toronto] [cover-title]
DESCRIPTION: 31.0 × 23.0 cm Pp 1–64 Paper; stapled
CONTENTS: 1 'The Housekeepers' Perfect Account Book // Published annually in December of each year at Toronto. Copies may be procured by writing to any of the advertisers. For advertising rates and method of distribution, address Geo. Shepard, publisher, 42 Colborne St., Toronto.' and ads; 2 ad; 3–63 weekly account tables, monthly calendars, recipes, and ads; 64 ad and 'Household List' [alphabetical list of household necessities from Abbey Effervescent Salt to Yeast (Royal)]
COPIES: *OKIT
NOTES: There are recipes on each weekly account page.

How we cook in Strathroy

O386.1 1917
How we cook / in / Strathroy / a selection of / tested recipes / compiled by / the Mary Armstrong Chapter / of the I.O.D.E. / "Now good digestion wait on appetite and health on both." – Shakespeare. / Strathroy, Ont. / Evans Brothers, printers and publishers / 1917
DESCRIPTION: 22.0 × 15.0 cm Pp [1] 2–72 Paper; stapled, and with two holes punched at left edge, through which runs the remnant of a cord
CONTENTS: 1 tp; 2 ad; 3–69 recipes credited with the

name of the contributor and ads; 70–1 'Laundry Notes'
and ad; 72 'Index' [i.e., table of contents] and list of
'Advertisements'
COPIES: *Private collection

The ideal cooking fat

O387.1   nd [about 1917]
The ideal / cooking fat / Half the cost of butter / In
frying / foods retain their / natural, dainty flavors /
In all baking / a rich shortening, always dependable
/ for cake, pie, bread, biscuits / See cook book offer
on last page / Made in Canada [cover-title]
DESCRIPTION: 12.5 × 8.5 cm   Pp [1] 2–31   Paper, with
image on front of a cylindrical container of Crisco;
stapled
CONTENTS: 1 cover-title; 2–3 'What This Booklet Tells';
4 'How Pure Crisco Is'; 5–6 'How Crisco Is Made';
7 'What This Means to You'; 8, 10 'Why Crisco Foods
Are Easy to Digest'; 9 'Buttermilk Biscuits'; 11 'Ontario
Doughnuts'; 12, 14 'Why Crisco Foods Are Appetizing'; 13 'Emily's White Cake'; 15 'Jelly Roll'; 16–17
'Why It Pays to Use Crisco'; 18 'Special Note on
Weight of Crisco'; 19 'Gingerbread'; 20, 22 'Why Crisco
Can Be Depended Upon'; 21 'Breakfast Muffins'; 23
'Plain Crisco Pastry'; 24 'Why Crisco Is Convenient
to Use'; 25 'French Fried Potatoes'; 26–8 'How to
Succeed with Crisco'; 29 'The Best Way to Buy Crisco';
30 'Cook Book Coupon' for *The Whys of Cooking, A
Calendar of Dinners,* and *Balanced Daily Diet*; 31 'Books
of the Crisco Library' and at bottom, 'Form 4. Canada'
COPIES: *QMM (RBD ckbk 1926)
NOTES: *The Ideal Cooking Fat* was published to promote Crisco shortening, made by Procter and Gamble
Distributing Company of Canada, to the Canadian
housewife. 'What This Booklet Tells' begins: 'The
building of a factory at Hamilton, Ont., to meet the
ever-increasing demand of the Canadian housewife
for Crisco ...' Crisco was introduced to the American
market in 1911, and the company officially opened its
first Canadian plant, in Hamilton, in 1915.

Of the books cited on p 30, *The Whys of Cooking* by
Janet McKenzie Hill (O363.2) is dated copyright 1916;
A 'Calendar of Dinners' with 615 Recipes by Marion
Harris Neil (O390.1) is dated copyright 1917 (there
were earlier American editions); and *Balanced Daily
Diet* by Janet McKenzie Hill (O362.1) was published
about 1916. The order of publication of the two un-
dated editions of *The Ideal Cooking Fat* is uncertain.
The text is printed in blue.

O387.2   nd [about 1917]
—The ideal / cooking fat / Better than the / best
leaf lard / Half the cost / of butter / See cook book
offer on last page [cover-title]
DESCRIPTION: 12.5 × 9.0 cm   Pp [1] 2–31   Paper, with
image on front of a cylindrical container of Crisco;
stapled
CONTENTS: 1 cover-title; 2–3 'What This Booklet Tells';
4 'How Pure Crisco Is'; 5–6 'How Crisco Is Made'; 7
'What This Means to You'; 8, 10 'Why Crisco Foods
Are Easy to Digest'; 9 'Buttermilk Biscuits'; 11 'Ontario
Doughnuts'; 12, 14 'Why Crisco Foods Are Appetiz-
ing'; 13 'Emily's White Cake'; 15 'Jelly Roll'; 16–17
'Why It Pays to Use Crisco'; 18 'Special Note on
Weight of Crisco'; 19 'Gingerbread'; 20, 22 'Why Crisco
Can Be Depended Upon'; 21 'Breakfast Muffins'; 23
'Plain Crisco Pastry'; 24 'Why Crisco is Convenient to
Use'; 25 'French Fried Potatoes'; 26–8 'How to Suc-
ceed with Crisco'; 29 'The Best Way to Buy Crisco'; 30
'Cook Book Coupon' with name and address of pub-
lisher: The Procter and Gamble Distributing Co. of
Canada Ltd, Hamilton; 31 [inside back face of bind-
ing] 'How to Get a Cook Book' includes a coupon for
ordering the cloth-bound *A Calendar of Dinners* by
Marion Harris Neil for $0.10 or the free paper-bound
250 Recipes (without *A Calendar of Dinners*), and at
bottom, 'Form 4. Canada'
CITATIONS: Simpson, p W17 (includes photograph)
COPIES: OH (R641.5 CRI CESH)   *Private collection
NOTES: The text is printed in blue.

Kinne, Helen (1861–1917), and Anna Maria Cooley (1874–)

*These American co-authors collaborated on other books
on household subjects.*

O388.1   [May] 1917
Foods and household / management / a textbook /
of the / household arts / by / Helen Kinne /
Professor of Household Arts Education / and /
Anna M. Cooley, B.S. / Assistant Professor of
Household Arts Education / Teachers College,
Columbia University / New York / The Macmillan
Company / 1917 / All rights reserved
DESCRIPTION: 18.5 × 12.5 cm   Pp [i–iv] v–ix [x] xi–xv
[xvi], 1–401, [i–vi]   Frontis is a reproduction of the
frontis 'From *The London and Country Cookbook*, 1770.
Courtesy of the Bryson Library,' 82 numbered
illus   Cloth
CONTENTS: i ht; ii 'The Macmillan Company New
York Boston Chicago Dallas Atlanta San Francisco //

Macmillan & Co., Limited London Bombay Calcutta Melbourne // The Macmillan Co. of Canada, Ltd. Toronto'; iii tp; iv 'Copyright, 1914, by the Macmillan Company. Set up and electrotyped. Published January, 1914. Reprinted February, June, August, October, 1914; February, June, October, 1915; April, August, 1916; May, 1917. Norwood Press J.S. Cushing Co. – Berwick & Smith Co. Norwood, Mass., U.S.A.'; v–vi preface; vii–ix 'Suggestions to Teachers'; x blank; xi–xv table of contents; xvi blank; 1–381 text; 382 blank; 383–6 'Appendix // Classification of Foodstuffs'; 387–90 'Appendix // Table 1'; 391–401 index; i blank; ii–vi ad and publ ads

COPIES: *OGU (CCC TX715.6 K55)

NOTES: The book was for use in 'high school and normal school' (p v). There are twenty-three chapters, to be followed in order through the school year: 'Food Materials and Foodstuffs'; 'Kitchen Furnishings'; 'Fuels and Stoves'; 'Food Preparation'; 'Water and Other Beverages'; 'Fruit and Its Preservation'; 'Vegetables and Vegetable Cookery'; 'Cereal Products'; 'Eggs, Milk, and Cheese'; 'The Fats and the Sugars'; 'Muffins, Biscuit, Cake, and Pastry'; 'Yeast Bread'; 'Meats and Poultry'; 'Fish and Shellfish'; 'Salads and Desserts'; 'Preparation of Meals and Table Service'; 'The Cost and the Purchase of Food'; 'Menus and Dietaries'; 'The Household Budget'; 'System in Management' [e.g., keeping accounts]; 'How to Buy'; 'Housewifery'; and 'Laundering and Dry Cleansing.' The chapter on 'Kitchen Furnishings' contains many illuminating diagrams and illustrations; for example, of cupboards, sinks, and ice-boxes. The chapter on 'Fuels and Stoves' is also well illustrated.

Macmillan advertised the book, possibly an earlier Canadian edition than that of 1917, on p 95 of O358.1, *Cook Book*, [1916]. The price quoted in the advertisement is $1.10.

AMERICAN EDITIONS: New York: Macmillan, 1914 (United States: DLC); New York: Macmillan, 1921 (OGU).

McCann, Alfred Watterson (1879–1931)

McCann's other works include: Starving America, *Cleveland, New York: F.M. Barton, c1913;* This Famishing World, *New York: George H. Doran Co., [c1918]; and* The Science of Eating; How to Insure Stamina, Endurance, Vigor, Strength and Health in Infancy, Youth and Age, *New York: George H. Doran Co., [c1919] (all at United States: DLC).*

O389.1 1917
[An edition of *Thirty Cent Bread: How to Escape a Higher Cost of Living,* Toronto: McClelland, Goodchild and Stewart, 1917, $0.50]
CITATIONS: BS, Vol. 33, No. 11 (November 1917), p 65 Spadoni/Donnelly No. 4321 ('Imprints Not Located')

AMERICAN EDITIONS: New York: George H. Doran Co., 1917 (United States: DLC).

Neil, Marion Harris

For information about this author and her other cookbooks, see O306.1.

O390.1 [copyright 1917]
A "calendar of dinners" / with 615 recipes / by Marion Harris Neil / including / The Story of Crisco [cover-title]
DESCRIPTION: 19.5 × 12.5 cm Pp [i–ii], [1–2] 3–231 [232–3] Illus Cloth, with pl col on front of four persons looking at a giant-size cookbook
CONTENTS: i endpaper recto; ii 'Copyright 1917 The Procter & Gamble Distributing Co. of Canada, Ltd. Hamilton, Canada // Price twenty-five cents ...'; 1 illustrated part-title with 'Form 81 The Story of Crisco' and at bottom right, the artist's name, 'Fred Pegram 1912'; 2 table of contents; 3–6 'Recipe Index'; 7 quotations; 8 introduction; 9–21 'The Story of Crisco'; 22 'Things to Remember in Connection with These Recipes'; 23 'Remember That – '; 24 'Hints to Young Cooks'; 25–30 'How to Choose Foods'; 31–8 'Methods of Cooking'; 39–40 'Time Table for Cooking'; 41 'Weights and Measures'; 42–4 'The Art of Carving'; 45–231 'Six Hundred and Fifteen Tested Recipes and a "Calendar of Dinners" by Marion Harris Neil'; 232 blank; 233 publ ad for *'The Whys of Cooking'* or *Questions Asked and Answered* by Janet McKenzie Hill, i.e., O363.1
CITATIONS: Ferguson/Fraser, p 232, illus col on p 35 of closed volume Simpson, p W17
COPIES: CIHM (66660) OH (R641.5 N317c CESH) OONL (TX715 N44 1917) *Private collection
NOTES: This is a deluxe, enlarged edition of O343.1, *The Story of Crisco: 250 Tested Recipes.*

O390.2 [copyright 1922]
—Form 81 / A calendar / of / dinners / with / 615 recipes / by / Marion Harris Neil
DESCRIPTION: 19.5 × 12.5 cm Pp [i–ii], [1–2] 3–231 Illus Cloth

CONTENTS: i endpaper recto; ii 'Copyright 1922 The Procter & Gamble Distributing Co. of Canada, Ltd. Hamilton, Canada // Price twenty-five cents'; 1 tp; 2 table of contents; 3–6 'Recipe Index'; 7 quotations; 8 introduction; 9–21 'The Story of Crisco'; 22 'Things to Remember ...'; 23 'Remember That – '; 24 'Hints to Young Cooks'; 25–30 'How to Choose Foods'; 31–8 'Methods of Cooking'; 39–40 'Time Table for Cooking'; 41 'Weights and Measures'; 42–4 'The Art of Carving'; 45–231 'Six Hundred and Fifteen Tested Recipes and a "Calendar of Dinners" by Marion Harris Neil'
COPIES: OHM (TX715 N45, missing)   OONL (TX703 N4)   OTNY (641.5 N)   OWTU (TX715 N4)   *Private collection

O390.3   [copyright 1923]
—Form C-81 / A calendar / of / dinners / with / 615 recipes / by / Marion Harris Neil
DESCRIPTION: 19.5 × 12.5 cm   Pp [i–ii], [1–2] 3–231 Illus   Cloth
CONTENTS: i endpaper recto; ii 'Copyright 1923 The Procter & Gamble Distributing Co. of Canada, Ltd. Hamilton, Canada // Price fifty cents The McDonald Printing Co. Cincinnati, Ohio'; 1 tp; 2 table of contents; 3–6 'Recipe Index'; 7 quotations; 8 introduction; 9–21 'The Story of Crisco'; 22 'Things to Remember ...'; 23 'Remember That – '; 24 'Hints to Young Cooks'; 25–30 'How to Choose Foods'; 31–8 'Methods of Cooking'; 39–40 'Time Table for Cooking'; 41 'Weights and Measures'; 42–4 'The Art of Carving'; 45–231 '615 Tested Recipes and a "Calendar of Dinners" by Marion Harris Neil'
CITATIONS: Barile, p 182
COPIES: SSWD   *OGU (UA s050 b15)

AMERICAN EDITIONS: The Story of Crisco, [Cincinnati: Procter and Gamble Co., copyright 1913], pp 231, 'Form 81' (United States: InU); A 'Calendar of Dinners' with 615 Recipes ... Including The Story of Crisco, [Cincinnati: McDonald Printing Co., c1913] (United States: DLC); [3rd ed.], [Cincinnati: McDonald Printing Co., c1914] (United States: DLC); 4th ed., Cincinnati: Procter and Gamble Co., copyright 1913, copyright 1914 (AHRMH); 7th ed., Cincinnati: Procter and Gamble Co., copyright 1913, copyright 1914 (Private collection); 8th ed., Cincinnati: Procter and Gamble Co., copyright 1913, copyright 1914 (OKITD); [8th ed.], [Richmond: L.H. Jenkins, printer, c1915] (United States: DLC); 9th ed., Cincinnati: Procter and Gamble, copyright 1915 (Private collection); 12th ed., Cincinnati: Procter and Gamble Co., 1916 (OBBM); 15th ed., Cincinnati: Procter and Gamble Co., c1920 (United

States: DLC); [19th ed., Cincinnati: Procter and Gamble Co., c1921] (United States: DLC); [20th ed., Cincinnati: Procter and Gamble Co., c1921] (United States: DLC).

O391.1   1917
[An edition of The Economy Cook Book, by Marion Harris Neil, Toronto: McClelland, Goodchild and Stewart, 1917, $1.50]
CITATIONS: BS, Vol. 33, No. 10 (October 1917), p 67   Spadoni/Donnelly No. 4329 ('Imprints Not Located')
NOTES: No corresponding American edition has been found, and the title is close to the same author's O425.1, Economical Cookery, published in 1918 in the United States, and in 1919 in Canada.

Purity Flour facts

For information about Western Canada Flour Mills and other cookbooks for Purity Flour, see O394.1, Warner, Miss E., Purity Flour Cook Book.

O392.1   nd [about 1917]
Purity Flour / facts / Some interesting information / on the world's most import- / ant food substance. A few / selections from the / latest publication / on the / economical preparation / of food. / The / Purity Flour Cook Book / and a variety of general and interesting / knowledge, of value to the housewife. / See last pages for Purity Flour Cook Book / coupons.
DESCRIPTION: 11.0 × 7.5 cm   Pp [1–3] 4–26 [27–30] Illus   Paper, with image on front of a woman holding a three-layer cake in her right hand and a loaf of bread in her left hand, and standing behind an oversize copy of Purity Flour Cook Book (O394.1) propped on sacks of flour; stapled
CONTENTS: 1 cover-title: 'Use Purity Flour for all Your Baking'; 2 'Distributed with the compliments of the Western Canada Flour Mills Co. Limited // Head office – Toronto ...'; 3 tp; 4–6 'Food Values'; 7–mid 25 'A Few Selections from the Purity Flour Cook Book'; bottom 25–30 'The Purity Flour Cook Book' [information about, and two coupons for ordering, 'this latest publication on the culinary art ... the work of Miss E. Warner ... only recently issued, ...']
COPIES: CIHM (9-92282)   *QMM (RBD ckbk 2101)
NOTES: The Purity Flour Cook Book by Miss E. Warner (O394.1), which is advertised on pp 25–30, was published in 1917. Purity Flour Facts was likely also published in 1917 because a stamped note on p 24

states, 'All premium plans cancelled by order of the Food Controller,' and the powers of the food controller were taken over by the Canada Food Board early in 1918, on 11 February. The printer, 'National Art Company, Toronto' (the same printer as for *The Purity Flour Cook Book*), is on the outside back face of the binding.

The thrift cook book

O393.1 1917
The thrift / cook book / Compiled by / a committee of the / War Relief Auxiliary / Price 50 cents / Net proceeds to be divided between the following: / The Brittany Hospitals Committee / The Serbian Aid Committee / The Blind Aid Committee / (for the National Library for the Blind) / Entered according to Act of Parliament, in the year one thousand nine hundred / and seventeen, by the Committee of the War Relief Auxiliary of Toronto, Canada, / in the office of the Minister of Agriculture.
DESCRIPTION: Tp illus of two male servants, each carrying a covered dish and walking toward the other, two potted trees behind each servant, and, in the centre, roast poultry on a platter
COPIES: *Private collection
NOTES: The volume has 59 pp. This copy is inscribed on the front face of the binding, in ink, 'Ethel M. Blake.'

Warner, Miss E.

The author of the cookbook has not been positively identified but she may be Miss Elizabeth A. Warner, who graduated in 1908 from the Macdonald Institute at the Ontario Agricultural College, in Guelph. In May 1912 she was working as an assistant flour tester with the Pillsbury Milling Co. in Minneapolis, Minnesota (report of the activities of Macdonald Institute graduates in O.A.C. Review Vol. 24, No. 8 (May 1912), p 468). Supporting the possibility that she was the cookbook's author are the facts that the cookbook was reviewed by staff of the Macdonald Institute and Elizabeth Warner had experience working in the flour industry. The Winnipeg city directory for 1917, the year that Purity Flour Cook Book was published, lists an Elizabeth Warner at 753 Wolseley, but no Elizabeth Warner for the years before or after. It is likely that she lived in Winnipeg at the time she compiled the book, in collaboration with the chemists in charge of the company's Winnipeg laboratory. A Miss Elizabeth Warner appears in a group

photograph of a 1934 Staff Conference of the Ontario Women's Institutes (Ambrose, p 118); further research may confirm that she is the same person as the 1908 graduate. More information about Elizabeth Warner, whose family lived in Coulson, Ontario, is in her Entrance Records at OGU (RE1 MAC A0003, Vols for 1903–5 and 1906–9, Registration Nos. 231 and 378). The 1901 Census gives her birth date, 20 January 1885.

Western Canada Flour Mills Co., the maker of Purity Flour, was formed in 1905, the result of a merger. Its new Winnipeg mill, which opened in 1906, was said to be the largest in Canada at the time (Monetary Times Vol. 40, No. 15 (12 October 1906), p 515). Head office was in Toronto. In 1945 the company became known as Purity Flour Mills Ltd. In 1961, Purity Flour Mills Ltd amalgamated with Toronto Elevators Ltd and Maple Leaf Milling Co. Ltd to create Maple Leaf Mills Ltd. In 1991, Maple Leaf Mills Ltd and Canada Packers Inc. merged to become Maple Leaf Foods, which no longer mills flour.

Miss Warner's Purity Flour Cook Book was the first cookbook promoting the use of Purity Flour. It was superseded by O504.1, The New Purity Flour Cook Book, in 1923, and then by O771.1, The Purity Cook-Book, in 1932.

For other cookbooks promoting the use of Purity Flour, see: O392.1, Purity Flour Facts; O543.1, For All Your Baking Use Purity Flour; O772.1, Recipes from One Friend to Another; Q222.1, Farine Purity, recettes anciennes et modernes; O931.1, Purity Flour Recipes and Menus; and O932.1, Purity Flour Tested Recipe Suggestions.

Western Canada Flour Mills also published a 12-page pamphlet entitled Holiday Recipes: Timely Suggestions for Special Occasions and Holidays, printed by the National Art Company, Toronto, nd [about 1920] (OGM (975.16.33)). On the inside front face of the paper binding, it is described as a 'supplement to the Purity Flour Cook Book,' i.e., O394.1. It contains recipes for Christmas Day, New Year's Day, Easter Season, Thanksgiving Day, Hallow Eve (31 October), St George's Day, St Andrew's Day, St Patrick's Day, St David's Day, Birthday, Weddings, and Picnics.

NFSG has a copy of the sixth edition, 'Special Newfoundland edition,' Purity 'Home-Helper' for 1950, Toronto: Purity Flour Mills Ltd, pp 32, of which only a few pages contain recipes and culinary information. NFSM has: 'Special Newfoundland edition,' Purity 'Home Helper' for 1947, Toronto: Western Canada Flour Mills, [1947]; fifth edition, 'Special Newfoundland edition,' Purity Home Helper for 1949, Toronto: Western Canada Flour Mills Co., 1949; Newfoundland edition, Purity Home Helper, 1951, [Toronto: Purity Flour Mills], 1951.

O394.1 [copyright 1917]
Purity Flour / cook book / A general purpose
publication on the culinary art, with / valuable
information and recipes on various methods / of
food preparation. Bread, rolls, buns, cakes, / pies,
fish, poultry, meats, vegetables, salads, / fruits,
pickles, sauces, beverages, / candies, preserves, etc.,
etc. / [symbol of Western Canada Flour Mills Co.] /
The text of this household reference book is the
work of / Miss E. Warner / in collaboration with
our two expert analytical chemists in charge / of our
Winnipeg laboratory. Miss Warner already has to /
her credit several notable publications on
food / preparation now in general circulation. /
The Purity Flour Cook Book carries a further /
recommendation to public favor in having been
reviewed and / approved by the teaching staff of
the / Domestic Science Department, Macdonald
Institute / National Art Company, Toronto.
DESCRIPTION: 22.0 × 20.0 cm   Pp [i–viii], 1–158, [i–ii]
5 pls col opp pp 8, 24, 32, 48, and 64; fp illus on pp 76–
7 of 'The Largest Mill of the Western Canada Flour
Mills Co., Limited ...'; a few illus   Paper, with hole
punched at top left corner for hanging
CONTENTS: i tp; ii untitled publisher's note and 'Copyright, Canada, 1917 Western Canada Flour Mills Company, Limited'; iii–iv 'Foreword'; v–vii 'Contents' [i.e.,
alphabetical index]; viii weights and measures; 1–158
text; i–ii six coupons for ordering the book at $0.20
per copy
CITATIONS: Driver 2001, All New Purity, inside front
cover   Driver 2001, Wellington County, p 95   Fergu-
son/Fraser, pp 65 and 233, illus col on p 35 of closed
volume   O'Neill (unpublished)
COPIES: ACG   ADTMP (641.5 W243)   AMHM
BCOM   BVMA   MBDHM   OAYM   OCOLM   OGU
(2 copies: CCC TX715.6 P87 1917, *UA s066
b03)   OKQ (F5012 1917 W281 Special Coll)
OMIHURM   OONL (TX715.6 W35 1917, 2 copies)
OWASRM   QMM (RBD ckbk 2099); Great Britain:
LB (not located)
NOTES: The 'Foreword' refers to 'two years ... taken to
prepare the Purity Flour Cook Book.'

The OGU copy in the Canadian Cookbook Collection has the colour plates opposite pp 8, 10, 20, 26,
and 32, and on the verso of each colour plate there is
a black-and-white advertisement for Western Canada
Flour Mills products; this copy also has an additional
leaf of advertisements for Western Canada Flour Mills
before the title-page, making a total of 10 unnumbered pages, [i–x], before the arabic sequence begins.

O'Neill's record for the book, based on copyright
material at the British Library, does not cite Warner as
the author.

O392.1, *Purity Flour Facts,* includes 'A Few Selections from the Purity Flour Cook Book' and coupons
for ordering copies of the book.

O394.2 facsimile ed., [copyright 1975]
—Purity Flour / Canadian / cook book / A general
purpose publication on the culinary art, with /
valuable information and recipes on various
methods / of food preparation. Bread, rolls, buns,
cakes, / pies, fish, poultry, meats, vegetables, salads,
/ fruits, pickles, sauces, beverages, / candies,
preserves, etc., etc. / Compiled by / Western
Canada Flour Mills Co. Ltd. / in 1917 / Equivalent
products may be substituted for brand names.
DESCRIPTION: 20.0 × 20.0 cm   Pp [i–vi], 1–158, [i–ii]
Fp illus on pp 76–7 of the largest mill of the Western
Canada Flour Mills Co. Ltd, illus   Paper, with image
on front of an aproned woman holding a plate of
baked goods
CONTENTS: i tp; ii introductory note and '© copyright
1975 and published by Coles Publishing Company
Limited Toronto – Canada'; iii–v table of contents; vi
'Weights and Measures'; 1–158 recipes and ads for
Western Canada Flour Mills Co. Ltd; i blank; ii 'Printed
in the United States'
CITATIONS: Carrière No. 174
COPIES: BWV   OONL (TX715 W43 1975, 2 copies)
*Private collection
NOTES: Miss Warner is not identified as the author.

Woodstock cook book

O395.1   1917
Woodstock / cook / book / 1917 [cover-title]
DESCRIPTION: 19.0 × 12.5 cm   Pp 1–176   Cloth
CONTENTS: 1–4 ads; 5 foreword signed 'The ladies of
St. Mary's Church'; 6 ad; 7–170 text and ads; 171 ad
and blank space for 'Special Recipes'; 172–3 blank for
'Special Recipes'; 174 ad; 175 index; 176 ads
COPIES: *OGU (UA s048 b17)

1917–18

Good things and how to cook them

*Three other cookbooks advertised Zam-Buk: O248.1,
O270.1, and O361.1.*

O396.1   nd [about 1917–18]
Good things / and / how to / cook / them / by /
"Chef." / Price 10¢ [cover-title]
DESCRIPTION: 20.0 × 12.5 cm   Pp 1–32   Illus on p 1

of a male chef Paper, with image on front of a male chef holding this cookbook; stapled
CONTENTS: Inside front face of binding 'A Valuable Book' [introductory text] signed C.E. Fulford Ltd, Toronto; 1–32 text; inside back face address of Zam-Buk Co., Dupont Street, Toronto, and 'Printed and published for C.E. Fulford, Limited'
COPIES: AEPMA MSM *Private collection
NOTES: The several undated editions are distinguished by the line endings of the first paragraph on p 1. In this edition, the line endings are: '... found useful in / ... lists of / ... unsuitable for / ... too / ... apply / ... cost of / ... working / ... easy to / ... good things / should be produced and enjoyed.' I have not determined the order of publication of all the editions. O396.1 was probably published toward the end of the First World War since there is a testimonial on p 4 from Captain Richard B. Nunn, who says that he has 'just returned from the Front where the men say [Zam-Buk] is invaluable.' Under 'A Valuable Book,' C.E. Fulford Ltd draws attention to the section of 'Invalid Cookery' and promotes the use of Zam-Buk herbal balm, Zam-Buk Soap, and Peps for coughs and colds.

O396.2 nd
—Good things / and / how to / cook / them / by / "Chef." / Price 10¢ [cover-title]
DESCRIPTION: 19.5 × 12.5 cm Pp 1–32 Illus on p 1 of a male chef Paper, with image on front of a male chef holding this cookbook; stapled
COPIES: *NSYHM Private collection
NOTES: The line endings of the first paragraph on p 1 are: '... found useful in / ... lists / ... unsuitable / ... good things / ... does not / ... The / ... reach of the / ... wholesome, and / ... good / things should be produced and enjoyed.' 'A Valuable Book,' on the inside front face of the binding, is signed the Zam-Buk Co.; 'Printed and published for C.E. Fulford, Limited' is on the inside back face. The private collector's copy has 'W.G. Smith, chemist & druggist // 139 Main St. East // Telephone 208. – Welland, Canada' stamped on the binding.

O396.3 nd
—[Cover-title of English face:] Good things / and / how to / cook / them / by / "Chef." / Price 10¢ [Cover-title of French face:] Bonnes choses / et / manière / de les / confectionner / par le / "Chef." / Prix 10¢
DESCRIPTION: 19.5 × 12.5 cm Pp English text: 1–16; French text: 1–16 Illus on p 1 of English and French texts of a male chef Paper, with same image on both

faces of a male chef holding this cookbook
CONTENTS: 1–16 English text; 1–16 French text
COPIES: QKB (87-74) *QSH (0430)
NOTES: The line endings of the first paragraph on p 1 of the English text are the same as in O396.2.

O396.4 nd
—[Cover-title of English face:] Good things / and / how to / cook / them / by / "Chef." / Price 10¢ [Cover-title of French face:] Bonnes choses / et / manière / de les / confectionner / par le / "Chef." / Prix 10¢
DESCRIPTION: 20.0 × 13.0 cm Pp English text: 1–16; French text: 1–16 Illus on p 1 of English and French texts of a male chef Paper, with same image on both faces of a male chef holding this cookbook; stapled
CONTENTS: 1–16 English text; 1–16 French text
COPIES: *Private collection
NOTES: The line endings of the first paragraph on p 1 of the English text are: '... found useful in every / ... lists of recipes / ... unsuitable for ordinary / ... too high for / ... apply to the / ... cost of none of / ... working man's purse. / ... wholesome, and easy to prepare, and / ... should be pro- / duced and enjoyed.'

This two-language edition does not include on p 1 information about 'Handy Weights and Measures'/ 'Poids et mesures d'accommodation' that appears on p 1 of the unilingual editions. 'Printed and published for C.E. Fulford, Limited' is printed opposite p 1 of the English text; 'Imprimé et publié pour C.E. Fulford, Limited' is opposite p 1 of the French text.

O396.5 nd
—Good things / and / how to / cook / them / by / "Chef." / Price 10¢ [cover-title]
DESCRIPTION: 20.0 × 12.5 cm Pp 1–32 Illus on p 1 of a male chef Paper, with image on front of a male chef holding this cookbook; stapled
CONTENTS: 1–32 text
COPIES: OGU (UA s070 b68) QMM (RBD ckbk 1441b) *Private collection
NOTES: The line endings of the first paragraph on p 1 are the same as for the English text of O396.4. 'A Valuable Book' on the inside front face of the binding is signed the Zam-Buk Co. 'Printed and published for C.E. Fulford, Limited' is on the inside back face of the binding. The OGU copy lacks its binding.

O396.6 nd [early 1920s]
—Good things / and / how to / cook / them / by / "Chef." / Price 10¢ [cover-title]
DESCRIPTION: 20.0 × 12.5 cm Pp 1–32 Illus on p 1

of a male chef   Paper, with image on front of a male chef holding this cookbook; stapled

CONTENTS: 1–32 text

COPIES: ACG AEUCHV AMHM ARDA (2 copies) BDUCVM BVIPM CIHM (79459) MCM OFERWM (A1983.8) OKITJS (999.24.5) OONL (TX715 Z36 1910za)   OTMCL (641.5971 H39 No. 8) OTNY (uncat)   OTUTF (uncat patent medicine) OWTU (F17104) QMM (RBD ckbk 1441a)   *Private collection

NOTES: The line endings of the first paragraph on p 1 are: '... found useful in / ... lists / ... unsuitable / ... good things / ... does not / ... The / ... reach of the / ... wholesome, / ... spread of / good things should be produced and enjoyed.' This edition was published after the First World War, likely in the early 1920s since there is an advertisement on p 13 featuring an illustration of Mr J. Gill and Mr Stevens, who took a 17,000-mile motorcycle adventure from England to Australia. The advertisement refers to advice from an 'R.A.F. officer from Iraq.' 'A Valuable Book' on the inside front face of the binding is signed the Zam-Buk Co., 310 Dupont Street, Toronto.

The OFERWM and OKITJS copies lack their bindings. The OFERWM copy also lacks pp 31–2.

OOWM has a copy (984.91.4) where the line endings of the first paragraph on p 1 are as described above; however, the museum reports that the book has only 16 pages.

O396.7   nd

—Bonnes choses / et / manière / de les / confectionner / par le / "Chef." / Prix 10¢ [cover-title]

DESCRIPTION: 20.0 × 12.5 cm   Pp 1–32   Illus on p 1 of a male chef   Paper, with image on front of a chef holding the English-language edition of this cookbook; stapled

CONTENTS: Inside front face of binding 'Un livre précieux' signed the Zam-Buk Co., 310 rue Dupont, Toronto; 1–30 text and publ ads; 31–2 publ ads

COPIES: CIHM (81741)   *OONL (TX715 B648)

Klim cook book

See O374.1 for information about Canadian Milk Products Ltd and the titles of other cookbooks published by the company. O913.1, Easy Recipes for Camp and Kitchen, *and O1171.1,* Skillet Skills for Camp and Cottage, *are later Klim recipe collections published by Borden Co. Ltd.*

O397.1   nd [about 1917–18]

Klim / Read it backward / For all uses / where milk is needed / cook book / Canadian / Milk Products Limited / 10–12 William St., Toronto [cover-title]

DESCRIPTION: 14.0 × 7.5 cm   Pp 1–30   Illus   Paper, with all-over blue chevron pattern; stapled

CONTENTS: 1 'Introduction'; 2 'Klim Recipes' [introductory information about measuring and methods]; 3–30 recipes using Klim as an ingredient

COPIES: *Private collection

NOTES: This booklet has a distinctive design: the binding, text, and illustrations are all printed in blue; and the binding's chevron pattern is used in the border around each text page. Unusually, the folios on the recto pages are even numbers, and the folios on the verso pages, odd numbers; the pagination begins on the inside front face of the binding.

Page 1 declares that Klim is guaranteed not to have any additives as 'proved by Government Bulletin of Inland Revenue Department No. 257' (a copy of this bulletin, dated [1913?], is at OOCIHM). Brands sold by Canadian Milk Products Ltd are listed on the outside back face of the binding: Klim, Milkstock, Trumilk, Modified Milk Powder (C.M.P.), Sweet Whey Powder (C.M.P.), and Trucream.

The company's address, 10–12 William Street, indicates that *Klim Cook Book* was published about 1917–18, the only two years for this address in Toronto directories (before 1917 the company was at 106 Bay Street; after 1918, it was at 10–12 St Patrick). The illustration on p 20 depicts a stove with an old-style range shape, rather than a more modern profile, and the recipes specify 'hot' or 'moderate' temperatures, rather than degrees Fahrenheit.

1918

Aunt Hanna's cook book

O398.1   nd [about 1918]

A Recipe for a Happy Life. / Take a large quantity of Cheerfulness and let it simmer without / stopping. Put with it a brimming basinful of Kindness, then add a full / measure of Thought for Other People. Mix into these a piling table- / spoonful of Sympathy. Flavor with essence of Charity. Stir well / together, and then carefully strain off any grains of Selfishness. Let / the whole be served with Love sauce, and Fruit of the Spirit. / Aunt Hanna's / cook book / compiled by the ladies of Ward 2 Patriotic Association / of Toronto. / Under the patronage of – / Lady Hendry, / Lady Hearst, / Lady Kemp, / Mrs. W.D. McPherson, / Mrs. R.A. Pyne, / Mrs. A.E. Gooderham, / Mrs. Charles Sheard, / Mrs. Mark H. Irish. [*sic*] / Mrs. E.B. Ryckman, / Mrs. H.C. Scholfield, [*sic*] / Proceeds to complete payment on motor ambulance purchased for / the Base Hospital and to aid in other / patriotic work.

DESCRIPTION: 23.5 × 15.5 cm   Pp 1–116   [$0.50, on binding]   Paper, with image on front of a brown beaver on a red-and-green maple leaf; stapled

CONTENTS: Inside front face of binding 'Index' [i.e., alphabetical list of section headings]; 1–2 ads; 3 tp; 4 ad; 5 'Foreword' signed the Committee; 6 ads; 7–113 text, with most recipes credited with the contributor's name, and ads; 114–16 ads

COPIES: *Private collection

NOTES: The cover-title of this First World War cookbook is 'Aunt Hanna's War-Time and Peace-Time Recipes.' *Aunt Hanna's Cook Book* was likely published about 1918: An advertisement on p 58 for Purity Flour refers to O394.1, *Purity Flour Cook Book*, published in 1917. The 'Foreword' states that the book is directed at those of 'average training and capabilities.' Page 5 carries the following exhortation to economy: 'Extravagance – always a folly – in these days becomes a crime; Thrift – always a virtue – in these days becomes a national duty.' This text is quoted (with credit to this book) in a Second World War cookbook, O1032.1, *The Village Cook Book*.

Canada, Canada Food Board

The Canada Food Board, which took over the powers of the food controller, existed for just over a year. It was created on 11 February 1918 and dissolved on 19 March 1919, when the Canadian Trade Commission took its place. In 1918, the Food Board published the 8-page Potatoes and How to Cook Them *(OGU, OONL) and the 4-page* Recipes for Jam-Making *(CIHM, OGU, OONL), concurrent with the following: O399.1,* Bread Recipes; *O401.1,* Fish Recipes; *O402.1,* Fruit and Vegetables: Canning, Drying, Storing; *O403.1,* Vegetable Recipes; *and probably the undated O400.1,* Fancy Meats in Newest Dishes.

O399.1   [1918]

Bread / recipes / which save food / for our soldiers / and allies [cover-title]

DESCRIPTION: 19.0 × 13.5 cm   Pp [1–2] 3–16   Paper, with image on front of a loaf of bread, sack of pota-

toes, and tins of barley flour, corn flour, and oatmeal; stapled

CONTENTS: Inside front face of binding 'Table of Equivalents'; 1 'Help to Save Wheat by Using Other Available Cereals' signed chairman, Canada Food Board, Ottawa, June 1918; 2 'Index' [i.e., table of contents]; 3–13 'Yeast and Quick Breads'; 14–16 'Miscellaneous Recipes'; inside back face list of uniform booklets available for $0.05 ('1. Fruit and Vegetables: Canning Drying, Storing. 2. Fish Recipes. 3. Vegetable Recipes. 4. Bread Recipes.') and 'Designed, engraved and printed by the Herald Press and Advertising Agency Montreal and Toronto'

CITATIONS: Cooke 2002, p 234   Golick, p 102 (note 19)

COPIES: MAUAM   OTMCL (641.5971 H39 No. 2) *QMM (RBD ckbk 1407); United States: DLC (TX769 C3)

O399.2   [1918]

—Recettes pour le / pain / qui sauvent / la nourriture / pour nos soldats / et nos alliés [cover-title]

DESCRIPTION: 19.0 × 13.5 cm   Pp [1–2] 3–16   Paper, with image on front of a loaf of bread, sack of potatoes, and tins of barley flour, corn flour, and oatmeal; stapled

CONTENTS: Inside front face of binding 'Table d'équivalents'; 1 'Contribuez à ménager le blé en vous servant d'autres céréales disponibles' signed président, Commission des vivres du Canada, Ottawa, June 1918; 2 'Index' [i.e., table of contents]; 3 'Notes explicatives'; 4–16 recipes

COPIES: OONL (COP.CA.2.1999-2550)   *Private collection

NOTES: No printer is named in the French-language edition.

O400.1   nd [about 1918]

Fancy meats / in newest / dishes

DESCRIPTION: 19.0 × 12.5 cm   Pp [1–3] 4–31   Illus of fancy meats   Paper, with image on front of six fancy meats; stapled

CONTENTS: 1 tp; 2 blank; 3–9 introductory text; 10–31 recipes grouped under headings for 'Brains,' 'Feet,' 'Fries,' 'Heads,' 'Hearts,' 'Kidneys,' 'Liver,' 'Lips, Ears and Tails,' 'Melts,' 'Ox Tails,' 'Sweetbreads,' 'Tongue,' 'Tripe,' and 'Miscellaneous'

COPIES: CIHM (9-01822)   OONL (COP.CA.2.1999-2052)   OTU (Gov. Doc. Can. F Gerstein, not located)   QMM (RBD ckbk 1405)   *Private collection

NOTES: Printed on the front face of the binding is the symbol for the Canada Food Board and 'Distributed by P. Burns & Company Limited' (the Calgary meat-packer; see A31.1). Another collector's copy has 'With the compliments of the Canada Food Board // Ottawa, Ont.' in place of the distributor Burns and Co. Another collector's copy has 'Distributed by Armour & Company' instead of Burns; according to information on the back face of the binding, Armour's Canadian office and plant were in Hamilton, Ontario, and its branches in Montreal, Toronto, Soo (i.e., Sault Ste Marie), and Sydney, Nova Scotia. Yet another collector's copy was distributed by Swift Canadian Co. Ltd, Toronto, Winnipeg, and Edmonton.

The book is undated, but it was published no earlier than 11 February 1918, when the Canada Food Board was created, and probably no later than the end of the First World War. The unnamed writer of the introductory text comments on p 4: 'There has been nothing sudden or dramatic about the dietetic changes that have taken place in Canada since war broke out. They have been gradual, almost imperceptible. The groundwork of food control has been the saving of meat, wheat, sugar and fats ... we are reverting inevitably from the extravagant habits of recent years to the thrifty ways of our grandmothers.' The text under 'By-products' on p 9 explains how the less desirable cuts of meat were promoted during wartime: 'There is protection for the housewife against the prices of the minor portions of meat going up, in the appointment of fair price list committees. It is for each municipality to see that meat by-products are popularized and that the prices are kept to a satisfactory scale. Packers are co-operating heartily with the Canada Food Board in bringing before the people the necessity of the purchase of these by-products ...'

O401.1 [1918]
Fish / recipes / Canadian fish and / how to cook them / [below image:] Design by courtesy of Forest and Stream [cover-title]
DESCRIPTION: 19.0 × 13.5 cm   Pp [1–4] 5–24   Illus of types of fish   [$0.05, on binding]   Paper, with image on front of a jumping fish on a line; stapled
CONTENTS: 1 'Eat More Fish' signed chairman, Canada Food Board, Ottawa, June 1918; 2 'Be Patriotic – Eat More Fish'; 3 'Canada Must Catch More Fish'; 4 index; 5 'Food Values of Fish'; 6 'Preparation of Fish'; 7 'Methods of Cooking'; top 8 'Best Methods of Cooking Different Fish'; mid 8–mid 17 'Canada's Chief Sea Fish'; mid 17–mid 18 'Canadian Shell Fish'; mid 18–21 'Canadian Fresh-Water Fish'; 22–mid 23 'General Sea Food Recipes'; mid 23–24 'Delicious Sauces for Fish'; inside back face of binding list of books uni-

form with *Fish Recipes* and 'Designed, engraved and printed by the Herald Press and Advertising Agency Montreal and Toronto'
CITATIONS: *Canadian Food Bulletin,* No. 20 (November 1918), p 20, illus
COPIES: AEPRAC   OONL (COP.CA.2.1999-2546) OTMCL (641.5971 H39 No. 5)   *Bookseller's stock
NOTES: The bookseller's copy has 'Benwell Fish Co.' stamped on the front face of the binding, and 'Compliments. Benwell Fish Co.' stamped on the back.

See also O377.1, Canada, Food Controller for Canada, *Eat More Fish,* for an earlier edition of 1917, and O467.1, for an edition of 1921 from the Department of Marine and Fisheries.

O401.2 [1918]
—Poissons / canadiens / et comment les apprêter / [below image:] Dessin dû à la gracieuseté de Forest & Stream [cover-title]
DESCRIPTION: 19.0 × 13.5 cm   Pp [1–4] 5–24   Illus of types of fish   Paper, with image on front of a jumping fish on a line; stapled
CONTENTS: 1 'Mangeons plus de poisson' signed président, Commission des vivres du Canada, Ottawa, June 1918; 2 'Soyez patriote – mangez plus de poisson'; 3 'Le Canada doit développer ses pêcheries'; 4 'Index' [i.e., table of contents]; 5 'Valeur nutritive du poisson'; 6–7 'Préparation du poisson'; 8–mid 18 'Meilleure méthode de faire cuire les différentes sortes de poisson'; mid 18–21 'Poissons canadiens d'eau douce'; 22–4 'Recettes diverses'
COPIES: OONL (COP.CA.2.1999-2549)   *Private collection

O402.1 [1918]
Fruit and / vegetables / canning / drying / storing [cover-title]
DESCRIPTION: 19.0 × 13.5 cm   Pp [1–2] 3–32   Illus [$0.05, on p 32]   Paper, with still-life on front of fruit and vegetables; stapled
CONTENTS: Inside front face of binding diagram of 'Steps in the Canning Process'; 1 'Save the Perishable Foods' signed chairman, Canada Food Board, Ottawa, June 1918; 2 table of contents; top–mid 3 'Home Canning Calendar'; bottom 3–mid 4 'Community Canning Calendar'; mid 4–mid 5 'Successful Canning'; mid 5–7 'Community Canning'; 8–20 'Part I. Canning in the Home'; 21–mid 24 'Part II. Drying Fruits and Vegetables'; bottom 24–32 'Part III. Winter Storage of Vegetables and Fruits' and at bottom p 32, list of books uniform with *Fruit and Vegetables;* inside back face '... Herald Press and Adv[ertising Agency]

Montreal and [Toronto]' [information partly cut off BKOM copy, but known from OTMCL copy]
COPIES: *BKOM   OTMCL (641.5971 H39 No. 43) QMM (RBD ckbk 1406); United States: DLC (TX601 G25)
NOTES: See also O376.1, Canada, Food Controller for Canada, *Can, Dry and Store for Victory*, an earlier edition of about 1917, and O495.1, Canada, Department of Agriculture, for later editions of the same title.

O402.2 [1918]
—[An edition of *Fruits et légumes: mise en conserves, dessiccation, mise en réserve*, Ottawa: Commission des vivres du Canada, [1918], pp 32]
CITATIONS: BouquinsCat 212, No. 387

O403.1 [1918]
Vegetable / recipes [cover-title]
DESCRIPTION: 19.0 × 13.5 cm   Pp [1–2] 3–16   Illus on inside front face of binding of 'Home-dried Vegetables' [$0.05, on binding]   Paper, with still-life on front of vegetables; stapled
CONTENTS: 1 'How Housewives Can Fulfill Work of the War Gardeners' signed chairman, Canada Food Board, Ottawa, June 1918; 2 'Index' [i.e., table of contents]; 3–16 'Vegetable Recipes // How to Make Appetizing and Nourishing Dishes Which Help to Save Essential Food for Our Soldiers and Allies'; inside back face of binding list of books uniform with *Vegetable Recipes* and 'Designed, engraved and printed by the Herald Press and Advertising Agency Montreal and Toronto'
COPIES: BPAM   BVAA   CIHM (9-01821)   MAUAM   MWPA   OGU (CCC CA1 DA845 18V26)   OONL (COP.CA.2.1999-2804)   OTMCL (641.5971 H39 No. 44) QMM (RBD ckbk 1409) *Private collection; United States: DLC (TX801 C3)
NOTES: The chairman states on p 1: 'Not only has farm production been largely augmented, but tens of thousands of war gardens and hundreds of thousands of war gardeners in all parts of the Dominion promise an important contribution to the National food supply ... It rests with the housewife to complete the work of our war gardeners by utilizing to the utmost this year's vegetable production.' The recipes are arranged alphabetically by vegetable, from asparagus to turnips, except for potato recipes, which begin the book 'because of the very great relative importance of this vegetable ...' (p 3). Following the recipes for turnips are sections for 'Greens' (spinach, beet tops, Swiss chard), 'Miscellaneous Vegetables,' 'Use of Dried Products,' and 'Individual Recipes.'

O403.2 [1918]
—Recettes pour / legumes [cover-title]
DESCRIPTION: 19.0 × 14.0 cm   Pp [1–2] 3–16   Paper, with still-life on front of vegetables; stapled
CONTENTS: Inside front face of binding illus of 'Légumes sechés à domicile'; 1 'Comment les ménagères peuvent compléter l'oeuvre des jardiniers de guerre' signed Commission des vivres du Canada, Ottawa, June 1918; 2 'Index' [i.e., table of contents]; 3–16 'Recettes pour légumes'
CITATIONS: BouquinsCat 212, No. 388
COPIES: OONL (COP.CA.2.1999-2548)   *Private collection
NOTES: No printer is named in the French-language edition.

Canada, Department of Agriculture

For other cookbooks published by the Department of Agriculture, see the following, all under Canada, Department of Agriculture: O495.1, Fruit and Vegetables: Canning, Drying, Storing; O496.1, Pommes cultivées au Canada; O1068.1, Wartime Canning: Jams and Jellies; O1069.1, Wartime Sugar Savers; O1087.1, Wartime Home Canning of Fruits and Vegetables; O1093.1, Recipe Book for Enjoying Canadian Apples; O1150.1, Cheese Dishes; O1151.1, Home Canning of Fruits and Vegetables; and O1205.1, Desserts You'll Like. The following were also published by the Department of Agriculture, but attributed to individual authors: O424.1, MacFarlane, Miss Margaret White, Preservation of Fruits and Vegetables for Home Use; O477.1, Campbell, Miss Helen Gertrude, Why and How to Use Cheese; O478.1, Campbell, Miss Helen Gertrude, Why and How to Use Milk; O599.1, Hamilton, Miss Ethel Watchorn, Preserving Fruits and Vegetables in the Home; O665.1, Elliot, Miss Edith L., Canadian Vegetables for Every Day; O666.1, Elliot, Miss Edith L., Canned Fruits and Vegetables for Variety in Everyday Meals; O676.1, Pepper, Miss Laura Christine, Milk Desserts; O679.1, Semple, Frank G., Beef: How to Choose and Cook It; O721.1, Elliot, Miss Edith L., Jams, Jellies, and Pickles; O770.1, Pepper, Miss Laura Christine, School Lunches; O819.1, Gooderham, Charles Benjamin, and Miss Mary Lilian Heeney, Honey and Some of the Ways It May Be Used; O926.1, Pepper, Miss Laura Christine, Cheese for Better Meals; O953.1, Pepper, Miss Laura Christine, Milk: The Food of Foods; and O1041.1, Atkinson, Francis Edward, and C.C. Strachan, Home Processing of Fruits and Vegetables. For the many Department of Agriculture recipe pamphlets too small to be included in this bibliography, see Ag 1867–1974.

O404.1 nd [1918]

160 / apple recipes / Issued by the Fruit Branch / Department of Agriculture / Ottawa / 46064–1

DESCRIPTION: 18.0 × 11.5 cm Pp [1–2] 3–40 Paper, with image on front of a red apple; stapled

CONTENTS: 1 tp; 2 blank; 3 'King Apple' by Minna Irving [a poem]; top 4 'Apple Recipes' [i.e., introductory text]; mid 4–top 5 'About the Apple'; mid–bottom 5 'Use Apples in Their Season'; 6–40 'Recipes'

CITATIONS: Ag 1867–1974, p 179

COPIES: *Private collection

NOTES: The cover-title is 'Eat Canadian Apples // 160 Apple Recipes.' The booklet is undated, but Ag 1867–1974 dates it 1918 and the introductory text on p 4 confirms that it was published during the First World War: 'The object in presenting this pamphlet to the consumers of Canada at this time is to awaken in their minds the great necessity of not only conserving food for the Allies in their great world struggle for liberty, but also to emphasize the great value of the apple as an article of food. Those who make a liberal use of apples will serve a dual purpose of saving for shipment overseas such articles of food as are fit for that purpose, and at the same time furnish a useful and valuable food for the household.' The introductory text states that the 'recipes have been tested by Miss L. Gertrude MacKay, Ph.G., B.S.B.A., Department of Domestic Economy, Washington, U.S.A.' The recipes in *160 Recipes* are reprinted from O323.1, MacKay, Miss Lucy Gertrude, *Two Hundred and Nine Recipes*, Ottawa: Department of Trade and Commerce, nd [about 1914], which itself may be an edition of MacKay's 1913 book, *Two Hundred and Nine Ways of Preparing the Apple ...*, Spokane: Shaw and Borden Co., printers, [c1913] (United States: DLC).

Some of the recipes in *160 Apple Recipes* were reprinted by the Fruit Branch in a later publication: O496.1, *Pommes cultivées au Canada*, 1923, and O496.2, *Canadian Grown Apples*, first English edition, 1924 (for example, Baked Apples, Creole Style on p 24 and Apples à la parisienne on p 13).

No copy of *160 Apple Recipes* was found at OOAG.

Cook book of St Quentin Chapter of I.O.D.E.

O405.1 nd [about 1918]

Cook book / of / St. Quentin Chapter / of / I.O.D.E.

DESCRIPTION: 23.0 × 15.0 cm Pp [1–11] 12–88, [i–viii] Paper, with image on front of the Union Jack; stapled

CONTENTS: 1–8 ads; 9 tp; 10 small decorative device of a pudding(?) flanked by two candelabra; 11–84 'Selected Recipes' credited with the name of the contributor and a few ads; 85–6 'Useful Hints'; 87 'Table of Weights and Measures'; 88 'Vegetables' (in two parts: 'Time Table for Cooking Vegetables in Water' and 'General Rules'); i–viii ads

COPIES: OGU (CCC TX715.6 S4328) *Private collection

NOTES: The St Quentin Chapter was located in Waterloo, Ontario. The printer, 'Chronicle-Telegraph Presses,' is on the outside back face of the binding. Advertisements indicate that the cookbook was published during the First World War. The advertisement on p 7 for Dietrich's Sanitary Bakery, for example, says: 'War more than doubles cost of home-made bread // The great conflict now raging in Europe is sending foodstuffs soaring.' The advertisement on p 8 for Toronto's Harris Abattoir Co. Ltd reminds the reader, 'Watchful care in the kitchen will help win the war.' The advertisement on p iii for Waterloo's Dominion Life Assurance Co. offers 'Evidence from the Front.' An advertisement on p 8 for Molsons Bank pinpoints the year of publication: It refers to 'Waterloo Branch in existance [sic] 37 years'; since Molsons Bank first opened a branch in Waterloo, in the Devitt Block, in March 1881 (see vertical file, local history room, OWT), the cookbook was published in 1918 (1881 + 37 years).

The recipes in *Cook Book of St Quentin Chapter of I.O.D.E.* were reprinted in O677.1, *Selected Recipes*, published by the Ontario Equitable Life and Accident Insurance Co., Waterloo, with an acknowledgment to the original cookbook and with the contributors of the recipes still credited.

The OGU copy is in poor condition and lacks the binding.

Evans, Mary Elizabeth
(Mrs Henry D. Sharpe)

This American author wrote My Candy Secrets, *New York: Frederick A. Stokes Co., [copyright 1919] (United States: DLC, InU). Concerning her family life, the start of her candy business, and her contribution to the war effort, see* Biographical Cyclopaedia, *Vol. 1, pp 252–4.*

O406.1 [copyright 1918]

Mary Elizabeth's / war time recipes / containing many simple but excellent recipes, for / wheatless cakes and bread, meatless dishes, sugar- / less candies, delicious war time desserts, and / many other delectable "economy" dishes / by / Mary

Elizabeth / With twenty-one illustrations / Toronto / McClelland, Goodchild & Stewart, Ltd. / publishers
DESCRIPTION: 19.0 × 12.5 cm   Pp [iii–iv] v–x [xi–xii], [1–2] 3–164   11 pls incl frontis portrait of author   Cloth
CONTENTS: iii tp; iv 'Copyright, 1918, by Mary Elizabeth Evans' and 'Made in the U.S.A.'; v–vi author's preface dated May 1918; vii–x table of contents; xi list of illustrations; xii blank; 1–18 I, 'Sugarless Candies'; 19–32 II, 'Soups'; 33–74 III, 'Meatless Recipes'; 75–92 IV, 'Salads in War Time'; 93–128 V, 'Wheatless Cakes, Breads and Pies'; 129–50 VI, 'War Time Desserts'; 151–64 VII, 'Beverages, Relishes, etc.'
CITATIONS: Bitting, p 149   Spadoni/Donnelly No. 386A
COPIES: *OGU (UA s048 b07); United States: DLC (TX715 M3734 1918)
NOTES: 'Stokes' is printed on the spine. According to Spadoni/Donnelly, the Canadian edition was made from the sheets of the Frederick A. Stokes Co. edition. Evans owned a food business. In the preface she comments, with regard to the soldiers' need for provisions, '... I then and there determined that I would sell and serve in my shops only foods that entirely conformed to the requirements of the United States Food Administration.'
    Cagle/Stafford No. 239 (the 1918 American edition at InU) refers to this Canadian edition.

AMERICAN EDITIONS: New York: Frederick A. Stokes Co., 1918 (United States: DLC, InU).

Helpful hints for housekeepers 1918

See O263.1 for information about the company and other issues of Helpful Hints for Housekeepers.

O407.1   1918
[Volume VIII of *Helpful Hints for Housekeepers,* Toronto: Dodds Medicine Co. Ltd, 1918]
COPIES: United States: Private collection

Hiller, Mrs Elizabeth O.

See Q80.1 for information about this American author.

O408.1   [copyright 1918]
The / corn / cook book / (War edition) / Compiled and arranged by / Elizabeth O. Hiller / formerly Principal of the Chicago Domestic/ Science Training

School, lecturer / on Household Economics / Published by / P.F. Volland Company / New York Chicago Toronto
DESCRIPTION: Cloth, with image on front of a cob of corn
CITATIONS: Bitting, p 230
COPIES: CIHM (9-91120)   OOAG; United States: DLC (TX809 M2 H6 1918)   NNNAM (S.21.B)
NOTES: Of the three places of publication printed on the title-page, Chicago is in the largest typesize. 'Copyright, 1918, P.F. Volland Company Chicago (All rights reserved)' is on the title-page verso. In the 'Preface,' which she signs Mrs Elizabeth O. Hiller, the author states: '"Save the wheat" is the call that has been sent out from Washington to the housekeepers of America. In response to this urgent plea, this new War Edition of the Corn Cook Book containing 200 recipes has been compiled, ...' The volume has 127 pp.

AMERICAN EDITIONS: Chicago: Rogerson Press, 1907 (United States: DLC).

The household helper

For information about McClary's and its cookbooks, see O162.1.

O409.1   nd [about 1918]
The household / helper / and catalogue of Florence / Automatic Oil Stoves / Recipes / and practical suggestions / for the home / Published by / McClary's / London / Toronto Montreal St. John, N.B., Hamilton Winnipeg / Vancouver Calgary Edmonton Saskatoon [cover-title]
DESCRIPTION: 19.5 × 12.5 cm   Pp [1] 2–32   Illus blue-and-black and illus of McClary Florence products, illus on p 26 of cuts of beef, illus on inside back face of binding of oil stove accessories   Paper; previously stapled, now sewn by library
CONTENTS: 1 'The Household Helper' signed McClary's and 'Table of Contents'; 2–25 'Recipes' and illus of Florence products; 26 'Parts of Beef to Select, and Their Uses'; 27 'Household Hints' and 'Some Ways to Remove Stains'; 28–30 'Household Remedies'; 31–2 'Florence Oil Cook Stoves'
COPIES: *OLU (TX657 S8 M325 1900z)
NOTES: The text on p 1 says that one of the messages of the book is 'to tell [the modern housewife] something about the Florence Automatic Wickless, Blue Flame Oil Cook Stove, the Success Asbestos-Lined Oven, and the Florence Oil Heater, ...' In the May 1918 issue of *Western Home Monthly*, McClary's ad-

vertised its Florence oil cookstove and a 'Booklet free.' The appearance of *The Household Helper* is consistent with publication in 1918.

Household science in rural schools

See also O364.1 in the same series.

O410.1 [copyright 1918]
Ontario / Teachers' Manuals / Household science / in / rural schools / Authorized by the Minister of Education / Toronto / William Briggs
DESCRIPTION: 19.0 × 12.0 cm   Pp [i–ii] iii–ix [x], 1–222   Illus   [$0.40, on binding]   Cloth
CONTENTS: i tp; ii 'Copyright, Canada, 1918, by the Minister of Education for Ontario'; iii–vi 'Contents'; vii–ix 'Preface'; x blank; 1–222 text
COPIES: CIHM (75794)   *OFERWM (A1980.85.4)   OONL (TX167 H65, 2 copies)
NOTES: According to the 'Preface,' the manual was published 'for the purpose of encouraging the introduction and furthering the progress of Household Science in the rural schools of [Ontario].' At the time of publication there were 903 urban and 5,697 rural schools, the latter having 45.87% of the school population. The 'Preface' suggests not only that the hot noon-day lunch is a convenient means of approaching the teaching of cookery in rural schools, but that such a meal 'greatly increases the efficiency of the pupil.' The text begins with 'Three Short Courses in Home-Making,' then follow 'Twenty Lessons in the Care of the Home,' 'Twenty Lessons in Cooking,' 'Twenty Lessons in Sewing,' 'Household Science Equipment,' 'The Rural School Lunch,' 'Serving a Hot Dish,' 'Recipes Suitable for the Rural School Lunch,' 'Household Science without School Equipment,' 'The Fireless Cooker,' 'Use of the Fireless Cooker in the Preparation of Lunches,' and 'Special Grants for Rural and Village Schools.'
NOTES: This book is not cited in Wallace. The OFERWM copy is inscribed on the front endpaper, in ink, 'Eunice E. Graham.'

O410.2 [2nd printing, 1921]
—Ontario / Teachers' Manuals / Household science / in / rural schools / Authorized by the Minister of Education / Toronto / The Ryerson Press
DESCRIPTION: 19.0 × 12.0 cm   Pp [i–ii] iii–ix [x], 1–222   43 numbered illus   [$0.40, on binding]   Cloth
CONTENTS: i tp; ii 'Copyrighted, Canada, 1918, by the Minister of Education for Ontario // Second print-ing, 1921.'; iii–vi table of contents; vii–ix preface; x blank; 1–222 text
COPIES: *Private collection

O410.3 [3rd printing, 1932]
—Ontario / Teachers' Manuals / Household science / in / rural schools / Authorized by the Minister of Education / Toronto / The Ryerson Press
DESCRIPTION: 19.0 × 12.0 cm   Pp [i–ii] iii–ix [x], 1–222   43 numbered illus   [$0.40, on binding]   Cloth
CONTENTS: i tp; ii 'Copyrighted, Canada, 1918, by the Minister of Education for Ontario // Second print-ing, 1921. Third printing, 1932.'; iii–vi 'Contents'; vii–ix 'Preface'; x blank; 1–222 text
COPIES: *OGU (CCC CA2ON DE 18H57)

The Metropolitan Life cook book

For information about Metropolitan Life Insurance Co. and its publications, see O373.1.

O411.1   1918
The / Metropolitan Life / cook book / Printed and distributed by the / Metropolitan Life Insurance Company / for the use of its industrial policy-holders / 1918
DESCRIPTION: 19.5 × 13.5 cm   Pp [1–2] [3–4 missing] 5–64   Paper, with red-and-green printing on front
CONTENTS: 1 tp; 2 'Contents'; 3–4 missing, but index indicates 'Our Daily Meals' and 'The Day's Food' on p 3, and 'Care of Food Materials' and 'Selection and Preparation of Food' on p 4; 5–62 text; 63–4 index
CITATIONS: Ferguson/Fraser, p 232, illus col on p 35 of closed volume   Neering, p 95
COPIES: AEUCHV (IC 2001.10.10)   ARDA   BBVM   BSORM   BVAMM   CIHM (75255)   MCM   MSOHM   NBFKL   NSPHM   OGU (CCC TX715.6 M477 1918)   OKELWM   OKQ (F5012 1918 M594)   OMAHM (993.16.12)   OMIHURM   OMMM   OONL (TX715 M578)   OTMCL (641.5971 M26 1918)   OTNY (uncat)   *Private collection
NOTES: The cover-title is 'Metropolitan Cook Book.' No place of publication is recorded and the Canadian head office was set up only in 1924; however, the French-language 1918 edition was printed in Canada and the many extant copies of the 1918 English-language edition in Canadian libraries and private collections suggest that it was widely distributed in Canada.

O411.2 1918

—Manuel de cuisine / de la / Compagnie d'assurance vie / "Metropolitan Life" / Imprimé et distribué par la / Metropolitan Life Insurance Company / pour l'usage des détenteurs de polices industrielles / 1918

DESCRIPTION: 19.5 × 13.5 cm   Pp [1–2] 3–64   Paper, with red-and-green printing on front; stapled, and with hole punched at top left corner, through which runs a string for hanging

CONTENTS: 1 tp; 2 'Table des matières'; 3–6 introductory text of 'Nos repas quotidiens,' 'La nourriture journalière,' 'Choix et préparation des aliments,' 'Soins à donner aux aliments,' 'Mesures,' 'Instructions générales,' and 'Équivalents'; 7–62 recipes; 63–4 'Index' and at bottom p 64, 'Printed in Canada.'

COPIES: CIHM (76430) *OONL (TX715 M57814) QMMMCM (AR-M2000.62.29)

NOTES: The cover-title is in English: 'Metropolitan Cook Book.'

O411.3 1922

—The / Metropolitan Life / cook book / Printed and distributed by the / Metropolitan Life Insurance Company / for the use of its industrial policy-holders / 1922

COPIES: OOAKM *Private collection

O411.4 nd [about 1924–6]

—The / Metropolitan / cook book / Published by / Metropolitan Life Insurance Company / Canadian head office, Ottawa, Ontario [cover-title]

DESCRIPTION: 19.5 × 13.0 cm   Pp 3–64   Paper, with image on front of an older woman stirring the contents of a steaming bowl

CONTENTS: 3 'The Food We Eat' and 'A Few Useful Suggestions'; 4–61 recipes; 62–4 index

COPIES: *Private collection

NOTES: This edition is undated and has no title-page. It was likely published about the same time as the three other editions featuring the older woman on the binding, i.e., O411.5, O411.6, and O411.7, dated 1924, 1925, and 1926. Like the 1924 edition, it has '331 86114 Printed in Canada' on the outside back face of the binding. It was published no earlier than 1924, when the company established the Ottawa head office (referred to in the cover-title). The company's building at 1 Madison Avenue, New York City, is depicted on the back face of the binding.

Ferguson/Fraser, p 233, cite an undated edition of *The Metropolitan Cook Book,* but do not distinguish between the various undated editions.

O411.5 1924

—The / Metropolitan Life / cook book / Cookery means carefulness and / inventiveness and willingness and / readiness of appliances. It means / the economy of your grandmothers / and the science of the modern chem- / ist; it means much testing and no / wasting; it means English thorough- / ness and French art and Arabian / hospitality. – Ruskin / Published by the / Metropolitan Life Insurance Company / Canadian head office, Ottawa, Ontario / 1924

DESCRIPTION: 19.5 × 13.0 cm   Pp [1–2] 3–64   Paper, with image on front of an older woman stirring the contents of a steaming bowl; stapled

CONTENTS: 1 tp; 2 untitled introductory note and table of contents; 3 'The Food We Eat' and 'A Few Useful Suggestions'; 4–61 recipes; 62–4 index

COPIES: APROM ARDA *BVIPM OKIT OONL (TX715 M578 1924)

NOTES: '331 86114 Printed in Canada' is on the outside back face of the binding.

O411.6 1925

—The / Metropolitan Life / cook book / Cookery means carefulness and / inventiveness and willingness and / readiness of appliances. It means / the economy of your grandmothers / and the science of the modern chem- / ist; it means much testing and no / wasting; it means English thorough- / ness and French art and Arabian / hospitality. – Ruskin / Metropolitan Life Insurance Company / 1925

DESCRIPTION: With image on front of an older woman stirring the contents of a steaming bowl; stapled

COPIES: *OOAKM

NOTES: The Canadian head office is not mentioned on the title-page, but the San Francisco, New York, and Ottawa offices are recorded on the front face of the binding; 'Metropolitan Life Press – (b) 331 LW – Printed in U.S.A.' is on the back face.

O411.7 1926

—The / Metropolitan Life / cook book / Cookery means carefulness and / inventiveness and willingness and / readiness of appliances. It means / the economy of your grandmothers / and the science of the modern chem- / ist; it means much testing and no / wasting; it means English thorough- / ness and French art and Arabian / hospitality. – Ruskin / Published by the / Metropolitan Life Insurance Company / Canadian head office, Ottawa, Ontario / 1926

DESCRIPTION: 19.5 × 13.5 cm   Pp [1–2] 3–64   Paper,

with image on front of an older woman stirring the contents of a steaming bowl; stapled
CONTENTS: 1 tp; 2 untitled introductory note and 'Table of Contents'; 3 'The Food We Eat' and 'A Few Useful Suggestions'; 4–61 recipes; 62–4 'Index'
COPIES: OMMM OONL (TX715 M578 1926) OTMCL (641.5971 M26 1926) *Private collection
NOTES: An illustration of the company's Ottawa building and '(a) 331 LW – Printed in Canada' are on the outside back face of the binding. The OTMCL copy is stamped on the title-page, 'Herbert W. Ware // representative Metropolitan Life // Hamilton.'

O411.8 1926
—Livre de cuisine / de la / Metropolitan / La cuisson demande du soin, de / l'intelligence, de la bonne volonté / et de la connaissance des appareils. / Vous devez posséder l'économie de / nos grand'mères et la science du / chimiste moderne; cela signifie des / expériences sans gaspillage; cela signi- / fie l'application anglaise, l'art français / et l'hospitalité arabe. – Ruskin / Metropolitan Life Insurance Company / Bureau-chef canadien, Ottawa / 1926
COPIES: *OOU (BRO 1926-20)

O411.9 1927
—The / Metropolitan Life / cook book / Cookery means carefulness and / inventiveness and willingness and / readiness of appliances. It means / the economy of your grandmothers / and the science of the modern chem- / ist; it means much testing and no / wasting; it means English thorough- / ness and French art and Arabian / hospitality. – Ruskin / Metropolitan Life Insurance Company / 1927
COPIES: *Private collection
NOTES: The Canadian head office is not mentioned on the title-page, but the San Francisco, New York, and Ottawa offices are recorded on the front face of the binding.

O411.10 nd [about 1928–9]
—The / Metropolitan Life / cook book / Cookery means carefulness and / inventiveness and willingness / and readiness of appliances. It means / the economy of your grandmothers / and the science of the modern chem- / ist; it means much testing and no / wasting; it means English thorough- / ness and French art and Arabian / hospitality. – Ruskin. / Metropolitan Life Insurance Company
DESCRIPTION: 19.0 × 13.5 cm   Pp [1–6] 7–64   Paper,

with image on front of a young woman stirring the contents of a bowl, watched by a girl and boy; stapled
CONTENTS: 1 tp; 2 blank; 3 untitled introductory note and table of contents; 4 blank; 5 'The Food We Eat'; 6 measures and weights, and oven temperatures; 7–61 recipes; 62–4 index
COPIES: AHRMH OGU (2 copies: *UA s070 b82, CCC TX715.6 M477 (d)) OONL (TX715 M578 1920z p***) OOWM (989.6.10) QMM (RBD ckbk 1827) SBIM SSWD Private collection
NOTES: O411.10 and O411.11 feature on the binding the image of a young woman, watched by a girl and boy. The introductory note on p 3 makes reference to another of the company's books, *Family Food Supply*, which is described as 'a companion book' to this one. The earliest edition of *Family Food Supply* is O619.1, copyright 1928. This edition of *The Metropolitan Life Cook Book*, therefore, was published no earlier than 1928. It was published no later than 1929 because a private collector has a copy signed with the original owner's name and the date April 1929.

The OGU copy catalogued here (UA) has a stamp, in purple ink, on the title-page: 'R.T. Mawhinney Field Repres., Metropolitan Life Port Williams, N.S.' The OOWM copy is faintly inscribed, 'OB White // Met office // Owen Sound.'

Printed on the outside back face of the binding of the AHRMH and the OOWM copies is '(b) 331 L.W. – Printed in Canada'; and on the OGU (UA), OONL, QMM, SBIM, and SSWD copies, '(d) 331 L.W. ...' Another private collector has a copy with 'M.L.I.Co. Press – (c) 331 L.W. – Printed in U.S.A.'

O411.11 nd [about 1928–9]
—Livre de cuisine / de la / Metropolitan / La cuisine demande du soin, de / l'intelligence, de la bonne volonté / et de la connaissance des appareils. / Vous devez posséder l'économie de / nos grand'mères et la science du / chimiste moderne; cela signifie des / expériences sans gaspillage; cela signi- / fie l'application anglaise, l'art français / et l'hospitalité arabe. – Ruskin. / Metropolitan Life Insurance Company
DESCRIPTION: Paper, with image on front of a young woman stirring the contents of a bowl, watched by a girl and boy; stapled
COPIES: *QSFFSC (3 copies)
NOTES: This edition has 64 pp. All the copies at QSFFSC have the following on the outside back face of the binding: '(d) 331 L.W. – French – Imprimé au Canada.' O411.11 was likely published about the same time as O411.10.

O411.12 nd [1930s]
—The / Metropolitan Life / cook book /
Metropolitan Life Insurance Company / (e) 331
L.W. – Printed in Canada
DESCRIPTION: 19.5 × 13.5 cm   Pp [1–4] 5–64   Paper,
printed with black diamond-shapes formed by diagonal crisscrossing yellow lines and with various
prepared dishes, one per diamond-shape; stapled
CONTENTS: 1 tp; 2 'Table of Measures and Weights'
and 'Oven Temperatures'; 3 untitled publ's note and
table of contents; 4 'A Few Useful Suggestions'; 5–61
recipes; 62–4 index
COPIES: OGM (985.82.102)   *Private collection
NOTES: All the editions with a binding featuring black
diamond shapes were likely published in the 1930s.
Chatelaine 1935, p 82, cites 'Metropolitan Cook Book,'
free upon request, but does not specify the edition.

O411.13 nd [1930s]
—The / Metropolitan Life / cook book /
Metropolitan Life Insurance Company / (f) 331 L.W.
– Printed in Canada
DESCRIPTION: 19.5 × 13.5 cm   Pp [1–4] 5–64   Paper,
printed with black diamond-shapes formed by diagonal crisscrossing yellow lines and with various
prepared dishes, one per diamond-shape; stapled
CONTENTS: 1 tp; 2 'Table of Measures and Weights'
and 'Oven Temperatures'; 3 untitled publ's note and
table of contents; 4 'A Few Useful Suggestions'; 5–61
recipes; 62–4 index
COPIES: QMM (RBD ckbk 1826b)   *Private collection

O411.14 nd [1930s]
—Le / livre de cuisine / de la Metropolitan /
Metropolitan Life Insurance Company / (f) 331 L.W.
– French – Imprimé au Canada
DESCRIPTION: Paper, printed with black diamond-
shapes and with various prepared dishes, one per
diamond-shape; stapled
COPIES: *QQUQT

O411.15 nd [1930s]
—The / Metropolitan Life / cook book /
Metropolitan Life Insurance Company / (g) 331
L.W. – Printed in Canada
DESCRIPTION: 19.5 × 13.5 cm   Pp [1–4] 5–64   Paper,
printed with black diamond-shapes formed by diagonal crisscrossing yellow lines and with various
prepared dishes, one per diamond-shape; stapled
CONTENTS: 1 tp; 2 'Table of Measures and Weights'
and 'Oven Temperatures'; 3 untitled publ's note and
table of contents; 4 'A Few Useful Suggestions'; 5–61
recipes; 62–4 index
COPIES: OKELWM   *QMM (RBD ckbk 1826a)

O411.16 nd [1930s]
—The / Metropolitan Life / cook book /
Metropolitan Life Insurance Company / (h) 331
L.W. – Printed in Canada
DESCRIPTION: 19.5 × 13.0 cm   Pp [1–4] 5–64   Paper,
printed with black diamond-shapes formed by diagonal crisscrossing yellow lines and with various
prepared dishes, one per diamond-shape; stapled
CONTENTS: 1 tp; 2 'Table of Measures and Weights'
and 'Oven Temperatures'; 3 untitled publ's note and
table of contents; 4 'A Few Useful Suggestions'; 5–61
recipes; 62–4 index
COPIES: *Private collection

O411.17 nd [1930s]
—Le / livre de cuisine / de la Metropolitan /
Metropolitan Life Insurance Company / (h) 331
L.W. – French – Imprimé au Canada
DESCRIPTION: 19.5 × 13.0 cm   Pp [1–4] 5–64   Lacks
binding; stapled
CONTENTS: 1 tp; 2 'L'équivalent de quelques mesures'
and 'Températures de cuisson au four'; 3 untitled
publ's note and 'Table des matières'; 4 'Quelques
suggestions utiles'; 5–61 recipes; 62–4 'Index'
COPIES: *QQS (218.4.29)   QSFFSC
NOTES: The QQS copy is stamped on the title-page,
'Ex-libris Rev. Mi Arthuri Maheux // Datis A.D. 1967'
and 'Albert Marier Rep. Metropolitan Life. Tél Bur.
3-0330 rue St-Louis Rés. 2-8018.' The QSFFSC copy
retains its paper binding printed with black diamond-
shapes formed by diagonal crisscrossing yellow lines
and with various prepared dishes, one per diamond.

O411.17a nd [1930s]
—The / Metropolitan Life / cook book /
Metropolitan Life Insurance Company / (i) 331 L.W.
– Printed in Canada
COPIES: *Private collection

O411.18 nd [1930s]
—The / Metropolitan Life / cook book /
Metropolitan Life Insurance Company / (j) 331 L.W.
– Printed in Canada
DESCRIPTION: 19.5 × 13.0 cm   Pp [1–4] 5–64   Paper,
printed with black diamond-shapes formed by di-
agonal crisscrossing yellow lines and with various
prepared dishes, one per diamond-shape; stapled
CONTENTS: 1 tp; 2 'Table of Measures and Weights'
and 'Oven Temperatures'; 3 untitled publ's note and
table of contents; 4 'A Few Useful Suggestions'; 5–61
recipes; 62–4 index
COPIES: BVIPM   QMMMCM   (AR-M2000.92.24)
*Private collection

O411.19   nd [1930s]
—Le / livre de cuisine / de la Metropolitan /
Metropolitan Life Insurance Company / (j) 331 L.W.
– French – Imprimé au Canada
DESCRIPTION: Paper, printed with black diamond-shapes formed by diagonal crisscrossing yellow lines and with various prepared dishes, one per diamond-shape; stapled
COPIES: *QSFFSC

O411.20   nd [1930s]
—The / Metropolitan Life / cook book /
Metropolitan Life Insurance Company / (k) 331
L.W. – Printed in Canada
DESCRIPTION: 20.0 × 13.5 cm   Pp [1–4] 5–64   Paper, printed with black diamond-shapes formed by diagonal crisscrossing yellow lines and with various prepared dishes, one per diamond-shape; stapled
CONTENTS: 1 tp; 2 'Table of Measures and Weights' and 'Oven Temperatures'; 3 untitled publ's note and table of contents; 4 'A Few Useful Suggestions'; 5–61 recipes; 62–4 index
COPIES: OGU (CCC TX715.6 M477 (k) cover b) OKIT   OTMCL (641.5971 M26)   *Private collection
NOTES: The OTMCL copy is rebound, with the front and back faces of the original paper binding applied to the new cloth.

O411.21   nd [1930s]
—The / Metropolitan Life / cook book /
Metropolitan Life Insurance Company / (l) 331 L.W.
– Printed in Canada
DESCRIPTION: 19.0 × 13.5 cm   Pp [1–4] 5–64   Paper, printed with black diamond-shapes formed by diagonal crisscrossing yellow lines and with various prepared dishes, one per diamond-shape; stapled
CONTENTS: 1 tp; 2 'Table of Measures and Weights' and 'Oven Temperatures'; 3 untitled publ's note and table of contents; 4 'A Few Useful Suggestions'; 5–61 recipes; 62–4 index
COPIES: *Private collection

O411.22   nd [about 1942–5]
—Metropolitan / cook book / Metropolitan Life
Insurance Company
DESCRIPTION: 19.5 × 13.5 cm   Pp [1–2] 3–56   Paper, printed with blue squares within a grid of red lines, recalling the pattern on earlier editions
CONTENTS: Inside front face of binding 'Table of Measures and Weights' and 'Oven Temperatures'; 1 tp; 2 foreword; 3 table of contents; 4 blank; 5–52 recipes; 53–6 index

COPIES: BVIPM   NSYHM   OGM (985.82.103)   OGU (CCC TX715.6 M572 No. 538)   QMMMCM (AR-M2000.92.22)   SWSLM   *Private collection
NOTES: The text is based on earlier editions, but it has been heavily revised for wartime conditions. The foreword states, '... never before in the history of our country has [food's] wise use been more important than it is at present, since we must feed our Army all over the world and our civilian population, and help to feed our allies.' The foreword refers to the need to know substitutes for rationed foods and for other foods in short supply; it thanks the Wheat Flour Institute, the Brooklyn Union Gas Company, the National Biscuit Company, and Sarah J. MacLeod, Frances Preston, and Helen Robertson, the authors of *What Do We Eat Now?*, for permission to use some of their material. Since *What Do We Eat Now?* was published in 1942 (Philadelphia: Lippincott), this edition of *Metropolitan Cook Book* was published no earlier than 1942 and no later than the end of the Second World War in 1945.

References to wartime difficulties are throughout the text; for example, on p 11 the introduction for cakes mentions limitations in supplies of sugar and shortening and the probability that fewer cakes will be baked during wartime, and on p 35 the introduction for vegetables notes the scarcity of commercially canned vegetables. Absent from this edition are an invalid cookery section and information about the lunch box, found in earlier editions.

'Metropolitan Life Insurance Company // Canadian head office Ottawa' is printed on the front face of the binding. The OGM and SWSLM copies and another private collector's copy have '[no letter in parentheses] 331 L.W. – Printed in Canada' on the outside back face; the OGU copy has '(n) 331 L.W. – Printed in Canada.'

The QMMMCM copy is stamped on the title-page, 'Bruce F. Bridle // Metropolitan Life Insurance Co. 235 Medland St., Toronto ...'; the printing information on the back face of the binding is unclear.

O411.23   nd [about 1942–5]
—Livre de cuisine / de la Metropolitan /
Metropolitan Life Insurance Company / Direction
générale au Canada: Ottawa
DESCRIPTION: 19.0 × 13.0 cm   Pp [1–2] 3–64   Paper, printed with blue squares within a grid of red lines, recalling the pattern on earlier editions; previously stapled, but now in new library cloth and sewn
CONTENTS: Inside front face of binding 'Table de correspondance' and 'Températures du four'; 1 tp;

2 'Préface'; 3 table of contents; 4 blank; 5–60 recipes; 61–4 'Table des matières'

COPIES: *OONL (TX715 M57814 1900z)

NOTES: The 'Préface' corresponds to the wartime preface of O411.22: 'La nourriture a toujours joué un rôle capital dans la vie des nations. Mais à aucune époque de l'histoire de notre pays, l'emploi rationnel des aliments n'a été aussi important qu'à l'heure actuelle, car il nous faut alimenter nos armées dans le monde entier, en même temps que notre population civile, ...' Printed on the outside back face of the binding is '(n) 331 L.W. (Fr.) – Imprimé au Canada.'

O411.24 nd [about 1945–7]
—Metropolitan / cook book / Metropolitan Life Insurance Company

DESCRIPTION: 19.5 × 13.5 cm   Pp [1–2] 3–56   Paper, printed with blue squares within a grid of red lines, recalling the pattern on earlier editions; stapled

CONTENTS: 1 tp; 2 foreword; 3 table of contents; 4 blank; 5–52 recipes; 53–6 index

COPIES: OGU (CCC TX715.6 M477 (n))   *Private collection

NOTES: As in O411.22, there are references to wartime conditions within the body of the text; however, there is no reference to war in the foreword. The foreword does include the same acknowledgments to the Wheat Flour Institute et al. This edition was likely published soon after 1945: it was easy to replace the wartime foreword with a new version; removing the references to rationing within the text only became necessary after rationing ended in Canada in 1947. A copy at QMM (RBD ckbk 1828) has '(N) 331 L.W. ...' on the outside back face of the binding.

O411.25 nd
—Livre de cuisine / de la Metropolitan / Metropolitan Life Insurance Company / Direction générale au Canada: Ottawa

DESCRIPTION: Paper, printed with blue squares within a grid of red lines, recalling the pattern on earlier editions; stapled

COPIES: *QSFFSC

NOTES: The following is printed on the outside back face of the binding: '(u) 331 L.W. (Fr.) – Imprimé au Canada.'

A private collector has a copy with '(n) 331 L.W. (Fr.) – Imprimé au Canada,' i.e., the same as O411.23, except there is no reference to war in the 'Préface,' which begins, 'Du point de vue économique, la nourriture est un des éléments principaux du budget familial.'

O411.26 February 1948
—Metropolitan / cook book / Edition of February 1948 / Metropolitan Life Insurance Company

DESCRIPTION: 20.0 × 13.5 cm   Pp [1–2] 3–56   Paper, printed with blue squares within a grid of red lines, recalling the pattern on earlier editions; stapled

CONTENTS: 1 tp; 2 'Foreword'; 3 'Table of Contents'; 4 'Table of Measures and Weights' and 'Oven Temperatures'; 5–52 recipes; 53–6 'Index'

COPIES: *Private collection

NOTES: All references to wartime conditions have been deleted. 'Metropolitan Life Insurance Company // Home office: New York // Pacific Coast head office: San Francisco // Canadian head office: Ottawa' is printed on the front face of the binding; 'P.F.M. – Printed in U.S.A. – (p) 331 L.W. – (Edition Feb. 1948)' is on the outside back face.

OTHER EDITIONS: The company continued to publish a cookbook under the English title *Metropolitan Cook Book*: November 1953 (Private collection); January 1954, copyright 1953 (OGU); copyright 1957 (Private collection); November 1957, copyright 1957 (OGU); 1970, copyright 1964 (OGU, OONL); retitled *New Metropolitan Cook Book*, copyright 1973. The cookbook also continued to be published under the French title *Livre de cuisine de la Metropolitan*: 1954 (Private collection); November 1957 (QMM).

AMERICAN EDITIONS: *Metropolitan Cookbook* [*sic*], 1914 (Dickinson, p 124); 1918 (Dickinson, p 122); *The Metropolitan Life Cook Book*, New York: Metropolitan Life Insurance Co., 1922 (WaiteCat 5, No. 352); [New York]: Printed and distributed by Metropolitan Life Insurance Co., 1924 (United States: DLC); New York: Metropolitan Life Insurance Co., nd, pp 64, paper binding printed with black background (OGU; United States: InU, MSaE); *Metropolitan Cook Book*, New York: Metropolitan Life Insurance Co., February 1948 (United States: InU); *Metropolitan Cookbook* [*sic*], 1953 (Dickinson, p 122); 1964 (Dickinson, p 124).

More eggs, sturdy chicks

The American company Ralston Purina was founded in 1894.

O412.1 1918
More / eggs / sturdy / chicks / 1918 Purina book / Compliments of – / [blank space] / Made in Canada by / Chisholm Milling Co., / Toronto. [cover-title]

DESCRIPTION: 23.0 × 10.0 cm   Pp 1–64   Illus col opp p 1 of a hen, illus   Paper, with stylized images on front of two eggs and a chick; stapled

CONTENTS: Inside front face of binding 'Copyright, 1912, Ralston Purina Co. Copyright, 1913, Ralston Purina Co. Copyright, 1914, Ralston Purina Co. Copyright, 1915, Ralston Purina Co. Copyright, 1916, Ralston Purina Co. Copyright, 1917, Ralston Purina Co.'; 1–52 information about the care of hens for the production of eggs; 53–9 'Cooking Recipes'; 60–3 information about Purina products; 64 order form for Purina books

COPIES: *Private collection

NOTES: The sources of the recipes, all American except for one, are acknowledged on p 53: Mrs T.E. Quisenberry, Mountain Grove, Mo.; *The Delineator*, New York City; Miss Fannie Merritt Farmer, from *The Woman's Home Companion*; Miss Helen T. Woods, from *American Poultry Journal*; *Today's Magazine*, New York City; and *The Canadian Poultry Review*.

Ontario, Department of Agriculture

For the titles of other cookbooks published by the Ontario Department of Agriculture, see O158.1.

O413.1   April 1918
Ontario Department of Agriculture / Women's Institutes / Circular No. 11 / Information / and recipes / on / war-time foods / and cooking / [Women's Institute symbol] / Toronto, Ontario, April, 1918 [cover-title]

DESCRIPTION: 22.0 × 14.5 cm   Pp [1] 2–32   Paper; stapled

CONTENTS: 1 cover-title; 2 'Information and Recipes on War-Time Foods and Cooking'; 3 'Common Foods Grouped According to Chief Food Constituents'; 4 information on substitutes for beef and pork, wheat, and sugar; 5–30 recipes for meat, poultry and game, fish, cereals, vegetables, fruit, eggs, milk, and cheese; 31 'How to Measure Food Values'; 32 table of calorie values

COPIES: *BVMA

NOTES: Page 2 describes the world shortage of food in graphic terms and concludes, 'The information and recipes contained in this booklet are prepared to assist the housewife in "doing her bit" to save the situation.' The 'McDonald [*sic*] Institute's Favourite Rule for Wheat Substitution' is on p 10.

Soon after the booklet's publication, Miss Margaret Smellie and Mrs T.M. Piper incorporated information from it in O417.1.

O414.1   July 1918
Ontario Department of Agriculture / Women's Institutes / Circular No. 12 / Drying of fruits and vegetables / and / preservation of vegetables by / fermentation and salting / [Women's Institute symbol] / Toronto, Ontario, July, 1918 [cover-title]

COPIES: *OGU (Rural Heritage Collection)

NOTES: The book has 23 pp.

Rockwell, Frederick Frye (1884–)

O415.1   [copyright 1918]
Save it for winter / modern methods of canning, dehydrating / preserving and storing vegetables / and fruit for winter use / with comments on / the best things to grow for saving / and when and how to grow them / by / Frederick Frye Rockwell / author of "Around the Year in the Garden," "Home Vegetable Gardening," etc. / Illustrated / Toronto / Frederick D. Goodchild / publisher

DESCRIPTION: 18.5 × 12.5 cm   Pp [i–vi] vii–xiii [xiv–xvi], 1–206   Frontis, pls, illus   Cloth, with image on front of jars of preserves

CONTENTS: i ht; ii blank; iii tp; iv 'Copyright, 1918, by Frederick A. Stokes Company ... Printed in U.S.A.'; v 'Acknowledgment' signed the author; vi blank; vii–viii table of contents; ix–xiii 'Preface' signed F.F.R., Fordhood Farms, May 1918; xiv blank; xv another ht; xvi blank; 1–202 text in nine chapters; 203–6 index

COPIES: *OONL (TX601 R63 1918 p***)

NOTES: In the 'Acknowledgment' Rockwell, an American author of gardening books, credits the following sources: publications of the United States Department of Agriculture, the National War Garden Commission, 'various Agricultural Colleges,' Ball Brothers Manufacturing Co., Kerr Manufacturing Co., Southern Canner and Evaporator Co., Home Canner Co., and Weis Fiber Manufacturing Co. In the 'Preface' he points out that the Great War has made the saving of food 'of even more importance than ever before, from every point of view: as a personal necessity; as the most commonsense kind of patriotism; and as a social obligation.'

AMERICAN EDITIONS: New York: Frederick A. Stokes Co., 1918 (United States: CU-A, CoDU, CoGrU, IaU, KMK, MChB, MU, MnSU, MoU-St, NN, NNNAM, OC, OCl, OO, PP, PPSJ, RCJW, TxAbC, TxCM, WU).

Selected recipes and household information

O416.1 nd [about 1918]
Selected recipes / and / household information / compiled and published / by / the Pansy Club / in aid of / the Children's Aid Society / Brantford / The MacBride Press, Limited
DESCRIPTION: 23.0 × 15.0 cm   Pp [1–6] 7–60 Paper; stapled
CONTENTS: 1 untitled poem; 2 blank; 3 tp; 4 blank; 5 foreword; 6 ad; 7–59 recipes credited with the name of the contributor and ads; 60 'Index' [i.e., table of contents]
COPIES: *Private collection
NOTES: The cover-title is 'The Pansy Club Cook Book.' Unusually, the compilers have chosen a poem that expresses regret for women's duty to prepare food for the family: 'What shall I have for dinner? / What shall I have for tea? / An omelet, a chop or two, / Or a savoury fricassee? / Dear, how I wish that nature / When she made her mighty plan / Hadn't given the task to woman / To care for hungry man.'

An advertisement on p 20 for Art Percy, hats and men's furnishings, 'new address 114 Colborne St,' indicates that the cookbook was published about 1918: In Brantford city directories, Percy's business is listed at 114 Colborne Street from 1918 onward.

Smellie, Miss Margaret (23 April 1882–), and Mrs T.M. Piper

Margaret Smellie was a member of a distinguished family in the twin cities of Fort William and Port Arthur (now Thunder Bay). Her father, Dr Thomas Smellie, was medical officer of health until 1897 and later an MPP for Fort William. Her younger sister, Colonel Elizabeth Smellie, had a remarkable career in the Canadian military (see Beeson, p 197, for her achievements and honours). Margaret graduated in 1910 from the Macdonald Institute in Guelph, with a Housekeeper Certificate (Entrance Record in RE1 MAC A0003, Vol. for 1907–10). The 1901 Census records her birth date. Mrs T.M. Piper is likely Margaret (March 1878–), wife of Thomas, a Fort William merchant (1911 Census).

O417.1 [1918]
Cook book / recipes of war time dishes / for the housewife / Compiled by / Miss Margaret Smellie, Port Arthur / Mrs. T.M. Piper, Fort William / At the request of / the Thunder Bay Production and Conservation Association / Fort William and Port Arthur / Office of Secretary: Grain Exchange, Fort William, Ont.

DESCRIPTION: About 21.5 × 14.5 cm [dimensions from photocopy] Pp [1–3] 4–96 Tp illus of a loaf of raisin(?) bread Paper(?), with tp illus on front; stapled
CONTENTS: 1 tp; 2 'Index' [i.e., table of contents]; 3 untitled introductory text; 4–96 text
CITATIONS: Beeson, p 197
COPIES: OTBH *OTBPM
NOTES: Page 4 is headed 'Twin Cities War Time Cook Book // A collection of the recipes of dishes shown at the food exhibits held in both cities, May 21st, 1918, supplemented by additional contributions.' The text includes suggestions on how to replace standard flour with other flour, taken from a Macdonald Institute leaflet, and information about sugar substitutes from the booklet 'War Time Foods and Cooking' by the Women's Institutes of Ontario, i.e., O413.1. The text on p 3 indicates that the aim of this compilation was 'to assist the housewife to alter her own home recipes to meet the need to substitute and preserve ...' The printer's name is on the front face of the binding: 'Times-Journal Presses, Fort William, Ont.'

War time cookery

For information about E.W. Gillett Co. and its other cookbooks, see O285.1.

O418.1 [1918]
War time / cookery / economy and / conservation / Published by / E.W. Gillett Co. Ltd. / Toronto, Canada / Winnipeg Montreal [cover-title]
DESCRIPTION: 15.0 × 8.5 cm Pp [1–3] 4–31 Paper; stapled
CONTENTS: 1 cover-title; 2 blank; 3 facsimile of letter dated 8 April 1918 from chairman of the Canada Food Board to Messrs E.W. Gillett Co. Ltd; 4 untitled introduction signed E.W. Gillett Co. Ltd; 5–29 recipes; 30 'Gillett's Goods'; 31 illus of 'Plant of E.W. Gillett Co. Ltd., Toronto, Ont. Erected 1912'
COPIES: CIHM (79081) OLU *Private collection
NOTES: The introduction states that the recipes are the 'result of an advertisement inserted in a number of papers offering cash prizes for the most practical recipes, by the use of which smaller quantities of eggs, butter, milk, lard, etc., could be used.' The contest closed on 25 March 1918 and the recipes were turned over to a 'committee of three competent judges.'

War-time cookery

The St Lawrence Chapter also produced O803.1, St Lawrence Cook Book.

O419.1 1918
War-time cookery / [IODE symbol] / Compiled by / St. Lawrence Chapter, I.O.D.E. / Cornwall, Ont. / Executive Committee / Regent – Miss B. Theobald. / First Vice-Regent – Miss M. Hermiston. / Second Vice-Regent – Miss A. Alguire. / Secretary – Miss L. Phillips. / Treasurer – Miss Eva Cumming. / Assistant Secretary – Miss M. Boyd. / Standard Bearer – Miss A. Mulhern. / Convenor of Work Committee – Miss B. Young. / Committee – Misses N. McFarlane, K. Alguire, A. Simp- / son, M. Whitham. / Committee in Charge of Book / Miss B. Young, Miss M. Hermiston, Miss H. Harkness, / Miss R. DeRochie. / Cornwall / Press of the Freeholder / 1918
DESCRIPTION: 22.5 × 15.0 cm   Pp [1] 2–74 [75]   Paper, with IODE symbol on front; stapled
CONTENTS: 1 tp; 2 ad; 3 'Index' [i.e., table of contents]; 4 ad; 5 'Abbreviations' and 'Comparison of Weights and Measures'; 6 ad; 7–74 text, mainly recipes credited with the name of the contributor, and ads; 75 ad and 'The paper in this book was made by the Toronto Paper Company, Cornwall, Ont.'
COPIES: CIHM (9-92245)   OONL (TX715.6 W349 1918)   *Private collection

The Women's Patriotic League cookery book

O420.1 1918
The / Women's / Patriotic League / cookery book / Brockville / 1918
DESCRIPTION: 23.0 × 15.0 cm   Pp [3–6] 7–160, [i–v]   Cloth
CONTENTS: 3 tp; 4 blank; 5 part-title: 'Good Things to Eat and How to Prepare Them'; 6 blank; 7 'Contents' [i.e., alphabetical list of chapters]; 8 blank; 9–160 text interleaved with blank leaves (included in the pagination) for manuscript recipes; i–v ads
COPIES: OBM   OOSS (TX715 W65)   OTMCL (641.5 W58205)   OTUTF (D-11 0982)   OTYA (TX715 W7 1918)   *Private collection
NOTES: There is a chapter of 'War Recipes' on pp 63–74, all for baked goods. The following is at the bottom of p [v]: 'This cookery book of tried and tested recipes is published by the Women's Patriotic League of Brockville, Ont., for the benefit of Red Cross Work, and is sold at $1.00. Copies may be had at the Recorder and Times office, or by mail, addressed to the Recorder Printing Company, Brockville, Ont., ...' Some of the recipes also appear in *The Brockville Cook Book* of 1923; see O232.2.

The private collector's copy is inscribed on the front endpaper, in black ink, 'Frances C. Simpson from Helen.' The OTUTF copy is inscribed on the front endpaper, in black ink, 'Eleanor E. Calvin // Christmas 1918 M.L.R.'

1919

Cook book

The same chapter produced O505.1, Official Cook Book.

O421.1 [June 1919]
Cook book / Published by / Mizpeh Chapter No. 56 / Order of the Eastern Star / Hamilton, Canada / Price 25c. [cover-title]
DESCRIPTION: Pp 1–68   With image on front of a star
CONTENTS: 1 'A selection of tested recipes compiled by the members of Mizpeh Chapter No. 56, O.E.S.,' list of officers, date of June 1919, plus two verses about the book; 2 ad; 3–61 recipes credited with the name of the contributor and ads; 62 'Weights & Measures'; 63 'Index' [i.e., table of contents] and untitled note by the Mizpeh Chapter; 64–8 blank for 'My Own Recipes'
COPIES: *Private collection
NOTES: The running head is 'Mizpeh Chapter Cook Book.' Of the seventeen officers listed on p 1, the first are Mrs Lulu B. Wood, worthy matron, Mr Percy Greenall, worthy patron, and Mrs Hannah Ackert, associate matron. The advertisement on p 2 is for Robert H. Ackert, stationer and tobacconist, Hannah's son (see 1901 Census). An unusual part of the 'Weights & Measures' is the table called 'For Fruits (Boil)' that shows how much sugar is required for each kind of fruit and the recommended time for boiling each fruit. The Mizpeh Chapter's note on p 63 comments: '[The book] will not only solve many difficulties in the domestic life, but will give many an opportunity to help on the work of this chapter.'

Famous Pointe Mouillée Club recipes

O422.1 [October 1919]
"Friendship is the most pleasant of all things, / and nothing more glads the heart of man." / Famous / Pointe Mouillée / Club recipes / [caption:] A.J.D., D.R. Pepin, C.M., Peter McK., "Blake." / The "Shanty," 1891

DESCRIPTION: 20.5 × 12.5 cm   Pp [i–ii], 1–19   Tp illus of five men at the door of the Shanty; frontis of 'The "Shanty," 1901'; illus on p ii of 'Our President,' on p 1 of 'It's me – the Chef,' on p 2 of 'D.R. on his way to the "Cathedral,"' on p 4 of 'A.J.D. taking a look round,' on p 8 of 'The club property from the bay,' on p 13 of 'C.M. and F.L.W. ...,' and on p 15 of 'D.R. and Joe coming in through the reeds'   Paper-covered boards; sewn

CONTENTS: i tp; ii illus of 'Our President' and dedication to 'my dear old comrade and brother "Muskrat" Duncan'; 1 'Author's Note' signed the chef, Pointe Mouillée Club, Bainsville, Ontario, October 1919, an illegible stamped signature, and illus of the chef; 2–19 text

CITATIONS: Driver 2003, 'Canadian Cookbooks,' illus p 26

COPIES: CIHM (75732)   *OONL (TX823 F36)   OTYA (CPC 1919 0151)

NOTES: See pl 30. Pointe Mouillée is on Lake St Francis (part of the St Lawrence River), near Bainsville, which is northeast of Cornwall and close to the Quebec border. The following history of the Point Mouillée Club is from Betty Peltier-York's 1989 typescript, *Pointe au Beaudette – A History of the Community 1784–1945*, Vol. 2, p 25 (copy at Glengarry Historical Society Archives): 'Around 1884 some wealthy men from Montreal selected it [Pointe Mouillée] as an ideal place for hunting ducks in the fall during their migration season and they decided to get together and form a club. Some distinguished Montreal names were to be found on the first roster, such as Molson and de Lotbinière-Harwood ... The club was to have a long history. It only ceased to exist in the last decade when the Ontario Government withdrew its lease as a private hunting preserve.' One of the men in the photograph on the title-page is Peter McKee, who ran a nearby inn.

If the membership of the club was cultured, the tone of the book evinces a sort of inverse sophistication. In the 'Author's Note,' for example, the chef professes, 'This booklet is not intended to rival the art of "Le grand Vatel," nor to eclipse "Ye Widdowe's Treasure," "Ye Accomplisht Cook," nor "Mrs. Beeton" of modern times. It is not in any sense a complete culinary compendium – just a small collection of recipes, the result of over 30 years experience ...' The recipes are set out attractively, one per page, and have characterful titles: A Pleasant Appetizer – Not hard to take; Pea Soup – 'Monkey' Brand; Finnan Haddie – à la 'President Robertson'; Shepherd's Pie; Irish Stew – 'Shanty' Style; Baked 'Sea Pie'; Minced Collops; Corned Beef Hash – 'Old Reliable' Brand; Rice Pudding; Bread and Butter Pudding; Omelets;

Welsh Rarebit (that won't be stringy); Fresh Mushrooms; and 'Muskrat' Cocktail (to be taken 15 minutes before retiring). The instructions are direct and often humorously tongue-in-cheek; for example, for Fresh Mushrooms, one is told to 'gather the right kind, usually found in old pasture fields, at sunrise'; after the cooking method, comes the advice, 'Don't try experiments unless you have a doctor and stomach pump handy.' 'Menus for a Week's Outing' are on p 16, and 'General Suggestions' on pp 17–19.

Famous Pointe Mouillée Club Recipes is not cited in MacGillivray.

O422.2   [2nd ed., October 1920]
—Famous / Pointe Mouillée / Club recipes / (2nd edition) / (All tried out and satisfaction guaranteed / if instructions are followed) / [caption:] A.J.D., D.R., [*sic*, comma] Pepin, C.M., Peter McK., "Blake" / The "Shanty" – 1891

DESCRIPTION: 20.5 × 12.5 cm   Pp [1–4] 5–31 [32]   Tp illus of five men; frontis of 'The "Shanty," Pointe Mouillée, as I first knew it – October, 1889'; illus of other members and club scenes; cartoon on p 32   Card; sewn

CONTENTS: 1 blank; 2 frontis; 3 tp; 4 illus of 'Our President'; 5 'Author's Note' signed the chef, Pointe Mouillée Club, Bainsville, Ontario, October 1919, and 'Preface to Second Edition' signed the chef, same place, October 1920; 6–32 text

COPIES: *Private collection

NOTES: In the 'Preface to Second Edition' the chef writes: 'When the original recipes were compiled and printed, it was my intention to send them as Xmas cards to a few intimate friends and brother sportsmen, some of whom had enjoyed the hospitality of Pointe Mouillée Club; ... I have had so many applications for copies that I feel compelled to bring out a second edition ... In this edition I have added some recipes ...'

Helpful hints for housekeepers 1919

See O263.1 for information about the company and other issues of Helpful Hints for Housekeepers.

O423.1   1919
1919 Volume IX. 1919 / Hang me in the kitchen / Helpful / hints / for housekeepers / Compliments of / the Dodds Medicine Co. / Limited / Toronto, Can. [cover-title]

DESCRIPTION: 15.5 × 10.5 cm   Pp 1–32   Paper; stapled, and with hole punched at top left corner for hanging

CONTENTS: 1–top 2 'Efficient Housekeeping'; mid–bottom 2 'Waste No Fat'; 3 'From Us to You' signed the Dodds Medicine Co. Ltd, Toronto; 4 'Left Over Meat, etc. '; 5, 7, 9, 11, 13, 15, 19, 21, 23, 25, 27, 29 entries for health issues, arranged alphabetically from Anaemia to Skin; 6 'Left Over Vegetables'; 8 'Cooking Different Fish'; 10 'Buying Your Vegetables'; 12 'Preserving Eggs'; 14, 18 'Things Worth Remembering'; 16–17 testimonials for Dodd's Kidney Pills; 20 'Points in Laundering'; 22 'The Removal of Stains'; 24, 26 'Points for the Kitchen'; 28 'The Care of Furniture'; 30 publ ad for Dodd's Dyspepsia Tablets; 31 'Weights and Measures'; 32 publ ad for Diamond Dinner Pills
COPIES: *MCM

Macfarlane, Miss Margaret White

Documents concerning Macfarlane's employment with the Department of Agriculture are at OOA (RG17 Records of the Department of Agriculture, Vol. 2795, File 248805). In a letter of 10 June 1918, J. Grisdale recommended that she be hired as an experimenter and demonstrator in canning. He describes her as 'a New Brunswick lady, who has been attending the School of Household Science at Macdonald College for the past two years.' She was appointed temporarily starting 2 July 1918. In a letter of 12 October 1918 W.T. Macoun requested of E.S. Archibald that her position be renewed so that she could write up the results of her summer work and also the work of her predecessor, Laura Kirby, in the form of a bulletin on the canning of fruits and vegetables (i.e., O424.1). Macoun wrote: 'I should like her to test, during the winter, the relative value of the different varieties of garden beans as baked beans, and the different varieties of garden peas for soups, as many people are now letting some beans and peas ripen in their gardens for use in the dry condition. There are also a great many recipes for the use of apples in combination with other things which we should get more information upon, and there would be other work also, so that her time would be fully employed ...' She was rehired for a further six months (E.S. Archibald to J.H. Grisdale, 16 November 1918), and renewed again from 1 August 1919 (Memorandum for the director of the Experimental Farm, 16 July 1919). She resigned her position at the end of October 1919 (E.S. Archibald to J.H. Grisdale, 30 October 1919). She may be Margaret W. McFarlane [sic], born 1 May 1894, recorded in the 1901 Census for Fredericton.

For a list of other cookbooks published by the Department of Agriculture, see O404.1.

O424.1 1919
Dominion of Canada / Department of Agriculture / Dominion Experimental Farms / Division of Horticulture / W.T. Macoun / Dominion Horticulturist / Preservation of fruits and / vegetables for home use / with results of experiments in canning, / drying, pickling and preserving at the / Central Experimental Farm, Ottawa, Ont. / By / Margaret Macfarlane / Bulletin No. 93 / Published by authority of Hon. T.A. Crerar, Minister of Agriculture / Ottawa, Ont. / 62008–1
DESCRIPTION: 24.5 × 16.5 cm   Pp [1–2] 3–32   Fp illus on p 4 of 'Public Demonstration in Canning, Experimental Farm ...'; fp illus on p 24 of nine bottles of preserves; 10 numbered illus on pp 9 and 11   Paper; stapled
CONTENTS: 1 tp; 2 blank; 3 letter to the minister of agriculture signed E.S. Archibald, director, Dominion Experimental Farms, Ottawa, May 1919; 4 fp illus; 5 table of contents; 6 blank; 7–32 text
CITATIONS: Ag 1867–1974, p 153   Ferguson/Fraser, p 232   Newman
COPIES: OBEHCM   OGU (Rural Heritage Collection uncat)   OOAG (630.4 C212 Exp. Farms Service Bul. 93, 4 copies)   *Private collection
NOTES: Archibald states in his letter, p 3: 'The information in this bulletin is based on that available from many sources in regard to the general principles underlying the successful preservation of food, on recipes found by long experience to be good, and on experimental work at the Central Experimental Farm in 1917 and 1918. The work in 1917 was in charge of Miss Laura Kirby, while Miss Macfarlane conducted the experiments in 1918. Both these ladies are graduates in Household Science of Macdonald College.' See also O599.1, for Ethel Hamilton's account of the experiments leading up to the publication of *Preservation of Fruits and Vegetables for Home Use*.

O424.2 1919
—[An edition of *Conserves de fruits et de légumes en bocaux, séchés, salés et confits, et résultats d'essais exécutés à la Ferme expérimentale centrale, Ottawa, 1919*]
CITATIONS: Ag 1867–1974, p 65
NOTES: No copy was found at OOAG.

O424.3 rev. ed., 1921
—Dominion of Canada / Department of Agriculture / Dominion Experimental Farms / Division of Horticulture / W.T. Macoun / Dominion Horticulturist / Preservation of fruits and / vegetables for home use / with results of experiments in canning, / drying, pickling and

preserving at the / Central Experimental Farm, Ottawa, Ont. / By / Margaret Macfarlane / Bulletin No. 93 / Revised 1921 / Published by authority of Hon. S.F. Tolmie, Minister of Agriculture, / Ottawa, Ont. / 24104–1

DESCRIPTION: 25.0 × 16.5 cm   Pp [1–2] 3–51   Fp illus on p 4 of 'Public Demonstration in Canning, Experimental Farm, Ottawa, Ont.'; fp illus on p 24 of nine bottles of preserves; 10 numbered illus   Paper; stapled

CONTENTS: 1 tp; 2 blank; 3 letter to the minister of agriculture signed E.S. Archibald, director, Dominion Experimental Farms, May 1921; 4 fp illus; 5 table of contents; 6 blank; 7–51 text

CITATIONS: Ag 1867–1974, p 153

COPIES: OGU (Rural Heritage Collection uncat) OOAG (630.4 C212 Exp. Farm Service Bul. 93, 3 copies)   QKB (80-7)   *Private collection

O424.4   rev. ed., 1921

—Ministère fédéral de l'agriculture – Canada / Fermes expérimentales du Dominion / Service de l'horticulture / W.T. Macoun / Horticulteur du Dominion / Conserves de fruits et de légumes / en bocaux, séchés, salés et confits, et résultats / d'essais exécutés à la Ferme expérimentale / centrale, Ottawa / Par / Margaret Macfarlane / Bulletin n° 93 / Traduit au Bureau de traduction du ministère / Revisé 1921 / Publié par ordre de l'hon. S.F. Tolmie, Ministre de l'agriculture, Ottawa, Ont.

DESCRIPTION: 24.0 × 16.0 cm   Pp [1–3] 4–52   Fp illus on p 4 of 'Démonstration publique d'emboîtage, Ferme expérimentale, Ottawa, Ont.'; fp illus on p 26 of nine bottles of preserves; 10 numbered illus   Paper; rebound in cloth, together with other bulletins

CONTENTS: 1 tp; 2 blank; 3 letter to the minister of agriculture signed E.S. Archibald, director, Dominion Experimental Farms, Ottawa, May 1919; 4 fp illus; 5 table of contents; 6 blank; 7–52 text

CITATIONS: Ag 1867–1974, p 65

COPIES: *OOAG (630.4 C212 Exp. Farms Service Bul. 93)

Neil, Marion Harris

For information about this author and her other cookbooks, see O306.1.

O425.1   1919

[An edition of *Economical Cookery,* by Marion Harris Neil, Toronto: McClelland and Stewart, 1919, $1.50]

CITATIONS: BS, Vol. 35, No. 4 (April 1919), p 73

Spadoni/Donnelly No. 4517 ('Imprints Not Located')

AMERICAN EDITIONS: Boston: Little, Brown and Co., 1918 (United States: DLC).

Recipes: Wholesome, nutritious, economical

For information about Gunns Ltd and its cookbooks, see O353.1.

O426.1   nd [about 1919]

Recipes / Wholesome / nutritious / economical [cover-title]

DESCRIPTION: 17.0 × 12.5 cm   Pp [1–2] 3–24   Illus   Paper, with black, vertical stripes on front; stapled

CONTENTS: 1 illus of Easifirst Shortening and 'Home Baking Made Easy // Use "Easifirst" // Gunns Limited Toronto – Montreal – St. John, N.B.'; 2 foreword; 3 '"Easifirst" Makes Delicious Pastry Economical for Every Cooking Use'; 4 'About the Economy of "Easifirst" for Shortening'; 5–6 'The Economical Way to Fry Foods'; 7–9 'Cakes'; 10–11 'Pies and Pastry'; 12–13 'Puddings'; 14–15 'For Afternoon Tea'; 16 'Salads'; 17–20 'Fish and Meat Dishes'; 21–2 'Vegetables'; 23 'Table of Weights and Measures'; 24 'Things You Should Know When Using Gunns "Easifirst"'

COPIES: *QMM (RBD ckbk 1626a)

NOTES: O426.1 and O426.2 are printed from different type settings. Here, the decorative border on pp 1 and 2 is made up of an alternating pattern of square shapes (formed by four corner dots and one centre dot) and oblong shapes (formed by four 0.5-cm-long straight lines, placed side by side); the heading on p 5 is '… Fry Foods,' not 'Fry Food.'

The foreword indicates a publication date of about 1919: 'In the spring of 1919 new buildings were constructed, practically doubling the capacity of the company's large plant in Toronto.' This book and another publication by Gunns Ltd, O560.1, *Recipes: Attractive, Nutritious, Economical*, could not have been published after 1927, the year that Gunns Ltd merged with the William Davies Co., the Canadian Packing Co. Ltd, and the Harris Abattoir Co. to form Canada Packers Ltd.

A private collector's copy differs from O426.1 in that the locations for Gunns Ltd on p 1 are 'Toronto and Montreal'; Saint John, New Brunswick, is not cited. In other respects, it appears to be the same.

The reference in Ferguson/Fraser, p 233, may be to O426.1 or O426.2.

O426.2 nd [about 1919]
—Recipes / Wholesome / nutritious / economical [cover-title]
DESCRIPTION: 17.0 × 13.0 cm   Pp [1–2] 3–24   Illus
Paper, with black, vertical stripes on front; stapled
CONTENTS: 1 illus of Easifirst Shortening and 'Home Baking Made Easy // Use "Easifirst" // Gunns Limited Toronto – Montreal – St. John, N.B.'; 2 foreword; 3 '"Easifirst" Makes Delicious Pastry Economical for Every Cooking Use'; 4 'About the Economy of "Easifirst" for Shortening'; 5–6 'The Economical Way to Fry Food'; 7–9 'Cakes'; 10–11 'Pies and Pastry'; 12–13 'Puddings'; 14–15 'For Afternoon Tea'; 16 'Salads'; 17–20 'Fish and Meat Dishes'; 21–2 'Vegetables'; 23 'Table of Weights and Measures'; 24 'Things You Should Know When Using Gunns "Easifirst"'
COPIES: *QMM (RBD ckbk 1626b)
NOTES: O426.2 and O426.1 are printed from different type settings. Here, the decorative border on pp 1 and 2 is made up of 1.1-cm-long lozenge-type shapes, placed end to end; the heading on p 5 is '... Fry Food,' not 'Fry Foods.' Like O426.1, the foreword refers to new buildings constructed in the spring of 1919.

1919–25

Alpha Audette(?) cook book

O427.1 [about 1919–25]
[An edition of *Alpha Audette(?) Cook Book*, Ottawa, Ont.]
COPIES: Private collection
NOTES: The book's owner reports that the binding and first pages are missing; only pp 5–88 remain. The advertisements are for Ottawa firms; for example, McCreary and McMonagle, real estate brokers, and J.H. Conner and Son, selling a Power Washer. The McCreary and McMonagle advertisement points to publication in the period 1919–25. In city and telephone directories before 1919, McCreary and McMonagle have separate listings at different addresses for individual real estate businesses. The first listing for McCreary and McMonagle as the same business, at 234 Bank Street, is in the 1919 city directory and September 1919 telephone directory; the joint business is listed up to 1925. From 1926, only McCreary is listed at 234 Bank.

1920

Book of latest and best recipes

The St Vincent branch of the Women's Institute was established in 1918 (Ambrose, p 235). See also O1029.1, 1941 Cook Book, by the same branch.

O428.1 1920
[An edition of *Book of Latest and Best Recipes*, alternative title: *Book of Household Helps*, North Grey Women's Institute, St Vincent branch, Grey County, Ontario, 1920, $0.50]
COPIES: Private collection

Canning, preserving and jelly making

Northern Aluminum Co. Ltd was chartered in 1902 as a Canadian subsidiary of Pittsburgh Reduction Co. (later Aluminum Co. of America or Alcoa). The Toronto Works opened in 1913, at 158 Sterling Road, as a foundry and plant making cooking utensils. On 8 July 1925 Northern Aluminum was renamed Aluminum Co. of Canada. In 1930, and still located on Sterling Road, Aluminum Goods Ltd was incorporated. (This history is from www.alcan.com, accessed in 2007.) For the titles of cookbooks advertising 'Wear-Ever' products under the name Aluminum Goods Ltd, see O807.1, The 'Wear-Ever' New Method of Cooking.

O429.1 nd [about 1920]
Canning / preserving & / jelly making / made easy by using a / "Wear-Ever" / Aluminum Canner / and a / "Wear-Ever" / Preserving Kettle [cover-title]
DESCRIPTION: 15.5 × 9.0 cm   Pp [1] 2–23   Illus
Paper, with image on front of a small boy licking a spoon and standing beside a table on which sits a preserving kettle; stapled
CONTENTS: 1 cover-title; 2 'The Principles of Canning'; 3–mid 4 'Utensils Needed for Canning // Preserving and Jelly Making'; mid 4–near bottom 5 'Methods of Canning – The Old Way – The Open Kettle Method'; bottom 5–mid 6 'The New Way – The Cold Pack Method'; mid–bottom 6 'Canning Outfits'; top–mid 7 'Cold Pack Canning – Explanation of Steps'; bottom 7–top 9 'General Precautions'; near top–mid 9 'Vegetables // Steps in Process'; mid 9–top 10 'Time for Scalding and Blanching'; mid 10–top 12 'Recipes for Cold Pack Canning'; mid 12 'Advantages of Canning Fruit by Cold-Pack Method' and 'Open Kettle Method of Canning'; bottom 12–top 13 'Syrups for

Canning'; mid–bottom 13 'Fruit Recipes for Cold Pack Canning'; 14–mid 17 'Jelly Making'; bottom 17–mid 22 'Preserving'; mid–bottom 22 'A Half Dozen "Don'ts"'; 23 'Replace utensils that wear out with utensils that "Wear Ever"' and 'The Aluminum Cooking Utensil Company // New Kensington, Pa. In Canada "Wear-Ever" Aluminum Cooking Utensils are made by Northern Aluminum Company, Ltd., Toronto'
COPIES: *OKIT
NOTES: 'Printed in U.S.A. ... The Corday & Gross Company, Cleveland' is printed on the outside back face of the binding. 'H. Wolfhard & Co. Hardware & Tinsmithing // Kitchener, Ontario 31 King St. W., – Phone 42' is stamped on the outside back face.

The book was published after September 1916, when Berlin was renamed Kitchener, and no later than 8 July 1925, when Northern Aluminum Co. Ltd was renamed the Aluminum Company of Canada. An advertisement in *Canadian Home Journal* Vol. 20, No. 4 (August 1923), p 55, for 'Wear-Ever' Aluminum Preserving Kettles by Northern Aluminum Co. Ltd, Toronto, does not mention a cookbook, evidence that *Canning, Preserving and Jelly Making* may have been published closer to 1925 than 1920.

Cooking recipes

An illustrated advertisement for Pfeffer Bros is in O191.1, The Bruce County Cook-Book.

O430.1   nd [about 1920]
Cooking recipes / Published by Pfeffer Bros., Milverton / Milverton Roller / Mills / Our brands / Banner / Jewel / Pfeffer Bros. [cover-title]
DESCRIPTION: 14.5 × 9.5 cm   Pp 1–15 [16]   Paper; stapled
CONTENTS: 1 cover-title; 2 'The Object of Presenting This Booklet'; 3–15 recipes, publ ads, and, on p 13, 'A Few Points to Remember' [about bread baking]; 16 [outside back face of binding] 'London Printing & Lithographing Co. London, Ont.'
COPIES: *OKITJS (991.23.5)
NOTES: The purpose of the book is given on p 2: '[The object] is to acquaint our customers with the facilities we have for manufacturing first-class flour; giving you a description at the same time of the different brands. We have also added a few recipes ...' The recipes are for baking bread, cake, cookies, and pastry. Milverton is north of Stratford, more than fifty km from London, where the book was printed. The OKITJS copy is inscribed on p 15, in ink, 'Mrs Hy Schiel.'

Cornforth, George E.

Cornforth also wrote O664.1, Better Meals for Less, *and a 16-page booklet,* Food Combinations and Methods of Cooking, *Washington, DC: Life and Health, [c1916] (United States: DLC).*

O431.1   [copyright 1920]
Good food / how to prepare it / the principles of cooking, and nearly five / hundred carefully selected recipes / By George E. Cornforth / Review and Herald Publishing Association / Washington, D.C. / New York, N.Y. Oshawa, Ontario, Canada / South Bend, Ind. Winnipeg, Manitoba, Canada
DESCRIPTION: 19.0 × 13.0 cm   Pp [1–3] 4–224   Frontis portrait on p 2 of George E. Cornforth, illus   Cloth
CONTENTS: 1 ht; 2 frontis; 3 tp; 4 'Preface' signed the author and 'Copyright, 1920 Review and Herald Publishing Association Washington, D.C.'; 5 'Table of Contents'; 6 fp illus of 'Nature's Bounties'; 7–218 text; 219–24 'Index'
CITATIONS: Wheaton/Kelly No. 1445
COPIES: *Private collection; United States: DLC (TX715 C815)   MCR (641.5 C81g)
NOTES: The preface states, '... there is a very close relation between diet and health, diet and efficiency, diet and morals.' The private collector's copy is inscribed on the front endpaper, in ink, 'Mrs Schorse // Chalmer Street // Galt [in Ontario].' Mrs Schorse was the owner's grandmother-in-law, and a member of the Seventh-Day Adventists church, which promotes vegetarianism for health reasons, believing that the human body is God's temple.

The Wheaton/Kelly entry, which cites only Washington as the place of publication, probably refers to the edition described here.

Dr Miles' cook book

To help market his proprietary medicines, such as Nervine, Dr Miles incorporated the Dr Miles Medical Co. in 1885. For the biography of this American medical man, see Martha M. Pickrell, Dr Miles: The Life of Dr Franklin Lawrence Miles, 1845–1929, *Carmel, Ind.: Guild Press of Indiana, 1997. There is no reference in the biography to O432.1,* Dr Miles Cook Book, *or to* Dr Miles Candy Book, *also published by Dr Miles Medical Co., but in Elkhart, Indiana, [about 1912] (Barile, p 187). Dickinson, p 96, cites* Dr Miles Hints to Housekeepers, *likely also published in the United States. In 1978 the Miles Medical Co. was acquired as a subsidiary of Bayer AG in Germany; in 1995 its name changed to Bayer.*

O432.1 nd [about 1920]

Dr. Miles' cook book [cover-title]

DESCRIPTION: 11.5 × 15.5 cm Pp [1] 2–32 Paper, with image on front of a boy watching his mother place a loaf(?) in the oven; stapled

CONTENTS: 1–2 'Dr. Miles' Cook Book' [information about cooking techniques]; 3–31 recipes and culinary information on versos, health information and testimonials for Dr Miles Medical Co. products on rectos; 32 list of 'Dr. Miles' Remedies'

COPIES: OHMB (Ephemera QV772 D755 D755d 1930) ONLAM (Walters-Wagar Collection, Box 20) OONL (TX715.6 D72 1920z p***) OTUTF (uncat patent medicine) QMM (RBD ckbk 1516) *Private collection

NOTES: The company name and city (Toronto) are on the inside back face of the binding. Most of the testimonials are from Canadians. Readers, however, are asked to send their letters to the company in Elkhart, Indiana.

'W.H. Winkler St. Jacobs – Ont.' is printed on the outside back face of the binding of the OHMB copy, in the blank space provided for the business name. 'Sold and guaranteed by Hooper's Drug Store // Knight's Pharmacy // Wallace's Drug Store // Napanee, Ont.' is printed in the same place on the ONLAM copy. 'Sold and guaranteed by Standard Drug Ltd. [four branch store addresses] London, Ont.' is printed in the same place on the OTUTF copy.

AMERICAN EDITIONS: Cure All Co., nd [about 1910] (Allen, p 104).

Favorite recipes

O433.1 nd [about 1920]

Favorite / recipes / The / Sweet / Oil of / Persica / W.J. Bush Citrus Products Co. Inc. / National City (California) / Distributed by / all Canadian wholesale grocers

DESCRIPTION: 15.5 × 8.5 cm Pp [1–2] 3–16 Illus Paper, with composite image on front of a railway freightyard, a woman carrying a basket of apricots or peaches, and a single large apricot or peach; stapled

CONTENTS: Inside front face of binding 'Copyright W.J. Bush & Co. (Canada) Limited'; 1 tp; 2 fp illus of Aprol; 3–8 'From California the Land of Sunshine'; 9–14 'Favourite [sic] Recipes'; 15–16 'What Your Neighbours Think about Aprol'

COPIES: *Private collection

NOTES: Aprol – 'The Sweet Oil of Persica' – was 'a pure and wholesome vegetable product – pressed from the ripe kernels of apricots and peaches (in Latin, the "Persica" family).' The oil is recommended for all table and culinary uses. The text says that it is 'now being introduced into Canada' and refers to tests on oils by the Inland Revenue Department, Ottawa, in 1918. The booklet was published shortly after the First World War, for the introduction to the recipes comments, '... even with our winning of the war, there did not come and will not come, for a long period, lack of necessity for conservation.' No place of publication is recorded, but the copyright holder, W.J. Bush and Co. (Canada) Ltd (described as 'chemists' in Toronto city directories), was located at 535 King Street West. The text and illustrations are printed in brown and green.

Good things to eat

O434.1 nd [about 1920]

Good things / to eat / Contributed by / Prescott ladies [cover-title]

DESCRIPTION: About 15.0 × 11.5 cm [dimensions from photocopy] Stapled

COPIES: *OPREFM

NOTES: The museum curator describes the book as 'a small gathering of "Receipes" printed locally by the *Prescott Journal* ... our local newspaper which first appeared in 1890.' She dates the cookbook 'early 20th century, possibly the 20's.'

Helpful hints for housekeepers 1920

See O263.1 for information about the company and other issues of Helpful Hints for Housekeepers.

O435.1 1920

1920 Volume X. 1920 / Hang me in the kitchen / Helpful / hints / for housekeepers / Compliments of / the Dodds Medicine Co. / Limited / Toronto, Can. [cover-title]

DESCRIPTION: 15.5 × 10.5 cm Pp 1–32 Paper; stapled, and with hole punched at top left corner for hanging

CONTENTS: 1–32 text

CITATIONS: Cooke 2002, p 234

COPIES: *NSWA OTUTF (uncat patent medicine) QMM (RBD ckbk 1503)

Hiller, Mrs Elizabeth O.

See Q80.1 for information about this American author.

O436.1 nd [about 1920]
The calendar of / cakes / fillings and frostings / recipes of 365 different cakes / and cookies, as well as / frostings and fillings / Compiled by / Elizabeth O. Hiller / Published and copyrighted / The P.F. Volland Company / Joliet, Illinois / New York Boston Toronto [cover-title]
DESCRIPTION: 28.0 × 14.0 cm Pp [1–119] Paper, with image on front of a woman poised to cut a cake; bound at top edge, and with two punched holes for hanging
CONTENTS: 1 'Foreword' signed E.O.H.; 2 blank; 3–5 'Cake Baking'; 6 blank; 7–105 recipe for every day in the year; 106 blank; 107–15 recipes for frostings and fillings; 116 blank; 117–19 'Index to Cake and Cookie Recipes' [keyed by date]
COPIES: *OGU (CCC TX715.6 H54)
NOTES: The verso pages are blank. The recipes include a birthday cake for each month, wedding and anniversary cakes, an appropriate cake for each holiday, ice-box cakes, and well-known cake recipes, such as Lady Baltimore Cake. In the 'Foreword' Hiller describes the latter as 'the original Lady Baltimore Cake, this recipe was copied from the original recipe which was presented to me by a former member of the Charleston, N.C., Woman's Exchange where the cake was sold.'

O437.1 nd [about 1920]
The calendar of / luncheons / teas and suppers / Compiled by / Elizabeth O. Hiller / [stamped?:] Published and copyrighted / The P.F. Volland Company / Joliet, Illinois / New York Boston Toronto [cover-title]
DESCRIPTION: 28.5 × 14.5 cm Pp [1–119] Paper, with image on front of three women having tea; stapled at top edge, and with two punched holes, through which runs a cord for hanging
CONTENTS: 1 'Foreword' signed Elizabeth O. Hiller; 2 blank; 3 'How to Measure Ingredients'; 4 blank; 5–109 menu and recipe for every day in the year; 110 blank; 111–13 'Meat and Fish Sauces'; 114 blank; 115–17 'Index to Luncheons and Teas'; 118 blank; 119 'The Six Famous Elizabeth O. Hiller Recipe Calendars'
COPIES: *QMM (RBD ckbk 1658)
NOTES: The verso pages are blank. The places of publication in the cover-title differentiate this edition from O437.2.

O437.2 nd [about 1920]
—The calendar of / luncheons / teas and suppers / Compiled by / Elizabeth O. Hiller / Published and copyrighted / P.F. Volland Company / Chicago / New York Boston Toronto [cover-title]
DESCRIPTION: 28.0 × 14.0 cm Pp [1–119] Paper, with image on front of three women having tea; bound at top edge and with two punched holes, through which runs a cord for hanging
CONTENTS: 1 'Foreword' signed Elizabeth O. Hiller; 2 blank; 3 'How to Measure Ingredients'; 4 blank; 5–109 menu and recipe for every day in the year; 110 blank; 111–13 'Meat and Fish Sauces'; 114 blank; 115–17 'Index to Luncheons and Teas'; 118 blank; 119 'The Six Famous Elizabeth O. Hiller Recipe Calendars'
COPIES: *Private collection
NOTES: The verso pages are blank. 'The Six Famous ... Recipe Calendars' listed on p 119 are 'Calendar of Cakes, Fillings, Frostings and Other Sweetmeats' (probably O436.1), 'New Calendar of Luncheons and Teas' (not O437.2?), 'New Dinners for All Occasions' (O440.1), 'The New Calendar of Desserts' (no edition found with a Canadian place of publication), 'Calendar of Sandwiches and Beverages' (O438.1), and 'The New Calendar of Salads' (O439.1).

AMERICAN EDITIONS: The following similarly titled work by Hiller may or may not be related to the two editions described above: *The Calendar of Luncheons: With 52 Practical Sunday Evening Suppers*, Chicago, New York: P.F. Volland, [1915?] (United States: MCR).

O438.1 nd [about 1920]
The calendar of / sandwiches / & beverages / 365 delicious, savory and sweet / sandwiches and beverages / Elizabeth O. Hiller / Published & copyrighted / P.F. Volland Company / New York Chicago Toronto [cover-title]
DESCRIPTION: 28.0 × 14.0 cm Pp [1–119] Paper, with image on front of a woman holding a cup of tea(?); bound at top edge, and with two punched holes, through which runs a cord for hanging
CONTENTS: 1 'Foreword' signed Elizabeth O. Hiller; 2 blank; top 3 'How to Measure' and 'Breads Used for Sandwiches'; mid 3–5 'Fancy Butters and Salad Dressings'; 6 blank; 7–105 menus and recipes for each day in the year; 106 blank; 107–15 'Hot and Cold Beverages'; 116 blank; 117–19 'Index to Recipes'
COPIES: *Private collection
NOTES: The form of the publisher's name and the places of publication differentiate this copy from O438.2.

O438.2 nd
—The calendar of / sandwiches / & beverages /
365 delicious, savory and sweet / sandwiches and
beverages / Elizabeth O. Hiller / Published &
copyrighted / The P.F. Volland Company / Joliet,
Illinois / New York Boston Toronto [cover-title]
DESCRIPTION: With image on front of a woman holding a cup of tea(?); bound at top edge, and with
two punched holes, through which runs a cord for
hanging
COPIES: *Private collection

AMERICAN EDITIONS: An edition is cited and illustrated in Longone/Longone R2.

O439.1 nd [about 1920]
New calendar of / salads / 365 answers to the daily
question / "What shall we have for salad?" /
Elizabeth O. Hiller / Published and copyrighted /
P.F. Volland Company / New York Chicago Toronto
[cover-title]
DESCRIPTION: With image on front of a woman mixing a bowl of salad; bound at top edge, and with
two punched holes, through which runs a cord for
hanging
COPIES: *Private collection

O440.1 nd [about 1920]
New / dinners / for all occasions / with
instructions for formal / and informal dinner
service / Elizabeth O. Hiller / Published and
copyrighted / The P.F. Volland Company / Joliet,
Illinois / New York Boston Toronto [cover-title]
DESCRIPTION: 28.0 × 14.0 cm   Pp [1–119]   Paper, with
image on front of a woman drawing apart drapes to
reveal a table set with two candles and a bowl of
fruit; stapled at top edge, and with two punched
holes, through which runs a cord for hanging
CONTENTS: 1 'Foreword' signed Elizabeth O. Hiller;
2 blank; 3–7 'Formal and Informal Dinners'; 8 blank;
9 'How to Measure Accurately'; 10 blank; 11–119
menus and recipes for special dinners (e.g., New
Year's, Thanksgiving) and for fifty numbered Sunday dinners
COPIES: *QMM (RBD ckbk 1657)
NOTES: The verso pages are blank.

O440.2 nd [about 1920]
—New / dinners / for all occasions including /
Sunday, holiday and anniversary dinners / with
instructions for formal / and informal dinner
service. / Compiled and arranged by / Elizabeth O.

Hiller / Published and copyrighted / P.F. Volland
Company / New York Chicago Toronto [cover-title]
DESCRIPTION: 28.0 × 14.0 cm   Pp [1–119]   Paper, with
image on front of a woman seated at a dinner table,
eating soup; stapled
CONTENTS: 1 'Foreword' signed Elizabeth O. Hiller;
2 blank; 3–7 'Formal and Informal Dinners'; 8 blank;
9 'How to Measure Accurately' and 'Methods of Cooking'; 10 blank; 11 'New Year's Dinner'; 12 blank; 13–
15 'Thanksgiving Dinner'; 16 blank; 17–19 'Christmas
Dinner'; 20 blank; 21–119 fifty numbered Sunday dinners (menus and recipes)
COPIES: *BKOM
NOTES: The verso pages are blank.

Kirk, Mrs Alice Gitchell

Also by this American author is Practical Food
Economy, *Boston: Little, Brown, 1917 (United States:
DLC).*

O441.1 1920
The people's / home recipe book / Book II / of the
/ People's / Home / Library / by / Mrs. Alice
Gitchell Kirk / lecturer and instructor / in domestic
science. / Author "Mrs. Kirk's Card Index /
Cooking Recipes" and "Handy / Expense Cards for
House Keepers." / Cleveland, Ohio. / Published
by / the R.C. Barnum Co. / Cleveland, Ohio –
Minneapolis, Minn. / Boston, Mass. / Imperial
Publishing Co. / Toronto, Canada / 1920
DESCRIPTION: 24.5 × 17.5 cm   Pp [1–2], i–iv, 1–238
2 tp illus black-and-brown of a woman with a bowl
and a woman carrying a tray; frontis portrait of the
author; 8 pls btwn pp iv and 1   Cloth
CONTENTS: 1 tp; 2 'Copyrighted 1910, by R.C. Barnum'
and copyright notice for the author's 'Card Index
Cooking Recipes,' earliest copyright date being 1906;
i–ii 'Author's Preface'; iii table of contents; iv 'List of
Illustrations'; 1–219 text; 220–2 blank for 'Supple-
ment. (Additional Recipes.)'; 223–38 'Culinary Index'
COPIES: *SR
NOTES: *The People's Home Recipe Book* was also pub-
lished as part of a larger volume, in various editions:
*The People's Home Library: A Library of Three Practical
Books*; see O348.1, under Ritter, T.J., Mrs Alice Gitchell
Kirk, and W.C. Fair.

AMERICAN EDITIONS: Cleveland: R.C. Barnum Co.,
1910 (United States: DLC).

Kitchen kraft

O442.1   nd [about 1920]
Kitchen / [same 1.6-cm initial 'K' as for 'Kitchen']raft / We may live without poetry, music and art; / We may live without conscience, and live without heart; / We may live without friends; we may live without books, / But civilized man can not live without cooks. / He may live without books – what is knowledge but grieving; / He may live without hope – what is hope but deceiving; / He may live without love – what is passion but pining; / But where is the man that can live without dining? / Compiled and published by the members of / the Argyll Chapter / Imperial Order Daughters of the Empire / Belleville – Ontario
DESCRIPTION: 22.5 × 15.0 cm   Pp [1–3] 4–56   Paper, with IODE symbol on front
CONTENTS: 1 tp; 2 'The Imperial Order Daughters of the Empire in Belleville' [a history of the Argyll Chapter]; 3 preface thanking those who assisted with the book and the advertisers; 4–55 recipes and ads; 56 index and ads
COPIES: *Private collection
NOTES: According to p 2, the Argyll Chapter was established on 1 November 1910, and since the war [i.e., the First World War], it 'has concentrated on more local social service work ...' The printer's name is on the outside back face of the binding: 'Ontario Intelligencer Print, Belleville.'

Nurses' cook book

The Royal Alexandra Hospital was founded by Abraham Groves, who purchased land for the hospital in 1901. From its beginnings (it was in operation by 1902), it was 'noted for [its] nurses-in-training program' (Looking Back: The Story of Fergus through the Years, Vol. 2, 1983, p 692).

O443.1   nd [about 1920 or earlier]
Nurses' / cook book / for the exclusive use of the / Royal Alexandra Hospital / Fergus, Ontario [cover-title]
DESCRIPTION: 22.5 × 15.0 cm   Pp [1] 2–20   Paper; stapled
CONTENTS: 1–18 recipes arranged in ten numbered lessons; 19–20 'Appendix' of additional recipes
CITATIONS: Driver 2001, Wellington County, p 90
COPIES: *OFERWM (A1996.86)
NOTES: The recipes are for invalid cookery and cover a wide variety of flavoured waters (for example, on

p 1, Oatmeal Water, Barley Water, Rice Water, Apple Water, and Toast Water), broths, gruels, beverages, soups, jellies, and other easily eaten dishes. OFERWM dates the book [1930], but from appearances, it was published about 1920 or earlier. The OFERWM copy is inscribed on the front face of the binding, in black ink, 'M. Thomson.'

Old homestead recipes

Maple Leaf Milling Co. was organized in 1910, taking over the assets of Maple Leaf Flour Mills Co. Head office was in Toronto. In 1961, the company amalgamated with Purity Flour Mills Ltd and Toronto Elevators Ltd to create Maple Leaf Mills Ltd. In 1991, Maple Leaf Mills Ltd and Canada Packers Inc. merged to become Maple Leaf Foods, which no longer mills flour. For a history of the business, see The Company That Grew with Canada, Maple Leaf Mills Ltd, *[about 1980].*

Another cookbook by Maple Leaf Milling Co. is O745.1, Recipes for Tea-Bisk. *For the titles of those published under the pseudonym of Anna Lee Scott, see O526.1.*

O444.1   nd [about 1920]
Old homestead / recipes / selected and compiled for users of / Monarch Pastry Flour by / Maple Leaf Milling / Company / Limited / Toronto Canada / Copyright Canada [cover-title]
DESCRIPTION: 22.5 × 14.5 cm   Pp [1–3] 4–78 [79–80]   Illus on p 1 of a house beside a tree, illus on p 3 of 'The Maple Leaf Mill at Port Colborne, Ont.'   Paper, with image on front of a house and two trees
CONTENTS: 1 publ's note 'To the Housewife:'; 2 blank; 3 information about Maple Leaf Milling Co.; 4 'Weights and Measures'; 5–76 recipes credited with the name of the contributor; 77–8 index; 79 blank; 80 'The Carswell Co., Limited printers – Toronto'
CITATIONS: Ferguson/Fraser, p 233, and illus col on p 57 of closed volume   Reitz, p [4]   Golick, p 101
COPIES: OGU (2 copies: *UA s066 b06, CCC TX715.6 O42)   OH (Special Collections Pamphlet File)   OKIT OKITD (968.137.021)   OKITJS (991.22.1)   OONL (AC901 A7 1930z No. 0020)   OSTPA   OTNY (uncat)   OWTU (G10576)   Company collection (Maple Leaf Mills Consumer Products Co.), in 1991; location now unknown   Private collection
NOTES: According to p 1, when compiling the book, the company 'had access – by means of a prize recipe contest – to the favorite recipes in over thirty thousand Canadian homes'; the judges were 'well-known domestic science experts.' The copy seen at Maple

Leaf Mills Consumer Products Co. in 1991 had the date '1920–21' pencilled on p 1. The private collector's copy has a loose, folded sheet inserted in the volume, headed 'Eighteen Prize Winning Recipes from the Cookies and Small Cakes Section of Our "Old Homestead Recipes" Book'; it says that *Old Homestead Recipes* was available on receipt of $0.25. A recipe from *Old Homestead Recipes* is reprinted in a Maple Leaf Milling Co. advertisement in O532.1, *305 Tested Recipes*, [about 1924–5].

Olive facts

William Gorman and D. Dyson established a spice company in 1883. When Dyson left in 1890, R.C. Eckert became Gorman's new partner. For other cookbooks by Gorman, Eckert and Co., see O1026.1, Gaige, Crosby, Season to Taste, and O1073.1, Delicious Mustard and Spice Recipes.

O445.1   nd [about 1920]
Olive / facts
DESCRIPTION: 9.5 × 7.0 cm   Pp [1] 2–23 [24]   Tp illus of a stylized olive tree, illus   Paper, with tp illus on front; stapled
CONTENTS: 1 tp; 2 'The Olive'; 3 fp illus; 4–6 'The Home of the Olive' and fp illus on p 5; 7 fp illus; 8–12 'The Olive Oil' and fp illus on pp 9 and 11; 13 fp illus; 14 'Imperial Club Salad'; 15 fp illus; 16 'Tomato Toast'; 17 fp illus; 18 'Stuffed Eggs'; 19 fp illus; 20 'Tomato Omelet'; 21 fp illus; 22 'French Fried Potatoes' and 'Stuffed Potatoes'; 23 'Potato Salad'; 24 'Gorman, Eckert and Company Limited London, Ont. Winnipeg, Man. Canada'
COPIES: *Private collection
NOTES: Gorman, Eckert and Co. sold olives under the Club House brand name. The title-page is printed in blue.

Ontario, Department of Agriculture

For the titles of other cookbooks published by the Ontario Department of Agriculture, see O158.1.

O446.1   August 1920
Ontario Department of Agriculture / Women's Institutes Branch / Circular No. 32 / Information and recipes / on / vegetables, fruits, / and salads. / [WI symbol] / Toronto, Ontario, August, 1920
CITATIONS: MacTaggart, p 37
COPIES: *OOAG
NOTES: The booklet has 16 pp.

Selected recipes

O447.1   1920
['Second number' of *Selected Recipes* by the Woman's Association of First Methodist Church, Hamilton, Ontario, 1920]
NOTES: This is the second of four cookbooks produced in the period 1914–48 by the women of First Methodist Church (called First United Church from 1925). The others are: O329.1, *Selected Recipes*; O799.1, *More Selected Recipes*; and O1178.1, *Cook Book*. No copies of the 1920 work were located, but it is referred to in O799.1 and in O1178.1; for more information, see those entries.

Selected recipes

O448.1   nd [about 1920]
Selected recipes / Published by / Falkland branch / of the / South Brant / Women's Institute / Motto: / "For home and country" [cover-title]
COPIES: *Private collection
NOTES: The recipes are credited with the name of the contributor. The last section in the book is 'Eggs and Omelets' on p 52. 'Walker Press, Limited, Paris, Ont.' is on the outside back face of the binding.

Some valuable recipes for canning fruits and vegetables

O449.1   nd [about 1920]
Some valuable recipes / for / canning fruits / and / vegetables / 10¢ / Compiled and published by / the T. Eaton Co Limited / Toronto and Winnipeg [cover-title]
DESCRIPTION: 15.5 × 11.5 cm   Pp [3] 4–29 [30–4]   Paper, with image on front of a woman holding a rack of bottled fruits and vegetables above a hot-water boiler; stapled
CONTENTS: Inside front face of binding 'Cook Books' [list of contemporary cookbooks, with prices, presumably available from Eaton's]; 3 'Instructions' and 'Blanching'; 4 'Simple Instructions for Canning Vegetables'; 5–22 recipes; 23–9 'The Drying of Fruits and Vegetables by M. Anna Hauser, Extension Specialist in Home Economics, State Agricultural College, New Brunswick, N.J.'; 30–4 blank for 'Memorandum'
COPIES: *QMM (RBD ckbk 1525)
NOTES: Of the cookbooks listed on the inside front face of the binding, only two are Canadian texts: *New Galt Cook Book*, $0.75 (one of O58.4–58.5); and *Home*

Cook Book, $0.90 (a later edition of O20.1). The rest are by American or British authors, but many were published in Canadian editions: *Boston Cooking School Cook Book,* by F.M. Farmer (O144.1); *White House Cook Book* [by Hugo Ziemann and Fanny Lemira Camp Gillette] (O93.1); *Mrs Rorer's New Cook Book* (O137.1); *Mrs Beeton's Cookery Book* (O256.1); *Cooking for Two,* by J.M. Hill; *Us Two Cook Book,* by Jennie B. Williams (O224.1); *Book of Entrees,* by J.M. Hill; *Salads, Sandwiches and Chafing Dish Dainties,* by J.M. Hill; *Canning, Preserving and Jelly-Making,* by J.M. Hill; *How to Cook in Casserole Dishes,* by M.H. Neil; *Canning, Preserving and Pickling,* by M.H. Neil (O325.1); *Mrs Rorer's Ice Creams, Water Ices, Frozen Puddings; Canning and Preserving,* by Mrs Rorer; *Sandwiches,* by Mrs Rorer; *Mrs Rorer's Cakes, Icings and Fillings; Home Candy Making,* by Mrs Rorer (O56.1); and *Candy Cook Book,* by Alice Bradley (O375.1).

Tried and tested recipes

O450.1   nd [about 1920]
Tried and tested / recipes / Christ Church / Cathedral / W A / Ottawa [cover-title]
DESCRIPTION: 16.5 × 10.0 cm   Pp [1–2] 3–61   Paper, with two small images on front: in centre, a covered platter from which steam escapes, and above, about nine standing books and one lying flat; stapled at top edge, and with two punched holes, through which is tied a brown cord for hanging
CONTENTS: 1 'These recipes have been contributed by the members of Christ Church Cathedral W.A. [i.e., Women's Association?] Ottawa'; 2 'Index' [i.e., table of contents]; 3 'Table of Measures and Weights'; 4 'Time Table for Cooking Meats and Vegetables'; 5–61 recipes
COPIES: *Private collection
NOTES: Since the book was designed to be hung, the verso pages are blank and not included in the pagination.

Tried and true recipes

The church is now known as St Andrew's Presbyterian Church.

O451.1   November 1920
Tried and true recipes / Compiled and arranged / by the / Girl's Club / of the / Willis Presbyterian Church / Clinton, Ontario / The officers and members of the Girl's Club / desire to thank the business and professional men / of Clinton and other places for the generous way / in which they have assisted them by contributing / advertisements. / [...] / Copies of this cook book may be obtained / from any of the members of the Girl's Club. / Clinton, Ontario, November 1920 / Ho! All Ye Poor Sinners. / [two-verse poem] / This page kindly donated by the Clinton News-Record. / [folio:] 1
COPIES: *Private collection

Valuable hints and helps for housekeepers

O452.1   nd [about 1920]
Valuable / hints and helps / for / housekeepers / Selected by the Ladies' Aid Society of Simpson Ave. Methodist / Church, for their tested value and usefulness in the homes of to-day. / Toronto: / The Armac Press, Limited
DESCRIPTION: 22.0 × 15.0 cm   Pp 3–144   Limp cloth; stapled
CONTENTS: 3–4 ads; 5 tp; 6 ads; 7 index of subject headings; 8 ads; 9 foreword signed the Committee; 10 ad; 11–143 text and ads; 144 ad
COPIES: *Private collection
NOTES: The running head is 'Simpson Avenue Methodist Church Cook Book.' The first leaf is missing in the private collector's copy, but the index of subject headings lists 'Church Directory' on 'cover page 2.' The wording of the foreword is nearly identical to the foreword in O497.1, *Cook Book,* published in Toronto, in 1923, by the Lord Salisbury Chapter of the IODE.

The wonderful story of Klim

See O374.1 for information about Canadian Milk Products Ltd and the titles of other cookbooks published by the company. O913.1, Easy Recipes for Camp and Kitchen, and O1171.1, Skillet Skills for Camp and Cottage, are later Klim recipe collections published by Borden Co. Ltd.

O453.1   nd [about 1920]
The wonderful story of / Klim [cover-title]
DESCRIPTION: 17.0 × 12.5 cm   Pp [1–2] 3–23   Illus col, illus   Paper, with image on front of cows under a tree, farm buildings in background, and a container of Klim in foreground; stapled
CONTENTS: 1 cover-title; 2 'Milk Is Food'; 3 'A Few Milk Facts'; 4 'The Ancients Used Dried Milk'; 5 'Present Day Manufacture of Powdered Milk in Sani-

tary Plants'; 6 'Where the Milk Comes From'; 7 'The Plants Are Scrupulously Clean'; 8–9 'Where Klim Is Made'; 10–11 'Comparative Food Values of Milk in the Diet'; 12–13 centre spread illus col of dishes made with Klim and a container of Klim; 14–21 'Recipes'; 22 'Standard Measurements and Tables'; 23 [inside back face of binding] index

COPIES: *Private collection

NOTES: The name of the Toronto manufacturer of Klim, Canadian Milk Products Ltd, appears on the Klim container depicted on the front face of the binding. The printer's name, 'R.C. Smith & Son, Limited Toronto,' is on the outside back face. Rubber-stamped above the printer's name is 'The T. Eaton Co Limited Toronto Canada.'

Four Klim plants are illustrated on pp 8–9, including 'First milk powder plant in Canada // Brownsville, Ont. (1903)' and 'Plant No. 1 Brownsville, Ont. (1919).' The text on p 2 states: 'The greatest development in the milk industry in the last ten years is the process of removing the water and fat from milk and drying into powder form the solids which have the flavor, the color and the body-building food value of separated milk. The result of this process is Klim – pure pasteurized separated milk in powder form.' From appearances, the book was published about the time of the illustration of Plant No. 1 dated 1919, perhaps in 1920.

1920s

[Title unknown]

O454.1   nd [about 1920s]
[An edition of a cookbook from Knox Church, Listowel, Ontario]

COPIES: Private collection

NOTES: The date is uncertain, but the owner describes it as 'very old.'

1920–2

Saving without sacrificing

The William Davies Co. was established in 1854, according to p 2 of Saving without Sacrificing. *In 1927 the firm merged with the Harris Abattoir Co. Ltd, the Canadian Packing Co. Ltd, and Gunns Ltd to form Canada Packers Ltd.*

O455.1   nd [about 1920–2]
Saving without / sacrificing / Contents / Meat and Its Nutrition 3 / How to Choose Meat 3 / Careful Marketing 4 / What Cuts of Meat to Ask For 5 / Inexpensive Cuts of Meat 6 / Meats – Their Care and Preparation 7 / Meats – How to Keep and Cook 8 / Carving 9 / To Carve a Roast of Beef 9 / To Serve a Leg of Lamb or Mutton 9 / Cuts of Beef Illustrated 10 16–17 / Recipes for Cooking Beef 11 / Cuts of Lamb and Mutton 18 / Recipes for Cooking Mutton 18 / Cuts of Pork Illustrated 21 / Recipes for Cooking Pork 21 / Fancy Meats – As Economical as They Are Good 25 / The / William Davies / Company / Limited / Toronto Montreal / Canada Food Packer's License No. 13–50

DESCRIPTION: 23.0 × 14.0 cm   Pp [1–2] 3–32   Illus col, illus   [$0.35, on binding]   Paper, with still-life on front of a basket of foods, a loaf of bread, and a brick-shaped package tied with string; stapled

CONTENTS: 1 tp; 2 publ's letter 'To the Canadian housewife'; 3–32 text

COPIES: *Private collection

NOTES: This item was published no later than 1922, when it was cited in the William Davies advertisement on p 251 of O294.2, *The Wimodausis Club Cook Book*: 'Free! Write for our booklet "Saving without Sacrificing."' There is an advertisement on p 29 of *Saving without Sacrificing* for Davies Peerless Oleomargarine. The margarine advertisement limits publication to the period 1917–23, when the 1886 ban on margarine was temporarily lifted because of food shortages during the First World War. Its appearance is consistent with publication in about 1920–2.

The running head is 'Food Economy' and the purpose of the book, according to p 2, was 'to preach and practise a doctrine of true economy ...' The following philosophy for meat-eating, possibly influenced by wartime experience, is offered on p 3: 'The aggressive, dominant nation is usually found to be a meat consuming nation. A people properly nourished – well-fed – healthy – will always be an aggressive nation: whereas ill-fed, under-nourished people lack enterprise and aggressiveness because of poor vitality which always handicaps efficiency.' There are illustrations of, and information about, Davies packaged meats and other products on pp 30–1.

1920–3

'Please make us a cake'

Also published by Harris Abattoir is O587.1, Rees, Margaret H., Tempting Domestic Recipes.

O456.1   nd [about 1920–3]
"Please make / us a cake" / Use / Domestic Shortening / Makes delicious pastry – lightest cakes / The Harris Abbatoir [*sic*] Company, Limited / Toronto, Canada [cover-title]
DESCRIPTION: 14.5 × 11.5 cm   Pp [3] 4–12 [13–14] Illus red, black, and yellow   Paper, with image on front of a girl and boy entreating their mother to make a cake with Domestic Shortening; stapled
CONTENTS: 3 'Domestic Shortening "Better than butter – cheaper than lard" What It Is – How to Use It' and at bottom, 'The Harris Abbatoir [*sic*] Company, Limited. Toronto, Canada'; 4–11 'Recipes'; 12 'Hints for the Housewife'; 13 testimonials for Domestic Shortening; 14 publ ad for H.A. [i.e., Harris Abattoir] Brand Oleomargarine; inside back face of binding order form for a free booklet that contains recipes for baking with H.A. Brand Oleomargarine [no copy located]
CITATIONS: Driver 2003, 'Canadian Cookbooks,' pp 24–5
COPIES: *OONL (TX763 P64 1920z p***)
NOTES: The booklet was published before the Harris Abattoir Co. Ltd merged in 1927 with the William Davies Co., the Canadian Packing Co. Ltd, and Gunns Ltd to form Canada Packers Ltd. The oleomargarine advertisement limits publication to the period 1917–23, when the 1886 ban on margarine was temporarily lifted because of food shortages during the First World War. From appearances the book was published about 1920–3.

1920–5

Care of the home and useful information

Dr Ray Vaughn Pierce (Starke, NY, 1840–) grew rich selling medicines made at his World's Medical Dispensary and running the Invalids' Hotel and Surgical Institute, both in Buffalo, New York, to which he had moved in 1867. See also O570.1, Good Cooking, another advertising booklet for his business.

O457.1   nd [about 1920–5]
Care of the home / and useful information [cover-title]

DESCRIPTION: 20.5 × 14.0 cm   Pp [1] 2–32
CONTENTS: top 1 'Hang Up This Booklet' signed World's Dispensary Medical Association, Bridgeburg, Ontario; mid 1–4 'Useful Recipes for the Household' and publ ad; 5 publ ad; 6–22 cooking information and recipes, and publ ads; 23 publ ad; 24–6 'First Aid to the Injured' and publ ad; 27–32 publ ads
COPIES: *OGU (CCC TX715.6 C38)
NOTES: The advertisements are for Dr Pierce's medicines. The advertisement on p 29 is for the Invalids' Hotel and Surgical Institute.

Cowan's book of jingles

See O336.1 for a list of other cookbooks by Cowan Co. Ltd.

O458.1   nd [about 1920–5]
Cowan's / book of / jingles [cover-title]
DESCRIPTION: 7.5 × 5.0 cm   Pp [1–15] 6 fp illus brown of nursery rhymes   Paper, with image on front of Miss Muffet spilling her curds and whey; stapled at top edge
CONTENTS: 1 cover-title; 2 'Cowan's Perfection Cocoa'; 3 'How to Make a Delicious Cup of Cocoa' and at bottom, 'The Cowan Co., Limited Toronto'; 4 fp illus of Red Riding Hood; 5 'Red Riding Hood' and recipe for Cocoa Cocoanut Cookies; 6 fp illus of Mary, Quite Contrary; 7 'Mary, Quite Contrary' and Cocoa Fudge; 8 fp illus of a sleeping baby in a tree top; 9 'Rock-a-Bye Baby' and Cocoanut Cream Ice; 10 fp illus of Jack and Jill tumbling downhill; 11 'Jack and Jill' and Cocoa Cup Cakes; 12 fp illus of Boy Blue sleeping in a haystack; 13 'Little Boy Blue' and Cocoa Cake; 14 fp illus of Simple Simon fishing; 15 'Simple Simon' and Chocolate Icing for Cakes
COPIES: *Private collection
NOTES: The text and illustrations are appropriately printed in brown. Each nursery rhyme has been re-written to incorporate a reference to Cowan's Cocoa; for example: 'Rock-a-bye Baby on the Tree Top, / The winds may whistle and blow so, / You're chubby and fat and can stand things like that, / Nourished on Cowan's Cocoa.'

Cowan's Cocoa insures a wealth of health

See O336.1 for a list of other cookbooks by Cowan Co. Ltd.

O459.1   nd [about 1920–5]
Cowan's / Cocoa / insures a wealth of health [cover-title]

DESCRIPTION: 15.5 × 11.0 cm Pp 1–14 Illus col, illus brown Paper, with image on front of a young child beside a sled, on a snow-covered hill; stapled
CONTENTS: 1 [inside front face of binding] 'Children Thrive on Cowan's Cocoa'; 2–14 [inside back face] recipes
COPIES: ONM *QMM (RBD ckbk 1463)
NOTES: The colour illustrations are of Cocoa Fruit Roll, Cocoa Float, Cocoa Layer Cake, and Cocoa Reception Cake. The centre spread on pp 7–8 is a colour illustration of Cowan's chocolate bars, all costing $0.05. 'Booklet -G-' is on the outside back face of the binding.

Cowan's Cocoa makes good things to eat

See O336.1 for a list of other cookbooks by Cowan Co. Ltd.

O460.1 nd [about 1920–5]
Cowan's / Cocoa / makes good things to eat [cover-title]
DESCRIPTION: 13.0 × 9.0 cm Pp [1–15] Illus brown of prepared dishes Paper, with image on front of two young children looking through a window at two cakes; stapled
CONTENTS: 1 cover-title; 2 'Children Thrive on Cowan's Cocoa' signed Cowan's, Toronto; 3–15 [inside back face of binding] recipes using Cowan's Cocoa as an ingredient
COPIES: *Private collection
NOTES: The text on p 2 states: 'Children do thrive on cocoa. Your doctor says so and every mother knows what an important part this food should play in the diet of the little ones ... Cakes, puddings, custards and other tempting dishes that have the delicious flavor which Cowan's Cocoa imparts will always be in great demand by the children.' The booklet includes recipes for cakes, puddings, and custards. The text and illustrations are appropriately printed in brown.

Cowan's Cocoa recipes

See O336.1 for a list of other cookbooks by Cowan Co. Ltd.

O461.1 nd [about 1920–5]
Cowan's / Cocoa recipes [cover-title]
DESCRIPTION: 10.5 × 8.5 cm Pp [1–2] 3–15 Illus brown Paper, with image on front of a three-layer cake; stapled
CONTENTS: 1 cover-title; 2 'Use More Cocoa,' 'Directions' [for substituting cocoa for squares of chocolate

in recipes], 'Free' [instructions for ordering 'a very interesting little booklet entitled "The Story of the Cocoa Bean"'], and 'Cowan's // The great chocolate industry of Canada // Toronto'; 3–14 recipes; 15 [inside back face of binding] fp illus of Cowan's Cocoa box and a cake
COPIES: SSWD *Private collection
NOTES: The text and illustrations are appropriately printed in brown. This little booklet is not to be confused with the 64-page cookbook of the same name, O468.1, 'Cowan's Cocoa Recipes,' of 1921.

Delicious marshmallow recipes

Willards Chocolates Ltd, first listed in Toronto city directories in 1913, was still in business in the last quarter of the twentieth century.

O462.1 nd [about 1920–5]
"Drum-Major" / Delicious / marshmallow / recipes. / Willards Chocolates Ltd. / Toronto, Canada / Marshmallows [cover-title]
DESCRIPTION: 8.5 × 6.5 cm Pp [1–16] Paper; stapled
CONTENTS: 1 cover-title; 2–15 recipes for cooking with marshmallows, credited with the initials of the contributor (e.g., L.R.)
COPIES: *Private collection
NOTES: Drum-Major was the brand name of the Toronto company's marshmallows.

The treasury cook book

Women from the same church (renamed Bathurst Street United Church) produced O763.1, Kitchen Lore.

O463.1 nd [about 1920–5]
[An edition of *The Treasury Cook Book,* published under the auspices of the Ladies' Aid Society of Bathurst Street Methodist Church, Toronto, nd, pp 112]
COPIES: Private collection

Tried and tested recipes

O464.1 nd [about 1920–5]
Tried and tested / recipes / [caption:] St. Paul's Church, Marmora / Compiled and arranged by / the Ladies' Guild / of / St. Paul's Church, Marmora
DESCRIPTION: Tp illus of the Anglican church
COPIES: *Private collection
NOTES: The last page, p 124, lists 'Names of Contributors of Recipes.' The private collector's copy is in-

scribed on the binding by her husband's grandmother, 'Bella Gray.' The family believes the cookbook was published about 1920. There is an advertisement for Deloro Chemical Co. Ltd, promoting its 'arsenate of lime' insecticide. Since Deloro's insecticide plant was built in 1920, the cookbook could not have been published before that date.

1921

Allen, Miss Olive

O465.1   nd [about 1921]
Form C-1521 / Miss Olive Allen's / tested recipes / 200 / selected from many hundreds / gathered from all over the world / The Procter & Gamble Manufacturing Co. / Hamilton, Canada
DESCRIPTION: 16.5 × 10.5 cm   Pp [1–3] 4–80   Tp illus of cake, a few small illus   Paper, with image on front of a mother sprinkling coconut on an iced cake, daughter to her right, holding empty icing bowl and licking spoon; stapled
CONTENTS: 1 tp; 2 'Pastry Hints,' 'Cake Hints,' 'Deep Frying Hints,' and 'Crisco is the trade mark for a superior shortening manufactured by the Procter & Gamble Company ...'; 3–6 'Miss Olive Allen's Tested Recipes' [introductory text]; 7–77 recipes; 78–80 index
COPIES: *Private collection
NOTES: The cookbook was published to promote the use of Crisco shortening, first marketed by Procter and Gamble in 1911. The introductory text offers the following information about Miss Allen and the recipe collection:

> [She is] a real home cook with many years' experience ... She has had charge of the food departments in family hotels, business men's clubs, canteens and army and navy clubs. She has catered to the tastes of business girls and college girls.
>
> Recently she has been gathering recipes and testing them in her unique skyscraper kitchen. These recipes have come from all over the world – ...
>
> From the many hundreds [*sic*, no 'of'] recipes received, Miss Allen has selected her favorite two hundred. These two hundred recipes have been appearing one each day in newspapers throughout the United States and Canada ... we have assembled them in this convenient book form.

Miss Allen has annotated each recipe with its source and with comments on the quality of the recipe.

Canadian recipes are included; for example, French Fried Potatoes from Canada, annotated 'This recipe won a prize in a Canadian recipe contest,' on p 21, Crisco Scones from Ontario, p 29, Fluffy Biscuits from Canada, p 30, A French Dainty from Alberta, p 47, Grandmother's Delicious Ginger Bread from Brantford, Ontario, p 70, and Cornflake Puffs from Ontario, p 71. Readers are advised to send any questions about Crisco to Home Economics Department, The Procter and Gamble Co., Cincinnati, Ohio.

O465.2   nd
—Form C-1521 / Miss Olive Allen's / tested recipes / 200 / selected from many hundreds / gathered from all over the world / The Procter & Gamble Manufacturing Co. / Hamilton, Canada / Printed in U.S.A.
DESCRIPTION: 16.5 × 10.5 cm   Pp [1–3] 4–80   Tp illus of a two-layer cake, a few small illus   Paper, with image on front of a mother sprinkling coconut on an iced cake, daughter to her right, holding empty icing bowl and licking spoon; stapled
CONTENTS: 1 tp; 2 'The McDonald Printing Co. Cincinnati, Ohio'; 3–6 'Miss Olive Allen's Tested Recipes'; 7–77 recipes; 78–80 index
COPIES: *APROM   OONL (TX715 A47 1920z p***)
NOTES: Unlike O465.1, this edition has 'Printed in U.S.A.' on the title-page and the printer's name on p 2 (instead of hints and copyright information).

AMERICAN EDITIONS: Form 1521, Cincinnati: Procter and Gamble Co., nd (OGU; United States: InU).

Caldwell, Miss Kathleen Mary Frances

For information about this author, known as Katherine or Kay, see O877.1, under the pseudonym Ann Adam, which she created for her own business purposes.

O466.1   [copyright 1921]
Form 852 / Recettes pour tous les jours / Compilées d'après la bibliothèque culinaire de Crisco / par / Katherine M. Caldwell, B.A. / The Procter & Gamble Manufacturing Co. / Hamilton, Canada
DESCRIPTION: 18.0 × 12.5 cm   Pp [1–2] 3–59   Tp illus col of three women seated at table, illus col   Thin card; stapled
CONTENTS: 1 tp; 2 introductory text and 'Copyright 1921, The Procter & Gamble Manufacturing Co.'; 3–4 'Connaissez-vous le Crisco?'; 5–8 'Emploi du Crisco pour toute cuisine' signed Procter and Gamble Manufacturing Co., Hamilton, Canada; 9 'Points à se

rappeler pour l'exécution des recettes'; 10–57 recipes; 58 'Mesures' and 'Comment mesurer'; 59 'Table des recettes'

COPIES: *Private collection

NOTES: The text on p 2 indicates that this edition of the book was produced specifically for the Quebec market, with reference to Quebec culinary authorities:

L'éditeur tient à exprimer sa gratitude à l'École ménagère de Montréal et l'École ménagère de Saint Pascal pour l'aimable empressement avec lequel ces institutions lui ont fourni des données intéressantes pour la composition de son petit livre de cuisine.

Le livre publié par les Dames de la Congrégation de Saint Pascal, La cuisine raisonnée [Q102.1, *Manuel de cuisine raisonnée,* first published in 1919], a été une aide précieuse tant au point de vue de la théorie culinaire que pour un certain nombre d'excellentes recettes.

Les remerciements de l'éditeur s'étendent aussi à l'École ménagère provinciale qui lui a donné des renseignements si complets sur les ressources et usages culinaires du Canada français et à Mademoiselle Aurore Bétournay pour ... un article intitulé 'Mets pour remplacer la viande' qui constitue le dernier chapitre de ce livre [i.e., pp 57–9].

Canada, Department of Marine and Fisheries

For the titles of other collections of fish recipes by the department, see O319.1.

O467.1 1921

Department of Marine and Fisheries / Ottawa, – Canada / Hon. C.C. Ballantyne, Minister / Eat more fish / hints to the cook on how it / should be treated / Bulletin No. 3 / Issued by Publicity Division of Fisheries Branch / Ottawa / F.A. Acland / printer to the King's Most Excellent Majesty / 1921 / 25216–1

DESCRIPTION: 20.0 × 10.0 cm   Pp [1] 2–24   Paper, with bar graph on front indicating average meat and fish consumption for 1920 and image on front of fish; stapled

CONTENTS: 1 tp; 2 'When Seafish Are Most Abundant'; 3–mid 4 'Why Is Fish Overlooked?'; mid 4–mid 5 'Fish Excellent Food and Cheap'; mid 5–mid 6 'Make Sure Fish Is Prime'; mid–bottom 6 'About Frozen Fish'; top–near bottom 7 'A Few General Rules'; bottom 7–mid 8 'How to Fry Fish'; mid 8–top 9 'How to Boil Fish'; mid 9–10 'Our Canned Sea Food'; 11–top 12 'About Fish Recipes'; near top 12–mid 22 recipes grouped by type of fish: cod, haddock, flatfish, fresh herring, kippered herring, bloaters, mackerel, halibut, salmon, and 'Other Fishes'; mid 22 'Canned Fish'; bottom 22–top 23 'Varieties of Salmon'; mid 23 'A Staple Preparation' [i.e., 'an improvement on the usual method of cooking fish' suggested by Mrs Evelene Spencer, 'who won considerable prominence a few years ago by her campaign to urge American people to eat more fish']; bottom 23–24 prize-winning recipes in a contest held by the Fisheries Branch

COPIES: BDEM   *Private collection

NOTES: See also O377.1, Canada, Food Controller for Canada, *Eat More Fish,* 1917, and O401.1, Canada, Canada Food Board, *Fish Recipes,* a retitled edition of 1918.

'Cowan's Cocoa recipes'

See O336.1 for a list of other cookbooks by Cowan Co. Ltd.

O468.1 nd [1921]

"Cowan's Cocoa recipes" / A book describing / new ways of using / cocoa in the making / of delicious things / to eat and drink. / Published and copyrighted by / the Cowan Company Limited / Toronto, Canada.

DESCRIPTION: 23.0 × 15.5 cm   Pp [1–6] 7–60 [61–4] Tp illus col, in circular frame, of a mother and child amidst maple leaves; centre spread double-sided pl col on pp 31–4; 5 double-sided pls col on pp 11–12, 21–2, 43–4, 53–4, and 63–4; illus col on p 2 of Cowan's factory; illus black-and-orange on p 4 of 'Cocoa // Food of the Gods'   Paper, with still-life on front of a three-layer cake with chocolate icing, and a coffee pot and cups; stapled

CONTENTS: 1 tp; 2 illus col; 3 'Historical'; 4 illus black-and-orange; 5 'Children Thrive on Cowan's Cocoa' and 'Ideal for Invalids'; 6 'Cooking with Cowan's Cocoa' and 'Cocoa Syrup'; 7–60 recipes; 61–top 62 index; mid–bottom 62 'Cowan's Table of Measurements'; 63–4 double-sided pl col

CITATIONS: Driver 2003, 'Canadian Cookbooks,' pp 36–7   O'Neill (unpublished)

COPIES: CIHM (85295)   OGU (CCC TX715.6 C688) OONL (TX715 C3465 No. 28 reserve)   OTNY (641.3374 C)   *Private collection; Great Britain: LB (Woolwich)

NOTES: O'Neill records 1921 as the year of publication, based on copyright records at the British Library. An advertisement for Cowan's '64-page recipe book' in the April 1922 issue of *Western Home Monthly* – just a few months into the next year – confirms 1921 as the likely date of publication.

The striking reproductions of watercolours are signed 'A. Helene Carter' (her signature is not legible on all the illustrations, but it is clear on p 44). Augusta Helene was born in 1889 to Louisa and Augustus Carter of Toronto (1901 Census). See pl 4.

The Cowan Company proudly promoted its goods as 'Made in Canada.' The colour plate on p 64 for Cowan's Maple Buds refers to the candy as 'the National Confection of Canada' and widely imitated.

The OGU and OONL copies lack their bindings.

MacMurchy, Dr Helen (Toronto, Ont., 7 January 1862–8 October 1953)

Helen MacMurchy was the daughter of Marjory Jardine Ramsay and Dr Archibald MacMurchy, principal of Jarvis Collegiate in Toronto. She and her sisters Bessie and Marjory (the latter was to become a noted writer and a proponent of women's rights) grew up in the family home at 122 South Drive in Toronto's Rosedale neighbourhood. Helen graduated from the University of Toronto in 1901, with First Class Honours in medicine and surgery. She was the first woman intern at Toronto General Hospital. After post-graduate work at Johns Hopkins Hospital in Baltimore, Maryland, under Sir William Osler, she set up private practice in Toronto. She served for a short time as medical officer to the Toronto Board of Education, where she battled publicly with the board over standards of medical inspection before resigning. In 1913 the Ontario government appointed her inspector of the feeble-minded. She wrote weekly articles for the Canadian Countryman *through 1914 and into 1915, sometimes discussing cookery (e.g., 'Cheese Dishes,' 'Fruits in Season,' 'Some Favorite Salads,' and 'School Lunches' on 31 January, 7 March, 21 March, and 9 May 1914). In 1920 she became chief of the Division of Child Welfare in the federal Department of Health, retiring from the position in November 1933. While at the Department of Health, she wrote* The Canadian Mother's Book *(first of several editions, 1921; 800,000 copies printed) and* The Little Blue Books, *of which* How We Cook in Canada *is No. 6. Earlier, as medical officer for Toronto schools, she wrote, with Henry W. Auden, principal of Upper Canada College,* Simple Rules of Health and Courtesy for Those at School, London, New York, Toronto, and Melbourne: Cassell and Co. Ltd, 1911 *(Private collection); Section II of this 16-page booklet covers 'Food and Drink,' discussing what to eat and how. For her pioneering work as a woman doctor,* she was granted many honours, including Commander of the British Empire (1934), life fellow of the Academy of Medicine (1939), and, from Hobart and William Smith College, the Elizabeth Blackwell citation as one of the ten leading women physicians of the Western World (1949). She is buried in Mount Pleasant Cemetery, Toronto.

For more information, see: Mary Josephine Trotter, 'Prominent Women,' Everywoman's World *(June 1914), p 6; Jean Bannerman,* Leading Ladies, Canada, 1639–1967, *Dundas, Ont., 1967, pp 98–100;* Canadian Women of Note No. 544; *Carlotta Hacker,* The Indomitable Lady Doctors, *Toronto: Clarke Irwin and Co. Ltd, 1974; Kathleen McConnachie, 'Methodology in the Study of Women in History: A Case Study of Helen MacMurchy, M.D.,'* Ontario History *Vol. 75, No. 1 (March 1983), pp 61–70; 'The MacMurchys' in Michael Kluckner,* Toronto the Way It Was, *Toronto: Whitecap Books (Toronto) Ltd, 1988; Dagg; and newspaper clippings on microfilm in TPL Scrapbooks.*

O469.1 1921
Department of Health, Canada / The Home Series / 6. – How we cook in Canada. / Issued by authority / Department of Health / Ottawa / Division of Child Welfare The Little Blue Books / Ottawa / F.A. Acland / printer to the King's Most Excellent Majesty / 1921 / 26621–1
DESCRIPTION: 20.5 × 12.5 cm   Pp [1–2] 3–35   Paper; stapled
CONTENTS: 1 tp; 2 quotations from B.M., Ruskin, Amiel, and George MacDonald; 3–35 text, and at bottom p 35, 'Helen MacMurchy.'
COPIES: *OTUTF (den/pam)
NOTES: The author writes in a cheerful and direct style about cooking in Canada, which, she says, 'is done, of course, by the same methods and on the same principles as in other countries, varying with the time of year, the climate, the food-supply, the kitchen equipment and the knowledge, resources, skill and interest of the mistress.' At the outset she describes the various types of stove Canadian housewives may have and explains the pros and cons of each, including wood, coal, coal-oil, gas, and electricity. For those with woodstoves, she suggests planting a wood lot on their farm: 'By the time the baby is ten years old and that is pretty soon a row of Manitoba maples will be big enough for firewood.'

Her advice is practical and her tone, encouraging. About 'Good Cooking' she writes, 'If you can bake bread, make porridge, cook eggs, fish, meat and vegetables and make good soup, tea and coffee you are "off to a good start." Perhaps we had better put in pie, too. Pies please people – especially apple pies, ...'

Supportive of women who may not have the newest equipment, she suggests that a double boiler is excellent for cooking oatmeal and explains exactly how, but then she reminds the reader that the Canadian pioneers made just as good porridge as anybody in the New or Old World without any such utensil: 'Their porridge pot was iron and do you remember how easy it was to scrape?' She gives extensive information about baking, including steps and a timetable for Baking Day, and various methods of making bread.

A reference on p 34 to eating pies on 19 February 1921 is evidence that this is the first edition. On the outside back face of the binding there is a list of the fourteen titles in 'The Little Blue Books // The Home Series' and the note: 'Mention whether the English or French edition is desired.' The series covers all sorts of domestic topics, from managing housework and waste disposal to building a house. Given the variety of topics, it is possible that the series was written by government staff, then published under MacMurchy's name.

Dagg, p 186, comments on the book, without citing the edition.

O469.2 1922
—Department of Health, Canada / The Home Series / 6. – How we cook in Canada. / Issued by authority / Department of Health / Ottawa / Division of Child Welfare The Little Blue Books / Ottawa / F.A. Acland / printer to the King's Most Excellent Majesty / 1922 / 33605–1
DESCRIPTION: 20.0 × 12.5 cm   Pp [1–2] 3–35   Paper; stapled
CONTENTS: 1 tp; 2 quotations from B.M., Ruskin, Amiel, and George MacDonald; 3–35 text, and at bottom p 35, 'Helen MacMurchy.'
CITATIONS: Ferguson/Fraser, p 233, illus col on p 57 of closed volume
COPIES: AHRMH (982-059-128)   *Private collection
NOTES: Like O469.1, there is a reference on the binding to 'the English or French edition.'

O469.3 1923
—Dominion of Canada / Department of Health / How we cook / in / Canada / by / Helen MacMurchy, M.D., (Tor.) / Chief of the Division of Child Welfare / [Canada's coat of arms] / The Little Blue Books / Household Series / Ottawa / F.A. Acland / printer to the King's Most Excellent Majesty / 1923
DESCRIPTION: 20.5 × 12.5 cm   Pp [3–4] 5–52   Frontis of 'Harvest-Time in Western Canada,' 6 fp illus Paper, with Canada's coat of arms on front; stapled
CONTENTS: 3 tp; 4 quotations from B.M., Ruskin,

Amiel, George MacDonald, and Marion Talbot; 5–52 text
CITATIONS: Dagg, p 187
COPIES: *ACG ACU OHM OONL (C.O.P. COP.CA.H. 464, 2 copies)   OWTU (F9397)
NOTES: In this edition and onward, MacMurchy's name is on the title-page. 'Publication No. 13' is on the front face of the binding.

O469.4 1925
—Dominion of Canada / Department of Health / How we cook / in / Canada / by / Helen MacMurchy, M.D., (Tor.) / Chief of the Division of Child Welfare / [Canada's coat of arms] / The Little Blue Books / Household Series / Ottawa / F.A. Acland / printer to the King's Most Excellent Majesty / 1925
DESCRIPTION: 20.5 × 12.5 cm   Pp [3–4] 5–52   Frontis, 6 fp illus   Paper, with Canada's coat of arms on front; stapled
CONTENTS: 3 tp; 4 quotations from B.M., Ruskin, Amiel, George MacDonald, and Marion Talbot; 5–52 text
COPIES: *BKOM   QMM (RBD TX681 M336 1925)
NOTES: 'Publication No. 13' is on the front face of the binding.

O469.5 1925
—[An edition of *La cuisine canadienne*, Ottawa: Ministère de la santé, 1925, pp 70, Les petits livres bleus, Collection domestique, Publication 13]
COPIES: OONL (C.O.P. COP.CA. H. 469, 2 copies)

O469.6 1927
—Dominion of Canada / Department of Health / How we cook / in / Canada / by / Helen MacMurchy, M.D., (Tor.) / Chief of the Division of Child Welfare / [Canada's coat of arms] / The Little Blue Books / Household Series / Ottawa / F.A. Acland / printer to the King's Most Excellent Majesty / 1927
DESCRIPTION: 20.5 × 12.5 cm   Pp [1–4] 5–52   Frontis of 'Harvest-Time in Western Canada,' 6 fp illus Paper, with Canada's coat of arms on front; stapled
CONTENTS: 1 tp; 2 quotations from B.M., Ruskin, Amiel, George MacDonald, and Marion Talbot; 5–52 text
COPIES: ABOM   *SRA

O469.7 1929
—Dominion of Canada / Department of Pensions and National Health / How we cook / in / Canada / by / Helen MacMurchy, M.D., (Tor.) / Chief of the Division of Child Welfare / [Canada's coat of arms]

/ The Little Blue Books / Household Series /
Ottawa / F.A. Acland / printer to the King's Most
Excellent Majesty / 1929
DESCRIPTION: 20.5 × 12.5 cm   Pp [3–4] 5–52   Frontis
of 'Harvest-Time in Western Canada,' 6 illus   Paper;
stapled
CONTENTS: 3 tp; 4 quotations from B.M., Ruskin,
Amiel, George MacDonald, and Marion Talbot; 5–52
text
COPIES: *NSHD
NOTES: 'National Health Publication No. 13' is on the
front face of the binding. On the back face there is a
reference to 'the English or the French edition.'

O469.8   1929
—Santé nationale / Publication nº 13 / Canada /
La cuisine / canadienne / par / Helen MacMurchy,
D.M., (Toronto) / Directrice du Service du bien-être
de l'enfance / (Traduit par Maurice Morisset) /
[Canada's coat of arms] / Les petits livres bleus /
Collection domestique / Ottawa / F.A. Acland /
imprimeur de sa très excellente majesté le roi / 1929
/ 83176–1
DESCRIPTION: 20.5 × 12.5 cm   Pp [3–4] 5–71   Frontis
of 'Le Temps de la moisson dans les prairies de l'ouest
canadien,' 6 fp illus   Paper, with Canada's coat of
arms on front; stapled
CONTENTS: 3 tp; 4 quotations from Amiel, Sénèque,
Brillat-Savarin, Ruskin, Le P. Buffier, and Franklin;
5–71 text
CITATIONS: BQ Exposition 1974, p 23   Carrière No.
260
COPIES: *QMBM (Env. 2130)   QMBN
NOTES: The French edition has a different selection of
quotations on p 4.

O469.9   1932
—Dominion of Canada / Department of Pensions
and National Health / How we cook / in / Canada
/ by / Helen MacMurchy, M.D., (Tor.) / Chief of the
Division of Child Welfare / [Canada's coat of arms]
/ The Little Blue Books / Household Series /
Ottawa / F.A. Acland / printer to the King's Most
Excellent Majesty / 1932
COPIES: *ACHP

O469.10   1932
— Santé nationale / Publication nº 13 / Canada /
La cuisine / canadienne / par / Helen MacMurchy,
D.M. (Toronto) / Directrice du Service du bien-être
de l'enfance / (Traduit par Maurice Morisset) / Les
petits livres bleus / Collection domestique / Ottawa
/ F.A. Acland / imprimeur de sa très excellente
majesté le roi / 1932 / 50337–1

DESCRIPTION: 20.5 × 12.5 cm   Pp [3–4] 5–71   Frontis
of 'Le temps de la moisson dans les prairies de l'ouest
canadien,' 6 fp illus   Paper; stapled
CONTENTS: 3 tp; 4 quotations from Amiel, Sénèque,
Brillat-Savarin, Ruskin, Le P. Buffier, and Franklin;
5–71 text
COPIES: *QSFFSC
NOTES: This copy is stamped on the binding, 'Rec'd
30 Sep 1932.'

The Magic way

*For information about E.W. Gillett Co. and its other
cookbooks, see O285.1.*

O470.1   nd [about 1921]
The / Magic / way [cover-title]
DESCRIPTION: 15.5 × 9.0 cm   Pp 3–31   Illus col
Paper, with image on front of a stout woman holding
a container of Magic Baking Powder in her left hand
and pointing to a plate of biscuits with her right
hand; stapled
CONTENTS: Inside front face of binding 'Published by
E.W. Gillett Company Limited Toronto, Ont. Winnipeg
Montreal'; 3–6 'The Magic Way'; 7–31 recipes and at
bottom of some pages, culinary hints
COPIES: OGU (CCC TX715.6 M36)   QMM (RBD ckbk
1603)   *Private collection
NOTES: Unlike O470.2 and O470.3, there is no edition
number opposite p 3. The QMM copy appears to be
identical to the private collector's copy catalogued
here, except that the information opposite p 3 reads,
'Published by E.W. Gillett Company Limited Toronto,
Canada Winnipeg Montreal' [i.e., 'Canada' is in place
of 'Ont.']. There is a recipe on p 8 for War Cakes,
indicating a publication date during or after the First
World War.

The binding design is a play on the word 'magic.'
The background is black, and the stout woman is
wearing a black dress so that only her head and
white collar and arms are visible, emerging from the
black background. (The binding design of the third
and fourth editions does not employ this conceit;
instead, these editions feature a younger woman
against a light-coloured background.) The binding
design offers a clue to the date of publication: There
is a Magic Baking Powder advertisement in the May
1921 issue of *Western Home Monthly* that shows the
same stout woman, looking at the reader and pointing to a copy of *The Magic Way* cookbook, on which is
depicted the stout woman herself pointing to a plate
of biscuits. Since this advertisement does not appear
in the April 1921 issue, or in an issue from the year

before, the first edition of *The Magic Way* was likely published in about May 1921.

O470.2 [3rd ed., nd, about 1924]
—The / Magic / way [cover-title]
DESCRIPTION: 15.0 × 9.0 cm   Pp 3–31   Illus col
Paper, with image on front of a woman holding up a chocolate cake; stapled
CONTENTS: Inside front face of binding 'Published by E.W. Gillett Company Limited Toronto, Canada Winnipeg Montreal 3rd edition 10082124'; 3–6 'The Magic Way'; 7–31 recipes and at bottom of some pages, culinary hints
COPIES: ACG QMM (RBD ckbk 1602) SSWD *Private collection
NOTES: There is no recipe for War Cakes in the third edition.

O470.3 [4th ed., nd, about 1925]
—The / Magic / way [cover-title]
DESCRIPTION: 15.0 × 9.0 cm   Pp 3–31   Illus col
Paper, with image on front of a woman holding up a chocolate cake; stapled
CONTENTS: Inside front face of binding 'Published by E.W. Gillett Company Limited Toronto, Canada Winnipeg Montreal 4th edition 10092925'; 3–6 'The Magic Way'; 7–31 recipes
COPIES: *AEUCHV (UV 85.264.25) ONM

Our favorites

O471.1 1921
Our favorites / Compiled / for the benefit of / Pembroke General Hospital / 1921 / Observer Print, Pembroke
DESCRIPTION: 21.5 × 15.0 cm   Pp [1–4] 5–38   Tp illus of the hospital   Paper; stapled
CONTENTS: 1 tp; 2 blank; 3 table of contents; 4 blank; 5–38 recipes credited with the name of the contributor
COPIES: *Private collection

Rawleigh's good health guide almanac cook book 1921

For information about Rawleigh's annual almanac cookbooks and other culinary publications, see M22.1.

O472.1 1921
Rawleigh's / Trade mark / good health guide / almanac cook book / 1889 1921 / [caption:] President founder / W.T. Rawleigh / Published by /

the W.T. Rawleigh Co. Ltd. / London, Ontario / Winnipeg Montreal
DESCRIPTION: 24.0 × 16.5 cm   Pp [1] 2–64   Tp illus portrait of W.T. Rawleigh, illus   Lacks binding; stapled
CONTENTS: 1 tp; 2 'Rawleigh's Good Health Service'; 3 'Rawleigh's Good Health Products'; 4 'Rawleigh's International Service'; 5–7 'Rawleigh's Foreign Buyers'; 8 'Selling Rawleigh Products in Cities, Towns and Villages'; 9 'Rawleigh Quality and Value'; 10 'Almanac Calculations'; 11 'The Rawleigh Retailer'; 12 'Eclipses for 1921'; 13 'How to Be Healthy'; 14–25 monthly calendars for January–December, weather forecasts, and information about Rawleigh products; 26 'Keeping Healthy and Vigorous'; 27 'Chronic Ailments'; 28 'Relief for Everyday Pains'; 29 'Good Health Requires Internal Cleanliness'; 30 'Ease the Pain – Prevent Infection'; 31 'Rawleigh's Factories and Branches'; 32–3 'Main Laboratories'; 34 'Rawleigh's Factories and Branches' continued; 35 'Made in Canada'; 36 'Guard against Minor Ills'; 37 'Exterminate Flies and Other Insects'; 38 'Rawleigh's Good Health Soaps'; 39 'Don't Neglect Coughs or Colds'; 40–1 'For Milady's Toilet'; 42 'Good Teeth – Good Health'; 43 'Rawleigh's Tested Spices'; 44 'Rawleigh's Pure Flavors'; 45–51 'Rawleigh's Good Health Recipes'; 52–3 'How Rawleigh's Pills & Tablets Are Made'; 54–5 'Rawleigh's Experimental Farms'; 56–7 'Farm Sanitation'; 58 'Veterinary Hints'; 59 'Thrifty Animals Pay Best'; 60–3 'Helps for Poultry Raisers'; 64 'In Account with the Rawleigh Man'
COPIES: *Bookseller's stock
NOTES: According to p 3, there were three lines in Rawleigh's products: the household line; the food products line, which included cocoa, Melomaze Dessert Powder, cereals, teas and coffees, and spices and extracts; and the veterinary line. The recipe section includes general information about 'What to Eat,' 'What Not to Eat,' 'How to Eat,' and 'When to Eat' on p 45; 'Invalid Cookery' on p 46; 'Meat and Fish' on p 47; 'Poultry and Game' on p 48; 'Pastry and Pies' on p 49; 'Jellies and Jams' on p 50; and 'Time Table for Cooking' on p 51.

Thorpe, Louisa

O473.1 1921
Bonbons / and simple sugar sweets / by / Louisa Thorpe / late staff teacher at the National Training School / of Cookery and Domestic Subjects, and present / teacher of bonbons-and-sweet making / With a foreword by / E. Gladys Clarke / Principal of the National Training School of Cookery / and

Domestic Subjects, Buckingham Palace Road, / London, S.W.1 / [IP & S symbol] / London / Sir Isaac Pitman & Sons[,] Ltd. / Parker Street, Kingsway, W.C.2 / Bath, Melbourne, Toronto, New York / 1921

DESCRIPTION: 18.0 × 11.5 cm   Pp [i–ii] iii [iv] v–viii, 1–81 [82–6], [i–ii]   Paper-covered boards, cloth spine
CONTENTS: i tp; ii 'Printed by Sir Isaac Pitman & Sons, Ltd. Bath, England'; iii 'Foreword' signed E. Gladys Clarke, 1921; iv blank; v–vi 'Preface' signed Louisa Thorpe, 1921; vii table of contents; viii 'List of Chief Materials Necessary'; 1–78 text in ten chapters (I, 'List of Necessary Utensils, Materials, and Useful Hints'; II, 'Sugar Boiling and Spun Sugar'; III, 'Fondant, and Its Uses'; IV, 'Marzipan, and Its Uses'; V, 'Crystallization'; VI, 'Chocolates'; VII, 'Caramels'; VIII, 'Nougat and Various Sweets'; IX, 'Toffees'; X, 'Sweets Made without the Use of a Thermometer'); 79–81 index; 82–6 blank for 'Notes and Recipes'; i–ii publ ads
COPIES: *OTMCL (641.85 T35); Great Britain: LB (07942.aa.87)
NOTES: In the 'Foreword' Gladys Clarke says that the book is useful for teachers, cooks, and private individuals. In the 'Preface' Louisa Thorpe comments that the recipes 'comprise methods for making every conceivable sweetmeat within the capacity of the amateur, from the homely toffee of our childhood's days to the more elaborate confectionery suitable for dessert bonbons.'

BRITISH EDITIONS: 1921 [described above]; London: Sir I. Pitman and Sons, 1929 (Great Britain: LB); [No place:] Pitman, 1929 (Great Britain: LB); 3rd ed., London: Sir Isaac Pitman and Sons Ltd, 1938 (Great Britain: LB).

1921–5

J.O.Y. Bible Class cook book

For other cookbooks from the same church, see O475.1, Selected and Tried Recipes, *O739.1,* Selected Recipes, *and O1103.1,* The Mixing Bowl.

O474.1   nd [about 1921–5]
J.O.Y. Bible Class / cook book / compiled by the ladies of the class
DESCRIPTION: 22.0 × 13.5 cm   Pp [1–2] 3–60   Tp illus of Zion Tabernacle Methodist Church, Hamilton, Ontario   Paper, with tp illus on front; stapled
CONTENTS: 1 tp; 2 blank; 3 'Greetings' signed the Committee and unattributed poem beginning, 'We

may live without poetry, music and art' [from *Lucile*, Part I, Canto ii, by Owen Meredith, pseudonym of Edward Robert Bulwer-Lytton]; 4 ads; 5–60 recipes credited with the name of the contributor and ads
COPIES: OH (R641.5 JOY)   *Private collection
NOTES: The name and location of the church – Zion Tabernacle Methodist Church at the corner of Pearl and Napier streets in Hamilton – is given below the illustration of the church on the binding. There is an advertisement for the printer of the book on the outside back face of the binding: 'Frederick G. Smith // Everything in job printing // 107 King St. West ... Hamilton ... This cook book printed by us.' There is a recipe for Victory Cake on p 45.

The cookbook was published before the Methodists joined with other denominations to form the United Church of Canada on 10 June 1925. An advertisement for Ontario Plate Glass Ltd, 112 King Street West, described as 'successors to Leeks & Potts,' limits publication to no earlier than about 1921: the last listing in Hamilton directories for Leeks and Potts is in 1919; in 1920, Edith Leeks (wife of the company owner) is listed as a widow; the first listing for Ontario Plate Glass is in 1921.

Selected and tried recipes

See O474.1 for the titles of other cookbooks from the same church.

O475.1   nd [about 1921–5]
Selected and tried / recipes / compiled by / Ladies' Aid Society / of / Zion Methodist Church / Hamilton Ontario / A good cook calls for / a generous spirit, a light hand and a large heart.
COPIES: *Private collection
NOTES: The cookbook was published before the Methodists joined with other denominations to form the United Church of Canada on 10 June 1925. From appearances, it was published in the 1920s, in the same period as O474.1.

1922

The bride's cook book

O476.1   nd [about 1922]
The bride's cook / book / Published by / Dominion Service Bureau / 138–140 Queen St., Ottawa. / [union symbol]
DESCRIPTION: 18.0 × 12.0 cm   Pp [1–5] 6–195   Fp illus on p 4 of a husband kissing his wife, while she

stirs the contents of a bowl   Paper-covered boards, with images on front of a bride at top left and a delivery boy carrying parcels at bottom right
CONTENTS: 1 tp; 2 ad; 3 'Table of Contents'; 4 fp illus; 5–195 recipes and ads
COPIES: *Private collection
NOTES: Information in advertisements for Dr Frederick C. Hagar and the business of Robertson, Pingle and Tilley matches that recorded in Ottawa city directories for 1921 and 1922, but not 1920 or 1923. The Dominion Service Bureau is not listed in Ottawa city directories; however, the Capital Publishing Co. was at the same address in 1922, but not before. *The Bride's Cook Book*, therefore, was most likely published in 1922. The recipe selection suggests that the text is American; for example, Old Virginia Waffles, Southern Waffles, Martha Washington Waffles, and Hominy Griddle Cakes on pp 132–3.

Campbell, Miss Helen Gertrude (5 December 1889–1970)

Helen was the daughter of Peter A. and Esther Ann Campbell, who farmed at Campbell's Cross, Ontario. The 1901 Census gives her first names as G. Nellie (nickname for Helen). She attended public school SS No. 12, Chinguacousy, and high school in Brampton. At the Macdonald Institute in Guelph, she completed the Short Course in Domestic Science, January–March 1910, then earned her Domestic Science Teacher Certificate, September 1911–June 1913. Her Entrance Record, Registration No. 1492, for the Macdonald Institute notes that she received her Household Science Teacher Certificate from the Ontario Education Department in 1913, and that she passed her first year of English at the University of Toronto in 1912, and her second year in 1913.

The 'Department of Agriculture Personnel Records 1920–47' at OOA record Campbell's employment with the federal government (see Finding Aid 17-59, arranged alphabetically by employee name). The first reference is to her 'promotion and transfer' as demonstrator and lecturer at the Dairy and Cold Storage Branch, on 22 October 1921, at the annual salary of $2,160 (File 281868). The last reference is to the acceptance of her resignation on 20 May 1930 (File 328287). During her nine years at the Department of Agriculture, she worked at exhibitions in Toronto, Ottawa, and Winnipeg, gave talks at schools in London and Windsor, attended various conventions in the United States, and took memberships in the Canadian Council of Child Welfare and the American Child Health Association, among other activities (see Files 282343, 283092, 283461, 286330, 287733, 288494, 288617,

289310, 289621, 291220, 293113, 294733, 295005, 303340, 309042, 309542, 317545, 317916, 321818).

Campbell wrote several publications for the federal Department of Agriculture, which are not described fully here because they are under 16 pages. Copies of all the following are at OOAG, unless another location is given: Why and How to Use Skim-Milk, *Circular 5, 1922, pp 4, and the French-language edition,* Consommons du lait écrémé, *1922, pp 4; not credited to Campbell, but the same work, is the renumbered edition, Publication 496, Circular 97, English reprint, March 1936, pp 3, and French reprint, May 1937, pp 4;* Why and How to Use Cream, *Circular 6, 1922, pp 4, and* Consommons de la crème, *1922, pp 4; not credited to Campbell, but the same work, is the renumbered edition, Publication 523, Circular 111, issued only in French, June 1936;* Why and How to Use Cottage Cheese, *Circular 7, 1922, pp 4, and 1927 (NSWA), and* Consommons du fromage cottage, *nd [1922?], pp 4; not credited to Campbell, but the same work, is the French reprint of Circular 7, 1935, pp 4; also not credited to Campbell, but the same work, is the renumbered edition, Publication 497, Circular 98, English reprint, March 1936, pp 4, and French reprint, May 1937;* Why and How to Use Buttermilk, *Circular 8, 1922, pp 4, and 1926 (NSWA), and* Consommons du lait de beurre, *nd [1922?], pp 4;* Milk Drinks, *Circular 43, 1926, pp 4, and* Boissons au lait, *1926, pp 4; not credited to Campbell, but the same work, is the renumbered edition, Publication 549, Circular 117, English reprint, December 1936, pp 4, and French reprint, May 1937, pp 4.* An Argument in the Kitchen; a Playlet for Children in One Act, *Pamphlet 67, 1926, and Publication 494, 1936, is about nutrition (both cited in Ag 1867–1974). With A.H. White, Campbell co-wrote* Home-made Frozen Desserts, *Pamphlet 49, New Series, 1924, pp 8, and the French edition,* Desserts gelés faits à la maison, *1924, pp 8. Not a recipe book is Campbell's* The Care of Milk in the Home, *Pamphlet 115, New Series, 1930, pp 16 (ARDA), and French edition,* Le soin du lait à la maison, *1930; this title was later renumbered as Publication 563, Household Bulletin 13, French edition, 1937, and English edition, 1938.*

Campbell's new position as director of the Chatelaine Institute was announced in the April 1930 issue of Chatelaine *magazine, p 88, a good month before her resignation was accepted by the Department of Agriculture and less than two years after* Chatelaine's *launch in March 1928. Issues of the magazine list her as director up to and including February 1946. She is not listed in the March and April 1946 issues, but from May 1946 to December 1949 she appears as consulting director, first to M. Lois Clipsham as the new director, then to Marie Holmes (for Holmes's cookbooks, see O854.1 and O1005.1).*

See also O1111.1, The Art of Entertaining, *under Campbell's name, and O881.1,* The Buying and Cooking of Meat, *S78.1,* The Doughnut Book of Recipes, *and O887.1,* Favorite Desserts of the Chatelaine Institute.

Campbell is buried in Dixon's Union Cemetery, Chinguacousy Township, Peel County, Ontario.

For a list of other cookbooks published by the Department of Agriculture, see O404.1.

O477.1   1922
Why and how / to / use cheese / by Helen G. Campbell / [caption:] Cut a 10 pound cheese in half. Paraffin the freshly cut end of one half and put away / for future use. Scoop from the other half the amount required each / day and then turn upside down when not in use. / Dominion of Canada / Department of Agriculture / Pamphlet No. 7 – New Series / The Dairy and Cold Storage Branch / J.A. Ruddick, Commissioner / Published by direction of the Hon. W.R. Motherwell, / Minister of Agriculture, Ottawa, 1922 / 39473–1 [cover-title]
DESCRIPTION: 22.0 × 15.0 cm   Paper, with image on front of a wheel of cheese being scooped
CONTENTS: 1 cover-title; 2 'Historical'; 3 recipes; 4 'Kinds of Cheese'; 5 recipes; 6 'Canadian Cheese'; 7 recipes; 8 'The Advantages of Cheese as Food'; 9 recipes; 10 'Cottage Cheese'; 11 recipes; 12 'Digestibility of Cheese' and 'Use of Cheese in the Diet'; 13 recipes; 14 'How to Buy and Keep Cheddar Cheese'; 15 recipes; 16 'Other Publications of the Dairy and Cold Storage Branch Relating to Dairy Manufactures'
CITATIONS: Ag 1867–1974, p 24
COPIES: *OOAG (630.4 C212 P7 N.S., 4 copies)
NOTES: 'Historical' relates the history of cheese in Canada. Unlike O477.3, there is no printer and publication date on p 16.

O477.2   1922
—Consommons du / fromage / par Helen G. Campbell / [caption:] Couper un fromage de 10 livres en deux moitiés. Paraffiner la surface fraîchement coupée d'une / moitié pour la conserver. Enlever à la cuiller de l'autre moitié la quantité nécessaire / pour la journée. Retourner cette moitié quand on ne s'en sert pas / Dominion du Canada / Ministère fédéral de l'agriculture / Feuillet no 7 – Nouvelle série / Traduit au Bureau de traduction du ministère / Division de l'industrie laitière et de la réfrigération / J.A. Ruddick, commissaire / Publié par ordre de l'honorable W.R. Motherwell, / ministre de l'agriculture, Ottawa, 1922 / 39474–1 [cover-title]

DESCRIPTION: 22.5 × 15.0 cm   Pp [1–2] 3–24   Paper, with image on front of a wheel of cheese being scooped; stapled
CONTENTS: 1 cover-title; 2 'Notes historiques'; 3–4 recipes; 5 'Sortes de fromages'; 6–7 recipes; 8 'Le fromage canadien'; 9–10 recipes; 11–12 'Les avantages du fromage dans l'alimentation'; 13–14 recipes; 15 'Fromage cottage'; 16–17 recipes; 18 'Digestibilité du fromage' and 'L'emploi du fromage dans l'alimentation'; 19–20 recipes; 21 'Comment acheter et comment conserver le fromage Cheddar'; 22–3 recipes; 24 'Autres publications de la Division de l'industrie laitière et de la réfrigération se rapportant à la fabrication de produits laitiers'
COPIES: *OOAG (630.4 C212 P7 N.S.)

O477.3   1922 [1923]
—Why and how / to / use cheese / by Helen G. Campbell / [caption:] Cut a 10 pound cheese in half. Paraffin the freshly cut end of one half and put away / for future use. Scoop from the other half the amount required each / day and then turn upside down when not in use. / Dominion of Canada / Department of Agriculture / Pamphlet No. 7 – New Series / The Dairy and Cold Storage Branch / J.A. Ruddick, Commissioner / Published by direction of the Hon. W.R. Motherwell, / Minister of Agriculture, Ottawa, 1922 [cover-title]
DESCRIPTION: 22.5 × 15.0 cm   Pp [1] 2–16   Paper, with image on front of a wheel of cheese being scooped; stapled
CONTENTS: 1 cover-title; 2 'Historical'; 3 recipes; 4 'Kinds of Cheese'; 5 recipes; 6 'Canadian Cheese'; 7 recipes; 8 'The Advantages of Cheese as Food'; 9 recipes; 10 'Cottage Cheese'; 11 recipes; 12 'Digestibility of Cheese' and 'Use of Cheese in the Diet'; 13 recipes; 14 'How to Buy and Keep Cheddar Cheese'; 15 recipes; 16 'Other Publications of the Dairy and Cold Storage Branch Relating to Dairy Manufactures' and at bottom, 'Ottawa F.A. Acland printer to the King's Most Excellent Majesty 1923'
COPIES: ARDA   *Private collection
NOTES: The cover-title is dated 1922, but p 16 bears the date 1923.

O477.4   1924
—Consommons du / fromage / par Helen G. Campbell / [caption:] Couper un fromage de 10 livres en deux moitiés. Paraffiner la surface fraîchement coupée d'une / moitié pour la conserver. Enlever à la cuiller de l'autre moitié la quantité nécessaire / pour la journée. Retourner cette moitié quand on ne s'en sert pas / Dominion

du Canada / Ministère fédéral de l'agriculture / Feuillet n° 7 – Nouvelle série / Traduit au Bureau de traduction du ministère / Division de l'industrie laitière et de la réfrigération / J.A. Ruddick, commissaire / Publié par ordre de l'honorable W.R. Motherwell, / ministre de l'agriculture, Ottawa, 1924 / 77059–1 [cover-title]
DESCRIPTION: 23.0 × 15.0 cm   Pp [1–2] 3–24   Paper, with image on front of a wheel of cheese being scooped; rebound in cloth, together with other Pamphlets
CONTENTS: 1 cover-title; 2 'Notes historiques'; 3–4 recipes; 5 'Sortes de fromages'; 6–7 recipes; 8 'Le fromage canadien'; 9–10 recipes; 11–12 'Les avantages du fromage dans l'alimentation'; 13–14 recipes; 15 'Fromage cottage'; 16–17 recipes; 18 'Digestibilité du fromage' and 'L'emploi du fromage dans l'alimentation'; 19–20 recipes; 21 'Comment acheter et comment conserver le fromage Cheddar'; 22–3 recipes; 24 [outside back face of binding] list of Bulletins and Circulars
CITATIONS: Ag 1867–1974, p 18
COPIES: *OOAG (630.4 C212 P7 Fr)

O477.5 1925
—Why and how / to / use cheese / by Helen G. Campbell / [caption:] Cut a 10 pound cheese in half. Paraffin the freshly cut end of one half and put away / for future use. Scoop from the other half the amount required each / day and then turn upside down when not in use. / Dominion of Canada / Department of Agriculture / Pamphlet No. 7 – New Series / The Dairy and Cold Storage Branch / J.A. Ruddick, Commissioner / Published by direction of the Hon. W.R. Motherwell, / Minister of Agriculture, Ottawa, 1925 [cover-title]
DESCRIPTION: 22.5 × 15.5 cm   Pp [1] 2–16   Paper, with image on front of a wheel of cheese being scooped; stapled
CONTENTS: 1 cover-title; 2 'Historical'; 3 recipes; 4 'Kinds of Cheese'; 5 recipes; 6 'Canadian Cheese'; 7 recipes; 8 'The Advantages of Cheese as Food'; 9 recipes; 10 'Cottage Cheese'; 11 recipes; 12 'Digestibility of Cheese' and 'Use of Cheese in the Diet'; 13 recipes; 14 'How to Buy and Keep Cheddar Cheese'; 15 recipes; 16 'Other Publications of the Dairy and Cold Storage Branch Relating to Dairy Manufactures' and at bottom, 'Ottawa F.A. Acland printer to the King's Most Excellent Majesty 1925'
COPIES: *Private collection

O477.6 1927
—Why and how / to / use cheese / by Helen G. Campbell / [caption:] Cut a 10 pound cheese in half. Paraffin the freshly cut end of one half and put away / for future use. Scoop from the other half the amount required each / day and then turn upside down when not in use. / Dominion of Canada / Department of Agriculture / Pamphlet No. 7 – New Series / The Dairy and Cold Storage Branch / J.A. Ruddick, Commissioner / Published by direction of the Hon. W.R. Motherwell, / Minister of Agriculture, Ottawa, 1927 [cover-title]
DESCRIPTION: 22.5 × 15.5 cm   Pp [1] 2–16   Paper, with image on front of a wheel of cheese being scooped; stapled
CONTENTS: 1 cover-title; 2 'Historical'; 3 recipes; 4 'Kinds of Cheese'; 5 recipes; 6 'Canadian Cheese'; 7 recipes; 8 'The Advantages of Cheese as Food'; 9 recipes; 10 'Cottage Cheese'; 11 recipes; 12 'Digestibility of Cheese' and 'Use of Cheese in the Diet'; 13 recipes; 14 'How to Buy and Keep Cheddar Cheese'; 15 recipes; 16 'Other Publications of the Dairy and Cold Storage Branch Relating to Dairy Manufactures' and at bottom, 'Ottawa F.A. Acland printer to the King's Most Excellent Majesty 1927'
COPIES: *NSWA

O477.7 1928
—[An edition of *Why and How to Use Cheese*, Department of Agriculture, 1928, pp 16]
CITATIONS: CCat No. 7, p I10
COPIES: Bookseller's stock

O477.8 1931
—Why and how / to / use cheese / by Helen G. Campbell / [caption:] Cut a 10 pound cheese in half. Paraffin the freshly cut end of one half and put away / for future use. Scoop from the other half the amount required each / day and then turn upside down when not in use. / Dominion of Canada / Department of Agriculture / Pamphlet No. 7 – New Series / The Dairy and Cold Storage Branch / J.A. Ruddick, Commissioner / Published by direction of the Hon. Robert Weir, / Minister of Agriculture, Ottawa, 1931 [cover-title]
DESCRIPTION: 22.5 × 15.0 cm   Pp [1] 2–16   Paper, with image on front of a wheel of cheese being scooped; stapled
CONTENTS: 1 cover-title; 2 'Historical'; 3 recipes; 4 'Kinds of Cheese'; 5 recipes; 6 'Canadian Cheese'; 7 recipes; 8 'The Advantages of Cheese as Food'; 9 recipes; 10 'Cottage Cheese'; 11 recipes; 12 'Digestibility of Cheese' and 'Use of Cheese in the Diet'; 13

recipes; 14 'How to Buy and Keep Cheddar Cheese'; 15 recipes; 16 'Other Publications of the Dairy and Cold Storage Branch Relating to the Food Value of Dairy Products' and at bottom, 'F.A. Acland, printer to the King's Most Excellent Majesty, Ottawa, 1931'
COPIES: *OGU (CCC CA1 DA3 22S07)
NOTES: This is the last edition attributed to Campbell, who left employment with the Department of Agriculture in May 1930.

O477.9 1934
—[An edition of *Why and How to Use Cheese,* 1934]
COPIES: Bookseller's stock
NOTES: There is no named author in O477.9 and O477.10.

O477.10 reprint, April 1936
—Publication 493 / Household Bulletin 4 / Issued April, 1936 / Reprint / Dominion of Canada, Department of Agriculture / Why and how / to / use cheese / [Caption:] Cut a 10-pound cheese in half. Paraffin the freshly cut end of one-half and put away / for future use. Scoop from the other half the amount required each / day and then turn upside down when not in use. / Dairy and Cold Storage / Branch / Published by authority of the Hon. James G. Gardiner, Minister of Agriculture / Ottawa, Canada [cover-title]
DESCRIPTION: 24.5 × 16.0 cm   Pp [1–2] 3–15   Paper, with image on front of a wheel of cheese being scooped; rebound
CONTENTS: 1 cover-title; 2 'Historical'; 3 recipes; 4 'Kinds of Cheese'; 5 recipes; 6 'Canadian Cheese'; 7 recipes; 8 'The Advantages of Cheese as Food'; 9 recipes; 10 'Cottage Cheese'; 11 recipes; 12 'Digestibility of Cheese' and 'Use of Cheese in the Diet'; 13 recipes; 14 'How to Buy and Keep Cheddar Cheese'; 15 recipes; outside back face of binding 'Other Publications ...' and 'Ottawa: Printed by J.O. Patenaude, I.S.O., printer to the King's Most Excellent Majesty, 1936.'
CITATIONS: Ag 1867–1974, pp 23 and 31
COPIES: OOAG (630.4 C212 P493, 3 copies, and 630.4 C212 HB4, 2 copies)   OONL (C.O.P. - COP.CA.A.1276, 2 copies)   *QMAC (S133 A346 No. 493 bound in QMAC volume labelled No. 1560)

O478.1 January 1922
Why and how / to / use milk / by Helen G. Campbell / [caption:] Wholesome food makes happy children / Dominion of Canada / Department of Agriculture / The Dairy and Cold Storage Branch / J.A. Ruddick, Commissioner /

Published by direction of the Minister of Agriculture / Ottawa, January, 1922 [cover-title]
DESCRIPTION: 22.5 × 15.0 cm   Pp [1] 2–31   Illus   Paper, with image on front of two girls drinking milk at table; stapled
CONTENTS: 1 cover-title; 2 untitled introductory text; 3 'Dairy Products,' 'Table of Weights and Measures,' and 'Abbreviations'; 4 'The Value of Milk'; 5 recipes; 6 'Protein in Milk'; 7 recipes; 8 'Mineral Matter in Milk'; 9 recipes; 10 'Carbohydrates in Milk'; 11 recipes; 12 'Vitamines in Milk'; 13 recipes; 14 'Digestibility of Milk'; 15 recipes; 16 'Care of Milk in the Home'; 17 recipes; 18 'Cream'; 19 recipes; 20 'Butter' and 'Skim-Milk'; 21 recipes; 22 'Sour Milk' and 'Buttermilk'; 23 recipes; 24 'Milk Powder,' 'Condensed Milk,' and 'Evaporated Milk'; 25 'Pasteurized Milk' and 'Cheese'; 26 'Ice Cream'; 27 recipes; 28 'Milk for Invalids'; 29 recipes; 30 'Milk for Babies'; 31 'Index to Subjects' and 'Index to Recipes'
CITATIONS: Ag 1867–1974, p 114   CCat No. 2, p D3
COPIES: OOAG (641.6371 C212)   *Private collection
NOTES: 'Ottawa F.A. Acland printer to the King's Most Excellent Majesty 1922' is on the outside back face of the binding. The photographic illustrations are charming. The illustration on p 26, for example, shows a child and a dog at table, with the caption, '"There'll be no leavins, Doggie, this is ice cream."'

O478.2 January 1922
—Consommons / du lait / par Helen G. Campbell / [caption:] Les enfants sainement nourris sont heureux / Ministère fédéral de l'agriculture / Canada / Division de l'industrie laitière et de la réfrigération / J.A. Ruddick, commissaire / Traduit au Bureau de traduction du ministère / Publié par ordre de l'hon. W.R. Motherwell, ministre de l'agriculture / Ottawa, janvier 1922 [cover-title]
DESCRIPTION: 22.0 × 15.0 cm   Pp [1–2] 3–39   Illus   Paper, with image on front of two girls drinking milk at table; rebound in cloth, together with other Pamphlets
CONTENTS: 1 cover-title; 2 blank; 3 untitled introductory text; 4 'Produits laitiers,' 'Tableau des poids et mesures,' and 'Abréviations'; 5 'La valeur du lait'; 6–top 7 recipes; mid 7–mid 8 'La protéine du lait'; mid 8–mid 9 recipes; mid 9–mid 10 'Matière minérale du lait'; mid 10–11 recipes; 12–top 13 'Les hydrates de carbone dans le lait'; mid 13–mid 14 recipes; mid 14–15 'Les vitamines du lait'; 16–mid 17 recipes; mid 17–mid 18 'Digestibilité du lait'; mid 18–mid 19 recipes; mid 19–mid 20 'Soin du lait à la maison'; bottom 20–21 recipes; 22–mid 23 'Crème'; mid 23–mid 24 recipes; mid 24–top 25 'Beurre'; mid 25 'Lait écrémé';

bottom 25–26 recipes; 27 'Lait sur' and 'Lait de beurre'; 28–top 29 recipes; mid–bottom 29 'Poudre de lait' and 'Lait condensé'; top 30 'Lait évaporé'; mid 30–top 31 'Lait pasteurisé'; bottom 31 'Fromage'; 32–top 33 'Crème à la glace'; mid 33–mid 34 recipes; mid 34–top 35 'Lait pour les invalides'; mid 35–mid 36 recipes; mid 36–37 'Lait pour les bébés'; 38 blank; 39 'Table alphabétique des sujets' and 'Table alphabétique des recettes'
CITATIONS: Ag 1867–1974, p 19
COPIES: *OOAG (630.4 C212 P36 N.S.)
NOTES: The Pamphlet number is not printed in the book; however, the OOAG copy is inscribed on p 1, in ink, 'Feuillet 36.' 'Ottawa F.A. Acland imprimeur ... 1922' is on the outside back face of the binding.

O478.3   rev. ed., 1923
— Why and how / to / use milk / (Revised edition) / by Helen G. Campbell / [caption:] Wholesome food makes happy children / Dominion of Canada / Department of Agriculture / Pamphlet No. 36 – New Series / The Dairy and Cold Storage Branch / J.A. Ruddick, Commissioner / Published by direction of the Hon. W.R. Motherwell, / Minister of Agriculture, Ottawa, 1923 [cover-title]
DESCRIPTION: 22.5 × 15.0 cm   Pp [1] 2–31   Illus   Paper, with image on front of two girls drinking milk at table; rebound in cloth, together with other Pamphlets
CONTENTS: 1 cover-title; 2 untitled introductory text; 3 'Dairy Products,' 'Table of Weights and Measures,' and 'Abbreviations'; 4 'The Value of Milk'; 5 recipes; 6 'Protein in Milk'; 7 recipes; 8 'Mineral Matter in Milk'; 9 recipes; 10 'Carbohydrates in Milk'; 11 recipes; 12 'Vitamines in Milk'; 13 recipes; 14 'Digestibility of Milk'; 15 recipes; 16 'Care of Milk in the Home'; 17 recipes; 18 'Cream'; 19 recipes; 20 'Butter' and 'Skim-Milk'; 21 recipes; 22 'Sour Milk' and 'Buttermilk'; 23 recipes; 24 'Milk Powder,' 'Condensed Milk,' and 'Evaporated Milk'; 25 'Pasteurized Milk' and 'Cheese'; 26 'Ice Cream'; 27 recipes; 28 'Milk for Invalids'; 29 recipes; 30 'Milk for Babies'; 31 'Index to Subjects' and 'Index to Recipes'
CITATIONS: Ag 1867–1974, p 25
COPIES: *OOAG (2 copies: 630.4 C212 P36 N.S., 641.6371)
NOTES: 'Ottawa F.A. Acland printer ... 1923' is on the outside back face of the binding.

O478.4   rev. ed., 1924
—Why and how / to / use milk / (Revised edition) / by Helen G. Campbell / [caption:] Wholesome food makes happy children / Dominion of Canada

/ Department of Agriculture / Pamphlet No. 36 – New Series / The Dairy and Cold Storage Branch / J.A. Ruddick, Commissioner / Published by direction of the Hon. W.R. Motherwell, / Minister of Agriculture, Ottawa, 1924 [cover-title]
DESCRIPTION: 23.0 × 15.0 cm   Pp [1] 2–31   Illus   Paper, with image on front of two girls drinking milk at table; stapled
CONTENTS: 1 cover-title; 2 untitled introductory text; 3 'Dairy Products,' 'Table of Weights and Measures,' and 'Abbreviations'; 4 'The Value of Milk'; 5 recipes; 6 'Protein in Milk'; 7 recipes; 8 'Mineral Matter in Milk'; 9 recipes; 10 'Carbohydrates in Milk'; 11 recipes; 12 'Vitamines in Milk'; 13 recipes; 14 'Digestibility of Milk'; 15 recipes; 16 'Care of Milk in the Home'; 17 recipes; 18 'Cream'; 19 recipes; 20 'Butter' and 'Skim-Milk'; 21 recipes; 22 'Sour Milk' and 'Buttermilk'; 23 recipes; 24 'Milk Powder,' 'Condensed Milk,' and 'Evaporated Milk'; 25 'Pasteurized Milk' and 'Cheese'; 26 'Ice Cream'; 27 recipes; 28 'Milk for Invalids'; 29 recipes; 30 'Milk for Babies'; 31 'Index to Subjects' and 'Index to Recipes'
COPIES: *NSWA
NOTES: 'Ottawa F.A. Acland printer to the King's Most Excellent Majesty 1924' is on the outside back face of the binding.

O478.5   January 1924
—Consommons / du lait / par Helen G. Campbell / [caption:] Les enfants sainement nourris sont heureux / Ministère fédéral de l'agriculture / Canada / Division de l'industrie laitière et de la réfrigération / J.A. Ruddick, commissaire / Traduit au Bureau de traduction du ministère / Publié par ordre de l'hon. W.R. Motherwell, ministre de l'agriculture / Ottawa, janvier 1924 / 77060–1 [cover-title]
DESCRIPTION: 22.5 × 15.5 cm   Pp [1–2] 3–39   Illus   Paper, with image on front of two girls drinking milk at table; stapled
CONTENTS: 1 cover-title; 2 blank; 3 untitled introductory text; 4 'Produits laitiers,' 'Tableau des poids et mesures,' and 'Abréviations'; 5 'La valeur du lait'; 6–top 7 recipes; mid 7–mid 8 'La protéine du lait'; mid 8–mid 9 recipes; mid 9–mid 10 'Matière minérale du lait'; mid 10–11 recipes; 12–top 13 'Les hydrates de carbone du lait'; mid 13–mid 14 recipes; mid 14–15 'Les vitamines du lait'; 16–mid 17 recipes; mid 17–mid 18 'Digestibilité du lait'; mid 18–mid 19 recipes; mid 19–mid 20 'Soin du lait à la maison'; bottom 20–21 recipes; 22–mid 23 'Crème'; mid 23–mid 24 recipes; mid 24–top 25 'Beurre'; mid 25 'Lait écrémé'; bottom 25–26 recipes; 27 'Lait sur' and 'Lait de beurre';

28–top 29 recipes; mid–bottom 29 'Poudre de lait' and 'Lait condensé'; top 30 'Lait évaporé'; mid 30–top 31 'Lait pasteurisé'; bottom 31 'Fromage'; 32–top 33 'Crème à la glace'; mid 33–mid 34 recipes; mid 34–top 35 'Lait pour les invalides'; mid 35–mid 36 recipes; mid 36–37 'Lait pour les bébés'; 38 blank; 39 'Table alphabétique des sujets' and 'Table alphabétique des recettes'
COPIES: *OOAG (630.4 C212 P36 N.S.)
NOTES: The Pamphlet number is not printed in the book; however, the OOAG copy is inscribed on p 1, in pencil, 'Feuillet #36.' 'Ottawa F.A. Acland imprimeur ... 1924' is on the outside back face of the binding.

O478.6 rev. ed., 1926
—Why and how / to / use milk / (Revised edition) / By Helen G. Campbell / [caption:] Wholesome food makes happy children / Dominion of Canada / Department of Agriculture / Pamphlet No. 36 – New Series / The Dairy and Cold Storage Branch / J.A. Ruddick, Commissioner / Published by direction of the Hon. W.R. Motherwell, / Minister of Agriculture, Ottawa, 1926 [cover-title]
DESCRIPTION: 22.5 × 15.5 cm Pp [1] 2–31 Illus Paper, with image on front of two girls drinking milk at table; stapled
CONTENTS: 1 cover-title; 2 untitled introductory text; 3 'Dairy Products,' 'Table of Weights and Measures,' and 'Abbreviations'; 4 'The Value of Milk'; 5 recipes; 6 'Protein in Milk'; 7 recipes; 8 'Mineral Matter in Milk'; 9 recipes; 10 'Carbohydrates in Milk'; 11 recipes; 12 'Vitamines in Milk'; 13 recipes; 14 'Digestibility of Milk'; 15 recipes; 16 'Care of Milk in the Home'; 17 recipes; 18 'Cream'; 19 recipes; 20 'Butter' and 'Skim-Milk'; 21 recipes; 22 'Sour Milk' and 'Buttermilk'; 23 recipes; 24 'Milk Powder,' 'Condensed Milk,' and 'Evaporated Milk'; 25 'Pasteurized Milk' and 'Cheese'; 26 'Ice Cream'; 27 recipes; 28 'Milk for Invalids'; 29 recipes; 30 'Milk for Babies'; 31 'Index to Subjects' and 'Index to Recipes'; outside back face of binding 'Ottawa F.A. Acland printer ... 1926'
CITATIONS: Ag 1867–1974, p 25
COPIES: *OOAG (641.6371)

O478.7 rev. ed., 1929
—[Revised edition of *Why and How to Use Milk*, by Campbell, Ottawa: Department of Agriculture, 1929]
CITATIONS: CCat No. 8, p J11

O478.8 rev. ed., 1931
—Why and how / to / use milk / (Revised edition) / By Helen G. Campbell / [caption:] Wholesome food makes happy children / Dominion of Canada /

Department of Agriculture / Pamphlet No. 36 – New Series / The Dairy and Cold Storage Branch / J.A. Ruddick, Commissioner / Reprinted by direction of the Hon. Robert Weir, / Minister of Agriculture, Ottawa, 1931 [cover-title]
COPIES: *OGU (Rural Heritage Collection)
NOTES: This is the last edition attributed to Campbell. It has 31 pp.

O478.9 1935
—Why and how / to / use milk / (Revised edition) / [caption:] Wholesome food makes happy children / Dominion of Canada / Department of Agriculture / Pamphlet No. 36 – New Series / The Dairy and Cold Storage Branch / J.F. Singleton, Commissioner / Reprinted by direction of the Hon. Robert Weir, / Minister of Agriculture, Ottawa, 1935 [cover-title]
DESCRIPTION: 22.5 × 15.0 cm Pp [1] 2–31 Illus Paper, with image on front of two girls drinking milk at table; stapled
CONTENTS: 1 cover-title; 2 untitled introductory text; 3 'Dairy Products,' 'Table of Weights and Measures,' and 'Abbreviations'; 4 'The Value of Milk'; 5 recipes; 6 'Protein in Milk'; 7 recipes; 8 'Mineral Matter in Milk'; 9 recipes; 10 'Carbohydrates in Milk'; 11 recipes; 12 'Vitamines in Milk'; 13 recipes; 14 'Digestibility of Milk'; 15 recipes; 16 'Care of Milk in the Home'; 17 recipes; 18 'Cream'; 19 recipes; 20 'Butter' and 'Skim-Milk'; 21 recipes; 22 'Sour Milk' and 'Buttermilk'; 23 recipes; 24 'Milk Powder,' 'Condensed Milk,' and 'Evaporated Milk'; 25 'Pasteurized Milk' and 'Cheese'; 26 'Ice Cream'; 27 recipes; 28 'Milk for Invalids'; 29 recipes; 30 'Milk for Babies'; 31 'Index to Subjects' and 'Index to Recipes'; outside back face of binding illus of child holding a milk bottle and 'Ottawa J.O. Patenaude printer to the King's Most Excellent Majesty 1935'
COPIES: OGU (CA1 DA9 35P92)   OOAG (630.4 C212 P N.S., 2 copies) *Private collection
NOTES: This and later editions are not attributed to Helen G. Campbell, who left employment with the Department of Agriculture in 1930.

O478.10 reprint, April 1936
—Publication 492 / Household Bulletin 3 / Issued April, 1936 / Reprint / Dominion of Canada, Department of Agriculture / Why / and how to use milk / Dairy and Cold Storage Branch / Published by authority of the Hon. James G. Gardiner, Minister of Agriculture / Ottawa, Canada [cover-title]
DESCRIPTION: 24.0 × 16.0 cm Pp [1] 2–23 Illus Paper, with image on front of two girls drinking milk at table; rebound

CONTENTS: 1 cover-title; 2 untitled introductory text; 3 'Dairy Products,' 'Table of Weights and Measures,' and 'Abbreviations'; top–mid 4 'The Value of Milk'; mid 4–mid 5 recipes; mid–bottom 5 'Protein in Milk'; top–mid 6 recipes; mid 6–top 7 'Mineral Matter in Milk'; near top–near bottom 7 recipes; bottom 7–top 8 'Carbohydrates in Milk'; bottom 8–mid 9 recipes; mid 9–top 10 'Vitamines in Milk'; near top–bottom 10 recipes; 11 'Digestibility of Milk' and recipes; top–mid 12 'Care of Milk in the Home'; mid 12–mid 13 recipes; mid 13–mid 14 'Cream'; mid 14 recipes; bottom 14–top 15 'Butter'; mid 15 'Skim-Milk'; bottom 15–mid 16 recipes; mid–bottom 16 'Sour Milk' and 'Buttermilk'; 17 recipes and 'Milk Powder'; 18 'Condensed Milk,' 'Evaporated Milk,' 'Pasteurized Milk,' and 'Cheese'; 19 'Ice Cream'; top–mid 20 recipes; bottom 20–top 21 'Milk for Invalids'; near top–bottom 21 recipes; 22 'Milk for Babies'; 23 [inside back face of binding] 'Index to Subjects' and 'Index to Recipes'; outside back face illus of child holding a milk bottle and 'Ottawa J.O. Patenaude, I.S.O. printer to the King's Most Excellent Majesty 1936'
CITATIONS: Ag 1867–1974, pp 23 and 31
COPIES: OGU (Rural Heritage Collection uncat) OOAG (630.4 C212 P492, 3 copies, and 630.4 C212 HB3, 3 copies)   *QMAC (S133 A346 No. 492)
NOTES: In this edition, there is no caption for the illustration on the front of the binding.

O478.11   reprint, April 1936
—Publication n° 492 / Bulletin de la ménagère n° 3 / Publié en avril 1936 / Réimpression / Dominion du Canada – Ministère de l'agriculture / Consommons du lait / Division de l'industrie laitière et de la réfrigération / Publié par ordre de l'hon. James G. Gardiner, ministre de l'agriculture, Ottawa, Canada [cover-title]
DESCRIPTION: 24.0 × 15.5 cm   Pp [1–2] 3–28   Illus   Paper, with image on front of two girls drinking milk at table; rebound in cloth, together with other Household Bulletins
CONTENTS: 1 cover-title; 2 'Version française par C.E. Mortureux, B.S.A.'; 3 untitled introductory text; 4 'Produits laitiers,' 'Tableau des poids et mesures,' and 'Abréviations'; top 5 'La valeur du lait'; mid 5–mid 6 recipes; mid 6–top 7 'La matière azotée ou "protéine" du lait'; near top–bottom 7 recipes; top 8 'Matière minérale du lait'; mid 8–mid 9 recipes; mid 9 'Les hydrates de carbone du lait'; bottom 9–mid 10 recipes; bottom 10–11 'Les vitamines du lait'; 12 recipes; top 13 'Digestibilité du lait'; mid 13–mid 14 recipes; mid 14–top 15 'Soin du lait à la maison'; near top–bottom 15 recipes; top 16 'Crème'; bottom 16–mid 17 recipes; bottom 17–top 18 'Beurre'; mid 18

'Lait écrémé'; bottom 18–mid 19 recipes; mid–bottom 19 'Lait sur' and 'Lait de beurre (ou babeurre)'; 20–top 21 recipes; mid 21 'Poudre de lait,' 'Lait condensé,' and 'Lait évaporisé'; 22 'Lait pasteurisé' and 'Fromage'; 23 'Crème à la glace'; top–mid 24 recipes; bottom 24–top 25 'Lait pour les invalides'; mid 25–mid 26 recipes; mid 26–27 'Lait pour les bébés'; 28 'Table alphabétique des sujets' and 'Table alphabétique des recettes'
CITATIONS: Ag 1867–1974, pp 6 and 24
COPIES: *OOAG (630.4 C212 HB3 Fr and 630.4 C212 P492 Fr)   QQLAS (S133 A346 F492)
NOTES: On the outside back face of the binding there is an illustration of a child holding a milk bottle and 'Ottawa J.-O. Patenaude, O.S.I. imprimeur ... 1936.'

O478.12   2nd reprint, May 1937
—Publication n° 492 / Bulletin de la ménagère n° 3 / Publié en mai 1937 / Deuxième réimpression / Dominion du Canada – Ministère de l'agriculture / Consommons du lait / Division de l'industrie laitière et de la réfrigération / Publié par ordre de l'hon. James G. Gardiner, ministre de l'agriculture, Ottawa, Canada [cover-title]
DESCRIPTION: 24.5 × 16.5 cm   Pp [1–2] 3–28   Illus   Paper, with image on front of two girls drinking milk at table; stapled
CONTENTS: 1 cover-title; 2 'Version française par C.E. Mortureux, B.S.A.'; 3 untitled introductory text; 4 'Produits laitiers,' 'Tableau des poids et mesures,' and 'Abréviations'; top 5 'La valeur du lait'; mid 5–mid 6 recipes; mid 6–top 7 'La matière azotée ou "protéine" du lait'; near top–bottom 7 recipes; top 8 'Matière minérale du lait'; mid 8–mid 9 recipes; mid 9 'Les hydrates de carbone du lait'; bottom 9–mid 10 recipes; bottom 10–11 'Les vitamines du lait'; 12 recipes; top 13 'Digestibilité du lait'; mid 13–mid 14 recipes; mid 14–top 15 'Soin du lait à la maison'; near top–bottom 15 recipes; top 16 'Crème'; bottom 16–mid 17 recipes; bottom 17–top 18 'Beurre'; mid 18 'Lait écrémé'; bottom 18–mid 19 recipes; mid–bottom 19 'Lait sur' and 'Lait de beurre (ou babeurre)'; 20–top 21 recipes; mid 21 'Poudre de lait,' 'Lait condensé,' and 'Lait évaporisé'; 22 'Lait pasteurisé' and 'Fromage'; 23 'Crème à la glace'; top–mid 24 recipes; bottom 24–top 25 'Lait pour les invalides'; mid 25–mid 26 recipes; mid 26–27 'Lait pour les bébés'; 28 'Table alphabétique des sujets' and 'Table alphabétique des recettes'
COPIES: *OOAG (630.4 C212 P492 Fr, 3 copies, and 630.4 C212 HB3)
NOTES: On the outside back face of the binding there is an illustration of a child holding a milk bottle and 'Ottawa J.-O. Patenaude, O.S.I. imprimeur ... 1937.'

Canadian home cook book

O479.1 1922
Canadian / home cook / book / St. Andrew's / Home and School Club / Port Arthur / Ontario / 1922 / For information pertaining to food values / and their application to the individual, we / are indebted to the Macdonald College, / St. Anne de Bellevue, Quebec; McDonald [*sic*] / Institute, Guelph, Ontario, and to / the Iowa State College, / Ames, Iowa. / Seventy-five cents
DESCRIPTION: 22.5 × 15.0 cm   Pp [1] 2–96   Paper, with image on front of a girl chef with an open book, against an over-size maple leaf; stapled
CONTENTS: 1 tp; 2 ad; 3–mid 5 'Cooking and Health' and ad; mid 5–7 'Children's Diet' and ad; 8 ad; 9 'Hints'; 10 ads; 11–87 'Tried and Tested Recipes' and ads; 88–92 ads; top 93 'Index to Recipes'; mid 93–95 'Classified Advertisers'; 96 ads and at bottom p 96, 'The Mortimer Co. Limited'
CITATIONS: Driver 2001, Wellington County, p 95
COPIES: *Private collection

Certo

For other books promoting Certo, see: O491.1, Recipes for Making Perfect Jams, Jellies and Marmalades; *O600.1,* How to Make Jams, Jellies, Marmalades; *O608.1,* Recipes for Making Better Jams, Jellies and Marmalades; *O714.1,* Certo Recipes; *O753.1,* 89 Tested Recipes; *O835.1,* 75 Tested Recipes; *and O905.1,* A Short Cut to Better Jams and Jellies.

O480.1 copyright 1922
Certo / Reg. Can. (Surejell) Pat. Off. / Makes / perfect / jams / and / jellies / without / boiling away / the flavor / Douglas Packing Co., Ltd. / Cobourg, Ont., Canada. / Registered Canada 1922 [cover-title]
DESCRIPTION: 16.5 × 10.0 cm   Pp 1–14   Paper, with image on front of stylized basket or bowl of fruit in a 3.4-cm circular frame; stapled
CONTENTS: 1 'Why the Certo Process Makes Perfect Preserves'; top 2 'A Government Expert's Opinion of the Short Process of Jam Making by the Use of Pectin'; mid 2–mid 3 'Important Instructions'; bottom 3 'Summary of Important Points'; 4–14 'Certo Process Recipes // Canada Patent No. 160137'
CITATIONS: O'Neill (unpublished)
COPIES: *Private collection; Great Britain: LB (Woolwich)

NOTES: Unusually, the recto pages are numbered with even numbers; the verso pages, with odd numbers. On the outside back face of the binding, there is an illustration of a jar of Certo, with the following printed below: 'Certo is made under the Douglas Patents // U.S.A. Dec. 30.1913 // Aug. 7.1917 // Canada No. 151079 // 163864 // Great Britain 12439-13 // 6497-15 // France 462044 // 478608 // and in other countries ...'
O491.1, *Recipes for Making Perfect Jams, Jellies and Marmalades,* is identified as a revised edition, copyright November 1922, and instructs the reader to 'Destroy previous editions.' I have not determined to what extent the text of O491.1 may be related to O480.1.

O480.2 1922
—[An edition of *Certo,* Cobourg, Ont.: Douglas Packing Co., 1922, in English and French, pp 14, 16]
CITATIONS: O'Neill (unpublished)
COPIES: Great Britain: LB (Woolwich 39881)

O480.3 1923
—[An edition of *Certo,* Cobourg, Ont.: Douglas Packing Co., 1923]
CITATIONS: O'Neill (unpublished)
COPIES: Great Britain: LB (Woolwich 41141, not located)

Cook book

The Avon Chapter was founded in 1915 and disbanded in 1971.

O481.1 1922
Cook book / compiled by / Avon Chapter. I.O.D.E. / Stratford, Ont. / [IODE symbol] / To the friends who have kindly given their assistance towards the / publication of this book the members of the chapter / extend their cordial thanks. / A.E. Taylor & Son, printers / Stratford. / 1922
DESCRIPTION: 17.0 × 13.0 cm   Pp [1–4] 5–165 [166]   Cloth; stapled
CONTENTS: 1 tp; 2 untitled verses; 3 'Abbreviations' and 'Table of Weights and Measures'; 4 ad; 5–165 recipes credited with the name of the contributor and ads; 166 index
COPIES: *OGU (UA s048 b43)
NOTES: The last recipe section, for beverages, includes instructions for homemade wines: dandelion (two versions), rhubarb, grape, clover, and elderberry.

Cook book

O482.1 February 1922
Cook book / collected and compiled by / Lt.-Col.
Campbell Becher Chapter / I.O.D.E. / London, Ont.
/ February, 1922 / The chapter wish to thank most
cordially all who have / assisted them in any way in
getting out this book. / London, Ont. / A. Talbot &
Co., printers and publishers / 1922
DESCRIPTION: 16.5 × 11.5 cm   Pp [i–ii], [1–3] 4–135
Cloth, with IODE symbol on front; stapled
CONTENTS: i ad; ii blank; 1 tp; 2 'Weights and Mea-
sures,' 'Liquids,' 'Times for Roasting,' and 'Index'
[i.e., table of contents]; 3–135 recipes credited with
the name of the contributor and ads
COPIES: *OTUTF (B-12 7866)

Cook book

*The Birr branch of the Women's Institute was established
in 1911 (Ambrose, p 237).*

O483.1 November 1922
Cook book / Collected and compiled by / Women's
Institute, / Birr, Ont. / November, 1922. / The
Institute wish to thank most cordially all who have
/ assisted them in any way in getting out this
book. / Price 50 cents / London, Ont. / Printed
by R.F. Fielding. / 1922
COPIES: OLU (Lloyd Walden Collection)   *Private
collection
NOTES: One purpose of the book's publication was to
'[form] the nucleus of a fund, for the beautifying of
our village cemeteries [sic] and social welfare in our
rural community' (quoted from 'Greetings' at the beginning of the text).

Fenwick, K.S.

O484.1 nd [about 1922]
A / valuable aid / to the / housewife who
appreciates / dainty dishes / for / breakfast /
luncheon / dinner and / supper / Compiled by
K.S. Fenwick, 109 Manning Chambers, Toronto
DESCRIPTION: 15.0 × 10.0 cm   Pp [1–3] 4–23 [24]
Paper, with image on front of a woman sipping
coffee(?); stapled
CONTENTS: 1 tp; 2 'A Useful Table'; 3–23 recipes for
'Soups,' 'Fish,' 'Game,' 'Meats,' 'Salads,' 'Pickles,'
'Eggs,' 'Vegetables,' 'Puddings,' 'Pies,' 'Bread and Bis-

cuits,' 'Cake Fillings,' 'Frostings,' 'Ice Cream,' and
'Candy'; 24 ad for the Elias Rogers Co. Ltd, Toronto
COPIES: *OGU (CCC TX715.6 V34)
NOTES: The cover-title is 'Dainty Dishes for the Home
// With the compliments of the Elias Rogers Co.,
Limited Toronto.' Elias Rogers Co. sold coal. The
'Game' section has recipes for Canvas Back Duck,
prairie chicken, quail, Squirrel Ragout, venison, and
woodcock. The compiler's address, '109 Manning
Chambers,' was probably an office in the impressive
Manning Arcade at 24–8 King Street West (built in
1884 to the design of E.J. Lennox, architect of Toronto's
City Hall; now demolished); however, the Toronto
city directory lists room numbers in the Manning
Arcade from No. 1 to No. 30 only, and no one by the
name of Fenwick is recorded in any room. Perhaps
'109' is a typographical error for 19: Room No. 19
accommodated United Publishers of Canada Ltd,
Manufacturers Press Ltd, and Empire Publications
Ltd. I could find no individual listing for K.S. Fenwick
in the Toronto city or suburbs directories for 1922.

The OGU copy is inscribed in pencil, on the title-
page, 'Dorothy Barber from mother 1922.' The recipi-
ent of the book may be Dorothy S. Barber, florist,
listed as living on College Street in the Toronto city
directory.

Fryer, Mrs Jane Eayre
(Philadelphia, Pa, 1876–)

Mrs Fryer also wrote The Mary Frances Cook Book,
*Philadelphia: John C. Winston Co., [copyright 1912]
(United States: DLC). See her biography in* Feeding
America.

O485.1 [copyright 1922]
Mrs. Fryer's / loose-leaf / cook book / a complete
cook book giving econom- / ical recipes planned
to meet the / needs of the modern housekeeper /
including chapters on / balanced rations /
entertaining // school lunches / diet for weight
control, etc. / Arranged by / Jane Eayre Fryer /
instructor of domestic science / author of The Mary
Frances Story-Instruction Books / With blank pages
for preserving personal recipes / and memoranda,
which can be inserted in any part / of the book
under the subjects to which they refer / Illustrated /
The John C. Winston Company / Chicago
Philadelphia Toronto
DESCRIPTION: 20.5 × 15.0 cm   Pp [1–2], [i–ii] iii–xi
[xii], [1] 2–475 [Frontis col, listed on p xi, is lacking

in this copy], 3 pls col, 16 pls, illus   Cloth; loose leaves held by screw posts and screws

CONTENTS: 1 'It Is a Matter of Only a Few Seconds to Insert Pages in Mrs. Fryer's Loose-Leaf Cook Book' [five numbered and illustrated steps]; 2 blank; [several blank leaves]; i tp; ii 'Copyright, 1922, by the John C. Winston Company Printed in U.S.A.'; iii Proverbs XXXI, 25–9; iv quotation from Ruskin; v–vi 'Preface'; vii–x table of contents; xi list of illustrations; xii blank; 1–452 text; 453–75 index

CITATIONS: Bitting, p 171

COPIES: BDEM   *OGU (CCC TX715.6 F79); United States: DLC (TX715 F88)

NOTES: In the 'Preface' Fryer acknowledges Miss Helen Cramp and Miss Ada Z. Fish for help with the recipes. O485.1 may be an earlier edition of O583.1, *The Winston Cook Book*. I have not compared the recipes, but the prefaces are identical.

Good things to eat and how to prepare them

O486.1   1922

[An edition of *Good Things to Eat and How to Prepare Them*, by the ladies of St George's Anglican Church, Sarnia, Ontario, 1922]

COPIES: Private collection

Jell-O

For the titles of other books for cooking with Jell-O, see O212.1.

O487.1   copyright 1922

Jell-O / Canada's most famous dessert / at home everywhere / © 1922, by the Genesee Pure Food Company [cover-title]

DESCRIPTION: With image on front of a bear beside a cabin in the mountains; stapled

COPIES: *OPETCM

NOTES: The publisher's name in the cover-title is Genesee Pure Food Co., but the name on the Jell-O box illustrated on the back face of the binding is Genesee Pure Food Co. of Canada Ltd, Bridgeburg, Ontario. The flavoured gelatine product was developed in the United States, where Jell-O cookbooks of the same period bear the recommendation 'Jell-O – America's most famous dessert' or 'America's most famous food' (Allen, p 198).

AMERICAN EDITIONS: *Jell-O America's Most Famous Dessert at Home Everywhere*, 1922 (Allen, p 198).

McClary's household manual

For information about McClary's and its cookbooks, see O162.1.

O488.1   [copyright 1922]

McClary's / household / manual / McClary's / London Toronto Montreal Winnipeg / Vancouver St. John, N.B. Hamilton Calgary / Saskatoon Edmonton

DESCRIPTION: 24.5 × 18.0 cm   Pp [1–4] 5–107 [108]   8 double-sided pls incl in pagination, rectos in col, versos b/w; 5 pls of cuts of meat, incl in pagination and with printing on other face; illus on pp 41, 43, 46, 47   Paper

CONTENTS: 1 ht; 2 blank; 3 tp with decorative border in col; 4 'Copyright, Canada, 1922 by the McClary Manufacturing Co. London, Ontario'; 5–12 'A Housewife's Opportunity // The Perfect Kitchen'; 13–14 'Bright and Shining Utensils Live Longest'; 15–18 'Giving a Good Stove Its Chance'; 19–20 double-sided pl; 21–3 'Care of Floors and Woodwork'; 24–5 'The Soft Glow of Well Kept Furniture'; 26–8 'The Table // Its Setting & Serving'; 29–30 double-sided pl; 31–8 'Some Laundry Secrets You Should Know'; 39–50 'Cuts of Meat and How to Choose Them'; 51–107 'McClary's Tested Household Recipes'; 108 index to recipes

CITATIONS: Ferguson/Fraser, p 233, illus col on p 57 of closed volume   Neering, pp 160, 161, 163, 164, 165   O'Neill (unpublished)

COPIES: BDEM   BVIPM   OL   OLU (TX145 M34 1922)   OONL (TX651 M33 1922)   QMM (RBD TX158 M23 1922)   *Private collection; Great Britain: LB (not located); United States: AzTeS

NOTES: See pl 5. 'The Perfect Kitchen' comments on the modern housekeeper's 'right' to a 'proper kitchen, properly equipped,' and goes on to discuss in detail the following topics: lighting; walls, woodwork, and ceiling; the floor; arranging the kitchen; the long or square kitchen; the stove; the sink; the table; the refrigerator ('Unless you are one of the very fortunate few who possess an electric refrigerator, study convenience of ice supply.'); the cabinet or pantry; kitchen utensils; and when meals are served in the kitchen. The business name of 'Humphry's Hardware, Viceroy, Sask.' is on the binding of the private collector's copy.

O488.2   [copyright 1923]

—McClary's / household / manual / McClary's / London Toronto Montreal Winnipeg / Vancouver St. John, N.B. Hamilton Calgary / Saskatoon Edmonton

DESCRIPTION: 24.5 × 17.5 cm   Pp [1–4] 5–91 [92]   4 pls col; 8 double-sided pls, rectos col, versos b/w; illus   Thin card; stapled
CONTENTS: 1 ht; 2 blank; 3 tp; 4 'Copyright Canada, 1923 by the McClary Manufacturing Co. London, Ontario'; 5–10 'A Housewife's Opportunity // The Perfect Kitchen'; 11–12 'Bright and Shining Utensils Live Longest'; 13–16 'Giving a Good Stove Its Chance'; 17–19 'Care of Floors and Woodwork'; 20–1 'The Soft Glow of Well Kept Furniture'; 22–4 'The Table // Its Setting & Serving'; 25–32 'Some Laundry Secrets'; 33–44 'Cuts of Meat and How to Choose Them'; 45–91 'McClary's Tested Household Recipes'; 92 index
COPIES: BVAMM   BVMA   OONL (TX651 M33 1923) SSWD   *Private collection
NOTES: The printer's name, 'A. Talbot & Co. printers London, Ont.' is on the outside back face of the binding.

O488.3   [1928]
—[An edition of *McClary's Household Manual,* published for General Steel Wares, [Toronto: 1928], pp 108]
CITATIONS: JPCat 130, No. 42
NOTES: This edition was published after McClary's merged in 1927 with four other companies to form General Steel Wares Ltd, which retained the McClary brand name.

One hundred tested recipes

For information about Carnation Milk Products Co., see O350.1.

O489.1   [copyright 1922]
One hundred / tested recipes [cover-title]
DESCRIPTION: 18.0 × 12.5 cm   Pp [1] 2–32   Illus col Paper, with images on front of two couples at table, and a carnation; stapled
CONTENTS: Inside front face of binding 'Table Setting and Service'; 1 untitled introductory note and 'All recipes tested by the School of Domestic Arts and Sciences Chicago, Ill. // Copyright 1922 Carnation Milk Products Company Seattle // Aylmer, Ont. Chicago C115'; 2 illus of 'A Modern Carnation Condensary'; 3–4 information about the production of Carnation Condensed Milk, about cooking with the milk, and about following the recipes in the book; 5–31 recipes; 32 timetables, temperatures, weights and measures; inside back face index
COPIES: *BVAMM   OONL (TX715.6 O544 1922)

NOTES: There is no named author in this selection of a hundred recipes for Carnation Condensed Milk. The introductory text on p 1 states that the recipes 'have been compiled especially for this book by many well known authorities.' The American printer is on the outside back face of the binding: 'Walton & Spencer Co. Chicago, Ill.' The book was advertised in the June 1922 issue of *Western Home Monthly* as 'new cook book containing 100 tested recipes.'

In 1924, the company published O515.1, *My Hundred Favorite Recipes,* attributed to the pseudonymous Mary Blake. I have compared only the first page of soup recipes in each book: in the later text, two recipes (Cream of Tomato Soup and Cream of Celery Soup) match, but have been revised; and the same illustration, a steaming bowl of soup, is printed at the top of the page.

Rawleigh's good health guide cook book almanac 1922

For information about Rawleigh's annual almanac cookbooks and its other culinary publications, see M22.1.

O490.1   1922
Rawleigh's / Trade mark reg. U.S. Pat. Off. / good health guide / 1889 cook book almanac 1922 / Published by / the W.T. Rawleigh Co. Ltd. / Winnipeg London Montreal / U.S. factories and branches / Freeport Memphis Chester Oakland Minneapolis
DESCRIPTION: 24.0 × 16.5 cm   Pp [1] 2–64   Tp illus portrait of W.T. Rawleigh, president and founder; illus   Paper, with image on front of a girl's face
CONTENTS: 1 tp; 2–3 'Pioneer Manufacturers in Canada'; 4 'Rawleigh's New Winnipeg Factory'; 5 'Rawleigh's Public Policies and Business Practices'; 6 'Almanac Calculations'; 7 'Equipped to Make Everything'; 8 January; 9 'The Rawleigh Organization'; 10 February; 11 'Trading in Foreign Countries'; 12 March; 13 'Why Scientific Tests Are Made'; 14 April; 15 'The World's Materials'; 16 May; 17 'An Interesting Pharmaceutical Science'; 18 June; 19–20 'How Fine Soaps Are Made'; 21 'Rawleigh's Printing Department'; 22 July; 23 'From Producer to Consumer'; 24 August; 25 'Service Makes Friends'; 26 September; 27 'Rawleigh's Good Health Service'; 28 October; 29 'Good Results Every Baking Day'; 30 November; 31 'Why Mothers Prefer Rawleigh's'; 32–3 'Rawleigh's Factories & Branches'; 34 December; 35 'How to Keep Fit'; 36–7 'From the Tropics to Your Table'; 38–9 'The Road to Health'; 40 'The Spice of Life'; 41–3 'Food for the

Family'; 44 'One Dish Meals'; 45 'Nourishing Soups'; 46 'When Company Comes'; 47 'Appetizing Salads'; 48 'Fruit Puddings and Sauces'; 49 'Drop Cakes'; 50 'Health Brings Beauty'; 51 'Trevere // The New Quality Line of Rawleigh Toilet Preparations'; 52 'The Need of Clean Teeth'; 53 'Salves and Ointments Needed Daily'; 54 'Friends of the Whole Family'; 55 'Constipation a Cause of Disease'; 56 'Rawleigh's Experimental Farms'; 57 'How to Prevent the Spread of Diseases'; 58 'Enormous Live Stock Losses'; 59 'The Care of Horses, Cattle, Hogs and Sheep'; 60–1 'Overcoming Poultry Losses'; 62–3 'Care of the Dairy Cow'; 64 'Complete List of Rawleigh's Good Health Products'

CITATIONS: Ferguson/Fraser, p 233
COPIES: ACG AMHM BBVM *Private collection
NOTES: Of the three Canadian places of publication, 'London' [in Ontario] is in the largest typeface. The cover-title is 'Rawleigh's Good Health Guide Almanac Cook Book 1922.' Page 2 states that the W.T. Rawleigh Co. Ltd is a 'Canadian corporation, incorporated in 1912.'

Recipes for making perfect jams, jellies and marmalades

For the titles of other Certo recipe collections, see O480.1.

O491.1   rev. ed., November 1922
Revised Nov. 1922. Destroy previous editions / Certo / Reg. Can. (Surejell) Pat. Off. / Recipes / for making perfect / jams / jellies / and / marmalades / The worlds [*sic*] new standard of quality / Douglas Packing Co. / Limited / Cobourg, Ont. / Canada. / Copyright 1922 [English cover-title on one face of binding] Revisé Nov. 1922. Détruisez les éditions précédentes / Certo / Reg. Can. (Surejell) Pat. Off. / Recettes / pour faire des / confitures / des gelees / et des / marmelades / La qualité suprême au monde / Douglas Packing Co. / Limited / Cobourg, Ont. / Canada. / Copyright 1922 [French cover-title on other face]
DESCRIPTION: 16.5 × 10.0 cm   Pp [English:] 1–14; [French:] 1–16   Paper, with image on front of a bottle of Certo; stapled
CONTENTS: [English:] 1 'What Is Certo?' and index; 2 'Why Certo Preserves Are Better and Cheaper'; top 3 'Why Use Certo?'; mid 3–4 'Instructions'; 5–14 recipes; [French:] 1 'Qu'est-ce que le Certo?' and index; top 2 'Pourquoi les confitures au Certo sont-elles

meilleures et moins chères?'; mid–bottom 2 'Pourquoi se servir du Certo?'; 3–mid 4 'Directions'; bottom 4–16 recipes
COPIES: QMM (RBD ckbk 1510)   *Private collection; Great Britain: LB (Woolwich 41414)
NOTES: In both the English and French texts, unusually, the recto pages have even numbers and the verso pages have odd numbers.

O'Neill (unpublished) records LB (Woolwich 41414) as dated 1923, but it is the 1922 edition described here.

O491.2   rev. ed., November 1922
—Revised Nov. 1922. Destroy previous editions / Certo / Reg. Can. (Surejell) Pat. Off. / Recipes / for making perfect / jams / jellies / and / marmalades / "The world's new standard of quality" / Douglas Packing Co., Ltd. / Cobourg, Ont., Canada. / Copyrighted 1922 [cover-title]
DESCRIPTION: 16.5 × 9.5 cm   Pp 1–14   Paper; stapled
CONTENTS: 1 [inside front face of binding] 'What Is Certo?' and 'Index'; 2 'Why Certo Preserves Are Better and Cheaper'; top 3 'Why Use Certo?'; mid 3–4 'Instructions'; 5–14 recipes
COPIES: *Private collection
CONTENTS: Unusually, the recto pages have even numbers and the verso pages have odd numbers. On the outside back face of the binding there is an image of a Certo bottle.

AMERICAN EDITIONS: *Certo // Recipes for Making Perfect Jams, Jellies and Marmalades*, rev. Nov. 1922, Rochester, NY: Pectin Sales Co. Inc., copyright 1922 (Dickinson, illus p 50).

St Andrew's cook book

O492.1   1922
St. Andrew's / cook / book / Compiled by the / Women of the Lake Section of / St. Andrew's Church, / Sudbury / Printed by / the Sudbury News / 1922
DESCRIPTION: Pp [1] 2–145
CONTENTS: 1 tp; 2 ad; 3–144 recipes credited with the name of the contributor and ads; 145 'Index' [i.e., table of contents]
COPIES: *Private collection
NOTES: The private collector's copy is inscribed on the title-page, 'To Bernice from Mrs White Xmas 1928.'

Salads and dressings

The Toronto city directory for 1922 lists Harold F. Ritchie and Co. Ltd as 'mfrs agts' at 10 McCaul; Harold F. Ritchie was the president.

O493.1 1922
[An edition of *Salads and Dressings*, Toronto: Harold F. Ritchie and Co., 1922]
CITATIONS: O'Neill (unpublished)
COPIES: Great Britain: LB (not located)
NOTES: O'Neill's record of British Library copyright information describes *Salads and Dressings* as a 'book,' but does not give the number of pages.

1923

Blake, Mary [pseudonym]

Mary Blake was the pseudonym used by the Carnation Co. on publications promoting Carnation Milk, from about 1923 onward. For later cookbooks by Blake, see: O515.1, My Hundred Favorite Recipes; *O660.1,* 100 Glorified Recipes; *and O844.1,* Carnation Cook Book. *O876.1,* The Carnation Year Book of Menus and Recipes, *and O1172.1,* The Velvet Blend Book, *also bear Blake's name. O350.1,* The Story of Carnation Milk, *and O489.1,* One Hundred Tested Recipes, *predate the Blake pseudonym. For information about Carnation Milk Products Co., see O350.1.*

O494.1 nd [about 1923]
A few of my / favorite recipes / Mary Blake [cover-title]
DESCRIPTION: Leaves graduate in size from 8.5 × 8.5 to 14.5 × 8.5 cm   Pp [1–16]   Paper, with image on front of carnation and, in oval frame, head-and-shoulders of Mary Blake(?); stapled at top edge, and with hole punched at top edge for hanging
CONTENTS: 1 cover-title; 2 foreword signed Mary Blake, Domestic Science Department, Carnation Milk Products Co. Ltd, and at bottom, 'CC-300'; 3 'Carnation Is Just –' and at bottom, 'Carnation Milk Products Company, Ltd. Aylmer, Ontario.'; 4–5 'Soups'; 6–7 'Fish – Meats'; 8–9 'Vegetables – Salads'; 10–11 'Icings – Fillings'; 12–13 'Puddings – Cakes'; 14–15 'Ice Cream – Candies'; 16 illus col of can of Carnation Evaporated Milk
COPIES: *Private collection
NOTES: This cookbook was published before standardization in the dairy industry guaranteed a uniform product. The text on p 3 describes Carnation as

a 'pure fresh milk – evaporated to double richness – kept safe by sterilization' and argues that many cooks use Carnation 'because experience has taught them that this milk never varies in its quality and richness,' unlike 'the big difference' found in other milk.

Blake writes in the foreword: '[The recipes are] arranged in an unusually convenient form. Just tie a string through the hole at the top of this folder and hang in the kitchen, ...' For easy reference, the section headings are printed at the bottom of each leaf, on the part that extends beyond the previous, shorter leaf.

Each of O494.1, O494.2, and O494.3 has a different image on the binding and a different number at bottom p 2 (CC-300, CC-300D, or CC-300E). From appearances, *A Few of My Favorite Recipes* was published in the 1920s. It may precede O515.1, *My Hundred Favorite Recipes,* [copyright 1924], which has the printer's mark 'CC-304A'; and it certainly follows O489.1, *One Hundred Tested Recipes,* [copyright 1922], not attributed to Blake.

O494.2 nd
—A few of my / favorite recipes / Mary Blake [cover-title]
DESCRIPTION: Leaves graduate in size from 8.5 × 8.5 to 15.0 × 8.5 cm   Pp [1–16]   Paper, with image on front of bowl of fruit, three-layer cake, and mug of coffee; stapled at top edge, and with hole punched at top edge for hanging
CONTENTS: 1 cover-title; 2 'Foreword' signed Mary Blake, Home Economics Department, Carnation Milk Products Co. Ltd, and at bottom,'CC-300D; 3 'Carnation Is Just –' and at bottom, 'Carnation Milk Products Company, Ltd. Aylmer, Ontario.'; 4–5 'Soups'; 6–7 'Fish – Meats'; 8–9 'Vegetables – Salads'; 10–11 'Icings – Fillings'; 12–13 'Puddings – Cakes'; 14–15 'Ice Cream – Candies'; 16 illus col of two cans (one large, one small) of Carnation Evaporated Milk
COPIES: *OWTU (E0914)

O494.3 nd
—A few of my favorite recipes / Mary Blake [cover-title]
DESCRIPTION: Leaves graduate in size from 8.5 × 8.5 to 15.0 × 8.5 cm   Pp [1–16]   Paper, with image on front of jellied salad, dessert, and floral arrangement; stapled at top edge, and with hole punched at top edge for hanging
CONTENTS: 1 cover-title; 2 foreword signed Mary Blake, Home Economics Department, Carnation Co. Ltd, and at bottom, 'CC-300E'; 3 'Carnation Is Just –' and at bottom, 'Carnation Company, Ltd. Aylmer,

Ontario.'; 4–5 'Soups'; 6–7 'Fish – Meats'; 8–9 'Vegetables – Salads'; 10–11 'Icings – Fillings'; 12–13 'Puddings – Cakes'; 14–15 'Ice Cream – Candies'; 16 illus col of two cans (one large, one small) of Carnation Evaporated Milk
COPIES: *Private collection

Canada, Department of Agriculture

For a list of other cookbooks published by the Department of Agriculture, see O404.1.

O495.1 1923
[An edition of *Fruit and Vegetables: Canning, Drying, Storing*, 1923]
COPIES: OONL (COP.CA.3.1999-470) Bookseller's stock
NOTES: See O402.1 for an earlier edition of the same title published in 1918 by the Canada Food Board.

O495.2 [1924]
—Fruit and / vegetables / canning / drying / storing [cover-title]
DESCRIPTION: 21.5 × 15.0 cm Pp [1–3] 4–26 10 numbered illus Paper, with still-life on front of fruit, vegetables, and preserves; stapled, and with hole punched at top left corner for hanging
CONTENTS: 1 untitled introductory note; 2 'Read These "Don'ts" before You Fail'; 3–top 19 'Successful Home Canning of Canadian Fruits and Vegetables'; bottom 19–21 'Home Drying'; 22–4 'Winter Storage of Vegetables and Fruits'; 25 'Time Table for Canning'; 26 'Time Table for Drying' and '"At a Glance" Storage Chart'
CITATIONS: Ag 1867–1974, p 3 Ferguson/Fraser, p 233
COPIES: ACG ACHP (HP 4628.12) OOAG (630.4 C212 B32 N.S., 3 copies, and 641.4) OONL (COP.CA.2.2000-343) SSWD (2 copies) *Private collection
NOTES: The following is on the outside back face of the binding: 'Dominion of Canada // Department of Agriculture // Fruit Branch // G.E. McIntosh Commissioner // Bulletin No. 32 Published by direction of the Hon. W.R. Motherwell, Minister of Agriculture, Ottawa, 1924 // Ottawa Government Printing Bureau 1924.'

O495.3 1924
—Conserves de fruits / et légumes / en bocaux, séchés, en cave / Dominion du Canada / Ministère fédéral de l'agriculture / Bulletin n° 32 – Nouvelle

série / Division des fruits / G.E. McIntosh, commissaire / Traduit au Bureau de traduction du ministère / Publié par ordre de l'hon. W.R. Motherwell, ministre de l'agriculture, / Ottawa, 1924 [cover-title]
DESCRIPTION: 21.0 × 15.0 cm Pp [1–3] 4–29 10 numbered illus Paper; with hole punched at top left corner for hanging; rebound in cloth, with other Bulletins
CONTENTS: 1 'Mangeons des fruits canadiens'; 2 'Ce qu'il ne faut pas faire'; 3–mid 6 'La fabrication à la maison des conserves de fruits et de légumes canadiens'; mid 6–20 'Recettes en détail'; 21–mid 23 'Dessiccation à la maison'; mid 23–26 'Conservation des légumes et des fruits en hiver'; 27 'Tableau indicateur de l'embouteillage'; 28 'Tableau indicateur de la dessiccation'; 29 'Tableau indicateur de la conservation'
CITATIONS: Ag 1867–1974, p 2
COPIES: *OOAG (630.4 C212 B32 N.S.)
NOTES: Unlike the English edition published in the same year, there is no image on the front face of the binding and the printer is not identified.

O495.4 [rev. ed., 1926]
—Fruit and / vegetables / canning / drying / storing [cover-title]
DESCRIPTION: 21.5 × 15.0 cm Pp [1–4] 5–32 14 numbered illus Paper, with still-life on front of fruit, vegetables, and preserves; stapled, and with hole punched at top left corner for hanging
CONTENTS: 1 untitled introductory note; 2 information about nutritional benefits of eating fruit and vegetables; 3 'Read These "Don'ts" before You Fail'; 4–top 13 'Successful Home Canning of Canadian Fruits and Vegetables'; mid 13–mid 25 'Canning Recipes in Detail'; bottom 25–mid 27 'Home Drying'; bottom 27–30 'Winter Storage of Vegetables and Fruits'; 31 'Time Table for Canning'; 32 'Time Table for Drying,' '"At a Glance" Storage Chart,' and 'Recipes by Ethel A. Preston, Assistant Demonstrator and Lecturer, Fruit Branch, Ottawa.'
CITATIONS: Ag 1867–1974, p 5 CCat No. 5, p G9
COPIES: MAUAM *NBFKL (Ruth Spicer Cookbook Collection) OOAG (630.4 C212 B65 N.S., 3 copies) OONL (COP.CA.2.1999-2026)
NOTES: The following is on the outside back face of the binding: 'Dominion of Canada Fruit Branch // Department of Agriculture // G.E. McIntosh Commissioner // Bulletin No. 65 (Revised edition) Published by direction of the Hon. S.F. Tolmie, Minister of Agriculture, Ottawa, 1926 // Ottawa Government Printing Bureau 1926.' This is the only edition in

which Preston is given credit for the recipes. She is also credited for the recipes in O496.3, the 1926 edition of *Canadian Grown Apples.* Preston is the author of the 2-page *Fruit and Vegetable Recipes,* Circular 17, Ottawa: Department of Agriculture, 1924 (OOAG). For biographical information about her, see O496.3.

O495.5 [rev. ed., 1929]
—Fruit and / vegetables / canning / drying / storing [cover-title]
DESCRIPTION: 21.5 × 15.0 cm   Pp [1–4] 5–32   14 numbered illus   Paper, with still-life on front of fruit, vegetables, and preserves; stapled, and with hole punched at top left corner for hanging
CONTENTS: 1 untitled introductory note; 2 information about nutritional benefits of eating fruit and vegetables; 3 'Read These "Dont's" [*sic*] before You Fail'; 4–top 13 'Successful Home Canning of Canadian Fruits and Vegetables'; mid 13–mid 23 'Canning Recipes in Detail'; mid 23–mid 24 'Other Methods of Canning'; mid 24–mid 25 'Jams and Jellies'; mid 25–mid 27 'Home Drying'; mid 27–30 'Winter Storage of Vegetables and Fruits'; 31 'Time Table for Canning'; 32 'Time Table for Drying' and '"At a Glance" Storage Chart'
CITATIONS: Ag 1867–1974, p 5   FitzPatrickCat 111 (April 1993) No. 3   Newman
COPIES: OOAG (641.634 1929)   *Private collection
NOTES: The following is on the outside back face of the binding: 'Dominion of Canada Fruit Branch // Department of Agriculture // G.E. McIntosh Commissioner // Bulletin No. 65 (Revised edition) Published by direction of the Hon. W.R. Motherwell, Minister of Agriculture, Ottawa, 1929 // Printed by F.A. Acland, King's printer // Ottawa, 1929.'

Lenore Newman, who worked under Edith Elliot in the Consumer Section of the Department of Agriculture in the 1940s, attributes the 1929 edition to Elliot.

O496.1 [1st ed., 1923]
Pommes / cultivées / au Canada / Chaque bouchée / est / un régal / Traduit au Bureau de traduction ministère / Division des fruits, / Ministère fédéral de l'agriculture, / Ottawa – Canada [cover-title]
DESCRIPTION: 21.5 × 15.5 cm   Pp 1–29 [30]   Paper; rebound in cloth, together with other Bulletins
CONTENTS: 1–near bottom 2 'La culture des pommes au Canada'; bottom 2–mid 4 'La loi des fruits'; mid 4 'Honneurs remportes'; bottom 4–top 5 'Que vaut la pomme'; mid 5 'Valeur nutritive de la pomme'; bottom 5–top 6 'Il faut employer les pommes dans leur saison'; near top 6–mid 11 'Recettes pratiques pour la

cuisson des pommes'; mid 11–mid 19 'Desserts et poudings aux pommes'; mid 19–mid 22 'Tartes aux pommes'; bottom 22–top 25 'Salades de pommes'; mid 25–mid 29 'Friandises aux pommes'; bottom 29–30 recipes for Pommes flottantes and Îles flottantes de pommes
CITATIONS: Ag 1867–1974, p 2
COPIES: *OOAG (630.4 C212 B35 N.S. Fr)
NOTES: No one is credited with the recipes. The following is on the outside back face of the binding: 'Recettes pour la cuisson des pommes ... Bulletin no. 35 Publié par ordre de l'hon. W. Motherwell, ministre de l'agriculture Ottawa, 1923.'

O496.2 [1924]
—Canadian / grown / apples / Delight / in every / bite / Fruit Branch / Department of Agriculture / Ottawa Canada [cover-title]
DESCRIPTION: 21.0 × 15.0 cm   Pp [1] 2–23   Paper, with image on front of apples in a bowl, half-apple beside bowl; stapled, and with hole punched at top left corner for hanging
CONTENTS: 1–mid 2 'Apple Culture in Canada'; mid 2–3 'The Fruit Act'; top–mid 4 'Awards,' 'About the Apple,' and 'Food Value of Apples'; bottom 4–5 'Use Apples in Their Season'; 6–mid 9 'Practical Apple Recipes'; mid 9–near bottom 15 'Apple Desserts and Puddings'; bottom 15–mid 18 'Apple Pies'; mid 18–19 'Apple Salads'; 20–near bottom 22 'Apple Relishes'; bottom 22 recipe for Apple Float; 23 recipe for Apple Floating Island and 'Ottawa: F.A. Acland, printer ... 1924'
CITATIONS: Ag 1867–1974, p 3   Driver 2003, 'Canadian Cookbooks,' p 37
COPIES: *OOAG (630.4 C212 B35 N.S., 3 copies)
NOTES: No one is credited with the recipes. The following is on the outside back face of the binding: 'Apple Recipes ... Bulletin No. 35 New Series Published by direction of the Hon. W. Motherwell, Minister of Agriculture Ottawa, 1924.'

O496.3 [rev. ed., 1926]
—Canadian / grown / apples / Delight / in every / bite / Fruit Branch / Department of Agriculture / Ottawa Canada [cover-title]
DESCRIPTION: 21.0 × 15.0 cm   Pp [1] 2–23   Paper, with image on front of apples in a bowl, half-apple beside bowl; stapled, and with hole punched at top left corner for hanging
CONTENTS: 1–mid 5 'Apple Culture in Canada'; mid 5–23 'Practical Apple Recipes by Ethel A. Preston' and at bottom p 23, 'Ottawa: F.A. Acland, printer to the King's Most Excellent Majesty, 1926'

COPIES: QMM (RBD ckbk 1392) *Private collection
NOTES: The following is on the outside back face of the binding: 'Apple Recipes ... Bulletin No. 35 (Revised edition) Published by direction of the Hon. S.F. Tolmie, Minister of Agriculture Ottawa, 1926.' 'Apple Culture in Canada' presents the history and current state of apple production in each province and discusses the Fruit Act, the grading of apples, their food value, and the seasons for particular varieties.

This is the only edition in which Preston is given credit for the 'Practical Apple Recipes.' She is also credited for the recipes in O495.4, the 1926 edition of *Fruit and Vegetables*. Preston is the author of *Fruit and Vegetable Recipes*, Circular 17, Ottawa: Department of Agriculture, 1924 (OOAG). This 2-page publication contains 'Food Value of Apples,' recipes for Apple Floating Island, Apple Sauce, Baked Apples, Apple Float, and three recipes using carrots.

Preston's original 'Application for Admission' in 1910 to the Faculty of Household Science at the University of Toronto is at OTUAR (A69-0008/172). In the application, she gives her full name, Ethel Ada Preston, and records that she was born in Napanee, Ontario, on 14 April 1886; her father, D.H. Preston, was a lawyer, and her family, Presbyterian.

O496.4 [rev. ed., 1929]
—Canadian / grown / apples / Delight / in every / bite / Fruit Branch / Department of Agriculture / Ottawa Canada [cover-title]
DESCRIPTION: 21.5 × 15.0 cm Pp [1] 2–23 Paper, with image on front of apples in a bowl, half-apple beside bowl; stapled, and with hole punched at top left corner for hanging
CONTENTS: 1–top 2 'Apple Culture in Canada'; mid 2–near bottom 3 'The Fruit Act'; bottom 3 'Buy Graded Apples'; top–mid 4 'About the Apple' and 'Food Value of Apples'; bottom 4–top 5 'Use Apples in Their Season'; mid 5–mid 9 'Practical Apple Recipes'; mid 9–15 'Apple Desserts and Puddings'; 16–mid 18 'Apple Pies'; mid 18–top 20 'Apple Salads'; near top 20–22 'Apple Relishes'; 23 recipes for Apple Float and Apple Floating Island and 'Ottawa: F.A. Acland, printer to the King's Most Excellent Majesty, 1929'
CITATIONS: Ag 1867–1974, p 3 CCat No. 8, p J10 FitzPatrickCat 111 (April 1993) No. 4
COPIES: OONL (COP.CA.2.1993-2657) *Private collection
NOTES: No one is credited with the recipes. The following is on the outside back face of the binding: 'Apple Recipes ... Bulletin No. 35 (Revised edition) Published by direction of the Hon. W.R. Motherwell, Minister of Agriculture Ottawa, 1929.' No copy was found at OOAG.

O496.5 [1929]
—Pommes / cultivées / au Canada / Chaque bouchée / est / un régal / Traduit au Bureau de traduction du ministère / Division des fruits / Ministère fédéral de l'agriculture, / Ottawa – Canada [cover-title]
COPIES: *Private collection
NOTES: The printer and year of publication are on p 24: 'Ottawa: F.A. Acland, imprimeur de sa très excellente majesté le roi, 1929.'

O496.6 [rev. ed., 1930]
—Canadian / grown / apples / Delight / in every / bite / Fruit Branch / Department of Agriculture / Ottawa Canada [cover-title]
DESCRIPTION: 21.0 × 15.0 cm Pp [1] 2–23 Paper, with image on front of apples in a bowl, half-apple beside bowl; stapled, and with hole punched at top left corner for hanging
CONTENTS: 1–top 2 'Apple Culture in Canada'; mid 2–near bottom 3 'The Fruit Act'; bottom 3 'Buy Graded Apples'; top–mid 4 'About the Apple' and 'Food Value of Apples'; bottom 4–top 5 'Use Apples in Their Season'; mid 5–mid 9 'Practical Apple Recipes'; mid 9–15 'Apple Desserts and Puddings'; 16–mid 18 'Apple Pies'; mid 18–top 20 'Apple Salads'; near top 20–22 'Apple Relishes'; 23 recipes for Apple Float and Apple Floating Island and 'Ottawa: Printed by F.A. Acland, printer to the King's Most Excellent Majesty, 1930.'
COPIES: OGU (2 copies: *CCC CA1 DA281 29B35, Rural Heritage Collection uncat)
NOTES: No one is credited with the recipes. The following is on the outside back face of the binding: 'Apple Recipes ... Bulletin No. 35 (Revised edition) Published by direction of the Hon. W.R. Motherwell, Minister of Agriculture Ottawa, 1930.'

O496.7 [rev. ed., 1931]
—Canadian / grown / apples / Delight / in every / bite / Fruit Branch / Department of Agriculture / Ottawa Canada [cover-title]
DESCRIPTION: 21.0 × 15.0 cm Pp [1] 2–23 Paper, with image on front of apples in a bowl, half-apple beside bowl; stapled, and with hole punched at top left corner for hanging
CONTENTS: 1–top 2 'Apple Culture in Canada'; mid 2–near bottom 3 'The Fruit Act'; bottom 3 'Buy Graded Apples'; top–mid 4 'About the Apple' and 'Food Value of Apples'; bottom 4–top 5 'Use Apples in Their Season'; mid 5–mid 9 'Practical Apple Recipes'; mid 9–15 'Apple Desserts and Puddings'; 16–mid 18 'Apple Pies'; mid 18–top 20 'Apple Salads'; near top 20–22 'Apple Relishes'; 23 recipes for Apple Float and Apple Floating Island and 'Ottawa: Printed by F.A. Acland,

printer to the King's Most Excellent Majesty, 1931.'
COPIES: *OAYM
NOTES: The following is on the outside back face of
the binding: 'Apple Recipes ... Bulletin No. 35 (Re-
vised edition) Published by direction of the Hon.
Robert Weir, Minister of Agriculture Ottawa, 1931.'

O496.8 [rev. ed., 1934]
—Canadian / grown / apples / Delight / in every /
bite / Fruit Branch / Department of Agriculture /
Ottawa Canada [cover-title]
DESCRIPTION: 21.0 × 15.0 cm   Pp [1] 2–26   Paper,
with image on front of apples in a bowl, half-apple
beside bowl; stapled, and with hole punched at top
left corner for hanging
CONTENTS: 1–7 'Apple Culture in Canada'; 8–26 'Prac-
tical Apple Recipes' and at bottom p 26, 'Ottawa:
Printed by J.O. Patenaude, printer to the King's Most
Excellent Majesty, 1934.'
CITATIONS: Ag 1867–1974, p 3
COPIES: BVAMM   *Private collection
NOTES: No one is credited with the recipes. No copy
was found at OOAG.

O496.9   1936
—Pommes / cultivées / au Canada / Chaque
bouchée / est / un régal / Division des fruits /
Ministère fédéral de l'agriculture / Ottawa – Canada
[cover-title]
COPIES: OONL (COP.CA.2.1999-1636)   *Private collection

O496.10   reprint, May 1937
—Publication 566 / Household Bulletin 14 / Issued
May, 1937 / Reprint Bulletin 35 / Dominion of
Canada, Department of Agriculture / Canadian
grown apples / apple recipes / Fruit Branch /
Published by authority of the Hon. James G.
Gardiner, Minister of Agriculture / Ottawa, Canada
DESCRIPTION: 21.5 × 15.0 cm   Pp [1–3] 4–28   Paper,
with image on front of apples in a bowl, half-apple
beside bowl; stapled, and with hole punched at top
left corner for hanging
CONTENTS: 1 tp; 2 blank; 3–9 'Apple Culture in
Canada'; 10–28 recipes and at bottom p 28, 'Ottawa:
Printed by J.O. Patenaude, I.S.O., printer to the King's
Most Excellent Majesty, 1937.'
CITATIONS: Ag 1867–1974, pp 23 and 34
COPIES: OOAG (630.4 C212 P566, 2 copies, and 630.4
C212 HB14)   *Private collection

O496.11   reprint, October 1937
—Publication 566 / Bulletin de la ménagère n° 14 /
Publié en octobre, 1937 / Réimpression Bulletin
n° 35 / Dominion du Canada – Ministère de
l'agriculture / Pommes cultivées au Canada /
recettes pour la cuisson / des pommes / Division
des fruits / Publiée [sic] par ordre de l'honorable
James G. Gardiner, ministre de l'agriculture, /
Ottawa, Canada.
DESCRIPTION: 21.0 × 15.0 cm   Pp [i–ii], [1] 2–29 [30]
Paper, with image on front of apples in a bowl, half-
apple beside bowl; rebound in cloth, together with
other Household Bulletins
CONTENTS: i tp; ii blank; 1–8 'La culture des pommes
au Canada'; 9–30 'Recettes pratiques pour la cuisson
des pommes' and at bottom p 30, 'Ottawa: J.-O.
Patenaude, O.S.I., imprimeur ... 1937.'
CITATIONS: Ag 1867–1974, pp 7 and 26   Ferguson/
Fraser, p 233
COPIES: *OOAG (630.4 C212 HB14 and 630.4 C212
P566)   OONL (COP.CA.2.2000-689)

O496.12   rev. ed., November 1938
—Publication 566 / Household Bulletin 14 / Issued
November, 1938 / Revised / Dominion of Canada,
Department of Agriculture / Canadian grown
apples / apple recipes / Marketing Service /
Published by authority of the Hon. James G.
Gardiner, Minister of Agriculture / Ottawa, Canada
DESCRIPTION: 21.5 × 15.0 cm   Pp [1–3] 4–24   Paper,
with image on front of apples in a bowl, half-apple
beside bowl; stapled, and with hole punched at top
left corner for hanging
CONTENTS: 1 tp; 2 blank; 3–7 'Apple Culture in
Canada'; 8–24 'Practical Apple Recipes' and at bot-
tom p 24, 'Ottawa: Printed by J.O. Patenaude, I.S.O.,
printer to the King's Most Excellent Majesty, 1938.'
CITATIONS: Ag 1867–1974, pp 23 and 34   Armstrong
2000, illus p F1
COPIES: ACG   OOAG (630.4 C212 P566 and 630.4
C212 HB14)   OONL (COP.CA.2.1999-2805)   QMAC
(S133 A346 No. 566 bound in volume labelled
No. 1560)   *Private collection

O496.13   rev. ed., 1939
—Publication 566 / Household Bulletin 14 / Issued
November, 1939 / Revised / Dominion of Canada,
Department of Agriculture / Canadian grown
apples / apple recipes / Marketing Service /
Published by authority of the Hon. James G.
Gardiner, Minister of Agriculture / Ottawa, Canada
/ 50M–3258–12-39

DESCRIPTION: 21.0 × 15.0 cm   Pp [1–3] 4–24   Paper, with image on front of apples in a bowl, half-apple beside bowl; stapled, and with hole punched at top left corner for hanging
CONTENTS: 1 tp; 2 blank; 3–7 'Apple Culture in Canada'; 8–24 'Practical Apple Recipes' and at bottom p 24, 'Ottawa: Printed by J.O. Patenaude, I.S.O., printer to the King's Most Excellent Majesty, 1939.'
COPIES: OGU (CCC TX715.6 M572 No. 500)   OOAG (630.4 C212 P566)   OONL (COP.CA.2.1994-521) *Private collection
NOTES: See pl 9.

O496.14   rev. ed., October 1941
—Publication 566 / Bulletin de la ménagère n° 14 / Publié en octobre 1941 / Édition revisée / Dominion du Canada – Ministère de l'agriculture / Pommes du Canada / recettes pour la cuisson / des pommes / Service des marchés / Publié par ordre de l'honorable James G. Gardiner, ministre de l'agriculture, / Ottawa, Canada. / 25M–5114–10:41
DESCRIPTION: 21.5 × 15.0 cm   Pp [1–3] 4–28   Paper, with image on front of apples in a bowl, half-apple beside bowl; stapled, and with hole punched at top left corner for hanging
CONTENTS: 1 tp; 2 blank; 3–7 'La culture des pommes au Canada'; 8–28 'Recettes pratiques pour la cuisson des pommes' and at bottom p 28, 'Ottawa: Edmond Cloutier, imprimeur ... 1941.'
COPIES: *OOAG (630.4 C212 P566)
NOTES: This edition has a new short-title on the title-page. The cover-title remains 'Pommes cultivées au Canada,' as in the first edition of 1923.

O496.15   rev. ed., August 1942
—Publication 566 / Household Bulletin 14 / Issued August, 1942 / Revised / Dominion of Canada, Department of Agriculture / Canadian grown apples / apple recipes / Marketing Service / Published by authority of the Hon. James G. Gardiner, Minister of Agriculture / Ottawa, Canada / 50M–6009–8-42
DESCRIPTION: 21.0 × 15.0 cm   Pp [1–3] 4–24   Paper, with image on front of a bowl of apples, half-apple beside bowl; stapled
CONTENTS: 1 tp; 2 blank; 3–mid 4 'Apple Culture in Canada'; mid–bottom 4 'The Fruit, Vegetables and Honey Act'; 5 'Food Value of Apples,' 'Buy Canadian Apples,' and 'Buy by Grade'; 6–7 'Some Leading Varieties of Canadian Apples'; 8–24 recipes
COPIES: ARDA   *Private collection

Cook book

O497.1   1923
Lord Salisbury Chapter / I.O.D.E. / Cook book / Compiled and published by the officers and members / of Lord Salisbury Chapter, I.O.D.E. / Toronto, Canada. / 1923
DESCRIPTION: 23.0 × 15.5 cm   Pp [1–10] 11–240   Fp illus portrait on p 5 signed Evelyn Byng of Vimy Cloth, with IODE symbol on front
CONTENTS: 1–3 ads; 4 blank; 5 fp illus portrait; 6 blank; 7 poem beginning, 'We may live without poetry, music and art' [from *Lucile*, Part I, Canto ii, by Owen Meredith, pseudonym of Edward Robert Bulwer-Lytton] and 'Sunshine Cake' contributed by Isabelle Cockshutt, Government House, Toronto; 8 ads; 9 tp; 10 blank; 11 foreword signed the Committee; 12 table of contents; 13 list of officers; 14 list of advertisers; 15–238 recipes credited with the name of the contributor and ads; 239–40 ads
CITATIONS: O'Neill (unpublished)   CCat No. 2, p D6   Rhodenizer, p 992
COPIES: OTMCL (641.5 I52)   OTYA (TX715 I46 1923)   *Private collection; Great Britain: LB (07942.c.28 destroyed)
NOTES: The cover-title is 'Cook Book'; the title on the spine and the running head is 'Lord Salisbury Chapter I.O.D.E. Cook Book.' The wording of the foreword is nearly identical to the foreword in O452.1, *Valuable Hints and Helps for Housekeepers*. CCat records the price of $1.00 for the book.

The Harrietsville cook book

The Harrietsville branch of the Women's Institute was established in 1908 (Ambrose, p 237).

O498.1   1st ed., nd [about 1923]
The / Harrietsville cook book / a selection of / tested recipes / Compiled by / the ladies of / the Women's Institute / Harrietsville, Ont. / First edition / The Aylmer Express / publishers, Aylmer, Ont.
DESCRIPTION: 20.5 × 13.5 cm   Pp [3–4] 5–123   Paper
CONTENTS: 3 tp; 4 'Preface'; 5–118 recipes credited with the name of the contributor and ads; 119–22 'Miscellaneous'; 123 'Index' [i.e., table of contents]
COPIES: *OONL (TX715 H38)
NOTES: There is an advertisement on p 32 for C.B. Adams, 'The Reliable Store,' Harrietsville, Ontario, 1885–1923 (presumably the current year).

Helpful hints for housekeepers 1923

See O263.1 for information about the company and other issues of Helpful Hints for Housekeepers.

O499.1 1923
1923 Volume XIII 1923 / Hang me in the kitchen / Helpful / hints / for housekeepers / Compliments of / the Dodds Medicine Co. / Limited / Toronto, Can. [cover-title]
DESCRIPTION: 15.5 × 10.5 cm Pp 1–32 Paper; stapled, and with hole punched at top left corner, through which runs a string for hanging
CONTENTS: 1 'The Kitchen Stove'; 2 'To You from Us'; 3 'Kitchen Scissors' and 'Measuring Butter Substitutes'; 4, 6, 8, 10, 12, 14, 18, 20, 22, 24, 26, 28 entries for illnesses and other medical information, arranged alphabetically from Anaemia to Skin; 5 continuation of 'Measuring Butter Substitutes' and 'Handy Measures'; 7 'How to Stop Small Leaks in the Kitchen' and 'Good Disinfectants'; 9 continuation of 'Good Disinfectants' and 'Durable Whitewash'; 11 'Some Egg Instructions'; 13 'Ways of Setting Colors Explained'; 15 'Removing Stains'; 16–17 publ ads for Dodd's Kidney Pills; 19 'To Get Rid of Pests'; 21, 23 'Things Worth Remembering'; 25 'Points for the Kitchen'; 27 'Points in Laundrying'; 29–30 .publ ads for Diamond Dinner Pills and Dodd's Dyspepsia Tablets; 31 'Care of Furniture'; 32 'Diet Rules'; inside back face of binding 'Self Examination Page'
COPIES: *OTUTF (uncat patent medicine)

How to cook with Moffats 'Electric' Range

For the titles of other cookbooks by the same manufacturer, see O342.1.

O500.1 [copyright 1923]
How / to cook / with / Moffats / "Electric" / Range [cover-title]
DESCRIPTION: 15.5 × 8.5 cm Pp [1–12] A few small illus of range parts Paper, with image on front of a woman stirring the contents of a saucepan on a range; stapled, and with hole punched at top left corner for hanging
CONTENTS: Inside front face of binding information about the 'Moffat set of porcelain enamelware' ('white to match the white splash and panels on range'); 1–mid 5 'Start Right // Important Information for Operating Moffats Electric Ranges' and at bottom

p 1, 'Copyright, Canada, 1923 by Moffats Limited Weston, Ont.'; bottom 5–12 recipes for baked goods, such as cookies, cakes, muffins, and pies
COPIES: *Private collection

The Ingersoll recipe book

O501.1 nd [about 1923]
The / Ingersoll / recipe / book [cover-title]
DESCRIPTION: 16.0 × 8.5 cm Pp [1–23] Illus brown-and-yellow Paper, with image on front of cows standing in a stream, a package of Ingersoll Cheese in the foreground; stapled
CONTENTS: 1 cover-title; 2–3 'Valuable Pointers by a Domestic Science Expert'; 4–23 recipes credited with the name of the contributor, for example, Mrs Norman Massey and Miss Jean Garrow (first prize winner)
CITATIONS: Chatelaine 1935, p 82
COPIES: AMHM *Bookseller's stock
NOTES: 'Manufactured by the Ingersoll Packing Co Ingersoll, Ontario, Canada' appears on the side of the cheese package on the binding. The text on p 2 begins: 'The recipes here given are the result of a contest conducted for the purpose of demonstrating the varied use of Ingersoll Cream Cheese in Canadian cookery. The competition was limited to domestic science graduates ...' The book is printed in brown ink.

An advertisement in the March 1923 issue of *Western Home Monthly* for 'The Book of Ingersoll Recipes free' probably refers to this cookbook. The appearance of *The Ingersoll Recipe Book* is consistent with publication in 1923.

A private collector has a copy of *The Ingersoll Recipe Book* that matches the description above, except that the lettering on the image of the cheese package on the binding says, 'Save this coupon // Premium list appears on inside wrapper // [lettering masked by the open end of the box] Cheese Co. Ltd. Ingersoll Ont.'

Another private collector has a copy of *The Ingersoll Recipe Book* that matches the description above, except that the lettering on the image of the cheese package on the binding is not clear and only 'soll Packing Co' is legible (some of the lettering is masked by the open end of the box). Another difference is that 'Valuable Pointers' is signed on p 3 by Miss K.A. Fisher. See O1046.1, *The Good Housekeeping Cook Book*, for a note about Katharine Anderson Fisher.

Jell-O

For the titles of other books for cooking with Jell-O, see O212.1.

O502.1   copyright 1923
"It's so simple" / Jell-O / Canada's most famous dessert / © 1923, by the Genesee Pure Food Company of Canada Ltd. [cover-title]
DESCRIPTION: 15.5 × 11.0 cm   Pp 1–14   Illus col, illus on p 1 of head-and-shoulders of a young girl   Paper, with image on front of a grandmother(?) adding hot water to an enamel jug, a boy and girl watching; stapled
CONTENTS: 1 'Introduction' signed Alice Bradley, principal, Miss Farmer's School of Cookery; 2, 5–6 'Jell-O Desserts'; 3 'First Lesson – Making Plain Jell-O'; 4 'Second Lesson – Layer Jell-O'; 7–8 centre spread illus col of six prepared Jell-O dishes; 9 'Delicious Whips'; 10, 13–14 'Jell-O Salads' and at bottom p 14, 'The Genesee Pure Food Company of Canada, Ltd. Bridgburg [sic], Ont.'; 11 'Third Lesson – Whipped Jell-O'; 12 'Fourth Lesson – Fruited Jell-O'
COPIES: AEUCHV (UV 85.264.29)   OONL (TX814.5 G4 J44 1923 p***)   OTMCL (641.5971 H39 No. 18A)   QMM (RBD ckbk 1597)   *Bookseller's stock
NOTES: The colour illustrations on the front and back faces of the binding are signed by the American illustrator Norman Rockwell. The printer's name is on the outside back face: 'Standard Litho. Co. Toronto, Can.' Unusually, p 1 is on the inside face of the binding so that even-numbered pages are on rectos and odd numbers, on versos.

The lessons are presented in numbered and illustrated steps, which Bradley describes in her 'Introduction' as 'Moving Pictures.' She explains that 'Jell-O is ... designed to meet the need of the modern housekeeper whose problem is to save time, energy, and money in doing her daily tasks.'

The copyright date in the QMM copy is difficult to read, but it is the same edition as that catalogued here.

AMERICAN EDITIONS: Probably 'It's So Simple' – Jell-O America's Most Famous Dessert, 1922 (Allen, p 198).

Jell-O rhymes

For the titles of other books for cooking with Jell-O, see O212.1. The editor of Jell-O Rhymes, Caroline Blanche King, also produced O670.1, Better Coffee Recipes.

O503.1   nd [about 1923]
Jell-O / rhymes / 10¢ / a package. / Canada's most famous dessert [cover-title]
DESCRIPTION: 15.5 × 10.5 cm   Pp [1] 2–19   Illus col   Paper, with image on front of three geese in the foreground and Mother Goose and two geese in the background; stapled
CONTENTS: 1 cover-title; 2–3 'Many Reasons for Jell-O // Edited by Caroline B. King'; 4 'How to Whip Jell-O' and 'How to Add Fruits to Jell-O Desserts'; 5 'Delicious Whips'; 6–mid 7 'New Recipes'; mid 7–8 'For Special Occasions'; 9 'Jell-O Recipes for the Children'; 10–11 centre spread illus col of 'Mary, Mary, quite contrary' growing 'rows of sweet Jell-O'; 12 'Jell-O for Convalescents'; 13–16 'Suggestions for Luncheons'; 17 'Dinner Suggestions'; 18 'The Easy Jell-O Way'; 19 'Facts about Jell-O'
COPIES: OKITJS (999.24.6)   OONL (TX773 J4)   QMM (RBD ckbk 1695)   *Bookseller's stock; United States: Company collection (Kraft Foods Inc., Archives Department, Morton Grove, Ill.)
NOTES: The text incorporates well-known nursery rhymes, adapted to refer to Jell-O. The illustrations are signed Lucile Patterson Marsh. Printed on the outside back face of the binding are the printer's name, 'Standard Litho. Co. Toronto, Can,' and an image of a Jell-O package with the maker's name, Genesee Pure Food Co. of Canada Ltd, Bridgeburg, Ontario. Although undated, the Canadian editions were likely published about the same year as the American edition, 1923.

The bookseller's copy is inscribed on the binding, 'Constance McKie, Paris, Ont.' The OKITJS copy lacks pp 1–2 and 19, but what remains matches the description here.

O503.2   nd [about 1923]
—Jell-O / rhymes / 10¢ / le paquet. / Le dessert le plus renommé au Canada [cover-title]
DESCRIPTION: 15.5 × 10.5 cm   Pp [1] 2–19   Illus col   Paper, with image on front of three geese in the foreground and Mother Goose and two geese in the background; stapled
CONTENTS: 1 cover-title; ... 19 [inside back face of binding] 'À propos de Jell-O'
COPIES: *QSFFSC
NOTES: The printer's name on the binding is illegible.

AMERICAN EDITIONS: Jell-O Rhymes – America's Most Famous Dessert, 1923 (Allen, p 198).

The new Purity Flour cook book

*For information about Western Canada Flour Mills and
other cookbooks for Purity Flour, see O394.1.*

O504.1 [copyright 1923]
Purity Flour / The new / Purity Flour / cook book
/ Contains the best recipes of our last book to /
which have been added the carefully tested / and
selected recipes of experts adapted to / the changes
and improvements in culinary / methods and
apparatus. / A book with valuable information on
the / preparation of a varied number of dishes /
and confections for all ordinary meals and / special
occasions. / Invaluable to the new – and helpful to
the / experienced housewife. / [symbol of Western
Canada Flour Mills Co.] / Better bread – delicious
pastry / [folio:] 3
DESCRIPTION: 22.5 × 15.5 cm   Pp 1–183 [184–92]   Illus
col   Paper
CONTENTS: 1 publ ad; 2 publ note commending 'this,
our Second Book'; 3 tp; 4 'Copyright, Canada, 1923
Western Canada Flour Mills Co., Limited // Head
office: Toronto, Canada' and 'National Art Co.,
Toronto'; 5–6 'Foreword'; 7–14 index; 15 four book-
order coupons; 16 note about the coupons; 17–183
text; 184–92 blank for 'Notes and Your Own Recipes'
CITATIONS: Driver 2001, All New Purity, inside front
cover   Ferguson/Fraser, pp 65 and 233
COPIES: AALIWWM   ACG   ACHP (HP 4628.7)
AEPRAC   AEUCHV   BVIPM   BVMA   NSHMS
(76.67.36)   OGU (CCC TX715.6 P87 1923, 2 copies)
OKELWM   OONL (TX715.6 N476 1923)   *Company
collection (Maple Leaf Mills Consumer Products Co.),
in 1991; location now unknown
NOTES: This book superseded O394.1, Warner, Miss
E., *Purity Flour Cook Book*, of 1917. In 1932 it was
replaced by O771.1, *The Purity Cook-Book*.
   The AALIWWM copy has only pp 9–178.

O504.2   [copyright 1925]
—Farine Purity / Le / livre de recettes / Farine
Purity / Contient les meilleures recettes de notre
dernier / livre auxquelles ont été ajoutées les
recettes / soigneusement choisies et vérifiées
d'experts, qui / ont été adaptées aux changements
et aux / améliorations des méthodes et des appareils
/ culinaires modernes. Un livre donnant des in- /
formations appréciables touchant la préparation /
d'un grand nombre de mets et de plats variés / pour
tous les repas ordinaires ainsi que pour les /
occasions spéciales. / D'une valeur sans bornes pour
la ménagère nou- / velle – et très utile aux

ménagères expérimentées. / Western Canada Flour
Mills Co., Limited / Siege social: Toronto /
Succursales a / Winnipeg, Calgary, Brandon,
Edmonton, Vancouver, New Westminster, Victoria, /
Nanaimo, Prince Rupert, Nelson, Rossland,
Goderich, Ottawa, / Montréal, St. John, N.B. /
Meilleur pain – délicieuse pâtisserie / [folio:] 1
DESCRIPTION: 22.5 × 15.0 cm   Pp 1–156   Illus blue on
p 2 of 'Notre installation à Winnipeg' and fp illus blue
on p 4 of 'Notre laboratoire à Winnipeg'   Paper, with
hole punched at top left corner for hanging; sewn
CONTENTS: 1 tp; 2 illus and 'Droits réservés, Canada,
1925 Western Canada Flour Mills Co., Limited //
Siège social: Toronto, Canada // Southam Press Lim-
ited Montréal et Toronto'; 3 'Avant-propos' signed
Western Canada Flour Mills Co. Ltd; 4 fp illus; 5–11
'Index'; 12 book-order coupons; 13 'Pour envoyer
Le livre de recettes Farine Purity à vos amis, faites
usage du coupon ...' [i.e., note about the coupons];
14–156 text
COPIES: OONL (TX715 L6914 1925 p***)   *QMBM
(Env. 7841)

Official cook book

See also O421.1, by the same group.

O505.1   nd [about 1923]
Official / cook book / Order of Eastern Star /
Mizpeh Chapter / No. 56 / [Ad in box:] French
gowns / Foster's / 30 King St. E. / Hamilton
[cover-title]
DESCRIPTION: 23.0 × 15.0 cm   Pp 1–61 [62–4]   Paper; stapled
CONTENTS: 1 ad for Eaton's New Gyrator [a wringer
washing machine]; 2 'Index' [i.e., table of contents]
and 'Printed by the Gardner Press // Phone Regent
2169'; 3 ad for McClary Electric Range; 4–55 recipes
and ads; 56 'Weights and Measures' and 'Time Table
for Baking'; 57 'Time Table for Cooking'; 58 'Linens';
59 'The Care of Furniture'; bottom 59–60 'The Removal of Stains'; 61 'Hints on Home Nursing'; 62–4
blank for 'Memorandum'
COPIES: *OH (R641.5 OFF CESH)
NOTES: There is an advertisement on p 23 for Finlay
Fish Co., successors to R.M. Cline. Hamilton city directories for 1922, and before, list Ransom Melvin
Cline, fish dealer or fish merchant, at 299 King Street
East. From 1923, Finlay Fish Co. is at this address,
and Cline is no longer listed as a fish dealer. The
cookbook, therefore, was published about 1923.

Pattinson, Miss Nellie Lyle (Bowmanville, Ont., 24 October 1879–30 April 1953, Toronto, Ont.)

See also O241.3, L.M.S. Book of Recipes, *edited by Annie L. Laird and Nellie Lyle Pattinson, under* Recipes in Individual and Large Amounts for Home and School; *O589.1,* New Recipes Baumert Cheese, *for which Pattinson approved the recipes; and O541.1,* Economical Recipe Book, *with which she may have been involved. She contributed a recipe for Fruit Jumbles to O294.2, the 1922 edition of* The Wimodausis Club Cook Book.

The 1901 Census gives Pattinson's birth date and records her as a student living in Bowmanville with her parents, Susana and Joseph, and her brothers, Edwin W. and Fredrick. She was a graduate of the Hamilton Normal School and of the Lillian Massey School of Household Science in 1907. She first taught at Brantford Collegiate, but after a year joined the staff of the Lillian Massey School. She exerted her greatest influence, however, at Toronto's Central Technical School, from the 1915–16 academic year as an instructor in cookery, then as director of domestic science from about 1920 until her retirement in June 1942 (the yearbook appreciation, cited below, says she became director in 1920; since the previous director, Miss Margaret Davidson, took another appointment in August 1919, Pattinson may have been appointed director in the autumn of 1919). While she was at Central Technical School, she wrote Canadian Cook Book, *which served not only as a culinary reference for housewives, but as a standard textbook for Household Science classes in secondary schools for well over thirty years. At the time of her death, she was living at 123 Imperial Street in Toronto, her residence of nearly twenty years. She is buried in Bowmanville Cemetery.*

For a photograph of Pattinson (pl 38 here), an appreciation of her upon her retirement, and a reprint of part of a review of her Canadian Cook Book *by Jean Brodie from the* Toronto Star Weekly *(5 December 1942), see* Vulcan *[Central Technical School yearbook],* Rainbow number *(January 1943), pp 28–9 (copy in school library). Regarding Brodie's review, see O506.14. Pattinson's obituary is in the* Globe and Mail *(Toronto) 1 May 1953.*

Information about four of Pattinson's five assistants named on the title-page of the first edition is held at OTUAR. Miss Helene Louise Wilkinson's 'Application for Admission' in 1910 to the Faculty of Household Science (A69-0008/172) says that she was born in Toronto on 28 August 1892 and lived at 53 Triller Avenue. Her father, B. Charles Wilkinson, was a wholesale jeweller; her family was Anglican. She had attended Queen Victoria School and Parkdale Collegiate Institute.

The 1901 Census gives her birth date as 28 August 1893 [sic], and her mother's name, Henrietta.

The OTUAR file (A73-0026/113 (53)) for Miss Myrtle Edith Gardiner (Mrs Newton Johnson Powell), the only daughter of Mr and Mrs David Gardiner, includes a clipping and photograph of her from Torontonensis, *1920. Gardiner was educated at Harbord Collegiate Institute, and graduated from Victoria College at the University of Toronto in 1920. In June 1922 she resigned her teaching job at Windsor Collegiate Institute and returned to Toronto, where she worked for a short time under Pattinson at Central Technical School. She later became head of the Household Science Department at Riverdale Technical School, resigning to marry in June 1928. The 1901 Census gives her birth date, 10 November 1898, and her mother's name, Victoria.*

Miss Ethel Louise Stockwell's 'Application for Admission' in 1909 to the University of Toronto Faculty of Arts (A69-0008/052 (02)) says that she attended George Street Public School for five years, then Moulton College, a private girls' school, for another five years. Her religious denomination was Baptist. Her English father, J.W. Stockwell, was a dyer and cleaner. Torontonensis, *1913, p 67, records her graduation in 1913 from University College with a BA, and reproduces a photograph of her. The 1901 Census gives her birth date, 16 August 1892, and her parents' names, Jno W. and Mary A. Her greatniece reports that she died in 1976.*

For information about Miss Alexandrina Denne at OTUAR, see the entry for her book, B37.1, Two Hundred and Fifty War-time Recipes, *published in 1918 for a British Columbia school, before she took up an appointment under Pattinson, in 1920.*

Miss Annie M. Gray may be the Miss Gray who contributed recipes to O124.1, The Spartan Cook Book, *1902.*

O506.1 [1923]
Canadian / cook book / by / Nellie Lyle Pattinson / Director of Domestic Science / Assisted by / Lexa Denne, B.A, [*sic,* comma] / Myrtle Gardiner, B.A. / Annie Gray / Ethel Stockwell, B.A. / Helene Wilkinson / teachers in Domestic Science / Central Technical School, Toronto / Toronto / The Ryerson Press

DESCRIPTION: 19.0 × 13.0 cm   Pp [i–ii] iii [iv] v–vii [viii] ix [x], 1–342 [343]   30 numbered illus   Cloth
CONTENTS: i tp; ii 'Copyright, Canada, 1923, by the Ryerson Press.'; iii unsigned 'Preface'; iv blank; v–vi table of contents; vii 'List of Tables'; viii blank; ix 'List of Diagrams'; x blank; 1–324 text; 325–6 blank for 'Notes'; 327–42 index; 343 'This book is a production of the Ryerson Press founded 1829'
CITATIONS: CCat No. 2, p D7   Cooke 2002, p 235

Driver 2003, 'Canadian Cookbooks,' p 38   Driver 2004, p vii   Driver 2005, letter   Ferguson/Fraser, pp 52 and 233   Goldenberg, pp 41–3   O'Neill (unpublished)   Rhodenizer, p 992   Wallace, p 69
COPIES: BLCK (998.38)   OKQ (TX715 P3234 1923) *Private collection; Great Britain: LB (7943.v.5 destroyed)
NOTES: The 'Preface' states: 'This book has been compiled, primarily, to satisfy a demand for a book of recipes conveniently arranged for use of teachers and students in technical schools. It is hoped that it may prove valuable also to all others who are interested in the preparation of food.' *Canadian Cook Book* was likely compiled in the 1922–3 school year, since that is the only year when all the assistants named on the title-page were on staff (commencement programs in the school library list Myrtle Gardiner for this one year only). CCat records the price of the first edition: $1.50. All editions before the Wattie/Donaldson revision of 1953 are bound in plain, blue cloth.

Incomplete publisher's records for *Canadian Cook Book* are at OTCC. On p 354 of 'Books for Sale 1904–1934' (Acc. 83.061C, UCC Board of Publication, Series III, Box 45), the entries begin with stock held February 1928 and carry forward to 18 November 1932. The following entry falls between April 1929 and September 1930: 'Sent to [illegible] Dec/4 [year not specified, but likely 1929] 84 [i.e., copies] Brides edition'; these may have been specially bound copies of the fifth edition of April 1928. At the head of the entries is the following information: 'Canadian Cook Book Miss N.L. Pattinson [$]2.25 List // 15% Royalty // 1% to Prof Peter Sandiford.' Dr Sandiford was a professor of educational psychology in the Faculty of Education at the University of Toronto; see his file at OTUAR (A73-0026/397 (14)).

Another individual who owns the 1923 edition reports, 'My copy is inscribed as a Christmas gift 1923 from Helene Wilkinson to Helen Wright, my mother, who was a domestic science teacher in various primary schools in Toronto until June 1924.'

The OKQ copy was donated to the library in 1992 by Bon Echo Provincial Park (on Lake Mazinaw, near Cloyne, Ontario). The copy likely belonged originally to Muriel Denison (born Jessie Muriel Goggin in Winnipeg; died 1954). A former employee of the park, who arranged the donation to OKQ, told Mary Savigny (author of *Bon Echo: The Denison Years*, Toronto: Natural Heritage/Natural History, 1997) that the copy was found in 1988, with other old books, in a closet at 'Greystones,' the largest of the original rental cottages at Bon Echo, which was operated as a resort in the 1920s by Muriel and her husband, Merrill.

Muriel first worked at Bon Echo in the summer of 1922, supervising food purchasing, preparation, and service (Savigny, p 16). She probably bought the 1923 edition of *Canadian Cook Book* as a reference for herself and the kitchen staff at Bon Echo. Although the copy does not bear Muriel's signature, she was not in the habit of inscribing her books (conversation with Mary Savigny, January 2001).

The illustrations in B59.3, *Foods, Nutrition and Home Management Manual,* published by the British Columbia Department of Education, are credited to Pattinson's *Canadian Cook Book* (edition not specified).

Carrière No. 169 cites the 1923 edition at QMBN, but the QMBN copy is O506.13.

O506.2   [2nd ed., December 1924]
—Canadian / cook book / by / Nellie Lyle Pattinson / Director of Domestic Science / Assisted by / Lexa Denne, B.A, [*sic,* comma] / Myrtle Gardiner, B.A. / Annie Gray / Ethel Stockwell, B.A. / Helene Wilkinson / teachers in Domestic Science / Central Technical School, Toronto / Toronto / The Ryerson Press
DESCRIPTION: 19.5 × 13.5 cm   Pp [i–ii] iii [iv] v–vii [viii] ix [x], 1–351 [352]   30 numbered illus   Cloth
CONTENTS: i tp; ii 'First edition, December, 1923 Second edition, December, 1924 Copyright, Canada, 1923, by the Ryerson Press. Printed and bound in Canada'; iii 'Preface' signed N.L.P.; iv blank; v–vi table of contents; vii 'List of Tables'; viii blank; ix 'List of Diagrams'; x blank; 1–332 text; 333–51 index; 352 'This book is a production of the Ryerson Press Toronto, Canada'
CITATIONS: Golick, p 108
COPIES: BVAU (Beatrice M. Millar Papers)   OTNY (uncat)   OTUTF (B-12 7852)   *Private collection
NOTES: The OTUTF copy has its original dust-jacket, which illustrates 'Specimen page showing method of presenting recipes.' The OTNY copy is inscribed on the front endpaper, in ink, 'May Wilson.'

O506.3   [3rd ed., December 1925]
—Canadian / cook book / by / Nellie Lyle Pattinson / Director of Domestic Science / Assisted by / Lexa Denne, B.A, [*sic,* comma] / Myrtle Gardiner, B.A. / Annie Gray / Ethel Stockwell, B.A. / Helene Wilkinson / teachers in Domestic Science / Central Technical School, Toronto / Toronto / The Ryerson Press
DESCRIPTION: 19.5 × 13.5 cm   Pp [i–ii] iii [iv] v–vii [viii] ix [x], 1–351 [352]   30 numbered illus   Cloth
CONTENTS: i tp; ii 'First edition, December, 1923 Second edition, December, 1924 Third edition, Decem-

ber, 1925 Copyright, Canada, 1923, by the Ryerson Press. Printed and bound in Canada'; iii author's preface; iv blank; v–vi table of contents; vii 'List of Tables'; viii blank; ix list of diagrams; x blank; 1–331 text; 332 blank for 'Notes'; 333–51 index; 352 'This book is a production of [Ryerson Press symbol] Toronto, Canada'

COPIES: AEU (TX715 P32)   *OGU (UA s048 b44) OTY (TX715 P37 1925)

O506.4   [4th ed., January 1927]
—Canadian / cook book / by / Nellie Lyle Pattinson / Director of Domestic Science / Assisted by / Annie Gray / Ethel Stockwell, B.A. / Helene Wilkinson / teachers in Domestic Science / Central Technical School, Toronto / Toronto / The Ryerson Press

DESCRIPTION: 19.5 × 13.0 cm   Pp [i–ii] iii [iv] v–ix [x], 1–416   Frontis of 'Reception Table,' 30 numbered illus, illus   Cloth

CONTENTS: i tp; ii 'First edition, December, 1923 Second edition, December, 1924 Third edition, December, 1925 Fourth edition, January, 1927 (revised and enlarged) Copyright, Canada, 1923, by the Ryerson Press. Printed and bound in Canada.'; iii 'Preface' signed N.L.P.; iv blank; v–vi 'Contents'; vii 'List of Tables'; viii 'List of Illustrations'; ix 'List of Diagrams'; x blank; 1–393 twenty-four chapters; 394–6 blank for 'Notes'; 397–416 index

CITATIONS: Eade, p E2 (wrong date cited; 1927 exhibited)

COPIES: OONL (TX715 P3234 1927)   *OTNY (uncat) Private collection

NOTES: The private collector reports that she received her copy as a prize on 20 April 1927 for highest standing that year in 'Housekeeping and Decoration' in a Home Economics course at the high school in Dunnville, Ontario.

CCat No. 5, p G4, cites a new edition of *Canadian Cook Book* published in 1926, at the price of $2.25; the number of pages is not recorded. The reference may be to the fourth edition.

O506.5   [5th ed., April 1928]
—Canadian / cook book / by / Nellie Lyle Pattinson / Director of Domestic Science / Assisted by / Annie Gray / Ethel Stockwell, B.A. / Helene Wilkinson / teachers in Domestic Science / Central Technical School, Toronto / Toronto / The Ryerson Press

DESCRIPTION: 19.0 × 13.0 cm   Pp [i–ii] iii [iv] v–ix [x], 1–416   Frontis of 'Reception Table,' 30 numbered illus, illus   Cloth

CONTENTS: i tp; ii 'First edition, December, 1923 Second edition, December, 1924 Third edition, December, 1925 Fourth edition, January, 1927 Fifth edition, April, 1928 (revised and enlarged) Copyright, Canada, 1923, by the Ryerson Press. Printed and bound in Canada'; iii preface signed N.L.P.; iv blank; v–vi table of contents; vii 'List of Tables'; viii 'List of Illustrations'; ix 'List of Diagrams'; x blank; 1–393 twenty-four chapters; 394–6 blank for 'Notes'; 397–416 index

COPIES: OGU (CCC TX715 P3 1928)   SSU (TX715 P32 1928, not on shelf)   *Private collection

NOTES: This edition may also have been specially bound in a 'Brides edition'; see 'Notes' for 506.1. The OGU copy is inscribed on the endpaper, in ink, 'Mary Park. Toronto 22 July 1930.'

The colour illustration of the closed volume in Ferguson/Fraser, p 57, is probably of the copy described here and the one consulted by the authors for their *A Century of Canadian Home Cooking.*

O506.6   [6th ed., May 1930]
—Canadian / cook book / by / Nellie Lyle Pattinson / Director of Domestic Science / Assisted by / Annie Gray / Ethel Stockwell, B.A. / Helene Wilkinson / teachers in Domestic Science / Central Technical School, Toronto / Toronto / The Ryerson Press

DESCRIPTION: 19.0 × 13.5 cm   Pp [i–ii] iii [iv] v–vi [vii–x lacking], [1–2 lacking] 3–408 [leaves lacking]   Frontis of 'Reception Table,' 30 numbered illus, illus   Cloth

CONTENTS: i tp; ii 'First edition, December, 1923 Second edition, December, 1924 Third edition, December, 1925 Fourth edition, January, 1927 Fifth edition, April, 1928 Sixth edition, May, 1930 (revised and enlarged) ... Printed and bound in Canada'; iii preface signed N.L.P.; iv blank; v–vi table of contents; vii–x lacking; 1–2 lacking; 3–396 twenty-four chapters; 397–408 index to 'Muffins, Butterscotch'; leaves lacking

COPIES: OGU (CCC TX715.6 P38 1930)   *Private collection

O506.7   [7th ed., October 1932]
—Canadian / cook book / by / Nellie Lyle Pattinson / Director of Domestic Science / Assisted by / Annie Gray / Ethel Stockwell, B.A. / Helene Wilkinson / teachers in Domestic Science / Central Technical School, Toronto / Toronto / The Ryerson Press

DESCRIPTION: 20.0 × 13.5 cm   Pp [i–ii] iii [iv] v–ix [x], 1–416   Frontis of 'Reception Table,' 30 numbered illus, illus   Cloth

CONTENTS: i tp; ii 'First edition, December, 1923 Second edition, December, 1924 Third edition, December, 1925 Fourth edition, January, 1927 Fifth edition, April, 1928 Sixth edition, May, 1930 (revised and enlarged) Seventh edition, October, 1932 ... Printed and bound in Canada'; iii preface signed N.L.P.; iv blank; v–vi table of contents; vii 'List of Tables'; viii 'List of Illustrations'; ix 'List of Diagrams'; x blank; 1–393 text; 394–6 blank for 'Notes'; 397–416 index
COPIES: OTUTF (B-12 7853)   OWTU (F15137)   *Private collection; United States: DLC (TX715 P3234 1932)

O506.8   [8th ed., March 1936]
—Canadian / cook book / by / Nellie Lyle Pattinson / Director of Domestic Science / Assisted by / Annie Gray / Ethel Stockwell, B.A. / Helene Wilkinson / teachers in Domestic Science / Central Technical School, Toronto / The Ryerson Press Toronto
DESCRIPTION: 20.0 × 13.5 cm   Pp [leaf lacking] [iii–iv] v [vi] vii–xi [xii], 1–414 [leaf lacking?]   Frontis lacking, 30 numbered illus, illus   Cloth
CONTENTS: i–ii lacking; iii tp; iv 'First edition, December, 1923 Second edition, December, 1924 Third edition, December, 1925 Fourth edition, January, 1927 Fifth edition, April, 1928 Sixth edition, May, 1930 (revised and enlarged) Seventh edition, October, 1932 Eighth edition, March, 1936 Copyright, Canada, 1923, by the Ryerson Press. Printed and bound in Canada'; v preface signed N.L.P.; vi blank; vii–viii table of contents; ix 'List of Tables'; x 'List of Illustrations'; xi 'List of Diagrams'; xii blank; 1–393 text; 394–6 blank for 'Notes'; 397–414 index; 415–16 index leaf lacking?
COPIES: *OGU (CCC TX715.6 P38 1936)   OONL (TX715 P3234 1936)   Private collection
NOTES: In the collector's copy, p i is the half-title; p ii, the frontispiece of 'Reception Table.'

O506.9   [rev. and enlarged ed., November 1937]
—Canadian / cook / book / by / Nellie Lyle Pattinson / Director of Domestic Science / Assisted by / Ethel Stockwell B.A. / Helene Wilkinson / teachers in Domestic Science / Central Technical School / Toronto / The Ryerson Press / Toronto
DESCRIPTION: 19.5 × 13.5 cm   Pp [i–iv] v [vi] vii–xi [xii], 1–441   Frontis of 'Reception Table,' 30 numbered illus, illus   Cloth
CONTENTS: i ht; ii frontis; iii tp; iv 'Copyright, Canada, 1923, by the Ryerson Press ... First edition, December, 1923 Second edition, December, 1924 Third edition, December, 1925 Fourth edition, January, 1927 Fifth edition, April, 1928 Revised and enlarged edition, May, 1930 Seventh edition, October, 1932 Eighth edi-

tion, March, 1936 Revised and enlarged edition, November, 1937 Printed and bound in Canada'; v preface signed N.L.P.; vi blank; vii–viii table of contents; ix 'List of Tables'; x 'List of Illustrations'; xi 'List of Diagrams'; xii blank; 1–420 text; 421–2 glossary; 423–41 index
CITATIONS: CCat No. 16, p R23   Cooke 2002, p 235
COPIES: OW (641.5 P27)   *Private collection
NOTES: CCat records the price: $1.75.

O506.10   [10th ed., March 1938]
—[Tenth edition, 1938]
CONTENTS: Tp verso 'Copyright, Canada, 1923, by the Ryerson Press ... First edition, December, 1923 Second edition, December, 1924 Third edition, December, 1925 Fourth edition, January, 1927 Fifth edition, April, 1928 Revised and enlarged edition, May, 1930 Seventh edition, October, 1932 Eighth edition, March, 1936 Revised and enlarged edition, November, 1937 Tenth edition, March, 1938 Printed and bound in Canada'
CITATIONS: Golick, p 110
COPIES: OGU (CCC TX715.6 P38)   OTNY (uncat)   *Private collection
NOTES: The collector comments: 'When I got married in 1938, this was the most popular cook book. It is ideal for a bride as receipes [sic] are basic ... It was my favourite gift to brides. Gave one in 1970, 71, 74, to daughters. They and I still [in 1991] use it.'

O506.11   [11th ed., April 1939]
—Canadian / cook / book / by / Nellie Lyle Pattinson / Director of Domestic Science / Assisted by / Ethel Stockwell B.A. / Helene Wilkinson / teachers in Domestic Science / Central Technical School / Toronto / The Ryerson Press / Toronto
DESCRIPTION: 20.0 × 13.5 cm   Pp [i–iv] v [vi] vii–viii [ix–x] xi [xii], 1–441   Frontis of 'Reception Table,' 30 numbered illus, illus   Cloth
CONTENTS: i ht; ii frontis; iii tp; iv 'Copyright, Canada, 1923, by the Ryerson Press ... First edition, December, 1923 Second edition, December, 1924 Third edition, December, 1925 Fourth edition, January, 1927 Fifth edition, April, 1928 Revised and enlarged edition, May, 1930 Seventh edition, October, 1932 Eighth edition, March, 1936 Revised and enlarged edition, November, 1937 Tenth edition, March, 1938 Eleventh edition, April, 1939 Printed and bound in Canada'; v preface signed N.L.P.; vi blank; vii–viii table of contents; ix 'List of Tables'; x 'List of Illustrations'; xi 'List of Diagrams'; xii blank; 1–420 text; 421–2 glossary; 423–41 index
CITATIONS: AbCat July 1976
COPIES: *Private collection

O506.12 [12th ed., May 1940]
—Canadian / cook / book / by / Nellie Lyle
Pattinson / Director of Domestic Science / Assisted
by / Ethel Stockwell B.A. / Helene Wilkinson /
teachers in Domestic Science / Central Technical
School / Toronto / The Ryerson Press / Toronto
DESCRIPTION: 20.0 × 13.5 cm   Pp [i–vi] vii–xi [xii],
1–441
CONTENTS: Tp verso 'Copyright, Canada, 1923, by the
Ryerson Press ... First edition, December, 1923 Sec-
ond edition, December, 1924 Third edition, Decem-
ber, 1925 Fourth edition, January, 1927 Fifth edition,
April, 1928 Revised and enlarged edition, May, 1930
Seventh edition, October, 1932 Eighth edition, March,
1936 Revised and enlarged edition, November, 1937
Tenth edition, March, 1938 Eleventh edition, April,
1939 Twelfth edition, May, 1940 Printed and bound in
Canada'
COPIES: *Private collection

O506.13 [13th ed., March 1941]
—Canadian / cook / book / by / Nellie Lyle
Pattinson / Director of Domestic Science / Assisted
by / Ethel Stockwell B.A. / Helene Wilkinson /
teachers in Domestic Science / Central Technical
School / Toronto / The Ryerson Press / Toronto
DESCRIPTION: 19.5 × 13.5 cm   Pp [i–vi] vii–xi [xii],
1–441   Frontis of 'Reception Table,' 30 numbered
illus, illus   Cloth
CONTENTS: i ht; ii frontis; iii tp; iv 'Copyright, Canada,
1923, by the Ryerson Press ... First edition, December,
1923 Second edition, December, 1924 Third edition,
December, 1925 Fourth edition, January, 1927 Fifth
edition, April, 1928 Revised and enlarged edition,
May, 1930 Seventh edition, October, 1932 Eighth edition, March, 1936 Revised and enlarged edition, November, 1937 Tenth edition, March, 1938 Eleventh
edition, April, 1939 Twelfth edition, May, 1940 Thirteenth edition, March, 1941 Printed and bound in
Canada'; v preface signed N.L.P.; vi blank; vii–viii
table of contents; ix 'List of Tables'; x 'List of Illustrations'; xi 'List of Diagrams'; xii blank; 1–420 text;
421–2 glossary; 423–41 index
CITATIONS: BQ Exposition 1974, p 15   Carrière No.
169
COPIES: QMBN (S641.5 P278c)   QMM (RBD ckbk 930)
*Private collection

O506.14 [14th ed., March 1942]
—Canadian / cook / book / by / Nellie Lyle
Pattinson / Director of Domestic Science / Assisted
by / Ethel Stockwell B.A. / Helene Wilkinson /
teachers in Domestic Science / Central Technical
School / Toronto / The Ryerson Press / Toronto

CITATIONS: AbCat March 1976   AbCat March 1977
COPIES: *ACG   OPEMO
NOTES: In December 1942, Jean Brodie reviewed
Pattinson's book in the *Toronto Star Weekly* ('These
Cook Books Can Help You,' 5 December 1942, Magazine Section No. 2, p 2). She does not give the edition,
but it was likely the most recent, that of March 1942.
Brodie's review is unequivocally positive: 'I've recommended this book to hundreds of young people
who have written to me for advice.' She praises
Pattinson as a teacher (Brodie had studied under her)
and emphasizes the quality of the text, despite the
plain appearance of the book. She explains that American cookbooks have colour photographs and other
attractive features because of the lower cost of production, but they are not written for Canadian households, as is Pattinson's.

O506.15 [15th ed., April 1943]
—[Fifteenth edition, Toronto: Ryerson Press, [April
1943]]
COPIES: Private collection
NOTES: Pattinson retired as director of domestic science in June 1942, but the title-pages of the fifteenth
to eighteenth editions, i.e., up to November 1945,
continued to describe her as director. Only the March
1947 and April 1949 editions describe her as 'formerly Director.'
   The private collector's father, Gus Cancilla, owned
the grocery store on Bloor Street West that supplied
food for Central Technical School's cooking classes
and lunch room. As a teenager, she worked in the
store, and Pattinson gave her a copy of the fifteenth
edition; it was her first cookbook.

O506.16 [16th ed., February 1944]
—Canadian / cook / book / by / Nellie Lyle
Pattinson / Director of Domestic Science / Assisted
by / Ethel Stockwell B.A. / Helene Wilkinson /
teachers in Domestic Science / Central Technical
School / Toronto / The Ryerson Press / Toronto
DESCRIPTION: 19.0 × 12.5 cm   Pp [i–vi] vii–viii [ix] x–
xi [xii], 1–441   Frontis, 30 numbered illus, illus   Cloth
CONTENTS: i ht; ii frontis; iii tp; iv 'Copyright, Canada,
1923, by the Ryerson Press ... First edition, December,
1923 Second edition, December, 1924 Third edition,
December, 1925 Fourth edition, January, 1927 Fifth
edition, April, 1928 Revised and enlarged edition,
May, 1930 Seventh edition, October, 1932 Eighth edition, March, 1936 Revised and enlarged edition, November, 1937 Tenth edition, March, 1938 Eleventh
edition, April, 1939 Twelfth edition, May, 1940 Thirteenth edition, March, 1941 Fourteenth edition, March,
1942 Fifteenth edition, April, 1943 Sixteenth edition,

February, 1944 Printed and bound in Canada'; v preface signed N.L.P.; vi blank; vii–viii table of contents; ix 'List of Tables'; x 'List of Illustrations'; xi 'List of Diagrams'; xii blank; 1–419 twenty-five chapters; 420 blank for 'Notes'; 421–2 glossary; 423–41 index
COPIES: *BVAU   OTNY (uncat)

O506.17   [17th ed., December 1944]
—Canadian / cook / book / by / Nellie Lyle Pattinson / Director of Domestic Science / Assisted by / Ethel Stockwell B.A. / Helene Wilkinson / teachers in Domestic Science / Central Technical School / Toronto / The Ryerson Press / Toronto
CONTENTS: Tp verso 'Copyright, Canada, 1923, by the Ryerson Press ... First edition, December, 1923 Second edition, December, 1924 Third edition, December, 1925 Fourth edition, January, 1927 Fifth edition, April, 1928 Revised and enlarged edition, May, 1930 Seventh edition, October, 1932 Eighth edition, March, 1936 Revised and enlarged edition, November, 1937 Tenth edition, March, 1938 Eleventh edition, April, 1939 Twelfth edition, May, 1940 Thirteenth edition, March, 1941 Fourteenth edition, March, 1942 Fifteenth edition, April, 1943 Sixteenth edition, February, 1944 Seventeenth edition, December, 1944 Printed and bound in Canada'
COPIES: OONL (TX715 P3234 1944)   OWTU (F15138)   *Private collection

O506.18   [18th ed., November 1945]
—Canadian / cook / book / by / Nellie Lyle Pattinson / Director of Domestic Science / Assisted by / Ethel Stockwell B.A. / Helene Wilkinson / teachers in Domestic Science / Central Technical School / Toronto / The Ryerson Press / Toronto
DESCRIPTION: 20.0 × 13.5 cm   Pp [i–vi] vii–xi [xii], 1–441   Frontis of 'Reception Table,' 30 numbered illus, illus   Cloth
CONTENTS: i ht; ii frontis; iii tp; iv 'Copyright, Canada, 1923, by the Ryerson Press ... First edition, December, 1923 Second edition, December, 1924 Third edition, December, 1925 Fourth edition, January, 1927 Fifth edition, April, 1928 Revised and enlarged edition, May, 1930 Seventh edition, October, 1932 Eighth edition, March, 1936 Revised and enlarged edition, November, 1937 Tenth edition, March, 1938 Eleventh edition, April, 1939 Twelfth edition, May, 1940 Thirteenth edition, March, 1941 Fourteenth edition, March, 1942 Fifteenth edition, April, 1943 Sixteenth edition, February, 1944 Seventeenth edition, December, 1944 Eighteenth edition, November, 1945 Printed and bound in Canada'; v 'Preface' signed N.L.P.; vi blank;

vii–viii table of contents; ix 'List of Tables'; x 'List of Illustrations'; xi 'List of Diagrams'; xii blank; 1–419 text; 420 blank for 'Notes'; 421–2 glossary; 423–41 index
COPIES: *BVICC   OGU (TX715 P3 1945)   Private collection
NOTES: The BVICC copy is inscribed on the front endpaper, in ink, 'M. Gloria John // Acadia Camp. Lab. E4.' The private collector, who graduated in 1949 from Macdonald College at McGill University, reports that this is the book that was used in the Food Lab during her studies there. Pattinson's text is recommended in O1095.1, *Canadian Cook Book for British Brides* of 1945.

O506.19   [rev. and enlarged ed., March 1947]
—Canadian / cook / book / by / Nellie Lyle Pattinson / formerly Director of Domestic Science, / Central Technical School, Toronto / The Ryerson Press / Toronto
DESCRIPTION: 19.5 × 13.5 cm   Pp [i–iv] v [vi] vii–xii, 1–451   30 numbered illus, illus   Cloth
CONTENTS: i ht; ii blank; iii tp; iv 'Copyright, Canada, 1923, by the Ryerson Press, Toronto ... First edition, December, 1923 Second printing, December, 1924 Third printing, December, 1925 Fourth printing, January, 1927 Fifth printing, April, 1928 Revised and enlarged edition, May, 1930 Seventh printing, October, 1932 Eighth printing, March, 1936 Revised and enlarged edition, November, 1937 Tenth printing, March, 1938 Eleventh printing, April, 1939 Twelfth printing, May, 1940 Thirteenth printing, March, 1941 Fourteenth printing, March, 1942 Fifteenth printing, April, 1943 Sixteenth printing, February, 1944 Seventeenth printing, December, 1944 Eighteenth printing, November, 1945 Revised and enlarged edition, March, 1947 Printed and bound in Canada by the Ryerson Press, Toronto'; v preface; vi blank; vii–viii table of contents; ix list of tables; x list of illustrations; xi–xii list of diagrams; 1–428 text; 429–30 glossary; 431–51 index
CITATIONS: CCat No. 26, p ZB13
COPIES: MW (641.5 PAT)   OGU (2 copies: CCC TX715 P38 1947, Rural Heritage Collection uncat)   *OONL (TX715 P3234 1947)   OPS   OSTC   OTMCL (641.5 P133)   QMM (TX715 P3234 1947); United States: DLC (TX715 P3234 1947)
NOTES: CCat records the price: $2.50. The OGU copy (CCC) has the property stamp of F.R. Close Technical Institute.

O506.20   [20th printing, April 1949]
—Canadian / cook / book / by / Nellie Lyle
Pattinson / formerly Director of Domestic Science, /
Central Technical School, Toronto / The Ryerson
Press / Toronto

CONTENTS: iii tp; iv 'Copyright, Canada, 1923, by the
Ryerson Press, Toronto ... First edition, December,
1923 Revised and enlarged edition, March, 1947 Twentieth printing, April, 1949 Printed and bound in
Canada by the Ryerson Press, Toronto'; v 'Preface'
signed N.L.P.; ...

COPIES: OOP   *Private collection

NOTES: In the 'Preface,' Pattinson comments, 'In the
war years we have come to realize the immense importance of food and nutrition in relation to national
economy. Naturally, the production of food comes
first to public attention, but, with greater knowledge
of food values, conservation of nutrients for the health
and well-being of each individual is receiving more
consideration.' She was still concerned to write the
text for Canadians specifically: 'Cooking and recipes
have, always, a local background of tradition and
custom, influenced by physical circumstances of food
supply and nutrition needs. We have tried to make
this book "Canadian" in content as well as in name.'

OTHER EDITIONS: In the early 1950s Ryerson Press
asked Pattinson to revise *Canadian Cook Book* to reflect
changing food fashions. She declined to make the
requested adaptations because she was unwell (she
died in April 1953) and because she felt that she was
not sufficiently up to date with the new ways of cooking. Instead, she accepted the suggestion of Cam
Hughes at Ryerson Press that it would be appropriate
for the text to be revised by two teachers at the Ryerson
Institute of Technology in Toronto, and she agreed
that any royalties from the revision would go to them:
Helen Wattie (a distant cousin of mine, born in
Bracebridge, Ontario, 1 September 1911) and Elinor
Donaldson (born Walkerville, Ontario, now part of
Windsor, 18 November 1926). In choosing Wattie and
Donaldson, Pattinson passed over two of her original
collaborators, Ethel Stockwell and Helene Wilkinson
of Central Technical School, and Edna Park, another
possible candidate. Before Pattinson died, Wattie and
Donaldson showed her the first draft of the revised
edition and won her approbation. The new edition,
retitled *Nellie Lyle Pattinson's Canadian Cook Book* and
described as 'Twenty-first printing Revised and enlarged, December, 1953,' was published in Toronto by
Ryerson Press in 1953 (AEU, AFFC, BVAU hard copy

and a sound recording, OGU, QMAC, QMBM, QMM
RBD uncat, OTMCL; United States: DLC). Wattie and
Donaldson omitted the individual portions that accompanied many recipes, in favour of 'the family
meal approach'; added chapters on appetizers, pressure cooking, oven-cooked meals, and freezing; enlarged the chapter on large-quantity recipes; and
included a chapter on 'Regional Dishes' – the first
attempt by anyone to define regional cooking in a
Canadian cookbook. Under the regional headings for
Newfoundland, the Maritime Provinces, Quebec,
Ontario, the Prairie Provinces, British Columbia, and
Yukon, there are references to the culinary history
and immigration patterns for the region; distinctive
dishes follow; for example, Danish and Swedish recipes for the Prairies, and for Ontario, Italian, Chinese,
Scottish, English, German, Irish, Dutch, and Jewish
recipes. The new edition was reprinted several times:
24th printing, October 1957 (Private collection);
Toronto: Ryerson Press, 1961 (OONL, QMM); Toronto:
Ryerson Press, [1963] (OGU); 29th printing, Toronto:
Ryerson Press, [1965] (QMBN); Toronto: Ryerson Press,
[1969] (United States: DLC); Toronto: Ryerson Press,
[1970], c1969 (OONL).

In 1977 Wattie and Donaldson (now Donaldson
Whyte) prepared the SI metric edition, in which the
regional dishes were no longer featured in a separate
section and the large-quantity recipes (found so use-
ful by church women's groups) were dropped:
Toronto and New York: McGraw-Hill Ryerson Ltd,
[copyright 1977] (AEU, BVAU, OONL, OTP, OTY;
United States: DLC); Toronto: McGraw-Hill Ryerson,
1978 (OONL, QMBM); large-print ed. photocopied
from McGraw-Hill Ryerson, 1978, 2 vols., Regina:
Saskatchewan Education, [19-] (OONL, SRED);
French-language ed. by Arlette and Edmond de
Meulemeester, *Les grandes recettes canadiennes de Nellie
Lyle Pattinson,* Toronto: McGraw-Hill Ryerson, 1984
(AEU, OONL); Toronto: McGraw-Hill Ryerson, copy-
right 1991 (OONL).

AMERICAN EDITIONS: The Wattie and Donaldson revi-
sion was published in the United States as *North
American Cook Book,* New York: Bouregy and Curl,
[c1954] (United States: DLC); an American bookseller
records *North American Cook Book,* New York: Ladies'
Home Journal Cook Book Club, by arrangement with
Thomas Bouregy and Co., 1954. The Wattie and
Donaldson revision was also published as *Guide to
Cooking: The Basic Cook Book,* New York: Airmont Pub-
lishing Co. Inc., 1968 (OONL).

Presbyterian cook book

O507.1 1923
[An edition of *Presbyterian Cook Book,* 1923, pp 46, typewritten, oil cloth and bound by black cord through two punched holes]
COPIES: Private collection
NOTES: Regarding the place of publication, the owner reported, 'probably Oshawa where my mother lived.' The recipes are credited with the name of the contributor.

Rawleigh's good health guide cook book almanac 1923

For information about Rawleigh's annual almanac cookbooks and other culinary publications, see M22.1.

O508.1 1923
Rawleigh's / Trade mark reg. U.S. Pat. Off. / good health guide / cook book almanac / 1889 1923 / Published by / the W.T. Rawleigh Co., Ltd. / Winnipeg London Montreal / U.S. factories and branches / Freeport, Memphis, Chester, Oakland, / Minneapolis, Denver
DESCRIPTION: Tp illus portrait of W.T. Rawleigh   With image on front of a seated woman and dog, in a mountain landscape; hole punched at top left corner for hanging
COPIES: AEEA *BBVM   OONL (RC81 R38)
NOTES: Of the three Canadian places of publication, 'London' is in the largest typeface.

O508.2 1923
—1923 / Guide de sante / et almanach / Rawleigh / Trade mark reg. U.S. Pat. Off. [cover-title]
DESCRIPTION: 24.0 × 16.5 cm   Pp 1–32   Illus   Paper, with image on front of a seated woman and dog, in a mountain landscape; stapled, and with hole punched at top left corner for hanging
COPIES: *QMM (RBD ckbk 1622)

Tara cook book

O509.1 1923
[An edition of *Tara Cook Book,* by Tara Women's Institute, Tara, Ontario, 1923, pp 68]
COPIES: Private collection

Thexton, A.G.

O510.1 1923
[An edition of *Autograph Recipes,* designed by A.G. Thexton, Toronto, Ont.: Hunter-Rose, 1923]
CITATIONS: O'Neill (unpublished)
COPIES: Great Britain: LB (Woolwich 41589)
NOTES: O'Neill's entry describes this item as a 'blank book.' It was designed to be filled by the owner with handwritten recipes. The unnumbered pages are divided into the following sections: 'Cold Desserts'; 'Cakes and Icings'; 'Cookies and Biscuits'; 'Pastries'; 'Puddings'; 'Candies'; 'Salads'; 'Jams and Jellies'; 'Pickles and Relishes'; and 'Miscellaneous.'

Three hundred tried and tested recipes

O511.1   September 1923
[An edition of *Three Hundred Tried and Tested Recipes,* compiled by the ladies of Central Avenue Methodist Church, Bridgeburg, Ontario, September 1923]
COPIES: Private collection
NOTES: Bridgeburg is now part of Fort Erie.

Tried recipes

O512.1   [December 1923]
[Cover-title lacking of *Tried Recipes*]
DESCRIPTION: 22.5 × 14.0 cm   Pp [1–2] 3–80 [81–2] Lacks binding; stapled
CONTENTS: 1(?) 'Index' [i.e., alphabetical list of sections]; 2(?) 'A New Recipe' [mock recipe] signed 'Selected // Mrs. Fred Willis'; 3–75 recipes credited with the name of the contributor and ads; 76 blank for 'This Space for Extra Recipes'; 77 thank-you from the members of the John Peel Chapter of the IODE to recipe contributors and advertisers, dated Uxbridge, December 1923; 78 ad; 79 'Tables of Weights and Measures'; 80 'What to Serve with Meats' and 'Printed at the office of the North Ontario Times // Uxbridge, Ontario'; 81–2 ads
CITATIONS: Wilson July 1991
COPIES: *Private collection
NOTES: The running head is 'John Peel Chapter I.O.D.E. Cook Book.' The binding was lacking in the copy examined; however, the cover-title is likely 'Tried Recipes,' the title cited in the Wilson article. The first leaf was loose; therefore, it is uncertain whether 'Index' is on p 1 and 'A New Recipe' is on p 2, or vice versa.

1924

Allen, Mrs Ida Cogswell Bailey (1885–1973)

For other titles by this American author, see O372.1.

O513.1 [1st ed.], 1924
Mrs. Allen on / cooking, menus, / service / 2500
recipes / by / Ida C. Bailey Allen / author – editor –
lecturer / international authority on foods / and
cooking / Illustrations posed by / Ida C. Bailey
Allen and Jack Wilbur / S.B. Gundy Toronto /
Doubleday, Page & Company / Garden City New
York / 1924
DESCRIPTION: Illus   Cloth
COPIES: *Bookseller's stock
NOTES: The bookseller describes the volume as hav-
ing 1,001 pp. The frontispiece is a portrait of Mrs
Allen.

AMERICAN EDITIONS: Garden City, NY: Doubleday,
Page and Co., 1924 (United States: DLC); *Ida Bailey
Allen's Modern Cook Book; 2500 Delicious Recipes, For-
merly Published as Mrs Allen on Cooking, Menus, Ser-
vice*, Garden City, NY: Garden City Publishing Co.
Inc., [c1935] (United States: DLC).

The basic sweet dough formula

*For the titles of other books about cooking with
Fleischmann's Yeast, see O131.1.*

O514.1 [8th ed., copyright 1924; about 1929]
The / basic sweet dough / formula / Presented to /
[blank space] / A / labor-saving development / in
the sweet goods market / Standard Brands Limited
/ Fleischmann's Yeast / Service Panomalt
DESCRIPTION: 25.0 × 17.5 cm   Pp [1–8] 9–45 Illus
Paper; stapled, and with hole punched at top left
corner for hanging, and also with two holes punched
at bound edge
CONTENTS: 1 tp; 2 'Copyright – 1924 Standard Brands
Limited Printed in Canada'; 3 'Index of Basic Sweet
Dough Products'; 4 'Basic Sweet Dough Formula';
5 'Successful Bakers Use the Basic Sweet Dough
Formula'; 6–7 'The Formula' [i.e., seven numbered
benefits of the formula]; 8 blank; 9–45 text
COPIES: *Private collection
NOTES: '8th edition of The Basic Sweet Dough For-
mula' is printed on the front of the binding. The text
on p 5 begins, 'Several years ago the makers of

Fleischmann's Yeast introduced the Basic Sweet
Dough Formula to the bakers of Canada.' Over fifty
products could be made with the dough; see p 4.
There is an illustration on p 45 of the advertising
material that was part of the 'National Advertising
Campaign' being run by Standard Brands, and bakers are encouraged to use the material 'to tie-up' with
the campaign.

There is no place of publication, but Standard
Brands Ltd was based in Toronto. Standard Brands
Ltd (Standard Brands Inc. in the United States) was
created by a merger of various companies, including
Fleischmann, and incorporated on 27 August 1929.
This edition was published no earlier than 1929, the
year of the merger.

Blake, Mary [pseudonym]

*For information about Mary Blake and her cookbooks, see
O494.1; for Carnation Milk Products Co., see O350.1.*

O515.1 [copyright 1924]
[Cover-title lacking of *My Hundred Favorite Recipes*]
DESCRIPTION: 17.5 × 12.5 cm   Pp [1] 2–32   Illus col
Stapled
CONTENTS: 1 untitled introductory note signed Mary
Blake, Domestic Science Department, Carnation Milk
Products Co. Ltd, Aylmer, Ontario, and 'Copyright
Carnation Milk Products Co., Ltd. 1924 Printed in
Canada'; 2–3 untitled text about milk and Carnation
Milk; 4 'Index – Table of Contents'; 5–32 recipes
COPIES: *Private collection
NOTES: On p 1, Blake says, 'My own favorite recipes
are contained herein, one hundred of them, ...' BSUM
and MSOHM each have a copy of the 1924 edition
with the cover-title 'My hundred / favorite recipes /
Mary Blake'; on the front face of the paper binding,
there is the image of a family at table, in silhouette,
and below, a carnation. On p 1, below 'Printed in
Canada,' there is the printer's mark 'CC-304A,' which
does not appear in the private collector's copy catalogued here. 'Standard Litho. Co. Limited Toronto'
is on the inside back face of the binding of both
museum copies.

Two years earlier, in 1922, Carnation Milk Products Co. published O489.1, *One Hundred Tested Recipes*, with no named author. *My Hundred Favorite
Recipes* attributed to Mary Blake is probably a revised
version of that text. In 1930, the company published a
new title by Blake, O660.1, *100 Glorified Recipes*, with
new recipes.

O515.2 [copyright 1926]
—My hundred / favorite recipes / Mary Blake [cover-title]
DESCRIPTION: 18.0 × 12.5 cm   Pp [1] 2–32   Illus col Paper, with image on front of a family at table, in silhouette, and a carnation; stapled
CONTENTS: Inside front face of binding 'Table Setting and Service'; 1 untitled introductory note signed Mary Blake, Domestic Science Department, Carnation Milk Products Co. Ltd, Aylmer, Ontario, and at bottom, 'Copyright Carnation Milk Products Co., Ltd. 1926 Printed in Canada CC-304-B'; 2–3 untitled text about milk and Carnation Milk; 4 'Index – Table of Contents'; 5–32 recipes; inside back face 'Time Table for Cooking' and at bottom, 'The London Print & Litho Co.'
COPIES: *BVAMM   OCHAK   OONL (TX715 C3465 No. 20)

O515.3 [copyright 1928]
—My hundred / favorite recipes / Mary Blake [cover-title]
DESCRIPTION: 18.0 × 12.5 cm   Pp [1] 2–32   Illus col, 1 illus on p 2   Paper, with image on front of a mother leading three children, each walking one behind the other and carrying a dish of food; stapled
CONTENTS: 1 untitled introductory note signed Mary Blake, Home Economics Department, Carnation Milk Products Co. Ltd, offices at Aylmer, Ontario, and at bottom, 'Copyright Carnation Milk Products Co., Ltd. 1928 CC485 – Printed in Canada'; 2–3 'The Delight of the New Cookery'; 4 'General Directions'; 5–32 recipes; inside back face of binding 'Table of Contents'
COPIES: *NBFKL (Ruth Spicer Cookbook Collection)   OGU (CCC TX715.6 B525)
NOTES: A private collector has a 1928 edition printed in the United States. On p 1 of her copy, the note is signed Mary Blake, Home Economics Department, Carnation Milk Products Co., offices at Oconomowoc, Wisconsin, Aylmer, Ontario, New York, and Seattle, Washington, and at bottom, 'Copyright Carnation Milk Products Co. 1928 C485B – Printed in U.S.A.' The printer 'Walton & Spencer Co. Chicago, Ill.' is below the 'Table of Contents.'

O515.4 [copyright 1929]
—My hundred / favorite recipes / Mary Blake [cover-title]
DESCRIPTION: Image on front face of binding of a mother leading three children, each walking one behind the other and carrying a dish of food; stapled
CONTENTS: 1 untitled introductory note signed Mary Blake, Home Economics Department, Carnation Milk

Products Co., offices at Oconomowoc, Wisconsin, Aylmer, Ontario, New York, and Seattle, Washington, and at bottom, 'Copyright Carnation Milk Products Co., Ltd. 1929 CC485A – Printed in Canada'
COPIES: *Private collection
NOTES: The owner reports that the book has 36 pp.

Chapman, Miss Ethel Matilda (Campbellville, Ont., 1888–28 August 1976, Toronto, Ont.)

See O379.1 for information about the author and her cookbooks. For the titles of other cookbooks published by the Ontario Department of Agriculture, see O158.1.

O516.1   January 1924
Ontario Department of Agricul[ture?] / Women's Institutes Branch / Toronto, Ontario, January, 1924 / Food for the family / by Ethel M. Chapman / [cover-title, followed by text]
DESCRIPTION: 23.5 × 15.5 cm   Pp [1] 2–39 [40]   Illus on p 1 of the food value of one quart of milk; illus on p 17 of 'Beef Cuts'   Paper; stapled
CONTENTS: top 1 cover-title; mid 1–40 text for 'Balancing the Family Ration' [about six classes of food], 'Vegetables,' 'Salads,' 'Fruits and Practical Fruit Dishes,' 'Eggs and Varied Ways of Cooking Them,' 'Milk and Its Miracles in Nutrition,' 'Cereals and Cheese,' 'Meat,' 'Meat Substitutes,' 'Yeast Bread,' 'Quick Breads,' 'Cake and Little Cakes,' 'Pastry,' 'Simple Desserts,' 'The School Lunch,' 'Meals for Young Children,' and 'Menu Planning'
CITATIONS: CCat No. 3, p E13   MacTaggart, p 27
COPIES: OGU (Rural Heritage Collection)   *Private collection

Choice recipes

See also O530.1, Cook Book of Practical Recipes, by No. 1 Circle of the same Windsor church. Giles Boulevard United Church (as it was named from 10 June 1925) closed about 1987.

O517.1   June–November 1924
Choice / recipes / by / members and friends / of / Circle No. 2 of Ladies Aid / Giles Boulevard / Methodist Church / June to November, 1924 / Price 25 cents [cover-title]
DESCRIPTION: About 22.0 × 14.5 cm [dimensions from photocopy]   Pp 1–36   Stapled
COPIES: *Private collection

NOTES: The pastor's name, T. Allen, and hours of service are on the outside back face of the binding. Advertisements in the cookbook are for Windsor and Walkerville businesses. The recipes are credited with the name of the contributor.

Cook book

In 1947, the Women's Auxiliary published another recipe collection, O1154.1, Cook Book.

O518.1 nd [about 1924]
A feast of good things / Cook book / compiled by / the Women's Auxiliary / of Hanover Memorial Hospital / Hanover, Ontario
DESCRIPTION: 22.0 × 15.0 cm Pp [1–5] 6–80 Illus on p 1 of Hanover Memorial Hospital Paper; stapled
CONTENTS: 1 illus of hospital; 2 'Dedication'; 3 tp; 4 'A Card' signed Committee, thanking advertisers; 5 'Index' [i.e., table of contents]; 6–80 recipes credited with the name of the contributor
COPIES: *OONL (TX715 H35 1920z)
NOTES: An advertisement on p 17 for Taylor's Bookstore indicates the cookbook's likely date of publication: '[the bookstore] started in Hanover in 1895 – 29 years ago' (1895 + 29 years = 1924). There is a full-page advertisement on p 10 for Knechtel Kitchen Kabinet Ltd in Hanover, which illustrates kitchen cabinet No. 203. The cookbook includes recipes contributed by Mrs D. Knechtel, and no doubt many local homes had Knechtel cabinets.

The book was reprinted two years later: OOWM has a copy (984.91.12) where the advertisement on p 17 for Taylor's Bookstore has been reset to read, 'started in Hanover in 1895 – 31 years ago.'

Cook book

O519.1 1924
Silver Chapter / I.O.D.E. / Cook book / Compiled and published by the officers and members / of Silver Chapter, I.O.D.E., Cobalt, / Ontario, 1924
DESCRIPTION: 21.0 × 15.0 cm Pp [1] 2–132 Illus of mines and mining scenes in the Cobalt area Thin card, with IODE symbol and text printed in silver on front; stapled
CONTENTS: 1 tp; 2 'List of Officers'; 3 'List of Advertisers'; 4 'Contents'; 5–132 recipes credited with the name of the contributor and her town, and ads
COPIES: *Private collection
NOTES: In the 'List of Officers,' the recipe convenor is

Miss Eileen Taylor and the recipe committee is Miss Laura Scott, Miss Anna Bell, and Miss Eleanor Wood. The illustrations show scenes such as the McIntyre Porcupine Mines Milling Plant and Shaft Houses, and the Lake Shore Mines new mill. The printer's name, 'Northern Miner Press Cobalt,' is on the outside back face of the binding; and there is an advertisement on p 42 for the *Northern Miner* and the *Northern News*. The attractive binding design of silver printed on dark blue card is an appropriate choice for the Silver Chapter based in the silver-mining town of Cobalt.

Currie, Margaret [pseudonym of] Mrs Irene Archibald, née Love (14 March 1880–1945)

This author wrote for the Montreal Star, *under the pen-name Margaret Currie. She married Eldred Archibald (18 October 1881–February 1958, St Lambert, Que.). Eldred had worked for the* Toronto Star, *but moved to the* Montreal Herald *in 1912, then to the* Montreal Star, *where he eventually became editor. The couple had no children.*

For information about Irene Archibald, see Dagg (who gives her husband's name incorrectly as Elfred); and Lang, p 42, and the group photograph on p 66, which includes Irene. See also Q170.1, St Barnabas Guild Cook Book, where Mrs Eldred Archibald is named on the title-page as president of the Guild. Her birth date is recorded in the 1901 Census.

O520.1 [copyright 1924]
Margaret Currie / her book / by / Margaret Currie / (Montreal Star) / Toronto / The Hunter-Rose Co., Limited
DESCRIPTION: 18.5 × 12.5 cm Pp [i–ix] x–xii, 1–352 Cloth
CONTENTS: i ht; ii blank; iii tp; iv 'Copyright, Canada, 1924 by the Hunter-Rose Co., Limited Toronto // Printed and bound by the Hunter-Rose Co., Limited'; v preface; vi blank; vii table of contents; viii blank; ix–xii index; 1–352 text
CITATIONS: CCat No. 3, p E2 Dagg, pp 76–7 Ferguson/Fraser, pp 54 and 233, illus col on p 57 of closed volume Rhodenizer, p 994
COPIES: *OGU (UA s045 b22) OMUC OTMCL (640 C79) OTUTF (B-12 7875, 2 copies) OWTU (TX144 C8x 1924)
NOTES: In the preface, the author refers to 'the ten years [she has] conducted [her] page on the Montreal Star ...' Cookery and household information make up about one hundred pages at the end of the volume

(pp 239–336); the other chapters are: 'Margaret Currie's Chats'; 'The Complete Wardrobe'; 'Would You Marry Young?'; 'The Spenders'; 'Suffer the Children'; 'The Philanderer'; 'Poor Mother'; 'Happy Ever After'; 'Husbands and Wives'; 'Food versus Rent'; 'Fathers, Provoke Not'; 'Envy, Malice and Gossip'; 'Films and Fiction'; 'The Family Grouch'; 'The Ontario Highlands'; 'Games'; 'Beauty'; and 'Laundry.' CCat records the price: $1.50.

The two OTUTF copies are identical except for differently coloured cloth bindings: brown cloth with blue lettering and blue cloth with gold lettering. The OWTU copy is bound in blue cloth with black lettering.

Fifty ways of serving Shredded Wheat

See O222.1 for information about the company and its other cookbooks for Shredded Wheat.

O521.1   copyright 1924
Fifty ways / of / serving / Shredded / Wheat / Copyright 1924 by / the Shredded Wheat Company / Niagara Falls, N.Y.
DESCRIPTION: 15.0 × 8.5 cm   Pp [1–2] 3–20   Paper, with image on front of a child seated at table, pouring milk onto a bowl of Shredded Wheat; stapled
CONTENTS: 1 tp; 2 'The Shredded Wheat Company, Niagara Falls, N.Y. Pacific Coast Shredded Wheat Company, Oakland, California. The Canadian Shredded Wheat Company, Ltd., Royal Bank Bldg., Toronto, Canada. Shredded Wheat Company, Ltd., General Bldgs., Aldwych, London, W.C., England. Additional copies of this booklet and samples of Shredded Wheat will be sent free on application to any one of the above companies.'; 3 'Is There a Perfect Food?'; 4 'A Perfect All-Day Food' and 'Shredded Wheat Prize Recipes'; 5–18 'Shredded Wheat Recipes'; 19–20 'Triscuit'
COPIES: OTMCL (641.5971 H39 No. 41)   *QMM (RBD ckbk 2017)
NOTES: Page 4 explains: 'The Shredded Wheat Company recently offered $1,500 in gold prizes for new ways of serving Shredded Wheat. In response to the advertising nearly one hundred thousand women sent in their favorite Shredded Wheat recipes ... We have printed fifty of these recipes, ...' The volume was printed in the United States: 'Printed in U.S.A. Series 419' is on the outside back face of the binding.
Longone/Longone Photo R illustrates the binding of an edition with the same title, which may be the same as the one catalogued here.

Haileybury cook book

O522.1   1924
Haileybury / cook book / 1924 / Tested recipes / compiled and published by / St. Paul's Parish Club
COPIES: *Private collection
NOTES: The Parish Club was part of St Paul's Anglican Church. The cookbook was probably a fundraiser to help rebuild the church after the Great Haileybury Fire destroyed most of the town on 4 October 1922.

Helpful hints for housekeepers 1924

See O263.1 for information about the company and other issues of Helpful Hints for Housekeepers.

O523.1   1924
1924 Volume XIV 1924 / Hang me in the kitchen / Helpful / hints / for housekeepers / Compliments of / the Dodds Medicine Co. / Limited / Toronto, Can. [cover-title]
DESCRIPTION: 15.5 × 10.5 cm   Pp 1–32   Paper; stapled, and with hole punched at top left corner, through which runs a string for hanging
CONTENTS: 1 'Various Uses for Salt'; 2 'To You from Us'; 3 'Keeping Fruit and Vegetables Fresh'; 4, 6, 8, 10, 12, 14, 18, 20, 22, 24, 26, 28 medical entries arranged alphabetically from Anaemia to Skin; 5 'Hints for Mothers'; 7 'How to Use "Leftovers"'; 9 'Care of Linoleum' and 'Combatting the Fly'; 11 'Care of the Eyes' and 'Potato as a Cleanser'; 13 'Ironing'; 15 'Removing Stains'; 16–17 testimonials; 19 'General Housekeeping Hints'; 21, 23 'Valuable Hints'; 25 'Suggestions for Simplifying Sewing and Knitting'; 27 'Safety First' and 'Equivalents'; 29–30 publ ad; 31 'Weights and Measures'; 32 'Diet Rules'
COPIES: *OHMB (Serial)   OTUTF (uncat patent medicine)

Jell-O book

For the titles of other books for cooking with Jell-O, see O212.1.

O524.1   copyright 1924
Canada's most famous dessert / Jell-O / This edition of the Jell-O Book [...]
DESCRIPTION: 15.5 × 11.0 cm   Pp 1–14   Illus col   Paper, with image on front of a box of Jell-O dropped on a railway track and a man running to rescue it

before a train comes; image on back of 'At Grand-mothers. The Jell-O Hour'; stapled
CONTENTS: 1 [inside front face of binding]–14 [inside back face] recipes
COPIES: ACG AMHM BDUCVM OKQ (F5012 1924 G327, missing) OMAHM (993.16.16) ONLAM (Walters-Wagar Collection, Box 20) OTYA (CPC 1924 0089) QMM (RBD ckbk 1598) *Private collection
NOTES: The year and publisher are on the front face of the binding: '© 1924 by the Genesee Pure Food Company'; the printer is on the outside back face: 'Printed in Canada // Standard Litho. Co. Limited Toronto.' The title transcription recorded above is at top p 1. 'The Genesee Pure Food Co. of Canada, Limited. Bridgeburg, Ont.' is on p 14.

AMERICAN EDITIONS: 1924 (Allen, p 198); 1925 (Allen, p 198).

Rawleigh's good health guide cook book almanac 1924

For information about Rawleigh's annual almanac cookbooks and other culinary publications, see M22.1.

O525.1 1924
Rawleigh's / Trade mark reg. U.S. Pat. Off. / good health guide / cook book almanac / 1889 1924 / Published by / the W.T. Rawleigh Co., Ltd. / Winnipeg London, Ont. Montreal / Freeport Memphis Chester / Oakland Minneapolis / Denver Richmond / Hayden Press, Ltd., London, Ont. / Printed in Canada
DESCRIPTION: 24.0 × 16.5 cm Pp [1] 2–64 Tp illus portrait of W.T. Rawleigh, illus yellowish-orange-and-black, illus Paper, with image on front of a boy on a river bank, catching fish; stapled, and with hole at top left corner for hanging
CONTENTS: 1 tp; 2 'Health // Prosperity and Hap-piness'; 3 'Largest and Most Complete Factories'; 4 'Almanac Calculations'; 5 'Service Comes First'; 6–63 monthly calendars, information about the com-pany and its products, health care, and recipes; 64 information about ordering Rawleigh products and paying accounts
COPIES: *SWSLM
NOTES: Of the three Canadian places of publication, 'London' is in the largest typeface.

O525.2 1924
—Guide de sante / et almanach / Rawleigh / Trade mark reg. U.S. Pat. Off. / 1889 1924 / Publié par / la cie W.T. Rawleigh, ltée / Winnipeg London, Ont.

Montreal / Freeport Memphis Chester / Oakland Minneapolis / Denver Richmond / Hayden Press, Ltd., London, Ont. / Printed in Canada
DESCRIPTION: Tp illus portrait of W.T. Rawleigh With image on front of a boy on a river bank, catching fish; hole at top left corner for hanging
COPIES: *BBVM

Scott, Anna Lee [pseudonym]

For information about Maple Leaf Milling Co., see O444.1. From the mid-1920s the company issued the following cookbooks under the pseudonym of Anna Lee Scott: O526.1, Cookery Arts and Kitchen Manage-ment; O531.1, The Maple Leaf Housekeeper; O554.1, When We Entertain; O773.1, The Easy Way Cake Book; O774.1, Maple Leaf Cooking School: Lessons 5–6–7–8; O775.1, Maple Leaf Cooking School: Les-sons 9–10–11–12; O776.1, Marketing and Meal Planning; O777.1, Planning the Party; O805.1, What Shall We Have for Dinner and How Much Will It Cost; O831.1, Christmas Recipes; O832.1, Cooking Secrets; O868.1, Four Star Recipes; O869.1, Happy 'Bakeday' to You!; O893.1, The Cook's Tour to the Realm of Cakes; O975.1, 51 Ways to a Man's Heart; O1170.1, Cooking Made Easy; O1191.1, The Mon-arch Mixing Bowl; and O1192.1, What's Cooking?

Several women wrote under Scott's name, over a period of several decades. In the French-language editions of the books, the pseudonymous author is sometimes called Marthe Miral. The identity of the real person(s) behind the pseudonym is not known conclusively for every book in the early years, but Katherine (Kay) Caldwell Bayley, with the assistance of her home econo-mists at Ann Adam Homecrafters, produced some of them. For Bayley and Ann Adam Homecrafters, see the biographical note at O877.1, Adam, Ann, 'Good Cook-ing.' Helen Gagen (born Helen Johanna Gegenschatz), who worked for Ann Adam Homecrafters from 1931 to 1942, stated that Bayley 'was consultant in a large way for Maple Leaf Mills' and that she did 'all home econom-ics work for Maple Leaf Mills – including the silver cook book [i.e., O832.1, Cooking Secrets]' (OGU, Helen Gagen Collection, XM1 MS A123, Box 44, File 9, 'Re: Katherine Caldwell Bayley, Ann Adam, Anna Lee Scott,' January 1987, p 1). Further evidence comes from the home economist Sara (Sally) Isabel Henry (died 1991), who told Carol Ferguson (co-author of A Century of Canadian Home Cooking) that the name Anna Lee Scott was first given to Bayley. Certainly, the way 'Anna Lee Scott' describes herself in O975.1, 51 Ways to a Man's Heart, of about 1939, matches Bayley perfectly: 'It is many years since I began as a dietitian lecturer and adviser on household science, and each year I have received thousands of letters through my magazine and radio work.' Bayley used her own image in advertisements for Ann Adam cooking demonstrations, and the drawn and photographed images of 'Anna Lee Scott' in advertisements for Anna Lee Scott cooking schools in the Hamilton Spectator *are clearly recognizable as Bayley (OGU, Helen Gagen Collection, XM1 MS A123, Box 44, File 6). The 1924 portrait of a young Anna Lee Scott on the binding of O526.1,* Cookery Arts and Kitchen Management, *however, does not appear to be Bayley.*

From 1945 to 1951 Grace Barbara Gray (West Flamborough, Ont., 23 October 1908–3 March 1977, Toronto, Ont.) was Anna Lee Scott. Gray was a graduate of the Macdonald Institute in Guelph. She joined Maple Leaf Milling Co. after serving as a dietitian in the Canadian Navy at Halifax, during the Second World War (she was a lieutenant). In 1948 she married Gordon Bourgard. A difficult pregnancy caused her to leave Maple Leaf Milling Co. in 1951 (the baby – her only child, Gordon – was born in 1952).

In 1951 Ethel Whitham 'temporarily' stepped into the fictional shoes of Anna Lee Scott, after Bourgard's departure. Whitham was not a home economist, but she had worked for the company for several years. She held the job until 1957, when Mary Adams took over the persona, until 1963. After Adams, Helen Gagen took the position for a short time, followed by Sally Henry (who had been 'Brenda York' at Canada Packers). Henry was the last Anna Lee Scott.

Also attributed to Scott and published by Maple Leaf Milling Co. are: Pastry Pointers, *nd [about 1925], pp 11, which specifies Monarch Flour in its recipes (Private collection);* Bake Day Delights, *nd [about 1925–30], pp 11, for Monarch Flour (Private collection);* Cakes for All Occasions, *nd [about 1935], pp 11 (Private collection); and* Anna Lee Scott Cooking School, *nd [1948 or later], pp 15 (Bookseller's stock).*

In the mid-1930s the Toronto Evening Telegram *published a column prepared by Anna Lee Scott called 'The Canadian Cooking School: A Complete Cookery Arts Course in 12 Lessons ...' I have compared Lesson No. 10 (19 March 1934, p 11) with the text of O526.5, the seventh edition of* Cookery Arts and Kitchen Management, *and they are not related.*

O526.1   copyright 1924
Cookery arts / and kitchen / management / Anna Lee Scott / Copyrighted, Canada, 1924 / Maple Leaf Milling Co., Limited [cover-title]
DESCRIPTION: 30.0 × 23.0 cm   Pp [1–80]   Card, with plaid pattern, and on front, in a circular frame, a portrait of Anna Lee Scott; bound by two metal fasteners

CONTENTS: 1–80 twenty numbered lessons and index on p 80
COPIES: *NSWA
NOTES: This is likely the first edition since there is no edition number. A note at the end of each lesson advises the reader to address all correspondence in connection with this cookery course to the Maple Leaf Club in Toronto.

Cookery Arts and Kitchen Management is mentioned in a 1927 advertisement for Anna Lee Scott's radio broadcast (*Daily Star* (Toronto) 3 February 1927, p 18), but the edition number is not given.

O526.2   3rd ed., 1924 [about 1925]
—[Third edition of *Cookery Arts and Kitchen Management*, 1924; card, with plaid pattern and portrait on front of Anna Lee Scott; bound by metal fasteners]
COPIES: Bookseller's stock
NOTES: Each of the twenty lessons invites the reader to write to the Maple Leaf Club, Maple Leaf Milling Co. Ltd, Winnipeg. There is a certificate of membership for the Maple Leaf Club slipped into the bookseller's copy, which is dated 11 March 1925 and bears the name of Mrs M. Mitrophen of Dumos, Saskatchewan.

O526.3   5th ed., copyright 1924
—Cookery arts / and kitchen / management / Fifth edition / Anna Lee Scott / Copyrighted, Canada, 1924 / Maple Leaf Milling Co., Limited [cover-title]
DESCRIPTION: 30.5 × 23.0 cm   Pp [1–80]   Card, with plaid pattern, and on front, in a circular frame, a portrait of Anna Lee Scott; bound by two metal fasteners
CONTENTS: 1–80 twenty numbered lessons and 'Index' on p 80
COPIES: *Private collection

O526.4   6th ed., copyright 1924
—Cookery arts / and kitchen / management / Sixth edition / Anna Lee Scott / Copyrighted, Canada, 1924 / Maple Leaf Milling Co., Limited [cover-title]
DESCRIPTION: With plaid pattern, and on front, in a circular frame, a portrait of Anna Lee Scott
COPIES: *Private collection

O526.5   7th ed., copyright 1924
—Cookery arts / and kitchen / management / Seventh edition / Anna Lee Scott / Copyrighted, Canada, 1924 / Maple Leaf Milling Co., Limited [cover-title]
DESCRIPTION: 30.0 × 23.0 cm   Pp [1–80]   Card, with plaid pattern, and on front, in a circular frame, a

portrait of Anna Lee Scott; bound by two metal fasteners
CONTENTS: 1–80 twenty numbered lessons and index on p 80
COPIES: *Private collection

O526.6   9th ed.
—Cookery arts / and kitchen / management / Ninth edition / Anna Lee Scott / [...] [cover-title]
DESCRIPTION: With portrait on front, in a circular frame, of Anna Lee Scott
COPIES: *Private collection

O526.7   10th ed., copyright 1924
—Cookery arts / and kitchen / management / Tenth edition / Anna Lee Scott / Copyrighted, Canada, 1924 / Maple Leaf Milling Co., Limited [cover-title]
DESCRIPTION: 30.0 × 23.5 cm
COPIES: *Private collection

O526.8   14th ed., copyright 1924
—Cookery arts / and kitchen / management / Fourteenth edition / Anna Lee Scott / Copyrighted, Canada, 1924 / Maple Leaf Milling Co., Limited [cover-title]
DESCRIPTION: 30.0 × 23.0 cm   Pp [1–80]   Thin card, with plaid pattern, and on front, in a circular frame, a portrait of Anna Lee Scott; bound by two metal fasteners
CONTENTS: 1–79 twenty numbered lessons; 80 index and 'Southam Press, Limited, Toronto'
COPIES: *MTM

O526.9   [copyright 1928]
—Cookery arts / and / kitchen / management / Anna Lee Scott [cover-title]
DESCRIPTION: 23.0 × 15.5 cm   Pp 1–8 ('Lesson One'), 1–7 [8] ('Lesson Two'), 1–8 ('Lesson Three'), 1–7 [8] ('Lesson Four'), 1–8 ('Lesson Five'), 1–8 ('Lesson Six'), 1–8 ('Lesson Seven'), 1–8 ('Lesson Eight'), 1–8 ('Lesson Nine'), 1–8 ('Lesson Ten'), 1–8 ('Lesson Eleven'), 1–8 ('Lesson Twelve'), 1–8 ('Lesson Thirteen'), 1–8 ('Lesson Fourteen'), 1–8 ('Lesson Fifteen'), 1–8 ('Lesson Sixteen')   Thin card, with the red checked pattern associated with Monarch Pastry Flour; bound by a shoelace through three punched holes
CONTENTS: Sixteen lessons paginated separately
CITATIONS: Ferguson/Fraser, pp 54 and 233, illus col on p 57 of closed volume   Powers/Stewart, p 292 (Bibliography)
COPIES: OWASRM   *Private collection; United States: MiEM (TX663 S3 1928)

NOTES: 'Copyright, Canada, 1928, by Maple Leaf Milling Co., Ltd.' is printed on the last page of each lesson. This edition has smaller dimensions than all those identified as copyright 1924, i.e., 23.0 × 15.5 cm rather than 30.0 × 23.0 cm. The recipes specify Monarch Pastry Flour and other brand-name products, such as Bobolink Corn Meal and Knighthood Brand Whole Wheat Flour.

Selected recipes and useful household information

See also O675.1, The Parkdale Baptist Cook Book, from the same church.

O527.1   nd [about 1924]
Selected recipes / and / useful household / information / [caption:] Parkdale Baptist Church, Toronto, Ont. / Compiled and published by / Young Women's Mission Circle / of the / Parkdale Baptist Church / for the benefit of / home and foreign missions
DESCRIPTION: 23.0 × 15.0 cm   Pp [1–4] 5–66 [67–8]   Tp illus of the church   Lacks paper binding; stapled
CONTENTS: 1 tp; 2 blank; 3 foreword; 4 index; 5–66 text; 67–8 blank for 'My Recipes'
COPIES: *Private collection
NOTES: An advertisement in the book for Garton Manufacturing Co., 210 Victoria Street, Toronto, points to publication in about 1924: the only listing in city directories for the company at the 210 Victoria address is in the directory for 1924 (the first listing is in 1923 at 62 Dundas Street East; the address in the 1925 directory is 215 Victoria).

Toronto, Board of Education

O528.1   1924
Handbook of / practical cookery / for the use of / household science classes / in the / public schools of Toronto / 1924
DESCRIPTION: 22.0 × 13.5 cm   Pp [1–3] 4–78   4 fp illus on pp 27, 29, 30, and 31 of 'meat cutting charts'   Thin card; stapled
CONTENTS: 1 tp; 2 'Produced by the United Press Limited Toronto Canada'; 3 'To the Teacher'; 4–63 text; 64 blank; 65–78 index
COPIES: OTSBM (TX663 T6 1924)   *Private collection
NOTES: Another collector's copy has a plate, printed in red and black, of 'Beef Cuts,' as a centre spread, which may be lacking in the copy described here.

There is no reference to Miss Margaret Davidson, supervisor of household arts, who is cited in later editions (O528.7–528.9) as having 'compiled and introduced [this book] into the Toronto Public Schools in 1924.' Davidson had been appointed director of household arts for Toronto public schools in 1919 (see 'Appointment of Miss Margaret Davidson,' *Mail and Empire* 16 August 1919, p 16). The same article reports that she was previously director of domestic science at Central Technical School in Toronto, where she had 'introduced every single phase of domestic science and housewifery'; the article also refers to her as a 'pioneer in the use of glucose as a sugar substitute,' who supplied the Canada Food Board with its information on the subject during the First World War. Davidson may also be the compiler of O342.1, *The Moffat Standard Canadian Cook Book.*

The 'Introduction' gives instructions for the care of the kitchen floor, stove, garbage can, sink, and refrigerator (i.e., ice-box), and information about personal cleanliness, dishwashing, and measurements. This Toronto school textbook was used by other Ontario school boards. See, for example, O528.5, an edition of the text published for Stratford schools, and O1090.1, Hamilton, Board of Education, *Handbook of Home Economics for Use in Elementary Schools of Hamilton.*

Ferguson/Fraser, p 233, refer incorrectly to an edition dated 1923.

O528.2 1925
—Handbook of / practical cookery / for the use of / household science classes / in the / public schools of Toronto / Board of Education / Toronto / 1925
CONTENTS: Tp verso 'Printed by the Industrial & Educational Publishing Co., Limited 263 Adelaide Street West Toronto'
COPIES: *OTSBM (TX663 T6 1925)

O528.3 1926
—Handbook of / practical cookery / for the use of / household science classes / in the / public schools of Toronto / Board of Education – Toronto / 1926
CONTENTS: Tp verso 'Produced by the United Press Limited Toronto Canada'
COPIES: *OTSBM (TX663 T6 1926)

O528.4 nd
—Handbook of / practical cookery / for the use of / household science classes / in the / public schools of Toronto / Board of Education – Toronto
DESCRIPTION: 21.0 × 13.5 cm   Pp [1–3] 4–78   Fp illus on pp 27, 29, 30, and 31 of cuts of meat   Thin card; stapled

CONTENTS: 1 tp; 2 'Produced by the United Press Limited Toronto Canada'; 3 'The spirit of thrift should be kept in view at all times. The pupil should be able to: [five numbered abilities]'; 4–63 text; 64 blank; 65–78 index
COPIES: *Private collection

O528.5 [Stratford ed.], nd
—Handbook of / practical cookery / for the use of / household science classes / in the / public schools of Stratford
DESCRIPTION: 21.5 × 13.5 cm   Pp [1–3] 4–78   Centre spread col of 'Beef Cuts,' fp illus on pp 27, 29, 30, and 31 of 'Meat Cutting' charts   Thin card; stapled
CONTENTS: 1 tp; 2 'Produced by the United Press Limited Toronto Canada'; 3 'The spirit of thrift should be kept in view at all times. The pupil should be able to: [five numbered abilities]'; 4–63 text; 64 blank; 65–78 'Index'
COPIES: *Private collection
NOTES: The private collector's copy is inscribed on the binding, in pencil, 'Kathleen Berry.'

O528.6 nd
—Handbook of / practical cookery / for the use of / household science classes / in the / public schools of Toronto / Board of Education – Toronto
DESCRIPTION: 21.0 × 14.0 cm   Pp [1–3] 4–78   4 fp illus on pp 27, 29, 30, and 31 of cuts of meat   Thin card; stapled
CONTENTS: 1 tp; 2 'Produced by Inland Printing House Limited Toronto Canada'; 3 'The spirit of thrift should be kept in view at all times. The pupil should be able to: [five numbered requirements]'; 4–63 text; 64 blank; 65–78 'Index'
COPIES: *OONL (TX663 H35 1930z)
NOTES: The printer, Inland Printing House Ltd, distinguishes this edition from earlier editions.

O528.7 [1931]
—Handbook of / practical cookery / for the use of / household science classes / in the / public schools of Toronto / Board of Education – Toronto
DESCRIPTION: 21.5 × 13.5 cm   Pp [1–3] 4–86   Centre spread col of beef cuts, 4 fp illus of cuts of meat   Thin card; stapled
CONTENTS: 1 tp; 2 'Printed by Inland Printing House Limited Toronto Canada ...'; 3 'Preface' signed D.D. Moshier, chief inspector; 4–73 text; 74 blank; 75–86 index
COPIES: *OONMS (TX66 T67 1931)   OTSBM (TX663 T6 1931)   Private collection
NOTES: The 'Preface' states: 'This book was compiled

and introduced into the Toronto Public Schools in 1924 by Miss Margaret Davidson, Supervisor of Household Arts. The subsequent editions and the present revision by Miss Kathleen Coggs, Supervisor of Household Arts, have been based on this first edition. It is intended to meet the need of a text book ... and at the same time to furnish them [children] with a simple recipe book for home use.' This is the first edition to acknowledge Margaret Davidson, and she is acknowledged only twice more, in O528.8 and O528.9. Kathleen Coggs is credited only in this edition and O528.8. Coggs's Entrance Record for the Macdonald Institute (OGU, RE1 MAC A0003, Registration No. 1280) states that she entered the HEI–Normal Domestic Science course on 15 September 1910, at the age of nineteen years, and left on 25 June 1912, having been granted the Certificate of Domestic Science Teacher. She matriculated from Havergal College in Toronto, 1901–8, and took a special course in sewing at a technical high school in 1910. There is also the added remark, 'Miss Coggs passed Toronto University 2nd year English – 1912.' Her mother's name was Mrs G.E. Coggs; her father was a clergyman; her religious denomination, Church of England. The family's permanent address was 54 Boswell Avenue in Toronto.

OONMS dates its copy [1931]. It is inscribed on the title-page, in pencil, 'Janet Somerville Christmas 1933. From Mary Gomer.' '1[0?]M–9-31' is on the front face of the binding of the private collector's copy. Only '–9-31' shows on the binding of the OTSBM copy; the first part is obscured by the museum's label. No such printer's mark is on the OONMS copy.

O528.8 [copyright 1932]
—Handbook / of / practical / cookery / for the use of / household science classes / in the / public schools of Toronto / Board of Education, Toronto
DESCRIPTION: 21.5 × 13.0 cm Pp [1–3] 4–86 Centre spread col of beef cuts, 4 fp illus of cuts of meat Thin card; stapled
CONTENTS: 1 tp; 2 'Copyright (Canada) 1932, by the Board of Education for the City of Toronto'; 3 'Preface' signed D.D. Moshier, chief inspector; 4–73 text; 74 blank; 75–86 'Index'
COPIES: *Private collection
NOTES: The 'Preface' is as O528.7.

O528.9 1935
—Handbook / of / practical / cookery / for the use of / household science classes / in the / public schools of Toronto / Board of Education, Toronto / 1935

DESCRIPTION: 21.5 × 13.0 cm Pp [1–3] 4–86 Centre spread col of 'Beef Cuts,' 4 fp illus on pp 30, 32, 33, and 34 of cuts of meat Paper; stapled
CONTENTS: 1 tp; 2 'Copyright (Canada) 1932, by the Board of Education for the City of Toronto Revised 1935'; 3 preface signed C.C. Goldring, superintendent of schools; 4–73 text; 74–86 index
COPIES: OTSBM (TX663 T6 1935) OTYA (CPC 1935 0121) *Private collection

O528.10 1937
—Handbook / of / practical / cookery / for the use of / household science classes / in the / public schools of Toronto / Board of Education, Toronto / 1937
DESCRIPTION: 21.5 × 13.0 cm Pp [1–3] 4–86 Centre spread col of 'Beef Cuts,' 4 fp illus on pp 30, 32, 33, and 34 of cuts of meat Paper; stapled
CONTENTS: 1 tp; 2 'Copyright (Canada) 1932, by the Board of Education for the City of Toronto Revised 1937.'; 3 'Preface' signed C.C. Goldring, superintendent of schools; 4–73 text; 74–86 'Index'
COPIES: OTSBM (TX663 T6 1937) *Private collection
NOTES: The 'Preface' states the book's 'two-fold purpose': 'It is intended to serve as a text-book for public school girls, and at the same time to furnish them with a simple recipe book for home use.'

O528.11 1939
—Form No. 13. / 10M-6-39. / Handbook / of / practical / cookery / for the use of / home economics classes / in the / public schools of Toronto / Board of Education, Toronto / 1939
DESCRIPTION: 21.5 × 13.5 cm Pp [1–3] 4–94 Centre spread col of 'Beef Cuts,' 4 fp illus on pp 37, 39, 40, and 41 of cuts of meat, illus on pp 78, 79, and 80 of place-settings
CONTENTS: 1 tp; 2 'Copyright (Canada) 1932, by the Board of Education for the City of Toronto Revised 1937. Revised 1939.'; 3 preface signed C.C. Goldring, superintendent of schools; 4–81 text; 82–94 index
COPIES: OTMCL (641.5 T583) *Private collection
NOTES: The title now refers to 'home economics classes,' instead of 'household science classes.'

The recipe for Oatmeal Date Cookies from a 1939 or later edition of the cookbook (i.e., 'home economics classes' edition) is reprinted in Barb Holland, 'Fare Exchange,' *Toronto Star* 19 December 2001.

O528.12 1942
—Form No. 13. / 11M-3-42 / Handbook / of / practical / cookery / for the use of / home economics classes / in the / public schools of

Toronto / Board of Education, Toronto / 1942
DESCRIPTION: 21.5 × 13.0 cm   Pp [1–3] 4–94   Centre spread col of 'Beef Cuts,' 4 fp illus on pp 37, 39, 40, and 41 of cuts of meat, illus on pp 78, 79, and 80 of place-settings   Paper; stapled
CONTENTS: 1 tp; 2 'Copyright (Canada) 1932, by the Board of Education for the City of Toronto Revised 1937. Revised 1939. Revised 1942.'; 3 preface signed C.C. Goldring, superintendent of schools; 4–81 text; 82–94 index
COPIES: OGU (CCC TX715.6 H36 1942)   OMATTM OONL (TX663 H35 1942 p***)   OOSS (TX663 H36) *Private collection
NOTES: The OGU copy is inscribed on the binding, in a student's hand, in pencil, 'Mabel Ethel Hurst.' The OONL copy lacks its title-page.

O528.13   1944
—Form No. 13 / 13M-1-44 / Handbook / of / practical / cookery / for the use of / home economics classes / in the / public schools of Toronto / Board of Education, Toronto / 1944
DESCRIPTION: 21.5 × 13.0 cm   Pp [1–3] 4–94   Centre spread col of 'Beef Cuts,' illus   Paper; stapled
CONTENTS: 1 tp; 2 'Copyright (Canada) 1932, by the Board of Education for the City of Toronto Revised 1937 Revised 1939 Revised 1942 Revised 1944'; 3 preface signed C.C. Goldring, superintendent of schools; 4–81 text; 82–94 index
COPIES: OTSBM (TX663 T6 1944)   *Private collection
NOTES: Another private collector reports that she used this edition as a student at Fern Avenue Public School in Toronto's west end.

O528.14   1946
—Form No. 13 / 13M-1-46 / Handbook / of / practical / cookery / for the use of / home economics classes / in the / public schools of Toronto / Board of Education, Toronto / 1946
DESCRIPTION: 22.0 × 13.5 cm   Pp [1–3] 4–94   Fp illus on pp 37, 39, 40, and 41 of cuts of meat, illus on pp 78, 79, and 80 of place-settings   Paper; stapled
CONTENTS: 1 tp; 2 'Copyright (Canada) 1932, by the Board of Education for the City of Toronto Revised 1937 Revised 1939 Revised 1942 Revised 1944 Revised 1946'; 3 'Preface' signed C.C. Goldring, director of education; 4–81 text; 82–94 index
COPIES: OTSBM (TX663 T6 1946)   OWTU (F13721) *Private collection
NOTES: The copy catalogued here, still in the hands of the original owner, was used at John Ross Robertson Public School in North Toronto, in the Grades 7 and 8 Home Economics class for girls, 'conducted by a doughty Scottish woman, Miss Robertson, ... sometime between September 1948 and June 1950.'

O528.15   1950
—Homemaking / and meals / for instruction in / home economic education / in Toronto schools / Copyright (Canada) 1932, by the Board of Education for the City of Toronto / Revised 1937, 1939, 1942, 1944, 1946, 1950.
DESCRIPTION: 23.0 × 15.0 cm   Pp [1–2] 3–155 [156–60]   3 pls col, illus on pp 23, 147, 148, and 149   Paper; spiral-bound
CONTENTS: 1 tp; 2 'Foreword' signed C.C. Goldring, director of education; 3–150 text; 151–5 index; 156–60 blank for 'Notes'
COPIES: OTMCL (640 T59)   *Private collection
NOTES: The OTMCL copy is rebound and lacks pp 155 onward. The OTSBM catalogue lists an edition with the same title; the description gives the publication date 1932, but the call number indicates 1957 (TX663 T62 1957).

1924–5

Cook book

For a later publication in support of the same hospital, see O940.1, The Heather Club Cook Book.

O529.1   nd [about 1924–5]
Cook book / tried – tested – proved / A collection of recipes / compiled by / the / Nurses' Alumnae / of the / the [*sic*] Public General Hospital / Chatham, Ont. / Baxter, printer, Chatham
DESCRIPTION: 20.0 × 13.5 cm   Pp [1–80]   Tp illus of Maltese cross   Paper, with tp illus on front; stapled, and with hole punched at top left corner for hanging
CONTENTS: 1 tp; 2 ads; 3–mid 79 recipes and ads; mid–bottom 79 'Useful Hints'; 80 ads
COPIES: *OGU (CCC TX715.6 C6617)
NOTES: The printer has over-printed all the folios with a black rectangle, perhaps to obscure errors in page-numbering.

Two advertisements point to publication in about 1924–5: one on p 78 for Archibald Park, which describes him as 'successor to Park Bros.'; another on p 68 for 'The New Hotel Garner,' which names J.B. Kerr. Chatham city directories first list Archibald Park as proprietor of Park Brothers Foundry in 1925. The 1924 program for 'The Old Boys Club Reunion' in Chatham contains an advertisement for the New Hotel Garner, along with a photograph of Kerr and the statement that 'complete renovation of the Old Garner House, inside and out, has been accomplished during the first year of the new management'; the first listing in city directories for the New Hotel Garner is in the volume for 1926. (OCHAK is the source of information for these businesses.) The cookbook was likely published in December, for Christmas sales: An advertisement on p 20 refers to 'Christmas gifts in leather' from Hammonds Leather Goods Store, and an advertisement on p 22 for Sulman's bookstore commands the reader to 'Give books this Xmas.'

Cook book of practical recipes

Circle No. 2 of the same church published O517.1, Choice Recipes.

O530.1 nd [about 1924–5]
Cook book / of / practical / recipes / presented by / No. 1 Circle of the / Giles Boulevard / Methodist Church / Windsor, Ont. / Price 25 cents. [cover-title]
DESCRIPTION: 17.5 × 12.0 cm   Pp [1] 2–36   Paper; stapled
CONTENTS: 1–36 recipes credited with the name of the contributor and ads
COPIES: *Private collection
NOTES: The first page is headed 'Practical Recipes.' The printer, 'W.T. Jacques & Sons, Windsor, Ont.,' is on p 36. The book was published before the creation of the United Church of Canada on 10 June 1925, when this church became known as Giles Boulevard United Church. An advertisement on the outside back face of the binding for Baum and Brody, 'the border cities [sic] largest home furnishers,' indicates publication no earlier than 1924: the company invites the reader 'to visit us in our new store, cor. Chatham and Ferry sts., Windsor, ...' In the 1923–4 Windsor city directory the company's address is listed as Sandwich Street; in the directory for 1924–5, updated to 1 September 1924, the address is at Ferry and Chatham.

Scott, Anna Lee [pseudonym]

For information about Anna Lee Scott and her cookbooks, see O526.1.

O531.1 nd [about 1924–5]
The / Maple Leaf / housekeeper / by / Anna Lee Scott / Published by / Maple Leaf Milling Company, Limited
DESCRIPTION: 23.0 × 15.0 cm   Pp [1] 2–128   Illus col
Thin card, with plaid pattern
CONTENTS: 1 tp; 2 'Table of Weights and Measures,' 'Oven Heats,' 'Time-Table for Roasting,' 'Time-Table for Broiling Meats'; 3 fp illus of 'The well-set dinner table ...'; 4–5 'The Well-Set Dinner Table'; 6–7 'To Serve When We Entertain'; 8–12 'The Helpful Kitchen'; 13–15 'Cleaning'; 16–19 'Laundering'; 20 illus of measuring methods; 21–124 recipes; 125–8 index
CITATIONS: *Daily Star* (Toronto) 3 February 1927, advertisement on p 18
COPIES: AHRMH (998-017-001)   MWASM   OFERWM (A1982.2)   OONL   (TX715 S36)   OSMFHHM   OTMCL (641.5971 S18)   *Private collection
NOTES: Scott is described as the author of *The Maple Leaf Housekeeper* on the title-page of O554.1, *When We Entertain,* copyright 1925, but not on the title-page of O526.1, *Cookery Arts and Kitchen Management,* copyright 1924; therefore, *The Maple Leaf Housekeeper* was published about 1924–5, but no earlier. No place of publication is recorded, but the head office of Maple Leaf Milling Co. Ltd was in Toronto.

The private collector's copy described here is inscribed on the title-page, in ink, 'To Mildred – Wishing you every success. Dorothy. 1934.' Another private collector's copy is stamped on the title-page, 'Menzies Bros. Limited.' The OTMCL copy has an extra 16-page section after p 128, titled 'Eastern Canada Section, Containing the Prize Recipes of the Ladies of the Maritime Provinces'; the recipes are credited with the name and town of the winner and the rank of her prize.

305 tested recipes

High Park Avenue Methodist Church was renamed High Park Avenue United Church on 10 June 1925, the date of the founding of the United Church of Canada. In 1970 the church amalgamated with Alhambra United Church. The congregation disbanded in 1996.

O532.1 nd [about 1924–5]
305 / tested / recipes / Published by / Mrs. J.W. Dodd's Unit / of the Ladies' Aid Society of High Park Avenue / Methodist Church [cover-title]
DESCRIPTION: 22.5 × 15.0 cm   Pp [i–ii], 1–89   Card, with image on front of the church; bound at top edge by two metal rings through punched holes
CONTENTS: Inside front face of binding 'Our Greetings'; i 'Index' [i.e., table of contents]; ii blank; 1 'Recipe for a Perfect Husband' by Mrs G.B. Ham; 2 ad; 3–89 recipes, most credited with the name of the contributor, and ads

COPIES: *OONL (TX715.6 T5556 1900 p***)
NOTES: 'Our Greetings' comments, 'We hope this book will ... be a souvenir of the many efforts made by our ladies to erect a new Sunday School building.' This cookbook was published before church union on 10 June 1925. An advertisement on p 80 for Fred Simmons and Son, 650 Runnymede Road, described as successors to York Heating, limits the time of publication to the period 1924–5: Toronto city directories list York Heating Co. at 650 Runnymede for only one year, in the volume for 1923; Fredk Simmons and Son is listed at 650 Runnymede in the 1924 volume as 'furnaces' and in the 1925 volume as 'tinsmiths' (another business is at the address in 1926).

An advertisement on p 10 for Maple Leaf Milling Co. Ltd reprints a recipe from O444.1, *Old Homestead Recipes*.

1925

[Title unknown]

O533.1   1925
[An edition of a cookbook from Wesley United Church, London, Ontario, 1925]
COPIES: Private collection

Camp cooking

See O374.1 for information about Canadian Milk Products Ltd and its other cookbooks. O913.1, Easy Recipes for Camp and Kitchen, *and O1171.1,* Skillet Skills for Camp and Cottage, *are later Klim recipe collections published by Borden Co. Ltd. The latter incorporates material from O534.1,* Camp Cooking.

O534.1   nd [about 1925]
Camp / cooking / Fresh milk in camp [cover-title]
DESCRIPTION: 16.5 × 10.5 cm   Pp 1–46 [47–8]   Illus   Paper, with image on front of a cow standing beside a tent and tethered to a can of Klim inside the tent door; stapled
CONTENTS: 1 'Foreword' signed Canadian Milk Products Ltd, Toronto, Montreal, Winnipeg, Vancouver; 2 illus showing the volume of liquid milk (16 quarts) that goes into a 5-lb can of Klim, and illus of Klim skimmed milk can and Klim whole milk can; 3–4 index; 5 'Charles S. Kirstead' [biographical notes]; 6 'How to Select Materials for the Camp Larder'; 7–16 'Klim Recipes by Charles S. Kirstead'; 17 'James Tandy Ellis' [biographical notes]; 18–25 'Klim Recipes by

James Tandy Ellis'; 26–7 'George L. Catton' [biographical notes]; 28–32 'Klim Recipes by George L. Catton'; 33–7 'Klim Recipes by Harry C. Phibbs'; 38–top 42 'Camp Food and Firewood'; mid–bottom 42 'Afterword' signed Canadian Milk Products Ltd, 347 Adelaide Street West, Toronto; 43 blank for 'Fishing Diary'; 44–5 blank for 'Your Own Recipes'; 46 ad for C.M.P. Powdered Lemon Juice; 47–8 blank for 'Your Own Supply List'
COPIES: *OTMCL (641.578 C117)
NOTES: The 'Foreword' comments: 'This is not a stereotyped recipe book. It is a book designed as a guide where cooking must be done with the primitive tools of the camp ... Canadian sportsmen will welcome the chapter of old Southern recipes contributed by Mr. James Tandy Ellis.' The 'Foreword' thanks the four men who contributed recipes: Kirstead, Tandy Ellis, Catton, and Phibbs. This edition has no recipes by Morris Ackerman; therefore, it precedes O534.2.

The address given for Canadian Milk Products is 347 Adelaide Street West, Toronto, indicating a publication date in the period 1925–7 (see the company listing in Toronto city directories). If O534.2 was published in 1925 (see that entry), then O534.1 was published no later than 1925. The blank leaf for 'Your Own Supply List' is perforated for tearing out.

O534.2   nd [about 1925]
—Camp / cooking / Fresh milk in camp
[cover-title]
DESCRIPTION: 16.5 × 10.5 cm   Pp 1–46   Illus   Paper, with image on front of a cow standing beside a tent and tethered to a can of Klim inside the tent door; stapled
CONTENTS: 1 'Foreword' signed Canadian Milk Products Ltd, Toronto, Montreal, Winnipeg, Vancouver; 2 illus showing the volume of liquid milk (16 quarts) that goes into a 5-lb can of Klim, and illus of Klim skimmed milk can and Klim whole milk can; 3–4 index; 5 'Morris Ackerman'; 6–9 'Ack's Chapter'; 10 'Charles S. Kirstead'; 11 'How to Select Materials for the Camp Larder'; 12–21 'Klim Recipes by Charles S. Kirstead'; 22 'James Tandy Ellis'; 23–30 'Klim Recipes by James Tandy Ellis'; 31–2 untitled biographical information about George L. Catton; 33–7 'Klim Recipes by George L. Catton'; 38–42 'Klim Recipes by Harry C. Phibbs'; 43–5 'Camp Food Lists'; 46 'Afterword' signed Canadian Milk Products Ltd, Toronto
COPIES: ABA (O2.7 C 16cc Pam)   QMM (RBD ckbk 1415)   *Bookseller's stock   Private collection
NOTES: New to this edition are recipes by Morris Ackerman. Biographical notes about him record his

birth date as 1883 and his age as forty-two years, evidence that this edition was published in 1925 (1883 + 42 years). The bookseller's copy is stamped on the front cover, 'George Boyd G.B. Jul 31 1934.'

The private collector's copy has a leaf of advertisements after p 46, with the address Canadian Milk Products Ltd, Fruit Juice Department, 347 Adelaide Street West, Toronto 2. The QMM copy also has a leaf of publisher's advertisements after p 46. The cataloguing record for the ABA copy gives 48 pp.

O534.3   nd [1934]
—Easy / camp cooking / recipes [cover-title]
DESCRIPTION: 16.0 × 10.0 cm   Pp [1] 2–55 [56]   Illus Paper, with image on front of a mountain-and-lake landscape with a tent and campfire by the shore; stapled
CONTENTS: 1 untitled introductory text signed the Borden Co. Ltd, Yardley House, Toronto; top 2 'Table of Contents'; mid 2–4 index; 5 'Morris Ackerman' [biographical notes]; 6–8 'Ack's Chapter'; 9 'Charles S. Kirstead' [biographical notes]; 10–19 'Klim Recipes' by Kirstead; 20 'James Tandy Ellis' [biographical notes]; 21–8 'Klim Recipes' by Ellis; 29 'W.H.H. Chamberlin' [biographical notes]; 30–3 'Klim Recipes' by Chamberlin; 34–8 'Klim Recipes by Harry C. Phibbs'; 39–40 'George L. Catton' [biographical notes]; 41–5 'Klim Recipes' by Catton; 46–8 'Camp Food Lists' [by Major Townsend Whelen, according to the 'Table of Contents']; 49 'How to Select Materials for the Camp Larder' by Kirstead; 50 'Afterword'; 51–4 blank, ruled leaves for 'Your Own Recipes'; 55 'Fishing Diary'; 56 'What Is Klim?'
CITATIONS: Chatelaine 1935, p 82
COPIES: *BBVM   OONL (TX823 E28 1900z p***)
NOTES: The introductory text explains that *Easy Camp Cooking* was 'designed as a reliable guide where you must cook with the primitive tools of the camp' and it was 'written by men who have cooked for the enjoyment of themselves and friends in any and all circumstances.' New to this edition are recipes by W.H.H. Chamberlin. 'Printed in Canada' is on the outside back face of the binding.

This edition was published after Borden bought Canadian Milk Products in 1928 (Thomas/Marchant, p 67). The first listing in Toronto city directories of Borden's Yardley House address (noted on p 1 in *Easy Camp Cooking*) is in 1934 (in 1932 and 1933 the company was at 115 George). The BBVM copy is inscribed on the front face of the binding, in ink, '[illegible initial] Morrow 1934.' This edition, therefore, was published in 1934. For information about the Borden Co. and its other books, see Q106.1.

Chase, Dr Alvin Wood (Cayuga County, NY, 20 March 1817–25 May 1885, Ohio)

For information about Dr Chase and his publications, see O8.1.

O535.1   1925
Hang me up / Dr. A.W. Chase's / calendar almanac / 1925 / for the / home, factory / farm, office / Published by / Dr. A.W. Chase Medicine Co / Toronto & Buffalo [cover-title]
DESCRIPTION: 21.0 × 15.5 cm   Pp [3] 4–50   Illus Paper, with image on front of Dr Chase and his signature; stapled, and with hole punched at top left corner, through which runs a string for hanging
CONTENTS: 3 zodiacal signs, festivals and anniversaries, stars, and eclipses for 1925; 4–5 'Again, We Greet You'; 6–50 monthly calendars, 'The Efficient Housekeeper' [includes many culinary recipes], medical information, and publ ads
COPIES: *OTUTF (jah patent medicine)
NOTES: The text on p 4 states, 'For nearly a quarter of a century Dr. Chase's Almanac has gone out ... With the single exception of one year during the war, Dr. Chase's Almanac has never failed to appear ...'

See also *Dr A.W. Chase's Calendar Almanac* for the years 1926, 1927, 1928, and 1935 (O578.1, O594.1, O613.1, O847.1). There is no cookery in the almanacs for 1904, 1906, 1907, 1908, 1909, 1911, 1913, 1915, 1916, 1917, [there was no issue in one of the war years, probably 1918], 1919, 1920, 1923, 1924, 1930, 1933, 1934, 1936, 1937, 1938, 1939 (thirty-fifth edition), 1941, 1942, 1943, 1946, 1947, 1948, 1949 (all at OTUTF, jah patent medicine). There were later issues, which I have not examined: 1951, 1952, 1954 (fiftieth anniversary edition), and 1959 (all at OTUTF; 1954 also at OKQ and QMM RBD uncat; 1959 also at OKQ).

Cook book

O536.1   [1925]
Women's Auxiliary / to / Canadian National Institute / for the Blind / [graphic symbol for 'Hope'] / Cook book
DESCRIPTION: 22.5 × 15.0 cm   Pp [1–7] 8–136   Fp illus on p 6 of Pearson Hall, 186 Beverley Street, Toronto, the CNIB head office; illus on pp 106, 111, 117, 123, 129   Paper, with tp symbol on front; sewn
CONTENTS: 1 tp; 2 'Toronto // The Macoomb Press 16 Johnston Street 1925'; 3 'Contents'; 4 'List of Advertisers'; 5 'Foreword' signed Toronto Women's

Auxiliary to the Canadian National Institute for the Blind; 6 fp illus; 7–102 recipes credited with the name of the contributor; 103–5 'Household Hints'; 106 two illus of Blind Craft Shop and Headquarters of the Women's Auxiliary; 107–10 ads; 111 illus of Basketry Workroom for blind men; 112–16 ads; 117 illus of Whitewear Shop for blind women and Clarkewood, a residence at 331 Sherbourne Street, Toronto; 118–22 ads; 123 illus of Broom Shop for blind men; 124–8 ads; 129 illus of Library and Publishing Department of CNIB; 130–2 ads; 133–6 blank for 'Notes'
COPIES: OFERWM (A1977.122.14)   OTMCL (641.5 C114)   *QMM (RBD ckbk 1417)   Private collection
NOTES: The 'Foreword' says that proceeds from the sale of the book will go to 'work for blind people.' The text is an enlarged version of O358.1, *Cook Book*, published by the St George Chapter of the Imperial Order Daughters of the Empire, in 1916. See the comments for that entry.

The private collector's copy of O536.1 is inscribed on the title-page, in ink, 'Marie Violet Reay. Sept. 12/ 25. Canadian National Exhibition.' (i.e., likely where Reay acquired her copy). The OFERWM copy lacks pp 1–6 and 127 onward (only part of one unidentified leaf from the end of the book remains).

Cook book: Containing many carefully-chosen practical recipes

The Glanford branch of the Women's Institute was established in 1904 (Ambrose, p 236).

O537.1   1925
[An edition of *Cook Book: Containing Many Carefully-Chosen Practical Recipes*, issued by the ladies of the Glanford Women's Institute, Glanford, Ontario, 1925, 22 cm, pp 91]
COPIES: OONL (TX715.6 C65645 1925, not on shelf)   Private collection
NOTES: The private collector reports a 1925 Glanford Women's Institute cookbook called *Selected Recipes*.

Cook book of selected recipes

See also O1022.1, Tested Recipes, from the same church.

O538.1   1925
Church of / St. John the Evangelist / Cook book / of / selected recipes / Compiled by the ladies / of the Guild / 1925 / [ad for Snowflake Ammonia] / [folio:] 1

DESCRIPTION: 22.5 × 14.5 cm   Pp 1–96   Cloth-covered card; stapled
CONTENTS: 1 tp; 2 ads; 3–95 recipes credited with the name of the contributor, menus, ads, and some blank leaves not included in the pagination; 96 'List of Contents' and ad
COPIES: *Private collection
NOTES: This book originally belonged to the present owner's mother, Mrs Clark. Both mother and daughter attended the Church of St John the Evangelist in London, Ontario. Mrs Clark contributed several recipes in the volume; for example, Veal Soufflé, Cabbage Salad, and Christmas Pudding.

Cooke, Mrs A.H., and J. Weston

O539.1   1925
Kiwanees' Kake Kontest / Recipes, 1925 / Timmins, Ontario [cover-title]
DESCRIPTION: With photograph on front of the Hollinger Consolidated Gold Mines; bound by string through two punched holes
COPIES: *OSPTM
NOTES: The following is on one of the introductory pages: 'The Kiwanee Kake Kontest Recipe Book // Compiled by Mrs A.H. Cooke and J. Weston in aid of the Kiwanee Club organized in February 1924. This club has always met with ever ready assistance in its work from the public in general and the members express their sincere thanks to people of Timmins and District for patronage of events given by them, and also to the Timmins Business College who so kindly printed the recipes herein.' Mrs A.H. Cooke is likely Mary C. Cooke, the wife of Albert H. Cooke, listed in the 1932, 1934, and 1936 Timmins city directories (Schumacher section) as a paymaster or accountant for the McIntyre Gold Mines. J. Weston may be John R. Weston, timberman, in the 1936 directory. The 37-page text is reproduced from typing; the cover-title is printed. The curator reports that many of the recipes are for fruitcakes.

Cooking and cake contests were apparently popular fund-raising tools for the Kiwanee Club. Two years after the publication of the 1925 cookbook, the 23 June 1927 issue of the *Porcupine Advance*, a Timmins newspaper, reported that the Kiwanee Club had great success with the cooking contest and cake auction held at the three-day Kiwanee Fair that year. The article lists categories and winners, and describes in detail the progress of the cake auction.

Craig, Verna Larrabee

Niagara Falls, Ontario, directories show Craig Bros (Flavoring Extracts) at 46 McRae in 1925 and at 1034 McRae in 1926. The business appears to have operated for only a few years. Mrs Verna L. Craig is listed as a representative of Mutual Life Assurance Co.; her husband was Vurnyer A. Craig. On the binding of some editions of Cook Book of Practical Recipes, *Verna Craig is described as from Niagara Falls, New York; on the binding of other editions, she is from Niagara Falls, Ontario.*

O540.1 nd [about 1925]
Cook book / of / practical recipes / [floral swags decorating a spherical shape] / compiled by / Verna Larrabee Craig / Niagara Falls, N.Y. / Price 25 cents / Craig Brothers / Manufacturers of concentrated flavors in tubes / Niagara Falls, N.Y. Niagara Falls, Ont. [cover-title]
DESCRIPTION: 22.5 × 15.0 cm   Pp [1–2] 3–31 [32]   Paper; stapled
CONTENTS: 1 'Introduction'; 2 blank; 3 'Notes'; 4 blank; 5–31 recipes; 32 index and publ ad
COPIES: *Private collection
NOTES: Although no street address is given in the various editions of *Cook Book of Practical Recipes* that would help determine the order or date of publication, they all appear to have been published in the mid-1920s. One differentiating feature of the editions is the decorative device on the front face of the binding. Here the decorative device (floral swags decorating a spherical shape) is exactly the same as that on B50.1, *Nakusp's Little Red Cook Book*, of May 1930.

'Notes' explains the benefit of Craig Brothers flavours, which were packaged in tubes: 'The principal feature of our flavors is the elimination of expensive alcohol which makes up from 80 to 90 per cent of all bottle flavors.' Most of the recipes use Craig flavours, such as celery, onion, sage, cloves, vanilla, lemon, nutmeg, ginger, cinnamon, maple, and orange. Housewives could sell Craig products on commission, according to the advertisement on p 32.

O540.2 nd [about 1925]
—Cook book / of / practical recipes / [basket of fruit, oak leaves, and acorns, in a triangular shape] / Compiled by / Verna Larrabee Craig / Niagara Falls, N.Y. / Price 25 cents / Craig Brothers / manufacturers of concentrated flavors in tubes / Niagara Falls, N.Y. Niagara Falls, Ont. [cover-title]
DESCRIPTION: Pp [1–2] 3–32   Paper; stapled

CONTENTS: 1 'Introduction'; 2 blank; 3 'Notes' and 'What Our Flavors Are'; 4 blank; 5–31 recipes; 32 index and publ ad
COPIES: *OONL (TX715 C65854 1930z p***)

O540.3 nd [about 1925]
—Cook book / of / practical recipes / [stylized vine forming a triangular shape] / Compiled by / Verna Larrabee Craig / Niagara Falls, N.Y. / Price 25 cents / Craig Brothers / manufacturers of concentrated flavors in tubes / Niagara Falls, N.Y. Niagara Falls, Ont. [cover-title]
DESCRIPTION: 22.5 × 15.0 cm   Pp [1–2] 3–31 [32]   Paper; stapled
CONTENTS: 1 'Introduction'; 2 blank; 3 'Notes' and 'What Our Flavors Are'; 4 blank; 5–31 recipes; 32 'Index' [i.e., alphabetical list of sections] and publ ad
COPIES: *Private collection

O540.4 nd [about 1925]
—Cook book / of / practical recipes / [thistle flower in a triangular shape] / Compiled by / Verna Larrabee Craig / Niagara Falls, Ontario / Price 25 cents / Craig Brothers / manufacturers of concentrated flavors in tubes / Niagara Falls, N.Y. Niagara Falls, Ont. [cover-title]
DESCRIPTION: 22.5 × 15.0 cm   Pp [1–2] 3–31 [32]   Paper; stapled
CONTENTS: 1 'Introduction'; 2 blank; 3 'Notes' and 'What Our Flavors Are'; 4 blank; 5–31 recipes; 32 index and publ ad
COPIES: *QMM (RBD ckbk 1470)

O540.5 nd [about 1925]
—Cook book / of / practical recipes / [0.8 × 1.6 cm image of roast poultry on a platter] / Compiled by / Verna Larrabee Craig / Niagara Falls, Ontario / [five-point star] / Price 25 cents / [five-point star] / Craig Brothers / manufacturers of concentrated flavors in tubes / Niagara Falls, N.Y. Niagara Falls, Ont. [cover-title]
DESCRIPTION: 22.5 × 15.0 cm   Pp [1–2] 3–31 [32]   Paper; stapled
CONTENTS: 1 'Introduction'; 2 'Below is a list of flavoring extracts manufactured by Craig Brothers ...' [twenty-two extracts listed alphabetically from Almond to Wintergreen]; 3 'Notes' and 'What Our Flavors Are'; 4 blank; 5–31 recipes; 32 'Index'
COPIES: *Private collection

Economical recipe book

In June 1925 the Toronto branch of the Canadian Red Cross opened a centre at 55 Beverley Street for training and supplying visiting housekeepers. Information about the centre is in various clippings in the file for Lexa Denne at OTUAR (A73-0026/082 (59)).

O541.1   nd [about 1925]
Economical / recipe book / Compiled by / the Visiting Housekeepers / Price 25 cents / Visiting Housekeepers Association / 55 Beverley Street, Toronto [cover-title]
DESCRIPTION: Pp [1] 2–36   Stapled
CONTENTS: 1 twelve numbered 'Cookery Suggestions' and abbreviations for teaspoon, tablespoon, and cup; 2–top 3 'Table of Weights and Measures,' 'Methods of Using Rice,' 'Methods of Using Rolled Oats,' and 'Methods of Using Beans'; mid 3–36 recipes
COPIES: *Private collection
NOTES: From appearances, the cookbook was published about 1925 or slightly later. No one is credited as the compiler, but three women whose cookbooks are described elsewhere in this bibliography may have been involved in some measure: Lexa Denne, who was the first director, from the centre's opening until her untimely death on 16 April 1930; and Nellie Lyle Pattinson and Annie Laird, both on the committee that established the centre. For information about Denne, see B37.1; for Pattinson, see O506.1; and for Laird, see O241.1.

Foods for fine fancies

O542.1   nd [about 1925]
Foods for / fine / fancies / Price fifty cents [cover-title]
DESCRIPTION: 21.5 × 13.5 cm   Pp [1–2] 3–104   Paper, with image on front of a plate carrying heart-shaped cookies and, beside the plate, a heart-shaped cake and a round cake, each decorated with hearts; stapled
CONTENTS: 1 'Foods for Fine Fancies compiled and published by C.E.E. Hospital Guild // Petrolia,' poem extolling cookbooks over other types of book, by Elsie Fowler (Mrs M.M.), and introductory note; 2 information about Charlotte Eleanor Englehart Hospital, owned by the town of Petrolia and opened 31 January 1911; 3–104 recipes credited with the name of the contributor and ads
COPIES: OCHAK   *Private collection
NOTES: The introductory note on p 1 says that the

object of the guild is 'the furnishing of linens and general upkeep of the Maternity Annex, as well as furnishing a part of the nurses' uniforms and helping ... to make the path of our nurses, a little smoother.' The note adds that copies of this cookbook may be procured from Mrs C. Umphrey, president, or Mrs Geo. Deacon, secretary, or from any member of the guild.

The reference on p 2 about previous hospital renovations ('from time to time the building has been enlarged by various additions ...') indicates that the book was published several years after the hospital's 1911 opening. The advertisement on p 7 for Walter Baker and Co. Ltd, the chocolate maker, suggests a publication date of 1925: It cites the establishment of the company in 1780 and refers to the 'more than 145 years' that the company's chocolate has set 'the standard.' The appearance of the book confirms 1925 as the approximate date of publication.

The OCHAK copy lacks its binding.

For all your baking use Purity Flour

For information about Western Canada Flour Mills and its cookbooks for Purity Flour, see O394.1.

O543.1   nd [about 1925]
For all your / baking / use / Purity / Flour / for bread, cakes and pastry [cover-title]
DESCRIPTION: 15.0 × 9.0 cm   Pp [1] 2–15   Paper; stapled
CONTENTS: 1 cover-title; 2 quotation from Dr Chas E. Saunders, former Dominion cerealist [and the discoverer of Marquis Wheat]; 3–4 'Home-made Bread in 4½ Hours // All the Drudgery Taken Out of Baking Bread at Home'; 5 'The Straight Dough Process // Make Bread This Way in 4½ Hours'; 6 'Home Made Yeast' and 'The Overnight Sponge Process'; 7 'The Value of a Fermenting Cupboard'; 8–14 'For All Your Baking Use Purity Flour' [recipes]; 15 [inside back face of binding] 'From Our Daily Mail' [testimonials]; outside back face publisher's name: Western Canada Flour Mills Co. Ltd, Toronto
COPIES: MCM   *Private collection
NOTES: The fermenting cupboard described on p 7 (in a quotation from Dr Saunders) had double walls filled with shavings or straw; heat was provided by a pan of hot water placed below the shelves that held the pans of dough. Such a cupboard solved the problem of maintaining a correct temperature for the rising bread: 'The main difficulty – indeed one is tempted

to say the only difficulty – encountered when bread is being made in an ordinary Canadian home is the lack of a warm place where the dough can be kept at a moderate suitable temperature without much variation throughout the whole period of fermentation.' The recipes are not exclusively for yeast goods, but also for sausage rolls, cakes, squares, cookies, muffins, doughnuts, pastry, and dumplings.

A testimonial on p 15 refers to the writer using Purity Flour 'for twenty years,' and in another testimonial, 'for the last twenty years.' If Purity Flour was introduced in 1905, the same year as the creation of Western Canada Flour Mills Co., then the booklet may have been published in about 1925.

The private collector's copy has 'For sale by Adam Brown & Sons' stamped on the back face of the binding.

O543.2   nd [about 1932]
—For all your / baking / use / Purity Flour [cover-title]
DESCRIPTION: 14.5 × 9.5 cm   Pp [1–2] 3–14   Paper; stapled
CONTENTS: 1 cover-title; 2 'Just a Word about Purity Flour'; 3–7 'Cakes and Pastry'; 8–13 'Simple Formulae for Home Bread Baking' [includes A Good Bread Recipe – Made in 4½ Hours]; 14 'Other Purity Products'; inside back face of binding coupon for ordering the 'Purity Flour Cook Book, containing 700 valuable recipes' addressed to Western Canada Flour Mills Co. Ltd, at Toronto, Montreal, Ottawa, Saint John, Winnipeg, or Calgary; outside back face publisher's name: Western Canada Flour Mills Co. Ltd, Toronto
COPIES: *Private collection
NOTES: The book-order coupon is probably for the 1932 edition of *The Purity Cook-Book* (O771.1), which has 743 numbered recipes.

Helpful hints for housekeepers 1925

See O263.1 for information about the company and other issues of Helpful Hints for Housekeepers.

O544.1   1925
1925 Volume XV 1925 / Hang me in the kitchen / Helpful / hints / for housekeepers / Compliments of / the Dodds Medicine Co. / Limited / Toronto, Can. [cover-title]
DESCRIPTION: 15.5 × 10.5 cm   Pp 1–32   Paper; stapled, and with hole punched at top left corner, through which runs a string for hanging

CONTENTS: 1 'A Message to You' signed the Dodds Medicine Co. Ltd, Toronto; 2 'Weights and Measures'; 3 'Hints on the Care of Brooms and Brushes'; 4, 6, 8, 10, 12, 14, 18, 20, 22, 24, 26, 28 entries for illnesses and other medical information, arranged alphabetically from Anaemia to Skin; 5 'Things Worth Knowing'; 7 'Combatting the Moth'; 9, top 11 'Avoid Mustiness'; mid–bottom 11 'Hints on Cleaning Gloves'; 13 'About Picture Hanging' and 'Equivalents'; 15 'The Medicine Chest' and 'To Extract a Splinter'; 16–17 publ ads for Dodd's Kidney Pills; 19 'Things Every Housewife Should Know'; 21 'A Kitchen Timetable'; 23, 25 'Valuable Hints'; 27 'Uses for the Lemon'; 29–30 publ ads; 31 'Rates of Postage'; 32 'Diet Rules'; inside back face of binding 'Self Examination Page'
COPIES: *OTUTF (uncat patent medicine)

Helpful hints for housewives

O545.1   nd [about 1925]
Helpful hints / for housewives / The / Provincial Natural Gas / & Fuel Company / of Ontario, Limited [cover-title]
DESCRIPTION: 23.0 × 15.0 cm   Pp 3–34   Illus of various manufacturers' gas appliances   Paper, with decorative border on front; stapled, and with hole punched at top left corner for hanging
CONTENTS: Inside front face of binding names of officers and agents of the Provincial Natural Gas and Fuel Company of Ontario and locations of its business offices; 3 'Foreword'; 4 'Index to Contents'; 5–34 text
COPIES: OONL (TX657 S6 H44 1900z p***)   *Private collection
NOTES: The text is composed of recipes and information about gas cooking and gas appliances. The 'Index to Contents' lists the following headings: 'Annex or Auxiliary Heaters'; 'Automatic Oven Control'; 'Broiler (In-a-Drawer)'; 'Clothes Dryer'; 'Furnaces'; 'Fireplaces'; 'Incinerators'; 'Incubators'; 'Laundry Plates'; 'Radiantfires'; 'Recipes'; 'Refrigeration'; 'Story, "The Bride's Return Home"'; 'Stoves'; 'Water Heaters (not automatic)'; 'Water Heaters (automatic)'; and 'Weights and Measures.' The illustrations of appliances include those from Beach Foundry Ltd, Ottawa, Findlay Bros Co. Ltd, Carleton Place, Moffats Ltd, Weston, Gurney, Whittaker Gas, and Payne Furnace and Supply Co. Inc., Beverley Hills, California. The printer of the cookbook is on the outside back face of the binding: 'The Review Company, printers // Bridgeburg, Ontario.'

Hip-o-lite professional recipes

The president of Bowron Bros Ltd, which made Hip-o-lite, was Arthur Ernest Bowron (Hamilton, Ont., 1881–16 March 1956, Hamilton, Ont.). He had started business in his mother's kitchen in 1910, with his two brothers Ralph and Walter. His one sister, Laura S. Bowron, is named in O546.2–546.3 as the person to whom readers should write about candy recipes (her later married name was Mrs Thomas Rhodes). From the mid-1920s, Bowron Bros Ltd is listed in Hamilton city directories as a manufacturer of grocers' specialties on Victoria Avenue North. It was 'the first firm in Canada to market an oil-less salad dressing and to use Canadian cherries for cake and confectionery decorations.' In 1939, the company moved to Aldershot and changed its name to Bowron Products Ltd.

Information about Arthur Bowron and the company is from two sources: Jesse Edgar Middleton, The Province of Ontario: A History, 1615–1927, *Vol. 4, Toronto: Dominion Publishing Co., [copyright 1927], p 461 (his middle name is spelled 'Earnest' here); and his obituary in the* Spectator *(Hamilton) 17 March 1956.*

See also O310.1, Snow-Mellow 'Goodies,' *an earlier book of recipes for Snow-Mellow, a marshmallow-like product.*

O546.1   nd [about 1925]
Hip-o-lite / The book of caterers and chefs / professional recipes / – which explains how madam herself may don an / apron and add a professional touch to home desserts. [cover-title]
DESCRIPTION: 17.5 × 13.0 cm   Pp [1–16]   Illus col Paper, with image on front of a woman topping tall-stemmed dessert cups with Hip-o-lite; stapled
CONTENTS: 1 'For the Tea Table'; 2 'Fruit Salads'; 3 'By Way of Making Simple Desserts Seem Elaborate'; 4–7 'Cake Frostings and Fillings'; 8–9 'Ice Creams and Ices'; 10–11 'Sauces'; 12 recipes for Marshmallow Meringue for pies and puddings; 13–16 illustrated ads for Bowron Bros products (Toro Tablets, a laundry soap; Aloha Glycerine Soap for skin; Dominica Lime Fruit Juice; Grenada Nutmegs; Dainty Lunch Mayonnaise; Bowron Cherries; Brillante Brand Olive Oil; Sure-Whip, 'assists in the whipping of cream')
COPIES: *Private collection
NOTES: Hip-o-lite was a marshmallow-like topping or creme. The following is on the outside back face of the binding: 'Products manufactured by Bowron Bros. Hamilton, Canada // The Moore Printery Hamilton, Ontario.'

O546.2   nd
—Hip-o-lite / The book of caterers and chefs / professional recipes / – which explains how madam herself may don an / apron and add a professional touch to home desserts. [cover-title]
DESCRIPTION: 17.0 × 13.0 cm   Pp [1–21]   Illus col [Free, on p 13]   Paper, with image on front of a woman topping tall-stemmed dessert cups with Hip-o-lite; stapled
CONTENTS: 1 'For the Tea Table'; 2 'Fruit Salads'; 3 'By Way of Making Simple Desserts Seem Elaborate'; 4–7 'Cake Frostings and Fillings'; 8–9 'Ice Creams and Ices'; 10–11 'Sauces'; 12 recipes for Marshmallow Meringue for pies and puddings; 13–17 '"Simplified Candy Making" as It Is Done with Hip-o-lite'; 18–21 ads for Bowron Bros Ltd, Hamilton, Ontario.
COPIES: *OH (R641.86 HIP CESH)
NOTES: This edition includes a section of candy recipes not found in O546.1. 'The Philip Davis Ptg. Co Limited // Hamilton, Ontario' is on the outside back face of the binding. On p 13, the reader is asked to write Laura S. Bowron, Educational Department, Bowron Bros Ltd, Hamilton, if she is having any difficulty with the candy recipes.

O546.3   nd
—Hip-o-lite / The book of caterers and chefs / professional recipes / – which explains how madam herself may don an / apron and add a professional touch to home desserts. [cover-title]
DESCRIPTION: 17.5 × 13.0 cm   Pp 1–5 [6–17], [i–vi] Illus col   Paper, with image on front of a woman topping tall-stemmed dessert cups with Hip-o-lite; stapled
CONTENTS: 1 'For the Tea Table'; 2 'Fruit Salads'; 3 'By Way of Making Simple Desserts Seem Elaborate'; 4–7 'Cake Frostings and Fillings'; 8–9 'Ice Creams and Ices'; 10–11 'Sauces'; 12 recipes for Marshmallow Meringue for pies and puddings; 13–17 '"Simplified Candy Making" as It Is Done with Hip-o-lite'; i–vi ads for Bowron Bros Ltd products
COPIES: *QMM (RBD ckbk 1343)
NOTES: This edition includes a section of candy recipes not found in O546.1. 'Hughes & Wilkins, Limited printers // Hamilton, Ontario' is on the outside back face of the binding. On p 13, the reader is asked to write Laura S. Bowron, Educational Department, if she is having any difficulty with the candy recipes.

How to prepare dainty desserts

The 1925 Toronto city directory records the Harry Horne factory at 1297–9 Queen Street West and Harry Horne's residence at 51 Sorauren Avenue.

O547.1 nd [about 1925]
How to prepare / dainty / desserts / quickly and / with least / expense / No eggs required / Published by. / The Harry Horne Company. Limited. / Toronto Canada. [cover-title]
DESCRIPTION: 19.0 × 12.0 cm   Pp [1] 2–48   Illus on p 1 of Harry Horne and three of his company's products (Double Cream Custard Powder, flavouring extract, and Nu-Jell jelly powder); many illus of products throughout; illus on inside back face of binding of the company's factory   Very thin card, with image on front of a bowl of custard, surrounded by fruit; stapled
CONTENTS: 1 letter to 'Madam' from Harry Horne, president; 2–15 information about, and recipes for, Double Cream Custard Powder; 16–26 information about, and recipes for, Nu-Jell; 27–40 'Other Recipes on Harry Horne's Pure Food Products' (e.g., Mello Cremo, puddings, ground rice, rice flour, potato flour, and others); 41–7 information about the company's coupons and premium offer; 48 'Important Notice' advising housewives who cannot buy Harry Horne products from their grocers to order from company
COPIES: *Private collection
NOTES: Page 28 refers to 'This new series of puddings ... introduced in Canada on May 1st, 1925, ...'

Maple leaf cook-book

O548.1 [1925]
Maple Leaf / cook-book / tested recipes / for housekeepers / Published under the auspices of / the Col. B.O. Hooper Chapter, I.O.D.E. / Hamilton Ontario [cover-title]
DESCRIPTION: 23.5 × 15.0 cm   Pp 1–116   Thin card; stapled
CONTENTS: 1 list of 'Officers for 1925' and ad; 2 ad; 3 'Index' [i.e., alphabetical list of headings] and ad; 4 ads; 5 'Table of Weights and Measures' and ad; 6–114 recipes and ads; 115 ad; 116 'List of Additional Friends'
COPIES: OKQ   OWTU (G6268)   *Private collection
NOTES: The OWTU cover-title differs from the private collector's in that 'Published under the auspices of / the Nina Louise Hooper Chapter, I.O.D.E. / Hamilton, Ontario' is printed on a label and glued in the place of 'Published ... Col. B.O. Hooper Chapter ...' The OKQ copy is catalogued as 'under the auspices of the Nina Louise Hooper Chapter.'

Moore Park Big Sister Circle cook book

O549.1 1925
Moore Park / Big Sister Circle / cook book / (well-proven recipes) / "In commencement, we thank you / For buying our book, / And hope it will help you, / And guide you to cook." / Toronto, Canada / 1925
DESCRIPTION: 21.5 × 14.5 cm   Pp [1–4] 5–87, [i–ix]   Small tp illus of a manservant carrying aloft a covered dish   Paper-covered thin card; stapled
CONTENTS: 1 tp; 2 symbol of W.S. Johnston and Co. Ltd, printers, and 'Made in Canada'; 3 'Sweet Disposition' [i.e., mock recipe], 'Preface,' and untitled four-line verse about the kitchen and its effect on the life of a man; 4 'Index' [i.e., alphabetical list of sections]; 5–87 text, mainly recipes credited with the name of the contributor, and blank pages for manuscript recipes; i–ix ads
CITATIONS: Crawford, p D1, illus col
COPIES: OTMCL (641.5971 C58)   *Private collection
NOTES: The 'Preface' says that the book was produced to raise funds for the Moore Park Circle of the Big Sister Association. Another private collector's copy is inscribed on the title-page, in pencil, 'Oct 26/ 25 Mrs Grubbe.'

101 prize recipes

O550.1 copyright 1925
101 / prize recipes / Printed from contest / conducted by / Postum Cereal Company, Inc. / Battle Creek, Mich. / Canadian Postum Cereal Co., Ltd. / Toronto, Ontario, Canada. / Grape-Nuts Company, Ltd./ London, England. / Copyright, 1925, by / Postum Cereal Company, Inc.
DESCRIPTION: 16.0 × 10.5 cm   Pp [1] 2–40   Illus brown   Paper; stapled
CONTENTS: 1 tp; 2 '$7550 in Prizes Was Given for These Recipes'; 3 'Food and Nourishment Are Two Very Different Things'; 4 'In Grape-Nuts Is Nourishment You Need in the Form Your Body Can Digest'; 5 'Table of Contents'; 6 'Measurements and Directions' and 'Suggestions'; 7–38 recipes credited with the name and address of the winner; 39 'From a Physician'; 40 'Post Health Products' and 'Printed in U.S.A.'
COPIES: *Private collection
NOTES: Over 80,000 recipes using Grape-Nuts cereal as an ingredient were submitted to the contest, which was judged by the Good Housekeeping Institute. Grape Nuts Omelet California was the first-prize winner. The text and illustrations are printed in brown.

O550.2 copyright 1928
—101 / prize recipes / Postum Company, Incorporated / Battle Creek, Mich. / Canadian Postum Company, Ltd. / Toronto, Ontario, Canada / Grape-Nuts Company, Ltd. / London, England / Copyright, 1928, by / Postum Company, Incorporated
DESCRIPTION: 15.9 × 10.4 cm   Pp [1] 2–40   Illus   Paper
CITATIONS: Cagle/Stafford No. 957
COPIES: United States: InU
NOTES: Information here is from Cagle/Stafford.

AMERICAN EDITIONS: Battle Creek, Mich.: Postum Cereal Co., 1924 (Barile, pp 144, 203, illus p 144).

Queen Anne cook-book

O551.1   [1925]
Queen Anne / cook-book / tested recipes / for housekeepers / Published under the auspices of / the Queen Anne Chapter I.O.D.E. / Kitchener, Ontario [cover-title]
DESCRIPTION: 23.0 × 15.0 cm   Pp [1–2] 3–80   Paper; stapled
CONTENTS: 1 'Queen Anne Chapter I.O.D.E. ... Officers for 1925' and ad; 2 ad; 3 index and ad; 4 ads; 5 'Table of Weights and Measures' and ad; 6–80 recipes and ads
CITATIONS: Bloomfield 3206   Ferguson/Fraser, p 233, illus col on p 57 of closed volume
COPIES: OKIT   OWTU (G6871)   *Private collection
NOTES: On p 77 is 'Copyright on this book applied for. If interested, write L.M. Brophy, 78 Dale Ave., Toronto.'

Rawleigh's good health guide cook book almanac 1925

For information about Rawleigh's annual almanac cookbooks and other culinary publications, see M22.1.

O552.1   1925
Rawleigh's / good health / guide / cook book / almanac / [caption for portrait:] 1889 W.T. Rawleigh 1925 / Published by / the W.T. Rawleigh Co., Ltd. / Winnipeg London, Ont. Montreal / Memphis Chester Oakland / Minneapolis Richmond / Printed in Canada
DESCRIPTION: Tp portrait of W.T. Rawleigh   With image on front of a Rawleigh factory scene

COPIES: *BBVM   OONL (RC81 R38 p***)
NOTES: 'London, Ont.' is the location in the largest typeface.

O552.2   1925
—1925 / Guide de bonne sante / Rawleigh / Trade mark reg. U.S. Pat. Off. / Almanach-livre de cuisine / [caption for portrait:] 1889 W.T. Rawleigh 1925 / Publié par / La cie W.T. Rawleigh, limitée / Winnipeg London Montreal / Manufactures et succursales dans les E.U. / Freeport Memphis Chester Oakland / Minneapolis Richmond / Imprime au Canada
DESCRIPTION: Tp portrait of W.T. Rawleigh, illus   Paper, with image on front of a Rawleigh factory scene
COPIES: *QMBN (Z-1466)
NOTES: Of the places of publication, London is in the largest typeface. There is a portrait on p 1 of W.T. Rawleigh at the age of eighteen years.

Recipes for desserts

Editions of this title were published by drugstores in New Brunswick, Ontario, and British Columbia. For the editions published in Port Arthur and Napanee, see NB35.3 and NB35.5.

Ruddy's Magic Ice Cream Freezer recipes

O553.1   nd [about 1925]
Ruddy's Magic / Ice Cream Freezer / recipes / Specially / prepared / Ruddy Manufacturing / Company, Limited / Brantford, Canada
DESCRIPTION: 17.0 × 11.0 cm   Pp [1] 2–16   Illus on p 14 of Ruddy's Kitchen Cabinet, on p 15 of Ruddy's Kitchen Table, and on p 16 of Brantford Refrigerator   Paper, with image on front of Ruddy's Magic Ice Cream Freezer; stapled
CONTENTS: 1 tp; 2 'Observations' [English]; 3 'Observations' [French]; 4 'Directions' [English]; 5 'Directions' [French]; 6–13 recipes for frozen desserts, in English; 14–16 publ ads
COPIES: *BSUM
NOTES: The 'Observations' and 'Directions' are given in English and French, but the recipes are in English only. The Brantford Refrigerator on p 16 is an ice-box, not an electric refrigerator.

The company's history helps to date the book. According to information at OBBM, Ruddy Manufacturing Co. was created in 1922, when Ham Brothers

Co. was divided and Ruddy Manufacturing took over the production of kitchen cabinets, bedsprings, and bee-keeping supplies. In 1925, Ruddy Manufacturing assumed the remaining interests of Ham Brothers, including the making of refrigerators. The appearance of the cookbook is consistent with publication in about 1925, but no later.

Scott, Anna Lee [pseudonym]

For information about Anna Lee Scott and her cookbooks, see O526.1.

O554.1   copyright 1925
When we / entertain / by / Anna Lee Scott / author of / "Cookery Arts and Kitchen Management" / and / "The Maple Leaf Housekeeper." / Price 25 cents / Published for users of / Monarch Flour / by / Maple Leaf Milling Co., Limited / Copyright, Canada, 1925.
DESCRIPTION: 22.5 × 15.0 cm   Pp [1] 2–32   Small tp illus of a steaming tea cup; fp illus on p 3 of a well-set dinner table; fp illus on p 25 of decoratively cut and shaped foodstuffs; illus on p 21 of Cocoanut Cake; all illus printed in blue and black   Paper; stapled
CONTENTS: 1 tp; 2–4 'The Well-Set Dinner Table'; 5–8 'The Dinner Party'; 9–11 'The Luncheon'; 12–14 'The Reception'; 15–17 'The Smaller Parties'; 18–20 'The Intimate Tea Party'; 21 'Cocoanut Cake'; 22–3 'The Children's Party'; 24 'Beverages'; 25 fp illus; 26–8 'Sandwiches'; 29–32 'Salads'
CITATIONS: Ferguson/Fraser, p 233, illus col on p 57 of closed volume
COPIES: *Private collection
NOTES: The cover-title is 'When We Entertain // What to Serve and How to Serve It.' All the sections from p 5 onward include recipes in addition to advice for entertaining.

O554.2   2nd ed., copyright 1925
—When we / entertain / by / Anna Lee Scott / author of / "Cookery Arts and Kitchen Management" / and / "The Maple Leaf Housekeeper." / Price 25 cents / Published for users of / Monarch Flour / by / Maple Leaf Milling Co., Limited / Copyright, Canada, 1925. / Second edition.
DESCRIPTION: 23.0 × 15.0 cm   Pp [1] 2–32   Small tp illus of a steaming tea cup; fp illus on p 3 of a well-set dinner table; fp illus on p 25 of decoratively cut and shaped foodstuffs; illus on p 21; all illus printed in blue and black

CONTENTS: 1 tp; 2–32 text
COPIES: *Private collection
NOTES: *When We Entertain* is mentioned in a 1927 advertisement for Anna Lee Scott's radio broadcast (*Daily Star* (Toronto) 3 February 1927, p 18), but the edition number is not given.

Tempting recipes of new and old-time treats; household hints

The Belle Ewart Ice Co. supplied Lake Simcoe ice for iceboxes in Toronto households. The company was founded in Bell Ewart in the 1890s by Alfred Chapman, who added the last vowel to Belle.

O555.1   [2nd ed.], nd [about 1925]
Tempting recipes / of new and / old-time treats / household hints / Your refrigerator is the guardian of your / table; keep all perishable foods on ice – / fresh and safe. / This booklet is published by the / Belle Ewart Ice Company / Chapmans Limited / and is dedicated to the woman in the home – the one who is in / charge of the greatest of all undertakings. It is sent forth in / appreciation of the patronage of our many customers and is / presented to you with the hope that we may serve you during the / coming year. / We trust that its contents may prove a real benefit to you. / A.W. Williams / General Manager
DESCRIPTION: 21.5 × 13.5 cm   Pp [1] 2–16   Tp illus green-and-black of a table set for three persons, illus green-and-black   Paper, with vertical green stripes on front; stapled
CONTENTS: 1 tp; 2–13 recipes and 'Household Hints'; 14 'Let Us Help You Enjoy Greatest Efficiency from Your Refrigerator' and illus of an ice-box; 15–top 16 'How to Choose and Care for the Refrigerator' courtesy of Mrs A.C. Hayward; mid–bottom 16 'Safeguard Your Baby's Health'; inside back face of binding seven numbered illus of the Belle Ewart organization, i.e., views of plants, office, ice harvesting, branch depots, horse-drawn van, truck, and the Belle Ewart Man carrying a block of ice held in tongs; outside back face addresses of 'Branch offices and yards' in Toronto and 'Printed in Canada'
COPIES: *Private collection
NOTES: 'Second edition' is on the front face of the binding. The women in the illustrations wear 1920s fashions.

Tried and true recipes

O556.1 1925

Tried and true recipes / 1854 [photograph of the church] 1925 / Arranged by the Ladies' Aid Society of / MacNab Street Presbyterian Church / Hamilton, Canada / Index / Soups Page 3 / Fish 4 / Meats 7 / Vegetables 9 / Salads 11 / Pickles 13 / Sauces 19 / Puddings 20 / Pastry 24 / Light desserts 28 / Bread and biscuits 31 / Cakes 35 / Small cakes 43 / Supper dishes 47 / Breakfast dishes 48 / Preserves 51 / Beverages 55 / Sandwiches 57 / Candy 59 / Table of measures 61 / Household hints 61 / Please favor our advertisers with your patronage / Heath & Fairclough, printers, 13 Charles Street.

DESCRIPTION: 23.0 × 14.5 cm   Pp [1] 2–64   Tp photograph of the church   Paper; stapled?

CONTENTS: 1 tp and 'Index' [i.e., table of contents]; 2 ads; 3–64 text and ads

COPIES: *OH (R641.5 H183 CESH)

NOTES: The cover-title is 'Choice Recipes.' The recipes are credited with the name of the contributor.

1925–6

New Jell-O recipes

For the titles of other books for cooking with Jell-O, see O212.1.

O557.1   copyright 1925–6

New / Jell-O / recipes / ©1925–1926 by the Jell-O Co Inc [cover-title]

DESCRIPTION: 11.0 × 15.5 cm   Pp 1–18   Illus col   Paper, with image on front of a woman removing a mould from jelly; stapled

CONTENTS: 1–15 recipes, and illus of prepared dishes on pp 3–4, 7–8, 11–12, and 15; 16 'Jell-O Perfection'; 17 'About the New Recipes'; 18 'Jell-O Rules'

COPIES: *ACG   OGU (CCC TX715.6 N485)   OONL (TX715 C3465 No. 12, 2 copies)

NOTES: The text contains twelve new recipes in amongst old familiar ones, according to p 17. Unusually, the odd-numbered pages are versos, the even-numbered pages, rectos. 'Printed in Canada // Standard Litho. Co. Limited Toronto' and the publisher, 'The Jell-O Company of Canada, Limited, Bridgeburg, Ont.,' are printed on the outside back face of the binding.

AMERICAN EDITIONS: 1925–6 (Allen, p 198).

Radio recipe note book

O558.1   nd [about 1925–6]

Radio / recipe / note / book / Radio Cooking School / each Friday at 11 a.m. / Reliable Battery Station C.K.C.L. / Prince George Hotel, Toronto / By the / Home Service Dept. / of the / Consumers' Gas Company / Toronto, Ontario / Telephone Main 8371 [cover-title]

DESCRIPTION: 18.5 × 11.5 cm   Pp 1–48   Paper, with image on front of a woman's head by a radio microphone; stapled

CONTENTS: 1–2 'Index' [headings, followed by spaces, for Cake, Confections, Cereals, Desserts, Drinks, Eggs, Fruits, Meats, Pastry, Pickles, Preserves, Salads, Sauces, Soups, Vegetables, and Miscellaneous]; 3–48 blank, ruled pages for manuscript recipes

COPIES: *Private collection

NOTES: This cookbook was to be used in conjunction with the Radio Cooking School; recipes were to be handwritten in the space provided. A note on the inside back face of the binding explains: 'All possessors of this note book are enrolled members of the [Radio Cooking] School. Miss Eaton will be glad to hear from her radio students.' Below this text there is an illustration of the 'C.K.C.L. Studio, Prince George Hotel, Toronto' from which the program was broadcast. On the inside front face of the binding, there is an advertisement for 'Lectures and Demonstrations for Home-makers' and for a 'Business Girls' Course.' At the head of some of the blank pages are aphorisms, e.g., 'Make him a contented man,' or 'A good breakfast is a good start,' or reminders such as 'Meet Miss Eaton at the Weekly Home Service Demonstration.'

Radio Recipe Note Book is undated and Miss Eaton's first name and position are not recorded in the booklet; however, the Home Service Department's first broadcast was aired on Toronto station CKCL on 22 May 1925 (a dated recipe sheet for Broadcast No. 1 is in a private collection), and Miss Gladys Eaton is named as director of the Home Service Department in articles and radio schedules in 1925 issues of Toronto's *Globe* newspaper. The Radio Cooking School was broadcast each Friday at 11 a.m. (see, for example, the radio schedules in the *Globe* for 1925; the first newspaper listing is for 29 May 1925, one week after the dated recipe sheet for Broadcast No. 1). According to the article 'A Cooking School of the Air' in the *Canadian Magazine* (September 1930), p 34, no trade names were used and 'a special recipe note book' was sent on request to every woman who wrote for it, 'a handy affair in which she can take down each lesson.' Beginning in November 1925, under Gladys Eaton, the Radio Cooking School hosted an annual dinner party for Toronto women (see 'Homemakers Attend Crowded Radio Party,' *Globe* 20 November 1925, p 14, and the photograph of Gladys Eaton addressing the throng of 1,400 women, p 15).

Some time in 1926, Miss Helen Wilson took over as director from Eaton; therefore, *Radio Recipe Note Book* was published about 1925–6. This approximate date of publication is confirmed by the telephone number in the cover-title – Main 8371. Toronto city directories list this telephone number for Consumers' Gas Co.'s domestic appliance showroom at 55 Adelaide Street East for the years 1925–8 (in 1924 and before, for the same address, the number was Adelaide 2180; in 1929 and later, it was Adelaide 9221).

On the outside back face of the binding, there is a note about 'the gas business,' which has 'served in Toronto for over seventy-five years ...' Consumers' Gas Co. was incorporated in 1848 and celebrated its seventy-fifth anniversary in 1923.

Wilson served as director of the Home Service Department from 1926 to 1928; she was succeeded by Jessie Read in 1929 (for Read's career, see O830.1).

1925–7

Bradbury, Adam H.

See O374.1 for information about Canadian Milk Products Ltd and its other cookbooks.

O559.1   nd [about 1925–7]
C.M.P. / bakery / formulas / compiled by / A.H. Bradbury / Toronto / Canadian Milk Products Limited / Head office 347 Adelaide St. West / Telephone Adelaide 0145 / Toronto 2, Canada. [cover-title]
DESCRIPTION: 15.5 × 9.0 cm   Pp [1–23]   Paper; hinged at top edge with two metal fasteners, each creating a hole for hanging
CONTENTS: 1 [recto] 'Method for Handling Doughs with Milk Powder'; all verso pages blank; 3 recipes for One Hour Dough, Two Hour Dough; 5 Three Hour Dough, Four Hour Dough; 7 Five Hour Dough; 9 'Condensed Milk'; 11 100% Whole Wheat Bread Two Hour Dough; 13 Sweet Dough Formulas for All Sweet Dough Goods; 15 Three Hour Bun Dough; 17 Custard Pie Filling; 19 Lemon Pie Filling, Lemon Jumbles; 21 Lemon Jelly Roll Two Pans, Lemon Cookies; 23 Lemon Layer Cake
COPIES: *Private collection

NOTES: All the recipes specify commercial quantities of ingredients. On the outside back face of the binding there are three cartoon characters, with the caption, 'John Dough and his two best friends [i.e., Milkstock and Trumilk].' The head office of Canadian Milk Products was at 347 Adelaide Street West from 1925 to 1927. The Toronto city directory for 1924 lists Adam H. Bradbury, salesman for the company, living at 74 Geary Avenue; the 1926 and 1927 directories give his home address as 6 Forsyth Road. The 1925 directory does not list Bradbury, but says of Forsyth Road, 'not built on'; Bradbury may have been moving to his new house on Forsyth when the 1925 directory was compiled.

The Chapleau cook book

See O567.1 for this book, which belongs here. The advertisement for Canadian Packing Co., which merged in 1927 with other firms to make Canada Packers Ltd, limits publication to no later than 1927.

Recipes: Attractive, nutritious, economical

For information about Gunns Ltd and its cookbooks, see O353.1.

O560.1   nd [about 1925–7]
Recipes / Attractive / nutritious / economical / Easifirst / Shortening / made by / Gunns Ltd. / Toronto [cover-title]
DESCRIPTION: 19.5 × 13.5 cm   Pp 1–32   Illus   Paper, with stylized image on front of two steaming bowls with handles; stapled
CONTENTS: 1 'A Foreword,' 'How to Measure,' 'Tables of Weights and Measurements,' and 'Abbreviations'; 2–27 recipes; 28–9 'Afternoon Tea Suggestions'; 30 'Table Service'; 31–2 'Index'
COPIES: *QMMMCM (AR-M2000.62.12)
NOTES: The 'Foreword' states that 'this little book of recipes ... has been prepared by a graduate of the Department of Household Science of the University of Toronto ...' From appearances, *Recipes: Attractive, Nutritious, Economical* was published later than another cookbook by the same company, O426.1, *Recipes: Wholesome, Nutritious, Economical*. I have not compared the texts of the two titles to determine whether they are related. Neither book was published after 1927, the year that Gunns Ltd merged with two other companies to form Canada Packers Ltd.

1925–8

Cook book souvenir of Manitoulin Island

In about 1950, the same Woman's Auxiliary published
Souvenir of Manitoulin Island (OONL).

O561.1   nd [about 1925–8]
Cook book / souvenir of / Manitoulin Island / Price
$1.00 / Compiled by / Women's Auxillary [*sic*] of
Little Current [cover-title]
DESCRIPTION: 22.5 × 15.0 cm   Pp [1] 2–170   1 fold-
out pl opp p 51 of 'Gore Bay as seen from the West
Bluff,' 10 fp illus of scenes of Manitoulin Island,
1 map of Manitoulin Island, illus   Cloth
CONTENTS: 1 endpaper ad glued to binding; 2–7 ads;
8 note about the importance of good cooking; 9 'Preface'; 10–146 recipes credited with the name of the
contributor; 147 ad; 148–52 'Diet' for fat persons; 153
ads; 154 'Butter Making'; 155 fp illus; 156–64 'Household Hints'; 165 ad; 166 'Time Table for Cooking,'
'Standardized Oven Temperatures,' and 'Weights
and Measures'; 167 blank for manuscript recipes;
168 index; 169–70 [endpaper glued to binding] ads
COPIES: *OGU (UA s045 b31)
NOTES: The cookbook was produced to raise money
'to aid in the work of the Woman's [*sic*] Auxiliary of
Holy Trinity Church, Little Current' (p 9). It must
have been published in the 1920s, before 1929: There
is an advertisement on p 170 for Byron H. Turner Co.,
'incorporated 1921'; and an advertisement on p 110,
placed by the Little Current Board of Trade, which
states, '... a motor road connecting the Manitoulin
with the great highway systems of the province at
Little Current will be completed in 1928.' A modern
facsimile was available for sale from the Michael's
Bay Historical Society in 2006.

1925–9

Brodie, Jean

The Toronto author Jean Brodie supervised the testing of
the recipes in Q203.1, A Guide to Good Cooking
published by Lake of the Woods Milling Co.

O562.1   nd [about 1925–9]
100 / tested / recipes / by / Jean Brodie / The /
Farmers / Dairy [cover-title]
DESCRIPTION: 17.0 × 12.5 cm   Pp [1–5] 6–25 [26–32]
Still-life on p 1 of a milk bottle, sifter, spoon, measur-
ing cup, and two eggs   Paper; stapled

CONTENTS: 1 untitled introductory text signed Jean
Brodie; 2 'Nature's Basic Food' [i.e., milk]; 3 'Milk in
Cooking'; 4–5 'The Farmers Dairy'; 6–25 recipes
using milk as an ingredient; 26–30 blank for 'Your
Favorite Recipes'; 31 'Measurements'; 32 'Index –
Table of Contents'
COPIES: *Private collection
NOTES: 'The Farmers Dairy' on pp 4–5 presents information about the publisher: 'A number of Ontario's
biggest and most progressive milk producing farmers own and control the Farmers Dairy ... The Farmers Dairy plant in Toronto covers a whole city block
... We are proud of our fine horses and of our clean
white wagons.' The plant referred to had been built
in 1915 at Walmer Road and Bridgman Street. According to Thomas/Marchant, pp 13–19, Farmers
Dairy was formed in 1909, and in 1929 consolidated
with two other dairies, at which point its name
changed to Acme Farmers Dairy. The cookbook, therefore, was published no later than 1929.

The Quaker method of easy bread baking

For other cookbooks promoting Quaker products, see
O699.1, Helpful Hints for the Housewife, and
O1113.1, Alden, Mary, 26 Delicious New Recipes.

The Quaker Oats Co. was incorporated in the United
States, in 1901, as a holding company for the American
Cereal Co., formed in 1888 by the amalgamation of seven
milling companies (one was the Quaker Mill Co., which
had registered the Quaker man as its trade mark in
1877). In the same year that Quaker Oats Co. was
incorporated – 1901 – it built a mill in Peterborough,
Ontario, and established its Canadian headquarters there.
In 1912, the company purchased a mill in Saskatoon,
Saskatchewan. Fire destroyed the Peterborough plant in
1916, but it was rebuilt in 1918. The Quaker Oats
Company of Canada Ltd was incorporated as an autono-
mously managed subsidiary of the American parent
company in 1943. In 2001 the company merged with
PepsiCo Inc.

Some editions of The Quaker Method of Easy Bread
Baking *ask the reader to send letters to Saskatoon; others*
give the Peterborough address. Entries for the book are
located in the Ontario section of this bibliography because
the head office was (and remains) in Peterborough.

O563.1   [1st ed.?], nd [about 1925–9]
New Quaker easy way / The / Quaker / method of
/ easy bread / baking / A / wonderful / new, easy,
/ quicker / way of / baking / delicious / bread and
/ Parker / House / rolls

DESCRIPTION: 16.5 × 12.5 cm   Pp [3] 4–18   Tp illus of the Quaker man's head, illus   Lacks paper binding; stapled
CONTENTS: 3 tp; 4–16 'The New Quaker Method' in text and illus; 17–mid 18 'An Army of Thrifty, Needle-wise Women Make Dainty, Useful Articles with the Generous Length of Fine Quality Cotton That Comes with Every Sack of Quaker Flour'
COPIES: *OONL (TX769 Q34 1920z copy 2)
NOTES: The text ends at middle p 18 with the following request: 'Perhaps you have found a use for Quaker Flour sacks which might interest other women ... Please send your letter [with ideas for uses] to: The Quaker Oats Company, Saskatoon, Sask.' In the later editions described below, some of the letters received in response to the company's appeal are printed on pp 18–19. Since the letters printed in O563.2 are dated March 1930, this edition, probably the first, was likely published in the late 1920s. OONL (TX769 Q34 1920z copy 1) is missing and may or may not match copy 2.

An order form for the cookbook is in a Quaker advertisement in *Nor'-West Farmer and Farm and Home* Vol. 50, No. 6 (20 March 1931), p 24, where the book is reported to have 'helped thousands of women'; there are order forms in other issues in 1931, but not in 1932. Chatelaine 1935, p 82, also lists this title, but does not specify the edition.

O563.2   nd [about 1930]
—New Quaker easy way / The / Quaker / method of / easy bread / baking / A / wonderful / new, easy, / quicker / way of / baking / delicious / bread and / Parker / House / rolls
DESCRIPTION: 16.5 × 12.5 cm   Pp [3] 4–19   Tp illus of the Quaker man's head, illus   Paper, with image on front of the man's head from Quaker packages; stapled
CONTENTS: 3 tp; 4–16 'The New Quaker Method' in text and illus; 17–mid 18 'An Army of Thrifty, Needle-wise Women Make Dainty, Useful Articles with the Generous Length of Fine Quality Cotton That Comes with Every Sack of Quaker Flour'; mid 18–19 [inside back face of binding] 'Letters from Enthusiastic Home-Bakers Using the Quaker Easy Method,' all dated March 1930 and addressed to the Quaker Oats Co., Peterborough, Ontario
COPIES: *Private collection
NOTES: A note printed on the inside front face of the binding states, 'Instructions on bread baking given in this booklet are included and printed by special arrangement with Mr. P.O. Walker, Denver, Colorado, U.S.A., and are taken from his booklet "Walker's Method of Easy Bread Baking," which booklet is copyrighted in both United States and Canada.'

O563.3   nd
—New Quaker easy way / The / Quaker / method of / easy bread / baking / A / wonderful / new, easy, / quicker / way of / baking / delicious / bread and / Parker / House / rolls
DESCRIPTION: 16.5 × 12.5 cm   Pp [3] 4–18   Tp illus of the Quaker man's head, illus   Lacks binding
CONTENTS: 3 tp; 4–16 'The New Quaker Method' in text and illus; 17–mid 18 'An Army of Thrifty, Needle-wise Women Make Dainty, Useful Articles with the Generous Length of Fine Quality Cotton That Comes with Every Sack of Quaker Flour'; mid–bottom 18 'Letters from Enthusiastic Home-Bakers Using the Quaker Easy Method' [two undated letters]
COPIES: *Private collection
NOTES: The reader is asked to send letters to Saskatoon, Saskatchewan.

O563.4   nd
—New Quaker easy way / The / Quaker / method of / easy bread / baking / A / wonderful / new, easy, / quicker / way of / baking / delicious / bread and / Parker / House / rolls
DESCRIPTION: 16.5 × 12.5 cm   Pp [3] 4–19   Tp illus of the Quaker man's head, illus   Paper, with image on front of the man's head from Quaker packages; stapled
CONTENTS: 3 tp; 4–16 'The New Quaker Method' in text and illus; 17–mid 18 'An Army of Thrifty, Needle-wise Women Make Dainty, Useful Articles with the Generous Length of Fine Quality Cotton That Comes with Every Sack of Quaker Flour'; mid 18–19 'Excerpts of Letters from Enthusiastic Home-Bakers Using the Quaker Easy Method' [eight undated letters, five of which are addressed to the the company's Peterborough location and three to the Saskatoon location]
COPIES: *NSWA
NOTES: This edition offers 'Excerpts of Letters from ...' on p 18, whereas O563.2 and O563.3 offer 'Letters from ...' Like O563.2, there is a note on the inside front face of the binding attributing the bread baking instructions to 'Walker's Method of Easy Bread Baking.'

O563.5   nd [about 1935–9]
—The / Quaker method / of / easy bread / baking / A wonderful new, easy, / quicker way of bak- / ing delicious bread and / Parker House rolls. / [across bottom of inside front face of binding and title-page:] Bake better bread and rolls ... the new Quaker easy way
DESCRIPTION: Pp [1–16]   Small tp illus of the Quaker Oats man, illus   With large image on front of baked

bread and rolls, and small tp illus above the bread and rolls; stapled

CONTENTS: 1 tp; 2–14 'The New Quaker Method' in text and illus; 15 'Here's What Enthusiastic Home Bakers Say about the Quaker Method of Easy Bread Baking' [testimonials from women in various Canadian provinces]; 16 'Look at the Many Lovely and Useful Things You Can Make with the Fine Quality Cotton You Get in Every Quaker Flour Sack'; inside back face of binding reference to Quaker Premium Catalogue No. 11

COPIES: *Company collection (Quaker Oats Company of Canada Ltd, Peterborough, Ontario)

NOTES: This is a later, redesigned and reset edition. The first two pages of introductory text after the title-page have been rewritten. Earlier editions feature a man demonstrating the cooking instructions; here the demonstrator is an aproned woman. As in earlier editions, there is a note on the inside front face of the binding attributing the bread baking instructions to 'Walker's Method of Easy Bread Baking.'

1925–30

After all it takes a baker

See also O575.1, Swift's Bakers' Pastry Shortening in the Bakeshop, *and O871.1,* Vreamay Icings and Fillings, *both by Swift Canadian Co. for professional bakers.*

O564.1   nd [about 1925–30]
After all it takes / a baker / [Swift Canadian Co. Ltd symbol] / Swift Canadian Co. / Limited / Canada
DESCRIPTION: About 18.0 × 12.5 cm [dimensions from photocopy]   Pp [1–2] 3–50 [51–2]   Illus   With image on front of a three-layer cake, a pie, and a plate of doughnuts; stapled
CONTENTS: 1 tp; 2 'Foreword'; 3–6 'Vream Bakery-Tested Formulas'; ...; 50 fp illus of 'Swift's Experimental Bakery'; 51 blank; 52 'Index'
COPIES: *Private collection
NOTES: No place of publication is recorded, but Swift Canadian Co.'s head office was in Toronto. The 'Foreword' states: 'This booklet has been prepared for bakers ... The formulas [i.e., the recipes] printed in this booklet have been developed about the qualities of Vream, the all hydrogenated vegetable shortening of Swift Canadian Co., Limited ... This booklet will be followed by others of like purpose furthering the

welfare of the baking industry ...' On p 3, the text refers to the installation 'some years ago' of 'an Experimental Bakery to be used in connection with the production and use of our various baking ingredient materials'; this bakery is illustrated on p 50. The 'Index' lists the following recipe sections, starting on p 7: '"Homemade" Cake from the Bake Shop'; 'Dressing the Cake – Changes in Icing Types'; 'Fruit Sauces'; 'Pie – A Dessert of Growing Popularity'; 'Pie Fillers and Pie Formulas'; and 'Doughnuts.' The recipes make commercial amounts.

Baumert Cheese recipes

For other cookbooks promoting Baumert Cheese, see O574.1, Recipes You Have Never Tried, *and O589.1,* New Recipes Baumert Cheese.

O565.1   nd [about 1925–30]
Baumert / Cheese recipes [cover-title]
DESCRIPTION: 16.5 × 12.0 cm   Pp [1–2] 3–30   Illus col of prepared dishes, centre spread illus col of 'Varieties of Baumert Cheese,' 5 illus on p 18 titled 'A Partial Group of Plants Owned and Operated by F.X. Baumert & Co. Inc.'   Paper, with image on front of a woman seated on a stool, holding a plate of food; stapled
CONTENTS: 1 cover-title; 2 table of contents; 3 'In Praise of Cheese'; 4–7 'Nourishing Cooked Dishes'; 8–11 'Cheese and Vegetable Salads'; 12–15 'Cheese and Fruit Salads' [p 14 incorrectly headed 'Cheese and Vegetable Salads']; 16–17 centre spread illus col; 18 illus of 'A Partial Group of Plants ...'; 19 'Why Baumert Cheese Is Better' and F.X. Baumert and Co.'s New York address and a list of its Canadian offices at Huntingdon, Que., Montreal, and Toronto; 20–3 'Tasty Cheese Sandwiches'; 24–7 'Appetizing Cheese Relishes'; 28–9 'Delicious Cheese Desserts'; 30 'Table of Weights and Measures'; inside back face of binding index of recipes arranged alphabetically under their section headings; outside back face 'Compliments of Chateau Cheese Co. Ltd. Ottawa'
CITATIONS: Chatelaine 1935, p 82
COPIES: *OTMCL (641.5971 H39 No. 1)
NOTES: The company history on p 19 refers to the establishment of F.X. Baumert and Co. Inc. in 1857. Its dairy herds were in Jefferson County, New York State.

Beach automatic oven cooking

The AutomatiCook was an oven heat controller for gas ranges, developed in the United States. Beach Foundry, an Ottawa company, likely distributed, rather than manufactured, the heat controller. Beach Foundry was established in 1894 in Winchester, Ontario, under the name B.C. Beach and Co.; it moved to Ottawa in about 1914 (see the 1941 issue of Hardware and Metal, *the Canadian trade magazine; copy at OTMCL). See also O591.1,* The AutomatiCook Book, *published about the same time as O566.1, and a later work, O842.1,* Beach Frozen Dainties and Other Recipes.

O566.1 nd [about 1925–30]
Beach / automatic / oven / cooking / Approved / times / temperatures/ and / tested recipes / Beach Foundry Limited / Ottawa / Toronto Winnipeg Calgary Vancouver
DESCRIPTION: 21.5 × 14.0 cm   Pp 1–16   Illus of Robertshaw AutomatiCook on each page   Paper, with image on front of a woman, dressed in coat and hat, adjusting her AutomatiCook; stapled
CONTENTS: 1 'Requires No Experience' and 'The AutomatiCook'; 2–mid 3 'Cooking Chart'; mid–bottom 3 'Hints for Cake Baking'; 4–5 'Automatic Cooking // Directions'; 6 'A Few Suggestions for Whole Meals'; 7 'Oven Canning Instructions'; 8 'Beach Oven Canning Chart'; 9–16 'Beach's Tested Time and Temperature Recipes'
COPIES: *AEEA   CIHM (81736)   OONL (TX657 O6 B43 1920z p***)

The Chapleau cook book

O567.1 nd
The / Chapleau / cook book / We thank one and all for their kind as- /sistance in the production of this / useful cook book, and specially commend / to the users the wares of the merchants / whose advertisements appear herein. [cover-title]
DESCRIPTION: 17.0 × 12.5 cm   Pp [1–2] 3–79   Paper, with small image on front of a male servant, in profile, carrying a covered dish; stapled
CONTENTS: 1 'Index' [i.e., table of contents]; 2 ads; 3–75 recipes credited with the name of the contributor and ads; 76–7 'Household Hints'; 78 'Table for Kitchen Use' and at bottom, 'Compiled and arranged by the Woman's Auxiliary of St. John's Church // Chapleau, Ont.'; 79 ad for Canadian Packing Co.
COPIES: *Private collection
NOTES: 'The Chapleau Printing Co.' is on the outside

back face of the binding. The advertisements refer to the industries that drove the economy of this Northern Ontario town; for example, that on p 17 for Crawley and McCracken Co. Ltd, 84 St Antoine Street, Montreal, boasts, 'We feed your men' in lumber camps, mining camps, and pulp mills; and that on p 37 is for Wm McLeod, general merchant, Chapleau: 'Dealer in raw furs // Canoes and guides furnished // Chestnut canoes always on hand // Special attention paid to survey parties.' The book was published about 1925–7; see cross-reference on p 645.

Favorite recipes

The Fairfield Women's Institute was founded in Wentworth County in 1919 and disbanded in 1963 (Ambrose, p 236).

O568.1 nd [about 1925–30]
Favorite recipes / Contributed by members and friends of / the Fairfield Women's / Institute / For home and / country / [introductory note of two paragraphs]
COPIES: *Private collection
NOTES: The cover-title is 'Selected Recipes.' The owner reports that the book has 95 pp and that the advertisements are for Hamilton businesses.

The Flesherton Advance cook book

O569.1 nd [about 1925–30]
The Flesherton / Advance / cook book / Compiled from recipes presented / by readers of the Advance / Price 10 cents [cover-title]
CONTENTS: 1st page 'Index' [i.e., table of contents]; ...
COPIES: *Private collection
NOTES: The book has 55 pp. The recipes are credited with the name of the contributor. A review of issues of the *Flesherton Advance* newspaper would reveal when the newspaper made an appeal for recipes and when the cookbook was published.

Good cooking

For information about Dr Pierce's medical business and another advertising booklet, see O457.1.

O570.1 nd [about 1925–30]
Good / cooking / Useful / information / Read / it. [cover-title]

DESCRIPTION: 18.0 × 12.5 cm   Pp [1] 2–32   Paper, with image on front of a woman and a girl looking at a boy sneaking a taste of a dish on a table; with hole punched at top left corner for hanging
CONTENTS: 1–32 text and ads
COPIES: AHRMH (994-001-072)   APROM   BBVM   CIHM (79790)   *OGU (UA s076 b26)   OMAHM (993.16.15)   OONL (RM671 A1 P38 No. 13, 2 copies)   OTMCL (641.5971 H39 No. 106)   OTUTF (uncat patent medicine)   OTYA (CPC 19-? 0072)   OWTU (F14224)   QMM (RBD ckbk 2122)   QSH (0425)   SSWD
NOTES: On p 1 there is a note signed 'World's Dispensary Medical Association, Bridgeburg, Ont.' There are advertisements and testimonials for Dr Pierce's health products. 'Murray Printing Co., Limited, Toronto' is on the outside back face of the binding.

Housser, Levi (South Cayuga, Ont., 1 January 1893–21 January 1983, Dunnville, Ont.)

Only the author's first initial is recorded in the book, but he was Levi Housser, the youngest of three children born to Sarah and Franklin Housser. Martha and Samuel were his older siblings, and he had a half-brother Jacob from Franklin's first marriage. The family was Mennonite and did not believe in formal education, but Levi is remembered as being especially clever. Although he was not a licensed medical doctor, he had strong opinions about health and diet, and he treated people in the community. A descendant has a painted sign announcing Dr L. Housser, chiropractor and natureology electric baths. In his early years he travelled to British Columbia, where he worked as a carpenter, suffering a fall that left one leg shorter than the other. Back in Ontario, he ran a peach farm near Beamsville. He also built a house near Dunnville and owned a few acres of bush in the country around Hawkesville (northwest of Kitchener), from which he harvested wood. Levi never married. He is buried in South Cayuga Mennonite Cemetery.

O571.1   nd [about 1925–30]
How / to / live / and keep / well / (Why be sick) / By L. Housser / Beamsville, Ont. [cover-title]
DESCRIPTION: 23.0 × about 15.0 cm   Pp 1–282 [283]   Thin card
CONTENTS: 1–7 'Introduction'; 8–281 text; 282–3 'Index' [i.e., table of contents]
COPIES: *OTUTF (jah)
NOTES: The title on the spine is 'Home Remedies.'

Housser promotes a diet based on nature and the Bible. In the section called 'Cooking,' on pp 57–62, he gives instructions and offers his thoughts on various cooking techniques. He is against the over-cooking of vegetables and advises never to use aluminium pots. There is a section on 'Herbs and Their Uses' on pp 158–98. On p 6 he refers to his special blood builder, Housser's Stomach, Liver and Blood Purifier; however, the book does not appear to have been written exclusively as a vehicle to promote the product.

How to Live and Keep Well was published after the announcement of the discovery of insulin in 1922, but likely before the new treatment for diabetes was well understood by the public. On p 62 Housser writes, 'Since the insulin has been given to the public, ...' He calls diabetes a 'money making disease' since, in his view, insulin doesn't effect a cure, but keeps the disease in a 'stagnant position'; he believed that proper diet is the answer.

The Markdale Standard cook book

O572.1   [about 1925–30]
[An edition of *The Markdale Standard Cook Book*, pp 74]
COPIES: Private collection
NOTES: The private collector's copy lacks its binding. The title is taken from the running head. The recipes are credited with the names of the contributors; for example, on p 3, Mrs Henry Yerkie, Mrs D. Heathers, Mrs J.W. Elliott, Nina Hutchinson, Mrs S.S. Burritt, and Mrs R.G. Snell, all of Markdale except for Mrs Burritt (the grandmother of the current owner of the book), who lived in Kimberley.

Ontario, Provincial Secretary's Department

O573.1   nd [about 1925–30]
[Provincial coat of arms] / Ontario / Standard recipes / used / in the / Ontario / reformatory / canning industry / at / Guelph / The Provincial Secretary's / Department / Parliament Buildings / Toronto, Ontario / Canada
DESCRIPTION: Paper; stapled
COPIES: *Private collection
NOTES: In the 2-page introduction, which he signs L. Goldie, provincial secretary, Lincoln Goldie explains how the institutional activity in the farms and gardens surrounding Ontario's public institutions not only lowers the cost of maintaining the institutions, but provides a healing value for those who are treated

there – a form of occupational therapy. He goes on to say that to secure the maximum use of the farm, orchard, and garden products, canning plants were established at the Ontario Reformatory in Guelph, the Ontario Hospital in London, and the Ontario Hospital in Whitby. The main canning plant was at Guelph, and although the goods were consumed only in the institutions and not sold, the public became aware of the quality of the goods and requested copies of the recipes. This 'pamphlet has been compiled by the officials in charge of the canning operations at the Ontario Reformatory, Guelph, ... [for] the general public ...'

Lincoln Goldie was provincial secretary and registrar for the Ontario Government from 16 July 1923 to 12 September 1930. The owner of the book comments that her mother 'used [this copy of *Standard Recipes*] for all canning and was always doing fruit for friends and relations – to perfection!' The home address inscribed on the binding is evidence that this copy came into her mother's possession in the period 1925–31. It has 16 unnumbered pp.

Recipes you have never tried

For the titles of other cookbooks promoting Baumert Cheese, see O565.1.

O574.1 nd [about 1925–30]
Recipes / you have / never tried / Baumert / Cream / Cheese [cover-title]
DESCRIPTION: 16.0 × 8.5 cm   Pp [1–3] 4–14   Illus on p 2 of the head-and-shoulders of a young girl(?) Paper, with image on front of a partly opened package of Baumert Cream Cheese; stapled
CONTENTS: 1 cover-title; 2 'Baumert Cheese sales office Ottawa Canada // manufacturers and importers of fancy cheese'; 3 'Foreword'; 4 untitled text about the packaging and manufacture of Baumert Cream Cheese; 5–top 7 'Suggested Breakfast Combinations' and 'Breakfast Main Dishes'; mid 7–mid 9 'Afternoon Tea Suggestions'; mid 9–11 'Salads'; 12–13 'Hot Sandwiches'; 14 'Supper Dishes'
CITATIONS: Chatelaine 1935, p 82
COPIES: *Private collection
NOTES: Chatelaine 1935 cites 'Recipes You Have Never Tried (French and English),' free upon request from Chateau Cheese Co. Ltd. I have not located a copy of the French-language version.

Swift's Bakers' Pastry Shortening in the bakeshop

See O564.1 for cookbooks by Swift Canadian Co. for professional bakers.

O575.1 nd [about 1925–30]
Swift's / Bakers' Pastry / Shortening / in the / bakeshop / for puff paste / and / French pastry / [symbol of Swift Canadian Co. Ltd] / Swift Canadian Co. / Limited / Bakery Research Laboratories
DESCRIPTION: 17.0 × 12.5 cm   Pp [1–2] 3–15   Illus of baked goods   Paper; stapled
CONTENTS: 1 tp; 2 'Introduction'; 3 'Swift's Bakers' Pastry Shortening'; 4–mid 6 'Puff Paste' recipe; mid 6–15 'Puff Paste Products Made with Swift's Bakers' Pastry' [i.e., recipes made with the shortening]
COPIES: *Private collection
NOTES: No place of publication is recorded, but the company's head office was in Toronto.

1926

The art of sandwich making

The Canada Bread Co. was formed in 1911, as a consolidation of several large Canadian bread manufacturing businesses, one of which was the Bredin Bread Co. of Toronto (see 'Bread Industry Revolutionized by Organization Here of Canada Bread Company, Ltd.,' Monetary Times Vol. 47, No. 7 (12 August 1911), p 726). The Canada Bread Co.'s head office was, and still is, in Toronto. For another cookbook by the company, see O765.1, Master Chef Recipes for the Use of Bread.

O576.1 nd [about 1926]
A collection of / famous – and / fashionable / sandwiches / The art / of / sandwich / making [cover-title]
DESCRIPTION: 15.0 × 11.5 cm   Pp [1–20]   Illus col, illus   Paper, with image on front of a maid carrying a tray of sandwiches and tea; stapled
CONTENTS: Inside front face of binding 'How It All Started'; 1 'And To-day'; 2 'Some Hints before You Begin'; 3–20 recipes; inside back face 'Canada Bread'
COPIES: QMM (RBD ckbk 1390)   *Private collection
NOTES: 'How It All Started' refers to the discovery of the sandwich by the Earl of Sandwich in 1758, 'only 168 years ago'; therefore, this booklet was published about 1926 (1758 + 168 years). Under 'Canada Bread,'

one learns that 'This great all-Canadian baking company is the out-growth of a business founded about 40 years ago by Mr. Mark Bredin, now President of the Canada Bread Company.' It was a national company with customers in 'eleven of the principal cities in Canada.'

See pl 8. The stylized image on the binding is dramatic: The stark black of the maid's dress contrasts with a bright yellow and orange background, framed by a purple border. The title is printed on the oversized skirt of the maid's dress, and the tail of the 'g' in 'Making' is exaggerated so that it echoes the round shape of the skirt. The illustrations are carefully composed still-lifes of sandwiches, and tea or coffee pots and cups, in shiny silver or patterned china. On the inside back face of the binding, there is a black-line illustration of a Canada Bread horse-drawn delivery cart.

On p 2 the cook is advised to remove all the crusts from the loaf before slicing because 'this prevents waste of butter and keeps the sandwiches in good shape.' The crusts are to be kept for breadcrumbs. There is a recipe for fashionable Club Sandwiches on p 7, which specifies three slices of toast per person, one layer of chicken (or pork), lettuce, and mayonnaise, and one layer of bacon, tomatoes, and mayonnaise.

O576.2 nd [about 1926]
—Recueil de / fameux et / fashionables / sandwiches / L'art / de / faire des / sandwiches [cover-title]
DESCRIPTION: 15.0 × 11.5 cm Pp [1–20] Illus col, illus Paper, with image on front of a maid carrying a tray of sandwiches and tea; stapled
CONTENTS: Inside front face of binding 'Son origine'; 1 'Et aujourd'hui'; 2 'Quelques conseils avant de commencer'; 3–20 recipes; inside back face 'Le pain "Canada Bread"'
COPIES: *Private collection
NOTES: The French-language edition was published about the same time as the English-language edition since 'Son origine' states, 'Toutefois il n'y a que 168 ans passés faisait le premier sandwich.'

Boy Scout home cooking recipes

The 3rd St Thomas Troop produced a cookbook with the same title about a year later, O592.1.

O577.1 nd [1926]
Boy Scout / home / cooking / recipes / Obtained from parents and friends of the boys / Price twenty-five cents / Issued by the / 1st Chatham Troop Boy Scouts / Chatham, Ontario [cover-title]
DESCRIPTION: Pp [1] 2–72 With image on front of the head of a Boy Scout; stapled
CONTENTS: 1–72 recipes and ads
COPIES: *Private collection
NOTES: The running head is 'Boy Scout Cook Book.' 'The News Job Printing Department' is on the outside back face of the binding. An advertisement on p 9 for William Rennie Co. Ltd, which cites *Rennie's 1926 Seed Annual*, points to publication of the cookbook in 1926.

Chase, Dr Alvin Wood (Cayuga County, NY, 20 March 1817–25 May 1885, Ohio)

See O535.1 for other years of the calendar almanac. For information about Dr Chase and his other publications, see O8.1.

O578.1 1926
Hang me up / Dr. A.W. Chase's / calendar almanac / 1926 / for the / home, factory / farm, office / Published by / the Dr. A.W. Chase Medicine Co. / Limited / Toronto Canada [cover-title]
DESCRIPTION: 21.0 × 15.0 cm Pp [3] 4–50 Illus Paper, with image on front of Dr Chase and his signature; stapled, and with hole punched at top left corner for hanging
CONTENTS: 3 zodiacal signs, festivals and anniversaries, stars, and eclipses for 1926; 4–5 'A Success Story'; 6–50 monthly calendars, 'Tested Recipes' (pp 7, 19, 31, 39), 'Helpful Suggestions' (p 29), 'How to Keep Foods' (p 43), 'The Kitchen Sink' (p 47), health and other information, jokes, and testimonials for the publisher's products
COPIES: *Private collection

Cook book

The Chesley branch of the Women's Institute was established in 1910 (Ambrose, p 235).

O579.1 1926
Cook book / compiled by / the Women's Institute / of Chesley, Ontario / 1926 / Officers / Honorary President Mrs. D.G. Leitch / President Mrs. F.A. MacLean / 1st Vice-President Mrs. C.R. Ankenman / 2nd Vice-President Mrs. W. Sutcliffe / Secretary-Treasurer Mrs. Wellington Krug / Press Secretary Mrs. J.E. Truemner / Directors – Mrs. G. Durst; Mrs. B. Wright; Mrs. F. Christoffer

DESCRIPTION: 22.5 × 15.0 cm   Pp [1–5] 6–67   Lacks binding; stapled
CONTENTS: 1 'The proceeds derived from the sale of this book are to be used to beautify Riverside Park.,' 'Institute Mottos and Quotations,' and 'The recipes contained in this book have been tested and are recommended by the contributors.'; 2 'A Card' thanking the advertisers; 3 tp; 4 ads; 5 'Index' [i.e., table of contents]; 6–65 recipes credited with the name of the contributor and ads; 66 ads; 67 'Tables of Weights and Measures'
CITATIONS: Driver 2001, Wellington County, p 97 (note 7)
COPIES: *Private collection
NOTES: This copy is inscribed by the owner, on the title-page, in ball-point pen, 'Mother's book Nelda Hopkins [i.e., the mother] / Hazel D. Wilson [i.e., her daughter].'

Davis dainty dishes

The roots of Davis Gelatine go back to 1881, in Auckland, New Zealand, when Charles George Davis started a small glue factory. The first gelatine plant was built in Christchurch, New Zealand, in 1913, followed in 1918 by the creation of Davis Gelatine Co. Ltd in the Australian state of New South Wales and the construction of a plant in Botany Bay. In 1925 Davis Gelatine (Canada) Ltd was formed to sell imports to Canada and the company is listed in Toronto city directories from 1926. Documents relating to the history of Davis Gelatine are at the Botany Bay Library in New South Wales.

O580.1   nd [1926 or 1929]
Davis / dainty / dishes / Price 25c. [cover-title]
DESCRIPTION: 18.5 × 12.5 cm   Pp [1] 2–48   Several small illus col of gelatine dishes; centre spread of 'The Home of Davis Gelatine, the Largest Works of Its Kind in the World'   Paper, with a checkerboard border and image on front of Asparagus Tip Salad; stapled
CONTENTS: Inside front face of binding 'Davis Gelatine (Canada) Ltd. Toronto 2, Ont. Vancouver, B.C.'; 1 'Foreword'; 2–3 table of contents; 4–45 recipes; 46–7 'Facts You May Not Know'; 48 'Let's Understand Gelatine'; inside back face 'Designed and lithographed in Canada by Smith-Moir Lithographing Co. Limited, Toronto'
COPIES: *Private collection
NOTES: There is no date or edition number; however, from appearances, this is one of the early Canadian editions (1926 or 1929) recorded in O580.2. It is likely

the 1926 edition because it does not have the four-layer 'jelly' Pavlova that appears in the 1927 New Zealand sixth edition (the first recorded instance of a dish called Pavlova, according to Helen Leach of the University of Otago, who has tracked the origins of the Pavlova dessert made with meringue) and in 1932 Toronto editions. Another private collector's copy of O580.1 (not the one described here) is inscribed on p 1, 'Thelma Briggs Mar 21. 1932.' O580.1 is revised for Canada; for example, recipes for peaches and rhubarb replace those for passionfruit and paw paw.

O580.2   [8th ed., 20,000 copies, 1932]
—Davis / dainty / dishes / Price 25 cents [cover-title]
DESCRIPTION: 18.0 × 12.5 cm   Pp [1] 2–48   Illus col of gelatine dishes; centre spread of 'The Home of Davis Gelatine, the Largest Works of Its Kind in the World'   Paper, with a checkerboard border and image on front of a savoury gelatine dish; stapled
CONTENTS: Inside front face of binding publishing history and 'Davis Gelatine (Canada) Limited Toronto 2, Ont. Montreal, Que. Vancouver, B.C.'; 1 'Foreword'; 2 'Let's Understand Gelatine'; 3–45 recipes; 46 'Hints That Will Help'; 47–8 'Contents'; inside back face 'Published by Davis Gelatine (Canada) Limited, ... Wholly set up and printed in Canada by the Hendrick-Jewell Co., Toronto.'
COPIES: OONL (TX715 D35 1932 copy 2)   QMMMCM (AR-M2000.62.9)   *Private collection
NOTES: The publishing history on the binding indicates that this edition is the eighth [i.e., third Canadian], published in 1932, in a run of 20,000 copies:

1st edition:	Australia	1922	– 30,000
	New Zealand	"	– 10,000
	South Africa	"	– 10,000
2nd edition:	Australia	1923	– 30,000
3rd edition:	Australia	1924	– 50,000
	South Africa	"	– 10,000
	New Zealand	"	– 10,000
4th edition:	Australia	1925	– 50,000
	New Zealand	"	– 10,000
5th edition:	Australia	1926	– 50,000
	South Africa	"	– 10,000
	New Zealand	"	– 10,000
	Canada	"	– 25,000
6th edition:	Australia	1927	– 50,000
	South Africa	"	– 10,000
	New Zealand	"	– 10,000

7th edition:	Australia	1929	– 50,000
	South Africa	"	– 20,000
	New Zealand	"	– 20,000
	Canada	"	– 20,000
8th edition:	Australia	1932	– 60,000
	South Africa	"	– 20,000
	New Zealand	"	– 20,000
	Great Britain	"	– 50,000
	Canada	"	– 20,000

O580.3   [8th ed., 40,000 copies, 1932]
—Davis / dainty / dishes / Price 25 cents [cover-title]
DESCRIPTION: 18.0 × 12.5 cm   Pp [1] 2–48   Illus col of gelatine dishes; centre spread of 'The Home of Davis Gelatine, the Largest Works of Its Kind in the World'   Paper, with a checkerboard border and image on front of a savoury gelatine dish; stapled
CONTENTS: Inside front face of binding publishing history and 'Davis Gelatine (Canada) Limited Toronto 2, Ont. Montreal, Que. Vancouver, B.C.'; 1 'Foreword'; 2 'Let's Understand Gelatine'; 3–45 recipes; 46 'Hints That Will Help'; 47–8 'Contents'; inside back face 'Wholly set up and printed in Canada by the Hendrick-Jewell Co., Toronto.'
COPIES: ONLAM (Walters-Wagar Collection, Box 20)   *Private collection
NOTES: The publishing history on the binding is as O580.2, except '8th edition: ... Canada " – 20,000' is replaced by '8th edition: ... Canada " – 40,000.'

O580.4   [8th ed., 60,000 copies, 1932]
—Davis / dainty / dishes / Price 25 cents [cover-title]
DESCRIPTION: 18.0 × 12.5 cm   Pp [1] 2–48   Illus col of gelatine dishes; centre spread of 'The Home of Davis Gelatine, the Largest Works of Its Kind in the World'   Paper, with a checkerboard border and image on front of a savoury gelatine dish; stapled
CONTENTS: Inside front face of binding publishing history and 'Davis Gelatine (Canada) Limited Toronto 2, Ont. Montreal, Que. Vancouver, B.C.'; 1 'Foreword'; 2 'Let's Understand Gelatine'; 3–45 recipes; 46 'Hints That Will Help'; 47–8 'Contents'; inside back face 'Published by Davis Gelatine (Canada) Limited, ... Wholly set up and printed in Canada by the Hunter-Rose Co., Limited, Toronto'
COPIES: *NBMOM   OGU (CCC TX715.6 D31) OONL (TX715 D35 1932 copy 1)
NOTES: The publishing history on the binding is as O580.2, except '8th edition: ... Canada " – 20,000' is replaced by '8th edition: ... Canada " – 60,000.' Note the different printer, Hunter-Rose Co. Ltd.

O580.5   [8th ed., 100,000 copies, 1932]
—Davis / dainty / dishes / Price 25 cents [cover-title]
DESCRIPTION: 18.0 × 12.5 cm   Pp [1] 2–48   Illus col of gelatine dishes; centre spread of 'The Home of Davis Gelatine, the Largest Works of Its Kind in the World'   Paper, with a checkerboard border and image on front of a savoury gelatine dish; stapled
CONTENTS: Inside front face of binding publishing history and 'Davis Gelatine (Canada) Limited Toronto 2, Ont. Montreal, Que. Vancouver, B.C.'; 1 'Foreword'; 2 'Let's Understand Gelatine'; 3–45 recipes; 46 'Hints That Will Help'; 47–8 'Contents'; inside back face 'Wholly set up and printed in Canada by the Murray Printing Co. Limited Toronto'
COPIES: QMM (RBD ckbk 1490)   *Private collection
NOTES: The publishing history on the binding is as O580.2, except '8th edition: ... Canada " – 20,000' is replaced by '8th edition: ... Canada " – 100,000.' Note the different printer, Murray Printing Co. Ltd.

Chatelaine 1935, p 82, cites 'Davis Dainty Dishes,' available upon request, but does not specify the edition.

O580.6   8th ed., 1932
—[Eighth edition of *Mets délicats 'Davis,'* Toronto, Montreal, and Vancouver: 1932, pp 48]
CITATIONS: BouquinsCat 229, No. 333

O580.7   rev. ed., 1938
—Davis dainty dishes / Published by / the Davis Gelatine Organization / Canada, Australia, New Zealand, South Africa, England / Editions 1–8 1922 to 1937 / Revised edition 1938
DESCRIPTION: 18.0 × 12.0 cm   Pp [1–3] 4–67 [68]   Illus col   [$0.50, on binding]   Paper, with image on front of a savoury gelatine dish; stapled
CONTENTS: 1 tp; 2 untitled remarks about the strength and measurement of Davis Gelatine; 3 untitled note about the company's product and this cookbook; 4–6 index; 7–67 text; 68 untitled remarks about the food value of Davis Gelatine and 'Wholly set up and printed in Canada by Brigdens Limited, for the publishers, Davis Gelatine (Canada) Limited'
COPIES: *OONL (TX715 D35 1938 p***)   OTMCL (641.5 D1353)
NOTES: The note on p 3 says of Davis Gelatine, '... for a score of years it has become known in the majority of homes of the chief countries of the British Empire and many lands beyond.' So popular has the gelatine been that 'it has been necessary to print this new Cookery Book in five different languages – English, French, German, Africaans, and Portuguese ...'

One learns on p 56 of the three ways in which gelatine may be set: 'Normally, without the aid of ice or refrigeration; in an ice-box; in a refrigerator.' Alternative instructions were necessary because not all households had ice-boxes or refrigerators in the late 1930s. The index lists recipes for invalid cookery and for children's desserts. On pp 34–5 there is an aerial view of the company's plant in Sydney, Australia, 'the largest gelatine factory in the world.'

Brigdens Ltd was a Toronto printer, at 160–4 Richmond Street West in 1938.

O580.8 rev. ed., 1938
—Mets délicieux Davis / Publié par / l'Organisation Davis Gelatine / Canada, Australie, Nouvelle-Zélande, Afrique-Sud, Angleterre / Éditions 1–8 1922 à 1937 / Édition revisée 1938
DESCRIPTION: With image on front of a savoury gelatine dish
COPIES: *Private collection

O580.9 reprint, 1939
—Davis dainty dishes / Published by / the Davis Gelatine Organization / Canada, Australia, New Zealand, South Africa, England. / Editions 1–8 1922 to 1937 / Revised edition 1938 / Reprinted 1939
DESCRIPTION: 18.0 × 12.0 cm   Pp [1–3] 4–67 [68]   Illus col   [$0.50, on binding]   Paper, with image on front of a savoury gelatine dish; stapled
CONTENTS: 1 tp; 2 untitled remarks about the strength and measurement of Davis Gelatine; 3 untitled note about the company's product and this cookbook; 4–6 index; 7–67 recipes; 68 untitled remarks about the food value of Davis Gelatine and 'Wholly set up and printed in Canada by Brigdens Limited, for the publishers, Davis Gelatine (Canada) Limited'
CITATIONS: Ferguson/Fraser, p 233, illus col on p 80 of closed volume
COPIES: ACG   OGU (CCC TX715.6 D31)   *Private collection

O580.10 rev. ed., 1941
—Davis dainty dishes / Published by / the Davis Gelatine Organization / Canada, Australia, New Zealand, South Africa, England / Editions 1–8 1922 to 1937 / Revised edition 1938 / Reprinted 1939 / Revised edition 1941
DESCRIPTION: 18.0 × 12.0 cm   Pp [1–3] 4–67 [68]   Illus col   [$0.50, on binding]   Paper, with image on front of a savoury gelatine dish; stapled
CONTENTS: 1 tp; 2 untitled remarks about the strength and measurement of Davis Gelatine; 3 untitled note about the company's product and this cookbook; 4–6 index; 7–67 text; 68 untitled remarks about the food value of Davis Gelatine and 'Wholly set up and printed in Canada by Brigdens Limited, for the publishers, Davis Gelatine (Canada) Limited'
COPIES: OGU (CCC TX715.6 D31 1941)   OONL (TX715 D35 1941)   *Private collection

O580.11 reprint, 1942
—Davis dainty dishes / Published by / the Davis Gelatine Organization / Canada, Australia, New Zealand, South Africa, England / Editions 1–8 1922 to 1937 / Revised edition 1938 / Reprinted 1939 / Revised edition 1941 / Reprinted 1942
DESCRIPTION: 18.0 × 12.0 cm   Pp [1–3] 4–67 [68]   Illus col   [$0.50, on binding]   Paper, with image on front of a savoury gelatine dish; stapled
CONTENTS: 1 tp; 2 'Important' [remarks about the strength and measurement of Davis Gelatine]; 3 untitled note about the company's product and this cookbook; 4–6 index; 7–67 text; 68 untitled remarks about the food value of Davis Gelatine and 'Wholly set up and printed in Canada by Brigdens Limited, for the publishers, Davis Gelatine (Canada) Limited'
COPIES: *Private collection

O580.12 reprint, 1945
—Davis dainty dishes / Published by / the Davis Gelatine Organization / Canada, Australia, New Zealand, South Africa, England / Editions 1–8 1922 to 1937 / Revised edition 1938 / Reprinted 1939 / Revised edition 1941 / Reprinted 1942 / Reprinted 1945
DESCRIPTION: 18.0 × 12.5 cm   Pp [1–3] 4–67 [68]   Illus col   [$0.50, on binding]   Paper, with image on front of a savoury gelatine dish; stapled
CONTENTS: 1 tp; 2 'Important' [remarks about the strength and measurement of Davis Gelatine]; 3 untitled introduction; 4–6 index; 7–67 recipes; 68 untitled remarks about the food value of Davis Gelatine and 'Wholly set up and printed in Canada by Brigdens Limited, for the publishers, Davis Gelatine (Canada) Limited'
COPIES: OONL (TX715 D35 1945 p***)   *Private collection

O580.13 English-language reprint, 1946
—Davis dainty dishes / Published by / the Davis Gelatine Organization / Canada, Australia, New Zealand, South Africa, England / Editions 1–8 1922 to 1937 / Revised edition 1938 / Reprinted 1939 / Revised edition 1941 / Reprinted 1942 / Reprinted 1945 / Reprinted 1946
DESCRIPTION: 18.0 × 12.0 cm   Pp [1–3] 4–67 [68]   Illus

col [$0.50, on binding] Paper, with image on front of a savoury gelatine dish; stapled
CONTENTS: 1 tp; 2 'Important' [remarks about the strength and measurement of Davis Gelatine]; 3 untitled note about the company's product and this cookbook; 4–6 index; 7–67 recipes; 68 untitled remarks about the food value of Davis Gelatine and 'Wholly set up and printed in Canada by Brigdens Limited, for the publishers, Davis Gelatine (Canada) Limited'
COPIES: *BVIPM   OGU (CCC TX715.6 D31)

O580.14   French-language reprint, 1946
—Mets délicieux Davis / Publié par /
l'Organisation Davis Gelatine / Canada, Australie, Nouvelle-Zélande, Afrique-Sud, Angleterre / Éditions 1–8 1922 à 1937 / Édition revisée 1938 / Réimprimé 1940 / Réimprimé 1946 / Réimprimé 1946 [sic, two reprints in 1946]
COPIES: *QSFFSC

O580.15   rev. ed., 1948
—Davis dainty dishes / Published by / the Davis Gelatine Organization / Canada, Australia, New Zealand, South Africa, England / Editions 1–8 1922 to 1937 / Revised edition 1938 / Reprinted 1939 / Revised edition 1941 / Reprinted 1942 / Reprinted 1945 / Reprinted 1946 / Revised edition 1948
DESCRIPTION: 18.0 × 12.0 cm   Pp [1–3] 4–67 [68]   Illus col [$0.50, on binding]   Paper, with image on front of a savoury gelatine dish; stapled
CONTENTS: 1 tp; 2 'Important' [remarks about the strength and measurement of Davis Gelatine]; 3 untitled note about the company's product and this cookbook; 4–6 'Index'; 7–67 recipes; 68 untitled remarks about the food value of Davis Gelatine and 'Printed in Canada by the Hugh Heaton Printing House Limited, for the publishers, Davis Gelatine (Canada) Limited'
COPIES: OGU (CCC TX715.6 D31 1948)   *Private collection

O580.16   reprint, 1949
—Davis dainty dishes / Published by / the Davis Gelatine Organization / Canada, Australia, New Zealand, South Africa, England / Editions 1–8 1922 to 1937 / Revised edition 1938 / Reprinted 1939 / Revised edition 1941 / Reprinted 1942 / Reprinted 1945 / Reprinted 1946 / Revised edition 1948 / Reprinted 1949
DESCRIPTION: 18.0 × 12.0 cm   Pp [1–3] 4–67 [68]   Illus col [$0.50, on binding]   Paper, with image on front of a savoury gelatine dish; stapled
CONTENTS: 1 tp; 2 untitled remarks about the strength

and measurement of Davis Gelatine; 3 untitled note about the company's product and this cookbook; 4–6 index; 7–67 text; 68 untitled remarks about the food value of Davis Gelatine and 'Printed in Canada by the Hugh Heaton Printing House Limited, for the publishers, Davis Gelatine (Canada) Limited'
COPIES: MBDHM   OFFRH   *Private collection

OTHER ENGLISH-LANGUAGE EDITIONS: Reprint, 1950 (Private collection); rev. ed., [printed by R.G. McLean Ltd, Toronto], 1955 (OGU, ONM, Company collection, Davis Germantown Inc., Toronto).

OTHER FRENCH-LANGUAGE EDITIONS: Rev. ed., [printed by R.G. McLean Ltd, Toronto], 1955 (Private collection).

Dowsett, Mrs C.W., and Mrs J.B. Hutchison

O581.1   [1926]
The / golden north / cook book / Compiled by / Mrs. C.W. Dowsett and Mrs. J.B. Hutchison / in aid of / St. Paul's Church / South Porcupine / Building Fund / To all those who assisted in the compilation of this book by / contributing recipes, and to those who helped make the publi- / cation possible by so generously subscribing for advertisements, / the compilors [sic] tender their sincere thanks. Users of the book / are requested to patronize the firms and individuals whose ad- / vertisements appear within its pages. / [folio:] 1
COPIES: OSPTM   *Private collection
NOTES: The 'Foreword,' on p 2, is signed J.E. Woodall, archdeacon, St Paul's Vestry, South Porcupine, 4 December 1926. He congratulates 'the two ladies who have undertaken to reduce the debt on our church building by publishing a cookery book.' The private collector reports that the volume has 225 pp; OSPTM reports 234 pp.

A few cooking suggestions

See also O332.1, A Few Cooking Suggestions, attributed to Mrs Mary Brown-Lewers, and O735.1, New Recipes, both Crisco cookbooks.

O582.1   [copyright 1926]
A few / cooking / suggestions [cover-title]
DESCRIPTION: 19.0 × 11.5 cm   Pp [1] 2–16   Illus Paper, with image on front of a woman working at a kitchen table, boy watching; stapled
CONTENTS: 1 cover-title; 2–top 3 'Hints for Simplifying Deep Fat Frying'; mid 3–16 recipes for 'Deep

Frying,' 'Pastry Making,' 'Cakes, Cookies and Quick Breads,' and 'Icing Recipes'

COPIES: ONM *Private collection

NOTES: The following is on p 2: 'Form C–1602–C'; and on p 16: 'Crisco is the trade-mark for a superior shortening manufactured by the Procter & Gamble Company of Canada, Ltd., Hamilton, Canada // Copyright, 1926 Procter & Gamble Cincinnati.'

In 1928 the company published a new selection of recipes in the United States: *New Cooking Suggestions*, [Cincinnati: Procter and Gamble Co., copyright 1928], 'T-2 Printed in U.S.A.' on p 19 (Private collection). This appears to have been distributed in Canada for the private collector's copy has a 'Made in Canada' product label mounted on p 19.

AMERICAN EDITIONS: *A Few Cooking Suggestions* by Della Stroud, Procter and Gamble Co., 1914, pp 16, may or may not be related to O582.1 (Barile, p 190); *A Few Cooking Suggestions*, [Cincinnati: Procter and Gamble, copyright 1927], on p 2: 'F. 1924' (Private collection).

Fryer, Mrs Jane Eayre (Philadelphia, Pa, 1876–)

For other cookbooks by this American author, see O485.1, which may be an earlier edition of O583.1.

O583.1 [copyright 1926]
The Winston / cook book / of guaranteed recipes / planned for a family of four / Economical recipes / designed to meet the / needs of the modern / housekeeper / With special chapters on / practical home economics / entertaining // diet for weight control / school lunches / balanced rations / proper meals for children / By / Jane Eayre Fryer / Instructor of Domestic Science / Illustrated / The John C. Winston Company / Chicago Philadelphia Toronto

DESCRIPTION: Pp [i–ii] iii–v ...

CONTENTS: i tp; ii 'Copyright, 1926, by the John C. Winston Co. Copyr., 1913–1922, The J.C.W. Co. Printed in U.S.A.'; iii 'The Housewife,' Proverbs XXXI, 25–9; iv quotation from Ruskin; v 'Preface'; ...

CITATIONS: Bitting, p 171

COPIES: *Private collection

NOTES: The book's owner reports that her copy was presented as a shower gift to her mother in 1932. Bitting records the pagination as xi + 3–533. In 1913 the Winston Co. published a cookbook of the same title, but under the name Helen Cramp; see O301.1.

Helpful hints for housekeepers 1926

See O263.1 for information about the company and other issues of Helpful Hints for Housekeepers.

O584.1 1926
1926 Volume XVI 1926 / Hang me in the kitchen / Helpful / hints / for housekeepers / Compliments of / the Dodds Medicine Co. / Limited / Toronto, Can. [cover-title]

DESCRIPTION: 15.5 × 10.5 cm Pp 1–32 Paper; stapled, and with hole punched at top left corner for hanging

CONTENTS: 1 'A Message to You'; 2 'Cleaning Recipes'; 3 'Weights and Measures'; 4, 6, 8, 10, 12, 14, 18, 20, 22, 24, 26, 28 entries on health-related topics, arranged alphabetically from Anaemia to Skin; 5 'Valuable Hints'; 7 'Avoid Waste'; 9 'Hints on Carving'; 11 'When Making Candy' and 'Safety First'; 13 'Wash Day Made Easy'; 15 'First Aid in the Home'; 16–17 testimonials for Dodd's Kidney Pills; 19, 21 'General Housekeeping Hints'; 23 'Timetable for Baking' and 'Timetable for Cooking'; 25 'Removing Stains'; 27 'Boots and Shoes'; 29 ad for Diamond Dinner Pills; 30 ad for Dodd's Dyspepsia Tablets; 31 'Rates of Postage'; 32 'Diet Rules'; inside back face of binding 'Self Examination Page'

COPIES: OFERWM (A1985.43) *Private collection

McGill, Mrs D.

See also O705.1, Moffats Cook Book, *a related text by Moffats Ltd. For the titles of other cookbooks by the same manufacturer, see O342.1.*

O585.1 copyright 1926
Moffats / cook / book / containing selected recipes / specially prepared for / cooking and baking and / giving all directions for / operating Moffats Electric / Ranges. / Copyright 1926 / Moffats Limited / Weston Ontario Canada

DESCRIPTION: 23.0 × 15.5 cm Pp [1–2] 3–96 3 fp illus, illus Paper-covered thin card, with image on front of a steaming dish; with hole punched at top left corner for hanging

CONTENTS: 1 tp; 2 fp illus of 'Canada's Model Stove Plant ...'; 3 manufacturer's guarantee for range; 4 fp illus of 'Awards of Mrs. D. McGill'; 5 the heading 'Moffats Cookery Book' and a fp illus with caption 'The author's recipes were all tried out on her own Moffat Electric Range.'; 6–9 'Start Right' [information about using the range]; 10–94 recipes and other items;

95 blank 'Space for Additional Recipes'; 96 'Contents' [i.e., index]
CITATIONS: Ferguson/Fraser, pp 65 and 233, illus col on p 57 of closed volume
COPIES: MWMM   OSTMYM   SBIHM   *Private collection
NOTES: The cover-title is 'Moffat's Cookery Book.' The title-page is printed in orange and black. Mrs McGill's awards, illustrated on p 4, were from Ontario fairs and exhibitions. One award, from the Canadian National Exhibition, 1925, bears her address: 141 Howard Park, Toronto. Mrs D. McGill was probably married to David McGill, who is listed in Toronto city directories as living at 141 Howard Park from 1925 to 1928. He is described as a traveller or, in 1927, as a rep for R.M. Ballantyne Ltd, whose product was knitted goods. Before 1925, 141 Howard Park is not listed in the street index, and David McGill is at 26 Mountview Avenue. From 1929 to 1931, he is at Glendonwynne Road. All these addresses are in the west end of Toronto, not far from Moffats Ltd in Weston.

The order of the two editions copyrighted 1926 is unknown.

O585.2   copyright 1926
—Moffats / cook / book / containing selected recipes / specially prepared for / cooking and baking and / giving all directions for / operating Moffats Electric / Ranges. / Copyright 1926 / Moffats Limited / Weston Ontario Canada
DESCRIPTION: 23.0 × 15.0 cm   Pp [1–2] 3–100   Illus
Paper-covered thin card, with a decorative pattern on the lower half of the front face; sewn, and with hole punched at top left corner for hanging
CONTENTS: 1 tp; 2 fp illus of 'Canada's Model Stove Plant ...'; 3 manufacturer's guarantee for range; 4 fp illus of 'Awards of Mrs. D. McGill.'; 5 fp illus with caption 'The author's recipes were all tried out on her own Moffat Electric Range.'; 6–8 'Start Right' [information about using the range]; 9–10 blank, but with note on p 9, 'This leaf may be removed and one replaced with your company's advertising.'; 11 'Contents' [i.e., index]; 12–96 recipes and other items; 97–100 blank 'Space for Additional Recipes'
COPIES: OBUJBM   OKQ   OTMCL (641.586 M57) *Private collection
NOTES: The cover-title is 'Moffats Cook Book for Moffats Ranges.' The title-page is printed in black only. 'West Toronto Printing House' is on the outside back face of the OTMCL copy (I may have missed this information on the private collector's copy).

Tried and tested receipts

The Inwood branch of the Women's Institute was established in 1909 (Ambrose, p 239).

O586.1   1926
For home and country / Tried and tested / receipts / carefully collected by / Inwood Branch of / the Women's Institute / Nineteen hundred and twenty-six / Officers / Hon. President Mrs. G.S. Courtright / President Mrs. A. Atkin / 1st Vice-President Mrs. Trowhill / 2nd Vice-President Mrs. S.S. Courtright / Sec'y.-Treasurer Mrs. W.A. Graham / Branch Directors Mesdames. Richardson, Urie / and S.S. Courtright. / Price 50c [cover-title]
DESCRIPTION: 21.5 × 14.5 cm   Pp 1–50   Paper; stapled
CONTENTS: 1 ad; 2–50 recipes credited with the name of the contributor and ads
COPIES: *Private collection
NOTES: 'This book was printed at Lillywhite's Print Shop // Brigden' is on the outside back face of the binding (for an earlier, but similarly titled, cookbook published in Brigden, see O331.1, *Tried and Tested Recipes*).

1926–7

Rees, Margaret H.

See also O804.1, Tasty Meals for Every Day, compiled under Rees's supervision. Also published by Harris Abattoir is O456.1.

O587.1   nd [about 1926–7]
Tempting / Domestic / recipes [cover-title]
DESCRIPTION: 16.5 × 12.5 cm   Pp [1–2] 3–48   Illus col   Paper; stapled
CONTENTS: 1 untitled introductory note signed Margaret H. Rees; 2 blank; 3 '"Domestic" ... the Perfect Shortening' signed Harris Abattoir Co. Ltd, Toronto and St Boniface; 4–38 recipes; 39–45 blank, except for running heads, for manuscript recipes; 46–7 'Table of Contents' [i.e., alphabetical index]; 48 'Table of Weights and Measures'
COPIES: *SSWD
NOTES: On p 1, Rees identifies herself as the author of the book: 'At the request of many of our users of "Domestic Shortening," I have prepared this book, ...' The running head is 'One Hundred Tested Recipes.' The recipes are arranged in chapters for 'Bread and Quick Bread,' 'Cakes and Cookies,' 'Pastry,' and 'Deep

Fat Frying.' Domestic Shortening was a 'purely vegetable' shortening.

Tempting Domestic Recipes was published about 1926–7, i.e., after Harris Abattoir's St Boniface location was established (Harris Abattoir (Western) Ltd is first listed in Winnipeg directories in 1926), and before Harris Abattoir Co. Ltd merged in 1927 with the William Davies Co., the Canadian Packing Co. Ltd, and Gunns Ltd to form Canada Packers Ltd.

1926–30

Splint, Miss Sarah Field (1883–1959)

Also by this American author, but published only in the United States, are: Time-Saving Cookery, New York: McCall's Magazine, [c1922]; The Art of Cooking and Serving, Cincinnati: 1926; Hawaiian Pineapple as One Hundred Good Cooks Serve It: ... Selection Made by Mildred Maddocks Bentley, Alice Bradley, Sarah Field Splint, San Francisco: Association of Hawaiian Pineapple Canners, 1927; and Smoothtop Cookery with Gas, the Modern Fuel, edited by Splint in collaboration with C.E. Fitchen, Cleveland: Standard Gas Equipment Corp., c1926 (all United States: DLC).

O588.1   nd [about 1926–30]
199 / selected recipes / by / Sarah Field Splint / The Procter & Gamble Co. of Canada, Ltd. / Hamilton, Canada
DESCRIPTION: 18.0 × 12.5 cm   Pp [1–4] 5–64   Lacks paper binding; stapled
CONTENTS: 1 tp; 2 'Crisco is the trade-mark for a superior shortening manufactured by the Procter & Gamble Co. of Canada, Ltd., Hamilton, Canada // C1793-A'; 3 '199 Selected Recipes by Sarah Field Splint' signed Procter and Gamble; 4 blank; 5–64 text in seventeen chapters
COPIES: *OTMCL (641.5971 H39 No. 59)
NOTES: The recipes specify Crisco as an ingredient. The introductory text on p 3 describes Splint's career. At the time of publication, she was editor of the Food Department of *McCall's Magazine*. During the First World War she was chief of the Division of Home Conservation in the US Food Administration. Her other positions included associate editor of the *Delineator* and editor of the *Woman's Magazine*. The four leaves between pp 32 and 33, which are not included in the pagination, are an advertisement for her widely distributed book, *The Art of Cooking and Serving*, first published in 1926.

AMERICAN EDITIONS: 1925 (Allen, p 183); Cincinnati: Procter and Gamble, [copyright 1926], '1793A' on copyright page (United States: InU; Cagle/Stafford No. 933 describes the 1926 edition as the first).

1926–34

New recipes Baumert Cheese

For the titles of other cookbooks promoting Baumert Cheese, see O565.1.

O589.1   nd [about 1926–34]
New / recipes / Baumert / Cheese / luncheons / teas – suppers [cover-title]
DESCRIPTION: 15.5 × 8.5 cm   Pp [1–2] 3–15   Illus col Paper; stapled
CONTENTS: 1 cover-title; 2 'Baumert Co. Limited // Factory Huntingdon, Que. // Montreal, Que. Toronto, Ont. // Manufacturers & importers of fancy cheese'; 3 'Foreword'; 4–7 'Salads'; 8–9 'Health Builder'; 10–mid 12 'Sandwiches'; mid 12–15 'Supper Dishes'; outside back face of binding 'Strathmore Press, Toronto.'
COPIES: *Private collection
NOTES: The 'Foreword' thanks 'Miss Jessie Reid [*sic*], of Consumers' Gas Co.; Miss Pattinson, of Central Technical School – who approved all recipes; Miss Margaret Milne and Miss Work.' Jessie Read worked for Consumers' Gas in Toronto from about 1926 to April 1934. *New Recipes Baumert Cheese* was published within this period. For further information about Read, see O830.1. For Pattinson, who was on staff at Central Technical School in Toronto from 1915 to 1942, see O506.1.

1927

All about milk

For information about Metropolitan Life Insurance Co. and its publications, see O373.1.

O590.1   [copyright 1927]
All about milk / our best / food
DESCRIPTION: 20.0 × 13.5 cm   Pp [1–2] 3–24   Tp illus of cow's head, illus orange-and-black   Paper, with image on front of boy and girl facing cow behind fence; stapled
CONTENTS: 1 tp; 2 'Copyright, Canada, 1927 Metropolitan Life Insurance Company'; 3–24 'Contents of

Milk,' 'Forms of Milk,' 'Milk Products,' 'Care of Milk,' and 'Milk for the Baby'

COPIES: OHMB (Ephemera QU145 M594a 1927) *QMM (RBD ckbk 1249)

NOTES: *All about Milk* with no named author, [copyright 1927], is a heavily revised version of *All about Milk* by Milton J. Rosenau, Canada: Metropolitan Life Insurance Co., 1922 [copyright 1923] (OHMB (Ephemera QU145 R813a 1922)). There was also a 1914 edition of Rosenau's book (Private collection). Rosenau was a professor of preventative medicine and hygiene at Harvard University.

O590.2 [copyright 1929]

—All about milk / our best / food

DESCRIPTION: 19.5 × 13.5 cm   Pp [1–2] 3–24   Tp illus of cow's head, illus orange-and-black   Paper, with image on front of boy and girl facing cow behind fence; stapled

CONTENTS: 1 tp; 2 'Copyright, 1929 Metropolitan Life Insurance Company'; 3–24 text

COPIES: *Private collection

NOTES: The text is written from an American perspective; for example, 'In the United States we use ...' Milk is recommended as a good food for adults, the sick, and children. Readers are advised to avoid 'Dip Milk' – milk dispensed by dippers from cans in grocery stores and small shops, a product which may be dirty or of poor quality. The process of pasteurization is explained, including how to pasteurize at home.

The AutomatiCook book

For information about Beach Foundry Ltd, its cookbooks, and the AutomatiCook, see O566.1.

O591.1 [copyright 1927]

The AutomatiCook / book / Selected recipes / for / time and temperature / oven cooking / Tire-less cooking [cover-title]

DESCRIPTION: About 25.5 × 17.0 cm [dimensions from photocopy]   [$0.50, on p 1]   With images on front of a table set for dinner and the Robertshaw AutomatiCook; stapled

CONTENTS: 1 'Introductory' and at bottom, 'Copyright 1927 Robertshaw Thermostat Company Youngwood, Pa. "Thermostats since 1899" The AutomatiCook Book – Price per copy fifty cents'; 2 'Cooking Chart'; ...; 55 recipes; 56 'Instructions for the Care and Adjustments of Gas Ranges Equipped with the AutomatiCook'; inside back face of binding 'Instructions for the Care and Adjustments of the

Robertshaw AutomatiCook'; outside back face 'Table of Contents' and at bottom, 'Beach Foundry, Limited Ottawa, Canada' and 'Printed in U.S.A.'

COPIES: *Private collection

O591.2 nd [about 1927–30]

—The AutomatiCook / book / Selected recipes / for / time and temperature / oven cooking / Price per copy twenty-five cents / Tire-less cooking [cover-title]

DESCRIPTION: 25.5 × 17.0 cm   Pp 1–60 Illus Paper, with images on front of a table set for dinner and the Robertshaw AutomatiCook; stapled

CONTENTS: 1 'Introductory' and at bottom, 'Beach Foundry Limited Ottawa Canada'; 2 'Cooking Chart'; 3–7 'General Cooking Information'; 8–57 recipes; 58 'Instructions for the Care and Adjustments of Gas Ranges Equipped with the AutomatiCook'; 59–60 blank for 'Notes'; inside back face of binding 'Instructions for the Care and Adjustments of the Robertshaw AutomatiCook' and at bottom, 'The Modern Press, Ottawa'; outside back face table of contents

COPIES: ACG *BVAU (Beatrice M. Millar Papers) OONL (TX657 O6 A87 1920z fol., 2 copies)

NOTES: This edition, which has Beach Foundry's name on p 1 and which was printed in Canada, probably follows O591.1, with Beach Foundry's name on the binding and printed in the United States.

Chatelaine 1935, p 82, cites the price of $0.10 for Beach Foundry's 'The Automatic Cook Book [*sic*].' The reference may be to this edition ($0.25 on the binding) or another, unidentified edition.

Boy Scout home cooking recipes

The 1st Chatham Troop published a cookbook of the same title, O577.1.

O592.1 nd [about 1927]

Boy Scout / home / cooking / recipes / obtained from parents and friends of the boys / Price twenty-five cents / Issued by the / 3rd St. Thomas Troop Boy Scouts / St. Thomas, Ontario / Charter No. 593 [cover-title]

DESCRIPTION: With image on front of a Boy Scout's head

CONTENTS: 1–2 recipes; ...

COPIES: *Private collection

NOTES: The volume has 72 pp. The running head is 'Boy Scout Cook Book.' Information on p 19 about the 3rd St Thomas Troop refers to a successful summer camp in July 1926 and 'a rule set down for 1927.'

Campbell, Walter Ruggles (Port Robinson, Ont., 1891–) and Mame Tanner Porter

Campbell co-authored, with John James Rickard, Insulin: Its Use in the Treatment of Diabetes, *Baltimore: Williams and Wilkins, 1925 (OONL; United States: DLC). The file for Campbell at OTUAR (A73-0026/050 (69)) contains biographical information about him and his photograph from* Torontonensis, 1915. *He matriculated from St Catharines Collegiate Institute, and earned his degrees at the University of Toronto: BA, 1911; MA, 1912; MB, 1915; and MD, 1917. OONL and the 1911 Census give 1890 as his birth date.*

Porter contributed to Lotta Jean Bogert's Dietetics Simplified ... with Laboratory Section by Mame T. Porter, *New York: Macmillan Co., 1937 (Great Britain: LB).*

O593.1   1927
[An edition of *A Guide for Diabetics*, Toronto: University of Toronto Press, 1927, 20 cm, pp 267, illus]
COPIES: OONL (RC909 C2 1927)

O593.2   4th ed., 1930
—A guide / for diabetics / by / Walter R. Campbell, M.A., M.D. (Tor.) / Associate in Medicine, University of Toronto / Assistant Physician, Toronto General Hospital / and / Mame T. Porter, B.Sc., M.A. / Chief Dietitian, Toronto General Hospital / Fourth revised edition / Toronto / The University of Toronto Press / 1930
DESCRIPTION: 19.5 × 13.0 cm   Pp [1–9] 10–272   Cloth
CONTENTS: 1 tp; 2 'Copyright, Canada 1925, 1930 W.R. Campbell and Mame T. Porter // Printed in Canada by the University of Toronto Press'; 3–4 'Preface' signed W.R.C. and M.T.P.; 5–6 'Contents'; 7 'List of Tables'; 8 blank; 9–269 text in eighteen chapters; 270–2 'Index'
COPIES: *OTMCL (616.46 C12)
NOTES: The 'Preface' states: 'The purpose of the Guide is to explain to the patient certain facts about diabetes and its dietetic control, which are essential foundations for his intelligent co-operation with his physician, and also to provide him with a number of tested recipes for suitable foods. Part of the book is devoted to the actual construction of menus ...' Chapter XVI, pp 131–236, is 'Recipes'; Chapter XVIII, pp 251–64, is 'Home Canning and Supplies.'

O593.3   5th ed., 1934
—A guide / for diabetics / by / Walter R. Campbell, M.A., M.D., F.R.C.P. (C), F.R.S.C. / Associate in Medicine, University of Toronto /

Assistant Physician, Toronto General Hospital / and / Mame T. Porter, B.Sc., M.A. / late Chief Dietitian, Toronto General Hospital / Fifth edition / Toronto / The University of Toronto Press / 1934
CONTENTS: Tp verso 'Copyright, Canada 1925, 1930, 1934 W.R. Campbell and Mame T. Porter // Printed in Canada by the University of Toronto Press'
COPIES: OONL (RC909 C2 1934)   *QMU

AMERICAN EDITIONS: Baltimore: Williams and Wilkins Co., 1926 (United States: DLC); 4th ed., Baltimore: Williams and Wilkins Co., 1930 (United States: DLC).

Chase, Dr Alvin Wood (Cayuga County, NY, 20 March 1817–25 May 1885, Ohio)

See O535.1 for other years of the calendar almanac. For information about Dr Chase and his books, see O8.1.

O594.1   1927
Hang me up / Dr. A.W. Chase's / calendar almanac / 1927 / for the / home, factory / farm, office / Published by / the Dr. A.W. Chase Medicine Co. / Limited / Toronto Canada [cover-title]
DESCRIPTION: 21.0 × 15.0 cm   Pp [3] 4–50   Illus   Paper, with image on front of Dr Chase and his signature; stapled, and with hole punched at top left corner, through which runs a string for hanging
CONTENTS: 3 zodiacal signs, festivals and anniversaries, stars, and eclipses for 1927; 4–5 publ ads; 6–50 monthly calendars, culinary recipes under various headings, medical information, publ ads, and humorous material
COPIES: *OTUTF (jah patent medicine)
NOTES: 'Murray Printing Co., Ltd., Toronto Can' is on the outside back face of the binding. The 1928 issue (O613.1) says that 1,733,000 copies of the 1927 issue were distributed.

Choice recipes

See also O165.1, Reliable Recipes, *by the same Ladies' Aid.*

O595.1   [1927]
Choice / recipes [cover-title]
DESCRIPTION: 22.5 × 14.5 cm   Pp 1–79 [80]   Paper; stapled
CONTENTS: 1–2 ads; 3 '"Good cooks are born, not made, they say, / The saying is most untrue; / Hard trying, and these fine recipes, / Will make good cooks

of you." Prepared for "The House Beautiful" Auspices Ladies' Aid Port Arthur General Hospital May, 1927.'; 4 ads; 5–79 recipes and ads; 80 'Conclusion // Community Pudding' [i.e., mock recipe, which begins, 'First, secure at small expense a little kindly feeling among your neighbors. Second, season with milk of human kindness ...']
COPIES: NBFY *Private collection

Cook book

The Maude Macdonald Chapter was founded on 15 February 1919 and disbanded in the period 1965–77. It was named in honour of a Brantford woman, who was the first Canadian nurse killed in the First World War.

O596.1 nd [about 1927]
Cook book / [IODE symbol] / Compiled by / Maude Macdonald Chapter / I.O.D.E. / Brantford, Ont.
DESCRIPTION: 22.0 × 14.0 cm Pp [1] 2–70 [71] Small illus on p 2 of a pudding, flanked by two candelabra Cloth-covered boards, with IODE symbol on front
CONTENTS: 1 tp; 2 'Before hand we thank you / for buying our book ...' and 'Sweet Disposition' [mock recipe]; 3 'Abbreviations' and 'Table of Weights and Measures'; 4–70 recipes credited with the name of the contributor; 71 'Index' [i.e., table of contents] and 'Moyer Printing Company 26 King St., Brantford'
COPIES: OBBM *Bookseller's stock Private collection
NOTES: The private collector's copy is inscribed 'From Effie Mayer, July–1927.' The appearance of the book is consistent with publication about that time.

CBCat 61, No. 90, lists a cookbook by the Maude Macdonald Chapter, no title given, nd [1920s], pp 114. Since the number of pages differs from that recorded here (and from the private collector's copy), it may be a different work or another edition. Alternatively, it may be the same work if the British bookseller made an error when cataloguing.

Cook book

The Prospect Hill Women's Institute was founded in Middlesex County in 1923 and disbanded in 1993 (Ambrose, p 237).

O597.1 1927
Cook book / Recipes / collected and compiled by / Women's Institute / Prospect Hill, – Ont. / Diamond

Jubilee of Confederation, 1927 / Price 60 cents / W. Sovereign & Sons, printers, Lucan, Ont. [cover-title]
COPIES: OSTMYM *Private collection
NOTES: The book has 148 pp.

Daisy recipe book No. 2

See also O346.1, by the same group.

O598.1 1927
Daisy recipe / book No. 2 / Compiled and arranged by the / the [sic] Daisy Bible Class / Hyatt Avenue United Church / London, Ontario / 1927 [cover-title]
DESCRIPTION: 22.0 × 14.5 cm Pp 1–104 [105–8] Card; bound by a cord running through two punched holes
CONTENTS: 1–2 ads; 3 quotations from Shakespeare, Ruskin, and two unidentified sources; 4 ad; 5 'Recipes Compiled and Arranged by the Daisy Bible Class ...,' 'Our Greeting,' 'Officers:,' and the year 1927; 6 ads; 7–104 text, mainly recipes credited with the name of the contributor; 105–7 blank; 108 'Index' [i.e., table of contents]
COPIES: *OLU (VF88)

Hamilton, Miss Ethel Watchorn (1892–1972)

'Department of Agriculture Personnel Records 1920–47' at OOA record Miss Ethel Watchorn Hamilton's employment with the federal government (see Finding Aid 17-59, arranged alphabetically by employee). The first reference is to her appointment as temporary assistant demonstrator and lecturer on 17 July 1923 at the annual salary of $1,440 (File 292314); her position was made permanent on 27 May 1927 (File 312485). Her resignation from the Experimental Farms Branch was authorized on 1 December 1931 (P.C. 1/2267). (Although she is still described as with the Branch in the 1933 reprint of Preserving Fruits and Vegetables in the Home (O599.5), it was a reprint from 1929.) Other files also record aspects of her employment (Files 297725, 312485, 315020, 320212, 325249, 339260). Miss Hamilton married Ray A. Ruggles. She is buried in Lakeview Cemetery, Tay Township, Simcoe County, Ontario.

For a list of other cookbooks published by the Department of Agriculture, see O404.1.

O599.1 1927
Preserving / fruits and vegetables / in the home / Results from experiments in canning, pickling and / preserving, at the Central Experimental / Farm,

Ottawa, Ontario. / By Ethel W. Hamilton / Assistant Demonstrator and Lecturer / Division of Horticulture / Dominion Experimental Farms / Dominion of Canada / Department of Agriculture / Bulletin No. 77 – New Series / Published by direction of the Hon. W.R. Motherwell, Minister of Agriculture, Ottawa, 1927. [cover-title]

DESCRIPTION: 25.0 × 16.5 cm   Pp [1] 2–46   Illus   Paper; stapled

CONTENTS: Inside front face of binding country-wide list of personnel in the Dominion Experimental Farms Branch; 1–2 table of contents; 3 'Preservation of Fruit [sic] and Vegetables in the Home' and 'Sterilization'; 4 fp illus of the experimental kitchen at the Central Experimental Farm; 5 'Appearance of Spoiled Canned Goods and Cause of Spoilage,' 'Equipment,' 'Containers,' 'Rubbers,' and 'Preparation of Utensils'; 6 illus numbered 2–5; 7 'Principal Methods of Canning'; 8 illus numbered 6–9; 9 'Scalding,' 'Blanching,' 'Cold Dip,' 'Syrups for Canning,' and 'General Rules for Canning Fruits by the Cold-Pack Method'; 10 illus numbered 10–13; top 11 continuation from p 9 of 'General Rules for Canning ...'; near top 11–mid 12 'Recommended Recipes for Canning Fruits'; mid 12 'General Rules for Canning Vegetables by the Cold-Pack Method'; bottom 12–mid 14 'Recommended Recipes for Canning Vegetables'; mid–bottom 14 'Fruit Jam'; top–mid 15 'Recommended Recipes for Fruit Jam'; bottom 15–top 18 'Jelly'; near top 18–top 19 'Marmalades'; mid 19–mid 20 'Conserves'; mid 20–mid 21 'Candied Fruit Peels'; mid 21–top 23 'Preservation of Vegetables by Fermentation and Salting'; near top 23–mid 27 'Pickles'; bottom 27 'Storage'; 28–46 timetables and other tables

CITATIONS: Ag 1867–1974, p 5   CCat No. 6, p H9   Rowe

COPIES: *OOAG (630.4 C212 B77 N.S., 2 copies)   OVOH

NOTES: The author recounts the history of the book on p 3: 'While the war was in progress, in 1917, it was decided to carry on experiments and demonstrations in the preservation of fruits and vegetables in order to assist in the conservation of food. The work begun then was continued in 1918 and 1919. At the close of the war operations were suspended for a time, but the experimental side of the work was again taken up in 1923. The work was in charge of Miss Laura Kirby in 1917 and Miss Margaret Macfarlane in 1918 and 1919. A bulletin entitled "Preservation of Fruits and Vegetables for Home Use" (Bull. No. 93), giving the results of the experiments with recommended recipes, was prepared by Miss Macfarlane and published in 1919 [see O424.1]. So popular was this that a new

edition had to be published in 1921. This bulletin being now practically exhausted and many additional experiments having been carried on, the author, who has had charge of the work since 1923, has prepared a new bulletin, in which are many new recipes, together with details of the more recent experimental work.' The following is on the outside back face of the binding: 'Printed at Government Printing Bureau Ottawa.'

O599.2   1927

—Conserves / de fruits et de légumes / faites à la maison / Résultats d'expériences faites à la Ferme expérimentale / centrale, Ottawa, Ontario / Par Ethel W. Hamilton / aide-démonstratice et conférencière / Service de l'horticulture / Fermes expérimentales fédérales / Ministère fédéral de l'agriculture / Canada / Bulletin no 77 – Nouvelle série / Traduit au Bureau de traduction du ministère / Publié par ordre de l'hon. W.R. Motherwell, ministre de l'agriculture, / Ottawa, 1927 [cover-title]

DESCRIPTION: 24.0 × 16.0 cm   Pp [1] 2–50   Illus   Paper; rebound in cloth, together with other Bulletins

CONTENTS: 1–2 table of contents; top–mid 3 'Conservation des fruits et des légumes à la maison'; bottom 3–top 5 'Stérilisation' and fp illus on p 4 of the experimental kitchen at the Central Experimental Farm; near top 5–top 7 'Apparence des conserves gâtées et cause de la fermentation,' 'Outillage,' 'Contenants,' 'Anneaux de caoutchouc,' and illus numbered 2–5 on p 6; near top 7 'Préparation des ustensiles'; mid 7–mid 9 'Principaux procédés pour les conserves' and illus numbered 6–9 on p 8; mid–bottom 9 'Ébouillantage' and 'Blanchiment'; 10 illus numbered 10–13; 11 'Trempage dans l'eau froide,' 'Sirops pour les conserves,' and 'Règles générales pour la conservation des fruits par l'embouteillage à froid'; 12–mid 13 'Recettes recommandées pour les conserves de fruits'; mid 13 'Règles générales pour conserver les légumes par l'embouteillage à froid'; bottom 13–mid 16 'Recettes recommandées pour la conservation des légumes'; mid 16 'Confitures de fruits'; bottom 16–mid 17 'Recettes recommandées pour les confitures de fruits'; bottom 17–mid 20 'Gelée'; mid 20–top 22 'Marmelades'; near top 22–top 23 'Conserves'; mid 23–mid 24 'Pelures de fruits confites'; bottom 24–mid 26 'Conservation des légumes par la fermentation et le salage'; mid 26–30 'Cornichons'; top 31 'Conservation'; mid 31–50 tables

CITATIONS: Ag 1867–1974, p 3

COPIES: *OOAG (630.4 C212 B77 N.S.)

NOTES: 'Imprimé par F.A. Acland, ... Ottawa, Canada' is on the outside back face of the binding.

O599.3 1928

—Preserving / fruits and vegetables / in the home / Results from experiments in canning, pickling and / preserving, at the Central Experimental / Farm, Ottawa, Ontario / By Ethel W. Hamilton / Assistant Demonstrator and Lecturer / Division of Horticulture / Dominion Experimental Farms / W.T. Macoun / Dominion Horticulturist / Dominion of Canada / Department of Agriculture / Bulletin No. 77 – New Series / Reprinted by direction of the Hon. W.R. Motherwell, Minister of Agriculture. / Ottawa, 1928 [cover-title]

DESCRIPTION: 25.0 × 16.5 cm   Pp [1] 2–54   Illus   Paper; stapled

CONTENTS: 1–2 table of contents; 3 'Preservation of Fruit [sic] and Vegetables in the Home' and 'Sterilization'; 4 fp illus of the experimental kitchen at Central Experimental Farm; 5 'Appearance of Spoiled Canned Goods and Cause of Spoilage,' 'Equipment,' 'Containers,' 'Rubbers,' and 'Preparation of Utensils'; 6 illus numbered 2–5; 7 'Principal Methods of Canning'; 8 illus numbered 6–9; 9 'Scalding,' 'Blanching,' 'Cold Dip,' 'Syrups for Canning,' and 'General Rules for Canning Fruits by the Cold-Pack Method'; 10 illus numbered 10–13; top 11 continuation from p 9 of 'General Rules for Canning ...'; near top 11–mid 12 'Recommended Recipes for Canning Fruits'; mid 12 'General Rules for Canning Vegetables by the Cold-Pack Method'; bottom 12–mid 14 'Recommended Recipes for Canning Vegetables'; mid–bottom 14 'Fruit Jam'; top–mid 15 'Recommended Recipes for Fruit Jam'; bottom 15–17 'Jelly'; 18–top 19 'Marmalades'; mid 19–mid 21 'Conserves'; mid 21–top 23 'Preservation of Vegetables by Fermentation and Salting'; near top 23–mid 27 'Pickles'; bottom 27 'Storage'; 28–54 timetables and other tables

COPIES: OOAG (630.4 C212 B77 N.S.)   *SSWD

NOTES: The same recipes are on pp 20–1 of the 1928 edition, but there is no heading for 'Candied Fruit Peels' as in the 1927 edition.

O599.4 1929

—Preserving / fruits and vegetables / in the home / Results from experiments in canning, pickling and / preserving, at the Central Experimental / Farm, Ottawa, Ontario. / By Ethel W. Hamilton / Assistant Demonstrator and Lecturer / Division of Horticulture / Dominion Experimental Farms / Dominion of Canada / Department of Agriculture / Bulletin No. 77. – New Series / Reprinted by direction of the Hon. W.R. Motherwell, Minister of Agriculture, Ottawa, 1929 [cover-title]

DESCRIPTION: 25.0 × 16.5 cm   Pp [1] 2–55   Illus   Paper; stapled

CONTENTS: Inside front face of binding country-wide list of personnel in the Dominion Experimental Farms Branch; 1–2 table of contents; top–mid 3 untitled introductory text relating book's history; bottom 3 'Sterilization'; 4 fp illus of the experimental kitchen at the Central Experimental Farm; 5 'Appearance of Spoiled Canned Goods and Cause of Spoilage,' 'Equipment,' 'Containers,' 'Rubbers,' and 'Preparation of Utensils'; 6 illus numbered 2–5; 7 'Principal Methods of Canning'; 8 illus numbered 6–9; top–mid 9 'Scalding,' 'Blanching,' 'Cold Dip,' and 'Syrups for Canning'; bottom 9 'General Rules for Canning Fruits by the Cold-Pack Method'; 10 illus numbered 10–13; top 11 continuation from p 9 of 'General Rules for Canning Fruits ...'; mid 11–mid 12 'Recommended Recipes for Canning Fruits'; mid 12 'General Rules for Canning Vegetables by the Cold-Pack Method'; bottom 12–mid 14 'Recommended Recipes for Canning Vegetables'; bottom 14 'Fruit Jam'; top–mid 15 'Recommended Recipes for Fruit Jam'; bottom 15–top 18 'Jelly'; near top 18–near bottom 19 'Marmalades'; bottom 19–top 21 'Conserves'; mid 21–mid 22 'Candied Fruit Peels'; bottom 22–top 24 'Preservation of Vegetables by Fermentation and Salting'; near top 24–mid 29 'Pickles'; mid–bottom 29 'Storage'; 30–55 tables; outside back face 'Printed by F.A. Acland, King's printer // Ottawa, Canada'

CITATIONS: CCat No. 8, p J11

COPIES: ADEAHM   OGU (Rural Heritage Collection uncat)   OKELWM   *Private collection

O599.5 reprint, 1933

—Preserving / fruits and vegetables / in the home / Results from experiments in canning, pickling and / preserving, at the Central Experimental / Farm, Ottawa, Ontario. / By Ethel W. Hamilton / Assistant Demonstrator and Lecturer / Division of Horticulture / Dominion Experimental Farms / Dominion of Canada / Department of Agriculture / Bulletin No. 77 – New Series / Reprinted by direction of Hon. Robert Weir, Minister of Agriculture, Ottawa, 1933. [cover-title]

DESCRIPTION: 24.5 × 16.5 cm   Pp [1] 2–56   Illus   Paper; stapled

CONTENTS: Inside front face of binding country-wide list of personnel in the Dominion Experimental Farms Branch; 1–2 table of contents; 3 'Preservation of Fruits and Vegetables in the Home' and 'Sterilization'; 4 fp illus of the experimental kitchen at the Central Experimental Farm; 5 'Appearance of Spoiled Canned Goods and Cause of Spoilage,' 'Equipment,' 'Containers,' 'Rubbers,' and 'Preparation of Utensils'; 6 illus numbered 2–5; 7 'Principal Methods of Can-

ning'; 8 illus numbered 6–9; top–mid 9 'Scalding,' 'Blanching,' 'Cold Dip,' and 'Syrups for Canning'; bottom 9 'General Rules for Canning Fruits by the Cold-Pack Method'; 10 illus numbered 10–13; top 11 continuation from p 9 of 'General Rules for Canning Fruits ...'; mid 11–mid 12 'Recommended Recipes for Canning Fruits'; mid 12 'General Rules for Canning Vegetables by the Cold-Pack Method'; bottom 12–mid 14 'Recommended Recipes for Canning Vegetables'; bottom 14 'Fruit Jam'; top–mid 15 'Recommended Recipes for Fruit Jam'; bottom 15–top 18 'Jelly'; near top 18–near bottom 19 'Marmalades'; bottom 19–top 21 'Conserves'; mid 21–mid 22 'Candied Fruit Peels'; bottom 22–top 24 'Preservation of Vegetables by Fermentation and Salting'; near top 24–mid 29 'Pickles'; mid–bottom 29 'Storage'; 30–55 tables; 56 'Oven Canning'
CITATIONS: Ag 1867–1974, p 5   Newman
COPIES: *OOAG (630.4 C212 B77 N.S.)
NOTES: There is a new section about 'Oven Canning' on the last page. 'Printed at Government Printing Bureau Ottawa' is on the outside back face of the binding.

How to make jams, jellies, marmalades

For the titles of other Certo recipe collections, see O480.1.

O600.1   [copyright 1927]
How to make / jams jellies marmalades / with one minute's boiling / New & tempting ways of serving them [cover-title]
DESCRIPTION: 17.5 × 12.0 cm   Pp [1–20]   Illus col Paper, with image on front of a woman holding up a jar of jam; stapled
CONTENTS: Inside front face of binding '© U.S.A., 1927, D.P. Corp. © Canada, 1927, D.P. Co., Ltd.'; 1–2 'Better Jams and Jellies'; 3–4 'Answers to Your Questions'; 5 'Handy Hints on Jam and Jelly Making by the Certo Short-Boil Method'; 6–9 descriptions and colour illus of preserves; 10–11 centre spread illus col of ways to serve jams and jellies; 12–15 continuation of material on pp 6–9; 16–17 'Jams, Jellies and Marmalades Can Now Be Made During the Winter Months'; 18–mid 19 'Suggestions for Serving Certo Jams and Jellies'; mid–bottom 19 'Jams and Jellies Are So Good for Children as Well as Grown-ups'; 20 'Home-made Jams and Jellies for Sale!!' and 'Jams and Jellies Make Such Nice Gifts'; inside back face 'Form 1016-500M-3-27-C.–Printed in U.S.A.'; outside back face 'Douglas-Pectin Corporation, Rochester,

N.Y., U.S.A. Douglas Packing Co., Ltd., Cobourg, Ont., Canada'
COPIES: OTMCL (641.5971 H39 No. 54)   *QMM (RBD ckbk 1511)

Instructions for operating Gurney Electric Ranges

For information about the company, see O172.1.

O601.1   1927
Instructions for operating / Gurney Electric Ranges / Manufactured / by / the Gurney Foundry Company / Limited / Toronto and Montreal / Winnipeg Vancouver / sole distributors / Northern Electric Company / Limited / Halifax Quebec Regina Montreal / Ottawa Edmonton Toronto / London Calgary Hamilton / Windsor Vancouver Winnipeg / C. 73-5M-2-27
DESCRIPTION: 16.0 × 9.0 cm   Pp [1–2] 3–25 [26]   Illus on p 26 of 'Installation of the Gurney Range'   Paper, with image on front of steaming tea biscuits on a napkin on a plate; stapled, and with hole punched at top left corner, through which runs a string for hanging
CONTENTS: 1 tp; 2 blank; 3–26 text for 'Switches,' 'Use of Surface Units,' 'Cooking in the Oven,' 'Utensils,' 'The Care of the Electric Range,' 'The Care of the Oven,' 'Roasting,' 'Baking,' 'Toasting,' 'Broiling,' 'Soups,' 'Meats,' 'Vegetables and Entrees,' 'Oven Chart,' 'Bread, Rolls and Breakfast Cakes,' 'Puddings,' 'Salads,' 'Electric Ovens for Oven Dinners,' 'Canning,' 'Fruits,' 'Green Vegetables,' 'General Rules for Jelly Making,' 'Measurements of Juice and Sugar,' and 'Installation of the Gurney Range'
COPIES: *Private collection
NOTES: The cover-title is 'Gurney Instruction Book // Electric Ranges.'

Jr Girl's Institute recipe book

O602.1   1927
[Unattributed poem beginning, 'We may live without poetry, music and art,' from *Lucile,* Part I, Canto ii, by Owen Meredith, pseudonym of Edward Robert Bulwer-Lytton] / Jr. Girl's Institute / recipe book / Teeswater, 1927
COPIES: *Private collection
NOTES: The owner reports that the book has 28 pp. The copy lacks its binding.

King's Daughters recipe book

The International Order of the King's Daughters and Sons, a philanthropic organization, was founded in New York in 1886.

O603.1 1927
Knox United Church / King's / Daughters / recipe / book / 1927 [cover-title]
DESCRIPTION: Pp 1–36   Stapled
CONTENTS: 1–34 recipes credited with the name of the contributor and ads; 35 ads; 36 'Officers'
COPIES: *Private collection
NOTES: Knox United Church is in Embro, and the advertisements are for Embro businesses.

Nestlé's Milky Way recipes

See also O851.1, Favourite Recipes of Canadian Women, advertising the same brand.

O604.1 copyright 1927
Nestlé's / Milky Way / recipes / delicious and / wholesome / dishes / Nestlé's Food Company / of Canada, Limited / Metropolitan Building / Toronto – Canada / Copyright Canada 1927
DESCRIPTION: 17.0 × 13.0 cm   Pp [1–2] 3–31 [32]   Illus col, illus on p 2 of constituents of Nestlé's Evaporated Milk   Paper, with image on front of a can of Nestlé's Evaporated Milk and a can of Nestlé's Sweetened Condensed Milk, and a woman stirring the contents of a bowl, behind her the Milky Way seen through a window; stapled
CONTENTS: 1 tp; 2 'What Nestlé's Evaporated Milk Is'; 3–4 'The Practical Kitchen'; 5–32 recipes and at bottom p 32, 'Printed in Canada by John Lovell & Son Limited Montreal'
COPIES: OTMCL (641.5971 H39 No. 26)   OTYA (CPC 1927 0112)   *Private collection
NOTES: Unlike O604.2, there is no reference on the front face of the binding to the edition. Here, the woman depicted on the binding is stirring the contents of a bowl; in O604.2, the woman is placing rolled dough into a pie plate.

O604.2 [new ed.], copyright 1927
—Nestlé's / Milky Way / recipes / delicious and / wholesome / dishes / Nestlé's Food Company / of Canada, Limited / Metropolitan Building / Toronto – Canada / Copyright Canada 1927 / [folio:] 1
DESCRIPTION: 17.0 × 13.0 cm   Pp 1–32   Illus col   Paper, with image on front of a can of Nestlé's Evaporated Milk and a can of Nestlé's Sweetened Con-

densed Milk, and a woman placing rolled dough into a pie plate, behind her the Milky Way seen through a window; stapled
CONTENTS: 1 tp; 2–3 'The Practical Kitchen'; 4–32 recipes
COPIES: MCM   OONL (TX715.6 N47 1927 p***) SSWD   *Private collection
NOTES: 'New edition' is on the front face of the binding.

Recipe book

O605.1 1927
Ladies Aid / of / Church of Christ / Recipe book / Windsor, Ontario / 1927
COPIES: *Private collection

Recipe book for modern waterless cooking

Toronto city directories indicate that Joseph Sully operated his brass foundry in the city's west end through the 1920s, and from 1929 to 1945, on Wabash Avenue, in the Parkdale area. The first listing in Long Branch is in the 1946 directory.

O606.1 nd [about 1927]
Sully / Aluminum / Recipe book / for modern / waterless / cooking / Made in Canada / by / Sully Aluminum / Company / Toronto [cover-title]
DESCRIPTION: With image on front of a Sully oval roaster, with rays of yellow, green, and blue radiating out from behind it; stapled
COPIES: *Private collection
NOTES: On the outside back face of the binding, the business is described as 'Sully Aluminum Co. operated by Sully Brass Foundry Limited Toronto Canada,' but no street address is noted. This copy is stamped on the binding, 'Modern Cookware Co. // G.W. Rowell // R.R. 2 London // Phone Met. 4182[0?]12.' Since George W. Rowell died on 13 December 1927, the cookbook was likely published before that time, unless his wife or their children carried on the business for a few years after his death. (Biographical information about Rowell is in the London Township history *Families Past and Present*, Vol. 2, in the London Room files at OL.)

O606.2 [1947]
—Sully / Aluminum / Recipe book / for modern / waterless / cooking / Made in Canada / by / Sully Aluminum / Company / Long Branch / Ont. [cover-title]

DESCRIPTION: 21.5 × 14.0 cm   Pp 3–18   Illus of Sully Aluminum Co. utensils   Paper, with image on front of a Sully oval roaster; stapled

CONTENTS: Inside front face of binding '"Waterless" Cooking Utensils' [introductory text] signed Sully Aluminum Co.; 3–17 information about Sully utensils and recipes; 18 'Facts to Ponder in Getting the Best Results from Your Sully Aluminum Equipment'; inside back face 'Instructions on Care of Sully Aluminum Equipment'; outside back face 'S1-2-47' [i.e., the year of publication, 1947]

COPIES: *Private collection

NOTES: The centre spread, pp 10–11, is an illustration of a variety of Sully Aluminum utensils. This copy is inscribed on the binding, in pencil, 'E. McCracken. 291 Lincoln // Windsor.'

Recipes for candy making

See also O693.1, [Title unknown], from the same church.

O607.1   1927

Recipes / for / candy making

DESCRIPTION: 14.0 × 10.5 cm   Pp [1–20]   Paper, with pl mounted on front, depicting a landscape; bound by a black cord through two holes

CONTENTS: 1 tp; 2 'Compiled by Hart Auxiliary, Chalmers Church // Guelph, 1927'; 3–19 one recipe per page; 20 blank for 'Additional Recipes'

CITATIONS: Driver 2001, Wellington County, pp 90–1

COPIES: *Private collection

NOTES: The cover-title is 'Sweet Sixteen.' The cover-title may refer to the number of recipes, although there are actually seventeen recipes, making a representative selection of 1920s favourites: Mexican Candy, Candied Orange Peel, Peanut Brittle, Glacé Fruit and Nuts, Turkish Delight, Sea Foam, Maple Cream, Fudge, Divinity Fondant, Cream Dates, Nut Creams, Cream Mints, Butter Taffy, Salted Almonds, Butter Scotch, Patience, and one simply called Delicious. The text is reproduced from typing.

Recipes for making better jams, jellies and marmalades

For the titles of other Certo recipe collections, see O480.1.

O608.1   copyright 1927

Recipes / © U.S.A. 1927, D.-P Corp. © Can. 1927, D. P Co. Ltd. / for making better / jams, jellies / & marmalades / with / Certo / from fresh, canned and dried / fruits, bottled fruit juices / and fruit syrups [cover-title]

DESCRIPTION: 15.5 × 8.0 cm   Pp [1] 2–35 [36]   Illus on p 17 of ways of serving jams and jellies   Paper, with image on front of an aproned woman holding up a jar of preserves; stapled at top edge

CONTENTS: 1 cover-title; 2–3 general information and instructions, and at bottom p 3, the reader is asked to send any questions or suggestions to Elizabeth Palmer, Home Service Department, at the American address, Douglas-Pectin Corp., Granite Building, Rochester, New York, or at the Canadian address, Douglas Packing Co. Ltd, Cobourg, Ontario; 4–16 recipes; 17 'Try These Attractive and Tempting Ways of Serving Jams and Jellies'; 18–19 'This Is the Story of Certo'; 20 'New Recipes for Jams and Jellies You Will Enjoy'; 21–35 recipes; 36 'Index,' the American company name and city and the Canadian company name and city, and 'Printed in U.S.A. ... R.R. Donnelley & Sons Co., Chicago'

COPIES: *Private collection; United States: CA-S   OTU

O608.2   copyright 1929

—Recipes / for making better / jams jellies / & marmalades / with / Certo / from fresh, canned and dried fruits, / bottled fruit juices and fruit syrups. / © U.S.A. 1929 C. Corp. © Can. 1929 D.P. Ltd. [cover-title]

DESCRIPTION: 15.5 × 8.0 cm   Pp [1] 2–35 [36]   Illus on p 17 of ways of serving jams and jellies   Paper, with image on front of a young woman holding up a jar of preserves, an older woman watching; stapled at top edge

CONTENTS: 1 cover-title; 2–3 general information and instructions, and at bottom p 3, the reader is asked to send questions or suggestions to Elizabeth Palmer, Home Service Department, Certo Corp., Rochester, New York, or to the Canadian branch, Cobourg, Ontario; 4–16 recipes; 17 'Try These Attractive and Tempting Ways of Serving Jams and Jellies'; 18–19 'This Is the True Story of Certo'; 20 'New Recipes for Jams and Jellies You Will Enjoy'; 21–35 recipes; 36 'Index' and 'Certo Corporation, Rochester, N.Y., U.S.A. // Canadian branch, Cobourg, Ont., Canada. Printed in U.S.A. B[in a circle] R.R. Donnelley & Sons Co., Chicago'

COPIES: *ONLAM (Walters-Wagar Collection, Box 20)

Selected recipes

O609.1   1927

Selected / recipes / 1835 1927 / Pilgrim United Church, Hamilton, Ont. / Compiled and published by / "The Guild" / of the / Pilgrim United Church / Heath & Fairclough, printers, 13 Charles Street.

DESCRIPTION: 23.5 × 15.0 cm   Pp [1] 2–64   Tp illus of Pilgrim United Church   Paper; stapled
CONTENTS: 1 tp; 2 'Index' [i.e., table of contents] and acknowledgment of advertisers' subscriptions; 3 ad; 4–64 recipes credited with the name of the contributor and ads
COPIES: *Private collection

Wilson, Anne Elizabeth (1901–46)

Wilson was the first editor of Chatelaine *magazine, launched in March 1928.*

O610.1   [copyright 1927]
MacLean's / surprise / recipes / compiled by / Anne Elizabeth Wilson / Selected from / cookery articles / in the Woman's section of / MacLean's magazine
DESCRIPTION: 17.0 × 12.5 cm   Pp [1–4] 5–63   Illus   Paper, with floral pattern; stapled
CONTENTS: 1 tp; 2 'Copyright, 1927, The MacLean Publishing Company, Limited.'; 3 untitled introductory note signed Anne Elizabeth Wilson; 4 'Index' [i.e., table of contents]; 5–63 'Spring-Time Recipes,' 'Hot Weather Dishes,' 'Interesting Dishes from Other Lands' (includes 'Old World' dishes, Mexican dishes, and Chinese cookery), 'Something New for the Hallowe'en Party,' 'Discoveries in Meat Dishes,' 'Hearty Fare for Thanksgiving,' 'Christmas as a Feast Day,' 'When You Entertain,' and 'Dishes That Tempt Children'
COPIES: *OTMCL (641.5971 W38); United States: IaU (SPEC SZAT TX715.6 M24 1927)
NOTES: No place of publication is cited, but the magazine was based in Toronto. On the title-page, MacLean's is spelled with a capital L, not the later spelling Maclean's. On p 3 Wilson says, 'This little book contains a representation of the many and varied dishes which have appeared in our pages [i.e., *MacLean's*] during the time of my supervision of our Women's Department.' The text examines subjects in detail, from making Maraschino Cherries to preparing dried corn to make Tortillas. The inclusion of recipes for Frijoles, Enchiladas, Tamales, and other Mexican dishes is, as the work's title suggests, 'surprising' for a Canadian cookbook of 1927. Parts of the text are credited to individual writers for the magazine: Ina Winnifred Colwell; Edythe Ann Palmer; Sybil Gayford Rhind; Estelle Carter MacPherson; Beatrice M. Hay-Shaw; Marjorie Elliott Wilkins; and Nellie Regan. Issues of *MacLean's* in 1927 contain a coupon for ordering the book at the price of $0.25.

The OTMCL copy is inscribed on the front face of the binding, in black ink, 'Helen B. Sulman.'

1927–8

The homemaker's comrade

The Kingsmill-Mapleton branch of the Women's Institute was established in 1907 (Ambrose, p 238).

O611.1   nd [1927 or 1928]
For home and country / The / homemaker's comrade / a cook book of home tested recipes / [Women's Institute symbol] / Compiled by / the Kingsmill-Mapleton / Women's Institute
DESCRIPTION: 22.0 × 13.0 cm   Pp [3–5] 6–107   Paper
CONTENTS: 3 tp; 4 'Your Assistance Is Appreciated'; 5 'Kingsmill-Mapleton Women's Institute' [list of officers, Mrs W. Orris as president]; 6 ads; 7–106 text, mainly recipes credited with the name of the contributor, and ads; 107 'Index'
COPIES: CIHM (49156)   OKQ (F5012 nd K55)   *OONL (TX715 H77)
NOTES: 'Printed at the Aylmer Express Office' is on the front face of the binding. The running head is 'Kingsmill-Mapleton W.I. Cook Book.' The advertisements are mainly for businesses in St Thomas and Aylmer, larger towns southwest and southeast of Mapleton. Kingsmill-Mapleton branch records show that Mrs Orris was president for one year, from April 1927 to April 1928. The cookbook, therefore, was published in 1927 or 1928.

The OKQ copy lacks p 107.

1928

A bookful of uses for vinegar

An article about Canada Vinegars Ltd in Saturday Night *Vol. 60, No. 21 (27 January 1945), p 32, refers to the company's history: 'The present company was incorporated in 1928 with a dominion charter to acquire a company of similar name. The origin of the business dates back to 1898. Canada Vinegars Limited is the largest producer in the Dominion of vinegar and allied products, ...' The reference to 1898 probably refers to the amalgamation in that year of various vinegar works in Ontario (see* Monetary Times *Vol. 32, No. 19 (4 November 1898), p 593).*

O612.1   nd [about 1928 or later]
A bookful of uses / for vinegar / culinary –
medicinal – general / including selected recipes for
pickles, / sauces, salads, catsups, etc. / Canada
Vinegars, Limited / 112 Duke St., Toronto, Canada /
the largest vinegar works in America. /
Manufacturers of / pure spirit, cider and malt /
vinegars / in bulk or in bottles. / Our Pure XXX
White Spirit is the very best / and most wholesome
vinegar that can possibly / be obtained anywhere.
[cover-title]
DESCRIPTION: 15.0 × 8.5 cm   Pp [1] 2–24   Paper, with
image on front of a bottle of Pure Spirit Vinegar and a
bottle of Pure Malt Vinegar; stapled
CONTENTS: 1 cover-title; 2–mid 3 'Pickled Fruits'; mid
3–top 6 'Tomato Products'; near top 6–mid 7 'Onion
Products'; mid 7–mid 9 'Sauces'; mid 9–mid 12 'Dressings'; mid 12–mid 17 'Pickles'; mid–bottom 17
'Catsups'; top 18 'Beverages'; mid 18–mid 19 'When
Cooking'; mid 19–22 'Miscellaneous'; 23 'Handy List
of Household Weights and Measures' and 'Time for
Cooking Vegetables'; 24 [outside back face of bind-
ing] three paragraphs of miscellaneous uses for vinegar, untitled note to the reader that the words 'Pure
Spirit Vinegar' in the recipes means a Canada Vin-
egars Ltd product and that the recipes are offered
with the company's compliments, blank space for
'Grocer's Name and Address,' 'Note to Retail Grocer' that on request the company will send 100 or
more copies of this cookbook if the grocer undertakes
the company's local distribution, 'Canada Vinegars
Limited Toronto,' and the printer's name, 'The Armac
Press, Limited Toronto – Canada'
COPIES: ONLAM (Walters-Wagar Collection, Box 20)
*OTMCL (641.5971 H39 No. 28)   Private collection
NOTES: This edition was published after the company's
incorporation in 1928 and before editions called *New
and Old Pickle Recipes*. In the blank space for 'Grocer's
Name and Address' on p 24 of the private collector's
copy, there is the stamp for Steel and Son, general
merchants, Erin, Ontario.

O612.2   nd [about 1933]
—New and old / pickle recipes / including selected
recipes for / sauces, salads, catsups, etc., / also
culinary, medicinal and / general uses for vinegar /
[caption:] The largest vinegar works in America /
Canada Vinegars / Limited / 112 Duke St., Toronto,
Canada / manufacturers of / pure spirit, cider and /
malt vinegars / under government supervision /
Delightful Canada beverages / Appleade for
summer season. / Sweet drinking cider for fall
and / winter months. [cover-title]

DESCRIPTION: 15.5 × 8.0 cm   Pp [1] 2–32   Illus
Paper, with image on front of Canada Vinegars Ltd
building; stapled
CONTENTS: 1 cover-title; 2–3 'Pickled Fruits'; 4–mid 6
'Tomato Products'; bottom 6–7 'Onion Products'; 8 fp
illus of woman dressing a salad; top 9 'Salad Suggestions'; mid 9–12 'Salad Dressings'; 13–14 'Sauces'; 15
illus of three barrels of malt, cider, and spirit vinegar
(the three kinds of Canada Vinegar); 16–17 illus of
'Canada Vinegars Limited Exhibit at Royal York Hotel, Toronto, Retail Grocers' Convention, March, 1933.';
18–top 22 'Pickles'; mid–bottom 22 'Catsups'; top 23
illus of three bottles of vinegar; bottom 23 'Beverages'; top–mid 24 'Candies'; bottom 24–29 'Helpful
Hints'; 30 'Handy List of Household Weights and
Measures' and 'Time for Cooking Vegetables'; 31 fp
illus of '"Canada Vinegars" Tractor and Tank'; 32 untitled note to grocers that the company will send 50
free copies of this book on request if the grocer undertakes local distribution of the book to 'lady customers who pride themselves in making the very
finest pickles' and 'Printed in Canada.'
COPIES: OGU (CCC TX715.6 N47387)   *Private collection
NOTES: This is a retitled edition of *A Bookful of Uses for
Vinegar*. A few recipes have been added, and the
order of the recipes has sometimes been changed. In
this edition, unlike those that follow, the Canada Vinegars Ltd Exhibit illustrated on pp 16–17 is dated
March 1933.

O612.3   nd
—New and old / pickle recipes / including selected
recipes for / sauces, salads, catsups, etc., / also
culinary, medicinal and / general uses for vinegar /
[caption:] The largest vinegar works in America /
Canada Vinegars / Limited / 112 Duke St., Toronto,
Canada / manufacturers of / pure spirit, cider and
/ malt vinegars / under government supervision /
Delightful Canada beverages / Appleade for
summer season. / Sweet drinking cider for fall
and / winter months. [cover-title]
DESCRIPTION: 15.5 × 7.5 cm   Pp [1] 2–32   Illus
Paper, with image on front of Canada Vinegars Ltd
building; stapled
CONTENTS: 1 cover-title; 2–3 'Pickled Fruits'; 4–mid 6
'Tomato Products'; bottom 6–7 'Onion Products'; 8 fp
illus of woman dressing a salad; top 9 'Salad Suggestions'; mid 9–12 'Salad Dressings'; 13–14 'Sauces'; 15
illus of three barrels of malt, cider, and spirit vinegar
(the three kinds of Canada Vinegar); 16–17 illus of
'Canada Vinegars Limited Exhibit at Royal York Hotel, Toronto, Retail Grocers' Convention.'; 18–top 22

'Pickles'; mid–bottom 22 'Catsups'; top 23 illus of three bottles of vinegar; bottom 23 'Beverages'; top–mid 24 'Candies'; bottom 24–29 'Helpful Hints'; 30 'Handy List of Household Weights and Measures' and 'Time for Cooking Vegetables'; 31 fp illus of '"Canada Vinegars" Tractor and Tank'; 32 untitled note to grocers that the company will send 50 free copies of this book on request if the grocer undertakes local distribution of the book to 'lady customers who pride themselves in making the very finest pickles' and 'Printed in Canada.'
COPIES: OTMCL (641.5971 H39 No. 118)   *QMM (RBD ckbk 1399)
NOTES: Unlike O612.2, the caption on pp 16–17 is undated. The QMM copy is stamped on p 32, 'Gillis for [g]ood [g]roceries // 160 Wortley Rd. Phone Met. 1397.'

O612.4   nd
—New and old / pickle recipes / including selected recipes for / sauces, salads, catsups, etc., / also culinary, medicinal and / general uses for vinegar / [caption:] The largest vinegar works in America / Canada Vinegars / Limited / 112 Duke St., Toronto, Canada / manufacturers of / pure spirit, cider and / malt vinegars / under government supervision / Delightful Canada beverages / Appleade for summer season. / Sweet drinking cider for fall and / winter months. / Allen's Apple Juice the year round. [cover-title]
DESCRIPTION: 15.0 × 7.5 cm   Pp [1] 2–32   Illus Paper, with image on front of Canada Vinegars Ltd building; stapled
CONTENTS: 1 cover-title; 2–3 'Pickled Fruits'; 4–mid 6 'Tomato Products'; bottom 6–7 'Onion Products'; 8 publ ad for Allen's Apple Juice; top 9 'Salad Suggestions'; mid 9–12 'Salad Dressings'; 13–14 'Sauces'; 15 illus of three barrels of malt, cider, and spirit vinegar (the three kinds of Canada Vinegar); 16–17 illus of 'Canada Vinegars Limited Exhibit at Royal York Hotel, Toronto, Retail Grocers' Convention'; 18–top 22 'Pickles'; mid–bottom 22 'Catsups'; top 23 illus of three bottles of vinegar; bottom 23 'Beverages'; top–mid 24 'Candies'; bottom 24–29 'Helpful Hints'; 30 'Handy List of Household Weights and Measures' and 'Time for Cooking Vegetables'; 31 fp illus of '"Canada Vinegars" Tractor and Tank'; 32 untitled note to grocers that the company will send 50 free copies of this book to grocers on request and 'Printed in Canada.'
CITATIONS: Driver 2001, Wellington County, p 98 (note 13)

COPIES: OFERWM (A1996.129 MU312)   OVOH *Private collection
NOTES: Unlike O612.3, the cover-title has the additional, final line, 'Allen's Apple Juice the year round.' The caption on pp 16–17 is undated. 'For sale by Steele Bros Fergus Ontario' is stamped on p 32 of the OFERWM copy.

O612.5   nd
—Pickling / recipes / Issued by / Western / Vinegars / Limited / manufacturers of / Vitalized Vinegars / pure spirit, malt / and cider / under government supervision [cover-title]
DESCRIPTION: 15.0 × 8.0 cm   Pp [1] 2–31 [32]   A few illus   Paper; stapled
CONTENTS: 1 cover-title; 2 'Selected Recipes for Pickles, Sauces, Salads // Catsups, etc.'; 3–4 'Pickled Fruits'; 5–mid 7 'Tomato Products'; bottom 7–8 'Onion Products'; 9 illus of woman dressing a salad; top 10 'Salad Suggestions'; mid 10–13 'Salad Dressings'; 14–15 'Sauces'; 16 'Vitalized Vinegars' and illus of three barrels; 17–top 21 'Pickles'; mid–bottom 21 'Catsups'; top 22 illus of bottles of spirit and malt vinegar; mid–bottom 22 'Beverages'; top–mid 23 'Candies'; bottom 23–30 'Helpful Hints'; 31 blank for 'Memo.'; 32 [outside back face of binding] blank space for grocer's name and address, and untitled note to grocers that company will send 50 free booklets
COPIES: *ACG
NOTES: The design of the book is newer than previously described editions, and there is no illustration on the front face of the binding.

O612.6   nd [about 1935–9]
—New and old / pickle recipes / including selected recipes for / sauces, salads, catsups, etc. / Also culinary, medicinal and / general uses for / Western / vitalized / vinegars / Western Vinegars / Limited / Winnipeg – Regina – Calgary / Edmonton – Vancouver / manufacturers of / pure spirit, cider and / malt vinegars / under government supervision / Delightful Western beverages / Appleade for summer season / Sweet drinking cider for fall / and winter months [cover-title]
DESCRIPTION: 15.0 × 7.5 cm   Pp [1] 2–31 [32]   Illus Paper; stapled
CONTENTS: 1 cover-title; 2–3 'Pickled Fruits'; 4–mid 6 'Tomato Products'; bottom 6–7 'Onion Products'; 8 publ ad for Vitalized XXX Spirit Vinegar; top 9 'Salad Suggestions'; mid 9–12 'Salad Dressings'; 13–14 'Sauces'; 15 illus of three barrels of malt, cider, and spirit vinegar; 16–top 20 'Pickles'; mid–bottom 20

'Catsups'; top 21 illus of three bottles of Western Vinegar; bottom 21 'Beverages'; top–mid 22 'Candies'; bottom 22–29 'Helpful Hints'; 30–1 blank, ruled leaves for 'Memo.'; 32 [outside back face of binding] blank space for grocer's name and address, and untitled note to grocers that company will send 50 free booklets
COPIES: *Private collection
NOTES: The cover-title is printed in red and black.

O612.7 nd [about 1935–9]
—New and old / pickle recipes / including selected recipes for / sauces, salads, catsups, etc. / Also culinary, medicinal and / general uses for vinegar / Western Vinegars / Limited / Winnipeg, Regina, Calgary, / Edmonton, Vancouver / manufacturers of / pure spirit, cider and / malt vinegars / under government supervision / Delightful Western beverages / Appleade for summer season. / Sweet drinking cider for fall / and winter months. [cover-title]
COPIES: *Private collection
NOTES: The cover-title is printed in red and black. In this edition Western Vinegar is not described as 'vitalized.'

For a later publication by Western Vinegars Ltd, see O1114.3, *Western Vinegars Recipe Book and Household Hints,* under *Canada Vinegars Recipe Book and Household Hints.*

Chase, Dr Alvin Wood (Cayuga County, NY, 20 March 1817–25 May 1885, Ohio)

See O535.1 for other years of the calendar almanac. For information about Dr Chase and his other publications, see O8.1.

O613.1 1928
Hang me up / Dr. A.W. Chase's / calendar almanac / 1928 / for the / home, factory / farm, office / Published by / the Dr. A.W. Chase Medicine Co. / Limited / Toronto Canada [cover-title]
DESCRIPTION: 21.0 × 15.5 cm Pp [3] 4–50 Illus Paper, with image on front of Dr Chase and his signature; stapled, and with hole punched at top left corner, through which runs a string for hanging
CONTENTS: 3 zodiacal signs, festivals and anniversaries, stars, and eclipses for 1928; 4 'Greetings'; 5 publ ad; 6–50 monthly calendars, culinary recipes under various headings, medical information, publ ads, and humorous material

COPIES: OKQ (F5012.1928 C487) *OTUTF (jah patent medicine)
NOTES: The 'Greetings' on p 4 refers to the sending out of 1,733,000 Almanacs in the previous year, i.e., 1927, 'one for almost every home in Canada.' It adds, 'In almost 100 per cent of rural homes you will find Dr. Chase's Almanac hanging on the kitchen window frame or kept in a handy place ... Mothers and daughters have learned to appreciate the section of the Almanac which is devoted to Tested Recipes.' The printer's name is on the outside back face of the binding: 'Murray Printing Co., Ltd., Toronto 2, Can.'

Come into the kitchen

Also by Lydia E. Pinkham Medicine Co. are: O685.1, Tested Recipes; O697.1, Food and Health; and O818.1, Favorite Recipes. The company was founded in 1873 by the children of Lydia Estes Pinkham (Lynn, Mass., 1819–1883) to market their mother's vegetable compound, a remedy for female illness. The business later expanded to Canada and Mexico, and the trademark was also registered in other parts of the world. The Canadian business was based in Cobourg, Ontario, in the old Model School for training teachers, on University Avenue, close to Spring Street (the building has since been demolished). The records of Lydia E. Pinkham Medicine Co. are at MCR (MC-181; B/L983; M-79) and hold, among other items, the 'complete series in various languages of Pinkham pamphlets.'

O614.1 1928
Come into / the / kitchen / A collection of / tested recipes for / busy housewives / Published by / Lydia E. Pinkham Medicine Co., / Lynn, Massachussetts, U.S.A. / and / Cobourg, Ontario, Canada / 1928
DESCRIPTION: 17.0 × 11.0 cm Pp [1] 2–32 Illus Paper, with image on front of an aproned young woman pouring liquid into a measuring cup; stapled
CONTENTS: 1 tp; 2–32 recipes, testimonials, and publ ads
COPIES: AEPMA OGU (CCC TX715.6 C645) OHMB (QV772 L983c 1928) OKELWM OONL (TX715 C65 copy 2) OTBPM *Private collection
NOTES: The title-pages of the two English editions, O614.1 and O614.2, are distinguished by the decorative brackets printed on each side of the subtitle, 'A collection of / tested recipes for / busy housewives.' In O614.1, the bracket is formed by a thin vertical line on its inside edge and two curved lines of varying

thickness on its outside edge (the top line curves outward and the bottom line inward). In O614.2, the bracket is formed by three thin vertical lines and there is a small decorative feature placed at the halfway point of the vertical lines. The order of publication of the two English editions is unknown.

The advertisement on p 5 recommends Lydia E. Pinkham's Vegetable Compound for working women: 'Hundreds of Canadian girls and women in offices, factories and stores are depending upon Lydia E. Pinkham's Vegetable Compound.' The testimonials for the Vegetable Compound in the advertisements are from Canadians. The Pinkham Sandwich on p 4 features a filling made of 2 cups boiled ham, ½ pound young American cheese, small bottle of stuffed olives, and one sweet pepper, put through a food chopper and moistened with salad dressing.

The OGU copy lacks its binding. QGMG has a copy of *Come into the Kitchen,* which may match O614.1 or O614.2.

O614.2   1928
—Come into / the / kitchen / A collection of / tested recipes for / busy housewives / Published by / Lydia E. Pinkham Medicine Co., / Lynn, Massachussetts, U.S.A. / and / Cobourg, Ontario, Canada / 1928
DESCRIPTION: 17.5 × 11.0 cm   Pp [1] 2–32   Illus Paper, with image on front of an aproned young woman pouring liquid into a measuring cup; stapled
CONTENTS: 1 tp; 2–32 recipes, testimonials, and publ ads
COPIES: *BDUCVM   OGU (CCC TX715.6 C645 copy 2)   OONL (TX715 C65)   OTMCL (641.5971 H39 No. 13)   QSH (0438)   SBIM   SSWD
NOTES: See O614.1 for a description of the brackets on the title-page of this edition.

O614.3   1928
—Venez / a la / cuisine / Une compilation de / recettes eprouvees pour / les menageres occupees / Publiee par / Cie de remedes Lydia E. Pinkham, / Lynn, Massachusetts, U.S.A. / et / Cobourg, Ontario, Canada / 1928.
DESCRIPTION: 17.5 × 11.0 cm   Pp [1] 2–32   Illus Paper, with image on front of an aproned young woman pouring liquid into a measuring cup; stapled
CONTENTS: 1 tp; 2–32 recipes and publ ads
COPIES: *OONL (TX715 C3465 No. 16 reserve)
NOTES: The brackets on the title-page of the French-language edition do not match those on either of the English editions.

Cook book

Glebe Road United Church is near the intersection of Mount Pleasant Avenue and Davisville.

O615.1   nd [about 1928]
A feast of good things / Cook book / compiled by / the Joy Givers' Class of / the Glebe Road United Church / Toronto
DESCRIPTION: 22.0 × 15.0 cm   Pp [1–5] 6–88   Fp illus on p 1 of Glebe Road United Church   Paper; stapled
CONTENTS: 1 fp illus of church; 2 'Dedication // To all the housewives throughout the land who are aiming at greater perfection in the art of cooking ...'; 3 tp; 4 'A Card' thanking the advertisers; 5 'Index' [i.e., table of contents]; 6–88 recipes credited with the name of the contributor, 'Tables of Weights and Measures,' 'Household Hints,' and ads
COPIES: *Private collection
NOTES: The cover-title is 'The Joy Givers' Cook Book.' 'Product of the Post Press // Hanover, Ont.' is printed on the outside back face of the binding. The book's owner has checked the advertisements against Toronto city directories and suggests a publication date of about 1928. This copy is inscribed on the binding, in ink, 'Jessie B. Graham.'

Cook book

For an earlier cookbook from the same church, then called Essex Methodist Church, see O176.1.

O616.1   nd [about 1928]
Cook book / compiled by / the Choir / of / the United Church / Essex, Ont.
DESCRIPTION: 23.0 × 15.0 cm   Pp [1–2] 3–168   Cloth
CONTENTS: 1 tp; 2 blank; 3 'Index' [i.e., table of contents]; 4 'Members of the United Choir'; 5 untitled four-line verse and 'Recipe for a Happy Life' by Edgar A. Guest; 6 'Abbreviations' and 'Table of Weights and Measures'; 7–165 recipes credited with the name of the contributor and ads; 166 ad; 167–8 'Hints to Housekeepers'
COPIES: *Private collection
NOTES: The cover-title is 'The Cook Book.' 'Members of the United Choir' lists the sopranos, contraltos, tenors, and bassos, and names Mrs Doris Brown as organist and choir leader. There is an advertisement on p 120 for a '1928 Rogers batteryless outfit,' indicating that the cookbook was published about 1928.

The collector's copy is inscribed on the front endpaper, in pencil, 'Gertrude L. Snell. 71 Regal Rd. Toronto, Ontario.'

Cook book of choice tested recipes

O617.1 1928
Cook book / of / choice tested recipes compiled by the / Parish Hall Guild / of / St. Thomas Church / St. Catharines / Ontario / [quotation from Ruskin] / 1928 / [folio:] 3
DESCRIPTION: 22.5 × 15.5 cm Pp 1–96 [97–100] Paper, with image on front of the church; stapled
CONTENTS: 1 'Preface' signed 'Committee on Cook Book'; 2 ads; 3 tp; 4 'Grace before Dinner'; 5–8 'Table Service,' 'Serving,' 'Vegetables Served with Meats,' 'Garnishes,' 'Tables of Weights and Measures,' 'Abbreviations of Cookery Terms,' and 'Oven Temperatures for Cookery Purposes'; 9–96 recipes and ads; 97 'Index' [i.e., table of contents]; 98–100 blank for manuscript 'Recipes'
COPIES: *OSTC (641.5 Coo M, 2 copies) OSTCM
NOTES: In the 'Preface' the 'ladies of St. Thomas Church Parish Hall Guild' thank 'the ladies of Knox Church, Winnipeg' for their assistance. The last advertisement is for the *St Catharines Standard* newspaper, which may be the printer of the cookbook.

Ellis, David (1874–1937), and Dugald Campbell

O618.1 1928
The / science and practice / of confectionery / By / David Ellis, D.Sc., Ph.D., F.R.S.E. / Professor of Bacteriology and Superintendent of the Scottish / School of Bakery, the Royal Technical College, Glasgow / and / Dugald Campbell / Chief Instructor of Confectionery in Evening Classes, / the Royal Technical College, Glasgow; Gold Medallist, London / winner of Scottish Champion Challenge Confectionery Cup 1913 / With diagrams / Longmans, Green and Co. Ltd. / 39 Paternoster Row, London, E.C.4 / New York, Toronto / Calcutta, Bombay, and Madras / 1928
DESCRIPTION: 18.5 × 12.5 cm Pp [i–iv] v–xii, 1–235 7 numbered illus Cloth
CONTENTS: i ht; ii blank; iii tp; iv 'Made in Great Britain. All rights reserved'; v–vi 'Preface' signed David Ellis and Dugald Campbell; vii–xii 'Contents'; 1–226 text in two parts (I, 'Raw Materials and Technic [sic],' and II, 'Practical Confectionery'); 227–35 'Index' and at bottom p 235, 'Printed in England by William Clowes and Sons, Limited, Beccles.'
COPIES: *OTMCL (641.85 E48) Private collection; Great Britain: LB (7941.de.17); United States: DLC (TX783 E5)

NOTES: The book is for the professional confectioner, but there is much of interest to the amateur. Part I has chapters for 'Eggs,' 'Chocolate Goods, Cream and Milk,' 'Oils and Fats,' 'Margarine,' 'Butter,' 'The Sugars,' 'Starch: Dried and Crystallized Fruits,' 'Jams, Jellies, Syrups, and Liquid Flavouring Agents,' 'Colouring Matters,' 'Fermentation,' 'Spices and Condiments,' and 'Final Report of Departmental Committee on Use of Preservatives and Colouring Matters.' Part II has chapters for 'Almond Goods, Marzipan and Its Uses,' 'Sugar Boiling,' 'Sponge Goods, Puff Paste, Short Paste,' 'Cakes,' 'Meringues,' 'Creams and Jellies: Ices,' and 'Chocolate Centres and Couvertures.' Pages 8–9 describe the grading of eggs in different countries, including Canada.

Family food supply

For information about Metropolitan Life Insurance Co. and its publications, see O373.1.

O619.1 [copyright 1928]
Family / food supply / What to buy and how / diet and marketing helps / for the housewife / Metropolitan Life Insurance Company / Canadian head office – Ottawa
DESCRIPTION: 19.5 × 13.5 cm Pp [1–2] 3–16 Illus orange-and-black Paper, with still-life on front, in a circular frame, of fruit; stapled
CONTENTS: 1 tp; 2 'Copyright, Canada, 1928 Metropolitan Life Insurance Company'; 3–16 text
COPIES: *OTMCL (641.5971 H39 No. 49)
NOTES: Printed on the outside back face of the binding is '(a) 439 L.W. – Printed in Canada.' *Family Food Supply* was a companion book to O411.1, *The Metropolitan Life Cook Book*, first published in 1918.

O619.2 [copyright 1930]
—Family / food supply / What to buy and how / diet and marketing helps / for the housewife / Metropolitan Life Insurance Company / Canadian head office – Ottawa
DESCRIPTION: 19.5 × 13.5 cm Pp [1–2] 3–16 Illus orange-and-black Paper, with still-life on front, in a circular frame, of fruit; stapled
CONTENTS: 1 tp; 2 'Copyright, Canada, 1930 Metropolitan Life Insurance Company'; 3–16 text
COPIES: *QMM (RBD ckbk 1824)
NOTES: Printed on the outside back face of the binding is '(a) 439 L.W. – Printed in Canada.' The text is organized under the following headings: 'The Food Needs of the Body'; 'Fuel Needs'; 'Building Needs';

'Regulating Needs'; 'Vitamins'; 'Calories'; 'What to Eat (and How to Buy It)'; 'How to Spend the Food Budget'; 'Meal Suggestions'; 'Further Guides to Food Thrift'; and 'Food Accounts.'

O619.3   [copyright 1934]
—Family / food supply / What to buy and why / food and marketing helps / for the homemaker / Metropolitan Life Insurance Company / Canadian head office – Ottawa
DESCRIPTION: 19.5 × 13.5 cm   Pp [1–2] 3–23   Illus red-and-black   Paper, with still-life on front of fruit and vegetables; stapled
CONTENTS: 1 tp; 2 'Copyright, Canada, 1934 Metropolitan Life Insurance Company'; 3–23 text
COPIES: OGU (CCC TX715.6 F343)   *Private collection
NOTES: Printed on the outside back face of the binding is '(h) 439 L.W. Printed in Canada.' The same collector has another copy, copyright 1934, but with '(f) 439 L.W. Printed in Canada'; it is inscribed on the title-page, 'Mr. Camyard(?) April 30/36.'

Chatelaine 1935, p 82, cites this title, but does not specify the edition.

O619.4   [copyright 1934]
—Alimentation / de la famille / Quoi acheter et pourquoi / conseils utiles à la ménagère / sur les aliments et leur achat / Metropolitan Life Insurance Company / Bureau chef canadien – Ottawa
DESCRIPTION: 19.5 × 13.5 cm   Pp [1–2] 3–23   Illus red-and-black   Paper, with still-life on front of fruit and vegetables; stapled
CONTENTS: 1 tp; 2 'Droits réservés au Canada, 1934 Metropolitan Life Insurance Company'; 3–23 text
COPIES: QQUQT   *QSFFSC
NOTES: Printed on the outside back face of the binding is '(h) 439 L.W. – French – Imprimé au Canada.' The QQUQT copy is inscribed on the title-page, in ink, 'P.A.P. [i.e., P.A. Picard, the name inscribed on the QQUQT copy of Q177.2, *Les meilleures recettes du Canada*, under *Canada's Prize Recipes*] août 1937.'

AMERICAN EDITIONS: New York: Metropolitan Life Insurance Co., 1927 (United States: MH); Newark: Metropolitan Life Insurance Co., [1934] (United States: MH).

Favorite recipes

O620.1   [1928]
Favorite recipes / contributed by members / and friends of / Loretto Academy / Alumnae / Hamilton, Canada / Mrs. Hugh C. Sweeney, President / [in left column:] Miss George Anne Dell / Miss Ann Clawsey / Miss Mary Jean Thompson / [in right column:] Mrs. Ed. Harris / Miss Madeline Yaldon / Miss Marie Campbell / Compiled by the executive
DESCRIPTION: 23.0 × 15.0 cm   Pp [leaf lacking] 3–116 [two leaves lacking]   Fp illus on p 8 of Niagara Falls with caption: 'Niagara Falls // Convention – Loretto Alumnae – August, 1928.'; fp illus on p 24 of Hamilton public buildings; fp illus on p 30 of Gore Park; illus on p 3 of Loretto Academy   Probably paper; stapled
CONTENTS: 3 'Loretto, Mount St. Mary' signed M.R. Campbell; 4 ad; 5–93 'Tested Recipes' credited with the name of the contributor and ads; 94 ads; 95 'What to Serve with What' and 'Table of Weights and Measures'; 96 ads; 97–mid 101 'When One Is Sick' [includes recipes]; mid 101–107 'How to Remove Spots with Home Remedies' and ads; 108–16 ads
CITATIONS: Simpson, p W17
COPIES: *OH (R641.5 LOR CESH)   Private collection
NOTES: The OH copy is incomplete. The title-page transcription is from a photocopy of the private collector's intact copy, where the title-page is on p 1 and an advertisement, on p 2; pp 117–20 are advertisements. The cover-title of the private collector's copy is 'Souvenir Cook Book' and the year of publication, 1928, is printed on the front face of the binding; the binding is inscribed, probably by the original owner, 'Mrs. Foster.' The printer, 'Flynn, printer, 33 John St. S.,' is on the inside back face of the binding. His advertisement (for Thos Flynn) is on p 118.

Fifty tested recipes

O621.1   1928
Fifty / tested recipes / Seaforth, Ontario, 1928 [cover-title]
DESCRIPTION: 21.0 × 15.0 cm   Pp [1–28]   Paper; stapled
CONTENTS: 1–8 blank pages headed 'Miscellaneous' for manuscript recipes; 9–20 recipes for 'Meats and Supper Dishes,' 'Miscellaneous,' 'Meats and Supper Dishes' [i.e., same title as first section], 'Salad and Salad Dressings,' 'Rolls and Small Cakes,' 'Pie and Puddings,' 'Miscellaneous Recipes,' and 'Desserts'; 21–8 blank for 'Miscellaneous' manuscript recipes

COPIES: *Private collection

NOTES: There are no advertisements. Although no group or association is identified as the author and the recipes are uncredited, the book conforms to the fund-raising type.

Fortier, Loftus Morton (26 April 1858–)

The 1901 Census records Fortier as a civil servant, living in Ottawa with his wife Fanny and seven children. He later moved his family to Annapolis Royal, Nova Scotia, and was instrumental in persuading the federal government to rebuild Fort Anne. He was made the first honorary superintendent of Fort Anne.

O622.1 1928

Champlain's / Order of Good Cheer / and / some brief notes relating to / its founder / by / L.M. Fortier / member of the Historical Association of Annapolis Royal / Toronto / Thomas Nelson & Sons Ltd. / 1928

DESCRIPTION: 21.5 × 14.0 cm   Pp [1–4] 5–28, [i–ii]   3 pls incl frontis, 1 fp illus of Port Royal   Paper-covered boards

CONTENTS: 1 ht; 2 blank; 3 tp; 4 'Copyright in Canada by L.M. Fortier'; 5 table of contents; 6 blank; 7 list of illustrations; 8 blank; 9–28 text; i publ ad for colour engravings of scenes from Canadian history; ii 'Warwick Bros. & Rutter Limited Toronto printers and bookbinders'

CITATIONS: JLCat 104

COPIES: ACU (FC332 F65 1928)   BVAU (F5061 F6) MWU (F1031.1 F67)   NBFU (FC2349 A55 F67) NBMOUA (060 B56f)   NBS (971.6 FOR)   NBSCU (971.601 F7412c)   NFSM (F1030 F6)   NSH (971.6 F741c)   NSHD (F1030.1 F67, 2 copies)   NSHV (F1030.1 F66)   NWSA (F1036 O74)   OGU (2 copies: *UA s066 b05, F5061.1 C5 F6)   OKQ (F1030.1 F7) OKR (F5061 F6)   OLU (F1030.1 F6)   OONG (N0 J45 F67 1928)   OONL (F5061.1 C5 F6, 4 copies)   OOSS (FC332 F67)   OSUL (92-1408 B41)   OTMCL (970.02 C34.01)   OTU (FC332 F67 1928)   OTY (CPC 1928 0022)   OW (R 971.01 F77)   OWTU (FC332 F67x 1928)   QMBN (971.601 F741c 1928)   QMM (2 copies: FC332 F66 1928, FC2349 A55 F67)   QQLA (FC332 F741 1928)

NOTES: The text comprises 'The Origin of the Order of Good Cheer' (p 9); 'L'Ordre de bon-temps' by William McLennan (a poem, p 13); 'Some Brief Notes on Champlain' (p 19); and 'Notes on the Picture by Charles W. Jefferys, A.R.C.A.' (p 23). The book is a celebration of Canada's first gastronomic society, established by Samuel de Champlain at Port Royal in the winter of 1606–7 to help his men survive the season. Members of the Order took turns as chief steward, the person charged with providing the food and with leading the procession of dishes to table, while wearing the symbol of the Order around his neck.

Helpful hints for housekeepers 1928

See O263.1 for information about the company and other issues of Helpful Hints for Housekeepers.

O623.1 1928

Hang up for handy reference / 1928 / edition / Helpful / hints / for housekeepers / Compliments of / the Dodds Medicine Co. Ltd. / Toronto – Canada [cover-title]

DESCRIPTION: 15.5 × 10.5 cm   Pp 1–40   Illus   Paper, with image on front of a woman consulting this book; stapled, and with hole punched at top left corner, through which runs a string for hanging

CONTENTS: Inside front face of binding calendars for 1927, 1928, and 1929, and a 5-inch ruler marked along the outside vertical edge of the page; 1 'A Message to You' signed the Dodds Medicine Co. Ltd, Toronto; 2–4 publ ads; 5 'Uses of Ammonia'; 6, 8, 10, 12, 14, 16, 18, 20, 22, 24, 26, 28 entries for illnesses and other medical information, arranged alphabetically from Anaemia to Skin; 7 'The Sick Room'; 9 'Taking Care of Blankets'; 11 'The Uses for Tea'; 13 'Stockings'; 15 'Facts about Fur' and 'Sandwiches' [recipes]; 17 'Clean Your Own Gloves'; 19 'Kitchen Equivalents'; 21 'The Care of Furniture'; 23 'Baking Hints'; 25 'Cleaning Saucepans' and 'A Word about Coal-Oil'; 27, 29 'Things Worth Remembering'; 30 'Rates of Postage'; 31 'To Prevent Juices from Running Out' and 'How to Keep Young'; 32 'Weights and Measures'; 33 'Laundering Silk'; 34 publ ad; 35 'Introductions'; 36 publ ad; 37 'Points for the Kitchen'; 38 publ ad; 39 'The Care of Flowers'; 40 'Diet Rules'; inside back face 'Self Examination Page'

COPIES: *OTUTF (uncat patent medicine)

Hunt, Mrs Clarry H., née Semple (Portsmouth, England, 1870–7 May 1950, Toronto, Ont.)

Clarry and her husband George had three children: Ernest W., killed at Amiens in 1918, and two daughters, Gwenyth and Frances Caroline. Clarry is buried in Park Lawn Cemetery in Toronto.

O624.1 [copyright 1928]
Modern / housekeeping / Arranged by / Mrs
Clarry Hunt / Published by / E.W. Gillett Company
Limited / Toronto Canada / Vancouver – Winnipeg
– Ottawa – Montreal – Quebec
DESCRIPTION: 20.5 × 15.0 cm   Pp [1–4] 5–352   Frontis
of author; 8 double-sided pls (rectos col, versos
b/w); 5 pls on pp 104–8 of cuts of meat   Washable
cloth
CONTENTS: 1 tp with decorative vertical band in green;
2 'Copyright Canada, 1928 E.W. Gillett Company Lim-
ited Toronto, Canada'; 3 'Foreword'; 4 blank; 5–339
text; 340–1 'Index' [i.e., table of contents]; 342 blank;
343–52 'General Index'
CITATIONS: Golick, pp 109–10
COPIES: BKM   *OGU (UA s045 b26)   OTNY (uncat)
NOTES: Clarry Hunt was the chief dietitian of E.W.
Gillett Co. Ltd, whose products are specified in the
ingredients lists of the recipes. The volume is bound
by two metal machine-threaded screws, allowing the
insertion of extra leaves. As the author explains in the
'Foreword,' 'This book is made in loose-leaf form so
that it can be kept perpetually up-to-date.' The OTNY
copy is inscribed on the front endpaper, in ink, 'Elsie
Woods.'

This edition was later distributed in two variant
bindings: one with 'Standard Brands Limited successor to E.W. Gillett Company Limited'; the other with
'Standard Brands Limited Gillett Products' (copies in
a bookseller's stock). These variants were produced
after 27 August 1929, when Standard Brands Ltd was
incorporated, but before the publication of O624.2,
where the title-page imprint reflects the new corporate identity.

O624.2 [copyright 1928; 1929 or later]
—Modern / housekeeping / Arranged by / Mrs
Clarry Hunt / Published by / Standard Brands
Limited / Montreal Toronto Winnipeg Vancouver
DESCRIPTION: 20.5 × 15.0 cm   Pp [1–4] 5–352   Frontis
of author; 8 double-sided pls (rectos col, versos
b/w)   Washable cloth
CONTENTS: 1 tp; 2 'Copyright Canada, 1928 Standard
Brands Limited'; 3 'Foreword' signed Clarry H. Hunt,
chief dietitian, Standard Brands Ltd; 4 blank; 5–339
text; 340–1 'Index' [i.e., table of contents]; 342 blank;
343–52 'General Index'
COPIES: ACG   OHWHH   QMM (RBD TX715.6 H86
1928)   *Private collection
NOTES: This edition was published after 27 August
1929, when Standard Brands Ltd was incorporated.

The model cook book

O625.1   nd [about 1928]
The / model cook / book / Under the auspices of /
the Ladies Guild of / the Trinity United Church /
[ad:] "Say it with flowers" / D.S. Kauffman / florist
/ 77 James St. North / Phone Regent 21 / Flowers
sent to all parts of the world. [cover-title]
DESCRIPTION: 22.0 × 14.0 cm   Pp [1–2] 3–46 [47–8]
Paper; stapled
CONTENTS: 1 preface; 2 'Things Worth Knowing'; 3–
46 recipes credited with the name of the contributor
and ads; 47–8 blank for 'Memorandum'
COPIES: *Private collection
NOTES: Trinity United Church is in Hamilton. There is
an advertisement on p 46 that includes a coupon
valid during the year 1928.

Motor picnic lunches

O626.1   nd [about 1928]
Motor picnic / lunches / with genuine Thermos
bottles and jars [cover-title]
DESCRIPTION: 16.5 × 12.5 cm   Pp 1–28   Illus   Paper,
with image on front of a mother, father, and three
children having a picnic; stapled
CONTENTS: 1 'Picnic Menus for Five Persons'; 2 'Picnic Menu for Four Persons' and 'Picnic Menu for
Three Persons'; 3 'Lunch Menu for Two Persons' and
'Lunch Menu for One Person'; 4–5 'New Thermos
Motor Outfit'; 6 'At School'; 7 'Sandwich Sugges-
tions'; 8 'For Verandah and Lawn Picnics'; 9 'Cake
Recipes'; 10 'Salads'; 11 Motor Outfit No. 260; 12 'Ther-
mos Jars for Different Purposes'; 13–15 'Menus for
Picnic Lunches'; 16 'Verandah or Lawn Picnic Menus';
17–18 'School Lunches'; top 19 'Salads – Continued
from page 10'; mid–bottom 19 'Meats for Picnic
Lunches'; 20–2 'Sandwich Fillings'; 23 'Thermos
Bottles // All Sizes and Finishes'; 24 'Nécessaire pour
l'auto – No. 247' and 'Menu pour cinq personnes'; 25
'Sac d'école – No. 168½' and 'Menus pour l'école'; 26
'Menus pour pique-niques'; 27 'Comment faire des
sandwiches'; 28 'Directions'; inside back face of binding 'Motor Rules' and 'Les commandements de
l'automobiliste'; outside back face 'Thermos Bottle
Co., Limited // 1239 Queen Street West // Toronto
3, Ontario // In United States: New York // In England: London'
COPIES: *QMM (RBD ckbk 2061)
NOTES: 'Recipes compiled by M.I. Nixon' is printed
on the inside front face of the binding. Not all of the
English text has been translated into French. The Ther-

mos Bottle Co. Ltd is listed at 1239 Queen Street West in the 1928 Toronto city directory (before 1928, the company was at 1303 Queen Street West and on other streets). After 1928, directories list the address as 1239–41 Queen Street West. The appearance of the book is consistent with publication in 1928.

Naomi cook book

O627.1   1928
Naomi cook book / Toronto, 1928
DESCRIPTION: 23.0 × 15.0 cm   Pp [1] 2–200   Cloth
CONTENTS: 1 tp; 2 ad; 3 note of thanks signed Committee and a list of committee members; 4 ad; 5 foreword signed Anna Selick; 6 ad; 7 'Index' [i.e., table of contents]; 8 ad; 9–174 text, mostly recipes credited with the name of the contributor, and ads; 175–6 ads; 177–200 blank for 'Memo'
CITATIONS: Ferguson/Fraser, p 233
COPIES: OTCJCA   *Private collection
NOTES: From its first edition in 1928, *Naomi Cook Book* served for decades as the standard source of recipes for Toronto's Jewish families. Selick writes in the foreword: 'Here in this book are the Old and the New. Here are strudle [sic] and, in the same breath, ice box cakes. Here, the homely dishes that Sarah must have prepared for angels, and here, too, the things that angels upon earth may prepare for modern and critical husbands ... the funds raised by the sale of this book will be employed in the immensely practical work of Hadassah in Palestine ... [I] recommend this book to the Jewish women of Canada ...' There is a chapter of 'Passover Dishes,' and the 'Household Hints' chapter has a recipe for Kosher Soap. The advertisements are for Toronto Jewish businesses, including several for Modern Laundry, 'a Jewish laundry.' The advertisement for Windsor Salt on p 33 describes the product as 'kosher to the utmost degree.'

The committee members listed on p 3 are: Mrs S.H. Adman, Mrs L. Berger, Mrs M.H. Bernstein, Mrs J. Broudy, Mrs M. Blackstone, Mrs J.D. Cadesky, Mrs L. Cadesky, Mrs A. Cohen, Mrs H. Cohen, Mrs L. Feinsod, Mrs M.C. Friedman, Mrs M. Greisman, Mrs M. Harlig, Mrs I.L. Himmelstein, Mrs A. Isaacson, Mrs H. Kaplan, Mrs L. Kert, Mrs J.S. Lavene, Mrs J. Rashkofsky, Mrs B. Sadowski, Mrs P. Salter, Mrs S. Sapera, Mrs E. Shapiro, Mrs M. Shulman, Mrs F. Silverman, Mrs E.F. Singer, Mrs A. Stock, Mrs L. Stossel, Mrs B. Vise, Mrs D. Vise, Mrs M.J. Weiss, and Mrs M. Wellman. The copy of the cookbook catalogued here belonged originally to committee member Mrs J.D. Cadesky. The make-up of the Committee changed for subsequent editions.

O627.2   2nd ed., 1934
—Naomi cook book / Second edition / Toronto 1934
DESCRIPTION: 23.0 × 15.0 cm   Pp [1] 2–200   Cloth
CONTENTS: 1 tp; 2 note of thanks signed Committee and a list of committee members; 3 ad; 4 'Index' [i.e., table of contents]; 5–6 ads; 7–177 text and ads; 178–200 blank for 'Memo'
CITATIONS: Landsberg
COPIES: OTCJCA   OWTU (G12668)   *Private collection
NOTES: This edition has no foreword. In this edition (and in 1948 and 1950), Mrs J.D. Cadesky's name appears as Cadesby.

O627.3   3rd ed., 1948
—The Naomi cook book / Third edition / Published by the Naomi Chapter of Hadassah to mark / the completion of 25 years of service in the interest / of Zion and the re-dedication of its efforts for the / welfare and upbuilding of the State of Israel. / Toronto, Canada / 1948–5708 / Additional copies of this book may be obtained by writing to the / Naomi Chapter, 651 Spadina Ave., Toronto.
DESCRIPTION: 22.5 × 15.0 cm   Pp [1–4] 5–200   Cloth
CONTENTS: 1 tp; 2 list of 'Naomi Chapter Members'; 3 'Foreword' signed 'Editorial Staff Mrs. B.W. Birn Mrs. Alfred Cohen Mrs. Bert Cooper Mrs. Max Cooper Mrs. Frank A. Silverman'; 4 ad; 5–6 index; 7–180 text and ads; 181–200 blank for manuscript recipes
COPIES: OONL (TX724 H23 1948)   OTCJCA   OWTU (TX651 N3 1948)   *Private collection
NOTES: The 'Foreword' (revised from the first edition) comments: 'Jews have carried with them, wherever they have wandered, styles of cookery prevailing in the countries from which they have migrated. This, together with the Dietary and Ceremonial Laws and the institution of the Passover, has contributed to make Jewish cookery distinctive.' This edition has a chapter of 'Purim Recipes' on pp 162–3.

One copy of the 1948 edition was sent on an unusual cross-cultural journey, when it was given as a gift by a Jewish family to its domestic employee, a gentile. The current owner of the book recounted its subsequent history, in a letter to me of 24 September 1991: 'Knowing nothing of Jewish culture or dietary laws, my grandmother did not hesitate to jot recipes for baked ham glaze or Mrs. Ladouceur's Christmas cake on the pages of the book.' When the granddaughter married a Jewish man, the cookbook was passed down to her, 'for its potential usefulness and as a keepsake.' Her husband especially appreciated the recipe for prune and potato tsimmies, which his own grandmother used to make.

OTHER EDITIONS: *The Naomi Cook Book*, 3rd ed., 2nd printing, 1950, 'Additional copies of this book may be obtained by writing to the Naomi Chapter, 32 Ardmore Road, Toronto' (Private collection); 4th ed., Toronto: Naomi Chapter, 1960, title-page lists the publications chairmen for the various editions: '1st edition – 1928 Mrs. Jacob Rash // 2nd edition – 1932 [*sic*] Mrs. David Vise // 3rd edition – 1948 Mrs. Max Cooper // 4th edition – 1960 Mrs. J.D. Cadsby' (OGU, OONL).

Tested recipes

O628.1 1928
Tested recipes / Compiled by / the Women's Association of / Trinity Church / Peterborough / 1928
DESCRIPTION: 23.0 × 14.5 cm   Pp [1–2] 3–133, [i]   Limp cloth; sewn?
CONTENTS: 1 tp; 2 'Dawe-Pearson Limited printers // 279 George St., Peterborough'; 3 table of contents; 4 blank; 5 'Measurements'; 6 blank; 7 'Foreword'; 8 blank; 9–132 recipes credited with the name of the contributor and ads; 133 'Household Hints'; i ads
COPIES: *OTYA (TX715.6 T73 1928)

The treasury cook book

The Micksburg branch of the Women's Institute was established in 1925 (Ambrose, p 230). Micksburg is south of Pembroke.

O629.1 1928
The / treasury / cook book / compiled by / the Girls' Circle / of the / Women's Institute / Micksburg / 1928
DESCRIPTION: [$0.40, on binding]
CONTENTS: Inside front face of binding 'Ye Cook Book' [i.e., introduction in the form of an eight-line verse] and 'Printed at Cobden, Ontario by the Cobden Sun'; 1 tp; 2 'How to Cook a Husband'; 3–78 recipes credited with the name of the contributor and ads; 79 'Miscellaneous'; 80–mid 82 'Hints and Suggestions' and ad; mid 82–mid 86 'Tips for Housekeepers'; mid 86–91 'Useful Information'; 92 'Antidotes for Poison'; 93 table of contents; 94–6 blank for 'Notes and Other Recipes'
COPIES: *Private collection

1928–9

Pollyanna glad book of recipes

O630.1 nd [about 1928–9]
Pollyanna / glad book / of / recipes / Collected and arranged by / the Pollyanna Class / of the / Centennial / United / Sunday School / London, Ontario [cover-title]
DESCRIPTION: 22.5 × 15.0 cm   Pp [1] 2–95 [96]   Paper, with image on front of a camel and mosque; stapled
CONTENTS: 1 'Be the Best of Whatever You Are,' a poem by Douglas Malloch, copyright 1926 by Scott Dowd; 2 ad; 3 'Index'; 4 'Helpful Hints' and 'Tables of Weights and Measures'; 5 '"Thank You"' and list of 'Pollyanna Glad Girls'; 6 ads; 7 'The Value of Food'; 8 ads; 9–93 recipes credited with the name of the contributor and ads; 94–5 'The Question of Food'; 96 'A Little Prayer' by S.E. Kiser
COPIES: *Bookseller's stock
NOTES: An advertisement on p 24 for Westervelt School in London states, 'June 1st, 1928 to October 1st, 1928, 188 graduates placed in positions,' evidence that the cookbook was likely published about 1928–9. 'Hayden Press, London' is on the outside back face of the binding.

1928–30

Three meals a day

For information about Metropolitan Life Insurance Co. and its publications, see O373.1.

O631.1 nd [about 1928–30]
Three meals / a day / Suggestions for good food at low cost / Metropolitan Life Insurance Company / Canadian head office – Ottawa [cover-title]
DESCRIPTION: 20.0 × 13.5 cm   Pp 1–16   Paper, with image on front of a single place-setting and a floral centrepiece
CONTENTS: 1 'Your Family Needs at Least These Foods'; 2 'A Week's Minimum Supply of Food'; 3 'Meals for the Whole Family'; 4–5 'For a Family of Three'; 6 'Market Order for Menus to Cost $6 per Week'; 7–8 'For a Family of Five'; 9 'Market Order for Menus to Cost $12 per Week'; 10–11 'For a Family of Seven'; 12 'Market Order for Menus to Cost $15 per Week'; 13–16 'Recipes'
COPIES: OTMCL (641.5971 H39 No. 16)   *Private collection
NOTES: A note on the inside front face of the binding

states, 'This material was prepared by the Food Committee of the New York Nutritionists, and the New York Nutrition Council to guide families in a choice of food which will help to maintain health ...' A note on the inside back face refers the reader to *The Metropolitan Cook Book* (O411.1) for recipes and *Family Food Supply* (O619.1) for information about food needs and marketing.

Metropolitan Life Insurance Co. established its Canadian headquarters in Ottawa in 1924; therefore, the cookbook was published no earlier than 1924. Since *Family Food Supply* was copyrighted in Canada in 1928, *Three Meals a Day* was likely published after it, in about 1928–30.

The following is on the outside back face of the binding: '(a) 468 L.W. – Printed in Canada.' There is a copy at OHMB (Ephemera QU145 M594t 1920) that appears to be the same as the private collector's and OTMCL copies except for '(c) 468 L.W.' on the binding. A copy at OONL (AC901 A7 1920z No. 0064) may match O631.1 or O631.2.

Chatelaine 1935, p 82, cites this title, but does not distinguish between editions.

O631.2 nd
—Three meals / a day / Suggestions for good food at low cost / Metropolitan Life Insurance Company / Canadian head office – Ottawa [cover-title]
DESCRIPTION: 19.5 × 13.5 cm   Pp 1–16   Paper, with image on front of a single place-setting and a floral centrepiece; stapled
CONTENTS: 1 'Your Family Needs at Least These Foods'; 2–3 'Suggested Adequate Food Budget for One Week'; 4 'Sample Budget,' 'Weekly Amount of Food,' and 'Sample for Calculating Daily Milk Allowance'; 5 'Food Budget for One Week' and 'Suggestions'; 6–7 'Menus to Be Used When the Amount to Spend Is Very Limited'; 8–9 'Menus Which Can Be Prepared from Food Suggested on Pages 2 and 3'; 10–11 'Slightly Higher Cost Menus Including More Fruit, Salads and Meat'; 12–13 'Weekly Menu Emphasizing Foods High in Minerals'; 14–16 'Recipes for Menus Suggested' [fourteen numbered recipes]
COPIES: *Private collection
NOTES: The following is on the outside back face of the binding: '(h) 468 L.W. – Printed in Canada.' Another private collector has a copy with '(f) 468 L.W. – Printed in Canada.'

O631.3 nd
—Three meals a day / Metropolitan Life Insurance Company / Canadian head office: Ottawa [cover-title]
DESCRIPTION: 20.0 × 14.0 cm   Pp 1–9   Paper, with image on front of a table set with three places and a plate of fruit; stapled
CONTENTS: 1–3 'Good Health Requires the Right Food'; 4–5 table of 'Weekly Food Needs for Individuals of Various Ages'; 6–7 'Sample Menus for One Week'; 8–9 [inside back face of binding] 'Menus Especially High in Minerals and Vitamins'
COPIES: *OGU (CCC TX715.6 T475 cover b)
NOTES: In the menus, recipes marked with an asterisk 'may be found in Metropolitan Cook Book.' In this later, shorter edition there are no recipes. The following is on the outside back face of the binding: '(m) 468 L.W. – Printed in Canada.'

AMERICAN EDITIONS: New York: Metropolitan Insurance Co., nd, pp 16, includes recipes, same image on binding as O631.3, '(l) 468 L.W.' on outside back face (OGU).

1928–33

The mixing bowl

O632.1 nd [about 1928–33]
The / mixing / bowl / St. Andrew's Presbyterian Church / Cobourg [cover-title]
DESCRIPTION: 22.5 × 15.0 cm   Pp 1–44   Paper
CONTENTS: 1 'Preface' signed 'Compiled by the Helping Circle of St. Andrew's Presbyterian Church // Cobourg, Ontario' and index; 2–37 recipes credited with the name of the contributor and ads; 38–9 'What to Serve with Meats'; 40 'Suggestions for Table Decorations'; 41 timetables for baking flour mixtures, for cooking vegetables in water, and for roasting; 42–3 'Large Amounts for Home Catering'; 44 'Equivalents'
CITATIONS: Driver 2001, Wellington County, p 86
COPIES: *Private collection
NOTES: This cookbook was produced when my great-aunt Ella's husband, Frank Harper, was minister of St Andrew's Presbyterian Church, in the period January 1928 to June 1933. The text includes Ella's recipes.

1929

Betty

O633.1 [copyright 1929]
Betty's home chats / and cook book / compiled and edited by / Betty / Listen to the Cooking School over the Cheerio / station, C.K.G.W., at Toronto, every morning / from ten to eleven o'clock. / Sponsored by / manufacturers of food products in

Canada / and / Radio Specialties of Canada, Ltd.
DESCRIPTION: 22.0 × 15.5 cm   Pp [i–iii], 1–39   Paper, with image on front of a woman tasting the contents of a steaming saucepan; top-hinged with two metal fasteners, and with cord for hanging
CONTENTS: i tp; ii–iii ads; 1 'Weights and Measures' and 'Table of Measure'; [two unnumbered leaves] ads; 2 'Combining Ingredients'; [unnumbered leaf] ad; 3–4 'Contents'; 5–39 recipes and unnumbered leaves of ads
COPIES: OONL (TX715.6 B494 1929, not on shelf) *Private collection
NOTES: The copyright date, 1929, is printed on the front face of the binding. CKGW was the radio station owned by Gooderham and Worts, the Toronto whisky distillery. In 1929 'Betty's Home Chats and Cooking School' was the first scheduled program on CKGW, Monday to Friday, at 10:00 a.m. 'Betty' is not identified by last name in the book, but she may be Mrs Betty D. Supplee, who is mentioned in a letter from M. Iola Plaxton [i.e., Miss Iola Meryl Russell Plaxton] of Radio Specialties of Canada Ltd to Mr Ashcroft of CKGW at the King Edward Hotel, Toronto, 30 May 1930 (letter in the Gooderham and Worts archives, owned by the developer of the historic distillery site, Cityscape Developments). Radio Specialties of Canada is described on the letterhead as 'Radio advertising consultants and specialists // Musical programmes planned and continuity written' and as 'Sponsors of Betty's Home Chats and Cooking School // Betty's Shopping Service // Betty's Children Hour // Betty's Holiday Hints.' In the letter Plaxton discusses payments made to CKGW, and says, 'You will also find that some allowance has been made to cover indebtedness owing by Mrs. Supplee.' There is no listing for Supplee in the Toronto city directory of 1929, but in 1930, Mrs Betty D. Supplee is listed as president of Radio Specialties of Canada Ltd and living at 6 St Thomas Street, the address of University Apartments.

The book was likely sponsored by the manufacturers of food products that are advertised on the unnumbered leaves. References to food companies also appear in the text; for example, pp 33–4 are headed 'Baking Experiences New and Delightful Tested with Purity Flour' and contain recipes using Purity products. Also, p 28 is 'Barron's [grocery store at 728 Yonge Street] Suggestion for an Emergency Shelf.'

The leaves are printed on the rectos only; the versos are not included in the pagination. The 'Contents' lists the final section as 'Special Recipes (pages 28–42)'; however, the private collector's copy ends at

p 39. Perhaps the last three leaves were removed. The same collector acquired (too late for an entry in this bibliography) *Marketing Guide and Economical Recipes*, by Betty D. Supplée [*sic*], nd, inscribed 'Christmas 1934,' pp 162, printed by Belgrave Press.

The Brantford Junior Hospital Aid cook book

O634.1   1929
The Brantford / Junior Hospital Aid / cook book / [within a circular wreath:] JHA / Produced by P. Ryan, printer / Brantford MCMXXIX
DESCRIPTION: 22.0 × 14.0 cm   Pp [3–4] 5–129   Boards
CONTENTS: 3 tp; 4 blank; 5 'Foreword' signed Phyllis Cockshutt, president; 6 blank; 7 'Table of Weights and Measures'; 8 ad; 9–119 recipes credited with the name of the contributor and ads; 120 ad; 121–8 blank for 'Special Recipes'; 129 'Index' [i.e., table of contents]
CITATIONS: JPCat 143, No. 27
COPIES: *OTYA (CPC 1929 0098)
NOTES: The OTYA copy has bare boards, probably originally covered in cloth since the copy cited in JPCat is described as having linen-covered boards. The 'Foreword' gives two purposes for publishing the book, the first of which was to raise money for a fund 'to [furnish and equip] new nursery wards in the General Hospital when the anticipated additions can be built.' The second aim refers to the way that fund-raising cookbooks bring together the cooking practices of a community: 'to give ... a collection of tested recipes, new and old, that may have been heretofore withheld or scattered through numbers of books and papers no longer in print. We hope that our book will thus be especially useful to the younger women who have not had the opportunity of owning the spendid books published in the past by our various sister-societies.'

Cattley, Jessie

O635.1   [copyright 1929]
The / blue book / a book on scientific home cooking / recipes guaranteed to please / by / Jessie Cattley / The Hunter-Rose Co., Limited / Toronto Canada [cover-title]
DESCRIPTION: 23.0 × 15.0 cm   Pp 1, [i], 2–34   Paper; stapled
CONTENTS: Inside front face of binding '[Copyright

(1929) by Jessie Cattley]'; 1 'Health and Efficiency'; i blank; 2–top 5 'What Domestic Science Teaches'; mid 5 'A Cook's Responsibility'; bottom 5 'Health Prescription for Women'; 6–mid 8 'Domestic Economy Helps'; bottom 8–34 'Recipes'
COPIES: *Private collection
NOTES: The text is an odd amalgam of scientific information, money-saving measures, health hints, and personal experience.

Cook book

O636.1 1929
Cook book / Rev. Jas. McCrea, B.A., – Minister / St. Andrew's United Church / Buxton, Ontario / 1929 / (Established by the late Rev. Wm. King in 1858) / Price 50 cents [cover-title]
DESCRIPTION: Pp 1–70   With image on front of the church; stapled
CONTENTS: 1 ad, 'Compiled by St. Andrew's Ladies' Aid,' and list of 'Officers'; 2–mid 8 'Golden Rules for the Kitchen,' 'Value in Foods,' 'General Cooking Information,' 'Tables of Weights and Measures,' 'Recipe for a Happy Life,' and ads; mid 8–70 recipes credited with the name of the contributor and ads
COPIES: *Private collection
NOTES: William King, the church's founder, played a key role in helping escaped slaves from the United States make their home in the area that became known as the Buxton Settlement.

The cook's companion

O637.1 1929
The cook's companion / compiled / by / Willing Workers Society / of / Knox Church / Belmont, Ontario. / 1929. [cover-title]
DESCRIPTION: 14.0 × 10.5 cm   Pp [1–36]   Paper; bound by a cord through two holes at the centre fold
CONTENTS: Inside front face of binding unattributed poem beginning, 'We may live without friends ... [from *Lucile*, Part I, part of Canto ii, by Owen Meredith, pseudonym of Edward Robert Bulwer-Lytton]; 1–36 recipes credited with the name of the contributor
COPIES: *OAYM
NOTES: The book appears to have been reproduced by making typed carbon copies; therefore, the number of copies made must be small.

Electric cookery on Hotpoint electric ranges

For other books about cooking with the Hotpoint Electric Range, see O658.1, [Title unknown], and O696.1, Electric Cookery by Hotpoint.

O638.1 copyright 1929
Electric cookery / on / Hotpoint / electric ranges / Copyright 1929 / Canadian / General Electric / Co. / Limited / Head office Toronto. Sales offices in all principal cities / Price fifty cents
DESCRIPTION: 23.0 × 15.0 cm   Pp [1] 2–104   Illus col   Paper, with image on front of a woman stirring the contents of a saucepan on an electric range; stapled
CONTENTS: 1 tp; 2 'Accurate Measurement an Essential // Do You Measure Accurately?'; 3 'Table of Measures and Weights'; 4–6 'Care and Operation of Ranges'; 7 'Cleaning and Care of Hotpoint Ranges'; 8–94 recipes; 95–104 'Index'
COPIES: MWMM   *OONL (TX715.6 E52 1929 p***)
NOTES: The cover-title is 'Electric Cookery.' The section of 'Oven Meals' on pp 73–94 presents menus where the dishes go into the oven all together, plus the accompanying recipes. 'A-100-1000-12-29-B.P.' is on the outside back face of the binding. A private collector has a copy that matches the description above, except that 'A-100-1500-7-30-B.P.' is on the outside back face.

Favourite recipes

O639.1 nd [about 1929]
Favourite recipes / compiled and arranged by / [Unit or Circle number in a wreath-shape:] 4 / Women's Association / of / Bethany United Church / Ottawa, Ont., Canada / [Unattributed poem beginning, 'We may live without poetry, music and art,' from *Lucile*, Part I, Canto ii, by Owen Meredith, pseudonym of Edward Robert Bulwer-Lytton] / All advertisers in this Favorite [*sic*] Recipe / Book are firms of the highest repute whose / productions can be relied upon as being absolutely / first class.
DESCRIPTION: 17.0 × 12.5 cm   Pp [1] 2–129, [i–iii], 130   Paper; stapled
CONTENTS: 1 tp; 2 ad; 3 'Foreword' and 'Weights and Measures'; 4 ad; 5–129 recipes credited with the name of the contributor and ads; i blank; ii 'These Recipes Inadvertently Omitted'; iii blank; 130 'Index' [i.e., table of contents]
COPIES: *Private collection
NOTES: The 'Foreword' refers to the book's fund-

raising purpose: 'We trust ... that our Church may greatly benefit by the sale of [this book].' On p 72 there is an advertisement for Findlay Bros Co. Ltd in Carleton Place (a maker of electric ranges) that includes a testimonial dated May 1929. The private collector's copy is inscribed on the binding, in ink, 'Mrs. R.H. Cram.'

Harrison, Mary

See Driver for descriptions and locations of this British author's other works: The Skilful Cook, *London: Sampson Low, Marston, Searle and Rivington, 1884;* Cookery for Busy Lives and Small Incomes, *London and New York: Longmans, Green and Co., 1892;* The School Cookery Book for Use in Elementary Schools and Technical Classes, *London: Macmillan and Co. Ltd, and New York: The Macmillan Co., 1898; and* Simple Lessons in Cookery for the Use of Teachers of Elementary and Technical Classes, *London: Macmillan and Co. Ltd, and New York: The Macmillan Co., 1898.*

O640.1 [rev. ed., 1929]
Mary Harrison's guide / to / modern cookery / by / the author of the "Skilful Cook" / London & Toronto / J.M. Dent and Sons Ltd.
CONTENTS: ...; v tp; vi 'All rights reserved // First published 1893 Revised edition 1929 Printed in Great Britain'; vii–? 'Contents'; ...
CITATIONS: Axford, p 262 Bitting, p 216 Driver 476.7
COPIES: Great Britain: LB LCS OB OPo(F) *WyLUB; United States: DLC NN NNNAM
NOTES: Although the title-page verso records 1893 as the year of the first edition, the first British edition was 1891 (see Driver, p 315). The title-page transcription and contents information are from a photocopy of the WyLUB copy.

The 1929 edition is the only one with Toronto as a place of publication. (AMICUS No. 2474228 describes a copy of the 1919 edition, published in London and Toronto, at NSHPL, but there is no such book at NSHPL; the AMICUS record refers to the Nova Scotia Union Catalogue of pre-1981 holdings, which gives NSHV as the location; there is *no* Toronto in the imprint of the NSHV copy of the 1919 edition.)

BRITISH EDITIONS: London: Sampson Low, Marston and Co. Ltd, 1891 (Driver 476.1); another ed., nd (Driver 476.2); another ed., 1900 (Driver 476.3); 4th ed., London: J.M. Dent and Co., 1905 (Driver 476.4);

5th ed., London: J.M. Dent and Co., 1906 (Driver 476.5); 7th ed., London: J.M. Dent and Sons Ltd, 1919 (NSHV; Driver 476.6). The 1919 edition at NSHV was originally in the collection of OTP; it is stamped on the title-page, 'Presented to Mount Saint Vincent College Library by the Toronto Public Libraries.'

Heywood, Mrs Margaret Weimer

O641.1 nd [about 1929]
The / Red & White Stores' / international / cook book / Totally different and complete with sug- / gested menus, rules for proper table service, / an abundance of practical recipes for every / need, famous international recipes, all home / tested, cookery technique and complete / indexing. / Completed and written by / Margaret Weimer Heywood / in co-operation with / the world's famous chefs / Illustrated in colors / Distributed by / the Red & White Corporation / an international organization / Buffalo Chicago San Francisco Toronto
DESCRIPTION: 19.5 × 13.0 cm Pp [i–vii] viii [ix] x [xi–xii] xiii–xv [xvi], [17–18] 19–383 10 pls col incl frontis, 2 double-sided pls col opp p 200, 2 double-sided pls opp p viii Cloth, with image on front of a kettle, saucepan, and three stars
CONTENTS: i ht: 'The International Cook Book'; ii blank; iii tp; iv blank; v dedication to 'the homemakers of the world'; vi blank; vii–viii 'The Authors'; ix–x 'Contents'; xi 'Illustrations'; xii blank; xiii–xv 'Introduction' signed the publishers; xvi blank; 17–372 text; 373–83 'Index'
COPIES: *Private collection
NOTES: 'The Authors' on p vii refers to co-author and compiler Mrs Margaret Weimer Heywood and says that she finished her home economics training in 1916 at the Stout Institute, Menomonie, Wisconsin, and has a Bachelor of Science degree from Columbia Teachers College. The many contributing chefs are listed on pp vii–viii, including these Canadian chefs: Louis Baltara, Château Frontenac, Quebec City; A. Franchi, Château Laurier, Ottawa; William Haag, The Macdonald Hotel, Edmonton; M. Kern, SS Empress of Australia, Canadian Pacific Railway Co.; John McGuire, Newfoundland Hotel, St John's; Henri Odiau, Banff Springs Hotel, Alberta; Carlo Scarabelli, Jasper Park Lodge, Alberta; Richard Simon, SS Empress of France, Canadian Pacific Railway Co.; and Maurice Vane, The Fort Garry Hotel, Winnipeg. Black-and-white photographs of Heywood and the chefs are on two double-sided plates opposite p viii. In

Section III, 'International Recipes,' the recipes are credited to individual chefs. The date of this edition is uncertain, but no earlier than the 1929 Boston edition.

AMERICAN EDITIONS: Boston: Merchandisers Inc., 1929 (United States: DLC); Boston: B. Humphries Inc., [1939] (United States: DLC).

Home economy

O642.1 1929
Home / economy / 1929 [cover-title]
DESCRIPTION: Stapled
CONTENTS: First page 'Compiled by the Ladies' Aid Society of the United Church // Preston, Ontario'
COPIES: *OWTU

The housekeepers' perfect account book 1930

See O145.1 for a list of other editions.

O643.1 [entered 1929]
[*The Housekeepers' Perfect Account Book,* with calendar for 1930]
CONTENTS: 1 'The Housekeepers' Perfect Account Book // Published annually in December of each year in Toronto. A copy may be procured by writing to any of the advertisers. For advertising rates and method of distribution, address Geo. Shepard, publisher, 92 Jarvis St Toronto // Entered according to Act of the Parliament of Canada, in the year nineteen hundred and twenty-nine, by Geo. Shepard, at the Department of Agriculture, Ottawa.' and ads; ...
COPIES: *MAUAM
NOTES: The MAUAM copy lacks the cover-title.

Mariposa cook book of choice and tested recipes

Zion Ladies' Aid was part of Zion United Church in Mariposa Township, Victoria County, south of the town of Little Britain. The church closed in the 1960s.

O644.1 1929
[An edition of *Mariposa Cook Book of Choice and Tested Recipes,* Zion Ladies' Aid, 1929]
COPIES: Private collection

The modern housekeepers' guide

O645.1 [copyright 1929]
The / modern housekeepers' / guide / with special reference / to coal and wood cookery / Price / one dollar / Published by / General Steel Wares / Limited / 25 branches across Canada: / Halifax, Saint John, Quebec City, Montreal (2), Ottawa, Toronto (4), Hamilton (2), Brantford, / London (2), Windsor, North Bay, Winnipeg (3), Regina, Saskatoon, Calgary, Edmonton, Vancouver
DESCRIPTION: 24.0 × 17.0 cm Pp [1–2], i–iii [iv], 1–110 [111–17] Tp illus red of a weeping willow tree, 6 pls col, 4 double-sided pls, illus Very thin card, with image on front of a woman holding an umbrella, standing outside a house and framed by trees, all in silhouette with a sunrise or sunset behind; stapled
CONTENTS: 1 tp; 2 'Copyright 1929 General Steel Wares Limited'; i–iii introductory text about using coal and wood ranges; iv small illus red of a woman in silhouette; 1–110 text; 111–13 index; 114–17 blank for 'Memoranda'
COPIES: AEUCHV (UV 85.132.2) *BDEM OONL (TX651 M62 1929 copy 1) SSWD
NOTES: The text covers kitchen design, equipment, dish washing and the care of utensils, laundry, the care of furniture and rugs, stain removal, floors and woodwork, table setting and service, and cookery.

In 1927, two years before this cookbook was published, the London, Ontario, firm of McClary's had amalgamated with four other firms to form General Steel Wares. *The Modern Housekeepers' Guide* has some of the same colour plates as O488.1, *McClary's Household Manual,* [copyright 1922]; for example, the one of Cocoanut Cake. General Steel Wares made the McClary Happy Thought and SMP coal and wood ranges.

No one place of publication is recorded and the book was distributed across Canada. Since the executive offices of General Steel Wares at this time were in Toronto (at 199 River Street) and since the company had the most branches in Ontario (twelve, including four in Toronto), the entries for the book are in the Ontario section of this bibliography.

An advertisement for McClary's ranges in *Nor'-West Farmer and Farm and Home* Vol. 51, No. 18 (October 1932), p 19, includes an order form for *The Modern Housekeepers' Guide* and illustrates the book. Chatelaine 1935, p 82, cites 'The Modern Housekeeper's [*sic*] Guide,' available from General Steel Wares for

$0.10, but does not distinguish between the editions for coal-and-wood, electric, and gas cookery.

For books about cooking with McClary appliances and for information about the company, see O162.1.

O645.2 [copyright 1929]
—The / modern housekeepers' / guide / with special reference / to electric cookery / Price / one dollar / Published by / General Steel Wares / Limited / 25 branches across Canada: / Halifax, Saint John, Quebec City, Montreal (2), Ottawa, Toronto (4), Hamilton (2), Brantford, / London (2), Windsor, North Bay, Winnipeg (3), Regina, Saskatoon, Calgary, Edmonton, Vancouver
DESCRIPTION: 24.5 × 17.5 cm   Pp [1–2], i–v [vi], 1–110 [111–17]   Tp illus red of a weeping willow tree, 6 pls col, 4 double-sided pls, illus   Very thin card, with image on front of a woman holding an umbrella, standing outside a house and framed by trees, all in silhouette with a sunrise or sunset behind; stapled
CONTENTS: 1 tp; 2 'Copyright 1929 General Steel Wares Limited'; i–v introductory text about using electric ranges; vi small illus red of a woman in silhouette; 1–110 text; 111–13 index; 114–17 blank for 'Memoranda'
COPIES: *Private collection
NOTES: General Steel Wares made the McClary Electric Range. Another collector's copy is inscribed 'From Betty Aug. 1st 1929.'

O645.3 [copyright 1929]
—The / modern housekeepers' / guide / with special reference / to gas cookery / Price / one dollar / Published by / General Steel Wares / Limited / 25 branches across Canada: / Halifax, Saint John, Quebec City, Montreal (2), Ottawa, Toronto (4), Hamilton (2), Brantford, / London (2), Windsor, North Bay, Winnipeg (3), Regina, Saskatoon, Calgary, Edmonton, Vancouver
DESCRIPTION: 24.0 × 17.5 cm   Pp [1–2], i–xii, 1–110 [111–17]   Tp illus red of a weeping willow tree, 6 pls col, 4 double-sided pls, illus   Thin card, with image on front of a woman holding an umbrella, standing outside a house and framed by trees, all in silhouette with a sunrise or sunset behind; stapled
CONTENTS: 1 tp; 2 'Copyright 1929 General Steel Wares Limited'; i–xii introductory text about cooking with McClary gas ranges, including information about 'Whole Meal Cooking' and 'Cold Pack Canning,' plus five menus with instructions for 'Typical All-Oven Dinners'; 1–110 text; 111–13 'Index'; 114–17 blank for 'Memoranda'
COPIES: *OONL (TX651 M62 1929 copy 2)

Recipe book

O646.1   1929
Pine Grove Women's Club / Recipe / book / Orillia, 1929 / Calvert-Maynard Job Press, Orillia [cover-title]
DESCRIPTION: 22.0 × 15.0 cm   Pp 1–32   Paper; stapled
CONTENTS: 1–2 ads; 3 'An Appreciation'; 4 'Recipe Book Compiling Committee'; 5–31 text and ads; 32 ad
COPIES: *Private collection
NOTES: On the 'Compiling Committee' were Mrs Wilbur Greer [no title given], Mrs Peter Gray, vice-president, Mrs James Strachan, secretary-treasurer, Miss Ruby Wyer, president, and sixteen other women listed as 'Members.'

Recipes

O647.1   1929
Recipes / compiled and arranged / by / Mrs. J.A. Rickaby's Group / in the interests of / the Women's Association / of / Kimbourne Park / United Church / Toronto, Canada / We have compiled and arranged this collection of recipes in the / hope that they will prove of service. We trust "Our Cook Book" will / provide often an answer to that vexing question "What shall I cook / to-day?" / We would appreciate your patronage of the firms who have so / graciously taken advertising space in our book. / Mrs. J.A. Rickaby's Group. / Kimbourne Park United Church. / Toronto, Canada. / July, 1929.
DESCRIPTION: 23.0 × 15.0 cm   Pp [1] 2–48 [49–52]   Paper, with image on front of Kimbourne Park United Church; stapled
CONTENTS: Inside front face of binding 'Church Calendar' and the name of the pastor, Rev. Ed. G. Robb; 1 tp; 2 'Index to Advertisers'; 3–4 ads; 5–48 recipes credited with the name of the contributor and ads; 49–52 blank for 'Notes'
COPIES: *BVAU
NOTES: The running head is 'Kimbourne Park United Church – Cook Book.' The last item in the text is 'What to Bring to Camp' on p 48.

Reliable recipes

O648.1   nd [about 1929]
Reliable recipes / by the / Women's Association of Kenyon / Presbyterian Church. / Dunvegan, Ontario. / [table of 'Weights and Measures']
DESCRIPTION: 17.0 × 13.0 cm   Pp [1] 2–95   Paper; stapled

CONTENTS: 1 tp; 2–95 recipes credited with the name of the contributor

CITATIONS: MacGillivray, p 42

COPIES: *Private collection

NOTES: 'Maxville Printing Office' is on the front face of the binding; 'Evelyn McEwen Maxville Ontario' is inscribed on the front face, in ink.

Entries for Maxville Printing in the *Dominion of Canada and Newfoundland Gazetteer and Classified Business Directory* indicate a publication date after 1915 and before 1935, and there is a recipe on p 18 for Canadian War Cake, a recipe that was reprinted in cookbooks through the 1920s. MacGillivray states, 'The "W.A. Cookbook" was long familiar in the Dunvegan-Skye-McCrimmon West area ... Possibly published 1929 as I have been informed ...' The appearance of the book is consistent with MacGillivray's suggested date.

The St John's Church Norway cook book

O649.1 [1929]

The / St. John's Church Norway / cook book / "Tested recipes for housekeepers" / Published under the auspices of / the Parish Association / of / St. John's Church Norway / Toronto [cover-title]

DESCRIPTION: With image on front of the church

CONTENTS: 1 'Index' [i.e., table of contents]; 2 [?]; 3 information about the Parish Association; ...

COPIES: *Private collection

NOTES: Page 3 refers to the reorganization of the Parish Association in 1919, and records the amount contributed by the ladies of the association to the church's mortgage for the years 1920–8, with the result that the sum of $50,000 had been reduced to $37,500 'to date, August 1929.' Presidents of the association are listed from 1920, the last being Mrs W.J. Stratton for 1929.

St John's Church Norway was designed by the same architect, C.J. Gibson, who designed Gravenhurst High School, illustrated on the binding of O98.1, *Gravenhurst Ladies' Cook Book*.

Selected recipes

The Women's Association also published O1015.1, The Pantry Shelf, and O1097.1, Helpful Household Hints.

O650.1 May 1929

Selected recipes / chosen by / the members of Group No. 1 / of the / Women's Association / of Metropolitan United Church / London, Ontario. / Our organization wishes to thank its members, friends / and especially the advertisers for their assistance, so gener- / ously given, in making this book. / May 1929 / "Let me cook the meals of my country, and I care not / who makes her laws." / [mock recipe for 'How to Preserve a Child' using ingredients of 6 children, 3 puppies, 1 field, 1 brook, 1 blue sky]

DESCRIPTION: 22.0 × 14.5 cm   Pp [1–2] 3–124   Paper, with image on front of a peacock

CONTENTS: 1 tp; 2 index; 3 'A Recipe for a Day'; 4 weights and measures; 5–6 ads; 7 'Correct Service for Dinner Table'; 8 ad; 9–121 recipes; 122–4 blank for 'Additional Recipes'

COPIES: OGU (2 copies: *UA s048 b48, CCC TX715.6 S433)   Private collection

NOTES: The cover-title is 'Metropolitan Church Cook Book.' On p 88 there is an advertisement for Kelvinator of Canada Ltd, and on p 89, 'Kelvinator Recipes' (Frozen Fruit Salad, Whipped Cream Dressing, Loganberry Sherbet, Frozen Apricots with Hot Caramel Sauce, and Golden Glow Salad) to be made using the company's electric refrigerators, which were first introduced to the Canadian market in the mid-1920s. Kelvinator of Canada had a manufacturing plant in London (for the company history, see O656.1, *The Miracle of Cold*).

Selected recipes

O651.1   nd [about 1929 or slightly later]

Selected recipes / by / the Ladies' Guild / of / St. Andrew's Church / Grimsby, Ont. / [caption:] St. Andrew's Parish Hall [cover-title]

DESCRIPTION: 21.5 × 15.0 cm   Pp [1–7] 8–67 [68]   Paper, with image on front of St Andrew's Parish Hall; stapled

CONTENTS: 1–2 ads; 3 'Foreword,' 'Abbreviations,' and 'Table of Weighths [*sic*] and Measures'; 4 ad; 5–67 recipes credited with the name of the contributor and ads; 68 blank for 'Memorandum'

COPIES: *OKQ (F5012 nd S133)

NOTES: The printer is identified on p 67: 'This book of recipes was printed by George Thompson ... Grimsby.' An advertisement on p 53 for the jeweller Thomas Lees, in business for 'over 67 years,' indicates that the cookbook was published about 1929 or later since the firm was established in 1861 (1861 + over 67 years; the year the Lees business started is recorded in the Hamilton city directory for 1911). An advertisement for Deloro Chemical Co. Ltd on the inside back face of the binding is evidence of the Depression era: 'Buy goods made in Canada – give more people work – bring better times.'

Tested and tried recipes

O652.1   nd [1929]

Tested and tried / recipes / Compiled by / Groups 2 & 3 of the Ladies' Aid of / Beecher United Church / London – Ontario / It Doesn't Take a Minute. / It doesn't take a minute / To speak a word of grace – / And yet it brings the sunshine / To another's face. / Just some appreciation, / A little word of praise – / A "thank you" kindly spoken, / May brighten someone's days. / It doesn't take a minute / To leave a smile behind – / And make some sad folks happier / To know the world is kind.

DESCRIPTION: 22.0 × 14.5 cm   Pp [1–2] 3–86   Paper; stapled

CONTENTS: 1 tp; 2 ad; 3 'Index' [i.e., table of contents]; 4 ads; 5–85 recipes credited with the name of the contributor and ads; 86 ads

COPIES: *Bookseller's stock

NOTES: The cover-title is 'The Family Favorite Cook Book.' The book is undated, but two advertisements are evidence that it was published in 1929: The advertisement on p 20 for Jas R. Haslett, 'plumbers for three generations 1856 – to – 1929'; and another advertisement on p 20, for J. Darch and Sons, '86 years in the business in London "since 1843"' (1843 + 86 years).

Tested recipe book

O653.1   1929

Tested / recipe book / All Nations' Bazaar / 1929 / District Union of Toronto / Woman's Christian Temperance / Union / "For God and home" [cover-title]

DESCRIPTION: 20.0 × 14.0 cm   Pp [i–vi], [1–59], [i–vii] Paper, with image on front of the WCTU's Willard Hall; stapled

CONTENTS: i ad for Willard Hall Recreation Club; ii–vi ads; 1–59 recipes credited with the name of the contributor; i–vii ads

COPIES: *Private collection

NOTES: The imposing Willard Hall stands on the north side of Gerrard Street East, just east of Yonge Street.

O653.2   nd [reprint, about 1939–45]

—Tested / recipe book / [On orange label, above illus of building:] Proceeds / for / W.C.T.U. War Service Fund / District Union of Toronto / Woman's Christian Temperance / Union / "For God and home" [cover-title]

DESCRIPTION: 20.5 × 14.0 cm   Pp [i–ii], [1–59], [i–iii] Paper, with image on front of the WCTU's Willard Hall; stapled

CONTENTS: i ad for Willard Hall Recreation Club; ii ads; 1–59 recipes credited with the name of the contributor; i–iii ads

CITATIONS: Crawford, p D1, illus col

COPIES: *Private collection

NOTES: This is a reprint of the 1929 edition. It is identical except for the label on the binding, which is applied over the 1929 bazaar name and date, and there are fewer leaves of advertisements.

Wigent, Zella

This American author also wrote Poultry for the Farm and Home, *International Harvester Company of New Jersey, Agricultural Extension Department, c1921 (United States: DLC).*

O654.1   1929

Home / canning / up-to-date / methods and equipment / by Zella Wigent / of the Agricultural Extension Department / This booklet succeeds our booklet "Canning" / by Grace Marian Smith, of this department. The / present writer has drawn freely from the material of / our former booklet and acknowledges herewith the / helpful suggestions which Miss Smith has given in / the preparation of this bulletin. / Presented with the compliments / of the / Bank of Montreal / Published 1929 by / International Harvester Company / of Canada Ltd. / Hamilton Canada / Western branches – Brandon, Winnipeg, Man., Calgary, Edmonton, Lethbridge, Alta. / Weyburn, N[no period] Battleford, Regina, Saskatoon, Swift Current, Yorkton, Sask. / Eastern branches – Hamilton, London, Ottawa, Ont., Montreal, Quebec, Que., St. John, N.B[no period] / AE–25L. 8-10-29. Printed in Canada.

DESCRIPTION: 23.0 × 15.5 cm   Pp [1] 2–70 [71–2]   Illus Paper, with image on front of a mother, father, and daughter in the process of canning at a kitchen table; stapled

CONTENTS: 1 tp; 2–69 text; 70 index; 71 'Make Use of Your Banker ...'; 72 'The IHC Agricultural Extension Department // What It Is – What It Does'

COPIES: AEPRAC   AHRMH (994-001-031)   ALAGM AMHM   ARDA   BSUM   OFERWM (A1996.52 MU306)   ONLAM (Walters-Wagar Collection, Box

20) OONL (TX603 W54 1929) OSGM OSTPA
*Private collection
NOTES: A synopsis is on p 2: 'This book discusses
from the farm-home standpoint the canning of – fruits
– vegetables – meats canned by the processed-in-the-
can method in open-top sealed-without-solder tin cans
and the more common types of glass jars cooked in
home-devised hot water outfits and home types of
pressure kettles.' A brief history of 'Progress in Home
Canning' on p 4 covers 'before 1860,' '1860–1910,'
and '1910–now.' The title-page reference to 'Canning'
by Grace Marian Smith is likely to Smith's *Home
Canning by the Cold Pack Method*, of which DLC has a
1917 edition.

The BSUM copy lacks its binding.

AMERICAN EDITIONS: Chicago: International Harvester
Co., copyright 1927 (Bookseller's stock).

1929–30

Choice tested recipes

O655.1   1929–30
Choice tested / recipes / Compiled and issued by /
the Ladies' Aid of St. Paul's United Church /
Brampton, Ont. / 1929–30 / Price 35 cents [cover-
title]
DESCRIPTION: With image on front of a smiling chef's
head, behind which is a large loaf of bread
COPIES: *Private collection

1929–32

The miracle of cold

*Kelvinator was the brand name of the Detroit, Michigan,
firm of Kelvinator Co., called after Lord Kelvin, the
English physicist. Incorporated in the United States in
May 1916 (for the first few months as Electro-Automatic
Refrigerating Co.), the company – a pioneer in the field –
began installing refrigeration units in Detroit homes in
the same year. In the beginning, the units were placed in
customers' existing ice-box cabinets: the cooling part of
the device went into the cabinet (usually a Leonard ice-box,
the most popular make in the United States), while the
other parts (motor, compressor, condensor) sat outside the
cabinet. The industry began to grow only after the First
World War, when difficulties in securing materials eased.
Kelvinator introduced the first self-contained unit to the
market in 1925 and soon after bought out the Leonard Co.*

*and organized a Canadian subsidiary called Kelvinator of
Canada Ltd (there had been a selling agency in Canada
from 1924). In 1937, Nash-Kelvinator Corp. was created
by the merger of Nash Motors and Kelvinator Co.*

*Kelvinator of Canada Ltd is first listed in Toronto city
directories in 1925; from 1926 to 1932, Toronto directories list Kelvinator Toronto Ltd; from 1933, the name
reverts to Kelvinator of Canada Ltd. City directories for
London, Ontario, where the company operated a plant,
list the company from 1927, as Kelvinator of Canada Ltd.*

*For a contemporary account of the refrigerator indus-
try in Canada, see 'Electric Refrigerator Industry Makes
Rapid Growth,' Monetary Times Vol. 79, No. 9 (26
August 1927), pp 3–4. For later Kelvinator cookbooks,
see O814.1, Cooking with Cold, and O920.1, The
Kelvinator Book of Kitchen Tested Recipes.*

O656.1   nd [about 1929–32]
The / miracle / of / cold / The modern home, year
by year, / has new devices, new luxuries, new /
aids to finer, better living, and at its / call undreamt-
of conveniences to / replace age-old makeshifts.
DESCRIPTION: 19.5 × 14.5 cm   Pp [3–4] 5–21 [22]   Illus
col   Paper, with image on front of two women and
two men about to sit down to a set table; stapled
CONTENTS: 3 tp; 4 fp illus col of a woman removing
ice cubes from the freezer compartment; 5 'To the
Home-makers of the World' signed Kelvinator of
Canada Ltd, London, Ontario; 6–21 recipes; 22 illus
of Kelvinator factory, information about Kelvinator
('tested by thousands upon thousands of women in
every part of the country since 1914'), and at bottom,
'Printed in U.S.A. The Stubbs Co. Detroit'; inside
back face of binding list of subjects and their page
numbers; outside back face 'Form No. 2058'
CITATIONS: Driver 2003, 'Canadian Cookbooks,' p 37
COPIES: *Private collection
NOTES: This collection of recipes is for use with refrigerators. The cover-title is 'For the Hostess.' The private collector's copy is stamped on the outside back
face of the binding, 'Kelvinator (Toronto) Limited //
11 Temperance St. Phone Ad. 2039.' Toronto city directories list the company's telephone number as
Adelaide 2039 for four years, 1929 to 1932 (before
1929, the number was Main 7037; from 1933, Adelaide
6435). From appearances, the cookbook was published before O814.1, *Cooking with Cold*.

The Miracle of Cold may be 'the interesting and
valuable 24-page recipe book prepared by Kelvinator
Corp.' advertised by Electrical Specialties Ltd of
Hamilton, Ontario, on p 20 of O620.1, *Favorite Recipes*, [1928]. If it is, this would push back the date of
publication of *The Miracle of Cold*.

The statement on p 22 of *The Miracle of Cold* that Kelvinator Refrigerators were first sold in Canada in 1914 is incorrect. The first experimental models of the refrigerator were developed in Detroit in 1914; units were first installed in Detroit homes only in 1916; Canadian sales were later, in the 1920s.

1929–35

A selection of favorite recipes

O657.1 nd [about 1929–35]
"But for life the universe were nothing, / And all that has life requires nourishment." / A selection of / favorite / recipes / Compiled by / the ladies of / the Women's Association / of the / Ottawa United Church, / Walkerville, Ont. / Now good digestion wait on appetite / And health on both. / – Shakespeare. / [folio:] 1
DESCRIPTION: Photograph on p 2 of the church
CONTENTS: 1 tp; 2 photograph of the church, list of 'Officers for the Year,' times of service, and 'Women's Activities'; ...
COPIES: *OCHAK
NOTES: The recipes are credited with the name of the contributor. OCHAK reports that the volume has 100 pp and the cover-title is 'Dietetics.' C.R. Durrant, listed on p 2 as pastor, held that position from 1929 to 1935. Walkerville is now part of the city of Windsor.

1930

[Title unknown]

For the titles of other cookbooks for the Hotpoint Electric Range, see O638.1.

O658.1 [about 1930]
[Title-page or cover-title lacking of cookbook for Hotpoint Electric Range]
DESCRIPTION: 23.0 × 15.0 cm   Pp [i–ii], [1] 2–90   Fp illus of Canadian General Electric factory on p i, illus   Lacks binding; stapled
CONTENTS: i fp illus; ii blank; 1 table of contents; 2 'Electric Cookery'; 3–4 'Why the Hotpoint Electric Range Is the Perfect Range'; 5 'Johnny Hotpoint Says:'; 6–9 'Care and Operation of the Hotpoint Electric Range'; 10 'Do You Measure Accurately?'; 11–90 fourteen chapters
COPIES: *Private collection
NOTES: From appearances, the book was published

about 1930. It was probably published in Toronto, where the head office of Canadian General Electric Co. was located.

The Barnet cook book

Alex Barnet started manufacturing wooden ice-boxes in Renfrew in 1907. Upon his death in 1917, the company was sold to new owners, who renamed it the Renfrew Refrigerator Co., but continued to make Barnet Refrigerators. In 1933, the factory changed to making steel refrigerators with equipment from the Renfrew Electric Co., at which point the company became the Renfrew Electric and Refrigerator Co. This history is from The Story of Renfrew, *edited by Carol Bennett, Renfrew: Juniper Books, 1984, and from information supplied by the McDougall Mill Museum, Renfrew.*

O659.1 nd [about 1930]
The Barnet / cook book / selected / recipes / Renfrew Refrigerator Co., Ltd. / Renfrew, Canada [cover-title]
DESCRIPTION: 22.0 × 15.0 cm   Pp [1–16]   Paper; stapled, and with hole punched at top left corner, through which runs a string for hanging
CONTENTS: 1–16 recipes
COPIES: *Private collection
NOTES: *The Barnet Cook Book* was published to encourage the sale of Barnet Refrigerators. The form of the company name on the title-page indicates that the book was published in the period 1917–33, likely about 1930 from appearances. The owner of the copy examined remembers that it came with a used refrigerator that her family acquired in 1934.

Blake, Mary [pseudonym]

For information about Mary Blake and her cookbooks, see O494.1; for Carnation Milk Products Co., see O350.1.

O660.1 [copyright 1930]
100 glorified recipes / by / Mary Blake [cover-title]
DESCRIPTION: 18.0 × 12.5 cm   Pp [1] 2–36   Illus col Paper, with image on front of three carnations tied with a red ribbon; stapled
CONTENTS: Inside front face of binding 'Table Setting and Service'; 1 untitled introductory text signed Mary Blake, Home Economics Department, Carnation Co. Ltd, offices at Oconomowoc, Wisconsin, Aylmer, Ontario, New York, and Seattle, Washington, and 'Copyright Carnation Company, Ltd. 1930 CC616 –

Printed in Canada'; 2–3 'The Delight of the New in Cookery' [about Carnation Milk]; 4–5 Carnation Milk as a food for babies; 6 'General Directions'; 7–36 recipes; inside back face 'Table of Contents'
COPIES: *Private collection
NOTES: This new title by Blake followed her *My Hundred Favorite Recipes,* editions of which appeared from 1924 to 1929 (O515.1–515.4). A comparison of the first few soup recipes in *100 Glorified Recipes* with those in *My Hundred Favorite Recipes* shows that, although recipe names may be the same (Cream of Tomato Soup and Cream of Celery Soup, for example), the ingredient amounts and instructions are different.

Chatelaine 1935, p 82, cites '100 Glorified Recipes (French and English) (limited supply),' but does not specify the copyright year(s). I have not located any copies of the French-language version.

O660.2 [copyright 1931]
—100 glorified recipes / by / Mary Blake [cover-title]
DESCRIPTION: 18.0 × 13.0 cm   Pp [1] 2–36   Illus col
Paper, with image on front of three carnations tied with a red ribbon; stapled
CONTENTS: Inside front face of binding 'Table Setting and Service'; 1 untitled introductory note signed Mary Blake, Home Economics Department, Carnation Co. Ltd, offices at Milwaukee, Wisconsin, Aylmer, Ontario, New York, and Seattle, Washington, and 'Copyright Carnation Company, Ltd. 1931 CC616A – Printed in Canada'; 2–3 'The Delight of the New in Cookery'; 4–5 Carnation Milk as a food for babies; 6 'General Directions'; 7–36 recipes; inside back face 'Table of Contents' [i.e., index]
COPIES: *Private collection

O660.3 [copyright 1932]
—100 glorified recipes / by / Mary Blake [cover-title]
DESCRIPTION: 18.0 × 12.5 cm   Pp [1] 2–36   Illus col
Paper, with image on front of three carnations tied with a red ribbon; stapled
CONTENTS: 1 untitled introductory note signed Mary Blake, Home Economics Department, Carnation Co. Ltd, offices at Milwaukee, Wisconsin, Aylmer, Ontario, New York, and Seattle, Washington, and 'Copyright Carnation Company, Ltd. 1932 CC616A – Printed in Canada'; 2–3 'The Delight of the New in Cookery'; 4–5 Carnation Milk as a food for babies; 6 'General Directions'; 7–36 recipes; inside back face 'Table of Contents' [i.e., index]
COPIES: OGU (UA s070 b02)   OONL (TX715 C3465 No. 21)   *Private collection

O660.4 [copyright 1933]
—100 glorified recipes / by / Mary Blake [cover-title]

DESCRIPTION: 18.0 × 13.0 cm   Pp [1] 2–36   Illus col
Paper, with image on front of three carnations tied with a red ribbon; stapled
CONTENTS: 1 untitled introductory note signed Mary Blake, Home Economics Department, Carnation Co. Ltd, offices at Milwaukee, Wisconsin, Aylmer, Ontario, New York, and Seattle, Washington, and 'Copyright Carnation Company, Ltd. 1933 CC616B – Printed in Canada'; 2–3 'The Delight of the New in Cookery'; 4–5 Carnation Milk as a food for babies; 6 'General Directions'; 7–36 recipes; inside back face 'Table of Contents' [i.e., index]
COPIES: *Private collection

O660.5 [copyright 1934]
—100 glorified recipes / by / Mary Blake [cover-title]
DESCRIPTION: 17.5 × 12.5 cm   Pp [1] 2–36   Illus col
Paper, with image on front of three carnations tied with a red ribbon; stapled
CONTENTS: 1 untitled introductory note signed Mary Blake, Home Economics Department, Carnation Co. Ltd, and 'Copyright Carnation Company, Ltd. 1934 CC616C – Printed in Canada'; 2–3 'The Delight of the New in Cookery'; 4–5 Carnation Milk as a food for babies; 6 'General Directions'; 7–36 recipes; inside back face 'Table of Contents' [i.e., index]
COPIES: MWPA   *NSLQCM

O660.6 [copyright 1935]
—100 glorified recipes / by / Mary Blake [cover-title]
DESCRIPTION: With image on front of three carnations tied with a red ribbon; stapled
CONTENTS: 1 untitled introductory note signed Mary Blake, Home Service Department, Carnation Co. Ltd, Toronto, and 'Copyright Carnation Company, Ltd. 1935 CC616D – Printed in Canada'; ...
COPIES: *Private collection
NOTES: In the same year, 1935, the company published O844.1, *Carnation Cook Book,* by Blake.

AMERICAN EDITIONS: Milwaukee: Carnation Co., 1932 (United States: CoDU, NcGU); Milwaukee: Carnation Co., 1934 (United States: NRMW, OTU).

Canada, Soldier Settlement Board of Canada

O661.1   1930
[Canada's coat of arms] / Useful hints on ... / home management / The / Soldier Settlement Board of Canada / Ottawa / Ottawa / F.A. Acland / printer to the King's Most Excellent Majesty / 1930
DESCRIPTION: 25.0 × 16.5 cm   Pp [1–4] 5–49   Very thin card; stapled

CONTENTS: 1 tp; 2 blank; 3 'Foreword' signed J.G. Rattray, chairman; 4 'Cooking Measurements'; 5 'Table of Contents'; 6 blank; 7 'Useful Hints on Home Management' [i.e., introductory text]; 8–34 culinary information and recipes; 35 'Vegetable Garden'; 36–mid 38 'Laundry'; mid 38–39 'Floor Finishes and Their Care'; 40–mid 46 'General Hints'; mid–bottom 46 'Children'; 47–9 'Decorating the Interior of the Home'
COPIES: NBFU   OONL (COP.CA.SO.13, 2 copies) OTU (Gov. Doc. Can S) QQS (missing) *Bookseller's stock
NOTES: Rattray says on p 3 that the material in the book 'has been collected by Mrs. Jean Muldrew who has been in charge of the Home Branch of the Soldier Settlement Board for ten years.' He adds that the book's title was chosen from forty-five titles submitted by members of the head office staff.

Cook book

Bealton is a small town south of Brantford. See also O1021.1, A Cook Book of Favorite Recipes, *by the Bealton Women's Institute.*

O662.1   December 1930
Cook book / by / Delta Alpha Class / of / Bealton United Church / teacher, Mrs. A. Jaffray / December 1930 / Price 50c [cover-title]
DESCRIPTION: 22.5 × 15.5 cm   Pp 1–11   Paper, with image on front of a small maple leaf; stapled
CONTENTS: 1–11 recipes, credited with the name of the contributor, for 'Bread and Buns,' 'Cookies,' 'Cookies and Drop Cakes,' 'Pies,' 'Desserts,' 'Supper Dishes,' 'Pickles,' 'Candy,' 'Cakes,' and 'Icings'
COPIES: *Private collection

Cook book

St Matthew's Church (Anglican) is in Ottawa, on First Avenue.

O663.1   [1930]
St. Anna's Guild of / St. Matthew's Church / Cook book / One dollar [cover-title]
DESCRIPTION: 23.0 × 15.0 cm   Pp [1–3] 4–129   Frontis of St Matthew's Church   Cloth
CONTENTS: 1 'Officers of St. Anna's Guild for 1930' and a thank-you from the 'Convenors of this book,' Mrs Thomas Cunningham and Mrs Frederic T. Gordon, to the ladies for their recipes and support, followed by a list of the ladies; 2 'Index' [i.e., alphabetical list of sections]; 3 'Weights and Measures'; 4 ads; 5–129 text, mainly recipes credited with the name of the contributor
COPIES: BCOM   *Private collection
NOTES: The advertisements are mainly for Ottawa businesses.

Cornforth, George E.

See O431.1 for the titles of Cornforth's other works.

O664.1   1930
[First printing of *Better Meals for Less*, 1930; cited in O664.2]
NOTES: A copy of this title at OONL (TX715 C6794 1930) is missing. 'Second printing' is not mentioned in the record for the book; therefore, the OONL copy may be the first printing.

O664.2   [copyright 1930, 2nd printing, 1934]
—Better meals for less / By George E. Cornforth / Chef for the New England Sanitarium / author of "Good Food: How to Prepare It" / Canadian Watchman Press / Oshawa, Ontario / Printed / in Canada / on Canadian / paper
DESCRIPTION: 19.0 × 13.0 cm   Pp [1–4] 5–128   Illus Paper, with image on front of a cornucopia of fruits and vegetables (foreground), a standing mother holding a steaming dish (middle ground), and a father and two children seated at table (background); stapled
CONTENTS: 1 ht: 'Better Meals for Less // BM-1'; 2 frontis of child playing grocer with caption 'The proper selection of foods is more than mere child's play'; 3 tp; 4 illus of 'Cantelopes,' table of contents, and 'Copyright, 1930, by the Canadian Watchman Press // Second printing, 1934'; 5 'Introduction'; 6–126 text; 127–8 index
COPIES: *Private collection
NOTES: The 'Introduction' explains the title: '"Better," especially in this respect that they [i.e., meals] will support better health. "For less," because expensive, unwholesome foods are omitted, and also because better health means less expense for medicine and doctors, and greater efficiency for work.' Cornforth recommends eating no meat, avoiding eating fruit and vegetables together at the same meal, limiting the amount of sugar used with milk, and avoiding food cooked in fat. In his view, alkali-forming foods should predominate over acid-forming foods such as cereals and breads, and bread should be wholewheat. There is no place for regular tea or coffee in the diet. Rather, he suggests hot drinks made from dried cel-

ery leaves, dried raspberry leaves, dried clover blossoms, and pine needles. Babies should be breast-fed.

AMERICAN EDITIONS: Takoma Park, Washington, DC: Review and Herald Publishing Association, [copyright 1930] (OGU); Washington, DC, Peekskill, NY [etc.]: Review and Herald Publishing Association, [c1930] (United States: DLC).

Elliot, Miss Edith L.

Edith L. Elliot is first listed in Ottawa city directories in 1930 (although her earliest pamphlet for the federal Department of Agriculture is dated 1929). For the next twenty years, city directories record her as working in the Department of Agriculture. From 1951, directories describe her as an administrative officer at the Department of Fisheries. Elliot was a founding member of the Canadian Home Economics Association and addressed its first convention in 1939 (We Are Tomorrow's Past, pp 3–5, and a photograph of her with four others, p 2). See also pl 42.

Also by Elliot is O721.1, Jams, Jellies and Pickles. *She wrote or co-wrote several publications for the federal Department of Agriculture, not described fully here because they are under 16 pages. She was sole author of* Salads That Are Different, *probably first published as nine unpaginated leaves printed on the rectos only and stapled to a folder at the top edge, nd [early 1930s], then as Publication 596, Household Bulletin 17, December 1937, pp 12; French-language edition,* Salades nouveau genre, *reprint, December 1938, pp 13. She was also sole author of* Home Preservation of Meats, Poultry and Soup, *Publication 628, Household Bulletin 18, 1st printing, September 1938, pp 6; French-language edition,* Conservation à la maison des viandes, volailles et soupes, *September 1940, pp 4. Although they are the same work, her name does not appear on the retitled later English editions,* Home Preservation of Meats, Poultry, Fish and Soups, *reprint, November 1940, and revised edition, January 1943, or on the French revised edition, September 1942. Also credited to her are:* Home Drying of Fruits and Vegetables, *[1934], pp 3;* Jams and Jellies Made from Garden or Wild Fruits, *[1936], pp 8; and* Wartime Pickles and Relishes, *nd.*

She shared authorship with Lilian Heeney on some editions of Canning Fruits and Vegetables *(French title,* Les conserves de fruits et de légumes*). The title was first issued as Pamphlet 109 under Elliot's name only: English edition, 1929, pp 13; French edition, 1930, pp 14. A few years later it was numbered Publication 534, Household Bulletin 8, and credited to both Elliot and Heeney: English edition, September 1936, pp 11;*

French edition, September 1936, pp 13. Later editions cite Elliot as sole author: in English, first revision, July 1938, pp 12, to revised edition, May 1942, pp 8; in French, revised edition, May 1942.

With Laura C. Pepper, Elliot co-wrote Healthful Meals at Low Cost, *Pamphlet 130, 1933, pp 4; French edition,* Repas sain [sic] à bas prix, *1933, pp 4. The work was later reprinted in English and French as Publication 510, Circular 100: English edition, June 1936, pp 4;* Repas sains à bas prix, *August 1936 (incorrectly numbered Publication 542 on p 1).*

Copies of all the above editions are at OOAG. For a list of other cookbooks from the Department of Agriculture, see O404.1.

O665.1   1930
Canadian vegetables / for every day / by / Edith L. Elliot / Fruit Branch / Department of Agriculture / G.E. McIntosh, Commissioner / Pamphlet No. 121 / Published by direction of Hon. Robert Weir, Minister of Agriculture, / Ottawa, 1930 [cover-title]
DESCRIPTION: 22.0 × 15.0 cm   Pp [1–3] 4–22   Illus   Paper, with image on front of bottled, fresh, and canned vegetables; rebound in cloth, together with other Pamphlets; with three punched holes for storing in a binder
CONTENTS: 1 cover-title; 2 blank; 3–mid 4 nutritional information about vegetables; mid 4–top 6 'General Preparation'; mid 6–8 'Cooking Vegetables'; 9–20 'Special Recipes'; 21 'Food Value of Vegetables'; 22 [outside back face of binding] 'Other Bulletins'
CITATIONS: Ag 1867–1974, p 29   CCat No. 9, p K10
COPIES: *OOAG (630.4 C212 P121, 4 copies)

O665.2   1931
—Légumes canadiens / pour tous les jours / par / Edith L. Elliot / Ministère fédéral de l'agriculture / Division des fruits / G.E. McIntosh, commissaire / Feuillet n° 121 / Publié par ordre de l'hon. Robert Weir, ministre de l'agriculture, / Ottawa, 1931 [cover-title]
DESCRIPTION: 22.0 × 15.0 cm   Pp [1–3] 4–22   Illus   Paper, with image on front of bottled, fresh, and canned vegetables; rebound in cloth, together with other Pamphlets; with three punched holes for storing in a binder
CONTENTS: 1 cover-title; 2 blank; 3–mid 4 nutritional information about vegetables; mid 4–top 6 'Préparation générale'; mid 6–8 'Cuisson des légumes'; 9–top 21 'Recettes spéciales'; mid–bottom 21 'Valeur nutritive des légumes'; 22 [outside back face of binding] 'Autres Bulletins'
CITATIONS: Ag 1867–1974, p 21
COPIES: *OOAG (630.4 C212 P121)

O665.3 1932
—Canadian vegetables / for every day / by / Edith
L. Elliot / Fruit Branch / Department of Agriculture
/ G.E. McIntosh, Commissioner / Pamphlet No. 121
/ Published by direction of Hon. Robert Weir,
Minister of Agriculture, / Ottawa, 1932 [cover-title]
CITATIONS: Ag 1867–1974, p 29
COPIES: Bookseller's stock   *Private collection
NOTES: No copy was found at OOAG.

O665.4 1934
—Canadian vegetables / for every day / by / Edith
L. Elliot / Fruit Branch / Department of Agriculture
/ G.E. McIntosh, Commissioner / Pamphlet No.
121 / Published by direction of Hon. Robert Weir,
Minister of Agriculture, / Ottawa, 1934 [cover-title]
DESCRIPTION: 22.5 × 15.0 cm   Pp [3] 4–22 Illus
Paper, with image on front of bottled, canned and
fresh vegetables; stapled, and with three punched
holes for storing in a binder
CONTENTS: 3–21 text; 22 'Other Bulletins'
COPIES: OGU (2 copies: *UA s052 b42, Rural Heritage
Collection uncat)
NOTES: 'Ottawa J.O. Patenaude, printer to the King's
Most Excellent Majesty 1934' is on the outside back
face of the binding.

O665.5 1934
—Légumes canadiens / pour tous les jours /
par / Edith L. Elliott [*sic*] / Ministère fédéral de
l'agriculture / Division des fruits / G.E. McIntosh,
commissaire / Feuillet no 121 / Publié par ordre de
l'hon. Robert Weir, ministre de l'agriculture, /
Ottawa, 1934 [cover-title]
DESCRIPTION: Paper, with image on front of bottled,
fresh, and canned vegetables; stapled
COPIES: *Private collection
NOTES: This is the only edition where Elliot's name is
incorrectly spelled in the cover-title.

O665.6 reprint, June 1936
—Publication 521 / Bulletin de la ménagère n° 6 /
Publié en juin 1936 / Réimpression du Feuillet
n° 121 / Dominion du Canada – Ministère de
l'agriculture / Légumes canadiens / pour tous les
jours / Edith L. Elliot / Division des fruits / Publié
par ordre de l'hon. James G. Gardiner, ministre de
l'agriculture / Ottawa, Canada [cover-title]
DESCRIPTION: 24.0 × 15.5 cm   Pp [1–3] 4–19 Illus
Paper; rebound in cloth, together with other publications
CONTENTS: 1 cover-title; 2 'Version française par C.E.
Mortureux, B.S.A.'; 3–mid 4 nutritional information

about vegetables; mid 4–mid 5 'Préparation générale';
bottom 5–mid 7 'Cuisson des légumes'; mid 7–mid
18 'Recettes spéciales'; bottom 18 'Valeur nutritive
des légumes'; 19 'Tableau de la proportion approximative d'hydrates de carbone,' 'Autres Bulletins,' and
'Ottawa: J.-O. Patenaude, O.S.I., imprimeur de sa très
excellente majesté le roi, 1936.'
CITATIONS: Ag 1867–1974, p 6
COPIES: *OOAG (630.4 C212 P521 Fr)   QQLAS (S133
A346 F521)

O665.7 reprint, July 1936
—Publication 521 / Household Bulletin 6 / Issued
July, 1936 / Reprint Pamphlet 121 / Dominion of
Canada, Department of Agriculture / Canadian
vegetables / for every day / Edith L. Elliot / Fruit
Branch / Published by authority of the Hon. James
G. Gardiner, Minister of Agriculture / Ottawa,
Canada [cover-title]
DESCRIPTION: 25.0 × 16.5 cm   Pp [1–3] 4–16 Illus
Paper; not stapled or sewn
CONTENTS: 1 cover-title; 2 blank; 3 nutritional infor-
mation about vegetables; 4–top 5 'General Prepara-
tion'; near top 5–6 'Cooking Vegetables'; 7–15 'Special
Recipes' arranged alphabetically by vegetable and
ending with recipes for 'Vegetable Combinations'; 16
'Food Value in Vegetables,' 'Other Publications,' and
'Ottawa: Printed by J.O. Patenaude, I.S.O., printer to
the King's Most Excellent Majesty, 1936.'
CITATIONS: Ag 1867–1974, pp 23 and 32
COPIES: *OOAG (630.4 C212 P521, 4 copies, and 630.4
C212 HB6, 3 copies)

O665.8 1st revision, September 1938
—Publication 521 / Household Bulletin 6 / Issued
September, 1938 / First revision / Dominion of
Canada – Department of Agriculture / Canadian
vegetables / for every day / Edith L. Elliot /
Marketing Service / Published by authority of the
Hon. James G. Gardiner, Minister of Agriculture /
Ottawa Canada [cover-title]
DESCRIPTION: 24.0 × 14.5 cm   Pp [1–3] 4–19 Illus on
pp 4 and 9   Paper; rebound in cloth, together with
other Household Bulletins
CONTENTS: 1 cover-title; 2 blank; 3–mid 6 nutritional
information about vegetables; mid 6–mid 7 'General
Preparation'; mid 7 'Vegetables Used without Cook-
ing'; bottom 7–top 9 'Cooking Vegetables'; near top–
bottom 9 'General Rules'; 10–19 'Special Recipes' and
at bottom p 19, 'Ottawa: Printed by J.O. Patenaude,
I.S.O., ...1938.'
COPIES: *OOAG (630.4 C212 HB6)
NOTES: The OOAG copy is inscribed on p 1, in pencil,
'not distrib[uted].'

O665.9   reprint, 1938
—[Reprint of *Légumes canadiens pour tous les jours*, 1938]
COPIES: QQLAS (S133 A346 F521 1938)

O665.10   reprint, June 1939
—[Reprint of *Canadian Vegetables for Every Day*, Ottawa: Department of Agriculture, June 1939, pp 19]
COPIES: Bookseller's stock

O665.11   reprint, June 1940
—Publication 521 / Household Bulletin 6 / Issued June, 1940 / Reprint / Dominion of Canada – Department of Agriculture / Canadian vegetables / for every day / Edith L. Elliot / Marketing Service / Published by authority of the Hon. James G. Gardiner, Minister of Agriculture, / Ottawa, Canada / 30M–4104–6:40 [cover-title]
DESCRIPTION: 24.0 × 16.0 cm   Pp [1–2] 3–19   Illus on pp 4 and 9   Paper; rebound
CONTENTS: 1 cover-title; 2 blank; 3–mid 6 nutritional information about vegetables; bottom 6–mid 7 'General Preparation'; mid 7 'Vegetables Used without Cooking'; bottom 7–top 9 'Cooking Vegetables'; near top–bottom 9 'General Rules'; 10–19 'Special Recipes' and at bottom p 19, 'Ottawa: Printed by J.O. Patenaude, I.S.O., printer to the King's Most Excellent Majesty, 1940.'
COPIES: *QMAC (S133 A346 No. 521)

O665.12   reprint, June 1941
—[Reprint of *Canadian Vegetables for Every Day*, Ottawa: Department of Agriculture, June 1941, pp 20]
COPIES: Bookseller's stock

O665.13   reprint, October 1941
—Publication 521 / Bulletin de la ménagère n° 6 / Publié en octobre 1941 / Réimpression / Dominion du Canada – Ministère de l'agriculture / Légumes canadiens / pour tous les jours / Edith L. Elliot / Service des marchés / Publié par ordre de l'hon. James G. Gardiner, ministre de l'agriculture, / Ottawa, Canada / 25M–5115–10:41 [cover-title]
DESCRIPTION: 25.0 × 16.5 cm   Pp [1–3] 4–21   Illus Paper; stapled
CONTENTS: 1 cover-title; 2 blank; 3–5 nutritional information about vegetables; 6 'Portions typiques de légumes avec leur valeur calorique' and 'Tableau de la proportion approximative d'hydrate de carbone'; 7 'Préparation générale'; top 8 'Légumes employés crus, sans cuisson préalable'; mid 8–top 9 'Cuisson des légumes'; near top–bottom 9 'Temps exigé pour la cuisson des légumes'; top–mid 10 'Règles générales';

bottom 10–21 'Recettes spéciales' and at bottom p 21, 'Autres Bulletins sur l'utilisation des fruits et des légumes' and 'Ottawa: Edmond Cloutier, imprimeur ... 1941'
COPIES: *OOAG (630.4 C212 P521 Fr 1941, 3 copies)

O665.14   reprint, June 1942
—Publication 521 / Household Bulletin 6 / Issued June, 1942 / Reprint / Dominion of Canada – Department of Agriculture / Canadian vegetables / for every day / Edith L. Elliot / Consumer Section / Marketing Service / Published by authority of Hon. James G. Gardiner, Minister of Agriculture, / Ottawa, Canada / 30M–5871–6:42 [cover-title]
DESCRIPTION: 24.5 × 16.5 cm   Pp [1–2] 3–20   Illus on p 4
CONTENTS: 1 cover-title; 2 blank; 3–20 text
COPIES: OGU (Rural Heritage Collection uncat) OOAG (630.4 C212 P521)   *Private collection

O666.1   1930
Canned / fruits and vegetables / for / variety in everyday meals / by / Edith L. Elliot / Fruit Branch / Department of Agriculture / G.E. McIntosh, Commissioner / Pamphlet No. 113 / Published by direction of Hon. W.R. Motherwell, Minister of Agriculture, / Ottawa, 1930 [cover-title]
DESCRIPTION: 22.5 × 15.0 cm   Pp [1–3] 4–15 [16]   Illus Paper, with image on front of jars of preserved fruit and vegetables, a basket of raw vegetables, and cans of tomatoes, all on a kitchen table; stapled, and with three punched holes for storing in a binder
CONTENTS: 1 cover-title; 2 blank; top–mid 3 introductory text; bottom 3–mid 6 'Regulations Regarding Canned Fruit and Vegetables in Canada'; bottom 6–top 7 'Ways of Serving Canned Vegetables'; near top 7–11 'Recipes for Use with Canned Vegetables'; top–mid 12 'Vegetable Mixtures'; mid 12–15 'Fruit Desserts'; 16 [outside back face of binding] 'Ottawa F.A. Acland printer ... 1930'
CITATIONS: Ag 1867–1974, p 28
COPIES: *OOAG (630.4 C212 P N.S., 3 copies)

O666.2   1930
—Comment apprêter / les / conserves de fruits et / de légumes / pour apporter de la variété aux repas / par / Edith L. Elliot / Division des fruits / Ministère de l'agriculture / G.E. McIntosh, commissaire / Feuillet n° 113 / Traduit au Bureau de traduction du ministère / Publié par ordre de l'hon. Robert Weir, ministre de l'agriculture, / Ottawa, 1930 [cover-title]
DESCRIPTION: 22.5 × 15.0 cm   Pp [1–3] 4–16   Illus

Paper, with image on front of jars of preserved fruit and vegetables, a basket of raw vegetables, and cans of tomatoes, all on a kitchen table; stapled, and with three punched holes for storing in a binder
CONTENTS: 1 cover-title; 2 'Ottawa F.A. Acland imprimeur ... 1930'; top–mid 3 introductory text; bottom 3–top 7 'Règlements touchant les conserves de fruits et de légumes au Canada'; mid 7 'Comment servir les conserves de légumes'; bottom 7–12 'Recettes pour la préparation des conserves de légumes'; top 13 'Mélanges de légumes'; mid 13–16 [outside back face of binding] 'Desserts aux fruits'
CITATIONS: Ag 1867–1974, p 21
COPIES: *OOAG (630.4 C212 P N.S.)

O666.3   1931
—Canned / fruits and vegetables / for / variety in everyday meals / by / Edith L. Elliot / Fruit Branch / Department of Agriculture / G.E. McIntosh, Commissioner / Pamphlet No. 113 / Published by direction of Hon. Robert Weir, Minister of Agriculture, / Ottawa, 1931 [cover-title]
DESCRIPTION: 23.0 × 15.0 cm   Pp [1–3] 4–15 [16]   Illus
Paper, with image on front of four cans of tomatoes (fancy quality, choice quality, standard quality, and second quality); stapled, and with three punched holes for storing in a binder
CONTENTS: 1 cover-title; 2 blank; top–mid 3 introductory text; bottom 3–mid 6 'Regulations Regarding Canned Fruit and Vegetables in Canada'; bottom 6–top 7 'Ways of Serving Canned Vegetables'; near top 7–11 'Receipts for Use with Canned Vegetables'; top–mid 12 'Vegetable Mixtures'; mid 12–15 'Fruit Desserts'; 16 [outside back face of binding] 'Ottawa F.A. Acland printer to the King's Most Excellent Majesty 1931'
COPIES: *Private collection

O666.4   1934
—Canned / fruits and vegetables / for / variety in everyday meals / by / Edith L. Elliot / Fruit Branch / Department of Agriculture / G.E. McIntosh, Commissioner / Pamphlet No. 113 / Published by direction of Hon. Robert Weir, Minister of Agriculture. / Ottawa, 1934 [cover-title]
DESCRIPTION: 22.5 × 15.0 cm   Pp [1–3] 4–15 [16]   Illus
Paper, with image on front of four cans of tomatoes (fancy quality, choice quality, standard quality, and second quality); stapled, and with three punched holes for storing in a binder
CONTENTS: 1 cover-title; 2 blank; top–mid 3 introductory text; bottom 3–mid 6 'Regulations Regarding Canned Fruit and Vegetables in Canada'; bottom 6–

top 7 'Ways of Serving Canned Vegetables'; near top 7–11 'Receipts for Use with Canned Vegetables'; top–mid 12 'Vegetables [sic] Mixtures'; mid 12–15 'Fruit Desserts'; 16 'Ottawa J.O. Patenaude printer to the King's Most Excellent Majesty 1934'
COPIES: *Private collection
NOTES: According to p 5, there were over thirty-five sizes of can on the market, only eleven of which were standardized.

O666.5   reprint, August 1936
—Publication 536 / Household Bulletin 10 / Issued August, 1936 / Reprint Pamphlet 113 / Dominion of Canada, Department of Agriculture / Canned / fruits and vegetables / for / variety in everyday meals / Edith L. Elliot / Fruit Branch / Published by authority of the Hon. James G. Gardiner, Minister of Agriculture / Ottawa, Canada [cover-title]
DESCRIPTION: 25.0 × 16.5 cm   Pp [1–2] 3–12   Illus
Paper; stapled
CONTENTS: 1 cover-title; 2 blank; top–mid 3 introductory text; mid 3–top 6 'Regulations Regarding Canned Fruit and Vegetables in Canada'; mid 6 'Ways of Serving Canned Vegetables'; bottom 6–9 'Receipts for Use with Canned Vegetables'; top 10 'Vegetables [sic] Mixtures'; mid 10–12 [outside back face of binding] 'Fruit Desserts' and at bottom p 12, 'Ottawa: Printed by J.O. Patenaude, ... 1936.'
CITATIONS: Ag 1867–1974, pp 23 and 33
COPIES: *OOAG (630.4 C212 P536, 3 copies, and 630.4 C212 HB10)

O666.6   reprint, August 1936
—Publication 536 / Bulletin de la ménagère n° 10 / Imprimé en août 1936 / Réimpression du Feuillet n° 113 / Dominion du Canada – Ministère de l'agriculture / Comment apprêter / les / conserves de fruits et de / légumes / par / Edith L. Elliot / Division des fruits / Publié par ordre de l'honorable James G. Gardiner, ministre de l'agriculture / Ottawa, Canada [cover-title]
DESCRIPTION: 25.0 × 16.5 cm   Pp [1] 2–12   Illus
Paper; stapled
CONTENTS: 1 cover-title; top–mid 2 introductory text; mid 2–mid 5 'Règlements touchant les conserves de fruits et de légumes au Canada'; bottom 5 'Comment servir les conserves de légumes'; 6–mid 9 'Recettes pour la préparation des conserves de légumes'; mid 9–top 10 'Mélanges de légumes'; near top 10–12 [outside back face of binding] 'Desserts aux fruits' and at bottom p 12, 'Ottawa: J.-O. Patenaude, O.S.I., imprimeur ... 1936.'
CITATIONS: Ag 1867–1974, pp 7 and 25
COPIES: *OOAG (630.4 C212 P536 Fr, 2 copies)

O666.7 2nd impression, July 1937
—Publication 536 / Bulletin de la ménagère n° 10 / Imprimé en juillet 1937 / Deuxième impression / Dominion du Canada – Ministère de l'agriculture / Comment apprêter / les / conserves de fruits et de / légumes / par / Edith L. Elliot / Division des fruits / Publié par ordre de l'honorable James G. Gardiner, ministre de l'agriculture / Ottawa, Canada [cover-title]
DESCRIPTION: 24.5 × 16.5 cm Pp [1] 2–12 Illus Paper; stapled
CONTENTS: 1 cover-title; top–mid 2 introductory text; mid 2–mid 5 'Règlements touchant les conserves de fruits et de légumes au Canada'; bottom 5 'Comment servir les conserves de légumes'; 6–mid 9 'Recettes pour la préparation des conserves de légumes'; mid 9–top 10 'Mélanges de légumes'; near top 10–12 [outside back face of binding] 'Desserts aux fruits' and at bottom p 12, 'Version française par C.E. Mortureux, B.S.A.' and 'Ottawa: J.-O. Patenaude, O.S.I., imprimeur ... 1937.'
COPIES: *OOAG (630.4 C212 P536 Fr, 3 copies, and 630.4 C212 HB10)

O666.8 rev. ed., July 1938
—Publication 536 / Household Bulletin 10 / Issued July, 1938 / Revision / Dominion of Canada, Department of Agriculture / Canned / fruits and vegetables / for / variety in everyday meals / Edith L. Elliot / Published by authority of the Hon. James G. Gardiner, Minister of Agriculture / Ottawa, Canada [cover-title]
DESCRIPTION: 24.5 × 16.5 cm Pp [1–3] 4–13 [14] Illus Paper; stapled
CONTENTS: 1 cover-title; 2 blank; top–mid 3 introductory text; mid 3–mid 4 'Regulations Regarding Canned Fruit and Vegetables in Canada'; mid 4–5 'Buying'; 6 'Storage,' 'Nutritional Value,' and 'Uses'; top 7 'Ways of Serving Canned Vegetables'; mid 7–10 'Receipts for Use with Canned Vegetables'; top 11 'Vegetable Mixtures'; mid 11–13 'Fruit Desserts'; 14 'Other Publications' and 'Ottawa: Printed by J.O. Patenaude, I.S.O., printer to the King's Most Excellent Majesty, 1938.'
COPIES: OOAG (630.4 C212 P536, 3 copies, and 630.4 C212 HB10) *Private collection

O666.9 rev. ed., April 1940
—Publication 536 / Household Bulletin 10 / Issued April, 1940 / Revision / Dominion of Canada, Department of Agriculture / Canned / fruits and vegetables / for / variety in everyday meals / Edith L. Elliot / Marketing Service / Published by

authority of the Hon. James G. Gardiner, Minister of Agriculture / Ottawa, Canada / 35M–3742–4:40 [cover-title]
DESCRIPTION: 24.0 × 16.0 cm Pp [1–3] 4–12 [13] Illus on pp 4 and 5 Paper; rebound
CONTENTS: 1 cover-title; 2 blank; top–mid 3 introductory text; mid–bottom 3 'Regulations Regarding Canned Fruit and Vegetables in Canada'; 4–5 'Buying'; top–mid 6 'Storage,' 'Nutritional Value,' and 'Uses'; bottom 6–top 7 'Ways of Serving Canned Vegetables'; near top 7–mid 10 'Receipts for Use with Canned Vegetables'; mid 10 'Vegetable Mixtures'; bottom 10–12 'Fruits [sic] Desserts'; 13 'Other Publications' and 'Ottawa: Printed by J.O. Patenaude, I.S.O., printer to the King's Most Excellent Majesty, 1940.'
COPIES: AEUCHV (UV 85.17.161) OOAG (630.4 C212 P536, 2 copies, and 630.4 C212 HB10) *QMAC (S133 A346 No. 536)

Favorite recipes

O667.1 nd [about 1930]
Favorite / recipes / "Nothing lovelier can be found / in woman than to study house- / hold good" – Milton
DESCRIPTION: 22.5 × 14.5 cm Pp [1–2] 3–99 Tp illus of a butler carrying a covered dish Lacks binding; stapled
CONTENTS: 1 tp; 2 blank; 3 'Index' [i.e., table of contents]; 4 'Weights and Measures,' 'Vegetables,' and 'Sauce for Vegetables'; 5–95 recipes credited with the name of the contributor and ads; 96–9 'Household Hints'
COPIES: *ABOM
NOTES: The name of the sponsoring organization was probably on the binding, which is lacking in this copy. The advertisements are for businesses in Hamilton, Dundas, St Catharines, and St George.

Favorite recipes

O668.1 1930
Favorite / recipes / 1930 / St. James United Church / Simcoe, Ontario [cover-title]
CONTENTS: First recto page 'Preface' and 'Compiled by the Woman's Association of the St. James United Church'
COPIES: *OSIDM
NOTES: The OSIDM copy is inscribed on the front face of the binding, in ink, 'Mrs. Gettas.'

Favorite recipes

O669.1 1930
Favorite recipes / 1930 / Sydenham United Church / Brantford Ontario / [ad:] When purchasing a gas appliance / consult your gas company / Gas ranges / equipped with oven heat control / assure you of perfect baking results / See our display of / Humphrey Radiant Fires – house heating units / automatic water heaters – room heaters / Brantford Gas Co. / 315 Colborne Street Phone 4120 [cover-title]
DESCRIPTION: 23.0 × 15.0 cm Pp 1–60 Paper; stapled
CONTENTS: 1 preface signed 'Compiled by the Ladies' Aid Society of the Sydenham United Church // Brantford, Ontario'; 2–57 recipes and ads; 58 'For Serving 100 People' and ads; 59 'Table Decoration Suggestions' and ads; 60 'Household Hints' and 'Kitchen' [i.e., kitchen hints]
COPIES: *Private collection
NOTES: An appropriate homily is printed at the beginning of the 'Jams and Jellies' chapter: 'Preserve an even temper and avoid family jars.'

King, Caroline Blanche, née Campion (1871–)

See also O503.1, Jell-O Rhymes, edited by King. Also by this American author, but published only in the United States, is Caroline King's Cook Book, Boston: Little, Brown and Co., 1918 (United States: InU).

O670.1 nd [1930]
Better / coffee / recipes / by Caroline B. King [cover-title]
DESCRIPTION: 13.0 × 8.0 cm Pp 1–20 Illus brown Paper, with image on front of a coffee pot and a filled coffee cup on a table; stapled
CONTENTS: 1 'Caroline B. King is a nationally known authority on foods and nutrition. She is the author of *Caroline B. King's Cook Book* and was Army Dietitian during the World War. Mrs. King is Woman's Editor of the *Country Gentleman* and her articles on cookery appear monthly in the *Ladies' Home Journal.*' and 'How to Make Good Coffee Taste Better' [four numbered steps]; 2 'The Old Fashioned Coffee Pot' and 'The Percolator Method'; 3 'The Drip Method Produces Fine Flavor'; 4 'Iced!'; 5 'Tempting Coffee Beverages'; 6 Coffee Spice Layer Cake and Mocha Icing; 7 Coffee Soufflé and Coffee Fudge Sauce; 8–9 'Delicious Coffee Desserts'; 10–11 map of South America indicating 'A & P's own branches and buyers in the important coffee markets'; 12 '5 Reasons Why A & P Coffees Are the Most Popular in the World'; 13 'Fine Flavor Depends on Freshness' and 'What Is the Answer?'; 14 'A World Wide Buying Organization' and 'World's Largest Distributors'; 15 'Roasting Plants in Every Section of U.S.' and 'Finest Roast Delivered from One to Three Times Each Week'; 16 'Every Roast Is Cup Tested'; 17 'Where the Best Coffee Comes From'; 18 'Again ... Bokar Coffee and Nectar Orange Pekoe Tea Are Honored' and 'A. & P. Tea and Coffee to Be Served to Hundreds of Thousands of Shriners at the Annual Convention in Toronto'; 19 'The World's Best Coffee Value'; 20 'The Selection of Bokar Coffee Endorses the Opinion of Ontario Women'
COPIES: *QMM (RBD ckbk 2140)
NOTES: The text and illustrations are appropriately printed in brown. 'Printed in Canada' is on the outside back face of the binding. The only printed date is on p 19 where the 1926 Sesqui-Centennial International Exposition in Philadelphia is mentioned; however, the reference on p 18 to the Shrine Convention 'to be held here [in Toronto] in June' fixes the book's year of publication in 1930. This huge gathering, hosted by Toronto's Rameses Shrine Temple, took place on 9–12 June 1930, in the Coliseum at the Canadian National Exhibition grounds. Nearby, Canadian Pacific Railway created Fez City on its land, to accommodate all the train cars carrying visiting Shriners from across North America.

The McClary Electric Range cook book

For other books about cooking with McClary appliances and for information about the company, see O162.1.

O671.1 nd [about 1930]
The / McClary / Electric Range / cook book / containing / tested recipes for cooking by / controlled heat / and / instructions for operating / the McClary Oven Heat Control / With the compliments of / General Steel Wares / Limited / 25 branches across Canada / Halifax, Saint John, Quebec City, Montreal (2), Ottawa, / Toronto (4), Hamilton (2), Brantford, London (2), Windsor, / North Bay, Winnipeg (3), Regina, Saskatoon, Calgary, / Edmonton, Vancouver. / Printed in Canada
DESCRIPTION: 17.0 × 12.0 cm Pp [1–2] 3–32 Tp illus of the McClary Oven Heat Control knob, small illus of kitchen scenes Paper; stapled
CONTENTS: 1 tp; 2 blank; 3–7 information about using the Oven Heat Control; 8–28 recipes; 29 blank for

'Notes'; 30 'Table of Measures and Weights'; 31 'Instructions for Using the McClary Electric Oven Heat Control'; 32 'Cooking Chart'

COPIES: *OGU (CCC TX715.6 M26)

NOTES: No one place of publication is recorded and the book was distributed across Canada. Since the executive offices of General Steel Wares at this time were in Toronto and since the company had the most branches in Ontario (twelve, including four in Toronto), the entries for the book are in the Ontario section of this bibliography.

The mixing bowl

O672.1   nd [about 1930]

The / mixing bowl / a selection of tried and tested / recipes / Compiled and published / by / the Ladies Aid / of / the Welland County General Hospital / Welland Ontario / [folio:] 1

DESCRIPTION: 23.0 × 15.5 cm   Pp 1–100   Tp illus of the Welland County General Hospital   Paper; stapled

CONTENTS: 1 tp; 2 'Printed in Canada on Canadian paper by the Welland Printing Company // Welland Ontario'; 3 preface signed the Committee; 4–99 recipes credited with the name of the contributor and ads; 100 'Index' [i.e., table of contents]

COPIES: *Private collection

Moonlight Mellos cook book

O673.1   nd [about 1930]

Moonlight / Mellos / cook book / The Patterson Candy Co Limited / makers of high grade chocolates and confections since 1888 / Toronto Canada [cover-title]

DESCRIPTION: 11.0 × 17.5 cm   Pp 1–28   Illus col, illus   Paper, with image on front of marshmallows floating on a moonlit sea, a fairy seated in the foreground; stapled

CONTENTS: 1 'To Those Who Love Dainty and Wholesome Delicacies'; 2–27 recipes and illus of prepared dishes; 28 'Suggestions for the Afternoon Party and Evening Bridge Game'

COPIES: *Private collection

NOTES: Moonlight Mellos marshmallows were sold in a round tin, which is illustrated on the back face of the binding. Recipes include Marshmallow Cream Pie, Moonlight Cake, Baked Apples with Moonlight Mellos, Moonlight Mello Fruit Salad, and other recipes using marshmallows as an ingredient.

Nationally known recipes

See O374.1 for information about Canadian Milk Products Ltd and its other cookbooks. O913.1, Easy Recipes for Camp and Kitchen, and O1171.1, Skillet Skills for Camp and Cottage, are later Klim recipe collections published by Borden Co. Ltd.

O674.1   nd [about 1930]

Nationally known / recipes / Compiled by / Canadian Milk Products / Limited / Toronto Ontario

DESCRIPTION: 17.0 × 12.5 cm   Pp [1] 2–47 [48]   Illus on tp and on p 48 of Klim container and various prepared dishes   Paper, with image on front of a woman holding this cookbook in her left hand and stirring the contents of a bowl with her right hand; stapled

CONTENTS: 1 tp; 2 'Introduction'; 3 'A Word of Explanation'; 4 'Klim'; 5 'Vitamins'; 6 'Suggestions' and 'Be Accurate'; 7–9 'Klim Mixing Tables'; 10–45 recipes; 46 acknowledgment; 47 'Index to Recipes'; 48 illus

CITATIONS: Chatelaine 1935, p 82

COPIES: *NSWA   OONL (TX759 N37 1940 p***)

NOTES: Klim (milk spelled backward) was a brand of powdered milk. The text on p 3 explains that Klim Brand Powdered Whole Milk is full cream and comes in a brown-and-yellow tin; Klim used to be powdered skim milk, but the skim milk product is now called C.M.P. Brand Powdered Skim Milk and is packed in a blue-and-white tin.

The 'Introduction' thanks 'the many manufacturers of nationally known and advertised food products whose copyrighted recipes are herein reproduced.' By reprinting recipes from 'nationally known' sources, Canadian Milk Products Ltd hoped to prove that 'Klim is milk and can be so used in any recipe and for any purpose for which fresh cow's milk is employed.' All the recipes are credited; for example, to the following cookbooks described in this bibliography (since specific editions are unknown, I have given the number for the first edition): *A Calendar of Dinners,* O390.1, by Marion Harris Neil; *Purity Flour Cook Book,* likely O504.1 of 1923; *Robin Hood Cook Book,* S16.1; *Easifirst Cookery Book,* Gunns Ltd, O426.1 or O560.1; *McClary's Household Manual,* O488.1; *Fish and How to Cook It,* Department of the Naval Service, O319.1; *Edwardsburg Recipe Book,* Canada Starch, Q83.1; *Dainty Desserts for Dainty People,* Knox, Q69.1; *Cowan's Cocoa Recipes,* Cowan Co. Ltd, O468.1; *Old Homestead Recipes,* Maple Leaf Milling Co., O444.1; *Reliable Recipes,* Egg-O Baking Powder Co., O288.1; and *Five Roses Cook Book,* Lake of the Woods Milling, Q79.1.

The design of *Nationally Known Recipes* suggests a publication date of about 1930. In 1928 Borden Co. Ltd acquired Canadian Milk Products, but continued to operate the business under its original name. Since the Borden name is nowhere in the book, it is possible the time of publication predates the Borden take-over.

The OONL copy matches the description for the NWSA copy except for the front face of the binding where, instead of a woman stirring, there is a still-life of a glass of milk, a plate of sandwiches, and a pot of flowers. OONL dates its copy [194-?], but it looks earlier.

The Parkdale Baptist cook book

See also O527.1 from the same church.

O675.1 [1930]
The / Parkdale Baptist Church / cook book / "Tested recipes for housekeepers" / Published under the auspices of / Ladies Aid / Parkdale Baptist Church / Toronto [cover-title]
DESCRIPTION: 23.0 × 15.0 cm   Pp 1–99   Paper, with image on front of the church; stapled
CONTENTS: 1 'Index' [i.e., table of contents]; 2 blank; 3 recommendation that church members patronize the book's advertisers; 4 list of executive of Ladies Aid Society of Parkdale Baptist Church, dated Toronto, 1930; 5–83 recipes credited with the contributor's name and ads; 84–99 ads and at bottom p 99, 'Printed by Printers Guild, Limited // 43 Victoria St. Toronto'
COPIES: *Private collection

Pepper, Miss Laura Christine (Ottawa, Ont., 11 March 1899–9 August 1982, Ottawa, Ont.)

See pl 43. Laura Pepper attended public and high school in Ottawa, where her father, C.G. Pepper, was secretary of the Children's Aid Society. She graduated from a two-year course at the Macdonald Institute, Guelph, Ontario, in 1926. After working as a dietetic intern at St Luke's Hospital in New York City and filling a dietetic position at Childs Restaurant in Toronto, she was assistant to Jessie Read, director of the Home Service Department at Consumers' Gas Co. in Toronto. In about 1930 she returned to Ottawa to join the Dairy Branch of the Department of Agriculture, as a lecturer and demonstrator. When the department was reorganized in 1939, Pepper was made chief of the Consumer Section. In 1946 she was appointed to the Most Excellent Order of the

British Empire in recognition of the Consumer Section's work during the war years (The London Gazette for the Year 1946, Vol. 3, supplement, p 3348). She retired from her position at the Department of Agriculture in June 1964. She was eighty-three years old when she died in 1982; therefore, she was born about 1899. The 1901 Census records L. Christina Pepper, Ottawa, born 11 March 1899.

O676.1, Milk Desserts, was Pepper's first cookbook for the Department of Agriculture. It was followed by O770.1, School Lunches, O865.1, Cream Desserts, O926.1, Cheese for Better Meals, and O953.1, Milk: The Food of Foods. She also wrote the 12-page Food Facts for Consumers, Ottawa: Department of Agriculture, November 1941 (OOAG). See also A98.1, Wartime Recipes and Food Rules, for which Pepper prepared the recipes.

With Edith L. Elliot, Pepper co-wrote the 4-page Healthful Meals at Low Cost, Pamphlet 130, 1933; French edition, Repas sain [sic] à bas prix, 1933. The work was later reprinted in English and French as Publication 510, Circular 100: English edition, June 1936; Repas sains à bas prix, August 1936. Copies of all these versions are at OOAG.

For a list of other cookbooks published by the Department of Agriculture, see O404.1.

Information about Pepper is from her Entrance Record for the Macdonald Institute at OGU (RE1 MAC A0003, Registration No. 3545); her obituary, 'Dr. Laura Pepper Dies,' Ag-Rapport [Agriculture Canada internal newsletter], September 1982, which includes a photograph of her; Doris Runciman's 1960 honorary degree citation for Pepper in the archives at NBSAM; and undated newspaper clippings in a family scrapbook belonging to Jessie Read's daughter.

O676.1 1930
[Title on p 1:] Milk desserts / by / Laura C. Pepper / Dairy and Cold Storage Branch, / Department of Agriculture, Ottawa, / Canada / [introductory text in four paragraphs]
DESCRIPTION: 28.0 × 21.5 cm   Pp [1] 2–14   Fourteen sheets stapled at top edge to a blue, thin-card folder, on which is printed 'Dairy and Cold Storage Branch // Department of Agriculture, Ottawa, Canada 1930'
CONTENTS: 1 title, author, publisher, and introductory text; 2–4 '"Starch" Desserts'; 5 'Junket'; 6–8 'Custards'; 9–10 'Crumb Puddings'; 11–14 'Cereal Desserts' and at bottom p 14, 'Abbreviations'
CITATIONS: Ag 1867–1974, p 113
COPIES: *OOAG (641.6371 C212)
NOTES: The Ag 1867–1974 entry describes the 1930 edition as 'Rev.,' but there is no such description on

the actual publication. This may be the first edition. The letters in the title 'Milk Desserts' are formed from milk-bottle shapes. Only the rectos of the sheets are printed and paginated; the versos are blank.

O676.2 [rev. ed., 1934]
—[Title on p 1:] Milk desserts / by / Laura C. Pepper / Dairy and Cold Storage Branch, / Department of Agriculture, Ottawa, / Canada. / [introductory text in four paragraphs]
DESCRIPTION: 28.0 × 21.5 cm   Pp [1] 2–14   Fourteen sheets stapled at top edge to a green, thin-card folder; typed on a label glued to the front of the folder: '641.5 School Lunches [corrected in pencil: 'Milk Desserts'] by Laura C. Pepper 1932 [last digit corrected in pencil to read '1934']'
CONTENTS: 1 title, author, publisher, and introductory text; 2–4 '"Starch" Desserts'; 5 'Junket'; 6–8 'Custards'; 9–10 'Crumb Puddings'; 11–14 'Cereal Desserts' and at bottom p 14, 'Abbreviations'
COPIES: *OOAG (641.6371)
NOTES: Unlike the 1930 edition, the letters in the title on p 1 are not composed of milk-bottle shapes. The introductory text has been revised and is closer to the introductory text in the March 1936 edition. Only the rectos of the sheets are printed and paginated.

O676.3   March 1936
—Publication 486 / Household Bulletin 1 / Issued March, 1936 / Dominion of Canada, Department of Agriculture / Milk / desserts / by / Laura C. Pepper / Dairy and Cold Storage Branch / Published by authority of the Hon. James G. Gardiner, Minister of Agriculture, / Ottawa, Canada [cover-title]
DESCRIPTION: 25.0 × 16.0 cm   Pp [1–3] 4–23   Paper, with still-life on front of two milk bottles and three milk desserts in front of a curtained window; stapled
CONTENTS: 1 cover-title; 2 table of contents; 3 'Milk Desserts' [introductory text]; 4 'Notes, Abbreviations and Measurements'; 5–22 recipes for 'Starch Desserts,' 'Junket,' 'Cereal Desserts,' 'Custards,' 'Crumb Puddings,' 'Moulded Milk Desserts,' 'Soufflés,' and 'Cream and Custard Pies'; 23 'Other Publications Dealing with the Food Value of Dairy Products Issued by the Dairy and Cold Storage Branch' and at bottom, 'Ottawa: Printed by J.O. Patenaude, I.S.O., printer to the King's Most Excellent Majesty, 1936.'
CITATIONS: Ag 1867–1974, pp 23 and 31
COPIES: OOAG (630.4 C212 HB1, 3 copies, and 630.4 C212 P486, 2 copies)

O676.4   reprint, March 1936
—Publication n° 486 / Bulletin de ménage n° 1 / Publié en mars 1936 / Réimpression / Dominion du Canada – Ministère de l'agriculture / Desserts / au lait / par / Laura C. Pepper / Division de l'industrie laitière / et de la réfrigération / Publié par ordre de l'hon. James G. Gardiner, ministre de l'agriculture, / Ottawa, 1936 [cover-title]
DESCRIPTION: 24.0 × 15.5 cm   Pp [1–3] 4–23   Paper, with still-life on front of two milk bottles and three milk desserts in front of a curtained window; rebound in cloth, together with other Household Bulletins
CONTENTS: 1 cover-title; 2 table of contents; 3 'Desserts au lait' [introductory text]; 4 'Notes, abréviations et mesures'; 5–mid 23 recipes; bottom 23 list of publications and 'Ottawa: J.-O. Patenaude, O.S.I., imprimeur ... 1936.'
COPIES: *OOAG (630.4 C212 HB1 Fr, 2 copies)

O676.5   reprint, April 1937
—Publication 486 / Household Bulletin 1 / Issued April, 1937 / Reprint / Dominion of Canada, Department of Agriculture / Milk / desserts / by / Laura C. Pepper / Dairy and Cold Storage Branch / Published by authority of the Hon. James G. Gardiner, Minister of Agriculture, / Ottawa, Canada [cover-title]
DESCRIPTION: 24.5 × 16.5 cm   Pp [1–3] 4–22 [23]   Paper, with still-life on front of two milk bottles and three milk desserts in front of a curtained window; stapled
CONTENTS: 1 cover-title; 2 table of contents; 3 'Milk Desserts' [introductory text]; 4 'Notes and Measurements'; 5–22 recipes; 23 'Other publications dealing with the food value and uses of milk and its products will be sent free upon request' and at bottom, 'Ottawa: Printed by J.O. Patenaude ... 1937.'
COPIES: *OOAG (630.4 C212 HB1, and 630.4 C212 P486, 3 copies)

O676.6   reprint, June 1938
—Publication n° 486 / Bulletin de la ménagère n° 1 / Publié en juin 1938 / Réimpression / Dominion du Canada – Ministère de l'agriculture / Desserts / au lait / par / Laura C. Pepper / Division de l'industrie laitière et de la réfrigération / Publié par ordre de l'hon. James G. Gardiner, ministre de l'agriculture, / Ottawa, 1938 [cover-title]
DESCRIPTION: 24.5 × 16.5 cm   Pp [1–3] 4–23   Paper, with still-life on front of two milk bottles and three milk desserts in front of a curtained window; stapled

CONTENTS: 1 cover-title; 2 table of contents; 3 'Desserts au lait' [introductory text]; 4 'Notes et mesures'; 5–23 recipes
COPIES: *OOAG (630.4 C212 P486 Fr, 3 copies)

O676.7   2nd printing, August 1938
—Publication 486 / Household Bulletin 1 / Issued August, 1938 / Second printing / Dominion of Canada – Department of Agriculture / Milk / desserts / by / Laura C. Pepper / Marketing Service / Dairy Products Division / Published by authority of the Hon. James G. Gardiner, Minister of Agriculture, / Ottawa, Canada [cover-title]
DESCRIPTION: 24.5 × 16.5 cm   Pp [1–3] 4–22 [23]   Paper, with still-life on front of two milk bottles and three milk desserts in front of a curtained window; stapled
CONTENTS: 1 cover-title; 2 table of contents; 3 'Milk Desserts' [introductory text]; 4 'Notes and Measurements'; 5–22 recipes; 23 'Other publications dealing with the food value and uses of milk and its products will be sent free upon request' and at bottom, 'Ottawa: Printed by J.O. Patenaude, I.S.O., printer to the King's Most Excellent Majesty, 1938.'
COPIES: *OGU (CCC CA1 DA9 35P86)

O676.8   reprint, March 1939
—Publication nº 486 / Bulletin de la ménagère nº 1 / Publié en mars 1939 / Réimpression / Dominion du Canada – Ministère de l'agriculture / Desserts / au lait / par / Laura C. Pepper / Service des marchés / Section des consommateurs / Publié par ordre de l'hon. James G. Gardiner, ministre de l'agriculture, / Ottawa, 1939 [cover-title]
DESCRIPTION: 25.0 × 16.5 cm   Pp [1–3] 4–23   Paper, with still-life on front of two milk bottles and three milk desserts in front of a curtained window; stapled
CONTENTS: 1 cover-title; 2 'Table des matières'; 3 'Desserts au lait' [introductory text]; 4 'Notes et mesures'; 5–23 [inside back face of binding] recipes; outside back face 'Ottawa J.-O. Patenaude, O.S.I. imprimeur de sa très excellente majesté le roi 1939'
COPIES: QQLAS (S133 A346 F486)   *QTS

O676.9   reprint, July 1939
—Publication 486 / Household Bulletin 1 / Issued July, 1939 / Reprint / Dominion of Canada – Department of Agriculture / Milk / desserts / by / Laura C. Pepper / Marketing Service / Consumer Service Section / Published by authority of the Hon. James G. Gardiner, Minister of Agriculture, / Ottawa, Canada / 35M–2428–7:39 [cover-title]
DESCRIPTION: 24.5 × 16.5 cm   Pp [1–3] 4–22 [23]   Paper, with still-life on front of two milk bottles and

three milk desserts in front of a curtained window; stapled
CONTENTS: 1 cover-title; 2 table of contents; 3 'Milk Desserts' [introductory text]; 4 'Notes and Measurements'; 5–22 recipes; 23 'Other publications dealing with the food value and uses of milk and its products will be sent free upon request' and at bottom, 'Ottawa: Printed by J.O. Patenaude, I.S.O., printer to the King's Most Excellent Majesty, 1939.'
COPIES: *Private collection

O676.10   reprint, November 1941
—Publication 486 / Household Bulletin 1 / Issued November, 1941 / Reprint / Dominion of Canada – Department of Agriculture / Milk / desserts / by / Laura C. Pepper / Marketing Service / Consumer Service Section / Published by authority of the Hon. James G. Gardiner, Minister of Agriculture, / Ottawa, Canada. / 15–5085-11-41 [cover-title]
DESCRIPTION: 25.0 × 16.5 cm   Pp [1–3] 4–22 [23]   Paper, with still-life on front of two milk bottles and three milk desserts in front of a curtained window; stapled
CONTENTS: 1 cover-title; 2 table of contents; 3 'Milk Desserts' [introductory text]; 4 'Notes and Measurements'; 5–22 recipes; 23 'Other publications dealing with the food value of milk and its products will be sent free upon request' and at bottom, 'Ottawa: Printed by Edmond Cloutier, printer to the King's Most Excellent Majesty, 1941.'
COPIES: *Private collection

Selected recipes

O677.1   nd [about 1930]
Selected / recipes / Most of the following recipes were contributed / by members of St. Quentin Chapter of the / Imperial Order of Daughters of the Empire, / and were published in a Cook Book which / the Chapter has very kindly permitted / the Ontario Equitable Life / and Accident Insurance / Company to reprint.
DESCRIPTION: 22.0 × 14.5 cm   Pp [1–2] 3–86 [87–96]   Paper, with small image on front, in a circular frame, of a lighthouse; stapled, and with hole punched at top left corner for hanging
CONTENTS: 1 tp; 2 blank; 3 'Index' [i.e., table of contents]; 4 'Table of Weights and Measures'; 5–86 text, including recipes credited with the name of the contributor, and on pp 79–mid 82, 'General Instructions for Weight Regulation,' and on pp bottom 82–85, 'Food Values'; 87–96 blank for 'Memo.'
CITATIONS: Bloomfield 3210

COPIES: *OGU (CCC TX715.6 S43288) OWTU (F3872)
NOTES: *Selected Recipes* is based on O405.1, *Cook Book of St Quentin Chapter of I.O.D.E.* The St Quentin Chapter was located in Waterloo.

The cover-title is 'Selected Recipes published by the Ontario Equitable Life & Accident Insurance Company // S.C. Tweed, President // Head office Waterloo, Ontario.' Sydney Charles Tweed was also president of the Universal Life Assurance and Annuity Co., Winnipeg, Manitoba, which published M82.1, *The Universal Cook Book.* His wife, Winnifred, was honorary president of the Queen Esther Auxiliary of First United Church, Waterloo, which published O690.1, *Favorite Recipes.*

Selected recipes

O678.1 [1930]
Selected / recipes / Stoney Creek / Women's Institute / F.G. Smith, printer, 107 King St. W., Hamilton [cover-title]
DESCRIPTION: 23.0 × 15.0 cm Pp [1–2] 3–64 Illus on p 3 of Mrs J.H. McNeilly, Miss M. Nash, Mrs E.D. Smith, the first officers elected to the Stoney Creek Women's Institute Paper; stapled
CONTENTS: 1 'The members of Stoney Creek Women's Institute the "Mother Institute" present these tested recipes to their many friends throughout the world'; 2 'A Card of Thanks' signed Stoney Creek Women's Institute, June 1930; 3–4 history of the Women's Institute; 5–64 text
COPIES: OSCELM *Private collection
NOTES: The Stoney Creek branch is the charter branch of the Women's Institute, founded on 17 February 1897. Mrs E.D. Smith was the branch's first president. 'A Card of Thanks' acknowledges 'Messrs E.D. Smith and Sons, Limited for their kindness in making this book possible.' The advertisements are for E.D. Smith and Sons, the manufacturer of preserves, based in Winona, Ontario. For information about the company and for a cookbook that contains recipes contributed by Mrs E.D. Smith, see O152.1.

Semple, Frank G.

Semple's given name is found in 1930s Ottawa city directories. He is likely Frank G. Semple, a farmer's son, born 10 July 1886 and living with his family in Waughs River, Nova Scotia, at the time of the 1901 Census. For a list of other cookbooks published by the Department of Agriculture, see O404.1.

O679.1 1930
Dominion of Canada / Department of Agriculture / Live Stock Branch / H.S. Arkell, Commissioner. R.S. Hamer, Chief of Cattle Division / Beef / how to choose and cook it / By / F.G. Semple / Dominion of Canada / Department of Agriculture / Bulletin No. 135 / Printed by direction of the Hon. Robert Weir, Minister of Agriculture, / Ottawa, 1930
DESCRIPTION: 25.0 × 16.5 cm Pp [1–4] 5–52 Frontis of 'Canadian Beef in the Making,' illus of beef cuts Paper; stapled
CONTENTS: 1 blank; 2 frontis; 3 tp; 4 'Printed by F.A. Acland, King's Printer Ottawa, Canada'; 5 'Introduction'; 6–7 'Food Value of Beef'; 8–10 'Selecting'; 11 'Higher-priced Cuts'; 12–13 'Lower-priced Cuts'; 14 'Care of Beef'; 15–22 'Cooking'; 23–4 'Fats'; 25–6 'Beef Soups'; 27–50 'Recipes'; 51–2 'Index to Recipes'
CITATIONS: Ag 1867–1974, p 8 CCat No. 9, p K11
COPIES: ACU (CA1 DA48 30B135) OOAG (630.4 C212 B135 N.S.) OONL (C.O.P. COP.CA.A.656, 2 copies) OTMCL (641.662 S25) SSU (CA1 DA7 1930B135) *Private collection
NOTES: The 'Introduction' says that copies of the colour 'Beef Chart' of cuts of beef and information about the 'Beef Grading Service' can be had from the Dominion Live Stock Branch, Ottawa.

O679.2 1931
—Dominion of Canada / Department of Agriculture / Live Stock Branch / H.S. Arkell, Commissioner. R.S. Hamer, Chief of Cattle Division / Beef / how to choose and cook it / By / F.G. Semple / Dominion of Canada / Department of Agriculture / Bulletin No. 135 / Printed by direction of the Hon Robert Weir, Minister of Agriculture, / Ottawa 1931
DESCRIPTION: 25.0 × 16.5 cm Pp [1–4] 5–52 Frontis of 'Canadian Beef in the Making,' illus Paper; stapled
CONTENTS: 1 blank; 2 frontis; 3 tp; 4 'Printed by F.A. Acland, King's Printer Ottawa, Canada'; 5 'Introduction'; 6–7 'Food Value of Beef'; 8–10 'Selecting'; 11 'Higher-priced Cuts'; 12–13 'Lower-priced Cuts'; 14 'Care of Beef'; 15–22 'Cooking'; 23–4 'Fats'; 25–6 'Beef Soups'; 27–50 'Recipes'; 51–2 'Index to Recipes'
COPIES: *BVIPM OOAG (630.4 C212 B135 N.S., 2 copies)

O679.3 1931
—Ministère fédéral de l'agriculture / Canada / Division de l'industrie animale / H.S. Arkell, commissaire. R.S. Hamer, chef du Service des bovins. / Le boeuf / choix et cuisson / Par / F.G. Semple / Ministère fédéral de l'agriculture / Canada / Bulletin n° 135 / Traduit au Bureau de

traduction du ministère / Publié par ordre de l'hon. Robert Weir, ministre de l'agriculture, / Ottawa, 1931

DESCRIPTION: 24.0 × 15.5 cm   Pp [1–4] 5–58   Frontis of 'Viande de boeuf en préparation au Canada,' illus   Paper; rebound in cloth, together with other Bulletins

CONTENTS: 1 blank; 2 frontis; 3 tp; 4 'Imprimé par F.A. Acland, ... Ottawa, Canada // Traduit par C.E. Mortureux, B.S.A.'; 5 'Avant-propos'; 6–7 'Valeur nutritive du boeuf'; 8–11 'Sélection'; 12 'Morceaux chers'; 13–14 'Morceaux bon marché'; 15 'Le soin du boeuf'; 16–24 'La cuisson'; 25–6 'Graisses'; 27–9 'Soupes ou bouillons'; 30–56 'Recettes'; 57–8 'Table alphabétique des recettes'

CITATIONS: Ag 1867–1974, p 5   BQ Exposition 1974, p 24

COPIES: *OOAG (630.4 C212 B135)

NOTES: BQ Exposition 1974 cites this edition with call number P641.3 Se5460, but the book was not found in the QMBN library catalogue.

O679.4   January 1934
—Dominion of Canada / Department of Agriculture / Live Stock Branch / Geo. B. Rothwell, Commissioner. R.S. Hamer, Assistant Commissioner / Beef / how to choose and cook it / By / F.G. Semple / Dominion of Canada / Department of Agriculture / Bulletin No. 135 / Printed by direction of the Hon. Robert Weir, Minister of Agriculture, / January, 1934

DESCRIPTION: 25.0 × 16.5 cm   Pp [1–4] 5–52   Frontis of 'Canadian Beef in the Making,' illus   Paper; stapled

CONTENTS: 1 blank; 2 frontis; 3 tp; 4 'Printed by J.O. Patenaude, King's Printer Ottawa, Canada'; 5 'Introduction'; 6–7 'Food Value of Beef'; 8–10 'Selecting'; 11 'Higher-priced Cuts'; 12–13 'Lower-priced Cuts'; 14 'Care of Beef'; 15–22 'Cooking'; 23–4 'Fats'; 25–6 'Beef Soups'; 27–50 'Recipes'; 51–2 'Index to Recipes'

COPIES: OWTU (G14561)   *QMM (RBD ckbk 1995)

O679.5   1934
—[An edition of *Le boeuf: choix et cuisson*, 1934, pp 58]
COPIES: Bookseller's stock

O679.6   reprint, December 1936
—Publication 547 / Bulletin de la ménagère n° 12 / Publié en décembre 1936 / Réimpression du Bulletin 135 / Dominion du Canada – Ministère de l'agriculture / Le boeuf / choix et cuisson / F.G. Semple / Services de campagne / Division de l'industrie animale / Publié par ordre de l'hon.

James G. Gardiner, ministre de l'agriculture, / Ottawa, Canada

DESCRIPTION: 25.0 × 16.5 cm   Pp [1–4] 5–58   Frontis of 'Viande de boeuf en formation au Canada,' illus of beef cuts   Paper; stapled

CONTENTS: 1 blank; 2 frontis; 3 tp; 4 'Imprimé par J.O. Patenaude ... Version française par C.E. Mortureux, B.S.A.'; 5 'Avant-propos'; 6–7 'Valeur nutritive du boeuf'; 8–11 'Sélection'; 12 'Morceaux chers'; 13–14 'Morceaux bon marché'; 15 'Le soin du boeuf'; 16–24 'La cuisson'; 25–6 'Graisses'; 27–8 'Soupes ou bouillons'; 29–56 'Recettes'; 57–8 'Table alphabétique des recettes'

CITATIONS: Ag 1867–1974, p 7

COPIES: OGU (CA1 DA9 36P47)   *OOAG (630.4 C212 P547 Fr, 2 copies)   OONL (COP.CA.2.1999-2003)

O679.7   reprint, March 1937
—Publication 547 / Household Bulletin 12 / Issued March, 1937 / Reprint Bulletin 135 / Dominion of Canada – Department of Agriculture / Beef / how to choose and / cook it / F.G. Semple / Field Services / Live Stock Branch / Published by authority of the Hon. James G. Gardiner, Minister of Agriculture / Ottawa, Canada

DESCRIPTION: 25.0 × 16.5 cm   Pp [1–4] 5–52   Frontis of 'Canadian Beef in the Making,' illus of beef cuts   Paper; stapled

CONTENTS: 1 blank; 2 frontis; 3 tp; 4 'Printed by J.O. Patenaude, I.S.O., King's Printer Ottawa, Canada'; 5 introduction; 6–7 'Food Value of Beef'; 8–10 'Selecting'; 11 'Higher-priced Cuts'; 12–13 'Lower-priced Cuts'; 14 'Care of Beef'; 15–22 'Cooking'; 23–4 'Fats'; 25–6 'Beef Soups'; 27–50 recipes; 51–2 'Index to Recipes'

CITATIONS: Ag 1867–1974, pp 23 and 33   CCat No. 16, p R23

COPIES: BDEM   OOAG (630.4 C212 P547, 3 copies, and 630.4 C212 HB12)   QMAC (S133 A346 No. 547 bound in volume labelled No. 1560)   SSU (CA1 DA9 P547)   *Private collection

O679.8   rev. ed., May 1938
—Publication 547 / Household Bulletin 12 / Issued May, 1938 / Revision / Dominion of Canada Department of Agriculture / Beef / how to choose and / cook it / Marketing Service / Published by authority of the Hon. James G. Gardiner, Minister of Agriculture / Ottawa, Canada [cover-title]

DESCRIPTION: 24.5 × 16.5 cm   Pp [1–2] 3–27   Foldout pl col between pp 14 and 15 of 'Beef Chart'   Paper; stapled

CONTENTS: 1 cover-title; 2 'Printed by J.O. Patenaude, I.S.O., King's Printer Ottawa, Canada'; 3–mid 6 'Food Value of Beef'; mid 6–mid 7 'Higher-priced Cuts'; mid 7–mid 8 'Lower-priced Cuts'; bottom 8 'Care of Beef'; 9–mid 14 'Cooking'; mid 14–mid 15 'Fats'; bottom 15–mid 16 'Beef Soups'; bottom 16–27 'Recipes'
COPIES: *OOAG (630.4 C212 P547, 3 copies, and 630.4 C212 HB12, 3 copies)
NOTES: Semple is not credited as the author in this and subsequent editions, which include the 'Beef Chart' as a fold-out colour plate.

O679.9 rev. ed., May 1939
—Publication 547 / Bulletin de la ménagère 12 / Publié en mai, 1939 / Revision / Dominion du Canada – Ministère de l'agriculture / Le boeuf / choix et cuisson / Service des marchés / Publié par ordre de l'honorable James G. Gardiner, ministre de l'agriculture / Ottawa, Canada / 10M88502-2-40 [cover-title]
DESCRIPTION: 25.0 × 16.5 cm Pp [1–2] 3–30 Fold-out pl col between pp 16 and 17 of 'Tableau du boeuf' Paper; stapled
CONTENTS: 1 cover-title; 2 'Imprimé par J.O. Patenaude ...'; 3–top 7 'Valeur nutritive du boeuf'; near top–bottom 7 'Morceaux chers'; 8 'Morceaux bon marché'; top 9 'Le soin du boeuf'; mid 9–mid 15 'La cuisson'; mid 15–top 17 'Graisses'; near top 17–mid 18 'Soupes ou bouillons'; mid 18–30 'Recettes'
CITATIONS: Ag 1867–1974, pp 7 and 26
COPIES: *OOAG (630.4 C212 P547 Fr, 3 copies) QQLAS (S133 A346 F547)

O679.10 reprint, January 1940
—Publication 547 / Household Bulletin 12 / Issued January, 1940 / Reprint / Dominion of Canada Department of Agriculture / Beef / how to choose / and cook it / Marketing Service / Published by authority of the Hon. James G. Gardiner, Minister of Agriculture / Ottawa, Canada / 25M–3250-1-40 [cover-title]
DESCRIPTION: 25.0 × 16.5 cm Pp [1–2] 3–27 Fold-out pl col between pp 14–15 of 'Beef Chart' Paper; stapled
CONTENTS: 1 cover-title; 2 'Printed by J.O. Patenaude, I.S.O., King's Printer Ottawa, Canada'; 3–mid 6 'Food Value of Beef'; mid 6–mid 7 'Higher-priced Cuts'; mid 7–mid 8 'Lower-priced Cuts'; bottom 8 'Care of Beef'; 9–mid 14 'Cooking'; mid 14–mid 15 'Fats'; bottom 15–mid 16 'Beef Soups'; bottom 16–27 'Recipes'
COPIES: OOAG (630.4 C212 P547, 3 copies, and 630.4 C212 HB12) *Private collection

NOTES: The private collector's copy is stamped on the binding, 'Health League of Canada 111 Avenue Rd., Toronto.'
In the 1950s, the Department of Agriculture adapted the title of Semple's book for Publication 971: *Meat: How to Buy, How to Cook.*

60 Marmite recipes

Marmite, a British product made from brewer's yeast and typically used as a spread on toast or crackers, was first made in 1902. The brand is now owned by Unilever. For more information, see The History of Marmite-Yeast Extract, *London: Marmite Food Extract Co., [1927] (Great Britain: LB), and the web site www.accomodata.co.uk/marmite.htm.*

O680.1 nd [about 1930]
60 / Marmite / recipes / The / Robert Simpson / Company / Limited [cover-title]
DESCRIPTION: About 19.0 × 12.5 cm [dimensions from photocopy] Pp 1–24 Illus With image on front of a saucepan; stapled
CONTENTS: 1 'Contents' and 'With the compliments of the Marmite Food Extract Co., Ltd., Mincing Lane House, 59, Eastcheap, London, E.C. 3; 2 'Introduction'; 3–23 recipes using Marmite as an ingredient; 24 'Index' and the printer's name, 'Maxwell, Love & Co., London.'
COPIES: *Private collection
NOTES: No Canadian place of publication is recorded in the book, but the Robert Simpson Co. was a Toronto department store.

Stevens, Mrs Alice

This author is likely the female member in the family buried in Dunnville Cemetery, marked by one headstone, with the following names and dates: Stevens, Robert E., 1865–1939; Alice M., 1869–1939; and Walter, 1892–1914.

O681.1 nd [about 1930]
Choice / recipes / collected and arranged by / Mrs. Alice Stevens / caterer of Dunnville, Ontario / 30 years experience in the catering business
DESCRIPTION: 22.5 × 15.5 cm Pp [i–iii], [1] 2–43 [44–5] Paper; stapled
CONTENTS: i tp; ii blank; iii 'Index' [i.e., table of con-

tents]; 1 blank; 2–42 recipes; 43 'Tables of Weights and Measures'; 44–5 blank for 'My Favorite Recipes'
COPIES: *OGU (CCC TX715.6 C48)
NOTES: The cover-title and running heads are 'Home Cook Book.'

Tested recipes

O682.1 nd [about 1930]
Tested recipes / compiled by / the Ladies' Aid Society / Bridge St. United Church / Belleville, Ont.
DESCRIPTION: 22.5 × 14.5 cm Pp [3–4] 5–154 Tp illus of the church Limp oil cloth; stapled
CONTENTS: 3 tp; 4 'The Ontario Printing & Publishing House // 166–168 Front Street Belleville'; 5 'Table of Contents'; 6 blank; 7 measurements and temperatures; 8 blank; 9 'Foreword'; 10 blank; 11–12 'List of Advertisers'; 13–148 recipes credited with the name of the contributor and ads; 149–50 running head and folio, otherwise blank for manuscript recipes; 151–3 'Household Hints'; 154 running head and folio, otherwise blank for manuscript recipes
COPIES: *Private collection
NOTES: There is an advertisement on p 54 for Tickell and Sons Co., 'Established 1858 // Seventy-two years continuous business ....,' which indicates the book was published in 1930 (1858 + 72 years).

Tested recipes

O683.1 nd [about 1930]
Tested recipes / [caption:] Chalmers' Church, Kingston / Compiled by / the Ladies' Aid Society / Chalmers' Church / Kingston, Ont.
DESCRIPTION: 22.5 × 15.0 cm Pp [1–2] 3–64 Tp photograph of Chalmers' Church Paper, with small image on front of the silhouette of a woman's head; stapled
CONTENTS: 1 tp; 2 blank; 3 table of contents; 4 blank; 5 'Measurements'; 6 blank; 7 'Foreword'; 8 blank; 9–10 'List of Advertisers'; 11–63 recipes credited with the name of the contributor and ads; 64 ads
COPIES: OGU (UA s070 b28) *OKQ (TX715 K44)
NOTES: 'Hanson & Edgar, printers, Kingston, Ontario' is on the outside back face of the binding. The OKQ copy is from the library of Dr J.A. Gray, 1967.

Tested recipes

O684.1 1930
Tested recipes / compiled by / the Women's Association of / First United Church / Lindsay, Ont. / 1930
DESCRIPTION: Pp [3–4] 5–68
CONTENTS: 3 tp; 4 blank; 5 'Table of Contents'; 6 'Measurements'; 7 ads; 8–68 recipes credited with the name of the contributor and ads
COPIES: *Private collection

Tested recipes

For information about Lydia E. Pinkham Medicine Co. and its cookbooks, see O614.1.

O685.1 nd [about 1930]
Tested / recipes [cover-title]
DESCRIPTION: 17.5 × 11.5 cm Pp 1–32 Illus Paper, with image on front of an aproned older woman carrying a bowl of steaming food; stapled
CONTENTS: 1 'Come into the Kitchen!' and testimonial for Lydia E. Pinkham's Vegetable Compound from Mrs Irvine, 34 Macklem Avenue, Toronto; 2 publ ad; 3–32 recipes and publ ads
COPIES: BBVM MCM NSWA OHMB (Ephemera QV772 L983t 1920) OKITD (989.045.002) OKITJS (999.24.9) OTMCL (641.5971 H39 No. 112) OTUTF (uncat patent medicine) OWTU (F17107) QMM (RBD uncat) SBIM SSWD *Private collection
NOTES: Despite the p 1 heading, 'Come into the Kitchen!,' *Tested Recipes* is a different selection of recipes from O614.1, *Come into the Kitchen,* also published to promote Lydia E. Pinkham's Vegetable Compound. *Tested Recipes* was likely published about 1930 since text on p 7 refers to over 10,000 bottles of Vegetable Compound sold per day during 1929. A less precise indication of the publication date is the reference on p 13 to 'over fifty years' that American and Canadian women have depended on the Vegetable Compound (according to this evidence, publication was after 1923, since the company was founded in 1873).

O685.2 nd
—D'excellentes / recettes [cover-title]
DESCRIPTION: 17.5 × 11.5 cm Pp 1–32 Illus Paper, with image on front of an aproned older woman carrying a bowl of steaming food; stapled
CONTENTS: 1 'Entrez dans la cuisine!' and testimonial for Lydia E. Pinkham's Composé végétal [Vegetable Compound]; 2 publ ad; 3–32 recipes and publ ads
COPIES: *OONL (TX715 C3465 No. 17 reserve)

Y.W.C.A. cook book

O686.1 nd [about 1930]
Y.W.C.A. / cook book / [YWCA symbol] /
Published by the / Y.W.C.A. of Owen Sound.
[cover-title]
COPIES: OOWM (988.18.1) *Private collection
NOTES: An advertisement on p 98 for Miss Helen
Moore's beauty shop includes the remark: ' – a host-
ess with straggling locks or unkept fingers? Not in
1930!' The volume has 192 numbered pages.

1930s

[Title unknown]

O687.1 nd [about 1930s]
[An edition of a cookbook from North Parkdale
Church, Toronto, Ontario, pp 52]
CITATIONS: CBCat 61, No. 90
NOTES: This cookbook and O688.1 were part of a lot
of 'Canadian charity cookbooks' in CBCat 61. The
suggested date is the bookseller's. The recipe collection likely originated from North Parkdale United
Church, which was known as North Parkdale Methodist Church from 1909 until church union in 1925. In
1961, the congregation amalgamated with another
church, changing its name and location.

[Title unknown]

O688.1 nd [about 1930s]
[An edition of a cookbook from Wanstead United
Church, Toronto, Ontario, nd, pp 55]
CITATIONS: CBCat 61, No. 90
NOTES: The suggested date of publication is the
bookseller's. Wanstead United Church is at 3340
Danforth Avenue.

The Lakefield Junior Institute cook book

O689.1 nd [about 1930s]
The Lakefield / Junior Institute / cook book /
Lakefield News Print
DESCRIPTION: 21.5 × 13.5 cm
COPIES: *Private collection
NOTES: The owner reports that the book has 39 pp.
Lakefield Junior Institute, part of the Women's Insti-
tutes, was founded in 1929 (two years after the local
adult group) and disbanded in 1945 (Ambrose, p 231).

1930–1

Favorite recipes

Also from the same church is O1203.1, A 1 Cook Book.

O690.1 1930–1
Favorite / recipes / 1930–1931 / First United
Church / Waterloo Ontario [cover-title]
DESCRIPTION: 23.0 × 15.5 cm Pp 1–52 Paper; stapled
CONTENTS: 1 'Preface' and 'Compiled by the Queen
Esther Auxiliary of the First United Church // Wa-
terloo, Ontario'; 2 'Officers Roster, 1930 // Queen
Esther Auxiliary of the First United Church ...'; 3–45
recipes credited with the name of the contributor and
ads; 46 'For Serving 100 People'; 47 ad and 'Table
Decoration Suggestions'; 48–9 'Gelatin Dishes' and
ads; 50–1 'Household Hints' and ads; 52 'Index' [i.e.,
table of contents]
CITATIONS: Bloomfield 3213
COPIES: *OWTU (G8271) Private collection
NOTES: The 'Officers Roster' on p 2 lists Mrs S.C.
Tweed as one of the two honorary presidents of the
Auxiliary. Winnifred was the wife of Sydney Charles
Tweed, president of the Ontario Equitable Life and
Accident Insurance Co. of Waterloo, whose adver-
tisement appears opposite p 1, on the inside face of
the binding. Interestingly, at about the same time as
Favorite Recipes appeared, the Ontario Equitable Life
and Accident Insurance Co. published O677.1, *Se-
lected Recipes*. Winnifred's sister also contributed reci-
pes, those credited to Olive H. Kyle; see, for example,
p 3. Olive later compiled M82.1, *The Universal Cook
Book*, published by the Universal Life Assurance and
Annuity Co., Winnipeg, another company of which
S.C. Tweed was president.

The 'Preface' explains how recipes were selected:
'No attempt to cover the entire field of cookery has
been made, but we have tried to include many dishes
for the hurried mid-day lunch and the hot summer
tea when light and easily prepared dishes are in order.' (This wording is echoed in the 'Preface' of another cookbook of the same title and of about the
same time, O729.1, *Favorite Recipes*, St James Anglican Church, 1931, and in various other church cookbooks of the same period.) Some recipes are not
credited to a specific person, but to an unidentified
'member,' or they are described as 'selected.'

The printer is on the outside back face of the binding (of the private collector's copy): 'Commercial
Printing Co., 20 Frederick St., Kitchener, Ont.'

The OWTU copy is inscribed on the front face of
the binding, in ink, 'R.E.S.'; and in pencil, 'Mrs. H.A.
Schondelmayer.'

1930–4

Cook book

O691.1 nd [about 1930–4]
The Mission Circle / Arva United Church / Cook
book [cover-title]
DESCRIPTION: With image on front of a woman's head,
in profile; probably stapled, and with hole punched
at top left corner, through which runs a string for
hanging
COPIES: *Private collection
NOTES: The 38-page booklet is reproduced from typed
copy. One page lists 'Officers': president, Gwen Mclary
[*sic*]; first vice-president, Mrs Fortner; second vice-
president, Edythe Wyatt; corresponding secretary,
Margaret Webb; recording secretary, Mrs Fletcher;
treasurer, Mrs Ironside; systematic giving treasurer,
Audrey Conner; and pianist, Marie Elson. Below the
'Officers' are the names of the 'Cook Book Commit-
tee': Verna McClary (convener), Audrey Conner,
Eileen Elson, and Margaret Webb. Arva is north of
London.

The cookbook could not have been published after
1934, when Gwen McClary married and took the
name Ironside (her son, Robert, gave me the marriage year, in conversation, February 2001). Verna
McClary, who married in 1939, was Gwen's older
sister. They were related to the family who manufactured McClary stoves.

Ontario, Department of Agriculture

*For the titles of other cookbooks published by the Ontario
Department of Agriculture, see O158.1.*

O692.1 nd [about 1930–4]
[Provincial coat of arms] / Recipes / for / Ontario /
fruits and vegetables / Compliments / of the /
Ontario Department of Agriculture/ Col. the Hon.
Thos. L. Kennedy / Minister of Agriculture. / James
B. Fairbairn / Deputy Minister. [cover-title]
DESCRIPTION: 17.0 × 10.0 cm Pp [1–44] Thin card
folder; leaves bound by two metal fasteners
CONTENTS: 1–44 information about, and recipes for,
grapes, peaches, plums, blueberries, raspberries, cauliflower, carrots, cabbage, beets, tomatoes, and corn
COPIES: *Private collection
NOTES: Each fruit or vegetable is allocated four pages
(on two leaves). The first of the four pages is identical
for each fruit and vegetable, and states: 'This folder is
one of a series containing recipes for fruits and vegetables and has been designed to assist consumers in

their better use. They are distributed through the
courtesy of retailers who also are interested in furthering the interests of Ontario products.'

Thomas Laird Kennedy was minister of agriculture from 12 September 1930 to 10 July 1934, and
from 17 August 1943 to 20 January 1953, when he
resigned his position. *Recipes for Ontario Fruits and
Vegetables* was published during his first time as
minister. James B. Fairbairn was deputy minister of
agriculture from 1 May 1930 to 18 October 1937.

1930–5

[Title unknown]

See also O607.1 from the same church.

O693.1 [about 1930–5]
[Title unknown of a cookbook compiled by the
Women's Association, Chalmers Church, Guelph,
Ontario]
DESCRIPTION: 22.5 × 14.5 cm Pp 1–56 Lacks bind-
ing; stapled
CONTENTS: 1 'Preface' and 'Compiled by the Women's
Association of the Chalmers Church // Guelph
Ontario'; 2 'Index' [i.e., table of contents]; 3–56 reci-
pes credited with the name of the contributor and ads
CITATIONS: Driver 2001, Wellington County, p 91
COPIES: *Private collection
NOTES: The 'Preface' has exactly the same text as
quoted for O690.1, *Favorite Recipes*, published by First
United Church, Waterloo, and other early 1930s cook-
books. The appearance of the book also supports an
approximate date of 1930–5.

Better cooking

The Guelph Stove Co. was incorporated in 1904.

O694.1 nd [about 1930–5]
Better cooking / Acme / Ranges / The / Guelph
Stove Co / Limited / Guelph Ontario / Printed / in
/ Canada
DESCRIPTION: 23.0 × 16.0 cm Pp [1–3] 4–34 Paper;
bound by a cord through three punched holes
CONTENTS: 1 tp; 2 blank; 3–4 'Instructions for Care
and Use of Electric Ranges'; 5–top 2nd column 8
'Meats'; near top 2nd column 8–10 'Whole Meal Cook-
ing in the Oven'; 11 'Meat Recipes'; 12 'Fish'; 13–14
'This Is What It Means' [i.e., glossary of cooking
terms]; 15 'Pastry'; 16–17 'Small Cakes'; 18–23 'Cakes';
24 'Icings'; 25–6 'Desserts'; 27–31 'Tea Biscuits, Rolls,

etc.'; 32 'Oven Canning'; top 33 'Canned Fruits and Vegetables'; bottom 33–34 'Beverages'
CITATIONS: Driver 2001, Wellington County, p 94
COPIES: *Private collection
NOTES: One would expect illustrations of the company's stoves, but there is none. A copy at OONL (TX657 S5 B47 1940z p***) has an extra leaf inserted between pp 4 and 5. The recto of the extra leaf is headed, 'Instructions for Use of Electric Range Features' (i.e., 'The Electric Timer Clock' and 'The Clock Selector Switch'); the verso is blank.

Better recipes with Jewel Shortening

For other recipe collections for Jewel Shortening, see: O863.1, 129 Prize Winning Recipes; O894.1, Tested Recipes: Wishes Come True for Cooks Who Use Jewel; O898.1, 43 Prize Winning Recipes; and O1018.1, Tested Recipes Selected from the Thousands of Interesting Recipes, ...

O695.1 nd [about 1930–5]
Better recipes / with / Jewel Shortening / These recipes were prepared by / Martha Logan's Test Kitchen / Swift Canadian Co. / Limited
DESCRIPTION: 21.0 × 12.5 cm Pp [3] 4–22 Illus col Paper, with image on front of a plate of apple fritters (?) and a package of Jewel Shortening; stapled
CONTENTS: 3 tp; 4–5 'Breads'; 6–mid 7 'Cake'; mid 7–9 'Cake in Small Forms'; 10–12 'Entrees and Luncheon Dishes'; 13–mid 15 'Meat, Poultry, Fish'; mid 15–16 'Miscellaneous'; 17–20 'Pastry'; 21 'Vegetables'; 22 'Desserts'; inside back face of binding 'Temperature Chart for Deep Fat Frying,' 'Equivalents,' and 'Lithographed in Canada'
COPIES: OGU (2 copies: UA s070 b54, CCC TX715.6 B45) OWTU (F13479) *Private collection
NOTES: No place of publication is recorded, but Swift Canadian Co.'s head office was in Toronto. For information about the pseudonym Martha Logan, see O1050.1, *Meat Complete,* under Logan.
The OGU copy is stamped on the front face of the binding, 'The T. Eaton Co Limited Toronto Canada.'

Electric cookery by Hotpoint

For the titles of other cookbooks for the Hotpoint Electric Range, see O638.1.

O696.1 nd [about 1930–5]
Electric / cookery / by / Hotpoint [English tp] La cuisine / à l'électricité / par / Hotpoint [French tp]
DESCRIPTION: 23.0 × 15.0 cm Pp [English:] [1–3] 4–

31 [32]; [French:] [1–3] 4–31 [32] Illus Paper, with same image on English and French faces of binding of an aproned woman carrying steaming poultry on a platter; stapled
CONTENTS: [English:] 1 tp printed in red and black; 2 blank; 3 illus of a woman holding a set of golf clubs and checking the timer on a Hotpoint Hi-Speed Range, and 'Introduction' signed Hotpoint Division, Canadian General Electric Co. Ltd; 4 illus of range parts; 5–mid 16 'The Hotpoint Oven' including information about the timer and cleaning; mid 16–17 'The Economy Cooker,' which is 'designed on the principle of the fireless cooker'; 18–21 'Service Helps'; 22 'Table of Measures and Weights' and 'Do You Measure Accurately?'; 23–31 recipes and cooking advice, including 'Baking,' 'Oven Meals,' 'Recipes for the Economy Cooker,' and 'Canning'; 32 'Instructions for Operating General Electric Hotpoint Hi-Speed Range' and 'The Following Temperatures and Times of Cooking Are Recommended'; [French:] 1 tp printed in red and black; 2 blank; 3 illus of a woman holding a set of golf clubs and checking the timer on a Poêle Hi-Speed Hotpoint General Electric, and 'Introduction' signed Division Hotpoint, Canadian General Electric Co. Ltd; 4 illus of range parts; 5–mid 16 'Le fourneau Hotpoint' including information about the 'Chronomètre-régulateur' and 'nettoyage'; mid 16–17 'La marmite combinée (cooker)'; 18–21 'Indications pratiques'; 22 'Table des poids et mesures' and 'Prenez-vous bien vos mesures?'; 23–31 recipes and cooking advice including 'Pâtisserie de ménage,' 'Repas cuits au fourneau,' and 'Mise en conserve'; 32 'Instructions sur la manière de se servir du fourneau Hotpoint Hi-Speed de General Electric' and 'On recommande les températures et les durées de cuisson suivantes'
COPIES: *Private collection
NOTES: The running foot is 'Designed by Women for Women.'

Food and health

For information about Lydia E. Pinkham Medicine Co. and its other cookbooks, see O614.1.

O697.1 nd [about 1930–5]
Food / [artist's initials below image:] KGH / and / health [cover-title]
DESCRIPTION: 18.0 × 11.5 cm Pp 1–32 Illus Paper, with image on front of a mother and young daughter at a kitchen table, the mother consulting a copy of this cookbook; stapled
CONTENTS: 1 'Hints for Mealtime'; 2–32 culinary text

and testimonials, most bearing Canadian addresses
COPIES: *OTUTF (uncat patent medicine)
NOTES: Although no Canadian address is given for the publisher, Lydia E. Pinkham Medicine Co., Lynn, Massachusetts, most of the testimonials are Canadian. The company's Canadian branch was in Cobourg, Ontario.

Health and happiness from whole meal waterless cooking

O698.1   nd [about 1930–5]
Health / and / happiness / from / whole meal / waterless / cooking / More nourishment Finer flavour / Lower cost / "Duro" Aluminum / Waterless Cooker
DESCRIPTION: 15.0 × 9.0 cm   Pp [1] 2–20   A few illus of the company's aluminium utensils   Paper; stapled, and with hole punched at top left corner, through which runs a cord for hanging
CONTENTS: 1 tp; 2 'Waterless Cooking // The Modern Healthful Way'; 3–near bottom 4 illus of 12-quart waterless cooker and 'Waterless Cooking'; bottom 4 'Cold Pack Canning'; 5–7 'General Directions for Use and Care of the "Duro" Aluminum Waterless Cooker'; 8–9 'Time Table for Cooking Foods in the Aluminum Cooker'; 10–11 'Advantages of Cooking in the Modern Healthful Way'; 12–top 17 'Recipes' [for main courses, cereal, and eggs]; near top 17–top 19 'Desserts'; mid–bottom 19 'Fruit'; 20 illus of, and information about, Aluminum Rack, Pudding Pan, and Duplicate Pans; inside back face of binding illus of, and information about, the waterless cooker; outside back face illus of '"Duro" Aluminum Waterless Cooker // 12 qt. size // Made in Canada by Duro Aluminum, Limited Hamilton, Ontario'
COPIES: *OH (641.73 HEA)
NOTES: In *Hamilton: Its Commerce and Industries 1933*, Hamilton, Ont.: Christian and Co., July 1933, p 71 (OH), there is an advertisement for Duro Aluminum Ltd that illustrates the company's 12-quart 'Duro' Aluminum Waterless Cooker, the same as illustrated in the cookbook. The company's 1936 catalogue (OH) also illustrates the 12-quart waterless cooker.

O698.2   nd [about 1930–5]
—Health / and / happiness / from / waterless / cooking / "Duro" Aluminum / Waterless Cooker
DESCRIPTION: 15.0 × 9.0 cm   Pp [1] 2–20   Illus of Duro Aluminum products   Paper; stapled, and with hole punched at top left corner for hanging
CONTENTS: 1 tp; 2–7 'Waterless Cooking'; 8–9 'Time

Table for Cooking Foods in the Aluminum Cooker'; 10–11 'Advantages of Cooking in the Modern Healthful Way in the "Duro" Aluminum Waterless Cooker'; 12–19 'Recipes'; 20 'Aluminum Rack,' 'Pudding Pan,' 'Duplicate Pans'; inside back face of binding illus of, and information about, the waterless cooker; outside back face illus of a waterless cooker and 'Made in Canada by Duro Aluminum, Limited // Hamilton, Ontario'
CITATIONS: Chatelaine 1935, p 82
COPIES: *APROM
NOTES: I have not compared the recipes in this book with those in O698.1, *Health and Happiness from Whole Meal Waterless Cooking*; however, since the format and pagination of the two booklets are the same and the text divisions appear to correspond, they are probably editions of the same work.

Helpful hints for the housewife

For information about the Quaker Oats Company of Canada and its cookbooks, see O563.1.

O699.1   nd [about 1930–5]
Helpful hints / for the / housewife / Quaker Mills / Saskatoon and Peterborough [cover-title]
DESCRIPTION: With image on front of a woman looking at a child on a chair (presumably modelling clothing made from a flour sack by the woman), and holding an empty Quaker Flour sack, her sewing basket beside her
COPIES: *BPAM
NOTES: Text on the inside front face of the binding explains the genesis of this 28-page publication: 'In this little book of Household Hints is published the result of a prize contest held for the purpose of discovering new and original uses for Quaker Flour sacks. It is a record of the resource and ingenuity of the Canadian housewife, ... Many of the articles mentioned in this booklet can be made from "Mother's Flour" gingham sacks, which, being made of good quality blue gingham in an attractive pattern, will also be found most useful for trimming articles made from Quaker Flour sacks.' The book was a response to the need for economy during the Depression and was likely published after O563.1, *The Quaker Method of Easy Bread Making*, where readers were asked to send in their ideas for using Quaker Flour sacks. The 'Table of Contents' lists the following text divisions: p 3, 'Preparation and Bleaching of Sacks'; p 5, 'Practical Uses for Quaker Flour Sacks'; p 16, 'Quaker Recipes'; and p 28, 'Testimonials from Our Friends.'

'Quaker Oats Company // Peterborough and Saskatoon' is printed on the empty flour sack depicted on the binding.

Household recipes

For a 1938 cookbook from the same church and also produced under M.E. Bradley's leadership, see O955.1, Selected Recipes.

O700.1   nd [about 1930–5]
Household recipes [cover-title]
DESCRIPTION: 23.0 × 15.0 cm   Pp [1–8] 9–119   Very thin card, with small image on front of church; stapled
CONTENTS: 1 'Introduction' signed M.E. Bradley, president Ladies' Aid, Simcoe Street United Church, Oshawa; 2 blank; 3 'Donations' and 'List of Advertisers'; 4 blank; 5 table of contents; 6 'Abbreviations' and 'Measurements'; 7–118 recipes credited with the name of the contributor and ads; 119 'Household Hints'
COPIES: *OTYA (CPC 19-? 0043)
NOTES: This book was published after the silent-film era, for there is an advertisement on p 99 for the New Martin Theatre, which presented 'High class talking pictures // Vaudeville and road shows.'

Kitchen lore

O701.1   nd [about 1930–5]
Kitchen lore / A collection / of / tested recipes / compiled and arranged / by / Mrs. M. Mathewson's Circle / of / the Ladies Aid Society / St. Paul's Eastern United Church / Ottawa Ontario / [folio:] 1
DESCRIPTION: 23.0 × 15.0 cm   Pp 1–84   Lacks binding; stapled
CONTENTS: 1 tp; 2 'Printed by the Dadson-Merrill Press // Ottawa, Ontario.'; 3 'Preface' signed 'The ladies of the Circle'; 4 blank; 5–83 text, mostly recipes credited with the name of the contributor, and ads; 84 ad and 'Index' [i.e., table of contents]
COPIES: *Private collection
NOTES: The writers of the 'Preface' argue that this book should become a valued possession if it meets the home-maker's need for 'a brief and authentic reference book on modern cooking ... [that] contains many new ways to serve, or prepare, old dishes, and above all [that is] made up of recipes which have been thoroughly tested.' At the end of the text there are sections on 'What to Serve with Meats,' 'Cottage Cheese Dishes,' 'Sauces,' 'Quantity Recipes,' 'Time Tables,' 'To Serve 100,' 'Gelatin Dishes,' and 'Table Decorations.'

The Magic cook book

For the titles of other cookbooks promoting Magic Baking Powder, see O285.1.

O702.1   nd [about 1930–5]
Presto! / The / Magic / cook book / Published by / Standard Brands Limited / Gillett Products / Toronto Montreal Winnipeg [cover-title]
DESCRIPTION: 20.0 × 13.0 cm   Pp 1–48   Paper, with image on front, against black background, of a woman lifting a napkin to reveal tea biscuits on a plate; stapled
CONTENTS: 1–4 'Biscuits'; 5–mid 2nd column 23 'Cakes'; mid 2nd column 23–mid 27 'Filling for Tarts'; mid 27–mid 30 'Bread and Rolls'; mid 30–32 'Soups'; 33–mid 34 'Fish'; bottom 34–near bottom 39 recipes for meat; bottom 39–mid 2nd column 41 'Salads'; mid 2nd column 41–top 2nd column 42 'Salad Dressings'; near top 2nd column 42–46 'Puddings'; 47 'Sauces'; 48 'Index'
COPIES: ACG   AMHM   ONM   OONL (TX715 C3465 No. 25 reserve copy 1)   QKB (87-74)   QMM (RBD ckbk 2033a)   SBIHM   SBIM   SMELM SRRPM   SSWD   *Private collection
NOTES: The earliest editions of *The Magic Cook Book* feature, on the front face of the binding, one woman against a black background; later editions have one woman against a green background; the latest editions have three female faces (a mother, grandmother, and daughter). The black-background design is a play on the word magic: Only the woman's head and arms emerge from the black background as she lifts the napkin to reveal the biscuits, just as a magician would remove a silk handkerchief with a flourish at the end of a trick, as he exclaimed, 'Presto!'

All the black-background editions were published after 27 August 1929, when Standard Brands Ltd was incorporated. The earliest was likely published in 1930 and certainly by February 1931: An advertisement for Magic Baking Powder in *Nor'-West Farmer and Farm and Home* Vol. 50, No. 4 (20 February 1931), p 21, has an order form for 'the new Magic Cook Book' and a small photograph of a black-background edition. The order of publication of the black-background editions is uncertain; however, the date of O702.4 is known since various printings have the month/year '11/32,' '4/33,' or '7/33.'

In O702.1, at top p 1, there is '[running head:] Magic Baking Powder contains no alum [folio:] 1'; also on p 1, there is no boxed text above 'All measurements are level'; the recipes in the first column on p 1 are Tea Biscuits, Cheese Biscuits – 1, Cheese Biscuits – 2, and in the second column, Potato Biscuits, Cinnamon Biscuits, Lemon Biscuits. The following recipes are on p 24: Cinnamon Buns, Chopped Pastry, Puff Paste, Custard Pie.

SWSLM has a copy that matches the above description, but lacks pp 23–6.

There is a colour illustration of an unidentified black-background edition in Rowe.

O702.2 nd [about 1930–5]
—Presto! / The / Magic / cook book / Published by / Standard Brands Limited / Gillett Products / Toronto Montreal Winnipeg [cover-title]

DESCRIPTION: 20.0 × 13.5 cm Pp [1] 2–48 Paper, with image on front, against black background, of a woman lifting a napkin to reveal tea biscuits on a plate; stapled

CONTENTS: 1–4 'Biscuits'; 5–mid 2nd column 23 'Cakes'; mid 2nd column 23–mid 27 'Filling for Tarts'; mid 27–mid 30 'Bread and Rolls'; mid 30–32 'Soups'; 33–mid 34 'Fish'; bottom 34–near bottom 39 recipes for meat; bottom 39–mid 2nd column 41 'Salads'; mid 2nd column 41–top 2nd column 42 'Salad Dressings'; near top 2nd column 42–46 'Puddings'; 47 'Sauces'; 48 'Index'

COPIES: AHRMH *Private collection

NOTES: In this edition, at top p 1, there is no running head and no folio; on p 1, above 'All measurements are level,' there is boxed text beginning, 'A better baking will result ...'; the recipes on p 1 are as O702.1. The following recipes are on p 24: Cinnamon Buns, Chopped Pastry, Puff Paste, Custard Pie.

O702.3 nd [about 1930–5]
—Presto! / The / Magic / cook book / Published by / Standard Brands Limited / Gillett Products / Toronto Montreal Winnipeg [cover-title]

DESCRIPTION: 20.0 × 13.0 cm Pp [1] 2–48 Paper, with image on front, against black background, of a woman lifting a napkin to reveal tea biscuits on a plate; stapled

CONTENTS: 1–4 'Biscuits'; 5–mid 2nd column 23 'Cakes'; mid 2nd column 23–mid 27 'Filling for Tarts'; mid 27–mid 30 'Bread and Rolls'; mid 30–32 'Soups'; 33–mid 34 'Fish'; bottom 34–near bottom 39 recipes for meat; bottom 39–mid 2nd column 41 'Salads'; mid 2nd column 41–top 2nd column 42 'Salad Dressings'; near top 2nd column 42–46 'Puddings'; 47 'Sauces'; 48 'Index'

COPIES: AEUCHV AWWDM BDEM BSUM BVAMM MAUAM MSOHM MWPA (MG14 C50 McKnight, Ethel) OFERWM (A1952x.419m) OGU (CCC TX715.6 M34) QMM (RBD ckbk 2033c) *Company collection (Nabisco Brands Ltd, Toronto, Ont.)

NOTES: See pl 7. In this edition, at top p 1, there is no running head and no folio; on p 1, above 'All measurements are level,' there is boxed text beginning, 'A better baking will result ...'; the recipes on p 1 are as O702.1. The following recipes are on p 24: Cheese Straws, Chopped Pastry, Flaky Pastry, Lemon Pie, Custard Pie.

O702.4 nd [1932–3]
—Presto! / The / Magic / cook book / Published by / Standard Brands Limited / Gillett Products / Toronto Montreal Winnipeg [cover-title]

DESCRIPTION: 20.0 × 13.0 cm Pp [1] 2–48 Paper, with image on front, against black background, of a woman lifting a napkin to reveal tea biscuits on a plate; stapled

CONTENTS: 1–4 'Biscuits'; 5–mid 2nd column 17 'Cakes'; mid 2nd column 17–near bottom 1st column 21 'Icings and Frostings'; bottom 1st column 21–mid 2nd column 24 'Cookies and Small Cakes'; bottom 2nd column 24–1st column 29 'Pastries and Fillings'; 2nd column 29–mid 1st column 32 'Bread and Rolls'; bottom 1st column 32–top 2nd column 33 'Soups'; mid 2nd column 33–34 'Fish'; 35 'Pickles'; 36–mid 1st column 40 'Meats'; mid 1st column 40–mid 2nd column 41 'Salads'; mid 2nd column 41–top 2nd column 42 'Salad Dressings'; near top 2nd column 42–46 'Puddings'; 47 'Sauces'; 48 'Index' and at bottom, '4/33'

COPIES: *AEPMA (2 copies: H79.114.191, H86.43.716) MWMM OONL (TX715 C3465 No. 25 copy 2) OOWM (984.91.3) QKB (87-74) QMM (RBD ckbk 2033b)

NOTES: In this edition, at top p 1, there is no running head and no folio; on p 1, above 'All measurements are level,' there is boxed text beginning, 'A better baking will result ...'; the recipes on p 1 are as O702.1. The following recipes are in the first column on p 24: Plain Rocks, Nut and Date Bars, Chinese Chews, and Almond Cakes; in the second column on p 24: Dainty Cheese Cakes, Spanish Cup Cakes, and, under the heading 'Pastries and Fillings,' Chopped Pastry.

The printing date differentiates the copies listed above: in the catalogued AEPMA copy and the OONL copy, '4/33' [i.e., April 1933] is on p 48; in MWMM and QMM, '7/33' is on p 48; and in QKB, '11/32' is on p 1.

O702.5   nd [about 1935]

—Presto! / The / Magic / Baking Powder / cook book / Published by / Standard Brands Limited / Gillett Products / Toronto Montreal Winnipeg Vancouver [cover-title]

DESCRIPTION: 23.0 × 15.5 cm   Pp [1] 2–32   Paper, with image on front, against green background, of a woman lifting a napkin to reveal tea biscuits on a plate; stapled

CONTENTS: 1–3 'Biscuits'; 4–5 'Cakes'; 6–7 '10 Famous Cakes ... Recipes That Brought Fame to Canada's Best Known Cookery Authorities'; 8–1st column 9 'Six Prize Winning Recipes ... National Mystery Cake Contest'; 2nd column 9–1st column 14 more cake recipes; 2nd column 14–16 'Icings and Frostings'; 17–18 'Cookies and Small Cakes'; 19–21 'Pastries and Fillings'; 22–1st column 23 'Bread and Rolls'; 2nd column 23 'Soups'; 24–5 'Meats'; 1st column 26 'Fish'; 2nd column 26–1st column 27 'Pickles'; 2nd column 27–1st column 28 'Salads'; 2nd column 28 'Salad Dressings'; 29–1st column 31 'Puddings'; 2nd column 31 'Sauces'; 32 'Index'

COPIES: AEUCHV APROM ARDA BVAMM OGU (CCC TX715.6 M33 cover b)   ONM   OONL (TX715 C3465 No. 24 reserve)   OTMCL (641.5971 H39 No. 67)   QMMMCM (AR-M2000.92.29)   SBIHM *Private collection

NOTES: The change from a black to a green background on the binding also marks a change of cover-title from 'The Magic Cook Book' to 'The Magic Baking Powder Cook Book.' The editions with the green background have larger dimensions (23.0 × 15.0 or 15.5 cm for green, 20.0 × 13.0 or 13.5 cm for black). The order of the green-background editions is uncertain, but those with four pastry recipes in the first column on p 19 likely precede those with three recipes (the latter are closer to the 'family tradition' editions (see O702.9 and following), which have the same three recipes in the first column on p 19).

In O702.5 there is no boxed text on p 1; the recipes in the first column on p 1 are Tea Biscuits, Cheese Biscuits – 1, Cheese Biscuits – 2, Potato Biscuits, Cinnamon Biscuits, Lemon Biscuits, and in the second column, Graham Biscuits, Golden Biscuits, Fruit Scone, Orange Biscuits – 1, Orange Biscuits –2, Emergency Biscuits, Fruit Biscuits. There are four recipes in the first column on p 19, under the heading 'Pastries and Fillings': Chopped Pastry, Flaky Pastry, Short Paste (Sweet), Puff Paste; recipes in the second column on p 19 are: Magic Baking Powder Flaky Pastry, Lemon Curd, Apricot Curd, Almond Cheese Curd, Cheese Straws.

Some copies correspond to the above description, except for a difference in the cover-title, where the places of publication are given as 'Montreal Toronto ...' instead of 'Toronto Montreal ...' These copies are at ACG, AEPMA, OFERWM (A1977.122.15), and SRRPM.

Chatelaine 1935, p 82, lists 'Magic Baking Powder Cook Book (English and French),' but does not specify which of the various editions with this title.

O702.6   nd [about 1935]

—Presto! / Le / livre culinaire / de la poudre a pate / "Magic" / Publié par / Standard Brands Limited / Produits Gillett / Montreal Toronto Winnipeg Vancouver [cover-title]

COPIES: *QSFFSC

NOTES: The following four recipes are on p 19, first column, under the heading 'Pâtes et garnitures': Pâte hachée, Pâte floconneuse, Pâte brisée (sucrée), and Pâte feuilletée; in the second column: Pâte floconneuse à la poudre à pâte 'Magic,' Gelée au citron, Gelée d'abricots, Gelée au fromage et aux amandes, and Pailles au fromage.

O702.7   nd [about 1935]

—Presto! / The / Magic / Baking Powder / cook book / Published by / Standard Brands Limited / Gillett Products / Toronto Montreal Winnipeg Vancouver [cover-title]

DESCRIPTION: 23.0 × 15.0 cm   Pp [1] 2–32   Paper, with image on front, against green background, of a woman lifting a napkin to reveal tea biscuits on a plate; stapled

CONTENTS: 1–3 'Biscuits'; 4–5 'Cakes'; 6–7 '10 Famous Cakes ... Recipes That Brought Fame to Canada's Best Known Cookery Authorities'; 8–1st column 9 'Six Prize Winning Recipes ... National Mystery Cake Contest'; 2nd column 9–1st column 14 more cake recipes; 2nd column 14–16 'Icings and Frostings'; 17–18 'Cookies and Small Cakes'; 19–21 'Pastries and Fillings'; 22–1st column 23 'Bread and Rolls'; 2nd column 23 'Soups'; 24–5 'Meats'; 1st column 26 'Fish'; 2nd column 26–1st column 27 'Pickles'; 2nd column 27–1st column 28 'Salads'; 2nd column 28 'Salad Dressings'; 29–1st column 31 'Puddings'; 2nd column 31 'Sauces'; 32 'Index'

COPIES: *Company collection (Nabisco Brands Ltd, Toronto, Ont.)

NOTES: In this edition, there is no boxed text on p 1; the recipes on p 1 are as O702.5. There are three recipes in the first column on p 19, under the heading 'Pastries and Fillings': Chopped Pastry, Short Paste (Sweet), Puff Paste; recipes in the second column on p 19 are: Magic Baking Powder Flaky Pastry, Lemon

Curd, Apricot Curd, Almond Cheese Curd, Cheese Straws.

Some copies correspond to the above description, except for a difference in the cover-title, where the places of publication are given as 'Montreal Toronto ...' instead of 'Toronto Montreal ...' These copies are at AEPMA, BSUM, OGU (CCC TX715.6 M33 cover a), OONL (TX765 S83 1920z), QMM (RBD Tudor Hart, ckbk 2034), and SBIM.

O702.8 nd [about 1935]
—Presto! / Le / livre culinaire / de la poudre a pate / "Magic" / Publié par / Standard Brands Limited / Produits Gillett / Montreal Toronto Winnipeg Vancouver [cover-title]
COPIES: *QSFFSC
NOTES: Only three recipes are on p 19, first column, under the heading 'Pâtes et garnitures': Pâte hachée, Pâte brisée (sucrée), and Pâte feuilletée; in the second column: the same recipes as O702.6.

O702.9 nd [about 1940]
—A family / tradition / The / Magic / Baking / Powder / cook book / Published by / Standard Brands Limited "Gillett Products" / Montreal Toronto Winnipeg Vancouver [cover-title]
DESCRIPTION: 23.0 × 15.0 cm   Pp [1] 2–16, [i–iv], 17–32   Paper, with image on front of three female faces (mother, grandmother, daughter) and a container of Magic Baking Powder; stapled
CONTENTS: 1–3 'Biscuits'; 4–5 'Cakes'; 6–7 '10 Famous Cakes ... Recipes That Brought Fame to Canada's Best Known Cookery Authorities'; 8–1st column 9 'Six Prize Winning Recipes ... National Mystery Cake Contest'; 2nd column 9–1st column 14 more cake recipes; 2nd column 14–16 'Icings and Frostings'; i 'Recipes for Good Home-made Bread and Sweet Goods'; ii–iii 'Special Recipes for Odd Occasions'; iv publ ad for Magic Soda; 17–18 'Cookies and Small Cakes'; 19–mid 1st column 20 'Pasteries [sic] and Fillings'; bottom 1st column 20–21 'Pie Fillings'; 22–1st column 23 'Bread and Rolls'; 2nd column 23 'Soups'; 24–5 'Meats'; 1st column 26 'Fish'; 2nd column 26–1st column 27 'Pickles'; 2nd column 27–1st column 28 'Salads'; 2nd column 28 'Salad Dressings'; 29–1st column 31 'Puddings'; 2nd column 31 'Sauces'; 32 'Index'
CITATIONS: Rowe, illus col
COPIES: ACG AEUCHV APROM BDEM BKOM BVIPM MAUAM MCM MSOHM MWMM OFERWM (A1978.189.41) *OGU (2 copies: CCC TX715.6 M33 cover c, CCC TX715.6 M572 No. 530) OKIT OPEMO OTMCL (641.5971 H39

No. 34) QKB (2 copies: 72-5, 87-74) QMM (RBD Vanna Garnier, ckbk 912) QMMMCM (ARM-2000.92.40) SBIHM SBIM SSWD SWSLM
NOTES: Editions where the binding has an image of three women and the slogan 'A family tradition' or 'Une tradition de famille' (O702.9, O702.10, O702.11, O702.12) were published about 1940. The evidence for this date is in a letter of 1 June 1991 to me, from an owner of one of these English editions (whether O702.9 or O702.11 is unknown): 'This last little cookbook was given to me while having lunch in Halifax while on our honeymoon in late July 1940. My husband who had a general store recognized the salesman from Standard Brands who was sitting near us. When he made himself known and said we were on our honeymoon, the salesman went out to his car and brought me the cookbook and some samples of their products. This started me cooking ...' Of the 'family tradition' editions, those with 'Gillett Products' in the cover-title precede those without.

There are three recipes in the first column on p 19, under the heading 'Pasteries [sic] and Fillings': Chopped Pastry, Short Paste (Sweet), Puff Paste; recipes in the second column on p 19 are: Magic Simplex Pastry, Lemon Curd, Apricot Curd, Almond Cheese Curd, Cheese Straws.

O702.10 nd [about 1940]
—Une tradition / de famille / Le / livre culinaire / de la poudre / a pate / "Magic" / Publié par / Standard Brands Limited "Gillett Products" / Montreal Toronto Winnipeg Vancouver [cover-title]
DESCRIPTION: 23.0 × 15.0 cm   Pp [1] 2–16, [i–iv], 17–32   Paper, with image on front of three female faces (mother, grandmother, daughter); stapled
CONTENTS: 1–3 'Biscuits'; 4–5 'Gâteaux'; 6–7 '10 gâteaux fameux ...'; 8–mid 9 'Six recettes primées'; mid 9–1st column 14 more cake recipes; 2nd column 14–16 'Glaçages et givres'; i 'Recettes pour faire du beau pain de ménage et des confiseries'; ii–iii 'Recettes spéciales pour occasions rares'; iv publ ad for 'Le Soda "Magic"'; 17–18 'Galettes et petits gâteaux'; 19–21 'Pâtes et garnitures'; 22–1st column 23 'Pain et petits pains'; 2nd column 23 'Soupes'; 24–5 'Viandes'; 1st column 26 'Poisson'; 2nd column 26–top 2nd column 27 'Marinades'; near top 2nd column 27–1st column 28 'Salades'; 2nd column 28 'Sauces à salades'; 29–1st column 31 'Poudings'; 2nd column 31 'Sauces'; 32 index
COPIES: *OONL (TX715 C3465 No. 26, 2 copies) QSFFSC Private collection
NOTES: There are three recipes in the first column on p 19, under the heading 'Pâtes et garnitures': Pâte

hachée, Pâte brisée (sucrée), and Pâte feuilletée; the second column begins with Pâte 'Magic Simplex.'

O702.11 nd [about 1940]
—A family / tradition / The / Magic / Baking / Powder / cook book / Published by / Standard Brands Limited / Montreal Toronto Winnipeg Van[couver] [cover-title]
DESCRIPTION: 23.0 × 15.0 cm   Pp [1] 2–32   Paper, with image on front of three female faces (mother, grandmother, daughter) and a container of Magic Baking Powder; stapled
CONTENTS: 1–3 'Biscuits'; 4–5 'Cakes'; 6–7 '10 Famous Cakes ... Recipes That Brought Fame to Canada's Best Known Cookery Authorities'; 8–1st column 9 'Six Prize Winning Recipes ... National Mystery Cake Contest'; 2nd column 9–1st column 14 more cake recipes; 2nd column 14–16 'Icings and Frostings'; 17–18 'Cookies and Small Cakes'; 19–mid 1st column 20 'Pastries and Fillings'; bottom 1st column 20–21 'Pie Fillings'; 22–1st column 23 'Bread and Rolls'; 2nd column 23 'Soups'; 24–5 'Meats'; 1st column 26 'Fish'; 2nd column 26–1st column 27 'Pickles'; 2nd column 27–1st column 28 'Salads'; 2nd column 28 'Salad Dressings'; 29–1st column 31 'Puddings'; 2nd column 31 'Sauces'; 32 'Index'
CITATIONS: Armstrong 2000, illus p F1   Ferguson/ Fraser, p 233, illus col on p 80 of closed volume
COPIES: AALIWWM   MBDHM   OGU (CCC TX715.6 M33 cover d)   QSH (0443)   Company collection (Nabisco Brands Ltd, Toronto, Ont.)   *Private collection
NOTES: Unlike O702.9, there is no 'Gillett Products' in the cover-title. There are three recipes in the first column on p 19, under the correctly spelled heading 'Pastries and Fillings': Chopped Pastry, Short Paste (Sweet), Puff Paste; recipes in the second column on p 19 begin with Magic Simplex Pastry.

The copy catalogued here is the one illustrated in Ferguson/Fraser.

O702.12 nd [about 1940]
—Une tradition / de famille / Le / livre culinaire / de la poudre / a pate / "Magic" / Publié par / Standard Brands Limited / Montreal Toronto Winnipeg Vancouver [cover-title]
DESCRIPTION: 23.0 × 15.0 cm   Pp [1] 2–32   Paper, with image on front of three female faces (mother, grandmother, daughter) and a container of Magic Baking Powder; stapled
COPIES: *QSFFSC
NOTES: Unlike O702.10, there is no 'Gillett Products' in the cover-title.

Meats and how to prepare them

Also by the London Life Insurance Co. are: O711.1, Salads for Health; O846.1, Canning Guide; O870.1, 300 Household Hints; O881.1, The Buying and Cooking of Meat; and O1058.1, Sugar-Saving Recipes.

O703.1 nd [about 1930–5]
Meats / and how to / prepare them / Printed and distributed by / the London Life Insurance Company / Head office: London, Canada [cover-title]
DESCRIPTION: 22.5 × 15.5 cm   Pp 3–14   Illus of cuts of meat   Paper, with image on front of roast meat on a platter and a vase of red roses; stapled
CONTENTS: Inside front face of binding 'Meat for Quick Energy' and 'Illustrations by courtesy of Chatelaine'; 3 'The Food Value of the Various Cuts of Meat'; 4 'Lamb and Mutton'; 5 'Lamb Recipes'; 6–7 'Beef'; 8 'Beef Recipes'; 9 'Veal' and 'Veal Recipes'; 10–top 11 'Pork'; mid–bottom 11 pork recipes; 12 'Miscellaneous Recipes'; 13–14 'How to Cook Meats'
CITATIONS: Chatelaine 1935, p 82   Golick, p 112
COPIES: *OTMCL (641.5971 H39 No. 110)
NOTES: The outside back face of the binding of the OTMCL copy is covered with the insurance salesman's pencilled notes and calculations, made during his pitch to the customer.

Moffats Blue Star cook book

For the titles of other cookbooks by the same manufacturer, see O342.1.

O704.1 nd [about 1930–5]
Moffats / Blue Star / cook book [cover-title]
DESCRIPTION: 16.0 × 8.5 cm   Pp 1–16   Illus on p 2 of a gas burner and on p 9 of a steamer   Paper, with image on front of a child reaching for a doughnut; stapled
CONTENTS: top 1 'Laboratory Seal of Approval ... trade mark registered 1927 – Canada'; bottom 1–mid 3 'Safety First!'; mid 3–mid 5 'Cooking Economies'; mid 5–mid 8 'Cooking Suggestions for Health'; bottom 8 'Canning'; top 9 'Moffats Steamer'; bottom 9–top 11 'Full Course Meal Cooking with Moffats Oven Control'; mid 11–16 recipes
COPIES: *OKQ (F5012 1927 M695)   OSMFHHM OTMCL (641.5971 H39 No. 117)   OWTU (E1022)
NOTES: Page 4 compares coal with gas: 'It is difficult for a cook who is used to a coal range to realize the

great intensity of a gas range heat.' The text is printed in brown. The place of publication is not recorded, but Moffats Ltd was based in Weston, Ontario.

Moffats cook book

For the titles of other cookbooks by the same manufacturer, see O342.1.

O705.1   nd [about 1930–5]
Monsieur Tournebroche / Moffats / cook / book / select recipe / guide [cover-title]
DESCRIPTION: 23.0 × 15.0 cm   Pp [1] 2–95 [96–7]
Frontis of 'The largest plant in the British Empire devoted exclusively to the manufacture of electric and gas ranges' with inset of 'Moffats, Limited, 1882 Markdale, Ont., Canada'; fp illus on pp 20, 22, and 24 of cuts of meat; illus   Paper-covered thin card, with image on front of head-and-shoulders of 'Monsieur Tournebroche'; with hole punched at top left corner for hanging
CONTENTS: 1 'Growth' [a history of Moffats Ltd that refers to the company's founding in 1882 at Markdale by Mr T.L. Moffat, Sr, and the company's move to Weston, Ontario, in 1892]; 2 'Monsieur Tournebroche'; 3–6 'Directions and Important Information for Operating Moffats Electric Ranges // Start Right'; 7–11 'Entertaining'; 12–95 recipes and other items; 96 index; 97 manufacturer's guarantee for the range
CITATIONS: FitzPatrickCat 111 (April 1993) No. 18
COPIES: OFERWM (A1978.189.43)   OONL (TX715 C674 copy 2)   OTMCL (641.5971 H39 No. 128)   *Private collection
NOTES: 'Monsieur Tournebroche' is explained on p 2 as 'a name affectionately applied by the old French families to their Chef.' The text is related to O585.1, McGill, Mrs D., *Moffats Cook Book*, by the same company, copyright 1926; however, in the 'Monsieur Tournebroche' editions, Mrs McGill is not identified as the author. Most of the recipes are word-for-word the same as in the McGill editions, but many of the recipes are placed in a different order. There is a new section called 'Entertaining.' The book is undated except for facsimiles of medals of 1925–6 on the binding; however, it was likely published about 1930–5. The text is printed in two tones of brown. The OFERWM copy lacks pp 1–2 and 95–7.

Chatelaine 1935, p 82, lists 'Moffat's Cook Book (free to purchasers of a Moffat range or owners of a used Moffat range on receipt of style and serial number. To others, 25c.)'; this reference likely refers to one of the 'Monsieur Tournebroche' editions.

O705.2   nd
—Moffats / cook book [cover-title]
DESCRIPTION: 23.0 × 15.0 cm   Pp [i–ii], 1–112, [i] Illus   Paper-covered thin card, with image on front of head-and-shoulders of 'Monsieur Tournebroche'
CONTENTS: i endpaper recto; ii untitled publ note; 1 'Moffats ... The World Over'; 2 'Monsieur Tournebroche'; 3–mid 7 'Directions and Important Information for Operating Moffats Electric Ranges and Cookers'; bottom 7 'Food Elements'; top 8 'Terms Relating to Cookery and Serving'; bottom 8–top 9 'Mixing of Food Ingredients'; bottom 9 'Weights and Measures'; 10 'Substitutes'; 11 'Temperature Chart' and 'Kitchen Hints'; 12–16 'Entertaining'; 17–111 recipes; 112 index; i Moffats Ltd guarantee
COPIES: *Private collection
NOTES: The untitled publisher's note on p ii explains how the book was produced: '... this cook book has been compiled with the help of our representatives from every corner of the earth. From over the seas came many tempting new recipes ... national dishes from far off countries where good cooking is traditional.' The illustration on p 1 shows the factory in Weston, and the factory in Blackburn, Lancashire, England. This edition has more pages than O705.1. The text is printed in black, and a green vertical band runs down the outer edge of each page. There are no dated facsimiles of medals on the binding.

O705.3   nd
—Moffats / cook book [cover-title]
DESCRIPTION: 23.0 × 15.0 cm   Pp [i–ii], 1–112, [i]   Illus printed in one or two colours   Paper-covered thin card, with image on front of head-and-shoulders of 'Monsieur Tournebroche'
CONTENTS: i endpaper recto; ii untitled publ note; 1 'Moffats ... The World Over'; 2 'Monsieur Tournebroche'; 3–6 'Directions and Important Information for Operating Moffats Electric Ranges and Cookers'; 7 'Food Elements' and 'Terms Relating to Cookery and Serving'; 8 'Mixing of Food Ingredients' and 'Weights and Measures'; top 9 'Table of Weights and Measures'; mid 9–top 10 'Substitutes'; mid 10 'Temperature Chart'; mid–bottom 10 'Kitchen Hints'; 11 'Household Hints' and 'Miscellaneous'; 12–16 'Entertaining'; 17–111 recipes; 112 index; i Moffats Ltd guarantee
COPIES: OONL (TX715 C674)   QMM (RBD ckbk 1836, 2 copies)   *Private collection
NOTES: In this edition, the introductory text has been reset so that, for example, 'Terms Relating to Cookery and Serving' starts partway down p 7, not at top p 8 as in O705.2. The text is printed in brown; there

are cream-coloured vertical bands at the outer edge of each page.

The OONL copy is rebound and lacks its cover-title.

The pantry shelf

O706.1 nd [about 1930–5]
The / pantry / shelf / St. George's Cathedral / Kingston, Ontario [cover-title]
DESCRIPTION: 23.5 × 15.5 cm Pp [1–3] 4–68 Photograph on p 1 of St George's Cathedral Thin card, with small image on front of a male servant carrying a covered dish, between two potted trees; stapled
CONTENTS: 1 photograph of church and 'A Collection of Tested Recipes compiled and arranged by the Church Women's Aid Society of St. George's Cathedral'; 2 'Printed in Canada on Canadian paper // Printed by Hanson & Edgar, Limited Kingston – Ontario'; 3 'Preface' signed the Ladies of the Church Women's Aid Society; 4–67 recipes credited with the name of the contributor, blank spaces for 'Notes' and 'My Own Recipes,' and ads; 68 'Index' [i.e., table of contents] and ads
COPIES: *Private collection
NOTES: 'Meatless Entrees' are on pp 43–4. O1030.1, *Victory Cook Book,* by the same printer, has a similar design.

The particular cook's cook book

For information about the company and its other books, see Q106.1.

O707.1 nd [about 1930–5]
The / particular cook's / cook book
DESCRIPTION: 19.0 × 13.5 cm Pp [1–2] 3–64 Tp illus blue of a can of Borden's St Charles Milk; illus col of prepared dishes Lacks paper binding; stapled
CONTENTS: 1 tp; 2 table of contents; 3–7 introductory text extolling the virtues of Borden's St Charles Milk; 8–63 recipes; 64 'Keep Your Larder Well Stocked' [illus and descriptions of six Borden's products] and at bottom, 'Serial No. 278 Litho in Canada'
CITATIONS: Chatelaine 1935, p 82 FitzPatrickCat 111 (April 1993) No. 2
COPIES: *Private collection
NOTES: Another collector owns a copy with the paper binding intact; on the front face there is a stylized image of various cooking utensils (a manual rotary beater, measuring cup, two spoons, and a bowl). No place of publication is recorded, but *The Particular*

Cook's Cook Book was probably published in Toronto, as were other Borden's cookbooks cited in Chatelaine 1935 (O784.2, *Magic!,* and O534.3, *Easy Camp Cooking Recipes*). The text is printed in blue and black.

Peters, Esther

O708.1 nd [about 1930–5]
Meals / in the modern manner / Photo by Chatelaine / Smart new notes on hospitality / by / Esther Peters [cover-title]
DESCRIPTION: 23.0 × 15.0 cm Pp [1] 2–15 Illus Paper, with three images on front: a tomato cocktail, a plate of cheese and crackers, and a woman lighting candles at a formally set dinner table; stapled
CONTENTS: 1 cover-title; 2 'Entertaining at Home'; 3 'The Tomato Cocktail'; 4–5 'Start the Meal with a Flourish'; 6 'Savory Accompaniments to the Tomato Cocktail'; 7 'Cheese Dessert Service'; 8–10 'The Dinner'; 11 'The Tea Hour'; 12 'The Late Snack' and 'To Grace Your Table'; 13 'A Tomato Juice with a Piquant Flavor'; 14 'The Choice of Cheese'; 15 [inside back face of binding] 'Choose the Right Crackers'
COPIES: OONL (AC901 A7 1930z No. 0034 p***) *Private collection
NOTES: The text tells how to entertain using the three products that are illustrated on the outside back face of the binding: Ingersoll Malted Cheese, Nature's Best Tomato Juice, and Weston's Soda Wafers. No place of publication is recorded, but the offices of Ingersoll Cream Cheese Co. Ltd and George Weston Ltd were in Toronto.

Tomato Cocktail, p 3, is described as 'a temperance cocktail of clear tomato juice.' Helen G. Campbell, director of the Chatelaine Institute, wrote an article about the same drink: 'A Temperance Cocktail,' *Chatelaine* Vol. 4, No. 1 (January 1931). *Meals in the Modern Manner* may have been published about the same time as Campbell's article, in the early 1930s; however, it is not listed in 'Build a Reference Library for Your Kitchen,' *Chatelaine* Vol. 8, No. 2 (February 1935), which names free publications available from food manufacturers.

Recipe and premium book for users of Karavan Stoneless Dates

O709.1 nd [about 1930–5]
Recipe and / premium book / for users of / Karavan / all / fruit / no / stones / Stoneless / Dates [cover-title]
DESCRIPTION: 19.0 × 12.5 cm Pp 1–16 Illus on

pp 11–15 of Karavan Stoneless Date premiums [Free, in Chatelaine 1935, p 82] Paper, with image on front of a man standing in front of a camel; stapled, and with hole punched at top left corner for hanging
CONTENTS: 1–3 'Karavan Stoneless Dates'; 4–9 recipes for 'Bread and Muffins,' 'Cookies and Cakes,' 'Desserts,' 'Salads,' 'Sandwiches,' 'Party Dainties,' 'For Children,' and 'School Lunch'; 10 'Conditions and Instructions Regarding Redemption of Karavan Stoneless Date Coupons'; 11–15 illus of premiums and number of coupons required for each item; 16 publ ad for Pyramid Brand Raisins
CITATIONS: Chatelaine 1935, p 82
COPIES: *Private collection
NOTES: The text on pp 1–3 gives information about date culture and the reasons why dates are a good food. The name of H.W. Grierson and Co., Toronto, is printed on the inside front face of the binding and both back faces, and on pp 3 and 16. 'Printed in Canada' is on the outside back face of the binding.

Recipes

O710.1   nd [about 1930–5]
[IODE symbol] / Recipes / compiled and arranged / by the members of / General Mercer Chapter / I.O.D.E. / Toronto [cover-title]
DESCRIPTION: 23.0 × 15.0 cm   Pp [i], 1–60 Paper; stapled
CONTENTS: i 'Index' [i.e., table of contents]; 1 'Table of Weights and Measures,' 'Time Table,' 'Baking Time and Temperatures,' and 'To Test Oven Heat without a Thermometer'; 2 ad; 3–60 recipes credited with the name of the contributor and ads
COPIES: *Private collection
NOTES: The running head is 'General Mercer Chapter, I.O.D.E. Cook Book.' The printer's name is on the outside back face of the binding: 'Booth Bros., printing, 64 Seaton Street.' Most of the advertisements are for businesses in the Beaches neighbourhood of East Toronto.

The tests for oven heat without a thermometer are as follows:

> Slow – Paper or flour slightly tinged with color in 20 minutes.
> Moderate – Paper or flour golden brown in 4 to 8 minutes.
> Hot – Paper or flour golden brown in 1½ to 3 minutes.
> Very hot – Paper or flour golden brown in ½ to 1 minute.

Salads for health

See O703.1 for other titles by the London Life Insurance Co.

O711.1   nd [about 1930–5]
Salads / for health / Printed and distributed by / the London Life Insurance Company / Head office: London, Canada [cover-title]
DESCRIPTION: 22.0 × 15.0 cm   Pp [1–2] 3–15 Paper, with image on front of a mother carrying a bowl of salad to the table, at which a father and daughter are seated
CONTENTS: 1 cover-title; 2 'Salads for Health'; 3 'Preparing the Salad'; 4–5 'Vegetable Salads'; 6–7 'Fruit Salads'; 8–mid 9 'Fish and Meat Salads'; bottom 9–10 'Molded Vegetable Salads'; 11 'Molded Fruit Salads'; 12–13 'Miscellaneous Salads'; 14 'Salad Dressings'; 15 'Index'
COPIES: *Private collection
NOTES: The binding is stamped 'Edgar [E.?] Petch // Kitchener Ph. office 206 Res. 2260-W.'

O711.2   nd [1936]
—Salads / for health / The London Life Insurance Company [cover-title]
DESCRIPTION: 22.5 × 15.5 cm   Pp [1–2] 3–15 Paper, with image on front of a bowl of salad; stapled
CONTENTS: 1 cover-title; 2 'Salads for Health'; 3 'Preparing the Salad'; 4–5 'Vegetable Salads'; 6–7 'Fruit Salads'; 8–mid 9 'Fish and Meat Salads'; mid 9–10 'Molded Vegetable Salads'; 11 'Molded Fruit Salads'; 12–13 'Miscellaneous Salads'; 14 'Salad Dressings'; 15 'Index'
COPIES: OGU (UA s070 b07)   *Private collection
NOTES: 'H5–5-36' is on the outside back face of the binding. OGU has another copy (UA s050 b26) with 'H5-4-38' on the binding. OONL (TX740 S25 1939 p***) has a copy with 'H5-3-39' on the back face of the binding and 'B.I. Barre // Office R2031 // Res. M3428' stamped on the front.

Tested recipes

Erskine Church School was part of Erskine United Church at the intersection of Roncesvalles and Wright avenues. Before church union in 1925, the church was called High Park Presbyterian Church, but it became Erskine United Church in 1925 to differentiate itself from High Park United Church. Although the congregation remains in the same location, amalgamations with other congregations led to further name changes (in 1961,

to Emmanuel United Church; in 1969, to Emmanuel–
Howard Park United Church). *The Women's Association
produced O1086.1,* Kitchen Kraft, *in the 1940s.*

O712.1   nd [about 1930–5]
Tested recipes / compiled by / primary teachers /
of / Erskine Church School / Toronto [cover-title]
DESCRIPTION: 22.5 × 14.0 cm   Pp [1–16]   Paper;
stapled
CONTENTS: 1 'Weights and Measures'; 2–3 'Cakes'; 4
'Frosting and Icing'; 5–6 'Cookies'; 7 'Afternoon Tea
Specials'; 8–9 'Sandwiches'; 10 'Pies'; 11 'Candy';
12 'Salad Dressing' and 'Marmalades'; 13 'Pickles';
14–16 blank for 'Extra Recipes'
COPIES: *Private collection
NOTES: The recipes are not credited and there are no
advertisements.

Tested recipes

*The Perth-upon-Tay Chapter was founded in 1915 and
disbanded in 1979.*

O713.1   [about 1930–5]
Tested recipes / Published by the members of the /
Perth-upon-Tay Chapter / Perth, Ontario, Canada /
Imperial Order Daughters of / the Empire /
Prefatory Note / [one-paragraph note]
COPIES: *Private collection

1931

Certo recipes

For the titles of other Certo recipe collections, see O480.1.

O714.1   copyright 1931
The short-boil method / Certo / recipes / For /
jams / jellies / marmalades / Notice! / If you live in
British countries other / than Canada, be sure to
read / pages 28–29 first! / Douglas-Pectin, Ltd.,
Cobourg, Ont., Canada / Distributed by / General
Foods Limited, Toronto, Ont., Canada / Grape-Nuts
Company, Ltd., London, England / © 1931, Canada
and Great Britain 8631 Printed in Canada [cover-
title]
DESCRIPTION: 15.0 × 8.0 cm   Pp [1] 2–31 [32]   Illus
Paper; stapled at top edge
CONTENTS: 1 cover-title; 2 'Why Certo and the Certo
Recipes Make Perfect Jams and Jellies'; 3 'Let the
Certo Short-Boil Method Save Fruit, Effort, Time, Fuel';

4 'The 5 Steps in Making Jelly'; 5 'The 5 Steps in
Making Jams, Marmalades, Conserves and Relishes';
6–8 'Hints on Jam and Jelly Making'; 9–27 'Certo
Recipes'; 28–9 'If You Live in British Countries Other
Than Canada, Be Sure to Read These Two Pages First!';
30–1 'Questions Which Jelly Makers Frequently Ask';
32 [outside back face of binding] 'Recipe Index,' Con-
sumer Service Department address of Douglas-
Pectin Ltd, Cobourg, and 'P-170-76588-1-32-M.P.CO'
COPIES: *Private collection
NOTES: Pages 28–9 explain the differences between
Canadian and British terms and offer advice regard-
ing British equipment and supplies.

Community cook book

*Ambrose, p 237, records the founding years for most of
the Women's Institute branches cited in the cookbook's
cover-title: St George, 1903; Paris, 1905; Onondaga,
1906; Cainsville, 1907; Echo Place, 1913. Ambrose lists
the Princeton and Woodbury branch in South Brant,
founded in 1919; there is no listing for Brantford and
Drumbo.*

O715.1   1931
Community / cook / book / 1931 / A goodly thing
it is to meet / In friendship's circle bright, / Where
nothing stains the pleasure sweet / Or dims the
radiant light. / No unkind word our lips shall pass
/ No envy sour the mind. / But each shall seek the
common weal / The good of all mankind. /
Compiled by Women's Institutes / of / [in left
column:] Brantford / St. George / Echo Place /
Cainsville / [in right column:] Paris / Princeton /
Drumbo / Onondaga [cover-title]
DESCRIPTION: 23.0 × 15.0 cm   Pp 1–68   Paper; stapled
CONTENTS: 1–2 ads; 3 'Preface'; 4 ad; 5–62 recipes
credited with the name of the contributor and ads; 63
'Longer Life for Cut Flowers' and ad; 64 ad; 65 'House-
hold Hints'; 66 'Index' [i.e., table of contents] and
'Table of Measurements'; 67–8 ads
COPIES: *OTYA (CPC 1931 0071)
NOTES: The 'Preface' presents information about the
North Brant Women's Institute, which, in 1931, was
made up of thirteen branches, of which eight are
listed in the cover-title as the compilers of *Community
Cook Book.*

A cook book of well proven recipes

O716.1   1931
A / cook book / of / well proven / recipes / collected by / the Mission Circle / of / Roys United Church / Russeldale [*sic*], Ontario / 1931
DESCRIPTION: About 21.0 × 14.0 cm [dimensions from photocopy]   Tp illus of a quill pen in an inkwell   Limp cloth; stapled
COPIES: *Private collection
NOTES: The cover-title is 'Selected Recipes.' The recipes, which are credited with the name of the contributor, are on pp 1–66. They are preceded by the title-page, advertisements, and the 'Index' [i.e., an alphabetical list of chapter headings]. Russelldale is west of Stratford, and north of London.

A cook's tour with Minute Tapioca

For another cookbook for Minute Tapioca, see O848.1, Easy Triumphs with the New Minute Tapioca.

O717.1   [copyright 1931]
A cook's tour with / Minute Tapioca / Published by Minute Tapioca Company, Inc. [cover-title]
DESCRIPTION: 17.0 × 12.0 cm   Pp 3–46   Illus col   Paper, with image on front of two tapioca desserts; stapled
CONTENTS: Inside front face of binding 'Minute Tapioca Company, Inc. Division of General Foods Corporation Orange, Mass. // In Canada: General Foods, Limited Sterling Tower, Toronto 2, Ontario // 7848 © 1931, G.F. Corp., printed in U.S.A.'; 3 'A Word in Advance'; 4–45 text; 46 'Recipe Index'
COPIES: *OKQ (F5012 1931 M668)
NOTES: The text begins with nine variations of the basic recipe: 'From this one simple recipe [for Minute Tapioca Cream] 9 Irresistible New Desserts.' There are also recipes for savoury dishes in the following sections: 'Minute Tapioca with Vegetables,' p 31; 'Sandwich Fillings,' pp 42–3; and 'Fish and Meat Dishes,' pp 32–8. The company was not successful in promoting tapioca in savoury dishes. Most Canadians think of tapioca only as a dessert.

AMERICAN EDITIONS: Minute Tapioca Co., 1929 (Vintage, May 2000).

Correct salads for all occasions

O718.1   [copyright 1931]
Correct salads / for all occasions [cover-title]
DESCRIPTION: Pp [1] 2–30   Illus on p 3 of a chef   With image on front of a man and a woman at a dining table, each eating a salad; stapled
CONTENTS: 1 cover-title; 2 [inside front face of binding] 'Double Whipped for Perfection' and '7807 © 1931 G.F. Corp. Litho. in U.S.A.'; 3 'Correct Salads for All Occasions' [introductory text]; ...; 30 recipes for 'Sandwiches'; inside back face 'Other Delicious Hellman Products You Will Want to Try' and 'Richard Hellman, Inc. Long Island City, N.Y. Division of General Foods Corporation // In Canada: General Foods, Limited Sterling Tower, Toronto 2, Ontario'
CITATIONS: Rowe, illus col
COPIES: *OKQ (F5012 1931 G326)   Private collection
NOTES: The recipes use Hellman's Mayonnaise and other Hellman's products, such as horse radish, as ingredients.

Daily wants

O719.1   [1931]
Daily wants
DESCRIPTION: 19.0 × 14.0 cm   Pp [i–ii], [1–2] 3–66   Fp illus on p 1 of interior of 'Southminster'   Limp cloth; stapled
CONTENTS: i tp; ii blank; 1 fp illus; 2 blank; 3 'Acknowledgement' dated by the anonymous compiler, 114 Cameron Street, February 1931; 4 'Miscellaneous – Kitchen Equivalents'; 5–55 recipes credited with the contributor's name and ads; 56 ad; 57–9 index; 60–6 blank for 'Memorandum'
COPIES: OOC   *Private collection
NOTES: *Might's Ottawa City Directory 1931* records J. Albert Ewart, an architect, and Alice, and two students, Helen and John Ewart, living at 114 Cameron Street. Alice Ewart was almost certainly the anonymous compiler of the book and the contributor of the nine recipes credited to A.G. Ewart (the first is Fruit Short Cake, p 13). In the 'Acknowledgement' she writes, 'The compiler of "Daily Wants" extends her most grateful acknowledgements to the ladies who have so kindly assisted her in sending in their recipes ...'

Although not explicitly stated, *Daily Wants* was likely published to raise funds to help pay for a new church building at 15 Aylmer Avenue, Ottawa, to accommodate two separate congregations that had joined in 1930 to form Calvin-Ottawa South United

Church. The cookbook's 'Acknowledgement' is dated February 1931, the same month as the amalgamated group renamed itself Southminster United Church on 4 February 1931 and a few months before the new structure's cornerstone was laid in May 1931. The church administration confirmed that J. Albert Ewart was the architect of the new building (communication to me, September 2004). There is a full-page advertisement on p 24 for Albert's architectural practice, and there are advertisements for various Ottawa building trades – for example, Alex Garvock, a general contractor – all likely business associates of Albert.

The Delta Rho cook book

O720.1   nd [1931]
The Delta Rho cook book / A selection of tried and tested recipes / compiled and published by / the ladies of Delta Rho / St. Andrew's United Church / London – Ontario
DESCRIPTION: 23.0 × 15.0 cm   Pp [1–3] 4–100   Tp illus of St Andrew's United Church   Paper
CONTENTS: 1 tp; 2 'Printed in Canada on Canadian paper'; 3 preface; 4–100 text and index
COPIES: *OGU (UA s066 b33)
NOTES: This book and its date of publication are mentioned in the 'Foreword' of *Our Best*, another cookbook compiled by the Evening Delta Rho of the same church (renamed First–St Andrew's) and published in about 1951–2: '... we are following in the footsteps of the members of the original Delta Rho who published "The Delta Rho Cook Book" in 1931. It was so successful that many brides, as well as homemakers of longer standing, looked on it as their culinary standby. We are happy to tell you that many whose recipes made that book so successful have contributed their up-to-date favourites to "Our Best."'

Elliot, Edith L.

For information about Elliot and her cookbooks, see O665.1. For a list of other cookbooks published by the Department of Agriculture, see O404.1.

O721.1   1931
Jams, / jellies and pickles / by / Edith Elliot / Fruit Branch / Department of Agriculture / G.E. McIntosh, Commissioner / Pamphlet No. 137 / Published by direction of Hon. Robert Weir, Minister of Agriculture, / Ottawa, 1931 [cover-title]
DESCRIPTION: 22.5 × 15.5 cm   Pp [1–2] 3–19   Illus on p 4 of a woman pouring paraffin, illus on p 6 of four shelves of preserves   Paper, with image on front of bottled preserves; stapled
CONTENTS: 1 cover-title; 2 blank; 3 introductory text including information about glass jars and sealing; 4–5 'Varieties of Fruit Confections'; 6–top 11 'Jams and Conserves, etc.'; mid 11 'Concentrated Pectins'; bottom 11–top 13 'Jellies'; mid 13–top 19 'Pickles and Relishes'; mid–bottom 19 scores for judging marmalades, conserves, jelly, and pickles, and 'The Sale of Home-made Jellies, Jams, and Pickles'
CITATIONS: Ag 1867–1974, p 29
COPIES: OOAG (630.4 C212 P N.S., 4 copies)   *Private collection
NOTES: Elliot presents a selection of classic Canadian recipes; see those listed at O721.9.

O721.2   1931
—Confitures, / gelées et marinades / par / Edith Elliot / Division des fruits / Ministère fédéral de l'agriculture / G.E. McIntosh, commissaire / Feuillet n° 137 / Traduit au Bureau de traduction du ministère / Publié par ordre de l'hon. Robert Weir, ministre de l'agriculture, / Ottawa, 1931 [cover-title]
DESCRIPTION: 22.5 × 15.5 cm   Pp [1–2] 3–22   Illus on p 4 of a woman pouring paraffin, illus on p 6 of four shelves of preserves   Paper, with image on front of bottled preserves; stapled
CONTENTS: 1 cover-title; 2 blank; 3–top 4 introductory text including information about glass jars and sealing; near top 4–5 'Modes de préparation des fruits'; 6–top 12 'Confitures, etc.'; mid 12 'Pectines concentrées'; mid 12–mid 14 'Gelées'; mid 14–21 'Marinades et condiments'; 22 scores for judging marmalades, conserves, jelly, and pickles, and 'Vente de conserves faites à la maison'
CITATIONS: Ag 1867–1974, p 22
COPIES: *OOAG (630.4 C212 P N.S., 2 copies)
NOTES: 'Ottawa F.A. Acland imprimeur ... 1931' is on the outside back face of the binding.

O721.3   1933
—Jams, / jellies and pickles / by / Edith Elliot / Fruit Branch / Department of Agriculture / G.E. McIntosh, Commissioner / Pamphlet No. 137 / Published by direction of Hon. Robert Weir, Minister of Agriculture, / Ottawa, 1933 [cover-title]
DESCRIPTION: 22.5 × 15.0 cm   Pp [1–2] 3–19   Illus on p 4 of a woman pouring paraffin, illus on p 6 of four shelves of preserves   Paper, with image on front of bottled preserves; stapled, and with three punched holes for storing in a binder
CONTENTS: 1 cover-title; 2 blank; 3 introductory text

including information about glass jars and sealing; 4–5 'Varieties of Fruit Confections'; 6–top 11 'Jams and Conserves, etc.'; mid 11 'Concentrated Pectins'; bottom 11–top 13 'Jellies'; mid 13–top 19 'Pickles and Relishes'; mid–bottom 19 scores for judging marmalades, conserves, jelly, and pickles, and 'The Sale of Home-made Jellies, Jams, and Pickles'; outside back face of binding 'Ottawa F.A. Acland printer to the King's Most Excellent Majesty 1933'
COPIES: *Private collection

O721.4 1934
—Jams, / jellies and pickles / by / Edith Elliot / Fruit Branch / Department of Agriculture / G.E. McIntosh, Commissioner / Pamphlet No. 137 / Published by direction of Hon. Robert Weir, Minister of Agriculture, / Ottawa, 1934 [cover-title]
COPIES: OVOH *Private collection
NOTES: The OVOH copy is inscribed on the binding, 'E.M. Stuart.'

O721.5 August 1936
—Publication 535 / Household Bulletin 9 / Issued August, 1936 / Dominion of Canada – Department of Agriculture / Jams, jellies and pickles / Lilian Heeney / and / Edith L. Elliot / Fruit Branch / and / Experimental Farms Branch / Published by authority of the Hon. James G. Gardiner, Minister of Agriculture / Ottawa, Canada [cover-title]
DESCRIPTION: 25.0 × 16.5 cm   Pp [1–3] 4–23   Illus on p 4 of a woman sealing jars with paraffin, illus on p 5 of bottles of preserves ready for storage   Paper; stapled
CONTENTS: 1 cover-title; 2 blank; top–mid 3 introductory text; bottom 3–4 'Varieties of Fruit Confections'; top–mid 5 'Concentrated Pectins'; bottom 5–top 11 'Jams and Conserves, etc.'; mid 11–12 'Jellies'; 13–mid 22 'Preservation of Vegetables by Fermentation and Salting'; mid 22 scores for judging marmalades, conserves, jelly, and pickles; 23 'The Sale of Home-made Jellies, Jams, and Pickles'
CITATIONS: Ag 1867–1974, pp 23 and 33
COPIES: ACG OGU (Rural Heritage Collection uncat) *NBFKL (Ruth Spicer Cookbook Collection) OOAG (2 copies: 630.4 C212 P535, 630.4 C212 HB9)
NOTES: 'Preservation of Vegetables by Fermentation and Salting' is new to this edition, which has larger dimensions than earlier editions. Lilian Heeney (i.e., Miss Mary Lilian Heeney, born 1907) is credited as a co-author in the 1936 edition (both languages) and in the 1937 French-language reprint. Her name is not cited in subsequent editions.
   Heeney also co-authored a pamphlet with Elliot:

Canning Fruits and Vegetables (French title, *Les conserves de fruits et de légumes*); for more information, see the biographical note for Elliot at O665.1. For another work co-authored by Heeney, see O819.1, Gooderham, Charles Benjamin, and Miss Mary Lilian Heeney, *Honey and Some of the Ways It May Be Used.*

O721.6 August 1936
—Publication nº 535 / Bulletin de la ménagère nº 9 / Publié en août 1936 / Dominion du Canada – Ministère de l'agriculture / Confitures, / gelées et marinades / Lilian Heeney / et / Edith Elliot / Division des fruits / et / Division des fermes expérimentales / Publié par ordre de l'hon. James G. Gardiner, ministre de l'agriculture, / Ottawa, Canada [cover-title]
DESCRIPTION: 24.0 × 15.5 cm   Pp [1–3] 4–25   Illus on p 4 of a woman sealing jars with paraffin   Paper, with image on front of bottled preserves; rebound in cloth, together with other Household Bulletins
CONTENTS: 1 cover-title; 2 blank; top–near bottom 3 introductory text; bottom 3–top 5 'Modes de préparation des fruits'; mid 5 'Pectines concentrées'; bottom 5–top 12 'Confitures, etc.'; near top 12–top 14 'Gelées'; near top 14–top 25 'Comment conserver les légumes par la fermentation et le salage'; mid–bottom 25 scores for judging marmalades, conserves, jelly, and pickles, 'Vente de conserves ou de confitures faites à la maison,' 'Version française par C.E. Mortureux, B.S.A.,' and 'Ottawa: J.-O. Patenaude, O.S.I., imprimeur ... 1936.'
CITATIONS: Ag 1867–1974, pp 6 and 25
COPIES: OOAG (2 copies: *630.4 C212 HB9 Fr, 630.4 C212 P535 Fr)
NOTES: The illustration on p 5 of the English-language edition (O721.5) is on the binding of the French edition.

O721.7 2nd impression, July 1937
—Publication nº 535 / Bulletin de la ménagère nº 9 / Publié en juillet 1937 / Deuxième impression / Dominion du Canada – Ministère de l'agriculture / Confitures, / gelées et marinades / Lilian Heeney / et / Edith Elliot / Division des fruits / et / Division des fermes expérimentales / Publié par ordre de l'hon. James G. Gardiner, ministre de l'agriculture, / Ottawa, Canada [cover-title]
DESCRIPTION: 25.0 × 16.5 cm   Pp [1–3] 4–25   Illus on p 4 of a woman sealing jars with paraffin   Paper, with image on front of various bottled preserves; stapled
CONTENTS: 1 cover-title; 2 blank; top–near bottom 3 introductory text; bottom 3–top 5 'Modes de pré-

paration des fruits'; mid 5 'Pectines concentrées'; bottom 5–top 12 'Confitures, etc.'; near top 12–top 14 'Gelées'; near top 14–top 25 'Comment conserver les légumes par la fermentation et le salage'; mid–bottom 25 scores for judging marmalades, conserves, jelly, and pickles, 'Vente de conserves ou de confitures faites à la maison,' 'Version française par C.E. Mortureux, B.S.A.,' and 'Ottawa: J.-O. Patenaude, O.S.I., imprimeur ... 1937.'
CITATIONS: Ag 1867–1974, pp 6 and 25
COPIES: *OOAG (630.4 C212 P535 Fr, 3 copies)

O721.8   reprint, January 1938
—Publication 535 / Household Bulletin 9 / Issued January 1938 / Reprint / Dominion of Canada – Department of Agriculture / Jams, jellies and pickles / Edith L. Elliot / Fruit Branch / Published by authority of the Hon. James G. Gardiner, Minister of Agriculture / Ottawa, Canada / 30M–874–1:38 [cover-title]
DESCRIPTION: 24.5 × 16.5 cm   Pp [1–3] 4–23   Illus on p 4 of a woman sealing jars with paraffin, illus on p 5 of bottled preserves ready for storage   Paper; stapled
CONTENTS: 1 cover-title; 2 blank; top–mid 3 introductory text; bottom 3–4 'Varieties of Fruit Confections'; top–mid 5 'Concentrated Pectins'; bottom 5–top 11 'Jams and Conserves, etc.'; mid 11–12 'Jellies'; 13–top 14 'Preservation of Vegetables by Fermentation and Salting'; mid 14 'Sauerkraut'; bottom 14–mid 22 'Pickles and Relishes'; bottom 22 scores for judging marmalades, conserves, jelly, and pickles; 23 'The Sale of Home-made Jellies, Jams, and Pickles'
COPIES: OVOH   *Private collection
NOTES: Another private collector's copy has 'Compliments of W.P. Mulock, M.P.' stamped on p 1.

O721.9   reprint, June 1939
—Publication 535 / Household Bulletin 9 / June, 1939 / Reprint / Dominion of Canada – Department of Agriculture / Jams, jellies and pickles / Edith L. Elliot / Marketing Service / Published by authority of the Hon. James G. Gardiner, Minister of Agriculture / Ottawa, Canada / 30M–2388–6-39 [cover-title]
DESCRIPTION: 25.0 × 16.5 cm   Pp [1–3] 4–23   Illus on p 4 of a woman sealing jars with paraffin, illus on p 5 of bottled preserves ready for storage   Paper; stapled
CONTENTS: 1 cover-title; 2 blank; top–mid 3 introductory text including comments about glass jars and sealing; bottom 3–4 'Varieties of Fruit Confections'; top–mid 5 'Concentrated Pectins'; bottom 5–top 11 'Jams and Conserves, etc.'; mid 11–12 'Jellies'; 13–mid 22 'Preservation of Vegetables by Fermentation

and Salting'; mid 22 scores for judging marmalades, conserves, jelly, and pickles; 23 [inside back face of binding] 'The Sale of Home-made Jellies, Jams, and Pickles' and 'Ottawa: Printed by J.O. Patenaude, I.S.O., printer to the King's Most Excellent Majesty, 1939.'
COPIES: *Private collection
NOTES: Blueberry and Apple Conserve, Apple Butter, Citron Preserve, Peach Conserve, Pear Marmalade, Wild Strawberry Preserve, Saskatoons and Rhubarb, and Rowanberry Jelly are among the classic Canadian recipes included by Elliot. There are also several recipes for cucumber pickle and chili sauce.

O721.10   reprint, June 1940
—Publication 535 / Household Bulletin 9 / June, 1940 / Reprint / Dominion of Canada – Department of Agriculture / Jams, jellies and pickles / Edith L. Elliot / Marketing Service / Published by authority of the Hon. James G. Gardiner, Minister of Agriculture / Ottawa, Canada / 50M–4105–6:40 [cover-title]
DESCRIPTION: 25.0 × 16.5 cm   Pp [1–3] 4–23   Illus on p 4 of a woman sealing jars with paraffin, illus on p 5 of bottled preserves ready for storage   Paper; stapled
CONTENTS: 1 cover-title; 2 blank; top–mid 3 introductory text including comments about glass jars and sealing; bottom 3–4 'Varieties of Fruit Confections'; top–mid 5 'Concentrated Pectins'; bottom 5–top 11 'Jams and Conserves, etc.'; mid 11–12 'Jellies'; 13–22 'Preservation of Vegetables by Fermentation and Salting'; 23 'The Sale of Home-made Jellies, Jams, and Pickles,' scores for judging marmalades, conserves, jelly, and pickles, and 'Ottawa: Printed by J.O. Patenaude, I.S.O., printer to the King's Most Excellent Majesty, 1940.'
CITATIONS: Newman
COPIES: AEAG   ARDA   *OGU (CCC CA1 DA9 36P35)
NOTES: Newman incorrectly refers to the 1940 edition as the first.

O721.11   reprint, August 1941
—Publication nº 535 / Bulletin de la ménagère nº 9 / Publié en août 1941 / Réimpression / Dominion du Canada – Ministère de l'agriculture / Confitures, / gelées et marinades / Edith Elliot / Service des marchés / Publié par ordre de l'hon. James G. Gardiner, ministre de l'agriculture, / Ottawa, Canada. / 25M–5111–8:41 [cover-title]
CONTENTS: 1 cover-title; 2 blank; top–near bottom 3 introductory text; bottom 3–near bottom 4 'Modes de préparation des fruits'; bottom 4–mid 5 'Pectines concentrées'; mid 5–mid 11 'Confitures, etc.'; mid 11–

mid 13 'Gelées'; mid 13–top 24 'Comment conserver les légumes par la fermentation et le salage'; mid–bottom 24 scores for judging marmalades, conserves, jelly, and pickles, 'Vente de conserves ou de confitures faites à la maison,' and 'Ottawa: Edmond Cloutier, imprimeur, ... 1941.'
COPIES: *OOAG (630.4 C212 P535 Fr, 3 copies)
NOTES: There are no illustrations in this edition.

Elliot's *Jams, Jellies and Pickles* was superseded in May 1943 when the Department of Agriculture published O1068.1, *Wartime Canning: Jams and Jellies*, Publication 751, Household Bulletin 20. In October 1956, it published an unrelated text with the same title, *Jams, Jellies and Pickles*, Publication 992; the French-language edition of this new work, *Confitures, gelées, marinades*, appeared in June 1957.

Favorite recipes

In the same year that this book was published, another United Church on Danforth Avenue published a cookbook with the same title; see O726.1.

O722.1 1931
Favorite / recipes / 1931 / Danforth Avenue United Church / Toronto, Ontario [cover-title]
CONTENTS: 1 'Preface,' 'Compiled by the Woman's Association of Danforth United Church, Danforth Ave. and Jackman Street, Toronto, Ontario,' and 'Index' [i.e., table of contents]; ...
COPIES: *Private collection
NOTES: The 'Preface' indicates that the book was designed to reflect new ways of cooking: 'The present members of the [Woman's] Association believe ... that the automatic refrigerator, the electric range and the many new foods introduced during the past few years, have made many changes in the Art of Cookerie [sic]. They feel, too, that a recipe book built around these developements [sic] will be gratefully received.'

Favorite recipes

See also O352.1, published by the same church (called Eglinton Methodist Church before 1925).

O723.1 1931
Favorite / recipes / 1931 / The Eglinton / United Church / Toronto / Ontario [cover-title]
DESCRIPTION: 23.0 × 15.0 cm   Pp 1–52   Photograph on p 2 of the church   Very thin card; stapled
CONTENTS: 1 'Preface,' 'Compiled by the Women's

Association of the Eglinton United Church // Sheldrake Boulevard Toronto, Ont.,' and 'Index' [i.e., table of contents]; 2 photograph of the church and 'Officers of the Women's Association 1931'; 3–50 recipes credited with the name of the contributor and ads; 51 timetables; 52 'For Serving 100 People'
COPIES: OTEUC (2 copies)   *Private collection

Favorite recipes

O724.1 1931
Favorite / recipes / 1931 / First United Church / Galt, Ontario [cover-title]
COPIES: *Private collection
NOTES: The book's owner reports that the volume has 40 pp. Printed on the first page are the 'Preface' and 'Compiled by the Ladies' Aid Society of the First United Church // Galt, Ontario'; the first page of the private collector's copy is inscribed 'With love Alice.' The recipes are credited with the name of the contributor. 'C.E. Knowles, printer, Dickson St., Galt' is on the outside back face of the binding.

Favorite recipes

O725.1 1931
Favorite / recipes / 1931 / First United Church / St. Catharines / Ontario [cover-title]
DESCRIPTION: 23.5 × 15.5 cm   Pp 1–40   Illus on p 2 of the church   Paper, with small image on front of a tray on which sits a steaming tea or coffee pot and other dishes; stapled
CONTENTS: 1 'Preface' signed First United Church, St Catharines, Ontario; 2–3 'First United Church, St. Catharines 1831–1931' [a history of the church and its women's organizations]; 4 'Index' [i.e., table of contents]; 5–35 recipes and ads; 36–mid 37 'Time Tables'; mid 37–38 'Household Hints'; 39 'For Serving 100 People'; 40 blank for 'Special Recipes'
COPIES: *OSTC (641.5 Fir M)
NOTES: The text on p 2 states, 'This recipe book is the fruit of the endeavours of the Women's Association of this church.'

Favorite recipes

In the same year that Favorite Recipes *was published, another United Church on Danforth Avenue published a cookbook with the same title; see O722.1. See also O872.1,* We Entertain, *another cookbook from Hope United Church.*

O726.1 1931
Favorite / recipes / 1931 / Hope United Church /
Danforth and Main / Toronto [cover-title]
DESCRIPTION: 23.0 × 15.5 cm Pp 1–56 Paper;
stapled, and with hole punched at top left corner for
hanging
CONTENTS: 1 preface signed 'Compiled by the
Women's Association of Hope United Church //
Danforth at Main St. Toronto, Ont.'; 2–55 text and
ads; 56 index
COPIES: *Private collection

Favorite recipes

O727.1 1931
Favorite / recipes / 1931 / The King Street Baptist
Church / Kitchener, Ontario [cover-title]
DESCRIPTION: 23.0 × 15.0 cm Pp 1–44 Paper; stapled
CONTENTS: 1 'Preface' and 'Compiled by the Women's
Association of the King Street Baptist Church //
Kitchener, Ontario'; 2–41 culinary text, mostly reci-
pes credited with the name of the contributor, and
ads; 42–3 'Household Hints' and ads; 44 'Index' [i.e.,
table of contents]
COPIES: *Private collection
NOTES: 'Commercial Printing Co., 20 Frederick St.,
Kitchener, Ont.' is on the outside back face of the
binding. This copy originally belonged to the owner's
mother, Mrs David Sim (Cora), whose mother's recipes are in the book.

Favorite recipes

*Sometime after 1950, the Woman's Association of
Melville United Church published another recipe collec-
tion,* Cook Book: A Collection of Choice Recipes
(OFERWM).

O728.1 1931
Favorite / recipes / 1931 / Melville United Church
/ Fergus Ontario [cover-title]
DESCRIPTION: 23.0 × 15.0 cm Pp 1–36 Paper
CONTENTS: 1 'A Prayer for the Kitchen Wall by Nancy
Bryd Turner,' untitled introductory text, and 'Com-
piled by the Women's Aid Association of the Melville
United Church // Fergus, Ontario'; 2–36 text, mainly
recipes credited with the name of the contributor and
including 'Table Decoration Suggestions,' 'For Serv-
ing 100 People,' 'Time Table for Roasting,' and 'Large
Amounts for Home Catering'
CITATIONS: Driver 2001, Wellington County, pp 91,
92–3, 97 (note 11)

COPIES: *OFERWM (A1996.129 MU312) Private collection
NOTES: 'Fergus News-Record Print' is on the outside
back face of the binding. There is an advertisement
on p 10 for Schultz Construction Ltd, Brantford, 'the
general contractors for the new Melville United
Church School.' Funds raised from the sale of the
cookbook may have gone toward this project. The
OFERWM copy is in poor condition: All leaves and
the binding are loose.

Favorite recipes

O729.1 1931
Favorite / recipes / 1931 / St. James Anglican
Church / Stratford, Ontario [cover-title]
DESCRIPTION: 23.0 × 15.0 cm Pp 1–48 Paper; stapled
CONTENTS: 1 'Preface' and 'Compiled by the Ladies'
Aid Society of St. James Anglican Church // Stratford,
Ontario'; 2–46 recipes credited with the name of the
contributor and ads; 47 'Suggestions for Table Decorations' and 'What to Serve with Meats'; 48 'Household Hints'
COPIES: OSTPA *Private collection
NOTES: The 'Preface' states: 'In compiling the book
only such recipes as were considered both useful and
practical have been included. No attempt to cover
the entire field of cookery has been made, but we
have tried to include many dishes for the hurried
mid-day lunch and the hot summer night tea when
light and easily prepared dishes are in order.' Regret
is expressed that 'a few omissions were found necessary due to duplications of recipes and the limitations of the printer's craft.' The wording of the
'Preface' is close to that of O690.1, *Favorite Recipes*,
First United Church, Waterloo, O693.1, [Title un-
known], Chalmers Church, Guelph, and O750.1, *The
Cook's Companion*, St Andrews Presbyterian Church,
Belleville. The same wording quoted here is also repeated in Q211.1, *The Mixing Bowl*, a 1933 cookbook
from Trinity United Church in Sherbrooke.

48 new Jell-O entrées, relishes, salads, desserts

*For the titles of other books for cooking with Jell-O,
see O212.1.*

O730.1 [copyright 1931]
Want / something different? / 48 / new / Jell-O /
Reg. U.S. Pat. Off. / entrées / relishes/ salads /
desserts [cover-title]

DESCRIPTION: Pp [1–2] 3–... Paper, with image on front of a moulded Jell-O dessert; stapled
CONTENTS: 1 cover-title; 2 'Insist on Genuine Jell-O' and '8101 © 1931 G.F. Corp. Litho'd in U.S.A.'; 3 'Want a Surprise Today?'; ...
COPIES: AEUCHV (UV 85.250.1); United States: *Company collection (Kraft Foods Inc., Archives Department, Morton Grove, Ill.)
NOTES: The Jell-O company's Toronto address is printed on the outside back face of the binding: 'The Jell-O Company, Inc. Division of General Foods Corporation Le Roy, N.Y. Los Angeles, Cal. // Canadian address: General Foods, Ltd., Sterling Tower, Toronto 2, Ontario.'

The housekeepers' perfect account book 1931

See O145.1 for a list of other editions.

O731.1   1931
The / housekeepers' / perfect account / book / 1931 / With compliments of / Standard Brands Limited / Gillett products / Fraser Avenue and Liberty Street / Toronto [cover-title]
COPIES: *MAUAM

The mixing bowl

O205.1 is from the same church, known as Parkdale Methodist Church before church union in 1925.

O732.1   1931
The / mixing / bowl / 1931 / Parkdale / United Church / Dunn Ave. and King St. / Toronto, Ont. [cover-title]
DESCRIPTION: 22.5 × 15.0 cm   Pp 1–52   Very thin card; stapled
CONTENTS: 1 'Preface,' 'Compiled by the Women's Association of Parkdale United Church ...,' and 'Index' [i.e., table of contents]; 2 'The Inner Radiance' by Margaret M. Howard [poem] and 'Roster of the Officers of the Woman's [sic] Association of the Parkdale United Church 1931'; 3–46 recipes credited with the name of the contributor and ads; 47–mid 52 'Time Tables and Useful Information'; bottom 52 'Patches' signed the Dorcas Society, Miss Eva Stevenson [poem]
COPIES: *Private collection

The mixing bowl

O733.1   1931
The / mixing bowl / 1931 / St. Paul's Presbyterian Church / Port Hope, Ontario [cover-title]
DESCRIPTION: 22.5 × 15.5 cm   Pp [1] 2–40   Paper; stapled
CONTENTS: 1 'Preface' signed the Ladies' Aid of St Paul's Presbyterian Church, Port Hope, and 'Index' [i.e., table of contents]; 2–40 recipes credited with the name of the contributor, other culinary text, and ads
COPIES: *Private collection
NOTES: On the outside back face of the binding, the printer's name, '"Guide" Print, Port Hope,' is below an advertisement for Port Hope's *Evening Guide* newspaper, proprietor Geo. Wilson.

The mixing bowl

O734.1   1931
The / mixing / bowl / 1931 / Compiled by the / Woman's Association / of / Westmoreland / United Church / Toronto, Ontario [cover-title]
COPIES: *Private collection

New recipes

See also O332.1 and O582.1, both Crisco booklets.

O735.1   nd [about 1931]
New / recipes / Every day dishes that are / new, simple, and different / See pages / 4–7–11–16–17 [cover-title]
DESCRIPTION: 21.0 × 12.5 cm   Pp [1] 2–18   Fp illus on p 2 of 'Deep Frying Hints' in six numbered steps, fp illus on p 9 of 'Pastry' in six numbered steps, fp illus on p 13 of 'Biscuits' in six numbered steps, fp illus on p 15 of 'Cake Making Simplified' in six numbered steps   Paper, with image on front of a cherry pie and one slice of the pie on a plate; stapled
CONTENTS: 1 cover-title; 2 fp illus; 3–7 'Hints for Frying' and recipes, and at bottom p 3, 'Printed in Canada Can. 160-T'; 8–11 'Pies and Pastry'; 12–18 'Cakes, Cookies, and Quick Breads'; inside back face of binding book-order coupon for *The Art of Cooking and Serving* by Miss Sarah Field Splint, copyright 1931, from the Procter and Gamble Company of Canada Ltd, Toronto
COPIES: OTMCL (641.5971 H39 No. 18)   *QMM (RBD ckbk 1927)   QMMMCM (AR-M2000.62.17)
NOTES: The recipes specify Crisco shortening made

by Procter and Gamble. *New Recipes* was likely published about the same time as the copyright date cited for Splint's book, 1931. The text and illustrations are printed in green.

A copy at OGU (CCC TX715.6 N486) is as described above, including 'Printed in Canada Can. 160-T' on p 3, except that the book-order coupon gives the American form of the company name, Procter and Gamble Co. (i.e., not 'of Canada').

Niagara community cook book

Ambrose, p 236, gives the founding dates for the Women's Institute branches: Smithville, 1904; Grimsby and Beamsville, 1905; Niagara-on-the-Lake, 1911; and Jordan Station Jr, 1926 (Vineland was established as a separate branch in 1940).

O736.1 1931
Niagara community / cook / book / 1931 / Compiled by the / Women's Institutes / of / Grimsby Beamsville / Vineland Jordan / Smithville / Niagara-on-the-Lake [cover-title]
DESCRIPTION: 23.0 × 15.0 cm Pp 1–102 Paper; stapled
CONTENTS: 1 'Preface'; 2 ads; 3–90 recipes credited with the name of the contributor and ads; 91–8 'Niagara-on-the-Lake Supplement' and ads; 99 ad and 'Longer Life for Cut Flowers'; 100–1 'Household Hints'; 102 'Index' [i.e., alphabetical list of sections] and 'Table of Measurements'
COPIES: *Private collection
NOTES: The 'Preface' states, 'Represented in the compilation of the book are the institutes in Grimsby, Beamsville, Union (Vineland and Jordan), and Smithville, ...' No mention is made in the 'Preface' of Niagara-on-the-Lake. Perhaps this branch joined the project at the last moment, which would explain its contribution added to the end of the text as a 'Supplement.' The 'Preface' refers to 1,150 individual 'institutes' in Ontario, having a total of 50,000 members, in 1931.

100 dainty dishes for your table

O737.1 copyright 1931
100 / dainty dishes / for / your table / Sponsored by / Betty / of-the-air / Published by / Appleford Paper Products Limited / Hamilton Vancouver Winnipeg / Toronto Montreal / Copyrighted 1931
DESCRIPTION: 22.0 × 14.5 cm Pp [1–2] 3–35 [36] Illus

on pp 18–19 of a woman wrapping food in waxed paper and of Appleford paper products Paper, with image on front of a bowl containing three cone-shaped croquettes; stapled
CONTENTS: 1 tp; 2 blank; 3–4 index; 5–35 101 numbered recipes or suggestions for using left-over food; 36 'Para-Sani Has Many Uses'
COPIES: ACG BTCA (77.74) OGU (CCC TX715.6 M572 No. 528) *Private collection
NOTES: The cover-title is 'Tempting Tidbits Made from Left-overs // 100 Dainty Dishes for Your Table.' Appleford Paper Products made waxed paper, one of the uses of which is to store left-over food. This collection of recipes for cooking with left-overs was a means of promoting the sale of its waxed paper. There is a recommendation on p 18 to use waxed paper on the table when preparing salads, juicy fruits, vegetables, and raw meats because it 'is sanitary and eliminates cleaning up' – an example of a wasteful habit one associates more with the second half of the twentieth century.

The BTCA copy is stamped, on the back face of the binding, 'G.C. Martin & Co. Calgary – Alta.'

Recipes

O738.1 nd [about 1931]
Recipes / compiled and arranged / by the / Guiders / of the / Wentworth Division / of / Canadian Girl Guides / who present this book of tested recipes to their many friends / Price 50 cents / Proceeds to be used for camp purposes
DESCRIPTION: 23.0 × 15.5 cm Pp [1] 2–128 Paper, with small image on front of the head-and-shoulders of a Girl Guide in profile; stapled
CONTENTS: 1 tp; 2 ads; 3 thanks from the district captain to the guiders of the Wentworth Division and to the seven named commercial companies who supported the project; 4 ads; 5 'Tree of Guiding'; 6 ads; 7 'The Guide Law,' 'The Guide Promise,' and 'The Brownie Promise'; 8 ads; 9 'Aims of the Girl Guides'; 10–11 ads; 12–13 'Origin of the Guide Movement'; 14 ads; 15 'Wentworth Division Girl Guides'; 16 ads; 17 'Directory of Wentworth Division Girl Guides'; 18–24 ads; 25 'Index' [i.e., table of contents]; 26 ads; 27–128 culinary text and ads; inside back face of binding 'Frederick G. Smith ... Job Printing // 107 King St. West Hamilton ...'
COPIES: *OH (R641.5 REC CESH, 2 copies)
NOTES: 'Camp Cookery' is on p 102. The book is undated, but there is a reference in the text to the first Guide World Camp held at Foxlease in 1924 and

there is an advertisement on p 14 for a De Forest Crosley Radio, '1931 Victory Series.' The appearance of the book is consistent with a publication date in the early 1930s.

Selected recipes

See O474.1 for the titles of other cookbooks from the same church.

O739.1   nd [about 1931]
J.O.Y. Bible Class / Selected recipes / Compiled by the ladies of the class / in the interests of / New Sunday School Building
DESCRIPTION: 23.0 × 13.5 cm   Pp [1] 2–57 [58–60]   Tp photograph of the church   Paper; stapled
CONTENTS: 1 tp; 2 'Foreword' signed the Committee and an invitation from the teacher R.M. Broadbent to all young ladies to join the JOY Bible Class; 3–4 ads; 5–57 recipes credited with the name of the contributor and ads; 58–60 blank for 'Memo'
COPIES: *OGU (CCC TX715.6 J16)
NOTES: The name of the church is not identified on the title-page or in the text; however, there is an advertisement on p 6 for the Pure Milk Co. that extends 'Best wishes to Zion United Church' and an inscription on the title-page, in pencil, 'Zion United Church // Pearl St N Hamilton.' An inscription on the binding gives the likely date of publication: 'Mary A. Graham (1931.).' The advertisement on p 6 for Frederick G. Smith, job printer, states, 'This book of recipes printed by us.'

The 'silent hostess' treasure book

O740.1   [1st ed.?], copyright 1931
The / "silent hostess" / treasure / book / [CGE symbol] / Copyright 1931 / Canadian General Electric Company Limited / Electric Refrigeration Division / Toronto, Canada
DESCRIPTION: 19.0 × 13.0 cm   Pp [1] 2–104   Illus col, illus   Thin card
CONTENTS: 1 tp; 2 table of contents and 'How to Use This Book'; 3 foreword; 4–96 text; 97 'The General Electric Company – An Organization'; 98–104 index and at bottom p 104, 'Form SP–257 Printed in Canada'
COPIES: OONL (TX715.6 S536 1931 p***)   *Private collection
NOTES: This is likely the first edition since the private collector's copy is inscribed on the binding with the same year as the copyright date: 'L. Herald /31.' The

OONL copy is signed on the front endpaper, in ink, 'F. Holmes.' The book was apparently distributed free by Toronto's municipal power company, for another private collector's copy is inscribed on the front endpaper, in ink, 'June 2nd 1932 Compliments of the Toronto Hydro System // JH Hoffruau[?].'

The foreword comments on how electric appliances have transformed the housewife's life: 'Fortunately, those days are past when the homemaker must sacrifice all outside interests for the sake of her home.' A list follows of labour-saving appliances, in the order of their invention: electric iron, electric washing machine, vacuum cleaner, and, most recently, the electric refrigerator.

Recipes from *The 'Silent Hostess' Treasure Book* were reprinted in O130.11, Denison, Mrs Grace Elizabeth, *The Canadian Home Cook Book*, 1932.

O740.2   [3rd ed.], copyright 1931
—The / "silent hostess" / treasure / book / [GE symbol] / Copyright 1931 / Canadian General Electric Company Limited / Electric Refrigeration Division / Toronto, Canada
DESCRIPTION: 19.0 × 13.0 cm   Pp [1] 2–106   Illus col, illus   Thin card
CONTENTS: 1 tp; 2 'Table of Contents' and 'How to Use This Book'; 3 'Foreword'; 4–96 text; 97 'The General Electric Company – An Organization'; 98–104 index; 105 blank; 106 '3-Year Guarantee' and 'Form SP–257 Third edition // Printed in Canada'
COPIES: AHRMH   OWTU (F3877)   *Private collection
NOTES: Unlike O740.1, where the publisher's symbol on the title-page incorporates three initials, here the symbol features only two initials, GE.

O740.3   [5th ed.], copyright 1933
—The / silent / hostess / treasure / book / [GE symbol] / Copyright 1933 / Canadian General Electric Company, Limited / Electric Refrigeration Division / Toronto, Ont.
DESCRIPTION: 19.0 × 13.0 cm   Pp [1] 2–104   Illus col, illus   Lacks binding
COPIES: *AALIWWM
NOTES: 'Form SP–257 Fifth edition // Printed in Canada' is on p 104. The fifth edition of *The Silent Hostess Treasure Book* was succeeded by O810.1, *The New Art of Buying, Preserving and Preparing Foods*, numbered as the sixth edition.

AMERICAN EDITIONS: *The Silent Hostess Treasure Book*, Cleveland: General Electric Co., Electric Refrigeration Department, c1931 (United States: DLC); Cleveland: General Electric Co., Electric Refrigeration Department, c1932 (United States: DLC); 5th ed., Cleveland: General Electric Co., copyright 1932 (Bookseller's stock).

Tested recipes

O741.1 1931
Tested / recipes / 1931 / Kew Beach United Church / Toronto, Ontario [cover-title]
COPIES: *Private collection
NOTES: The owner reports that the recipes were compiled by the Women's Association of the church.

This book contains many of ye recipes for cooks

O742.1 1931
This book contains / many of / ye recipes / for cooks / which have been truely tried, tested and found / excellent by ye ladies of ye church. / Placed in print in the year / 1931 A.D. / Centre Street United Church / Oshawa, Ontario [cover-title]
DESCRIPTION: 23.0 × 15.0 cm Pp [1] 2–48 Very thin card; stapled
CONTENTS: 1 'To All Our Friends Greeting' signed Woman's Association, Centre Street United Church, Oshawa, Ontario; 2 'Index' [i.e., table of contents] and note about the advertisers; 3–48 text, mainly recipes credited with the name of the contributor, and ads
COPIES: *OONL (TX715.6 T55 1931 p***) OTYA (CPC 1931 0069)

Tried and tested recipes

O743.1 1931
[In a shield-shape:] T.W.I. / "For home and country" / Thorndale Women's Institute / 1931 / Tried and tested recipes [cover-title]
DESCRIPTION: Pp 1–40
CONTENTS: 1 'Beforehand we thank you / For buying our book / 'Twill teach and guide you / And help you to cook.' and 'Sweet Disposition' [mock recipe]; 2 'Table of Weights & Measures' and 'Abbreviations'; 3–40 recipes credited with the name of the contributor
COPIES: *Private collection
NOTES: The text is reproduced from typing. The out-side back face of the cover is numbered as p 41 and lists the names of 'Officers,' 'Board of Directors,' 'Auditors,' and 'Conveners' for the Thorndale Women's Institute.

1931–5

Campbell's Condensed Tomato Soup

Campbell Soup Co. Ltd built its first Canadian plant in 1931, in New Toronto. At the time, the factory was close to local market gardens and farm land; New Toronto is now part of the larger conurbation of Toronto. See also O746.1, Rhymes and Recipes, *and O1214.1,* Easy Ways to Good Meals, *other Campbell's cookbooks.*

O744.1 nd [about 1931–5]
Campbell's / Condensed / Made / in Canada / Tomato / Soup / Campbell Soup Company Ltd. / New Toronto, Ontario, Canada [cover-title]
DESCRIPTION: 12.0 × 7.0 cm Pp [1–20] Several amusing illus col of the Campbell Soup boy and girl; centre spread illus of Campbell Soup Co. Ltd factory in New Toronto, entitled 'New Canadian Kitchens' Paper; stapled
CONTENTS: 1–2 'Soups' [i.e., introductory text]; 3–9 entries for different flavours of Campbell's soup, arranged alphabetically from Asparagus to Printanier; 10–11 centre spread illus; 12–14 entries for soups from Tomato to Vermicelli-Tomato; 15–20 'Recipes' using Campbell's soups as an ingredient
COPIES: *Private collection
NOTES: The booklet's leaves are cut in the shape of a soup can, and the front face of the binding is printed to look like a can of Tomato Soup. 'Twenty-one tempting soups' are listed on the inside front face of the binding. Chatelaine 1935, p 82, cites 'Campbell's Soup Recipe Booklets' as free upon request, but does not identify specific titles. From appearances, *Campbell's Condensed Tomato Soup* was published about the time of the *Chatelaine* reference, but no earlier than 1931, the year the company came to New Toronto.

Recipes for Tea-Bisk

*Tea-Bisk was first made by Maple Leaf Milling Co. in 1931 (*The Company That Grew with Canada, *Maple Leaf Mills Ltd, [about 1980], p 19). See O1192.1, Scott, Anna Lee,* What's Cooking?, *for a later collection of recipes for cooking with Tea-Bisk.*

O745.1 nd [about 1931–5]
Recipes for / Tea-Bisk / Maple Leaf Milling
Company, Limited / Toronto
DESCRIPTION: 23.0 × 15.0 cm   Pp [1] 2–15   Paper,
with images on front of a Tea-Bisk package and various foods made with Tea-Bisk, such as tea biscuits,
waffles, and pancakes; stapled
CONTENTS: 1 tp; 2–15 recipes
COPIES: *Private collection
NOTES: The cover-title is 'Tea-Bisk // The quick way
to chicken pie // pancakes // shortcake // waffles
// delicious dumplings // tea biscuits // – lots of
other good things.'

O745.2 nd [about 1931–5]
—Tea-Bisk / The quick way / to / chicken pie /
pancakes / shortcake / waffles / delicious /
dumplings / tea biscuits / – lots of other / good
things [cover-title]
DESCRIPTION: 18.5 × 12.0 cm   Pp [1] 2–15   Paper,
with images on front of a Tea-Bisk package and various foods made with Tea-Bisk; stapled
CONTENTS: 1 cover-title; 2–15 [inside back face of bind-
ing] recipes
COPIES: OGU (CCC TX715.6 T425)   *Private collection
NOTES: The text is the same as O745.1, but it is printed
on smaller-sized leaves. The binding design is identical to O745.1, but reduced in size to fit the smaller
format. This edition has no title-page.

Rhymes and recipes

*See O744.1 for the titles of other Campbell's soup
cookbooks.*

O746.1 nd [about 1931–5]
Rhymes and / [same initial 'R' as 'Rhymes']ecipes /
I'm the Campbell's farmer-man, / So jolly, plump
and hearty – / Please thank me for such gorgeous
soup / And ask me to your party! [cover-title]
DESCRIPTION: 12.5 × 7.0 cm   Pp [1–24]   Illus col,
illus   Paper, with image on front of the Campbell's
boy carrying a basket of tomatoes; stapled
CONTENTS: 1 list of the twenty-one flavours of
Campbell's soup; 2–23 amusing illus col of a girl or
boy and a verse on versos, recipes on rectos, and
centre spread illus col of the Campbell's girl and boy,
and two bowls of soup, with caption 'Eat soup and
keep well'; 24 'Look for the Red-and-White Label'
CITATIONS: FitzPatrickCat 158 (September 2001)
COPIES: OONL (TX715 C3465 No. 30 reserve)   QMM

(RBD ckbk 1387)   *Private collection
NOTES: 'Printed in Canada' is on the outside back face
of the binding; on the inside back face there is an
illustration of the Campbell Soup Co. Ltd's factory
in New Toronto. The booklet's leaves are cut in the
shape of a soup can. Chatelaine 1935, p 82, cites
'Campbell's Soup Recipe Booklets' as free upon request, but does not identify specific titles. From appearances, *Rhymes and Recipes* was published about
the time of the *Chatelaine* reference, but no earlier
than 1931, when the company built the New Toronto
factory.

O746.2 nd [about 1931–5]
—Recettes et / [same initial 'R' as 'Recettes']imes /
Et pour Campbell's mon beau jardin / Fournit de
superbes légumes! / Alors, prenez donc la coutume
/ De m'inviter à vos festins. [cover-title]
DESCRIPTION: 12.5 × 7.0 cm   Pp [1–24]   Illus col,
illus   Paper, with image on front of the Campbell's
boy carrying a basket of tomatoes; stapled
CONTENTS: 1 list of the twenty-one flavours of
Campbell's soup; 2–23 amusing illus col of a girl or
boy and a verse on versos, recipes on rectos, and
centre spread illus col of the Campbell's girl and boy,
and two bowls of soup, with the caption 'Mangez
de la soupe et portez-vous bien'; 24 'Recherchez
l'étiquette rouge-et-blanche'
COPIES: *Private collection
NOTES: 'Imprimé au Canada' is on the outside back
face of the binding; on the inside back face there is an
illustration of the company's factory in New Toronto.
The booklet's leaves are cut in the shape of a soup
can.

1932

Baker's best chocolate recipes

*For the titles of earlier books by Walter Baker and Co., see
Q52.1.*

O747.1 [copyright 1932]
Baker's / best chocolate / recipes / Walter Baker &
Company, Inc. / Division of General Foods
Corporation / Dorchester, Massachusetts, U.S.A.
Established 1780 [cover-title]
DESCRIPTION: 17.5 × 12.0 cm   Pp [1–2] 3–60   Tp illus
of La belle chocolatière, illus col   Paper, with image
on front of La belle chocolatière; stapled
CONTENTS: 1 'Copyright, 1932, by General Foods Cor-
poration' and 'Walter Baker & Co., Inc. of Dorchester,

Mass. Canadian address: General Foods, Ltd., Sterling Tower, Toronto 2, Ontario'; 2 order form for *General Foods Cook Book* [O760.1] from General Foods, Battle Creek, Michigan; 3 'Four Hundred Years of Popularity'; 4–7 'Walter Baker Introduces Chocolate and Cocoa to America'; 8–12 'Beverages'; 13–29 'Chocolate Cakes ... Cookies ... Éclairs'; 30–1 centre spread illus col of Walter Baker products; 32–40 'Frostings ... Fillings ... Sauces'; 41–9 'Chocolate Desserts // Frozen Desserts ... Puddings ... Pastries'; 50–8 'Candies'; 59–60 'Index of Recipes' and at bottom p 60, '9328 – Litho. in U.S.A.'
CITATIONS: Cagle/Stafford No. 907   Chatelaine 1935, p 82
COPIES: ARDA OGU (CCC TX715.6 B234) OPETCM *Private collection; United States: InU
NOTES: Chatelaine 1935 cites 'Baker's Best Chocolate Recipes (free on receipt of end flap from a package of Baker's Premium No. 1 chocolate).' Many of the recipes in *Baker's Best Chocolate Recipes* are the same as those in Q173.1, with only slight revisions.

AMERICAN EDITIONS: *Baker's Best Chocolate Recipes,* Walter Baker and Co., copyright 1930 (Barile, p 180); *Best Chocolate and Cocoa Recipes,* Dorchester, Mass.: Walter Baker and Co. Inc., copyright 1931 (OGU); *Baker's Best Chocolate Recipes,* Dorchester, Mass.: Walter Baker and Co. Inc., copyright 1932 (AWWDM, BSUM).

Claire, Mabel

O748.1   [copyright 1932]
Smallman & Ingram's / cook book / for the busy woman / including a complete guide to / kitchen management / by Mabel Claire / Greenberg Publisher / New York
DESCRIPTION: Cloth, with grid pattern
CONTENTS: 1 tp; 2 'Copyright, 1932 by Greenberg, Publisher, Inc. New York // Manufactured in the United States of America by H. Wolff, New York, N.Y.'; 3–? 'Contents'; ...; 405–16 'Index'
COPIES: *Private collection
NOTES: Smallman and Ingram was a London, Ontario, department store, founded in 1877.

AMERICAN EDITIONS: *Busy Woman's Cook Book; or, Cooking by the Clock,* 1925 (United States: DLC); *Macy's Cook Book for the Busy Woman,* 1932 (United States: DLC); *World's Modern Cook Book for the Busy Woman,* 1941 (United States: DLC).

Cook book and homemakers' guide

The newspaper published a tabloid supplement cookbook in 1941 (when it was called the Standard-Freeholder*), and in 1942 and 1943 (as the* Daily Standard-Freeholder*); see O1025.1, O1044.1, and O1072.1. A scan of runs of issues of the newspaper might identify others.*

O749.1   12 March 1932
The Cornwall Freeholder / Cook book / and homemakers' guide / Containing more / than / five hundred / favorite recipes / of housewives in / all portions of the / United Counties / March / 1932 [cover-title]
DESCRIPTION: With image on front of a woman demonstrating cooking before an audience of other women
CITATIONS: MacGillivray, p 46
COPIES: *OC (micro)
NOTES: This is the first cookbook supplement published by the newspaper. 'Our Thanks and Our Apologies' (on the second page) states: 'The Cornwall Freeholder to-day presents its first Cook Book and Home-Makers' Guide. A few weeks ago, the Freeholder sent out a thousand or more forms, asking women in the various sections of the United Counties to send in recipes for use in the Freeholder's cook book. The response was simply overwhelming ... It is the hope of the management ... to publish another cook book [not located], in about six months' time in which will appear the recipes submitted this time, which were not published [i.e., for lack of space].' The recipes are credited with the name of the contributor.

The cook's companion

O750.1   1932
The cook's / companion / 1932 / St. Andrews Club / of / St. Andrews Presbyterian Church / Belleville – Ontario [cover-title]
DESCRIPTION: About 23.0 × 15.0 cm [dimensions from photocopy]   Stapled
CONTENTS: 1 'Preface' and 'Compiled by the ladies of St. Andrews Club of St. Andrews Presbyterian Church ...'; 2–55 recipes (according to the 'Index'); 56 'Index' [i.e., table of contents] and ads
COPIES: *Private collection
NOTES: The printer of the cookbook, 'Ontario Intelligencer Print, Belleville,' is on the outside back face of the binding. There is an advertisement on p 56

for 'social and commercial printing of any description' by the Job Printing Department of the *Ontario Intelligencer*. See O729.1 regarding the wording of the 'Preface.'

Dean, Miss Charlotte Ruth, and Miss Elspeth Munro Middleton (Toronto, Ont., 7 December 1893–5 September 1962, Victoria County, Ont.)

Ruth Dean graduated with a BA from the University of Toronto in 1920, then worked at St Luke's Hospital in New York City for a year, and the Psychiatric Institute, Morristown, New Jersey. In May 1923 she took the job of dietitian at the hospital in Cochrane in Northern Ontario. She then taught at Kitchener-Waterloo Collegiate for three years, from September 1925 to May 1928, after which she moved to Central Technical School in Toronto. She enrolled at Teachers College, Columbia University, in 1931, and received her MA degree from that institution in December 1934. In 1942 she became an associate professor of home economics at the Ontario College of Education, and in 1950, a full professor. She retired in 1963. Dean was a founding member of the Canadian Home Economics Association, formed in 1939 (We Are Tomorrow's Past, p 5; a photograph of Dean and two others, taken at the association's first convention, is on p 2). Career information for Dean is at OTUAR (A73-0026/081 (21); staff card; and Torontonensis, 1920, with a photograph).

Elspeth Middleton also co-wrote, with Miss Muriel Eleanor Ransom and Albert Vierin, O1078.1, The Cook's Recipe Manual, and O1187.1, 100 to Dinner. For biographical information about Middleton, see O1078.1.

O751.1 [1st ed., copyright 1932]
Junior / home economics / by / Ruth Dean, B.A. / and / Elspeth Middleton, B.A. / [Ryerson Press symbol] / The Ryerson Press, Toronto
DESCRIPTION: 19.5 × 13.5 cm   Pp [i–iv] v [vi] vii–viii, 1–206 Illus Cloth
CONTENTS: i ht; ii blank; iii tp; iv 'Copyright, Canada, 1932, by the Ryerson Press, Toronto Printed and bound in Canada by the Ryerson Press, Toronto'; v 'Foreword' signed the authors; vi blank; vii–viii 'Contents'; 1–199 text in three parts (I, 'Food and Health'; II, 'Measures and Abbreviations,' 'Lessons in Cookery – A,' and 'Lessons in Cookery – B'; III, 'Care of the House'); 200–1 'Books for Reference'; 202 blank for 'Notes'; 203–6 'Index'
CITATIONS: CCat No. 11, p M38   Wallace, p 89

COPIES: *OTU (TDS – D)
NOTES: Dean and Middleton state their purpose on p v: 'This book is submitted in an attempt to meet a recognized need in the teaching of Household Economics in the secondary schools in Canada. It is intended for the use of beginners, and covers work that the authors consider suitable for the first and second forms.' There are small, attractive, and sometimes amusing illustrations throughout the text, but the artist is not identified. CCat records the price of $1.00. Dean likely participated in the writing of the text before commencing her studies at Columbia University in autumn 1931.

O751.2 [reprint, 1939]
—Junior / home economics / lessons in cookery / by / Ruth Dean, M.A. / and / Elspeth Middleton, B.A. / Central Technical School, Toronto / [Ryerson Press symbol] / The Ryerson Press – Toronto
DESCRIPTION: 19.5 × 13.5 cm   Pp [i–iv] v [vi] vii–viii, 1–206   A few small illus (e.g., illus on p 15 of measurements), decorative head- and tail-pieces for chapters   Cloth
CONTENTS: i ht; ii list of books in 'The Ryerson Technical Series,' of which this is one title; iii tp; iv 'Copyright, Canada, 1932, by the Ryerson Press, Toronto ... Published 1932 Reprinted 1937 Reprinted 1938 Reprinted 1939 ...'; v 'Foreword' signed the authors; vi blank; vii–viii table of contents; 1–199 text in three parts; 200–1 'Books for Reference'; 202 blank for 'Notes'; 203–6 'Index'
COPIES: *Private collection
NOTES: This copy is inscribed in pencil, on the front endpaper, by a student: 'June Ruse 9D 301 Kingswood Rd.' (in the Beaches area of Toronto, near Malvern Collegiate Institute).

O751.3 [rev. ed., 1941]
—Junior / home economics / lessons in cookery / by / Ruth Dean, M.A. / Bloor Collegiate Institute, Toronto / and / Elspeth Middleton, B.A. / Central Technical School, Toronto / The Ryerson Press – Toronto
DESCRIPTION: 19.5 × 13.0 cm   Pp [i–iv] v [vi] vii–viii, 1–208 Illus Cloth
CONTENTS: i ht; ii list of books in 'The Ryerson Technical Series,' of which this is one title; iii tp; iv 'Copyright, Canada, 1932, by the Ryerson Press, Toronto ... Published 1932 Reprinted 1937 Reprinted 1938 Reprinted 1939 Revised 1941 Printed and bound in Canada by the Ryerson Press, Toronto'; v foreword; vi blank; vii–viii table of contents; 1–13 Part I, 'Food and Health'; 14–182 Part II, 'Lessons in Cookery';

183–99 Part III, 'Care of the House'; 200–4 Part IV, 'Home Laundry'; 205–8 index
COPIES: *Private collection

O751.4 [reprint, 1943]
—[Reprint of *Junior Home Economics,* Toronto: Ryerson Press, [1943]]
COPIES: Private collection

O751.5 [rev. ed., 1946]
—Junior / home economics / lessons in cookery / by / Ruth Dean, M.A. / Associate Professor of Home Economics, / Ontario College of Education, / formerly Bloor Collegiate Institute, Toronto / and / Elspeth Middleton, B.A. / Head of Household Science Department, / Central Technical School, Toronto / The Ryerson Press – Toronto
DESCRIPTION: 19.5 × 13.5 cm   Pp [i–iv] v [vi] vii–viii, 1–208 Illus Cloth
CONTENTS: i ht; ii list of books in 'The Ryerson Technical Series,' of which this is one title; iii tp; iv 'Copyright, Canada, 1932, by the Ryerson Press, Toronto ... Published 1932 Reprinted 1937 Reprinted 1938 Reprinted 1939 Revised 1941 Reprinted, 1943 Revised, 1946 Printed and bound in Canada by the Ryerson Press, Toronto'; v 'Foreword'; vi blank; vii–viii table of contents; 1–13 Part I, 'Food and Health'; 14–182 Part II, 'Lessons in Cookery'; 183–99 Part III, 'Care of the House'; 200–4 Part IV, 'Home Laundry'; 205–8 index
COPIES: *Private collection

Each taste a treat: 87 delicious recipes

This booklet was given as a gift by four dairy companies. Other dairies likely also used it as a promotional tool.

O752.1 [copyright 1932]
Each taste a treat / 87 / delicious recipes [cover-title]
DESCRIPTION: 19.5 × 12.0 cm   Pp 1–36 Illus col signed 'CEH' Paper, with image on front of a table set and served for tea or coffee and a sweet bun; stapled
CONTENTS: Inside front face of binding 'Copyrighted 1932 // Printed in Canada on Canadian paper'; 1 'Milk and Some of Its Uses'; 2–3 'Index' [i.e., table of contents] listing headings for 'Soups,' 'Entrées,' 'Vegetables,' 'Puddings,' 'Desserts,' 'Bread and Cakes,' 'Sauces and Dressings,' and 'Miscellaneous'; 4–28 recipes; 29–36 blank for 'Add your Own Recipes'; inside back face 'This Recipe Booklet is presented with the compliments of the City Dairy // Kingsdale 6151'

COPIES: OH (R641.5 EAC CESH)   OTMCL (2 copies: 641.5971 H39 No. 63 and No. 105)   *Bookseller's stock   Private collection
NOTES: The OH copy has a different dairy on the inside back face of the binding: 'This Recipe Booklet is presented with the compliments of Hamilton Dairies Limited // 100 Vine Street Regent 9440.' One private collector's copy has Borden's Farm Products Co. Ltd and Montreal telephone numbers; another private collector's copy has '... compliments of Borden's Niagara Dairies Limited // Niagara Falls, Ont. Phone 50.' One OTMCL copy (No. 63) has '... compliments of the Pure Milk Company Limited // 181 John Street North // Hamilton, Ont. Regent 8600'; the other copy (No. 105) matches that in the bookseller's stock (i.e., '... City Dairy // Kingsdale 6151'). No place of publication or printing is given; however, since most of the dairies that distributed the book were in Ontario, the entry is in the Ontario section.

The same artist's initials – CEH – are in O761.1, *The Good Provider's Cook Book,* of about the same date.

89 tested recipes

For the titles of other Certo recipe collections, see O480.1.

O753.1   copyright 1932
89 / tested / recipes / ... for making / jams, jellies / & marmalades / with / Certo / and the short-boil method / General Foods Corporation (Certo Division) / Fairport, N.Y., U.S.A. / Douglas-Pectin, Ltd., Cobourg, Ont., Canada / © 1932. U.S.A. & Canada. G.F. Corp. [cover-title]
DESCRIPTION: About 14.0 × 8.0 cm (dimensions from photocopy)   Top-hinged
COPIES: United States: *Private collection

Favorite recipes

O754.1   1932
Favorite / recipes / 1932 / Central United Church / Barrie, Ontario [cover-title]
DESCRIPTION: With image on front of a woman standing beside a stove and a kitchen table
CONTENTS: First page 'Preface' and 'Compiled by Women's Association of Central United Church // Barrie Ontario'
COPIES: *Private collection
NOTES: The book has 50 pp and was printed by the 'Press of the Northern Advance' (printer's name on outside back face of binding).

Favorite recipes

In 1954, 'in response to continued demands for "our favourite" recipes [likely O755.1],' the church published Our Favourites, *a new selection of recipes contributed by the Women's Association (Private collection).*

O755.1 1932
Favorite / recipes / 1932 / Deer Park United Church / Toronto Ontario [cover-title]
DESCRIPTION: 23.0 × 15.0 cm   Pp 3–60   Paper; stapled
CONTENTS: 3–60 recipes credited with the name of the contributor and ads
COPIES: *OGU (CCC TX715.6 D39)
NOTES: Mrs Harry Baldwin Hall (Alice), a member of the church who lived on Farnham Avenue from 1914 to 1936, contributed the recipe for Lima Bean Scallop on p 12, the same recipe that she contributed to O1183.1, *Favorite Recipes from American Kitchens.* Mrs Hall's daughter was the donor of the OGU copy of the Deer Park cookbook.

Favorite recipes

O756.1 1932
Favorite / recipes / 1932 / Queen St. United Church / Kingston, Ontario [cover-title]
COPIES: *Private collection
NOTES: At the beginning of the book there is a photograph of the church and 'Roster // Officers of Women's Association of Queen Street United Church 1932.' The volume has 72 pp, reports the private collector.

Favorite recipes

O757.1 1932
Favorite / recipes / 1932 / [compiler's name(?) obscured by brown paper tape] [cover-title]
DESCRIPTION: 23.0 × 15.0 cm   Pp [1] 2–28   Paper; stapled
CONTENTS: 1 'Preface' and 'Compiled by Catholic Women's Auxiliary of St. Patrick's Church Galt, Ontario'; 2–28 recipes credited with the name of the contributor and ads
COPIES: *Private collection
NOTES: The following pencil inscription is on the binding, on the paper tape that obscures what is probably the compiler's name: 'Miss Mary Rattray // Overland Hotel // Galt. Ont.'

Favorite recipes cook book

O758.1 1932
Favorite / recipes / cook / book/ Price 50 cents / Compiled and published by / the Ladies' Aid of Bromley United Church, / Bromley, Ontario / Nineteen hundred and thirty-two [cover-title]
DESCRIPTION: With small image on front of a male servant carrying a covered dish, two small potted trees behind
COPIES: *Private collection

48 new Jell-O recipes

For the titles of other books for cooking with Jell-O, see O212.1.

O759.1 [copyright 1932]
Try / the new Jell-O / You make it without boiling water! / 48 new Jell-O recipes [cover-title]
DESCRIPTION: 14.5 × 10.0 cm   Pp [1–2] 3–23   Illus col   Paper, with image on front of a moulded Jell-O dessert and six packages of Jell-O; stapled
CONTENTS: 1 cover-title; 2 'A Marvelous New Product in a Bright New Package!' and at bottom, '8893 © 1932 G.F. Corp. Litho'd in U.S.A.'; 3 'Want a Surprise Today?'; 4–20 recipes; 21–2 'Jell-O Rules' and information about ordering 'Jell-O Molds'; 23 [inside back face of binding] 'And Have You Ever Tried Jell-O Ice Cream Powder?' and three recipes; outside back face 'Canadian address: General Foods, Ltd., Sterling Tower, Toronto 2, Ontario'
COPIES: AEUCHV (UV 85.250.2) *BPM OONL (TX715 C3465 No. 8 reserve)

General Foods cook book

O760.1 [1st ed., 1932]
General Foods / cook book / Consumer Service Department / General Foods Corporation / New York / A key to the question of three meals a day
DESCRIPTION: 21.3 × 13.9 cm   Illus   Cloth
CONTENTS: Tp verso: 'Copyright 1932 by General Foods Corporation All rights reserved Manufactured in the U.S.A. Form 8140 // First edition [General Foods monogram] General Foods Corporation New York, N.Y. // General Foods, Ltd. Toronto 2 Ontario, Canada // Grape-Nuts Company, Ltd. London, England'

CITATIONS: Axford, p 179   Barile, p 192   Bitting, p 556   Cagle/Stafford No. 950   Dickinson, p 84
COPIES: *Private collection; United States: DLC (2 copies: TX715 G34, TX715 G34 1932a)   InU

O760.2   [4th ed., January 1935]
—General Foods / cook book / Consumer Service Department / General Foods Corporation / New York / A key to the question of three meals a day
CONTENTS: Tp verso: 'Copyright 1932 by General Foods Corporation All rights reserved Manufactured in the U.S.A. Form 1164 // First edition, August 1932 // Second edition, November 1932 // Third edition, April 1934 // Fourth edition, January 1935 [General Foods monogram] General Foods Corporation New York, N.Y. // General Foods, Ltd. Toronto 2 Ontario, Canada // Grape-Nuts Company, Ltd. London, England'
CITATIONS: Chatelaine 1935, p 82
COPIES: *SSWD
NOTES: Chatelaine 1935 records the price of $1.50, but does not specify the edition.

O760.3   [5th ed., October 1937]
—General Foods / cook book / Consumer Service Department / General Foods Corporation / New York / A key to the question of three meals a day
DESCRIPTION: 21.5 × 14.0 cm   Pp [i–viii] ix [x] xi [xii], 1–370   Frontis on p iv of 'General Foods Offers over Twenty Famous Products for Your Well-Stocked Pantry Shelf,' illus   Cloth
CONTENTS: i ht; ii–iii blank except for a vertical rule in the margin of each page and a dot in the centre of each page; iv frontis; v tp; vi 'Copyright 1932 by General Foods Corporation ... Manufactured in the U.S.A. Form 3162 // First edition, August 1932 // Second edition, November 1932 // Third edition, April 1934 // Fourth edition, January 1935 // Fifth edition, October 1937 [General Foods monogram] General Foods Corporation New York, N.Y. // General Foods, Ltd. Toronto 2 Ontario, Canada // Grape-Nuts Company, Ltd. London, England'; vii dedication 'To the American homemaker'; viii blank except for a vertical rule in each margin and a dot in the centre; ix table of contents; x blank except for a vertical rule in each margin and a dot in the centre; xi list of illustrations; xii blank except for a vertical rule in each margin and a dot in the centre; 1–4 'About This Cook Book'; 5–62 'This Question of Three Meals a Day // A Subject Index'; 63–6 'General Foods Corporation'; 67–88 'Know the Products on Your Pantry Shelf'; 89–96 'Doing the Job – The Modern Way'; 97–102 'An

Adequate Diet'; 103–6 'Seasoned and Sauced – and Served with Grace'; 107–16 'Planning Menus of Interest'; 117–330 'Tested Recipes'; 331–6 'Tables for Convenience'; 337–62 'Market Lore'; 363–70 'General Index'
COPIES: *Private collection

The good provider's cook book

For information about the company and its other books, see Q106.1.

O761.1   nd [about 1932]
The / good provider's / cook / book
DESCRIPTION: 20.0 × 12.5 cm   Pp [1–4] 5–78 [79–80]   Tp still-life col of a bowl, pitcher, measuring cup, spoon, rotary beater, and can of Borden's St Charles Evaporated Milk; illus col   Paper, with all-over pattern on front of recipe names; stapled
CONTENTS: 1 tp; 2 blank; 3 table of contents; 4 'Borden's Evaporated Milk // St. Charles Unsweetened Milk are identical'; 5–12 foreword; 13 'Evaporated Milk Recipes' and 'Standard Recipes'; 14–78 recipes; 79 'Keep Your Larder Well Stocked!'; 80 'Borden's Evaporated Milk // St. Charles Unsweetened Milk are identical' and at bottom, 'Printed in Canada Serial No. 500'
COPIES: ONLAM (Walters-Wagar Collection, Box 20)   *Private collection
NOTES: The foreword begins by referring to 'wartime thrift,' when it was patriotic and fashionable to be economical. It adds: 'Many people never went back to the old ways of eating. High food prices were one reason. The vogue for extreme slenderness among women was another. After the war, too, women were all so busy with outside activities that it was a temptation to make meals as simple as possible.' Now, however, there is 'a swing back to more normal food habits – a decided turn away from too-meagre diets.'

The private collector's copy is inscribed on the title-page, in pencil, 'Thelma Briggs. Feb 13. 1932.' The attractive colour illustrations are signed by the artist, 'CEH.' The same artist's initials are in O752.1, *Each Taste a Treat: 87 Delicious Recipes,* copyright 1932.

No place of publication is recorded, and in the early 1930s, Borden had offices in Montreal and Toronto; however, I have positioned *The Good Provider's Cook Book* in the same section as O752.1, which has the same illustrator and was published in the same period.

The housekeepers' perfect account book 1932

See O145.1 for a list of other editions.

O762.1   1932
[*The Housekeepers' Perfect Account Book,* with calendar for 1932]
COPIES: MAUAM
NOTES: The MAUAM copy lacks the cover-title and pp 1–2. The text includes recipes.

Kitchen lore

See also O463.1 from the same church.

O763.1   1932
Kitchen / lore / 1932 / Compiled by / the Women's Association / of / Bathurst Street United Church / Bathurst & Lennox streets / Toronto, Ontario [cover-title]
DESCRIPTION: Pp 1–76   With image on front of steaming food on a dining table
CONTENTS: 1 'Foreword' and 'Index' [i.e., table of contents]; 2–76 recipes credited with the name of the contributor, 'For Serving 100 People,' 'Suggestions for Table Decorations,' and ads
COPIES: *Private collection

Kitchen secrets

O764.1   1932
Kitchen / secrets / 1932 / The Children's Aid Society / (Women's Auxiliary) / Brockville Ontario [cover-title]
CONTENTS: 1 'Preface' and 'Compiled by the Women's Auxiliary of the Children's Aid Society Brockville Ontario'; ...
COPIES: *OBM

Le pâtissier Magic

For the edition published in Toronto, see Q207.4, under Royal Cook Book.

Magic cook book

For the edition published in Toronto, see Q207.3, under Royal Cook Book.

Master chef recipes for the use of bread

For information about Canada Bread Co., see O576.1, The Art of Sandwich Making.

O765.1   [copyright 1932]
Master / chef / recipes / for the use of / bread [cover-title]
DESCRIPTION: 17.0 × 10.5 cm   Pp [1–3] 4–30   Illus col   Paper, with image on front of a male chef moving his hands above a loaf of bread as if to conjure a variety of dishes from it; stapled
CONTENTS: 1 cover-title; 2 'The Courteous Canada Bread Man' and at bottom, 'Copyright, 1932, by Arthur Guest, Toronto'; 3 'How to Make Meals More Interesting'; 4 'The Bread Is Very Important' signed Victor Loftus, general manager, Canada Bread Co. Ltd; 5–29 100 numbered recipes; 30 'Measurements for These Recipes'
COPIES: QMM (RBD ckbk 1931)   *Private collection
NOTES: Arthur Guest, who held the copyright, is likely the Arthur Guest listed in the 1932 Toronto city directory as a caterer, living at 287 Jarvis Street.

The mixing bowl

O766.1   1932
[An edition of *The Mixing Bowl,* King Street United Church, Trenton, Ontario, 1932, pp 32]
COPIES: Private collection

The mixing bowl

O767.1   1932
The / mixing / bowl / 1932 / St. Paul's United Church / Midland [cover-title]
DESCRIPTION: 23.0 × 15.5 cm   Pp 3–40   Paper, with small image on front of a piece of pie; stapled
CONTENTS: 3–36 recipes credited with the name of the contributor and ads; 37 'For Serving 100 People'; 38 'Professional Directory,' 'Time Table,' and 'Roasting'; 39 ad and 'Table Decoration Suggestions'; 40 'Index' [i.e., table of contents] and ads
COPIES: *OWTU (G14565)
NOTES: The OWTU copy is in poor condition: The leaves are loose because the staples are missing; the first leaf is probably lacking; and the outside back face of the binding is lacking.

A new way of living

For other Kellogg books about All-Bran, see O795.1, Keep on the Sunny Side of Life; O837.1, The Sunny Side of Life Book; O918.1, The Housewife's Year Book of Health and Homemaking 1937; and O943.1, The Housewife's Almanac 1938.

O768.1   copyright 1932
A new / way of / living / Copyright 1932 / by / the Kellogg Company of Canada, Ltd. / Come over to the sunny side of life / No. C-233 Printed in Canada
DESCRIPTION: 19.0 × 14.0 cm   Pp [1] 2–32   Illus col Paper, with image on front of a father, mother, and son in a sunbeam; stapled
CONTENTS: 1 tp; 2 foreword; 3 table of contents; 4–31 text in ten chapters; 32 'References'
CITATIONS: Ferguson/Fraser, p 234, illus col on p 80 of closed volume
COPIES: OTUTF (uncat patent medicine)   QMM (RBD ckbk 1704)   *Private collection
NOTES: Chapter VIII, 'Suggestions for Serving All-Bran,' pp 20–6, has recipes using Kellogg's All-Bran Cereal as an ingredient and 'A Week of Menus for Correction of Constipation.' Page 23 lists additional booklets available upon request from the Home Economics Department of the Kellogg Company of Canada Ltd, London, Ontario.

O768.2   copyright 1932
—Une / nouvelle / manière / de vivre / Copyright 1932 / by / the Kellogg Company of Canada / Limited / Soyez parmi les heureux de la vie / No. F-233 Imprimé au Canada
DESCRIPTION: 19.0 × 14.0 cm   Pp [1] 2–31   Illus col Paper, with image on front of a father, mother, and son in a sunbeam; stapled
CONTENTS: 1 tp; 2 'Préface'; 3 table of contents; 4–31 text in ten chapters
COPIES: *OKQ (F5012 1932 K29)
NOTES: There are no 'References' in the French-language edition; p 32 is blank.

Norge kitchen companion

O769.1   [1932]
[Symbol of Consolidated Industries: initials CI in a circle] / Norge / kitchen / companion [cover-title]
DESCRIPTION: Pp [1–12]   Illus of Norge appliances Stapled
CONTENTS: Inside front face of binding 'Lady of the House' signed Consolidated Industries; 1 'Appetizers – Soup Recipes'; 2 'Salad Recipes'; 3 'Appetizing Desserts'; 4 'Vegetable Cooking Table'; 5 'Useful Hints for Kitchen'; 6 illus of Norge Refrigerator; 7 'Cooling Drinks'; 8 illus of Norge electric washer and iron; 9 'Helpful Household Hints'; 10 'More Helpful Hints'; 11 'Hints on Health'; 12 'Just for Fun'; inside back face 'Why Electric Refrigeration?' and information about a contest, answers to be sent to Norge Corp. in Toronto by 31 August 1932
COPIES: *Private collection
NOTES: The text under 'Lady of the House' states that 'Norge and the related C.I. products ... are all-Canadian.'

Pepper, Miss Laura Christine (Ottawa, Ont., 11 March 1899–9 August 1982, Ottawa, Ont.)

For information about Pepper and her other books, see O676.1.

O770.1   1932
School lunches / by Laura C. Pepper / Dominion of Canada / Department of Agriculture / Pamphlet No. 148 / The Dairy and Cold Storage Branch / J.F. Singleton, Commissioner / Published by direction of the Hon. Robert Weir, Minister of Agriculture, / Ottawa, 1932 [cover-title]
DESCRIPTION: 22.0 × 15.0 cm   Pp [1–3] 4–16   Paper, with image on front of children walking toward a schoolhouse; rebound in cloth, together with other Pamphlets
CONTENTS: 1 cover-title; 2 blank; 3–12 untitled introductory text, 'Improving the Lunch in the Rural School,' 'The Requirements of a Good School Lunch,' 'Classification of Foods,' 'Milk in the School Lunch,' 'The Lunch Box,' 'Lunch Box Menus' for four weeks, 'Reheating Food Brought from Home,' 'Preparing Hot Food at School,' and 'Menus for Lunches Containing One Hot Dish' for four weeks; 13–15 recipes and at bottom p 15, 'Abbreviations and Measurements'; 16 [outside back face of binding] list of 'Other publications dealing with the food value of dairy products ...'
CITATIONS: Ag 1867–1974, pp 30 and 114
COPIES: *OOAG (630.4 C212 P148 N.S.)
NOTES: No printer is recorded.

O770.2   1932 [1933]
—Le dîner à l'école / par Laura C. Pepper / Ministère fédéral de l'agriculture / Canada / Feuillet nᵒ 148 / Division de l'industrie laitière et de la réfrigération / J.F. Singleton, commissaire /

Publié par ordre de l'hon. Robert Weir, ministre de l'agriculture, / Ottawa, 1932 [cover-title]
DESCRIPTION: 22.0 × 15.5 cm   Pp [1–3] 4–16   Paper, with image on front of children walking toward a schoolhouse; rebound in cloth, together with other Pamphlets
CONTENTS: 1 cover-title; 2 'Ottawa F.A. Acland imprimeur ... 1933 // Version française par C.E. Mortureux, B.S.A.'; 3–12 untitled introductory text, 'Comment améliorer le dîner à l'école rurale,' 'Ce qu'il faut pour avoir un bon dîner à l'école,' 'Classification des aliments,' 'L'importance du lait,' 'La cantine,' 'Menus' for four weeks, 'Comment réchauffer les aliments apportés par les écoliers,' 'Préparation des mets chauds à l'école,' and 'Menus pour les repas qui contiennent un mets chaud' for four weeks; 13–15 recipes and at bottom p 15, 'Abréviations et mesures'; 16 [outside back face of binding] 'Autres publications traitant de la valeur alimentaire des produits laitiers, ...'
CITATIONS: Ag 1867–1974, p 22
COPIES: *OOAG (630.4 C212 P148 N.S.)   QQS (missing)

OTHER EDITIONS: *Le dîner à l'école,* Household Bulletin 5, Publication 495, 1936, 12 pp (OOAG); *School Lunches,* Household Bulletin 5, Publication 495, 1938, 11 pp (OOAG).

The Purity cook-book

For information about Western Canada Flour Mills and other cookbooks for Purity Flour, see O394.1.

O771.1   [copyright 1932]
The / Purity / cook-book / A publication of / Western Canada Flour Mills Co. Limited / Head office: Toronto, Canada / Millers of Purity Flour, Purity Oats and Hovis Flour / Mills at: / Goderich Winnipeg Brandon Calgary Victoria / Offices at: / Saint John Montreal Ottawa Toronto Winnipeg Calgary / Vancouver New Westminster Victoria
DESCRIPTION: 24.0 × 17.5 cm   Pp [1–202]   10 fp illus col, 1 fp illus, illus col   Cloth, with small oval portrait on front of the head-and-shoulders of a woman
CONTENTS: 1 blank; 2 'Copyright, Canada, 1932 Western Canada Flour Mills Co., Limited // Head office: Toronto, Canada // Designed and produced by the Hendrick-Jewell Co., Toronto, Canada'; 3 tp; 4 fp illus of 'One of the Company's Modern Flour Mills Located at Winnipeg, Manitoba'; 5 letter from the publisher; 6 'The Masterpiece of Modern Kitchen Lore';

7 ad for 'Ruddy Kitchen Units'; 8 ad for Purity Salt; 9 table of contents; 10 table of equivalents and temperature chart; 11–top 13 'The Art of Making Bread'; 13–190 743 numbered recipes; 191–3 'Menu Suggestions'; 194 'Home Nursing'; 195–200 'Index of Recipes'; 201 cut-out coupons for ordering the 1932 edition; 202 'Certificate of Approval' for Purity Flour dated 26 May 1932
CITATIONS: Driver 2001, All New Purity, inside front cover   Driver 2003, 'Canadian Cookbooks,' p 36   Ferguson/Fraser, p 234, illus col on p 80 of closed volume
COPIES: ACG   OONL (TX715.6 P87 1932, 2 copies)   OSTMYM   *Company collection (Maple Leaf Mills Consumer Products Co.), in 1991; location now unknown
NOTES: This new publication by Western Canada Flour Mills superseded O504.1, *The New Purity Flour Cook Book,* of 1923. The year 1932 also saw the publication of Q203.1, *A Guide to Good Cooking,* which promoted Five Roses Flour, in effect creating a battle for popularity between the flour cookbooks.

In the copy catalogued here (company collection), the book-order coupons are stamped 'DeLuxe Presentation Edition $2.00 per copy,' i.e., the regular edition was free upon receipt of $0.50 for postage and handling, but the presentation edition cost extra. The ACG copy – the free, regular edition – is bound in black paper, with a rectangular image on the front featuring sun rays and coloured circles (another copy with the same design is reproduced in a photograph in Mairlyn Smith, 'Musing on Cookbooks,' *Toronto Star* 5 March 2003, p D4). The OONL copy is bound in black-paper-covered card.

O772.1, *Recipes from One Friend to Another,* published by Western Canada Flour Mills Co. Ltd at about the same time, reprints some recipes from *The Purity Cook-Book.* See also the notes for Q222.1, *Farine Purity, recettes anciennes et modernes,* a French-language cookbook published by Western Canada Flour Mills in about 1934–5.

O771.2   [rev. ed., 1937]
—The / Purity / cook-book / A publication of / Western Canada Flour Mills Co., Limited / Head office: Toronto, Canada / Millers of Purity Flour, Purity Oats and Hovis Flour / Mills at: / Goderich Winnipeg Brandon Calgary / Offices at: / Saint John Montreal Ottawa Toronto Winnipeg Calgary / Vancouver New Westminster Victoria
DESCRIPTION: 23.0 × 16.0 cm   Pp [1–202]   10 fp illus col, 4 fp illus, many illus col   Cloth
CONTENTS: 1 blank; 2 'Copyright, Canada, 1932 (Re-

vised, 1937) Western Canada Flour Mills Co., Limited // Head office: Toronto, Canada // Printed by Murray Printing Company, Limited, Toronto, Canada'; 3 tp; 4 fp illus of mills; 5 letter from publisher; 6 fp illus of a table setting; 7 notice about Purity Flour, on a pink leaf glued to the gutter; 8 blank; 9 table of contents; 10 table of equivalents; 11–top 13 'The Art of Making Bread'; 13–191 742 numbered recipes; 192–4 'Menu Suggestions'; 195–200 'Index of Recipes'; 201 cut-out coupons for ordering the 1937 edition of the book; 202 facsimile of 'Certificate of Approval' for Purity Flour from *Canadian Home Journal*
CITATIONS: *National Home Monthly* (November 1938)
COPIES: *OGU (UA s045 b29) SSWD
NOTES: The letter from the publisher, p 5, states that 'this work was undertaken by a practical housekeeper – an experienced dietitian.'

O771.3 [2nd rev. ed., January 1945]
—Purity / cook / book / A publication of / Purity Flour Mills / Limited / Head office: / Toronto, Canada / Millers of: Purity Flour Purity Oats / Hovis Flour Pioneer Feeds / Mills at: / Goderich Winnipeg Calgary / Offices at: / Saint John Montreal / Ottawa Toronto Winnipeg / Calgary Vancouver
DESCRIPTION: 23.5 × 16.0 cm Pp [1–2] 3–209 [210] 12 fp illus col; 2 fp illus on pp 128 and 129 of cuts of meat; illus Cloth
CONTENTS: 1 tp; 2 Purity Flour Mills Ltd symbol and 'Copyright, Canada, 1932 (Revised, 1937) (Second revision, January, 1945) ... Designed and lithographed by Sampson-Matthews Limited, Toronto // Colour illustrations by A.J. Casson, R.C.A.'; 3 'Introduction'; 4 'Important': ten notes about learning to cook well for those with limited experience; 5 'Oven Temperature Chart,' 'Table of Equivalents,' and 'Measuring Flour and Shortening'; 6–7 'Planning Meals for Health' based on six food groups; 8 cross-reference to the book-order coupons on p 209; 9 table of contents; 10–199 text, including 875 numbered recipes; 200–8 index; 209 six book-order coupons, asking for $1.00 per copy; 210 facsimile of 'Home Bureau Certificate of Approval' for Purity Flour and Purity Oats from *Canadian Home Journal*
CITATIONS: Armstrong 2000, p F2, illus p F1 Crawford, p D1, illus col of pp 76–7 (raspberry pie) Driver 2001, Wellington County, pp 88, 94 Ferguson/Fraser, p 234, illus col on p 103 of closed volume
COPIES: AEPMA AEPRAC BKOM MTM MWMM NBFY OGU (CCC TX715.6 P87 1945, 2 copies) OLU (TX715.6 P87 1945) OOWM (989.6.13) OPETCM OTR (TX715 P95 1945) OWTU (G12906)

QMM (RBD Vanna Garnier, ckbk 596) *Private collection
NOTES: The 'Introduction' states: 'More than twenty-five years have passed since the first Purity Cook Book [i.e., O394.1] ... The present edition has been largely re-written and re-arranged by Mrs. Kathleen M. Watson, a graduate in Home Economics of the University of Manitoba and now a member of the teaching staff of that institution and a housewife as well. In spite of numerous difficulties caused by food rationing and shortages, she has personally tested and carefully selected all the recipes.' The cookbook's illustrations are by Arthur Joseph Casson (1898–1992), an artist who had been a member of the Group of Seven, then of the Canadian Group of Painters. Casson worked as a graphic artist for Sampson-Matthews Ltd from 1926 to 1958, where he produced designs and illustrations for books, posters, magazine covers, packaging, and a wide variety of advertising material, including O1230.1, *Margene Recipe Book*.

O771.4 [2nd rev. ed., January 1945]
—Livre de / cuisine / Purity / Publié par: / Purity Flour Mills / Limited / Bureau chef: / Toronto, Canada / Les meuniers de: La farine Purity / La farine d'avoine Purity La farine Hovis / Nourritures Pioneer / Moulins à: / Goderich Winnipeg Calgary / Bureaux à: / Saint-Jean Montréal / Ottawa Toronto Winnipeg / Calgary Vancouver
DESCRIPTION: 23.5 × 16.0 cm Pp [1–2] 3–209 [210] Illus col, illus Cloth
CONTENTS: 1 tp; 2 translator's note signed Rose C. Lacroix; 3 'Avant-propos'; 4 'Principes généraux concernant la bonne cuisine'; 5 'Tableau des températures,' 'Tableau des équivalences,' and 'Mesurage de la farine et du shortening'; 6–7 'Menus rationnels'; 8 'Pour copies additionnelles'; 9 'Table des matières'; 10–199 text; 200–8 'Index'; 209 book-order coupons; 210 'Droits réservés, Canada, 1932 (Revisé, 1937) (Seconde revision, janvier, 1945) Purity Flour Mills Limited // Bureau chef: Toronto, Canada // Dessins et lithographies par Sampson-Matthews Limited, Toronto // Illustrations coloriées par A.J. Casson, R.C.A.'
CITATIONS: BQ Exposition 1974, p 3 Carrière No. 175
COPIES: OONL (TX715 L6914 1945, 3 copies) QMBM (641.5 P985Li) QMBN (TX715 L58 1945 and 181021 CON) QMM (RBD Soeur Berthe, ckbk 436) QSFFSC (641.5 P985L) *Private collection
NOTES: According to p 2, Rose C. Lacroix was 'directrice de "Les écoles ménagères provinciales"' and 'auteur d'un recueil de recettes intitulé "Le menu du jour" ...' No copies of *Le menu du jour* have been

located, but OONL has a bilingual cookbook by Mme Rose Lacroix: *Cuisine typiquement canadienne/Traditional Canadian Recipes,* illustrations by M. Jean Simard, Montmagny: Edited and distributed by A. Bélanger limitée, [between 1940 and 1952], 34 pp of French text and 34 pp of English text.

OTHER EDITIONS: *The Pocket Purity Cook Book,* Harlequin No. 51, 'This Harlequin Book edition is published by special arrangement with Purity Flour Mills Ltd., Toronto Canada // Copyright Canada, 1950 // Harlequin edition published May, 1950 Printed in Canada' (Private collection); *Livre de cuisine Purity: petit format,* Harlequin, [copyright 1950], translated by Rose Lacroix (OONL, QMM); 3rd rev. ed., *Purity Cook Book,* [January 1954] (OGU); 4th rev. ed., *The New Purity Cook Book,* Toronto: Purity Flour Mills Ltd, [June 1959] (QMM); rev. centennial ed., retitled *The All New Purity Cook Book,* Maple Leaf Mills Ltd, 1967 (Private collection; Great Britain: OPo(F)); 'toute nouvelle édition,' *Livre de recettes Purity,* nd [1974], 'Avant-propos' signed Stéphanie Boivin refers to more than fifty years since 'notre premier livre Purity' (OONL); *The New Purity Cook Book,* nd, 'Foreword' signed Anna Lee Scott refers to 'more than fifty years ...' (OGU); facsimile of 1967 centennial ed., Vancouver: Whitecap Books, 2001, Classic Canadian Cookbooks Series, includes 'Historical Notes' by Elizabeth Driver, reviewed by John Allemang, 'Back to Backburner Basics,' *Globe and Mail* (Toronto) 17 March 2001 (OONL).

Recipes from one friend to another

For information about Western Canada Flour Mills and other cookbooks for Purity Flour, see O394.1.

O772.1   nd [about 1932]
Recipes / from / one friend / to another [cover-title]
DESCRIPTION: 23.0 × 10.0 cm   Pp [1–16]   Illus col
Paper; metal spiral
CONTENTS: 1 untitled introductory note signed Western Canada Flour Mills Co. Ltd, three book-order coupons for *Recipes from One Friend to Another* and the 200-page edition of 'Purity Cook Book' (i.e., O771.1), and 'Spirax Binding patented Canada 1932 No. 326518'; 2 blank; 3–16 seven envelopes [an eighth is lacking in this copy], with recipes and illus on rectos and blank 'List of Recipes' on versos
COPIES: OGU (CCC TX715.6 R44)   *Private collection
NOTES: The introductory note refers to *Recipes from*

One Friend to Another as 'this unique pocket file' for storing handwritten recipes and newspaper and magazine clippings. The book-order coupons instruct the reader to send the coupon to Western Canada Flour Mills Co.'s nearest office, and they list the offices from east to west: Saint John, New Brunswick; Montreal; Ottawa; Toronto; Goderich; Winnipeg; Calgary; and Brackman-Ker Milling Co. Ltd in Vancouver, New Westminster, and Victoria, British Columbia. Although not stated, head office was in Toronto.

The envelopes are arranged alphabetically by subject: 'Bread and Rolls'; 'Cakes'; 'Canning'; 'Desserts'; 'For the Dinner'; 'For the Lunch'; ['For the Party' lacking in the copy catalogued here]; and 'Miscellaneous.' The recipes printed on the rectos of the envelopes are identified by their number in the 200-page edition of *The Purity Cook-Book* (O771.1, copyright 1932). The blank 'List of Recipes' on the envelope versos was to be filled in by the owner as she filed her manuscript recipes and clippings. *Recipes from One Friend to Another* is bound in black paper, matching some copies of O771.1, which are bound in black paper or black-paper-covered card.

The book-order coupons have been removed from the OGU copy.

Royal cook book

For an edition published in Toronto by Standard Brands Ltd, see Q207.2.

Scott, Anna Lee [pseudonym]

For information about Anna Lee Scott and her cookbooks, see O526.1.

O773.1   nd [about 1932]
The easy way / cake book / for beginners and / the best of cooks / by / Anna Lee Scott / Maple Leaf Milling Co., Limited / Toronto Winnipeg [cover-title]
DESCRIPTION: 23.0 × 15.0 cm   Pp [1] 2–32   Paper; stapled
CONTENTS: 1 'The Easy Way Cake Book' [introductory comments] signed Anna Lee Scott; 2 'Cake Making – Step by Step' and 'To Judge When a Cake Is Baked'; 3 'General Directions for Cakes with Shortening'; 4 'If Butter Cake Has These Faults –'; 5 'General Directions for Sponge Cakes'; 6 'If Your Sponge Cake Has These Faults –'; 7–28 'Recipes'; 29–32 index

COPIES: *NSWA OGU (CCC TX715.6 M572 No. 357)
NOTES: The three titles in 'The Easy Way Series' (*The Easy Way Cake Book;* O776.1, *Marketing and Meal Planning;* and O777.1, *Planning the Party*) were distributed by Maple Leaf Milling Co. itself and through newspapers in various cities, likely in conjunction with a series of cooking lessons printed in the individual newspapers (see O773.7). I have not determined the order of publication of the English-language editions of *The Easy Way Cake Book,* but some likely appeared about 1932, when the series was advertised in O774.1 and O775.1, Anna Lee Scott's *Maple Leaf Cooking School: Lessons 5–6–7–8* and *Lessons 9–10–11–12.* A search of the various newspapers in the period 1932–4 might locate the series of cooking lessons and identify the year of publication of each associated cookbook. I have arranged the newspaper editions in alphabetical order, by newspaper name.

O773.15, the French-language edition, titled *L'art de réussir des gâteaux* and copyright 1934, is attributed to the pseudonymous author Marthe Miral, not Scott.

O773.2 nd
—[An edition of *The Easy Way Cake Book,* Barrie, Ont.: Barrie Examiner, nd]
COPIES: Bookseller's stock

O773.3 nd
—The easy way / cake book / for beginners and / the best of cooks / by / Anna Lee Scott / "The Easy Way Series" / Bowmanville Statesman [cover-title]
DESCRIPTION: 23.0 × 15.0 cm Pp [1] 2–32 Paper; stapled
CONTENTS: 1 'The Easy Way Cake Book' [introductory comments] signed Anna Lee Scott and 'General Rules for All Cakes'; 2 'Cake Making – Step by Step' and 'To Judge When a Cake Is Baked'; 3 'General Directions for Cakes with Shortening'; 4 'If "Butter" Cake Has These Faults –'; 5 'General Directions for Sponge Cakes'; 6 'If Your Sponge Cake Has These Faults –'; 7–28 'Recipes'; 29–32 index
COPIES: *Private collection

O773.4 nd
—The easy way / cake book / for beginners and / the best of cooks / by / Anna Lee Scott / "The Easy Way Series" / The Daily Colonist. / The oldest daily newspaper on the Pacific Coast / Victoria, B.C. [cover-title]
COPIES: *Private collection

O773.5 nd
—The easy way / cake book / for beginners and /

the best of cooks / by / Anna Lee Scott / "The Easy Way Series" / Edmonton Journal / "One of Canada's great newspapers" [cover-title]
COPIES: *ACG

O773.6 nd
—The easy way / cake book / for beginners and / the best of cooks / by / Anna Lee Scott / "The Easy Way Series" / The Expositor [cover-title]
DESCRIPTION: 23.0 × 15.5 cm Pp [1] 2–32 Paper; stapled
CONTENTS: 1 'The Easy Way Cake Book' [introductory comments] signed Anna Lee Scott and 'General Rules for All Cakes'; 2 'Cake Making – Step by Step' and 'To Judge When a Cake Is Baked'; 3 'General Directions for Cakes with Shortening'; 4 'If "Butter" Cake Has These Faults –'; 5 'General Directions for Sponge Cakes'; 6 'If Your Sponge Cake Has These Faults –'; 7–28 'Recipes'; 29–32 index
COPIES: *Private collection
NOTES: No place of publication is given and 'Expositor' was a popular name for Ontario newspapers. The book's owner lives halfway between Seaforth and Brantford, both of which have *Expositors.* Since Brantford is the larger place, it is likely the book was published by the Brantford *Expositor.*

O773.7 nd [about 1933–4]
—The easy way / cake book / for beginners and / the best of cooks / by / Anna Lee Scott / "The Easy Way Series" / Family Herald and Weekly Star / Montreal, Canada [cover-title]
DESCRIPTION: 22.5 × 15.0 cm Pp [1] 2–32 Paper; stapled
CONTENTS: 1 'The Easy Way Cake Book' [introductory comments] signed Anna Lee Scott and 'General Rules for All Cakes'; 2 'Cake Making – Step by Step' and 'To Judge When a Cake Is Baked'; 3 'General Directions for Cakes with Shortening'; 4 'If "Butter" Cake Has These Faults –'; 5 'General Directions for Sponge Cakes'; 6 'If Your Sponge Cake Has These Faults –'; 7–28 'Recipes'; 29–32 index
COPIES: ASPMHC *OGU (CCC TX715.6 S36)
NOTES: A private collector writes of her copy: 'These books [O773.7, *The Easy Way Cake Book;* O776.6, *Marketing and Meal Planning;* and O777.3, *Planning the Party*] were bought in 1933 or 1934 in conjunction with a series of cooking school lessons appearing in the Family Herald. I participated in the lessons and have a "Diploma" from them saying I have successfully completed the course. The diploma is dated August, 1934. I was 11 years old.'

There is a recipe on p 10 for Tomato Soup Cake,

which calls for ²/₃ cup tomato soup, but not the proprietary canned variety, such as Campbell's Soup. Recipes for Tomato Soup Cake still circulate among home cooks, almost three-quarters of a century later.

OGU has a second, unidentified edition of *The Easy Way Cake Book,* which lacks its binding.

O773.8 nd
—The easy way / cake book / for beginners and / the best of cooks / by / Anna Lee Scott / "The Easy Way Series" / Kitchener Daily Record [cover-title]
DESCRIPTION: 23.0 × 15.0 cm   Pp [1] 2–32   Paper; stapled
CONTENTS: 1 'The Easy Way Cake Book' [introductory comments] signed Anna Lee Scott and 'General Rules for All Cakes'; 2 'Cake Making – Step by Step' and 'To Judge When a Cake Is Baked'; 3 'General Directions for Cakes with Shortening'; 4 'If "Butter" Cake Has These Faults –'; 5 'General Directions for Sponge Cakes'; 6 'If Your Sponge Cake Has These Faults –'; 7–28 'Recipes'; 29–32 index
COPIES: *OKIT

O773.9 nd
—The easy way / cake book / for beginners and / the best of cooks / by / Anna Lee Scott / "The Easy Way Series" / The Leader-Post / Regina, Sask. [cover-title]
DESCRIPTION: 22.5 × 15.0 cm   Pp [1] 2–32   Paper; stapled
CONTENTS: 1 'The Easy Way Cake Book' [introductory comments] signed Anna Lee Scott and 'General Rules for All Cakes'; 2 'Cake Making – Step by Step' and 'To Judge When a Cake Is Baked'; 3 'General Directions for Cakes with Shortening'; 4 'If "Butter" Cake Has These Faults –'; 5 'General Directions for Sponge Cakes'; 6 'If Your Sponge Cake Has These Faults –'; 7–28 'Recipes'; 29–32 index
COPIES: *OONL (TX771 S46 1900z p***)   QMM (RBD ckbk 1990)

O773.10 nd
—The easy way / cake book / for beginners and / the best of cooks / by / Anna Lee Scott / "The Easy Way Series" / The Montreal Daily Star [cover-title]
DESCRIPTION: 23.0 × 15.0 cm   Pp [1] 2–32   Paper; stapled
CONTENTS: 1 'The Easy Way Cake Book' [introductory comments] signed Anna Lee Scott and 'General Rules for All Cakes'; 2 'Cake Making – Step by Step' and 'To Judge When a Cake Is Baked'; 3 'General Directions for Cakes with Shortening'; 4 'If "Butter" Cake Has These Faults'; 5 'General Directions for

Sponge Cakes'; 6 'If Your Sponge Cake Has These Faults'; 7–28 'Recipes'; 29–32 index
CITATIONS: BQ 24-4878
COPIES: *QMM (RBD ckbk 1221)

O773.11 nd
—The easy way / cake book / for beginners and / the best of cooks / by / Anna Lee Scott / "The Easy Way Series" / The Oshawa Daily Times / The Cobourg Sentinel-Star / The Whitby Gazette & Chronicle [cover-title]
DESCRIPTION: 22.5 × 15.0 cm   Pp [1] 2–32   Paper; stapled
CONTENTS: 1 'The Easy Way Cake Book' signed Anna Lee Scott and 'General Rules for All Cakes'; 2 'Cake Making – Step by Step' and 'To Judge When a Cake Is Baked'; 3 'General Directions for Cakes with Shortening'; 4 'If "Butter" Cake Has These Faults –'; 5 'General Directions for Sponge Cakes'; 6 'If Your Sponge Cake Has These Faults –'; 7–28 'Recipes'; 29–32 'General Index,' index for 'Cakes,' and index for 'Frostings and Fillings'
COPIES: *Private collection

O773.12 nd
—The easy way / cake book / for beginners and / the best of cooks / by / Anna Lee Scott / "The Easy Way Series" / The Review-Reporter / Bruce County's best newspaper / Kincardine, Ontario [cover-title]
COPIES: *Private collection

O773.13 nd
—The easy way / cake book / for beginners and / the best of cooks / by / Anna Lee Scott / "The Easy Way Series" / The Sun Publishing Company, Limited / Brandon, Man. [cover-title]
COPIES: *Private collection

O773.14 nd
—[An edition of *The Easy Way Cake Book,* Vancouver Daily Province, nd]
COPIES: Private collection

O773.15 [copyright 1934]
—L'art de reussir / les gateaux / methode facile pour les / debutantes et les cuisinieres / experimentees / par / Marthe Miral / "La méthode à portée de tous" / La presse Montreal [cover-title]
DESCRIPTION: 22.5 × 15.0 cm   Pp [1] 2–32   Paper; stapled
CONTENTS: top 1 'L'art de réussir les gâteaux' signed

Marthe Miral and 'Tous droits réservés, Ottawa, 1934.'; mid 1 'Règles générales pour tous les gâteaux'; bottom 1–top 2 'Manière de procéder'; mid 2 'Comment reconnaître qu'un gâteau est cuit' and 'Indications générales touchant les gâteaux au beurre'; bottom 2–near bottom 3 'Les défauts des gâteaux au beurre'; bottom 3–top 4 'Indications générales touchant les gâteaux éponge (gâteaux de Savoie)'; mid 4 'Les défauts des gâteaux éponge'; bottom 4–30 'Recettes'; 31–2 'Table des matières'

CITATIONS: Bédard, p 3

COPIES: *QMBN (127695 CON)

NOTES: In this French-language edition, the company names the author Marthe Miral, not Anna Lee Scott. QMBN has a second copy (127696 CON) that varies from the one described above in that there is no horizontal rule below the running head and folio on each page, and throughout the text there is less leading between the lines of type.

O774.1 [copyright 1932]

The true fundamentals of good cooking / Maple Leaf / Cooking / School / That / every girl / may learn / to cook / Directed by / Anna Lee Scott / A complete home study course / for beginners and others in / twelve easy lessons // Lessons 5–6–7–8 [cover-title]

DESCRIPTION: 23.0 × 15.0 cm   Pp 1–8, 1–8, 1–8, 1–8 Paper; stapled

CONTENTS: 1–8 'Lesson 5 Meat, Poultry, Fish' and at bottom p 8, 'Copyright, Canada, 1932, by Maple Leaf Milling Co., Ltd.'; 1–8 'Lesson 6 Vegetables' and at bottom p 8, 'Copyright, Canada, 1932, ...'; 1–8 'Lesson 7 Eggs and Cheese' and at bottom p 8, 'Copyright, Canada, 1932, ...'; 1–8 'Lesson 8 How to Make Good Bread' and at bottom p 8, 'Copyright, Canada, 1932, ...'

CITATIONS: Ferguson/Fraser, p 234, illus col on p 80 of closed volume

COPIES: *NSWA   OGU (CCC TX715.6 M3665 v. 2)

NOTES: On the inside front face of the binding, there is an advertisement for Maple Leaf Milling Co.'s 'The Easy Way Series' (see notes for O775.1). The NSWA copy includes the loose leaf 'Examination Paper.' No copy of *Lessons 1–2–3–4* has surfaced.

O775.1 [copyright 1932]

The true fundamentals of good cooking / Maple Leaf / Cooking / School / That / every girl / may learn / to cook / Directed by / Anna Lee Scott / A complete home study course / for beginners and others in / twelve easy lessons // Lessons 9–10–11–12 [cover-title]

DESCRIPTION: 23.0 × 15.0 cm   Pp 1–8, 1–8, 1–8, 1–8

Paper; stapled

CONTENTS: 1–8 'Lesson 9 Cake Making' and at bottom p 8, 'Copyright, Canada, 1932, by Maple Leaf Milling Co., Ltd.'; 1–8 'Lesson 10 Fillings and Frostings' and at bottom p 8, 'Copyright, Canada, 1932, ...'; 1–8 'Lesson 11 (a) Cookies, and (b) Sweet Sauces' and at bottom p 8, 'Copyright, Canada, 1932, ...'; 1–8 'Lesson 12 Desserts' and at bottom p 8, 'Copyright, Canada, 1932, ...'

COPIES: *NSWA   OGU (CCC TX715.6 M3665 v. 3)

NOTES: On the inside front face of the binding, the reader is advised: 'All enrolled students who have sent in a total of 8 coupons from Maple Leaf Flour bags and 25c. will receive their Examination Paper along with the three books of The Easy Way Series // "Marketing and Meal Planning" "The Easy Way Cake Book" and "Planning the Party."' See O773.1, O776.1, and O777.1 for these three titles.

O776.1 nd [about 1932]

Marketing and / meal planning / most of the best for / your time and money / by / Anna Lee Scott / Maple Leaf Milling Co., Limited / Toronto Winnipeg [cover-title]

DESCRIPTION: 23.0 × 15.0 cm   Pp [1] 2–32   Paper; stapled

CONTENTS: 1–2 'Marketing and Meal Planning' signed Anna Lee Scott; 3–top 15 entries for meat, fish, poultry, milk, cheese, fats, eggs, canned foods, flour, prepared biscuit flour [Tea-Bisk], breakfast cereals including Maple Leaf brands, miscellaneous cereals, leavening agents, sugars, salt, spices, fruits, dried fruits, and vegetables; mid 15–24 'To Plan Meals Wisely' including 'Group I. Foods That Are Regulating,' 'Group II. The Building Foods,' and 'Group III. The Fuel Foods'; 25–top 26 'Vitamins'; mid 26–mid 29 'When Economy Is Vital'; mid 29–top 30 'When the Budget Is Bigger'; near top 30–bottom 30 'When There Are Children'; top 31 'When Constipation Enters'; mid 31–32 'When You Would Change Weight'

COPIES: *NSWA

NOTES: The text on p 1 refers to *Marketing and Meal Planning* as one of 'The Easy Way Series.' I have not determined the order of publication of the various editions of this title. Some were likely published about 1932, when 'The Easy Way Series' was advertised in O774.1 and O775.1, Anna Lee Scott's *Maple Leaf Cooking School: Lessons 5–6–7–8* and *Lessons 9–10–11–12*. O776.1 was published after the introduction of Tea-Bisk to the marketplace in 1931. I have arranged the newspaper editions in alphabetical order by newspaper name. The other two titles in 'The Easy Way Series' are O773.1, *The Easy Way Cake Book*, and O777.1, *Planning the Party*.

O776.2 nd
—Marketing and / meal planning / most of the best for / your time and money / by / Anna Lee Scott / "The Easy Way Series" / Bowmanville Statesman [cover-title]
DESCRIPTION: 23.0 × 15.0 cm   Pp [1] 2–32   Paper; stapled
CONTENTS: 1–2 'Marketing and Meal Planning' signed Anna Lee Scott; 3–14 entries for meat, fish, poultry, milk, cheese, fats, eggs, canned foods, flour, breakfast cereals, miscellaneous cereals, leavening agents, sugars, salt, spices and flavourings, fruits, dried fruits, and vegetables; 15–24 'To Plan Meals Wisely' including 'Group I. Foods That Are Regulating,' 'Group II. The Building Foods,' and 'Group III. The Fuel Foods'; 25–top 26 'The Vitamins'; mid 26–mid 29 'When Economy Is Vital'; mid 29–top 30 'When the Budget Is Bigger'; near top 30–bottom 30 'When There Are Children'; top 31 'When Constipation Enters'; bottom 31–32 'When You Would Change Weight'
COPIES: *Private collection
NOTES: Unlike O776.1, there is no separate entry for prepared biscuit flour and Maple-Leaf-brand names are not cited in the text; however, the text on p 7, under 'Flour,' refers to 'prepared biscuit flour' as 'very new – very useful.'

O776.3 nd
—Marketing and / meal planning / most of the best for / your time and money / by / Anna Lee Scott / "The Easy Way Series" / Prepared by Anna Lee Scott for the / Calgary Herald [cover-title]
DESCRIPTION: 23.0 × 15.0 cm   Pp [1] 2–32   Paper; stapled
CONTENTS: 1–2 'Marketing and Meal Planning' signed Anna Lee Scott; 3–14 entries for meat, fish, poultry, milk, cheese, fats, eggs, canned foods, flour, breakfast cereals, miscellaneous cereals, leavening agents, sugars, salt, spices and flavourings, fruits, dried fruits, and vegetables; 15–24 'To Plan Meals Wisely' including 'Group I. Foods That Are Regulating,' 'Group II. The Building Foods,' and 'Group III. The Fuel Foods'; 25–top 26 'The Vitamins'; mid 26–mid 29 'When Economy Is Vital'; mid 29–top 30 'When the Budget Is Bigger'; near top 30–bottom 30 'When There Are Children'; top 31 'When Constipation Enters'; mid 31–32 'When You Would Change Weight'
COPIES: *OONL (TX651 S46 1900z p***)

O776.4 nd
—Marketing and / meal planning / most of the best for / your time and money / by / Anna Lee Scott /

"The Easy Way Series" / Edmonton Journal / "One of Canada's great newspapers" [cover-title]
COPIES: *ACG

O776.5 nd
—Marketing and / meal planning / most of the best for / your time and money / by / Anna Lee Scott / "The Easy Way Series" / The Expositor [cover-title]
DESCRIPTION: 23.0 × 15.5 cm   Pp [1] 2–32   Paper; stapled
CONTENTS: 1–2 'Marketing and Meal Planning' signed Anna Lee Scott; 3–14 entries for meat, fish, poultry, milk, cheese, fats, eggs, canned foods, flour, breakfast cereals, miscellaneous cereals, leavening agents, sugars, salt, spices and flavourings, fruits, dried fruits, and vegetables; 15–24 'To Plan Meals Wisely' including 'Group I. Foods That Are Regulating,' 'Group II. The Building Foods,' and 'Group III. The Fuel Foods'; 25–top 26 'The Vitamins'; mid 26–mid 29 'When Economy Is Vital'; mid 29–top 30 'When the Budget Is Bigger'; near top 30–bottom 30 'When There Are Children'; top 31 'When Constipation Enters'; mid 31–32 'When You Would Change Weight'
COPIES: *Private collection
NOTES: No place of publication is given. See O773.6, *The Easy Way Cake Book,* regarding the possible place of publication.

O776.6 nd [about 1934]
—Marketing and / meal planning / most of the best for / your time and money / by / Anna Lee Scott / "The Easy Way Series" / Family Herald and Weekly Star / Montreal, Canada [cover-title]
COPIES: OGU (TX715.6 S37)   *Private collection
NOTES: The private collector's copy is inscribed on the binding, 'Annabell McLennan. Jan–Apr. 19[34?].' See O773.7, *The Easy Way Cake Book,* for the comments of another owner of this edition.

O776.7 nd
—Marketing and / meal planning / most of the best for / your time and money / by / Anna Lee Scott / "The Easy Way Series" / Kitchener Daily Record [cover-title]
DESCRIPTION: 22.5 × 15.0 cm   Pp [1] 2–32   Paper; stapled
CONTENTS: 1–2 'Marketing and Meal Planning' signed Anna Lee Scott; 3–14 entries for meat, fish, poultry, milk, cheese, fats, eggs, canned foods, flour, breakfast cereals, miscellaneous cereals, leavening agents, sugars, salt, spices and flavourings, fruits, dried fruits, and vegetables; 15–24 'To Plan Meals Wisely' includ-

ing 'Group I. Foods That Are Regulating,' 'Group II. The Building Foods,' and 'Group III. The Fuel Foods'; 25–top 26 'The Vitamins'; mid 26–mid 29 'When Economy Is Vital'; mid 29–top 30 'When the Budget Is Bigger'; near top 30–bottom 30 'When There Are Children'; top 31 'When Constipation Enters'; bottom 31–32 'When You Would Change Weight'
COPIES: *OKIT

O776.8 nd
—Marketing and / meal planning / most of the best for / your time and money / by / Anna Lee Scott / "The Easy Way Series" / The Leader-Post / Regina, Sask. [cover-title]
COPIES: *Private collection

O776.9 nd
—Marketing and / meal planning / most of the best for / your time and money / by / Anna Lee Scott / "The Easy Way Series" / The Montreal Daily Star [cover-title]
DESCRIPTION: 22.5 × 15.0 cm   Pp [1] 2–32   Paper; stapled
CONTENTS: 1–2 'Marketing and Meal Planning' signed Anna Lee Scott; 3–14 entries for meat, fish, poultry, milk, cheese, fats, eggs, canned foods, flour, breakfast cereals, miscellaneous cereals, leavening agents, sugars, salt, spices and flavourings, fruits, dried fruits, and vegetables; 15–24 'To Plan Meals Wisely' including 'Group I. Foods That Are Regulating,' 'Group II. The Building Foods,' and 'Group III. The Fuel Foods'; 25–top 26 'The Vitamins'; mid 26–mid 29 'When Economy Is Vital'; mid 29–top 30 'When the Budget Is Bigger'; near top 30–bottom 30 'When There Are Children'; top 31 'When Constipation Enters'; mid 31–32 'When You Would Change Weight'
CITATIONS: BQ 24-4879
COPIES: *QMM (2 copies: RBD ckbk 1991, RBD ckbk 1223)

O776.10 nd
—Marketing and / meal planning / most of the best for / your time and money / by / Anna Lee Scott / "The Easy Way Series" / The Review-Reporter / Bruce County's best newspaper / Kincardine, Ontario [cover-title]
DESCRIPTION: 23.0 × 15.0 cm   Pp [1] 2–32   Paper; stapled
CONTENTS: 1–2 'Marketing and Meal Planning' signed Anna Lee Scott; 3–14 entries for meat, fish, poultry, milk, cheese, fats, eggs, canned foods, flour, breakfast cereals, miscellaneous cereals, leavening agents, sug-

ars, salt, spices and flavourings, fruits, dried fruits, and vegetables; 15–24 'To Plan Meals Wisely' including 'Group I. Foods That Are Regulating,' 'Group II. The Building Foods,' and 'Group III. The Fuel Foods'; 25–top 26 'The Vitamins'; mid 26–mid 29 'When Economy Is Vital'; mid 29–top 30 'When the Budget Is Bigger'; near top 30–bottom 30 'When There Are Children'; top 31 'When Constipation Enters'; bottom 31–32 'When You Would Change Weight'
COPIES: *Private collection

O776.11 nd
—Marketing and / meal planning / most of the best for / your time and money / by / Anna Lee Scott / "The Easy Way Series" / The Sun Publishing Company, Limited / Brandon, Man. [cover-title]
COPIES: *Private collection

O776.12 nd
—[An edition of *Marketing and Meal Planning,* 'The Easy Way Series,' Winnipeg: Winnipeg Evening Tribune, nd]
COPIES: Bookseller's stock

O777.1 nd [about 1932]
Planning / the party / entertaining ideas / for the smart hostess / by / Anna Lee Scott / "The Easy Way Series" / Bowmanville Statesman [cover-title]
DESCRIPTION: 23.0 × 15.0 cm   Pp [1] 2–31 [32]   Paper; stapled
CONTENTS: 1 'Planning the Party' signed Anna Lee Scott; 2–11 entries for 'Afternoon Tea,' 'Sunday Suppers,' 'The Bridge Supper,' 'The Luncheon,' 'The Dinner Party,' 'The Children's Party,' 'Fireside Suppers,' 'The Spread-Your-Own Party,' 'The Big Reception,' 'Bridal Showers and Announcements,' and 'The Wedding Reception'; 12–mid 13 'Colour Schemes for the Party'; mid 13 'Smart Canapes'; bottom 13–mid 14 'Spreads'; mid 14–top 15 'Sandwiches in General'; mid–bottom 15 'Sandwich Spreads'; 16–31 'Recipes to Aid the Hostess' [fifty-six numbered recipes]; 32 index
COPIES: *Private collection
NOTES: Some English-language editions of *Planning the Party* were likely published about 1932, when the series was advertised in O774.1 and O775.1, Anna Lee Scott's *Maple Leaf Cooking School: Lessons 5–6–7–8* and *Lessons 9–10–11–12.* The French-language edition, O777.9, titled *L'art de recevoir,* is dated copyright 1934 and attributed to Marthe Miral, not Scott. I have not located an edition published by Maple Leaf Milling Co., as there was for other titles in 'The Easy Way

Series,' but there undoubtedly was one. The English-language newspaper editions are arranged in alphabetical order by newspaper name.

O777.2 nd
—Planning / the party / entertaining ideas / for the smart hostess / by / Anna Lee Scott / "The Easy Way Series" / Edmonton Journal / "One of Canada's great newspapers" [cover-title]
COPIES: *ACG

O777.3 nd
—[An edition of *Planning the Party,* 'The Easy Way Series,' Montreal: Family Herald and Weekly Star, nd]
COPIES: OGU (CCC TX715.6 S375)   Private collection
NOTES: See O773.7, *The Easy Way Cake Book,* for the comments of another owner of this edition.

O777.4 nd
—Planning / the party / entertaining ideas / for the smart hostess / by / Anna Lee Scott / "The Easy Way Series" / Kitchener Daily Record [cover-title]
DESCRIPTION: 22.5 × 15.0 cm   Pp [1] 2–31 [32]   Paper; stapled
CONTENTS: 1 'Planning the Party' signed Anna Lee Scott; 2–11 entries for 'Afternoon Tea,' 'Sunday Suppers,' 'The Bridge Supper,' 'The Luncheon,' 'The Dinner Party,' 'The Children's Party,' 'Fireside Suppers,' 'The Spread-Your-Own Party,' 'The Big Reception,' 'Bridal Showers and Announcements,' and 'The Wedding Reception'; 12–mid 13 'Colour Schemes for the Party'; mid 13 'Smart Canapes'; bottom 13–mid 14 'Spreads'; mid 14–top 15 'Sandwiches in General'; mid–bottom 15 'Sandwich Spreads'; 16–31 'Recipes to Aid the Hostess' [fifty-six numbered recipes]; 32 index
COPIES: *OKIT

O777.5 nd
—Planning / the party / entertaining ideas / for the smart hostess / by / Anna Lee Scott / "The Easy Way Series" / The Leader-Post / Regina, Sask. [cover-title]
DESCRIPTION: 23.0 × 15.0 cm   Pp [1] 2–31 [32]   Paper; stapled
CONTENTS: 1 'Planning the Party' signed Anna Lee Scott; 2–11 entries for 'Afternoon Tea,' 'Sunday Suppers,' 'The Bridge Supper,' 'The Luncheon,' 'The Dinner Party,' 'The Children's Party,' 'Fireside Suppers,' 'The Spread-Your-Own Party,' 'The Big Reception,' 'Bridal Showers and Announcements,' and 'The Wed-

ding Reception'; 12–mid 13 'Colour Schemes for the Party'; mid 13 'Smart Canapes'; bottom 13–mid 14 'Spreads'; mid 14–top 15 'Sandwiches in General'; mid–bottom 15 'Sandwich Spreads'; 16–31 'Recipes to Aid the Hostess' [fifty-six numbered recipes]; 32 index
COPIES: *OONL (TX731 S36 1950z p***)

O777.6 nd
—Planning / the party / entertaining ideas / for the smart hostess / by / Anna Lee Scott / "The Easy Way Series" / The Lethbridge Herald [cover-title]
COPIES: *Private collection

O777.7 nd
—Planning / the party / entertaining ideas / for the smart hostess / by / Anna Lee Scott / "The Easy Way Series" / The Montreal Daily Star [cover-title]
DESCRIPTION: 22.5 × 15.0 cm   Pp [1] 2–31 [32]   Paper; stapled
CONTENTS: 1 'Planning the Party' signed Anna Lee Scott; 2–11 entries for 'Afternoon Tea,' 'Sunday Suppers,' 'The Bridge Supper,' 'The Luncheon,' 'The Dinner Party,' 'The Children's Party,' 'Fireside Suppers,' 'The Spread-Your-Own Party,' 'The Big Reception,' 'Bridal Showers and Announcements,' and 'The Wedding Reception'; 12–mid 13 'Colour Schemes for the Party'; mid 13 'Smart Canapes'; bottom 13–mid 14 'Spreads'; mid 14–top 15 'Sandwiches in General'; mid–bottom 15 'Sandwich Spreads'; 16–31 'Recipes to Aid the Hostess'; 32 index
CITATIONS: BQ 24-4880
COPIES: QMBN (120288 CON)   *QMM (2 copies: RBD ckbk 1989, RBD ckbk 1222)

O777.8 nd
—Planning / the party / entertaining ideas / for the smart hostess / by / Anna Lee Scott / "The Easy Way Series" / The Review-Reporter / Bruce County's best newspaper / Kincardine, Ontario [cover-title]
DESCRIPTION: 23.0 × 15.0 cm   Pp [1] 2–31 [32]   Paper; stapled
CONTENTS: 1 'Planning the Party' signed Anna Lee Scott; 2–11 entries for 'Afternoon Tea,' 'Sunday Suppers,' 'The Bridge Supper,' 'The Luncheon,' 'The Dinner Party,' 'The Children's Party,' 'Fireside Suppers,' 'The Spread-Your-Own Party,' 'The Big Reception,' 'Bridal Showers and Announcements,' and 'The Wedding Reception'; 12–mid 13 'Colour Schemes for the Party'; mid 13 'Smart Canapes'; bottom 13–mid 14 'Spreads'; mid 14–top 15 'Sandwiches in General'; mid–bottom 15 'Sandwich Spreads'; 16–31 'Recipes

to Aid the Hostess' [fifty-six numbered recipes]; 32 index
COPIES: *Private collection

O777.9   [copyright 1934]
—L'art / de recevoir / suggestions aux / maitresses de maison / par / Marthe Miral / "La méthode à portée de tous" / La presse Montréal [cover-title]
DESCRIPTION: 22.5 × 15.0 cm   Pp [1] 2–31   Paper; stapled
CONTENTS: top 1 'L'art de recevoir' signed Marthe Miral and at bottom, 'Tous droits réservés, Ottawa, 1934.'; mid 1–mid 11 entries for 'L'heure du thé,' 'Le souper du dimanche soir,' 'Après le bridge,' 'Le déjeuner,' 'Le dîner,' 'Les réunions d'enfants,' 'Souper improvisé "au coin du feu,"' 'Les réceptions "sans-façon,"' 'Les grands réceptions,' 'Réceptions à la future mariée,' and 'Réception de noces'; mid 11–top 13 'Le rôle des couleurs dans les réceptions'; mid 13 'Canapés élégants,' 'La base du canapé,' and 'Garnitures'; bottom 13–mid 14 'Sandwichs'; bottom 14–mid 15 'Garnitures de sandwichs'; mid 15–30 'Recettes à l'usage de la maîtresse de maison' [fifty-six numbered recipes]; 31 'Table des matières'
CITATIONS: Bédard, p 3
COPIES: *QMBN (127694 CON)
NOTES: In this French-language edition (as in O773.15), the company names the author Marthe Miral, not Anna Lee Scott.

Sparkman, Edna I.

Canadian Westinghouse Co. was founded in Hamilton in 1904.

O778.1   copyright 1932
Tested recipes / suggestions for food preservation / directions for the care of / your Westinghouse Refrigerator / Prepared by Edna I. Sparkman, / Supervisor of Westinghouse Refrigeration Home Economics / Glassware, china and silver by courtesy / of the Kinney and Levan Co. / [across bottom of inside front face of binding and tp:] Copyright 1932 by Canadian Westinghouse Company, Limited Merchandising Department, Hamilton, Canada
DESCRIPTION: 21.5 × 14.0 cm   Pp [1–2] 3–76   Illus col, illus   Paper, with image on front of a woman carrying a container of pink liquid toward a refrigerator; stapled
CONTENTS: Inside front face of binding 'Contents' and 'Price $1.00'; 1 tp; 2 'Foreword'; 3 'The Westinghouse

Refrigerator Protects Your Food and Your Family's Health' and 'Temperature Selector'; 4–mid 5 'Conditions Which Determine Freezing Time'; mid–bottom 5 'Cleaning Your Westinghouse'; 6–7 'Defrosting'; 8–mid 10 'General Directions'; mid 10–12 'Economy Buying'; 13–mid 14 'Ice Cubes'; mid–bottom 14 'Hints for Preparing Frozen Desserts'; 15–16 'Directions for Freezing Desserts'; 17 'Suggestions for Serving Frozen Desserts'; 18–33 'Frozen Desserts'; 34–7 'Refrigerator Cakes and Puddings'; 38–9 'Ice Cream and Pudding Sauces'; 40–3 'Beverages'; 44–9 'Baked Goods'; 50–4 'Canapes and Cocktails'; 55–9 'Left Overs'; 60–1 'Sandwiches'; 62–71 'Salads'; 72–3 'Salad Dressings'; 74–5 'Refrigerator Meals'; 76–inside back face 'Index of Recipes'; outside back face '11 C-51 Printed in U.S.A.'
COPIES: *OONL (TX830 S63 1932 p***)
NOTES: The cover-title is 'The Westinghouse Refrigerator Book.' One year later, the company published the first of various editions of a book also called *The Westinghouse Refrigerator Book,* but not attributed to Edna I. Sparkman and with fewer pages (see O808.1–808.8). The later books are probably related to the Sparkman text: The recipes in the Sparkman version begin with Angel Parfait, Fruit Delight, Butterscotch Parfait, Chocolate Mousse, and Economy Mousse; O808.1 begins with White or Angel Parfait, Golden Parfait, Butterscotch Parfait, Mousses [basic recipe and variations], Fruit Delight, and Economy Mousse.

Tested recipes: Oven meals and other menus

O779.1   nd [about 1932]
Tested / recipes / Oven meals / and / other menus / Dedicated to our patrons / and the / homemakers of Ottawa / By / the Home Service / Department / of / the Ottawa Electric Company / The Ottawa Gas Company / Ottawa / Canada
DESCRIPTION: 22.5 × 15.5 cm   Pp [1] 2–174   Paper-covered card
CONTENTS: 1 tp; 2 table of contents; 3 foreword signed M.P. Richardson, superintendent, Home Service Department; 4 'Care of a Gas Range'; 5 'Advantages of an Automatic Heat Controlled Gas Range'; 6 'Care of a Refrigerator'; 7 'Tables of Measures and Equivalents'; 8–11 menus; 12–167 recipes; 168–70 'Useful Hints'; 171–2 'Removal of Stains'; 173–4 'Spices and Flavors' and at bottom p 174, 'Printed in Canada'
COPIES: OONL (TX715 O87 1930z)   *Private collection
NOTES: In the foreword, Richardson refers to the 'many lecture-demonstrations since the inauguration of the

[Home Service] Department, four years ago.' Marcella P. Richardson is listed as superintendent of the Home Service Department in Ottawa city directories from 1928; therefore, the cookbook's likely year of publication was 1932 (1928 + 4 years), a date which conforms with the appearance of the volume. Oven meals (where all the dishes of a meal were put into the oven together) were a fashion of the 1930s.

Another private collector's copy has a label over the title-page imprint: 'Robertson Pingle & Tilley, Limited // 58 Sparks Street // Ottawa 2-1581 // Everything electric.'

Waite, Sheridan C.

O780.1 [3rd ed., pocket ed., 1932]
"The / food pilot" / a / balanced / meal / Pocket / edition / By Sheridan C. Waite, D.D.S., M.S.D. / The Food Pilot Company // Springville, Erie County, N.Y. / Canadian distributors: Health Service, 634 Confederation / Life Building, Toronto, Canada
DESCRIPTION: 17.0 × 10.0 cm   Pp [1–4] 5–39   Tp illus of a man holding a set of scales, on which are balanced a whole chicken on one side and an equal weight of fruit and vegetables on the other   Cloth, with image on front of the head-and-shoulders of a boat's pilot dressed in rain gear, i.e., the 'food pilot'
CONTENTS: 1 ht; 2 'All rights reserved // Third edition (revised) 1932 // Copyright Canada – 1932 by F.A. Robinson. Printed in Canada'; 3 tp; 4 'Chinese Dictum' and 'Old Arabian Proverb'; top–mid 5 introductory text; mid 5–38 text in six chapters and, at bottom p 38, author's acknowledgment signed S.C.W. and a note that Canapar, Pecano, Marmite, Savita, and 'other articles and foods' may be bought at large stores or at Health Service, 634 Confederation Life Building, Toronto; 39 publ ad for *The Secret of Health* and *The Medical Millenium* [*sic*], two books by Dr William Howard Hay
COPIES: *Private collection
NOTES: The introductory text, p 5, comments on this Canadian edition: 'Some slight changes have been made in the manner of printing. Nothing has been omitted that is contained in the former United States edition. All the contents of the paper chart which formerly accompanied the Food Pilot have been embodied throughout the eight additional pages of the present book. The new Kitchen Disc-Chart is supplementary to the present volume ... (See description on the back of jacket).' The dust-jacket advertises the 'Food Pilot Kitchen Disc' chart and a 'Kitchen Chart,' which helped plan meals. As the first chapter ex-

plains, 'The Food Pilot is a simplified treatise on how to select and combine foods properly, so as to insure freedom from incompatible digestive tasks ... [It] is not a diet, but teaches by a simplified technique how to eat a wholesome enjoyable and adequate meal ... Wrong habits of feeding and devitalized foods are responsible for many of the physical ills of civilization, ...' The text includes recipes for starch meals, protein meals, and fruit meals, and for vegetables, salads, and candy. The title-page and text are printed in red and green.

On p 38 Waite acknowledges the 'cooperation of his friend, Dr. F.A. Robinson of Toronto, Canada, in the preparation of the United States edition of The Food Pilot for the press and for his careful revision of the Canadian edition.' The Toronto city directory lists Rev. Frank A. Robinson as secretary, Missions of Biblical Education and Evangelism and Health Service.

See also O792.1, *Health Service Cook Book*, from the same publisher, which may or may not be a related text.

AMERICAN EDITIONS: Pocket ed., Springville, NY: Food Pilot Co., [1932] (United States: DLC).

Westinghouse dual-automatic flavor-zone cookery

As home economist for Canadian Westinghouse, Miss Cornell's name is associated with several of the company's cookbooks through the 1930s and 1940s. See O790.1, 1092 Meals and How to Save 20% of Their Cost!; O959.2, Yours ... for Better Meals, under Westinghouse Electric Roaster Recipe Book; O1115.1, Recipe and Use Book; O1132.1, Delicious Foods and How to Cook Them with Your Westinghouse Electric Range; and O1225.1, Recipes ... Care ... Use: Westinghouse Refrigerators. Miss Cornell also edited the Westinghouse Home Service Bulletin (undated sheet of 'Summer Drinks' in a private collection). Photographs of her (younger and older) are in O790.1, O1115.1, and O1225.1.

No clear matches were found for Anna May Cornell in Hamilton city directories. One company employee who can be identified with certainty is Miss Edith Coombes, whose photograph appears in Chatelaine (October 1937), p 74, where she is described as 'Home Economist for the Canadian Westinghouse Company' (Coombes had visited the Chatelaine Test Kitchen). Coombes may have been involved in some way with the various Westinghouse cookbooks. (Hamilton city directories for 1938 and 1940 give the spelling Coombs.)

O781.1 nd [about 1932]
Westinghouse / dual-automatic / flavor-zone / cookery / Selected recipes / tested by / Anna May Cornell / Home Economist / Canadian Westinghouse Co. Ltd.

DESCRIPTION: 22.5 × 14.5 cm Pp [i] ii–xvi, 1–138 [139–44], paper pocket Tp illus of the head-and-shoulders of two male chefs, several illus accompanying the instructions for use of the Westinghouse Range Paper-covered card, with tp illus (enlarged and in colour) on front; spiral-bound

CONTENTS: i tp; ii table of contents; iii 'Your Dual Automatic Range'; iv–v 'The Cooking Surface'; vi–vii 'The Flavor-Zone Oven'; viii–ix 'Dual Automatic Cookery ...'; x–xiv 'General Instructions on Shelf Position in Your Westinghouse Oven'; xv illus of cleaning 'Pyrox Speedway elements' and of removing 'interchangeable oven heating elements'; xvi 'Keeping Your Westinghouse Range Like New'; 1–132 recipes; 133–8 index; 139–44 blank for 'Memorandum'; paper pocket for the 'Range Instruction Card That Comes with Your Range'

COPIES: AEPMA *Private collection

NOTES: According to p vi, the oven allowed three methods of cooking: 'dual-automatic method'; 'Dutch-oven method'; and 'maintained heat method.' Printed at bottom p 144 of the AEPMA copy is 'Spirax Canada Pat. 326.518 Form No. 32-V-6,' which indicates a likely publication date of 1932.

A booklet with a similar title was published earlier in the United States: *Flavor Zone Electric Cookery*, Mansfield, Ohio: Westinghouse Electric Co., [about 1925], pp 70 (Barile, p 190).

A private collector has a book, copyright 1937 and supplied with Model SA-4 Dual Automatic, which has the same title-page illustration of the two chefs, but a different title on the first page: Westinghouse / electric cookery / Selected recipes / tested by / Anna May Cornell / Home Economist / Canadian Westinghouse Co. Ltd. / Hamilton, Canada

White, Miss Florence (Peckham, a suburb of London, England, 20 June 1863–1940)

Florence White, who had earlier worked as a private teacher, freelance journalist, and in domestic service, founded the English Folk Cookery Association in 1928 when she realized how ignorant people were of the history and quality of English food. In her autobiography, she relates the story of how she struck the rich line of research into English food history, commenting, 'In 1926 no one had any idea that England possessed any national cook-ery beyond roast beef, Yorkshire pudding, and Christmas pudding ... We had the finest cookery in the world, but it had been nearly lost by neglect' (A Fire in the Kitchen: The Autobiography of a Cook, London: J.M. Dent and Sons, 1938, p 317).

See also O839.1, Flowers as Food, compiled by White. Her other food-related works are: How to Cook Well and Cheaply, No. 3 in the Home Series, [April 1901] (Great Britain: LB, OB); Good Food Register, Ringwood: Albany Press, [1934] (Great Britain: LB), a later edition retitled Where Shall We Eat or Put Up?; and Good English Food, Local and Regional, London: Jonathan Cape, [1952] (OGU; Great Britain: LB; United States: DLC). A photograph of White is reproduced in A Fire in the Kitchen. Her death date is recorded in the 1968 edition of O782.1.

O782.1 3rd impression, 1932
Good things in England / a practical cookery book / for everyday use / containing traditional and regional / recipes suited to modern tastes con- / tributed by English men and women / between 1399 and 1932 and edited by / Florence White ('Mary Evelyn') / founder of the English Folk Cookery Association / member of the American Home Economics Association / practical cook (English, American / and French cookery) / London Jonathan Cape Toronto

DESCRIPTION: 20.0 × 13.5 cm Pp [1–4] 5–392 4 pls incl frontis Cloth

CONTENTS: 1 ht; 2 blank; 3 tp; 4 'First published 1932 // Second impression July, 1932 // Third impression October, 1932,' publisher's London and Toronto addresses, and 'Printed in Great Britain in the city of Oxford at the Alden Press ...'; 5 table of contents and 'Note // The cloth in which this book is bound is fast to light, is washable, and may be cleaned with petrol or benzine.'; 6 blank; 7 two quotations; 8 blank; 9–18 introductory matter; 19–378 text in seven chapters; 379–92 index

COPIES: *OGU (UA s012 b16) OTMCL (641.5 W338) QMM (TX717 W47 1932b); United States: DLC (TX717 W47 1932b)

NOTES: White comments, 'This book is an attempt to capture the charm of England's cookery before it is completely crushed out of existence.' She collected the recipes from ordinary people across the country. The seven chapters cover 'English Breakfasts,' 'Home-made Bread, Huffkins, Wiggs, Oatcakes, etc.,' 'Luncheon, Dinner and Supper Dishes,' 'Country and Schoolroom Teas,' 'Some Local and National Specialities,' 'Some Simple English Dinners for Every Month in the Year,' and 'Authorities on English Food and Cookery.' On p 13 she gives British, Empire, and American weights and measures: American pint, 16 fluid ounces; British pint before 1878, 16 fluid ounces; British pint by the Act of 1878, 20 fluid ounces.

In *A Fire in the Kitchen*, pp 320–1, she credits Hamish Miles of Jonathan Cape Ltd for approaching her with the idea of publishing her discoveries in book form. She refers to a leading article in *The Times* marking the publication of *Good Things in England* on 23 May 1932.

There is no impression number in the OTMCL copy; therefore, it is the first. The QMM copy is the third impression. I have not seen the DLC copy.

BRITISH EDITIONS: London: Jonathan Cape, 1932 (Great Britain: LB); London: Jonathan Cape, 1951 (OWTU; Great Britain: LB); with a revised index, London: 1962 (Great Britain: LB); London: Cookery Book Club, 1968 (United States: Private collection).

1932–3

Favorite recipes

O783.1   1932–3
Favorite / recipes / 1932–1933 / The United Church / Smiths Falls – Ontario / Printed / in Canada / on Canadian / paper [cover-title]
DESCRIPTION: 23.0 × 15.0 cm   Pp [1] 2–36   Illus on p 1 of the United Church   Paper; stapled
CONTENTS: 1 'The United Church of Canada // Smiths Falls' [information about church services and church groups], 'Preface,' and 'Compiled by the Women's Association of the United Church, Smiths Falls, Ontario'; 2–35 text, including recipes credited with the name of the contributor, blank spaces for 'Memorandum' and 'New Recipes,' and ads; 36 'Index' [i.e., table of contents] and ads
COPIES: *OSMFHHM
NOTES: The 'Preface' leaves no doubt about the importance of a cook's work: 'The ladies of the Women's Association of the United Church believe that there is a constant and growing demand for tried and tested recipes and information concerning "The Nation's Greatest Industry," the Kitchen.' The printer is on the outside back face of the binding: 'Record-News Press.' This copy is inscribed on the binding, in ink, 'Mrs. R.W. Lumsden.'

Magic!

In 1999 Eagle Family Foods Inc. (new owners in 1998 of the Eagle Brand Sweetened Condensed Milk brand) celebrated the product's hundredth year. By 1999 the product was sold in a can with a 'pull top,' which meant that it was no longer possible to caramelize the milk by boiling the unopened can in water ('Still Another Magic Trick!' on pp 10–11 of Magic!*); apparently, women in Quebec and South Africa especially regretted that they could no longer make the caramelized milk treat. Another 1990s innovation was the introduction of a low-fat version of the product.*

For information about the company and its other books, see Q106.1.

O784.1   nd [about 1932–3]
Magic! / The most / amazing / short-cuts / in cooking / you ever heard of [cover-title]
DESCRIPTION: 26.0 × 20.0 cm   Pp [1] 2–37   Many illus brown   Paper, with images on front of prepared dishes; stapled
CONTENTS: 1 untitled introductory note beginning 'Goodbye, forever, to humdrum cooking!'; 2–3 'Here's What Happens when 38,000 Women Put on Their Aprons'; 4–5 'Here's Magic Trick No. 1' [salad dressing]; 6–7 'Here's Another Magic Trick!' [adding chocolate]; 8–9 'And Look at This Magic Trick!' [adding lemon juice]; 10–11 'Still Another Magic Trick!' [caramelized sweetened condensed milk]; 12–13 'And Here's Magic Trick No. 5' [cookies]; 14–top 15 recipes for salad dressings; mid–bottom 15 quick breads; 16–17 puddings; 18 custards; 19 sauces; 20–1 ice-box cakes; 22–5 ice creams and sherbets; 26–7 pies and tarts; 28–top 30 cakes and cookies; mid 30–31 frostings; 32–3 candies; 34 beverages; 35 '3 New Ways to Surprise Them' [recipes for Marvel Cheese Spread, Fish Steaks, and Spanish Corn Pudding]; 36 index; 37 [inside back face of binding] 'Do You Know the Answer?' and at bottom, 'Printed in Canada'
COPIES: ACG   OGU (CCC TX715.6 M32)   OMAHM (983.48.73)   QMM (RBD ckbk 1337)   *Private collection
NOTES: The recipes use Eagle Brand Sweetened Condensed Milk as an ingredient. The text on p 1 refers to how the recipes were collected: 'Last year, when we announced that we'd pay $25 each for new recipes using Eagle Brand Sweetened Condensed Milk, we didn't dream we'd uncover so much that is really new! ... When the offer had terminated, over 38,000 women had sent in recipes – in all, over 81,000 recipes ...'

On p 36, the reader is advised that she may write

for a copy of the book to the Borden Co. Ltd, 115 George Street, Toronto. City directories list the company at this address in 1932 and 1933 (before 1932, the company was on Richmond Street West; from 1934, its address was Yardley House, as printed in O784.2). This edition, therefore, was published about 1932–3. The text and illustrations are printed in brown.

I have seen in another private collection a single sheet (35.5 × 13.0 cm) promoting Eagle Brand Sweetened Condensed Milk. Printed on one side is a 'Molly Magic' cartoon and a book-order coupon for 'Free! A Roto-Picture Cook Book of Magic Short-Cut Recipes'; on the other side, recipes for Eagle Brand Magic Milk, the notice 'Free! Beautiful Cook Book of Magic Recipes,' and 'Compliments of,' below which is stamped 'Dominion Stores Limited // Main Street // Yarmouth N.S.'

The OGU copy lacks the cover-title and p 37.

O784.2 nd [about 1933–4]
—Magic! / The most / amazing / short-cuts / in cooking / you ever heard of [cover-title]
DESCRIPTION: 26.0 × 20.0 cm   Pp [1] 2–37   Many illus brown   [Free, on p 37]   Paper, with image on front of prepared dishes; stapled
CONTENTS: 1 'This Is No Ordinary Cook Book!'; 2–3 'You Won't Believe It ... Till You See It, But ...'; 4–5 'Here's Magic Trick No. 1 ...' [adding chocolate]; 6–7 'And Look at This Magic Trick!' [adding lemon juice]; 8–9 'Here's Another Magic Trick!' [salad dressing]; 10–11 'Still Another Magic Trick!' [caramelized sweetened condensed milk]; 12–13 'And Here's Magic [sic, no 'Trick'] No. 5' [cookies]; 14–top 15 recipes for salad dressings; mid–bottom 15 quick breads; 16–17 puddings; 18 custards; 19 sauces; 20–1 refrigerator cakes; 22–5 ice creams and sherbets; 26–7 pies and tarts; 28–top 30 cakes and cookies; mid 30–31 frostings; 32–4 candies; 35 beverages; 36 index; 37 [inside back face of binding] 'Do You Know the Answer?' and at bottom, 'Printed in Canada'
CITATIONS: Chatelaine 1935, p 82
COPIES: ARDA BVIPM OKQ (F5012 1935 B728) OTMCL (641.5971 H39 No. 33) *Private collection
NOTES: Page 1 illustrates the recipe pages of various magazines, one of which is dated 16 April 1933. Readers could write to the Borden Co. Ltd, Yardley House, Toronto, for a free copy of the book (p 37); Yardley House, at the southwest corner of Harbour and York streets, is listed as the company address in Toronto city directories from 1934 onward. This edition of *Magic!*, therefore, was published about 1933–4. The text and illustrations are printed in brown.

At Christmas, copies of this edition were distributed with an additional special cover, which reads, 'Amazing / Short-cut / Recipes/ Featuring / Christmas / Candies'; a holly-and-red-ribbon design decorates the front. Recipes for Christmas candies are printed on the inside front and back faces of the cover and there is a cross-reference to pp 32 and 33 of the book for 'more Christmas candy recipes.' The BVIPM copy has the Christmas cover.

The ARDA copy is incomplete (pp 3–34 only).

O784.3 [about 1934]
—[An edition of *Magie! Les plus étonnants raccourcis*]
CITATIONS: *Revue moderne* (November 1934)

AMERICAN EDITIONS: *Amazing Short-cuts*, 1932 (Allen, p 202). Barile, p 99, illustrates an undated edition with a binding design uniform with the two Canadian editions, O784.1 and O784.2; her citation on p 199 dates the book 1920s, probably incorrectly.

Tested recipes

O785.1 1932–3
Tested / recipes / 1932–1933 / St. Paul's United Church / Perth, Ontario [cover-title]
CONTENTS: First page 'Preface' and 'Compiled by the Women's Association of St. Paul's United Church // Perth, Ontario'
COPIES: *Private collection

1932–9

Uneeda cook book

In the 1960s, the North Gower United Church Women produced An Autographed Album of Recipes.

O786.1 nd [about 1932–9]
Uneeda / cook book / Compiled by / the Women's Association / of / North Gower United Church / Rev. H.M. Servage, Pastor [cover-title]
COPIES: *Private collection
NOTES: The cookbook was published when Harvey Servage was pastor, in the period 1932–9. The names of the women on the Recipe Committee are listed below the 'Preface': Mrs A. McFarlane, Mrs Russell Wallace, Mrs I.C. Wiltse, Mrs Geo. Stone, Mrs B.H. Craig, Mrs P. McGibbon. The women on the Advertising Committee are also named.

1933

The basic cake formula

O787.1   2nd ed., 1933

The basic / cake formula / Compiled by the / Bakery Research Department / Standard Brands Limited / Second edition 1933

DESCRIPTION: 25.5 × 17.5 cm   Pp [1–2] 3–63   Illus   Paper, with hole punched at top left corner, through which runs a string for hanging, and with two holes punched at left edge for storing in a binder

CONTENTS: 1 tp; 2 'Index'; 3–15 'The Basic Cake Formula'; 16–20 'Material Cost Calculation'; 21–5 'Producing Additional Bases by Re-mixing Other Ingredients with White or Yellow Basic Cake Mixtures'; 26–54 recipes for, and illus of, various sweet baked goods; 55–6 'Mixtures, Pastes and Fillings'; 57–mid 61 'Stock Icings'; mid–bottom 61 'Treating Dry Cocoanut'; 62–3 'Quality and Variety Is Not Enough – Merchandising Is Necessary to Win Cake Market'

COPIES: *Private collection

NOTES: 'Standard Brands Limited // Fleischmann's Baking Powder Service' is printed on the front face of the binding; 'Printed in U.S.A.' is on the outside back face. The Canadian operation of Standard Brands was based in Toronto.

Cook book

O788.1   nd [about 1933]

St. Thomas Memorial Hospital / Woman's Hospital Aid / Cook book [cover-title]

DESCRIPTION: 21.0 × 14.5 cm   Pp 1–148 [149]   Paper, with image on front of the hospital; stapled

CONTENTS: 1 'Introduction'; 2 blank; 3 'Dedication'; 4 blank; 5 'Table of Weights and Measures' and 'Fruit Chart'; 6 ads; 7–136 recipes credited with the name of the contributor, blank spaces for 'Special Recipes,' and ads; 137–45 'First Aid and Home Nursing,' blank space for 'Notes,' and ads; 146–8 'Household Hints'; 149 'Index' [i.e., table of contents]

COPIES: OONL (TX715.6 C65558 1930z, not on shelf)   *Private collection

NOTES: The 'Introduction' states: 'This book of recipes is published under the auspices of the Woman's Hospital Aid of Memorial Hospital, St. Thomas, in the hope that its sale will add considerably to the funds of the Auxiliary. Built in 1924 ... our hospital was formally dedicated at its opening, as a memorial to the men and women of St. Thomas and Elgin County who served and died in the Great War.'

An advertisement on p 76 for F. Steele refers to offering optical service 'for the past 10 years'; the first listing for F. Steele in St Thomas directories is in 1923, pointing to 1933 as the most likely year of publication. An advertisement on p 98 for W. McPhillips Ltd, which 'established a new high sales record for 1932 ...' is further evidence that the book was published in 1933.

There is an advertisement for 'Sid Gilbert // job printer,' the probable printer of the cookbook, on the inside front face of the binding. Page 136 is incorrectly numbered 137; p 137 is incorrectly numbered 136.

Cooking craft

The Port Credit branch of the Women's Institute was founded in 1910 (Ambrose, p 233).

O789.1   1933

Cooking / craft / Compiled by / Port Credit Women's Institute / 1933 [cover-title]

DESCRIPTION: 22.0 × 15.0 cm   Pp [1] 2–48   Paper, with image on front of two cakes, a loaf, and a pie; stapled

CONTENTS: 1 'Foreword' signed Committee, Mrs C.A. McLean, Mrs F.B. Pense, and Mrs J.J. Jamieson, and 'Index' [i.e., table of contents]; 2–48 recipes credited with the name of the contributor, ads, and on p 48, 'Helpful Hints,' 'Handy Table of Weights and Measures,' and 'For Serving 100 People'

COPIES: *OTYA (CPC 1933 0083)

Cornell, Miss Anna May

For Cornell's other cookbooks, see O781.1.

O790.1   [1933]

1092 / meals / and how / to save / 20% / of their cost! / By / Anna May Cornell / Home Economist / Canadian Westinghouse Co. Limited [cover-title]

DESCRIPTION: 23.5 × 31.0 cm   Pp [1–28]   Illus   Paper, with image on front of a curving line of 'meals' (i.e., the same prepared dishes) disappearing into the distance; stapled

CONTENTS: Inside front face of binding 'Feeding a Family of Four for a Year! An Experiment of Intense Interest to Every Home-Manager' and photograph of the house that contained the Westinghouse Experimental Kitchen, 'the domestic "proving ground" for Westinghouse home appliances'; 1 'Facts ... Not Theories ... Guide the Westinghouse Department of Home Economics,' 'An Astonishing Comparison,' and photograph of Miss Anna May Cornell, director of the Westinghouse Home Economics Department, at work in the Experimental Kitchen; 2–27 on versos, menus for each day in a month, and on the rectos, daily shopping lists to match those menus for housewives without a Westinghouse Refrigerator [i.e., without refrigerator storage] and weekly shopping lists for housewives with a Westinghouse Refrigerator, showing the actual savings of weekly shopping; 28 'How the Westinghouse Refrigerator Simplifies Menu Planning'; inside back face 'How to Utilize Left Overs,' 'Special Notes Regarding Menus by Anna May Cornell,' and letter from the sales manager of the Hamilton A and P Store to Miss Cornell, Canadian Westinghouse Co. Ltd, Hamilton, Ontario, dated 14 December 1933, thanking her for making her purchases at the store as part of her research for this book; outside back face 'No. 33-V-7'

CITATIONS: Chatelaine 1935, p 82

COPIES: *Private collection

NOTES: This book presents the results of the author's research into how much could be saved by shopping weekly and using a Westinghouse Refrigerator for storage, versus the costs of shopping daily for a person without a refrigerator.

Gibson, Josephine

Gibson edited O1074.1, Wartime Canning and Cooking Book. *Also by this author is* The Heinz Book of Meat Cookery, *[Pittsburgh: H.J. Heinz Co., c1934] (United States: DLC). The H.J. Heinz Co. Collection of corporate records is at the Benson Ford Research Center, Henry Ford Museum, Dearborn, Michigan.*

O791.1   nd [about 1933]
The / Heinz / salad / book / 57 / Something new in / salad books for the / woman who likes / to make every meal /a culinary triumph / Published by H.J. Heinz Company Pittsburgh Toronto London / [in circle, to left of subtitle:] The / one recipe / for all salads / ... Buy only fresh greens / Keep refrigerated in vegetable pan / Make dressing in advance ... / ... Use the very best ingredients / Make salad just before serving / ... then listen to them rave

DESCRIPTION: 22.0 × 15.0 cm   Pp [1] 2–99 [100]   Illus   Paper, with image on front of a bowl of green salad; stapled

CONTENTS: 1 tp; 2 'Here Is a Picture Book of Salad Making' signed Josephine Gibson, director, Home Economics Department, H.J. Heinz Co., Pittsburgh, Pennsylvania; 3 table of contents; 4 'We're Off to a New Adventure in Salad Making'; 5–18 'Salad Dressings'; 19–24 'Green Salads'; 25–36 'Vegetable Salads'; 37–46 'Fruit Salads'; 47–54 'The 57 Varieties,' including centre spread illus col, on pp 50–1, of Heinz products; 55–62 'Meat and Fish Salads'; 63–70 'Molded and Frozen Salads'; 71–5 'Miscellaneous Salads'; 76–83 'Canapés // Cocktails and Hors-d'oeuvres'; 84–7 'Sandwiches'; 88–90 'Equipment for Salad Making'; 91 'The Etiquette of Salad Service'; 92 'What to Serve with Salads'; 93–9 'Index'; 100 quotation from Howard Heinz, president, and at bottom right, 'Printed in U.S.A. 12333'

COPIES: *Private collection

NOTES: On p 100 Howard Heinz refers to the company's growth 'for sixty-four years'; since the company was founded in 1869, the book was published in about 1933 (1869 + 64 years). This publication date is confirmed by the printer's mark of '12333' (p 100).

O791.2   nd [about 1935]
—The Heinz book of / salads and meat recipes / Salads / appetizers / and sandwiches / for all occasions / Meat dishes to / everyone's / taste / By / Josephine Gibson / 25¢ [cover-title]

DESCRIPTION: 22.0 × 15.0 cm   Pp [1–3] 4–108   Illus   Paper, with image on front of a bowl of green salad; stapled

CONTENTS: 1 table of contents; 2 'A Picture Book of Salads and Meat Dishes' signed Josephine Gibson, director, Home Economics Department, H.J. Heinz Co.; 3–10 'Salad Dressings'; 11–12 'Green Salads'; 13–20 'Vegetable Salads'; 21–8 'Fruit Salads'; 29–34 'Meat and Fish Salads'; 35–40 'Moulded and Frozen Salads'; 41–4 'Miscellaneous Salads'; 45–9 'Canapés, Hors-d'oeuvres'; 50–2 'Sandwiches'; 53–5 'The 57 Varieties' [centre spread illus col of Heinz products]; 56–106 'Heinz Meat Recipes'; 107 list of 'The 57 Varieties Heinz Pure Foods'; 108 'A 66 Year Tradition'; inside back face of binding 'Copyright Canada, H.J. Heinz Co., Toronto Printed in Canada – 22335'

COPIES: ACG   BVAU (Beatrice M. Millar Papers) OONL (2 copies: TX807 H45 1900z copy 2, TX807 P53 1900z p***)   *Private collection

NOTES: Since the heading on p 108 refers to a sixty-six-year tradition, this edition was published about

1935 (1869 + 66 years), a date confirmed by the printer's mark, '22335.'

An advertisement on p 34 of O916.1, *Flavour Magic 57*, published by H.J. Heinz Co. in 1937, gives the price for *The Heinz Book of Salads and Meat Recipes* as $0.25 or only $0.10 if accompanied by three labels from Heinz soups.

Chatelaine 1935, p 82, cites 'Heinz Book of Salads,' available from the company for $0.10. The reference is unlikely to be for O791.2, since another reference follows to 'Heinz Book of Meat Cookery,' also for $0.10. I found no Canadian edition of the meat recipes treated in a separate volume, although there was an edition published in Pittsburgh, Pennsylvania, in 1934 (United States: DLC).

An advertisement in the February 1937 issue of *National Home Monthly* for *The Heinz Book of Salads and Meat Recipes* may refer to this or another edition.

OONL (TX807 P53 1900z p***) lacks its binding; the library has catalogued it by the heading on p 2, 'A Picture Book ...'

O791.3 [about 1935]
—[French-language edition of *The Heinz Book of Salads and Meat Recipes*]
COPIES: Private collection
NOTES: The private collector's copy is incomplete, but the last page is headed 'Une tradition qui date de 66 ans'; therefore, it was published in the same year as O791.2.

O791.4 nd [about 1937–8]
—The Heinz book of / salads and meat recipes / Salads / appetizers / and sandwiches / for all occasions / Meat dishes to / everyone's / taste [cover-title]
DESCRIPTION: 22.0 × 15.0 cm   Pp [1–3] 4–107 [108] Illus   Paper, with image on front of a bowl of green salad; stapled
CONTENTS: Inside front face of binding 'Copyright Canada, H.J. Heinz Co., Toronto Printed in Canada 20937'; 1 table of contents; 2 introduction signed Home Economics Department, H.J. Heinz Co.; 3–10 'Salad Dressings'; 11–12 'Green Salads'; 13–20 'Vegetable Salads'; 21–8 'Fruit Salads'; 29–34 'Meat and Fish Salads'; 35–40 'Moulded and Frozen Salads'; 41–4 'Miscellaneous Salads'; 45–9 'Canapés, Hors-d'oeuvres'; 50–2 'Sandwiches'; 53 'Toast to Canadian Tomatoes'; 54–5 'The 57 Varieties of Heinz Pure Foods' [centre spread illus col of Heinz products]; 56–106 'Heinz Meat Recipes'; 107 list of 'The 57 Varieties Heinz Pure Foods'; 108 'A 69 Year Tradition'

CITATIONS: Ferguson/Fraser, p 233
COPIES: OAUH   OONL (TX807 H45 1900z copy 1) QMM (RBD ckbk 1645)   *Private collection
NOTES: Josephine Gibson is not identified as the author. The reference on p 108 to 'A 69 Year Tradition' points to a publication date of about 1938 (1869 + 69 years). The printer's mark '20937' indicates printing in 1937. The book is advertised in the February 1938 issue of the *National Home Monthly*; the June 1938 issue illustrates the binding.

The QMM copy lacks its binding.

O791.5 nd [about 1937–8]
—Le livre Heinz avec / recettes de salades et de viandes / Salades / apéritifs / et sandwiches / pour / toutes occasions / Plats de viande / au goût de / tout le monde [cover-title]
DESCRIPTION: 22.5 × 15.0 cm   Pp [1–3] 4–107 [108] Illus   Paper, with image on front of a bowl of green salad; stapled
COPIES: *QSFFSC
NOTES: 'Une tradition qui date de 69 ans' suggests a publication date of about 1938. 'Copyright Canada, H.J. Heinz Co., Toronto Imprimé au Canada 20937' is on the inside front face of the binding, indicating printing in 1937. The QSFFSC copy is inscribed, on the binding, '11 avril 1946.'

AMERICAN EDITIONS: The following may or may not be related to the Canadian editions: *Heinz Book of Salads*, H.J. Heinz Co., 1925 (Dickinson, p 96, illus p 95; Vintage, May 2000); *The Heinz Salad Book*, H.J. Heinz Co., [1930s] (Vintage, May 2000).

Health Service cook book

O792.1 [copyright 1933]
Health / Service / cook / book / Foods and combinations of foods have more to do / with our physical constitutions than any / other known cause. / Prepared with the supreme desire to promote / good health / Health Service / Confederation Life Building / Toronto, Canada
DESCRIPTION: 21.5 × 13.5 cm   Pp [1–2] 3–143   Cloth
CONTENTS: 1 tp; 2 'Copyright, 1933 // Printed in Canada by the Mundy-Goodfellow Printing Co., Ltd. Toronto, Canada'; 3 'Foreword' signed Health Service; 4 'The Health Service Cook Book'; 5–137 text; 138–42 index; 143 publ ad
COPIES: OONL (TX715 H43, 2 copies)   *Private collection

NOTES: The 'Foreword' thanks Mrs F.L. Hilliard, a Toronto dietitian, for having 'given several weeks of earnest care and thought to collecting, correcting and also to furnishing many original recipes,' and Mrs H.B. Dunnington [*sic*]-Grubb of Toronto, 'a well-known student of healthful living,' for contributing several recipes. The text on p 4 stresses the importance of natural, unprocessed foods. Lorrie Alfreda Dunington (1877–1945) and her husband were English landscape architects, who established a well-known practice in Toronto after immigrating in 1911.

See also O780.1, Waite, Sheridan C., '*The Food Pilot*,' which may or may not be a related text.

O792.2 [copyright 1945]
—Food / pilot / cook / book / with which is embodied a guide to / compatible eating. / Foods and combinations of foods have more to do / with healthy bodies than any other / known cause. / Prepared with the supreme desire to promote / good health / Health Book Supply Co. / Confederation Life Building / Toronto 1, Canada
DESCRIPTION: 21.5 × 13.5 cm   Pp [1–2] 3–190   Cloth
CONTENTS: 1 tp; 2 'Copyright, 1945 Printed in Canada by the Mundy-Goodfellow Printing Co., Ltd. Toronto, Canada'; 3 'Foreword'; 4 'The Food Pilot Cook Book'; 5–173 text; 174 blank for 'Notes'; 175–84 index; 185–6 blank for 'Notes'; 187 publ ad; 188–9 ads; 190 publ ad
COPIES: OONL (TX715.6 F6415 1945)   *Private collection
NOTES: The 'Foreword' states that this is a 'revised and enlarged cook book under the new title of The Food Pilot' and that it will 'especially appeal to those who are disciples of Tilden, Hay, Jackson and others [i.e., various physicians].' In this edition, the 'Foreword' describes Mrs F.L. Hilliard as formerly of Johns Hopkins Hospital and Cleveland Clinic Hospital. The text on p 4 lists the parts of a health-giving diet in the order of their relative importance: fruits and milk; leafy greens and all raw vegetable salads; root vegetables; cereals; and high protein foods. The recipe collection is not vegetarian: There are recipes for meats, poultry, and fish, but p 88 advises that 'not more than two ounces of proteins daily are required by the normal average adult.'

The housekeeper's companion

O793.1 1933
[An edition of *The Housekeeper's Companion*, by the Ladies' Aid Society of Emmanuel Church, Belleville, Ontario, 1933]
COPIES: Private collection

The housekeepers' perfect account book 1933

See O145.1 for a list of other editions.

O794.1 1933
[*The Housekeepers' Perfect Account Book*, with calendar for 1933]
COPIES: MAUAM
NOTES: The MAUAM copy lacks the cover-title and pp 1–2. The text includes recipes.

Keep on the sunny side of life

For the titles of other Kellogg books about All-Bran, see O768.1.

O795.1 [copyright 1933]
Keep on the sunny side of life / A new way of living / [artist's signature:] F. S[?] Br[?]er [cover-title]
DESCRIPTION: 18.5 × 13.5 cm   Pp [1–2] 3–31 [32]   Illus col   Paper, with image on front of a mother, father, and son carrying a dog, all walking forward, stylized rays of sunshine in background; stapled
CONTENTS: Inside front face of binding 'Copyright 1933 by the Kellogg Company, Ltd.'; 1 'Keep on the Sunny Side of Life // A New Way of Living' signed W.K. Kellogg; 2 fp illus col of a family in a car; 3 table of contents; 4–5 'Public Enemy Number 1' [i.e., constipation]; 6–8 'What Happens to the Food You Eat'; 9 'The Dangers of Cathartics'; 10–11 'How Bran Came into General Use as a Laxative Food'; 12–14 'What Bran Adds to Your Menu'; 15 'What Is a "Bulkless" Meal?'; 16–17 'How to Serve All-Bran in Tempting Ways'; 18 fp illus col of a woman taking a box of All-Bran from a cupboard; 19–21 'The 7 Day Diet for Correcting Constipation'; 22 fp illus col of three slim women; 23 'Dieting for Charm and Chic'; 24 fp illus col of three women at a weight scale; top 25 'Ideal Weight, According to Height'; mid 25–26 '5 Rules for Reducing'; 27 fp illus col of women and a man at a swimming pool; 28–9 'One Hundred Calorie Portions of Some Commonly Used Foods'; 30–1 'A Simple Reducing Diet for One Week'; 32 'Don't Be Confused by Misleading Claims'; inside back face 'Printed in Canada.'
CITATIONS: Chatelaine 1935, p 82
COPIES: *MWPA (MG14 C50 McKnight, Ethel) ONLAM (Walters-Wagar Collection, Box 20)   OONL (TX355 K44 1933)
NOTES: No place of publication is recorded, but in 1933 the Canadian arm of Kellogg's (Kellogg Company of Canada Ltd) was based in London, Ontario, at 1097 Dundas.

Kitchen lore

O796.1 1933
Kitchen / lore / 1933 / Grace Church / (Anglican) / King Street and Grosvenor Avenue, Hamilton, Ontario / Printed / in Canada / on Canadian / paper [cover-title]
DESCRIPTION: 23.0 × 15.0 cm   Pp 1–44   Paper; stapled
CONTENTS: 1 'Preface' and 'Compiled by the Ladies' Guild of Grace Anglican Church ...'; 2–43 recipes credited with the name of the contributor, 'Suggestions for Table Decorations,' 'For Serving One Hundred People,' and ads; 44 'Index' [i.e., table of contents] and ad
COPIES: *OTNY (uncat)
NOTES: 'Heath & Fairclough Press' is on the outside back face of the binding.

Kitchen tested recipes

The Sunbeam Mixmaster (an electric mixer) was invented by Ivar Jepson, head designer for the Chicago Flexible Shaft Co. It was patented in the United States in 1928 and 1929 and first sold on the mass market in 1930. The first Canadian patent was granted in 1931 (see O919.6). For another publication about cooking with the Sunbeam Mixmaster, see O919.1, How to Get the Most Out of Your Mixmaster.

O797.1   nd [1933]
Kitchen tested / recipes / by the home economists of the famous / Sunbeam / Mixmaster / the king of food mixers / With the compliments of / [blank space for dealer's name] / We sell the Mixmaster / Price 50 cents [cover-title]
DESCRIPTION: 22.5 × 15.0 cm   Pp 1–40   Illus   Paper; stapled, and with hole punched at top left corner for hanging
CONTENTS: 1–40 recipes interspersed with information about the Mixmaster and at bottom p 40, 'Printed in Canada 1040T'
COPIES: QMM (RBD ckbk 1562)   *Private collection
NOTES: On p 19 there is a coupon for 'Free attachment for you // Not good after December 31, 1933,' indicating a publication date of 1933. There are illustrations of, and information about, attachments and accessories on pp 10–12. The name of the Canadian maker – Flexible Shaft Co. Ltd, Toronto – is on p 40.

In the QMM copy, 'Public Utilities Commission of Cobourg // Cobourg, Ontario' is printed in the space in the cover-title for the dealer's name. A copy in a bookseller's stock had 'Hatt's Hardware // Victoria, B.C.' in the space.

The mixing bowl

O798.1   1933
The / mixing / bowl / 1933 / Renfrew Presbyterian Church / Renfrew, Ont. [cover-title]
DESCRIPTION: 23.0 × 15.0 cm   Pp [1] 2–44   Paper, with image on front of a two-layer cake; stapled
CONTENTS: 1 'Preface' and 'Compiled by the Ladies' Aid of the Presbyterian Church // Renfrew, Ontario'; 2–43 recipes credited with the name of the contributor and ads; 44 ad and 'Index' [i.e., table of contents]
COPIES: *QMM (RBD ckbk 1950)   Private collection
NOTES: A small slip of 'Corrections' is glued to the gutter of p 1. 'Renfrew Mercury Print' is on the inside back face of the binding.

More selected recipes

O799.1   [1933]
More / selected recipes / [caption:] First United Church / Rev. J.E. Hughson Rev. C.C. Murray / A selection of tried and tested recipes / compiled and published / by / the Woman's Association / of / First United Church / King and Wellington streets / Hamilton Ontario
DESCRIPTION: Pp [1] 2–108   Tp illus of First United Church
CONTENTS: 1 tp; 2 'Officers' Roster // Woman's Association // First United Church Hamilton, Ontario'; 3 'Preface' signed ladies of the Woman's Association; 4–105 recipes credited with the name of the contributor and ads; 106 blank for 'My Own Recipes'; 107 ad and 'Table Decorations'; 108 'Index' [i.e., table of contents] and ads
COPIES: *Private collection
NOTES: The year of publication, 1933, is on the front face of the binding; the printer, 'Heath & Fairclough Press,' is on the back face. The 'Preface' refers to two earlier cookbooks: 'Our first effort of this kind was made in the far-off days of 1914 [O329.1] ... six years later, in 1920, we issued the second number of "Selected Recipes" [O447.1].' The 'Preface' also comments on the many culinary developments since 1920, namely 'the electric range, the mechanical refrigerator and the ready availability of exotic fruits, vegetables and materials.' See also a fourth recipe collection from the same church, O1178.1, *Cook Book*.

The O.E.S. cook book

O800.1   nd [about 1933]
The / O.E.S. / cook book / favorite recipes for your mixing bowl / We may live without poetry, music and art, / We may live without conscience and live without heart: / We may live without friends, we may live without / books, / But civilized man cannot live without cooks. / He may live without books – what is knowledge but / grieving? / He may live without hope – what is hope but deceiving? / He may live without love – what is passion but pining? / But where is the man who can live without dining? / – Lord Lyton [*sic*]. / Arranged and published by the ladies / of / Hamilton Chapter / The Order of the Eastern Star / Hamilton, Ontario
DESCRIPTION: 22.5 × 15.5 cm   Pp [1] 2–48   Thin card; stapled
CONTENTS: 1 tp; 2 'Printed in Canada on Canadian paper by the Fairclough Printing Co. Hamilton, Ontario.'; 3 preface signed Edith Dalton, W.M. [i.e., worthy matron], William Powell, W.P. [i.e., worthy patron], and Carolyn Morris, convenor; 4–45 recipes and ads; 46 'To Serve 100 People'; 47 'Time Tables'; 48 ad and index
COPIES: *Private collection
NOTES: There is an advertisement on the binding for Bryans-Currie, optometrists and opticians, succeeding I.B. Rouse, 52 King Street East, Hamilton. The city directories for 1932, and several years before, list Globe Optical (I.B. Rouse) on King Street. The 1933 directory has listings for Globe Optical (Bryans-Currie) and for Bryans-Currie (successors to I.B. Rouse), at the same address. The cookbook, therefore, was published about 1933.

The Hamilton Chapter published another cookbook, called *Recipe Book* (Private collection), for which Carolyn Morris was also the convenor. *Recipe Book* is undated, but there is an advertisement on p 34 for Wm K. Anderson, 'Radios – Television ...,' indicating publication no earlier than the 1950s.

The pantry shelf

See also O28.1, The Canadian Economist, *from the same church, when it was called Bank Street Church.*

O801.1   nd [about 1933]
The / pantry / shelf / Our tested recipes / The cook may be a scientist, / Who measures as she makes; /

And she may be an artist, / Creating as she bakes. / Her busy heart and brain and hand / May think and feel and do; / A kitchen is a happy place / To make these dreams come true. / Compiled by / the Women's Association / of / Chalmer's [*sic*] United Church / Ottawa Canada
DESCRIPTION: 23.0 × 15.5 cm   Pp 1–128   Paper; stapled
CONTENTS: 1 tp; 2 preface signed the Committee; 3–127 text; 128 index
COPIES: *OGU (UA s045 b43)
NOTES: The recipes are credited with the name of the contributor. An advertisement on p 56 for R. Brown and Son, a memorial manufacturer, suggests that the cookbook was published in 1933: 'It will be to your advantage to see our stock before placing your order for 1933.' An advertisement on p 95 for Reid's Exclusive Stove Store illustrates a 1932 model gas stove.

Rotary Ann recipe book

O802.1   [1933]
[In Rotary symbol:] Rotary International / Rotary Ann / recipe book [cover-title]
DESCRIPTION: 21.0 × 13.5 cm   Pp [1–2] 3–55   Thin card, with Rotary International symbol on front; bound by three large metal rings through punched holes
CONTENTS: 1 dedication dated Toronto, Canada, 1933; 2–55 recipes credited with the name of the contributor
CITATIONS: Ferguson/Fraser, p 234
COPIES: *OTYA (CPC 1933 0084)
NOTES: Only the recto pages are numbered; the versos are not included in the pagination. The dedication is to the Layette Workers, 'whose co-operation in [the book's] preparation is deeply appreciated'; the dedication is followed by the statement, 'Collected and compiled in the years of Bennie McTavish and Agnes Hutchinson by Tweed Williams.' The recipe for Ginger Snaps on p 14 is from Mrs Frank Stollery, wife of the owner of Stollery's, the Toronto men's clothing store at 1 Bloor Street West.

The OTYA copy is stamped on the title-page, 'Lennox and Addington Historical Society Napanee Ontario'; and inscribed on the title-page, in ink, 'The Walters' Collection.'

St Lawrence cook book

See also O419.1 by the same chapter.

O803.1 1933
[An edition of *St Lawrence Cook Book,* by the St Lawrence Chapter of the Imperial Order Daughters of the Empire, Cornwall, Ontario, 1933]
COPIES: Private collection

Rees, Margaret H.

See also O587.1, Tempting Domestic Recipes, prepared by Rees for the Harris Abattoir Co. Ltd. Rees worked as the plant dietitian at Canada Packers Ltd's head office until her retirement in the 1950s (e-mail from Kay Hodgins to Elizabeth Driver, 18 June 2001).

O804.1 copyright 1933
Tasty meals / for every day / Information about the buying, preparation and / cooking of meats, and the making of a wide / variety of tempting dishes for the home; from / tested recipes / [Canada Packers symbol] / Compiled and published under the supervision of / Margaret H. Rees, dietitian / Copyright, Canada, 1933 / Canada Packers Limited / Head office – Toronto / Plants at / Toronto – Montreal – Winnipeg – Peterborough – Hull
DESCRIPTION: 20.0 × 13.5 cm   Pp [1] 2–51 [52]   Illus col, illus   Paper, with image on front of Canada Packers Ltd's maple leaf and 'Canada Approved' symbol; stapled
CONTENTS: 1 tp; 2 'A Guide Book for Every Canadian Home' and 'The Brand of Quality'; 3 '"Canada Approved" Your Protection'; 4–5 'Meat'; 6–11 'Beef'; 12–13 'Veal at Its Best'; 14–16 'Lamb and Mutton'; 17–23 'Canadian Pork'; 24 'Fancy Meats'; 25 'Gold Cake'; 26–7 centre spread illus col of Canada Packers Ltd's products; 28 'Veal and Chicken Croquettes'; 29–mid 30 'Left Over Meats'; bottom 30 'Maple Leaf Lard'; 31–mid 32 'Pork Sausage'; bottom 32 'Cooked and Jellied Meats'; 33–4 'Pasteurized Cheese'; 35 'Domestic Shortening' and 'How to Measure'; top 36 'For Baking'; bottom 36–40 'Biscuits and Quick Breads'; 41–6 'Cakes and Cookies'; 47–8 'Pies and Pastry'; 49–50 'Deep Fat Frying'; 51 'Table of Weights and Measures'; 52 index
CITATIONS: Ferguson/Fraser, p 234, illus col on p 80 of closed volume
COPIES: MWMM   OONL (TX749 T37 1933 p***) OTMCL (641.5971 H39 No. 129)   *Private collection
NOTES: On the title-page of the OONL copy, the final

't' did not print in the line 'Plants at.' The colour illustration in Ferguson/Fraser is of the copy catalogued here. Chatelaine 1935, p 82, cites this title, but does not distinguish between the editions.

O804.2 copyright 1933
—Repas savoureux / pour tous les jours / Ce livre traite de l'achat, de la préparation et / de la cuisson des viandes. Il explique aussi la / manière de faire une grande variété de mets / appétissants pour le foyer / [Canada Packers symbol] / Préparé et publié sous la direction de / Margaret H. Rees, / autorité en diététique / Tous droits réservés, Canada, 1933 / Canada Packers Limited / Siège social – Toronto / Etablissements à / Toronto – Montréal – Winnipeg – Peterborough – Hull
DESCRIPTION: 19.5 × 13.5 cm   Pp [1] 2–51 [52]   Illus col, illus   Paper, with image on front of Canada Packers Ltd's maple leaf and 'Canada approved' symbol; stapled
CONTENTS: 1 tp; 2 'Un guide pour tous les foyers canadiens' and 'Le marque de qualité'; 3 '(Approuvé par le gouvernement) "Canada Approved" votre protection'; 4–5 'La viande'; 6–11 'Le boeuf'; 12–13 'Le meilleur veau'; 14–16 'L'agneau et le mouton'; 17–23 'Porc canadien'; 24 'Viandes de fantaisie'; 25 'Gâteau d'or'; 26–7 centre spread illus col of Canada Packers Ltd's products; 28 'Croquettes de veau et de poulet'; 29–mid 30 'Restes de viandes'; bottom 30 'Le saindoux Maple Leaf'; 31–mid 32 'Saucisse'; bottom 32 'Viandes cuites et en gelée'; 33–4 'Le fromage pasteurisé'; 35 'Shortening Domestic' and 'Comment mesurer les ingrédients'; top 36 'Pour la cuisson au fourneau'; bottom 36–40 'Biscuits et gâteaux rapides'; 41–6 'Gâteaux et biscuits'; 47–8 'Tartes et pâtisserie'; 49–50 'Grande friture'; 51 'Table de poids et mesures'; 52 'Table des matières'
COPIES: *QSFFSC

O804.3 [copyright 1933]
—Tasty meals / for every day / Information about the buying, preparation and / cooking of meats, and the making of a wide / variety of tempting dishes for the home; from / tested recipes / [Canada Packers symbol] / Compiled and published under the supervision of / Margaret H. Rees, dietitian / Canada Packers Limited / Head office – Toronto / Plants at / Toronto – Montreal – Winnipeg – Peterborough – Hull
DESCRIPTION: 19.5 × 13.5 cm   Pp [1] 2–51 [52]   Illus col, illus   Paper, with image on front of Canada Packers Ltd's maple leaf and 'Canada Approved' symbol; stapled

COPIES: *NSYHM   QMM (RBD ckbk 1388)
NOTES: There is no date on the title-page. Printed on the inside front face of the binding is 'Copyright, Canada, 1933 Canada Packers Limited.'

O804.4   copyright 1938
—Tasty meals / for every day / Information about the buying, preparation and / cooking of meats, and the making of a wide / variety of tempting dishes for the home; from / tested recipes / [Canada Packers symbol] / Compiled and published under the supervision of / Margaret H. Rees, dietitian / Copyright, Canada, 1938 / Canada Packers Limited / Head office – Toronto / Plants at / Toronto – Montreal – Winnipeg – Peterborough – Hull / Edmonton – Vancouver
DESCRIPTION: 20.0 × 13.5 cm   Pp [1] 2–51 [52]   Illus col, illus   Paper, with image on front of Canada Packers Ltd's maple leaf and 'Canada Approved' symbol; stapled
CONTENTS: 1 tp; 2 'A Guide Book for Every Canadian Home' and 'The Brand of Quality'; 3 '"Canada Approved" Your Protection'; 4–5 'Meat'; 6–11 'Beef'; 12–13 'Veal at Its Best'; 14–16 'Lamb and Mutton'; 17–23 'Canadian Pork'; 24 'Fancy Meats'; 25 'Gold Cake'; 26–7 centre spread illus col of Canada Packers Ltd's products; 28 'Veal and Chicken Croquettes'; 29–mid 30 'Left Over Meats'; bottom 30 'Maple Leaf Lard'; 31–mid 32 'Pork Sausage'; bottom 32 'Cooked and Jellied Meats'; 33–4 'Pasteurized Cheese'; 35 'Domestic Shortening' and 'How to Measure'; top 36 'Approximate Time and Temperature for Baking Pastry and Pies'; bottom 36–40 'Biscuits and Quick Breads'; 41–6 'Cakes and Cookies'; 47–8 'Pies and Pastry'; 49–50 'Deep Fat Frying'; 51 'Table of Weights and Measures'; 52 index
COPIES: OONL (TX749 T37 1938)   OPEMO   *Private collection

OTHER EDITIONS: *Tasty Meals for Every Day ... Margaret H. Rees*, Toronto: Canada Packers Ltd, 1953 (QMM RBD uncat).

Scott, Anna Lee [pseudonym]

For information about Anna Lee Scott and her cookbooks, see O526.1.

O805.1   [1933]
What / shall we have / for / dinner / and how much / will it cost / by / Anna Lee Scott [cover-title]

DESCRIPTION: 24.0 × 16.5 cm   Pp 1–28   Paper; stapled
CONTENTS: Inside front face of binding introductory note and 'Presented by the Maple Leaf Milling Company, Limited ... Toronto Winnipeg'; 1–28 a menu and recipes, plus their cost, for each day in the week for four weeks, one day per page; inside back face 'Special Recipes for "Tea-Bisk"' by Anna Lee Scott, in English and French
COPIES: *Private collection
NOTES: The introductory note indicates that the recipes are designed to feed a family of four adults and that 'the prices are those prevailing in Toronto in the early months of 1933, ...' There are advertisements for Maple Leaf Milling Co. products at the bottom of each page.

Tested recipes

O806.1   1933
Tested / recipes / 1933 / Women's Association / Grace–St. Andrew's United Church / Arnprior, Ontario [cover-title]
DESCRIPTION: 23.0 × 15.0 cm   Pp [1] 2–48   Small illus head some chapters   Paper, with image on front of the church
CONTENTS: 1 'Preface' and 'Index' [i.e., table of contents]; 2–48 text
COPIES: *OGU (UA s070 b49)

The 'Wear-Ever' new method of cooking

For an earlier cookbook promoting 'Wear-Ever' products, see O429.1. For other publications by Aluminum Goods Ltd, see O966.1, Cooking Made Easy with a Wear-Ever Pressure Cooker, *and O1195.1,* The 'Wear-Ever' PM Recipe Booklet.

O807.1   [1933]
[Wear-Ever Aluminum trademark symbol] / The / "Wear-Ever" / new method of / cooking / health / flavor / economy / Aluminum Goods Limited / 158 Sterling Road / Toronto 3, Ontario
DESCRIPTION: 23.0 × 15.5 cm   Pp [1] 2–47 [48]   Illus col, illus   Paper, with image on front of the front-facing silhouette of a woman in a full-length dress, carrying a covered dish; stapled
CONTENTS: 1 tp; 2 'Contents'; 3–4 'Health'; 5 'Origin of New Method of Cooking'; 6–8 'The "Wear-Ever" New Method of Cooking'; 9 'Suggestions'; 10–44 recipes; 45 'Vitamins'; 46 'Auxiliary Items of New Method Equipment'; 47 'The Care of "Wear-Ever" Utensils';

48 'For Over a Third of a Century "Wear-Ever" Has Given Satisfactory Service ...' and at bottom, 'Form C.U. 120–100M–12-33. Printed in U.S.A.'

CITATIONS: Chatelaine 1935, p 82

COPIES: *Private collection

NOTES: The title-page is printed in blue and black. The 'Origin of New Method Cooking' on p 5 refers to the research of Margaret Mitchell of the 'Wear-Ever' Test Kitchen. The text is addressed to American housewives. The printer's mark on p 48 records 1933 as the year of publication.

A Canadian private collector has a 48-page book, which, at first glance, appears to be an earlier American edition, except that almost none of the recipes matches those in the 1933 Canadian edition described here. The title-page reads: 'The / "Wear-Ever" / new method of cooking / and / 100 tested recipes / from the / Priscilla Proving Plant / Copyright 1929 / [on label applied over a mostly illegible, but American, imprint:] Aluminum Goods Limited / 158 Sterling Road, Toronto, Ontario / [printed upside down: illegible numbers and] U.S.A.' On p 48, there is a reference to twenty-nine years of the 'Wear-Ever' trademark, indicating that the trademark was registered in 1900 [1929 – 29 years]; a list of branch sales offices, all in the United States; and 'Form No. CU-120 Printed in U.S.A. William G. Johnston Company Pittsburgh, Pa.' On p 43 there is a 'Modern Priscilla Certificate of Approval' certifying that 'Wear-Ever' products were tested from 1 January to 1 May 1927 at the Priscilla Proving Plant, of which Della Thompson Lutes [1872–1942] was director.

O807.2   copyright 1935

—[Wear-Ever Aluminum trademark symbol] / The / "Wear-Ever" / new method of / cooking / health / flavor / economy / Aluminum Goods Limited / 158 Sterling Road / Toronto, Canada / Copyright 1935

DESCRIPTION: 23.0 × 15.0 cm   Pp [1] 2–48 [49–51] Illus col, illus   Paper, with image on front of the front-facing silhouette of a woman in full-length dress, carrying a covered dish; stapled

CONTENTS: 1 tp; 2 'Contents'; 3–4 'Health'; 5 'Origin of New Method of Cooking'; 6–8 'The "Wear-Ever" New Method of Cooking'; 9 'Suggestions'; 10–44 recipes; 45 'Vitamins'; 46–7 'Auxiliary Items of "Wear-Ever" New Method Equipment'; 48 'The Care of "Wear-Ever" Utensils'; 49 'For Over a Third of a Century "Wear-Ever" Has Given Satisfactory Service in Millions of Homes' and at bottom, 'Form C.U. 120–

5M–4-35 Printed in U.S.A. by William G. Johnston, Co., Pittsburgh, Pa.'; 50 blank; 51 blank, ruled lines for customers to request 'additional information about "Wear-Ever" ...'

COPIES: *Private collection

NOTES: This copy is stamped on the outside face of the binding, front and back, 'R.H. Thaler // Kitchener Ont // 146 Lancaster St. East.'

The Westinghouse Refrigerator book

O808.1   nd [about 1933]

The / Westinghouse Refrigerator book / [Canadian Westinghouse symbol] [cover-title]

DESCRIPTION: 21.5 × 14.0 cm   Pp 1–48   Illus col, illus Paper, with image col on front of a woman carrying a rectangular container of pink liquid toward a refrigerator; stapled

CONTENTS: Inside front face of binding table of contents; 1 'Your Westinghouse Refrigerator // What It Is and What It Does' signed Department of Home Economics, Canadian Westinghouse Co. Ltd; 2 'Why It Is Hermetically Sealed' and 'Sealed for Lifetime Efficiency'; 3 'Why It Is Dual-Automatic' and 'The Priceless Boon – Peace of Mind'; 4 'The Seven Point Temperature Selector' and 'The Scrupulous Sanitation of Spotless Porcelain'; 5 'The Ageless Beauty of Its Appearance,' 'Lifetime Dulux Finish,' and 'Even in Details ... Perfection'; 6–7 'The Extra Conveniences That Mean So Much'; 8 'How It Saves You Money'; 9 'How It Protects Your Health' and 'How It Saves You Work and Worry'; 10 'How It Safeguards Your Investment' and 'How It Makes Meals More Tempting'; 11–17 'Frozen Desserts'; 18–20 'Refrigerator Cakes and Puddings'; 21–2 'Ice Cream and Pudding Sauces'; 23–5 'Beverages'; 26–8 'Baked Goods'; 29–31 'Canapés and Cocktails'; 32–6 'Left Overs'; 37–44 'Sandwiches Salads'; 45 'Salad Dressings'; 46 'Temperature Selector' and 'Cleaning'; top–mid 47 'Defrosting' and 'Food Arrangement'; bottom 47–mid 48 'Food Storage'; mid–bottom 48 'Dessert Making'; inside back face 'Suggestions'

COPIES: *Private collection

NOTES: Printed on the outside back face of the binding is '33V3 Printed in Canada.' No specific place of publication is cited, but Canadian Westinghouse Co. Ltd was based in Hamilton.

See also O778.1, likely an earlier version of this text. This edition of *The Westinghouse Refrigerator Book* has the same image on the binding as O778.1.

O808.2   nd [about 1933]

—The / Westinghouse owner's / refrigerator book [cover-title]

DESCRIPTION: With image on front of an open refrigerator; stapled

CONTENTS: Inside front face of binding 'Contents'; 1 'Your Westinghouse Refrigerator // What It Is and What It Does' signed Department of Home Economics, Canadian Westinghouse Co. Ltd; ...

COPIES: *Private collection

NOTES: The 48-page volume has 'Printed in Canada – 33-V-3' on the back face of the binding. This edition, therefore, was likely published about the same time as O808.1. The image on the binding is different from O808.1: There is no figure and the refrigerator appears larger since it is seen close-up. This is the only edition called *The Westinghouse Owner's Refrigerator Book*.

O808.3   1936

—The / Westinghouse / Refrigerator / book [cover-title]

DESCRIPTION: With two circles on front: one circle with the letter W in the centre surrounded by the words 'Westinghouse Golden Jubilee 1886 1936' and the other circle with a refrigerator in the centre surrounded by 'The new [bra]nd of refrigerator value'; stapled

COPIES: *Private collection

NOTES: The book's owner reports that it has 47 pp.

O808.4   nd

—The / Westinghouse / Refrigerator / book [cover-title]

DESCRIPTION: 21.0 × 14.0 cm   Pp 1–35 [36]   A few small illus   Paper, with images on front of two cold desserts, each in a circular frame; stapled

CONTENTS: 1 'Your Westinghouse Refrigerator // What It Is and What It Does' signed Department of Home Economics, Canadian Westinghouse Co. Ltd; 2 'How It Saves You Money'; 3 'How It Safeguards Your Investment,' 'How It Protects Your Health,' and 'How It Makes Meals More Tempting'; 4 'New Convenience' and 'Cleaning'; top–near bottom 5 'Temperature Selector'; bottom 5–mid 6 'Defrosting'; mid 6 'Food Arrangement'; bottom 6–top 7 'Food Storage'; mid–bottom 7 'Dessert Making'; 8 'Suggestions'; 9–13 'Frozen Desserts'; 14–15 'Refrigerator Cakes and Puddings'; 16–17 'Ice Cream and Pudding Sauces'; 18–19 'Beverages'; 20–1 'Baked Goods'; 22–3 'Canapés and Cocktails'; 24–5 'Left Overs'; 26 'Meat Left-overs' and 'Fish Left-overs'; 27 'Vegetable Left-overs,' 'Fruit Left-overs,' and 'Ice Cream Left-overs'; 28–34 'Sand-

wiches Salads'; 35 'Salad Dressings'; 36 blank for 'Memorandum'

COPIES: *ACG   OONL (TX830 W47 1900z, 2 copies)

NOTES: This is the only 36-page edition where 'Salad Dressings' is on p 35 (in O808.5 and O808.6, 'Salad Dressings' is on p 36). A pocket is bound in at the back of the book, following p 36, to hold a leaflet. The ACG and OONL copies retain the instruction leaflet for Westinghouse Model 'G' Refrigerator. The location of Canadian Westinghouse Co. Ltd, Hamilton, is recorded on the pocket of the ACG copy. Printed on the outside back face of the binding is 'Form No. 6006.'

O808.5   nd

—The / Westinghouse / Refrigerator / book [cover-title]

DESCRIPTION: 21.5 × 14.0 cm   Pp 1–36   A few small illus   Very thin card, with images on front of two cold desserts, each in a circular frame; stapled

CONTENTS: 1 'Your Westinghouse Refrigerator // What It Is and What It Does' signed Department of Home Economics, Canadian Westinghouse Co. Ltd, and at bottom, 'No. 6016'; 2 'How It Saves You Money'; 3 'How It Safeguards Your Investment,' 'How It Protects Your Health,' and 'How It Makes Meals More Tempting'; 4 'Installing Your New Refrigerator'; 5 'Cleaning and Maintenance of Cabinet' and 'Food Arrangement'; 6 'Temperature Selector'; top–mid 7 'Defrosting'; mid 7–top 8 'Cleaning Condenser'; mid 8–9 'Dessert Making'; 10–14 'Frozen Desserts'; 15–16 'Refrigerator Cakes and Puddings'; 17–18 'Ice Cream and Pudding Sauces'; 19–20 'Beverages'; 21–2 'Baked Goods'; 23–4 'Canapés and Cocktails'; 25–6 'Left Overs'; 27 'Meat Left-overs' and 'Fish Left-overs'; 28 'Vegetable Left-overs,' 'Fruit Left-overs,' and 'Ice Cream Left-overs'; 29–35 'Sandwiches Salads'; 36 'Salad Dressings'

COPIES: *Private collection

NOTES: In this 36-page edition, 'Salad Dressings' is on p 36, but, unlike O808.6, there is no title-page.

O808.6   nd [about 1941]

—The Westinghouse / Refrigerator / recipe book / Recipes tested and recommended / by / Department of Home Economics, / Canadian Westinghouse Co. Ltd., / Hamilton, Canada / No. 6037-J

DESCRIPTION: 21.0 × 14.5 cm   Pp [1] 2–36   A few small illus   Paper, with images on front of two cold desserts, each in a circular frame; stapled

CONTENTS: 1 tp; 2 'Your Westinghouse Refrigerator // What It Is and What It Does' [unsigned]; 3 'How

It Saves You Money'; 4 'How It Safeguards Your Investment,' 'How It Protects Your Health,' and 'How It Makes Meals More Tempting'; 5 'Index' [i.e., table of contents] and 'Cleaning and Maintenance of Cabinet'; 6 'Food Arrangement'; 7 'Temperature Selector'; top 8 'Defrosting'; mid 8–9 'Dessert Making'; 10–14 'Frozen Desserts'; 15–16 'Refrigerator Cakes and Puddings'; 17–18 'Ice Cream and Pudding Sauces'; 19–20 'Beverages'; 21–2 'Baked Goods'; 23–4 'Canapés and Cocktails'; 25–6 'Left Overs'; 27 'Meat Left-overs' and 'Fish Left-overs'; 28 'Vegetable Left-overs,' 'Fruit Left-overs,' and 'Ice Cream Left-overs'; 29–35 'Sandwiches Salads'; 36 'Salad Dressings'

CITATIONS: Simpson, p W17

COPIES: *OGU (CCC TX715.6 W48)   OH (R641.5 WES CESH)

NOTES: In this 36-page edition, 'Salad Dressings' is on p 36, and there is a title-page. The original owner of the OGU copy writes in an accompanying note, 'This book came with our first refrigerator in 1941.' A copy in a private collection confirms this date; it is inscribed on the title-page, 'July 11th. 1941.'

ACG and OWTU have copies where the only apparent difference is '151 P734' instead of 'No. 6037-J' on the title-page. A private collector has a copy where the only apparent difference is 'Form B.H. 7061 // 705-P8122' instead of 'No. 6037-J.'

O808.7   nd
—[An edition of *Le livre de recettes du réfrigérateur Westinghouse*, nd, pp 36]
CITATIONS: BouquinsCat 212, No. 383

O808.8   nd
—The / Westinghouse / Refrigerator / book [cover-title]
DESCRIPTION: 21.5 × 14.0 cm   Pp 1–47   Illus col, illus Paper, with images on front of two cold desserts, each in a circular frame; stapled
CONTENTS: 1 'Your Westinghouse Refrigerator // What It Is and What It Does' signed Department of Home Economics, Canadian Westinghouse Co. Ltd; 2 'How It Saves You Money'; 3 'How It Protects Your Health' and 'How It Saves You Work and Worry'; 4 'How It Safeguards Your Investment' and 'How It Makes Meals More Tempting'; 5 'Cleaning' and 'Temperature Selector'; 6 'Defrosting' and 'Food Arrangement'; bottom 6–top 7 'Food Storage'; 7 'Dessert Making'; 8 'Suggestions'; 9–15 'Frozen Desserts'; 16–18 'Refrigerator Cakes and Puddings'; 19–20 'Ice Cream and Pudding Sauces'; 21–3 'Beverages'; 24–6 'Baked Goods'; 27–9 'Canapés and Cocktails'; 30–4 'Left Overs'; 35–42 'Sandwiches Salads'; 43 'Salad

Dressings'; 44–7 blank for 'Additional Recipes May Be Written or Pasted Here'
COPIES: OGU (CCC TX715.6 W48)   *Private collection
NOTES: In this edition, 'Salad Dressings' is on p 43.

In Ferguson/Fraser, the reference on p 233 and the colour illustration on p 57 of the closed volume are probably of this edition, the one consulted by the authors for *A Century of Canadian Home Cooking*.

AMERICAN EDITIONS: *The Westinghouse Refrigerator Book*, Westinghouse Electric and Manufacturing Co., copyright 1933, 'Printed in U.S.A. 50M–7-33 (BVAMM); Westinghouse Electric and Manufacturing Co., copyright 1934, '50M–4-35 Printed in U.S.A.' (BVAMM).

1933–4

Milligan, Madeleine L.

O809.1   nd [about 1933–4]
Frozen delicacies / and / chilled salads / prepared by / Madeleine L. Milligan, B.Sc. / home economist / with suggestions for the care / and most satisfactory use / of your Universal Cooler. / Universal Cooler Corporation / Detroit, U.S.A. Windsor, Canada
COPIES: *Private collection
NOTES: The 'Foreword,' signed Universal Cooler Corporation, states that the recipes in the book 'will offer further evidence of the convenience and economy of electrical refrigeration.' The staple-bound book has 31 pp. The title-page is stamped at bottom, 'Printed in U.S.A.,' and at top, 'The R.W. Bierwagen Electric Co. 357 King St. W. Phone 3290 Kitchener Ontario.' Kitchener city directories list this form of the Bierwagen name at 357 King Street West for 1933 and 1934.

1933–5

The new art of buying, preserving and preparing foods

O810.1   6th ed., nd [about 1933–5]
The new art / of buying, preserving / and preparing foods / Presented by / General Electric / Kitchen Institute / Canadian General Electric / Co. / Limited / Price $1.00 Printed in Canada / Form No. SP-257-6th edition

DESCRIPTION: 19.0 × 13.5 cm Pp [1–3] 4–112 Illus col, illus Very thin card, with image on front of an artist's palette, a wooden fork and spoon in place of brushes, and prepared dishes in place of dabs of paint; sewn

CONTENTS: 1 tp; 2 'In the Kitchens of the G-E Institute'; 3 table of contents; 4–106 text; 107–12 index

COPIES: *AHRMH (987-035-007) OSGM

NOTES: Page 9 illustrates 'Before ... The old-fashioned kitchen' and 'After ... The modern General Electric Kitchen –' No place of publication is recorded, but Canadian General Electric Co. was based in Toronto.

The New Art of Buying, Preserving and Preparing Foods, numbered as the sixth edition, was preceded by five editions of O740.1, *The 'Silent Hostess' Treasure Book*. The fifth Canadian edition of *The 'Silent Hostess' Treasure Book* bears the copyright date 1933. The earliest identified American edition of *The New Art of Buying, Preserving and Preparing Foods* was published in 1933. Chatelaine 1935, p 82, cites 'The New Art (cook book), 25c.,' but does not specify the edition. The sixth edition of *The New Art ...*, therefore, was published about 1933–5.

Ferguson/Fraser, p 234, cite an edition of about 1935, but do not specify the edition number.

O810.2 7th ed., nd

—The new art / of buying, preserving / and preparing foods / Presented by / General Electric / Kitchen Institute / Canadian General Electric / Co. / Limited / Price $1.00 Printed in Canada / Form No. SP-257-7th edition

DESCRIPTION: 19.0 × 13.5 cm Pp [1–3] 4–112 Illus col, illus Very thin card, with image on front of an artist's palette, a wooden fork and spoon in place of brushes, and prepared dishes in place of dabs of paint; sewn

CONTENTS: 1 tp; 2 'In the Kitchens of the G-E Kitchen Institute'; 3 'Table of Contents'; 4–106 text; 107–12 'Index'

COPIES: *Private collection

O810.3 8th ed., nd

—The new art / of buying, preserving / and preparing foods / Presented by / General Electric / Kitchen Institute / Canadian General Electric / Co. / Limited / Price $1.00 Printed in Canada / Form No. SP-257-8th edition

DESCRIPTION: 19.0 × 13.5 cm Pp [1–3] 4–112 Illus col, illus Thin card, with image on front of an artist's palette, a wooden fork and spoon in place of brushes, and prepared dishes in place of dabs of paint; sewn

CONTENTS: 1 tp; 2 'In the Kitchens of the G-E Kitchen Institute'; 3 'Table of Contents'; 4–106 text; 107–12 'Index'

COPIES: *OGU (CCC TX715.6 G452 1933) ONM

O810.4 9th ed., 1936

—The new art / of buying, preserving / and preparing foods / Presented by / General Electric / Kitchen Institute / Canadian General Electric / Co. / Limited / Price $1.00 Printed in Canada / Form No. 257-36-9th edition

DESCRIPTION: 19.0 × 13.0 cm Pp [1–3] 4–112 Illus col, illus Very thin card, with image on front of an artist's palette, a wooden fork and spoon in place of brushes, and prepared dishes in place of dabs of paint; sewn

CONTENTS: 1 tp; 2 'In the Kitchens of the G-E Kitchen Institute'; 3 table of contents; 4–106 text; 107–12 index

COPIES: *Private collection

NOTES: The text on p 4 states, 'Electricity has made possible many new and better methods of kitchen management and it is the purpose of the [General Electric Kitchen] Institute to study, develop and perfect these methods ...'

O810.5 10th ed., 1936

—The new art / of buying, preserving / and preparing foods / Presented by / General Electric / Kitchen Institute / Canadian General Electric / Co. / Limited / Price $1.00 Printed in Canada / Form No. 257-36-10th edition

DESCRIPTION: 19.0 × 13.0 cm Pp [1–3] 4–112 Illus col, illus Very thin card, with image on front of an artist's palette, a wooden fork and spoon in place of brushes, and prepared dishes in place of dabs of paint; sewn

CONTENTS: 1 tp; 2 'In the Kitchens of the G-E Kitchen Institute'; 3 table of contents; 4–106 text; 107–12 index

COPIES: *Private collection

O810.6 11th ed., 1937

—The new art / of buying, preserving / and preparing foods / Presented by / General Electric / Kitchen Institute / Canadian General Electric / Co. / Limited / Price $1.00 Printed in Canada / Form No. 257-37 11th edition 20M 1-37

DESCRIPTION: 19.0 × 13.0 cm Pp [1–3] 4–114 Illus col, illus

CONTENTS: 1 tp; 2 'In the Kitchens of the G.E. Kitchen Institute'; 3 table of contents; 4–108 text; ...

COPIES: *Private collection

O810.7   12th ed., 1938
—The new art / of buying, preserving / and preparing foods / Presented by / General Electric / Kitchen Institute / Canadian General Electric / Co. / Limited / Price $1.00 Printed in Canada / Form No. 257-37 12th edition 25M 1-38
COPIES: *Private collection

O810.8   13th ed., 1939
—The new art / of buying, preserving / and preparing foods / Presented by / General Electric / Kitchen Institute / Canadian / General Electric / Company Limited / Price $1.00 Printed in Canada / Form 300-39, 13th edition, 25M 1-39.
DESCRIPTION: 19.0 × 13.5 cm   Pp [1–3] 4–124   Illus col, illus   Thin card, with image on front of a table set with prepared dishes for a buffet meal; bound by a metal clasp through slots in the paper
CONTENTS: 1 tp; 2 'In the Kitchens of the G-E Kitchen Institute'; 3 table of contents; 4–118 text; 119–24 index
COPIES: *MWMM   OGU (CCC TX715.6 N474 1939)   OONL (TX715.6 N474 1940z)

O810.9   14th ed., 1940
—The new art / of buying, preserving / and preparing foods / Presented by / General Electric / Kitchen Institute / Canadian / General Electric / Company Limited / Price $1.00 Printed in Canada / Form 300-40, 14th edition, 3-40
DESCRIPTION: 19.0 × 13.5 cm   Pp [1–3] 4–128   Illus col, illus   Card, with image on front of a table set with prepared dishes for a buffet meal; bound by a metal clasp through slots in the paper
CONTENTS: 1 tp; 2 'In the Kitchens of the G.E. Kitchen Institute'; 3 'Table of Contents'; 4–119 text; 120–2 blank for 'Notes'; 123–8 index
COPIES: *Private collection

O810.10   15th ed., 1941
—GE / The new art / of / modern cooking / A complete book of favorite recipes and suggested menus / with helpful hints for modern preservation and preparation / of food as tested and tasted by the Home Service Division of / Canadian General Electric Co. Limited, Toronto, Canada / Canadian General Electric Co. Limited / Price $1.00 Printed in Canada / Form 300-41, 15th edition, 1-41
DESCRIPTION: 19.0 × 13.5 cm   Pp [1–3] 4–128   Illus col, illus   Card, with image on front of a table set with prepared dishes for a buffet meal; bound by a metal clasp through slots in the paper
CONTENTS: 1 tp; 2 'In the Kitchens of the G.E. Kitchen Institute'; 3 'Table of Contents'; 4–119 text; 120–2 blank for 'Notes'; 123–8 index

COPIES: *Private collection
NOTES: This and subsequent editions are retitled *The New Art of Modern Cooking*.

O810.11   5th ed., 1941
—L'art nouveau / dans l'achat, la conservation / et la preparation des aliments / Tel qu'exposé par / l'Institut culinaire / General Electric / Canadian / General Electric / Company Limited / Prix $1.00 Imprimé au Canada / Montreal, P.Q. / Forme no. 300-41F. 5ième edition
DESCRIPTION: 19.0 × 13.0 cm   Pp [1–3] 4–105   Illus Paper; stapled
CONTENTS: 1 tp; 2 'Dans les cuisines de l'Institut culinaire General Electric'; 3 'Table des matières'; 4–96 text; 97–8 blank for 'Notes'; 99–105 'Index'
COPIES: *QSFFSC
NOTES: The numbering of the French-language editions is separate from that of the English-language editions. There are no colour illustrations. This copy is inscribed on the title-page and on the binding, in ink, '30 juillet 1945.'

O810.12   16th ed., 1942
—GE / The new art / of / modern cooking / A complete book of favorite recipes and suggested menus / with helpful hints for modern preservation and preparation / of food as tested and tasted by the Home Service Division of / Canadian General Electric Co. Limited, Toronto, Canada / Canadian General Electric Co. Limited / Printed in Canada / Form 300-42, 16th edition, 6-42 / Wire-O Binding, patented 1936
DESCRIPTION: 19.0 × 13.5 cm   Pp [1–2] 3–140   Illus col, illus   Thin card, with image on front of a table set with prepared dishes for a buffet meal; Wire-O binding
CONTENTS: 1 tp; 2 table of contents; 3–132 text; 133–4 blank for 'Notes'; 135–40 index
COPIES: ACG   QSFFSC   QSTHS   *Private collection

O810.13   17th ed., 1945
—GE / The new art / of / modern cooking / A complete book of favorite recipes and suggested menus / with helpful hints for modern preservation and preparation / of food as tested and tasted by the Home Service Division of / Canadian General Electric Co. Limited, Toronto, Canada / Canadian General Electric Co. Limited / Form 300-45, 17th edition, 2-45 Printed in Canada / Price $1.00 / Wire-O Binding, Patented 1936
DESCRIPTION: 19.0 × 13.5 cm   Pp [1–2] 3–140   Illus col, illus   Very thin card, with image on front of a

table set with prepared dishes for a buffet meal; Wire-O binding
CONTENTS: 1 tp; 2 table of contents; 3–132 text; 133–4 blank for 'Notes'; 135–40 index
COPIES: *Private collection

O810.14   18th ed., 1946
—GE / The new art / of / modern cooking / A complete book of favorite recipes and suggested menus / with helpful hints for modern preservation and preparation / of food as tested and tasted by the Home Service Division of / Canadian General Electric Co. Limited, Toronto, Canada / Canadian General Electric Co. Limited / Form 300-46, 18th edition, 2-46 Printed in Canada / Price $1.00
DESCRIPTION: 19.0 × 13.0 cm   Pp [1–2] 3–140   Illus col, illus   Thin card, with image on front of a table set with prepared dishes for a buffet meal; wire
CONTENTS: 1 tp; 2 'Table of Contents'; 3–132 text; 133–4 blank for 'Notes'; 135–40 'Index'
COPIES: *QMM (RBD ckbk 1411)

AMERICAN EDITIONS: *The New Art of Buying, Preserving and Preparing Foods,* Cleveland: General Electric Kitchen Institute, 1933 (United States: DLC, MCR); Cleveland: General Electric Kitchen Institute, 1935 (Vintage, May 2000); *The New Art of Modern Cooking ... as Tested by the Home Service Division of the General Electric Institute, Nela Park, Cleveland, Ohio,* [Cleveland: Institute], c1937 (United States: MCR).

1933–6

Kitchen craft

O811.1   nd [about 1933–6]
Kitchen craft / A / selection of tested recipes / compiled and published by the ladies of / the Admiral Collingwood Chapter / of / the Imperial Order Daughters of the Empire / Collingwood Ontario / Foreword [two paragraphs follow]
DESCRIPTION: About 23.0 × 15.5 cm [dimensions from photocopy]   Pp [1] 2–28   With IODE symbol on front; stapled
CONTENTS: 1 tp; 2–27 recipes credited with the name of the contributor; 28 ad and 'Index' [i.e., table of contents]
COPIES: *Private collection
NOTES: 'This book was printed by the Enterprise-Bulletin ... Simcoe Street // Collingwood' is on the outside back face of the binding. On the inside front face, there is an advertisement for 'Trott's // over 70 years

in Collingwood.' Trott's was a home furnishing and funeral business. OCOLM reports that Trott's celebrated its seventy-fifth anniversary on 12 March 1937 (a photograph of the event is at the museum); therefore, its seventieth anniversary was in 1932. The cookbook was published sometime between these two anniversaries.

1934

[Title unknown]

O812.1   1934
[Title unknown of a cookbook published by the Church of St Clement's Eglinton [Anglican], Toronto, Ontario, Parochial Guild, in 1934, as a fund-raising project]
NOTES: Joyce Lewis, a food historian and member of St Clement's Eglinton, knows about the publication of this book from her research into the history of the church. No copy has been located.

Community Service Club recipe book

O813.1   1934
Community Service / Club / recipe book / 1934 / Timothy Eaton Memorial Church / Toronto, Ontario [cover-title]
CITATIONS: CBCat 61, No. 90
COPIES: *Private collection
NOTES: CBCat 61 records the book as having 100 pp.

Cooking with cold

See O656.1 for information about Kelvinator of Canada Ltd and its cookbooks.

O814.1   nd [about 1934]
Cooking / with cold / To the modern woman who / looks on home-making as both / a science and an art .. [sic, only two ellipsis points] who / appreciates the importance of / good foods and attractive / meals appetizingly served ... / the makers of Kelvinator / dedicate this book ... in the / hope that she will find in it / much to help her in the fulfill- / ment of her undertakings. / Kelvinator of Canada Limited / London, Ontario
DESCRIPTION: 14.0 × 19.0 cm   Pp [1] 2–55 [56]   Illus col, illus   Paper; stapled

CONTENTS: 1 tp; 2–3 'Index' [i.e., table of contents]; top 4 'Correct Food Placement'; bottom 4–5 'Food Storage'; 6–7 'Some Important Kelvinator Features ... and How to Use Them'; 8–9 'How to Care for ... Your Kelvinator'; 10–11 'General Suggestions for ... Cooking with Cold'; 12–13 'The Care and Use ... of Leftovers'; 14–41 recipes for appetizers, entrees, salads, ices, sherbets, mousses, parfaits, ice creams, sponges, miscellaneous desserts, iced beverages, baking, sandwiches, and hors d'oeuvres; 42–3 'Suggestions for ... the Modern Hostess'; 44–5 'Bridge Luncheon'; 46–7 'Afternoon Tea'; 48–9 'Informal Dinner'; 50–1 'Buffet Supper'; 52–3 'For the Woman ... with Small Children'; 54–5 'Children's Party'; 56 illus of Kelvinator factory in London, Ontario, and at bottom, 'Printed in Canada Form C 2596'
CITATIONS: FitzPatrickCat 111 (April 1993) No. 11
COPIES: OL (London Room Box 338)   OONMS   *Private collection
NOTES: Another collector's copy (not the one catalogued here) has '... Form C 2596 5M-7-34' on p 56, and a leaf of two perforated, book-order forms (postcards), at the front and back of the volume.

Chatelaine 1935, p 82, lists this title as available upon request for $0.15, but does not indicate the number of pages; therefore, the reference may refer to O814.1 or O814.2.

O814.2   [1935]
—Cooking / with cold / To the modern woman who / looks on home-making as both / a science and an art ... who / appreciates the importance of / good foods and attractive / meals appetizingly served ... / the makers of Kelvinator / dedicate this book ... in the / hope that she will find in it / much to help her in the fulfill- / ment of her undertakings. / Kelvinator of Canada Limited / London, Ontario
DESCRIPTION: 14.0 × 19.5 cm   Pp [i–ii], [1] 2–51 [52], [i–ii]   Illus col, illus   Paper; stapled
CONTENTS: i–ii book-order forms [i.e., two postcards]; 1 tp; 2–3 'Index' [i.e., table of contents]; top 4 'Correct Food Placement'; bottom 4–5 'Food Storage'; 6–7 'General Suggestions for ... Cooking with Cold'; 8–9 'The Care and Use ... of Left-overs'; 10–37 recipes for appetizers, entrees, salads, ices, sherbets, mousses, parfaits, ice cream, sponges, miscellaneous desserts, iced beverages, baking, and sandwiches; 38–9 'Suggestions for ... the Modern Hostess'; 40–1 'Bridge Luncheon'; 42–3 'Afternoon Tea'; 44–5 'Informal Dinner'; 46–7 'Buffet Supper'; 48–9 'For the Woman ... with Small Children'; 50–1 'Children's Party'; 52 illus of Kelvinator factory in London, Ontario, and at bottom, 'Printed in Canada Form C 2596 5M-4-35'; i–ii book-order forms [two postcards]

COPIES: *Private collection
NOTES: This edition has fewer pages. The title-page has been reset, but the line endings remain the same. Whereas on the title-page of O814.1, the first ellipsis is formed of only two points and the company name is in capital letters in the phrase 'makers of KELVINATOR,' here the first ellipsis is formed of three points and the company name is in upper- and lower-case letters.

De Wolfe, Ellen Anderson (Elsie) (New York City, 20 December 1865–12 July 1950, Versailles, France)

Elsie de Wolfe is recognized as the first female professional interior decorator in the United States. She married Sir Charles Mendl in 1926. For her autobiography, see After All, *New York: Harper and Brothers, 1935; reprint, New York: Arno Press, 1974.*

O815.1   [1934]
[First edition of *Recipes for Successful Dining* by Elsie de Wolfe (Lady Mendl), London, England, and Toronto: William Heinemann Ltd, [1934], pp ix, 116]
DESCRIPTION: Frontis portrait
CITATIONS: Bitting, p 124
COPIES: Great Britain: LB (7942.s.36); United States: DLC (TX715 D496 1934a)

O815.2   1947
—[Another edition of *Recipes for Successful Dining*, London, England, and Toronto: W. Heinemann Ltd, 1947, pp 116]
CITATIONS: Axford, p 344

AMERICAN EDITIONS: *Elsie de Wolfe's Recipes for Successful Dining*, New York: D. Appleton-Century Co. Inc., 1934 (United States: DLC); New York: William-Frederick Press, January 1947, reprinted May 1947 (Bookseller's stock).

Favorite recipes

O816.1   [1934]
Favorite recipes / a collection / of / tested recipes / compiled and published / by / the ladies / of / Christ Church Guild / Christ's Church / (Anglican) / River Road Niagara Falls, Ont.
DESCRIPTION: Stapled
COPIES: *ONF (LHC 641.5 Chr)
NOTES: The year of publication, 1934, is printed on the front face of the binding.

Favorite recipes

O817.1   1934
Favorite recipes / a collection / of / tested recipes / compiled and arranged / by / the Young Womens' [*sic*] Society / of / Knox United Church / London, Ontario
DESCRIPTION: 23.0 × 15.0 cm   Pp [1–3] 4–64   Thin card; stapled
CONTENTS: 1 tp; 2 'Printed in Canada on Canadian paper // Hayden Press, Limited London, Ontario'; 3 'Thank You' signed Helen M. Elliott, president, and Evelyn McLachlan, secretary; 4–63 text, blank spaces for 'New Recipes,' and ads; 64 'Index' [i.e., table of contents]
COPIES: OL (London Room Box 179b)   *Private collection
NOTES: The year of publication, 1934, is printed on the front face of the binding. The recipes are credited with the name of the contributor. There is a section of 'Quantity Recipes' on pp 57–8, which includes, for example, Potato Salad for 50 People, Pie Crust for 14 Pies, and 100 Baking Powder Biscuits.

Favorite recipes

For information about Lydia E. Pinkham Medicine Co. and its cookbooks, see O614.1.

O818.1   nd [about 1934]
Favorite / recipes / Save time and money [cover-title]
DESCRIPTION: 17.5 × 11.0 cm   Pp [1] 2–32   Illus Paper, with image on front of an aproned woman stirring the contents of a bowl; stapled
CONTENTS: 1 'A Word to Women Readers' signed Lydia E. Pinkham Medicine Co., Lynn, Massachusetts, and Cobourg, Ontario; 2 testimonials; 3–31 recipes, testimonials, and publ ads; 32 publ ad
COPIES: *MBDHM   OKQ (F5012 1919 L983)   OONL (TX715 L94 1930z)   OTUTF (uncat patent medicine)
NOTES: A publisher's advertisement on p 17 says, 'If Lydia E. Pinkham were alive today she would be 115 years old.' Since Lydia Estes Pinkham was born in 1819, the date of publication is about 1934. There is a recipe for Depression Sponge Cake on p 3.

O818.2   nd [about 1934]
—Recettes / favorites / Épargnez du temps et de l'argent [cover-title]
DESCRIPTION: 17.5 × 11.5 cm   Pp [1] 2–32   Illus Paper, with image on front of an aproned woman stirring the contents of a bowl; stapled

CONTENTS: 1 'Un mot à nos lecteurs' signed Lydia E. Pinkham Medicine Co., Lynn, Massachusetts, and Cobourg, Ontario; 2 testimonials; 3–31 recipes, testimonials, and publ ads; 32 publ ad
COPIES: *QSFFSC
NOTES: As in the English-language edition, there is a publisher's advertisement on p 17 that says, 'Si Lydia E. Pinkham vivait aujourd'hui elle aurait 115 ans.'

AMERICAN EDITIONS: There is an American edition at OTUTF (uncat patent medicine): only the Lynn, Massachusetts, address is on p 1; the cookery text, illustrations, and cover design are the same as the Canadian edition described above, but the type setting is different, as are the publisher's advertisements and the testimonials.

Gooderham, Charles Benjamin (1883–), and Miss Mary Lilian Heeney (1907–)

For another work co-authored by Heeney, see O721.5. For a list of other cookbooks published by the Department of Agriculture, see O404.1.

O819.1   1934
Honey / and some of the ways it may be used / by / C.B. Gooderham / Dominion Apiarist / and / M.L. Heeney / specialist in cooking and preserving of foods / Bee Division / Dominion Experimental Farms / Dominion of Canada / Department of Agriculture / Pamphlet No. 161 – New Series / Published by direction of the Hon. R. Weir, Minister of Agriculture, / Ottawa, 1934 [cover-title]
DESCRIPTION: 24.0 × 16.0 cm   Pp [1–2] 3–15   Paper; rebound in cloth, together with other Pamphlets
CONTENTS: 1 cover-title; 2 blank; 3 table of contents; 4 blank; 5–6 'Honey and Some of the Ways It May Be Used'; top–mid 7 'The Use of Honey in Home Cooking'; mid 7–15 recipes and at bottom p 15, 'Ottawa: Printed by J.O. Patenaude, ... 1934.'
CITATIONS: Ag 1867–1974, p 30   CCat No. 13, p O24
COPIES: *OOAG (630.4 C212 P161 N.S.)

O819.2   1934
—Le miel / et quelques façons de l'utiliser / par / C.B. Gooderham / Apiculteur du Dominion / et / M.L. Heeney / spécialiste en cuisson et en conservation des aliments / Service de l'apiculture / Fermes expérimentales fédérales / Ministère fédéral de l'agriculture / Canada / Feuillet n° 161 – Nouvelle série / Publié par ordre de l'hon. R. Weir, ministre de l'agriculture, / Ottawa 1934 [cover-title]

DESCRIPTION: 23.5 × 16.0 cm   Pp [1–2] 3–16   Paper; rebound in cloth, together with other Pamphlets
CONTENTS: 1 cover-title; 2 table of contents and 'Version française par C.E. Mortureux, B.S.A.'; 3–6 'Le miel et quelques façons de l'utiliser'; top–mid 7 'L'emploi du miel dans la cuisine'; mid 7–16 [outside back face of binding] recipes and at bottom p 16, 'Ottawa: J.-O. Patenaude, imprimeur ... 1934'
CITATIONS: Ag 1867–1974, p 22
COPIES: *OOAG (630.4 C212 P161 N.S.)
NOTES: On p 6 Gooderham refers to 'Miss' Heeney's recipes, evidence that his co-author was an unmarried woman.

O819.3   1st revision, April 1936
—Publication 501 / Household Bulletin 2 / Issued April, 1936 / First revision / Dominion of Canada, Department of Agriculture / Honey and some of the / ways it may be used / by / C.B. Gooderham / and / M.L. Heeney / Bee Division / Dominion Experimental Farms / Published by authority of the Hon. James G. Gardiner, Minister of Agriculture / Ottawa, Canada [cover-title]
DESCRIPTION: 25.0 × 16.5 cm   Pp [1–4] 5–20   Fp illus on p 2 of a table set with dessert dishes   Paper; stapled
CONTENTS: 1 cover-title; 2 fp illus; 3–4 table of contents; 5–6 'Honey and Some of the Ways It May Be Used'; top–mid 7 'The Use of Honey in Home Cooking'; mid 7–20 recipes
CITATIONS: Ag 1867–1974, p 23
COPIES: *BSUM   OOAG (630.4 C212 P501, 2 copies)   QMAC (S133 A346 No. 501)
NOTES: The recipes were 'tested and proved by the writer [i.e., Heeney] in the Central Experimental Farm kitchen at Ottawa' (p 7).

O819.4   1st revision, April 1936
—Publication n° 501 / Bulletin de la ménagère n° 2 / Publié en avril 1936 / Première revision / Dominion du Canada – Ministère de l'agriculture / Le miel / et quelques façons de l'utiliser / par / C.B. Gooderham / et / M.L. Heeney / Service de l'apiculture / Fermes expérimentales fédérales / Publié par ordre de l'hon. James G. Gardiner, ministre de l'agriculture. / Ottawa, 1936 [cover-title]
DESCRIPTION: 24.0 × 15.5 cm   Pp [1–3] 4–23   Fp illus on p 6 of a table set with dessert dishes   Paper; rebound in cloth, together with other Household Bulletins
CONTENTS: 1 cover-title; 2 blank; 3–4 table of contents and at bottom p 4, 'Version française par C.E. Mortureux, B.S.A.'; 5–7 'Le miel et quelques façons

de l'utiliser'; top–mid 8 'L'emploi du miel dans la cuisine'; mid 8–23 recipes
CITATIONS: Ag 1867–1974, pp 6 and 24
COPIES: *OOAG (630.4 C212 HB2 Fr)

O819.5   2nd revision, April 1937
—Publication 501 / Household Bulletin 2 / Issued April, 1937 / Second revision / Dominion of Canada, Department of Agriculture / Honey and some of the / ways it may be used / by / C.B. Gooderham / and / M.L. Heeney / Bee Division / Dominion Experimental Farms / Published by authority of the Hon. James G. Gardiner, Minister of Agriculture / Ottawa, Canada [cover-title]
DESCRIPTION: 24.5 × 16.5 cm   Pp [1–3] 4–23   Fp illus on p 6 of a table set with dessert dishes   Paper; stapled
CONTENTS: 1 cover-title; 2 blank; 3–4 table of contents; 5–7 'Honey and Some of the Ways It May Be Used'; top–mid 8 'The Use of Honey in Home Cooking'; mid 8–23 recipes and at bottom p 23, 'Ottawa: Printed by J.O. Patenaude, I.S.O., printer to the King's Most Excellent Majesty, 1937.'
COPIES: *OOAG (630.4 C212 P501, 3 copies)

O819.6   1937
—[An edition of *Le miel et quelques façons de l'utiliser*, 1937]
COPIES: QQLAS (S133 A346 F501)

O819.7   3rd revision, March 1938
—Publication 501 / Household Bulletin 2 / Issued March, 1938 / Third revision / Dominion of Canada, Department of Agriculture / Honey and some of the / ways it may be used / by / C.B. Gooderham / and / M.L. Heeney / Bee Division / Dominion Experimental Farms / Published by authority of the Hon. James G. Gardiner, Minister of Agriculture, / Ottawa, Canada [cover-title]
DESCRIPTION: 25.0 × 16.5 cm   Pp [1–3] 4–23   Fp illus on p 6 of a table set with dessert dishes   Paper; stapled
CONTENTS: 1 cover-title; 2 blank; 3–4 table of contents; 5–7 'Honey and Some of the Ways It May Be Used'; top–mid 8 'The Use of Honey in Home Cooking'; mid 8–23 recipes and at bottom p 23, 'Ottawa: Printed by J.O. Patenaude, I.S.O., ... 1938.'
CITATIONS: Ag 1867–1974, p 32
COPIES: *OOAG (630.4 C212 P501, 3 copies, and 630.4 C212 HB2)

O819.8   reprint, September 1938
—Publication 501 / Household Bulletin 2 / Issued

September, 19[torn off, but likely '38'] / Reprint / Dominion of Canada – Department of Agriculture / Honey and some of the / ways it may be used / by / C.B. Gooderham / and / M.L. Heeney / Bee Division / Dominion Experimental Farms / Published by authority of the Hon. James G. Gardiner, Minister of Agriculture, / Ottawa, Canada [cover-title]
DESCRIPTION: 25.0 × 16.5 cm   Pp [1–3] 4–23   Fp illus on p 6 of a table set with dessert dishes   Paper; stapled
CONTENTS: 1 cover-title; 2 blank; 3–4 table of contents; 5–7 'Honey and Some of the Ways It May Be Used'; top–mid 8 'The Use of Honey in Home Cooking'; mid 8–23 recipes and at bottom p 23, 'Ottawa: Printed by J.O. Patenaude, I.S.O., ... 1938.'
COPIES: *Private collection

O819.9   reprint, March 1940
—Publication 501 / Household Bulletin 2 / Issued March, 1940 / Reprint / Dominion of Canada – Department of Agriculture / Honey and some of the / ways it may be used / by / C.B. Gooderham / and / M.L. Heeney / Bee Division / Experimental Farms Service / Published by authority of the Hon. James G. Gardiner, Minister of Agriculture / Ottawa, Canada / 20M–3636-3-40 [cover-title]
DESCRIPTION: 25.0 × 16.5 cm   Pp [1–3] 4–23   Fp illus of a table set with dessert dishes   Paper; stapled
CONTENTS: 1 cover-title; 2 blank; 3–4 table of contents; 5–7 general information about honey; top–mid 8 'The Use of Honey in Home Cooking'; bottom 8–23 recipes and at bottom p 23, 'Ottawa: Printed by J.O. Patenaude, I.S.O., printer to the King's Most Excellent Majesty, 1940.'
COPIES: OGU (CCC TX715.6 M572 No. 521)   *Private collection
NOTES: According to p 5, Canada produced 37,819,900 pounds of honey in 1938.

O819.10   reprint, March 1940
—Publication nº 501 / Bulletin de la ménagère nº 2 / Publié en mars 1940 / Réimpression / Dominion du Canada – Ministère de l'agriculture / Le miel / et quelques façons de l'utiliser / par / C.B. Gooderham / et / M.L. Heeney / Division de l'apiculture / Service des fermes expérimentales fédérales / Publié par ordre de l'hon. James G. Gardiner, ministre de l'agriculture. / Ottawa, 1940 [cover-title]
DESCRIPTION: 25.0 × 16.5 cm   Pp [1–3] 4–24   Fp illus on p 6 of a table set with dessert dishes   Paper; stapled
CONTENTS: 1 cover-title; 2 blank; 3–4 table of contents; 5–7 'Le miel et quelques façons de l'utiliser'; top–mid 8 'L'emploi du miel dans la cuisine'; mid 8–24 recipes and at bottom p 24, 'Ottawa: J.-O. Patenaude, O.S.I., imprimeur ... 1940.'
COPIES: OOAG (630.4 C212 P501 Fr, 3 copies, and 630.4 C212 HB2)

O819.11   reprint, April 1942
—Publication 501 / Household Bulletin 2 / Issued April, 1942 / Reprint / Dominion of Canada – Department of Agriculture / Honey / and some of the ways / it may be used / by / C.B. Gooderham / and / M.L. Heeney / Bee Division / Experimental Farms Service / Published by authority of the Hon. James G. Gardiner, Minister of Agriculture / Ottawa, Canada / 20M–5556-4-42 [cover-title]
CITATIONS: Ag 1867–1974, p 32
COPIES: OGU (CCC CA1 DA9 36P01)   *Private collection
NOTES: No copy was found at OOAG, despite the citation in Ag 1867–1974.

Helpful hints for housekeepers [about 1934]

See O263.1 for information about the company and other issues of Helpful Hints for Housekeepers.

O820.1   nd [about 1934]
Dodd's / helpful / hints / for / housekeepers [cover-title]
DESCRIPTION: 18.0 × 12.5 cm   Pp 1–32   Illus   Paper, with image on front, in oval frame, of a woman's head; stapled, and with hole punched at top left corner, through which runs a string for hanging
CONTENTS: 1–32   culinary, entertaining, and housekeeping information, jokes and games, publ ads, health advice, and rules of etiquette
COPIES: *OTUTF (uncat patent medicine)
NOTES: A testimonial on p 16 indicates that the book was published about 1934: 'I was farming up to 1926 but for the past 8 years have been Postmaster here.' For culinary information, see: 'When You Entertain,' p 1; 'A Few Useful Hints,' p 6; 'Weights and Measures,' p 10; 'Use Lemons,' p 11; 'Grapefruit,' p 15; untitled text, pp 20 and 21; and 'Kitchen Equivalents,' p 29.

Home-proved baking recipes [Blossom of Canada Flour]

See also O971.1, Home-Proved Baking Recipes, which may or may not be a related text. Lakeside Milling Co. Ltd, founded in 1928, was bought by Maple Leaf Milling Co. in 1950.

O821.1 [copyright 1934]
Blossom / of / Canada / Home-proved / baking / recipes / Issued by / the Lakeside Milling Co. Limited / Princess St. Toronto [cover-title]
DESCRIPTION: With image on front of a large head of wheat and kitchen utensils; stapled
COPIES: *Private collection
NOTES: The first page is headed, 'Home-Proved Baking Recipes by and for Canadian Women' and is signed the Lakeside Milling Co. Ltd, Princess Street, Toronto, 'Copyright, 1934, by Lakeside Milling Co., Limited // Printed in Canada.' It reads, 'The thought was to take the ripe experience of good home-bakers, add the expert knowledge of a group of dietitians of first rank, and blend both into a handy-size, convenient-form volume ...'

The Hostess blue book

O822.1 copyright 1934
The / Hostess / blue / book / Price 65 cents / Copyrighted, 1934 / Presented by / Hostess Corporation Limited / Head office: Toronto / Montreal Halifax Winnipeg / Calgary Vancouver
DESCRIPTION: 19.5 × 13.5 cm   Pp [1] 2–63 [64]   Illus col, illus   Paper, with image on front of a plate, glass, cutlery, and flowers; stapled
CONTENTS: 1 tp; 2 fp illus of 'An Average Family Size Hostess Servador Refrigerator Showing the Proper Cabinet Location of Food'; 3 foreword by Jay Margaret Laws, director of home economics, Hostess Corp. Ltd, and a portrait of Laws; 4–5 introduction; 6–7 'Index to Contents'; 8 'Index to Illustrations'; 9 fp illus of 'Table Set for Formal Luncheon'; 10–11 'Menu Suggestions'; 12–61 recipes; 62 'Practical Hints'; 63 'Weights and Measures,' 'Substitutions,' and 'Sizes of Cans'; 64 blank for 'Memoranda'
COPIES: OONL (TX715.6 H67 1934)   *Private collection
NOTES: Hostess Corp. was a 'wholly owned subsidiary of International Metal Industries Limited, a Canadian company ... with executive and head offices located at Toronto' (p 4). The Hostess Servador

Refrigerator was 'designed and developed in [the company's] Experimental and Engineering Departments at Toronto' and introduced to the public 'several years ago' (p 5).

O822.2 copyright 1936
—The / Hostess / bluebook [*sic*] / Price 65 cents / Copyrighted, 1936 / Presented by / Hostess Corporation Limited / Head office: Toronto / Montreal Moncton Winnipeg / Calgary Vancouver
DESCRIPTION: 19.5 × 13.5 cm   Pp [1–3] 4–63 [64]   Tp illus blue-and-black of a refrigerator, illus col, illus   Very thin card, with image on front of a plate, glass, cutlery, and flowers; stapled
CONTENTS: 1 tp; 2 illus of Hostess Servador Refrigerator; 3 untitled and unsigned foreword; 4–5 'Introduction'; 6–7 'Index to Contents'; 8 'Index to Illustrations'; 9 fp illus of 'Table Set for Formal Luncheon'; 10–11 'Menu Suggestions'; 12–61 recipes; 62 'Practical Hints'; 63 'Weights and Measures'; 64 fp illus of the company's main plant and head office, 101 Hanson Street, Toronto
COPIES: *QMMMCM (AR-M2000.92.38)
NOTES: The 'Introduction' begins, 'Hostess Corporation Limited is a wholly owned subsidiary of International Metal Industries Limited, a Canadian company ...'

O822.3 copyright 1937
—The / Hostess / blue book / Price 65 cents / Copyrighted, 1937 / Presented by / Hostess Corporation Limited / Head office: Toronto / Montreal Moncton Winnipeg / Calgary Vancouver
DESCRIPTION: 19.5 × 13.5 cm   Pp [1–3] 4–63 [64]   Tp illus blue-and-black of a refrigerator, illus col, illus   Very thin card, with image on front of a plate, glass, cutlery, and flowers; Wire-O binding
CONTENTS: 1 tp; 2 fp illus of Hostess Servador Refrigerator; 3 untitled and unsigned foreword; 4–5 'Introduction'; 6–7 'Index to Contents'; 8 'Index to Illustrations'; 9 fp illus of 'Table Set for Formal Luncheon'; 10–11 'Menu Suggestions'; 12–61 recipes; 62 'Practical Hints' and 'Important Essentials'; 63 'Weights and Measures,' 'Substitutions,' and 'Sizes of Cans'; 64 fp illus of the company's main plant and head office, 101 Hanson Street, Toronto
COPIES: *OONL (TX715.6 H67 1937 p***)
NOTES: The 'Introduction' begins, 'Hostess Servador Refrigerators are truly Canadian! Hostess Corporation Limited is a wholly owned subsidiary of International Metal Industries Limited, a Canadian company ...'

Kitchen lore

Parkdale Presbyterian Church, now called Bonar-Parkdale, is on Dunn Avenue.

O823.1   nd [1934]
Kitchen / lore – / A collection of / tried and tested recipes / compiled and published by the / members of / the Ladies Aid Society / Parkdale Presbyterian Church / Toronto, Ontario / [caption:] Parkdale Presbyterian Church / organized 1879.
DESCRIPTION: Tp illus of the church
COPIES: *Private collection
NOTES: There is a list of officers for 1934 on p 3. The volume has 58 pp. 'Table Decorations' are on p 56; 'New Recipes,' on p [57]; and 'Index,' p [58].

Kitchen lore

O824.1   [1934]
Kitchen / lore / A collection of / tried and tested recipes / compiled and published by the members of / the Women's Association / of / Zion United Church / Brantford Ontario
DESCRIPTION: 23.0 × 15.5 cm   Pp 1–72   Tp illus of Zion United Church   Paper; stapled
CONTENTS: 1 tp; 2 'Printed in Brantford // Made in Canada'; 3 preface signed the Committee; 4 'Roster of Officers and Members of the Executive Committee of the Women's Association of Zion United Church 1934'; 5–71 text and ads; 72 'Index' [i.e., table of contents]
COPIES: *Private collection
NOTES: Following the recipes there are sections for 'To Serve 100 People' on p 67, 'Gelatin (How to Use It)' on p 68, 'Time Tables' on p 69, 'Which Vegetable Is Best with That Meat' on p 70, and 'Suggestions for Table Decorations' on p 71.

Magic recipes

For information about the company and its other books, see Q106.1.

O825.1   nd [about 1934]
Magic / recipes / Quicker, easier / surer to succeed / [caption:] Did you ever hear of a lemon pie filling – / creamy and lemon-y and smooth – that is / made without cooking? See pages 28 to 31 / for this and other truly amazing pie recipes. / [caption:] A miracle here! Every / lovely candy pictured / at the

right is made / without going near a / stove! See pages 32 to 34. / [caption:] And who said ice cream / making is lots of trou- / ble? Expensive? Better / see pages 15 to 17! [cover-title]
DESCRIPTION: 25.5 × 20.0 cm   Pp [3] 4–34   Many illus brown   Paper, with six images on front and back of dishes made with Eagle Brand Sweetened Condensed Milk
CONTENTS: 3 'It's Thrilling for Beginners!,' 'It's Marvellous in Emergencies!,' and 'It's Soul-Satisfying to a Seasoned Cook!'; 4 'If You Skip This Page You May Fail with These Recipes!' [explanation of the difference between sweetened condensed milk and evaporated milk]; 5–7 recipes for salad dressings; 8 custards; 9–11 puddings incl 'Magic Caramel Pudding' on p 11; 12 sauces; 13–14 refrigerator cakes; 15–17 ice cream; 18–19 'Five-Star Successes for Your Parties ...'; 20 beverages; 21–4 cakes and cookies; 25–7 frostings; 28–31 pies; 32–4 candies; inside back face of binding index, 'Some Eagle Brand Left Over?' and at bottom, 'Printed in Canada // Photo-Engravers and Electrotypers Ltd. Toronto'
COPIES: QMMMCM (AR-M2000.92.37)   *Private collection
NOTES: On p 3 and opposite, there are illustrations of recipe columns in various magazines, one of which (*Delineator*) is dated 1934.

O825.2   nd [about 1940]
—Magic recipes / Quicker, easier; / surer to succeed / [caption:] Old-fashioned ice cream made / a new-fashioned way! ... See / page 4 / [caption:] Creamy lemon filling made / without cooking! ... See page 17 [cover-title]
DESCRIPTION: 20.5 × 12.5 cm   Pp [1] 2–23   Illus brown   Paper, with images on front of ice cream sundae and lemon pie; stapled
CONTENTS: 1 cover-title; 2 'What Does It Mean ... Cooking by Magic?'; 3 'If You Skip This Page You May Fail With These Recipes!'; 4–6 'The Best Ice Creams an Automatic Refrigerator Ever Made!'; 7 'Magic Milk Makes Perfect Freezer Ice Creams!'; 8 'Sauces Made in a Twinkling!'; 9 'Salad Dressings!'; 10–11 'Work a Few Miracles with Custards and Puddings'; 12–13 'A Ten-Year-Old Can Make Cookies with Magic!'; 14 'Tea Specialties'; 15 'Hot and Cold Beverage Secrets'; 16–17 'Hard to Make Good Pies?'; 18 filling and frosting recipes; 19–21 'Let's Make Candy!'; 22 information about Borden's Eagle Brand Sweetened Condensed Milk; 23 [inside back face of binding] index and at bottom, 'Printed in Canada E540'
COPIES: *ACG   OGU (CCC TX715.6 M357)

NOTES: From appearances, this edition was published later than O825.1, likely about 1940.

AMERICAN EDITIONS: 1932 (Allen, p 202); [New York: Borden Co., 1939] (United States: DLC).

The mixing bowl

O826.1   [December 1934]
The / mixing / bowl / A selection of tried and tested / recipes / compiled and published by / the Governor Simcoe Chapter of the / Imperial Order, Daughters of the Empire / Simcoe Ontario
DESCRIPTION: 23.0 × 15.0 cm   Pp [1] 2–48   Thin card, with IODE symbol on front
CONTENTS: 1 tp; 2 'Imperial Order Daughters of the Empire in Simcoe'; 3 'Preface,' 'Compiled by the Imperial Order, Daughters of the Empire in Simcoe December 1934,' 'Officers of Chapter for 1934,' and 'Life Members'; 4–46 recipes credited with the name of the contributor, blank spaces for 'Memoranda,' and ads; 47 ad and 'Suggestions for Table Decorations'; 48 ad and 'Index' [i.e., table of contents]
COPIES: *OGU (CCC TX715.6 M5737)
NOTES: The history on p 2 states that the IODE was organized in Simcoe on 15 August 1914 and describes the chapter's achievements to date. 'Reformer Printing Shop, Simcoe' is on the outside back face of the binding.

The mixing-bowl

O827.1   [1934]
The / mixing-bowl / A collection of / tried and tested recipes / A Recipe for a Happy Day / [twelve-line verse beginning, 'A little dash of water cold, ...'] / – Selected by Mrs. T.S. McGillivray. / Compiled / by / the Ladies' Association / of / St. Paul's Presbyterian Church / Hamilton Ontario
DESCRIPTION: Pp [1–2] 3–76   Stapled
CONTENTS: 1 tp; 2 'Preface' signed the Committee; 3–73 recipes credited with the name of the contributor and ads; 74 'Home Catering in Large Amounts'; 75 ad and 'Table Decorations'; 76 'Index' [i.e., table of contents] and ads
COPIES: *Private collection
NOTES: The year of publication, 1934, is printed on the front face of the binding.

The mystery chef's own cook book

The 'mystery chef' was John MacPherson, a cooking star on American radio in the 1930s.

O828.1   1st ed., 1934
[First edition of *The Mystery Chef's Own Cook Book*, New York and Toronto: Longmans, Green and Co., 1934, 21.0 cm, pp xviii, 366, frontis]
CITATIONS: Bitting, p 580
COPIES: United States: CLob COMC CTo CU CU-SB CoDU CtNh DLC FTaSU IEuC ILfB IaU IdU KMK MCR MiD MnM MoK NBPu NBuBE NIC NNStJ NRRI NcMoB NcSppA NjN OC OCl OKentU ScCJW (TX715 M2 1934) ScRhW SdB TxCM (TX715 M2) TxDaM TxLoL TxSmS ViSwC WM WU
NOTES: No copies have been found in Canada, which suggests the book was not sold here, despite the Toronto place of publication. Yet, it is advertised in the IODE magazine *Echoes* (October 1934), p 31: 'The famous radio star who has done revolutionary things for the "Art of excellent cooking" presents his own cook book, a really explicit exposition for the beginner, ...'

O828.2   1935
—[Another edition of *The Mystery Chef's Own Cook Book*, New York and Toronto: Longmans, Green and Co., 1935, 21.0 cm, pp xviii, 366, frontis, cloth]
CITATIONS: Bitting, p 580
COPIES: United States: NN   OC

AMERICAN EDITIONS: New York: Longmans, 1940 (Barile, p 201); reprint, Garden City, NY: Garden City Publishing Co., 1943 (United States: CoDJW, ScCJW, ViNJW); reprint, Philadelphia: Blakiston Co., [1945] (BVA); 8th printing, Garden City, NY: Garden City Publishing Co., 1949 (Bookseller's Stock).

The pantry shelf

O829.1   [1934]
The / pantry / shelf / 1934 / Trinity United Church / Kitchener Ontario [cover-title]
DESCRIPTION: 22.5 × 15.0 cm   Pp [leaf lacking] 3–72   Paper
CONTENTS: 3 preface signed 'Ladies of the Women's Association'; 4–67 recipes and ads; 68 'Time Tables'; 69 'Household Hints'; 70 ad and blank space for 'New Recipes'; 71 ad and 'Table Decorations'; 72 ad and

'Index' [i.e., list of recipe sections in alphabetical order, plus the concluding topics]

COPIES: *Private collection

NOTES: The copy catalogued here is in poor condition. Another collector's copy retains the first leaf, where p 1 is the undated title-page:

The / pantry / shelf / A selection of tried and tested recipes / compiled and published by / the Women's Association of / Trinity United Church / Kitchener Ontario

Page 2 has 'Made in Canada // Merchants Printing Co. Limited Kitchener, Ontario.' 'Large Quantity Recipes' begin on p 60; 'To Serve 100' is on p 63.

Read, Miss Jessica (Jessie) Madeline (Mrs Robert Stuart Hately) (Lucan, Ont., 15 February 1905–8 April 1940, Toronto, Ont.)

Although born in Lucan, Ontario, Jessie Read grew up in Toronto. She was educated at Fern Avenue Public School, Parkdale Collegiate, and Central Technical School, where she studied dietetics and from which she graduated in 1925. After training in dietetics at the Royal Victoria Hospital in Montreal, she returned to Toronto to work for the Home Service Department of Consumers' Gas Co., first under Miss Helen Wilson, then, from 1929, as director, assisted by Miss Laura Pepper and, later, Miss Helen Bates (Pepper later worked for the federal Department of Agriculture; for her cookbooks, see O676.1). Read became well known through her cooking demonstrations for Consumers' Gas Co.; regarding her evening lectures, see Dorothy Dignam, 'Mama's Night Out,' Gas Age–Record Vol. 70, No. 26 (24 December 1932), pp 669–71. One private collector reported to me that, when she was a girl, she attended Consumers' Gas classes on Saturdays in February 1932, with other members of her Girl Guide troop; she still owns the 'Free Recipe Sheets,' which were handed out each week, to be kept bound by two rings in a cover titled Tested Recipes from the Home Service Department of the Consumers' Gas Company. *Read also gained a wide audience through her weekly broadcasts for the company's Radio Cooking School on CKCL. (For information about the Radio Cooking School, see O558.1,* Radio Recipe Note Book, *published when Miss Gladys Eaton was director of the Home Service Department.) Some time in the period 1925–34, Read was associated with a Bloor Street West restaurant called the Diet Kitchen Tea Room (see her obituary, cited below.) Also in this period, she contributed to O589.1,* New Recipes Baumert Cheese, *the 'Foreword' of which thanks her and others.*

In April 1934, Read left Consumers' Gas to write daily columns for the Toronto Evening Telegram, *called 'Three Meals a Day' (a full-page advertisement in the* Telegram *of 28 March 1934, p 48, with a photograph of Read, announces the start of the column on 2 April). The recipes in these columns were subsequently gathered together and published as books.*

In spring 1936 she starred in 'the first cooking school talking picture to be made in Canada,' called Kitchen Talks. *Made by Commercial Talking Pictures Ltd of Toronto, it was backed by national advertisers and sponsored by the Provincial Council of Women of Ontario (part of the National Council of Women). The* Telegram *ran stories chronicling the making of the film, from Read's signing of the contract in March to the film's preview at the Royal York Hotel on 9 June, and newspaper photographs show long queues of women waiting to enter cinemas in the over three hundred Ontario cities and towns where the film was screened (see, for example, the following* Telegram *articles: 'Telegram Dietician Signs Film Contract,' 11 March 1936, p 14; 'On the Set,' 17 April 1936, p 9; 'The Final Set ...,' 9 May 1936, p 10; 'The Last Day of Shooting,' 14 May 1936, p 3; 'At the Movies,' a report of the film's preview by Helen Allen, 10 June 1936, p 36).*

*In summer 1939, Read travelled to the New York World's Fair and reported in a full-page article, with photographs, on all the food-related exhibits (*Evening Telegram, *8 July 1939, p 11).*

Jessie Read was the daughter of Isabella (née McGlinch) and William Read, and she belonged to a large family. She had two siblings (Alma and Charles). Her mother had four children (Eva, Mary, William Arthur, and Violet) by a previous marriage; her father had one son (Clarence) by a previous marriage. On 16 September 1933, at the Church of the Epiphany in Toronto, she married Robert Stuart Hately. Both Jessie and her husband were well known in Toronto musical circles. Robert, a baritone, sang as a guest artist with the Toronto Symphony Orchestra, and he founded the Toronto Philharmonic Choir; Jessie was a member of the Conservatory Choir, the Women's Musical Club, and the Junior Symphony Association, and sang in several of the city's operatic productions. For a photograph of her, see pl 41. She died young, leaving one daughter, Heather Ann (Mrs Claggett). The Evening Telegram *printed an obituary, 'Noted Expert on Meals Jessie Read Succumbs,' on 9 April 1940, p 3. She is buried in Park Lawn Cemetery in Toronto (Section A, Lot 50).*

I am grateful to Jessie Read's daughter, Mrs Heather Claggett, for sharing with me scrapbooks about her mother's career, compiled by Eva Carter.

O830.1 [1934]
Three meals a day / recipe review / by / Jessie
Read / Home Economist of / the Evening Telegram
/ "Toronto's most interesting newspaper" / Price /
25 / cents [cover-title]
DESCRIPTION: 25.5 × 17.5 cm   Pp [1–2] 3–96   Illus on
p 1 of the author   Paper; stapled
CONTENTS: 1 foreword signed Jessie M. Read; 2 ad for
Evening Telegram; 3–93 text; 94–6 'Index' and on p 96,
'Cross-Index to Assist in Menu Planning'
COPIES: *OGU (UA s066 b01)   OONL (TX715.6 R35
1934, 2 copies)
NOTES: Read writes on p 1, '... you will find new ideas
in meal planning and household management to-
gether with a review of "Three Meals a Day for 1934."
Next year we shall give you another "Three Meals a
Day" review for 1935.'

She welcomes new ideas for cooking with manufactured food products on p 63: 'Cornflake cookery
[i.e., cooking with Kellogg's Corn Flakes] is one of
the modern cookery tricks that is so interesting. You
know for years we have gone along serving the same
things and ... getting into a nice old rut. However,
thanks to the very clever home economists with various commercial companies we have been shaken out
of our lethargy.'

O830.2   2nd ed., nd [about 1935]
—3 / meals / a / day / recipe / review / (Second
edition) / By / Jessie / Read / Home Economist of
/ the Evening Telegram / "Toronto's most
interesting newspaper" / Price twenty-five cents
[cover-title]
DESCRIPTION: 25.5 × 17.5 cm   Pp [1–2] 3–96   Illus on
p 1 of the author, illus   Paper, with image on front of
a woman in silhouette, carrying a steaming casserole
dish, the steam rising to form the number '3' in the
title; stapled
CONTENTS: 1 'Foreword' signed Jessie M. Read; 2 ad
for the *Evening Telegram*'s Woman's Page; 3–93 text
and ads; 94–6 'Index'
CITATIONS: Ferguson/Fraser, p 234, illus col on p 80
of closed volume
COPIES: OKQ   *Private collection
NOTES: Read writes on p 1, '... this is the second edition of "Three Meals a Day Recipe Review", with
more – many more – new recipes for you. Since it is a
review of recipes given in the Evening Telegram, it
does not mean it is a complete recipe book, but with
your previous edition [O830.1] and ones to follow – it
will eventually make a complete recipe set.' The first
edition was dated 1934 and promised a second review in 1935; therefore, this undated second edition

was likely published in 1935. 'All food photos courtesy of General Foods Limited' is on p 94, below the
'Index' title.

In 1938, Read produced another, larger book,
under the same, but shortened, title; see O954.1.

Scott, Anna Lee [pseudonym]

*For information about Anna Lee Scott and her cookbooks,
see O526.1.*

O831.1   nd [about 1934]
Christmas / recipes / Anna Lee Scott [cover-title]
DESCRIPTION: 30.5 × 22.5 cm   Pp [1–12]   Illus   Paper, with images on front of a poinsettia blossom
and five reindeer; stapled
CONTENTS: 1–inside back face of binding recipes and
menus
COPIES: *Private collection
NOTES: Unlike O831.2 and O831.3, where the booklet
is designed to look like a gift-wrapped Christmas
present, here the volume is in a magazine-style format: It has larger dimensions, semi-gloss paper, and
black-and-white illustrations. The text closely mirrors that in O831.2 and O831.3; however, one notable
difference is that this edition includes a recipe on p 8
for Shortcut Christmas Pudding, which uses Tea-Bisk
as an ingredient. Illustrations of Maple Leaf Milling
Co. Ltd's products are on the outside back face of
the binding, including a package of Tea-Bisk, with
the comment, 'Special recipes on the package and in
the new book – Cooking Secrets.' The company introduced Tea-Bisk to the marketplace in 1931 (see *The
Company That Grew with Canada*, Maple Leaf Mills
Ltd, [about 1980], p 19). O832.1, *Cooking Secrets*, by
Anna Lee Scott, bears the copyright date of 1934. This
edition of *Christmas Recipes*, therefore, was published
about 1934. The order of publication of the various
editions of *Christmas Recipes* is uncertain.

O831.2   nd
—Christmas / recipes / from Anna Lee Scott
[cover-title]
DESCRIPTION: 23.0 × 15.0 cm   Pp 1–16   Paper, with
binding and leaves trimmed, and binding printed, to
resemble a Christmas present with red wrapping
paper and a white bow; stapled
CONTENTS: Inside front face of binding 'First! Read
This Page' signed Anna Lee Scott; 1–3 three numbered menus for Christmas dinner; 4 menu for 'Buffet Christmas Supper'; 5–16 recipes
COPIES: QMM (RBD ckbk 1988)   *Private collection

NOTES: 'Read This Page' explains the difference between 'a pastry flour and a bread flour – sometimes referred to as an all-purpose flour' and tells how 'to adjust your favourite hard wheat flour recipes to Monarch Flour.'

The binding of the QMM copy is also red.

O831.3   nd
—Christmas / recipes / from Anna Lee Scott [cover-title]
DESCRIPTION: 23.0 × 15.0 cm   Pp [1–4] 5–16   Paper, with binding and leaves trimmed, and binding printed, to resemble a Christmas present with green wrapping paper and a yellow bow; stapled
COPIES: *AEPRAC
NOTES: The pagination and binding colour distinguish this edition from O831.2.

O832.1   copyright 1934
Cooking / secrets / by / Anna Lee Scott / Maple Leaf Milling Co. Limited / Toronto Winnipeg
DESCRIPTION: 22.5 × 15.0 cm   Pp [1–2] 3–127 [128]   Illus col   Thin card; spiral-bound
CONTENTS: 1 tp; 2–119 text; 120–8 index, and at bottom p 128, 'Copyright. Canada, 1934 Maple Leaf Milling Co. Limited // Southam Press Toronto Limited'
CITATIONS: CCB
COPIES: *OONL (TX715 S418 1934, 2 copies)   Private collection
NOTES: An advertisement for *Cooking Secrets* in another publication by Maple Leaf Milling Co. says: 'For only 50¢ you can obtain a copy of this wonderful book, postage paid. Simply write ... mentioning the type of flour you use. There are two editions – Maple Leaf Flour edition for users of bread flour for all their baking, and Monarch Pastry Flour edition for users of pastry flour. You only need one edition. The pastry flour edition includes the Bread Section, calling for the use of a bread flour.' (The preceding text is printed on the outside back face of an 11-page pamphlet with the running head 'Short Cuts with Tea-Bisk by Anna Lee Scott,' at OGU.) The OONL copies are identified as the Maple Leaf Flour edition by the following phrase on the front face of the binding: 'For the users of Maple Leaf Flour'; the private collector's copy has 'For the users of Monarch Flour.'

Selected recipes

O833.1   [1934]
Selected recipes / [IODE symbol] / The Princess of Wales Chapter / Imperial Order / Daughters of the Empire / Kitchener Ontario [cover-title]
DESCRIPTION: 23.0 × 15.0 cm   Pp [1] 2–48   Thin card; stapled
CONTENTS: 1 'Foreword,' 'Compiled by the Princess of Wales Chapter Imperial Order Daughters of the Empire Kitchener, Ontario,' and 'Roster of Officers 1934'; 2–3 history of the Princess of Wales Chapter, organized on 12 March 1903; 4–46 recipes credited with the name of the contributor and ads; 47 'Table Decorations' and ads; 48 ad and 'Index' [i.e., table of contents]
COPIES: *OGU (CCC TX715.6 S4329)
NOTES: A private collector owns a variant copy with typographical errors, where the cover-title is 'Selected Receipes [*sic*]' and p 1 reads, 'Compiled by the Prince [*sic*] of Wales Chapter.'

Selected recipes

O834.1   1934
Selected recipes / 1934 / The Livingston United Church / corner Barton St. and Sanford Ave. / Hamilton Ontario
DESCRIPTION: 22.5 × 15.0 cm   Pp [1] 2–40   Tp illus of the church, illus on p 3 of Rev. I.G. Bowles, pastor   Paper; stapled
CONTENTS: 1 tp; 2 'Preface' signed Mrs Wm Vasey, captain; 3 illus of Rev. I.G. Bowles and list of 'Officers 1934'; 4 ads; 5–mid 39 recipes credited with the name of the contributor and ads; mid–bottom 39 blank for 'Memorandum'; 40 blank for 'My Recipes'
COPIES: *Private collection
NOTES: The 'Preface' declares, 'The Captain and members of Division No. 3 of the Woman's Association of Livingston United Church submit this book ...' An advertisement on p 12 for York Press states, 'This book was printed by the York Press // George Thompson, prop. ... 311 York St.'

75 tested recipes

For the titles of other Certo recipe collections, see O480.1.

O835.1   copyright 1934
75 / tested / recipes / ... for making / jams, jellies / & marmalades / with / Certo / and the short-boil method / Douglas-Pectin, Ltd., Cobourg, Ont., Canada / © 1934, Canada [cover-title]
DESCRIPTION: 14.5 × 8.0 cm   Pp [1] 2–30   Illus   Paper; stapled at top edge
CONTENTS: 1 cover-title; 2 'Recipe Index' and address for advice (Jane Taylor Allen, Douglas-Pectin Ltd, Cobourg); 3 'Why Scores of Jelly Champions Follow

the Certo Method'; 4 '5 Simple Steps in Making Perfect Jelly'; 5 'Jams, Marmalades, Conserves, and Relishes Just as Easy!'; 6–22 'Certo Recipes'; 23–mid 27 'How to Make Sure of Perfect Jams and Jellies'; bottom 27–30 '"Questions I Am Often Asked by Jelly Makers" by Jane Taylor Allen'; inside back face of binding 'Old Fashioned? Or Modern!,' a coupon for a free copy of *Secrets of the Jam Cupboard* ('new dessert and salad recipes using jams and jellies') from General Foods Ltd, Cobourg, and 'P-466-95560-3-34-M.P.Co. Printed in Canada'
COPIES: *Private collection

The Sudbury cook book

O836.1 1934
The Sudbury / cook book / Compiled and published / by / the Woman's Auxiliary / Church of the Epiphany / Sudbury, Ont. / 1934 / Officers of the Woman's Auxiliary / 1934 / Sudbury, Ontario / Mrs. James Purvis / Honorary President / Mrs. C.J. Wood / President / 1st Vice-Pres., Mrs. W.A. Evans; 2nd Vice-Pres., Mrs. J.R. Wainwright; / Secretary, Mrs. W.H. Riddell; Treasurer, Mrs. O. Anderson; Dorcas / Secretary, Mrs. W. Greenwood; Thankoffering Secretary, Mrs. D.H. / Bowen; Little Helpers' Secretary, Mrs. James Boydell; Hon. Pres. G.A., / Mrs. T.C. Young; Advertising Manager, Mrs. D.H. Andress; / Recipe Convener, Mrs. W.H. Riddell
COPIES: *Private collection

The sunny side of life book

For the titles of other Kellogg books about All-Bran, see O768.1.

O837.1 [copyright 1934]
The sunny side of life / book / To keep happy, / keep well / – a new way of living [cover-title]
DESCRIPTION: 18.5 × 13.5 cm Pp [1–32] Illus col, illus Paper, with image on front of a family (dog, son, father, mother, daughter), holding hands and running by a sundial; stapled
CONTENTS: Inside front face of binding 'Copyright 1934, by Kellogg Company of Canada, Ltd., London, Ontario'; 1 'Do You Know – the Answers to These Important Questions?'; 2–3 '"We Kept Well Last Year"'; 4 'Make Happiness a Habit' signed W.K. Kellogg; 5–10 'The Road to Regularity'; 11–18 'How

to Keep Fit'; 19–28 'Cook Book' of recipes and menus featuring Kellogg's All-Bran cereal; 29–32 'Beauty Aids'; inside back face list of 'additional literature from the Kellogg Kitchen' and at lower left, 'No. C-429'
COPIES: QMM (RBD ckbk 1705) *Private collection

Titus, Miss Zorada Z.

O838.1 copyright 1934
Better / cooked foods / by / Zorada Z. Titus / food economist / A series of recipes especially / compiled and tested on Coleman / Instant-Gas Stoves. Their purpose / is – / (1) To show the wide range of cooking / to which the Coleman is adapted. / (2) To show how the Coleman supplies / modern gas service for every cooking need / for any home anywhere. / (3) To show how it cooks foods so that / they retain their natural, delicious flavors / – makes it possible for you to place on / your table better cooked foods. / Price 25¢ / Copyright 1934 by / the Coleman Lamp and Stove Company / General offices: Wichita, Kansas, U.S.A. / Sales branches: Philadelphia, Chicago, Los Angeles / Factories: Wichita, Kansas and Toronto, Canada / Form A225. Printed in U.S.A.
DESCRIPTION: Pp [1] 2–38 [39–40] Illus portrait on p 2 of Miss Zorada Z. Titus, illus on p 38 of Coleman products, illus on p 39 of the Coleman factory in Toronto and in Wichita, Kansas Binding with all-over plaid pattern; stapled
CONTENTS: 1 tp; 2 'A Booklet for Homemakers' [i.e., biographical information about the author]; ...; 39 'For 30 Years the Name Coleman Has Stood for Quality'; 40 'Index'
COPIES: *Private collection
NOTES: The cover-title is 'Better Cooked Foods the Coleman Way.' According to p 2, Miss Zorada Z. Titus was director of the Household Searchlight, the national testing service of *The Household Magazine*. 'Reared in the Central West,' she was a graduate of Kansas State College and held a Master's degree in nutrition from Iowa State College.

By the end of the twentieth century in Canada, Coleman stoves were associated almost exclusively with camping and with cottages without electricity.

White, Miss Florence (Peckham, a suburb of London, England, 20 June 1863–1940)

For information about White, see O782.1.

O839.1 [1934]
Flowers as food / Receipts and lore from / many sources, compiled by / Florence White / author of Good Things in England / founder of the English Folk Cookery Association / London Jonathan Cape Toronto
DESCRIPTION: 19.0 × 12.5 cm Pp [1–4] 5–154 Cloth
CONTENTS: 1 ht; 2 blank; 3 tp; 4 'First published 1934 Jonathan Cape Ltd. 30 Bedford Square, London and 91 Wellington Street West, Toronto // Printed in Great Britain in the city of Oxford at the Alden Press // Paper made by John Dickinson & Co., Ltd. Bound by A.W. Bain & Co. Ltd., in cloth, fast to light and washable, made by Morton Sundour Fabrics Ltd.'; 5 'Contents'; 6 blank; 7 dedication to Delitia and Katharine Hinxman; 8 quotation from William Lawson, *A New Orchard and Garden*, 1618; 9–19 'Prologue' signed Florence White, The Albany, Ringwood, Hants, 8 December 1933; 20 blank; 21–38 'Part One // General Directions for 1. Crystallizing Flowers 2. Flowers Preserved with Vinegar for Salads 3. Making Flower Syrups 4. Flower Teas or Tisanes 5. Wines Made from Flowers'; 39–143 'Part Two // Fifty-four Flowers Arranged in Alphabetical Order with Recipes for Food Delicacies in Which They Play a Part'; 144 blank; 145–50 'Epilogue'; 151–4 'Books Recommended'
COPIES: AEU (TX396 W58); Great Britain: LB (7943.p.35); United States: DLC (TX396 W4)
NOTES: In most cases, White gives the printed or manuscript source for each recipe. She makes a passing reference to *Flowers as Food* in her autobiography, *Fire in the Kitchen*, p 321.

Woodman, Mary

O840.1 [1934]
Foulsham's cloth-bound Pocket Library / 100 varieties / of / sandwiches / How to prepare them / By / Mary Woodman / For the picnic, / the Bridge party, / the dance buffet, / the motorist's wayside meal, / the rambler and the cyclist, / the impromptu supper, / the drawing room tea, / and other occasions. / London / W. Foulsham & Co., Ltd. / New York Toronto Cape Town Sydney
COPIES: *Private collection; Great Britain: LB (12209.ppp.8/65)
NOTES: LB records the book as having 92 pp.

1934–5

The pantry shelf

O841.1 1934–5
The / pantry / shelf / 1934–1935 / St. John's Anglican Church / Smiths Falls, Ont. [cover-title]
DESCRIPTION: Pp [1] 2–24 Stapled
CONTENTS: 1 'Preface' and 'Compiled by the Women's Guild of St. John's Anglican Church // Smiths Falls, Ont.'; 2–23 recipes credited with the name of the contributor, 'Table Decorations,' 'For Serving 100 People,' and ads; 24 'Index' [i.e., table of contents] and ads
COPIES: *Private collection
NOTES: The printer's name, 'Standard Press, Smiths Falls,' is on p 23.

1935

Beach frozen dainties and other recipes

For information about Beach Foundry Ltd and its cookbooks, see O566.1.

O842.1 nd [about 1935]
Beach / frozen dainties / and / other recipes
DESCRIPTION: 19.0 × 13.5 cm Pp [1] 2–24 Illus of Beach kitchen range and electric refrigerator Paper, with image on front of a male cook holding a tray
CONTENTS: Inside front face of binding illus of a Beach range; 1 tp; 2 note from Beach Foundry; 3 table of contents; 4 preface; 5 'Beach Cold Control'; 6 'Vegetable Crisper'; 7 'Care of Vegetables'; 8 'How to Arrange Foods in the Beach Electric Refrigerator'; 9 'General Hints'; 10–23 recipes; 24 blank for 'Notes'; inside back face 'Designed and produced by the Runge Press Limited Ottawa Canada'; outside back face 'Beach Foundry Limited Ottawa Canada'
CITATIONS: Ferguson/Fraser, p 233
COPIES: *Private collection
NOTES: The recipes are arranged under the following headings: 'Frozen Creams'; 'Sauces for Ice Cream'; 'Sherbets and Ices'; 'Chilled Desserts'; 'Chilled Appetizers'; 'Salads'; 'Salad Dressings'; and 'Cold Beverages.' From appearances, the book was published about 1935.

'Be prepared'

O843.1   nd [about 1935]
"Be prepared" / – with these favourite recipes, /
– and the services advertised. [cover-title]
DESCRIPTION: 23.0 × 15.0 cm   Pp [1] 2–96   Illus
Paper, with image on front of a Boy Scout's head-and-shoulders
CONTENTS: 1 blank; 2 index of chapter headings; 3
'"Be Prepared"' [i.e., preface]; 4–88 recipes credited
with the name of the contributor and ads; 89–mid 90
'Quantities to Serve 50 Persons'; bottom 90 'Weights
and Measures' and 'Temperature Chart'; 91 'Food
Equivalents'; 92–3 'Calories Chart'; 94–5 'Index to
Advertisers'; 96 'Mother's Promise'
COPIES: *Private collection
NOTES: The text on p 3 states, 'The members of the
various Boy Scout Auxiliaries in the Lakeshore, ...
take pleasure in presenting this little volume of recipes.' The Lakeshore is a community in Etobicoke,
now part of Toronto. There are advertisements for
businesses in Port Credit, Lakeview, New Toronto,
Mimico, Streetsville, and Toronto. The illustrations
are amusing and show Boy Scouts in action, such as
carrying a large fish, photographing a posing bear,
whistling while hiking, cooking over a campfire, and
eating at table. The book's owner remembers her
mother having the book in the 1930s.

Blake, Mary [pseudonym]

*For information about Mary Blake and her cookbooks, see
O494.1; for Carnation Milk Products Co., see O350.1.*

O844.1   copyright 1935
Carnation / cook book / by Mary Blake / The
Carnation Company Ltd. / Toronto, Ont. /
Copyright 1935, The Carnation Company Ltd. /
Printed in Canada CC943
DESCRIPTION: 23.5 × 15.5 cm   Pp [1–2] 3–93 [94–
6]   Tp illus green of basket of fruit and vegetables,
15 fp illus col, centre spread illus col of petits fours,
illus   Paper, with title and author's name represented
in cross-stitching; stapled
CONTENTS: 1 tp; 2 'Letter by Mary Blake,' director,
Home Economics Department, Carnation Co. Ltd;
3 table of contents; 4–7 'Introduction // Irradiated
Milk'; 8–9 'Rules'; 10–93 text; 94–6 index
COPIES: ACG   NBCOM   OAYM   *Private collection
NOTES: On p 2, Mary Blake refers to 'this new cook
book' and comments that 'just as this cook book is

new, so is Irradiated Carnation Milk.' She says that
Grace Viall Gray, of the Gray Institute of Home Economics, 'collaborated with [her] in the preparation of
this book.' Irradiated Carnation Milk is described on
p 4 as 'simply rich whole milk, evaporated to double
richness, irradiated for "sunshine" Vitamin D,
homogenized to break up the cream particles, and
sterilized for safe keeping.' The company began irra-
diating the milk product in 1934. The text covers
'Menus,' 'Child Feeding, Recipes, Menus,' 'Invalid
Cookery,' and 'International Recipes.'

O844.2   copyright 1937
—Carnation / cook book / by Mary Blake / The
Carnation Company Ltd. / Toronto, Ont. /
Copyright 1937, The Carnation Company Ltd. /
Printed in Canada CC943AA
DESCRIPTION: 23.5 × 15.5 cm   Pp [1–2] 3–93 [94–6]
Tp illus green of basket of fruit and vegetables, 15 fp
illus col, centre spread illus col of petits fours,
illus   Paper, with title and author's name represented
in needlework; stapled
CONTENTS: 1 tp; 2 'Letter by Mary Blake,' director,
Home Economics Department, Carnation Co. Ltd;
3 table of contents; 4–7 'Introduction // Irradiated
Milk'; 8–9 'Rules'; 10–93 text; 94–6 index
CITATIONS: Crawford, p D1, illus col
COPIES: AEPMA   AWWDM   QMM (RBD ckbk
1326)   *Private collection
NOTES: Another private collector's copy has 'CC943A'
on the title-page (not 'CC943AA'), but otherwise appears to be identical to the copy catalogued here.

O844.3   copyright 1939
—Carnation / cook book / by Mary Blake / The
Carnation Company Ltd. / Toronto, Ont. /
Copyright 1939, The Carnation Company, Ltd. /
Printed in Canada CC333
DESCRIPTION: 23.5 × 15.5 cm   Pp [1–2] 3–93 [94–
6]   Tp illus green of basket of fruit and vegetables,
15 fp illus col, centre spread illus col of petits fours,
illus   Paper, with image on front of carnation tied
with red ribbon; stapled
CONTENTS: 1 tp; 2 'Letter by Mary Blake,' director,
Home Economics Department, Carnation Co. Ltd;
3 table of contents; 4–7 'Introduction // Irradiated
Milk'; 8–9 'Rules'; 10–93 text; 94–6 index
COPIES: BSORM   MWMM   OGU (CCC TX715.6 B52
1939)   OONL (TX715.6 B534 1939)   QMM (2 copies:
RBD ckbk 2295; RBD Vanna Garnier, ckbk 749)   *Private collection

O844.4 copyright 1941
—Carnation / cook book / by Mary Blake / The Carnation Company Ltd. / Toronto, Ont. / Copyright 1941, The Carnation Company Ltd. / Printed in Canada CC497

DESCRIPTION: 23.5 × 15.5 cm Pp [1–2] 3–93 [94–6] Tp illus green of basket of fruit and vegetables, 15 fp illus col, centre spread illus col of petits fours, illus Lacks binding; stapled

CONTENTS: 1 tp; 2 'Letter by Mary Blake,' director, Home Economics Department, Carnation Co. Ltd; 3 table of contents; 4–7 'Introduction // Irradiated Milk'; 8–9 'Rules'; 10–93 text; 94–6 index

COPIES: BVMA *OGU (CCC TX715.6 B52 1941) QMMMCM (AR-M2000.92.41)

NOTES: The binding of the QMMMCM copy matches O844.5, i.e., paper, with an open-work crochet pattern, title and author's name in embroidery.

O844.5 copyright 1942
—Carnation / cook book / by Mary Blake / The Carnation Company / Toronto, Ont. / Copyright 1942, The Carnation Company Ltd. / Printed in Canada CC497A

DESCRIPTION: 23.0 × 15.5 cm Pp [1–2] 3–93 [94–6] Tp illus green of basket of fruit and vegetables, illus col Paper, with open-work crochet pattern, title and author's name in embroidery; stapled

CONTENTS: 1 tp; 2 'Letter by Mary Blake'; 3 table of contents; 4–7 'Introduction // Irradiated Milk'; 8–9 'Rules'; 10–93 text; 94–6 index

COPIES: OGU (CCC TX715.6 B52 1942) SEEK *Private collection

O844.6 copyright 1943
—Carnation / cook book / by Mary Blake / The Carnation Company / Toronto, Ont. / Copyright 1943, The Carnation Company Ltd. / Printed in Canada CC497C

DESCRIPTION: 23.5 × 15.5 cm Pp [1–2] 3–93 [94–6] Tp illus green of basket of fruit and vegetables, centre spread illus col of three dishes of food on a sideboard decorated with two vases of carnations, illus col Paper, with open-work crochet pattern, title and author's name in embroidery; stapled

CONTENTS: 1 tp; 2 letter signed Mary Blake, director, Home Economics Department, Carnation Co. Ltd; 3 table of contents; 4–7 'Introduction // Irradiated Milk'; 8–9 'Rules'; 10–93 text; 94–6 index

CITATIONS: Ferguson/Fraser, p 234, illus col on p 103 of closed volume

COPIES: OGU (ES XR1 MS A700052) OMIHURM

OTMCL (641.5 B47) *Private collection

NOTES: Marnie Derksen refers to her copy of the 1943 edition of *Carnation Cook Book* in 'Season to Taste: Cookbooks Often Serve Up Much More Than Just Recipes,' *Globe and Mail* 18 August 2000, p A18 (Derksen incorrectly spelled Derkson in the article). Another private collector has a copy dated copyright 1943, but with 'CC497B' on the title-page.

O844.7 copyright 1944
—Carnation / cook book / by Mary Blake / The Carnation Company / Toronto, Ont. / Copyright 1944, The Carnation Company Ltd. / Printed in Canada CC497D

DESCRIPTION: 23.0 × 16.0 cm Pp [1–2] 3–93 [94–6] Tp illus green of basket of fruit and vegetables, centre spread illus col of three dishes of food on a sideboard decorated with two vases of carnations, illus col Paper, with open-work crochet pattern, title and author's name in embroidery; stapled

CONTENTS: 1 tp; 2 letter signed Mary Blake, director, Home Economics Department, Carnation Co. Ltd; 3 table of contents; 4–7 'Introduction // Irradiated Milk'; 8–9 'Rules'; 10–93 text; 94–6 index

COPIES: *NBDKH QMM (RBD Soeur Berthe, ckbk 55) Private collection

NOTES: The private collector's copy has 'CC497E' on the title-page.

O844.8 copyright 1947
—Carnation / cook book / by Mary Blake / Carnation Company, Ltd. / Toronto, Ont. / Copyright 1947, Carnation Company, Ltd. / Printed in Canada CC497F

DESCRIPTION: 23.5 × 16.0 cm Pp [1–4] 5–93 [94–6] Tp illus red of basket of fruit and vegetables, 15 fp illus col, centre spread illus col of three dishes of food on a sideboard decorated with two vases of carnations Paper, with open-work crochet pattern, title and author's name in embroidery; stapled

CONTENTS: 1 tp; 2 'An Invitation from Carnation' signed Mary Blake, Home Service Department, Carnation Co. Ltd; 3 table of contents; 4–7 'Introduction'; 8–9 'Rules'; 10–93 text; 94–6 index

CITATIONS: Cooke 2003, p 201

COPIES: MBDHM MWMM OONL (TX715.6 B534 1947) OTBPM QMM (RBD Soeur Berthe, ckbk 2532) *Private collection

AMERICAN EDITIONS: 1942 (Allen, p 204); 1943 (Dickinson, p 46, illus p 47).

Boulestin, Xavier Marcel (France, 1878–1943)

The French chef Boulestin worked for much of his career in London, England, where he opened his famed Restaurant Boulestin in 1925, taught cooking at the luxury provisioners Fortnum and Mason, and recorded the BBC's first television cooking show in 1937. In addition to O845.1, The Evening Standard Book of Menus, *and O906.1,* The Finer Cooking, *he wrote several English-language books on food and cooking, and a cookery column for* Vogue *magazine. The following titles were all published by William Heinemann, London:* Simple French Cooking for English Homes, *1923 (also at OGU);* The Conduct of the Kitchen, *1925; A Second Helping; or, More Dishes for English Homes, *1925;* Herbs, Salads and Seasonings, *1930;* What Shall We Have To-day?, *1931;* Eggs: One-Hundred-and-Twenty Ways of Cooking, *1932; Potatoes: One-Hundred-and-One Ways of Cooking, *1932;* Savouries and Hors-d'oeuvre, etc., *1932;* What Shall We Have to Drink?, *1933;* Having Crossed the Channel, *1934 (all Great Britain: LB).*

O845.1 [1935]
The / Evening Standard / book of menus / containing / economical menus for all the days in the / year and recipes for the dishes / by / X.M. Boulestin / William Heinemann Ltd / London Toronto
DESCRIPTION: 19.5 × 13.0 cm   Pp [i–vi], 1–294   Patterned cloth
CONTENTS: i ht; ii list of ten books 'also by X. Marcel Boulestin'; iii tp; iv 'First published 1935 // Printed in Great Britain at the Windmill Press, Kingswood, Surrey'; v table of contents; vi blank; 1–284 text; 285–9 'Descriptive Index'; 290–4 'Alphabetical Index'
COPIES: *OGU (UA s002 b27); Great Britain: LB (7943.v.7)
NOTES: The text is in three sections: 'Our Daily Food'; 'Menus for the Fifty-two Weeks of the Year'; and 'Recipes.'

Canning guide

See O703.1 for other titles by the London Life Insurance Co.

O846.1 [1935]
Canning / guide / Published and distributed by / the London Life Insurance Company [cover-title]
DESCRIPTION: 22.5 × 15.5 cm   Pp [1–3] 4–15   Illus green   Paper, with image on front of a woman screwing a top on a jar; stapled
CONTENTS: 1 cover-title; 2 index; 3–15 text
COPIES: *Private collection
NOTES: The text is printed in brown; the illustrations, in green. 'H8-7-35' is on the outside back face of the binding, and from appearances, the book was published in 1935.

O846.2 nd [about 1945]
—Canning / guide / Compliments of the London Life Insurance Company [cover-title]
DESCRIPTION: 23.0 × 15.5 cm   Pp [1–3] 4–15   Illus blue   Paper, with image on front of a woman holding up grapes in her right hand, a jar in her left hand; stapled
CONTENTS: 1 cover-title; 2 index; 3–15 text
COPIES: *Private collection
NOTES: The text and illustrations are printed in blue. The binding design indicates a date of publication considerably later than O846.1, likely about 1945. 'H-8' is on the outside back face of the binding.

Chase, Dr Alvin Wood (Cayuga County, NY, 20 March 1817–25 May 1885, Ohio)

See O535.1 for other years of the calendar almanac. For information about Dr Chase and his publications, see O8.1.

O847.1 1935
Hang me up / Dr. A.W. Chase's / calendar almanac / 1935 / for the / home, factory / farm, office / Published by / the Dr. A.W. Chase Medicine Co. / Limited / Toronto, Canada [cover-title]
DESCRIPTION: 21.0 × 15.0 cm   Pp [3] 4–50   Illus   Paper, with image on front of Dr Chase and his signature; stapled, and with hole punched at top left corner for hanging
CONTENTS: 3 'The Family Doctor'; 4–50 monthly calendars, culinary recipes, medical information, zodiacal signs and astronomical information on p 6, publ ads, and humorous material
COPIES: *OTUTF (jah patent medicine)
NOTES: 'Murray Printing Co. Ltd., Toronto, Canada' is on the outside back face of the binding.

Easy triumphs with the new Minute Tapioca

For another cookbook for Minute Tapioca, see O717.1.

O848.1 [about 1935]
[An edition of *Easy Triumphs with the New Minute Tapioca*]
CITATIONS: Chatelaine 1935, p 82
NOTES: *Easy Triumphs with the New Minute Tapioca* is advertised on p 15 and on the outside back face of the 15-page booklet *Delicious, Nourishing Foods That Will Delight Your Entire Family*, [Cobourg, Ont.: General Foods Ltd, nd, about 1935] (OGU). The publisher's notice refers to 'the new 48-page Minute Tapioca Recipe Book' that is 'fully illustrated in colours'; an image of the book shows the cover-title to be 'Easy / Triumphs / with the / New / Minute Tapioca / 85 recipes / with / glad news / in them'; readers were to send the book-order coupon to General Foods Ltd, Cobourg, Ontario.

Chatelaine 1935 cites 'Easy Triumphs with the New Minute Tapioca (free on receipt of the minute man trade mark from a regular sized package of this tapioca),' available from General Foods Ltd.

Fancy meats

O849.1 nd [about 1935]
Fancy / meats / Swift Canadian Co. / Limited / Canada [cover-title]
DESCRIPTION: 17.0 × 12.0 cm Pp [1] 2–20 Centre spread illus of 'A Few of Swift's Fancy Meat Packages' Paper, with two images on front: a set table and, in an oval frame, an aproned woman consulting this(?) cookbook; stapled
CONTENTS: 1 introductory text; 2 'Brains'; 3 'Calf's Head'; 4 'Pork Cutlets'; 5 'Kidneys'; 6–7 'Liver'; 8–mid 9 'Sweetbreads'; bottom 9–mid 12, excluding centre spread 'Ox Tails'; mid 12–top 13 'Hearts'; mid–bottom 13 'Tongues'; top 14 'Lamb Plucks'; mid 14 'Melts'; bottom 14–mid 15 'Pork Feet'; bottom 15 'Pork Tails'; top 16 'Pork Lacones'; mid 16 'Pork Lips'; bottom 16–top 17 'Pork Ears'; mid 17 'Tripe'; bottom 17–top 18 'Pork Snouts'; near top 18 'Beef Hanging Tender'; mid 18 'Lamb Fries'; bottom 18–top 19 'Lamb Heads'; mid 19 'Pork Heads'; bottom 19 'Beef Stew Meat'; 20 'Table of Contents' [i.e., index]
COPIES: *Private collection
NOTES: The introductory text recommends this book to the housewife 'to help vary your menus, at a de-cided saving and with an increase in nutritional value.' No place of publication is recorded, but Swift Canadian Co.'s head office was in Toronto.

Favorite recipes

O850.1 nd [about 1935]
Favorite / recipes / Tested recipes / selected and arranged for / publication by / the Young Married Women's Group / of / Park Road Baptist Church / Park Road Toronto, Ontario [cover-title]
DESCRIPTION: 22.5 × 15.0 cm Pp [1] 2–48 Paper
CONTENTS: 1 'Favorite Recipes' [i.e., introductory note] signed the Committee; 2–46 recipes credited with the name of the contributor and ads; 47 'Table Decorations'; 48 index
COPIES: *OGU (UA s045 b42)
NOTES: There is an advertisement on the inside front face of the binding for City Dairy milk, 'the milk chosen by the guardians of the Dionne quintuplets.' The world's first surviving quintuplets were born on 28 May 1934, near Callendar, Ontario. They were placed under the care of four guardians in July 1934, by a judicial order obtained by the attorney general. In spring 1935, they were made wards of the Crown under a Guardianship Bill passed by the provincial legislature.

Favourite recipes of Canadian women

For an earlier cookbook for the same product, see O604.1.

O851.1 [February 1935]
Favourite / recipes / of / Canadian / women / [caption:] Mrs. W.D. Herridge / wife of Canada's Minister to / United States and sister of / Canada's Prime Minister the / Right Hon. R.B. Bennett. [cover-title]
DESCRIPTION: 16.5 × 11.0 cm Pp 3–31 Illus of Canada's society women and finished dishes Paper, with portrait on front of Mrs W.D. Herridge; stapled
CONTENTS: 3 publisher's note and 'Index' [i.e., table of contents]; 4–30 recipes using Nestlé's Evaporated Milk as an ingredient; 31 [inside back face of binding] 'What Nestlé's Evaporated Milk Is'; outside back face 'February 1935 Printed in Canada'
CITATIONS: Ferguson/Fraser, illus on p 78 of front face of binding FitzPatrickCat 111 (April 1993) No. 20

COPIES: *OGU (CCC TX715.6 F385)   SSWD
NOTES: The publisher's note begins: 'Nestlé's Home Economics Bureau take great pleasure in presenting you with this book ... In the following pages you will find a selection of recipes which have proved to be favourites with representative women throughout Canada, many of whom are of first importance in the social life of the Dominion.' On each of pp 4, 6, 8, 12, 16, 20, 24, and 28, there is a portrait of a prominent Canadian woman and her favourite recipe using Nestlé's Evaporated Milk. In addition to Mrs William D. Herridge, the contributors were Miss Martha Allan ('founder and director of Montreal's distinguished Repertory Theatre and daughter of Sir Montague Allan, C.V.O., and Lady Allan, Ravenscrag, Montreal'), Mrs John V. Casgrain (wife of the 'prominent Montreal barrister and member of one of Canada's oldest and best-known French-Canadian families' and 'daughter-in-law of the Hon. Senator Colonel J.P.B. Casgrain'), Mrs Hugh H. McLean Jr ('daughter-in-law of Major-General, the Honourable Hugh Havelock McLean, K.C., V.D., L.L.D., Lieutenant-Governor of New Brunswick, 1928–1935'), Mrs W.H. Covert ('wife of Nova Scotia's Lieutenant-Governor, social leader of Halifax and the Maritimes, and well known patroness of the Victorian Order of Nurses'), Mrs J.A. McAvity, formerly Miss Marjorie Mills ('member of one of the Maritimes [sic, no apostrophe] best known families and granddaughter of the Honourable William F. Todd, former Lieutenant-Governor of New Brunswick'), Miss Betty Sandford Smith ('well-known member of Toronto's famous Skating Club, of the Toronto Junior League and of the Eglinton Hunt Club'), and Mrs G.A.P. Brickenden ('one of Canada's foremost horsewomen, a prominent member of the London [Ontario] Hunt Club and wife of G.A.P. Brickenden, owner of the famous Brickenden Stables'). The recipes may have been the favourites of these women, but it was their family or embassy cooks who prepared them. Each cook is quoted above the featured recipe; for example, Emelda Normand, the Casgrains' cook, says, 'One of Mrs. John V. Casgrains [sic] favourite Lenten dishes is Haddock Steamed in Milk, and here is how I make it.'

No place of publication is recorded, but Nestlé's Canadian head office was in Toronto. The text and illustrations are printed in brown.

The health of your family depends entirely upon you

See also O1147.1, Super Health Aluminum, by the same company, which refers to the origination of the Super Health process of cooking in 1927. The company also published the 11-page booklet Super-Health Aluminum Guarantees Better Cooked Foods, Less Labor, Less Cost, Better Health *[cover-title], nd [about 1930] (OTMCL).*

O852.1   nd [about 1935]
The health / of your / family / depends entirely / upon you / Super Health Aluminum Co. Limited / Head office and factory: / 107 McGill Street, Toronto, Ontario / Branches throughout Canada
DESCRIPTION: 22.5 × 14.5 cm   Pp [1–2] 3–32   Illus of utensils   Paper, with light-and-dark-purple image on front of a mother bringing a covered aluminium pot to table, at which a child sits; stapled
CONTENTS: 1 tp; 2 blank; 3 'The Super Health Waterless (Vapor) Process of Cooking'; 4 'General Directions as to Use of Super Health Cooking Units'; 5–mid 9 'The Three-in-One Set' and recipes for its use; mid 9–11 '"Super Health" Oval Roaster' and recipes; 12–mid 13 '"Super Health" Oblong Roaster' and recipes; mid 13–14 '"Super Health" Casserole' and recipes; 15–16 '"Super Health" Reversible Griddle' and recipes; 17–18 '"Super Health" Double Fry Pan – The Handy Unit' and recipes; 19–mid 20 '"Super Health" Coffee Pot or Beverage Urn' and recipes; bottom 20 information about the 8-quart preserving kettle; 21 'Pastry'; 22–3 '"Super Health" Preserving Kettles' and recipes; 24 '"Super Health" Tea Kettle'; 25 '"Super Health" Saucepans'; 26–7 '"Super Health" Fry Pans' and recipes; 28–top 29 fp illus of 'The Super Health Household Line' and key to the illus; mid–bottom 29 'Care of Super Health Cooking Equipments'; 30 'To Enjoy Satisfaction and Long Service ...'; 31 'Approximate Time for Cooking Fruits and Vegetables the Super Health Way'; 32 'Aluminum Cookware Is the Safest to Use' and 'Super Health Service'
COPIES: *ACG   OONL (TX657 C74 H43 1930z copy 1)
NOTES: This edition has a title-page, unlike O852.2 and O852.3. Super Health Aluminum Co. is first listed in the Toronto city directory for 1929, at 370 Bloor Street West. In the directories for 1930–42, it is listed at 107 McGill Street; for 1943–5, at 107 McGill and the foundry at 348 Greenwood Avenue; from 1946 on, only the Greenwood address is given. Since all the editions described here cite the McGill address for

the head office and factory, they were all published before 1943. The graphic design is typical of the 1930s. The order of the editions is uncertain; however, O852.1, which has a title-page, but no untitled introduction, may be the earliest. The cover-title of O852.1 matches O852.2–852.3.

The ACG copy is inscribed on the inside front face of the binding, 'ca 1932/33.' The OONL copy is inscribed on the title-page, in ink, 'H.F. Henner 219 McLeod Bldg Edmonton.' Since this is the company address stamped in OONL copy 2 (O852.2), Henner was probably a salesman for the company's products.

There is a variant at OWTU (G11374) that matches the above description except that the heading on p 4 is 'General Instructions as to Use of Super Health Cooking Units' not 'General Directions ...' Three of the company's leaflets accompany the OWTU copy, one of which refers to recipes devised by the company's test kitchen: 'Dear customer: ... Each month we issue two tested recipes from our own Experimental Kitchen and if you wish to be placed on our list for a period of one year, please write us. Super Health Aluminum Co., Ltd.'

O852.2   nd
—Less labor / less cost / in the cooking of / your daily food / The health / of your / family / depends entirely / upon you / Super-Health / Aluminum / guarantees / better health [cover-title]
DESCRIPTION: 23.5 × 15.5 cm   Pp [1–2] 3–32   Illus of Super Health Aluminum Co.'s products   Paper, with blue-and-green image on front of a mother bringing a covered aluminium pot to table, at which a child sits; stapled
CONTENTS: 1 untitled introduction and at bottom, 'Super Health Aluminum Co. Limited // Head office and factory: 107 McGill Street, Toronto, Ontario ...'; 2 blank; 3–5 'The Super Health Waterless (Vapor) Process of Preparing Foods'; 6–27 recipes interspersed with illus of, and information about, specific models of Super Health Equipment: Triplicate or Vegetable Health Set, Oval Roaster, Casserole, Griddle and Broiler, Omelette or Double Fry Pan, Coffee Pot or Beverage Urn, Tea Pot, Preserving Kettles and Bake Ovens, Pie Plates, Combination Unit, Saucepans, Fry Pans, and Tea Kettle; 28 'The Super Health Household Line'; 29 'Super Health Cooking Equipment for Hotels, Institutions, Restaurants, etc.'; 30 'To Enjoy Satisfaction and Long Service ...'; 31 'Aluminum Cookware Is the Safest to Use' and 'Super Health Service';

32 'Approximate Time for Cooking Fruits and Vegetables the Super Health Way'
COPIES: *OONL (TX657 C74 H43 1930z copy 2)   Private collection
NOTES: Like O852.3, this edition has an untitled introduction, but it does not quote Dr Wodehouse.

The OONL copy is stamped, opposite p 1, 'Superhealth [sic] Aluminum Co., Ltd. 219 McLeod Building Phone 21762 Edmonton, Alta.' The binding of the private collector's copy is printed in light and dark blue.

O852.3   nd [about 1938–9]
—Less labor / less cost / in the cooking of / your daily food / The health / of your / family / depends entirely / upon you / Super-Health / Aluminum / guarantees / better health [cover-title]
DESCRIPTION: 23.0 × 15.5 cm   Pp [1–2] 3–30 [31–2] Illus   Paper, with dark-and-light-blue image on front of a mother bringing a covered aluminium pot to table, at which a child sits; stapled
CONTENTS: 1 untitled introduction and at bottom, 'Super Health Aluminum Co. Limited Head office and factory: 107 McGill Street, Toronto, Ontario ...'; 2 blank; 3–7 'The Super Health Waterless (Vapor) Process of Preparing Foods'; 8–mid 10 '"Super Health" Wonder Electric Cooker'; mid 10–29 recipes interspersed with illus of, and information about, specific models of Super Health equipment; 30 'Approximate Time Table "Super Health" Vapor Process'; 31 publ ad; 32 guarantee
COPIES: *Private collection
NOTES: The introductory text on p 1 quotes Dr Wodehouse, deputy minister of health, who refers to the establishment of the Canadian National Council on Nutrition. Wodehouse was deputy minister of health from 1934 to 1944, and the Canadian National Council of Nutrition held its first meeting on 19 February 1938, with Dr Wodehouse as the first chairman. This edition, therefore, was published in 1938 or later, but likely not in the 1940s since there is no reference to the Second World War.

The company promoted aluminium cookware as healthful because it was designed to limit the destruction of vitamins by heat and by boiling. The 'Four "Super Health" Fundamentals' (pp 4–5) were that no water or a minimal amount of water was used, very little heat was needed, no grease was used, and the cover was kept on through cooking.

Helpful hints for housekeepers [about 1935]

See O263.1 for information about the company and other issues of Helpful Hints for Housekeepers.

O853.1   nd [about 1935]
Dodd's / helpful / hints / for / housekeepers [cover-title]
DESCRIPTION: 18.0 × 12.0 cm   Pp 1–32   Illus   Paper, with image on front, in oval frame, of a woman's head; stapled, and with hole punched at top left corner, through which runs a string for hanging
CONTENTS: 1 publ ad for the book *Sunny Memories* by 'Old Man Sunshine,' 1934–5 edition; 2–32 culinary and housekeeping information, health advice, 'Naming the Baby' on p 17, jokes, and publ ads
COPIES: *OTUTF (uncat patent medicine)
NOTES: For culinary information, see: 'More Helpful Hints,' p 5; 'Several Ways to Use Rice,' p 9; 'Weights and Measures,' p 10; 'Eat More Fish,' p 12; 'Uses for Mint,' p 14; 'More Useful Hints,' p 15; untitled text, p 20; 'Some Hints on Buying Meat,' p 21; 'A Few Egg Hints,' p 22; and 'More Helpful Hints,' p 31.

Holmes, Marie [pseudonym of] Mrs William Wallace, née Marie Thompson (Toronto, Ont.–2 February 1974, Toronto, Ont.)

After graduating from the Toronto Normal School, Marie taught household science in schools for several years, before joining the Toronto Star. *For her 'Cooking Chat' columns at the* Star *and for other professional work she always used the pseudonym Marie Holmes – a combination of her two grandmothers' names (THEA 1988, p 8). Her photograph was reproduced at the head of each column (for example, the issue for 5 December 1942, p 24).*

The 'Cooking Chat' column of 11 December 1942 asks readers to write for her new leaflet, called 'Cooking in Wartime,' in which recipes 'suitable for packing in overseas boxes are specially indicated' (no copy located). Both her Entertaining at the Tea Hour (1935) *and* O1005.1, Food from Market to Table (1940), *were published while she was at the* Star. *From September 1947 to August 1956 she was director of the Chatelaine Institute (see 'Introducing the New Director of Chatelaine Institute,'* Chatelaine *(September 1947), p 32). Also by her, but not a cookbook, is* Glamour and the Hostess: A Guide to Canadian Table Setting, Toronto: *Distributed by Northumbria Sterling, nd [194-?] (OONL).*

She was a founding member of the Toronto Home Economics Association in 1938 and its third president; and she was a founding member of the Canadian Home Economics Association in 1939 (We Are Tomorrow's Past, p 5; on p 2 she appears in a group photograph taken at the association's first convention). A brief biography and photograph is in THEA 1988, pp 8–9; and she is in a group photograph on p 13. Her obituary is in the Star *7 February 1974, p B7.*

O854.1   [copyright 1935]
Entertaining at the / tea hour / by / Marie Holmes / Home Economics Editor / The Toronto Daily Star [cover-title]
DESCRIPTION: 15.0 × 9.0 cm   Pp [1] 2–20   Paper, with portrait on front of the author; stapled
CONTENTS: 1 cover-title; 2 directions for obtaining additional copies of this booklet or the author's 'booklet on "Special Cakes for Special Occasions"' and '(Printed in Canada) Copyright, 1935, Star Newspaper Service'; 3–mid 4 introductory comments and 'Tea Service'; mid 4–top 5 'Tea Menus'; near top 5–20 recipes
COPIES: *Private collection

Jubilee cook book

O855.1   nd [about 1935]
Jubilee / cook book / This cook book we sell, / To let you all know / How best to knead / And cook the dough. / Cakes, jams and fancy cookies / Learn how to make these lovely goodies, / Doughnuts, pies and a juicy ham / Would win the heart of any man. / These recipes are especially nice, / If you eat them once, you'll bake them twice, / Try them all, and you will see, / That you'll be as pleased as you can be. / (Composed by Miss Dolce Russell.) / Issued by / Group No. 3, of Women's Association
DESCRIPTION: 23.0 × 15.0 cm   Pp [1] 2–40   Paper, with photograph on front of St Paul's United Church, Carp, Ontario; stapled
CONTENTS: 1 tp; 2 ads; 3–39 recipes credited with the name of the contributor and ads; 40 'Household Hints' and ad
COPIES: *Private collection
NOTES: The book was published about 1935 since there is an advertisement on p 6 for Rivington's Bakery, Carp, 'established 1883–1935.' The title of the cookbook may refer to the twenty-fifth anniversary of the reign of George V, who ascended the throne in 1910. There is a recipe on p 7 for Meat Loaf that 'took first prize, Carp Fair, 1932.'

Jubilee hostess

O856.1   nd [about 1935]
Jubilee hostess / a collection of / tested recipes /
compiled and arranged / by / Ottawa Chapter No.
37 / Order of the Eastern Star / Ottawa – Canada
DESCRIPTION: 22.0 × 14.5 cm   Pp [1–2] 3–72   Paper;
stapled
CONTENTS: 1 tp; 2 blank; 3 'Introduction' [i.e., poem
beginning, 'We may live without poetry, music and
art,' from *Lucile,* Part I, Canto ii, by Owen Meredith,
pseudonym of Edward Robert Bulwer-Lytton]; 4
blank; 5–69 recipes and ads; top–mid 70 'Quantities
for Serving Fifty People' and 'Time for Cooking
Meats'; bottom 70–71 'Household Hints'; 72 'Index'
[i.e., table of contents]
COPIES: OONL (TX715.6 J83 1935)   *Bookseller's
stock   Private collection
NOTES: The OONL copy is inscribed on the title-page,
in ink, 'Em Roy 17.1.36 [i.e., 17 January 1936] From
sis S. Butler.' The title of the cookbook may refer to
the twenty-fifth anniversary, in 1935, of the reign of
George V.

The Junket book

Several years earlier, in the June 1919 issue of
Everywoman's World, *Hansen's Laboratory advertised
a Junket recipe booklet (no copy located).*

O857.1   nd [about 1935]
Cool – creamy – desserts / The Junket book
[cover-title]
DESCRIPTION: 19.5 × 13.0 cm   Pp [1] 2–23   Illus col
Paper, with image on front of three junket desserts;
stapled
CONTENTS: 1 cover-title; 2 'Cool – Creamy – Desserts
// Quick and Easy to Make'; 3 'See How Easy It Is to
Make Junket! Follow Directions Carefully'; 4–21 recipes; 22 list and illus of Junket products (Junket Powder, Junket Tablets, Flavotint, Junket Food Colors); 23
[inside back face of binding] 'Index' and 'Lithographed in Canada // Harris Litho Co.'
CITATIONS: Chatelaine 1935, p 82
COPIES: QMM (RBD ckbk 1699)   *Private collection
NOTES: Junket is the name for a dessert made by the
addition of rennet (a preparation made from a cow's
stomach) to sweetened, flavoured milk. The rennet
causes the milk to form a soft curd. It was considered
an especially suitable food for children, infants, and
invalids. 'Copyright applied for' is on p 2. The

publisher's name and address are on p 22: The Junket Folks, Hansen's Laboratory Inc., 201 Church Street,
Toronto, Ontario.

Kitchen gems

O858.1   1935
Kitchen gems / Compiled by / the Women's
Association / Hensall, [*sic*, comma] United Church
/ 1935 / Cooks are born not made, they say, /
Which saying is not true / These recipes without
much trying / Will make good cooks of you. /
Methuselah ate what he found on his plate, / And
never as people do now, / Did he note the amount
of the calorie count. / He ate it because it was chow.
/ He wasn't disturbed as at dinner he sat, /
Destroying a roast or a pie, / To think it was lacking
in granular fat, / Or a couple of vitamines shy. /
He carefully chewed every species of food /
Untroubled by worries or fears, / Lest his health
might be hurt by some fancy dessert, / And he lived
over nine hundred years.
DESCRIPTION: Illus of the church above 'Our Greeting'
COPIES: OONL (TX715.6 K585 1935, not on shelf)
*Private collection
NOTES: The 'Index,' i.e., table of contents, shows
'Soups' beginning on p 1. 'Household Hints' on p 80
is the last text page, followed by several pages of
advertisements. The recipes are credited with the
name of the contributor. 'Our Greeting' acknowledges
the 'generous assistance of the McDonald [*sic*] Institute, Guelph.'

Kitchen lore

O859.1   [1935]
Kitchen / lore / Tested recipes / collected and
published by / the members of / Major George
Smith Chapter / Imperial Order / Daughters of the
Empire / of / Chatham, Ontario
DESCRIPTION: 23.5 × 15.5 cm   Pp [1] 2–68   Paper,
with IODE symbol on front; stapled
CONTENTS: 1 tp; 2 'Preface' and 'The Officers for 1935–
36'; 3 brief history of the Major George Smith Chapter, the second IODE chapter in Chatham, formed in
1915, and a report of its work to date; 4–61 recipes
credited with the name of the contributor, blank spaces
for 'Memoranda,' and ads; 62 'To Serve 100'; 63 'Large
Quantity Recipes'; 64 'Jelly Making'; 65 ad and 'Oven

Canning'; 66 'Time Table for Vegetables'; 67 blank for 'My Own Recipes'; 68 ad and 'Index' [i.e., table of contents]
COPIES: *OTMCL (641.5971 K39)

The latest cake secrets

Swans Down Cake Flour is an American product, first produced by Igleheart Bros Inc. of Evansville, Indiana, in 1896. Igleheart Bros later became part of General Foods Corp. Other cookbooks promoting the flour, published in the United States and predating The Latest Cake Secrets, *include* Cake Secrets *and* New Cake Secrets *(see Allen, p 157). I have seen copies of* Cake Secrets *and* New Cake Secrets *in Canadian homes, which indicates that they were distributed in Canada (for example, the 1925, 1926, and 1928 editions of* Cake Secrets, *and the 1931 edition of* New Cake Secrets*). For other Swans Down Cake Flour cookbooks, see Q131.1,* Cake Secrets, *published by Carnol Ltd, and O895.1,* Bake Like a Champion.

O860.1 nd [about 1935]
The latest / cake secrets / About forty years ago, the first cheery package of Swans Down / Cake Flour appeared to show women a wonderful new way to per- / fection in baking. This new kind of flour made friends fast. Women / tried it and marveled at the wonders it performed. The news flew / from kitchen to kitchen – to millions of homes. / "It makes cakes lighter ... tenderer ... more delicious." "It / gives cakes a fineness you simply can't get with ordinary flour." / Today, Swans Down, the original cake flour, is the most popular / and successful cake flour used in the land. / One glorious proof of it comes straight from the countless blue / ribbons that Swans Down cakes capture at fairs all over the / country. At state and county fairs, more prize-winning cakes are / made with Swans Down than with any other cake flour! / The "reason why" – the secret of this matchless Swans Down / perfection – makes a fascinating story. Before you reach for a / mixing bowl and spoon, before you try any of the tempting / recipes given in this book, be sure to turn to page 45. Read the / story of Swans Down. Here you will learn just how to make every / cake a blue-ribbon success. / And this is only one of the important sections in this helpful book, / for The Latest Cake Secrets includes the following sections: / Good Recipes Page 3 / A Hostess Calendar Page 39 / For Perfect Cakes

Page 43 / General Index Page 62 / Cake Set Offer Page 64 / Consumer Service Department / General Foods Limited / 1801 Sterling Towers Toronto
DESCRIPTION: 20.5 × 13.5 cm   Pp [1–3] 4–64   Illus col, illus   Paper, with image on front of a three-layer chocolate cake; stapled
CONTENTS: 1 tp; 2 untitled introductory note and '587 Printed in Canada'; 3–38 'Good Recipes ...'; 39–42 'A Hostess Calendar'; 43–61 'For Perfect Cakes ...'; 62–3 'General Index'; 64 order form for 'Swans Down Cake Set' and 'A Reliable Oven Thermometer' from Jane Taylor Allen, General Foods Ltd, Cobourg, Ontario, and at bottom, 'Produced in Canada by R.G. McLean Limited Toronto'
CITATIONS: Chatelaine 1935, p 82
COPIES: OGU (CCC TX715.6 L365 1930)   *Private collection
NOTES: This edition was likely published about 1935. The order form on p 64 for the cake set and thermometer says, 'Offer expires December 31, 1936,' and another private collector's copy is inscribed on the title-page, in ink, 'Thelma Briggs. Sept 6. 1935.' Chatelaine 1935, p 82, cites this title, available on request, for $0.10.

The 'Cake Score Card' on p 44 allocates 20% for general appearance, 35% for flavour, 15% for lightness, and 30% for crumb.

O860.2 nd
—[An edition of *The Latest Cake Secrets*]
COPIES: Private collection
NOTES: This edition appears to match the one above except that no expiry date is cited on p 64 for the cake set and thermometer offer.

AMERICAN EDITIONS: 3rd printing, General Foods Corp., 1934 (Allen, p 157); 4th printing, New York: General Foods Corp., [copyright 1934, cake set and thermometer order form on p 64 with expiry date of 31 December 1940] (OGU (CCC TX715.6 L365 1934)).

The mixing bowl

See also O991.1, Victory Cook Book, *from the same church.*

O861.1 1935
The mixing bowl / Preface / [three paragraphs of 'Preface'] / Compiled in 1935 by the / Women's Association / of / Calvin Presbyterian Church / Delisle Avenue – Toronto, Ont. / [folio:] 1

DESCRIPTION: 23.0 × 15.0 cm   Pp 1–88   Paper, with image on front of a bowl on a stand
COPIES: Great Britain: *OPo(F)
NOTES: The recipes are credited with the name of the contributor.

The mixing-bowl

O862.1   nd [about 1935]
The / mixing-bowl / A collection of / tried and tested / recipes / A Recipe for a Happy Day / A little dash of water cold, / A little leaven of prayer, / A little bit of sunshine gold, / Dissolved in morning air, / Add to your meal some merriment, / Add thought for kith and kin, / And then as a prime ingredient / A plenty of work thrown in. / Flavor it all with essence of love, / And a little dash of play; / Then a nice old book and a glance / above / Complete the happy day. / Compiled by / the members of / Pro Patria Chapter / Imperial Order Daughters of the Empire / Sarnia Ontario
DESCRIPTION: 22.5 × 14.5 cm   Pp [1–4] 5–64   Card, with IODE symbol on front; stapled
CONTENTS: 1 tp; 2 'Printed in Canada on Canadian paper by Canadian Printing Company // Sarnia, Ont.'; 3 'The Imperial Order Daughters of the Empire in Sarnia' [a history of the chapter]; 4 'Preface' signed the Committee; 5–61 recipes, most credited with the name of the contributor, a few blank spaces for 'Memorandum,' and ads; 62 'To Serve 100 People'; 63 ad and 'Table Decorations'; 64 ad and 'Index' [i.e., table of contents]
COPIES: *Private collection
NOTES: The history on p 3 records the chapter's creation in 1915 and refers to activities 'during the years of peace,' indicating a publication date after the First World War. An advertisement on p 12 for Doherty Mfg Co. Ltd, 'makers of good stoves for 53 years,' points to publication in about 1935 since the company, originally known as the Doherty-Barton Stove Works, was established in 1882 (1882 + 53 years; date of founding in Glen C. Phillips, *Sarnia: A Picture History of the Imperial City*, Sarnia, Ont.: Iron Gate Publishing Co., 1990). Further evidence of the date of publication is an advertisement on p 44 for the Clark Coal Co. Ltd, established in 1846, which boasts 'over 85 years of good service'; and an advertisement on p 35 for the Westinghouse Dual Automatic Refrigerator, a refrigerator design featured in O808.1, *The Westinghouse Refrigerator Book*, [about 1933].

129 prize winning recipes

For the titles of other Jewel Shortening cookbooks, see O695.1.

O863.1   copyright 1935
129 / prize winning recipes / from the / Jewel Shortening recipe contest / Published by / Swift Canadian Co., Limited / Toronto / Copyright, 1935
DESCRIPTION: 19.5 × 13.0 cm   Pp [1–2] 3–96   Illus   Paper; stapled
CONTENTS: 1 tp; 2–93 text; 94 'Canadian Home Journal Home Service Bureau Certificate of Approval' dated 2 December 1935 and overprinted '1936–37'; 95 publ ad for Jewel Shortening; 96 index
COPIES: OCHAK   OGU (CCC TX715.6 O545)   *Private collection
NOTES: The cover-title is '129 Winners!' The title-page is printed in red and black. The recipes are credited with the name of the winner.

O863.2   copyright 1935
—Recettes primées / 129 / au / concours de recettes du Shortening bijou / Livre publié par la / Swift Canadian Co., Limited / Toronto / Copyright, 1935
DESCRIPTION: 19.5 × 13.0 cm   Pp [1–2] 3–100   Illus   Paper; stapled
CONTENTS: 1 tp; 2–98 text; 99 publ ad for 'Bijou – le shortening moderne'; 100 'Table des matières'
COPIES: *OONL (TX767 S45 C4514 1935)
NOTES: The cover-title is '129 gagnantes!' The recipes are credited with the name of the winner.

The pantry shelf

O864.1   nd [about 1935]
The pantry shelf / A selection of / tried and tested recipes / Compiled and published / by the members of / the Ladies' Aid / of / St. Paul's United Church / Orillia, Ontario
DESCRIPTION: About 23.0 × 15.0 cm [dimensions from photocopy]   Pp [1–3] 4–56   Tp photograph of the church   Stapled
CONTENTS: 1 tp; 2 'Printed in Canada on Canadian paper // Packet-Times Press, Limited // Orillia, Ontario'; 3 'Preface' signed members of the Ladies' Aid; 4 'A Table of Weights and Measures'; 5–55 recipes credited with the name of the contributor and ads; 56 ad and 'Index' [i.e., table of contents]
COPIES: *Private collection

NOTES: This copy is inscribed on the binding, '1935.' An advertisement on the inside front face of the binding for H.A. Raney comments, 'for 29 years we have satisfied our customers with famous Reading Anthracite.' Knowing when the business started would confirm the cookbook's date of publication.

Pepper, Miss Laura Christine (Ottawa, Ont., 11 March 1899–9 August 1982, Ottawa, Ont.)

For information about Pepper and her other cookbooks, see O676.1.

O865.1 [1935]
Cream desserts / by / Laura C. Pepper / Dairy and Cold Storage Branch / Issued by the / Dominion Department of Agriculture / Ottawa, Canada [cover-title]
DESCRIPTION: 21.5 × 14.0 cm   Pp 1–24   Very thin card; stapled
CONTENTS: 1 'Cream Desserts' [i.e., introductory text]; 2 'Contents,' 'Abbreviations & Measurements,' and 'Notes'; 3–6 'Whipped Cream Desserts'; 7–14 'Moulded Cream Desserts'; 15–24 'Frozen Cream Desserts' and at bottom p 24, '2000.7.35'
CITATIONS: Ag 1867–1974, p 112
COPIES: *OOAG (641.637148 C212)   Private collection
NOTES: The private collector's copy has only '2000.' on p 24.

Recipes and pictures of famous movie stars

O866.1 nd [about 1935]
Price / $1.00 / Recipes / and pictures / of / famous movie / stars / featured in / Capitol Entertainment / Theatres / "Canada's finest" / Revealing the culinary secrets of the / screen idols of the world / Compliments of / Baker Brothers Cleaners / co-operating / with / St. Clair Theatre [cover-title]
DESCRIPTION: 23.0 × 15.5 cm   Pp [1–80]   Illus on p 1 of a Famous Players Theatre, many photographic portraits of movie stars   Paper, with design on front featuring scenes associated with the movie industry arranged around a large central star; stapled
CONTENTS: 1 ad for Capitol Entertainment Theatres operated by Famous Players' Canadian Corp. Ltd and 'Copright [sic] applied for. Printed in Canada.'; 2–80 photographs of movie stars, each accompanied by a recipe, and at bottom p 80, 'Douglas & Irving, printers – Toronto'
COPIES: *OKQ (F5012 nd F198)
NOTES: Chatelaine 1935, p 82, lists 'Favorite Foods of Famous Stars (limited supply),' free upon request from Rogers-Majestic Ltd, possibly the same book as O866.1.

AMERICAN EDITIONS: One or both of the following works may be related to the Canadian title: [Knight, Midge], *Hollywood's Famous Recipes of the Movie Stars, in Which 100 Screen Favorites Reveal Their Culinary Secrets,* Los Angeles: [1932] (United States: DLC); [Schulman, B. Donald], editor, *Favorite Recipes of the Famous Movie Stars ...,* [Milwaukee:] c1934 (United States: DLC).

Recipes and suggestions for serving Libby's 100 foods

Mary Hale Martin, who contributed the text on p 4 of O867.1, is the author of My Best Recipes, *Chicago: Libby, McNeill and Libby, 1934 (United States: DLC).*

O867.1   nd [about 1935]
Recipes and / suggestions / for serving / Libby's / 100 / foods / Presented with compliments / by / Libby, McNeill & Libby / of Canada, Limited / Chatham, Ontario
DESCRIPTION: 21.0 × 13.5 cm   Pp [1] 2–19   Illus on p 2 of Libby's factory; illus of Libby's products   Paper; stapled
CONTENTS: 1 tp; 2 illus of Libby's factory and information about company policy; 3 'Index' and 'Can Sizes'; 4 'Everyday Dishes for Everyday Table' signed Mary Hale Martin; 5–15 recipes using Libby's canned foods as ingredients; 16 'Libby's Foods and Where They Come From'; 17 'The Following Foods are Offered by Libby to Canadian Housewives' [i.e., list of products]; 18 'Mothers! Bring This Page to the Attention of Your Boy' [promotion where boys save labels to exchange for prizes listed in a catalogue]; 19 'Revolutionary Change in Baby Feeding' [ad for Libby's Baby Food]
CITATIONS: Chatelaine 1935, p 82
COPIES: ACG   *Private collection
NOTES: Chatelaine 1935 cites 'Suggestions for Serving Libby's 100 Foods (in preparation),' indicating a publication date of about 1935.

Scott, Anna Lee [pseudonym]

For information about Anna Lee Scott and her cookbooks, see O526.1.

O868.1   nd [about 1935]
Anna Lee Scott's personal selection / Four star recipes / chosen by Canada's foremost food authority / for the users of Monarch Flour [cover-title]
DESCRIPTION: 24.0 × 17.0 cm   Pp 1–16   Paper, with image on front of a tray of pastries; stapled
CONTENTS: Inside front face of binding 'Monarch Flour' and the manufacturer's name, Maple Leaf Milling Co. Ltd, Toronto and Winnipeg; 1 'All Measurements True and Level'; 2–3 'Biscuits, Muffins, Fancy Quick Breads'; 4–5 'Pastry and Fillings for Pies and Tarts'; 6–11 'Cakes'; 12–14 'Small Cakes and Cookies'; 15–16 'Fillings and Frostings'
COPIES: *NBMOM
NOTES: 'Oven Temperatures' on p 1 offer specific Fahrenheit degrees plus descriptive temperatures for housewives whose stoves do not have thermometers; for example: slow oven, 250° to 325°, hot enough to brown a spoonful of Monarch Pastry Flour very delicately in five minutes.

O869.1   nd [about 1935]
Happy "bakeday" to you! / For pastry and cakes / Monarch Flour / makes baking a pleasure [cover-title]
DESCRIPTION: 22.5 × 15.0 cm   Pp 1–16   Paper, with image on front of five singing blue birds; stapled
CONTENTS: Inside front face of binding 'First! Read This Page' signed Anna Lee Scott, explaining the difference between pastry flour and bread flour and telling how 'to adjust your favourite hard wheat flour recipes to Monarch Flour'; 1 untitled information about measuring, 'How to Measure – Important!,' and 'Oven Temperatures'; 2–16 recipes; inside back face publ's note signed Maple Leaf Milling Co. Ltd that says: 'The recipes in this book have all been carefully tested. They are the very cream of Anna Lee Scott's tremendous collection which she has been years in creating, accumulating, classifying and testing.'
CITATIONS: BouquinsCat 229, No. 343
COPIES: ACG   AEPMA   *NSLQCM   OGU (CCC TX715.6 H36)   OONL (TX763 H36 1900z, 2 copies) QMMMCM (2 copies: AR-M2000.62.18, AR-M2000 .92.36)
NOTES: The text is printed in blue throughout. Oven temperatures are described three ways: in Fahrenheit

degrees; in terms of speed, such as 'slow'; and in time taken to colour a spoonful of pastry flour. From appearances, the book was published about 1935. No place of publication is recorded, but in 1934 Maple Leaf Milling Co. moved its headquarters from West Toronto to the Dominion Bank Building in Toronto.

O869.2   nd [about 1935]
—"Délices de la cuisine" / Farine à pâtisserie et gâteaux / Monarch / pour une cuisine délectable [cover-title]
DESCRIPTION: 22.5 × 15.0 cm   Pp 1–16   Paper, with image on front of five singing blue birds; stapled
CONTENTS: Inside front face of binding 'En premier lieu – Lisez cette page!' signed Anna Lee Scott; 1 untitled information about measuring, 'Comment mesurer – Important!,' and 'Températures du four'; 2–16 recipes; inside back face publ's note signed Maple Leaf Milling Co. Ltd
COPIES: OONL (TX763 D44 1950z p***)   *QMBM (Env. 7839)   QSFFSC
NOTES: The text is printed in blue.

300 household hints

See O703.1 for other titles by the London Life Insurance Co.

O870.1   [1935]
300 / household / hints / Published and distributed by / [the] London Life Insurance Company – Head office London, Can. [cover-title]
DESCRIPTION: 23.0 × 15.5 cm   Pp [1–2] 3–19   Paper, with flower pattern on front; stapled
CONTENTS: 1 cover-title; 2–4 index; 5–19 300 numbered hints
COPIES: OTNY (uncat)   *Private collection
NOTES: 'H-10–6-35' is printed on the outside back face of the binding, indicating a publication date of 1935. The index lists hints for bread, butter, cake, cream and milk, eggs, the cooking of fish, fowl, and meat, flour, fruit, jams and jellies, lemons, measuring, nuts, pickles, potatoes, puddings and pies, salt and its uses, soup making, vegetables, vinegar, and for other subjects associated with cooking, such as cleaning and preventing and removing odours. The text is printed in brown throughout.

The book was reprinted in 1936 and 1937: QMM (RBD ckbk 1776) has a copy with 'H-10–7-36' on the outside back face of the binding; OONL (AC901 A7 1937 No. 0062) has a copy with 'H-10–2-37.'

O870.2 nd
—300 / household hints / Presented with the compliments of / the London Life Insurance Company / Head office: London, Canada [cover-title]
COPIES: *Private collection
NOTES: The binding is plain; there is no floral pattern.

Vreamay icings and fillings

See also O564.1, After All It Takes a Baker, *promoting the use of Vream, the company's vegetable shortening, and O575.1,* Swift's Bakers' Pastry Shortening in the Bakeshop, *another cookbook for professional bakers.*

O871.1 nd [about 1935]
Vreamay / icings / and / fillings / Prepared by / Research Bakery Division / Swift Canadian Company / Limited / Toronto
DESCRIPTION: About 21.5 × 14.0 cm [dimensions from photocopy]
CONTENTS: 1 tp; 2 'Eye Appeal'; 3 'Icing Pointers'; 4–28 recipes for icings and fillings; 29 'Index' [i.e., table of contents]; 30–1 blank for 'Your Own Formulas'
COPIES: *Private collection

O871.2 7th ed., nd
—[Seventh edition of *Vreamay Icings and Fillings,* Toronto: Research Bakery Division, Swift Canadian Co., nd, pp 31]
COPIES: Bookseller's stock
NOTES: The bookseller judges the date of publication to be 1940s.

We entertain

See also O726.1 from the same church.

O872.1 1935
We / entertain / with / salads sandwiches / cakes cookies desserts / supper dishes / 1935 / Compiled by / the Woman's Association / Hope United Church / Danforth Avenue at Main St. / Toronto, Ontario [cover-title]
DESCRIPTION: 22.5 × 15.0 cm   Pp 1–60   Paper; stapled
CONTENTS: 1 'We Entertain // A Collection of Tested Recipes for Salads Sandwiches Cakes Cookies Desserts and Supper Dishes' and untitled preface; 2–59 text and ads; 60 index
COPIES: *Private collection
NOTES: In the same year, North Broadview United

Church, also in the east end of Toronto, published a cookbook with an identical title and the same number of pages (O873.1).

We entertain

O873.1 1935
We / entertain / with / salads sandwiches / cakes cookies desserts / supper dishes / 1935 / Compiled by / the Woman's Association / North Broadview United Church / Dearbourne and Broadview avenues / Toronto, Ontario [cover-title]
DESCRIPTION: 23.0 × 15.0 cm   Pp 1–60   Thin card; stapled
CONTENTS: 1 untitled introductory text; 2–57 recipes credited with the name of the contributor and ads; 58 'Household Hints'; 59 'Suggestions for Table Decorations'; 60 ad and 'Index' [i.e., table of contents]
COPIES: *Private collection
NOTES: In the same year, Hope United Church, also in the east end of Toronto, published a cookbook with an identical title and the same number of pages (O872.1).

Weston's modern recipes for delicious desserts

O874.1 nd [about 1935]
Weston's / modern / recipes / for / delicious / desserts / quickly and / easily / prepared / George Weston Ltd. / 134 Peter St. Toronto [cover-title]
DESCRIPTION: 16.5 × 9.0 cm   Pp [1–2] 3–15   Paper, with four images on front: an aproned woman setting a dessert on a table, and three different desserts; stapled
CONTENTS: 1 cover-title; 2 'Index to Recipes'; 3–15 forty-two numbered recipes using Weston's Honey Graham Wafers, Weston's 'Frigid-Icies' Biscuits, and Weston's Summertime Crackers
COPIES: ACG   MWPA   *Private collection
NOTES: The text is printed in red and black.

What you should know about economical cooking

O875.1 1935
What you should know about / economical cooking / No. 2 in the "What You Should Know / About –" Series / Under the general editorship of / Grant Fleming, M.C., M.D., D.P.H., F.R.C.P. (C.). / ['The

Macmillans in Canada' symbol] / Toronto: The Macmillan Company of / Canada Limited, at St. Martin's House / 1935
DESCRIPTION: 15.5 × 10.0 cm   Pp [i–x] xi [xii–xiv], 1–82   Paper-covered boards
CONTENTS: i ht; ii list of titles in the 'What You Should Know About' Series (*Cancer, Economical Cooking,* and *Your Heart*); iii tp; iv 'Copyright, Canada, 1935 by the Macmillan Company of Canada, Limited ... Printed in Canada T.H. Best Printing Co., Limited Toronto, Ont.'; v–vii 'Contents'; viii blank; ix 'Foreword' signed Grant Fleming; x blank; xi 'Introduction'; xii blank; xiii part-title; xiv blank; 1–81 text in fifteen chapters; 82 'Postscript'
CITATIONS: Whiteman et al., No. 666
COPIES: OH (R641.5 C161 CESC)   OHM (TX715.6 C36 1935)   OONL (TX715 W4347 1935)   OTTHOCI (641.5 C212 missing)   *QMM (TX715 C2121W 1935 Health Sciences); United States: NNNAM (S.21.B)
NOTES: The first chapter presents general information about 'Feeding the Family,' 'Food for Health,' 'The Kinds of Food,' 'What to Eat,' and 'How Much to Eat,' etc. Chapters 2–14 include recipes. The last chapter, 'Budgetting,' shows how to budget on an annual income of $1,000 for a family of five. The QMM copy has a presentation plate that states, 'Presented to Medical Library of McGill University by Dr A.G. Fleming' [i.e., Albert Grant Fleming, the general editor].

1935–7

The Carnation year book of menus and recipes

Mary Blake, the name on p 2 of O876.1, was the pseudonym used by the company on publications promoting Carnation Milk, from the 1920s. For information about Blake and her cookbooks, see O494.1; for the company, see O350.1.

O876.1   nd [about 1935–7]
The / Carnation / year book / of menus and / recipes / [circling the title:] spring summer autumn winter [cover-title]
DESCRIPTION: 23.0 × 15.5 cm   Pp [1] 2–44 [45–7] 9 fp illus, a few illus   Paper; stapled
CONTENTS: 1 cover-title; 2 'Seasonable Menus and Dishes for Your Table' signed Mary Blake, home counselor, Carnation Co. Ltd, Toronto, Ontario; 3 'It's a Joy to Cook This Easy, Economical Way'; 4–12 menus and recipes for spring; 13–21 menus and recipes for

summer; 22–30 menus and recipes for autumn; 31–9 menus and recipes for winter; 40–1 'Ideal for Babies and Growing Children'; 42 'Menus for Children'; 43 'Children's Recipes'; 44 'Cookery Advice'; 45–6 'Send for This De Luxe Cook Book' [i.e., *Carnation Cook Book* by Mary Blake]; 47 [inside back face of binding] 'Index' and at bottom p 47, 'Printed in Canada CC-964'
COPIES: OONL (TX759.5 M54 C37 1900z, 2 copies) *OGU (CCC TX715.6 B523)
NOTES: The illustration on p 45 of the *Carnation Cook Book* by Mary Blake is of one of the editions where the title and author's name are shown in needlework, possibly the 1935 or 1937 edition (O844.1 or O844.2); therefore, the undated *Carnation Year Book of Menus and Recipes* was likely published about those years.

O876.2   nd [about 1935–7]
—Le livre / de menus et recettes / Carnation / pour toute / l'année / [circling the title:] printemps été automne hiver [cover-title]
DESCRIPTION: 23.5 × 15.5 cm   Pp [1] 2–44 [45]   9 fp illus, a few illus   Paper; stapled
CONTENTS: 1 cover-title; ...; 45 'Table des matières' and at bottom, 'Imprimé au Canada CC-964F-C'
COPIES: *QSFFSC

1935–9

Adam, Ann [pseudonym]

Kathleen Mary Frances Bayley, née Caldwell and known as Katherine or Kay (10 September 1889–1976), created the pseudonym Ann Adam and the business called Ann Adam Homecrafters, which she operated out of her home at 42 Roselawn Avenue, in Toronto. Her husband, Walter Silliman Bayley (1886–1959), served as business manager. The couple had no children. Katherine, the eldest of five sisters, graduated with a BA from the University of Toronto in 1911. Under the pseudonym Ann Adam, she wrote cookery columns for the Mail and Empire, *from 1936 called the* Globe and Mail. *(In later years, Mary Adams, an employee of Ann Adam Homecrafters, wrote the last Ann Adam columns in the* Globe and Mail.) *For about thirty years Katherine was the host of the Ann Adam Cooking School of the Air on CFRB. Ann Adam Homecrafters acted as consultants to many food companies, including Standard Brands and Maple Leaf Milling Co., so that Katherine and the home economists she employed wrote many of the cookbooks produced by these client companies; for example, early cookbooks by Maple Leaf Milling Co. published under the pseudonym Anna Lee Scott (see the history of Scott at O526.1).*

See also the following by Ann Adam: O1065.1, The Lunch Box and Food Saver Book; *O1066.1,* The Meat Extender Book; *O1067.1,* New Ideas for Praise Winning Meals and Parties; *and O1149.1,* De la magie dans les menus avec le nouveau 'Handi-Chef.' *Ann Adam contributed 'Food Forecast for 1944' to O1091.1,* Household Helps for 1944.

Under her own name, Katherine wrote for the 'Household Department' of Everywoman's World *in the period November 1916–December 1920, and she was the food editor of the* Canadian Home Journal, *from the 1920s until the last issue of June 1958 (after which the magazine merged with* Chatelaine). *She wrote O466.1,* Recettes pour tous les jours, *1921, for Procter and Gamble Manufacturing Co., and she 'judged and approved' the recipes in O898.1,* 43 Prize Winning Recipes, *for Swift Canadian Co. in 1936. She contributed recipes to S78.1,* The Doughnut Book of Recipes.

For a first-hand account of the activities of Ann Adam Homecrafters, see a 4-page document at OGU by the home economist Helen Gagen, who worked for Katherine from 1931 to 1942, when Katherine's sister Lois Caldwell succeeded her (Helen Gagen Collection, XM1 MS A123, Box 44, File 9, 'Re: Katherine Caldwell Bayley, Ann Adam, Anna Lee Scott,' January 1987). Information in this entry also comes from a personal communication with Mary Adams, June 2001. See also: 1901 Census; and 'Honor Food Columnist. For 50 Years' Service,' Globe and Mail *(Toronto) 27 February 1963, which includes Katherine's photograph, and photographs of her in* THEA *1988, p 2 (about 1934, at Massey Hall) and p 37 (at the 1963 reception in her honour). A picture of her in her graduation year is in* Torontonensis *(University of Toronto yearbook), 1911. She is buried in Mount Pleasant Cemetery in Toronto.*

O877.1   nd [about 1935–9]
[Northern Electric symbol] / "Good cooking" / by / Ann Adam / with the / Northern Electric / Range [cover-title]
DESCRIPTION: 22.5 × 15.5 cm   Pp [1–2] 3–96   Illus
Paper; stapled
CONTENTS: 1 'Foreword' signed Ann Adam; 2 blank; 3–7 information about the range; 8 blank; 9–90 recipes; top 91 'General Index of Subjets'; mid 91–96 'Index'
COPIES: *OGU (CCC TX715.6 A3)
NOTES: According to p 3, Northern Electric ranges were 'designed and built in Canada by Canadians.' Page 4 refers to models No. 800 and No. 1800. 'Printed in Canada by Southam Press Toronto Limited' is on the outside back face of the binding.

O878.1   nd [about 1935–9]
Meat / cookery / by / Schneiders [cover-title]
DESCRIPTION: 20.0 × 12.5 cm   Pp [1] 2–16   Illus col
Paper, with image on front of plump gnome-like chefs carrying over-sized sausages, hams, and other meats; stapled
CONTENTS: Inside front face of binding illus of factory (caption: 'The home of Schneiders quality meat products // Established 1890') and portrait of J.M. Schneider, founder and president; 1 'Schneider's "For Every Meal of the Day,"' introductory note signed Ann Adam, and 'J.M. Schneider Limited Kitchener, Ontario.'; 2 'Meat in Daily Meals' and 'This Book to Aid You'; 3 'Canada Approved Protection' and '"Schneider's" Protection'; 4–5 recipes; 6 pork cuts; 7–10 illus of Schneider's meat products; 11 beef cuts; 12–16 recipes, and at bottom p 16, 'Artindale & Shantz Ltd.' [i.e., printer]; inside back face Seal of Approval No. 120 from the Home Service Bureau of *Canadian Home Journal*
COPIES: OGU (CCC TX715.6 A29)   QMMMCM (AR-M2000.62.16)   *Private collection
NOTES: The title on p 1 and the running head is 'Schneider's "For Every Meal of the Day."' Government strip brands are explained on p 3: blue strip means '"Schneider's Good" quality'; red strip means '"Schneider's Choice."'

The OGU copy matches the description above except that the caption for the factory does not include 'Established 1890.'

Attractive recipes for Canadian households

O879.1   nd [about 1935–9]
Attractive recipes / for Canadian households [cover-title]
DESCRIPTION: 19.0 × 12.5 cm   Pp 1–19   Paper, with image on front of mother kangaroo and two joeys at a kitchen table where the mother has rolled out pastry in the shape of Australia and bags of currants and raisins sit open on the table; stapled
CONTENTS: 1 'Sunshine Recipes' [i.e., introductory text]; 2–mid 19 recipes for 'Breads (Hot),' 'Cakes (Small),' 'Cakes (Large),' 'Desserts,' 'Meats,' 'Miscellaneous,' 'Pastry,' 'Salads,' 'Sandwiches,' and 'Sauces' (some recipe sections are followed by tips for making that type of recipe); bottom 19 'General Hints'
COPIES: *Private collection
NOTES: 'Index,' i.e., the table of contents, is on the outside back face of the binding. 'Sunshine Recipes,' p 1, makes clear that *Attractive Recipes* was published to promote the use by Canadians of Australian rai-

sins and currants, although no sponsoring organization or publisher is named: 'This booklet contains simple and inexpensive recipes specially prepared by a leading Canadian dietitian. All these recipes require the use of raisins or currants. Australian raisins and currants are sun-dried grapes, full of rich flavours, abounding in nourishment and free from injurious chemicals. Australian raisins and currants are meatier, more flavoury and richer in natural grape sugar than competing products.' Many of the recipe names make reference to Australia: Australian Sultana Tea Ring, Murray River Raisin Bread, Australian Fruit Drops, Anzac Tea Cakes, Captain Cook Christmas Cake, Melbourne Sultana Cake, Brisbane Rice and Raisin Pudding, Renmark Raisin Whip, Sydney Sultana Sponge Pudding, Australian Meat Loaf, Derwent River Chutney, Mildura Mincemeat, Adelaide Pie, Bush Tartlets, Fish Salad, Australian Style, and Swan River Salad. There is also a recipe for Commonwealth Tea Scones, a reference to the British Commonwealth to which both Canadians and Australians belong.

The same private collector owns a 12-page booklet, with an identical binding design, titled *Attractive Recipes for the Canadian Bakery Trade.* On the inside back face of the binding, bakers are advised that 'Further copies of this booklet may be obtained on application to: The Australian Trade Commissioner in Canada // 15 King Street West, Toronto, Ont.' The introductory text, headed 'Sunshine Recipes for the Canadian Bakery Trade,' states: 'This book contains simple and inexpensive recipes specially designed by a Canadian dietitian as being suitable for the Canadian trade. They have been examined, revised and approved by practical Canadian bakers. All of these recipes require the use of raisins and currants.' The recipes are for making large amounts, for sale. *Attractive Recipes for Canadian Households* was probably also published by the Australian Trade Commissioner in Toronto.

Budget recipes for every day of the year

St Lawrence Starch Co., Port Credit, Ontario, incorporated in 1889. Its archives are at OTAR.

O880.1   nd [about 1935–9]
Budget / recipes / for every day of the year / All measurements level, using / standard measuring spoons & cup / Page [i.e., heading for column of page numbers] / [untitled index of 34 items with corresponding page numbers] / St. Lawrence Starch Co. Limited / Port Credit Ontario

DESCRIPTION: 16.5 × 8.0 cm   Pp [3] 4–23 Illus col   Paper, with image on front of upside-down cake, and on back, slice of lemon meringue pie; stapled
CONTENTS: 3 tp and index; 4–14 recipes using Bee Hive Golden Corn Syrup and on pp 12–13, 'Health Value of Bee Hive Corn Syrup'; 15–19 recipes using Durham Corn Starch; 20–1 recipes using St Lawrence Refined Corn Oil; 22–3 [inside back face of binding] instructions for Ivory Starch
COPIES: *Private collection
NOTES: 'Tested and approved by the Home Bureau, Canadian Home Journal' is on the front face of the binding. The date of publication is uncertain; *Budget Recipes* may have appeared as late as O1054.1, *The Bee Hive Cook Book,* [copyright 1942], another company publication.

The buying and cooking of meat

See O703.1 for other titles by the London Life Insurance Co.

O881.1   nd [about 1935–9]
The buying and cooking of / meat / Presented with the compliments of / the London Life Insurance Company [cover-title]
DESCRIPTION: 23.0 × 15.0 cm   Pp [1–2] 3–23 Illus   Paper, with image on front of a mother preparing a pot roast as daughter watches; stapled
CONTENTS: 1 cover-title; 2 table of contents and 'The London Life [*sic*, abbreviated name] acknowledges the valuable assistance of Miss Helen G. Campbell, Director of Chatelaine Institute, in the preparation and editing of this booklet. The illustrations were provided through the courtesy of Swift Canadian Company. The London Life Insurance Company // Head office: London, Canada'; 3–17 general information about the buying and cooking of meat; 18–22 recipes for beef, veal, pork, and lamb; 23 [inside back face of binding] 'Time Table for Meat Roasting'; outside back face 'H-9' and the stamp 'Harry M. Philbrook // Office phone N.W. 939 // 306 Westminster Trust Block'
COPIES: OGU (CCC TX715.6 B99)   *OONL (TX749 B89 1940z p***)   OTMCL (641.5971 H39 No. 89)
NOTES: From appearances, the book was published in the late 1930s. It could not have been published after 1946, the last year that Helen Campbell was director of the Chatelaine Institute. For the titles of Campbell's cookbooks and information about her, see O477.1. 'D. Kewin representing London Life Insurance Co.' is stamped on the outside back face of the OTMCL copy.

Cook book

Bellingham United Church is part of the Iron Bridge pastoral charge in Northern Ontario, midway between Thessalon and Blind River.

O882.1 [about 1935–9]
Cook / book / By the / Bellingham United Church W.A. [cover-title]
DESCRIPTION: Paper, with image on front of a cake with slice removed; stapled
COPIES: *Private collection
NOTES: The binding is inscribed 'Mrs Lynn Forder.'

Cook book

O883.1 nd [about 1935–9]
Empress Avenue United Church / London – Canada / Cook book / All recipes tested and proven // Compiled by Group IV W.A. / All proceeds for Church Building Fund [cover-title]
DESCRIPTION: 15.0 × 21.0 cm   Pp [i–ii], 1–64   Paper; stapled
CONTENTS: i 'Index' [i.e., alphabetical list of sections]; ii blank; 1–64 recipes credited with the name of the contributor
COPIES: *Private collection
NOTES: The arabic-numbered pages are printed on the rectos only; the versos are blank and not included in the pagination. This copy is inscribed on p i: 'From Rosalia Nov. 20. 1953. Susan Axford 738 Elias St London Ont.'

Cook book

O884.1 nd [about 1935–9]
First United Church / Circle "4" / Cook / book / We may live without friends, / We may live without books; / But civilized man – / Cannot live without cooks. / Price: 50c [cover-title]
DESCRIPTION: 21.5 × 14.0 cm   Pp [i–ii], [1] 2–68 [69–70]   Paper; stapled
CONTENTS: i 'Index' [i.e., table of contents]; ii blank; 1–68 recipes; 69 blank; 70 blank for 'Memorandum'
COPIES: *Private collection
NOTES: The cover-title is printed on the paper binding; the interior text pages are typed. On the inside faces of the binding and on the outside back face, there are advertisements for Ottawa businesses. The advertisement on the outside back face is for the company that likely printed this cookbook: Progres-sive Printers, 430 Gladstone Avenue, Ottawa, telephone 5-1437, 'church printing a specialty.'

Dumont-Lespine, Gabriel

The French author Gabriel Dumont-Lespine, known as an expert in electric cookery, wrote: Mes recettes de cuisine électrique, *Paris: Impr. française de l'édition, Société Als-Thom, 1933;* Nos recettes au four électrique, *Paris: Compagnie parisienne de distribution d'électricité, [1943]; and* Mes recettes de pâtisserie, *Paris: Éditions de la couronne, 1948 (all France: PBNF).*

O885.1 nd [about 1935–9]
Entremets / et boissons / glacés / par / l'appareil / réfrigérateur / Recettes par / G. Dumont-Lespine / Illustrations de / M.A.B. Campbell
DESCRIPTION: 21.0 × 14.0 cm   Pp [3–9] 10–183 [184]   Illus red-and-black   Paper-covered boards; sewn
CONTENTS: 3 ht; 4 'Les recettes ont été exécutées dans le réfrigérateur Général électrique de la Canadian General Electric Co Ltd, King & Silcoe [*sic*; should be Simcoe] streets, Toronto, Ontario, Canaca [*sic*].'; 5 tp; 6 blank; 7 'Note de l'auteur' signed G. Dumont-Lespine, 'Rédacteur en chef de "Culina", vice-président de l'Association des gastronomes régionalistes, professeur de cuisine et de pâtisserie à la Compagnie parisienne de distribution d'électricité'; 8 blank; 9–180 text; 181–3 'Table des matières' and at bottom p 183, 'Printed in France'
CITATIONS: BQ 10-0986
COPIES: QMBN (202779 CON) *QSFFSC (641.5 D893e)
NOTES: This is a beautifully produced book, with the exception of the typographical errors on p 4.

Electric cookery by Westinghouse

O886.1 nd [about 1935–9]
Electric cookery / by / Westinghouse [cover-title]
DESCRIPTION: [$1.25, on p i]
CONTENTS: i 'Your Westinghouse Range' signed Canadian Westinghouse Co. Ltd, Hamilton, Ontario, the price, and 'No. 6020 RM'; ii 'Keeping Your Westinghouse Range Like New'; ...
COPIES: *Private collection
NOTES: The introductory note about 'Your Westinghouse Range' is the same as O886.2, except that there is no reference to wartime. The owner of the book reports that it came with a new stove that her

parents purchased in the late 1930s. The main text of 144 pp is followed by a 15-page 'Meat Selection and Cookery Guide,' copyright 1937, which suggests that this entry belongs later in the bibliography. Another collector has a copy where the text is identical on p i except for the mark 'Form 6021A–A4M.'

O886.2   nd [about 1939–45]
—Electric cookery / by / Westinghouse [cover-title]
DESCRIPTION: 22.5 × 14.5 cm   Pp [i] ii–xii, 1–144 [$1.25, on p i]   Illus   Card; bound with a form of metal clasp
CONTENTS: i 'Your Westinghouse Range' signed Canadian Westinghouse Co. Ltd, Hamilton, Ontario, the price, and 'Form 6020B–RM, CM & A4M'; ii 'Keeping Your Westinghouse Range Like New'; iii 'Cleaning Your Oven'; iv 'The Cooking Surface'; v 'Care of Elements'; vi 'The Westinghouse Oven'; vii 'Broiling'; viii 'Mixed Grills'; ix 'Oven Dinners Are Delicious and Save Time'; x 'Oven Temperature Guide for Meat'; xi 'Oven Temperature Guide for Baking'; xii 'Substitutions'; 1–137 recipes; 138–44 'Index' and at bottom p 144, '32 V. Form No. 6014 Printed in Canada [paper abraded]'
COPIES: *OH (R641.5 COR CESH)
NOTES: The text on p i indicates that the book was published during wartime: 'The range which you have purchased is precious. The use, in war industry, of much of the material required to build ranges means that future production is very problematical.'

I have not compared, side by side, the texts of *Electric Cookery by Westinghouse* and O1132.1, *Delicious Foods and How to Cook Them with Your Westinghouse Electric Range*, by Anna May Cornell; however, *Delicious Foods* may be a later edition of *Electric Cookery*: The headings of the roman-numbered pages correspond, except that *Electric Cookery* has a page headed 'Care of Elements' but no title-page, whereas *Delicious Foods* has a title-page but no page devoted to elements; each has the same number of arabic-numbered pages where the recipes are on pp 1–137 and the index on pp 138–44; and *Delicious Foods* shares the same cover-title, *Electric Cookery by Westinghouse*. The earliest identified edition of *Delicious Foods* is the revised of June 1946. Whether Anna May Cornell was involved in the wartime production of *Electric Cookery* (or of O886.1) is unknown. Although her name is not cited in its pages, she was the home economist for Canadian Westinghouse, and she is connected with several of the company's cookbooks through the 1930s and 1940s. (OH has catalogued O886.2 as the same as O1132.1.) For Cornell's cookbooks, see O781.1.

Favorite desserts of the Chatelaine Institute

O887.1   nd [about 1935–9]
Chatelaine Service Bulletin Number 2201 / Favorite desserts / of the / Chatelaine Institute / Helen G. Campbell, Director [cover-title]
DESCRIPTION: 22.5 × 15.0 cm   Pp [1] 2–16   Illus   Paper, with image on front of desserts in stemmed glasses; stapled
CONTENTS: 1 cover-title; top 2 'Favorite Desserts' [i.e., introductory text]; mid 2–16 recipes for 'Cold Desserts,' 'Hot Desserts,' 'Jellied Desserts,' 'Frozen Desserts,' 'Fruit Desserts,' and 'Pastry Desserts,' and at bottom p 16, the Chatelaine 'Tested and approved' symbol and 'Chatelaine Service Bulletin No. 2,201 // Price 15 cents'
COPIES: *Private collection
NOTES: From appearances, *Favorite Desserts* was published in the late 1930s. It could not have been published after 1946, the last year that Campbell was director of the Chatelaine Institute. Other Service Bulletins include No. 2200, *28 Cookie Recipes*, pp 8, $0.10 (Private collection), and *Wedding Etiquette*, $0.05 (noted on p 8 of *28 Cookie Recipes*). No place of publication is recorded, but the *Chatelaine* office was in Toronto.

Favorite recipes

O888.1   nd [about 1935–9]
Favorite recipes / A selection of tried and tested recipes / compiled and published by / the Ladies Aid / of / Norfolk Street United Church / Guelph Ontario / [folio:] 1
DESCRIPTION: 23.0 × 15.0 cm   Pp 1–48   Tp photograph of the church   Lacks binding; stapled
CONTENTS: 1 tp; 2 'Preface' and 'Officers of Ladies' Aid Norfolk Street United Church' (lists Mrs W.H. Beattie as honorary president and Mrs Wm C. Wyles as president); 3–46 recipes credited with the name of the contributor and ads; 47 'For Serving 100'; 48 ad and 'Index' [i.e., table of contents]
COPIES: *Private collection

Findlay cooking guide

David Findlay, the original founder, died in 1890; David Findlay, his eldest son, died in 1934. Findlays Ltd was purchased by a larger company in 1968; the business closed in 1974.

O889.1   nd [about 1935–9]
Findlay / cooking / guide / Findlays Limited /
Carleton Place – Ontario [English cover-title on one
face of binding] Guide / Findlay / pour la /
cuisiniere moderne / Findlays Limited / Carleton
Place – Ontario [French cover-title on other face]
COPIES: *Private collection
NOTES: There are 18 pp of English text and 18 pp of
French text. The 'Foreword' for the English text states:
'Findlay Stoves have been giving service in Canadian
homes for more than fifty years. From the small
foundry built in 1860 by the late David Findlay, the
business has grown to such an extent that the plant
has floor space of five acres and employs three hundred men ... Findlays Limited takes pride in offering
... a complete line of coal and wood ranges, gas ranges,
electric ranges, combination ranges, heaters for coal,
wood and oil, warm air furnaces, and air condition-
ing systems.' The reference to the 1860 foundry and
over fifty years of service is evidence of publication
after 1910. From appearances, the book was published about 1935–9, but the actual date may be a
little earlier, before the death of the second David
Findlay in 1934.

The good luck cook book

*The White Oak Chapter was established in 1921 and
disbanded in 2000.*

O890.1   nd [about 1935–9]
The / good luck / cook book / A Kitchen Prayer /
[poem beginning, 'Lord of all pots and pans and
things, ...' by 'Anon.'] / A collection of tried and
tested recipes / arranged and published by / White
Oak Chapter / Imperial Order Daughters of the
Empire / Oakville Ontario
DESCRIPTION: 23.0 × 15.0 cm   Pp [1–3] 4–48   Thin
card, with IODE symbol on front; stapled
CONTENTS: 1 tp; 2 'Index' [i.e., table of contents] and
the printer's name, 'The Oakville Record Ltd.,
Oakville, Ont.'; 3 'Preface'; 4–top 47 recipes credited
with the name of the contributor and ads; mid–
bottom 47 'Household Hints'; 48 'Time Tables'
COPIES: *Private collection

The pantry shelf

O891.1   nd [about 1935–9]
The / pantry shelf / A / collection / of / tried and
tested recipes / selected and arranged for

publication / by / the members of / the Ladies' Aid
/ of / St. Paul's Presbyterian Church /
Peterborough Ontario
DESCRIPTION: 22.5 × 15.5 cm   Pp [1–2] 3–84   Thin
card; stapled
CONTENTS: 1 tp; 2 'Officers of St. Paul's Ladies' Aid'
[lists Mrs R. Stewart and Mrs W.H. Hill as honorary
presidents, and Mrs H.G. McKenzie as president]; 3
'Preface' signed Ladies' Aid of St Paul's Presbyterian
Church; 4–83 text, mainly recipes credited with the
name of the contributor, blank spaces for 'My Own
Recipes' and 'New Recipes,' and ads; 84 'Index' [i.e.,
table of contents] and ads
COPIES: *Private collection
NOTES: The text includes recipes from Mrs Barr, wife
of Dr A.T. Barr, minister of St Paul's from 1931 to
1941. The appearance of the book suggests publication about 1935–9.

Recipe clippings

O892.1   nd [about 1935–9]
Recipe / clippings [cover-title]
DESCRIPTION: 20.5 × 13.5 cm   [Nine envelopes]   Thin
card; Cercla binding (patent 337087)
CONTENTS: Inside front face of binding 'Recipe Clip-
ping Book // For Successful Cooking [six numbered
steps] Cercla bound ... Book No. C53 Warwick Bros.
& Rutter, Limited Toronto, Canada'; envelope [env.] 1
'Cakes'; env. 2 'Desserts'; env. 3 'Fish'; env. 4 'Meats';
env. 5 'Pies'; env. 6 'Soups'; env. 7 'Salads'; env. 8
'Sweets'; env. 9 'Miscellaneous'; inside back face
'Cooking Tables and Charts'
COPIES: *Private collection

Scott, Anna Lee [pseudonym]

*For information about Anna Lee Scott and her cookbooks,
see O526.1.*

O893.1   nd [about 1935–9]
The cook's tour / to the realm of / cakes / Fine cake
recipes for / Maple Leaf Cake Flour / Anna Lee
Scott [cover-title]
DESCRIPTION: 18.5 × 12.0 cm   Pp [1–2] 3–15   Paper,
with image on front of a box of Maple Leaf Cake
Flour; stapled
CONTENTS: 1 cover-title; 2 index; 3–15 recipes
CITATIONS: Ferguson/Fraser, p 234, illus col on p 103
of closed volume
COPIES: OAUH   OGU (3 copies: CCC TX715.6 S352,

TX715.6 M572 Nos. 177 and 303) OONL (TX765 S46 1940z copy 1; copy 2 missing) *Private collection
NOTES: On the box of Maple Leaf Cake Flour (illustrated on the binding) Anna Lee Scott is depicted holding up a box of the Cake Flour, i.e., the box design features an image within an image. On the outside back face of the binding there are illustrations of packages of Tea-Bisk, Maple Leaf Cream of the West Flour, Monarch Pastry Flour, and Red River Cereal, plus the manufacturer's name, Maple Leaf Milling Co. Ltd, which was based in Toronto. Ferguson/Fraser suggest a date of about 1945, but the image of Anna Lee Scott is the one used in the late 1930s; for example, on the outside back face of the binding of O975.1, *51 Ways to a Man's Heart*.

Tested recipes: Wishes come true for cooks who use Jewel

For the titles of other Jewel Shortening cookbooks, see O695.1.

O894.1 nd [about 1935–9]
Tested recipes / Wishes come true / for cooks who use / Jewel [cover-title]
DESCRIPTION: 16.5 × 8.0 cm Pp 1–16 Illus Paper, with image on front of a mother watching her son blow out four candles on a birthday cake; stapled
CONTENTS: 1–6 'Jewel Makes Excellent Cakes, Cookies, Desserts'; 7–11 'Jewel Makes Pastry News'; 12–14 'Practical and Perfect Jewel Doughs'; 15–16 'Jewel ... Unrivalled for Successful Frying'
COPIES: *Private collection
NOTES: No place of publication is recorded, but Swift Canadian Co. Ltd, which made Jewel Shortening, had its head office in Toronto. From appearances, *Tested Recipes* was published about 1935–9.

1936

Bake like a champion

See O860.1 for information about Swans Down Cake Flour and other cookbooks for the flour.

O895.1 [copyright 1936]
Bake like a / champion / cakes pies muffins biscuits cookies [cover-title]
DESCRIPTION: 14.5 × 10.0 cm Pp [1–2] 3–22 Illus col Paper, with image on front of two-layer cake; stapled

CONTENTS: 1 cover-title; 2–3 'Would You Like to Know?' and at bottom p 2, '2401 – © 1936, G.F. Corporation – Litho in U.S.A.'; 4–14 'Swans Down Cakes'; 15–18 'Frostings and Fillings'; 19–22 'Other Uses of Swans Down'; inside back face of binding 'Three Wonderful Bargains from the Swans Down Kitchens' and the instruction to send your order to 'Frances Lee Barton, General Foods, Battle Creek, Michigan // In Canada, address: General Foods, Ltd., Cobourg, Ontario'
COPIES: OGU (CCC TX715.6 M572 No. 210) *QMM (RBD ckbk 1593)
NOTES: The recipes are for baking with Swans Down Cake Flour.

Canada, Department of Fisheries

For the titles of other collections of fish recipes by the department, see O319.1.

O896.1 1936
Department of Fisheries / Ottawa, Canada / Minister: / Hon. J.E. Michaud, M.P. / Any day / a / fish day / A booklet dealing with the preparation of / Canadian fish foods for the table / (Previous editions of this booklet have been issued under the title / "Fish and How to Cook It") / Ottawa / J.O. Patenaude, I.S.O. / printer to the King's Most Excellent Majesty / 1936
DESCRIPTION: 19.0 × 12.0 cm Pp [1–3] 4–52 Very thin card, with image on front of four larger fish and three smaller fish; stapled
CONTENTS: 1 tp; 2 blank; 3 'The Value of Fish in the Diet' by Dr R.E. Wodehouse; 4–8 'Fish Foods and Health'; 9 'The Purpose of "Any Day a Fish Day"'; 10–11 'Marketing Notes'; 12–17 'General Talk on Fish Cookery' [includes recipes for Court Bouillon on p 16 and Spiced Pickling Vinegar on p 17]; 18–50 recipes; 51–2 index
COPIES: QMMMCM (AR-M2000.62.14) *Private collection
NOTES: Pages 6–8 list Canada's fish and shellfish, indicating the forms in which they are marketed (fresh, pickled, smoked, canned, dried, dry-salted, paste, roe, etc.) and whether they are from the Atlantic or Pacific coast. There are special sections for sauces and dressings, and for the cooking of salt or dried fish and specific shellfish. The recipes are 'suitable for use in the average home.'

The title-page refers to previous editions published by the Department of the Naval Service in 1914 and 1915 (O319.1–319.3), and a second, revised edition issued in 1932 by the Department of Fisheries (O319.4). In 1938 *Any Day a Fish Day* was superseded by O936.1, *100 Tempting Fish Recipes.*

O896.2   1936
—[An edition of *Du poisson pour n'importe quel jour: opuscule traitant de la préparation des produits canadiens de la pêche pour la table,* Ottawa: Ministère des pêcheries, 1936, pp 62]
CITATIONS: BouquinsCat 228, No. 298

O896.3   1937
—Department of Fisheries / Ottawa, Canada / Minister: / Hon. J.E. Michaud, M.P. / Any day / a / fish day / A booklet dealing with the preparation of / Canadian fish foods for the table / (Previous editions of this booklet have been issued under the title / "Fish and How to Cook It") / Ottawa / J.O. Patenaude, I.S.O. / printer to the King's Most Excellent Majesty / 1937
DESCRIPTION: 19.5 × 12.0 cm   Pp [1–3] 4–52   Paper, with image on front of four larger fish and three smaller fish; stapled
CONTENTS: 1 tp; 2 blank; 3 'The Value of Fish in the Diet' by Dr R.E. Wodehouse; 4–8 'Fish Foods and Health'; 9 'The Purpose of "Any Day a Fish Day"'; 10–11 'Marketing Notes'; 12–17 'General Talk on Fish Cookery' [includes recipes for Court Bouillon on p 16 and Spiced Pickling Vinegar on p 17]; 18–50 recipes; 51–2 index
COPIES: NBCOM   OGU (CCC CA1 FS 37A52) OONL (COP.CA.3.1996-56, 2 copies)   *Private collection
NOTES: *Any Day a Fish Day* (edition not identified) is advertised in the January 1938 issue of *National Home Monthly.*

O896.4   1938
—Ministère des pêcheries, / Ottawa, Canada. / Le ministre: / l'hon. J.-E. Michaud, M.P. / Le poisson / au / menu du jour / Opuscule traitant de la cuisine des / produits canadiens de la pêche / (Déjà publié sous le titre: "Du poisson n'importe quel jour") / Ottawa / J.-O. Patenaude, O.S.I. / imprimeur de sa très excellente majesté le roi / 1938
COPIES: OONL (COP.CA.2.2003-585)   *Private collection

Cooking craft

O897.1   1936
Cooking craft / A Kitchen Prayer / Lord of all pots and pans and things, since I've no time to be / A saint by doing lovely things, or watching late with Thee, / Or dreaming in the dawnlight, or storming heaven's gates, / Make me a saint by getting meals, and washing up the plates. / Although I must have Martha's hands, I have a Mary mind; / And when I black the boots and shoes, Thy sandals, Lord, I find. / I think of how they trod the earth, what time I scrub the floor; / Accept this meditation, Lord, I haven't time for more. / Warm all the kitchen with Thy love, and light it with Thy peace; / Forgive me all my worrying, and make all grumbling cease. / Thou who didst love to give men food, in room, or by the sea, / Accept this service that I do – I do it unto Thee. Anon. / A collection of favorite recipes / selected and arranged for publication / by members of the / Women's Hospital Auxiliary / of / the Niagara Falls General Hospital / Niagara Falls – Ontario
DESCRIPTION: 22.5 × 15.0 cm   Pp [1–3] 4–68   Illus of the hospital, Jepson Street, Niagara Falls, Ontario Thin card, with image on front of a woman using an electric mixer; stapled
CONTENTS: 1 tp; 2 'Official Roster of Women's Hospital Auxiliary of the Niagara Falls General Hospital ... Officers 1936 ...'; 3 'Preface'; 4–67 recipes credited with the name of the contributor and ads, incl ad on p 56: 'This book is the product of F.H. Leslie, Limited commercial printers ...'; 68 'Index' [i.e., table of contents] and ad
CITATIONS: Crawford, p D1, illus col
COPIES: *Private collection

43 prize winning recipes

For the titles of other Jewel Shortening cookbooks, see O695.1.

O898.1   copyright 1936
43 / prize winning recipes / from the / Manitoba and Saskatchewan / Jewel Shortening Recipe Contest / supplemented by / 54 of the best recipes from the / Eastern Canada Jewel Contest / These prize-winning Western recipes / were judged and approved by: Miss Esther / Thompson, Director, Women's Work Ex- / tension Service, Department of

Agriculture, / Government of Manitoba; Professor Mary / Hiltz, Faculty of Agriculture and Home / Economics, Manitoba University; Miss / Gertrude Dutton, National Home Monthly; / and Miss Katherine Caldwell, Canadian / Home Journal. / Published by / Swift Canadian Co., Limited / Copyright, 1936

DESCRIPTION: 19.5 × 13.5 cm   Pp [1–2] 3–77 [78–80]   Illus   Lacks paper(?) binding; stapled

CONTENTS: 1 tp; 2–77 recipes and illus; 78 Canadian Home Journal Home Service Bureau Certificate of Approval dated 2 December 1935 and '1936–37'; 79 index; 80 publ ad for Jewel Shortening

COPIES: MWMM   MWPA   OONL (TX715.6 F667 1936)   *Private collection

NOTES: The text is printed in red and black. There is no place of publication, but Swift Canadian Co. was based in Toronto. For information about Mary Hiltz, see M37.1; for Gertrude Dutton, see O1001.1; and for Katherine Caldwell, see O877.1, under Ann Adam.

The I.O.D.E. cook book

O899.1   nd [1936]
The / I.O.D.E. / cook / book / [IODE symbol] / The Municipal Chapter / of / Imperial Order Daughters of the Empire / Kingston Ontario [cover-title]

DESCRIPTION: 23.0 × 15.5 cm   Pp [3] 4–62   Thin card; stapled

CONTENTS: 3 preface signed the Committee; 4–62 recipes credited with the name of the contributor and ads

COPIES: *Private collection

NOTES: The date of the book is determined by advertisements: On p 18 an advertisement for Beach Electric Stoves sold by Jos. Abramsky and Sons Ltd says, 'See our new 1936 display'; and on p 24 an advertisement for a refrigerator states, 'Kelvinator "Standard of the World" 1914–1936.' Large-quantity recipes and large-quantity serving instructions are on pp 61–2.

The jubilee cook book

O900.1   1936
The jubilee cook book / A collection of / tested recipes / compiled and arranged / by / the Woman's Auxiliary of / St. George's Church / on the occasion of the completion of its fiftieth year / 1886–1936

DESCRIPTION: 23.0 × 15.0 cm   Pp [1] 2–64   Illus on p 3 of St George's Church, Church Street, St Catharines, Ontario   Paper; stapled

CONTENTS: 1 tp; 2 'Officers of the Woman's Auxiliary... 1886,' 'Presidents of the Woman's Auxiliary, 1886–1936,' and 'Officers of the Woman's Auxiliary ... 1936'; 3 preface; 4–63 text; 64 index

CITATIONS: Ferguson/Fraser, p 234

COPIES: *OGU (UA s066 b02)   OONL (TX715 J79 1936)

NOTES: The preface comments, 'Many of the recipes have been "handed down" from the earliest members of the Woman's Auxiliary ...'

The mixing bowl

See also O44.1 from the same church.

O901.1   nd [1936]
The / mixing bowl / A selection of / tested recipes / compiled and published / by / a group of members of / the Elizabeth Lyle Auxiliary / Central Presbyterian Church / Hamilton – Ontario

DESCRIPTION: 23.0 × 15.0 cm   Pp [1] 2–64   Paper; stapled

CONTENTS: 1 tp; 2 list of the seven ladies who carried out 'the preparation and publication' of the book: Miss Ida Fairgrieve, Miss Edith Small, Mrs F.L. Britton, Mrs Wm Stewart, Mrs Gordon Stewart, Mrs Gordon McLandlish, and Mrs Charles Ogilvie; 3 preface; 4–61 recipes credited with the name of the contributor and ads; 62 'To Serve 100 People'; 63 'Time Tables'; 64 ad and 'Index' [i.e., table of contents]

COPIES: OH (R641.5 MIX CESH, 2 copies)   OONL (TX715.6 M59 1900z)   *Private collection

NOTES: There is an advertisement on p 34 for Powell and Co. Ltd, 'Fifty-seven years in business 1879–1936'; therefore, *The Mixing Bowl* was published in 1936. The two OH copies are identical except that one has a blue-paper binding, the other, yellow.

'My favorite recipe'

O902.1   [1936]
"My / favorite / recipe" / From the Sarnia / Canadian Observer / Presented with the compliments of Sarnia merchants and / the Sarnia Canadian Observer / Lambton County's only daily [cover-title]

DESCRIPTION: 27.0 × 21.0 cm   Pp [1] 2–48   Paper, with image on front of a mother mixing the contents of a bowl and a girl watching; stapled

CONTENTS: 1–39 recipes and ads; 40 'Index to Advertisers'; 41–mid 42 'Index to Recipes'; mid–bottom 42 'Helpful Hints'; 43–8 blank for the reader to 'List Your Favorite Recipes Here'
COPIES: OMMM *Private collection
NOTES: An advertisement on p 39 for the W.B. Clark Co. Ltd bears the dates 1846 and 1936 and the phrase 'The House of Quality for over ninety years'; therefore, the date of publication was 1936. 'Cookery Section // Supplement to the Sarnia Canadian Observer' is on p 1.

The Nugget cook book

O903.1 [about 1936]
[An edition of *The Nugget Cook Book*]
NOTES: An article in North Bay's *Nugget* newspaper of 9 September 1936 is headed 'Select Recipes Submitted for the Nugget Cook Book.' The text introducing the recipes says, 'The Nugget presents more recipes selected by women of North Bay for The Nugget Cook Book.'

Beginning on 30 September 1952, the newspaper began a series of annual recipe collections, also called *Nugget Cook Book*, printed on newsprint as a supplement to the periodical.

The pantry shelf

O904.1 [1936]
The / pantry shelf / A collection of / tried and tested recipes / compiled and published by / the Women's Association / of / Queen Street United Church / Lindsay, Ont.
DESCRIPTION: 23.0 × 15.0 cm Pp [1–2] 3–44 Thin card; stapled
CONTENTS: 1 tp; 2 'Printed in Canada by Watchman-Warder // Lindsay, Ont.'; 3 'Preface' signed members of the Women's Association, Queen Street United Church; 4–43 recipes credited with the name of the contributor, blank space on p 6 for 'Memorandum' and on p 31 for 'New Recipes,' and ads; 44 ad and 'Index' [i.e., table of contents]
COPIES: *Private collection
NOTES: The year of publication, 1936, is on the front face of the binding. In the 'Preface' the Women's Association members comment, 'We know that "Our Church" will be benefited by the sale [of this book].'

A short cut to better jams and jellies

For the titles of other Certo recipe collections, see O480.1.

O905.1 copyright 1936
A / short cut / to / better jams and jellies / Perfect jams and jellies Pages 2–3 / Steps to follow 4–5 / Jam recipes 6–14 / Jelly recipes 15–23 / Marmalades and relishes 23–25 / Do's and Don't's 27–31 / Douglas-Pectin, Ltd., Cobourg, Ont., Canada. / © 1936, Canada. [cover-title]
DESCRIPTION: 14.0 × 8.0 cm Pp [1] 2–32 Illus Paper, with image on front of a Certo bottle and two jars of preserves; stapled at top edge
CONTENTS: 1 cover-title and table of contents; 2 'Perfect Jams and Jellies'; 3 'Certo Short-Boil Method'; 4–5 'The Steps to Follow'; 6 'Index to Jam Recipes'; 7–14 jam recipes; 15 'Index to Jellies // Marmalades // Relishes'; 16–mid 23 jelly recipes; mid 23–24 marmalade recipes; 25 relish recipes; 26 'How to Seal Jam and Jellies for Perfect Protection'; 27–8 'Important Do's and Don't's for Jelly Makers'; 29–31 '"Questions I Am Often Asked by Jelly Makers" by Jane Taylor Allen'; 32 [outside back face of binding] 'Mrs. A Shows Mrs. B That Certo Pays for Itself' and 'P-615-30009-1-36-M.P.Co. Printed in Canada.'
COPIES: *Private collection

O905.2 copyright 1936
—Un / raccourci / pour de / meilleures confitures et gelées / Méthode Certo à courte ébullition Pages 2 / Marche à suivre 4–5 / Recettes de confitures 6–10 / Marmelades 11 / Recettes de gelées 11–16 / Ce qu'il faut ou ne faut pas faire 17–18 / Lorsque vous employez Certo, ayez / toujours soin de suivre attentivement / les instructions données dans cette / brochure. C'est le seul moyen d'obtenir / de bons résultats. / Douglas-Pectin, Ltd., Cobourg, Ont., Canada. / (c) 1936, Canada. [cover-title]
DESCRIPTION: 15.5 × 8.0 cm Pp [1] 2–20 Illus on pp 4–5 of 'Marche à suivre' Paper, with image on front of a Certo bottle and two jars of preserves; stapled at top edge
CONTENTS: 1 cover-title and table of contents; 2 'Méthode Certo à courte ébullition'; 3 'Index des recettes'; 4–5 'Marche à suivre'; 6–10 jam recipes; 11 marmalade and jelly recipes; 12–16 jelly recipes and at bottom p 16, recipe for Assaisonnement de piments; 17–18 'Ce qu'il faut ou ne faut pas faire'; 19 'Comment sceller les confitures et les gelées pour les protéger parfaitement'; 20 'Mme. A démontre à Mme. B comment Certo se paie de lui-même' and 'P800-30007-1-36-M.P.Co. Imprimée [*sic*] au Canada.'
COPIES: *QMM (RBD ckbk 1513)

O905.3 copyright 1938

—A / short cut / to / better jams and jellies / Perfect jams and jellies Pages 2–3 / Steps to follow 4–5 / Jam recipes 6–14 / Jelly recipes 15–23 / Marmalades and relishes 23–26 / Do's and don't's 28–31 / Douglas-Pectin, Ltd., Cobourg, Ont., Canada. / © 1938, Canada. [cover-title]

DESCRIPTION: 14.5 × 8.0 cm   Pp [1] 2–32   Illus on pp 4–5 of 'The Steps to Follow'   Paper, with image on front of a Certo bottle and two jars of preserves; stapled at top edge

CONTENTS: 1 cover-title and table of contents; 2 'Perfect Jams and Jellies'; 3 'Certo Short-Boil Method'; 4–5 'The Steps to Follow'; 6 'Index to Jam Recipes'; 7–14 jam recipes; 15 'Index to Jellies // Marmalades // Relishes'; 16–mid 23 jelly recipes; mid 23–25 marmalade and fruit butter recipes; 26 relish recipes; 27 'How to Seal Jams and Jellies for Perfect Protection'; 28–9 'Important Do's and Don't's for Jelly Makers'; 30–1 '"Questions I Am Often Asked by Jelly Makers" by Jane Taylor Allen'; 32 'Mrs. A Shows Mrs. B That Certo Pays for Itself' and at bottom, 'P-1481-64382-1-40-M.P.Co. Printed in Canada.'

COPIES: *QMM (RBD ckbk 1512a)

NOTES: QMM has another copy with 'P-1481-70020-12-40-M.P.Co.' at bottom p 32 (RBD ckbk 1512b).

O905.4 copyright 1943

—A / short cut / to / better jams and jellies / Perfect jams and jellies Pages 2–3 / Steps to follow 4–5 / Jam recipes 6–14 / Jelly Recipes 15–23 / Marmalades and relishes 23–26 / Do's and don't's 28–31 / Douglas-Pectin, Ltd., Cobourg, Ont., Canada. / © 1943, Canada. [cover-title]

DESCRIPTION: 14.0 × 8.0 cm   Pp [1] 2–32   Illus   Paper, with image on front of a Certo bottle and two jars of preserves; stapled at top edge

CONTENTS: 1 cover-title; 2 'Perfect Jams and Jellies'; 3 'Certo Short-Boil Method'; 4–5 'The Steps to Follow'; 6–32 text and at bottom p 32, 'P-3031-4097-10-44-M.P.Co. Printed in Canada.'

COPIES: *NBFKL (Ruth Spicer Cookbook Collection)

O905.5 copyright 1946

—A / short cut / to / better jams and jellies / Perfect jams and jellies Page [*sic,* singular] 2–3 / Steps to follow 4–5 / Jam recipes 6–14 / Jelly recipes 15–23 / Marmalades and relishes 23–26 / To seal jams and jellies 27 / Do's and don't's 28–31 / Douglas-Pectin, Limited, Cobourg, Ontario. / (c) 1946, Canada. [cover-title]

DESCRIPTION: 14.0 × 8.0 cm   Pp [1] 2–32   Illus on pp 4–5 of 'The Steps to Follow,' illus on p 32 of 'Mrs. A

Shows Mrs. B That Certo Pays for Itself'   Paper, with image on front of a Certo bottle; stapled at top edge

CONTENTS: 1 cover-title; 2 'Perfect Jams and Jellies'; 3 'Certo Short-Boil Method'; 4–5 'The Steps to Follow'; 6 'Index to Jam Recipes'; 7–14 jam recipes; 15 'Index to Jellies // Marmalades // Relishes'; 16–mid 23 jelly recipes; mid 23–25 marmalade and fruit butter recipes; 26 relish recipes; 27 'To Seal Jams and Jellies'; 28–9 'Important Do's and Don't's for Jelly Makers'; 30–1 '"Questions I Am Often Asked by Jelly Makers" by Jane Taylor Allen'; 32 'Mrs. A Shows Mrs. B That Certo Pays for Itself' and 'P-4165-5050-1-47-M.P.Co. Printed in Canada.'

COPIES: *Private collection

1937

Boulestin, Xavier Marcel (France, 1878–1943)

For information about Boulestin and his cookbooks, see O845.1.

O906.1 [1937]

The finer cooking / or / dishes for parties / by / X.M. Boulestin / With decorations by / J.E. Laboureur / Cassell & Company Limited / London, Toronto, Melbourne / and Sydney

DESCRIPTION: 18.5 × 12.0 cm   Pp [i–vi] vii [viii] ix [x] xi [xii], 1–131 [132], [1–2] 3–198   Frontis, 4 fp illus and illus in the first sequence of pages   Cloth

CONTENTS: i ht; ii–iii blank; iv frontispiece; v tp; vi 'First published 1937 Printed in Great Britain by T. and A. Constable Ltd. at the University Press, Edinburgh F. 437'; vii table of contents; viii blank; ix 'Note // It is intended that this volume should stand among the cookery books of the hostess's library. It contains all the recipes which are in the companion volume, and in designing a meal it is necessary only to quote the numbers of the dishes that are required. The smaller book is intended for the cook.' and 'Special Note' indicating that the first sequence of page numbers (1–131) is in roman type, the second (3–198) in italic; x blank; xi 'All the recipes for dishes mentioned in these pages will be found at the end ...'; xii illus; 1–132 text; 1–186 308 numbered recipes; 187–98 index to recipes and general index

COPIES: *OGU (UA s018 b05); Great Britain: LB (7941.ppp.43); United States: DLC (TX651 B6)

O906.2 [1937]

—The finer cooking / or / dishes for parties / by / X.M. Boulestin / The recipes / Cassell & Company

Limited / London, Toronto, Melbourne / and Sydney

DESCRIPTION: 18.5 × 12.0 cm   Pp [i–iv] v [vi] vii [viii], [1–2] 3–198   Cloth

CONTENTS: i ht; ii blank; iii tp; iv 'First published 1937 Printed in Great Britain by T. and A. Constable Ltd. at the University Press, Edinburgh F. 437'; v 'Note // This book contains all the recipes which appear in Part 2 of the companion volume. They are numbered in the same order ...'; vi blank; vii table of contents; viii blank; 1–186 308 numbered recipes; 187–98 index to recipes and general index

COPIES: *OGU (UA s013 b08); Great Britain: LB (7941.ppp.44); United States: DLC (TX651 B62)

NOTES: This volume contains only recipes. There are no illustrations.

Cook book

The Scarboro Junction branch of the Women's Institute was founded in 1909 (Ambrose, p 232). The first Junior Institutes in Ontario were organized in 1915 (Ambrose, p 124).

O907.1   1937

Cook book / compiled by / the Scarboro Junction Junior / Women's Institute / 1937 / [Women's Institute symbol] / It's easy enough to be pleasant / When life flows on like a song; / But the cook worth while is the cook who can smile / When everything goes dead wrong.

DESCRIPTION: About 22.5 × 15.5 cm [dimensions from photocopy]   Pp [i–ii], [1–2] 3–33   Stapled

CONTENTS: i blank; ii untitled four-line verse and 'Star Print, Port Perry, Ont.'; 1 tp; 2 blank; 3–33 recipes credited with the name of the contributor

COPIES: *Private collection

The coronation cook book

O908.1   1937

The / coronation / cook book / Tested recipes / selected and published by / Earl Grey Chapter / Imperial Order Daughters of the Empire / Owen Sound, Ontario

DESCRIPTION: 22.0 × 15.0 cm   Pp [1–2] 3–55 [56]   Tp illus of four small crowns   Thin card, with IODE symbol on front; stapled

CONTENTS: 1 tp; 2 'Printed in Canada by the Bates Advertising and Printing Service // Owen Sound Ontario'; 3 'Preface'; 4–53 recipes credited with the name of the contributor, blank spaces for 'New Recipes,' and ads; 54 'Time Tables'; 55 ad and 'Table Decorations'; 56 ad and 'Index' [i.e., table of contents]

COPIES: *Private collection

NOTES: The date of publication, 1937, is printed on the front face of the binding. *The Coronation Cook Book* marked the coronation of King George VI on 12 May 1937. Page 54 is incorrectly numbered 56. There is an advertisement for the printer on the outside back face of the binding, which gives the proprietor's name, C. Roger Bates.

The coronation cook book

In the year 2000, the Victoria Guelph Chapter published One Hundredth Birthday Cookbook *to celebrate the centenary of the Imperial Order Daughters of the Empire (founded in 1900), the ninetieth anniversary of the Victoria Guelph Chapter, and the millennium.*

O909.1   [1937]

The / coronation / cook book / A Housewife's Prayer / [five verses of the poem] / [poet:] Margaret Peake Benton. / Tested recipes / selected and published by the ladies of / Victoria-Guelph Chapter / Imperial Order Daughters of the / Empire / Guelph Ontario

DESCRIPTION: 23.0 × 15.0 cm   Pp [1–2] 3–68   Card, with IODE symbol on front; stapled

CONTENTS: 1 tp; 2 'Preface' and 'Officers Roster, Victoria Guelph Chapter, I.O.D.E. 1937'; 3 'The Victoria-Guelph Chapter' [history of the chapter, formed 4 December 1909]; 4–67 text, mainly recipes credited with the name of the contributor, blank spaces for 'New Recipes,' and ads; 68 'Index' [i.e., table of contents] and ads

CITATIONS: Bloomfield/Stelter 1164, p 200   Driver 2001, Wellington County, p 91 (note 7)

COPIES: *OG (P00173)

NOTES: King George VI's coronation was on 12 May 1937. The book was likely published at the end of 1937, or early 1938, since there is an advertisement opposite the title-page for Bond Hardware Co., Guelph, that says, '1868 1938 // January first, nineteen thirty-eight completes 70 years of hardware service ...' It was certainly published after June 1937 as one of the councillors, Mrs Dunbar, is listed on p 2 as '(deceased) June.'

The OG copy has an address label on the title-page for a previous owner of the book, Mrs Donald D. Fowke, 336 Gordon Street, Guelph, Canada N1G 1X6.

The coronation cook book

O910.1 [1937]

The / coronation / cook book / A Housewife's Prayer / [five verses of the poem] / [poet:] Margaret Peake Benton. / Tested recipes / selected and published by the ladies of / Women's Auxiliary of Victoria Hospital / London Ontario / [folio:] 1

DESCRIPTION: 23.5 × 15.5 cm   Pp 1–100   Paper, with portraits on front of King George VI and Queen Elizabeth; stapled

CONTENTS: 1 tp; 2 'Printed in London // Selby Young Printing Co.'; 3 'Preface' signed Mrs J.F. Giffin, convenor; 4 'Roster of Officers and Members'; 5 blank except for folio; 6–99 text, mainly recipes credited with the name of the contributor, and ads; 100 'Index' [i.e., table of contents]

CITATIONS: Ferguson/Fraser, p 233   RushCat List 1, 2002, No. 84

COPIES: OGU (2 copies: *UA s066 b04, CCC TX715.6 C67823)   Private collection

NOTES: The year of publication, 1937, is printed on the front face of the binding. *The Coronation Cook Book* marked the coronation of King George VI on 12 May 1937. The private collector's copy is inscribed on the binding, 'Miss Helen James. ACM July 29/39.'

Coronation historical review and cook book

O911.1 [1937]

Coronation / historical review and / cook book / Price 25c. [cover-title]

DESCRIPTION: 23.0 × 15.0 cm   Pp [1–36]   Illus on p 1 of King George VI and Queen Elizabeth   Paper; stapled

CONTENTS: 1 illus of King George VI and Queen Elizabeth and below, 'Coronation – May 12th, 1937'; 2 blank; 3–5 'The New King,' 'The Coronation Church,' 'The King's Crowns,' 'Coronation Chair,' and ad; 6 ads; 7 'Foods and Their Relative Values' and 'A Few Reminders'; 8 ad; 9 'Tables of Measures and Equivalents,' 'List of Calories Contained in One Pound,' and 'Causes of Failure in Making Cake'; 10 ad; 11–1st column 32 recipes credited with the name of the contributor and ads; 2nd column 32 'The Coronation Colors'; 33–6 'The Coronation Ceremony in Westminster Abbey'

COPIES: *OTYA (CPC 1937 0105)   Private collection

NOTES: No group is named as the compiler of the book. The advertisements are for businesses in Prescott and Belleville, Ontario, and the recipe contributors came from those two towns plus other smaller places, such as Spencerville, Johnstown, Tincap, Maynard, and Shanly. The private collector, who lives in Prescott, wrote to me in the early 1990s: 'No one seems to know who gathered recipes and had them printed – thought to be a Women's Institute project.'

Coronation souvenir book

O912.1 [1937]

[Title-page lacking; see notes]

DESCRIPTION: 23.5 × 15.0 cm   Pp [1–2 lacking] 3–100   Illus   Paper, front face lacking; stapled

CONTENTS: 3 illus of 'Their Majesties King George VI and Queen Elizabeth crowned at Westminster Abbey May 12, 1937'; 4 preface signed ladies of the Friendship Circle; 5 'Coronation // The Inspired Word Concerning Kingship' from the *Christian Science Monitor*; 6 'The British Empire' [quotations from Emerson and Milton]; 7–9 'The Romance of Kirkland Lake' and ads; 10–11 ads; 12–13 illus of 'The First United Church in Kirkland Lake' built July 1920, illus of 'The New Trinity United Church' completed in 1935, and messages from the past and present ministers; 14 individual photographs of the present minister and three past ministers of Trinity United Church; 15 photograph of the Friendship Circle, Trinity United Church, with members identified; 16 photograph of 'First Ladies' Aid of Trinity United Church Taken During the Winter of 1920' with members identified, and an account of the organizational structure of Trinity Women's Association; 17–34 photographs of Kirkland Lake, past and present; 35 photograph of 'The Choir of Trinity United Church' with members identified; 36–8 ads; 39 part-title: 'Kitchen Lore Presenting Several Pages of Recipes Compiled by the Ladies of the Friendship Circle // These recipes have all been tried and tested and will give interest to well-planned meals ...' and illus of an aproned woman stirring the contents of a saucepan; 40 'Table Service'; 41 ad; 42 'Correct Table Etiquette' and ad; 43–92 recipes and ads; 93 ads; top–mid 94 'Table Decorations'; bottom 94–top 95 'Time Tables'; bottom 95 blank for 'Memorandum'; 96–7 ads; top–mid 98 'Carving'; mid 98–99 'Household Hints' and ads; 100 'Index to Recipe Section'

COPIES: *Private collection

NOTES: In the preface, thanks are given to the recipe contributors, the advertisers, and the *Northern News* of Kirkland Lake for providing 'the plates depicting old Kirkland Lake.'

Another private collector's copy retains its title-

page and paper binding. The title-page, which has an illustration of a crown reads:
Coronation / souvenir book / with views of / Kirkland Lake / and a selection of / tried and tested recipes / by the / Friendship Circle / Trinity United Church / Kirkland Lake, Ontario / Officers of the Friendship Circle / President Mrs. W.A. Faire / First Vice-President Mrs. R.A. Trussler / Second Vice-President Mrs. W. Scott / Secretary Mrs. J. McDonald / Treasurer Mrs. S. Last / Book Convener – Mrs. T.A. Jeacle / [folio:] 1
The year of publication, 1937, and the Canadian coat of arms are on the front face of the binding.

Easy recipes for camp and kitchen

For other Klim recipe collections, see: O397.1, Klim Cook Book; O453.1, The Wonderful Story of Klim; O534.1, Camp Cooking; O674.1, Nationally Known Recipes; and O1171.1, Skillet Skills for Camp and Cottage. For information about the Borden Co. and its other books, see Q106.1.

O913.1 [1937]
Easy recipes / for camp and kitchen [cover-title]
DESCRIPTION: 19.0 × 12.5 cm   Pp [1–2] 3–64   Illus part-titles, illus   Paper, with image on front of four persons dining on a cottage verandah and, below this image, prepared dishes of biscuits, pancakes, fish, etc.; stapled
CONTENTS: top–mid 1 'Index to Camp Cooking Recipes'; mid 1–2 'Index to Kitchen Cooking Recipes'; 3 'Whether You're an – Outdoor Cook or an – Indoor Cook'; 4–7 'Meet the Star of Our Story' [i.e., information about Klim]; 8–9 'Cooking with Klim'; 10 'Time Saving Ideas for Kitchen or Camp'; 11–24 'Camp Cookery'; 25–61 'Kitchen Cookery'; 62–3 blank 'For Your Own Notes, Reminders and Favourite Recipes'; 64 'And So – Bon Voyage!'
COPIES: OGU (CCC TX715.6 E289)   *Bookseller's stock   Private collection
NOTES: In addition to its camping uses, Klim, a milk powder, is said to be 'excellent for infants' (p 7). 'Printed in Canada 12-37-K-393' is on the outside back face of the binding, indicating publication in 1937; on the inside back face are a list of Borden Co. Ltd's products and the company's Toronto address of Yardley House (this address is in Toronto city directories from 1935 on; the company had moved from 115 George Street). Unlike editions of an earlier Klim cookbook – O534.1, *Camp Cooking* – no experts are credited with the recipes.

A copy in a private collection varies from the description above in a few ways. On the front face of the paper binding there is an image, at top, of a tent beside a lake, with a woman cooking at a campfire and a man returning with fish; and at bottom, there is a family seated at a dinner table. 'Printed in Canada 7-37-K-37-1' is on the outside back face. The heading on p 64 has ellipses, not a dash: 'And So ... Bon Voyage!'

A copy in another private collection is with its original envelope, addressed to a woman in Brockville, Ontario, and postmarked 6 August 1938.

Favorite recipes

O914.1   nd [about 1937]
Favorite recipes / presented / by / George Griffiths Limited / 1470 Queen St. W at Lansdowne / LA 1211 LA 2222 [cover-title]
DESCRIPTION: 20.5 × 16.0 cm   Pp [1–16]   Paper; stapled
CONTENTS: Inside front face of binding 'Salads'; 1 publ ad; 2 'Appetizers' and 'Cocktails'; 3–5 publ ads; 6–7 'Soups,' 'Salads,' and 'Meats'; 8–9 publ ads; 10–11 'Meats,' 'Thrift Cooker,' and 'Frozen Desserts'; 12–13 publ ads; 14–inside back face 'Meats,' 'Thrift Cooker,' 'Pastries,' 'Sandwich Suggestions,' 'Cookies and Cake,' and 'Cocktails'
COPIES: *Private collection
NOTES: George Griffiths Ltd was a Toronto store in the Parkdale area that sold stoves, refrigerators, and wringer washing machines. An advertisement on p 12 for 'General Electric Hotpoint Ranges for 1937' suggests a publication date of 1937. According to an advertisement on p 13, Griffiths had '25 years of sound business experience in Parkdale.'

Favorite recipes

O915.1   nd [about 1937]
Favorite recipes / A selection of / tried and tested / recipes / arranged for publication / by / the Ladies' Aid / of / St. John's Anglican Church / St. Thomas Ontario
DESCRIPTION: 23.0 × 15.0 cm   Pp [1–3] 4–64   Thin card; stapled
CONTENTS: 1 tp; 2 'Printed in St. Thomas by the Sutherland Press, Limited'; 3 'Preface' signed members of the Ladies' Aid; 4–63 culinary text, mainly recipes credited with the name of the contributor, blank spaces for 'My Own Recipes' and 'New Reci-

pes,' and ads; 64 'Index' [i.e., alphabetical list of topics] and ads

COPIES: *OSTT (R641.5 FAV)

NOTES: There is an advertisement for Alma College, which boasts 'education for girls and young women for sixty years in St. Thomas.' The college was established in 1877; therefore, the book's date of publication is about 1937. The appearance of the book confirms a date in the 1930s.

Flavour magic 57

O916.1 nd [1937]

Flavour / magic / 57 [cover-title]

DESCRIPTION: 15.0 × 9.0 cm   Pp [1–2] 3–34   Illus   Paper, with image on front of a bottle's contents being poured into a glass; stapled

CONTENTS: 1 cover-title; 2 table of contents; 3–4 'Pour Some Heinz Vinegar into a Glass ...'; 5–33 recipes; 34 'Heinz Vinegars' and publ ad for *The Heinz Book of Salads and Meat Recipes* [i.e., O791.2 or O791.3]

COPIES: *Private collection

NOTES: The caption on pp 18–19 for the illustration of the H.J. Heinz Co. plant in Leamington, Ontario, reads, 'Established in Leamington, Canada in 1909 – more than a quarter century ago – ...,' indicating that *Flavour Magic 57* was published after 1934 (1909 + 25 years). The printer's mark of '11637,' opposite p 34, confirms a publication date of 1937.

According to p 3, 'Heinz Vinegar is made as the French create their finest wines.' An illustration on the same page shows a couple in evening clothes smelling wine (or vinegar!) in a wine glass.

Haines, Mrs Edith Key (1882–)

Also by this American author are Tried Temptations, *[No place: c1916], and* Tried Temptations Old and New, *New York: Farrar and Rinehart, [c1931] (both United States: DLC).*

O917.1 1937

[An edition of *Edith Haines' Cook Book*, New York and Toronto: Farrar and Rinehart, 1937, pp vii, 655, illus]

COPIES: United States: DLC (TX715 H13)   MCR (641.5 H15)

AMERICAN EDITIONS: *Wonderful Ways to Cook; Formerly Edith Key Haines' Cook Book*, New York: Rinehart, [1951] (United States: DLC).

The housewife's year book of health and homemaking 1937

For the titles of other Kellogg books about All-Bran, see O768.1.

O918.1 1937

The housewife's / year book / of health and / homemaking / 1937 / being, until July 1st, the 70th year / of Canadian Confederation / and containing / a calendar for the year with / important historical events, / astronomical data and sun and / moon rise and set times; valu- / able advice on food and its re- / lation to health; new recipes; / meal planning; housekeeping; / how to gain weight; how to / reduce; horoscopes; games for / children; home entertain- / ment; first aid; and much / other useful information. / Published by / Kellogg Company / of Canada Limited / London, Ontario / No. 7171 Copyright, Kellogg Co. Printed in Canada

DESCRIPTION: 20.5 × 14.0 cm   Pp [1] 2–36   Illus col, illus   [Free, on inside front face of binding]   Paper, with image on front of a mother, father, son, and daughter

CONTENTS: 1 tp; 2 'The Zodiac'; 3 'Important Information about the Neglected Ailment' [i.e., constipation]; 4 'Horoscopes'; 5 'January 1937'; 6 'What Constipation Means'; 7 'February 1937'; 8 'How to Keep the Children Busy'; 9 'March 1937'; 10 '16 Rules for Safe Reducing'; 11 'April 1937'; 12 'Data for the Home Gardener'; 13 'May 1937'; 14 'All-Bran Cleanses like a Water-Softened Sponge'; 15 'June 1937'; 16 'Financial House-keeping'; 17–20 'Six Tempting Ways to Serve Kellogg's All-Bran'; 21 'Answers to Questions People Ask about Bran'; 22 'Ten Helpful Beauty Hints'; 23 'July 1937'; 24 'The Stain Remover'; 25 'August 1937'; 26 'The Cathartic Habit'; 27 'September 1937'; 28 'Some Ideas in Home Entertainment'; 29 'October 1937'; 30 'How Can I Gain Weight?'; 31 'November 1937'; 32 'Handy Facts on How to Fix It'; 33 'December 1937'; 34 'How to Plan Health Meals'; 35 'The Information Desk' [includes kitchen measures]; 36 'Modern First Aid'

CITATIONS: Ferguson/Fraser, p 233

COPIES: ONM   QMM (RBD ckbk 1673; 2 copies)   *Private collection

NOTES: The Edith Adams page of the *Vancouver Sun*, 19 March 1937, p 14, reported the distribution of O918.1 in British Columbia: 'Vancouver Housewives Receive Year Books ... The Kellogg Company of Canada is doing a great service for the Canadian housewife ... in the form of the "Houswife's Year Book of Health and Homemaking."'

How to get the most out of your Mixmaster

*For information about the Sunbeam Mixmaster and an
earlier Mixmaster cookbook, see O797.1.*

O919.1 [1937]
How / to get the most / out of your / Mixmaster /
[captions for ten illus, from top left to bottom right:]
It chops food / grinds meat / It slices, shreds / and
grates / It extracts / fruit juices / It peels potatoes /
It mixes drinks / It grinds coffee / It opens cans /
It turns my / ice cream freezer / It polishes /
silverware / It sharpens / knives, scissors [cover-
title]
DESCRIPTION: 23.0 × 15.0 cm Pp [1–4] 5–38 Illus
Paper, with ten images on front of a woman using a
Mixmaster; stapled
CONTENTS: 1 cover-title; 2–3 'Now That You Have
Your Automatic Mixmaster'; 4–37 recipes and publ
ads; 38 publ ad
COPIES: *AHRMH
NOTES: The cookbook gives instructions for preparing food with a Sunbeam Mixmaster. The advertisement on p 38 illustrates 'Parts for No. 3A Automatic
Mixmaster.' On the outside back face of the binding,
there are calendars for 1937 and 1938, the company's
name and address (Flexible Shaft Co. Ltd, Toronto),
the statement '47 years making quality products,'
and seals of approval from the Chatelaine Institute,
the Canadian Home Journal Home Service Bureau,
and the Good Housekeeping Institute. There is a loose
leaf inserted in the AHRMH copy that states, '48
years making quality products.'

O919.2 nd [about 1939]
—How to get / the most out of / your Sunbeam /
Mixmaster / Hydro-Electric / Power Commission /
Approval Number / 3100 / [seals of approval of
Canadian Home Journal / Good Housekeeping
Institute / and Chatelaine Institute] / Sunbeam /
Mixmaster / is endorsed by the / authorities whose
/ seals of approval are / shown and other / home
service labor- / atories as well as / domestic science
ex- / perts and cooking / authorities every- /
where. [cover-title]
DESCRIPTION: 23.0 × 15.0 cm Pp [1–3] 4–39 [40]
Illus Paper, with image on front of the Mixmaster
and a woman holding up a cake; stapled
CONTENTS: 1 cover-title; 2–3 'Now That You Have
Your Automatic Mixmaster ...'; 4–33 'Tested Recipes
for the Sunbeam Automatic Mixmaster' and instructions for various functions of the Mixmaster; 34 'Special 3-quart Aluminum Bowl and Cover ...' and 'Other

Practical Mixmaster Accessories'; 35–9 ads for other
Sunbeam products; 40 'Things to Remember in the
Use of Your Mixmaster' and, at bottom, 'Made and
guaranteed by Flexible Shaft Company Limited ...
321 Weston Road South Toronto, Can. 49 Years Making Quality Products // Printed in Canada No. 1530T'
COPIES: *Private collection
NOTES: This edition was published two years after
O919.1, likely in 1939 (it has '49 Years Making Quality Products' instead of 47 years). There is a loose-
leaf, product-order form in the private collector's copy,
on which is printed the date '193_' where the last
digit is left blank for the year.

O919.3 nd [early 1940s]
—How to get the most out of your / Sunbeam /
Mixmaster / [Good Housekeeping Institute symbol]
/ All recipes in this book / tested and approved /
by Good House- / keeping Institute. [cover-title]
DESCRIPTION: 23.0 × 15.5 cm Pp 3–42 Illus Paper,
with image on front of seven women, each holding a
prepared dish, and behind them, a giant Mixmaster;
stapled
CONTENTS: 3 'Now That You Have Your Sunbeam
Mixmaster'; 4–top 8 'Suggestions for the Use of Sun-
beam Mixmaster' [for models 5 or 5B]; mid–bottom 8
'Before Using'; 9–mid 13 'Cakes and Cookies'; mid
13–14 'Frostings'; top 15 'Candies'; bottom 15–mid 16
'Mashed Potatoes, Vegetables, etc.'; mid 16–mid 17
'Mayonnaise & Salad Dressings'; mid 17–mid 19
'Breads and Biscuits'; mid 19–21 'Desserts & Miscellaneous'; 22 'The New Automatic Mix-Finder'; 23–36
'How to Get the Most Out of Mixmaster Attachments!'
and recipes; 37 'Mixmaster Accessories'; 38–42 publ
ads for other Sunbeam appliances
COPIES: *Private collection
NOTES: 'Printed in Canada // Guaranteed by Flexible
Shaft Company Limited ... Over 50 years making
quality products' is on the inside back face of the
binding. This edition was published a year or more
after O919.2, which has the reference '49 Years Making Quality Products'; and it precedes O919.4, which
refers to models 7 or 7B. A photograph of an edition
with the same binding design (seven women and a
giant Mixmaster) and the instruction 'Send for the
new 1940 Sunbeam Recipe Book' is in *Home Service
News* [BC Electric's customer newsletter] Vol. 13, No.
12 (May 1940), p 7 (copy at BBH); therefore, O919.3
may have been published in 1940.

O919.4 nd [1945 or before]
—How to get the most out of your / Sunbeam /
Mixmaster / [Good Housekeeping Institute symbol]

/ All recipes in this book / tested and approved / by Good House- / keeping Institute. [cover-title]
DESCRIPTION: 23.0 × 15.0 cm   Pp 3–42   Illus   Paper, with image on front of seven women, each holding a prepared dish, and behind them, a giant Mixmaster; stapled
CONTENTS: 3 'Now That You Have Your Sunbeam Mixmaster'; 4–7 'Suggestions for the Use of Sunbeam Mixmaster' [for models 7 or 7B]; 8 'Before Using'; 9–mid 13 'Cakes and Cookies'; mid 13–14 'Frostings'; top 15 'Candies'; bottom 15–mid 16 'Mashed Potatoes, Vegetables, etc.'; mid 16–mid 17 'Mayonnaise & Salad Dressings'; mid 17–mid 19 'Breads and Biscuits'; mid 19–21 'Desserts & Miscellaneous'; 22 'The New Automatic Mix-Finder'; 23–36 'How to Get the Most Out of Mixmaster Attachments!' and recipes; 37 'Mixmaster Accessories' including 'Parts for Model 7 and 7B ...'; 38–42 publ ads for other Sunbeam appliances (toaster, iron, shaver, heating pad, another iron, Coffeemaster)
COPIES: *BVIPM
NOTES: 'Guaranteed by Flexible Shaft Company Limited ... Over half a century making quality products 1812T' is on the outside back face of the binding. This edition was published before 6 November 1945, when Flexible Shaft Corporation of Canada Ltd was incorporated.

O919.5   nd [about 1945–7]
—How to get the most out of your / Sunbeam / Mixmaster / [Good Housekeeping Institute symbol] / All recipes in this book / tested and approved / by Good House- / keeping Institute. [cover-title]
DESCRIPTION: 23.0 × 15.0 cm   Pp 3–42   Illus   Paper, with image on front of seven women, each holding a prepared dish, and behind them, a giant Mixmaster; stapled
CONTENTS: Inside front face of binding 'Index to Recipes'; 3 'Now That You Have Your Sunbeam Mixmaster'; 4–7 'Suggestions for the Use of Sunbeam Mixmaster' [for model 7B]; 8 'Before Using'; 9–mid 13 'Cakes and Cookies'; mid 13–14 'Frostings'; top 15 'Candies'; bottom 15–mid 16 'Mashed Potatoes, Vegetables, etc.'; mid 16–mid 17 'Mayonnaise & Salad Dressings'; mid 17–mid 19 'Breads and Biscuits'; mid 19–21 'Desserts & Miscellaneous'; 22 'The New Automatic Mix-Finder'; 23–36 'How to Get the Most Out of Mixmaster Attachments!' and recipes; 37 'Mixmaster Accessories' including 'Parts for Model 7B ...'; 38–42 publ ads for other Sunbeam appliances (waffle iron, toaster, Coffeemaster, iron, shaver)
COPIES: *BVIPM

NOTES: This edition refers only to model 7B (O919.4 refers to models 7 and 7B). 'Guaranteed by Sunbeam Corporation (Canada) Ltd. formerly Flexible Shaft Company Limited ... Over half a century making quality products 2117T' is on the outside back face of the binding. This edition was published after O919.4 and before O919.6, which refers to 'Model 9 Automatic Mixmaster.'

O919.6   [copyright 1948]
—How to get the most out of your / Sunbeam / Automatic / Mixmaster / Instructions / for use and care of your Sunbeam Mixmaster / see pages forty-one to forty-three. [cover-title]
DESCRIPTION: 23.0 × 15.5 cm   Pp [1] 2–44   Illus col on pp 21–4 of Sunbeam appliances, illus   Paper, with image on front of a three-layer cake and a Sunbeam Mixmaster; stapled
CONTENTS: Inside front face of binding 'Index' [i.e., table of contents] and 'Copyright 1948, Sunbeam Corporation (Canada) Ltd. International copyright 1948, all rights reserved'; 1 'You Now Have the Finest Food Mixer Made' signed Sunbeam Home Economics Department; 2–3 illus and captions for mix-finder dial, bowl-speed control, beater ejector, and juice extractor; 4 'How to Get the Most Out of Your Mixmaster'; 5–20 recipes; 21–4 publ ads; 25–33 recipes; 34–40 illus and captions for various attachments (meat grinder/food chopper, drink mixer, slicer and shredder, butter churn, colander, can opener, bean slicer, ice cream freezer, coffee grinder, knife sharpener, polisher, pea sheller, and potato peeler); 41–2 'General Information'; 43 'Care' and dates of Sunbeam Mixmaster Canadian patents (1931, 1934, 1935, 1936, 1939, 1942, 1944); 44 'Parts for Model 9 Automatic Mixmaster'
COPIES: *OGU (CCC TX715.6 H678)   QMM (RBD uncat)
NOTES: The Mixmaster allowed for faster mixing of cake batters, as the first page of the 'Cakes' chapter explains: 'The new "short-cut" recipes on pages 5, 6 and 7 were developed and tested to give greater baking efficiency. Most recipes require only the use of one bowl, measuring cup, measuring spoons and a rubber spatula. Mixing time requires only three to four minutes in most cases.'

O919.7   [copyright 1948]
—How to get the most out of your / Sunbeam / Automatic / Mixmaster [cover-title]
DESCRIPTION: 22.5 × 15.0 cm   Pp [1] 2–44   Illus col on pp 21–4 of Sunbeam appliances, illus   Paper, with image on front of a Mixmaster and a three-layer cake; stapled

CONTENTS: Inside front face of binding 'Index' [i.e., table of contents] and 'Copyright 1948, Sunbeam Corporation (Canada) Ltd. International copyright 1948, all rights reserved.'; 1 'You Now Have the Finest Food Mixer Made'; 2–3 illus and explanation of Mixmaster features; 4 'How to Get the Most Out of Your Mixmaster'; 5–20 recipes; 21–4 publ ads; 25–33 recipes; 34–40 illus and explanation of various attachments; 41–2 'General Information // Operation of Model 9 Automatic Mixmaster'; 43 'Care of Model 9 Automatic Mixmaster'; 44 'Parts for Model 9 Automatic Mixmaster'
COPIES: *Private collection
NOTES: 'Printed in Canada' is on the inside back face of the binding. In the cover-title of this edition there is no reference to pp 41–3 (as there is in O919.6). The order of publication of O919.6 and O919.7 is unknown.

OTHER EDITIONS: *How to Get the Most Out of Your Sunbeam Automatic Mixmaster*, [Sunbeam Corporation (Canada) Ltd, copyright 1950] (Private collection); *How to Get the Most Out of Your New Sunbeam Automatic Mixmaster De Luxe*, 1957 (QMM).

The Kelvinator book of kitchen tested recipes

See O656.1 for information about Kelvinator of Canada Ltd and its cookbooks.

O920.1   nd [about 1937]
The / Kelvinator / book / of / kitchen tested / recipes / Price twenty-five cents / Published by / Kelvinator of Canada / Limited / London ... Canada
DESCRIPTION: 24.0 × 16.0 cm   Pp [1] 2–32   Small illus red   Paper, with image on front of stylized dishes; stapled
CONTENTS: 1 tp; 2–32 text and, at bottom p 32, 'Form No. K-3804 Part No. 03637 Printed in Canada'
COPIES: *Private collection
NOTES: The cookbook was published to promote the use of Kelvinator Refrigerators. The graphic design looks late 1930s, and the printer's mark on p 32 may indicate publication in 1937.
   O947.1, *The Leonard Book of Kitchen Tested Recipes*, published by the Leonard Refrigerator Co., features the same binding design as the Kelvinator book. Leonard was a division of the Kelvinator company, and the two titles may be editions of the same text.

O920.2   nd
—Kelvinator / présente un choix / de / recettes / vérifiées en cuisine / Prix vingt-cinq cents / Publié par / Kelvinator of Canada / Limited / London Canada
DESCRIPTION: 23.0 × 15.5 cm   Pp [1] 2–32   Illus pink   Very thin card, with image on front of stylized dishes; stapled
CONTENTS: 1 tp; 2–32 text and, at bottom p 32, 'Form No. K 3804 F Imprimé au Canada'
COPIES: *QTS

AMERICAN EDITIONS: *Kelvinator Book of Kitchen Tested Recipes*, Kelvinator Corp., nd [1930s] (Barile, p 198).

Kitchen craft

O921.1   nd [about 1937]
Kitchen craft / A selection / of / tried and tested recipes / compiled and published / by / the Women's Association / of / Mark Street United Church / Peterborough, Ontario
DESCRIPTION: Pp [1–3] 4–64
CONTENTS: 1 tp; 2 'Printed by the Peterborough Review Co., Limited Peterborough, Ont.'; 3 'Preface' signed ladies of the Women's Association; 4–63 recipes credited with the name of the contributor and ads; 64 ad and 'Index' [i.e., table of contents]
COPIES: *Private collection
NOTES: An advertisement on p 38 for H. Florence's Home Furnishing Co., '25 years in the furniture business in Peterboro,' is evidence of *Kitchen Craft*'s date of publication. The earliest identified listing for Home Furnishing Co. in Peterborough city directories is in the volume for 1912; the first listing in Bell Telephone Co. directories (Peterborough section, Ontario Central) is in the volume for August 1912. The cookbook, therefore, was published in 1937 (1912 + 25 years). The appearance of the book is consistent with this date.

Kitchen gems

O922.1   1937
Kitchen / gems / Compiled by the "A" Group of the / Women's Association of United Church / Waubaushene, Ontario / 1937 [cover-title]
DESCRIPTION: 22.0 × 15.0 cm   Pp [i–iv], [1] 2–54 [55], [i]   Illus on p i of the church   Limp cloth; stapled
CONTENTS: i illus of the church, 'Our Greeting,' and eight-line untitled verse; ii ad; iii 'Index' [i.e., table of

contents] and ad; iv ads; 1–55 recipes credited with the name of the contributor and ads; i ads

COPIES: *BVIPM

NOTES: 'Our Greeting' includes acknowledgments and comments, 'We trust ... our church may greatly benefit by the sale of [this book].'

The mixing bowl

O923.1   nd [about 1937]
The / mixing bowl / A selection of / tested recipes / compiled and published / by the members of / the Women's Association / of / St. John's United Church / Stratford – Ontario

DESCRIPTION: Pp [1–2] 3–56   Stapled

CONTENTS: 1 tp; 2 'Printed in Canada on Canadian paper // The B-H Press // Stratford'; 3 'Preface'; 4–54 recipes credited with the name of the contributor and ads; 55 'Table Decoration'; 56 ad and 'Index' [i.e., table of contents]

COPIES: *Private collection

NOTES: There is an advertisement on p 32 for '1937 Majestic Radios.'

The modern Canadian cake baker, Part 3

Love flavours – the only emulsion-type, non-alcoholic flavours on the Canadian market – were developed by Robert W. Love, a chemist. He started the business in Saskatoon, but then moved to Victoria. After his first wife died, he and his four children (George Stewart, Phyllis, William Gordon, and Frederick Douglas) moved from Victoria to Winnipeg, from Winnipeg to Windsor, then, in about 1935, to Toronto, a better base from which to manage the Canada-wide distribution of the flavours. His second wife, Jean (Jenny) P. Love, to whom one of the company's cookbooks is dedicated (O1001.1, Questing, by Miss Gertrude Dutton), also helped with the business, and all the children (the first four, plus Frances and Robert H. borne by Jean) eventually joined in the family enterprise in one capacity or another. W. Gordon was the last owner of the business.

The company sold a commercial and a domestic line of flavours. Of the several cookbooks that the company published, the following were aimed at the commercial market: O924.1, The Modern Canadian Cake Baker, Part 3; O1052.1, Loves Standard Canadian Baker; O1188.1, Middleton, Sidney, The Pastry Chef's Helper; and O1198.1, Carter, Charles A., Food for Thought. Only Questing was compiled for the home cook.

O924.1   Part 3, 1937
The modern / Canadian / cake / baker / Part 3, 1937 / Published in four parts / and presented / to our customers / by / Love / The Flavor Man [cover-title]

DESCRIPTION: About 18.5 × 8.5 cm [dimensions from photocopy]   [38 unnumbered leaves, possibly some lacking]   Stapled

CONTENTS: 1 blank; 2 'Food for Thought'; 3 'The Modern Canadian Cake Baker // Part 3, 1937' signed Love – The Flavor Man; 3 ...

COPIES: *Private collection

NOTES: 'Food for Thought' discusses the importance of attractiveness, variety, and quality in cakes for winning customers. The text on p 3 states: 'As in Book 2, every second page is left blank for your own notes and formulae ... The first part of this cook book, up to and including Fruit Puree, is compiled by Bonnie Dundee [who also contributed text to O1052.1], and any questions as to this list will be cheerfully answered by the author care of Love – The Flavor Man, 62 Lombard Street. Balance of book is made up from [secret for]mula offered in many localities by friendly [user]s of our products, ... At the request of many customers Book 3 is largely devoted to cookies.' The recipes are for commercial amounts. At the end of the book there is a list of 'Representatives' in different parts of Canada: Toronto (Fruit Product Distributors, 62 Lombard Street, i.e., the office for Love – The Flavor Man); Ontario (Love Brothers, W. Gordon Love, 62 Lombard Street); Montreal (George P. Coghill); Winnipeg (Weidman Brothers); Regina (Love Brothers, G. Stewart Love); Calgary (Donald MacAlister); Vancouver (Love Brothers, Wm Ketchen); and Victoria (Cyril Buhlin).

The old home cook book

Before church union in 1925, Trinity United Church was the Methodist Church. For an earlier cookbook by the same congregation, see O98.1.

O925.1   1937
The old home cook book / compiled by / the Women's Association of / Trinity United Church, Gravenhurst / 1937 / [caption below photograph of the church:] Trinity United Churcr [sic], Gravenhurst, Ont. / Rev. J.G. Gorwill, Minister. / Our Greetings / We wish to thank all those who have helped by the giving of recipes / and by friendly advice [...] We trust this book may be use- / ful and our church may greatly benefit by the sale of it.

DESCRIPTION: 22.0 × 14.5 cm   Pp [i–vi], [1] 2–65, [i–ii]   Tp illus of the church   Patterned oil cloth

CONTENTS: Inside front face of binding 'Index' [i.e., table of contents]; i–ii ads; iii tp; iv–vi ads; 1–mid 63 recipes credited with the name of the contributor and ads; mid 63–65 'Household Hints' and ads; i–ii ads

COPIES: *OGU (CCC TX715.6 G7347)

NOTES: The pages of advertisements within the body of the text are not included in the pagination, i.e., there are more than 65 pages in the run [1] 2–65.

Pepper, Miss Laura Christine (Ottawa, Ont., 11 March 1899–9 August 1982, Ottawa, Ont.)

For information about Pepper and her other books, see O676.1.

O926.1   1st printing, July 1937

Publication 586 / Household Bulletin 16 / Issued July, 1937 / First printing / Dominion of Canada, Department of Agriculture / Cheese / for better meals / by / Laura C. Pepper / Dairy and Cold Storage Branch / Published by authority of the Hon. James G. Gardiner, Minister of Agriculture, / Ottawa, Canada [cover-title]

DESCRIPTION: 24.5 × 16.5 cm   Pp [1–3] 4–16   Paper, with image on front of a steaming casserole, a wedge of cheese on a plate, and three small plates with lettuce; stapled

CONTENTS: 1 cover-title; 2 untitled list of the advantages and characteristics of cheese; 3 'Cheese Making in Canada'; 4 'Branding and Grading of Cheese'; 5 'Buying and Storing Cheese'; 6 'Value of Cheese in the Diet'; 7 'Varied Uses of Cheese'; 8–12 'Cheese Luncheon and Supper Dishes'; 13 'Cheese Salads'; 14 'Salad Accompaniments'; 15 'Cheese Sandwiches'; 16 [outside back face of binding] 'Ottawa: Printed by J.O. Patenaude, ... 1937.'

CITATIONS: Ag 1867–1974, pp 23 and 35

COPIES: AEPMA (H86.43.717)   *OOAG (630.4 C212 P586, 3 copies, and 630.4 C212 HB16)   QMAC (S133 A346 No. 586)

O926.2   July 1937

—Publication 586 / Bulletin de la ménagère nᵒ 16 / Publié en juillet 1937 / Dominion du Canada – Ministère de l'agriculture / Repas au fromage – meilleurs repas! / Par / Laura C. Pepper / Division de l'industrie laitière et de la réfrigération / Publié par ordre de l'hon. James G. Gardiner, ministre de l'agriculture / Ottawa, Canada [cover-title]

DESCRIPTION: 24.0 × 15.5 cm   Pp [1–3] 4–16   Paper,

with image on front of a steaming casserole, a wedge of cheese on a plate, and three small plates with lettuce; rebound in cloth, together with other Household Bulletins

CONTENTS: 1 cover-title; 2 untitled list of the advantages and characteristics of cheese; 3 'La fabrication du fromage au Canada'; 4 'Le marque et le classement du fromage'; 5 'L'achat et la conservation du fromage'; 6–top 7 'Valeur du fromage dans le régime alimentaire'; near top–bottom 7 'Emplois variés du fromage'; 8–12 'Mets au fromage pour le lunch et le souper'; 13 'Salades au fromage'; 14–top 15 'Plats pour servir avec salade'; near top 15–16 [outside back face of binding] 'Sandwichs au fromage' and at bottom p 16, 'Version française par C.E. Mortureux, B.S.A. Ottawa: J.-O. Patenaude, O.S.I., imprimeur ... 1937.'

COPIES: *OOAG (630.4 C212 HB16 and 630.4 C212 P586)   QQLAS (S133 A346 F586)

O926.3   2nd printing, August 1938

—Publication 586 / Household Bulletin 16 / Issued August, 1938 / Second printing / Dominion of Canada – Department of Agriculture / Cheese / for better meals / by / Laura C. Pepper / Marketing Service / Dairy Products Division / Published by authority of the Hon. James G. Gardiner, Minister of Agriculture, / Ottawa, Canada [cover-title]

DESCRIPTION: 24.5 × 16.5 cm   Pp [1–3] 4–15 [16]   Paper, with image on front of a steaming casserole, a wedge of cheese on a plate, and three small plates with lettuce; stapled

CONTENTS: 1 cover-title; 2 untitled list of the advantages and characteristics of cheese; 3 'Cheese Making in Canada'; 4 'Branding and Grading of Cheese'; 5 'Buying and Storing Cheese'; 6 'Value of Cheese in the Diet'; 7 'Varied Uses of Cheese'; 8–12 'Cheese Luncheon and Supper Dishes'; 13 'Cheese Salads'; 14 'Salad Accompaniments'; 15 'Cheese Sandwiches'; 16 [outside back face of binding] 'Ottawa: Printed by J.O. Patenaude, I.S.O., printer to the King's Most Excellent Majesty, 1938.'

COPIES: ACG   *ARDA   OOAG (630.4 C212 P586, 3 copies)

O926.4   reprint, March 1939

—Publication 586 / Bulletin de la ménagère nᵒ 16 / Publié en mars 1939 / Réimpression / Dominion du Canada – Ministère de l'agriculture / Repas au fromage – meilleurs repas! / Par / Laura C. Pepper / Service des marchés / Section des consommateurs / Publié par ordre de l'hon. James G. Gardiner, ministre de l'agriculture / Ottawa, Canada [cover-title]

DESCRIPTION: 24.0 × 15.5 cm   Pp [1–3] 4–16   Paper, with image on front of a steaming casserole, a wedge of cheese on a plate, and three plates with lettuce; rebound in cloth, together with other Household Bulletins

CONTENTS: 1 cover-title; 2 untitled list of the advantages and characteristics of cheese; 3–top 4 'La fabrication du fromage au Canada'; mid 4–mid 5 'Le marque et le classement du fromage'; mid–bottom 5 'L'achat et la conservation du fromage'; 6–top 7 'Valeur du fromage dans le régime alimentaire'; near top–bottom 7 'Emplois variés du fromage'; 8–12 'Mets au fromage pour le lunch et le souper'; 13 'Salades au fromage'; 14–top 15 'Plats pour servir avec salade'; near top 15–16 [outside back face of binding] 'Sandwichs au fromage' and at bottom p 16, 'Version française par C.E. Mortureux, B.S.A. Ottawa: J.-O. Patenaude, O.S.I., imprimeur ... 1939.'

COPIES: *OOAG (630.4 C212 HB16)

O926.5   reprint, July 1939
—Publication 586 / Household Bulletin 16 / Issued July, 1939 / Reprint / Dominion of Canada – Department of Agriculture / Cheese / for better meals / by / Laura C. Pepper / Marketing Service / Consumer Service Section / Published by authority of the Hon. James G. Gardiner, Minister of Agriculture, / Ottawa, Canada / 35M–2427–7:39 [cover-title]

DESCRIPTION: 25.0 × 16.5 cm   Pp [1–3] 4–15 [16]   Paper, with image on front of a steaming casserole, a wedge of cheese on a plate, and three plates with lettuce; stapled

COPIES: *OOAG (630.4 C212 P586, 3 copies)

CONTENTS: 1 cover-title; 2 untitled list of the advantages and characteristics of cheese; 3 'Cheese Making in Canada'; 4 'Branding and Grading of Cheese'; 5 'Buying and Storing Cheese'; 6 'Value of Cheese in the Diet'; 7 'Varied Uses of Cheese'; 8–12 'Cheese Luncheon and Supper Dishes'; 13 'Cheese Salads'; 14 'Salad Accompaniments'; 15 'Cheese Sandwiches'; 16 [outside back face of binding] 'Ottawa: Printed by J.O. Patenaude, ... 1939.'

Purser, Mrs Mona Hazelwood Cleaver (Toronto, Ont., 5 May 1885–12 August 1954, Toronto, Ont.)

The daughter of Solomon Cleaver, a Methodist and later United Church minister, Mona Cleaver grew up in Winnipeg, Victoria, and Toronto. Before her marriage in 1920 to Harold M. Purser, she was a reporter in the women's department of the Globe *newspaper, writing under the pen name of Polly Peel. In 1925 Purser returned to the* Globe *to edit the Homemaker Page and to write the Homemaker column, for many years anonymously. Her last Homemaker column appeared on 4 June 1954, making an almost thirty-year run of columns. Her work elicited a huge correspondence from readers, including many from other provinces, who were apparently often moved by her campaigns for various good causes. From about 1933, clippings of Purser's Homemaker's Page could be collected in a special binder distributed by the newspaper and titled 'The Homemaker Kitchen Library' (Private collection).*

Purser was a member of the Toronto Women's Press Club, the Heliconian Club, and Sherbourne United Church. She was likely also a member of the Wimodausis Club because her recipes are included, with her mother's, in O294.1, The Wimodausis Club Cook Book, *first edition, 1912 or 1913. At the time of her death, she lived at 85 Glen Road in Toronto's Rosedale. (For more information, see newspaper clippings on microfilm in TPL Scrapbooks and the 1911 Census, which records her birth date and also her mother's name, Ida.)*

O927.1   nd [about 1937]
The homemaker's / guide book / short cuts to household / efficiency gleaned from / the Homemaker Page of / the Globe and Mail / Compiled by / Mona Cleaver Purser / The Homemaker / Price 35 cents / Address: / The Homemaker, the Globe and Mail / Toronto – Canada

DESCRIPTION: 23.0 × 15.0 cm   Pp [1–4] 5–63 [64]   Illus   Paper; stapled

CONTENTS: 1 tp; 2 'Portrait sketch of the Homemaker by Maida Knowles [i.e., the Toronto artist Maida Doris Parlow Knowles (1891–)]; 3 'What It Means to Be a Homemaker ...' signed the Homemaker; 4 table of contents; 5–63 text; 64 'To the Women of Ontario:' signed the Globe and Mail, Toronto

COPIES: *Private collection

NOTES: 'Chiefly Culinary' on pp 9–16 and 'Kitchen and Cupboard' on pp 17–20 are the only sections to do with food and cooking; the rest of the text is about housekeeping topics, such as laundry, baby care, the sick room, care of clothes, sewing, insect pests, care of floors, housecleaning, repairs and renovations, and the garden.

CCat No. 16, p R23, cites *The Homemaker's Guide Book*, Toronto: Mundy-Goodfellow, 1937, pp 64, compiled by the Homemaker Page of the Toronto *Globe and Mail*. The reference may be for O927.1 or O927.2, although the Mundy-Goodfellow name appears on neither. The order of publication of the two editions is unknown.

O927.2   nd [about 1937]
—The homemaker's / guide book / short cuts to household / efficiency gleaned from / the Homemaker Page of / the Globe and Mail / Compiled by / Mona Cleaver Purser / The Homemaker / Address: / The Homemaker, the Globe and Mail / Toronto – Canada
DESCRIPTION: 23.0 × 15.0 cm   Pp [1–4] 5–63 [64] Illus   Thin card; stapled
CONTENTS: 1 tp; 2 'Portrait sketch of the Homemaker by Maida Knowles'; 3 'What It Means to Be a Homemaker ...' signed the Homemaker; 4 table of contents; 5–63 text; 64 'To the Women of Ontario:' signed the Globe and Mail, Toronto
COPIES: *OGU (CCC TX715.6 P877)
NOTES: There is no price on the title-page of this edition.

Tested recipes

O928.1   1937
Tested recipes / compiled by / the Woman's Association / of / Turin United Church / 1937 / [caption:] Turin United Church / We desire to thank all whose liberal patronage in advertising / matter has made this book possible. We sincerely hope our / friends will freely patronize those who have patronized us. / Printed by the Shepherd Printing Company, Chatham, Ont.
DESCRIPTION: 24.5 × 16.0 cm   Pp [1–2] 3–77 [78–84] Tp illus of the church and a beaver superimposed on a maple leaf   Paper, with images on front of a crown at top left and at bottom right; stapled
CONTENTS: 1 tp; 2 ad; 3–77 recipes credited with the name of the contributor and ads; 78 ads; 79 blank for 'Memorandum'; 80 ads; 81 blank for 'Memorandum'; 82 ads; 83 'Index' [i.e., table of contents] and 'Miscellaneous'; 84 ads
COPIES: *Private collection
NOTES: The cover-title is '1937 Coronation Cook Book sponsored by Women's [sic] Association of Turin United Church'; the running head is 'Turin United Church Cook Book.' The church is near Ridgetown.

Another private collector has a copy with a variant binding design: There is no crown at top left, only at bottom right.

Tried and tested recipes

The Crumlin Women's Institute published another cookbook with the same title in 1949; see O1228.1. The branch was established in 1924 (Ambrose, p 237).

O929.1   1937
Tried and tested / recipes / compiled by / the Crumlin / Women's Institute / 1937 / R.F. Fielding Co., printers, London [cover-title]
DESCRIPTION: 22.5 × 15.0 cm   Pp [i–iv], 1–44, [i–iv] Paper, with image on front of a woman stirring the contents of a bowl; stapled
CONTENTS: i–iv ads; 1 'Crumlin Women's Institute officers 1936–37' and ad; 2 'Table of Measurements' and ads; 3–44 recipes and household hints; i–iv ads
CITATIONS: Ferguson/Fraser, p 234
COPIES: *Private collection
NOTES: The advertisements are for businesses in Crumlin, London, Dorchester, and Ingersoll.

The West End Circle recipe book

O930.1   [1937]
The / West End Circle / recipe book / Central / (Presbyterian) / Church / A collection of / tested recipes / published by / the ladies of the West End Circle / Central Presbyterian Church / Queen's Square Galt, Ontario
DESCRIPTION: 23.0 × 15.0 cm   Pp [1] 2–52   Tp illus of the church   Thin card, with image on front of a red star; stapled
CONTENTS: 1 tp; 2 'Preface' signed members of West End Circle; 3 'Roster of the Members of West End Circle of the Ladies' Aid of Central Presbyterian Church 1937'; 4–49 recipes credited with the name of the contributor, blank spaces for 'Memoranda,' and ads; 50 'Household Hints'; 51 'Table Decorations' and ad; 52 ad and 'Index' [i.e., table of contents]
COPIES: *Private collection
NOTES: Oddly, there is no reference in the 'Preface' or elsewhere to the church's famous publication, O58.1, *The Galt Cook Book*, first published in 1892, then in several later editions.

1937–9

Purity Flour recipes and menus

For information about Western Canada Flour Mills and other cookbooks for Purity Flour, see O394.1.

O931.1   nd [about 1937–9]
Purity Flour / recipes and menus [cover-title]
DESCRIPTION: 15.0 × 10.0 cm   Pp [1–16]   Several small illus of a cartoon-like woman with an over-size head, in various poses in a kitchen setting   Paper, with image on front of an aproned woman holding a layer cake and standing behind a kitchen table on which sits a loaf of bread and a bag of Purity Flour; stapled
CONTENTS: 1 cover-title; 2 'To Help You with Your Baking'; 3–7 'Recipes'; 8–12 'Menus'; 13 'Children's Parties'; 14 'Children's Lunch Box'; 15 'A Cook Book Every Woman Should Own' and order form for *Purity Cook Book*; 16 [outside back face of binding] list of Purity products produced by Western Canada Flour Mills Co. Ltd, Toronto, Montreal, Ottawa, Winnipeg, Calgary, Vancouver, New Westminster, Victoria, and Saint John
COPIES: SSWD   *Private collection
NOTES: The description on p 15 for the 'Purity Cook Book' (742 recipes, blue cloth, and 'run into two editions') corresponds to O771.2, dated 1937. Since there is no mention of wartime, O931.1 was likely published about 1937–9. The recipes in the menus are identified by their number in *The Purity Cook-Book*.

Purity Flour tested recipe suggestions

For information about Western Canada Flour Mills and other cookbooks for Purity Flour, see O394.1.

O932.1   nd [about 1937–9]
Here's / home baking / made easy! / Purity Flour / tested recipe suggestions [cover-title]
DESCRIPTION: 9.0 × 16.0 cm   Pp [1–16]   Illus brown of prepared dishes and a cartoon-like woman with over-size head (the Purity Maid)   Paper, with image on front of the Purity Maid and a two-layer cake; stapled
CONTENTS: 1 cover-title; 2 introductory text signed Western Canada Flour Mills Co. Ltd; 3–12 recipes; 13 'Hints for Best Success in Baking Cakes with Purity Flour'; 14 'How to Make the Most Successful Pastry with Purity Flour'; 15 [inside back face of binding] coupon for ordering *The Purity Cook-Book* and illus of the 1937 edition (O771.2); 16 [outside back face] publisher's name: Western Canada Flour Mills Co. Ltd, Toronto, Ottawa, Montreal, Saint John, New Brunswick, Winnipeg, Calgary, and Vancouver
COPIES: *Private collection

1938

The blue water cook book

O933.1   1938
The / blue water / cook / book / Price 50c / Printed 1938 / Compiled by / Woman's Auxiliary / Church of the Messiah / Kincardine, Ontario
COPIES: *Private collection
NOTES: The owner reports that the volume has 63 pp. The town of Kincardine looks out on the 'blue water' of Lake Huron.

Brown, Cora Lovisa Brackett (1861–1939), Rose Johnston Brown, née Watson (1883–1952), and Robert (Bob) Carlton Brown (Chicago, Ill., 14 June 1886–7 August 1959, New York City)

This American family trio – mother Cora, son Bob, and his second wife, Rose – co-wrote twelve cookbooks, all published in the period 1934–40. Of these, two are known to have Toronto as a place of publication: O934.1 and O962.1, The Vegetable Cook Book. After Cora's death, Bob and Rose produced only one more cookbook, which suggests that Cora, always named first on the title-page, was the 'driving force' behind these culinary works (see Andrew F. Smith's entry for Bob Brown in Arndt, p 82). Bob was a widely travelled fiction and non-fiction writer and poet, and his experience in the publishing sphere undoubtedly also contributed to the success of their enterprise. After Rose died, Bob married Eleanor Parker, and together they began the bibliography Culinary Americana: Cookbooks Published in the Cities and Towns of the United States of America during the Years from 1860 through 1960, *which Eleanor completed and had published in 1961.*

O934.1   [copyright 1938]
Salads and / herbs / Cora, Rose and Bob Brown / Philadelphia New York / J.B. Lippincott Company / London Toronto
DESCRIPTION: 19.6 × 13.1 cm   Pp [1–8] 9–274   Cloth
CONTENTS: Tp verso: 'Copyright, 1938, by Cora, Rose and Robert Carlton Brown // Made in the United States of America'
CITATIONS: Arndt, p 82 (Andrew F. Smith, 'Bob Brown')   Axford, p 355   Cagle/Stafford, No. 114
COPIES: OGU (UA s055 b21); United States: InU
NOTES: Information about this book is from the Cagle/ Stafford entry.

Brown, Cynthia [pseudonym of] Mrs Rose Marie Claire Armstrong Christie (Ottawa, Ont., 18 February 1894–1939, Toronto, Ont.)

Rose Marie Armstrong, whose nickname was Jane, married the Canadian diplomat Loring Christie. It was after her separation from Christie, in the last eleven years of her life, that she took up the pseudonym Cynthia Brown. In Saturday Night *she also sometimes used the pseudonym Marie-Claire (see Grace F. Heggie and Gordon R. Adshead, eds,* An Index to Saturday Night: The First Fifty Years, 1887–1937, *Toronto: Micromedia Ltd, 1987). On the dust-jacket of* Cooking – with a Grain of Salt, *the last sentence in the blurb about the author alludes to Brown being a pseudonym. The blurb states, in its entirety: 'She began her career in Ottawa, the only daughter in an otherwise satisfactory family of boys. Her first headmistress jumped off a bridge, but her last, at Bishop Strachan's [a Toronto private school for girls], merely retired. She has tried art, matrimony, parenthood, living abroad and writing advertising copy, and enjoyed them all. She now keeps house, writes a daily column of cheerful reflections on fashionable merchandise for a big store, two weekly columns of varied degrees of literary merit, suffers from writer's cramp and a sense of the futility of all human endeavour. Her name is not Cynthia Brown.'*

She was the first of other food journalists in her family. When Rose Marie suffered ill health from heart disease (from which she eventually died), her sister-in-law Agnes (nickname Polly) took over her 'Concerning Food' col-umn in Saturday Night, *writing under the pseudonym Janet March. In the 1950s, after the 'Concerning Food' column was discontinued, Agnes wrote for the women's section of the* Globe and Mail, *still under the pseud-onym Janet March. And Rose Marie's niece, Julian Armstrong, is food editor of the* Montreal Gazette *(1957–64 and 1979 to the present), and she held the same position at the* Montreal Star *from 1964 until the paper ceased publication in 1979. She is also the author of* A Taste of Quebec *(Toronto: Macmillan of Canada, 1990; 2nd ed., 2001), published in French under the title* Au goût du Québec *(Éditions du Trécarré, 1992).*

For another cookbook by a female columnist for Satur-day Night, *see O130.1, Denison, Grace Elizabeth,* The New Cook Book.

O935.1 1938
Cooking – / with a grain of salt / by / Cynthia Brown / With an introduction by / Bernard K. Sandwell / Decorations by / Ann Monkman / Toronto: The Macmillan Company of / Canada Limited, at St. Martin's House / 1938

DESCRIPTION: 20.5 × 14.0 cm   Pp [i–ix] x [xi] xii–xiii [xiv–xvi], [1–2] 3–382   Several fp illus incl one opp tp of chef and over-sized cookbook   Cloth
CONTENTS: i ht; ii fp illus; iii tp; iv 'Copyright, Canada, 1938 by the Macmillan Company of Canada ... Printed in Canada'; v dedication to 'E.A. "Whose daughter I am ..."'; vi blank; vii acknowledgments; viii blank; ix–x 'Introduction' signed B.K. Sandwell; xi–xiii table of contents; xiv blank; xv 'Illustrations'; xvi blank; 1–353 text; 354 blank; 355–82 'Index'
CITATIONS: CCat No. 17, p S22   Ferguson/Fraser, p 233   Rhodenizer, p 992   Whiteman et al., No. 788
COPIES: BKOM   OONL (TX651 B76 1938)   OTMCL (641.5 B68)   OWTU (F14980)   QMM (RBD ckbk 1371)   *Private collection
NOTES: Bernard Sandwell was the editor of *Saturday Night*, for whom Rose Marie Armstrong wrote her food column. In his 'Introduction' he remarks that the author's 'formulae [i.e., the recipes] are imbed-ded in the most perfect prose lyrics about food and drink that have ever been executed in Canada – a country not distinguished for lyrical feeling about either drink or food.' He adds: '... that which inspires her to write is not – please note this! – the mere pleasure of the palate; it is the social quality of the food and drink she is discussing. There is nothing here for that ineffably selfish beast, the solitary gour-mand or guzzler.' CCat records the price of the book: $2.75.

The copy catalogued here belongs to Julian Armstrong. It is inscribed by her father, on the front endpaper, 'To the author's niece and gastronomic lega-tee from the author's brother and niece's father 25.xii.58.' The copy was bought second-hand; hence, the year of inscription is later than the year of publi-cation. It was likely purchased from the famous Cor-ner Book Shop at 102 Fourth Avenue in New York City since it has that store's label.

Another private collector has a copy with the origi-nal dust-jacket, which features, on the front face, a large red spoon against a black background.

Canada, Department of Fisheries

On 29 April 1933, Miss Estelle LeBlanc and two other women judged a Robin Hood Flour baking contest at the Capitol Theater in Quebec City; in an article about the contest, 'Robin Hood Stages Popular Baking Contest in Quebec and Ontario,' Grist *[Robin Hood Mills Ltd in-house magazine] (July 1933), pp 10–11, LeBlanc is described as an official instructor in domestic economy for the Province of Quebec and she is in a photograph of the judges and organizers in the exhibition hall. LeBlanc's name is associated with a Quebec government cookbook, Q251.1, Mangeons plus de légumes.*

For the titles of other collections of fish recipes by the federal department, see O319.1.

O936.1   1938
100 / tempting / fish recipes / Issued by the department of / Fisheries Ottawa, Canada / Honourable J.E. Michaud, M.P., Minister / Prepared under the direction of the Depart- / ment's lecturer-demonstrators / Miss Estelle LeBlanc / Miss Hazel J. Freeman, B.Sc. in Hm. Ec. / Ottawa / J.O. Patenaude, I.S.O. / printer to the King's Most Excellent Majesty / 1938
DESCRIPTION: 19.5 × 12.0 cm   Pp [1–2] 3–56   Tp illus of five fish, illus   Paper [front face lacking]; stapled
CONTENTS: 1 tp; 2 blank; 3–5 'The Value of Fish in the Daily Diet'; 6–8 'Canadian Fish in Wide Variety'; 9–top 10 'Buying Fish'; mid 10 'Keeping Fresh or Frozen Fish'; 11–top 12 'Preparing Fish for Cooking'; mid 12 'Cooking Fish'; bottom 12 'Overcoming Odours'; 13–47 '100 Tempting Fish Recipes'; 48–52 'Sauces'; 53–6 index
CITATIONS: Armstrong 2000, p F2, illus p F2   *National Home Monthly* (January 1938)
COPIES: ARDA   OONL (COP.CA.2.1994-530, 2 copies)   *Private collection

O936.2   1939
—100 / tempting / fish recipes / Issued by the Department of / Fisheries Ottawa, Canada / Honourable J.E. Michaud, M.P., Minister / Prepared under the direction of the Depart- / ment's lecturer-demonstrators / Miss Estelle LeBlanc / Miss Hazel J. Freeman, B.Sc. in Hm. Ec. / Ottawa / J.O. Patenaude, I.S.O. / printer to the King's Most Excellent Majesty / 1939
DESCRIPTION: 19.5 × 12.0 cm   Pp [1–2] 3–56   Tp illus of five fish, illus   Paper, with image on front of tp illus and a fish on a platter; stapled
CONTENTS: 1 tp; 2 blank; 3–5 'The Value of Fish in the Daily Diet'; 6–8 'Canadian Fish in Wide Variety'; 9–top 10 'Buying Fish'; mid 10 'Keeping Fresh or Frozen Fish'; 11–top 12 'Preparing Fish for Cooking'; mid 12 'Cooking Fish'; bottom 12 'Overcoming Odours'; 13–47 '100 Tempting Fish Recipes'; 48–52 'Sauces'; 53–6 index
COPIES: BLCK (983.13)   OONL (COP.CA.2.1999-1534) *Private collection

O936.3   1940
—100 / tempting / fish recipes / Issued by the Department of / Fisheries Ottawa, Canada / Honourable J.E. Michaud, M.P., Minister / Prepared under the direction of the Depart- / ment's lecturer-demonstrators / Miss Estelle LeBlanc / Miss Hazel J. Freeman, B.Sc. in Hm. Ec. / Ottawa / J.O. Patenaude, I.S.O. / printer to the King's Most Excellent Majest [*sic*] / 1940
DESCRIPTION: 19.5 × 12.0 cm   Pp [1–2] 3–56   Tp illus of five fish, illus   Paper, with image on front of tp illus and a fish on a platter; stapled
CONTENTS: 1 tp; 2 blank; 3–5 'The Value of Fish in the Daily Diet'; 6–8 'Canadian Fish in Wide Variety'; 9–top 10 'Buying Fish'; mid 10 'Keeping Fresh or Frozen Fish'; 11–12 'Preparing Fish for Cooking'; 13–47 '100 Tempting Fish Recipes'; 48–52 'Sauces'; 53–6 index
COPIES: *Private collection

O936.4   1940
—100 / délicieuses / recettes de poisson / Opuscule émané du Ministère des / pêcheries Ottawa, Canada / Honorable J.E. Michaud, M.P., ministre. / Rédigé sous la direction des conférencières- / démonstratices au service du / département / Mlle Estelle LeBlanc / Mlle Hazel J. Freeman, B.Sc., Hm. Ec. / Ottawa / Edmond Cloutier / imprimeur de sa très excellente majesté le roi / 1940
DESCRIPTION: 19.5 × 12.0 cm   Pp [1–2] 3–63   Tp illus of five fish, illus   Paper, with image on front of tp illus and a fish on a platter; stapled
CONTENTS: 1 tp; 2 blank; 3–5 'La valeur du poisson dans la régime alimentaire quotidien'; 6–8 'Diversité des produits de la pêche au Canada'; 9–top 10 'Achat du poisson'; mid 10 'Conservation du poisson frais'; 11–12 'Préparation du poisson pour la cuisson'; 13–top 52 '100 délicieuses recettes de poisson'; mid 52–57 'Sauces'; 58 blank; 59–63 'Index'
COPIES: *QSFFSC

O936.5   1941
—100 / tempting / fish recipes / Issued by the Department of / Fisheries Ottawa, Canada / Honourable J.E. Michaud, M.P., Minister / Prepared under the direction of the Depart- / ment's lecturer-demonstrators / Miss Estelle LeBlanc / Miss Hazel J. Freeman, B.Sc. in Hm. Ec. / Ottawa / Edmond Cloutier, / printer to the King's Most Excellent Majesty / 1941
DESCRIPTION: 19.0 × 12.0 cm   Pp [1–2] 3–56   Tp illus of five fish, illus   Paper, with image on front of tp illus and a fish on a platter; stapled

CONTENTS: 1 tp; 2 blank; 3–5 'The Value of Fish in the Daily Diet'; 6–8 'Canadian Fish in Wide Variety'; 9–top 10 'Buying Fish'; mid 10 'Keeping Fresh or Frozen Fish'; 11–12 'Preparing Fish for Cooking'; 13–47 '100 Tempting Fish Recipes'; 48–52 'Sauces'; 53–6 index
COPIES: *Private collection

O936.6 1942
—100 / tempting / fish recipes / Issued by the Department of / Fisheries Ottawa, Canada / Honourable J.E. Michaud, M.P., Minister / Prepared under the direction of the Depart- / ment's lecturer-demonstrators / Ottawa / Edmond Cloutier / printer to the King's Most Excellent Majesty / 1942
DESCRIPTION: 19.0 × 12.0 cm Pp [1–2] 3–56 Tp illus of five fish, illus Paper, with image on front of tp illus and a fish on a platter; stapled
CONTENTS: 1 tp; 2 blank; 3–5 'The Value of Fish in the Daily Diet'; 6–8 'Canadian Fish in Wide Variety'; 9–top 10 'Buying Fish'; mid 10 'Keeping Fresh or Frozen Fish'; 11–12 'Preparing Fish for Cooking'; 13–47 '100 Tempting Fish Recipes'; 48–52 'Sauces'; 53–6 index
COPIES: *OGU (2 copies: CCC CA1 FS 42O53)

O936.7 1946
—100 / tempting / fish recipes / Issued by the Department of / Fisheries – Ottawa, Canada / Hon. H. Francis G. Bridges, M.P., Minister / Miss Hazel J. Freeman, B.A., B.Sc., in Hm. Ec. / Miss Estelle LeBlanc / Ottawa / Edmond Cloutier / printer to the King's Most Excellent Majesty / 1946
DESCRIPTION: 19.0 × 12.0 cm Pp [1–2] 3–56 Tp illus of five fish, illus Paper, with image on front of tp illus and a fish on a platter; stapled
CONTENTS: 1 tp; 2 blank; 3–5 'The Value of Fish in the Daily Diet'; 6–8 'Canadian Fish in Wide Variety'; 9–top 10 'Buying Fish'; mid 10 'Keeping Fresh or Frozen Fish'; 11–12 'Preparing Fish for Cooking'; 13–47 '100 Tempting Fish Recipes'; 48–52 'Sauces'; 53–6 index
COPIES: *Private collection

O936.8 1946
—100 / tempting / fish recipes / Issued by the Department of / Fisheries – Ottawa, Canada / Hon. H. Francis G. Bridges, M.P., Minister / Ottawa / Edmond Cloutier / C.M.G., B.A., L.Ph. / printer to the King's Most Excellent Majesty / Controller of Stationery / 1946
DESCRIPTION: 19.0 × 12.0 cm Pp [1–2] 3–56 Tp illus of five fish, illus Paper, with image on front of tp illus and a fish on a platter; stapled
CONTENTS: 1 tp; 2 blank; 3–5 'The Value of Fish in the

Daily Diet'; 6–8 'Canadian Fish in Wide Variety'; 9–top 10 'Buying Fish'; mid 10 'Keeping Fresh or Frozen Fish'; 11–12 'Preparing Fish for Cooking'; 13–47 '100 Tempting Fish Recipes'; 48–52 'Sauces'; 53–6 index
COPIES: OONL (COP.CA.2.1994-171) *Private collection
NOTES: Unlike the other 1946 edition, O936.7, Freeman and LeBlanc are not credited on the title-page.

O936.9 1948
—100 / tempting / fish recipes / Issued by the Department of / Fisheries – Ottawa, Canada / Ottawa / Edmond Cloutier, C.M.G., B.A., L.Ph. / printer to the King's Most Excellent Majesty / Controller of Stationery / 1948
COPIES: *Private collection

O936.10 1949
—100 / tempting / fish recipes / Issued by the Department of / Fisheries – Ottawa, Canada / Ottawa / Edmond Cloutier, C.M.G., B.A., L.Ph. / printer to the King's Most Excellent Majesty / Controller of Stationery / 1949
DESCRIPTION: 19.0 × 12.0 cm Pp [1–2] 3–56 Tp illus of five fish, illus Paper, with image on front of tp illus and a fish on a platter; stapled
CONTENTS: 1 tp; 2 blank; 3–5 'The Value of Fish in the Daily Diet'; 6–8 'Canadian Fish in Wide Variety'; 9–top 10 'Buying Fish'; mid 10 'Keeping Fresh or Frozen Fish'; 11–12 'Preparing Fish for Cooking,' 'Cooking Fish,' and 'Overcoming Odours'; 13–47 '100 Tempting Fish Recipes'; 48–52 'Sauces'; 53–6 'Index'
COPIES: *Private collection
NOTES: This copy is inscribed on the binding, 'Nov 21/50.'

O936.11 1949
—100 / délicieuses / recettes de poisson / Opuscule émané du Ministère des / pêcheries Ottawa, Canada / Rédigé sous la direction des conférencières- / démonstratices au service du / département / Ottawa / Edmond Cloutier / imprimeur de sa très excellente majesté le roi / 1949
DESCRIPTION: Tp illus of five fish Stapled
COPIES: *Private collection

Cook book

O937.1 reprint, 1991, of 1938
Cook book / in aid of the Women's / Association Fraternity United Church / Creighton Mine Ontario / Originally printed in 1938 / A reproduction

project / of / the Anderson Farm Museum / (c) The Anderson Farm Museum/ 1991 / [folio:] 1
DESCRIPTION: 21.5 × 14.0 cm Pp 1–36 [$0.50, on binding] Paper, with small image on front of a family at table; stapled
CONTENTS: 1 tp; 2 'Foreword' signed Jim Fortin, curator, Anderson Farm Museum; 3–33 recipes credited with the name of the contributor and ads; 34 blank for 'Additional Recipes' and, at bottom, inscription reproduced: '1938 Cook Book donated by John Dingwall Aug. 1989.'; 35–6 ads for 1991 businesses
COPIES: OLIAF *Private collection
NOTES: The 'Foreword' relates the history of Fraternity United Church, which began in 1899 as a Presbyterian congregation, with services in tents and log cabins. A church building was constructed in 1916; the last service held in the church was on 25 June 1973. The village of Creighton Mine is now a ghost town located within the political boundary of Greater Sudbury. The date of the cookbook is known from an advertisement that is reprinted on the inside front face of the binding: 'Again in 1938 Universal Cooler [a type of refrigerator] leads them all in value ...'

The 1991 reprint was made from a copy of the original book at OLIAF. The cover-title of the 1938 book is:
Cook book / in aid of / the Women's Association / Fraternity United Church / Creighton Mine, Ontario / Price 50c

Frances Willard centenary cook book

See also O970.1, The Frances Willard Memorial Cook Book, another Ontario anniversary compilation.

O938.1 1938
Frances Willard centenary / cook / book / Tried and tested / recipes / Compiled and published by / the Woman's Christian Temperance Unions / of / Leeds and Frontenac counties / in 1938 / Price 25c [cover-title]
DESCRIPTION: With small image on front of a ribbon tied in a bow
COPIES: *OBM
NOTES: The production of this cookbook anticipated the celebration in 1939 of the hundredth anniversary of the birth of Frances Willard (1839–1898), the famous American temperance leader and one-time president of the WCTU. The OBM copy is inscribed on the binding, 'Evelyn McRory 1944 // [added at a later date:] McGreer.'

Golden jubilee cook book

O939.1 1938
Perth Avenue / United Church / Golden / jubilee / cook / book / Issued by the ladies of / Perth Ave. United Church / Toronto / 1938 [cover-title]
DESCRIPTION: With small image on front of the church
COPIES: *Private collection
NOTES: The owner reports that the book has 40 pp.

The Heather Club cook book

For a cookbook by the hospital's Nurses' Alumnae, see O529.1.

O940.1 [March 1938]
The Heather Club / cook book / Tested recipes // household hints / menu suggestions / Arranged and published / by / the Heather Club / of / the Public General Hospital / Chatham Ontario
DESCRIPTION: 22.5 × 15.0 cm Pp [1–2] 3–84 Tp illus of the hospital entrance (?) Paper; stapled
CONTENTS: 1 tp; 2 'Preface' signed ladies of the Heather Club and 'Printed in Chatham by the Shepherd Printing Company'; 3 'Foreword' by superintendent of the Public General Hospital, dated March 1938; 4–77 recipes credited with the name of the contributor and ads; 78–80 'Menu Suggestions' and ad; 81–2 'Miscellaneous' and ads; 83 'Table Decorations' and ad; 84 'Index' [i.e., table of contents] and ads
COPIES: *OGU (CCC TX715.6 H4255)
NOTES: The year of publication, 1938, and 'Chatham General Hospital' are printed on the front face of the binding. In the 'Foreword' the superintendent explains that the Heather Club was organized in 1909 by 'a group of public-spirited women,' following a 'Fair of Nations' held in aid of the hospital work, and he goes on to describe the club's significant contributions to the hospital. In the 'Preface' one learns that the compilers have 'tried to include a large number of recipes of other types [than cake and cookies]' because most housewives already have their own favourite recipes for these.

Helpful hints for housekeepers [1938]

See O263.1 for information about the company and other issues of Helpful Hints for Housekeepers.

O941.1 [1938]
Dodd's / helpful / hints / for / housekeepers [cover-title]

DESCRIPTION: 17.5 × 12.5 cm   Pp 1–32   Illus   Paper, with image on front, in oval frame, of a woman's head; stapled, and with hole punched at top left corner, through which runs a string for hanging
CONTENTS: 1 'Some Helpful Hints,' jokes, and a 1938 calendar; 2–32 culinary and housekeeping information, health advice, jokes, 'How to Forecast the Weather' on p 20, and publ ads
COPIES: *OTUTF (uncat patent medicine)
NOTES: For culinary information see: 'Some Helpful Hints,' p 1; 'A French Chef Tells Us How to Make an Omelette,' p 5; 'Weights and Measures,' p 10; 'Kitchen Equivalents,' p 17; untitled text, p 18; 'More Useful Hints,' p 25; and 'To Make Oyster Stew' and 'To Select Meats,' p 27.

The Home and School Council cook book

O942.1   [1938]
The Home and School Council / cook book / Tested recipes / household helps // menus / Arranged and published by / the members of / the Home and School Council / Windsor Walkerville Sandwich / Ontario / [folio:] 1
DESCRIPTION: Pp 1–76
CONTENTS: 1 tp; 2 'Officers of Home and School Council,' 'Executive Committee,' 'Conveners of Standing Committees,' and 'Presidents of Associations'; 3 'Preface'; 4 'Each Days [sic] Meals Should Contain:'; 5–74 recipes credited with the name of the contributor and ads; 75 'Household Hints'; 76 'Index' and ads
COPIES: *Private collection
NOTES: The year of publication, 1938, is printed on the front face of the binding. 'Printed by the Windsor Daily Star' is on the outside back face.

The housewife's almanac 1938

For the titles of other Kellogg books about All-Bran, see O768.1.

O943.1   1938
The housewife's / almanac / a book for homemakers / 1938 / A compilation of information / for everyday use containing: / a calendar for the year with important historical events; / astronomical data; sun, moon rise and set times; / valuable / advice on keeping fit; tempting recipes; / outdoor and indoor / games; interesting facts for movie and radio fans; time table / for baking and roasting; interesting facts about Canada; /

horoscopes; pointers for safe driving; and much other useful / and entertaining information. / Published by Kellogg Company of Canada Ltd. / London, Ontario / C-8171 Printed in Canada
DESCRIPTION: 20.0 × 13.5 cm   Pp [1] 2–36   Tp illus of a mother, father, and two children beside a car and looking at a mountain scene, illus col   Paper, with image on front of a mother, father, son, and dog; stapled
CONTENTS: 1 tp; 2 'Calendar for 1938'; 3 'Do You Ever Feel Listless and Played Out?'; 4 'Interesting Facts for Radio and Movie Fans'; 5 January; 6 'What to Do about Common Constipation'; 7 February; 8 'Time Table for Baking and Roasting and Weights and Measures'; 9 March; 10 'How to Acquire and Develop Winning Ways ...'; 11 April; 12 'Amusing and Helpful Facts from the World of Science'; 13 May; 14 'What Is Meant by "A Natural Laxative Food"?'; 15 June; 16 'The Canadian Wedding'; 17–20 'Try These Recipes Made with Kellogg's All-Bran'; 21 'How All-Bran Works to Keep You "Regular"'; 22 'Where to Go and What to See'; 23 July; 24 'Dreams and Their Meaning'; 25 August; 26 'It's Fun to Keep "Regular"'; 27 September; 28 'Outdoor and Indoor Games'; 29 October; 30 'Interesting Facts about Canada'; 31 November; 32 'Handy Facts for Those Who Figure'; 33 December; 34 'Answers to Questions about All-Bran'; 35 'Pointers for Safe Driving'; 36 'Horoscopes'
CITATIONS: Cooke 2002, p 234
COPIES: MCM   OGU (CCC TX715.6 H6774)   QMM (RBD ckbk 1674)   *Private collection

O943.2   1938
—L'almanach / de la menagere / un manuel pour le foyer / 1938 / Compilation de renseignements / pour usage journalier comprenant: / un calendrier avec importants évènements historiques; indications astrono- / miques; lever et coucher du soleil et de la lune; bons conseils sur la marche / à suivre pour bien se porter; recettes appétissantes; jeux de grand air et / d'intérieur; informations intéressantes pour les amateurs de cinéma et de / radio; tableau de cuisson; renseignements intéressants sur le Canada; horo- / scope de l'année; memento de l'automobiliste; et maintes autres informations / utiles et amusantes. / Publié par Kellogg Company of Canada Ltd. / London, Ontario / C-8171
DESCRIPTION: 20.0 × 13.5 cm   Pp [1] 2–36   Tp illus of a mother, father, and two children beside a car and looking at a mountain scene, illus col   Paper, with image on front of a mother, father, son, and dog; stapled
COPIES: *QSFFSC

Instructions for care and operation of Canadian Cookware health equipment

O944.1 [copyright 1938]
Instructions for / care and operation of / Canadian Cookware / health equipment / It is very important to / read these instructions / carefully before using / your new equipment. / Canadian Cookware Limited / 251 Queen Street East / Toronto / Phone: Elgin 8602 [cover-title]
DESCRIPTION: Pp [1–2] 3–18 Fp illus on p 1 of 'The Canadian Cookware Economy Health Set,' i.e., the saucepans and other utensils made by the company Stapled
CONTENTS: Inside front face of binding introductory text and 'Copyright 1938'; 1 illus; 2 blank; 3 'Twin Set'; 4–7 recipes for 'Vegetables,' 'Puddings,' and 'Baking'; 8–10 'Roaster,' plus instructions and recipes for 'Steaming,' 'Preserving,' and 'Baking'; 11–12 'Griddle' and recipes; 13 'Beverage Server' and recipe; 14 'Care of Utensils'; 15–17 'Vitamins'; 18 'Acid-Forming Foods'
COPIES: *Private collection
NOTES: The text opposite p 1 describes the company's cookware as 'equipment for waterless and low temperature cooking ... the latest, most efficient and easiest to use health utensils ... [that] will automatically save the health-giving elements of natural foods while you use any recipe you wish and season to suit yourself.' The instructions call for cooking the food in a small amount of water, in a covered saucepan, at a low temperature, so as not to destroy vitamins.

The jubilee Service book

O945.1 nd [about 1938]
The jubilee / Service book / by the Service Club / of / St. John's Presbyterian Church / Toronto
DESCRIPTION: 22.5 × 15.0 cm Pp [1] 2–40 Small tp illus of a boar's(?) head on a platter Paper, with tp illus on front; stapled
CONTENTS: 1 tp; 2 'Preface' and 'A Recipe for a Happy Life'; 3 ads; 4–35 recipes credited with the name of the contributor and ads; 36 'Table of Measures,' 'Table Decorations,' and 'Index' [i.e., table of contents]; 37 ads; 38–40 blank for 'Memoranda,' and at bottom p 40, 'Printed by F.W. Duggan, Toronto'
COPIES: *Private collection
NOTES: St John's Presbyterian Church, at 415 Broadview Avenue, was founded in 1888. 'Jubilee' in the cookbook's title may refer to the church's fiftieth anniversary celebrations in 1938. An advertisement

on p 28 for Rexall Drug Store reproduces an image of the Dionne quintuplets, who were born in 1934, looking about four years old. Further evidence pointing to publication in about 1938 is an advertisement on p 25 for Hasting's Linden Dairy, 970 Broadview, 'established over 40 years'; the first listing in Toronto city directories for Linden Dairy is in the classified section of 1898 (1898 + 40 years = 1938).

The kitchen crusade

O946.1 1938
The / kitchen / crusade / 1938 / Compiled and published by / Sixth Line of Moore United Church [cover-title]
DESCRIPTION: About 23.0 × 15.0 cm [dimensions from photocopy] Stapled
COPIES: *OMMM

The Leonard book of kitchen tested recipes

For a later cookbook from the same company, see O1173.1, Your Leonard Refrigerator.

O947.1 nd [about 1938]
The / Leonard / book / of / kitchen tested / recipes / Price twenty-five cents / Published by / Leonard Refrigerator / Company / London Canada
DESCRIPTION: 24.0 × 16.0 cm Pp [1] 2–32 Illus green Paper, with image on front of stylized dishes; stapled
CONTENTS: 1 tp; 2–32 text and at bottom p 32, 'Form No. L-3804 Part No. 03638 Printed in Canada'
COPIES: OONL (AC901 A7 1940z No. 0085) OTNY (uncat) *QMM (RBD ckbk 1766)
NOTES: The cover-title is 'The Leonard Book of Recipes.' The recipes are organized in the following sections: 'Appetizers,' pp 2–4; 'Beverages,' pp 5–6; 'Baking,' pp 7–10; 'Casserole Dishes,' pp 11–13; 'Ice Cream,' pp 14–15; 'Ices,' p 16; 'Sherbets,' p 17; 'Mousses,' p 18; 'Parfaits,' p 19; 'Sauces,' p 20; 'Miscellaneous,' p 21; 'Pies ... Cakes ... Puddings,' pp 22–4; 'Soups,' pp 25–7; 'Salads,' pp 28–30; 'Salad Dressings,' p 31; and 'Equivalent Measures,' p 32.

The OTNY copy is as described for the QMM copy except that it has no 'Part No. 03638' on p 32.

The Leonard Book of Kitchen Tested Recipes may be an edition of the same text as O920.1, *The Kelvinator Book of Kitchen Tested Recipes*, published about 1937; see the notes at that entry. *The Leonard Book* was likely published about the same time, perhaps in 1938, given the form and part numbers on p 32.

Maltby, Lucy Mary

O948.1 [copyright 1938]
It's fun to / cook / by / Lucy Mary Maltby /
Drawings by / Ruth King / The John C. Winston
Company / Chicago Philadelphia Toronto
DESCRIPTION: 22.0 × 15.5 cm   Pp [i–iv] v [vi] vii [viii]
ix–xiv [xv–xvi], 1–399 [400–2]   Frontis brown of
'Cooking is fun,' tp illus brown of the head-and-
shoulders of a young woman holding a measuring
cup and spoon, illus brown, illus   Cloth
CONTENTS: i ht; ii frontis; iii tp; iv 'Copyright, 1938, by
the John C. Winston Company // Copyright in Great
Britain // the British Dominions and Possessions ...
Printed in the U.S.A. ...'; v 'Foreword'; vi illus; vii
'Acknowledgment'; viii illus; ix–x 'Contents'; xi–xiv
'Illustrations'; xv–xvi blank; 1–383 text; 384 blank;
385–99 'Index'; 400–2 blank for 'My Own Collection
of Recipes'
COPIES: AEU (TX652.5 M35 1938)   BVA (641.5
M26I)   NSHV (652.5 M3)   *OGU (CCC TX715.6
M364); United States: DLC (TX652.5 M3)
NOTES: The 'Foreword' explains that the cookbook
was written for 'young people' and that the easiest
recipes are starred with an asterisk for young girls
and boys. On the title-page, Philadelphia is in the
largest typeface. The endpapers are illustrated.

Menus and budgets for economy buying and cooking

O949.1   5th printing, February 1938
To protect health / be sure to use these foods daily /
Milk [...] / Bread and cereal [...] / Vegetables [...] /
Fruits [...] / Eggs, meat, fish [...] / Butter, lard [...] /
Sugar, molasses [...] / Children under 2 years need
from 1 to 2 teaspoonfuls of / Cod Liver Oil daily.
Give it to all children, if possible. / Menus and
budgets / for economy buying and cooking / The
Canadian Welfare Council / Council House /
Ottawa / Reprint from publ'n No. 66. / 5th
printing, Feb. 1938. [cover-title]
DESCRIPTION: 22.5 × 15.0 cm   Pp [1] 2–15   Illus on
p 1   Paper
CONTENTS: 1 cover-title; 2–3 'Suggested Menus'; 4
'Suggested Menus for One Week'; 5 'Suggested Menus
for Two Adults'; 6–15 'Recipes'
COPIES: *Private collection
NOTES: The book was written for families on extremely
limited budgets. A footnote on p 3 advises: 'Honey or
jam for the use of adults only at breakfast. Milk to
drink for children only at breakfast and supper.'

Menus and recipes feature mainly potatoes, turnips,
cabbage, beets, onions, beans, rice, carrots, parsnips,
stews and soups, porridges, and prune and apple
desserts. The first four printings likely appeared before 1938.

O949.2   1942
—[An edition of *Menus and Budgets for Economy Buying and Cooking*, Ottawa: Canadian Welfare Council,
1942, pp 16]
Copies: MWU

The mixing bowl

O950.1   1938
[An edition of *The Mixing Bowl: A Guide to Good Cooking Written by the Housewives of Little Britain*, Women's
Association of the United Church, Little Britain,
Ontario, 1938]
CITATIONS: Wilson May 1991
NOTES: The Wilson article features a photograph of
the book's owner, Laura Kirkwood, holding her copy
of *The Mixing Bowl*, and it reprints recipes from the
book, including English Plum Pudding that her
mother contributed.

Modern mixes for bakers

O951.1   [copyright 1938]
Modern mixes / for / bakers / [Sunsoy symbol
incorporating the phrase 'Sunsoy Reg'd'] / Sunsoy
Products Limited / 468 Queen Street East / Toronto
Canada
DESCRIPTION: About 20.0 × 12.0 cm [dimensions from
photocopy]   Pp [1] 2–56   [Free, on binding]   Metal-
spiral bound
CONTENTS: Inside front face of binding 'Copyright,
Canada, 1938 by Sunsoy Products Limited Toronto,
Canada'; 1 tp; 2 company guarantee; 3–4 'The Soya
Bean'; 5– 'A Few Facts about Bread and Bread Mak-
ing'; ...; 56 blank for 'Memorandum'; inside back face
'Mundy Brothers Limited Toronto Canada'
COPIES: *Private collection
NOTES: The cover-title is 'Bakers Manual.' The recipes
use the publisher's soya bean products to make a
variety of goods, in commercial amounts; for example,
Sunsoy Cereal Loaf and Sunsoy Plum Pudding. The
versos of the leaves are blank and not included in
the pagination, except at the end of the book, where
the 'Memorandum' page is printed on the verso.

Osborne, Mabel

Also by Osborne are Meatless Dishes for Hay Dieters, *London: G.G. Harrap and Co., 1937 (Great Britain: LB), and* Bakes, Buns and Biscuits, *London: G.G. Harrap and Co., 1940 (Great Britain: LB).*

O952.1 [1st ed., 1938]
Hors-d'oeuvres / for Hay dieters / light luncheon or supper dishes / By / Mabel Osborne / author of / "Meatless Dishes for Hay Dieters" / George G. Harrap & Co. Ltd. / London Toronto Bombay Sydney

DESCRIPTION: 18.5 × 12.5 cm   Pp [1–4] 5–94 [95]   [3s 6d, on dust-jacket]   Cloth

CONTENTS: 1 ht; 2 blank; 3 tp; 4 'First published 1938 by George G. Harrap & Co. Ltd. ... London ... Made in Great Britain. Printed at the St Ann's Press, Timperley, Cheshire'; 5–8 foreword signed Mabel Osborne; 9–12 table of contents; 13 'General Notes on Ingredients for Hors-d'oeuvres'; 14 blank; 15–95 recipes

COPIES: *Private collection; Great Britain: LB (7944.r.20)

NOTES: The foreword comments: '[The recipes] will tend to reduce the protein or starch content of the meal. The letters P., S., and A. after each heading indicate the type of meal (Protein, Starch, and Alkaline) at which the recipe may be used ... Raw vegetables and raw salads, and of course raw fruit, are an integral part of the Hay system of eating ...' The Hay System books, many written by Dr William Howard Hay, are listed on the back of the dust-jacket.

Pepper, Miss Laura Christine (Ottawa, Ont., 11 March 1899–9 August 1982, Ottawa, Ont.)

For information about Pepper and her other books, see O676.1.

O953.1 1st printing, December 1938
Publication 635 / Household Bulletin 19 / Issued December, 1938 / First printing / Dominion of Canada – Department of Agriculture / Milk / the food of foods / by / Laura C. Pepper / Marketing Service / Dairy Products Division / Published by authority of the Hon. James G. Gardiner, Minister of Agriculture, / Ottawa, Canada [cover-title]

DESCRIPTION: 24.0 × 15.0 cm   Pp [1–3] 4–22 [23]   Paper, with image on front of milk bottles lined up in a V-shape; rebound in cloth, together with other Household Bulletins

CONTENTS: 1 cover-title; 2 list of the advantages and characteristics of milk; 3–5 'The Value of Milk in the Diet'; 6–9 'Milk in Various Forms'; 10–12 'Care of Milk from Producer to Consumer'; 13–14 'Consumption and Uses of Milk'; 15–23 recipes for 'Soups and Chowders,' 'Luncheon and Supper Dishes,' 'Cream Sauces,' 'Milk Drinks,' and 'Milk Dishes for the Convalescent,' and at bottom p 23, 'Ottawa: Printed by J.O. Patenaude, ... 1938.'

CITATIONS: Ag 1867–1974, pp 23, 37

COPIES: OGU (Rural Heritage Collection uncat) *OOAG (630.4 C212 HB19, 2 copies; 630.4 C212 P635, 5 copies)

O953.2 1st printing, April 1939
—Publication 635 / Bulletin de la ménagère 19 / Publié en avril 1939 / Première impression / Dominion du Canada – Ministère de l'agriculture / Le lait / l'aliment par excellence / par / Laura C. Pepper / Service des marchés / Section des produits laitiers / Publié par ordre de l'hon. James G. Gardiner, ministre de l'agriculture, / Ottawa, Canada [cover-title]

DESCRIPTION: 24.0 × 15.5 cm   Pp [1–3] 4–24   Paper, with image on front of milk bottles lined up in a V-shape; rebound in cloth, together with other Household Bulletins

CONTENTS: 1 cover-title; 2 list of the advantages and characteristics of milk; 3–5 'La valeur du lait dans l'alimentation'; 6–10 'Les différentes formes de lait'; 11–13 'Le soin du lait par le producteur et le consommateur'; 14–15 'Consommation et emplois du lait'; 16–24 recipes for 'Soupes et marmites ou chaudronnées (Chowders),' 'Plats pour le lunch et le souper,' 'Sauces blanches dites "Sauces à la crème,"' 'Boissons au lait,' and 'Mets au lait pour le convalescent,' and at bottom p 24, 'Ottawa: J.-O. Patenaude, O.S.I., imprimeur ... 1939.'

CITATIONS: Ag 1867–1974, pp 7, 28

COPIES: *OOAG (630.4 C212 HB19, 630.4 C212 P635)

NOTES: QQLAS (S133 A346 F635) has one of the 1939 French-language printings.

O953.3 reprint, July 1939
—Publication 635 / Household Bulletin 19 / Issued July, 1939 / Reprint / Dominion of Canada – Department of Agriculture / Milk / the food of foods / by / Laura C. Pepper / Marketing Service / Consumer Service Section / Published by authority of the Hon. James G. Gardiner, Minister of Agriculture, / Ottawa, Canada [cover-title]

DESCRIPTION: 24.5 × 16.5 cm   Pp [1–3] 4–23   Paper, with image on front of milk bottles lined up in a V-shape; stapled

CONTENTS: 1 cover-title; 2 list of the advantages and

characteristics of milk; 3–5 'The Value of Milk in the Diet'; 6–9 'Milk in Various Forms'; 10–12 'Care of Milk from Producer to Consumer'; 13–14 'Consumption and Uses of Milk'; 15–23 recipes for 'Soups and Chowders,' 'Luncheon and Supper Dishes,' 'Cream Sauces,' 'Milk Drinks,' and 'Milk Dishes for the Convalescent,' and at bottom p 23, 'Ottawa: Printed by J.O. Patenaude, ... 1939.'

COPIES: *OOAG (630.4 C212 P635, 2 copies)

O953.4   reprint, November 1939

—Publication 635 / Bulletin de la ménagère 19 / Publié en novembre 1939 / Réimpression / Dominion du Canada – Ministere de l'agriculture / Le lait / l'aliment par excellence / par / Laura C. Pepper / Services [sic] des marchés / Division des produits laitiers / Publié par ordre de l'hon. James G. Gardiner, ministre de l'agriculture, / Ottawa, Canada [cover-title]

DESCRIPTION: 25.0 × 16.5 cm   Pp [1–3] 4–23 [24]   Paper, with image on front of milk bottles lined up in a V-shape; stapled

CONTENTS: 1 cover-title; 2 list of the advantages and characteristics of milk; 3–5 'La valeur du lait dans l'alimentation'; 6–10 'Les différentes formes de lait'; 11–13 'Le soin du lait par le producteur et le consommateur'; 14–15 'Consommation et emplois du lait'; 16–24 recipes for 'Soupes et marmites ou chaudronnées (Chowders),' 'Plats pour le lunch et le souper,' 'Sauces blanches dites "Sauces à la crème,"' 'Boissons au lait,' and 'Mets au lait pour le convalescent,' and at bottom p 24, 'Ottawa: J.-O. Patenaude, O.S.I., imprimeur ... 1939.'

COPIES: *OOAG (630.4 C212 P635 Fr, 3 copies)

Read, Miss Jessica (Jessie) Madeline (Mrs Robert Stuart Hately) (Lucan, Ont., 15 February 1905–8 April 1940, Toronto, Ont.)

For information about the author, see O830.1, Three Meals a Day. *The 1934 collection of recipes has one-quarter the number of pages of the 1938 book of the same title (O954.1).*

O954.1   1938

Three meals a day / by / Jessie Read / Canadian home economist, / Food Editor, "Toronto Telegram" / Toronto / The Musson Book Company Ltd. / 1938

DESCRIPTION: 21.5 × 14.0 cm   Pp [i–iv] v–vii [viii–x], 1–435   2 tp illus: woman at a stove, above, and one place-setting, below; 13 pls incl frontis   Cloth

CONTENTS: i ht; ii blank; iii tp; iv 'Copyright, Canada, 1938 by the Musson Book Company Ltd. Toronto'; v–vi table of contents; vii foreword signed Jessie Read; viii blank; ix ht; x blank; 1–417 text; 418–19 glossary; 420–35 index

CITATIONS: CCat No. 17, p S23   Driver 2004, p vii   Ferguson/Fraser, p 234

COPIES: OGU (CCC TX715.6 R3965)   OTMCL (641.5 R24)   *Private collection

NOTES: The photographic plates of table settings feature Read's own china and silverware (conversation with the author's daughter, May 2001). For an illustration of the book with its dust-jacket, see the review by Doris Berry, *Narrator* [publication of the Literary Guild in Canada] Vol. 5, No. 7 (July 1938), p 9. An advertisement for the book on the outside back face of *Musson's Spring Catalogue 1938* gives the price of $1.75. CCat identifies Jessie Read as Mrs Robert Hately and records a higher price: $2.00.

The OGU copy is inscribed on the front endpaper, in ink, 'Oct 30th/40 To Marg With every good wish for your happiness – And mind you use this book & feed him good // A.A. Knowles // 832 Burrard St.' The OTMCL copy lacks pp 377–92.

O954.2   [copyright 1940]

—The Dominion / cook book of / tested recipes / by / Jessie Read / Canadian home economist / The Dominion Book and Bible House / Toronto Canada

DESCRIPTION: 21.5 × 14.0 cm   Pp [3–4] 5–6, 8 [9], 13–16, 19 [20], 23–6, 29, 32, 39, 44–6, 55, 58, 63, 66, 71–2, 83–4, 87, 90, 93–4, 101, 106, 117, 120, 122, 124–5, 128, 135–6, 144, 146, 163–5, 170, 191, 194, 197, 200, 235, 240, 245, 248, 263, 266, 269, 272, 291, 302, 311, 328–9, 346, 351, 354, 357, 368, 373–4, 383, 394, 397, 408, 411–12, 415, 418, 429, 432, 435–6, 448, 450, 453–4, 456, 464, 479 [480]   10 pls incl frontis of 'A Modern Kitchen' [$2.50, on p 480]   Cloth

CONTENTS: 3 tp; 4 'Copyright, Canada, 1940 Dominion Book and Bible House // Copyright, 1938, M.B. Co. Ltd.'; 5–6 'Contents'; 8 'Foreword' signed Jessie Read; 9 blank; 13–453 text; 454 'Glossary'; 456–79 'Index'; 480 ad for this book

COPIES: *OTUTF (D-11 0985)

NOTES: This is a retitled edition of *Three Meals a Day*, from a different publisher, the Dominion Book and Bible House, instead of Musson. The table of contents matches O954.3.

The OTUTF copy may be a publisher's sample volume. Many pages are not bound in; for example, p 464 of the index, which ends at 'Sole,' is followed by p 479, which begins at 'Veal.' The advertisement for the book on p 480 refers to Read as the 'former

Food Editor of the Toronto Evening Telegram,' evidence that this volume was produced after Read died in April 1940. Tipped in on the back endpaper is a 'Certificate of Membership in the International Institute' located in Room 402, 60 Front Street West, Toronto. The certificate allowed the member to secure information or advice on questions pertaining to the culinary art or home economics.

O954.3 [2nd ed.], 1941
—Three meals a day / by / Jessie Read / Canadian home economist, / Food Editor, "Toronto Telegram" / New and revised edition / Toronto / The Musson Book Company Ltd. / 1941
DESCRIPTION: 21.5 × 14.0 cm   Pp [1–4] 5–480   2 tp illus: woman at a stove and one place-setting; 15 pls incl frontis   Cloth
CONTENTS: 1 ht; 2 blank; 3 tp; 4 'Copyright, Canada, 1938, 1941 by the Musson Book Company Ltd. Toronto // Second edition'; 5–6 table of contents; 7 'Preface to the New Edition'; 8 blank; 9 'Preface to the First Edition'; 10 acknowledgment; 11 ht; 12 blank; 13–455 text; 456–80 index
CITATIONS: CCat No. 20, p V15
COPIES: *OGU (UA s045 b27)
NOTES: *Three Meals a Day* was recommended, along with O506.1, Nellie Pattinson's *Canadian Cook Book,* as a useful Canadian cookbook in Brodie 5 Dec 1942. Brodie says of the author, 'Jessie Read was one of the most popular demonstrators of cookery methods that Toronto has ever known.'

O954.4 [3rd ed.], 1943
—Three meals a day / by / Jessie Read / Canadian home economist, / Food Editor, "Toronto Telegram" / New and revised edition / Toronto / The Musson Book Company Ltd. / 1943
DESCRIPTION: 21.5 × 14.0 cm   Pp [1–4] 5–480   2 tp illus: woman at a stove and one place-setting; 15 pls incl frontis
CONTENTS: 1 ht; 2 blank; 3 tp; 4 'Copyright, Canada, 1938, 1941 by the Musson Book Company Ltd. Toronto ... Third edition'; 5–6 table of contents; 7 'Preface to the New Edition' signed Jessie Read; 8 blank; 9 'Preface to the First Edition' signed Jessie Read; 10 'Acknowledgment' to *Evening Telegram,* Toronto, for releasing the book's copyright; 11–455 text; 456–80 index and at bottom p 480, symbol of 'The Hunter-Rose Co. Limited Toronto printers-bookbinders'
CITATIONS: CCat No. 23, p Y17
COPIES: *OTMCL (641.5 R24.11)   Private collection
NOTES: CCat records the price: $2.00.

O954.5 [4th ed.], 1945
—Three meals a day / by / Jessie Read / Canadian home economist, / Food Editor, "Toronto Telegram" / New and revised edition / Toronto / The Musson Book Company Ltd. / 1945
DESCRIPTION: 21.5 × 14.0 cm   Pp [1–4] 5–480   2 tp illus: woman at a stove and one place-setting; 15 pls incl frontis   Cloth
CONTENTS: 1 ht; 2 blank; 3 tp; 4 'Copyright, Canada, 1938, 1941 by the Musson Book Company Ltd. Toronto ... Fourth edition'; 5–6 table of contents; 7 'Preface to the New Edition' signed Jessie Read; 8 blank; 9 'Preface to the First Edition' signed Jessie Read; 10 'Acknowledgment'; 11–455 text; 456–80 index and at bottom p 480, 'The Hunter-Rose Co. Limited Toronto printers-bookbinders'
COPIES: *Private collection
NOTES: *Three Meals a Day* is recommended in O1095.1, *Canadian Cook Book for British Brides.*

O954.6 [5th ed.], 1946
—Three meals a day / by / Jessie Read / Canadian home economist, / Food Editor, "Toronto Telegram" / New and revised edition / Toronto / The Musson Book Company Ltd. / 1946
DESCRIPTION: 21.5 × 14.0 cm   Pp [1–4] 5–480   2 tp illus: woman at a stove and one place-setting; 15 pls incl frontis   Cloth
CONTENTS: 1 ht; 2 blank; 3 tp; 4 'Copyright, Canada, 1938, 1941 by the Musson Book Company Ltd. Toronto ... Fifth edition'; 5–6 table of contents; 7 'Preface to the New Edition' signed Jessie Read; 8 blank; 9 'Preface to the First Edition' signed Jessie Read; 10 'Acknowledgment'; 11–455 text; 456–80 index and at bottom p 480, 'The Hunter-Rose Co. Limited Toronto printers-bookbinders'
COPIES: OOWM (989.6.12)   *Private collection

O954.7 [6th ed.], 1949
—Three meals a day / by / Jessie Read / Canadian home economist, / Food Editor, "Toronto Telegram" / New and revised edition / Toronto / The Musson Book Company Ltd. / 1949
DESCRIPTION: 21.5 × 14.0 cm   Pp [1–4] 5–480   2 tp illus: a woman at a stove and one place-setting; frontis and pls   Cloth
CONTENTS: 1 ht; 2 blank; 3 tp; 4 'Copyright, Canada, 1938, 1941 by the Musson Book Company Ltd. Toronto [Musson symbol] Sixth edition'; 5–6 table of contents; 7 'Preface to the New Edition' signed Jessie Read; 8 blank; 9 'Preface to the First Edition' signed Jessie Read; 10 'Acknowledgment'; 11–455 text; 456–80 in-

dex and at bottom p 480, symbol of Hunter-Rose Co.
Ltd, printers-bookbinders
COPIES: OKQ (TX715 R4 1949t)   OONL (TX715.6 R35
1949)   *OTNY (uncat)

Selected recipes

*For an earlier cookbook from the same church and also
under M.E. Bradley's leadership, see O700.1.*

O955.1 [1938]
Selected / recipes [cover-title]
DESCRIPTION: About 22.5 × 15.0 cm [dimensions from
photocopy]   Pp [1–4] 5–127 [128]   Stapled
CONTENTS: 1 'Preface' signed M.E. Bradley, con. [i.e.,
convenor], W.A. Group, 1938, Simcoe Street United
Church; 2 ads; 3 'Table of Contents,' 'Abbreviations,'
and 'Measurements'; 4 ads; 5–126 recipes credited
with the name of the contributor and ads; 127 'Household Hints' and ad; 128 ad
COPIES: *Private collection
NOTES: The advertisements are for Oshawa businesses.
There is an advertisement on the outside back face of
the binding for the *Oshawa Daily Times,* the likely
printer of the book.

Tested recipes

*Staffa Junior Institute, part of the Women's Institutes,
was founded in 1929 and disbanded in 1945 (Ambrose,
p 238).*

O956.1 1938
[An edition of *Tested Recipes,* by Staffa Junior Insti-
tute, 1938]
COPIES: Private collection

The Thousand Island cook book

O957.1 2nd ed., 1938
[Second edition of *The Thousand Island Cook Book,*
Gananoque, Ontario, 1938]
CITATIONS: Garrett, pp 105, 131
NOTES: Garrett reprints the recipe for Raspberry
Vinegar.

The W.A. cook book

O958.1 1938
[An edition of *The W.A. Cook Book,* by the Women's
Association of the United Church, Spencerville,
Ontario, 1938]
COPIES: Private collection

Westinghouse Electric Roaster recipe book

O959.1 nd [about 1938]
Westinghouse / Electric Roaster / recipe book /
Canadian Westinghouse Company Limited /
Hamilton Ontario / Every house needs
Westinghouse [cover-title]
DESCRIPTION: 21.0 × 13.5 cm   Pp 3–28 [29–30]   Illus
Paper, with image on front of the Electric Roaster;
stapled, and with hole punched at top left corner for
hanging
CONTENTS: 3–4 'A Word of Introduction to the User of
the Westinghouse De Luxe Adjustomatic Roaster'; 5–
8 'General Instructions'; 9–26 recipes, including
'Roaster Meal Combinations' [nine numbered meals
on pp mid 11–14]; 27–8 'General Directions for Canning'; 29 'Index' [i.e., table of contents]; 30–inside
back face of binding '"Kitchen-Proved" Appliances
by Westinghouse'; outside back face 'Form 924 Printed
in Canada'
COPIES: *OONL (TX827 W47 1900z p***)
NOTES: This edition has no introductory comments
by Anna May Cornell. In 'A Toast to the Roaster,'
Chatelaine (April 1938), pp 75, 78, Helen G. Campbell
refers to the appliance as 'this newcomer to the
kitchen.' Electric roasters, therefore, had been introduced to the marketplace by 1938; however, since
Campbell does not discuss a particular make of the
appliance, the article provides only a guide to the
date of publication of *Westinghouse Electric Roaster
Recipe Book.*

O959.2 [rev. ed.], nd [about 1940]
—Yours ... for / better meals / this easier time
saving way / Westinghouse De Luxe /
Adjustomatic Electric / Roaster [cover-title]
DESCRIPTION: 21.5 × 13.5 cm   Pp 1–36   Paper, with
image on front of the roaster; stapled, and with hole
punched at top left corner for hanging
CONTENTS: Inside front face of binding 'Enjoy Electric
Cooking at Its Delicious Best with the Westinghouse

DeLuxe Adjustomatic Roaster' signed Anna May Cornell, home economist, Canadian Westinghouse Co. Ltd; 1 'Cooks Complete Delicious Meals ... All at One Time!'; 2 'How to Use the Westinghouse Roaster'; 3 'General Cooking Hints and the Care of the Roaster'; 4–12 'Meal Combinations' [i.e., seventeen numbered menus with corresponding recipes]; 13–17 'Meats'; 18–19 'Fish'; 20 'Fried Foods'; 21–2 'Vegetables'; 23–34 'Baked Foods'; 35 'Canning'; 36 'Soups, Chowders'; inside back face 'Index' [i.e., table of contents]; outside back face 'Canadian Westinghouse Company Limited // Head office, Hamilton, Ontario Form 924. Revised.'

COPIES: *Private collection

NOTES: Anna May Cornell comments opposite p 1, 'Please don't look upon the Roaster as something to be used only on rare occasions.' 'Roaster Meal Combinations' is explained on p 4: '[The term] refers to the preparation of a whole meal at one time. It means economy of electricity and release of time.' For Cornell's other cookbooks, see O781.1.

This is a heavily revised and retitled edition of O959.1. New 'Meal Combinations' have been added, making a total of seventeen combinations. The numbering of the 'Meal Combinations' does not match O959.1; for example, in the earlier edition, Meal No. 1 of Meat Loaf, Potatoes, and Butterscotch Pudding is Meal No. 10 in *Yours ... for Better Meals*. The 'Fish' section has been expanded by the addition of new recipes.

A Westinghouse advertisement in *Chatelaine* (December 1940), p 51, illustrates the same model of roaster as in *Yours ... for Better Meals*. This edition, therefore, was likely published about 1940.

1938–9

Home and School cook book

For a later cookbook by the association, see O1049.1, Home and School Cook Book.

O960.1 [about 1938–9]
[An edition of *Home and School Cook Book: A Selection of Tested Recipes,* by Home and School Association, Aylmer, Ontario, list on p 3 of officers for 1938–9]
COPIES: Private collection

1939

Berolzheimer, Ruth

O961.1 [copyright 1939]
The / Canadian woman's / cook book / edited and revised by / Ruth Berolzheimer / Director, / Culinary Arts Institute / from the / Delineator Cook Book / edited by / Delineator Institute, / Mildred Maddocks Bentley, Director / Martha Van Rensselaer and Flora Rose / Directors, College of Home Economics / Cornell University / Published for / McLean Publishers Syndicate / 29 Melinda Street / Toronto 2, Ontario
DESCRIPTION: 20.0 × 13.0 cm   Pp [i–ii] iii–vi, 1–815 Many pls col, many illus   Rebound
CONTENTS: i tp; ii 'Copyrighted Dominion of Canada 1939 // Copyrights of previous works in which certain parts of this book appeared // Copyright, MCMXXVIII MCMXXXIV by Butterick Publishing Company // Entered at Stationers' Hall, London, England // Copyright, MCMXXXVIII by Consolidated Book Publishers, Incorporated // Manufactured in the United States of America by the Cuneo Press, Inc.'; iii 'Table of Contents'; iv–vi 'List of Illustrations' and at bottom p vi, 'The illustration on the jacket is by courtesy of Land O'Lakes Creameries // At Your Service' and information about the number of servings in each recipe (six) and how to increase or decrease that number; 1–758 text; 759–815 index
CITATIONS: CCat No. 18, p T18
COPIES: *OTMCL (641.5 C12)
NOTES: The title implies that the cookbook was prepared for Canadian women, but it was an American production aimed at American readers. See 'American editions,' below, for the story of this book's evolution. Martha van Rensselaer (1864–1932), who is cited on the title-page as director of the College of Home Economics at Cornell, was deceased at the time of publication of this edition. The volume is thumb-indexed. CCat records the price: $3.00.

O961.2 [copyright 1939]
—[An edition of *The Canadian Woman's Cook Book,* published for the Stratford Beacon-Herald by Atlantis Book Co. of Canada Ltd, copyright 1938 by Consolidated Book Publishers Inc., Dominion copyright 1939, with image on front of four maple leaves]
COPIES: eBay on-line auction, October 2002

O961.3 [copyright 1941]
—The / Canadian woman's / cook book / edited and revised by / Ruth Berolzheimer / Director, /

Culinary Arts Institute / from the / Delineator Cook Book / edited by / Delineator Institute, / Mildred Maddocks Bentley, Director / Martha van Rensselaer and Flora Rose / Directors, College of Home Economics / Cornell University / Atlantis Book Co. of Canada Ltd. / 111 Richmond St. East / Toronto, Ont.

DESCRIPTION: 20.5 × 13.5 cm   Pp [i–ii] iii–vi [vii–viii], 1–816   Many pls col, many illus   Cloth, with image on front of four maple leaves

CONTENTS: i tp; ii 'The material in this book has been copyrighted in the United States of America in 1938, 1939, 1940 and 1941 by Consolidated Book Publishers, Inc., as The American Woman's Cook Book. Certain parts of this book protected by the following previous copyrights: MCMXXVII [sic] MCMXXXIV by Butterick Publishing Company // Entered at Stationers' Hall, London, England // Printed in U.S.A.'; iii 'Table of Contents'; iv–vi 'List of Illustrations'; vii 'The Color Plates'; viii acknowledgment of those who supplied photographs for the book; 1–758 text; 759–816 index

COPIES: *OH (R641.5971 CAN CESC)

NOTES: The OH copy is inscribed on the title-page, 'Mary M. Douglas.' The front and back endpapers are printed with a colour illustration of petits fours on a silver tray. The volume is thumb-indexed.

O961.4   special ed., nd

—The / St. Catharines Standard / Special edition of the / Canadian woman's / cook book / edited and revised by / Ruth Berolzheimer / Director, Culinary Arts Institute / Entered at Stationers' Hall, London. [sic, period] England / Copyright, MCMXXXVIII / by / Consolidated Book Publishers, Incorporated / Dominion copyright, MCMXXXIX / Published for / the St. Catharines Standard / by / Atlantis Book Co. of Canada Ltd. / 111 Richmond St. E. Toronto

DESCRIPTION: Pp [i–ii] iii–vi [vii–viii], 1–...   With image on front of four maple leaves

CONTENTS: i tp; ii blank; iii 'Table of Contents'; iv–vi 'List of Illustrations'; vii 'The Color Plates'; viii acknowledgment of those who supplied photographs for the book; 1– text; ...

COPIES: *Bookseller's stock

NOTES: The endpapers are printed with a colour illustration of petits fours on a silver tray. The volume is thumb-indexed.

AMERICAN EDITIONS: In *America's Collectible Cookbooks*, pp 90–1, DuSablon explains the evolution of the text of *The American Woman's Cook Book* from a series of pamphlets published by the Butterick Publishing Co. Ltd in the 1890s (for more information about these pamphlets, see DuSablon and Driver 176.1):

The pamphlets [with various titles, such as *Correct Cookery* or *The Perfect Art of Canning and Preserving*] were well received and bound together to be sold in one volume after the turn of the century.

Then, in 1911, the cooking topics were removed and elaborated upon by Helen Judson for a new publication titled *The Butterick Cook Book* (360 pages) ... *The New Butterick Cook-Book* (733 pages) was an enlarged version of the book, revised, and with all recipes retested by Flora Rose, co-head of the School of Home Economics at Cornell University ...

In 1928 the volume was once again revised as the *Delineator Cook Book*, this time by the Delineator Home Institute under the direction of Mildred Maddocks Bentley, edited by Flora Rose and Martha Van Rensselaer, ... with Butterick still the publisher.

As its next incarnation the book was titled *The American Woman's Cook Book*, edited and revised by Ruth Berolzheimer, whose title was director of a nebulous enterprise called the Culinary Arts Institute, and published by Consolidated Book Publishers, Inc., Chicago, Illinois in 1938 ... A unique feature of this edition, and probably the biggest reason this book finally caught the fancy of the public at the time, was the thumb-indexing of chapters, which gave it the subtle authority of a reference work. Indeed, in 1941 and 1947 it was retitled *The Encyclopedic Cook Book*.

Berolzheimer's signature and the Culinary Arts Institute cameo would be connected with hundreds of titles based on these same and similar recipes – and numerous new ones – during the next two decades, with scores of industries – ...

DuSablon's publishing history does not mention the text's publication as *The Canadian Woman's Cook Book*.

The following American editions, all titled *The American Woman's Cook Book*, were found in Canadian collections: Chicago: Consolidated Book Publishers Inc., 1939 (Private collection); Chicago: Consolidated Book Publishers Inc., 1943 (OFERWM); Chicago: Consolidated Book Publishers, 1946 (OWTU); Garden City, NY: Garden City Publishing Co. Inc., 1947 (OTR); Chicago: Culinary Arts Institute, 1947 (Private collection); Chicago: Culinary Arts Institute, 1948 (OTSHH); Chicago: Culinary Arts Institute, 1949 (Private collection); Chicago: Culinary Arts Institute, 1956 (OTSHH); New York: Doubleday and Co., copyright 1972 (Private collection). A copy of the 1949 American edition in an Ontario home has the following label on the title-page: 'Special edition of *The American Woman's Cook Book* // Supplied by your hometown weekly the *Peterboro Review*.'

Brown, Cora Lovisa Brackett (1861–1939), Rose Johnston Brown, née Watson (1883–1952), and Robert (Bob) Carlton Brown (Chicago, Ill., 14 June 1886–7 August 1959, New York City)

See O934.1 for information about the authors.

O962.1 [copyright 1939]
The / vegetable / cook book / from trowel to table / Cora, Rose and Bob Brown / J.B. Lippincott Company / Philadelphia / New York London Toronto
DESCRIPTION: 19.7 × 13.6 cm   Pp [1–6] 7–279 [280] Cloth, with dust-jacket
CONTENTS: Tp verso: 'Copyright, 1939, by Cora, Rose and Robert Carlton Brown // Made in the United States of America'
CITATIONS: Arndt, p 82 (Andrew F. Smith, 'Bob Brown')   Axford, p 408   Cagle/Stafford, No. 116
COPIES: United States: InU
NOTES: Information about this book is from the Cagle/Stafford entry.

Cook book

O963.1 1939
Cook book / Tested recipes / Compiled and arranged by / Group 6 of / the Women's Association of the / King Street United Church / 1939, London, Ont. [cover-title]
DESCRIPTION: 23.0 × 15.0 cm   Pp [1] 2–72   Illus on p 1 of a male chef carrying a pig's head on a platter, a few other illus   Very thin card, with p 1 illus also on front; stapled, and with hole punched at top left corner for hanging
CONTENTS: Inside front face of binding '"I Guessed"' [poem]; 1 illus, book title, and 'Our Greeting'; 2–66 recipes, most credited with the name of the contributor, ads, and spaces for 'New Recipes or Memorandum'; 67 'Helpful Hints for the Home'; 68 'Time Table for Fruits'; 69 'Table of Measurements'; 70 'Index' [i.e., table of contents] and 'Index to Advertisers'; 71–2 space for 'New Recipes or Memorandum'
COPIES: *OL (London Room Box 180)

NOTES: 'Printed by Middlesex Printing Co., 557 Dundas St., London, book & catalog printers' is on the outside back face of the binding. O1070.1, *Cook Book*, by another London church, has the same image on the binding.

Cook book

O964.1 [1st ed.], 1939
United Church Ladies' Aid / Cook book / Kapuskasing, Ontario, Canada – 1939
CITATIONS: CBCat 61, No. 90
COPIES: *Private collection
NOTES: The volume has 98 pp.

O964.2 [2nd ed., 1943]
—United Church Ladies' Aid / Cook book / Kapuskasing / Ontario Canada [cover-title]
DESCRIPTION: 22.5 × 15.0 cm   Pp [i–vi], 1–93   Fp illus on p i of Kapuskasing United Church   Thin card; Cirlox-bound
CONTENTS: i fp illus; ii blank; iii 'Preface' signed 'The United Church Ladies Aid – 1943'; iv blank; v 'Table of Contents'; vi blank; 1–93 recipes credited with the name of the contributor
COPIES: *Private collection
NOTES: The 'Preface' states: 'We present this second edition of our Cook Book ... In this edition all advertising has been omitted. In all other respects the contents are exactly the same as in the 1939 edition. The decision to omit the advertising and the increased cost of print and paper has made it necessary to mimeograph recipes instead of having them printed ... To Mr. Dalton J. Caswell whose untiring efforts made the first publication possible ... we extend our thanks. The sketch of the church which appears on the first page was drawn by Mr. John Straiton.'

OTHER EDITIONS: 3rd ed., 1950, compiled by United Church Women's Association, likely printed by Lawson and Farrow, whose advertisement appears at the foot of most pages (Private collection).

Cook book of favorite tested recipes

O965.1 1939
The Pembroke Standard-Observer / 1939 edition Thursday, May 11th, 1939 / Cook book / of favorite tested recipes / Recipes contributed by women readers of the Pembroke Standard-Observer [cover-title]

DESCRIPTION: 28.0 × 23.0 cm   Pp [1–2] 3–60   Paper, with circular image on front of an aproned woman removing roast meat from oven; stapled
CONTENTS: 1 cover-title; 2 'An Appreciation and Explanation' and 'Table of Contents' [i.e., alphabetical list of section headings]; 3–59 text and ads; 60 ad
COPIES: *Private collection
NOTES: Page 2 acknowledges recipe contributions from readers and from specific Women's Institute branches.

Cooking made easy with a Wear-Ever Pressure Cooker

For the titles of other cookbooks by Aluminum Goods Ltd, see O807.1.

O966.1   nd [about 1939]
Cooking made / easy / with a / Wear-Ever / Pressure Cooker [cover-title]
DESCRIPTION: 17.5 × 13.5 cm   Pp [i–ii], 1–32   Illus   Paper, with image on front of a pressure cooker; stapled
CONTENTS: Inside front face of binding table of contents; i 'Our Warranty' by Aluminum Goods Ltd, 158 Sterling Road, Toronto 3, Ontario; ii blank except for 'T-390' at bottom left corner; 1 'These Six Advantages Are Yours with the Wear-Ever Pressure Cooker'; 2–5 'How Easy It Is to Use' [eight numbered and illustrated steps]; 6 'Important // Be Sure to Read This Page before Using ...'; 7 'General Instructions'; 8–32 recipes
COPIES: *Private collection

O966.2   nd [about 1939]
—Cooking made / easy / with a / Wear-Ever / Pressure Cooker [cover-title]
DESCRIPTION: 17.5 × 13.5 cm   Pp 1–32   Illus   Paper, with image on front of a pressure cooker; stapled
CONTENTS: Inside front face of binding table of contents; 1 'These Six Advantages Are Yours with the Wear-Ever Pressure Cooker'; 2–5 'How Easy It Is to Use' [eight numbered and illustrated steps]; 6 'Important // Be Sure to Read This Page before Using ...'; 7 'General Instructions'; 8–32 recipes
COPIES: *Private collection
NOTES: In this edition 'Our Warranty' is printed on the inside back face of the binding. 'T-390 Printed in Canada' is on the outside back face. The order of publication of O966.1 and O966.2 is unknown.

The Elmvale community cook book

O967.1   1939
The / Elmvale community / cook book / 1939 / Published by / the Elmvale Lance Press
DESCRIPTION: 22.0 × 14.5 cm   Pp [1–2] 3–52   Paper; stapled
CONTENTS: 1 tp; 2 'Index' [i.e., table of contents]; 3–52 recipes credited with the name of the contributor
COPIES: *OGU (TX 715.6 G7347)
NOTES: No organization is identified as the compiler of the book. The OGU copy is inscribed by the original owner, on the binding, in ink, 'Mrs Edgar Campbell' [i.e., Hazel Maud Shaw]. Hazel (born 1896) married Edgar Campbell in 1918 and moved with him to a farm on the third concession in Tiny Township, where they lived until 1965.

Favorite recipes

O968.1   1939
[An edition of *Favorite Recipes*, by the Women's Association of Knox United Church, Agincourt, Ontario, 1939]
COPIES: Private collection

Favorite recipes

O969.1   1939
UCA / Favorite recipes / submitted by / the Women's Association of / Teeswater United Church / 1939 [cover-title]
DESCRIPTION: Stapled
COPIES: *Private collection

The Frances Willard memorial cook book

See also O938.1, Frances Willard Centenary Cook Book, by the Unions of Leeds and Frontenac counties.

O970.1   [1939]
The / Frances Willard / memorial / cook book / Compiled and arranged / by the / Woman's Christian / Temperance Union / of / Middlesex County / 1939 [cover-title]
COPIES: OL (uncat)   *Private collection
NOTES: There is a portrait of Frances E. Willard on p 3, and a biography entitled 'Frances E. Willard: Story of the Famous Founder of the W.C.T.U.' by Mrs M. Hawkin on pp 3, 5–7, and 12. 'Our Greeting' and a list of 'Officers' is on p 9 (president, Mrs A. Tutt,

London; secretary, Mrs D. Cottam, London; treasurer, Mrs M. Hawkin, London). The recipes are credited with the name of the contributor. The text includes: 'Household Hints,' p 65; 'Cooking Time Table,' p 66; 'Cookery Hints,' pp 67–8; 'Foods to Be Avoided in the Cure of Alcoholics,' p 69; 'Hints on Serving,' p 70; 'Practical Hints for the Housekeeper,' p 71; and 'Index,' p 72. The book was printed by the McGuire Printing Co., 318 Rectory Street, London.

Home-proved baking recipes
[Blossom of Canada Flour]

See O821.1, Home-Proved Baking Recipes, which may or may not be a related text. See also another collection of recipes published by Lakeside Milling Co., but for Campbells Flour: O1006.1, Home Tested Recipes.

O971.1 [copyright 1939]
Blossom / of / Canada / Home-proved / baking recipes / The Lakeside Milling Co. Limited [cover-title]
DESCRIPTION: 20.5 × 13.5 cm   Pp [1] 2–68   Paper, with image on front of a large head of wheat; metal-spiral bound
CONTENTS: 1 'Home-Proved Baking Recipes by and for Canadian Women' signed Lakeside Milling Co. Ltd, Princess Street, Toronto, and 'Copyright, 1939, by Lakeside Milling Co., Limited Printed in Canada'; 2 '[Help]ful Information [for the Home-Baker]'; 3–66 recipes; 67–8 index and at bottom p 68, '16–1–39–5M'
COPIES: OONL (TX765 L35 1939)   *Private collection
NOTES: This cookbook promotes the use of Lakeside Milling Co.'s Blossom of Canada Flour. On p 1, the publisher offers 'thanks to all women who contributed home-used recipes and to the food experts who home-tested these, and compiled their selections in the form herein presented.' The OONL copy is rebound in cloth.

O971.2 [copyright 1941]
—Ye olde baker / Blossom / of / Canada / Quality Flour / by Campbells / Selected hard wheat flour / Home tested recipes / for breads, rolls, pastry, cakes, cookies, / frostings, icings, fillings and puddings [cover-title]
DESCRIPTION: 20.5 × 13.5 cm   Pp 1–84   Paper, with image on front of a baker's head and heads of wheat; metal-spiral bound
CONTENTS: Inside front face of binding 'Copyright 1941 by Lakeside Milling Co., Limited Printed in Canada'; 1 'Home Tried and Proved Baking Recipes by and for Canadian Women' signed Lakeside Mill-

ing Co. Ltd, Princess Street, Toronto; 2 'Helpful Information for the Home-Baker'; 3–78 recipe chapters, each chapter followed by a blank page for manuscript recipes; 79–80 'Well-Stocked Kitchen'; 81 'Reasons Why Blossom of Canada Flour Gives Such Wonderful Results' and a book-order coupon; 82 blank for 'Your Own Special Recipes'; 83–4 index and at bottom p 84, '"Spirax" Patent Canada 1932 No. 326518'
COPIES: *Private collection

O971.3 [copyright 1945]
—Ye olde baker / Blossom / of / Canada / Quality Flour / by Campbells / Selected hard wheat flour / Home tested recipes / for breads, rolls, pastry, cakes, cookies, / frostings, icings, fillings and puddings [cover-title]
DESCRIPTION: 20.0 × 13.5 cm   Pp [i–ii], 1–91   Illus   Thin card; spiral bound
CONTENTS: Inside front face of binding 'Copyright 1945 by Lakeside Milling Co., Limited Printed in Canada'; i–ii 'Statement by Ruth Hudson' on a pink leaf; 1 'Home Tried and Proved Baking Recipes by and for Canadian Women' signed Lakeside Milling Co. Ltd, Princess Street, Toronto; 2–87 text; 88 'Blossom of Canada Cook Book Coupon'; 89–91 'Index' [i.e., table of contents] and at bottom p 91, '5M – July 1945'
CITATIONS: Ferguson/Fraser, p 234, illus col on p 103 of closed volume
COPIES: *Company collection (Maple Leaf Mills Consumer Products Co.), in 1991; location now unknown
NOTES: Ruth Hudson was the dietitian at the Lakeside Home-Baking Service Bureau, established 'some time ago' by Mr Campbell, president of Lakeside Milling Co. Hudson comments on p i that 'this book was originally printed before shortages of sugar, nuts, chocolate, flavourings, shortening, eggs, butter and many other items were apparent'; she includes 'some general wartime substitute hints.' The text on p 1 refers to the book as *The Blossom of Canada Home-Proved Recipe Book*.

Kitchen chatter

St Clair Avenue United Church later amalgamated with St Matthew's United Church; the combined congregation remains at St Clair's original location, 729 St Clair Avenue West.

O972.1 1939
Kitchen / chatter / 1939 / St. Clair Avenue United Church / Toronto Canada [cover-title]

DESCRIPTION: 23.0 × 15.5 cm   Pp [1] 2–64   Illus on p 1 of the church   Paper; stapled
CONTENTS: 1 untitled four-line verse and illus of the church; 2 'The ladies of Circle 8 of the W.A. of the St. Clair United Church wish to thank all those who contributed to the success of our cook book.,' list of 'Officers' and 'Phoning Captains,' and 'Index' [i.e., table of contents]; 3–60 text, mostly recipes credited with the name of the contributor, and at bottom p 60, ads; 61–4 blank for 'Additional Recipes'
COPIES: *Private collection
NOTES: 'Large Amounts for Home Catering' is on p 55; '30 Household Hints' is on pp 58–60.

CBCat 61, No. 90 lists, in a group of 'Canadian Charity Cookbooks,' 'St Clair Ave Church, Toronto, nd, c1920's, 64 pp.' Although described as undated, the number of pages matches. The citation may or may not refer to the edition described here.

The pantry shelf

O973.1   [1939]
The / pantry shelf / A / collection of / tested recipes / selected and arranged for publication / by the members of / Admiral Vansittart Chapter / Imperial Order Daughters of the Empire / Woodstock Ontario
DESCRIPTION: 23.0 × 15.0 cm   Pp [1] 2–64   Thin card, with IODE symbol on front; stapled
CONTENTS: 1 tp; 2 ads; 3 'Officers Roster, 1939 // Admiral Vansittart Chapter I.O.D.E.'; 4–5 history of the chapter, which received its charter on 26 October 1903; 6–61 recipes credited with the name of the contributor and ads; 62 'To Serve 100 People'; 63 ads and 'Table Decorations'; 64 ad and 'Index' [i.e., table of contents]
COPIES: *Private collection

The royal visit souvenir cook book

O974.1   1939
The royal visit / souvenir / cook book / 1939 / Aughrim Women's Guild / Aughrim / Ontario [cover-title]
DESCRIPTION: 25.0 × 16.5 cm   Pp 1–76   A few illus   Paper, with image on front of a crown; stapled
CONTENTS: 1–76 recipes credited with the name of the contributor, space for 'Memoranda,' and ads
COPIES: *Private collection
NOTES: *The Royal Visit Souvenir Cook Book* marked the visit to Canada in 1939 of King George VI and Queen Elizabeth. There is a 'Children's Department' by Mrs L.V. Pocock on pp 70–2, which presents recipes that would appeal to a child's palate. On p 69 a 'thank you' from the Aughrim Women's Guild includes the time of the guild's meetings, a notice that supplies of aprons, fancy work, and quilts are for sale at all times, and the names of the guild's four officers. Two mock recipes, 'How to Preserve a Wife' and 'How to Preserve a Husband,' are on p 76; whereas the version offering advice on how to keep one's husband is commonly found in cookbooks, 'How to Preserve a Wife' is an unusual variation. Below the mock recipes is 'Printed by Alvinston Free Press, Alvinston, Ont.'

Scott, Anna Lee [pseudonym]

For information about Anna Lee Scott and her cookbooks, see O526.1.

O975.1   nd [about 1939]
51 ways / to a man's heart / by Anna Lee Scott [cover-title]
DESCRIPTION: 24.0 × 16.5 cm   Pp [1] 2–16   Paper, with image on front of the head-and-shoulders of a man who is winking and holding up a fork in his right hand; stapled
CONTENTS: 1 dedication 'to wives whose husbands appreciate good food, and to all women who like to please their men'; 2–16 fifty-one numbered recipes
CITATIONS: Ferguson/Fraser, p 234, illus col on p 103 of closed volume
COPIES: BVAU   NBDKH   OGU (CCC TX715.6 S363)   OONL (TX715.6 S353 1900z, 2 copies)   QKB (87-74)   SELH   *Private collection
NOTES: The cookbook promotes the use of Maple Leaf Cream of the West Flour, milled by Maple Leaf Milling Co. Ltd, whose head office was in Toronto. On the outside back face of the binding, there is a 1930s-style portrait of Anna Lee Scott above her letter to 'Dear friend,' in which she writes: 'It is many years since I began as a dietitian lecturer and adviser on household science, and each year I have received thousands of letters through my magazine and radio work ... Each [recipe] was prepared with Maple Leaf "Cream of the West" Flour.'

Another private collector's copy is inscribed on the binding, 'Doris Sokolotosky Sept. 17th, 1939.' The NBDKH copy is inscribed on the title-page, 'Eileen Palmer 1940,' and it is stamped on the binding, 'Herbert G. Palmer general merchant Dorchester, N.B.,' indicating that the cookbook was probably given away at the local store.

ONTARIO 1939–42 / 829

O975.2 nd

—Les mets qui lui / plairont / par / Anna Lee Scott [cover-title]

DESCRIPTION: With image on front of the head-and-shoulders of a man who is winking and holding up a fork in his right hand

COPIES: *Private collection

NOTES: Another individual (now deceased) reported in her possession a French-language edition titled *51 façons d'atteindre le coeur d'un homme*, which may or may not correspond to O975.2.

A selection of tested recipes

O976.1 [1939]

A selection of / tested / recipes / Compiled by / St. George's / Parochial Guild / Trenton, Ontario / [folio:] (2)

DESCRIPTION: About 22.5 × 14.5 cm [dimensions from photocopy] Pp [1] 2–56 Illus on p 1 of the church Stapled

CONTENTS: 1 'St. George's Church // Trenton, Ontario 1939' and illus of the church; 2 tp; 3 ad and 'Preface'; 4 ads and 'Table of Contents'; ...

COPIES: *Private collection

NOTES: The cover-title is 'The Cook's Delight.' Unusually, the title-page is on a verso page. A 'Short History of St. George's Church' is on p 29. 'A Weekly Menu for Children' and 'First Aid to the Injured' end the text. There is an advertisement on the inside back face of the binding for the *Quinte Sun*, which did '"Quality" job printing' – the likely printer of the cookbook. St George's Church is Anglican.

Tested recipes

O977.1 1939

Tested recipes / Published by / the Women's Guild / of / All Saints Church – Ottawa / 1939 / [quotation from Ruskin]

DESCRIPTION: 22.5 × 15.0 cm Pp [1–5] 6–133 [134–6] Card; stapled

CONTENTS: 1 tp; 2 'Prefatory Note'; 3 'Contents'; 4 ads; 5–133 text, mostly recipes credited with the name of the contributor; 134–6 'Index'

COPIES: *OOC (641.5 A416) OWTU

NOTES: Page 5 is headed 'Recipes Used on the Royal Train' and signed Thomas G. Gear, chef, Royal Train. The three recipes presented (Chicken Indian Style, Cheese Pudding, and Corn Waffles) may have been served during the visit to Canada of King George VI

and Queen Elizabeth in 1939. The OOC copy is inscribed on the binding, in ink, 'M.J [*sic*, no period] Hennessy, Christmas 1939.'

Yorke, Elizabeth

See also O1146.1, Canada's Famous Foods, by Yorke.

O978.1 nd [about 1939]

Snacks / Answers your menu problems. / 10¢ / By / Elizabeth Yorke / The Hostess Shop / The T. Eaton Co Limited / Toronto Canada [cover-title]

DESCRIPTION: With image on front of snacks on a table, with a woman partly visible behind the table

COPIES: *Private collection

NOTES: The owner reports that her copy is inscribed with the date 18 August 1939 and has 37 pp.

O978.2 rev. ed., nd

—Eaton's / Snacks / Revised edition / By / Elizabeth Yorke / The Hostess Shop / [1?]5¢ / The T. Eaton Co Limited [cover-title]

DESCRIPTION: With stylized image on front of various ingredients

COPIES: *Private collection

1939–42

Taylor, Demetria M. (1903–)

Taylor, an American, wrote: The Nutrition Handbook, *Garden City, NY: Doubleday, Doran and Co. Inc., 1942;* Complete Book of Home Canning, *New York: Greenberg, [1943];* Ration Cook Book, *New York, NY: Reklam Press, c1943;* Square Meals on Short Rations, *New York: Home Guide Publications, c1943;* The New Century Cook Book, *based on* Good Food and How to Cook It, *by Phyllis Krafft Newill, New York: Appleton-Century-Crofts, [1949];* Family-Favorite Meat Cook Book, *New York: Bartholomew House, [1958];* Rawleigh's Picture Treasury of Good Cooking, *[Long Island City, NY: Published by Tested Recipe Institute] for W.T. Rawleigh Co., Freeport, Ill., [1959];* Roundup of Beef Cookery, *New York: Sterling Pub. Co., [1960];* The Cook's Blessings, *New York: Random House, [1965];* Apple Kitchen Cook Book, *New York: Popular Library, [1971]. She co-authored, with Jean I. Simpson,* The Frozen Food Cook Book, *New York: Simon and Schuster, [1948]. She co-authored, with Lillian C. Ziegfeld,* A Picture Treasurey of Good Cooking, *[Long Island City, NY: Tested Recipe Institute,*

1953]. She tested the recipes for The Sugar-Free Cookbook, *by William Irving Kaufman, Garden City, NY: Doubleday, [1964]. (All the above are at DLC in the United States.)*

O979.1   [about 1939–42]
[An edition of *The Day-by-Day Cook Book*, Toronto: McClelland and Stewart]
CITATIONS: Brodie 5 Dec 1942
NOTES: The Canadian edition was published some time after the first American edition (1939) and before Jean Brodie's December 1942 review. It probably has the same number of pages (367) as the American edition. Brodie describes the text as covering 'the entire year – day-by-day, with a menu for every meal and three or four recipes for each day.' She names two authors, Demetria Taylor and Gertrude Lynne, 'two well-known home economists'; the latter is not cited in the DLC record for the book.

AMERICAN EDITIONS: *The Day by Day Cook Book*, New York and London: Harper and Brothers, 1939 (United States: DLC); Garden City, NY: Halcyon House, [1950] (United States: DLC).

1939–45

Choice recipes

Allenby School is a public elementary school on St Clements Avenue in Toronto.

O980.1   nd [about 1939–45]
Choice / recipes / collected and arranged by the / pupils of Room 24 / Allenby School / [over the column of page numbers:] Page / Breads, Muffins, etc. 3, 4, 42 / Cakes 6–9, 35, 36 / Candy 11, 12 / Cookies, etc. 14–19, 39 / Desserts 21–28, 40, 41 / Icings 37, 38 / Miscellaneous 36, 43 / Supper Dishes 30–33 / Time Table for Vegetables 44
DESCRIPTION: 17.5 × 21.5 cm   Pp [1–2] 3–44 [45]   Paper, with symbol on front of letter V for victory and a torch; stapled
CONTENTS: 1 tp and table of contents; 2 '"Who Can Live without Dining?"' [from *Lucile,* Part I, Canto ii], by Owen Meredith [pseudonym of Edward Robert Bulwer-Lytton]; 3–43 recipes; 44 'Time Table for Boiling Vegetables'; 45 untitled six-line verse by Cowper
COPIES: *Private collection
NOTES: The cover-title is 'On the Kitchen Front.' The text is mimeographed on the rectos of differently coloured leaves; the versos are blank and not included in the pagination.

Circle (1) recipes

Centenary United Church is at 24 Main Street West.

O981.1   nd [about 1939–45]
Circle (1) recipes / Tested recipes household hints / general information / Arranged for publication / by / the ladies of Circle (1) / of / Centenary United Church / Main St. West / Hamilton – Ontario
DESCRIPTION: Pp [1] 2–76   Stapled
CONTENTS: 1 tp; 2 'Compliments of Friends' [i.e., the page was paid for by supporters of the church] and 'Printed in Canada on Canadian paper'; 3 'Preface' signed members of Circle 1; ...
COPIES: *Private collection
NOTES: The recipes are credited with the name of the contributor. There is an advertisement on p 14 for Canadian Fanner Ltd that confirms a publication date during the Second World War: 'Our materials are serving on the War Front // Our men 100% War Loan subscribers.'

East York schools win-the-war cook book

O982.1   nd [about 1939–45]
East York schools / win-the-war / cook book / [symbol for 'The Board of Education // Township of East York // 1937']
DESCRIPTION: 21.0 × 15.0 cm   Pp [1–5] 6–104   Tp illus of a Union Jack, Red Ensign, crown, and beaver; fp illus on p 2 of King George VI, Queen Elizabeth, and their daughters Elizabeth and Margaret Rose; centre spread col on pp 52–3 of beef cuts   Paper, with image on front of the Union Jack and Red Ensign; stapled
CONTENTS: 1 tp; 2 fp illus of royal family; 3 foreword signed Walter Stewart, chairman, East York Schools Win-the-War Fund Committee; 4 'Committees' [list of executive members of East York Schools Win-the-War Fund Committee, Home and School Associations, and Cook Book Committee]; 5 table of contents and acknowledgments; 6 'Township of East York Telephone Listings'; 7–97 text; 98–103 blank for 'Additional Recipes'; 104 'Donations' [list of donors]
COPIES: OGU (CCC TX715.6 E28)   QMM (RBD ckbk 1523)   *Private collection
NOTES: The foreword states: 'The purchase and sale of this cook book is part of a campaign being carried out by the boys and girls of our East York schools to achieve a new financial objective, which will permit the purchase of a Mobile Canteen. This equipment will be given to the Canadian Legion for use over-

seas ...' Recipes for War-Time Spice Cake and War Cake are on p 29. East York is now part of Toronto.

Favoured foods

The Scandinavian Canadian Club of Toronto was founded in the 1930s. Records of the club, 1937–61, are at OOA (MG28 V77).

O983.1 nd [about 1939–45]
Favoured / foods / compiled by / the Fireside Group / of / the Scandinavian Canadian Club / Toronto / Proceeds from the sale of this book to / be used for war and welfare work of / the Fireside Group. / Copyright applied for
DESCRIPTION: 17.5 × 12.5 cm Pp [i–ii], 1–169 Card, with image on front of a Viking ship with the initials S.C.C. on its sail; bound by two metal rings through punched holes
CONTENTS: i tp; ii blank; 1 'Introduction' signed the Committee; 2 untitled text about Scandinavian food (i.e., of Denmark, Finland, Norway, and Sweden); 3–147 395 numbered recipes; 148–50 'Measurements,' 'Approximate Weight of Some Foods,' and 'Amounts for 100 Servings' numbered 396, 397, and 398; 151–6 'Household Hints' numbered 399; 157–69 'Index' keyed by recipe number and, at bottom p 169, lines from 'Kalevala,' the Finnish national epic poem
COPIES: *OGU (CCC TX715.6 S3442)
NOTES: This is the only cookbook about Scandinavian cooking in this bibliography. The text on p 2 comments on Scandinavian cooking generally, and on Danish, Norwegian, and Swedish cooking specifically (but not on Finnish). A review of the club's minutes and financial records at OOA may produce a reference to the cookbook and pinpoint the date of publication.

Favourite recipes

O984.1 nd
Canadian Red Cross / Milton Branch / Favourite recipes / [poem:] I hope that a great many copies of me / Will be sold to the people. Because / Don't you see – / My reason for living at all is two-fold, / And that's why I'm anxious that I / may be sold. / Though I say it myself, I'm a very / nice book! / Ostensible object – to teach you to / cook. / But there's much better reason, much / higher by far – / All proceeds from my sale go to help / win the war. / I.R. McK. [cover-title]

DESCRIPTION: 23.0 × 15.0 cm Pp [1–3] 4–56 Very thin card, with image on front of a red cross, at top, and a woman holding a covered roasting pan, below; stapled
CONTENTS: 1 'Preface' signed Mrs W.I. Dick, convener, Mrs Gordon MacKenzie, Mrs Carl Martin, Miss Charlotte Campbell, and Miss Laura Chisholm; 2 ads; 3–56 recipes credited with the name of the contributor and ads
COPIES: *Private collection
NOTES: The advertisement on the outside back face of the binding for P.L. Robertson Mfg Co. Ltd refers to 'thirty-three years of sustained effort.' Since this famous screw-making company was founded in 1907, this Second World War cookbook was likely published about 1940 [1907 + 33 years]. The private collector's copy is inscribed on the binding, 'Mrs W.N. Brownridge // Georgetown Ont.'

Favourite recipes

See also the Lady Grey Chapter's second and third books of Favourite Recipes, *O1136.1 and O1217.1.*

O985.1 nd [about 1939–45]
[First book of *Favourite Recipes,* Lady Grey Chapter, IODE, Fort William, Ontario, nd, cover-title, stapled]
COPIES: Bookseller's stock
NOTES: According to the foreword, net proceeds from the sale of the book were to go 'solely for our war effort.' The foreword also comments: 'You will note that various recipes stress Canadian foods, such as cheese, apples, fish, bacon, honey, maple syrup and sugar.' The 'Index' [i.e., table of contents], which is on the last page of the volume, lists recipes on pp 4–87. There are blank pages for 'Memo' between p 87 and the 'Index.' The IODE symbol is on the binding.

June Frost's recipe book

O986.1 nd [about 1939–45]
[At left:] Frozen foods are better foods / It's patriotic to save food / [At right:] June Frost's / recipe book / With our compliments / Barrie Frosted Foods / Registered / Individual lockers / 29 Collier Street, / Dial 3750 Barrie, Ontario [cover-title]
DESCRIPTION: 12.5 × 21.0 cm Pp 1–32 Illus headpieces Paper, with still-life on front, in a frosted circular frame, of a whole fowl, leg of ham, cut of beef, two peaches, two strawberries, ear of corn, bundle of asparagus, and bunch of cherries; stapled

CONTENTS: 1–2 introductory text headed 'June Frost's Frozen Food Recipe Book'; 3–12 'How to Use Locker Meats'; 13–17 'Preparing Fish for the Table'; 18–19 'Preparing Frozen Fowl'; 20–3 'Preparing Vegetables for the Locker'; 24–6 'Preparing Fruits for the Locker'; 27–32 'Delicious Desserts with Frozen Foods'; inside back face of binding 'Index' [i.e., table of contents]

COPIES: *Private collection

NOTES: Locker plants (rented spaces for freezing foods) were introduced to Canadian cities and towns in the 1930s as a way for families to freeze large amounts of food, usually meat. The introductory text refers to the rise of locker plants: Ten years before the publication of this cookbook there were 'no locker plants'; five years before, 'only a few hundred'; at the time of publication of this book, there were 'more than 4,500' in the United States, and in Ontario, '240 locker depots, most of them located in the western part of the province.' The cookbook was published during the Second World War, for the introductory text states: 'Now, in wartime, the locker plant is as important to the national economy as to that of the individual. By processing locally grown foods and making them available for later use in the community in which they are produced, the locker plant saves much transportation ...' The introductory text ends with the exhortation, 'Food for freedom!' As Canadian families began to buy large chest freezers from about the 1960s, locker plants lost business and many closed.

A copy at OGU (CCC) has a variation in the cover-title: Instead of the Barrie Frosted Foods information, it has 'Welland Provision Co. / 66 Hellems Avenue / Dial 5657 Welland, Ontario.'

Kitchen kraft

O987.1   nd [about 1939–45]

Kitchen kraft / Tested recipes and / cooking aids / A Beautiful Recipe / [fifteen-line prayer beginning, 'A beautiful turning to God in prayer,' and signed:] – Mrs. J.C. Robbins / Collected and arranged by / the members of / the Phyllis Fletcher Guild / McNab Street Presbyterian Church / Hamilton Ontario

DESCRIPTION: 22.5 × 15.0 cm   Pp [1] 2–100   Thin card, with small image on front of a five-pointed star; stapled

CONTENTS: 1 tp; 2 'Printed in Canada' and ad; 3 'Preface' signed members of the Phyllis Fletcher Guild; 4–99 text, including recipes credited with the name of the contributor, blank spaces for 'My Own Recipes' or 'New Recipes,' and ads; 100 'Index' [i.e., table of contents] and ads

COPIES: *OH (R641.5 KIT CESH)

NOTES: The 'Preface' refers to the 'marked change in cooking habits' during wartime and describes some of the new ways: 'The lunch box has definitely entered our lives, ... The use of substitutes for many of the old stand-bys of cookery is required. The day worker wants a lunch in mid-morning and something at noon that will carry him through to the hot night meal. The night worker wants something hot in the morning and a good lunch for midnight. Our times have changed and our material and people are on a war time footing.' The text includes sections for 'To Serve 100 People,' 'Cottage Cheese Dishes,' 'How to Use Honey,' 'Lunch Box Hints,' 'Canning,' and 'Table Decorations.' The entire text is printed in blue. The typeface of the title 'Kitchen Kraft' on p 1 is the same as that used for 'Kitchen Kraft' on p 1 of O1086.1.

The pantry shelf

O988.1   nd [about 1939–45]

The / pantry shelf / A collection / of / tested recipes / Selected and arranged for publication by / Group 8 of the Women's Aid / Victoria Presbyterian Church / Toronto – Ontario

DESCRIPTION: 23.0 × 15.0 cm   Pp [1–2] 3–52   Thin card; stapled

CONTENTS: 1 tp; 2 blank; 3 'Preface' signed Mrs J.A. Wenger and Mrs W.J. Scott, captains, and Mrs R.S. Hutcheon, convenor; 4–49 recipes and ads; 50 'To Serve Fifty People'; 51 ad and 'Table Decorations'; 52 ads and 'Index'

COPIES: *Bookseller's stock

NOTES: The cover-title is 'The Mixing Bowl.' An advertisement on p 14 for Purity Bread Ltd indicates a publication date during the Second World War: 'Ask about our lectures and bakery tours to assist your war funds.'

Recipes

O989.1   nd [about 1939–45]

Recipes / JRR [cover-title]

DESCRIPTION: 16.0 × 21.5 cm   Pp [i–x], 1–46   Paper; stapled

CONTENTS: i 'Oven Temperatures,' 'Table of Approximate Equivalents,' and 'Household Hints' numbered 1–3; ii blank; iii continuation of 'Household Hints' numbered 4–7 and 'Cooking Hints'; iv blank; v continuation of 'Cooking Hints'; vi blank; vii continuation of 'Cooking Hints'; viii blank; ix continuation of 'Cooking Hints'; x blank; 1–46 recipes credited with the name of the contributor

COPIES: *Private collection

NOTES: The leaves are mimeographed on the rectos only; the blank versos are not included in the arabic pagination. 'JRR' stands for John Ross Robertson Public School in Toronto. There are recipes for War Fruit Cake, War Cake, and War Icing, and some recipes reflect wartime restrictions, e.g., Meat Saving Recipe and Meat Stretcher Dish. Some 'Cooking Hints' also point to publication during the Second World War, e.g., 'Stretching Butter' and 'Whipping Cream,' which gives five methods, one using gelatine, another called Mock Whipped Cream.

Selected recipes

O990.1   nd [about 1939–45]
Selected / recipes / [YWCA symbol] / Compiled by / Y.W.C.A. Swimming Club / Toronto, Canada / Printed in Canada
DESCRIPTION: 22.5 × 15.0 cm   Pp [1–2] 3–60   Paper; stapled
CONTENTS: 1 tp; 2 ads; 3 ads and table of contents; 4 ads and 'Table of Measurements'; 5–59 recipes credited with the name of the contributor, 'Servings for Fifty Persons,' and ads; 60 blank for 'Memorandum'
COPIES: *Private collection
NOTES: There is an advertisement opposite p 1 for the Young Women's Christian Association, 21 McGill Street, Toronto, and its gym and swimming classes and Camp Tapawingo, on Georgian Bay near Parry Sound, Ontario. An advertisement on p 4 for Echo Naptha Soap, which exhorts the reader to 'Help Canada's war effort,' confirms a publication date during the Second World War. The text is arranged in the following sections: 'Table of Measurements,' 'Soups,' 'Meats, Fish and Supper Dishes,' 'Salads and Salad Dressings,' 'Quick Breads,' 'Pies and Tarts,' 'Puddings and Desserts,' 'Cakes and Icings,' 'Small Cakes and Cookies,' 'Pickles and Preserves,' 'Beverages,' 'Candy,' and 'Miscellaneous.'

Victory cook book

See also O861.1 from the same church.

O991.1   nd [about 1939–45]
Victory / cook book / Tested and proven / recipes / [two-verse poem beginning, '"I guessed the pepper; ...'] / – From an Irish recipe book / Published by / the Moore Park Group / of / the Women's Association / Calvin Presbyterian Church / Toronto Ontario

DESCRIPTION: With image on front of the letter V and Morse code symbol for V
COPIES: *Private collection

Victory cook book

O992.1   nd [about 1939–45]
Victory / cook book / Tested recipes and cooking aids / Complied [*sic*] / by / the members / of / the Ladies Aid / of / Knox Presbyterian Church / Woodstock, Ontario
DESCRIPTION: 23.0 × 15.0 cm   Pp [1] 2–80   Thin card, with image on front of a male servant carrying a tray; stapled
CONTENTS: 1 tp; 2 'Roster of the Executive of Knox Presbyterian Church Ladies' Aid'; 3 'Preface' signed ladies of the Women's Association, Knox Presbyterian Church, Woodstock, Ontario; 4–79 text, mostly recipes credited with the name of the contributor, blank space for 'My Own Recipes,' and ads; 80 'Index' [i.e., table of contents] and ads
COPIES: *ONDA (89.0005)
CONTENTS: The 'Preface' comments: '... we had constantly in mind the desirability of including a great many "made dishes" for the hurried mid-day lunch or the summer night supper. We have also tried to include a number of recipes designed for use with the electric range, the electric ice box, and a number of others which are best prepared with strictly Canadian products.' On pp 70–1 there is a section headed 'How to Use Honey,' which explains its use as a substitute for sugar or molasses. An advertisement on p 56 for H.A. Berlette and Son, appliances, refers to 'our 29th year at 528 Dundas St.' Identifying the business's first year at this address would confirm the cookbook's year of publication.

Victory cook book

O993.1   nd [about 1939–45]
–... V ...– / Victory / cook / boo[same 'k' as in 'cook'] / St. Paul's United Church / Sarnia – Ontario [cover-title]
DESCRIPTION: About 22.5 × 15.0 cm [dimensions from photocopy]   With small image on front of a Union Jack
COPIES: *OWYL
NOTES: In the cover-title, the words 'Cook Book' are arranged in a V-shape and share the letter k at the bottom of the V. The word 'Victory' is positioned horizontally, above the V-shape. The Union Jack sits within the triangular space created by the three words.

1940

Book of tested recipes

O994.1 [April 1940]
Thamesford / Westminster United / W.A. / Book of / tested recipes [cover-title]
DESCRIPTION: 22.5 × 15.5 cm   Pp [1] 2–40   Paper, with photograph on front of the church; stapled
CONTENTS: 1 'Westminster United Church // Thamesford, Ontario April 29th, 1940' signed R. Watson Langdon [commendation of the work of the church's Women's Association] and 'Women's Association Executive' [list of officers]; 2 'Recipe for Happiness,' 'Index' [alphabetical list of sections], and ad; 3 'The Thamesford Ladies' Cook Book' [poem about the making of this cookbook] and ad; 4 ads; 5–39 recipes credited with the name of the contributor, 'Miscellaneous,' and ads; 40 ads
COPIES: *OONL (TX715.6 B64 1940 p***)
NOTES: The printer may have been Embro Printing Shop, whose advertisement appears on the outside back face of the binding.

Cake-bakers special recipes

O995.1 [copyright 1940]
Cake-bakers / special / recipes / Note how they are / balanced / to produce the type [sic, no 'of'] icings and fill- / ings most in demand – in every / district – to help get your share / of the housewife's budget dollar. / G.C. Bear & Company / manufacturing food chemists to bakers / Windsor, Ontario [cover-title]
COPIES: *OGU (UA s070 b51)
NOTES: The copyright date is on the inside front face of the binding.

Canada, Department of Fisheries

O996.1 nd [about 1940]
Economical / lobster / recipes [cover-title]
DESCRIPTION: 19.0 × 12.0 cm   Pp 3–18 [19]   Illus col Paper, with image on front of a red lobster; stapled
CONTENTS: 3 introductory text; 4–18 recipes; 19 'Recipe Index' and at bottom p 19, 'Department of Fisheries, Ottawa // Hon. J.E. Michaud, Minister'
Citations: Chatelaine Nov 1940
COPIES: OGU (CCC CA1 FS 42E14, 2 copies)   *Private collection

NOTES: The introductory text describes three brands of lobster (fancy, choice, and standard) and encourages the reader to buy the product: 'Your purchases of Canadian canned lobster help the lobster industry, and aid in strengthening Canada's economic power to meet war-time needs.' On the inside front face of the binding, there is an illustration of Canada Brand Lobster, which was sold in tins of several sizes, including 'Ones' (not less than 12 ounces) and 'Halves' (not less than 6 ounces).

O996.2 nd [about 1940]
—Le / homard / recettes / économiques [cover-title]
DESCRIPTION: 19.0 × 12.0 cm   Pp 3–18   Illus col Paper, with image on front of a red lobster; stapled
CONTENTS: 3 introductory text; 4–18 recipes; inside back face of binding 'Index' and at bottom, 'Ministère des pêcheries, Ottawa // Hon. J.E. Michaud, ministre'
COPIES: *QSFFSC
NOTES: This copy is stamped on the binding, 'Rec'd 24 Oct 1940.'

Canada, Department of National Defence

O997.1 1940
[An edition of *Cooking for the General Mess, a Canadian Supplement (1940) to B.R. 5, Admiralty Manual of Naval Cookery (1936)*, Ottawa: Edmond Cloutier, printer to the King's Most Excellent Majesty, 1940]
COPIES: BPSIC
NOTES: This is a Canadian supplement to a British publication, *Manual of Naval Cookery, 1936*, London: 1937, pp 223 (Great Britain: LB); the previous British edition was *B.R. 5 Manual of Naval Cookery ... 1930* (Great Britain: LB microform, OB). There are no copies of O997.1 at OONL, OONMC, or OONDH.

Cook book

O998.1 nd [about 1940]
Ekfrid / Eureka / Community / Club / Cook book / A fine collection of / proven and tested recipes [cover-title]
DESCRIPTION: Pp 1–90 [91–2]   Purple paper, with gilt lettering
CONTENTS: 1 'Thank You!,' 'Compliments' [list of names and each person's financial contribution], 'Recipe for Happiness' [mock recipe], and 'Guess-

work' [poem]; 2 'To Help You Slect [*sic*] Your Mineral and Vitamin Menu' and 'Approximate Measures of Hundred Calorie Portions'; 3–4 'Kitchen Helps'; 5 'To Serve in Quantities'; 6 ads; 7 'Do You Know?'; 8 'Hints'; 9–89 recipes credited with the name of the contributor; 90 'Weights and Measures,' 'Roasting,' 'How Many Cups to a Can,' and 'Abbreviations'; 91–2 blank for 'Memorandum'

COPIES: *Private collection

NOTES: An advertisement on p 6 is a clue to the date of publication: T. Hockin Co. Ltd, a department store in Dutton, with '58 years of service.' In September 1882, James Pool and Thomas Hockin took over Dutton's general store from C. Turpain and the store became known as Hockin and Pool. In 1895, the store was renamed T. Hockin Co. when James Pool left to go into banking full-time. When Thomas's grandson Donald Hockin finally sold the business, the family had run the store in Dutton for over a century. The cookbook was likely published in 1940, counting the years of service from Thomas Hockin's co-ownership with Pool (1882 + 58 years). The appearance of the book is consistent with publication in 1940, not the 1950s if one counted from 1895.

There is no place of printing or publication in the volume, and the location of the club is unknown. The advertisements are for businesses in Glencoe, Strathroy, Appin, Melbourne, Mt Brydges, and Dutton, all southwest of London. Today there is no village called Ekfrid, but there is an Ekfrid Township, southwest of London. (In 1832, a post office named Ekfrid was opened in Ekfrid Township, but it was renamed Longwood in 1857.)

The cook's delight

O999.1   [1940]

The / cook's / delight / Foreword / [twelve-line verse signed A.M.T.] / A collection of tried and tested recipes / Compiled by / the Ladies' Guild / of / St. John's Church / Antrim, Ont.

DESCRIPTION: Tp illus of a Union Jack   With image on front of the church

COPIES: *Private collection

NOTES: The owner of the book reports that it was published in 1940 and has 68 pp. 'Compliments of G. Russell Boucher, M.P. Ottawa, Ontario' is printed on the inside front face of the binding. Boucher was a member of Parliament from 19 August 1940 to 1 November 1948.

The culinary art perfected to pleasing certainty

For the titles of other cookbooks by the same manufacturer, see O342.1.

O1000.1   [copyright 1940]

The / culinary art / perfected to pleasing certainty / with a new / Moffat / Roper / Gas Range [cover-title]

DESCRIPTION: 19.0 × 13.5 cm   Pp [1] 2–31 [32]   Illus Paper, with image on front of several cooked dishes; stapled

CONTENTS: 1 'The Wonders of Modern Gas Cookery'; 2 'Culinary Success Depends on Control of Ingredients, Time, Temperature'; 3 'Located and Controlled Heat for Ideal Top Burner Cooking'; 4 'Flavor-Seal "Waterless" Cooking Offers You Many Advantages'; 5 chart for 'waterless' cooking of vegetables, giving weight, water, and time for each vegetable; 6–8 '... Full Meal Oven Cookery ...'; 9 'What to Serve with Meat'; 10–11 'Broiled Foods Are Healthful // Modern Broiling'; 12–28 recipes for bread, cakes and icings, pies, fillings, custards, cookies, biscuits and muffins, puddings, sauces, meats, fish and stuffings, and vegetables and fruits; 29 'Oven Canning Instructions'; 30 oven-canning chart; 31 'Correct Table Service'; 32 'Moffat Roper Scientific Broiling Chart' and below chart, 'This chart is intended as a general guide only // Copyright 1940 Patent pending'; inside back face of binding 'Moffat Roper Scientific Cooking Chart' and below chart, 'Copyright 1938'

COPIES: *Private collection

NOTES: 'Moffats Limited Weston, Ont. Litho in Canada CBI-6-40-5M' is on the outside back face of the binding.

O1000.2   [about 1943]

—The / culinary art / perfected to pleasing certainty / with a new / Moffat / gas range [cover-title]

DESCRIPTION: 18.5 × 13.0 cm   Pp [1] 2–31 [32]   Illus Paper, with image on front of several prepared dishes; stapled

CONTENTS: 1 'The Wonders of Modern Gas Cookery'; 2 'Culinary Success Depends on Control of Ingredients, Time, Temperature'; 3 'Located and Controlled Heat for Ideal Top Burner Cooking'; 4 'Flavor-Seal "Waterless" Cooking Offers You Many Advantages'; 5 'Moffat Flavor-Seal "Waterless" Cooking Chart'; 6–8 'The Ease and Advantages of Full Meal Oven Cookery ...'; 9 'What to Serve with Meat'; 10 'Broiled Foods

Are Healthful'; 11 'Modern Broiling'; 12–28 recipes for 'Bread,' 'Cakes,' 'Cakes and Icings,' 'Pies, Fillings, Custards, etc.,' 'Cookies,' 'Biscuits and Muffins,' 'Custards, Puddings, Sauces,' 'Meats, Fish and Stuffings,' and 'Vegetables and Fruits'; 29 'Oven Canning Instructions'; 30 'Oven Canning' [chart]; 31 'Correct Table Service'; 32 'Moffat Roper Scientific Broiling Chart ... Copyright 1940'; inside back face of binding baking chart and 'Copyright 1938'
COPIES: *OONL (TX657 O6 C85 1938 p***)
NOTES: Unlike the cover-title of O1000.1, here there is no 'Roper' before 'gas range.' 'Moffats Limited Weston, Ont. Litho in Canada CBI-8-43-2200' is o the outside back face of the binding; therefore, the date of publication is likely 1943. A private collector has a copy identical to that at OONL, except the printer's mark on the binding is 'CBI-3-44-3500.'

Dutton, Miss Gertrude

For information about Dutton and her cookbooks, see M70.1, Specially Selected Recipes. *For a history of* Love – The Flavor Man *and the titles of its other cookbooks (all for professional bakers), see O924.1.*

O1001.1 [1940 or later]
Questing / a book of a thousand and one delights / In memory of her constant inspiration / and untiring efforts in helping to make / these flavors what they are, this book / is dedicated / to / Jean Love / Published by R.W. Love, Toronto, Ontario / Price 50 cents
DESCRIPTION: 23.0 × 15.5 cm   Pp [1–4] 5–126 [lacking 127–8]   Tp illus brown of a ship at sea, many illus brown   Paper, with image on front of a man on a camel; stapled
CONTENTS: 1 tp; 2 foreword by Gertrude Dutton; 3 'Questing compiled and edited by Gertrude Dutton, B.Sc. Illustrations and cover, J. Compton Smith,' index, and 'This is a publication of Love – The Flavor Man, 62–68 Lombard Street ... Toronto, Ontario'; 4 'Questing' signed E.G.R.; 5–117 recipes; 118–mid 119 'Measurements'; mid 119–122 timetables and temperatures; 123–mid 124 'Terms Used in Cooking'; mid 124–126 condiments and herbs
COPIES: OWTU (G11253)   *Private collection
NOTES: In this edition, the address on p 3 for Love – The Flavor Man is 62–8 Lombard Street. The two editions with the Lombard address precede O1001.3 with the 111 Bathurst Street address (first recorded in the 1950 Toronto city directory). In 'Questing' E.G.R. comments, 'Loves list of flavors is the largest ever

put on the commercial market up to the present year (1940).' Since this statement also appears in O1001.2, either O1001.1 or O1001.2 is the first edition, published in 1940.

There are chapters for appetizers, beverages, breads, cakes, candies, condiments, desserts, frostings and fillings, frozen dishes, gelatine desserts, jellies and conserves, pies and pastry, sauces, and small cakes and cookies. The text and illustrations are printed in brown. The book is dedicated to Robert W. Love's second wife, Jean, who had recently died.

In the foreword, Dutton refers to using Love's flavours in her practical work in the Homecraft Theatre in Winnipeg. It is not surprising that the Toronto-based company chose this Winnipeg cooking expert to compile the recipes. Love's domestic line of flavours was more popular in the West, and Robert W. Love, the inventor of the flavours, had once lived in Winnipeg and knew Dutton as a customer. She used to promote the company's products on her radio show, running recipe contests where the winners received Sunbeam Mixmasters as prizes.

O1001.2 [1940 or later]
—Questing / a book of a thousand and one delights / In memory of her constant inspiration / and untiring efforts in helping to make / these flavors what they are, this book / is dedicated / to / Jean Love / Published by R.W. Love, Toronto, Ontario / Price 50 cents
DESCRIPTION: 23.0 × 15.0 cm   Pp [1–4] 5–128   Tp illus brown of a ship at sea, many illus brown   Paper, with image on front of a man on a camel; stapled
CONTENTS: 1 tp; 2 'Foreword' by Gertrude Dutton; 3 'Questing' signed E.G.R.; 4 'Questing compiled and edited by Gertrude Dutton, B.Sc. Illustrations and cover J. Compton Smith,' index, and 'This is a publication of Love – The Flavor Man, 62–68 Lombard Street ... Toronto, Ontario'; 5–117 recipes; 118–mid 119 'Measurements'; mid 119–122 timetables and temperatures; 123–mid 124 'Terms Used in Cooking'; mid 124–126 condiments and herbs; 127 'Food for Fifty'; 128 'General Information on Loves Fruit Products'
COPIES: OONL (TP419 D87 1940, 2 copies)   *QMM (RBD Vanna Garnier, ckbk 598)
NOTES: In this edition the address for Love – The Flavor Man is 62–8 Lombard Street (as O1001.1), but it appears on p 4; 'Questing' is on p 3. OKCKT (Lady Eaton Estate Collection) owns a variant where p 4 has the index (as O1001.2), but no statement about the compiler and illustrator and no address; however, the Lombard Street address appears on p 128.

O1001.3 [about 1950]
—Questing / a book of a thousand and one delights / In memory of her constant inspiration / and untiring efforts in helping to make / these flavors what they are, this book / is dedicated / to / Jean Love / Published by R.W. Love, Toronto, Ontario / Price 50 cents
DESCRIPTION: 23.0 × 15.5 cm   Pp [1–4] 5–128   Tp illus brown of a ship at sea, many illus brown   Paper, with image on front of a man on a camel; stapled
CONTENTS: 1 tp; 2 foreword by Gertrude Dutton; 3 'Questing compiled and edited by Gertrude Dutton, B.Sc. Illustrations and cover, J. Compton Smith,' index, and 'This is a publication of Love – The Flavor Man, 111 Bathurst Street ... Toronto, Ontario'; 4 'Questing' signed E.G.R.; 5–117 recipes; 118–mid 119 'Measurements'; mid 119–122 timetables and temperatures; 123–mid 124 'Terms Used in Cooking'; mid 124–126 condiments and herbs; 127 'Food for Fifty'; 128 'General Information on Loves Fruit Products'
COPIES: OTMCL (641.5 D79)   *Private collection
NOTES: In this edition the address on p 3 for Love – The Flavor Man is 111 Bathurst Street. The company is listed in Toronto city directories at this address from 1950 on. The reference on p 4 to 'the present year (1940)' is misleading.

The epicurean treasury

The same group produced O1133.1, Favorite Recipes.

O1002.1 [1940]
The / epicurean / treasury / St. Peter's Church / Young Women's Club / Madoc – Ontario / Review Print, Madoc, Ont. [cover-title]
DESCRIPTION: Pp 1–48   Fp illus on p 1 of the church   Stapled
CONTENTS: 1 illus of the church and the date '1940'; 2 'A Selection of Tested Recipes // Compiled by St. Peter's Church // Madoc, Ont.'; 3 'Preface' and ad; 4 'Table of Contents' and ads; 5 'Temperatures' and ads; 6 ads; 7–48 recipes credited with the name of the contributor, 'Brief History of St. Peter's Church' on pp 23–4, and ads
COPIES: *Private collection

Favourite recipes

See O984.1 for a book likely published in 1940 by the Milton Branch of the Canadian Red Cross.

Favourite recipes for morning, noon and night

O1003.1 [1940]
Favourite / recipes / for / morning / noon / and / night [cover-title]
DESCRIPTION: 17.0 × 11.0 cm   [66 leaves, printed on rectos only]   Paper; bound at top edge by two metal rings through punched holes
CONTENTS: 1st leaf table of contents; leaves 2–66 recipes credited with the name of the contributor; inside back face of binding 'The recipes in this booklet have been contributed by members and friends of the Toronto Theosophical Society, 52 Isabella Street, Toronto, and compiled by the Ladies' Committee of the society. Price: Twenty-five cents 1940'
COPIES: *Private collection
NOTES: There is a section of vegetarian recipes.

Food for health in peace and war

See also O1020.1, War Economy Nutrition, which was intended to be used in conjunction with Food for Health in Peace and War.

O1004.1 [copyright 1940]
Keep this book in your kitchen / Food / for / health / in peace and war / What Canadian doctors / suggest for wholesome meals / at low cost / Prepared by the / Canadian Medical Association [cover-title]
DESCRIPTION: 19.0 × 12.5 cm   Pp 3–19   Illus   Paper; stapled
CONTENTS: Inside front face of binding 'Why This Book Was Prepared' signed Canadian Medical Association; 3 'Food for Health'; 4–5 'What to Buy'; 6 'Family Food Lists'; 7 'How to Use Your Family Food List'; 8–17 family food lists for 'Small Families,' 'Families with Two Children,' 'Families with Three Children,' 'Families with Four Children,' and 'Families with Five Children'; 18 'Suggestions for Meals'; 19 [inside back face] 'Shopping Hints' and 'Cooking Hints'; outside back face acknowledgment of the Canadian Red Cross Society for aid in distributing the book and of the life insurance companies of Canada for their assistance in the book's publication, and 'Canadian Medical Association // 184 College Street, Toronto Copyright, 1940 Lithographed in Canada'
COPIES: ACG   BVAMM   QMM (RBD ckbk 1564)   *Private collection
NOTES: 'Why This Book Was Prepared' states: '[This book] is published at this particular time because

history shows that in times of war tuberculosis, influenza and many other diseases may spread rapidly, claiming the lives of men, women and children who have become slowly weakened from lack of the right kind of food ...' According to p 3, when money is limited, 'first on the shopping list should be milk or cheese, potatoes and whole grain products (rolled oats, rolled wheat and whole wheat bread).' The food lists on pp 8–17 record each food, the amount per week, and the cost per week. The Canadian Dietetic Association assisted in the preparation of the food lists, which were tested by Canadian families under the supervision of the Visiting Homemakers Association (p 19).

Holmes, Marie [pseudonym of] Mrs William Wallace, née Marie Thompson (Toronto, Ont.–2 February 1974, Toronto, Ont.)

For information about the author and her other books, see O854.1.

O1005.1 1940
Food / from market to table / A complete guide to buying and cooking for / every day and special occasions / By / Marie Holmes / With a foreword by / Margaret Lawrence / Toronto: The Macmillan Company of / Canada Limited, at St. Martin's House / 1940
DESCRIPTION: 21.0 × 13.5 cm   Pp [i–iv] v–ix [x], [1–2] 3–560 [561–6] Frontis of 'Table Correctly Set for Lunch,' illus   Cloth; matching box
CONTENTS: i ht; ii frontis; iii tp; iv 'Copyright, Canada. [*sic*, period] 1940 by the Macmillan Company of Canada Limited ... Printed in Canada'; v–vi foreword; vii–viii table of contents; ix author's preface; x blank; 1 ht; 2 blank; 3–529 forty-three numbered chapters; 530 blank; 531–60 index; 561–3 blank for 'My Favourite Recipes'; 564–6 blank for 'Dishes My Friends Like'
CITATIONS: Brodie 5 Dec 1942   CCat No. 19, p U16 'Introducing the New Director of Chatelaine Institute,' *Chatelaine* (September 1947), p 32   Ferguson/ Fraser, pp 100 and 234, illus col on p 103 of closed volume in original dust-jacket   Spadoni 1989 No. 874B   THEA 1988, p 9
COPIES: BVAU   OHM (TX715 H75)   OOAG (641.5 H752 1940)   QMM (TX715 H75)   *Private collection
NOTES: The Macmillan Co. papers at OHMA record that the book, which Marie Wallace began writing in April 1937, was published on 11 March 1940. The total number of copies printed was 1,009 and production costs came to $2,290.79. CCat records the retail

price of the book: $2.00. The contributor of the foreword, Margaret Lawrence, was the literary editor of the *Canadian Home Journal*. The first chapter is devoted to 'Food Conservation and Meal Planning in Wartime.'

When the author asked the publisher about the possibility of reprinting the book or preparing a revised edition, she was informed that the stock was exhausted, the type was broken up, and that a new edition was financially unrealistic. In June 1950 she asked if Macmillan Co. would allow the Chatelaine Institute to publish another edition, and again was rebuffed. A letter from Frank Upjohn to John Gray of 22 June 1950 reveals the publisher's lack of enthusiasm for the author and her work: 'I think at sometime in the future, we ought to explore the whole cookbook market carefully, with the idea of having the best Canadian book on the market. The field is a very competitive one, and I rather doubt if Marie Holmes would be up with the leaders. So, I am all for letting this one go, with a view to having a really first-rate book at some later date.'

Food from Market to Table is recommended in O1095.1, *Canadian Cook Book for British Brides*. Wallace, writing as Marie Holmes in her 'Cooking Chat' columns in the Toronto *Daily Star*, also referred readers to *Food from Market to Table*; see, for example, the issue for 2 January 1945, p 18.

Home tested recipes [Campbells Flour]

O1006.1 [copyright 1940]
Campbells / Flour / Lakeside Milling Co. Limited / Home tested recipes / for cakes, cookies, quick-breads, sauces, / pies, frostings, fillings, desserts and tarts [cover-title]
DESCRIPTION: 20.0 × 13.5 cm   Pp 1–84 Illus Paper, with image on front of a gold crest and thistle for Campbells Flour; metal-spiral bound
CONTENTS: Inside front face of binding 'Copyright 1940 by Lakeside Milling Co., Limited'; 1 'Home Tried and Proved Baking Recipes by and for Canadian Women' signed Lakeside Milling Co. Ltd, Princess Street, Toronto; 2–3 'Helpful Information'; 4–76 recipes; 77–8 lacking in this copy; 79–80 'Well-Stocked Kitchen'; 81–2 lacking; 83–4 index
COPIES: OGU (CCC TX715.6 H663)   OONL (TX765 C35 1940)   *Private collection
NOTES: In the OGU copy, pp 77–8 are blank for 'Your Own Pastry, Pie, Tart and Pie Filling Recipes on This Page'; p 81 is a book-order coupon for *Campbell's Flour Cook Book*, i.e., this book; p 82 is a book-order

coupon for *Blossom of Canada Flour Cook Book*, i.e., likely O971.1, *Home-Proved Baking Recipes* [Blossom of Canada Flour].

The OONL copy is stamped with the Library of Parliament copyright stamp, in which is inscribed the deposit number 1424. OONL's book plate is applied over the spot where the copyright date is printed.

O1006.2   1947
—1947 edition / Campbells / Flour / Lakeside Milling Co. Limited / Home tested recipes / for cakes, cookies, quick-breads, sauces, / pies, frostings, fillings, desserts and tarts [cover-title]
DESCRIPTION: 20.5 × 13.5 cm   Pp [i–ii], 1–123 [124]   Illus   [Free, on p 119]   Thin card; Wire-O-Binding
CONTENTS: Inside front face of binding 'Copyright 1940 and 1947 by Lakeside Milling Co., Limited ...'; i–ii 'Statement by Ruth Hudson' printed on a pink leaf; 1 'Home Tried and Proved Baking Recipes by and for Canadian Women' signed Lakeside Milling Co. Ltd, Princess Street, Toronto; 2–118 text; 119 'Campbells Flour Cook Book Coupon'; 120 'Blossom of Canada Flour Cook Book Coupon'; 121–3 'Index' [i.e., table of contents]; 124 'Wire-O-Binding, Patented 1936'
CITATIONS: Ferguson/Fraser, p 234, illus col on p 103 of closed volume
COPIES: *Company collection (Maple Leaf Mills Consumer Products Co.), in 1991; location now unknown
NOTES: Ruth Hudson was the dietitian at the Lakeside Home-Baking Service Bureau, established 'some time ago' by Mr Campbell, president of Lakeside Milling Co. Hudson comments on p i that 'the first edition of this book was originally printed before shortages existed of sugar, nuts, chocolate, flavourings, shortening, eggs, butter and many other items'; she includes 'some general substitute hints.' The text on p 1 refers to the book as *The Campbells Home-Tested Recipe Book*.

A kitchen bouquet

The Kippen East Women's Institute was founded in 1934 (Ambrose, p 238). Kippen is near Seaforth, northwest of Stratford.

O1007.1   1940
Kippen East Women's Institute / presents / A kitchen bouquet / gathered / from the culinary gardens / of its members and friends / Arranged by / Mrs. James Finlayson, Mrs. George Glenn, / Mrs. Robert Simpson, Mrs. John Sinclair, / and Miss Grace Tremeer. / 1940 / Appreciation / To the

members, who gave us whole- / hearted support and co-operation; to the / friends outside the Institute, who responded / so graciously to requests for special recipes, / and to the publishers, who were never too / busy to give information and timely counsel, / we say a grateful Thank You!
DESCRIPTION: Pp [1–5] 6–76   Paper, with image on front of a bouquet of flowers; stapled
CONTENTS: 1 tp; 2 'A Recipe for a Day' selected by Mrs Archie Hoggarth; 3 'Index' [i.e., table of contents]; 4 'Weights and Measures'; 5–76 recipes, some credited with the name of the contributor, and at bottom p 76, 'Expositor Print // Seaforth'
COPIES: *Private collection

The kitchen guide

O1008.1   [1940]
The kitchen guide / Curries United Church / Curries, Ontario / Minister Rev. E.J. Wolland B.D., Th.M. / The Women's Association of Curries United Church of Canada / submits this cook book of tested recipes to the public, in the / hope that it may prove beneficial in many homes. / [folio:] 1
DESCRIPTION: 23.0 × 15.0 cm   Pp 1–48   Tp illus of the church   Paper; stapled
CONTENTS: 1 tp; 2 ads; 3 list of 'Helping Hand Club Executive' and thank-you to advertisers; 4 ads; 5–47 text and ads; 48 index and ad
COPIES: *Private collection
NOTES: The year of publication, 1940, is printed on the front face of the binding. The first recipe on p 5 is Recipe for a Sweet Disposition: '3 grains of common sense, 1 good liver, 1 bushel of contentment, 1 good husband, 1 large heart, plenty of fresh air and sunshine. Do not bring to a boil. – Mrs. Geo. Easton.' Another mock recipe, How to Cook a Husband, is on p 12. The first section of recipes is for pickles and relishes.

The mixing bowl

O1009.1   [1940]
The / mixing / bowl / A collection of / tried and / tested / recipes / Compiled and tested by the / members of / the Young Married Women's Group / of First Baptist Church / Guelph, Ontario
DESCRIPTION: 23.0 × 15.5 cm   Pp [1] 2–52   Paper; stapled
CONTENTS: 1 tp; 2 'Printed in Guelph by Guelph Print-

ing Service // 47 Cork St. E.'; 3 preface; 4–49 recipes and ads; 50 'To Serve in Quantities'; 51 'Weights and Measures'; 52 index and ads
CITATIONS: Driver 2001, Wellington County, pp 91–2
COPIES: *Private collection
NOTES: The date of publication, 1940, is printed on the front face of the binding. 'The Use of Honey in Home Cooking' is on pp 48–9.

Ontario, Department of Agriculture

For the titles of other cookbooks published by the Ontario Department of Agriculture, see O158.1.

O1010.1   1940
25M-3-40–P. 4954. / Bulletin 408 April, 1940 / Ontario Department of Agriculture / Statistics and Publications Branch / Toronto, Ontario / Conserve / by canning [cover-title]
DESCRIPTION: 24.0 × 16.5 cm   Pp [1–2] 3–43 [44]   Illus   Paper, with image on front of a woman adding sugar to a preserving kettle; stapled
CONTENTS: Inside front face of binding 'This bulletin has been prepared by the Women's Institute Branch, Department of Agriculture, Toronto // In co-operation with MacDonald Institute, Guelph // Ontario Agricultural College, Guelph // Home Economics School of the Kemptville Agricultural School'; 1 table of contents; 2 blank; 3–43 text; 44 'References'
CITATIONS: CCat No. 19, p U16   Driver 2001, Wellington County, p 95
COPIES: OGU (Rural Heritage Collection uncat) OVOH   OWTU   *Private collection

O1010.2   reprint, March 1941
—25M-3-41 R. 4337. / Bulletin 408 Reprint March 1941 / Ontario Department of Agriculture / Statistics and Publications Branch / Toronto, Ontario / Conserve / by canning [cover-title]
DESCRIPTION: 24.0 × 16.5 cm   Pp [1–2] 3–43 [44]   Illus   Paper, with image on front of a woman adding sugar to a preserving kettle; stapled
CONTENTS: Inside front face of binding 'This bulletin has been prepared by the Women's Institute Branch, Department of Agriculture, Toronto // In co-operation with MacDonald Institute, Guelph // Ontario Agricultural College, Guelph // Home Economics School of the Kemptville Agricultural School'; 1 table of contents; 2 blank; top–mid 3 'Conserve by Canning' [introductory text]; bottom 3–mid 5 'Food Spoilage'; mid 5–top 10 'Canning Methods'; mid 10–mid 13 'Canning Step-by-Step'; mid 13–14 'The Use of Tin

Cans'; 15–21 'Canning of Fruit'; 22–4 'Canning of Vegetables'; 25–31 'Jelly'; 32–4 'Jams, Marmalades and Conserves'; 35–43 'Pickles'; 44 'References'
CITATIONS: Driver, Wellington County, p 95
COPIES: OGU (Rural Heritage Collection uncat)   *Private collection

Orono recipe book

O1011.1   1940
[An edition of *Orono Recipe Book,* compiled by the Orono branch of the Women's Institute, printed by the Orono Weekly Times office, 1940, stapled]
COPIES: Private collection
NOTES: The recipes are credited with the name of the contributor.

Our favorite recipes

O1012.1   nd [1940]
Our / favorite / recipes / Arranged for publication by / the ladies of / St. Matthews Missionary Society / Church and Benton streets / Kitchener, Ontario [cover-title]
DESCRIPTION: 23.0 × 15.5 cm   Pp [1–60]   Paper; stapled
CONTENTS: 1 'Recipe for a Happy Year of Cooking' [mock recipe] signed H.M.S.; 2 ad; 3 'Entree' [i.e., introductory text], 'Mud Pies' by Florence A. Jones [poem], and 'For Moulding a Kitchen Mechanic' [mock recipe]; 4–60 recipes credited with the name of the contributor and ads
COPIES: *OTYA (CPC 1940 0085)
NOTES: An advertisement on p 2 for Tavistock Milling Co. Ltd sends congratulations to 'the Mission [*sic*] Society of St. Matthews Lutheran Church.' The 'Entree' on p 3 refers to the long-held 'reputation for good home cooking' and 'the unrivalled excellence of [the] cuisine' of Waterloo County housewives. Waterloo County is still renowned for its cooking and the high quality of food available in its farmers' markets. An advertisement on p 35 for Goudies Department Store indicates that *Our Favorite Recipes* was published in 1940; it says, 'To-day in 1940, ...'

Our favorite recipes

O1013.1   [1940]
Our favorite recipes / [caption:] Temple Baptist Church / Selected and arranged by the members of

/ the Women's Association / We present this carefully selected group of recipes to our / readers with the hope that they will help to provide many tasty / dishes for the home. / The ladies of the church have been most helpful and we thank / them heartily. / The advertisers have made the publication possible and we / recommend that you patronize them on every possible occasion. / The Women's Association / Temple Baptist Church / Dewhurst Avenue / Toronto Ontario / [folio:] 1
COPIES: *Private collection
NOTES: The owner gives 1940 as the date of publication.

Our favourite recipes

O1014.1   nd [about 1940]
Our / favourite recipes / A / collection of / tried and tested / recipes / Selected and arranged / for publication / by / the Talent Workers / of / St. Andrew's Presbyterian Church / Lindsay Ontario
COPIES: *Private collection
NOTES: This copy is inscribed by the original owner, on the binding, 'Mrs. J.W. Rabbie 1940.'

The pantry shelf

See O650.1 for the titles of two other cookbooks from the same church.

O1015.1   nd [about 1940]
The / pantry shelf / A collection of / tested recipes / Compiled and published by / the Women's Association of / Metropolitan United Church / London Ontario
DESCRIPTION: 23.0 × 15.0 cm   Pp [1] 2–76   Thin card; stapled
CONTENTS: 1 tp; 2 'Printed in Canada on Canadian paper // R.F. Fielding Co. printers London Ontario'; 3 'Preface' signed ladies of the Woman's [sic] Association; 4–75 text, mainly recipes credited with the name of the contributor, blank spaces for 'My Own Recipes,' and ads; 76 'Index' [i.e., table of contents] and ads
COPIES: *OL (London Room Box 179b)
NOTES: There is an advertisement on p 20 for Hunt Milling Corp. Ltd, London, 'millers for over 85 years'; since Hunt Milling was established in 1854, *The Pantry Shelf* was likely published about 1940 or slightly later (1854 + 'over 85 years'). The date for Hunt Milling is in Benjamin Samuel Scott, 'The Economic and Industrial History of the City of London, Canada,' Master's thesis, University of Western Ontario, 1930, p 225 (OL).

Selected recipes

See also O1157.1, Cook Book Containing Many Carefully-Chosen Practical Recipes, by the Presbyterian Young Women's Club at St Andrew's Church.

O1016.1   nd [about 1940]
Selected recipes / A selected group / of / tested recipes / Arranged for publication by / the Ladies' Aid / of / St. Andrews' [sic] Presbyterian Church / Weber and Queen streets / Kitchener, Ontario
DESCRIPTION: 23.0 × 15.0 cm   Pp [1] 2–76   Thin card; stapled
CONTENTS: 1 tp; 2 ads; 3 'Preface' signed the Committee; 4 'Printed in Canada on Canadian paper // Commercial Printing Company Kitchener, Ontario'; 5–75 recipes credited with the name of the contributor, blank pages and a space for 'My Own Recipes,' and ads; 76 'Index' [i.e., table of contents] and ads
COPIES: *OTYA (CPC 19-? 0056)
NOTES: There is an advertisement on the outside back face of the binding for the Economical Mutual Fire Insurance Co., which refers to 'serving the public for over 69 years' and has the company symbol incorporating the phrase 'Established 1871'; therefore, the date of publication of *Selected Recipes* is about 1940 (1871 + 69 years). This date is supported by the advertisement on p 26 for Rickert Dairy ('for over 30 years a "Buy" word ...') because the very same Rickert Dairy advertisement is in O1012.1, *Our Favorite Recipes*, another Kitchener cookbook that was certainly published in 1940.

Tested recipes

O1017.1   nd [about 1940]
Tested / recipes / East Plains United Church / Aldershot, Ontario [cover-title]
DESCRIPTION: Pp 1–64
CONTENTS: 1 'Foreword' and 'Sweet Disposition' [mock recipe]; 2 ads; 3–63 recipes credited with the name of the contributor, 'How to Serve 100 People,' and ads; 64 ad and 'Index' [i.e., table of contents]
COPIES: *Private collection
NOTES: The 'Foreword' extends thanks from the Women's Association of the church. A quarter-page advertising space on p 46 was purchased 'Compli-

ments of Premier Hepburn'; therefore, *Tested Recipes* was published in the period 1934–42, when Hepburn was premier. The design of the 'modern kitchen' illustrated in the advertisement opposite p 1 points to publication toward the end of the 1930s or later, but since there is no mention of the Second World War, perhaps in about 1940, before wartime conditions became most acute.

Tested recipes selected from the thousands of interesting recipes

For the titles of other Jewel Shortening cookbooks, see O695.1.

O1018.1   copyright 1940
Tested / recipes / selected from the thousands of interesting / recipes, entered in our recent / Jewel Shortening recipe contest. / Published by / Swift Canadian Co., Limited / Toronto / Copyright, 1940
DESCRIPTION: 19.5 × 13.5 cm   Pp [1–2] 3–96   Illus
Paper; stapled
CONTENTS: 1 tp; 2–89 recipes; 90 *Canadian Home Journal* Home Bureau Certificate of Approval dated 19 June 1940; 91 ad for Jewel Shortening; 92–6 index
COPIES: *OGU (CCC TX715.6 T46, 3 copies)   OONL (TX715.6 T47 1940)   QMM (RBD Vanna Garnier, ckbk 646)   SSWD
NOTES: The company produced another book of the same title, copyright 1950, which has a different selection of recipes from the 1940 edition (copies at OGU and OONL).

O1018.2   copyright 1940
—Recettes / essayées / choisies parmi les milliers de recettes / intéressantes qui nous ont été envoyées lors de / notre récent concours de / recettes au Shortening bijou. / Livre publié par la / Swift Canadian Co., Limited / Toronto / Droits réservés, 1940
COPIES: *Private collection
NOTES: A bookseller reports that his copy of O1018.2 has 104 pp.

Truscott, J.H.L.

See also O1229.1, Frozen Foods, by Truscott, E.C. Stillwell, and E.S. Snyder. For the titles of other cookbooks published by the Ontario Department of Agriculture, see O158.1.

O1019.1   June 1940
Bulletin 412 June, 1940 / Ontario Department of Agriculture / Statistics and Publications Branch / Toronto, Ontario / Quick frozen / fruits / and / vegetables / in / locker storages / By / J.H.L. Truscott, Ph.D. / Department of Horticulture / Ontario Agricultural College / Guelph, Ontario / R. 1031–18M. [cover-title]
DESCRIPTION: Pp 3–12
CONTENTS: Top 3 'Quick Frozen Fruits and Vegetables' [introductory text]; mid 3–top 4 'The Use of Quick-Frozen Fruits and Vegetables'; mid 4 'Varieties Suitable for Freezing'; bottom 4–top 5 'Packages'; mid 5 'Method of Packing'; bottom 5 'Speed Is Essential'; 6–8 'Fruits'; 9–12 'Vegetables'
COPIES: *OSUL (CA2 ON AF6 B412)

O1019.2   reprint, June 1942
—Bulletin 412 Reprinted June, 1942 / Ontario Department of Agriculture / Statistics and Publications Branch / Toronto, Ontario / Quick frozen / fruits / and / vegetables / in / locker storages / With an appendix / on / frozen meats / By / J.H.L. Truscott, Ph.D. / Department of Horticulture / Ontario Agricultural College / Guelph, Ontario / B 556–20M. [cover-title]
COPIES: *OGU (Rural Heritage Collection)
NOTES: The reprint has 16 pp.

War economy nutrition

O1020.1   nd [about 1940]
War / economy / nutrition / Help make Canada strong / [credit for photograph of man:] Courtesy of "Consumers' Guide" / Issued by the Canadian Red Cross / 95 Wellesley Street – Toronto, Ontario / Price 10c [cover-title]
DESCRIPTION: 22.5 × 15.0 cm   Pp 1–23   Very thin card, with images on front of a red cross and a man carrying a heavy object; stapled
CONTENTS: Inside front face of binding 'Foreword' and note about the *Consumers' Guide* photograph; 1–23 text in eight lessons (I, 'The Market Basket'; II, 'How Does Your Milk Measure Up?'; III, 'Our Garden Friends'; IV, 'Salads That Are Different'; V, 'The Fruit Basket'; VI, 'Variety and Flavour in Our Diet'; VII, 'The Grain Field'; VIII, 'Other Foods and Flavourings')
COPIES: *OGU (CCC TX715.6 W27)
NOTES: The 'Foreword' states, 'This pamphlet can be used by women in conjunction with "Food for Health in Peace and War,"' i.e., O1004.1. The pamphlet was

designed as a teaching aid by a 'teacher of nutrition.' Each lesson gives information about nutrition, prices for a family of five, and recipes. The date of publication was likely about the same time as O1004.1, copyright 1940.

1940s

A cook book of favorite recipes

The Bealton branch of the Women's Institute was founded in 1914 and was still active in 1996 (Ambrose, p 237). See also O662.1, from Bealton United Church.

O1021.1   nd [about 1940s]
[An edition of *A Cook Book of Favorite Recipes*, compiled by the members of Bealton Women's Institute, [1940s]]
COPIES: eBay on-line auction, July 2001

1940–5

Tested recipes

See also O538.1 from the same church.

O1022.1   nd [about 1940–5]
Tested recipes / Household hints // general information / Arranged for publication by / the ladies of the Womens [*sic*] Guild / of / the Church of St. John the Evangelist / St. James and Wellington streets / London – Ontario / A Recipe for a Day / [six-line verse beginning:] Take a little dash of water cold, and a little laven [*sic; i.e.,* leaven] of prayer, / [...]
DESCRIPTION: 22.5 × 15.0 cm   Pp [1–2] 3–75 [76] Card, with image on front of letter V and Morse Code symbol for V; stapled
CONTENTS: 1 tp; 2 'Printed in Canada // Printed in Canada on Canadian paper // R.F. Fielding Company London, Ont.'; 3 'Preface' signed members of the Women's Guild; 4–75 recipes credited with the name of the contributor, 'Use of Honey in Home Cooking,' 'Table Decorations,' 'Miscellaneous,' 'Time Tables,' 'Weights and Measures,' blank spaces for 'My Own Recipes,' and ads; 76 ads and 'Index' [i.e., table of contents]
COPIES: *Private collection
NOTES: 'Church of St. John the Evangelist (Anglican)' is on the front face of the binding. The letter V for victory on the binding indicates publication during the Second World War. An advertisement on p 7 for

Hunt Milling Corp. Ltd in London describes the firm as 'millers for over 85 years'; since this milling business started in 1854, the cookbook was published about 1940 or later (O1015.1, by the same printer, also has a Hunt Milling Corp. advertisement referring to 'over 85 years'). The 'Preface' says that the purpose of the book 'was to make available to a great number of our friends some recipes which have been proven through long use by our members.' Curiously, a 1947 IODE cookbook from Orillia, O1158.1, *Cooking Craft*, repeats this phrasing and has 'Tested recipes / household hints / general information' as its subtitle. The private collector's copy of *Tested Recipes* is inscribed on the binding, 'Dorothy Burns.'

1941

Bakery formulae

O1023.1   [1941]
Bakery formulae / tested and approved / by the / Bakery Research Laboratory / Canada Packers Limited [cover-title]
DESCRIPTION: 21.5 × 14.0 cm   Pp 1006, 1008–26, 1028–43, 8P5, [i–xviii], 2000–19, 8P5, 3000–21, [i–xl], 5000–5, 4000–9, 6000–3, [i–iv], 7000–6, 8000–5, [i–ii] Cloth-covered, three-ring binder
CONTENTS: Recipes on all rectos and a few versos
COPIES: *Private collection
NOTES: The leaves are numbered on the rectos only, and the versos are not included in the printer's pagination; however, in the 'Description' above, where I have supplied page numbers in square brackets, the roman numbers count rectos and versos (i.e., i–ii = one leaf).

Most leaves are dated at the top with different days in 1941. 'Sven Young // Baking Research Laboratory // Canada Packers Limited' is at the bottom of the first recto page and most other rectos; 'Sven Young // Mark Rey ...' is at the bottom of others. No place of publication is given, but the book was likely published in Toronto, where Canada Packers was located.

This copy originally belonged to A.W. Burns, a cook on a Royal Canadian Navy ship; it is now owned by his daughter. A copy at OGU (CCC TX715.6 B25) is in the same three-ring binder, but some of the contents differ. The initial leaf is headed 'Service and Research' and there are sub-dividers for 'Cakes,' 'Icings,' 'Cookies,' 'Pies – Pastries,' 'Bread // Sweet Dough,' 'Doughnuts,' 'Fillings,' and 'Miscellaneous.' Most of the leaves are dated 1941, but a few are 1942 and 1943.

Cook book

O1024.1 [1941]
A.W. Circle / Knox Church Ladies' Aid / Cook book / [caption:] Knox Presbyterian Church / St. Catharines, Ontario
DESCRIPTION: Pp [1–3] 4–48 Tp illus of the church
CONTENTS: 1 tp; 2 ads; 3 'The A.W. Circle of Knox Presbyterian Church is glad to present a cook book ...' [introductory text]; 4–? recipes credited with the name of the contributor and ads; 48 blank space for 'New Recipes' and 'Index' [i.e., table of contents]
COPIES: *Private collection
NOTES: The cover-title is 'Centennial Cook Book 1841–1941.' The introductory text states that the cookbook is 'the means of providing revenue for the Association.'

Cook book edition

See O749.1 regarding other cookbooks by the same newspaper.

O1025.1 24 February 1941
The Standard-Freeholder / Cornwall, Ontario, Monday, February 24, 1941 / 1941 / We are taking this opportunity / to extend thanks to all Cornwall / and district women who so kind- / ly submitted to us cooking re- / cipes of the highest quality. As / a matter of fact our cook book / edition contains recipes repre- / senting all classifications of dish / and food preparations. [...] / Response to the request for re- / cipes has been so enthusiastic / that all of them cannot be print- / ed in this edition. As far as pos- / sible we have followed the "first / come, first served" rule. To / those whose recipes do not ap- / pear, we submit our apologies. / They will appear in the regular / columns of this paper later. / 1941 / Cook book / edition [cover-title]
DESCRIPTION: Pp [1] 2–24 Illus Paper, with image on front, in a circular frame, of a mother holding a joint of meat in a roasting pan, and around this image four other images: the mother lifting the lid of the roasting pan, the father and son at table, and two scenes of the mother and father together
CONTENTS: 1 cover-title; 2 ad; 3–23 recipes credited with the name and town of the contributor, articles about food during wartime, and ads; 24 ad
CITATIONS: MacGillivray, p 46
COPIES: *OONL (microfilm)

Gaige, Crosby (1882–1949)

Other food- and drink-related books by this American author include: Food at the Fair, *New York: Exposition Publications Inc., c1939;* New York World's Fair Cook Book, the American Kitchen, *New York: Doubleday, Doran and Co., 1939;* Crosby Gaige's Cocktail Guide and Ladies' Companion, *New York: M. Barrows and Co., incorporated at the Fireside Press, 1941;* The Standard Cocktail Guide, *New York: M. Barrows, 1944;* Macaroni Manual, *[New York:] M. Barrows, 1947; and* Dining with My Friends; Adventures with Epicures, *New York: Crown Publishers, [1949] (all United States: DLC). Gaige 'adapted for America'* Madame Prunier's Fish Cookery Book, *selected, translated, and edited by Ambrose Heath, New York: J. Messner Inc., [c1939], and he prepared the revised edition of André Simon's* French Cook Book, *Boston: Little, Brown, 1948 (both United States: DLC).*

For the titles of other cookbooks published by Gorman, Eckert and Co., see O445.1.

O1026.1 [copyright 1941]
Season to taste / dishes of glamour and how to prepare them / with accent on spice / Edited by / Crosby Gaige
DESCRIPTION: 19.5 × 14.0 cm Pp [1–5] 6–47, [i] Illus of individual spices and of scenes of harvesting various spices; world map on inside faces of binding showing where spices grow [$0.25, on binding] Paper, with image on front of a sailing ship and compass; stapled
CONTENTS: 1 tp; 2 'Copyright 1941 by the American Spice Trade Association // Printed in U.S.A.'; 3 'Good Cooking' signed Crosby Gaige; 4 'Table of Contents'; 5–9 'Flavor ... "The Soul of Food"'; 10–16 spice chart indicating uses; 17–43 recipes using herbs and spices; 44–5 'Savory Hints for Housewives'; 46–7 'Index'; i ad for Club House Brand Spices made by Gorman, Eckert and Co. Ltd, London, Ontario
CITATIONS: CCat No. 21, p W17
COPIES: *Private collection
NOTES: 'Compliments of Gorman, Eckert & Co., Ltd. London, Canada' is printed on the front face of the binding, i.e., the London, Ontario, spice company used the American Spice Trade Association's *Season to Taste* for its own promotional purposes. CCat gives 1942 as the year of publication.

Hints that are golden

O1027.1 [1941]
Hints that are / golden / Specially compiled by / Davis Gelatine (Canada) Ltd. / 27 Front Street East / Toronto, Canada [cover-title]
DESCRIPTION: 11.0 × 7.0 cm   Pp 1–16   Gold paper; stapled
CONTENTS: Inside front face of binding 'If you are interested in gelatine cookery, secure a copy of our large recipe book, Davis Dainty Dishes [O580.1] ...'; 1–16 information about gelatine and cooking with gelatine, in a question-and-answer format, and at bottom p 16, '40M-6-41'; inside back face 'Davis Gelatine is the finest and most widely used gelatine in the Empire ...' and the company's Toronto, Montreal, and Vancouver addresses
COPIES: *Private collection
NOTES: The text is printed in blue.

Home-tested recipes

O1028.1 [1941]
Home-tested recipes / compiled and arranged by / Circle 2 / of / Women's Association / of / Parkdale United Church / Ottawa, Ont., Canada / To our advertisers we extend our grateful appre- / ciation. Your generous contributions have made our book / possible, and we trust your gains shall be as great as ours.
DESCRIPTION: 20.5 × 13.5 cm   Pp [3–4] 5–94 [95–6] Paper, with image on front of a woman tossing a salad; stapled
CONTENTS: 3 tp; 4 'Foreword'; 5–89 recipes credited with the name of the contributor and ads; 90–4 'Miscellaneous,' 'Table of Measurements,' and ads; 95 blank for 'Memorandum'; 96 ads; inside back face of binding 'Index' [i.e., table of contents]
COPIES: *Private collection
NOTES: The year of publication, '1941,' is printed on the outside back face of the binding.

1941 cook book

For a 1920 cookbook by the St Vincent branch, see O428.1.

O1029.1 1941
The St. Vincent / [Women's Institute symbol] / Women's Institute / 1941 / cook book / Tested recipes / selected by the women of the Institute [cover-title]

DESCRIPTION: Metal spiral
COPIES: *OOWM
NOTES: Printed on the first page is the 'Preface' and 'Published by the Hart Advertising Agency – Owen Sound for the St. Vincent Women's Institute // Printed in Meaford by the Meaford Express.' OOWM reports that the volume has 62 pp and cost $0.50.

Victory cook book

O1030.1 1941
Victory / cook book / 1941 / V / ...– [i.e., Morse Code for V] / The Young Women Church Workers / of St. James' Church / Kingston, Ontario [cover-title]
DESCRIPTION: 22.5 × 15.5 cm   Pp [1–3] 4–72   Photograph on p 1 of St James' Church   Very thin card; stapled
CONTENTS: 1 photograph of church and 'A Collection of Tested Recipes compiled and arranged by the Young Women Church Workers of St. James' Church'; 2 thank-you for buying the book and 'Printed by Hanson & Edgar, Ltd. Kingston, Ontario'; 3 'Foreword' signed J.D. Mackenzie-Naughton [rector of St James' Church]; 4–72 text, mainly recipes credited with the name of the contributor, blank spaces for 'New Recipes,' 'My Own Recipes,' or 'Notes,' ads, and blank space on p 72 for 'Index'
COPIES: *Private collection
NOTES: Page 1 (design and text) mirrors p 1 of an earlier Kingston cookbook from the same printer, O706.1. 'Meatless Entrees' are on pp 47–9. This copy is signed by the original owner of the book, 'Marjorie Simmons. Mar. 17/42.'

'Victory' recipe book

Jackson is west of Owen Sound, near Paisley. The Jackson branch of the Women's Institute, which published the 1986 facsimile, was organized in 1963 (Ambrose, p 235).

O1031.1 1941
[First edition of 'Victory' Recipe Book, by Jackson's School War Workers, 1941]
NOTES: The first edition is cited in O1031.2.

O1031.2 facsimile ed., 1986
—"Victory" recipe book / Favorite recipes / by / Jackson's School War Workers / U.S.S. [i.e., Union School Section] No. 8 Greenock & Elderslie / 1941 / This is being reprinted as a project by the Jackson / Women's Institute, 1986. / Index / Beverages 1 /

Bread 3 / Buns and Fancy Breads 4 / Canning and Preserving 8 / Candy 10 / Cakes 12 / Cookies 22 / Desserts 29 / Additional Recipes 33 / Jams, Jellies and Conserves 35 / Pies and Tarts 38 / Pickles 43 / Salads and Dressings 47 / Supper and Luncheon Dishes 49 / Miscellaneous 53 / Helpful Household Hints 55
DESCRIPTION: 21.5 × 13.5 cm   Pp [i–ii], [1] 2–56 [57–8]   Small tp illus (0.8 cm high) of a maple leaf   Paper, with Union Jack on front and the caption 'There'll always be an England'; stapled
COPIES: *Private collection

The village cook book

O1032.1   May 1941
The village / cook book / compiled by the members of / Forest Avenue / Home and School Association / Port Credit – Ontario / May 1941
DESCRIPTION: 22.5 × 15.5 cm   Pp [i–ii], 1–67, [i]   Paper
CONTENTS: i tp on blue leaf; ii blank; 1 'A Recipe for a Happy Life' and 'The Aims and Policies of Our Organization Are: –'; 2–61 text; 62 ads; 63–4 blank for 'Extra Recipes'; 65 'Thank You!,' 'Our Advertisers,' and 'Officers for 1940–41'; 66 blank for 'Favourite Dishes'; 67 ads; i 'You too can serve – by saving! Buy War Savings Stamps'
COPIES: *OGU (UA s048 b38)
NOTES: *The Village Cook Book* quotes, with credit, a passage about economy from O398.1, *Aunt Hanna's Cook Book*, published during the First World War (see that entry for the text of the quotation).
  'Mexican Recipes' are on pp 51–2, including Chili con Carne, Mock Enchiladas, Sopa de Arros, Real Mexican Chili Sauce, Green Chili Sauce, Spanish Liver, Mexican Chicken Mole, Chili con Queso, and Mexican Chocolate. 'Health and Patriotism' on pp 59–60 lists food requirements recently published by the Canadian Medical Association and comments on the patriotic task of Canadian housewives during wartime, to 'fight against poor foods, minimum efficiency, sickness, [poor] nutrition and disease.'

1941 or 1942

Batchelder, Ann (1885–1955)

Also by this American author are Cookery for Today, *[New York:] Butterick Publishing Co., c1932, and* Start to Finish; Ideas Old and New for Cook and Hostess ..., *Woodstock, Vt: 1954 (both United States: DLC).*

O1033.1   [1941 or 1942]
[An edition of *Ann Batchelder's Own Cook Book,* Toronto: McClelland and Stewart]
CITATIONS: Brodie 5 Dec 1942
NOTES: The Canadian edition was published either in the year of the first American edition (1941) or in the year of Brodie's review (1942). It probably had the same number of pages – 232 – as the American edition.

AMERICAN EDITIONS: *Ann Batchelder's Own Cook Book,* New York: M. Barrows and Co. Inc., 1941 (United States: DLC); *Cookbook,* [completely rev.], New York: M. Barrows, [1949] (OPAL, QMAC; United States: DLC).

Better homes and gardens cook book

O1034.1   [1941 or 1942]
[An edition of *Better Homes Cook Book* [sic], Toronto: City News Co., Canadian agents, $2.00]
CITATIONS: Brodie 5 Dec 1942
NOTES: Jean Brodie reviews what she calls the *Better Homes Cook Book,* probably *Better Homes and Gardens Cook Book,* the first American edition of which was published in 1941. Brodie describes the book as 'a substantial, loose-leaf book with plenty of space for extra pages and with an excellent index.' The Canadian edition was published either in the year of the first American edition or in the year of Brodie's review.

AMERICAN EDITIONS: *Better Homes and Gardens Cook Book,* [Des Moines, Iowa: Meredith Publishing Co., c1941] (United States: DLC); [Des Moines, Iowa: Meredith Publishing Co., 1946] (United States: DLC); [Des Moines, Iowa: Meredith Publishing Co., 1947] (United States: DLC); [Des Moines, Iowa: Meredith Publishing Co.], 1951 (United States: DLC); Des Moines, Iowa: Meredith Publishing Co., c1962 (BVA); [Des Moines, Iowa:] Meredith Publishing Co., c1965 (SSU).

Diat, Louis (Montmarault, France, 1885–29 August 1957, New York, NY)

Diat worked at the Ritz hotels in Paris and London, before becoming the first chef of the Ritz Carlton Hotel in New York City at its opening in 1910. He is famed for his invention of the cold leek-and-potato soup, Crème Vichyssoise. Diat also wrote: Louis Diat's Home Cookbook, *Philadelphia, New York: J.B. Lippincott Co.,*

[1946] (Great Britain: LB; United States: DLC); Sauces, French and Famous, *New York: Rinehart, [1951]* (United States: DLC); and Gourmet's Basic French Cookbook, *published posthumously, [New York:] Gourmet, [1961] (Great Britain: LB; United States: DLC).*

O1035.1 [1941 or 1942]
[An edition of *Cooking à la Ritz,* Toronto: Longmans, Green and Co., $3.00]
CITATIONS: Brodie 12 Dec 1942
NOTES: The Canadian edition was published either in the year of the first American edition (1941) or in the year of Jean Brodie's review (1942). It probably had the same number of pages – 524 – as the American edition. The American and British editions include a portrait of the author; in 'To My Readers,' pp xi–xx, he tells the story of his life. The recipes are Diat's, from the Ritz Carlton Hotel, but he has assembled the collection for the American home cook.

AMERICAN EDITIONS: Philadelphia, London, and New York: J.B. Lippincott Co., [copyright 1941] (Great Britain: LB; United States: DLC, MiD).

BRITISH EDITIONS: London, New York [etc.]: Restaurant Trade Journal Ltd, [1945] (Great Britain: LB; United States: DLC).

Hibben, Sheila

This American author also wrote: The National Cookbook, *New York, London: Harper and Brothers, 1932;* The AGA Cook Book, *New York: A.G.A. Co., [c1934];* and American Regional Cookery, *Boston: Little, Brown and Co., c1946 (all United States: DLC). She co-authored, with Sara Murray Jordan,* Good Food for Bad Stomachs, *Garden City, NY: Doubleday, 1951 (United States: DLC).*

O1036.1 [1941 or 1942]
[An edition of *A Kitchen Manual,* Toronto: Collins, $3.00]
CITATIONS: Brodie 12 Dec 1942
NOTES: The Canadian edition was published either in the year of the first American edition (1941) or in the year of Jean Brodie's review (1942). It probably had the same number of pages – 231 – as the American edition. Brodie describes Hibben as 'the author of a popular food and cookery column in a New York paper.'

AMERICAN EDITIONS: New York: Duell, Sloan and Pearce, [c1941] (United States: DLC).

Platt, Mrs June, née Evans

Other cookbooks by this American author are: June Platt's Party Cookbook, *Boston: Houghton Mifflin Co., [1936];* June Platt's Dessert Cookbook, *Boston: Houghton Mifflin, 1942;* The Best I Ever Ate, *New York: Rinehart, [1953]; and* June Platt's New England Cook Book, *New York: Atheneum, 1971 (all United States: DLC).*

O1037.1 [1941 or 1942]
[An edition of *June Platt's Plain and Fancy Cook Book,* Toronto: Ryerson Press, $2.50]
CITATIONS: Brodie 5 Dec 1942
NOTES: In Brodie's review of the Canadian edition of this American text, she refers to the book as 'new.' It was published either in the year of the first American edition (1941) or in the year of Brodie's review (1942). It probably had the same number of pages – 356 – as the American edition.

AMERICAN EDITIONS: Boston: Houghton Mifflin Co., 1941 (United States: DLC).

1941–5

Eagle Brand recipes

For information about the company and its other books, see Q106.1.

O1038.1 nd [about 1941–5]
[In cartoon dialogue bubble, spoken by Elsie, the Borden cow:] This is my book / of magic recipes / [title:] Eagle / Brand / recipes / © The Borden Co. Ltd. / We regret that due to paper shortage / we were unable to produce our usual / illustrated cookbook. Nevertheless, / this booklet contains all of the / popular Eagle Brand recipes. [cover-title]
DESCRIPTION: Pp [1] 2–15 [16]   Paper, with image on front of Elsie, the Borden cow; stapled
CONTENTS: 1 cover-title; 2–15 [inside back face of binding] recipes for ice cream, sauces, cookies, 'Tea Time Treats,' beverages, frostings, candies, pies, custards, puddings, and salad dressings; 16 [outside back face] 'Cooking by Magic: What Does it Mean?' and 'How to Measure Eagle Brand'
COPIES: *Private collection
NOTES: The company introduced the advertising character, Elsie, the Borden cow, in the late 1930s, and began to transport a real cow named Elsie to cities and towns across North America, attracting huge crowds. Elsie first visited Canada in 1941, at the

Canadian National Exhibition in Toronto; and she came to Canada again in 1943 (Thomas/Marchant, p 38).

Although there is no mention of the Second World War, the reference to a 'paper shortage' indicates that the cookbook was published during that conflict, but which year is unknown. Initiatives to limit the domestic use of paper and to recycle began early on (paper drives by groups, such as the Boy Scouts, for example, started in autumn 1940 and became more frequent by summer 1941); however, the demand for paper was greatest toward the end of the war, in 1944–5.

On the outside back face of the binding, there is a reference to 'a few years ago, [when] the Borden Kitchen started experimenting with the use of Sweetened Condensed Milk in short-cut recipes ...' The short-cut recipes were published in O784.1, *Magic!*, nd [about 1932–3], which is sub-titled, 'The most amazing short-cuts in cooking ...' Many of the recipes in *Eagle Brand Recipes* are revised versions of dishes in the earlier book.

There is no place of publication, but Borden's Canadian headquarters moved from Montreal to Toronto in 1931.

Victory cook book

O1039.1 [about 1941–5]
Victory / cook book / Tested recipes and cooking aids / Compiled / by / the members / of / the Ladies [*sic*, no apostrophe] Aid / of / Alexandra Presbyterian Church / Colborne and Peel streets / Brantford Ontario
DESCRIPTION: About 23.0 × 15.0 cm [dimensions from photocopy] Pp [1] 2–100 With image on front of letter V and Morse Code symbol for V; stapled
CONTENTS: 1 tp; 2 'Printed in Brantford by Mercantile Press'; 3 'Preface' signed 'The ladies of the Women's Association ...'; 4–mid 95 recipes; bottom 95–6 blank for 'My Own Recipes'; 97 'Home Catering in Large Amounts'; 98 'Time Tables'; 99 ad and 'Table Decorations'; 100 'Index' [i.e., table of contents] and ads
COPIES: *Private collection
NOTES: An advertisement exhorting readers to buy Victory Bonds indicates that the book was published during the Second World War, but no earlier than June 1941, the launch of the first of nine official victory loan drives (the last was in November 1945, after the cessation of hostilities). 'How to Use Honey' on p 85 includes seven general rules and recipes for Honey Graham Bread, Honey Angel Cake, Honey Cream

Filling, and Honey Pecan Pie. Cooks turned to honey as a sugar substitute in the war years.

1942

Allen, Mrs Ida Cogswell Bailey (1885–1973)

For other titles by this American author, see O372.1.

O1040.1 [1942]
[An edition of *Successful Entertaining*, Toronto: McClelland and Stewart, $3.50]
CITATIONS: Brodie 12 Dec 1942
NOTES: The Canadian edition probably had the same number of pages – 500 – as the American edition.

AMERICAN EDITIONS: Garden City, NY: Doubleday, Doran and Co. Inc., 1942 (United States: DLC).

Atkinson, Francis Edward (1905–), and C.C. Strachan

Atkinson is also the author of the 8-page A Home Cider Press, *Publication 530, Circular 112, Ottawa: Department of Agriculture, September 1936, and the French-language edition,* Un pressoir à cidre fait chez soi, *September 1936 (copies at OOAG). For a list of other cookbooks published by the Department of Agriculture, see O404.1.*

O1041.1 1st printing, November 1942
Publication 744 / Farmer's Bulletin 114 / Issued November, 1942 / First printing / Dominion of Canada – Department of Agriculture / Home processing of fruits / and vegetables / F.E. Atkinson and C.C. Strachan / Summerland Experimental / Station / Experimental Farms / Service / Published by authority of the Hon. James G. Gardiner, Minister of Agriculture, / Ottawa, Canada / 5M–6217–11:42 [cover-title]
DESCRIPTION: 24.0 × 15.5 cm Pp [1–4] 5–27 13 numbered illus Paper, rebound in cloth, together with other publications
CONTENTS: 1 cover-title; 2 blank; 3 'Table of Contents' and 'List of Illustrations'; 4 blank; top 5 'Introduction'; mid 5–near bottom 12 'Drying Fruits and Vegetables'; bottom 12–mid 13 'Sun Drying Apricots'; mid 13 'Cherry Raisins'; bottom 13–mid 14 'Candying Fruit'; mid 14–top 15 'Maraschino Cherries'; mid 15–mid 16 'Apple Juice'; bottom 16 'Grape Juice'; 17–mid 18 'Juices with Suspended Pulp (Tomato, Apri-

cot, and Prune)'; mid 18–mid 19 'Apple Syrup'; mid 19 'Pectin from Apples'; bottom 19–mid 20 'Vinegar'; mid 20–27 'Juice Press'

CITATIONS: Ag 1867–1974, pp 20 and 41   CCat No. 21, p W3

COPIES: *OOAG (630.4 C212 1942–50)

NOTES: There are detailed instructions and illustrations for making a fruit-and-vegetable drier and a juice press.

O1041.2   reprint, September 1943

—Publication 744 / Farmer's Bulletin 114 / Issued September, 1943 / Reprint / Dominion of Canada – Department of Agriculture / Home processing of fruits / and vegetables / F.E. Atkinson and C.C. Strachan / Summerland Experimental / Station / Experimental Farms / Service / Published by authority of the Hon. James G. Gardiner, Minister of Agriculture, / Ottawa, Canada / 10M–6895–9-43 [cover-title]

DESCRIPTION: 24.5 × 16.5 cm   Pp [1–4] 5–28   13 numbered illus   Paper; stapled

CONTENTS: 1 cover-title; 2 blank; 3 table of contents; 4 'List of Illustrations'; top 5 'Introduction'; mid 5–near bottom 12 'Drying Fruits and Vegetables'; bottom 12–mid 13 'Sun Drying Apricots'; mid 13 'Cherry Raisins'; bottom 13–mid 14 'Candying Fruit'; mid 14–top 15 'Maraschino Cherries'; mid 15–top 17 'Apple Juice'; mid 17–top 18 'Grape Juice'; near top–bottom 18 'Juices with Suspended Pulp (Tomato, Apricot, and Prune)'; 19 'Apple Syrup'; top 20 'Pectin from Apples'; mid 20–mid 21 'Vinegar'; mid 21–28 'Juice Press'

COPIES: *AEAG   OOAG

Centenary cook book

O1042.1   [1942]

Church of / St. John the / Evangelist / Centenary / cook book / Compiled by members of / Junior Women's Guild / Strathroy [cover-title]

DESCRIPTION: 22.5 × 14.5 cm   Pp 1–92   Illus on p 1 of the church   Silver paper; stapled

CONTENTS: Inside front face of binding 'The Centenary Cook Book' [i.e., a poem about the cookbook in the voice of the 'married men of Strathroy']; 1–top 4 'Brief History of St. John the Evangelist Church 1842 1942 Strathroy' and on p 1, illus of the church; mid 4 'A Word of Appreciation'; 5 'Index' [i.e., table of contents]; 6–mid 87 recipes credited with the name of the contributor and ads; bottom 87–8 'Household Hints' and ad; 89 'Wartime Conservation' and 'Quantities to Serve 100'; 90 ad; 91 'Foods for Health'; 92 'Equiva-

lents,' 'Substitutions,' 'Baking Time for Cakes,' and 'Cooking Temperatures'

COPIES: *OTYA (CPC 1942 0120)

Cook book

O1043.1   1942

Hamilton 1. / [illus of house] / The Homestead / Home League / [Salvation Army symbol] / Cook / book / 1942 [cover-title]

DESCRIPTION: 21.5 × 13.5 cm   Pp [i–iv], 1–72, [i–iv] Photograph on p i of Amy G. Richie, Mrs Lieutenant-Colonel, Divisional Home League Secretary   Paper, with image on front of a house; stapled

CONTENTS: i statement of the purpose of the Salvation Army Home League and a poem signed Amy G. Richie; ii–iv blank, ruled leaves for 'Memo'; 1–64 129 numbered recipes credited with the name of the contributor, mostly women from Hamilton; 65–6 twelve numbered 'Penny Stretchers'; 67 ten numbered 'Household Hints'; 68 table of equivalent measures, 'Temperature Chart,' and ad; 69–72 'Index' [i.e., list of the recipes in the order in which they appear in the book, which is alphabetically by name within each section]; i–iv blank, ruled leaves for 'Memo'

COPIES: *Private collection

NOTES: On p i, Amy Richie states, 'The Salvation Army Home League, as it's [sic] name implies, centres around the family of the Nation, and it's [sic] purpose is to show that the humblest dwelling-place may become the "home beautiful" where love and happiness may always abound.'

The design of the text is distinctive: The recipe numbers and names are printed in a large face; the ingredients, instructions, and contributors' names look 'typed.'

The economy cook book

See O749.1 regarding other cookbooks by the same newspaper.

O1044.1   30 May 1942

Daily Standard-Freeholder / Cornwall, Ontario, Saturday, May 30, 1942 / War time edition / The economy / cook book / Dedicated to wives and mothers – on / whose wise and thrifty management / of our household food budgets, will de- / pend the health and strength of the / men and women behind the lines – and / that of our children, too, for whose future / we seek to make a better world.

/ The aim of the cook book is to help / homemakers prepare and serve nutri- / tious, well balanced, vitamin-filled meals, / temptingly and economically. / Featuring "My Favorite Low Cost Meal" / by nationally famous writers on home economy [cover-title]

DESCRIPTION: Pp [1] 2–24 Illus Paper, with image on front of a woman holding a basket of groceries

CONTENTS: 1 cover-title; 2–23 articles about food, nutrition, and budgeting during wartime, recipes (some credited with the name of the contributor), and ads; 24 ad

CITATIONS: MacGillivray, p 46

COPIES: *OONL (microfilm)

NOTES: Photographs of the 'nationally famous writers on home economy' are reproduced.

Food facts

O1045.1 1942

[An edition of *Food Facts*, Runnymede Presbyterian Church, Toronto, 1942]

COPIES: Private collection

The Good Housekeeping cook book

O1046.1 [copyright 1942]

The / Good / Housekeeping / cook book / Farrar & Rinehart, Inc. / New York Toronto

DESCRIPTION: 21.0 × 14.0 cm Pp [i–iv] v–x, [1–2] 3–947 Frontis col of roast beef, pls col, illus Cloth, with plaid-like pattern

CONTENTS: i ht; ii blank; iii tp; iv 'Copyright, 1942, by Farrar & Rinehart, Inc. Printed in the United States of America by J.J. Little and Ives Company, New York ...'; v–vi 'Preface' signed Katharine Fisher and Dorothy B. Marsh; vii–viii 'How to Use the Index'; ix–x 'Contents'; 1 part-title; 2 blank; 3–877 text; 878 blank; 879–947 'Index'

CITATIONS: Brodie 5 Dec 1942

COPIES: *OTR (TX715 G624 1942)

NOTES: In her review of the Canadian edition, Jean Brodie describes the book as 'almost a library in one cover.' Brodie gives Oxford University Press as the publisher and $3.00 as the price.

Although *The Good Housekeeping Cook Book* originated in the United States, it has a Canadian connection: Miss Katharine Anderson Fisher, director of New York's Good Housekeeping Institute from 1924 to 1953, hailed from Stratford, Ontario, and was a graduate of the Ontario Normal School of Domestic Science and Art in Hamilton, Ontario (DCB, Vol. 13, p 490).

From 1910 to 1917 Fisher was head of the School of Household Science at Macdonald College in Montreal; she then moved to New York City to take up a position first at Teachers College, Columbia University, and then at the Good Housekeeping Institute (John Ferguson Snell, *Macdonald College of McGill University: A History from 1904–1955*, Montreal: McGill University Press, 1963, p 66).

O1046.2 1944

—The / Good / Housekeeping / cook book / Completely revised / edition / Toronto / Oxford University Press / 1944

DESCRIPTION: 21.0 × 14.5 cm Pp [i–iv] v–x, [1–2] 3–981 8 pls col incl frontis Cloth, with plaid-like pattern

CONTENTS: i ht; ii blank; iii tp; iv 'Copyright, 1942, 1944, by Farrar & Rinehart, Inc. Copyright, Canada, 1944 by Oxford University Press // Printed in Canada'; v–vi 'Preface to the 7th Edition (Revised)' signed Katharine Fisher and Dorothy B. Marsh; vii–viii 'How to Use the Index'; ix–x table of contents; 1–917 text; 918 blank; 919–81 index

COPIES: *Private collection

O1046.3 [copyright 1944]

—The / Good / Housekeeping / cook book / Edited by Dorothy B. Marsh / Food Editor, Good Housekeeping Magazine / Completely revised / edition / Rinehart & Company, Inc. / New York Toronto

COPIES: BVAU (missing) *Private collection; United States: DLC (TX715 G624 1944)

NOTES: There is no date on the title-page. The following is on the verso of the title-page: 'Copyright, 1942, 1944, by Farrar & Rinehart, Inc. Printed in the United States of America by J.J. Little and Ives Company, New York.'

O1046.4 [copyright 1949]

—The / Good Housekeeping / cook book / Edited by / Dorothy B. Marsh / Food Editor, Good Housekeeping Institute / Rinehart & Company, Inc. / New York and Toronto

DESCRIPTION: 21.0 × 13.5 cm Pp [i–iv] v–x, [1–2] 3–1014 Frontis col, 9 double-sided pls col, a few small illus Cloth

CONTENTS: i ht; ii blank; iii tp; iv 'Copyright, 1942, 1944, 1949, by Hearst Magazines, Inc. ... Printed in the United States of America'; v–vi 'Preface to New Edition' signed Katharine Fisher, director, Good Housekeeping Institute; vii–viii 'How to Use the Index'; ix–x table of contents; 1–936 text; 937–1014 index

COPIES: *Private collection; United States: DLC (TX715 G623 1949)

AMERICAN EDITIONS: *Good Housekeeping Cook Book,* New York: Good Housekeeping, [c1933] (United States: DLC); 4th ed., 1935 (Dickinson, p 87); *The Good Housekeeping Cook Book,* New York: International Readers League, Periodical Publishers Service Bureau Inc., [1942] (United States: DLC); [new ed.], New York: Stamford House, [1949] (United States: DLC); New York: Rinehart, [1955] (United States: DLC).

Growing up with milk

For the company history, see O350.1.

O1047.1   [copyright 1942]
Growing up with milk / eating and drinking / the Carnation way [cover-title]
DESCRIPTION: 23.0 × 15.0 cm   Pp [3] 4–47   Illus brown and blue-green   Paper, with image on front of a girl feeling a boy's biceps; stapled
CONTENTS: 3 'Foreword' signed Carnation Co. Ltd, Toronto, Ontario, and 'Copyright 1942, Carnation Company, Ltd. CC-641 Lithographed in Canada'; 4–45 text; 46–7 [inside back face of binding] index
COPIES: *Private collection
NOTES: See O1047.2 for comment.

O1047.2   [copyright 1943]
—Growing up with milk / eating and drinking / the Carnation way [cover-title]
DESCRIPTION: 23.0 × 15.0 cm   Pp [3] 4–47   Illus brown and blue-green   Paper, with image on front of a girl feeling a boy's biceps; stapled
CONTENTS: 3 'Foreword' and 'Copyright 1943 Carnation Company, Ltd. CC-641A Lithographed in Canada'; 4–6 'Drink and Eat ... and Be Merry'; 7–8 'Bottle Days Are Over!'; 9 'Menus Age 1 Year'; 10–11 'Toddlers on the March!'; 12 'Menus Ages 2 and 3'; 13–14 'A Man-Sized Diet for a Man-Sized Boy!'; 15 'Menus Ages 4, 5, and 6'; 16–17 'For the Rip-Roaring Hungry School Days'; 18 'Menus Ages 7 to 13'; 19–20 'So Big ...'; 21 'Menus Age from 13 on'; 22 'Milk-Rich Recipes'; 23–45 recipes; 46–7 [inside back face of binding] 'Index to Recipes'
COPIES: *BDEM   OONL (TX715 C3465 No. 29)
NOTES: The recipes are for cooking with the company's evaporated milk. The 'Foreword' states: 'In preparing this booklet, we have secured the cooperation of Ruth Holt Crowley, R.N. Mothers who have read our booklet, "Your Contented Baby," or the one for expectant mothers, "Two to Feed," will remember Mrs.

Crowley as the author.' The office of Carnation Co. was in Toronto (p 3). A notice is stapled to the binding of the BDEM copy: 'You may have a copy of this book free.'

O1047.3   1944
—[Another edition of *Growing Up with Milk,* Toronto: Carnation Co. Ltd, 1944]
COPIES: Bookseller's stock

AMERICAN EDITIONS: 1942 (Allen, p 204).

Hawkins, Nancy (1914–)

This American author co-wrote the following with Arthur Hawkins: The Low-Cost Meat Book, *Garden City, NY: Doubleday, 1973;* The American Regional Cookbook, *Englewood Cliffs, NJ: Prentice-Hall, c1976; and* The Shellfish Cookbook, *New York: Hastings House, c1981 (all United States: DLC).*

O1048.1   [1942]
[An edition of *Let's Cook,* Toronto: Ryerson Press, $2.25]
CITATIONS: Brodie 5 Dec 1942
NOTES: In her review of the Canadian edition of this American book, Jean Brodie comments: '[It] is ... intended for beginners. This ... is a book that would prove invaluable to the bride who has had no previous experience in cooking.' The Canadian edition was probably the same length as the American edition – 219 pp.

AMERICAN EDITIONS: *Let's Cook; a Cookbook for Beginners of All Ages,* New York: A.A. Knopf, 1942 (United States: DLC).

Home and School cook book

For an earlier cookbook by the association, see O960.1.

O1049.1   1942
Home and School / cook book / 1942 edition / A selection of / tested recipes / Compiled by / the Aylmer Home and School Association / Aylmer, Ontario. [cover-title]
DESCRIPTION: 23.5 × 15.5 cm   Pp 3–82   Paper; stapled
CONTENTS: Inside front face of binding 'The Home and School Creed'; 3 'Preface' signed members of the Home and School Association, and 'Ten Commandments for Parents' reprinted from *Parents' Magazine*; 4 'Recipe for a Good Home and School Association' and 'Helpful Hint for Teachers and Mothers' by Miss

Ruby Stuart, from Report at Teachers' Convention; 5–80 culinary text, mainly recipes credited with the name of the contributor, and ads; 81 'Index of Advertisers'; 82 'Index' [alphabetical list of topics]
COPIES: *OSTT (R641.5 HOM)
NOTES: In the 'Preface' the compilers refer to this as a 'souvenir cook book' and express the hope that 'it will be of daily value to busy mothers and others who so faithfully and cheerfully prepare the food for their households.'

Logan, Martha [pseudonym]

Other cookbooks attributed to Martha Logan are: O1119.1, Handibook of Meat Cookery; O1120.1, Queens of Cuisine with Swift'ning; O1185.1, Captivating Cookery with Allsweet; and O1186.1, Sweets with Allsweet. See also O695.1, Better Recipes with Jewel Shortening, prepared by Martha Logan's Test Kitchen. Also attributed to Martha Logan, but outside the bounds of this bibliography, are: 77 Recipes Using Swift'ning Make-Your-Own Mix, [Toronto, Ont.: Swift Canadian Co. Ltd, copyright 1950] (OGU, OONL), and a French-language edition (BouquinsCat 229, No. 341); and probably Tempting Ways to Serve Swift's Premium Ham, nd.

The character of Martha Logan was created by Swift and Co., the American parent company of Swift Canadian Co. Answering the question 'Who is Martha Logan?,' Swift and Co. gave this explanation in Martha Logan's Meat Cook Book, by Beth Bailey McLean and Thora Hegstad Campbell, New York: Pocket Books Inc., [1952]: 'The Martha Logan name represents the combined meat-cooking knowledge and practical experience of the entire Swift & Company Home Economics Staff. Hundreds of Swift & Company food-experts, who have been serving American housewives for almost 35 years [i.e., from about 1918], have assumed the proud title of Martha Logan in their work on the radio and television, in the women's magazines and newspapers.' In Canada, before 1945, American home economists from Swift's Chicago test kitchen were the public face of Martha Logan; for example, the photographic portrait of the real person behind the pseudonym in O1050.1, Meat Complete, of 1942, is Beth Bailey McLean (1892–), who ran the Chicago kitchen from 1937 to the mid-1950s.

From 1945, Swift Canadian Co. employed a series of Canadian home economists to be Martha Logan. Part of the job was to adapt American material from the Chicago office to Canadian conditions (for example, ingredients), and to do promotional work, such as cooking demonstrations, across the country. The first Canadian Martha

Logan was Miss Marjorie Josephine Ellis, who joined Swift in 1945, after receiving a Bachelor of Science in Home Economics degree from the University of Manitoba in the same year. Ellis had to leave the job in 1956 after suffering a brain aneurism, which left her disabled. She returned to Winnipeg and died there some years later. Ellis was president of the Toronto Home Economics Association for two terms, 1953–4 and 1954–5.

Mrs Christine Robb Hindson became the new Martha Logan in 1956. She had been hired as an assistant to Ellis in 1954 after graduating from the Macdonald Institute. Hindson was succeeded in about 1960–1 by Greta Wiener (later Elgis).

O1050.1   copyright 1942
Meat / complete / A handbook of meat cookery / By Martha Logan / Swift Canadian Co., / Limited / General office: / Toronto Canada / Home Economics Division – Research Laboratories / Copyright 1942
DESCRIPTION: 21.5 × 15.0 cm   Pp [1] 2–54 [55–6]   Illus col on pp 52–3 of Swift products, illus   Thin card, with image on front of seven stylized clock faces; Cirlox-bound
CONTENTS: Inside front face of binding table of contents; 1 tp; 2 illus of 'Martha Logan Test Kitchen,' two women performing an experimental test, and Martha Logan giving a talk to homemakers; 3 untitled introductory note signed Martha Logan, Home Economist, Swift Canadian Co. Ltd, and illus portrait of Martha Logan; 4–53 text; 54 'Cooking Time Index' [i.e., recipes categorized by cooking time, from 5 minutes to 3½ hours]; 55 order form for a year's supply of 'Right Foods Check Charts' as described on pp 6–7 of the book; 56 order form for this book at $0.10 per copy; inside back face 'Meat Index' [i.e., recipes organized by type of meat]
CITATIONS: CCat No. 22, p X17   Cooke 2003, p 207
COPIES: OGU (CCC TX715.6 L627 copy 1)   OONL (TX749 L64 1942)   QMM (RBD ckbk 1775)   *Private collection
NOTES: The title-page is printed in blue and black. Meat rationing was introduced in May 1943, after this cookbook was published; hence, there are no comments about conserving meat during wartime. In the Canadian edition, Martha Logan addresses her note on p 3 to the 'queens of your modern Canadian castles'; in the American edition, she uses the phrase 'modern American castles.'

The photograph of 'Martha Logan' on p 3 is actually Beth Bailey McLean from Swift's Chicago test kitchen, according to Christine Robb Hindson (conversation with me, October 2001).

O1050.2   copyright 1942

—Viandes / un manuel / pour la cuisson des viandes / Par Martha Logan / Swift Canadian Co., / Limited / Siège social: / Toronto Canada / Service de l'économie ménagère – Laboratoires des recherches / Droits réservés 1942

DESCRIPTION: 21.5 × 15.0 cm   Pp [1] 2–54 [55–6]   Illus col on pp 52–3 of Swift products, illus   Card, with image on front of seven stylized clock faces; Cirlox-bound

CONTENTS: Inside front face of binding table of contents; 1 tp; 2 illus of 'Une des Cuisines d'essai de Martha Logan,' two women performing an experimental test, and Martha Logan giving a talk to homemakers; 3 untitled introductory note signed Martha Logan and illus portrait of Martha Logan; 4–53 text; 54 'Table de cuisson'; 55 order form for a year's supply of 'Tableaux de vérification des aliments convenables' as described on pp 6–7; 56 order form for this book; inside back face 'Tables de viandes'

COPIES: *OONL (TX749 L642 1942 p***)

NOTES: The title-page is printed in blue and black.

AMERICAN EDITIONS: *Meat Complete: A Handbook of Meat Cookery,* Chicago: Swift and Co., copyright 1942 (OGU); Chicago: Swift and Co., Home Economics Division, Research Laboratories, c1943 (recorded in DLC catalogue, but no holdings information).

Lohman, Mrs Tina

O1051.1   [copyright 1942]

Book of Jewish recipes / Edited by / Mrs. Tina Lohman / Published by / the Jewish Standard / Toronto Montreal

DESCRIPTION: 23.5 × 15.5 cm   Pp [1–4] 5–98   Paper, with Star of David on front; stapled

CONTENTS: 1 tp; 2 'Copyright 1942 ...'; 3–4 'Foreword'; 5–98 text

COPIES: *Private collection

NOTES: The 'Foreword' describes Tina Lohman as a 'qualified dietitian' and records the dual purpose of the book, written for Jewish families across Canada: 'to provide the young and comparatively inexperienced housewife with a manual of instruction in the art of Jewish cookery, and at the same time to provide the older and experienced housewife with a compendium of more or less complicated recipes suitable for special occasions.' There is no table of contents or index. Recipes are arranged under the following chapter headings: 'Appetizers'; 'Soups'; 'Soup Accessories' [i.e., dumplings, noodles, croutons, meat marbles,

etc.]; 'Fish'; 'Meats'; 'Poultry'; 'Stuffings'; 'Pastries'; 'Passover Recipes'; and 'Purim Recipes.'

Loves standard Canadian baker

In 1937 Love – the Flavor Man published O924.1, The Modern Canadian Cake Baker, Part 3, which also included material by Bonnie Dundee. See that entry for information about the company and its cookbooks.

O1052.1   1942

Loves / standard / Canadian / baker / with which is incorporated / The / Modern / Method / by / Bonnie Dundee / 1942 / Published and presented to / our customers by / Love / the Flavor Man / Church and Lombard sts., Toronto, Ont.

DESCRIPTION: 18.0 × 12.5 cm   Pp [1] 2–72   Paper; stapled

CONTENTS: 1 tp; 2–6 'Index' [i.e., table of contents]; 7–9 'The Modern Method' by Bonnie Dundee; 10–70 text for 'Loves Standard Canadian Cake Baker'; 71 address for Love in Toronto, eastern distributor in Toronto, and western distributor in Regina, Saskatchewan; 72 'War Time Frostings and Glazes'

COPIES: *Private collection

NOTES: 'Copyrighted' is stamped on the title-page. Bonnie Dundee explains that the 'modern method' was 'developed so that the smaller baker could successfully compete against factory manufactured cakes ...'

Moffat cook book

O1053.5, Moffat Cook Book, was superseded in 1949 by a new text with the same title, O1221.1, Moffat Cook Book. For the titles of other cookbooks by the same manufacturer, see O342.1.

O1053.1   nd [1942]

Moffat / cook / book / We hope this Moffat Cook Book, with its / rich collection of recipes, suggestions / and instructions, will add to the pleasure / you will enjoy through the ownership of / a Moffat Electric Range ... and so con- / tribute to the art of good living which / plays such an important part in the / march of human progress. / Moffats Limited / Weston / Ont., Canada / Blackburn / Lancs., England

DESCRIPTION: 22.5 × 15.0 cm   Pp [1] 2–72   Tp illus of a woman bringing a spoon to her lips (shows head and hand only), illus purplish brown, illus   Paper, with tp illus on front; stapled

CONTENTS: 1 tp; 2 'Model 924 Moffat Electric Range'; 3–7 'Moffat Electric Ranges and Cookers // General Instructions'; 8 'Substitutes'; 9 'Measuring'; 10 'Food Elements' and 'Terms Relating to Cookery and Serving'; 11–72 recipes; inside back face of binding 'Index' and 'No. 173 7M-9-42 B.L.'
COPIES: *OONL (TX715.6 M64 1940z p***)
NOTES: There is an illustration of Model 924 on p 2, Model 914 on p 6, and Model E30-M on p 7. The printer's mark on the inside back face of the binding establishes the year of publication of the various editions.

O1053.2 nd [1944]
—Moffat / cook / book / We hope this Moffat Cook Book, with its / rich collection of recipes, suggestions / and instructions, will add to the pleasure / you will enjoy through the ownership of / a Moffat Electric Range ... and so con- / tribute to the art of good living which / plays such an important part in the / march of human progress. / Moffats Limited / Weston / Ont., Canada / Blackburn / Lancs., England
DESCRIPTION: 21.5 × 14.0 cm   Pp [1] 2–72   Tp illus of a woman bringing a spoon to her lips (shows head and hand only), illus brown, illus   Paper, with tp illus on front; stapled
CONTENTS: 1 tp; 2 'Model 985 Moffat Electric Range'; 3–7 'Moffat Electric Ranges and Cookers // General Instructions'; 8 'Substitutes'; 9 'Measuring'; 10 'Food Elements' and 'Terms Relating to Cookery and Serving'; 11–72 recipes; inside back face of binding 'Index' and 'No 173 7M–7–44 B.L.'
COPIES: QMMMCM (AR-M2000.92.35)   *SWSLM   Private collection
NOTES: There is an illustration of Model 985 on p 2, Model 914 on p 6, and Model E46-M on p 7.

The private collector's copy appears to be identical except for the printer's mark on the inside back face of the binding, 'No 173 5M–11 45 B.L.' The QMMMCM copy lacks its binding.

O1053.3 nd [1947]
—Moffat / cook / book / We hope [...]
DESCRIPTION: 23.0 × 15.0 cm   Pp [1] 2–72   Illus brown, illus   Paper, with image on front of a woman bringing a spoon to her lips (shows head and hand only); stapled
CONTENTS: 1 tp; 2 'Model 1225 Moffat Electric Range'; 3–7 'Moffat Electric Ranges and Cookers // General Instructions'; 8 'Substitutes'; 9 'Measuring'; 10 'Food Elements' and 'Terms Relating to Cookery and Serving'; 11–72 recipes; inside back face of binding

index and 'No. 115 10M 9-47 B.L.'
COPIES: *Private collection
NOTES: There is an illustration of Model 1225 on p 2, Models 1054 and 1144 on p 6, and Model E46-M on p 7.

O1053.4 nd [1948]
—Moffat / cook / book / We hope this Moffat Cook Book, with its / rich collection of recipes, suggestions / and instructions, will add to the pleasure / you will enjoy through the ownership of / a Moffat Electric Range ... and so con- / tribute to the art of good living which / plays such an important part in the / march of human progress. / Moffats Limited / Weston / Ont., Canada / Blackburn / Lancs., England
DESCRIPTION: 23.0 × 15.5 cm   Pp [1] 2–72   Tp illus brown of a woman bringing a spoon to her lips (shows head and hand only), illus brown   Paper, with tp illus on front; stapled
CONTENTS: 1 tp; 2 'Model 1225 Moffat Electric Range'; 3–7 'Moffat Electric Ranges and Cookers // General Instructions' [includes specifications for Model Nos. 1054, 1144, and E46-M]; 8 'Substitutes'; 9 'Measuring'; 10 'Food Elements' and 'Terms Relating to Cookery and Serving'; 11–72 recipes; inside back face of binding 'Index' and 'No. 115 10M 1-48-B.L.'
COPIES: AHRMH (987-035-005)   QMM (RBD ckbk 1837)   *Private collection
NOTES: The AHRMH copy appears to be identical to the private collector's except that the printer's mark on the binding reads, 'No. 115 10M 9-48 B.L.' [i.e., printed in the ninth, not the first, month]. In the QMM copy, the printer's mark after '10M' is torn off.

O1053.5 nd [1949]
—Moffat / cook / book / We hope this Moffat Cook Book, with its / rich collection of recipes, suggestions / and instructions, will add to the pleasure / you will enjoy through the ownership of / a Moffat Electric Range ... and so con- / tribute to the art of good living which / plays such an important part in the / march of human progress. / Moffats Limited / Weston / Ont., Canada / Blackburn / Lancs., England
DESCRIPTION: 23.0 × 15.5 cm   Pp [1] 2–72   Tp illus reddish-brown of a woman bringing a spoon to her lips (shows head and hand only), illus reddish-brown   Paper, with tp illus on front; stapled
CONTENTS: 1 tp; 2 'Model 1225 Moffat Electric Range'; 3–7 'Moffat Electric Ranges and Cookers // General Instructions' [includes specifications for Model Nos. 1054, 1144, and E46-M]; 8 'Substitutes'; 9 'Measur-

ing'; 10 'Food Elements' and 'Terms Relating to Cookery and Serving'; 11–72 recipes; inside back face of binding 'Index' and 'No. 115 10M 4-49 B.L.'
COPIES: *OTMCL (641.586 M57 1949)
NOTES: This edition is differentiated from O1053.4 by the printer's mark on p 72, which establishes 1949 as the date of publication. The OTMCL copy has an inscription by the original owner of the book, on the binding, that confirms the year of publication: 'June 23rd, 1949. Stove installed.'

Moore, Mary Allen (Mrs Harry Forrester Moore, divorced), née Clark (Hamilton, Ont., 21 February 1903–22 May 1978, Hamilton, Ont.)

For information about the author and her other cookbooks, see Q189.1. See also O880.1, another book from St Lawrence Starch Co. Ltd.

O1054.1   [copyright 1942]
The / Bee Hive / cook book / 90 new ways to add delightful variety to your daily menus [cover-title]
DESCRIPTION: 16.5 × 12.0 cm   Pp [1–2] 3–31   Illus col   Paper, with image on front of a slice of Perfect Lemon Pie; stapled
CONTENTS: 1 cover-title; 2 'Contents' [i.e., index] and 'Copyright, 1942 St. Lawrence Starch Company, Limited Port Credit, Ont.'; 3 'Corn Syrup Cookery Can Be Fun'; 4–31 [inside back face of binding] 'Recipes' and at bottom p 31, 'Sampson-Matthews Limited, Toronto'
CITATIONS: Canadian Women of Note No. 634
COPIES: *ACG (2 copies)   ARDA   MWPA (MG14 C50 McKnight, Ethel)   NSHMS (88.74.5)   OGU (2 copies: CCC TX715.6 B425, TX715.6 M572 No. 533) OONL (TX715.6 B44 1942)
NOTES: Mary Moore is not credited as the author; the text on p 3 says only that '[t]he recipes in this book were compiled, tested and approved by two of Canada's foremost cooking experts.' However, the article 'Meet Mary Moore' by Carroll Allen, *Homemaker's Digest* Vol. 7, No. 4 (July/August 1972), pp 54 and 56, tells the story of *The Bee Hive Cook Book:*

Because sugar was on the rationed list, during World War II, the editor of the Windsor Star asked Mary to develop some recipes using syrup or honey for sweetening. She spent a couple of days experimenting with cake recipes and when she was satisfied that cake and icing were delicious using only corn syrup, she plunked the cake in a dishpan,

grabbed some plates and forks and drove to the offices of the St. Lawrence Starch Co. where she fed samples to the president and his staff.

'St. Lawrence offered me $1,200 if I could come up with a booklet of recipes using Bee Hive Corn Syrup instead of sugar – inside of three weeks.' Mary flew into a cooking frenzy and with the help of her sisters [Pearl and Doris] met the deadline ...

[']The fee was used as down payment on a small four-room bungalow on Hamilton's mountain [where she still lived in 1972] ...'

In the 'Foreword' to *The Mary Moore Cookbook,* 1978, she also referred to her authorship of this unattributed publication: 'During the Second World War, with sugar rationed, I was asked to write a cookbook using corn syrup instead of sugar, ...'
In *The Bee Hive Cook Book,* p 3, Moore explained the benefits of cooking with corn syrup:

Glazed savoury foods profit by the use of Bee Hive Golden Corn Syrup, and its mild sweetness and smooth consistency 'touch up' a vegetable or meat flavour to just the right degree. Remember always that Bee Hive Golden Corn Syrup is more easily digested than most forms of sugar and like other St. Lawrence products is 100% Canadian, being made from corn grown and planted in Canada. It is not expensive, is a good mixer and is altogether a valuable health addition to the family diet.

As well as corn syrup, St Lawrence Starch Co. made cornstarch and corn oil, and these ingredients are also called for in the recipes.

100 sugarless recipes

O1055.1
[First edition of *100 Sugarless Recipes* by the Fort William Women's Air Force Auxiliary, likely 1942]
NOTES: Two women's groups in Manitoba and one in Saskatchewan reprinted a cookbook compiled by the Fort William Women's Air Force Auxiliary. No copy of the original book has been located.

O1055.2   nd [1942]
—100 / sugarless / recipes / compiled by the / Fort William / Women's Air Force Auxiliary / [caption:] The Hawker Hurricane IIC has a greater fire power than any other / single-engine fighter in service anywhere. Fitted with a more / powerful Rolls-Royce Merlin engine, it has an extraordinary rate /

of climb and ceiling. Manufactured in Fort William, Canada. / Erickson Ladies' Auxiliary / Canadian Legion, B.E.S.L. [i.e., British Empire Service League] / Price 25c [cover-title]

DESCRIPTION: 20.5 × 13.5 cm   Pp [1–2] 3–26 [27]   Paper, with image on front of a Hawker Hurricane IIC; stapled

CONTENTS: 1 'A Hymn for Today'; 2 'Dear Friend:' signed Fort William Women's Air Force Auxiliary; 3–26 recipes and poems; 27 'High Flight' by John Gillespie Magee, Jr

COPIES: *OGU (CCC TX715.6 O5274)   SSWD

NOTES: The text accompanying the poem 'High Flight' says that 'Magee was killed last December 11th in action with the Royal Canadian Air Force.' Magee died on 11 December 1941; therefore, the cookbook was likely published in 1942.

The text on p 2 indicates that the cookbook was compiled by one group, but sold by another: 'This book ... being sold by the Erickson Ladies' Auxiliary Canadian Legion, B.E.S.L. through the kind permission of the Fort William Women's Air Force Auxiliary.' Fort William is now part of Thunder Bay, Ontario. The Erickson Ladies' Auxiliary of the Canadian Legion is based in Erickson, Manitoba. Appropriately for an air force publication, the binding is printed in blue ink on blue paper.

O1055.3

—100 sugarless / recipes / Price 25¢ / Presented by / Winnipeg Women's / Air Force Auxiliary [cover-title]

DESCRIPTION: 20.5 × 13.5 cm   Pp [1–2] 3–26 [27]   Paper, with small image on front of a fighter plane that has just completed a loop and the book's title printed in the trace of the loop; stapled

CONTENTS: 1 'A Hymn for Today'; 2 'Dear Friend:' signed Fort William Women's Air Force Auxiliary; 3–26 recipes and poems; 27 'High Flight' by John Gillespie Magee, Jr

COPIES: *Bookseller's stock

NOTES: The text on p 2 reads, 'This book ... being sold by the Winnipeg Women's Air Force Auxiliary, through the kind permission of the Fort William Women's Air Force Auxiliary.' The binding is printed in red and blue on white paper; the interior text is in black on white paper.

O1055.4

—100 / sugarless / recipes / compiled by the / Fort William / Women's Air Force Auxiliary / [caption:] The Hawker Hurricane IIC has a greater fire power than any other / single-engine fighter in service

anywhere. Fitted with a more / powerful Rolls-Royce Merlin engine, it has an extraordinary rate / of climb and ceiling. Manufactured in Fort William, Canada. / Officer's [sic] Wives Auxiliary / No. 11, S.F.T.S. – Yorkton, Saskatchewan / Price 25c [cover-title]

DESCRIPTION: With image on front of a Hawker Hurricane IIC

COPIES: *Private collection

NOTES: SFTS stands for Saskatchewan Flight Training School, which was part of the British Commonwealth Air Training Programme during the Second World War. The binding design is uniform with O1055.2.

Our pet recipes

The Venerable Order of the Blue Goose, now called the Honorable Order of the Blue Goose International, is an insurance industry association founded in 1906 near Milwaukee, Wisconsin. In the 1940s, the Toronto Women's Auxiliary met monthly in the Round Room at Eaton's department store.

O1055a.1   [about 1942]

[An edition of *Our Pet Recipes*, by the Venerable Order of the Blue Goose, Toronto, [about 1942]]

NOTES: A notice in the *Globe and Mail* (Toronto), 20 January 1943, headed 'Blue Goose Cook Book Adds $500 to Treasury,' reported: 'More than $300 was realized from the sale of the cook book *Our Pet Recipes* published by the auxiliary.' It is possible that the text was not compiled in Ontario, but produced by the American members of the Order.

Perkins, Wilma Lord (1897–)

Wilma Perkins, an American, prepared the 1930 revision of Fannie Farmer's The Boston Cooking-School Cook Book *(O144.4). She was married to Herbert Perkins, the son of Fannie's sister Cora.*

O1056.1   [1942]

[An edition of *The Fanny* [sic] *Farmer Junior Cook Book*, Toronto: McClelland and Stewart, $2.35]

CITATIONS: Brodie 5 Dec 1942

NOTES: In her review of the Canadian edition, Jean Brodie comments, '[It] was intended for children but will be found most helpful by the young bride who has had little experience in cookery.' The Canadian edition was probably the same length as the American first edition – 208 pp – and also illustrated by Martha Powell Setchell.

AMERICAN EDITIONS: Boston: Little, Brown and Co., 1942 (NSWA, QMU; United States: DLC); Boston: Little, Brown, [1957] (NSH, NWY, OOC; United States: DLC); [Braille ed., transcribed from 1957 ed.], Washington, DC: Library of Congress, [197-?] (OTBNL).

Rombauer, Irma, née von Starkloff (St Louis, Mo., 30 October 1877–4 October 1962)

In 1931, after her husband had committed suicide, Irma Rombauer self-published the first edition of The Joy of Cooking, *as a means of making income for her family. Bobbs-Merrill published subsequent editions of* The Joy of Cooking, *and by 1943 it was an American best-seller. From 1944 it outsold Fannie Farmer's* The Boston Cooking-School Cook Book (O144.1) *in the United States. Rombauer also wrote* Streamlined Cooking, *Indianapolis and New York: Bobbs-Merrill, [1939] (United States: NN), and* A Cookbook for Girls and Boys, *Indianapolis and New York: Bobbs-Merrill Co., [1946] (United States: DLC). In* Little Acorn: Joy of Cooking, the First Fifty Years, 1931–1981, *Indianapolis and New York: Bobbs-Merrill Co., copyright 1981, Marion Rombauer Becker tells the story of her mother's life and describes the evolution of the various editions of* The Joy of Cooking. *See also Anne Mendelson,* Stand Facing the Stove: The Story of the Women Who Gave America the Joy of Cooking, *New York: H. Holt, 1996, a more comprehensive and accurate account, but which does not mention the Canadian printings.*

O1057.1 [about 1942]
[An edition of *The Joy of Cooking*, Toronto: McClelland and Stewart]
CITATIONS: Brodie 5 Dec 1942
NOTES: In her December 1942 review, Jean Brodie was enthusiastic about *The Joy of Cooking:* 'It's a grand book, written in a friendly, intimate style.'

O1057.2 [copyright 1945]
—The / joy of / cooking / A compilation of reliable recipes / with an occasional culinary chat / by / Irma S. Rombauer / Illustrations by / Marion Rombauer Becker / The Bobbs-Merrill Company / Indianapolis // publishers // New York
DESCRIPTION: 20.5 × 14.0 cm   Pp [1–10] 11–884   Illus headpieces for chapters   Cloth, with diamond pattern
CONTENTS: 1 ht; 2 blank; 3 tp; 4 'Copyright, 1931, 1936, 1941, 1942, 1943 by the Bobbs-Merrill Company // Copyright, Canada, 1945 by McClelland & Stewart Limited // Printed in Canada T.H. Best Printing Co.,

Limited, Toronto'; 5 dedication to 'my friend Mary Whyte Hartrich'; 6 blank; 7 'Foreword' signed I.S.R.; 8 blank; 9 'Preface to the 1943 Edition' signed I.S.A.; 10 blank; 11–14 'Table of Contents'; 15 half-title; 16 blank; 17–822 text; 823–84 'Index'
COPIES: *Private collection
NOTES: In the 'Preface to the 1943 Edition' Rombauer refers to 'a number of emergency chapters added' because of wartime conditions and the introduction of ration cards in the United States. She also describes the book as a 'record of our American way of life.' There is a chapter of sugarless and sugar-saving recipes and a chapter about meat-stretching.

The copy of the 1945 Canadian edition described here has the label of the original bookseller (a Montreal department store) affixed to the front endpaper: 'Henry Morgan & Co. Limited Book Dept.' Another private collector has a copy of the 1945 McClelland and Stewart edition, where the information on p 4 differs slightly: Instead of 'Printed in Canada' by T.H. Best, it reads 'Printed and bound in Canada' by Best.

Another private collector reports in his possession a 1947 reprint of the McClelland and Stewart 1945 edition. This suggests that McClelland and Stewart did not pick up the new American 1946 edition, where Rombauer replaced the war-ration recipes with other material (although most of the book was printed from the 1943 plates). On the other hand, Spadoni/Donnelly No. 1641 (which describes a 1967 reprint) refers to an advertisement in the McClelland and Stewart Spring 1946 catalogue for a 'new completed [*sic*] revised edition,' a description that seems to refer to the American 1946 edition.

OTHER EDITIONS: Irma S. Rombauer and Marion Rombauer Becker, Toronto: McClelland and Stewart, Indianapolis: Bobbs-Merrill, [1967, c1964] (QMJ; United States: DLC); Toronto: T. Allen, [1972] (NSDB).

AMERICAN EDITIONS: *The Joy of Cooking: A Compilation of Reliable Recipes with a Casual Culinary Chat,* by Irma S. Rombauer, illus by Marion Rombauer, [St Louis: A.C. Clayton Printing Co., c1931], 3,000 copies printed (United States: DLC); [2nd ed.], Indianapolis and New York: Bobbs-Merrill Co., [c1936] (Great Britain: LB; United States: DLC); reprints in 1938, 1939, 1940, 1941 (United States: DLC), and possibly 1942 (all cited by Mendelson, pp 169, 170–1); retitled *The Joy of Cooking: A Compilation of Reliable Recipes with an Occasional Culinary Chat,* Indianapolis and New York: Bobbs-Merrill Co., [1943] (Great Britain: LB); Indianapolis and New York: Bobbs-Merrill Co., [c1946] (United States: DLC).

The Joy of Cooking, by Irma S. Rombauer and Marion Rombauer Becker, Indianapolis: Bobbs-Merrill, [1951] (United States: DLC); Indianapolis: Bobbs-Merrill, [1952] (United States: DLC); Indianapolis: Bobbs-Merrill, [1953] (United States: DLC); retitled *Joy of Cooking,* Indianapolis: Bobbs-Merrill, [1962] (AE, MW, OOSH; United States: DLC); Indianapolis: Bobbs-Merrill, [1963] (United States: DLC); Indianapolis: Bobbs-Merrill, [1964] (United States: DLC); New American Library, [c1964] (NFSG, OW); New York: New American Library (Signet), 1973 (NSHPL, NSHV); 1974 printing (NSH, NSKR); Indianapolis: Bobbs-Merrill, [1975] (NSHPL, NSKKR, OOP, OWA, QMBM; United States: DLC); New York: Macmillan, 1975 (AMICUS No. 6961440); Penguin Putnam, c1975 (NBS).

Joy of Cooking, by Irma S. Rombauer, Marion Rombauer Becker, and Ethan Becker, New York: Scribner, c1997 (United States: DLC).

Facsimile of the 1931 ed., with 'Foreword' by Edgar R. Rombauer, Jr, [New York: Scribner, copyright 1998] (United States: DLC, NNU).

75th anniversary ed., New York: Scribner, 2006 (OTMCL).

BRITISH EDITIONS: *The Joy of Cooking,* London and Toronto: J.M. Dent and Sons, [1945] (Great Britain: LB); adapted for use in England by M. Baron Russell, London: J.M. Dent and Sons, 1948 (Great Britain: LB); adapted for use in England by M. Baron Russell, London: J.M. Dent and Sons, 1952 [1953] (Great Britain: LB); 4th ed., London: J.M. Dent and Sons, 1963 (Great Britain: LB); London: Dent, 1974 (Great Britain: LB); *Joy of Cooking,* 5th ed., London: Dent, 1980 (AEU, BVA, OTMCL; Great Britain: LB).

Sugar-saving recipes

See O703.1 for other titles by the London Life Insurance Co.

O1058.1 [October 1942]
Sugar-saving / recipes / The London Life Insurance Company [cover-title]
COPIES: *Private collection
NOTES: The note on the first page, which is signed 'The London Life Insurance Company October, 1942,' refers to 'today's conditions of reduced sugar supplies' and states that the recipes have been tested by the Chatelaine Institute. 'Printed by the London Life Insurance Company, London, Canada' is on the back face of the binding.

The universal cookery book

O1059.1 1942
The / universal / cookery / book / over 1000 / tested and inexpensive / recipes including / many French dishes / and / how to mix cocktails / Toronto / The Musson Book Company Ltd. / 1942
COPIES: *Bookseller's stock
NOTES: 'Copyright, Canada, 1942 by the Musson Book Company Ltd. Toronto // Published by arrangement with W. Foulsham & Co., Ltd., London, England' is on the title-page verso. There are 1,017 recipes in twenty-one chapters.

BRITISH EDITIONS: *Foulsham's Universal Cookery Book,* London: W. Foulsham and Co., [about 1930] (Great Britain: LB); *The Universal Cookery Book,* London: W. Foulsham and Co., [1931] (Great Britain: LB); London: W. Foulsham and Co., [1935] (Great Britain: LB); 35th ed., London: W. Foulsham and Co., [1950] (Great Britain: LB).

Victory cook book

O1060.1 nd [1942]
V [Morse Code symbol '...–' superimposed over the letter V] / Victory cook book / tested recipes / Compiled / by / the Ladies' Aid / of / Central United Church / Stratford Ontario
DESCRIPTION: 23.0 × 15.0 cm   Pp [1–2] 3–52   Thin card; stapled
CONTENTS: 1 tp; 2 'Printed in Canada on Canadian paper // The B-H Press // Stratford, Ont.'; 3 'Preface' signed members of the Ladies' Aid; 4–51 text, including recipes credited with the name of the contributor, blank spaces for 'My Own Recipes,' and ads; 52 'Index' [i.e., table of contents] and ads
COPIES: *OTU (TX717 V53 1942 PAM VUAR)
NOTES: Advertisements on p 16 indicate that the book was published in 1942: One advertisement is for 'Mansion House for home cooked meals // J.H. Killer and Sons 1895 1942'; the other, for Stratford Tri-Pure Ice Co. Locker Service, announces that 'New Locker Room will be open March 1, 1943.' The OTU copy is signed on the title-page, in ink, 'Mrs. T.E. Dunn.'

Vitamins for victory

O1061.1 [1942]
"Vitamins for victory" / A collection of recipes compiled by / the St. Andrew's Club / of / Grace

United Church / Port Dover, Ontario / The thanks of the members of the club is extended to all who / assisted in making it possible to publish this book. / Price 35c / [ad for Patterson's Drug Store]

DESCRIPTION: 22.5 × 15.5 cm   Pp [1–2] 3–64   Paper; stapled

CONTENTS: 1 tp; 2 'Executive of St. Andrew's Club 1942' [list of names and positions], 'Cook Book Committee' [convenors: Mrs J.H. Misner and Mrs H.A. Guiler; advertising: Mrs J.H. Misner, Mrs H.A. Guiler, Mrs J.D. Struthers, Mrs T.G. Caley; recipes: Mrs W. Waters, Mrs L. Parker, Mrs G.W. Slocombe; compiling: Mrs M. Woodger, Mrs E. Hind, Miss E.C. Kolbe], and '"Beforehand we thank you / For buying our book; / 'Twill teach you and guide you / In learning to cook."'; 3 'Table of Weights and Measures'; 4 ads; 5 'Menu Hints' [in poem-form] and 'Index'; 6 ads; 7–63 recipes credited with the name of the contributor and ads; 64 blank for 'Memorandum' and poem beginning, 'We may live without poetry, music and art, ...' [from *Lucile*, Part I, Canto ii, by Owen Meredith, pseudonym of Edward Robert Bulwer-Lytton]

COPIES: *OWTU (G11240)

NOTES: The publication date, 1942, is on the front face of the binding; the printer, 'The Reformer Press, Simcoe,' is on the outside back face.

Wallace, Mrs Lily Haxworth (born London, England)

Wallace graduated from the National Training School for Cookery in London, England, and worked for the Rumford Chemical Works in London before moving to the United States (Allen, p 59). Wallace also wrote: The Modern Cook Book and Household Recipes, *revised and edited by Wallace, New York: Warner Library Co., 1912 (United States: DLC);* The Rumford Complete Cook Book, *Providence, RI: Department of Home Economics of the Rumford Co., [c1918] (United States: DLC);* The Woman's World Cook Book, *Chicago: Reilly and Lee Co., [1921] (Bitting, p 483);* Rumford Fruit Cook Book, *1927 (Allen, p 59);* Carving the Easy Way, *New York: M. Barrows and Co. Inc., 1941 (United States: DLC);* The New American Cook Book, *Wallace as editor-in-chief, New York: Books Inc., 1941 (United States: DLC);* The New American Etiquette, *Wallace as editor-in-chief, New York: Books Inc., 1941 (United States: DLC);* The Complete Vitamin Cook Book, *Jay Morton as editor-in-chief and Wallace as associate editor, New York: Books Inc., 1943 (United States: DLC);* Sea Food Cookery, *New York: Barrows and Co. Inc., [1944] (United States: DLC);* Egg Cook-

ery, *New York: M. Barrows and Co. Inc., [1945] (United States: DLC); and* Soups, Stews and Chowders, *New York: M. Barrows and Co. Inc., [1945] (United States: DLC);* Egg Cookery, *London: Cassell and Co., 1951 [1952] (Great Britain: LB).*

O1062.1   [1942]

[An edition of *Just for Two*, Toronto: McClelland and Stewart, $2.50]

CITATIONS: Brodie 12 Dec 1942

NOTES: The Canadian edition was probably the same length as the first American edition – 311 pp.

AMERICAN EDITIONS: *Just for Two*, New York: M. Barrows, 1942; *Just for Two Cookbook*, New York: M. Barrows, 1949; reprint of 1949, *Good Cooking for Two*, New York: Dover Publications, 1984 (all United States: DLC).

Wartime economy cook book

O1063.1   1942

Wartime / economy / cook book / compiled and published / by the / Ladies' Auxiliary / to / Barrie Lions Club / Our thanks are due to those who contributed / recipes, to all who in any way made pos- / sible the publication of this book, and especial- / ly to our advertisers, for whom we would ask / your generous patronage. / The entire proceeds from the sale of this / book are to be devoted to welfare projects [...] / Barrie, 1942

DESCRIPTION: About 23.0 × 15.0 cm [dimensions from photocopy]   Pp [1] 2–60   Stapled

CITATIONS: Sullivan 102

COPIES: OMSA   *Private collection

NOTES: The first section is recipes for cooking with honey. The recipes are credited with the name of the contributor. The cookbook was probably printed by Barrie Business College, whose advertisement on the outside back face of the binding describes the college as 'educators and printers.'

1942–5

A venture in fun

O1064.1   nd [about 1942–5]

A / venture / in fun [cover-title]

DESCRIPTION: 23.0 × 15.5 cm   Pp [i–ii], 1–46   Paper; stapled

CONTENTS: i untitled introductory note signed Venture Club of Toronto; ii 'Index'; 1 'On Being a Hostess'; 2–45 recipes, ideas and advice for entertaining, games, decorations, and ads; 46 untitled end note signed Venture Club of Toronto

COPIES: *Private collection

NOTES: The introductory note refers to this book, which brings new ideas for entertaining, as 'our debut in the editorial field.' Sales of the book were to make it possible for the Venture Club 'to bring ventures in fun to our girls in the Women's Royal Canadian Naval Service.' The note on p 46 states, 'Now that you have the necessary "passport," in the form of ideas, for your cruise of fun and laughter, nought remains for us but to bid you bon voyage ...'

There is a recipe on p 4 for Cheese Delights (Made with Unrationed Ingredients), which indicates that *A Venture in Fun* was published in the period when rationing was in place in Canada, from 1942 to 1947. An advertisement on p 13 suggests that the book appeared before the war ended: It asks those willing to rent space in their homes 'to the family of a soldier or a war worker' to contact the Toronto Housing Registry.

1943

Adam, Ann [pseudonym]

See O877.1 for information about Ann Adam and her books.

O1065.1   copyright 1943

The lunch box and / food saver / book / by Ann Adam / With foreword to / The Lunch Box Book / by Lionel Bradley Pett, Ph.D., M.D. / Director, Nutrition Services, / Department of Pensions and National Health / Published in support of / the Canadian Nutrition Programme / by / Appleford Paper Products Limited / Hamilton – Canada / Copyright, 1943

DESCRIPTION: 23.0 × 15.0 cm   Pp [1–3] 4–68   Fp illus col on p 66 of Appleford paper products; illus   Paper, with illus col on front of lunch box surrounded by lunch box foods; stapled

CONTENTS: 1 tp; 2 untitled publisher's introductory note; 3 foreword by Lionel Bradley Pett; 4 '"Eat Right to Feel Right"'; 5 'Canada's Official Food Rules'; 6–35 'Out with Monotony ... Bane of the Lunch Box!'; 36–63 'The Book of Left-overs'; 64–5 'Other Uses for ... Appleford Waxed Paper'; 66 fp illus col; 67–8 index

COPIES: *OGU (CCC TX715.6 A31)

NOTES: The note on p 2 makes the connection between nutritious lunches and good war work: 'The woman who packs a lunch box which nutrition experts would rate "Good," and which the war-worker or the child who carries it would rate as highly in terms of "good eating," is doing a genuine war job ...' Bradley Pett reports on p 3 that 'only 15 in every 100 lunch boxes examined by field workers ... could be rated "Good," when Nutrition Services made a survey of some 30 war plants in 1942.'

O1066.1   copyright 1943

The / meat extender / book / with roasting chart / and / Department of Agriculture cooking guide / also / a full color "pin-up" coupon value chart / All recipes tested in the / Homecraft Kitchens of / Ann Adam / Published in support of the Gov't. Meat Rationing Plan / by / Appleford Paper Products Limited / Hamilton Canada / Copyright, 1943

DESCRIPTION: 22.0 × 15.0 cm   Pp [1] 2–35 [36]   1 fp illus col on p 34 of Appleford paper products, illus   Thin card; stapled

CONTENTS: 1 tp; 2 untitled publisher's introduction; 3–5 'Meat Is Valuable – Make the Most of It!' signed Ann Adam; 6–33 recipes with cooking guide on pp 18–19; 34 fp illus col; 35 index; 36 blank for 'Other Meat Recipes'

COPIES: *OGU (CCC TX715.6 A315)

NOTES: The publisher's introduction explains why it is necessary to ration meat in Canada, tells where Canadian meat goes to help the war effort, and says that 'Planning ... selecting ... storing ... cooking ... extending' are all things which will help to make the most of a family's meat supply. The recipe titles are followed by the stretching agent, for example, 'Double-Crust Meat Pie // Stretching Agent // gravy, pastry, vegetables' or 'Kidney Loaf // Stretching Agent // bread.' The 'pin-up' coupon chart, cited on the title-page, was probably not bound into the volume, and is missing from the OGU copy.

O1067.1   nd [about 1943]

New / ideas / for / praise winning / meals and / parties / by / Ann Adam [cover-title]

DESCRIPTION: 18.0 × 12.5 cm   Pp [1–2] 3–13 [14]   Illus col, illus   Paper, with image on front of a woman holding a cheese tray; stapled

CONTENTS: 1 cover-title; 2 'For the Queen of the Party or ... the Man of the House ...'; 3 introductory text, 'The Ingersoll Cream Cheese Co. Limited Ingersoll Ontario Canada // The oldest Canadian manufacturer of packaged cheese,' and index; 4 'Salads'; 5 'Party Recipes'; 6–7 'The Hostess Tray Says "Help

Yourself"'; 8–9 centre spread illus col of various prepared cheese dishes; 10–11 'A Party in Itself! Or Prelude to a Grand Affair ... The Trayful of Hors d'Oeuvres That Go 'Round and 'Round'; 12–13 'For Budget Menus'; 14 'Ingersoll // The Pioneer Cheese District'; inside back face of binding map of Oxford County, Ontario, 'Home of Ingersoll Cheese'

COPIES: OGU (2 copies: CCC TX715.6 A316, TX715.6 M572 No. 6) QMM (RBD ckbk 1243) *Private collection

NOTES: This book about cooking with cheese was likely published about 1943: The text on p 14 refers to Farrington, Adams, and Andes Smith being responsible for starting the art of cheese-making in Canada, then comments, 'which in the last seventy-seven years has grown to be one of Canada's most important industries'; and there is an illustration of the mammoth cheese made in 1866 at the Harris factory (1866 + 77 years = 1943). The subject of parties, however, suggests publication outside wartime.

Canada, Department of Agriculture

For a list of other cookbooks published by the Department of Agriculture, see O404.1.

O1068.1 May 1943
Publication 751 / Household Bulletin No. 20 / Issued May, 1943 / Dominion of Canada – Department of Agriculture / Wartime canning / jams and jellies / Consumer Section / Marketing Service / Published by authority of the Hon. James G. Gardiner, Minister of Agriculture, / Ottawa, Canada / 200M–6720–5:43 [cover-title]
DESCRIPTION: 24.5 × 16.5 cm Pp [1–2] 3–15 Paper; stapled
CONTENTS: 1 cover-title; 2 'Steps in Canning'; 3 'Home Canning of Fruits and Vegetables' [introductory text about the importance of home canning in wartime] and 'Spoilage of Canned Foods'; top–mid 4 'Steps in Canning'; bottom 4–5 'Preparation'; top–mid 6 'Canning Fruit without Sugar,' 'Methods of Packing,' and 'Filling Sealers'; bottom 6–top 8 'Processing or Sterilizing'; mid 8 'Sealing'; bottom 8–mid 9 'Storing'; mid–bottom 9 'Approximate Yield of Canned Fruit – Jam – Jelly'; 10 'Time Table for Fruits'; 11 'Time Table for Vegetables'; top 12 'General Directions for Making Jam'; mid 12–mid 14 'Recipes'; mid 14–top 15 'General Directions for Making Jelly'; near top 15–bottom 15 'Rose Hip Juice,' 'Pectin Test,' 'Beans in Brine,' 'Sauerkraut,' and 'Storing, Home Drying and Freezing'

CITATIONS: Ag 1867–1974, pp 23 and 42 CCat No. 22, p X4
COPIES: *AEAG MWPA (MG14 C50 McKnight, Ethel) OKITJS (992.11.4) OOAG (630.4 C212 P751, 3 copies; 630.4 C212 HB20, 3 copies) OONL (COP.CA.A.3684, 2 copies)
NOTES: This is likely the 'Wartime Jams, Jellies and Pickles leaflet' cited by Newman as produced in 1944.

O1068.2 May 1943
—Publication 751 / Bulletin de la ménagère n° 20 / Publié en / mai 1943 / Dominion du Canada – Ministère de l'agriculture / Conserves de guerre / confitures et gelées / Section des consommateurs / Service des marchés / Publié par ordre de l'hon. James G. Gardiner, ministre de l'agriculture / Ottawa, Canada / 75M–6720–7:43 [cover-title]
DESCRIPTION: 24.0 × 15.5 cm Pp [1–3] 4–16 Paper; rebound in cloth, together with other Household Bulletins
CONTENTS: 1 cover-title; 2 blank; top 3 'Mise en conserve de fruits et de légumes'; mid 3–top 4 'Décomposition des conserves'; mid 4 'La fabrication des conserves'; bottom 4–top 6 'Préparation'; near top–bottom 6 'Conserves de fruits sans sucre,' 'Mise en conserves,' and 'Remplissage des bocaux'; 7–mid 8 'Traitement ou stérilisation'; mid–bottom 8 'Bouchage' and 'Mise en réserve'; 9 'Tableau de la durée de la stérilisation pour les fruits'; 10 'Tableau de la durée de la stérilisation pour les légumes'; top 11 'Rendement approximatif des conserves de fruits – confitures – gelées'; mid 11–top 12 recipes for Jus de rhubarbe, Jus de raisins, Jus de tomates, and Soupe aux tomates; mid 12 'Instructions générales pour faire les confitures'; bottom 12–mid 15 'Recettes'; mid–bottom 15 'Instructions générales pour faire la gelée'; 16 recipes for Essai de pectine, Haricots (fèves) conservés dans la saumure, and Choucroute, 'Encavage, dessiccation et congélation,' and at bottom p 16, 'Ottawa: Edmond Cloutier, imprimeur ... 1943.'
CITATIONS: Ag 1867–1974, pp 7 and 31
COPIES: *OOAG (630.4 C212 HB20)

O1069.1 rev. ed., October 1943
Wartime sugar savers / Issued by / Consumer Section – Marketing Service / Dominion Department of Agriculture / [introductory text beginning, 'These practical, wartime recipes have been "tested / and approved" in Canada's Kitchen ...'] / Revised October 1943 Ottawa, Canada [cover-title]
DESCRIPTION: 21.5 × 14.0 cm Pp [1] 2–16 Paper; stapled

CONTENTS: 1 cover-title and introductory text; 2 'Tips to Save Sugar'; 3–16 recipes

CITATIONS: Ag 1867–1974, p 174

COPIES: *OOAG (641.55 C212)

NOTES: The text on p 1 says: 'Alternatives for sugar are not suggested. Designed to stretch your sugar ration, each recipe calls for only a moderate amount of sugar.' It adds, 'Butter rationing has been taken into account in these recipes'; and butter is 'only included where the butter flavour is especially desirable.'

An earlier, undated edition of this booklet at OOAG (641.55 C212), also called *Wartime Sugar Savers*, is only 11 pp on six sheets of paper, stapled once at the top left corner.

I have also seen a 12-page publication called *Sugar Savers*, issued by the Consumer Section, Marketing Service, Department of Agriculture, and described as 'Revised, January 1946,' where the sheets are folded in thirds and stapled at one edge to the cover.

O1069.2 1947

—"Sugar / savers" / kitchen-tested / ration stretchers / Prepared by / Consumer Section, Marketing Service, / Department of Agriculture, Ottawa. [cover-title]

DESCRIPTION: 21.5 × 14.0 cm   Pp [1] 2–15   Paper, with plaid pattern and image on front of 1946–7 calendar and two faceless, miniature, aproned women stretching a ration book across the calendar; stapled

CONTENTS: 1 cover-title; 2 'Sugar Savers' and 'To Save Sugar'; 3–mid 15 recipes; bottom 15 index; outside back face of binding 'Ottawa // Edmond Cloutier ... King's Printer and Controller of Stationery 1947 // 9919–30M–1246'

CITATIONS: Ag 1867–1974, p 174   Ferguson/Fraser, p 234, illus col on p 103 of closed volume

COPIES: AEAG   OOAG (641.55 C212)   SMELM *Private collection

NOTES: The selection of recipes closely follows O1069.1. 'Wartime' has been dropped from the title, but rationing was still in place. Unlike the plain earlier versions, this post-war edition is attractively designed: It has a pink-plaid pattern on the binding, pink recipe titles, and better-quality paper.

Cook book

O1070.1   nd [about 1943]

Cook book / tested recipes / Price 25¢ / Compiled and arranged by / the Ladies Guild of / the Church of / St. Andrew Memorial / Wellington Rd. S. London, Ont. [cover-title]

DESCRIPTION: 22.5 × 15.0 cm   Pp 1–48   Photograph on p 1 of the interior of the Church of St Andrew Memorial, a few other illus   Very thin card, with image on front of a male chef carrying a pig's head on a platter; stapled

CONTENTS: Inside front face of binding 'Weights and Measures,' 'Roasting,' and 'How Many Cups to a Can'; 1 'Thank You' and below the photograph of the church interior, 'Erected 1941, Wellington Road at Foxbar // Rev. Alford Abraham, Lth. ...'; 2–48 recipes credited with the name of the contributor, other culinary and household information, blank space for 'Memorandum or New Recipes,' and ads; inside back face 'Table of Measurements' and recipe for 'Hard Soap'

COPIES: *OL (London Room Box 179b)

NOTES: An advertisement on p 29 for 'Willmots' jewellery and gift shop refers to '50 years in business.' London city directories first list Norman F. Willmot, jeweller, in the volume for 1893; therefore, the cookbook was published about 1943 [1893 + 50 years]. The image on the binding is the same as O963.1, *Cook Book,* from another London church.

Cook book

O1071.1   1943

Lynrock Chapter / No. 154 / Order of the Eastern Star / Cook book / 1943 / Officers of chapter / [Left column:] Worthy Matron – Jeanetta Sager / Worthy Patron – Stanley Edworthy / Associate Matron – Bessie Knox / Associate Patron – Arthur Mannen / Secretary – Agnes Robertson / Treasurer – Jean Braithwaite / Conductress – Muriel Thompson / Associate Conductress – Lois Archer / Chaplain – Eunice Patrick / [Right column:] Marshall – Mabel Dewel / Organist – Vera Wood / Adah – Hattie Hunt / Ruth – Belle Robertson / Esther – Clara Edworthy / Martha – Evelyn Dayman / Electa – Pearl Weaver / Warder – Elizabeth Lawrason / Sentinel – Kathleen Nisbit

DESCRIPTION: 23.0 × 15.0 cm   Pp [1] 2–58   Paper, with image on front of Union Jack and Red Ensign; stapled

CONTENTS: 1 tp; 2 'Weights and Measures,' 'A Beautiful Recipe' [i.e., poem by Mrs Pearl Weaver], and 'Appreciation' [acknowledgments]; 3–56 recipes credited with the name of the contributor and ads; 57–8 'Household Hints' credited with the name of the contributor

COPIES: *Private collection

NOTES: There are several recipes adapted to food short-ages: Wartime Dinner, Wartime Recipe, and Wartime Meat Dish (p 7); Wartime Butter (p 33), made from butter, Crisco shortening, salt, and cream; Canada War Cake (p 35); and Sugarless Cake (p 40). No place of publication is recorded, but the advertisements are for businesses in Troy, Galt, Dundas, Waterdown, St George, Lynden, Ancaster, and Hamilton, Ontario.

Cook book edition

See O749.1 regarding other cookbooks by the same newspaper.

O1072.1   29 May 1943

Daily Standard-Freeholder / Cornwall, Ontario, Saturday, May 29, 1943 / 1943 / Cook book / edition / The war will never be won / without you Mrs. Housewife! / You're the woman behind the / meals at your house. Food is your / ammunition – know how to use / it, for good foods – the right / foods – are brawn, brain and / beauty. Food can make our nation / strong – but it's up to you. / In presenting this annual cook / book edition, the Daily Stand- / ard-Freeholder has endeavoured to / feature a variety of wartime recipes / – many contributed by our own / subscribers – to aid you in serv- / ing nutritious and well balanced / meals. / Buy wisely – Cook carefully / – Do with less so they'll have enough [cover-title]

DESCRIPTION: Pp [1] 2–20   Illus   Paper, with image on front of a woman pouring liquid into a saucepan and, below right of this image, individual dishes, such as a pie, loaf, casserole, doughnuts, cake, etc.

CONTENTS: 1 cover-title; 2–20 recipes, some credited with the name and address of the contributor, and ads

CITATIONS: MacGillivray, p 46

COPIES: *OONL (microfilm, AMICUS No. 8445734)

NOTES: Most of the captions to the illustrations exhort the reader to help the war effort: 'Serve him fighting foods'; 'Fight the Axis with recipes as well as rifles' with the image of a woman carrying an over-size wooden spoon on her shoulder, like a rifle; 'Waste helps the Axis! Be a waste-warden'; and 'The kitchen moves up to the battle front' with a line of women carrying wooden-spoon 'rifles' advancing toward artillery and fighter planes.

Delicious mustard and spice recipes

For the titles of other cookbooks by Gorman, Eckert and Co., see O445.1.

O1073.1   nd [about 1943]

Delicious mustard and / spice recipes / compiled by / Gorman, Eckert & Co. Ltd. / Index: / Page [above column of page numbers] / Introduction 1 / Mayonnaise Dressings 3 / Mayonnaise Sauces 8 / Salads 10 / Pickles 12 / Sandwiches 16 / Various Dishes 18 / Spices and Condiments 29 / For the medicinal uses of Gorman's Mustard / see page 24

DESCRIPTION: 15.0 × 9.5 cm   Pp [i–ii], 1–46   Paper, with image on front of a bottle of Club House Cinnamon and a container of Gorman's Mustard; stapled

CONTENTS: i tp and 'Index' [i.e., table of contents]; ii blank; 1–45 text; 46 list of Club House products and at bottom, 'Gorman, Eckert & Co., Ltd. London – Canada'

COPIES: OAYM   OONL (TX715.6 C58 1940z p***) *Private collection

NOTES: The cover-title is 'Club House Brand Canadian Housewife Recipe Book // Delicious Mustard and Spice Recipes.' The following is on the outside back face of the binding: 'For 60 years // Gorman, Eckert & Co. Ltd. London 1883 Canada.' This indicates a publication date of 1943 (1883 + 60 years).

Economy recipes for Canada's 'housoldiers'

See Q284.1 for this cookbook published simultaneously in Montreal and Toronto.

Gibson, Josephine

See O791.1 for Gibson's other works.

O1074.1   copyright 1943

Wartime canning / and / cooking book / Dedicated to the Canadian / homemaker whose time / is so generously devoted / to the war effort / Learn how to make cooking and / canning easy! / Substitutions! Balanced menus! / Meatless meals! Ingenious Menus! / Preserving and Canning!

DESCRIPTION: 22.5 × 14.5 cm   Pp [1] 2–64   Tp illus of 1-cm-high maple leaf, illus   [$0.25, on binding]   Paper, with small still-life on front of foodstuffs; stapled

CONTENTS: Inside front face of binding 'Foreword' and at bottom, 'Copyright 1943 Vital Publications,

206 Dundas St. W., Toronto'; 1 tp; 2–mid 4 'Keeping Your Family Fit in Wartime'; bottom 4 'Planning Rationed Menus'; 5 'A Week's Menus for a Family of Four'; 6–8 'Hearty Soups in Rationed Menus'; 9–11 'The Wartime Lunch Box'; 12–20 'Meat Stretching Dishes'; 21–9 'Meals without Meat Conserve Ration Coupons'; 30–2 'Colorful Salads of Vitamins and Victory'; 33–4 'Bread and Rolls in the Wartime Menu'; 35 'Wartime Substitutions and Helps'; 36–44 'Tempting Desserts Despite Rationing'; 45–64 'Canning, etc.'; inside back face table of contents; outside back face 'Wartime Substitutions'
CITATIONS: Ferguson/Fraser, p 234, illus col on p 103 of closed volume
COPIES: *Private collection
NOTES: 'How to Eat Well though Rationed // Edited by Josephine Gibson // Wartime Canning and Cooking Book // Printed in Canada 25c' is on the front face of the binding.

The golden anniversary cook book library

See also O207.1 from the same church.

O1075.1   1943
[An edition of *The Golden Anniversary Cook Book Library*, presented by the Women's Association, St Giles United Church, Hamilton, Ontario, 1943]
COPIES: Private collection

Helpful hints for housekeepers [1943]

See O263.1 for information about the company and other issues of Helpful Hints for Housekeepers.

O1076.1   1943
Dodd's / helpful / hints / for / housekeepers [cover-title]
DESCRIPTION: 18.0 × 12.5 cm   Pp 1–32   Illus   Paper, with image on front, in oval frame, of a woman's head; stapled, and with hole punched at top left corner for hanging
CONTENTS: 1 'Home Hints' and 'Handy Household Calendar 1943–4'; 2–32 recipes, health advice, household information, and publ ads
COPIES: *AEEA   OTUTF (uncat patent medicine)
NOTES: 'CE-43' is printed on the outside back face of the binding.

London Home and School Council cook book

O1077.1   nd [about 1943]
London / Home and School / Council / cook book / A collection of tried and / tested recipes / selected and arranged for publication / by / the members of the London / Home and School Council / affiliated with the Ontario and National and International / Federation of Home and School Associations. / London – Ontario
DESCRIPTION: 22.5 × 15.0 cm   Pp [1] 2–112   Paper; stapled
CONTENTS: 1 tp; 2–3 'Roster of London Home and School Council Executive,' 'Conveners,' 'Representatives,' and 'Association Presidents'; 4 'Printed in London by R.F. Fielding Co.'; 5 'Preface'; 6–111 text, mainly recipes credited with the name of the contributor, blank spaces for 'New Recipes,' and ads; 112 'Index' [i.e., table of contents] and ads
COPIES: *OL (London Room Box 369)
NOTES: This cookbook was not apparently published to raise money for the Home and School Council, but 'to make available ... some recipes which have been proven through long use by our members' (p 5). There is an advertisement on p 24 for Gorman's Pure Mustard, 'for 60 years Gorman's Pure Mustard has set the standard for all Canada,' and the advertisement records 1883 as the year that Gorman Eckert and Co. Ltd of London, Ontario, was established; therefore, the cookbook was published about 1943 (1883 + 60 years). The wartime publication date is confirmed by the advertisement on p 30 that exhorts the reader to 'buy more bonds for victory!'

Middleton, Miss Elspeth Munro (Toronto, Ont., 7 December 1893–5 September 1962, Victoria County, Ont.), Miss Muriel Eleanor Ransom [Mrs Robert Clifford Carter] (1912–), and Albert Vierin (Romanel, Switzerland, 10 April 1893–28 May 1976, East York, Ont.)

Middleton, Ransom, and Vierin also co-wrote O1187.1, 100 to Dinner.

Elspeth Middleton, the daughter of Mr and Mrs Lilias Middleton, received her BA in household science from the University of Toronto in 1915. In 1943, she left her teaching post at Toronto's Central Technical School to be an 'instructor in the new cooking school at H.M.C.S. Cornwallis, Nova Scotia, where classes include both sailors and Wrens' ('Plotting Way to Navy's Heart,'

Evening Telegram (Toronto) 20 December 1943, includes a photograph of Middleton). She 'died suddenly as the result of an accident' on Highway 35 North in Victoria County, Ontario. She is buried in the Necropolis in Toronto. Her obituary is in the Toronto Star, 8 September 1962, and in the Globe and Mail on the same date. See also her file at OTUAR (A73-0026/321 (33)). For a book co-written by Elspeth Middleton and Miss Charlotte Ruth Dean, see O751.1, Junior Home Economics.

Muriel Ransom was the daughter of J. Milton Ransom and Jennie B. Weston, and wife of Robert Clifford Carter. She received her BA in home economics from Victoria College, University of Toronto, in 1934. After graduating, she worked for a summer at the Bigwin Inn in Muskoka, north of Toronto, followed by seven months as a dietitian at the Montreal General Hospital, then two and a half years in charge of the Men's Grill at Eaton's department store in Toronto, working under Miss Violet Ryley. In fall 1938, still only in her twenties, she became supervisor of the Great Hall at Hart House, University of Toronto, at that time an institution exclusively for male students. An article in the Varsity about her appointment refers to the invasion by a female of 'the last stronghold of masculinity on the university campus.' Another Varsity article quotes her as saying that the masculine appetite was easy to satisfy: 'It is really no trouble preparing meals for men.' On 22 May 1939 she was in charge when King George VI and Queen Elizabeth dined at Hart House during their tour of Canada. See articles about Ransom, including photographs, at OTUAR in file A73-0026/372 (80).

Albert Vierin was born in a mountain village, a few kilometres from Lausanne, and had two brothers and one sister. Their father, who was a contractor, moved the family to France, where Albert found a job as a messenger boy in a restaurant, started an apprenticeship as a cook, and later worked in resort hotels in Europe. In April 1914, Albert emigrated to New York City. He worked at the Waldorf, the Claridge, and the Beaux Arts hotels, before, as a French-speaker, being drawn to Montreal, where he met his future wife Letitia Frances Piton and worked at the St James Club. This was followed by a stint as chef at the Rideau Club in Ottawa, and a job at the Bigwin Inn. By 1920 Vierin had moved to Toronto, where he had a varied career: first chef at the Georgian Room at Eaton's, with Violet Ryley; chef to King George VI and Queen Elizabeth during their 1939 tour of Canada; in 1945, organizing cooking classes at a rehabilitation centre for returning servicemen, to train them as bakers and cooks; catering for Trans-Canada Air Lines; and running the Skipper Restaurant at Queen's Quay, as a part-owner

with Paul Phelan. In addition to contributing to The Cook's Recipe Manual, Vierin wrote articles on culinary subjects for the Canadian Hotel Review and Restaurant, a trade paper for chefs. The Vierins had three children, Robert, Norman, and Victor, and two grandchildren, Karen and Douglas. Husband and wife are buried in Pine Hills Cemetery in Toronto. For photographs of Albert and information about him, see Betty Laidlaw, 'Liberty Profile: Albert Vierin,' Liberty Vol. 22, No. 15 (14 April 1945), pp 12–13; and Anderson/Mallinson, p 49. His obituary is in the Toronto Star, 1 June 1976.

O1078.1 [January 1943]
The cook's / recipe manual / by / Miss E. Middleton, B.A. / member of the Home Economics Dept. / Central Technical School, Toronto / in charge of classes for army cooks / Miss M. Ransom, B.A. / Superintendent of the Great Hall / Hart House, University of Toronto / Albert Vierin / Chef of the Georgian Room / The T. Eaton Co. Ltd., Toronto / Toronto / The Ryerson Press
DESCRIPTION: 20.0 × 12.0 cm   Pp [1–8] 9–225 [226] Illus of cuts of meat   Thin card; Wire-O Binding
CONTENTS: 1 tp; 2 'Copyright, Canada, 1943, by the Ryerson Press, Toronto ... Published January, 1943 ... Acknowledgments ... to Miss J. Lambden, B.A., Director of the R.C.A.F. School of Cookery, Guelph; to Mr. J.R. Gilley of Hart House, University of Toronto; to the Home Economics Association of Toronto; ... Printed and bound in Canada by the Ryerson Press, Toronto'; 3 'Foreword'; 4–220 text; 221–5 index; 226 'Wire-O Binding Patented 1936'
CITATIONS: CCat No. 21, p W18   Driver 2001, Wellington County, p 95   Ferguson/Fraser, illus col on p 100 of front face of binding   THEA 1988, pp 10–11, illus
COPIES: AEU   OH (R641.57 M584 CANA)   *Private collection
NOTES: The 'Foreword' states: 'This book is designed as a guide for cooks in the armed forces, munition plants, industrial plants and camps – or wherever large numbers are served. The tested recipes are based primarily on foods provided in the army rations ... Each recipe yields 100 servings ...'

Some of the recipes in the book came from a project run by the Toronto Home Economics Association in 1939, to develop recipes based on the standard army ration. The project was initiated when Miss Middleton was asked to run an experimental course for training army chefs, at Brampton, Ontario, by Lieutenant-Colonel Louis Keene, who was concerned about the nutritional value of army rations and that army cooks have proper training. Information about the project and an illustration of the binding of *The Cook's Recipe Manual* are in THEA 1988, pp 10–11.

The publisher's record for the cookbook is at OTCC (Acc. 83.061C, UCC Board of Publication Series I, Box 3, File 2, 'Notebook, 1940–1942'). Under the title, 'The Cook's Recipe Book,' is the specification for the book, dated December 1942, which includes information about authors' royalties and that two thousand copies were to be printed.

CCat records 1942 as the year of publication, and $2.00 as the price. The book is not cited in Wallace.

The catalogues of MWU and, in the United States, MCR (641.57 M62) record a 1943 edition, but do not specify which printing. The MWU copy was not on the shelf in June 1993.

In Wilson July 1991, one learns that Lorna Burchell Hicks's daughter Beth used *The Cook's Recipe Manual* when she cooked for Camp Allsaw.

O1078.2 [reprint, June 1943]
—The cook's / recipe manual / by / Elspeth Middleton, B.A. / member of the Home Economics Dept. / Central Technical School, Toronto / in charge of classes for army cooks / Muriel Ransom, B.A. / Superintendent of the Great Hall / Hart House, University of Toronto / Albert Vierin / Chef of the Georgian Room / The T. Eaton Co. Ltd., Toronto / The Ryerson Press
DESCRIPTION: 19.5 × 11.0 cm   Pp [1–8] 9–225 [226] Illus of cuts of meat   Thin card
CONTENTS: 1 tp; 2 'Copyright, Canada, 1943, by the Ryerson Press, Toronto ... Published January, 1943 // Reprinted June, 1943 // Acknowledgments ... to Miss J. Lambden, B.A., Director of the R.C.A.F. School of Cookery, Guelph; to Mr. J.R. Gilley of Hart House, University of Toronto; to the Home Economics Association of Toronto; ... Printed and bound in Canada by the Ryerson Press, Toronto'; 3 foreword; 4–220 text; 221–5 index; 226 'Canadian Patent 334331 License A'
COPIES: *OONL (TX820 M5)

Muskoka recipes old and new

O1079.1 1943
[An edition of *Muskoka Recipes Old and New*, Women's Association of Port Carling United Church, Port Carling, 1943, pp 80]
COPIES: Private collection

Practical cookery

O1080.1 February 1943
Practical cookery / In presenting this collection of prac- / tical, tested recipes, the Service Group of / the Women's Association, Trinity United / Church, Smiths Falls, desires to assist in the / national campaign for better nutrition. / Most of the recipes have been chosen with / a view to their nutritive value and their / adaptability to the restrictions on foods, / which are essential in this time of war, but / a few others, especially recommended, will, / we hope, prove useful as soon as a wider / variety of foods is available. / To the business men of our town, whose / generosity has made possible the publication / of this book, we express our sincere thanks, / and our hope that they will receive the pat- / ronage of all who benefit by the book. / [first column of names:] Mrs. Harold Amy / Mrs. O.C. Connerty / Mrs. A.E. Dobbie / Mrs. J.A.B. Dulmage / Mrs. R.E. Helmer / Mrs. L.A. Hetanen / Mrs. Chas. Henniger / Mrs. A.D. Hudson / Mrs. J.C. Ketchum / Mrs. J.G. Maxwell / Miss Mary McCallum / [second column of names:] Mrs. A.J. McCaw / Mrs. C.H. McKimm / Mrs. G.W. Mulligan / Mrs. R.J. Prescott / Mrs. R.H. Purcell / Mrs. H.G. Robertson / Mrs. H. Shane / Mrs. P. Strader / Mrs. H.A. Stewart / Mrs. W.R. Tanton / Mrs. A.J. Whalen / Smiths Falls, Ontario. February, 1943. / [folio:] 1
DESCRIPTION: 20.0 × 15.0 cm   Pp 1–64   Paper, with image on front of large letter V for victory; stapled
CONTENTS: 1 tp; 2 ad; 3 'Index' and 'Grace before Meals'; 4 ads; 5–64 recipes and ads
COPIES: *Private collection   OSMFHHM

Recipes for today

O1081.1 [copyright 1943]
Recipes / for today [cover-title]
DESCRIPTION: 20.0 × 11.0 cm   Pp [1–2] 3–31 [32]   Illus red-and-black   Paper, with image on front of a woman carrying a steaming bowl and a cat walking beside her; stapled
CONTENTS: 1 cover-title; 2 fp illus of a woman reaching for Swans Down Cake Flour among several other General Foods products on shelves; 3 'Staunch Friends for Today's Kitchens' and at bottom, 'General Foods, Limited, Toronto, Ontario // 6917 Copyrite. [*sic*] 1943 General Foods, Ltd. Ptd. in Canada 38M.E. 8.43CC'; 4–31 recipes; 32 index
COPIES: *Private collection
NOTES: The text on p 3 turns the housewife's war-

time difficulties to General Foods Ltd's advantage: 'Today we are on rations! And because we must buy and use less, we cannot afford to invest in mistakes. So today's kitchens turn to dependable products – ' Other war-related sections are 'Main Dishes without Meat' on pp 14–15, 'Substitution Rules' on p 28, and 'Wartime Food Rules' on p 30.

O1081.2 [copyright 1943]
—Recettes / d'aujourd'hui [cover-title]
DESCRIPTION: 20.5 × 11.0 cm   Pp [1–2] 3–31 [32]   Illus red-and-black   Paper, with image on front of a woman carrying a steaming bowl and a cat walking beside her; stapled
CONTENTS: 1 cover-title; 2 fp illus of a woman reaching for Swans Down Cake Flour among several other General Foods products on shelves; 3 'Produits alimentaires qui ont fait leurs preuves' and at bottom, 'General Foods, Limited – Toronto, Ontario 6917 Droits réservés 1943 General Foods Ltd. Imprimé au Canada 17'M.F. 8.43CC'; 4–31 recipes; 32 index
COPIES: *OONL (TX715.6 R39 1943 p***)

Taylor, Mary Lippincott Richards (1874–)

O1082.1   1943
Economy for epicures / A practical menu and recipe / book / Mary L.R. Taylor / Oxford University Press 1943 / New York London Toronto
DESCRIPTION: Tp illus of foodstuffs
COPIES: *Private collection; Great Britain: LB (7946.b.42); United States: DLC (TX715 T247)
NOTES: DLC describes the book as having 511 pp. The second edition of 1947 was published only in New York.

AMERICAN EDITIONS: 2nd ed., New York: Oxford University Press, 1947 (Great Britain: LB; United States: DLC).

Victory cook book

See also O1155.1, Cook Book, *from the same church.*

O1083.1   [1943]
Victory / cook book / Our / favorite recipes / selected / by / the members / of / the Women's Association / of / St. James' United Church / Peterborough Ontario
DESCRIPTION: Pp [i–ii], [1] 2–92 [93]   Fp illus on p i of St James' United Church, corner Romaine and Aylmer

streets   With image on front of letter V for victory and the Morse Code symbol for V
CONTENTS: i fp illus of the church; ii blank; 1 tp; 2 'Roster // Officers of the Women's Association // St. James' United Church Peterborough, Ontario 1943'; 3 'Preface' signed the Committee; 4–90 recipes, some credited with the name of the contributor, and ads; 91 ad and 'Table Decorations'; 92 'Index' and ads; 93 blank for 'Victory Recipes'
COPIES: *Private collection

Victory recipes

O1084.1   nd [1943]
Victory recipes / Compiled by / the members of / the Women's Association / of / Knox Presbyterian Church / Guelph Ontario / [four paragraphs of introductory text] / [signed:] The members / [folio:] 1
DESCRIPTION: Pp 1–72   Stapled
CONTENTS: 1 tp and untitled introductory text; 2–70 recipes and ads; 71 blank for 'New Recipes'; 72 'Index' [i.e., table of contents] and ads
COPIES: *Private collection
NOTES: The text on p 1 refers to rationing, which began in 1942 in Canada. An advertisement on the inside back face of the binding pinpoints 1943 as the cookbook's year of publication: 'Robert Stewart Limited // lumber millwork // 1854–1943 ... founded 13 years before Confederation.'

Wartime suggestions

O1085.1   [copyright 1943]
Wartime / suggestions / to help you get the / most out of your / refrigerator / How to store and keep food properly under today's / conditions. Easy ways to give your refrigerator the best / of care. Tested recipes. Read and keep for future / reference. Published for all refrigerator users by Frigidaire / Division of General Motors. / Contains no advertising / (except on pages 32–33) [cover-title]
DESCRIPTION: 15.0 × 11.0 cm   Pp [1] 2–32   Illus   Paper, with small, stylized image on front of an eagle; stapled, and with hole punched at top left corner for hanging
CONTENTS: Inside front face of binding 'Contents' and 'Copyright 1943, Frigidaire Division, General Motors Corporation'; 1 'Foreword' signed Frigidaire Products of Canada Ltd, Toronto, Ontario, and Frigidaire Division, General Motors Corporation, Dayton, Ohio;

2 'Make Better Use of What You Have'; 3–24 text for 'Use of the Refrigerator' [includes recipes]; 25–31 text for 'Care of the Refrigerator'; 32 'Advertisement'
CITATIONS: CCat No. 22, p X17
COPIES: *Private collection
NOTES: 'HA 1259-1 1,000M – Printed in U.S.A.' is printed on the outside back face of the binding; 'Frigidaire Sales and Service // W.W. Hawley // Eastern Ontario distributor // 272 Princess St. – Kingston, Ont.' is stamped on the outside back face.

1943–4

Kitchen kraft

In the 1930s Erskine Church School compiled O712.1, Tested Recipes. Slipped into the back of the catalogued copy of O1086.1 is a later publication from the same church: 'Supplement to the Noble Workers' Cook Book // Erskine United Church 1955.'

O1086.1 nd [about 1943–4]
Kitchen kraft / A large and varied group of / carefully selected / recipes / arranged for publication by / the members of / the Women's Association / Erskine United Church / Roncesvalles and Wright / Toronto Ontario
DESCRIPTION: 22.5 × 15.0 cm Pp [1–3] 4–48 Thin card, with small image on front of an aproned woman consulting a cookbook, with bowl and ingredients before her; stapled
CONTENTS: 1 tp; 2 'Printed in Canada'; 3 'Preface'; 4–46 recipes credited with the name of the contributor, blank spaces for 'My Own Recipes,' and ads; 47 ad and 'Table Decorations'; 48 ads and 'Index' [i.e., table of contents]
COPIES: *Private collection
NOTES: The 'Preface' states that the cookbook is a 'means of providing revenue for the Association, whose object is to help the Board of Managers of our Church.' The typeface of the title 'Kitchen Kraft' on p 1 is the same as that used for 'Kitchen Kraft' on p 1 of O987.1.

An advertisement on p 20 for Hooker the Mover, 275 Roncesvalles Avenue, limits the time of publication to about 1943–4: Toronto directories list George A. Hooker at 275 Roncesvalles for only 1943 and 1944 (before 1943 he was on Dundas Street; after 1944, he was at 465 Roncesvalles). An advertisement on p 16 for Guest Hardware, which refers to a fuel-saving government measure, confirms publication during the Second World War: 'Owing to the government ruling all orders must be $1.00 or over.'

1944

Canada, Department of Agriculture

For a list of other cookbooks published by the Department of Agriculture, see O404.1.

O1087.1 [1944]
Wartime / home / canning / of fruits & vegetables / Prepared by the Consumer Section / Marketing Service / Dominion Department of Agriculture / Ottawa / Honourable James G. Gardiner, Minister [cover-title]
DESCRIPTION: 24.5 × 16.5 cm Pp [1] 2–15 [16] Illus Paper; stapled
CONTENTS: 1 cover-title; 2 'The Importance of Home Canning in Wartime' and 'Approximate Yields of Canned Fruits'; 3 'Quality of Fruits and Vegetables' and 'Equipment'; 4–11 'Steps in Canning'; 12–13 'Time Table for Fruits'; 14–15 'Time Table for Vegetables'; 16 [outside back face] 'Spoilage of Canned Food' and '200M–6-44 (A7542) K.P. 9718'
CITATIONS: Ag 1867–1974, p 174 Newman
COPIES: AEAG AHRMH (983-081-001) ARDA AWWDM BVAA (1944-103) OGU (CCC CA1 DA77 44W13, 2 copies) OOAG (641.634 C212) OONL (COP.CA.A.4379) *Private collection; United States: MCR (641.56 C2 and micro SLC #139)
NOTES: The text and illustrations are printed in the patriotic colours of red and blue. Newman states that the book was produced under the direction of Laura Pepper and that 200,000 copies of the 1944 edition were distributed within the first twelve months.

Canadian favourites

O1088.1 [1944]
Canadian favourites / cook book / compiled by a committee of C.C.F. / women from favourite recipes sub- / mitted by housewives across the country / Published under the auspices / of the / C.C.F. National Council / 56 Sparks St., Ottawa / [printer's union symbol] 100
DESCRIPTION: 23.0 × 15.0 cm Pp [i–iv] v [vi] vii [viii] ix–xii, 1–252 Paper, with small image on front of maple leaf
CONTENTS: i ht; ii blank; iii tp; iv blank; v 'Foreword' signed Lucy L. Woodsworth, Winnipeg, Manitoba, 1944; vi blank; vii 'Préface' [i.e., French translation of 'Foreword'] signed Lucy L. Woodsworth, but not dated; viii blank; ix–x 'Preface'; xi 'Contents' [i.e., chapter headings arranged alphabetically]; xii ad for Crystal Lake Campsite, C.C.F. Summer School; 1–242

text; 243 ad; 244–52 blank 'For Additional Recipes'
CITATIONS: Barss 1980, pp 40, 41, 72, 97, 101, 104–5, 111, 116, 117   Carrière No. 103   CCat No. 24, p Z20   Driver 2003, 'Canadian Cookbooks,' p 35   Ferguson/ Fraser, p 234   Garrett, pp 71, 131   Golick, pp 100–1   COPIES: AC (Pam file 641.5 Can)   BVIV   OGU (CCC TX715.6 C36, 2 copies)   OONL (TX715.6 C36 1944)   OTMCL (641.5 C585)   OTNY (uncat)   *Private collection
NOTES: Lucy Woodsworth was the wife of James S. Woodsworth, who had founded the Co-operative Commonwealth Federation in 1932. In the 'Foreword' Lucy explains the ideals that lie behind the book:

> The publication of Canadian Favourites under the auspices of the Co-operative Commonwealth Federation is a matter of more than passing interest. Ours is a people's movement organized to make Canada a land in which opportunity for real living shall be the birthright of all her citizens.
>
> It is recognized that in this undertaking one of our immediate aims must be to develop a high standard of health. Hence quite naturally, our C.C.F. women have chosen to centre their first united effort upon food. This is a field in which woman has long had especial responsibility ...

The 'Preface' reiterates that the production of this cookbook is 'the first time in ... C.C.F. history when the women members of the party have undertaken a project on a national scale.' The Book Committee, named on p x, was composed of Mrs A.M. Nicholson, Mrs Stanley H. Knowles, Mrs David Lewis, Mrs Walter B. Mann, and Mrs P.E. Wright. The Book Committee admits that 'a number of the recipes may not be practicable during the war, owing to shortages and rationing'; however, the women point out that in a country the size of Canada, the shortages are not uniform, and they hope for peace soon. The text begins on pp 1–2 with a short section called 'Nutrition and the Good Daily Diet' by Margaret S. McCready.

The 'Foreword' is dated 1944; however, CCat records 1945 as the year of publication and $1.00 as the price. Barss 1980 reprints several recipes.

O1088.2   2nd ed., 1947
—Canadian favourites / cook book / compiled by a committee of CCF / women from favourite recipes sub- / mitted by housewives across the country. / First edition, 1944 / Second edition, 1947 / Published under the auspices / of the / CCF National Council / Woodsworth House / 301 Metcalfe St., Ottawa / [printer's trade symbol] 100
DESCRIPTION: 22.5 × 15.0 cm   Pp [i–iv] v [vi] vii–xi

[xii], 1–301   Tp illus of maple leaf   Thin card, with image on front of maple leaf; sewn
CONTENTS: i ht; ii blank; iii tp; iv blank; v 'Preface to Second Edition' dated Ottawa, May 1947; vi blank; vii–viii 'Preface to First Edition' signed CCF Cook Book Committee [names of five members listed], Ottawa, 1944; ix 'Foreword' signed Lucy L. Woodsworth, Winnipeg, Manitoba, 1944; x 'Préface' [i.e., French translation of 'Foreword']; xi 'Contents' [i.e., chapter headings arranged alphabetically]; xii blank; 1–285 text and ads; 286 ads; 287–99 index; 300–1 blank 'For Additional Recipes'
COPIES: *BVAU   OONL (TX715.6 C36 1947)   SR (641.5 C)   SSA   SSWD   Private collection
NOTES: The 'Preface to Second Edition' says that 10,000 copies of the first edition 'were printed and sold in record time.' Regarding the second edition, it comments: 'No new recipes have been added, although a few changes have been made. The introductory article on "Nutrition and the Good Daily Diet" has been rewritten and brought up to date. The most useful feature added to this edition is a full index of all recipes, ...'

The SSA and SSWD copies are bound in cloth. The SSA copy, which was donated by a member of the original Book Committee, is inscribed on the front endpaper, in ink, 'Presented to the Saskatchewan Archives // Marion L. Nicholson // Convener, Canadian Favourites C.C.F. Cook Book Committee p. viii June 2, 1970.'

57 ways to use Heinz condensed soups

Regarding the H.J. Heinz Co., see O791.1.

O1089.1   [copyright 1944]
57 ways to use / Heinz / condensed soups [cover-title]
DESCRIPTION: 15.0 × 8.0 cm   Pp [1–3] 4–38   Illus   Paper, with photograph on front of a woman pouring a can of soup into a mixing bowl; stapled
CONTENTS: 1 cover-title; 2 'Copyright 1944 H.J. Heinz Company of Canada Ltd. 420 Dupont St. Toronto 4, Canada'; 3 untitled introductory text; 4–38 fifty-seven numbered recipes; inside back face of binding 'Index' [i.e., table of contents] and 'Litho in Canada 100M 3308'
COPIES: BNEM   *OTMCL (641.6 F57)
NOTES: The text on p 3 says of canned soup, 'Formerly served strictly as a first course, versatile soup now appears as an important ingredient in dozens of dishes – dressings, meat loaves, rarebits, casseroles ...' Recipe No. 57 is Tomato Soup Cake, still in

the repertoire of some twenty-first-century home cooks.

The BNEM copy has 'Printed in Canada 100M–3101' on the outside back face of the binding. In a variant at OGU (CCC TX715.6 F48), the printing information is 'Litho in Canada 100M 2746' and it appears on p 2, below the copyright information, not below the 'Index.' In another variant, at QMM (RBD ckbk 1660), 'Litho in Canada 100M 1215' is on p 2. In yet another variant, in a private collection, 'Printed in Canada 100M–1802' appears on the outside back face of the binding.

OTHER EDITIONS: *57 Ways to Use Heinz Condensed Soups*, [Leamington, Ont.: H.J. Heinz Company of Canada Ltd, copyright 1953] (QMMMCM).

AMERICAN EDITIONS: Pittsburgh: H.J. Heinz Co., nd [about 1947], 'SO-134/1047' on inside front face of binding (Private collection).

Hamilton, Board of Education

O1090.1   1944

Handbook / of / home / economics / for use in / elementary schools / of Hamilton / Hamilton Board of Education / 1944
DESCRIPTION: 22.0 × 13.5 cm   Pp [1–2] 3–62, [1–2], i–vii   Illus on p 9 of 'Breakfast Cover' and 'Luncheon Cover,' illus on p 12 of teaspoon and tablespoon measurements   Very thin card; stapled
CONTENTS: 1 tp; 2 'Foreword' signed Frank E. Perney, superintendent of schools; 3–62 text; 1 'Index' part-title; 2 blank; i–vii 'Index'
COPIES: *Private collection
NOTES: The 'Foreword' states, 'This booklet on Home Economics is intended primarily for the use of Grades VII and VIII students at school and at home.' Some of the recipes are the same as in O528.7, Toronto, Board of Education, *Handbook of Practical Cookery for the Use of Household Science Classes in the Public Schools of Toronto*; for example, Foamy Omelet and French Omelet (I was unable to compare the Hamilton book with the Toronto edition of the same year, O528.13).

Household helps for 1944

O1091.1   1944

Household / helps / for / 1944 / Published in the interests of / better housekeeping by / Tintex / the world's largest selling tints and dyes / Sold at drug, department and 10c. stores everywhere [cover-title]
DESCRIPTION: 21.5 × 14.0 cm   Pp [3] 4–47 [48–50]   Illus   Paper, with image on front of a woman carrying a broom and wearing a sandwich board on which the short-title is printed; stapled, and with hole punched at top left corner for hanging
CONTENTS: 3 'Introduction' and 'Index'; 4–7 'New Clothes for Old' by Kate Aitken, supervisor of conservation, Consumers Branch, Wartime Prices and Trade Board; 8–11 'Household Hints Start Here (336 of 'em!)'; 12–15 'Food Forecast for 1944' by Ann Adam, director of Ann Adam Homecrafters; 16–19 household hints; 20–2 'Don't Phone Mother' by Isobel Morrell, RN; 23–6 household hints; 27–30 publ ad for Tintex; 31 household hints; 32–5 'New Rooms for Old!' by Monica Mugan, CBC commentator; 36–9 household hints; 40–2 'Learn to Save Yourself' by Ethel Chapman, editor, Home Section, *The Farmer's Magazine*; 43–5 household hints; 46–7 continuation of 'Food Forecast for 1944'; 48–50 blank for '... Your Own Favourite Recipes'
COPIES: *Private collection
NOTES: A note on p 47 says that copies of the book will be sent free to women's clubs with a membership of fifteen or more; orders were to be addressed to Tintex, 159 Bay Street, Toronto. For cookbooks by Kate Aitken, Ann Adam, and Ethel Chapman, see the Name Index.

1944–5

Erskine cook book

O1092.1   nd [about 1944–5]

Erskine / cook book / Erskine Presbyterian Church / Hamilton, Ontario [cover-title]
DESCRIPTION: 22.0 × 15.0 cm   Pp [1] 2–52   Very thin card, with image on front of the church; stapled
CONTENTS: Inside front face of binding untitled four-line verse; 1 'Foreword'; 2–3 quotations from Shakespeare and Proverbs, three unattributed quotations, and poem beginning, 'We may live without poetry, music and art' [from *Lucile*, Part I, Canto ii, by Owen Meredith, pseudonym of Edward Robert Bulwer-Lytton]; 4–52 recipes credited with the name of the contributor, ads, and spaces for 'Memoranda' or 'My Own Recipes'
COPIES: *Private collection
NOTES: The 'Foreword' is a thank-you from the Ladies' Association. Advertisements on p 20 for Ryan's Flower Shoppe, 104 King Street West, and Toddle House, 545 York Street, suggest that the cookbook

was published about 1944–5. Mary Ryan's flower shop is listed in Hamilton city directories for 1942 through to 1944. The first listing for Toddle House restaurant is in the directory for 1945, in the street index; in previous directories, a restaurant is at the same address, but no name is recorded.

1945

Canada, Department of Agriculture

For a list of other cookbooks published by the Department of Agriculture, see O404.1.

O1093.1 nd [about 1945]
Recipe book / for / enjoying Canadian / apples / "The world's finest fruit" [cover-title]
DESCRIPTION: 15.0 × 15.0 cm   Pp [1–16] Illus Paper, cut in the shape of an apple and printed to resemble an apple; stapled
CONTENTS: 1–16 recipes
CITATIONS: FitzPatrickCat 111 (April 1993) No. 5
COPIES: ARDA BSUM OAYM ONM OTMCL (641.5971 H39 No. 107) *Private collection
NOTES: Printed on the outside back face of the binding is 'Serve apples daily and you serve your country too // Marketing Service // Dominion Department of Agriculture, Ottawa // Honourable James G. Gardiner Minister.' The OAYM copy is stamped on p 1, 'Vote Duncan G. Ross // Compliments Duncan G. Ross, M.P.' Another private collector's copy has 'Compliments Harold W. Timmins, M.P. Parkdale' stamped on p 1.

The stamps for Ross and Timmins help to determine the date of publication. Duncan Graham Ross was first elected to the House of Commons in 1935, re-elected in 1940, and defeated in 1945; therefore, his stamp, which asks the receiver of the book to vote for him, was made in 1935, 1940, or 1945, i.e., *Recipe Book for Enjoying Canadian Apples* was published no later than 11 June 1945, the date of Ross's last election. Harold Aberdeen Watson Timmins was elected in a by-election on 21 October 1946, and defeated in the election of 1949; therefore, he stamped the book in the period 1946–9. (James G. Gardiner was minister of agriculture from 4 November 1935 to 21 June 1957 – no help in pinpointing the year of publication.) The patriotic comment to 'serve your country' by serving apples daily suggests that the book was published in the war period; however, there is no specific reference to the war and the quality of the paper and colour printing seem an unlikely choice for the middle

of the war period. *Recipe Book for Enjoying Canadian Apples* was likely published about 1945.

This edition is not cited in Ag 1867–1974.

OTHER EDITIONS: Ottawa: Printed by Edmond Cloutier, King's Printer, for Consumer Section, Marketing Service, Department of Agriculture, 1950 (OGU, OONL).

Canada, Royal Canadian Air Force

O1094.1 1945
C.A.P. 434 / The Royal Canadian Air Force / recipe / manual / 1945 / "The health of the people is really the founda- / tion upon which all their happiness and all / their powers as a state depend." – Disraeli. / Ottawa / Edmond Cloutier / printer to the King's Most Excellent Majesty
DESCRIPTION: 21.5 × 14.0 cm   Pp [1–2] 3–244 Illus Cloth
CONTENTS: 1 tp; 2 blank; 3 preface signed Robert Leckie, air marshal, chief of the staff; 4 blank; 5 table of contents; 6 illus of 'Testing the Products at No. 1 R.C.A.F. Test Kitchen'; 7–236 text; 237–44 index
COPIES: QMAC (UC723 C35) *Private collection
NOTES: See also O1206.1, Canada, Department of National Health and Welfare, *Recettes – 100 portions pour les hommes qui travaillent dur*, which uses material from this book.

OTHER EDITIONS: *Royal Canadian Air Force Recipe Manual 1945*, Ottawa: Royal Canadian Air Force, 1956, 'Reprinted 1953, 1956' (OONL).

Canadian cook book for British brides

O1095.1 [1945]
Canadian cook book / for British brides / [symbol of Women's Voluntary Services, Canada] [cover-title]
DESCRIPTION: 21.5 × 14.0 cm   Pp [1] 2–32 Illus Paper; stapled
CONTENTS: 1 'A Word of Welcome' signed Women's Voluntary Services Division, Department of National War Services; 2 'New Lands // New Ways'; 3–top 5 'Canadian Meal Pattern'; mid 5–mid 6 'Appointments for Your Table'; bottom 6–top 8 'What You'll Need in the Kitchen'; mid 8–top 12 'To Help You When You Shop'; mid 12–14 'Measurements of a Good Cook'; 15–29 recipes; 30–1 'Where Can I Find Out'; 32 'Index to Recipe Section'
CITATIONS: Ferguson/Fraser, p 234, illus col on p 103 of closed volume

COPIES: OGU (UA s070 b89) *Private collection
NOTES: The date of publication is printed on the outside back face of the binding: 'Issued by Division of Women's Voluntary Services under the authority of the Hon. J.J. McCann // Minister of National War Services 1945.' 'A Word of Welcome' states: 'Now that thousands of you [British women], as wives of our sons and brothers, are coming from the old land to make your home in Canada we are anxious to extend a welcome – ... A practical form of welcome to the Canadian way of life is this little book which has been prepared in collaboration with the Consumer Sections of the Wartime Information Board and the Department of Agriculture.' Under 'New Lands // New Ways,' the text points out the differences from Britain of the Canadian kitchen, aspects of shopping (the way goods are displayed, the type of goods available and when available), names for familiar foods (for example, treacle/molasses, scrag end of lamb/neck of lamb), ways of cooking and serving, recipes, and foods. 'The Canadian Meal Pattern' offers illuminating detail about Canadian food habits; for example: 'Don't be surprised to see marmalade being eaten with bacon. It is one of those odd combinations of foods which taste so much better than they sound.'; or 'Canadians are very fond of all sorts of pickles and relishes ...'

'Where Can I Find Out' lists the names and addresses of provincial government services and refers to organizations in 'almost every town and city' that run 'special cookery classes for British brides or regular classes.' Four cookbooks are recommended: Nellie Lyle Pattinson's *Canadian Cook Book* (an eighteenth edition of which was published in November 1945, O506.18); Miss Jessie M. Read's *Three Meals a Day* (a fourth edition was published in 1945, O954.5); Marie Holmes's *Food from Market to Table*, 1940 (O1005.1); *Food and the Family Income* (1945 printing, Q272.2).

In 2005 Library Services of Citizenship and Immigration Canada published an edition with images and stories from Pier 21 Society, Halifax (OONMC).

Elm Grove Women's Institute recipe book

O1096.1 [1945]
Elm Grove Women's Institute / recipe book / Price 25c copy [cover-title]
DESCRIPTION: 17.5 × 14.0 cm   Pp [1–2] 3–112 Paper, with image on front of a woman breaking an egg into a bowl; stapled
CONTENTS: 1 'Being a collection of tested favourite

recipes of Institute members and friends. Elm Grove Women's Institute // Organized in 1939 with a membership of 18 // Present membership (1945) 44 // Printed by the Reporter, Sutton West' and poem beginning, 'We may live without poetry, ...' [from *Lucile*, Part I, Canto ii, by Owen Meredith, pseudonym of Edward Robert Bulwer-Lytton]; 2 ads; 3–106 text and ads; 107–12 blank for 'Personal Recipes'; inside back face of binding index
COPIES: *Private collection
NOTES: These recipes are characteristic of a book published at the end of the Second World War: Overseas Cake [fruit cake], p 3; War Cake, p 4; Pre-War Chocolate Cake, p 9; and Overseas Fruit Cake, p 14. Sutton West (so named in 1885, now called Sutton) is near Georgina, on the south side of Lake Simcoe.

Helpful household hints

See O650.1 for the titles of two other cookbooks by the same church.

O1097.1   1945
Helpful household / hints / Compiled by / Group Four / of the / Women's Association / of / Metropolitan United Church / London, Ontario / 1945
DESCRIPTION: 23.0 × 14.0 cm   Pp [1] 2–72 Paper; stapled
CONTENTS: 1 tp; 2 ad; 3 'Foreward' [*sic*]; 4 ads; 5 table of contents; 6 ads; 7–69 text and ads; 70–2 blank for 'Memo'
COPIES: *Private collection
NOTES: The text is organized alphabetically by topic, from 'Bathroom' to 'Woodwork.' Sections with culinary information include: 'Cooking,' pp 7–19; 'Canning,' p 19; 'Eggs,' pp 23–5; 'Fowl,' p 27; 'Fruit,' pp 27–9; 'Kitchen,' pp 33–6; 'Meat,' pp 39–41; 'Picnics,' p 47; 'Storage,' p 63; and 'Utensils,' pp 65–7. The printer's name, 'The Ledger Publishing Company Ltd.,' is on the outside back face of the binding.

Home feeding in emergency

O1098.1   nd [about 1945]
The / Canadian Red Cross Society / Ontario Division / Home feeding / in / emergency / Issued by / the Canadian Red Cross Society, Ontario Division / Toronto 5 [cover-title]
DESCRIPTION: 22.5 × 15.5 cm   Pp [1–3] 4–26 Paper; stapled

CONTENTS: 1 cover-title; 2 'Acknowledgement'; 3 'Unless otherwise stated, recipes make from 5 to 6 servings.' and list of abbreviations; 4–19 lessons numbered I–IX; 20–6 'Substitutes Which Can Be Used in Menus'
COPIES: *Private collection
NOTES: In 1945 the book's owner took a course, for which she received a dated certificate, that trained pupils to go into the home to nurse the sick when no professional nurses were available. *Home Feeding in Emergency* was the textbook for the course. There is a reference on p 5 to Q272.1, *Food and the Family Income*, second edition, which was copyrighted in 1941.

Kaye-Smith, Sheila (1887–1956)

This prolific English author wrote novels and books on literary subjects. There is a Sheila Kaye-Smith Society, based in the United Kingdom.

O1099.1 1945
Kitchen fugue / by / Sheila Kaye-Smith / Cassell / and Company, Ltd. / London, Toronto, Melbourne / and Sydney
DESCRIPTION: 18.5 × 12.0 cm Pp [i–iv] v [vi], 1–210 Cloth
CONTENTS: i ht; ii list of other titles written by the author; iii tp; iv 'Book production war economy standard // This book is produced in complete conformity with the authorized economy standards // First published ... 1945 Printed in Great Britain by Butler and Tanner Ltd., Frome and London F.945'; v table of contents; vi dedication; 1–210 text
COPIES: *OGU (UA s022 b20) OWTU (PR6021 A8K5 1945); Great Britain: LB (12359.f.46); United States: DLC (PR6021.A8 K5 1945a)
NOTES: The cookbook was published after the Second World War, but the recipes reflect the ongoing food shortages in Britain. Kaye-Smith comments on p 1: '... my subject, ... is cooking in war-time – rather, I should say war conditions, for peace does not have the same immediate effect in the kitchen as on the battlefield.'

AMERICAN EDITIONS: New York and London: Harper and Brothers, 1945 (United States: DLC).

Kitchen kraft

O1100.1 nd [1945]
Kitchen kraft / A collection of / tested recipes / Arranged and published by / the members of / the Home and School Council / Chatham Ontario
DESCRIPTION: 23.0 × 15.0 cm Pp [1] 2–96 Small tp illus of a woman's head Very thin card, with image on front of a wife serving her husband at the dining table; stapled
CONTENTS: 1 tp; 2 'Executive Roster of Chatham Home and School Council'; 3 'Preface'; 4–90 recipes credited with the name of the contributor; 91 ad and blank space for 'My Own Recipes'; 92 ads; 93 'Weights and Measures'; 94 ad and 'Time Tables'; 95 ad and 'Table Decorations'; 96 'Index' [i.e., table of contents] and ads
COPIES: *OGU (CCC TX715.6 H6369)
NOTES: There is an advertisement on p 38 for Maxwell and Co., which pinpoints the year of publication: '1919 – We are experts in keeping clothes new – 1945.'

MacFarlane, Miss Eva (16 July 1891– 1 January 1982)

Eva MacFarlane held the position of dietitian at the United Church Training School from 1927 to 1954, when she retired (see her file at OTCC). At the time the cookbook was published, the Training School was at 214 St George Street, Toronto. The institution was later renamed Covenant College, then, in 1970, the Centre for Christian Studies (after amalgamation with the Anglican Women's Training College). In 1998, it moved to Winnipeg.

O1101.1 1945
Fiftieth / anniversary / Cook book / United / Church / Training / School / Compiled by Eva MacFarlane, House Director / Mimeographed for the 50th anniversary / by the class of 1945 [cover-title]
DESCRIPTION: 14.0 × 21.5 cm Pp [1–34] Paper; bound with piece of wool through two punched holes
CONTENTS: 1–34 recipes
COPIES: *Private collection

The mixing bowl

O1102.1 nd [about 1945]
The / mixing bowl / Compiled by / the Almonte Farm Women's Club / Almonte – Ontario [cover-title]
DESCRIPTION: With border on front of alternating maple leaves and Union Jacks; stapled
COPIES: *Private collection

The mixing bowl

See O474.1 for the titles of other cookbooks from the same church.

O1103.1   nd [about 1945]
The / mixing bowl / Tested recipes / Our Greeting / To all women interested in the art of cooking, / these pages are offered by the compilers in the / hope that they may make the task of cooking a / joy and not a perplexing problem. / We desire to thank all kind contributors and / especially those who have advertised with us. We / would ask you to patronize these merchants as / it is their contributions that have made our under- / taking an assured financial success. / This book was compiled by the ladies of the / J.O.Y. Bible Class of Zion United Church, / Hamilton, Ont. / "I Guessed" / [poem beginning, 'I "guessed my pepper, / My soup was too hot."']
DESCRIPTION: 22.5 × 15.0 cm   Pp [1] 2–52   Paper; stapled
CONTENTS: 1 tp; 2 ads; 3–51 text, including recipes credited with the name of the contributor, and ads; 52 'Index' [i.e., table of contents]; inside back face of binding information about the church, including the name of the minister, George R. Service; outside back face 'Hamilton Printing Service, 83 John St. S.'
COPIES: *OH (R641.5 MIX CESH)   Private collection
NOTES: The cookbook was published when George Service was minister, from 1939 to 1947. It was likely published about 1945, since a private collector's copy is inscribed 'From Edie, March 2, 1945.'

Moore, Mary Allen (Mrs Harry Forrester Moore, divorced), née Clark (Hamilton, Ont., 21 February 1903–22 May 1978, Hamilton, Ont.)

For information about the author and her other cookbooks, see Q189.1.

O1104.1   nd [about 1945]
Fruit-Kepe / Reg'd / recipes / by / Mary A. Moore / This preserving process / was perfected by the National Fruit Research Station in Great Britain, / and officially introduced – by the Station's expert on preserving – over / the British Broadcasting Corporation's network in July, 1940. / In August, 1941, this same British formula was introduced to / Canadians at the Canadian National Exhibition (in the Governments' / Building – British Section).

Since that time the Fruit-Kepe method / has been widely used by many thousands throughout the Dominion, [...] Price 10c / Astone Products Company – Toronto 5, Canada / Printed in Canada [cover-title]
DESCRIPTION: 18.5 × 13.5 cm   Pp [1] 2–15 [16]   Illus Paper, with photograph on front of Mary A. Moore; loose leaves, not bound
CONTENTS: 1 cover-title; 2–mid 4 general instructions for preserving with Fruit-Kepe; mid 4–16 [outside back face] 'Recipes'
COPIES: *QMM (RBD ckbk 1842)
NOTES: The author's son confirmed that *Fruit-Kepe Recipes* was by his mother and that the photograph is of her (conversation, May 2001). The QMM copy retains the envelope in which the booklet was sent to the original owner: Mrs G.R. England, Sunset Cottage, Knowlton, Quebec.

National Presto Cooker

See also O1163.1, Instructions for Cooking and Canning, by the same company.

O1105.1   [copyright 1945]
National / Presto / Cooker / Its care and operation / with / cooking instructions / time tables and recipes
DESCRIPTION: 17.0 × 12.5 cm   Pp [1–2] 3–70   Tp illus of a National Presto Cooker, illus of cooker and parts   Paper, with pattern of horizontal wavy lines; stapled
CONTENTS: 1 tp; 2 table of contents and 'Copyright 1945 Copyright under the International Copyright Union by National Pressure Cooker Co. (Canada) Ltd. Printed in Canada'; 3 'Factory Warranty'; 4–14 'Chapter I // General Instructions to the New Users of This Wonderful Cooker'; 15–68 Chapters II–X of recipes; 69 'Using the Cooker as a Sterilizer'; 70 'Cooker Parts'
COPIES: OGU (CCC TX715.6 M572 No. 498)   OONL (TX840 P7 C8313 1945, 2 copies)   *Private collection
NOTES: The cover-title is 'National / Presto / Cooker / Recipe book / Instructions and / cooking time tables / National Pressure Cooker Company (Canada) Limited / Wallaceburg Ontario'; no model number is cited. The cookbook was distributed with new pressure cookers, as the 'Factory Warranty' makes clear: 'This Cooker was thoroughly tested ...'
   Editions with the wavy-line pattern on the binding (O1105.1–1105.4) precede all others. Of the wavy-line editions, O1105.1 and O1105.2 are likely the earliest

because no model number is cited, there is no reference to 'Trade mark registered' on the title-page, and they have fewer pages.

O1105.2   nd [about 1946]
—National / Presto / "Makes cooking a snap!" / Cooker / Its care and operation / with / cooking instructions / time tables and recipes
DESCRIPTION: 17.0 × 12.0 cm   Pp [1–2] 3–71   Tp illus of a National Presto Cooker, illus   Paper, with pattern of horizontal wavy lines; stapled
CONTENTS: 1 tp; 2 table of contents; 3 'Factory Warranty'; 4–14 'Chapter I // General Instructions to the New Users of This Wonderful Cooker'; 15–68 Chapters II–X of recipes; 69 'Using the Cooker as a Sterilizer'; 70 'Cooker Parts'; 71 blank except for folio
COPIES: *Private collection
NOTES: No model number is cited on the binding or elsewhere, and there is no copyright date; however, the private collector's copy is annotated on p 70, in ink, with the prices of the various cooker parts and '1946' is written on the title-page in the same hand and with the same pen.

O1105.3   [copyright 1945]
—National / Presto / Trade mark registered / Cooker / (Model "40") / Its care and operation / with / cooking instructions / time tables and recipes / Canning procedure
DESCRIPTION: 17.0 × 12.0 cm   Pp [1–2] 3–78   Tp illus of National Presto Cooker, illus   Paper, with pattern of horizontal wavy lines; stapled
CONTENTS: 1 tp; 2 'Table of Contents' and 'Copyright 1945 Copyright under the International Copyright Union by National Pressure Cooker Co. (Canada) Ltd. Printed in Canada'; 3 'Factory Warranty'; 4–14 'Chapter I // General Instructions to the New Users of This Wonderful Cooker'; 15–68 Chapters II–X of recipes; 69–77 'Introduction to Canning in a Presto Cooker (Model "40")'; 78 'Cooker Parts'
COPIES: *Private collection
NOTES: Page 78 lists 'Recipe Book' at the price of $0.25.

O1105.4   nd
—National / Presto / Trade mark registered / Cooker / (Model "40") / Recipe book / Instructions and / cooking time tables / National Pressure Cooker Company (Canada) Limited / Wallaceburg Ontario [cover-title]
DESCRIPTION: 17.0 × 12.5 cm   Pp [1–2] 3–78   Illus of cooker and parts   Paper, with pattern of horizontal wavy lines; stapled
CONTENTS: 1–2 'Important // Recipe Instructions for

the 2½ Quart (Model "40A") Presto Cooker' numbered 1–6 and printed in red ink; 3 'Factory Warranty'; 4–14 'Chapter I // General Instructions to the New Users of This Wonderful Cooker'; 15–68 Chapters II–X of recipes; 69–77 'Introduction to Canning in a Presto Cooker (Model "40")'; 78 'Cooker Parts'
COPIES: *Private collection
NOTES: This edition, which refers to Models 40 and 40A, has no title-page and no copyright date. Page 78 lists 'Recipe Book' at the price of $0.25.

O1105.5   [copyright 1945]
—National / Presto / Trade mark registered / Cooker / Recipe book / Instructions and / cooking time tables / including special instructions for the / use of the new 406 Presto Cooker / Although recipes in this book have been tested for / the Presto Cooker (3-½-qt. size) they are all appli-/ cable to the 406 Presto Cooker (5-qt. size). All the / necessary instructions for changes of ingredients / are clearly shown throughout the book. / National Pressure Cooker Company (Canada) Ltd. / Wallaceburg, Ontario [cover-title]
DESCRIPTION: 17.0 × 12.0 cm   Pp [1] 2–128   Illus   Thin card, with doily border incorporated in the cover design; stapled
CONTENTS: 1 'Your Presto Cooker Warranty'; 2–3 table of contents and 'Copyright, 1945, National Pressure Cooker Company (Canada) Ltd.'; 4–5 'The Modern Way to Cook for Family Health and Pleasure'; 6–7 'How to Use and Care for Your Presto Cooker'; 8–12 'A Simple Demonstration in the Use of a Presto Cooker'; 13–mid 14 'In Cooking Meats ...'; bottom 14 'Care of Cooker'; 15 'Instructions for Reversing Sealing Ring of Presto Cooker'; 16 'Read This Page Carefully before Using Your Cooker'; 17 'Presto Recipes'; 18 'Some Hints on Food Selection'; 19 'Food Preparation' and 'Seasoning'; 20–106 recipes; 107 'Your Presto Cooker as a Sterilizer'; 108 'Some Hints on Meal Planning'; 109 'Save More of the Good in the Foods You Eat!'; 110–11 'Food Value Chart'; 112–13 'Some Hints on Table Setting'; 114–17 'Simple Answers to Your More Important Questions about Presto Cooking'; 118–19 'Introduction to Canning in the Presto Cooker'; 120–5 canning recipes; 126 'How to Obtain the Best Service from Your Presto Cooker' and 'How to Obtain Prompt Repair Service for Your Presto Cooker'; 127 'Cooker Parts'; 128 'For Canning or Cooking ... National Pressure Cooker' and 'Printed in Canada'
COPIES: *BVAU (Beatrice M. Millar Papers)   QSH (0442)
NOTES: O1105.5–1105.7 have a doily border on the binding.

O1105.6 [copyright 1945]
—Le cuiseur / National / Presto / Marque déposée / Livre de / recettes / Instructions et / tableaux de cuisson / Instructions spéciales pour / l'usage du nouveau Cuiseur Presto 406 / Bien que les recettes de ce livre aient été éprouvées / pour le Cuiseur Presto de 3½ pintes, elles s'appliquent / toutes au Cuiseur Presto no. 406 (5 pintes). Le livre / indique, partout où il le faut, les transpositions de / quantités des ingrédients. / National Pressure Cooker Company (Canada) Ltd. / Wallaceburg, Ontario [cover-title]
DESCRIPTION: Doily border on binding
COPIES: *Private collection
NOTES: 'Tous droits réservés 1945, National Pressure Cooker Company (Canada) Ltd.' is at top p 2. The table of contents is on pp 2–3. There are 128 pp.

O1105.7 [copyright 1947, copyright 1948]
—National / Presto / Trade mark registered / Cooker / Recipe book / Instructions and / cooking time tables / including special instructions for the / use of the new 406 Presto Cooker / Although recipes in this book have been tested for / the Presto Cooker (3½-qt. size) they are all appli-/ cable to the 406 Presto Cooker (5[paper crease obscures hyphen?]qt. size). All the / necessary instructions for changes of ingredients / are clearly shown throughout the book. / National Pressure Cooker Company (Canada) Ltd. / Wallaceburg, Ontario [cover-title]
DESCRIPTION: 17.0 × 12.0 cm   Pp [1] 2–128   Illus   Thin card, with doily border incorporated in the cover design; stapled
CONTENTS: 1 'Your Presto Cooker Warranty'; 2–3 table of contents and 'Copyright, 1947, National Pressure Cooker Company (Canada) Ltd.'; 4–5 'The Modern Way to Cook for Family Health and Pleasure'; 6–7 'How to Use and Care for Your Presto Cooker'; 8–12 'A Simple Demonstration in the Use of a Presto Cooker'; 13–mid 14 'In Cooking Meats ...'; bottom 14 'Care of Cooker'; 15 'Instructions for Reversing Sealing Ring of Presto Cooker'; 16 'Read This Page Carefully before Using Your Cooker'; 17 'Presto Recipes'; 18 'Some Hints on Food Selection'; 19 'Food Preparation' and 'Seasoning'; 20–106 recipes; 107 'Your Presto Cooker as a Sterilizer'; 108 'Some Hints on Meal Planning'; 109 'Save More of the Good in the Foods You Eat!'; 110–11 'Food Value Chart'; 112–13 'Some Hints on Table Setting'; 114–17 'Simple Answers to Your More Important Questions about Presto Cooking'; 118–19 'Introduction to Canning in the Presto Cooker'; 120–5 canning recipes; 126 'How to Obtain

the Best Service from Your Presto Cooker' and 'How to Obtain Prompt Repair Service for Your Presto Cooker'; 127 'Cooker Parts'; 128 'For Canning or Cooking ... National Pressure Cooker' and at bottom, 'Copyright 1948 Printed in Canada'
COPIES: OKELWM   *Private collection
NOTES: The copyright date on p 128 (1948) is a year later than the copyright date on p 2 (1947).

O1105.8 [copyright 1948]
—National / Presto / Trade mark registered / Cooker / Instructions / recipes / time tables / Important / Be sure to read and follow directions on pages 5 through 16 before using / your Presto Cooker for the first time. / National Pressure Cooker Company (Canada) Limited.
DESCRIPTION: 21.0 × 13.5 cm   Pp [1] 2–127, [i]   Illus   Paper, with image on front of vegetables, shrimp, and meat; stapled
CONTENTS: 1 tp; 2 'Table of Contents' and 'Copyright 1948, National Pressure Cooker Company (Canada) Limited'; 3–4 'The Modern Way to Cook for Family Health and Pleasure'; 5–6 'How to Use and Care for Your Presto Cooker'; 7–10 'A Simple Demonstration in the Use of a Presto Cooker'; 11–mid 12 'When Cooking Meats ...'; mid–bottom 12 'Care of Cooker'; 13 'Instructions for Reversing Sealing Ring'; 14 'How to Obtain the Best Service from Your Presto Cooker' and 'Caution ... Read This Carefully before Preparing Recipes'; 15 'Read This Page Carefully before Using Your Cooker'; 16 'Food Preparation and Seasoning'; 17–105 recipes; 106–7 'Cooking for Baby'; 108–10 'Answers to Your More Important Questions about Presto Cooking'; 111–12 'An Introduction to Canning in a Presto Cooker'; 113–20 canning recipes; 121–3 'Answers to Your More Important Questions about Presto Canning'; 124 'How to Obtain Prompt Repair Service for Your Presto Cooker'; 125 'Cooker Parts'; 126–7 'Recipe Index'; i publ ad
COPIES: QMM (RBD ckbk 1923)   *Private collection
NOTES: The cover-title is 'National Presto ... Cooker // Recipe Book // Instructions and cooking time tables for Presto Cooker Models 402, 404, and 406 ...' O1105.8–1105.12 have an image of vegetables, shrimp, and meat on the binding. O1105.8 and O1105.9 have 127 pp.

The QMM copy lacks its binding.

O1105.9 [copyright 1948]
—Cuiseur / National / Presto / Marque enregistrée / Instructions / recettes / tables de cuisson / Important / S'assurer de lire et de suivre les instructions sur les pages 5 à 16 avant / de se servir

de son Cuiseur Presto pour la première fois. / National Presto Cooker Company (Canada) Limited
DESCRIPTION: 21.0 × 13.0 cm   Pp [1] 2–127, [i]   Illus   Thin card, with image on front of vegetables, shrimp, and meat; stapled
CONTENTS: 1 tp; 2 'Table des matières // Tous droits réservés 1948, National Pressure Cooker Company (Canada) Limited'; 3–4 'La façon moderne de cuire pour le plaisir et la santé de votre famille'; 5–6 'Comment employer et prendre soin de votre Cuiseur Presto'; 7–10 'Démonstration simple sur l'emploi d'un Cuiseur Presto'; 11–mid 12 'Pour la cuisson des viandes ...'; mid–bottom 12 'Le soin du cuiseur'; 13 'Instructions pour retourner la rondelle de caoutchouc'; 14 'Comment obtenir bon rendement de votre Cuiseur Presto' and 'Attention ... Lire attentivement avant de préparer une recette'; 15 'Lisez cette page attentivement avant d'employer votre cuiseur'; 16 'Préparation des aliments et assaisonnement'; 17–105 recipes; 106–7 'En cuisant pour bébé'; 108–10 'Réponses à vos questions importantes sur la cuisine au Presto'; 111–12 'Introduction à la mise en conserve dans un Cuiseur Presto'; 113–20 canning recipes; 121–top 124 'Réponses simples à vos questions importantes sur la mise en conserve au Presto'; near top–bottom 124 'Comment obtenir réparation prompte de votre Cuiseur Presto'; 125 'Pièces du cuiseur'; 126–7 'Recette index'; i publ ad
COPIES: *OONL (TX840 P7 C83 1948)   QSFFSC
NOTES: The cover-title is 'Cuiseur National Presto ... Livre de recettes // Instructions et tables de temps de cuisson pour Cuiseur Presto, modèles 402, 404 et 406 ...'

O1105.10   [copyright 1948]
—National / Presto / Trade mark registered / Cooker / Instructions / recipes / time tables / Important / Be sure to read and follow directions on pages 5 through 16 before using / your Presto Cooker for the first time. / National Pressure Cooker Company (Canada) Limited
DESCRIPTION: 21.0 × 13.5 cm   Pp [1] 2–79, [i]   Illus   Paper, with image on front and back of vegetables, shrimp, and meat; stapled
CONTENTS: 1 tp; 2 table of contents and 'Copyright 1948, National Pressure Cooker Company (Canada) Limited'; 3–77 text; 78–9 'Recipe Index'; i ad for Presto iron
CITATIONS: Ferguson/Fraser, p 234, illus col on p 103 of closed volume
COPIES: OTYA (CPC 1948 0078)   QMM (RBD uncat) *Private collection
NOTES: 'Recipe Book' is the cover-title. 'Instructions

and cooking time tables for Presto Cooker Models 402, 404, and 406 National Pressure Cooker Co. (Canada) Ltd. Wallaceburg, Ontario' is printed on the front face of the binding, at the bottom. O1105.10–1105.12 have 79 pp.

O1105.11   [copyright 1948]
—Cuiseur / National / Presto / Marque enregistrée / Instructions / recettes / tables de cuisson / Important / S'assurer de lire et de suivre les instructions sur les pages 5 à 16 avant / de se servir de son Cuiseur Presto pour la première fois. / National Pressure Cooker Company (Canada) Limited
DESCRIPTION: 21.0 × 13.0 cm   Pp [1] 2–79, [i]   Illus   Paper, with image on front and back of vegetables, shrimp, and meat; stapled
CONTENTS: 1 tp; 2 'Table des matières' and 'Droits réservés 1948, National Pressure Cooker Company (Canada) Limited'; 3–77 text; 78–9 'Index des recettes'; i ad
COPIES: *Private collection
NOTES: The cover-title is 'Cuiseur National Presto ... Livre de recettes // Instructions et tables de temps de cuisson pour Cuiseur Presto, modèles 103, 104 et 106 ...'

O1105.12   [copyright 1948]
—National / Presto / Trade mark registered / Cooker / Instructions / recipes / time tables / Important / Be sure to read and follow directions on pages 5 through 16 before using / your Presto Cooker for the first time. / National Presto Industries of Canada Limited
DESCRIPTION: 21.0 × 13.5 cm   Pp [1] 2–79, [i]   Illus   Paper, with image on front and back of vegetables, shrimp, and meat; stapled
CONTENTS: 1 tp; 2 'Table of Contents' and 'Copyright 1948, National Presto Industries of Canada Limited'; 3 'How to Use Your New 200 Series Presto Cooker'; 4 'Instructions for Reversing Sealing Ring'; 5–6 'How to Use and Care for Your Presto Cooker'; 7–10 'A Simple Demonstration in the Use of a Presto Cooker'; 11–mid 12 'When Cooking Meats ...'; bottom 12 'Care of Cooker'; 13–14 'Suggestions That Will Help You to Obtain the Best Service from Your Presto Cooker'; 15 'Read This Page Carefully before Using Your Cooker'; 16 'Food Preparation and Seasoning'; 17–61 recipes; 62–4 'Answers to Your More Important Questions about Presto Cooking'; 65–6 'An Introduction to Canning in a Presto Cooker'; 67–72 canning recipes; 73–5 'Answers to Your More Important Questions about Presto Canning'; 76 'How to Obtain Prompt Repair

Service for Your Presto Cooker'; 77 'Cooker Parts';
78–top 79 'Recipe Index'; bottom 79 ad for Presto
Cooker–Canner; i ad for Presto iron
COPIES: *Private collection
NOTES: Editions published by National Presto Indus-
tries of Canada Ltd follow those by National Presto
Cooker of Canada Ltd. The cover-title is 'New Presto
Cooker // Recipe Book // Instructions and cooking
time tables for Presto Cooker Models 204, 206 ...'

OTHER EDITIONS: *Presto Cooker: Instructions, Recipes,
Time Tables*, National Presto Industries of Canada Inc.,
copyright 1962 (Private collection); *Presto Cooker: Instructions, Recipes, Time Tables/Cuiseur Presto: instructions, recettes, tableaux de cuisson*, Scarborough, Ont.:
Supreme Aluminum Industries Ltd, nd (Private
collection).

AMERICAN EDITIONS: *National Presto Cooker: Its Care
and Operation with Cooking Instructions, Time Tables
and Recipes*, Eau Claire, Wis.: National Pressure Cooker
Co., nd (Private collection); *National Presto Cooker
(Model '40') Recipe Book ...*, Eau Claire, Wis.: [National
Pressure Cooker Co., copyright 1946] (NBCOM); *Na-
tional Presto Cooker (Model '40') Recipe Book ...*, Eau
Claire, Wis.: [National Pressure Cooker Co., 1947]
(United States: DLC); *National Presto Cooker (Model
'60') Recipe Book*, Eau Claire, Wis.: National Pressure
Cooker Co., [1946] (WaiteCat 5, No. 355); *National
Presto Cooker: Instructions, Recipes, Time Tables* [for
Cooker Models 103, 104, and 106], [Eau Claire, Wis.:]
National Presto Industries Inc., [copyright 1953]
(Private collection).

Old favorite honey recipes

O1106.1 [rev. ed.], copyright 1945
Old favorite / honey / recipes / [American Medical
Association Council on Foods and Nutrition
symbol] / The nutritional statements in this booklet
have been found / acceptable to the Council on
Foods and Nutrition of the / American Medical
Association. / American Honey Institute / Madison
3, Wisconsin / Copyright, 1945
DESCRIPTION: 23.0 × 15.5 cm   Pp [1] 2–52   Tp illus of
a woman and a girl at table, executed in a cross-stitch
pattern; illus headpieces in a cross-stitch
pattern   Paper, with image on front of a woman,
girl, and dog, in a cross-stitch pattern; stapled
CONTENTS: Inside front face of binding 'Distributed
in Canada by the Canadian Beekeepers' Council //

Printed in U.S.A.'; 1 tp; 2–5 'Honey Hints'; 6–51 reci-
pes; 52 index
CITATIONS: Brown/Brown
COPIES: *Private collection
NOTES: 'Revised and enlarged' is on the binding. No
place of publication is recorded, but the Canadian
Beekeepers' Council, founded in 1940, had its na-
tional office in Ottawa in the 1940s.

OTHER EDITIONS: Copyright 1945, 16th printing, 1957,
'Compliments of Clover Crest Honey, Winnipeg,
Man.' (Private collection).

AMERICAN EDITIONS: *Old Favorite Honey Recipes*, Madi-
son, Wis.: American Honey Institute, copyright 1941
(United States: DLC, InU); *American Honey Institute's
Old Favorite Honey Recipes and the Honey Recipes Book
of the Iowa Honey Producers Association*, Glenwood, Ill.:
Meyerbooks, c1988 (United States: DLC).

Souvenir cook book

O1107.1 1945
[An edition of *Souvenir Cook Book*, compiled at St
Paul's Presbyterian Church golden anniversary by
the Agnes Glassford Auxiliary, Winchester, Ontario,
1945]
COPIES: Private collection
NOTES: The cookbook includes a letter to 'Dear Friend'
from (Mrs A.G.) Mary E. Suffel, president, Winchester, Ontario, 10 June 1945, relating the history of the
Agnes Glassford Young Women's Auxiliary, organized
in February 1943.

Tried and tested recipes

O1108.1 nd [about 1945]
R•O•F / Royal Order Friends / Tried and tested /
recipes / Selected / arranged and published / by /
the members and friends / of / the Women's
Assisting Board / for / Restall Camp / Hamilton,
Ontario
DESCRIPTION: 22.5 × 15.0 cm   Pp [1] 2–64   Photographs on p 3 of a group scene of campers and of a
young boy in a swimming suit   Thin card, with small
image on front of a torch and an open book; stapled
CONTENTS: 1 tp; 2 'Roster // The Women's Assisting
Board of Restall Camp' [names of officers and members of the Board]; 3 'This cook book is compiled by
the Women's Board of St. Christopher Church. The

Board ... takes this means of raising funds for – Restall Camp' and information about the camp; 4–63 text, including recipes credited with the name of the contributor, blank spaces for 'My Own Recipes,' and ads; 64 'Index' [i.e., table of contents] and ads
COPIES: *OH (R641.5 TRI CESH)
NOTES: The cover-title is 'Tested Recipes.' Restall Camp, through its Royal Order of Friends, provided ten days of 'happy, healthful rest for mothers and children from All People's (Mission) churches.' The camp's director was the Rev. W.H. Pike, of All People's United Church, 187 Sherman North, Hamilton.

On p 18 there is an advertisement for the printer of the cookbook, the Seagers Press, 25 Vine Street, Hamilton.

The book is undated; however, there is an advertisement on p 20 for the funeral directors Blachford and Wray, which boasts, 'Have served Hamilton and vicinity for nearly 100 years.' OH, which holds Blachford and Wray's papers, reports that the funeral business started in 1851, but that the firm did some cabinetry work before this date. An advertisement for Blachford and Wray in another Hamilton cookbook (O901.1, *The Mixing Bowl*, [1936]) states that the business was 'Established 1843.' A publication date of about 1945, give or take a few years, therefore, seems likely; and the appearance of the book is clearly pre-1950.

Victory cook book

O1109.1 [about 1945]
Victory / cook book / A collection of / tested recipes / Contributed and published by / the ladies of the church / Arranged by / the members of the Ladies' Aid / First Presbyterian Church / Brockville Ontario / Page one
COPIES: *OBM
NOTES: The 'Preface' is on p 3. OBM reports that the book was printed by Farrow Brothers in Brockville. The museum's copy is signed and dated on the binding, 'Nellie Campbell 45.'

Victory cook book

O1110.1 nd [about 1945]
Victory / cook book / Our / favorite recipes / Selected by the members of / the St. Thomas Home and / School Council / St Thomas – Ontario
DESCRIPTION: Pp [1] 2–88
CONTENTS: 1 tp; 2 'Printed in Canada on Canadian

paper'; 3 'Preface' signed members of the Home and School Council; 4–87 text, mostly recipes credited with the name of the contributor, and ads; 88 'Index' [i.e., table of contents] and ads
COPIES: *Private collection
NOTES: An advertisement on p 88 for Steele Optical Co., Cyril H. Clarke, optometrist, described as 'Opposite Capitol Theatre for 22 years,' is evidence of the date of publication. The first listing in St Thomas city directories for the optical business is in the volume for 1923, where F. Steele and C.H. Clarke are at 557½ Talbot; therefore, the cookbook was published about 1945 [1923 + 22 years]. In 2007, the Capitol Theatre was still operating at 560 Talbot.

1945–6

Campbell, Miss Helen Gertrude (1889–1970)

For information about this author and her other cookbooks, see O477.1.

O1111.1 nd [about 1945–6]
The art of / entertaining / Published by the London Life Insurance Company / Written by / Helen G. Campbell / Director of Chatelaine Institute / [table of contents:] Page 2 The art of entertaining / 4 Invitation to dinner / 7 Holiday morning "brunch" / 8 Drop in for tea / 10 Fireside suppers / 12 Special occasions / 14 A buffet party / 16 Bridge and after / 19 Stag party / 20 Showers / 22 Wedding anniversary / 24 Games for your party
DESCRIPTION: 23.0 × 15.0 cm   Pp [1] 2–24   Tp illus of three stylized flowers, several illus of social scenes   Paper, with image on front of a set table; stapled
CONTENTS: 1 tp and table of contents; 2–24 text and at bottom p 24, 'Form No. H-12'
COPIES: *OGU (CCC TX715.6 C34923)   OONL (TX731 C35, 2 copies)
NOTES: For each occasion, Campbell offers a menu, recipes, and advice about entertaining. No place of publication is recorded, but it was probably London, Ontario. Since Campbell was last director of the Chatelaine Institute in 1946, *The Art of Entertaining* was published no later than that year. The appearance of the volume and the nature of the subject matter suggest a date after the Second World War.

The OGU copy is stamped on the binding, probably by a London Life Insurance agent, 'For further information phone A.J. Penfold // Office 2-1346 Res. 2-0159.'

1945–7

Cooking lore

The Rudyard Kipling Chapter was founded in 1923 and disbanded in 1973.

O1112.1   nd [about 1945–7]
Cooking / lore / Rudyard Kipling Chapter / I.O.D.E. – Toronto [cover-title]
DESCRIPTION: 21.5 × 13.5 cm   Pp 1–40   Very thin card, with IODE symbol on front; stapled
CONTENTS: 1 'Preface' signed 'Compiled by the Rudyard Kipling Chapter, Imperial Order, Daughters of the Empire // Toronto, Ontario' and 'Cooking Index' [i.e., table of contents]; 2 ad; 3–40 recipes and ads
COPIES: *Private collection
NOTES: There is an advertisement on p 4 for Purity Flour Mills, which illustrates the January 1945 edition of *Purity Cook Book;* therefore, *Cooking Lore* was published no earlier than 1945. An advertisement on p 20 for Love – The Flavor Man, at 62–8 Lombard Street, Toronto, limits publication to before 1950, when the company was at a different address. The advertisement on p 26 for Tea-Time Flour, a soft wheat flour 'for cakes and pastry' made by Robin Hood Flour Mills, suggests publication before 5 June 1947, when the company launched the Velvet brand of cake and pastry flour. The recipes are not credited.

Maguire, Mrs Vera C., née Walt

See A111.1.

1945–9

Alden, Mary

For information about the Quaker Oats Company of Canada and its cookbooks, see O563.1.

O1113.1   nd [about 1945–9]
26 / delicious new recipes .. / featuring healthful / Quaker Oats / Breakfast-to-dinner collection of / Mary Alden's favorite tested recipes [cover-title]
DESCRIPTION: 15.5 × 10.5 cm   Pp [1] 2–18   Illus brown   Paper, with image on front of Quaker Oats man pointing to a variety of prepared dishes behind him; stapled
CONTENTS: 1 cover-title; 2 'Every Day Can Be a Quaker Oats Day in a Different Way! ... "Quaker Oats still

costs less than 1¢ a Serving"'; 3 'Preparation of Oatmeal and Variations'; 4–5 menus; 6–11 'Booty in the Cookie Jar!'; 12–13 '"Satisfy That Sweet Tooth"'; 14–15 'Muffins and Bread Put on a Party Dress ...'; 16–18 'Magic with Your Main Dishes'
COPIES: *Private collection
NOTES: The text and illustrations are printed in brown. The food producer's name is recorded as the Quaker Oats Company of Canada Ltd, the name under which the Canadian branch of the American company was incorporated in 1943. The cookbook, therefore, was published no earlier than 1943. There are no text references to wartime and the appearance of the book points to publication about 1945–9. On the inside back face of the binding there is a note advising the reader to 'Get Grand New Premiums,' using Quaker Oats package tops as part payment; requests were to be sent to the Canadian company's Peterborough, Ontario, headquarters.

Canada Vinegars recipe book and household hints

An earlier Canada Vinegars recipe book is O612.1.

O1114.1   nd [about 1945–9]
The new and improved / Canada / Vinegars / recipe book / and / household hints / This book of recipes has been designed to aid you in / preparing a great variety of delicious preserves, relishes, / tasty dishes and menus, with the aid of vinegar. It also / contains many valuable and surprising hints on how / vinegar can help you in your household. / Published by and presented / with the compliments of / Canada Vinegars / 112 Duke Street Toronto
DESCRIPTION: 23.0 × 15.0 cm   Pp [1–4] 5–31   Tp illus of two bottles of Canada White Vinegar, illus of animated vegetables and vinegar bottle, and an animated salad   [Free, on p 3]   Paper, with image on front of prepared salads and jars of pickles; stapled
CONTENTS: 1 tp; 2 'Contents'; 3 'Preface'; 4 'Facts You Should Know about Vinegars'; 5–23 'Recipes'; 24 'Weights, Measures and Times'; 25–9 'General Household Hints on Uses of Vinegar'; 30–top 31 'Hints on Preparing Vegetables and Fruits'; mid–bottom 31 blank for 'Memoranda'
COPIES: *Private collection
NOTES: The order of the Canada Vinegars, Kent Vinegars, and Western Vinegars editions is unknown; they may have been published at the same time. The book's design is more modern (probably post–Second World War) than many of the household hints,

and medical and toilet uses for vinegar (pp 25–9), which are from an earlier era (for example, restoring isinglass in the side curtains of cars, or deodorizing the sick room with cider vinegar boiled with myrrh).

O1114.2 nd
—The new and improved / Kent / Vinegars / recipe book / and / household hints / This book of recipes has been designed to aid you in / preparing a great variety of delicious preserves, relishes, / tasty dishes and menus, with the aid of vinegar. It also / contains many valuable and surprising hints on how / vinegar can help you in your household. / Published by and presented / with the compliments of / Kent Vinegars / Canning, N.S.
DESCRIPTION: 23.0 × 15.0 cm Pp [1–4] 5–31 Tp illus of two bottles of Kent Cider Vinegar, illus of animated vegetables and vinegar bottle, and an animated salad [Free, on p 3] Paper, with image on front of prepared salads and jars of pickles; stapled
CONTENTS: 1 tp; 2 table of contents; 3 preface; 4 'Facts You Should Know about Vinegars'; 5–23 'Recipes'; 24 'Weights, Measures and Times'; 25–9 'General Household Hints on Uses of Vinegar'; 30–1 'Hints on Preparing Vegetables and Fruits'
COPIES: *Private collection

O1114.3 nd
—The new and improved / Western / Vinegars / recipe book / and / household hints / This book of recipes has been designed to aid you in / preparing a great variety of delicious preserves, relishes, / tasty dishes and menus, with the aid of vinegar. It also / contains many valuable and surprising hints on how / vinegar can help you in your household. / Published by and presented / with the compliments of / Western Vinegars / 109 Higgins Avenue Winnipeg / 1906-10th Ave. West Calgary / 1057-98th Street Edmonton / 1055 E. Cordova Vancouver
DESCRIPTION: 22.5 × 15.0 cm Pp [1–4] 5–31 Tp illus of bottle of Western White Vinegar and jug of Western Pickling Vinegar, illus of animated vegetables and a vinegar bottle, and an animated salad Lacks paper binding; stapled
CONTENTS: 1 tp; 2 table of contents; 3 'Preface'; 4 'Facts You Should Know about Vinegars'; 5–23 'Recipes'; 24 'Weights, Measures and Times'; 25–9 'General Household Hints on Uses of Vinegar'; 30–1 'Hints on Preparing Vegetables and Fruits'
COPIES: *Private collection
NOTES: For an earlier publication by Western Vinegars, see O612.5, *Pickling Recipes,* and O612.6 and O612.7, *New and Old Pickle Recipes.*

Cornell, Miss Anna May

For Cornell's other cookbooks, see O781.1.

O1115.1 nd [about 1945–9]
Here is your / Westinghouse Food Mixer / It beats anything for saving work / Recipe and use book / prepared by the Westinghouse Home Economics Department [cover-title]
DESCRIPTION: 22.5 × 15.0 cm Pp 1–24 Illus Paper, with image on front of young girl tasting icing from the mixer bowl, an iced cake in foreground; stapled
CONTENTS: Inside front face of binding 'Your Westinghouse Food Mixer Is Sensationally New ... Thoroughly Tested' [introductory text] signed Anna May Cornell, director, Home Economics Department, and a photograph of Cornell; 1–7 information about the Food Mixer; 8–24 'Recipes'; inside back face 'Index'
COPIES: *Private collection
NOTES: The order of publication of the two, differently titled editions is uncertain, but the text opposite p 1 of *Recipe and Use Book* suggests that it may be the first edition. It refers to 'all the months we spent in testing this new Food Mixer,' whereas *Instructions and Recipes Westinghouse Food Mixer* refers to 'all the months we spent in testing the Westinghouse Food Mixer.'

O1115.2 nd [about 1945–9]
—Instructions / and / recipes / Westinghouse / Food Mixer [cover-title]
DESCRIPTION: 23.0 × 15.5 cm Pp 1–24 Illus Paper, with image on front of a woman pouring liquid into the bowl of a Westinghouse Food Mixer; stapled
CONTENTS: Inside front face of binding 'Your Westinghouse Food Mixer Is Sensationally Modern and Thoroughly Tested' [introductory text] signed Anna May Cornell, director, Home Economics Department, and a photograph of Cornell, and 'Si vous préférez avoir une version française de ce livre de recettes, prière d'en adresser la demande à: Canadian Westinghouse Co. Ltd. 4102-ouest, rue Ste-Catherine, Montréal, P.Q. ...'; 1 'Get Acquainted with Your Food Mixer'; 2–3 'Your Food Mixer Is Simple to Operate'; 4–5 'You'll Truly Enjoy These Westinghouse Advantages'; 6–7 'It Mixes ... It Beats ... It Blends ... It Juices ... So Much Better!'; 8–9 'Helpful Hints You Will Appreciate'; 10–24 recipes; inside back face 'Index'
COPIES: *Private collection
NOTES: 'Canadian Westinghouse Company Limited // Hamilton Canada' is on the outside back face of the binding.

Delicious, nourishing dishes

See O222.1 for information about the company and for the titles of other cookbooks promoting Shredded Wheat.

O1116.1 nd [about 1945–9]
Delicious, / nourishing dishes / for breakfast ... for luncheon ... for dinner [cover-title]
DESCRIPTION: 21.0 × 14.0 cm   Pp 1–22 [23–4]   Illus   Paper, with image on front of a bowl of Shredded Wheat and strawberries; stapled
CONTENTS: Inside front face of binding publisher's note signed Canadian Shredded Wheat Co. Ltd; 1–5 'Breakfast Suggestions' including 'Nabisco Family Favorite' on p 1 and 'New Twists for a Breakfast Favorite' on p 2; 6–9 'Luncheon Treats'; 10–16 'Dinner Dishes'; 17–23 'Desserts'; 24 'How Nabisco Shredded Wheat Is Made'
COPIES: *Private collection
NOTES: Shredded Wheat was an invention of the 1890s. The publisher's note opposite p 1 refers to Nabisco Shredded Wheat as 'famous for more than half a century'; therefore, *Delicious, Nourishing Dishes* was likely published sometime in the 1940s, and the appearance of the book indicates about 1945–9. The city in which Canadian Shredded Wheat Co. Ltd was situated – Niagara Falls, Ontario – is printed on the box of Shreddies illustrated opposite p 24.

O1116.2 nd [about 1945–9]
—Mets délicieux / et nourrissants / pour le déjeuner ... le lunch ... le dîner [cover-title]
DESCRIPTION: 21.0 × 14.0 cm   Pp 1–22 [23–4]   Illus   Paper, with image on front of a bowl of Shredded Wheat and strawberries; stapled
CONTENTS: Inside front face of binding publisher's note signed Canadian Shredded Wheat Co. Ltd; 1 'Nabisco – Favori de la famille'; 2–5 'Nouvelles idées pour le déjeuner'; 6–9 'Pour lunch'; 10–16 'Pour dîner'; 17–23 'Desserts'; 24 'Comment le Nabisco Shredded Wheat est fait'
COPIES: *QMBM (Env. 7866)

OTHER EDITIONS: *Delicious Nourishing Dishes for Breakfast, Luncheon and Dinner,* Nabisco Foods Ltd, nd [no earlier than 1954, when Canadian Shredded Wheat Co. Ltd changed its name to Nabisco Foods] (OTMCL).

AMERICAN EDITIONS: *Delicious Nourishing Dishes for Breakfast, Luncheon and Dinner,* Nabisco Co. Inc., 1950 (Allen, p 211).

I.O.D.E. cook book

The Capt. Wm F. Owen Chapter received its charter in 1936 and disbanded in 2003.

O1117.1 nd [about 1945–9]
I.O.D.E. cook book / compiled and edited by / members of / Capt. Wm. F. Owen Chapter / Owen Sound, Ontario / Our sincere thanks to those who in any / way made possible the publication / of this book; and especially to / our advertisers for whom / we would ask your / generous patronage.
DESCRIPTION: 23.0 × 15.0 cm   Pp [1] 2–60   Paper, with small label on front of IODE symbol; stapled
CONTENTS: 1 tp; 2 ads; 3 'Index' [i.e., table of contents] and 'Printed by – The Georgian Press, Owen Sound'; 4 ads; 5–56 recipes credited with the name of the contributor and ads; 57–60 blank 'For Your Favorite Receipt'
COPIES: *OGU (CCC TX715.6 I69)

Kitchen craft

O1118.1 nd [about 1945–9]
Kitchen craft / A selection of our / tried and tested recipes / arranged and published / by / the Ladies Guild / of / St. Paul's Anglican Church / Arden Ontario / [folio:] 1
DESCRIPTION: With image on front of an older woman lifting the lid from a steaming casserole dish
COPIES: United States: MCR (641.6971 89-B220-704)
NOTES: The MCR catalogue describes the volume as having 64 pp. The MCR copy is inscribed on the binding, 'Tompkins.' Arden is north of Napanee, close to Highway 7.

Logan, Martha [pseudonym]

For information about the real women behind the pseudonym Martha Logan and for the titles of other cookbooks attributed to Logan, see O1050.1.

O1119.1 nd [about 1945–9]
By Martha Logan / Home Economist / Swift Canadian Co. / Limited / Handibook of meat cookery [cover-title]
DESCRIPTION: 12.0 × 16.5 cm   Pp [1] 2–15   Illus portrait on p 3 of Martha Logan(?)   Paper, with stylized images on front of a woman's head, a cleaver, and a skewer(?); stapled at top edge
CONTENTS: 1 cover-title; 2 'Index' [i.e., table of con-

tents]; 3 introductory note signed Martha Logan; 4 'Meat Cookery'; 5 'Dry Heat // Roasting'; 6–7 'Roasting Schedule – Fresh Meats'; 8 'Roasting Schedule – Cured and Smoked Pork'; 9 'Roasting Schedule – Poultry'; top 10 'Dry Heat, Too! Broiling'; mid 10–mid 11 'Broiling Schedule'; mid 11–bottom 11 'Pan-Frying' and 'Sausage and Bacon Cookery'; 12–13 'Moist Heat – Slow and Easy Does It ... Braising' and 'Braising Schedule'; 14–15 'More Moist Heat Cookery! Water Cooking' and 'Water Cooking Schedule'
COPIES: OGU (CCC TX715.6 L6266)   *Private collection
NOTES: The text is printed in purple. No place of publication is recorded, but the company's head office was in Toronto.

O1120.1   nd [about 1945–9]
Queens of / cuisine / with / Swift'ning / Swift's shortening / by Martha Logan / Home Economist for Swift Canadian Co. Limited [cover-title]
DESCRIPTION: 19.5 × 13.5 cm   Pp [1–4] 5–58 [59–64]   Illus part-titles   Very thin card; stapled
CONTENTS: Inside front face of binding untitled introductory note signed Martha Logan; 1 'Baking Ingredient Hints'; 2–3 'Index' [i.e., table of contents]; 4–58 recipes; 59–63 blank for 'Notes'; 64 'Accurate Measurements Are Important' and 'Measurement of Ingredients'
COPIES: OAYM   OGU (CCC TX715.6 L629)   OONL (TX715.6 L63 1900z p***)   *Private collection
NOTES: The note opposite p 1 states, 'Queens of Cuisine ... Aristocrats of the Kitchen ... are these recipes for cakes, cookies, pies, and other baked and fried foods,' i.e., 'Queens' in the title refers to the recipes, not to cooks. No place of publication is recorded, but the company's head office was in Toronto. *Queens of Cuisine with Swift'ning* is cited in *77 Recipes Using Swift'ning Make-Your-Own Mix*, [Toronto: Swift Canadian Co. Ltd, copyright 1950].

Old Colony cook book

The Strathroy Flour Mills had its start in 1836 when John Stewart Buchanan built a grist mill in the new settlement. In 1846 the mill was bought by James Keefer and Timothy Cook, who sold it to Richard Pincombe in about 1862. Already an experienced miller, he had emigrated from England in 1832, where he had worked with his father (also Richard) in a mill in the Parish of Peters Marland. In Upper Canada he first worked at the Hunt Milling Co. in London, then at a mill in Napier and a mill on Longwood's Road (now Highway 2), before

buying the Strathroy business. The family connection with the business was severed when it was sold to a larger producer in 1969 or 1970.

Sources consulted at OL include Clifford R. Cox, History of Strathroy, 1989, pp 6, 8; and 1868–9 City of London and County of Middlesex General Directory.

O1121.1   nd [about 1945–9]
Old Colony / cook book / Compliments of / the Strathroy Flour Mills / R.M. Pincombe & Sons / Strathroy Ontario / "millers for over 100 years" [cover-title]
DESCRIPTION: 23.0 × 14.5 cm   Pp [1–24]   Card; stapled, and with hole punched at top centrefold, through which runs a string for hanging
CONTENTS: Inside front face of binding publ ad for Old Colony Flour milled by Strathroy Flour Mills; top 1 'Introductory'; mid 1–2 'Useful Information'; 3–14 recipes; 15–22 blank for 'My Favorite Recipes'; 23–4 blank for 'Memorandum'; inside back face publ ad for Drummer Pastry Flour milled by Strathroy Flour Mills
COPIES: *Private collection
NOTES: The 'Introductory' refers to the cookbook as 'this permanent collection of truly Canadian recipes.' On the outside back face of the binding, under the heading 'Over 100 Years of Milling Service' (a reference to the family's long experience, not to the length of ownership of the Strathroy Flour Mills), is the statement: 'Three generations of the Pincombe Family have contributed to the development of their flour products, until today, Old Colony and Drummer brands are justly recognized as a standard of quality.' Old Colony was the company's bread flour; Drummer, the pastry flour. Richard G. Pincombe, the great-grandson of the first Richard Pincombe to own the Strathroy Flour Mills and the last president of the family company, stated that the cookbook was published in the 1940s and that recipes were collected from the local community (conversation, July 2000). The Meat Loaf recipe on p 5 is his mother's.

Recipes

O1122.1   nd [about 1945–9]
Recipes / prepared and tested / by / Consumer Service Dept. / Silverwood Dairies / Limited [cover-title]
DESCRIPTION: 21.5 × 14.0 cm   Pp 1–16   Illus on p 8 of the 'Cream Top Bottle' and on p 9 of 'How to Take the Cream Off'   Paper, with stylized image on front of the 'Cream Top Bottle'; stapled

CONTENTS: 1 list of Silverwood's products; 2–3 recipes using buttermilk; 4–7 recipes using sour cream; 8–9 illus, and information about, the 'Cream Top Bottle'; 10–14 recipes using cottage cheese; 15 recipes using Dari-Rich [a chocolate drink] and the London, Ontario, address of Silverwood's Consumer Service Department; 16 'How Each Day's Requirement Is Met'

COPIES: *Private collection

NOTES: Silverwood's acquired the Ontario rights for the Cream Top Bottle in 1928, and by 1942 the bottle's body had an octagonal shape, as seen in the book illustration; the last Cream Top Bottle design appeared in 1953 (Thomas/Marchant, pp 107, 120). *Recipes* was published after the company name changed to Silverwood Dairies Ltd in 1936, and likely in the late 1940s from the appearance of the volume. Bert Williams, who worked for Silverwood Dairies Ltd from 1949, reports that copies of this cookbook were passed out to customers by the men who built the company's home-service business.

There is a copy of *Recipes* at OONL (TX759 S5 R4) that matches the description above, except that it has no printed page numbers; it is rebound in cloth.

Selected recipes

In 1953 the name Phillipston-Zion changed to Bethel-Zion Women's Institute. The branch is in Hastings County.

O1123.1   nd [about 1945–9]
Selected / recipes / [Women's Institute symbol] / Compiled by the / Phillipston-Zion Institute members [cover-title]
COPIES: *Private collection

Sugar and spice

Anderson United Church, a rural church near St Marys (fourth line of Blanchard), was closed in the 1960s.

O1124.1   nd [about 1945–9]
Sugar and spice / Prepared by / Anderson W.M.S. [i.e., Women's Missionary Society] / Arranged by / Mrs. Ed. [corrected by hand, in ink, 'Eu.'] Stephens / Mrs. Theodore Stephens / Mrs. R.G. Ratcliffe / In appreciation / To the members, who gave us whole- / hearted support and co-operation; to the / friends outside the Institute ['the Institute' corrected by hand, in ink, 'W.M.S.'], who responded / so

graciously to requests for special recipes, / and to the publishers, who were never too / busy to give information and timely counsel, / we say a grateful Thank You!

DESCRIPTION: 23.5 × 15.5 cm   Pp [1–2] 3–60   Paper, with image on front of Anderson United Church; stapled

CONTENTS: Inside front face of binding 'Index' [i.e., table of contents] and 'Expositor Print, Seaforth'; 1 tp; 2 'The Heart of the Home' by Ethel Romig Fuller [poem]; 3–38 recipes credited with the name of the contributor; 39–60 ads

COPIES: *Bookseller's stock   Private collection

NOTES: The recipes, which are for both sweet and savoury dishes, are arranged under the following headings: 'Cakes'; 'Cookies'; 'Desserts and Puddings'; 'Jams and Jellies'; 'Pies and Tarts'; 'Supper Dishes'; and 'Pickles and Relishes.'

Wake up appetites

O1125.1   nd [about 1945–9]
Wake up / appetites / with / Shakespeare's / best recipes / Presbyterian Church / Shakespeare Ontario [cover-title]
DESCRIPTION: 23.0 × 15.0 cm   Pp 1–36   Paper, with image on front of a mother serving father, son, and daughter at table; stapled

CONTENTS: Inside front face of binding 'Recipe for a Home' and 'A Recipe for Happiness'; 1–34 recipes credited with the name of the contributor and 'Household Hints –'; 35–6 blank for 'Notes'; inside back face 'Index' [i.e., table of contents]

COPIES: *OONL (TX715.6 W34 1900z p***)

NOTES: In October 1999 I tried to trace four of the recipe contributors (Mrs Glen Fryfogel, Mrs Edwin Pines, Mrs Lincoln Biehn, Mrs B[ertha] McClurg); however, all were dead. Apparently, the recipes were solicited from the wider community, since not all the contributors belonged to the Shakespeare Presbyterian Church.

1946

Borden's Eagle Brand magic recipes

For information about the company and its other books, see Q106.1.

O1126.1   [copyright 1946]
Borden's / Eagle Brand / magic recipes [cover-title]

DESCRIPTION: 22.0 × 16.5 cm   Pp [1] 2–27   7 fp illus, illus   Paper, with image on front of desserts

CONTENTS: 1 cover-title; 2–3 'Let's Start by Explaining Eagle Brand "Magic"' and at bottom p 2, 'Copr. – The Borden Company – 1946'; 4–5 'Pies'; 6–7 'Puddings'; 8–9 'Custards'; 10–11 'Frostings'; 12–17 'Ice Creams'; 18 'Sauces'; 19 'Desserts'; 20–1 'Cookies'; 22–3 'Candies'; 24 recipes for mayonnaise and cooked salad dressing; 25 recipes for hot drinks; 26 'Hints'; 27 [inside back face of binding] index and 'E-58–Rev.'

CITATIONS: Ferguson/Fraser, p 234, illus col on p 103 of closed volume

COPIES: ACG   MCM   OGU (2 copies: CCC TX715.6 M572 No. 26, *UA s070 b96)   OONL (TX759.5 M54 B67 1946 p***)

AMERICAN EDITIONS: 1946 (Allen, p 202).

Canada, Department of National Health and Welfare

O1127.1   1st ed., 1946
[First edition of a 'mimeographed manual on camp feeding,' 1946]
NOTES: This edition is cited in later editions. No copy surfaced.

O1127.2   rev. ed., 1948
—[Folio:] 2 / Feeding fifty campers / [four paragraphs of introductory text] / Nutrition Division / Department of National Health and Welfare / Revised, 1948. / L.B. Pett, Ph.D., M.D., / Chief of the Division. / Miss Margaret Lock, / Supervisor of the / Group Feeding Section. / 1585 / 12.47
DESCRIPTION: Pp 2–47   Rebound
COPIES: *OGU (CA1 HW22 48F22)
NOTES: There may have been a cover-title, but the OGU copy is rebound. As Canada found peace and prosperity after the Second World War, many new children's summer camps opened. The introductory text explains the aim of *Feeding Fifty Campers*, to provide advice on holiday camp cooking: 'Little information has been published on this type of group feeding but the demand for material on camp equipment, supplies, menus and recipes for different sized camps has been increasing. As a result, the Nutrition Division, Department of National Health and Welfare first published a mimeographed manual on camp feeding in 1946, and this present issue is the result of further study on the subject.' The text covers 'Caloric Requirements of Different Age Groups in Holiday Camps,' 'Helpful Hints,' 'Pre-Camp Routine,' 'Suggested Kitchen Equipment for Camp Serving 50 People,' 'Supply List,' and 'Daily Master Menu Pattern & Supply Order // 50 People'; then follow 'Recipes for 50 Servings' (85 numbered recipes) on pp 23–47.

OTHER EDITIONS: *Feeding Fifty Campers*, rev. ed., Ottawa: Nutrition Division, Department of National Health and Welfare, 1953 (NBFU, OTMCL); Ottawa: Department of National Health and Welfare, 1954 (ACU, BVA, BVAU, NBFL, OONL, OOU, OWTU, SRL).

Also *Feeding Twenty Campers*, Department of National Health and Welfare, 1954 (ACU, OONL, OTU); the 'Introduction' on p 3 refers to the 'mimeographed manual' of 1946, the revised edition of 1947 [*sic*], the revised edition of 1949 [*sic*], and this 1954 revision; the title-page refers to the revised edition of 1953.

O1128.1   [rev. ed.], January 1946
Menus et recettes / economiques / Protegez votre sante / en mangeant ces aliments tous les jours / [suggested daily servings of 'lait,' 'pain et céréales,' 'légumes,' 'fruits,' and 'viande – poisson,' plus advice about serving cod liver oil and iodized salt] / Brochure n° 66B / Janvier 1946. / Publié par / le Conseil canadien du bien etre social / 245, rue Cooper / Ottawa, Canada / Prix: .05 [cover-title]
DESCRIPTION: 28.0 × 21.5 cm   Pp [1–2] 3–22   Very thin card; stapled
CONTENTS: 1 cover-title; 2 'Suggestions pour menus à prix modique' and 'Cette brochure a été revisée par la Division de nutrition // Ministère de la santé nationale et du bien-être social 1946'; 3–6 'Menus pour une semaine'; 7 'Index alphabétique des recettes'; 8–22 recipes
COPIES: *OONL (TX715.6 M45 1946 fol., 2 copies)
NOTES: Pages 3–22 are printed on the rectos only; the blank versos are not included in the pagination. Page 2 begins, 'Pour avoir une bonne santé et afin de suivre les règles officielles d'alimentation canadienne, les repas doivent être projetés soigneusement.'

The centennial cook book

O1129.1   1946
The / centennial / cook book / St. Paul's Cathedral / London / 1846–1946 / Compiled by / Evening Branch W.A. [cover-title]
DESCRIPTION: 22.5 × 15.0 cm   Pp 1–80   Illus on p 1 of the cathedral   Very thin card; stapled

CONTENTS: 1–top 2 history of the cathedral signed G.N.L.; bottom 2 'A Word of Appreciation' signed Evening Branch W.A.; 3–78 recipes credited with the name of the contributor and ads; 79 'How to Grow the African Violet' and 'A Few Tips on Moving Perennials'; 80 'Index' [i.e., table of contents; the text is arranged alphabetically by heading, from 'Beverages' to 'Vegetables']
COPIES: *OL (London Room Box 179b)

Central's choice cookery

O1130.1 [1946]
Central's / [same letter C as 'Central's']hoice / [same letter C]ookery [cover-title]
DESCRIPTION: Stapled
CONTENTS: First page 'Central United Church,' photograph of the church, and 'Windsor – Ontario 1946'
COPIES: *Private collection
NOTES: The recipes are credited with the name of the contributor. The volume has 96 pp.

Clover Leaf cook book

O1131.1 November 1946
[Lacks cover-title]
DESCRIPTION: Illus on p 1 of a three-leaf clover (not four-leaf) and a photograph of the church   Lacks binding; stapled
COPIES: *Private collection
NOTES: The following is on p 1: 'Compiled by the Cloverleaf [sic, one word] Society of St. Mark's Lutheran Church // King & Green sts. Kitchener, Ontario November, 1946.' The three-leaf clover is above the photograph of the church, where the edition information is in the second and third editions.

O1131.2 [2nd ed., March 1948]
—Clover Leaf / [on four leaves of clover, reading clockwise from bottom left:] C L S '21 / cook / book [cover-title]
DESCRIPTION: 22.0 × 15.0 cm   Pp [1] 2–54   Photograph on p 1 of St Mark's Lutheran Church   Yellow paper, with clover-leaf shape and green vertical stripes on front; stapled
CONTENTS: 1 'Second edition printed March, nineteen hundred and forty-eight' and 'Compiled by the Cloverleaf [sic] Society of St. Mark's Lutheran Church // King & Green sts. Kitchener, Ontario November, 1946'; 2 'Essential Ingredients!' by Clara Bernhardt and 'Printed in St. Jacobs by the St. Jacobs Printery.'; 3 'Index' [i.e., table of contents] and 'For extra copies of

this book // Mrs. E.G. Knarr // 475 Wendell Ave. Dial 20488'; 4–54 recipes credited with the name of the contributor
COPIES: *Private collection
NOTES: The first letters of the list of 'Essential Ingredients!' on p 2 (for example, Cleanliness ..., Labour ...) spell 'CLOVERLEAF.'

Marnie Derksen refers to her copy of the second edition in 'Season to Taste: Cookbooks Often Serve Up Much More Than Just Recipes,' *Globe and Mail* (Toronto) 18 August 2000, p A18 (Derksen incorrectly spelled Derkson in the article). Her grandmother noted on the binding, 'Plum Pudding is in this book.'

O1131.3 [3rd ed., November 1948]
—Clover Leaf / [on four leaves of clover, reading clockwise from bottom left:] C L S '21 / cook / book [cover-title]
DESCRIPTION: 22.5 × 15.0 cm   Pp [1] 2–54   Photograph on p 1 of St Mark's Lutheran Church   Yellow paper, with clover-leaf shape and dark blue-green vertical stripes on front; stapled
CONTENTS: 1 'Third edition printed November, nineteen hundred and forty-eight' and 'Compiled by the Cloverleaf [sic] Society of St. Mark's Lutheran Church // King & Green sts. Kitchener, Ontario November, 1946'; 2 'Essential Ingredients!' by Clara Bernhardt and 'Printed in St. Jacobs by the St. Jacobs Printery.'; 3 'Index' [i.e., table of contents] and 'For extra copies of this book // Mrs. E.G. Knarr // 475 Wendell Ave. Dial 20488'; 4–54 recipes credited with the name of the contributor
COPIES: *Private collection

Cornell, Miss Anna May

For Cornell's other cookbooks, see O781.1.

O1132.1 rev. ed., June 1946
Delicious / foods / and how to cook them / with your / Westinghouse / Electric Range / By / Anna May Cornell / Home Economist / Canadian Westinghouse Company Limited / Price $1.25 / 153–P512–A / Rev. June, 1946
DESCRIPTION: 22.0 × 14.5 cm   Pp [i–ii] iii–xii, 1–144   Illus of electric range   Thin card; bound with a form of metal clasp
CONTENTS: i tp; ii 'Your Westinghouse Electric Range'; iii 'Keeping Your Westinghouse Range Like New'; iv 'Cleaning Your Oven'; v 'The Cooking Surface'; vi 'The Westinghouse Oven'; vii 'Broiling'; viii 'Mixed Grills'; ix 'Oven Dinners Are Delicious and Save Time'; x 'Oven Temperature Guide for Meat'; xi 'Oven Tem-

perature Guide for Baking'; xii 'Substitutions'; 1–137 recipes; 138–44 index and on p 144, 'Printed in Canada'
CITATIONS: Ferguson/Fraser, p 234
COPIES: OH (641.5 COR)   *Private collection
NOTES: The cover-title is 'Electric Cookery by Westinghouse'; the running foot is 'Westinghouse Cook Book.' See O886.2, *Electric Cookery by Westinghouse,* for a discussion of whether *Delicious Foods* is a later edition of that text.

O1132.2   [rev. index, June 1948]
—Delicious / foods / and how to cook / them / by / Anna May Cornell / Home Economist / Canadian Westinghouse Company, Limited / Si vous parlez français / Le livre de recettes en langue anglais qui / accompagne ce poêle pourra être échangé / contre une copie en français si on le retourne à / Canadian Westinghouse Co. Limited / 400 McGill Montreal P.Q. / Price $1.25
DESCRIPTION: 22.0 × 14.5 cm   Pp [i–ii] iii–xii, 1–139, [i–xiii]   Tp illus of foodstuffs   Card
CONTENTS: i tp; ii 'Your New Westinghouse Electric Range' signed Anna May Cornell; iii 'Your Westinghouse Provides a Proper Heat for Every Food'; iv 'There Is Measured Heat in Your Westinghouse True-Temp Oven'; v 'How Your Oven Brings Out the Best in Every Food'; vi–ix 'How to Use Your Oven'; x–xi 'How to Care for Your Range'; xii 'Useful Information'; 1–132 recipes; 133–9 index and on p 139, 'Index revised June, 1948'; i–v blank; vi–xiii blank for 'My Favourite Recipes'
COPIES: OGU (CCC TX715.6 C675)   QMM (RBD ckbk 1419)   *Private collection
NOTES: The cover-title is 'Electric Cookery by Westinghouse.' In the QMM copy, some pages are obscured by clippings.

Favorite recipes

O1133.1   [1946]
Favorite / recipes / St. Peter's Church / Young Women's Club / Madoc – Ontario / Review Print, Madoc, Ont. [cover-title]
DESCRIPTION: 23.0 × 15.5 cm   Pp 1–48   Fp illus on p 1 of St Peter's Church   Paper; stapled
CONTENTS: 1 illus of the church and the date 1946; 2 table of contents and 'Temperatures'; 3–48 recipes credited with the name of the contributor
COPIES: *Private collection
NOTES: Oddly, no mention is made of a 1940 cookbook by the same group, O1002.1, *The Epicurean Treasury.*

Favorite recipes

O1134.1   nd [1946]
Just a Little Kindness / [sixteen-line verse] / Favorite recipes / Arranged for publication / by / the Central Group / of / Trinity Church Ladies' Aid / The members of the Central Group of Trinity Church Ladies' Aid wish / to express their thanks to all who assisted in making this recipe book a / success. / Publication has been made possible by the generous support of the / merchants, and the professional men, whose advertisements appear in this / book. Show your appreciation by patronizing them whenever possible.
DESCRIPTION: 23.5 × 15.0 cm   Pp 1–64   Very thin card, with image on front of Trinity Anglican Church, St Thomas, Ontario, Wellington and Southwick streets; stapled
CONTENTS: 1 tp; 2 'Weights and Measures'; 3–59 recipes credited with the name of the contributor, blank spaces for 'My Own Recipes,' and ads; 60 blank; 61–4 blank for 'Memorandum'
COPIES: *OSTT (R641.5 MY)
NOTES: The cover-title is 'My Favorite Cook Book.' There is an advertisement on the inside back face of the binding for Andersons, 'Our fiftieth anniversary in St. Thomas 1896–1946,' indicating a publication date for the book of 1946.

Favourite recipes

O1135.1   1946
Favourite / recipes / "Of all appeals – although / I grant the power of pathos, and of gold, / Of beauty, flattery, threats, a shilling – no / Method's more sure at moments to take hold / Of the best feelings of mankind, which grow / More tender, as we every day behold, / Than that all-softening, overpowering knell, / The tocsin of the soul – the dinner bell." / – Byron / Women's Auxiliary / of / Sudbury District Hospital / 1946 edition [cover-title]
DESCRIPTION: 23.5 × 15.5 cm   Pp [1] 2–116   Illus on pp 4, 5, and 6 of Sudbury scenes   Paper; stapled
CONTENTS: 1 table of contents; 2 'Printed in Canada by the Victoria Publishing Co. Ltd. Lindsay, Ontario'; 3 'Foreword'; 4–6 'Sudbury' [a brief history of Sudbury and three scenes]; 7 ad; 8–116 recipes credited with the contributor's name, 'Miscellaneous,' and ads
COPIES: *Private collection
NOTES: The running head is 'Women's Auxiliary Sudbury Hospital Cook Book.'

Favourite recipes, Book No. 2

See also the Lady Grey Chapter's first and third books of
Favourite Recipes, *O985.1 and O1217.1.*

O1136.1   [January 1946]
Favourite recipes / Book No. 2 / [IODE symbol] /
Lady Grey Chapter / I.O.D.E. / Fort William, Ont.
[cover-title]
DESCRIPTION: 23.5 × 15.5 cm   Pp 1–104   Illus   Paper,
with IODE symbol on front; stapled
CONTENTS: 1 ad; 2 'Index' [i.e., table of contents] and
'Published January, 1946 by Consolidated Press Fort
William, Ontario'; 3 'Foreword'; 4–5 'Fort William'
[a brief history of the city] and two views of the city;
6–104 text and ads
COPIES: OTBH   *Private collection
NOTES: The 'Foreword' states: 'We are happy that we
can call this our Victory Issue. In addition to many
recipes that give consideration to war time restrictions still with us, there are many others you will be
trying out as soon as certain scarcities are no more ...
we are sure that [the book] will be of distinct interest
to tourists as a souvenir of Fort William, Canada.'
The running head is 'I.O.D.E. Cook Book.'

Gougeon, Hélène Carroll (Ottawa, Ont., 13 September 1924–12 May 2000, Toronto, Ont.)

*Christened Hélène, but usually called Helen, this author
began working as a reporter for the* Ottawa Journal *at
the age of eighteen. She attended, but did not graduate
from, Queen's University in Kingston, where she was in
Arts and Science, class of 1950. In 1950 she moved to
Montreal to join* Weekend Magazine *as food editor.
After* Cooking with an Accent, *she wrote one other
cookbook,* Helen Gougeon's Good Food, *Macmillan
Company of Canada Ltd, 1958 (NBFU, OHM, OONL,
OTNY uncat; Great Britain: OPo(F)). In 1975 new
material was added and the book republished by Tundra
Books in Montreal, as* Helen Gougeon's Original
Canadian Cookbook. *She opened a kitchen store in
Montreal, in 1968, called La Belle Cuisine, and hosted a
weekly CBC television show,* Bon Appétit. *She married
the playwright and historian Joseph Schull in 1955, and
they had three children, Christiane, Joseph, and Michael.
Her obituary is in the* Globe and Mail *(Toronto) 17 May
2000, p R10.*

O1137.1   [copyright 1946]
Cooking .... / with an accent / By / Helen C.
Gougeon [cover-title]

DESCRIPTION: 20.0 × 14.5 cm   Pp [i–ii], 1–28   Paper;
stapled
CONTENTS: i blank; ii 'Acknowledgment' and 'Copyright, 1946'; 1–2 'Introduction' signed Helen C.
Gougeon, Canada, April 1946; 3 'Australia'; 4 'Belgium'; 5–6 'Brazil'; 7 'Britain'; 8–9 'Chile'; 10–11 'Cuba';
12 'Czechoslovakia'; 13–14 'France'; 15–16 'Peru';
17–18 'Poland'; 19–20 'Russia'; 21–2 'South Africa';
23–4 'Sweden'; 25 'Turkey'; 26 'United States'; 27–8
'Yugoslavia'
COPIES: OGU (2 copies: *CCC TX715.6 G68, UA s063
b03)   OONL (TX725 A1 G69 1946)   Private collection
NOTES: Gougeon had become interested in national
cuisines as she covered events at embassies in Ottawa, on her reporter's beat for the *Ottawa Journal*.
She wrote a series of columns for the newspaper,
headed 'Recipes from Ottawa's Diplomatic Row,'
that appeared almost every day from 9 January to
19 February 1946. The columns were so well received
that she decided to self-publish a pamphlet that would
feature the best of the material. She paid for the printing of *Cooking with an Accent* with a loan from the
bank of about $350, and distributed copies for sale as
she moved about the city on her beat; 2,000 copies
were sold at $0.25 each (conversation with the au-
thor, March 2000). In the introductory text for each
country, Gougeon discusses the national cuisine and
identifies the diplomatic family that shared recipes
with her.
   The private collector's copy is inscribed, 'To Sheila
Orr, sincerely, Helen C. Gougeon, Queen's /47' (the
date refers to the year of the inscription, not of her
class at Queen's).

Hadassah cook book

O1138.1   1946
Hadassah / Sonya Kaplan Chapter / Kirkland Lake,
Ontario / Cook / book / First edition / 1946
DESCRIPTION: 23.0 × 15.5 cm   Pp [1–4] 5–106 [107–8]
Paper; stapled
CONTENTS: 1 tp; 2 acknowledgments and names of
cookbook conveners and committee members; 3 table
of contents; 4 ad; 5–106 text and ads, with chapters
for 'Appetizers,' 'Soups and Garnishes,' 'Fish and
Sauces,' 'Meats,' 'Luncheon and Supper Dishes and
Vegetables,' 'Salads and Salad Dressings,' 'Pies, Pud-
dings and Desserts,' 'Buns, Biscuits and Rolls, etc.,'
'Cakes and Icings,' 'Ice Box Pastries,' 'Cookies, Squares
and Strudels,' 'Jams and Jellies,' 'Pickles and Relishes,' 'Passover and Purim Recipes,' 'Candies,' and
'Household Hints'; 107–8 blank for 'Memorandum'

CITATIONS: Ferguson/Fraser, p 234

COPIES: *Private collection

NOTES: The title on the spine and the running head is 'Hadassah Cook Book.' The book offers a window on the Jewish community in Kirkland Lake: There are many Jewish recipes, some for Passover and Purim, the recipes are credited with the name of the contributor, and many of the advertisements are for Jewish businesses.

Laverty, Mrs Maura, née Kelly (Rathangan, County Kildare, Ireland, 1907–1966)

Maura Laverty was a well-known Irish broadcaster and a writer of novels, plays, children's books, and cookbooks. She also contributed to the periodical Model Housekeeping. *The dust-jacket of O1139.1 says of her, 'for nearly six years she has been broadcasting weekly Cooking Talks from RADIO EIREANN, ...' Her other cookbooks are:* Flour Economy: Practical Recipes for Breads, Cakes, etc. Based on Potatoes and Oatmeal, *Dublin: Browne and Nolan, [1941] (Great Britain: LB);* Full and Plenty (Complete Guide to Good Cooking), *[Dublin:] Irish Flour Millers Association, 1960 (Great Britain: LB); and* Feasting Galore: Recipes and Food Lore from Ireland, *New York: Holt, Rinehart and Winston, 1961 (United States: DLC).*

O1139.1 [reprint, July 1946]

Maura Laverty's / cookery book / With a section on diet / by Sybil Le Brocquy / Decorations by Louis Le Brocquy / Longmans, Green and Co. / London – New York – Toronto

DESCRIPTION: 21.5 × 13.5 cm   Pp [i–vi], 1–133   Tp illus black-and-yellow, chapter headpieces black-and-yellow   [10s 6d, on dust-jacket]   Cloth

CONTENTS: i ht; ii list of titles 'By the same author'; iii tp; iv publisher's addresses in London, India (three cities), New York, and Toronto, 'First published 1946 // Reprinted July 1946. Code number: 16406 Printed in Eire by the Kerryman Ltd., Tralee.'; v–vi 'Contents'; 1–130 text; 131–3 'Index'

COPIES: *QMM (RBD ckbk 1759)

NOTES: The writing is lively, anecdotal, and personal. What may be the first printing is at DLC in the United States (TX717 L38 1946).

O1139.2 1947

—Maura Laverty's / cookbook / With a section on diet by / Sybil Le Brocquy / Decorations by / Louis Le Brocquy / Longmans, Green and Co. / New York Toronto / 1947

DESCRIPTION: 20.0 × 13.5 cm   Pp [i–iv] v–vi [vii–viii], 1–149   Tp illus black-and-orange, chapter headpieces black-and-orange   Cloth

CONTENTS: i ht; ii 'Other Books by Maura Laverty'; iii tp; iv publisher's addresses in New York and Toronto and '... Copyright 1947 by Maura Laverty ... Published simultaneously in the Dominion of Canada by Longmans, Green and Co., Toronto // Originally published by the Kerryman, Tralee, Ireland, for Maura Laverty Miscellanies, under the title of Kind Cooking // First edition // Printed in the United States of America'; v–vi table of contents; vii 'Maura Laverty's Cookbook'; viii blank; 1–140 text; 141–9 index

COPIES: *OTMCL (641.5 L135, 2 copies); United States: DLC (TX717 L38 1947)

O1139.3 [3rd impression, 1948]

—Maura Laverty's / cookery book / With a section on diet / by Sybil Le Brocquy / Decorations by Louis Le Brocquy / Longman's, Green and Co. / London – New York – Toronto

DESCRIPTION: 21.5 × 13.5 cm   Pp [i–vi], 1–133   Tp illus black-and-orange, chapter headpieces black-and-orange   [10s 6d, on dust-jacket]   Cloth

CONTENTS: i ht; ii list of titles 'By the same author'; iii tp; iv publisher's addresses in London, India (three cities), New York, and Toronto, 'This edition // First published 1946 // Reprinted July 1946 // New impression 1948,' and 'Printed in Eire by the Kerryman Ltd., Tralee.'; v–vi table of contents; 1–130 text; 131–3 index

COPIES: *OGU (UA s013 b27)

NOTES: 'Third impression' is printed on the dust-jacket.

IRISH EDITIONS: *Kind Cooking*, [Dublin:] Electricity Supply Board, [1955] (Great Britain: AnB, LB).

A modern kitchen guide

O1140.1 copyright 1946

A modern / kitchen guide / This book will be found to contain an / excellent collection of practical re- / cipes. / Beginners will value it because of its / simplicity; experienced cooks will use / it to refresh their memories of for- / gotten dishes. / Copyrighted, 1946 / The Bunting Publications, Inc. / North Chicago, Illinois / Printed in U.S.A.

DESCRIPTION: 18.5 × 13.5 cm   Pp [1–4] 5–255   Illus on pp 1 and 4, tailpiece on p 255   Paper

CONTENTS: 1 illus of an open book, candle, and three acorns; 2 blank; 3 tp; 4 illus of four faceless chefs; 5–241 text; 242–55 'Contents – Index'

COPIES: *NBFKL (Ruth Spicer Cookbook Collection) OGU (CCC TX715.6 M626) OPETCM OTYA (TX715 M64 1946)
NOTES: The cover-title is 'A Modern Kitchen Guide // A Complete Book of Up-to-Date Recipes and Household Hints // Farmer's Advocate and Canadian Countryman // London, Canada.'

AMERICAN EDITIONS: North Chicago: Bunting Publications Inc., [c1934] (United States: DLC).

Notes on spices

O1141.1 1946
Notes on spices / [symbol of Canadian Spice Association] / Canadian Spice Association / 1946 [cover-title]
DESCRIPTION: 23.0 × 15.0 cm   Pp 1–16   Paper; stapled
CONTENTS: Inside front face of binding 'Foreword'; top 1 'Notes on Spices'; bottom 1–top 8 'Spices'; mid 8–10 'Seeds'; 11–top 13 'Herbs'; bottom 13–mid 14 'Secondary Products'; bottom 14–16 untitled general remarks
CITATIONS: CCat No. 25, p ZA3
COPIES: OONL (TX406 C3)   *Private collection
NOTES: *Notes on Spices* was published by the Canadian Spice Association for distribution by Canadian companies, as the 'Introduction' to the 1957 edition explains: 'When the [1946] booklet was published, quantities were purchased by the great majority of the firms engaged in the spice business in Canada. They distributed them to schools, clubs, newspapers and magazine editors and to many housewives and other individuals ...'
The 'Foreword' of O1141.1 states: 'During the war, there is evidence of a definitely increasing general interest in seasonings for food. This is quite logical for a great many items have been absent from our normal diet and the interest in seasonings has developed in an effort to make the food at our disposal more zestful.' There are entries for individual seasonings, identifying the part of the plant from which it comes and other botanical information, past and present uses of the seasoning, the form in which it is marketed, and the sources of supply for Canada. The concluding general remarks, p 15, refer to spice milling in Canada as an old and historic business and to the 'several firms of spice millers in Canada which have celebrated their hundredth birthday, and many that are at least half a century old.' The American Spice Trade Association is thanked on p 16 'for some of the material herein contained.'

Questions regarding spices are directed, on p 16, to 'the firm whose name appears on the back cover of this booklet.' In the copy catalogued here, the firm is Griffith Laboratories Ltd, Toronto (founded in Chicago in 1919, a worldwide business in 2007); in the OONL copy, it is McLarens Ltd, Hamilton, a company that sold spices; in other private collectors' copies, it is the spice-seller Gorman, Eckert and Co. Ltd, London; Glenwood Products Ltd, Toronto and Montreal, manufacturers, importers, and millers of spices and other products; and Condor brand products, Montreal.
The book was likely produced in Toronto because the CCat entry includes the name and Toronto address of the secretary-treasurer of the Canadian Spice Association: L.G. Rector, Griffith Laboratories, 109–17 George Street.

O1141.2 1946
—Histoire abrégée des / épices / [symbol of Canadian Spice Association] / Canadian Spice Association / 1946 [cover-title]
DESCRIPTION: 23.0 × 15.0 cm   Pp [i–ii], 1–17   Paper; stapled
CONTENTS: i 'Avant-propos'; ii blank; top 1 'Notes sur les épices'; mid 1–top 9 'Épices'; mid 9–mid 12 'Graines'; mid 12–top 15 'Herbes'; near top 15–mid 16 'Produits secondaires'; mid 16–17 untitled general remarks
CITATIONS: CCat No. 25, p ZA3
COPIES: *QSFFSC (641.338309 C212h)

OTHER EDITIONS: 2nd ed., Canadian Spice Association, 1957 (company collection of Halford-Lewis Ltd, Montreal).

The secret of seasoning

See also an earlier book promoting Lea and Perrins Sauce, Q111.1.

O1142.1 copyright 1946
The / secret / of ... / seasoning / With illustrated / lessons in carving / [On label mounted over original New York imprint:] Lea & Perrins Sauce / is made in Worcester, England. / Bottled and distributed in Canada by / E.D. Smith & Sons, Limited / Winona, Ontario / Printed in U.S.A.
DESCRIPTION: 17.5 × 9.5 cm   Pp [1–2] 3–96   Illus blue-green, illus   Paper, with image on front of a male chef holding a frying pan; stapled
CONTENTS: 1 tp; 2 blank; 3 table of contents, note

about the number of servings per recipe, and 'Copyright 1946 Lea & Perrins, Inc., New York, N.Y.'; 4 'The Englishman's Secret'; 5 'Preparing Flavorful Meals'; 6 'The Table Trio ...'; 7–71 recipes; 72–84 'On Carving ...'; 85–6 index; 87–96 blank for 'Recipe Scrapbook'
COPIES: OGU (CCC TX715.6 S43)   *Private collection
NOTES: A copy at QMMMCM (AR-M2000.92.9) has brown illustrations (not blue-green) and a slightly different text on the title-page label: 'Lea & Perrins Sauce / is bottled and distributed / in Canada by / E.D. Smith & Sons, Limited / Winona, Ontario, Canada / by authority of / Lea & Perrins Limited / Worcester, England.'

Selected recipes

O1143.1 [1946]
Selected recipes / [caption:] The Church of St. James the Apostle – Established 1890 / A collection of tested recipes / selected and arranged for / publication by the members / of the / Parish Guild of / the Church of St. James the Apostle
DESCRIPTION: 23.0 × 15.5 cm   Pp [1] 2–80   Tp photograph of the church   Paper
CONTENTS: 1 tp; 2 ad; 3 'Preface' and 'Members of St. James Parish Guild 1946'; 4 'The Woman Who Cooks' [poem]; 5 ads; 6–79 recipes credited with the name of the contributor and ads; 80 'Index' [i.e., table of contents] and ads
CITATIONS: Driver 2001, Wellington County, p 97 (note 7)
COPIES: *Private collection
NOTES: The cover-title is '1946 / Around the / Clock / Favourites / Parish Guild of / the Church of St. James the Apostle / Guelph, Ontario.'

Silver jubilee souvenir cook book

O1144.1 1946
Silver jubilee / souvenir / cook book / 1921–1946 / A collection of / tested recipes / contributed and published / by / members and friends / of / Star of the Mountain Lodge No. 408, L.O.B.A. [i.e., Ladies' Orange Benevolent Association] / Hamilton, Ontario / We strongly recommend that the ladies consult the advertising pages / of the book before making purchases and that they mention to the / merchant that they have noticed his advertisement in the book. / The members.
DESCRIPTION: 23.0 × 15.0 cm   Pp [1–6] 7–85   Individual photographs of various officers in the organization and a group photograph of 'Officers of L.O.B.A. No. 408, 1946'   Paper; stapled
CONTENTS: 1 tp; 2 blank; 3–6 individual photographs of various officers, including M.W. Sister Phebe Hoey, who 'organized' Star of the Mountain Lodge No. 408 in 1921, and Mrs Florence Burrows-Adam, who 'instituted' No. 408 in the same year; 7 'Provincial Grand Lodge Officers Elected at Hamilton in 1945'; 8 group photograph; 9 'Past Worthy Mistresses of No. 408, L.O.B.A.' [from 1921 to 1946]; 10 blank for 'My Favorite Recipe'; [11–12] [duplicate of pp 9–10, numbered 9–10]; 13 menus for Friday and Saturday meals, 'Lunch Box Menus for Fall and Winter,' and 'For Health, Every Lunch Should Contain:'; 14 ads; 15–80 'Recipes' credited with the name of the contributor and ads; 81 'Household Hints'; 82 'Index' [i.e., table of contents]; 83 'Amount to Serve One Hundred'; 84 'Weights and Measures' and 'Oven Temperatures'; 85 'Wedded Bliss' [mock recipe]
COPIES: *OH (R641.5 SIL CESH)

The well-groomed cookie

O1145.1 nd [about 1946]
The well-groomed / cookie [cover-title]
DESCRIPTION: 10.0 × 13.5 cm   Pp [1–64]   Red paper, with image on front of a woman looking through her lorgnette at a plate of cookies; stapled
CONTENTS: 1–64 sixty-three numbered recipes for cookies, credited with the name of the contributor (Nos. 1–42 for baked cookies, 43–63 for unbaked cookies)
COPIES: OTSCE   *Private collection
NOTES: The title of the book is a play on the name of the group that compiled the recipes, which is printed on the outside back face of the binding: 'St. Clement's Parochial Guild // Groome Group // Convener, Mrs. N. [i.e., Nicholls] Holt, Hudson 8-3957.' The group belonged to St Clement Eglinton Anglican Church at 59 Briar Hill in Toronto. The text is reproduced from typing and the copies were likely home-made by the group rather than professionally printed. The copy catalogued here is inscribed on the binding, in ink, with the year '1946.' The original owner (now deceased) of this copy lived in Toronto in the 1940s.

The Martha Group at the same church also produced a collection of cookie recipes, in the same format as O1145.1, with the same title (*The Well-Groomed Cookie*), and with recipes from many of the same contributors – even, in some cases, the same recipe (copy at OTSCE). The Martha Group publication has a blue-paper binding, with no image. Perhaps the Martha Group's book was a sequel to the Groome Group's.

Yorke, Elizabeth

See also O978.1 by Yorke.

O1146.1   copyright 1946
Canada's / famous / foods / The T. Eaton Co
Limited / Canada Copyright, 1946
DESCRIPTION: About 14.5 × 15.0 cm [dimensions from
photocopy]   [$0.25, on binding]   With image on
front of a lobster
COPIES: *Private collection
NOTES: The cover-title is 'Canada's Famous Foods
and How to Serve Them! ... by Elizabeth Yorke.' This
60-page book about Canadian food was published by
Eaton's, the national chain of department stores. The
following code is on p 60: '8072-5/46-10,900 bks.'
There is no place of publication, but Eaton's was
based in Toronto and O978.1, *Snacks*, another title by
Elizabeth Yorke, was published in Toronto.

1946–9

Super Health Aluminum

O1147.1   nd [about 1946–9]
Less labour less cost / in the cooking of your daily
food / [Super Health Cookware symbol] / A
guaranty of better health / Super Health /
Aluminum [cover-title]
DESCRIPTION: 23.0 × 15.5 cm   Pp [1] 2–30   Illus on
pp 15–18 of 'Super Health Cookware Cast Line'   Pa-
per; stapled
CONTENTS: 1 'The Super Health Process of Cooking'
and at bottom, 'Super Health Aluminum Company
Limited 348 Greenwood Avenue, Toronto'; 2–4 'Gen-
eral Directions for Cooking Vegetables and Fresh
Fruits by the Super Health Process'; 5–8 'General In-
structions for Super Health Method of Roasting'; 9
'Instructions for Using the Super Health Combina-
tion Units'; 10–12 'General Instructions for Baking
Pies, Tarts, Tea Biscuits, Cookies, Cakes, on Top of the
Stove'; 13–14 'Baking Cakes Made in Super Health
Saucepans'; 15–18 illus of Super Health Cookware;
19–21 'Cake Mixes'; 22 'Easy Luncheon Rolls' and
'Fresh Meat Loaf'; 23–top 27 'Grilling and Frying
Pancakes and Steaks the Healthful Way'; mid 27–28
'Super Health Preserving Kettles'; 29 'To Enjoy Satis-
faction and Long Service with Super Health Cooking
Equipment'; 30 'Approximate Time Table "Super
Health" Vapor Process'
COPIES: *Private collection
NOTES: According to p 1, the Super Health process of

cooking, which 'first originated in 1927,' is founded
on two main features, 'healthful food and ... economy
in cooking.' By cooking fruits and vegetables in practically their own moisture and at a low temperature,
more natural goodness is retained than by boiling.

The earliest references to *Super Health Aluminum
Co.'s* Greenwood address in Toronto city directories
is for the years 1943–5, when the company is listed at
107 McGill Street and the foundry at 348 Greenwood.
From 1946, only the Greenwood address is given.
The cookbook was likely published about 1946–9.

Super Health Aluminum Co. published O852.1,
The Health of Your Family Depends Entirely upon You, in
the 1930s. I have not compared the texts of the two
titles to determine whether they are related.

1947

[Title unknown]

O1148.1   [about 1947]
[Title unknown]
DESCRIPTION: 22.5 × 15.0 cm   Pp [leaves lacking]
7–82 [leaves lacking?]   Stapled
CONTENTS: 7–82 recipes credited with the name of the
contributor and ads for Welland, Ontario, businesses
COPIES: *Private collection
NOTES: The original owner reports that the cookbook
was published by Trinity Anglican Church in Welland.
An advertisement on p 40 for W.G. Somerville and
Sons refers to 'the old firm, 1881–1947.'

Adam, Ann [pseudonym]

*See O877.1 for information about Ann Adam and her
books. For the titles of other cookbooks by Moffats Ltd,
see O342.1.*

O1149.1   [1947]
De / la / magie / dans / les / menus / avec le
nouveau / "Handi-Chef" Moffat / par / Ann Adam
/ autorité en matière de cuisine / de renommée
internationale [cover-title]
DESCRIPTION: 23.0 × 15.5 cm   Pp [1–2] 3–23   Illus
Paper, with image on front of the 'Handi-Chef';
stapled, and with two holes punched at left edge for
storing in a ring-binder
CONTENTS: 1 cover-title; 2 untitled general information about operating the 'Handi-Chef'; 3 introductory text signed Ann Adam; 4–22 text; 23 publ ad;
outside back face of binding 'Moffats Limited //

Weston Ontario Canada // F 08100-5M-8-47'
COPIES: *OONL (TX715.6 A366 1947 p***)
NOTES: The 'Handi-Chef' was a compact, electric cooking appliance that sat on a countertop or table. A publisher's advertisement on p 23 refers to sixty-five years since the first Moffat stove was constructed. Since the company was founded in 1882 (see the company history in O705.1, *Moffats Cook Book*), this book was published in 1947. The printer's mark on the binding confirms 1947 as the year of publication.

Canada, Department of Agriculture

For a list of other cookbooks published by the Department of Agriculture, see O404.1.

O1150.1 1947
[First edition of *Cheese Dishes,* 1947; see notes for O1150.2]

O1150.2 [rev. ed.], nd [about 1950]
—Consumer Section – Marketing Service / Department of Agriculture / Ottawa – Canada / Cheese / dishes / Published by authority of the Rt. Hon. James G. Gardiner, / Minister of Agriculture, [*sic,* comma] [cover-title]
DESCRIPTION: 22.0 × 10.5 cm   Pp 3–19   Paper; stapled
CONTENTS: 3 'Canadian Cheese'; 4 'Cheese – A Healthful Food'; 5 'Many Uses for Cheese' and 'How to Cook Cheese'; 6 'How to Store Cheese'; 7–19 recipes
COPIES: *OOAG (641.6373 C212 rev., 2 copies)
NOTES: Ag 1867–1974, p 172, cites this title, 1947 and revised 1950, 1957. The edition described here is undated; however, the OOAG call number indicates that it is a revised edition. The booklet's design is similar (but not identical) to that of another Department of Agriculture booklet from about the same time, O1205.1, *Desserts You'll Like.*

O1151.1 April 1947
Home canning / of fruits / and / vegetables / Prepared by / Consumer Section, Marketing Service / Dominion Department of Agriculture / Right Honourable James G. Gardiner, Minister / Publication 789 Consumer Bulletin 1 // April, 1947. [cover-title]
DESCRIPTION: 23.0 × 15.0 cm   Pp [1] 2–32   Paper, with vertical band at left that has a scalloped edge punctuated by cherries and other fruit; stapled
CONTENTS: 1 cover-title; 2 'Approximate Yields of Canned Fruit'; 3 'Canning Fruits and Vegetables'; 4–5 'Equipment for Canning'; 6–13 'Steps in Canning'; 14–16 'Processing Time Table for Fruits'; 17 'Special Methods of Canning Fruits'; 18–19 'Processing Time Table for Vegetables'; 20–mid 23 'Jams and Conserves'; mid 23–25 'Jellies'; 26–9 'Pickles and Relishes'; 30–2 [outside back face of binding] 'Questions and Answers'
CITATIONS: Ag 1867–1974, p 43
COPIES: AMHM   OOAG (630.4 C212 P789, 2 copies) *Private collection

O1151.2 May 1948
—Home canning / of fruits / and / vegetables / Prepared by / Consumer Section, Marketing Service / Dominion Department of Agriculture / Right Honourable James G. Gardiner, Minister / Publication 789 Consumers [*sic,* plural] Bulletin 1, May 1948 [cover-title]
DESCRIPTION: 23.0 × 15.0 cm   Pp [1] 2–32   Paper, with vertical band at left that has a scalloped edge punctuated by cherries and other fruit; stapled
CONTENTS: 1 cover-title; 2 'Approximate Yields of Canned Fruit'; 3 'Canning Fruits and Vegetables' and 'Steps in Canning'; 4–5 'Equipment for Canning'; 6–13 'Steps in Canning'; 14 'Special Methods of Canning Fruits'; 15–17 'Processing Time Table for Fruits'; 18–19 'Processing Time Table for Vegetables'; 20–mid 23 'Jams and Conserves'; bottom 23–25 'Jellies'; 26–9 'Pickles and Relishes'; 30–2 'Questions and Answers'
CITATIONS: Ag 1867–1974, p 43   Newman
COPIES: *AEAG   OOAG (2 copies: 630.4 C212 P789, 630.4 C212 CB1)
NOTES: The text is printed in green and black.

O1151.3 rev. ed., May 1949
—Home canning / of fruits / and / vegetables / Prepared by / Consumer Section, Marketing Service / Dominion Department of Agriculture / Right Honourable James G. Gardiner, Minister / Publication 789 Consumer Bulletin 1, Revised May 1949 [cover-title]
DESCRIPTION: 22.5 × 15.0 cm   Pp 3–34   Paper, with vertical band at left that has a scalloped edge punctuated by cherries and other fruit; stapled
CONTENTS: 3 'Canning Fruits and Vegetables' and 'Steps in Canning'; 4–5 'Equipment for Canning'; 6–13 'Steps in Canning'; 14–15 'Processing Time Table for Vegetables'; 16 'Approximate Yields of Canned Fruit'; 17 'Special Methods of Canning Fruits'; 18–20 'Processing Time Table for Fruits'; 21–3 'Jams and Conserves'; 24 'Jams and Conserves – Jellies'; 25–6 'Jellies'; 27–31 'Pickles and Relishes'; 32–4 'Questions and Answers'
CITATIONS: Ag 1867–1974, p 43

COPIES: OGU (2 copies: Rural Heritage Collection uncat, CCC CA1 DA9 47P89 rev. 1949) *OOAG (630.4 C212 P789, 2 copies; 630.4 C212 CB1, 2 copies)
NOTES: The text is printed in green and black. '40M. 12617. 5:49' is on the outside back face of the binding.

O1151.4 rev. ed., May 1949
—Conserves / de fruits / et de / légumes / Préparé par / la Section des consommateurs / Service des marchés / Ministère fédéral de l'agriculture / le très honorable James G. Gardiner, ministre / Publication numéro 789 Bulletin du consommateur – 1 // mai 1947 / Publication numéro 789 Bulletin du consommateur 1. Revisé mai, 1949 [cover-title]
DESCRIPTION: 23.0 × 15.0 cm Pp 3–35 Paper, with vertical band at left that has a scalloped edge punctuated by cherries and other fruit; stapled
CONTENTS: 3 'Conserves de fruits et de légumes'; 4–5 'Matériel de mise en conserves'; 6–13 'Marché à suivre pour la mise en conserves'; 14–15 'Tableau de la durée de stérilisation pour les légumes'; 16 'Quantité approximative des fruits en conserves'; 17 'Procédés spéciaux pour la mise en conserves des fruits'; 18–20 'Tableau de la durée de stérilisation pour les fruits'; 21–mid 24 'Confitures'; mid 24–26 'Gelées'; 27–31 'Marinades et condiments'; 32–5 [inside back face of binding] 'Questions et réponses sur la mise en conserves'
CITATIONS: Ag 1867–1974, p 32
COPIES: *OOAG (630.4 C212 CB1, 2 copies)
NOTES: The text is printed in green and black. '15M – 12617. 5-49.' is on the outside back face of the binding.

OTHER EDITIONS: *Home Canning of Fruits and Vegetables*, rev. ed., February 1950 (OOAG); June 1952 (OOAG); March 1954 (OOAG, OONL); rev. ed., June 1956 (OOAG, OONL); 1959 (OONL); [rev. ed.], 1965 (OOAG, OONL); [1966] (OONL); 1968 (OONL); 1972 reprint of 1965 (OOAG, OONL). The 1972 reprint also lists reprints in 1967 and 1969.
Conserves de fruits et de légumes, rev. ed., April 1950; rev. ed., June 1956; reprint, November 1959; reprint, 1966, 1967, 1969, 1972 (all at OOAG). The 1972 reprint gives the following publishing history: 'Imprimé 1947 Revisé 1953, 1959, 1966 Réimprimé 1966, 1967, 1968, 1972.'

Canada, Department of National Defence, Royal Canadian Navy

See also a related manual, O1175.1, Canada, Department of National Defence, Royal Canadian Navy, The R.C.N. Recipe Manual, 1948.

O1152.1 [December 1947]
B.R.C.N. 3103 / Department of National Defence / The instructional manual / of / naval cookery
DESCRIPTION: 20.5 × 17.5 cm Pp [i–viii], [unpaginated leaves of text numbered as 28 chapters in numbered paragraphs] Illus Card; bound with two metal fasteners
CONTENTS: i tp; ii blank; iii 'B.R.C.N. 3103 The Naval Service of Canada // The first day of December, 1947 // The instructions contained in this publication, ... are issued under the authority of the Minister within his power under the Naval Service Act, 1944 ...'; iv blank; v–viii 'Table of Contents'; unpaginated leaves of text
COPIES: OONL (COP.CA.D.2267) *QMAC (VC375 C2A53)
NOTES: Paragraph 1.03 states, 'The purpose of this manual ... is to assist you in becoming and continuing to be an efficient Cook rating.' There are no recipes. The instruction is on general principles and methods of cooking, and there is information about running a navy kitchen and mess.

A collection of tested recipes

O1153.1 nd [1947]
A collection of / tested recipes / We may live without poetry, music and art; / We may live without conscience and live without heart; / We may live without friends, we may live without books; / But civilized man cannot live without cooks. / – Owen Meredith. / Sponsored by / St. Peter's Parish Guild / of / St. Peter's Church / Brockville, Ontario / [folio:] Page one
DESCRIPTION: Pp 1–88 With image on front of the church
CONTENTS: 1 tp; 2 'Index' [i.e., alphabetical list of sections]; 3 'Foreword' signed John L. Hutchinson, rector; 4 ad; 5–mid 86 recipes credited with the name of the contributor and ads; mid 86–87 'Household Hints'; 88 blank for 'My Own Recipes'
COPIES: *Private collection
NOTES: The cover-title is 'Cook Book.' An advertisement on p 48 is evidence of the date of publication: '1869 – seventy-eight years – 1947 Mutual Life of Canada.'

Cook book

See also O518.1, by the same group.

O1154.1 1947
Cook book / Compiled and published by / the Women's Auxiliary of Hanover Memorial Hospital [cover-title]
DESCRIPTION: 23.0 × 15.5 cm Pp [1] 2–108 'View of Hanover Memorial Hospital' on p 1 Paper; stapled
CONTENTS: 1 illus of hospital and a list of Hanover Hospital Auxiliary members; 2 'Foreword' signed John A. Paterson, president of the Board, and acknowledgment; 3 'Weights and Measures,' 'Other Equivalents,' and 'Table Decorations'; 4 ad; 5 'How Much Does It Take to Serve 50?'; 6 ads; 7–103 recipes and ads; 104–5 'Household Hints'; 106 ad; 107 'Index' [i.e., table of contents]; 108 blank for 'My Own Recipes' and at bottom, 'The Hanover Post Press – June, 1947'
COPIES: *Private collection

Cook book

O1155.1 [1947]
Cook book / Our / favorite recipes / Selected / by / the members / of / the Women's Association / of / St. James' United Church / Peterborough Ontario
DESCRIPTION: About 22.0 × 13.0 cm [dimensions from photocopy] With photograph on front of the church; stapled
CONTENTS: 1 tp; 2 'Roster // Officers of the Woman's [*sic*] Association // St. James United Church // Peterborough, Ontario 1947' [list of positions and names]; 3 'Preface' signed the Committee; ...
COPIES: *Private collection
NOTES: The owner reports that the book was printed by Baker Printing Co., Peterborough. Her copy is inscribed on the title-page, in ink, 'With best wishes from the Womans Association of St. James Church // Mrs. G. Harris Pres. June 7 1947.' The cookbook is titled and organized following the pattern set by an earlier publication from the same church, O1083.1.

Cook book

Horton Township is in Renfrew County, west of Ottawa. The North Horton branch of the Women's Institute was established in 1915 (Ambrose, p 230).

O1156.1 1947
It's fun / to bake it yourself / North Horton Women's Institute / Cook book / 1947 / For home and country [cover-title]
DESCRIPTION: 23.0 × 15.5 cm Pp [1] 2–87 Paper, with small image on front of baked goods; stapled
CONTENTS: 1 'Our Appreciation' and an untitled verse (in mock-recipe form), beginning 'Take one whole pound of kindliness'; 2 'Weights and Measures' and 'Oven Temperatures'; 3–84 recipes credited with the name of the contributor and ads; 85–7 'Household Discoveries'
COPIES: *Private collection
NOTES: There are recipes on p 6 for To Cure Meat (For each 100 lbs. meat) and Dry Cure (For 100 lbs meat).

Cook book containing many carefully-chosen practical recipes

See also O1016.1, by the Ladies' Aid of St Andrew's Church.

O1157.1 1947
Cook book / containing many carefully-chosen practical / recipes / Issued by / the Presbyterian Young Women's / Club / Kitchener, Ontario. / 1947 / Cober Printing Service
DESCRIPTION: 21.5 × 14.5 cm Pp [1–2] 3–64 Tp illus of a manservant carrying aloft a covered dish, two potted fruit trees behind him Paper, with image on front of a church (unidentified, but St Andrew's Presbyterian Church at the corner of Queen and Weber streets); stapled
CONTENTS: 1 tp; 2 'Index' [i.e., table of contents] and 'Introductory' signed Presbyterian Young Women's Club, Kitchener, Ontario, November 1947'; 3–64 recipes, 'Helpful Hints,' 'Removing Stains,' 'Household Hints,' and ads
CITATIONS: Bloomfield 3212
COPIES: *OWTU (2 copies: F6987, F14676)
NOTES: The cover-title is 'Our Best Recipes.' On p 3 the recipes are headed 'Selected Recipes.' There is an advertisement on p 64 for the printer, Cober Printing Service, 85 Samuel Street, Kitchener.

Cooking craft

The Lady Margaret Alexander Chapter was formed on 2 April 1946; it disbanded in 1990.

O1158.1 [20 February 1947]
Cooking craft / Tested recipes / household hints / general information / Our intention in the

preparation of this book was / to make available some recipes which have been / proven through long use by our members and / friends. / Some of the recipes are old, some of them are new, / but we feel sure that the quantities indicated and / the methods suggested will produce excellent / results. / The advertisers have helped materially in the pub- / lication. We suggest that the reader consult the / advertising pages and patronise these advertisers. / [IODE symbol] / Lady Margaret Alexander Chapter / Imperial Order / Daughters of the Empire / Orillia, Ontario.

DESCRIPTION: Pp [1–2] 3–88

CONTENTS: 1 tp; 2 ad; 3–87 recipes credited with the name of the contributor, 'Invalid Cookery,' 'Simple Remedies,' 'Table Setting and Service,' 'Equivalents and Anniversaries,' 'For Serving 100 People,' and ads; 88 'Index' [i.e., table of contents], 'Printed in Canada on Canadian paper,' and 'This book was printed at the office of the *Packet and Times*, which is in Orillia, in the Province of Ontario, this twentieth day of February, which is Thursday, in the year one thousand nine hundred and forty-seven, anno domini.'

COPIES: *Private collection

NOTES: The year of publication, 1947, is printed on the front face of the binding, and on p 88, with the day and month. The cover-title is 'Cook Book.' On the outside back face of the binding, under the heading 'This Cook Book Is an Exchange of Ideas,' an advertisement for the *Packet and Times* states, 'The chief appeal of the recipes in this cook book to most women, is in the fact that they are "home tested" – that other women have tried them and found them good. This habit of exchanging ideas is probably the basic reason why women can create so much pleasing variety with the same ingredients, year after year, ...'

See also the notes for O1022.1, *Tested Recipes*.

Favorite recipes

O1159.1 [1947]

Favorite recipes / Bethel United Church / Kinburn, Ontario [cover-title]

DESCRIPTION: 22.0 × 15.0 cm   Pp [1–2] 3–102   Paper, with image on front of Bethel United Church; stapled

CONTENTS: 1 'Foreword' signed Mrs H.W. Mayhew, president; 2 'W.A. [i.e., Women's Association] Bethel United Church, Group I – 1947,' list of officers and members and the name of the minister; 3–102 recipes and ads; inside back face of binding 'Prensler Press

// commercial printers Phone 9 142 John St. P.O. Box 463 Arnprior, Ontario'

COPIES: *Bookseller's stock

NOTES: The bookseller's copy is inscribed on p 1, in ink, 'Happy Birthday Bessie. Love, mother. 1947.'

Favourite recipes

O1160.1   1947

[IODE symbol] / Favourite recipes / prepared and compiled by / members of / Angela Bruce Chapter / Imperial Order / Daughters of the Empire / Oakville Ontario / Index appears on page 161 / 1947 / Acknowledgments / The officers and members of the Angela Bruce / Chapter, I.O.D.E., wish to express their appreciation to / the friends and advertisers who have helped with advice, / recipes and donations to make this book possible. / [folio:] 1

DESCRIPTION: 23.0 × 15.5 cm   Pp 1–164   Paper, with IODE symbol on front; Semi-exposed Wire-O Binding patented 1939

CONTENTS: 1 tp; 2 ad; 3 'Angela Bruce Chapter, I.O.D.E.' [a history]; 4 list of mayor and Council and the town officials of Oakville, 1947; 5 'The Town of Oakville' [historical sketch and important telephone numbers]; 6 ads; 7–160 text, mostly recipes credited with the name of the contributor, and ads; 161 'Where to Find It' [i.e., alphabetical list of sections]; 162–3 'Telephone Directory of Local Advertisers'; 164 ad

CITATIONS: CCat No. 26, p ZB13

COPIES: *Private collection

NOTES: The Angela Bruce Chapter was organized on 4 May 1933; the text on p 3 records the chapter's accomplishments to date. CCat records the price: $1.00.

Freeman, Mae Blacker (1907–)

This American author wrote many books for children, mostly on science topics.

O1161.1   copyright 1947

Fun with / cooking / by / Mae Blacker Freeman / New revised edition / Random House New York

DESCRIPTION: 25.5 × 18.0 cm   Pp [1–4] 5–60 [61]   Many fp illus and illus   Cloth, with image on front of a girl serving a boy and girl seated at table

CONTENTS: 1 tp; 2 'Copyright 1947 by Random House, Inc. ... Published in New York by Random House, Inc. and simultaneously in Toronto, Canada, by Random House of Canada, Ltd. 1947. Printed in the United States of America ...'; 3 table of contents; 4 blank; 5 'Introduction'; 6–61 text

COPIES: *Private collection; United States: DLC (TX652.5 F7)

NOTES: The cookbook is for children. Generally, there is one recipe per page, with an illustration on the facing page. The recipes are predominantly for sweet dishes, such as Mickey Mouse Salad (a pear is the mouse head) and Root Beer Float, but there are also savoury dishes, such as Surprise Meatloaf (with a hard-boiled egg in the centre) and Tuna Casserole (canned mushroom soup, tuna, and crushed potato chips).

The private collector's copy is stamped 'Withdrawn from North York Public Library' [i.e., OTNY].

Friendly favorites for bachelor apartments

O1162.1 [1947]
Friendly favorites / for / bachelor apartments / Chi Eta Chapter / of / Alpha Iota Sorority / Westervelt School / London, Ontario / The cup of friendship, filled with cheer, / Grand things to eat, to each heart dear, / Break down all barriers and reserve, / And shared – shall peace and joy preserve.

DESCRIPTION: 23.0 × 15.5 cm Pp [1–4] 5–35 Paper; stapled

CONTENTS: 1 tp; 2 'Index' [i.e., table of contents]; 3 'A Recipe for a Day,' three untitled verses, and 'Our Greeting'; 4 blank; 5–35 recipes credited with the name of the contributor

COPIES: *Private collection

NOTES: The book's owner reports that it was published as a fund-raiser for the Alpha Iota International Convention held in Winnipeg in 1947. 'Our Greeting' expresses the hope that the 'sorority may greatly benefit by the sale of [the book].' The verses are about cooking and cooks, written in a moralistic, but amusing, vein. 'Hunter Printing Company // London Ontario' is on the outside back face of the binding.

Instructions for cooking and canning

See also O1105.1, by the same company.

O1163.1 copyright 1947
Reg[.?] / trade mark / National / Trade mark reg / Pressure Cooker / Instructions for cooking and canning / A complete manual on the science of canning and cooking / under steam pressure / Directions Time tables Recipes / The Consumer Section of the Dominion / Department of Agriculture at Ottawa / recommends the pressure cooker for / the canning of all vegetables (except / tomatoes), meat, fish and poultry. / Copyright 1947, National Pressure Cooker Co. (Canada) Ltd., Wallaceburg, Ontario

DESCRIPTION: 23.0 × 15.0 cm Pp [1] 2–85 [86–8] Small tp illus of the dome of the Capitol in Washington, DC, illus Paper, with small image on front of the dome of the Capitol; stapled

CONTENTS: 1 tp; 2 'Warranty' and 'Repair and Replacement Information'; 3 table of contents; 4–5 'Know Your Cooker and the Pressure Cooking Method Thoroughly ...'; 6 'Instructions for the Use and Care of the Pressure Cooker'; 7 'The How and Why of Your Canning Budget'; 8 'Table of Approximate Yield // Fruits'; 9 'Table of Approximate Yield // Vegetables'; 10 'Why Can at Home ...?'; 11–13 'Know the Parts of Your Pressure Cooker before You Put It to Use'; 14 'How to Care for Your Cooker'; 15 'Filling, Sealing & Testing Glass Sealers'; 16 'Tin Cans' and 'Sealing Machine'; 17 'If Canning in Tin, Follow These Important Instructions'; 18 'Other Helpful Equipment' and 'The Theory of Pressure Canning'; 19 'Principles of Food Preservation'; 20 'Important Instructions for Opening and Closing Your Cooker'; 21–5 'Steps in Canning'; 26 'Use of Cooker with Different Types of Fuel'; 27–48 'Canning Directions'; 49–83 'General Cooking with a Pressure Cooker'; 84 'Other Pressure Cooker Uses'; 85 'Repair Parts Price List'; 86–8 blank for 'Memoranda'

COPIES: AEPMA *Bookseller's stock

NOTES: The cover-title is 'Modern Guide to Home Canning // Instructions Recipes'; printed below the cover-title is '2-47.' The recipes are for cooking with the National Pressure Cooker. In the United States, National Pressure Cooker Co. was based in Eau Claire, Wisconsin. The text makes an American reference on p 72: 'In the not-too-distant past, poultry and game was served by most American families as holiday treats ...'

O1163.2 copyright 1947
—Le cuiseur a pression / National / Trade mark reg / Instructions pour la cuisine et la mise en conserves / Un manuel complet sur le procédé scientifique de mise en / conserves et de cuisson sous pression de vapeur. / Directions Tables de temps Recettes / Le ministre fédéral de l'agriculture recom- / mande le cuiseur à pression pour la mise en / conserves de tous les légumes (sauf les /

tomates), la viande, le poisson / et la volaille. / Tous droits réservés 1947 par National Pressure Co. [*sic*] (Canada) Ltd., / Wallaceburg, Ontario.

COPIES: *QSFFSC (2 copies)

NOTES: The cover-title is 'Guide moderne pour la mise en conserves chez-soi.' The company name is incorrectly printed on the title-page: 'National Pressure Co.' instead of National Pressure Cooker Co. The publication date, '2-47,' is printed below the cover-title. One copy at QSFFSC is inscribed on the binding, '25 juillet 1947,' and stamped, 'Rec'd 25 Jul 1947'; the other copy is inscribed on the title-page, '15 aout 1947.'

Jubilee cook book

Byron became part of the city of London in 1961.

O1164.1   nd [1947]

Jubilee / cook book / [Women's Institute symbol] / Compiled by / Byron Women's Institute [cover-title]

DESCRIPTION: About 23.0 × 15.0 cm   Pp 1–68   Paper or card?; probably stapled

CONTENTS: 1 'Foreword' and 'Officers of Byron Women's Institute'; 2 ads and 'Thanks'; 3–67 culinary text, mainly recipes credited with the name of the contributor, blank spaces for 'My Own Recipes,' and ads; 68 ad and 'Index' [i.e., table of contents]

COPIES: *OL (R641.5971325 JUB, photocopy)

NOTES: The 'Foreword' relates the history of the Women's Institute, from its establishment on 19 February 1897 in Saltfleet Township, Wentworth. It says that the Byron branch was 'organized in 1922 [Ambrose, p 237, records the same year], just 25 years after Stoney Creek and thus we celebrate our Silver Jubilee,' and it refers to the Women's Institute as a whole preparing to celebrate its Golden Jubilee in February 1947; therefore, the date of publication of the cookbook is 1947 (1897 + 50 years or 1922 + 25 years) or possibly late 1946. The names of the first president and other officers of the Byron branch are given and the locations of past meetings are recorded.

King Cole cook book

O1165.1   nd [about 1947]

King Cole / cook book / "Recipes fit for a king" / The Church of St. Jude, Toronto [cover-title]

DESCRIPTION: 22.5 × 15.0 cm   Pp 1–48   Very thin card, with image on front of a crown; stapled

CONTENTS: 1 'The Church of St. Jude, Toronto' [a history]; 2–47 recipes, some of which are credited with the name of the contributor, occasional blank spaces for 'My Own Recipes,' 'To Serve 100 People' on p 42, 'Suggestions for Table Decorations' on p 45, and ads; 48 ad and 'Index' [i.e., table of contents]

COPIES: *Private collection

NOTES: The church history on p 1 begins in the summer of 1888, when 'the name of St. Jude was given to what had previously been known as the Howard Street Mission in St. Anne's Parish.' The cornerstone of a small church was laid on 24 May 1889, and the foundation stone of the new church, on 13 September 1911. The last rector mentioned in the history is 'the fourth and present Rector, Rev. R.J. Shires, [who] took charge on August 1st, 1933.'

An advertisement on the inside back face of the binding, for Alfred H. Owen Ltd, a maker of interior furnishings, suggests a publication date for the cookbook of 1947. The advertisement records the establishment of the business in 1922 and refers to 'our 25th year selling direct to you.'

No particular group within the church is officially identified as the compiler of the cookbook; however, there is an advertisement on p 3 for Francis G. Stevens, seller of real estate insurance, that offers 'congratulations to St. Jude's Parish Guild in their latest venture.' The printer, 'Amherst Card Guild, 8 Caithness Ave. GE, 4323,' is on the outside back face of the binding. The advertisements are for businesses in the Roncesvalles area of Toronto.

Memorial book

O1166.1   1947

Memorial book / As an added feature / tested recipes / Compiled and published by / the Snye Women's Patriotic League. / 1947

DESCRIPTION: 23.5 × 15.5 cm   Pp [1] 2–88   Many illus   Paper; stapled

CONTENTS: 1 tp; 2 'Executive of Snye Patriotic League 1947'; 3 'Preface'; 4 fp illus of a gathering of the Snye Patriotic League; 5 'Dedication'; 6–7 'Baldoon Settlement and Snye Ecarte [i.e., Écarté]' and landscape scene of 'At the point'; 8 fp illus of 'Our own H.M.C.S. Wallaceburg'; 9 fp illus of 'Beautiful scene going through the cut into the river'; 10 'In Flanders Fields' [poem by John McCrae]; 11–14 ads; 15 'Knox Presbyterian Church' [illus and history]; 16 ads; 17 fp illus of 'Children of Union School No. 15, Chatham and Dover, 1947'; 18 'Recessional 1897' by Rudyard

Kipling; 19 ads; 20 'History of Wallaceburg Parish' by Rev. R.A. Van Vynckt; 21 illus of 'The Palms and Catholic Church' and 'Crossing the Snye to Walpole Island in ferry'; 22 'History of Wallaceburg Anglican'; 23 fp illus of Wallaceburg Anglican Church; 24 ads; 25 fp illus of 'Some trouble – boats getting crossways of the river – needed help'; 26 ads; 27 fp illus of 'George Arnold crossing the Snye in his boat'; 28 ads; 29 fp illus of 'The New Snye Union School'; 30 ads; 31 fp illus of 'The Old Snye School'; 32 'Chanel E'Carte [sic] (The Lost Channel)' by George H. Taylor; 33 'Wallaceburg Baptist Church' [illus and information]; 34 ads; 35 fp illus of 'Coming home from Walpole Island on the ferry'; 36 ads; 37–82 recipes, many credited with the name of the contributor; 83 'Household Hints'; 84–7 blank for 'Memorandum'; 88 'Index' [i.e., table of contents] and ad
COPIES: *OTNY (971.333 MEM)
NOTES: The cover-title is 'Memorial Book // 14–18 39–45.' The dedication is 'to the memory of the boys of this community who made the supreme sacrifice in World Wars I and II, and to all boys and girls who helped to keep the home land safe from the invader.'

My favourite recipes

O1167.1   [1947]
My favourite / recipes / Compiled and published / by the / Woman's Association / St. Paul's United Church / New Liskeard – Ontario / Printed by the Temiskaming Printing Co. Ltd., New Liskeard, Ont.
DESCRIPTION: Tp illus of a plate of cookies
COPIES: *Private collection
NOTES: The 'Preface' on p 2 is dated 1947. This is the first of a series of St Paul's cookbooks identified by the colour of their bindings. As the 'Forward' [sic] of 100th Anniversary: 98 and Growing Great explains: 'With great joy, we bring this cookbook in celebration of 100 years 1898–1998 for the congregation of St. Paul's // We have brought recipes from our previous cookbooks, ... There were 3 cookbooks, the "brown" book 1947, the grey book 50's, and the yellow 1983.' In the list of 'Colour Coded Sections' below the foreword, the undated grey cookbook (called Recipes for Every Day) is assigned the year 1957. On p 8 of the centennial cookbook there is a list of the 1947 members who prepared the first cookbook; on p 18, there is a list of the members who prepared the grey one. Copies of all four cookbooks are at the church.

Preparing foods for storage in your Massey-Harris Home Freezer

O1168.1   nd [about 1947]
Preparing foods for storage / in your / Massey-Harris Home Freezer [cover-title]
DESCRIPTION: 23.0 × 15.0 cm   Pp 1–18   Illus   Paper, with images on front of foodstuffs and of two scenes of a hunter shooting game; stapled, and with hole punched at top left corner for hanging
CONTENTS: 1 'Acknowledgments' signed Massey-Harris Co. Ltd; 2 'The Home Preparation of Frozen Foods' and 'Suggestions for Satisfaction'; 3–5 'Packaging Foods for Freezing'; 6–9 'Vegetables'; 10–12 'Fruits'; 13–17 'Meat'; 18 'Keeping an Inventory of Your Frozen Foods' and 'Servicing the Home Freezer'
COPIES: *Private collection
NOTES: The collector's copy is dated on p 1, with ball-point pen, 'Nov. 1948.' No place of publication is recorded, but the Massey-Harris Co. was based in Toronto. The text is probably by Elaine Collett, who is reported to have 'produced a freezer book for farm women' in the period she worked for Massey-Harris, about 1945 to 1947. In light of the dated inscription in the collector's copy, the cookbook was likely published about 1947. For biographical information about Collett, see O1221.1, Moffat Cook Book.

Recipes from Muskoka

O1169.1   nd [about 1947]
Recipes from Muskoka / A selection of tried and tested recipes, / compiled and published by the members of / the Parish Guild of / All Saints Anglican Church, / Huntsville, Ontario, / Canada
DESCRIPTION: 23.5 × 15.5 cm   Pp [1–6] 7–76   Illus on p 1 of All Saints Anglican Church   Lacks paper binding; stapled
CONTENTS: 1 tp; 2 'Ray Ball Job Press // Huntsville, Ontario'; 3 preface signed members of All Saints Parish Guild; 4 ads; 5 'Index' [i.e., table of contents]; 6 blank; 7–73 recipes and ads; 74 blank for 'Notes' and ad; 75 'Household Hints' and ad; 76 'A Table of Weights and Measures' and ad
COPIES: *Private collection
NOTES: This copy is inscribed on p 3, in ink, 'To Jean // Love from mother // Easter 1947.'

Scott, Anna Lee [pseudonym]

For information about Anna Lee Scott and her cookbooks, see O526.1.

O1170.1 [copyright 1947]
Cooking / made easy / Anna Lee Scott / A home economics course / for users of / Monarch Pastry Flour
DESCRIPTION: 22.5 × 14.5 cm   Pp [i–iii], [1] 2–132   Paper, with red-and-white checked pattern associated with Monarch Pastry Flour; spiral-bound
CONTENTS: i tp; ii–iii ad for Maple Leaf Milling Co.'s products; 1 introduction signed Anna Lee Scott; 2–126 seventeen numbered lessons with recipes; 127–32 index, and at bottom p 132, 'Copyright Canada 1947 Maple Leaf Milling Co. Ltd. // Printed in Canada by the Copp Clark Co. Ltd.'
COPIES: BVAU (Beatrice M. Millar Papers)   NSHMS (88.74.13)   QMM (RBD ckbk 1992)   *Private collection
NOTES: Unusually, the recto pages have even numbers; the versos, odd numbers. The private collector's copy is inscribed on the binding, in ink, 'Beverley Jenkins – 12D Room – 211,' evidence that this promotional cookbook was used in a public school classroom. Another private collector's letter confirms this: '... my cookbook which I received when taking my Home Economics class in High School, Dryden, Ont.' And another owner inscribed her copy as a girl, 'Rose Marie Liznick – Grade 9 // Home Economics – 1953–1954 // Teacher – Miss Dora Wilson.'

O1170.2 [copyright 1947]
—Cooking / made easy / Anna Lee Scott / A domestic science course for users of / Monarch Pastry Flour [cover-title]
DESCRIPTION: 22.5 × 15.0 cm   Pp [i], 1–132   Paper-covered boards, with red-and-white checked pattern associated with Monarch Pastry Flour; sewn
CONTENTS: i blank; 1 introduction signed Anna Lee Scott; 2–126 seventeen numbered lessons with recipes; 127–32 index, and at bottom p 132, 'Copyright Canada 1947 Maple Leaf Milling Co. Ltd. // Printed in Canada by the Copp Clark Co. Ltd.'
COPIES: *OGU (CCC TX715.6 S35)   OONL (TX715.6 S35 1947, 3 copies)   SRRPM
NOTES: Unusually, the recto pages have even numbers; the versos, odd numbers. In this edition, the cover-title refers to 'domestic science course,' not 'home economics course.'

O1170.3 [copyright 1947]
—La cuisine / rendue facile / Anna Lee Scott / Cours de science culinaire pour celles qui emploient / la farine à pâtisserie Monarch [cover-title]
DESCRIPTION: 22.0 × 15.0 cm   Pp 1–129   Paper-covered boards, with red-and-white checked pattern associated with Monarch Pastry Flour
CONTENTS: 1 unsigned 'Introduction'; 2–126 seventeen numbered lessons with recipes; 127–9 'Table des matières,' and at bottom p 129, 'Tous droits réservés, Canada 1947 Maple Leaf Milling Co. Ltd. Imprimé au Canada par The Copp Clark Co. Ltd.'
COPIES: OONL (TX715.6 S35 1947b)   QMM (2 copies: *RBD Soeur Berthe, ckbk 294; RBD TX715 S26 Joubert)   QQSCA
NOTES: A photocopy of the cover-title of the QQSCA copy shows what is probably a label applied to the binding, below Scott's name, which warns: 'Attention! Lisez les pages 1-19-20 avant d'appliquer les recettes.'

O1170.4 [copyright 1947]
—Cooking / made easy / by Anna Lee Scott / Maple Leaf Milling Co. Limited / Toronto Canada
DESCRIPTION: 21.5 × 14.5 cm   Pp [i], [1] 2–123 [124–7]   Tp still-life of a sifter, bowl, and measuring cup   Thin silver card, with tp still-life on front
CONTENTS: i tp; 1 introduction signed Anna Lee Scott; 2–123 text; 124–7 index, and at bottom p 127, 'Copyright Canada 1947 Maple Leaf Milling Co. Ltd. // Printed in Canada by the Copp Clark Co. Ltd.'
COPIES: *Private collection
NOTES: Unusually, the recto pages have even numbers; the versos, odd numbers. Unlike previous editions, the chapters are not numbered as lessons. The text is printed in blue and black.

O1170.5 nd
—Cooking / made easy / by Anna Lee Scott / Maple Leaf Milling Co. Limited / Toronto Canada
DESCRIPTION: 21.5 × 14.5 cm   Pp [i], [1] 2–123 [124–7]   Tp still-life of a sifter, bowl, and measuring cup   Thin silver card
CONTENTS: i tp; 1 introduction signed Anna Lee Scott; 2–123 text; 124–7 index
COPIES: OONL (TX715.6 S35 1950z, 2 copies)   *Private collection
NOTES: 'Copyright Canada' is on p 127, but no date is recorded. Unusually, the recto pages have even numbers; the versos, odd numbers. The chapters are not numbered as lessons.

Skillet skills for camp and cottage

Jack Hambleton (1901–61), a fishing enthusiast, wrote outdoor columns for the Toronto Daily Star *and later the* Globe and Mail. *Cartoonist Jim Frise (Scugog Island, Ont., 1891–13 June 1948, Toronto, Ont.) was noted for his collaboration with the humorous writer Gregory Clark and for his 'Birdseye Centre' cartoons in the* Toronto Star. *A collection of Frise's original works and a historical plaque commemorating the cartoonist are at OPPSSHM. For information about the Borden Co. and its other books, see Q106.1. See O534.1 for the titles of other Klim recipe collections.*

O1171.1 [copyright 1947]
"Skillet / skills for / camp and / cottage" / Feature by Jack Hambleton / Cartoons by Jim Frise [cover-title]
DESCRIPTION: 15.5 × 10.0 cm   Pp [1] 2–63   Illus   Paper, with images on front of a fisherman, a man kneeling before a camp fire, and a hunter with a gun, all against a birch-bark pattern background; stapled
CONTENTS: Inside front face of binding 'Copyright, 1947, by the Borden Company, Limited ... Printed in Canada.'; 1 notice about a free booklet called *Reinforced Diet Recipes* and a folder called 'Milk Magic for Everyone,' and the imprint 'The Borden Company, Limited. Spadina Crescent, Toronto 4, Ontario.'; top 2 table of contents; mid 2–4 index; 5 biographical notes for Jack Hambleton and Jim Frise, and their portraits; 6–14 Chapter I by Jack Hambleton, an anecdotal account of his camping experiences, mainly in Northern Ontario, extolling Klim powdered whole milk for camping; 15 biographical notes for Charles S. Kirstead and his portrait; 16–27 Chapter II, 'Klim Recipes by Charles S. Kirstead'; 28 biographical notes for W.H.H. Chamberlin and his portrait; 29–32 Chapter III, 'Klim Recipes by W.H.H. Chamberlin'; 33–8 Chapter IV, 'Klim Recipes by Harry C. Phibbs' and Phibbs's portrait on p 33; 39–45 Chapter V, 'Klim Recipes by George L. Catton'; 46–7 'Two Campers' Grub Lists'; top–mid 48 'Cooking Utensils to Take Along'; mid 48–top 51 'Camping Tips'; mid 51–52 blank for 'Your Own Recipes'; 53–9 blank for 'Daily Notes' [spaces for fourteen days]; 60–3 blank for 'Memos'; inside back face list of 'Borden Products' and the printer's mark '5-K-47E'
COPIES: OKQ (TX823 S53 1947t Special Coll)   OONL (TX840 S55 1947 p***)   OPPSSHM   *Private collection

NOTES: *Skillet Skills for Camp and Cottage* incorporates material from O534.1, *Camp Cooking;* however, the publisher refers to the 1947 publication as 'Borden's new Klim booklet.' Jack Hambleton, author of the first chapter, and Jim Frise, illustrator, are new contributors. The text and illustrations are highly amusing.

The OONL copy has no blank pages for 'Memos' after p 59.

The Velvet Blend book

For information about Carnation Co. Ltd, see O350.1. Mary Blake was the pseudonym used by the company on publications promoting Carnation Milk, from the 1920s. For other titles by Mary Blake, see O494.1, A Few of My Favorite Recipes.

O1172.1   nd [about 1947]
The / Velvet Blend book / Milk-rich / Carnation recipes [cover-title]
DESCRIPTION: 23.0 × 15.0 cm   Pp 3–29 [30]   Illus col, illus   Paper, with images on front of a carnation and a woman adding Carnation Milk to a double-boiler; stapled
CONTENTS: Inside front face of binding 'An Invitation from Carnation' signed Mary Blake; 3 'Good Nutrition Is Right on Your Pantry Shelf ... with "Velvet Blend" Carnation Milk'; 4 'Quick Tricks ... and a "Velvet Blend" ... with Carnation'; 5 'Box Lunches'; 6–29 recipes; 30 publ's name, Carnation Co. Ltd, Toronto, and publ ad for Mary Blake's De Luxe *Carnation Cook Book,* a revised edition containing 'many more tempting recipes' than could be included in this book; inside back face 'Index' [i.e., table of contents]
CITATIONS: Chatelaine (May 1947), p 42
COPIES: OGU (CCC TX715.6 V438)   OONL (TX759.5 M54 V44 1900z p***)   QMMMCM (ARM2000.92.31)   *Private collection
NOTES: Printed at bottom p 30 is 'CC907E Litho in Canada'; in the OONL copy, there is 'CC907'; in the QMMMCM copy, 'CC907A'; in the OGU copy, 'CC907B'; and in another private collector's copy, 'CC907D.' An advertisement in *Chatelaine* Vol. 20, No. 5 (May 1947), p 42, asks readers to 'Write for the new "Velvet Blend Book" of milk-rich Carnation dishes.'

AMERICAN EDITIONS: nd [1940s] (Allen, p 204).

Your Leonard Refrigerator

For another cookbook from the same company, see O947.1.

O1173.1   nd [about 1947]
Your / Leonard / Refrigerator [cover-title]
CONTENTS: First page 'First in Canada's Kitchens' [introductory note] and 'Leonard Refrigerator Company, Limited // London Canada Part No. 1101621KC'
COPIES: *Private collection
NOTES: The owner reports that the cookbook came with her parents' new refrigerator in 1947, and that the recipes are on pp 18–45.

1947–9

Cook book

O1174.1   nd [about 1947–9]
Cook / book / There are no "experiments" in this cook book. They / are the cherished recipes from the kitchens of / the homes of the district. / Compiled by the Women's Association of Trinity / United Church. [cover-title]
DESCRIPTION: 23.0 × 15.0 cm   Pp 1–87 [88]   Card, with image on front of a mother, father, and child at table
CONTENTS: 1 'Preface'; 2 'Trinity United Church // Grimsby Ontario // Rev. A. Leonard Griffith, B.A. Minister' and information about the church; 3 'Index' [i.e., table of contents]; 4 'Oven Temperatures, Abbreviations, Measurements, Time Tables, etc.'; 5 'For Cooking Vegetables in Water' and 'Substitutions'; 6 ads; 7–87 recipes credited with the name of the contributor and ads; 88 blank for 'Additional Recipes'
COPIES: *Private collection
NOTES: 'Printed by the Grimsby Independent' is on the outside back face of the binding. Leonard Griffith was the church's minister from 1947 to 1949.

1948

Canada, Department of National Defence, Royal Canadian Navy

O1175.1   [May 1948]
B.R.C.N. 3102 / Department of National Defence / The R.C.N. / recipe manual / (N.S. Req. 1834-121-3102) ['Req.' crossed out in ink; label with new number glued at right: 'Req. 575-119/47-(1000)']
DESCRIPTION: 21.0 × 15.0 cm   Pp [i–iv], 1–475 [476], i–xiv   Illus   Cloth
CONTENTS: i tp; ii 'B.R.C.N. 3102 The Naval Service of Canada // The first day of May, 1948 // The instructions contained in this publication ... are issued under the authority of the Minister within his power under the Naval Service Act, 1944 ...'; iii–iv 'Table of Contents'; 1–475 text; 476 blank; i–xiv 'Index' on green leaves
COPIES: *QMAC (VC375 C2A54)
NOTES: 'How to Use This Manual' on p 1 states, 'The R.C.N. Recipe Manual (B.R.C.N. 3102) is closely related to The Instructional Manual of Naval Cookery (B.R.C.N. 3103) [i.e., O1152.1].' The recipes make large amounts, usually specified as 100 servings of so many ounces or sometimes as, for example, 33 pounds of cake.

Cochrane's choice cookery

O1176.1   [November 1948]
Cochrane's / choice / cookery / [caption:] The Lady Minto Hospital / [caption:] The Annex / Established / 1915 / Bed capacity / 60 / [caption:] Nurses' Residence / Compiled and published by the / Ladies' Auxiliary / of the / Lady Minto Hospital at Cochrane, Ont.
DESCRIPTION: 3 tp illus
CONTENTS: 1 tp; 2 'A Gift from the Gods' signed the Committee, and 'Appreciation' signed the Ladies' Auxiliary, Cochrane, Ontario, November 1948; ...
COPIES: *Private collection

Cook book

O1177.1   1948
Cook book / First Presbyterian / Church / St. Mary's – Ontario / Centennial year / 1848–1948 / Rev. Scott Duncan, B.A. / Minister / A.A. Armitage & Son, printers, St. Mary's, Ont. [cover-title]
DESCRIPTION: 23.0 × 15.0 cm   Pp [1] 2–140   Fp illus on p 1 of the church   Paper; stapled
CONTENTS: 1 fp illus of the church; 2 'First Presbyterian Church Ladies' Aid Centennial Cook Book' [i.e., introductory text]; 3–4 [torn out]; 5–115 recipes credited with the name of the contributor, blank pages for 'Receipts // Memorandum Notes,' and ads; 116 ads; 117–18 blank for 'Receipts // Memorandum Notes';

119–22 [torn out]; 123–32 'Complete Calories'; 133–5 blank for 'Memorandum Notes'; 136–7 ads; 138 'A Recipe for a Day' by Mrs Henry Ullyott; 139 ads; 140 blank except for page number and the church name as running head

COPIES: *Private collection

NOTES: The pages that are lacking (3–4, 119–22) have been cleanly torn out. Where these pages are lacking, there is no apparent interruption in the text. Perhaps a printer's error necessitated removal of the pages.

Cook book

O1178.1   1948
Cook book / First United Church / 1948 [cover-title]
DESCRIPTION: 22.5 × 15.0 cm   Pp 1–116 [117–28]   Illus on p 1 of the church   Paper, with image on front of two nearly identical, 5.5-cm-high women, each woman holding up a bowl in right hand, left hand on hip; stapled
CONTENTS: 1 illus of church, 'Arranged for publication by the Business Woman's Division No. 6 of the Woman's Association of First United Church ... Hamilton, Ontario,' publishing history of the cookbook, and acknowledgments; 2 'Index' [i.e., alphabetical list of sections]; 3–115 recipes credited with the name of the contributor and ads; 116 ad; 117–28 blank for 'Favourite Recipes'
COPIES: *Private collection

NOTES: The text on p 1 refers to four cookbooks published by First United Church: '... in 1914, ... "Selected Recipes" [O329.1] was compiled and published by the "Gleaners' Mission Band of First Methodist Church". In 1920, the Woman's Association issued the second number of "Selected Recipes" [O447.1] ... In 1933, "More Selected Recipes" was published [O799.1], ... Now, 15 years later, we present to you Cook Book "Number Four".'

O1178.2   2nd ed., 1950
—Cook book / First United Church / Second edition / 1950 [cover-title]
DESCRIPTION: 23.0 × 15.0 cm   Pp 1–88 [89–96]   Illus on p 1 of the church   Paper, with image on front of two nearly identical, 5.5-cm-high women, each woman holding up a bowl in right hand, left hand on hip; stapled
CONTENTS: 1 illus of church, 'Arranged for publication by the Business Woman's Division No. 6 of the Woman's Association of First United Church ... Hamilton, Ontario,' publishing history of the cook-

book, and acknowledgments; 2 'Index' [i.e., alphabetical list of sections]; 3–88 recipes credited with the name of the contributor; 89–96 blank for 'Favourite Recipes'
COPIES: *Private collection

Cook book

O1179.1   1948
Heroes / of / Ancaster / Chapter / [IODE symbol printed on paper label mounted on binding] / Cook book / 1948 [cover-title]
DESCRIPTION: 28.5 × 14.5 cm   Pp [1–57]   Paper; bound at top edge, through two punched holes, probably by a cord or two rings (now lacking)
CONTENTS: 1–2 'Preface' [a brief history of Ancaster] dated Ancaster, 26 November 1948; 3–55 recipes credited with the name of the contributor and ads; 56 'Household Hints' credited with the name of the contributor; 57 ads
COPIES: *OH (R641.5 Im7 CESH)

Cook book

O1180.1   1948
Friendship Group / Cook book / 1948 / Maple Leaf Chapter No. 3 / Order of the Eastern Star / St. Thomas [cover-title]
DESCRIPTION: 23.0 × 15.0 cm   Pp 1–104   Fp illus on p 1 of 'Mr. and Mrs. David Meadows,' fp illus on p 2 of 'Meadows Home'   Paper; stapled
CONTENTS: 1 fp illus; 2 fp illus; 3 'Kitchen Chant' [poem] and acknowledgments; 4 'Weights and Measures,' 'Baking Time and Temperature,' and 'Abbreviations ...'; 5–8 'Favorite Recipes of Mrs. Alice Meadows' and ads; 9–14 'Favorite Recipes of Some of the Presiding Matrons and Patrons of 1948' and ads; 15–103 recipes and ads; 104 ad, index, and untitled four-line verse
COPIES: *Private collection

NOTES: On the inside front face of the binding, under the heading 'Sixty-fifth Wedding Anniversary,' there is a dedication in honour of Alice and David Meadows's anniversary, and biographical information about Alice, who was a member of this OES chapter and the first worthy grand matron of the Province of Ontario. This copy is inscribed on p 1, in pencil, 'Sister Meadows passed away Jan 1st 1955 at the age of 92.'

Cooking the modern way!

O1181.1   copyright 1948
Cooking / the modern way! / 129 / home tested
and proved / recipes / to please your family /
Published by the manufacturers / Planters Edible
Oil Company / Suffolk, Va. – Wilkes-Barre, Pa. –
Toronto, Ontario / San Francisco, Calif. / Copyright
1948 – Printed in U.S.A. / [folio:] 3
DESCRIPTION: Paper, with image on front of a series of
six prepared dishes, from salad at top to cake at
bottom; stapled
COPIES: *Private collection
NOTES: The book's owner reports that it has 39 pp.

Dover daily dainties

O1182.1   1948
Dover / daily / dainties / 1948 [cover-title]
DESCRIPTION: 23.0 × 15.0 cm   Pp [1–2] 3–144   Fp illus
on p 1 of 'United Church of Canada // Dover
Centre'; small illus head some chapters   Paper;
stapled
CITATIONS: Ferguson/Fraser, p 234
CONTENTS: 1 fp illus; 2 foreword signed Woman's
Association, Dover Centre United Church, Dover
Centre, Ontario; 3 'Substitutions, Equivalents, Yields'
and 'Weights and Measures'; 4–5 'Measured Heat
Chart // Temperature and Time for Oven Cooking';
6 ad; 7–140 recipes and ads; 141 'Helpful Hints'; 142–
3 'Preparing Fruits and Vegetables for Cold Storage';
144 'Index' [i.e., table of contents]
COPIES: *Private collection
NOTES: In the cover-title, the words 'Dover Daily Dain-
ties' all share the same 6.3-cm-high 'D.'

Favorite recipes from American kitchens

*The American Women's Club of Toronto was founded in
1917. One of the founders and an early president was
Alice Baldwin Hall (Columbus, Ohio, 1890–1981), the
mother of Ruth W. McCuaig, of Hamilton, who donated
a copy of the third edition of the book to OGU. Ruth
writes of her mother and the club: 'In 1912 she married a
Canadian. Torontonian, Harry Bell Hall ... But my
mother was rather lonely and very conscious of an anti-
American feeling (partly due to the recent "reciprocity"
fight and then later, when the Americans did not enter
the Great War until 1917). She was college-educated with
a number of talents and youthful enthusiasm. She met a
few similarly stranded American-born wives – some were
married to American men who were in Toronto as the*

*employees of American companies with branch plants
being built in Canada. This handful of women decided to
form the American Women's Club ... They usually met in
what had been an elegant family home on Sherbourne
Street – known as Sherbourne House. Then, having
outgrown that, they met regularly for luncheon meetings
in the Eaton's College Street store Round Room [opened
1930].' Alice Hall contributed the recipe for Lima Bean
Scallop on p 334 of Favorite Recipes from American
Kitchens (the same recipe she had contributed to O755.1,
Favorite Recipes, a 1932 book by the Women's Association of Deer Park United Church in Toronto).*

O1183.1   1st ed., 1948
Favorite recipes / from / American / kitchens /
Compiled by / the American Women's Club / of
Toronto / First edition / Copyrited [sic] 1948
COPIES: *Private collection

O1183.2   2nd ed., 1949
—Favorite recipes / from / American / kitchens /
Compiled by / the American Women's Club / of
Toronto / Second edition / Copyright 1949
DESCRIPTION: 22.0 × 14.0 cm   Pp [3–9] 10–448   1 fp
illus on p 6 of a woman consulting this book by a
stove; illus part-titles; many small illus   Paper, with
image on front of compass points (N, S, E, W); metal
clasp (?)
CONTENTS: 3 tp; 4 untitled acknowledgments signed
the Committee; 5 dedication to the women who
founded the American Women's Club of Toronto in
1917; 6 fp illus; 7 table of contents; 8 'Recipe for a
Day'; 9–378 text; 379–81 ads; 382–410 index on versos,
ads on rectos; 411–16 'Helpful Hints' on versos, ads
on rectos; 417–48 ads
COPIES: *Private collection

O1183.3   3rd ed., 1949
—Favorite recipes / from / American / kitchens /
Compiled by / the American Women's Club / of
Toronto / Third edition / Copyright 1949
DESCRIPTION: 21.5 × 14.0 cm   Pp [3–9] 10–448   1 fp
illus on p 6 of a woman consulting this book by a
stove; illus part-titles; many small illus   Paper, with
image on front of compass points (N, S, E, W); metal
clasp
CONTENTS: 3 tp; 4 untitled acknowledgments signed
the Committee; 5 dedication to the women who
founded the American Women's Club of Toronto in
1917; 6 fp illus; 7 table of contents; 8 'Recipe for a
Day'; 9–377 text; 378–9 'Advertisers' Index'; 380–1
ads; 382–410 index on versos, ads on rectos; 411–15
ads; 416 'Helpful Hints'; 417–46 ads; 447 three recipes; 448 ad

COPIES: OGU (CCC TX715.6 F74 1949)   *Private collection

NOTES: The illustrated part-titles were drawn by Murray McLean.

Kulinary kapers

O1184.1   1948

Kulinary / [same 'K' as Kulinary]apers / Published by / the Union Street Home and School Association / 1948 [cover-title]

DESCRIPTION: With cartoon image on front of a stout, grinning chef, standing on a stool and adding a large bone to a saucepan

COPIES: *Private collection

NOTES: 'The Jackson Press, Kingston, Ont.' is on the outside back face of the binding. Perhaps the association's location in Kingston was the motivation for the spelling of *Kulinary Kapers*.

Logan, Martha [pseudonym]

For information about the real women behind the pseudonym Martha Logan and for the titles of other cookbooks attributed to Logan, see O1050.1.

O1185.1   nd [1948 or later]

Captivating cookery / with / Allsweet / by Martha Logan Home Economist / Swift Canadian Co., Limited [cover-title]

DESCRIPTION: 10.0 × 15.0 cm   Pp [1] 2–26   Illus col, illus   Paper, with image on front of five prepared dishes; stapled

CONTENTS: 1 cover-title; 2 'Hello, homemakers!' signed Martha Logan; 3–26 recipes

COPIES: ACG   BKOM   *OGU (CCC TX715.6 M3955)

NOTES: Allsweet was a margarine. The earliest that *Captivating Cookery with Allsweet* could have been published is the end of 1948, when margarine was legalized in Canada (the 1886 ban on margarine was enforced until 1917, then temporarily lifted until 1923 because of food shortages during the First World War). A note on the outside back face of the binding states, 'Allsweet is sold yellow where laws permit, elsewhere white.' Laws requiring margarine to be white were to prevent the consumer confusing the product with butter. There is no place of publication, but the company's head office was in Toronto. See also O1186.1, another Allsweet cookbook.

AMERICAN EDITIONS: nd (Dickinson, p 46).

O1186.1   nd [1948 or later]

Cakes / cookies / desserts candies / Sweets with Allsweet / by Martha Logan, Home Economist / Swift Canadian Co. Ltd. Toronto, Ont. [cover-title]

DESCRIPTION: 10.0 × 15.0 cm   Pp [1] 2–19   Illus Paper, with image on front of a plate of cookies; stapled

CONTENTS: 1 cover-title; 2 'Hello!' signed Martha Logan; 3–18 recipes and at bottom p 18, 'Litho in Canada 69289'; 19 'What Wins and Holds Users for Allsweet?'

COPIES: QMMMCM (AR-M2000.92.12)   *Private collection

NOTES: The earliest that *Sweets with Allsweet* could have been published is the end of 1948, for the same reason as stated in O1185.1.

Middleton, Miss Elspeth Munro (Toronto, Ont., 7 December 1893–5 September 1962, Victoria County, Ont.), Miss Muriel Eleanor Ransom [Mrs Robert Clifford Carter] (1912–), and Albert Vierin (Romanel, Switzerland, 10 April 1893–28 May 1976, East York, Ont.)

Middleton, Ransom, and Vierin also co-wrote O1078.1, The Cook's Recipe Manual. For biographical information about these authors, see O1078.1.

O1187.1   1948

100 / to / dinner / by / Elspeth Middleton, B.A. Director of the / Household Science Department, Central / Technical School, Toronto / Muriel Ransom, B.A. Superintendent / of the Great Hall, Hart House, University of / Toronto / Albert Vierin. Executive Chef, Aero- / caterers supplying Trans-Canada Air Lines / University of Toronto Press: 1948

DESCRIPTION: 19.5 × 12.0 cm   Pp [i–vi], 1–342   Illus of cuts of meat   [$3.50, in CCat and in *Globe and Mail* review]   Paper-covered boards, cloth spine

CONTENTS: i tp; ii 'Copyright, Canada, 1948 // University of Toronto Press // Printed in Canada'; iii 'Preface' signed E.M., M.R., and A.V.; iv blank; v table of contents; vi blank; 1–338 text; 339–42 index

CITATIONS: CCat No. 27, p ZC13   MacTaggart, p 224

COPIES: *AEU   MWU   NSWA (TX820 M5)   OOAG (641.572 M628 1948)   OTL (not on shelf)   OTU (TDS M)   QMBM (641.5 M6281on)

NOTES: The 'Preface' states, 'This recipe manual is planned to serve as a guide to better cooking in clubs, schools, camps, factories, offices, institutions, tourist resorts – in fact, wherever large numbers of people are served. It is the result of research undertaken by the authors during World War II ...' The text is a reworking of the authors' earlier book, O1078.1, *The Cook's Recipe Manual*. For a brief review of *100 to Dinner*, see 'Quantity Meals,' *Globe and Mail* (Toronto) 30 October 1948.

MacTaggart, p 224, states of the 1948 edition: '[T]his edition has been specially prepared for distribution by the Development Branch [of the Department of Travel and Publicity of the Ontario Government]. Reprinted 1949, 1954.'

The MWU copy lacks the title-page.

OTHER EDITIONS: *100 to Dinner: Better Cooking for: Clubs, Camps and Resorts, Institutions, Industrial Plants, and All Public Dining Places*, Toronto: University of Toronto Press, 1960 (AC, AEAG, AEU, BVAU, BVAUW, NBFU, NFSCF, NFSG, NSAS, NSH, NSHPL, OCHA, OLU, OOC, OOCC, OONL, OOU, OTB, OTMCL, OTR, OW, OWYL, PCU, QMBM, SRU, SSU; United States: MCR); Toronto: University of Toronto Press, 1972 (AMICUS No. 22776775).

Middleton, Sidney

For information about Love – The Flavor Man and its other cookbooks, see O924.1.

O1188.1   1948
The pastry chef's helper / Compiled by / Sidney Middleton / 1948 / Published by / Love the Flavor Man / Toronto Canada / Copyrighted
DESCRIPTION: About 18.0 × 11.0 cm [dimensions from photocopy] [48 unnumbered leaves] Tp photograph of the author, illus
CONTENTS: 1 tp; 2–3 'Foreword // Love's Pastry Chef's Helper' signed Sidney Middleton; 4–5 'Index' and at bottom p 5, table of Canadian and American measurements; ...; last page recipes and 'Cercla Binding – Canada Binding Limited // Printed by F.W. Barrett Company Ltd.'
COPIES: *Private collection
NOTES: In the 'Foreword,' Middleton refers to this publication as 'my sixth.' He says that his association with the profession of pastry chef started in 1904, and that he has been a pastry chef in a 'leading hotel' (unidentified). He also mentions that some pastry chefs and pastry bakers have been using Love's flavours for twenty-five years, i.e., since 1923. There are 145 numbered recipes, plus two unnumbered recipes on the last page, making commercial amounts.

Our favourite recipes

O1189.1   nd [about 1948]
Our / favourite / recipes / Kenilworth United Church / Hamilton – Ont. [cover-title]
DESCRIPTION: 22.5 × 14.0 cm Pp 1–60 Very thin card, with image on front of flowers (tulip, hyacinth, and lilies); stapled
CONTENTS: 1 'Preface' and 'Compiled by Junior Women's Association of Kenilworth United Church // Hamilton, Ont.'; 2–59 recipes credited with the name of the contributor and ads; 60 'Index' [i.e., table of contents] and ads
COPIES: *Private collection
NOTES: The printer's name is on the outside back face of the binding: 'Printed by – Amherst Card Guild, 8 Caithness Ave. – Toronto.' An advertisement on p 24 is evidence of the cookbook's year of publication: 'Visit new modern Marigold Coffee Shop and Soda Bar, 37 Kenilworth Ave. North ...' The 1947 Hamilton city directory lists a 'new building' at 37 Kenilworth Avenue, but there is no name entry for Marigold Coffee Shop; however, the 1948 directory lists the coffee shop at that address. *Our Favourite Recipes*, therefore, was published about 1948. Also supporting publication in about 1948 is an advertisement on p 58 for Florence Young, 'ladies' and children's wear ... 1524 King Street East (late of 1369 Main)'; the first listing for the Florence Young Shop at 1524 King Street East is in the 1947 directory.

Pellegrini, Angelo M. (Casabianca, Italy, 1904–91)

Pellegrini wrote about his Italian heritage and the pleasures of eating. See, for example: Wine and the Good Life, *New York: Knopf, c1965;* The Food-Lover's Garden, *New York: Knopf, 1970; and* Vintage Pellegrini: The Collected Wisdom of an American Buongustaio, *Seattle: Sasquatch Books, c1991 (all United States: DLC).*

O1190.1   1948
The / unprejudiced / palate / by / Angelo M. Pellegrini / I could write a better book about cookery / than has ever been written: It should be a / book upon philosophical principles. / Dr. Johnson / New York / The Macmillan Company / 1948
DESCRIPTION: 20.5 × 12.0 cm Pp [i–viii], [1–2] 3–235 Paper-covered boards, cloth spine
CONTENTS: i ht; ii publisher's symbol and 'The Macmillan Company New York Boston Chicago

Dallas Atlanta San Fransisco // Macmillan and Co., Limited London Bombay Calcutta Madras Melbourne // The Macmillan Company of Canada, Limited Toronto'; iii tp; iv 'Copyright, 1948, by the Macmillan Company ... First printing ...'; v dedication 'To Virginia ...'; vi blank; vii 'Contents'; viii blank; 1–235 text

COPIES: *OONL (TX633 P38); United States: DLC (TX633 P38)

NOTES: Pellegrini, an Italian immigrant to the United States, discourses on American food and eating habits, and his native Italian traditions. The text is in two parts – 'Bread and Wine in Perspective' and 'Bread and Wine in Good Taste,' followed by a Conclusion, 'Toward Humane Living.'

AMERICAN EDITIONS: San Francisco: North Point Press, 1984 (United States: DLC); New York: Lyons and Burford, [1996?], c1984 (recorded in DLC catalogue); edited by Ruth Reichl, Random House, 2005 (OTMCL).

Scott, Anna Lee [pseudonym]

For information about Anna Lee Scott and her cookbooks, see O526.1.

O1191.1   nd [about 1948]
The / Monarch / mixing / bowl [cover-title]
DESCRIPTION: 22.0 × 14.0 cm   Pp [1–2] 3–23   Paper, with image on front of a stylized spoon and bowl; stapled
CONTENTS: 1 cover-title; 2 'Maple Leaf Milling Company, Limited // Dear friend:' signed Anna Lee Scott; 3–6 recipes for 'White Cake Mix'; 7–8 'Chocolate Cake Mix'; 9–11 'Monarch Golden Yellow Cake Mix'; 12–14 'Monarch Angel Food Cake Mix'; 15 'Monarch Cherry Pound Cake Mix' and 'Monarch Fruit Cake Mix'; 16–17 'Gingerbread Mix'; 18–19 'Pie Crust Mix'; 20 'Cookie Short-Cuts with Monarch Mixes'; 21–top 22 'Tea-Bisk Short Cuts'; near top 22–23 [inside back face of binding] 'Muffins' and 'For 101 tempting Tea-Bisk recipes write for our free book "What's Cooking". Address // Monarch // Box 52, Toronto 9, Ont.'
COPIES: *OGU (CCC TX715.6 M572 No. 274)
NOTES: The text is printed in red and black. The order of the three editions, all undated, is uncertain, but this may be the first. Monarch cake mixes were put on the market in 1948, according to the corporate history (*The Company That Grew with Canada*, Maple Leaf Mills Ltd, [about 1980], p 20).
   Both O1191.1 and O1191.2 have a binding design

with a yellow background; in the cover-title, the word 'Monarch' has a block-capital M filled in with the red-and-white checked pattern associated with Monarch Flour, and the rest of the word is solid-red, lower-case letters.

O1191.2   nd
—The / Monarch / mixing / bowl [cover-title]
DESCRIPTION: 22.0 × 14.0 cm   Pp [1–2] 3–23   Paper, with image on front of a stylized spoon and bowl; stapled
CONTENTS: 1 cover-title; 2 'Maple Leaf Milling Company, Limited // Dear friend:' signed Anna Lee Scott; 3–6 recipes for 'White Cake Mix'; 7–8 'Chocolate Cake Mix'; 9–11 'Monarch Golden Yellow Cake Mix'; 12–14 'Monarch Angel Food Cake Mix'; 15 'Monarch Cherry Pound Cake Mix' and 'Monarch Fruit Cake Mix'; 16–17 'Gingerbread Mix'; 18–19 'Pie Crust Mix'; 20–2 'Monarch Cookie Mix'; 23 [inside back face of binding] 'Tea-Bisk Short Cuts' and at bottom, 'For 101 tempting Tea-Bisk recipes write for our free book "What's Cooking". Address // Monarch // Box 52, Toronto 9, Ont.'
COPIES: *Private collection
NOTES: The contents of pp 20–3 distinguish this edition from O1191.1. The binding is identical to O1191.1.

O1191.3   nd
—The / Monarch / mixing / bowl [cover-title]
DESCRIPTION: 23.0 × 15.0 cm   Pp [1–2] 3–31   Paper, with image on front of a stylized spoon and bowl; stapled
CONTENTS: 1 cover-title; 2 'Maple Leaf Milling Co. Limited // Dear friend:' signed Anna Lee Scott; 3–4 recipes for 'Chocolate Cake Mix'; 5–10 'White Cake Mix'; 11–12 'Pie Crust Mix'; 13–14 'Gingerbread Mix'; 15–26 'Tea-Bisk Short Cuts'; 27–31 [inside back face of binding] 'Glamour Cakes for Which You Mix Your Own Batter'
COPIES: NSHMS (88.74.12) *OONL (TX763 M65 1950z, 2 copies)
NOTES: This edition begins with recipes for Chocolate Cake Mix, not White Cake Mix. The front face of the binding has a brown background, and all the letters in the word 'Monarch' are block capitals filled in with the red-and-white checked pattern associated with Monarch Flour.

O1192.1   nd [about 1948]
What's / cooking? / Biscuits / cakes / cookies / desserts / dumplings / meat dishes / meatless dishes / muffins / pancakes and waffles / quick breads and buns / 101 short-cuts with / Tea-Bisk [cover-title]

DESCRIPTION: 21.5 × 14.5 cm   Pp [1–28]   Paper; stapled

CONTENTS: Inside front face of binding 'Dear friend:' signed Anna Lee Scott; 1–28 101 numbered recipes

COPIES: OFERWM (A1978.189.45)   OGU (2 copies: CCC TX715.6 S379, TX715.6 M572 No. 356)   OONL (TX767 T42 W43)   *Private collection

NOTES: Tea-Bisk was made by Maple Leaf Milling Co. Ltd of Toronto. The letter opposite p 1, probably referring to an earlier pamphlet, says, 'The original "dozen 'n one" baking short-cuts now stand at 101 quick, easy ways ...' The text is printed in red and blue. Monarch cake mixes, which are advertised on the outside back face of the binding, were introduced to the market in 1948. *What's Cooking?* is advertised in O1191.1 and O1191.2, *The Monarch Mixing Bowl*.

See O745.1 for the first collection of recipes for cooking with Tea-Bisk.

Speed cooking

O1193.1   [1948]

Speed cooking / with your new / General GE Electric / range / Instructions recipes menus [cover-title]

DESCRIPTION: 23.0 × 15.5 cm   Pp 1–64   Illus   Very thin card; stapled

CONTENTS: 1 'Table of Contents'; 2 'These Advantages Are Now Yours with Electric Cooking'; 3 'Know Your Range' and 'Measured Heat'; 4–5 'Convenience Features'; 6–18 'Section 1 Surface Cooking'; 19–29 Section 2 Thrift Cooker'; 30 and 35–56 'Section 3 Oven Cooking'; 31–4 'Warranty'; 57–61 'Section 4 Broiling'; 62–3 'Section 5 Care and Cleaning'; 64 'Index to Recipes'; inside back face of binding 'Form 100-48'

COPIES: *Bookseller's stock

NOTES: The printer's mark, 'Form 100-48,' points to publication in 1948, a date confirmed by the 'Warranty,' which in the bookseller's copy is inscribed with the date the range was delivered: 'April 24th [19]48.' Copies at OONL (TX715.6 S644 1949 p***) and QMM (RBD ckbk 1412) have 'Form 100-49.' Cooke 2002, p 234, records an edition of 1940 [sic].

Treasured recipes

St Paul's Ladies' Aid published another cookbook with a similar title, Tasty Treasures *(Private collection). The 'Acknowledgments' describe it as 'our new cook book' and it likely appeared in the 1950s because of the section called 'T.V. Snack,' which has only one recipe, Nuts and Bolts.*

O1194.1   nd [about 1948]

Treasured / recipes / Compiled by / St. Paul's Ladies' Aid / Queen St. South / Kitchener [cover-title]

DESCRIPTION: 22.0 × 14.5 cm   Pp [1] 2–98   Photograph on p 1 of the church   Paper, with image on front of a plate of bread slices being placed on a set table; stapled

CONTENTS: 1 address of St Paul's Evangelical Lutheran Church (corner of Queen and Church streets), pastor's name (Arthur Eissfeldt), service times, illus of church, and 'Published by St. Paul's Ladies' Aid // The executive // Mrs. H. Zohr, President // Mrs. C. Stevens, 1st Vice-President // Mrs. C.J. Rockel, 2nd Vice-President // Mrs. W. Strome, Secretary // Mrs. K. Orzen, Assistant Secretary // Mrs. H. Huber, Treasurer // Mrs. A. Eissfeldt, member Ex-officio'; 2 quotation from the Bible; 3 'Foreword' signed St Paul's Ladies' Aid; 4 'Index' [i.e., table of contents]; 5–6 ads; 7–94 recipes credited with the name of the contributor and ads; 95–6 'Household Hints'; 97 ads; 98 'Quantities to Serve 100'

COPIES: *OGU (CCC TX715.6 T743)

NOTES: The running head is 'St Paul's Ladies' Aid Cook Book.' The date, price, and print run are inscribed on p 1, in pencil: '1948 $.50 4,000 copies.' It may have been published a little earlier than this inscription suggests, since the daughter of the original owner of another copy reported that her mother married in 1946 and she had the cookbook then.

The 'Wear-Ever' PM recipe booklet

For the titles of other cookbooks by Aluminum Goods Ltd, see O807.1.

O1195.1   nd [about 1948]

The / "Wear-Ever" / PM / recipe booklet / [Wear-Ever trademark symbol] / Made in Canada / Aluminum Goods Limited / 158 Sterling Road Toronto 3 Ont. [cover-title]

DESCRIPTION: 28.5 × 22.5 cm   Pp 1–21, [i–ii]   Illus   Paper, with several small images on front of saucepans and an aproned woman, and a large image (10.3 × 18.2 cm) of a covered casserole on which the title appears; stapled at top edge

CONTENTS: Inside front face of binding 'How to Care for Your New "P.M." Aluminum Utensils'; top–mid 1 'Proper Cooking Essential to Health' and 'Aluminum Is Friendly to Foods'; mid 1–2 'How to Cook by the "Wear-Ever" P.M. Method'; 3–6 'Utensils for Cooking Vegetables and Fruits,' information about cooking vegetables and fruits, information about a fruit and

vegetable press, and vegetable recipes; 7–8 'Dried Foods'; 9 and unnumbered verso publ ad; 10–mid 13 utensils, instructions, and recipes for cooking meat; bottom 13–mid 14 'The Griddle'; mid 14–15 'Direct Top-Stove Baking'; 16–17 'How to Bake the New Method Way' and recipes; 18–19 'Canning'; 20 'How to Use the No. 990 "Wear-Ever" French Drip Filtrater Coffee Maker'; 21 'The P.M. and Northumbria Sterling Bonus Club Plan'; i publ ad; ii 'How You May Acquire "Wear-Ever" Specials on the "Wear-Ever" P.M. Bonus Club Plan'
COPIES: *Private collection
NOTES: The owner acquired the book with her aluminium saucepans, received as a wedding gift in 1948.

Westdale United Church cook book

O1196.1   nd [about 1948]
Westdale United Church / cook book / The Woman Who Cooks / "Some women are loved because of good looks, / But every one loves the woman who cooks, / Now, the secret of being an excellent cook / Lies in the possession of a reliable book. / The recipes which are here offered you / We are happy to state are all tried and true, / And, if you will follow with care and precision, / We're sure naught but praise will be your decision. [no closing quotation-marks]
DESCRIPTION: 22.5 × 15.0 cm   Pp [1–4] 5–96   Paper, with image on front of Westdale United Church; stapled
CONTENTS: 1 tp; 2 ads; 3 'Preface' signed W.A. [i.e., Woman's Association], Group 13, and at bottom, 'Printed by Hamilton Printing Service'; 4 ad; 5–mid 96 text, including recipes credited with the name of the contributor, and ads; mid–bottom 96 'Index' [i.e., table of contents]
COPIES: *OH (R641.5 WES CESH)
NOTES: '1948' is marked in pencil on the front face of the OH copy, and the book appears to have been published about that date. The OH copy is also inscribed in pencil, on the front face, by a previous owner of the book, 'E.L.E.'

Zion Line Women's Institute cook book

Zion Line Women's Institute in Renfrew County was formed in 1919 (Ambrose, p 230).

O1197.1   1948
Recipes / to please the / whole family / Zion Line

Women's Institute / cook book / 1948 / "For home and country" / Renfrew Advance Print [cover-title]
DESCRIPTION: With image on front of a single place-setting and a woman carrying a tray; stapled
COPIES: *Private collection

1948–9

Carter, Charles A.

For information about Love – The Flavor Man and its other cookbooks, see O924.1.

O1198.1   1948–9
Food for thought / by / the master baker / 1948–49 / Published by / Love the Flavor Man / Toronto Canada / Copyrighted
DESCRIPTION: About 21.5 × 14.0 cm [dimensions from photocopy]   Pp [i–viii], 1–106
CONTENTS: i tp; ii photograph of 'The author Charles A. Carter // proprietor, "Carter Family" Bakery // member of Advisory Committee of the School of Food Technology, Toronto // Secretary, I.M.B.A.'; iii–v 'Preface'; vi–vii 'Index' [i.e., table of contents]; viii chart of 'Composition and Relative Sweetness of Sweetening Agents'; 1–106 recipes and baking information in twelve numbered parts and, at bottom p 106, 'Errata'
CITATIONS: CCat No. 28, p ZD22
COPIES: *Private collection
NOTES: The recipes are for professional bakers. As the author explains on p iii, 'What has been attempted here is a continuity of proven recipes and instructions that cover the general daily procedure of the average good class bakery across the Dominion ...'

Favorite recipes

O1199.1   1948–9
Favorite / recipes / I guessed the pepper; the soup was too hot! / I guessed the water; it dried in the pot! / I guessed the salt; and – what do you think? / We did nothing else the whole day but drink / I guessed the sugar; the sauce was too sweet! / And so by my guessing I spoiled our treat / And now I guess nothing, for cooking by guess / Is sure to result in a terrible mess. / Published by / Women's Hospital Aid of the / Norfolk General Hospital / Simcoe – Ontario
DESCRIPTION: 22.0 × 14.5 cm   Pp [1–70]   Paper, with image on front of Norfolk General Hospital; stapled
CONTENTS: 1 tp; 2 blank; 3 'Preface' and the names of 'Officers (June) 1948–1949,' including Mrs S. Castle,

convenor of cook book; 4–66 recipes and ads; 67 ads and space for 'My Own Recipes'; 68–9 ads; 70 'Index' [i.e., table of contents] and ad
COPIES: OCHAK   OKQ (F5012 194- N835)   OSIDM *QMM (RBD ckbk 1870)
NOTES: 'Simcoe Job Print' is on the outside back face of the binding.

Tested tasty treats

O1200.1   nd [about 1948–9]
Tested tasty / treats / Salford United Church [cover-title]
DESCRIPTION: 21.0 × 14.5 cm   Pp [1] 2–80   Paper; stapled
CONTENTS: 1 'Foreword'; 2 'Index' [i.e., alphabetical list of sections] and ad; 3 ads; 4–80 recipes credited with the name of the contributor, other culinary information, blank spaces for 'Extra Recipes,' and ads
COPIES: *Private collection
NOTES: The 'Foreword' refers to 'all the girls of the Junior Bible Class who are responsible for compiling and arranging this book' and thanks 'all the ladies who so liberally donated their best and tried recipes.' On p 20, at the head of the 'Candy' section, is the rhyme 'The sugar ration is no more, / So don't go without the candy you adore.' Since sugar rationing ended in Canada in November 1947, the cookbook was published about 1948 or slightly later. The name of the printer, 'Tillsonburg News Presses,' is on the outside back face of the binding.

1948–50

How to use your Admiral Refrigerator

For How to Use Your Admiral Refrigerator, *published in London, Ontario, see* Q311.2, *under* How to Use Your McClary Refrigerator.

How to use your Multart Pressure Cooker

O1201.1   nd [about 1948–50]
How to use your / Multart / Pressure / Cooker [cover-title]
DESCRIPTION: 23.0 × 15.0 cm   Pp 1–27 [28–32]   Illus [$0.25, on p 27]   Paper, with image on front of a pressure cooker; stapled
CONTENTS: 1–top 2 'A Miracle Comes to Your Kitchen!'; mid–bottom 2 'Pressure Cooking Is Economy Cooking 5 Ways!'; 3 'Open and Close This Easy Way'; 4 'So

Easy to Cook With ...'; 5 '... In a Nutshell'; 6 'Cooking by Electricity'; 7 'Before You Start to Cook May We Say a Word on Cooking Time'; 8–11 'Cooking of Vegetables'; 12–15 'Cooking of Meats and Poultry'; 16–17 'Cooking of Soups'; 18–19 'Cooking of Fish and Seafoods'; 20–3 'Cooking of Cereals'; 24–5 'Meals in Minutes'; 26 'Care of Your Multart Pressure Cooker'; 27 order form for parts; 28 blank; 29–32 blank for 'Recipes'
COPIES: *Private collection
NOTES: Page 27 records Multart Co. of Canada's address as 350 Wallace Avenue, Toronto. Since this number on Wallace Avenue is not listed in the Street Index of city directories until 1948, the cookbook was likely published no earlier than that year. There are no entries for Multart in city directories, but J.D. Tolton Co. Ltd, described as manufacturers' agents in the 1950 and 1951 volumes, may be connected to the book. The printer, 'Northern Miner Press Limited // Toronto, Ontario,' is on the outside back face of the binding. The book belonged to the current owner's aunt, who married in the late 1930s.

1949

[Title unknown]

O1202.1   [1949]
[Title unknown of a cookbook with running head 'Knox Church Woman's Association']
DESCRIPTION: 23.0 × 14.5 cm   Pp [Lacks leaves] 5–112 [lacks leaves]   Lacks binding; stapled
CONTENTS: 5–110 recipes credited with the name of the contributor and ads; 111 'Household Hints'; 112 ads
COPIES: *Private collection
NOTES: There is an advertisement on p 104 for the Corporation of the City of Port Arthur that lists the mayor as Fred O. Robinson and the aldermen as E.V. Anten, T.J. McAuliffe, R.A. Robinson, W.E. Riddell, W.R. Brown, Eunice M. Wishart, J. Styffe, A.J. Hinton, Geo. Wardrope, and C. Dilley. Fred Robinson was mayor from 1949 to 1951 and 1953 to 1955, but 1949 was the only year that all the named aldermen served together with Mayor Robinson; therefore, this cookbook was published in 1949. There are two Knox United Churches in what is now Thunder Bay: 1 Shuniah Street in the former Port Arthur and 303 Pruden Street in the former Fort William. The copy examined lacked its binding and pages that might identify which church published the book; however, the City of Port Arthur advertisement suggests that it was the Shuniah Street church.

A 1 cook book

See also an earlier cookbook from the same church, O690.1.

O1203.1 1949
A 1 / cook book / 1949 / Sunday School Auxiliary / First United Church / Waterloo, Ontario [cover-title]
DESCRIPTION: 21.5 × 15.0 cm   Pp [1] 2–95 [96]   Illus on p 1 of the church   Paper, with image on front of the church; stapled
CONTENTS: 1 name of the minister (Rev. A.R. Cragg), hours of Divine Service and Church School, 'Published by Sunday School Auxiliary,' and names of the Auxiliary's charter members (Mrs J.H. Bullard, president; Mrs W.E. Totten, vice-president; Mrs J.R. Walker, secretary; Mrs L. Boehmer, treasurer; Mrs H. Greig; Mrs C. Klinck; Mrs J.O. Anderson; Mrs J. Crawford; Mrs Wm Smith; Mrs Fred Snyder; Mrs G. Neill; Mrs J. Close; Mrs L. Sprung; Mrs P. Littler; Mrs W.B. Brant; Mrs Morris Hallman); 2 untitled comments about cooking by Mrs Garfield Bender and 'Ten Commandments for Parents' reprinted from *Parents' Magazine*; 3 several mock recipes about living a Christian life, contributed by the ministers of local churches in Kitchener and Waterloo; 4 ad; 5–90 recipes credited with the name of the contributor and ads; 91 ad; 92 'Household Hints' and 'Tea for 100'; 93–6 ads
COPIES: *Private collection
NOTES: 'Acme Printers' is on the outside back face of the binding. In July 2002, Mrs J.H. Bullard (Alice), charter member of the Sunday School Auxiliary and the first president, told me that the Sunday School Auxiliary was formed in 1949 with the purpose of improving the conditions for the Sunday School children, who were taught in the church's basement. She reported that they raised over $5,000 through sales of the *A 1 Cook Book* and advertisements, which went toward renovations and the purchase of books and equipment. *A 1 Cook Book* (known as 'the red book') was apparently more successful than their second publication, *A Collection of Tried and Tested Recipes*, nd [1950 or 1951] ('the blue book') (Private collection).

The Baptist ladies' cook book

O1204.1 1949
The Baptist ladies' / cook book / [quotation from Ruskin] / Compiled and published by the members of the / Winnifred Paskall Mission Circle / of the First Baptist Church / Leamington Ontario
DESCRIPTION: 23.0 × 15.5 cm   Pp [1–2] 3–158   Paper; stapled
CONTENTS: 1 tp; 2 'Our Greeting' signed the Committee; 3–152 recipes credited with the name of the contributor, ads, and blank pages for adding manuscript recipes or clippings; 153–8 'Index'
COPIES: *Private collection
NOTES: The cover-title is 'The Baptist Cook Book // 1949 // Selected recipes ...' The printer's name is on the outside back face of the binding: 'Printed by the Widmeyer Press – Leamington, Ontario.' Several recipes are credited to two, and sometimes three persons – possibly a diplomatic gesture by the Committee to avoid causing offence by rejecting duplicate recipes.

The title-page of this copy is inscribed, 'Carolyn Baldwin // Compliments of Gertrude Hewer'; Gertrude may be Mrs J.F. Hewer, who contributed Chocolate Layer Cake on p 27, or Mrs A.H. Hewer, who contributed Salad on p 145, or a relative of these two women.

Canada, Department of Agriculture

For a list of other cookbooks published by the Department of Agriculture, see O404.1.

O1205.1 nd [1949]
Consumer Section – Marketing Service / Department of Agriculture / Ottawa – Canada / Desserts / you'll like / Published by authority of the Rt. Hon. James G. Gardiner, Minister of Agriculture. [cover-title]
DESCRIPTION: 22.0 × 10.5 cm   Pp 3–19   Paper; stapled
CONTENTS: 3–19 recipes
CITATIONS: Ag 1867–1974, p 172
COPIES: *Bookseller's stock
NOTES: The year of publication is from Ag 1867–1974. No copy was found at OOAG.

O1205.2 nd [about 1949]
—Section des consommateurs / Service des marches / Ministere de l'agriculture / Ottawa – Canada / Les / desserts / que vous / aimerez / Très Honorable James G. Gardiner, ministre de l'agriculture. [cover-title]
DESCRIPTION: 22.0 × 10.0 cm   Pp 3–19   Paper; stapled
CONTENTS: 3–19 recipes
COPIES: *OOAG (641.5 C212)

Canada, Department of National Health and Welfare

For an earlier book on the same subject, see Q238.1, Feeding Men in Camps.

O1206.1 [1949]
Recettes – 100 portions / pour les hommes qui / travaillent dur / Numéro IV. / Série Services alimentaires collectifs / Publiées par / le Service de l'hygiène alimentaire, / Ministère de la santé nationale et du bien-être social / Ottawa, Canada
DESCRIPTION: 27.5 × 20.5 cm   Pp [i–x], 1–170 [171] Paper, with image on front of two men cutting down a tree with a cross-cut saw; rebound in cloth
CONTENTS: i tp; ii blank; iii 'Avant propos'; iv blank; v 'Remerciements' signed L.B. Pett, le chef du Service de l'hygiène alimentaire; vi blank; vii 'Table des matières'; viii blank; ix 'Abréviations' and 'Mesures'; x blank; 1–2 'Températures'; 3–163 recipes; 164–70 'Index'; 171 'Série Services alimentaires // I. Chef et cuisine II. Achat et emmagasinage des aliments dans les camps de bûcherons III. Préparation des aliments en grande quantité et soin du matériel IV. Recettes – 100 portions pour les hommes qui travaillent dur // On peut obtenir des exemplaires de ce manuel en s'adressant à l'imprimeur du roi, Ottawa (Prix: $1.00)'
COPIES: *QMBM (641.57 C212re)
NOTES: The date of publication, 1949, is on the front face of the binding. Under 'Remerciements,' Pett says that the book was published at the request of the 'Section des chantiers' of the Canadian Pulp and Paper Association. He credits Miss Margaret Lock for most of the compiling and editing, and thanks the Royal Canadian Air Force for permission to use material from 'Manuel de recettes C.A.P. 434 du Corps d'aviation royal canadien,' i.e., O1094.1, *Royal Canadian Air Force Recipe Manual 1945.*

OTHER EDITIONS: Ottawa: [1954] (OONL).

Centennial cook book

O1207.1   1949
1849 – Centennial – 1949 / cook book / Compiled and edited by the / Women's Circle / Trinity Church / Mooretown Ontario [cover-title]
DESCRIPTION: About 23.0 × 15.5 cm [dimensions from photocopy]   With image on front of a woman holding a cookbook in her left hand and a wooden spoon in her right hand; stapled
COPIES: *OWYL

Clinton Hospital Aid cook book

Clinton is southeast of Goderich.

O1208.1   1949
Clinton Hospital Aid / cook book / Compiled and published by the members / of the / Hospital Aid / Clinton Public Hospital / 1949 / [Paragraph beginning, 'Our sincere thanks to the many friends who have contributed recipes ...'] / ['Index,' i.e., table of contents] / Press of Clinton News-Record
DESCRIPTION: 23.0 × 15.0 cm   Pp [1–2] 3–61, [i–iii] Very thin card; stapled
CONTENTS: 1 tp; 2 ads; 3–61 recipes credited with the name of the contributor and ads; i–iii ads
COPIES: *Private collection

Cook book

O1209.1   1949
1949 / Cook book / Compiled and published by / Group 3, Women's Association / Oakdale United Church / Notice / [two paragraphs of introductory text] / Index / [table of contents] / [folio:] 3
DESCRIPTION: 22.0 × 14.5 cm   Pp 3–86   Paper, with photograph on front of Oakdale United Church; stapled
CONTENTS: 3 tp; 4 ad; 5–86 recipes credited with the name of the contributor and ads
COPIES: OWYL   *Private collection
NOTES: '1879 Seventieth anniversary 1949' is on the front face of the binding, at top; 'Petrolia Advertiser-Topic Print' is at bottom. Oakdale is south of Petrolia, where the book was printed. This copy is inscribed on the binding, 'Mrs Gordon Dawson.'

Cook book

Campbell's Cross is northwest of Toronto, in Peel Region, at the intersection of Kennedy Road and King Street. The Campbell's Cross branch of the Women's Institute was established in 1935 (Ambrose, p 232).

O1210.1   1949
Cook book / [Women's Institute symbol] / Compiled and tested / by the members of / Campbell's Cross / Women's Institute / 1949–1950 [cover-title]
DESCRIPTION: About 22.0 × 14.5 cm [dimensions from photocopy]   With image on front of a woman setting a table

CONTENTS: 1 Women's Institute symbol, poem beginning, 'We may live without poetry, music and art' [from *Lucile,* Part I, Canto ii, by Owen Meredith, pseudonym of Edward Robert Bulwer-Lytton] signed '(Quotation from "Lucille" [*sic*]) Mrs. A.L. Armstrong,' and thank-you from the Campbell's Cross Women's Institute; 2 'Index' [i.e., alphabetical list of subjects]; ...
COPIES: *Private collection
NOTES: The book has 88 pp. Another private collector's copy is inscribed, 'Bought this book Oct. 8, 1949.'

Cook book

O1210a.1   April 1949
Niagara / Women's Institute / [Women's Institute symbol] / Cook book / [Ontario coat of arms] / Ontario / Compiled April, 1949 / from recipes donated by members and friends of / Niagara, Port Dalhousie, Queenston–St. Davids / and Virgil Women's Institutes [cover-title]
DESCRIPTION: Stapled
CONTENTS: 1 'List of Officers, 1949–50' and 'Foreword' signed Anna P. Lewis, director, Women's Institutes of Ontario, in which she congratulates the Niagara-on-the-Lake Women's Institute; ...; inside back face of binding 'Index' [i.e., table of contents]
COPIES: *Private collection
NOTES: There are 53 numbered pp. The recipes are credited with the name of the contributor.

Cook book

O1211.1   1949
North Waterloo / Women's Institute / [Women's Institute symbol] / 1949 / Cook book [cover-title]
DESCRIPTION: About 22.0 × 14.5 cm [dimensions from photocopy]   Pp [1] 2–28   Stapled
CONTENTS: 1 'North Waterloo Women's Institute,' Women's Institute symbol, year of publication, and 'Index' [i.e., table of contents]; 2 ads; 3–27 recipes credited with the name of the contributor; 28 ads
COPIES: *Private collection
NOTES: The 'Index' lists the following sections: 'Candy,' p 3; 'Miscellaneous,' p 4; 'Pies,' p 5; 'Supper Dishes,' p 5; 'Cookies,' p 9; and 'Cake,' p 17. Most of the advertisements are for businesses in Linwood, which is northwest of Kitchener, beyond St Jacobs. The cookbook was probably compiled by the Linwood branch of the Women's Institute, founded in 1907 (Ambrose, p 233). 'Printed in St. Jacobs' is on the outside back face of the binding.

A cook book of well proven recipes

O1212.1   1949
A / cook book / of / well proven recipes / Collected by / the Women's Association / of / Blakes United Church / Ashfield / 1949
DESCRIPTION   22.5 × 15.0 cm   Pp [1–4] 5–113 [114–16]   Tp illus of a woman carrying a tray of food in each hand   Thin card; stapled
CONTENTS: 1 tp; 2 'Guess Work' [poem] and 'Foreword'; 3 'Index' [i.e., table of contents] and ad; 4 ads; 5–113 recipes credited with the name of the contributor and ads; 114–15 ads; 116 'Household Hints' and ads
COPIES: *OGU (CCC TX715.6 C66)
NOTES: The cover-title is 'Selected Recipes.' An advertisement on p 116 for the *Lucknow Sentinel* says that the cookbook was printed on the Sentinel's 'New Heidelberg Press'; 'Printed by the Lucknow Sentinel' is on the outside back face of the binding.

Cooking with joy!

O1213.1   [1949]
Cooking / with / joy! [cover-title]
DESCRIPTION: Pp 1–127   Photograph on p 1 of the church
CONTENTS: 1 untitled introductory note signed Gwynneth M. Hoag, 1949; 2 'Preface' signed Committee, 'Recipe for a Happy Day,' and 'Table of Weights and Measures'; 3 'Index' [i.e., table of contents]; 4 ad; 5–121 recipes credited with the name of the contributor; 122–3 thirty-six numbered 'Household Hints'; 124–top 126 'Large Quantity Cookery // Food Weights and Measures'; mid–bottom 126 'Anniversaries'; 127 'Average Can Sizes'
CITATIONS: FitzPatrickCat 111 (April 1993) No. 12
COPIES: *Private collection
NOTES: On p 1 Hoag explains that the members of the Joy Unit of Kingsway-Lambton Women's Association compiled and edited the book, and 'the proceeds from its sale may enable them to contribute more generously to the many worthwhile projects supported by their church [i.e., Kingsway-Lambton United Church in Etobicoke, now part of Toronto].'

Easy ways to good meals

For the titles of other cookbooks for Campbell's soups, see O744.1.

O1214.1   copyright 1949
Easy ways to good meals / Contents / From soup to cake, Campbell's soups can play their / part in adding fresh interest to your lunches, dinners / and suppers. A glance below will give you an idea of / the many aids to interesting meals this book contains. / For further ideas – just turn the pages! / Because Campbell's soups are condensed 2 / Menus 3 / Main course dishes 4 / Leftovers – how to use them 10 / Casserole dishes 14 / Fish dishes 18 / Cheese and egg dishes 20 / Vegetable dishes 23 / Sauces and gravies 27 / Salads, salad dressings and jellied dishes 30 / Desserts 36 / Soup combinations 38 / New soups to try 41 / Soup garnishes 43 / Party patterns with soup 45 / Meal-planner's guide 46 / Index 48 / Campbell Soup Company / Camden Chicago Sacramento New Toronto / [folio:] 1 / Copyrighted, 1949, Campbell Soup Company
DESCRIPTION: 19.0 × 13.0 cm   Pp 1–48   Tp illus col of a table setting and a moulded salad, illus col, illus   Paper, with image on front of 'Beef Stew with Vegetables and Dumplings'; stapled
CONTENTS: Inside front face of binding 'From One Good Cook to Another' signed Anne Marshall, home economist; 1 tp; 2 'Because Campbell's Soups Are Condensed'; 3 'Menus'; 4–42 recipes; 43 'Soup Garnishes'; 44–5 'Party Patterns with Soup'; 46–7 'Meal-Planner's Guide'; 48 index
COPIES: *Private collection
NOTES: The sub-title on the binding is '99 Delicious Dishes Made with Campbell's Soups.'

Favourite recipes

Marathon is on the north shore of Lake Superior, east of Thunder Bay.

O1215.1   1949
Favourite recipes / Collected / by / Group IV / from members of / Women's Association / Trinity Church / Marathon, Ontario. / 1949 / [folio:] 1
DESCRIPTION: 23.0 × 15.0 cm   Pp 1–44   Paper, with image on front of a woman with an over-size head, holding up a cake in one hand and a pie in the other; stapled
CONTENTS: 1 tp; 2 'Basic Measurements,' 'For Serving 100 People' [i.e., quantities of rolls, coffee, milk, meat, potatoes, soup, butter, loaves of bread, ham, ice cream, cakes, and pies], and 'Recipes for Serving 50 People' [i.e., recipes for Coffee, Cocoa, Mashed Potatoes, Biscuits, and Baked Beans]; 3 'Baking Hints'; 4–41 recipes credited with the name of the contributor and ads; 42 ad; 43 'Doubling Butter' and 'Suggested Cold Lunches'; 44 'Index'
COPIES: *Private collection
NOTES: The cover-title is 'Meals from Marathon Kitchens.' The text is printed in blue.

Favourite recipes

O1216.1   1949
Favourite recipes / Compiled by the / Junior Women's Association / for the / Building Fund / of / Westminster Presbyterian Church / Westboro, Ontario / 1949
DESCRIPTION: 22.0 × 15.0 cm   Pp [1] 2–99 [100]   Tp illus of a sandwich on a plate   Paper, with image on front of an aproned woman stirring the contents of a bowl; stapled
CONTENTS: 1 tp; 2 ads; 3 'Foreword'; 4 ad; 5 'Helpful Food Table'; 6 ad; 7–100 recipes and ads
COPIES: *Private collection
NOTES: The 'Foreword' warns the reader: 'It has not been possible to test every recipe in this book. They have been submitted, in good faith by friends to whom we hereby express our thanks.' The printer's name is on the outside back face of the binding: 'Flora Printers – Ottawa.'

Favourite recipes, Book No. 3

See also the Lady Grey Chapter's first and second books of Favourite Recipes, O985.1 and O1136.1.

O1217.1   [December 1949]
Favourite recipes / Book No. 3 / [IODE symbol] / Lady Grey Chapter / I.O.D.E. / Fort William, Ont. [cover-title]
DESCRIPTION: 23.5 × 15.0 cm   Pp 1–100   Illus   Paper, with IODE symbol on front; stapled
CONTENTS: 1 'Index' [i.e., table of contents]; 2 introductory note signed Hubert Badanai, mayor; 3 'Foreword'; 4–97 text and ads; 98 ads; 99–100 blank for 'Menus'
CITATIONS: Armstrong 2000, illus p F2
COPIES: OTBH   *Private collection
NOTES: The 'Foreword' states, 'This issue ... marks the

fortieth anniversary of our chapter – December 9, 1909 to December 9, 1949 ... Book No. 3 Favourite Recipes will make an ideal gift, and as a souvenir of Fort William it has particular merit.'

From Trinity kitchens

O1218.1 [1949]
From / Trinity kitchens / A / collection of / choice recipes / presented by / Women's Association / Trinity United Church / Burlington, Ont. / Index on page 9 / Printed by the Burlington Gazette
DESCRIPTION: 22.5 × 15.0 cm Pp [1] 2–132 [133–4] Fp illus on p 3 of Trinity United Church by J.T. Kirby, fp illus on p 5 of 'Burlington – Cradled by the Hills,' fp illus on p 12 of 'Burlington – Lake Shore' Paper, with image on front of a covered casserole bowl; Cirlox-type binding
CONTENTS: 1 tp; 2 untitled note and 'Appreciation'; 3 fp illus; 4 'The Town of Burlington'; 5 fp illus; 6 continuation of 'The Town of Burlington' and ads; 7–8 ads; 9 'Index' [i.e., table of contents], four-line verse, and 'Copies of this book will be mailed on request to Trinity Church Secretary, Mrs. McKeen, Burlington, Ont. Price $1.00 October, 1949'; 10–11 'Treasured Recipes'; 12 fp illus; 13 continuation of 'Treasured Recipes'; 14 ads; 15–126 recipes and ads; 127 'Helpful Hints'; 128–9 ads; 130 blank 'For Your Favourite Recipes'; 131–2 'Telephone Directory'; 133–4 ads
COPIES: OBUJBM   OH (R641.5 T736 CESH)   *Private collection
NOTES: The note on p 2 states: 'Trinity United Church, Burlington, Ontario, which was erected in 1886 and rebuilt in 1895, has planned to install a new organ console. Proceeds from this book will be contributed to the fund.' The 'Appreciation' acknowledges the recipe contributors and Mr Kirby of King's Road, Burlington, for the illustrations.

Handy household hints

O1219.1 1949
Handy household / hints .... / all material originally published in / Chatelaine / the Canadian woman's magazine / published by Maclean-Hunter Publishing Company Limited / 481 University Avenue, Toronto 2, Canada
DESCRIPTION: 25.5 × 16.5 cm Pp [i–ii], [1–2] 3–42 [43–50] Many illus Paper, with four photographs on front of household scenes; stapled
CONTENTS: i tp; ii 'Copyright 1949 Maclean-Hunter

Publishing Company Limited // 481 University Avenue, Toronto 2, Canada'; 1 foreword; 2 table of contents, which lists 'In the Kitchen,' 'Quiz,' 'Around the Home,' and 'Miscellaneous'; 3–42 text; 43–50 blank for 'Additional Tips'
COPIES: *OGU (UA s070 b34)   OTNY (uncat)
NOTES: The book is printed in blue and black.

Meeting over tea

O1220.1 [1949]
Meeting over tea / A guide to the proper preparation and serving of / tea for women's organizations, church groups, etc. / with / a selection of quick tea-time snacks. / A Tea Bureau Publication / The Tea Bureau / Head office / Toronto / Bank of Montreal Building / Branch offices / Montreal / 2027 Mansfield St. / Winnipeg / 144 Lombard St. / Vancouver / 640 Burrard St. / Page 3
DESCRIPTION Frontis of a women's group at tea-time
COPIES: OONL (TX817 T3 M44 1950z, 2 copies)   *Private collection
NOTES: A typed letter from Frank A. Healy, director of information for the Tea Bureau, dated 20 June 1949, is inserted in one of the OONL copies. He writes: 'We are enclosing a copy of a booklet entitled "Meeting over Tea" which has just come off the press ... The booklet was made possible by the co-operation of a number of food editors whose recipes you will find in the latter pages of the booklet. Copies may be obtained, free of charge, ...' There are recipes from Kate Aitken, from the *Canadian Home Journal,* and from Marie Holmes of the Chatelaine Institute. The volume has 20 pp.

Moffat cook book

For the titles of other cookbooks by the same manufacturer, see O342.1.

Elaine Collett was educated in Toronto at Davisville Public School and North Toronto Collegiate Institute. For financial reasons, her subsequent studies in home economics at Central Technical School lasted only one year, after which she supervised the cafeteria at the National Life Assurance Co., then the dining rooms at the Royal Bank of Canada head office. During the Second World War, she took a course in dietetics at the University of Toronto, and from 1942 to 1944 she worked at Chatham General Hospital. Her next job was at Massey-Harris, where she 'produced a freezer book for farm women,' according to the tribute paid to her in 1992 when she was inducted into the Hall of Fame of the Association of Ontario Home Economists in Business; this publication is likely O1168.1, Preparing Foods for Storage in Your Massey-Harris Home Freezer, *although Collett's name does not appear in the volume. In 1947, she joined Moffats Ltd, for which she prepared O1221.1,* Moffat Cook Book. *She served as director of the Chatelaine Institute from November 1956 to 1975, and wrote* The Chatelaine Cookbook, *first published in 1965. Following her retirement from the Chatelaine Institute, she continued to work in a variety of capacities. She married George Marvin Drury in 1950, but kept her maiden name in her professional life. She died on 5 September 2002.*

O1221.1 [miniature ed., 1949]
Moffat / cook / book [cover-title]
DESCRIPTION: 15.0 × 10.0 cm   Pp [i], 1–16   [Free, on inside front face of binding: 'Compliments of Moffats Limited Weston Ontario']   Paper; stapled
CONTENTS: i untitled introductory text signed Elaine Collett, Moffat home economist, and order coupon for 'New 1950 deluxe edition // Moffat Cook Book // Special exhibition price 50c. post paid ... Available October 15, 1949'; 1–16 recipes
COPIES: *Bookseller's stock
NOTES: In the introductory text Collett states: 'This is a miniature edition of the new Moffat Cook Book. In this little booklet, we are bringing you a few of the many special recipes which are included in this big new 1950 edition.' All but one of the recipes in the miniature edition are for sweet dishes. For the larger edition (English and French), see O1221.2 and O1221.3. The miniature and larger editions have the same binding design: a geometric pattern of diamond shapes in the background, with the title in a frame created by organic, scroll-like shapes.

Unusually, the page numbering begins on the verso of the first leaf so that the odd numbers are on the versos and even numbers, on the rectos. Also unusual is the orientation of the recipes on the page: Whereas the cover-title and the introductory text are positioned conventionally on the portrait-format page, to read the recipes one must turn the booklet by 90° and flip what are now top-hinged pages. The text is printed in blue throughout.

O1221.2   nd [15 October 1949]
—Moffat / cook / book [cover-title]
DESCRIPTION: 23.0 × 15.0 cm   Pp [1] 2–105 [106–8]   Illus   Thin card; Cirlox-type binding
CONTENTS: 1 foreword signed Elaine Collett, director,

Home Service Department, Moffats Ltd; 2 'Index' [i.e., table of contents]; 3–105 text; 106–8 blank for 'Notes'
CITATIONS: Possibly Ferguson/Fraser, p 234
COPIES: OGU (CCC TX715.6 M63, 2 copies)   OONL (TX715.6 M64 1950z copy 2)   QMM (RBD ckbk 1835)   *Private collection
NOTES: This is a new text and not related to earlier cookbooks by the same company, such as O1053.1, *Moffat Cook Book.* This edition is undated; however, in O1221.1 it is described as the '1950 edition, available 15 October 1949.' 'Canadian Patent No. 334331' is on the inside back face of the binding of the OGU and QMM copies, but not of the OONL copy.

O1221.3   nd [about 1949]
—Livre de / cuisine / Moffat [cover-title]
DESCRIPTION: 23.0 × 15.0 cm   Pp [1] 2–105 [106–8]   Illus   Thin card; Cirlox-type binding
CONTENTS: 1 'Avant-propos' signed Elaine Collett and 'Canadian Patent No. 334331'; 2 'Index' [i.e., table of contents]; 3–105 text; 106–8 blank for 'Notes'
COPIES: *QSFFSC

OTHER EDITIONS: *Moffat Cook Book,* nd [1950s], 'Foreword' signed Denyse Pesant, director, Home Service Department, Moffats Ltd, and outside back face of binding with two company names: Moffats Ltd, Weston, Ontario, and Avco of Canada Ltd (BKOM).

Ontario, Department of Agriculture

For the titles of other cookbooks published by the Ontario Department of Agriculture, see O158.1.

O1222.1   August 1949
Canning / Ontario's / fruits and / vegetables / Ontario Department of Agriculture / Statistics and Publications Branch Toronto / Bulletin 468 August 1949 [cover-title]
CITATIONS: AnderCat April 2001, No. 13835   MacTaggart, p 33
COPIES: *OGU (2 copies: Rural Heritage Collection, CA2ON AF6 B468)   Bookseller's stock
NOTES: The book has 40 pp and illustrations.

OTHER EDITIONS: Rev. ed., 1968 (OGU).

O1223.1   April 1949
Salads / – all the year 'round / The objective of "Salads All / the Year 'Round" is to prove / to you and your family that / salads are full of zip and /

may begin ... accompany ... / end ... or make a meal! Serve / good salads in all seasons! / When should you start? / Today! / Prepared by / Women's Institute Branch / and / Home Economics Service / Ontario Department of Agriculture

DESCRIPTION: 23.0 × 15.0 cm Pp [1] 2–16 Illus green Paper, with image on front of salad in a bowl; stapled

CONTENTS: 1 tp; 2–3 'Rabbit Food?,' 'Seasonings to Enliven Flavour,' 'Measurements,' and 'Important Points in Salad Making'; 4–5 'Surprise Flavour with ... Salad Dressings'; 6–13 recipes for salads, including 'Salad Accompaniments' on p 12; 14–15 'Salad Garnishes'; 16 'Help Yourself to Health ... Canada's Food Rules Approved by the Canadian Council on Nutrition, 1944'

CITATIONS: MacTaggart, p 33

COPIES: OGU (Rural Heritage Collection) *Private collection

NOTES: 'Ontario Department of Agriculture // Statistics and Publications Branch, Toronto, Ontario // Bulletin 466 April, 1949' is on the front face of the binding. The text is printed appropriately in green.

OTHER EDITIONS: Reprint, September 1958 (Private collection).

O1224.1 [1949]

Your money's / worth in food. / 120 / tested recipes / and / money saving / food facts / [Ontario coat of arms] / Ontario / Department of Agriculture / Women's Institute Branch / and Home Economics Service / Published by authority of Hon. Thomas L. Kennedy / Minister of Agriculture [cover-title]

DESCRIPTION: 23.0 × 15.0 cm Pp [1–2] 3–64 Illus brown Thin card, with image on front of a piggy bank into which are falling coins inscribed with the names of various dishes, such as meats or desserts; stapled

CONTENTS: Inside front face of binding 'Abbreviations' and 'Equivalents'; 1 'Index of Recipes'; 2–3 'Let's Face the Facts about High Food Prices!' [prices cited for January 1949]; 4–5 'Canada's Food Rules'; 6–7 'Meal Planning' [prices cited for January 1949]; 8 'Dollars and Sense [sic] with Food'; 9 'How Does Your Garden Grow?' and 'To Market! To Market!'; 10 'Making Use of Leftovers'; 11–64 recipes

COPIES: *Private collection

NOTES: The text and illustrations are printed in brown. The text on p 3 explains that the book was published in response to the reduction in the purchasing power of the dollar; it contrasts the prices of 1937 and April 1946 with those of January 1949, for basic foodstuffs,

and exhorts the reader to 'Budget first for health foods!' There is no Bulletin number, and this edition is not recorded in MacTaggart.

OTHER EDITIONS: *Your Money's Worth in Food: 120 Tested Recipes,* Bulletin 470, April 1950, Statistics and Publications Branch (Private collection); reprinted October 1955 (OGU); revised September 1958 (OGU).

Recipes ... care ... use: Westinghouse refrigerators

For Cornell's other cookbooks, see O781.1.

O1225.1 [copyright 1949]

Recipes ... care ... use / Westinghouse / refrigerators [cover-title]

DESCRIPTION: 22.5 × 15.0 cm Pp 1–40 Illus Thin card, with fanciful image on front of a woman in a snowy landscape, storing food in a hole in the snow; stapled

CONTENTS: Inside front face of binding 'Things You'll Want to Know' [i.e., table of contents] and 'Copyright, 1949 – Canadian Westinghouse Company, Limited // Prepared by Canadian Westinghouse Company Limited, Hamilton, Ontario'; 1 'Now You Have a New "Maid"!' signed Anna May Cornell, director, Home Economics Department, and a photograph of Cornell; 2–15 information about using refrigerators; 16–39 'Refrigerator Recipes'; 40 'Westinghouse Refrigerator Warranty'; inside back face space for 'model no.,' 'cabinet serial no.,' and 'date of purchase'; outside back face '705P945 // BH7100'

COPIES: *Private collection

Tasty, easy and different

O1226.1 1949

[An edition of *Tasty, Easy and Different,* Wellington Square Church, Burlington, Ontario, 1949, [printed by?] James Kemp Co.]

COPIES: Private collection

Tried and tested recipes

O1227.1 [1949]

Tried & tested / recipes / [British Empire Service League symbol] / Compiled by the Ladies Auxiliary to the / Canadian Legion, B.E.S.L., / Palmerston Branch / One dollar per copy [cover-title]

DESCRIPTION: 23.0 × 15.5 cm   Pp 1–91 [92]   Thin card; stapled
CONTENTS: 1 'The Woman Who Cooks' [poem], 'In Appreciation,' and ad; 2–90 text, mostly recipes credited with the name of the contributor, and ads; 91 ad; 92 'Index' [i.e., table of contents]
CITATIONS: Driver 2001, Wellington County, p 93
COPIES: *OFERWM (A1984.51)
NOTES: Evidence that the book appeared in 1949 is in two places: on p 60, where the Canadian Legion wishes the compilers 'Every success in the publishing of your new cook book' and lists 'Officers for year 1949'; and on the outside back face of the binding, where there is a car advertisement that refers to 'the 1949 Ford' and illustrates a gold medal awarded in 1949.

Tried and tested recipes

The Crumlin Women's Institute published another cookbook with the same title in 1937; see O929.1.

O1228.1   1949
Tried and tested / recipes / Crumlin Women's Institute / 1949 [cover-title]
DESCRIPTION: Pp 1–68   With image on front of a woman carrying a tray of food
CONTENTS: Inside front face of binding 'Handy Weights and Measures,' 'Substitutes,' and 'Sauces for Meat and Fish'; 1–68 recipes and 'Hints' credited with the name of the contributor, and ads; inside back face 'Officers 1948–1949' and 'Thanks'
COPIES: *Private collection

Truscott, J.H.L., E.C. Stillwell, and E.S. Snyder

Also by Truscott is O1019.1. For the titles of other cookbooks published by the Ontario Department of Agriculture, see O158.1.

O1229.1   June 1949
Frozen foods / by J.H.L. Truscott, E.C. Stillwell and E.S. Snyder / Ontario Agricultural College / Guelph, Ontario / Ontario Department of Agriculture / Statistics and Publications Branch, Toronto, Ontario / Bulletin 467 June, 1949 [cover-title]
DESCRIPTION: 24.0 × 16.5 cm   Pp [1–2] 3–45   Illus Paper, with image on front of various foodstuffs viewed from above; stapled

CONTENTS: 1 introductory text; 2 blank; 3–8 Section I, 'Problems in the Freezing of Foods'; 9–21 Section II, 'Frozen Fruits and Vegetables'; 22–35 Section III, 'Frozen Poultry'; 36–45 Section IV, 'Meat for the Locker'
CITATIONS: MacTaggart, p 33
COPIES: *Private collection
NOTES: The introductory text states, 'This bulletin is intended for householders who use the freezing method for the preservation of part of their food supply.' Truscott was with the Department of Horticulture at the Ontario Agricultural College; Stillwell was with the Department of Animal Husbandry; and Snyder, with the Department of Poultry Husbandry. The private collector's copy is inscribed in a child's hand, 'Lloyd Douglas Irwin ... Leslie Charles Irwin.'

York, Brenda [pseudonym]

The pseudonym Brenda York was created by Canada Packers Ltd in 1947. The name was inspired by the company's York Brand of canned fruits and vegetables. Kathleen Hodgins, who was the first Brenda York, writes, 'I was hired in 1947 ... It was a very high profile job – teaser bill boards promoting the name, recipe contests monthly, lots of food photography, cooking schools in church basements and school auditoriums and recipe development for product promotions and advertising ... I left in 1951, [I was] followed by Jean Trenholme (from the Maritimes) and then Joan Fielden (U[niversity] of T[oronto]) [died 2000]. Sally Henry [died 1991] came about 1954 and stayed until 1963 when she went to Maple Leaf Mills [to be 'Anna Lee Scott'] ... By that time the name Brenda York was used less, although there still were recipes in promotions under the name. Jean Patterson worked with Sally for a couple of years before Sally left and then she stayed on until the company was sold' (e-mail to Elizabeth Driver, 18 June 2001).

Kathleen Mary Hodgins, née Watson (born 25 April 1923, Toronto, Ontario), graduated from the University of Toronto with a BA in 1945 and was awarded her MA in food chemistry in 1947. Immediately after graduation and unmarried, she joined Canada Packers, where she was known as Kay Watson (not to be confused with Mrs Kathleen M. Watson of the University of Manitoba, who revised the 1945 edition of O771.3, Purity Cook Book). In her last year at Canada Packers, she married Eric Hodgins. They later divorced; she married Peter Williams; they divorced, and Kathleen reunited with Eric Hodgins and legally reverted to her first married name.

O1230.1 nd [1949]

Margene / recipe book / by / Brenda York / [Chatelaine Institute 'Tested and approved' symbol]

DESCRIPTION: 13.0 × 21.5 cm Pp [i–ii], [1–4] 5–40, [i–ii] Tp illus of a letter addressed 'Dear Madam,' signed Brenda York, and on Canada Packers Ltd, Toronto, stationery; illus col Paper, with image on front of a package of Margene; stapled

CONTENTS: i–ii foil leaf with 'Margene' impressed in all-over regular pattern on recto, and 'New Margene is foil-wrapped to protect the flavour' printed on verso; 1 tp; 2–3 table of contents; 4–39 recipes; 40 'How to Colour Margene a Golden Yellow in 3 Minutes'; i–ii foil leaf with 'New Margene is foil-wrapped to protect the flavour' printed on recto, and 'Margene' impressed in all-over pattern on verso

CITATIONS: Driver 2003, 'Canadian Cookbooks,' pp 25, 36 FitzPatrickCat 111 (April 1993) No. 27

COPIES: ACG OGU (CCC TX715.6 M572 No. 245) OONL (TX715.6 Y67 1900z p***) OTMCL (641.6 Y59) QMM (2 copies: RBD ckbk 1073, RBD ckbk 2124) *Private collection

NOTES: Margarine was legalized in Canada at the end of 1948 (the 1886 ban on margarine was enforced until 1917, then temporarily lifted until 1923 because of First World War food shortages). The first advertisement in *Chatelaine* magazine for Margene, Canada Packers' new brand, is in Vol. 22, No. 6 (June 1949), p 65. In the September issue (Vol. 22, No. 9), there are advertisements on p 73 announcing the 'free Margene Recipe Book ... containing 60 tested Margene recipes, and illustrated in full colour.' On p 77, Brenda York launches a new form of her monthly advertising column, retitled 'Brenda York's "Here's How" Cookery Column,' which she devotes to Margene, 'the first margarine sold in Canada.' She offers $100 to the reader who submits the best recipe for using Margene, and she asks readers to send for the 'new "Margene" Cook Book' of sixty recipes.

According to Kay Hodgins, the printer of the book was the Toronto firm Sampson-Matthews, and the art director, A.J. Casson (of Group of Seven fame). Casson's distinctive design incorporated foil leaves at front and back, mimicking Margene's foil wrapper; on the front face of the binding, part of the image of the block of margarine is cut out, revealing the foil leaf behind. See pl 11. See also Casson's illustrations in O771.3, *Purity Cook Book*, and O771.4, the French translation.

Late 1940s

HHEA cook book

O1231.1 nd [late 1940s]

HH / EA / cook book / Hamilton Home Economics Association [cover-title]

DESCRIPTION: 23.0 × 15.5 cm Pp [1] 2–104 Thin card; plastic Cirlox-type binding

CONTENTS: 1 'Introduction' [eight-line verse]; 2–104 text and ads; inside back face of binding 'Thank You!' signed Hamilton Home Economics Association, and below, 'Central Press Commercial Printing'

COPIES: *OH (R641.5 HHE CESH)

1949–50

The favourite cook book

O1232.1 [1949 or 1950]

The favourite cook book / A collection of / tried and tested / recipes / compiled and published by / the members of / the Friendship Circle / South Porcupine United Church / Bloor Avenue, South Porcupine

DESCRIPTION: [$0.50, on binding]

COPIES: *Private collection

NOTES: The title-page is inscribed '1949 or 1950.'

The pantry shelf

O1233.1 [rev. ed., 1949–50]

The pantry shelf / (revised edition) / A collection of home-proven / recipes / compiled and published / by / [IODE symbol] / Alexander Graham Bell Chapter / Imperial Order Daughters of / the Empire / Brantford Ontario / Page 1

DESCRIPTION: 23.5 × 15.5 cm Pp 1–96 Portrait on p 3 of Alexander Graham Bell Very thin card, with portrait on front of Alexander Graham Bell, and IODE symbol on front; stapled

CONTENTS: 1 tp; 2 history of Alexander Graham Bell Chapter; 3 portrait of Bell, untitled acknowledgments, and 'Officers for the Year 1949–50,' which includes 'Co-Convenors of Revised "Pantry Shelf" Mrs. J.W. Merklinger and Mrs. A.J. Craven'; 4–95 recipes credited with the name of the contributor and ads; 96 'Index' [i.e., table of contents]

COPIES: *QMM (RBD Vanna Garnier, ckbk 581)

NOTES: 'Quantity Cookery to Serve 100 People' is on p 94; 'Quantity Cookery to Serve 50 People' is on p 95.

Manitoba

Vínarterta

¾ cup butter
2 cups sugar
4 eggs
1 cup shelled blanched almonds
1 teaspoon shelled and ground cardamoms
½ teaspoon vanilla
4 cups flour; 1 cup flour for handling it
3 teaspoons baking powder
1 tablespoon water

Cream butter and sugar. Beat eggs and add to mixture, also add cardamoms, vanilla and almonds finely ground. Add water and flour sifted with baking powder. Cut in as cockie paste. Divide into 6 portions and roll as cookies. Place each portion in a layer cake pan, having cut it to the same shape as the pan. Bake in oven 450°F., and put in filling:

1 lb. prunes
½ cup sugar
Salt
½ teaspoon vanilla

Cook prunes in water until tender and stone. Put through meat chopper. Add sugar and flavoring and cook a few minutes more.
Remarks: I make cookies out [of] what is left. I reserve 1 white of an egg to spread on cookies and sprinkle with sugar before baking.

Mrs Finnur Johnson

M54.1, *Cook Book*, by the Ladies' Aid of First Lutheran Church, Winnipeg, [1929]

In 1882, twelve years after the founding of the province of Manitoba on 2 May 1870, the Canadian Pacific Railway reached Winnipeg. The city quickly became the gateway for east-west trade and for the flood of new settlers to the West in the period 1897–1930. Between 1881 and 1901, Manitoba's population grew from 62,260 to 255,211; by 1911, the province had reached 461,394, and Winnipeg, 157,000. The city was the largest in the West and it remained the pre-eminent urban centre for a long time. The strength of Winnipeg's industrial and commercial sector, its well-established press, the influence of the Manitoba Agricultural College, and the role of the provincial government in rural education (the latter two institutions both based in Winnipeg) are all reflected in the body of cookbooks published in Manitoba before 1950 – 157 titles in total.[1] Many community cookbooks, which make up over half the total (54%), emanated from the small towns in the hinterlands of Winnipeg and Brandon, the province's other urban centre. In no other province was the variety of immigrant cultures expressed so clearly through cookbooks as in Manitoba before 1950, where one finds Icelandic, Jewish, Scottish, Ukrainian, and German recipe collections. No French-language cookbooks written specifically for the Franco-Manitoban population surfaced, possibly because French cookbooks from outside the province were available;[2] however, the provincial government did publish at least one title in the *Manitoba Farmers' Library* series in English and French.[3]

The earliest book recorded here, *Home and Health* (O32.3), was issued in 1884, two years after the arrival of the railway, by the Winnipeg publishers of the monthly periodical *Nor'West Farmer*. It was an American 'compendium of useful knowledge' that contained some information about food and cooking; the text had also been published in Ontario. Likewise, the recipe collections published by the Winnipeg druggist J.H. Rose in the 1890s (O68.4) and by the Red Cross Pharmacy in Portage la Prairie in 1904 and 1906 (M6.1, M7a.1) were likely American texts. Winnipeg's Royal Crown Soap Co. distributed American cookbooks as premiums to their customers, in exchange for soap wrappers (see M1.1 and the notes for B2.1).

The first cookbook written in Manitoba – *The Souvenir Cook Book* (M2.1) by the Ladies' Aid Society of Grace Church, Winnipeg – was published in 1896. Its title-page boasted that the recipes were 'Tried! Tested! Proved!,' copying Toronto's best-selling *The Home Cook Book,* the first Canadian fund-raiser, published in 1877 and issued in a Winnipeg edition in about 1901 (O20.38). In the first decade of the twentieth century, when immigration to the province was booming, other community cookbooks were compiled in Brandon in 1901 (M3.1, *The Wheat City Cook-Book,* by the ladies of the Methodist Church), in Winnipeg in 1902 (M4.1, by the ladies of St Stephens Church), in Neepawa in 1903 (M5.1, from the Lucile-Davidson Mission Circle), in Winnipeg in 1910 (M12.1, for St Luke's Church Organ Fund), and in Souris in about 1910 (M11.1, by the Young Ladies' Guild of the Fifth Avenue Methodist Church). *The Wheat City Cook-Book,* which went through three editions by 1910, and *St Luke's Organ Fund Recipe Book,* enlarged for a second edition in 1910, were especially popular in their respective cities. Other early titles that were also issued in multiple editions are the *Dauphin Ladies' Cook Book*

(M18.1, no sponsoring organization identified), published in 1913 and in 1923, and *The Minnedosa Cook Book* (M20.1, by the Women's Hospital Aid), a second edition of which appeared in 1914. These local recipe collections were clearly welcomed by Manitobans.

In 1914, the year that war broke out in Europe, the Sir Edward Grey Chapter of the Imperial Order Daughters of the Empire was organized in Winnipeg. Toward the end of the war, the chapter published *War Recipes* (M29.1) to raise money to buy 'comforts' for Canadian prisoners of war. At about the same time, ladies in Reston and vicinity produced a cookbook to benefit the Red Cross (M24.1). Another work that may have been a fund-raiser for the Red Cross is the 1914 *Selkirk Cook Book* (M21.1), a sophisticated production from the town's Anglican church, that reproduced on the binding a painting by local artist Marion Hooker and carried a 'Prologue' by the Winnipeg writer Valance Patriarche. During the Second World War, the Women's Auxiliary of the Fort Garry Horse published a fund-raiser 'to provide comforts for the troops' (M117.1), and the Erickson Ladies' Auxiliary of the Canadian Legion and the Winnipeg Women's Air Force Auxiliary reprinted an Ontario compilation of sugarless recipes to help the housewife at a time when there was a reduced supply of sugar for the domestic market (O1055.2, O1055.3). The Greenway Ladies' Aid called their 1940s recipe collection *Victory Cook Book,* like many wartime fund-raisers in other provinces (M110.1).

Community cookbooks continued to flow from church groups and other women's organizations after the First World War. The history of Winnipeg's imposing Knox Presbyterian Church (now Knox United Church) stretches back to 1868. *Knox Church Cook Book* (M30.1), of about 1917–20, included a 'Preface' by the wife of its distinguished first minister, Dr George Bryce, who had established Manitoba College and helped to found the University of Manitoba. In the 'Preface' Mrs Bryce, who was active in the Local Council of Women and in the Women's Christian Temperance Union, argues for the 'cultivated woman' and against critics of the expansion of women's education. Reflecting a different sentiment, the women of St Mark's Anglican Church and Regent's Park United Church in St Vital, in about 1925, joined across denominations to co-compile a cookbook whose title advised that *Wise Wives Keep Husbands Happy* (M48.1). Probably to support the local hospital, the Brandon Graduate Nurses Association published two editions of *The New Hospital Cook Book* in about 1922 and about 1930 (M38.1, M38.2); the Girls' Auxiliary of the Women's Hospital Aid Society in

Neepawa compiled *Cook Book* (M43.1) in 1924 for the Neepawa General Hospital; the Harmsworth Auxiliary produced *Harmsworth Community Cook Book* in 1924 (M44.1) and in 1941 (M120.1), in aid of Virden Hospital; and the PEO Sisterhood in Selkirk compiled a cookbook to help furnish the town's hospital in 1929 (M56.1). In 1926 the League of Winnipeg, a women's volunteer service organization, was founded; the very next year they published *The League Cook Book* (M52.1). In 1926, and again ten years later, the American Women's Club in Winnipeg (formed in 1917) put together a collection called *A Cook Book of Tested Recipes* (M49.1, M89.1). From the United Farm Women of Manitoba in 1929 came *Recipes* (M57.1), probably following the example of *Recipes* (A59.1) by the United Farm Women of Alberta in 1928. Nine years later, in 1938, the United Farm Women produced another recipe collection, *The Manitoba Health Cook Book* (M103.1). By 1930, community cookbooks were so commonplace in Manitoba that a Winnipeg firm, calling itself the Canadian Cook Book Company of Canada, capitalized on their popularity by publishing *All Tested Recipes* or *The Church Cook Book* (cover-title, M59.1), which the company described as 'contributed by the most famous chefs in the world,' by which it meant mothers.

In about 1934, in the depth of the Depression, the Commercial Girls' Club of Winnipeg published a cookbook (M75.1) that is an emblem of the resourcefulness of the women who faced hard times. The club had been formed in 1931 to help those who had lost their jobs or who couldn't find work. Only unemployed 'commercial girls' could register as members, and money raised by the club was dispensed as wages for work done. The book refers to one of their fundraising ventures, 'the most astounding tea party ever put on in Winnipeg' on 14 October 1932, at Eaton's department store, and offers economical and time-saving recipes, plus menus suitable for a business woman's bridge party. Other women's organizations that wrote cookbooks through the 1930s and 1940s, in addition to the many active church groups, include the Women's Institute (branches in Dugald, M61.1, and in Moline, M66.1; curiously, only these two cookbooks surfaced from the Manitoba Women's Institute, whose beginnings go back to 1910 in Morris);[4] Lions Club of Winnipeg (M77.1); Rebekah Lodges of Greater Winnipeg (M97.1), Colfax Rebekah Lodge No. 39, in Crystal City (M137.1), and Sunshine Rebekah Lodge No. 43, Winnipeg (M138.1); Ladies' Orange Benevolent Association, Victory Lodge No. 240, Winnipeg (M112.1); Order of the Eastern Star, Elm Creek Chapter (M133.1); and Guild of Ravenscourt School (now St John's Ravenscourt School) in Fort Garry (M140.1).

Icelandic, Jewish, and Scottish women gathered together recipes from their own communities. The Icelandic congregation of First Lutheran Church on Victor Street in Winnipeg published three editions of a work called simply *Cook Book,* in 1929, about 1938, and 1950 (M54.1), which includes a variety of Icelandic recipes, such as Pönnukökur, Rulla Pylsa, Livra Pylsa, and several versions of Vínarterta (the recipe especially associated with Canadian Icelanders),[5] plus favourite Canadian recipes, such as Butter Tarts. Regrettably, only one publicly held copy (1938 edition) was located. From Winnipeg's Hadassah Council came an annual series of a 'Souvenir Book' that contained information about the city's Jewish organizations and their activities, advertisements for Winnipeg businesses, and recipes. The series began in about 1928 and continued into the 1960s, and the nearly complete run of issues held in the archives of the Hadassah-Wizo Council of Winnipeg is an invaluable historical record of this vibrant community (see M73.1 for a list of issues). In 1934, the Sons of Scotland Benevolent Association, which ran the Winnipeg Camps, published *The Waverley Cook Book* (M78.1). Its compiler, May McMillan, included a range of recipes from Scotland's national cuisine, from Scotch Broth and Haggis to Dundee Cakes (there is also an article about the place of local Manitoba lake fish in the daily menu).

Cookbooks were also produced for the Ukrainian and German populations, but these were not of the community type.[6] In 1937 the Ukrainian Book Store at 660 Main Street in Winnipeg published, in the Ukrainian language, a collection of recipes for the preservation of fruits and vegetables from Mary Hiltz, a well-known professor at the Manitoba Agricultural College (M96.1). After the Second World War, the same business published two recipe books: *Ukrainian-English Cook Book* (M128.1), in Ukrainian except for bilingual recipe titles, to help immigrants learn about cooking in Canada, where the expectations were different from those for peasant families in the old country; and a shorter text, *Domashnie miasovyrobnytstvo ta konservuvannia ovochiv i iaryn* (M129.1), about meat processing and preserving at home. In the same period, National Publishers Ltd in Winnipeg published *,Nordwesten'-Kochbuch* (M127.1) for the German-Canadian housewife, also with bilingual recipe titles.

After 1882, Winnipeg quickly developed as the manufacturing and supply centre for the West. Royal Crown Soap Co.'s book premiums have already been mentioned. Three Winnipeg-based companies that made their own brand of food products (tea, coffee, spices, flavouring extracts, baking powder, jelly powders, etc.) also published and widely distributed cookbooks for advertising purposes: Blue Ribbon Manufacturing Co., later Blue Ribbon Ltd (Blue Ribbon brand); Codville-Georgeson Co., later Codville Co. Ltd (Gold Standard brand); and Western Pure Foods Ltd (Eclipse brand). The earliest, longest-lasting, and most famous of the three firms was Blue Ribbon Manufacturing Co., owned by the cousins George and John Galt, who had started in the grocery business in Winnipeg in 1882. Many thousands of copies of the *Blue Ribbon Cook Book* (M7.1) were printed, in multiple editions, from 1905 to 1970, and although the very early editions are rare, the book is still often found in Canadian homes. At first it was sub-titled 'especially for every-day use in Western homes' and later sometimes 'for everyday use in Canadian homes,' but despite the sub-title, some early editions include material extracted from an American text, Horace Kephart's *Book of Camping and Woodcraft* (for example, M7.2). In 1932, the company employed Mary Hiltz and Mary Moxon (like Hiltz, a professor at the Manitoba Agricultural College) to prepare a revised edition. Blue Ribbon products were sold at all Red and White stores in Manitoba, and in the 1930s the Point du Bois Supply Co. distributed free copies of *Red and White Health, Diet and General Recipe Book* (M84.1) that advertised both Blue Ribbon and Red and White brands.

Within a year or two of the appearance of the *Blue Ribbon Cook Book*, Codville-Georgeson Co. published *Tried, Tested and True Recipes for the Practical Everyday Use of Gold Standard Goods*, dedicated to 'the ladies of the Canadian Northwest' (M8.1). There were several later editions, some retitled *Practical Selected Recipes by Noted Cooks* and published by Gold Standard Manufacturing Co., which began to be listed in Winnipeg city directories in 1914. For the last edition (M8.7), published no later than 1920, the company hired Echlin Studios in Toronto to design the art nouveau–style binding and title-page.

In 1931, when Blue Ribbon was still the dominant brand, Western Pure Foods Ltd published *Eclipse Tempting Recipes* (M72.1), written by Miss Dickson Riley, 'well known in Western Canada as a lecturer' and a former student of the American health-food writer Eugene Christian. Although the binding featured a striking red, yellow, and black abstract representation of the moon crossing the sun, and the book went through three editions, it failed to 'eclipse' the success of the *Blue Ribbon Cook Book*.

During the Second World War, Winnipeg's Newport Cereal Co. Ltd issued *The Newport Book of Recipes* by Dorothy Faulconer, to promote Newport Fluffs, 'the cereal sensation of the nation' made of popped wheat (M118.1). Recipes using Newport Fluffs were also printed on the cereal boxes and given out over the company's radio programs. Faulconer also produced a canned-meat cookbook for Canada Packers at war's end (M125.1) and recipe leaflets for the biscuit-manufacturer Paulin Chambers Co. Ltd, which had been founded in Winnipeg in 1876 as Chambers' Steam Biscuit Factory. In the late 1940s, Paulin Chambers turned to radio personality Corinne Jordan, whose 'beautiful, familiar voice' was heard on stations across the prairies, to produce two promotional vehicles for its products: *From Me to You* (M132.1), a collection of 'poetry recipes tidbits shorties'; and *Between Ourselves* (M136.1), another compilation of verses, homilies, and recipes.

From the agricultural sector came cookbooks by two of the province's major seed producers: A.E. McKenzie Co. (now called McKenzie Seeds) of Brandon, which published *Favorite Vegetable Recipes* in about 1935–9 (M87.1), and McFayden Seed Co. of Winnipeg, which hired Katharine Middleton, then food editor at the *Winnipeg Tribune*, to write the 1941 *Vegetable Cook Book* (M121.1). When McFayden Seed Co. republished the book in 1948, it added instructions for freezing vegetables, a new trend for preserving food at home. Frank Skinner, the founder of Manitoba Hardy Plant Nursery in Dropmore, had become famous in the province for developing plant varieties that would thrive in the prairie environment. In about 1940 his business issued a recipe booklet about preserving hardy home-grown fruits (M113.1). Five Roses Flour was made from Manitoba wheat, but the cookbooks promoting the flour were mostly published in Montreal (see the titles listed at Q58.1, *Get Flourwise*).

One surprising local business to publish a recipe collection was the Winnipeg Laundry Ltd. Its service manageress, Mrs Anna S. Welch, a widow, compiled and edited *The Bride's Cook Book* of about 1930 (M64.1). The Universal Life Assurance and Annuity Co. published three editions of *The Universal Cook Book* in the 1930s (M82.1). Although the company's offices were in the Paris Building in Winnipeg, Olive Kyle, the cookbook's author and company president's sister-in-law, lived in Waterloo, Ontario. From the Great-West Life Assurance Co., whose head office was in Winnipeg, came *Mrs Becker's Favorite Recipes*, in about 1939–41 (M108.1).

Winnipeg's press served the city and, in the case of

some periodicals, the entire West. Recipes and household hints were staple fare in newspapers and magazines, but their publishers also occasionally printed cookbooks on their presses. From *Farmers' Weekly Telegram* came two editions of *Western Farmers' Handbook* (M10.1) in 1909 and 1910, a compendium in which Part II was devoted to 'Household Information.' *Western Home Monthly* (from October 1932 called *National Home Monthly*) produced three cookbooks: *A World of Useful Information in a Nutshell*, about 1920–5 (M35.1); several editions of *Specially Selected Recipes* (M70.1), the first in about 1931, written by Gertrude Dutton, the person in charge of the periodical's 'Better Cookery Department'; and a 'Better Cookery clipping book,' in the late 1930s (M99.1), also Dutton's creation. The *Grain Growers' Guide* had been founded in 1908 as the official organ of the Manitoba Grain Growers' Association and soon also represented the interests of the Saskatchewan Grain Growers' Association and the United Farmers of Alberta.[7] Two cookbooks bore its imprint in 1922: the first edition of what was to become both a standard home economics textbook in schools and a kitchen bible in Western homes – *The Country Cook or the M.A.C. Cook Book* (M37.1) by Mary Hiltz and Mary Moxon; and *The Country Homemaker* (M39.1) compiled by Margaret Speechly, which reprinted articles from the *Grain Growers' Guide*. In addition to the 1884 edition of *Home and Health*, the owners of *Nor'West Farmer* (and *Farm and Home*) published *Betty's Scrapbook of Little Recipes for Little Cooks* in 1931 (M67.1). This is one of the handful of Canadian cookbooks designed for children: the first twelve pages of the large-format scrapbook were already printed with recipes; the child was instructed to paste into the remaining pages recipes cut out each month from a special page in the magazine's 'Home Section.' In 1935, the *Free Press* opened a model kitchen in its Carlton Street building and began to issue a series of annual cookbooks by the columnist Madeline Day, featuring recipes tested in the model kitchen or demonstrated at the Cooking School held in the newspaper's auditorium (M80.1, M90.1, M94.1, M101.1). The 1937 issue featured both 'foreign recipes' and an illustration of pioneer women cooking over a campfire in 1850. Whereas the *Free Press* cultivated the profile of its own cookery expert, the *Tribune* first turned, in 1936, to an American celebrity, Jessie Marie DeBoth, to write *Party Entertaining and New Menus for the Winter Season* (M91.1), but two years later it issued *The Winnipeg Home Cook Book* (M104.1) by its own columnist, Katharine Middleton.

Beginning in 1916, the Department of Agriculture and Immigration published a new title each month in the Manitoba Farmers' Library, which was 'distributed free among the people of Manitoba who make application for it.' The series was 'devoted to the extension of information on agricultural and sanitary matters,' and several of the bulletins in the period 1917–26 contained detailed information on culinary topics, as some titles illustrate: *Cookery Recipes* (M25.1); *Canning by the Cold Pack Method* (M26.1); *The Potato* (M27.1); *Cheese-Making on the Farm* (M28.1); *Asparagus* (M31.1); *Practical Cookery* (M32.1); *The Beef Ring* (M42.1), which explains the system where farming families take turns butchering an animal and sharing the carcass; *Home Cheese Making* (M40.1); and *Canning, Pickling and Preserving* (M50.1). Later, in 1939, the provincial government, in collaboration with staff at the University of Manitoba, investigated how the mullets in Lake Winnipegosis could be canned at home, with the hope of creating a domestic market for the overabundance of fish. Mary Hiltz's recipes for five different canning methods are printed in the published report (M114.1).

The Household Science Department of the Manitoba Agricultural College was for the West what the Macdonald Institute at the Ontario Agricultural College in Guelph, the Lillian Massey School of Household Science at the University of Toronto, and Macdonald College at McGill University in Montreal were for the East: a major centre for training women in the new discipline. The faculties in the East had all been established in the period 1902–7. Although household science students were enrolled at MAC (its familiar name) from 1910, the first degrees were conferred only in 1918.[8] The teachers were influential. Annie Bessie Juniper, who directed the the college's first household science program, was instrumental in founding the Manitoba Household Science Association in January 1911 and was its first president. Later that year she moved to Victoria, British Columbia, where she wrote the first home economics textbook for British Columbia in 1913 (B28.1). Mary Hiltz and Mary Moxon were both on staff for over three decades, until the early 1950s. Their *M.A.C. Cook Book* went through multiple editions, from 1922 to 1951, and gave the college a national reach: By the sixth edition of 1941 it was retitled *Home Economics Cook Book (Canada)* and the 1947 edition is known to have been used in Nova Scotia classes. Hiltz also wrote, or revised editions of, several other cookbooks. Another professor, Ethel M. Eadie, supplied recipes for bulletins in the Manitoba Farmers' Library (M27.1, M31.1), as did women connected with MAC's Extension Service; for example, Elizabeth Crawford (M25.1), Miss R.M. Atkinson (M26.1), and Helen MacDougall

(M26.2). Gertrude Dutton at the *Western Home Monthly* had been a cookery demonstrator at MAC early in her professional career. The women who graduated from MAC went on to become cookery teachers, food journalists, and cookbook writers in Manitoba and beyond, among them, Margaret Speechly, compiler of *The Country Homemaker*, Alice Stevens, author of *Apple Secrets* (B77.1) for the Associated Growers of British Columbia Ltd and *Home Canning Ration Guide* (B115.1) for BC Tree Fruits Ltd, June Horne, who revised *A Diary of Celebrated Christmas Recipes* for Lake of the Woods Milling Co. (M102.4) and who supervised the model kitchen at the *Winnipeg Free Press* (see M101.1, by Madeline Day), Katharine Middleton, author of *Vegetable Cook Book* and later the host of a television cooking show in Chicago, and Kathleen Watson, who prepared the 1945 edition of the *Purity Cook Book* (O771.3). Other graduates went on to teach in Winnipeg schools, where they would have used as a classroom guide *Winnipeg High School Domestic Science Note Book* in the 1920s (M46.1) and *Theory and Practice in Household Science* in the 1930s and 1940s (M98.1).

The largest publicly held collection of pre-1950 Canadian cookbooks in Manitoba is at the Provincial Archives of Manitoba. Modest collections are at the following institutions: Manitoba Agricultural Museum in Austin, Carberry Plains Museum, Daly House Museum, Winnipeg's Museum of Man and Nature, Le musée de Saint-Boniface, and the Hillcrest Museum. For a full list of Manitoba locations, see 'Abbreviations,' pp xlii–xliii.

NOTES

1 There are 144 numbered entries and one late addition, M7a.1, in the Manitoba section, plus twelve titles that were published in Manitoba but whose entries are in British Columbia (possibly an edition cited in the notes for B2.1; B21.5), in Ontario (O32.3; O68.4; O20.38 and O20.43; O130.8; O612.5, O612.6, and O612.7; O773.13; O776.11 and O776.12; O1055.2 and O1055.3; O1114.3), and in Quebec (Q224.2).

2 Many Canadian companies translated their English-language advertising cookbooks into French for the Quebec market, and these were also distributed to French-speaking populations outside Quebec. A copy of *Le livre culinaire de la poudre à pâte 'Magic'*

(O702.10), for example, was found in the home of a Franco-Manitoban. French-speaking Manitobans are mostly Catholic and, for Canada generally, only a small number of community cookbooks by Catholic women's groups surfaced in the course of my research; for a discussion of this phenomenon, see p 76.

3 See, for example, I. Villeneuve, *Fabrication du fromage à la ferme* (M28.2). Perhaps this author, who, from the evidence of his last name, was probably French-speaking, did his own translation.

4 *The Great Human Heart: A History of the Manitoba Women's Institute, 1910–1980*, [Winnipeg:] Manitoba Women's Institute, 1980. The history of the next twenty years is told in *The Great Human Heart II: A History of the Manitoba Women's Institute, 1980–2000*, edited by Dianne C. Kowalchuk, [Winnipeg:] Manitoba Women's Institute, 2000. Until 23 March 1919, the groups in Manitoba were called Home Economics Societies; from that date, they were called Women's Institutes.

5 For the history of the recipe in Canada, see Jim Anderson, 'The Vinarterta Saga,' *Petits Propos Culinaires* No. 67 (June 2001), pp 97–101. Concerning Icelandic cooking in Canada, see Kristin Olafson-Jenkyns, *The Culinary Saga of New Iceland: Recipes from the Shores of Lake Winnipeg*, Guelph, Ont.: Coastline Publishing, 2001.

6 Although no Ukrainian fund-raisers were found to have been published in Manitoba before 1950, what was to become a classic text for Ukrainian Canadians in the second half of the twentieth century was first published by Winnipeg's Trident Press in 1957: *Traditional Ukrainian Cookery* by Savella Stechishin (first edition located in bookseller's stock). It was a national project of the Ukrainian Women's Association of Canada.

7 The periodical was called *Grain Growers' Guide*, June 1908–15 March 1928; then *Country Guide*; then *Country Guide and Nor'West Farmer*, June 1936–February 1942. An account of its early history and information about the editors of the woman's page and other female contributors is in *'Country Homemakers': A Selection of Letters and Editorials from the Woman's Page of the Grain Growers' Guide 1908–1928*, compiled and introduced by Angela E. Davis, Winnipeg, 1989.

8 In 1924 the Manitoba Agricultural College came under the administration of the University of Manitoba.

1884

Home and health

Home and Health *was an American book, subsequently published in Ontario. For the edition published in 1884 by the Nor' West Farmer Publishing House in Winnipeg, see O32.3.*

1894

The modern home cook book and family physician

M1.1   [about 1894 or later]
[An edition of *The Modern Home Cook Book and Family Physician,* No. 25 in 'The Royal Crown Series,' published for the Royal Crown Soap Co., Winnipeg, Manitoba, [about 1894 or later]]
NOTES: There is a full-page advertisement for *The Modern Home Cook Book and Family Physician* in a promotional leaflet for Winnipeg's Royal Crown Soap Co. (OONL), which says, 'This book, in paper cover, mailed free for 25 Royal Crown Soap wrappers, or 15 Royal Crown Washing Powder packages; or cloth bound for fifty Royal Crown Soap wrappers or 30 Royal Crown Washing Powder packages.' Under a heading for 'The Royal Crown Series' is the phrase 'Entered at the New York Post Office as Second-Class Matter,' evidence that the books in the series originated in the United States. Most of the soap testimonials in the leaflet are dated 1893 or 1894, the latest being 12 November 1894; therefore, the cookbook was published about 1894 or later. No copy of the cookbook has been found. The Steam Soap Works of the Royal Crown Soap Co. were at 289–99 King Street in Winnipeg.

Library records for the American editions attribute the book to Frank M. Lupton (1854–1910).

AMERICAN EDITIONS: *The Modern Home Cook Book and Family Physician: Embracing More Than One Thousand Selected Recipes and Practical Suggestions to Housekeepers,* Stratford ed., New York: F.M. Lupton Pub. Co., [about 1890–9], an expanded edition of *The Modern Cook Book and Medical Guide,* 1889 (United States: IaU, MnHi, NIC, NNF, NRM); New York: Federal Book Co., [about 1900–20], Golden Rod Series (United States: IaU, NNNAM).

1895

[Title unknown]

An edition of a cookbook published about 1895 by the Winnipeg druggist J.H. Rose. The text is the same as three Ontario editions called Gems of Fancy Cookery. *See O68.4.*

1896

The souvenir cook book

M2.1   1896
Tried! Tested! Proved! / The souvenir / cook book. / Compiled by / the Ladies' Aid Society of / Grace Church, Winnipeg, / Winnipeg: / The Consolidated Stationery Co., Ltd. / 1896.
DESCRIPTION: 20.5 × 14.5 cm   Pp [1–3] 4–242   Cloth; sewn
CONTENTS: 1 tp; 2 blank; 3–230 recipes credited with the name of the contributor; 231–42 table of contents
COPIES: CIHM (95417)   *OGU (CCC TX715.6 S6583) SSWD
NOTES: This is Manitoba's first community cookbook. Although not explicity stated in the text, it was likely published to raise funds for Grace Church. 'Tried! Tested! Proved!' at the head of the title copies a phrase from many nineteenth-century editions of Canada's first and best-selling fund-raising cookbook, O20.1, *The Home Cook Book,* first published in 1877.

The Souvenir Cook Book features in Susan Coyne's memoir, *Kingfisher Days,* Toronto: Random House Canada, 2001, pp 87–96. The memoir captures one summer at Coyne's cottage on Lake of the Woods, and is based on her childhood correspondence with R.C. Moir, an elderly neighbour, who leaves letters for her, purportedly from Princess Nootsie Tah. Three of the letters concern *The Souvenir Cook Book* and candy recipes contributed by Coyne's great-aunt, Miss Mabel Elliott. In the play that Coyne subsequently wrote, based on the book and also called *Kingfisher Days,* she dramatized the part of the story about *The Souvenir Cook Book* and the candy recipes. The play ran at the Tarragon Theatre in Toronto, from 18 February to 30 March 2003, with Coyne in the role of herself as a child.

The OGU copy of *The Souvenir Cook Book* is inscribed, in ink, 'To dear Sara from sister Mary.'

1901

The home cook book

The Home Cook Book, *published in Toronto in 1877, was the first fund-raising cookbook in Canada. For the edition published in Winnipeg in about 1901, see O20.38, and for another Winnipeg edition, by another publisher, see O20.43.*

The wheat city cook-book

M3.1   1901
The wheat city / cook-book / Compiled by the ladies of the / Methodist Church, Brandon. / "Let me cook the meals of our country and I care not / who makes her laws." / Brandon: / Record Printing House. / 1901.
DESCRIPTION: 17.0 × 12.5 cm   Pp [i–x], [1] 2–82, [i–iv] Paper, punched with two holes and bound with string
CONTENTS: i–viii ads; ix tp; x ad; 1–82 recipes; i–iv ads
CITATIONS: Ferguson/Fraser, p 232, illus col on p 11 of the volume opened at the title-page
COPIES: *Private collection
NOTES: One of the advertisements on the front face of the binding is for 'Twentieth Century Fair 1901 Western Manitoba's Big Fair // Brandon July 23 to 26 ...'

M3.2   3rd ed., 1910
—The wheat city / cook book / Compiled by the ladies of the / First Methodist Church, Brandon / "Let me cook the meals of our / country and I care not who makes / her laws." / (Third edition, fourth thousand) / Brandon: / Record Printing House. / 1910
DESCRIPTION: 16.0 × 11.5 cm   Pp [leaf(ves) lacking?] [i–x], [1] 2–92, [i–xi]   Paper, front face lacking; stapled
CONTENTS: i–viii ads; ix tp; x ad; 1–92 text and ads; i–ix ads; x blank; xi ads
COPIES: *MBDHM
NOTES: The recipes are credited with the name of the contributor. The text is printed in blue. MBDHM has a second copy lacking more leaves.

A recipe from this cookbook may have been reprinted in S13.1, *Cook Book,* compiled by the Ladies' Aid Society of Metropolitan Methodist Church, Watrous, Saskatchewan, 1913. See that entry.

Then and Now Cookery Book 1882–1957, produced by the Brandon Quota Club to mark its seventy-fifth anniversary (MBDHM), reprints twelve recipes from *The Wheat City Cook-Book.* The introduction refers to 'two editions – 1903 and 1905.' The first page lists 'The Advertisers in "The Wheat City Cook Book" –

1905.' Perhaps 1903 is an error for 1901 (M3.1) and the second edition was published in 1905.

1902

One hundred selected recipes

St Stephen's Church (Presbyterian) was established in the early 1890s and known as the 'West End' Church in its early years. In 1925 it became St Stephen's United Church. The church building, located at the corner of Spence and Portage, was sold in 1928 and renamed Elim Chapel by the new congregation.

M4.1   1902
[An edition of *One Hundred Selected Recipes,* Winnipeg, Man.: St Stephens Church Ladies Association, 1902]
CITATIONS: O'Neill (unpublished)
COPIES: Great Britain: LB (not located)

1903

Good recipes

M5.1   1903
1903 / Good / recipes / recommended and / tested by the / ladies of Neepawa / Neepawa Register Print [cover-title]
DESCRIPTION: 22.0 × 15.0 cm   Pp [i–ii], 1–20   Fp illus child portrait on p i of 'Lucile Davidson. President Lucile-Davidson Mission Circle; through whose efforts this book was compiled.'   Paper; stapled
CONTENTS: i fp illus; ii blank; 1–20 'Selected Recipes' credited with the name of the contributor
COPIES: *MNBPM

1904

Taylor's 1904 calendar cook book

See also M7a.1, The Red Cross Almanac and Cook Book 1906, *from the same pharmacy.*

M6.1   1904
[An edition of *Taylor's 1904 Calendar Cook Book,* Portage la Prairie, Man.: Red Cross Pharmacy, 1904, pp [1–3] 4–32, 'W.A. Vrooman, pharmaceutical chemist']
CITATIONS: Peel's Bibliography 2793
NOTES: See notes for O140.1.

1905

Blue Ribbon cook book

Blue Ribbon Cook Book *was published by the company that made Blue Ribbon brand products, such as tea, coffee, spices, extracts, and baking powder. The owners of Blue Ribbon Manufacturing Co. (which registered the cookbook's copyright) and G.F. and J. Galt Ltd, a wholesale grocery business, were the cousins George Frederick Galt (Toronto, Ont., 1855–15 April 1928, Winnipeg, Man.) and John Galt (Montreal, Que., 29 September 1856–1932, Victoria, BC), both of whom came from illustrious families. George was the son of Chief Justice Sir Thomas Galt; he married Margaret Smith in 1883 and had four children. John was the son of Sir Alexander Tilloch Galt, a father of Confederation, and grandson of the author John Galt; he married Mabel Patton Henderson in 1890, after his first wife died.*

George and John established their wholesale grocery business in Winnipeg in 1882. The first listing for Blue Ribbon Manufacturing Co. in Winnipeg directories is in 1898; however, since the directories were published at the beginning of the year, the company existed in 1897. Although there is no record of the Blue Ribbon Manufacturing Co. at the Companies Office of the Manitoba government, there are records for the following: Corporation No. 83B, Blue Ribbon Ltd, incorporated under the laws of Manitoba on 27 December 1905, cancelled in 1929; Corporation No. 380, Blue Ribbon Ltd, incorporated under the laws of Canada on 11 April 1928, registered in Manitoba on 5 October 1932, cancelled in Manitoba on 24 November 1960; and Corporation No. 7817, Blue Ribbon Corporation Ltd, incorporated under the laws of Canada on 25 March 1930, registered in Manitoba on 29 December 1949, cancelled in Manitoba on 24 November 1960. The statement in John's obituary (MWPA) that the Blue Ribbon Co. Ltd was formed in 1907 as a subsidiary of the grocery business is inaccurate, based on the evidence above. The obituary adds that 'in 1910, the firm wound up the grocery side of their business and merg[ed] with the Blue Ribbon company, ...'

In Toronto, the cousins had a business called Blue Ribbon Tea Co., first listed in city directories in 1899, at 42 Scott Street (in the two previous years, 1897 and 1898, the name index lists G.F. and J. Galt at 42 Scott, but not Blue Ribbon Tea Co.; in 1896, the address is vacant). From 1900 to 1908, Blue Ribbon Tea Co. was at 12 Front Street East (there is no listing after 1908).

In the Monetary Times *Vol. 83, No. 26 (27 December 1929), p 15, it was reported that western-based Blue Ribbon Ltd and Pure Gold Manufacturing Co. of Toronto, which sold its products in the eastern part of*

Canada, would form a holding company and each would market the other's products in its own particular territory, while remaining separate entities. This union of the two companies for sales purposes explains the change in cover-title in 1932 (M7.6) from 'Everyday Use in Western Homes' to 'Everyday Use in Canadian Homes.' It also explains the appearance of the Pure Gold name on later editions of the cookbook titled Blue Ribbon and Pure Gold Cook Book *or* Livre culinaire Blue Ribbon et Pure Gold, *all published in the 1940s (M7.11, M7.13, M7.14, M7.15, and M7.16). Like Blue Ribbon, Pure Gold had been founded in the nineteenth century. Its last listing in Toronto city directories is in 1946.*

See also M9.1, A Few Selected Recipes from the Blue Ribbon Cook Book.

For information about, and photographs of, George Galt, see The Newspaper Reference Book of Canada, *Toronto: Press Publishing Co. Ltd, 1903, p 141, and his obituary in* Beaver, *Outfit 259, No. 1 (June 1928), pp 6–7. For John Galt, see his* Winnipeg Free Press *obituary on file at MWPA and 'New President of the Union Bank of Canada,'* Monetary Times *Vol. 49, No. 8 (24 August 1912), p 334.*

M7.1 [1st ed.], entered 1905
Blue Ribbon / cook book / Prepared especially for every-day use in Western homes / [4 paragraphs of introductory text] / Entered according to Act of the Parliament of Canada, in the year one thousand / nine hundred and five by the Blue Ribbon Manufacturing Company, / Winnipeg, at the Department of Agriculture.
DESCRIPTION: 17.5 × 12.0 cm   Pp [1–2] 3–154 [leaf lacking?]   Cloth, with image on front of a blue ribbon tied in a bow
CONTENTS: 1 tp; 2–mid 4 'Tables of Weights and Measures'; mid 4–mid 6 'Time Tables for Cooking'; mid–bottom 6 'Table of Proportions'; 7 'Intoxicating Liquors Avoided' and 'Principal Methods of Cooking'; 8–146 recipes; 147–8 lacking; 149–54 continuation of index
CITATIONS: O'Neill (unpublished)
COPIES: AEUCHV *BKOM MAUAM (72.532.3) MWPA OFERWM (A1996.98)   Private collection; Great Britain: LB (07943.g.75 destroyed)
NOTES: See pl 27. This is the earliest known edition. It has no illustrations. The BKOM copy, the one catalogued here, lacks pp 147–8, but an examination of other copies reveals that p 146 is the last page of recipes and p 148, the first page of the index.

Variants of this edition are distinguished by the end pagination. The AEUCHV copy, which is in excellent condition, ends at p 154. It is inscribed on the front endpaper, in ink, 'May Speers. Oak Lake Man.

1905.' The inscription confirms that the year of publication was 1905, the same year as the copyright date recorded on the title-page (editions as late as the 1950s record the copyright date of 1905, but not the actual year of publication, and, consequently, 1905 is often incorrectly given by libraries or booksellers as the year of publication for later editions).

The MWPA copy has publisher's advertisements at the back of the book, which are included in the pagination, i.e., Pp [1–2] 3–160, where pp 155–60 are advertisements. The advertisement for Blue Ribbon Tea on p 160 includes a testimonial dated 12 September 1907. This variant, therefore, is likely a reprinting two years after the first issue.

The OFERWM copy ends at p 154. It is inscribed on p 1, in ink, 'Mundell's book. Cook book. Blue Ribbon Cook Book ...'; and on p 3, in pencil, 'Mrs. [M.?] Mundell.'

The private collector's copy has one unnumbered page after p 154, on which appears 'Printed and published by the Farmer's Advocate Printing Company of Winnipeg Limited.'

LB's destroyed copy is described as having 154 pp.

Barss 1980, p 54, reprints Restoring Tainted Game from an unidentified edition of Blue Ribbon Cook Book.

M7.2 [rev. ed., about 1910]
—[No tp; cover-title worn away]
DESCRIPTION: 17.5 × 11.5 cm   Pp [leaf lacking], [i] ii–v [vi] vii–xii, [1–2] 3–147, 147a–147c, [148–54], [i–iii]   Cloth
CONTENTS: i–v 'Food and Its Uses'; vi–viii 'Table Setting'; ix–xii 'Common Mistakes in Cooking'; 1 'Blue Ribbon Cook Book Revised edition Prepared especially for everyday use in Western homes' and at bottom, 'Entered according to Act of the Parliament of Canada, in the year one thousand nine hundred and five, by the Blue Ribbon Manufacturing Company, Winnipeg, at the Department of Agriculture.'; 2–mid 4 'Tables of Weights and Measures'; mid 4–mid 6 'Time Tables for Cooking'; mid 6–top 7 'Table of Proportions'; mid–bottom 7 'Principal Methods of Cooking'; 8–147c recipes; 148–54 index; i–iii publ ads
COPIES: *AEUCHV (IC 90.19.1)   Private collection
NOTES: The text on p 1 points to a publication date of about 1910: 'In revising the book for this edition, after five years' practical use all over Western Canada [1905 + 5 years = 1910], but little alteration is required in the recipes or general arrangement. To make it still more worthy of its position as the standard cook book of the West, however, a section on bachelor cookery has been added, also a few pages on the different classes of foods ...; table setting; common mistakes in cooking; hints on carving, etc.' The new section of 'Bachelor Cookery' is on pp 144–147c, and there is a footnote on p 144 acknowledging Kephart's Book of Camping and Woodcraft, published by Musson Book Co., Toronto. The first edition of Book of Camping and Woodcraft by Horace Kephart appeared in 1908 (see the preface to the 1916–17 New York edition at DLC).

The leaf lacking before p i was likely a leaf of perforated coupons. Apparently, there was no title-page in this edition.

The AEUCHV copy is inscribed on the front face of the binding, 'Mrs. S.G. Stephenson.'

M7.3 [rev. ed., about 1924]
—Blue Ribbon / cook book / For everyday use / in Western homes [cover-title]
DESCRIPTION: 16.5 × 12.5 cm   Pp [i–x], [3–4] 5–156 [157–8, corner where folio would be printed is torn off]   A few small illus   Cloth, with image on front of a bow
CONTENTS: i–iv publ ads in colour; v–x index; 3 'Blue Ribbon Cook Book Revised edition Prepared especially for everyday use in Western homes'; 4–8 'Food and Its Uses'; 9–11 'Table Setting'; 12–15 'Common Mistakes in Cooking'; 16–mid 18 'Blue Ribbon Cook Book // Tables of Weights and Measures'; mid 18–20 'Time Tables for Cooking'; 21 'Table of Proportions'; 22 'Intoxicating Liquors Avoided' and 'Principal Methods of Cooking'; 23–157 text; 158 blank for 'Memorandum'
COPIES: *Private collection
NOTES: No copyright date is recorded and, unlike M7.2, there is no indication of the actual date of publication; instead, the text on p 3 begins, 'In revising the book for this edition, but little alteration is required in the recipes or general arrangement.' The text on p 3 states that there is a 'Complete Index in back of book'; however, in this copy it is positioned at the front. 'Bachelor Cookery,' with acknowledgment of Kephart's Book of Camping and Woodcraft, is on pp 152–7. The private collector's copy is inscribed, 'Elsie Dreger. 1924.'

M7.4 [rev. ed., about 1925]
—[No tp; title on coupons and on p 3: 'Blue Ribbon Cook Book']
DESCRIPTION: 16.5 × 12.5 cm   Pp [i–ii], [1–4] 5–157 [158–76]   Fp illus on p 1 of G.F. and J. Galt Ltd building, small illus   Cloth [in poor condition, no legible lettering]
CONTENTS: i–ii four coupons: 'Please send me Blue Ribbon Cook Book at special reduced price of 25c.';

1 fp illus of building with caption: 'G.F. & J. Galt Limited manufacturers and packers of Blue Ribbon Tea, Coffee, Baking Powder, Extracts, Spices, etc.'; 2 'Entered according to Act of the Parliament of Canada, in the year one thousand nine hundred and five, by the Blue Ribbon Manufacturing Company, Winnipeg, at the Department of Agriculture.'; 3 'Blue Ribbon Cook Book Revised edition Prepared especially for everyday use in Western homes'; 4–157 text; 158–9 blank for 'Memorandum'; 160–6 publ ads, some in colour; 167–76 index

COPIES: ABOM ACG (641.5 B658b) AEPMA (H85.1210.6a) AMHM APROM ARDA (82.65.29) BBVM BCOM BNEM CIHM (78121) OAYM *OGU (UA s045 b39) OONL (TX715 B58 1910z p***) SBIM SSU (TX715 B58 1905)

NOTES: The caption on p 1 distinguishes this edition from M7.5. The copies listed in the 'Copies' line have one of two different settings of type on p 3. In one setting, the lines of the second paragraph begin, 'To ... / Cook ... / has ... / Foods ... / Common ... / blank ... / the back.' (AEPMA, AMHM, APROM, BCOM); in the other, 'To ... / Cook ... / Cookery ... / Classes ... / Table ... / Carving ... / recipes have been added in the back.' (ACG, ARDA, BNEM, OGU, OONL, SSU). The latter setting is also found in M7.3.

Printing on the front face of the binding of the OGU copy is worn away or obscured by newspaper adhering to the surface. A blue bow and 'Blue Ribbon / cook book / For everyday use / in Western homes' are on the binding of the OONL copy.

The BBVM copy is inscribed on the front endpaper, in ink, 'C.J. Caunt Jan 27/25 Vancouver, B.C.' The AEPMA copy is inscribed on the front endpaper, in ink, 'Marion Bode. Sept. 27th Calgary 1926.'

The OAYM copy probably matches the OGU copy; however, its front cover is badly worn, it lacks pp 3–4 and the last leaf of the index, and it may lack a leaf of publisher's advertisements between the end of the text and the index.

A copy at BFSJNPM (983.14.14) may be a variant of this edition. The caption on p 1 reads, 'G.F. & J. Galt Limited manufacturers of Blue Ribbon Tea, Coffee, Baking Powder, Extracts, Spices, etc.' (note that there is no reference to 'packers'). The copy is inscribed 'Mildred I. Hart. 1922.'; and below this, inscribed later, 'Baldonnel B.C., Nov. 14th/31,' and above the name Hart, '(Hazlett).'

A copy at SSWD may match this edition, but it lacks the leaf of coupons and pp 1–2. The BVAMM catalogue records a copy that may match this edition, but the volume was not on the shelf.

M7.5 [rev. ed.]
—Blue Ribbon / cook book / For everyday use / in Western homes [cover-title]

DESCRIPTION: 16.5 × 12.5 cm Pp [coupon leaf lacking?], [1–4] 5–157 [158–76] Fp illus on p 1 of 'Blue Ribbon Limited' building, small illus Cloth, with image on front of a blue bow

CONTENTS: 1 fp illus of building with caption: 'New home of Blue Ribbon Limited, Winnipeg, containing two acres of floor space. The largest establishment of its kind in the Dominion of Canada.'; 2 'Entered according to Act of the Parliament of Canada, in the year one thousand nine hundred and five, by the Blue Ribbon Manufacturing Company, Winnipeg, at the Department of Agriculture.'; 3 'Blue Ribbon Cook Book Revised edition Prepared especially for everyday use in Western homes'; 4–157 text; 158–9 blank, ruled leaves for 'Memorandum'; 160–6 publ ads in colour; 167–76 index

COPIES: ARDA (74.186.1) BBVM *MWMM SBIN

NOTES: The caption on p 1 distinguishes this edition from M7.4.

M7.6 rev. ed., [1932]
—Revised edition / Blue Ribbon / cook book / For everyday use in Canadian homes [cover-title]

DESCRIPTION: 16.0 × 12.5 cm Pp [i–ii], [1–4] 5–144 [145–67] Fp illus on p 1 of Blue Ribbon Ltd building, fp illus of 'Diagram of table laid for home dinner (without service of maid),' illus Cloth, with image on front of a blue bow

CONTENTS: i–ii four coupons: 'Special Coupon. Price 25c. Blue Ribbon Limited, Winnipeg. Please send Blue Ribbon Cook Book to'; 1 fp illus; 2 'Entered according to Act of the Parliament of Canada, in the year one thousand nine hundred and five, by the Blue Ribbon Manufacturing Company, Winnipeg, at the Department of Agriculture'; 3 'Blue Ribbon Cook Book Revised edition – 1932 Prepared especially for everyday use in Western homes // Foreword' signed Blue Ribbon Ltd; 4–144 text; 145–9 blank, ruled leaves for 'Memorandum'; 150–6 publ ads in colour; 157–67 index

COPIES: ACG AHRMH (997-028-001) OKELWM *Private collection

NOTES: The 'Foreword' refers to this as a 'new and revised edition' and acknowledges 'the editors of the M.A.C. Cook Book [i.e., Miss Mary Catherine Hiltz and Miss Mary Caroline Moxon; see M37.1] and ... Florence H. Howden, B.Sc. (H.Ec.), Teacher of Home Economics in King Edward High School, Vancouver, B.C., for their assistance in the preparation of the manuscript.' The cover-title describes the book as for 'Canadian homes'; p 3 says for 'Western homes.'

M7.7 rev. ed.
—Revised edition / Blue Ribbon / cook book / For everyday use in Canadian homes [cover-title]
DESCRIPTION: 16.0 × 12.5 cm Pp [leaf lacking] [3–4] 5–144 [145–66] Fp illus on p 10 of 'Diagram of table laid for home dinner (without service of maid),' illus Cloth, with image on front of a blue bow
CONTENTS: 3 'Blue Ribbon Cook Book Revised edition Prepared especially for everyday use in Western homes //Foreword' signed Blue Ribbon Ltd; 4–144 text; 145–7 blank, ruled leaves for 'Memorandum'; 148–54 publ ads in colour; 155–66 index
COPIES: ARDA BBVM BKM *OGU (CCC TX715.6 B57)
NOTES: This edition matches M7.6, except there is no year 1932 on p 3. The cover-title describes the book as for 'Canadian homes'; p 3 says for 'Western homes.'

In the BKM copy, the contents of the last pages are: 145–9 blank, ruled leaves for 'Memorandum'; 150–6 publ ads in colour; 157–68 index.

M7.8 15th ed., [about 1936]
—Blue / Ribbon / Fifteenth edition / cook / book / For / everyday / use in / Canadian / homes [cover-title]
DESCRIPTION: 16.0 × 12.5 cm Pp [i–ii], [1–4] 5–144 [145–68] Fp illus on p 1 of Blue Ribbon Ltd building, fp illus on p 10 of 'Diagram of table laid for home dinner (without service of maid),' illus [$0.25, on p i] Cloth, with image on front of a blue bow
CONTENTS: i–ii perforated leaf of book-order coupons; 1 fp illus; 2 'Entered according to Act of the Parliament of Canada, in the year one thousand nine hundred and five, by the Blue Ribbon Manufacturing Company, Winnipeg, at the Department of Agriculture.'; 3 'Blue Ribbon Cook Book Fifteenth edition Prepared especially for everyday use in Western homes // Foreword'; 4–144 text; 145–9 blank, ruled leaves for 'Memorandum'; 150–6 publ ads in colour; 157–68 index
COPIES: AALIWWM ACG BDUCVM *BVAMM CIHM (78120) OONL (TX715 B58 1905) SBIHM
NOTES: The cover-title describes the book as for 'Canadian homes'; p 3 says for 'Western homes.'

The BVAMM copy is inscribed on the inside front face of the binding, in ink, 'Feb 25 – 1936 A. Hillier, 1637 Victoria Drive.' The BDUCVM copy is in the original box in which it was sent by the company to Mr R.A. Colvin, Cowichan Station, British Columbia;

the box is postmarked 1936. The AALIWWM copy is inscribed on the front endpaper, in pencil, 'Edith Holsworth 1936.'

M7.9 16th ed., [about 1940]
—Blue / Ribbon / Sixteenth edition / cook / book / For / everyday / use in / Canadian / homes [cover-title]
DESCRIPTION: 16.0 × 12.5 cm Pp [i–ii], [1–4] 5–144 [145–66] 1 fp illus on p 1 of Blue Ribbon Ltd building, fp illus of 'Diagram of table laid for home dinner (without service of maid),' illus Cloth, with image on front of a blue bow
CONTENTS: i–ii perforated leaf of book-order coupons; 1 fp illus; 2 'Entered according to Act of the Parliament of Canada, in the year one thousand nine hundred and five, by the Blue Ribbon Manufacturing Company, Winnipeg, at the Department of Agriculture.'; 3 'Blue Ribbon Cook Book Sixteenth edition Prepared especially for everyday use in Western homes // Foreword'; 4–144 text; 145–9 blank, ruled leaves for 'Memorandum'; 150–6 publ ads in colour; 157–66 index
COPIES: *Private collection
NOTES: The cover-title describes the book as for 'Canadian homes'; p 3 says for 'Western homes.' The book's owner writes, 'I think I remember using this copy as a child at home in the early '40s.' The date of publication can be no later than 1940, the inscribed date on the seventeenth edition, M7.11.

M7.10 17th ed.
—Blue / Ribbon / Seventeenth edition / cook / book / For / everyday / use in / Canadian / homes [cover-title]
DESCRIPTION: 16.0 × 12.5 cm Pp [i–ii], [1–4] 5–144 [145–68] 1 fp illus on p 1 of Blue Ribbon Ltd building, fp illus on p 10 of 'table laid for home dinner (without service of maid),' illus Cloth, with image on front of a blue bow
CONTENTS: i–ii book-order coupons; 1 fp illus; 2 'Entered according to Act of the Parliament of Canada, in the year one thousand nine hundred and five, by the Blue Ribbon Manufacturing Company, Winnipeg, at the Department of Agriculture.'; 3 'Blue Ribbon Cook Book Seventeenth edition Prepared especially for everyday use in Western homes // Foreword'; 4–6 'Food and Its Uses'; 7 'Meal Planning'; 8–13 'Table Service'; 14–16 'Common Mistakes in Cooking'; 17–144 'Blue Ribbon Cook Book'; 145–9 blank for 'Memorandum'; 150–6 publ ads in colour; 157– index
COPIES: *Private collection

NOTES: The cover-title describes the book as for 'Canadian homes'; p 3 says for 'Western homes.'

M7.11   17th ed., [about 1940]
—Blue Ribbon / and / Pure Gold / cook / book / Seventeenth edition / For everyday use / in Canadian homes [cover-title]
DESCRIPTION: 16.0 × 12.0 cm   Pp [i–ii], [1–4] 5–144 [145–72]   1 fp illus on p 1 of Pure Gold Manufacturing Co. Ltd building, fp illus on p 10 of 'Diagram of table laid for home dinner (without service of maid),' illus   Cloth, with image on front of containers of Blue Ribbon Coffee, Baking Powder, and Tea, and a blue bow
CONTENTS: i–ii four coupons: 'Please send the Blue Ribbon and Pure Gold Cook Book at the special price of 25c. to'; 1 fp illus; 2 'Entered according to Act of the Parliament of Canada, in the year one thousand nine hundred and five, by the Blue Ribbon Manufacturing Company, Winnipeg, at the Department of Agriculture.'; 3 'Blue Ribbon Cook Book Seventeenth edition Prepared especially for everyday use in Western homes // Foreword' signed Pure Gold Manufacturing Co. Ltd; 4–144 text; 145–53 publ ads, some in colour; 154 blank; 155–66 index; 167–72 blank, ruled leaves for 'Memorandum'
COPIES: OAYM   OGU (2 copies: CCC TX715.6 B57 1905, *UA s030 b05)   OTMCL (641.5971 B494)   OWTU (F14504)   QKB (79-21)   Private collection
NOTES: The title – *Blue Ribbon and Pure Gold Cook Book* – distinguishes this seventeenth edition from the other seventeenth edition, M7.10, *Blue Ribbon Cook Book*. The cover-title describes the book as for 'Canadian homes'; p 3 says for 'Western homes.'

The OGU copy in the Canadian Cookbook Collection is inscribed on the front endpaper, in ink, 'Mrs. Jas. W. Rogers // Salem Ont. Nov. 27/40.' The OTMCL copy is inscribed on the front endpaper, in ink, 'Mrs. R. Swanson, 3257 Dundas St. W., Toronto, 9, Ont. Aug. 6, 1944.' The private collector received her copy as a gift in 1941.

M7.12   18th ed., [about 1944]
—Blue / Ribbon / Eighteenth edition / cook / book / For / everyday / use in / Canadian / homes [cover-title]
DESCRIPTION: 16.0 × 12.5 cm   Pp [i–ii], [1–4] 5–144 [145–68]   Fp illus on p 1 of Blue Ribbon Ltd building, fp illus on p 10 of 'Diagram of table laid for home dinner (without service of maid),' small illus   Cloth, with image on front of a blue bow
CONTENTS: i–ii four coupons; 1 fp illus; 2 'Entered according to Act of the Parliament of Canada, in the

year one thousand nine hundred and five by the Blue Ribbon Manufacturing Company, Winnipeg, at the Department of Agriculture.'; 3 'Blue Ribbon Cook Book Eighteenth edition Prepared especially for everyday use in Western homes // Foreword' signed Blue Ribbon Ltd; 4–144 text; 145–9 blank for 'Memorandum'; 150–6 publ ads in colour; 157–68 index
COPIES: *Private collection
NOTES: The cover-title describes the book as for 'Canadian homes'; p 3 says for 'Western homes.' Another private collector's copy is inscribed on the endpaper, 'Margaret Mitchell // Elkhorn Man[itoba] Feb 17th 1944.'

M7.13   18th ed., [about 1945]
—Blue Ribbon / and / Pure Gold / cook / book / Eighteenth edition / For everyday use / in Canadian homes [cover-title]
DESCRIPTION: 20.5 × 13.0 cm   Pp [i–ii], [1–4] 5–145 [146], [i–vi], 147–58 [159–62]   Fp illus on p 1 of company buildings in Vancouver, Winnipeg, and Toronto, fp illus on p 10 of 'Diagram of table laid for home dinner (without service of maid),' small illus   Cloth, with image on front of containers of Blue Ribbon Coffee, Baking Powder, and Tea, and a blue bow
CONTENTS: i–ii four coupons: 'Please send the Blue Ribbon and Pure Gold Cook Book at the special price of 25c. to'; 1 fp illus; 2 'Entered according to Act of the Parliament of Canada, in the year one thousand nine hundred and five, by the Blue Ribbon Manufacturing Company, Winnipeg, at the Department of Agriculture.'; 3 'Blue Ribbon Cook Book Eighteenth edition Prepared especially for everyday use in Canadian homes // Foreword' signed Pure Gold Manufacturing Co. Ltd; 4–145 text; 146 blank, ruled page for 'Memorandum'; i–vi publ ads in colour; 147–58 index; 159–62 blank, ruled pages for 'Memorandum'
COPIES: *Private collection
NOTES: The title – *Blue Ribbon and Pure Gold Cook Book* – distinguishes this eighteenth edition from the other English-language eighteenth edition, M7.12, *Blue Ribbon Cook Book*.

Another private collector has a copy that appears to match the one described here, except for the illustration on p 1 that shows only the building in Toronto, not buildings in Vancouver, Winnipeg, and Toronto. Another private collector reports that her mother purchased this edition on 14 May 1945.

M7.14   18th ed.
—Livre / culinaire / Blue Ribbon / et / Pure Gold / Édition dix-huit / Pour employer tous les jours / dans les ménages canadiens [cover-title]

DESCRIPTION: Cloth, with image on front of containers of Blue Ribbon Coffee, Baking Powder, and Tea, and a blue bow

CONTENTS: ...; 2 'Entré selon l'Acte du Parlement du Canada pendant l'année mil neuf cent cinq par Blue Ribbon Manufacturing Company, Winnipeg, au département d'Agriculture.'; 3 'Livre culinaire Blue Ribbon Édition dix-huit Préparé spécialement pour employer tous les jours dans les ménages canadiens / / Préface'; ...

COPIES: *Private collection

NOTES: The collector's copy belonged originally to her mother, who lived in Quebec City. Another collector has what is probably the same edition, where p 1 is a full-page illustration of Pure Gold Manufacturing Co. buildings in Vancouver, Winnipeg, and Toronto.

M7.15 19th ed. on binding [18th ed. on p 3], [about 1946]

—Blue Ribbon / and / Pure Gold / cook / book / Nineteenth edition / For everyday use / in Canadian homes [cover-title]

DESCRIPTION: 20.0 × 13.5 cm   Pp [i–ii], [1–4] 5–145 [146], [i–vi], 147–58 [159–62]   Fp illus on p 1 of Pure Gold Manufacturing Co. Ltd building, fp illus on p 10 of 'Diagram of table laid for home dinner (without service of maid),' illus   Cloth, with image on front of containers of Blue Ribbon Coffee, Baking Powder, and Tea, and a blue bow

CONTENTS: i–ii four perforated book-order coupons; 1 fp illus; 2 'Entered according to Act of the Parliament of Canada, in the year one thousand nine hundred and five, by the Blue Ribbon Manufacturing Company, Winnipeg, at the Department of Agriculture.'; 3 'Blue Ribbon Cook Book Eighteenth edition Prepared especially for everyday use in Canadian homes // Foreword' signed Pure Gold Manufacturing Co. Ltd; 4–145 text; 146 blank, ruled page for 'Memorandum'; i–vi publ ads in colour; 147–58 index; 159–62 blank, ruled leaves for 'Memorandum'

COPIES: OAYM OTNY (uncat) *Private collection

NOTES: M7.15 and the French-language nineteenth edition were published no later than 1946, the last year that Pure Gold Manufacturing Co. is listed in the Toronto city directory.

M7.16 19th ed. on binding [18th ed. on p 3], [about 1946]

—Livre / culinaire / Blue Ribbon / et / Pure Gold / Édition dix-neuf / Pour employer tous les jours / dans les ménages canadiens [cover-title]

DESCRIPTION: 20.0 × 13.0 cm   Pp [1–4] 5–174 [175–6], [i–vi], 177–89 [190–4]   Fp illus on p 1 of Pure Gold Manufacturing Co. Ltd building in Toronto, fp illus on p 10 of 'Dessin d'une table qui est mise pour un dîner chez-soi,' illus   Cloth, with image on front of containers of Blue Ribbon Coffee, Baking Powder, and Tea, and a blue bow

CONTENTS: 1 fp illus; 2 'Entré selon l'Acte du Parlement du Canada pendant l'année mil neuf cent cinq par Blue Ribbon Manufacturing Company, Winnipeg, au département d'Agriculture.'; 3 'Livre culinaire Blue Ribbon Édition dix-huit Préparé spécialement pour employer tous les jours dans les ménages canadiens // Préface' signed Pure Gold Manufacturing Co. Ltd; 4–174 text; 175–6 blank, ruled leaf for 'Memorandum'; i–vi publ ads in colour; 177–89 'Index'; 190–4 blank, ruled leaves for 'Memorandum'

COPIES: *OONL (TX715 B5814 1940) QSFFSC (641.5 P985L)

NOTES: The initial leaf of book-order coupons is torn out of the OONL copy.

M7.17 19th ed.

—Blue / Ribbon / Nineteenth edition / cook / book / For / everyday / use in / Canadian homes [cover-title]

DESCRIPTION: 16.0 × 12.5 cm   Pp [i–ii], [1–4] 5–144 [145–68]   Fp illus on p 1 of Blue Ribbon Ltd building, fp illus on p 10 of 'Diagram of table laid for home dinner (without service of maid),' illus   Cloth, with image on front of a blue bow

CONTENTS: i–ii perforated book-order coupons; 1 fp illus; 2 'Entered according to Act of the Parliament of Canada, in the year one thousand nine hundred and five by the Blue Ribbon Manufacturing Company, Winnipeg, at the Department of Agriculture.'; 3 'Blue Ribbon Cook Book Nineteenth edition Prepared especially for everyday use in Western homes' and foreword; 4–144 text; 145–9 blank, ruled leaves for 'Memorandum'; 150–6 publ ads in colour; 157–68 index

COPIES: BVIPM *OONL (TX715 B58 1920z p***)

NOTES: The cover-title describes the book as for 'Canadian homes'; p 3 says for 'Western homes.'

M7.18 20th ed., [about 1947]

—Blue / Ribbon / Twentieth edition / cook / book / For / everyday / use in / Canadian / homes [cover-title]

DESCRIPTION: 16.5 × 12.5 cm   Pp [i–ii], [1–4] 5–144 [145–68]   Fp illus on p 1 of Blue Ribbon Ltd building, fp illus on p 10 of 'Diagram of table laid for home dinner (without service of maid),' illus   Cloth, with image on front of a blue bow

CONTENTS: i–ii perforated, book-order coupons; 1 fp illus; 2 'Entered according to Act of the Parliament of Canada, in the year one thousand nine hundred and five by the Blue Ribbon Manufacturing Company, Winnipeg, at the Department of Agriculture.'; 3 'Blue Ribbon Cook Book Twentieth edition Prepared especially for everyday use in Western homes // Foreword' signed Blue Ribbon Ltd; 4–144 text; 145–9 blank, ruled leaves for 'Memorandum'; 150–6 publ ads in colour; 157–68 index

COPIES: MSOHM   *Private collection

NOTES: Another private collector reports that she 'just happened to write [her] name and the year 1947 in it when [she] received it as a gift from [her] mother.'

M7.19   21st ed.
—Blue / Ribbon / Twenty first edition / cook / book / For / everyday / use in / Canadian / homes [cover-title]
DESCRIPTION: 16.0 × 12.5 cm   Pp [i–ii], [1–4] 5–144 [145–68]   Fp illus on p 1 of Blue Ribbon Ltd building, fp illus on p 10 of 'Diagram of table laid for home dinner (without service of maid),' illus   Cloth, with image on front of a blue bow
CONTENTS: i–ii book-order coupons, torn out in this copy; 1 fp illus; 2 'Entered according to Act of the Parliament of Canada, in the year one thousand nine hundred and five by the Blue Ribbon Manufacturing Company, Winnipeg, at the Department of Agriculture.'; 3 'Blue Ribbon Cook Book Twenty-first edition Prepared especially for everyday use in Western homes // Foreword'; 4–144 text; 145–9 blank, ruled leaves for 'Memorandum'; 150–6 publ ads in colour; 157–68 index
COPIES: AHRMH (980-031-002) MTM OKELWM *Private collection
NOTES: The cover-title describes the book as for 'Canadian homes'; p 3 says for 'Western homes.'

Ferguson/Fraser, p 232, cite *Blue Ribbon Cook Book,* Winnipeg: Blue Ribbon Ltd, 1905; the reference likely refers to the twenty-first edition illustrated in colour on p 11. Comments on p 21 may refer to the same edition.

M7.20   22nd ed.
—Blue / Ribbon / Twenty second edition / cook / book / For / everyday / use in / Canadian / homes [cover-title]
DESCRIPTION: 16.0 × 12.5 cm   Pp [i–ii], [1–4] 5–144 [145–68]   Fp illus on p 1 of Blue Ribbon Ltd building, fp illus on p 10 of 'Diagram of table laid for home dinner (without service of maid),' illus   Cloth, with image on front of a blue bow

CONTENTS: i–ii book-order coupons; 1 fp illus; 2 'Entered according to Act of the Parliament of Canada, in the year one thousand nine hundred and five by the Blue Ribbon Manufacturing Company, Winnipeg, at the Department of Agriculture.'; 3 'Blue Ribbon Cook Book Twenty-second edition Prepared especially for everyday use in Western homes // Foreword'; 4–144 text; 145–9 blank, ruled leaves for 'Memorandum'; 150–6 publ ads in colour; 157–68 index
COPIES: OCALNHM   OTMCL (641.5971 B494) OTSHH *Private collection
NOTES: The OTMCL copy is inscribed on the front end paper, in ink, 'Margaret Newall.'

M7.21   23rd ed., [about 1948–50]
—Blue / Ribbon / Twenty third edition / cook / book / For / everyday / use in / Canadian / homes [cover-title]
DESCRIPTION: 16.0 × 12.5 cm   Pp [i–ii], [1–4] 5–144 [145–68]   Fp illus on p 1 of Blue Ribbon Ltd building, a few illus   Cloth, with image on front of a blue bow
CONTENTS: i–ii four book-order coupons; 1 fp illus; 2 'Entered according to Act of the Parliament of Canada, in the year one thousand nine hundred and five by the Blue Ribbon Manufacturing Company, Winnipeg, at the Department of Agriculture.'; 3 'Blue Ribbon Cook Book Twenty-third edition Prepared especially for everyday use in Western homes'; 4–144 text; 145–9 blank, ruled leaves for 'Memorandum'; 150–6 publ ads in colour; 157–68 index
COPIES: *AEUCHV OKELWM   Private collection
NOTES: One private collector reports, 'I acquired [the twenty-third edition] as a curling prize in about 1948–1950 ...' Another collector writes: '[The twenty-third edition was] probably published after 1950, since it was given to the Dean of Women at U. of Manitoba in 1952 for her comments. I was her assistant at the time.' Yet another collector has a copy that is inscribed on the front endpaper, 'Laura Bray[rest of name torn off] // Hartney, Manitoba 1953.'

OTHER EDITIONS: *Blue Ribbon Cook Book,* 26th ed., [after 1950] (OKELWM); 27th ed., 'All recipes in this book fully tested and approved by Norah Cherry // home economist,' Toronto, Winnipeg, and Vancouver: Lithographed by Bulman Bros Ltd, Winnipeg, for Blue Ribbon Ltd, nd (Private collection); 29th ed., Montreal: Brooke Bond Canada, copyright 1961 (NBSAM missing, OONL); 30th ed., [Montreal: Brooke Bond Foods Ltd, copyright 1970] (OONL, Private collection).

1906

Denison, Mrs Grace Elizabeth

For the 1906 Winnipeg edition of Grace Denison's The New Cook Book, *see O130.8.*

The Red Cross almanac and cook book 1906

See also M6.1, Taylor's 1904 Calendar Cook Book, from the same pharmacy.

M7a.1   1906
Hang this up for reference. / The Red Cross / almanac and / cook book / 1906 / Published by / the / Red Cross Pharmacy / W.A. Vrooman, Ph.B. / dispensing chemist, / Pratt Opera / House Block / Portage la Prairie. / Telephone No. 18. / [in column at left of title:] It will pay you to read / this almanac carefully / Mail or telephone / orders / promptly delivered / Satisfaction guaranteed / The best of everything / usually found in / first-class drug stores / we always / carry in stock. / [across bottom:] Opal Suds, the perfect washing powder [cover-title]
DESCRIPTION: 17.5 × 13.0 cm   Pp [1–3] 4–32   Illus of astrological symbols   Paper, with Red Cross symbol on front; stapled, and with hole punched at top left corner, through which runs a string for hanging
CONTENTS: 1 'This Is Important. Don't Skip It.' [information about the drugstore]; 2 publ ad for Oxygen Pills; 3–32 astronomical information, recipes, monthly calendars, 'Practical Breaks' [i.e., jokes], publ ads, and blank spaces for 'Memoranda'
COPIES: *Bookseller's stock
NOTES: The text on the inside front face of the binding, headed 'Vrooman's Drug Store / / "The Red Cross Pharmacy" Pratt Block,' refers to the store's 'past twenty years' and to the store being 'formerly owned by Jos. Taylor.' The recipes begin on p 4 with Ginger Bread, Neapolitan Cake, Nut and Raisin Cake, and Plain Cake.

1906–7

Tried, tested and true recipes for the practical everyday use of Gold Standard goods

In the January 1919 and February 1920 issues of Western Home Monthly, *the makers of Gold Standard Baking Powder advertise 'A big 110-page Cook Book sent free upon request.' None of the editions described below has this many pages, yet no other cookbooks for Gold Standard Baking Powder have been identified. The free offer may have been for an edition not yet located or for another cookbook altogether.*

M8.1   nd [about 1906–7]
[Cover-title lacking]
DESCRIPTION: 17.0 × 12.5 cm   Pp [1] 2–78 [leaf(ves) lacking]   Lacks binding
CONTENTS: 1 dedication to 'the ladies of the Canadian Northwest' by the manufacturers of Gold Standard goods; 2 publ ad for Gold Standard goods 'packed by the Codville-Georgeson Co., Limited Winnipeg, Man.'; 3–76 'Tried, Tested and True Recipes for the Everyday Use of Gold Standard Goods' and publ ads; 77–8 'Helpful Hints to the Housewife'
COPIES: *SSWD (Domestic cookbooks No. 21)
NOTES: This is an earlier edition of M8.4, *Practical Selected Recipes by Noted Cooks* (copies of M8.1 and M8.4 compared at SSWD): Many of the recipes are the same and there are other parallels in the text. Codville-Georgeson Co. Ltd is listed in Winnipeg city directories for 1906 and 1907 (before 1906 the company is called Codville and Co.; after 1907, it is called Codville Co. Ltd and John J. Codville's and William Georgeson's names are no longer listed with the company entry or separately). The text is printed in green.

SSWD has another copy, probably of M8.1, that could not be found at the time of my visit. Photocopies of pp 2–3 of the missing copy, supplied before my research trip, appear to match the copy catalogued here; the cover-title is 'Tried tested / and / true / recipes / for the practical / everyday use / of / Gold / Standard / goods / "Guaranteed-the-best"' and there is an image on front of a woman in a dark, ankle-length dress and spotted apron, holding up a plate of baked goods with her left hand.

M8.2   1911
—[An edition of *Gold Standard Cook Book. Practical Selected Recipes by Noted Cooks.*, Winnipeg, Man.: Codville Co., 1911]
CITATIONS: O'Neill (unpublished)
COPIES: Great Britain: LB (not located)
NOTES: The variant title, *Gold Standard Cook Book*, recorded in O'Neill's entry, may indicate a distinct edition.

M8.3   nd [about 1912–13]
—[Trademark symbol] / Selected / recipes / by noted cooks / for everyday use / in the home / Compliments of / the Codville Co. Ltd. / Winnipeg. [cover-title]
DESCRIPTION: 17.0 × 13.0 cm   Pp [1–6] 7–78 [79–80]

Illus Paper, with a decorative border on front composed of heads of grain; stapled, and with hole punched at top left corner for hanging

CONTENTS: 1 trademark symbol; 2 'Index' [i.e., table of contents]; 3 'To the ladies of Canada ... with the compliments of the Codville Company, Ltd. sole manufacturers Gold Standard Pure Food Products'; 4 fp illus of general offices, factory, and warehouse of Codville Co. Ltd, Winnipeg; 5–6 'Gold Standard Our Trade Mark and What It Means to You' signed Codville Co. Ltd; 7–69 'Selected Recipes for Everyday Use in the Home'; 70–2 'Helpful Hints to the Housewife'; 73–4 'Letters of Appreciation'; 75 'You Can Purchase Gold Standard Food Products at Almost Every First-Class Grocery'; 76 fp illus of Gold Standard products in the foreground, the globe behind; 77 complete list of Gold Standard food products; 78 'We Will Send Your Friends a Copy of This Book'; 79 illus of three toddlers, each holding a candle; 80 trademark symbol

COPIES: *MWPA (MG14 C50 McKnight, Ethel)

NOTES: The dedication is now to the 'ladies of Canada,' not 'ladies of the Canadian Northwest,' as in M8.1. Page 5 states, 'Only six years ago we began manufacturing these products ...' Since the earliest edition of the cookbook, M8.1, was published about 1906–7, this edition was likely published about 1912–13 (1906 or 1907 + 6 years), one year before M8.4, which refers to 'seven years ago.'

A copy at SBIM appears to be the same as that at MWPA except that p 1 is blank and there are no printed pages 79–80; 'Presented by A,H, [sic] Nichol General Merchant Nokomis Sask,' is stamped in purple ink on p 1 of the SBIM copy.

M8.4 nd [about 1913–14]
—Practical / selected recipes / by / noted / cooks / Compliments of / the Gold Standard Manfg. Co., / Winnipeg, Man. [cover-title]

DESCRIPTION: 17.0 × 12.5 cm Pp [1–2] 3–95 [96] 3 pls col, illus Paper, with image on front of Gold Standard products on a table top; stapled, and with hole punched at top left corner for hanging

CONTENTS: 1 Gold Standard symbol; 2 'Index' [i.e., table of contents]; 3 dedication to the 'ladies of Canada' by the Gold Standard Manufacturing Co.; 4 fp illus of general offices, factory, and warehouse of Codville Co. and Gold Standard Manufacturing Co., Winnipeg; 5–6 'Gold Standard Our Trade Mark and What It Means to You'; 7–87 'Selected Recipes for Everyday Use in the Home'; 88–90 'Helpful Hints to the Housewife'; 91–2 'Letters of Appreciation'; 93 'You Can Purchase Gold Standard Food Products at Almost

Every First-Class Grocery'; 94 fp illus of Gold Standard products in the foreground, the globe behind; 95 complete list of Gold Standard products; 96 'We Will Send Your Friends a Copy of This Book' and at bottom, 'Bulman Bros. Ltd., printers, Winnipeg'

COPIES: *SSWD

NOTES: Page 5 states, 'Only seven years ago we began manufacturing these products, and in that short space of time our business has grown into the largest institution of its kind in the West, with an output extending over the entire Dominion.' Gold Standard Manufacturing Co. is listed in Winnipeg city directories from 1914 to 1917. Since the earliest edition of the cookbook, M8.1, was published about 1906–7, this edition was likely published about 1913–14 (1906 or 1907 + 7 years). (The 1914 directory listing for Gold Standard suggests that the company existed in 1913.)

M8.5 nd [about 1913–14]
—Trade mark / [trademark symbol] / Selected / recipes / by noted cooks / for everyday use / in the home / Compliments of / the Gold Standard Manfg. Co. / Winnipeg. [cover-title]

DESCRIPTION: 17.0 × 13.0 cm Pp [1–6] 7–78 [79–80] Illus of the Gold Standard factory and scenes in the factory, Gold Standard products, and on p 41, a cake Paper, with a decorative border on front composed of heads of grain; stapled

CONTENTS: 1 trademark symbol; 2 'Index' [i.e., table of contents]; 3 [obscured by newspaper clippings in this copy]; 4 fp illus of Winnipeg factory; 5–6 'Gold Standard Our Trade Mark and What It Means to You'; 7–69 'Selected Recipes'; 70–2 'Helpful Hints to the Housewife'; 73–4 'Letters of Appreciation'; 75 'You Can Purchase Gold Standard Food Products at Almost Every First-Class Grocery'; 76 fp illus of Gold Standard products in the foreground, the globe behind; 77 complete list of Gold Standard food products; 78 'We Will Send Your Friends a Copy of This Book'; 79 three toddlers, each holding a candle; 80 trademark symbol

COPIES: OVOH SBIHM *Private collection

NOTES: The cover-title and the pagination distinguish M8.5 from M8.4. Like M8.4, p 5 states, 'Only seven years ago we began manufacturing these products, and in that short space of time our business has grown into the largest institution of its kind in the West, with an output extending over the entire Dominion.' The recipes in this book proved so useful and popular, so states p 78, that 'many of the ladies who received a copy of the first edition, requested that we [the publisher] send copies to their friends.'

This edition was likely published about 1913–14 for the same reasons given for M8.4.

M8.6   nd [about 1916–17]
—Practical / selected recipes / by / noted / cooks / [trademark symbol] / Gold Standard Mf'g Co. / Winnipeg Canada
DESCRIPTION: 17.0 × 12.5 cm   Pp [1–2] 3–95 [96]   Centre spread pl col btwn pp 48 and 49 of 'Gold Standard Palate Pleasures' [i.e., prepared dishes], illus of Gold Standard factory, scenes in factory, and company products, illus headpieces for recipe sections   Lacks paper binding; stapled, and with hole punched at top left corner for hanging
CONTENTS: 1 tp; 2 'Index' [i.e., table of contents]; 3 'To the ladies of Canada ... this little volume is respectfully inscribed // With the compliments of the Gold Standard Manufacturing Co ...'; 4 fp illus of 'General offices, factory and warehouse of the Codville Co., Limited, and the Gold Standard Manufacturing Co., Winnipeg, Man.'; 5–6 'Our Trade Mark and What It Means to You'; 7–87 'Selected Recipes'; 88–90 'Helpful Hints to the Housewife'; 91–2 'Letters of Appreciation'; 93 'You Can Purchase Gold Standard Food Products at Almost Every First-Class Grocery'; 94 fp illus of Gold Standard products in the foreground, the globe behind; 95 complete list of Gold Standard food products; 96 'We Will Send Your Friends a Copy of This Book'
COPIES: *Private collection
NOTES: Page 5 states, 'It is only about ten years ago that we began manufacturing these products, ...'; therefore, this edition was published three years later than M8.5, in about 1916–17. The title-page of this edition has the same decorative flower-and-leaf border as M8.7.

M8.7   nd [about 1916–17]
—Practical / selected recipes / by / noted / cooks / [trademark symbol] / Gold Standard Mf'g Co. / Winnipeg Canada
DESCRIPTION: 17.0 × 12.5 cm   Pp [1–2] 3–80   Centre spread pl col between pp 40–1 of 'Gold Standard Palate Pleasures,' illus of Gold Standard factory, scenes in factory, and company products, illus headpieces for recipe sections   Paper, with image on front of a woman holding a moulded jelly on a platter; copy 1 previously stapled, now sewn and in new library cloth; with hole punched at top left corner for hanging
CONTENTS: 1 tp; 2 'Index' [i.e., table of contents]; 3 'To the ladies of Canada ... this little volume of useful recipes is respectfully inscribed // With the compli-

ments of the Gold Standard Manufacturing Co. ...'; 4 fp illus of 'General offices, factory and warehouse of the Codville Co., Limited, and the Gold Standard Manufacturing Co., Winnipeg, Man.'; 5–6 'Our Trade Mark and What It Means to You'; 7–top 73 'Selected Recipes'; mid 73–75 'Helpful Hints to the Housewife'; 76–7 'Letters of Appreciation'; 78 fp illus of Gold Standard goods in the foreground, the globe behind; 79 complete list of Gold Standard food products; 80 'You Can Purchase Gold Standard Food Products at Almost Every First-Class Grocery'; inside back face of binding 'The Echlin Studios Toronto'
COPIES: *OONL (TX715 P73, 2 copies)   Private collection
NOTES: Page 5 states, 'It is only about ten years ago that we began manufacturing these products, ...' The title-page has the same decorative flower-and-leaf border as M8.6. The text is printed in dark brown ink (the private collector's copy is printed in black).

Echlin Studios, run by John A. Echlin, is listed in Toronto city directories from 1916 to 1920 (before 1916, John A. Echlin is listed as president of Advertising Designers; after 1920, there is no listing for him or the Studios); therefore, this edition was published in the period 1916–20. Note, however, that the last listing in Winnipeg directories for Gold Standard Manufacturing Co. is in the volume for 1917. The image on the binding is signed with the artist's monogram 'AD.'

1907

A few selected recipes from the Blue Ribbon Cook Book

M9.1   nd [about 1907]
A few / selected / recipes / from the / Blue Ribbon Cook Book [cover-title]
DESCRIPTION: 18.5 × 12.0 cm   Pp 1–10, 1-P–12-P, 11–18   Paper, with image on front of a blue ribbon tied in a bow; stapled, and with hole punched at top left corner for hanging
CONTENTS: Inside front face of binding 'You Need This Book' [i.e., *Blue Ribbon Cook Book*], orders to be sent to Blue Ribbon Ltd, Department S.R., Winnipeg; 1–10 recipes and publ ads; 1-P–12-P 'How to Get Blue Ribbon Premiums' and a catalogue of the premiums; 11–16 recipes and publ ads; 17 'An Easily Made Dessert'; 18 'Why Blue Ribbon Tea Is So Good' and a testimonial dated 12 September 1907
COPIES: *AALIWWM   OONL (TX715.6 F485 1900z p***)   SSWD

NOTES: M7.1, *Blue Ribbon Cook Book*, the source of the selected recipes, was first published in 1905 and went through many subsequent editions.

The SSWD copy has an extra leaf of 'Beverages' on pp 19–20. The OONL copy, which also has the extra leaf, has no catalogue of premiums between pp 10 and 11.

1909

Western farmers' handbook

M10.1   nd [about 1909]
Western farmers' / handbook / The Winnipeg Telegram's compendium of / household, / legal and veterinary / information / Price net: Paper cover $1.00; in cloth $1.50
CITATIONS: Watier, p 7
COPIES: *OONL (S508 A1 W48 1910)   SSU (S522 C2 W47 1910)
NOTES: There is no indication of the date or edition number. 'With the compliments // The Farmers' Weekly Telegram Winnipeg' is on the front face of the OONL binding. 'Published by the Farmers' Weekly Telegram // Winnipeg, Canada' is on the front of the SSU copy. Since the *Farmers' Weekly Telegram* began publication on 27 January 1909 (continuing the *Weekly Telegram*, which ceased the week before), this edition was published no earlier than 1909, and it likely pre-dates the 1910 revised edition. The index begins on p 197.

M10.2   rev. ed., 1910
—Western farmers' / handbook / The Winnipeg Telegram's compendium of / household, / legal and veterinary / information / Revised edition, 1910 / Price net: Paper cover $1.00; in cloth $1.50
DESCRIPTION: 22.5 × 14.5 cm   Pp [1–6] 7–208 [leaf lacking]   Lacks paper(?) binding; stapled
CONTENTS: 1 tp; 2 ads; 3 'Preface' signed Telegram Printing Co.; 4 table of contents; 5–53 'Part I. Legal Information ... Compiled and copyrighted by J. Robert Long, J.P. // Caron, Sask. With numerous additions'; 54 ads; 55–77 'Part II. Veterinary Information'; 78 ad; 79–199 'Part III. Household Information'; 200–8 index
COPIES: *MSM
NOTES: Recipes are on pp 91–179.

1910

The new cook book

M11.1   nd [about 1910]
The new / cook book / compiled by / the Young Ladies' Guild / Fifth Avenue / Methodist / Church / Souris Manitoba
DESCRIPTION: 16.5 × 12.0 cm   Pp [1–2] 3–79   Paper, with image on front of the church; stapled
CONTENTS: 1 tp; 2 blank; 3–79 recipes credited with the name of the contributor and ads
COPIES: BTCA (77.73)   *MSOHM
NOTES: The date '1910' is inscribed on the front face of the binding, in ink. The BTCA copy lacks its binding and the lower half of the title-page.

St Luke's Organ Fund recipe book

See also M62.1, Favorite Recipes, *from the same church.*

M12.1   [1st ed.?], 1910
St. Luke's Organ Fund / recipe book / Winnipeg / Stovel Company, printers / 1910
DESCRIPTION: 17.5 × 12.0 cm   Pp [i–ii], [1–5] 6–144, [i–viii]   Fp illus on p 2 of St Luke's Church   Striped blue cloth, with paper label mounted on front, on which is printed the title and the last four lines from *Lucile*, Part I, Canto ii, by Owen Meredith, pseudonym of Edward Robert Bulwer-Lytton: '"He can live without love; / What is passion but pining; / But where is the man / That can live without dining."'
CONTENTS: i tp; ii blank; 1 'This book is published for the purpose of applying the proceeds of its sale to the Organ Fund of St. Luke's Church, Winnipeg' and a note that 'recipes in the book are either original or else they have been tried and found successful by those whose names are appended'; 2 fp illus of the church; 3 'Index' [i.e., alphabetical list of sections]; 4 blank; 5–144 recipes, most credited wih the name of the contributor, and ads; i–viii ads
CITATIONS: Duncan, pp 127, 181
COPIES: CIHM (77974)   *OONL (TX715.6 S235 1910 p***)
NOTES: The illustration of the church on p 2 confirms that the cookbook was produced by St Luke's Anglican Church on Nassau Street North, founded in 1897.

M12.2   1910
—St. Luke's Organ Fund / recipe book / Winnipeg, Man. / Henderson Brothers, printers / 1910

DESCRIPTION: 17.5 × 12.5 cm   Pp [1–3] 4–192   Tp illus of St Luke's Church   Cloth; sewn

CONTENTS: 1 tp; 2 'This book is published for the purpose of applying the proceeds of its sale to the Organ Fund of St. Luke's Church, Winnipeg' and a note that recipes are 'either original, or else they have been tried and found successful ...'; 3 'Index' [of subject headings] and 'Advertisements' [i.e., index of advertisers]; 4 ad; 5–192 recipes credited with the name of the contributor and ads

COPIES: *MSM

NOTES: The cover-title is 'The Recipe Book for St Luke's Organ Fund.' Since M12.2 has more pages, it probably follows M12.1.

1910–14

[Title unknown]

M13.1   nd [about 1910–14]
[Title-page lacking]
DESCRIPTION: 20.5 × 12.5 cm   Pp [two leaves lacking] [5] 6–78 [leaves lacking]   Paper binding lacking; stapled
CONTENTS: 5–78 recipes credited with the name of the contributor and ads
COPIES: *Private collection
NOTES: The advertisements are mainly for Hartney businesses. An older resident of Hartney reports that most of the businesses were from the period before his early childhood in the late 1910s and early 1920s. There is an advertisement on p 44 for Robin Hood Flour, which does not mention the company's cookbook, S16.1, *Robin Hood Flour Cook Book,* by Mrs Sarah Tyson Rorer, of about 1915. The Hartney cookbook, therefore, was likely published before *Robin Hood Flour Cook Book,* and, from appearances, about 1910–14.

1911

Knox Church cook book

In 1925, Knox Presbyterian Church became Knox United Church.

M14.1   nd [about 1911]
Knox Church / cook book / Compiled by / the Willing Workers / The Record Printing Co. [cover-title]
DESCRIPTION: 21.5 × 14.5 cm   Pp [1] 2–60   Illus blue on p 1 of Knox Presbyterian Church, Brandon   Paper; stapled
CONTENTS: 1 illus of the church and 'Contents' [i.e., alphabetical list of chapter headings]; 2 ad; 3–60 recipes credited with the name of the contributor and ads
COPIES: *MBDHM
NOTES: The text and illustration are printed in blue ink. An advertisement on p 50 for Campbell and Campbell, a furniture store, includes an illustration that incorporates the phrase 'Copyright 1911 by C.E. Zimmerman[?] Co.,' which suggests a publication date of about that year. No reference is made to the First World War, supporting a date before the outbreak of war in 1914.

Knox Presbyterian Church was built in 1910. The illustration shows the church not long after construction, for there is a ladder against the side of the building and what look like piles of bricks at the front.

The Souris almanac and cook book 1911

M15.1   1911
The Souris / almanac / and / cook book / 1911 / Published by / Sherrin & Co. / chemists and druggists / Souris Manitoba
DESCRIPTION: 17.5 × 13.5 cm   Pp [1–3] 4–32   Illus of astrological signs and symbols   Paper; stapled
CONTENTS: Inside front face of binding untitled introduction signed Sherrin and Co.; 1 tp; 2 publ ad; 3 'Eclipses, 1911,' 'Morning and Evening Stars, 1911,' and 'Chronological Cycles, 1911'; 4–29 recipes, monthly calendars, humour (jokes), and publ ads; 30 menus for breakfast, luncheon, dinner, Thanksgiving dinner, and Christmas dinner; 31–2 'Superstitions'
COPIES: *MSOHM
NOTES: Sherrin and Co. likely also published an edition in 1910, since the text opposite p 1 refers to M15.1 as 'this second edition of the Souris Almanac and Cook Book.'

1912

Cook book

Westminster Presbyterian Church held its first service in 1893. In 1912 it finished construction of a new building (depicted on the binding of M16.1) at 745 Buell (now Westminster) Avenue. In 1925 the congregation joined the United Church of Canada.

M16.1   [1912]
Cook book / published by / the Young Ladies' Club / of / Westminster Church / "All human history attests that happiness for man – / the hungry sinner – / Since Eve ate apples, much depends on dinner." / – Byron. [cover-title]
DESCRIPTION: 21.0 × 14.0 cm   Pp 3–98   Paper, with image on back of Westminster Church, Winnipeg, dated 1912; stapled
CONTENTS: 3 ads; 4 'Index' [i.e., table of contents]; 5 ads; 6 '300 Tried and True Recipes Arranged by the Young Ladies' Club of Westminster Church,' list of officers, and untitled five-line verse; 7–8 ads; 9–95 recipes credited with the name of the contributor and ads; 96–7 blank for 'My Favorite Recipes'; 98 'Tables of Weights and Measures'
COPIES: *MWPA (MG14 C50 McKnight, Ethel)

The reliable cook book

M17.1   Christmas 1912
The reliable / cook book / Compiled by / the Ladies Aid of the Methodist Church / Foxwarren, Man. / Christmas 1912 / The turnpike road to people's hearts, I find, / Is through their mouths, or I mistake mankind.
COPIES: *Private collection

1913

Dauphin ladies' cook book

M18.1   1st ed., November 1913
Dauphin / ladies' / cook / book / A / valuable collection of recipes / contributed by the ladies of / Dauphin, Man. / First edition published November 1913 / Dauphin Herald Print [cover-title]
CONTENTS: 1 'We ask you cooks to patronize those men who in our Cook Book advertise,' 'Table of Weights and Measures,' 'Miscellaneous // Equivalents in Weights for Measure,' and 'Time Table for Cooking' by Mrs E.C. McLeod; ...
COPIES: *MAUAM

M18.2   2nd ed., 1923
—Dauphin ladies' / cookery book / Useful / hints / Aug. / 1923 / Tried / recipes / A valuable collection of recipes / contributed by the ladies of / Dauphin, Manitoba. / First edition published November, 1913 / Second edition published August, 1923 / [ad:] You will get better results by /

using ingredients supplied by – / Ramsay-Wright Ltd. / Dauphin / Phone – 22 / for quick service / Manitoba / [below ad:] Dauphin Herald Print [cover-title]
DESCRIPTION: 22.5 × 15.5 cm   Pp 1–88   Thin card; stapled
CONTENTS: 1 'We ask you cooks to patronize those men who in our Cook Book advertise,' 'Table of Weights and Measures,' 'Miscellaneous,' 'Time Table for Cooking,' and ad; 2 ad; 3–83 text, including recipes credited with the name of the contributor, and ads; 84–8 blank for 'Memorandum'
COPIES: *Private collection
NOTES: There is no indication of a particular group to which the Dauphin ladies might have belonged, such as a church. 'Carnation Milk Recipes' are on p 75; 'Schedule of Infectious Diseases' on pp 80–3 presents information about Chicken Pox, Diphtheria, German Measles, Measles, Mumps, Scarlet Fever, Smallpox, Typhoid Fever, and Whooping Cough.
   The copy catalogued here originally belonged to the owner's mother, who resided in Dauphin all her married life.

Riverview Presbyterian Church cook book

M19.1   1913
[An edition of *Riverview Presbyterian Church Cook Book,* 'a valuable collection of recipes compiled by the Ladies Aid of Riverview Church, Fort Rouge, Winnipeg,' 1913, pp 146]
COPIES: Bookseller's stock

1914

The Minnedosa cook book

M20.1   2nd ed., 1914
Tried tested proved / The Minnedosa cook / book / compiled from recipes contributed / by the ladies of Minnedosa and vici- / nity, and published in [sic] behalf of the / Women's Hospital Aid, Minnedosa, / Manitoba. / "We may live without books – what is knowledge but grieving? / We may live without hope – what is hope but deceiving? / We may live without love – what is passion but pining? / But where is the man who can live without dining? [sic, no closing quotation-marks] / Second edition 1000 copies / 1914 / Price 50 cents. / W.G. Pickell, / Book and Job Printing, / Portage la Prairie, / Man. [cover-title]

DESCRIPTION: 20.0 × 13.5 cm   Pp [1] 2–75 [76]   Paper; stapled

CONTENTS: 1 cover-title; 2–3 'Household Hints'; 4–75 recipes; 76 'Index' [i.e., table of contents]

COPIES: *Private collection

NOTES: There are decorative tailpieces for each section; for example, a cherub pulled by two doves on p 3 and two hatching chicks on p 45.

The real home-keeper

The earliest edition of this title was published in Vancouver. For the edition published in Winnipeg in 1914, see B21.5.

Selkirk cook book

M21.1   1914
Selkirk / cook book [cover-title]

CITATIONS: Hughes, Mary Jo, *Marion Nelson Hooker: Two Lives – One Passion,* Winnipeg Art Gallery, 1999, p 46

COPIES: *Bookseller's stock

NOTES: The bookseller reports that the volume has 54 pp and is stapled. This community cookbook has contributions from a Canadian artist and a Canadian novelist, both women. The reproduction of a painting applied to the front face of the binding is by Mrs Marion Hope Nelson Hooker (27 March 1866–29 May 1946). The 'Prologue' on p 1 is by Mrs Valance St Just Patriarche, née Berryman (1875–18 January 1970). Below the 'Prologue' is the alternative title, the name of the group that produced the book, and the date of publication: 'Tested Recipes // Compiled and arranged by the W.A. [probably Women's Auxiliary] of Christ Church // Selkirk, Man. 1914.' Christ Church was Anglican, and although Marion Nelson married into a Methodist family, she herself was Anglican, as was Valance Patriarche. The recipes are credited with the name of the contributor. The original Christ Church building is no longer standing.

The watercolour painting, which is signed and dated 1914, depicts the ferry crossing the Red River, at the foot of McLean Avenue in Selkirk, with the town's church spires visible against the sky on the other bank (a bridge was built later, during the Depression). Notes made by the artist's granddaughter, Helen Ruth Robinson, about the painting, which she calls *The Old Ferry,* state: 'Location of the original watercolour is not known. Painted as a project for the Red Cross for purposes of raising money for the war

effort. It was printed on the cover of cook books sold by the Anglican Church.' One Selkirk resident wrote (correspondence with the author, 23 September 2002): 'The story goes ... that Marion produced little approx. 4" × 6" prints of a painting she did of the ferry ... She allowed Christ Church Anglican ladies to attach a print to every copy of their cookbook (and probably to charge a bit more and make a bit more profit, I'd imagine) in such a way that the print could be removed without damaging it or the cookbook. My mother-in-law framed her copy [of the print].' (The resident, who inherited her mother-in-law's copy of the cookbook, *sans* print, intends to donate the volume to Selkirk's local archives, which, in 2005, were in the planning stage.) Marion Nelson grew up in St Catharines, Ontario, and studied art there and in Buffalo, New York, and Europe, eventually exhibiting with the Royal Canadian Academy and the Ontario Society of Artists. One of her childhood friends had married a Selkirk businessman, and in 1907, a year after the friend's death, Marion moved to Selkirk from Ontario to marry the widowed husband, Frank W. Hooker, and care for his six children. She lived in Selkirk for the next three decades, pursuing her painting career and contributing to numerous fund-raising projects in the town. For further information about the artist, see the exhibition catalogue *Marion Nelson Hooker: Two Lives – One Passion,* by Mary Jo Hughes, Winnipeg Art Gallery, 1999.

In the 'Prologue' Valance Patriarche makes the following comments about the cookbook and Selkirk's citizens: 'This is a cook book for "just folks" // It was not compiled for the use of two-hundred-a-month chefs, for dyspeptic millionaires ... or haughty brides who only intend to cook fifty-seven varieties of ice cream ... When you come to think of it the descendants of Selkirk's hardy pioneers should be peculiarly fitted to produce a cook book. The same spirit of intrepid daring and enterprise which animates the lonely settler is ever to be found in the breast of a good cook. Perhaps the strongest recommendation that can be offered for this little volume is that any number of hale and hearty men and women may be seen in Selkirk – any time between the hours of 8 a.m. and 11 p.m. – who have broken their fast, lunched and dined on the dishes described herein all the days of their lives.' Valance was an author, journalist, public speaker, and, after the First World War, a film censor for the province of Manitoba (the first female censor in Canada). Her writing career began in Toronto, where she was born (as a schoolgirl, she was already having articles published in *Saturday Night* magazine), and in Chicago, but by the time of the cookbook's publication, she was living in Winnipeg, her home until 1960. For more information about her, see: *The Canadian Who's Who, 1938–9*, p 533; her obituary, 'Author Dies at 94,' *Winnipeg Free Press* 23 January 1970; No. 514 in *Canadian Children's Books, 1799–1939*, in the *Special Collections and University Archives Division, the University of British Columbia Library: A Bibliographical Catalogue*, compiled by Sheila A. Egoff, Vancouver: University of British Columbia Library, 1992; and Lang, pp 85, 110, 120, 131, and 237.

1916

Rawleigh's 1916 almanac, cook book and medical guide

The 1916 issue is the earliest known Canadian-published Rawleigh almanac cookbook. There were earlier editions published in the United States. Although the company's first Canadian factory opened in Winnipeg in 1912, it was not until 17 August 1915 that the W.T. Rawleigh Co. Ltd was incorporated in Canada. For later almanac cookbooks, some of which were also published in French, see: M33.1, for 1919; O472.1, 1921; O490.1, 1922; O508.1, 1923; O525.1, 1924; O552.1, 1925; Q155.1, 1926; Q163.1, 1927; Q168.1, 1928; Q175.1, 1929; Q188.1, 1930; Q197.1, 1931; Q206.1, 1932; Q213.1, 1933; Q230.1, 1935; Q239.1, 1936; Q245.1, 1937; Q250.1, 1938; Q260.1, 1939; Q269.1, 1940; Q274.1, 1941; Q281.1, 1942; Q286.1, 1943; Q288.1, 1944; Q301.1, 1946; Q313.1, 1948; and Q317.1, 1949. There were also issues in the 1950s: 1950 (AEUCHV, ARDA, BDEM, OTUTF uncat patent medicine); 1951 (OKQ); 1952 (AEUCHV); 1953 (OONL); 1954 (BVIPM, OWTU); 1955 (OONL); 1956 (OGU, OONL); 1957 (OONL); 1958 (Private collection); and 1959 (Private collection). Also published by Rawleigh are Q157.1, Rawleigh Recipe Book, and Q280.1, Rawleigh's Consumers Catalog with Cooking Recipes.

Since Rawleigh's first Canadian factory opened in Winnipeg, entries for the earliest almanac cookbooks are in the Manitoba section of this bibliography. Those for 1921–5 are in the Ontario section because 'London' is in the largest typeface in the imprints. The Montreal factory opened in 1926; almanac cookbooks from 1926 onward are in the Quebec section because, in their imprints, 'Montreal' is either the first city recorded or in the largest typeface. The company's history is recounted in Q260.1, the fiftieth anniversary issue.

M22.1   1916
27th year / Rawleigh's / Trade mark / 1916 / almanac, cook book / and medical guide / Published annually for gratuitous distribution / into rural homes throughout North America. / [caption:] Hon. W.T. Rawleigh / President and founder / Printed in Canada for / the W.T. Rawleigh Co., Ltd. / Hamilton – Winnipeg – Toronto / Freeport Memphis Chester Oakland
DESCRIPTION: 22.0 × 14.5 cm   Pp [1] 2–67 [68]   Tp illus portrait of W.T. Rawleigh, illus   Paper, with image on front of a mother holding a baby; stapled, and with hole punched at top left corner for hanging
CONTENTS: 1 tp; 2 'A Country Girl's Creed'; 3–68 monthly calendars for 1916, astrological and weather information, publ ads, health care, and recipes
COPIES: *AEEA
NOTES: In the title, '27th year' refers to the number of years in business since Rawleigh started selling products in 1889. The AEEA copy is stamped on the outside back face of the binding, under 'Compliments of': 'A.L. Briggs // The Rawleigh Man // Shepard, Alta.'

M22.2
—[French-language edition, *Rawleigh's almanach, livre de cuisine et guide medical*, Hamilton [etc.]: W.T. Rawleigh, 1916]
COPIES: OKQ (F5012 1916 R258)

AMERICAN EDITIONS: *Rawleigh's 1916 Almanac Cook Book and Medical Guide* (Dickinson, p 149, illus p 150).

1916–20

Norwood Methodist souvenir cook book

M23.1   nd [about 1916–20]
Norwood Methodist / souvenir / cook book / Prepared by / the Ladies' Aid [cover-title]
COPIES: *Private collection
NOTES: The owner reports that the book dates from when her grandfather, Thomas Neville, was pastor at Norwood Methodist Church. Reverend Neville is listed in the book. He was at Norwood, Manitoba, from 1916 to 1920 (Douglas Walkington, *Methodist Ministers in Canada, 1903–1925*, Toronto: United Church of Canada Archives, nd [198–]).

1917

[Title unknown]

M24.1 [1917]

[Cover-title lacking?; running head: 'The Red Cross Cook Book']

DESCRIPTION: 22.0 × 14.5 cm   Pp [i], [1] 2–101, [i] Lacks binding; stapled

CONTENTS: i 'Index' [i.e., table of contents] printed in blue; 1 'To the ladies of Reston and vicinity and the enterprising business men whose kindness and co-operation made this publication possible, this book is respectfully decicated [sic]. Mrs. Thomas Mutter. Mrs. Colin C. Campbell. Miss Raechel [sic] Guthrie.' and untitled verse; 2–top 100 recipes credited with the name of the contributor and ads; near top 100–101 'Household Hints'; i ad

COPIES: *Private collection

NOTES: The book was a fund-raiser for the Red Cross. An advertisement on p 65 for a '1917 Ford Touring Car' and an advertisement on p 91 that gives an insurance company's statement for 'year ending December 31st 1916' indicate that the book was published in 1917. Page 2 begins with a mock recipe for 'How to Cook Husbands to Make Them Tender and Good.' Unusually, the odd-numbered pages are versos and the even-numbered pages, rectos.

Crawford, Miss Elizabeth

Elizabeth Crawford likely emigrated to Canada from Britain. Her National Union Cookery Diploma was a British qualification conferred by the Northern Union of Training Schools of Cookery. This institution was founded in 1876 by the Liverpool School of Cookery and other cookery schools in the north of England and Scotland to set a uniform standard for teacher training.

For other culinary titles in the Manitoba Farmers' Library, see: M26.1, Lee, Charles Henry, and Miss R.M. Atkinson, Canning by the Cold Pack Method; M27.1, Neilson, James A., V.W. Jackson, and Miss Ethel M. Eadie, The Potato; M28.1, Villeneuve, I., Cheese-Making on the Farm; M31.1, Neilson, James A., and Miss Ethel M. Eadie, Asparagus; M32.1, MacDougall, Miss Helen, Practical Cookery; M40.1, Brown, Reuben Wesley, Home Cheese Making; M42.1, Sommerfeld, H.B., The Beef Ring; and M50.1, Manitoba, Department of Agriculture and Immigration, Canning, Pickling and Preserving.

M25.1   July 1917

Manitoba Farmers' Library / Published monthly by the Manitoba Department of Agriculture and Immigration / Winnipeg, Canada, July, 1917 / The Manitoba Farmers' Library is devoted to the extension of information on agri- / cultural and sanitary matters, and is distributed free among the people of Manitoba / who make application for it. Request to have one's name entered on the mailing / list should be addressed to the Publications Branch, Department of Agriculture, / Winnipeg. If any particular bulletin is wanted, ask for it as Extension Bulletin / No. ... / Extension Bulletin No. 16 / Cookery recipes / Compiled by / Miss Elizabeth Crawford / (holder of National Union Cookery Diploma) / Cookery Demonstrator, / Extension Service, Manitoba Agricultural College, / Winnipeg, Manitoba. / Published by authority of Hon. Valentine Winkler, Minister of Agriculture and Immigration [cover-title]

DESCRIPTION: 22.0 × 15.0 cm   Pp [1–3] 4–53 [54–5] Paper, with image on front of utensils and ingredients on a kitchen table; stapled

CONTENTS: 1 cover-title; 2 'Introduction'; 3–53 recipes; 54–5 index

COPIES: *MWP

NOTES: The 'Introduction' states, 'The continuous demand upon the Manitoba Agricultural College for these recipes, many of which have been demonstrated by the author before audiences of Manitoba women, is the reason for publishing them in bulletin form.' The basic ingredients of the recipes 'are [those] largely produced by Manitoba farms and gardens.'

Lee, Charles Henry, and Miss R.M. Atkinson

For other culinary titles in the Manitoba Farmers' Library, see M25.1. C.H. Lee was also a co-author of M50.1 in the same series.

M26.1   2nd ed., June 1917

Manitoba Farmers' Library / Published monthly by the Manitoba Department of Agriculture and Immigration / Winnipeg, Canada, March, 1917. / (Revised and enlarged June, 1917.) / The Manitoba Farmers' Library is devoted to the extension of information on / agricultural and sanitary matters, and is distributed free among the people of / Manitoba who make application for it. Request to have one's name entered on / the mailing list

should be addressed to the Publications Branch, Department of / Agriculture, Winnipeg. If any particular bulletin is wanted, ask for it as / Extension Bulletin No. ... / Extension Bulletin No. 12 – (Second edition). / Canning / by the / cold pack method / [caption:] Peas, beans, corn, carrots and cauliflower as canned at Manitoba Agricultural College. / C.H. Lee, / Professor of Bacteriology / Manitoba Agricultural College / and / Miss R.M. Atkinson, / of the Extension Service. / Published by authority of Hon. Valentine Winkler, Minister of Agriculture and Immigration, / and Hon. R.S. Thornton, Minister of Education. [cover-title]
DESCRIPTION: 22.0 × 15.0 cm   Pp [1–7] 8–31   Many illus of preserving equipment   Paper, with image on front of five jars of vegetables; stapled
CONTENTS: 1 cover-title; 2 fp illus of canning utensils; 3 'Introduction'; 4 fp illus of a 'home-made canning outfit'; 5 'Leading Points'; 6 'Fruit and Vegetable Canning Chart'; 7–31 text
COPIES: *MWP
NOTES: The book presents instructions for preserving vegetables, fruits, and meats in jars and cans.

M26.2   3rd ed., August 1918
— Manitoba Farmers' Library / Published monthly by the Manitoba Department of Agriculture and Immigration / Winnipeg, Canada, March, 1917 / Reprinted, August, 1918 / The Manitoba Farmers' Library is devoted to the extension of information on / agricultural and sanitary matters, and is distributed free among the people of Manitoba / who make application for it. Request to have one's name entered on the mailing list / should be addressed to the Publications Branch, Department of Agriculture, Winnipeg. / If any particular bulletin is wanted, ask for it as Extension Bulletin No. ... / Extension Bulletin No. 12 – (Third edition) / Canning / by the / cold pack method / [caption:] Peas, beans, corn, carrots and cauliflower as canned at Manitoba Agricultural College / C.H. Lee / Professor of Bacteriology / Manitoba Agricultural College / and / Miss Helen MacDougall / of the Extension Service / Published by authority of Hon. Valentine Winkler, Minister of Agriculture and Immigration [cover-title]
COPIES: *OGU (Rural Heritage Collection)
NOTES: In this edition Helen MacDougall is credited, not R.M. Atkinson. See also M32.1, by MacDougall, in the same series.

Neilson, James A., V.W. Jackson, and Miss Ethel M. Eadie

For other culinary titles in the Manitoba Farmers' Library, see M25.1.

M27.1   May 1917
Manitoba Farmers' Library / Published monthly by the Manitoba Department of Agriculture and Immigration / Volume II Winnipeg, Canada, May 1917 No. 5 / The Manitoba Farmers' Library is devoted to the extension of information on agricul- / tural and sanitary matters, and is distributed free among the people of Manitoba / who make application for it. Request to have one's name entered on the mailing list / should be addressed to the Publications Branch, Department of Agriculture, Winnipeg. / If any particular bulletin is wanted, ask for it as Extension Bulletin No. ... / Extension Bulletin No. 14 / The potato / [caption:] A model type of tuber / Part I – Potato growing and storing – J.A. Neilson, B.S.A., Lecturer, Horticultural Dept. / Part II – Potato diseases in Manitoba – V.W. Jackson, B.A., Professor of Botany. / Part III – Potatoes as food – Miss Ethel M. Eadie, / Professor of Household Science. / Manitoba Agricultural College / Winnipeg, Manitoba / Published by authority of Hon. Valentine Winkler, Minister of Agriculture and Immigration. [cover-title]
DESCRIPTION: 22.5 × 15.0 cm   Pp [1–5] 6–27   14 numbered illus   Paper, with image on front of a potato; stapled
CONTENTS: 1 cover-title; 2 letter from J.B. Reynolds, president, Manitoba Agricultural College, to Valentine Winkler, minister of agriculture and immigration, 17 April 1917; 3–4 'Leading Points'; 5–16 'Part I Potato Growing and Storing by J.A. Neilson'; 17–24 'Part II Potato Diseases in Manitoba by Prof. V.W. Jackson'; 25–7 'Part III Potatoes as Food by Miss Ethel M. Eadie'
COPIES: *MWP

Villeneuve, I.

For other culinary titles in the Manitoba Farmers' Library, see M25.1.

M28.1   November 1917
Manitoba Farmers' Library / Published monthly by the Manitoba Department of Agriculture and Immigration / Winnipeg, Canada, November, 1917. / The Manitoba Farmers' Library is devoted to the

extension of information / on agricultural and sanitary matters, and is distributed free among the / people of Manitoba who make application for it. Request to have one's / name entered on the mailing list should be addressed to the Publications / Branch, Department of Agriculture, Winnipeg. If any particular bulletin / is wanted, ask for it as Extension Bulletin No. ... / Extension Bulletin No. 20. / Cheese-making on the / farm / (with especial reference to the making of soft cheese for war-time consumption) / By / I. Villeneuve, / Instructor in Cheese Making. / Dairy Branch, Dept. of Agriculture, / Winnipeg, Manitoba. / Published by authority of Hon. Valentine Winkler, Minister of Agriculture and Immigration, [sic] [cover-title]
DESCRIPTION: 22.5 × 15.0 cm   Pp [1–2] 3–19   Illus   Paper, with image on front of stacked wheels of cheese; stapled
CONTENTS: 1 cover-title; mid 2 'Economy of Cheese in the Dietary'; bottom 2–3 'Some Essentials'; 4–top 8 'Fancy Skim-Milk Cheese'; mid 8–mid 10 'Coulommier Cheese'; mid 10–mid 14 'Cream Cheese'; mid 14–16 'Cheddar Cheese Making on the Farm'; top–mid 17 'Buttermilk Cottage Cheese'; bottom 17–18 'Neufchatel Cheese'; 19 'Cottage Cheese'
CITATIONS: Driver 2003, 'Canadian Cookbooks,' p 37
COPIES: *MWP

M28.2   February 1918
—Edition française février, 1918 / Département d'agriculture, Manitoba / Fabrication du fromage / à la ferme / (avec explication spéciale sur la fabrication des fromages mous pour la consommation / en temps de guerre) / Traduction du bulletin anglais no 20 / Par / I. Villeneuve / professeur pour la fabrication du fromage / Branche de l'industrie laitière / Département d'agriculture / Winnipeg, Manitoba / Publié par ordre de l'hon. Valentine Winkler, ministre d'agriculture et d'immigration [cover-title]
DESCRIPTION: 22.5 × 15.0 cm   Pp [1–2] 3–19   9 numbered illus   Paper, with image on front of stacked wheels of cheese; stapled
CONTENTS: 1 cover-title; top 2 'Utilité du fromage dans l'économie domestique'; bottom 2–3 'Points importants'; 4–7 'Fromage de lait écrémé délicieux'; 8–mid 10 'Fromage de Coulommiers'; mid 10–top 14 'Fromage à la crème'; mid 14–mid 16 'Fromage Cheddar fabriqué à la ferme'; mid 16–mid 17 'Fromage "cottage" obtenu du lait de beurre'; mid 17–mid 18 'Fromage de Neufchâtel (Van Slyke & Publow)'; mid 18–19 'Fromage cottage'
COPIES: *MWP

M28.3   4th ed., April 1935
—Price of this bulletin for distribution outside Manitoba, ten cents per copy. / Manitoba Farmers' Library / Published by the Manitoba Department of Agriculture and Immigration. / Winnipeg, Canada, April, 1935 / The Manitoba Farmers' Library is a series of bulletins that are devoted / to the extension of information on agricultural and home economics / subjects, and that are distributed free among the people of Manitoba / who make application for them. All requests should be addressed to: / The Publications Branch, Department of Agriculture, Winnipeg. / Extension Bulletin No. 20. – Fourth edition / Cheese-making / on the farm / By / I. Villeneuve / Instructor in Cheese Making / Dairy Branch, Department of Agriculture / Winnipeg, Manitoba / Published by authority of Hon. D.G. McKenzie, Minister of Agriculture / and Immigration. [cover-title]
DESCRIPTION: 23.0 × 15.0 cm   Pp [1] 2–15   9 numbered illus   Paper, with image on front of stacked wheels of cheese; stapled
CONTENTS: 1 cover-title; top 2 'The Food Value of Cheese'; mid 2–top 3 'Some Essentials'; mid 3–6 'Skim-Milk Cheese'; 7–mid 8 'Manitoba Soft Cheese'; bottom 8–11 'Cream Cheese'; 12–13 'Cheddar Cheese-Making on the Farm'; 14 'Neufchatel Cheese (Van Slyke and Publow)'; 15 'Cottage Cheese' and 'Preparing Cheddar Cheese for Sandwiches'
COPIES: *MWP
NOTES: The following message is stamped on the binding: 'Please // Do not throw this away; if of no value to you, pass on to someone else who may be interested in the subject.'

1917–18

War recipes

M29.1   nd [about July 1917–11 November 1918]
War recipes / These recipes have been collected by the members of the Juvenile / "Prisoners of War" Club, under the auspices of the Sir Edward Grey / Chapter, I.O.D.E. All proceeds will be used for comforts / for Canadian Prisoners of War. / Price 25 cents [cover-title]
DESCRIPTION: 23.0 × 15.0 cm   [4 leaves printed on rectos only]   Thin card, with plate mounted on front of head-and-shoulders portrait of Currie with caption: 'General Sir Arthur Currie // Commander of the Canadian Forces in France // Sir Arthur went to France with the original Canadian contingent, and

has had a part in all the principal engagements of the Corps. He is the first Canadian to be given the Chief Command of the Canadian forces.'; bound at top edge by a cord through two punched holes

CONTENTS: 1–4 recipes credited with the name of the contributor for 'Bread,' 'Soups,' 'Savories,' 'Fish,' 'Meat Substitutes,' 'Puddings,' 'Cakes and Buns,' and 'Potato Recipes'

COPIES: *Private collection

NOTES: Arthur William Currie became head of the famed Canadian Corps on 9 June 1917 and was knighted in the field in the same month. The cookbook was published after these events and before the end of the war, on 11 November 1918. The text is printed in dark brown on light brown paper. The location of the Sir Edward Grey Chapter is not given in the book, but it was organized in Winnipeg, in 1914, and disbanded in 1967.

1917–20

Knox Church cook book

For a history of the church, see A Celebration of People: 125 Years, 1868 1993, Knox United, Winnipeg, [Winnipeg: Printed by Christian Press].

M30.1   nd [about 1917–20]
Knox / Church / cook / book [cover-title]
DESCRIPTION: 17.0 × 13.0 cm   Pp [1–4] 5–96   1 pl opp p 2 of Knox Church; 1 pl opp inside back face of binding of an illustrated publ ad for Royal Crown Soaps Ltd, Winnipeg   Cloth
CONTENTS: 1 'Preface' signed Mrs George Bryce; 2 blank; 3 'Index' [i.e., table of contents]; 4 'Grace before Dinner' by Burns and eight other verses by Shakespeare, Cowper, Dryden (two), Wm King, Massinger, B. Franklyn, and one unattributed; 5–84 recipes credited with the name of the contributor; 85–8 'Hints' and ad; 89–96 ads
COPIES: *MWMM
NOTES: Knox Presbyterian Church, which became Knox United Church in 1925, had its beginnings in 1868. The construction of its current home – the imposing structure at 400 Edmonton Street, illustrated in the cookbook – started in 1914 and the opening service was in March 1917. The cookbook was published after completion of the new building, about 1917–20 from appearances.

In the 'Preface' Mrs George Bryce (née Marion Samuel) says that the book was 'published under the

auspices of the ladies of Knox Presbyterian Church, Winnipeg,' and 'contains about 600 well selected cooking recipes.' She then comments: 'The fear has been expressed perhaps selfishly that the present expansion of women's education and the study she is making of public questions might militate against the comforts of home life; but so far, this case against the cultivated women has not been proven.' She goes on to discuss the developing relationship of science to housekeeping and the resulting demand for new books and new ideas in cooking. The Bryces were prominent members of the community. She was vice-president of the Local Council of Women and president of the Women's Christian Temperance Union in Winnipeg. Dr Bryce organized Knox Church and served as its first minister, and in 1902 became moderator of the General Assembly of the Presbyterian Church in Canada. He helped to established Manitoba College and the University of Manitoba.

1918

The 'home queen' World's Fair souvenir cook book

This 1893 American cookbook was offered as a premium by Royal Crown Soaps in 1918; see B2.1 for comment.

Neilson, James A., and Miss Ethel M. Eadie

For other culinary titles in the Manitoba Farmers' Library, see M25.1.

M31.1   January 1918
Manitoba Farmers' Library / Published monthly by the Manitoba Department of Agriculture and Immigration. / Winnipeg, Canada, January, 1918 / The Manitoba Farmers' Library is devoted to the extension of information / on agricultural and sanitary matters, and is distributed free among the / people of Manitoba who make application for it. Request to have one's / name entered on the mailing list should be addressed to the Publications / Branch, Department of Agriculture, Winnipeg. If any particular bulletin is / wanted, ask for it as Extension Bulletin No. ... / Extension Bulletin No. 22 / Asparagus / [caption:] Ready for market. / Part I – Asparagus culture – J.A. Neilson, B.S.A., Lecturer in Horticulture. / Part II – Preparation and use of asparagus – Miss E.M. Eadie, / Professor of

Household Science. / Manitoba Agricultural College, / Winnipeg, Man. / Published by authority of Hon. Valentine Winkler, Minister of Agriculture and Immigration. [cover-title]

DESCRIPTION: 22.5 × 15.0 cm   Pp [1–3] 4–15   Illus Paper, with image on front of a bunch of asparagus; stapled

CONTENTS: 1 cover-title; 2 'Leading Points'; 3–13 'Part I Asparagus Culture by Jas. Neilson, B.S.A., Lecturer in Horticulture, Manitoba Agricultural College'; 14–15 'Part II Preparation and Use of Asparagus by Miss E.M. Eadie, Professor of Household Science, Manitoba Agricultural College' (recipes for Sauce for Vegetables, Cream of Asparagus Soup, For a Salad, Boiled Dressing, and Drying)

COPIES: *MWP

1919

MacDougall, Miss Helen

For other culinary titles in the Manitoba Farmers' Library, see M25.1. MacDougall is credited as the author of the third edition of Canning by the Cold Pack Method, *M26.2.*

M32.1   May 1919

Manitoba Farmers' Library / Published monthly by the Manitoba Department of Agriculture and Immigration / Winnipeg, Canada, May, 1919. / The Manitoba Farmers' Library is devoted to the extension of information on / agricultural and sanitary matters, and is distributed free among the people of / Manitoba who make application for it. Request to have one's name entered on / the mailing list should be addressed to the Publications Branch, Department of / Agriculture, Winnipeg. If any particular bulletin is wanted, ask for it as / Extension Bulletin No. ... / Extension Bulletin No. 38 / Practical cookery / Miss Helen MacDougall / Agricultural Extension Service / Department of Agriculture / Winnipeg, Manitoba. / Published by authority of Hon. Valentine Winkler, Minister of Agriculture and Immigration [cover-title]

DESCRIPTION: 22.5 × 15.0 cm   Pp [1] 2–71   Paper, with still-life on front of a loaf of bread, muffins, cookies(?), and a bowl of porridge(?); stapled

CONTENTS: 1 cover-title; 2 'Abbreviations,' 'Table of Measurements,' and 'Approximate Measure of One Pound'; 3–4 'How to Select Foods'; 5–69 recipes; 70–1 index

COPIES: *MWP

M32.2   2nd ed., August 1923

—Price of this bulletin for distribution outside Manitoba: Twenty cents per copy / Manitoba Farmers' Library / Published by the Manitoba Department of Agriculture and Immigration / Winnipeg, Canada, May, 1919 / Revised and reprinted, August, 1923 / The Manitoba Farmers' Library is a series of bulletins that are devoted to the / extension of information on agricultural and home economics subjects, and / that are distributed free among the people of Manitoba who make application / for them. If any particular bulletin is wanted, ask for it as Extension Bulletin / No. ... All requests should be addressed to: / The Publications Branch, Department of Agriculture, Winnipeg / Extension Bulletin No. 38 – Second edition / Practical cookery / Department of Agriculture / Winnipeg, Manitoba. / Published by authority of Hon. Neil Cameron, Minister of Agriculture and Immigration. [cover-title]

DESCRIPTION: 22.5 × 15.0 cm   Pp [1] 2–71   Illus Paper, with still-life on front of a loaf of bread, muffins, cookies(?), and a bowl of porridge(?); stapled

CONTENTS: 1 cover-title; 2 'Abbreviations,' 'Table of Measurements,' and 'Approximate Measure of One Pound'; 3–4 'How to Select Foods'; 5–69 recipes; 70–1 index

COPIES: *MSM

NOTES: Helen MacDougall is not identified as the author in this edition.

M32.3   3rd ed., 1926

—[Third edition of *Practical Cookery*, Extension Bulletin 38, 1926]

COPIES: Private collection

Rawleigh's almanac cook book and guide to health 1919

For information about Rawleigh's annual almanac cookbooks and other publications, see M22.1.

M33.1   1919

Rawleigh's / Trade mark / almanac / cook book and / guide to health / W.T. Rawleigh / President & founder / 1919 / The W.T. Rawleigh Co Ltd. / Winnipeg Toronto / Canada / Freeport Memphis Chester / Oakland Minneapolis USA / Our 30th year

DESCRIPTION: 22.0 × 14.5 cm   Pp [1–2] 3–64   Tp illus portrait of W.T. Rawleigh; illus col on inside front face of binding of 'Rawleigh Factories & Branches';

illus   Paper, with image on front of a boy with dog and a girl with doll, consulting this edition of the almanac cookbook; stapled, and with hole punched at top left corner for hanging

CONTENTS: 1 tp; 2 'The W.T. Rawleigh Co.'; 3 'Almanac Calculations'; 4 'Jan' [sic]; 5 'February'; 6 'March'; 7 'April'; 8 'May'; 9 'June'; 10 'July'; 11 'August'; 12 'September'; 13 'October'; 14 'November'; 15 'December'; 16 'Eclipses for 1919 and Other Astronomical Information'; 17 'Rawleigh Service Direct to You'; 18 'Good Health // How to Obtain It by Wholesome Food // Fresh Air, Exercise, Rest & Baths'; 19 'Wholesome Food'; 20 'Fresh Air, Ventilation and Rest'; 21 'Baths and Exercise'; 22–3 'A Study of Foods' and on p 23, 'How to Make Lye Hominy'; 24–6 'Meatless Cookery for Health and Economy'; 27 'Spices'; 28–9 'Extracts and Flavors'; 30 'Substitutes for Wheat Flour'; 31–4 [lacking in private collector's copy]; 35–6 information about feeding babies and children; 37–8 'Thin and Fat Persons'; 39 'Constipation // Its Cause, Effect and Correctives'; 40 'The Blood'; 41–3 'Common Diseases & Ailments'; 44–5 'Making Fluid Extracts and Tinctures'; 46–7 'Salves, Ointments and Pomades'; 48–9 'Liniment // Anti-Pain Oil // Camphor Balm'; 50 'Dental Hygiene'; 51 'Toilet Helps'; 52–3 'Making Toilet Articles at Rawleigh's Factories'; 54–5 'Making Toilet Soap'; 56 'Of Particular Interest to Stock and Poultry Raisers'; 57 'The Largest Line // The Best Products // Superior Service'; 58 'Some Startling Facts about Loss // Human Life & Animal Life'; 59 'How to Choose Dips & Disinfectants'; 60 'Making Rawleigh's Dip and Disinfectant'; 61 'Insecticides and Fungicides'; 62–3 'Poultry Raising'; 64 list of products and customer's account forms

COPIES: MSOHM   OHMB (Serial)   *Private collection

NOTES: A footnote on p 24 says that the meatless recipes are from 'New Cookery – Lenna F. Cooper – Sanatarium, B.C.' Before the publication of the almanac cookbook in 1919 there were at least three editions of *The New Cookery*, by Lenna Frances Cooper (1884–), including: Battle Creek: Good Health Publishing Co., [copyright 1913], and third edition, [copyright 1916], by the same publisher (both, United States: DLC).

There are comments about 'Drinking Ice Water' on p 9, and about 'Proper Food of Utmost Importance' on p 12. According to p 28, flavours made without alcohol and sold in tubes were introduced by the company in 1917; the US government had specified non-alcoholic flavours for the army and for Indian Reservations.

On the title-page, the first two digits of the year 1919 are to the left of the imprint, and the second two digits are to the right of the imprint.

1920

Meat and its substitutes

M34.1   nd [about 1920]
Circular No. 10 Extension Service / Meat and its / substitutes / Extension Service / Manitoba Agricultural College / Winnipeg, Canada / Published by the authority of Hon. Valentine Winkler, Minister of Agriculture [cover-title]
DESCRIPTION: 23.0 × 15.0 cm   Pp [1–3] 4–14   Illus on outside back face of binding of cuts of beef   Paper, with image on front of cuts of meat on a butcher's block; stapled
CONTENTS: 1 cover-title; 2 list of 'Home Economics Literature' free from Extension Service of Manitoba Agricultural College; 3–mid 4 'General Rules for Meat'; mid–bottom 4 'Cooking of Tough Meats'; 5–mid 6 recipes; mid–bottom 6 'Made-Over Meat Dishes'; 7–mid 8 recipes; mid 8–mid 9 recipes for 'Meat Substitutes' [e.g., Walnut Sausages and other nut- and bean-based dishes]; bottom 9–mid 11 'Eggs'; mid 11–top 13 'Cheese'; mid 13–14 'Cuts of Meat and Their Uses'; inside back face of binding list of bulletins and circulars from Manitoba Agricultural College
COPIES: *MWP
NOTES: Valentine Winkler served as minister of agriculture from 15 May 1915 to 7 June 1920. The appearance of the booklet suggests a publication date of about 1920.

1920–5

A world of useful information in a nutshell

M35.1   nd [about 1920–5]
A world of useful / information in / a nutshell
DESCRIPTION: 21.5 × 14.0 cm   Pp [1–6] 7–93 [94–6]   Paper; stapled
CONTENTS: 1 tp; 2 blank; 3 table of contents; 4 blank; 5–16 Chapter I, 'Budgeting and Marketing'; 17–40 Chapter II, 'Cooking Secrets'; 41–50 Chapter III, 'Plain Sewing'; 51–8 Chapter IV, 'Hygiene in the Home'; 59–78 Chapter V, 'Health and Beauty'; 79–93 Chapter VI, 'Hints on the Mental Care of Children'; 94–6 blank for 'Memoranda' and at bottom p 96, 'Stovel Company Limited Winnipeg'
COPIES: *Private collection

NOTES: 'The Western Home Monthly' is printed on the front face of the binding. The book was published before *Western Home Monthly* was renamed *National Home Monthly* in October 1932, and not long after the end of the First World War, as the text on p 19 reveals: 'Gauffres [one of 'Ten Famous Recipes'] // an unusual tea or supper cake ... Many whose fortunes placed them around Brussels after the Armistice will recall them with delight, for they were generally obtainable in estaminets and various popular haunts.'

1921

Better baking

The J.R. Watkins Co. was established in Winona, Minnesota, in 1868. The company made flavourings, baking powder, spices, and other food products, which were sold door-to-door. See also: Q147.1, Watkins Cook Book; NP14.1, Watkins 1868 1937 Almanac Home Book; and Q298.1, Allen, Elaine, Watkins Salad Book.

M36.1   nd [about 1921]
Better / baking / The J.R. Watkins Company / Winona, Minnesota, U.S.A. / New York Memphis San Francisco Winnipeg Hamilton [cover-title]
DESCRIPTION: 12.5 × 20.0 cm   Pp 1–16   2 double-sided pls col, small illus   Paper, with image on front of a woman adding baking powder to a bowl, and in the foreground, a large container of Watkins Baking Powder; stapled
CONTENTS: 1 'Watkins Baking Powder'; 2–3 'A.B.C. of Cake Making'; 4–15 recipes; 16 list of Watkins products
COPIES: *Private collection
NOTES: There are colour illustrations of the company's factories in various cities on the inside front and back faces of the binding. According to p 3, the recipes in this booklet were 'prepared ... by the eminent culinary authority, Marian Cole Fisher, ...' Fisher was an American domestic science teacher and cookbook author.

The only Canadian place-names in the imprint are Winnipeg and Hamilton; therefore, *Better Baking* was published before Q147.1, *Watkins Cook Book* of 1925, where Montreal is the first recorded Canadian city in the imprint, before Hamilton, Winnipeg, and Vancouver. *Better Baking* was likely published before the first listing for J.R. Watkins Co. in Montreal city directories in the volume for 1922–3. The company is listed in the Winnipeg and Hamilton city directories for 1921.

1922

Hiltz, Miss Mary Catherine (1890–), and Miss Mary Caroline Moxon

Both Hiltz and Moxon were from Nova Scotia. A photograph of the two women, in a faculty group picture, is in Ec-Ho: Home Economics Annual – 1950, University of Manitoba, 1950, p 8. Both were founding members of the Canadian Home Economics Association in 1939 (We Are Tomorrow's Past, pp 3–5).

Mary Hiltz was a native of Dartmouth. After teaching school for over four years at Mill Village and Dartmouth, she took a one-year course at the Macdonald Institute in Guelph, Ontario, earning a Household Science Teacher Certificate in June 1914 (Entrance Record, Registration No. 1866, at OGU). She then taught at Kamsack High School in Saskatchewan and worked for the Saskatchewan Department of Education as an itinerant teacher of home economics, mainly in non-English-speaking school districts (see Peterat/DeZwart, pp 55–6, regarding Hiltz's work in the Ruthenian settlements, establishing hot-lunch programs as a means of cultural transmission). After receiving her BS degree in 1920 from Teachers College, Columbia University, New York, she joined the Department of Household Science at the Manitoba Agricultural College. She retired from the University of Manitoba in 1955.

Mary Moxon was from Truro. After a two-year course at the Macdonald Institute in Guelph, she graduated with a Domestic Science Teacher Certificate in June 1916, with the highest standing of any student to date (Entrance Record, Registration No. 2004, notes her marks). She taught at the high school in Truro and was an instructor in household science at Truro's Normal College. In 1919 she began teaching at the Manitoba Agricultural College. She helped to revise the public school home economics curriculum for the Manitoba Department of Education. She retired in 1952.

Also by Hiltz are M96.1, Prezervovannia ovochiv i iaryn, and M107.1, Low Cost Recipes. She contributed to M114.1, University of Manitoba, with Manitoba Department of Mines and Natural Resources, The Commercial and Home-Canning Possibilities of Mullets. See also M50.1, Manitoba, Department of Agriculture, Canning, Pickling and Preserving, 'revised from former editions by Miss Mary C. Hiltz ... and C.H. Lee.' Hiltz, with others, 'judged and approved' the recipes in O898.1, 43 Prize Winning Recipes, for Swift Canadian Co. Hiltz and Moxon assisted in the preparation of M7.6, the 1932 edition of Blue Ribbon Cook Book.

For articles about Hiltz and Moxon when they joined

the Manitoba Agricultural College, see the college journal Managra *Vol. 13, No. 1 (November 1919), p 28, for Moxon (includes her photograph), and Vol. 14, No. 1 (November 1920), p 34, for Hiltz.*

M37.1 1922
The country cook / or / the M.A.C. cook book / Edited and compiled by / Mary C. Hiltz, B.S. / Professor of Household Science / Manitoba Agricultural College / and / Mary C. Moxon / Lecturer in Household Science / Manitoba Agricultural College / The Grain Growers' Guide Limited / Winnipeg, Canada / 1922
DESCRIPTION: 19.0 × 14.0 cm   Pp [1–4] 5–128   Cloth
CONTENTS: 1 tp; 2 'Copyright, Canada, 1922 by the Grain Growers' Guide Limited'; 3 'Foreword' signed Mrs Mary L. Kelso Guild, director of home economics, Manitoba Agricultural College; 4 blank; 5–9 table of contents; 10 abbreviations, and weights and measures; 11–128 recipes
CITATIONS: Driver 2003, 'Canadian Cookbooks,' p 38 O'Neill (unpublished)
COPIES: MCM   *OGU (UA s043 b30); Great Britain: LB (7943.t.23 destroyed)
NOTES: There is a chapter of 'Recipes for Fifty Servings.' Only the first edition was called *The Country Cook*; then the sub-title became the main title until 1941, when the book was renamed *Home Economics Cook Book (Canada)*.

M37.2 1924
—[An edition of *The M.A.C. Cook Book*, Manitoba Agricultural College, 1924]
CITATIONS: AbCat April 1976

M37.3 [3rd ed.], 1926
—The / M.A.C. cook book / Edited and compiled by / Mary C. Hiltz, B.S. / Professor of Nutrition / Manitoba Agricultural College / and / Mary C. Moxon, Ph.B. / Lecturer in Home Economics / Manitoba Agricultural College / Published by / the M.A.C. Co-operative Association Limited / Manitoba Agricultural College, / Winnipeg. / 1926
DESCRIPTION: 18.5 × 13.5 cm   Pp [1–4] 5–128   Cloth
CONTENTS: 1 tp; 2 'Third edition, (revised). Copyright, Canada, 1926, The M.A.C. Co-operative Association Limited Man Agr. College, Winnipeg.'; 3 'Foreword' signed Mrs Mary L. Kelso Guild, former director of home economics, Manitoba Agricultural College; 4 blank; 5 table of contents; 6–9 index; 10 'Abbreviations,' 'Weights and Measures,' 'Oven Temperatures for Baking Different Products,' and 'Sugar Temperatures'; 11–128 recipes

COPIES: *MWP   OGU (CCC CA2MA U20 26M11) OTUTF (B-12 7859)
NOTES: The MWP copy is stamped on the front endpaper, 'Boys & Girls Clubs // Department of Education.' The OGU copy has a label on the front endpaper identifying the book as used by Irene Campbell Adams, a MAC graduate.

M37.4 [4th ed.], 1929
—The / M.A.C. cook book / Edited and compiled by / Mary C. Hiltz, M.A. / Assistant Professor of Nutrition / Manitoba Agricultural College / and / Mary C. Moxon, Ph.B. / Lecturer in Home Economics / Manitoba Agricultural College / Published by / the M.A.C. Co-operative Association Limited, / Manitoba Agricultural College / Winnipeg. / 1929
DESCRIPTION: 18.5 × 13.5 cm   Pp [1–4] 5–128   Cloth
CONTENTS: 1 tp; 2 'Fourth edition, (revised) Copyright, Canada, 1929, The M.A.C. Co-operative Association Limited Man. Agr. College, Winnipeg'; 3 'Acknowledgements' signed the authors; 4 blank; 5 table of contents; 6–9 index; 10 'Abbreviations,' 'Weights and Measures,' 'Oven Temperatures for Baking Different Products,' and 'Sugar Temperatures'; 11–128 recipes
COPIES: AMHM   *Private collection

M37.5 [5th ed.], 1932
—The / M.A.C. cook book / Edited and compiled by / Mary C. Hiltz, M.A. / Assistant Professor of Foods and Nutrition / Manitoba Agricultural College / and / Mary C. Moxon, Ph.B. / Lecturer in Home Economics / Manitoba Agricultural College / Published by / the M.A.C. Co-operative Association, Limited, / Manitoba Agricultural College, / Winnipeg. / 1932
COPIES: *Private collection
NOTES: The following is on the title-page verso: 'Fifth edition, (revised) Copyright, Canada, 1932, The M.A.C. Co-operative Association Limited, Manitoba Agricultural College, Winnipeg, Manitoba Printed in Canada.' Another private collector reports that she used this edition in the Provincial Normal College in Truro, Nova Scotia, in the 1930s; and another owner of the 1932 edition wrote in a letter of 14 October 1991: 'This was the cookbook required for the "Domestic Science" class at the Provincial Normal College (now the Nova Scotia Teachers' College) in 1940. Am not sure of the number of years it served this purpose, but all teachers (N.S.) of my vintage are familiar with it ... I had really never noticed until now

that our instructions were from a book published in Manitoba!' Neither did she realize that the authors were originally from Nova Scotia.

M37.6 [6th ed.], 1941
—Home economics / cook book / (Canada) / Edited and compiled by / Mary C. Hiltz, B.S., M.A. / Assistant Professor of Foods and Nutrition / University of Manitoba / and / Mary C. Moxon, Ph.B., M.A. / Lecturer in Home Economics / University of Manitoba / Published by / the University of Manitoba / Book Department / Winnipeg / 1941
DESCRIPTION: 18.5 × 13.0 cm   Pp [i–ii], [1–2] 3–145   Cloth
CONTENTS: i tp; ii 'Sixth edition, (revised) Copyright, Canada, 1941 The University of Manitoba Book Department // Winnipeg, Man. Printed in Canada // T.H. Best Printing Co., Limited Toronto, Ont.'; 1 'Preface' signed the authors; 2 blank; 3 table of contents; 4 blank; 5–9 index; 10 'Abbreviations,' 'Weights and Measures,' 'Oven Temperatures for Baking Different Products,' and 'Sugar Temperatures'; 11–145 recipes
CITATIONS: CCat No. 21, p W17
COPIES: *MWU   Private collection
NOTES: In the 'Preface' the authors explain the changes in the sixth edition: '... we have attempted to make a complete revision of the recipes included in The M.A.C. Cook Book. While a new name has been adopted for the book it is hoped that the compilation will be of service to any student of home-making. Only those recipes which seem basic and fundamental will be found here.' The private collector reports that she bought her copy in Truro, Nova Scotia, in 1945.

M37.7 [6th ed.], 1947
—Home economics / cook book / (Canada) / Edited and compiled by / Mary C. Hiltz, B.S., M.A. / Associate Professor of Foods and Nutrition / University of Manitoba / and / Mary C. Moxon, Ph.B., M.A. / Associate Professor in Home Economics and Education / University of Manitoba / Published by / the University of Manitoba Press / 1947
COPIES: *Private collection
NOTES: The following is on the title-page verso: 'Sixth edition, (revised) Copyright, Canada, 1947 The University of Manitoba Press // Winnipeg, Man. Printed and bouned [sic] in Canada // T.H. Best Printing Co., Limited, Toronto.' The owner used the book in home economics class at the Provincial Normal School in Truro, Nova Scotia, in 1947–8.

M37.8 [7th ed.], 1951
—Home economics / cook book / (Canada) / Edited and compiled by / Mary C. Hiltz, B.S., M.A. / Associate Professor of Foods and Nutrition / University of Manitoba / and / Mary C. Moxon, Ph.B., M.A. / Associate Professor in Home Economics and Education / University of Manitoba / Published by / the University of Manitoba Press / Winnipeg / 1951
DESCRIPTION: 18.5 × 13.5 cm   Pp [i–ii], [1–2] 3–145   Cloth
CONTENTS: i tp; ii 'Seventh edition, copyright, Canada, 1951 The University of Manitoba Press // Winnipeg, Man. Printed and bound in Canada // T.H. Best Printing Co., Limited, Toronto'; 1 'Preface' signed the authors; 2 blank; 3 table of contents; 4 blank; 5–9 'Index'; 10 'Abbreviations,' 'Weights and Measures,' 'Oven Temperatures for Baking Different Products,' and 'Sugar Temperatures'; 11–145 recipes
COPIES: *OONL (TX715.6 H53 1951, 2 copies)
NOTES: OONL copy 2 has its original dust-jacket.

The new hospital cook book

M38.1   nd [about 1922]
The new hospital / cook / book / Compiled by / the Brandon Graduate Nurses / Association
DESCRIPTION: 22.0 × 14.0 cm   Pp [1] 2–116   Paper, with image on front of 'The New Hospital'; stapled, and with hole punched at top left corner for hanging
CONTENTS: 1 tp; 2 ad; 3 untitled introductory text; 4 ads; 5–99 recipes credited with the name of the contributor and ads; 100–7 'Invalid Cooking'; top–mid 108 'Diabetic Recipes'; bottom 108–115 'Useful Household Hints' and ads; 116 ad
CITATIONS: Peel's Bibliography 4565
COPIES: *Private collection
NOTES: The recipes were 'contributed by the members of the Graduate Nurses' Association, Brandon, and their many friends,' according to p 3. The cookbook was likely published in 1922: An advertisement on p 34 suggests that customers buy 'a new 1922 Ford'; and the new, 200-bed, Brandon General Hospital was opened on 11 May 1922 (Madeline H. Perry, *BGH – 100, a History of the Brandon General Hospital, 1883–1983*, Brandon: The Hospital, [1983]). The printer of the cookbook, 'Sun Job Print, Brandon, Man.,' is on the outside back face of the binding.

M38.2   nd [about 1930]
—[Running head and folio:] The hospital cook book 1 / The hospital / cook book / Compiled by / Brandon Graduate Nurses / Association

DESCRIPTION: 22.0 × 14.0 cm   Pp 1–128   Paper, with image on front of the General Hospital, Brandon; stapled

CONTENTS: 1 tp; 2 ad; 3 untitled introductory text; 4 ads; 5–mid 113 recipes credited with the name of the contributor and ads; bottom 113–mid 120 'In-valid Cooking'; mid 120–mid 122 'Liver Recipes in Anaemia'; mid 122–mid 123 'Diabetic Recipes'; bottom 123–125 'Useful Household Hints'; 126–7 blank for 'Memoranda'; 128 ads

CITATIONS: Peel's Bibliography 4565

COPIES: MAUAM   MBDHM   *Private collection

NOTES: According to p 3, 'The receipes [sic] found in this volume have been contributed by the members of the Graduate Nurses' Association, Brandon, and their many friends.'

Speechly, Miss Margaret Mary (21 May 1896, Neston, Cheshire, England–3 June 1990, Winnipeg, Man.)

Margaret Speechly immigrated to Canada with her parents, who settled in Pilot Mound when she was six years old. Educated at Havergal College, Winnipeg, she entered the Manitoba Agricultural College in 1914 and graduated in 1919, with a degree in home economics. She then worked for the Extension Service of the Manitoba Department of Agriculture, organizing boys' and girls' clubs. In 1920, she joined the editorial staff of the Grain Growers' Guide, where she was responsible for the periodical's new, monthly 'Household Numbers,' and she also wrote for the regular numbers (her arrival was announced in 'Bigger and Better: An Enlarged Women's Department and the Guide's New Editor,' 13 October 1920, p 43). In 1922 she produced a compilation of articles from the periodical, M39.1, The Country Homemaker. On 10 September 1924, the monthly Household Number became the Magazine Number, and she was named household editor (with Amy J. Roe). She left the Grain Growers' Guide in 1926 to wed Jack Stansfield, a master registered seed grower in Atwater, Saskatchewan, and moved to that province, where they worked together on the farm and she wrote freelance articles. Upon retirement, they built a house in Fort Garry, south of Winnipeg, where she volunteered for the Consumers' Association of Canada. Among her several awards were the first annual Consumer of the Year award from the Manitoba government in 1985, an Honorary Doctor of Laws Degree from the University of Manitoba in 1977, and the YWCA Woman of the Year Award for community service. She had no children. A friend, Ruth

E. Berry, described her as 'humble and self-effacing but [having] a great sense of humour' (personal communication, August 2002).

Her university-educated mother, Mary, was well known for her work with women's groups in Winnipeg, an early advocate for birth control, and the first woman appointed to the University of Manitoba's Board of Governors. Her father, Harry M. Speechly, was a medical doctor and later provincial coroner. She had two brothers, William Grove and Leslie.

See the Manitoba Agricultural College journal Managra Vol. 12, No. 3 (March 1919), pp 49–50, for Margaret Speechly's entry and photograph, on the occasion of her graduation. Concerning her career at the Grain Growers' Guide, see Angela E. Davis, 'Country Homemakers': A Selection of Letters and Editorials from the Woman's Page of the Grain Growers' Guide 1908–1928, Winnipeg, 1989, pp 3, 35–6, 39–40, 41.

M39.1   1922

The / country homemaker / Edited and compiled / by / Margaret M. Speechly, B.H.Ec. / Associate Editor, The Grain Growers' Guide / The Grain Growers' Guide Limited, / Winnipeg, Canada, / 1922

DESCRIPTION: 19.0 × 14.0 cm   Pp [1–6] 7–132   Illus   Thin card; sewn and glued

CONTENTS: 1 tp; 2 'Copyright, Canada, 1922 by the Grain Grower's [sic] Guide, Limited'; 3 'Index' [i.e., table of contents]; 4 blank; 5 'Introduction' signed the publishers; 6 blank; 7–132 thirty-five chapters organized under headings for 'Clothing,' 'Laundry,' 'Furnishings,' 'Labor Saving,' and 'Miscellaneous'

CITATIONS: Ferguson/Fraser, pp 52 and 54   O'Neill (unpublished)

COPIES: *OONL (TX321 S64 1922); Great Britain: LB (7943.t.24 destroyed)

NOTES: The 'Introduction' explains: 'During the last two years there has been a great demand for the articles which have appeared in the Grain Growers' Guide. We are therefore publishing them in book form and are giving some information about each writer.' Information about each contributor, except for Speechly, follows. Food-related text is in chapters called 'My Labor Saving Kitchen' by Eva Jacobs, 'A Home-Made Dish Drier' and 'The Food Chopper' by Speechly, 'Trying Out Hot Luncheons' [i.e., in schools, not homes] by Mabel E. Finch, and 'Feeding the Threshers' edited by Speechly (Ferguson/Fraser, p 52, quote farm women's suggestions from 'Feeding the Threshers').

1923

Brown, Reuben Wesley

For other culinary titles in the Manitoba Farmers' Library, see M25.1.

M40.1   June 1923
Price of this bulletin for distribution outside Manitoba: Ten cents per copy / Manitoba Farmers' Library / Published by the Manitoba Department of Agriculture and Immigration / Winnipeg, Canada, June, 1923 / The Manitoba Farmers' Library is a series of bulletins that are devoted to the / extension of information on agricultural and home economics subjects, and that / are distributed free among the people of Manitoba who make application for them. / If any particular bulletin is wanted, ask for it as Extension Bulletin No. [blank space] / All requests should be addressed to: / The Publications Branch, Department of Agriculture, Winnipeg / Extension Bulletin No. 72 / Home cheese making / [caption:] Necessary utensils / By R.W. Brown, B.S.A., / Professor of Dairy Husbandry, / Manitoba Agricultural College / Winnipeg, Manitoba / Printed by authority of Hon. Neil Cameron, Minister of Agriculture and Immigration [cover-title]
DESCRIPTION: 22.0 × 15.0 cm   Pp [1–2] 3–15   Illus on p 2 of dairy cattle at waterhole, 7 numbered illus   Paper, with image on front of 'Necessary Utensils'; stapled
CONTENTS: 1 cover-title; 2 illus; 3–11 'Part I. Making of Soft Cheese'; 12–15 'Part II. Gouda Cheese'
COPIES: *MWP
NOTES: Brown writes on p 4: 'The following varieties of soft cheeses are the simplest to make. They require no utensils or materials other than those found in the average household, ...' Part I includes directions for making Neufchatel Cheese, Pimento Cheese, Olive Cream Cheese, Sandwich Nut Cheese, Cream Cheese, Club Cheese, Cottage Cheese, Cottage Cheese from Buttermilk, and Sweet Buttermilk.

N.P.L.A. cook book

M41.1   1923
N.P.L.A. / cook book / Compiled by / the Home-Cooking Circle / of the / Norwood Presbyterian Ladies' Aid / 1923 [cover-title]
DESCRIPTION: 22.5 × 15.0 cm   Pp [3–4] 5–90   Photograph on p 3 of Rev. D. McIvor   Paper; stapled

CONTENTS: 3 'Our Church' [church history and the meeting times of current groups]; 4 ads; 5 'Weights and Measures' and 'Table of Proportions'; 6 ads; 7–84 recipes credited with the name of the contributor, other culinary information, and ads; 85–top 89 'Laundry Hints' and ads; mid 89–top 90 'Household Hints'; mid–bottom 90 'Index' [i.e., table of contents]
COPIES: *Private collection
NOTES: 'Norwood Presbyterian Church held its first meeting on May 1st, 1904,' states p 3.

Sommerfeld, H.B.

For other culinary titles in the Manitoba Farmers' Library, see M25.1.

M42.1   January 1923
Price of this bulletin for distribution outside Manitoba: Ten cents per copy / Manitoba Farmers' Library / Published by the Manitoba Department of Agriculture and Immigration / Winnipeg, Canada, January, 1923 / The Manitoba Farmers' Library is a series of bulletins that are devoted to the extension of information / on agricultural and home economics subjects, and that are distributed free among the people of Manitoba / who make application for them. If any particular bulletin is wanted, ask for it as Extension Bulletin / No. ... All requests should be addressed to: / The Publications Branch, Department of Agriculture, Winnipeg. / Extension Bulletin No. 65 / The beef ring / [caption:] Utilizing beef – Chuck: Roast, steak, boiling beef. Ribs: Roasts. Loin: Porterhouse, / sirloin and tenderloin steaks, choice roasts. Rump: Roast, corned beef. Round: Steak, roast, dried / beef, pot roast. Plate: Stew, Hamburg steak, corned beef. Flank: Stew, Hamburg steak, corned beef, / flank steak. / By H.B. Sommerfeld, M.S. / Animal Husbandry Department / Manitoba Agricultural College / Winnipeg, Manitoba / Published by authority of Hon. Neil Cameron, Minister of Agriculture and Immigration. [cover-title]
DESCRIPTION: 22.5 × 15.0 cm   Pp [1–2] 3–14 [15]   7 numbered illus, illus on p 15 of a dehorned animal   Paper, with illus on front of cuts of beef; stapled
CONTENTS: 1 cover-title; top 2 'The Beef Ring' [introductory text]; mid 2–top 6 'Organization of the Beef Ring'; near top 6–top 8 'Method of Dividing the Carcass'; near top 8–top 10 'Selection and Preparation of Animal for Slaughter'; mid 10 'Method of Keeping Record'; bottom 10–11 'Legislation'; 12 'Table 1. Record Farmers' Beef Ring, May 20th–Sept. 2nd.'; 13 'Reci-

pes for Curing Beef' [i.e., two numbered recipes for Corned Beef and Dried Beef]; 14 'Tools Required,' 'How to Determine the Age of an Ox from the Teeth,' and 'Yield from Cattle'; 15 'Dehorning Cattle Pays'
CITATIONS: Driver 2003, 'Canadian Cookbooks,' p 37
COPIES: *MWP

M42.2 3rd ed., January 1936
—Price of this bulletin for distribution outside Manitoba, ten cents per copy. / Manitoba Farmers' Library / Published by the Manitoba Department of Agriculture and Immigration. / Winnipeg, Canada, January, 1923 / Revised and reprinted, January, 1936. / The Manitoba Farmers' Library is a series of bulletins that are devoted to the / extension of information on agricultural and home economics subjects, and / that are distributed free among the people of Manitoba who make application / for them. All requests should be addressed to: / The Publications Branch, / Department of Agriculture, Winnipeg. / Extension Bulletin No. 65 – Third edition / The beef ring / (including also meat curing recipes) / Part I – The beef ring / Part II – Meat curing recipes / [caption:] Utilizing beef – Chuck: Roast, steak, boiling beef. Ribs: Roasts. Loin: Porterhouse, sirloin / and tenderloin steaks, choice roasts. Rump: Roast, corned beef. Round: Steak, roast, dried beef, pot / roast. Plate: Stew, Hamburg steak, corned beef. Flank: Stew, Hamburg steak, corned beef, flank steak. / Animal Husbandry Department and / Home Economics Department, University of Manitoba, / Winnipeg, Manitoba. / Published by authority of Hon. D.G. McKenzie, Minister of Agriculture and Immigration. [cover-title]
DESCRIPTION: 23.0 × 15.5 cm   Pp [1–2] 3–15   7 numbered illus   Paper, with image on front of cuts of beef; stapled
CONTENTS: 1 cover-title; 2–12 'Part I – The Beef Ring'; 13–15 'Part II – Meat Curing Recipes'
COPIES: *MWP
NOTES: Sommerfeld is not named as the author in this edition.

1924

Cook book

M43.1 1924
Cook book / in aid of / the Girls' / Auxiliary / of the W.H.A.S. / Neepawa, Man. 1924 [cover-title]
DESCRIPTION: 23.0 × 15.0 cm   Pp 1–88   Limp oil cloth; stapled

CONTENTS: 1 title and 'Preface'; 2 'Index' [i.e., table of contents] and 'Weights and Measures'; 3–88 text and ads
COPIES: *MNBPM
NOTES: 'W.H.A.S.' stands for the Women's Hospital Aid Society. The 'Preface' states that funds raised by the sale of the book were to assist the new wing of the Neepawa General Hospital. The recipes are credited with the name of the contributor.

Harmsworth community cook book

Harmsworth is a district northwest of Virden. See also M120.1, Harmsworth Community Cook Book, which may or may not be related to M44.1.

M44.1 1924
Harmsworth / community / cook book / 1924 / Man cannot live by bread alone, / He wants a menu good; / He wants a wife who is not above / Preparing a dainty food. / Profits in aid of the Virden Hospital / Empire-Advance Print, Virden, Man. [cover-title]
DESCRIPTION: 20.5 × 13.5 cm   Pp 1–52   Paper; stapled
CONTENTS: 1 ad; 2 'Introduction' and 'Preface' signed Harmsworth Auxiliary; 3–52 recipes and ads
COPIES: MVPHM *Private collection
NOTES: The preface states, 'This book was compiled and published for the benefit of the Virden Hospital by the members of Harmsworth Auxiliary.' The recipe for Choke Cherry Drink on p 52 is described as 'delicious in hot weather': Grind ripe choke cherries, pits and all, in a meat chopper; put in a crock and cover with white wine vinegar; let stand 3 days; strain and add ¾ cup white sugar to each cup liquid; boil 15–20 minutes and bottle; use 1 tablespoon per glass of water.

Tested recipes

M45.1 1924
Tested recipes / contributed / by / the ladies / of / Greenwood Church / Published by / the Adult Bible Class / 1924 / If soups you want or fowl or meats, / Jams, jellies, cakes or other sweets, / Just search within, you'll surely find, / The very things you have in mind. / – Lorna M. Cook.
DESCRIPTION: 21.5 × 13.0 cm   Pp [1–6] 7–127, [i]   Tp illus of a manservant carrying a covered platter, and behind him, two small potted fruit trees   Card, with image on front of an aproned woman carrying a pie;

probably originally stapled, but now in new library cloth

CONTENTS: 1 tp; 2 'Forward' [*sic*] dated 2 April 1924; 3 'Index to Recipes' [i.e., table of contents listing 'Table of Weights and Measures,' 'Soup,' 'Fish,' 'Meats and Poultry,' 'Vegetables,' 'Salads,' 'Salad Dressing,' 'Luncheon Dishes,' 'Bread,' 'Biscuits and Muffins,' 'Cakes,' 'Icings,' 'Small Cakes and Cookies,' 'Puddings,' 'Light Desserts,' 'Pies and Tarts,' 'Preserves and Jams,' 'Ices,' 'Candy,' 'Beverages,' 'Pickles and Sauces,' and 'Miscellaneous']; 4 'Greenwood Methodist Church' [address at Greenwood Place near Portage Avenue, pastor's name (Rev. R.E. McCullagh), and a list of church activities]; 5–6 'Index to Advertisers'; 7 'Table of Weights and Measures'; 8 ads; 9–127 recipes credited with the name of the contributor and ads; i ads

COPIES: *OTMCL (641.5 G6678)   Private collection

NOTES: The 'Forward' says that the Adult Bible Class published the book to raise funds to finance a Sunday Bulletin for the church; and it lists the names of all the women on the cookbook committee.

Winnipeg high school domestic science note book

M46.1   [about 1924]
Winnipeg high school / domestic science / note book / Price 50 cents / Russell, Lang & Co., Ltd. / Somerset Bldg., Winnipeg. [cover-title]

DESCRIPTION: About 24.0 × 17.0 cm [dimensions from photocopy]

COPIES: *Private collection

NOTES: This is a form of textbook where printed text pages (called 'cards') and blank sheets for handwritten notes were inserted by the student on the instruction of the teacher. This copy first belonged to the present owner's aunt, Helen MacLennan, when she attended Daniel McIntyre High School in Winnipeg. The volume contains her notes for 'Lesson Plan 1924–5,' which includes item 16, 'Placing cards in Books,' and her comments on various recipes under headings for date, dish, result, and remarks. Each of the cards is headed 'Winnipeg Technical High Schools // Household Science Department' and has a number or letter at the top left corner, to indicate the position within the lesson plan or volume. Some instructions required more than one card, such as 'General Rules for Canning' where 'Continued on card 2' is printed at the bottom of the page.

Versions of M46.1 appeared earlier than 1924: MWPA (MG14 C17) has Dora Dibney's school scrap-

book in which she pasted Household Science Department cards for Winnipeg Public Schools, bearing the printed date '1908–1909'; also at MWPA (Ethel M. Brown collection, P4901 f. 3) is a *Domestic Science Note Book* used at Lord Selkirk School, 1928–9. The material in M46.1 was used later in M98.1, a bound volume titled *Theory and Practice in Household Science.*

OTHER EDITIONS: *Original Winnipeg Schools Household Science Recipes* [cover-title], Winnipeg: Grant Park High School Press, copyright 1981, 'Originally published as Winnipeg Technical Schools, Household Science Department, Recipe Sheets #1–54, Theory Sheets A–Z, circa 1909' (MWU); the 'Foreward' [*sic*] states that School District Winnipeg No. 1 established a Household Science Department in 1905, according to the Minutes of 5 May 1905.

1925

Ranchvale Ladies Aid cook book

The building site for Ranchvale Presbyterian Church, located in NE 26-20-25 in the Rural Municipality of Rossburn, was purchased in 1911. In 1925, the church became known as Ranchvale United Church. It closed in 1952. See On the Sunny Slopes of the Riding Mountains: A History of Rossburn and District, *Vol. 2, Rossburn, Man.: Rossburn History Club, 1984.*

M47.1   nd [about 1925]
Ranchvale / Ladies Aid / cook book. / The Review Job Print, Rossburn, Man. [cover-title]

DESCRIPTION: 18.0 × 12.0 cm   Pp [1–18]   Thin card, with two small images on front: three maple leaves on a single stem and a decorated Christmas tree; stapled

CONTENTS: 1–18 recipes credited with the name of the contributor

COPIES: *Private collection

NOTES: The owner reports that the cookbook was sent as a gift to her family, shortly after they moved away from the Ranchvale area in 1922. The reference to 'Ladies Aid' in the title is evidence that the cookbook was published by the local Presbyterian/United church, although no institution is named in the publication.

Wise wives keep husbands happy

The Evening Branch of St Mark's Woman's Auxiliary compiled M130.1, Fancy Fare.

M48.1 nd [about 1925]
Wise wives / keep / husbands happy / by using this / good guide / to / wholesome cookery / Produced by the ladies of St. Vital / The proceeds of the sale of this book will be divided / between St. Mark's and Regent's Park churches. / St. Mark's Church Pastor – Rev. Arthur Wiley. / Regent's Park United Church – Rev. C.I. Mason. / Price 50 cents. [cover-title]
DESCRIPTION: 22.0 × 15.5 cm   Pp [1–2] 3–61 [62]   Paper; stapled
CONTENTS: 1 quotation submitted by Arthur S. Wiley and 'My Prayer' submitted by C.I. Mason; 2 ads; 3–61 recipes credited with the name of the contributor and ads; 62 'Index' [i.e., table of contents]
CITATIONS: Crawford, p D1, illus col
COPIES: *Private collection
NOTES: This is an unusual example of two churches of different denominations (Anglican and United Church of Canada) co-operating to produce a cookbook. C.I. Mason was minister at Regent's Park United Church from 1925 to 1927; therefore, *Wise Wives* was published in that period. It could not have been published before 1925, the year of union for the United Church of Canada. An advertisement on p 6 for Crescent Creamery Co. Ltd points to publication in 1925: The advertisement refers to 'Twenty years leadership as purveyors of pure dairy products to the people of Greater Winnipeg' and the first listing for the dairy in Winnipeg city directories is in the volume for 1905 (1905 + 20 years = 1925).

1926

A cook book of tested recipes

Ten years later the American Women's Club published another cookbook of the same title, M89.1.

M49.1 1926
A cook book of / tested recipes / Compiled by / the members of the American / Women's Club / Winnipeg, Manitoba / 1926
DESCRIPTION: Pp [3] 4–160   Cloth, with small image on front of a mother, father, and child seated at a dining table
CONTENTS: 3 tp; 4 ad; 5 'Preface' signed Mrs A.M. Dafoe, president, Mrs S.A. Burpe, convener, Mrs C.A.

Baird, Mrs W.E. Buck, Mrs L.R. Clements, Mrs L.E. Frost, Mrs E.F. Hurd, Mrs C.J. Lee, Mrs W. Pickup, and Mrs G.S. Wickman, followed by unattributed poem beginning, 'We may live without poetry, music and art' [from *Lucile*, Part I, Canto ii, by Owen Meredith, pseudonym of Edward Robert Bulwer-Lytton]; ...; 9–? recipes credited with the name of the contributor; 159 'Index' [i.e., alphabetical list of sections] and 'Household Hints'; 160 ad
COPIES: *Private collection
NOTES: The private collector's copy is inscribed on the front endpaper, 'Merry Christmas and Happy New Year for Liza, from Mrs. R.R. Winslow. Winnipeg – Dec. 1927.'

Manitoba, Department of Agriculture and Immigration

For other culinary titles in the Manitoba Farmers' Library, see M25.1.

M50.1 rev. ed., June 1926
Price of this bulletin for distribution outside Manitoba: Ten cents per copy / Manitoba Farmers' Library / Published by the Manitoba Department of Agriculture and Immigration / Winnipeg, Canada, June, 1926 / The Manitoba Farmers' Library is a series of bulletins that are devoted to the extension of information / on agricultural and home economics subjects, and that are distributed free among the people of Manitoba / who make application for them. If any particular bulletin is wanted, ask for it as Extension Bulletin / No. ... All requests should be addressed to: / The Publications Branch, Department of Agriculture, Winnipeg. / Extension Bulletin No. 82 / Canning, pickling / and preserving / Revised from former editions by / Miss Mary C. Hiltz, B.S. / Assistant Professor of Nutrition / and / C.H. Lee, M.A. / Professor of Bacteriology / Manitoba Agricultural College, Winnipeg, Man. / Published by authority of Hon. A. Prefontaine, Minister of Agriculture and Immigration. [cover-title]
DESCRIPTION: 22.5 × 15.0 cm   Pp [1] 2–23   8 numbered illus on pp 2–3 of 'Successive Steps in the Cold Pack Method,' illus   Paper, with image on front of a woman holding a jar; stapled
CONTENTS: 1 cover-title; 2–3 illus; 4 'Fruit and Vegetable Canning Chart'; top–mid 5 'Canning'; mid 5–mid 6 'Bacteria, Yeasts and Moulds'; mid–bottom 6 'Open Kettle and Cold Pack Methods Compared'; 7–10 'Cold Pack Process'; 11 'Pressure Cooker'; 12 'Canning Fruits'; 13–14 'Canning Vegetables – Individual

Recipes'; 15–top 17 'Pickling'; mid–bottom 17 'Preserves, Jams, etc.' and 'Marmalade'; 18–19 'Jellies'; 20–1 'Relish'; 22 'Canning Meats'; 23 'Canning Fish'
COPIES: *MWP   OGU (Rural Heritage Collection)

M50.2 3rd ed., June 1932
—Price of this bulletin for distribution outside Manitoba: Ten cents per copy / Manitoba Farmers' Library / Published by the Manitoba Department of Agriculture and Immigration / Winnipeg, Canada, June, 1926. / Revised and reprinted, June, 1932. / The Manitoba Farmers' Library is a series of bulletins that are devoted to the extension of / information on agricultural and home economics subjects, and that are distributed free / among the people of Manitoba who make application for them. All requests should be addressed / to: The Publications Branch, Department of Agriculture, Winnipeg. / Extension Bulletin No. 82 – Third edition / Canning, pickling and / preserving / Revised from former editions by / Miss Mary C. Hiltz, M.A. / Assistant Professor of Foods and Nutrition, / Manitoba Agricultural College / Winnipeg, Man. / Published by authority of Hon. D.G. McKenzie, Minister of Agriculture and Immigration. [cover-title]
DESCRIPTION: 23.0 × 15.0 cm   Pp [1–3] 4–15   Illus Paper, with image on front of two girls in a classroom kitchen; stapled
CONTENTS: 1 cover-title; 2 'Time Table for Canning Tomatoes and Other Fruits'; 3 'Time Table for Canning Non-Acid Vegetables and Meats'; 4–10 'Canning'; 11–12 'Pickling'; 13–15 'Preserving'
COPIES: *MSM   MWU

M50.3 4th ed., July 1934
—[Fourth edition of *Canning, Pickling and Preserving*, revised from former editions by Miss Mary C. Hiltz, Extension Bulletin 82, revised and reprinted July 1934, pp 15]
COPIES: Bookseller's stock

1927

Cook book

M51.1 1927
[An edition of *Cook Book: A Collection of Tested Recipes*, compiled by the Ladies' Aid Society of Home Street United Church, Winnipeg, Manitoba, pp 64, illus on front of the church, list of officers for 1927 on p 2]
COPIES: Bookseller's stock

The League cook book

M52.1 1927
The League / cook book / Winnipeg, Canada, 1927
DESCRIPTION: 17.0 × 12.5 cm   Pp i–xv [xvi], [1–4] 5–135, xvii–xxv [xxvi]   2.2-cm-high tp illus of a male servant carrying a tray, illus headpieces to chapters Cloth, with image on front, in a rectangular frame, of kitchen utensils
CONTENTS: i–xvi ads; 1 tp; 2 blank; 3 'Preface' signed Mildred Kidder Heffelfinger, president; 4 table of contents; 5–132 recipes; 133–5 'Hints for the Careful Housewife'; xvii–xxvi ads
CITATIONS: Golick, p 107
COPIES: *MWPA (P3846 f. 1 Junior League of Winnipeg) OTUTF (B-12 7854)
NOTES: Heffelfinger states on p 3 that the League of Winnipeg was formed in the spring of 1926 with the purpose of 'fostering interest among its members in the social, economic, educational, and civic conditions of their community and to make efficient their volunteer service.' She lists the activities of the League, which at the time of the book's publication had seventy-five members. The recipes are organized in the following chapters: 'To Tempt the Appetite'; 'Dinner Is Served'; 'What Shall We Have for Luncheon'; 'The Tea Table'; 'The Well Stocked Larder'; and 'Appealing to the Invalid.'

The OTUTF copy is inscribed on the front end paper, in ink, 'June 2. 1928. Hope this little book may solve some of your problems. Very much love Helen // Waterloo – June 2.'

1928

A cook book of favorite recipes

M53.1 1928
A cook book of / favorite recipes / Compiled by members of the / Woman's Association of / Crescent United Church / Winnipeg, Manitoba / 1928
DESCRIPTION: 22.5 × 15.0 cm   Pp [1–3] 4–88 [89–94] Tp illus of Crescent United Church   Paper, with image on front of the church; stapled
CONTENTS: 1 tp; 2 'Index' [i.e., table of contents] and 'List of Abbreviations'; 3–85 recipes credited with the name of the contributor and ads; 86–7 'Household Hints'; 88 'Kitchen Time Table'; 89 ads; 90–4 blank for 'Memorandum'
COPIES: *Private collection
NOTES: The cover-title is 'Cook Book.' An advertisement on p 89 states, 'This cook book is a product of our plant // Farmer's Advocate of Winnipeg, Ltd.'

1929

Cook book

M54.1 [1929]
Cook book / Published by the Ladies' Aid / of the / First Lutheran Church / Victor Street / Winnipeg / All of the recipes in this book are not necessarily original. / They have been widely used by the contributors / to whom we are gratefully indebted / Price: One dollar
DESCRIPTION: Tp illus of a maple leaf   With image on front of a maple leaf
CITATIONS: Barss 1980, pp 102, 103
COPIES: *Private collection
NOTES: The congregation of Winnipeg's First Lutheran Church was composed of immigrants from Iceland. Many of the recipes are Icelandic, such as those on p 83 for Skyr contributed by Mrs Sigridur Sigurdson and Misu Otur (Whey Cheese) from Mrs J. Johannesson, plus four recipes on pp 20–1 for Vínarterta, a special favourite among Icelanders in Canada.

The printer and date of publication are on the back face of the binding: 'Printed by the Columbia Press, Ltd. Winnipeg, Canada. 1929.' Two advertisements confirm the publication date of 1929: on p 91, one for the New York Life Insurance Co. cites 'Assets (December 31, 1928)' and 'Dividends apportioned to policy holders 1928'; and on p 100, Canadian Pacific Steamships announces 'Icelandic Excursion 1930,' a trip to Iceland on the occasion of the thousandth anniversary of the Icelandic Parliament. The private collector's copy has 109 pp.

I have examined an incomplete copy (stapled) at the home of a member of the church. It measures 24.5 × 17.0 cm, and the contents are: [lacks leaves]; 7–84 recipes credited with the name of the contributor; 85 ad; 86 'Index' [i.e., table of contents]; 87 ad; 88–9 'Household Hints'; 90 'Table of Weights and Measures'; 91–102 ads; [lacks leaves]. The same Icelandic recipes carry forward to M54.2.

Barss 1980 reprints Mrs J.K. Johnson's recipe for Skyr and a recipe for Cranberry Catsup, but inaccurately gives the book title as 'Icelandic Lutheran Church Cook Book.'

M54.2   nd [about 1938]
—Cook book / Published by the Ladies' Aids [sic] / of the / First Lutheran Church / Victor Street / Winnipeg / All of the recipes in this book are not necessarily original. / They have been widely used by the contributors / to whom we are gratefully indebted / Price: One dollar

DESCRIPTION: 25.0 × 17.0 cm   Pp [1–4] 5–132   Fp illus on p 3 of the church   Paper; stapled
CONTENTS: 1 tp; 2 'Thanksgiving at Table' by Björn Bo Jonsson, pastor, First Lutheran Church; 3 fp illus of 'First Lutheran Church (Icelandic) Victor Street, Winnipeg, Manitoba'; 4 thanks 'To the Advertisers'; 5–112 text; 113–mid 128 ads; bottom 128 'Table of Weights and Measures'; 129 'Index' [i.e., table of contents]; 130–2 blank 'For Extra Recipes'
COPIES: OKCKT (KING-BKS-0022, Lady Eaton Estate Collection)   *Private collection
NOTES: The copy examined was in a home-made dust-jacket obscuring any text on the original binding. The recipes are credited with the name of the contributor. There is an advertisement on p 120 for a Stromberg-Carlson furniture radio, 1938 model, which suggests the book was published about that year.

This is the edition seen by Kristin Olafson-Jenkyns and cited in *The Culinary Saga of New Iceland*, p 234. She reprints several recipes from the book (reprinted recipes are listed on p 235). The OKCKT copy was part of Lady Eaton's cookbook collection, about which see Anderson/Mallinson, pp 139–40.

OTHER EDITIONS: *Cook Book*, published by the Dorcas Society of the First Lutheran Church, Victor Street, Winnipeg, 1950 (Private collection; Olafson-Jenkyns, pp 14 and 234, incorrectly described as 2nd ed.).

A cook book of tested recipes

Gordon United Church later amalgamated with another congregation to become Gordon-King Memorial United Church.

M55.1 [1929]
A cook book of / tested recipes / Compiled by / members of Group Number Three / Gordon United Church / Ladies Aid / Ladies: / Mrs. J.R. Leitch, Convener / Phone 501 771 / Mrs. A.E. Boyd / Mrs. R.G. Henderson / Mrs. L. Root / Mrs. F. Osbourne
DESCRIPTION: 22.5 × 15.0 cm   Pp [1] 2–48   [$0.25, on binding]   Paper; stapled, and with hole punched at top left corner, through which runs a string for hanging
CONTENTS: 1 tp; 2 'Abbreviations,' 'Index' [i.e., table of contents], and acknowledgment; 3–44 recipes credited with the name of the contributor and ads; 45–8 blank for 'My Favorite Recipes'
COPIES: *Private collection
NOTES: The year of publication and the printer – 1929, 'Reynolds Printing C[rest of name obscured]' – are on the front face of the binding. The advertisements are for Winnipeg businesses.

P.E.O. cook book

The PEO Sisterhood is an international society of women, founded in 1869 on the campus of Iowa Wesleyan College, Mount Pleasant, Iowa. PEO stands for Philanthropic Educational Organization. The Sisterhood has a strong presence in Selkirk: In 2005 there were four active chapters.

M56.1 [1929]
P.E.O. / cook book / Compiled by members of Chapter "A" / P.E.O. Sisterhood Selkirk, Man. / ['P.E.O.' within a star] / The proceeds of this cook book will be used to defray ex- / penses of furnishing the Surgical Ward of the Selkirk / General Hospital.
DESCRIPTION: 22.0 × 14.0 cm   Pp [1] 2–106   Paper; stapled
CONTENTS: 1 tp; 2 quotation from Ruskin; 3 'Preface'; 4 'Recipe for a Happy New Year'; 5 'Abbreviations Used' and 'Table of Measurements and Weights'; 6 ad; 7–101 recipes, most credited with the name of the contributor, and ads; 102–6 'Household Hints'
COPIES: *OONL (TX715.6 P25 1929 p***)
NOTES: The year of publication, 1929, is printed on the front face of the binding. On p 85, the recipe title Jam Cake has been corrected by hand to read June Cake.

Recipes

M57.1 1929
Recipes / contributed by the members / of the / United Farm Women / of Manitoba / Compiled by the executive / 1929
DESCRIPTION: 22.0 × 15.0 cm   Pp [1–2 lacking] [3] 4–172   Tp illus of a girl and boy holding roast poultry   Cloth
CONTENTS: 1–2 lacking; 3 tp; 4 ad; 5 'United Farm Women of Manitoba // 306 Bank of Hamilton Bldg., Winnipeg, Man. October 14, 1929.' [list of officers and directors, and an explanation of the organization's purpose]; 6 ads; 7 'Co-operation' signed United Farm Women of Manitoba; 8 ads; 9–166 recipes credited with the name of the contributor and ads; 167–72 blank for 'Notes and Your Own Recipes'; inside back face of binding table of contents
CITATIONS: Peel's Bibliography 5388
COPIES: *BVIV   MSOHM   MVPHM   MWMM
NOTES: The cover-title is 'United Farm Women of Manitoba Cook Book'; the running head is 'U.F.W.M. Cook Book.' The text on p 7 refers to 'this our first cook book.' *Recipes* appears to have been modelled

after A59.1, *Recipes*, by the members of the United Farm Women of Alberta, published the year before.

The Young Woman's Auxiliary cook book

M58.1 1929
[An edition of *The Young Woman's Auxiliary Cook Book*, Roland United Church, Roland, Manitoba, 1929, printed by R.E. Buffy, Roland, $0.35]
COPIES: Private collection
NOTES: The 'Preface' states that the cookbook was 'made by the members of the Young Woman's Auxiliary, a branch of the Woman's Missionary Society of Roland United Church.'

1930

All tested recipes

M59.1 1930
All tested / recipes / contributed by / the most famous chefs / in the world / Compiled and published by / the Canadian Cook Book Company / of Canada / Head office – Winnipeg / 1930
DESCRIPTION: 22.0 × 15.5 cm   Pp [1–4] 5–207 [208]   Tp illus of a woman's head-and-shoulders and a tea tray loaded with éclairs, loaf of bread, and china [$1.00, on binding]   Cloth, with two scenes on front: above title, church beside a river with bridge; below title, chef stirring contents of a bowl
CONTENTS: 1 tp; 2 'This volume is affectionately dedicated to "my mother" T.D.B.'; 3 'Who Are These Famous Chefs?' signed the Canadian Cook Book Co. of Canada; 4 'Table of Weights and Measures' and 'Time Table for Roasting Meats'; 5–207 recipes; 208 index
COPIES: OTUTF (D-11 0981)   OVOH   QMM (RBD uncat 0781)   *Private collection
NOTES: The cover-title is 'The Church Cook Book // Secrets of a Famous Chef.' The running head is 'The Church Cook Book.' T.D.B., who signs the dedication, may be the author. According to p 3, 'This tested Canadian Cook Book contains only favorite recipes of someone's Mother, every recipe throughout was signed by someone's Mother, the publishers of this book kept this foremost in their minds when having it compiled; not highly seasoned indigestible dishes, but Canadian Home Cooking that some Canadian husband, boy or girl has enjoyed in their Canadian Home.' In this introductory text and in the use of the title 'The Church Cook Book,' the publisher models the cookbook after the fund-raising genre produced by church women's groups; however, none of the

recipes is credited to an individual. S63.1, *All-Tested Recipes*, published in Regina in 1934, has the same form of title and the same title-page illustration.

The Canadian bride's reference book

M60.1 [copyright 1930]
The Canadian / bride's / reference / book / Published by / Merton Corporation Limited / publishers of "Baby's Health and Record" / Toronto General Trusts Bldg. / Winnipeg
DESCRIPTION: 25.5 × 16.5 cm   Pp [1–4], 4a–5a, 5–203   A few, small illus   Cloth, with alligator pattern
CONTENTS: 1 tp; 2 'Copyright 1930 by Merton Corporation Limited Winnipeg, Canada Printed by the Hignell Printing Co., Winnipeg'; 3 'To the Bride' signed the publishers; 4 blank; 4a–5a ads; 5 'Index to Advertisers'; 6 poem by Sir Philip Sidney; 7–197 text; 198–202 'Index to Recipes'; 203 'Index to Special Articles'
COPIES: *OONL (TX145 C36 1930 fol.)   Private collection
NOTES: There are articles, a table of weights and measures, some menu ideas, and many recipes, separately indexed.

The Dugald Women's Institute cook book

M61.1 1930
[An edition of *The Dugald Women's Institute Cook Book*, 1930, pp 79, stapled]
COPIES: Private collection
NOTES: There is a list of officers for 1930.

Favorite recipes

See also M12.1, from the same church.

M62.1 1930
Favorite recipes / 1930 / With grateful thanks / to the contributors, / advertisers and others, / whose kind assistance / has made possible the / publication of this / book. / St. Luke's Parish Guild / Winnipeg Canada
DESCRIPTION: 22.5 × 15.0 cm   Pp [1–4] 5–100   Cloth-covered boards, bound by two rings
CONTENTS: 1 tp; 2 'The Willson Stationery Co. Limited printers and stationers Winnipeg Manitoba'; 3 table of contents; 4 quotation from Brillat-Savarin; 5–100 text
COPIES: *Private collection

140 good recipes

M63.1 nd [about 1930]
140 good recipes / contributed by the women of / Augustine / Church / Winnipeg / How to Cook a Husband / A good many husbands are entirely spoiled by mis- / management in cooking, and so are not tender and / good. Some women keep them too constantly in hot water, / others freeze them, others put them in a stew, others / keep them constantly in a pickle. It cannot be supposed / that any husband will be good and tender if managed in / this way, but they are truly delicious if properly treated. / Don't keep him in the kettle by force, as he will stay there / himself if proper care is taken. If he should sputter and / fizz, don't be anxious, some husbands do this. Add a little / sugar, the variety that confectioners call "kisses," but on no / account add any vinegar or pepper. A little spice improves / him, but it must be used with judgment. Do not try him / with something sharp to see if he is becoming tender. Stir / him gently lest he lie too long in the kettle and become / flat and tasteless. If you follow these directions, you will / find him very digestible, agreeing nicely with you, and he / will keep as long as you want to have him.
DESCRIPTION: 23.0 × 15.0 cm   Pp [1–2] 3–39 [40]   Tp illus of the church   Paper; stapled
CONTENTS: 1 tp; 2 ad; 3–38 recipes and ads; 39 ad; 40 'Index' [i.e., table of contents]
COPIES: *OGU (CCC TX715.6 O52)
NOTES: From appearances, the book was published about 1930.

Welch, Mrs Anna S.

Mrs Anna S. Welch was the widow of Leonard Welch, according to the 1929 Winnipeg city directory.

M64.1 nd [about 1930]
Winnipeg Laundry cook book / Introduction / [18-line introductory paragraph beginning, 'Among the arts of home-making, ...'] / Compiled and edited by / Anna S. Welch / Service Manager, Winnipeg Laundry Limited / Printed by Public Press Limited, Winnipeg / Copyright applied for
DESCRIPTION: 23.5 × 15.0 cm   Pp [1] 2–16   Paper, with image on front of a bride; stapled
CONTENTS: 1 tp; 2–16 recipes
COPIES: *MSM
NOTES: The cover-title is 'The Bride's Cook Book // Compliments of Winnipeg Laundry Limited.' In

Winnipeg city directories, Mrs Anna S. Welch is listed as service manageress at Winnipeg Laundry Ltd for only one year, in the volume for 1930. The appearance of the cookbook is consistent with publication in 1930. Before this date she worked as a stenographer for other employers; in the 1931 directory she is listed as a visitor with the Manitoba government, and in later directories, as working for the Children's Bureau.

1930s

Good things to eat

M65.1   nd [about 1930s]
[An edition of *Good Things to Eat,* by the ladies of St Ignatius Church, Winnipeg, Manitoba, nd, pp 114, 24.0 cm]
COPIES: OONL (TX715.6 G673 1930z, not on shelf)

1930–5

The community cook book

M66.1   nd [about 1930–5]
The / community / cook book / Compiled by the members of / Moline Women's Institute / Men may come or men may go / but meals go on for ever [cover-title]
DESCRIPTION: 23.0 × 15.0 cm   Pp 1–23 [24]   Paper; stapled
CONTENTS: Inside front face of binding ad for the Moline Co-operative Ltd and a list of the officers and directors in the Moline Women's Institute; 1–23 recipes credited with the name of the contributor; 24 'Saults & Pollard Limited, printers, Winnipeg'
COPIES: *Private collection
NOTES: The president of the Moline Women's Institute was Mrs A. Coutts when the cookbook was published. The Moline branch was organized in 1916.

1931

Betty's scrapbook of little recipes for little cooks

M67.1   nd [1931]
Betty's / scrapbook / of / little recipes / for little cooks / saved from / the Nor'-West / Farmer / and Farm & Home / Winnipeg – Canada / The pioneer / farm journal of / Western Canada [cover-title]

DESCRIPTION: 35.5 × 26.0 cm   Pp [1–24]   Many illus of Little Betty cooking   Paper
CONTENTS: Inside front face of binding 'The Story of Betty' signed Mrs R.C. Dahlberg, 'Betty's mother,' and 'Betty's Scrapbook of "Little Recipes for Little Cooks"' [i.e., introductory text] signed the Nor'-West Farmer and Farm and Home; 1–24 twenty-four numbered cooking lessons for children; inside back face 'Things That Every Little Cook Should Know' [i.e., measurements and 'Rules for Working'] and 'How to Keep This Scrap Book'
COPIES: Bookseller's stock   *Private collection
NOTES: The publisher's note on the inside front face of the binding comments that 'the first twelve pages of recipes are already printed in this scrapbook, so that you will not have to put them in ...' The text on the inside back face, 'How to Keep This Scrap Book,' explains that there will be one page per month printed in the 'Home Section' of the magazine, to be cut out and pasted in the scrapbook by the child.

There is no date printed in the scrapbook and no evidence of the date of individual clippings in the collector's copy; however, the scrapbook was announced in the 'Editorial' of 5 January 1931, Vol. 50, No. 1, p 10 ('"Little Recipes" for little girls, appearing once each month beginning February 5, ...'). The following lessons and other information were found in issues of *Nor'-West Farmer and Farm and Home,* through the years 1931 and 1932, to January 1933: Lesson 1, 5 February 1931, p 19; Lesson 2, 5 March 1931, p 12 (includes a photograph of Little Betty holding the scrapbook); Lesson 3, 6 April 1931, p 14; Lesson 4, 5 May 1931, p 14; Lesson 5, 5 June 1931, p 12; Lesson 6, 6 July 1931, p 14; Lesson 7, 5 August 1931, p 12; Lesson 8, 5 September 1931, p 12; Lesson 9 and Betty's request that readers send in snapshots of themselves, 5 October 1931, p 12; Lesson 10, 20 October 1931, p 14; snapshots of 'little cooks' requested by Betty (i.e., photographs of prairie children, with their names and towns), 5 November 1931, p 7; letters to Betty, 20 November 1931, p 26; Lesson 11, 5 December 1931, p 14; more snapshots of 'Little Cooks Who Use Betty's Recipes and Scrap Books,' 21 December 1931, p 14; Lesson 12, 5 January 1932, p 12; Lesson 13, 5 February 1932, p 14; Lesson 14, 5 March 1932, p 14; 'Letters to Betty,' 20 March 1932, p 14; Lesson 15, 5 April 1932, p 12; Lesson 16, 5 May 1932, p 14; snapshots of 'Little Cooks,' 20 May 1932, pp 16–17; Lesson 17, 20 June 1932, p 31; Lesson 18, 5 and 20 July 1932, p 14; Lesson 19, 5 and 20 August 1932, p 14; Lesson 20, September 1932, p 14; Lesson 21, October 1932, p 14; Lesson 22, November 1932, p 14; Lesson 23, December 1932, p 16; and Lesson 24, January 1933, p 16. If a reader missed ordering the scrapbook when it was first published at the beginning of 1931, she could order it at any time and the newspaper would supply the missed lessons. A note in Lesson 8, for example, stated: 'Betty's Scrap Book now has seven lessons in it – and here is Number Eight! It sure is a fine book now. If you have not seen one send 15 cents for one (with all the previous lessons) to Betty, c/o ...'

The collector's copy is inscribed on the binding, 'Jean Ann Jamieson // Hamiota, Manitoba, Canada. 1933.' The dated inscription marks the end of the run of lessons.

The OONL microfilm of the above-cited issues of *Nor'-West Farmer and Farm and Home* reproduces copies of issues that must have belonged originally to the periodical's publisher because many of the recipes in the 'Home Section' have been annotated by an editor or other employee with the name of the recipe contributor – valuable evidence of the provenance of the culinary material.

Cook book and household budget

M68.1   nd [1931]
Cook book / and / household budget / with / notes on domestic science / by Miss Rhela Leslie, B.Sc. / Published and distributed by / Ladies' Aid Society / Fort Rouge United Church [cover-title]
DESCRIPTION: 23.0 × 15.5 cm   Pp [1] 2–62   Thin card, with image on front of the church; stapled?
CONTENTS: 1 'Introductory' signed Mrs J.B. Parkin, president, and 'Appreciation' signed Thomas C. Mackey, publicity; 2 ads; 3–26 'Household Budget' for twelve months [i.e., a blank form], menus, and recipes (all on rectos), and ads (on versos); 27–35 'Domestic Science' by Miss Rhela Leslie and ads; 36 ads; 37–61 'Recipes' and ads; 62 ads
COPIES: *Private collection
NOTES: The recipes are credited with the name of the contributor. Miss Leslie's section covers 'Household Hints,' 'Oven-Cooked Meals,' 'Household Helps,' 'Meal Planning,' and 'Care of the Furnace.' There is an advertisement on p 54 for Melvin's Ltd, headed 'Vanities of 1931.'

Cook book and household budget

East Kildonan is part of the city of Winnipeg. The church, now called John Black Memorial United Church, is at 898 Henderson Highway.

M69.1   nd [about 1931]
Cook book / and / household budget / with / notes on domestic science / Published and distributed by / John Black United Church / Ladies' Aid Society [cover-title]
DESCRIPTION: 20.5 × 14.0 cm   Pp [1] 2–63   Illus on p 1 of John Black United Church, East Kildonan   Very thin card; stapled
CONTENTS: 1 illus of the church and 'Introductory' signed Ladies' Aid Society; 2–13 'Domestic Science' by Miss Rhela Leslie, B.Sc., six blank tables for monthly 'Household Budget,' blank spaces for 'Memorandum,' 'Oven Temperature for Baking Different Products,' 'Weights and Measures,' and ad; 14–63 'Recipes' credited with the name of the contributor, six blank tables for monthly 'Household Budget,' blank spaces for 'Memorandum,' and ads
COPIES: *Private collection
NOTES: The 'Introductory' describes the contents of the book: 'The first section of the publication consists of articles on domestic science and useful household helps. The Budget consists of twelve pages – one for each month – where housewives can keep their monthly expenses. The third section consists of a great number of tried recipes by the Ladies' Association, to suit all meals, at all seasons and, we hope, to suit all tastes.' 'Evans Printing Company Winnipeg – Manitoba' is on the back cover. This book was likely published about the same time as M68.1.

Dutton, Miss Gertrude

Dutton was the cookery expert for Western Home Monthly. *Her first column appeared in the February 1920 issue, where she is described as a demonstrator in domestic science at the Manitoba Agricultural College. An article about her in the retitled* National Home Monthly *(January 1938), p 40, reports: '... it is only a mere eighteen years since Miss Dutton joined forces with the National Home Monthly [i.e., in 1920], ... Miss Dutton held important posts both in Canada and the United States where her work was greatly appreciated. Not so long ago, the Manitoba School Board retained her services in connection with the evening extension classes for the unemployed ... she was invited to become Director of the Homecraft Theatre, an institute which is maintained by National advertisers for the housewife, ...' The article goes on to discuss Dutton's idea for a 'Better Cookery clipping book,' now available from the magazine; see M99.1. In about 1940 she was commissioned to prepare O1001.1,* Questing, for Love – The Flavor Man,*

Toronto. Dutton, with others, 'judged and approved' the recipes in O898.1, 43 Prize Winning Recipes, for Swift Canadian Co. For her photograph, see pl 40.

M70.1   nd [about 1931]
Specially / selected / recipes / The / Western / Home / Monthly [cover-title]
DESCRIPTION: 20.5 × 13.5 cm   Pp [1–4] 5–102   Fp illus portrait on p 1 of Miss Gertrude Dutton   Paper
CONTENTS: 1 illus of 'Miss Gertrude Dutton nationally known dietitian who is in charge of "The Western Home Monthly" Better Cookery Department'; 2–3 'Preface'; 4 'Abbreviations'; 5–94 recipes; 95–102 'Contents'
CITATIONS: Ferguson/Fraser, p 233
COPIES: ABOM BSUM MCM OGU (CCC TX715.6 S6594) OKQ (F5012 nd W527) OTYA (CPC 1930 0095) QMM (RBD ckbk 2102) *Private collection
NOTES: The book was intended for western housewives, as the 'Preface' states: 'It has always been our aim, in "Better Cookery," to keep in mind the many problems confronting the women of our western country, ... We endeavor to make the fullest possible use of the many food products which are readily available to us here, especially the products of our own farms, without giving much consideration to the more costly luxuries, and what is usually known as "Fancy Cookery," which we can well forego.' The Western Home Monthly was published in Winnipeg by Home Publishing Co., beginning in 1899. From October 1932, it was called National Home Monthly.

The text of the private collector's copy described here is printed in black ink; the text of another private collector's copy is printed in green ink. The QMM copy is inscribed, on the binding, 'Florence Dunwoody October 19th 1931.'

M70.2   nd [October 1932 or later]
—Specially / selected / recipes / National / Home / Monthly [cover-title]
DESCRIPTION: 21.0 × 13.5 cm   Pp [1–4] 5–102   Fp illus portrait on p 1 of Miss Gertrude Dutton   Paper; stapled
CONTENTS: 1 illus of 'Miss Gertrude Dutton celebrated dietitian who is in charge of "The National Home Monthly" Better Cookery Department'; 2–3 preface; 4 'Abbreviations'; 5–94 recipes; 95–102 'Contents'
COPIES: BDEM BDUCVM MAUAM OONL (TX715.6 S64 1920z, 2 copies) QMMMCM (Old information file – cookery)   *Private collection
NOTES: All editions bearing the name National Home Monthly were published after September 1932, the date of the last issue called Western Home Monthly.

M70.3   nd [about 1933]
—Specially / selected / recipes / The / National / Home / Monthly [cover-title]
DESCRIPTION: 20.5 × 13.5 cm   Pp [1–4] 5–102   Fp illus portrait on p 1 of Miss Gertrude Dutton   Paper; stapled
CONTENTS: 1 illus of Dutton; 2–3 preface; 4 'Abbreviations'; 5–94 recipes; 95–102 table of contents
COPIES: OGU (CCC TX715.6 S659) *Private collection
NOTES: Unlike M70.2, 'The' precedes 'National Home Monthly' in the cover-title. The private collector's copy is inscribed on p 1, 'Oct. 18 – 1933.'

M70.4   10th ed., nd [about 1937]
—Specially / selected / recipes / National / Home / Monthly / Tenth edition [cover-title]
DESCRIPTION: 19.0 × 13.0 cm   Pp [1–4] 5–102   Fp illus portrait on p 1 of Miss Gertrude Dutton   Paper; stapled
CONTENTS: 1 illus of 'Miss Gertrude Dutton celebrated dietitian who is in charge of "National Home Monthly" Better Cookery Department'; 2–3 'Preface'; 4 'Abbreviations'; 5–94 recipes; 95–102 'Contents'
COPIES: *QMM (RBD ckbk 1856)
NOTES: The QMM copy is inscribed on the binding, in ink, 'Mary. Wheeler. 1937.'

M70.5   nd [late 1930s]
—National / Home Monthly / Specially / selected / recipes [cover-title]
DESCRIPTION: 20.0 × 13.0 cm   Pp [1–4] 5–102   Fp illus portrait on p 1 of Miss Gertrude Dutton   Paper, with image on front of a crown roast of lamb; stapled
CONTENTS: 1 illus of Dutton; 2–3 'Preface'; 4 'Abbreviations'; 5–94 recipes; 95–102 'Contents'
COPIES: *Private collection
NOTES: The bindings of the other editions are plain, with lettering only. The copy described here has a colour illustration of a sophisticated main-course dish seen against diagonal bands of black, blue, and yellowish brown.

Recipes old and new, tried and true

M71.1   1931
King Memorial / United Church / Recipes / old and new / tried and true / Compiled by / the ladies of the Business Women's Group / Mrs. H.D. Beattie, Convener // Miss I. Smith, Secretary
DESCRIPTION: 23.5 × 15.0 cm   Pp [1] 2–64   Tp illus of church   Paper; stapled

CONTENTS: 1 tp; 2 'Recipe for a Happy Day' and acknowledgment; 3–59 recipes and ads; 60–4 blank for 'Favorite Recipes'

COPIES: *Private collection

NOTES: Printed on the front face of the binding is 'Compiled by the Business Women's Group // Winnipeg // 1931 // Reynolds Printing Co. Limited.' The running head is 'King Memorial Cook Book.'

Riley, Miss Dickson

In the introductory text of M72.1, Miss Riley is described as a 'former pupil of Eugene Christian, food specialist and author,' and as 'well known in Western Canada as a lecturer … [with] 10 year's [sic] experience.' (For Christian's Eat and Be Well, *see O357.1.) Riley also wrote the 11-page* Lallemand's Tested Baking Recipes, *Montreal, Toronto, and Winnipeg: Fred A. Lallemand Refining Co. Ltd, nd [about 1930–5], for a company that made yeast cakes (Private collection).*

Western Pure Foods Ltd was incorporated in Manitoba on 29 January 1895, and the Department of Consumer and Corporate Affairs, Companies Office, has a second entry for the firm dated 20 August 1930.

M72.1   copyright 1931

Eclipse / tempting / recipes / Western / Pure Foods Ltd. / Winnipeg – Canada / Copyright 1931

DESCRIPTION: 17.0 × 13.0 cm   Pp [1–3] 4–32   Tp illus bold col of fruits and vegetables, illus bold col   [$0.05, on binding]   Paper, with stylized image on front of an eclipse of the sun; stapled

CONTENTS: Inside front face of binding illus of the company's Winnipeg factory; 1 tp; 2–3 untitled introductory text signed Western Pure Foods Ltd; 4–32 recipes; inside back face 'Measurements'

COPIES: ACG   *AEUCHV (UV.85.17.134)   MAUAM MCM   MWMM   MWPA (MG14 C50 McKnight, Ethel)   OONL (TX715.6 E35 1931 p***)   SBIHM

NOTES: The cookbook was published to promote the use of Eclipse-brand food products, such as baking powder, yeast cakes, jelly powders, extracts, and spices. The order of publication of the various editions is unknown. This edition differs from M72.2 and M72.3 in that the fruits and vegetables on the title-page are boldly coloured instead of rendered in pastel colours and, although similarly arranged, the fruits and vegetables are differently drawn; for example, here the pineapple has eight to nine leaves and the pumpkin sits on leaves. Unlike M72.3, the author is not cited on the title-page and there is no index. A comparison of the text of this edition and

M72.3 reveals that, although the introductions appear to be the same, they are printed from different settings of type; also, the recipes have been revised and rearranged; for example, p 7 of this edition gives recipes for Welsh Buns and Butterscotch Buns, whereas M72.3 offers Welsh Buns and three different recipes for types of 'Baking Powder Bread.'

The colour of the text on the title-page of M72.1 varies between copies: for example, in those at ACG, AEUCHV, MWPA, and OONL, the brand name 'Eclipse' and the company name 'Western Pure Foods Ltd.' are in a dark colour (red for OONL) that contrasts with 'tempting recipes' and 'Winnipeg – Canada Copyright 1931' in a lighter colour (light blue for OONL); in the MWMM copy, the dark and light colours are reversed.

Ferguson/Fraser, p 233, cite *Eclipse Tempting Recipes,* but do not distinguish between the three editions.

M72.2   copyright 1931

—Eclipse / tempting / recipes / Western / Pure Foods Ltd. / Winnipeg – Canada / Copyright 1931

DESCRIPTION: 17.0 × 13.0 cm   Pp [1–3] 4–32   Tp illus pastel col of fruits and vegetables, illus pastel col   Paper, with stylized image on front of an eclipse of the sun; stapled

CONTENTS: Inside front face of binding illus of the company's Winnipeg factory; 1 tp; 2–3 untitled introductory text signed Western Pure Foods Ltd; 4–32 recipes; inside back face 'Measurements'

COPIES: AHRMH (2 copies)   ARDA   BTCA (77.72) MBDHM   OONL (TX715.6 E35 1931 copy 2)   SBIM *Private collection

NOTES: Like M72.3, the fruits and vegetables on the title-page are printed in pastel colours, the pineapple has only five leaves, and there are no leaves under the pumpkin. Unlike M72.3, the author is not cited on the title-page, p 7 gives recipes for Welsh Buns and Butterscotch Buns, and there is no index. There is no price on the binding.

M72.3   copyright 1931

—Eclipse / tempting / recipes / By / Miss Dickson Riley / Western / Pure Foods Ltd. / Winnipeg – Canada / Copyright 1931

DESCRIPTION: 17.0 × 13.0 cm   Pp [1–3] 4–32   Tp illus pastel col of fruits and vegetables, illus pastel col   Paper, with stylized image on front of an eclipse of the sun; stapled

CONTENTS: 1 tp; 2 untitled introductory text signed Western Pure Foods Ltd; 3–30 recipes; 31–2 'Index'; inside back face of binding 'Measurements'

COPIES: *AEUCHV (UV.85.17.135) MCDHM OKELWM

NOTES: Like M72.2, the fruits and vegetables on the title-page are printed in pastel colours, the pineapple has only five leaves, and there are no leaves under the pumpkin. Unlike M72.1 and M72.2, here the author is cited on the title-page, p 7 has Welsh Buns and three different recipes for types of 'Baking Powder Bread,' and there is an index. There is no price on the binding.

AEUCHV has a second copy of this edition (UV.85.17.136), which lacks its binding. The OKELWM copy is inscribed on the title-page, 'E. Barnett 177 Perth.'

1932

A guide to good cooking

Q203.1, A Guide to Good Cooking, was published simultaneously in Montreal and Winnipeg.

Scott, Anna Lee [pseudonym]

See O773.13 for the edition of Scott's The Easy Way Cake Book *published by the Sun Publishing Co., Brandon, and O776.11 and O776.12 for editions of her* Marketing and Meal Planning *published by the Sun Publishing Co., Brandon, and the Winnipeg Evening Tribune.*

Souvenir book and shoppers' guide 1932

The Winnipeg Hadassah Council produced annual versions of this work, from about 1928 up to at least 1968, although copies have not been found for every year. See also: M74.1, Souvenir Book and Shoppers Guide 1933–1934; M79.1, Souvenir Book and Shoppers Guide 1934–1935; M81.1, Hadassah Souvenir Book and Shoppers Guide 1935–1936; M95.1, Hadassah Souvenir Book Shopper's Guide 1937; M106.1, Hadassah Souvenir Book Shoppers Guide 1939; M111.1, Hadassah Souvenir Book and Shopper's Guide 1940; M119.1, Hadassah Souvenir Programme and Shoppers' Guide 1941; M122.1, Souvenir Book and Shoppers' Guide 1942; M123.1, Souvenir Book and Shoppers' Guide 1943; M124.1, Hadassah Souvenir Book and Shoppers' Guide 1944; M126.1, Hadassah Shoppers Guide and Cook Book 1945; M131.1, Hadassah Shoppers' Guide and Cook Book 1946; *M135.1, Hadassah Shoppers' Guide and Cook Book 1947.*

M73.1   1932
Souvenir book / and / shoppers' guide / Winnipeg / Hadassah Council / December, 1932 [cover-title]
DESCRIPTION: 22.0 × 15.5 cm   Pp 3–90   Illus   Paper; stapled
CONTENTS: Inside front face of binding untitled thanks to the advertisers and to the compilers, signed (Mrs I.R.) Rose Slavin, program chairman, Winnipeg Hadassah Council, and table of contents; 3 'Greetings from President Canadian Hadassah' signed Lillian Freiman, and her portrait; 4–89 text, including messages and greetings from other Jewish organizations, recipes credited with the name of the contributor, ads, and miscellaneous information; 90 blank for 'Memorandum'
COPIES: *MWHWC
NOTES: The 'Message to Hadassah' by (Mrs J.M.) Sara Bernstein, president, Winnipeg Hadassah Council, on p 11, implies that the first souvenir book was published in 1928: She refers to 'this present Souvenir Book, our fifth annual one'; since the fifth is dated 1932, the first annual was 1928. In her message she also '[looks] back upon twelve years of Hadassah history in Winnipeg.' The printer's name is on the outside back face of the binding: 'Printed for the Hadassah by the Jewish Post Printing Dept.'

1933

Souvenir book and shoppers guide 1933–1934

For a list of the annual editions in this series, see M73.1.

M74.1   1933
Souvenir book / and / shoppers guide / Winnipeg Hadassah Council / 1933–1934 [cover-title]
DESCRIPTION: 22.0 × 15.0 cm   Pp 1–102   Illus   Paper, with image on front of a uniformed man holding up an over-size, stylized copy of this cookbook; stapled
CONTENTS: Inside front face of binding untitled thanks to the advertisers and the contributors signed (Mrs F.) Bessie Buchwald, programme chairman, Winnipeg Hadassah Council, and ad; 1 'Greetings from President Canadian Hadassah' signed Lillian Freiman, and her portrait; 2–102 text, including greetings and messages from other Jewish organizations, recipes credited with the name of the contributor, ads, and miscellaneous information
COPIES: *MWHWC

1934

All tested recipes

M75.1   nd [about 1934]
All tested recipes / To a Cook Book / We may live without poetry, music, / and art; / We may live without conscience and live / without heart; / We may live without friends; / we may live without books; / But civilized man cannot live without / cooks. / He may live without books – / What is knowledge but grieving? / He may live without hope – / What is hope but deceiving? / He may live without love, / What is passion but pining? / But where is the man that can live / without dining? / Compiled and issued by / the Commercial Girls' Club / Winnipeg, Man. / 1934 / [folio:] 1
DESCRIPTION: 22.5 × 15.0 cm   Pp 1–108   Thin card; stapled
CONTENTS: 1 tp; 2 ad; 3 list of Commercial Girls' Club officers, board of directors, advisory board, and staff; 4 ad; 5–6 'History of Our Club'; 7–106 text and ads; 107 'Table of Weights and Measures'; 108 'Index' [i.e., table of contents] and ads
COPIES: OTYA (CPC 1934 0125)   *Private collection
NOTES: The cover-title is 'Cookery Book'; the running head is 'The Commercial Girls' Club Cookery Book.' According to the history on pp 5–6, the Commercial Girls' Club was founded in 1931 in response to the large numbers of Winnipeg women who had lost their jobs or were unable to find employment. Only unemployed commercial women were eligible to register with the club. The history refers to 'the most astounding tea party ever put on in Winnipeg' on 14 October 1932, at the T. Eaton Co. store, as a fundraising event for the club. All money raised by club activities was disbursed in the form of wages for work done, as a way of creating employment for its members. A club room was opened in the Alexandria Block in February 1934.

In addition to the usual recipes, there are sections for 'Tea and Bridge Dishes' on pp 89–99 and 'The Business Women's Bridge Party' on pp 101–6. The latter gives different menus for producing a party with the minimum expenditure of time and effort.

Choice recipes

M76.1   nd [about 1934]
Choice / recipes / Preface / [three paragraphs of 'Preface'] / Committee / [first column:] Mrs. J.H.C. Lawrence / Mrs. C.P. Banning / Mrs. J.M. Davidson / Mrs. R. Fry / Mrs. A. MacLean / [second column:] Mrs. G. Goodall / Miss L. Ashdown / Mrs. F.J. Bainard / Mrs. A.E. Duff / Mrs. S.G. Wark / Compiled by / the Women's Association / St. Stephens-Broadway United Church / Winnipeg
DESCRIPTION: 22.0 × 15.0 cm   Pp 1–84   Thin card, with image on front of the church; stapled
CONTENTS: 1 tp; 2 ads; 3–77 recipes credited with the name of the contributor and ads; 78–9 'Household Hints' and ad; 80 'Time Tables' and ad; 81 'For Serving 100 People'; 82 ad; 83 'Weights & Measures'; 84 'Index' [i.e., table of contents] and ad
COPIES: *Private collection
NOTES: An advertisement on p 12 for Wilson Furniture Ltd points to publication of the cookbook in 1934. It describes the company as 'Established 1883 – Incorporated 1921 // Fifty-one years furnishing Winnipeg homes ...' [1883 + 51 years = 1934]. Another advertisement, on p 24, confirms the date of publication; it is for Henry Brothers Ltd, 'Established 1900 ... the experience of 34 years ...'

Household hints – cooking recipes

The Winnipeg chapter of Lions Clubs International was founded on 12 December 1921.

M77.1   [about 1934]
[An edition of *Household Hints – Cooking Recipes*, Lions Club of Winnipeg, [about 1934], pp 63]
COPIES: Private collection

McMillan, May

There is no information about May McMillan in The Waverley Cook Book, *but she may be the person listed in the Winnipeg city directory for 1935 (Mrs Mae McMillan, 191 Colony), for 1936 (Mrs May McMillan, 10 Whitehall), and for 1937 (May McMillan, 100 Osborne). No May McMillan is listed for 1933 or 1934, when the cookbook was published.*

The author is probably not May MacMillan, lecturer at the University of Manitoba, listed in the directories from 1937 onward. This person, Annie May McMillan (sometimes found spelled MacMillan), was from Jacquet River, New Brunswick. She received a Bachelor of Science degree in home economics from Mount Allison University in May 1929, and a Master of Arts degree in education and practical arts from Columbia University, New York City, in June 1933. At the time the cookbook was published, she was at Mount Allison University, teach-

ing in the Department of Home Economics for the second term of the 1933–4 academic year, and for the next two years (see Mount Allison University, Annual Report of the President, 23 May 1934 and 31 October 1934; and University Calendar for 1935–6). In spring 1936, she was offered the position of lecturer in Foods and Nutrition at the University of Manitoba (see Mount Allison University, Annual Report of the President to the Board of Regents, 30 October 1936); she held the job from 1936 to 1950.

M78.1   nd [1934]
The / Waverley cook book / and / housewife's purchasing guide / Compiled and arranged by / May McMillan / "Scot's wha hae been often fed / On oatmeal, scones and gingerbread; / Let it noo be truly said / That we hae variety." / Price 50 cents / Issued under the auspices of the / Sons of Scotland Benevolent Association / Winnipeg Camps
DESCRIPTION: 27.0 × 19.5 cm   Pp [1] 2–72   Illus on p 3 of a seated woman consulting this book(?)   Paper, with image on front of ¾-length view of a woman standing behind a table on which are arrayed cooking utensils, containers, and food stuffs; stapled
CONTENTS: 1 tp; 2 'Simple, Accurate Measures' and 'Suggestions on Arranging the Dinner Table'; 3 'A Word to the Cooks about This Magazine of Recipes and How You Can Use Them to Best Advantage' signed May McMillan; 4 ad; 5–top 6 'The Food the Human Body Requires' by John Ferguson; mid 6–70 recipes, other culinary text, and ads; 71 'Index to Recipes,' 'Index to Articles,' and ads; 72 'Directory of Winnipeg Camps // Sons of Scotland Benevolent Association,' and invitation from Wm D. Morrison, grand organizer, to join the association, and ads
COPIES: MWMM   *Private collection
NOTES: There are many Scottish recipes; for example, Scotch Haggis, Scotch Fancies, Scotch Shortbread, Scotch Trifle, Dundee Biscuits, Scotch Pork Sandwich, and Scotch Meat Pie. On p 13 there is an article called 'The Daily Menu Should Include Manitoba Lake Fish.' An advertisement on p 10 exhorts the reader to 'come to the Winnipeg Exhibition August 4 to 11 1934'; therefore, the book was published in the first half of 1934.
The Sons of Scotland Benevolent Association is a Canadian organization. Morrison's invitation to join the Sons of Scotland, on p 72, explains that it was formed on 27 June 1876 'to foster a feeling of kinship among Scots in Canada, with the further object of cultivating a taste for things typically Scottish, and a love for its music, poetry, literature, history, costume and sports.'

The image of the woman on the binding is unlikely to be May McMillan because the same image is used in an advertisement in S71.1, a mid-1930s Prince Albert, Saskatchewan, cookbook, unless McMillan was then working for Waskesiu Mills Ltd and offered the flour miller the same picture of herself.

Roy A. McLeod of the Sons of Scotland searched the association's Winnipeg District Archives and found references to the cookbook (letter, 14 March 2005): Minute Book, Camp St Andrew's, Monday, 16 November 1934, Cook Book Committee, Sister Selkirk reported receipts of $10.75 to date; Minute Book, Camp St Andrew's, Monday, 25 February 1935; and camp reports from Mearns Camp about sales of cookbooks.

Souvenir book and shoppers guide 1934–1935

For a list of the annual editions in this series, see M73.1.

M79.1   1934
Souvenir book / and / shoppers guide / Winnipeg Hadassah Council / 1934–1935 [cover-title]
DESCRIPTION: With image on front of a uniformed man holding up an over-size, stylized copy of this cookbook; stapled
COPIES: *MWHWC

1935

Day, Mrs Madeline

See also Day's other annual cookbooks for the Winnipeg Free Press: M90.1; M94.1; and M101.1. Her portrait is reproduced on a Vancouver Sun poster for 'Canadian Cookery' presented by Mrs Madeline Day, lecturer for School of Canadian Cookery Ltd, second session on 19 October 1938 at the Orpheum Theatre (the poster is reproduced in Ferguson/Fraser, p 77). OONL has a pamphlet by Day, My Favorite Pickle Recipes [cover-title], Winnipeg: School of Canadian Cookery, nd.

M80.1   1935
Free Press cook book – 44 pages / Winnipeg Free Press / Winnipeg, Saturday, September 28, 1935. / To our readers / [thirteen lines of introductory text] [cover-title]
DESCRIPTION: 41.0 × 28.0 cm   Pp [1–2] 3–44   Illus Paper, with image on front of Mrs Day in the newspaper's model kitchen; rebound in card with *Winnipeg Free Press* cookbook supplements for 10 October 1936, 12 October 1937, and 18 October 1938

CONTENTS: 1 cover-title; 2 ad; 3 'Popular Recipes in Permanent Form Are Gathered in New Free Press Cook Book // By Mrs. Madeline Day' and 'Index to Cook Book'; 4–43 text and ads; 44 publ ad

COPIES: *MNBPM

NOTES: 'To our readers' states: 'As a special supplement of today's paper, the Winnipeg Free Press presents its readers with a Cook Book ... This is a new departure for the Free Press. The picture on this page shows the new model kitchen, on the fourth floor of its building on Carlton Street.' A note on p 3 adds, 'The recipes used in the Free Press Cooking School in the Auditorium, of April of this year, are all contained in this Cook Book and are indicated by the caption, "Cooking School Recipe."'

Hadassah souvenir book and shoppers guide 1935–1936

For a list of the annual editions in this series, see M73.1.

M81.1 1935

Hadassah / souvenir book / & / shoppers / guide / Winnipeg / Hadassah / Organization / 1935–1936 [cover-title]

COPIES: *MWHWC

NOTES: The text includes recipes.

Kyle, Mrs Olive, née Hobson (Mrs William A. Kyle) (11 September 1886–1955)

Sydney Charles Tweed (born in Winnipeg, 1886) had offices in Winnipeg, where he was president of the Universal Life Assurance and Annuity Co., which published The Universal Cook Book *and M109.1,* Honey and Sugarless Recipes, *and in Waterloo, Ontario, where he was president of the Ontario Equitable Life and Accident Insurance Co., which published O677.1,* Selected Recipes.

Mrs Olive Kyle, compiler of The Universal Cook Book, *was the younger sister of Tweed's wife, Winnifred. Waterloo city directories for the period 1927–40, which includes the year* The Universal Cook Book *was published, show her living at 4 Willow Street, a property owned by Tweed and one of the city's finer homes. Winnifred is also recorded at this address from 1935. Given that Olive was a graduate of the Fannie Farmer School of Cookery in Boston (so states p 1 of the cookbook), perhaps she played the role of resident cook. In directories for 1929–35, she is described as widow of Wm A. Kyle, and the 1936 volume gives her middle initial H.*

She is buried in Grove Cemetery, Flamborough West, Wentworth County, with her parents Amelia and Oliver Hobson. See also O690.1, Favorite Recipes, *which has recipes credited to Olive.*

Although S.C. Tweed is listed in the 1940 Waterloo city directory, his company's office, which had been at 18 Queen North, is vacant in 1940. The 1941 volume has no listing for Kyle or Tweed, and the property at 4 Willow is owned by another person.

Olive and Winnifred's family relationship is identified in Winnifred's obituary in the Kitchener Daily Record, *20 November 1948, p 3, and confirmed by the 1881 Census and Grove Cemetery gravestone transcriptions.*

M82.1 nd [about 1935]

The Universal / cook book / Issued by / the Universal Life Assurance / and Annuity Company / (Established 1902) / S.C. Tweed, President / Hon. J.T. Haig, K.C., Vice-President / Paris Building Winnipeg, Man. [cover-title]

DESCRIPTION: 22.0 × 15.0 cm   Pp [1–4] 5–48   Paper, with image on front of two views of the globe; stapled

CONTENTS: 1 'Selected Recipes' [i.e., introductory text]; 2 blank; 3 'To Policyholders and Friends of the Universal Life Assurance and Annuity Company:' signed S.C. Tweed; 4 blank; 5–37 recipes; 38 'Did You Know –'; 39–41 'Endowment Annuities'; 42–7 blank for 'Memo'; 48 testimonials

COPIES: *MSM

NOTES: The text on p 1 states, 'This book has been compiled [for the company] by Mrs. Olive Kyle, a graduate of the Fannie Farmer School of Cookery, Boston, Mass.' There are testimonials dated 1935 throughout the text and on p 39 the reader is referred to figures on the following pages for 'actual cash results paid on policies that matured in the years 1928 to 1934, inclusive.'

M82.2 nd [about 1936]

—The Universal / cook book / Issued by / the Universal Life Assurance / and Annuity Company / (Established 1902) / S.C. Tweed, President / Hon. J.T. Haig, K.C., Vice-President / Paris Building Winnipeg, Man. [cover-title]

DESCRIPTION: 21.5 × 14.5 cm   Pp [1–4] 5–48   Paper, with image on front of two views of the globe; stapled

CONTENTS: 1 'Selected Recipes' [i.e., introductory text]; 2 blank; 3 'To Policy Holders and Friends of the Universal Life Assurance & Annuity Company:' signed S.C. Tweed; 4 blank; 5–37 recipes; 38 'Do You Know –'; 39–48 'Buying Dollars for Future Delivery' [information about company services]

COPIES: *MWPA (MG14 C50 McKnight, Ethel)

NOTES: Page 40 quotes cash results paid on contracts that matured 1928–36 and there are testimonials dated 1935 throughout the text; therefore, the date of publication is about 1936. The text on p 1 states, 'This book has been compiled for the Universal Life Assurance and Annuity Company by Mrs. Olive Kyle, a graduate of the Fannie Farmer School of Cookery, Boston, Mass. ... requests for [culinary] information, addressed to Mrs. Kyle, in care of the company, will receive prompt attention.'

M82.3   nd [about 1939]
—The Universal / cook book / Issued by / the Universal Life Assurance / and Annuity Company / (Established 1902) / S.C. Tweed, President / Hon. J.T. Haig, K.C., Vice-President / Paris Building Winnipeg, Canada [cover-title]
DESCRIPTION: 21.5 × 14.5 cm   Pp [1–4] 5–48   Paper, with image on front of two views of the globe; stapled
CONTENTS: 1 'Selected Recipes' [i.e., introductory text]; 2 untitled text beginning, 'For the past ten years I've been planning and hoping ...'; 3 'To Policyholders and Friends of the Universal Life Assurance & Annuity Company:' signed S.C. Tweed; 4 letter to the company dated 1 September 1938; 5–37 recipes; 38 'Do You Know –'; 39 letter to the company dated 16 June 1939; 40 'The Endowment Annuity Plan'; 41 table for payments made in 1908, 1910, 1912, 1914, 1916, and 1918; 42 information about annuity plans and a letter to the company dated 16 September 1935; 43 'An Actual Result 1939'; 44–7 'Questions and Answers ...'; 48 'An Endowment Annuity Contract'
COPIES: *Private collection
NOTES: The reference on p 43 to 'An Actual Result 1939' points to publication about 1939 or a little later.

Newman, F.

M83.1   [copyright 1935]
The guide / for kitchen and table / Use "Foam Lake" Flour / for baking and / cooking ... / biscuits / buns / muffins / cookies / pastry / cakes, etc. / Over 200 recipes! / Foam Lake Flour Mills / flour and feed / millers of / "Foam Lake" Flour / Rolled Whole Wheat Porridge / K.R. Barkman / proprietor / Phone 75-2   Foam Lake, Sask. [cover-title]
DESCRIPTION: Paper(?), with several images on front of prepared dishes
CONTENTS: First page 'The Banner Cook Book // General Guide for Kitchen and Table compiled by F. Newman Published by Bulman Bros. Paper & Envelope Co. Ltd., Winnipeg, Manitoba Copyright Canada,

1935' and, below this boxed text, 'Causes of Failure in Baking Bread (Excerpts from radio address by Miss Hazel McIntyre, Department of Household Economics, University of Alberta.)'
COPIES: *SFLM
NOTES: The order of publication of the two editions is unknown.

M83.2   [copyright 1935]
—The banner / cook book / Use "Kernel" Flour / for baking and / cooking ... / biscuits / buns / muffins / cookies / pastry / cakes, etc. / Over 200 recipes! / For quality bread use / Kernel / ['K' in a circle] / Flour / Krause Milling Co. / for better results on baking day / Milled by / Krause Milling Co. / Radway, Alberta [cover-title]
DESCRIPTION: 22.5 × 14.5 cm   Pp [1] 2–40   Paper, with several images on front of prepared dishes; stapled, and with hole punched at top left corner for hanging
CONTENTS: top 1 'The Banner Cook Book // General Guide for Kitchen and Table compiled by F. Newman Published by Bulman Bros. Paper & Envelope Co. Ltd., Winnipeg, Manitoba Copyright Canada, 1935'; near top 1–top 2 'Causes of Failure in Baking Bread (Excerpts from radio address by Miss Hazel McIntyre, Department of Household Economics, University of Alberta.)'; near top 2–top 3 'Helpful Suggestions for Making and Baking Bread'; near top 3–mid 38 recipes; mid–bottom 38 'Heat Testing for Baking'; 39–40 'Index'
COPIES: *OONL (TX715.6 B35 1935 p***)

Red and White health, diet and general recipe book

M84.1   nd [about 1935]
Red & White / health, diet and general recipe book / tested recipes / [on ribbon wrapped around left classical column:] quality / uniformity / dependability / service / [on ribbon wrapped around right classical column:] economy / profit / security / success / [in space between columns:] Every housewife is naturally / interested in good foods. / Foods that are high in quality / yet low in price. Foods that / contribute to the nourishment / and enjoyment of every mem- / ber of the family. / This book contains many / popular tested recipes that only / need to be tried to be fully / appreciated. / [on base supporting columns:] Compliments of / Point du Bois Supply Co Point du Bois, Man. [cover-title]

DESCRIPTION: 22.5 × 15.0 cm   Pp [1] 2–48   Illus on p 1 of Red and White products   Paper, with small image on front, between two columns, of a Red and White store; stapled

CONTENTS: 1 introductory text; 2 publ ads; 3–5 'Health and Diet' and ad; 6 ad; 7–47 recipes and ads; 48 'Index' [i.e., alphabetical list of sections], 'Weights and Measures,' 'Oven Temperatures for Baking Different Products,' and ad for Kleerex, a healing salve made in Winnipeg by Kleerex Mfg Co.

COPIES: *Private collection

NOTES: 'An History Note' on p 27 about Robertson's marmalade states, 'The firm was founded over 70 years ago by the late Mr. James Robertson, ...' Since the company was established in 1864, the cookbook was published a little later than 1934 [1864 + 'over 70 years'].

1935–9

Choice tested recipes

See also two cookbooks by the Harmsworth Auxiliary of Virden hospital, M44.1 and M120.1.

M85.1   nd [about 1935–9]
Choice tested / recipes / A Toast / Take the name of Virden, mix well with an / equal amount of love and loyalty; season with / the spirit of the pioneers, stir in a hearty co- / operation in all good works. Raise it with the / hope of future beauty and usefulness, and bake / it in an oven fired with desires that – though / fashions in cooking may change, our children's / children will follow this formula to the great / benefit of our beloved town. / Recipes given by the / women of Virden Hospital Aid / and their friends

DESCRIPTION: 15.0 × 9.0 cm   Pp [i–ii], 1–57   Illus on p 1 of a loaf of bread   Bound at top edge by a cord through two punched holes

CONTENTS: i tp; ii untitled verse beginning, 'I "Guessed my pepper –,' and 'Index' [i.e., table of contents]; 1–56 recipes credited with the name of the contributor; 57 'Household Hints'

COPIES: *Private collection

NOTES: The printer's name is on the front face of the binding: 'Empire-Advance Print.Virden.' The leaves are printed on the rectos only; the versos are blank and not included in the pagination. The title-page of another private collector's copy is inscribed, 'Dora L Bray.'

Diet facts and health cookery

M86.1   nd [about 1935–9]
Diet facts / and / health cookery / Latest information on the science / and art of eating for the sake of / good health and long life. / [three stars] / "The food we eat is as important / as the most potent medicine, even / more so. For what we eat / becomes part of us, part of our / blood, our heart, our brain." / Price: 50 cents / Published by / the Health Supply Centre / 264 Portage Avenue / Winnipeg, Canada [cover-title]

DESCRIPTION: 15.0 × 8.0 cm   Pp [1–2] 3–51 [52]   Paper; stapled

CONTENTS: 1 cover-title; 2 'Table of Contents'; 3–51 text; 52 [outside back face of binding] 'Community Printers, Winnipeg'

COPIES: *OHMB (Ephemera WB400 H434d 1940)

NOTES: The text discusses mainly diet, but there is culinary information under the headings 'Rules for Healthful Cooking' on pp 23–4, 'Salads and Salad Dressings' on pp 30–mid 32, and 'Whole Wheat Bread Recipes' on pp mid 32–mid 33.

The book is undated; however, there is a reference on p 24 to Mrs Madeline Day's *Winnipeg Free Press Cook Book*, the first annual edition of which appeared in 1935 (M80.1) and the fourth, in 1938 (M101.1). There are also references to unidentified editions of *The Handy Home Doctor*. OONL has the seventh (1937) and eighth (1940) editions of *The Handy Home Doctor*, both published by Health Supply Centre, the same publisher as *Diet Facts and Health Cookery*; both are copyrighted 1935. Since there is no mention of the Second World War in *Diet Facts and Health Cookery*, it was likely published about 1935–9. OHMB dates it 1940.

Favorite vegetable recipes

The Brandon Seed House (from 1906, A.E. McKenzie Co. Ltd, now McKenzie Seeds) was founded by Dr Albert Edward McKenzie in Brandon, Manitoba, in 1896. The company papers are in the S.J. McKee Archives at Brandon University.

M87.1   nd [about 1935–9]
Favorite / vegetable recipes / by / Western Canada / housekeepers / Published by / A.E. McKenzie Co. Ltd. seedsmen / Brandon Moose Jaw / Saskatoon Edmonton Calgary [cover-title]

DESCRIPTION: 15.0 × 11.0 cm   Pp [1] 2–47   Paper, with image on front of a woman peeling vegetables; stapled, and with a hole punched at top left corner, through which runs a string for hanging

CONTENTS: 1 cover-title; 2 'Thanks to You and Thousands of Other McKenzie Customers'; 3 'Abbreviations Used in This Book,' 'Time Table for Boiling Vegetables,' and 'General Rules for Cooking Vegetables in Water'; 4 'Vegetable and Fruit Canning Chart'; 5 'The Cold Pack Process of Canning' and 'Just Where to Find' [i.e., table of contents]; 6–42 'Favorite Vegetable Recipes'; 43–6 'Vegetable Combinations'; 47 [inside back face of binding] 'Vegetable Puddings'

COPIES: *ACG

NOTES: 'Thanks to You ...' thanks the 'upwards of two thousand customers' who sent in recipes in response to a request in the company's seed catalogue. The recipes are credited with the contributor's name. The text is printed in orange and green.

Home curing and preparing of meats

M88.1 nd [about 1935–9]

Home curing / and / preparing of meats / Recipes and / household hints [cover-title]

DESCRIPTION: 19.5 × 13.5 cm   Pp [1–2] 3–32, [i–ii] Illus [Free, on p i]   Paper, with image on front of a family eating at table; stapled, and with hole punched at top left corner, through which runs a string for hanging

CONTENTS: Inside front face of binding 'Important Hints on Home Curing'; 1 introductory text signed Standard Chemical Co. Ltd, Toronto, Winnipeg, and Montreal; 2 'Contents'; 3–20 culinary text; 21–31 'Household Hints'; 32 'Table of Weights and Measures'; i–ii book-order coupons addressed to the company's Winnipeg office

COPIES: *Private collection

NOTES: The company made Standard Liquid Smoke, bottles of which are illustrated throughout. The introductory text states: 'This booklet has been prepared to provide you with information on curing meats at home ... It contains directions for the selection, butchering, cutting and curing of pork, hints on preserving other meats for use as food on the farm, recipes for cooking cured meats, and information which will be found useful in the home.'

Pickling recipes

For a cookbook advertising the products of Western Vinegars Ltd, Winnipeg, see O612.5, Pickling Recipes, *and* O612.6 *and* O612.7, *retitled* New and Old Pickle Recipes.

1936

A cook book of tested recipes

See also M49.1 from the same club.

M89.1 1936

A cook book of / tested recipes / Compiled by members of the / American Women's Club / Winnipeg / Winnipeg, Manitoba / 1936

DESCRIPTION: 22.5 × 15.0 cm   Pp [1–2] 3–197 [198–201]   Cloth

CONTENTS: 1 tp; 2 blank; 3 'Preface' and 'Announcement'; 4 'Table of Weights and Measures'; 5 'Abbreviations Used,' 'Measurements,' and 'How to Measure'; 6 ad; 7–193 recipes credited with the name of the contributor and ads; 194 'Miscellaneous and Hints'; 195 ad for De Montfort Press, Winnipeg, the printer of this cookbook; 196 'Provisions for 40 People'; 197 'Index' [i.e., table of contents]; 198 blank; 199 'The following blank pages can be used for writing additional recipes.'; 200 blank; 201 blank for 'Additional Recipes'

CITATIONS: Ferguson/Fraser, p 233

COPIES: OGU (CCC TX715.6 C6586)   *OONL (TX715 C668 1936, 2 copies)

NOTES: The running head is 'American Women's Club Cook Book.' The 'Preface' explains that the American Women's Club was organized in 1917 for the purpose of assisting in 'war work.'

Day, Mrs Madeline

For information about Day and references to her other annual cookbooks for the Winnipeg Free Press, *see* M80.1.

M90.1 1936

Winnipeg Free Press / Winnipeg, Saturday, October 10, 1936. / Cook book / Around the clock with the / Free Press Kitchen [cover-title]

DESCRIPTION: 41.0 × 28.0 cm   Pp [1] 2–72   Illus   Paper, with image on front of Madeline Day in the kitchen, pouring boiling water from a kettle into a saucepan on the stove, and a clock dial superimposed over this image; rebound in card, with *Winnipeg Free Press* cookbook supplements for 28 September 1935, 12 October 1937, and 18 October 1938

CONTENTS: 1 cover-title; 2 ad; 3 'Practical Tested Recipes Are Contained in Second Edition Free Press Cook Book // By Mrs. Madeline Day' and 'Index to Cook Book' [i.e., table of contents]; 4–71 text and ads; 72 ad

COPIES: *MNBPM   MTM

NOTES: This is the second annual cookbook. Under 'Practical Tested Recipes ...,' Day writes: '[This book is] a collection, in permanent form, of those [recipes] which have appeared during the past year. The recipes used at the Free Press Cooking School are so marked, as are those which have been tried and tested here in the Model Kitchen.' She also comments, 'This year we have added a section devoted to the needs of the small families, and also some space to those of you who are interested in losing or gaining weight.'

In the previous month, the *Winnipeg Tribune* had published a cookbook supplement by an American author; see M91.1.

DeBoth, Miss Jessie Marie

This American author also wrote: Food for Family, Company and Crowd, *Chicago: 1936 (United States: DLC), in which she is described as director of Homemakers' Schools of Chicago, New York, and Canada;* Famous Sportsmen's Recipes for Fish, Game, Fowl and Fixin's, *Chicago: c1940 (United States: DLC, MCR);* Jessie Marie DeBoth's Cook Book, *Racine, Wisc.: Whitman Publishing Co., 1940 (United States: DLC);* Modern Household Encyclopedia, *Chicago: J.G. Ferguson and Associates, 1946 (United States: DLC, MCR);* Modern Guide to Better Meals; with Calendar of Dinners and Abstinence Schedules, 1940 to 1946, *[Chicago: Printed by Cuneo Press], c1939 (United States: DLC).*

M91.1   1936

Party entertaining / and / new menus / for the / winter season / Tested recipes / by / Jessie Marie / DeBoth / specially prepared for / the Winnipeg Tribune / The Winnipeg Tribune / Volume XLVII   No. 220 / Winnipeg, Manitoba, Sept. 12, 1936

DESCRIPTION: 42.5 × 30.5 cm   Pp [1] 2–32   Illus   Paper, with image on front of a woman in a kitchen (Jessie Marie DeBoth?); not bound

CONTENTS: 1 tp; 2–31 text and ads; 32 ad

COPIES: *MTM

NOTES: The 'Foreword' on p 2 states, 'The recipes in this cook book have all been collected by Miss Jessie Marie DeBoth, head of the famous Homemakers Schools bearing her name and all are copyrighted.' A month later, the *Winnipeg Free Press* published its annual cookbook supplement by the newspaper's resident cookery writer; see M90.1.

Everyday recipe book

M92.1   1936

Everyday / recipe book / 1936 / Published by / "Willing Workers" / Circle No. 2 / of the Ladies Aid Society of / Roblin United Church [cover-title]

DESCRIPTION: 21.5 × 14.0 cm   Pp [1–42]   Paper; stapled

CONTENTS: 1 'How to Cook Husbands' [i.e., mock recipe] and 'A Word of Thanks' [to the advertisers]; 2 ads; 3–41 recipes credited with the name of the contributor and ads; 42 ads

COPIES: *Private collection

NOTES: 'Printed by "The Review" Roblin Man.' is on the outside back face of the binding.

1937

Cook book

Chesley Methodist Church was built in 1898 on the Chesley Road, 3 miles west and ¾ mile south of Wawanesa.

M93.1   1937

Cook book / Compiled and published by / Chesley Ladies' Aid / 1937 [cover-title]

DESCRIPTION: 22.5 × 14.5 cm   Pp 1–47   Thin card; stapled

CONTENTS: 1 blank; 2–47 recipes credited with the name of the contributor and town, and ads

COPIES: *OONL (TX715.6 C6557 1937)   Private collection

NOTES: This slim cookbook was almost completely homemade: The cover-title is professionally printed, but the text pages are typed carbon copies; some of the advertisements incorporate precise handwriting. Lorna McKibbon, née Patterson (letter to author, July 2006), remembers that her mother helped to type the book because she had worked as a typist for Wawanesa Mutual before marrying, and that she herself 'work[ed] away on the old manual typewriter, making two or three carbon copies. It was quite an undertaking. I was eight at the time and I imagine quite a nuisance.' The OONL copy is inscribed on p 1, in ink, 'I. Poole.'

Day, Mrs Madeline

For information about Day and references to her other annual cookbooks for the Winnipeg Free Press, *see M80.1.*

M94.1 1937

Winnipeg Free Press / Winnipeg, Tuesday, October 12, 1937 / Cook book / 1937 / [caption for portrait of author:] Mrs. Madeline Day / lecturer and columnist / [subtitle:] Recipes / old / and / new / [caption for illus:] Pioneer cooking – 1850 [cover-title]

DESCRIPTION: 41.0 × 28.0 cm   Pp [1] 2–72   Illus   Paper, with images on front of a kitchen, portrait of the author in an oval frame, and a pioneer scene of women cooking over a campfire; rebound in card, with *Winnipeg Free Press* cookbook supplements for 28 September 1935, 10 October 1936, and 18 October 1938

CONTENTS: 1 cover-title; 2 ads; 3 'Third Edition of Free Press Cook Book Has New and Enlarged Sections of Great Value // By Mrs. Madeline Day' and 'Index to Cook Book'; 4–71 text and ads; 72 ad

COPIES: *MNBPM   MTM

NOTES: The introductory text explains the innovations in this third annual recipe collection: 'The section devoted to foreign recipes is a new classification ... We have enlarged the section dealing with canning, preserving and pickle-making, ... We have tried also to include a greater number of casserole or whole meal suggestions, ...'

Hadassah souvenir book shopper's guide 1937

For a list of the annual editions in this series, see M73.1.

M95.1 1937

Hadassah / 1937 / Hadassah souvenir book shopper's guide [cover-title]

DESCRIPTION: With image on front face of two flags (Zionist flag and the Red Ensign); stapled

COPIES: *MWHWC

NOTES: The text includes recipes.

Hiltz, Miss Mary Catherine (1890–)

For information about Hiltz and her other cookbooks, see M37.1.

M96.1 1937

Prezervovannia / ovochiv i iaryn / nainovishym i nailekshym sposobom / pislia / Meri S. Hilts, / Asyst. Profesorky pohzysy na Universyteti / Manitoby, i druhykh avtoriv. / Tsina 25 tsentiv. / 1937. / Nakladom Ukr[...] Knyharni / 660 Main St., Winnipeg, Man.

Tp translation: Preservation / of fruits and vegetables / newest and best way / after / Mary C. Hiltz, / Assistant Professor working at University / [of] Manitoba, and other authors. / Price 25 cents. / 1937. / Published by Ukrainian Book Store / 660 Main St., Winnipeg, Man.

DESCRIPTION: 21.0 × 14.5 cm   Pp [1–3] 4–43 [44–8]   Illus   Paper; stapled

CONTENTS: 1 tp; 2 blank; 3–43 text; 44–8 blank for 'Misce na inshi prypysy.' ['Space for different recipes.']

COPIES: *OONL (TX601 H5 1937)

Rebekah cook book

M97.1 1937

Rebekah / cook / book / Combined / F L T / 1937 / Winnipeg / Manitoba [cover-title]

DESCRIPTION: 22.5 × 15.0 cm   Pp [1] 2–156 [157–60]   Paper; stapled

CONTENTS: 1 'Rebekah Lodges of Greater Winnipeg // Mrs. Mabel Sommerville President of the Rebekah Assembly of Manitoba 1935–1936' [list of lodges and meeting times and places]; 2–140 recipes credited with the name of the contributor and ads; 141 'Table of Weights and Measures' and ads; 142 ads; 143 'Table of Weights and Measures' and ads; 144–6 'Household Hints' and ads; 147 'To Remove Stains' and ads; 148–52 ads; 153–4 'Index' [i.e., table of contents] and ads; 155–6 ads; 157–60 blank for 'Memoranda'

COPIES: OONL (TX715.6 R37 1937)   *Private collection

Winnipeg Public Schools

M98.1 1937

Theory and Practice / in / Household Science / Winnipeg Public Schools / 1937

COPIES: *MWE   Private collection

NOTES: The book uses material from M46.1, *Winnipeg High School Domestic Science Note Book*, produced by what was then called Winnipeg Technical High Schools Household Science Department.

M98.2 1939

—Theory and practice / in / household science / Winnipeg Public Schools / 1939

DESCRIPTION: 22.0 × 14.5 cm   Pp [1–2] 3–169   A few illus   Cloth

CONTENTS: 1 tp; 2 blank; 3 'Index to Theory'; 4 'Index to Recipes'; 5 'Cleaning'; 6 'Cleaning of Woods and Metals'; 7 'Weights and Measures'; 8 'Fuels and Stoves'; top–mid 9 'Control of Electric and Gas

Ovens'; mid 9–mid 10 'Methods of Cooking Food'; mid 10–11 'Food: Its Uses and Composition'; 12–13 'Vitamins'; top–mid 14 'Preservation of Foods'; mid 14–mid 15 'Vegetables, Fruits and Nuts'; mid 15–mid 16 'Cereals'; mid 16–mid 17 'Flour'; mid 17–top 18 'Carbohydrates – (1) Starches – (2) Dextrins'; mid–bottom 18 'Carbohydrates – (3) Sugars'; 19 'Eggs'; 20 'Milk'; 21 'Cheese'; 22 'Meat – Structure and Food Value'; 23 'Meat – Experiments and Beef Chart'; 24 'Cuts of Meat and Their Uses'; 25 'Lamb and Pork Standard Cuts'; 26 'Fish'; 27 'Batters – Doughs – Leavens'; 28 'Flour Mixtures'; 29 'Cakes and Temperature Guide for Baking'; 30 'Yeast'; 31 'Table Service I – Preparation for a Meal'; 32 'Table Service II – Rules for Serving and Removing Dishes'; 33 'Table Service III – Rules for Table Setting'; 34 blank; 35–169 'Recipes'
COPIES: *OONL (TX651 T43 1939 p***)
NOTES: For pp 35–169, the versos are blank. The OONL copy is inscribed on the binding, in ink, in a child's hand, 'Nancy Pearce.'

M98.3 1944
—Theory and practice / in / household science / Winnipeg Public Schools / 1944
DESCRIPTION: 22.0 × 14.5 cm   Pp [1–2] 3–169   A few illus   Cloth
CONTENTS: 1 tp; 2 blank; 3 'Index to Theory'; 4 'Index to Recipes'; 5 'Cleaning'; 6 'Cleaning of Woods and Metals'; 7 'Weights and Measures'; 8 'Fuels and Stoves'; top–mid 9 'Control of Electric and Gas Ovens'; mid 9–mid 10 'Methods of Cooking Food'; mid 10–11 'Food: Its Uses and Composition'; 12–13 'Vitamins'; top–mid 14 'Preservation of Foods'; mid 14–mid 15 'Vegetables, Fruits and Nuts'; mid 15–mid 16 'Cereals'; mid 16–mid 17 'Flour'; mid 17–top 18 'Carbohydrates – (1) Starches – (2) Dextrins'; mid–bottom 18 'Carbohydrates – (3) Sugars'; 19 'Eggs'; 20 'Milk'; 21 'Cheese'; 22 'Meat – Structure and Food Value'; 23 'Meat – Experiments and Beef Chart'; 24 'Cuts of Meat and Their Uses'; 25 'Lamb and Pork Standard Cuts'; 26 'Fish'; 27 'Batters – Doughs – Leavens'; 28 'Flour Mixtures'; 29 'Cakes and Temperature Guide for Baking'; 30 'Yeast'; 31 'Table Service I – Preparation for a Meal'; 32 'Table Service II – Rules for Serving and Removing Dishes'; 33 'Table Service III – Rules for Table Setting'; 34 blank; 35–169 'Recipes'
COPIES: *Private collection
NOTES: The contents of the 1944 edition are the same as the 1939 edition. For pp 35–169, the versos are blank.

1937–8

[Title unknown]

M99.1   [about 1937–8]
[Title unknown of an edition of a 'Better Cookery clipping book' published by National Home Monthly, [about 1937–8]]
CITATIONS: *National Home Monthly* (Jan 1938), p 40
NOTES: An article in the January 1938 issue of *National Home Monthly* about Miss Gertrude Dutton, the magazine's cookery expert, credits her with the idea for a 'clipping book for pasting in favorite recipes.' It was designed to take the recipes marked by dotted lines in the pages of the magazine. The article illustrates the book, which was available free upon request, and describes it as having 72 pp and a 'spiral back' that allows it to lie flat. *National Home Monthly* was published in Winnipeg.

For more information about Gertrude Dutton, see O1001.1, under her name.

1938

Community cook book

M100.1   1938
Community cook book / Compiled and published by the / Crandall Mission Band. / 1938 [cover-title]
DESCRIPTION: 20.5 × 13.5 cm   Pp [1–27]   Very thin card; stapled
CONTENTS: Inside front face of binding list of 'Mission Band Members'; 1–26 recipes credited with the name of the contributor and ads; 27 ads
COPIES: *Private collection
NOTES: The heading on p 1 is 'Community Cook Book Compiled by Crandall United Church Mission Band.' On p 3 there is an 'Appreciation' thanking the businessmen of the town of Crandall.

Day, Mrs Madeline

For information about Day and references to her other annual cookbooks for the Winnipeg Free Press, *see M80.1.*

M101.1   1938
Winnipeg Free Press / Winnipeg, Tuesday, October 18, 1938 / 1938 cook book / 4th annual edition / "Let the stoics say what / they please, we do not / eat for the good of / living, but because / the meat

is savory / and the appetite / is keen." / – Emerson [cover-title]

DESCRIPTION: 41.0 × 28.0 cm   Pp [1] 2–64   Illus   Paper, with image on front of a woman directing (like an orchestra conductor) five women with utensils or foodstuffs, who surround an over-size bowl, in which is printed the Emerson quotation; rebound in card, with *Winnipeg Free Press* cookbook supplements for 28 September 1935, 10 October 1936, and 12 October 1937

CONTENTS: 1 cover-title; 2 ad; 3 'Free Press Cook Book Is Based on Simple and Practical Recipes // By Mrs. Madeline Day,' 'Free Press Model Kitchen,' and 'Index to Cook Book'; 4–63 text and ads; 64 ad

COPIES: *MNBPM

NOTES: On p 3 there are photographs of Mrs Day and Miss June Horne, a graduate in home economics of the University of Manitoba, who is described as supervising the model kitchen. A note on p 3 states that recipes demonstrated at the March 1938 Winnipeg Free Press Cooking School are marked as such.

A diary of celebrated Christmas recipes

For the titles of other cookbooks advertising Five Roses Flour, see Q58.1.

M102.1   nd [1938 or later]
The makers of / Five Roses Flour / present / A diary of / celebrated / Christmas / recipes [cover-title]

DESCRIPTION: 15.0 × 7.5 cm   Pp 3–31   Illus opp p 3 of a candle in a window   Paper, with image on front of three candles; stapled

CONTENTS: 3–5 'Christmas Cake Making'; 6–7 'Christmas Cakes'; 8 'Icings'; 9 'Christmas Pudding'; 10 'Shortbread Making'; 11 'Shortbreads'; 12–17 'Christmas Dainties'; 18 'Desserts'; 19–20 'Sweets'; 21 'Mincemeat'; 22 'Roasting'; 23–4 'Sauces and Stuffings'; 25–8 'Helpful Hints'; 29–30 blank for 'Notes'; 31 [inside back face of binding] 'Important // How to Get Your Copy of ... 191 Pages // "A Guide to Good Cooking"'

COPIES: *ACG   OONL (TX715.6 D52 1900z p***)

NOTES: The 191-page edition of *A Guide to Good Cooking* (Q203.3), advertised on p 31, was copyrighted in 1938; therefore, this edition of *A Diary of Celebrated Christmas Recipes* was published in 1938 or later (as was M102.2 and M102.4). The order of the various editions, however, is uncertain.

The ACG copy has a red paper cover, and the text is printed in red and green. The OONL copy lacks pp 29–30.

M102.2   nd [1938 or later]
—The makers of / Five Roses Flour / present / A diary of / celebrated / Christmas / recipes [cover-title]

DESCRIPTION: 15.5 × 7.5 cm   Pp 3–31   Illus red opp p 3 of a candle in a window   Paper, with image on front of poinsettias; stapled

CONTENTS: 3–4 'Christmas Cake Making'; 5–7 'Christmas Cakes'; 8–9 'Icings'; 10 'Christmas Pudding'; 11 'Pudding Sauce'; 12 'Shortbread'; 13–19 'Christmas Dainties'; 20–1 'Sweets'; 22 'Mincemeat'; 23 'Roasting'; 24 'Stuffings'; 25 'Relishes'; 26–9 'Helpful Hints'; 30 blank for 'Notes'; 31 [inside back face of binding] notice about the 191-page edition of *A Guide to Good Cooking*, published by Lake of the Woods Milling Co. Ltd, Winnipeg

COPIES: *ACG

NOTES: For the same reason as discussed in M102.1, this edition was published in 1938 or later. The ACG copy has a green paper cover, and the text is printed in red and green.

M102.3   [1941]
—The makers of / Five Roses Flour / present / A diary / of / celebrated / Christmas / recipes [cover-title]

DESCRIPTION: 15.0 × 7.5 cm   Pp 3–30   Illus red-and-green of holly   Paper, with image on front of holly; stapled

CONTENTS: 3–5 'Christmas Cake Making'; 6–7 'Christmas Cakes'; 8 'Icings'; 9 'Christmas Pudding'; 10 'Shortbread Making'; 11 'Shortbreads'; 12–16 'Christmas Dainties'; 17 'Desserts'; 18–19 'Sweets'; 20 'Mince Meat'; 21 'Roasting'; 22–3 'Sauces and Stuffings'; 24–7 'Helpful Hints'; 28–9 blank for 'Notes'; 30 'Important // How to Get Your Copy of the Famous Five Roses Cook Book' from Lake of the Woods Milling Co. Ltd, Winnipeg; inside back face of binding '1941 Calendar'

CITATIONS: AnderCat No. 20977

COPIES: ARDA (2 copies)   *BDEM

NOTES: The text is printed in red and green.

M102.4   nd [mid-1940s]
—The makers of / Five Roses / Flour / present / A diary of / celebrated / Christmas / and party / recipes [cover-title]

DESCRIPTION: Pp 3–31   Illus opp p 3 of a candle   With image on front of a carriage pulled by four horses; stapled

CONTENTS: Inside front face of binding 'Christmas Recipes // Revised by June Horne home economist'; 3 'Christmas Preparations'; ...; 30 blank for 'Notes'; 31

[inside back face] 'Important // How to Get Your Copy of ... 191 pages "A Guide to Good Cooking"'
COPIES: *Bookseller's stock
NOTES: This edition, revised by June Horne, was published in 1938 or later because of the reference to the 191-page edition of *A Guide to Good Cooking*, but nearer to 1948 because of the title that is similar to M102.5. It was likely published before M102.5, which has a newer-looking design. Horne appears in a photograph in M101.1.

M102.5   rev. ed., nd [about 1948]
—A / new / revised / Diary / of / celebrated / Christmas / and / party / recipes / by the makers of / Five Roses / Flour [cover-title]
DESCRIPTION: 15.0 × 7.5 cm   Pp [1–2] 3–30   Illus orange on p 2 of Santa's sleigh above houses, many illus purple-and-orange of candles   Paper, with image on front of a candle; stapled
CONTENTS: 1 cover-title; 2 'Christmas Recipes // Compiled by Norah Cherry home economist'; 3 'Merry Christmas'; 4–6 'Christmas Cakes'; 7–9 'Icings'; 10–12 'Christmas Puddings'; 13 'Pudding Sauce'; 14–15 'Christmas Breads'; 16–20 'Christmas Dainties'; 21–4 'Christmas Entertainment'; 25 'Doughnuts'; 26 'Dressing – Gravy'; 27 'Relishes – Pie'; 28 'Ham Glaze – Salad'; 29–30 'The Festive Bird'
CITATIONS: AnderCat No. 20978
COPIES: ACG   *BSUM
NOTES: This edition is credited to Norah Cherry. On p 3 she comments, 'As is the custom of the makers of Five Roses Flour at Yuletide we have gathered together our favorite recipes ... We have added a Quick-Mix white cake ...' Cherry was a founding member of the Canadian Home Economics Association, formed in 1939, and she served on the 1946–8 Executive (We Are Tomorrow's Past, p 5; Cherry in group photograph, p 31).

Page 9 states that 'Five Roses Flour has been the reliable stand-by for Christmas baking in Canada for over 60 years.' Since Lake of the Woods Milling Co. was formed in 1887 (*Monetary Times* Vol. 20, No. 49 (3 June 1887), p 1432), this edition was published after 1947 (1887 + over 60 years).

The Manitoba health cook book

M103.1   1938
The Manitoba / health / cook book / Issued by / the United Farm Women / of the province / Officers / President Mrs. E.L. Johnson, Arborg. / Vice-Pres.

Mrs. F. Owen, Miami. / Secretary Mrs. M.A. Elwood, Winnipeg / 1207 Union Trust Building / Winnipeg, Manitoba / 1938
DESCRIPTION: 22.5 × 15.0 cm   Pp [1] 2–176   Paper; stapled
CONTENTS: 1 tp; 2 ad; 3 'Foreword'; 4 'Patronize Our Advertisers,' 'Abbreviations as Used in This Book,' and 'Convenient Weights and Measures'; 5 'Culinary Terms Convenient to Know'; 6 ads; 7–171 text in twenty chapters; 172–4 blank for 'Favorite Recipes'; 175–6 table of contents
CITATIONS: Peel's Bibliography 6237
COPIES: OONL (TX715.6 U53 1938)   *Private collection
NOTES: 'This book is designed to give practical every day service in the kitchen of the average Manitoba home,' according to the 'Foreword.' Chapter 20, 'Storage of Vegetables,' gives detailed information for storing vegetables in different ways: in outside pits, inside and outside cellars, and above-ground houses.

Middleton, Miss Katharine (Kay) Major S. (Toronto, Ont., 1906–2 June 1987, Chicago, Ill.)

See also M121.1, for this author's Vegetable Cook Book. *Katharine Middleton graduated from the University of Manitoba with a Bachelor of Science degree in home economics in 1929, after which she worked as a dietitian at Kahler Hospital, Rochester, Minnesota, and in Manitoba at Morden Hospital and for the T. Eaton Co., Winnipeg. From 1935 to 1948, she was food editor at the* Winnipeg Tribune, *and she was a founding member of the Canadian Home Economics Association at its formation in 1939 (We Are Tomorrow's Past, pp 3–5). She moved to Chicago in 1948 to be editor of the Consumer Education Department of the Household Finance Corp. In 1950 she joined Harvey and Howe Inc. She became well known as the host, for two years, of a television cooking show called 'Chicago Cooks with Kay Middleton.' She retired from Harvey and Howe in 1961. With Mary Abbott Hess, she co-authored* The Art of Cooking for the Diabetic, *Chicago: Contemporary Books, 1978. She is buried in Mount Pleasant Cemetery in Toronto.*

Information about her life is from her obituary in the Toronto Star, *7 June 1987, p A18, and from 'A Tribute to Katharine Middleton' in* We Are Tomorrow's Past, *p 1, which includes a photograph of her (another photograph is on p 51). See also Lang, p 184.*

M104.1   5 November 1938
The Winnipeg home / cook book / Selected recipes / This cook book contains / a collection of popular / recipes which have / already appeared in the / Tribune's Winnipeg Home / column. They are published / in this form in response to / requests from many readers. / That they may be of interest / to all is my sincere wish, and / it is my hope that Tribune / readers may continue to find / the Winnipeg Home column / of value to them in solving / their culinary problems. / Katharine Middleton/ The / Winnipeg / Tribune / Saturday, November 5th, 1938 [cover-title]
DESCRIPTION: 42.0 × 29.0 cm   Pp [1] 2–48   Illus   Paper, with image on front of a woman, surrounded by a variety of kitchen objects (rolling pin, stove, etc.), who is looking upward to a giant open book of 'Selected Recipes' that has a photograph of Middleton on its left page and her introductory note on the right page; stapled
CONTENTS: 1 cover-title; 2 ad; 3 'Favorite Suggestions for Various Meats' and 'Index to Cook Book Departments'; 4–47 recipes and ads; 48 [outside back face of binding] ad
COPIES: *Bookseller's stock

1939

Favorite recipes of the Woman's Missionary Society Teulon United Church

M105.1   1939
Favorite recipes / of / the Woman's Missionary / Society / Teulon United Church / 1939 / We may live without conscience / and live without heart; / We may live without poetry, / music and art: / We may live without friends: we / [sic, no 'may'] live without books: / But civilized man cannot live / without cooks. / Page 1
DESCRIPTION: 17.0 × 9.5 cm   Pp 1–37 [versos blank and not included in the pagination]   Small tp illus of Holy Bible and roast poultry   Limp black oil cloth; stapled at top edge
CONTENTS: 1 tp; 2 'Large Amounts for Home Catering'; 3–37 recipes credited with the name of the contributor
COPIES: *MTM   OGU (CCC TX715.6 F384)

Hadassah souvenir book shoppers guide 1939

For a list of the annual editions in this series, see M73.1.

M106.1   January 1939
Hadassah / souvenir / book / shoppers / guide / January / 1939 [cover-title]
DESCRIPTION: Stapled
COPIES: *MWHWC
NOTES: The text includes recipes.

Hiltz, Miss Mary Catherine (1890–)

For information about Hiltz and her other cookbooks, see M37.1.

M107.1   1939
Low cost / recipes / January, 1939 / Mary C. Hiltz, M.A. / Assistant Professor of Foods and Nutrition, / University of Manitoba / Winnipeg, Man. [cover-title]
DESCRIPTION: With small image on front of a woman holding a knife in one hand, pie(?) in the other
COPIES: *MWPA
NOTES: The booklet has 23 pp. It is stamped on the binding, 'Provincial Library Manitoba.' *Low Cost Recipes* is referred to in *Fiftieth Anniversary – School of Home Economics, University of Manitoba, 1910–1960*, Winnipeg: Public Press Ltd, 1960, p 15: 'A small book of low-cost recipes, high in nutritive content was compiled at the request of the Family Bureau and used for many years by the housekeeper service of the Family Bureau.'

1939–41

Becker, Mrs

M108.1   nd [about 1939–41]
Mrs. Becker's favorite recipes / The Great-West Life / Assurance Company / Head office – Winnipeg / P.V. Bond Branch Manager / Lombard St. Winnipeg / A manual of tasty cookery [cover-title]
DESCRIPTION: 21.0 × 27.5 cm   Pp 1–23   Illus   Thin card, with image on front of 'The Cutty Sark // Copyright The Gerlach Barklow Co. Joliet, Ill. U.S.A.'; stapled at top edge and with two holes punched at top edge, through which runs a cord for hanging
CONTENTS: 1 'How to Use Calendar,' 'Index to Calendar,' and 'Household Data'; 2 'Before You Marketing

Go'; 3–16 recipes; 17 'How Shall I Entertain (With Menus)'; 18 'Carefully Planned Guest Menus'; 19 'Carefully Planned Menus for Sunday Night Guest Suppers'; 20 'Limited Club Menus'; 21 'Planning Breakfast Menus'; 22 'Needed Equipment for Your Kitchen'; 23 'To Help You Select Your Mineral and Vitamin Menu'
COPIES: *Bookseller's stock
NOTES: The reference on p 2 to the Dairy Branch of the Department of Agriculture in Ottawa suggests that the text was written in Canada or revised for Canada. The name of the branch manager on the binding points to publication in the period 1939–41: Percival V. Bond is listed in Winnipeg city directories through the 1930s, but the first description of him as agency or branch manager is in the volume for 1939, and the last, in 1941. The colour image of the Cutty Sark was printed separately and tipped onto the binding.

M108.2   nd
—Mrs. Becker's favorite recipes / The Great-West Life / Assurance Company / Head office –
Winnipeg / A manual of tasty cookery [cover-title]
DESCRIPTION: With image on front of 'Last of the Wind-jammers'; hinged at top edge
COPIES: *Private collection
NOTES: This edition has been reset. In M108.1, for example, the 'Index to Calendar' on p 1 is arranged in four columns; here, it is in three columns. Although the order of publication of the two editions is uncertain, M108.2 appears newer. Unlike M108.1, no branch manager is named as evidence of the date. The binding depicts a different sailing ship.

1939–42

Honey and sugarless recipes

Universal Life Assurance and Annuity Co. also published M82.1.

M109.1   nd [about 1939–42]
[An edition of *Honey and Sugarless Recipes*, issued by the Universal Life Assurance and Annuity Co., Paris Building, Winnipeg, through the courtesy of the Manitoba Co-operative Honey Producers Ltd]
COPIES: Private collection
NOTES: The last listing in Winnipeg city directories for Universal Life Assurance and Annuity Co. is in the volume for 1942; therefore, this wartime cookbook was published about 1939–42, but most likely in 1942, when sugar rationing started.

1939–45

Victory cook book

M110.1   nd [about 1939–45]
Victory / cook book / Compiled by / the Greenway Ladies' Aid [cover-title]
DESCRIPTION: 19.5 × 13.5 cm   Pp [1–2] 3–30 [i.e., 32] Paper, with a large, red V and blue Morse Code symbol for V printed on front; stapled
CONTENTS: 1–32 recipes credited with the name of the contributor and ads
COPIES: *Private collection
NOTES: An advertisement on p 6 for the *Baldur Gazette* states, 'This booklet was printed by the Baldur Gazette.' There are printing errors in the pagination; the last page should be numbered 32. The heading on p 1 and the running heads are 'Victory Recipe Book.' The advertisements are for businesses in Greenway, Baldur, Belmont, and Mariapolis. The text is printed in blue.

1940

Hadassah souvenir book and shopper's guide 1940

For a list of the annual editions in this series, see M73.1.

M111.1   1940
Hadassah / souvenir book / and / shopper's / guide / 1940 [cover-title]
DESCRIPTION: With image on front of a skyscraper reaching up to a cloud whose outline encloses the word 'Hadassah'; stapled
COPIES: *MWHWC
NOTES: The text includes recipes.

Orange Lodge cook book

M112.1   1940
Orange / Lodge / cook / book / 1940 / Winnipeg, Man. [cover-title]
DESCRIPTION: 25.5 × 17.0 cm   Pp [1] 2–128   Paper, with symbol of Ladies' Orange Benevolent Association printed three times on front; stapled
CONTENTS: 1 'Victory Lodge No. 240 // Executive Officers for 1940' and the names of those holding executive and other positions; 2 ads; 3–111 recipes and ads; 112–13 'Cow's Milk as a Food for Children' by Dr Burton and 'Health Menu'; 114–18 'Classified

Directory' [i.e., ads]; 119–20 'Household Hints,' 'Relief from Asthma,' 'Cure for Pimples,' and ads; 121 'Vegetable Hints' and ads; 122 'For Quantity Servicing [*sic*]' and ads; 123–4 'Table of Weights and Measures' and ads; 125–6 'Index' [i.e., table of contents] and ads; 127–8 ads
COPIES: *Bookseller's stock

Preserving recipes for hardy home grown fruits

Manitoba Hardy Plant Nursery, established by Frank Skinner on his Dropmore homestead by 1925, was renamed Skinner's Nursery Ltd in 1949.

M113.1 nd [about 1940]
[An edition of *Preserving Recipes for Hardy Home Grown Fruits*, Dropmore, Man.: Manitoba Hardy Plant Nursery, nd [about 1940], pp [16]]
CITATIONS: Peel's Bibliography 6383

University of Manitoba, with Manitoba Department of Mines and Natural Resources

For information about Miss Mary Catherine Hiltz, see M37.1.

M114.1 1939 [1940]
Economic Research, 1939. Report No. 1 / The commercial / and home-canning possibilities / of mullets / Departments of Political Economy & Home Economics, University of Manitoba, / in co-operation with the Game and Fisheries Branch, / Department of Mines and Natural Resources, / Province of Manitoba.
DESCRIPTION: 28.0 × 21.5 cm   Pp [i–iv], [1] 2–18   Card; stapled
CONTENTS: i tp; ii blank; iii letter from H.C. Grant to Hon. John Bracken, premier, dated 11 January 1940, Winnipeg; iv blank; 1–6 'Preliminary Report, June, 1939' signed H.C. Grant; 7–15 'The Commercial and Home-Canning Possibilities of Mullets' by Mary C. Hiltz; 16–18 'Appendix // Home Recipes for Using Canned Mullet'
COPIES: *MWU
NOTES: In his letter to the premier, Grant gives the reasons for undertaking the investigation into canning mullets: The catch of mullets in Lake Winnipegosis was increasing and there was a need to find a market for the fish. He refers to prairie farmers of Central European origin canning mullets at home. He names Miss Iva Halsall as Hiltz's assistant, and thanks various organizations for their help. In Hiltz's section of the book, she discusses her experimental method and provides recipes for five canning methods. The arabic-numbered leaves have blank versos, which are not part of the pagination. The book is multigraphed from typed text.

1940s

Favorite recipes of the parents and friends of the members of the Lake Max Branch of the Canadian Junior Red Cross

M115.1 nd [early 1940s]
Favorite recipes / of the / parents and friends / of the members / of the / Lake Max Branch / of the / Canadian / Junior Red Cross. / Proceeds from the sale of / these recipe books are to be / used for Red Cross activities
DESCRIPTION: 21.5 × 14.0 cm   [28 leaves]   Lacks binding; leaves punched with two holes at left edge
CONTENTS: 1 tp; leaves 2–28 text on rectos only
COPIES: *Private collection
NOTES: The copy described here is the master copy of the text, which was reproduced by hectograph. It is owned by Eileen Brake, who, as a teacher in the early 1940s at Lake Max School, organized the pupils to collect recipes from family and friends. The rural school was located southwest of Boissevain, in the southeast quarter section of 12-2-21 WPM.

Harrow United Church cook book

M116.1 nd [1940s]
[An edition of *Harrow United Church Cook Book*, nd [1940s], pp 60, mimeographed, recipes credited with the name of the contributor]
COPIES: Private collection
NOTES: There is a Harrow United Church in Winnipeg and in Harrow, Ontario, but the cookbook was likely produced in Winnipeg, where the owner of this copy lived. The Winnipeg congregation took the name Harrow in 1930, when it built a new church at the intersection of Harrow and Fleet streets. In 1949 it moved again to another new church at Harrow and Mulvey. The book's owner suggested the 1940s publication date.

1940–2

Cook book

The Regiment of the Fort Garry Horse, which originated in 1912, is based in Winnipeg. During the Second World War, the Regiment left for the United Kingdom late in 1941 and took part in the D-Day Landing in Normandy on 6 June 1944.

M117.1   nd [about 1940–2]
Women's Auxiliary / Fort Garry Horse / Cook / book / Published by the Women's Auxiliary of the Fort Garry / Horse to raise funds to provide comforts for the troops / Price 50 cents
DESCRIPTION: 20.0 × 12.5 cm   Pp [1–2] 3–76   Very thin card, with image on front of the Regiment's symbol (Fort Garry Gate superimposed on a maple leaf); wire spiral–bound
CONTENTS: 1 tp; 2 'Thanks! To the advertisers ...'; 3–69 recipes credited with the name of the contributor and ads; 70 'Meal Planning' and ad; 71–2 'Sample Menus'; 73 'Sample Luncheon Menus'; 74 'Household Hints' and ad; 75 'Index' [i.e., table of contents] and ads; 76 blank for 'Memo' and printer's symbol for Winnipeg Saturday Post Ltd
COPIES: *Bookseller's stock   Private collection
NOTES: There is an advertisement on p 18 for the Universal Life Assurance and Annuity Co., Winnipeg, that quotes from the April 1940 issue of a periodical called *Health*. The last listing in Winnipeg city directories for Universal Life is in the volume for 1942.

1941

Faulconer, Dorothy

See also M125.1, Canned Meat Recipes, by Faulconer. Her photograph appears on a leaflet (single sheet, folded three times) called Tasty Dishes Easily Made Using 16 Tempting Recipes Tested and Approved by Dorothy Faulconer, *Winnipeg: Paulin Chambers Co. Ltd, nd [about 1930s] (Private collection). Unrelated to* M118.1, *but also containing recipes using Newport Fluffs as an ingredient, is* Kitchen Tested Recipes *by Ann Adam Homecrafters of Toronto, London, Ont.: The Newport Cereal Co. Ltd, nd, pp 4 (Private collection).*

M118.1   copyright 1941
The Newport / book of recipes / by / Dorothy Faulconer / Compiled and tested for / Newport Cereal Co. Limited / Winnipeg / Copyright 1941, Newport Cereal Co. Limited

DESCRIPTION: 17.5 × 12.0 cm   Pp [1–2] 3–62 [63]   Illus
Paper; stapled
CONTENTS: 1 tp; 2 'Foreword' signed Dorothy Faulconer, October 1941; 3 'Equivalent Weights and Measures'; 4 chemical analysis of Newport Fluffs by B. Guy Hunt and Co., Winnipeg, 10 October 1941; 5 note about storing Newport Fluffs and 'Temperature Chart'; 6–59 recipes using Newport Fluffs as an ingredient, and illus of Newport glassware and of scenes incorporating Newport Fluffs; 60–2 'Index' and at bottom p 62, 'Printed by Bulman Bros. Ltd., Winnipeg'; 63 three order forms for *The Newport Book of Recipes*
COPIES: OONL (TX715.6 F375 1941)   QMM (RBD ckbk 1862)   *Private collection
NOTES: Newport Fluffs were a breakfast cereal made of roasted popped wheat. An item of glassware, such as a fruit nappie or a glass, came in each package of Newport Fluffs. In her 'Foreword,' Faulconer describes the product as 'now famous as the cereal sensation of the nation' and mentions that cereals head the list of wartime foods in *Foods for Home Defence*, a booklet recently issued by the Dominion Department of Agriculture (Ag 1867–1974, p 173, lists the 1941 edition of this 9-page leaflet; OOAG also has 1942 and 1943). *The Newport Book of Recipes*, Faulconer says, was published in response to the many requests for copies of the recipes broadcast on the company's radio programs and included recipes that appeared on packages of Newport Fluffs.

Hadassah souvenir programme and shoppers' guide 1941

For a list of the annual editions in this series, see M73.1.

M119.1   1941
Hadassah / souvenir programme / and / shoppers' guide / 1941 [cover-title]
DESCRIPTION: With image on front of a standing woman, seen in profile against two flags (Union Jack and Zionist flag); stapled
COPIES: *MWHWC
NOTES: The text includes recipes.

Harmsworth community cook book

See also M44.1, Harmsworth Community Cook Book, which may or may not be related to M120.1.

M120.1   1941
Harmsworth / community / cook / book / Man cannot live by bread alone, / He wants a menu

good, / He wants a wife not above / Preparing dainty food. / Published / May, nineteen-forty-one / Elkhorn Mercury Print [cover-title]
DESCRIPTION: 22.5 × 13.5 cm Pp [i–vi], 1–48 Card, with small image on front of a woman stirring the contents of a bowl; bound by metal rings through two punched holes
CONTENTS: i 'Index' [i.e., table of contents]; ii–vi ads; 1–48 recipes credited with the name of the contributor and ads
COPIES: *Private collection
NOTES: The text is printed on card leaves, not paper.

Middleton, Miss Katharine (Kay) Major S. (Toronto, Ont., 1906–2 June 1987, Chicago, Ill.)

For another work by this author and information about her life, see M104.1.

M121.1 [copyright 1941]
Vegetable / cook / book / McFayden / Seed Co. Winnipeg [cover-title]
DESCRIPTION: 21.0 × 13.0 cm Pp [1] 2–37 [38–9] Illus Paper, with image on front of a woman seated at a kitchen table, preparing vegetables; stapled
CONTENTS: Inside front face of binding 'From the Plant Breeder to the Cook'; 1 'Introduction' signed 'Katharine Middleton // The author. Material for this publication prepared by Katharine Middleton, Home Economics Editor, Winnipeg Tribune, by special permission.'; 2–3 'Vegetables'; 4–20 individual entries for vegetables arranged alphabetically from asparagus to turnips and describing preparation and cooking; 21–4 'Canning'; 25 'Household Storage of Vegetables'; 26–31 'Pickles'; 32–mid 35 'Salads'; mid 35–7 'Herbs'; 38 blank for 'Memo'; 39 four book-order coupons, book sent upon receipt of $0.10
COPIES: ACG AEPMA (H86.43.720) NSYHM OONL (TX801 M52 1941, 2 copies) SWSLM *Private collection
NOTES: The text is printed in red and black ink on orange paper. 'Copyright 1941, McFayden Seed Co.' is on the outside back face of the binding. In this edition there is no 'Ltd.' in the cover-title or in the copyright information on the binding.

A variant at SBIHM has the same cover-title, but the copyright information on the back face of the binding includes the word 'Ltd.': 'Copyright 1941, McFayden Seed Co. Ltd.' Also, although the interior leaves are orange paper, the paper binding is green.

The order of the editions bearing the 1941 copyright date is uncertain.

M121.2 [copyright 1941]
—Vegetable / cook / book / McFayden / Seed Co. Ltd. Winnipeg [cover-title]
DESCRIPTION: 21.0 × 13.0 cm Pp [1] 2–37 [38–9] Illus Paper, with image on front of a woman seated at a kitchen table, preparing vegetables; stapled
CONTENTS: Inside front face of binding 'You have to enjoy [our seeds] or we do not get repeat orders, and so – our Vegetable Cook Book; ...'; 1 'Introduction' signed 'Katharine Middleton // The author. Material for this publication prepared by Katharine Middleton, Home Economics Editor, Winnipeg Tribune, by special permission.'; 2–3 'Vegetables'; 4–20 individual entries for vegetables arranged alphabetically from asparagus to turnips and describing preparation and cooking; 21–4 'Canning'; 25 'Household Storage of Vegetables'; 26–31 'Pickles'; 32–mid 35 'Salads'; mid 35–7 'Herbs'; 38 blank for 'Memo'; 39 four book-order coupons, book sent upon receipt of $0.10
COPIES: OTMCL (641.5971 H39 No. 123) *Private collection
NOTES: The text is printed in red and black ink on orange paper. 'Copyright 1941, McFayden Seed Co. Ltd[.?]' is on the outside back face of the binding.

M121.3 [copyright 1948]
—Vegetable / cook / book / McFayden / Seed Co. Ltd. Winnipeg [cover-title]
DESCRIPTION: 21.0 × 13.0 cm Pp [1] 2–37 [38–9] Illus Paper, with image on front of a woman seated at a kitchen table, preparing vegetables; stapled
CONTENTS: Inside front face of binding 'New Ways for Vegetables All-the-Year-Round' [information about quick-freezing vegetables]; 1 'Introduction' signed 'Katharine Middleton // The author. Material for this publication prepared by Katharine Middleton, Home Economics Editor, Winnipeg Tribune, by special permission.'; 2–3 'Vegetables'; 4–20 individual entries for vegetables arranged alphabetically from asparagus to turnips and describing preparation and cooking; 21–4 'Canning'; 25 'Household Storage of Vegetables'; 26–31 'Pickles'; 32–mid 35 'Salads'; mid 35–7 'Herbs'; 38 blank for 'Memo'; 39 four book-order coupons, book sent upon receipt of $0.10
COPIES: OONL (TX801 M52 1948) *Private collection
NOTES: The text is printed in red and black ink on orange paper. 'Copyright 1948 McFayden Seed Co. Ltd.' is on the outside back face of the binding.

A copy at MWMM matches the above description in every respect except that the text is printed in orange and blue ink on white paper.

1942

100 sugarless recipes

For editions of 100 Sugarless Recipes *published by the* Erickson Ladies' Auxiliary, Canadian Legion, *and by the* Winnipeg Women's Air Force Auxiliary, *see O1055.2 and O1055.3.*

Souvenir book and shoppers' guide 1942

For a list of the annual editions in this series, see M73.1.

M122.1   1942
Work for victory through / Hadassah / [caption:] Hadassah ward / in London / [caption:] Palestine / refugees / [caption:] Military hospital / for British soldiers / [caption:] Soldiers' huts / [caption:] Ambulance / [caption:] Youth aliyah / Souvenir book and shoppers' guide / 1942 [cover-title]
DESCRIPTION: With six small images on front; stapled
COPIES: *MWHWC

1943

Souvenir book and shoppers' guide 1943

For a list of the annual editions in this series, see M73.1.

M123.1   1943
Hadassah / War Services edition / [illustrator's name below image:] Harry Gutkin / For Canada, Palestine and the Empire / Souvenir book / and / shoppers' guide / 1943 [cover-title]
DESCRIPTION: With image on front of the head-and-shoulders of a sailor, airman, soldier, and member of the women's force, above whom fly three flags (Red Ensign, Zionist flag, and Union Jack)
COPIES: *MWHWC

1944

Better meat curing

For a copy of Better Meat Curing *distributed by Deleau Cons. Co-op., see Q224.2.*

Hadassah souvenir book and shoppers' guide 1944

For a list of the annual editions in this series, see M73.1.

M124.1   1944
Hadassah / souvenir book / and / shoppers' guide / War Services edition / 1944 [cover-title]
DESCRIPTION: With image on front of the head-and-shoulders of a sailor, airman, soldier, and member of the women's force
COPIES: *MWHWC
NOTES: The text includes recipes.

1945

Faulconer, Dorothy

See also M118.1 by Faulconer.

M125.1   nd [about 1945]
Canada Packers Limited / Canned meat / recipes / Klik / Kam / York / brand / canned / meats [cover-title]
DESCRIPTION: 13.0 × 20.5 cm   Pp [1] 2–20   Illus of Klik, Kam, and York brand products, dishes made with those products, and family scenes   Paper, with image on front of a mother carrying a steaming casserole toward the dining table at which her husband and son are seated; stapled
CONTENTS: Inside front face of binding 'Index'; 1 'Introduction' signed Canned Meat Division, Canada Packers Ltd; 2 definitions of Klik, Kam, and York Spiced Ham; 3–19 recipes using Klik, Kam, and York brand products; 20 'List of Products'; inside back face 'Equivalent Weights and Measures'
COPIES: *Bookseller's stock
NOTES: The 'Introduction' refers to the tremendous war demand for canned meats and states that 'in 1944 Canada Packers St. Boniface Plant shipped to England over thirty million cans of Kam.' It adds, 'We have just completed the construction of a new Canning Department, with a weekly capacity of three million cans'; and it identifies the compiler of the recipe collection as Dorothy Faulconer, 'one of the leading dietitians.' No place of publication is recorded, but the reference to the St Boniface plant and the fact that Faulconer produced recipe collections for Winnipeg businesses indicate that *Canned Meat Recipes* was published in Manitoba. The headquarters of Canada Packers was in Toronto, but each plant was treated as a separate business (see the company's explanation of 'departmentalization' in *The Story of Our Products: Canada Packers Limited*, Kingston, Ont.: Jackson Press, 1943, pp 49–51).

The text on p 2 explains that Klik 'is an all-pork product ... in the modern square can'; Kam 'is a similar product to Klik, but is packed in a round can'; and

York Spiced Ham 'is practically identical to both Klik and Kam, but is made entirely from ham meat.' The recipes are organized in sections for 'Breakfast,' 'Noon or Evening Dinner,' 'Lunches, Parties, Midnight Snacks,' and 'Sauces, Toppings, Dressings, etc.'

Hadassah shoppers guide and cook book 1945

For a list of the annual editions in this series, see M73.1.

M126.1 victory ed., 1945
Hadassah / shoppers guide / and / cook book / 1945 / Victory / edition [cover-title]
DESCRIPTION: 25.0 × 17.5 cm   Pp 1–168   Illus of Winston Churchill, Franklin Delano Roosevelt, Dr Chaim Weizmann, Mr A.J. Freiman, Anna Raginsky, Sarah Gottlieb, Leni Jacobson, Esther Kahanovitch, the Canadian Hadassah Agricultural School at Nahalal, Palestine, and Nahalal pupils in the Lillian Freiman Orchard   Paper, with image on front of a woman in a flowing gown, and doves; stapled
CONTENTS: 1 'Hadassah Organization of Canada' [list of officers]; 2 'Advisory Board and All Past Presidents of Council' and ad; 3–4 'Hadassah War Time Activities' and ad; 5 'We Salute the Jewish Brigade' and illus of Winston Churchill; 6 ad; 7 'President Roosevelt's Historic Address'; 8 ads; 9 'Winnipeg Hadassah Pays Tribute ... Dr. Chaim Weizmann ...'; 10 ad; 11 'In Memoriam ... Mr. A.J. Freiman ...'; 12 'We Congratulate Hadassah!' signed Sharon Zionist Club and Chaim Weizman [*sic*] Club; 13 'A Message to Hadassah' from Anna Raginsky and Sarah Gottlieb; 14 'The Canadian Hadassah Agricultural School at Nahalal, Palestine'; 15 'Greetings from the Presidents,' Leni Jacobson and Esther Kahanovitch; 16 ads; 17 'Thanks to Our Advertisers and Loyal Workers' signed Sara Bernstein, chairman souvenir book; 18–129 greetings from individuals, organizations, and businesses, plus ads; top 130 'Foreword' signed (Mrs M.H.) Rose Halparin, chairman; mid 130–147 recipes credited with the name of the contributor; 148–66 ads; 167 blank for 'Memo's'; 168 ads
COPIES: *Bookseller's stock
NOTES: The printer's name, 'Baker & Sons Ltd.,' is on the outside back face of the binding.

‚*Nordwesten'-Kochbuch*

M127.1 new, enlarged ed., [1945]
Der deutsch-canadischen [*sic*] Hausfrau / gewidmet! / „Nordwesten"- / Kochbuch /

Neue vergrößerte Ausgabe / Kaufpreis $1.00
Tp translation: To the German-Canadian housewife / dedicated! / "Northwest"- / cookbook / New enlarged edition / Purchase price $1.00
DESCRIPTION: 20.5 × 13.0 cm   Pp [1–3] 4–239   Very thin card; stapled
CONTENTS: 1 tp; 2 blank; 3–225 text; 226–39 index
COPIES: *OONL (TX721 N6 1945, 2 copies)
NOTES: OONL copy 1 is rebound; it has 'Elfriede Niessen' stamped on the title-page. The following is printed on the front face of the binding of copy 2: 'Das neue Nordwesten Kochbuch // Neue vergrößerte Ausgabe 1945 // Druck und Verlag: National Publishers Limited Winnipeg, Canada'; copy 2 is inscribed on the verso of p 239, in ink, 'Freue Nordwich Sept. 1952.'

The German on the title-page has been anglicized (or 'Canadianized') in one respect: The correct form of 'kanadischen' for 'Canadian' is modified to read 'canadischen.' The text is in German except for English translations of the recipe names. Pages 3–11 are headed 'Wie wir uns richtig ernähren' ['How We Nourish Ourselves Correctly']; pp 12–14, 'Winke für die Hausfrau' ['Hints for the Housewife']; pp 15–18, 'Vorbereitungen' ['Preparations']; pp 19–220 contain the recipes with German and English names; and p 224 is 'Deutsch-englisches Wörter-Verzeichnis' [a list of German and English words for various foodstuffs].

'Wie wir uns richtig ernähren' asserts that nourishment following scientific principles is necessary for health. This section lists the essential components of food – water, egg white (i.e., protein; the word for egg white is sometimes used in colloquial German to mean protein), fat, carbohydrate, minerals, and vitamins – and suggests that, although diets may vary because of income level or taste, it is the lack of any one of these elements that leads to serious health problems. See also S97.1, *Deutsch-Canadisches Kochbuch*, for another German-language text that presents nutritional information.

Ukrainian-English cook book

M128.1 nd [about 1945]
Ukrainian-English cook book / Ukraiins'ko-angliys'ka / kukharka / Praktychni porady i poiasnennia v Ukraiins'kiy / movi iak varyty i pechy na angliys'kiy sposib. / II. / Starokraieva domashnia kukhnia / III. / Vkazivky dlia zdorovlia. / Nakladom Ukraiins'koi Knyharni i Nakladni / 660 Main Street Winnipeg, Man.
Tp translation: Ukrainian-English cook book /

Ukrainian-English / cook / Practical suggestions and explanations in Ukrainian / language how to cook and bake in English way / II. / Old-Country-style domestic kitchen / III. / Direction for health. / Published by Ukrainian Book Store and Press / 660 Main Street Winnipeg, Man.

DESCRIPTION: 20.0 × 14.5 cm   Pp [1–3] 4–220   Thin card, with image on front of a woman, in a floor-length dress, carrying a covered soup tureen, wood stove in background; stapled

CONTENTS: 1 tp; 2 blank; 3–4 introduction, in Ukrainian, signed by the publisher, *Canadian Farmer*; 5–206 text; 207–14 index of Ukrainian headings; 215–20 index of English headings

CITATIONS: Nakonechny/Kishchuk, pp 163, 1081

COPIES: AEUCHV (UV 85.3.3)   MG   *SSUMC

NOTES: The following is stamped on the title-page: 'Ukraiins'ka Torhovlia [i.e., Ukrainian Trading Company] 788 Main Street Winnipeg, Manitoba.' Page 3 is inscribed, in ink, probably by a previous owner of the book, 'Vasyl' Turetzkyi.' Although the image on the binding shows an early-twentieth-century scene, the book was published much later, about 1945.

The text is in Ukrainian, except for the recipe titles, which are in English, followed by the Ukrainian name. The English terms for certain ingredients, such as baking powder, have been used, but in the Ukrainian alphabet, i.e., they have been rendered phonetically, not translated.

Although the periodical *Canadian Farmer* is cited in the introduction as the organization that financed and published the cookbook, its name does not appear on the title-page. The introduction refers to the need for a good Ukrainian-language manual for cooking in the English way. Peasants in the Old Country, the introduction says, worked so hard in the fields that they cooked only to meet the need for food. This cookbook was designed to help Ukrainians in Canada to learn about the cooking and baking expected of North American women. The introduction states that some of the text is translated from *The White House Cook Book*, 'popular with Americans.' O93.1, *The White House Cook Book*, by Hugo Zieman and Mrs Fanny Lemira Camp Gillette, was an American cookbook, but it was widely distributed in Canada. Part II of the text is Old-Country-style recipes prepared by Leontyna Luchakivs'ka, but with recipe names in English.

See also A34.1, Belegai, Michael M., *Ukrains'ko-angliiskyi kukhar* [Ukrainian-English cook], which also features recipes by Leontyna Luchakivs'ka and material from *The White House Cook Book*. I have not com-

pared A34.1 and M128.1 to see whether they are related.

OTHER EDITIONS: 4th ed., Winnipeg, Man.: Ukraiins'koi Knyharni, nd [1950s] (OONL, SSUMC).

1945–9

Domashnie miasovyrobnytstvo ta konservuvannia ovochiv i iaryn

M129.1   [rev. ed.], nd [about 1945–9]
Domashnie miasovyrobnytstvo / ta / konservuvannia ovochiv i iaryn / zbirka nainovishykh prypysiv dlia miasnykh / vyrobiv doma, konservuvannia miasa ta / ovochiv i iaryn / [...] 660 Main Street Winnipeg, Man., Canada
Tp translation: Domestic meat processing and preserving fruits and vegetables // Gathering the best recipes for meat products at home, preserving meat and fruits and vegetables // Published by Ukrainian Book Store 660 Main Street Winnipeg, Man., Canada

DESCRIPTION: 20.0 × 13.0 cm   Pp [1–3] 4–93   Paper, with two images on front: at bottom left, a woman with a spoon in her left hand, saucepan in her right hand; at top right, fruit and vegetables; stapled?

CONTENTS: 1 tp; 2 blank; ...

CITATIONS: Nakonechny/Kishchuk pp 162, 207

COPIES: *OONL (TX601 D6 1930)   SRP (Ukr 641.4 Dom)   SSUMC (TX723.5 U5D6)

NOTES: The text is in Ukrainian. Only the Winnipeg address of the publisher (Nakladom Ukr. knyharni) is in English. OONL dates the book [193–?], but the style of the woman's dress and the design of the stove indicate publication about 1945–9. 'Revised edition,' in Ukrainian, is on the front face of the binding. The title-page transcription here follows OONL's translation of the Cyrillic characters to the roman alphabet in the library's catalogue.

The publisher's introductory note explains that the book is mainly about meat processing at home. Knowing how to slaughter, process, and preserve meat by salting, drying, and smoking helps farmers make the most economical use of their animals. Farmers can sell the animals live at market or process the meat at home for their own use or for sale later. The publisher comments on Ukrainians' love of pork and smoked meat. He mentions the importance of meat protein for energy, but also advises the reader to eat bread, vegetables, fruit, and milk.

Western Vinegars recipe book and household hints

See O1114.3, Western Vinegars Recipe Book and Household Hints, *other editions of which were published in Ontario and Nova Scotia.*

1946

Fancy fare

The ladies of St Mark's co-operated with the ladies of Regent's Park United Church to publish M48.1.

M130.1 nd [about 1946]
[An edition of *Fancy Fare*, by the Evening Branch, Woman's Auxiliary, St Mark's Anglican Church, St Vital, Manitoba, nd, pp 96]
COPIES: Private collection
NOTES: An advertisement in the book for Stanley's Shoe Repair Shop, 576 St Mary Road, refers to the business serving St Vital for sixteen years. The earliest listing for Stanley Werbitski as a shoemaker on St Mary Road is in the 1930 Winnipeg city directory (the spelling of his last name varies, as does his street number on St Mary Road); therefore, the cookbook was published about 1946 (1930 + 16 years).

Hadassah shoppers' guide and cook book 1946

For a list of the annual editions in this series, see M73.1.

M131.1 1946
Hadassah / shoppers' / guide / and / cook / book / The pendulum / is swinging / to a Jewish / commonwealth / in Palestine ... / 1946 [cover-title]
DESCRIPTION: 25.0 × 17.5 cm Pp 3–190 Illus Paper, with image on front of a stylized pendulum decorated with the Star of David; stapled
CONTENTS: 3 'Value beyond Price' signed Winnipeg Hadassah Council [states the book's fund-raising purpose]; 4 'Winnipeg Hadassah Council 1945–1946'; 5 message from Dr Chaim Weizmann, president of World Zionist Organization and of Jewish Agency, and obituary for Henrietta Szold; 6 'Our First Post-War Building Project'; 7 'Greetings from the Presidents'; 8 ads; 9 'Your $2 Dues Keep the Hadassah Production Line Moving'; 10 ads; 11 'Children of the Ghettos Rescued through Youth Aliyah'; 12 ads; 13

'We Congratulate Hadassah'; 14 ad; 15 'Zionist Quiz'; 16–54 ads; 55 'Jewish Brigade' and ad; 56–68 ads; 69 'The Bible'; 70–95 ads; 96 'Our Grateful Thanks' and ads; 97–9 ads; 100–20 culinary text, 'Household Helps,' and ads; 121–9 ads; 130 'At the Baby Creche in Jerusalem' and ads; 131–2 ads; 133 'Answers to Quiz'; 134–72 ads; 173 'Saved through Youth Aliyah' and ads; 174 'Henrietta Szold' and ads; 175–8 ads; 179–87 'The President, officers and members of the Winnipeg Chapter Hadassah extends greetings and good wishes to Hadassah ...'; 188 'Index to Cook Book Section' and 'Thank You Ever So Much'; 189–90 blank for 'Additional Recipes'
COPIES: MWHWC *OONL (TX724 H22 1946 fol.)

Jordan, Corinne

For another cookbook published by Paulin Chambers and featuring Corinne Jordan, see M136.1, Between Ourselves. *Newspaper clippings about the firm are at MWP,* History Scrapbooks, *M16, p 110, and M28, pp 284, 293.*

M132.1 nd [about 1946]
From me to you / Corinne Jordan / Poetry recipes tidbits shorties [cover-title]
DESCRIPTION: 22.5 × 15.5 cm Pp [1–3] 4–31 Illus on pp 2 and 3 of Corinne Jordan Paper, with image on front of Corinne Jordan; stapled
CONTENTS: 1 cover-title; 2 'This little booklet compiled by Corinne Jordan is sent to you with the compliments of Paulin Chambers Co. Ltd. Winnipeg – Canada manufacturers of fine quality biscuits and candies for 70 years' and list of times on Sunday evenings that Jordan could be heard on radio stations in Winnipeg, Regina, Lethbridge, Calgary, Edmonton, and Saskatoon; 3 Jordan's thanks to those who compiled the book; 4–30 poems, recipes using Paulin Chambers products as ingredients, stories, aphorisms; 31 [inside back face of binding] 'Recipe Index'
COPIES: *MWMM OONL (PS8519 O6 F7 1930z)
NOTES: Jordan was a radio personality. The illustration on p 2 shows her singing into a microphone, with the caption, 'soothing, relaxing music played as only Corinne Jordan can play it ... Poems, recipes, tidbits, shorties and poetry in the beautiful, familiar voice of Corinne Jordan.'
The Paulin Chambers Co. celebrated its centenary in 1976. As Chambers' Steam Biscuit Factory, it produced its first batch of biscuits on 18 May 1876. Since the text on p 2 refers to seventy years' production, the cookbook was published about 1946. There is a hand-

written note on p 2 of the MWMM copy: 'Paulin Chambers closed Wpg plant 1991. Bought out by Quebec firm ...'

Star recipes

M133.1 1946
[An edition of *Star Recipes*, Order of the Eastern Star, Elm Creek Chapter, Elm Creek, Manitoba, 1946]
CITATIONS: Garrett, pp 125, 131
NOTES: Garrett reprints the recipe for Green Tomato Mince Meat contributed by Mrs Carrie Watchorn.

1947

Cook book

M134.1 1947
Knox / Church / Junior / Aid / Cook / book / Selkirk, Manitoba – 1947 [cover-title]
DESCRIPTION: 15.0 × 11.0 cm Pp [i–iv], 1–166 Card; Cirlox-style metal
CONTENTS: i 'Index' [i.e., table of contents] and 'Printed by the Selkirk Enterprise'; ii blank; iii part-title for 'Salads'; iv blank; 1–166 recipes credited with the name of the contributor, 'Quantity Servings,' 'Sandwich Quantities,' and 'Household Hints'
COPIES: *Bookseller's stock
NOTES: The text is printed in blue. The part-titles are printed on pink leaves and not included in the pagination. The same bookseller held *Knox Church Junior Aid Cook Book*, Vol. 2, Selkirk, Manitoba, Knox Church Guild, 1950.

Hadassah shoppers' guide and cook book 1947

For a list of the annual editions in this series, see M73.1.

M135.1 1947
Hadassah / shoppers' / guide / and / cook / book / The goal that / was made / cannot be / countermanded / Walt Whitman / 1947 [cover-title]
DESCRIPTION: With image on front of a stylized pendulum decorated with the Star of David
COPIES: *MWHWC

Jordan, Corinne

For information about Corinne Jordan and another cookbook by Paulin Chambers, see M132.1.

M136.1 nd [about 1947]
Between / ourselves [cover-title]
DESCRIPTION: 25.5 × 17.0 cm Pp [1–32] Illus brown Paper, with photograph on front of Corinne Jordan, playing the piano and singing into a radio microphone; stapled
CONTENTS: 1 'We send you this little booklet ...' and publ's name, 'The Paulin Chambers Company Limited,' across bottom p 1 and inside front face of binding; 2 'This little book holds bits of this and that, collected here, there, and everywhere' and thank-you signed Corinne Jordan; 3–21 verses, homilies, and a prayer, plus photographs of Jordan on the centre spread, including two of her in her farm kitchen; 22–9 'Some of My Favorite Recipes'; 30–1 'Common Mistakes in Cooking'; 32 publ ad; inside back face of binding photographs of the biscuit factory floor
COPIES: *Bookseller's stock Private collection
NOTES: The recipes use Paulin's Biscuits as an ingredient. The publisher's advertisement on p 32 refers to Paulin Chambers 'serving the West for over 70 years,' evidence that *Between Ourselves* was published no earlier than 1947 because the business was founded in 1876 (as Chambers' Steam Biscuit Factory) (1876 + over 70 years). The publication date was likely 1947 because a Paulin Chambers advertisement in a cookbook dated that year, A116.1, asks readers to 'Write Paulin's for booklet "Between Ourselves" giving additional recipe.' Another reference to *Between Ourselves* appears in an advertisement for Paulin's Biscuits on p 83 of M137.1, *Favorite Recipes for Home Cooking*.

1947–9

Favorite recipes for home cooking

M137.1 nd [about 1947–9]
Favorite / recipes / for / home / cooking
DESCRIPTION: 23.0 × 15.5 cm Pp [3–4] 5–93 Paper; stapled
CONTENTS: 3 tp; 4 blank; 5–78 recipes credited with the name of the contributor; 79 'Time Table for Vegetables'; 80 'Time Table for Fruits' and 'Amounts for Serving a Crowd'; 81 'Weights of Common Articles of Food,' 'Measures,' and 'Measurements'; 82–93 ads
COPIES: *MWMM

NOTES: 'Published by Colfax Rebekah Lodge, No. 39 // Crystal City, Manitoba' is on the front face of the binding; the printer is on the back face: 'Deloraine Times Publishing Company Limited, Deloraine, Manitoba.' There is an advertisement on p 83 for Paulin's Biscuits that refers to M136.1, *Between Ourselves,* by Corinne Jordan, which was likely published in 1947; therefore, *Favorite Recipes for Home Cooking* appeared no earlier than 1947. Since the volume's graphic design is close to that of another cookbook printed by the Deloraine Times, which is dated 1949 (M144.1, *Tested Recipes for Home Cooking*), *Favorite Recipes for Home Cooking* was likely published in the period 1947–9.

1948

Sunshine snacks

M138.1   1948
Sunshine / snacks / R / Compiled / by / Sunshine Rebekah Lodge No. 43 / Winnipeg 1948
DESCRIPTION: 22.0 × 18.0 cm   Pp [1–61]   Tp illus of the sun peeking out from behind clouds   Patterned plastic tablecloth; stapled
CONTENTS: 1 tp; 2 blank; 3–61 on rectos, recipes credited with the name of the contributor, versos blank
COPIES: *Bookseller's stock
NOTES: The recipes are mostly for sweet baked goods, such as cookies, cakes, and loaves.

1948–50

The Evening Circle cook book

M139.1   nd [about 1948–50]
[An edition of *The Evening Circle Cook Book,* by the Evening Circle of St Vital United Church, St Vital, Manitoba, pp 48, stapled]
COPIES: Private collection
NOTES: The owner reports that the cover-title is 'The Evening Circle Cook Book: Favorite Recipes of Members of the Evening Circle St. Vital United Church' and that there is an image on the front face of the binding of an aproned woman operating a mixing bowl. 'Introduction' is on the first page. The recipes are credited with the name of the contributor. The text is reproduced from typing.

The advertisement on p 12 for Dodds' Drug Store, Ron Dodds and Roy Breed pharmacists, 'Established over 25 years,' is evidence of the date of publication.

The first listing in Winnipeg city directories for a drugstore run by a member of the Dodds family is in the volume for 1922, where G.C. Gordon Dodds is listed as a druggist. If the business was founded 'over 25 years' after 1922, then the cookbook was published in 1948 or slightly later.

Ravenscourt recipes

Ravenscourt School, a day and boarding school, opened in 1929 in Thompson House in Fort Garry, south of Winnipeg. In 1951 Ravenscourt amalgamated with St John's School to become St John's Ravenscourt School.

M140.1   nd [about 1948–50]
Ravenscourt / recipes / Published by / Ravenscourt School Guild
DESCRIPTION: 23.0 × 15.0 cm   Pp 1–40   Paper, with image on front of the school crest; stapled
CONTENTS: Inside front face of binding 'Index' [i.e., table of contents]; 1–39 recipes credited with the name of the contributor and ads; 40 ads
COPIES: *Private collection
NOTES: *Ravenscourt Recipes* was published before the amalgamation with St John's School and after the legalization of margarine in Canada at the end of 1948 since there is an advertisement on p 40 for Canada Packers Ltd's Margene. From appearances, the book was published in the late 1940s, likely no earlier than June 1949 when Margene was first advertised in *Chatelaine* magazine.

1949

Cook book

M141.1   1949
Westminster United Church / Women's Association / Cook book / Compiled and published / by Circle 3 / 1949 [cover-title]
DESCRIPTION: 23.5 × 15.5 cm   Pp [1] 2–39   Paper; stapled
CONTENTS: 1 'Preface' [mock recipe]; 2 ad; 3–39 recipes credited with the name of the contributor and ads, and at bottom p 39, a thank-you from Circle 3 to 'all who helped make possible the publication of this book'
COPIES: *Private collection
NOTES: Most of the advertisements are for businesses in Shoal Lake, the location of Westminster United Church.

Morden cook book

M142.1 2nd ed., 1949
[Second edition of *Morden Cook Book*, by the WA of the United Church, Morden, Manitoba, printed by the Morden Times, 1949]
COPIES: Private collection
NOTES: Another collector reports that the running head on p 8 is 'United Church Cook Book'; and on p 120, 'Morden Cook Book // Second edition.' The church has no record of the first or second edition.

OTHER EDITIONS: 3rd ed., compiled by the UCW [i.e., United Church Women] of St Paul's United Church, 1963 (Private collection).

The St James' Women's Auxiliary cook book

M143.1 February 1949
The St. James' Womens [*sic*, no apostrophe] Auxiliary / cook / book / Flin Flon Nineteen forty nine [cover-title]
DESCRIPTION: 21.5 × 16.5 cm   Pp [i–ii], 1–80   Very thin card, with image on front of the church; stapled
CONTENTS: i introductory text signed R.B. Horsefield, Flin Flon, Manitoba, February 1949, and 'Index' [i.e., table of contents]; ii blank; 1–76 recipes credited with the name of the contributor; 77 blank; 78–80 blank for 'Memo'
COPIES: *Bookseller's stock
NOTES: On p i, Horsefield states, 'Compiled by the Uptown Branch of the Anglican W.A., [this book] is being sold for the Building Fund of St. James' Church.' He thanks Mrs A.D. Cressy and Mrs Harvey Stevens, 'who typed the stencils' and 'the "Daily Reminder" press, who reproduced them.'

Tested recipes for home cooking

M144.1 October 1949
Tested / recipes / for / home / cooking / Published October, 1949, by / the Young Women's Association / of Waskada United Church / Waskada, Manitoba
DESCRIPTION: 22.5 × 15.0 cm   Pp [1–2] 3–46   Paper, with image on front of a cake; stapled
CONTENTS: 1 tp; 2 blank; 3–38 recipes credited with the name of the contributor; 39 'Time Table for Vegetables'; 40 'Time Table for Fruits' and 'Amounts for Serving a Crowd'; 41 'Weights of Common Articles of Food,' 'Measures,' and 'Measurements'; 42–6 ads
COPIES: *Private collection
NOTES: The running head is 'Favorite Recipes for Home Cooking.' The printer's name is on the outside back face of the binding: 'Printed by Deloraine Times Publishing Company, Ltd.' The same printer produced other cookbooks in a similar graphic style: M137.1, *Favorite Recipes for Home Cooking*; and an undated publication, likely early 1950s, *Tested Recipes for Home Cooking*, by the Women's Association of King's United Church, Margaret, Manitoba (Private collection).

Thirtieth anniversary cook book 1919–1949

Recipes contributed by the Manitoba circuit of the Women's Missionary Federation are in S116.1, Thirtieth Anniversary Cook Book 1919–1949.

Saskatchewan

We clasp your unseen hands in a silent token of appreciation across the border of our workday world, and feel that as this book goes into your home it will become one of the best friends the housewife has, and the pride of her kitchen.

Saskatoon Jam

4 cups saskatoons, 1½ cups sugar, 1 cup water

Pick over and wash the berries, put in a saucepan with the water and boil for 5 minutes. Add sugar and stir until dissolved. Boil 1 minute, pour into sterilized jars and seal at once.

S100.1, *Co-op Cook Book,* Outlook Women's Co-operative Guild, 1946, 'Foreword' and recipe, p 165

The pattern of cookbook publishing in Saskatchewan is distinct from that of the neighbouring provinces of Manitoba and Alberta. The story begins in 1901, after the earliest cookbooks published in Manitoba, which appeared in the nineteenth century, but a few years before the first Alberta cookbook, an evolution in step with the westward migration of new settlers. A total of 126[1] different culinary titles were found to have been published in Saskatchewan before 1950. Although this number is close to that for Alberta, the proportions of types published differ. In Saskatchewan, an astonishing 104 of 126, or 83%, were community cookbooks, and only 15 titles, or 12%, were advertising cookbooks. In contrast, in Alberta and Manitoba community cookbooks made up 61% and 54% of the total, respectively. The Saskatchewan statistics and the fact that many of the province's community cookbooks emerged from small rural towns reflect the agricultural base of the economy. The many fund-raisers are also evidence of the impulse within Saskatchewan society to strive for the collective good.

The Souris Branch Cook Book (S1.1), by the Ladies' Aid Society of Carnduff and dated 1901, is the earliest culinary manual found to be compiled in Saskatchewan. It appeared four years before the creation of the provinces of Saskatchewan and Alberta on

1 September 1905. At the time of its publication, the population was 91,279; by 1911, the population had grown to 492,432, more than either Manitoba, Alberta, or British Columbia; by 1921, it had reached 757,510. *The Souris Branch Cook Book* was printed in Melita, just over the border in Manitoba. Three other early cookbooks were also printed outside of the province: *Tested Recipes* (S4.1), by a member of Wanakipew Church at the File Hills Indian Colony in 1907, was printed in Goderich, Ontario; *Two Hundred Tested Recipes* (S6.1), by the ladies of the Chancel Guild of St John's Church in Saskatoon, 1910, was printed in Saint John, New Brunswick; and *Cook Book* (O 300.1), by the Woman's Auxiliary of St Michael and All Angels' Anglican Church in Grenfell, came off a newspaper press in Smiths Falls, Ontario. There was no shortage of print shops closer to home, but the ladies may have chosen to rely instead on their distant church connections.

By the start of the First World War, the practice of publishing cookbooks to raise funds was well established in the province. Most of the earliest ones were compiled by church women's groups: the Carnduff Ladies' Aid, Wanakipew Church, and St John's Church, likely the unidentified organization in Arcola in about 1905 (S2.1), plus the Presbyterian Guild in

Semans in 1910 (S5.1), Regina's First Baptist Church in about 1910–14 (S7.1), Regina's Metropolitan Methodist Church in 1911 (S8.1), the 'Methodist Maids' in Indian Head (S10.1) and the Union Church Ladies' Aid in Forget (S11.1) in 1912, Saskatoon's First Baptist Church in about 1912–14 (S12.1), and Watrous Ladies' Aid Society (S13.1), the Anglican women of Grenfell's St Michael and All Angels' Church, and Rosetown Presbyterian ladies (S14.1) in 1913. In the period up to 1949, about half of all Saskatchewan's community cookbooks came from religious sources. Although the groups were almost all Christian, and usually Protestant, three Jewish cookbooks surfaced, one from the Regina Chapter of Hadassah in about 1929 (S53.1) and two from the Lillian Freiman Chapter of Hadassah in Moose Jaw in 1943 and 1948 (S89.1, S107.1).

Saskatchewan's growing population needed medical facilities and the publication and sale of two cookbooks in Moose Jaw, in 1905 and 1914, supported new institutions there, the General Hospital (S3.1) and Providence Hospital (S15.1). By mid-century, women's groups at nine other hospitals had compiled cookbooks to support medical services in Regina (S22.1, S63.1), Yorkton (S25.1), Assiniboia (S72.1), Rose Valley (S75.1), Prince Albert (S94.1), Saskatoon (S95.1), Wolseley (S104.1), and Tisdale (S117.1).

In 1926, the United Farmers of Canada (Saskatchewan Section) emerged out of the earlier Farmers' Union of Canada and the Saskatchewan Grain Growers' Association as a new and radical force. The Women's Section of the organization lobbied hard on all matters affecting the lives of rural women. Every June, a Farm Women's Week was held at the University of Saskatchewan, and at the June 1939 gathering delegates asked the executive of the Women's Section of the UFC to prepare a cookbook (S82.1), which appeared in 1940 and included a forceful message from Mrs Bradley, the president. Two local lodges are also known to have published cookbooks: 'Prairie Rose' Cook Book by the lodge of that name in Craik, about 1934 (S68.1); and a recipe collection by the Colonsay group, published to commemorate the royal visit of King George VI and Queen Elizabeth to Saskatchewan in 1939 (S80.1).

The cookbook that best represents the spirit of Saskatchewan's farming communities, and which must rank as one of the most popular in Saskatchewan at about mid-century, is the Co-op Cook Book (S100.1). First published in 1946 by the Outlook Women's Co-operative Guild, it went through several revisions and reprintings in the 1950s. The compilers aimed 'to aid the housewives [across the prairies and beyond] by making the experience of others available to them, to add to their storehouse of good recipes, to brighten their hours with pleasant thoughts and lay the foundation of a better today and a brighter tomorrow, by acquainting them with the different phases of the co-operative movement.' The compilers achieved both their culinary and educational aims admirably. The recipe selection is extensive and chosen from contributions from many different locations in the province (the contributor's name and town are appended to each recipe). The text offers a representative sampling of local delicacies (Roast Wild Duck, Saskatoon Jam), everyday recipes (Shepherd's Pie, Washday Dinner, Macaroni and Tomatoes), old favourites (Lemon Squares, Oatmeal Cookies), and newer fashions (Pineapple Meat Loaf, Barbecued Spareribs), plus recipes throughout the book reflecting the ethnic mix of the population, especially those in the section of 'Foreign Recipes' where one finds, for example, Norwegian Lefse, Swedish Limpa, Finnish Herring Salad, Ukrainian Pyrohy, German Berlinerkranser, and Italian Ravioli. There are also detailed instructions for baking bread, the care of eggs, the care and feeding of poultry, and freezing food (home freezer units were new on the market), plus a page of recipes for making homemade soap. The book is also a treasure trove of information about the co-operative movement. The compilers give the origin, and aims and objectives, of the world-wide Co-operative Women's Guilds, of which they were a part. They also include brief essays about the history, functions, and objectives of other co-operative organizations: the Saskatchewan Federated Co-operatives Ltd, Consumers' Co-operative Mills, British Columbia Co-operative Wholesale Society, Alberta Co-operative Wholesale Association Ltd, Saskatchewan Co-operative Credit Society Ltd, Consumers' Co-operative Refineries, Canadian Co-operative Implements Ltd, Saskatchewan Co-operative Producers Ltd, and Manitoba Co-operative Wholesale Ltd. And they solicited advertisements from numerous co-operative associations, large and small. The Co-op Cook Book was dedicated to the housewives of Canada because it is they 'who destines [sic] human welfare by designating our purchasing power.' The book is at once instructive and uplifting.

Another Saskatchewan organization committed to the concept of mutual help and community betterment was the Homemakers' Clubs, a non-partisan and non-sectarian body founded in January 1911, at a conference held at the University of Saskatchewan in Regina, in emulation of the Women's Institutes of Ontario.[2] In 1919 the Saskatchewan Homemakers'

Clubs joined with the Women's Institutes in other provinces to form the Federated Women's Institutes of Canada. Several local clubs produced cookbooks, in Richard in 1925 (S36.1), Saskatoon in 1933 (S60.1), Conquest in 1936 (S73.1), Yorkton in about 1940 (S84.1), Simpson in 1940 (S85.1, which includes a town history), Shaunavon in 1947 (S103.1), and Quill Lake in 1949 (S113.1).

Saskatchewan women also joined groups with a patriotic purpose. The first Saskatchewan chapter of the Imperial Order Daughters of the Empire, the Duchess of York Chapter, was formed in Moose Jaw in 1901 (one and a half years after the beginning of the organization in Fredericton in 1900), and it was this chapter that published the 1905 *Moose Jaw Hospital Cook Book* (S3.1). In 1916, an unidentified chapter produced *War-Time Cook Book,* compiled by Mrs J. MacGregor Smith (S18.1). Like other First World War cookbooks, it aimed to '[help] the housewife to reduce the high cost of living and to conserve wheat, beef, bacon and sugar.' Toward the end of the war, the Regina Boat Club Girls' Auxiliary of the Salisbury Chapter produced the aptly titled *Food Conservation Cook Book* (S20.1). In 1924, two IODE cookbooks were published, by the Fitzgerald Chapter in Saskatoon (S30.1) and the Capt. McNair Chapter in Biggar (S31.1). No further IODE cookbooks have been identified until 1949, when the Governor Laird Chapter in North Battleford published *Favourite Recipes* (S114.1). The Princess Patricia Club, which had been founded in 1916 as a girls' auxiliary to the 195th CEF Battalion, remained active, and in 1933 published a cookbook to fund its charitable work (S61.1). Also during the First World War, the Great War Veterans Association in Swift Current compiled *War-Time Cook Book* (S21.1). The GWVA became part of the Canadian Legion of the British Empire Services League in 1926, and during the Second World War, the Eston Ladies' Auxiliary of this new entity published *Hostess Book* (S86.1). In 1943, to help the war effort, the Duff Patriotic Club produced the humble, 40-page *Souvenir Cook Book* (S91.1) and the Officers Wives' and Mothers' Auxiliary of HMCS Unicorn compiled the *Navy Cook Book of Tested Recipes* (S90.1) – an unexpected title for a prairie cookbook until one remembers that a division of the Royal Navy Canadian Volunteer Reserve has been based in Saskatoon since the First World War. Also during the Second World War, in Yorkton, the Officer's [sic] Wives Auxiliary of Saskatchewan Flight Training School No. 11 reprinted a compilation produced by the Fort William Women's Air Force Auxiliary in Ontario, called *100 Sugarless Recipes* (O1055.4), a useful resource while sugar rationing was in effect in Canada from 1942 to 1947.

Several other service and social clubs in Saskatchewan wrote cookbooks, some of which reveal the depth of philanthropic work in the province through printed lists of organizations and officers: the Empire Rebekah Lodge No. 43 in Regina in about 1923 (S29.1; in 2006 this lodge was still active, catering banquets and fund-raising suppers); the Alpha Guild in aid of the Red Cross Society in about 1925 (S35.1; the book names the officers for many charitable groups in Regina); Unity Lodge 499 of the Ladies' Orange Benevolent Association, in Tuxford, in about 1928–9 (S47.1 illustrates the Orange Home at Indian Head, which offered refuge to any dependent Protestant child in Saskatchewan); the Regina Local Council of Women in 1935 (S70.1; *Souvenir Cookery Book* celebrated forty years since the founding of the group and listed forty-two affiliated women's societies in Regina); the Wa Wa Shrine Ladies' Auxiliary of Melfort during the Second World War (S81.1 explained how to use honey, syrup, and molasses in home cooking so that sugar was saved for the armed forces); Acacia Chapter No. 3, Order of the Eastern Star, in Biggar in the late 1940s (S96.1); and Regina Lodge No. 4, Order of the Royal Purple, in the Benevolent and Protective Order of Elks in the late 1940s (S112.1 was sold to raise money for medical care and research).

In the second decade of the century, there was concern about the 'noon lunch problem': How could one ensure that children were fed a nourishing lunch in the middle of the school day? In 1916 the Saskatchewan Department of Education answered this question by publishing *The Rural School Luncheon* (S19.1) by Fannie Twiss – well ahead of texts on the same topic from the Ontario and Alberta governments.[3] Twiss, an Ontarian who, only the year before, had been appointed Saskatchewan's first director of household science, believed that making a hot school lunch was a wonderful opportunity to teach children about cooking and nutrition. In her booklet, of which 6,000 copies were printed in the first of two print-runs, she presents all the information necessary to run a successful school lunch program, from descriptions of equipment and recipes to advice on the selection of food. In the early 1920s, the Department of Education issued another booklet on school lunches (S27.1) and *Recipes for Household Science Classes* (S28.1). The latter, in addition to the recipes, set out the expectations for schoolchildren in these classes, including 'Rules for Working,' 'Dishwashing,' and even how to sew the 'Uniform for Cookery Classes' (the photograph of the 'Youthful Homemaker' in her uniform is charming).

From the Department of Natural Resources and Industrial Development, in about 1946, came *Saskatchewan Fish Cookery*, written by Lena Phelps (S101.1). It appeared at about the time the author's husband, Joseph Phelps, minister of the department, was in the process of establishing the Saskatchewan Fish Board.

Cookbooks published for advertising purposes were few in Saskatchewan. The earliest one here is *McCuaig's Year Book 1912* (S9.1), a calendar-type cookbook that reproduces text from elsewhere, likely from an American source. *Robin Hood Flour Cook Book* (S16.1) by Mrs Rorer, of about 1915, is an early publication by Robin Hood Mills Ltd, which had been established in Moose Jaw in 1908 (originally under the name Saskatchewan Flour Mills Co.), by the American owner of its parent company, International Milling Co. of New Prague, Minnesota. The Canadian branch created its own brands and quickly gained a national market for its Robin Hood Flour. *Robin Hood Flour Cook Book* was likely conceived as competition for the already immensely successful 1913 *Five Roses Cook Book* (Q79.1) from Lake of the Woods Milling Co.: $10,000 was spent on the production, which featured specially commissioned colour artwork and text by one of the most famous American cookbook authors of the time. *Robin Hood Flour Cook Book* is the only Saskatchewan-published work that was distributed nationally in large numbers. (Robin Hood Mills went on to publish many more cookbooks, but these are in the section for Quebec, where the main sales office was located in later years.) Another Saskatchewan-based flour company, but a locally owned enterprise, was Arcola Flour Mills Ltd. In about 1928 it published *Golden West Cook Book and Recipes*, which followed the system of the community cookbook by featuring recipes credited to individuals (S45.1). Quaker Oats Co., based in Peterborough, Ontario, also had a Saskatoon office and readers of some editions of *The Quaker Method of Easy Bread Baking* of about 1925–9 were asked to write to the Saskatoon address (O563.1, O563.3). From the Saskatoon Dairy Pool, which made Primrose-brand products, came

One Hundred Tested Cheese Recipes (S59.1) in about 1930–5. Two 1934 recipe collections, both titled *Community Booster Cook Book*, were published as promotional vehicles for the businessmen of 'the Battlefords' (S64.1) and of Melfort (S65.1).

One Saskatchewan cookbook that deserves special mention is Mary Berkner's *Country Cook Book* of 1935 (S69.1), in which she describes her 'improved method of making sugar-beet syrup' and gives recipes using the syrup in place of sugar. She hoped that her sugar-beet syrup would be an economical alternative for families unable to afford cane sugar during the difficult Depression years.

The 'foreign' and other European recipes in the 1946 *Co-op Cook Book* have been mentioned. Also published in the 1940s was *Deutsch-Canadisches Kochbuch* or, as translated in the cover-title, *German-Canadian Cook Book*, one of only two Canadian German-language cookbooks that surfaced in the course of my research (S97.1).

The Western Development Museum in Saskatoon is the richest source in the province for pre-1950 Canadian cookbooks, followed by the Soo Line Historical Museum in Weyburn. Smaller collections are at the Biggar Museum (privately owned), Homestead Museum in Biggar, Regina Plains Museum, Saskatchewan Archives Board, and University of Saskatchewan. For a full list of Saskatchewan locations, see 'Abbreviations,' pp xlvii–xlviii.

NOTES

1 There are 118 numbered titles in the Saskatchewan section, plus Saskatchewan editions of seven books in the Ontario section (O48.18; O300.1; O563.1 and O563.3; O773.9; O776.8; O777.5; O1055.4) and one book in the Alberta section (A111.2).
2 A detailed history of the clubs, including the founding and disbanding dates of individual clubs, is in SWI.
3 See O410.1 and A37.1.

1901

The Souris Branch cook book

S1.1 1901
Tried! Tested! Proved! / The Souris Branch / cook book / Compiled by / the Ladies' Aid Society, / of / Carnduff. / Melita: / Enterprise Printing House. / 1901.
DESCRIPTION: 16.5 × 12.5 cm   Pp [3–7] 8–198 [199] Cloth-covered boards; stapled
CONTENTS: 3 tp; 4–5 blank; 6 ad; 7–197 recipes credited with the name of the contributor and ads; 198–9 ads
COPIES: *Private collection
NOTES: See pl 26. Carnduff is in the southeast corner of what became the province of Saskatchewan in 1905. Melita, where the book was printed, is in the southwest corner of Manitoba. 'Tried! Tested! Proved!' at the head of the title is the same phrase found on the title-page of Canada's nineteenth-century bestseller, O20.1, *The Home Cook Book*.

1905

The Arcola cook book

S2.1 nd [about 1905]
The Arcola / cook book / [rest of cover-title indecipherable]
DESCRIPTION: 15.0 × 12.0 cm   Pp [i–ii], [1] 2–88, [i–iii] Paper; metal fastening(?)
CONTENTS: i–ii ads; 1–84 recipes credited with the name of the contributor; 85 'Weights and Measures'; 86–8 'Household Hints'; i–iii ads
COPIES: *SSU
NOTES: The advertisements are for Arcola businesses; for example, on p 28, W.H. Montgomery, blacksmith, and Arcola Carriage Shop. The printer of the cookbook was likely the job printing office of the *Moose Mountain Star*, the newspaper 'published at Arcola every Friday' and advertised on p [iii]. *The Arcola Cook Book* could not have been published before the first issue of the *Moose Mountain Star* on 19 September 1902.

Hospital cook book

S3.1 1905
Hospital / cook book / Compiled by / the Daughters of the Empire / Moose Jaw, Sask.: / The Leader-Times Company Limited / 1905

DESCRIPTION: Fp illus on p 4 of Moose Jaw Hospital
CITATIONS: Peel's Bibliography 2860
COPIES: *SMJ (Canadiana 641.5 Hos)
NOTES: The cover-title is 'Moose Jaw Hospital Cook Book.' No IODE chapter name is recorded in the book, but in 1905 there was only one chapter in Moose Jaw, the Duchess of York Chapter, formed in August 1901. From the beginning, the members devoted their efforts to raising funds to build a hospital. The cookbook was published after the hospital's cornerstone was laid in 1904 and before the official opening in spring 1906. The 'Preface' states that money from the book's sale was intended 'to purchase the many comforts necessary to aid the sick and suffering while they are patients in our hospital.' The recipes are credited with the name of the contributor.

Sometime after the cookbook's publication, the Duchess of York Chapter disbanded to become the auxiliary to the hospital; however, in 1909 the group reorganized as the Prairie Chapter. In 1913 it took the new name of Moose Jaw Chapter. From 1912, the hospital was run by the city of Moose Jaw and called the Union Hospital.

1907–8

Tested recipes

The Presbyterian congregation of Wanakipew Church was based on the File Hills Indian Colony, northeast of Balcarres (in 1925 they joined the United Church of Canada). Wanakipew Church was built in 1907. The building project was proposed at the congregation's annual meeting in 1907, and the wooden structure completed in the same year. Information about the church and a recipe contributor, Kate Gillespie, is in L.L. Dobbin, 'Mrs. Catherine Gillespie Motherwell, Pioneer Teacher and Missionary,' Saskatchewan History (Winter 1961), pp 17–26.

S4.1 nd [about 1907–8]
Tested recipes / Compiled by a member of C.E. of "Wanakipew / Church," interpreted "Sitting Place of Angels," / File Hills Indian Colony, in aid of the / Building Fund.
DESCRIPTION: 19.5 × 14.0 cm   Pp [1–4] 5–44 [45–6] Small tp illus of a female cook working at a kitchen table; illus tailpieces to each chapter   Cloth; stapled
CONTENTS: 1 tp; 2 blank; 3 'Index' [i.e., table of contents]; 4 blank; 5–44 recipes credited with the name and place of the contributor, and at bottom p 44, 'The Signal Press, Goderich'; 45–6 blank for 'Memo.'
COPIES: *SRA (R-E3383)

NOTES: The cookbook's compiler, a member of the 'C.E.' – probably Church Executive – has not been identified. The recipe contributors are from several places in Saskatchewan and from other towns in Canada; for example: Miss K.J. Gillespie, File Hills, Indian Mission; Mrs McWhinney, Crowstand Indian Mission; Mrs R.B. Heron, Indian School, Regina; Mrs T. Lines and others, from Graytown, Saskatchewan; Victoria, British Columbia; Killarney, Manitoba; and from St Helens, Dunlop, Sheppardton, Toronto, Nairn, Port Albert, Westfield, Dungannon, Carlow, Goderich, and St Augustine, in Ontario. Most, if not all, of the recipe contributors probably came from within the Presbyterian community, especially those involved in missionary work. Miss K.J. Gillespie is Catherine (Kate) Jane Gillespie, principal of the File Hills boarding school from 1901 to 1908. She had previously taught at the Crowstand Mission, where Mrs McWhinney, another contributor, was located. The cookbook was likely published about 1907–8, after the church was built in 1907 and before Kate Gillespie moved to Regina upon her marriage in August 1908 to W.R. Motherwell (then Saskatchewan's minister of agriculture and later federal minister of agriculture).

1910

The guild cook book

S5.1 1910
Tried / tested / proved / The / guild cook book / "We may live without books – / What is knowledge but grieving? / We may live without hope – / What is hope but deceiving? / We may live without love – / What is passion but pining? / But where is the man – / Who can live without dining? [sic, no closing quotation-marks] / 1910 / "And we'll mend our dinners here." – Byron. / Gazette Print, Semans.
DESCRIPTION: 20.0 × 14.5 cm   Pp [i–ii], [1–5] 6–78   Cloth, with image on front of a sheaf of grain
CONTENTS: i–ii ads; 1 tp; 2 'Index to General Subjects'; 3 'Our Advertisers'; 4 'Weights and Measures,' 'Proportions,' and 'Boiling'; 5–7 'Table Service'; 8 ad; 9–76 recipes credited with the name of the contributor and ads; top 77 'Miscellaneous'; bottom 77–78 'Facts Worth Knowing'
COPIES: CIHM (80110)   *OONL (TX715.6 G85 1910 p***)
NOTES: The cover-title is 'Cook Book.' Also printed on the binding is 'Compiled by the ladies of the Semans Presbyterian Guild'; inscribed there, in ink, is 'Donald Clancy April 10th 1927.'

Two hundred tested recipes

S6.1 1910
Two hundred / tested recipes / Compiled by the / ladies of the Chancel Guild / of St. John's Church, / Saskatoon. / St. John, N.B.: / Barnes & Co., Ltd., printers, 84 Prince Wm. Street. / 1910.
DESCRIPTION: 18.5 × 12.0 cm   Pp [i–iii] iv–v [vi–viii], 1–74   Cloth
CONTENTS: i tp; ii blank; iii–v 'Index' [i.e., table of contents]; vi 'Table of Measures and Weights'; vii–viii blank; 1–74 recipes
CITATIONS: Ferguson/Fraser, p 233
COPIES: *OGU (UA s048 b12)
NOTES: Remarkably, this cookbook was printed in New Brunswick for a Saskatoon church.

1910–14

First Baptist Church Ladies' Aid cook book

S7.1 nd [about 1910–14]
First Baptist Church / Ladies' Aid / cook book / What shall I have for dinner? / What shall I have for tea? / An omelette, a chop or two / Or a savory fricassee? / Dear! How I wish that Nature / When she made her mighty plan / Hadn't given the task to woman / To care for hungry man. / Regina Saskatchewan
DESCRIPTION: 22.0 × 15.0 cm   Pp [i–xiv], [1–5] 6–165, [i–xix]   Frontis of 'Saskatchewan Beach // A Splendid Spot for an Outing. McKillop, Benjafield & Co'   Cloth, with pl on front of First Baptist Church
CONTENTS: i–xiii ads; xiv frontis; 1 tp; 2 'A Dinner from the Bible' [i.e., mock menu featuring Bible verses for the various courses]; 3 table of contents; 4 blank; 5–157 recipes credited with the name of the contributor; 158–9 blank for 'Notes'; 160–mid 162 'Helpful Hints'; mid 162–164 'Miscellaneous' [running head]; 165 blank for 'Notes'; i–xix ads
COPIES: *SRRPM
NOTES: The SRRPM catalogue card states, 'The First Baptist Church Ladies [sic] Aid Cook Book was published between 1910 and 1916, while Mr. Farmer was Minister.' There is no reference in the book to the First World War, which suggests a publication date before August 1914.

1911

Recipes

The Metropolitan Methodist Church, which in 1925 became Metropolitan United Church, merged in 1951 with Knox United Church (previously Presbyterian) to become Knox Metropolitan United Church. Knox Presbyterian also produced a cookbook: S34.1, The Knox Church Cook Book.

S8.1 1911
Recipes / Compiled and arranged by / the Ladies' Aid Society / of / Metropolitan Methodist / Church / Regina, Saskatchewan / 1911
DESCRIPTION: 21.0 × 13.5 cm Pp [1–2] 3–101 Paper, with image on front of the church; stapled
CONTENTS: Inside front face of binding ad for Saskatchewan Publishing Co. Ltd, Regina; 1 tp; 2 table of contents and 'Table of Weights and Measures'; 3–101 'Recipes' credited with the name of the contributor and ads
COPIES: SRA *Private collection
NOTES: The cover-title is 'Metropolitan Cook Book.' The SRA copy lacks its binding.

1912

McCuaig's year book 1912

See also B21a.1, Atkinson's Year Book 1912, and B23.1, Jackson's Imperial Cook Book and Calendar 1912, which are likely related.

S9.1 1912
Hang me up in a handy place. I'm worth while. / McCuaig's / year book / 1912 / A valuable book / containing / tested recipes for tasty / dishes / Canadian facts, information / for your health. Also, a / monthly calendar and / birthday horoscope / Geo. A. McCuaig / druggist, jeweler and optometrist / Lang, – Sask. [cover-title]
DESCRIPTION: 18.0 × 13.5 cm Pp [1] 2–32 Illus of zodiac signs and illus headpieces for the monthly calendars Paper; stapled
CONTENTS: 1 'Calendar for 1912'; 2 'This Little Book'; 3–29 recipes, monthly calendars, and horoscopes; 30 'Table of Weights and Measures,' 'Facts about Canada,' and information about teething trouble and hygiene; 31–2 'Household Hints'
COPIES: *SSWD

NOTES: The booklet is printed on yellow paper. Page 2 states: 'This little book is presented to remind you throughout the coming year of our store ... The occasional references to Nyal Remedies we would commend particularly to your attention ...' The SSWD copy is inscribed on the binding, 'Mrs Todd // Lang, Sask.'

'Methodist Maids' cook book

S10.1 1912
"Methodist Maids" / cook book / Indian Head / Saskatchewan / 1912
DESCRIPTION: 17.0 × 12.0 cm Pp [1–2] 3–44 [45–6] Paper; sewn(?)
CONTENTS: 1 tp; 2 blank; 3–46 recipes credited with the name of the contributor
COPIES: *SSWD
NOTES: No institution is named, but the cookbook was likely produced by the women of Indian Head's Methodist Church, built in 1898. The SSWD copy is in poor condition and may be lacking leaves at the back.

The reliable cook-book

S11.1 1912
The reliable / cook-book / Compiled by the Ladies' Aid of Forget Union Church. / "Let me cook the meals of my country, and I / care not who makes her laws." / December / tenth. / Nineteen / hundred / and / twelve / [caption:] The / Union / Church / Forget
DESCRIPTION: About 15.5 × 11.5 cm [dimensions from photocopy] Pp [i–vi], [1] 2–90 [91–2] Tp photograph of the church
CONTENTS: i tp; ii blank; iii–iv 'Table of Equivalents' and 'Table of Proportions'; top–mid v 'To Be a Good Cook' quoted from Ruskin; bottom v–vi 'Golden Rules for the Kitchen'; 1–90 recipes credited with the name of the contributor and ads; 91–2 'The Care of Silverware'
COPIES: *Private collection
NOTES: The name of the printer, 'Stoughton Times Print,' is on the front face of the binding. The running head is 'Forget Ladies' Aid Cook Book.'

1912–14

Saskatoon souvenir cook book

S12.1   nd [about 1912–14]
Saskatoon souvenir / cook book / First Baptist
Church / 4th Avenue at 25th Stree [*sic*] / Users of
this book are asked to patronize our / advertisers /
Published by / Philathea Class / First Baptist
Church / Perry & Anderson [union label] printers,
Saskatoon
DESCRIPTION: Pp [1] 2–32   Tp illus of the church
Stapled
CONTENTS: 1 tp; 2 ad; 3–28 recipes credited with the
name of the contributor; 29 blank; ...; 32 ad
COPIES: *Private collection
NOTES: The church building illustrated on the title-
page was dedicated on 3 December 1911 and burnt
down in 1943. Advertisements point to publication in
the first years after the church's construction, about
1912–14: The Saskatoon Pure Milk Co. Ltd (advertised on outside back face of binding) was incorporated in 1912; the last listing in city directories for
Saskatoon Trading Co. Ltd (advertised on inside back
face) is in the volume for 1914.

1913

Cook book

*Watrous was founded in 1906. The Methodist Church
was built in 1909 on the corner of Third Avenue East and
Second Street. In 1919, the Methodist and Presbyterian
congregations amalgamated to form the Union Church,
at which point the Presbyterian Church was used for
worship; the Methodist building was later sold. For a
cookbook published by the Union Church, see S24.1,
Cook Book. The church history is in* Prairie Reflections: Watrous, Venn, Manitou Beach, Renown,
Amazon and District, *published by Watrous and
District History Committee, copyright 1983, first printing 1984, pp 91–2.*

S13.1   1913
Metropolitan Methodist Church / Cook / book /
Compiled and arranged by the / Ladies' Aid Society
/ Price 50 cents. / Watrous, Sask., 1913
DESCRIPTION: 20.0 × 14.0 cm   Pp [1–4] 5–82   Illus on
p 82 of Manitou Mineral Lake   Very thin card; stapled
CONTENTS: 1 tp; 2 'Food Definition'; 3 'Contents' and
'Table of Weights and Measures'; 4 'How to Cook a
Husband' [mock recipe]; 5–82 recipes credited with
the name of the contributor and ads
COPIES: *Private collection

NOTES: 'Watrous Post Job Print' is on the outside back
face of the binding. The recipe for Turkish Delight on
p 80 is credited to Brandon Methodist Cook Book.
This is probably a reference to M3.1, *The Wheat City
Cook-Book*, compiled by the ladies of the Methodist
Church, Brandon, three editions of which were published from 1901 to 1910. The collector's copy of S13.1
is inscribed on the title-page, 'Mrs. J.E. Charlesworth
// Blyth Ont.'

Cook book

*See O300.1, Cook Book, for the work produced by the
Woman's Auxiliary of St Michael and All Angels'
Anglican Church in Grenfell, Saskatchewan, but printed
by a newspaper in Smiths Falls, Ontario. Unusual for a
community cookbook, there are several advertisements for
distant businesses (for example, the jam maker E.D.
Smith in Winona, Cowan Co. in Toronto, and Kaufman
Rubber Co. in Berlin, all in Ontario); however, the
advertisement on p 34 for the Windsor Hotel, Grenfell,
Saskatchewan, confirms that the book is from that town,
which has a church called St Michael and All Angels'
(there is no church of that name in Grenfell, Ontario).*

Rosetown Presbyterian ladies cook book

S14.1   1913
Rosetown / Presbyterian ladies / cook book /
Rosetown / Printed by the Rosetown Eagle / 1913
DESCRIPTION: 18.5 × 13.5 cm   Pp [1] 2–57   No bind-
ing?; stapled
CONTENTS: 1 tp; 2 ad; 3 'Preface'; 4 ad; 5–57 recipes
credited with the name of the contributor and ads
COPIES: CIHM (78241)   *OONL (TX715 R67)
NOTES: The running head is 'R.P.L. Cook Book.' This
volume may never have had a binding; the title-
page/cover-title is on the same paper as the text
pages. The ladies belonged to the Presbyterian
Church, one of only two churches in Rosetown in
1913 (the other was Methodist).

1914

Providence Hospital cook book

*Providence Hospital opened in November 1912. It was
run by the Sisters of Providence of St Vincent de Paul.*

S15.1   1914
Providence / Hospital / cook / book / Moose Jaw,
January, 1914 / Price fifty cents [cover-title]

DESCRIPTION: 17.5 × 14.5 cm   Pp [1–5] 6–118, [i–ii]
Fp illus on p 1 of Providence Hospital   Paper, with
image on front of books on a shelf; stapled
CONTENTS: 1 fp illus; 2 ad; 3 'Index'; 4 ad; 5 'Preface'; 6
'How to Cook a Husband' [mock recipe]; 7–113 reci-
pes credited with the name of the contributor; 114
'Table for Kitchen Use'; 115 'Weights and Measures';
116–18 'Helpful Hints to the Housewife'; i–ii ads
COPIES: *Private collection
NOTES: The 'Preface' refers to the Ways and Means
Committee of Providence Hospital, organized 21 April
1913, 'to devise ways and means to procure money.'
The 'Preface' comments: 'The "Cook Book money
making scheme" is not new, but ... we found courage
to try the Cook Book scheme ... we now modestly
launch the first edition ...' The printer's name, 'Times
Job Dept., Moose Jaw,' is on the outside back face of
the binding.

1915

Rorer, Mrs Sarah Tyson, née Heston (Richboro, Bucks County, Pa, 1849–1937, Colebrook, Lebanon County, Pa)

For information about this American author and the titles of her other books, see O56.1.

Robin Hood Mills Ltd had its beginnings in Moose
Jaw, Saskatchewan, in July 1908, when Francis Atherton
Bean, Sr (1840–1930) bought Moose Jaw Milling Co.
from a local firm, Donald McLean and Son. Bean, Sr
(affectionately known in later years as Grandfather Bean)
was the American owner of International Milling Co.,
which he had founded in New Prague, Minnesota, in
1892. On 27 January 1909, the modernized and enlarged
mill began producing flour, under the new American
ownership and the name Saskatchewan Flour Mills Co.
Ltd. Robin Hood was one of the four new brand names
introduced at the outset and it was exclusive to the
Canadian market (the other brand names were Radium,
Keynote, and Saskania). A disastrous fire at the Moose
Jaw mill in December 1911 spurred on the company's
plans for expansion: In 1912, it purchased another mill in
Calgary (from Calgary Milling Co.; see that company's
cookbook, A20.1, Woolley, E.S., The Mainstay of Multitudes), rebuilt the Moose Jaw mill, and on 12 April 1912,
incorporated the business as Robin Hood Mills Ltd. The
Canadian entity grew rapidly as sales offices were established nation-wide. Whereas the American parent company, in the period up to 1945, focused on products for
commercial bakers, the growth of the Canadian branch of
the business was through the sale of family flour under
the Canadian brand Robin Hood. By 1932 Robin Hood

Mills Ltd produced the most flour for home use in
Canada. In the 1930s, massive audiences attended Robin
Hood Cooking Schools in cities across the country, hosted
by local women's charitable groups; and the company
boasted of the many users of Robin Hood Flour who won
top prizes at the popular baking contests held at fairs and
exhibitions (see, for example, Grist (October 1933), p 12,
and (April 1936), p 24). Cookbooks and other printed
material helped to advertise the brand, as did 'Robin
Hood the Answer Man,' a radio personality in Quebec
City, played by the actor J.R. Coutlee (see Grist (April
1936), p 8). The image of Robin Hood on the binding of
Robin Hood Flour Cook Book was painted by Arthur
H. Hider before the company's 1912 name change (see
unsourced publication in Canadian Artists Files,
OTMCL) and used in promotions for many years.
The Moose Jaw mill was famous for the 80-foot-high
figure of Robin Hood painted on its side in 1922 by
Harry Bell, a local sign painter. Following the release
of the film The Adventures of Robin Hood in 1938,
starring Errol Flynn as Robin, the flour company
capitalized on the film's popularity by obtaining permission to use Flynn's likeness for Robin on all its
products.

Robin Hood's success in Canada was due in large part
to the leadership of the dynamic Canadian salesman
Charles Ritz, who had started with the company in Moose
Jaw on 16 October 1910, set up the eastern sales office in
Montreal in 1915, and, from about 1937, directed Canadian and American sales from the Minneapolis office. In
1955 he became chairman of the Board of International
Milling. It was Ritz who introduced Robin Hood Flour to
the American market in the late 1930s, possibly first in
Greenville, Texas; however, family flour was a small part
of International Milling's business and Robin Hood Flour
was sold only in regional markets in the United States up
to 1945. At the end of the Second World War, Ritz
spearheaded an initiative to increase the American
company's family flour business, jettisoning unsuccessful
brands and aggressively marketing the Robin Hood
brand. By 1950, Robin Hood was the 'third largest selling
brand of family flour in the United States.' (For Ritz's
career, see Grist Vol. 16, No. 17 [Special Issue, October
1960], celebrating his fifty years with the company.)

Although the Canadian branch of the business had
started in Moose Jaw and Moose Jaw remained Canada's
head office on paper until the flour mill closed there in
1966, the Montreal sales office became the de facto Canadian headquarters. About 1936–8, the company changed
its name from Robin Hood Mills Ltd to Robin Hood Flour
Mills Ltd. In 1952 the company bought St Lawrence
Flour Mills Ltd and Brodie and Harvie Ltd, both
Montreal-based flour producers (cookbooks by both
companies are in this bibliography). Robin Hood Flour

Mills Ltd became a public company in January 1964. In 1970 it was renamed Robin Hood Multifoods Ltd.

Robin Hood Flour Cook Book is located in the Saskatchewan section of this bibliography because Moose Jaw, the first city recorded in the imprint, was the company's head office then. Other cookbooks promoting Robin Hood Flour are located in the Quebec section because, at the time of their publication, headquarters was in Montreal. These are: Q176.1, 77 Winning Recipes; Q247.1, Baking Made Easy; Q285.1, Ration Recipes; and the titles listed in Q249.1, Simplified Method for Making Refrigerator Sweet Dough, under Rita Martin, one of the pseudonyms used by the company to market its products, from about 1938.

The above history of Robin Hood Mills and International Milling Co. is gleaned from issues of Grist *(OMARH corporate archives and a former employee's private collection; copies of* Grist, *from April 1942, are also at the Minnesota Historical Society), and from clippings about the company's Moose Jaw mill, on file at SMJ (see especially 'Saskatchewan Flour Mills Opened Today,'* Moose Jaw Evening Times, *27 January 1909).*

S16.1   nd [about 1915]
Robin Hood / Flour / cook / book / Robin Hood Mills Ltd / Moose Jaw Calgary Canada
DESCRIPTION: 26.5 × 19.0 cm   Pp [1–6] 7–78 [79–80]
Pls col on pp 3–4, 35–6, 45–8; illus green and two shades of brown   Paper, with image on front of Robin Hood about to shoot an arrow, and cloth spine
CONTENTS: 1 tp; 2 blank; 3–4 pl col (verso blank); 5 'Table of Contents'; 6 'The recipes in this cook book were prepared and written for our special use by Mrs. S.T. Rorer, are copyrighted, and are published by permission of her publishers, Arnold & Company, Philadelphia, Pa. // Bulman Bros. Limited, printers, Winnipeg, Man.'; 7–8 'Introductory // Foreword'; 9–72 recipes; 73–4 blank for 'Grandmother's Recipes'; 75–6 blank for 'Mother's Recipes'; 77–8 blank for 'Auntie's Recipes'; 79–80 instructions and coupons for ordering the cookbook
CITATIONS: Cooke 2003, p 213   Crawford, p D1, illus col of pl col of woman and sack of flour   Driver 2003, Ogilvie's Book, inside front cover   Ferguson/Fraser, p 233, illus col on p 34 of pl col, illus col on p 35 of closed volume
COPIES: AC (Pam file 641.5971 Ror)   ACG   AEUCHV (UV 85.312.12)   AHRMH   BVAMM (NN482) *BVMA   MCDHM   MWMM   OKITJS (991.39.3) SELH
NOTES: This is the first of several cookbooks, in the period to 1950, produced by Robin Hood Mills to promote its products. Opposite p 34 there is an illus-

tration of a container of Robin Hood Porridge Wheat; printed on the container's label is 'Copyright Canada 1914 by Robin Hood Mills.' The cookbook was likely published about 1915 since the copy at SELH is identified as 'brought by Mrs. Adam Kelsey to the homestead in 1915.' The cookbook is advertised in the November 1919 issue of *Western Home Monthly,* although the edition is not specified: 'Get the $10,000 Robin Hood Cook Book ... it's a handsome book by Mrs. Rorer, one of the best known authorities on cooking.'

Robin Hood Flour Cook Book is notable for its lavish colour illustrations. As the 'Introductory // Foreword' states:

> This is not an ordinary advertising Cook Book ... Nearly two years of preparatory work and $10,000.00 in money was spent on the first edition of this book ... No pains have been spared to make the Robin Hood Cook Book the finest example of modern printing. Note particularly the seven beautiful three-color process plates showing the Robin Hood products in their natural color. This is the first time this expensive process has been used in any cook book in Canada. There are in addition about forty illustrations, also in three colors, showing scenes from the life of Robin Hood. One of the leading American artists, Mr. Moen, has been engaged for the past year gathering material and drawing this beautiful series of illustrations.

Many of the images are signed with the artist's monogram, 'L.M.' The unattributed painting of Robin Hood reproduced on the binding is by the Canadian artist Arthur Hider (see p 997).

It is not surprising that an American author was chosen to write *Robin Hood Flour Cook Book* since Robin Hood Mills was privately owned by an American at the time. Mrs Rorer was already in her mid-sixties and the author of about forty titles when she compiled *Robin Hood Flour Cook Book,* whose text embodies her many years of experience as a cookery writer and lecturer. In particular, the organization of the chapters, the selection of recipes, and the phrasing of the instructions show many parallels with her major reference work, *Mrs Rorer's New Cook Book,* first published in Philadelphia in 1902 (and in Toronto a year later, O137.1). Sometimes, the wording of recipes in the Robin Hood book is virtually identical to that in her 1902 work (Home Made Yeast, English Plum Pudding), or the instructions for the same recipe are abridged (for Chicken Croquettes she specifies cooked-and-chopped chicken, instead of explaining how to boil the poultry first). In other instances, she recasts two recipes from *New Cook Book* as one recipe (Cream of Green Pea Soup and Cream of Pea Soup from Canned Peas become Cream of Pea Soup, incorporating directions for both fresh and canned peas). In only 78 pp, she offers a wide range of dishes, from sophisticated to the humblest. Many recipes bear American names (Eggs Jefferson, Carolina Snow), but there are also ones from other national cuisines, such as Mexico, the West Indies, France, and England. Although her selection was generally familiar to Canada's home cooks, the American author inadvertently omitted some Canadian favourites, such as Butter Tarts, Maple Syrup Tarts, Maple Syrup Pie, and doughnuts (all found in Q79.1, *Five Roses Cook Book,* by a competing flour miller).

In this edition of *Robin Hood Flour Cook Book*, the last section listed in the 'Table of Contents' is 'Auntie's Recipes,' pp 77–8. There are variant editions distinguished by the typesetting of the Rorer/Arnold and Co. information on p 6. One variant has this information in a two-line box, all lines of text justified right and left; in the last line, there is no decorative space-filling device between the words 'Company,' and 'Philadelphia' (AEUCHV, MWMM, OKITJS). Another variant has the information in a two-line box, all lines of text justified right and left; in the last line there is a decorative device of four dots between the words 'Company,' and 'Philadelphia' (AC, ACG, AHRMH, SELH). Another variant has the information in a one-line box, all lines of text justified right and left; in the last line, there is no decorative space-filling device in the last line (BVMA). Another variant has the information in a one-line box, all lines of text justified right and left, except the first line is indented and the last line is not justified right; there is no decorative space-filling device in the last line (BVAMM, MCDHM). OONL (TX714 R66 1930z fol.) and SBIM, and DLC (TX714 R64 1930z Bitting Coll) in the United States, have a copy of *Robin Hood Flour Cook Book* that may match S16.1 or S16.2. There were no American editions of the cookbook because Robin Hood Flour was distributed only in Canada in the early years.

A letter from a user of Robin Hood Flour (Mrs G.B. Thrasher), dated 30 September 1931, Bull River, British Columbia, is reprinted on p 18 of the January 1932 issue of *Grist,* the company's in-house magazine. In the letter, she refers to using Robin Hood Flour since 1914. She says that she has lost everything in a forest fire, and requests 'another Cook Book,' as she is 'utterly at a loss without it now after using it in so many years.' She probably owned Rorer's *Robin Hood Flour Cook Book,* the only cookbook published in Canada by

the company until Q176.1, *77 Winning Recipes,* of 1929. A British Columbia owner of *Robin Hood Flour Cook Book* reported (letter of 25 March 1992), 'My husband's oldest brother used it as a Camp Cook when he was picked up for fire fighting forestry camp about 1920.'

S16.2   nd
—Robin Hood / Flour / cook / book / Robin Hood Mills Ltd. / Moose Jaw Calgary Canada
DESCRIPTION: 1 pl col on p 3   Cloth-covered boards, with hole punched at top left corner for hanging
COPIES: *MWPA (MG14 C50 McKnight, Ethel)
NOTES: This edition appears to be identical to the BVMA copy described above, except for the following differences: There is no image on the front face of the binding; on the title-page 'Ltd.' has a period; pp 79–80 are blank for 'Friend's Recipes' instead of containing instructions and coupons for ordering the book, and the table of contents reflects this difference by listing 'Friend's Recipes 79–80'; there is only one colour plate, on p 3 (although the 'Foreword' still refers to the 'seven beautiful three-color process plates'). On p 6, the Rorer/Arnold and Co. information is set in a one-line box, all lines justified right and left, except the first is indented and the last is not justified right; there is no decorative space-filling device of four dots in the last line (i.e., the setting matches the edition at MCDHM; see S16.1).

Copies at AEU (TX714 R787 1930), BDEM, and BDUCVM match the description for the copy at MWPA, but instead of a plain cover, the figure of Robin Hood is depicted. The AEU copy was donated by Lilian Leversedge, September 1991, and is inscribed on the front endpaper, 'Kate Isabel (Ramsey) Leversedge (1873–1944) Used 1917 –.' A copy at AHRMH lacks its binding.

S16.3   facsimile of S16.1, [copyright 2003]
—Robin Hood / Flour / cook / book / Robin Hood Mills Ltd / Moose Jaw Calgary Canada / Historical Notes by Elizabeth Driver / Whitecap
DESCRIPTION: 26.5 × 19.0 cm   Pp [1–6] 7–72 [73–83], [i–v]   Fp illus col on pp 3, 35–6, 45–8; illus green and two shades of brown   Card, with image on front of Robin Hood about to shoot an arrow
CONTENTS: 1 tp; 2 blank; 3 fp illus col; 4 'This edition copyright © 2003 Robin Hood Multifoods Inc. Whitecap Books'; 5 'Table of Contents'; 6 'The recipes in this cook book were prepared and written for our special use by Mrs. S.T. Rorer, are copyrighted, and are published by permission of her publishers, Arnold & Company, Philadelphia, Pa. // Bulman Bros. Limited, printers, Winnipeg, Man.'; 7–8 'Introduc-

tory // Foreword'; 9–72 recipes; 73–6 blank for 'Grandmother's Recipes'; 77–80 blank for 'Mother's Recipes'; 81–3 blank for 'Auntie's Recipes'; i–v 'Historical Notes by Elizabeth Driver'
COPIES: BVA   OGU   OONL (2 copies: TX715.6 R64 2003 fol., Preserv C-44572)   *Private collection
NOTES: The leaf of book-order coupons is omitted, and extra blank leaves are added for grandmother's, mother's, and auntie's recipes.

Weyburn cook book

S17.1   1915
Weyburn / cook / book / Woman's Auxiliary / of / All Saints' Church / 1915
DESCRIPTION: 20.5 × 13.5 cm   Pp [1] 2–82 [83–4, folio may be torn off]   Paper; stapled
CONTENTS: 1 tp; 2 ad; 3–84 text and ads
COPIES: *SWSLM
NOTES: The running head is 'W.A. of All Saints' Church Cook Book.' The recipes are credited with the name of the contributor.

1916

Smith, Mrs J. MacGregor

S18.1   [1916]
War-time cook book / I.O.D.E. [cover-title]
DESCRIPTION: 22.0 × 15.0 cm   Pp [1] 2–39   Illus on p 23 of cuts of beef   Paper, with three horizontal bands on front, in the patriotic colours of red, white, and blue; stapled
CONTENTS: 1 'A Patriotic Call'; 2 ads; 3 'Tested Recipes // War Time Cook Book Compiled by Mrs. J. MacGregor Smith'; 4–mid 5 'A Call to Housewives'; bottom 5 'All along the Line'; 6 ads; 7–37 recipes and ads; 38 'Menus January 14th to 20th, 1916'; 39 'A Week's Menu'
COPIES: *SSA (Cameron Mackintosh papers)
NOTES: 'A Patriotic Call' states that the purpose of the book is to '[help] the housewife to reduce the high cost of living and to conserve wheat, beef, bacon and sugar, ...' On p 3 there is a list of books from which the recipes were taken. All the listed books are American government publications; however, the writer comments that, according to the food controller's office in Ottawa, 'recipes suitable to the times are being prepared and can be procured upon application.' The names of the five members of the cookbook committee are recorded on p 3. No specific chapter of the IODE is identified. The printer's name is on the outside back face of the binding: 'The Saskatoon Daily Star Job Print.'

Twiss, Miss Fannie Adelia (12 January 1875–)

Fannie Twiss, daughter of Eliza J. and James Bond Twiss, was from Woodburn, Ontario, south of Hamilton, where her Irish ancestors had settled in the 1830s. She graduated from the Ontario Normal College in Hamilton in 1900, then taught in Galt, before studying domestic science at the Macdonald Institute in Guelph, graduating in 1907 (Entrance Record in RE1 MAC A0003, Vol. for 1906–9, Registration No. 417).

In 1915 Twiss was made the first director of household science for the Saskatchewan government. Her job entailed overseeing the teaching of the subject in high schools, teacher-training, and developing a program for rural schools, where she focused on the role of the hot school lunch for learning about cookery and nutrition. Selections from her writings on school lunches are reprinted, with a biography, in Peterat/DeZwart. Twiss is noted for producing the first Canadian film on home economics (Household Science in Saskatchewan Schools), which was shown at a summer school in Victoria, British Columbia, in 1922.

Twiss studied at Teachers College, Columbia University, in New York City, for the academic years 1918–19, 1922–3, 1923–4, and 1924–5, receiving her Bachelor of Science in 1920 and her Master's degree in 1923. By the second half of the 1920s, she had moved back to Ontario: Hamilton city directories list her living at 87 Victoria Avenue South from 1927 to 1940, with sister Helena and brother George. The 1929 directory gives her occupation as teacher at the Hamilton Technical Institute on Wentworth North.

For more information about the author, see: 1901 Census; and Mary Leah DeZwart, 'Fannie Twiss,' Canadian Home Economics Journal Vol. 49, No. 1 (1998), pp 32–3. Columbia University Archives is the source for her middle name.

In about 1919–20, the Alberta Department of Education published a book on the same subject as S19.1 – A37.1, Rural School Lunches; and in about 1923, the Saskatchewan Department of Education produced S27.1, The School Lunch in Saskatchewan, covering the same topics as S19.1. For another title by the Saskatchewan Department of Education, see S28.1, Recipes for Household Science Classes.

S19.1 1916
Household Science Circular No. 1 / The rural / school luncheon / Department of Education, Saskatchewan / Regina: / J.W. Reid, King's printer / 1916
DESCRIPTION: Pp [1–6] 7–39 [40] Illus
CONTENTS: 1 tp; 2 blank; 3 'Contents'; 4 blank; 5 fp illus of 'A visit from the School Inspector, the School Board and the mothers ...'; 6 blank; 7–38 text; 39 'Bibliography'; 40 'Index of Recipes'
COPIES: *CIHM (85130) OOAG SSU (LB3475 S25)
NOTES: Twiss is not named as the author in the book; however, in *Annual Report of the Department of Education of the Province of Saskatchewan 1916,* Regina: 1917, p 54, Twiss, as director of household science, writes about her publications for the year: 'During 1916 a few articles were written for the *Agricultural Gazette,* the *Public Service Monthly,* and the local newspapers. In the latter part of the year I wrote Household Science Circular No. 1, entitled "The Rural School Luncheon," six thousand copies of which were distributed in the province. Another edition is to be printed. The circular is written especially to help the teacher, mothers and school boards to solve the noon lunch problem.' The text covers the following topics: 'The School Luncheon a Problem of Education'; 'The Necessity for Its Consideration in Our Province'; 'The Agencies Concerned in the Problem of the School Luncheon'; 'The Duty of the School Board'; 'Equipment for Noon Lunch'; 'The Duty of the Teacher'; 'Organisation'; 'Utensils'; 'Recipes'; 'Benefit the Child Derives from the Noon Lunch'; 'The Duty of the Mothers'; 'Selection of Food for the Lunch'; 'Packing the Lunch'; 'The Lunch Box'; 'Schedule of Menus'; 'Abbreviations and Tables of Weights and Measures'; 'Recipes Suitable for Noon Lunch'; 'Directions for Work'; 'The Hektograph' [a method of copying before the invention of photocopy machines]; 'The Fireless Cooker'; 'Home Project Work'; and 'Educational Value of the Rural School Luncheon.'

S19.2 4th ed., 1920
—[Fourth edition of *The Rural School Luncheon,* Household Science Circular 1, Regina: Department of Education, Saskatchewan, 1920, pp 32]
COPIES: OONL (COP.SA.2.1999–153)

1917

Rexall cook book

The first two editions of this cookbook were published in Toronto and in Stratford, Ontario, in 1890, under the title The Art of Cooking Made Easy. *For the edition of* Rexall Cook Book *distributed in Saskatoon, in about 1917, see the notes for O48.18.*

1918

Food conservation cook book

S20.1 1918
R.B.C. Girls' Auxiliary / Food conservation / cook book / [IODE symbol] / Compiled by / Regina Boat Club Girls' Auxiliary / of / the Salisbury Chapter, I.O.D.E. / March, 1918. / A collection of tried and economical / recipes / Executive Committee: / Regent: Mrs. E.C. Rossie. Vice-Regent: Miss B. Pearl Dowswell. / 2nd Vice-Regent: Miss Marie Cathro. / Treasurer: Mrs. Gladys Laird. Rec. Sec.: Miss Eva Creighton. / Cor. Sec.: Miss Mabel Macfarlane. / Organized, September, 1915.
DESCRIPTION: 21.0 × 13.0 cm Pp [1–2] 3–118 [$0.50, on binding] Paper; stapled
CONTENTS: 1 tp; 2 blank; 3–110 recipes credited with the name of the contributor and ads; 111–13 'A Week of War Menus' and ads; 114 ad; 115 'Index of Chapters' [i.e., table of contents]; 116–18 ads
COPIES: *SRA
NOTES: There is an advertisement on p 117 for the University Press Ltd, Regina, the likely printer of the cookbook.

War-time cook-book

The initials GWVA stand for Great War Veterans Association, which was formed in 1917 to assist Canadians returning from the conflict overseas. A meeting in 1925 of the GWVA and similar organizations resulted in the founding of the Canadian Legion of the British Empire Services League, which issued its first charter in 1926.

S21.1 nd [about 1918]
War-time / cook-book / Compiled by / G.W.V.A. / Swift Current [cover-title]
DESCRIPTION: 22.5 × 14.5 cm Pp 1–36 Paper, with Union Jack on front; stapled

CONTENTS: 1–35 recipes credited with the name of the contributor and ads; 36 ad

COPIES: *Private collection

NOTES: 'War-time Cooking // New Ways of Cooking Rice' is on pp 9–top 13. The printer's name is on the outside back face of the binding: 'Sun Print.' The title *War-time Cook-Book* suggests that the book was published before the First World War ended.

War-time recipe book

S22.1 1918

1918 / War-time / recipe book / Compiled by Lady Patronesses of / Regina Hospital, Grey Nuns / To the business men who have given advertisements, to the / ladies who have given recipes, and to all who may purchase / copies of this book, we tender our most grateful thanks, on / behalf of the Society / Ella Patricia Boegel / President / Kathllen [*sic*] O'Phelan / Secretary

DESCRIPTION: 21.0 × 13.5 cm   Pp [1] 2–104   [$0.25, on binding]   Paper, with image on front of the hospital; stapled

CONTENTS: 1 tp; 2 ad; 3–101 recipes credited with the name of the contributor and ads; 102 ad; 103 'Index' [i.e., table of contents]; 104 ads

COPIES: *Bookseller's stock

NOTES: The cover-title is 'War-time Cook Book // 250 Tested Recipes.' Printed below the cover-title is 'Copies of this book may be had from the sisters at the Grey Nuns' Hospital.' The last two sections of text are 'Beverages and Invalid Dishes' and 'War-time Economies.' The printer, 'The University Press, Limited, Regina,' is on the outside back face of the binding.

1920

Tried and tested recipes

S23.1   nd [1920]

Tried and tested recipes / Compiled and arranged by the / Presbyterian Ladies Aid Society / Penzance, Saskatchewan / "We may live without poetry, music and art, / We may live without conscience, and live without heart, / We may live without friends, we may live without books, / But civilized man cannot live without cooks." / Issued in connection with the Church Fund. / For sale by the members of the Society. / [folio:] 1

DESCRIPTION: 21.0 × 15.0 cm   Pp 1–112 [113–15]   Tp illus of Penzance Presbyterian Church   [$1.00, on p 3]   Card, with tp illus on front; stapled

CONTENTS: 1 tp; 2 ad; 3 'Why Not a Cook Book // For a Christmas gift. These books are for sale at $1.00 each ...'; 4 ad; 5–109 recipes credited with the name of the contributor and ads; 110 'Thanks'; 111–12 ads; 113 'Index' [i.e., alphabetical list of sections]; 114 ad; 115 blank for 'Recipes'

COPIES: *Bookseller's stock

NOTES: On p 12 there is information about 'Village of Penzance, Sask. Population 250.' The advertisement on p 112 is for the Job Printing Department of the *Craik Weekly News*, the likely printer of the cookbook. Regarding the date of publication, see S23.2.

S23.2   [1980, facsimile of 1920 ed.]

—Tried and tested recipes / Compiled and arranged by the / Presbyterian Ladies Aid Society / Penzance, Saskatchewan / "We may live without poetry, music and art, / We may live without conscience, and live without heart, / We may live without friends, we may live without books, / But civilized man cannot live without cooks." / Issued in connection with the Church Fund. / For sale by the members of the Society. / [folio:] 1

DESCRIPTION: Tp illus of Penzance Presbyterian Church   [$1.00, on p 3]

CONTENTS: 1 tp; 2 ad; 3 'Why Not a Cook Book // For a Christmas gift. These books are for sale at $1.00 each ...'; 4 ad; 5–109 recipes credited with the name of the contributor and ads; 110 'Thanks'; 111–12 ads; 113 index; 114 ad; 115 blank for 'Recipes'; 116 'Introduction'

COPIES: *OGU (TX715.6 P729 1920a)

NOTES: The 'Introduction' for the facsimile on p 116 states, 'We, the United Church Women of Penzance, have decided to republish this delightful recipe book and dedicate it, in the year of 1980 to all participants in the Penzance Celebrate Saskatchewan Homecoming.' The secretary of the Penzance United Church Women reported (personal correspondence, 1991) that the facsimile was made from a copy of the original book in the local community. She writes that, although the original was undated, 'we know from our church history book that it was published in 1920 and we believe it may have been done by the Craik Weekly News which has an ad in the book [p 112] and also did the reprint ...'

1920–5

Cook book

For a cookbook by the Ladies' Aid Society of the former Methodist Church, see S13.1.

S24.1 nd [about 1920–5]
Cook / book / Compiled and arranged by the / Ladies' Aid Society / Union Church[,?] Watrous, Sask. / Price 75 cents / Watrous Signal Print [cover-title]
COPIES: *ACHP (HP 3594.1)
NOTES: According to the church history in *Prairie Reflections*, p 93 (citation at S13.1), the Ladies' Aid Society of the Union Church was formed on 18 June 1919, with Mrs J.A. Findlay as president, and the constitution accepted on 16 July (the same year the Methodist and Presbyterian churches amalgamated to form the Union Church). *Prairie Reflections*, p 94, states that the Ladies' Aid made the first large donation to the building fund for a new church, an amount of $2,700, in 1923. The cookbook was likely part of the fundraising drive for the new church. It was published before 10 June 1925, when the Union Church joined the Canada-wide church union and was renamed Watrous United Church.

1922

Cook book

S25.1 nd [about 1922]
Cook book / containing over / 295 true and tried recipes / Published at Yorkton, / Saskatchewan, by the / Hospital Ladies' Aid / in aid of the / Queen Victoria Hospital. / Index to Recipes / Soups Pages 3–7 / Eggs and potatoes 7–13 / Bread 15–18 / Meats 18–26 / Salads 26–29 / Pickles 29–33 / Relishes and sauces 33–37 / Pastry and pies 37–45 / Cakes 46–60 / Puddings 60–64 / Desserts 64–69 / Candies 70–71 / Miscellaneous 71–72
DESCRIPTION: 21.0 × 13.0 cm Pp [i–ii], 1–72 Paper, with image on front of Queen Victoria Hospital; stapled
CONTENTS: i tp and 'Index to Recipes'; ii blank; 1 'Measures and Abbreviations' and 'Equivalents'; 2 ad; 3–72 recipes credited with the name of the contributor and ads
COPIES: *Private collection
NOTES: The printer's name, 'Yorkton Enterprise Print,'

is on the front face of the binding. The private collector's copy is inscribed by her grandmother, on the front endpaper, 'Mrs A Walker Dec 1922.'

1923

[Title unknown]

S26.1 1923
[An edition of a cookbook by the Union Ladies' Aid Society, Valparaiso, Saskatchewan, 1923, pp 118]
CITATIONS: CBCat 61, No. 90

Saskatchewan, Department of Education

For another publication from the Department of Education, see S19.1.

S27.1 5th ed., 1926
Home Economics Bulletin No. 4 / The / school lunch / in / Saskatchewan / Authorised by / the Minister of Education / Saskatchewan / Fifth edition / Regina: / J.W. Reid, King's printer / 1926 / [union label]
DESCRIPTION: 22.5 × 15.0 cm Pp 2–23 Fp illus on p 2 of a girl holding a glass of milk, on p 4 of 'The lunch hour at Saskatoon Normal School,' and on p 14 of 'Serving the lunch'; illus of a food poster and of 'A typical school lunch' Very thin card; stapled
CONTENTS: 2 fp illus; 3 tp; 4 fp illus; 5–top 6 'The School Lunch'; mid 6–13 'The School Board,' 'Noon Lunch Equipment,' 'The Teacher and Pupils,' 'The Mothers,' 'Lunch Box Requirements,' 'Contents of Lunch Box,' 'Packing the Lunch,' 'The Desk Covers,' 'The Dishes,' 'The Supplies,' and 'Directions for Work'; 14 fp illus; 15–top 16 'Suggestions,' 'Table of Measurements,' 'General Rules for Working,' and 'Dishwashing'; mid 16–mid 22 'Recipes,' making 25 servings each, for beverages, fruits, cereals, vegetables, white sauces, and cream soups; mid 22–23 'The Daily Diet Should Contain' [seven constituents] from *Dietetics for High Schools*, Willard and Gillett
COPIES: *Private collection
NOTES: The text on p 5 states that 59% of Saskatchewan schoolchildren attend rural schools and the majority of these carry lunches to be eaten at noon. The private collector's copy is inscribed on the binding, 'F. Gilbert.'
No copy of the first edition of Household Science Bulletin No. 4 has surfaced, but the first edition of

No. 4 would have preceded No. 5, S28.1; therefore, it was published in 1923 or slightly earlier. Like S28.1, the series name for the earliest editions likely referred to 'Household Science,' rather than 'Home Economics.'

S27.2 6th ed., 1929
—[Sixth edition of *The School Lunch,* Bulletin 4, 1929, pp 23]
COPIES: SRA

S28.1 1923
Household Science Bulletin No. 5 / Recipes / for / household science classes / Government of the Province of Saskatchewan / Department of Education / Authorised by the Minister of Education / Regina: / J.W. Reid, King's printer, / 1923.
DESCRIPTION: About 22.5 × 15.5 cm [dimensions from photocopy]
CITATIONS: AnderCat May 2000, No. 7563
COPIES: OONL (COP.SA.2.2001-2) *Bookseller's stock
NOTES: OONL records 48 pp.

S28.2 1925
—[An edition of *Recipes for Household Science Classes,* Household Bulletin 5, Regina, Sask.: Department of Education, 1925, pp 47]
CITATIONS: AnderCat May 2000, No. 7452
COPIES: Bookseller's stock

S28.3 1926
—Home Economics Bulletin No [*sic,* no period] 5 / Recipes / for / home economics classes / Government of the Province of Saskatchewan / Department of Education / Authorised by the Minister of Education / Regina: / J.W. Reid, King's printer / 1926
DESCRIPTION: 22.0 × 15.0 cm Pp [1–2] 3–48 Pl opp p 2 of 'A Youthful Homemaker,' pl opp p 48 of 'Fruit and Vegetables Canned by Saskatoon Public School Children,' illus on p 5 of a place-setting Paper; stapled
CONTENTS: 1 tp; 2 blank; 3 'Suggestions for Saskatchewan School Children'; 4–5 'Table Setting and Serving'; 6 'Table of Measurements,' 'Rules for Working,' 'Dishwashing,' and 'Uniform for Cookery Classes'; 7–44 'Recipes'; 45–8 'Index'
COPIES: *SWSLM
NOTES: The SWSLM copy is inscribed on the binding, 'Jessie Darby.'

S28.4 1929
—Home Economics Bulletin No. 5 / Recipes / for / home economics classes / Government of the Province of Saskatchewan / Department of Education / Authorised by the Minister of Education / Regina: / J.W. Reid, King's printer / 1929
DESCRIPTION: 22.5 × 15.5 cm Pp [1–2] 3–48 Pl opp p 2 of 'A Youthful Homemaker,' pl opp p 48 of 'Fruit and Vegetables Canned by Saskatoon School Children,' illus on p 5 of a place-setting Paper; stapled
CONTENTS: 1 tp; 2 blank; 3 'Suggestions for Saskatchewan School Children'; 4–5 'Table Setting and Serving'; 6 'Table of Measurements,' 'Rules for Working,' 'Dishwashing,' and 'Uniform for Cookery Classes'; 7–44 'Recipes'; 45–8 'Index'
CITATIONS: Ferguson/Fraser, reproduction on p 53 of pl of 'A Youthful Homemaker'
COPIES: *Private collection
NOTES: Printed at the bottom left corner of the plate opposite p 48 is '5,000 – Oct., 1929.' The 'Suggestions for Saskatchewan School Children' presents eleven points regarding nutrition, fresh air, and amount of sleep. The private collector's copy is inscribed on the binding, probably by the original owner, 'Luella Miness.'

Tried recipes

S29.1 nd [about 1923]
Tried recipes / Compiled and arranged by / the members of / Empire Rebekah / Lodge No. 43 / Regina, Sask. / To the ladies who have given us recipes, and to / the business firms who have given advertise- / ments, we tender our thanks.
DESCRIPTION: 22.5 × 15.0 cm Pp [1] 2–27 [28] Tp illus of three rings (symbol of Independent Order of Odd Fellows), a dove, a beehive, and two flowers [$0.50, on binding] Paper, with small image on front of a woman's head-and-shoulders, in profile; stapled
CONTENTS: 1 tp; 2 ad; 3 'Index' [i.e., table of contents]; 4 ad; 5–26 recipes credited with the name of the contributor and ads; 27 'Helpful Hints,' 'Weights and Measures,' and ad; 28 blank for 'My Recipes'
COPIES: *OTMCL (641.5971 H39 No. 41B)
NOTES: The cover-title is 'Recipes.' An advertisement on p 5 for Eilers, 1849 Scarth Street, which describes the jewellery business as 'successors to Hicks and Pentz,' is evidence that the cookbook was published about 1923: The 1922 Regina city directory lists Hicks and Pentz at the Scarth Street address; the 1923 directory lists Eilers there.

1924

Cook book

The Fitzgerald Chapter was founded in 1911 and disbanded in 1949.

S30.1 1924
[IODE symbol] / Cook book / Compiled and published by / Fitzgerald Chapter I.O.D.E. / Saskatoon, Sask. / December, 1924
DESCRIPTION: 23.0 × 15.0 cm   Pp [1–3] 4–77 [78] Lacks binding
CONTENTS: 1 tp; 2 ads; 3 'The Menu Maker' [a poem]; 4 ads; 5–75 recipes credited with the name of the contributor and ads; 76 ads; 77 'Contents,' 'Comparative Measurements,' and ads; 78 blank for 'Additional Recipes'
COPIES: *OONL (TX715 I52)

I.O.D.E. cook book

The Capt. McNair Chapter, named in honour of a captain killed in action in 1916, was founded in 1922 and dissolved in 1975.

S31.1 [1924]
I.O.D.E. / cook book / Capt. McNair Chapter / Biggar, Sask. [cover-title]
DESCRIPTION: 21.5 × 15.5 cm   Pp [1] 2–43 [44] Paper; stapled
CONTENTS: 1–43 recipes credited with the name of the contributor and ads; 44 blank for 'Additional Recipes' and at bottom, 'Printed by the Independent // Biggar 1924'
COPIES: *SBIM

1925

[Title unknown]

S32.1 [about 1925]
[Title unknown]
DESCRIPTION: Pp [1] 2–62 Lacks binding; stapled
CONTENTS: 1 [top half of leaf lacking], 'Recipe for Happiness All the Year Round' contributed by Rev. F.A. Healey, C.Ss.R. [mock recipe]; 2 [top half of leaf lacking], ad for Kelly Drug Co. Ltd; 3–61 recipes credited with the name of the contributor and ads; 62 'The Christmas Pudding (A Recipe)' contributed by Rev. F.A. Healey, C.Ss.R. [mock recipe in five verses]
COPIES: *SMM

NOTES: An advertisement on p 50 for a Catholic college points to publication in about 1925. It states: 'Campion College // Conducted by the Jesuit Fathers Regina, Sask. ... 1924–25 ... the College, availing itself of the privilege granted by the University of Saskatchewan, is this year taking up 2nd year Arts.' Now part of the University of Regina, Campion College confirms that it began offering its second year arts program in 1924, likely in September.

The name of the organization that compiled the cookbook is not recorded in the text pages, although it may have been printed on the binding; however, the cookbook was likely compiled by the women of Regina's Holy Rosary Cathedral. Father Francis Healey, who contributed the mock recipes, was rector of Holy Rosary Cathedral from 1924 to 1927. In the same period he also served as superior of the Redemptorist priests who ministered to the cathedral parish (*Archdiocese of Regina: A History*, Muenster, Sask.: St Peter's Press, 1988, p 275).

Friendship cook book

S33.1 nd [about 1925]
Friendship / cook book / Published under the auspices of the / Watson United Church Ladies' Aid / Watson, Sask. / Naicam Progoess [*sic*] Print, Naicam, Sask.
DESCRIPTION: 21.5 × 14.0 cm   Pp [1–2] 3–52 Paper; stapled
CONTENTS: 1 tp; 2 'Index' [i.e., table of contents] and 'Our Advertisers'; 3–4 ads; 5–51 recipes credited with the name of the contributor and ads; 52 ads
COPIES: *BVIV
NOTES: The book was published after church union on 10 June 1925.

The Knox Church cook book

In 1951 Knox United Church amalgamated with Metropolitan United Church (previously Methodist) to become Knox-Metropolitan United Church, at the Metropolitan church building, 2340 Victoria Avenue. The Knox church was subsequently torn down. Metropolitan Methodist Church also produced a cookbook: S8.1, Recipes.

S34.1 1925
Tried and proven / The Knox Church / cook book / Happiness in man – the hungry sinner – / Since Eve ate apples – depends on the dinner. / Regina, 1925 / McInnis Brothers, Limited, printers, Regina.

DESCRIPTION: 22.5 × 14.5 cm   Pp [1–5] 6–116 [117]
Photograph on p 1 of Knox Church   Cloth
CONTENTS: 1 photograph of the church; 2 blank; 3 tp;
4 blank; 5 'Our Advertisers'; 6 ad; 7 'Index' [i.e., table
of contents]; 8 ad; 9 unattributed poem beginning,
'We may live without poetry, music and art' [from
Lucile, Part I, Canto ii, by Owen Meredith, pseudo-
nym of Edward Robert Bulwer-Lytton]; 10 ads; 11–
116 recipes credited with the name of the contributor
and ads; 117 blank for 'Memoranda'
CITATIONS: Peel's Bibliography 5025
COPIES: *OONL (TX715.6 K66 1925, 2 copies)   SRL
(641.5 K77 missing)
NOTES: The SRL catalogue card records the book as
from Knox Presbyterian Church. On 10 June 1925
Knox Presbyterian Church became Knox United
Church. There is no evidence in the book itself as to
whether it was published before or after church union.
Recipes from *The Knox Church Cook Book* were reprinted in S57.1, *Cook Book and Homemakers Guide*.

An olio of tried recipes and domestic wrinkles

S35.1   nd [about 1925]
An olio of / tried recipes and domestic / wrinkles /
Compiled by the / Alpha Guild / in aid of the Red
Cross Society / Price 50 cents. / The Alpha Guild
was organized Sept. 4th, 1914, to do relief work / of
any kind during the war. The membership is limited
to twenty.
DESCRIPTION: 21.5 × 14.0 cm   Pp [1–4] 5–100   Paper; stapled
CONTENTS: 1 tp; 2 blank; 3 'Index' [i.e., table of con-
tents]; 4 blank; 5–78 recipes credited with the name of
the contributor and ads; 79 blank; 80–4 'The Diet of a
Child ... as suggested by Rose McElhone, Child Welfare Nurse' and ads; 85 ads; 86–8 'Household
Wrinkles'; 89–91 blank; 92 ads; 93 officers of the Saskatchewan Provincial Branch of the Red Cross Society; 94 officers of Imperial Order Daughters of the
Empire, various Saskatchewan branches; 95 officers
of Local Council of Women, Alpha Guild, Aberdeen
Association, and Local Red Cross Association; 96
officers of Women's Musical Club, Equal Suffrage
League, Alexandra Club, and Home Makers; 97 officers of YWCA, West End WCTU, Central WCTU, and
North Side WCTU; 98 officers of St Paul's WA, St
Mary's WA, Qu'Appelle Association, and Holy Rosary Altar Society; 99 officers of Westminster Women's
Guild, St Andrew's Ladies Aid, Metropolitan Ladies

Aid, and St Andrew's WMS; 100 meeting times for
Knox Church societies
CITATIONS: Peel's Bibliography 4245
COPIES: CIHM (9-92260)   SR   *SRA
NOTES: The title-page refers to the Alpha Guild's
founding in 1914, but the cookbook was published
after the First World War. An advertisement on p 92
for Heintzman and Co. Ltd, maker of Heintzman
pianos, boasts that the company has been 'Canada's
standard for sixty-five years.' Theodore Heintzman
established his piano company in Toronto in 1866,
but had been making pianos in the city since about
1860; therefore, the cookbook was published about
1925 (1860 + 65 years).
   'Fireless Cooking,' edited by Dr Grace Armstrong,
is on p 70. 'Invalid Cookery,' edited by Miss Nora
Armstrong, is on pp 75–8. The officers of the Alpha
Guild are listed on p 95: Miss Eva Clare, president;
Miss Winifred Styles, secretary-treasurer; and Dr Grace
Armstrong, Miss Miles, Miss Dibblee, and Miss
McElhone, the executive. 'Saskatchewan Publishing
Co. Limited' is on the outside back face of the bind-
ing. A British cookbook by Miss L. Sykes of 1905
(editions to 1914) has a similar title, *An Olio of Proved
Recipes and Domestic Wrinkles* (Driver 1043.1); perhaps
someone in the Alpha Guild had a copy and the
Guild adapted the title for its own publication.
   The SRA copy is inscribed on the title-page, 'EA
Patton // Regina Sask.'; this may be the Mrs Patton
listed on p 95 as on the Executive of the local Red
Cross Association. The SR copy is incomplete, retaining only pp 7–96.

Tried and true recipes

*The Richard Homemakers Club was organized in 1922
(SWI, pp 129, 152).*

S36.1   1925
Richard / Homemakers / Club / Tried & true /
recipes / "Cookery is a refined labor / of love" –
Dodin-Bouffant / Christmas 1925 Price 25c. [cover-
title]
DESCRIPTION: 14.5 × 9.5 cm   Pp 1–23 [24]   Paper,
with ribbon-and-holly border on front; stapled
CONTENTS: 1–23 recipes and ads; 24 'Household Hints'
COPIES: *Private collection
NOTES: The recipes are arranged in sections for 'Cakes,'
'Small Cakes,' 'Cookies,' 'Bread and Parkin,' 'Des-
serts,' 'Pickles and Chutneys,' 'Odds and Ends,' and
'Candies.'

1925–6

Assiniboia cook book

S37.1   1st ed., [about 1925–6]
Assiniboia / cook book / Tested / and selected / recipes / First edition / "He may live without books – what is knowledge but grieving? / He may live without hope – what is hope but deceiving? / He may live without love – what is passion but pining? / But where is the man who can live without dining?" / Compiled and published by / the Women's Association of the / St. Paul's United Church / Assiniboia, Sask.
DESCRIPTION: 19.5 × 12.5 cm   Pp [1–8] 9–187   Oil cloth
CONTENTS: 1 ads; 2 blank; 3 tp; 4 untitled introduction; 5 duplicate tp; 6 duplicate untitled introduction; 7 'Index' [i.e., table of contents]; 8 blank; 9–187 recipes credited with the name of the contributor and ads
CITATIONS: Peel's Bibliography 4968
COPIES: *Private collection
NOTES: The untitled introduction states, 'This work was done in the first year of the history of St. Paul's United Church Assiniboia.' St Paul's was founded in 1913 as a Methodist church. The cookbook was published within twelve months of 10 June 1925, when St Paul's joined the United Church of Canada. Peel's Bibliography refers to an insurance advertisement on p 56 that cites statistics for 1925; the cookbook was likely published in 1926, after the collection of statistics in 1925. Another copy seen in a bookseller's stock did not have the duplicate title-pages and introductions.

1925–9

The Quaker method of easy bread baking

See O563.1 and O563.3 for editions of The Quaker Method of Easy Bread Baking *where the reader is asked to send letters to the Saskatoon address of Quaker Oats Co.*

1926

Souvenir programme and recipe book of the Cosmopolitan Fair

S38.1   1926
[Ad for J.G. Jackson, men's outfitter, above title] / [ad for King George Hotel, left of title] / Souvenir / programme & / recipe book / of / the / Cosmopolitan / Fair / under the auspices of / All Saints' Church / held in the / Town Hall, Melville / December 1st & 2nd, 1926 / [ad for Smith's Book Store, right of title] / [ad for Pioneer Store, below title] [cover-title]
DESCRIPTION: 21.0 × 13.5 cm   Pp 1–42   Paper; stapled
CONTENTS: Inside front face of binding two recipes for Lemon Curd and ads; 1 '$5.00 Reward' for the reader finding the most spelling errors in the book, and 'Foreword' signed Executive Committee; 2–mid 41 recipes credited with the name of the contributor, ads, and program information for the fair; mid 41–42 'Index to Recipes'; inside back face recipes and ads
COPIES: *SMELM
NOTES: The 'Foreword' states: 'The Cosmopolitan Fair is a combined effort of the congregation and various organizations of All Saints' Church, Melville, together with kind assistance promised from Duff, Fenwood, Cana and Bangor, ... to pay off some pressing debts and to help towards the furnishing of our church.' Within a year, this cookbook was out of print, prompting All Saints' Church to produce S40.1, *My Best Recipe Book*, for the Maple Leaf Fair in 1927.

1927

Cook book

S39.1   [1927]
['B.B. Circle / Women's Guild, Westminster Church' obscured by paper glued over the printing] / Cook book / The members of the B.B. Circle of Westminster Guild / desire to thank the business men of Regina for the generous / way in which they assisted them by contributing adver- / tisements.
DESCRIPTION: 23.0 × 15.0 cm   Pp [1–48]   Tp illus of the church   Paper, with symbol on front of the Saskatchewan Curling Association; stapled
CONTENTS: 1 tp; 2 blank; 3–45 recipes credited with the name of the contributor and ads; 46–8 blank for 'Memorandum'

CITATIONS: Peel's Bibliography 5191
COPIES: *Bookseller's stock   Private collection
NOTES: There is an advertisement on p 4 for Cockshutt Implements that refers to 'Better Farm Equipment Week // March 21st to 26th, 1927.'

My best recipe book

S40.1   1927
[Ad for Anderson's, a hardware store] / My best recipe book / together with / programme / of / the Maple Leaf Fair / under the auspices of / All Saints' Church / held in the Town Hall, Melville / November 16th and 17th, 1927 / [ad for Pioneer Store] [cover-title]
DESCRIPTION: 21.5 × 13.5 cm   Pp 1–44   Paper; stapled
CONTENTS: Inside front face of binding recipe for Baked Bean Soup and ads; 1 '$5.00 Reward' for the reader discovering the most spelling errors in the book, and 'Foreword' signed Executive Committee; 2–42 recipes credited with the name of the contributor, program information for the fair, and ads; 43–4 'Index to Recipes'; inside back face recipe for White Wine Vinegar and ads
COPIES: *SMELM (2 copies, one incomplete)
NOTES: The 'Foreword' states: 'Owing to the numerous requests that have been made for a copy of the Cosmopolitan Fair souvenir recipe book [S38.1] and same being out of print, the committee ... felt that it would be advisable to print a souvenir of the Maple Leaf Fair ... The returns from this book enable the committee to launch the Maple Leaf Fair which has a three-fold object: 1. To raise funds for the payment of some pressing debts and help towards some necessary furnishings of our church. 2. To be an instrument of education as to the vastness of this great Dominion which is now celebrating its Jubilee of Confederation. 3. To provide healthy fun and amusement.'

Wilkinson, Mrs J., Mrs M. Staples, Mrs W. Wilkinson, and Mrs J. MacLennan

S41.1   1982, facsimile of 1927
Reliable / receipes [*sic*] / Compiled by / Mrs. J. Wilkinson / Mrs. M. Staples / Mrs. W. Wilkinson / Mrs. J. MacLennan / Talent money / for Ladies' Aid 1927 of United Church, / Aberdeen, Sask. / Pastor, Rev. H.A. MacManus
CONTENTS: 1 tp; 2 'Index,' 'Table of Weights and Measures,' and dedication 'to those housekeepers whose patience has often been tried, and their materials wasted in attempts to follow impractical directions

contained in cookery books'; 3–52 recipes credited with the name of the contributor and ads
NOTES: The cookbook is reproduced on pp 293–306 of *Aberdeen, 1907–1981*, Aberdeen, Sask.: Aberdeen Historical Society, 1982.

1928

Cook book

S42.1   [modern reprint of 1928]
Eastend / United Church / Ladies' Aid / Cook book / 1928 / Happiness in man – / The hungry sinner – / Since Eve ate apples – / Depends on the dinner. [cover-title]
DESCRIPTION: Pp [i–ii], 1–40   Fp illus on p i of United Church of Canada, Eastend   Paper, with small image on front of roast poultry on a platter; stapled
CONTENTS: i fp illus; ii 'Preface,' 'Table Blessing,' poem beginning, 'We may live without poetry, music and art' [from *Lucile*, Part I, Canto ii, by Owen Meredith, pseudonym of Edward Robert Bulwer-Lytton], and 'Index' [i.e., table of contents]; 1–40 text, mainly recipes credited with the name of the contributor, and ads
COPIES: *Private collection
NOTES: The printer's name is on the outside back face of the binding: 'The Eastend Enterprise, Eastend, Sask.' The copy catalogued here appears to be a modern reprint.

Cook book

S43.1   1928
The / Ladies Aid / of the / United Church / Cook / book / December 1928 / The welfare of the family is largely in / the hands of the one who provides the / "Three Meals a Day." / Bonnie View, Sask. / Loreburn P.O. [cover-title]
DESCRIPTION: 20.0 × 13.5 cm   Pp [1–2] 3–80   Paper; stapled
CONTENTS: 1 'The Ladies Aid of the United Church // We've tried the things you all like best, / And are willing now to stand the test. / The proof of the pudding is in the eating; / These recipes here will stand no beating. // Bonnie View, Sask. Loreburn P.O.'; 2 'Index to Contents' [i.e., table of contents] and 'Abbreviations'; 3–75 recipes and ads; 76 'Miscellaneous'; 77–8 'Weights and Measures'; 79 blank; 80 'Conclusion // Community Pudding'
CITATIONS: CBCat 61, No. 90
COPIES: SSWD   *Private collection

Every woman's cook book

S44.1 nd [about 1928]

Preeceville United Church / Every woman's / cook book. / All tried and tested recipes [cover-title]

DESCRIPTION: 20.5 × 13.0 cm   Pp [i–iv], 1–63, [i]   Paper; stapled

CONTENTS: i–ii ads; iii 'The Advertisers,' 'Index of Contents,' and ad; iv ads; 1 quotation from Charles Kingsley, 'Abbreviations,' and 'This recipe book is published by the Preeceville United Chch [sic] ladies'; 2–63 recipes and ads; i ad and 'The Enterprise Print, Preeceville'

COPIES: *Private collection

NOTES: The collector's copy is inscribed 'Mrs. R.B. Paterson Oct 30/28.'

Golden West cook book and recipes

S45.1 nd [about 1928]

Golden West / cook book / and / recipes / With the compliments of the / Arcola Flour Mills, Ltd. / Arcola Sask. [cover-title]

DESCRIPTION: 19.5 × 11.0 cm   Pp [i–ii], 1–18   Illus Paper, with image on front of the Arcola Mills; stapled, and with hole punched at top left corner for hanging

CONTENTS: i list of officers and members of the Executive Committee of Arcola Flour Mills Ltd; ii 'To Our Readers'; 1–top 2 'Table of Equivalents'; mid–bottom 2 'Table of Proportions'; top 3 'To Be a Good Cook' [quotation from Ruskin]; bottom 3–4 'Golden Rules for the Kitchen'; 5–18 recipes credited with the name of the contributor, testimonials for Golden West Flour, jokes, and ads

COPIES: *Private collection

NOTES: 'To Our Readers' promotes Golden West Flour and explains that the Arcola Flour Mill is 'owned by a number of people in the neighbourhood.' Most of the testimonials are dated January or February 1928; the latest testimonial is dated 3 March 1928. 'The Star-Standard, printers, Arcola, Sask.' is on the outside back face of the binding.

Recipe book

S46.1 1928

Recipe book / Compiled by the / United Church Ladies' Aid / Strasbourg, Saskatchewan / Price 50 cents / The Menu Maker / [twenty-three-line verse] / [signed:] Mrs. W.D. McKay. / 1928 / The Strasbourg Mountaineer / Strasbourg, Sask.

DESCRIPTION: Pp [1–2] 3–36

CONTENTS: 1 tp; 2–35 ads on even-numbered pages and recipes credited with the name of the contributor on odd-numbered pages; 36 recipes credited with the name of the contributor

COPIES: *Private collection

1928–9

The Unity Lodge cook book

S47.1 nd [about 1928–9]

The / Unity Lodge cook / book / Recipes tried and / proved / Tuxford Saskatchewan [cover-title]

DESCRIPTION: 22.0 × 14.0 cm   Pp [1–4] 5–115, [i]   Illus on p 3 of Pavilions 1 and 2 of the Orange Home at Indian Head, Saskatchewan, 'for any dependent Protestant child in Saskatchewan'   Cloth

CONTENTS: 1–2 ad; 3 'Compiled and published by Unity Lodge 499, L.O.B.A. [i.e., Ladies' Orange Benevolent Association] Tuxford Sask. The Executive Committee of the Tuxford L.O.B.A. No. 499 who compiled this book thank the advertisers, those who contributed recipes, ...'; 4 ads; 5 'How to Preserve a Husband' [mock recipe] and 'Weights and Measures'; 6–110 recipes and ads; 111–15 blank for 'Additional Recipes'; i ad

CITATIONS: Ferguson/Fraser, p 233, illus col on p 57 of closed volume

COPIES: OONL (TX715.6 U54 1920z)   *Private collection

NOTES: There are recipes for Dry Curing Meat, Pickle for Beef, Ham or Bacon, and Curing Hams and Shoulders. Two advertisements point to publication in 1928: The advertisement for Fred Ivay, optometrist, refers to '15 years experience'; that for Success Business College says the school 'has been tried and tested for 15 years.' Since the Moose Jaw city directory for 1913 contains the first listing for Fred Ivay as an optometrist and the first listing for Success Business College, the cookbook was published about 1928 (1913 + 15 years). Another advertisement, on p 22, suggests a year later. Headed 'The Call of Osteopathy,' it refers to osteopathy as 'practised and developed for fifty-five years.' The basic principles of osteopathy were first announced in 1874 by the American medical practitioner Andrew Taylor Still, which indicates publication in about 1929 (1874 + 55 years).

1929

Cook book

S48.1 1929
[An edition of *Cook Book,* compiled and published by the Women's Association of the United Church, Delisle, Saskatchewan, 1929]
COPIES: Private collection

Cook book

S49.1 1929
Cook / book / Published by / the Women's Association of the / United Church, Kinley, Sask. / 1929 / Price per copy, / 50 cents
DESCRIPTION: 22.0 × 15.0 cm   Pp [1] 2–48   Paper; stapled
CONTENTS: 1 tp; 2 ads; 3–48 recipes credited with the name of the contributor and ads
COPIES: *SBIHM
NOTES: 'G.W. Norman, printer, Saskatoon' is on the front face of the binding.

Cook book

The same circle of women produced S88.1, Westminster Cook Book.

S50.1 nd [1929]
Westminster Church / Cook / book / Idylwyld Circle / (Saskatoon) [cover-title]
DESCRIPTION: 22.0 × 15.0 cm   Pp 3–100   Paper; stapled
CONTENTS: 3–mid 99 recipes credited with the name of the contributor and ads; mid–bottom 99 'Table of Weights and Measures'; 100 'Index' [i.e., table of contents]
COPIES: *Bookseller's stock
NOTES: Three advertisements point to publication in the last quarter of 1929. The advertisement on p 8 for Robin Hood Flour boasts of '46 first prizes ... at Saskatoon and other provincial 1929 exhibitions.' Another on p 14 for Saskatoon-Success Business College gives enrolment numbers for the periods 27 August 1928–25 August 1929 and 26 August 1929–20 September 1929, and refers to staff for the 1929–30 academic year. Another on p 88 for Birks jewellers encourages 'a visit to our new store (after November 1st, 1929).' The copy described here is lacking the back face of the binding, which may name the printer, possibly the Modern Press Ltd on Second Avenue North, whose advertisement is on p 94.

The Maple Creek cook book

S51.1 1929
The / Maple Creek / cook book / This book of tested receipts was compiled / and published by the ladies of / St. Lawrence's Church, / Maple Creek, / Sask. / 1929. [cover-title]
DESCRIPTION: Pp [1–2] 3–?
CONTENTS: 1 'Preface'; 2 'Index to Recipes' and 'Index to Advertisers'; 3 recipes credited with the name of the contributor; ...
COPIES: *Bookseller's stock
NOTES: The 'Preface' states that proceeds from the book's sale will be contributed to St Lawrence's Catholic Church. The bookseller reports that the volume has 68 pp.

Star City cook book

S52.1 1929
Star City / cook book / Issued by / the Ladies' Aid / of the / Star City United Church / 1929 / Star City Echo
DESCRIPTION: 24.5 × 18.0 cm   Pp [1] 2–120   Paper; stapled
CONTENTS: 1 tp; 2 ad; 3 'Index' [i.e., table of contents]; 4 ad; 5 'Preface'; 6 ads; 7–9 'General Rules' and ads; 10 ads; 11–117 recipes credited with the name of the contributor; 118–20 blank for 'Notes'
CITATIONS: Peel's Bibliography 5382
COPIES: *Bookseller's stock
NOTES: The date '1929–30' is printed on the binding. The 'Preface' lists the members of the Ladies' Aid Executive Committee and the Star City Town Council for 1929.

Tried and tested recipes

Hadassah was organized in Regina in 1921.

S53.1 [1st ed.], nd [about 1929]
Tried and tested / recipes / Issued by the / Regina Chapter of / Hadassah / Commercial Printers, Ltd., Regina, Sask. [cover-title]
DESCRIPTION: Pp 1–64   Stapled

CONTENTS: 1 'This book is dedicated to Mrs. A.J. Freiman // mother of Canadian Hadassah // Compiled by Mrs. L. Epstein Mrs. M.A. Rose Mrs. J. Mael Mrs. J.M. Diamond Mrs. I. Reinhorn'; 2 'Appetizers' [recipes credited with the name of the contributor]; ...; 60–1 'Greetings and Good Wishes to the Hadassah Organization of Regina from [list of names, the first being Rabbi and Mrs Kalef]'; ...; 64 'Contents'
COPIES: *OOJA

NOTES: 'Passover Dishes' start on p 51. Mrs Isadore Reinhorn (named on the title-page) and her husband were among the earliest Jewish settlers in Regina, having moved from one of the Jewish farm colonies. Rabbi Kalef (the first-named person on p 60) was the rabbi of the Regina synagogue and lived in the city from 1920 until his death in 1946.

The OOJA copy was part of the personal effects of Edith Chernick Singer (Winnipeg, Man., 1908–Las Vegas, Nev., 2001). Edith moved from Winnipeg to California in 1926, but often returned home for visits. She may have acquired the cookbook from her Regina relatives. The year '1929' is inscribed on the binding in ballpoint pen.

S53.2 2nd ed., nd [about 1934–5]
—Tried and tested / recipes / Second edition / Issued by the / Regina Chapter of / Hadassah [cover-title]
DESCRIPTION: 23.0 × 15.0 cm   Pp [1] 2–64   Paper; stapled
CONTENTS: 1 'Regina Chapter of Hadassah Cook Book // Second edition,' table of contents, and untitled acknowledgments signed Regina Chapter of Hadassah, Mrs Martin A. Rose, president; 2–61 recipes and ads; 62–3 'Greetings and Good Wishes to the Hadassah Organization of Regina from [list of individual and company names]' and ads; 64 ads
COPIES: *OGU (CCC TX715.6 T75 19-)   SRBJ

NOTES: There is a chapter of 'Passover and Purim Dishes.' The printer's name is on the outside back face of the binding: 'Commercial Printers, Ltd., Regina, Sask.' The book was published about 1934–5 since those are the only years when Mrs Martin Rose was president of the chapter and when all the advertised businesses were in the locations listed. When the book was donated to SRBJ, the librarian (Roberta Swetlow) consulted with members of the community about its date of publication. Abe Safian, whose family had owned Paramount Cleaners, one of the advertisers, remembered the cookbook's publication in 1934 or 1935, a date agreed with by others consulted.

1930

[Title unknown]

S54.1 [about 1930]
[Cover-title lacking?]
DESCRIPTION: 23.0 × 14.5 cm   Pp [1–2] 3–12   Lacks binding
CONTENTS: 1 'Meats' [i.e., recipes]; 2 'Index' and 'Printed by "The Independent" Biggar, Sask.'; 3–12 recipes credited with the name of the contributor and ads
COPIES: *SBIM

NOTES: The museum's copy may lack leaves. It is inscribed on p 1, in ink, 'Florence I. White // Biggar March 25/1930.'

Choice, tested recipes

S55.1 nd [1930]
Choice, tested / recipes / collected by / the Heather Circle / of / First Presbyterian Church / Regina / Price 50 cents / Commercial Printers, Ltd., Regina, Sask. [cover-title]
DESCRIPTION: 22.5 × 15.0 cm   Pp [1] 2–96   Photograph on p 1 of First Presbyterian Church   Very thin card; stapled
CONTENTS: 1 'First Presbyterian Church // Regina, Sask. Corner 14th and Albert St.' and a thank-you to the recipe contributors and advertisers; 2 ad; 3–93 text, including recipes credited with the name of the contributor, and ads; 94–5 blank for 'Memo'; 96 'Index' [i.e., alphabetical list of sections]
COPIES: *OONL (TX715.6 C55 1900z, 2 copies)   QMU (Collection John H. Archer 0179)

NOTES: The book is undated, but there is an advertisement on p 7 for Mutual Life of Canada that cites '1870 – Diamond Jubilee – 1930' and an advertisement on p 10 for Robin Hood Flour that refers to medals won 'at 1929 exhibitions.' Page 85 presents 'quantities [to] serve one hundred persons at social gatherings.' On pp 86–9 there are menus, including those for 'Wedding Luncheons,' 'Wedding Breakfast,' and 'Evening Party or Afternoon Tea.' 'Little Knacks of Cookery' are on pp 91–mid 92.

Cook book

S56.1   1930
Cook book / Hoosier / Ladies' Aid / 1930 /
Pric[e $1.00]
DESCRIPTION: 22.0 × 14.5 cm   Pp [i–iv], 1–39   Tp
illus of the church   Paper, with tp illus on front;
stapled
CONTENTS: i tp; ii blank; iii 'Index' [i.e., table of con-
tents]; iv ads; 1–39 text and ads
COPIES: *Private collection
NOTES: The book was produced by the Ladies' Aid of
the United Church in Hoosier. 'Printed by the
Kerrobert Citizen // Kerrobert, Sask.' is on the out-
side back face of the binding.

Cook book and homemakers guide

S57.1   [1930]
The Leader-Post / Regina, Sask. Thursday, June 26
Twenty pages / Cook book / and / homemakers /
guide [cover-title]
DESCRIPTION: 46.0 × 29.0 cm   Pp [1] 2–19 [20]   Illus
Paper, with image on front of a set table
CONTENTS: 1 cover-title; 2–19 recipes and ads; 20 [out-
side back face of binding] ad
COPIES: *Private collection
NOTES: The running heads include the year of publi-
cation, 1930. On p 3, 'Repertoire of Knox Church
Cooks in Choice' reproduces recipes from S34.1, *Knox
Church Cook Book*.

Wallard Ladies' Aid cook book

S58.1   nd [1930]
Cook book / Contains over two hundred / and
thirty carefully selected / recipes / Compiled and
published by the / Wallard Ladies Aid Society /
Wallard, Sask. [cover-title]
DESCRIPTION: Pp [1] 2–36   Stapled
CONTENTS: 1 'Wallard Ladies' Aid Cook Book,' 'Dedication,' 'Committee' [i.e., the names of Mrs L. Turner,
Mrs F. Grills, and Mrs B. Grills], 'How to Cook a
Husband' [mock recipe], 'Weights and Measurements,' and 'Syrups for Fruit'; 2–34 recipes credited
with the name of the contributor and ads; 35 'Canning Chart'; 36 'Table of Contents' and 'News Magnet Print, Aneroid, Sask.'
COPIES: *Private collection
NOTES: An advertisement on the outside back face of
the binding for Robin Hood Flour cites prizes and

medals won at prairie exhibitions in 1929, evidence
that the cookbook was likely published in 1930. Most
advertisements are for businesses in Aneroid and
Ponteix, south of Swift Current. Wallard no longer
exists.

1930–5

One hundred tested cheese recipes

The Saskatoon Dairy Pool was formed in 1927.

S59.1   nd [about 1930–5]
One hundred tested / cheese recipes / Issued by /
Saskatoon Dairy Pool / Saskatoon, Canada /
manufacturers of / Primrose Dairy Products /
butter cheese / skim milk powder
DESCRIPTION: 20.0 × 13.0 cm   Pp [1–2] 3–44   Paper,
with images on front of a block of Harvest Loaf Canadian Cheddar Cheese and of a mother serving a block
of the cheese to her family at the dining table; stapled
CONTENTS: 1 tp; 2 'Index' [i.e., alphabetical list of
sections]; 3–42 recipes using cheese and information
about cheese; 43 'A Week's Meals'; 44 blank for
'Additional Recipes'
COPIES: *OONL (TX759.5 C48 O54 1930z, 2 copies)
NOTES: 'Printed by the Saskatoon Star-Phoenix Ltd.'
is on the outside back face of the binding. There is a
quotation on p 29 that is dated April 1929. The cookbook was likely published about 1930 or slightly later.

1932

Scott, Anna Lee [pseudonym]

See O773.9, O776.8, and O777.5, for editions of Scott's
The Easy Way Cake Book, Marketing and Meal
Planning, *and* Planning the Party, *published by the*
Leader-Post in Regina.

1933

The Floral Homemakers cook book

S60.1   1933
The / Floral / Homemakers / cook book / Tested
recipes / 1933 / Price $1.00 [cover-title]
DESCRIPTION: Pp 1–57   Stapled
CONTENTS: 1 'Recipe Book published and for sale by
the Floral Homemakers Club,' 'Index' [i.e., table of

contents], and Yeast Cake Recipe; 2 ads; 3–57 recipes and ads

COPIES: *Private collection

NOTES: 'Printed by the Nutana Herald Saskatoon' is on the inside back face of the binding; the printer's name is also on the outside back face.

Patricia Club cook book

S61.1 1933

Patricia Club / cook book / 1933 / Published by / the Princess Patricia Club / Regina

DESCRIPTION: 22.5 × 15.0 cm   Pp [1–3] 4–56   PPC fleur-de-lis symbol on tp   Paper; stapled

CONTENTS: 1 ad; 2 table of contents; 3 tp; 4 'Members Princess Patricia Club 1932–33'; 5 'A Foreword'; 6 'Weights and Measures' and 'Vitamins'; 7–56 recipes credited with the name of the contributor and ads

COPIES: OONL (TX715.6 P37 1933)   *SRA

NOTES: The 'Foreword' relates the history of the club, which was founded in April 1916 as an auxiliary of girls to the 195th CEF Battalion. The object of the club was 'to make life less difficult for others.' The purpose of the cookbook was to raise funds for the club's charitable activities.

Silver jubilee cook book

St Thomas–Wesley United Church is the result of an amalgamation in 1930 of Wesley United Church (founded in 1907) and St Thomas United Church (founded in 1908).

S62.1   nd [about 1933]

Silver jubilee / cook book / Recipes compiled by the / ladies of / St. Thomas–Wesley / United Church / Saskatoon, Sask.

DESCRIPTION: 23.5 × 15.5 cm   Pp [1–4] 5–64   Tp illus of St Thomas–Wesley United Church   Paper, with tp illus on front; stapled

CONTENTS: 1 tp; 2 blank; 3 'Foreword' signed Central Circle, St Thomas Wesley [sic, no dash] Church W.A., Saskatoon, Saskatchewan; 4 blank; 5–56 recipes credited with the name of the contributor and ads; 57 'Household Hints'; 58 'Weights and Measures'; 59–63 blank for 'Recipes'; 64 ad; inside back face of binding 'F.W. Fowler & Sons printers Saskatoon, Sask'

COPIES: *OONL (TX715 S354)

NOTES: The appearance of the volume suggests that it was published in the mid-1930s. It was likely produced to commemorate the church's twenty-fifth an-

niversary, given 'silver jubilee' in the title and the advertisement on p 12 for Monarch Lumber Co. that says, 'Congratulations to St. Thomas–Wesley.' Since the amalgamated congregation counts church anniversaries from St Thomas's founding in 1908, the cookbook was published about 1933 (1908 + 25 years).

1934

All-tested recipes

S63.1   1934

All-tested / recipes / Contributed by friends of / Regina General Hospital / Women's Auxiliary / 1934 / [folio:] 1

DESCRIPTION: 22.5 × 15.0 cm   Pp 1–72 [73–80]   Tp illus of a woman holding the edges of a tray, on which sit éclairs, a loaf, and dishes; photograph on p 2 of Regina General Hospital   Card; stapled

CONTENTS: 1 tp; 2 photograph of the hospital, 'Officers – 1934,' and 'Councillors'; 3–62 recipes credited with the name of the contributor and ads; 63 'Index' [i.e., table of contents] and ad; 64 'Table of Weights and Measures' and 'Time Table'; 65–72 'Feeding the Children'; 73–80 blank for 'My Favorite Recipes'

COPIES: *OONL (TX715.6 C66739 1934 p***)

NOTES: The cover-title is 'Cookery Book [in a diamond-shape:] RGHA.' The text includes information about breast-feeding. The form of the title ('All-Tested Recipes contributed by ...') and the title-page illustration match the title and title-page illustration of M59.1, *All Tested Recipes*. The OONL copy is inscribed on the title-page, in ink, 'Mrs A.R. Donnelly.'

The community booster cook book

See also S65.1, The Community Booster Cook Book.

S64.1   1934

The / community / booster / cook book / Published by the business men / of the Battlefords / 1934 / Printed at the office of the North Battleford News [cover-title]

DESCRIPTION: 21.5 × 14.0 cm   Pp 1–16   Paper, with image on front of a woman holding a plate, on which sits an unidentified prepared dish; stapled

CONTENTS: 1 ads and 'Foreword'; 2 ads; 3–15 recipes and ads; 16 ads

COPIES: *OONL (TX715.6 C6513 1934 p***)

NOTES: The 'Foreword' states, 'The businessmen of Battleford and North Battleford have taken this opportunity of placing these valuable books in every household in this vicinity, and through their sincere co-operation it has been made possible to mail you one of the books absolutely free. Our aim is given in the name: "Community Booster" ...' The first few recipes are Fruit Salad, Jellied Tomato and Olive Salad, Salad, and Stuffed Tomato Salad.

The community booster cook book

S65.1   1934
The / community / booster / cook book / Published by the business men / of / Melfort / 1934 / With our compliments [cover-title]

DESCRIPTION: 21.5 × 14.0 cm   Pp [1–16]   Paper, with image on front of a man seated at table; stapled
CONTENTS: 1 ad and 'Forward' [sic]; 2 ads; 3–15 recipes credited with the name of the contributor and ads; 16 ads
CITATIONS: Ferguson/Fraser, p 233
COPIES: *SSWD
NOTES: Page 1 echoes the wording of S64.1, published by the businessmen of the Battlefords: 'The business men of Melfort have taken this opportunity of placing these valuable books in every household in the vicinity, and through their sincere co-operation it has been possible to mail you one of the books absolutely free. Our aim is given in the name: "Community Booster" ...' Unlike S64.1, the first recipes in the Melfort cookbook are for cakes, and there are no salad recipes.

Hostess recipe book

S66.1   1934
Hostess / recipe book / 1934 / Published by / Friendship Circle of St. Andrew's / United Church / Yorkton, Saskatchewan [cover-title]

DESCRIPTION: 20.5 × 13.5 cm   Pp 1–44   Paper; stapled
CONTENTS: 1 book title, date of publication, 'A Word of Thanks,' '"Who have to scheme and plan and matters onward force; and praise, and pay and smile as well? The Ladies' Aid, of course!,"' and 'How to Preserve a Husband' [mock recipe]; 2 ads; 3–44 recipes credited with the name of the contributor and ads
COPIES: *Private collection
NOTES: 'Printed by Commercial Press, 8 First Avenue, Yorkton' is on the outside back face of the binding.

Household manual

S67.1   nd [about 1934]
Household / manual / Preface / The ladies who compiled this book tender their / most grateful thanks to the business firms who / so materially assisted them with the advertise- / ments, also the ladies who sent in their / recipes, and the young women who / did typing. The recipes are / all tested and used / continually by / the donors. / Committee / [Left column:] Mrs. David Lawrence, Pres. / Mrs. L.F. Heartwell, Sec'y. / Mrs. Gilbert Gordon, Treas. / Mrs. David McConnell / Mrs. Percy Smith / [right column:] Mrs. Joseph Smith / Mrs. Harry Anderson / Mrs. David Geddes / Mrs. Dewey Lamborn / Mrs. Robt. Higgins / [centred below columns:] Women's Association / United Church / Rosetown, Saskatchewan

DESCRIPTION: 21.0 × 15.5 cm   Pp [i–ii], 1–103 [104]   Thin card, with small image on front of a chef holding a tray; stapled
CONTENTS: i tp; ii 'Abbreviations' and 'Weights and Measures'; 1–103 recipes credited with the name of the contributor and ads; 104 ads
COPIES: *Bookseller's stock
NOTES: Advertisements fix the date of publication in about 1934. An advertisement on p 37 for Borden and Co. Ltd, the maker of sweetened condensed milk, includes a book-order coupon for *Magic! The Most Amazing Short-Cuts,* to be sent to Yardley House in Toronto; this address indicates the edition published in about 1933–4 (O784.2). An advertisement on p 60 for Prairie Mutual Benefit Association gives 1924 as its year of incorporation and refers to 'Over $150,000.00 distributed to beneficiaries ... during the past ten years' [1924 + 10 years = 1934]. *Household Manual* was likely printed by the Service Printing Co. (Saskatoon) Ltd, whose advertisement is on p 102.

'Prairie Rose' cook book

S68.1   nd [about 1934]
"Prairie Rose" cook book / Recipes tried and true / of / United Farmers of Canada / (Women's Section) / Craik, Sask. / Compiled and arranged by the women / of Prairie Rose Lodge / Craik. / Joy, temperance and repose, / Slam the door on the doctor's nose. / Gone your temper, fret and woes, / When using recipes from the Prairie Rose.

DESCRIPTION: 21.0 × 14.0 cm   Pp [1] 2–89   Thin card; stapled

CONTENTS: 1 tp; 2 'Table of Weights and Measures'; 3–82 recipes credited with the name of the contributor and ads; 83 'Hints for the Home'; 84 'The Cook' and 'Receipt for Kisses' [mock recipe]; 85 'Husbands' [mock recipe]; 86 'Membership of Prairie Rose Lodge // United Farmers' [*sic*] of Canada'; 87–8 blank for 'Memo'; 89 'Index'

CITATIONS: Ferguson/Fraser, p 233

COPIES: *SRA

NOTES: The cookbook was published no earlier than 1926, the year that the United Farmers of Canada was established. An advertisement on p 20 for Hotel Champlain, which refers to the hotel's '20 years in Regina,' points to publication in 1934: Hotel Champlain was run by Wesley and David Champ, and Regina directories list Champ's Cafe and Hotel, run by the Champ family, from 1914 (1914 + 20 years = 1934). The cookbook was published no earlier than 1932 since the first listing for Champ in Regina directories is in 1912 (for Wesley as a bookkeeper). The appearance of the cookbook is consistent with publication in 1934.

There is an advertisement on p 72 for the Craik Weekly News, possibly the printer of the cookbook. The SRA copy is inscribed on the inside front face of the binding, 'Hazel M. White.'

1935

Berkner, Mrs Mary (Mrs J. Berkner)

S69.1 [1935]

Country / cook book / with special recipes for / making cookies and an / improved method of / making sugar-beet syrup / by / Mrs. Mary Berkner / Price 25¢ [cover-title]

DESCRIPTION: 22.0 × 18.0 cm   Pp [i–iii], 1–19   Paper; stapled

CONTENTS: Inside front face of binding 'To Whom It May Concern' signed Mrs M. Berkner; i letter from Mrs Ethel B. Rutter per N.M., head, School of Household Science, University of Saskatchewan, Saskatoon, to Dr Frank Hoffman, Saskatoon, 22 April 1935, recommending Mrs Berkner's recipes, especially her directions for preparing sugar-beet syrup; ii–iii 'Pure Sugar Beet Syrup'; 1 'Mrs. J. Berkner's Cook Book' [i.e., author's introduction]; 2 'Uses of Sugar Beet Syrup,' 'Making Sugar Beet Syrup,' and 'Method of Procedure'; top 3 'Useful Hints'; mid 3–19 recipes for 'Jams,' 'Pastry,' 'Cookies,' and 'Soups,' plus other culinary information

COPIES: *OONL (TX819 S94 B47 1935 p***)

NOTES: Mrs Berkner's note opposite p [i] identifies Dr Frank Hoffman as the 'Editor of "Az Otthon" Hungarian monthly, who was kind enough to encourage [the author] to publish this booklet which is the summary of [her] long years experience in cooking.' On p 1 she refers to her four years experimenting on Sugar Beet Syrup and its uses. Her aim was to find a good alternative to cane sugar, which was expensive for many families during the Depression. She asks, 'Why do without pastry, cakes, cookies, etc., on account of hard times, and high price of sugar, when we can have the best of results using Sugar Beet Syrup in place of sugar.' On p 1 she quotes the price of the book as $1.00, but $0.25 is printed on the front of the binding. The book is reproduced from typewritten copy.

Souvenir cookery book

S70.1 1935

Souvenir / cookery / book / Compiled by / Regina Local Council of Women / 1895 1935 [cover-title]

DESCRIPTION: 23.0 × 15.0 cm   Pp [1] 2–78 [leaf lacking]   Illus portrait on p 1 of Helen W. Horne   Paper; stapled

CONTENTS: Inside front face of binding 'Officers, 1935 Local Council of Women Regina, Sask.'; 1 'In Appreciation!' signed Helen W. Horne, president, LCW, thanking the advertisers in this 'Souvenir Recipe Book'; 2–5 'Regina Local Council of Women' signed Elizabeth G. Cameron, first vice president, Regina LCW, December 1935; 6 'Affiliated Societies Regina Local Council of Women 1935' [list of forty-two women's societies in Regina]; 7 two untitled poems; 8 'Table of Abbreviations,' 'Table of Measures,' 'Weights and Measures re Liquids,' 'Approximate Contents of Canned Foods,' and ad; 9 'Weights and Measures' and ad; 10 'Oven Temperatures for Baking Different Products,' 'Sugar Temperatures,' and 'What Goes with What'; 11–top 12 'Meats, Dressings and Vegetables'; mid–bottom 12 'Menu Planning'; 13–top 14 'Rules for Planning and Measuring Menus'; mid–bottom 14 'Menus for Special Occasions'; 15–16 'A Week's Menus for Family Use' and ad; 17–78 recipes and ads

COPIES: OONL (TX715.6 S63 1935)   *SRRPM

NOTES: Elizabeth Cameron comments on p 5, '... through the sale of [this book] they hope to finance several delegations to conventions and to expand the work of the Council.' The souvenir cookbook marked forty years since the founding of the Regina Local Council of Women.

Valuable recipes

S71.1 nd [about 1935]
Valuable / recipes / Keep this useful / cook book
// You'll / find it helpful / every day of / the year
/ Presented with the compliments of / the firms
whose advertisements / appear within [cover-title]
DESCRIPTION: Pp 1–24 Stapled
CONTENTS: 1–2 'Index' and ads; 3–19 recipes, some
credited with the name of the contributor, and ads;
20 ad; 21–3 'Household Hints' and ads; 24 'Index to
Advertisers'
COPIES: *Private collection (photocopy)
NOTES: The advertisements are for Prince Albert businesses. The book is undated, but the image in the
advertisement on p 12 for Waskesiu Mills Ltd (¾-
length view of a woman standing behind a table on
which are arrayed cooking utensils, containers, and
food stuffs) is the same as on the binding of M78.1,
The Waverley Cook Book, published in Winnipeg in
1934. The printer's name is on the outside back face
of the binding: 'The Herald Job Print // Prince Albert
Sask.'

There are only three named recipe contributors:
Mrs J. Bartle (*Henderson's Prince Albert Directory 1934*
lists John L. Bartle as a CNR foreman); Mrs F.D. Culp
(Frank D. Culp was an optometrist); and Mrs A.E.
Doak, credited with the most recipes (Hon. Algernon
E. Doak was a District Court judge).

1936

All tested recipes

S72.1 1936
All tested / recipes / Happiness in man – the
hungry sinner – / Since Eve ate apples – depends on
the dinner. / Contributed by the members of /
Assiniboia Union Hospital / Women's Auxiliary /
1936 / [folio:] 1
DESCRIPTION: 23.0 × 15.5 cm Pp 1–72 Illus on p 2 of
the hospital Thin card; stapled
CONTENTS: Inside front face of binding 'Index' [i.e.,
table of contents] and poem beginning, 'We may live
without poetry, music and art' [from *Lucile*, Part I,
Canto ii, by Owen Meredith, pseudonym of Edward
Robert Bulwer-Lytton]; 1 tp; 2 illus of the hospital and
list of 'Officers of Auxiliary, 1936' and 'Members of
Hospital Board'; 3 'Table of Weights and Measures'
and 'Time Table'; 4–68 recipes credited with the name
of the contributor and ads; 69–72 blank for 'My Favorite Recipes'

CITATIONS: Peel's Bibliography 5976
COPIES: *OGU (CCC TX715.6 C664)

An original cook book

S73.1 1936
An original / cook book / We may live without
friends, we may live without books, / But civilized
man cannot live without cooks, / He may live
without love – what is passion but pining? / But
where is the man that can live without dining? /
Compiled in the year 1936 / by the / Homemakers'
Club / Conquest, Sask.
CONTENTS: 1 tp; 2 'Table of Contents' [i.e., alphabeti-
cal list of sections]; 3–? recipes credited with the name
of the contributor; ...
COPIES: *Bookseller's stock
NOTES: The running head is 'Conquest Homemakers'
Club Cook Book.' The bookseller reports 82 pp.

1937

Rosemont coronation year cook book

S74.1 nd [1937]
Rosemont / coronation year / cook book /
Published by the Ladies' Aid of / Rosemont United
Church, Regina, Sask. / Officers and past officers /
Past Presidents: / Mrs. Charles Shawcross, Mrs.
H.C. Duck, Mrs. E. Bentley, / Mrs. G. Robinson. /
Hon. President Mrs. S.B. East / President Mrs. J.R.
Dutton / Secretary Mrs. John McLintock / Treasurer
Mrs. R. Miles
DESCRIPTION: With image on front of the church
CITATIONS: Peel's Bibliography 6121
COPIES: *SSU (TX715.6 R67 1937)
NOTES: The cookbook marked the coronation of George
VI on 12 May 1937.

1938

Cook book

S75.1 [1938]
Compiled by Rose Valley Ladies Hospital Aid /
Cook book / Tried and tested receipes [*sic*] from the
ladies / of the Ponass Lake Municipality. / Price
40 cents [cover-title]

DESCRIPTION: 22.5 × 15.0 cm   Pp [1–60]   Very thin card, with image on front of two flags, the Union Jack and Red Ensign; stapled
CONTENTS: 1 'Hospital Aid Officers,' 'Hospital Board,' 'Hospital Staff,' and 'Council of R.M. Ponass Lake'; 2 'Index' [i.e., table of contents], thanks to businessmen and friends for facilitating printing, and 'The proceeds will be used for the safety and comfort of your sick.'; 3 'How to Roast a Husband' signed M.M.M., and printer's name and date of publication – Radio Printers, Kelvington, Saskatchewan, 1938; 4–60 recipes credited with name of the contributor and ads
CITATIONS: FitzPatrickCat 110 (February 1993) No. 146   FitzPatrickCat 111 (April 1993) No. 21   Peel's Bibliography 6217
COPIES: *Private collection
NOTES: The text is printed in blue ink.

St Andrew's cook book

S76.1   1938
1938 / St. Andrew's / cook book / Sponsored by / the Heather Unit / Saskatoon, Canada [cover-title]
DESCRIPTION: Pp [1–2] 3–56
CONTENTS: 1 introductory note signed the Heather Unit, St Andrew's Church, and a poem by Edgar A. Guest; 2 'Index' [i.e., table of contents]; 3–56 recipes and ads, and at bottom p 56, 'Recipe for Good Printing ... National Job Printers' and its Saskatoon address
COPIES: *Private collection

St Henry's jubilee cook book

Also from St Henry's Roman Catholic Church is S110.1, St Henry's 40th Anniversary Cook Book.

S77.1   1938
[Ad:] Princess Theatre / Melville, Sask. / The home of the very / latest & best / pictures / [title:] St. Henry's / jubilee cook book / 1908–1938 / Compiled / by / Ladies / Altar / Society / Melville, Sask. [cover-title]
DESCRIPTION: 22.5 × 14.5 cm   Pp 1–80   Illus on p 57 of a miniature chef carrying roast poultry on a platter above his head   Paper, with still-life on front of a bowl of cereal(?), cream, and sugar; stapled
CONTENTS: 1 'Recipe for Preserving Children' and ads; 2–77 recipes credited with the name of the contributor and ads; 78 ad for Marian Press, Regina, the likely printer of the cookbook; 79–80 blank for 'Memo'
COPIES: *SMELM

1938–9

The doughnut book of recipes

For cookbooks by Aitken, Bayley, and Campbell, see the Name Index.

S78.1   nd [about 1938–9]
4X / bread – cakes – rolls / from your store or from our / salesman / The / doughnut book / of / recipes [cover-title]
DESCRIPTION: 20.0 × 25.0 cm   Pp [1–32]   Paper; bound by a cord through two punched holes
CONTENTS: 1 heads of two bakers, peeping through the hole of one doughnut, below which are a quotation from Samuel Johnson and the 'Tested and approved' seals of Good Housekeeping Bureau (Serial No. 4584) and Chatelaine Institute (Serial No. 159); 2 'Favorite Recipes of Mrs. H.M. Aitken, Canadian National Exhibition'; 3 'Favorite Recipes of Helen G. Campbell, Director Chatelaine Institute'; 4 'Favorite Recipes of Katherine Caldwell Bayley, Canadian Home Journal'; 5–28 blank; 29–30 'Suggested Summer Menus by Chatelaine'; 31–2 'Suggested Winter Menus by Chatelaine' and at bottom p 32, 'Form No. 103 Printed in Canada Toronto – Alger Press Limited – Oshawa'
COPIES: *Private collection
NOTES: On p 2, Aitken is described as director of women's activities at the Canadian National Exhibition, a position she held from 1938. From appearances, the cookbook was likely published about 1938–9. There are some blank pages impressed with 'Seal Farmers Cattle Exchange Ltd. Saskatoon.'

1939

Cook book

S79.1   1939
Bracken / Ladies' Aid / Cook book / 1939 [cover-title]
DESCRIPTION: 15.5 × 10.5 cm   Pp [i], 1–30   Card; bound at top edge by a ribbon through two punched holes
CONTENTS: i 'Index' [i.e., table of contents]; 1 ten numbered 'Health Rules'; 2–4 'Household Hints' credited with the name of the contributor; 5–30 recipes credited with the name of the contributor
COPIES: *Private collection
NOTES: The leaves are printed and numbered on the rectos only; the versos are not included in the pagination. The first item on p 5, the start of the 'Cakes'

section, is Golden Rule Cake, a mock recipe calling for 1 cup Zeal, 1 teaspoon Forbearance, 1 cup milk of Human Kindness, 1 cup Faith, and 1 cup Charity.

Cook book of selected recipes

S80.1 [1st ed.], 1939
United / Farmers of Canada / (Woman's Section) / Cook book / of / selected recipes / Price 25 cents / June 1939 / Colonsay / Saskatchewan [cover-title]
DESCRIPTION: 22.5 × 15.5 cm   Pp [1] 2–32   Portraits on p 1 of King George VI and Queen Elizabeth   Paper; stapled
CONTENTS: 1 'Welcome to Their Majesties! Commemorating the visit of Their Majesties King George VI and Queen Elizabeth to Saskatchewan May 25th and June 3rd, 1939'; 2 'Appreciation,' 'Index' [i.e., table of contents], and 'Printed by W.T. Morphy, Viscount, Sask.'; 3–30 recipes credited with the name of the contributor and ads; 31–2 blank for 'Memo'
COPIES: *SSWD

NOTES: The 'Appreciation' on p 2 refers to the cookbook as 'the first edition of Selected Recipes' and lists the names of the recipe contributors. An advertisement on p 26 illustrates a mug made by Henry Birks and Sons – a 'free souvenir of the royal visit' that would be mailed 'to every farmer who pays his membership fee of two dollars ($2.00) in full [to the United Farmers] between the first of May and the first of July, inclusive, 1939.'

1939–45

War time cook book

S81.1   nd [about 1939–45]
War time / cook book / Save sugar / by using honey, syrup / and molasses / Edited and compiled by the / Wa Wa Shrine Ladies' Auxiliary of Melfort / Price 25 cents [cover-title]
DESCRIPTION: 22.0 × 18.5 cm   Pp 1–24   Paper, with still-life on front of baked goods; stapled
CONTENTS: 1 'The Use of Honey, Syrup and Molasses in Home Cooking' and 'Index' [i.e., table of contents]; 2–24 recipes for 'Breads,' 'Cakes and Icing,' 'Pies and Filling,' 'Cookies,' 'Muffins & Pancakes,' 'Pudding, Dessert and Sauce,' 'Fruit, Relishes, Pickles,' 'Miscellaneous,' and 'Ice Cream'
COPIES: *Private collection
NOTES: 'Melfort Moon Print, Melfort' is on the outside back face of the binding.

1940

Cook book

S82.1   1940
United Farmers of Canada / Saskatchewan Section Limited / [symbol of UFC, Saskatchewan Section Ltd] / (Women's Section) / Cook book / 1940
DESCRIPTION: Small tp illus of a woman's head in silhouette, in an oval (like a cameo); photograph on p 2 of 'The Executive of the U.F.C. Women's Section'   Oil cloth
CONTENTS: 1 tp; 2 photograph of the executive; 3 untitled note from the executive, signed Mrs Mabel Bradley, president; 4 'A Message' signed Mrs Mabel Bradley; 5–? recipes credited with the name and town of the contributor; ...
COPIES: *Bookseller's stock
NOTES: There are 158 pp. On p 3, Mrs Bradley says that this cookbook was prepared by the Women's Section executive, at the request of delegates to Farm Women's Week at the University of Saskatchewan in June 1939, and she thanks the commercial co-operatives and others who have paid for advertising in the book. On p 4, she outlines the aims and objectives of the Women's Section: 'Home conditions, after all, on the farm form the basis of the entire agricultural industry, ... The women membership of the U.F.C. and the officials seek legislative and economic changes which will make improvement in our home life possible ... We believe that every farm home should be equipped with all available modern conveniences; that social, educational and health services should be within the reach of every farm family; that our boys and girls should have equal opportunity with others to enter the higher educational institutions, and that there should be a place for them upon the farm where they can establish their home.' The cookbook was likely published in Saskatoon, the location of the organization's Central Office.

Favorite recipes

LLCC stands for the Landrose Ladies Community Club formed on 7 February 1940. The Landrose School District is east of Lloydminster in the east half of Section 8-50-26 W⅓. For information about the club and photographs, see East of Lloydminster: A Historical Review *by the East of Lloydminster Historical Society, edited by Eunice Hawkins, printed by the Lloydminster Times, May 1979, pp 193–53. Although the club's activities are recorded, there is no mention of the cookbook.*

S83.1 nd [about 1940]
[An edition of *Favorite Recipes*, by the LLCC, Landrose, nd, pp 38]
COPIES: Private collection
NOTES: The owner reports that the volume includes a photograph taken at Banff Springs Hotel in 1939, during the visit of King George VI and Queen Elizabeth. The cookbook was likely an early project of the club, whose first few years were given to war work. The recipes are credited with the name of the contributor. There are advertisements from businesses in nearby Lloydminster and Marshall.

Homemaker's cook book

The Yorkton club was organized in 1932 and disbanded in 1954 (SWI, p 153).

S84.1 nd [about 1940]
[Saskatchewan Homemakers' Club symbol] / Homemaker's / cook / book / Yorkton District Homemaker's [sic] / Clubs / Price 25 cents [cover-title]
DESCRIPTION: 23.0 × 15.0 cm Pp [1–2] 3–57 [58–60] Paper; stapled
CONTENTS: 1 'Foreword' signed Mrs E.L. Fowler; 2 'A Timely Hint' [poem]; 3 'Abbreviations,' 'Weights and Measures,' and 'Quantities Needed for 50 or More People'; 4 'Index' [i.e., table of contents]; 5–57 recipes credited with the name of the contributor and ads; 58–60 blank for 'My Own Recipes'
COPIES: *Private collection
NOTES: The advertisement for Robin Hood Flour on the inside back face of the binding gives the flour's '1939 Record' for baking competitions. This copy is inscribed on the binding, 'From Mrs. Thompson // Bredenbury Sask. Betty [Curll?] August 29/40.'

Simpson Homemakers' Club cook book

The Simpson club was founded in 1921 (SWI, p 152).

S85.1 1940
[An edition of *Simpson Homemakers' Club Cook Book*, Simpson, Sask.: Homemakers' Club, 1940, pp 80]
CITATIONS: AnderCat April 2001, No. 14473
COPIES: Bookseller's stock
NOTES: There is a page devoted to the local history of the community. The recipes are credited with the name of the contributor.

1940s

Hostess book

S86.1 nd [about 1940s]
[An edition of *Hostess Book*, Eston, Sask.: Canadian Legion BESL [i.e., British Empire Services League], Ladies' Auxiliary, nd, pp 69, 23 cm]
COPIES: OONL (TX715.6 H673 1940z missing)

1941

Sutherland cook book

S87.1 1941
Sutherland / cook book / Compiled and published by the / Sutherland Circle of St. Joseph's Altar Society / Sutherland / 1941 / V [for victory] ...– [i.e., Morse Code symbol for V] / Price 55¢ [cover-title]
DESCRIPTION: 22.0 × 15.0 cm Pp [1] 2–112 Paper, with image on front of a woman stirring the contents of a bowl; stapled
CONTENTS: 1 'Foreword' and 'Committee'; 2 ads; 3 'Index' [i.e., table of contents]; 4–111 recipes credited with the name of the contributor and ad; 112 ads; inside back face of binding 'Compliments of the Federal Printing Company "Printers of the Sutherland Cook Book" 107 Third Avenue North // Saskatoon Sask.'
CITATIONS: Peel's Bibliography 6467
COPIES: OONL (TX715.6 S87 1941) *Private collection
NOTES: Sutherland, which used to be on the outskirts of Saskatoon, is now incorporated as part of the city. Mrs A.J. McIntosh, named on p 1 as president of St Joseph's Altar Society, was also, at one time, an alderman for Sutherland.

1942

100 sugarless recipes

For editions of 100 Sugarless Recipes *published by the Officer's [sic] Wives Auxiliary of Saskatchewan Flight Training School No. 11, in Yorkton, see O1055.4.*

Westminster cook book

In 1968 Westminster Church amalgamated with another congregation and was renamed Grace-Westminster United Church.

S88.1 nd [about 1942]
Westminster cook book / Idylwyld Circle / We may live without poetry, music and art, / We may live without conscience, and live without heart, / We may live without friends, we may live without books, / But civilized man cannot live without cooks. / The members of Idylwyld Circle wish to take this opportunity to / thank all those who sent in recipes for this book, also the adver- / tisers, who by their support, have helped make our book possible. / We hope our readers will see fit to patronize our advertisers, or / specify their products whenever possible.
DESCRIPTION: 23.0 × 15.0 cm Pp [1–2] 3–84 Paper; stapled
CONTENTS: 1 tp; 2 'Index' [i.e., table of contents]; 3–84 recipes credited with the name of the contributor, ads, and on p mid 84, 'Table of Weights and Measures'
CITATIONS: Ferguson/Fraser, p 234
COPIES: SSU (TX715.6 I39 1961)   *Private collection
NOTES: The cover-title is 'Westminster Cook Book // Idylwyld Circle // New book // Saskatoon, Sask.' This 'new book' offers a different selection of recipes from S50.1, from the same church. Another private collector's copy of *Westminster Cook Book* is inscribed on the binding, 'January 28th, 1942.' The appearance of the book is consistent with publication in 1942. There are advertisements for National Job Printers, 334 Twentieth Street West, on pp 4, 22, 44, 52, and 78; this company is likely the printer of the cookbook.

1943

Cook book

In 1948 the same chapter published another Cook Book, *numbered Vol. 2, S107.1.*

S89.1 1943
Hadassah / Lillian Freiman Chapter / Moose Jaw / 1943 / Cook / book / V [for victory] / ...– [i.e., Morse Code symbol for V] / Tried and tested recipes [cover-title]
DESCRIPTION: 22.0 × 15.0 cm Pp [i–ii], [1] 2–80 Portrait on p 1 of Mrs A.J. Freiman, president, Hadassah Organization of Canada, 1923–40 Paper; stapled, and with hole punched at top left corner for hanging
CONTENTS: i blank; ii 'Canadian Hadassah's War Effort'; 1 'In tribute to the sacred memory of our late beloved leader Mrs. A.J. Freiman, O.B.E. ...' and her portrait; 2 poem beginning, 'We may live without poetry, music and art' [from *Lucile,* Part I, Canto ii, by Owen Meredith, pseudonym of Edward Robert Bulwer-Lytton] and list of officers of the Moose Jaw Chapter of Hadassah, including members of the Cook Book Committee, whose chairman was Mrs Arthur I. Lerner; 3 table of contents and 'Thank You ...' from the Moose Jaw Chapter of Hadassah; 4 'Greetings and Good Wishes to the Lillian Freiman Chapter of Hadassah, Moose Jaw from [lists thirteen western Hadassah chapters]'; 5–78 text; 79 'Greetings to Moose Jaw Chapter of Hadassah from [list of names of individuals]'; 80 'Jewish Holy Days' [calendar of holy days for 1943, 1944, and 1945]
COPIES: *Private collection
NOTES: 'Passover and Purim Dishes' are on pp 67–70. The printer, 'The Times Company Limited, Moose Jaw, Sask.,' is on the inside back face of the binding.

Navy cook book of tested recipes

S90.1 1943
Navy / cook book / of / tested recipes / [crest and motto of HMCS Unicorn] / Compiled by / Officers Wives' and Mothers' Auxiliary / H.M.C.S. "Unicorn" / Saskatoon / 1943
DESCRIPTION: About 22.5 × 15.5 cm [dimensions from photocopy]
COPIES: *Bookseller's stock
NOTES: The bookseller reports that the volume has 80 pp, the recipes are credited with the name of the contributor, the table of contents is on p 80, and there are advertisements for local businesses.

Souvenir cook book

S91.1 1943
[Ad for Walters' Garage, Melville, Saskatchewan] / Souvenir / cook book / published by / Duff Patriotic Club / 1943 / Duff Sask. / [ad for J.W. Redgwick, Melville] [cover-title]
DESCRIPTION: 22.0 × 15.0 cm Pp 1–40 Paper; stapled
CONTENTS: 1–39 recipes, most credited with the name of the contributor, ads, and on p mid 39, a small Union Jack and blank space for 'Memo'; 40 'Index to Contents' [i.e., table of contents] and blank space for 'Memo'
COPIES: *OONL (TX715.6 S629 1943 p***)

1944

Victory cook book

S92.1 nd [1944]

Victory cook book / I promise to / 1. Follow rules of nutrition. / 2. Buy wisely – not waste. / 3. Save time for war work. / 4. Be neighborly – hospitable. / 5. Build morale at home. / V V V / Published by / Friendship Circle / Knox United Church / Regina, Sask. / Price 50 cents

DESCRIPTION: 23.0 × 15.5 cm   Pp [1] 2–104   Tp illus of a saluting housewife, her long spoon positioned as a rifle; small illus   Paper, with small image on front of an RCMP rider on horseback; stapled

CONTENTS: Inside front face of binding recipe for Honey Feather Cake, a 'wartime cake,' in ad for Jewel Shortening made by Swift Canadian Co. Ltd; 1 tp; 2 ads; 3 'Foreword' by W.A. Riddell, chairman, Saskatchewan Nutrition Committee; 4 ads; 5 'Canada's Official Food Rules' and ad; 6 ad; 7 'Supper Dish' courtesy of Mrs A.P. McNab, chatelaine of Government House; 8 ads; 9–104 text

CITATIONS: Peel's Bibliography 6525

COPIES: *OGU (CCC TX715.6 V53)   OONL (AC901 A7 1940z No. 0084)   QMM (RBD ckbk 1949)   SRA

NOTES: There is an advertisement on p 50 for Mid-West Creameries Ltd, which places the book's publication after 1942; it refers to 'two successive wins, 1941–2 for highest consistent quality [of butter-making] throughout the year.' The year of publication is limited to 1944, by the description of W.A. Riddell as chairman of the Saskatchewan Nutrition Committee. This committee was created by the Department of Health in 1944. Miss Jean Oddie, who contributed 'School Lunches' on p 81 and 'The War Worker's Lunch' on p 83, is described as director of Junior Red Cross, evidence that the cookbook was published before November 1944, when Oddie was appointed the first provincial nutritionist for Saskatchewan. (In the 1945 annual report of the Department of Health, Oddie mentions producing a publication entitled 'Better School Lunches' with assistance from Dr Riddell; I have not located a copy of this title.)

'Nutrition for Older Women' by Hope Hunt, dean, College of Household Science, University of Saskatchewan, is on p 21. 'Nutrition in the Rural Home' by Bertha G. Oxner, director of women's work, University of Saskatchewan, is on p 38. Margaret Racine contributed 'Cooking for One in War Time' on p 98.

The printer's name is on the back face of the binding: 'Commercial Printers, Limited Regina, Sask.'

The OGU copy is inscribed on the title-page, in ink, 'Merry Christmas and Happy New Year. Ruth and Phil.'; and there are two Christmas stickers applied to the title-page. The volume was a gift to the person who later donated it to OGU.

1945

Cook book

S93.1 1945

Cook / book / recipes / old and new / Published by / Young Matrons' District / C.W.L. / Moose Jaw, Sask. / 1945 [cover-title]

DESCRIPTION: 22.0 × 15.0 cm   Pp [1] 2–80   Paper, with image on front of a woman combining ingredients in a bowl

CONTENTS: 1 'Thank You' signed 'Young Matrons' District, Catholic Women's League,' untitled poem, and 'Index' [i.e., table of contents]; 3 ads; 4–80 text and ads

COPIES: *Private collection

NOTES: There is a section of 'Recipes from Other Lands' on pp 72–4, which includes recipes for Norwegian Fish Pudding, Crepes French Pancakes, Polish Zraziki, Spitzbub, Czech Meat Rolls, Danish Pastry, Real Scotch Haggis, and Butter Kringle.

Favorite recipes cook book

S94.1 nd [about 1945]

Holy Family Hospital / Favorite recipes / cook / book / Patronesses' Auxiliary [cover-title]

DESCRIPTION: 23.0 × 15.5 cm   Pp 1–91 [92]   Illus on p 1 of Holy Family Hospital, 15th Street West, Prince Albert   Paper; stapled

CONTENTS: 1 illus and history of Holy Family Hospital; 2 foreword; 3 'Index' [i.e., table of contents]; 4 ads; 5–89 recipes; 90–2 ads

COPIES: *Private collection

NOTES: The book is undated, but a former member of the Auxiliary remembers that it was published in 1945. The history on p 1 states that the hospital was founded in 1910 by the Sisters of Charity of Saint John, New Brunswick. The text begins with 'Where to Find Your Vitamins' on p 5 and '"The Bride" Cooking for Two' on p 6 (the same headings as in S95.1). 'Herald Job Print, Prince Albert, Sask.' is on the outside back face of the binding. In 1992 I was served Log Cabin Potatoes, p 72, and Orange Tarts, p 56, from this book; they were delicious.

1945–9

The auxiliary cook book

S95.1 nd [about 1945–9]
The auxiliary / cook / book / Compiled by / the Women's / Auxiliary / of / St. Paul's / Hospital / Price $1.00 [cover-title]
DESCRIPTION: 24.0 × 17.0 cm   Pp [1–3] 4–108   Illus on p 1 of St Paul's Hospital   Paper; stapled
CONTENTS: 1 illus; 2 foreword; 3 'Index' [i.e., table of contents]; 4 'Where to Find Your Vitamins'; 5–106 recipes and ads; 107–8 ads
COPIES: *OGU (CCC TX715.6 A99)   OONL (TX715.6 A96 1950z p***)
NOTES: 'Midwest Litho Printing Ltd., Saskatoon' is on the outside back face of the binding. The caption for the illustration on p 1 records the following history: 'In 1906, during a serious typhoid epidemic, two Sisters of Charity (Grey Nuns) opened a temporary nursing home. Petitioned by a large group of Saskatoon citizens, a permanent hospital was established by the Order in 1907. The present building, appearing above, was opened in 1913.' The first section of recipes is '"The Bride", Cooking for Two' (this heading and that on p 4 are the same as in S94.1). There is a section of 'Meatless Casseroles and Soups.' Recipes from immigrants not of British extraction include Kamoish Broit contributed by Mrs D.M. Baltzan, Melomacarona (Honey-Dipped Cookies) and Karidato (Walnut Sponge Cake) by Mrs Sam Girgulis, and Halvas by Mrs A. Barootes.

Cook book

S96.1 nd [about 1945–9]
Cook / book / Compiled by / Acacia Chapter No. 3 / Order of the Eastern Star / Biggar / Sask. [cover-title]
DESCRIPTION: 23.5 × 14.5 cm   Pp 1–100   Photograph on p 68 by Yousuf Karsh of M.J. Coldwell, a politician; photograph on p 72 of Woodrow S. Lloyd, minister of education, Saskatchewan   Paper; stapled
CONTENTS: Inside front face of binding 'Printed by the Independent, Biggar, Sask.'; 1 'Foreword' signed O.E.S. Cook Book Committee and six names, and 'Index'; 2–100 recipes credited with the name of the contributor and ads
COPIES: OONL (TX715.6 C656 1950z)   *SBIHM
NOTES: W.S. Lloyd was minister of education from 10 July 1944 to 1 August 1960; therefore, the cookbook was published no earlier than 1944. M.J. Coldwell was member of Parliament for Rosetown-Biggar from 1935 to 1958.

Deutsch-Canadisches Kochbuch

S97.1 nd [about 1945–9]
Deutsch-Canadisches / Kochbuch / Herausgegeben von: / Western Printers Ass'n, Ltd. / Regina, Sask.
DESCRIPTION: Tp illus of a giant milk bottle and a woman at a kitchen table who is mixing the contents of a bowl   [$1.00, on binding]   With image on front of a woman fastening the lid of a preserving jar, with other jars and a preserving kettle on the counter before her
CONTENTS: 1 tp; 2–3 'Inhaltsverzeichnis // Deutsche Abteilung'; 4 'English Section // Index'; 5 'Die Ernährung des Menschen' ...
COPIES: *OONL (B-15979)
NOTES: The cover-title is 'German-Canadian Cook Book / Deutsch-Canadisches / Kochbuch / in deutscher und englischer sprache ...' The first and largest part of the text is in German; 'Inhaltsverzeichnis // Deutsche Abteilung' lists the topics covered, beginning on p 5, the last topic beginning on p 210. 'English Section // Index' lists the topics covered, beginning on p 213; the last topic is 'One Hundred Calorie Portions of Some Commonly Used Foods' on p 271. All the German recipes have the recipe name in German and English; the English recipes have only English names.

Peter Duchesne, collections librarian at OONL, dates the book late 1930s or early 1940s, based on the style of the book and the fact that an advertisement for Eaton's uses fraktur script, which he has not seen in advertisements for a national company past the end of the Second World War. Other evidence points to publication in about 1945–9: the illustration on the binding, and the final part of the English text that presents 'Rules for Reducing,' 'Ideal Weight, According to Height,' and 'One Hundred Calorie Portions ...'

The nutritional information on p 5 recalls 'Wie wir uns richtig ernähren' ['How We Nourish Ourselves Correctly'] in M127.1, *Nordwesten'-Kochbuch*; however, I have not compared the two texts to see if there is a connection.

Favorite recipes

S98.1 nd [about 1945–9]

Favorite recipes / Compiled by / Northwest District Women's Association / St. Andrew's United Church [cover-title]

DESCRIPTION: 22.5 × 15.0 cm Pp [1] 2–77 [78–80] Very thin card, with image on front of the church; stapled

CONTENTS: 1 'Thank you' signed Mrs Edmund R. Wyatt, cook book convener, untitled introductory text, and 'Index'; 2 ad; 3–74 recipes, most credited with the name of the contributor, and ads; 75 'Your Church Supper,' courtesy of Canada Starch Home Service Department; 76–7 'Household Hints'; 78–80 blank, ruled leaves for 'Memorandum'

COPIES: OGU (CCC TX715.6 F379) *OONL (TX715.6 F3862 1950z p***)

NOTES: St Andrew's United Church is in Moose Jaw. An advertisement on p 24 for Galt Coal, 'mined for more than fifty years,' limits the date of publication. Sir Alexander Galt organized the North Western Coal and Navigation Co. in 1882 to mine coal deposits in Lethbridge, Alberta (then called Coalbanks). Sales of coal started after the train line to Lethbridge was established in 1885. Based on the evidence of the advertisement, *Favorite Recipes* may have been published as early as 1936 (1885 + 'more than fifty years'). The appearance of the book, however, suggests about 1945–9, i.e., about sixty years after mining started.

Favorite recipes

S99.1 nd [about 1945–9]

Favorite / recipes / Issued by / the Evening Branch / Women's Auxiliary / Wilkie United Church [cover-title]

DESCRIPTION: 23.5 × 15.5 cm Pp 1–32 Paper, with image on front of the church; stapled

CONTENTS: 1 blank for 'Memo'; 2–30 recipes credited with the name of the contributor and ads; 31 'Helpful Household Hints'; 32 blank for 'Additional Recipes'

COPIES: *Bookseller's stock

NOTES: 'This cook book was printed by the Wilkie Press' is on p 17.

Maguire, Mrs Vera C.

For an edition of her Honey Sunday 'n' Monday 'n' All through the Week *distributed in Fort Qu'Appelle, see A111.2.*

1946

Co-op cook book

S100.1 [1st ed., 1946]

Co-op / cook book / with / kitchen tested recipes / [symbol of two clasped hands and the motto 'Each for all and all for each'] / Dedicated to the housewives of / Canada, who destines [*sic*] human / welfare by designating our / purchasing power.

DESCRIPTION: 22.5 × 15.0 cm Pp [1–2] 3–208 Cloth, with the year of publication (1946) on front; sewn

CONTENTS: 1 tp; 2 blank; 3 'Foreword' signed Outlook Women's Co-operative Guild; 4 information about Saskatchewan's 'Co-op Family'; 5 'Creed,' 'Ode,' 'Prayer,' and 'Little Kitchen' [poem]; 6 ad for Consumers' Co-operative Mills Ltd; 7 'Co-operative Women's Guild' [information about this international organization] signed Saskatchewan Women's Co-operative Guilds; 8–9 'Nutrition Facts' by Jean Oddie, provincial nutritionist; 10 'Saskatchewan Federated Co-operatives Limited'; 11–202 culinary text, including many recipes credited with the name and city or town of the contributor, and information about the co-operative movement; 203 'Table of Contents'; 204–8 blank for 'Favorite Recipes'

CITATIONS: Landsberg

COPIES: *Private collection

NOTES: In the 'Foreword' the Outlook Guild explains why they produced this cookbook: 'By the distribution of this book into the various homes across the prairies and beyond, we hope to aid the housewives by making the experience of others available to them, to add to their storehouse of good recipes, ... and lay the foundation of a better today and a brighter tomorrow, by acquainting them with the different phases of the co-operative movement.' The text is an ambitious collection of practical information, from nutritional facts to meat and menu charts, and the recipes, some of which have been gathered together in a section called 'Foreign Recipes,' reflect the immigrant makeup of the prairie population. The printer's name, 'Modern Press Limited, Saskatoon,' is on the outside back face of the binding, and there is an advertisement on p 32 that states, 'This excellent cook book was printed by Modern Press Limited Saskatoon // publishers of Canada's leading co-operative newspaper the Western Producer.' According to the 'Foreword' of the 1952 edition, the women of Outlook were 'aided [in their production of the 1946 edition] by the manager and staff of the first Co-operative Flour Mill in Canada, which was then located at Outlook, ...' *Co-op Cook Book* was a tremendous success, and was revised and reprinted several times in the decade following its first publication.

Ferguson/Fraser, p 234, cite the 1946 edition, but incorrectly give the title as *Cooking the Co-op Way* (the 1960s title) and the publisher as Federated Co-operatives Ltd (the latter was formed in January 1955).

OTHER EDITIONS: Rev. ed., 1952, committee in charge of revision: Violet M. Johnsrude, Ann E. Poth, Rennie M. Fast, and Amelia A. Lawrence (OONL); reprint, March 1953 and September 1953; rev. ed., 1954 (OONL); rev. ed., 1955; reprint, June 1956 and September 1956 (the latter, Private collection).

A new 'Co-op' cookbook, incorporating recipes from former editions of *Co-op Cook Book* and from the Manitoba Women's Co-operative Guild's *For Tasteful Living*, was issued as *Cooking the Co-op Way*, recipes selected and tested by J.A. Penny, edited by Donna Rochdale, [Regina, Sask.?]: Manitoba Women's Co-operative Guild, Saskatchewan Co-operative Women's Guild, 1959 (OGU, OONL).

Phelps, Mrs Lena Mae, née Ackerman (Mrs Joseph Lee Phelps) (farm near Saskatoon, Sask., 14 October 1909– 13 September 1952)

Lena married Joseph Lee Phelps on 14 February 1931. Joseph, a member of the Co-operative Commonwealth Federation, represented the Saltcoats constituency in the Saskatchewan Legislature from 1938 to 1948; he was minister of natural resources, 10 July 1944–13 November 1944, and minister of natural resources and industrial development, 13 November 1944–4 August 1948. One of the notices at the time of Lena's death described her as 'one of [Saskatchewan's] brightest and most outstanding personalities' and commented that 'it used to be said Mrs. Phelps was the real minister, such was her interest and enthusiasm in her husband's job.' She was a great support to him, writing speeches, researching issues, co-authoring legislation, and sometimes standing in for him at events. Employees at the Legislative Library named her 'honorary librarian' for her extensive use and promotion of the library. Lena died on a Saskatoon-bound train, on her way back from Montreal where she had received treatment from the famous neurosurgeon Dr Wilder Penfield. Lena and Joseph had five children: George Lee, Ella Josephine, Donald Bruce, a daughter, Leila, who died in infancy, and Gordon Wayne.

Information about the author is from her daughter, Ella Little, and gleaned from records for her husband at SRL and from three articles at the time of her death, in the Leader Post*: 'Mrs. J.L. Phelps Dies aboard Train,'*

15 September 1952, p 1; 'A Bright Spirit Passes,' 16 September 1952, p 11; J.R. Bothwell, 'Lena Phelps – Tireless Researcher: The Library Knew Her Well,' 25 September 1952, p 17.

S101.1 nd [about 1946]
Saskatchewan / fish / cookery / Guide to cooking Saskatchewan's / high quality fish products [cover-title]
DESCRIPTION: 22.0 × 14.0 cm   Pp [1] 2–20   Illus headpieces to chapters   Paper, with image on front of a box of SFP [i.e., Saskatchewan Fish Products] Whitefish Fillets; stapled
CONTENTS: Inside front face of binding 'Processing Our Northern Fish'; 1 'Delicious Fish Dishes You Can Prepare' [i.e., table of contents]; 2 'Foreword' signed Jean Oddie, provincial nutritionist; 3 'What You Should Know about Fish'; 4 'Preparation of Fish for Cookery'; 5–8 'Tasty Baked Fish'; 9 'Boiled Fish Is a Favorite'; 10 'Everyone Enjoys Broiled Fish'; 11 'Fry Your Fish'; 12–13 'Fish Dishes That Are Different'; 14 'What to Serve with Fish'; 15–16 'Home Canned Fish'; 17–18 'Developing Saskatchewan's Fishing Industry'; 19–20 'Processing Saskatchewan's Quality Fish'; inside back face 'Produced by: The Bureau of Publications // Legislative Building Regina for the Department of Natural Resources and Industrial Development ...'
COPIES: *Private collection
NOTES: This unnumbered edition is probably the first. The 'Foreword' names Mrs J.L. Phelps as the compiler of the book. Jean Oddie, who wrote the 'Foreword,' was made the first provincial nutritionist for Saskatchewan in November 1944 (she held the position until 1951). Jean (now Mrs Wenhardt) remembers that the cookbook was first published about 1946 (conversation, October 2001). At war's end, Saskatchewan experienced a sharp decline in prices and in demand for its fish products, especially in the United States, which had introduced strict quality controls. Lena Phelps compiled the cookbook at about the same time as Joseph Phelps was working to establish the Saskatchewan Fish Board, as a way to revitalize the province's fishing industry.

S101.2 [3rd ed., 1948]
—Saskatchewan / fish / cookery / Guide to cooking Saskatchewan's / high quality fish products [cover-title]
DESCRIPTION: 21.5 × 14.0 cm   Pp [1] 2–20   Illus headpieces to chapters   Paper, with image on front of a box of SFP Whitefish Fillets; stapled
CONTENTS: 1 'Delicious Fish Dishes You Can Prepare' [i.e., table of contents]; 2 'Foreword' signed Jean Oddie,

provincial nutritionist; 3 'What You Should Know about Fish'; 4 'Preparation of Fish for Cookery'; 5–8 'Tasty Baked Fish'; 9 'Boiled Fish Is a Favorite'; 10 'Everyone Enjoys Broiled Fish'; 11 'Fry Your Fish'; 12–13 'Fish Dishes That Are Different'; 14 'What to Serve with Fish'; 15–16 'Home Canned Fish'; 17–18 'Developing Saskatchewan's Fishing Industry'; 19–20 blank for 'Your Favorite Fish Recipes'
COPIES: SSU   *SWSLM
NOTES: The edition number and date are on the outside back face of the binding: 'Produced by: The Bureau of Publications // Legislative Building Regina for the Department of Natural Resources and Industrial Development // Natural Resources Building // Regina, Saskatchewan // Third edition 1948.'

1947

Kindersley cook book

S102.1   1947
Kindersley / cook book / Compiled and published by the Guild of / St. Mary's Anglican Church / Kindersley, Sask. 1947 / Price $1.00 [cover-title]
DESCRIPTION: 22.5 × 15.5 cm   Pp [1–2] 3–52 [53]   Paper, with 3.5-cm-high image on front of a woman, standing behind a counter on which are placed various foodstuffs; stapled
CONTENTS: 1 acknowledgments and list of the Guild executive; 2 blank; 3–52 recipes; 53 'Index' [i.e., table of contents] and ads
COPIES: *Private collection

Shaunavon Homemakers' Club cook book

The Shaunavon club was organized in 1944 (SWI, p 152).

S103.1   1947
Shaunavon / Homemakers' Club / cook book / 1947 / [Women's Institute symbol] [cover-title]
DESCRIPTION: 21.0 × 14.5 cm   Pp [1] 2–56   Paper; stapled
CONTENTS: 1 'Shaunavon Homemakers Cook Book,' unattributed poem beginning, 'We may live without poetry, music and art' [from Lucile, Part I, Canto ii, by Owen Meredith, pseudonym of Edward Robert Bulwer-Lytton], 'Index' [i.e., table of contents], and ad; 2 ad; 3–56 recipes credited with the name of the contributor
COPIES: *OONL (TX715.6 S428 1947 p***)

1947–9

Cook book

Wolseley Memorial Union Hospital accepted its first patient on 3 July 1947, and was officially opened on 11 November 1947 (Bridging the Past: Wolseley and District, 1880–1980, Wolseley, Sask.: Wolseley and District History Book Committee, 1981, p 31).

S104.1   nd [about 1947–9]
Cook book / [caption:] Wolseley Memorial Union Hospital / Tested recipes / Women's Hospital Auxiliary / Wolseley, Saskatchewan [cover-title]
DESCRIPTION: Pp [1] 2–?   With photograph on front of the hospital
CONTENTS: 1 'Foreword // Tried and tested recipes compiled and arranged by the ladies of the district of the Wolseley Memorial Union Hospital // Price – $1.00' and unattributed poem beginning, 'We may live without music, poetry and art' [from Lucile, Part I, Canto ii, by Owen Meredith, pseudonym of Edward Robert Bulwer-Lytton; 'poetry' and 'music' transposed from original]; 2 ad; 3 'Index' [i.e., table of contents]; ...
COPIES: *Bookseller's stock
NOTES: The 'Index' lists: 'Breads and Fancy Breads,' p 5; 'Supper Dishes,' p 7; 'Salads,' p 11; 'Cakes,' p 13; 'Cookies,' p 25; 'Pies and Tarts,' p 37; 'Desserts, Puddings and Frozen Desserts,' p 41; 'Pickles,' p 47; 'Marmalade, Jams, etc.,' p 51; 'Candy,' p 55; 'Miscellaneous,' p 57; and 'Household Hints,' p 59. From appearances, the cookbook was published in the late 1940s.

1948

The Carievale Willing Workers cook book

S105.1   [1948]
The Carievale Willing Workers / cook / book / 247 tried and true recipes and / 108 time and worry saving hints / Compiled by the members of the Willing / Workers Group of Carievale, / Sask., and their lady friends! / Obtainable from: – / Mrs. A.W. Fuller, President / Mrs. Arthur Burke, Secretary / or any other member.
DESCRIPTION: 20.0 × 12.5 cm   Pp [i–iv], 1–65, [i–xi] Paper; stapled
CONTENTS: i tp; ii 'Gazette-Post-News congratulates the Willing Workers of Carievale in gathering and publishing this booklet ...'; iii–iv ads; 1–65 recipes

credited with the name of the contributor, and at bottom p 65, 'Printed by the Gazette-Post-News, Carnduff, Sask. for the Carievale, Sask., News – 1948'; i–xi ads

COPIES: *Private collection

NOTES: The year of publication, 1948, is printed on the front face of the binding and also recorded on p 65.

Cook book

S106.1   nd [about 1948]

Cook / book / Tested recipes / Compiled by the / Organ Guild / of / First United Church / Melville – Sask. [cover-title]

DESCRIPTION: 21.0 × 15.0 cm   Pp [i–iv], 1–128   Paper; stapled

CONTENTS: i 'Foreword' thanking recipe contributors and advertisers; ii blank; iii 'Index' [i.e., table of contents]; iv ads; 1–124 recipes credited with the name of the contributor and ads; 125–8 ads

COPIES: *SMELM   Private collection

NOTES: On p 90 there is an advertisement for the Melville Advance Publishing Co. Ltd, which says, 'This book printed and published in our plant at Melville, Sask.' The private collector reports that she purchased her copy in 1948.

Cook book, Volume two

The Lillian Freiman Chapter also published S89.1.

S107.1   1948

Hadassah / Lillian Freiman / Chapter / Moose / Jaw / Cook / book / Volume two / 1948 [cover-title]

DESCRIPTION: With small image on front of a menorah

COPIES: *Private collection

NOTES: The owner reports that the book has 102 pp.

Garvagh Circle recipe book

S108.1   1948

Garvagh Circle / recipe book / Plenty United Church / 1948 [cover-title]

DESCRIPTION: 23.0 × 15.0 cm   Pp 1–80   Paper, with image on front of the church; stapled

CONTENTS: Inside front face of binding 'Index' [i.e., table of contents]; 1 'Garvagh Circle Members 1948' [twenty-one names]; 2 'Let Me Taste Your Wares'

[poem]; 3 'The Eleven Ages of Man (expressed in menu style)'; 4 thank-you from Garvagh Circle; 5–80 recipes credited with the name of the contributor and ads

COPIES: *Bookseller's stock

NOTES: On the inside back face of the binding is 'Congratulations to the ladies of Garvagh Circle' from the *Rosetown Eagle* (possibly the printer of the cookbook).

A practical guide to good cooking

S109.1   [1948]

A practical guide / to good cooking / by the Kennedy / United Church Choir [cover-title]

DESCRIPTION: About 22.5 × 15.0 cm [dimensions from photocopy]   Card, with image on front of a mother, father, and son being served soup by a waitress; metal-spiral-bound

COPIES: *Bookseller's stock

NOTES: The bookseller reports that the volume has 103 pp and the recipes are credited with the name of the contributor. The 'Foreword,' which is signed and dated the Committee, United Church Choir, Kennedy, Saskatchewan, 1948, states, 'This book has been published for the building of our church and for the upbuilding of the constitutions of the people whom it serves.'

St Henry's 40th anniversary cook book

See also S77.1 from St Henry's Roman Catholic Church. The parish women also published Catholic Women's League Cook Book *in 1961 (OONL).*

S110.1   1948

St. Henry's / 40th anniversary / cook book / 1908 1948 / Compiled / by / Ladies' / Altar / Society / Melville, Sask. [cover-title]

COPIES: *Private collection

Souvenir cook book

Christ Church Anglican was founded in 1907. The new cathedral-style building depicted on the cookbook's title-page was not erected. Instead, a new church was completed in 1957 to a different design.

S111.1   1948

Souvenir / cook book / [caption:] Proposed Memorial Church / Published by / the Wednesday

Evening Circle / of Christ Church / Saskatoon, Sask. February, 1948

DESCRIPTION: 24.5 × 17.0 cm   Pp [1–2] 3–59 [60]   Tp illus of the proposed church   Paper-covered card

CONTENTS: 1 tp; 2 'Foreword' signed Herbert Bowles, canon and rector, and 'List of Circle Members' [twelve names]; 3–58 recipes credited with the name of the contributor and ads; 59 'Quantities to Serve Fifty'; 60 'Index' [i.e., alphabetical list of sections]

COPIES: *Bookseller's stock

NOTES: In the 'Foreword' Bowles says, '[This cookbook] represents [the ladies'] endeavour on behalf of a great venture in faith, that of completing the building of Christ Church ... [which] will perpetuate the honour and sacrifice of the many men and women who, in the course of two great wars, left their homes and families ...' The book was likely printed by Midwest Litho Printing Ltd, Saskatoon, whose advertisement is on p 58.

1949

Cook book

S112.1   nd [about 1949]

Benevolent and Protective / Order of Elks / [BPOE symbol] / Cook book / Order of the Royal Purple / Regina Lodge No. 4 / Price $1.00

DESCRIPTION: 23.0 × 15.0 cm   Pp [i–vi], 1–104 [105–6] Paper, with image on front of a pansy; stapled

CONTENTS: i tp; ii–iii blank; iv 'Foreword' signed Mrs Anne Thunberg, Honoured Royal Lady, Regina Lodge No. 4, OORP, and thanks to the ladies of the Royal Purple No. 4 signed S.F. Otto, Exalted Ruler, BPOE, Regina Lodge No. 9; v 'Greetings to Our Friends' signed ladies of Regina Lodge No. 4; vi 'Remember in Using This Book,' 'Helpful Hints,' and 'Equivalents for Sugar'; 1–103 recipes and ads; 104 'Table of Measures'; 105 'Index' [i.e., table of contents] and thanks to the printer of the cookbook; 106 blank 'For Your Own Favorite Recipes'

COPIES: OGU   (CCC   TX715.6   B44314) *SRRPM   Private collection

NOTES: The 'Foreword' says that the cookbook was published to raise funds for 'the post-care of infantile paralysis and also for cancer research.' 'Greetings' refers to the publication as the 'Royal Purple Cook Book.' The private collector reports that she bought her copy from her landlord's wife in December 1949. An advertisement on p 64 for Dad's Place, 2039 Broad Street, 'Oldest established Tire Shop in Regina – over 25 years,' suggests a later date because Regina city

directories first list Dad's Place and 2039 Broad Street in the volume for 1930 (1930 + 25 years = 1955); however, the tire shop may have had another name and been at another address before 1930.

Cook book

The Quill Lake club was organized in 1914 and disbanded in 1971 (SWI, pp 128, 152).

S113.1   1949

The Quill Lake Homemakers' Club / Cook book / 1949 / Homemakers' Creed / Keep, us, O Lord, from pettiness; let us be large in thought, in word, / and deed. / Let us [...] – Mary Stewart. / Reprinted by permission / of the Associated Country Women of the World. [cover-title]

DESCRIPTION: 22.0 × 14.0 cm   Pp 1–128   Chapter headpieces   Paper, with image on front of bowl of fruit; stapled

CONTENTS: 1 'Household Measurements and Weights' and 'Substitutions'; 2–125 recipes credited with the name of the contributor and ads; 126–7 blank for 'Memo'; 128 'Index' [i.e., table of contents]

CITATIONS: Peel's Bibliography 7135

COPIES: *Private collection

NOTES: On the outside back face of the binding there is an advertisement for the Wadena News that states, 'This cook book is a product of our Job Printing Department.'

Favourite recipes

The Governor Laird Chapter was organized on 9 November 1909 and disbanded in the 1980s.

S114.1   nd [1949]

[IODE symbol] / Governor Laird Chapter / I.O.D.E. / Favourite / recipes / North Battleford / Saskatchewan [cover-title]

DESCRIPTION: 23.0 × 15.5 cm   Pp [1] 2–72   Paper, with images on front of IODE symbol and two flags; stapled

CONTENTS: 1 'Foreword'; 2 ad; 3–67 recipes credited with the name of the contributor, 'Household Hints,' and ads; 68 ads; 69 'Catering // Provisions for 40 People' and 'Measures'; 70 ads; 71 'Index' [i.e., alphabetical list of sections] and ads; 72 'Directory' [of businesses]

COPIES: *Bookseller's stock

NOTES: 'Printed by the North Battleford Optimist' is

on the outside back face of the binding. Two advertisements point to publication in 1949: one on p 52 for Sterling Hardware and Millwork Ltd, '1907 ... 1949'; and one on p 56 for Bert McMullin that gives a figure for payments made in 1948 by the Metropolitan Life Insurance Co. The cookbook was likely published late in 1949: There is an advertisement on p 64 for Zeal and Hallis that commands the reader to 'See our exciting 1950 Fur Fashion Preview.'

Friendly Circle cook book

S115.1 1949

Friendly Circle cook book / 1949 / Choice recipes / The members of the Friendly Circle, United / Church of Craik, Sask., take pleasure in present- / ing to you our recipe book. We especially wish / to commend to you the merchants whose / advertisements have made this issue possible. / We are sure that your patronage of them, and / their products, will justify their faith in us. / Thanks to the advertisers, recipe givers, T. / Eaton Co., and any others who have con- / tributed in any way to make this undertaking a / success. / [poem beginning, 'We may live without poetry, music and art,' from *Lucile*, Part I, Canto ii, by Owen Meredith, pseudonym of Edward Robert Bulwer-Lytton] [cover-title]
DESCRIPTION: About 21.0 × 14.0 cm [dimensions from photocopy] With image on front and on p 1 of a woman rolling dough Stapled
COPIES: *OONL (B-20194 p***)
NOTES: The 'Index' [i.e., table of contents] on p 1 lists recipes on pp 2–62 and 'Miscellaneous' on pp 63–4.

Thirtieth anniversary cook book 1919–1949

S116.1 1949

Thirtieth anniversary / cook book / 1919–1949 / "As for me and my house, we will serve the Lord." / – Joshua 24: 15 / ['WMF' in triangle shape] / Canada District / Women's Missionary Federation / Evangelical Lutheran Church [cover-title]
DESCRIPTION: 22.5 × 14.5 cm Pp 1–64 Paper, with image on front of a roast ham; stapled
CONTENTS: 1 'Foreword' signed Women's Missionary Federation, Canada District; 2 '1919 Officers,' '1949 Officers,' and 'Edited by Mrs. J.B. Haave // Admiral, Saskatchewan // Printed by the Wadena News // Wadena, Saskatchewan'; 3–61 recipes identified as

contributed by local societies of the WMF, sometimes followed by information about the particular local society; 62–3 blank for 'Memo'; 64 'Index' [i.e., table of contents]
COPIES: *OONL (TX715.6 T545 1949 p***)
NOTES: The running head is 'W.M.F. Thirtieth Anniversary Cook Book.' The genesis of the book is explained in the 'Foreword': 'The Women's Missionary Federation of the Evangelical Lutheran Church in Canada, sought a way to commemorate the Thirtieth Anniversary since its organization in the District. At the Workers' Conference and Board Meeting in 1948, the suggestion that we print a cook book was well received.' All the local WMF societies in Canada were invited to contribute. A total of 193 recipes were chosen, each section of recipes being organized by a particular circuit: 'Meats and Vegetables' by the Camrose circuit; 'Salads and Salad Dressings' by Edmonton; 'Pickles and Relishes' by Manitoba; 'Frostings, Icings and Candies' by Moose Jaw; 'Jams, Jellies and Preserves' by Peace River; 'Cakes and Cookies' by Prince Albert; 'Biscuits and Small Cakes' by Saskatoon; 'Pastries and Puddings' by Southern Alberta; 'Bread and Rolls' by Swift Current; and 'Christmas Section' by Yorkton.

Tisdale favorites

The hospital used to be owned and managed by the Sisters of Charity of Our Lady of Evron, France.

S117.1 1949

[Running head:] Tisdale favorites / [title:] Tisdale / favorites / Compiled and published by / Tisdale Hospital Aid / Tisdale, Saskatchewan / April 1949 / [caption:] The St. Therese Hospital / Tisdale, Saskatchewan / Printed by the Tisdale Recorder, Tisdale, Saskatchewan / [folio:] 1
DESCRIPTION: 22.0 × 14.5 cm Pp 1–50 Tp illus of St Therese Hospital Very thin card, with image on front, at top, of a woman adding an ingredient to a bowl, and at bottom, of a cup and saucer, meal on a plate, and soup in a bowl; stapled
CONTENTS: 1 tp; 2 'Foreward' [*sic*], 'Officers of the Tisdale Hospital Aid, 1948–1949,' and 'Life Members'; 3 'Moral: Don't Guess' and 'Methuselah' [poems]; 4–45 recipes credited with the name of the contributor; 46–7 ads; 48–50 blank for 'Memo'
COPIES: *OONL (TX715.6 T57 1949 p***) Private collection
NOTES: The 'Index,' i.e., table of contents, is printed

on the front face of the binding. On the outside back face, there is a mock recipe under the heading 'Tisdale Hospital Aid Cook Book // Cooking a Husband.'

Women's Association cook book

S118.1   1949
Women's Association / cook book / United Church / Frobisher, Sask. / 1949 / (All recipes approved by members) [cover-title]
DESCRIPTION: 15.5 × 11.5 cm   Pp 1–42   Paper, with image on front of the United Church; stapled
CONTENTS: Inside front face of binding thanks to advertisers, and a list of 'Officers' in the Women's Association; 1–2 ads; 3–42 recipes credited with the name of the contributor and ads
COPIES: MWPA (MG14 C50 McKnight, Ethel)   *SRA
NOTES: The last committee recorded under 'Officers'
is 'Committee in Charge,' i.e., probably the group in charge of the cookbook; the names listed are Mrs Timlin, Mrs A. Brandon, Mrs R.R. Deyell, Mrs Mawhinney, and Mrs L.E. Rennie.

S118.2   1989
—Women's Association / cook book / United Church / Frobisher, Sask. / 1949 / (All recipes approved by members) [cover-title]
DESCRIPTION: 15.0 × 10.5 cm   Pp [i–ii], 1–42 [43–6] Paper, with image on front of the United Church; stapled
CONTENTS: i thanks to advertisers, and a list of 'Officers'; ii 'Republished by: Frobisher United Church Women 1989' and a list of officers; 1–2 ads; 3–43 reprint of original recipes and ads; 44–6 recipes new to the 1989 edition
COPIES: *Private collection

Alberta

Orange Charlotte

½ box gelatine, or 1⅓ tablespoons granulated gelatine, ⅓ cup cold water, ⅓ cup boiling water, 1 cup sugar, 3 tablespoons lemon juice, 1 cup orange juice and pulp, whites of 3 eggs, 2 cups cream well whipped.

Soak gelatine in cold water, dissolve in boiling water, strain, and add sugar, lemon juice, orange juice and pulp. Chill in pan of ice water. When quite thick, beat with wire spoon and whisk until frothy, then add whites of eggs, beaten stiff, and fold in cream. Line a mould with sections of oranges, turn in mixture, smooth evenly and chill.

Mrs Macleod [wife of Colonel Macleod, who signed Treaty No. 7 with Chief Crowfoot]

A18.1, *The W.A. Cook Book,* by Mary Pinkham, [about 1910], p 50

The first cookbooks compiled in Alberta appeared after full provincial status came into force on 1 September 1905: at least three were published in 1907; one undated work may be from 1906. Earlier cookbooks have surfaced, but they were editions of texts produced outside the province, the first being one published in Medicine Hat in 1904, when Alberta was still part of the North-West Territory. As the population boomed – growing from 73,022 to 374,295 between 1901 and 1911, and to 588,454 by 1921 – the province's charitable groups, private companies, and government departments began to produce a steady stream of cookbooks specifically for Albertans. Although the recipe collections reflected primarily British food traditions, especially at the beginning, evidence of the varied strands in Alberta's ethnic mix is increasingly seen in later books, where Cabbage Rolls, Cornish Pasties, and Chop Suey may happily co-exist on the same pages with Foothills Pot Roast. And by 1947 or so, adventurous Calgarians could prepare dishes such as Won Ton Soup or Cantonese Shrimp from *Chinese Recipes*, a free promotional booklet for Rosedale Cleaners run by brothers in the Ho Lem family (A116a.1).

The earliest cookbooks published in Alberta were almanac or calendar cookbooks distributed by druggists to boost their business. Examples have been found for the years 1904 to 1910, from drugstores in Medicine Hat (1904, A1.1), Edmonton (1905, A2.1), Innisfail (1906, A3.1), Strathcona (1907 and 1910, A9.1 and A15.1), Lethbridge (1909, A11.1), Taber (1909, A12.1), and Calgary (1910, A16.1). It is likely that proprietors published a new recipe collection each year, and other issues in the series remain to be discovered. These annuals reprinted texts that originated elsewhere, probably the United States. The recipes in *Pingle's 1904 Calendar Cook Book* (A1.1), for example, also appear in two Ontario almanac cookbooks of the same year. About 1910, two Alberta druggists issued a non-calendar type of cookbook in which a text from another source is reprinted: *Calgary's Domestic Science Cook Book* (A14.1) and *Cowles' Domestic Science Cook Book* (A15.1).

In the course of research for this bibliography, 127[1] different culinary titles were found to have been published in Alberta before 1950. The largest category is community cookbooks: 61% of the total number, with 29% of the total produced by church women's groups, almost all of them Protestant. The three earliest positively dated community cookbooks appeared in 1907, all from churches: The only publicly held copy of *Clever Cooking* (A5.1), from Holy Trinity Anglican Church in Strathcona, has disappeared since it was deaccessioned by Royal Tyrrell Museum of Palaeontology, but a photocopy of a privately held copy may be consulted at the Glenbow Museum; also at the Glenbow Museum is the only known copy of *Cook Book* (A6.1) from Calgary's Knox Presbyterian Church, a fund-raiser for a Home Mission Station; *High River Cook Book* (A7.1), from First Chalmer's Presbyterian Church, survives in several copies. Another early title, *The W.A. Cook Book* (A18.1), compiled in about 1910 by Mary Pinkham, president of the Woman's Auxiliary of Calgary's Pro-Cathedral Church of the Redeemer, features recipes from the families of Colonel Macleod, Bishop Pinkham (Mary's father), the architect William S. Bates, and other families whose members played important roles in the city's early history. A 1923 'Cook Book' (A49.1) by the Lethbridge Stake Relief Society is the only recipe collection from a Mormon church group. *Cook Book* (A48.1), published in aid of St Stephen's Church Memorial Hall in Calgary, was popular in the 1920s, going through three editions, in 1923, 1924, and 1927. Although *Cook to Win* (A100.1), by the Good Cheer Club of Calgary's Wesley United Church, appeared in only one 1943 edition, several copies have survived in public and private collections, evidence that it was printed in larger than usual numbers. Contributing to its success were the eye-catching binding and title-page illustrations, the war-related aphorisms on many of the text pages ('A stamp a day will keep Hitler away'), and recipes contributed by Princess Alice and by suffragist, legislator, and author Nellie McClung.

Between 1941 and the mid-1950s, the Ukrainian Catholic women of St Josaphat's Ladies' Auxiliary in Edmonton produced four editions of *Tested Recipes* (A95.1). This cookbook is an invaluable record of the people and food of the community, with Ukrainian 'national' recipes and special Christmas fare. Some recipes are identified as belonging to other Eastern European cultures: Czech, Hungarian, Slovak, and Jewish. Much earlier, in 1917, Michael Belegai had published a collection of Ukrainian and 'Anglo-American' recipes for Ukrainian immigrants to Alberta: *Ukrains'ko-angliiskyi kukharare* (A34.1). The whole text was in the Ukrainian language, except for English titles for the New World recipes, which he chose from the popular 1913 *Five Roses Cook Book* (Q79.1) by Lake of the Woods Milling Co. and from the American *White House Cook Book* (O93.1, published in several Canadian editions). Only two of the Alberta titles here come from a Jewish group, both from chapters

of Hadassah, in Edmonton in 1946 (A114.1) and Medicine Hat in 1947 (A115.1), although Jewish recipes are included in *Tested Recipes* (A95.1) by St Josaphat's Ladies' Auxiliary.

The community cookbook that had the longest run of editions and the farthest reach was *Recipes* (A59.1), compiled by members of the United Farm Women of Alberta from all over the province. There were five numbered editions in the period covered by this bibliography, from 1928 to 1946. The 1946 edition was apparently produced 'in response to many requests from all over Canada.' The 1989 version, called *Country Classics,* by the renamed Women of Unifarm, refers to cumulative sales from all editions of 125,000 copies. Branches of the UFWA in Alix (Local No. 1, A41.1) and Arrowwood (A57.1) also compiled cookbooks, with the Alix cookbook adding information about Alberta women's voting rights. The UFWA had emerged in 1915 as an auxiliary of the United Farmers of Alberta and was reorganized a year later as the UFWA. The women were committed to the improvement of rural life, and these recipe books served the dual purpose of raising money for the cause as well as offering practical help with daily living.

The Domestic Science Department of the American Women's Club of Calgary was responsible for another influential and popular community cookbook: *Favorite Recipes* (A28.1), later called *The Blue Bird Cook Book.* It went into several editions, the first in 1913, then in 1923–4, 1928, and about 1960. Members of the club demonstrated recipes regularly at their meetings, and their cookbook introduced a 'south-of-the-border' flavour to Calgary kitchens: Waldorf Salad, Philadelphia Scrapple, and Southern Spoon Bread, directions for Mexican Chili Con Carni [*sic*] and Chinese Chop Suey, plus an ancient recipe for a British Wassail Bowl from overseas. Cookbooks were published by the American Women's Club in Winnipeg in 1926 and 1936 (M49.1, M89.1) and in Toronto in 1948 (O1183.1), but the Calgary group seems to have made the greatest local culinary impact.

In 1909 the first branch of the Alberta Women's Institutes (WI) was established at Lea Park, and the organization grew rapidly after 1912, with the support of the provincial Department of Agriculture.[2] Individual branches produced cookbooks as fundraisers from the earliest period: in Queenstown, about 1914–18, to support the war effort (A29.1); Brooks in about 1920 (A39.1); Alliance in 1921 (A45.1); Vulcan in 1923 (A50.1); Barons in 1925 (A53.1); Stony Plain in 1930 (A63.1); Drumheller and Hand Hills in about 1945–9 (A109.1); and Botha in 1948 (A120.1). The WI Branch of the Department of Agriculture published

Home Canning of Fruits, Vegetables, Meats (A36.1), which instructed Alberta women in the rudiments of this essential skill. Written by Bessie McDermand, the assistant superintendent in charge of the WI Branch, it went through three editions from about 1918 to 1922.

Chapters of the Imperial Order Daughters of the Empire were a force in Calgary and Edmonton, producing two cookbooks in each city: from Calgary's Armistice Chapter, *The Modern Cook Book* in 1923 (A51.1) and *Seen through the Pantry Keyhole* in about 1935 (A76.1), for which special cover art was commissioned; from Edmonton's Alex. McQueen Chapter, *War-Time Cook Book* (A30.1), which appeared between 1914 and 1918 with the patriotic object of 'helping the housewife to reduce the high cost of living, and to conserve wheat, beef, bacon and sugar'; and from the Dr David George McQueen Chapter, the self-titled *Dr McQueen Chapter I.O.D.E. Cook Book* in 1935 (A75.1). In 1918 another patriotic Calgary group, the Friday Unit of the Daughters of the Allies, had published the *Conservation Cook Book* (A35.1), and two branches of the Red Cross Society compiled cookbooks during the Second World War (A90.1, A93.1). It appears that some copies of *CJCJ's Radio Cook Book* (A92.1), by Pats Parker, editor of the Calgary radio station's Woman's Program, were sold by the IODE to raise money for the war effort.

Many other Alberta volunteer associations produced cookbooks, including a 'Ladies' Hospital Aid' (A24.1 and A60.1, for Edmonton's Royal Alexandra Hospital, in 1912 and about 1928), supporters of the Boy Scouts (A74.1, A99.1), Little Red Deer Dorcas Society (A89.1), Order of the Royal Purple (A81.1, A110.1), Canadian Daughters League (A96.1), Independent Order of Odd Fellows (A118.1), and the Women's Guild of Robertson College in Edmonton (A44.1). The latter has full directions for preparing wild ducks. From the province's Social Credit Women's Auxiliaries, in the late 1940s, came *The Alberta Home Maker* (A108.1), proudly featuring recipes for Alberta Gold Medal Ranch Steak and Veal Albertan, but also including European recipes, such as Perishki.

Cookbooks issued by Alberta food businesses for advertising purposes make up 29% of the total number of titles. *Rising Sun Cook Book* (A8.1) by Calgary's Western Milling Co., 1907, and *The Mainstay of Multitudes* (A20.1) by E.S. Woolley, Calgary Milling Co.'s advertising manager, 1910, highlight the growing importance of wheat in the economy and are early examples of the flour-company cookbook, a significant type of Canadian culinary manual.

Another Alberta industry with early roots was the production of livestock and the associated activity, meat processing. P. Burns and Co. Ltd, established in Calgary as a meat packer since before the turn of the last century, first published *The Shamrock Cook Book* in about 1915 (A31.1). One edition amused the harassed cook with cartoons featuring two Irish characters, tall-and-thin Shamrock and short-and-stout Weaney (A31.4). The company turned for assistance to an unnamed lady who held a cookery diploma from the Board of Education in London, England, and the recipe selection reflects British tastes. Other Burns and Co. publications followed in about 1922–3 (A47.1, *Helpful Hints for the Preparation of Meals*); in the 1930s (one to promote Bakeasy Shortening, one for Shamrock Ham and Bacon, and two with recipes for Shamrock-brand products and Hormel canned meats; A62.1, A77.1, A78.1, A79.1); and during the Second World War (for Spork, the firm's canned spiced pork, A102.1).

Canadian Sugar Factories, which had begun processing beets into sugar in Raymond in 1925 and later in Picture Butte in 1936, published three cookbooks, each with attractively illustrated bindings and each telling the story of Alberta sugar: *'Sweet' Dreams Come True* (A69.1) and *Alberta Sugar Makes 'Delicious' Things to Eat* (A85.1) in the 1930s, and *Smart Ways to Make a Cook's Life Sweeter* (A106.1) in about 1945–7.

Other cookbooks promoted the consumption of bread, fish, and dairy products. Two small items came from the McGavin family bakery in Edmonton (A54.1, *Good Bread*, about 1925–9, and A91.1, *Menu Magic*, about 1939–45). Calgary's Billingsgate Fish Co. (founded in 1907 and still in business) published *Billingsgate Fish Facts* (A88.1), copyright 1938, although the text may be reprinted from an American source. Edmonton's Woodland Dairy produced *Wartime Recipes and Food Rules* (A98.1) during the Second World War, with the co-operation of the federal Department of Agriculture.

In 1929 the Home Service Department of the Canadian Western Natural Gas, Light, Heat and Power Co. Ltd was organized in Calgary. Soon after, the department produced *Home Canning with the Modern Gas Range* (A68.1), followed by frequent editions in Calgary and Edmonton of a new version called simply *Home Canning* (A83.1), all of which were probably handed out at cooking classes and demonstrations.

Although the number of culinary titles published by provincial government departments was small, copies were distributed widely and served an educational purpose, especially for rural women. McDermand's *Home Canning of Fruits, Vegetables, Meats* has already been mentioned in connection with Women's Institute cookbooks, and the Department of Agriculture published another cookbook on the theme in 1934, *The Preservation of Fruits, Vegetables and Meats* (A72.1). Many Alberta children must have learned to prepare food and have eaten their mid-day meal based on the precepts and recipes printed in *Rural School Lunches* (A37.1), published by the Department of Education in about 1919–20. Likewise, *Cooking Manual, Second Year* (A38.1), published no later than 1919–20, served as the textbook for the second year of the two-year household science course offered throughout the province at the Alberta Schools of Agriculture. During both World Wars, the Alberta and federal governments promoted honey as a substitute for sugar, which was being diverted to feed the armed forces; despite wartime, the Alberta Department of Agriculture paid careful attention to the design of the 1942 recipe collection, *Honey Helpings* (A97.1) by Vera D. Richards: the booklet is trimmed in a circular shape and a stylized beehive is the focus of the front cover. *Farm Cheesemaking* (A104.1), a 1945 book from the Department of Agriculture, offered detailed instructions on a specialized subject.

E. George Barber, a Claresholm baker, wrote a text called 'Pastry Recipes' (A21.1) and tried to secure a publisher in Toronto. Records for the Methodist Book and Publishing House in that city reveal that Barber's manuscript was passed from its office to Maclean Publishing Co., also in Toronto. Although no further evidence of the book has surfaced and it may or may not have been printed, it is included in this bibliography because it highlights the skills and ambitions of a local professional who seems to have established a national reputation for his confectionery work: one of his decorated cakes was illustrated in a Montreal manual for commercial bakers (Q129.1, *The Masterpiece*).

The most important collection in Alberta of pre-1950 Canadian cookbooks is at the Library of the Glenbow Museum in Calgary, followed by those at the Provincial Museum of Alberta in Edmonton, Medicine Hat Museum and Art Gallery, and Red Deer and District Museum and Archives. Other significant resources are at the Ukrainian Cultural Heritage Village east of Edmonton, City of Edmonton Archives, Calgary's Heritage Park Historical Village, Museum of the Highwood in High River, Alix Wagon Wheel Museum, and Calgary Public Library. For a full list of Alberta locations, see 'Abbreviations,' pp xli–xlii.

NOTES

1 There are 122 numbered titles in the Alberta section, plus one late addition (A116a.1), an Alberta edition of a work in the Manitoba section (M83.2), and Alberta editions of three works in the Ontario section (O773.5, O776.3 and O776.4, O777.2 and O777.6).
2 For a history of the Women's Institutes, see Cole/Larmour.

1904

Pingle's 1904 calendar cook book

A1.1 1904
Pingle's / 1904 / calendar / cook book / Published
by / Chas. S. Pingle, / druggist and stationer, /
Medicine Hat, Assa. [i.e., Assiniboia]
DESCRIPTION: 17.5 × 13.0 cm   Pp [1–3] 4–32   Illus of
astrological symbols   Paper; stapled, and with string
through top left corner for hanging
CONTENTS: 1 tp; 2 publ ad; 3–29 astronomical information, recipes, monthly calendars, 'Comical Conversations,' and publ ads; 30 'As to Diet'; 31 'Weights
and Measures,' 'Terms Used in French Menus Explained for the Benefit of the Canadian Hostess,' and
'Language of the Eyes'; 32 'Children and the Moon'
and 'How to Sleep'
COPIES: *OTUTF (uncat patent medicine)
NOTES: This cookbook was published before Alberta
became a province on 1 September 1905. The recipes
begin with Velvet Cake, Birthday Cake, and Walnut
Cakes on p 4, Indian Pound Cake, Spice Cake, and
Layer Cake on p 6, and Plain Sponge Cake, Hickory-
Nut Cake, Invalids' Cake, and Spanish Bun on p 8 –
the same as two Ontario almanac cookbooks, O140.1,
Almanac of Dr Mack's Pills 1904, published in St
Catharines, and O149.1, *Tuthill's Almanac and Cook
Book 1904,* published in Toronto. M6.1, *Taylor's 1904
Calendar Cook Book,* may also be related.

1905

Almanac and cook book 1905

A2.1 1905
1905 / 1905 [these two years in column to left of the
following text:] / Graydon's / Northern Alberta. /
Almanac / and / cook / book / Published by /
G.H. Graydon / King Edward Pharmacy /
Edmonton, Alberta. [cover-title]
DESCRIPTION: 17.5 × 13.5 cm   Pp [1–3] 4–32   Illus of
astrological symbols and, on p 28, 'Map of the Hand,'
and on p 32, 'Classes of Hands and What They
Imply'   Paper; stapled
CONTENTS: 1–2 publ ads; 3–27 astronomical informa-
tion, recipes, monthly calendars, 'Jokes and Breaks,'
and publ ads; 28–32 information about palmistry
COPIES: *OTUTF (uncat patent medicine)
NOTES: On p 1 the druggist is referred to as Geo. H.
Graydon. The recipes are the same as described for
NF2.1, *McMurdo's 1905 Calendar Cook Book,* published
in St John's.

1906

Geary's 1906 Central Alberta almanac and housewife's and bachelor's favorite cook book

A3.1 1906
Geary's 1906 / Central Alberta / almanac / and
housewife's and bachelor's favorite / cook / book /
Published by / William Geary, / druggist, stationer
and seedsman, / Innisfail, Alberta.
DESCRIPTION: 17.5 × 13.5 cm   Pp [1–3] 4–32   Illus of
astrological symbols and, on p 29, three hand-
shapes   Paper, with image on front of a boy-baker
carrying a loaf of bread under each arm; stapled, and
with hole punched at top left corner, through which
runs a string for hanging
CONTENTS: 1 tp; 2 'To My Customers' signed William
Geary; 3–28 astronomical information, recipes,
monthly calendars, 'Practical Breaks' [i.e., jokes], and
publ ads; 29–32 'Character Reading from the Hand'
COPIES: *OTUTF (uncat patent medicine)
NOTES: The recipes begin on p 4 with Sponge Cake,
Spice Cake, Plain Fruit Cake, Muffins, and Neapoli-
tan Cake, and continue on p 6 with Sally Lunns,
Spanish Bun, Jelly or Layer Cake, Scones, and Corn
Muffins. The p 6 recipes match those listed in NB22.1,
Brown's New Brunswick Almanac and Cook Book 1906.
Oddly, the p 4 recipes do not match.

1906–10

A book of cookery

*In 1906 the Presbyterian and Methodist congregations of
Lamont, which had been holding their services separately
in local schools, decided to construct a common church
building; the new wood church was opened on 18 November 1906. Although the congregations still had separate
ministers at this time, there was one Union Ladies' Aid,
one Sunday school, and one choir. In 1925 the church
became Lamont United Church, part of the United
Church of Canada. Lamont is 56 km northeast of
Edmonton. For information about the church, see Irene
Hackett Stainton and Elizabeth Course Carlsson, eds,
Lamont and Districts along Victoria Trail, Edmonton:
Lamont and District Historian, 1978.*

A4.1   nd [about 1906–10]
A book of / cookery / Compiled by Union Ladies'
Aid / Lamont, Alberta. [cover-title]
DESCRIPTION: 16.0 × 12.5 cm   Pp [3–7] 8–126   Cloth
CONTENTS: 3–4 ads; 5 'Index of Cookery' [i.e., table of

contents]; 6 ad; 7–126 recipes credited with the contributor's name and ads
COPIES: *AEUCHV (UV 85.17.142)
NOTES: From appearances, the cookbook dates from the early period of the Union Church's history, about 1906–10.

1907

Clever cooking

The Anglican parish of Holy Trinity was founded in 1893. In 1906, having moved from another site, it dug a basement for a new church and erected upright steel beams. A downturn in the economy prompted the parishioners to temporarily roof over the basement and stop further construction, but they continued to raise funds for the project. Clever Cooking was published at this critical juncture. Rebuilding began in summer 1913 and the first service was held in the new church in October of the same year. A mortgage of $35,000 remained on the church when the First World War broke out in 1914.

A5.1 1907
Clever / cooking / Woman's Guild of Holy Trinity Church, / Strathcona, Alberta / A.D. 1907 / Printed by the Chronicle Co., Strathcona, Alberta / Committee / Mrs. Skinner Mrs. Frederick Jamieson
DESCRIPTION: About 22.0 × 13.5 cm [dimensions from photocopy and from ADTMP catalogue description] Pp [1–107] Oil cloth; stapled
CONTENTS: 1 tp; 2 ad; 3–98 recipes credited with the name of the contributor and ads; 99–105 'Hints and Helps' credited with the name of contributor; 106 blank; 107 'Table of Weights and Measures'
COPIES: *ACG (photocopy) ADTMP (641.5 St82 deaccessioned) Private collection

Cook book

At the time of the cookbook's publication, Knox Presbyterian Church was at the corner of Centre and 7th Avenue, but the building is no longer standing. Known as Knox United Church since church union in 1925, the congregation now worships at 506 4th Street SW. For another cookbook from the church, see A119.1, Club Cookery.

A6.1 nd [1907]
Knox / Church / Cook book / Ladies' / Branch "E" Aid / [ad:] Calgary Furniture Store, Limited /

F.F. Higgs, Manager / High-class furniture and house furnishings [cover-title]
DESCRIPTION: 21.0 × 13.5 cm Pp 1–104 Cloth-covered card; stapled
CONTENTS: 1–4 ads; 5 'Preface'; 6 'Table of Weights and Measures'; 7–8 ads; 9–101 recipes and ads; 102–4 ads
CITATIONS: Bly
COPIES: *ACG
NOTES: The 'Preface' lists the names of thirty-three recipe contributors. 'Hammond Litho. Co., Ltd., Calgary' is on the outside back face of the binding. The cookbook's date of publication is known from the *Twenty-Fourth Year Book of Knox Presbyterian Church for the Year 1907* (copy in the church's archives), in which the report of Branch E of the Ladies' Aid Society states: 'This Branch undertook to raise funds for the support of a Home Mission Station. For this purpose there has been a Cook Book published and offered for sale. The ladies have also held a Ten Cent Tea and a sale of work, the results of which will be shown below.' The report lists the following receipts: Donations, $2.50; Proceeds of Tea, Sale of Work and Cook Book, $237.85; Advertisements for Book, $267.50; and Interest on Deposit, $0.95. Expenditures related to the cookbook included a payment to Hammond Lithographing Co. of $248.70 and 'Material for and expenses of sale' of $5.50.

High River cook book

The full name of the church was First Chalmer's Presbyterian Church.

A7.1 1907
High River cook book / Collected and compiled by the / Ladies' Aid of Chalmer's Church, / High River. / August / Nineteen hundred and seven. / The Ladies' Aid wish to thank most cordially all who / have assisted them in any way in getting out this book, / which they hope will prove of practical assistance to all / who are interested in the "Good Food" problem. / Herald Company Ltd. / Calgary, Alta.
DESCRIPTION: 16.0 × 12.0 cm Pp [1–3] 4–81, [i–xiv] Cloth
CONTENTS: 1 tp; 2 blank; 3–81 recipes credited with the name of the contributor; i–iii blank; iv–xiv ads
CITATIONS: Peel 1933 micro Peel's Bibliography 3067
COPIES: *ACG ACU AHCESM AHRMH (3 copies: 987-035-004, 979-026-002, 975-024-002)

A7.2   reprint, 1994

—High River cook book / Collected and compiled by the / Ladies' Aid of Chalmer's Church, / High River. / August / Nineteen hundred and seven. / The Ladies' Aid wish to thank most cordially all who / have assisted them in any way in getting out this book, / which they hope will prove of practical assistance to all / who are interested in the "Good Food" problem. / Herald Company Ltd. / Calgary, Alta. / Reprinted by / Friends of the Bar U Historic Ranch Association / November / Nineteen hundred and ninety-four / Quebecor Printpak

DESCRIPTION: 16.5 × 12.0 cm   Pp [1–3] 4–81, [i–xvi] Very thin card, with image on front of the Bar U Historic Ranch; plastic coil

CONTENTS: 1 tp; 2 blank; 3–81 recipes credited with the name of the contributor; i–iii blank; iv–xiv ads; xv blank; xvi book-order form addressed to Friends of the Bar U Historic Ranch Association, Nanton, Alberta

COPIES: AC (641.5 CHA)   *Private collection

NOTES: The Bar U Ranch is near High River. This reprint was a fund-raiser for the ranch, which is now a national historic site.

Rising Sun cook book

A8.1   copyright 1907

Western Milling Co., Limited / New / Rising Sun cook book / Important notice / Each owner of a Rising Sun Cook Book is / entitled to four additional copies without any / cost whatever. These copies may be obtained in / the following manner: / Please turn to page 71 where you will find four / coupons. As fast as you desire to use your privi- / lege for four additional copies cut out the coupon, / fill in your friend's address and mail to us. No / postage is required for these extra copies. / We trust you will avail yourself of this privilege / immediately. / Address all communications to Western Milling / Co., Limited, Calgary, Alberta. / Be sure and read the article on white bread appearing on page 70 / Copyright, 1907. / Western Milling Co., Limited / Calgary, Alberta.

DESCRIPTION: 27.5 × 20.0 cm   Pp [1–5] 6–71 [72]   Illus chapter heads   Paper, with image on front of a sack of Rising Sun Flour; stapled

CONTENTS: Inside front face of binding illus of Western Milling Co. grain elevator and 'Entered according to Act of Parliament of Canada in the year 1907, by the Western Milling Co., Limited, of Calgary, Alberta, in the office of the Minister of Agriculture.'; 1 tp;

2 'Tables'; 3 table of contents and 'This book has been carefully revised, rearranged and amplified by the best talent obtainable.'; 4 blank; 5–69 recipes; 70 'White Bread'; 71 'Send a Cook Book to Your Friends' and four coupons; 72 publ ad stating that the capacity of the Western Milling Co. mill is 500 barrels per day

CITATIONS: O'Neill (unpublished)

COPIES: AC (Pam file 641.597123 Ris)   ACG   *Private collection; Great Britain: LB (not located)

NOTES: The running head is 'Western Milling Co., Limited, New Cook Book.' In the first few decades of the twentieth century, all the major Canadian flour companies began to publish cookbooks to promote their brands of flour. *The Rising Sun Cook Book* is an early example; it follows O85.1, about 1898, O95.1, about 1900, and Q55.1, 1905, and precedes Q79.1, *Five Roses Cook Book*, 1913, by several years. It is uncertain whether *Rising Sun Cook Book* was compiled locally or not.

Thomson and Co.'s 1907 almanac and every day cook book

A9.1   1907

Thomson & Co.'s / 1907 almanac 1907 / and every day / cook book / Published by / Thomson & Co. / chemists and druggists / Corner Drug Store, Strathcona, Alta.

DESCRIPTION: Pp [1–3] 4–?   Stapled

CONTENTS: 1 tp; 2 publ ad; 3 'Eclipses, 1907,' 'Morning and Evening Stars, 1907,' and 'Chronological Cycles, 1907'; 4 'Cakes, etc.' and publ ad; 5 calendar for January 1907 and 'Practical Breaks and Monologues'; ...

COPIES: *Private collection

NOTES: The recipes on p 4 are Cornstarch Cake, Macdonald Cake, Spice Cake, Cookies, and Ribbon Cake. There are 32 pp.

1908

Savory selections from Edmonton ladies

A10.1   1908

Savory selections / from / Edmonton ladies. / For the benefit of the / Grace Methodist Church / 1908.

DESCRIPTION: 16.0 × 12.0 cm   Pp [1] 2–84 [85–109] Tp illus of the church   Paper, with tp illus on front; bound by a cord through two punched holes

CONTENTS: Inside front face of binding 'The Cross of Christ'; 1 tp; 2 ad; 3–109 recipes credited with the name of the contributor and ads; [blank page]; inside back face 'Recipe for a Happy Day' and 'Sweet Disposition' [mock recipes]

COPIES: *Private collection

NOTES: The cover-title states that the book was 'Compiled by the Ladies' Aid of Grace Methodist Church.' The text and title-page illustration are printed in blue ink.

1909

The Alberta almanac and cook book

A11.1 1909

Please hang me up where I can be found when wanted / The Alberta / almanac and cook book / 1909 / Published by the pioneer chemists / J.D. Higinbotham & Co., Limited / Established 1884 / wholesale and retail / chemists and druggists / Lethbridge – Alberta / Two resident assistants. Dispensing by graduates / Telephone 49 Night bell / Sunday hours: – 10.30 to 11 a.m. 12.30 to 1 p.m. 4 to 4.30 p.m. 8.30 to 9 p.m. [cover-title]

DESCRIPTION: 17.0 × 13.0 cm   Pp [1–3] 4–32   Illus of astrological symbols   Paper, with illus on front of drugstore interior; stapled, and with hole punched at top left corner for hanging

CONTENTS: 1–2 publ ads; 3 'Eclipses, 1909,' 'Morning and Evening Stars, 1909,' and 'Chronological Cycles, 1909'; 4 recipes and publ ad; 5–27 monthly calendars, jokes, recipes, and publ ads; 28–top 1st column 30 'Poisons and Antidotes'; mid 1st column 30–bottom 2nd column 30 'Relation of a Pulse to Temperature,' first aid information, and 'Handy Household Drugs'; 1st column 31–mid 2nd column 31 'Worth Knowing'; bottom 2nd column 31–32 'Things to Remember'

COPIES: *ACG

NOTES: The publisher's note on the inside front face of the binding indicates that there were previous issues of the book: 'We take great pleasure in again presenting our Alberta Almanac and Cook Book, ...'

The Taber calendar cook book 1909

A12.1 1909

The Taber / calendar / cook book / 1909 / Published by / the Alberta Drug & Stationery Co. / Limited / Taber Alberta

DESCRIPTION: 17.0 × 13.5 cm   Pp [1–3] 4–32   Illus of astrological symbols   Paper, with image on front of

a mortar and pestle; stapled, and with hole punched at top left corner, through which runs a string for hanging

CONTENTS: 1 tp; 2 introductory note signed Alberta Drug and Stationery Co. Ltd; 3–27 astronomical information, recipes, monthly calendars, 'Practical Breaks' [i.e., jokes], and publ ads; 28–mid 1st column 30 'Poisons and Antidotes'; mid 1st column 30–2nd column 30 medical information; 1st column 31–mid 2nd column 31 'Worth Knowing'; bottom 2nd column 31–32 'Things to Remember'

COPIES: *OTUTF (uncat patent medicine)

NOTES: The recipes are the same as listed for NB25.1, *Brown's New Brunswick Almanac and Cook Book 1909*, and for other titles cited in that entry.

1910

[Title unknown]

A13.1 [about 1910]

[Title unknown]

COPIES: *ARDA (photocopy)

NOTES: ARDA identifies the book as 'Red Deer Women's Cook Book.' The photocopy comprises one opening of advertisements and pp 5–75 of recipes and advertisements. The recipes on p 5 are To Cure Ham or Pork, Spiced Beef, Beef Loaf, and Beef Loaf, No. 2. The recipes are credited with the name of the contributor, and the names are old ones from the community; for example, Mrs H.H. Gaetz and Mrs Thos Gaetz (a street in Red Deer bears their last name). From appearances, the book was published about 1910, and a comparison of some contributors' names and advertisements with directories for the province (and earlier territory) confirms publication about this time.

Calgary's domestic science cook book

A14.1 nd [about 1910]

Calgary's / domestic / science / cook book / containing only / reliable / recipes / Published by / MacFarlane & White / prescription druggists / 124 8th Ave. East Calgary, Alta. / Phone 1298 [cover-title]

DESCRIPTION: 17.5 × 13.0 cm   Pp [1] 2, 5–32   Thin card; stapled, and with hole punched at top left corner, through which runs a string for hanging

CONTENTS: 1 'To Our Customers' signed MacFarlane

and White; 2 publ ad; 5–6 tables for broiling, baking, and frying; 7–32 recipes and publ ads
COPIES: *Private collection
NOTES: The following are likely related publications issued in the same year: O230.1, Armstrong, George S., *Domestic Science Cook Book, Containing Only Reliable Recipes;* A15.1, *Cowles' Domestic Science Cook Book Containing Only Reliable Recipes;* and B16.1, *Gillanders' Domestic Science Cook Book Containing Only Reliable Recipes.*

Cowles' domestic science cook book

A15.1   nd [about 1910]
Cowles' / domestic / science / cook book / containing only / reliable / recipes / Published by Frank Cowles druggist / Strathcona, Alta. [cover-title]
DESCRIPTION: 17.5 × 13.0 cm   Pp 3–30   Card; stapled, and with hole punched at top left corner for hanging
CONTENTS: 3 'Spoon and Cup Measure' and 'Table of Proportions'; 4–6 'Timetables for Cooking'; 7–30 recipes and publ ads
CITATIONS: Peel 2127 micro   Peel's Bibliography 3403
COPIES: ACG (641.5 C875d)   ACU (micro)   ALU (micro)
NOTES: See A14.1.

Findlay's calendar cook book for 1910

A16.1   1910
Findlay's / calendar / cook book / for / 1910 / The / Jas. Findlay Drug Co. / Limited / prescription druggists / opp. Royal Hotel. Calgary, Alta. [cover-title]
DESCRIPTION: 17.0 × 13.5 cm   Pp [1–3] 4–32   A few illus of zodiac signs and symbols   Paper; stapled, and with hole punched at top left corner, through which runs a string for hanging
CONTENTS: 1 'To the Public' signed Jas Findlay Drug Co. Ltd; 2 publ ad; 3–32 monthly calendars, recipes, and ads
COPIES: *Private collection
NOTES: 'To the Public' on p 1 implies that the company published one or more other annual editions: 'We present you with the 1910 edition of our Calendar Cook Book, ...'

Good things from the mountains

A17.1   nd [about 1910]
Good things / from the / mountains
DESCRIPTION: 23.0 × 9.0 cm   Pp 1–22   Paper, with four circular photographs of Rocky Mountain scenes mounted on front: Glacier House, Mount Stephen, Lake Louise, and Banff Springs Hotel; stapled
CONTENTS: 1 tp; 2–3 'Contents'; 4 'Savouries'; 5 'Soups'; 6–8 'Fish'; 9–11 'Entrées'; 12–13 'Salads'; 14–15 'Puddings'; 16 'Cheese'; 17–18 'Ices'; 19–20 'Cakes'; 21–2 'Candies'
COPIES: *QMM (RBD ckbk 1615)
NOTES: Only the recto pages are printed; the versos are blank and not included in the pagination. The name of a British Columbia printing company, 'Evans & Hastings, printers,' is on the front face of the binding. The same company, which was in business by 1891, printed B8.1, *The Great West Cook Book,* copyright 1908. Glacier House was built in 1886; Banff Springs, in 1888. From appearances, the cookbook was published about 1910.

Pinkham, Miss Mary Isabel Ross (St James Rectory [a suburb of Winnipeg], Man., 20 December 1878–23 April 1964, Calgary, Alta)

Mary Pinkham was one of three daughters of Bishop William Cyprian Pinkham, the first Anglican Bishop of Calgary, and his wife, Mrs Jean Anne Drever Pinkham. Mary's obituary in the Calgary Herald, 24 April 1964, *describes her as belonging to 'one of Calgary's best known pioneer families and a noted social worker.' In 1935 she received the Order of the British Empire for her community service, which embraced church women's organizations and the Red Cross. She never married. For more information about her, see her file at ACG. For information about her family, see Sherrill MacLaren,* Braehead: Three Founding Families in Nineteenth Century Canada, *Toronto: McClelland and Stewart, 1986.*

A18.1   nd [about 1910]
Tried tested proved / The W.A. / cook book / Compiled by / Mary Pinkham / President, Pro-Cathedral Branch Woman's Auxiliary / The proceeds of the sale of this book are to be devoted / to missionery [*sic*] work in the Diocese of Calgary.
DESCRIPTION: 21.5 × 14.5 cm   Pp [leaf lacking?] [3–11] 12–63, [leaves lacking] [i–iii]   Cloth
CONTENTS: 3–8 ads; 9 tp; 10 dedication 'to all those

who have so kindly given their valuable assistance in compiling it' and 'Hints for Cooking'; 11–63 recipes credited with the name of the contributor; i blank; ii–iii ads

CITATIONS: 'Favorite Recipes in Calgary Homes: Old Recipes from W.A. Still Good,' *Calgary Herald* 15 November 1958

COPIES: ACHP (HP 4105.8) ACU (TX714 P56) *ARDA Private collection

NOTES: The 1958 *Calgary Herald* article, which includes a photograph of Mary Pinkham, refers to her compiling *The W.A. Cook Book* 'nearly 50 years ago,' which suggests a publication date of about 1910. Members of the Woman's Auxiliary of the Pro-Cathedral Church of the Redeemer submitted their favourite recipes to Mary, who then selected and classified them for the book. She included recipes from her mother Jean and from Jean's sister, Mrs Mary Drever Macleod of Winnipeg, the wife of Colonel James Macleod, who signed Treaty No. 7 with Chief Crowfoot of the Blackfoot Nation (see Orange Charlotte, p 1030 of this bibliography). Another recipe contributor was Mrs W.S. Bates, wife of the Calgary architect William S. Bates and mother of the artist Maxwell Bates; her several recipes are on pp 26, 27, 28, 42, 44, 51, 71, 73, and 90. The *Calgary Herald* article reprints recipes for Spiced Beef and Chutney.

The ARDA copy is loose from its binding and lacks leaves; three loose leaves of recipes (one numbered p 67) are slipped between pp 42 and 43. One private collector reports that her copy has eight pages of advertisements before the title-page, recipes on pp 11–90, an index on two pages, and more advertisements. Another copy of the book has been passed down in the family to the great-granddaughter of Mary Macleod.

Tried and true cook book

A19.1 1910
We may live without poetry, music and art, / We may live without conscience and live without heart, / We may live without friends, we may live without books, / But civilized man cannot live without cooks. / Owen Meredith. / Tried & true / cook book / A selection of tested recipes compiled by the / ladies and friends of the First Con- / gregational Church, Calgary, Alta., / contributed by the ladies of / the congregation. / 1910

DESCRIPTION: 17.5 × 12.5 cm Pp [1] 2–68 [69] Paper, with image on front of a cherub in an apron and chef's hat, carrying a covered platter; stapled

CONTENTS: 1 tp; 2 ads; 3–66 recipes credited with the name of the contributor and ads; 67 'Household Hints'; 68 'Weights and Measures' and ad; 69 'Index' [i.e., table of contents]

CITATIONS: Peel 2104 micro Peel's Bibliography 3380

COPIES: *ACG (Pam 641.5 C151t)

NOTES: The printer's name, 'McAra Presses,' is on the front face of the binding; and there is an advertisement on p 48 for J.D. McAra, 'the office which designed and produced this book.' There are a few errors for French food terms; for example, on p 5, 'Crontons' should be Croutons, and on p 13, 'Egg Bondons' should be Egg Bonbons.

Woolley, Ernest S. (June 1886–)

The Calgary city directory for 1910 gives E.S. Woolley's occupation as advertising manager, Calgary Milling Co. His first name and birth date are recorded in the 1911 Census under the spelling Wooley. In 1912, two years after the publication of The Mainstay of Multitudes, *Calgary Milling Co. Ltd's Calgary mill was bought by the American owners of Robin Hood Mills Ltd (for the history of the latter, see S16.1).*

A20.1 [1910]
The / mainstay / of / multitudes / "Some books are to be tasted, / Others to be swallowed, / Some few to be chewed and digested" / – Bacon / [in column at left:] On / the / flour / the / bread / depends / [in column at right:] On / the / bread / the / world / depends [cover-title]

DESCRIPTION: 22.0 × 14.5 cm Pp 1–24 Illus Paper, with image on front of a globe of the world sitting on a loaf of bread, which sits on a sack of flour; stapled

CONTENTS: Inside front face of binding table of contents and 'Written and designed by E.S. Woolley // The Calgary Milling Co. Limited. Calgary and Vancouver Canada.'; 1–2 'To the Agriculturist'; 3–10 'Trip around the Mill'; 11 publ ad; 12–14 'The Housewife'; 15–21 'Recipes'; 22–4 'The Children'

COPIES: ACG (Pam 641.5 C151c photocopy) *Private collection

NOTES: The cookbook was published early in 1910 since there is a notice on p 24 about a contest that closes on 30 April 1910. Further evidence of a 1910 publication date is a note on p 14: 'The Alberta Provincial Exhibition is to be held in Calgary this year, 1910, from June 30th to July 7th, ...' On the outside back face of the binding there is a poem titled 'The Ruling Virtue of Mankind' and the printer's name: 'Printed by the Herald-Western Co., Ltd., Calgary.'

1911

Barber, E. George (died December 1924)

One of George Barber's decorated cakes, made in 1922, is illustrated in Q129.1, The Masterpiece. Information about Barber and his wife, Emma, is in Where the Wheatlands Meet the Range *(Claresholm, Alta: Claresholm History Book Club, 1974):*

> Mr. and Mrs. Barber came from Brighton, England to Claresholm in 1909, where they purchased the bakery business of L. De Forest. They continued in this business until 1924 when they sold to Mr. Brooker. Mr. Barber passed away in December 1924 and in January 1924 [sic; likely 1925] Mrs. Barber and her mother, Mrs. Matthew McClean, left Claresholm and settled in Ottawa to be near her daughter, Mrs. Willard McKinney. Mrs. Barber passed away in 1959 in Sault Ste. Marie where the McKinneys were then living. There were two daughters in the Barber family: Edith (Mrs. O.S. Longman) of B.C. and Mabel (Mrs. J. Willard McKinney) of Sault Ste. Marie.

A21.1   [about 1911]
[Manuscript of 'Pastry Recipes (Everyday Cakes for Everyday Bakers)']
NOTES: The following handwritten notation is in the papers of the Methodist Book and Publishing House at OTCC (Acc. 83.061C, UCC Board of Publication Series I, Box 3, File 5, 'Publications Record, 1910–1913'): 'Ms. [i.e., manuscript] E.G. Barber // Claresholm Alta // Pastry Recipes (Everyday Cakes for Everyday Bakers) Ms. rec'd 24/11/10 // Sent to Maclean Pub Co on author's orders.' I have not found a copy of the book, which may or may not have reached publication.

Women's Exchange cook book

Located in Calgary on the corner of 12th Avenue and 1st Street West, the Pryce Jones department store opened on 14 February 1911 and stayed in business for about five years.

A22.1   [copyright 1911]
Women's / Exchange / cook book / Souvenir from / Pryce Jones (Canada) Limited / departmental store & mail order house / "The metropolitan store for the metropolis of the last West" / This store does not base its claims to public confidence and patronage solely / upon the magnitude or diversity of its stocks but upon the unquestioned high / character of its merchandise. / Shop by mail – You are just as safe in shopping with us by mail as if you / were buying in person. All orders promptly and intelligently attended to, and / satisfaction guaranteed with every purchase. Send for our catalogue. [cover-title]
DESCRIPTION: 23.5 × 15.0 cm   Pp [1] 2–32   Paper; stapled
CONTENTS: 1 'Index' [i.e., table of contents] and 'Copyrighted 1911 by W.C. & F.D. Burgess Co.'; 2–32 recipes
COPIES: *AHRMH
NOTES: 'Published by W.C. & F.D. Burgess, Newark, New York' is on the outside back face of the binding. Although the publisher was American, the cookbook was a souvenir from a Calgary store and the advertisements are for Canadian products.

1912

Classified collection of tested recipes

A23.1   nd [about 1912]
"Now good digestion wait on appetite and health on both." – Shakespeare / Classified collection of / tested recipes / Lethbridge, Alberta: / The Herald Book and Job Department [cover-title]
COPIES: *Private collection
NOTES: There is an advertisement on p 74 for 'Cadillac 1912' sold by T.S. Mackenzie, general agent for the cars. An advertisement on p 44 for the Union Bank of Canada reports profits as of 30 June 1911. The book's owner reports that the volume has 128 pp.

Royal Alexandra cook book

The Royal Alexandra Hospital is in Edmonton. See also A60.1, Royal Alexandra Book of Household Science, *by the same group.*

A24.1   [1912]
Royal Alexandra / cook book / Published under the auspices of / the Ladies Hospital Aid of the / Royal Alexandra Hospital
DESCRIPTION: 21.0 × 14.0 cm   Pp 1–64 [65–72]   Paper, with image on front of the hospital; stapled
CONTENTS: 1–2 ads; 3 tp; 4 ads; 5 thank-you to recipe contributors and to advertisers, signed Mrs A.E.

Braithwaite, president, November 1912; 6 ad; 7–63 recipes and ads; 64 ads; 65–71 blank for 'Your Additional Recipes'; 72 ad and 'Index' [i.e., table of contents]

COPIES: ABARRCM *AEARN AEU (TX715.6 R888 1912)

NOTES: The ABARRCM copy lacks its binding.

1913

The Alix recipe book

A25.1 [1913]

The Alix recipe book / Practical cookery / household hints / and / ideas for entertaining / Compiled by / the Women's Guild of the / Presbyterian Churbh [sic] / Alix Alberta

DESCRIPTION: 21.0 × 13.0 cm Pp [1–10] 11–74 Paper, with flaming torch on front; stapled

CONTENTS: 1 tp; 2 blank; 3 dedication to those who 'endeavour to create of the erstwhile drudgery of housekeeping, an art' and thanks to the recipe contributors and the advertisers, signed the committee, Mrs Jas Hall, president, Mrs Geo. Ross, Mrs H.G. Finch, Mrs F.R. Mitchell, Mrs E.L. Trickey, and Mrs J.H. Williamson; 4 ad; 5 'The Alix Presbyterian Women's Guild' [poem about this book]; 6 ads; 7 'Index'; 8 ad; 9 'Weights and Measures'; 10 ad; 11–21 'Household Hints' and ads; 22 ad; 23–64 recipes credited with the name of the contributor and ads; 65–73 'Ideas for Entertaining' and ads; 74 ads

CITATIONS: Bly

COPIES: *AALIWWM (2 copies) ACG

NOTES: The year of publication is printed on the front face of the binding. On pp 58–9 there is a map and information about the town of Alix.

Cook book

A26.1 1913

Cook / book / Presbyterian Church / Wetaskiwin Alberta / 1913 / Price 25 cents / Free Press Print, Wetaskiwin [cover-title]

DESCRIPTION: 17.0 × 12.5 cm Pp 1–57 Paper; stapled

CONTENTS: 1 'Thanks' signed 'The Willing Workers, of the Presbyterian Church'; 2 ads; 3–57 recipes credited with the name of the contributor and ads

COPIES: *AWWDM CIHM (73438) OONL (TX715.6 C665 1913)

Cook book in aid of the Organ Fund of St Barnabas Church

St Barnabas Church assisted in the production of A43.1, A Booke of Recypies.

A27.1 1913

Cook book / in aid of the / Organ Fund of / St. Barnabas Church / Medicine Hat, 1913 / D & A Print [cover-title]

DESCRIPTION: 15.0 × 11.0 cm Pp [1–2 lacking] 3–167 [168] Limp oil cloth; stapled

CONTENTS: 1–2 tp lacking; 3 ad; 4 preface; 5–156 text; 157–67 'Write your additional recipes on these pages.'; 168 index

COPIES: AMHM *Private collection

NOTES: The AMHM copy retains the title-page: 'Cook book / in aid of the / Organ Fund of St. / Barnabas Church / Medicine Hat, 1913'; p 2 is an advertisement.

Favorite recipes

A28.1 [1st ed.], nd [1913]

Favorite / recipes / Domestic Science / Department / American / Women's Club

DESCRIPTION: 22.5 × 14.5 cm Pp [1–3] 4–78 [79–80 lacking?] Tp illus of a bluebird Paper, with image on front of a bluebird; stapled

CONTENTS: 1 tp; 2 blank, with running head 'Favorite Recipes'; 3 'Dedicated to the American Woman's [sic] Club of Calgary, Canada, whose members, midst their many broad interests, consider their chief concern to be the welfare of the home and family – woman's dearest possession.'; 4 blank, with running head 'Favorite Recipes'; 5 'Index' [i.e., table of contents]; 6 'Recipe for a Perfect Husband' signed Mrs A.M. Moline; 7 ad for Pryce-Jones (Canada) Ltd; 8 'Weights, Measures and Time Table,' 'Baking,' and 'Boiling'; 9 blank, with running head 'American Women's Club'; 10 ads; 11–78 recipes, most credited with the name of the contributor, ads, and blank pages for manuscript recipes

COPIES: *ACG

NOTES: Many of the recipes are American – for example, Waldorf Salad, New England Boiled Dinner, Philadelphia Scrapple, and Southern Spoon Bread – but there are also recipes from other places. Mrs Florence A. Wade contributed British recipes, such as 'Ye Wassail Bowl,' which she describes as 'used 600 years ago in Kent,' and 'Ye Syllabub' 1621 AD, and

Appledoor Flapjacks – 1700 AD. There are also recipes for Real Mexican Chili Con Carni [*sic*] and Chop Suey. The printer was likely the Morning Albertan Job Department, whose advertisement is on p 42.

The 'Foreword' of the 1960s edition includes publishing information about what became known as *The Blue Bird Cook Book* under a 'History of the American Woman's Club of Calgary': The club was organized on 29 March 1912 and in 'the second year [i.e., 1913] ... Domestic Science [a department of the club] published its first cook book, a paper-covered volume selling for twenty-five cents. In 1923–24 a cook book was published again by Domestic Science Department. The sale of this book raised sufficient funds to purchase the club house and furnish it. In the term of [President] Mrs. R.H. Beavers, 1927–1929, more cook books were published.'

A28.2   [2nd ed.], nd [1923–4]
—The blue bird / cook book / Domestic Science Department / American Woman's Club / of Calgary [cover-title]
DESCRIPTION: 22.5 × 14.5 cm   Pp 1–184   Cloth, with image on front of a blue bird
CONTENTS: 1–2 ads; 3 'Dedication' to the American Woman's Club of Calgary; 4 ads; 5 'Domestic Science Department'; 6 ads; 7 'Announcement' of thanks to advertisers; 8 ads; 9–183 text and ads; 184 'Index' [i.e., table of contents]; inside back face of binding 'S.A. Hynd Litho-Print Limited 603 Centre Street, Calgary, Alberta'
COPIES: ACG   *BVMA
NOTES: Information on p 5 confirms the publication date of 1923–4 given in the 1960s edition: 'The Domestic Science Department of the American Woman's Club was organized in 1912. A monthly meeting is held during the club year and one or two recipes are demonstrated at each meeting. We feel that the twelve years of practical demonstrations are worthy of your special consideration ...' (1912 + 12 years = 1924). The second edition, retitled *The Blue Bird Cook Book*, is heavily revised. Some of the recipes are the same (for example, Codfish Balls, Finnan Haddie, two Fruit Punch recipes), but many new ones have been added; the 'Beverages' section is now near the back of the book. Unlike A28.1, this and later editions use only the singular form: Woman's Club.

A28.3   nd [about 1928]
—The blue bird / cook book / Domestic Science Department / American Woman's Club / of Calgary [cover-title]
DESCRIPTION: 22.5 × 14.0 cm   Pp 1–240   Cloth, with image on front of a blue bird

CONTENTS: 1–2 ads; 3 dedication to the American Woman's Club of Calgary; 4 ads; 5 'Domestic Science Department'; 6 ads; 7 'Announcement' of thanks to 'the merchants who have contracted for advertising space'; 8 ads; 9–239 text and ads; 240 'Index' [i.e., table of contents]; inside back face of binding 'Hickey & Dyke printers Phone M2961 // 114 7th Avenue East – Calgary, Alta.'
COPIES: ABA (Pearl Brewster Moore home, uncat) ACG   *Private collection
NOTES: The text on p 5 refers to the organization of the Domestic Science Department in 1912 and 'sixteen years of practical demonstrations' since then; therefore, this edition was published about 1928, a date consistent with the publishing history recorded in the 1960s edition (and quoted in A28.1). Another private collector's copy was presented as a gift to her mother-in-law in 1928.

'Menus and Suggestions for Occasions' on pp 9–18 covers Thanksgiving, Christmas, A Game Dinner, St Patrick's Dinner, One-Plate Meal Menus, Luncheon Menu, Inexpensive Family Luncheon Menus, Menus for Card Parties, and An Easter Company Breakfast.

OTHER EDITIONS: *The Blue Bird Cook Book,* by the American Woman's Club of Calgary, Albertan Printers, nd [about 1960 because the list of past presidents says that the last president's term ran until May 1960] (OONL).

1914–18

The Red Cross cook book

The Queenstown branch of the Women's Institute was established in 1913 (Cole/Larmour, p 129).

A29.1   nd [about 1914–18]
The / Red Cross / cook book / Compiled and issued by the / Queenstown Women's Institute / Queenstown Alberta [cover-title]
DESCRIPTION: 21.5 × 14.5 cm   Pp [1–128]   Cloth, with small image on front of a red cross
CONTENTS: 1 dedication 'To the "Lords of Creation" dear to us as fathers, brothers, husbands or sons ...'; 2 ad; 3 'Preface'; 4 'How to Cook a Husband' [mock recipe]; 5–8 ads; 9–120 text, ads, and blank leaves for manuscript recipes; 121–4 blank; 125–8 ads
COPIES: *AHRMH (977-075-001)   ARDA (incomplete)
NOTES: The 'Preface' explains how *The Red Cross Cook Book* will help Albertan women contribute to the war effort:

... the aim [of the book] has been not only to help the inexperienced but to help all others in these trying times. First by substituting other cereals in the place of white flour for the making of many kinds of delicious bread. Second to eliminate waste by providing many ways to serve left overs in an attractive and appetising manner ... The custom of our grandmothers of keeping the bread board on the dining table should be revived, that all may have plenty, but waste nothing. Bones, bits of meat, a tea spoon of vegetables will all help to keep the old fashioned 'stockpot' filled. And then, the slogan 'Eat what you can, and what you can't, CAN.' We all remember the bountiful supplied tables of long ago with dried vegetables and berries and home canned fruits and preserves. These women of long ago met the same conditions that confront house keepers today and surely there is greater efficiency now and determination among women to do their bit to 'HELP WIN THE WAR.'

In addition to the usual sections of recipes, there are 'Children's Dishes' and sections on 'The Dining Room,' 'Hog Killing at Home Saves Money,' and 'Home Made Soap from Refuse Fat.' Each recipe section is credited to an individual.

War-time cook book

The Alex. McQueen Chapter was organized on 11 February 1914 (the chapter name is Alec [sic] McQueen in the records of the IODE national office, Toronto). It should not be confused with another Edmonton chapter, called after Dr David George McQueen, which compiled A75.1.

A30.1   [about 1914–18]
We have prepared this cook book, with the object of helping / the housewife to reduce the high cost of living, and / to conserve wheat, beef, bacon and sugar, / thus rendering a patriotic service to the / country at this critical time / War-time / cook book / Compiled by / Alex. McQueen Chapter, I.O.D.E. / Edmonton, Alberta / Metropolitan Press, Edmonton [cover-title]
COPIES: *AEPMA
NOTES: The title-page transcription is from a photocopy supplied before my visit to the museum, when the cookbook could not be found.

1915

The Shamrock cook book

Patrick Burns, in later life a senator, established his meat-packing business in Calgary in 1890. In spring 1923, the company was reorganized and the name changed from P. Burns and Co. Ltd to Burns and Co. Ltd. The business expanded across Canada and encompassed fruit (from 1920, under a subsidiary company), cheese production (beginning in 1922; processed cheese from 1925), other dairy (from 1923, under the name Palm Dairies Ltd), meat canning (from 1929), eggs (from 1940), and live-stock feed. For a company history, see The Story of Burns and Co. Limited: Pioneer Meat Packers of Canada, *[1943]. For other cookbooks published by the company see: A47.1,* Helpful Hints for the Preparation of Meals; *A62.1,* Appealing Recipes; *A77.1,* 60 Ways to Serve Burns' Shamrock Ham and Bacon; *A78.1,* Tempting Recipes for Hot Weather Meals; *A79.1,* Tempting Recipes for Quick Tasty Meals; *and A102.1, Henderson, Mrs Margaret,* How to Save in Your Kitchen. *The company distributed copies of O400.1,* Fancy Meats in Newest Dishes.

A31.1   nd [about 1915]
The / Shamrock / cook book / "Cookery means [..., quotation from Ruskin] / Published by / P. Burns & Company, Limited / Calgary, Edmonton, Vancouver / Copyright applied for [cover-title]
DESCRIPTION: 15.0 × 11.0 cm   Pp [1–32]   Paper, with shamrock border on front; stapled
CONTENTS: Inside front face of binding 'These Requisites'; 1 'Introduction' and other introductory text signed P. Burns and Co. Ltd; 2–inside back face recipes
COPIES: *Bookseller's stock
NOTES: The 'Introduction' states that the book 'has been compiled with the assistance of a lady holding a First Class Diploma of Cookery (Board of Education, London, England), and the Diploma of the Royal Sanitary Institute (London, England).' Recipes such as Queen Cakes, Toad in the Hole, Raised Pork Pies, and Sausage Rolls show the compiler's English roots. The cookbook is titled after the company's Shamrock Brand products. The untitled note on p 1 points out that 'the chief ingredients of each recipe are one or more of the products of our Calgary, Edmonton and Vancouver packing houses.' The printer's name is on the outside back face of the binding: 'S.A. Hynd Litho-Print Limited, Calgary.'

This is the earliest of all the versions because, as the cover-title states, copyright was 'applied for,' but not yet acquired. Since A31.1 is identical to A31.2 except for the copyright line in the cover-title, it was likely published in the same year as A31.2, 1915.

A31.2   copyright 1915
—The / Shamrock / cook book / "Cookery means [..., quotation from Ruskin] / Published by / P. Burns & Company, Limited / Calgary, Edmonton, Vancouver / Copyright, Canada, 1915, by P. Burns & Company, Limited [cover-title]
DESCRIPTION: 15.0 × 11.0 cm   Pp [1–32]   Paper, with shamrock border on front; stapled
CONTENTS: Inside front face of binding 'These Requisites'; 1 'Introduction' and other introductory text signed P. Burns and Co. Ltd; 2–inside back face recipes
COPIES: Bookseller's stock   *Private collection
NOTES: The printer's name is on the outside back face of the binding: 'S.A. Hynd Litho-Print Limited, Calgary.'

A31.3   copyright 1915
—The / Shamrock / cook book / "Cookery means [..., quotation from Ruskin] / Published by / P. Burns & Company, Limited / Calgary, Edmonton, Vancouver / Copyright Canada 1915 [cover-title]
DESCRIPTION: Pp [1–32]   Paper, with shamrock border on front
CONTENTS: Inside front face of binding 'These Requisites'; 1 'Introduction' and other introductory text signed P. Burns and Co. Ltd; ...
COPIES: *AC (Pam file 641.5971 Sha)
NOTES: The cover-title is differentiated from A31.2 by the copyright line, where there are no commas, and the company name is not repeated; otherwise, the inside and outside face of the binding and p 1 are identical to A31.2.

A31.4   nd [about 1918]
—The "Shamrock" girl / With compliments of / P. Burns & Company, Limited / Calgary, Alberta [cover-title]
DESCRIPTION: 17.0 × 12.0 cm   Pp [1–32]   6 fp cartoons, 2 Union Jacks at head of 'Special War Time Recipes' section   Paper, with image on front of 'The "Shamrock" Girl'
CONTENTS: Inside front face of binding ad for Tisgood Golden Shortening; 1 'Introduction,' untitled note signed P. Burns and Co. Ltd, Calgary, Edmonton, and Vancouver, and 'Canada Food Board License No. 113'; 2 'Note Specially: These Requisites' [measurements, ingredients, and abbreviations]; 3 'Soups'; 4–12

'Meats'; 13–14 'Fish'; 15–25 'Cakes'; 26–32 'Special War Time Recipes'
CITATIONS: Driver 2003, 'Canadian Cookbooks,' illus p 34
COPIES: ACG (photocopy)   ACHP (HP 3446.27) BVIPM (986.22.1c)   *Private collection
NOTES: See pl 29. This is the only edition with 'Special War Time Recipes' and cartoons. The cartoons feature two Irish characters, Shamrock (tall and thin) and Weaney (short and stout). In one cartoon, the two are leaning over a bull pen and looking at a snorting bull. Shamrock asks Weaney to inspect the bull: 'Go down und look im over sausage!'; Weaney replies, 'Divil a look ye yillow strake! – It's the rale inspector ye are yoursilf. Sure und he looks hilthy from hare.' In another cartoon, Shamrock says, 'Faith Weaney wer'e [sic] chosen by the people to inspict the famous Shamrock Brand hams bacon, lard etc. made by our old frind P. Burns and his company'; Weaney answers, 'Hoot! Mon! Whatever Burns makes needs no inspictin.' Quotations from *Paradise Lost*, Herrick, Pliny, Cicero, Shakespeare, and others are printed along the top edge of the pages. The printer's name is on the outside back face of the binding: 'J.D. McAra printer Calgary.'

Canada Food Board Licence No. 113, noted on p 1, limits the date of publication to after the creation of the Canada Food Board on 11 February 1918 and before the Board's replacement on 19 March 1919 by the Canadian Trade Commission. The Board began issuing licences to persons slaughtering livestock and to meat packers on 3 May 1918 (*Food Laws: Manual of Orders in Council and Orders of the Canada Food Board Relating to the Production, Conservation and Distribution of Food*, Ottawa: Canada Food Board, June 1918, p 44). Licence No. 113 was issued in 1918 because a total of 480 licences were issued to packers in 1918 (*Report of the Canada Food Board, February 11–December 31, 1918*, Ottawa: [1919], p 39).

A31.5   nd [about 1919–23]
—The / Shamrock cook book / Compliments of / P. Burns & Company, Limited / Limited [sic] [cover-title]
DESCRIPTION: 17.5 × 10.0 cm   Pp [1–24]   Paper, with image on front of the Shamrock Girl; stapled
CONTENTS: 1 'Introduction' and information about company products signed 'P. Burns & Company, Limited Plants at Calgary Edmonton Vancouver Regina Prince Albert'; 2 'Note Specially: These Requisites'; 3–24 recipes
COPIES: *AMHM

NOTES: On the outside back face of the binding there is a photograph of the Calgary head office and employees dated 15 June 191[9?]. This edition and A31.6 were published no later than spring 1923, when the company changed its name from P. Burns and Co. Ltd to Burns and Co. Ltd.

A31.6   nd [about 1919–23]
—The / Shamrock cook book / Compliments of / P. Burns & Company / Limited [cover-title]
DESCRIPTION: 17.5 × 10.0 cm   Pp [1–24]   Paper, with image on front of the Shamrock Girl; stapled
CONTENTS: 1 'Introduction' and untitled note signed P. Burns and Co. Ltd, plants at Calgary, Edmonton, Vancouver, Regina, and Prince Albert; 2 'Note Specially: These Requisites'; 3 'Soups'; 4–10 'Meats'; 11 'Fish'; 12–mid 18 'Cakes'; bottom 18–24 'Puddings'
COPIES: *ACG
NOTES: On the outside back face of the binding there is a photograph of the Calgary head office dated 1919.

1916

Deachman, Elizabeth Grant [Mrs Robert John Deachman] (1872–1952)

Elizabeth's husband, Robert John, was the Calgary publisher of a commercial journal for merchants and manufacturers ('They Have to Be Good to Handle Deachman,' Toronto Star, 30 August 1931). In 1926 the couple moved to Ottawa. They are buried in Ottawa's Beechwood Cemetery.

A32.1   nd [about 1916]
Home / canning / By / Mrs. R.J. Deachman / President Calgary Consumers' League / Price 15 cents [cover-title]
DESCRIPTION: 22.0 × 14.0 cm   Pp [3] 4–30   Paper; stapled
CONTENTS: 3–top 4 'Home Canning'; mid 4–top 6 'Jams and Butters'; mid 6–mid 8 'Jelly Making'; mid 8–top 10 'Sugarless Canning'; mid 10–mid 11 'Open Kettle Preserving'; bottom 11–mid 13 'Closed Boiler Fruit Canning'; bottom 13–top 15 'Canning Fruit Juices and Cordials'; mid 15–16 'Marmalades'; 17–mid 20 'Canning Vegetables and Greens'; bottom 20–mid 22 'Canning Corn and Tomatoes'; bottom 22–mid 25 'Pickles and Sauces'; mid 25–top 27 'Canning Soups and Broths'; near top 27–mid 28 'Canning Puddings, Left-overs, etc.'; mid 28–mid 30 'Canning Meats, Fowl, Fish and Game'; bottom 30 'Calgary Public Market'

COPIES: *ACG
NOTES: On p 3, Deachman offers the following reasons for home canning: 'Home canning is thrift. It keeps down food bills. It gives variety to the diet all the year round. It is a time saver. It induces home gardening. It gives the girls interesting home work. It preserves garden and orchard culls. It offers an opening for a new industry among women.' Text on p 4 indicates that the booklet was published during the First World War: 'We must feed ourselves, feed our soldiers, and help feed our Allies. The need is greater in 1916 than in 1915.'

1917

Anderson, Hans Steele (1877–)

A33.1   [4th ed.], 1917
Food and / cookery / By / H.S. Anderson / Food Expert, Loma Linda / Sanitarium, California / 1917 / Pacific Press Publishing Association / Mountain View, California / Kansas City, Mo. Portland, Ore. Brookfield, Ill. / Calgary, Alberta, Canada Cristobal, Canal Zone
DESCRIPTION: 18.0 × 12.0 cm   Pp [1–2] 3–163   Illus on p 62 of loaf of bread indicating its constituent parts (gas, water, carbohydrates, proteid, fat, mineral matter)   Cloth, with image on front of a woman stirring the contents of a bowl
CONTENTS: 1 tp; 2 'Copyright 1915 by the College Press Loma Linda, California Revised fourth edition copyright 1917 by Pacific Press Publishing Assn.'; 3 'Publishers' Preface'; 4–6 author's preface; 7–8 table of contents; 9–159 text; 160–3 index
COPIES: CIHM (9-90234)   OOAG   *Private collection
NOTES: I have found no earlier Canadian editions. The author describes his approach to diet on p 4: 'While we have not attempted to write a treatise on vegetarianism, we do advocate the total disuse of the flesh of animals as food, and a more extensive use of grains, fruits, nuts, and other products of the vegetable kingdom.' In reference to the restricted food supply during the First World War, the 'Publishers' Preface' points out the 'moral demand for the information [the book] contains, in these days of world food scarcity and the need of wise food conservation, ...' About H.S. Anderson, the 'Publishers' Preface' says: 'He has served for years under German and Swiss and Spanish and English and French chefs. For a year, he was second cook in the Calumet Club of Chicago, where he served European royalty; and for nearly the same length of time, in the California

Club of Los Angeles; and he has also served in like capacity in many leading hotels in various cities. For the last ten years, Mr. Anderson has given himself to the better side of the question, – healthful, palatable, scientific, economical cookery.'

Belegai, Michael M.

Under the name Michael M. Bellegay, this author wrote a number of Ukrainian- and English-language books, on subjects other than cookery, through the first half of the twentieth century.

A34.1 [reprint, rev. ed.], 1917
M.M. Belegai / Ukrains'ko-angliiskyi / kukhar / Starokraieva chast' zladzhena pislia / Leontyny Luchakivs'koi. / Angliis'ka chast' pislia / "Vait Havz Kuk Buk" / i / "Faif Rozes Kuk Buk." / Nakladom / "Ukr. Vydavnychoii Spilky" / "Pros'vita" / Box 22 Edmonton, Alberta. / 1917.
Tp translation: M.M. Belegai / Ukrainian-English cook / Ukrainian part How to prepare dishes in an Old Country way after / Leontyny Luchakivs'ka. / English part / "White House Cook Book" / and / "Five Roses Cook Book." / Publisher / "Ukr. Publishers Co-operation" / "Pros'vita" [i.e., Ukrainian organization for the promotion of education and culture among the people] / Box 22 Edmonton, Alberta. / 1917.
DESCRIPTION: 20.5 × 14.5 cm   Pp [1–5] 6–223 [224] Marbled-paper-covered boards, cloth spine; stapled
CONTENTS: 1 tp; 2 blank; 3 ['From the Publisher']; 4 blank; 5–124 ['Part I, Old Country']; 125–220 ['Part II, Anglo-American']; 221 blank; 222–3 ['Alphabetical Index']; 224 ['Reprint // Revised.']
COPIES: *OONL (TX723.5 U5 B4 1917)
NOTES: Apart from the publisher's address in English on the title-page, the book is in Ukrainian; in the 'Contents' section, above, English translations of the Ukrainian headings are in square brackets. The publisher's note on p 3 refers to an earlier Ukrainian-language cookbook published in Winnipeg, Manitoba, that was difficult to understand because it used an older, pre–First World War form of the language (I have not identified this work, which would be the first Ukrainian cookbook published in Canada). The publisher explains that this new book is easy to understand and presents both Old Country recipes and 'Anglo-American' recipes based on the two cookbooks named on the title-page. He adds that the recipes chosen are basic ones for the most important dishes, they cover cooking and baking, and are economical.

Another advantage, he asserts, is that the book uses the exact recipe names for the Canadian or American recipes, put into the Ukrainian alphabet.

The two North American books used as sources for the recipes were both successful publications. *Five Roses Cook Book* (Q79.1), which supplied the 'Anglo' recipes, was first published in Montreal in 1913 and, by the time of the 1915 edition, it boasted a copy in over 950,000 Canadian homes; it was a promotional vehicle for Five Roses Flour made by Lake of the Woods Milling Co. in Winnipeg. *The White House Cook Book*, by Hugo Zieman and Mrs Fanny Lea Camp Gillette, first published in Chicago in 1887, had been through numerous American editions by the time of Belegai's Ukrainian cookbook. American editions were commonly owned by Canadians and there was a Canadian edition published in Toronto, copyright 1899 (O93.1). See also M128.1, *Ukrainian-English Cook Book*, which also features recipes by Luchakivs'ka and material from *The White House Cook Book*.

1918

Conservation cook book

A35.1   1918
Daughters of / the Allies / Conservation / cook book / A collection of tested recipes / compiled by the Friday Unit / Calgary Alberta / June, 1918
DESCRIPTION: 22.0 × 15.0 cm   Pp 1–159 [160]   [$1.00, on binding]   Cloth
CONTENTS: 1–2 ads; 3 tp; 4 ad; 5 'Announcement' signed Friday Unit of the Daughters of the Allies; 6 'Regular Eating' signed C.S. Mahood, Department of Public Health, Calgary; 7 'Appreciation' thanking advertisers and recipe contributors; 8 Canada Food Board request to not use wheat; 9 dedication to 'the soldiers of the Allies'; 10 ad; 11–157 recipes credited with the name of the contributor and ads; 158 ad; 159 'Index'; 160 'The Avenue Press printers and publishers Calgary Alberta'
CITATIONS: Axford, p 78   Barss 1980, pp 76, 116   Peel 2620   Peel's Bibliography 4376
COPIES: ACHP (HP 3480)   *ACU (TX357 D38 1918 mph)   CIHM (9-92264); United States: DLC (TX715 D228)
NOTES: The 'Announcement' states that the book 'is offered to the public as an aid in the conservation of beef, bacon, sugar, and animal fats, which are needed by our soldiers ...'

1918–20

McDermand, Miss Bessie Cameron

McDermand attended the Macdonald Institute at the Ontario Agricultural College in Guelph from 17 September 1913 to 29 June 1915, earning the Certificate of Domestic Science Teacher. Her Entrance Record at OGU (RE1 MAC A0003, Registration No. 1834) states that her permanent address at that time was Lakeview, Ontario, which is south of Aylmer, on Lake Erie; her father, Sydney McDermand, was a farmer; and her religious denomination, Baptist. Since she entered the course at age twenty years, she was born about 1893, but the 1901 Census gives 8 December 1894. The Entrance Record also states that she went to SS #3 Malahide public school, 1900–8; worked in Port Burwell, Ontario, 1908–11, and in Aylmer, Ontario, 1912–13; and matriculated from Moulton College in Toronto, after studying there from 1911 to 1912. There is an added remark that she 'passed Toronto University 1st year English 1914 // 2nd year English 1915.' Sometime after her stint at the Macdonald Institute, she travelled to Alberta. McDermand left her position at the Women's Institute Branch of the Alberta Department of Agriculture in 1922 (see A36.3). From 1934 she served as the first female superintendent of the Ontario Women's Institutes. She resigned in fall 1938, to marry Guy Skinner and move to New England. She is reported to have had experience of 'extension service in New York State,' before her Ontario appointment (Ambrose, p 120). For her accomplishments as Ontario superintendent and her photograph, see Ambrose, pp 120–4. A photograph of her is also in Chatelaine (October 1937), p 74.

For other cookbooks published by the Alberta Department of Agriculture, see A72.1, The Preservation of Fruits, Vegetables and Meats; A97.1, Richards, Vera D., Honey Helpings; and A104.1, Farm Cheesemaking.

A36.1 nd [about 1918–20]
Women's Institute Branch / Department of Agriculture / Province of Alberta / Home canning / of / fruits / vegetables / meats / By / Bessie McDermand / Assistant Superintendent of / Women's Institutes / [Alberta Women's Institute symbol] / Published by the direction of / Hon. Duncan Marshall, Minister of Agriculture
DESCRIPTION: 23.0 × 15.0 cm   Pp [1–3] 4–15   5 numbered illus   Paper; stapled
CONTENTS: 1 tp; 2 blank; 3 'Home Canning Instructions'; 4–top 6 'Canning Outfits'; mid 6 'General Rules'; bottom 6–top 9 'Methods'; mid 9–mid 11 'Spe-

cial Directions for Canning Vegetables'; bottom 11–13 'Special Directions for Canning Fruits'; 14–top 15 'Canning of Meats'; mid–bottom 15 'Difficulties' and 'Printed by J.W. Jeffery, King's printer, Edmonton, Alta.'
COPIES: *ACG
NOTES: In this edition, there is no 'Cameron' in McDermand's name. Marshall was minister of agriculture from 1909 to 1920, but the cookbook was published in 1912 or later, because it was in 1912 that the Department of Agriculture established the position of superintendent to help organize the growing number of Women's Institute branches (Cole/Larmour, p 18). The cookbook was likely published no earlier than 1918: Bessie McDermand is listed in the Edmonton city directory for 1919 as assistant superintendent of Women's Institutes, but she is not listed in the directories for 1917 or before (no directory was published in 1918).

A36.2 nd [about 1918–20]
—Women's Institute Branch / Department of Agriculture / Province of Alberta / Home canning / of / fruits / vegetables / meats / By / Bessie Cameron McDermand / Assistant Superintendent and Director / of Household Economics / [Alberta Women's Institute symbol] / Published by the direction of / Hon. Duncan Marshall, Minister of Agriculture
DESCRIPTION: 23.0 × 15.0 cm   Pp [1–3] 4–16   5 numbered illus   Paper; stapled
CONTENTS: 1 tp; 2 blank; 3 'Home Canning Instructions'; 4–top 6 'Canning Outfits'; mid 6 'General Rules'; bottom 6–top 9 'Methods'; mid 9–mid 11 'Special Directions for Canning Vegetables'; bottom 11–mid 14 'Special Directions for Canning Fruits'; mid 14–mid 15 'Canning of Meats'; bottom 15–16 'Difficulties' and at bottom p 16, 'Edmonton: Printed by J.W. Jeffery, King's printer.'
COPIES: *ACG
NOTES: In this edition 'Cameron' is given as part of McDermand's name and she is described as director of household economics.

A36.3 nd [about 1920–2]
—Women's Institute Branch / Department of Agriculture / Province of Alberta / Home canning / of / fruits / vegetables / meats / By / Bessie Cameron McDermand / Assistant Superintendent and Director of / Household Economics / [Alberta Women's Institute symbol] / Published by the direction of / Hon. George Hoadley, Minister of Agriculture

DESCRIPTION: 23.0 × 15.0 cm   Pp [1–3] 4–16   4 numbered illus   Paper; stapled
CONTENTS: 1 tp; 2 blank; 3 'Home Canning Instructions'; 4–top 6 'Canning Outfits'; mid 6 'General Rules'; bottom 6–top 9 'Methods'; mid 9–mid 11 'Special Directions for Canning Vegetables'; bottom 11–mid 14 'Special Directions for Canning Fruits'; mid 14–mid 15 'Canning of Meats'; bottom 15–16 'Difficulties' and on p 16, 'Edmonton: Printed by J.W. Jeffery, King's printer.'
COPIES: *AMHM
NOTES: Hoadley was minister of agriculture from 1920 to 1933. Cole/Larmour, p 19, recount how Mary MacIsaac, superintendent of the Alberta Women's Institute, was dismissed from her job in September 1921, and that extension officer Bess McDermand left the WI Branch six months later [i.e., in 1922]. This edition, therefore, was published about 1920–2.

The AMHM copy includes two loose leaves from the Department of Agriculture, Horticultural Branch, one headed 'Can. Cir. "A" 17/7/16.'

1919–20

Alberta, Department of Education

A37.1   nd [about 1919–20]
Rural school / lunches / Province / of / Alberta / Published by direction of Hon. Geo. P. Smith, / Minister of Education
COPIES: AEE (LB3479 A4 A333 1920)   BVAU (LB3479 A4 A333 1920)
NOTES: The text of *Rural School Lunches* is arranged under the following headings: 'Introduction,' p 5; 'Agencies,' p 7; 'Supplies,' p 9; 'Classes of Supplies,' p 9; 'Equipment,' p 10; 'Suitable Dishes,' p 12; 'General Directions for Cooking,' p 12; 'Dishes Made with White Sauce as Basis,' p 14; 'Preparation of Vegetables,' p 14; 'Fresh Fruit,' p 19; 'Table of Suggested Hot Dishes for Rural Schools,' p 21; 'General Plan of the Hot Lunch,' p 26; 'Suggestions for a Rural School Demonstration,' p 29; 'Demonstration,' p 29; 'The Mother's Part,' p 30; and 'Bibliography,' p 31.
Fourteenth Annual Report of the Department of Education of the Province of Alberta 1919, Edmonton: 1920, p 30, states:

Early in the year there was issued a bulletin entitled 'Rural School Lunches,' giving specific instructions to the teachers and boards of trustees as to the best procedure in organizing for the lunch as well as complete information as to the equipment

and supplies needed. Copies of this bulletin were sent to the normal schools, the inspectors, the teachers in training, school boards and others interested. So great was the demand for this bulletin from Women's Institutes, United Farm Women, and other organizations of rural women, that by September the first edition was exhausted. Certain revisions to make it more complete were then made and a second and larger edition has just been received from the press.

It is uncertain whether A37.1 is the shorter, first edition published 'early in the year,' i.e., 1919, or the larger, second edition, 'just ... received from the press,' i.e., likely in 1920. George P. Smith was minister of education from 22 August 1918 to 13 August 1921. There is no reference to *Rural School Lunches* in *Fifteenth Annual Report*.

The Saskatchewan Department of Education had published a book on the same subject in 1916; see S19.1.

Cooking manual, second year

The Alberta Schools of Agriculture were organized by the provincial government. They began as demonstration farms in 1911, and in 1913 schools opened at the sites (at Vermilion, Olds, and Claresholm in the first year, then in other rural centres). All the schools offered courses in household science. The Schools of Agriculture calendar for 1925–6, pp 11–12 (copy at AC), states that the two-year home economics course covered a period of two sessions of five months each. After completing the two years, students could go on to take home economics at university. Records relating to the schools, including calendars and yearbooks, are at AEPAA.

A38.1   nd [about 1919–20]
Alberta Schools / of Agriculture / Cooking manual / second year / Household Science Department
DESCRIPTION: Stapled
COPIES: *AC (Pam file 641.597123 Coo)
NOTES: The volume has 55 pp. No place of publication is recorded, but the Department of Agriculture was in Edmonton. AC dates the book about 1926, based on a dated inscription on the inside front face of the binding; however, it was likely published no later than about 1919–20, when the Alberta Schools of Agriculture began to use the term home economics instead of household science. A search of school calendars at AEPAA (1974.294) revealed that the calendar for 1916–17 used household science and the

calendars for 1920–1 and after used home economics; AEPAA does not have the calendars for the intervening years, but *ASA Magazine* for 1918 referred to household science. No manual for the first year has been located.

1920

Handy cook book

Cole/Larmour, p 126, record 1917–about 1933 as the years of operation of the Brooks branch of the Women's Institute.

A39.1 nd [about 1920]
Handy / cook book / Compiled by members of the / Brooks Women's / Institute / A collection of every-day, tried recipes / Bulletin – Brooks [cover-title]
DESCRIPTION: 17.5 × 13.0 cm Pp [i–iv], 1–32, [i–iv] Paper; stapled
CONTENTS: i–iii ads; iv 'Weights and Measures' and ad; 1–28 recipes credited with the name of the contributor; 29–32 ads; i–iv ads
COPIES: *APROM
NOTES: The running head is 'Brooks Women's Institute Cook Book.'

Walsh Ladies' Aid cook book

Walsh is east of Medicine Hat, near the Saskatchewan border. Information about the Methodist Church Ladies' Aid is in Walsh and District Pioneers, *Walsh, Alta: Walsh and District History Book Committee, 1997.*

A40.1 nd [about 1920]
Walsh / Ladies' Aid / cook book [cover-title]
DESCRIPTION: Pp 1–20
CONTENTS: 1–18 recipes credited with the name of the contributor and ads; 19 ad and 'Household Hints'; 20 ads
COPIES: *Bookseller's stock (photocopy) Private collection
NOTES: Although the church is not identified, the Ladies' Aid was a group at Walsh Methodist Church. An advertisement on p 20 for the Medicine Hat News Ltd reveals that the cookbook was printed on the newspaper's presses: 'Look it over again! Go through the book once more and size up the printing, style and general appearance of the book. We printed it.' The book's owner reports that two recipe contribu-

tors, who give their married names, are known to have married in 1918; therefore, the cookbook was published no earlier than that year. The only date in the volume is in an advertisement opposite p 20 for M.S. Schroder, the Ranchers' Store, 'Established 1907.'

1920–1

Cook book

For information about the United Farm Women of Alberta, see A59.1.

A41.1 [1920–1]
United Farm Women / Cook book / We may live without poetry, music and art; / We may live without conscience and live without heart; / We may live without friends; we may live without books; / But civilized man cannot live without cooks. / He may live without books – what is knowledge but grieving? / He may live without hope – what is hope but deceiving? / He may live without love – what is passion but pining? / But where is the man that can live without dining? / Published under the auspices of / Alix Local / United Farm Women of Alberta / [folio:] 3
DESCRIPTION: 23.0 × 15.0 cm Pp 1–104 [leaves lacking] Fp illus on p 7 of 'U.F.W.A. Board, 1921,' illus portrait on p 8 of Mrs A.C. Mull Paper; stapled
CONTENTS: 1 'Preserving' [ad for Sun Life Assurance Company of Canada]; 2 names of president and secretary of the United Farm Women of Alberta 'for 1920' and 'Doors of Opportunity Open to Alberta Women' [information about voting rights at different levels of government]; 3 tp; 4 ad for the *Journal*; 5–6 'A Few Practical Achievements of the U.F.W.A.'; 7–8 illus; 9 'Hints on Serving'; 10 'Bills of Fare for Special Days'; 11–16 ads; 17–103 recipes and ads; 104 ad
COPIES: AALIWWM *Private collection
NOTES: The AALIWWM copy, which is complete, has 130 pp; the contents of the last pages run: 105–17 recipes and ads; 118 ads; 119–23 'Household Notes' and ads; 124 ads; 125–7 'The Use of Salt' and ads; 128 ads; 129 'Index' [i.e., table of contents]; 130 ad. The printer, 'S.A. Hynd Litho-Print, Limited, Calgary,' is on the outside back face of the binding. The cookbook was published no later than October 1921 since there is an advertisement on p 104 that states, 'The Provincial School of Agriculture at Olds will commence its eighth year's work on Wednesday, Oct. 26th, 1921.'

1920–5

[Title unknown]

A42.1 [about 1920–5]
[An edition of a cookbook with running head 'Cook Book Reciepts [*sic*]' or 'Cook Book Receipts' and with recipes contributed by residents of Brownfield, Puffer, Battle Ridge, and Coronation, Alberta]
COPIES: Private collection
NOTES: The copy originally belonged to the present owner's mother, who came to Brownfield in 1917. The place of publication is unknown, but Coronation is the one town on a main route (between Stettler and Consort).

1921

A booke of recypies

See also A46.1, [Title unknown], published for the 1922 fair. St Barnabas Church also produced A27.1.

A43.1   1921
A / booke / of / recypies / Souvenir of / the Old Country Fair / June 30th, July 1st and 2nd, 1921 / under the auspices of / Holy Trinity Church, Medicine Hat / assisted by / St. Barnabas Church, Medicine Hat and / St. Ambrose Church, Redcliff. [cover-title]
DESCRIPTION: 22.5 × 15.0 cm   Pp [1] 2–44   Paper; stapled
CONTENTS: 1 cover-title; 2 [inside front face of binding] ads and recipe for Mexican Date Pie; 3 '$5.00 Reward' for discovering the most spelling errors in this book, 'Foreword' signed the Committee, and a list of Executive Committee members; 4–41 recipes credited with the name of the contributor, ads, and program information for the fair; 42 'To Readers:' [request that readers patronize advertisers] and 'Index'; 43–4 [outside back face] ads
COPIES: ACG   *AMHM
NOTES: The 'Foreword' gives two aims of the fair: '1. To raise funds to clear our church of debt. 2. To make some necessary improvements to our present building and provide for further accommodation.' The ACG copy is inscribed on the binding, 'Mrs Maud Bell.'

Cook book

Robertson College was a Presbyterian seminary. In 1925, at the time of church union and the creation of the United Church of Canada, it merged with Alberta College South, a Methodist institution, to become the United Theological College; two years later, in 1927, it was renamed St Stephen's College.

A44.1   nd [about 1921]
Cook book / Published under the auspices of / the Women's Guild of Robertson / College / Edmonton, Alberta
DESCRIPTION: 20.5 × 14.0 cm   Pp [1] 2–126 [127]   Illus on pp 4 and 127   Paper, with decorative border on front that features foodstuffs, including a turkey; stapled
CONTENTS: 1 tp; 2–4 'Index'; 5–126 recipes credited with the name of the contributor; 127 three images of an elf-cook
COPIES: *OONL (TX715.6 C653 1920z p***)
NOTES: The cookbook predates the college's name change in 1925. There is an advertisement opposite p 84 for Swans Down Cake Flour, 'the grocers' choice for 25 years.' This brand of cake flour was developed in 1896 (Allen, p 157); therefore, the cookbook was published about 1921 (1896 + 25 years), a date consistent with the appearance of the volume. On p 64 there is a recipe for Wild Ducks, which offers full instructions on their preparation and cooking, and includes a comment as to the relative quality of mallard, teal, and widgeon.

Tested recipes

The Argyle branch of the Women's Institute was founded in 1913 (Cole/Larmour, p 125); the Excelsior branch operated from 1915 to about 1926 (Cole/Larmour, p 127). Scottish immigrants settled in and around the town of Alliance; hence, the name Argyle.

A45.1   1921
Tested recipes / from / Argyle Excelsior / W.I. / Girls' Club / 1921 [cover-title]
DESCRIPTION: 15.0 × 10.0 cm   Pp [i–iv], 1–44   Paper; stapled
CONTENTS: i 'Greeting' and poem beginning, 'We may live without poetry, music and art' [from *Lucile*, Part I, Canto ii, by Owen Meredith, pseudonym of Edward Robert Bulwer-Lytton]; ii 'Introduction' [i.e., a poem about this book, 'The Girls' Club Cook Book']; iii 'Table of Contents' [i.e., alphabetical list of head-

ings]; iv 'Handy Weights and Measures' and 'Time Table for Cooking Vegetables'; 1–43 recipes credited with the name of the contributor; 44 'Household Hints' COPIES: *AEEA

NOTES: The 'Greeting' says, 'Our cook book has been compiled ... with the object of forming a nucleus of a fund for the interests of social welfare in our rural community.' The printer's name is on the outside back face of the binding: 'Printed for Argyle Excelsior Girls' Club by the Alliance Times // Alliance Alberta.'

1922

[Title unknown]

See also A43.1, published for the 1921 fair.

A46.1 1922
[Cover-title lacking]
DESCRIPTION: 22.5 × 14.0 cm   Pp 1–32   Red paper, mostly lacking; stapled
CONTENTS: 1 '$5.00 Reward' for the reader discovering the most spelling errors in this book, 'The Cosmopolitan Fair December 1st and 2nd, 1922 // Foreword,' recipes, and ads; 2–31 recipes, program information for the fair, and ads; 32 'To readers:' requesting patronage of advertisers, and 'Index to Recipes'; inside back face of binding ads and recipe for Angel Cake
COPIES: *AMHM

NOTES: The 'Foreword' states, 'We thank you for your kind support at the Old Country Fair last year which enabled us to pay off in full the mortgage on our church building. The Cosmopolitan Fair is an effort to clear a small deficit caused mainly by the unemployment in the earlier part of the year and for extension work.' The recipes are credited with the name of the contributor.

1922–3

Helpful hints for the preparation of meals

For information about the company and its cookbooks, see A31.1.

A47.1   nd [about 1922–3]
Helpful / hints ... / for the preparation / of meals / Compliments of / P. Burns & Co., / Limited [cover-title]
DESCRIPTION: 16.5 × 9.5 cm   Pp [1–2] 3–22 [23–4]
Illus   Card; stapled

CONTENTS: 1 'Foreword' signed P. Burns and Co. Ltd, Service Department; 2 'Contents' listing 'Quick Suppers,' 'Salads,' 'Sausage Dishes,' 'Lamb and Mutton,' 'Beef and Pork,' 'Ham and Bacon,' 'Cheese Dishes,' and 'Picnic Suggestions'; 3–24 text
COPIES: CIHM (79446)   *OONL (TX749.5 P67 H45 1920z p***)

NOTES: Some of the company's products are illustrated: Burns Goldenloaf Cheese, Glendale Brand Fancy Creamery Butter, Shamrock Ham, Shamrock Bacon, and White Carnation Brand Shortening. The company began producing cheese in 1922, and in spring 1923 it changed its name from P. Burns and Co. Ltd to Burns and Co. Ltd (*The Story of Burns and Co. Limited*, [1943], pp 12–13); therefore, the booklet was published about 1922–3. No place of publication is given, but P. Burns and Co. Ltd's head office was in Calgary.

1923

Cook book

A48.1   [1923]
Cook book / in aid of / St. Stephen's Memorial Hall / [ad for Hammond Floral Co.] [cover-title]
DESCRIPTION: 22.5 × 15.0 cm   Pp [1–2] 3–95 [96]   Paper, with image on front of St Stephen's Memorial Hall; stapled
CONTENTS: 1 'An Appreciation' signed Mrs George Nickle; 2 blank; 3 address of St Stephen's Church in Calgary, rector's name, times of service, and Holy Communion, and 'This book is printed under the auspices of – St. Stephen's Guild // Officers selected, 1923: [names of officers]'; 4 quotation from James Whitcombe Riley; 5–95 recipes credited with the name of the contributor and ads; 96 ads and at bottom, 'The Quick Print // Calgary, Alberta'
COPIES: *ACG

NOTES: Barss 1980, p 125, reprints Lemon Juice to Drink, identified as from St Stephens [*sic*] Guild, Calgary; the recipe is likely from one of the three editions of this book.

A48.2   2nd ed., [1924]
—Cook book / Second edition / in aid of / St. Stephen's Memorial Hall / [ad for Hammond Floral Co., Calgary] [cover-title]
DESCRIPTION: 22.5 × 15.0 cm   Pp [1–2] 3–108 [109–11], [i]   Paper, with image on front of St Stephen's Memorial Hall; stapled
CONTENTS: 1 'An Appreciation' signed Mrs Geo.

Nickle and 'Foreword' signed Mrs George Nickle, Calgary, Alberta, 1924; 2 blank; 3 rector's name, times of service and Holy Communion, '1924 edition,' and illus of St Stephen's Memorial Hall; 4 quotation from James Whitcombe Riley; 5–108 recipes and ads; 109–11 blank for additional recipes; i ads and at bottom, 'The Quick Print Calgary, Alberta'
COPIES: *AHRMH (987-035-001)

A48.3 3rd ed., [1927]
—Cook book / Third edition / [caption:] St. Stephen's [*sic*, spacing of period] Memorial Hall / Erected 1923 / [ad:] Buy at / Hollinsworth's & Co. / Limited / who have a marvellous assortment of coats, suits, / dresses and fur coats, and their prices are so / reasonable. [cover-title]
DESCRIPTION: 22.0 × 14.5 cm   Pp [1–2] 3–109 [110–12] Illus on p 3 of St Stephen's Memorial Hall   Paper, with illus on front of the hall; stapled
CONTENTS: 1 'An Appreciation' signed Mrs Geo. Nickle, 'Foreward' [*sic*] signed Mrs George Nickle, Calgary, Alberta, 1924, and 'Third edition – 1927' signed Mrs George Nickle; 2 blank; 3 church address, rector's name, times of service and Holy Communion, '1927 edition,' and illus of the hall; 4 'For Thou Art with Me!' by James Whitcombe Riley; 5–109 text and ads; 110–11 blank 'For Additional Recipes'; 112 ads and at bottom, 'The Quick Print, Calgary, Alta.'
COPIES: AC (Pam file 641.5971 Coo 1927)   ACG   *Private collection

'Cook book'

The Stake Relief Society is a women's organization in the Church of Jesus Christ of Latter-Day Saints that dates back to the beginning of the denomination.

A49.1 nd [1923]
"Cook / book" / Compiled and / edited by the / Lethbridge Stake / Relief Society / [artist's signature, lower right:] D Ursenbach [cover-title]
DESCRIPTION: 22.5 × 15.0 cm   Pp 1–136   Paper, with image on front of a bowl and milk bottle sitting in front of a window; stapled
CONTENTS: 1–2 ads; 3 'Officers of the Lethbridge Stake Relief Society'; 4 ads; 5 'A Few General Rules' and 'Recipe for Home Comfort'; 6 ads; 7–132 recipes credited with the name of the contributor and ads; 133 'Index' [i.e., table of contents]; 134–5 blank; 136 ad
COPIES: *Bookseller's stock
NOTES: The following names are listed on p 3 as

officers of the Lethbridge Stake Relief Society: Mildred Cluff Harvey, president; Mary E. Nalder Green, first councillor; Annie Craven Lingard, second councillor; Olivia M. Thornhill Green, secretary-treasurer; and, as Board members, Hannah Child Russell, Afton Hauser Elton, Elizabeth Layne Wilcox, and Hattie Walton Heninger. Some recipes are credited to Mrs Hannah Ursenbach, presumably related to D. Ursenbach, who designed the binding. The cookbook's date of publication is known from an advertisement on p 44, which features a letter dated 1 July 1923 from Ellison Milling and Elevator Co. Ltd 'To the users of this cook book.'

Cook book

The Good Deeds branch of the Women's Institute was founded in Vulcan in 1923 (Cole/Larmour, p 127).

A50.1 1923
Cook book / Compiled and arranged by members of the / Good Deeds Woman's [*sic*] / Institute / October / nineteen hundred and twenty-three / The members of the Good Deeds Institute wish / to thank most cordially all who have assisted / them in any way in getting out this cook book.
DESCRIPTION: 16.5 × 12.0 cm   Pp [1–2] 3–120 [121–8] Cloth
CONTENTS: 1 tp; 2 blank; 3–117 recipes credited with the name of the contributor and ads; 118 'Helpful Hints'; 119 table of contents and 'A Toast'; 120 ad for the Vulcan Advocate, 'We Specialize in fine job printing'; 121–8 blank for 'Memorandum'
COPIES: *Private collection
NOTES: The cover-title is 'The Good Deeds Institute Cook Book.' Most of the advertisements are for businesses in Vulcan and Nanton.

The modern cook book

The Armistice Chapter was founded in 1921 and disbanded in 1979. See also A76.1, Seen through the Pantry Keyhole, *by the same chapter.*

A51.1 nd [1923]
The modern / cook book / containing / many carefully selected and tested recipes, / household hints, table of equivalents / and other useful suggestions / [IODE symbol] / 35 cents per copy / Compiled and issued by / Armistice Chapter I.O.D.E. / Calgary, Alberta [cover-title]

DESCRIPTION: 22.5 × 15.0 cm   Pp 1–88   Paper, with IODE symbol on front; stapled
CONTENTS: 1–2 ads; 3 'Foreword'; 4–82 text and ads; 83–8 blank for 'Additional Recipes'; inside back face of binding table of contents; outside back face ad and 'Canniff-O'Brien Printing Co., Calgary, Alta.'
CITATIONS: Bly
COPIES: *ACG (2 copies)
NOTES: There is an advertisement on p 2 for Henry Birks and Sons Ltd, Calgary, that points to publication of *The Modern Cook Book* at the end of 1923: 'Simplifying Christmas shopping // Our 1924 Year Book is now ready for distribution.'

1925

Cook book

A52.1   [1925]
Cook book / in aid of / South Calgary United Church / [ad for Wilkinson Electric Co.] [cover-title]
DESCRIPTION: 22.0 × 14.0 cm   Pp [1] 2–47   Paper, with image on front of South Calgary United Church; stapled
CONTENTS: 1 church address, pastor's name, hours of service, and 'This book is printed under the auspices of South Calgary United Church Ladies' Aid 1925' followed by names of members of the executive; 2 dedication to 'the late Mrs. Joseph Brown, of this church,' thoughts on the role of the housewife, and 'An Appreciation' signed Mrs W. Worsnop, president of the Ladies' Aid; 3–47 recipes credited with the name of the contributor and ads
COPIES: *ACG
NOTES: The cookbook was published after the founding of the United Church of Canada on 10 June 1925.

Mother's favorite recipes

Cole/Larmour, p 127, give 1925–33 as the approximate dates of operation of the Garden Prairie branch.

A53.1   1925
Mother's / favorite recipes / Garden Prairie Women's / Institute / Girl's Club / Barons, Alberta / Canada / 1925 [cover-title]
DESCRIPTION: 20.5 × 13.5 cm   Pp [1–4] 5–48 [49]   Paper, with image on front of wild roses(?); stapled
CONTENTS: 1 blank; 2 'Introduction'; 3 'Officers,'
'Directors,' 'Auditors,' 'Motto,' 'Flower' [wild rose], and 'Colors' [pink and white]; 4 'A.W.I. Girls' Club Code'; 5–44 recipes credited with the name of the contributor; 45 'Soap'; 46–8 'Removal of Stains'; 49 'Index' [i.e., table of contents]
CITATIONS: Bly
COPIES: *ACG
NOTES: The 'Introduction' dedicates the book to the mothers of the community.

1925–9

Good bread

Before 1916 the firm was known as McGavin Bros Bakery (James and Alan McGavin, proprietors). McGavin Ltd is first listed in Edmonton city directories in 1916. From 1935 the name is McGavin's Bakeries Ltd. For a later cookbook by the company, see A91.1, Menu Magic.

A54.1   nd [about 1925–9]
Good bread / the most important / of all / foods / Published by / McGavin Limited / bakers of Butter Krust Bread / Edmonton / Phone 6828 [*sic*; '6820' on binding] Phone 1444
DESCRIPTION: 14.5 × 11.0 cm   Pp [1–2] 3–16   Illus of bread-making machines   Paper, with image on front of a baker holding a loaf in his hand; stapled
CONTENTS: 1 tp; 2 blank; 3–16 recipes, text about the quality of the company's bread, and illus of company machines
COPIES: *AEPMA
NOTES: The recipes use bread as an ingredient. The McGavin bakery is described on p 4 as 'a civic institution employing over 90 persons and ... recognized as the only large fair wage bake shop west of Winnipeg.' Prizes won by the company's president, Jim McGavin, in England and Scotland, from 1908–12, are listed on p 6.

The identification of Jim McGavin as president and the telephone numbers limit the date of publication to the period 1921–9. Edmonton city directories record James McGavin as manager, then president, of McGavin Ltd from 1916 to 1929; from 1930, James McGavin's name disappears from the directories. The first reference to the telephone numbers 6820 and 1444 is in the 1921 directory (in 1920, the numbers were 6820 and 72491). From appearances, *Good Bread* was likely published in the second half of the 1920s.

1927

Cook book

A55.1 [1927]
Cook book / Banff / United Church / Ladies' Aid
[cover-title]
DESCRIPTION: 21.5 × 15.0 cm [dimensions from photo-
copy]   With image on front of a Banff street scene;
stapled, and with string through top left corner for
hanging
COPIES: *ACHP (HP 4628.8)
NOTES: The following is on the first page: 'Printed
under the auspices of the Ladies' Aid. Officers: – 1927
// President Mrs. W.E.C. Richards // Vice-President
Mrs. H.W. McConnell // Secretary-Treasurer Mrs.
J.M. Dignall.' Also on the first page is information
about church services and a dedication to those who
helped compile the cookbook.

The Military Chapter cook book

The Military Chapter is still active in Calgary.

A56.1   nd [about 1927]
The / Military Chapter / [IODE symbol] / cook
book / "We may live without poetry, music and art;
/ We may live without conscience and live /
without heart; / We may live without friends, we
may live / without books – / But civilized man
cannot live without cooks."
DESCRIPTION: 22.0 × 15.0 cm   Pp [1] 2–96   Cloth,
with IODE symbol on front
CONTENTS: 1 tp; 2 'Weights and Measures,' 'Avoirdu-
pois Weight,' 'Dry Measure,' and 'Liquid Measure';
3–mid 4 'Household Hints' and ads; mid 4–92 recipes
credited with the name or initials of the contributor
and ads; top 93 ad; mid 93–96 index and at bottom
p 96, 'Quick Print // Calgary, Alta.'
CITATIONS: Peel's Bibliography 4996
COPIES: ACG   BTCA (77.76)   *Private collection
NOTES: There is an advertisement on p 14 for Star
Cycle Co., bicycle specialists, 'Established 19 years.'
Since Star Cycle Co. is first listed in the Calgary city
directory for 1908, the cookbook was published about
1927 (1908 + 19 years). Barss 1980, p 126, reprints
Parsnip Wine from 'I.O.D.E. Military Cook Book,'
probably A56.1.

1928

Buffalo Hill U.F.W.A. cook book

*For information about the United Farm Women of
Alberta, see A59.1.*

A57.1   nd [about 1928]
Buffalo Hill / U.F.W.A. / cook book / Arrowwood,
Alberta
DESCRIPTION: 22.0 × 14.5 cm   Pp [1] 2–104   Limp
cloth; stapled
CONTENTS: 1 tp; 2 'United Farm Women of Alberta'
[i.e., invitation to join the organization and a list of
the organization's aims]; 3 'Preface' signed the Committee; 4 ad; 5–103 text and ads; 104 ad
COPIES: *ACG
NOTES: An advertisement on p 6 for the Alberta Wheat
Pool cites expenses for 1926–7, which indicates a publication date for the cookbook of about 1928. The
'Preface' is an original poem, thanking those who
provided material for the book and dedicating the
book to 'maids and housewives.' The recipes are credited with the name of the contributor. The printer is
on the outside back face of the binding: 'Albertan Job
Press Limited.'

Cook book in aid of St Joseph's Cathedral

A58.1   1928
Cook book / in aid of / St. Joseph's Cathedral /
Thanking all who have contributed to / the success
of this book / Promoter / Mrs. R. McDonald /
Assisted by / Mrs. Irwin Mrs. Murray Mrs. Boyle /
Secretary / Mrs. Pratley / December 1st, 1928 /
I commend the sale of this book, which the /
promoters have so kindly compiled, in the interests
/ of St. Joseph's Cathedral. I hope that their efforts /
will meet with generous support on the part of /
every well-wisher of our new cathedral. / Signed: /
Henry J. O'Leary, / Archbishop of Edmonton.
DESCRIPTION: 22.0 × 14.5 cm   Pp [3] 4–118   Fp illus
on p 6 of St Joseph's Cathedral, Edmonton   Oil cloth,
with image on front of a pedestal bowl filled with
fruit
CONTENTS: 3–5 ads; 6 fp illus; 7 tp; 8 ads; 9–117 text
(recipes credited with the name of the contributor)
and ads; 118 'Index to Contents' and ad
COPIES: ACG   OOA   *Private collection

NOTES: The cover-title is 'Cathedral Housewives Guide'; the running head is 'Cathedral Cook Book.' The OOA copy was transferred from the collection of the Canadian Home Economics Association (MG 28 I 359).

Recipes

In 1915 the Women's Auxiliary of United Farmers of Alberta was created, at the invitation of the men's organization. In 1916 the Auxiliary was reorganized as the United Farm Women of Alberta, with the purpose of bringing about positive changes in rural schools and improving the social and cultural conditions of rural Albertans. In 1949 the women renamed their organization the Farm Women's Union of Alberta. In 1970 the name changed to Women of Unifarm, when the Farmers' Union of Alberta and the Alberta Federation of Agriculture amalgamated to form Unifarm. Langford is an authoritative source of information about the organization.

A59.1 1928
Recipes / contributed by the / members of the / United Farm Women / of Alberta / Compiled by the executive, / 1928. / Phoenix Press Co., 408–7th Ave. West, / [printers' trade symbol] / Calgary, Alta.
DESCRIPTION: 22.0 × 15.0 cm Pp [1] 2–220 Cloth
CONTENTS: 1 tp; 2 ads; 3 'This book has been compiled in the hope that it may be of service to the farm women of the province, whose co-operation has made possible its publication. Appreciation is tendered to those who have contributed advertising ...'; 4 ad; 5 'A Few Practical Achievements of the U.F.W.A.' and 'Aims of the U.F.W.A.'; 6 ad; 7–219 recipes credited with the name of the contributor and ads; 220 blank for 'Notes and Your Own Recipes'
CITATIONS: Peel's Bibliography 5291 Landsberg Langford, pp xiv, 105
COPIES: AC (641.597123 Rec) *ACG ACHP AEEA
NOTES: The cover-title is 'United Farm Women of Alberta Cook Book'; the running head is 'U.F.W.A. Cook Book.' Langford, p 105, writes of the *U.F.W.A. Cook Book*: 'One of the best money makers, and one that became a tradition over the years, was the organization's cookbook. First produced in 1928 from recipes donated by members from all over the province, the organization published the book themselves, with assistance from Co-op Press. In total they produced eight editions over five decades.' For the year 1989, under 'Significant Dates' on p xv, Langford

records the publication of the 'eighth' edition and states, 'Over 100,000 copies of the cookbook (all editions) are sold.'

A59.2 2nd ed., 1930
—Recipes / contributed by the members / of the / United Farm Women / of Alberta / Compiled by the executive / 1-9-2-8 / Second edition, 1930 / West Printing Company, Limited, 225A–7th Ave. W. / [printers' trade symbol] / Calgary, Alberta
DESCRIPTION: 22.0 × 15.0 cm Pp [1] 2–220 Cloth, with UFA [i.e., the men's organization] symbol on front
CONTENTS: 1 tp; 2 ads; 3 untitled introductory note; 4 ad; 5 'A Few Practical Achievements of the U.F.W.A.' and 'Aims of the U.F.W.A.'; 6 ad; 7–215 recipes credited with the name of the contributor and ads; 216 ad; 217–18 index; 219–20 blank for 'Notes and Your Own Recipes' and at bottom p 220, 'West Printing Co. Limited Calgary'
CITATIONS: Peel's Bibliography 5291
COPIES: AALM ABARRCM ACG *BVABSM OONL (TX715.6 R433 1930)
NOTES: Barss 1980, pp 52–3, reprints a recipe for Sugar Cured Hams and Bacons contributed by Mrs W.L. Barker to *U.F.W.A. Cook Book*, West Printing Co. Ltd, Calgary, 1928 [*sic*]; Barss's reference is likely to the 1930 or 1940 editions by the same printer (Phoenix Press printed the first edition).

A59.3 3rd ed., 1936
—Recipes / contributed by the members / of the / United Farm Women / of Alberta / Compiled by the executive / 1-9-2-8 / Second edition, 1930 / Third revised edition, 1936 / The Institute Press, Ltd. / Edmonton / [Allied Printing Trades symbol]
DESCRIPTION: 22.0 × 14.5 cm Pp [1] 2–224 Illus chapter heads Cloth
CONTENTS: 1 tp; 2 ads; 3 untitled introductory note; 4 ad; 5 'A Few Practical Achievements of the U.F.W.A.'; 6–220 recipes; 221–4 index
COPIES: AEPMA *Private collection
NOTES: The cover-title is 'United Farm Women of Alberta // Cook Book // Anniversary Number.' In 1936 the organization was twenty-one years old. This copy is inscribed on the inside front face of the binding, by the owner's mother: 'Mrs. Ray Ure.'

A59.4 4th ed., 1940
—Recipes / contributed by the members / of the / United Farm Women / of Alberta / Compiled by the executive / 1-9-2-8 / Second edition, 1930 /

Third revised edition, 1936 / Fourth revised edition, 1940 / West Printing Co., Limited / Calgary [printers' trade symbol] Canada
DESCRIPTION: 21.5 × 14.5 cm   Pp [1] 2–224   Illus chapter heads   Cloth
CONTENTS: 1 tp; 2 ad; 3 'The preparation of this fourth edition of the U.F.W.A. Cook Book has been a pleasure, and we issue it with perfect confidence that it will prove of valuable assistance ...' and a thank-you to advertisers; 4 ad; 5 'Some Aims of the U.F.W.A.'; 6–219 recipes; 220–4 index
CITATIONS: Peel's Bibliography 5291
COPIES: AC (641.597123 Rec 1940)   *ACG

A59.5   5th ed., 1946
—Recipes / contributed by the members / of the / United Farm Women / of Alberta / Compiled by the executive / 1-9-2-8 / Second edition, 1930 / Third revised edition, 1936 / Fourth revised edition, 1940 / Fifth revised edition, 1946 / [printers' trade symbol] / John D. McAra, printer and bookbinder / Calgary Alberta
DESCRIPTION: 23.0 × 15.0 cm   Pp [1] 2–240   Illus chapter heads   Cloth
CONTENTS: 1 tp; 2 ad; 3 untitled preface to fifth edition and a thank-you to advertisers; 4 'Some Aims of the U.F.W.A.'; 5 'The Art of Cooking'; 6–225 recipes and ads; 226 ad; 227–37 index and ads; 238–40 ads
CITATIONS: Peel's Bibliography 5291
COPIES: AC (641.597123 Rec 1946)   OONL (TX715.6 R433 1946, 2 copies)   *Private collection

OTHER EDITIONS: The numbering of editions after 5th ed., 1946, is inconsistent with the earlier numbering: *Cook Book,* 2nd ed., 3rd printing, 'compiled 1952,' list of officers for 1954, Farm Women's Union of Alberta (Bookseller's stock); *Cook Book,* 3rd ed., [Edmonton:] Farm Women's Union of Alberta, [1956] (OONL).
Retitled ed., *Country Classics,* cover-title: *Canadian Farm Women's Country Classics,* 2nd ed., Edmonton: Plains Publishing, 1989 (OONL); 2nd printing, 1990 (OTP). In the 'Foreword' of this 'second edition,' the Women of Unifarm state: 'We have come a long way since 1928 when we first started our collection of farm women's favorite recipes. Who would have thought that 60 year's [sic] later our cookbook would still be in such demand? Our first edition was reprinted eleven times and sold more than 125,000 copies ... Along with the traditional favorites, *Country Classics* features more than 250 new recipes, many of them for microwave cooking.' Langford, p 105, writes of this new edition: 'The organization sought a pub-

lisher for the eighth edition in 1989 and produced a new, updated version of the cookbook, complete with microwave recipes and information about environmentally friendly cleaning products. Although some long-time members were concerned about giving up the publication rights to the cookbook, it once again proved to be a popular publication, and the royalties have provided the organization with much needed funds.'

Royal Alexandra book of household science

See also A24.1, by the same group.

A60.1   nd [about 1928]
Royal / Alexandra / book of / household / science [cover-title]
DESCRIPTION: 22.0 × 14.5 cm   Pp [1] 2–144   Cloth
CONTENTS: 1–2 ads; 3 'Royal Alexandra Hospital Ladies' Aid dedicate this book to the Children's Department' and a thank-you signed Mrs W.A. Wilson, president, Mrs Thos Cox, secretary, and Mrs W. Boyt, treasurer; 4–138 text, mainly recipes credited with the name of the contributor, and ads; 139–43 'Index'; 144 blank for 'Memorandum'
COPIES: *OONL (TX715.6 R69 1920z p***)
NOTES: The 'Children's Department' on pp 4–23 includes information about appropriate foods for children and recipes for children's foods. Under each section heading is the name of the woman who, one assumes, organized that section (for example, 'Cakes // Mrs C.E. Archer'); the individual recipes that follow are credited to various contributors, including usually also the organizer of the section. An advertisement on p 34 for 'Higham's Market (late Horne's)' at 9940 101st Avenue, Edmonton, is evidence that the cookbook was published about 1928: The first listing in Edmonton city directories for Higham's Market is in 1928; there is no listing in the 1927 directory for Higham's or Horne's meat business; the 1926 directory lists Hornes [sic, no apostrophe] Meat Market.

1929

Tested recipes with practical references

A61.1   1929
Tested recipes / with practical references / 1929 / Published by the Ladies' Aid of / Bethel Lutheran Church / Wetaskiwin, Alberta, Canada [cover-title]

DESCRIPTION: 21.0 × 15.0 cm   Pp [1] 2–94 [95–6]
Card; bound by two metal rings through punched
holes
CONTENTS: 1 'Foreword' thanking the support of
Wetaskiwin businessmen, dedication 'to the cause of
better cooking,' and 'The Wetaskiwin Times Presses';
2 ads; 3–80 recipes credited with the name of the
contributor and ads; 81 'General Rules for Serving';
82–top 84 'The Cold Pack Method'; near top–bottom
84 'Wear Garments Longer; Set Colors While New'
and ads; 85 'Table of Weights, Measures and Abbreviations' and ads; 86–mid 87 'First Aid Hints' and
ads; mid 87–88 'Infant Feeding and Care of the Baby';
89–mid 90 'Household Hints'; mid 90–mid 92 'Practical Dietetics'; mid 92–top 93 'Care of Food'; mid–
bottom 93 'Cooking of Food' and 'Objective Points in
Cooking'; 94 ads; 95 'Index to Recipes'; 96 'Index to
Advertisements'
COPIES: *AWWDM

1930

Appealing recipes

*For information about the company and its cookbooks,
see A31.1.*

A62.1   nd [about 1930]
Appealing / recipes [cover-title]
DESCRIPTION: 22.5 × 15.0 cm   Pp 1–32   Paper, with
image on front of various ingredients and utensils,
plus a pail of Burns' Bakeasy Shortening, sitting on a
table; stapled, and with hole punched at top left
corner for hanging
CONTENTS: 1 'Foreword'; 2 'Index'; 3 'Weights and
Measures'; 4–30 recipes; 31 'Afternoon Tea Sugges-
tions'; 32 'Table Service' and at bottom, 'John D. McAra
Limited printers Calgary'
COPIES: ACG   BSUM   OONL (TX715 A557 1930z
missing)   *Private collection
NOTES: *Appealing Recipes* promoted the use of Burns'
Bakeasy Shortening made by Burns and Co. Ltd of
Calgary. The 'Foreword' tells the reader how she can
adapt her other recipes that may specify butter or
lard: double the amount of salt and less Bakeasy
Shortening than lard or butter (for example, 12–14
ounces to replace 16 ounces of lard or butter). 'Little
Knacks of Meat Cookery,' i.e., hints, are on the out-
side back face of the binding.

The cook's friend

A63.1   [1930]
The cook's friend / By / the Stony Plain / Women's
Institute / President: / Mrs. R.E. Wood / 1st Vice-
President: / Mrs. F.W. Yeats / 2nd Vice-President: /
Mrs. J.H. Lory / Secretary: / Mrs. R.M. Oatway /
Treasurer: / Mrs. H. Oppertshauser
DESCRIPTION: 17.0 × 12.0 cm   Pp [1–3] 4–99 [100]
Cloth, with image on front of a boy and girl holding
up roast poultry on a platter
CONTENTS: 1 tp; 2 'Printed by the Willson Stationery
Co., Ltd. Winnipeg to Vancouver'; 3 'Preface' signed
Stony Plain Women's Institute, 1 January 1930; 4 ad; 5
'Contents'; 6 'Boost Canada' signed Stony Plain
Women's Institute members; 7–100 recipes credited
with the name of the contributor and ads
COPIES: *Private collection
NOTES: 'Boost Canada' encourages readers to buy
Canadian and Albertan products.

Evening Auxiliary cook book

A64.1   nd [about 1930]
Nec tamen consumebatur [i.e., Burning but not
consumed] / Evening Auxiliary / cook / book /
St. Andrew's / Presbyterian Church / Edmonton –
Alberta
DESCRIPTION: Tp illus of a burning bush
COPIES: *Private collection
NOTES: The book's owner reports that it has 88 pp
and is 'believed to be about 1930.'

Recipes and health guide

A65.1   nd [about 1930]
Recipes / and / health guide / Compliments of /
United Dairies Ltd. / Union Milk Co. Ltd. / Phone
M 4686 / Crystal Dairy Ltd. / Phone M 2003 /
Central Creameries Ltd. / Phone M 9591 [cover-
title]
DESCRIPTION: 15.0 × 8.5 cm   Pp [1–16]   Paper, with
image on front of a toddler drinking a glass of milk;
stapled
CONTENTS: 1 cover-title; 2 ad for Crystal Dairy Ltd;
3 'The Protective Foods'; 4 'Christmas Pudding'
and 'Dark Christmas Cake'; 5–top 6 'Soups'; mid 6–
mid 10 'Desserts'; mid 10–12 'Miscellaneous'; 13–14
'Delicious Milk Drinks'; 15 'Contents of a Bottle of
Milk'; 16 [outside back face of binding] ad for Central
Creameries Ltd
COPIES: *ACG

NOTES: No place of publication is cited, but United Dairies Ltd was in Calgary. The first listing in city directories for United Dairies is in the volume for 1930, and the appearance of the booklet is consistent with publication about that year. The text is printed in brown.

Tested and selected recipes

A66.1 1930
Tested and selected / recipes / Issued by / the Ladies' Aid Society / Mundare United Church / 1930
COPIES: *Private collection
NOTES: The book has 99 pp.

1930–5

Cook book

A67.1 2nd ed., nd [about 1930–5]
Tested recipes / Cook book / Second edition / Complied [sic] by members of the / Evening Branch of / St. Michael's W.A. / Calgary Alberrta [sic]
DESCRIPTION: 17.5 × 10.0 cm   Pp [i–ii], 1–32, [i–ii] Limp oil cloth; stapled
CONTENTS: i tp; ii blank; 1–mid 30 recipes credited with the name of the contributor; mid 30–31 'Household Hints'; 32 'Useful Information,' 'Knitting Hints,' and 'A Prize Recipe'; i [blank?]; ii 'West Printing Co., Limited Calgary Canada'
COPIES: *Private collection
NOTES: The book's owner told me that it had been in the possession of her elderly friend many years before the 1950s. From appearances, it was published in the early 1930s. Although numbered as the second edition, it was published much earlier than another cookbook by the Evening Branch, A117.1. The first edition of A67.1 has not surfaced.

Home canning with the modern gas range

The Canadian Western Natural Gas Co. Ltd was incorporated on 19 July 1911, and the Home Service Department organized in 1929. A pamphlet published on the occasion of the company's seventy-fifth anniversary states: 'The thirties featured new promotional campaigns ... The Home Service Department ... introduced cooking schools and demonstrations of new appliances' (ACG, Pam 338.2728 C212C 1987, p 7). See also A83.1, Home Canning, *by the same company.*

A68.1 nd [about 1930–5]
Home / canning / with the / modern / gas range / Compiled and tested by the / Home Service Department / The Canadian Western Natural Gas, / Light, Heat and Power Co., Limited / Calgary Alberta
DESCRIPTION: 22.5 × 15.0 cm   Pp [1] 2–16   Illus Paper; stapled
CONTENTS: 1–6 'Home Canning'; 7–mid 8 'Jelly Making'; mid 8–11 'Jams and Conserves'; 12–14 'Pickles and Relishes'; 15–16 blank for 'Your Own Recipes'
COPIES: *ACG
NOTES: 'The Albertan Publishing Co., Ltd., Calgary' is on the outside back face of the binding. *Home Canning with the Modern Gas Range* was likely produced under the leadership of Hesperia Lee Aylsworth, the Home Service Department's first director, 1929–34.

'Sweet' dreams come true

Canadian Sugar Factories Ltd was established in 1925, when the Utah-Idaho Sugar Co. moved its sugar-processing operation from Sunnyside, Washington, to Raymond, Alberta. In 1931, BC Sugar Refining Co. Ltd of Vancouver bought the Raymond factory, but continued to operate it under the Canadian Sugar Factories name. A second plant was built in Picture Butte to process the 1936 beet crop. See also A85.1, Alberta Sugar Makes 'Delicious' Things to Eat, *and A106.1,* Smart Ways to Make a Cook's Life Sweeter, *by the same company.*

A69.1 nd [about 1930–5]
"Sweet" / dreams / come true / Recipes you'll relish [cover-title]
DESCRIPTION: 17.0 × 11.5 cm   Pp 1–16   Illus on inside back face of binding of the Raymond plant of Canadian Sugar Factories Ltd   Paper, with image on front of a girl sitting in bed, with a bowl of sweet food on her lap; stapled
CONTENTS: Inside front face of binding 'Foreword' and 'Index' [i.e., table of contents]; top 1 'Hints for Successful Preserving'; mid 1–2 'Unusual Preserves with Alberta Sugar'; 3–4 'Jellies and Jams'; 5–6 'Cakes, Puddings and Pies'; 7–9 'Frostings and Icings'; 10–12 'Candies and Confections'; 13–14 'Vegetables'; 15 'The Story of Alberta Sugar'; 16 'Beet Sugar Is Cane Sugar – Sucrose Is Sucrose'
COPIES: *ACG   OONL (TX819 S94 S84 1940z p***)
NOTES: The 'Foreword' lists 'Western Canada's leading dieticians' who contributed recipes to the book: Caroline B. King, Sugar Institute of America; Hesperia Lee Aylesworth [sic, should be Aylsworth], home ser-

vice director, Canadian Natural Gas, Light, Heat and Power Co., Calgary; Mrs N. Hampton, Saskatoon and Regina; Mrs Wm Wallace Wilson, dietitian, Calgary; and Mrs W.J. Thorne, preserves prize winner, Calgary Exhibition. Most of the recipes in the book are credited to one of the women in this list.

'Sweet' Dreams Come True was published about 1930–5, before A85.1, Alberta Sugar Makes 'Delicious' Things to Eat, of about 1936–9. In 'Sweet' Dreams Come True, 'The Story of Alberta Sugar,' p 15, relates that 'Sugar has been manufactured in Alberta, from Sugar Beets, successfully, since 1925, ...,' and says that there are over 800 farms growing sugar beets in Alberta. Only one plant, the Raymond plant, is identified, and it uses 150,000 tons of beets (see text on inside back face of binding). In A85.1, 'The Story of Alberta Sugar,' p 12, cites factories at Raymond and Picture Butte, which process together 200,000 tons of sugar beets from over 1,000 farms.

1931

Kitchen tested recipes

A70.1   1931
Kitchen tested recipes / [caption:] St. John's Presbyterian Church / Medicine Hat, Alberta / Built 1902 / First Street Circle / St. John's Church / 1931
DESCRIPTION: Tp photograph of the church   Stapled
COPIES: *Private collection
NOTES: The cover-title is 'Cook Book // Kitchen Tested Recipes.' The printer's name is on the front face of the binding: 'E.N. Dowson, printer, Medicine Hat, Alta.' The copy is inscribed on the title-page, by the owner's mother, 'Muriel A. Hargrave Sept. 7 1933.' The cookbook was likely a gift before her wedding on 23 September that year.

1932

Scott, Anna Lee [pseudonym]

See O773.5, O776.4, and O777.2, for editions of Scott's The Easy Way Cake Book, Marketing and Meal Planning, and Planning the Party, published by the Edmonton Journal; see O776.3, for Marketing and Meal Planning published by the Calgary Herald; and see O777.6, for Planning the Party published by the Lethbridge Herald.

1933

Cook book

A71.1   1932 [1933]
Cook book / Compiled and arranged by members / of the / Ladies' Circle / of the Church of Christ / Vulcan, Alberta / November / Nineteen hundred and thirty-two / The members of the Ladies' Circle wish / to thank all those who have assisted / them in any way in compiling this / cook book.
DESCRIPTION: 18.0 × 13.0 cm   Pp [1] 2–100 [101] Cloth
CONTENTS: 1 tp; 2–4 'Table Service'; 5 ads; 6–91 recipes credited with the name of the contributor and ads; 92 ads; 93–5 'Helpful Hints'; 96 ad; 97 'Icings for All Kinds of Cakes'; 98–100 ads; 101 table of contents
COPIES: *Private collection
NOTES: The title-page refers to the book being compiled in November 1932; the cover-title reads, 'Ladies' Missionary Circle // Cook Book // Issued 1933.' The section on 'Table Service' is 'by courtesy of the Blue Ribbon Ltd.' It is not a coincidence, therefore, that the phrase 'For everyday use in Canadian homes' that appears after the date in the cover-title is the same phrase used in editions of the company's Blue Ribbon Cook Book from 1932 (see, for example, M7.6).

1934

Alberta, Department of Agriculture

For the titles of other cookbooks published by the Alberta Department of Agriculture, see A36.1.

A72.1   1934
Alberta Department / of Agriculture / The preservation of / fruits, vegetables / and meats / Issued by direction of / Hon. F.S. Grisdale, Minister of Agriculture / Printed by W.D. McLean, King's printer / 1934 [cover-title]
COPIES: *Private collection
NOTES: There is no mention of this publication in the Alberta Public Accounts books or the province's Annual Reports for the early 1930s. In the Annual Report of the Department of Agriculture, 1935, under new projects for the year, there is a reference to 'Revision of the Canning Bulletin' that may concern The Preservation of Fruits, Vegetables and Meats.

A72.2 1938
—Alberta Department / of Agriculture / The preservation of / fruits, vegetables / and meats / Issued by direction of / Hon. D.B. Mullen, Minister of Agriculture / Edmonton: / Printed by A. Shnitka, King's printer / 1938 [cover-title]
DESCRIPTION: 25.5 × 16.5 cm   Pp [3–4] 5–30   3 numbered illus   Paper; stapled
CONTENTS: 3 'Index to Contents'; 4 'Directory // Alberta Department of Agriculture'; 5 'The Preservation of Fruits // Vegetables and Meats' [about spoilage of food by micro-organisms]; top 6 'Methods of Preserving Foods'; mid 6–top 8 'Canning Outfits'; mid 8 'Containers for Canning'; bottom 8–mid 12 'Methods of Canning'; mid 12–top 15 'Special Directions for Canning Vegetables'; near top 15–mid 16 'Special Directions for Canning Fruits'; bottom 16–top 18 'Canning of Meats'; mid 18–mid 19 'Other Methods of Preserving Food // A. Jelly Making'; mid 19–mid 21 'B. Tested Recipes for Jams, Marmalades, Conserves and Preserves'; mid 21 'C. Pickling'; bottom 21–24 'Pickles and Relishes'; 25–top 26 'Vinegar Making'; mid 26–mid 28 'F. Preserving Meat Products'; mid 28–top 29 'G. Salting Vegetables'; mid 29–30 'H. Drying Vegetables and Fruits'
COPIES: *AEAG
NOTES: There is an omission in the text headings: 'Pickles and Relishes' and 'Vinegar Making' should be lettered D and E, respectively. The 1939 Annual Report of the Department of Agriculture (which covers 1938) lists 'Preservation of Fruits, Vegetables and Meats (reprint)' under 'Publications and Statistics.' The Annual Report for the previous year does not cite the booklet, but does refer to various day-long projects offered around the province, one of which was Project No. 1, Foods and Nutrition, which included 'The Preservation of Fruits, Vegetables and Meats.' The book was likely used as part of the course.

Alberta Avenue community cook book

A73.1   nd [about 1934]
Alberta Avenue / community / cook book / Edmonton, Alberta [cover-title]
DESCRIPTION: 23.0 × 15.0 cm   Pp 1–74   Paper, with image on front of a cartoon-like girl-chef carrying a plate of steaming food; stapled
CONTENTS: 1 ad; 2–mid 71 recipes and ads; mid 71–mid 72 'Household Hints'; mid–bottom 72 'Kitchen Helps' [i.e., equivalent measures]; 73 'Index' [i.e., table of contents]; 74 ad
COPIES: *Private collection

NOTES: The cookbook was likely published in 1934 since there is an advertisement on p 36 for Blue Willow Pure Baking Powder, which 'secured 100% of all the prizes awarded in five classes at the Edmonton 1933 Exhibition.' An advertisement on p 3 for Edmonton's Gas Co. includes a photograph of Miss Kathleen Esch, B.Sc., home service director.

1935

Culinary creations by careful cooks

The Red Deer Troop, likely the first scout troop in Alberta, was organized in 1910.

A74.1   nd [about 1935]
Culinary / creations / by / careful cooks / Issued by the Red Deer Troup [sic] / Boy Scouts / Advocate Press [cover-title]
DESCRIPTION: 23.0 × 15.0 cm   Pp 1–18   Paper; stapled
CONTENTS: top 1 untitled introductory text signed First Red Deer Troop of Boy Scouts; mid 1–18 recipes
COPIES: *Private collection
NOTES: The running head is 'Boy Scout Cook Book.' The introductory text states, 'Knowing from the delicacies produced for the various "Bun Feeds" held at our shack down by the river that exceptionally tasteful culinary creations are produced by the careful cooks in our homes, we feel that we are doing the community a service in offering the best of these to all.' There are 'Outdoor Cooking Recipes (for cooking over an open fire)' on pp mid 16–17. The recipes are not credited with the name of the contributor.

The Dr McQueen Chapter I.O.D.E. cook book

The Dr David George McQueen Chapter (not to be confused with the Alex McQueen Chapter that compiled A30.1) was formed on 9 December 1931 and disbanded on 10 January 1955 (a few years later, in 1958, another Edmonton chapter started, taking the name Dr D.G. McQueen).

A75.1   nd [1935]
The / Dr. McQueen Chapter / I.O.D.E. / cook book
DESCRIPTION: 22.5 × 15.0 cm   Pp [1] 2–60   Paper, with three horizontal, coloured bands (red, white, and blue) and IODE symbol on front; stapled
CONTENTS: 1 tp; 2 'Table of Weights and Measures'; 3–57 recipes and ads for Edmonton businesses; 58–9 blank for 'Memorandum'; 60 'Index'

COPIES: *AEPMA

NOTES: On p 36 there is an advertisement for the Imperial Bank of Commerce that asks readers to 'Join our 1935 Xmas Club now and be sure of money for next Xmas.'

Newman, F.

For an edition of The Banner Cook Book, *by F. Newman and published to promote Kernel Flour milled by Krause Milling Co., Radway, Alberta, see M83.2.*

Seen through the pantry keyhole

See also A51.1, by the same chapter.

A76.1   nd [about 1935]
Seen through the / pantry keyhole / Favorite recipes of the members of the / Armistice Chapter I.O.D.E. Calgary Alberta [cover-title]
DESCRIPTION: 20.0 × 12.5 cm   Pp [1] 2–52   Very thin card, with image on front of prepared dishes within a keyhole-shaped frame; stapled
CONTENTS: 1 'Foreward' [sic] signed regent and members, Armistice Chapter, IODE, Calgary, Alberta; 2–50 recipes credited with the name of the contributor, blank spaces for 'Memo,' and ads; 51 ads; 52 'Index' [alphabetical list of sections]
COPIES: *OONL (TX715.6 S38 1900z p***)
NOTES: The foreword states, '... the committee in charge has endeavored to select recipes that are new and that are not found in the ordinary cook books ... The proceeds of the sale of the book will be devoted to the charitable work of the chapter.' Mr B. Mannix is identified in the foreword as the designer of the cover, where the short-title wraps around the top of a keyhole-shape enclosing images of prepared dishes; the binding is printed in a striking, deep blue. 'This recipe book printed by Commonwealth Press Ltd., Calgary, Alta' is on the outside back face of the binding. The book was likely published later in the year, to take advantage of Christmas gift-giving. The first section is 'Yuletide Cookery' and the OONL copy is inscribed, on p 1, 'Merry Christmas to Frances.'

The appearance of the book suggests publication in the 1930s. There is a note on p 19, preceding the fish recipes by Calgary's Billingsgate Fish Co., which refers to the company's '26 years in the business in Canada.' The first listing in Henderson's Calgary city directories for Ernest F. Trigg and Alfred [sic] Malthouse, the early proprietors of the Billingsgate

Fish Co., is in the volume for 1909, where they are described as fish dealers. The directory listing suggests that the cookbook was published about 1935 (1909 + 26 years); however, the company web site (June 2007) refers to Bert Malthouse, a new immigrant from England, purchasing a horse and trap to start up his seafood business in 1907, which points to 1933 as the year of publication.

60 ways to serve Burns' Shamrock ham and bacon

For information about the company and its cookbooks, see A31.1.

A77.1   nd [about 1935]
60 ways / to serve / Burns' / Shamrock / registered / ham & / bacon / Compliments / Burns & Co. Limited / Canada [cover-title]
DESCRIPTION: 21.5 × 14.5 cm   Pp [1] 2–19 [20]   Illus of company products   Paper, with image on front of one large and four small shamrocks; stapled, and with hole punched at top left corner for hanging
CONTENTS: 1 illus of Shamrock ham; 2 'Shamrock Ham Delicious the Year 'Round'; 3–9 recipes for ham; 10–11 illus of Shamrock bacon; 12 'Shamrock Bacon'; 13–19 recipes for bacon; 20 publ ad for the company's canned meats
COPIES: *ACG   APROM   AWWDM
NOTES: From appearances, *60 Ways to Serve Burns' Shamrock Ham and Bacon* was published about 1935. No place of publication is given, but Calgary was the location of the company's head office.

Tempting recipes for hot weather meals

For information about the company and its cookbooks, see A31.1.

A78.1   nd [about 1935]
Tempting / recipes / for / hot / weather / meals [cover-title]
DESCRIPTION: 22.0 × 14.5 cm   Pp 1–20   Illus of Burns and Co. Ltd products   Paper; previously stapled, now sewn in new library cloth
CONTENTS: Inside front face of binding 'Compliments of Burns & Co. Limited'; 1 'Burns' Sausage and Cooked Meats for Every Taste'; 2 'Sausage Saves Time' and recipes using Shamrock Sausage and Shamrock Bologna; 3 recipes using Burns' Shamrock Weiners and Frankfurters and Burns' Liver Sausage; 4 'Sau-

sage and Ready-to-Serve Meats in Sandwiches' [recipes]; 5 'Sausage and Cooked Meats for School Lunches,' recipes using Head Cheese, and 'A Partial List of Burns' Sausage and Cooked Meats'; 6 'Sausage and Ready-to-Serve Meats in Salads' [recipes]; 7 publ ad for Burns' Shamrock and Hormel Brand ready-to-serve canned meats; 8 publ ad for Burns' Shamrock Pure Pork and Sausage; 9 'Burns' Shamrock Baked Pork Sausage' [recipes]; 10 publ ad for Burns' Hormel Ham; 11 recipes using Burns' Hormel Ham; 12 publ ad for Burns' Hormel Spiced Ham; 13 recipes using the Spiced Ham; 14 publ ad for Burns' Hormel Boneless Chicken; 15 'Burns' Hormel Brand Flavor Sealed Boneless Chicken' [recipes]; 16 publ ad for Burns' Hormel Milk-Fed Whole and Half Chicken; 17 'Quick Ways to Serve Burns' Hormel Brand Flavor Sealed Whole and Half Canned Chicken' [recipes]; 18 publ ad for Burns' Hormel Chicken a la King; 19 recipes using the canned Chicken a la King; 20 'A Partial List of Burns' Shamrock and Other Branded Products'

COPIES: *OONL (TX749 T45)

NOTES: 'John D. McAra Limited printers, Calgary' is on the outside back face of the binding. In 1929 Burns and Co. Ltd secured from the American firm George A. Hormel and Co. the exclusive right to use the Hormel formulae for canning meats (see *The Story of Burns and Co. Limited*, [1943], p 36). From appearances, *Tempting Recipes for Hot Weather Meals* was published about 1935. A79.1 also promotes Hormel canned meats.

Tempting recipes for quick tasty meals

For information about the company and its cookbooks, see A31.1.

A79.1 nd [about 1935]
Tempting / recipes / for / quick / tasty / meals [cover-title]
DESCRIPTION: 23.0 × 15.0 cm   Pp 1–20   Paper; stapled
CONTENTS: Inside front face of binding 'Compliments of Burns & Co. Limited'; 1 'Burns' Sausage and Cooked Meats for Every Taste'; 2–3 'Sausage Saves Time'; 4 'Sausage and Ready-to-Serve Meats in Sandwiches'; 5 'Sausage and Cooked Meats for School Lunches'; 6 'Sausage and Ready-to-Serve Meats in Salads'; 7 publ ad for 'Burns' Shamrock and Hormel Brand Ready-to-Serve Canned Meats'; 8 publ ad; 9 'Burns' Shamrock Baked Pork Sausage'; 10–12 publ ads; 13 'Burns' Hormel Brand Spiced Ham'; 14 publ ad; 15 'Burns' Hormel Brand Boneless Chicken'; 16

publ ad; 17–19 'Quick Ways to Serve Burns' Hormel Brand Flavor Sealed Whole and Half Canned Chicken' and publ ad; 20 publ ad

COPIES: *APROM

NOTES: 'John D. McAra Limited printers, Calgary' is on the outside back face of the binding. Regarding the introduction of Hormel products, see A78.1. From appearances, *Tempting Recipes for Quick Tasty Meals* was published about 1935.

Tested recipes

A80.1   1935
Tested recipes / [caption:] Gordon Memorial United Church / Redcliff, Alberta / Built 1920 / Young People's Society / 1935
DESCRIPTION: 22.0 × 14.5 cm   Pp [1–6] 7–46 [47–8] Tp illus of the church   Paper; stapled
CONTENTS: 1 tp; 2 blank; 3–5 'Index to Recipes'; 6 ads; 7–46 recipes credited with the name of the contributor and ads; 47 blank for 'Memorandum'; 48 'Kitchen Rules'
COPIES: *Private collection
NOTES: The title-page is inscribed, 'M. Jean Pow // Jean Turnbull.' [i.e., maiden name, followed by married name]; and below the married name, '176 Aubrey St. // 1045 Wolseley Ave.' Jean Turnbull's father, Rev. Dr R.E. Pow, was the minister of Gordon Memorial United Church. The text includes recipes by her mother, Mrs R.E. Pow (p 26) and her brother, C.G. Pow (Bachelor's Supper Dish, p 35). Jean was a member of the Young People's Society.

1935–6

Kellett, V., and W. Kellett

A81.1   1935–6
Royal Purple / Lodge No. 22 / 1935–1936 / cook book / Edmonton, Alberta [cover-title]
DESCRIPTION: 23.5 × 15.5 cm   Pp 1–110 [111–12]   Paper, with image on front of an elk head; stapled
CONTENTS: 1 'Ladies of the Royal Purple // Executive Committee 1934–1935' [list of executive]; 2–108 text and ads; 109 'Index' [i.e., table of contents] and ad; 110 ad; 111 blank; 112 'Jenvrin Printing Company Edmonton // Advertising solicited and book compiled by V. and W. Kellett'
COPIES: *Private collection
NOTES: The compilers named on p 112 are not listed as members of the Executive Committee.

1935–9

Cook book

A82.1 nd [about 1935–9]
Highlands United / Church / Edmonton, Alberta / [illus of the church] / Cook book / Compiled by / Women's Association of the / Highlands United Church [cover-title?]
CONTENTS: 2 untitled four-line verse, 'Index' [i.e., alphabetical list of section headings], and 'An Appreciation' thanking the recipe contributors and advertisers
COPIES: *Private collection

Home canning

A83.1 nd [about 1935–9]
Home / canning / Tested and compiled by the / Home Service Dept. / Elsie Mae Currie, B.H.Sc. / Director / Dorothy Griffith, B.Sc. / Assistant / With the / compliments / of / your gas company – Calgary [cover-title]
DESCRIPTION: 23.0 × 15.0 cm Pp 1–20 Illus Paper, with image on front of a stylized female figure in a kitchen, the figure composed of the letters G, A, and S; stapled
CONTENTS: 1 table of contents; 2 'Tested and compiled by the Home Service Dept. Elsie Mae Currie, B.H.Sc. Director // Dorothy Griffith, B.Sc. Assistant'; 3–top 4 'Processing to Destroy Enzymes and Micro-Organisms'; mid 4 'Acid and Non-Acid Foods Defined'; mid 4–top 5 'Seasons'; mid–bottom 5 'Equipment for Canning'; 6 'Methods of Canning'; 7–top 8 'General Procedure for Canning'; near top–bottom 8 'Time Table for Canning of Fruits'; 9 'Syrup for Fruits,' 'Canning Fruit without Sugar,' and 'Canning of Vegetables'; 10 'Time Table for Canning of Vegetables'; 11 'Time Table for Processing Vegetables (Pressure Cooker)'; 12–13 'Jellies'; 14–16 'Jams // Jellies // Preserves // Conserves and Marmalades'; 17–20 'Pickles'
COPIES: *ACG
NOTES: One of the distinguishing features of the editions of *Home Canning* is the name of the director of the Home Service Department and her assistant. Knowing when the different women held their positions, whether in Calgary for Canadian Western Natural Gas or in Edmonton for Northwestern Utilities, indicates the approximate date of publication of the various editions. The names of the Calgary directors and their years of office appear in *Western Favourites:*

A Golden Anniversary Selection of Favourite Recipes by the Home Service Department of Canadian Western Natural Gas Co. Ltd, 1979 (Private collection): Hesperia Aylsworth, 1929–34; Elsie Mae Currie, 1934–41; Dorothy Griffith, filled in for Currie for part of 1939; Jessie Skene, 1941–2; Claire Abbott, a few months in 1942; Muriel Roberts, née Pettigrew, 1942–4; Frances Harkness, 1944–5; Elizabeth McCaffrey, 1946–50; Joan Ross, née Venini, 1951–4; Margaret Hall, née Scougall, 1954–5; Mona Cox, née Breton, 1955–7; and Evelyn Erdman, 1957–90. A list of 'Edmonton Staffing' in the Atco Gas archives, Edmonton, records Marianne Linnell as director of the Home Service Department of Northwestern Utilities in 1944 and 1945; and Margaret Dulmage as assistant in 1946 and director in 1947. City directories for Calgary and Edmonton provide additional information.

In A83.1, Elsie Mae Currie is director, and Dorothy Griffith, assistant. Calgary city directories list Currie as 'Miss' and confirm her years as director as recorded in *Western Favourites*, i.e., 1934–41; however, no listings were found in city directories for Griffith. Since Griffith filled in as director for Currie for part of 1939 and since Jessie Skene is listed as assistant dietitian in city directories for 1940 and 1941, Griffith likely preceded her as assistant, but for how many years is unknown. The Currie/Griffith edition, therefore, was published about 1935–9, perhaps as early as 1934.

This edition of *Home Canning* uses some of the illustrations and a few of the pickle recipes from an earlier cookbook, A68.1, *Home Canning with the Modern Gas Range*, published by the Canadian Western Natural Gas, Light, Heat and Power Co. Ltd, Calgary. The gas company is not named in *Home Canning*, but the same telephone number is given as in A68.1. For information about the company, see A68.1.

A83.2 nd [about 1940–1]
—Home / canning / Tested and compiled by the / Home Service Dept. / Elsie Mae Currie, B.H.Sc. / Director / Jessie Skene, B.Sc. / Assistant / With the / compliments / of / your gas company – Calgary [cover-title]
DESCRIPTION: 23.0 × 15.5 cm Pp 1–20 Illus Paper, with image on front of a stylized figure composed of the letters G, A, and S; stapled
CONTENTS: 1 table of contents; 2 'Tested and compiled by the Home Service Dept. Elsie Mae Currie, B.H.Sc. Director // Jessie Skene, B.Sc. Assistant'; ...
COPIES: *Private collection
NOTES: The Calgary city directory for 1939 lists Jessie Skene as stenographer at the gas company; the vol-

umes for 1940 and 1941 list her as assistant dietitian; she was Director for part of 1941–2, according to *Western Favourites.* This edition, therefore, was published about 1940–1.

A83.3   nd [about 1941–2]
—Home / canning / Tested and compiled by / Home Service Department / With the / compliments of / your gas company – Calgary [cover-title]
DESCRIPTION: 23.0 × 15.5 cm   Pp [1–2] 3–28 [29–32] Illus on p 13 of 'The "Sheeting-Off" Test for Jelly' Paper, with all-over pattern of blue dots; stapled
CONTENTS: Inside front face of binding 'Tested and compiled by the Home Service Dept. Jessie Skene, B.Sc. Director'; 1 'Table of Contents'; 2 blank; 3–top 4 'Processing to Destroy Enzymes and Micro-Organisms'; mid 4 'Acid and Non-Acid Foods Defined'; mid 4–top 5 'Seasons'; mid–bottom 5 'Equipment for Canning'; 6 'Methods of Canning'; 7–top 8 'General Procedure for Canning'; mid–bottom 8 'Time Table for Canning of Fruits'; 9 'Syrup for Fruits,' 'Canning Fruit without Sugar,' and 'Canning of Vegetables'; 10 'Time Table for Canning of Vegetables'; 11 'Time Table for Processing Vegetables (Pressure Cooker)'; 12–mid 13 'Jellies'; mid–bottom 13 'Jelly Table'; 14–top 17 'Jams'; mid 17–mid 18 'Marmalades'; mid 18–19 'Conserves'; 20 'Preserves'; 21–mid 22 'Pickles (Whole)'; mid 22–mid 24 'Pickles (Sliced)'; mid 24–mid 26 'Chopped Relishes'; mid 26–mid 27 'Sweet Fruit Pickles'; mid–bottom 27 'Ketchups and Chutneys'; 28 'Assorted Pickles'; 29–32 blank for 'Additional Recipes'
COPIES: *OONL (TX603 H56 1940z copy 2)
NOTES: This edition follows A83.2 where Jessie Skene is named assistant; here Skene is director, a position she held for part of 1941–2. The OONL copy is inscribed on the binding, 'Merle Crozier.'

A83.4   nd [1942]
—Home / canning / Tested and compiled by / Home Service Department / With the / compliments of / your gas company – Calgary [cover-title]
DESCRIPTION: 23.0 × 15.5 cm   Pp [1–2] 3–28 [29–32] Illus on p 13 of 'The "Sheeting-Off" Test for Jelly' Paper, with all-over pattern of blue dots; stapled
CONTENTS: Inside front face of binding 'Tested and compiled by the Home Service Dept. Claire Abbott, B.Sc., Director'; 1 'Table of Contents'; 2 blank; 3–top 4 'Processing to Destroy Enzymes and Micro-Organisms'; mid 4 'Acid and Non-Acid Foods Defined'; mid 4–top 5 'Seasons'; mid–bottom 5 'Equipment for

Canning'; 6 'Methods of Canning'; 7–top 8 'General Procedure for Canning'; mid–bottom 8 'Time Table for Canning of Fruits'; 9 'Syrup for Fruits,' 'Canning Fruit without Sugar,' and 'Canning of Vegetables'; 10 'Time Table for Canning of Vegetables'; 11 'Time Table for Processing Vegetables (Pressure Cooker)'; 12–mid 13 'Jellies'; mid–bottom 13 'Jelly Table'; 14–top 17 'Jams'; mid 17–mid 18 'Marmalades'; mid 18–19 'Conserves'; 20 'Preserves'; 21–mid 22 'Pickles (Whole)'; mid 22–mid 24 'Pickles (Sliced)'; mid 24–mid 26 'Chopped Relishes'; mid 26–mid 27 'Sweet Fruit Pickles'; mid–bottom 27 'Ketchups and Chutneys'; 28 'Assorted Pickles'; 29–32 blank for 'Additional Recipes'
COPIES: *OONL (TX603 H56 1940z copy 1)
NOTES: Claire Abbott is named director in this edition. Calgary city directories list Abbott as stenographer with the gas company in the volumes for 1940 and 1941, and dietitian in 1942. According to *Western Favourites,* she was director for only a few months in 1942. The recipes are the same as A83.3.

A83.5   nd [about 1944–5]
—Home canning / Recipes tested and compiled / by the / Home Service Dept. / Marianne E. ['L' handwritten in black ink]innell, B.Sc. / Director / With the compliments of / Northwestern Utilities Limited / Phone 22121
DESCRIPTION: 23.5 × 15.0 cm   Pp [1–4] 5–39 [40]   Illus on pp 6–7 of jar types; on p 11 of a woman peeling fruit(?); on p 23 of jelly test   Lacks paper binding; stapled
CONTENTS: 1 tp; 2 blank; 3 table of contents; 4 blank; 5–39 text; 40 [outside back face of binding] 'John D. McAra, printer, Calgary.'
COPIES: *Private collection
NOTES: 'Wartime Jam and Jelly Recipes' are on pp 38–9, indicating a publication date during the Second World War. The book was published no earlier than 1944, the year that Marianne Linnell joined Northwestern Utilities in Edmonton, and no later than 1945, the year she moved to Vancouver. On p 1, the first letter of her last name has been rubbed out and corrected by hand to read Linnell. See B128.1, under Adams, Miss Edith, for books published during Linnell's time at the *Vancouver Sun*'s Edith Adams Cottage and for biographical information about her.

A83.6   nd [about 1947]
—Home canning / Recipes tested and compiled / by the / Home Service Dept. / Margaret Dulmage, B.H.Sc. / Director / With the compliments of / Northwestern Utilities Limited / Phone 22121

COPIES: *Private collection

NOTES: The 1947 Edmonton city directory lists Mrs H.M. Dulmage, dietitian, Northwestern Utilities; her name and position do not appear in earlier or later volumes. The list of 'Edmonton Staffing' in the Atco Gas archives records her as assistant in 1946 and director in 1947. The last section in the 'Table of Contents' is 'Sugar Saving Jams and Jellies' starting on p 37.

A83.7   nd [about 1949]
—Home canning / Recipes tested and compiled / by the / Home Service Dept. / Elizabeth McCaffrey, B.Sc. / Director / With the compliments of / your gas company – Calgary / Phone R2091

DESCRIPTION: Paper, with image on front of a gas flame against a fruit-and-vegetable pattern

COPIES: *ACG

NOTES: The front face of the binding is inscribed with the date 'June 1949,' the possible date of publication, although McCaffrey had been director since 1946. There was another edition bearing McCaffrey's name, but it has the printed date 1950 (see 'Other editions').

OTHER EDITIONS: *Home Canning ... Elizabeth McCaffrey Director 1950*, compliments of Canadian Western Natural Gas Co. Ltd, Calgary (ACG, OONL); *Home Canning ... Doreen Thomson, B.Sc. Director 1950*, compliments of Northwestern Utilities Ltd, Edmonton (AEAG); *Home Canning ... Doreen Thomson, B.Sc. Director 1951*, compliments of Northwestern Utilities Ltd, Edmonton (Bookseller's stock); *Home Canning*, [no named director], compliments of Canadian Western Natural Gas Co. Ltd, Calgary, nd [1950s], pp 61 (Canadian Western Natural Gas corporate archives, Calgary).

1936

Recipes

A84.1   1936
Recipes / 1936 / Ladies Aid / of / Spring Bank United Church [cover-title]

DESCRIPTION: 16.0 × 11.5 cm   Pp 1–80   Illus   Paper; stapled

CONTENTS: 1 'Members of Ladies' Aid Spring Bank United Church'; 2 'Recipe for Preserving Children'; 3–79 recipes credited with the name of the contributor and ads; 80 'Index' and a thank-you to advertisers

COPIES: *ACG

1936–9

Alberta sugar makes 'delicious' things to eat

See A69.1 for information about Canadian Sugar Factories Ltd and its cookbooks.

A85.1   nd [about 1936–9]
Alberta / sugar / makes / "delicious" / things to eat [cover-title]

DESCRIPTION: 16.5 × 11.5 cm   Pp [1] 2–24   Illus brown-and-yellow   Paper, with image on front of a woman measuring sugar into a spoon; stapled

CONTENTS: Inside front face of binding 'Index' [i.e., table of contents]; 1 'Foreword'; 2 'Hints for Successful Preserving'; 3–4 'Preserves'; 5–7 'Jams and Jellies'; 8–10 'Cakes and Pies'; 11 'Cookies'; 12–13 'The Story of Alberta Sugar'; 14–16 'Frostings and Icings'; 17–20 'Candies, Confections'; 21–2 'Vegetables'; 23 'Pie Fillings'; 24 'Pudding Sauces'; inside back face 'Alberta Sugar Is Now Produced at These Two Alberta Factories' and illus of factories at Raymond and Picture Butte

COPIES: OONL (TX819 S94 A53 1930z, 2 copies) OOWM (984.91.1)   *SBIM

NOTES: The publisher's name, Canadian Sugar Factories Ltd, Raymond, Alberta, is visible on illustrations of bags of the sugar; for example, on the front face of the binding and on p 4. The 'Foreword' states, 'Pure Alberta Sugar has been used with complete success by Western Canadian housewives for more than ten years ... This new edition of exclusive recipes, has been prepared by leading dieticians ...' The book was likely published about 1936–9 since there is a reference on p 12 to Alberta Sugar having been 'grown and manufactured since 1925' (1925 + 'more than ten years' = 1936 or later). 'The Story of Alberta Sugar,' p 12, states that the two factories in Raymond and Picture Butte together 'transform over 200,000 tons of sugar beets [from over one thousand farms] into over 60,000,000 lbs. of Pure Alberta Sugar every year.' Since the Picture Butte plant was built to process the 1936 crop, the cookbook was published after the opening of the plant. The appearance of the book confirms a publication date in the second half of the 1930s.

1937

Consort United Church Ladies' Aid cook book

A86.1 nd [about 1937]
Consort / United Church Ladies' Aid / cook book [cover-title]
DESCRIPTION: 22.0 × 15.0 cm   Pp 1–42   Paper; stapled
CONTENTS: 1–42 recipes credited with the name of the contributor and ads
COPIES: AEPMA   *Private collection
NOTES: The printer is on the outside back face of the binding: 'Printed by "The Enterprise" Consort, Alta.' The section on 'Meats and Miscellaneous Dishes,' on pp 22–3, includes the following large-quantity recipes: Beef Cure for 12 lbs.; Dry Cure for Pork (for 100 lbs of meat); and Egg Preservative for 14 Dozen Eggs. The private collector's copy is inscribed on the binding, by the present owner's mother, 'Greta Ure' (Mrs Greta A. Ure, née Isaac). Greta, who grew up in Consort, married in 1937, and this cookbook may have been a bridal shower gift.

Cook book

A87.1 1937
[Captions to portraits:] King George VI. Queen Elizabeth / Coronation, May 12th, 1937 / Cook book / Compiled by / Young Women's Auxiliary / Medicine Hat Presbyterial of the / United Church of Canada. [cover-title]
DESCRIPTION: 22.0 × 15.0 cm   Pp [1–6] 7–50 [51–2]   Paper, with portraits on front of King George VI and Queen Elizabeth, and image of crossed flags; stapled
CONTENTS: 1 'A Recipe for a Happy Day' [poem]; 2–4 'Index to Recipes'; 5–6 ads; 7–50 recipes credited with the name of the contributor and ads; 51 blank for 'Memorandum'; 52 'Weights and Measures' and 'E.N. Dowson, printer, Medicine Hat, Alta.'
COPIES: *ACG   AMHM
NOTES: The running head is 'Coronation Cook Book.'

1938

Billingsgate fish facts

Recipes from Billingsgate Fish Co. are in A76.1, Seen through the Pantry Keyhole. *See that entry for the company history.*

A88.1 [copyright 1938]
Billingsgate / fish / facts / With the compliments of / the Billingsgate Fish Company / Calgary, Alberta, Canada / 222-8th Ave., E. / Phone M 1089 / and / 107-7th Ave., W. / Phone M 9230 [cover-title]
DESCRIPTION: 18.5 × 10.0 cm   Pp 1–32   Paper, with image on front of a fishing boat and net; stapled
CONTENTS: Inside front face of binding 'Why Fish Is a Health-Building Food'; top 1 'Why You Should Eat Plenty of Fish'; mid 1–mid 2 'How to Buy Fish'; mid–bottom 2 'How to Serve Fish'; 3 'Practical Fish Guide'; 4 'How to Dress Fish for Cooking'; top 5 'Hints on Cooking Fish'; mid 5–inside back face recipes under headings for 'Fried Fish,' 'Boiled Fish,' 'Baked Fish,' 'Broiled Fish,' 'Flaked Fish Recipes,' 'Fish Soups,' 'Oysters,' 'Clams,' 'Lobsters,' 'Crabs,' 'Shrimp,' 'Scallops,' 'Sauces,' and 'Fish Stuffings'
COPIES: *OONL (TX747 B55 1936 p***)
NOTES: Printed on the outside back face of the binding is 'Copyright 1938 Ronald Lichter // Made in U.S.A.' and the printer's name, 'Lawson & Jones, Ltd., London, Canada.' The text is printed in green. The order of publication of A88.1 and A88.2 is unknown.

A88.2 [copyright 1936 or 1938?]
—Fish / facts / Silverstein's / Where they specialize in / lake and sea foods / [on label that conceals previous address, which begins, '135 [street name illegible]':] 54 Market St. Phone 801 [cover-title]
DESCRIPTION: 18.5 × 10.0 cm   Pp 1–32   Paper, with image on front of a boat and net; stapled
CONTENTS: Inside front face of binding 'Why Fish Is a Health-Building Food'; top 1 'Why You Should Eat Plenty of Fish'; mid 1–mid 2 'How to Buy Fish'; mid–bottom 2 'How to Serve Fish'; 3 'Practical Fish Guide'; 4 'How to Dress Fish for Cooking'; top 5 'Hints on Cooking Fish'; mid 5–inside back face recipes under headings for 'Fried Fish,' 'Boiled Fish,' 'Baked Fish,' 'Broiled Fish,' 'Flaked Fish Recipes,' 'Fish Soups,' 'Oysters,' 'Clams,' 'Lobsters,' 'Crabs,' 'Shrimp,' 'Scallops,' 'Sauces,' and 'Fish Stuffings'
COPIES: *Private collection
NOTES: 'Copyright 193[unclear, 6 or 8?] Ronald Lichter Printed in U.S.A.' is on the outside back face of the binding. The text is printed in green.

1939

Tested recipes

A89.1 1939
Tested recipes / By / Little Red Deer / Dorcas Society / 1912–1939 / [artist's signature:] M. Thomson [cover-title]
DESCRIPTION: 28.0 × 21.5 cm Pp [i–iv], 1–32 Illus chapter heads Paper, with image on front of a house in a landscape; stapled
CONTENTS: i 'This book is dedicated to all the good cooks in the Dorcas Society and especially to the memory of our first beloved President: Mrs. Anne Calder and to the women associated with her in founding the society in 1912: [list of ten names]'; ii blank; iii 'Little Red Deer Dorcas Society' by Marie Travers Briggs; iv blank; 1–32 recipes
COPIES: *ARDA
NOTES: The history of the Little Red Deer Dorcas Society on p iii names the members of the cookbook committee: Mrs Margaret Thompson, Mrs Bertha Lind, Miss Isobel MacDougall, and Miss Minnie Mackay.

1939–42

Cook book

A90.1 nd [about 1939–42]
Cook book / Dog Pound Branch / Canadian Red Cross / Alberta [cover-title]
DESCRIPTION: 23.0 × 15.0 cm Pp [1] 2–32 Paper, with image on front of a woman watching milk pouring from a giant milk bottle into a mixing bowl; stapled
CONTENTS: 1 'Sugar Substitute' and ad; 2–32 recipes and ads
COPIES: AHRMH *BKOM OONL (TX715.6 C6565 1940z)
NOTES: The cookbook was published during the Second World War, likely in the period before rationing was first introduced in April 1942. An advertisement on the inside back face of the binding states, 'During the critical times upon which we, as Canadians have entered, we must expect more and more shortages of very essential goods.' Page 1 tells how to use honey as a sugar substitute. The advertisements are for businesses in Calgary, Crossfield, Madden, Cremona, Bottrel, and other Alberta towns.

1939–45

Menu magic

For an earlier cookbook from the same business, then called McGavin Ltd, and for information about the company, see A54.1.

A91.1 nd [about 1939–45]
Menu magic / McGavin's Bakeries [cover-title]
DESCRIPTION: 9.0 × 14.5 cm Pp 1–20 Illus col Very thin card, with image on front of a stylized magic lamp (like Aladdin's) emitting smoke within which the short-title is printed; stapled
CONTENTS: 1 'Contents'; 2–6 recipes; 7–10 'Decorative Tables for All Occasions'; 11–13 'Menus'; 14 'Household Hints'; 15–19 recipes; 20 'Quick Bread Snacks'
COPIES: *Private collection
NOTES: No place of publication is recorded, but McGavin's Bakeries Ltd was based in Edmonton. *Menu Magic* was published during the Second World War: 'Bread to the Fore!' on the inside front face of the binding states, '... we hope this booklet proves ... no small contribution to war-time cookery.'

Parker, Pats

A92.1 nd [about 1939–45]
[Part of title likely obscured by pl col mounted at top edge] Cook / book / Compiled by / Pats Parker / from home-tested / recipes contributed / by the / housewives / of Alberta [cover-title]
DESCRIPTION: 25.5 × 17.0 cm Pp [1–2] [3–4 lacking] 5–292 Fp portrait on p 2 of 'Pats Parker // Editor of CJCJ's Woman's Program,' small illus chapter heads Cloth, with two pls col: one (8.2 × 14.3 cm) mounted at top edge, featuring a Union Jack, an airplane, IODE symbol, and the phrase '"Help win the war"'; the other (2.1 × 14.3 cm) mounted at bottom edge, with phrase '"For King and Empire"'; the top plate obscures the image of what is likely a radio transmission tower
CONTENTS: 1 'Your Cook Book' by Wilma Ohler, Carmangay [poem beginning, 'I'm Alberta's Cook Book, / You housewives did suggest.']; 2 portrait of Pats Parker; 3–4 lacking; 5–6 ads; 7–270 recipes credited with the name of the contributor; 271–4 'Miscellaneous Helps and Recipes'; 275–92 'Short Cuts for Busy Housewives'
COPIES: *BKOM OONL (TX715.6 C19 1900z)

NOTES: The running head is 'Radio Recipes.' The OONL copy is bound in paper, with an image on front of a radio transmission tower. The cover-title is 'CJCJ's Radio Cook Book.' The pagination runs [1–2] 3–292. Advertisements are on p 3; the table of contents, on p 4.

Tested recipes

A93.1   nd [about 1939–45]
[An edition of *Tested Recipes* compiled by the Red Cross Society of Wainwright and District, Wainwright, Alta: 'Star' Job Print, nd, cover-title: 'Selected Recipes,' pp 71]
COPIES: OGU (CCC TX715.6 T4623)
NOTES: An advertisement exhorts the reader to 'Send the boys over there,' indicating publication during wartime – the Second World War from other evidence. There are Ukrainian recipes for 'Haloopsie' and Cabbage Rolls, and recipes for Cornish Pasties, Date Duff, Carrot Pudding, Saskatoon Pie, Butter Tarts, and Short Bread (five versions).

1940s

Cook book

Central Church of Christ (Disciples) was at 702 15th Avenue West from the 1920s to the 1960s.

A94.1   nd [1940s]
Cook book / Compiled by / the Alpha Girls' Club
DESCRIPTION: With photograph on front of Central Church of Christ (Disciples), 702 15th Avenue West, Calgary; stapled
COPIES: *AC (Pam file 641.5971 Cen)
NOTES: The book has 51 pp.

1941

Tested recipes

A95.1   nd
Tested / recipes / Edited by / St. Josaphat's Ladies' Auxiliary / Edmonton, Alberta [cover-title]
DESCRIPTION: 23.0 × 15.0 cm   Pp [1–2] 3–104   Paper, with small image on front of a manservant carrying a covered dish; stapled
CONTENTS: 1 'A cook book containing recipes tested and proven by the Ukrainian Ladies' Good Will Or-

ganization and friends. Edmonton, Alberta, Canada' and list of nine committee members: Mrs F. Montaine, Mrs M. Sawchukevich, Mrs M. Melnychuk, Mrs A. Pryma, Mrs A. Demco, Mrs E. Zarski, Mrs E. Swistowich, Mrs M. Basarab, and Mrs O. Esaiw; 2 ad; 3 'An Appreciation' thanking recipe contributors, advertisers, and individuals who made cash donations [list of eleven names]; 4 ads; 5–8 'Bread, Rolls, etc.' and ads; 9–27 'Cakes' and ads; 28–top 45 'Cookies' and ads; mid 45–46 'Soups' and ad; 47–8 'Fish'; 49–51 'Meat Dishes' and ads; 52–4 'Supper Dishes' and ad; 55–6 'Vegetables'; 57–8 'Fruit and Vegetable Salads' and ad; 59–61 'Desserts and Puddings' and ad; 62–4 'Pies' and ads; 65–77 'Pickles' and ads; 78 'Sandwiches' and ad; 79–80 'Jams and Marmalades' and ad; 81–2 'Canning' and ad; 83–top 86 'War Time Recipes' and ad; mid–bottom 86 'Beverages' and ad; 87–93 'National Recipes' and ads; 94–7 'Ukrainian Christmas Eve Dinner' and ads; 98 ad; 99–103 'Household Hints' and ads; 104 'Index' [i.e., table of contents]
COPIES: *OGU (CCC TX715.6 T459)
NOTES: There are many Ukrainian recipes, credited with the contributor's name. There are also recipes identified as Czech, Hungarian, Slovak, and Jewish.

The donor of the OGU copy reports the following publishing history for *Tested Recipes,* presumably taken from a later edition in her possession: 'Composed by the Goodwill Club – U.C.W.L.C. [i.e., Ukrainian Catholic Women's League of Canada] Printed by Ukrainian News in Edmonton // Printed in 1941 – 5000 copies // Three other editions followed. Sold throughout Can., U.S.A. and England.' A95.1 or A95.2 may be the first edition of 1941. The only numbered editions are the third and fourth.

A95.2   nd
—Tested / recipes / Edited by / St. Josaphat's Ladies' Auxiliary / Edmonton, Alberta [cover-title]
DESCRIPTION: Pp [1–2] 3–108   Paper, with small image on front of a manservant carrying a covered dish; stapled
CONTENTS: 1 'A cook book containing recipes tested and proven by the Ukrainian Ladies' Good Will Organization and friends. Edmonton, Alberta, Canada' and list of seven committee members: Mrs Geo. Woytkiw, Mrs F. Montaine, Mrs M. Sawchukevich, Mrs Wm Sereda, Mrs G. Skwarok, Mrs M. Luchkovich, and Mrs J. Baron; 2 ad; 3 'An Appreciation' thanking recipe contributors, advertisers, and individuals who made cash donations [list of twelve names]; 4 ad; 5 recipes for 'Bread, Rolls, etc.' credited with the name of the contributor; ...; 106 ad; 107 'Index' [i.e., table of

contents]; 108 blank for 'Memoranda'
COPIES: *Private collection
NOTES: The 'Index' lists 'Greek Easter Dinner' on pp 100–1.

A95.3   3rd ed., nd [about 1954]
—Tested / recipes / Third edition / Published by / Ukrainian Catholic Ladies' Goodwill [sic] Club / of St. Josaphat's Parish / Edmonton, Alberta [cover-title]
DESCRIPTION: Illus on p 2 of the church   Paper, with small image on front of a manservant carrying a covered dish
CONTENTS: 1 'A cook book containing recipes tested and proven by the Ukrainian Ladies' Good Will Organization and friends. Edmonton, Alberta, Canada' and list of ten committee members: Mrs T. Petaske, Mrs P. Greszchuk, Mrs M. Sawchukewich (only this edition has this spelling), Mrs J. Pryma, Mrs H. Demco, Mrs P. Swist, Mrs J. Baron, Mrs G. Woytkiw, Mrs J. Melnychuk, and Mrs O. Zarsky, and note that additional copies available from Mrs J. Melnychuk; 2 illus of the church and Ukrainian text; 3 'An Appreciation'; ...
COPIES: *Bookseller's stock   Private collection
NOTES: There is an advertisement on p 106 for Dominion Furriers, 'in business 20 years.' The first reference found in city directories was for Dominion Fur, exporters, in *Henderson's Greater Edmonton Directory 1934,* which suggests publication of the third edition in about 1954 (1934 + 20 years).

A95.4   4th ed., nd [1950s]
—Tested / recipes / Fourth edition / Published by / Ukrainian Catholic Ladies' Goodwill [sic] Club / of St. Josaphat's Parish / Edmonton, Alberta [cover-title]
DESCRIPTION: 23.0 × 15.5 cm   Pp [1] 2–129 [130]   Illus on p 2 of the church   Paper, with small image on front of a manservant carrying a covered dish; stapled
CONTENTS: 1 'A cook book containing recipes tested and proven by the Ukrainian Ladies' Good Will Organization and friends. Edmonton, Alberta, Canada.' and list of sixteen committee members: Mrs J. Semkow, Mrs P. Swist, Mrs M. Burtnick, Mrs T. Petaske, Mrs W. Sereda, Mrs T. Koziak, Mrs J. Krywko, Mrs J. Pryma, Mrs M. Basarab, Mrs P. Walusko, Mrs O. Zarsky, Mrs E. Wolansky, Mrs J. Starko, Mrs L. Melnychuk, Mrs M. Demco, and Mrs M. Muzyka, and 'For additional copies: Mrs. T. Koziak, 11708–135B Street // Edmonton Alberta'; 2 illus of the church and Ukrainian text; 3 'In Appreciation'; 4 'Recipe for Happiness in the New Year'; 5–17 'Breads, Rolls, etc.'

and ads; 18–47 'Cakes' and ads; 48–9 'Icings' and ad; 50–mid 68 'Cookies'; mid 68–76 'Desserts & Puddings' and ads; 77–8 'Soups' and ad; 79–92 'Meats' and ads; 93–5 'Fish'; 96–9 'Salads' and ad; 100–2 'Appetizers'; 103–mid 109 'Pickles'; mid 109–top 111 'Jams & Marmalades'; mid 111–mid 112 'Canning'; mid 112–115 'Ukrainian Christmas Eve Supper'; 116 ad; 117–21 'National Recipes'; 122 ad; 123–7 'Miscellaneous' and ad; 128 'Weights and Measures Chart'; 129 'Household Hints'; 130 'Index' [i.e., table of contents]
COPIES: *OONL (TX715.6 T468 1940z)
NOTES: The OONL copy has an errata slip and handwritten corrections. The recipes are credited with the name of the contributor.

1941–2

Recipes and penny stretchers

The Canadian Daughters League was founded in 1923.

A96.1   nd [about 1941–2]
Recipes / and / penny stretchers / [Canadian Daughters League symbol] / From CJCAV Good Morning / [Neighbor?] Programme [cover-title]
CITATIONS: Veronica Hill, 'Canadian Daughters League Cookbook Offers Penny-Stretching Tips,' web site of the *Daily Press*, Victorville, California, 30 June 2002, illus (http://www.vvdailypress.com/food/vintage/canadian/)
COPIES: *Private collection
NOTES: The web site text says that the cookbook was published in Edmonton.

1942

Richards, Vera D.

Vera D. Richards is almost certainly the same person as Mrs Vera Richards MacDonald (Mrs Vincent MacDonald), supervisor of women's extension work, Alberta Department of Agriculture, who contributed 'Cheese Recipes' to A104.1, Farm Cheesemaking. *Vera Richards MacDonald also wrote* The Salad Bowl, *cited as a new publication, Bulletin 57, in* Annual Report *of the Department of Agriculture of the Province of Alberta for the Year 1942 (too few pages for inclusion in this bibliography). Cole/Larmour, p 49, state that Vera Macdonald [sic] was appointed head of the Women's Extension Program in 1940. If Vera D. Richards is Vera Richards MacDonald, it is odd that her position with the*

Women's Extension Program is not mentioned in Honey Helpings.

Mrs Vincent MacDonald was still living in Edmonton in 1955. There is no record of her in the Edmonton cemetery listings, but BVIPA records Vera MacDonald and Vincent MacDonald dying in British Columbia in 1979, Vera at the age of seventy-nine.

For the titles of other cookbooks published by the Alberta Department of Agriculture, see A36.1.

A97.1   nd [1942]
Honey helpings / By / Vera D. Richards / Issued by direction of / Hon. D.B. MacMillan / Minister of Agriculture / Agricultural Extension Service / Department of Agriculture / Edmonton, Alberta [cover-title]
DESCRIPTION: 11.5 × 11.0 cm [leaves trimmed to form a circular shape]   Pp [1–16]   Paper, with image on front of a beehive; stapled
CONTENTS: 1 cover-title; 2 'Honey Helpings' [general information about using honey]; 3–16 [outside back face of binding] recipes and at bottom p 16, 'Produce your own honey! Write for "Beekeeping for Beginners" from Agricultural Extension Service, ...'
COPIES: *AEPMA
NOTES: *Honey Helpings* is listed as a 'special leaflet' (no author named) in *Annual Report of the Department of Agriculture of the Province of Alberta for the Year 1942*, Edmonton: 1943, p 66 (along with *Canning and Preserving with Honey*, which I have not seen). D. Bruce MacMillan, named in the cover-title, was minister of agriculture from December 1940 to 1947.

1942–5

Wartime recipes and food rules

A98.1   nd [about 1942–5]
Wartime / recipes / and / food rules / V [i.e., for victory] / Woodland Dairy Limited / Edmonton, Alberta
DESCRIPTION: 20.0 × 13.0 cm   Pp [1] 2–36   Paper, with image on front, within a giant letter V, of a hand stirring the contents of a bowl; stapled
CONTENTS: 1 tp; 2 'Foreword' signed Woodland Dairy Ltd, Edmonton, Alberta; 3–4 'Food Rules' by Dr L.B. Pett, director, Nutrition Services, Department of Pensions and National Health; 5–16, 21–35 'Wartime Recipes' prepared by Consumer Section, Marketing Service, Department of Agriculture, Ottawa; 17 'Milk and Dairy Products Are in the Front Line of Canada's

Nutrition Program'; 18–19 'Food for Health' by Dr L.B. Pett; 20 'Tips to Save Sugar'; 36 blank for 'Memoranda'
COPIES: OONL (TX715.6 W663 1940 p***)   *Private collection
NOTES: The 'Foreword' states: 'This booklet ... has been issued with the co-operation of Dr. L.B. Pett, Director of Nutrition Services of the Department of National Pensions and Health, and Miss Laura Pepper, Chief of the Consumer Section, Marketing Service, of the Department of Agriculture. The purpose ... is to assist housewives in the task of adjusting their menus to wartime conditions. The recipes have all been prepared by Miss Pepper, or under her direction, to fit into the national nutrition program.' There is a reference on p 20 to 'your sugar ration,' which indicates a publication date of April 1942 or later. Canada's 'Official Food Rules' were introduced to the public in 1942. 'Commercial Printers Ltd. Edmonton' is on the outside back face of the binding. The design of the binding features the patriotic colours of red, blue, and white. For information about Pepper and cookbooks by her, see O676.1, *Milk Desserts*.

1943

Cook book

A99.1   1943
Cook book / Presented by / the Women's Auxiliary of the 8th Group / Boy Scout Parent Association / Calgary – Alberta / June, 1943 / Price 25 cents [cover-title]
DESCRIPTION: 15.5 × 10.0 cm   Pp [1–2] 3–60   Paper; stapled
CONTENTS: 1 list of Women's Auxiliary executive including the cook book conveners, Mrs R.W. Holmes and Mrs A. Stephen, and note about the Boy Scouts signed C.R. Patterson, DC; 2 blank; 3 'When It's Honey,' 'When It's Molasses or Maple Syrup,' and 'When It's Corn Syrup'; 4 'Know Your Measurements?' and 'Index' [i.e., table of contents]; 5–60 recipes credited with the name of the contributor and ads
COPIES: *Private collection
NOTES: 'West Printing Co., Limited Calgary Canada' is on the outside back face of the binding. Honey, molasses, maple syrup, and corn syrup were used as substitutes for sugar during the Second World War.

Cook to win

A100.1 1943
Cook to win / Compiled by / the "Good Cheer Club" / of Wesley United Church / First published – April, 1943 / Calgary, Alberta, / Canada
DESCRIPTION: 22.5 × 15.0 cm   Pp [1] 2–112   Tp illus of a woman pointing to a 'Family Nutrition Chart,' illus chapter heads   Paper, with image on front of four flags; stapled
CONTENTS: Inside front face of binding 'Contents' [i.e., alphabetical list of headings] and the book's price, $0.50; 1 tp; 2 ads; 3 'Foreword' signed Good Cheer Club of Wesley United Church; 4 'Canada's Official Food Rules Outlined'; 5 'War Pudding' by permission of Princess Alice; 6 ads; 7 'Good Health and Your Diet' signed Mrs Kenneth Seaborne, nutritionist, Calgary Branch, Canadian Red Cross; 8 ad; 9 'Where to Find Your Vitamins'; 10 ads; 11–107 recipes and ads; 108 'Notes from the Blood Donor Clinic,' 'Health Porridge,' and ad; 109–10 ads; 111–12 'Household Hints'
CITATIONS: Ferguson/Fraser, p 234
COPIES: AC (Pam file 641.5971 Coo)   ACG   *ACU   ARDA   BTCA (77.75)   OONL (TX715.6 C66735 1943)   Private collection
NOTES: The 'Foreword' describes the purpose of the cookbook: 'You [the housewives of Alberta] have so cheerfully accepted wartime restrictions already imposed, and are willing to accept the challenge of further rationing. The pioneer spirit that is your Western inheritance will see your families well nourished and happy no matter what the future holds. To that end the Good Cheer Club has compiled this cookbook.' Princess Alice's War Pudding was a potato-and-treacle mixture. The 'Meat Stretchers' section starts with the recipe Serve Stew to Your Company, courtesy of Mrs Nellie L. McClung, i.e., the advocate for women's rights and one of the 'Famous Five' who, in 1929, won the Persons Case. There are recipes for Large Victory Cake, Victory Roast, and Victory Meat Loaf; and several recipes are sugarless and eggless. Aphorisms are printed at the bottom of many text pages, such as 'Fats in the garbage won't win the war' and 'Saving bones is a terrible chore, but better than the War at your door.'

GWG household handbook

A101.1 [1943]
GWG / household / handbook / Recipes / home information / handy tables / breeding records / clothing / catalog / G.W. West & Son / Innisfail Alberta [cover-title]
DESCRIPTION: 22.5 × 15.0 cm   Pp [1] 2–63 [64]   Illus   Paper; stapled, and with hole punched at top left corner for hanging
CONTENTS: Inside front face of binding 'Price Ceiling,' 'Style Changes,' and 'Where No Price Is Quoted'; 1 'GWG Household Handbook' [introduction]; 2–3 'Food for Health'; 4–15 'Home-Tested Recipes'; 16 'Household Hints'; 17–48 lacking; 49–52 'Facts for Farmers'; 53–6 'Feeding of Dairy Cows' and information about feed for lambs and horses; 57–1st column 58 'Household Hints'; 2nd column 58–top 60 information about feeding poultry; near top–bottom 60 'Shampoo Rugs'; 61–4 tables for recording crops, eggs, and stock breeding; inside back face 'Contents'; outside back face calendar for 1943
COPIES: *ABOM
NOTES: The initials GWG stand for Great Western Garment Co. Ltd. The text on p 1 says that the first sixteen pages are information for women; the last sixteen pages are for the farmer; and the intervening pages (lacking in this copy) 'display in full color some of the garments manufactured by Great Western Garment Company Limited for Western Canadians.'

Henderson, Mrs Margaret

For information about Burns and Co., see A31.1.

A102.1 nd [about 1943]
How to save / in your kitchen / Burns' tested wartime recipes & thrift hints [cover-title]
DESCRIPTION: 21.0 × 15.0 cm   Pp [1] 2–24   Illus portrait on p 1 of the author, illus of prepared dishes   Paper, with image on front of a tray of food (Spork, cauliflower, and peas); stapled
CONTENTS: 1 'Introduction,' note about Mrs Margaret Henderson and her image, and 'Burns & Co. Limited'; 2–20 recipes; 21–4 'Thrifty Hints to Help You Save in Kitchen and Home'
COPIES: *Bookseller's stock
NOTES: The cookbook promotes the use of Burns and Co.'s products, especially Spork, canned spiced pork described as 'the new meat sensation of the day.' The

'Introduction' states that '[t]he contents of this book were prepared by Mrs. Margaret Henderson.' Evidence of the date of publication is in the caption to her portrait: 'Mrs. Henderson has been Director of the Modern Kitchen of the Vancouver Daily Province since its inception eight years ago.' Since the Modern Kitchen began in 1935, *How to Save in Your Kitchen* was published in about 1943 (1935 + 8 years) (for information about Henderson and the Modern Kitchen, see B104.1). No place of publication is recorded, but Burns and Co.'s head office was in Calgary.

Tested recipes

A103.1 1943

[Running head:] Alliance Ladies' Aid – cook book – 1943 / [title:] Tested recipes / Compiled by / the Ladies' Aid of / Alliance United Church / 1943 / Page 1

CONTENTS: 1 tp; 2 blank; 3 'A Note of Appreciation'; 4 'Index to Recipes' [i.e., table of contents listing section headings, which run alphabetically fom 'Breads and Buns' to 'Supper Dishes']; 5–40 recipes credited with the name of the contributor and ads; 41 ad; 42–7 blank for 'Additional Recipes'

COPIES: *Private collection

NOTES: 'Printed at the office of "The Enterprise" Alliance, Alberta' is on the outside back face of the binding. An advertisement for the *Enterprise*, run by R.E. Matthews, is on p 40.

1945

Alberta, Department of Agriculture, and University of Alberta

For the titles of other cookbooks published by the Alberta Department of Agriculture, see A36.1.

A104.1 1945

Joint Series / Publication No. 5 / Province of Alberta / Department of Agriculture / June, 1945 / University of Alberta / Faculty of Agriculture / Farm cheesemaking / By / the staffs of / the Dairy Branch / Department of Agriculture / Edmonton / and / the Department of Dairying / University of Alberta / Edmonton / Authorized by / Hon. D.B. MacMillan / Minister of Agriculture / Prepared under the direction of / the Publications Committee / University of Alberta and Alberta Department of

Agriculture / Photographs by courtesy of / Publicity and Travel Bureau, Department of / Trade and Industry / Edmonton, Alberta

DESCRIPTION: 23.0 × 15.0 cm   Pp [3] 4–23 Illus Paper, with image on front of four plates of cheese; stapled

CONTENTS: 3 tp; 4 table of contents; 5 'Introduction'; top–mid 6 'Selecting the Milk'; bottom 6–7 'Heat-Treatment of the Milk'; 8 'Setting or Coagulating the Milk' and 'Starters'; 9–top 13 'Soft Cheese'; near top 13–17 'Farm Dairy Cheese'; 18 'Nutritive Value of Cheese'; 19–mid 22 'Cheese Recipes by Vera Richards MacDonald, Supervisor of Women's Extension Work, Department of Agriculture'; mid–bottom 22 'Helpful Information'; 23 [inside back face of binding] 'Activities of the Department of Dairying // University of Alberta'; outside back face 'Activities of the Dairy Branch, Department of Agriculture' and at bottom, 'Edmonton: Printed by A. Shnitka, King's printer'

COPIES: *AEAG

NOTES: Vera D. Richards, author of A97.1, *Honey Helpings,* is likely the same person who contributed 'Cheese Recipes' on p 19. For information about her, see that entry.

1945–6

800 favorite recipes

Patricia Myers gives 1940 as the founding year of the CAVU Club (see her Sky Riders: An Illustrated History of Aviation in Alberta, 1906–1945, *Fifth House, 1995, p 143).*

A105.1 nd [about 1945–6]

C.A.V.U. Club / (Ceiling and Visibility Unlimited) / 800 / favorite recipes / The favorite recipes used by club members and their / friends

DESCRIPTION: Tp illus of an airplane   Paper, with image on front of a flying airplane seen against the Edmonton skyline; stapled

CONTENTS: 1 tp; 2 'Foreword' signed the CAVU Club, Mrs Frank English, recipe book convener; 3 'Club History'; 4 'Table of Contents'; 5 'Weights and Measures Chart'; 6 'Temperature Chart'; 7–108 recipes credited with the name of the contributor; 109 book-order coupons

COPIES: *Private collection (photocopy)

NOTES: According to the 'Club History,' this service club, registered under the War Charities Act, was organized in the early days of the war by a 'group of girls' connected with flying. They chose the name Ceiling and Visibility Unlimited Club because its short form, CAVU, was a welcome signal of good weather for their pilot husbands. The club's purpose was to provide mutual support to its members and to raise money for the war effort. The 'Club History' names the many charitable organizations that benefited from the club's fund-raising efforts and lists the club's executive and membership.

Mrs English's 'Foreword' indicates that the cookbook's date of publication was shortly after the end of the Second World War. She writes, 'Now that the war is over our thoughts turn naturally to those many unfortunate children who have been left fatherless in our midst and to those unhappy mothers with a double load to carry.' She goes on to say that the proceeds from the cookbook's sale will go to the club's Child Welfare Fund. 'Distributed by Sunland Biscuit Company' is on the front face of the binding, and readers were to send book-order coupons (on p 109) to CAVU Favorite Recipes Committee, c/o Sunland Biscuit Co., Edmonton, with $1.00 per copy requested. The cookbook title printed on the book-order coupons is 'C.A.V.U. Favorite Recipes.' In addition to the usual recipe sections, there are seasonal recipes in 'At Christmas,' pp 95–7, and recipes from other countries in 'Round the World with the Chef,' pp 98–108, such as Norwegian Fattig Mans Bakels and Gai Lan Soong. The striking cover design is reported to be printed in royal blue (the airplane) and orange (the sun streaks in the sky).

1945–7

Smart ways to make a cook's life sweeter

See A69.1 for information about the company and its cookbooks.

A106.1 nd [about 1945–7]
Smart ways / to make a / cook's life / sweeter / Published by / Canadian Sugar Factories Limited / Raymond, Alberta [cover-title]
DESCRIPTION: 16.5 × 11.5 cm   Pp 1–32   Illus   Paper, with image on front of a miniature male chef pouring granulated sugar to form the letters of the short-title; stapled
CONTENTS: Inside front face of binding index and at bottom, 'Recipes by: Mrs. Jane M. Wilson, Alberta Sugar Dietician'; 1 illus of the sugar refining plant at

Picture Butte; 2 'Why We Need Sugar'; 3–6 'Preserving and Canning'; 7–15 'Jellies, Conserves, Jams, Marmalades'; 16–17 'The Story of Alberta Sugar ...'; 18 'Alberta Sugar and Cane Sugar Are Identical'; 19–22 'Candy'; 23–8 'Cakes, Cookies, Icings, Sauces'; 29–31 blank for 'Extra Recipes'; 32 illus of 'The Parent Plant' at Raymond
COPIES: ARDA   OONL (AC901 C3 Pt 640 No. 523)   SWSLM   *Private collection
NOTES: 'The Story of Alberta Sugar,' p 16, states: 'Today, over 1,250 farms grow sugar beets under the ideal conditions of Southern Alberta. Their annual production of over 300,000 tons of sugar beets is transformed into ... well over 80,000,000 pounds [of sugar] annually.' The cookbook's date is uncertain, but it was likely published after the end of the Second World War and before the opening of the company's Taber plant in 1947 (the caption for the illustration of the Picture Butte plant, p 1, describes it as 'one of two [sugar refining plants] operated by the company; the other plant was in Raymond).

1945–8

Our favorite recipes

A107.1 nd [about 1945–8]
Our / favorite / recipes / First Auxiliary / First Presbyterian Church
DESCRIPTION: 22.5 × 15.0 cm   Pp [1–2] 3–104   Paper; stapled
CONTENTS: 1 tp; 2 table of contents; 3–104 recipes, most credited with the name of the contributor, and ads
COPIES: *Private collection
NOTES: There is an advertisement for Mike's News Agency, on Jasper Avenue in Edmonton, 'your magazine store ... for more than 30 years.' Since the store is first listed in the Edmonton city directory for 1914 (under the same proprietor, John Michaels, but then called the Provincial News Co.), the cookbook was published in 1945 or later (1914 + 'more than 30 years'). In this copy, the recipe for English Fruit Cake on p 80 is annotated 'Xmas 1948.' The printer's name is on the outside back face of the binding: 'The Douglas Printing Co., Ltd., Edmonton, Alta.'

1945–9

The Alberta home maker

A108.1   nd
The Alberta / home maker [cover-title]
DESCRIPTION: 22.5 × 15.0 cm   Pp [1] 2–112   Paper, with image on front of the head and upper body of a woman holding a pencil(?) and a sheet of paper on which is written 'recipes for better eating,' and behind the woman, the shape of the province of Alberta; stapled
CONTENTS: 1 'In Appreciation' signed Mrs F.M. Baker, provincial president; 2 table of contents; 3–4 'Index to Household Hints' and ad; 5–mid 13 151 numbered 'Household Hints' and ads; mid–bottom 13 'Horticulture'; 14 'Beauty Hints,' 'Nutrition' signed Hon. Dr W.W. Cross, minister of public health and welfare, and 'Canada's Food Rules'; 15–111 recipes and ads; 112 'Weights and Measures' and 'Comparative Table for Thickeners'
CITATIONS: Gladys A. Willison, *Stars in Time: A History of the Alberta Social Credit Women's Auxiliaries*, Edmonton: 1973, p 22
COPIES: *OGU (CCC TX715.6 A43)
NOTES: Mrs Baker signs her 'Appreciation' on behalf of the Social Credit Women's Auxiliaries of Alberta, the compilers of the cookbook. The 'Household Hints' are featured prominently at the beginning of the book and cover a variety of topics, from cleaning and ironing, and lamps and lanterns, to furniture care and care of rubber bathing caps. The recipe section presents seasonal information for 'The Christmas Season' on pp 106–11, including a recipe on p 111 for Holiday Delight from Mrs Ernest Manning (née Muriel Preston), wife of Social Credit leader Ernest C. Manning, who served as premier of Alberta from 1943 to 1968. The meat recipes feature Alberta products; for example, Alberta Gold Medal Ranch Steak on p 29, Foothills Pot Roast on p 30, Outdoor Cooking – Alberta Steak on p 31, and Veal Albertan on p 32. There are also recipes of European origin, such as Perishki submitted by Mrs F. Hannochko, p 88, and To Keep Sauer Kraut Fresh submitted by Jennie Lopatka, p 28. The printer's name is on the back of the binding: 'The Douglas Printing Co. Limited, Edmonton.'

From appearances, *The Alberta Home Maker* was published in the late 1940s. Willison, p 22, pinpoints the date: 'One of the first [money-making projects of the SCWA] was "The Alberta Homemaker [*sic*]" ... It was ready for distribution at the Convention in November, 1947, priced at $1.00.' (This entry belongs on p 1076.)

OTHER EDITIONS: *The Alberta Homemaker: 450 Choice Recipes*, 2nd ed., Edmonton: Alberta Social Credit League, nd (Private collection); Muriel Manning wrote the 'Foreword,' where she states, 'So some years ago, as a service to all who are interested in good cooking, the Social Credit Women's Auxiliaries published the first edition of "The Alberta Homemaker [*sic*]", a collection of recipes and household hints for our Alberta women.'

Cook book

Cole/Larmour record founding dates for the branches of the Drumheller and Hand Hills Constituency that are slightly at odds with the dates in the cookbook: Drumheller, 1922–43 (p 126); Hand Hills, 1925–disbanded (p 127); Verdant Valley, 1912–about 1943, merged (p 131); Munson, 1912–current (p 129); Rosedale, 1922–71 (p 130); Horseshoe Canyon, 1921–81 (p 128); and Majestic–Farrell Lake (Delia), 1919–disbanded (p 128).

A109.1   nd [about 1945–9]
[Alberta Women's Institute symbol] / Cook book / Compiled by / Drumheller and Hand Hills Constituency / Women's Institute [cover-title]
COPIES: *Private collection
NOTES: In the 'Foreword,' Isabel J. Sharp, home economics convenor, offers a brief sketch of the activities of each of the five branches of the Drumheller–Hand Hills Constituency of the Alberta Women's Institute: Verdant Valley, organized in May 1912; Munson, December 1914; Rosedale, 1921; Horse Shoe Canyon, 1921; and Majestic–Farrell Lake, 1925. Her statement in the 'Foreword' is evidence that the cookbook was published after the Second World War: 'War-work, during both world conflicts, was carried on ...' The recipes are credited with the name of the contributor.

Leduc cook book

A110.1   nd [about 1945–9]
[Diamond-shape with each of the initials 'OORP' in one of four corners and BPOE elk head in centre] / Leduc / cook / boo[same 'k' as in 'cook'] [cover-title]
COPIES: *Private collection
NOTES: The book was produced by the Benevolent and Protective Order of Elks, Order of the Royal Purple, in Leduc.

Maguire, Mrs Vera C., née Walt (Midhurst, Ont., 31 August 1906–1 June 1987)

It was after marrying R. Wilbert Maguire, a beekeeper, in 1931, that Vera became involved in apiculture. From May 1947 to April 1958 (and possibly later) she wrote the 'Hello Folks' column in the Canadian Bee Journal (an Ontario beekeepers' publication), and she gave demonstrations about cooking with honey at fairs and Women's Institute meetings throughout Ontario. She was a force behind the Food Committee at the Barrie Fair and president of the Minesing Women's Institute. She had one son, Robert C. Maguire. In 1992, she was inducted into the Ontario Agricultural Hall of Fame.

A111.1 nd [about 1945–9]
Honey / Sunday 'n' Monday 'n' / all through / the week / Published by / Canadian Beekeepers' Council / Recipes edited and tested by / Mrs. Vera C. Maguire / Distributed by / Alberta Beekeepers' Association / Terrace Building, Edmonton
DESCRIPTION: 21.5 × 14.0 cm   Pp [1–4] 5–24   Paper; stapled
CONTENTS: 1 tp; 2 dedication 'to the homemakers'; 3 'Dear reader:' signed Vera; 4 'Some Rules That Will Simplify the Using of Honey'; 5–6 'Breakfast'; 7–10 'Dinner'; 11–15 'Supper or Lunch'; 16–17 'Toppings and Fillings'; 18–19 'Confections'; 20–1 'Canning'; 22–3 'Honey Sweet Beverages'; 24 'For Infants'
COPIES: *ACG   OONL (TX767 H7 H65 1940z copy 1)
NOTES: An edition 'distributed by the Ontario Beekeepers' Association, O.A.C., Guelph, Ontario,' surfaced as this bibliography went to press. Vera's reference on p 3 to 'sharing from the same meagre sugar bowl' indicates a publication date before sugar rationing ended in 1947, although her file at the Hall of Fame suggests the 1950s.

A111.2 nd [about 1945–9]
—Honey / Sunday 'n' Monday 'n' / all through / the week / Published by / Canadian Beekeepers' Council / Recipes edited and tested by / Mrs. Vera C. Maguire / Distributed by / Saskatchewan Honey Producers Co-operative / Fort Qu'Appelle, Saskatchewan
DESCRIPTION: 21.5 × 14.0 cm   Pp [1–4] 5–24   Paper; stapled
CONTENTS: 1 tp; 2 dedication 'to the homemakers'; 3 'Dear reader:' signed Vera; 4 'Some Rules That Will Simplify the Using of Honey'; 5–6 'Breakfast'; 7–10 'Dinner'; 11–15 'Supper or Lunch'; 16–17 'Toppings and Fillings'; 18–19 'Confections'; 20–1 'Canning'; 22–3 'Honey Sweet Beverages'; 24 'For Infants'
COPIES: *OONL (TX767 H7 H65 1940z copy 2)

1946

Cook book

The Fort Normandeau Chapter received its charter on 11 December 1946 and disbanded on 8 December 1952.

A112.1 nd [about 1946 or later]
Cook book / presented by / Imperial Order / Daughters of the Empire / [IODE symbol] / Fort Normandeau Chapter / Red Deer, Alberta [cover-title]
DESCRIPTION: 22.5 × 14.5 cm   Pp 1–72   Paper; stapled
CONTENTS: Inside front face of binding 'Index' and 'A Thank You Note' to the ladies of Red Deer who contributed recipes and to the advertisers; 1–69 recipes credited with the name of the contributor and ads; 70–1 ads; 72 'Her Day' [poem about a housewife's day] and ad
COPIES: *ARDA (3 copies)   Private collection
NOTES: From appearances, the cookbook was published in the 1940s, but no earlier than 1946, the year the chapter was founded.

Glenmore District Association cook book

A113.1 1946
Glenmore District / Association / cook book / 1946 / Compiled by the / ladies of the District [cover-title]
DESCRIPTION: 22.5 × 15.0 cm   Pp 1–92   Illus chapter heads   Paper; stapled
CONTENTS: Inside front face of binding table of contents; 1 'General Food and Kitchen Hints'; 2 ad; 3 'Foreword' signed Glenmore District Association; 4 ad; 5 'Canada's Official Health Rules'; 6 ads; 7–85 recipes and ads; 86 ad; 87–92 blank for manuscript recipes
COPIES: *ACG
NOTES: Glenmore is now part of the city of Calgary.

Hadassah cook book

A114.1 [1946]
Hadassah / cook / book / Edmonton Chapter of Hadassah / Tried and tested recipes [cover-title]
DESCRIPTION: 23.5 × 15.5 cm   Pp [1–2 torn out] 3–80   Photograph on p 3 of Mrs D.P. (Sarah) Gotlieb, Hadassah Western vice president, 1935–46 [i.e., the current vice president]   Card, with image on front of Star of David; stapled

CONTENTS: [1–2 lacking]; 3 photograph of Mrs D.P. Gotlieb, dedication of the cookbook to her, and 'Thank You' signed Mrs E. Wershof, cook book chairman, Edmonton Chapter of Hadassah; 4 ad; 5 'Contents' [i.e., alphabetical list of sections] and 'Greetings and Good Wishes to the Edmonton Chapter of Hadassah from [the names of various couples follow, for example, Mr and Mrs A. Brody, and Mr and Mrs M. Bornstein]; 6 ads; 7–79 recipes credited with the name of the contributor and ads; 80 'Table of Time, Weights and Measures'

COPIES: Bookseller's stock *Private collection

NOTES: The bookseller's copy retains the first leaf, which has the following printed on p 2: 'Greetings and Good Wishes to the Edmonton Chapter of Hadassah from [the names of various groups, for example, Rose Bricker Chapter of Hadassah, Vegreville, and Pioneer Women's Organization].' The bookseller reports that there is a short history of the Edmonton Chapter (presumably on p 1). 'Passover Cookery' is on pp 76–9. The printer's name is on the outside back face of the binding: 'The Metropolitan Printing Company Limited.'

1947

The Alberta home maker

See A108.1, which should be positioned here.

Hadassah cook book

A115.1   1947
Hadassah / cook book / Lillian Freiman Chapter / Medicine Hat – 1947 [cover-title]

DESCRIPTION: 23.0 × 15.5 cm   Pp 1–92   Very thin card; stapled

CONTENTS: 1 'Hadassah Cook Book // Lillian Freiman Chapter 1947 Medicine Hat, Alta.,' 'Contents,' and 'In Appreciation' signed Fanny Keel Veiner, president and cook book convenor; 2 'Greetings and Good Wishes to the Lillian Freiman Chapter of Hadassah // Medicine Hat' from various other Hadassah chapters; 3–89 recipes credited with the name of the contributor and ads; 90 'Greetings from' various named individuals, and ads; 91 'Household Hints'; 92 blank for 'Memorandum'

COPIES: *Bookseller's stock

NOTES: 'Holiday Recipes (Passover and Purim)' are on pp 81–4. The printer, 'News Print // Medicine Hat,' is on the outside back face of the binding.

The star cook book

A116.1   [April 1947]
The star cook book / Convened by: / Mrs. J.C. Leslie / Mrs. Harry Coombs / Mrs. Arthur Gregory / We ask you to patronize our advertis- /ers, who, through their help, have / made this book possible. / Index / Bread, buns and scones 3 / Cakes, icings and frostings 15 / Cookies 35 / Pastries, luncheon dishes 57 / Salads 67 / Marmalade, pickles and relishes 69 / Miscellaneous 72 / A woman's arm can work a charm / As well as woman's looks, / For though we praise her winsome ways, / She's fairest when she cooks.

DESCRIPTION: 15.0 × 10.0 cm   Pp [1–2] 3–74 [75–6] Paper, with image on front of a star; stapled

CONTENTS: 1 tp; 2 ad; 3–73 recipes and ads; 74 ads; 75–6 blank for 'Recipes – My Friends [sic] and My Own'

COPIES: *ACG

NOTES: The date of publication, April 1947, is on the front face of the binding. There is no indication of the sponsoring organization or of the place of publication; however, most of the recipes are contributed by Calgary residents.

1947–50

Chinese recipes

Rosedale Cleaners, named after its Calgary neighbourhood, belonged to two sons of Mr Ho Lem (c. 1870–1960, known by his last name only). Mr Ho Lem was the leader of Calgary's Chinese community from his arrival in the city in 1901, and was on the Board of Elders of Knox United Church, reputedly the first Chinese person in Canada to serve in this position. A record of the Service of Remembrance for Mr Ho Lem's son David, at Knox United Church in 2000, relates that in 1947 David returned to Calgary and with his brother George purchased the dry-cleaning shop. City directories for 1945–7 give Lloyd R. Sage as the owner; the directory for 1948 gives David Ho Lem.

A116a.1   nd [about 1947–50]
Chinese / recipes / [Chinese characters for:] Kitchen / book [cover-title]

DESCRIPTION: 11.5 × 7.0 cm   Pp [1–16]   Illus on inside front cover of a Chinese waitress and other Chinese images, such as a dragon, farmer in a rice paddy, and junks under sail   [Free, on outside back cover]   Very thin card; stapled

CONTENTS: Inside front cover 'This booklet is published through the courtesy of Rosedale Cleaners ... Three stores to serve you // 916-Centre St. N. // 832-16 Ave. N.W. // 712-2nd St. E. M6446'; 1 'This booklet is printed in this handy 3 × 5 inch size in order that it may fit into the average recipe card file.'; 2 How to Cook Rice; 3 Almond Chicken Chop Suey; 4 Tomato and Chicken; 5 Cantonese Shrimp; 6 Beef Chop Suey; 7 Sweet and Sour Spare Ribs; 8 Melon Soup and Chinese Greens Soup; 9 Fried Rice; 10 Fried Won Ton; 11 Won Ton Soup and Won Ton Noodles; 12 Chow Yuk; 13 Barbecued Spareribs; 14 Tomato Chicken Fritters; 15 Pineapple Chicken Fritters; 16 fp illus; inside back cover publ ad and 'Copies will be mailed to your friends upon request.'
COPIES: *ACG
NOTES: The record of David Ho Lem's Service of Remembrance states that Rosedale Cleaners' 'promotional trademark was a tiny bottle of soya sauce and a little Chinese cook book as a give-away to their customers.' A116a.1 is the free cookbook and likely the source of the Chinese recipes in A117.1. It was published no earlier than 1947, when the Ho Lem family acquired Rosedale Cleaners, and likely before 1951, when that year's city directory had a new address for one of the three stores.

Cook book

See A67.1, also by the Evening Branch.

A117.1   nd [about 1947–50]
Tested recipes / Cook book / Compiled by members of the / Evening Branch of the / St. Michael's W.A. / Calgary, Alberta
DESCRIPTION: 17.5 × 10.0 cm   Pp [1] 2–48   Limp oil cloth, with child's pattern of teddy bears, rabbits, elephants, and ducklings; stapled
CONTENTS: 1 tp; 2 ad; 3–47 text, including recipes credited with the name of the contributor, and ads; 48 ad
COPIES: *OONL (TX715.6 C667 1930z p***)
NOTES: 'Chinese Dishes (courtesy J. [i.e., Jack, brother of David and George] Ho Lem, Rosedale Cleaners)' is on pp 38–9. This section has recipes for How to Steam Rice, Sweet and Sour Spareribs, Beef Chop Suey, and Almond Chicken Chop Suey, which likely come from A116a.1, *Chinese Recipes*. A117.1 was published no earlier than 1947, when the Ho Lem family purchased Rosedale Cleaners. The appearance of the volume is consistent with publication about that time, notwithstanding the date assigned by OONL. The text ends

with 'How to Defrost Frozen Meat' on p 45, 'Household Hints' on p 46, and 'Useful Information' and 'A Prize Recipe' [i.e., mock recipe for orderly management of the kitchen] on p 47.

Specialty cook book

St George Lodge No. 39 received its charter from the Independent Order of Odd Fellows in 1908. Naomi Lodge No. 12 was instituted in 1910.

A118.1   nd [about 1947–50]
Specialty cook book / Compiled by: / Naomi No. 12 and St. George No. 39 / Building and Finance Committee / Calgary, Alberta, Canada / The proceeds from the sale of these cook books is to be used / in furthering the construction of a new hall. / The interest and assistance of our friends is most deeply / appreciated. We wish to thank all those who have given or helped / in any way. / The firms who have advertised in our book are worthy of / your support, and we thank them for their co-operation. – Building / and Finance Committee.
DESCRIPTION: 22.0 × 15.0 cm   Pp [i–ii], [1–2] 3–116 [117–18]   Card; stapled
CONTENTS: i tp; ii 'How to Cook a Husband' signed Mrs N.L. Bird and 'For Orderly Management'; 1 ad; 2 table of contents; 3–118 text and ads
COPIES: *Private collection
NOTES: 'Specialty Cook Book containing the pick of the best Canadian, British and American recipes' and the IOOF name are on the front face of the binding. This edition and A118.2 were published in 1947 or slightly later, when the Naomi and St George lodges instituted a joint building project. Although the history behind the new hall is not told in the cookbook, the Grand Lodge of Alberta reported (personal communication, November 2002) that in 1947 the St George Lodge appointed a Ways and Means Committee to meet with a similar committee from its sister lodge, to explore the possibility of obtaining suitable property on which to build a new hall. Subsequently, the St George and Naomi Building Committee was formed to raise money to finance and build the new hall at 1435 – 9th Avenue SE. Meetings began to be held in the new building in September 1952. The structure was later sold because of rising costs and declining membership.

The private collector has two copies, the one described here bound in green card, the other in red card.

A118.2 nd

—Specialty cook book / Compiled by: / Naomi No. 12 and St. George No. 39 / Building and Finance Committee / Calgary, Alberta, Canada / The proceeds from the sale of these cook books is to be used / in furthering the construction of a new hall. / The interest and assistance of our friends is most deeply / appreciated. We wish to thank all those who have given or helped / in any way. / The firms who have advertised in our book are worthy of / your support, and we thank them for their co-operation. – Building / and Finance Committee.

DESCRIPTION: 22.5 × 15.0 cm   Pp [i], 6, 3, 8, 7, 4, 9–112 [113–14]   Card; stapled

CONTENTS: i tp; 6 recipes; 3 recipes; 8 ad; 7 recipes; 4 recipes and ad; 9–112 text and ads

COPIES: *Private collection

NOTES: The pagination of this edition is odd, especially at p 100 where it runs 100, 100b [recto page], [i] [verso page], [ii] [recto page], 100a [verso page]. This may be a badly produced first edition, later corrected as A118.1. This copy is bound in yellow card.

1948

Club cookery

Knox United Church is in Calgary. Its congregation compiled one of the earliest of Alberta's community cookbooks, A6.1.

A119.1 1948

COMET / Count on me every time / Club / cookery / Knox (United) Church / 1948

DESCRIPTION: 22.5 × 15.0 cm   Pp [1–2] 3–41   Paper; stapled

CONTENTS: 1 tp; 2 'Index' [i.e., alphabetical list of section headings], 'Equivalents,' and 'Acknowledgement'; 3–41 recipes, many credited with the name of the contributor, and ads

COPIES: *OGU (CCC TX715.6 C576)   OONL (TX715.6 C57 1948 p***)

NOTES: Pp 1–2 are typeset and printed; pp 3–41 are reproduced from typing. 'Printed by: Northwest Printing & Lithographing Phone H4947' is on the outside back face of the binding.

A119.2 1949

—COMET / Count on me every time / Club cookery / Knox United Church / 1949 [cover-title]

DESCRIPTION: 23.0 × 15.0 cm   Pp 3–41   Paper; stapled

CONTENTS: Inside front face of binding 'Index' [i.e., table of contents], 'Equivalents,' and 'Acknowledgement'; 3–41 recipes credited with the name of the contributor and ads

COPIES: *OONL (TX715.6 C57 1949 p***)

NOTES: The 1949 edition has no title-page.

Cook book

The Botha branch of the Women's Institute was founded in 1915 (Cole/Larmour, p 125).

A120.1 1948

Botha / Women's / Institute / [chapter part-title:] Meats / Cook book / 1948

DESCRIPTION: 22.0 × 15.0 cm   Pp [1–83]   Lacks paper binding; stapled

CONTENTS: 1–81 text and ads; 82–3 ads

COPIES: *Private collection

NOTES: The chapter part-titles are printed on blue leaves. Each chapter part-title is as p 1, except that the subject is changed from 'Meats' to, for example, 'Vegetables.' The recipes are credited with the name of the contributor. There is an insert of three loose leaves, headed 'Corrections for Cook Book – Botha.'

Kitchen capers

A121.1 nd [about 1948]

Kitchen / capers [cover-title]

DESCRIPTION: 22.5 × 14.5 cm   Pp 1–148   Illus on p 2 of a mother serving a father, son, and daughter   Thin card, with image on front of a dancing male chef, signed 'M.E. Mohl'; stapled

CONTENTS: 1 'Foreword' signed the Committee; 2 two untitled verses and illus; 3 'Index' [i.e., table of contents]; 4–148 recipes credited with the name of the contributor, 'Household Hints,' blank pages for the reader's own notes, and ads

COPIES: *OONL (TX715.6 K57 1900z p***)

NOTES: The 'Foreword' says that the cookbook was 'compiled by Group 6 of the Women's Auxiliary of the First United Church, Hanna, Alberta ... The cover of the book was designed by Mrs. Betty Mohl, ...' (Many families with the name Mohl still live in Hanna.) The printer is on the outside back face of the binding: 'Printed at the office of the Drumheller Mail, Clarke Brothers, publishers, Drumheller, Alta.'

From appearances, the book was published in the late 1940s. An advertisement on p 131 for the *Hanna Herald* and *East Central Alberta News* gives the description 'serving the District and community for 36 years.' The town of Hanna was established in 1912 (and incorporated on 14 April 1914) and the earliest *Hanna Herald* at AEPAA is dated 24 December 1912; therefore, the cookbook was published about 1948 (1912 + 36 years). Further evidence pointing to publication about 1948 is the advertisement on p 90 for Odell's Ltd: 'We have been serving the people of Hanna and District for the past 36 years with groceries, ...'

1949

Favorite recipes of Canadian woman

A122.1   nd [about 1949]
Favorite / recipes / of / Canadian / woman [*sic*] / Published by / Favorite Recipes / Committee / Bishop Gray / Convalescent Home / Bessie B. Winspear, Convenor
DESCRIPTION: 23.0 × 14.5 cm   Pp [i–iv], 1–91, [i] Card, with image on front of a woman carrying a covered platter; bound at top edge by two rings through two punched holes
CONTENTS: i tp; ii 'Foreword' and 'Dedication' to 'Our Husbands' signed Favorite Recipes Project Committee, Bessie B. Winspear, convenor; iii 'Table of Contents' [i.e., alphabetical list of sections] and ad; iv ad; 1–91 recipes and ads; 92 ad

COPIES: AEU (TX715.6 F275)   *Private collection
NOTES: The 'Foreword' sets out the purpose of the book: 'The net proceeds from the sale of this cook book will help to swell a fund already established for the building of a convalescent home in memory of the late Bishop Gray.' Harry Gray, the first Anglican Bishop of Edmonton, died on 12 December 1939. Readers are asked to write to an Edmonton address for more information about the convalescent home project.

Two advertisements in the cookbook indicate a publication date about ten years after Bishop Gray's death. One on p 17 is for McClary stoves, 'Canada's favorite ranges for over 100 years.' Since McClary's was founded in London, Ontario, in 1847, the book was published after 1947. Another on p 9 is for Margene, a margarine made by Canada Packers and first advertised in *Chatelaine* magazine in June 1949 (see comments about Margene in O1230.1, York, Brenda, *Margene Recipe Book*).

Thirtieth anniversary cook book 1919–1949

Recipes contributed by various Alberta circuits of the Women's Missionary Federation are in S116.1, Thirtieth Anniversary Cook Book 1919–1949.

British Columbia

During the calm, warm days of August and September came the Sun-artist. Daily he toiled with his vermilions and crimsons and carmines to make the apple a masterpiece. Every day the 'Yello-fello' sat and watched, while the apple glowed redder and redder, until at last it was finished, round and red – a perfectly formed, beautifully colored, luscious O.K. apple ...

Apple Whip

Pare, quarter and core four sour O.K. Apples; steam until tender, and rub through a sieve; there should be three-quarters of a cup of pulp. Beat on a platter the whites of three eggs; gradually add the apple pulp sweetened to taste, and continue beating. Pile lightly on a serving dish, and chill. Serve with cream or soft custard.

B46.1, *Yello Fello, the Apple Elf*, Okanagan United Growers Ltd, Vernon, [about 1920–5]

British Columbia was created as Canada's westernmost and third-largest province on 20 July 1871. After the last spike was driven in the transcontinental CPR rail line at Craigellachie on 7 November 1885 (realizing the promise made at Confederation), growing numbers of people arrived at the terminus in Vancouver, on their way to settle mainly in the southwest corner of the province, a region blessed with natural resources, especially the bounty of the sea and rich agricultural land with a long frost-free growing season. The Okanagan Valley in the interior was another destination by the 1890s (although the orchards only flourished there after the introduction of irrigation in the 1930s). Between 1891 and 1901 the province's population increased from 98,173 to 178,657; by 1911, it had ballooned to 392,480, and by 1951, it had reached 1,165,210. Many of the 149[1] cookbooks in the British Columbia section of this bibliography were published to advertise the province's fruits, vegetables, fish, and dairy products, while others promoted local or provincial utility companies or Vancouver businesses, including its thriving newspapers. Whereas most advertising cookbooks emanated from Vancouver and government publications from Victoria, 44% of the total number of culinary

titles before 1950 were community cookbooks and many of these were published in small towns in the interior, especially in Kamloops and in towns in the Okanagan Valley, but also farther east in Revelstoke, Rossland, Trail, Nelson, Creston, and Cranbrook, up the coast in Powell River, and as far north as Prince Rupert, Prince George (B127.1 proudly called itself *The Northern Interior Cook Book*), and Fort St John (B113.1 commemorated the Alaska Highway in its title). Size of town was not the determining factor, as the spirited residents of Nakusp, in the Arrow Lakes Valley, showed by producing four cookbooks between 1922 and 1949 (see B50.1, B101.1, B143.1).

In the early part of the twentieth century more than 75% of British Columbians were of British origin, and most of the recipe collections in this section reflect this cultural make-up. In one case, *English Recipes* (B100.1), by a Victoria chapter of the Imperial Order Daughters of the Empire in 1939, most of the pages were devoted to English cuisine, including a table of Canadian equivalents for English measurements and terms, and the front cover was decorated with the image of a medieval thatched-roof cottage (despite the antique feel of the binding design, the text includes sophisticated advice about pairing wines with food and temperatures for the serving of wine). Two authors, Alice Ravenhill (of Shawnigan Lake), who prepared the first Women's Institutes publications for the Department of Agriculture, and Bessie Juniper (of Victoria), who wrote the province's first household science textbook, had both made their careers in England before emigrating to Canada.[2] A small but concentrated Chinese population lived in Vancouver, the earliest residents having arrived in Canada to labour on the railway, and some cookbooks occasionally include recipes from their cuisine (adapted for North American tastes), such as the brief section of 'Chinese Cookery' in a Vancouver Gas Co. publication of about 1909, *Modern Household Cookery Book* (B13.1).[3] From the turn of the century, Japanese immigrants came to British Columbia to work in the fishing industry, for Vancouver businesses, or on Fraser Valley farms. Partly for these men (the book contains references specific to British Columbia), but also for all Japanese immigrants to 'Amerika,' J.S. Watanabe wrote *An English-Japanese Conversational Guide and Cook Book,* a third edition of which was published in Oakland, California, in 1901 (US3.1).

The earliest cookbooks published in British Columbia were editions of American texts: *The Handy Reliable Cook Book* by Jane Warren, about 1892 (B1.1); and *The 'Home Queen' World's Fair Souvenir Cook Book,* copyrighted 1893 (B2.1). Other American authors were Annie Gregory, who wrote *Woman's Favorite Cook Book* (O119.5) published in Vancouver in 1902 (and in Ontario editions), and Felix Mendelsohn, who wrote *The Cook Book De Luxe* (B24.1), copyright 1912, which advertised a Kelowna business. Also probably from the United States were the texts of the annual 'calendar cookbooks' issued by Vancouver, Victoria, and Ladner druggists in the first twelve years of the new century (these were also reprinted by druggists in other parts of Canada). The run begins with one for 1900 published by Duncan Campbell (B3.1), who started his store at the corner of Fort and Douglas streets in Victoria in 1882. *Gillanders' Domestic Science Cook Book* (B16.1) from Central Drug Store on Cordova Street in Vancouver in about 1910 also reprinted text from another source. The only example to surface of a British cookbook published in the province was Fanny Lea Gillette's *The New Temperance Cookery Book* of about 1911–12 (B18.1). Grace Denison was the well-known writer of the society pages in *Saturday Night* magazine and her *The New Cook Book,* first published in Toronto in 1903, was popular enough to be reprinted in Victoria in 1906 (O130.7).

At the same time as these foreign texts and the lone Ontario author's work were available, British Columbians began to produce their own cookbooks, both the advertising and community types, educational texts, plus some titles that are not easily categorized, all of which together made the cookbook-publishing landscape in British Columbia especially varied and interesting in the period up to the outbreak of the First World War in 1914. The earliest recipe collection compiled in the province appeared in 1904 in Victoria: *The King's Daughters Cookery Book* (B5.1) by Mrs McMicking, probably a fund-raiser for her circle of the King's Daughters based at St Andrew's Presbyterian Church. Mrs McMicking clearly saw a need for a local cookbook and met it with this substantial volume of 228 pages, which was so successful that it was revised and enlarged to 287 pages in 1911. Like her husband, who brought telephones and street lighting to Victoria, Mrs McMicking worked for the betterment of her society through the avenues available to her, by serving as a member of various women's groups, and her cookbook, even if the effect was unintended, may have served to launch a succession of community cookbooks by women in other parts of the province: in the period 1908–12, the ladies of St Andrew's Church in Kamloops (B9.1, called *Kamloops Cook Book,* a title embracing all the town's citizens); the ladies of Westminster Presbyterian Church in South Vancouver (B12.1); an unidentified group in Chase or Kamloops (B14.1); the ladies of Zion Presbyterian Church in Armstrong (B17.1); the ladies of St John's Church, Vancouver (B26.1); and the Woman's Hospital Aid Society in Nelson (B22.1). From the First World War onward, community cookbooks emanated from a variety of other groups, in addition to churches, among them the Women's Institutes (B35.1, B36.1, B54.1, B56.1, B70.1), Victoria's Shamrock Club (B43.1), Imperial Order Daughters of the Empire (B51.1, B75.1, B96.1, B100.1, B102.1, B109.1),[4] Vancouver Section of the National Council of Jewish Women (B67.1, B141.1), Arrow Lakes Agricultural and Industrial Association (B50.1, B101.1), Boy Scout Association (B52.1, B78.1) and Girl Guides (B79.1), Ladies' Orange Benevolent Association (B57.1), the interdenominational Girls' Corner Club (B61.1), Order of the Royal Purple (B69.1), the PEO Sisterhood (B89.1), several hospital auxiliaries (B91.1, B111.1, B126.1, B132.1, B136.1), Local Council of Women in Vancouver, to celebrate the city's 1936 golden jubilee (B93.1), the Stagette Club (B134.1), and a Parent Teachers Association (B143.1). Vancouver's golden jubilee was the cause for another recipe collection, *Vincent Galleries Book of Cookery* (B92.1) published by an antique store in the city.

In the educational realm, Bessie Juniper has been

mentioned as the author of the province's first household science textbook, the 1913 *Girls' Home Manual of Cookery, Home Management, Home Nursing and Laundry* (B28.1), which she wrote when she was supervisor of household science for the public schools of Victoria and which was authorized by the minister of education for British Columbia. Although Juniper's career eventually led her back to England, she was apparently well loved and well remembered by her pupils in Victoria. The outbreak of war in 1914 affected the teaching of cookery in schools: in 1918 Lexa Denne, an instructor in household science at the Victoria Normal School, had published by the government printer her collection of wartime recipes used in the 'Normal War Demonstration classes' (B37.1). In 1927 Juniper's text was superseded by the provincial Department of Education's *Recipes for Home Economics Classes* (B59.1, no named author), which in 1931 was revised and retitled *Foods, Nutrition and Home Management Manual,* and reprinted many times up to 1955. Its influence extended into Alberta and Ontario classrooms (see B59.5, B59.6, B59.14).

The two bulletins on *The Preparation of Food* (B20.1) and *The Preservation of Food* (B25.1) that Alice Ravenhill produced in 1911 and 1912 for the Department of Agriculture on behalf of the Women's Institutes also had an educational purpose. The reputation she carried with her from England as a pioneer in the fields of public health and household science helped her to win the commission for these and other bulletins in the series; however, the work did not lead to her holding any official position in British Columbia (perhaps her profile was too high and the province's institutions too undeveloped to make a good fit; she has been characterized as not suffering fools gladly).[5] Ravenhill's booklet on food preservation was superseded by the Department of Agriculture's *Preservation of Food* (B49.1), issued in multiple editions through the 1920s, 1930s, and 1940s.

Recipe collections came from the province's rapidly growing energy sector, beginning in about 1909 with the Vancouver Gas Co.'s 172-page *Modern Household Cookery Book* (B13.1), which featured a cosmopolitan selection of recipes from the famed National Training School for Cookery in London, England, the School of Cookery in Dundee, Scotland, dishes from France, India, and Spain, and from famous chefs, plus sections of vegetarian and Chinese cookery. Two small, undated booklets of about 1920 may also have been aimed at new gas customers (B41.1, B42.1). The British Columbia Electric Railway Co. Ltd (owner of Vancouver Gas from 1904) established a Home Service Department in 1917 and its first two directors,

Agnes Reed and the long-serving Jean Mutch, became well known to BC home cooks. The company's *Hints for the Housewife* (B58.1) offered all kinds of advice for using gas and electric appliances, including comments on the 'Correct Gas Flame' and an admonition about the 'False Economy of Cheap Tubing.' In the 1940s, it published *Refrigerator Recipes* (B105.1), *Home Preservers' Handbook* (B107.1), *B.C. Electric Meat Book* (B116.1), and another recipe collection also called *Home Preservers' Handbook* (B118.1).

Vancouver's port was an ideal location for the West's first sugar refinery, started by the Rogers family in 1890. Their firm, BC Sugar Refining Co., published the first of several editions of *The Great West Cook Book* in 1908 (B8.1). Later, to promote Rogers' Golden Syrup (still sold today), they produced *Golden Recipes* in the 1920s (B45.1), with directions for such wonderfully sweet delights as Divinity Fudge and Golden Suet Pudding (a traditional British steamed pudding), and in about 1938, *Rogers' Golden Recipes* (B98.1). In 1931 the company bought the Raymond, Alberta, plant of Canadian Sugar Factories, which processed beet, as opposed to cane, sugar, so the various cookbooks published in Alberta in the 1930s and 1940s (A69.1, A85.1, A106.1), still under the Canadian Sugar Factories name, were, in fact, part of the BC company's corporate activities.

As the commercial centre for the province, Vancouver spawned three cookbooks in the second decade of the twentieth century that were designed as advertising vehicles for local businesses. More compendia than cookbooks, each contained recipes, general household information, a 'Business Directory,' and many advertisements. The first, *The Real Home-Keeper* (B21.1), sub-titled 'a perpetual honeymoon for the Vancouver bride,' was published in about 1911–13 by the Real Home-Keeper Publishing Co., 417 Granville Street, the interim copyright held by George A. Brandow. Another Vancouver edition appeared in 1913, then Brandow Publishing Co. Ltd repeated the successful formula in cities across the country (Winnipeg, Hamilton, Toronto, and French and English editions in Montreal); from 1928, editions were retitled *The Bride's Book*. Although Vancouver was the launching pad for Brandow's series, it is possible that the culinary text was from an American source, as yet unidentified. In 1914, soon after the first edition of *The Real Home-Keeper*, the second example of this type appeared, *The Vancouver Home-Builder and Home-Keeper* (B30.1) from the Dominion Publishing Co., and in about 1920, the third such compendium, the 'British Columbia edition' of *The Bride's Book of Household Management* (B44.1), compiled by Frank

R. Thompson and Lila May Geddis, which carried the confidence-inspiring recommendation 'approved by [Vancouver's] Board of Trade.' The idea still held appeal in 1930 when Progress Publishing Co. issued *The Vancouver Bride* (B74.1), mimicking community cookbooks by printing recipes contributed by the city's housewives; the 'Introduction' reassuringly commented, 'Many of these ladies will be known to Vancouver brides.'

It is also interesting to note the concentration of medical services in Vancouver, and that by the mid-teens the city could support a *Nurses' Year Book and Directory 1913* (B29.1), probably a money-making venture on the part of the printer or possibly a fundraiser of some sort, although which is not clear. Along with recipes, there are illustrations of the Vancouver General Hospital, New St Paul's Hospital, and Fairview Nurses Home, articles about nursing and symptoms, a list of doctors and surgeons, and hospitals and asylums, and advertisements for health practitioners and funeral directors.

It is uncommon in Canada in the first half of the twentieth century to find an individual woman writing and having published her own cookbook, outside of a charitable group or corporate entity, but in about 1920, Annie Langhout, who is reported to have had a bakery on Broadway Street in Vancouver, showed just that entrepreneurial spirit when she compiled *Economy's Friend* (B40.1).

The recipe books promoting the province's fruit, vegetables, dairy products, and seafood are especially attractive. During the First World War, the BC Fruit Growers' Association, established in 1889 and still the voice for the industry today, published, for free distribution, *British Columbia Fruit* (B33.1), a collection of 225 recipes for a huge variety of fruit, from apples, rhubarb, and strawberries to cantaloupes, plums, and pears, and including celery, onion, and tomatoes. Some fruits are illustrated in the text, but it is the single, red apple depicted on the front cover that begs to be eaten. The crossed Union Jack and Red Ensign on the back cover signified wartime, but the dedication to the 'patriotic housewives of Western Canada' was more an appeal for British Columbians to buy from local growers than a comment on their sense of loyalty to either Canada or the Mother Country. Not long after the war, the Okanagan United Growers Ltd produced the delightful story of *Yello Fello, the Apple Elf* – 'The Guardian Elf of the O.K. Apple,' illustrated by Helen Dickson and incorporating apple recipes (B46.1). In 1931 Alice Stevens, editor of the Women's Section of *Country Life in British Columbia* (the BC Fruit Growers' magazine), wrote *Apple Secrets* (B77.1). Depicted on the front cover were orange rings of light emanating from the OK apple symbol printed on a map of the province. Probably because of Depression-era conditions, Stevens touted apples as 'the least expensive of all health foods.' In 1943, during the Second World War, Stevens compiled, for BC Tree Fruits Ltd, the first of what were to become annual home-canning guides (B115.1), some of which bear the image of a bright-eyed girl, with braids, holding apples in the skirt of her dress or held aloft in a bowl. The booklet promoting Pacific Brand Evaporated Milk (B62.1), by the Fraser Valley Milk Producers' Association in about 1927, is trimmed in the shape of a can of milk and the front cover shows a rural scene of cows in a field. Also in the late 1920s, the Broder Canning Co. Ltd of New Westminster, purveyors of Royal City brand, published *Peas in the Diet* (B63.1), the pages of which were decorated with pea-pod borders; on the front cover, a steaming tureen of peas sits at the centre of radiating bands of alternating colours. A leaping salmon decorates the cover of *25 Recipes for Canned Salmon* (B72.1, about 1930), probably from British Columbia Packers Ltd, while a can of Cloverleaf and canned salmon on a plate are on the company's *Sea Food Recipes* (B84.1, about 1935). Although Kelly, Douglas and Co. Ltd (Nabob-brand foods) and W.H. Malkin Co. (own-name label) also published cookbooks (B66.1, B88.1), they were not as visually appealing as those for the province's fruit, vegetables, fish, and dairy products.

The women's pages of newspapers were an important forum for sharing recipes and learning about new trends. Margaret Henderson, director of the Daily Province Modern Kitchen since its inception in 1935, was behind several cookbooks from that paper (B104.1, B117.1, B122.1, B138.1), but the person who really caught the public's imagination long-term was the fictional Edith Adams, food editor of the *Vancouver Sun* from 1924, when her name was dreamed up by the circulation manager at the time, until 1999. Starting in the 1930s, the *Vancouver Sun* published, under Edith Adams's name, annual collections of 'prize recipes,' i.e., ones contributed by readers, who won $1.00 for each recipe selected (B81.1 lists the annual issues). Edith Adams's popularity soared when the *Sun* opened the Edith Adams Cottage, with its own separate door at 510 Beatty Street, on 1 February 1947. Women, properly attired in gloves and hats, eagerly attended the regular cooking demonstrations held there under the supervision of Marianne Linnell as Edith.

The British Columbia Archives in Victoria has the largest collection of pre-1950 Canadian cookbooks in the province, followed by the collections at the Royal British Columbia Museum, Victoria, and Burnaby Village Museum. Other local museums have modest numbers, including the Delta Museum and Archives, Cowichan Valley Museum in Duncan, Kamloops Museum and Archives, Kelowna Centennial Museum, Summerland Museum, Vancouver Museum, and Greater Vernon Museum and Archives. Small, but still useful collections, are at the University of British Columbia (Beatrice M. Millar Papers), University of Victoria, and Vancouver Public Library. For a full list of British Columbia locations, see 'Abbreviations,' p xlii.

NOTES

1 There are 143 numbered entries and one late edition, B21a.1, in the British Columbia section, plus cross-references to British Columbia editions of four works in the Ontario section (O48.19, O119.5, O130.7, O773.4) and one work in the New Brunswick section (NB35.2, NB35.4).

2 For Ravenhill, see B20.1; for Juniper, B28.1.

3 A copy of a cookbook in Chinese characters, but called *Tom Wone Cook Book: A Selection of Dishes // Chef's Reminder* on the title-page, has found its way into the collection of the Kelowna Centennial Museum, evidence that it may have been used in the province. The date is uncertain, but possibly about 1920. Whether the cookbook was published in Canada or mentions Canada has not been determined.

4 The Coronation Chapter, founded in Vancouver in 1902, was the first in British Columbia, but no cookbook by this chapter was found.

5 Christine E.J. Daniels and Robert A. Bayliss, 'Alice Ravenhill, Home Economist, 1859–1954,' *Westminster Journal of Education* Vol. 8 (1985), p 26.

1892

Warren, Mrs Jane

Also by Warren is NB10.1, The Ladies' Own Home Cook Book.

B1.1 nd [about 1892]
The / handy reliable cook book. / A / practical and comprehensive manual / of commonsense cookery. / Showing / how to buy, dress, cook, serve and / carve every kind of meat, game, / fish, fowl and vegetable. / Also giving plain directions for preserving, / pickling, canning and drying all kinds of / berries, fruits, meats, game, etc. / and also / instructions for making in the best style all varieties / of candies, ice creams, cakes and pastry. / By Mrs. Jane Warren. / Published expressly for this hous[e?] / See covers of this book.
DESCRIPTION: 18.0 × 12.5 cm   Pp [3–26] 27–124, [5–6] 7–100 [101–6]   Illus   Paper; stapled
CONTENTS: 3 tp; 4 blank; 5 'Preface'; 6 blank; 7–117 text; 118–24 'Contents' [i.e., index]; 5 part-title: 'The Art of Canning, Smoking, Pickling, Drying, and Otherwise Preserving Meats, Fowl, Game, Fruit and Berries; Also, How Pickles Are Made and the Process of Candying, Described in a Plain, Practical Manner for Home Use'; 6 blank; 7–96 text; 97–100 index; 101–6 'Ready Reckoner'
COPIES: *BBVM   OFERWM (A1982.88)
NOTES: Some of the initial folios of the first part of the book did not register and there are only traces of ink where the page number should be; I have recorded such pages as unpaginated if there is no legible number.

The running head of the first part of the book is 'The Young Wife's Own Cook Book.' The following is printed on the front face of the binding: 'The Handy Reliable Cook Book // Published by Thomson Bros'. Booksto[re?] 108 Cordova St., Vancouver, B.C[.?] Fine stationers and printers.'

The OFERWM copy lacks its binding.

OTHER EDITIONS: Pinestar Publishing of Alberta Beach, Alberta, published a reset edition, copyright 1990, of a text by Jane Warren, which it titled *Yesterday's Cookbook 1885 (History in Cooking): Over 700 Recipes and Instructions on How to Buy, Dress, Cook, Serve and Carve – Forming an Encyclopedic Cookbook As It Was in 1885* (OONL). Taped to the inside front face of the binding is a 'Certificate of Authenticity' dated 17 March 1993 in which a commissioner for oaths in Alberta certifies that she has examined '"An Economical Cookbook",

"The Young Wives' Cookbook" and "A Practical Cookery Book of Today", originally published in 1891–1893' and found the contents to be an authentic reproduction of the original. It is unclear which original edition Pinestar Publishing has reset and reprinted.

AMERICAN EDITIONS: *The Handy Reliable Cook Book,* New York: Hurst and Co., 1892 (United States: DLC).

The second section of *The Handy Reliable Cook Book,* i.e., the last pp 7–96 of B1.1, plus the carving information (but repositioned), also appeared in Jane Warren's *The Economical Cook Book. Practical Cookery Book of Today with Minute Directions How to Buy, Dress, Cook, Serve and Carve and 300 Standard Recipes for Canning, Preserving, Curing, Smoking, and Drying Meats, Fowl, Fruits and Berries – a Chapter on Pickling and Candying,* New York: Hurst and Co., nd (OFERWM); however, the first section of *The Economical Cook Book,* which is in fifteen parts, differs from *The Handy Reliable Cook Book* and may be the same as the first section of NB10.1, *The Ladies' Own Home Cook Book.*

I have not examined *San Francisco Economical Cook Book; a Practical Guide to Everyday Cookery, with Minute Directions How to Buy, Dress, Cook, Serve, and Carve, and 300 Standard Recipes ...,* San Francisco: Sullivan, Burtis and Dewey, [1891?], pp 120, 96 (United States: DLC), but the title and pagination indicate that it is another edition of Hurst and Co.'s *Economical Cook Book.*

1893

The 'home queen' World's Fair souvenir cook book

B2.1 [copyright 1893]
The / "home queen" / World's Fair / souvenir / cook book, / two thousand valuable recipes / on / cookery and household economy, menus, / table etiquette, toilet, etc. / Contributed by over two hundred World's Fair lady / managers, wives of governors and other ladies / of position and influence. / Illustrated. / J.M. MacGregor Publishing Co., / Vancouver, B.C.
CONTENTS: Tp verso 'Copyright secured, 1893.'
COPIES: *BCOM
NOTES: This American cookbook was originally published on the occasion of the Chicago World's Fair in 1893. The 'Introductory,' which is opposite the copyright page, states that the aim of the book was 'to secure a few choice and well-tried recipes from each

of hundreds of individuals scattered throughout every State and Territory in the Union, thus giving all the benefit of the prevailing styles of cooking in every section of the country, ...' The Vancouver edition may have appeared in 1893 or later.

An advertisement for Royal Crown Soaps of Winnipeg in the *Western Home Monthly* (November 1918), p 29, offers 'The Home Queen Cook Book over 600 pages' as a free premium on submission of 200 soap wrappers.

AMERICAN EDITIONS: [White, James Edson, ed.], New York, Chicago: G.F. Cram, 1893 (United States: DLC); Chicago: John F. Waite Publishing Co., [copyright 1893, 1894, 1895] (Private collection).

1900

Campbell's calendar cook book 1900

Duncan E. Campbell (born in Fingal, Ontario; died in Victoria, British Columbia, in September 1937, at eighty-one years old) established his Victoria drugstore at the northwest corner of Fort and Douglas streets in 1882. In 1912 he built an eight-storey building for his business at the southwest corner of the same intersection. In September 1921 he sold out to the Owl Drug Co. and retired. For Campbell's other calendar cookbooks, see B6.1 for 1907; B7.1 for 1908; B11.1 for 1909; and B15.1 for 1910. Campbell also published O48.19, Rexall Cook Book.

B3.1   1900
Campbell's / 1900 / calendar / cook book / 1900 / Published by / D.E. Campbell, / family chemist / Cor. Fort and Douglas streets, / Victoria, – B.C.
DESCRIPTION: 17.5 × 13.5 cm   Pp [1–3] 4–32   Illus of astrological symbols   Paper; stapled, and with hole punched at top left corner for hanging
CONTENTS: 1 tp; 2 publ ad; 3 'Eclipses, 1900' and 'Morning and Evening Stars'; 4–29 recipes, publ ads, monthly calendars, and jokes; 30–2 'Useful Information,' which includes a recipe for Everton Toffee
COPIES: *BDUCVM
NOTES: There is an illustration of the interior of Campbell's Prescription Store on the outside back face of the binding.

1900–5

Hall's tested recipes

See also O105.1, Coate's Tested Recipes, which has the same subtitle.

B4.1   nd [about 1900–5]
Hall's / tested / recipes / A practical everyday / cook book / Published by / Hall & Co. / Central Drug Store, / Clarence Block, corner Yates and Douglas streets, / Victoria, B.C.
DESCRIPTION: Pp [1–5] 6–32
CONTENTS: 1 tp; 2 'To Our Lady Patrons and Friends' signed Hall and Co.; 3 'Our Baking Powder' and 'Spices'; 4 'Spoon and Cup Measure' and 'Table of Proportions'; 5–32 'Tested Recipes' and publ ads
COPIES: BVAU   *CIHM (98401)
NOTES: BVAU dates the book between 1900 and 1911. From appearances, both editions were published about 1900–5, although the order of publication is unknown. The title-page of B4.1 differs from B4.2 in minor ways; for example, here 'corner' and 'streets' are spelled out. In both B4.1 and B4.2, the recipes begin on p 5 with Frozen Beef Tea, Indian Pea Soup, Macaroni and Tomatoes, and Eggs, with Cream. The binding of B4.1 survives, on which is printed the word 'Copyrighted.'

B4.2   nd [about 1900–5]
—Hall's / tested / recipes / A practical everyday / cook book / Published by / Hall & Co., / Central Drug Store, / Clarence Block, cor. Yates & Douglas sts., / Victoria, B.C.
DESCRIPTION: 16.5 × 12.0 cm   Pp [1–5] 6–32   Lacks paper binding?; originally stapled?
CONTENTS: 1 tp; 2 'To Our Lady Patrons and Friends' signed Hall and Co.; 3 'Our Baking Powder' and 'Spices'; 4 'Spoon and Cup Measure' and 'Table of Proportions'; 5–32 'Tested Recipes' and publ ads
COPIES: *BVIPM

1902

Gregory, Annie R.

Gregory was an American author. See O119.5 for an edition of her Woman's Favorite Cook Book *published in Vancouver by J.M. MacGregor Publishing Co., [copyright 1902]. Other Canadian editions, called* Woman's Favorite Cook Book *or* Canada's Favorite Cook Book, *were published in Brantford or Guelph, Ontario.*

1904

McMicking, Mrs Margaret Leighton (Mrs Robert Burns McMicking) (Garmouth, Morayshire, Scotland, 1845–1940)

Margaret McMicking was well known in Victoria social circles. She volunteered her time with the King's Daughters, after which the cookbook was named, the Victoria Literary Society, IODE, Historical Society, Burns Club, Friendly Help, Local Council of Women, and Alexandra Club; and she was decorated for her contribution to the Belgian Relief effort during the First World War. Her husband, Robert Burns McMicking, who had made his way to the West Coast as one of the famous group of 'Overlanders,' established the Victoria and Esquimalt Telephone Co. and built the electric street lighting system for the city. For more information about Margaret, see the 1979 edition of the cookbook. The International Order of the King's Daughters and Sons, a philanthropic organization, was founded in New York in 1886.

B5.1   [1st ed.], 1904
Each recipe is plain and tried, / And some good housewife's honest pride; / Some home's delight. / And should your effort bring no prize, / I'll say not where the trouble lies – / t'were [*sic*] impolite. / [IOKDS symbol, i.e., initials IHN, for 'In His Name,' within a Maltese cross] / The King's Daughters / cookery book / Compiled by / Mrs. R.B. McMicking. / We may live without friends, we may live without books, / But civilized man cannot live without cooks! / He can live without books – what is knowledge but grieving? / He may live without hope – what is hope but deceiving? / He may live without love – what is passion but pining? / But where is the man that can live without dining? / – Owen Meredith. / Victoria, B.C. / Chas. F. Banfield, printer. / 1904
DESCRIPTION: 21.0 × 14.0 cm   Pp [i–x], [1] 2–226 [227]   Cloth
CONTENTS: i–ii ads; iii tp; iv 'To Mrs. George C. Shaw Provincial Secretary for British Columbia this book is affectionately dedicated.'; v 'Preface'; vi quotation from Ruskin; vii–ix 'Introduction // Food in Its Relation to Life. (By Miss McKeand.) Teacher of Domestic Science Victoria Public Schools'; x 'Table of Weights and Measures'; 1–226 recipes credited with the contributor's name and ads; 227 table of contents
CITATIONS: Cooke 2002, p 234
COPIES: *BVIPA BVIPM BVIV CIHM (75568)
NOTES: The cookbook was likely published to raise money for the circle of the King's Daughters to which

Margaret McMicking belonged. Her group was associated with the Ministering Circle of St Andrew's Presbyterian Church in Victoria (the dedication in the 1911 edition makes reference to the Ministering Circle, but the church is not named).

In the BVIPA copy, the first three lines of the 'Preface' are corrected in ink. The BVIPM copy lacks pp [i–vi] and pp 217 onward.

B5.2   2nd ed., 1911
—[IOKDS symbol] / The King's Daughters / cookery book / Compiled by / Mrs. Robert Burns McMicking / Each recipe is plain and tried, / And some good housewife's honest pride; / Some home's delight. / And should your effort bring no prize, / I'll say not where the trouble lies – / 'twere impolite. / 1st edition 1904 / 2nd edition 1911 / Victoria, B.C.
DESCRIPTION: 21.0 × 14.0 cm   Pp [1–15] 16–286 [287]   Frontis portrait of author, illus on p 153 of plum pudding, illus on p 191 of a table set with frozen desserts   Cloth, with image on front of three maids walking one behind the other, the first carrying plates, the others carrying finished dishes
CONTENTS: 1–2 ads; 3 tp; 4 'To Mrs. George C. Shaw our beloved "old leader" of the Ministering Circle this book is affectionately dedicated'; 5 'Preface' dated Victoria, March 1911; 6 quotation from Ruskin, poem by Owen Meredith; 7–12 'Household Department' described as 'Written for the Woman's Edition of the "Colonist" by Mrs. R.B. McMicking, Nov. 6th, 1909.'; 13–14 'A Culinary Dictionary'; 15 'Table of Weights and Measures'; 16–279 recipes, many credited with the name of the contributor, and ads; 280–1 'Selected Menus'; 282–6 'The Wisdom of Many' described as 'Written for the Women's Edition of the Colonist, Nov. 6th, 1909, by Mrs. R.B. McMicking'; 287 table of contents
COPIES: BLCK (990.43)   BVAU (TX715 M33 1911, not on shelf) BVIP BVIPA *BVIPM CIHM (75603) OONL (TX715 K4996 1911)   OWTU (F9428)
NOTES: The author's printed signature, Margaret Leighton McMicking, is under the frontispiece portrait. The 'Preface' refers to this as 'the second and enlarged edition.'

B5.3   3rd ed., 1st printing, November 1979
—The King's Daughters / cook book / Compiled by / Mrs. Robert Burns McMicking / of Victoria, B.C. / and originally published in 1904. / Third edition / Published by / the Unusual House, Inc. / Vancouver, B.C., Canada / First printing November 1979.

DESCRIPTION: 21.5 × 13.5 cm   Pp [i] ii–iv [v] vi–viii, [1–15] 16–286   Fp illus portrait on p v of the author, illus on p 153 of plum pudding, illus on p 191 of a table set with frozen desserts   Soft cover

CONTENTS: i tp; ii 'Compiled by Margaret Leighton McMicking. First edition published Victoria, B.C., 1904. Second edition published Victoria, B.C., 1911. Editors: Third edition, Wilson, Stuart Renwick, and Hastings, Margaret Edna. ISBN 0-920226-00-0 (soft cover edition) ISBN 0-920226-01-9 (hard cover edition) ... McMicking, Margaret Leighton, 1845–1940'; iii introduction; iv 'This third edition ... is dedicated to six great ladies ... Margaret Leighton McMicking (Mrs. R.B. McMicking), her eldest daughter, Maude Leighton McMicking (Mrs. R.A. Renwick), and the four daughters of Mr. and Mrs. Renwick; Myra Leighton Balagno, Kate Kelman Foot, the late Marjorie McMicking Wilson, and Maude Daugherty Church, ...'; v fp illus portrait; vi–viii 'A Wee Bit of the McMicking Story' and at bottom p viii, 'Metric Measures'; 1 tp of second edition, 1911; 2 dedication to Mrs George C. Shaw, '"old leader" of the Ministering Circle'; 3 table of contents; 4 blank; 5 preface dated Victoria, March 1911; 6 quotations from Ruskin and Owen Meredith; 7–286 text

CITATIONS: Ferguson/Fraser, p 232, illus col on p 11 of closed volume

COPIES: BVIPA   OONL (TX715 K4996 1979, 2 copies) *Private collection

1906

Denison, Mrs Grace Elizabeth

For the 1906 Victoria edition of Grace Denison's The New Cook Book of 1903, see O130.7.

1907

Campbell's calendar cook book 1907

For a history of D.E. Campbell's business and his other cookbooks, see B3.1.

B6.1   1907
Campbell's Prescription Store / 1907 1907 / Campbell's / calendar / cook book / Published by / D.E. Campbell / family chemist / cor. Fort and Douglas sts. Victoria, B.C. / We are prompt We are careful / [along left edge:] Pure drugs and chemicals / [along right edge:] Your physician will be pleased with our work [cover-title]

DESCRIPTION: 17.5 × 13.5 cm   Pp [1–3] 4–32   Illus of astrological symbols, illus on pp 29 and 32 of hand with palm lines   Paper, with small image on front of a camel on which is printed 'D.E. Campbell family chemist Victoria B.C.'; stapled, and with hole punched at top left corner, through which runs a string for hanging

CONTENTS: 1–2 publ ads; 3 'Eclipses, 1907,' 'Morning and Evening Stars, 1907,' and 'Chronological Cycles, 1907'; 4–27 recipes, publ ads, monthly calendars, and 'Practical Breaks and Monologues'; 28–32 'Palmistry'

COPIES: *OTUTF (uncat patent medicine)

1908

Campbell's calendar cook book 1908

For a history of D.E. Campbell's business and his other cookbooks, see B3.1.

B7.1   1908
Campbell's Prescription Store / Campbell's / calendar / cook book / 1908 / Published by / D.E. Campbell / family chemist / Cor. Fort and Douglas sts. / Victoria – B.C. / We are prompt We are careful / [along left edge:] Pure drugs and chemicals / [along right edge:] Your physician will be pleased with our work [cover-title]

DESCRIPTION: 17.0 × 13.5 cm   Pp [1–3] 4–32   Illus of astrological symbols   Paper, with image on front of a camel on which is printed 'D.E. Campbell family chemist Victoria B.C.'; stapled, and with hole punched at top left corner for hanging

CONTENTS: 1–2 publ ads; 3 'Eclipses, 1908,' 'Morning and Evening Stars, 1908,' and 'Chronological Cycles, 1908'; 4–28 recipes, publ ads, monthly calendars, and jokes; 29 'Proper Sauces for Meats,' 'Frost on Windows,' and 'Magic Age Table'; 30 'Foods for Dyspeptics' and 'Antidotes for Common Poisons'; 31 'Human Models,' 'Cold Feet and Sleepy Hands,' and 'Hints for the Home'; 32 'Hints for the Home,' 'The Family Medicine Chest,' and 'Number of Trees on an Acre'

COPIES: *BDUCVM

The great west cook book

The Rogers family started building its first sugar refinery in 1890, in Vancouver – the first such plant in western Canada. Production began the next year. For other cookbooks from BC Sugar Refining Co. Ltd, see B45.1, Golden Recipes, and B98.1, Rogers' Golden Recipes.

B8.1 entered 1908

The great west / cook book / A help to housewives / Presented with the compliments of the / B.C. Sugar Refining Co. / Limited / Vancouver British Columbia / Entered according to Act of the Parliament of Canada in the year 1908 by the / British Columbia Sugar Refining Co., Limited, at the Department of Agriculture.

DESCRIPTION: 22.5 × 15.0 cm   Pp [1–2] 3–40   Tp illus red-and-black of a manservant striding to the right and carrying a tray on which sits a wine glass and a container   Paper; stapled

CONTENTS: 1 tp; 2 blank; 3 table of contents; 4 'Tables of Weights and Measures'; 5–40 recipes

CITATIONS: O'Neill (unpublished)

COPIES: ACG   BVABSM   MWPA   *Private collection; Great Britain: LB (07945.k.30 destroyed)

NOTES: 'Evans & Hastings, printers' is on the front face of the binding. The title-page and text are printed in red and black. LB's destroyed copy was likely this one since it has the subtitle 'a help to housewives.'

B8.2 nd [about 1913 or later]

—The / great west / cook book / Do you want / your / preserves / to keep? / Use / B.C. / cane sugar / Presented with the compliments of the / B.C. Sugar Refining Co. / Limited / Vancouver, B.C. / A.H. Timms, printer [printers' trade symbol] Vancouver, B.C. [cover-title]

DESCRIPTION: 22.0 × 15.0 cm   Pp [1–4] 5–40   Paper; stapled

CONTENTS: 1 'This trade mark [trade mark printed in red, blue, and green] stands for perfection'; 2 'Contents'; 3 'A Table of Weights and Measures'; 4 'Analysis of British Columbia Cane Granulated Sugar' dated 30 August 1913; 5–40 recipes

COPIES: AALIWWM   AEUCHV (UV 84.332.2) ARDA   *BVABSM   OGU (UA s048 b20)   OWTU (G10988)

NOTES: In this edition, the printer is named on the binding and the heading on p 5 ('The Great West Cook Book // A Help to Housewives') is set in italic. B8.3 and B8.4 have no named printer and the heading is in roman.

B8.2 and B8.3 have the 1913 'Analysis of British Columbia Cane Granulated Sugar' on p 4; however, each is printed from a different setting of type. One difference is that in B8.2 '[Signed]' is in square brackets; in B8.3, '(Signed)' is in parentheses. Another difference is the line endings in the four-line certification statement: B8.2 has '... analysed / ... Sugar / ... in / ... sugar.'; B8.3 has '... samples / ... Refining / ... to / ... sugar.' The BVABSM copy is inscribed on the binding, 'James Fowler // Chef.'

B8.3 nd [about 1913 or later]

—The / great west / cook book / Do you want / your / preserves / to keep? / Use / B.C. cane sugar / Presented with the compliments of the / B.C. Sugar Refining Co. / Limited / Vancouver, B.C. [cover-title]

DESCRIPTION: 23.0 × 15.5 cm   Pp [1–4] 5–40   Paper; stapled

CONTENTS: 1 'This trade mark [trade mark printed in red, green, and blue] stands for perfection'; 2 'Contents'; 3 'A Table of Weights and Measures'; 4 'Analysis of British Columbia Cane Granulated Sugar' dated 30 August 1913; 5–40 recipes

COPIES: BDUCVM   *BVABSM   BVIPA

NOTES: Ferguson/Fraser, p 232, may be B8.3 or B8.4.

B8.4 nd

—The / great west / cook book / Do you want / your / preserves / to keep? / Use / B.C. cane sugar / Presented with the compliments of the / B.C. Sugar Refining Co. / Limited / Vancouver, B.C. [cover-title]

DESCRIPTION: 23.0 × 15.0 cm   Pp [1–5] 6–40   Paper; stapled

CONTENTS: 1 'This trade mark [trade mark printed in red, green, and blue] stands for perfection'; 2 'Contents'; 3 'A Table of Weights and Measures'; 4 blank; 5–40 recipes

COPIES: *BVABSM   BVAMM

NOTES: Unlike B8.3, there is no 'Analysis' of the company's cane sugar on p 4, which is blank.

1908–10

Kamloops cook book

B9.1 nd [about 1908–10]

Kamloops / cook book / Kamloops Standard Presses [cover-title]

DESCRIPTION: 22.0 × 14.5 cm   Pp [1–2] 3–99   Paper, with 4.2-cm-high image on front of flowers in a vase; stapled

CONTENTS: 1 'Cooking Recipes // Compiled by the Willing Workers of St. Andrew's Church // Preface' and 'Weights and Measures'; 2 'Time for Cooking'; 3–97 recipes credited with the name of the contributor and ads; 98–9 'Hints' and at bottom p 99, 'Finale' [four lines from poem beginning, 'We may live without poetry, music and art,' from *Lucile,* Part I, Canto ii, by Owen Meredith, pseudonym of Edward Robert Bulwer-Lytton]

COPIES: *BKM

NOTES: The object of the cookbook was 'to gather

together and present in a handy form a number of the best recipes of the housewives of Kamloops, ... a neighborly exchange, as it were.' There is an advertisement on p 72 for the Hotel Leland, 'this new hotel.' In 1908 the Hotel Leland (previously run under a different name) was reopened after extensive renovations. The cookbook, therefore, was published some time after the reopening.

1909

Calendar cook book 1909

B10.1   1909
Knowlton's Drug Store / Calendar / cook book / 1909 / Published by / Knowlton's Drug Store / 1 Hastings Street E. / Vancouver British Columbia / Always open
DESCRIPTION: 17.5 × 13.5 cm   Pp [1–3] 4–32   Illus of astrological symbols   Paper; stapled, and with hole punched at top left corner, through which runs a string for hanging
CONTENTS: 1 tp; 2 publ ad; 3–27 astronomical information, recipes, monthly calendars, 'Practical Breaks' [i.e., jokes], and publ ads; 28–mid 1st column 30 'Poisons and Antidotes'; mid 1st column 30–bottom 2nd column 30 medical information; 1st column 31–mid 2nd column 31 'Worth Knowing'; bottom 2nd column 31–32 'Things to Remember'
COPIES: *OTUTF (uncat patent medicine)
NOTES: The recipes are the same as listed for NB25.1, *Brown's New Brunswick Almanac and Cook Book 1909* (see that entry for the titles of other cookbooks with the same recipes).

Campbell's calendar cook book 1909

For a history of D.E. Campbell's business and his other cookbooks, see B3.1.

B11.1   1909
Campbell's Prescription Store / Campbell's / calendar / cook book / 1909 1909 / Published by / D.E. Campbell / family chemist / Cor. Fort and Douglas sts. Victoria, B.C. / We are prompt We are careful / [along left edge:] Pure drugs and chemicals / [along right edge:] Your physician will be pleased with our work [cover-title]
DESCRIPTION: Pp [1–3] 4–32   Illus of astrological symbols   Paper, with image on front of a camel on which is printed 'D.E. Campbell family chemist Victoria B.C.'

CONTENTS: 1–2 publ ads; 3 'Eclipses, 1909,' 'Morning and Evening Stars, 1909,' and 'Chronological Cycles, 1909'; 4–27 recipes, publ ads, monthly calendars, and 'Practical Breaks' [i.e., jokes]; 28–mid 1st column 30 'Poisons and Antidotes'; bottom 1st column 30–2nd column 30 'Relation of a Pulse to Temperature,' 'Handy Household Drugs,' and items that appear to be part of 'Worth Knowing' on opposite page; 1st column 31–mid 2nd column 31 'Worth Knowing'; bottom 2nd column 31–32 'Things to Remember'
COPIES: *CIHM (80166)   OONL (D11.5 C28 1909)
NOTES: The recipes on p 4 are the same as listed for NB25.1, *Brown's New Brunswick Almanac and Cook Book 1909* (see that entry for the titles of other cookbooks with the same recipes).

Cookery book of tried and approved recipes

Westminster Presbyterian Church was dedicated in 1909. In June 1925 it was renamed Westminster United Church, then Bethany United Church in November 1925. In 1928, Bethany United was amalgamated into Mountain View United Church. The municipality of South Vancouver is now part of Vancouver. For a later cookbook by Westminster Presbyterian Church, see B53.1, Three Hundred Dainty Recipes.

B12.1   nd [about 1909]
Westminster / Presbyterian Church, / South Vancouver. / In aid of the funds of the / Ladies' Aid. / Cookery book / of / tried and approved / recipes. / Price, 25 cents. [cover-title]
DESCRIPTION: 21.0 × 13.5 cm   Pp 1–64   Paper; stapled
CONTENTS: 1–4 ads; 5–59 recipes credited with the name of the contributor and ads; 60 'Household Hints'; 61–4 ads
COPIES: *BVIPA
NOTES: The cookbook appears to have been published about the time of the church's dedication in 1909.

Modern household cookery book

Incorporated in 1886, the Vancouver Gas Co. was acquired in 1904 by British Columbia Electric Railway Co., which ran it as a subsidiary until 1926, when it became part of a new holding company, British Columbia Electric Power and Gas. For other titles from Vancouver Gas, see B41.1, Recipes, and B42.1, [Recipes?].

B13.1   nd [about 1909]
Modern household / cookery book / with
numerous recipes / Learn to read your gas meter
regularly / and so prevent waste. / Published by /
Vancouver Gas Co., Limited / 435 Carrall St. and
779 Granville St. / Phone 5000
DESCRIPTION: 22.0 × 14.0 cm   Pp [1–9] 10–162, 163–
72   3 fp illus on pp 1, 3, and 5; many illus of gas
appliances in publ ads   Cloth
CONTENTS: 1 caption to fp illus: '"It raised the ire of
Mr. Squire / To have to light the kitchen fire."'; 2 publ
ad; 3 caption to fp illus: '"His wife said, 'John, / You
silly ass, / Stay with the mass / And cook with
gas'."'; 4 publ ad; 5 caption to fp illus: '"Then John
got wise / And bought a range. / This then explains
/ The reason why / This wise old guy / Now wears a
smile. / Broad? Half a mile."'; 6 publ ad; 7 tp; 8 blank;
9 'Preface'; 10–12 'A Few Words about Cooking and
Heating by Means of Gas' and other introductory
material; 13–145 recipes and hints; 146–7 'How to
Use a Gas Range'; 148 blank; 149–62 index; 163–72
publ ads
CITATIONS: Ferguson/Fraser, p 232   Hale 2061
COPIES: BVAMM   BVAU   BVIPA   OGU (2 copies:
*UA s066 b34, CCC TX715.6 M625)   OTNY (uncat)
NOTES: The 'Preface' gives the source of the recipes:
'[Some are] from a series of practical lessons given at
the South Kensington National Training School of
Cookery, London [England]; others dedicated to the
Right Honourable the Earl of Shaftesbury by the fa-
mous French chef, Alexis Soyer, and others, handed
down in families, old-fashioned, but really good.
These recipes are from the Mother Country, France,
India and Spain, and the School of Cookery, Dundee,
Scotland.' There is a section of 'Chinese Cookery' on
pp 125–7 and a section of 'Vegetarian Dishes.' Testimonials in the publisher's advertisements at the back
of the book are dated September 1909. The OGU
copy is inscribed 1914, but it is unknown who wrote
the date and when.

B13.2   nd [about 1910]
—Modern household / cookery book / with
numerous recipes / Learn to read your gas meter
regularly / and so prevent waste / Published by /
Victoria Gas Company, Limited / Cor. Fort and
Langley sts. / Victoria, B.C. / Phone 123
DESCRIPTION: 22.0 × 14.0 cm   Pp 3–170 [171–2]   Fp
illus on p 171   Cloth
CONTENTS: 3 'Don't Overlook Our Customers' Letters'; 4–6 'What Prominent Victorians Think of Gas'
[testimonials dated 1910]; 7 tp; 8 blank; 9 'Preface';
10–mid 11 'A Few Words about Cooking and Heating
by Means of Gas'; mid 11–top 12 'How to Measure';

mid 12 'Table of Measures and Weights'; 13–133 culinary text; 134–7 'The Baby'; 138–9 'Personal Hints';
140–5 'Household Hints'; 146–7 'How to Use a Gas
Range'; 148 blank; 149–62 index; 163–70 publ ads;
171 fp illus with caption: '"It raised the ire / of Mr.
Squire / To have to light / the kitchen fire."'; 172 illus
[in BVIPA copy, clipping glued over illus]
CITATIONS: Golick, p 102
COPIES: *BVIPA   OTNY (uncat)
NOTES: The binding design and the 'Preface' are the
same as for the Vancouver edition, B13.1. Whereas
the testimonials in the Vancouver edition are dated
1909, those in the Victoria edition are dated 1910.

1910

[Title unknown]

B14.1   [about 1910]
[Title-page and cover-title lacking?]
DESCRIPTION: 22.5 × 14.0 cm   Pp [first leaf lacking?]
[2–149] [leaves lacking]   Limp cloth; top hinged
CONTENTS: 3 'Index' [i.e., table of contents without
page numbers]; 4 blank; 5 'Weights and Measures'
and 'Time for Cooking'; 6 blank; 7–13 'Soups'; 14 ad
for Hudson's Bay Co., Kamloops; 15–top 21 'Fish &
Oysters' and ads for businesses in Chase, BC; mid 21–
35 'Salads and Dressing'; 36 ads; 37–43 'Game & Poultry'; 44 ads; 45–55 'Meat' and ad; 56 ad; 57–73
'Vegetables & Potatoes'; 74 ads; 75–93 'Bread & Biscuits'; 94 ads; 95–103 'Puddings'; 104 blank; 105–top
113 'Pies'; mid 113–125 'Cakes' and ads; 126 blank;
127 'Cookies & Doughnuts'; 128 blank; 129 'Pickles';
130 blank; 131 'Preserves'; 132 blank; 133–5 'Hot &
Cold Desserts'; 136 blank; 137–49 'Candy'
COPIES: *BKM
NOTES: The recipes are credited with the name of the
contributor. The 'Index' lists sections for 'Miscellaneous' and 'Household Hints,' but these pages are
lacking in the BKM copy. From appearances, the book
was published about 1910.

Campbell's calendar cook book 1910

*For a history of D.E. Campbell's business and his other
cookbooks, see B3.1.*

B15.1   1910
Campbell's Prescription Store / / Pure drugs and
chemicals / Campbell's / calendar cook book /
1910 / 1910 / Published by / D.E. Campbell /
family chemist / Cor. Fort and Douglas sts. –

Victoria, B.C. / We are prompt / Your physician will be pleased / with our work / We are careful [cover-title]

DESCRIPTION: 17.0 × 13.0 cm   Pp [1–3] 4–32   Illus of astrological symbols   Paper, with image on front of a camel on which is printed 'D.E. Campbell family chemist Victoria B.C.'; stapled, and with hole punched at top left corner for hanging

CONTENTS: 1–2 publ ads; 3 'Eclipses, 1910,' 'Morning and Evening Stars, 1910,' and 'Chronological Cycles, 1910'; 4–29 recipes, publ ads, monthly calendars, and jokes; 30 'Facts about Canada' and 'What Is Canada's Population'; 31 'Grand Trunk Pacific Railway,' 'Rates of Postage,' 'How Occupation Affects Life,' and 'Wedding Anniversaries'; 32 'Language of Flowers,' 'Original Homes of Plants,' and 'Weights of the Sexes at Different Ages'

COPIES: BDUCVM   *BVIPA   CIHM (84429)

Gillanders' domestic science cook book

B16.1   nd [about 1910]
Gillanders' / domestic / science / cook book / containing only / reliable / recipes / Published by / Central Drug Store / C.D. Gillanders / 16 Cordova St. West / Vancouver, B.C. / Copyrighted [cover-title]

DESCRIPTION: 17.0 × 12.5 cm   Pp [1] 2–32   Thin card; stapled, and with hole punched at top left corner, through which runs a string for hanging

CONTENTS: 1 'To Our Customers' signed C.D. Gillanders, Vancouver, BC; 2 publ ads; 3 'Spoon and Cup Measure' and 'Table of Proportions'; 4–6 'Time-tables for Cooking'; 7–32 recipes and publ ads

COPIES: *BDEM

NOTES: The following are likely related publications issued in the same year: O230.1, Armstrong, George S., *Domestic Science Cook Book, Containing Only Reliable Recipes*; A14.1, *Calgary's Domestic Science Cook Book Containing Only Reliable Recipes*; and A15.1, *Cowles' Domestic Science Cook Book Containing Only Reliable Recipes*.

Tried and true recipes

The first service was held at Zion Presbyterian Church on 5 January 1902.

B17.1   nd [about 1910]
Tried and true / recipes / Compiled by the Ladies' Aid Society / Zion Presbyterian Church / Armstrong, British Columbia / "Let me cook the

meals of our country and I care not who / makes her laws." / Okanagan [printers' trade symbol] Advertiser

DESCRIPTION: 21.0 × 13.5 cm   Pp [1] 2–33 [34]   Tp illus of a pedestal dish overflowing with fruit and, below, holly or oak(?) leaves   Paper, with tp illus on front; sewn

CONTENTS: 1 tp; 2–33 recipes credited with the name of the contributor; 34 'Index' [i.e., table of contents], 'Measuring Table,' and poem beginning, 'We may live without poetry, music or art' [from *Lucile*, Part I, Canto ii, by Owen Meredith, pseudonym of Edward Robert Bulwer-Lytton]

COPIES: *BVAMM

NOTES: BVAMM dates the book [about 1910?].

1910–11

Gillette, Mrs Fanny Lea

This author (probably British) should not be confused with the American Mrs Fanny Lemira Camp Gillette, co-author with Hugo Zieman of O93.1, The White House Cook Book.

B18.1   nd [about 1911–12]
The new / temperance cookery / book / By / Mrs. Fanny Lea Gillette / author of / "The Model Housewife," "Economy and Comfort at Home," etc. / Illustrated / The Thomson Stationery Co., Limited / Gaskell-Odlum-Stationers [*sic*, two hyphens], Limited / Vancouver New Westminster

DESCRIPTION: 18.0 × 12.0 cm   Pp [i–vii] viii [ix] x–xx, [21] 22–337   Frontis of cuts of 'Beef,' a few illus of cuts of meat   Cloth

CONTENTS: i ht; ii–iii blank; iv frontis; v tp; vi blank; vii–viii 'Preface'; ix–xx table of contents; 21–337 text in thirty-nine chapters

COPIES: *BVIPA

NOTES: The 'Preface' states, 'The book embodies many original and commendable features among which is the elimination of the use of alcohol.' The name Gaskell-Odlum Stationers Ltd indicates publication in about 1911–12. This form of the company name appears only in Henderson's Vancouver business directory for 1911 (introduction dated June 1911). The 1910 directory (introduction, 24 June 1910) lists Gaskell, Odlum and Stabler, proprietors, Thomson Stationery Co. Ltd. The 1912 directory lists Gaskell Book and Stationery Co. Ltd. Gaskell-Odlum-Stabler Ltd was incorporated under the BC Companies Act on 16 March 1910 (incorporation No. 2925), and when it was dissolved it was under the name Gaskell Book and Stationery Co. Ltd. It appears that Stabler left the business sometime between June 1910 and June 1911, and that the name Gaskell-Odlum Stationers Ltd was used no later than about June 1912. The Corporate Registry file for the company (on microfilm at BVIPA) may pinpoint the date of the name changes more accurately.

BRITISH EDITIONS: London: Simpkin, Marshall, Hamilton, Kent and Co., and Glasgow: Thomas D. Morison, nd (Great Britain: OPo(F)).

1911

Delta calendar cook book, 1911

B19.1   1911
Hang me up in a handy place. / Delta / calendar / cook book, 1911 / Specialties: / Fragrant Carbolic Tooth Wash / Thoroughly cleanses the teeth, strengthens the gums and / sweetens the breath. 25 cents. / Melba's Skin Food / This is an ideal preparation for the skin and especially / delightful after shaving. 25 and 50 cents. / Lyster's Solution / The original antiseptic solution, 25, 50 and 75 cents. / Fisher's Drug and Book Store / Ladner, B.C. / Kindly let us know when goods fail to please. / [along right edge:] Qualified people wait on you here. / [along left edge:] We aim to assist in every way we can. [cover-title]
DESCRIPTION: 17.5 × 14.0 cm   Pp 1–32   Illus on p of signs of zodiac, illus calendar heads   Paper; stapled, and with hole punched at top left corner for hanging
CONTENTS: Inside front face of binding 'Delta Directory' [information about Delta and Ladner]; 1 'Calendar for 1911. Eclipses ...,' 'The Twelve Signs of the Zodiac,' 'The Seasons,' and 'Morning and Evening Stars'; 2 'Just about This Book' and 'Correct Kitchen Measurements'; 3–32 recipes, monthly calendars, and some publ ads
COPIES: *BDEM

Ravenhill, Miss Alice (Snaresbrook, Essex, England, 31 March 1859–27 May 1954, Victoria, BC)

In Alice Ravenhill – The Memoirs of an Educational Pioneer, Toronto and Vancouver: J.M. Dent and Sons (Canada) Ltd, 1951, the author recounts how she blazed a trail for English women in the field of public health by earning a National Health Society diploma and begin-

ning work in 1893 as a County Council lecturer on home nursing, first aid, and healthy homes. In 1901 she was asked by the Board of Education to travel to the United States to investigate school sanitation and the teaching of hygiene, and in 1904 she was elected the first woman fellow of the Royal Sanitary Institute. In 1908 she was instrumental in launching the first degree course in social and household science at the University of London. These were but a few of her achievements before she and her sister Edith left England for Shawnigan Lake on Vancouver Island in November 1910, for what they thought was a short period, to help her brother and nephew establish their lives in Canada. The start of the First World War disrupted her plans, and she never returned to England.

Soon after her arrival in Shawnigan, she was lecturing to British Columbia Women's Institutes on food and home management, and writing the following bulletins for the Women's Institutes, published by the provincial Department of Agriculture: No. 35, The Place and Purpose of Family Life, 1911 (CIHM, OOAG); No. 36, The Preparation of Food, 1911 (B20.1); No. 37, The Preservation of Food, 1912 (B25.1); No. 41, Labour-Saving Devices in the Household, 1912 (BVAU, CIHM, OOAG); Nos. 46–7, Food and Diet, two volumes, 1912 and 1913 (BVAU, CIHM, OOAG); No. 50, The Art of Right Living, 1913 (CIHM, OOAG); and No. 53, The Care of Young Children, 1914 (CIHM, OOAG). In her Memoirs, p 191, she recalls being commissioned in August 1911 to prepare the series of bulletins: 'The remuneration offered was ... so inadequate that I called personally on the Minister of Agriculture to enter a protest, ... With complete frankness he told me that as all I needed for the job was a pair of scissors and a pot of paste he thought my remonstrance quite unreasonable! However, thanks to Mr. W.E. Scott, a firm supporter of the Women's Institute movement, a compromise was effected. The bulletins had a warm reception. They were well illustrated and printed, but so restricted in numbers that the supply was exhausted in a year or two. The type had been broken up and they were never reprinted, though they were reproduced by request in Nova Scotia.' In 1911 she had published in Toronto, by McClelland and Goodchild Ltd, a book that had been published the year before in London, by Sidgwick and Jackson: Household Foes: A Book for Boys and Girls (OHM; Spadoni/Donnelly No. 27). Her lecturing expanded to other parts of Canada and the United States, including, in 1913, Toronto, where she gave the inaugural address at the official opening of the new Household Science Building at the University of Toronto; Annie Laird was her hostess during this trip (about Laird, see O241.1). In 1917 she was made director of home economics at the State College in Utah, but ill health forced her *retirement and she returned to live in Victoria from 1919. In her later years she became an advocate for BC native arts and crafts. In 1941 she was presented with an award from the Canadian Home Economics Association (We Are Tomorrow's Past, p 54). In 1948, the University of British Columbia conferred on her the degree of Doctor of Science, honoris causa.*

Ravenhill's Memoirs *includes photographs of her and a list of her published works. Christine E.J. Daniels and Robert A. Bayliss assess her achievements in 'Alice Ravenhill, Home Economist, 1859–1954,'* Westminster Journal of Education *Vol. 8 (1985), pp 21–36. See also Mary Gale Smith, 'Alice Ravenhill: International Pioneer in Home Economics,'* Illinois Teacher of Home Economics *Vol. 33, No. 1 (1989), pp 10–14; and Dagg, pp 250–1.*

B20.1 1911
Province of British Columbia. / Department of Agriculture / (Women's Institutes). / Bulletin No. 36. / The preparation of food. / By / Miss Alice Ravenhill, / Fellow of the Royal Sanitary Institute, etc., etc. / [provincial coat of arms] / The Government of / the Province of British Columbia. / Printed by authority of / the Legislative Assembly of British Columbia. / Victoria, B.C.: / Printed by William H. Cullin, printer to the King's Most Excellent Majesty. / 1911.
DESCRIPTION: Pp [1–5] 6–20 Illus
CONTENTS: 1 tp; 2 blank; 3 letter from Wm E. Scott, deputy minister of agriculture, to Price Ellison, minister of agriculture, 7 November 1911; 4 blank; 5–19 text; 20 'Notice' of bulletins prepared by Miss Ravenhill of Shawnigan Lake to be issued by the Department of Agriculture for distribution to members of the Women's Institutes
COPIES: *CIHM (84065) OOAG
NOTES: On p 3 Scott states that the book was 'compiled under the auspices of the Women's Institutes.' Ravenhill discusses boiling, steaming, paper-bag cookery, the fireless cook-stove, and frying. In Ravenhill's *Memoirs*, p 240, she incorrectly dates Bulletin 36 1912.

1911–13

The real home-keeper

See also later cookbooks for Vancouver brides: B44.1, Thompson, Frank R., and L.M. Geddis, The Bride's Book of Household Management, *and B74.1,* The Vancouver Bride.

B21.1 Vancouver ed., interim copyright [about 1911–13]
If you would enjoy distinction / As a cook for the elite, / Just turn the leaves of R.H.K.; / Your success will be complete. / The / real home-keeper / Published by / the Real Home-keeper Publishing Co. / 417 Granville Street / Vancouver, B.C. / The firms that advertise in this book / are all reliable, representing the best / stores in our city, and they will accord / you the fairest kind of treatment if you / will patronize them. The gift of this book / to you is from them collectively. Please / mention this book when you patronize / them. / Interim copyright by Geo. A. Brandow / Brand & Perry, printers [printers' trade symbol] 629 Pender Street West
DESCRIPTION: 25.0 × 17.0 cm Pp [1–7] 8–240 Paper-covered boards, with image on front, in an oval frame, of a bride
CONTENTS: 1–4 ads; 5 tp; 6 ad; 7–11 'Business Directory' and ads; 12 ad; 13–16 table of contents and ads; 17 ad; 18–240 text and ads
CITATIONS: Probably Ferguson/Fraser, pp 32 and 233, colour illus on p 35 of closed volume Hale 2391
COPIES: BRMA BVA (641.59 Ca2R28r) BVAA BVAU (Beatrice M. Millar Papers) BVIPM *OGU (UA s043 b38)
NOTES: 'Copyright, Canada 1913 by George A. Brandow' is stamped on the title-page. B21.3 and other later editions give 1911 as the year of George Brandow's copyright. The cover-title's sub-title is 'A Perpetual Honeymoon for the Vancouver Bride.' The text is mainly culinary recipes, but there is also other household information. Recipes for Huckleberry Cake, Baltimore Chicken, and others (recipes noted from 'Contents' of B21.4) suggest an American source for the text, as yet unidentified.

B21.2 Vancouver ed., copyright 1913
—If you would enjoy distinction / As a cook for the elite, / Just turn the leaves of R.H.K.; / Your success will be complete. / The / real home-keeper / The firms that advertise in this book / are all reliable, representing the best / stores in our city, and they will accord / you the fairest kind of treatment if you / will patronize them. The gift of this book / to you is from them collectively. Please / mention this book when you patronize / them. / Published by / the Real Home-keeper Publishing Co. / 417 Granville Street / Vancouver, B.C. / Copyrighted in Canada, 1913, by Geo. A. Brandow / Saturday Sunset Presses Vancouver, B.C.
DESCRIPTION: 25.0 × 16.5 cm Pp 1–184 Rebound
CONTENTS: 1–2 ads; 3 tp; 4 ad; 5–7 'Business Direc-

tory' and ad; 8–10 ads; 11–15 'Contents' [i.e., index] and ads; 16–18 ads; 19–184 text and ads
CITATIONS: Hale 2390
COPIES: *BVA BVAMM BVIPA CIHM (78449) Likely Neering, pp 96, 98, 99
NOTES: The BVAMM copy is bound in paper-covered boards, with an oval-shaped plate mounted on the front of a woman, her right hand raised, her left hand touching a stand bearing a plate of food(?).

B21.3 Hamilton ed., copyright 1914
—The / real home-keeper / Published by / the Brandow Publishing Co., / Limited / Geo. A. Brandow, President. Geo. G. McKenzie, Sec.-Treas. / L.A. Kennedy, Res. Manager. / 36 Rebecca Street. / Phone 6899 / The firms that advertise in this book are all / reliable, representing the best stores in our city, / and they will accord you the fairest kind of treat- / ment if you will patronize them. The gift of / this book to you is from them collectively. Please / mention this book when you patronize them. / Copyright 1911 / by / Geo. A. Brandow / Copyright 1914 / by / the Brandow Publishing Co. Ltd / Notice is hereby given of the above copyrights / under which all rights are reserved. / [folio:] 5
CITATIONS: Simpson, pp W16–17 (includes two photographs)
COPIES: CIHM (78541) *OH (R640 REA CESH) OONL (TX145 R42 1911 fol.)

B21.4 Toronto ed., copyright 1914
—The / real home-keeper / Published by / the Brandow Publishing Co., / Limited / Geo. A. Brandow, President. Geo. G. McKenzie, Sec.-Treas. / Toronto, Canada. / The firms that advertise in this book are all / reliable, representing the best stores in our city, / and they will accord you the fairest kind of treat- / ment if you will patronize them. The gift of / this book to you is from them collectively. Please / mention this book when you patronize them. / Copyright 1911 / by / Geo. A. Brandow / Copyright 1914 / by / the Brandow Publishing Co., / Limited / Notice is hereby given of the above copyrights / under which all rights are reserved. / [folio:] 5
DESCRIPTION: 25.5 × 17.0 cm Pp 3–144 Paper-covered boards, with oval pl col mounted on front of a woman wearing a flower-decorated straw hat and carrying a bouquet of violets
CONTENTS: 3–4 ads; 5 tp; 6 ad; 7–13 table of contents and ads; 14–16 'Business Directory' and ad; 17 ad; 18–top 123 culinary text and ads; mid 123–mid 142 information about household topics and ads; bottom 142–144 'How to Bake Bread' and other recipes

COPIES: CIHM (77867) OH (R640 R229 CESC) OONL (TX651 R42 1914 fol. p***) *Private collection
NOTES: The cover-title's sub-title is 'A Perpetual Honeymoon for the Toronto Bride.' The endpaper glued to the inside back face of the binding is numbered as p 145.

B21.5 Winnipeg ed., copyright 1914
—The / real home-keeper / Published by / the Brandow Publishing Co. Ltd. / Geo. A. Brandow, President Geo. G. McKenzie, Sec.-Treas. / W.C. Vincent, Res. Manager / 842 Grosvenor Avenue / Phone Ft. Rouge 584 / The firms that advertise in this book are / all reliable, representing the best stores / in our city, and they will accord you the / fairest kind of treatment if you will / patronize them. The gift of this book / to you is from them collectively. Please / mention this book when you patronize them. / Copyright 1911 / by / Geo. A. Brandow / Copyright 1914 / by / the Brandow Publishing Co. Ltd. / Notice is hereby given of the above copyrights / under which all rights are reserved / [folio:] 5
DESCRIPTION: 25.0 × 17.0 cm Pp 1–224 Cloth, with oval plate on front of a bride (the same bride as B21.1)
CONTENTS: 1–4 ads; 5 tp; 6 ad; 7–11 'Contents' [i.e., index] and ads; 12 ad; 13–16 'Business Directory' and ads; 17 ad; 18–224 text and ads
COPIES: *AEU (TX158 R28 1914) CIHM (84926) MWMM MWU (TX158 R28 1914)
NOTES: 'The Story of Winnipeg' by Chas F. Roland (i.e., Charles Franklin Roland, 1870–1936?) is on p 162. The cover-title's sub-title is 'A Perpetual Honeymoon for the Winnipeg Bride.'

The MWMM copy lacks the last leaf. A copy at BPORH has the lower right part of the title-page torn off, but it is likely this edition.

B21.6 Montreal ed., English, copyright 1928
—The / bride's book / Published by / the Brandow Publishing / Company / of Canada, Limited / publishers of household books for brides / 610 Shaughnessy Building / 407 McGill Street / Montreal / Geo. A. Brandow President / G.D. Evans Vice-President / T.J. Coulter Treasurer / W. Gosling Secretary / Copyright 1911 by Geo. A. Brandow / Copyright 1928 by Geo. A. Brandow / Foreign copyrights / All rights reserved / Publication whole or in part of the contents of this book prohibited by the / terms of the above copyrights / [folio:] 3
DESCRIPTION: 25.5 × 17.0 cm Pp 1–352 [Free, on p 8] Cloth simulating leather
CONTENTS: 1–2 ads; 3 tp; 4 'An Introduction'; 5–6 ads;

7 'To the Husband' [unsigned poem]; 8 'Foreword to the Bride'; 9 ad; 10–344 text; 345–7 'Index to Contents'; 348–50 'Business Directory'; 351–2 ads

COPIES: *OGU (UA s049 b22)

NOTES: 'A Perpetual Guide for the Montreal Bride' is printed on the front face of the binding. The 'Foreword to the Bride' says, 'This beautiful and exceedingly useful book is a gift to you, ... from the manufacturers and other business concerns whose announcements appear within its covers.' The 'Introduction' describes the contents of the book: 'One hundred and nine pages are devoted to the food problem ... Pages on the home itself include articles on home decorating, selection and care of rugs, home equipment, flowers, pictures, care of canaries, etc. There is also a splendid treatise on bridge ... [health and beauty] are given much space.' This edition also contains an article by the secretary of the Province of Quebec about Quebec's marriage laws. There are blank, ruled, yellow leaves throughout for 'My Personal Recipes.'

B21.7 Montreal ed., French, copyright 1930
—Le livre / de la / nouvelle / mariée / Publié par / The Brandow / Publishing Company / of Canada, Limited / éditeurs de livres domestiques / pour les nouvelles mariées / 610, édifice Shaughnessy / 407, rue McGill / Montréal / Droits réservés par Geo. A. Brandow / Canada, 1930 / Droits réservés à l'étranger / Tous droits réservés / La reproduction en entier ou en partie du contenu de ce livre est interdite / par les droits réservés ci-dessus.

DESCRIPTION: 25.0 × 17.0 cm   Pp [i–ii], [1–3] 4–208, [i–ii]   Frontis of 'Sa sainteté Pie XI,' pl on p 8 of Monseigneur Georges Gauthier   Cloth, with image on front, in an oval frame, of a bride

CONTENTS: i–ii endpaper ads; 1–2 frontis; 3 tp; 4 'Introduction'; 5 'Résumé de la table des matières'; 6 'Un mot à la mariée'; 7–8 pl of Georges Gauthier; 9 'Ce que dit l'église' signed Adélard Dugré; 10 'Au mari'; 11 'Notre certificat de mariage' [in this copy, the certificate is filled out for Monsieur J. Albini Rochon and Mademoiselle Jeanne Vachon, married 7 February 1931 at Église de Ste Anne de Prescott, Ontario]; 12–200 text and ads (the leaves of ads are not included in the pagination); 201–5 'Index du contenu'; 206–8 'Index des annonces' [i.e., business directory]; i–ii ads

COPIES: *QMBN (204487 CON)

B21.8 Montreal ed., English, copyright 1932
—The / bride's / book / Published by / the Brandow / Publishing Company / of Canada, Limited / publishers of household books for brides

/ 610 Shaughnessy Building / 407 McGill Street / Montreal / Copyright 1932 by Geo. A. Brandow / Foreign copyrights / All rights reserved / Publication whole or in part of the contents of this book prohibited by the / terms of the above copyrights.

DESCRIPTION: 25.0 × 17.0 cm   Pp [i–ii], [1] 2–224, [i–ii]   A few small illus   Cloth, with image on front of a bride

CONTENTS: i–ii endpaper ads; 1 tp; 2 'Summary of Contents'; 3 'An Introduction'; 4 'Foreword to the Bride'; 5 'To the Husband' by G.A.B. [poem, likely by George A. Brandow]; 6 'A Message from the Editor // Go to Church'; 7 'Our Marriage Record'; 8 'Bridal Party'; 9 'Guests and Autographs'; 10 'Our Wedding Presents'; 11 'The Honeymoon'; 12 'Wedding Anniversaries,' 'Precious Stones,' and 'Birthday Flowers'; 13–216 culinary text followed by sections on other household topics, graphology (i.e., interpreting handwriting), bridge, information for expectant mothers, and other diverse topics, and ads; 217–18 'List of Recommended Products'; 219–24 'Index of Contents'; i–ii endpaper ads

COPIES: QMM (RBD ckbk 1347)   *Private collection

B21.9 Montreal ed., French, copyright 1934
—Le livre / de la / nouvelle / mariée / Publié par / La compagnie de / publicité Brandow / de Montréal / éditeurs de livres domestiques / pour les nouvelles mariées / 610, édifice Shaughnessy / 407, rue McGill / Montréal / Droits réservés par The Brandow Publishing Co. of Canada, Limited. / Canada, 1934 / Droits réservés à l'étranger / Tous droits réservés / La reproduction en entier ou en partie du contenu de ce livre est interdite / par les droits réservés ci-dessus.

DESCRIPTION: 25.0 × 17.0 cm   Pp [i–ii], [1–5] 6–199 [200–2]   3 portraits on pp 3–5 of Roman Catholic Church figures   Cloth simulating leather

CONTENTS: i–ii ads; 1 tp; 2 biographical information for 'le pape Pie XI'; 3 portrait of Pie XI; 4 portrait of Villeneuve, 'archevêque de Québec'; 5 portrait of 's. ex. mgr Georges Gauthier' and biographical information; 6 'Ce que dit l'église'; 7 introduction; 8 'Au mari' [poem]; 9 'Un mot à la mariée' signed Geo. A. Brandow; 10 'Résumé de la table des matières'; 11 'Notre certificat de mariage'; 12 list of marriage anniversaries, precious stones for the months, and flowers for the months; 13–193 text; 194–8 'Index du contenu'; 199 'Index des annonces' [i.e., business directory]; 200–2 ads

COPIES: *OGU (UA s017 b23)   QMBN (99509 CON and MIC/B5883 GEN)   QVMVS

NOTES: 'Un guide général pour la mariée de Montréal'

is printed on the front face of the binding. There are blank, ruled leaves throughout for 'Mes recettes personnelles.'

1912

Atkinson's year book 1912

See also B23.1, Jackson's Imperial Cook Book and Calendar 1912, *and S9.1,* McCuaig's Year Book 1912, *which are likely related.*

B21a.1   1912
Hang me up in a handy place. I'm worth while. / Atkinson's year book / 1912 / A valuable book / containing / tested recipes for tasty / dishes / Canadian facts, information / for your health. Also, a / monthly calendar and / birthday horoscope / Atkinson's Drug Store / 955 Nicola St., near No. 6 Fire Hall / Phone Seymour 2459 Vancouver, B.C. [cover-title]
DESCRIPTION: 18.0 × 13.5 cm   Pp [1] 2–32   Zodiac signs, astronomical symbols, and illus calendar heads   Paper; stapled, and with hole punched at top left corner for hanging
CONTENTS: 1 'Calendar for 1912,' 'The Twelve Signs of the Zodiac,' 'The Seasons,' and 'Morning and Evening Stars'; 2 'This Little Book'; 3–29 recipes, monthly calendars, monthly birthday horoscopes, and publ ads; 30 'Table of Weights and Measures,' 'Facts about Canada,' and medical advice; 31–2 'Household Hints'
COPIES: *Private collection
NOTES: Page 2 states, 'This little book is presented to you to remind you throughout the coming year of our store ... The occasional references to Nyal Remedies we would commend particularly to your attention.' The recipes on p 3 are Pork and Beans, How to Cook Young Chicken, Mock Duck, Chicken Pie, Curry Sauce, and Mint Sauce. The leaves and binding are orange paper.

Buchan, Mrs, Mrs A.L. McCulloch, and Mrs N.A. Cummins

Mrs A.L. McCulloch was the wife of Andrew Lake McCulloch, listed in the Nelson section of Henderson's and Wrigley's British Columbia directories variously as a civil or hydraulic engineer and as a provincial land surveyor. In the 1901 Census she is recorded as Annie B. McCulloch, born 14 April 1874. Mrs Buchan may have been the wife of John L. Buchan, manager of the Canadian Bank of Commerce in Nelson.

B22.1   nd [about 1912]
[Running head:] The Hospital Aid cook book.
[folio:] 9 / The / Hospital Aid / cook book / Nelson, B.C. / Compiled by / Mrs. Buchan // Mrs. A.L. McCulloch / Mrs. N.A. Cummins
DESCRIPTION: Tp illus of a cross   With image on front of a cross
CONTENTS: ...; 8 ad for Joy's Cash Grocery; 9 tp; 10 ad for 'The Hume'; 11 'Preface'; ...
COPIES: *BNEM
NOTES: BNEM reports that the volume has 83 pp, 'plus empty pages for additions.' In the 'Preface' the Woman's Hospital Aid Society refers to 'publishing this book to raise funds for their work.' The Hospital Aid Society was associated with Nelson's hospital. The suggested date of publication, about 1912, is BNEM's, based on the advertisement for 'The Hume,' which names Geo. P. Wells as proprietor of the hotel. A search of British Columbia directories to determine the period when George P. Wells was proprietor was inconclusive because no complete run of directories could be located; however, he was not listed as proprietor in the volume for 1905 (Henderson's directory lists J. Fred Hume), or in the volume for 1918 (Wrigley's directory lists George Benwell), but he was listed as proprietor in Henderson's directory for 1910.

Jackson's Imperial cook book and calendar 1912

See also B21a.1, Atkinson's Year Book 1912, *and S9.1,* McCuaig's Year Book 1912, *which are likely related.*

B23.1   1912
Hang me up in a handy place. I'm worth while. / Jackson's / Imperial / cook book / and calendar / 1912 / Wm. Jackson & Co. / family druggists / Established 1875 / Waverly Building, – Douglas St. / near Johnston / Victoria, B.C. / We handle the largest and newest stock / on [sic] Nyal goods in British Columbia / manufacturers / Imperial Family Remedies [cover-title]
DESCRIPTION: Pp [1] 2–32   Paper(?); stapled, and with hole punched at top left corner for hanging
CONTENTS: 1 'Calendar for 1912'; 2 'This Little Book'; 3–29 recipes, monthly calendars, and monthly horoscopes; 30 'Table of Weights and Measures' and 'Facts about Canada'; 31–2 'Household Hints'; inside back face of binding list of 'Imperial Preparations'
COPIES: *BVIPM (photocopy)
NOTES: The cookbook promotes Nyal products.

Mendelsohn, Felix (1876–)

This author also compiled Favorite Recipes of Famous People, *Chicago: F. Mendelsohn, [c1936] (United States: DLC).*

B24.1 [copyright 1912]
The / cook book / de luxe / containing over 600 / "recipes of quality" / Published by / Felix Mendelsohn / People's Gas Building / Chicago
DESCRIPTION: With image on front of a maid carrying a steaming joint of meat on a platter
CONTENTS: Tp verso unattributed poem beginning, 'We may live without poetry, music and art' [from *Lucile*, Part I, Canto ii, by Owen Meredith, pseudonym of Edward Robert Bulwer-Lytton] and 'Copyright 1912, by Felix Mendelsohn'
CITATIONS: Bitting, p 320
COPIES: BKOM   *Private collection; United States: DLC (TX715 B647 1912b)
NOTES: This American book was used by two Canadian businesses as a promotional tool. The following is on the binding of the BKOM copy: 'Recipes of Quality // A Cook Book De Luxe // A "National" Range and A Cook Book De Luxe solve your cooking problems // Dalgleish & Harding Kelowna, B.C.' The private collector's copy has compliments of the *Edmonton Journal* on the binding.

AMERICAN EDITIONS: *The Blue and Gold Cook Book; Recipes of Quality*, Oakland, Calif.: Oakland Brewing and Malting Co., [1912], author not named (United States: DLC); *Recipes of Quality*, [Washington?:] c1912 (United States: DLC). *Sonia's Cook Book; a Cook Book De Luxe of Tested and Selected Recipes*, Chicago: F. Mendelsohn, [c. 1920] (Bitting, p 320), may be an edition of *The Cook Book De Luxe* described here.

Ravenhill, Miss Alice (Snaresbrook, Essex, England, 31 March 1859–27 May 1954, Victoria, BC)

For information about the author and her other publications, see B20.1.

B25.1 1912
Province of British Columbia. / Department of Agriculture / (Women's Institutes). / Bulletin No. 37. / The preservation of food. / By / Miss Alice Ravenhill, / Fellow of the Royal Sanitary Institute, etc., etc. / [British Columbia coat of arms] / Printed by authority of / the Legislative Assembly of British Columbia. / Victoria, B.C. / Printed by William H.

Cullin, printer to the King's Most Excellent Majesty. / 1912.
DESCRIPTION: Pp [1–3] 4–19   10 numbered illus
CONTENTS: 1 tp; 2 letter from Wm E. Scott, deputy minister of agriculture, superintendent of [Women's] Institutes, to Price Ellison, minister of agriculture, 26 February 1912; 3–18 'Desire for Food a Fundamental Instinct,' 'Mankind Thrives on Varied Forms of Food,' 'Three Factors in Healthful Diet,' 'Some Results of Monotonous Food,' 'This Variety Should Be Sought,' 'Association between Flavour and Digestion,' 'Some Reasons Why Meals Are Monotonous,' 'Food-Preservation an Important Factor in Wholesome Variety,' 'An Important Point in Food-Preservation,' 'Methods of Food Preservation in General Use,' 'What Decay Is,' 'Why Decay Spreads So Rapidly,' 'Micro-Organisms, Good and Bad,' 'What Is Fermentation?,' 'Moulds and Yeasts as Agents of Decay,' 'Summary,' 'The Prevention of Decay,' 'The Preservation of Food' (on pp 8–mid 15), 'The Preservation of Groceries, Fruit, Vegetables, etc., in the Home' (on pp bottom 15–top 18), and 'Conclusion'; 19 'Notice' of bulletins to be prepared by Ravenhill and issued by the Department of Agriculture, 'Bulletins Issued by the Department of Agriculture,' 'Alice Ravenhill' [her qualifications and publications], and 'Victoria, B.C.: Printed by William H. Cullin, ... 1912.'
COPIES: BVAU   *CIHM (84067)   OOAG
NOTES: The first part of the text, pp 3–7, is mostly about decay; the second part, pp 8–18, is about preservation. B49.1, British Columbia, Department of Agriculture, *Preservation of Food*, Bulletin 83, is not attributed to Ravenhill and is likely a new text.

Selected recipes

B26.1 1912
Selected / recipes / Compiled by / the ladies of St. John's Church / Vancouver, B.C. / 1912 / "She looketh well to the ways of her household"
DESCRIPTION: 21.0 × 13.0 cm   Pp [1–8] 9–95 [96] Paper-covered boards, cloth spine; stapled
CONTENTS: 1–6 ads; 7 tp; 8 'Preface' signed the Committee; 9 menus for Christmas Dinner, Easter Dinner, and Thanksgiving Dinner; 10 ads; 11–81 recipes credited with the name of the contributor and ads; 82 ads; 83–94 lacking; 95 table of contents; 96 'Saturday Sunset Presses Vancouver, B.C.'
COPIES: AMHM   BVAU (TX715 S449 1912 ACA-9002) *BVIPA   CIHM (80438)   OONL (AC901 A7 1912 No. 0055)   OTNY (uncat pamphlet file – cookery)
NOTES: The cover-title is 'St. John's Church Woman's Aid Cook Book'; the 'Preface' uses the title 'St. John's

Presbyterian Church Cook Book.' The 'Preface' echoes the text of the 'Preface' of O86.2, the 1905 edition of *Public School Household Science*, co-authored by Mrs Adelaide Sophia Hoodless and Miss Mary Urie Watson, when it states: '... the mental, moral and physical well-being of our families depends largely not so much on the quantity but the quality of the food set before them.'

The BVIPA copy lacks pp 83–94, but the BVAU copy has the following contents on these pages: 83–5 'Candies'; 86 ads; 87–90 'Invalid Cooking'; 91–2 'Practical Hints'; 93 'Table of Measures,' 'Table of Weights and Measures,' and 'Spoon and Cup Measure'; 94 ads.

1913

Elkins, Mrs F. Mitchell

Henderson's Vancouver city directory for 1913 lists F. Mitchell Elkins, the author's husband, as a notary public, living at 1037 Thurlow. Saturday Sunset Presses printed Saturday Sunset, *the Vancouver weekly that ran from 1907 to 1915.*

B27.1   1st ed., 1913
Saturday Sunset / cook book / by / Mrs. F. Mitchell Elkins / prepared specially / for / British Columbia / use / First edition / Vancouver / Saturday Sunset Presses / publishers / 1913
DESCRIPTION: 22.5 × 15.0 cm   Pp [i–vi], [1] 2–175 [176]   Cloth, with image on front of a woman carrying a covered dish; stapled
CONTENTS: i ht; ii blank; iii tp; iv blank; v–vi 'Contents' [i.e., alphabetical list of headings]; 1–3 'Time Required for Cooking'; 4–12 'Combinations for Serving'; 13–168 recipes; 169–75 menus; 176 blank for 'Recipes'
COPIES: *BVMA
NOTES: 'Christmas Puddings' are on pp 66–74. There is a leaf between pp 96–7 that is not included in the pagination; on the recto is 'Cook with Gas,' and on the verso, 'Electrical Appliances in the Modern Home.'

Juniper, Miss Annie Bessie
(died December 1933)

Annie Juniper graduated from Norfolk and Norwich School of Household Science, then taught for six years in England and Wales. Her career in Canada followed a path from the East to the West Coast, and advanced in step with the growth of domestic science in this country.

Her first two jobs in Canada were as a domestic science teacher at the Macdonald School in Middleton, Nova Scotia, then at Hillsboro Consolidated School in Prince Edward Island. From October 1908 to 1910 she served as the second head of household science at Macdonald College in Ste Anne de Bellevue, Quebec (the school had opened only one year before her appointment). In 1910, she moved to Winnipeg to direct the first program in household science at the Manitoba Agricultural College. When not teaching at the college, she demonstrated and lectured throughout Manitoba to thousands of people (sometimes in an equipped car on the Better Farming Train), and encouraged the formation of Home Economics Societies (the name for Women's Institutes in Manitoba until 1919). She was the founding president of the Manitoba Household Science Association at its inception in January 1911. Later that year she left Winnipeg to become supervisor of household science for Victoria schools. She returned to England during the First World War to help with the war effort, but came back to Victoria when the war ended to teach summer school classes for teachers, followed by a stint teaching home economics in New Zealand. In 1923 she was appointed principal of the Yorkshire Training College of Housecraft in Leeds, England (now the Tourism, Hospitality and Events School at Leeds Metropolitan University). She was affectionately remembered by Victoria citizens, and her vacation in the city in 1926 was reported in an article in the Daily Colonist *of 26 August ('Former Victoria Teacher Now English Principal,' p 1). When she died, the newspaper printed an obituary (11 February 1934, p C7).*

For more information about Juniper, see contemporary accounts of her work in the M.A.C. Gazette: *'Household Science Convention' and 'Men and Home Development,' Vol. 1, No. 7 (March 1911), pp 67–9; and 'An Appreciation,' Vol. 1, No. 8 (February 1912), p 73. See also John Ferguson Snell,* Macdonald College of McGill University: A History from 1904–1955, *Montreal: McGill University Press, 1963, p 66;* Fiftieth Anniversary of the School of Home Economics – University of Manitoba (1910–1960), *Winnipeg: 1960, pp 11, 26–7, 40 (a photograph of her is on p 26); The Great Human Heart: A History of the Manitoba Women's Institute 1910–1980, MWI, 1980, p 3; and Mary Leah DeZwart, 'Annie B. Juniper: Home Economics Pioneer,'* Canadian Home Economics Journal *Vol. 48, No. 3 (summer 1998), pp 101, 103, which includes references to other sources.*

For another book authorized by the minister of education, see B59.1, Recipes for Home Economics Classes.

B28.1   1913
Girls' home manual / of / cookery / home management / home nursing / and / laundry /

by / Annie B. Juniper / Supervisor of Household Science, Public Schools, Victoria, B.C.; / late Dean of Household Science, Macdonald College, Ste. Anne de Bellevue; / and Professor of Household Science, Manitoba Agricultural College, Winnipeg / [provincial coat of arms] / The Government of / the Province of British Columbia / Issued under the authority of the Minister of Education / for British Columbia / Victoria, B.C. / Printed by W.H. Cullin, printer to the King's Most Excellent Majesty / 1913
DESCRIPTION: 26.0 × 17.0 cm   Pp [1–3] 4–187 [188–200]   Illus   Lacks paper(?) binding; stapled
CONTENTS: 1 tp; 2 dedication to Mrs Margaret Jenkins 'whose interest, sympathy and help have done so much to further the Home Economic Movement in British Columbia' and 'Preface' signed Annie Bessie Juniper; 3–4 table of contents; 5–122 'Cookery'; 123–44 'House Management'; 145–52 'Home Nursing'; 153–80 'Laundry Work'; 181–7 index; 188–200 blank for 'Memorandum'
CITATIONS: Neering, pp 93–4, 99, 100–1, 105, 106–7, 108   O'Neill (unpublished)
COPIES: BDEM *BVICC BVIP CIHM (66186); Great Britain: LB (07944.k.24 destroyed)
NOTES: This is the first household science textbook written for British Columbia schools. In the 'Preface,' Juniper states that the book covers a three-year course in household science, and comments, 'On investigation, it was found that only a small percentage of housekeepers possess any library bearing on their work, with the exception of an occasional cook-book and manufacturers' sample cook-books.' There are chapters for 'Fireless Cookery,' 'Paper-Bag Cookery,' 'House Plans and Furniture,' and 'Cookery Uniform.' When Juniper returned for a vacation in Victoria in 1926, the *Daily Colonist* referred to the book in the article 'Former Victoria Teacher Now English Principal,' 26 August 1926, p 1: 'An enduring souvenir of her connection with the department may still be found in many Victoria homes in the form of a cookbook which is regarded by its owners as a standard and invaluable work.'

Nurses' year book and directory 1913

B29.1   1913
Nurses' / year book and / directory / 1913 edition
DESCRIPTION: 22.0 × 14.5 cm   Pp [1–10] 11–57, [i–xiv]   Illus on p 7 of Vancouver General Hospital, New St Paul's Hospital in Vancouver, and Fairview Nurses Home   Cloth
CONTENTS: 1–4 ads; 5 tp; 6 ads; 7 illus; 8 ads; 9–11

'The Royal Victoria Order of District Nurses of Canada' and ads; 12 ads; 13–25 'What Does Cookery Mean // Soup, Meat and Pudding Recipes' and ads; 26–8 ads; 29–39 'Hints on Nursing the Sick' and ads; 40–2 ads; 43–7 'Symptoms, General Duration and Special Dangers of the Different Infectious Diseases' and ads; 48 ads; 49 'The Care of Infants'; 50–2 ads; 53–7 list of 'Physicians and Surgeons' and 'Hospitals and Asylums,' and ads; i–xiv ads
COPIES: *Private collection
NOTES: Surprisingly, the recipes are for general use, not for invalids. The printer's name, 'Commercial Print, Ltd.,' is on the inside back face of the binding. The advertisements are for Vancouver businesses, including medically related ones, such as ambulance services, surgical supplies, and – ominously – funeral directors.

1914

The Vancouver home-builder and home-keeper

B30.1   1914
[Running head:] Vancouver home-builder and home-keeper [folio:] 3 / [title:] The Vancouver / home-builder and / home-keeper / The gift of this book to you is from the / advertisers collectively. All firms whose / advertisements you see are reliable, and / by patronizing them when possible and / mentioning this publication you will / receive in many cases better prices, / courteous treatment and better service / than you can obtain elsewhere. / This publication has been compiled with / much trouble and time, and the informa- / tion we furnish you herein is as near / authentic as possible. No doubt you will / receive many hints and save much time / and trouble by perusing this valuable / information. In order for you to show / your appreciation we might suggest again / that you keep the names of the advertisers / before you and by patronizing them it / will mean money in your pocket. / Published by / the Dominion Publishing Company / 114 Yorkshire Building Seymour 2611 / Vancouver, B.C. / Copyright applied for November, 1914
DESCRIPTION: 24.5 × 17.0 cm   Pp 1–118   A few illus   Paper-covered boards; stapled
CONTENTS: 1–2 ads; 3 tp; 4 ads; 5 table of contents and ad; 6 ad; 7 'Business Directory'; 8–10 ads; 11–117 text and ads; 118 ads
CITATIONS: Hale 3125

COPIES: *BVIPA

NOTES: 'The Home-Keeper' section of the book is on pp 81–117; pp 83–100 of this section are recipes. About a year or so before, another company had published a promotional vehicle for Vancouver businesses, B21.1, *The Real Home-keeper*. The title-pages of both books express the same sentiment about patronizing the reliable firms advertised within to ensure the best service. I have not compared the two texts.

1914–18

Cookery book

B31.1   nd [about 1914–18]

The Soldiers' Comforts / Club / Cookery / book / Kamloops, B.C. / Printed by the Inland Sentinel and / published by the Soldiers' / Comforts Club

DESCRIPTION: 22.0 × 15.0 cm   Pp [1–3] 4–44   Paper, with image on front of two Union Jacks; stapled

CONTENTS: 1 tp; 2 'Foreword'; 3–44 recipes credited with the name of the contributor; inside back face of binding 'Printed by "The Inland Sentinel" Job Department, Kamloops, B.C.'

COPIES: *BDEM   BKM

NOTES: The object of the book is stated on p 2: 'to enable the publishers to sell it for the benefit of the funds for the purchase of field comforts for the men of Kamloops and district who are serving their King and country in the various war theatres.'

Patriotic cook book

B32.1   nd [about 1914–18]

Patriotic / cook book / Isaiah 58: 10, 11 / War recipes / collected and compiled by / Women's Auxiliary / Pioneers of Vancouver / The Auxiliary are indebted to Mrs. Philip A. Wilson for many of / the recipes contained in this book, given to her by / members of the Women's Committee on Food / Conservation in her home state, Missouri. / [printers' trade symbol] / A.H. Timms, printer / Vancouver, B.C.

DESCRIPTION: 22.5 × 15.0 cm   Pp [1–2] 3–64   Tp illus of a wheat sheaf   Thin card, with image on front of a Union Jack, Red Ensign, and crown; stapled

CONTENTS: 1 tp; 2 'Your Country Calls'; 3 'Let Us Remember,' 'Meat Plans,' and 'Helps to a Wise Choice'; 4 ads; 5 'Directions' and 'Protein Foods'; 6 ads; 7–62 recipes, tables, and ads; 63 'Table of Contents' [i.e., alphabetical list of headings]; 64 ads

COPIES: *BVAU (Beatrice M. Millar Papers)

NOTES: Text on the binding states, 'Profits from the sale of this book go to the Prisoners of War Fund.'

1915

British Columbia fruit

B33.1   nd [1915]

British Columbia / fruit / Two hundred and twenty-five / recipes / Dedicated to the patriotic housewives / of Western Canada / in the full confidence that they will give British / Columbia fruit that practical preference which / a grown-in-Canada product of established merit / deserves, that they will ask for it persistently, / and spare no effort to impress their dealers with / the reality of their demand for a Canadian-grown / article. / Issued by the / British Columbia Fruit Growers' Association / Members of this association are fruit growers / from all parts of the province of British Columbia, / and the object of the association is the advance- / ment of the industry in the province. Its / directors are representative men from every fruit / growing district of the province. / Copies of this booklet free / on request

DESCRIPTION: 11.5 × 17.5 cm   Pp [1–2] 3–78   Illus of fruit   Paper, with image on front of a red apple; stapled

CONTENTS: 1 tp; 2 blank; 3–4 'Contents' [i.e., alphabetical index]; 5–11 introductory text including 'Why B.C. Fruit?,' 'Inter-provincial Trade,' 'How to Buy B.C. Fruit,' 'Best Time to Buy B.C. Fruits,' 'Watch for the B.C. Brand on the Box,' 'Preserve Your Fruits without Sugar,' 'Confectioners, Make Your Own Fruit Flavorings,' 'General Canning and Jam-Making Methods,' and 'The British Columbia Potato'; 12–78 information about, and recipes for, apples, rhubarb, strawberries, raspberries, black and red currants, tomatoes, cherries, apricots, gooseberries, blackberries, onions, peaches, cantaloupes, celery, plums, and pears

COPIES: ACG   *BDEM (DE 969.42.20)   BNEM   BVIP   BVIPA   CIHM (76210)   OONL (TX811 B75 1910z p***)

NOTES: The cover-title is 'British Columbia Fruit // Delicious Canadian home-grown // Two hundred and twenty-five recipes.' On the back face of the binding, below two crossed flags (Union Jack and Red Ensign), is the exhortation 'Canada first! Buy home-grown fruit!' This edition is undated and has no place of publication; however, BVIPA dates its copy [Victoria, 1915].

A private collector has a copy of this edition that is stamped on p 6, 'W.E. McTaggart 328a 8th Avenue West Calgary,' a new BC markets commissioner, to supersede L. Forsythe Smith, 632 10th Street, Sunnyside, Calgary. McTaggart is the commissioner named on the title-page of the 1916 edition. The collector's copy of the 1915 edition, however, has a design on the binding that is different from, and looks newer than, the bindings seen on other copies of the 1915 and 1916 editions: The cover-title is 'What Do You Know about Apples?' and below there is a large red apple at left and a woman in a yellow apron at right. From appearances, the design dates from the 1930s, suggesting that leftover copies of the 1915 edition were rebound in an updated paper cover.

B33.2 [new ed.], 1916
—British Columbia / fruit / (1916 edition) / Dedicated to the patriotic housewives / of Western Canada / in the full confidence that they will give British / Columbia fruit that practical preference which / a grown-in-Canada product of established merit / deserves, that they will ask for it persistently, / and spare no effort to impress their dealers with / the reality of their demand for a Canadian-grown / article. / Issued by the / British Columbia Fruit Growers Association / Members of the association are fruit growers / from all parts of the province of British Columbia, / and the object of the association is the advance- / ment of the industry. Its directors are repre- / sentative men from every fruit growing district / of the province. / Copies of this booklet free / on request / from / R.M. Winslow, / Secretary B.C. Fruit Growers' Association / Victoria, B.C. / W.E. McTaggart, / B.C. Markets Commissioner / Calgary, Alta. / R.C. Abbott, / Coast Markets Commissioner / Bank of Ottawa Bldg. / Vancouver, B.C.
DESCRIPTION: 17.0 × 11.5 cm   Pp [1–2] 3–80   Illus of fruit   Paper, with image on front of a red apple; stapled
CONTENTS: 1 tp; 2 blank; 3–4 'Contents' [i.e., alphabetical list of headings]; 5–6 'British Columbia Fruit'; 7 'Best Time to Buy B.C. Fruits'; top 8 'Watch for the B.C. Brand on the Box'; mid 8–9 'Preserve Your Fruits without Sugar'; 10 'Confectioners, Make Your Own Fruit Flavorings'; 11 'General Canning and Jam-Making Methods'; 12–80 recipes for, and information about, rhubarb, strawberries, gooseberries, raspberries, blackberries, black currants, red currants, cherries, apricots, peaches, cantaloupes, plums, pears, apples, potatoes, celery, tomatoes, onions
COPIES: BVAU (SPAM 14395)   *BVIP   OONL (TX811 B75 1916 p***)

NOTES: The cover-title is 'British Columbia Fruit // Its qualities and uses // Two hundred and twenty-five recipes (New edition).' The apple recipes begin on p 52, under the heading '108 Apple Recipes.'

B33.3 [new ed.], 1918
—British Columbia / fruit / Its qualities and uses / Two hundred and twenty-five / recipes
DESCRIPTION: 17.0 × 11.5 cm   Pp [i–ii], [1–4] 5–80, [i–ii]   Illus of fruit   Paper, with image on front of a red apple; stapled
CONTENTS: i tp; ii ad; 1 'British Columbia Fruit (1918 edition) Dedicated to the patriotic housewives of Western Canada ... Issued by the British Columbia Fruit Growers' Association ... Copies of this booklet free on request ...'; 2 blank; 3 'Contents' [i.e., alphabetical list of headings]; 4 blank; 5–6 'British Columbia Fruit'; 7 'Best Time to Buy B.C. Fruits'; top 8 'Watch for the B.C. Brand on the Box'; mid 8–9 'Fruits Can Be Preserved without Sugar'; 10 'Confectioners, Make Your Own Fruit Flavorings'; 11 'General Canning and Jam-Making Methods'; 12–80 information about, and recipes for, rhubarb, strawberries, black currants, gooseberries, blackberries, raspberries, red currants, apricots, cantaloupes, cherries, peaches, plums, pears, apples, potatoes, celery, tomatoes, and onion; i–ii ads
CITATIONS: Ferguson/Fraser, p 232
COPIES: *BSUM   BVIP   BVIPA
NOTES: 'New edition' is on the outside front face of the binding; 'The Sun Job Presses Vancouver, B.C.' is on the outside back face. The text on p 8 refers to the high wartime price of sugar, which 'has possibly led some economical housewives to consider curtailing the quantities of fruit they will put up this year ...'; the text goes on to persuade the reader that sugar is not necessary for preservation and that it is still advantageous to can fruit despite sugar shortages.

1915–18

Hayes, Olive E.

Hayes's Entrance Record for the Macdonald Institute at the Ontario Agricultural College, at OGU (RE1 MAC A0003, Registration No. 1991), states that she entered the Normal Household Science Course on 17 September 1914 and left on 29 June 1915, having been granted the Certificate of Household Science Teacher. The document reveals that she was twenty-eight years old when she applied for the course in June 1914 (therefore, she was born about 1886), her permanent address was Parkhill, Ontario, her mother's name was Mrs E.J. Hayes, her father was deceased, and her religious denomination was

Methodist. She attended public school and high school in Parkhill, 1895–1901 and 1901–6, and Normal School in London, Ontario, 1907–8, after which she taught for six years in Ontario and Alberta. The 1911 Census records her as a teacher in Nipigon, Ontario, born September 1887.

B34.1 nd [about 1915–18]
War-time recipes / by / Olive E. Hayes / Government Food Specialist / Compliments of / Lorne A. Campbell / Rossland. B.C. [cover-title]
DESCRIPTION: 15.0 × 11.0 cm   Pp [1–16]   Paper; stapled
CONTENTS: 1–top 10 'War Breads'; mid 10–mid 14 'Meat Substitutes and Meat Dishes'; mid 14–16 'Desserts'
COPIES: *BVIPA
NOTES: Publication of this First World War–period text must have followed Hayes's graduation from the Macdonald Institute in June 1915. BVIPA's date of [1939–45] is incorrect. War bread recipes substitute ingredients such as cornmeal, rice, oatmeal, and mashed potato for wheat flour. The text on p 1 begins, 'War Breads // Corn meal yeast bread, satisfactory in texture and mild in flavor, ...'

B34.2 nd [about 1915–18]
—War-time recipes / by / Olive E. Hayes / Government Food Specialist / Printed and published by the Kamloops Telegram [cover-title]
DESCRIPTION: 14.5 × 12.0 cm   Pp [1–32]   Paper, with image on front of two Union Jacks; stapled
CONTENTS: 1 'Foreword'; 2 blank; 3–32 recipes and ads
COPIES: *BVAU (Beatrice M. Millar Papers)
NOTES: The 'Foreword' says that the book is 'furnished to the housewives of the Kamloops district without charge.'

1916

Book for a cook

B35.1   15 June 1916
Cranbrook / Women's Institute / Book for a / cook / Motto / "For home and country" / June 15th, 1916 [cover-title]
DESCRIPTION: 23.0 × 15.0 cm [dimensions from photocopy]   Stapled
CONTENTS: 1 ad for Little and Atchison; ...
COPIES: *ACHP

Kaslo Women's Institute cook book

B36.1   1916
[Women's Institute symbol] / Kaslo Women's / Institute / cook / book / Kaslo, B.C. 1916 [cover-title]
DESCRIPTION: 17.5 × 12.0 cm   Pp 1–40   Paper; stapled
CONTENTS: 1–40 recipes credited with the name of the contributor
COPIES: *BSUM   BVIPA   CIHM (83302)

1917

Rexall cook book

The first two editions of this cookbook were published in Toronto and in Stratford, Ontario, in 1890, under the title The Art of Cooking Made Easy. *For the edition distributed in Victoria, British Columbia, in about 1917, see O48.19.*

1918

Denne, Miss Alexandrina (Lexa) (died 16 April 1930, Toronto, Ont.)

Denne graduated from Victoria College, University of Toronto, in 1912, with a degree in household science and arts. Her file at OTUAR (A73-0026/082 (59)) contains newspaper clippings relating to aspects of her career, photographs of her, and obituaries. Following graduation, she taught at the Victoria Normal School in British Columbia, where she had published Two Hundred and Fifty War-Time Recipes. *In 1920 she returned to Toronto to take up the job of assistant teacher of domestic science at Central Technical School on 1 December of that year (see 'Appointments Recommended,'* Telegram *(Toronto) 7 October 1920). While at Central Technical School, she assisted Nellie Pattinson with what was to become a classic text, O506.1,* Canadian Cook Book, *first published in 1923. Obituaries for her reveal that she was best known, however, for her work as director of the Visiting Housekeepers' Centre on Beverley Street in Toronto, which she supervised from its opening in 1925 until her premature death in 1930. Although not named in the volume, she must have been involved in the production of O541.1,* Economical Recipe Book, *which, from appearances, was published about 1925. She was the eldest daughter of Thomas Henry Gerald Denne and Anna May Denne of Peterborough, Ontario, and she is buried in Little Lake Cemetery in Peterborough.*

B37.1   [1918]

Two hundred and fifty / war-time recipes / Food / Buy it carefully. Cook it well / Eat what you need / Save all you can / We save food when we make the best / possible use of every particle of it / Compiled by / Lexa Denne, Instructor in Household Science / Victoria Normal School [cover-title]

DESCRIPTION: 17.0 × 11.5 cm   Pp [3–5] 6–99   Paper; stapled, and with hole punched at top left corner for hanging

CONTENTS: 3 table of contents; 4 'Acknowledgments,' 'Abbreviations,' and 'Measurements'; 5–99 [inside back face of binding] text, and at bottom p 99, 'Victoria, B.C.: Printed by William H. Cullin, printer to the King's Most Excellent Majesty. 1918.'

COPIES: *BVMA   OOAG (641.55 P186)

NOTES: 'The majority of these recipes have been tested by the Victoria Normal School students and have been used in the Normal War Demonstration classes,' states a note on p 3. The introductory text offers advice on such topics as 'The Family Balanced Ration,' 'Budget for a Family of Five,' food conservation, 'Ways of Fixing Cakes without Icing,' and substitutes for sugar, meat, wheat, and butter. The recipes are organized by ingredient (rice, oatmeal, cornmeal, rye, barley, buckwheat, meat, meat substitutes, vegetables), followed by a group of miscellaneous recipes, and canning and preserving recipes. The cover-title is decorated with two small swastika-shapes, an ancient symbol of good luck, which in 1918 did not have the sinister implications now associated with the Nazis' use of it.

Selected recipes for home cooking

B38.1   1918

Selected / recipes / for / home cooking / Compiled and arranged by / the Home Comfort Club / Summerland, B.C. / 1918 / Review Presses, Summerland

DESCRIPTION: 21.0 × 13.5 cm   Pp [1–4] 5–24   Lacks paper binding; stapled

CONTENTS: 1 tp; 2 'The Home Comfort Club // Summerland, B.C. Organized December 8, 1915. Officers: [list of five names]'; 3 'The Home Comfort Club Cook Book,' poem beginning, 'We may live without poetry, music or art' [from *Lucile*, Part I, Canto ii, by Owen Meredith, pseudonym of Edward Robert Bulwer-Lytton], and 'Summerland, B.C., 1918.'; 4 'Abbreviations'; 5–24 recipes credited with the name of the contributor

COPIES: BPM   *BSUM   CIHM (77810)   OONL (TX715 S456 1918)

1920

Economy cook book

B39.1   nd [about 1920]

Mt. Pleasant Methodist Church / Economy / cook book / Losesa Auxiliary [cover-title]

DESCRIPTION: 23.0 × 15.0 cm   Pp [1] 2–94 [95]   Paper; stapled

CONTENTS: 1 tp; 2–94 text and ads; 95 'Order of Contents'

COPIES: *BVIPA

NOTES: No place of publication is given, but the advertisements are for Vancouver businesses. The book was published before 10 June 1925, the date when the Methodists joined with other denominations to form the United Church of Canada; the book's appearance suggests about 1920.

Langhout, Annie (Holland, 1894–24 February 1924, Weyburn, Sask.)

According to Arie Langhout, the author's brother, Annie used to have a bakery on Broadway Street in Vancouver. Annie was named after her mother, Annie Langhout, widow of G.M. Langhout, who, with Arie and other family members, is listed in the Wrigley-Henderson BC directories as living in Vancouver during the 1920s. The 1911 Census records seventeen-year-old 'Anniqje' and family resident in Weyburn. At the time of her death, at only thirty years old, she was working as a nurse at Weyburn General Hospital. She is buried in Weyburn Hillcrest Cemetery.

B40.1   nd [about 1920]

Economy's / friend / Tried and / economical / recipes / for / cooking / By / Annie Langhout / Price – $1.25 [cover-title]

DESCRIPTION: 23.0 × 14.5 cm   Pp [1–2] 3–68   Thin card; stapled at top edge

CONTENTS: 1 tp; 2 preface signed 'The writer'; 3–63 'Recipes'; 64 ad for W.H. Malkin Co. products; 65–8 'Contents' [i.e., index] and at bottom p 68, 'Quality Press Victoria B.C.'

COPIES: *Private collection

NOTES: Annie Langhout says in the preface: '... I hope to fill a long felt need for a cook book that supplies good, substantial, and economical recipes. The recipes ... have all been tried and tested by myself, and I have carefully selected the best recipes from many different homes. Having had twelve years of experience in cooking, ...' The recipe directions are confidence-inspiring and full of Annie's personal hints and opinions. Arie Langhout believes that Annie published the book about 1920.

Recipes

For another cookbook by the Vancouver Gas Co., see B13.1.

B41.1   nd [about 1920]
Recipes [cover-title]
DESCRIPTION: 15.0 × 11.0 cm   Pp [1] 2–16   Thin card; stapled
CONTENTS: 1–4 'Soups'; 5–7 'Meats'; 8–12 'Entrees'; 13–16 'Salads'
COPIES: *BVAA (PAM und. 290)
NOTES: No date, no publisher, and no place of publication are cited; however, BVAA catalogues the book as published by the Vancouver Gas Co.(?). The first recipe is Brown Soup Stock; the last is Lettuce and Walnut Salad. The collection of recipes was continued in a separately bound booklet, also held by BVAA (B42.1).

The recipe for Waldorf Salad on p 15 may (or may not) help date the book. Waldorf Salad was created by Oscar Tschirky at the Waldorf-Astoria Hotel in New York City in the 1890s. He first published the recipe in *The Cook Book by 'Oscar' of the Waldorf*, Chicago and New York: Werner Co., [1896]. His original version had celery, apples, and mayonnaise. According to John F. Mariani, *The Encyclopedia of American Food and Drink*, New York: Lebhar-Friedman Books, 1999, walnuts became a standard ingredient only in the 1920s. If this is the case, the British Columbia book was likely published in the 1920s since its recipe has walnuts. Determining, with certainty, the history of Waldorf Salad is beyond the scope of the research for this bibliography, but it is interesting to note that B5.1, the 1904 edition of *The King's Daughters Cookery Book* compiled by Mrs McMicking, has a recipe on p 63 for Apple, Celery and Nut Salad – a turn-of-the-century Victoria, British Columbia, recipe for Waldorf Salad in everything but name (the kind of nut is not specified; no dressing is given, but recipes for a cooked and a mayonnaise dressing immediately follow). In the 1911 edition, the Apple, Celery and Nut Salad is replaced with an equivalent one called Apple Salad, p 102, that specifies apples, celery, walnuts, and a mayonnaise-type dressing – again, a nut version of a Waldorf Salad well before the 1920s, the period indicated by Mariani. S16.1, *Robin Hood Flour Cook Book*, by the American Mrs Rorer and published about 1915

in Moose Jaw, for national distribution, has a Waldorf Salad recipe on p 34 that calls for chopped almonds or English walnuts to be 'dusted thickly' on the dish. Whatever the truth about the walnut version of Waldorf Salad, the appearance of *Recipes* suggests publication in about 1920. *Recipes* is similar in format and design to a slightly later gas cookery book: B58.1, *Hints for the Housewife*, from the British Columbia Electric Gas Department.

[Recipes?]

B42.1   [about 1920]
[Cover-title lacking, likely *Recipes*(?)]
DESCRIPTION: 14.5 × 10.5 cm   Pp 17–31   Lacks paper(?) binding; stapled
CONTENTS: 17–top 19 'Pastry'; mid 19–20 'Cakes'; 21–top 24 'Made Dishes'; mid 24–27 'Luncheon and Supper Dishes'; 28–31 'Confections, Sandwiches and Canapes'
COPIES: *BVAA (PAM und. 291)
NOTES: This is a continuation of B41.1, *Recipes*, with the pagination running on from the last page of that book, p 16. No date, no publisher, and no place of publication are cited; however, like B41.1, it was likely published by the Vancouver Gas Co.

Shamrock kitchen movies

B43.1   1920
Shamrock kitchen movies / A shower of recipes / old and new, / tried and true, / with helpful hints for you / borrowed from the experience / of / the Shamrock Club / Victoria, B.C. / to / Phoebe. A. Rae – June 1920 / Revised and edited by K. Healy and F.K. Healy.
DESCRIPTION: 33.0 × 20.0 cm   Pp [i–xxii], 1–159 [versos of arabic-numbered leaves not incl in pagination] Green-paper shamrock mounted on tp   Limp green cloth
CONTENTS: i tp; ii–iv blank; v table of contents; vi blank; vii–xxi index, versos blank; xxii blank; 1–6 'The Bride's New Work'; 7–159 recipes
COPIES: *BVIPA
NOTES: The book was reproduced as carbon copies of typed text, and was intended for the new bride. British Columbia marriage records identify the bride as Phoebe Agnes Tourigny, who married Andrew John Ferguson Rae on 6 April 1920, in Prince George. 'Washing // Sister K. Healy's Formula for "P.D.Q. [i.e., 'pretty damned quick'] Washing"' is on p 159.

Thompson, Frank R., and Lila May Geddis

Henderson's Vancouver city directory for 1919 records Frank R. Thompson as living at 1406 Alberni Street and the manager of Business Development Co. Ltd, 'financial and fiduciary agents, organizers, incorporaters, underwriters.' In the 1920 directory, he is manager of Industrial Development Securities Corporation Ltd. In the volume for 1921, there is no entry for Frank, but Mrs Bella Thompson is at 1406 Alberni. Lila May Geddis, editor, Educator of Canada, is listed in the 1919 directory, but not 1920 or 1921. She was born in Vancouver on 5 May 1891 (Pedigree Resource File, Church of Jesus Christ of Latter-day Saints, www.familysearch.org). The 1911 Census records her as a teacher in Slocan.

B44.1   nd [about 1920]
British Columbia edition / The bride's book of / household / management / Compiled and edited by / Frank R. Thompson / and / L.M. Geddis / Approved by / Board of Trade / Vancouver, B.C. / Published for the / merchants, manufacturers and business houses whose / advertisements appear in this edition / Interim copyright by Frank R. Thompson / The Sun Job Presses Vancouver, B.C.
DESCRIPTION: 24.5 × 17.0 cm   Pp [1–7] 8–305 [306] Cloth
CONTENTS: 1 tp; 2 blank; 3 'This volume is respectfully dedicated to the brides of British Columbia by the merchants, manufacturers and business houses of the province'; 4 blank; 5 'Introduction'; 6 blank; 7, 9, 11, 13, 15–16 'Contents' [i.e., index]; 8, 10, 12, 14, 17–18 ads; 19 'Business Directory'; 20 ad; 21 continuation of 'Business Directory'; 22 'Patronize Our Local Industries'; 23–4 ads; 25 'Marriage' by Samuel Rodgers; 26–302 text and ads; 303–5 ads; 306 blank for 'New Recipes'
COPIES: *ACG   BVAMM   BVIPA   SSWD
NOTES: On the binding, *The Bride's Book of Household Management* is described as 'A perpetual reference book of efficient housekeeping.' The 'Introduction' gives the publishers' aim, 'to provide the bride with a compact, convenient and beautiful volume, covering ... the whole field of domestic knowledge, from the kitchen to the nursery.' Two advertisements are evidence that the book was published about 1920: On p 100, for the Phonola 'registered July 11th, 1919'; on p 106, for beds, where the text comments, 'Whether it is a four-poster heirloom or a 1920 model, ...'

The Bride's Book of Household Management was published as a promotional vehicle for Vancouver businesses, like B21.1, *The Real Home-keeper*, which is similarly subtitled 'A perpetual honeymoon for the Vancouver bride' and later retitled *The Bride's Book*. Despite these parallels, the texts are not related.

1920–5

Golden recipes

For the titles of other cookbooks from BC Sugar Refining Co. Ltd, see B8.1.

B45.1   nd [about 1920–5]
Golden recipes / Index / Page [above page numbers] / Apple Pudding 7 / Baked Custard 19 / Chocolate Fudge 26 / Coconut Macaroons 27 / Corn Bread 29 / Dainty Spice Cakes 10 / Date and Nut Blanc Mange 25 / Divinity Fudge 24 / Diplomatic Bread Pudding 6 / Fondant 20–21 / Frozen Pudding 14 / Fudge Frosting 32 / Gingerbread 12 / Golden Suet Pudding 9 / (Continued over leaf)
DESCRIPTION: 8.0 × 6.5 cm   Pp [1–2] 3–32   Thin card, printed front and back to look like a 2-pound can of Rogers' Golden Syrup made by the BC Sugar Refining Co. Ltd; stapled
CONTENTS: 1 title and index to Golden Suet Pudding; 2 index from Golden Suet Pie to Vanilla Caramels; 3–32 recipes
COPIES: BVABSM   *Private collection

Yello Fello, the apple elf

See also B77.1, Stevens, Mary Alice, Apple Secrets, another cookbook promoting OK Apples.

B46.1   nd [about 1920–5]
Yello Fello / the apple elf [cover-title]
DESCRIPTION: 11.5 × 15.5 cm   Pp [1–28]   Fp illus col   Paper, with image on front of Yello Fello sitting on the branch of an apple tree watching the Sun-artist paint an apple red; stapled
CONTENTS: Inside front face of binding information about the Okanagan United Growers Ltd, a co-operative association whose members produce OK Apples; 1 'The Guardian Elf of the O.K. Apple' [introductory text]; 2–inside back face of binding fairy story about Yello Fello who cares for OK Apples, illustrated by fp illus col on each recto page, plus information about the British Columbia apple-growing industry and about the cultivation of apples, and fifteen apple recipes (one per text page)
COPIES: *OTNY (641.6411 Y)
NOTES: The attractive full-page colour illustrations are by Helen Dickson. 'Issued by Okanagan United Growers, Limited, Vernon, B.C.' is on the outside back face of the binding. The following reference on p 24 indicates that the book was likely published

shortly after the First World War: 'During the World War, Christmas week always ushered many boxes of the O.K. specimens into the French farms and villages of the British battlefront.'

1921

The Kerrisdale cook book

B47.1 1921
The Kerrisdale cook book / Compiled by / the ladies' [*sic*] of St. Mary's Church / Kerrisdale / November 1921 / The Kerrisdale Cook Book / A woman there was and she wrote for the press / (As you or I might do) / She told how to cut and fit a dress / And how to stew many a savoury mess, / But she never had done it herself, I guess, / (Which none of her readers knew) / A woman there was and she had her fun / (Better than you or I), / She wrote out receipts and sampled none, / But the Kerrisdale woman [*sic*] have tried every one, / And have told us to do just what they have done, / (And we intend to try).
DESCRIPTION: 20.5 × 14.0 cm   Pp [1] 2–48   Paper; stapled
CONTENTS: 1 tp; 2 ads; 3–48 recipes credited with the name of the contributor and ads, and at bottom p 48, 'Harvey Bawden, printer, Vancouver, B.C.'
CITATIONS: Hale 5729
COPIES: *BVIPA
NOTES: Kerrisdale is now a part of Vancouver.

St Mark's Parish Guild cook book

B48.1 nd [about 1921]
St. Mark's / Parish Guild / cook / book / Vancouver / British Columbia [cover-title]
DESCRIPTION: 22.5 × 15.0 cm   Pp [1] 2–128   Limp cloth; stapled
CONTENTS: 1 'Introduction' signed the convenors; 2 ad; 3–125 recipes credited with the name of the contributor and ads; 126 ads; 127 'Household Economies and Hints'; 128 'Table of Weights and Measures' and 'Index' [i.e., table of contents]
COPIES: *Private collection
NOTES: There is a recipe on p 114 for Turkish Delight (Now Known as Allies' Delight) and an advertisement on p 32 for Geo. T. Wadds, portrait photographer, who offers 'special discount to military men.' This evidence and the appearance of the book indicate a publication date sometime after the First World War. It is no later than 1921 since there is an adver-

tisement on p 40 for Morrow and Deane, grocers with 'eight years' experience in this district,' and Morrow and Deane are listed in the 1913 Vancouver city directory (1913 + 8 years).

The recipes specify Royal Standard Flour produced by the Vancouver Milling and Grain Co., whose advertisement is printed on the outside back face of the binding. In the advertisement the milling company refers to its own cookbook, *Better Baking,* mailed free, upon request: 'We have just issued this interesting booklet which contains the famous Royal Standard Bread Recipe and other information ...' No copy of this booklet has surfaced. The Vancouver Milling and Grain Co. was established in 1906; it converted from a public to a private company in 1929.

1922

British Columbia, Department of Agriculture

B49.1   2nd ed., 1922
Province of British Columbia / Department of Agriculture / Preservation of food / home canning, preserving / jelly-making, pickling / drying / Bulletin No. 83 / 2nd edition / Victoria, B.C.: / Printed by William H. Cullin, printer to the King's Most Excellent Majesty. / 1922.
DESCRIPTION: 22.5 × 15.0 cm   Pp [1–5] 6–46   Illus   Paper; stapled
CONTENTS: 1 tp; 2 blank; 3 'Table of Contents' [i.e., alphabetical list of sections]; 4 blank; 5–21 'Home Canning'; 22–5 'Preserves, Conserves, etc.'; 26–8 'Jelly-Making'; 29–35 'Pickling'; 36–mid 37 timetables for canning fruits, vegetables, and meats; mid 37–38 'Storing Canned Goods'; 39–40 'Fermentation and Salting'; 41–6 'Home Drying' and at bottom p 46, '5,000-12-22–9863'
COPIES: *BDEM
NOTES: Text opposite p 1 states, 'This manual is based on research and experience, supplemented by information procured from the Ontario Agricultural College, Guelph, New York State College of Agriculture, Columbia University, and from other sources.' The Department of Agriculture published an earlier similarly titled booklet, B25.1, Bulletin 37, by Alice Ravenhill, called *The Preservation of Food.* I have not compared the two similarly titled Bulletins side by side, but the text of No. 83 is likely mostly or all new.

B49.2   1942
—[An edition of *Preservation of Food,* 1942]
COPIES: BVAU (Beatrice M. Millar Papers)
NOTES: The BVAU copy is in poor condition: The title-

page and table-of-contents page are incorrectly taped to a copy of another unidentified preserving book in a file in the Millar Papers; the remainder of the book is separated from these two pages, but is held in the same file. The printer and date on the title-page is Victoria, BC: Charles F. Banfield, 1942; '5M-142-5890' is at the bottom of the table of contents.

B49.3 1945
—Province of British Columbia / Department of Agriculture / Preservation of food / home canning, preserving / jelly-making, pickling, drying / meat-preserving, and / bacon-curing / Bulletin No. 83 / [BC coat of arms] / Victoria, B.C.: / Printed by Charles F. Banfield, printer to the King's Most Excellent Majesty. / 1945.
DESCRIPTION: 22.0 × 14.5 cm   Pp [1–3] 4–46 [47]   8 numbered illus   Paper; stapled
CONTENTS: 1 cover-title; 2 blank; top–near bottom 3 'Home Canning'; bottom 3–mid 19 'Methods of Canning'; bottom 19–mid 23 'Preserves, Conserves, etc.'; bottom 23–top 26 'Jelly-Making'; mid 26–top 33 'Pickling'; mid 33 'Storing Canned Goods'; bottom 33–34 'Fermentation and Salting'; top 35 'Salting without Fermentation'; mid 35–near bottom 40 'Home Drying'; bottom 40–mid 42 'The Preservation of Meat'; bottom 42–mid 45 'The Home-Curing of Bacon'; mid 45 'Fish'; mid 45–46 timetables; 47 [inside back face of binding] 'Table of Contents' [i.e., alphabetical list of subjects] and at bottom p 47, '5M–445–6074'
COPIES: *Private collection

Nakusp's little red cook book

B50.1   [2nd ed.,] May 1930
Nakusp's / little red / cook book / Issued by the / Arrow Lakes Agricultural & Industrial / Association, Nakusp, B.C. / May, 1930 / President [sic, no colon] B. Parkinson / Vice-President: Kay Johnson. / Secretary-Treasurer: H. Kershaw / The success of "Nakusp's Little Red Cook Book," we owe to the / numerous friends who contributed the recipes, proved by them and / appreciated by all who have tasted them. / The success of our first issue in 1922 was so great that we here- / with republish it with some additions. / Support local industries and assist at Fall Fair and so build up / the town in which you live.
DESCRIPTION: 17.0 × 11.5 cm   Pp [1–32]   Paper, with decorative device on front (floral swags decorating a spherical shape, identical to that on O540.1); stapled

CONTENTS: 1 tp; 2–8 'Cakes'; 9–13 'Cookies and Small Cakes'; 14–16 'Pies and Pastries'; 17 'Bread'; 18–19 'Desserts and Puddings'; 20–1 'Meat'; 22 'Egg Recipes'; 23 'Breakfast and Supper Dishes'; 24–6 'Preserves and Pickles'; 27–31 'Miscellaneous'; 32 'Arrow Lakes News, Nakusp, B.C.' [i.e., the printer]
COPIES: *Private collection
NOTES: The recipes are credited with the name of the contributor. 'E [second initial illegible] Bailey' is inscribed on the binding. This edition of the cookbook was published eight years after the 'first issue' of 1922.

Reliable recipes

B51.1   nd [about 1922]
Reliable / recipes / [IODE symbol] / Triple Entente Chapter / Vancouver, B.C.
DESCRIPTION: 22.0 × 11.5 cm   Pp 1–108   Cloth-covered boards, with IODE symbol on front
CONTENTS: 1–4 ads; 5 tp; 6 ad; 7 'Preface'; 8 ad; 9 'Index' [i.e., table of contents] and 'Errata' slip glued to the gutter; 10 ad; 11 'Measures and Weights in Ordinary Use'; 12 ad; 13–mid 101 recipes credited with the name of the contributor and ads; mid 101–102 blank for 'Memorandum'; 103–4 'Useful Hints'; 105–8 ads
CITATIONS: Hale 2406
COPIES: *BVA   BVAU   BVIPA
NOTES: 'Evans & Hastings, printers' is on the front face of the binding, and there is an advertisement for the printer on p 108. The 'Preface' recounts the history of the chapter and its activities: 'The Triple Entente Chapter ... was formed in August, 1914, and has thirty members. Approximately ten thousand dollars has been raised in the past eight years, and has been expended on Field Comforts during the period of war, and on relief among soldiers' families and the education of soldiers' dependents since the armistice.' If the chapter was formed in 1914 and money was raised for eight years, then the cookbook was published about 1922.

The Scout Auxiliary cook book

B52.1   nd [about 1922]
The / Scout Auxiliary / cook book / Compiled by / the Ladies' Auxiliary to the / Boy Scout Association / Kelowna, B.C.
DESCRIPTION: 22.0 × 14.5 cm   Pp [1–7] 8–82   Tp illus

of Boy Scout Hall   Paper, with tp illus on front; stapled

CONTENTS: 1 'Table of Measures'; 2 ad; 3 tp; 4 blank; 5 'Foreword' and table of contents; 6 ad; 7–82 recipes and ads

COPIES: *BKOM   OONL (TX715.6 S36 1920z)

NOTES: 'Kelowna Printing Co.' is on the front face of the binding. The recipes were contributed by 'mothers of Boy Scouts and Cubs and the members of the Ladies' Auxiliary to the Boy Scout Association, Kelowna, B.C., and their friends,' according to the 'Foreword.'

BKOM reports that the Boy Scout Hall opened in June 1922, and that aspects of the photograph of the building on the title-page and binding are a close match with another image of the building made at the opening; therefore, the cookbook was likely published close to the hall's opening date.

On p 28 there is an advertisement for Carnation Milk that refers to a free 'book of 100 tested recipes.' This could be O489.1, *One Hundred Tested Recipes*, [copyright 1922]; O515.1, Blake, Mary, *My Hundred Favorite Recipes*, [copyright 1924]; or O660.1, Blake, Mary, *100 Glorified Recipes*, [copyright 1930]; however, it is most likely the first-cited, *One Hundred Tested Recipes*, published before Mary Blake represented the company. If so, then *The Scout Auxiliary Cook Book* was published about 1922, a date consistent with the appearance of the volume and the evidence provided by the photograph of the Boy Scout Hall.

Three hundred dainty recipes

For another cookbook from the same church, see B12.1.

B53.1   nd [about 1922]

Three / hundred / dainty / recipes / Compiled and published / by / the Willing Workers' Guild / of Westminster Presbyterian Church / South Vancouver, B.C. [cover-title]

CONTENTS: 1 'Willing Workers' Cook Book,' poem beginning, 'We may live without poetry, music and art' [from *Lucile*, Part I, Canto ii, by Owen Meredith, pseudonym of Edward Robert Bulwer-Lytton], and 'Boden Press – 30th and Main'; 2 ad for Victory Flour Mills Ltd, Vancouver; 3 'Foreword' signed the Committee; 4 ads; 5 'Table of Contents'; 6 ad; 7 'Table of Measures,' 'Table of Weights and Measures,' and 'Spoon and Cup Measure'; 8 information about Westminster Presbyterian Church, at the corner of

Sophia and 26th Avenue; 9 menus for Christmas, Easter, and Thanksgiving dinners; 10 ad; 11–99 recipes, some credited with the name of the contributor, and ads; 100–1 'Household Hints' and ad; 102 ad

COPIES: *Private collection

NOTES: On p 8 there is a reference to the first in a series of 'visitors' nights' held at the Church Hall on 29 October 1922. The cookbook, therefore, was published about 1922, and no later than June 1925, when the church became Westminster United Church.

1924

Women's Institute cook book

B54.1   1 July 1924

Women's Institute / cook book / July 1st, 1924 / The welfare of the family is largely in / the hands of the one who provides the / "three meals a day." / Nelson and District / Women's Institute / Mrs. Hector MacKenzie, / Sec.-Treasurer / Mrs. W. Garland Foster, / President [cover-title]

DESCRIPTION: 22.0 × 9.5 cm   Pp [1–11] 12–78 [79–100] Card, with image on front of a Christmas pudding and roast poultry; stapled

CONTENTS: 1–8 ads; 9 'Introductory' signed Mrs Stanley Horswill, and 'Prepared by the Home Economics Committee:' followed by the names of ten women, the first being Mrs W.H. Smedley, convener; 10 'Weights and Measures'; 11–78 recipes credited with the name of the contributor, and ads on centre spread; 79 'Conclusion // Community Pudding' [mock recipe] signed Mrs Stanley Horswill; 80–8 ads; 89–100 blank, ruled leaves for 'Recipes – My Friends [*sic*, no apostrophe] and My Own'

COPIES: BNEM   *BVAU

NOTES: The cookbook was likely printed by the Daily News, Nelson, for which an advertisement appears on the inside back face of the binding.

1925

Recipes for desserts

Editions of this title were also published by drugstores in New Brunswick and Ontario. For the editions published by drugstores in New Westminster and Kelowna, see NB35.2 and NB35.4.

Tested recipes and household business directory

Fairfield is a neighbourhood in Victoria.

B55.1 nd [about 1925]
Tested recipes / and / household / business directory / Indexed / Compiled by / Fairfield Young Ladies' / Service Club / We would call your attention to the / splendid advertisements in this book / and ask for them your generous patronage
DESCRIPTION: 22.5 × 15.5 cm Pp [1] 2–100 Paper; stapled
CONTENTS: 1–2 ads; 3 tp; 4 ad; 5 'Hints for Brides' [i.e., mock recipes: 'A Recipe for a Happy Day' and 'How to Cook a Husband']; 6 ad; 7 'Tables of Weights'; 8 ad; 9–97 recipes and ads; 98–9 'Household Hints'; 100 table of contents and 'Business Directory'
COPIES: BVICC *BVIPA
NOTES: 'Clarke Ptg. Co. Victoria, B.C.' is on the outside back face of the binding. From appearances, the book was published about 1925.

1925–30

Cook book

B56.1 nd [about 1925–30]
Westbank / Women's Institute / cook book / To the many friends / who have in their kindness / contributed to its success / this book is dedicated. / Home Economics / Committee / Westbank Women's Institute / Mrs. J.L. Dobbin, Convener / Mrs. D. Mackay Smith / Mrs. W.D. Gordon / Mrs. S.J. Hewlett / Mrs. H. Duggan / Mrs. S.K. Mackay
DESCRIPTION: 20.5 × 13.0 cm Pp [1] 2–40 Tp illus of coffee pot, cup, and plate of sandwiches Paper, with image on front of a woman bringing a tray of sandwiches and coffee to two women seated at table; stapled
CONTENTS: 1 tp; 2 ad; 3–40 recipes credited with the name of the contributor and ads
COPIES: *BVABSM Private collection
NOTES: The private collector's copy has 'Kelowna Printing Co.' on the binding. From appearances, the book was published about 1925–30.

1926

Orange cook book

B57.1 1926
Orange / cook book / Proceeds from sale of this book to be / devoted to the Children's Protestant / Home, New Westminster, now in course / of erection. / Compiled and published / by the / Daughters of Derry No. 646 / Ladies' Orange Benevolent Association / Vancouver, British Columbia / December, 1926 [cover-title]
DESCRIPTION: 23.0 × 15.5 cm Pp [1–8] 9–96 Paper, with images on front of a Union Jack and Red Ensign, a boy and girl, and a building; stapled
CONTENTS: 1 'Foreword' signed the Committee; 2 ad; 3 table of contents; 4 ads; 5 'L.O.B.A. Daughters of Derry No. 646' [information about the lodge]; 6 ads; 7 untitled verse beginning, 'Preserve an even temper and avoid family jars,' and 'Recipe for a Day' [mock recipe]; 8 ads and space for 'Memoranda'; 9–94 recipes, ads, and space for 'Memoranda'; 95–6 'Household Hints' and space for 'Memoranda'; inside back face of binding 'A.H. Timms printer Vancouver, B.C.'
CITATIONS: Hale 2194
COPIES: *BVIPA
NOTES: Page 5 states, 'This lodge [i.e., Daughters of Derry No. 646] is the baby lodge of Vancouver. It was organized on January 15, 1925, in the K.P. Hall, Mount Pleasant.'

1926–30

Hints for the housewife

B58.1 nd [about 1926–30]
Hints for the / housewife – / This booklet will save you / money. Keep it handy. / Compliments of / British Columbia Electric Gas / Department [cover-title]
DESCRIPTION: 14.0 × 10.0 cm Pp [1–2] 3–16 Illus brown Paper, with image on front of a man pointing to a woman working at a kitchen table; stapled
CONTENTS: 1 table of contents; 2 'Foreword'; top 3 'Clean Appliances Are All Important'; bottom 3–mid 4 'Correct Gas Flame'; mid 4–top 5 'Gas-Saving Utensils'; mid 5–7 'Cooking Economics'; 8–mid 12 'Cooking Suggestions'; bottom 12–13 'Oven Temperature'; 14 'Hints on Gas Lighting'; top 15 'False Economy of Cheap Tubing'; mid 15–16 'Things to Remember'
COPIES: *BVAMM

NOTES: From appearances, *Hints for the Housewife* was likely published about 1926–30, after British Columbia Electric Railway Co. created British Columbia Electric Power and Gas Co. as a holding company in 1926. Several references in the text are to the increasing use of gas in British Columbia; for example, on p 8: 'Today we are using three times as much gas as we did twenty years ago and double the amount used ten years ago.'

1927

British Columbia, Department of Education

See also B28.1, another book authorized by the minister of education.

B59.1 1927
Government of the Province of British Columbia / Department of Education / Recipes / for / home economics / classes / Home Economics Circular No. 1 / Price, 25 cents / [BC coat of arms] / Authorized by the Minister of Education / Victoria, B.C.: / Printed by Charles F. Banfield, printer to the King's Most Excellent Majesty. / 1927. [cover-title]
DESCRIPTION: 23.0 × 15.0 cm   Pp [1–5] 6–90   Illus
Paper; stapled
CONTENTS: 1 ht; 2 blank; 3 'Preface'; 4 'Rules for Healthy, Happy B.C. School-Children'; 5–85 text; 86 blank; 87–90 index and at bottom p 90, '15M–827–8916'
COPIES: *BBVM   BVAU   BVIPA
NOTES: The 'Preface' states, 'This book is intended for use in the teaching of foods and cookery in the elementary and junior high schools.'

B59.2 rev. ed., 1931
—Government of the Province of British Columbia / Department of Education / Foods, nutrition / and / home management / manual / Home Economics Circular No. 1 / (Revised) / [BC coat of arms] / Authorized by the Minister of Education / Victoria, B.C.: / Printed by Charles F. Banfield, printer to the King's Most Excellent Majesty. / 1931.
DESCRIPTION: 22.5 × 15.0 cm   Pp [1–5] 6–156   Illus
Cloth-covered boards
CONTENTS: 1 tp; 2 blank; 3 'Foreword. To the teacher:' signed Jessie L. McLenaghen, provincial director of home economics; 4 table of contents; 5–150 text in five units; 151–6 index and at bottom p 156, '5M–931–6862'
COPIES: BPGRM (989.43.01)   *Private collection

NOTES: I have not compared the text of this retitled edition of Circular 1 with the 1927 edition to determine the extent of the revisions. The 'Foreword' states, 'This manual is intended for the use of the students of Home Economics in elementary and junior high school classes.' Children and teachers referred to the many editions of *Foods, Nutrition and Home Management Manual* as the 'Red Book' because of the red-coloured binding.

B59.3 1933
—Government of the Province of British Columbia / Department of Education / Foods, nutrition / and / home management / manual / Home Economics Circular No. 1 / (Revised) / [BC coat of arms] / Authorized by the Minister of Education / Victoria, B.C.: / Printed by Charles F. Banfield, printer to the King's Most Excellent Majesty. / 1933.
DESCRIPTION: 22.5 × 15.0 cm   Pp [1–5] 6–156   Illus
Very thin card; stapled
CONTENTS: 1 tp; 2 blank; 3 'Foreword. To the teacher:' signed Jessie L. McLenaghen, provincial director of home economics; 4 table of contents; 5–150 text in five units; 151–6 index and at bottom p 156, '2M–433–3053'
COPIES: ACG   *BDEM
NOTES: The illustrations are credited to an unidentified edition of O506.1, *Canadian Cook Book*, by Nellie Lyle Pattinson.

B59.4 1935
—[Another edition of *Foods, Nutrition and Home Management Manual*, Victoria: 1935]
COPIES: BVAUW (TX167 B7 AEG-0647)

B59.5 1936
—Government of the Province of British Columbia / Department of Education / Foods, nutrition / and / home management / manual / Home Economics Circular No. 1 / (Revised) / [BC coat of arms] / Authorized by the Minister of Education / Victoria, B.C.: / Printed by Charles F. Banfield, printer to the King's Most Excellent Majesty. / 1936.
DESCRIPTION: 22.0 × 15.0 cm   Pp [1–5] 6–173   Illus
Cloth-covered boards
CONTENTS: 1 tp; 2 blank; 3 'Foreword. To the teacher:' signed Jessie L. McLenaghen, provincial director of home economics; 4 table of contents; 5–160 text in five units; 161–2 'Appendix A. Chemical Tests for Foodstuffs'; 163–5 'Appendix B. Additional Recipes'; 166 blank; 167–73 index and at bottom p 173, '7,500–1236–3666'
COPIES: *BVIPM

NOTES: The BVIPM copy is inscribed by two male students: on the front endpaper, 'Graham McCall // Victoria Provincial Normal School Class C // 534 Trutch St. Victoria B.C.' [crossed out]; and opposite this inscription, on the inside face of the binding, 'Lewis C. Phillips // Victoria Normal School, Class D.' An individual who owns a copy of this edition reports: 'The home management manual, although published in B.C., was used by the Edmonton Schools for their Home Economics classes. Mine was purchased in 1937.'

B59.6   1938
—Government of the Province of British Columbia / Department of Education / Foods, nutrition / and / home management / manual / Home Economics Circular No. 1 / (Revised) / [BC coat of arms] / Authorized by the Minister of Education / Victoria, B.C.: / Printed by Charles F. Banfield, printer to the King's Most Excellent Majesty. / 1938.
COPIES: *Private collection
NOTES: The owner used this book in her Grade 8 class in Edmonton, Alberta.

B59.7   1939
—Government of the Province of British Columbia / Department of Education / Foods, nutrition / and / home management / manual / Home Economics Circular No. 1 / (Revised) / [BC coat of arms] / Authorized by the Minister of Education / Victoria, B.C.: / Printed by Charles F. Banfield, printer to the King's Most Excellent Majesty. / 1939.
DESCRIPTION: 22.0 × 15.0 cm   Pp [1–5] 6–173   Illus Cloth-covered boards; stapled
CONTENTS: 1 tp; 2 blank; 3 'Foreword. To the teacher:' signed Jessie L. McLenaghen, provincial director of home economics; 4 table of contents; 5–160 text in five units; 161–2 'Appendix A. Chemical Tests ...'; 163–6 'Appendix B. Additional Recipes'; 167–73 index and at bottom p 173, '8,250–1239–2678'
CITATIONS: CCat No. 19, p U15
COPIES: MWU (TX167 F66 1939)   OGU (CA2BC ED1 39C01C)   OTMCL (641.1 B67)   *Private collection

B59.8   1941
—Government of the Province of British Columbia / Department of Education / Foods, nutrition / and / home management / manual / Home Economics Circular No. 1 / (Revised) / [BC coat of arms] / Authorized by the Minister of Education / Victoria, B.C.: / Printed by Charles F. Banfield, printer to the King's Most Excellent Majesty. / 1941.

COPIES: OONL (COP.BC.2.1987-614, 2 copies)   *Private collection

B59.9   1942
—Government of the Province of British Columbia / Department of Education / Foods, nutrition / and / home management / manual / Home Economics Circular No. 1 / (Revised) / [BC coat of arms] / Authorized by the Minister of Education / Victoria, B.C.: / Printed by Charles F. Banfield, printer to the King's Most Excellent Majesty. / 1942.
DESCRIPTION: 22.0 × 14.5 cm   Pp [1–5] 6–175   Illus Cloth-covered boards
CONTENTS: 1 tp; 2 blank; 3 'Foreword. To the teacher:' signed Jessie L. McLenaghen, provincial director of home economics; 4 table of contents; 5–161 text in five units; 162–3 'Appendix A. Chemical Tests ...'; 164–8 'Appendix B. Additional Recipes'; 169–75 index and at bottom p 175, '6,500–1042–9974'
COPIES: ACG   *Private collection
NOTES: The private collector's copy has a label for Lord Byng High School in Vancouver.

B59.10   1943
—Government of the Province of British Columbia / Department of Education / Foods, nutrition / and / home management / manual / Home Economics Circular No. 1 / (Revised) / [BC coat of arms] / Authorized by the Minister of Education / Victoria, B.C.: / Printed by Charles F. Banfield, printer to the King's Most Excellent Majesty. / 1943.
COPIES: *Private collection

B59.11   1944
—Government of the Province of British Columbia / Department of Education / Foods, nutrition / and / home management / manual / Home Economics Circular No. 1 / (Revised) / [BC coat of arms] / Authorized by the Minister of Education / Victoria, B.C.: / Printed by Charles F. Banfield, printer to the King's Most Excellent Majesty. / 1944.
DESCRIPTION: 22.0 × 15.0 cm   Pp [1–5] 6–177   Illus of set tables on pp 46 and 47, from an unidentified edition of O506.1, *Canadian Cook Book,* by Nellie Lyle Pattinson; illus of the divisions of a measuring spoon on p 49; illus of cuts of meat on pp 122, 123, 124, and 125   Cloth-covered boards
CONTENTS: 1 tp; 2 blank; 3 foreword signed Jessie L. McLenaghen, provincial director of home economics; 4 table of contents; 5–161 text in five units; 162–3 'Appendix A. Chemical Tests for Foodstuffs'; 164–9 'Appendix B. Additional Recipes'; 170 'Canada's Official Food Rules'; 171–7 index and at bottom p 177,

place of publication, printer, date, and '7,500–1144–3792'
COPIES: AEU   BLCK (989.53)   *Private collection
NOTES: The five text units are 'Home Management,' 'Nutrition,' 'Meal-planning and Table Service,' 'Food Preparation,' and 'Sources of Food Products.' The longest is 'Food Preparation,' pp 49–155, and includes information about 'Lunch-Box,' 'Invalid Cookery,' and 'Infant-Feeding.'

B59.12   1946
—Government of / the Province of British Columbia / Department of Education / Foods, nutrition and / home management / manual / Home Economics Circular No. 1 / (Revised) / [BC coat of arms] / Authorized by the Minister of Education / Victoria, B.C.: / Printed by Charles F. Banfield, printer to the King's Most Excellent Majesty. / 1946.
DESCRIPTION: 22.0 × 14.5 cm   Pp [1–5] 6–177   Illus   Cloth-covered boards
CONTENTS: 1 tp; 2 blank; 3 'Foreword. To the teachers:' signed Jessie L. McLenaghen; 4 table of contents; 5–161 text in five units; 162–3 'Appendix A. Chemical Tests …'; 164–70 'Appendix B. Additional Recipes'; 171–7 index and at bottom p 177, '7M–1046–7196'
COPIES: *Private collection
NOTES: The owner's copy was used at Lord Byng High School.

B59.13   1947
—[Another edition of *Foods, Nutrition and Home Management Manual,* Victoria: Government of the Province of British Columbia, Department of Education, 1947]
COPIES: OONL (COP.BC.2.2001-63)

B59.14   1949
—Government of / the Province of British Columbia / Department of Education / Foods, nutrition, and / home management / manual / Home Economics Circular No. 1 / (Revised) / [BC coat of arms] / Authorized by the Minister of Education / Victoria, B.C.: / Printed by Don McDiarmid, printer to the King's Most Excellent Majesty. / 1949.
COPIES: OWTU (G11251)   *Private collection
NOTES: Another private collector reports that she used this text at the Guelph Collegiate and Vocational Institute, in Guelph, Ontario, in Grade 9, in 1950–1.

OTHER EDITIONS: Rev. ed., 1950 (Private collection); rev. ed., Victoria: Don McDiarmid, printer, 1951 (OONL); rev. ed., 1953 (OONL); rev. ed., Victoria: Don McDiarmid, printer, 1955 (Private collection).

Cook book

B60.1   1927
Cook / book / 1927 / Compiled by / Young Ladies' Club / of / First United St. Andrews Church / Nanaimo, B.C. [cover-title]
DESCRIPTION: 21.5 × 14.0 cm   Pp 1–104   Illus on inside front face of binding of St Andrews Church   Thin card
CONTENTS: 1 list of club's officers, poem beginning, 'We may live without friends' [from *Lucile*, Part I, Canto ii, by Owen Meredith, pseudonym of Edward Robert Bulwer-Lytton], and mock recipe 'How to Cook a Husband'; 2 ad; 3–104 recipes credited with the name of the contributor and ads
COPIES: *OONL (TX715 C665)   OWTU (G11427)
NOTES: The running head is 'Tested Household Recipes.'

Souvenir cook book

B61.1   1927
Souvenir / cook book / 1927 / [initials in a diamond-shape:] V. / C.C. / G. / Vancouver / Girls' Corner / Club / Compiled by the Women's Advisory Board
DESCRIPTION: 22.5 × 15.0 cm   Pp [3–4] 5–127   Cloth
CONTENTS: 3 tp; 4 'Motto'; 5–6 ads; 7 untitled introductory note signed Women's Advisory Board; 8 'Women's Advisory Board' [list of members] and 'Girls' Executive Branch' [list of members]; 9 untitled text signed Isobel S. Miller, superintendent; 10 ads; 11 table of contents; 12 ads; 13–126 text and ads; 127 ads
CITATIONS: Ferguson/Fraser, p 233   Hale 2606
COPIES: *BVAMM   BVIPA   OONL (TX715 S684)
NOTES: The note on p 7 refers to the Vancouver Girls' Corner Club as an interdenominational Christian club organized in 1917, and states that the book was published 'to preserve the recipes of the delicious cakes served by the ladies of the various church organizations at the Tuesday night suppers of the club,' which had been held since the club's inception ten years before.

Unsweetened Pacific Brand Evaporated Milk

A dairy cooperative, formed in 1913, began operating as the Fraser Valley Milk Producers' Association in 1917. See also B87.1.

B62.1   nd [about 1927]
Unsweetened / Pacific / Brand / Evaporated / Milk [cover-title]

DESCRIPTION: 13.5 × 7.5 cm   Pp [1–24]   Illus   Paper; leaves and binding are trimmed in a curve at top and bottom, to resemble the shape of a can; with image on front of cows in a field; stapled

CONTENTS: Inside front face of binding 'Pacific Milk Valuable as a Baby Food'; 1 illus of 'The Abbotsford Plant' and 'The Factory at Ladner, B.C.'; 2 'Pacific Milk // A Superior Product'; 3, 5, 7, 9, 11, 13, 15, 17, 19, 21 'Recipes for Pacific Milk Selected by Our Own Dietitian'; 4 'Pacific Milk // Milk from Healthy Cattle'; 6 'Clipping the Cows'; 8 'Clean Cows Mean Clean Milk'; 10 'Milking Time'; 12 'The Farm Milk House'; 14 'A Daily Delivery of Fresh Milk from the Farm'; 16 'Grading and Sampling'; 18 'The Bacterial Test'; 20 'Evaporation'; 22 'Process of Homogenization'; 23 'Sterilizing and Canning'; 24 'When You Buy "Pacific Milk" You Are Helping to Increase the Prosperity of British Columbia'; inside back face 'How to Prepare "Pacific" Milk for Infant Feeding' and the printer's name, 'The Columbian Co., Ltd.'

COPIES: *BVIPA

NOTES: The Fraser Valley Milk Producers' Association manufactured Pacific Milk, according to p 24. There is a reference on p 2 to an award won at the British Empire Exhibition, Wembley, England, 1925–6, and a reference on p 24 to 'Nearly four million dollars ... distributed in 1926'; therefore, the booklet was published about 1927. The text and illustrations are printed in brown ink.

1928

Peas in the diet

B63.1   nd [about 1928]

Peas / in the diet [cover-title]

DESCRIPTION: 20.5 × 12.5 cm   Pp [i–ii], 1–18 [19–21] Paper, with image on front of a dish of peas, above which is a scene of a woman standing in front of a field of peas; stapled

CONTENTS: i blank; ii 'Why Use Canned Peas?' and 'Packed' [i.e., list of pea sizes]; 1–4 'Peas in the Diet'; 5–14 recipes for soups, vegetable dishes, main dishes, salads, breads; 15 'Foreign Recipes'; 16–18 'Ancient Use of Peas'; 19 'Reasons Why "Royal City" Canned Peas Are the Best'; 20 blank; 21 'This book ... is presented with the compliments of the Broder Canning Company, Ltd., of New Westminster, B.C., and Edmonton, Alta., proprietors of "Royal City" Brand of canned fruits, vegetables, and jams. Robt Broder President ...'

COPIES: ACG   *BDEM (969.42.4)   BVIPA   BVIPM

NOTES: The text pages are decorated with a pea-pod border. 'Printed and distributed by the Broder Canning Co., Ltd. New Westminster, B.C. Edmonton, Alta.' is on the outside back face of the binding. *Peas in the Diet* was published no earlier than 1928, when the British Columbia company opened a new plant in Edmonton (see 'Broder Canning Company to Operate in Edmonton,' *Monetary Times* Vol. 80, No. 20 (18 May 1928), p 40). The plant was to begin operations on 1 June, and that spring 1,000 acres of leased land had been seeded with vegetables to supply the plant. The appearance of the book is consistent with publication in the late 1920s.

The BDEM copy has a label from Royal City Size 3 Sweet Peas glued to the inside back face of the binding. The BVIPA copy has the same label glued to the inside margin of p 9.

1929

Souvenir cook book

B64.1   1929

Souvenir / cook book / 1929 / Issued by / We Try Club / Sidney, B.C. / Index / [first column:] Biscuits 3 / Breads 3 / Cakes 5 / Candies 9 / Cookies 11 / Desserts 12 / Dumplings 13 / Fillings 14 / [second column:] Meats 15 / Pickles 15 / Pies 17 / Potatoes 19 / Puddings 21 / Salad dressings 21 / Recipe for a day 23 / We Try motto 23 / [folio:] 1

DESCRIPTION: 16.0 × 12.5 cm   Pp 1–24   Thin card; stapled

CONTENTS: 1 tp and 'Index'; 2 ad; 3–23 text and ads; 24 ad

COPIES: *BVIPA

NOTES: The text is printed in blue. The recipes are credited with the name of the contributor. 'Printed by the Review, Sydney, B.C.' is on the outside back face of the binding.

Tested recipes

B65.1   [1929]

Tested recipes / Compiled by / Ladies' Aid Society / Canadian Memorial Church / Vancouver, B.C.

DESCRIPTION: 22.0 × 15.0 cm   Pp 2–127   Illus on p 5 of 'Canadian Memorial Hall – The Parish House' Cloth

CONTENTS: 2 endpaper ad glued to inside front face of binding; 3 blank except for running head 'Tested Recipes' and folio; 4 ad; 5 illus of Canadian Memorial Hall and 'Canadian Memorial Ladies' Aid 1929' [i.e.,

list of executive, 'Circle Convenors,' and 'Committees']; 6 blank except for running head and folio; 7 tp; 8 blank except for running head and folio; 9 'Index to Our Advertisers'; 10 ad; 11 'Index to Tested Recipes' [i.e., table of contents]; 12 ads; 13 quotations from Ruskin and De Penesy [sic; i.e., Henrion De Pensey]; 14 ads; 15–127 [endpaper glued to inside back face] recipes credited with the name of the contributor and ads, and at bottom p 127, 'Printed by Pacific Printers, Ltd. 500 Bekins Building Sey. 9592'
COPIES: *BVIPA   OTMCL (641.5 V123)

A worth-while recipe book

The Nabob Brand included canned fruit, fish, and vegetables, baking powder, and coffee.

B66.1   nd [1929]
A / worth-while / recipe book / A concise compend of tested / recipes which make delicious / dishes, together with a com- / pilation of helps and hints of / value to every housekeeper. / Published by / Kelly, Douglas & Co. Ltd. / manufacturers of "Nabob" / Brand / pure food products / Vancouver, B.C. New Westminster, B.C. / Victoria, B.C. / Price twenty-five cents
DESCRIPTION: 20.0 × 14.5 cm   Pp [1–2] 3–48   Paper; stapled
CONTENTS: 1 tp; 2 'Recipe for a Happy Day'; 3 'How to Cook a Husband'; 4 'Table of Weights and Measures'; 5–45 recipes, other culinary information, and information about Nabob products; 46 'Dietetic Suggestions'; 47–8 blank, ruled leaves for 'Memorandum'
COPIES: *BBVM   BVIPA
NOTES: The book is not dated, but on p 4 there is a notice about a company contest: 'The final contest ends July, 1929, or sooner, without notice.' (The person sending in the most complete set of Nabob labels each month won a prize.)

1929–30

Council's choice cookery

The Vancouver Section of the National Council of Jewish Women of Canada was formed in 1924. The first Section was established in Toronto in 1897.

B67.1   [about 1929–30]
Council's / choice cookery / Compiled by / Vancouver Section / National / Council of Jewish

Women / [Council symbol] / Vancouver, B.C. [likely the title-page, transcribed from a photocopy of another copy of the book]
DESCRIPTION: 21.5 × 13.5 cm   Pp [leaves lacking] 7–90   Bound by two metal rings through punched holes
CONTENTS: 7–15 recipes for cakes; 16–24 'Squares'; 25–42 'Cookies & Dainties'; 43–7 'Rolls & Buns'; 48–51 'Pies & Fillings'; 52–4 'Desserts'; 55–7 'Miscellaneous'; 58–9 'Soups'; 60–5 'Fish'; 66–70 'Meat & Fowl'; 71–7 'Puddings, Pancakes, etc.'; 78–80 'Vegetable Dishes'; 81–3 'Egg Dishes'; 84–9 'Passover Recipes'; 90 'Hints'
COPIES: *Private collection
NOTES: The versos are blank and not included in the pagination. The recipes are not credited with the name of the contributor. Mrs Sue Abramson, who compiled later cookbooks for the Vancouver Section (see B141.1), reports that this first cookbook was published in 1929. I have a photocopy of what is likely the title-page of another copy of the book, plus what is likely the second leaf, on which is printed 'This is the first copy of Council's Choice Cookery and is presented to Mrs. Harry Rosenbaum by the Vancouver Section Council of Jewish Women in appreciation of her excellent work in procuring the advertising and compiling this volume'; the second leaf is inscribed with the date '1930.' Sue Abramson reports that Mrs Rosenbaum's given name was Dorothy and that some time after the publication of *Council's Choice Cookery* she moved to Denver, Colorado, at which point the Vancouver Section lost touch with her. The cookbook could still be purchased in 1932, according to a notice that year in the *Vancouver Sun,* 4 November, p 12: 'One of the most telling accomplishments of the Jewish Council of Women, Vancouver Branch is the compilation of several hundred selected recipes in a loose leaf cook book entitled "Council's Choice Cookery." Today on this page [the Edith Adams page] appear but a few of the recipes from that book, which is on sale at B.C. Electric.'
   The recipe for Rice Krispie Dainties on p 21 of the book indicates that it could not have been published before 1928, the year that Rice Krispies cereal was introduced to the market by Kellogg. Rice Krispie Dainties (which has for ingredients sugar, oil, cocoa, salt, corn syrup, Kellogg's Rice Krispies, raisins, and nuts) is not the same recipe as the more familiar Rice Krispies Squares Marshmallow Bars, which was first tested and published by the Kellogg Test Kitchen in Battle Creek, Michigan, in 1941.

1930

[Title unknown]

B68.1   nd [about 1930]
[An edition of a cookbook by the ladies of St Cecilia Review, Nanaimo, British Columbia, nd, pp 48]
CITATIONS: CBCat 61, No. 90
NOTES: The suggested date of publication is the bookseller's. No information surfaced about St Cecilia Review at the Vancouver Island Regional Library, the Nanaimo Museum, or through telephone calls to Catholic churches in Nanaimo.

A cook book containing recipes tested and proven

B69.1   [1930]
A cook book / containing recipes tested / and proven by the / ladies of the Order of the / Royal Purple Lodge No. 8 / Prince Rupert, B.C. / Rose, Cowan & Latta Limited / printers / Prince Rupert, B.C.
DESCRIPTION: 23.0 × 15.0 cm   Pp [1] 2–72   OORP symbol on tp   [$0.50, on binding]   Paper, with image on front of an elk's head; stapled
CONTENTS: 1 tp; 2 'An Appreciation' signed Mrs G.E. Gulick, Miss Amelia Gurvich, Mrs G.C. Arseneau, Mrs G.E. Phillipson, Mrs W.E. Williscroft [i.e., the Committee]; 3 table of contents and 'Table of Weights and Measures'; 4 ads; 5–72 recipes credited with the name of the contributor and ads
COPIES: *BVIPA
NOTES: The cover-title is '1930 // Royal Purple Cook Book No. 2' (no copy of Book No. 1 has surfaced). The interior text is printed in purple ink.

The cook book of the Creston and District Women's Institute

B70.1   1930
The / cook book / of the / Creston and District / Women's Institute / 1930 [cover-title]
DESCRIPTION: 24.0 × 15.0 cm   Pp 1–52   Paper, with small image on front, in a square frame, of a four-person family at table; stapled
CONTENTS: 1 untitled verse, five numbered requirements for successful baking, and 'Index' [i.e., table of contents]; 2 ad; 3–51 recipes credited with the name of the contributor and ads; 52 'Useful Hints' and 'Correct Sauces for Meats'
COPIES: BCVM   *Private collection

NOTES: The running head is 'Creston and District Women's Institute Cook Book.' The BCVM copy lacks the front face of the binding.

Tested recipes

B71.1   June 1930
Tested recipes / as / compiled by / the Ladies' Aid of / Richmond United Church / June, 1930
DESCRIPTION: 20.0 × 13.5 cm   Pp [i–ii], 1–32   Tp illus of two maids, each carrying a steaming dish, and below, a shield-shape featuring a crossed rolling pin and spoon at centre and a salt-shaker above top edge of shield-shape; a few small illus   Thin card, with image on front of a shield-shape similar to the tp illus; sewn
CONTENTS: i tp; ii blank; 1–30 recipes credited with the name of the contributor and ads; 31 'Index' [i.e., table of contents]; 32 blank for 'Memoranda'
COPIES: *BRMA
NOTES: The cookbook is multigraphed. The BRMA copy is inscribed on the title-page, at top, 'Mrs Fessenden,' and below, 'Bridge Port 1930.'

25 recipes for canned salmon

B72.1   nd [about 1930]
25 / recipes for / canned / salmon [cover-title]
DESCRIPTION: Pp [1–15]   Illus   Paper, with two images on front: a salmon leaping to pass over a waterfall and a plate of cooked salmon; stapled
CONTENTS: 1 cover-title; 2 'The Best Way to Open a Can of Salmon'; 3–13 twenty-five numbered recipes for canned salmon; 14–15 [inside back face of binding] 'Consider the Five Varieties of Salmon' and at bottom p 15, 'McC – F Vancouver'
COPIES: *Private collection
NOTES: No publisher is named, but the cookbook may have been produced by British Columbia Packers Ltd, Vancouver, which published B84.1, *Sea Food Recipes.*

1930s

Pollyanna's tried and true cook book

B73.1   nd [1930s]
[An edition of *Pollyanna's Tried and True Cook Book,* Vancouver]
COPIES: Private collection
NOTES: The approximate date is the owner's suggestion.

1930–1

The Vancouver bride

Earlier cookbooks for Vancouver brides are B21.1 and B44.1.

B74.1 1930–1
The Vancouver bride [folio:] 5 / The Vancouver bride / 1930–31 edition / A wedding present to brides of Greater Vancouver / from the advertisers and the publisher. / The contents of this book represent a very con- / siderable expenditure of time and money, every / care having been taken to include only the most / authentic information obtainable. / The publisher [*sic*, singular] will protect their copyright in- / terest to the full, and reproduction without per- / mission is strictly prohibited in Canada and the / United States. / Progress Publishing Company, Ltd. / (Established 1913) / Marine Building Vancouver, British Columbia
DESCRIPTION: 25.0 × 17.5 cm   Pp 3–246   Illus   Cloth
CONTENTS: 3 endpaper ad; 4 blank; 5 tp; 6 ad; 7 'Record of My Wedding'; 8 'Record of Wedding Presents' and 'Wedding Anniversary'; 9 'Introduction' signed the publishers; 10–241 text; top 242 'Index'; mid 242–244 'List of Recipes'; 245 'List of Advertisers'; 246 'Insurance'
COPIES: *Private collection
NOTES: The 'Introduction' states: 'The recipes have mainly been tested by Vancouver housewives, whose names are appended to each recipe, ... Many of these ladies will be known to Vancouver brides.' There are sections for 'The Household Budget,' 'The Home – Buy or Build' (including photographs and plans), 'Things Worth Knowing,' and other topics before the recipes.

1930–5

Favourite recipes

The Ganges Chapter received its charter in 1914; the group changed its name to HMS Ganges Chapter in 1954.

B75.1 nd [about 1930–5]
Imperial Order / Daughters of the Empire / [IODE symbol] / Favourite recipes / Ganges Chapter / Ganges, B.C.
DESCRIPTION: 22.5 × 14.5 cm   Pp [1–2] 3–32   Paper; stapled

CONTENTS: 1 tp; 2 ads; 3–30 recipes credited with the name of the contributor; 31 ad; 32 'Index' [i.e., table of contents]
COPIES: *BVIPM

Tested recipes

Cedar Cottage is a historic area of East Vancouver, located south of Trout Lake. Cedar Cottage United Church was founded in 1908, as Cedar Cottage Presbyterian Church.

B76.1 nd [about 1930–5]
Tested / recipes / Compiled by the / Women's Association of / Cedar Cottage United Church [cover-title]
DESCRIPTION: 21.0 × 14.0 cm   Pp [i–ii], 1–66   Paper; stapled
CONTENTS: i 'Index' [i.e., table of contents] and 'This book contains 260 tested recipes, compiled by the Women's Association of the Cedar Cottage United Church.'; ii 'A Martha' contributed by Mrs J. Warnock [poem]; 1–66 recipes credited with the name of the contributor
COPIES: *Private collection
NOTES: The text is multigraphed. The advertisements on the binding are for Vancouver businesses.

1931

Stevens, Miss Mary Alice (20 March 1900–1952)

Also by this author is B115.1, Home Canning Ration Guide. Mary Alice Stevens was the daughter of William and Jane Stevens of Hamiota, Manitoba, where she attended high school. In 1923, she received a Bachelor of Science in Home Economics degree from the University of Manitoba, having spent her undergraduate summers in British Columbia at her father's irrigation camp in the mountains. In November 1923 she moved to Guelph, Ontario, to become head of the Department of Home Economics at the new Guelph Collegiate Vocational Institute. She resigned in late 1926 and moved to Vernon, British Columbia, to take up the position of domestic science teacher. She was a founding member of the Canadian Home Economics Association, established in 1939 (We Are Tomorrow's Past, p 5). In 1947, she was appointed assistant director of Women's Extension Programs at the University of Sakatchewan, and in 1949 she became an associate professor at that university. She contributed text to B125.1, Dehydrated Vegetables.

Her 'Values in Home Economics,' 1936, is reprinted in Peterat/DeZwart.

Information about Stevens is from the 1901 Census and from the Manitoba Agricultural College journal, Managra *Vol. 16, No. 5 (March 1923), p 5 (includes her photograph); Vol. 17, No. 1 (November 1923), p 35; Vol. 18, No. 4 (February 1925), pp 26–7 (reprints her photograph); Vol. 19, No. 3 (January 1926), p 43; and Vol. 20, No. 1 (November 1926), p 42. In 'The Okanagan Valley,'* Managra *Vol. 20, No. 5 (March 1927), pp 52–4, Stevens discusses fruit growing and domestic science teaching in the Okanagan Valley, and the state of British Columbia's teacher training in domestic science.*

See also B46.1, another cookbook for OK Apples.

B77.1   [1931]
Apple secrets / Apples for health and / thrift – how to serve / this least expensive of / all health foods. / Associated Growers of British Columbia Ltd. [OK Apples symbol] / Apple recipes compiled by / Alice Stevens, B.Sc. (H.E.) / Editor, Women's Section, / Country Life in British Columbia / (official organ of the British Columbia / Fruit Growers' Association.)
DESCRIPTION: 16.0 × 10.5 cm   Pp [1] 2–16   Tp illus col of an apple hanging from a branch, a few small illus col   Paper, with the following on front: the shape of the province of British Columbia, OK Apples symbol, and publication date of 1931; stapled
CONTENTS: 1 tp; 2 untitled note about how apples get from orchard to grocer; 3 'How to Keep Healthy with OK Apples'; 4 'General Rules for the Cookery of Apples'; 5–15 recipes under the headings 'Beverages,' 'Desserts,' 'Flour Mixtures,' 'Miscellaneous,' 'Salads,' and 'Supper Dishes'; 16 'Variety, Season and Uses of OK Apples'; inside back face of binding table of contents and at bottom, the printer, 'Mc.–F., Vancouver'
CITATIONS: Ferguson/Fraser, p 233, illus col on p 80 of closed volume
COPIES: ACG   MWPA   OONL (TX813 A6 S73 1931, 2 copies)   SSWD   *Private collection
NOTES: The following is on the inside front face of the binding: 'This booklet is presented to the users of OK Apples with the compliments of 2,000 co-operative fruit growers, known as the Associated Growers of British Columbia Limited ... Further copies of this booklet may be had from the Associated Growers of British Columbia Ltd. Vernon, B.C.'

1932

Cub camp cook book

B78.1   1932
First Pack, Vernon Wolf Cubs / 1932 / Cub camp cook book / Only 35 cents / If you buy me, it means – / camp and good scouting for us / and / good value for you [cover-title]
DESCRIPTION: 17.0 × 12.0 cm   Pp 3–12 [versos not incl in pagination]   Card, with image on front of a man carrying a steaming or flaming Christmas pudding; punched with two holes at top edge and tied together with string
CONTENTS: 3–12 recipes credited with the name of the contributor
COPIES: *BVMA
NOTES: The recipes, which are printed in two columns per page, are for home use, not for camp cooking. They are in random order: Matrimony Cake, for example, is next to Best Sweet Pickled Cherries. An initial leaf may be lacking from the BVMA copy.

Girl Guide cook book

B79.1   nd [about 1932]
Girl Guide cook / book / compiled and arranged by / the Guides of Greater / Vancouver / British Columbia [cover-title]
DESCRIPTION: 22.0 × 14.5 cm   Pp [1–6] 7–95 [96]   Illus portrait on p 1 of Mrs Alan Morkill, provincial commissioner for British Columbia   [$0.50, on inside front face of binding]   Paper, with image on front of three Girl Guides walking toward the reader, a globe of the world behind them
CONTENTS: 1 illus portrait, 'The Guide Law,' 'The Guide Promise,' and 'The Brownie Promise'; 2–3 'Aims of the Girl Guides' and 'Origin of the Guide Movement'; 4 'The Beauty of Order,' a verse by M.B. Paxton from *Woman's Magazine,* and a quotation from Daniel Willard; 5 'Household Hints' and 'Table of Weights and Measures'; 6 'Index' [i.e., table of contents]; 7–95 text; 96 blank for 'My Recipes'
COPIES: BVIPA   OONL (TX715.6 G59 1920z)   *Private collection
NOTES: Text on p 74 states, 'The Guides of Greater Vancouver celebrated the 21st birthday of Guiding on May 28th, 1932, with a rally.' The cookbook was likely published about the same year. Edith Chesman was the convenor for the cookbook; in her acknowledgments (inside back face of binding), she thanks

friends and fellow Guiders in the province and also Mrs Harold Dickinson, 'who helped [her] gather and arrange the copy.' The proceeds from the sale of the book were 'to be used for camp purposes' (inside front face of binding).

'Recipes by Famous Chefs of Canadian Pacific Hotels across Canada' are on pp 59–63. 'Camp Cookery' on p 93 describes how to roast or bake eggs, potatoes or corn by covering the food with a thick layer of wet mud and burying it in hot ashes; and the section has recipes for Indian Bacon and Eggs (a heated, flat stone is the cooker) and for Dampers (dough wrapped around sticks and cooked over the fire, after which jam or butter is pushed down the hole left by the stick). 'Camp Expedients' on p 95 gives directions for Cake without an Oven, for Stew (when the meat supply fails), and for making a homemade grater and a homemade egg slicer.

Scott, Anna Lee [pseudonym]

See O773.4 for an edition of Scott's The Easy Way Cake Book published by the Daily Colonist, Victoria.

1933

Choice, tested recipes

B80.1   1933
Choice, tested / recipes / collected by / Relief Committee / Young People's Society / Revelstoke United Church, / Revelstoke, B.C. / The members of the Relief Committee / of the Young People's Society of the / Revelstoke United Church desire to / thank all those who have contributed / recipes and advertisements, thus mak- / ing possible the publishing of this little / book. We hope it will be of great ser- / vice to the purchasers. / A copy of this recipe book will be delivered to any address / upon the receipt of 50 cents. Address the Secretary-Treasurer / Young People's Society, Revelstoke United Church, Revelstoke. / British Columbia.
DESCRIPTION: 21.0 × 14.0 cm   Pp [1] 2–41   Paper; stapled
CONTENTS: Inside back face of binding 'Printed by the Revelstoke Review'
CITATIONS: Ferguson/Fraser, p 233
COPIES: *OGU (UA s045 b32)

1934

Adams, Edith [pseudonym]

The first column attributed to Edith Adams ('Rhubarb Is Best Dessert for Spring') appeared in the Vancouver Sun newspaper on 4 April 1924, p 17 (the microfilm of the Vancouver Sun by Commonwealth Microfilm Library is missing this issue, but a paper copy is at BVIP). There was no announcement in preceding issues of the paper or fanfare related to the appearance of the new name, and only in the next issue, 11 April, was her page identified by the banner headline 'Edith Adam's [sic] Cookery Page.' At the beginning, her name was variously spelled Adams or Adam, but eventually it stayed Adams. The pseudonym was coined by Herb Gates, circulation manager (reported in an article celebrating the opening of the Edith Adams Cottage in Sun Spots, February 1947, an in-house publication). The person behind the pseudonym before 1947 is unknown, but from 1947 to the 1960s it was Marianne Linnell (see pl 46). (Eve Johnson is incorrect when she implies, in Five Star Food, Vancouver: Pacific Press, 1993, pp 7 and 8, that Edith Adams first appeared in the Vancouver Sun in 1912, which is actually the first year the paper was published, on 12 February; she repeats the error in 'Her Life Was a Lie ...,' Vancouver Sun, 30 October 1999, p E4.) Edith Adams last appeared in the Vancouver Sun in 1999.

From the mid-1930s to the 1950s, the newspaper published cookbooks, under the Edith Adams name, nearly every year. Each issue reproduced a selection from the readers' 'prize recipes' that had been printed daily in the pages of the newspaper over the preceding twelve months or so, winning a $1 prize for the contributor. The first two issues, which contained the same text, are described below. For later collections, see: B82.1, Edith Adams Prize Winners Third Annual Cook Book; B94.1, Edith Adam's Prize Winners 4th Annual Cook Book; B97.1, Prize Winners 5th Annual Cook Book; B99.1, Sun Prize Winners 6th Annual Cook Book; B103.1, Edith Adams 7th Annual Cook Book; B110.1, Edith Adam's 8th Annual Prize Winners' Cook Book; B114.1, 9th Annual Edith Adam's Wartime Cook Book; B119.1, The Vancouver Sun's 10th Annual Cook Book; B124.1, The Vancouver Sun's 11th Annual Cook Book; and B133.1, Edith Adams' Twelfth Annual Prize Cook Book. See also the following, which are not part of the numbered sequence: B128.1, Edith Adams' Cooking under Pressure (biographical information about Linnell is here); B129.1, Modern Guide to Home Canning; B139.1, Globe

Trotting Gourmet; *and B140.1,* Successful Home Canning.

The Vancouver Sun *owns copies of the third, fifth, sixth, tenth, eleventh, thirteenth, and fourteenth annual cookbooks. At the newspaper's office there is a file card headed 'Edith Adams' Prize Cook Books' that lists numbers 3 to 14 with a year beside each number. Beside the column of numbers and years is a note: 'Earlier books have been lost – fire – and dates are uncertain –.' In my entry for each annual, I give the reasons for my assigned date and note the instances where the file card is incorrect.*

Edith Adams Omnibus, compiled by Elizabeth Driver, Vancouver: Whitecap Books, 2005, is an abridged edition of the first thirteen issues. It reproduces the front covers and includes an introduction, photographs of Edith Adams Cottage activities and staff, and an index to the recipes.

The pseudonymous Edith Adams of the Vancouver Sun *should not be confused with Edith Adams (1891–1957) who wrote the social notes for various Toronto newspapers from 1928.*

B81.1   [1st ed., about 1934 or earlier]
[Title-page lacking of the first edition of '$100.00 Cook Book' by Edith Adams]
DESCRIPTION: Pp 1–96   Illus   Lacks binding; stapled
CONTENTS: 1 'To Our Readers:' signed the Vancouver Sun; 2 'Here's to Your Health' by Dr Frank McCoy; 3–96 recipes
COPIES: *Private collection
NOTES: Although the recipes and illustrations are the same as B81.2, the wording of 'To Our Readers' makes no mention of an edition number: 'In keeping with the custom of the Vancouver Sun to offer to its readers services over and above those found within its daily pages, this $100 Cook Book – so called because of the hundred prize recipes included in its contents – ...' The private collector's copy, therefore, is likely the first edition in what was to become a series of annual cookbooks.

If the third annual cookbook was published at the end of 1935, the first annual and its second edition likely appeared in 1934 or slightly earlier. The file card at the newspaper office does not list the first and second issues.

The copy at BVAMM, which has pp 3–92 only and lacks its binding, may be B81.1 or B81.2.

B81.2   [2nd ed., about 1934]
—The Vancouver Sun / $100.00 / cook / book / [artist's signature:] Callan / Compiled / by / Edith Adams / Department [cover-title]

DESCRIPTION: 25.5 × 17.5 cm   Pp 1–96   Illus   Paper, with image on front of a mother working at a kitchen table, her young daughter standing on chair at table and stirring contents of bowl; stapled
CONTENTS: Inside front face of binding 'Index' and 'Presented with the compliments of the Vancouver Sun ...'; 1 'To Our Readers:'; 2 'Here's to Your Health' by Dr Frank McCoy; 3–96 recipes and articles of general interest
COPIES: *BVAA
NOTES: 'To Our Readers' refers to this publication as 'this second edition of our $100 Cook Book – so called because of the hundred prize recipes included in its contents – ...' According to text below the 'Index,' the '100 prize recipes [were] from subscribers, who were each awarded $1.00 for a recipe.' The 'second edition' is a reprint of the recipe pages of B81.1. In B81.1 and B81.2 the prize recipes, which are credited to individual readers, with their addresses, are in the minority; unattributed recipes make up the larger part of the text. In subsequent issues, most of the text is prize recipes.

1935

Adams, Edith [pseudonym]

For information about the pseudonym and a list of the annual recipe collections published under the Edith Adams name, see B81.1.

B82.1   nd [1935]
Edith / Adams / prize / winners / third annual / cook book / The / Vancouver / Sun [cover-title]
DESCRIPTION: 24.5 × 14.5 cm   Pp [1] 2–64   Illus   Paper, with image on front of a mother working at a kitchen table, her young daughter standing on chair at table and stirring contents of bowl
CONTENTS: 1 untitled introductory note signed Edith Adams; 2–63 recipes; 64 'Index'
COPIES: *BVA   BVAMM   BVIPM   OONL (TX715 P754 fol.)   Company collection (Vancouver Sun) Private collection
NOTES: The text states on p 1: 'Once again the Vancouver Sun is happy to accede to the demand of its readers and to present herewith its Third Annual Cook Book ... a collection of prize winning dishes devised by some of the most successful home cooks of British Columbia and carefully tested out in scientific culinary laboratories ... This Prize Winners' Cook Book is ... the concrete result of a year's successful kitchen experimentation on the part of British

Columbia's most deft and inventive housewives.' At bottom p 1 is the note 'Edith Adams ... offers a daily prize of $1 for the best recipe submitted by readers.' The image on the binding is a redrawn version of that on B81.2.

The third annual cookbook was advertised in the *Vancouver Sun* on 6 December 1935: 'Did you get a copy of the Vancouver Sun's Third Annual Cook Book? It contains about 180 tested prize winning recipes which have been published during the past year. Send in your order today to the Recipe Editor and enclose 6c to cover mailing charges.' Copies of the third annual were still available for sale early in the new year, according to a notice in the newspaper on 14 February 1936, p 9: 'There are still some of the Third Annual Cook Books left.' On 27 March 1936, p 20, the reader was instructed '[t]o get a copy of the Vancouver Sun's Third Annual Prize Recipe Book send 6c to cover cost of mailing to the Recipe Editor.' The only date printed in the book is on p 5, in the note for Mrs Drewery's Inexpensive Christmas Cake that says, 'The ingredients cost about sixty-one cents for this cake in December, 1934.' The file card at the *Sun* office for the annual prize cookbooks incorrectly dates the third annual cookbook 1938.

Cookery book

St Andrew's was established in 1904 as a Presbyterian church. It became St Andrew's United Church after church union on 10 June 1925.

B83.1 nd [about 1935]
St. Andrew's United Church / Women's Association, Circle No. 5 / Cookery book / North Shore [printers' trade symbol] Press, Ltd. [cover-title]
DESCRIPTION: 23.0 × 14.5 cm   Pp [1] 2–30   Paper, with image on front of St Andrew's United Church; stapled
CONTENTS: 1–30 recipes and ads
COPIES: *BVAMM
NOTES: An advertisement on p 4 points to publication in the mid-1930s. The advertisement is for Avenue Barber Shop, 1535 Lonsdale Avenue; the proprietor is named as W.J. Colwill, and the shop described as 'Established over 5 years.' *Wrigley's British Columbia Directory* for 1929 and 1930 list M. Whitaker as proprietor; *Wrigley's Greater Vancouver and New Westminster (British Columbia) Directory 1933* lists W.J. Colwill.

Sea food recipes

British Columbia Packers Ltd had its start in 1902, as the British Columbia Packers' Association, when a majority of the independent salmon canneries amalgamated to create a centralized system for processing and marketing canned fish. The association's history to the 1920s is documented in Dianne Newell, The Development of the Pacific Salmon-Canning Industry: A Grown Man's Game, *Montreal and Kingston: McGill-Queen's University Press, 1989.*

B84.1 nd [about 1935]
Sea food / recipes [cover-title]
DESCRIPTION: 8.5 × 15.0 cm   Pp [1] 2–23   Centre spread illus col of a horizontal band of ocean at top, a shelf of seven canned seafood products at middle, and six prepared dishes on a chequered tablecloth at bottom, with the caption 'From the sea // to your shelf // to your table'; illus col of prepared dishes Paper, with image on front of a can of Clover Leaf salmon packed by British Columbia Packers Ltd, Vancouver, and the contents of a can of salmon on a dinner plate, garnished with lemon slices and olives; stapled
CONTENTS: 1 cover-title; 2–3 'From the Sea to Your Shelf to Your Table' [description of seven canned seafood products: Sockeye salmon, Cohoe salmon, Pink salmon, Pilchard, Herring, Clams, Oysters]; 4–5 'Appetizers'; 6–7 'Soups'; 8–9 'Salads'; 10–11, 14–21 'Supper and Luncheon Dishes'; 12–13 centre spread illus col; 22 'Sandwiches'; 23 [inside back face of binding] 'Index Recipes'
COPIES: ONM   *OTMCL (641.5971 H39 No. 14)
NOTES: From appearances, *Sea Food Recipes* was published about 1935.

Supper menus

B85.1 1935
Supper / menus / Issued by / Circle No. 2 / Trinity United Church, Nelson, B.C. / 1935 edition / Fifty cents [cover-title]
DESCRIPTION: With small image on front of a cornucopia
COPIES: *Private collection

1935–8

The Province cook book

B86.1 nd [about 1935–8]
The / Province cook book / Published by the / Household Service Department of the / Vancouver Daily Province
DESCRIPTION: 25.0 × 17.5 cm Pp [1–4] 5–52 [$0.25, on binding] Paper, with a vertical band on front, at left, featuring images of various foodstuffs (e.g., roast poultry, pumpkin, pie); stapled
CONTENTS: 1 tp; 2 blank; 3 untitled introductory note; 4 'Table of Measurements'; 5–50 recipes; 51–2 index
COPIES: *BVAU OONL (TX715 P76)
NOTES: Page 3 refers to free cooking lessons at the Province Modern Kitchen. Since the Modern Kitchen began in 1935 (see B104.1), this edition is no earlier than 1935.

B86.2 rev. ed., July 1939
—The / Province cook book / Published by the / Household Service Department of the / Vancouver Daily Province / Revised July, 1939.
DESCRIPTION: 25.5 × 17.0 cm Pp [1–4] 5–52 [$0.25, on binding] Paper, with image on front of a woman leaning on a kitchen table, on which sits a bowl of eggs, salt and pepper, milk, and a box of sugar(?); stapled
CONTENTS: 1 tp; 2 blank; 3 untitled introductory note; 4 'Table of Measurements'; 5–50 recipes; 51–2 index
COPIES: *BVAA

B86.3 rev. ed., July 1941
—The / Province cook book / Published by the / Household Service Department of the / Vancouver Daily Province / Revised July, 1941.
DESCRIPTION: [$0.25, on binding] Paper, with image on front of a woman leaning on a kitchen table, on which sits a bowl of eggs, salt and pepper, milk, and a box of sugar(?); stapled
COPIES: *Vancouver Sun (company collection)
NOTES: The Vancouver Sun copy is inscribed on the title-page, 'E Norman,' i.e., Eileen Norman, who worked for the newspaper (see B128.1).

1935–9

Creamed cottage cheese

See also B62.1.

B87.1 nd [about 1935–9]
The health food / Creamed / cottage / cheese / Sixty-two practical tested / ways to serve / Fraser Valley Milk Producers' Association / Vancouver, B.C.
DESCRIPTION: 17.0 × 12.5 cm Pp [i–ii], [1–2] 3–30 [31–8] Paper, with image on front of cottage cheese on a lettuce-lined plate; stapled
CONTENTS: i tp; ii blank; 1–2 table of contents; 3–4 untitled text about the food value of cottage cheese; 5–30 sixty-two numbered recipes; 31–8 blank 'For Your Own Recipes' and at bottom p 38, 'Wrigley Printing Co. Ltd. 578 Seymour Street, Vancouver, B.C.'
COPIES: *BVIPM
NOTES: The cover-title is 'Recipes // Creamed Cottage Cheese.' From appearances, B87.1 and B87.2 were published before the start of the Second World War.

B87.2 nd [about 1935–9]
—The health food / Creamed / cottage / cheese / Eighty-six practical tested / ways to serve / Fraser Valley Milk Producers' Association / Vancouver, B.C.
DESCRIPTION: 16.0 × 12.0 cm Pp [i–ii], [1–2] 3–38 Paper, with image on front of cottage cheese on a lettuce-lined plate; stapled
CONTENTS: i tp; ii blank; 1–2 table of contents; 3–4 untitled text about the food value of cottage cheese; 5–38 eighty-six numbered recipes
COPIES: *BVAMM
NOTES: The cover-title is 'Creamed Cottage Cheese Recipes.' This edition has more recipes.

Malkin's best handy book

B88.1 nd [about 1935–9]
Malkin's / best / handy / book. [cover-title]
DESCRIPTION: 22.5 × 14.5 cm Pp [1] 2–47 [48] Illus of Malkin's products Paper, with image on front of four hands reaching for the title; stapled
CONTENTS: Inside front face of binding name of W.H. Malkin Co. Ltd, Vancouver, Victoria, Prince Rupert, and Nanaimo; 1 'Index'; 2–47 text; 48 'Glimpse of "The House behind the Goods"'; inside back face list of Malkin's products and at bottom, 'Sun Publishing Co. Ltd. Vancouver, B.C.'
COPIES: *BVIPA
NOTES: The text includes recipes, twenty-three num-

bered 'Quality Hints' about Malkin products on the rectos of pp 3–47, and information about reading tea-cups, making tea and coffee, first aid, canned foods, company premiums, and stain removal. On p 48 there is a reference to the company's 'nearly half a century of effort.' Since the business was established in 1895 (see the W.H. Malkin Co. fonds at BVAA), the cookbook was published in the late 1930s or early 1940s, but likely before the war since there are no references to wartime conditions.

'101' tested recipes

The PEO Sisterhood is an international society of women, founded in 1869 on the campus of Iowa Wesleyan College, Mount Pleasant, Iowa. PEO stands for Philanthropic Educational Organization.

B89.1 nd [about 1935–9]
"101" / tested / recipes / [Initials PEO in a star-shape] / Chapter O // Vancouver, B.C. [cover-title]
DESCRIPTION: Stapled
COPIES: *Private collection
NOTES: From appearances, the book was published about 1935–9.

Selected recipes

The church is in Vancouver.

B90.1 nd [about 1935–9]
Selected / recipes / by the / members of Devonshire Circle / and their friends / Shaughnessy Heights United Church [cover-title]
COPIES: *Private collection
NOTES: The owner dates the book as 'prior to 1940,' and the appearance of the cover-title is consistent with publication in the 1930s.

1936

The Kelowna Hospital Women's Auxiliary cook book

B91.1 1936
The / Kelowna Hospital Women's Auxiliary / cook book / A collection of tried and tested / recipes / We may live without poetry, music, and art; / We may live without conscience, and live without heart; / We may live without friends, and live without books; / But civilized man cannot live without cooks. / We may live without books – what is knowledge but grieving? / We may live without hope – what is hope but deceiving? / We may live without love – what is passion but pining? / But where is the man that can live without dining? / Compiled and published by / the Kelowna Hospital Women's Auxiliary / Kelowna, B.C. / November, 1936 Kelowna Printing Co.
DESCRIPTION: 21.5 cm × 13.5 cm Pp [1] 2–120 Tp illus of Kelowna Hospital [$0.50, on binding] Thin card, with tp illus on front; stapled
CONTENTS: 1 tp; 2 'Table of Measures' and 'Table Decorations'; top 3 untitled acknowledgments; mid 3–4 'A Short History of the Kelowna Hospital'; 5 'Large Quantity Recipes'; 6 'To Serve 100 People'; 7–mid 118 recipes and ads; mid 118–119 'Household Hints'; 120 'Index' and ad
CITATIONS: Edwards 1974 Neering, p 157
COPIES: BVIPA *Private collection

Stewart, Florence Elizabeth, née Sharp (Scotland, 30 June 1883–23 May 1973, Vancouver, BC), and Gretchen Day Ross (Wausau, Wisc., 7 October 1887–22 June 1973, Vancouver, BC)

Vincent Galleries, at 821 Howe Street, sold antiques, tableware, and home furnishings to a rich clientele. Gretchen Day Ross, the store owner and co-compiler of the cookbook, was the daughter of Richard Vincent Day and Cordellia Noble. She came to Vancouver in 1894. At the time of the cookbook's publication, she and her husband, stockbroker John Campbell Ross, were living at the Vancouver Hotel.

Marian Laing, who wrote the cookbook's foreword, was probably related to Gretchen, perhaps a cousin: Marian was born on 18 July 1886, in the United States, to John Day and Elizabeth Noble. Her husband, George Frederick Laing, was a bank manager, and they lived in Shaughnessy, an upscale Vancouver neighbourhood.

Florence Elizabeth Stewart, co-compiler, is likely the same person as the contributor of recipes signed Mrs F.E. Stewart, F.E. Stewart, and Mrs Angus Stewart. If so, she is Florence Elizabeth Sharp, who married Angus Stewart on 9 December 1908 at St Andrew's Manse, New Westminster. At the time of the cookbook's publication, Florence and Angus lived in the Shaughnessy Crescent Apartments, opposite the home of A.D. McRae and his wife, both also recipe contributors.

B92.1 1936

Vincent Galleries / book of cookery / Vancouver / Canada / Compiled and edited / by / Florence Elizabeth Stewart / and / Gretchen Day Ross / 1936

DESCRIPTION: 22.5 × 15.5 cm   Pp [1–5] 6–222 [223–4] Cloth, with check pattern

CONTENTS: 1 tp; 2 foreword signed Marian Laing; 3 editors' acknowledgments; 4 'Index to Advertisers'; 5 ad for celebration of Vancouver's golden jubilee, 1886–1936; 6 ad; 7–215 text and ads; 216 ad; 217–22 'Index' [i.e., recipes listed in the order in which they appear, under chapter headings]; 223 blank; 224 'Printed by the Clarke & Stuart Co. Ltd. Vancouver, B.C. 1936'

CITATIONS: Ferguson/Fraser, p 234, illus col on p 80 of closed volume   Hale 3186

COPIES: BVIPA   OONL (TX715.6 V55 1936)   *Private collection

NOTES: The foreword refers to 'cosmopolitan Vancouver, where the population comprises citizens from every province in Canada, every state in the Union, and many from Europe and Asia.' The recipes are attributed to well-known Vancouver residents, likely customers of Vincent Galleries.

Vancouver's golden jubilee cook book

B93.1 1936

Vancouver's golden / jubilee / cook book / Edited by the / Local Council of Women / Vancouver / British Columbia / 1936 [cover-title]

DESCRIPTION: 17.5 × 12.5 cm   Pp 1–60 [61–4]   Illus portrait on p 1 of T. Jean Rolston   Paper; stapled

CONTENTS: 1 untitled introduction signed T. Jean Rolston; 2 ad and 'Officers for 1936–37' [list of executive of Local Council of Women]; 3 verses, provided 'Compliments of Miss Winnifred Kydd, O.B.E., M.A. President of National Council of Women'; 4 ad; 5–59 recipes credited with the name of the contributor and ads; 60 ads; 61–3 blank; 64 'Printed by Ward & Phillips Ltd.'

CITATIONS: Hale 3163

COPIES: *BVIPA

NOTES: On p 1, Jean Rolston refers to this as the Local Council's 'first cook book.' On p 2 her name is listed as Mrs F.J. Rolston. The year 1936 marked the fiftieth anniversary of the incorporation of the City of Vancouver.

1937

Adams, Edith [pseudonym]

For information about the pseudonym and a list of the annual recipe collections published under the Edith Adams name, see B81.1.

B94.1 nd [about 1937]

Edith / Adam's [*sic*] / prize / winners / 4th / annual / cook / book / Compliments of [artist's signature at far right:] Wilson / The Vancouver Sun [cover-title]

DESCRIPTION: 27.5 × 17.0 cm   Pp 1–96   Illus   Paper, with image on front of a woman holding up a lattice-top pie; stapled

CONTENTS: 1 untitled note signed Edith Adams; 2 'Index' [i.e., table of contents]; 3–91 recipes; 92–6 publ ads

COPIES: *BVAA   BVAMM   BVIPA

NOTES: According to p 95, 'The recipes in this book all represent prize selections ... recipes for which the Sun has paid a dollar ...' Jubilee Cake, on p 9, is described as having 'won a prize during Vancouver's Golden Jubilee,' i.e., in 1936. Recipes in the fourth annual cookbook appeared in the newspaper through 1936 and as late as 26 February 1937; recipes in the fifth annual cookbook appeared in the newspaper from 4 March 1937 onward. The fourth annual, therefore, was likely published in 1937, although I have not found a publication notice to confirm the date. There was a fire at the *Sun* in March 1937, which may have delayed the cookbook's production. The fifth annual was published in late 1938. The file card at the *Sun* office for the annual prize cookbooks incorrectly dates the fourth, 1939.

The artist is Fraser Wilson, who drew cartoons for the *Vancouver Sun* and *Daily Province* up to 1947. His art is also featured on B97.1 and B114.1.

The BVAMM copy is in poor condition.

Coronation cook book

B95.1 1937

Coronation / 1937 / cook book / Prince George, B.C. [cover-title]

DESCRIPTION: With image on front of King George VI's head between two open curtains

COPIES: *BPGRM (992.02.01)

NOTES: The museum names the Professional and Business Women of Prince George as the book's compilers. King George VI was crowned on 12 May 1937.

Coronation number cook book

The Dr O.M. Jones Chapter, in Victoria, received its charter in 1918 and disbanded in 1960.

B96.1 1937
[IODE symbol] / Dr. O.M. Jones Chapter / I.O.D.E. / Coronation number / cook book / May 12th, 1937 / Including recipes gathered by Radio Station CFCT / on the Friendly Hour [cover-title]
DESCRIPTION: 25.5 × 17.0 cm Pp [1] 2–64 Paper, with images on front of IODE symbol (at top) and Union Jack, Red Ensign, maple leaf, and beaver (at centre); stapled
CONTENTS: 1 'Dr. O.M. Jones Chapter I.O.D.E.' [history of the chapter]; 2 'Patrons' and ad; 3 'Tables of Weights' [measure, time for vegetables, proportions, time for broiling] and recipe for Hand Lotion; 4 ad; 5 'Household Hints'; 6 ads; 7 'Sandwich Fillings' and ads; 8 ads; 9–64 recipes credited with the name of the contributor and ads
COPIES: BVIPA *Private collection
NOTES: *Coronation Number Cook Book* was named for the coronation of King George VI on 12 May 1937.

1938

Adams, Edith [pseudonym]

For information about the pseudonym and a list of the annual recipe collections published under the Edith Adams name, see B81.1.

B97.1 nd [1938]
Prize / winners / 5th annual / cook book / By / Edith / Adams / [artist's signature:] Wilson / Compliments / of / the Vancouver Sun. [cover-title]
DESCRIPTION: 27.5 × 17.0 cm Pp 1–64 Illus Paper, with image on front of a mother and daughter at oven door, mother holding rectangular pan; stapled
CONTENTS: 1 untitled introduction signed Edith Adams; 2–64 recipes
COPIES: Company collection (Vancouver Sun) *Private collection
NOTES: The introductory text states, 'These prize-winning recipes, which were selected from many thousand submitted by Vancouver Sun readers, have been carefully tested in scientific laboratories.' The text also calls the reader's attention 'to the daily prize recipes as they appear in the Vancouver Sun and also

the weekly cookery section which appears every Thursday.' This cookbook, it adds, is 'the direct creation of our capable and inventive housewives of British Columbia.'

The fifth annual cookbook was published in late 1938 and was still available for sale in early 1939. It was advertised in the *Vancouver Sun*, 8 December 1938, p 11: 'Get a Cook Book // To get your copy of the Prize Winners Fifth Annual Cook Book send me your name and address and 10c to cover cost of mailing. Edith Adams.' The same advertisement was repeated on 12, 19, and 26 January and 2 and 9 February 1939. The file card at the *Sun* office for the annual prize cookbooks incorrectly dates the fifth cookbook 1940.

See B94.1 regarding the artist Fraser Wilson.

Rogers' Golden recipes

For the titles of other cookbooks from BC Sugar Refining Co. Ltd, see B8.1.

B98.1 nd [about 1938]
Chef tested / Rogers' Golden / recipes / The cake reproduced on the cover is the "Cake Box" Light Fruit Cake page 5
DESCRIPTION: 17.0 × 11.5 cm Pp [1–3] 4–32 Tp illus green of a male chef holding up a can of Rogers' Golden Syrup in his right hand Very thin card, with image on front of a white-iced fruit cake on which is written, in red and yellow icing, 'Rogers' Golden Syrup Recipes'; stapled
CONTENTS: 1 tp; 2–3 index; 4–32 recipes, mainly for desserts
COPIES: BSUM *BVABSM MWPA (MG14 C50 McKnight, Ethel) OONL (TX819 S94 C44 1940z p***; copy 2 missing) SSWD
NOTES: The cover-title is 'Rogers' Golden Syrup Recipes.' A can of Rogers' Golden Syrup is illustrated on the outside back face of the binding (the illustration is cut out of the BVABSM copy). The syrup was – and still is – made by the BC Sugar Refining Co. in Vancouver.

The cookbook was published about 1938 since there is a photograph of its front cover in a Rogers' syrup advertisement on p 23 of M104.1, Middleton, Miss Katharine Major S., *The Winnipeg Home Cook Book*, published on 5 November 1938. The advertisement exhorts the reader to 'Mail this coupon today!' for a free copy of the book.

1939

Adams, Edith [pseudonym]

For information about the pseudonym and a list of the annual recipe collections published under the Edith Adams name, see B81.1.

B99.1 nd [1939]
Sun / prize winners / 6th / annual / cook / book / By / Edith / Adams. / Compliments of / The Vancouver Sun / Vancouver owned. [cover-title]
DESCRIPTION: 28.0 × 22.0 cm Pp 1–64 Illus Paper, with image on front of six smiling male chefs in a large cauldron over a fire; stapled
CONTENTS: 1 'Concerning Culinary Art' signed Edith Adams; 2 'Table of Measurements'; 3 'One Hundred Calorie Portions of Some Commonly Used Foods'; 4–60 recipes; 61–2 'Home Handies'; 63–4 blank for 'Paste Your Additional Recipes from the Vancouver Sun Here'
COPIES: *BVAA BVAMM BBVM Company collection (Vancouver Sun)
NOTES: In 'Concerning Culinary Art,' Adams writes, 'The main object in presenting the Sixth Annual Prize Winner's Cook Book is to show you how to save money by way of the kitchen.' This annual was advertised in the *Vancouver Sun* on 16 November 1939, p 11: 'Get a Cook Book // To get your copy of the new Prize-Winner Sixth Annual Cook Book, send me your name and address and 10c to cover the cost of mailing. Edith Adams.' The file card at the *Sun* office for the annual prize cookbooks incorrectly dates the sixth annual cookbook 1941.

English recipes

The Major John Hebden Gillespie Chapter received its charter on 24 February 1930, replacing a junior chapter called the Daisy Chain Chapter, which had been organized in June 1911. The Gillespie Chapter disbanded in 1995.

B100.1 nd [about 1939]
English / recipes / Published by the / Major John Hebden Gillespie Chapter / Imperial Order Daughters of the Empire / Victoria, B.C. / Price: Twenty-five cents [cover-title]
DESCRIPTION: 23.0 × 15.0 cm Pp 1–24 Paper, with image on front of an English cottage drawn on an unscrolled piece of paper or vellum, from which hangs the IODE symbol; image initialled by artist, 'L.S.Y.'; stapled

CONTENTS: 1 note about proceeds from the book, thank-you to advertisers and recipe contributors, 'Weights and Measures for English Cooking,' 'Wines and Menu,' and 'Temperature for Wines'; 2–22 recipes and ads; 23–4 blank for 'Own Recipes'
COPIES: *Bookseller's stock
NOTES: According to p 1, 'Proceeds from this book will be used for the purpose of caring for the indigent out-patients of the Tuberculosis Clinic of the Province of British Columbia.' The table of weights and measures offers Canadian equivalents for standard English measurements and terms, e.g., 4 tablespoonfuls equals ½ gill; 1 heaping quart of sifted flour equals 1 lb flour; Castor sugar is Berry sugar. The suggestions for matching wines with food and the wine temperatures are unusual features in a Canadian cookbook of this period. The recipes are, as the title indicates, mostly from England; for example, Lancaster Stew, Crumpets, and Chester Pudding. 'Printed by Diggon-Hibben Ltd.' is on the outside back face of the binding.

Two advertisements point to publication in about 1939. An advertisement on p 7 for Old British Fish and Chips, 1316 Broad Street, describes the business as 'Established 21 years'; the first listing for the business in *Wrigley's British Columbia Directory* is in the volume for 1929 (1929 + 21 years = 1940, but the directory would have been compiled the year before). An advertisement on p 10 for Nixon's Ltd, offering 'complete electrical service,' states that the business is 'now in our new location, 1205 Douglas.' BVIPA reports that Thomas M. Nixon's company was incorporated on 13 January 1938, at which time he was at 833 Yates Street, but on 6 December 1938 he filed a change of office address, 1205 Douglas Street, as advertised in the cookbook. The Douglas Street address, therefore, was a 'new location' in late 1938 and also continuing into 1939.

Mutch, Miss Jean E.

See B107.1 concerning 1939 and 1940 editions of Home Preservers' Handbook.

Nakusp souvenir cook book

B101.1 [1939]
Nakusp souvenir / cook book / Sponsored by / the Evening Auxiliary / of the / United Church / President: Mrs. E.J. Oxenham / Vice President: Mrs [sic, no period] J. Motherwell / Secretary: Mrs. R.S. LaRue / Treasurer: Miss G.E. Johnson / Supply

Secretary: Mrs. R. McCulloch / "If I cannot do great things, I can do small things in a / great way." – James Freeman Clarke.

DESCRIPTION: 17.0 × 11.0 cm Pp [1–40] Paper, with image on front of 'Lake Scene below Nakusp' and the date 1939; stapled

CONTENTS: 1 tp; 2–3 'Table of Measurements,' 'Substitutions,' 'Timetable for Roasting,' and 'Timetable for Cooking Vegetables'; 4–5 'Breads'; 6–7 'Fish Dishes'; 8–10 'Meats'; 11 'Vegetables'; 12–14 'Luncheon or Supper Dishes'; 15–16 'Salads and Salad Dressings'; 17–20 'Puddings and Desserts'; 21–3 'Pies'; 24–7 'Cakes and Frostings'; 28–31 'Cookies'; 32–3 'Pickles'; 34 'Jams and Jellies'; 35–7 'Candies'; 38–40 blank for 'Memorandum'

COPIES: *OGU (CCC TX715.6 E9)

NOTES: The recipes are credited with the name of the contributor. There is a recipe on p 10 for Brine for Preserving Meats of All Kinds, and on p 11 for a dish with the amusing name of Vegetable Aeroplane, made from Vegetable Marrow.

Late 1930s

Tested recipes and kitchen lore

The HMS Lion Chapter disbanded in 1957.

B102.1 nd [late 1930s]
H.M.S. Lion Chapter / Imperial Order, Daughters of the Empire / Chilliwack B.C. / Tested recipes and / kitchen lore / "We may live without poetry, music and art; / We may live without conscience and live / without heart, / We may live without friends, we may live / without books / But civilized man cannot live without / cooks" / We wish to express our thanks and appreciation / to all those who assisted in making this recipe / book a success. We wish to express our gratit- / ude particularly to the city merchants and / business houses, whose generous support has / made the publication of this book possible. In / recognition of their co-operation, we would / urge that our members and friends reciprocate / by patronising those places of business whose / advertisements appear in this book. / Mimeographed by Chilliwack News

DESCRIPTION: 21.0 × 15.0 cm Pp [1] 2–63 Paper, with images on front of a male chef's head and IODE symbol; stapled

CONTENTS: 1 tp; 2 table of contents, 'Measurements,' and 'Oven Temperatures'; 3–62 recipes credited with the name of the contributor and ads; 63 'Kitchen Lore'

COPIES: *BCHM

NOTES: There is an advertisement on p 49 for 'Langley Greenhouses (1930) Ltd.,' which places publication no earlier than that year, and the BCHM archivist suggests a publication date in the late 1930s, based on other advertisements. The cover-title is 'Recipe Book.'

B102.2 nd [late 1940s]
—H.M.S. Lion Chapter / Imperial Order, Daughters of the Empire / Chilliwack, B.C. / Tested recipes & / kitchen lore / [no opening quotation-marks] We may live without poetry, / music and art; / We may live without conscience / and live without heart, / We may live without friends, / We may live without books / But civilized man cannot / live without cooks." / We wish to express our thanks and apprec- / iation to all those who assisted in making / this recipe book a success. We wish to / express our gratitude particularly to the / city merchants, and business houses, whose / generous support has made the publication / of this book possible. In recognition of / their co-operation, we would urge that our / members and friends reciprocate by patron- / izing those places of business whose adv- / ertisements appear in this book.

DESCRIPTION: 21.0 × 15.5 cm Pp 1–64 Illus Paper, with images on front of a male chef carrying a steaming dish in each hand and IODE symbol; stapled

CONTENTS: 1 tp; 2 table of contents, 'Oven Temperatures,' and 'Measurements'; 3–63 recipes and ads; 64 'Kitchen Lore'

COPIES: *BCHM BVIPA

NOTES: In this later edition, some recipes are retained, some new recipes are added, and there are illustrations. There is an advertisement on the outside back face of the binding for the Canadian Legion BESL, inviting 'all ex-Service Men' to visit, which suggests a publication date after the Second World War.

1940

Adams, Edith [pseudonym]

For information about the pseudonym and a list of the annual recipe collections published under the Edith Adams name, see B81.1. See B107.1 for information about Jean Mutch and the BC Electric Home Service Department.

B103.1 nd [1940]
Compliments / of ... / The / Vancouver / Sun / Edith / Adams / 7th annual / cook / book / Prize recipes [cover-title]

DESCRIPTION: 28.0 × 22.0 cm   Pp [1] 2–64   Illus   Paper, with image on front of an animated sun-cook consulting *Edith Adams 7th Annual Cook Book*; stapled
CONTENTS: 1–2 'Meal Planning in Wartime'; 3–59 recipes and ads; 60–1 'Kitchen Handies'; 62 blank for 'Paste Your Additional Recipes from the Vancouver Sun Here'; 63 'Table of Measurements'; 64 'Index' [i.e., table of contents] and 'We acknowledge ... the assistance of Miss Jean Mutch and her staff in the Home Service Kitchen of the B.C. Electric for testing the readers' prize recipes appearing in this Seventh Annual Cook Book.'
COPIES: *BSUM   BVIPA
NOTES: This annual was advertised in the *Vancouver Sun* on 21 November 1940, p 10, and again a week later: 'Get a Cook Book // To get your copy of the new Prize Winner Seventh Annual Cook Book, send me your name and address and 10c to cover the cost of mailing. Edith Adams.' The file card at the *Sun* office for the annual prize cookbooks incorrectly dates the seventh annual 1942.

1940–5

Henderson, Mrs Margaret

Henderson was the first director of the Modern Kitchen of the Vancouver Daily Province *newspaper (see p 1 of A102.1,* How to Save in Your Kitchen, *which she compiled for the Calgary meat packer Burns and Co. Ltd). Before joining the newspaper, she was the 'home economics head' of the General Electric kitchen at Clarkson's Ltd, 401 West Hastings, where, in summer 1934, she tested recipes for a weekly contest run by the newspaper (see 'The Province to Pay for Recipes Tested by Expert,'* Vancouver Daily Province, *5 July 1934, p 10, also 19 and 26 July). There is no reference to the Modern Kitchen in the January 1935 food pages, but by May 1935 the public could attend cooking demonstrations at the kitchen and receive loose-leaf recipe sheets for 'The Province Modern Kitchen Recipe Book' (see 'Salads on Latest Cook Book Page,'* Vancouver Daily Province, *20 July 1935). Henderson's name appeared only occasionally in the food pages in the Modern Kitchen's first years; for example, on 6 January 1938, p 8, where she is identified as conducting cooking classes, assisted by Miss Ruth Hamlin. Her name is not cited in the earliest work published by the Modern Kitchen, B86.1,* The Province Cook Book, *but she is identified in B104.1, below, and in B117.1,* Tested Recipes for Canning, Jams, Jellies*

and Pickles, B122.1, ABC of the Kitchen, *and the later Christmas issues noted at B138.1,* Tested Christmas Recipes. *She contributed to B125.1,* Dehydrated Vegetables, *B115.7,* Home Canning of B.C. Fruits, *and B143.1,* Practical Tested Approved Recipes. *Her photograph is in* Home Service News *[BC Electric's customer newsletter] Vol. 15, No. 11 (April 1942), p 4 (copy at BBH).*

B104.1   nd [about 1940–5]
The Daily Province / Modern Kitchen / Wartime / recipes / Compiled by / Mrs. Margaret Henderson / Director of the Vancouver Daily Province / Modern Kitchen.
DESCRIPTION: 20.0 × 13.0 cm   Pp [1–3] 4–54 [55]   Rebound; original paper(?) binding mounted on new boards; image on front of a man admiring woman's freshly baked cake
CONTENTS: 1 tp; 2 blank; 3 'Introduction'; 4 'Abbreviations Used in This Book,' 'Table of Measurements,' 'Substitutions,' and 'Time Table for Roasting'; 5 'Weights and Measures,' 'Oven Temperatures ...,' and 'Cooking Temperatures'; 6 blank; 7–54 'Tested Recipes'; 55 'Index' [i.e., table of contents]
COPIES: *BVA
NOTES: The running head is 'The Vancouver Daily Province Modern Kitchen Recipes.'

Refrigerator recipes

B105.1   nd [about 1940–5]
Refrigerator / recipes / B.C. Electric [cover-title]
DESCRIPTION: 17.0 × 10.5 cm   Pp [1–17]   3 numbered illus on p 15 of folding flaky pastry   Paper, with image on front of a penguin, wearing a sailor's hat and holding up a Union Jack; stapled
CONTENTS: Inside front face of binding 'We Must All Save Food'; 1–3 'Refrij Refresher // Some Do's and Dont's about Your Refrigerator'; 4–17 [inside back face] 'Recipes' under the headings of 'Frozen Desserts,' 'Refrigerator Cakes,' 'Salads,' 'Rolls,' 'Cookies,' and 'Beverages'
COPIES: BVAU   *Private collection
NOTES: 'We Must All Save Food' suggests how the reader can 'wage war against waste' with refrigerators: 'You can help the country's war effort by conserving food ... cutting down on deliveries ... and by taking the utmost care of your appliances.' The text is printed in green. The Home Service Department and its director Jean Mutch are not named in the booklet.

1941

Handbook and guide to canning and pressure cooking

B106.1   nd [about 1941 or later]
The / "Ideal" / Safety Seal Steam / Pressure / Cooker / Handbook and guide / to canning / and pressure cooking / Price 25 cents / Ideal Utensil Company Limited / Vancouver, B.C. [cover-title]
DESCRIPTION: 23.0 × 15.0 cm   Pp 1–20   Paper, with image on front of a woman and a pressure cooker; stapled
CONTENTS: 1 'Complete Directions for Canning Foods and Preparing Meals under Steam Pressure' and 'Warranty'; 2–near bottom 3 'Advantages of Steam Pressure Cooking the "Ideal" Way'; bottom 3–mid 5 'Sterilizing'; mid 5–near bottom 6 'Instructions for Operating the "Ideal" ...'; bottom 6–7 'Preparing Meals the "Ideal" Way'; 8–19 timetables and recipes; 20 'Price List of Parts of the "Ideal" Safety Seal Pressure Cooker'
COPIES: *BVAMM
NOTES: The printer's name is on the outside back face of the binding: 'Halsall Printing Co. – 319 E. Broadway, Vancouver, B.C.' Arthur E. Halsall, printer, appears in city directories in the 1930s, but the first listing for the business as Halsall Printing is in the 1941 *British Columbia and Yukon Directory*, published by Sun Directories Ltd. By 1949 the company had moved to 903 East Hastings.

Mutch, Miss Jean E.

A graduate of Macdonald College in Montreal, Mutch worked as a dietitian at Vancouver General Hospital, then, from the late 1920s until her retirement in 1968, for BC Electric's Home Service Department (established 1917). She became director of the department in 1932, after the sudden death of the first director, Miss Agnes M. Reed. For Mutch's other books, see B116.1, B.C. Electric Meat Book, and B118.1, Home Preservers' Handbook (same title as B107.1, but with a different design and more pages). Her name is also associated with B103.1, Edith Adams 7th Annual Cook Book, and B110.1, Edith Adam's 8th Annual Prize Winners' Cook Book. For more information about Reed and Mutch, including their photographs, and for the names and photographs of Mutch's assistants, see BC Electric's customer newsletters (at BBH), in particular: Utility Topics Vol. 4, No. 8 (April 1931), pp 8, 12–13, and No. 10 (August 1931), pp 6–9; and Home Service News Vol. 6, No. 5 (October 1932), p 5, Vol. 13, No. 6 (Novem-

ber 1939), p 9, Vol. 14, No. 8 (January 1941), p 2, and Vol. 15, No. 8 (January 1942), p 3. For information about BC Electric's Home Service Department, see 'Home Service – from the '20's to the '80's,' Intercom [published by British Columbia Hydro and Power Authority, Public and Customer Relations Division] Vol. 20, No. 18 (18 September 1981).

B107.1   [1941]
Home / preservers' / handbook / Jellies / pickling / canning / jams / marmalades / conserves / Home Service Department / British Columbia Electric / Railway Company Limited [cover-title]
DESCRIPTION: 23.0 × 14.5 cm   Pp [1–2] 3–15   Paper, with image on front of a jar of cherries; stapled
CONTENTS: 1 cover-title; 2 publ ad for 'CP Gas Ranges'; 3–4 'Jelly Making'; 5–8 'Pickling'; 9–11 'Canning'; 12 publ ad for hot water heater: 'Are you living in 1941 with a 1921 hot water system?'; 13–mid 14 'Jams'; mid–bottom 14 'Marmalades'; 15 'Conserves'
COPIES: *BVAA   BVAU (2 copies: Special Collections, Beatrice M. Millar Papers)
NOTES: The advertisement on p 12 dates the book 1941. The BVAA copy is printed on orange paper. No author is named, but a photograph in *Home Service News* Vol. 15, No. 4 (September 1941), p 3, shows Jean Mutch pointing at what appears to be a copy of this edition held by her assistant, and the caption refers to 'Our Home Preservers' Handbook, compiled by Jean E. Mutch, ... It's free.'

There were earlier editions of *Home Preservers' Handbook*. In *Home Service News* Vol. 13, No. 1 (June 1939), p 6, Mutch writes, 'The 1939 edition of our "Home Preservers' Handbook" will be in our B.C. Electric stores after the first of May.' In Vol. 14, No. 4 (September 1940), p 3, she refers again to 'our "Home Preservers' Handbook."' Perhaps the latter reference is to the copy at OONL (TX603 B75 1940z), which differs in minor ways from B107.1: page 12 is an advertisement for a '1940 "refrij!"'; and the book is printed on blue paper.

B107.2   nd [about 1942–5]
—Home / preservers / handbook / Canning, jams, marmalades / jellies, pickling, conserves / Home Service Department / British Columbia Electric Railway Company Limited [cover-title]
DESCRIPTION: 23.5 × 15.5 cm   Pp [1–15]   2 illus on p 2 of Union Jack and still-life of preserving equipment and fruit   Paper, with image on front of a preserving kettle sitting on a stove top; stapled, and with hole punched at top left corner for hanging
CONTENTS: 1 cover-title; 2 'Save Food // Save Sugar

and Save Up Energy!'; 3–4 'Jelly Making'; 5–9 'Pickling'; 10–12 'Canning'; 13–14 'Jams'; 15 [inside back face of binding] 'Marmalades'

COPIES: BVAU   BVIPM   OONL (TX603 B75 1940zb) *Private collection

NOTES: This edition was published during wartime because p 2 comments, 'Our knowledge of nutrition has advanced further since the beginning of the war than it would have done, under normal circumstances, in fifty years ... Fruit is an important aid in a sugar-rationed country ...' Sugar was rationed from April 1942 to 1947; therefore, this edition was published about 1942–5. The private collector's and OONL copies are printed on blue leaves.

BKOM has a copy where the front face of the binding is identical to the private collector's copy, but the advertisement on the outside back face of the binding differs: Instead of an advertisement for BC Electric Stores, urging maintenance of existing appliances as part of the war effort, the BKOM advertisement is for BC Electric Home Service News, a radio program.

B107.3   nd [about 1942–5]
—Home / preservers / handbook / Canning, jams, marmalades / jellies, pickling, conserves / Home Service Department / British Columbia Electric Railway Company Limited [cover-title]
DESCRIPTION: 22.0 × 15.0 cm   Pp [1–2] 3–19   2 illus on p 2 of Union Jack and still-life of preserving equipment and fruit   Paper, with image on front of a preserving kettle sitting on a stove top; stapled, and with hole punched at top left corner for hanging
CONTENTS: 1 cover-title; 2 'Save Food // Save Sugar and Save Up Energy!'; 3–mid 5 'Jelly Making'; mid 5–9 'Pickling'; 10–14 'Canning'; 15 'Canning Fish and Meat'; 16–17 'Jams'; 18 'Marmalades' and 'Conserves'; 19 'Dehydrated Foods'
COPIES: *OONL (TX603 B75 1940za)
NOTES: The text on p 2 is the same as on p 2 of B107.2. The folios are printed at the bottom of the page; some folios were partly cut off when the leaves were trimmed.

The Powell River cook book

The pulp and paper mill at Powell River was the first in British Columbia, starting operation in 1912. At the time the cookbook was published, Powell River Townsite was still a company-owned settlement.

B108.1   [1941]
The / Powell River / cook book / Entire proceeds to the Red Cross [cover-title]
DESCRIPTION: 22.0 × 15.5 cm   Pp 3–72   Paper, with image on front of the Powell River pulp and paper mill; stapled
CONTENTS: 3–4 ads; 5–mid 70 recipes credited with the name of the contributor and ads; bottom 70 'Acknowledgements'; 71 'Table of Abbreviations,' 'Important Equivalents to Memorize,' and 'Directions for Measuring'; 72 'Index' [i.e., table of contents]
COPIES: *Private collection
NOTES: The year of publication, 1941, is printed at the top of most pages. It was wartime and there is a recipe on p 33 for Soldier's Cake, described as 'a good moist cake to send overseas.' There is a recipe on p 7 for Ukrainian Pyrohy from Mrs H. Skuhra and a recipe on p 69 for Norwegian Benlose Fugle from Mrs A. Helland. The group that produced the cookbook is not identified.

Victory cook book

B109.1   [October 1941]
[IODE symbol] / Navy League Chapter / I.O.D.E. / V / [Morse Code symbol for V: dot, dot, dot, dash] / Victory cook book [cover-title]
DESCRIPTION: 23.5 × 15.5 cm   Pp [1] 2–88   Paper; stapled
CONTENTS: 1 'Navy League Chapter I.O.D.E. (October, 1941)' [history of the chapter and acknowledgment]; 2 'Patrons' and ad; 3 'A Word of Appreciation,' 'Table of Measurements,' and 'What to Serve with Meats, Fish, etc.'; 4 ads; 5 'A Modern Kitchen Helps to Plan a Week of Meals' [menus]; 6 ads; top 7 'Kitchen Hints'; mid 7–mid 8 'How to Remove Stains'; mid 9–88 recipes credited with the name of the contributor and ads
COPIES: *BVIPA
NOTES: The history of the Navy League Chapter, p 1, says that the chapter was organized on 24 September 1912 in Victoria and 'has always made the interests of the Navy foremost in its work.' It adds that, since the outbreak of the Second World War, the chapter has raised and spent an average of $100 per month on war work and 'the members have collected these tested recipes in an endeavour to raise more money.'

1942

Adams, Edith [pseudonym]

For information about the pseudonym and a list of the annual recipe collections published under the Edith Adams name, see B81.1. See B107.1 for information about Jean Mutch and the BC Electric Home Service Department.

B110.1   nd [1942]

Vitamins / for / victory! / Edith Adam's [*sic*] / 8th / annual / prize winners' / cook book / With choice / recipes from / the Vancouver Sun [cover-title]

DESCRIPTION: 28.0 × 22.0 cm   Pp [1] 2–64   Amusing illus chapter heads   Paper, with image on front of a woman carrying a full shopping basket, seen against a Union Jack; stapled

CONTENTS: 1 'Preface' signed Edith Adams; 2 'Table of Measurements'; 3 'One Hundred Calorie–Portion Foods'; 4 'Substitutions,' 'Methods of Cooking,' 'Food Equivalents,' 'Oven Temperatures for Baking,' and 'How to Make 1 Pound of Butter into 2'; 5–63 recipes; 64 'Index' [i.e., table of contents] and acknowledgment of the assistance of Miss Jean Mutch and her staff in the Home Service Kitchen of BC Electric for testing the recipes

COPIES: *BVAA   BVAMM

NOTES: The 'Preface' comments, 'This Eighth Annual Edition ... appears in a world that is vastly different in outlook from that of previous editions ... the preserving season of 1941 took on a new and deeper significance.' This annual was advertised in the *Sun* on 26 February 1942, p 11: 'Get a Cook Book // To get your copy of the new Prize-Winner Eighth Annual Cook Book, send me your name and address and 10 cents to cover cost of mailing. Edith Adams.' The file card for the annual cookbooks at the *Sun* office incorrectly notes 1943 for the eighth annual.

Recipes can help Allies

B111.1   [1942]

[Along left arm of V-shape, from top down to point:] R / C / H / A / [along right arm of V-shape, from top down to point:] Recipes / Can / Help / [same initial A as for 'RCHA']llies [cover-title]

DESCRIPTION: 23.5 × 15.5 cm   Pp [1–3] 4–64   Paper; stapled

CONTENTS: 1 'Sponsored by the Royal Columbian Hospital Auxiliary // First published Dec. 1942 New Westminster, B.C. Canada'; 2 'Canada's Official Food Rules Outlined'; 3 'Foreword' signed Muriel Wilson, president; 4 ad; 5–62 text and ads; 63–4 ads

COPIES: BNW   *Private collection

NOTES: The first letter of each word in the title matches the initials of the sponsoring group, RCHA. The 'Foreword' states that the book has two purposes: 'First, to raise funds to carry on our work as Auxiliary to the Royal Columbian Hospital, ... Second, we hope the collected recipes and penny-saving ideas will help the housewife in these days of shortages.' On p 62, 'Victory Tips' give ideas for cooking and grooming. The printer's name is on the outside back face of the binding: 'The Columbian Co. Ltd., New Westminster, B.C.'

Wright, Julia Lee

The Safeway Homemakers' Bureau in Vancouver also published Julia Lee Wright's Step-by-Step Canning Guide, an 11-page, undated, top-hinged booklet of about 1945; a private collector's copy has the original address label for a Saskatoon woman, bearing a 14 June 1945 postmark.

B112.1   [copyright 1942]

Julia Lee Wright's / Kitchen course / in nutrition / a simplified course of study of the principles of nutrition / and how to apply them in planning, cooking, and serving / everyday meals. Containing the latest findings in the field / of nutrition, it is designed to help Canadian homemakers / solve special wartime food problems. / Wartime edition [cover-title]

DESCRIPTION: 28.0 × 21.5 cm   Pp [1] 2–99   Illus red-and-blue   Paper, with image on front of maple leaves; stapled, and punched with three holes (this copy tied with a shoe lace through the holes)

CONTENTS: 1 cover-title; 2 'To order this course: Send ... 25 cents in coin to Julia Lee Wright, Director, Safeway Homemakers' Bureau, Box 519, Vancouver, B.C., and the entire series of ten lessons will be mailed to you, one each week, for ten weeks,' note about Nutrition Classes: 'Any group wishing to use the "Kitchen Course in Nutrition" as a text book for class work may obtain complete sets ... at one time (100 pages in all) by sending 25 cents ...,' table of contents for the ten lessons, and 'Copyright 1942, Julia Lee Wright'; 3–96 ten numbered lessons; 97 'Suggested Reading'; 98–9 index

COPIES: AEU (RM219 W95) *BVAMM

NOTES: The text is printed in red and blue. There are many recipes in addition to the nutritional information.

AMERICAN EDITIONS: *Kitchen Course in Nutrition*, Oakland, Calif.: Safeway Homemakers' Bureau, [c1941] (United States: DLC).

1942–5

Alaska Highway cook book

B113.1 nd [about 1942–5]

Alaska Highway / cook book / St. Martin's W.A. / Fort St. John, B.C. [cover-title]

DESCRIPTION: 22.5 × 15.0 cm Pp 1–71 Paper, with image on front of bridge spanning river; stapled

CONTENTS: 1 'Church Notices // North Peace River Parish // St. Martin's Church, Fort St. John'; 2 table of contents; 3–71 recipes credited with the name of the contributor and ads

COPIES: *BVIPA

NOTES: 'Distributed by the Fellowship of the West // 1440 Union Avenue Montreal, – Que.' is stamped on the front face of the binding. 'Printed by the Douglas Printing Co., Ltd., Edmonton, Alta.' is on the outside back face. The cookbook was published during the Second World War, as the following advertisement on p 30 for Gething Mines in Hudson Hope makes clear: '"King Coal" has gone to war // 80% of our entire output is pledged to the armed forces but ... some day, soon we shall be at your service.' Since the Alaska Highway was completed in November 1942, the cookbook was published about 1942–5.

1943

Adams, Edith [pseudonym]

For information about the pseudonym and a list of the annual recipe collections published under the Edith Adams name, see B81.1.

B114.1 nd [1943]

The / Sun / Prize winning / wartime recipes / substitutions / lunch boxes / budget stretching / wartime canning / The / Vancouver / Sun / 9th / annual / Edith Adam's [sic] / wartime / cook book / [artist's signature:] Wilson [cover-title]

DESCRIPTION: 27.5 × 22.0 cm Pp 1–32 Paper, with image on front of animated Sun building pointing to a blackboard on which is printed the contents of the cookbook; stapled

CONTENTS: 1 'Preface' and 'Index' [i.e., table of contents]; 2 'Sugar Substitution,' 'Shortening Substitution,' and 'Table of Substitution'; 3 'Substitutions' [e.g., recipes for Mock Whipped Cream and Coffee Substitute]; 4–32 recipes

COPIES: BCOM *BVAA (1941-126)

NOTES: See pl 32. The 'Preface' states: 'The recipes in this book were chosen because they call for only materials available on our markets. A section is devoted to the current problem of packing lunch buckets and parcels for men in service, both overseas and in Canada. A large section is devoted to home canning, a chore which has become of greater importance since we cannot depend on the buying of commercially canned foods.'

Edith Adams announced the upcoming printing of the ninth annual cookbook on 3 December 1942, p 8: 'New Cookbook Soon // The new wartime edition of the Vancouver Sun's cookbook will be off the press in a few weeks. It contains many sugar saving recipes, substitutions for material which is off the market this year, and tips on wartime cooking. In the meantime I am completely out of the eighth annual edition and am keeping names and addresses of all of you who have written for cookbooks, until the new book is ready. So, if your cookbook doesn't arrive, be patient for a little while and you will receive one of the newest ninth annual edition [sic], as soon as it is printed. – Edith Adams.' Although she does not give the number of the 'new wartime edition' in the announcement, it clearly followed the eighth annual. The next mention of the ninth annual, on 21 January 1943 and repeated a week later, marked its publication in the new year: 'Announcement // Because of a limited supply of Edith Adams' Wartime Cook Books, we advise you to send for your copy immediately. With your name and address enclose 10 cents to cover cost of mailing.' A similarly worded notice about the limited supply of the 'Wartime Cook Book' appeared on 4 November 1943. It was offered for sale again a year later, on 2 November 1944, in a notice that identified it as the ninth: 'Wartime Cook Book // Because of a limited supply of Edith Adams' Wartime Cook Book (ninth annual), we advise you to send for your copy immediately.' Perhaps the wartime shortage of newsprint restricted the number of copies that could be printed at any one time.

See B94.1 regarding the artist Fraser Wilson.

Stevens, Miss Mary Alice
(20 March 1900–1952)

For biographical information about Stevens and her earlier cookbook, see B77.1.

B115.1 June 1943
Here's / your / Home / canning / ration / guide / Prepared for Western Canada housewives / by / Alice Stevens / B.Sc. (U. of Man.) / and published in the interests of maximum / results in home canning with available sugar / by / B.C. Tree Fruits Ltd. / Canada's finest / fruits and vegetables / Kelowna British Columbia / June 1943 [cover-title]
DESCRIPTION: 17.5 × 12.5 cm   Pp [1–2] 3–19   Illus red-and-green   Paper, with image on front of a female cook standing at attention and saluting, while holding a saucepan in her other hand; stapled
CONTENTS: 1 cover-title; 2 'Time Table for Processing (Cooking) Fruits'; 3 'Here Are the Answers to Your War-Time Home Canning Problems'; 4–7 'Canning without Sugar'; 8–9 'B.C. Cherries'; 10 'B.C. Apricots'; 11 'B.C. Peaches'; 12 'B.C. Crabapples'; 13 'B.C. Grapes'; 14–15 'Prunes and Plums'; 16 'Pears'; 17 'Canned Applesauce'; 18 'Hints to Beginners'; 19 'Canning Budget'
COPIES: AEPMA   *Bookseller's stock

B115.2 [1944]
—Wartime / home / canning / of / B.C. / fruits / Prepared by / Alice Stevens / B.Sc. (H.Ec.) / (University of Manitoba) / B.C. Tree Fruits Ltd. [on apple:] B.C. / Kelowna / B.C. / Growing and distributing / Canada's finest foods [cover-title]
DESCRIPTION: 20.5 × 14.5 cm   Pp [1] 2–15   Illus blue-and-orange   Paper, with image on front of a girl holding fruit in the skirt of her dress; stapled
CONTENTS: 1 cover-title; 2 'Successful Home Canning with Limited Sugar Ration'; 3 'Basic Principle of Canning'; 4–5 'Methods of Canning'; 6 'B.C. Apricots'; 7 'B.C. Cherries'; 8–9 'British Columbia Peaches'; 10 'B.C. Transcendent and Hyslop Crabapples'; 11 'B.C. Prunes and Plums'; 12–13 'B.C. Pears'; 14 'B.C. Grapes'; 15 'B.C. Canned Applesauce'; outside back face of binding 'Home Canning Guide 1944'
COPIES: BVIPM OONL (AC901 A7 1944 No. 0122)   *Private collection
NOTES: According to p 2, 'Food is considered as important as munitions and fruit is one of the "musts" in your war-time diet.' See CHO No. 53 (Summer 2007), pp 7–10, for discussion and illustrations of B115.2, B115.5, and two 1950s editions.

B115.3 [1945]
—Home / canning / of / B.C. / fruits / Prepared by / Alice Stevens / B.Sc. (H.Ec.) / (University of Manitoba) / B.C. Tree Fruits Ltd. / [on apple:] B.C. / Kelowna / B.C. / Growing and distributing / Canada's finest fruits [cover-title]
DESCRIPTION: 20.5 × 14.5 cm   Pp [1] 2–15   Illus red-and-blue   Paper, with image on front of a girl holding fruit in the skirt of her dress; stapled
CONTENTS: 1 cover-title; 2 'Successful Home Canning with Limited Sugar Ration'; 3 'Basic Principle of Canning'; 4–5 'Methods of Canning'; 6 'B.C. Apricots'; 7 'B.C. Cherries'; 8–9 'British Columbia Peaches'; 10 'B.C. Transcendent and Hyslop Crabapples'; 11 'B.C. Prunes and Plums'; 12 'B.C. Pears'; 13 'Try These B.C. Pear Recipes'; 14 'B.C. Grapes'; 15 'B.C. Canned Applesauce'; outside back face of binding 'Home Canning Guide 1945'
COPIES: *Bookseller's stock
NOTES: The text on p 2 gives the sugar allowance in 1945, ten pounds per person, and explains the system for that year: 'Canadians will use two types of coupons for the purchase of sugar, – the regular sugar coupon good for one pound of sugar and the preserves coupon good for half a pound of sugar or the alternative value in preserves. Twenty extra preserves coupons will be available for the purchase of sugar for canning. Each will purchase ½ pound of sugar. The first two of the twenty extra preserves coupons (Numbers 43 and 44) became valid March 15 ... On May 17, the next eight (Numbers 49 to 56 inclusive) became available for the purchase of home canning sugar and the remaining ten (P4 to P13) may be used on and after July 19.'

B115.4 [1946]
—Home / canning / of / B.C. / fruits / Prepared by / Alice Stevens / B.Sc. (H.Ec.) / (University of Manitoba) / B.C. Tree Fruits Ltd. / Head office / Kelowna / British Columbia / Growing and distributing / Canada's finest fresh fruits [cover-title]
DESCRIPTION: 19.5 × 11.5 cm   Pp [1] 2–15   Illus green and red-and-green   Paper, with image on front of a girl holding up a bowl of apples; stapled
CONTENTS: 1 cover-title; 2 'Successful Home Canning with 1946 Sugar Ration'; 3 'Basic Principles of Canning'; 4–5 'Methods of Canning'; 6 'Frosted Foods'; 7 'B.C. Cherries'; 8–9 'British Columbia Peaches'; 10 'B.C. Canned Applesauce'; 11 'B.C. Prunes and Plums'; 12–13 'B.C. Pears'; 14 'B.C. Transcendent and Hyslop Crabapples';15 'B.C. Grapes'; outside back face of

binding 'Home Canning Guide 1946'
COPIES: OONL (TX603 H565 1948 copy 2) *Bookseller's stock
NOTES: The war was over, but sugar rationing continued until 1947. The text on page 2 explains: 'Home canning sugar allowance for Canadians in 1946 is ten pounds per person. The sugar and preserve rations are combined now; the same coupons are available for either preserves or sugar.' OONL copy 2 is the 1946 edition, despite the 1948 call number.

B115.5 [1947]
—Home / canning / of / B.C. / fruits / Prepared by / Alice Stevens / B.Sc. (H.Ec.) / (University of Manitoba) / B.C. Tree Fruits Ltd. / Head office / Kelowna / British Columbia / Growing and distributing / Canada's finest fresh fruits [cover-title]
DESCRIPTION: 20.0 × 11.5 cm Pp [1] 2–15 Illus Paper, with image on front of a girl holding up a bowl of apples; stapled
CONTENTS: 1 cover-title; 2 'Successful Home Canning'; 3 'Basic Principles of Canning'; 4–5 'Methods of Canning'; 6 'B.C. Cherries'; 7 'B.C. Apricots'; 8–9 'British Columbia Peaches'; 10–11 'B.C. Prunes and Plums'; 12 'B.C. Pears'; 13 'Frosted Foods'; 14 'B.C. Transcendent and Hyslop Crabapples'; 15 'B.C. Grapes'; outside back face of binding 'Home Canning Guide 1947'
COPIES: ACG *OGU (CCC TX715.6 S739)
NOTES: According to p 2, 'The "squirrel" instinct to "store up for the winter" is strong and is to be encouraged in the Canadian housewife.' See B115.2 notes.

B115.6 [1948]
—Home canning / of / B.C. fruits / Compiled by one of Canada's / leading authorities on Home Economics / This year – plenty of fruit ... plenty of sugar! / B.C. Tree Fruits Ltd. / Head office / Kelowna / British Columbia / Growing and distributing / Canada's finest fresh fruits [cover-title]
DESCRIPTION: Pp [1] 2–16 Illus blue Paper, with image on front of a woman holding up a jar of Fruit Salad, seven other jars of bottled fruit in front of her; stapled
CONTENTS: 1 cover-title; 2 'Successful Home Canning'; 3 'Basic Principles of Canning'; 4–5 'Methods of Canning'; 6 'B.C. Cherries'; 7 'B.C. Apricots'; 8–9 'British Columbia Peaches'; 10–11 'B.C. Prunes and Plums'; 12 'B.C. Transcendent and Hyslop Crabapples'; 13 'B.C. Grapes'; 14 'B.C. Pears'; 15 'Home Canning Guide 1948'; 16 'How to Select Apples'

COPIES: *OONL (TX603 H565 1948 copy 1 p***)
NOTES: This edition celebrates the end of sugar rationing. Page 2 exclaims: 'Sugar scarcity ... and hence, sugar rationing ... are past history! The 1948 supply of sugar in Canada is ample – and what a difference this will make in your home canning of fruits ... During rationing, a thin syrup (1 cup sugar to 2 cups water) was used and now the medium syrup (1 cup sugar to 1 cup water) can be restored.'

Stevens is not credited as author in the 1948 and later editions, likely because she had moved from British Columbia in 1947, to work at the University of Saskatchewan (see the biographical notes at B77.1).

B115.7 1949
—Home canning / of B.C. fruits / 1949 / [BC Tree Fruits Ltd symbol] B.C. Tree Fruits Ltd. / Head office / Kelowna / British Columbia / Growing and distributing / Canada's finest fresh fruits [cover-title]
DESCRIPTION: 20.0 × 11.5 cm Pp [1] 2–16 Illus Paper, with image on front of a woman removing processed jars of preserves from a hot-water bath; stapled
CONTENTS: 1 cover-title; 2 'Successful Home Canning'; 3 'Basic Principles of Canning'; 4–5 'Methods of Canning'; 6 'B.C. Cherries'; 7 'B.C. Apricots'; 8–9 'British Columbia Peaches'; 10–11 'B.C. Prunes and Plums'; 12 'B.C. Transcendent and Hyslop Crabapples'; 13 'B.C. Pears'; 14 'B.C. Grapes'; 15 untitled note signed Margaret Henderson, director, Daily Province Modern Kitchen, and her photograph, and 'Fresh Fruit in Our Daily Diet'; 16 [outside back face of binding] 'Home Canning Guide 1949'
COPIES: *Private collection
NOTES: For other books with which Margaret Henderson's name is connected, see B104.1.

OTHER EDITIONS: BC Tree Fruits Ltd continued to publish versions of the cookbook into the 1950s, all undated: *B.C. Home Canning and Fruit Recipe Booklet*, with image on front of the head-and-shoulders of a smiling woman (AALIWWM, ACG), and another version with the same title, but with image on front of a woman holding up a preserving jar, an orchard in the background (AALIWWM, OONL); *B.C. Fruit Preserving Guide*, 'edited by one of Canada's foremost cooking experts,' with image on front of a woman holding a jar of Prune Plums, shelves of preserves behind her (BKOM, OONL, SBIM); *B.C. Fruit Preserving Guide*, edited by Miss Dorothy Britton, with same image on front of a woman holding a jar of Prune Plums (ACG).

1943–6

Mutch, Miss Jean E.

See B107.1 for information about Jean Mutch and the Home Service Department.

B116.1   nd [about 1943–6]
B.C. Electric / meat / book / Issued with the compliments of the B.C. Electric / Home Service Department [cover-title]
DESCRIPTION: 22.0 × 12.0 cm   Pp [1–16]   Illus   Paper, with image on front of a butcher sharpening a knife; stapled
CONTENTS: Inside front face of binding photograph of Jean Mutch and untitled note signed Jean Mutch, BC Electric home service director; 1–5 'Beef'; 6 'Lamb'; 7 'Pork'; 8–9 'Standard Cutting Chart // Retail Primary Cuts'; 10 continuation of 'Pork'; 11–mid 12 'Poultry'; mid 12–mid 13 'Meat Specialties'; bottom 13–top 14 'Extend Your Ration'; mid 14 'To Store Meat' and 'Soup from Bones and Trimmings'; bottom 14–16 'Meat Carving'; inside back face 'Meat Rationing'
COPIES: *BVAMM   OONL (TX749 B2)
NOTES: The book was published when meat rationing was in force, from May 1943 to March 1947, but before the company name-change noted in B118.4.

1944

Henderson, Mrs Margaret

For other books with which Henderson's name is connected see B104.1.

B117.1   nd [about 1944]
The Vancouver / Daily Province / Modern Kitchen / Tested recipes / for / canning, jams, / jellies and pickles / Compiled by / the Modern Kitchen / The Vancouver Daily Province [cover-title]
DESCRIPTION: Pp [1–2] 3–39 [40]   Stapled
CONTENTS: 1 'Introduction' signed Margaret Henderson, director, Province Modern Kitchen; 2 blank; 3–39 text in four sections ('Canning,' 'Jams,' 'Jellies,' 'Pickles'); 40 'Index'
COPIES: *Bookseller's stock   Private collection
NOTES: On p 1 Henderson refers to the first five 'F' canning sugar coupons becoming valid on 25 May, and the second set on 6 July. The canning sugar coupons, she explains, could be exchanged for preserves coupons for those women who prefer to buy preserves rather than make their own (one F coupon in exchange for one preserves coupon). Establishing when the F coupons were issued would pinpoint the date of publication. Sugar rationing was in place in Canada from April 1942 to November 1947. Annual booklets published by BC Tree Fruits Ltd during wartime reveal that in 1945 the government issued separate coupons for sugar and preserves, but by 1946 there was one combined coupon (see B115.3 and B115.4); therefore, this edition of *Tested Recipes for Canning, Jams, Jellies and Pickles* was published no later than 1945. A clipping from an unidentified issue of the *Daily Province* newspaper indicates that it was likely published in 1944: The clipping is of an article by Margaret Henderson ('Many Delicious Small Fruits Ready for Home Preserving') that bears the copyright date 1944 and that refers to 'the new Modern Kitchen Canning Book,' price $0.25.

B117.2   [rev. ed.], 1947
—The Vancouver / Daily Province / Modern Kitchen / Tested recipes / for / canning, jams, / jellies and pickles / 1947 / Compiled by / the Modern Kitchen / The Vancouver Daily Province / Price 25c / [printers' trade symbol] [cover-title]
DESCRIPTION: 21.0 × 13.5 cm   Pp 1–70 [71–2]   Paper; stapled
CONTENTS: 1–2 'Introduction' signed Margaret Henderson, director, Daily Province Modern Kitchen; 3–mid 69 text; mid 69–70 blank 'For Your Own Recipes'; 71–2 'Index'
COPIES: *Bookseller's stock
NOTES: Henderson begins the 'Introduction': 'This little book on preserving and pickling has been revised, with the addition of several new recipes. It includes information on canning with your pressure cooker, and the use of cans, as well as the preparation of frozen foods for the locker plant.'

B117.3   [rev. ed.], 1948
—The Vancouver / Daily Province / Modern Kitchen / Tested recipes / for / canning, jams, / jellies and pickles / 1948 / Compiled by / the Modern Kitchen / The Vancouver Daily Province / Price 25c / [printers' trade symbol]
DESCRIPTION: 21.0 × 13.0 cm   Pp [i–ii], 1–77   Paper; stapled
CONTENTS: i tp; ii blank; 1–2 'Introduction' signed Margaret Henderson, director, Daily Province Modern Kitchen; 3–71 text; 72–5 blank 'For Your Own Recipes'; 76–7 index
COPIES: *Private collection
NOTES: Henderson states in the 'Introduction': 'This

little book on preserving and pickling has been revised, with the addition of several new recipes. It
includes information on canning with your pressure
cooker, and the use of cans, as well as the preparation
of frozen foods for the locker plant.'

B117.4 1949
—The Vancouver Daily Province / Modern Kitchen
/ Tested recipes / for / canning, jams, jellies / and
pickles / 1949
DESCRIPTION: 20.5 × 14.0 cm   Pp [1–3] 4–87   Tp illus
of a chef tasting from a spoon   [$0.25, on binding]
Thin card, with tp illus on front; stapled
CONTENTS: 1 tp; 2 blank except for printers' union
label; 3–4 'Introduction' signed Margaret Henderson,
director, Daily Province Modern Kitchen; 5–80 text;
81–5 blank 'For Your Own Recipes'; 86–7 index
COPIES: *Private collection
NOTES: Page 3 of the 'Introduction' states, 'This little
book on preserving and pickling has been revised
with addition of several new recipes.'

OTHER EDITIONS: *The Vancouver Daily Province Modern
Kitchen Tested Recipes for Canning, Jams, Jellies and
Pickles*, 1950, with an 'Introduction' by Margaret
Henderson: 'This year our Canning Book has been
completely revised, with the addition of many new
and interesting recipes, ...' (OONL).

1944–5

Mutch, Miss Jean E.

*See B107.1 for information about Jean Mutch and the
Home Service Department.*

B118.1   nd [about 1944–5]
Home preservers' handbook / British Columbia
Electric Railway Company Limited [cover-title]
DESCRIPTION: Paper, with image on front of two
women, one of whom is holding up a jar of preserves
CONTENTS: Inside front face of binding 'Table of
Contents'; top–mid 1 'There Are Three Methods of
Canning:'; mid 1–? 'Jars'; ...; 22 'Drying Chart' and
publ ad suggesting that the reader contact Miss Mutch
at the Home Service Department of BC Electric; 23
[lacking in BDEM copy, but 'Table of Contents' lists
as 'Canning Quiz']
COPIES: *BDEM   OONL (TX603 P74 1940z copy 1,
missing)
NOTES: This undated edition looks earlier than the
dated editions of 1945, 1946, and 1948. During the
Second World War, BC Electric published B107.1, *Home*

Preservers' Handbook – another cookbook by Mutch
with the same title, but with fewer pages and a plainer
design (there is no photograph on the binding, as in
B118.1–118.5, for example). Whether B118.1 was published in the late 1930s, before the shorter, plainer,
wartime *Home Preservers' Handbook*, or after, in about
1944–5, is unknown, although the later date seems
more likely.

B118.2 1945
—Home preservers' handbook / 1945 edition /
British Columbia Electric Railway Company Limited
[cover-title]
DESCRIPTION: 22.0 × 15.0 cm   Pp [1–3] 4–30 [31]   Illus
on p 2 of greengrocer's display of mainly vegetables
Paper, with image on front of a woman holding a jar
of preserves in each hand, five bottles on the table in
front of her and a flowering fruit tree behind
CONTENTS: 1 cover-title; 2 'Table of Contents'; 3–30
text; 31 [inside back face of binding] 'Canning Quiz'
COPIES: *OONL (TX603 B74 1945)

B118.3 1946
—Home preservers' handbook / 1946 edition /
British Columbia Electric Railway Company
Limited [cover-title]
DESCRIPTION: 22.5 × 15.0 cm   Pp [1–3] 4–30 [31]   Illus
blue   Paper, with image on front of a woman hold-
ing a bushel basket of vegetables and, to her right,
four jars of preserves; stapled
CONTENTS: 1 cover-title; 2 table of contents; 3–29 text;
30 'Free B.C. Electric Services' and 'Make Every Foot
Count in Your New Kitchen'; 31 [inside back face of
binding] 'Canning Quiz'
COPIES: OONL (TX603 B74 1946)   *Private collection

B118.4 1948
—Home preservers' handbook / 1948 edition /
British Columbia Electric Company Limited [cover-
title]
DESCRIPTION: 22.5 × 15.0 cm   Pp [1–3] 4–30 [31]   Illus
blue   Paper, with image on front of a woman holding a bushel basket of vegetables and, to her right,
four jars of preserves; stapled
CONTENTS: 1 cover-title; 2 table of contents; 3–29 text;
30 'Free B.C. Electric Services' and 'Down in Blue and
White' [about the company's planning service and
blueprints for kitchens and laundry rooms]; 31 'Canning Quiz'
COPIES: *OGU (CCC TX715.6 B7394)
NOTES: British Columbia Electric Co. was the name
adopted by British Columbia Electric Power and Gas
Co. in December 1946, when a reorganization resulted
in this entity handling all electric power and gas

activities and British Columbia Electric Railway retaining transportation only.

B118.5   nd [about 1949 or later]
—Home preservers' handbook / British Columbia Electric Company Limited [cover-title]
DESCRIPTION: 22.5 × 15.0 cm   Pp [1–3] 4–30 [31]   Illus blue   Paper, with image on front of a woman holding a bushel basket of vegetables and, to her right, four jars of preserves; stapled
CONTENTS: 1 cover-title; 2 table of contents; 3–29 text; 30 'An Invitation' signed Jean E. Mutch, home service supervisor, BC Electric, Vancouver; 31 [inside back face of binding] 'Canning Quiz'
COPIES: BVAMM   BVIPM   *Private collection
NOTES: BVAMM has a second copy that matches the above description, except that p 30 is 'The B.C. Electric Invites You ...,' instead of 'An Invitation.'

1945

Adams, Edith [pseudonym]

For information about the pseudonym and a list of the annual recipe collections published under the Edith Adams name, see B81.1.

B119.1   nd [1945]
The / Vancouver Sun's / 10th annual / cook book / Edited by / Edith Adams / Including: Prize winning recipes / canning, calorie chart, entertaining [cover-title]
DESCRIPTION: 27.0 × 22.0 cm   Pp 1–32   Paper; stapled
CONTENTS: Inside front face of binding 'Teen-age and Junior Cooks'; 1 'Measurements ... Cooking for a Crowd,' untitled introduction signed Edith Adams, and 'Cook Book Index' [i.e., table of contents]; 2–32 recipes; inside back face continuation from p 16 of 'Ps-s-s-st – Your Calories Are Showing'
COPIES: Company collection (Vancouver Sun)   *Private collection
NOTES: Despite the reference on p 1 to 'the war-time newsprint shortage' that confined this issue of the annual cookbook to only 32 pp, the tenth annual cookbook was published after the Second World War ended on 15 May 1945. It was advertised in the *Sun* on 11 October 1945, p 14: 'New Cook Book: It's ready – The Vancouver Sun's Tenth Annual Cook Book, edited by Edith Adams.' Whereas the ninth annual cookbook had been devoted to sugar saving and meat stretching, the tenth is concerned with entertaining and calorie counting.

1945–9

The Aristocrat way to better cooking better health

B120.1   nd [about 1945–9]
The / Aristocrat / way / to / better cooking / better health / Aristocrat Cookware Ltd. / Vancouver, Canada [cover-title]
DESCRIPTION: 23.0 × 15.0 cm   Pp [1–3] 4–30 [31–4] Illus   Paper, with image on front of raw vegetables; stapled
CONTENTS: 1 letter to the reader signed Louise Hayward, home economics director, Aristocrat Cookware Ltd; 2 guarantee; 3 table of contents; 4 'Protect Your Life-long Investment with Proper Care'; 5 'Amounts of Food Required Weekly by Different Types of People'; 6–7 'What to Eat to Be Healthy' excerpted from address by Frederick F. Tisdall, director of Research Laboratories, Hospital for Sick Children, Toronto; top 8 'Give Your Equipment the Care and Protection It Deserves'; bottom 8–top 9 'Cooking Instructions'; mid–bottom 9 'General Instructions'; 10–15 recipes; 16–17 'Biological Food Chemistry'; 18–30 recipes; 31–2 blank for 'Additional and Favorite Recipes'; 33–4 prepaid postcards for sending in names and addresses of friends interested in Aristocrat cookware
COPIES: *OGU (CCC TX715.6 A75)
NOTES: The company made stainless steel utensils, such as saucepans, deep fryers, poachers, and steamers, many of which are illustrated on the inside front and back faces of the binding, which fold out. Printed on the outside back face is 'Printed in Canada Copyright pending // [printer's name:] Bulman Bros. B.C. Ltd. Van.' The book is undated, but Tisdall, whose address is reproduced on pp 6–7, died in 1949.

Family favorites

B121.1   nd [about 1945–9]
Family favorites / A book of proven / recipes / compiled by / the Evening Group / First United Church / Woman's Association / Victoria, B.C.
DESCRIPTION: 18.0 × 12.5 cm   Pp [1–2] 3–51 [52]   Paper, with image on front of three children 'cooking' at a kitchen table; stapled
CONTENTS: 1 tp; 2 'This book was made possible by the kind co-operation of all the groups of the Woman's Association of the First United Church and the advertisers'; 3 'Household Hints' and 'Stretched Butter'; 4 ads; 5 'Index'; 6–49 recipes and ads; 50–2 blank

for 'Recipes' and at bottom p 52, 'Clarke Ptg. Co. Ltd. Victoria, B.C.'
COPIES: *BVIPA
NOTES: 'Meals for Young Children' are on pp 44–9. BVIPA dates the book [1940–2]; however, there is no mention of the Second World War and the volume looks later, possibly about 1945–9. An advertisement on p 38 for Owl Drug Co. Ltd, at the corner of Fort and Douglas streets, in the Campbell Building, describes the company as 'prescription specialists for over fifty years'; however, this advertisement is not conclusive evidence of the date of publication. Owl Drug Co. was established on 13 October 1910, pointing to publication after 1960 (1910 + 50 years). On the other hand, in 1921 Owl Drug Co. took over a well-known Victoria drugstore owned by D.E. Campbell, who had been in business at that intersection since 1882. If one takes 1882 as the start for 'prescription specialists' and adds 'over fifty years,' the book was published in the 1940s (1882 + about 63 years = 1945). It was certainly published before 1962, when the Woman's Association became known as the United Church Women.

Henderson, Mrs Margaret

For other books with which Henderson's name is connected see B104.1.

B122.1 nd [about 1945–9]
The Vancouver / Daily Province / ABC / of the kitchen / for / course on cookery and / kitchen management / [printers' trade symbol] / Compiled by / the Modern Kitchen / The Vancouver Daily Province / Price 25c
DESCRIPTION: 20.5 × 13.0 cm   Pp [i–iv], 1–116   Fp portrait on p iii of Margaret Henderson, director, Daily Province Modern Kitchen   Paper; stapled
CONTENTS: i tp; ii blank; iii fp portrait; iv blank; 1 'Preface' signed Margaret Henderson; 2 'Index'; 3–116 nineteen numbered lessons
COPIES: *Private collection
NOTES: On p 1 Henderson thanks Maple Leaf Milling Co. for 'material assistance included in this book.'

1946

[Title unknown]

B123.1   1946
[An edition of a cookbook, by the Women's Auxiliary to the Canadian Legion, British Empire Service League, Branch No. 11, Trail, British Columbia, 1946]
COPIES: Private collection

Adams, Edith [pseudonym]

For information about the pseudonym and a list of the annual recipe collections published under the Edith Adams name, see B81.1.

B124.1   [1946]
The / Vancouver Sun's / 11th annual / cook book / Edited by / Edith Adams / Including: Prize winning recipes / canning, calorie chart, entertaining [cover-title]
DESCRIPTION: 27.5 × 22.0 cm   Pp 1–32   Three small illus on p 16   Paper; stapled
CONTENTS: Inside front face of binding ''Teen-age and Junior Cooks'; 1 'Measurements and Substitutions,' 'Sun Readers Can Aid World's Starving Millions' signed Edith Adams, cookery editor, 'Cook Book Index,' and 'Cooking for a Crowd'; 2 'Home-made Biscuits, Buns and Bread'; 3 'Easy Ways to Use Up Bread Crumbs'; 4 '1946 Cakes, Icings and Tea Loaves'; 5 'Ingenious Cooks Manage Pies, Tarts'; 6 '"Shortage" Cookies Hit a New High'; 7 'Toothsome Squares from What-Have-You'; 8 'No-Shortening Recipes, Butter Stretchers'; 9 'No-Sugar Treats for a Sweet Tooth'; 10 'Ice-Cold Desserts for Hot Days'; 11 'A Pudding's as Good as Its Sauce'; 12 'Appetizing Meat Makes the Meal'; 13 'Make Use of "No Token" Meats'; 14 'More Fish at Home – More Meat Abroad'; 15 'Wild Game Helps Out the Meat Ration'; 16 'Ps-s-s-st – Your Calories Are Showing'; 17–18 'A Calorie Chart for Losing Weight'; 19 'Green Salads Are Vitamin-Rich'; 20 'Appetite-Appeal for Vegetables'; 21 'Soups, Casseroles, Use Up Left-overs'; 22 'Hallowe'en Follows Thanksgiving'; 23 'An Old-fashioned Yuletide'; 24 'Easy Refreshments for the Hostess'; 25 'Serving the Wedding Breakfast'; 26 'Cocktails and Punches'; 27 'Special Canning'; 28 'Timetable for Canning Fruits'; 29 'Timetable for Canning Vegetables'; 30–1 'Sugar-Shortage Jams and Jellies'; 32 'Sugar-Shortage Pickles, Relishes'; inside back face continuation from p 16 of 'Ps-s-s-st – Your Calories Are Showing'

CITATIONS: Ferguson/Fraser, p 234, illus col on p 103 of closed volume

COPIES: BVAU (Beatrice M. Millar Papers) Company collection (Vancouver Sun) *Private collection

NOTES: The eleventh annual was advertised in the *Sun* on 7 November 1946, p 25: 'Cook Books: Eleventh Annual Cook Book is now available. In gay scarlet cover, its pages are filled with recipes and cooking instructions especially adapted to British Columbia conditions. Persons interested may obtain them by sending 10 cents each for mailing charges to Cook Book, care of Edith Adams, the Vancouver Sun.' The binding design is identical to B119.1, *The Vancouver Sun's 10th Annual Cook Book*; only the annual number changes.

Dehydrated vegetables

For other books with which Margaret Henderson's name is connected, see B104.1; for Alice Stevens, see B77.1.

B125.1   nd [about 1946]
Dehydrated vegetables / Tastes good – good for you [cover-title]
DESCRIPTION: 15.0 × 11.5 cm   Pp [1–20]   Illus blue-and-black   Paper, with image on front of a can of Bulmans Dehydrated Vegetable Mix against a background of vegetables; stapled
CONTENTS: 1–2 'A Proud Achievement' signed T.R. Bulman, president, and at bottom p 2, 'The recipes in this booklet have been tested and approved by Mrs. Margaret Henderson, Province Modern Kitchen, Vancouver Daily Province, Vancouver, B.C.'; 3 'From the Garden to Your Table' signed Alice Stevens and Phyllis P. Wardle, home economists; 4 'Cooking Directions'; 5 beet recipes; 6 'Food Values'; 7 recipe for Jellied Salad; 8 'School Lunches'; 9 soup recipes; 10–11 'Vegetable Mix' recipes; 12–13 'Supper Dishes'; 14 potato recipes; 15 carrot recipes; 16 onion recipes; 17 cabbage recipes; 18 parsnip recipes; 19 turnip recipes; 20 'Tables of Equivalents'
COPIES: AEPMA *BVIPA
NOTES: *Dehydrated Vegetables* was likely published after the Second World War, in about 1946: The text on p 1 refers to '30 years of scientific research,' beginning 'on one of the Bulman farms near Vernon, B.C., in 1916'; and p 2 refers to developments 'early in the war.' The booklet was free: 'Compliments of Bulmans Limited Vernon, B.C.' is printed on the outside back face of the binding.

LA to RIH cook book

B126.1   1946
L / A / to / RIH / cook / book / Compiled and published by the / Ladies' Auxiliary / to the / Royal Inland Hospital / 1946 Price $1.00 [cover-title]
DESCRIPTION: 22.0 × 14.0 cm   Pp 1–132   Paper, with image on front of a stylized window, awning, and row of nine small tulips; metal spiral
CONTENTS: 1 'Over 60 years service' [history of the Kamloops Hospital, founded in 1885 (name changed in 1896 to Royal Inland Hospital), and of the Ladies' Auxiliary, organized on 11 November 1899]; 2 ad; 3–129 recipes credited with the name of the contributor and ads; 130 ads; 131 'Home Canning Guide'; 132 'Index' and 'Table of Measurements'
COPIES: *BKM
NOTES: The running head is 'Ladies' Auxiliary to Royal Inland Hospital Cook Book.' The printer, 'Kamloops Sentinel Limited,' is on the inside front face of the binding.

The northern interior cook book

B127.1   [about 1946]
The northern interior / cook / book/ Prepared by / Prince George & District Hospital W.A. [cover-title]
DESCRIPTION: With image on front of a woman adding ice cubes(?) to a bowl
COPIES: *BPGRM (992.02.02)
NOTES: 'W.A.' stands for Women's Auxiliary. BPGRM dates the book [1946?].

1947

Adams, Edith [pseudonym]

For information about the pseudonym and a list of the annual recipe collections published under the Edith Adams name, see B81.1. From 1 February 1947 to the 1960s, Edith Adams was Marianne Linnell, née Marion Elizabeth Pearson (in adulthood she officially changed her first name). She took up the position concurrent with the opening of the Edith Adams Cottage, a demonstration kitchen attached to the Sun building, with its own separate entrance at 510 Beatty Street. The newspaper introduced its new employee to staff in 'Edith Adams Takes Over Sun Cottage,' Sun Spots [in-house periodical] February 1947. For a photograph of visitors entering the new Cottage, see Vancouver Sun 20 March 1947, p 10. For Linnell in 1950 see pl 46. She was assisted by

Eileen Norman, Marion McGill, and Mary Hult. The Sun's women's editor and administrative head of the Cottage was Myrtle Patterson Gregory.

Linnell was born in Calgary in October 1914, but raised in Edmonton, where her father was a member of the Alberta Legislature. She studied home economics at the University of Alberta in Edmonton and served as vice-president of the university's student body. After graduation in 1935, she worked for Calgary Power, doing cooking demonstrations from a mobile trailer throughout Alberta as part of the utility's rural electrification program. In 1942, after her husband, an RCAF pilot, left for overseas, she supervised a staff of 175 at the Montreal Eaton's department store lunch counter. In 1944, the year her husband was killed in action (she was only twenty-nine years of age at the time of his death and the mother of a two-month-old infant), she joined Northwestern Utilities in Edmonton. As the Utilities' director, she was credited with compiling A83.5, Home Canning. In 1945 she moved to Vancouver, beginning her career as Edith Adams in 1947. In the 1960s, she left the newspaper to work in real estate, then in civic politics. Linnell never remarried. She died on 6 June 1990. Her son, Robert Linnell, has saved his mother's scrap book and audio tapes on which she recorded, later in life, her memories of working at the Edith Adams Cottage.

B128.1   copyright 1947
Edith Adams' / cooking under pressure / A modern guide to pressure cooking / and canning / Designed for the modern pressure cooker, these recipes, / nevertheless, lend themselves admirably to general cooking, / with or without the use of a pressure cooker. Should ordinary / heat be used, longer cooking time will be required. / Note / Recipes contained in this book are designed for standard / pressure cookers and have been carefully checked for / safety in temperature and pressure. They should be fol- / lowed *exactly* if full success is to be achieved. Users / must take full responsibility. / Edith Adams' Cottage / (510 Beatty Street) / Homemakers' Service / The Vancouver Sun / Vancouver, B.C. / Copyright, Canada, 1947
DESCRIPTION: 22.5 × 15.0 cm   Pp [1] 2–65   Tp illus of a woman carrying a bag of groceries   Paper, with image on front of the Sun building
CONTENTS: Inside front face of binding table of contents; 1 tp; 2–mid 3 'Introduction'; bottom 3–60 text; 61–5 [inside back face of binding] index
CITATIONS: Ferguson/Fraser, pp 105 and 234
COPIES: OONL (TX840 P7 A32 1947)   *Private collection

NOTES: This title and B129.1, *Modern Guide to Home Canning*, were published in the year between B124.1, *The Vancouver Sun's 11th Annual Cook Book*, and B133.1, *Edith Adams' Twelfth Annual Prize Cook Book*, and they signalled the beginning of special subject cookbooks issued under the Edith Adams name.

B128.2   copyright 1947
—Edith Adams' / cooking under pressure / A modern guide to pressure cooking / and canning / Adapt these recipes to the ordinary kitchen range by cooking / approximately three times as long as specified for the pressure / cooker and adding more liquid to make up for evaporation. / Note / Recipes contained in this book are designed for standard / pressure cookers and have been carefully checked for / safety in temperature and pressure. They should be fol- / lowed *exactly* if full success is to be achieved. Users / must take full responsibility. / Copyright, Canada, 1947
DESCRIPTION: Tp illus of a woman carrying a bag of groceries   [$0.35, on binding]
COPIES: *Vancouver Sun (company collection)
NOTES: Unlike B128.1, there is no image on the binding and no Cottage address on the title-page. The order of publication of the two editions is unknown.

B129.1   1947
[An edition of *Modern Guide to Home Canning*, by Edith Adams, Vancouver: Sun Publishing Co., 1947, pp 40, $0.26]
CITATIONS: CCat No. 28, p ZD13
NOTES: This title is listed on the inside front face of the binding of B133.1, the twelfth annual cookbook, copyright 1948, for $0.25, and on the inside back face of *Edith Adams' Thirteenth Prize Cook Book,* copyright 1950.

Cook book

Hollyburn, the location of St Christopher's Anglican Church, is now part of West Vancouver.

B130.1   1947
Cook book / 1947 / Compiled by / St. Christopher's W.A. / Hollyburn, B.C. [cover-title]
DESCRIPTION: 20.5 × 15.5 cm   Pp [1–3] 4–64   Paper, with image on front of church; stapled
CONTENTS: 1 ads; 2 'St. Christopher's W.A. wishes to thank all merchants, business houses and friends ... the proceeds from the sale of [the book] is to go

towards our church building fund ... Also we wish to thank Captain and Mrs. Lovegrove, who have given us such great help.' and table of contents; 3 ads; 4–60 recipes and ads; 61 ad; 62 'Home Hints'; 63 ad; 64 'Oven Temperatures,' 'Measurements,' and 'Large Amounts for Catering'
COPIES: *BVIPA
NOTES: The printer, 'Shoemaker, McLean & Veitch (1945) Ltd.,' is on the outside back face of the binding.

Jubilee cook book

B131.1 [June 1947]
Jubilee cook book / Compiled by / the Union Avenue Circle of the / Women's Association / St. Andrew's United Church / Rossland, B.C. / The members of the Union Avenue Circle tender their / most grateful thanks to all those who so materially assisted / them with the advertisements, also the ladies whose recipes / made this book possible. / This book is not intended to be a complete line of all recipes / but presents the favorite recipes of many of the women and some / of the men in Rossland.
DESCRIPTION: Pp [1–2] 3–82 [83–4] Small tp illus of a man carrying a steaming dish With photograph on front of 'Columbia Avenue, looking west, in the spring of 1896' [$1.00, on binding] Stapled
CONTENTS: 1 tp; 2 'Grace' by Robert Burns; 3 'Recipes for Living'; 4–81 recipes credited with the name of the contributor and ads; 82 'Household Hints'; 83 'Table of Weights and Measures'; 84 'Index' [i.e., table of contents]
COPIES: *Private collection
NOTES: The printer is identified on the outside back face of the binding: 'This book was printed by Rossland Miner [i.e., the local newspaper].' The years 1897 and 1947 flank the word 'Jubilee' in the cover-title. St Andrew's Presbyterian Church (founded in 1895), was united in 1917 with Rossland Methodist Church (founded in 1897). The cookbook marks the fiftieth anniversary of the latter entity.

B131.2 2nd ed., [1948]
—Favourite recipes from the Golden City / [caption and credit for photograph:] Rossland's famous ski lift // Pat Archibald / Jubilee / cook book / Compiled and published by / the Union Avenue Circle / of / St. Andrew's United Church / Rossland, B.C. / Second edition Price one dollar [cover-title]
DESCRIPTION: Illus of Rossland's ski lift, the store-

front of Hunter Brothers Ltd, and the fleet of cars of the Rossland Co-operative Transportation Society
COPIES: *Bookseller's stock
NOTES: The volume has 88 pp. The front matter indicates the second edition was published in 1948. The front matter includes a note from Hunter Brothers Ltd, its years of operation, '1895–1948,' and a list of its 'Trained and Courteous Staff'; thanks from the Union Avenue Circle to those who assisted with advertisements and to the ladies who contributed recipes; information about the Rossland Co-operative Transportation Society, organized in 1932, and a reference to the growth of Rossland 'in the past fifteen years'; and a history of the Red Mountain Ski Club, formed in spring 1947 by the amalgamation of the Trail and Rossland ski clubs. The ski club history refers to the main skiing event in 1949, which 'will take place in the week of February 5 to 13.'

The pot o' gold

B132.1 [copyright 1947]
The / pot / o' gold / A treasure chest / of selected recipes / Compiled / by the / Junior / Auxiliary / of / St. Joseph's / Hospital [cover-title]
DESCRIPTION: 23.0 × 15.0 cm Pp [i–iv], 1–276 Illus Paper, with image on front of a pirate and an open chest of gold; metal spiral
CONTENTS: i illus of proposed addition to St Joseph's Hospital, Victoria, B.C., and 'Junior Auxiliary of St. Joseph's Hospital Victoria, B.C. Copyright 1947 – '; ii dedication to the people of Victoria, statement that the proceeds from the book's sale will go toward the new hospital wing, and acknowledgments; iii table of contents; iv 'Mystery Chef's Recipe for Baked Sliced Ham'; 1 ad; 2–275 recipes credited with the name of the contributor and ads; 276 'Oven Temperatures for Baking' and 'Equivalent Measures & Weights'
COPIES: *BVIPA Private collection
NOTES: The text is reproduced from hand-writing. The acknowledgments give 'special thanks to Diggon-Hibben for their wonderful co-operation.' Diggon-Hibben Ltd is described in the company's advertisement on p 107 as selling books, stationery, and office supplies.

1948

Adams, Edith [pseudonym]

For information about the pseudonym and a list of the annual recipe collections published under the Edith Adams name, see B81.1. Marianne Linnell was Edith Adams in 1948; for information about her, see B128.1.

B133.1 copyright 1948
Edith Adams' / twelfth annual / prize cook book / For more than twenty years, Western Canada's most versatile home cooks have / been sending their favorite recipes to Edith Adams, and this well-known / food authority has been publishing one of them each day, with a dollar prize / award, in her regular newspaper column. Women everywhere have liked the / practical recipes and many of them, by popular demand, have been compiled / into a number of Edith Adams' Prize Cook Books. This is the twelfth of the / series and, with more than 550 readers' recipes and basic cookery recipes / from Miss Adams' own file, easily becomes the largest of them all. Each / recipe on the following pages will be found to have a certain "different" / quality that will delight homemakers. Indeed, the entire book will serve as a / good basis for practising that most satisfying of all domestic arts – home cooking. / Copyright, Canada, 1948 / [printers' trade symbol]
DESCRIPTION: 22.0 × 14.5 cm   Pp [1] 2–96   Tp illus of father and son at table   [$0.25, on binding]   Paper, with images on front, reversed out of blue, of various kitchen utensils; originally stapled, but BVA copy sewn between new boards
CONTENTS: Inside front face of binding table of contents; 1 tp; 2 'Weights and Measures' and 'Equivalents'; 3–96 recipes; inside back face 'Temperature Chart,' 'Deep Fat Frying Chart,' and at bottom, 'Sunprinting'
COPIES: AEPMA *BVA BVAMM BVAU
NOTES: The next annual prize cookbooks in the series were the thirteenth, dated 1950, and the fourteenth, dated 1953.

Cook book

B134.1 [June 1948]
Cranbrook Stagette Club / Cook book / Cranbrook, B.C. [cover-title]
DESCRIPTION: With image on front of stag's head; stapled
COPIES: *Bookseller's stock

NOTES: The 'Acknowledgment' (on the first page) is dated June 1948 and states: 'This little book has been compiled to aid the Cranbrook Stagettes in raising money for their Banff School of Fine Arts Scholarship Fund, and to make possible a substantial donation to the Cranbrook Girl Guides in the erection of a building for their use, ...' The 'Index' lists 'Beverages and Cocktails,' 'Cakes,' 'Candy,' 'Cookies and Muffins,' 'Frostings and Icings,' 'Luncheon Dishes,' 'Pickles and Preserves,' 'Pies and Pastries,' 'Puddings and Desserts,' and 'Salad Dressings, Sauces and Stuffings.' The text is reproduced from typed copy.

Favorite recipes

Henderson-Jubilee Church is now called West Burnaby United Church.

B135.1 1948
Favorite / recipes / by the / Agenda Circle / of / Henderson-Jubilee Church / 1948
DESCRIPTION: 18.0 × 10.5 cm   Pp [i–ii], 1–68   Limp plastic(?); bound at top edge by a cord through two punched holes
CONTENTS: i tp; ii blank; 1–68 recipes on rectos only (versos not included in the pagination)
COPIES: *Private collection

Revelstoke recipes

B136.1 nd [1948]
Revelstoke / [same initial 'R' as 'Revelstoke']ecipes / Junior / Auxiliary / to Queen Victoria / Hospital Revelstoke / British Columbia [cover-title]
DESCRIPTION: 23.0 × 15.0 cm   Pp 1–97   Paper; metal spiral
CONTENTS: 1 'Revelstoke Recipes' signed the Committee and 'Index' [i.e., table of contents]; 2 'Table of Weights and Measures,' 'Sandwich Quantities,' and 'Large Amounts for Catering'; 3–97 recipes credited with the name of the contributor and ads
COPIES: *Private collection
NOTES: The book was likely published in 1948: An advertisement on p 36 for the Revelstoke Co-op. Society refers to the beginning of the society in 1921 and to the growth of the membership 'during the twenty-seven years that have elapsed since that time.'

Streamline your canning the Burpee way

B137.1 [32nd ed., copyright 1948]
Streamline / your/ canning / the / Burpee / way /
Letson & Burpee Ltd., Vancouver, Canada / In
United States: – The Burpee Can Sealer Co.,
Barrington, Illinois [cover-title]
DESCRIPTION: With image on front of an elf carrying a
basket of tomatoes(?), an elf sealing a can, and an elf
holding up a sealed can
CONTENTS: Inside front face of binding ad for Burpee
Aristocrat Pressure Pan; 1 'What You'll Find Inside'
[i.e., table of contents] and 'Thirty-second edition.
Copyright 1948'; ...
COPIES: *BLCK (983.13)
NOTES: The book has 78 pp.

Tested Christmas recipes

B138.1 nd [about 1948]
Vancouver Daily Province / Modern Kitchen /
Tested / Christmas recipes / Compiled by / the
Vancouver Daily Province / Modern Kitchen
DESCRIPTION: 20.0 × 13.0 cm   Pp [1–3] 4–16   Small
tp illus of a Christmas bell   Paper, with tp illus on
front; stapled
CONTENTS: 1 tp; 2 blank; 3 'Our Service to You'; 4–13
Christmas recipes; 14–16 blank 'For Your Own Recipes'
COPIES: *OONL (TX715 T436 1900z p***)
NOTES: 'Our Service to You' outlines the culinary re-
sources offered by the newspaper: 'Our library is at
your disposal, containing information on foreign
receipes [sic], cooking in large quantities, etiquette,
planning weddings and parties. We also invite you to
read the Thursday cookery page and daily Kitchen
Column regularly, and to listen to the radio broad-
casts each Tuesday and Wednesday morning at 10:30
over station CKWX.' The book contains recipes for
Fish Cocktail Sauce for Christmas, Preparing and
Roasting the Turkey, Stuffing for 10-Pound Turkey,
Cranberry Sauce, Century Plum Pudding, Carrot Pudding, Hard Sauce, Butter or Suet Mincemeat, Century
Christmas Cake, Angel Fruit Cake, Old-fashioned
Southern Fruit Cake, Golden Fruit Cake, Almond
Paste, Icing for Chrismas Cakes, Scotch Shortbread
(Brown Sugar), Scotch Shortbread (Icing Sugar), and
Basic Punch for Christmas. The OONL copy has two
handwritten recipes on p 16, the first dated 'Xmas.
1948' and the second, '1949,' which suggests a publication date for the book of about 1948.
   The Daily Province published three other undated
collections of Christmas recipes that are likely later
than B138.1 because they have more pages. All three
have the title 'The Vancouver / Daily Province /
Modern Kitchen / Tested / recipes / Christmas edition / Compiled by / the Vancouver Daily Province
/ Modern Kitchen' and a small image of a Christmas
bell on the title-page, but each has different pagination. The copy owned by the Vancouver Sun and
stamped 'Edith Adams' Cottage Homemakers Service' has 48 pp; the 'Preface' is signed Margaret
Henderson; the 'Index' on p 48 lists sections for
'Cakes,' 'Cakes, Small,' 'Cookies,' 'Frostings,' and 'Traditional Christmas Recipes.' A private collector has
an incomplete copy where the 'Index' and space 'For
Your Own Recipes' are on p 56, presumably the last
page; the last item in the 'Index' is Punch, p 55. BVIPA
has a copy of 72 pp. In the BVIPA copy, Margaret
Henderson's 'Preface' refers to sixteen years of readers' letters, which suggests a publication date of 1951
since the Modern Kitchen began in 1935 (1935 + 16
years). This 'Preface' confirms that there were earlier,
shorter issues before 1951 since it states, 'Once again
your Daily Province Modern Kitchen presents your
guide to successful Christmas baking, revised and
considerably increased in volume. In this new Christmas edition you will find ...' The BVIPA title-page has
a printers' trade symbol, not found in the 48- and 56-
page issues.

1949

Adams, Edith [pseudonym]

*For information about the pseudonym and a list of the
annual recipe collections published under the Edith
Adams name, see B81.1. Marianne Linnell was Edith
Adams in 1949; for information about her, see B128.1.*

B139.1 nd [about 1949]
Globe / trotting / gourmet / Menus and / recipes
of / England / Scotland / France / Spain / Italy /
Germany and / central Europe / Denmark /
Norway / Sweden / Russia / Balkans / India /
China / Japan / Australia and / New Zealand /
Dutch East Indies / Hawaii / South America /
Mexico / Southern United / States / Edith Adams'
foreign cook book [cover-title]
DESCRIPTION: With image on front of a woman carry-
ing a tray of fruit on her head, a map of the world
behind her; stapled
CITATIONS: CCat No. 28, p ZD13
COPIES: *ACU

NOTES: This 48–page book was produced by the Edith Adams' Cottage Homemakers' Service at the *Vancouver Sun*. 'Wines' are on p 48. CCat records 1949? as the year of publication, and the price of $0.36. The title is listed on the inside back face of the binding of *Edith Adams' Thirteenth Prize Cook Book,* copyright 1950. The ACU copy is inscribed on p 1, in ink, 'Compliments of the author.'

B140.1 nd [about 1949]
Successful / home canning / By / Edith Adams / The Vancouver / Sun / 36¢ / This is an Edith Adams' / Cottage Publication [cover-title]
DESCRIPTION: 28.0 × 21.5 cm Pp [i–ii], 1–70 Paper front, card back; with image on front of a cornucopia filled with fruit and vegetables; stapled at top edge
CONTENTS: i note about canning at various altitudes and index; ii 'L'Envoi' by Margery Vanderburgh and 'Useful Weights and Measures'; 1–70 text
COPIES: *BVIPA
NOTES: *Successful Home Canning* was published after the opening of the Edith Adams Cottage in 1947. It may have been published in 1949, after *Edith Adams' Twelfth Annual Prize Cook Book,* copyright 1948, and before *Edith Adams' Thirteenth Prize Cook Book,* copyright 1950. The text is reproduced from typed copy.

Council's choice cookery

B141.1 nd [about 1949]
Council's choice / cookery / Vancouver Sub-Senior Section / National Council of Jewish Women / of Canada
DESCRIPTION: 22.5 × 15.0 cm Pp [1] 2–168 NCJW symbol on tp Paper; wire spiral
CONTENTS: 1 tp; 2 ad; 3 'Card of Thanks' signed Mrs H. Lauer, president, Mrs S. Malkin, cook book chairman, and Mrs A. Herstein, recipe chairman; 4 ad; 5 'Contents'; 6 ad; 7–165 recipes credited with the name of the contributor and ads; 166–8 ads
CITATIONS: Rome et al., No. 61
COPIES: SRBJ *Private collection
NOTES: The cover-title is 'Council Cook Book.' About twenty years before, the Vancouver Section had published its first cookbook, under the same title (B67.1). This is a completely new selection of recipes. Mrs Sue Malkin (born 1914; later Mrs Abramson) was the cook book chairman, having been asked to take on the job shortly after she moved to Vancouver from Winnipeg. She reports that the book was published in about 1949. 'Jewish Cookery' starts on p 133; 'Jewish Holiday Dishes,' on p 143; and 'Foreign Cookery,' on p

153. (According to Sue Abramson, the publishing history given in the fourth edition is not correct for B141.1; it states, 'The first edition was printed in 1929 and subsequent editions were printed in 1943 [*sic*] and 1953.')

OTHER EDITIONS: *New Council Cook Book,* 3rd ed., 1953, and reprint of 3rd ed. after first printing sold out (Private collection); 4th ed., nd [1960s] (Private collection). Sue Abramson was not involved with the following subsequent editions of *The Council Cookbook:* 5th ed., Vancouver: November House, 1974 (OONL), and 6th ed., Richmond, BC: S. and T. Stereo Printers Ltd, nd (Private collection), which are completely new texts. Half a century after launching *Council's Choice Cookery* in about 1949, eighty-six-year-old Sue Abramson, in collaboration with two other NCJW members, prepared another cookbook for the Vancouver Section, *Bubbe's Kitchen,* Vancouver: Raincoast Books, 2000.

The new thrills of freezing with your Frigidaire Food Freezer

B142.1 [copyright 1949]
The new thrills of freezing / with your / Frigidaire Food Freezer / Instructions for preparing, packaging, and freezing food the / easy Frigidaire way. [cover-title]
DESCRIPTION: 20.0 × 15.0 cm Pp 1–40 Illus Thin card, with image on front of a woman's hands pressing a meatloaf-mixture into an oblong glass pan; stapled
CONTENTS: Inside front face of binding 'Index' [i.e., table of contents]; 1–39 text and at bottom p 1, 'Copyright 1949, Frigidaire Division, General Motors Corporation, (1752)'; 40 blank, ruled page for 'Notes'
COPIES: *BVAMM
NOTES: 'Artic [*sic*] Frozen Food Lockers ... Bill Webber, Manager 1320 Commercial Dr. Hastings 3748 / / FA–2248–11/49 PC. No. 5884456 Litho in U.S.A.' is on the outside back face of the binding.

Practical tested approved recipes

B143.1
[An edition of *Practical Tested Approved Recipes,* also known as *The PTA Cook Book,* by members of Nakusp United District Parent Teachers Association, Nakusp, BC, 1949]

NOTES: The date of the first edition is from the Arrow Lakes Historical Society.

B143.2   facsimile, [1993]
—A memento for good cooking / Practical / tested / approved / recipes / By / members of the / Nakusp United District / Parent-Teachers Association [cover-title]
DESCRIPTION: 22.0 × 14.5 cm   Pp [1–4] 5–104   2 photographs on p 2 of 'A group of P.T.A. members' and 'Looking west over Nakusp'   Thin card, with image on front of a cook carrying roast poultry on a platter; Cirlox-bound
CONTENTS: 1 'A Word from Our Committee' signed PTA Cook Book Committee, Nakusp, BC; 2 photographs; 3 'Foreword' signed Rev. B. Hartley; 4 ad; 5–97 recipes credited with the name of the contributor and ads; 98 'Miscellaneous Hints, etc.'; 99 'Kitchen Weights and Measures' and ad; 100 'Grocery List for the New Homemaker' and 'Simple Table Service for

the Beginner'; 101 'Substitutions or Equivalents' and 'Recipe Neighbours'; 102–3 blank for 'Additional Recipes'; 104 'Table of Contents'
COPIES: *Private collection
NOTES: In the cover-title, which is a 1993 design, the first letters of 'Practical, tested, approved' are the initials of the Parent-Teachers Association; hence, 'P.T.A. Recipe Book' is the alternative title. This is a facsimile of the 1949 edition, although the year of the first edition is not recorded. 'Reprinted (November, 1993) by the Arrow Lakes Historical Society Box 584, Nakusp, B.C. V0G 1R0' is on the outside back face of the binding. The Committee states on p 1, 'This book has been published to help equip our new school now being erected.' There is a drawing of 'The New Elementary School' on the inside back face of the binding. The selection of 'Apple Recipes' on pp 7–12 is introduced by text about apples by Margaret Henderson of the Province Modern Kitchen.

Yukon Territory

Crab Casserole

In layers as given:
4 sliced hard boiled eggs
Cream sauce made with flour, butter and 2 cups milk
1 can shredded crab
Minced onion browned in butter
1 tin green asparagus
Buttered bread crumbs
Salt and pepper

Hazel Gloslie

Lumberjack Macaroni

¼ lb. macaroni (cooked in boiling salted water)
2 cups grated nippy cheese
¼ cup Lea & Perrins Sauce
¼ cup Chili sauce
¾ cup melted butter

Have large platter very hot, and spread macaroni on this. Sprinkle with cheese and sauce which has been slightly heated. Pour melted butter over all. Serve at once.

Esther Rogers

Y1.1, *Choice Recipes*, both recipes p 51

The Yukon Territory was established in 1898, soon after the discovery of gold in 1896 at Bonanza Creek brought thousands of people to the area and an instant town was born – Dawson, which became the first capital (in 1953, the capital moved to Whitehorse). A San Francisco company published US1.1, *Helpful Hints for Klondike Gold Hunters,* probably at the height of the Gold Rush, which contained culinary, medical, and other 'useful information.' Only one cookbook was found from the Yukon in the period covered by this bibliography, and it was published in 1942, the same year as the Alaska Highway was completed, connecting the Territory with the rest of Canada by road for the first time.

1942

Choice recipes

Y1.1   1942
Choice recipes / Compiled by / the Women of
Yukon Chapter No. 1 / Order of the Eastern Star /
Dawson, Yukon Territory / For the benefit of the
war work / Dawson, Y.T., 1942 / This book contains
many of the favorite recipes of Dawson housewives
/ who have no slight reputation as cooks. / The
members of Yukon Chapter No. 1, O.E.S., herein
express their appreciation to / the committee who
have so zealously collected, assorted, copied and
arranged the / recipes for this collection; to the
advertising committee; to the advertisers who
have / so generously responded; to all those who
contributed recipes and to all others / who helped
in any capacity.
DESCRIPTION: 23.0 × 15.0 cm   Pp [3–6] 7–71 [72]
Card, with star-shape on front; stapled
CONTENTS: 3 'Recipe for a Happy Day'; 4 blank except for typed(?) name 'Mrs Olive A.K. Powesrs [first
's' scored through with a dry pen to correct spelling;
should be Powers] // Tacoma Washington'; 5 tp; 6
blank; 7 'Table of Weights and Measures,' 'Oven
Chart,' and 'Roast Meats'; 8 blank; 9 'Table of Contents' [i.e., alphabetical list of subjects]; 10 ad; 11–70
recipes credited with the name of the contributor and
ads; 71 'To Make a Good Housekeeper' [mock recipe];
72 'Printed by the Clarke & Stuart Co. Limited
Vancouver, B.C.'
COPIES: *ACG
NOTES: The cover-title is 'The Star Cook Book.' There
are no distinctively northern recipes, featuring local
ingredients. The text is a typical collection of recipes
for biscuits, hot breads, and doughnuts, cakes, frostings and fillings, candy, cookies, frozen desserts, luncheon dishes, marmalade, pickles, puddings and
sauces, salads and salad dressings, sandwiches, cocktails, and sauces and garnishes for meats. The 'Luncheon Dishes' section features hearty casseroles of
meat or canned fish, root vegetables, and canned corn.

Northwest Territories

Bannock

(1 cup of flour per person, all the other ingredients apply to 1 cup of flour)

1 cup of flour, 1 teaspoon of baking powder, 1 teapsoon [sic] salt, 1 tablespoon sugar. Mix dry ingredients well, add about ⅓ cup water, stir with spoon until dough becomes too thick to stir, knead dough until it is stiff and will no longer stick to the fingers. More flour may be dusted on the dough, in order to fetch it to the correct consistency. Place dough in a well greased pan and bake in a medium oven, a sliver of wood or wire tester should come out clean when inserted in the centre of the Bannock.

To bake Bannock on an open camp fire: Dust the frying pan with flour, press the dough firmly into the pan and place onto the camp fire until a slight crust is formed on the bottom. The pan is then taken from the fire, and propped up at an angle of 45° facing the fire. Some coals are taken from the fire and placed behind the pan. It is necessary to shift the Bannock around while baking. This is done by twitching your wrist while holding the pan steady. This will move the Bannock inside the frying pan. With a little practice one becomes quite efficient. Bake the Bannock in this manner until it is brown and inserted sliver comes out clean. Frequently it will be found necessary to puncture the crust with the point of a hunting knife so as to be able to insert the sliver or cake tester.

Jake Woolgar

Caribou a la Mode

Mix 1 tsp. salt, ½ tsp. pepper, ¼ tsp. each cloves, mace and cinnamon, 4 tbsps. vinegar, 1 tbsps. melted butter. Rub a thick round steak thoroughly with this mixture, roll, bind with twine and let stand overnight. Then roast.

Margaret Oldenburg

Both recipes, NWT2.1, *D M S Cook Book,* by Daughters of the Midnight Sun, Yellowknife, [1947], pp 67, 69

The Northwest Territories was created on 15 July 1870 from land previously owned by the Hudson's Bay Co. and Great Britain. Between 1870 and 1912, parts of the huge swath of land were reassigned to form the new prairie provinces and the Yukon Territory, and to add to the areas of Ontario and Quebec. In 1999 the eastern part of the Northwest Territories became a new territory called Nunavut. There were few non-native inhabitants until the 1930s, when mineral exploration attracted more settlement, but even so, by 1941, the population was only 12,028, and by 1951, only 16,004. The only two cookbooks from the Northwest Territories to surface in the course of my research were published in the 1940s in Yellowknife, the largest urban centre and, from 1967, the seat of the territorial government (before 1967, the Northwest Territories was governed by a commissioner and Council based in Ottawa).

1941–2

D M S

NWT1.1   nd [about 1941–2]
D M S [cover-title]
COPIES: *NWYWNH (N92-079)
NOTES: The archives reports that the book has 11 leaves, with 19 printed pages. The text is reproduced from typing and the block-letter initials that form the cover-title have a 'home-made' quality. The first page presents a history of the club, the Daughters of the Midnight Sun, known as the Yellowknife DMS, which was formed on 11 November 1938 'to fill the need of a woman's social organization in the small but growing settlement of Yellowknife.' The history explains that until the end of 1940, the DMS took an active part in welfare work, making donations of money to the Red Cross and the local school board, but in January 1941, the DMS 're-organized as a social club only, the members feeling that the Red Cross needed any financial support that the community could give.' The reorganization, however, 'did not put an end to the annual banquet and party held at midnight of June twenty-first, when the Daughters of the Midnight Sun leave their husbands at home and have fun on their own!' The club offered the cookbook as 'a souvenier [*sic*] of the only club of its kind in the Northwest Territories.' At the bottom of the first page there is a letter V and the Morse code symbol for V, indicating that the cookbook was published during the Second World War. This is followed by lists of the names of the women in the first four executives. If the club began in November 1938 and there were four executives to date, then the cookbook was published about 1941–2. Part of NWT1.1 was reprinted in a 1984 cookbook; see the notes for NWT2.1.

1947

D M S cook book

NWT2.1   [1947]
[Initials in column at top left:] D / M / S / New / recipe / Yk. [i.e., Yellowknife] / cook book / [artist's name:] R. Stanton [cover-title]
DESCRIPTION: 22.5 × 15.0 cm   Pp [i–ii], 1–96 [97–8] Very thin card, with image on front of two polar bears, nose to nose and standing on top of an ice-covered half-sphere representing the planet Earth; stapled
CONTENTS: i–ii ads; 1 'The Daughters of the Midnight Sun' [i.e., history of the club and list of members in January 1947]; 2 ad; 3 How to Preserve a Husband [mock recipe] contributed by Leila Barwise; 4 ads; 5–96 recipes credited with the name of the contributor and ads; 97 ad; 98 'Index to Sections' [i.e., table of contents] and 'General Index'
COPIES: *Private collection
NOTES: See pl 12. On the binding, 'Yk.' is next to a shape indicating the location of Yellowknife on the stylized planet Earth; and 'R. Stanton' is likely Ruth Stanton, one of the DMS members listed on p 1. The club history on p 1 refers to the construction of a new hospital building to be started in Yellowknife 'this summer, 1947,' and states that money raised from the publication of the cookbook was to go to this project. Membership in January 1947 totalled almost fifty persons.

There is a section of 'Northern Recipes' on pp 67–73 with instructions for the following dishes: Baked Northern Fish, Bannock, Canned Caribou and Beef, Canned Ducks, Caribou, Caribou a la Mode, Caribou Hamburger, Dehydrated Carrots (not dried for preserving, but boiled until the water has evaporated, then dressed with butter, pepper, and salt), Dehydrated Potatoes (boiled till tender and drained, then fried in butter, pepper, and salt, or mashed with butter and canned milk), Hints for Northern Cooking, Dressed Moosemeat Roast, Fish Pie, Mock Strawberry Shortcake (in place of strawberries are cranberries, apples, and canned pineapple, all put through a meat grinder), Ptarmigan en Casserole, Rose Hip Juice, Comments on Sour Dough, Whipped Cream (the directions are not for fresh cream, but for evaporated, powdered, and condensed milk), Wild Game Sauce, Wild Cranberry Jelly, and Wild Cranberry Sauce.

The copy described here is inscribed on p i, 'Maybe this will help you remain a social success. From your nurses Kay // Eileen // Anne. // Mary // "Amitty" [M?]uyres.' The book's owner reports that the volume was given to her then-husband, Harry Madden, when he was a patient in hospital.

In 1984, to mark the fiftieth anniversary of the Gold Rush and first settlement of Yellowknife in 1934, the Daughters of the Midnight Sun compiled a 'Special Edition' cookbook for the city's 'Homecoming 1984' (Private collection). The 1984 volume reprinted parts from all the cookbooks produced by the organization over the years: NWT1.1, NWT2.1, 1955, 1960, 1970, 1982, plus a final section of recipes contributed in 1984. Each reprinted part begins with a reproduction of the front face of the original binding (except for NWT1.1) and the original introductory text.

No Province of Publication

1879

Tyree, Marion Fontaine Cabell
(Va, 1826–1912)

See this American author's biography in Feeding America.

NP1.1   [facsimile ed., 1980]
Old-time / recipes / and / remedies / M.C. Tyree / Coles
CONTENTS: Tp verso 'This book, originally published in 1879, suggests remedies and household formulas which may be considered harmful today ... © copyright 1980 and published by Coles Publishing Company Limited Toronto – Canada Printed in Canada'
COPIES: *OONL (TX715 O43 1980, 2 copies)
NOTES: The 1980 Coles edition of this American text is retitled to disguise its Virginia origins, and there is no indication of whether the 1879 edition on which it is based was Canadian or American. No Canadian edition has surfaced. The Coles facsimile may have been made from the 1879 Louisville edition, a copy of which is at OTAG.

AMERICAN EDITIONS: *Housekeeping in Old Virginia*, edited by Marion Cabell Tyree, New York: G.W. Carleton and Co., 1877 (United States: DLC); Richmond, [Va]: J.W. Randolph and English, 1878 (United States: KMK); Louisville, Ky: J.P. Morton and Co., 1878 (United States: DLC); Louisville, Ky: John P. Morton, 1879 (OTAG; United States: KMK, 2 copies); Louisville, Ky: J.P. Morton and Co., 1890 (United States: DLC).

1904

The Canadian home cook book

NP2.1   nd [about 1904]
The / Canadian / home / cook book / containing / 739 valuable recipes / This cook book contains 739 tested and tried recipes for breakfast dishes, / soups, fish, meats and poultry, cakes, pies, puddings, fancy dishes / ice creams, summer drinks and confectionery. [cover-title]
DESCRIPTION: 21.0 × 14.0 cm   Pp [1] 2–64   Limp cloth; stapled
CONTENTS: 1–64 recipes
COPIES: *NBFKL (Ruth Spicer Cookbook Collection) QKB   QMM (RBD ckbk 1414)
NOTES: There is no place of publication. A comparison of photocopies of p 1 and pp 40–1 of NP2.1 and NP2.2 indicates that the text is identical in both; only the cover-titles differ. The order of publication of the two versions is unknown.

The NBFKL copy is inscribed on the inside front face of the binding, in ink, 'Eva Mills // Sussex NB // August 1904 // From Mamma and Edna. Kings Co. Canada.' The QKB copy lacks pp 1–4.

NP2.2   nd
—The latest and best / The / Canadian / home / cook book / 739 / valuable / recipes / Breakfast dishes, soups, fish, meats and / poultry, cakes, pies, puddings, / fancy dishes, ice creams, / summer drinks, con- / fectionery, etc. [cover-title]
DESCRIPTION: 21.0 × 14.0 cm   Pp [1] 2–64   Paper; stapled
CONTENTS: 1–64 recipes
COPIES: OGU (CCC TX715.6 C364)   OKELWM ONLAM   *Private collection

1910

Fleischmann's booklet

For the titles of other books about cooking with Fleischmann's Yeast, see O131.1.

NP3.1   copyright 1910
Form No. 902, Rev. 1-'10. (12-'09) / Fleischmann's / booklet / Devoted to / the interests of / good baking / and containing / some valuable hints / pertaining thereto / Copyright 1910, by the Fleischmann Co. [cover-title]
DESCRIPTION: 15.5 × 11.0 cm   Pp [1–2] 3–18 [19]   Paper; stapled
CONTENTS: 1 cover-title; 2 'Do You Know That' signed 'The Fleischmann Co. Only successors to Fleischmann & Co. Original manufacturers, introducers and distributers in the United States and Canada of Fleischmann's Yeast' ; 3 'A Few Pertinent Remarks on the Subject of Good Bread and Yeast'; 4 'General Hints upon Baking with Fleischmann's Yeast'; 5–17 recipes; 18 '"Cup and Spoon" Measures'; 19 [inside back face of binding] 'Plain Facts'
COPIES: *Private collection
NOTES: No place of publication is recorded, but Canada is mentioned on p 2 as a country where the product is distributed. In the period 1909–10, the Fleischmann Co. had an office in both Toronto and Montreal, and a 'factory depot' in Montreal. An earlier Fleischmann cookbook (O131.1, 1903) was published in Toronto, according to British Library copyright records; in a later Fleischmann cookbook (Q87.1, copyright 1915), Montreal is the first-listed location for the company.

1912

A book for the cook

NP4.1   nd [about 1912]
Edwards' / Desiccated / Soup / – and all / about it / Made in / Ireland / A book for the cook. [cover-title]
DESCRIPTION: 12.5 × 8.5 cm   Pp 1–16   Illus on inside front and back faces of binding of publisher's Irish and English offices   Paper, with image on front of a woman carrying a covered soup tureen; stapled
CONTENTS: 1–3 'A Book for the Cook' [introductory text about Edwards' Soup]; 4–15 'Every-day Recipes'; 16 untitled text about Edwards' Soup
COPIES: *QMM (RBD ckbk 1529)

NOTES: The text on p 3 describes the three varieties of Edwards' Desiccated Soup: Brown, Tomato, and White. No place of publication is recorded in the volume, but the price of the soup packets is quoted in cents, not in British currency.

An advertisement for Edwards' Desiccated Soup in *Canadian Courier* Vol. 13, No. 2 (14 December 1912), p 40, refers to 'lots of dainty new dishes in our new cook book.' Although the title is not identified, the reference is likely to *A Book for the Cook*, the appearance of which is consistent with publication about that time. Advertisements for the soup in earlier issues (2 December 1911, 20 January 1912, and 23 March 1912) make no mention of a cookbook, confirming 1912 as the likely year of publication. The 14 December 1912 advertisement names three distributors of the soup: W.G. Patrick and Co., Toronto and Vancouver; Wm H. Dunn, Montreal; and Escott and Harmer, Winnipeg. The next month, in the new year, another advertisement for the soup repeated the reference to 'lots of dainty new dishes in our new cook book' (*Toronto Daily News* 24 January 1913, p 7).

1918

Win-the-war suggestions and recipes

NP5.1   nd [about 1918]
Win-the-war / suggestions / and / recipes / Sold for / the benefit of returned soldiers / Price 15 cents. [cover-title]
DESCRIPTION: Pp [1] 2–39   Paper
CONTENTS: 1–mid 9 introductory text and at bottom p 1, '31752–1'; mid 9–mid 34 recipes; mid 34–39 'Suggestions'
CITATIONS: PAC Pamphlets, Vol. II, No. 4435, p 374
COPIES: CIHM (80585)   *OONL (reserve, uncat)
NOTES: No author or place of publication is given, but the text is addressed to Canadian women and exhorts them to be economical so as to free up resources for the war effort. The introductory text begins, 'This is not a cookery book, only a few recipes and some sketchy hints to help those who want to do more towards economizing our food supply ... Food *must* be conserved; the Government *must* have our money; women *must* sacrifice their vanity, their mean self-indulgence and criminal selfishness on the altar of their country's safety.' The reference on p 38 to a population of 7,000,000 Canadians indicates the First World War period. The year of publication was likely 1918, as the following quotation indicates: 'Our loyal

neighbours [i.e., the Americans] have profited by our hopeful, but sadly mistaken and optimistic rulers, who so flattered us – and, with their usual push, have started right in at a point we have not yet reached after three and a half years' (August 1914 + 3½ years = 1918). PAC Pamphlets No. 4435 places the title with publications dated 1916.

Selections from the book are reprinted in *Ontario and the First World War 1914–1918: A Collection of Documents,* edited by Barbara M. Wilson, Toronto: Champlain Society for the Government of Ontario, University of Toronto Press, 1977, as D6, from p 124 onward.

1920–5

Home cooking suggestions

NP6.1   nd [about 1920–5]
Home cooking / suggestions [cover-title]
COPIES: *Private collection
NOTES: The Ontario owner reports that this 16-page booklet belonged to her husband's mother. She adds, 'Book doesn't s[ay] who its published by or any date.'

1922

New Royal cook book

For the titles of other Royal Baking Powder cookbooks, see Q71.1.

NP7.1   [copyright 1922]
New / Royal / cook book / Royal Baking Powder Co., / New York, U.S.A. / Made in Canada [cover-title]
DESCRIPTION: 20.5 × 13.0 cm   Pp [i–ii], [1–2] 3–49, [i]
Paper, with image on front of tea biscuits, pancakes, strawberry shortcake, and doughnuts; stapled
CONTENTS: Inside front face of binding untitled introductory text and 'Copyright, 1922, by Royal Baking Powder Co.'; i–ii 'Index to Recipes'; 1 publ ad; 2 'General Suggestions'; 3–49 recipes; i publ ad
COPIES: AEPMA AMHM ARDA AWWDM BSUM *NBFKL (Ruth Spicer Cookbook Collection) NSWA OBBM OGU (CCC TX715.6 N487) OTBPM OTMCL (641.5971 H39 No. 39) QKB (87-74) QMM (RBD ckbk 1978) SBIHM SSWD SWSLM
NOTES: *New Royal Cook Book* is advertised in the No-

vember 1922 issue of *Western Home Monthly.* The OTMCL copy is inscribed on the inside front face of the binding, 'Helen B. Sulman.'

AMERICAN EDITIONS: USA, [copyright 1920] (QMM); 1922 (Allen, p 145).

1925–30

Tried and tested recipes

NP8.1   nd [about 1925–30]
Adelaide / McLaurin Mission Circle / Tried and tested / recipes [cover-title]
DESCRIPTION: With silhouette on front of two women seated before a window, a cat at each side; stapled
COPIES: *OBUJBM (974.015.14i)
NOTES: There are no advertisements to help establish the place and date of publication. The book was donated to OBUJBM in 1974 by a woman from London, Ontario. The recipe for Shortbread (at the centre fold) specifies Five Roses Flour, a Canadian brand. Baking temperatures are given in the form of 'slow oven' or 'hot oven,' not degrees. It is possible that the Adelaide McLaurin Mission Circle was a Baptist organization because members of a McLaurin family were instrumental in the early development of the Baptist church in Canada; however, no reference to the Mission Circle was found in the Canadian Baptist Archives at McMaster University, Hamilton.

1927

Fowler, Arthur L. (1881–)

NP9.1   3rd ed., [copyright 1927]
Hang this book up in kitchen for handy reference / Fowler's blue book / of selected / household helps / and guide to / household economy / Brimful of "tried and true" helps about the / home, carefully compiled, classified and in- / dexed in convenient form for frequent use / Saves food, time and money / Third edition / revised and enlarged / With such a book of "helps" as this, / Housekeeping should not go amiss; / So, housewives, all – and others, too, / Prove how each "does its bit" for you. / Each "help" herein is "true and tried" / And some good housewife's honest pride – / Some home's delight; / Yet should your effort prove in vain; / We'll say not where to put the blame – / 'T were impolite! /

This booklet has some imitators, but no equals [cover-title]

DESCRIPTION: 21.5 × 14.0 cm   Pp [1] 2–64   Paper; stapled

CONTENTS: Inside front face of binding recipes; 1 'Introduction // Mrs. Housewife, everywhere:' signed 'A.L. Fowler, author and compiler // Published by Household Publishing Co. 214 West 34th Street, New York City, N.Y.,' warning about imitations, and 'Copyright, 1916, 1918, 1923, 1924, 1925, by A.L. Fowler Copyright, Canada, 1927, by A.L. Fowler (Printed in U.S.A.)'; 2–mid 23 'In the Kitchen'; bottom 23–top 25 'In the Sewing Room'; mid 25 'In the Bedroom'; bottom 25–mid 26 'In the Parlor'; mid 26–mid 27 'In the Bathroom'; mid 27–30 'In the Laundry'; 31 'Salads and Dressings'; 32 'Household Weights and Measures,' 'To Serve with Meats, Fish, etc.,' and 'How to Serve Potatoes'; 33 'Time Table for Baking,' 'Time Table for Cooking,' 'Time Table for Cooking Fish,' and 'Canning Time Table'; top–mid 34 continuation of 'Salads and Dressings'; mid 34–mid 35 'Sandwiches'; bottom 35–top 36 'Selected Candy Recipes'; mid 36–top 37 continuation of 'In the Laundry'; mid 37–near bottom 40 'To Remove Stains, etc.'; bottom 40–top 55 'Miscellaneous'; mid 55–62 'In the Sick Room // Also Miscellaneous Beauty Helps'; 63–4 index; inside back face recipes

COPIES: *Private collection

AMERICAN EDITIONS: *Fowler's Household Helps,* rev. ed., Albany, NY: Household Publishing Co., [c1918] (United States: DLC).

1930

Getting the most out of foods

NP10.1   [1930]
Getting the / most out of / foods [cover-title]
DESCRIPTION: 17.5 × 13.0 cm   Pp 1–32   Illus   Paper, with image on front of a woman holding a covered Pyrex casserole dish; stapled
CONTENTS: Inside front face of binding 'A Few Simple Rules That Will Give You a Lifetime of Service from Your Pyrex Glassware:' and 'Form B-29–200M 9-30 Canadian // Printed in U.S.A.'; 1–mid 2 'Oven Cookery Conserves the Nutritive Juices and Healthful Minerals of Foods'; mid 2–14 'Thirty Fuel-Saving Menus' [including cooking instructions]; 15–16 'Thousands of Women Tell Why They Prefer Pyrex Dishes for Baking and Serving'; 17–32 illustrations, descriptions,

and prices of various Pyrex products, including suggested cooking uses for them; inside back face 'Guarantee' and the printer's name, 'J.W. Clement Co., Buffalo'; outside back face 'Corning Glass Works // Corning, N.Y.'

COPIES: *OSMFHHM

NOTES: The text is printed in red and black.

1930–5

[Title unknown]

NP11.1   [about 1930–5]
[Title-page lacking?]
COPIES: Private collection
NOTES: A private collector reports in her possession a 108-page cookbook, lacking binding and title-page. A photocopy of p 101 shows a page of recipes for 'Candy' (Maple Cream, Turkish Delight, Fudge, Fudge Nougat, and Sea Foam); at top of page: 'Fine pastry – Made for King George and Queen Mary is made from Royal Household Flour. The Gourlie-Grenier Co.'; at bottom: 'Buy your groceries from the Gourlie-Grenier Co.' The recipes are credited with the name of the contributor; for example, J.L. Ross for Maple Cream and Turkish Delight; Mrs Jas Scott for Fudge Nougat, and Mrs Goodeve for Sea Foam. The reference to King George V and Queen Mary indicates a publication date during their reign, 1910–36. From the appearance of the photocopied page, the book was published about 1930–5. Royal Household Flour was made by Ogilvie Flour Mills Co. Ltd., Montreal.

1936

Herbert, Claire

NP12.1   copyright 1936
Time-tried / recipes / Compiled by / Claire Herbert / Copyright, Canada / 1936
DESCRIPTION: 19.0 × 12.5 cm   Pp [1–2] 3–27   Paper; stapled
CONTENTS: 1 tp; 2 'Index'; 3–27 recipes
COPIES: *OONL (TX715 H47 1936 p***)
NOTES: Most of the recipes are identified as from various counties in Britain. The majority are from Yorkshire, but there are also some from Cumberland, Lincolnshire, and Lancashire; some are labelled 'Scotch' or Aberdeen. The Cabbage Roll recipe is described as Greek; Rose-Hip Jam, as Swiss. There is a

Chutney described as a Manitoba recipe. Some recipes are credited with the initials S.S., M.B., C.S., L.S., or 'D.A. – Yorkshire.' The OONL copy is stamped on the outside back face of the binding 'The property of the Library of Parliament.'

103 ways to serve bread

NP13.1   copyright 1936
103 / ways to serve / bread / Published by / Canadian Bakers' Association / Copyright 1936
DESCRIPTION: 18.0 × 12.5 cm   Pp [1–4] 5–47 [48]   Illus   [$0.25, on binding]   Paper, with image on front of loaves of bread; stapled
CONTENTS: 1 tp; 2 illus of sliced and unsliced loaves of bread; 3 'Today ... Your Baker Offers ... Bread in Variety'; 4 'Seven Reasons Why You Should Eat More Bread'; 5–47 recipes; 48 index
CITATIONS: Rowe
COPIES: ACG   ARDA   BNEM   OGU (CCC TX715.6 O53)   OMIHURM   OONL (TX769 O54 1936)   *Private collection
NOTES: The title-page and text are printed in red and black. No place of publication is recorded. The ACG copy has 'National System of Baking Per [dotted line]' stamped on the title-page. Applied to the title-page of the BNEM copy is a slip of paper on which is printed 'With the compliments of Choquette Bros. [a bakery] Nelson – B.C. Phone 258.'

NP13.2   copyright 1936
—103 / façons de servir / le pain / Publication de / l'Association des boulangers du Canada / Droits réservés 1936
DESCRIPTION: 20.5 × 15.0 cm   Pp [1–4] 5–47 [48]   Illus   [Price on binding obscured by library label]   Paper, with image on front of loaves of bread; stapled
CONTENTS: 1 tp; 2 illus of sliced and unsliced loaves of bread; 3 'Aujourd'hui ... votre boulanger vous offre le pain sous formes variées'; 4 'Sept raisons pour lesquelles vous devriez manger plus de pain'; 5–47 recipes; 48 'Index'
COPIES: *OONL (TX715 C46)

1937

Watkins 1868 1937 almanac home book

For information about the J.R. Watkins Co. and its cookbooks, see M36.1.

NP14.1   1937
Watkins / 1868 / 1937 / almanac / home book [cover-title]
COPIES: *SSWD
NOTES: On the front face of the binding, there is an image of a girl watching her mother add Watkins flavouring to a bowl; on the outside back face, there is a 1937 calendar and 'Printed in Canada.'
   Allen, p 175, lists *Watkins Almanac and Home Book 1868–1936,* likely an American issue of the previous year.

1945

Hunt, Elma

NP15.1   copyright 1945
Elma Hunt's / cooking service / Salads / Copyright 1945, U.S.A. and Canada by Elma Hunt
DESCRIPTION: 14.5 × 11.0 cm   Pp [1] 2–32   [$0.35, on binding]   Paper, with portrait on front of the author(?); stapled
CONTENTS: 1 tp; 2 'Foreword'; 3–31 text; 32 'Index' [i.e., table of contents] and 'Copyright 1945, by Elma Hunt'
COPIES: *Bookseller's stock
NOTES: In the 'Foreword' the American author says she has been the owner/operator of a delicatessen, bakery, cafeteria, and tea room, a teacher of cookery, a caterer, and a newspaper columnist, writing under the pseudonym of Patsy Pantry. On the outside back face of the binding, there is a 'Complete List of Booklet [*sic*] to Be Published for Beginners ...'; *Salads* is the second of fifteen titles. Book orders were to be sent to Elma Hunt, PO Box 2227, Hollywood 28, California. 'Printed in U.S.A.' is also on the back face.

The modern hostess cook book for this season

NP16.1   [about 1945]

The modern hostess / cook book / for this season / 10¢ No. 2 / February / Hundreds of tested recipes – interesting m[eal]s / for / your budget, party and everyday winter meals [cover-title]

DESCRIPTION: 24.0 × 16.5 cm   [All leaves lacking] Paper, with images on front, in a circular frame divided by a fork and spoon into four sections; within each section there is a woman carrying out a kitchen task (serving, carrying groceries, mixing the contents of a bowl, carrying a steaming casserole)

COPIES: *Private collection

NOTES: 'Measurements and Temperatures' are on the inside front face of the binding.

1945–9

Choice recipes

NP17.1   nd [about 1945–9]

[Hand-lettered:] Choice / recipes [cover-title]

DESCRIPTION: Leaves of varying sizes, most about 17.5 × 14.0 cm   [14 unnumbered leaves with text on rectos only, leaves 12 and 13 lacking]   Paper; bound by cord through four holes

CONTENTS: One recipe on the recto of each leaf: I.C. Salad contributed by Miss Lynch and 'guaranteed by Dr. H.R. Casgrain'; Cucumber Salad contributed by Mrs P.A. Belleperche; Spaghetti a l'Italienne, Mrs V. Fenech; Fruit Salad, Mrs Mahoney; Devils Food Cake, Mrs J.O. Reaume; Boiled Frosting Sponge Cake, Mrs C.A. McIntosh; Marguerites, Mrs Bourke; Quick German Coffee Cake, Mrs Albert Drouillard; Horseshoe Soft Ginger-bread, Mrs J.C. Peters, Horseshoe Hotel; Christmas Cake, Mrs DeGurse; [2 leaves lacking]; A Dainty Dessert, Mrs A.J.E. Belleperche

COPIES: *OTNY (uncat)

NOTES: No place of publication is given, but the French and English names of the contributors suggest Quebec, Northern Ontario, or Manitoba. This is truly a 'homemade' cookbook: The recipes were typed by various persons (evident from the inconsistencies in style) and multiple copies made using carbon paper. The date of publication is uncertain.

1946

Your Philco Freezer

NP18.1   nd [about 1946]

Your / Philco / Freezer / How to prepare, freeze, / store and cook / frozen foods [cover-title]

DESCRIPTION: 22.0 × 14.5 cm   Pp 1–63 [64]   Illus Thin card, with image on front of an aproned woman carrying a covered platter; stapled

CONTENTS: 1 'Table of Contents'; 2–3 'A New Way of Life'; 4–13 'General Hints on the Use of Your Philco Freezer'; 14–15 'The Storage of Packaged Frozen Foods in Your Philco Freezer'; 16–23 'How to Freeze and Store Meat, Poultry and Fish in Your Philco Freezer'; 24–33 'How to Freeze and Store Vegetables in Your Philco Freezer'; 34–43 'How to Freeze and Store Fruits and Berries in Your Philco Freezer'; 44–7 'How to Freeze and Store Dairy Products in Your Philco Freezer'; 48–55 'How to Freeze and Store Baked Goods, Cooked Foods, Leftovers in Your Philco Freezer'; 56–61 'How to Thaw and Cook Frozen Foods from Your Philco Freezer'; 62–4 'The Operation and Care of Your Philco Freezer'

COPIES: *QMM (RBD ckbk 1909)

NOTES: 'Printed in U.S.A.' is on the outside back face of the binding. An extra, unpaginated leaf, glued to the gutter of p 5, reads: 'For Canadians // On pages 17 and 20 reference is made to the U.S. Department of Agriculture, Washington, D.C. Similar bulletins and information may be secured by writing the dominion Department of Agriculture, Ottawa; or the Department of Agriculture of the province in which you reside ...' The book is undated, but several illustrations show foods labelled with the date 15 May 1946, 10 July 1946, or August 1946.

Great Britain

1846

Cobbett, Mrs Anne, née Reid (1774–1848)

Anne Reid (called Nancy) spent part of her childhood in New Brunswick, when her father, Thomas Reid, a British artillery sergeant in the 54th Regiment, was stationed there. In 1787, at age thirteen years, she became engaged to William Cobbett (1763–1835), who at the time was stationed in New Brunswick with the same regiment as her father. Within six months of her engagement, her father returned to England with the family, including Anne. In 1891 William was able to return to England; he obtained a discharge from the army and married Anne, in Woolwich, on 5 February 1792. The couple had seven children. Anne never lived in the Maritimes again, but she passed through Halifax in June 1800, when she and William were en route from New York to England.

William was to become famous as a journalist and politician, whose radical views attracted controversy and forced the family to move several times. The first such instance was shortly after their marriage, when William took Anne to France to escape reprisals for trying to have his former officers court-martialled. The upheaval of the revolution in France soon led the couple to move to the United States. After thirteen months in Wilmington on the Delaware River, they settled in Philadelphia, Pennsylvania, in early 1794; then in New York, in 1797. In 1800 they returned to England. When, in 1817, William had to flee England again, for the United States, Anne went too, but only for about a year. In 1819, William made a final return to England, to join Anne.

Although William is best known for his Rural Rides *(London: 1830), cookbook collectors and food historians have a special interest in two books, in which he sought to persuade rural people to revive the self-sufficient ways of earlier times:* Cottage Economy: Containing Information Relative to the Brewing of Beer, Making of Bread, Keeping of Cows, Pigs, Bees, Ewes, Goats, Poultry and Rabbits, and Relative to Other Matters Deemed Useful in the Conducting of the Affairs of a Labourer's Family, *London: C. Clement, 1822; and* A Treatise on Cobbett's Corn ... and Also an Account of the Several Uses to Which the Produce Is Applied, with Minute Directions Relative to Each Mode of Application, *London: 1828. Anne's 'Instructions for Using Meal and Flour of Indian Corn' were added to later editions of* Cottage Economy *(for further details, see notes in the entry below).*

For an account of Anne as a person and as a good wife and mother, see George Spater, William Cobbett, the Poor Man's Friend, *2 vols, Cambridge University Press, 1982, pp 162–5; this is also the best source of information about Anne's and William's lives, and includes a silhouette of Anne made in Philadelphia in 1818 (p 374) and a painting of her in about 1830 (p 517). For a perspective on William in New Brunswick, see Wallace Brown's entry for William Cobbett in DCB, Vol. 6, pp 154–6, and his article 'William Cobbett in the Maritimes,'* Dalhousie Review *Vol. 56, No. 3 (Autumn 1976), pp 448–61. For the Cobbett family's life, as told by the eldest daughter, see* An Account of the Family, *by Anne Cobbett, William Cobbett Society, 1999.*

GB1.1 1846
[An edition of *Instructions for Using Meal and Flour of Indian Corn*, London: 1846]
CITATIONS: Arndt, p 109 (Sandra L. Oliver, 'William Cobbett')   MacFarlane, p 20
NOTES: In *New Brunswick Bibliography: The Books and Writers of the Province*, MacFarlane records *Instructions for Using Meal and Flour of Indian Corn*, by Mrs Ann Read [*sic*] Cobbett, London: 1846, and describes the work as 'the result of her New Brunswick experience.' Although MacFarlane records the title in a separate entry, without reference to any other work, no copy has surfaced of the text published on its own.

Anne Cobbett's 'Instructions for Using Meal and Flour of Indian Corn' is an additional section in posthumous editions of William Cobbett's *Cottage Economy*, which were published by the couple's eldest child, also called Anne (1795–1877). Morris

Leonard Pearl, in *William Cobbett: A Bibliographical Account of His Life and Writings*, London: 1953, and reprint, Greenwood Press, 1971, No. 115, pp 119–21, documents the following: fifteenth edition, published by Anne Cobbett (daughter), 1838 (Great Britain: LaOP); sixteenth edition, London: Anne Cobbett, 1843 (Great Britain: NtU(S)), seventeenth edition, London: Anne Cobbett, 1850 (OTU; Great Britain: LB); nineteenth edition, 'with recipes for using Indian Corn Meal in the Making of Bread, &c.,' London: Charles Griffin and Co., [1865?] (OTU); reprint of seventeenth edition, 'with an introduction by G.K. Chesterton,' London: Douglas Pepler, 1916 (Great Britain: BeRU, LoEN); 'with a preface by G.K. Chesterton,' London: Peter Davies, 1926 (OTU, 2 copies, and OTUTF; Great Britain: BeRU, OPo(F)). In 1979 the 1926 edition was reprinted by Oxford University Press (OTU).

MacFarlane's reference to an 1846 edition may be based on the heading for the added section (pp 201–17) in the seventeenth edition of *Cottage Economy*: 'Instructions for Using the Meal & Flour of Indian Corn, Published by the Late Mrs. Cobbett in 1846.' This heading and the common first name of mother and daughter may be the reason some twentieth-century sources incorrectly identify Mrs Cobbett as the publisher. The 'Publisher's Note' to the 1979 reprint, for example, states that the seventeenth edition (the text used for the 1979 reprint) was 'published by Cobbett's wife Anne in 1850,' but she had died in 1848. Also incorrectly, S.D. Scott, in 'William Cobbett,' *Acadiensis* Vol. 5 (1905), p 201, refers to the nineteenth edition thus: '[Anne] outlived her husband ... and when she had been a widow eleven years [i.e., in 1846], published an addition to his work on Cottage Economy, ...'

Anne must have had assistance in compiling her 'Instructions' because Spater, p 30, notes that she never learned to read or write. It is reasonable to assume that daughter Anne helped her mother. For years Anne, the daughter, had served as scribe to her father; she was the publisher of *Cottage Economy* and other of his titles, after his death; and at about the time that she took on the role of publisher, she herself wrote a household manual, *The English Housekeeper*, London, [183-?] (United States: DLC), which she published in several editions (Great Britain: WyLUB).

The extent to which Mrs Cobbett's 'Instructions' are based on her New Brunswick experience (as reported by MacFarlane) is an open question. In the first recipe, for Indian Corn Bread, she begins by referring to her 'residence in America, from 1792 to 1800.' This was the period, immediately after her marriage, when she and William moved to Philadel-

phia, then New York. Elsewhere in the text, she refers to customs in 'America' and in Italy, but she does not mention New Brunswick or Nova Scotia specifically, where she was first exposed to North American ways. Although at the time she was only a girl growing into womanhood, she would undoubtedly have gained some experience in New Brunswick kitchens, which, in the 1780s, were being transformed by Yankee cooking brought by the influx of Loyalists to the colony. Determining the degree to which her early life in New Brunswick influenced the 'Instructions' is a matter for culinary historians and falls outside the realm of bibliographical research.

Attar 46 records various editions of *Cottage Economy*, but incorrectly locates William Cobbett in Florida from 1784 to 1791.

1931

Bowker, Mrs Kathleen Kirkhoffer (15 October 1881–3 March 1958, St Thomas, Ont.)

The 1901 Census records Kathleen Kirkhoffer living in Brandon, Manitoba, with her parents, John N. and Clara. She contributed an article to Chatelaine *Vol. 8, No. 6 (June 1935). In the introduction to this issue of the magazine, the editor writes, under the heading 'She Makes Friends for Canada': 'Kathleen Bowker, who tells the story of Mrs. G. Howard Ferguson's responsibilities as wife of the Canadian High Commissioner, lives within walking distance of Westminster Abbey. She has made a name for herself as a Canadian woman who has done a great deal in "selling" Canada to England.' Her obituary in the Toronto* Globe and Mail *of 6 March 1958 refers to her as 'widow of Edward C. Bowker, formerly of Toronto and Montreal.' She is buried in Mount Pleasant Cemetery in Toronto.*

GB2.1 London, nd [about 1931]
The / maple leaf / Canadian / recipe book / Issued by the / Director of Canadian Trade Publicity, / British Columbia House. / 3, Regent Street, London, S.W. 1. / This book is printed on Canadian-made paper [cover-title]
DESCRIPTION: 19.5 × 13.5 cm Pp 1–72 Centre spread col, between pp 36 and 37, of prepared dishes within a maple-leaf border and the caption 'Canada // The Empire's larder'; photograph on p 1 of H.H. Stevens Paper, with image on front of autumn-coloured maple leaves against a blue background; stapled

CONTENTS: 1 'Message to the British Housewife' signed H.H. Stevens, minister of trade and commerce for Canada; 2 'The Author's Preface' signed Kathleen K. Bowker, British Columbia House, London; top 3 'Please Read This' [note about obtaining Canadian products]; mid 3–4 'The Can in Canada'; 5–8 'Canadian Canned Soup'; 9 'Fish from Canada'; 10–14 'Canadian Lobster, Salmon, and Chicken Haddie Recipes'; 15–19 'Canadian Canned Vegetables'; 20–4 'Canadian Macaroni // Canadian Shelloni // Canadian Baked Beans // Canadian Spaghetti in Sauce'; 25–8 'Canadian Ham – Bacon – Chicken – Canned Meats'; 29–36 'Canadian Cookery Section'; 37 'Canadian Apples'; 38–mid 40 'The Canadian Apple'; mid 40–44 'Canadian Apple Recipes'; 45 'Canadian Breakfast Foods'; 46–7 'The Modern Milk-Made // Canadian Condensed // Canadian Evaporated // Canadian Powdered Milk'; 48–9 'Canadian Honey'; 50 'Canadian Fruit Pectin'; 51–4 'Canadian Fruits – Bottled or Canned'; 55–60 'Canadian Scones, Bread, Cake'; 61–2 'Puddings and Pastry'; 63–4 'Pastry'; 65–7 'Sauces à la Canada'; 68–70 'Canadian Cheeses'; 71–2 'Canadian Cocktails and "Ceteras"' and at bottom p 72, the printer's name, 'Goddard, Walker & Brown, Ltd., Hull & London'

CITATIONS: Driver 2003, 'Canadian Cookbooks,' p 37 (publisher incorrectly cited)

COPIES: *Private collection; Great Britain: OPo(F)

NOTES: See pl 10. *The Maple Leaf Canadian Recipe Book* was first published in Britain to encourage British housewives to cook with Canadian products, then published later in Canada in response to demand for the book (GB2.4). On p 1 Herbert Stevens states, '[This book] is intended to provide several more links in the chain of distribution between the Canadian producer and the British consumer.' On the outside back face of the binding there is a list of Canadian government trade commissioners in the British Isles, and this copy is stamped, 'Canadian Trade Commissioner, 44 Ann Street, Belfast, N.I.' Most of the recipes are named after a Canadian place; for example, Athabasca Cookies, Halifax Half-Hour Jelly Roll, and Prince Albert Potato Cakes.

The book is undated; however, there is a recipe on p 71 for The '1931' Cocktail. A reference on p 39 to the first Fruit Mark Act confirms a publication date of about 1931: 'It is thirty years since Canada passed its first Fruit Mark Act [i.e., in 1901], making the grading of apples compulsory.' Stevens was minister of trade and commerce from August 1930 to December 1934; therefore, this edition could not have been published after 1934. This edition has no 'Index,' which suggests that it is earlier than those described below.

This edition is also differentiated by the address in the cover-title; here it is British Columbia House, 3 Regent Street, London, SW 1.

GB2.2   London, nd [about 1931–4]
—The / maple leaf / Canadian / recipe book / Issued by the / Director of Canadian Trade Publicity, / Canadian Building, / Blackburn Road, London, N.W. 6. / This book is printed on Canadian-made paper [cover-title]

DESCRIPTION: 19.5 × 13.5 cm   Pp 1–73 [74]   Illus on p 1 of H.H. Stevens   Paper, with image on front of autumn-coloured maple leaves against a blue background; stapled

CONTENTS: 1 'Message to the British Housewife' signed H.H. Stevens, minister of trade and commerce for Canada; 2 'The Author's Preface' signed Kathleen K. Bowker; i ad; top 3 'Please Read This' [note about obtaining Canadian products]; mid 3–4 'The Can in Canada'; 5–8 'Canadian Canned Soup'; 9 'Fish from Canada'; 10–14 'Canadian Lobster, Salmon, and Chicken Haddie Recipes' and ad; 15–19 'Canadian Canned Vegetables'; 20–4 'Canadian Macaroni // Canadian Shelloni // Canadian Baked Beans // Canadian Spaghetti in Sauce'; 25–8 'Canadian Ham – Bacon – Chicken – Canned Meats'; 29–36 'Canadian Cookery Section'; 37 'Canadian Apples'; i ads; 38–mid 40 'The Canadian Apple'; mid 40–44 'Canadian Apple Recipes'; 45 'Canadian Breakfast Foods'; i ad; 46–7 'Canadian Condensed // Canadian Evaporated // Canadian Powdered Milk' and ad; 48–9 'Canadian Honey'; 50 'Canadian Fruit Pectin'; 51–4 'Canadian Fruits – Bottled or Canned'; 55–60 'Canadian Scones, Bread, Cake'; 61–2 'Puddings and Pastry'; 63–4 'Pastry'; 65–7 'Sauces à la Canada'; 68–70 'Canadian Cheeses'; 71–2 'Canadian Cocktails and "Ceteras"'; 73 'Canadian Tobacco'; 74 'Index' [i.e., table of contents] and at bottom, the printer's name, 'Goddard, Walker & Brown, Ltd., Hull & London'

COPIES: *Private collection

NOTES: This edition has an 'Index,' and the address in the cover-title is Canadian Building, Blackburn Road, London, NW 6. The pages of advertisements are not included in the pagination.

GB2.3   London, nd
—The / maple leaf / Canadian / recipe book / Issued by / the High Commissioner for Canada / Canada House London S.W. 1 [cover-title]

DESCRIPTION: 21.0 × 14.0 cm   Pp [1] 2–68   Brown paper, with image on front of darker-brown maple leaves; stapled

CONTENTS: 1 unsigned 'Message to British House-

wives by the High Commissioner for Canada'; 2 'The Author's Preface' signed Kathleen K. Bowker, Canadian Building, Blackburn Rd, London NW 6; 3–4 'The Can in Canada'; 5–66 recipes; 67–8 'Index to Recipes'
COPIES: *Private collection
NOTES: This 68-page edition was issued by the high commissioner for Canada at Canada House, instead of the director of Canadian trade publicity.

GB2.4 Ottawa, nd [about 1932–4]
—The / maple leaf / Canadian / recipe book / Issued by / Department of / Trade and Commerce / Ottawa, Canada / Hon. H.H. Stevens / Minister / Jas. G. Parmelee / Deputy Minister [cover-title]
DESCRIPTION: 21.0 × 14.0 cm Pp 1–68 Portrait of H.H. Stevens on p 1 Paper, with abstract maple-leaf pattern on front; stapled, and with hole punched at top left corner for hanging
CONTENTS: 1 'Message to the Canadian Housewife' signed H.H. Stevens, minister of trade and commerce; 2 'The Author's Preface' signed Kathleen K. Bowker; 3–4 'The Can in Canada'; 5–66 recipes; 67–8 index
CITATIONS: Armstrong 2000, illus p F1 Ferguson/Fraser, p 234, illus col on p 80 of closed volume
COPIES: *Private collection
NOTES: Under the 'Message to the Canadian Housewife' on p 1, there is an additional note: 'The book was prepared originally for use in Great Britain, but so many requests for copies have been received from our own Dominion that it has been decided to issue a Canadian edition.' The Canadian edition was published after James G. Parmelee became deputy minister of trade and commerce in November 1931 (he held the position until September 1940), but not later than 1934, the last year that Stevens was minister of trade and commerce. The printer is on the outside back face of the binding: 'Printed by F.A. Acland, King's printer // Ottawa, Canada.' The colour illustration in Ferguson/Fraser is of the copy catalogued here.

1945–7

The Anglo-Canadian cook book

GB3.1 nd [about 1945–7]
The / Anglo-Canadian / cook book / Two shillings and sixpence [cover-title]
DESCRIPTION: 21.5 × 14.0 cm Pp [3–4] 5–48 Paper; stapled

CONTENTS: 3 'Index' [i.e., table of contents]; 4 blank; 5–47 recipes, including 'Seven Layer Dinner ($100.00 prize-winning recipe)' on p 23; 48 'Measurements'
COPIES: *Private collection
NOTES: No date or place of publication is recorded, and no publisher or sponsoring organization named; however, since the price is quoted in pounds sterling, *The Anglo-Canadian Cook Book* was probably published in Great Britain. The 'Measurements' text on p 48 appears to be directed at British cooks who must adapt to Canadian ways of measuring, likely 'war brides,' who had met and married Canadian servicemen during the war and were about to emigrate to Canada to begin a new life there. For example, detailed instructions are given for measuring dry ingredients, such as flour and sugar, by volume using the 8-ounce cup (instead of by weight, as in Britain). To stress the importance of the cup as the basic unit of measurement, 'The cup is equal to 8 ounces' is printed in bold type. At the foot of every recipe page, the reader is reminded to 'Read carefully comments on page 48.' The modest production of the book (plain grey paper binding) accords with the economic restrictions still in place in Britain after the end of the Second World War. The Canadian government offered free patriation to dependants of Canadian servicemen beginning in 1942, but most British war brides and their children emigrated between August 1944 and January 1947, travelling to Halifax, Nova Scotia, on ships organized by the Department of National Defence.

The Anglo-Canadian Cook Book is a rare example of a cookbook published outside of Canada that presents Canadian cooking to non-Canadian readers. The choice of recipes encompasses typical family fare and includes several meat casseroles, meat loaf, and egg dishes, Baking Powder Biscuits, Date and Nut Bread, Date Squares, Lemon Squares, Chinese Chews, Strawberry Shortcake (with the comment: 'Old-fashioned shortcake is always made with a biscuit mixture rather than cake.'), and such classic candy recipes as Divinity Fudge and Brown Sugar Fudge. There are also American recipes popular in Canada; for example, Rice Krispies (the cereal-and-marshmallow square first tested and published by the Kellogg Test Kitchen in Battle Creek, Michigan, in 1941, and which the company has called by various names over the years, such as Kellogg's Rice Krispies Treats in 2006), Club Sandwich, and Toll House Cookies (chocolate chip cookies). See also O1095.1; *Canadian Cook Book for British Brides*.

United States

1900

Helpful hints for Klondike gold hunters

US1.1   nd [about 1900]
Helpful hints / for / Klondike / gold hunters /
Tillmann & Bendel / importers, manufacturers,
wholesale grocers / 318–327 Battley St., San
Francisco / Established 1852 [cover-title]
DESCRIPTION: Pp [1] 2–24   Fp illus on pp 12–13 of
'Tillmann & Bendel's Establishments'; illus on pp 2
and 5 of cartoon bear digging and cartoon bear wield-
ing a pickaxe   With image on front of a cartoon bear
panning for gold
CONTENTS: 1 untitled note; 2 'To Prospective Miners'
signed Tillmann and Bendel; 3–4 'One Year's Supply
of Provisions'; 5 'As to Other Necessary Supplies'; 6–
mid 10 'A Few Simple Cooking Receipts'; bottom 10
'Weights and Measures for Cooks, etc.'; 11 'Percentage of Nutrition in Various Articles of Food'; 12–13 fp
illus; 14–17 'Medicinal'; 18–23 'Miscellaneous Useful
Information'; 24 'Pea Sausage // A Miner's Luxury'
COPIES: *YWA (pam nd-546, photocopy of MnHi copy);
United States: MnHi (Alexander Whyte papers, P1062)
NOTES: The booklet was published after the discovery
of gold in 1896, in what is now the Yukon Territory,
and the ensuing rush of prospectors to the area. The
note on p 1 comments, 'You cannot afford to take
inferior goods, whether in clothing or provisions, to
the far and frigid Klondike. It costs as much to transport chaff as grain.' Tillmann and Bendel's Pea Sausage is described on p 24 as 'a composition of pea
meal with bacon and potatoes, and finely seasoned
with the best spices'; it was Pea Soup in concentrated
form, 'made instantly by cutting slices into soup plates
or bowls, and pouring on boiling water.' The 'Medicinal' section includes a 'Cure for Drunkenness.'

Parsons, Miss Catharine E. (6 February 1876–)

*The title-pages of the 1907 and 1909 editions of her
cookbook are likely incorrect in giving the author's last
name as Parson. The earlier edition (US2.1) gives Parsons, and* Alma College: Centennial Book, 1877–1977
*(OSTT) lists Miss Parsons. She was on the faculty for
1900 only, according to the centennial history. The St
Thomas city directory for 1900 lists her as a teacher of
domestic science, resident at Alma College. The 1901
Census also gives the last name Parsons, records her birth
date, and describes her as an American, born in the
United States, lodging with Catharine and Robert I.
Warner.*

*I have not been able to confirm what may be a family
connection with Catharine D. Warner, née Parsons, the
wife of Alma College's principal (Robert Ironsides
Warner, on staff from 1881, principal from 1898 to
1919). Mrs Warner and her sister Mrs W.W. Smith were
the daughters of Robert Campbell Parsons (1829–1912)
and Sarah Jane Griffin. Robert Parsons also had a connection with Alma College; he was sub-treasurer from
1879 to 1881. After his superannuation in 1896, he spent
a year in California (possibly visiting his daughter since
Mrs W.W. Smith is described as of Ontario, California),
then he settled in St Thomas, as a member of Central
Church (Methodist). No connection could be found with
families called Parsons in South Bend, Indiana.*

*The Malleable Steel Range Manufacturing Co. was
founded in 1898 in South Bend. Canada was an important market for the company's products. The article
'Malleable Steel Range Co. Enjoys Rapid Growth to
Prominence since 1898,'* South Bend News Times
*23 February 1919, stated, 'The ranges now manufact-
ured are shipped to all parts of the world, but chiefly to
Canada.' The company was later renamed Southbend,
which in 2007 was a division of the Middleby Corp.*

US2.1   nd [about 1900]

Harry A. Engman, Jr., President / Irving A. Sibley, Vice-President / Wm. L. Kizer, Secretary / Jacob Woolverton, Treasurer / "The Malleable" / cookbook / Compiled by / Miss Catharine E. Parsons / Instructor of Domestic Science, Alma College, / St. Thomas, Ont. / Issued by / The Malleable Steel Range Mfg. Co. / South Bend, Indiana

DESCRIPTION: With image on front of a woman feeding coal to the range and a man raising a large mallet

COPIES: *Bookseller's stock

NOTES: This may be the first edition, perhaps issued during the one year that Catharine Parsons was a teacher at Alma College. Although all editions of the book were published in South Bend, Indiana, the author is described on the title-page as a teacher at an Ontario college, copies of all the editions described here have been found in Canada, and Canada was a major market for Malleable Steel Ranges. The bookseller reports that the volume has 80 pp and was printed by R.R. Donnelley and Sons of Chicago. This edition is almost square in format, in contrast to the 1907 and 1909 editions, which are taller and thinner. The first twenty-four pages are devoted to attributes of the range, pp 25–79 are recipes, and p 80 is an illustrated advertisement for the range. The text includes a one-page 'Announcement' signed the Malleable-Steel Range Mfg Co., South Bend, Indiana, which states that '"The Malleable" was placed on the market in response to a strong demand for a range which combines, with the "sterling" malleable construction, exquisite finish, and the latest and best modern improvements.' Opposite is a page headed 'Description,' which comments, 'Malleable iron is the very highest grade of gray iron, submitted, after casting, to an annealing process.'

US2.2   [copyright 1907]

—Kitchen / economy / comfort / cooking / Select cooking receipts compiled by / Miss Catharine E. Parson [sic], Instructor / of Domestic Science, Alma College, / St. Thomas, Ontario / Especially for / the Malleable Steel Range Mfg. Co. / South Bend, Indiana, U.S.A. / Harry A. Engman, Jr., Pres. Wm. L. Kizer, Sec. / J. Woolverton, Vice-Pres. and Treas. / The Cargill Co., printers, Grand Rapids

DESCRIPTION: 22.0 × 9.5 cm   Pp [1] 2–80   Illus brown Paper, with image on front of a woman, seated in front of a Malleable Range, reading a cookbook; stapled

CONTENTS: 1 tp; 2 'Copyright 1907 by the Malleable Steel Range Mfg. Co. South Bend, Indiana'; 3–5

'Kitchen Economy or, the Story of the Development of the Malleable Range'; 6–9 'A Few Reasons Why the Malleable Range Is the Best Range in the World'; 10–15 information about, and illus of, various models; 16–22 'Directions for Setting Up and Operating the Malleable Range'; 23–79 'Select Cooking Receipts'; 80 illus of '17 Piece Set of Kitchenware Complete'

COPIES: *MWPA   Private collection

NOTES: Despite the different title, this is likely another edition of The 'Malleable' Cook-Book, which has the same number of pages. The text on pp 3–5 describes the evolution of cooking devices, from an outside wood fire, to the Roman brazier, then an open fireplace, a fireplace with an oven, the old Hathaway, cast iron, and finally the Malleable Range (made from malleable iron and steel). The text and illustrations are printed in brown.

The private collector's copy is stamped, on the outside back face of the binding, 'H.S. Price, Boissevain, Manitoba.'

US2.3   [copyright 1909]

—Cook book / Select cooking receipts compiled by / Miss Catharine E. Parson [sic], Instructor / of Domestic Science, Alma College / St. Thomas, Ontario / Especially for / the Malleable Steel Range Mfg. Co. / South Bend, Indiana / U.S.A. / Harry A. Engman, Jr., Pres. Wm. L. Kizer, Secretary / J. Woolverton, Vice Pres. and Treas. / L.P. Hardy Co. Press, South Bend, Ind.

DESCRIPTION: 22.0 × 9.5 cm   Pp [1] 2–80   Illus brown Paper, with image on front of a woman carrying roast poultry on a tray, and behind her, a range in a heart-shape frame; stapled

CONTENTS: 1 tp; 2 'Copyright 1909 by the Malleable Steel Range Mfg. Co. South Bend. Indiana'; 3–5 'Kitchen Economy or, the Story of the Development of the Malleable Range'; 6–9 'A Few Reasons Why the Malleable Range Ranks First in the Heart of the Home'; 10–15 information about, and illus of, various models; 16–22 'Directions for Setting Up and Operating the Malleable Range'; 23–77 'Select Cooking Receipts Compiled Especially for the Malleable Steel Range Mfg. Co. South Bend, Ind.'; 78 illus of '18-Piece Set of High Grade Kitchenware'

COPIES: *MCDHM

NOTES: This is a retitled edition of Kitchen Economy Comfort Cooking. The cover-title is 'Cook Book // The Malleable Range made in South Bend ranks first in the heart of the home.' The text and illustrations are printed in brown.

US2.4   modern facsimile, nd

—Kitchen / economy / comfort / cooking / Select cooking receipts compiled by / Miss Catharine E. Parson [*sic*], Instructor / of Domestic Science, Alma College, / St. Thomas, Ontario / Especially for / the Malleable Steel Range Mfg. Co. / South Bend, Indiana, U.S.A. / Harry A. Engman, Jr., Pres. Wm. L. Kizer, Sec. / J. Woolverton, Vice-Pres. and Treas. / A.B. Morse Company, St. Joseph, Mich / [folio:] 1

DESCRIPTION: 21.5 × 9.0 cm   Pp 1–79   Illus   Very thin card, with image on front of a woman carrying roast poultry on a tray, and behind her, a range in a heart-shape frame; stapled

CONTENTS: 1 tp; 2 illus of the company's factory; 3–5 'Kitchen Economy or, the Story of the Development of the Malleable Range'; 6–9 'A Few Reasons Why the Malleable Range Is the Best Range in the World'; 10–15 information about, and illus of, various models; 16–22 'Directions for Setting Up and Operating the Malleable Range'; 23–79 'Select Cooking Receipts Compiled Especially for the Malleable Steel Range Mfg. Co. South Bend, Ind.'

COPIES: *Private collection

NOTES: There is no sign in the volume of the printer or publisher of this modern facsimile, or of the year it was printed, although it was offered for sale by an Omaha, Nebraska, book dealer in 2002. The facsimile is of an edition different from the three described above. The printer of the original edition, A.B. Morse Co. (named on the title-page), was in business in St Joseph in the period 1897 to 1918 (publications by Morse in St Joseph, in this span of years, are at DLC); however, the year 1898 on the binding may be a fabrication of the printer of the facsimile, not the actual date of the original edition. Unlike US2.2 and US2.3, there is no copyright date on p 2, but various aspects of the facsimile correspond to either (or both) of the 1907 and 1909 editions. The image on the binding is as US2.3, but the title on p 1 and the heading for pp 6–9 are as US2.2. The format is the same as both (tall and thin). Perhaps the year 1898 on the binding was meant as a reference to the founding year of the Malleable Steel Range Manufacturing Co.

1901

Watanabe, Shirō (1882–)

The Japanese author Watanabe also wrote on non-culinary topics (see, for example, his titles at DLC, in the United States).

US3.1   [3rd. ed., 1901]

An / English-Japanese / conversational / guide & cook book. / By / J.S. Watanabe. / [two columns of Japanese characters, giving the author's name, title, and 'expanded edition']

CITATIONS: Driver, Liz, 'An English-Japanese Cookbook for "Amerika"' in CHO No. 44 (Spring 2005), p 11   Nishimura, Sakuya, and Susan Michi Sirovyak, 'A Guidebook to Living in Canada – 1906 Style,' *New Canadian*, 28 June 2001, p E9, reprinted from *Nikkei Images* [Japanese Canadian National Museum newsletter] (Summer 2001)

COPIES: *BBJCNM (Mariko Kitamura Collection)

NOTES: Watanabe wrote *An English-Japanese Conversational Guide and Cook Book* for Japanese men immigrating to 'Amerika' – the Japanese term at the time for both Canada and the United States. Although most of the references to government offices and examples of workplaces are for California, especially San Francisco, there are references to Vancouver businesses on Georgia, Powell, and Robson streets, and to the temporary summer work of salmon fishing on the Fraser River. The BBJCNM copy was used in Canada by its original owner, Yotaro Kosaka, who emigrated from Japan in 1907, moving first to Hawaii, then settling in Vancouver in 1914.

The 554-page text is mainly in Japanese. One page has the imprint: The publisher's name is at the top, in the Roman alphabet: 'Domoto & Co. No. 1317, 26th St., Oakland, Cal.,' followed by the publisher's name and address in Japanese characters. Opposite the title-page, in Japanese characters, there is an 'Afterword' to the third, expanded edition, by Kyōsuke Ueda (born 1871), American Literature, Ph.D., dated spring 1901, in America. (The *New Canadian* article incorrectly gives the edition number as thirteen, and the date as 1906.)

The first section of the main body of the text presents lessons in the English language and covers conversation and correspondence on such important topics as communicating with immigration authorities, looking for employment, and buying groceries. The second section includes sample conversations for different jobs. The third section has recipes for cooking Western-style dishes, such as Mock Turtle Soup, Veal Croquettes, Scrambled Eggs, and Strawberry Short-Cake. The instructions are in Japanese, but the recipe names are in English. Watanabe provides three levels of recipes, for cooks of different abilities: the schoolboy; the half-day worker; and the all-day worker. There are menus for breakfast, lunch, and dinner, for a week.

I have not determined whether these other editions of *An English-Japanese Conversational Guide and Cook Book* have Canadian content: *Eigo kaiwa to shokugyō hen: katsuyō jizai: shintobeisha risshin no moto / Watanabe Shirō henjutsu*, Sōkō [Calif.]: Watanabe Shirō, Meiji 33 [1900] (United States: DLC); *Eigo kaiwa to shokugyō hen: katsuyō jizai = An English-Japanese Conversational Guide and Cook Book / Watanabe Shirō henjutsu*, Kaisei zōho, dai 11-han, Tokyo, Japan: Unteisha; San Francisco: Daihanbaijo Dōmoto Shōkai, Meiji 37 [1904] (United States: DLC).

1939

Renaud, Helena

US4.1   copyright 1939
The / Canadian home / cook book / By / Helena Renaud / Grosset & Dunlap / publishers / New York
DESCRIPTION: 21.0 × 14.0 cm   Pp [i–iv] v–x [xi–xii],

1–394   Tp illus of measuring spoons, 6 pls col incl frontis, 5 double-sided pls, 2 pls   Cloth, with image on front of measuring spoons
CONTENTS: i ht; ii blank; iii tp; iv 'Copyright, 1939, by Grosset & Dunlap, Inc. Printed in the United States of America'; v–viii table of contents; ix–x 'List of Illustrations'; xi 'The Canadian Home Cook Book'; xii blank; 1–372 text; 373–94 index
CITATIONS: CCat No. 19, p U16
COPIES: OONL   (TX715.6   R47   1939)   OTNY (uncat)   *Private collection; Great Britain: LB
NOTES: CCat records the price: $1.00. This is likely an American book, retitled for distribution in Canada.

AMERICAN EDITIONS: *The American Home Cook Book*, New York: Grosset and Dunlap, [copyright 1939] (United States: DLC); *The American Home Cook Book*, New York: Grosset and Dunlap, [copyright 1941] (United States: DLC); retitled *The Cook Book of the Stars*, New York: Windsor Editions, [1942] (United States: DLC).

Subject Index

The category 'General' is for books whose texts treat cooking in general and where no other classification could be assigned. There are many other cookbooks with general texts, which may be found under such headings as 'Community cookbooks,' 'Compendia,' or 'Household guides.'

    Advertising cookbooks are arranged by the product or business being promoted. A book that promotes, for example, the products of a cheese company and that uses cheese as an ingredient is listed under 'Advertising cookbooks, cheese.' The book is not listed again under 'Cheese' later in the index, so when searching for a particular subject, it may be useful to check both 'Advertising cookbooks' and other headings in the index. If the product or business being promoted is not the subject of the text, then there is one or more other listings for the book later in the index; for example, M87.1, Favorite Vegetable Recipes published by A.E. McKenzie Co. Ltd, seedsmen, is listed first under 'Advertising cookbooks, seed company' and later under 'Vegetables.'

O1018.1; Swift'ning O1120.1; Swift's Bakers'
Pastry Shortening O575.1; Vream O564.1,
O871.1
– Soap company NB6.1, NB10.1, NB15.1, Q24.1,
O35.6–35.7, O35.10, O71.1
– Soup: canned O744.1, O746.1, O1089.1, O1214.1;
desiccated NP4.1
– Soya bean products O951.1
– Spice company or association O1026.1, O1073.1,
O1141.1
– Stoves O324.4, O342.1, O488.1, O705.1, O889.1,
O1221.1, B24.1; coal O53.1, O645.1; Coleman
O838.1; electric Q256.1, Q256.6, O500.1, O585.1,
O601.1, O638.1, O645.2, O658.1, O671.1, O694.1,
O696.1, O781.1, O877.1, O886.1, O1053.1, O1132.1,
O1193.1 (*see also* Appliances, electric); gas Q256.2,
Q256.5, O53.1, O72.1, O162.1, O169.1, O200.1,
O322.1, O334.1, O645.3, O704.1, O1000.1; iron
O64.1, O172.1, O179.1, O283.1, US2.1; oil O164.1,
O409.1; wood O53.1, O645.1; *see also* Oven heat
controller
– Sugar Q97.1, Q107.1, Q108.1, O255.1, A69.1, A85.1,
A106.1, B8.1; brown Q98.1
– Syrup: maple Q121.1, Q152.1; Rogers' Golden
B45.1, B98.1
– Tapioca O717.1, O848.1
– Tea NB36.1 (Red Rose), O54.1, O1220.1
– Tea-Bisk: *see* Flour company, Maple Leaf
– Thermos bottles O626.1
– Tomato juice O708.1
– Utensil manufacturer O944.1; aluminium O429.1,
O606.1, O698.1, O807.1, O852.1, O1147.1, O1195.1;
enamelware Q126.1; Pyrex glass NP10.1; stainless
steel B120.1
– Vegetable mix, dehydrated B125.1
– Vinegar Q186.1, Q297.1, O612.1, O916.1, O1114.1
– Waxed paper O737.1, O1065.1, O1066.1
– Yearbook cookbooks B29.1
– Yeast Q87.1, Q103.1, Q124.1, Q150.1, Q231.1,
O131.1, O369.1, O514.1, NP3.1; extract (Marmite)
O680.1
– Zam-Buk [skin ointment] O248.1, O270.1, O361.1,
O396.1
Air force, cooking in O1078.1, O1094.1
Apples NS62.1, O323.1, O404.1, O496.1, O1093.1; *see
also* Advertising cookbooks, apples
Army, cooking in O356.1, O1078.1
Artists or cartoonists (professional, Canadian) as
illustrators of cookbooks: André Bieler Q314.1; Les
Callan B81.2; A. Helene Carter O468.1; A.J. Casson
O771.3–771.4, O1230.1; initials A.D. M8.7; Helen
Dickson (Cdn?) B46.1; Jim Frise O1171.1; Mrs
Edward Hart (likely Sarah Stewart Hart, teacher

of fine arts and crafts at Mount Allison University)
NB47.1; Marion Hooker M21.1; Frederick Palmer
Kirby NB39.1, NB41.1; Maida Knowles O927.1;
M.C. Perley (Cdn?) Q79.4; A.G. Racey et al. Q86.1;
Annie Louise Ricker NS67.1; Lorne Kidd Smith
Q221.1; Irene Tuzo Q314.1; Fraser Wilson B94.1,
B97.1, B114.1; Rex Woods Q306.1, Q308.1; V.C.
Wynn-Edwards Q314.1; as authors of cookbooks:
Kate Hill and Florence Seeley NS8.1; *see also*
Writers or journalists (Canadian) as cookbook
authors
Asparagus M31.1

Babies: breast-feeding: *see* S63.1; cooking for NB15.1,
Q10.1, Q11.1, O10.1, O876.1; preparing milk for:
see B62.1; *see also* Children, cooking for
Bachelor apartment, cooking in: *see* Cooking for
one
Baking Q166.1, Q176.1, Q191.1, Q214.1, Q247.1,
Q249.1, Q261.1, Q263.1, O25.1, O172.1, O369.1,
O821.1, O869.1, O895.1, O932.1, O1006.1, M36.1,
M138.1; *see also* Advertising cookbooks: Baking
powder, Baking soda, Flour company, Shortening,
Yeast; Bread; Cakes; Cookies
Baking, commercial/professional Q129.1, Q187.1,
Q205.1, Q209.1, Q268.1, O367.1, O374.1, O514.1,
O559.1, O564.1, O575.1, O951.1, O995.1, O1023.1,
O1198.1; *see also* Advertising cookbooks:
Nulomoline, Panomalt; Pastry chef, cookbook for
Beef ring: *see* Meat
Beets, sugar syrup from S69.1
Belgium, cooking of Q95.1
Beverages: *see* Drinks
Biscuits: *see* Advertising cookbooks, biscuit com-
pany; Cookies
Bread O389.1; brown Q105.1; cooking with Q103.1,
O765.1, A54.1, A91.1, NP13.1; war Q99.1, O380.1,
O399.1; yeast Q87.1, Q150.1, Q214.1, Q218.1,
Q220.1, Q243.1?, Q296.1, O41.1, O42.1, O236.1,
O321.1, O563.1; *see also* Advertising cookbooks,
yeast; Yeast
Breakfast: *see* Meals, breakfast
Bridal showers: *see* Weddings and bridal showers
Brides, cookbooks for NS67.1, O193.1, O476.1,
M60.1, B21.1, B43.1, B44.1, B74.1
Brides, war, cookbooks for NB57.1, O1095.1, GB3.1
Budgeting Q204.1, Q272.1, O389.1, O790.1, O875.1,
O949.1, O1004.1, O1020.1, O1224.1; *see also* Meal
planning, low-cost

Cakes Q131.1, Q150.1, Q215.1, Q264.1, Q308.1, O4.1,
O80.1, O173.1, O341.1, O436.1, O539.1, O773.1,
O860.1, O893.1, O895.1, O1186.1; commercial/

professional O787.1, O924.1, O1052.1, A21.1; *see also* Icing

Camp cooking: Q270.1; for Boy Scouts, Girl Guides O738.1, A74.1, B79.1; for lumber business Q238.1, O1206.1; for prospectors US1.1; recreational, for individuals Q132.1, O133.1, O534.1, O913.1, O1171.1; residential, catering for large groups O1127.1; *see also* Catering

Canada, cooking of [selection of books identifying themselves as Canadian, compiled in Canada or by a Canadian; does not include American books retitled as 'Canadian'] Q2.1, Q3.1, Q6.1, Q62.1, Q162.1, Q177.1, Q292.1, O5.1, O6.1, O9.1?, O34.1, O35.1 (later editions called 'dominion' or 'new Canadian'), O43.1, O54.1, O190.1, O469.1, O479.1, O506.1, O1146.1, NP2.1?, GB2.1, GB3.1

Canada, cooking of Lower Q3.1; of Upper O2.1

Canada, early food history Q287.1, O622.1

Candy-making: home Q47.1, Q153.1, Q185.1, O56.1, O206.1, O302.1, O306.1, O307.1, O375.1, O473.1, O607.1, O1186.1; professional O74.1, O157.1, O237.1, O618.1

Canned fruits and vegetables, cooking with: *see* Fruit; Vegetables

Canning [i.e., preserving food, such as fruit, vegetables, meat, and soup, in glass jars; books about canning sometimes also include sections for other types of preserving, such as jams or pickles] Q96.1, Q154.1, Q184.1, Q212.1, Q310.1, O376.1, O402.1, O429.1, O449.1, O495.1, O654.1, O846.1, O1010.1, O1087.1, O1151.1, O1163.1, O1222.1, M114.1, A32.1, A36.1, A83.1, B106.1, B115.1, B129.1, B140.1; cold-pack method M26.1; in reformatories O573.1; *see also* Advertising cookbooks, pressure canners; Fruit, canned, cooking with; Preserving and canning; Vegetables, canned, cooking with

Catering O1023.1, O1078.1, O1187.1, O1220.1; *see also* Air force, cooking in; Army, cooking in; Camp cooking; Navy, cooking in; Tourism, cookbooks for the trade

Cereal, breakfast, cooking with O222.1, O242.1, O521.1

Champlain, Samuel de, Order of Good Cheer O622.1

Cheese: cooking with Q137.1, O477.1, O926.1, O1150.1, A104.1 (*see also* Advertising cookbooks, cheese); making Q68.1, M28.1, M40.1, A104.1

Chefs, male, in Canada: *see* Men

Chicken: *see* Poultry

Children, cooking for O857.1, O876.1, O931.1, O1047.1; *see also* Babies, cooking for; Meals, lunch: for schools, for rural schools, lunch boxes

Children and young people, cookbooks for O948.1, O1048.1, O1056.1, O1161.1, M67.1, B46.1

China, cooking of: *see* O610.1, B13.1

Chinese Canadians, cooking of A116a.1

Christmas, cooking for O831.1, M102.1, B138.1; *see* pp 277, 555, NF5.4, NS37.2, NB4.1, Q65.1, Q79.4, Q216.4, Q237.1, Q242.1, O20.1 (p 323), O46.1, O234.1, O262.1, O440.2, O610.1, O627.3, M15.1, S116.1, A28.3, A65.1, A76.1, A95.1, A105.1, A108.1, B26.1, B27.1, B53.1, B82.1, B124.1, NP17.1

Christmas, Ukrainian A95.1

Christmas presents, cookbooks as O154.1, O168.1, O196.1, O202.1, O257.1, O420.1, O506.1, O528.7, O529.1, M17.1, M47.1, M49.1, S23.1, S36.1, S92.1, A76.1

Christmas pudding, mock recipe S32.1

Clippings, books for: *see* Manuscript cookbooks

COMMUNITY COOKBOOKS [Arranged by compiling organization or organization represented by the author, not necessarily by the beneficiary of funds raised]

– [Organization unknown or uncertain] NS61.1, O177.1, O226.1, O254.1?, O312.1, O427.1, O667.1, O957.1, M13.1, S2.1, S54.1, A13.1, A42.1, B14.1, B73.1, NP11.1

– [No named organization, often attributed to 'ladies of' a town] NB2.1, Q70.1, O67.1, O83.1, O121.1, O123.1, O167.1, O279.1, O434.1, O621.1, O967.1, M18.1, A73.1, A116.1, B108.1, NP17.1; *see* O130.1

– [No organization, compiled by Grace Clergue Harrison and Gertrude Clergue from contributed recipes, for war relief] Q95.1

– [Several organizations in one book] NS24.1, NB31.1, NB37.1 (Catholic), NB45.1 (hospitals)

– Ancient Arabic Order of the Nobles of the Mystic Shrine Q240.1, S81.1

– Association: Arrow Lakes Agricultural and Industrial B50.1; Big Sister O549.1; Brandon Graduate Nurses M38.1; Columbus Ladies' NF6.1; Glenmore District A113.1; Great War Veterans S21.1; Hamilton Home Economics O1231.1; Ladies' Orange Benevolent O1144.1, M112.1, S47.1, B57.1; Montreal Amateur Athletic Q142.1; Sons of Scotland Benevolent M78.1; Ward 2 Patriotic, Toronto O398.1; Young Men's Christian, Ladies' or Women's Auxiliary NS70.1, O161.1, O210.1, O247.1; Young Women's Christian O203.1, O686.1, O990.1

– Benevolent and Protective Order of Elks, Order of the Royal Purple S112.1, A81.1, A110.1, B69.1

– Bishop Gray Convalescent Home, Edmonton A122.1

M26.1, M27.1, M28.1, M31.1, M32.1, M40.1, M42.1, M50.1; Manitoba Agricultural College M34.1; Mines and Natural Resources M114.1

– New Brunswick, Agriculture NB57.1
– Newfoundland, Agriculture and Rural Reconstruction NF9.1
– Nova Scotia: Agriculture NS41.1; Highways NS46.1, NS50.1; Land Settlement Board NS53.1
– Ontario: Agriculture O158.1, O236.1, O379.1, O380.1, O413.1, O414.1, O446.1, O516.1, O692.1, O1010.1, O1019.1, O1222.1, O1223.1, O1224.1, O1229.1; Education O364.1; Provincial Secretary O573.1
– Prince Edward Island P6.1
– Quebec: Agriculture Q48.1, Q68.1, Q74.3, Q96.1, Q99.1, Q109.1, Q123.1, Q137.1, Q184.1, Q220.1, Q251.1, Q259.1; Colonization, Game and Fisheries NS27.4–27.6; Roads Q162.1
– Saskatchewan: Education S19.1, S27.1; Natural Resources and Industrial Development S101.1

Great Britain, cooking of [books that specifically refer to the cooking of Great Britain in the title or text] Q51.1, Q95.1, O317.1, O1099.1, NP12.1; *see* O610.1; *see also* England, cooking of ('British editions' recorded at the end of an entry generally represent British cooking if the work was compiled in Britain.)

Hallowe'en, cooking for: *see* Q237.1, O184.1, O262.1, O610.1, B124.1
Herbs, cooking with O571.1; *see* O934.1, M121.1; *see also* Spices and seasonings
High-class cooking NB13.1, O184.1
Home economics NB54.1, NB63.1, O528.11–528.15, O751.1, O1090.1, O1170.1, M37.1, S27.1, S28.3–28.4, B28.1, B59.1; *see also* Domestic economy, Domestic science, Household management, Household science, Scientific cooking, Systematic cooking
Honey, cooking with Q109.1, O158.1, O819.1, M109.1, A97.1; *see also* Advertising cookbooks, honey; Sugar, saving in wartime; Wartime cooking
Hors-d'oeuvres O952.1
Hotels, cooking in: *see* Tourism, cookbooks for the trade
Household exhibition, Toronto O384.1
Household guides or manuals NB4.1, NB5.1, NB17.1, O5.1, O16.1, O17.1, O18.1, O24.1, O37.1, O38.1, O39.1, O46.1, O55.1, O59.1, O70.1, O110.1, O132.1, O216.1, O339.1, O348.1, O488.1, O520.1, O927.1, M35.1, S67.1; for farms M10.1, M39.1, NP9.1
Household hints O870.1, O1091.1, O1097.1, O1219.1, M77.1; *see also* Advertising cookbooks, vinegar
Household management O364.1, O388.1; *see also* Domestic economy, Domestic science, Home economics, Household science, Scientific cooking, Systematic cooking
Household science Q275.1, Q276.1, O86.2–86.3, O126.1, O241.1, O410.1, O528.1–528.10, M98.1, S19.1, S28.1–28.2, A38.1; *see* S27.1; *see also* Domestic economy, Domestic science, Home economics, Household management, Scientific cooking, Systematic cooking
Housekeeping: *see* Household guides or manuals

Ice-boxes, recipes for O555.1; *see also* Frozen dishes
Ice-cream making, professional O237.1
Icelandic Canadians, cooking of M54.1
Icing Q205.1, Q215.1; commercial/professional O871.1
Illustrated cookbooks: *see* Artists or cartoonists
Immigrants, cookbooks for O5.1, O469.1, M127.1, M128.1, S97.1, A34.1, US3.1; *see also* Brides, war, cookbooks for; German-language cookbooks; Ukrainian-language cookbooks
Infants: *see* Babies
International cooking [i.e., books about national cuisines] Q257.1, O212.1, O320.1, O641.1, O1137.1, B139.1 (*see* A105.1, B13.1); *see also* 'Foreign recipes'
Invalid cooking Q10.1, Q11.1, Q35.1, Q56.1, Q69.1, Q161.1, O36.1, O78.1, O129.1, O180.1, O443.1, O857.1, O1098.1
Italy, cooking of Q95.1, O1190.1

Jams, jellies, and marmalades Q108.1, Q157.1, O355.1, O429.1, O480.1, O491.1, O600.1, O608.1, O714.1, O721.1, O753.1, O835.1, O905.1, O1068.1; *see also* Canning; Preserving and canning
Japanese-language cookbooks US3.1
Jewish cooking NS68.1, NB58.1, Q127.1, Q319.1, O337.1, O627.1, O1051.1, O1138.1, M73.1, M74.1, M79.1, M81.1, M95.1, M106.1, M111.1, M119.1, M122.1, M123.1, M124.1, M126.1, M131.1, M135.1, S53.1, S89.1, S107.1, A114.1, A115.1, B67.1, B141.1; *see* Q7.1, A95.1, p 621

Kitchen, ideal O148.1, O488.1
Kitchenette, cooking in O382.1
Klondike, cooking in US1.1

Land settlement for unemployment relief, cookbooks for NS53.1
Left-overs, cooking with O361.1, O737.1, O1065.1; *see also* Economical cooking
Lobster O996.1
Lunch: *see* Meals, lunch

Magazine cookbooks [i.e., produced by staff of magazine] Q291.1, O257.1, O610.1, O887.1,

O1219.1, M35.1, M39.1, M67.1, M70.1, M99.1; *see also* Newspaper cookbooks

Manuscript cookbooks [for the purpose of this index, printed volumes designed for handwritten recipes or clippings] NS67.1, Q9.1, Q51.1, O510.1, O772.1, O892.1, M99.1

Maple sugar, cooking with Q109.1; *see also* Advertising cookbooks, syrup, maple

Maritime provinces, cooking of Q258.1, O531.1

Marketing [i.e., buying food for home cooking] O619.1, O631.1, O776.1, O790.1, O1004.1, O1005.1, O1020.1

Marmalades: *see* Jams, jellies, and marmalades

Meal planning O304.1, O338.1, O516.1, O619.1, O776.1, O780.1; low-cost Q204.1, Q272.1, O631.1, O664.1, O949.1, O1004.1, O1020.1, M107.1, A111.1; *see also* Entertaining

Meals: breakfast O111.1, O182.1 (*see also* Advertising cookbooks: Cereal, Oatmeal); dinner Q80.1, Q279.1, O22.1, O139.1, O183.1, O440.1; lunch O115.1, O125.1, O183.1, O437.1, O626.1, O952.1; lunch boxes O1065.1; lunch for rural schools S19.1, A37.1; lunch for schools S27.1 (*see* O485.1, O583.1, O770.1); picnic O626.1; snack O978.1, M138.1; supper Q233.1, Q279.1, O184.1, O437.1, O952.1, B85.1; tea NB36.1, O182.1, O437.1, O854.1, O1220.1; *see also* Railway dining

Measurements (different national practices) Q156.1, O935.1 (pp 46–9), GB3.1

Meat: beef ring M42.1; butchering M129.1; butchering pork M88.1; carving Q126.1; cooking Q126.1, O703.1, O791.2–791.5, O881.1, O886.1, M34.1, B116.1; cooking beef O679.1; cooking offal O400.1, O849.1; cooking pork A77.1; cooking with canned M125.1; cooking with cured M88.1; curing M42.1, M129.1; freezing O1019.2; saving in wartime Q99.1, O400.1, O1066.1, A30.1; substitutes M34.1; *see also* Advertising cookbooks: Liquid smoke, Meat cure, Meat packer

Men, cooking for O975.1

Men, professional Canadian cooks, as authors NB13.1, Q67.1, Q166.1, Q235.1, O25.1, O1078.1; as recipe contributors Q95.1, O641.1

Men's culinary writing, humorous O133.1, O204.1 (captions to illustrations by men?), O422.1, O1171.1

Menus Q195.1, Q204.1, Q237.1, Q253.1, Q299.1, O22.1, O46.1, O234.1, O262.1, O316.1, O357.1, O362.1, O370.1, O440.1, O513.1, O631.1, O790.1, O805.1, O845.1, O876.1, O931.1, O949.1, O1111.1, O1128.1, M91.1, B85.1; *see also* Meal planning; Meals

Mexico, cooking of: *see* O610.1, O1032.1

Military cooking: *see* Air force; Army; Navy

Milk: artificial human O10.1; cooking with O478.1, O590.1, O676.1, O953.1; *see also* Advertising cookbooks, milk

Movie stars, recipes of O866.1

Native cooking, Iroquois O371.1

Navy, cooking in O997.1, O1078.1, O1152.1, O1175.1; *see* O1023.1

New Brunswick, cooking of NB47.1

Newspaper cookbooks [produced by a newspaper, sometimes as a supplement to the newspaper; not books printed by a newspaper for another author] NS5.1, NB28.1, Q292.1, O139a.1, O202.1, O316.1, O569.1, O572.1, O830.1, O902.1, O903.1, O927.1, O965.1, O1051.1, S57.1; Cornwall Freeholder O749.1, O1025.1, O1044.1, O1072.1; Daily Province B86.1, B104.1, B117.1, B122.1, B138.1; Family Herald Q66.1, Q125.1; Vancouver Sun B81.1, B82.1, B94.1, B97.1, B99.1, B103.1, B110.1, B114.1, B119.1, B124.1, B128.1, B129.1, B133.1, B139.1, B140.1; Winnipeg Free Press M80.1, M90.1, M94.1, M101.1; Winnipeg Telegram M10.1; Winnipeg Tribune M91.1, M104.1; *see also* Magazine cookbooks

Norwegian Canadians, cooking of: *see* Scandinavian Canadians

Novelists: *see* Writers or journalists (Canadian) as cookbook authors

Nutrition NS56.1, P8.1, Q161.1, Q204.1, Q272.1, Q283.1, Q299.1, O271.1, O362.1, O365.1, O619.1, O631.1, O949.1, O1004.1, O1020.1, O1080.1, O1128.1, M107.1, A98.1, B112.1; *see also* Food and health; Food as medicine

Offal: *see* Meat, offal

Outdoor cooking: *see* Camp cooking

Oven cooking O566.1, O591.1, O779.1; *see also* Whole-meal cooking

Paper-bag cooking O290.1

Parties: *see* Entertaining

Pastry chef, cookbook for O1188.1; *see also* Baking, commercial/professional

Pickles O60.1, O325.1, O721.1, M50.1; *see also* Advertising cookbooks, vinegar; Preserving and canning

Picnic: *see* Meals, picnic

Pies and pastry Q219.1, Q266.1, Q308.1

Poetry, original, written for a cookbook NS1.1, NS29.1, NS30.1, NS32.1, NS38.1, NS66.1, NB53.1, NB57.1, Q41.1?, Q131.1, O28.1, O296.1, O308.1, O421.1, O458.1, O629.1, O746.1, O994.1, O1042.1, A25.1, A45.1, A57.1, A92.1

Porridge Q190.1; *see also* Advertising cookbooks, oatmeal

Potatoes M27.1

Poultry Q259.1, O412.1

Preserving and canning Q75.1, Q107.1, Q157.1, Q212.1, O60.1, O109.1, O325.1, O379.1, O415.1, O424.1, O429.1, O599.1, O1041.1, O1068.1, O1074.1, M50.1, M96.1, M113.1, M129.1, A72.1, B25.1, B49.1, B107.1, B117.1, B118.1; *see also* Advertising cookbooks, vinegar; Canning; Drying food; Fermenting vegetables; Freezing food for preservation; Fruit, canned; Jams, jellies, and marmalades; Pickles; Salting vegetables; Storing food; Vegetables, canned

Pressure cookers, cooking with B128.1; *see also* Advertising cookbooks, pressure cookers

Printers, nineteenth century, as cookbook compilers NB3.1, O6.1

Puddings Q216.1, O173.1, O238.1

Quebec, cooking of [books that specifically refer to the cooking of Quebec in the title or text] Q222.1, Q235.1, Q287.1, Q314.1

Radio cookbooks [associated with radio shows] O558.1, O633.1, O737.1?, O828.1, M132.1, M136.1, A92.1

Railway dining Q112.1

Raisins and currants, cooking with O879.1

Ranges: *see* Advertising cookbooks, stoves

Rationing: *see* Wartime rationing

Recipe clippings, books for: *see* Manuscript cookbooks

Recipes, low-cost: *see* Meal planning, low-cost

Refrigerators, preparing food with: *see* Advertising cookbooks, refrigerators

Reprints and facsimiles, modern NS9.2, NB15.4, NB31.2, P3.1?, P5.1, Q3.12, Q53.3, Q55.19–55.21, Q79.6, Q112.1, Q177.3, Q204.2, Q292.2, of O5.3 (p 299), O20.49–20.52, O55.2, O58.6–58.7, O70.14–70.15, of O124.1 (p 423), O169a.1, O241.6, of O371.1 (p 545), O394.2, O1031.2; of O1095.1 (p 872), S16.3, S23.2, S118.2, A7.2, B5.3, B143.1, NP1.1, US2.4

Royal jubilee cookbooks: Queen Victoria P1.1, O83.1; George V Q227.1, O855.1, O856.1; *see also* Coronation cookbooks

Royal visit cookbooks (King George VI and Queen Elizabeth to Canada in 1939) Q258.1, O974.1, S80.1; *see also* Coronation cookbooks

Royalty, cooking for: *see* Q258.1, O977.1

Russia, cooking of Q95.1

Salads Q167.1, Q185.1, Q244.1, Q298.1, O305.1, O439.1, O446.1, O493.1, O711.1, O718.1, O791.1, O809.1, O934.1, O1223.1, NP15.1; *see also* Advertising cookbooks: Gelatine, Jell-O, Vinegar

Salting vegetables O414.1

Sandwiches Q244.1, O305.1, O438.1, O576.1, O840.1

Scandinavian Canadians, cooking of O983.1

Scientific cooking O335.1, O635.1; *see also* Domestic economy, Domestic science, Home economics, Household management, Household science, Systematic cooking

Scotland, cookbooks of Q4.1

Scottish Canadians, cooking of M78.1

Seasons, cooking for: all O935.1; summer O57.1, A78.1; winter NP16.1

Settlers: *see* Immigrants; Land settlement; Soldier settlement

Seventh Day Adventists, cooking of O431.1, O664.1

Shellfish: *see* Lobster

Sickroom cooking: *see* Invalid cooking

Snack: *see* Meals, snack

Soda fountain, recipes for O157.1

Soldier settlement, cookbooks for O661.1

Souvenir cookbooks with images of local scenes and people: Grand Pre NS52.1; Sutton Q41.1; Cobalt O204.1, O519.1; Essex O176.1; Fort William O1136.1; Hamilton O620.1; Kirkland Lake O912.1; Winnipeg, Jewish community M73.1, M74.1, M79.1, M81.1, M95.1, M106.1, M111.1, M119.1, M122.1, M123.1, M124.1, M126.1, M131.1, M135.1; Rossland B131.2; *see also* Tourism, cookbooks for the public

Spices and seasonings, cooking with: *see* Advertising cookbooks: Seasoning sauces, Spice company or association; Herbs, cooking with

Storing food O376.1, O402.1, O495.1; vegetables M103.1

Sugar, cooking with: *see* Advertising cookbooks, sugar

Sugar, saving in wartime Q278.1, O1055.1, O1058.1, O1069.1, M109.1, A30.1, B33.1

Sugar-beet syrup, recipe for, and cooking with S69.1

Summer cooking: *see* Seasons

Supper: *see* Meals, supper

Swedish Canadians, cooking of: *see* Scandinavian Canadians

Systematic cooking Q156.1; *see also* Domestic economy, Domestic science, Home economics, Household management, Household science, Scientific cooking

Tea: drink (*see* Advertising cookbooks, tea); meal (*see* Meals, tea)

Temperance cooking O49.1, O970.1, B18.1; *see also* Community cookbooks: Woman's Christian Temperance Union, Women's Temperance Auxiliary

Place-of-Publication Index

In the case of a title with a run of editions that are all published in the same place, the index lists only the entry for the first or earliest known edition. In the case of a run of editions where subsequent editions were published in other places (in the same province or outside the province), the index usually also lists entries for those other places; for example, O20.5–20.6, O20.8, for the Saint John, New Brunswick, editions of The Home Cook Book, *first published in Ontario. For cookbooks where the title-page records corporate offices in more than one city, the first-recorded city is generally taken as the place of publication. The index does not list places of publication for facsimiles or other editions published after 1949.*

Fort St John B113.1
Ganges B75.1
Hollyburn: *see* Vancouver
Kamloops B9.1, B31.1, B34.2, B126.1
Kaslo B36.1
Kelowna NB35.4, B24.1, B52.1, B91.1, B115.1
Kerrisdale: *see* Vancouver
Ladner B19.1
Nakusp B50.1, B101.1, B143.1
Nanaimo B60.1, B68.1
Nelson B22.1, B54.1, B85.1
New Westminster NB35.2, B63.1, B111.1
North Vancouver B83.1
Powell River B108.1
Prince George B95.1, B127.1
Prince Rupert B69.1
Revelstoke B80.1, B136.1
Richmond B71.1
Rossland B34.1, B131.1
Sidney B64.1
South Vancouver: *see* Vancouver
Summerland B38.1
Trail B123.1
Vancouver (incl Hollyburn, Kerrisdale, South Van-
 couver) O119.5, O773.14, B1.1, B2.1, B8.1, B10.1,
 B12.1 (South Vancouver), B13.1, B16.1, B18.1, B21.1,
 B21a.1, B26.1, B27.1, B29.1, B30.1, B32.1, B39.1,
 B41.1, B42.1, B44.1, B45.1, B47.1 (Kerrisdale), B48.1,
 B51.1, B53.1 (South Vancouver), B57.1, B61.1, B62.1,
 B65.1, B66.1, B67.1, B72.1, B73.1, B74.1, B76.1, B79.1,
 B81.1, B82.1, B84.1, B86.1, B87.1, B88.1, B89.1, B90.1,
 B92.1, B93.1, B94.1, B97.1, B98.1, B99.1, B103.1,
 B104.1, B106.1, B110.1, B112.1, B114.1, B117.1,
 B119.1, B120.1, B122.1, B124.1, B128.1, B129.1,
 B130.1 (Hollyburn), B133.1, B137.1, B138.1, B139.1,
 B140.1, B141.1, B142.1; *see also* North Vancouver
Vernon B46.1, B77.1, B78.1, B125.1
Victoria O130.7, O773.4, B3.1, B4.1, B5.1, B6.1, B7.1,
 B11.1, B13.2, B15.1, B20.1, B23.1, B25.1, B28.1,
 B33.1, B37.1, B40.1, B43.1, B49.1, B55.1, B59.1,
 B96.1, B100.1, B109.1, B121.1, B132.1; *see also*
 O48.19
Westbank B56.1

Manitoba

Brandon O773.13, O776.11, M3.1, M14.1, M38.1,
 M87.1
Crandall M100.1
Crystal City M137.1
Dauphin M18.1
Deleau Q224.2
Dropmore M113.1
Dugald M61.1

East Kildonan: *see* Winnipeg
Elm Creek M133.1
Erickson O1055.2
Flin Flon M143.1
Fort Garry M140.1
Fort Rouge: *see* Winnipeg
Foxwarren M17.1
Greenway M110.1
Hartney M13.1
Lake Max M115.1
Minnedosa M20.1
Moline M66.1
Morden M142.1
Neepawa M5.1, M43.1
Norwood M23.1, M41.1
Point du Bois M84.1
Portage la Prairie M6.1, M7a.1
Ranchvale M47.1
Reston M24.1
Roblin M92.1
Roland M58.1
Rossburn: *see* Ranchvale
St Boniface M125.1
St Vital M48.1, M130.1, M139.1
Selkirk M21.1, M56.1, M134.1
Shoal Lake M141.1
Souris M11.1, M15.1
Teulon M105.1
Virden M44.1, M85.1, M120.1
Waskada M144.1
Wawanesa (Chesley Rd, west of Wawanesa) M93.1
Winnipeg (incl East Kildonan, Fort Rouge) O20.38,
 O20.43, O32.3, O68.4, O130.8, O612.5–612.7,
 O776.12, O1055.3, O1114.3, M1.1, M2.1, M4.1,
 M7.1, M8.1, M9.1, M10.1, M12.1, M16.1, M19.1
 (Fort Rouge), M22.1, M25.1, M26.1, M27.1, M28.1,
 M29.1, M30.1, M31.1, M32.1, M33.1, M34.1, M35.1,
 M36.1, M37.1, M39.1, M40.1, M42.1, M45.1, M46.1,
 M49.1, M50.1, M51.1, M52.1, M53.1, M54.1, M55.1,
 M57.1, M59.1, M60.1, M62.1, M63.1, M64.1, M65.1,
 M67.1, M68.1 (Fort Rouge), M69.1 (East Kildonan),
 M70.1, M71.1, M72.1, M73.1, M74.1, M75.1, M76.1,
 M77.1, M78.1, M79.1, M80.1, M81.1, M82.1, M83.1,
 M86.1, M88.1, M89.1, M90.1, M91.1, M94.1, M95.1,
 M96.1, M97.1, M98.1, M99.1, M101.1, M102.1,
 M103.1, M104.1, M106.1, M107.1, M108.1, M109.1,
 M111.1, M112.1, M114.1, M116.1, M117.1, M118.1,
 M119.1, M121.1, M122.1, M123.1, M124.1, M126.1,
 M127.1, M128.1, M129.1, M131.1, M132.1, M135.1,
 M136.1, M138.1, B21.5; *see also* O70.7, B2.1

New Brunswick

[Place of publication unknown] NB8.1, NB45.1

Newfoundland

Northwest Territories

Nova Scotia

Ontario

Yukon Territory

Great Britain

United States

Name Index

This index lists the names of individual, corporate, and institutional authors, and significant persons or organizations associated with a text. It also includes culinary brand names where the brand name of the product featured in the book (usually an ingredient or utensil) differs from the manufacturing company that produced it; for example, there are listings for both 'Princess' Baking Powder and its maker, Wm Lunan and Son, but no separate listing for Egg-O Baking Powder, the references for which are under Egg-O Baking Powder Co. Printers and trade publishers are included only if there is a possibility that they helped to shape the text in some way.

A., Mme M.H. Q59.1
Abbott, Claire A83.4
Abbs and McNamara, druggists O321.1
Abell, Mrs L.G. Q5.1
Aberdeen Hospital, Ladies' Aid NS24.1
Acadia brand fish NS12.1, NS39.1
Ackerman, Morris O534.2–534.3
Acme Food Choppers O106.3
A.C. Miller and Co. O61.1
Adam, Ann [pseudonym] O877.1, O878.1, O1065.1, O1066.1, O1067.1, O1091.1, O1149.1; see also Ann Adam Cooking School of the Air; Ann Adam Homecrafters; Bayley, Mrs Kathleen Mary Frances; Caldwell, Miss Kathleen Mary Frances
Adams, Edith [pseudonym] B81.1, B82.1, B94.1, B97.1, B99.1, B103.1, B110.1, B114.1, B119.1, B124.1, B128.1, B129.1, B133.1, B139.1, B140.1
Adelaide McLaurin Mission Circle NP8.1
Admiral refrigerators Q311.2
A. Dulmage Ltd O48.18
A.E. McKenzie Co. Ltd, seedsmen M87.1
Aitken, Mrs Katherine (Kate) May (Mrs H.M. Aitken) Q214.1, Q215.1, Q216.1, Q217.1, Q218.1, Q263.1, Q264.1, Q265.1, Q266.1, Q277.1, Q278.1, Q292.1, O1091.1, S78.1
A.J. White and Co. Q22.1
Alberta:
– Department of Agriculture: A72.1; Agricultural Extension Service A97.1; Dairy Branch A104.1; Women's Institute Branch A36.1
– Department of Education A37.1
Alberta Avenue, Edmonton A73.1
Alberta Beekeepers' Association A111.1

Alberta Drug and Stationery Co. Ltd A12.1
Alberta Schools of Agriculture, Household Science Department A38.1
Alden, Mary O1113.1
Alexandra Presbyterian Church, Brantford, Women's Association O1039.1
All-Bran cereal O768.1, O795.1, O837.1, O918.1, O943.1
Allen:
– Elaine Q147.5–147.7, Q298.1
– Mrs Ida Cogswell Bailey O372.1, O513.1, O1040.1
– Jane Taylor O835.1, O860.1, O905.1
– Miss Olive O465.1
– Mrs Sarah Q27.1
Allenby School, Toronto, pupils of Room 24 O980.1
Alliance United Church, Ladies' Aid A103.1
All Saints Anglican Church:
– Huntsville, Parish Guild O1169.1
– Montreal: see Q200.1
All Saints Cathedral, Halifax, Diocesan Women's Cathedral League NS17.1
All Saints Church:
– Bedford, Guild, ladies NS10.1, NS11.1
– Ottawa, Women's Guild O977.1
All Saints' Church:
– East Saint John, ladies NB38.1
– Melville S38.1, S40.1
– Weyburn, Woman's Auxiliary S17.1
Allsweet margarine O1185.1, O1186.1
Almonte Farm Women's Club O1102.1
Alonzo O. Bliss Medical Co. Q92.1, Q93.1
Alpha Audette(?), Ottawa O427.1
Alpha Guild, Regina S35.1

Chester Kent and Co., Windsor, Ont. NB35.4

C.H. Gunn and Co., drugstore O178.1, O215.1

Children's Aid Society, Brockville, Women's Auxiliary O764.1

Chipman United Church, Guild NB62.1

Chisholm Milling Co. O412.1

Choquette Bros, Nelson NP13.1

Christ Church:
– East Angus, Ladies' Guild Q158.1
– Saskatoon, Wednesday Evening Circle S111.1
– Selkirk, WA [likely Women's Auxiliary] M21.1

Christ Church Cathedral, Ottawa, WA [Women's Association?] O450.1

Christ Church Parish Church, Fredericton, Senior WA [Women's Association?] NB48.1

Christ's Church (Anglican), Niagara Falls, Christ Church Guild, ladies O816.1

Christian, Eugene O357.1

Christian Church, Newmarket, Ladies' Aid O258.1

Christie, Mrs Rose Marie Claire Armstrong: *see* Brown, Cynthia [pseudonym]

Church and Dwight Co. O82.1

Church and Dwight Ltd Q130.1, Q210.1, Q312.1, O82.7–82.10

Churchill and Co., maker of Breadmakers' goods O41.1, O42.1

Church of Christ:
– Vulcan, Ladies' Missionary Circle A71.1
– Windsor, Ladies Aid O605.1

Church of England Institute, Woman's Auxiliary NS1.1

Church of Jesus Christ of Latter-Day Saints: *see* Lethbridge Stake Relief Society

Church of St Andrew and St George, Baie Comeau, Ladies' Guild Q271.1

Church of St Andrew Memorial, London, Ladies Guild O1070.1

Church of St Clement's Eglinton, Toronto, Parochial Guild O812.1

Church of St James the Apostle, Guelph, Parish Guild O1143.1

Church of St John the Evangelist:
– London: Guild O538.1; Women's Guild O1022.1
– Montreal, ladies Q21.1
– Shawinigan Falls, Ladies' Guild Q242.1
– Strathroy, Junior Women's Guild O1042.1

Church of St Jude, Toronto, Parish Guild O1165.1

Church of the Ascension, Montreal, Women's Guild Q179.1

Church of the Epiphany, Sudbury, Woman's Auxiliary O836.1

Church of the Messiah, Kincardine, Woman's Auxiliary O933.1

Church of the Redeemer (Anglican), Montreal: *see* Q200.1

Citadelle Maple Syrup Q152.1–152.4

City Dairy O752.1

CJCAV radio station A96.1

CJCJ radio station, Calgary, Woman's Program A92.1

CKCL radio station, Toronto, Radio Cooking School O558.1

CKGW radio station, Toronto, Betty's Home Chats and Cooking School O633.1

Claire, Mabel O748.1

Clark:
– Doris Q204.1
– Miss Margaret Alice NB7.1

Clarke, Mrs Anne O35.1

Clark's prepared foods Q159.1, Q180.1

Clément, Marie-Blanche Q253.1

Clergue, Miss Alice Gertrude Q95.1, Q119.1, Q236.1, O84.1

Clinch, Peter NB31.1

Clinton Public Hospital, Hospital Aid O1208.1

Clover Leaf salmon B84.1

Club House brand olives, spices, mustard: *see* Gorman, Eckert and Co. Ltd

CMP Powdered Milk O374.1

Coate, W.E., Medical Hall O105.1

Cobbett:
– Mrs Anne GB1.1
– Mrs Ann Read [*sic*]: *see* Cobbett, Mrs Anne
– William: *see* GB1.1

Cobourg Congregational Church, Ladies' Aid O209.1

Codville Co. Ltd M8.2–8.7

Codville-Georgeson Co. Ltd M8.1

Coggs, Miss Kathleen O528.7–528.8

Cole, Miss Rose Owen O35.1

Coleman Lamp and Stove Co., Wichita, Kans. O838.1

College Street Methodist Church, Toronto, Adult Bible Class, ladies O229.1

Collett, Elaine O1168.1, O1221.1

Colman-Keen (Canada) Ltd Q139.1, Q167.1, Q193.1, Q248.1

Colman's Mustard Q139.1

Columbus Ladies' Association, St John's NF6.1

Commercial Girls' Club, Winnipeg M75.1

La compagnie de publicité Brandow de Montréal B21.9

La compagnie de publicité nationale Q82.2

La compagnie des farines naturelles enrg. Q105.1

La compagnie Pastene ltée Q307.1

La cie [i.e., compagnie] W.T. Rawleigh ltée: *see* W.T. Rawleigh Co. Ltd

Norge Refrigerators O769.1
North Broadview Presbyterian Church, Toronto,
    Junior Bible Class O286.1
North Broadview United Church, Toronto, Woman's
    Association O873.1
Northern Aluminum Co. Ltd O429.1
Northern Electric stoves O877.1
North Gower United Church, Women's Association
    O786.1
North Parkdale United Church, Toronto O687.1
Northrop and Lyman [later Northrop and Lyman
    Co. Ltd], maker of patent medicine O7.1
Northwestern Utilities Ltd A83.5–83.6
Nor'-West Farmer and Farm and Home [newspa-
    per], Winnipeg M67.1
Norwood Methodist Church, Ladies' Aid M23.1
Norwood Presbyterian Church, Ladies' Aid, Home-
    Cooking Circle M41.1
Nourse, Mrs Elizabeth Q4.1
Nova Scotia: Bureau of Information NS46.1; Depart-
    ment of Agriculture NS41.1; Government Bureau
    of Information and Publicity NS50.1; Land Settle-
    ment Board NS53.1
Nova Scotia Fruit Growers Association NS41.1
Noyan, ladies Q70.1
Nugget [newspaper], North Bay O903.1
Nukraft Cheese Q115.5
Nulomoline Ltd Q205.1, Q209.1, Q268.1

Oakdale United Church, Women's Association,
    Group 3 O1209.1
Oddie, Miss Jean S92.1, S100.1, S101.1
Odiau, Henri, chef O641.1
OES: see Order of the Eastern Star
Ogilvie Flour Mills Co. Ltd Q55.1, Q214.1, Q215.1,
    Q216.1, Q217.1, Q218.1, Q219.1, Q261.1
Okanagan United Growers Ltd B46.1
OK Apples B46.1, B77.1
Old Colony Flour O1121.1
Old Country Fair, Medicine Hat, 1921 A43.1
Oliphant, Mrs Nelson B. Q51.1
O'Mara's Drug Store, St John's NF O48.9
Ontario:
– Department of Agriculture: O158.1, O692.1;
    Ontario Agricultural College O236.1 (see also
    Ontario Agricultural College and Experimental
    Farm); Statistics and Publications Branch O1010.1,
    O1019.1, O1222.1, O1229.1; Women's Institute
    Branch O1010.1; Women's Institute Branch and
    Home Economics Service O1223.1, O1224.1;
    Women's Institutes O158.2–158.3, O379.1, O380.1,
    O413.1, O414.1; Women's Institutes Branch
    O446.1, O516.1

– Department of Land and Forests, Relief Land
    Settlement Committee: see NS53.1
– Minister of Education O19.1, O364.1, O410.1
– Provincial Secretary's Department O573.1
Ontario Agricultural College and Experimental
    Farm, Guelph O120.1; see also Ontario, Depart-
    ment of Agriculture, Ontario Agricultural College
Ontario Canning Co. O61.1
Ontario Equitable Life and Accident Insurance Co.
    O677.1
Ontario Reformatory, Guelph O573.1
Orange Order: see Ladies' Orange Benevolent Asso-
    ciation
Order of the Eastern Star: Acacia Chapter No. 3,
    Biggar S96.1; Elm Creek Chapter M133.1;
    Hamilton Chapter O800.1; Lynrock Chapter No.
    154, near Hamilton O1071.1; Maple Leaf Chapter
    No. 3, St Thomas, Friendship Group O1180.1;
    Mizpeh Chapter No. 56, Hamilton O421.1, O505.1;
    Ottawa Chapter No. 37 O856.1; Yukon Chapter
    No. 1, Dawson Y1.1
Order of the Royal Purple: see Benevolent and
    Protective Order of Elks
Osborne, Mabel O952.1
Ottawa Electric Co. O779.1
Ottawa Gas Co. O225.1, O779.1
Ottawa Ladies Hebrew Benevolent Society O337.1
Ottawa United Church, Walkerville, Women's
    Association O657.1
Outlook Women's Co-operative Guild: see Women's
    Co-operative Guild, Outlook
Owens, Mrs Frances Emugene Q29.1, Q30.1
Oxner, Bertha G. S92.1
Oxo (Canada) Ltd Q229.1
Oxo Ltd Q148.1, Q172.1

P., C. de: see De Pratz, Madame Claire
Pacific Brand Evaporated Milk B62.1
Packert, Herman N., chemist and druggist O68.2
Packert's Baking Powder O68.2
Palmer:
– Mrs Ida M. O147.1
– Miss Lilian L. Q190.1
Panomalt Q187.1
Pansy Club, Brantford O416.1
Paré, Eugénie Q220.1
Parent, Roméo Q226.1, Q232.1
Park, Edna W. O241.4–241.6
Parkdale Baptist Church, Toronto: Ladies Aid Soci-
    ety O675.1; Young Women's Mission Circle O527.1
Parkdale Methodist Church, Toronto, Bascom Mis-
    sion Band O205.1; see also Parkdale United
    Church, Toronto

St George's Guild, Owen Sound: *see* St George's Church, Owen Sound

St Giles' Presbyterian Church, Hamilton, Ladies' Aid and friends O207.1; *see also* St Giles United Church

St Giles United Church, Hamilton, Women's Association O1075.1; *see also* St Giles' Presbyterian Church

St Henry's Roman Catholic Church, Melville, Ladies' Altar Society S77.1, S110.1

St Ignatius Church, Winnipeg, ladies M65.1

St James' Anglican Church, Flin Flon, Women's Auxiliary, Uptown Branch M143.1

St James Anglican Church, Stratford, Ladies' Aid Society O729.1

St James Church:
– Hamilton, [Anglican], Women's Auxiliary O328.1
– Ingersoll, Ladies Guild O214.1
– Port Colborne, Woman's Auxiliary O169a.1

St James' Church, Kingston, Young Women Church Workers O1030.1

St James Methodist Church, Montreal, ladies Q23.1

St James' United Church, Peterborough, Women's [or Woman's] Association O1083.1, O1155.1

St James United Church, Simcoe, Woman's Association O668.1

Saint John: Board of School Trustees NB54.1; city schools, teachers of Home Economics Department NB54.2

Saint John, ladies NB2.1

St John Ambulance Brigade, Montreal Q198.1

St John Presbyterian Church, Hamilton, Laurel Mission Circle O217.1

St John's Anglican Church:
– St Thomas, Ladies' Aid O915.1
– Smiths Falls, Women's Guild O841.1
– Truro, Woman's Auxiliary, branch of NS15.1
– Winona, Women's Auxiliary O152.1

St John's Church:
– Antrim, Ladies' Guild O999.1
– Bridgewater, Managers' Auxiliary NS14.1
– Chapleau, Woman's Auxiliary O567.1
– Fairview, Evening Guild NS69.1
– North Bay, ladies O91.1
– Preston, Women's Guild and Home Mission O239.1
– Saskatoon, Chancel Guild, ladies S6.1

St John's Church Norway, Toronto, Parish Association O649.1

St John's Presbyterian Church:
– Medicine Hat, First Street Circle A70.1
– Toronto, Service Club O945.1
– Vancouver, Woman's Aid B26.1

St John's United Church:

– Moncton, Young Ladies' [Association or Auxiliary?] NB43.1, NB60.1
– Stratford, Women's Association O923.1

St Johns United Church, Unity Group Q255.1

St John the Evangelist Church, Strathroy: *see* Church of St John the Evangelist

St Josaphat's Parish, Edmonton: Ladies' Auxiliary, Ukrainian Ladies' Good Will Organization A95.1–95.2; Ukrainian Catholic Ladies' Goodwill [*sic*] Club A95.3–95.4

St Joseph's Altar Society, Sutherland Circle S87.1

St Joseph's Cathedral, Edmonton A58.1

St Joseph's Hospital, Victoria, Junior Auxiliary B132.1

St Lawrence Flour Mills Co. Ltd Q88.1, Q143.1, Q160.1, Q191.1

St Lawrence Refined Corn Oil O880.1

St Lawrence's Catholic Church, Maple Creek, ladies S51.1

St Lawrence Starch Co. Ltd O880.1, O1054.1

St Luke's Anglican Cathedral, Sault Ste Marie, Woman's Auxiliary O84.1

St Luke's Anglican Church:
– Magog, Women's Guild Q117.1
– Montreal: *see* Q200.1

St Luke's Church [Anglican], Winnipeg [Nassau Street North]: M12.1; Parish Guild M62.1

St Luke's United Church, Montreal, Women's Association Q199.1

St Margaret's Church, Midland, Women's Auxiliary O265.1

St Margaret's College, Toronto, Household Science Department O351.1

St Mark's Anglican Church, St Vital: ladies M48.1; Woman's Auxiliary, Evening Branch M130.1

St Mark's Church, Vancouver, Parish Guild B48.1

St Mark's Lutheran Church, Kitchener, Cloverleaf Society O1131.1

St Martin's Church, North Peace River Parish, Fort St John, WA B113.1

St Mary Edith, Sister: *see* Sainte-Marie Edith, soeur

St Mary's Anglican Church:
– Kindersley, Guild S102.1
– Montreal: *see* Q200.1

St Mary's Church:
– Kerrisdale, ladies B47.1
– Woodstock, ladies O395.1

St Matthews Anglican Church, Hampstead: *see* Q200.1

St Matthew's Church, Ottawa, St Anna's Guild O663.1

St Matthews Lutheran Church, Kitchener, Missionary Society, ladies O1012.1

St Matthews Missionary Society, Kitchener: *see* St Matthews Lutheran Church

St Matthew-Wesley United Church, North Sydney, Ladies Guild NS47.1

St Matthias' Church, Westmount, ladies Q76.1

St Michael and All Angels' Church, Grenfell, Sask. O300.1

St Michael's, Calgary: *see* St Michael's and All Angels Anglican Church

St Michael's and All Angels Anglican Church, Calgary, WA, Evening Branch A67.1, A117.1

St Patrick's Church, Galt, Catholic Women's Auxiliary O757.1

St Paul's Anglican Church:
– Arden, Ladies Guild O1118.1
– Haileybury, Parish Club O522.1

St Paul's Cathedral, London, WA, Evening Branch O1129.1

St Paul's Church:
– Fort William O298.1
– Ingersoll, young ladies O109a.1; *see also* St Paul's Presbyterian Church, Ingersoll
– Kentville, ladies NS18.1
– Marmora, Ladies' Guild O464.1
– Rothesay, Sewing Society, ladies NB18.1
– South Porcupine O581.1

St Paul's Eastern United Church, Ottawa, Ladies Aid Society, Mrs M. Mathewson's Circle O701.1

St Paul's Evangelical Lutheran Church, Kitchener, Ladies' Aid O1194.1

St Paul's Hospital, Saskatoon, Women's Auxiliary S95.1

St Paul's Parish Club, Haileybury: *see* St Paul's Anglican Church

St Paul's Presbyterian Church:
– Hamilton, Ladies' Association O827.1
– Ingersoll, young ladies O66.1; *see also* St Paul's Church, Ingersoll
– Peterborough, Ladies' Aid O891.1
– Port Hope, Ladies Aid O733.1
– Thornbury and Clarksburg, ladies O175.1
– Winchester, Agnes Glassford Young Women's Auxiliary O1107.1

St Paul's Service Club: *see* St Paul's United Church, Fredericton

St Paul's United Church:
– Assiniboia, Women's Association S37.1
– Brampton, Ladies' Aid O655.1
– Carp, Women's Association, Group No. 3 O855.1
– Fredericton, Service Club NB61.1
– Midland O767.1
– New Liskeard, Woman's Association O1167.1
– Orillia, Ladies' Aid O864.1

– Perth, Women's Association O785.1
– Sarnia O993.1

St Peter's Church:
– Brockville, Parish Guild O1153.1
– Madoc, Young Women's Club O1002.1, O1133.1

St Philips Church: Montreal West, Ladies' Guild Q116.1; Westville, Pictou Co., Young Ladies' Branch NS19.1

St Phillip's Anglican Church, Montreal West: *see* Q200.1

St Stephens–Broadway United Church, Winnipeg, Women's Association M76.1

St Stephen's Church, Calgary, Guild A48.1

St Stephens Church, Winnipeg, Ladies Association M4.1

St Therese Hospital, Tisdale, Tisdale Hospital Aid S117.1

St Thomas Church, St Catharines, Parish Hall Guild, ladies O617.1

St Thomas Memorial Hospital, Woman's Hospital Aid O788.1

St Thomas–Wesley United Church, Saskatoon, WA, Central Circle S62.1

St Vincent's Orphanage, St Elizabeth's Aid Society P5.1

St Vital United Church, Evening Circle M139.1

Salford United Church, Junior Bible Class, girls O1200.1

Salvation Army, Home League, Hamilton 1 O1043.1

Sandwell, Bernard K. O935.1

Sangster, Margaret Elizabeth Munson O148.1

Sargent and Co., New York O118.1

Saskatchewan: Department of Education S19.1, S27.1, S28.1; Department of Natural Resources and Industrial Development S101.1

Saskatchewan Curling Association S39.1

Saskatchewan Fish Products S101.1

Saskatchewan Flight Training School No. 11, Yorkton, Sask., Officer's [*sic*] Wives Auxiliary O1055.4

Saskatchewan Homemakers' Clubs: *see* Homemakers' Clubs, Sask.

Saskatchewan Honey Producers Co-operative, Fort Qu'Appelle, Sask. A111.2

Saskatoon Dairy Pool S59.1

Saturday Sunset Presses, Vancouver (as publisher) B27.1

Saunders, Dr Chas E. O543.1

Savard, Napoléon, illustrator Q86.1

Scandinavian Canadian Club, Toronto, Fireside Group O983.1

Scarabelli, Carlo, chef O641.1

Scarlett, R.A., chemist O68.3

Short-Title Index

This index lists the titles of all works featured as numbered entries in Culinary Landmarks, including alternative titles (such as a cover-title or running head that differs from the title found on the title-page) and new titles for subsequent editions. With a few exceptions, the index does not include the titles of other books by a person, company, institution, or association that may be recorded after the main heading for a work. Alternative titles are cross-referenced to the entry number; for example: Corner Brook's favourite recipes: see NF11.1. In the case of multiple editions of a work with the same title, only the entry number of the first-recorded edition is given here, but where the title or language of a work varies according to the edition, each variant is listed with its corresponding entry number or run of numbers; for example, these English and French titles: The truth about baking powder O354.1, O354.3; La vérité sur la poudre à pâte O354.2. New titles of 1950 and later editions ('other editions' at the end of a run of entries) and of non-Canadian editions (usually American or British editions at the end of a run of entries) are located by page number in most cases. References to works in the general and provincial introductions are also located by page number or, if cited in another entry, by a cross-reference to that entry (in the case of works published in both English- and French-language editions, most references are to the English version of the title). In the case of multiple works with the same title, distinguishing information precedes the entry number. The short-title index also includes series titles. If you do not find a title in the alphabetical run below, be sure also to check under '[Title unknown]' at the start of the list.

As explained on p xxxv, entries for editions of a work published in more than one province are located in the section for the province of the first edition (or other appropriate edition). In these occasional instances, an edition published in one province may have an entry number starting with the letter for another province (for example, B21.3 published in Hamilton, Ontario). In the index below, if you find a title that matches the work for which you are searching, but the entry number is for a different province, check the entry itself.

[Title unknown]: 'Legion Ladies' NF10.1; St Philip's Church, Pictou County NS19.1, p 11; Halifax NS61.1, p 11; 'Modern Recipes' NB8.1; Saint John NB16.1, p 38; P4.1, p 67; Amherst Manufacturing Co., Montreal Q24.1; National Drug and Chemical Co. of Canada Ltd, Montreal Q65.1; 'Les épiciers modernes ltée en coopération avec Magasins E-M Stores' Q262.1, p 77; St Paul's Presbyterian Church, Ingersoll O66.1, p 277; N.C. Polson and Co., Kingston O113.1; Echo newspaper, Wiarton O139a.1, p 278; St John's Anglican Church, Winona O152.1; Burrow, Stewart and Milne Co. Ltd O179.2; North Bay O226.1, p 278; WI?, Palermo area O227.1; Princess Street Methodist Church, Kingston O228.1; Knox Church, Listowel O454.1; Wesley United Church, London O533.1; Hotpoint Electric Range, Canadian General Electric Co. O658.1; North Parkdale United Church, Toronto O687.1; Wanstead United Church, Toronto O688.1; Chalmers Church, Guelph O693.1 (see also O729.1); Church of St Clement's Eglinton, Toronto O812.1; 'manual on camp feeding' O1127.1, p 283; Trinity Anglican Church, Welland O1148.1; Knox Church Woman's Association, Port Arthur? O1202.1; Hartney M13.1; 'The Red Cross Cook Book' (running head), Reston M24.1, p 921; 'Better Cookery clipping book' M99.1, p 924; Union Ladies' Aid Society, Valparaiso S26.1; Holy Rosary Cathedral?, Regina S32.1; Biggar S54.1; 'Red Deer Women's Cook Book' A13.1; recipes from Brownfield, Puffer, Battle Ridge, and Coronation A42.1; Cosmopolitan Fair, Medicine Hat A46.1; ads for Chase and Kamloops B14.1, p 1081; St Cecilia's Review, Nanaimo B68.1; British Empire Service League, Canadian Legion, Branch No. 11, Trail B123.1; Gourlie-Grenier Co. ad NP11.1

ABC of the kitchen B122.1, p 1083

The accomplished family cook p 83

Adult Bible Class cook book O229.1

After all it takes a baker O564.1, p 280

World-famous chocolate and cocoa recipes: *see* Q173.1

A world of useful information in a nutshell M35.1, p 924

World's modern cook book for the busy woman p 729

The world's most popular chocolate and cocoa recipes: *see* Q173.1

A worth-while recipe book B66.1, p 1083

Wright's golden recipes O112.1

Wrigley's practical receipts in the arts, manufactures, trades, and agriculture O13.1, p xxiii

Yeast and its household use O120.1

Yello Fello, the apple elf B46.1, pp xxvii, 1080, 1083

Ye old miller's household book O35.11–35.12

Ye recipes: *see* O742.1

Yesterday's cookbook 1885 (history in cooking) p 1085

YLA recipes: St John's United Church, Moncton NB43.1, NB60.1

YMCA cook book: Owen Sound O247.1

The young housekeeper's guide NB12.1, p 39

The young wife's own cook book: *see* B1.1

The Young Woman's Auxiliary cook book M58.1

Your Leonard Refrigerator O1173.1

Your money's worth in food O1224.1, p 284

Your Philco Freezer NP18.1

Yours ... for better meals O959.2

YWCA cook book: Owen Sound O686.1

The YWCA cook book: St Thomas O203.1

The Zam-Buk book of cookery recipes O248.1

Zion Line Women's Institute cook book O1197.1

STUDIES IN BOOK AND PRINT CULTURE

General editor: Leslie Howsam